THE COMPLETE BIBLE

AN AMERICAN TRANSLATION

THE COMPLETE BIBLE

AN AMERICAN TRANSLATION

THE OLD TESTAMENT

Translated by

J. M. POWIS SMITH

AND A GROUP OF SCHOLARS

THE APOCRYPHA

AND

THE NEW TESTAMENT

Translated by

EDGAR J. GOODSPEED

THE UNIVERSITY OF CHICAGO PRESS
CHICAGO · ILLINOIS

THE UNIVERSITY OF CHICAGO PRESS, CHICAGO 37
Cambridge University Press, London, N.W. 1, England
W. J. Gage & Co., Limited, Toronto 2B, Canada

 Published 1939. Fifteenth impression 1951
Composed and printed by The University of Chicago Press
Chicago, Illinois, U.S.A.

THE rapid advance of learning in recent years in the fields of history, archaeology, and language has thrown new light upon every part of the Bible. At the same time our changing English speech has carried us farther and farther from the sixteenth-century diction in which all our standard versions of it are clothed. Yet the great messages of the Old and New Testaments were never more necessary than in our present confused and hurried life. We have, therefore, sought to produce a new translation of them, based upon the assured results of modern study, and put in the familiar language of today. We do this in the hope that, through its use, the literary appreciation, the historical understanding, and the religious influence of the Bible may be furthered in our generation.

It has been truly said that no one can have the complete Bible, as a source book for the cultural study of art, literature, history, and religion, without the Apocrypha. From the earliest Christian times down to the age of the King James Version, they belonged to the Bible; and, while modern critical judgments and religious attitudes deny them a position of equality with the Old and New Testament scriptures, historically and culturally they are still an integral part of the Bible. A new translation of the Apocrypha, the first ever made of them throughout from the most ancient languages in which they are preserved, is accordingly included in this edition.

Dr. Smith and I felt that in introducing the American translation to the public we could not do better than to repeat some sentences from the noble Preface of the King James Version of 1611, which was the third Authorized Version, and the sixth revision of the English Bible:

"We are so farre off from condemning any of their labours that traueiled before vs in this kinde, either in this land or beyond sea . . . . that we acknowledge them to have beene raised vp of God, ... and that they deserue to be had of vs and of posteritie in everlasting remembrance. . . . . Therefore blessed be they, and most honoured be their name, that breake the yce and give the onset vpon that which helpeth forward to the saving of soules. Now what can bee more auaileable thereto, than to deliuer Gods booke vnto Gods people in a tongue which they vnderstand? . . . .

"So, if we building vpon their foundation that went before vs, and being holpen by their labours, doe endeavour to make that better which they left so good; no man, we are sure, hath cause to mislike vs; they, we perswade ourselues, if they were aliue, would thanke vs.

"For is the kingdome of God become words or syllables? Why should wee be in bondage to them if we may be free. . . . .?"

EDGAR J. GOODSPEED

TABLE OF CONTENTS

THE OLD TESTAMENT

PART I

THE PENTATEUCH

PART II

THE HISTORICAL BOOKS

PART III

THE POETICAL BOOKS

PART IV

THE BOOKS OF THE PROPHETS

THE APOCRYPHA

Translated by Edgar J. Goodspeed

THE NEW TESTAMENT

Translated by Edgar J. Goodspeed

TABLE OF CONTENTS

THE OLD TESTAMENT

AN AMERICAN TRANSLATION

By

ALEXANDER R. GORDON · THEOPHILE J. MEEK
J. M. POWIS SMITH · LEROY WATERMAN

Edited by
J. M. POWIS SMITH

Revised by
THEOPHILE J. MEEK

PREFACE

WHY should anyone make a new English translation of the Old Testament? With the Authorized Version of King James and the British and American revisions, to say nothing of unofficial renderings, have we not enough? This question may quite fairly be asked. The only possible basis for a satisfactory answer must be either in a better knowledge of Hebrew than was possible at the time when the earlier translations were made, or in a fuller appreciation of fundamental textual problems, or in a clearer recognition of poetic structures, or in such a change in our own language as would render the language of the older translations more or less unintelligible to the average man of our day. As a matter of fact, our answer is to be found in all of these areas.

The most urgent demand for a new translation comes from the field of Hebrew scholarship. The control of the Hebrew vocabulary and syntax available to the scholar of today is vastly greater than that at the command of the translators of the Authorized Version or of its revisers. This is due partly to the greater degree of scientific methodology now practiced in the study of language in general and of Hebrew in particular, and partly to the contributions made to our knowledge of Hebrew by the decipherment of the hieroglyphic and cuneiform writings. The first requirement of a translation is that it should reproduce as fully and accurately as possible the meaning of the original documents. To this end the translators should know the language of the original as well as it can be known.

Modern studies of textual problems reinforce the need for a new rendering. These have brought out more and more clearly the uncertain state of the Hebrew text and have perfected the technique of critical method. The science of textual criticism has made great progress in recent years, and no translation of the Old Testament can afford to ignore its results. Our guiding principle has been that the official Massoretic text must be adhered to as long as it made satisfactory sense. We have not tried to create a new text; but rather to translate the received text wherever translation was possible. Where departure from this text was imperative we have sought a substitute for it along generally approved lines, depending primarily upon the collateral versions, having recourse to scientific conjecture only when the versions failed to afford adequate help. If the number of such passages seems to him unduly large, he should bear in mind certain facts. The oldest known Hebrew manuscript of the Old Testament dates from the ninth century A.D. This means that at least eighteen centuries elapsed between the earliest Hebrew written documents and our oldest manuscript; and that between the latest Hebrew document now found in the Old Testament and our oldest manuscript there was a lapse of approximately eleven centuries. Moreover, the original Hebrew text included only the consonants. The vowels were not added until about the seventh century A.D.[1]

[1] There is a fragment of papyrus, found in Egypt about 1901 A.D., which contains the Hebrew text of the Decalogue and the Shema (Deut. 6:4 f.). It is pre-Massoretic and probably dates from about the second century A.D.

Naturally many more errors are found in the vocalic part of the text than in the much older consonantal element. A vowel change naturally involves a very much slighter correction than is involved in a change of consonants. Anyone who has had experience in handling ancient manuscripts will be surprised, not that there are so many corrupt passages, but rather that under the circumstances there are so few. We trust that our attitude in this fundamentally important matter will commend itself to careful and cautious scholars.

The last half-century has developed a great interest in the stylistic qualities of Hebrew poetry. Much of the text that had long passed for prose is now recognized as really poetic in both form and spirit. This adds to the necessity for a new translation. Poetry should not be printed as prose. The present translation brings into clear light many of the hidden beauties of Hebrew poetry. The text is printed in poetic lines as clearly indicated by the parallelism of the structure. In cases where the elegiac measure is employed in Hebrew, the text indicates it by a deep indentation of the second or short line. Where the content and the form both point to the presence of strophes the text has been printed in stanzas. Where such structure is not clearly shown the poetic lines are left to follow one another without a break.

The English of King James's day is not wholly natural or clear to the average man at the present time. In common everyday speech "thou," "thee," and "thy" are no longer used; they have been retained here when they occur in language addressed to God, since they convey a more reverent feeling than the blunt "you." The endings "est" for the second person and "eth" for the third person singular of verbs are now archaic. The same holds true of "ye" for "you," "waxen" for "waxed," and "lade" for "load." The use of "vinegar" in the sense of a wine or liquor for drinking has long since ceased to be recognized. "To ear" in the sense of "to plow" or "to till" is obsolete; so are "marish" for "marsh," "scrabble" for "scratch," "in the audience of" for "in the hearing of," "all to" for "altogether," and many others like them. Time has wrought changes in the usage of words. The translators of the King James Version were casting no aspersion upon the character of womankind in general when they said, "Who can find a virtuous woman?" The word "virtuous" for them had its old force brought over from the Latin *virtus*. But today, when applied to woman, the word will almost inevitably be taken in a more specialized sense, and so be misunderstood. The same charge lies against "virtuously." The word "prevent" once meant "to anticipate," but is now used in the sense of "to hinder"; consequently its old usage in passages like Psalms 119:147 f. puzzles modern readers. Facts like these make the reading of the Bible a scholarly rather than a religious exercise, and clearly point toward the need of a new translation.

The translator to do his best work must be in sympathy with his subject matter and be able to put himself into mental and spiritual contact with its authors. From this side of his work the demand made upon him is a very heavy one. On the other hand, a translation should read well. It should be in a vocabulary and style appropriate to the thought which it is designed to express. If the original be dignified, impressive, and eloquent, those qualities must not be lacking in the translation; if it be trivial, commonplace, and prosaic, the translation must take on the same character. The content of the Old Testament is, with little exception, upon a high literary plane. The language of the translation, therefore, cannot be allowed to fall to the level of the street. In this translation the foregoing principles have been kept constantly in mind. It tries to be American in the sense that the writings of Lincoln, Roosevelt, and Wilson are American. This does not imply any limitation of our mother-tongue, but if anything an enrichment of it. Least of all does it mean that the translation is for Americans only; it aims at being easily understood wherever English is spoken. In general we have been loyal to the Hebrew in its use of symbolic and figurative language; occasionally where such figures would not be clear to the reader, we have translated the figure into more familiar terms.

One detail of the translation which requires explanation is the treatment of the divine name. As nearly as we can now tell, the Hebrews called their Deity by the name Yahweh, and in a shorter form, Yah, used in relatively few cases. In course of time they came to regard this name as too sacred for utterance. They therefore substituted for it the Hebrew word for "Lord." When vowels were added to the text, the consonants of "Yahweh" were given the vowels of "Lord." Somewhere in the fourteenth century A.D. Christian scholars, not understanding this usage, took the vowels and consonants exactly as they were written and produced the artificial name "Jehovah" which has persisted ever since. In this translation we have followed the orthodox Jewish tradition and substituted "the Lord" for the name "Yahweh" and the phrase "the Lord God" for the phrase "the Lord Yahweh." In all cases where "Lord" or "God" represents an original "Yahweh" small capitals are employed. Anyone, therefore, who desires to retain the flavor of the original text has but to read "Yahweh" wherever he sees LORD or GOD.

The translators and the University Press have sought to give this work the appearance of a modern book. This purpose has determined the make-up of the page and has led to the addition of headings for paragraphs, and to the insertion of some half-titles. It has also kept the verse numbers out of the text and relegated them to the margin, so that the reading of the text may not be interrupted.

The work of translation has been shared by four men: Professor Alex. R Gordon, of the United Theological College and McGill University, Montreal; Professor Theophile J. Meek, of the University of Toronto; Professor Leroy Waterman, of the University of Michigan; and the Editor. Each of them carries the primary responsibility for his own work. The Editor has left his fellow-workers free to express themselves as they would, and has aimed at uniformity only in the most essential matters. If it be felt that each translator has his own style, this should not be regarded as a defect, for each document in the Old Testament has a style of its own, and the extent to which such stylistic characteristics are ignored by translators is a measure of their failure. Each book ought to speak its own message in its own way, even in a translation.

The Editor wishes to express his appreciation of the self-sacrificing labor of his fellow-translators, of their conscientious devotion to the work and of their prompt responsiveness to his few suggestions. Only by such faithful and hearty co-operation could our common task have attained any measure of success.

We are well aware that in undertaking the task of presenting the Old Testament to the modern world in its own speech we have undertaken the impossible. No translation can preserve intact the full content and the symmetrical beauty of the original; in the transition from the old language to the new, much must be lost by the way. We can but hope that we have not fallen too far short of the summit of perfection; and that our work may at least serve as a stepping-stone toward those greater translations which time will surely bring.

THE EDITOR

University of Chicago
March 8, 1927

PUBLISHER'S NOTE

FOR the revision of the translation of the Old Testament we are indebted to Professor Theophile J. Meek of the University of Toronto. In the first edition Professor Meek translated the Pentateuch and contributed to the translation of the Historical Books, the Poetical Books, and the Books of the Prophets. He knows the whole translation as only a participant can, and with the co-operation of Professor Leroy Waterman of the University of Michigan, also one of the original translators, he has applied his special knowledge of the problems of this translation and his wide familiarity with the Hebrew language, literature, and institutions to the work of revision. In it he has followed two principal lines: on the one hand he has established a greater degree of uniformity of style and expression in the versions of the four translators; and on the other, he has used the results of the most recent investigations in the interpretation of doubtful passages. Hebrew scholarship is moving fast, and even the few years that have elapsed since the first edition was issued in 1931 have seen contributions to the subject that neither translator nor publisher can ignore. We are under special obligation to Professor Meek for undertaking so exacting a task at a time when he was already actively engaged in other important work.

THE UNIVERSITY OF CHICAGO PRESS

July 12, 1935

PART I

THE PENTATEUCH

GENESIS, EXODUS, LEVITICUS, NUMBERS, AND DEUTERONOMY

Translated by Theophile J. Meek

THE BOOK OF GENESIS

THE STORY OF CREATION, 1:1—2:3

1 WHEN God began to create
the heavens and the earth,
2 the earth was a desolate
waste, with darkness covering the abyss and a tempestuous wind
raging over the surface of the waters.
3 Then God said,
"Let there be light!"
4 And there was light; and God saw
that the light was good. God then separated the light from the darkness.
5 God called the light day, and the darkness night. Evening came, and morning, the first day.
6 Then God said,
"Let there be a firmament in the
middle of the waters to divide the waters in two!"
7 And so it was. God made the firmament, dividing the waters that were
below the firmament from those that
8 were above it; and God called the firmament sky. Evening came, and morning, the second day.
9 Then God said,
"Let the waters below the sky be
gathered into one place so that the dry
land may appear!"
10 And so it was. God called the dry
land earth, and the gathered waters
seas. God saw that it was good.
11 Then God said,
"Let the earth produce vegetation,
seed-bearing plants and the various
kinds of fruit-trees that bear fruit containing their seed!"
12 And so it was. The earth brought
forth vegetation, the various kinds of
seed-bearing plants and the various
kinds of trees that bear fruit containing
their seed. God saw that it was good.
13 Evening came, and morning, the third
day.
14 Then God said,
"Let there be luminaries in the firmament of the sky to separate day from
night; let them serve for signs, for fixed
15 times, and for days and years; and let
them serve as luminaries in the firmament of the sky to shed light on the
earth!"
And so it was. God made the two 16
great luminaries, the greater luminary
to rule the day and the smaller one to
rule the night—and the stars also. God 17
set them in the firmament of the sky to
shed light on the earth, to rule by day 18
and by night, and to separate the light
from the darkness. God saw that it was
good. Evening came, and morning, the 19
fourth day.
Then God said, 20
"Let the waters teem with shoals of
living creatures, and let birds fly over
the earth across the firmament of the
sky!"
And so it was. God created the great 21
sea-monsters and all the various kinds
of living, gliding creatures with which
the waters teem, and all the various
kinds of winged birds. God saw that it
was good, and God blessed them, say- 22
ing,
"Be fruitful, multiply, and fill the
waters in the seas; and let the birds
multiply on the earth!"
Evening came, and morning, the 23
fifth day.
Then God said, 24
"Let the earth bring forth the various kinds of living creatures, the various kinds of domestic animals, reptiles,
and wild beasts of the earth!"
And so it was. God made the various 25
kinds of wild beasts of the earth, the
various kinds of domestic animals, and
all the various kinds of land reptiles;
and God saw that it was good.
Then God said, 26
"Let us make man in our image, after
our likeness, and let him have dominion
over the fish of the sea, the birds of the
air, the domestic animals, the wild
beasts, and all the land reptiles!"
So God created man in his own im- 27
age; in the image of God he created
him; he created both male and female.
Then God blessed them, and God said 28
to them,

"Be fruitful, multiply, fill the earth,
and subdue it; have dominion over the
fish of the sea, the birds of the air, the
domestic animals, and all the living
things that crawl on the earth!"
29 Further, God said,
"See, I give you all the seed-bearing
plants that are found all over the earth,
and all the trees which have seed-bear-
30 ing fruit; it shall be yours to eat. To all
the wild beasts of the earth, to all the
birds of the air, and to all the land reptiles, in which there is a living spirit, I
give all the green plants for food."
31 And so it was. God saw that all that
he had made was very good. Evening
came, and morning, the sixth day.
2 Thus the heavens and the earth were
2 finished, and all their host. On the seventh day God brought his work to an
end on which he had been engaged, de-
sisting on the seventh day from all his
3 work in which he had been engaged. So
God blessed the seventh day, and consecrated it, because on it he had desisted
from all his work, in doing which God
had brought about creation.

THE CREATION AND FALL OF MAN, 2:4—3:24

4 The following are the origins of the
heavens and the earth in their creation.
At the time when the LORD God made
the earth and the heavens, there were
5 as yet no field shrubs on the earth, and
no field plants had as yet sprung up; for
the LORD God had sent no rain on the
earth, and there was no man to till the
6 soil—although a flood used to rise from
the earth and water all the surface of
7 the ground. Then the LORD God molded man out of the dust of the ground,
and breathed into his nostrils the
breath of life, so that man became a
8 living being. Then the LORD God
planted a garden in Eden, to the east,
and put there the man whom he had
9 molded. Out of the ground the LORD
God made all sorts of trees grow that
were pleasant to the sight and good for
food, as well as the tree of life in the
middle of the garden, and the tree of
the knowledge of good and evil.
10 There was a river flowing out of Eden
to water the garden, and leaving there
11 it divided into four branches; the name
of the first being Pishon (the one which
encircles all the land of Havilah, where
there is gold—the gold of that land is 12
fine—and bdellium and onyx stone);
the name of the second river, Gihon 13
(the one which encircles all the land of
Cush); the name of the third river, the 14
Tigris (the one which flows east of Ashur); and the name of the fourth river,
the Euphrates.
The LORD God took the man and 15
put him in the garden of Eden to till it
and look after it; and the LORD God 16
laid this command upon the man:
"From every tree in the garden you
are free to eat; but from the tree of the 17
knowledge of good and evil you must
not eat; for the day that you eat of it
you shall certainly die."
Then the LORD God said, 18
"It is not good for the man to be
alone; I must make a helper for him
who is like him."
So the LORD God molded out of the 19
ground all the wild beasts and all the
birds of the air, and brought them to
the man to see what he would call
them; whatever the man should call
each living creature, that was to be its
name. So the man gave names to all the 20
domestic animals, the birds of the air,
and all the wild beasts; but for man
himself no helper was found who was
like him. Then the LORD God had a 21
trance fall upon the man; and when he
had gone to sleep, he took one of his
ribs, closing up its place with flesh. The 22
rib which he took from the man the
the LORD God built up into a woman,
and brought her to the man, whereupon 23
the man said,
"This at last is bone of my bone,
And flesh of my flesh;
She shall be called woman,
For from man was she taken."
(That is why a man leaves his father 24
and mother, and clings to his wife, so
that they form one flesh.)
Both of them were naked, the man 25
and his wife, but they felt no shame.
Now the serpent was the most clever **3**
of all the wild beasts that the LORD
God had made.
"And so God has said that you are
not to eat from any tree of the garden?"
he said to the woman.
"From the fruit of the trees of the 2
garden we may eat," the woman said to
the serpent; "it is only concerning the 3
fruit of the tree which is in the middle
of the garden that God has said, 'You

may not eat any of it, nor touch it, lest
you die.' "
4 But the serpent said to the woman,
5 "You would not die at all; for God
knows that the very day you eat of it,
your eyes will be opened, and you will
be like gods who know good from evil."
6 So when the woman realized that the
tree was good for food and attractive to
the eye, and further, that the tree was
desirable for its gift of wisdom, she took
some of its fruit, and ate it; she also
gave some to her husband with her, and
7 he ate. Then the eyes of both of them
were opened, and they realized that
they were naked; so they sewed fig-
leaves together, and made themselves
8 girdles. But when they heard the sound
of the LORD God taking a walk in the
garden for the breezes of the day, the
man and his wife hid themselves from
the LORD God among the trees of the
9 garden. The LORD God called to the
man.

"Where are you?" he said to him.

10 "I heard the sound of thee in the garden," he replied, "and I was afraid, because I was naked; so I hid myself."

11 "Who told you that you were naked?" he said. "Have you eaten from the tree from which I commanded you not to eat?"

12 The man said,

"The woman whom thou didst set at my side, it was she who gave me fruit from the tree; so I ate it."

13 Then the LORD God said to the woman,

"What ever have you done?"

The woman said,

"It was the serpent that misled me, and so I ate it."

14 So the LORD God said to the serpent,

"Because you have done this,
The most cursed of all animals shall you be,
And of all wild beasts.
On your belly you shall crawl, and eat dust,
As long as you live.
15 I will put enmity between you and the woman,
And between your posterity and hers;
They shall attack you in the head,
And you shall attack them in the heel."

16 To the woman he said,

"I will make your pain at child-birth very great;
In pain shall you bear children;
And yet you shall be devoted to your husband,
While he shall rule over you."

And to the man he said, 17

"Because you followed your wife's suggestions, and ate from the tree from which I commanded you not to eat,
Cursed shall be the ground through you,
In suffering shall you gain your living from it as long as you live;
Thorns and thistles shall it produce for you, 18
So that you will have to eat wild plants.
By the sweat of your brow shall you earn your living, 19
Until you return to the ground,
Since it was from it that you were taken;
For dust you are,
And to dust you must return."

The man called his wife's name Eve 20
[mother], because she was the mother
of all living beings.

The LORD God made skin tunics for 21
the man and his wife, and clothed
them.

Then the LORD God said, 22

"See, the man has become like one of us, in knowing good from evil; and now, suppose he were to reach out his hand and take the fruit of the tree of life also, and eating it, live forever!"

So the LORD God expelled him from 23
the garden of Eden, to till the ground
from which he had been taken; he 24
drove the man out, and stationed the
cherubim east of the garden of Eden,
with the flaming, whirling sword to
guard the way to the tree of life.

THE EARLY DESCENDANTS OF ADAM, 4:1—5:32

The man had intercourse with his 4
wife Eve; so she conceived and bore
Cain. Then she said,

"I have won back my husband; the LORD is with me!"

Later she bore his brother, Abel. 2
Abel was a shepherd, while Cain was a
tiller of the soil.

In the course of time Cain brought 3
some produce of the soil as an offering
to the LORD, while Abel on his part 4
brought some firstlings from his flock,

that is, some fat pieces from them. The
LORD took notice of Abel and his offer-
5 ing; but of Cain and his offering he took
no notice. So Cain became very angry
6 and downcast. Then the LORD said to
Cain,
7 "Why are you angry, and why are
you downcast? If you have been doing
right, should you not be happy? But if
you have not, sin will be lurking at the
door. And yet he is devoted to you,
while you rule over him."
8 Then Cain said to his brother Abel,
"Let us go off into the country."
When they were out in the country,
Cain attacked his brother Abel, and
murdered him.
9 Then the LORD said to Cain,
"Where is your brother Abel?"
"I do not know," he said. "Am I my
brother's keeper?"
10 Whereupon he said,
"What have you done? Hark, your
brother's blood is crying to me from the
11 ground! And now, cursed shall you be
in banishment from the soil which has
opened its mouth to receive your
brother's blood from your hand.
12 Though you were to till the soil, never
again would it yield you its full produce;
a vagrant and vagabond shall you be on
the earth."
13 Cain said to the LORD,
14 "My punishment is too great to bear.
Seeing that thou hast today driven me
off the soil, I must remain hidden from
thee; I must be a vagrant and a vagabond in the earth, and then anyone
who comes across me will kill me."
15 So the LORD said to him,
"In that case, sevenfold vengeance
shall be taken on anyone who kills Cain."
Then the LORD prescribed a mark
for Cain, to prevent anyone who
chanced upon him from hurting him.
16 So Cain left the presence of the LORD,
and settled in the land of Nod, east of
Eden.
17 Cain had intercourse with his wife;
so she conceived and bore Enoch. Then
he became the builder of a city, and
named the city after his son, Enoch.
18 To Enoch was born Irad; and Irad was
the father of Mehujael. Mehujael was
the father of Methushael, and Methu-
19 shael of Lamech. Lamech married two
wives, the name of one being Adah, and
20 the name of the other Zillah. Adah
bore Jabal, who was the ancestor of
those who live in tents as shepherds;
his brother's name was Jubal, who was 21
the ancestor of all who play the lyre and
pipe. Zillah in turn bore Tubal-cain, 22
the forger of bronze and iron utensils;
and the sister of Tubal-cain was Naamah.
Lamech said to his wives, 23
"Adah and Zillah, hear my voice,
You wives of Lamech, give ear to my
words:
I kill a man for wounding me,
And a boy for striking me.
If Cain is to be avenged sevenfold, 24
Then Lamech seventy and sevenfold!"
Adam again had intercourse with his 25
wife, who bore a son, and called his
name Seth, saying,
"God has given me another child in
place of Abel; since Cain slew him."
Seth in turn had a son born to him, 26
and called his name Enosh. It was then
that men began to call upon the name
of the LORD.

The following is the list of Adam's 5
descendants.
When God created man, it was in the
likeness of God that he made him; both 2
male and female he created; he blessed
them, and at the time of their creation
he called them man.
After living one hundred and thirty 3
years Adam had a child born to him in
his own likeness, resembling himself,
and he called his name Seth. Adam 4
lived eight hundred years after the
birth of Seth, and was the father of
other sons and daughters. Thus Adam 5
lived altogether nine hundred and thirty years; and then he died.
After living one hundred and five 6
years Seth became the father of Enosh;
Seth lived eight hundred and seven 7
years after the birth of Enosh, and was
the father of other sons and daughters.
Thus Seth lived altogether nine hun- 8
dred and twelve years; and then he
died.
After living ninety years Enosh be- 9
came the father of Kenan; Enosh lived 10
eight hundred and fifteen years after
the birth of Kenan, and was the father
of other sons and daughters. Thus 11
Enosh lived altogether nine hundred
and five years; and then he died.
After living seventy years Kenan be- 12
came the father of Mahalalel; Kenan 13
lived eight hundred and forty years

after the birth of Mahalalel, and was
the father of other sons and daughters.
14 Thus Kenan lived altogether nine hundred and ten years; and then he died.
15 After living sixty-five years Mahala-
16 lel became the father of Jared; Mahalalel lived eight hundred and thirty years after the birth of Jared, and was the father of other sons and daughters.
17 Thus Mahalalel lived altogether eight hundred and ninety-five years; and then he died.
18 After living one hundred and sixty-two years Jared became the father of
19 Enoch; Jared lived eight hundred years after the birth of Enoch, and was the father of other sons and daughters.
20 Thus Jared lived altogether nine hundred and sixty-two years; and then he died.
21 After living sixty-five years Enoch became the father of Methuselah;
22 Enoch walked with God for three hundred years after the birth of Methuselah, and was the father of other sons
23 and daughters. Thus Enoch lived altogether three hundred and sixty-five
24 years. Enoch walked with God, and then he disappeared; for God took him away.
25 After living one hundred and eighty-seven years Methuselah became the
26 father of Lamech; Methuselah lived seven hundred and eighty-two years after the birth of Lamech, and was the father of other sons and daughters.
27 Thus Methuselah lived altogether nine hundred and sixty-nine years; and then he died.
28 After living one hundred and eighty-two years Lamech had a son born to
29 him, and called his name Noah, saying,

"This is the one, after our work and the labor of our hands, to bring us consolation from the very soil which the LORD cursed."

30 Lamech lived five hundred and ninety-five years after the birth of Noah, and was the father of other sons and
31 daughters. Thus Lamech lived altogether seven hundred and seventy-seven years; and then he died.
32 After Noah had become five hundred years old, he became the father of Shem, Ham, and Japheth.

THE ORIGIN OF THE GIANTS, 6:1–4

6 Presently when men began to grow numerous over the earth, and had
daughters born to them, the sons of the 2
gods noticed that the daughters of men were attractive; so they married those
whom they liked best. Then the LORD 3
said,

"My spirit must not remain in man forever, inasmuch as he is flesh. Accordingly, his lifetime shall be one hundred and twenty years."

In those days, as well as afterward, 4
there were giants on the earth, who were born to the sons of the gods whenever they had intercourse with the daughters of men; these were the heroes who were men of note in days of old.

THE STORY OF THE FLOOD, 6:5—9:17

When the LORD saw that the wicked- 5
ness of man on the earth was great, and that the whole bent of his thinking was
never anything but evil, the LORD re- 6
gretted that he had ever made man on the earth, and he was grieved to the
heart. So the LORD said, 7

"I will blot the men that I have created off the face of the ground, both men and animals, reptiles, and birds of the air; for I regret that I ever made them."

Noah, however, had found favor 8
with the LORD.

The following are the descendants of 9
Noah. Noah alone among his contemporaries was a pious and exceedingly good man; Noah walked with God.
Noah had three sons born to him, 10
Shem, Ham, and Japheth. Now in 11
God's sight, the earth was corrupt; the
earth was full of wrong-doing; God saw 12
that the earth was corrupt; for every mortal on the earth had corrupted his
life. So God said to Noah, 13

"I have resolved on the extermination of all mortals; for the earth is full of wrong-doing through them; I am going to exterminate them from the
earth. Make yourself an ark of olean- 14
der wood; make the ark with cabins, and smear it with bitumen inside and
out. This is how you are to make it: 15
the length of the ark is to be three hundred cubits, its breadth fifty cubits,
and its height thirty cubits; you are to 16
make a roof for the ark, finishing it off on top to the width of a cubit; and the doorway of the ark you are to put in its side; you are to make it with lower, sec-

17 ond, and third decks. I on my part am
about to bring a flood upon the earth,
to destroy every mortal from under the
heavens, who has the breath of life in
him; everything that is on the earth
18 shall perish. But with you I will make
a covenant; you shall enter the ark, accompanied by your sons, your wife, and
19 your sons' wives. Also, of all living
creatures, of all animals, you must have
two of every kind enter the ark, to keep
them alive with you; they are to be a
20 male and a female. Of the various kinds
of birds, the various kinds of animals,
and all the various kinds of reptiles,
two of every kind are to join you, that
21 you may keep them alive. Take also
some of every kind of edible food, and
store it by you, to be food for yourself
and them."

22 Noah did so; he did just as God had
commanded him.

7 The LORD said to Noah,

"Enter the ark, with all your household; for you alone of the present age
2 have I found righteous. Of all clean animals, you are to take seven pairs, a
male with its mate; but of the animals
that are not clean a pair, a male with its
3 mate; likewise, of the birds of the air
seven pairs, a male and a female—to
keep their kind alive all over the earth.
4 For in seven days' time I am going to
make it rain for forty days and nights
on the earth, to blot off the face of the
earth every living thing that I have
made."

5 Noah did just as God had commanded him.

6 Noah was six hundred years old
when the flood came on the earth.

7 Noah, with his sons, his wife, and his
sons' wives, went into the ark to escape
8 the waters of the flood. Of the clean
animals and of those that were not
clean, of the birds, and of all the rep-
9 tiles, a pair of each, a male and a female, joined Noah in the ark, as God
10 had commanded Noah. Then, at the
end of the seven days the waters of the
flood came on the earth.

11 In the six hundredth year of Noah's
life, on the seventeenth day of the second month, on that very day the fountains of the great abyss were all broken
open, and the windows of the heavens
12 were opened. (The rain fell on the earth
13 for forty days and nights.) That same
day Noah, with Shem, Ham, and
Japheth, Noah's sons, and Noah's wife,
and the three wives of his sons accompanying them, went into the ark, to- 14
gether with all the various kinds of wild
beasts, all the various kinds of domestic
animals, all the various kinds of land
reptiles, and all the various kinds of
birds, everything with feathers and
wings; of all creatures in which there
was the breath of life, a pair of each 15
joined Noah in the ark. Those that en- 16
tered were a male and a female of every
kind of animal, as God had commanded
him. Then the LORD shut him in.

The flood continued for forty days 17
upon the earth. The waters mounted,
and lifted the ark so that it rose above
the earth. The waters rose and in- 18
creased greatly on the earth, so that the
ark floated on the surface of the waters.
The waters rose higher and higher on 19
the earth, until the highest mountains
everywhere under the heavens were all
covered. Fifteen cubits above them the 20
waters rose, so that the mountains were
covered. Every creature that moved on 21
the earth perished, including birds, domestic animals, wild beasts, all the land
reptiles, and all mankind. Of all that 22
was on the land, everything in whose
nostrils was the breath of life died; ev- 23
ery living thing was blotted off the face
of the earth, both men and animals and
reptiles and birds; they were blotted
off the earth, so that Noah alone was
left, and those that were with him in
the ark. The waters rose on the earth 24
for one hundred and fifty days.

Then God remembered Noah, and all 8
the wild and domestic animals that
were with him in the ark; so God made
a wind blow over the earth, and the
waters subsided. Likewise, the foun- 2
tains of the abyss and the windows of
the heavens were closed. The rain from
the heavens ceased, and the waters 3
abated steadily from the earth. At the
end of one hundred and fifty days the
waters subsided, so that on the seven- 4
teenth day of the seventh month the
ark grounded on the mountains of
Ararat. The waters subsided steadily 5
until the tenth month; and on the first
day of the tenth month the tops of the
mountains became visible.

At the end of forty days Noah 6
opened the window that he had made
in the ark, and released a raven, which 7
went flying back and forth until the

8 waters had dried off the earth. Then he
released a dove, to see whether the waters had subsided from the surface of
9 the land; but the dove could find no
resting-place for the sole of her foot, so
she came back to him into the ark; for
there was water all over the earth. He
put out his hand, and catching her,
10 drew her into the ark with him. After
waiting another seven days, he again
11 released the dove from the ark; in the
evening the dove came back to him,
and there, in her beak, was a freshly
picked olive leaf! So Noah knew that
the waters had subsided off the earth.
12 After waiting another seven days, he
released the dove, but she never came
13 back to him. By the first day of the
first month of the six hundred and first
year of Noah's life the waters had dried
off the earth. So Noah removed the
covering of the ark and found that the
surface of the ground was quite dry.
14 By the twenty-seventh day of the second month the earth was dry.
15 Then God said to Noah,
16 "Come out of the ark, your wife,
your sons, and your sons' wives accom-
17 panying you; bring out with you every
animal of every sort that is with you,
birds, quadrupeds, and all land reptiles,
that they may breed freely on the
earth, and be fruitful and multiply on
the earth."
18 So Noah came out, his sons, his wife,
and his sons' wives accompanying him.
19 Every animal, every reptile, and every
bird, everything that moves on the
earth came out of the ark by their
species.
20 Then Noah built an altar to the
LORD, and taking some clean animals
and birds of every kind, he offered
them as burnt-offerings on the altar.
21 When the LORD smelled the soothing
odor, the LORD said to himself,
"I will never again curse the soil because of man, though the bent of man's
mind may be evil from his very youth;
nor will I ever again destroy all life, as
22 I have just done. As long as the earth
endures, seedtime and harvest, cold and
heat, summer and winter, day and
night, shall never cease."
9 God blessed Noah and his sons, and
said to them,
2 "Be fruitful, multiply, and fill the
earth. The fear and dread of you shall
be on every wild beast of the earth and
on every bird of the air; as in the case
of all the reptiles on the ground and all
the fish of the sea, they have been delivered into your power. Everything 3
that moves, that is alive, is to be food
for you; as I once gave you the green
plants, I now give you everything.
Only, you must never eat flesh with the 4
life (that is, the blood) in it. For your 5
own life-blood, however, I will require
an account; I will hold every animal accountable for it, and I will hold men
accountable for one another's lives;
whoever sheds the blood of man, by 6
man shall his blood be shed; for God
made man in his own image. As for you 7
then, be fruitful, and multiply; be prolific in the earth and multiply in it."
God then said to Noah and to his 8
sons with him,
"As for me, I do hereby establish my 9
covenant with you and your descendants after you, and with every living 10
creature that is with you, the birds, the
domestic animals, and all the wild
beasts with you, as many of them as
came out of the ark; I establish my 11
covenant with you, that never again
shall all flesh be destroyed by the waters of a flood, and never again shall
there be a flood to ravage the earth."
Further, God said, 12
"This shall be the symbol of the covenant which I am making between myself and you and every living creature
that is with you, to endless generations:
I put my rainbow in the clouds, and it 13
shall be a symbol of the covenant between myself and the world. Whenever 14
I bring clouds over the earth, the rainbow will appear in the clouds, and then 15
I will remember my covenant, which
obtains between myself and you and
every living creature of every sort, and
the waters shall never again become a
flood to destroy all flesh. When the 16
rainbow appears in the clouds, I will
see it, and remember the everlasting
covenant between God and every living creature of every sort that is on the
earth."
God said to Noah, 17
"This shall be the symbol of the covenant which I am making between myself and all flesh that is on the earth."

Symbol of Covenant

THE CURSE OF CANAAN, 9:18–29

18 The sons of Noah who came out of
the ark were Shem, Ham, and Japheth;
and Ham was the father of Canaan.
19 These three were the sons of Noah, and
from them sprang the whole world.
20 Now Noah was the first farmer to plant
21 a vineyard. Having drunk some of the
wine, he became intoxicated, and lay
22 uncovered in his tent. When Ham, the
father of Canaan, saw his father lying
naked, he told his two brothers outside;
23 whereupon Shem and Japheth took a
robe, which they put on their shoulders,
and walking backward, they covered up
their father's nakedness, their faces being turned away so that they could not
24 see their father's nakedness. When
Noah awoke from his wine, and learned
what his youngest son had done to him,
25 he said,

"Cursed be Canaan!
The meanest of slaves shall he be to
his brothers."

26 Also he said,

"Blessed of the LORD my God may
Shem be;
And let Canaan be his slave!
27 May God expand Japheth, and dwell
in the tents of Shem;
But let Canaan be his slave!"

28 Noah lived three hundred and fifty
29 years after the flood; thus Noah lived
altogether nine hundred and fifty years,
and then he died.

THE TABLE OF NATIONS, 10:1–32

10 The following are the descendants of
Noah's sons, Shem, Ham, and Japheth,
who were born to them after the flood.
2 The descendants of Japheth were
Gomer, Magog, Madai, Javan, Tubal,
3 Meshech, and Tiras. The descendants
of Gomer were Ashkenaz, Riphath, and
4 Togarmah. The descendants of Javan
were Elishah, Tarshish, Kittim, and
Rodanim. It was from these that the
coast-lands of the nations were popu-
lated, country by country, each with
its respective language, according to
the various clans, nation by nation.
6 The descendants of Ham were Cush,
Egypt, Put, and Canaan. The descendants of Cush were Seba, Havilah, Sab-
tah, Raamah, and Sabteca. The de- 7
scendants of Raamah were Sheba and
Dedan. Cush was the father of Nim- 8
rod, who was the first person on the
earth to be a despot. He was a mighty 9
hunter in the sight of the LORD; hence
the saying, "As mighty a hunter in the
sight of the LORD as Nimrod." The 10
nucleus of his kingdom was Babylon,
Erech, and Accad, all of them in the
land of Shinar; from that region he 11
pushed out into Assyria, and built Nine- 12
veh, Rehoboth-ir, Calah, and Resen,
the large city lying between Nineveh
and Calah. Egypt was the father of Lu- 13
dim, Anamim, Lehabim, Naphtuhim,
Pathrusim, Casluhim, and Caphtorim, 14
from whom the Philistines sprang.
Canaan was the father of Sidon, his 15
first-born, and then of Heth—also the 16
Jebusites, the Amorites, the Girgashites, the Hivites, the Arkites, the 17
Sinites, the Arvadites, the Zemarites, 18
and the Hamathites. Later the Canaanite clans scattered, until the territory of 19
the Canaanites extended from Sidon in
the direction of Gerar, as far as Gaza,
and in the direction of Sodom, Gomorrah, Admah, and Zeboiim, as far as
Lasha. These were the descendants of 20
Ham, by clans and languages, country
by country, nation by nation.
Children were also born to Shem, the 21
ancestor of all the Hebrews, and the
older brother of Japheth. The sons of 22
Shem were Elam, Assyria, Arpachshad,
Lud, and Aram. The sons of Aram 23
were Uz, Hul, Gether, and Mash. Ar- 24
pachshad was the father of Shelah, and
Shelah of Eber. To Eber were born two 25
sons, the name of the one being Peleg
[division] (for in his time the world was
divided), and the name of his brother
Joktan. Joktan was the father of Al- 26
modad, Sheleph, Hazarmaveth, Jerah, 27
Hadoram, Uzal, Diklah, Obal, Abima- 28
el, Sheba, Ophir, Havilah, and Jobab— 29
all these were sons of Joktan, and the 30
region inhabited by them extended
from Mesha in the direction of Sephar,
to the mountains of the East. These 31
were the descendants of Shem, by clans
and languages, country by country, nation by nation.
These were the clans descended from 32
Noah, arranged according to their descendants by nationalities; and from
these the nations of the earth were pop-
ulated after the flood.

THE TOWER OF BABEL, 11:1–9

11 Now the whole earth used only one
2 language, with few words. On the occasion of a migration from the east, men
discovered a plain in the land of Shinar,
3 and settled there. Then they said to
one another,

"Come, let us make bricks, burning
them well."

4 So they used bricks for stone, and
bitumen for mortar. Then they said,

"Come, let us build ourselves a city
with a tower whose top shall reach the
heavens (thus making a name for ourselves), so that we may not be scattered
all over the earth."

5 Then the LORD came down to look
at the city and tower which human be-
6 ings had built. The LORD said,

"They are just one people, and they
all have the same language. If this is
what they can do as a beginning, then
nothing that they resolve to do will be
7 impossible for them. Come, let us go
down, and there make such a babble of
their language that they will not understand one another's speech."

8 Thus the LORD dispersed them from
there all over the earth, so that they
9 had to stop building the city. That was
why its name was called Babel, because
it was there that the LORD made a babble of the language of the whole earth,
and it was from there that the LORD
dispersed them all over the earth.

THE DESCENDANTS OF SHEM, 11:10–26

10 The following are the descendants of
Shem.

When Shem was one hundred years
old, he became the father of Arpach-
11 shad, two years after the flood. Shem
lived five hundred years after the birth
of Arpachshad, and was the father of
other sons and daughters.

12 After living thirty-five years Arpach-
13 shad became the father of Shelah. Arpachshad lived four hundred and three
years after the birth of Shelah, and was
the father of other sons and daughters.

14 After living thirty years Shelah be-
15 came the father of Eber. Shelah lived
four hundred and three years after the
birth of Eber, and was the father of
other sons and daughters.

16 After living thirty-four years Eber
became the father of Peleg. Eber lived 17
four hundred and thirty years after the
birth of Peleg, and was the father of
other sons and daughters.

After living thirty years Peleg be- 18
came the father of Reu. Peleg lived two 19
hundred and nine years after the birth
of Reu, and was the father of other sons
and daughters.

After living thirty-two years Reu be- 20
came the father of Serug. Reu lived 21
two hundred and seven years after the
birth of Serug, and was the father of
other sons and daughters.

After living thirty years Serug be- 22
came the father of Nahor. Serug lived 23
two hundred years after the birth of
Nahor, and was the father of other sons
and daughters.

After living twenty-nine years Nahor 24
became the father of Terah. Nahor 25
lived one hundred and nineteen years
after the birth of Terah, and was the
father of other sons and daughters.

After living seventy years Terah be- 26
came the father of Abram, Nahor, and
Haran.

THE DESCENDANTS OF TERAH, 11:27–32

The following are the descendants of 27
Terah.

Terah was the father of Abram, Na-
hor, and Haran, and Haran of Lot.
Haran died during the lifetime of his 28
father Terah in the land of his birth,
the Chaldean city of Ur. Abram and 29
Nahor both married, the name of
Abram's wife being Sarai, and that of
Nahor's Milcah, the daughter of Har-
an, the father of Milcah and Jiscah.
Sarai was barren; she had no children. 30

Terah took his son Abram, his grand- 31
son Lot, the son of Haran, and his
daughter-in-law Sarai, the wife of his
son Abram, and emigrated with them
from the Chaldean city of Ur, to go to
the land of Canaan. But when they
reached Haran, they settled there. The 32
life time of Terah was two hundred and
five years; then Terah died in Haran.

THE STORY OF ABRAHAM, 12:1—25:18

The LORD said to Abram, 12
"Leave your land, your relatives, and
your father's home, for the land that I

2 will show you; and I will make a great
nation of you; I will bless you, and
make your name so great that it will be
3 used for blessings. I will bless those
who bless you, and anyone who curses
you I will curse; through you shall all
the families of the earth invoke blessings on one another."

4 So Abram departed, as the LORD
had told him, and Lot went with him.
Abram was seventy-five years old when
5 he left Haran. Abram took his wife
Sarai and his nephew Lot, with all the
property that they had accumulated,
and the persons that they had acquired
in Haran, and they started out for the
land of Canaan; and to the land of Canaan they came.

6 Abram traveled through the land as
far as the sanctuary of Shechem at the
terebinth of Moreh, the Canaanites be-
7 ing then in the land. Then the LORD
appeared to Abram, and said,

"To your descendants I am going to
give this land."

So he built an altar there to the
LORD, who had appeared to him.
8 From there he moved on to the hills
east of Bethel, and pitched his tent,
with Bethel on the west and Ai on the
east. There he built an altar to the
LORD, and called upon the name of the
9 LORD. Then Abram set out, continuing on his way to the Negeb.

10 Now there came a famine in the land;
and because the famine was so severe
in the land, Abram went down to
11 Egypt to reside there. When he was on
the point of entering Egypt, he said to
his wife Sarai,

12 "See now, I know that you are such
a beautiful woman that when the Egyptians see you, they will say, 'This is his
wife,' and then they will kill me in order
13 to keep you. Please say that you are
my sister, so that I may be well treated
for your sake, and my life spared
through you."

14 When Abram arrived in Egypt, the
Egyptians saw that the woman was
15 very beautiful. Pharaoh's courtiers also
saw her, and praised her so highly to
Pharaoh that the woman was taken
16 into Pharaoh's household. Abram, too,
was well treated for her sake, and was
the recipient of sheep, cattle, he-asses,
male and female slaves, she-asses, and
camels.

17 The LORD, however, struck Pharaoh
and his household with severe diseases
because of Abram's wife, Sarai. So 18
Pharaoh summoned Abram, and said,

"What a way for you to treat me!
Why did you not tell me that she was
your wife? Why did you say, 'She is 19
my sister,' and let me marry her? Well,
there is your wife; take her and begone!"

Then Pharaoh ordered an escort for 20
him, to see him off, with his wife and all
that belonged to him.

So Abram went up from Egypt to the 13
Negeb, accompanied by his wife and all
that belonged to him, and Lot. Abram 2
was now very rich in cattle, silver, and
gold. From the Negeb he journeyed by 3
stages as far as Bethel, to the place
where his tent had previously been, between Bethel and Ai, to the site of the 4
altar which he had previously erected
there, and where he had called upon the
name of the LORD.

Lot, who accompanied Abram, also 5
had flocks and herds, as well as tents.
The land could not support them both; 6
for their possessions were so great that
they could not live together. Trouble 7
arose accordingly between the herdsmen of Abram's stock and those of
Lot's. (The Canaanites and Perizzites
were living in the land at that time.)

"There simply must be no quarrel 8
between you and me," Abram said to
Lot, "nor between your herdsmen and
mine; for we are kinsmen. The whole 9
land is open to you, is it not? Please
part from me then. If you go to the
left, I will go to the right; or if you go
to the right, I will go to the left."

Then Lot looked out, and saw that 10
the whole basin of the Jordan was well
watered everywhere (this was before
the LORD destroyed Sodom and Gomorrah) like the LORD'S own garden,
like the land of Egypt in the vicinity of
Zoar. So Lot chose the whole Jordan 11
basin. Lot set off eastward, and thus
they parted from each other. Abram 12
settled in the land of Canaan, while
Lot settled in the cities of the basin, extending his tents as far as Sodom.
(Now the men of Sodom were wicked, 13
being great sinners against the LORD.)

After Lot had parted from him, the 14
LORD said to Abram,

"Raise your eyes now, and look out
from the place where you are, north,
south, east, and west; for all the land 15

that you see, I am going to give to you
16 and your descendants for all time. I
am going to make your descendants like
the dust of the earth, so that it will be
as possible to count the dust of the
17 earth as to count your descendants. Go
and travel the length and breadth of
the land; for I am giving it to you."
18 So Abram moved his tent, and went
to live beside the terebinth of Mamre
at Hebron, where he built an altar to
the LORD.

14 It was in the time of Amraphel, king
of Shinar, Arioch, king of Ellasar, Chedorlaomer, king of Elam, and Tidal,
2 king of Goiim, that war was made by
them with Bera, king of Sodom, Birsha,
king of Gomorrah, Shinab, king of Admah, Shemeber, king of Zeboiim, and
3 the king of Bela (that is, Zoar), all of
whom had gathered in alliance at the
valley of Siddim (that is, the Salt Sea).
4 For twelve years they had been subject
to Chedorlaomer, but in the thirteenth
5 year they revolted. So in the fourteenth year there came Chedorlaomer
and his confederate kings. They
crushed the Rephaim at Ashteroth
and Karnaim, then the Zuzim at Ham,
the Emim at Shaveh and Kirjathaim,
6 and the Horites in the highlands of
Seir, penetrating as far as Elparan,
7 which is close to the desert. Retracing
their steps, they reached En-mishpat
(that is, Kadesh), and ravaged all the
country of the Amalekites, and likewise
that of the Amorites who were living at
8 Hazazon-tamar. Thereupon the king
of Sodom marched forth, along with
the king of Gomorrah, the king of Admah, the king of Zeboiim, and the king
of Bela (that is, Zoar). They drew up
in battle array against them in the val-
9 ley of Siddim, against Chedorlaomer,
king of Elam, Tidal, king of Goiim,
Amraphel, king of Shinar, and Arioch,
king of Ellasar—four kings against
10 the five. The valley of Siddim was
so full of bitumen wells that on the
flight of the kings of Sodom and Gomorrah some fell into them, but the sur-
11 vivors fled to the hills. The victors captured all the goods and provisions of
Sodom and Gomorrah, and then made
12 off. They also carried off Lot, the nephew of Abram, and his goods, since he
was living in Sodom.
13 A fugitive came and told Abram, the
Hebrew. who was living beside the terebinth of Mamre, the Amorite, a kinsman of Eshcol and Aner, who were allies of Abram. When Abram heard that 14
his kinsman had been taken prisoner,
he called out his retainers, his household slaves, to the number of three hundred and eighteen, and went in pursuit
as far as Dan. With his slaves he fell 15
upon them at night, and defeated them.
After pursuing them as far as Hobah,
which is north of Damascus, he recov- 16
ered all the goods; he also recovered his
kinsman Lot and his goods, together
with the women and the rest of the
people.
On his return from the defeat of 17
Chedorlaomer and his confederate
kings, the king of Sodom came out to
the valley of Shaveh (that is, the king's
valley) to meet him, while Melchizedek, 18
king of Salem, brought out bread and
wine, and, as priest of God Most High,
blessed him, saying, 19

"Blessed be Abram by God Most High,
The creator of the heavens and the
earth!
And blessed be God Most High, 20
Who delivered your foes into your
power!"

Thereupon he gave him a portion of
everything.
The king of Sodom said to Abram, 21
"Give me the people, but keep the
goods yourself."
But Abram said to the king of So- 22
dom,
"I have sworn by uplifted hand to
the LORD, God Most High, the creator
of the heavens and the earth, that I 23
would not take anything that belongs
to you, not even so much as a thread or
a sandal-lace, lest you should say, 'It 24
was I who made Abram rich.' Apart
from what my servants have eaten, let
the men who accompanied me, Aner,
Eshcol, and Mamre, take their share."
After these events the word of the 15
LORD came to Abram in a vision,
"Do not be afraid, Abram; I am your
shield; your reward shall be very
great."
But Abram said, 2
"O Lord GOD, what canst thou give
me, seeing that I am childless, and that
my heir is a Damascene, Eliezer?"
"Since you have given me no poster- 3
ity, my household slave will be my
heir," said Abram.

4 But there came to him this message
from the LORD,
"No such person is to be your heir,
but one born of your own body is to be
your heir."
5 Then he took him outside, and said,
"Now look at the sky, and count the
stars if you can." "So shall be your descendants," he said to him.
6 And he trusted the LORD, who
7 counted it to his credit, and said to
him,
"I am the LORD, who brought you
out of the Chaldean city of Ur to give
you possession of this land."
8 But he said,
"O Lord GOD, how am I to know
that I shall possess it?"
9 So he said to him,
"Procure a three-year-old heifer, a
three-year-old she-goat, a three-year-
old he-goat, a dove, and a young
pigeon."
10 Procuring all these, he cut them in
two—but not the birds—and placed the
11 pieces opposite each other. The birds
of prey swooped down on the carcasses,
12 but Abram drove them off. Then, as
the sun was going down, a trance fell
on Abram; indeed a great and awful
13 gloom fell upon him. Then the LORD
said to Abram,
"Know of a surety that your descendants shall be immigrants in a land
not their own, where they shall be
slaves, and be oppressed for four hun-
14 dred years; but I will in turn bring
judgment upon the nation that made
slaves of them, after which they shall
15 escape with great wealth. (As for yourself, you shall join your fathers in
peace, and be buried at a ripe old age.)
16 It will only be in the fourth generation,
however, that they will return here; for
the guilt of the Amorites is not yet
complete."
17 When the sun had set and it was
quite dark, there appeared a smoking
fire-pot and a blazing torch that passed
18 between the pieces. That day the
LORD made a covenant with Abram,
saying,
"To your descendants I give this
land, from the River of Egypt as far as
the Great River, the river Euphrates—
19 that of the Kenites, Kenizzites, Kad-
20 monites, Hittites, Perizzites, Rephaim,
21 Amorites, Canaanites, Girgashites, and
Jebusites."

Abram's wife Sarai had borne him no 16
children, but she had an Egyptian maid
whose name was Hagar. So Sarai said 2
to Abram,
"Seeing now that the LORD has prevented me from having children, suppose you marry my maid; I might perhaps build up a family through her."
Abram agreed to the suggestion of 3
Sarai; so Abram's wife Sarai took Hagar, her Egyptian maid (it was after
Abram had been living in the land of
Canaan for ten years), and gave her in
marriage to her husband Abram. He 4
had intercourse with Hagar, and she
conceived. When she found that she
had conceived, she looked with disdain
upon her mistress. So Sarai said to 5
Abram,
"May the wrong done me fall on you!
It was I who put my maid in your arms,
but when she found that she had conceived, she looked with disdain upon
me. May the LORD judge between you
and me!"
"Your maid is in your power," 6
Abram said to Sarai; "do what you like
with her."
Then Sarai treated her so cruelly
that she ran away from her. But the 7
angel of the LORD came upon her beside a spring in the desert (the spring
on the road to Shur), and said, 8
"Hagar, maid of Sarai, where have
you come from, and where are you going?"
"I am running away from my mistress Sarai," she said.
The angel of the LORD said to her, 9
"Return to your mistress, and submit to her authority."
Further, the angel of the LORD said 10
to her,
"I will make your descendants so numerous that they will be too many to
count."
The angel of the LORD also said to 11
her,
"You are with child, and are going to
bear a son; you are to call his name
Ishmael [God heard], because the
LORD has heard of your ill-treatment.
He shall be a wild-ass of a man, with his 12
hand against everyone, and everyone's
hand against him; he shall live on the
outskirts of all his kindred."
So she named the LORD who spoke 13
to her El-roi [a God who can be seen].
"For," said she, "I have actually

seen God, and am still alive after seeing him."
14 That was how the spring came to be
called Beer-lahai-roi [the spring where
one saw (God) and still lived]; it is between Kadesh and Bered.
15 So Hagar bore a son to Abram, and
Abram gave the name of Ishmael to his
16 son, whom Hagar bore. Abram was
eighty-six years old when Hagar bore
Ishmael to him.
17 When Abram was ninety-nine years
old, the LORD appeared to Abram, and
said to him,
"I am God Almighty; conduct your-
2 self before me so as to be blameless, and
then I will establish my covenant between you and me, and will make you
grow more and more numerous."
3 Thereupon Abram fell on his face;
and God said to him,
4 "This is my covenant with you: you
shall be the ancestor of a company of
5 nations. Accordingly, your name shall
no longer be called Abram, but your
name shall be Abraham; for I am making you the ancestor of a company of
6 nations. I will make you more and
more prolific, and will make nations of
you, and kings shall spring from you.
7 I am establishing my covenant between myself and you and your descendants after you throughout their
generations as a perpetual covenant, to
be God to you and your descendants.
8 I will give you and your descendants
after you the land in which you are now
only an immigrant, the whole of the
land of Canaan, as a possession for all
time, and I will be their God."
9 Further, God said to Abraham,
"You on your part must keep my
covenant, and likewise your descendants after you throughout their genera-
10 tions. The covenant between myself
and you and your descendants after
you which you are to keep is this:
everyone of your males must be circum-
11 cized; you are to be circumcised in your
foreskin, and this shall be the symbol
of the covenant between you and me.
12 At the age of eight days, every male
among you, from generation to generation, must be circumcised, as well as the
slaves born in the house or purchased
from any foreigner who is not of your
13 race—slaves, whether born in your
house or purchased by you, are to be
circumcised. Thus shall my covenant
stand imprinted on your flesh as a perpetual covenant. If there is an uncir- 14
cumcised male, one who has not been
circumcised in the foreskin, that person
must be cut off from his people, in that
he has broken my covenant."
God also said to Abraham, 15
"As for your wife Sarai, you are not
to call her Sarai, but Sarah. I will 16
bless her, and furthermore, I will give
you a son by her; I will bless her, so
that she shall become the mother of nations, with kings of peoples coming
from her."
Then Abraham fell on his face and 17
laughed, saying to himself,
"Can he who is one hundred years
old become a father, or can Sarah at the
age of ninety bear a child?"
So Abraham said to God, 18
"May Ishmael live in thy favor!"
But God said, 19
"No, it is a fact; your wife Sarah is to
bear you a son, and you are to call his
name Isaac [laughter]; I will establish
my covenant with him as a perpetual
covenant for his descendants after him.
With reference to Ishmael, I have heard 20
you, and will indeed bless him; I will
make him prolific, and will make him
grow more and more numerous; he shall
be the ancestor of twelve princes; I will
make a great nation of him. I will like- 21
wise establish my covenant with Isaac,
whom Sarah shall bear to you at this
time next year."
Having finished speaking with him, 22
God left Abraham.
Then Abraham took his son Ishmael 23
and all the slaves born in his house and
all those purchased by him—every
male in Abraham's household—and
circumcised them in the foreskin that
very same day, as God had commanded
him. Abraham himself was ninety-nine 24
years old when he was circumcised in
the foreskin, while his son Ishmael was 25
thirteen when he was circumcised.
That very day was Abraham circum- 26
cised, as well as his son Ishmael; and all 27
the men of his household, the slaves
born in the house and those purchased
from foreigners, were circumcised with
him.
The LORD appeared to him at the **18**
terebinth of Mamre, as he was sitting
at the doorway of his tent in the heat of
the day. Raising his eyes, he saw three 2
men standing near him. On seeing

them, he ran from the door of his tent
to meet them, and bowing to the earth,
3 said,
"O sirs, if perchance I find favor
with you, please do not pass by without
4 stopping with your servant. Let a little
water be brought to wash your feet, and
stretch yourselves out under the tree,
5 while I fetch a bit of food that you may
refresh yourselves. Afterward you may
proceed on your way, since you will
then have paid your servant a visit."
"Do as you propose," they said.
6 So Abraham hurried into the tent to
Sarah, and said,
"Quick, three seahs of the best flour!
Knead it, and make it into cakes."
7 Abraham then ran to the herd, and
picked out a bullock, tender and plump,
which he gave to a servant, who quick-
8 ly prepared it. Then, taking curds and
milk and the bullock that he had prepared, he set them before them, and as
he waited on them under the tree, they
ate.
9 "Where is your wife Sarah?" they
said to him.
"Inside the tent there," said he.
10 Then he said,
"I will come back to you at the time
for life to appear, when your wife Sarah
shall have a son."
11 Now Sarah was behind the door of
the tent listening. Since both Abraham
and Sarah were old, being well advanced in life, and woman's periods had
12 ceased with Sarah, Sarah laughed to
herself, saying,
"Now that I am worn out and my
husband old, can there be marriage
pleasure for me?"
13 The LORD said to Abraham,
"Why is it that Sarah laughs, saying,
'Can I really bear a child when I am so
14 old?' Is anything too wonderful for the
LORD? I will come back to you at the
appointed time, at the time for life to
appear, and Sarah shall have a son."
15 Because she was afraid, Sarah denied
it, saying,
"I did not laugh."
"No, but you did laugh," he said.
16 Setting out from there, the men directed their steps toward Sodom, while
Abraham went with them to see them
17 off. Then the LORD thought,
"Shall I hide what I am about to do
18 from Abraham, seeing that Abraham is
bound to become a great and powerful
nation, and through him all the nations
of the earth will invoke blessings on one
another? No, I will make it known to 19
him, in order that he may give instructions to his sons and his family after
him to keep to the way of the LORD by
doing what is good and right, so that
the LORD may fulfil for Abraham what
he promised him."
So the LORD said, 20
"Because the outcry against Sodom
and Gomorrah is great, and their sin
very grave, I must go down and see 21
whether or not their conduct entirely
answers to the outcry against them
that has reached me; I would know."
So the men departed from there, and 22
went off to Sodom, while the LORD remained standing before Abraham.
Abraham then went up to him, and 23
said,
"Wilt thou really sweep away good
along with bad? Suppose there are fifty 24
good men in the city, wilt thou really
sweep it away, and not spare the place
for the sake of the fifty good men that
are in it? Far be it from thee to do such 25
a thing as this, to make the good perish
with the bad, so that good and bad fare
alike! Far be it from thee! Shall not
the judge of the whole earth himself act
justly?"
So the LORD said, 26
"If I find in Sodom fifty good men,
within the city, I will spare the whole
place for their sake."
Abraham rejoined, 27
"Here I am venturing to speak to the
LORD, and I mere dust and ashes! Sup- 28
pose there are five short of the fifty
good men; wouldst thou destroy the
whole city by reason of the five?"
"I will not destroy it, if I find forty-
five there," he replied.
Once more he said to him, 29
"Suppose only forty are to be found
there?"
"I will not do it for the sake of the
forty," he replied.
Then he said, 30
"Pray, let not my Lord be angry if
I should say: suppose only thirty are
to be found there?"
"I will not do it, if I find thirty
there," he said.
"Here I am venturing to speak to the 31
LORD; suppose only twenty are to be
found there?" he said.

"I will not destroy it for the sake of
the twenty," he said.
32 Then he said.
"Pray. let not my Lord be angry if I
should speak just once more; suppose
only ten are to be found there?"
"I will not destroy it for the sake of
the ten," he said.
33 As soon as he finished speaking to
Abraham, the LORD went away, while
Abraham returned home.
19 The two angels arrived at Sodom in
the evening while Lot was sitting at the
gate of Sodom. When Lot saw them,
he rose to greet them, bowing his face
2 to the ground, and saying,
"If you please, sirs, come over to
your servant's house to pass the night
and wash your feet; in the morning you
may rise early, and go on your way."
But they said,
"No, we will pass the night in the
open."
3 He pressed them so strongly, however, that they went over to his home
and entered his house, where he prepared a feast for them, and baked un-
4 leavened cakes for them to eat. Before
they lay down, the townsmen, the men
of Sodom, from the youngest to the
oldest, all the people to the last man,
5 surrounded the house, and shouted to
Lot,
"Where are the men who came to
your house tonight? Bring them out to
us that we may have intercourse with
them."
6 Then Lot went out to the doorway to
them, and shutting the door after him,
7 said,
"Please, my friends, do not be so de-
8 praved. See, I have two daughters who
have never had intercourse with a man;
let me bring them out to you to do
what you like with them; only do nothing to these men, inasmuch as they
have come under the shelter of my
roof."
9 But they said,
"Get out of the way!"
"This fellow came in as an immigrant," they said, "and now he would
make himself a judge! Here, we will
treat you worse than them!"
Then they pressed hard against the
man, Lot, and tried to reach the door to
10 break it in; but the men reached out
their hands, and pulling Lot into the
11 house with them, shut the door; while
those who were at the entrance to the
house, from the least to the greatest,
they struck with blindness, so that they
searched in vain for the entrance. Then 12
the men said to Lot,
"If there is anyone else belonging to
you here, sons-in-law, sons, daughters,
or anyone at all that belongs to you in
the city, take them out of the place; for 13
we are about to destroy this place, because the outcry against it that has
come to the LORD is so great that the
LORD has sent us to destroy it."
So Lot went out, and said to his sons- 14
in-law who had married his daughters,
"Leave this place at once; for the
LORD is about to destroy the city."
But his sons-in-law thought that he
was jesting.
When dawn appeared, the angels 15
urged Lot on, saying,
"Bestir yourself; take away your wife
and the two daughters that are at hand,
lest you be swept away in the punishment of the city."
When he hesitated, the men, because 16
of the LORD'S pity on him, seized his
hand and those of his wife and two
daughters, and bringing him out, they
left him outside the city. After they 17
had brought them outside, they said,
"Fly for your life; do not look behind
you, nor stop anywhere in the valley;
fly to the hills, lest you be swept away."
Lot said to them, 18
"O no, sirs! Your servant has indeed 19
found favor with you, and great is the
kindness that you have done me in
saving my life, but I cannot possibly
fly to the hills, lest the disaster overtake me and I perish. Here is this town 20
near enough to fly to, and quite small;
pray, let me fly there (is it not small?)
to save my life."
The LORD said to him, 21
"See, I grant you this request as well,
in that I will not overthrow the town
of which you speak. Hurry and fly 22
there; for I can do nothing until you
reach there."
Thus the name of the town came to
be called Zoar [small].
Just as the sun rose over the earth 23
and Lot entered Zoar, the LORD rained 24
sulphur and fire from the sky on Sodom
and Gomorrah, devastating those cities 25
and all the valley, with all the inhabitants of the cities and the vegetation on

26 the land. And Lot's wife had looked
back, and had become a pillar of salt.
27 Next morning when Abraham went
early to the place where he had stood
28 before the LORD, he gazed toward
Sodom and Gomorrah, and all the region of the valley, and saw smoke from
the land rising like smoke from a kiln.
29 Thus it was that God remembered
Abraham when he destroyed the cities
of the valley, by sending Lot away from
the catastrophe when he devastated the
cities where Lot lived.
30 Accompanied by his two daughters,
Lot left Zoar to go up and live in the
hills; for he was afraid to live in Zoar;
and he lived in a cave with his two
31 daughters. The older one said to the
younger,
"Since our father is old, and there is
no one in the land to marry us, as is
32 customary for all the earth, come, let
us make our father drunk with wine,
and then lie with him, and so preserve
our race through our father."
33 So that night they made their father
drunk with wine, and the older one
went in and lay with her father, but he
was unaware of her lying down or get-
34 ting up. Next morning the older said
to the younger,
"I lay with my father last night: let
us make him drunk with wine again
tonight, and then you go in and lie with
him, so that we may preserve our race
through our father."
35 So that night too they made their
father drunk with wine, and the younger went and lay with him, but he was
unaware of her lying down or getting
36 up. Thus the two daughters of Lot
37 were with child by their father. The
older bore a son, and called his name
Moab (he is the ancestor of the present-
38 day Moabites). The younger also bore
a son, and called his name Ben-ammi
(he is the ancestor of the present-day
Ammonites).
20 From there Abraham set out for the
region of the Negeb, and settling between Kadesh and Shur, he established
2 himself as an immigrant at Gerar. Since
Abraham had said of his wife Sarah,
"She is my sister," Abimelech, king of
3 Gerar, had sent and taken Sarah; but
God came to Abimelech in a dream by
night, and said to him,
"You are going to die because of the
woman whom you have taken, since
she is married."
Now Abimelech had not approached 4
her, so he said,
"O Lord, wilt thou slay one who is
clearly innocent? Did he not himself 5
say to me, 'She is my sister,' while she
herself said, 'He is my brother'? In purity of heart and innocence of hand have
I done this."
Then God said to him in the dream, 6
"I do indeed know that it was in purity of heart that you did this; and furthermore, it was I who kept you from
sinning against me. That is why I did
not let you touch her. Now then, re- 7
store the man's wife, and so save your
life; for he is a prophet, and will intercede for you. But if you do not restore
her, be assured that you and all who belong to you shall die."
So next morning Abimelech rose 8
early, and summoning all his slaves, he
recounted all these words to them, so
that the men were much terrified.
Abimelech then summoned Abraham, 9
and said to him,
"What have you done to us? What
harm have I done to you that you
should bring such a great sin on me and
my kingdom? You have done to me
things that should not be done."
"What ever possessed you to do 10
this?" Abimelech said to Abraham.
Abraham said, 11
"I simply thought that, since there
was no reverence for God in this place,
I should be slain for the sake of my
wife. Besides, she really was my sister 12
when I married her, being the daughter
of my father, but not of my mother.
Accordingly, when God sent me wan- 13
dering from my father's home, I said
to her, 'This is the kindness that you
must do me: at every place to which
we come, say of me, "He is my brother."'"
Thereupon Abimelech took sheep, 14
oxen, and male and female slaves, and
gave them to Abraham, and restored
his wife Sarah to him.
"My country is at your disposal," 15
said Abimelech; "settle wherever you
like."
To Sarah he said, 16
"See, I have given your brother a
thousand shekels of silver; it shall com-
pensate you for all that has befallen

you, and you yourself shall be completely exonerated."
17 Then Abraham prayed to God, and
God cured Abimelech, as well as his
wife and female slaves, so that they
18 could bear children; for the LORD had
completely closed the wombs of all in
Abimelech's household on account of
Sarah, Abraham's wife.
21 The LORD dealt with Sarah, as he
had said; the LORD did to Sarah as he
2 had promised. Sarah conceived, and at
the time that God had indicated she
bore Abraham a son in his old age.
3 Abraham gave the name of Isaac to his
son that had been born to him, whom
4 Sarah bore him; and as God had commanded him, Abraham circumcised his
son Isaac when he was eight days old,
5 Abraham himself being one hundred
years old when his son Isaac was born
to him.
6 "God has made me a laughing-stock;
everyone that hears of it will laugh at
7 me," Sarah said. "Who ever would
have ventured to tell Abraham," she
added, "that Sarah would be giving
suck to children? And yet I have borne
him a son in his old age!"
8 So the child grew and was weaned;
and on the day that Isaac was weaned
9 Abraham held a great feast. But Sarah
noticed the son of Hagar, the Egyptian,
whom she had borne to Abraham, play-
10 ing with her son Isaac; so she said to
Abraham,
"Get rid of this slave-girl and her
son; for this slave-girl's son must not
share the inheritance with my son
Isaac."
11 The proposal, however, was very displeasing to Abraham, for his son's sake;
12 but God said to Abraham,
"Do not be distressed for the boy
and your slave; follow Sarah's bidding
in all that she tells you; for it is
through Isaac that you are to have de-
13 scendants bearing your name. As for
the slave-girl's son, I will make a nation of him too, because he is your
child."
14 So next morning Abraham rose early,
and taking some bread and a skin of
water, he gave them to Hagar, along
with her son, and putting them on her
shoulder, he sent her away. So she departed, and wandered about in the des-
15 ert of Beersheba. Then the water in the
skin became exhausted, and throwing
the child under one of the bushes, she 16
went and sat down about a bowshot
away; "For," said she, "I cannot bear
to see the child die!" So she sat down
some way off, and lifted up her voice in
weeping.
God, however, heard the boy's cry, 17
and the angel of God called from the
heavens to Hagar, and said to her,
"What is the matter with you, Hagar? Fear not; for God has heard the
boy's cry, even here where he is. Come, 18
pick up the boy, and hold fast to him;
for I am going to make a great nation of
him."
Then God opened her eyes, and she 19
saw a well of water, whereupon she
went and filled the skin with water, and
gave the boy a drink. So God was with 20
the boy, and he grew up. He lived in
the desert, and became expert with the
bow. He settled in the desert of Paran, 21
and his mother got a wife for him from
the land of Egypt.
It was at that time that Abimelech 22
and the general of his army, Phicol, said
to Abraham,
"God is with you in all that you do;
swear by God to me here, then, that 23
you will never be false to me, nor to my
children, nor to my descendants, but
that you will treat me and the land in
which you have settled as an immigrant
as kindly as I have treated you."
"I swear it," said Abraham. 24
So Abraham took some sheep and 27
oxen, which he gave to Abimelech, and
the two of them made a covenant.
Hence that place came to be called 31
Beersheba [well of the oath], because
it was there that the two took the
oath.
Abraham kept making complaints to 25
Abimelech about a well which the
slaves of Abimelech had seized; but 26
Abimelech said,
"I do not know who did this. Neither
have you informed me of it, nor have I
heard of it, until today."
Then Abraham set seven ewe lambs 28
apart by themselves, whereupon Abim- 29
elech said to Abraham,
"What is the significance of these
seven ewe lambs which you have set
apart?"
"You will accept the seven ewe 30
lambs from my hand," he said, "to
serve as witness for me that I dug this
well."

32 So they made a covenant at Beersheba. Then Abimelech and the general of his army, Phicol, proceeded to
return to the land of the Philistines,
33 while Abraham planted a tamarisk at
Beersheba, and there called upon the
name of the LORD, the eternal God.
34 Abraham resided for a long time in the
land of the Philistines.

22 Some time after this God put Abraham to the test.

"Abraham!" he said to him.

"Here am I," he said.

2 "Take your son," he said, "your only
son, whom you love, Isaac, and go to
the land of Moriah, and there offer him
as a burnt-offering on one of the hills
which I shall designate to you."

3 So next morning Abraham rose early,
and harnessing his ass, he took two of
his servants with him and his son Isaac,
and having cut wood for the burnt-
offering, he started off for the sanctuary
4 which God had designated to him. On
the third day, when Abraham raised his
eyes, he saw the sanctuary in the dis-
5 tance. So Abraham said to his servants,

"Stay here with the ass, while I and
the boy go yonder to perform our devotions, after which we shall return to
you."

6 So Abraham took the wood for the
burnt-offering and put it on the back of
his son Isaac, while he carried in his
own hand the fire and the knife. So the
two of them went off together.

7 "Father!" said Isaac to his father
Abraham.

"Yes, my son," he responded.

"Here are the fire and the wood,"
he said, "but where is the sheep for a
burnt-offering?"

8 "God will provide himself with the
sheep for a burnt-offering, my son,"
said Abraham.

Thereupon the two of them proceeded on their way together.

9 When they arrived at the sanctuary
which God had designated to him, Abraham built the altar there, arranged the
wood, and binding his son Isaac, laid
him on the altar on top of the wood.
10 But as Abraham put out his hand to
11 grasp the knife to slay his son, the angel
of the LORD called to him from the
heavens,

"Abraham, Abraham!"

"Here am I," he replied.

"Do not lay hands on the boy," he 12
said, "do nothing of the sort to him; for
I know now that you revere God, in
that you have not withheld your son,
your only son, from me."

When Abraham raised his eyes, he 13
saw behind him a ram caught in the
brushwood by its horns! So Abraham
went and took the ram, and offered it
up as a burnt-offering in place of his
son. Then Abraham called the name of 14
that sanctuary Yahweh-jireh, which is
today interpreted as "At the hill of the
LORD provision is made."

A second time the angel of the LORD 15
called to Abraham from the heavens,

"I swear by myself"—it is the oracle 16
of the LORD—"that since you have
done this, and have not withheld your
son, your only son, I will indeed bless 17
you, and will surely make your descendants as numerous as the stars of
the sky, or the sands that are on the
seashore, so that your descendants
shall take possession of the cities of
their enemies, and through your de- 18
scendants all the nations of the earth
shall invoke blessings on one another—
just because you heeded my injunction."

Abraham then returned to his serv- 19
ants, and together they started off for
Beersheba; and in Beersheba Abraham
made his home.

Some time after this word came to 20
Abraham as follows: "Milcah, too, has
borne children to your brother Nahor:
Uz, the first-born, Bus, his brother, 21
Kemuel (the ancestor of the Arameans),
Chesed, Hazo, Pildash, Jidlaph, and 22
Bethuel"—which Bethuel became the 23
father of Rebekah. These eight did
Milcah bear to Nahor, Abraham's
brother. Moreover, his consort, whose 24
name was Reumah, also bore Tebah,
Gaham, Tahash, and Maacah.

The length of Sarah's life was one 23
hundred and twenty-seven years. Sa- 2
rah died at Kirjath-arba (that is, Hebron), in the land of Canaan, and Abraham proceeded to wail and weep for
Sarah. Rising from the side of his dead, 3
Abraham said to the Hittites,

"Since I am an immigrant and a serf 4
under you, give me some property with
you as a burial-ground, that I may in-
ter my dead."

The Hittites answered Abraham, 5
"Listen, sir; you are a mighty prince 6

among us; bury your dead in the choicest of our sepulchres; none of us will deny you his sepulchre for the burial of your dead."
7 Abraham rose, and bowing to the
8 Hittites, the natives of the land, he said to them,
"If your consent to the burial of my dead is assured, listen to me; approach Ephron, the son of Zohar, on my behalf,
9 that he may give me the cave of Machpelah which belongs to him, on the edge of his field. Let him sell it to me in your presence for its full value, as a burial-ground of my own."
10 Now Ephron was sitting among the Hittites. So Ephron, the Hittite, answered Abraham in the hearing of the Hittites, namely all those accustomed to enter the gates of his city,
11 "Not at all, sir; listen to me; I make you a present of the field; I make you a present of the cave as well; in the presence of my fellow-countrymen I present it to you; bury your dead in it."
12 Bowing to the natives of the land,
13 Abraham said to Ephron in the hearing of the natives of the land,
"If really you are so obliging, please listen to me; I offer you money for the field; accept it from me, that I may bury my dead there."
14 Ephron answered Abraham,
15 "Sir, listen to me; a piece of land worth four hundred shekels of silver—what is that between us? Bury your dead in it."
16 So Abraham accepted Ephron's terms, and Abraham paid over to Ephron the sum which he had named in the hearing of the Hittites, four hundred shekels of silver of commercial standard.
17 Thus the field of Ephron at Machpelah, which faces Mamre, the field together with the cave in it and all the trees that were in the field, throughout
18 its whole area, was conveyed in the presence of the Hittites, namely all those accustomed to enter the gates of his city, to Abraham as his property.
19 Following that Abraham buried his wife Sarah in the cave in the field of Machpelah, facing Mamre (that is,
20 Hebron), in the land of Canaan. Thus the field with the cave that was in it passed from the possession of the Hittites to that of Abraham for use as a burial-ground.

Now that Abraham was old and well 24
advanced in life, having been blessed
by the LORD in all things, Abraham 2
said to the oldest slave of his household, who had charge of everything that belonged to him,
"Put your hand under my thigh,
while I make you swear by the LORD, 3
the God of the heavens and the earth, that you will not marry my son to a daughter of the Canaanites, among
whom I am living, but that you will go 4
to my own land and kindred to get a wife for my son Isaac."
The slave said to him, 5
"Suppose the woman is unwilling to follow me to this land; am I to take your son back to the land that you left?"
Abraham said to him, 6
"See to it that you do not take my
son back there! It was the LORD, the 7
God of the heavens, who took me from my father's home and the land of my birth, who spoke to me and made me this promise, 'It is to your descendants that I am going to give this land'—it is he who will send his angel ahead of you, so that you shall get a wife for my
son there. But if the woman should be 8
unwilling to follow you, then you will be absolved from this oath to me; only you must never take my son back there."
So the slave put his hand under the 9
thigh of his master, Abraham, and swore to him to this effect.
The slave took ten of his master's 10
camels, and set out on his journey, taking with him all kinds of valuables from his master; he started off, and eventually arrived at Aram-naharaim, the city
of Nahor. Toward evening, at the time 11
that the women came out to draw water, he made the camels kneel by the well outside the city.
"O LORD, the God of my master 12
Abraham," he said, "pray give me success today, and so be gracious to my
master Abraham. Here I am taking 13
my stand beside the spring, as the daughters of the townsmen come out to
draw water. Let the girl, then, to 14
whom I say, 'Will you please let down your pitcher for me to drink?' and who says, 'Drink, and let me water your camels as well'—let her be the one whom thou hast allotted to thy servant Isaac. By this I shall be assured

that thou wilt really be gracious to my
master."
15 Before he had finished speaking, out
came Rebekah, the daughter of Bethuel, the son of Milcah, the wife of Abraham's brother Nahor, with her pitcher
16 on her shoulder. The girl was very
beautiful, a virgin with whom no man
had ever had intercourse. She went
down to the spring to fill her pitcher,
17 and when she came up, the slave ran to
her and said,
"Will you please let me drink a little
water from your pitcher?"
18 "Drink, sir," she said; and quickly
lowering the pitcher to her hand, she
19 gave him a drink. When she had finished giving him a drink, she said,
"For your camels, too, I will draw
water, until they finish drinking."
20 So she quickly emptied her pitcher
into the trough, and ran back to the
well to draw more water. Thus she drew
21 water for all his camels, while the man
gazed after her, eager to learn whether
the LORD had brought his errand to a
22 successful issue or not. Accordingly, as
soon as the camels finished drinking,
the man took a gold ring weighing half a
shekel, and put it in her nose, as well as
two gold bracelets weighing ten shekels
23 on her wrists. Then he said,
"Whose daughter are you? Pray tell
me. Is there room in your father's
house for us to spend the night?"
24 "I am the daughter of Bethuel, the
son of Milcah, whom she bore to Na-
25 hor," she replied. "We have plenty of
both straw and fodder," she added,
"and there is also room to spend the
night."
26 Thereupon the man bowed in hom-
27 age to the LORD, and said,
"Blessed be the LORD, the God of
my master Abraham, who has not failed
to be gracious and true to my master. I
am on the right road; the LORD has led
me to the home of my master's kinsfolk."
28 Then the girl ran, and gave an account of these things to her mother's
29 household. Now Rebekah had a brother, whose name was Laban. So Laban
30 ran out to the man at the spring, when
he saw the ring and the bracelets on his
sister's wrists and heard his sister Rebekah saying, "This is what the man
said to me." When he reached the man,
there he was, standing beside the camels near the spring.
"Come in, you blessed of the LORD," 31
he said. "Why do you stand outside,
when I have the house ready, as well as
a place for the camels?"
So he brought the man into the 32
house, and unharnessed the camels. He
brought straw and fodder for the camels, and water for him and the men that
were with him to wash their feet. Food 33
was then set before him to eat, but he
said,
"I will not eat until I have told my
story."
"Say on," he said.
So he said, 34
"I am Abraham's slave. The LORD 35
has richly blessed my master, so that he
is a great man; he has given him flocks
and herds, silver and gold, male and female slaves, camels and asses. Now 36
Sarah, my master's wife, after she was
quite old, bore a son to my master, and
to him he is leaving everything that belongs to him. My master made me take 37
this oath: 'You must not marry my son
to any daughter of the Canaanites in
whose land I am living; but you must 38
go to my father's home and my own
kindred to get a wife for my son.' I said 39
to my master, 'Suppose the woman will
not follow me?' He said to me, 'The 40
LORD, in whose favor I have lived, will
send his angel along with you, and will
bring your errand to a successful issue,
so that you shall get a wife for my son
from my own kindred and my father's
home. Then you shall be absolved from 41
the oath to me; when you come to my
kindred, if they refuse you, you shall be
absolved from the oath to me.' So to- 42
day when I came to the spring, I said,
'O LORD, God of my master Abraham,
if thou wouldst really bring success to
this errand in which I am engaged,
grant that, as I stand beside the spring, 43
the girl who comes out to draw water,
and to whom I say, "Will you please
give me a little water to drink out of
your pitcher?" and who says to me, 44
"Not only drink yourself, but let me
draw water for your camels as well"—
let that woman be the one whom the
LORD has allotted to my master's son.'
Before I could finish my meditations, 45
out came Rebekah, with her pitcher on
her shoulder, and went down to the
spring to draw water. So I said to her,

'Will you please give me a drink?'
46 whereupon she quickly lowered her
pitcher from her shoulder, and said,
'Drink, and let me water your camels as
well.' So I drank, and she gave the
47 camels a drink too. Then I asked her,
'Whose daughter are you?' and she
said, 'The daughter of Bethuel, the son
of Nahor, whom Milcah bore to him.'
Then I put the ring in her nose, and the
48 bracelets on her wrists; and I bowed in
homage to the LORD, blessing the
LORD, the God of my master Abraham,
who had led me by the right road to get
the daughter of my master's kinsman
49 for his son. Now then, tell me whether
you are ready to treat my master kindly
and honorably or not, so that I may
turn one way or the other."
50 Laban and Bethuel answered,
"This is the LORD'S doing; we dare
not answer you adversely or favorably.
51 Here is Rebekah for you; take her and
go; let her become the wife of your master's son, as the LORD has signified."
52 As soon as the slave of Abraham
heard their words, he bowed to the
53 earth before the LORD. The slave then
brought out articles of silver and gold,
and clothing, which he gave to Rebekah; he also gave costly presents to
54 her brother and mother. Then he and
the men that were with him had something to eat and drink, and retired for
the night.
When they rose next morning, he said,
"Let me go to my master."
55 But her brother and mother said,
"Let the girl stay with us a while
longer, or at least ten days, after which
she may go."
56 "Do not hinder me," he said to them;
"since the LORD has brought my errand to such a successful issue, let me go
that I may return to my master."
57 "We will call the girl, and consult
her wishes," they said.
58 So they called Rebekah, and said to
her,
"Will you go with this man?"
"I will," said she.
59 So they let their sister Rebekah go,
and her nurse, and Abraham's slave
60 and his men. They blessed Rebekah,
saying to her,
"May you, our sister, become a thousand myriads!
And may your descendants conquer
the cities of their foes!"

Then Rebekah started off with her 61
maids, and riding on the camels, they
followed the man. Thus the slave took
Rebekah and departed.
Now Isaac had moved from the 62
neighborhood of Beer-lahai-roi, and was
living in the land of the Negeb. One 63
evening Isaac went out to stroll in the
fields, and raising his eyes, he saw
camels coming. Rebekah too raised 64
her eyes, and seeing Isaac, she dismounted from her camel, saying to the 65
slave,
"Who is the man yonder that is walking through the field toward us?"
"He is my master," said the slave.
Then she took her veil, and covered
herself.
The slave told Isaac all that he had 66
done; so Isaac brought her into his tent. 67
He married Rebekah and she became
his wife; and in loving her, Isaac found
consolation for the death of his mother.
Abraham married another wife whose 25
name was Keturah, who bore him Zim- 2
ran, Jokshan, Medan, Midian, Ishbak,
and Shuah. Jokshan was the father of 3
Sheba and Dedan. The descendants of
Dedan were the Ashurim, the Letushim, and the Leummim, while the 4
descendants of Midian were Ephah,
Epher, Hanock, Abida, and Eldaah. All
these were Keturah's children. To Isaac 5
Abraham gave everything that he had,
while to the children that Abraham had 6
by consorts, while he was still alive,
Abraham gave presents, and sent them
away eastward to the land of Kedem, so
that they might not interfere with his
son Isaac.
This was the total length of Abra- 7
ham's life—one hundred and seventy-
five years. So Abraham came to his 8
death, dying at a ripe old age, an old
man, satisfied with life; and he was
gathered to his fathers. His sons, Isaac 9
and Ishmael, buried him in the cave of
Machpelah, in the field of Ephron, the
son of Zohar, the Hittite, which faces
Mamre, the field which Abraham had 10
bought from the Hittites. There Abraham was buried, along with his wife
Sarah. After the death of Abraham, 11
God blessed his son Isaac, who made his
home close to Beer-lahai-roi.
The following are the descendants of 12
Ishmael, the son of Abraham, whom
Hagar, the Egyptian, Sarah's maid,
bore to Abraham; the following are the 13

names of the sons of Ishmael, named in
the order of their birth: Nebaioth, Ishmael's first-born, Kedar, Adbeel, Mib-
14 sam, Mishma, Dumah, Massa, Hadad,
15 Tema, Jetur, Naphish, and Kedemah.
16 These were the sons of Ishmael; these
were their names as arranged by villages and encampments—twelve princes
arranged by peoples.
17 This was the length of Ishmael's life
—one hundred and thirty-seven years.
So he came to his death; he died, and
18 was gathered to his fathers. He inhabited the region from Havilah as far as
Shur, which is on the border of Egypt,
in the vicinity of Ashur, having settled
on the outskirts of all his kindred.

THE STORY OF JACOB,
25:19—37:1

19 The following are the descendants of
Isaac, the son of Abraham. Abraham
20 was the father of Isaac, and Isaac was
forty years old when he married Rebekah, the daughter of Bethuel, the
Aramean of Paddan-aram, and the sis-
21 ter of Laban, the Aramean. Isaac besought the LORD on behalf of his wife,
because she was barren; so the LORD
yielded to his entreaty, and his wife
22 Rebekah conceived. While in her
womb, the children jostled each other,
so that she said,
"If it is to be thus, on whose side am
I to be?"
So she went off to consult the LORD,
23 and the LORD said to her,
"Two nations are in your womb,
And the two peoples have been hostile
ever since conception in you;
The one people shall master the other,
And the older shall serve the younger."
24 When the time of her delivery came,
there were indeed twins in her womb.
25 The first one was born red, his whole
body like a hairy garment; so his name
26 was called Esau [hairy(?)]. Then his
brother was born, with his hand gripping Esau's heel; so his name was called
Jacob [heel-gripper]. Isaac was sixty
years old when she bore them.
27 The boys grew up. Esau became a
skilful hunter, a man of the open country, while Jacob became a man of
peaceful pursuits, making his home in
28 tents. Isaac favored Esau, because he
was fond of game, while Rebekah favored Jacob.
Once when Jacob was making a stew, 29
Esau came in from the fields famishing;
whereupon Esau said to Jacob, 30
"Let me have a swallow of that red
stuff there; for I am famishing."
(That was how his name came to be
called Edom [red].)
"First sell me your birthright," said 31
Jacob.
So Esau said, 32
"Here I am at the point of death; so
of what use is a birthright to me?"
"First give me your oath," said Ja- 33
cob.
So he gave him his oath, and sold his 34
birthright to Jacob. Jacob then gave
Esau bread and stewed lentils. He ate
and drank; then rose and went away.
Thus lightly did Esau value his birthright.
A famine occurred in the land—a dif- 26
ferent one from the first famine which
occurred in the time of Abraham—so
Isaac went to Gerar, to Abimelech, king
of the Philistines. The LORD then ap- 2
peared to him, and said,
"Do not go down to Egypt; settle in
the land that I shall designate to you.
If you establish yourself as an immi- 3
grant in this land, I will be with you,
and bless you; for to you and your descendants I am going to give this whole
country, and so fulfil the oath which I
made to your father Abraham. I will 4
make your descendants as numerous as
the stars in the sky, and I will give your
descendants this whole country, so that
all the nations of the earth will invoke
blessings on one another through your
descendants—just because Abraham 5
heeded my instructions and kept my
charge, my commands, statutes, and
laws."
So Isaac settled at Gerar. When the 6 7
men of the place asked him about his
wife, he said,
"She is my sister."
For he was afraid to say, "She is my
wife," lest the men of the place should
slay him for the sake of Rebekah, because she was good-looking.
When he had been there a long time, 8
Abimelech, king of the Philistines,
looked out of his window, and saw Isaac
fondling his wife Rebekah. Sc Abim- 9
elech summoned Isaac, and said,

"So she really is your wife; then why
did you say, 'She is my sister'?"
"I said so, that I might not lose my
life through her," Isaac said to him.
10 "What a way to treat us!" said Abimelech. "One of my people might easily
have lain with your wife, and then you
would have brought guilt on us."
11 So Abimelech warned all his people,
"Anyone laying hands on this man or
his wife shall be put to death."
12 Isaac sowed a crop in that land, and
he obtained that year one hundred
13 measures of barley. The LORD blessed
him, so that the man grew rich, and
kept on growing richer and richer, until
14 he became very rich indeed; he had
flocks of sheep and herds of cattle, and
so many work-animals that the Phi-
15 listines vented their spite on him. All
the wells which his father's slaves had
dug in the time of his father Abraham,
the Philistines stopped up and filled
16 with dirt. Accordingly, when Abimelech
said to Isaac, "Leave our midst; for you
17 are much too powerful for us," Isaac
left there, and camping in the valley of
18 Gerar, he settled there. Isaac then reopened the wells which had been dug
in the time of his father Abraham, but
which the Philistines had stopped up
after Abraham's death; and he gave
them the same names as his father had
19 given them. But when Isaac's slaves
dug in the valley, and found a well of
20 running water, the shepherds of Gerar
got into a dispute with Isaac's shepherds, saying, "The water is ours."
Hence the name of the well came to be
called Esek [trouble], because they got
21 into trouble with him. Then they dug
another well, but they got into a dispute over that too; so its name came to
22 be called Sitnah [hostility]. Moving
from there, he dug another well, and
there was no dispute over this; so he
called its name Rehoboth [room], saying, "At last the LORD has made room
for us, so that we shall become numerous in the land."
23 From there he went up to Beersheba;
24 and that very night the LORD appeared
to him, saying,
"I am the God of your father Abraham; do not be afraid; for I am with
you. I will bless you and make your descendants numerous, for the sake of my
servant Abraham."
25 So Isaac built an altar there, and
called upon the name of the LORD. He
pitched his tent there, and there also
his slaves dug a well.
Then Abimelech came to him from 26
Gerar, with Ahuzzath, one of his ministers, and Phicol, the general of his
army. Isaac said to them, 27
"Why have you come to me, seeing
that you hate me, and drove me from
your midst?"
They said, 28
"We see very clearly that the LORD
is with you, so we make this proposal:
'Let there be an oath between us—between ourselves and you; let us reach
an agreement with you that you will do 29
us no harm, since we did not hurt you,
but only did you good, and let you go
amicably.' You are indeed the blessed
of the LORD."
Thereupon he made a feast for them, 30
at which they ate and drank. Rising 31
early next morning, they took oath
with each other, and then Isaac let
them go, and they departed from him
on friendly terms. It was that same day 32
that Isaac's slaves came and told him
about the well that they had dug; "We
have found water," they told him. So 33
he called it Shibah [oath]. That is why
the name of the city is Beersheba [the
well of the oath] to this day.
When Esau was forty years old, he 34
married Judith, the daughter of Beeri,
the Hittite, and Basemath, the daughter of Elon, the Hittite; and they were
a source of distress to Isaac and Rebekah.
One day, when Isaac had become old **27**
and his eyes so dim that he could not
see, he called his older son Esau.
"My son!" he said to him.
"Here I am," he replied.
He said, 2
"Here I am an old man, not knowing
what day I may die. Get your weapons, 3
then, your quiver and bow, and go out
into the fields, and hunt some game for
me. Then make me a tasty dish, such 4
as I like, and bring it to me to eat, that
I may give you my blessing before I
die."
Now Rebekah was listening when 5
Isaac spoke to his son Esau; so when
Esau went off to the fields to hunt game
for his father, Rebekah said to her son 6
Jacob,
"I have just heard your father say to
your brother Esau, 'Bring me some 7

game, and make me a tasty dish to eat,
that I may bless you before the LORD
8 before I die.' Now then, my son, obey
9 me in the charge that I give you. Go to
the flock and get two fat kids for me
there, that I may make them into a
tasty dish for your father, such as he
10 likes. Then you shall take it to your
father to eat, that he may bless you before he dies."

11 But Jacob said to his mother Rebekah,

"Ah, but my brother Esau is a hairy
12 man, while I am smooth. Suppose my
father were to feel me? I should look like an impious person to him, and bring a curse on myself, and not a blessing."

13 "Let any curse for you, my son, fall on me!" his mother replied. "Only obey me, and go and get them for me."

14 So he went and got them, and
brought them to his mother. His mother then made a tasty dish, such as his
15 father liked; and taking the best clothes
of her older son Esau, which she had in
the house, Rebekah dressed her young-
16 er son Jacob in them; she put the skins
of the kids on his hands and on the
17 smooth parts of his neck, and committed the tasty dish and bread which
she had made into the hands of her son
18 Jacob. Then he went in to his father,
and said,

"Father!"

"Yes," he said. "Who are you, my son?"

19 Jacob said to his father,

"I am Esau, your first-born; I have done as you told me; now sit up and eat once more of my game, that you may give me your blessing."

20 But Isaac said to his son,

"How ever did you come to find it so quickly, my son?"

"Because the LORD your God brought it in my path," he said.

21 Isaac then said to Jacob,

"Come up close that I may feel you, my son, to see whether you really are my son Esau or not."

22 So Jacob went up to his father Isaac, who felt him, and said,

"The voice is Jacob's voice, but the hands are those of Esau."

23 Hence he did not detect him, because his hands were hairy, like those of his brother Esau; so he blessed him.

"Are you really my son Esau?" he 24
said.

"I am," he replied.

So he said, 25

"Bring me some of your game to eat, my son, that I may give you my blessing."

So he brought it to him, and he ate;
he also brought him wine, and he
drank. Then his father Isaac said to 26
him,

"Come here and kiss me, my son."

So he went up and kissed him; and 27
when he smelt his clothes, he blessed
him, saying,

"Ah, my son's smell is like that of a
field that the LORD has blessed.
May God give you of the heavens' dew, 28
Of earth's fatness, with plenty of grain
and wine!
Nations shall serve you, 29
And peoples bow down to you.
Be master of your brothers,
And let your mother's sons bow down
to you!
Cursed be they who curse you,
And blessed be they who bless you!"

No sooner had Isaac finished blessing 30
Jacob, indeed Jacob had just left the
presence of his father Isaac, when his
brother Esau came in from his hunt.
He too made a tasty dish, and brought 31
it to his father.

"Let my father sit up," he said to his father, "and eat some of his son's game, that you may give me your blessing."

"Who are you?" his father Isaac said 32
to him.

"I am your son," he said, "your first-born, Esau."

Thereupon Isaac was very greatly 33
agitated, and said,

"Who was it then who got some game and brought it to me? I ate heartily of it before you came, and blessed him, so that he is indeed blessed."

On hearing his father's words, Esau 34
cried loud and bitterly, and said to his
father,

"Bless me also, my father!"

But he said, 35

"Your brother came under false colors, and stole your blessing."

"Is it because he is named Jacob that 36
he has twice now got the better of me?" he said. "He stole my birthright, and now he has stolen my blessing!" "Have you not kept a blessing for me?" he added.

37 But Isaac in reply said to Esau,
"Since I have made him master over you, and have made all his brothers his slaves, and have provided grain and wine for his sustenance, what then is there that I can do for you, my son?"
38 Esau said to his father,
"Have you only one blessing, my father? Bless me too, my father."
Whereupon Esau lifted up his voice
39 in weeping. So his father Isaac complied, and said to him,
"Away from the fat of the earth shall your dwelling be,
Away from the dew of the heavens on high.
40 By your sword you shall live,
And your brother you shall serve;
But when you become restive,
You shall break his yoke off your neck."
41 So Esau had a grudge against Jacob because of the blessing which his father had bestowed on him.
"It will soon be time to mourn for my father," Esau said to himself, "and then I will slay my brother Jacob."
42 But Rebekah was informed of the designs of her older son Esau, so she sent for her younger son Jacob, and said to him,
"Here is your brother Esau threatening to take revenge on you by murder-
43 ing you! Now, my son, listen to me; flee at once to my brother Laban at
44 Haran, and stay awhile with him, until
45 your brother's anger subsides—until your brother's wrath against you relents, and he forgets what you have done to him; then I will send and fetch you from there. Why should I be bereft of both of you on the same day?"
46 So Rebekah said to Isaac,
"I am tired to death of the Hittite women. If Jacob marries a Hittite woman like these, one of the natives of the land, what good will life be to me?"
28 So Isaac called Jacob, and blessing him, gave him this charge:
"You must not marry any Canaanite
2 woman; go at once to Paddan-aram, to the home of Bethuel, your mother's father, and procure a wife there from the daughters of Laban, your mother's
3 brother. May God Almighty bless you, and make you prolific, and so numerous that you become a company of peoples!
4 May he bestow the blessing vouchsafed to Abraham on you, and likewise on your descendants after you, that you may take possession of the land in which you are now only an immigrant, which God gave to Abraham."
So Isaac sent Jacob away, and he 5
went to Paddan-aram, to Laban, the son of Bethuel, the Aramean, the brother of Rebekah, the mother of Jacob and Esau.
When Esau discovered that Isaac had 6
blessed Jacob, and had sent him off to Paddan-aram to get a wife there, and on blessing him, had charged him not to
marry any Canaanite woman, and that 7
Jacob had obeyed his father and mother and had gone to Paddan-aram,
Esau realized that his father Isaac dis- 8
liked Canaanite women, so he went to 9
Ishmael, and married Mahalath, the daughter of Abraham's son Ishmael, the sister of Nebaioth, in addition to the wives that he had.
Leaving Beersheba, Jacob set out for 10
Haran. Reaching a certain sanctuary, 11
he spent the night there; for the sun had set. He took one of the stones of the sanctuary, and using it for a pillow,
he lay down in that sanctuary. He had 12
a dream in which he saw a ladder set up on the earth, with its top reaching the sky, and angels of God were ascending
and descending on it. Then the LORD 13
stood over him, and said,
"I am the LORD, the God of your father Abraham and of Isaac. The land on which you are lying, I am going to give to you and your descendants.
Your descendants shall be like the dust 14
on the ground; you shall spread to the west, to the east, to the north, and to the south, so that all races of the earth will invoke blessings on one another
through you and your descendants. I 15
will be with you, and guard you wherever you go, and bring you back to this land; for I will never forsake you, until I have done what I have promised you."
When Jacob woke from his sleep, he 16
said,
"The LORD must surely be in this place—and I did not know it!"
He was awe-struck, and said, 17
"What an awesome place this is! This can be nothing other than the house of God, and that the gate of the sky."
Accordingly, he called the name of 19
that sanctuary Bethel [house of God],

whereas the earlier name of the city had
been Luz.
18 So when Jacob rose in the morning,
he took the stone which he had used as
a pillow, and setting it up as a sacred
20 pillar, he poured oil on its top. Jacob
then made this vow:
"If God will go with me, and watch
over me on this journey that I am making, and give me food to eat and clothes
21 to wear, so that I come home safely to
my father's house, then the LORD shall
22 be my God, and this stone which I have
set up as a sacred pillar shall be God's
house, and I will give to thee a portion
of everything that thou givest me."
29 Jacob then continued his journey,
and came to the land of the Kedemites.
2 Looking around, he saw a well in the
open, with three flocks of sheep lying
beside it; for it was from this well that
3 the flocks were watered, but the stone
over the mouth of the well was so large
that it was only after all the shepherds
had collected there that they could roll
the stone off the mouth of the well, and
water the sheep, after which they would
replace the stone over the mouth of the
well.
4 "My friends, where do you come
from?" Jacob said to them.
"We come from Haran," they said.
5 "Do you know Laban, the son of Nahor?" he said to them.
"We do," said they.
6 "Is he well?" he said to them.
"He is," they said, "and here is his
daughter Rachel coming with his sheep!"
7 "Why," said he, "the day has still
long to run! It is not yet time for the
live stock to be gathered in; water the
sheep, and go on pasturing them."
8 But they said,
"We cannot until all the shepherds
assemble, and roll the stone off the
mouth of the well so that we can water
the sheep."
9 While he was still talking with them,
Rachel arrived with her father's flock;
10 for she was a shepherdess. As soon as
Jacob saw Rachel, the daughter of Laban, his mother's brother, with the
flock of Laban, his mother's brother,
Jacob went up, and rolling the stone off
the mouth of the well, watered the flock
11 of Laban, his mother's brother. Then
Jacob kissed Rachel, and lifted up his
voice in weeping.
12 When Jacob told Rachel that he was
a relative of her father and the son of
Rebekah, she ran and told her father.
As soon as Laban heard about Jacob, 13
his sister's son, he ran to meet him, embraced him, kissed him, and brought
him home. Jacob then told Laban his
whole story, whereupon Laban said to 14
him,
"You are my very own flesh and
blood!"
So he stayed with him for a whole
month.
Then Laban said to Jacob, 15
"Should you, just because you are a
relative of mine, work for me for nothing? Let me know what your wages
should be."
Now Laban had two daughters, the 16
name of the older being Leah, and that
of the younger Rachel; Leah had weak 17
eyes, while Rachel was beautiful and
lovely. Jacob had fallen in love with 18
Rachel, so he said,
"I will work seven years for you in
return for Rachel, your younger daughter."
Whereupon Laban said, 19
"It is better for me to give her to you
than to anyone else; stay with me."
So Jacob worked seven years for 20
Rachel, and they seemed to him but a
few days, because he loved her. Then 21
Jacob said to Laban,
"Give me my wife; for my time is up,
and I want to marry her."
So Laban gathered all the men of the 22
place, and held a feast; but in the 23
course of the evening he took his daugh-
ter Leah and brought her to Jacob,
who married her. Laban gave his slave 24
Zilpah to his daughter Leah as her
maid.
Next morning, however, Jacob dis- 25
covered that it was Leah! So he said to
Laban,
"What a way for you to treat me!
Did I not work with you for Rachel?
Why then have you cheated me?"
"It is not customary in our country 26
to marry the younger daughter before
the older," Laban said. "Finish the 27
week's festivities for this one, and then
I will give you the other also, in return
for another seven years' service with
me."
Jacob did so; he finished her week's 28
festivities, and then Laban gave him
his daughter Rachel in marriage; and to 29
his daughter Rachel he gave his slave

30 Bilhah as her maid. So he married Rachel also, and besides, he loved Rachel
more than Leah. Thus he had to work
with Laban another seven years.
When the LORD saw that Leah was
31 slighted, he made her pregnant, while
32 Rachel remained barren. So Leah conceived and bore a son, whom she named
Reuben [behold a son]; "For," said she,
"the LORD has taken note of my distress; now my husband will love me."
33 Again she conceived and bore a son;
so she said,
"Because the LORD heard that I was
slighted, he has given me this one also."
Hence she called his name Simeon
[hearing].
34 Again she conceived and bore a son;
"This time," she said, "my husband
will surely become attached to me, seeing that I have borne him three sons."
That was how he came to be called
Levi [attachment].
35 Once more she conceived and bore a
son, whereupon she said,
"Now do I praise the LORD!"
That was why she called his name
Judah [praise].
Then she stopped bearing children.

30 When Rachel realized that she was
not bearing children to Jacob, she became jealous of her sister, and said to
Jacob,
"Give me children, or else I die!"
2 Jacob blazed with anger against Rachel, and said,
"Can I take the place of God, who
has kept you from having children?"
3 Then she said,
"Here is my slave Bilhah; have intercourse with her, that she may bear children for my knees, and that I too may
build up a family through her."
4 So she gave him her maid Bilhah in
marriage, and Jacob had intercourse
5 with her. Bilhah conceived and bore
6 Jacob a son, whereupon Rachel said,
"God brought judgment upon me,
but now he has heeded my cry and giv-
en me a son."
That was why she called his name
Dan [he brought judgment].
7 Again Rachel's maid, Bilhah, conceived and bore Jacob a second son.
Then Rachel said,
8 "It was a clever trick that I played
my sister, and I succeeded too!"
So she called his name Naphtali
[trick].

When Leah discovered that she had 9
stopped bearing children, she took her
maid Zilpah and gave her to Jacob in
marriage. Zilpah, Leah's maid, bore 10
Jacob a son, whereupon Leah said, 11
"How lucky!"
So she called his name Gad [luck].
Zilpah, Leah's maid, bore Jacob an- 12
other son. So Leah said, 13
"How fortunate I am; for women will
certainly call me fortunate!"
So she called his name Asher [for-
tune].
At the time of the wheat-harvest 14
Reuben went out into the fields, where
he found some mandrakes which he
brought home to his mother Leah.
"Please give me some of your son's
mandrakes," Rachel said to Leah.
But she said to her, 15
"Is the fact that you took away my
husband such a trifle that you should
want to take my son's mandrakes as
well?"
"Well then," said Rachel, "he may
lie with you tonight in exchange for
your son's mandrakes."
So when Jacob came home from the 16
fields in the evening, Leah went out to
meet him, and said,
"You must come home with me; for
I have hired you with my son's mandrakes."
So he lay with her that night.
God gave heed to Leah, so that she 17
conceived and bore a fifth son to Jacob,
whereupon Leah said, 18
"God has given me my reward for
giving my maid to my husband."
So she called his name Issachar [re-
ward].
Again Leah conceived and bore a 19
sixth son to Jacob. Then Leah said, 20
"God has made me a magnificent
present; my husband will surely stay
with me now; for I have borne him six
sons."
So she called his name Zebulun
[abode].
She afterward bore a daughter, 21
whom she named Dinah.
God also remembered Rachel; God 22
gave heed to her, and made her pregnant, so that she conceived and bore 23
a son, whereupon she said,
"God has taken away my reproach."
So she called his name Joseph [may 24
he add], saying,

"May the LORD give me another
son!"
25 It was after Rachel had given birth
to Joseph that Jacob said to Laban,
"Let me go, that I may depart for my
26 own home and country. Give me my
wives and children, for whom I have
worked for you, that I may go; for you
know how well I have worked for you."
27 But Laban said to him,
"If I may have your permission to
say so, I have learned from the omens
that the LORD has blessed me because
28 of you." "Name me your wage," he
added, "and I will pay it."
29 But he said to him,
"You know yourself how I have
worked for you, and what your stock
30 has become under my care; for it was
little that you had before I came,
whereas now it has expanded into a
great deal, since the LORD blessed you
upon my arrival. But when am I to
make provision for my own household?"
31 "What should I give you?" he said.
"Give me nothing of the sort," said
Jacob. "I will go on pasturing and
tending your flock, if you will do this
32 for me: go through all the flock today,
and remove from it every speckled
and spotted sheep, every one of the
lambs that is black, and any of the
goats that is spotted and speckled; such
33 shall be my pay. At some future time,
whenever you may come, my honesty
toward you will answer for me in the
matter of my hire; if there is any one
among the goats that is not speckled
and spotted, or among the lambs that is
not black, it came into my possession
by theft."
34 "Good," said Laban, "let it be as you
say."
35 So that day he removed the striped
and spotted he-goats, all the speckled
and spotted she-goats, every one with
white on it, and all of the lambs that
were black; and handing them over to
36 his sons he put a distance of three days'
journey between himself and Jacob,
while Jacob remained in charge of the
rest of Laban's flock.
37 Then Jacob procured some fresh
boughs of poplar, almond, and plane,
and peeled white stripes in them, thus
laying bare the white on the boughs.
38 He then placed the boughs which he
had peeled in front of the sheep in the
troughs, that is, the water-troughs,
where the sheep came to drink. Since 39
they bred when they came to drink, the
sheep bred among the boughs, and so
had lambs that were striped, speckled,
and spotted. Jacob set the lambs apart, 40
and so added the best sheep in Laban's
flock to those that were striped and all
black. He put his own flock off by
themselves, and did not add them to
Laban's flock. Whenever the hardier 41
ewes were breeding, Jacob used to put
the boughs in the troughs in front of the
flock so that they might breed among
the boughs, but not in the case of the 42
weaker ones. Thus the weaker ones fell
to Laban, and the hardier to Jacob.
The man, accordingly, grew richer and 43
richer, and had large flocks, as well as
male and female slaves, camels and
asses.

Now Jacob heard Laban's sons say- 31
ing, "Jacob has taken all that our father had; it is out of what our father
had that he has acquired all this
wealth." Jacob saw too that the atti- 2
tude of Laban toward him was not
what it used to be; so the LORD said to 3
Jacob,
"Return to the land of your fathers
and to your relatives; I will be with
you."
So Jacob sent for Rachel and Leah to 4
come to his flock in the fields, and said 5
to them,
"I see that your father's attitude toward me is not what it used to be. However, the God of my father is with me.
You know yourselves that I have worked 6
for your father to the best of my ability,
whereas your father has cheated me, 7
and has changed my wages ten times.
But God has not allowed him to do me
any harm. Whenever he said, 'The 8
speckled animals are to be your wage,'
then all the sheep had speckled lambs;
and whenever he said, 'The striped animals are to be your wage,' all the sheep
had striped lambs. Thus God has taken 9
away your father's stock, and given it
to me.
"Once when the sheep were breeding, 10
I had a dream, and raising my eyes, I
saw that the rams that were leaping on
the goats were striped, speckled, and
mottled. Then the angel of God said to 11
me in the dream, 'Jacob!' 'Here I am,'
said I. Whereupon he said, 'Raise your 12
eyes, and look; all the rams that are

leaping on the goats are striped,
speckled, and mottled—for I have seen
all that Laban has been doing to you.
13 I am the God who appeared to you at
Bethel, where you anointed a sacred
pillar and made a vow to me. Come
then, leave this land, and return to the
land of your birth.' "
14 In response Rachel and Leah said to
him,
"Is there any share or heritage left to
15 us in our father's house? Are we not
considered foreigners by him? For he
sold us, and has enjoyed the usufruct
16 of our dowry as well. All the property which God has taken from our father
really belongs to us and our children;
so do just what God has told you to
do."
17 So Jacob proceeded to mount his
18 sons and wives on camels, and drove off
all his stock, all the live stock which he
had acquired, his accumulated stock,
which he had acquired in Paddan-aram,
to go home to his father Isaac in the
land of Canaan.
19 When Laban was away shearing his
sheep, Rachel stole the household gods
20 that belonged to her father; and Jacob
outwitted Laban, the Aramean, by not
telling him that he was going to flee.
21 So he fled, with all that belonged to
him; starting forth, he crossed the River, and set his face toward the highlands of Gilead.
22 Three days later Laban was told that
23 Jacob had fled; so he took his fellow-
tribesmen with him, and pursued him
for seven days, overtaking him in the
24 highlands of Gilead. But God had come
to Laban, the Aramean, in a dream one
night, and had said to him, "Take care
to say nothing to Jacob, either good or
25 bad." So when Laban came up with
Jacob, Jacob having pitched his tent on
Mount Mizpeh, and Laban having encamped with his fellow-tribesmen on
26 Mount Gilead, Laban said to Jacob,
"What do you mean by outwitting
me, and carrying off my daughters like
27 prisoners of war? Why did you flee in
secret without telling me, and rob me?
I would have sent you off with mirth
and songs, with tambourine and lyre.
28 You did not even allow me to kiss my
grandsons and daughters goodbye!
29 How foolishly you have acted! I had it
in my power to do you harm, but the
God of your father said to me the other
night, 'Take care to say nothing to Jacob, either good or bad.' So now you 30
are off, because of course you longed for
your father's home! But why did you
steal my gods?"
In reply Jacob said to Laban, 31
"I was afraid; for I thought that you
would take your daughters from me by
force. The one in whose possession you 32
find your gods shall not live; in the
presence of our tribesmen identify
whatever is yours among my belongings, and take it."
(But Jacob did not know that Rachel
had stolen them.)
So Laban went into the tent of Jacob, 33
the tent of Leah, and that of the two
maids, but found nothing. Leaving
Leah's tent, he went into Rachel's.
Now Rachel had taken the household 34
gods, and putting them in the camel's
saddle, had sat down on them. So when
Laban had felt all over the tent without
finding anything, she said to her father, 35
"Let not my lord be angry that I
cannot rise in your presence; for the ail-
ment common to women is on me."
So he searched thoroughly, but did
not find the household gods.
Then Jacob grew angry, and took 36
Laban to task; Jacob spoke up, and
said to Laban,
"What is my offense; what is my
misdeed, that you should have come
raging after me, and have felt all
through my goods? Whatever goods 37
you have found belonging to your
house, set out here in the sight of my
tribesmen and yours, that they may decide the issue between us two. For the 38
past twenty years I have been with
you; your ewes and she-goats have never miscarried; and I have never eaten
the rams of your flock. I never reported 39
to you the animals torn by wild beasts
—I bore the loss myself. You held me
responsible for anything stolen by day
or night. It was my lot to have the heat 40
wear me out in the day-time, and the
cold at night, and to lose my sleep. For 41
twenty years now I have been a member of your household; I worked fourteen years for you for your two daughters, and six years for your sheep. Ten
times you changed my wages; and if the 42
God of my father, the God of Abraham
and the Awe of Isaac, had not been on
my side, you would now have sent me
away empty-handed. God saw my suf-

fering and the fruits of my toil, and he
has just recently set it right."
43 In reply Laban said to Jacob,
"The girls are my daughters, the
children are my grandchildren, the
flocks are my flocks—indeed everything that you see is mine; but what
can I do now about these daughters of
mine, or the children that they have
44 borne? Come then, let us make a covenant, you and me, and let the LORD
be witness between us."
45 So Jacob took a stone and set it up as
a sacred pillar.
46 Jacob said to his men,
"Gather stones."
So they procured stones, and made a
cairn. Then they had a meal there be-
47 side the cairn. Laban called it Jegar-
sahadutha [Aramaic for "cairn of witness"], while Jacob called it Galeed
[Hebrew for "cairn of witness"].
48 "This cairn," said Laban, "is a witness between you and me today."
That was how it came to be named
49 Galeed. Of the sacred pillar he said,
"May the LORD keep watch between
you and me when we are out of one an-
50 other's sight. If you ill-treat my daughters, or marry other wives beside my
daughters, although there may be no
man to watch us, remember that God
is witness between you and me."
51 Further, Laban said to Jacob,
"See, this cairn and the sacred pillar
which I have erected stand between
52 you and me. This cairn is a witness,
and the sacred pillar a witness that I
will not pass this cairn to harm you,
and that you will not pass this cairn
53 and sacred pillar to harm me. May the
God of Abraham and the God of Nahor
(the gods of their ancestors) be judge
between us!"
54 So Jacob swore to it by the Awe of
his father Isaac. Jacob then offered a
sacrifice on the hill, and invited his relatives to partake of the meal. They did
so, and then spent the night on the hill.
55 Next morning Laban rose early, and
after kissing his grandchildren and his
daughters, and giving them his blessing, he left and went home, while Jacob
32 resumed his journey. Then the angels
2 of God encountered him; and as soon as
he saw them, Jacob said, "This is God's
camp," and so called the name of that
place Mahanaim [camps].
3 Jacob sent messengers ahead of him
to his brother Esau in the land of Seir,
the country of Edom, commanding 4
them as follows:
"Thus shall you speak to my lord
Esau: 'Thus says your servant Jacob:
"I have been residing with Laban, and
having stayed right up to now, I have 5
oxen, asses, flocks, male and female
slaves; so I am sending to tell my lord
in the hope of finding favor with
you."'"
The messengers returned to Jacob, 6
saying,
"We came to your brother Esau as he
was on his way to meet you, accompanied by four hundred men."
Very much terrified and distressed, 7
Jacob divided the people that were
with him into two companies, as well
as the flocks, herds, and camels. "If 8
Esau comes on one company and destroys it," he thought, "then the remaining company can escape."
Then Jacob said, 9
"O LORD, God of my father Abraham and my father Isaac, who didst
say to me, 'Return to your country and
your kindred, and I will make you
prosperous,' I do not deserve all the 10
acts of kindness and fidelity that thou
hast shown thy servant; for with nothing but my staff I crossed the Jordan
here, but now I have become two companies. Save me, I beseech thee, from 11
the power of my brother Esau; for I am
afraid that he will come and slay me, as
well as the mothers and children. But 12
thou didst say, 'I will be sure to make
you prosperous, and I will make your
descendants like the sands of the sea,
which are too numerous to count.'"
So Jacob stayed there that night. 13
From what he had at hand he selected a present for his brother Esau: two 14
hundred she-goats and twenty he-
goats, two hundred ewes and twenty
rams, thirty milch camels with their 15
colts, forty cows and ten bulls, twenty
she-asses and ten he-asses. Putting 16
them in charge of his slaves, with each
drove by itself, he said to his slaves,
"Proceed ahead of me, and leave a
space between one drove and another."
To the leader he gave this order: 17
"When my brother Esau meets you,
and asks you, 'To whom do you belong;
where are you going; and to whom do
these animals belong that you are driving?' say, 'To your servant Jacob; they 18

are a present, sent to my lord Esau,
while he himself is just behind us.' "
19 He gave the same orders to the second, and the third, and to all the others
who were driving the droves, saying,
"Give this same message to Esau,
20 when you meet him. Also be sure to
say 'Your servant Jacob is just behind
us.' "
"For," thought he, "I may appease
him with the present that precedes me,
and then when he does see me, he may
perhaps receive me kindly."
21 So the present went on ahead of him,
while he himself spent that night in the
camp.
22 That same night he rose, and taking
his two wives, his two female slaves,
and his eleven children, he sent them
23 across the ford of the Jabbok. He took
them, and sent them across the stream,
and sent everything that belonged to
24 him across. Jacob himself was left behind all alone. Then a man wrestled
25 with him until daybreak, and when
he found that he could not master him, he touched the socket of his
thigh, so that the socket of Jacob's
thigh was dislocated as he wrestled
26 with him. Then he said,
"Let me go; for the dawn is breaking."
But he replied,
"I will not let you go, unless you
bless me."
27 "What is your name?" he said to
him.
"Jacob," he replied.
28 Then he said,
"Your name shall no longer be Jacob,
but Israel [wrestler with God], because
you have wrestled with God and man,
and have been the victor."
29 "Please tell me your name," requested Jacob.
"Why is it that you ask for my
name?" he replied; nevertheless he
blessed him there.
30 So Jacob called the name of that
place Peniel [face of God]; "For," said
he, "I have seen God face to face, and
yet my life has been spared."
31 The sun rose on him just as he passed
Penuel, limping because of his thigh.
32 That is why to this day the Israelites do
not eat the hip muscle which is on the
socket of the thigh; for the socket of
Jacob's thigh was touched on the hip
muscle.

Raising his eyes, Jacob saw Esau 33
coming, accompanied by four hundred
men; so he divided the children among
Leah, Rachel, and the two maids, and 2
put the maids with their children in
front, then Leah with her children, and
finally Rachel and Joseph in the rear,
while he himself went on ahead of 3
them, bowing seven times to the earth
until he reached his brother. Then 4
Esau ran to meet him, and embracing
him, fell on his neck, and kissed him, so
that they wept. When he raised his 5
eyes, he saw the women and children,
and said,
"What relation are these to you?"
"The children whom God has graciously bestowed on your servant," he
replied.
Whereupon the maids came up with 6
their children and bowed; and likewise 7
Leah with her children came up and
bowed; and then Joseph and Rachel
came up and bowed.
"What do you mean by all this com- 8
pany that I met?" he said.
"To win my lord's favor," he replied.
"I have plenty, my brother," said 9
Esau; "keep what you have."
But Jacob said, 10
"Not at all; if perchance I find favor
with you, accept my present from me,
since it is like seeing the face of God for
me to see your face, in that you have
received me favorably. Please accept 11
my gift of greeting that has been
brought to you; for God has been good
to me, and I have all I need."
Thus he urged him until he took it,
whereupon he said, 12
"Let us set out on our way; I will go
alongside you."
But he replied, 13
"My lord can see for himself that the
children are frail, and that the sheep
and cattle giving suck are a care to me;
if they were to be over-driven a single
day, the whole flock would die. Pray 14
let my lord go on ahead of his servant,
and I will proceed leisurely, at the pace
of the stock that I am driving, and at
the pace of the children, until I join my
lord at Seir."
"At least," said Esau, "let me leave 15
with you some of the troops accompanying me."
"How can I thank my lord?" he said.
So Esau started back that day on his 16
way to Seir, while Jacob set out for Suc- 17

coth, where he built a house for himself, and constructed sheds for his cattle. That was how the place came to be
named Succoth [sheds].
18 In the course of his journey from
Paddan-aram, Jacob arrived safely at
the city of Shechem, which is in the
land of Canaan, and camped in front of
19 the city. For one hundred kesitas he
bought the piece of ground on which he
had pitched his tent from the sons of
20 Hamor, the father of Shechem. There
he erected an altar, which he called El-
elohe-Israel [El, the God of Israel].
34 Now Dinah, the daughter that Leah
had borne to Jacob, went out to visit
2 the women of the district. When Shechem, the son of Hamor, the Hivvite,
the prince of the district, saw her, he
seized her, and lay with her, and rav-
3 ished her. He had a passionate longing
for Dinah, the daughter of Jacob; he
loved the girl, and spoke endearingly to
4 her. So Shechem said to his father Hamor,

"Get this girl for me in marriage."
5 Jacob heard that his daughter Dinah
had been violated, but since his sons
were out in the country with the stock,
Jacob took no action until their return.
6 Hamor, the father of Shechem, went
7 to Jacob to speak with him. The sons
of Jacob had come in from the country
as soon as they heard the news, and the
men were distressed and very angry
that such a shameless act had been
committed in Israel as the violation of
Jacob's daughter—which thing ought
8 not to be done. But Hamor said to
them,

"My son Shechem has set his heart
on your daughter; pray give her to him
9 in marriage. Intermarry with us, giving us your daughters in marriage, and
10 marrying ours. If you will make your
home with us, the land will be at your
disposal; settle down, engage in trade,
and acquire property in it."
11 Shechem said to her father and
brothers,

"If I may find favor with you, I will
pay anything that you demand of me.
12 Ask me ever so much in the way of marriage-price and presents, and I will pay
you just what you demand of me; only
give me the girl in marriage."
13 But the sons of Jacob answered
Shechem and his father Hamor craftily,
and refused, because he had violated
their sister Dinah; and they said to 14
them,

"We cannot do such a thing as to
give our sister to a man that is uncircumcised; for that would be a disgrace
to us. Only on this condition will we 15
accede to your requests, that you become like us, every male among you becoming circumcised. Then we will give 16
you our daughters in marriage, and
marry yours; we will make our home
with you, and become a single people.
If you will not agree to our proposal to 17
become circumcised, we will take our
daughters and go away."

The proposal was agreeable to Ha- 18
mor, and to Shechem, the son of
Hamor.

The young man made no delay in 19
carrying the matter through; for he
was in love with Jacob's daughter, and
he himself was the most important of
his father's family.

So Hamor and his son Shechem came 20
to their city gate, and said to their fellow-citizens,

"These men are well disposed to- 21
ward us; let them make their home in
the land, and engage in trade in it,
since the land is quite spacious enough
for them; let us marry their daughters,
and give them our daughters in marriage. It is only on this condition, how- 22
ever, that the men will agree to make
their home with us, and form a single
people: that all the males among us become circumcised as they are. Will not 23
their live stock and possessions and all
their cattle be to our advantage? If we
will but agree to their proposal, they
will make their home with us."

All those accustomed to go out 24
through the gates of his city agreed
with Hamor and his son Shechem, and
all the males were circumcised, namely,
all those accustomed to go out through
the gates of his city.

On the third day, when they were 25
sore, the two sons of Jacob, Simeon and
Levi, Dinah's brothers, each took his
sword, and advancing boldly against
the city, they slew every male. Hamor 26
and his son Shechem they put to the
sword, and taking Dinah from the house
of Shechem, they made off. Coming 27
upon the slain, the sons of Jacob sacked
the city that had violated their sister,
taking its flocks, herds, and asses, what 28
was in the city and in the fields; all its 29

wealth, and all its women and children
they captured, and took as spoil everything that was in the houses.
30 Then Jacob said to Simeon and Levi,
"You have brought trouble on me by
bringing me into bad odor with the inhabitants of the land, the Canaanites
and Perizzites. My numbers are small,
and if they combine against me and
attack me, I shall be destroyed, both I
and my family."
31 But they replied,
"Could our sister be treated like a
harlot?"
35 Then God said to Jacob,
"Rise, go up to Bethel to live, and
construct an altar there to the God who
appeared to you when you fled from
your brother Esau."
2 So Jacob said to his household and all
who were with him,
"Get rid of the foreign gods that are
in your midst, purify yourselves, and
3 change your garments. Then we shall
set out and go up to Bethel, where I am
to construct an altar to the God who
answered me at the time of my distress,
and has accompanied me wherever I
have gone."
4 So they handed over to Jacob all the
foreign gods that they had, as well as
rings that were in their ears, and Jacob
buried them at the foot of the terebinth
5 near Shechem. Then they set out, and
so great was the terror of God on the
cities around them that they did not
6 pursue the sons of Jacob. So Jacob and
all the people that were with him
reached Luz (that is, Bethel), which is
7 in the land of Canaan, and there he
built an altar, calling the sanctuary El-
Bethel, because it was there that God
had revealed himself to him when he
fled from his brother.
8 When Deborah, Rebekah's nurse,
died, she was buried below Bethel, at
the foot of the oak; so it came to be
named the Oak of Weeping.
9 On his journey from Paddan-aram,
God again appeared to Jacob, and
10 blessed him. God said to him,
"Your name has been Jacob; you
shall no longer be called Jacob, but Israel is to be your name."
So he came to be named Israel.
11 Further, God said to him,
"I am God Almighty; be fruitful and
multiply; a nation, or rather a company
of nations shall come from you, and
kings shall spring from you. The land 12
which I gave to Abraham and Isaac, I
will give to you, and to your descendants after you I will give it."
God then left him at the place where 13
he spoke with him, whereupon Jacob 14
erected a sacred pillar at the place
where he spoke with him, a pillar of
stone, poured a libation on it, and
anointed it with oil. So Jacob called 15
the name of the place where God spoke
with him Bethel.
They then set out from Bethel, and 16
while it was still some little distance to
the vicinity of Ephrath, Rachel gave
birth to a child, with terrible labor. In 17
the midst of her labor, the midwife said
to her,
"Do not be afraid; for here is another
son for you."
Just as her spirit left her (for she 18
died), she called his name Benoni, but
his father called him Benjamin. Thus 19
Rachel died, and was buried on the
way to Ephrath (that is, Bethlehem).
At her grave Jacob set up a sacred pil- 20
lar; it remains to this day as the Pillar
of Rachel's Grave.
Israel then moved on, and pitched 21
his tent on the further side of Migdal-
eder. It was while Israel was living in 22
that land that Reuben went and lay
with Bilhah, his father's consort; and
Israel heard of it.
The sons of Jacob were twelve in
number: the sons of Leah: Reuben, Ja- 23
cob's first-born, Simeon, Levi, Judah,
Issachar, and Zebulun; the sons of Ra- 24
chel: Joseph and Benjamin; the sons of 25
Bilhah, Rachel's maid: Dan and Naphtali; and the sons of Zilpah, Leah's 26
maid: Gad and Asher. These were the
sons of Jacob that were born to him in
Paddan-aram.
Then Jacob joined his father Isaac at 27
Mamre or Kirjath-arba (that is, Hebron), where Abraham and Isaac had
settled as immigrants. The length of 28
Isaac's life was one hundred and eighty
years; then Isaac came to his death; he 29
died and was gathered to his fathers, an
old man, satisfied with life; and his
sons, Esau and Jacob, buried him.
The following are the descendants of 36
Esau (that is, Edom). Esau married 2
Canaanite women: Adah, the daughter
of Elon, the Hittite, Oholibamah, the
daughter of Anah, the son of Zibeon,
the Hivvite, and Basemath, the daugh- 3

ter of Ishmael, the sister of Nebaioth.
4 Adah bore Eliphaz to Esau, Basemath
5 bore Reuel, and Oholibamah bore Jeush, Jalam, and Korah. These were the
sons of Esau that were born to him
in the land of Canaan.

6 Then Esau took his wives, his sons,
his daughters, all the members of his
household, his flocks, all his cattle, and
all the property that he had acquired in
the land of Canaan, and went away to
another land out of the way of his
7 brother Jacob; for their possessions
were too great for them to live together,
and the land in which they were living
as immigrants could not support them
8 because of their live stock. So Esau
made his home in the highlands of Seir
(Esau being Edom).

9 The following are the descendants of
Esau, the ancestor of Edom in the high-
10 lands of Seir; the following are the
names of the sons of Esau: Eliphaz, the
son of Esau's wife Adah, and Reuel,
11 the son of Esau's wife Basemath. The
sons of Eliphaz were Teman, Omar,
12 Zepho, Gatam, and Kenaz; while Timna was a consort of Esau's son Eliphaz,
and bore Amalek to Eliphaz. These
were the descendants of Esau's wife
Adah.

13 The following are the sons of Reuel:
Nahath, Zerah, Shammah, and Miz-
zah. These were the descendants of
Esau's wife Basemath.

14 The following are the sons of Esau's
wife Oholibamah, the daughter of
Anah, the son of Zibeon: she bore
Jeush, Jalam, and Korah to Esau.

15 The following are the chieftains of
the Esauites. The sons of Eliphaz, the
first-born of Esau: the chieftains of
16 Teman, Omar, Zepho, Kenaz, Korah,
Gatam, and Amalek. These were the
chieftains of Eliphaz in the land of
Edom, the same being the descendants
of Adah.

17 The following are the sons of Esau's
son Reuel: the chieftains of Nahath,
Zerah, Shammah, and Mizzah. These
were the chieftains of Reuel in the land
of Edom, the same being the descendants of Esau's wife Basemath.

18 The following are the sons of Esau's
wife Oholibamah: the chieftains of Jeush, Jalam, and Korah. These were the
chieftains of Esau's wife Oholibamah,
the daughter of Anah.

These were the sons of Esau (that is, 19
Edom), and these their chieftains.

The following are the sons of Seir, the 20
Horite, the inhabitants of the land: Lotan, Shobal, Zibeon, Anah, Dishon, 21
Ezer, and Dishan. These were the
chieftains of the Horites, the descendants of Seir in the land of Edom. The 22
sons of Lotan were Hori and Hemam,
while Lotan's sister was Timna. The 23
following are the sons of Shobal: Al-
van, Manahath, Ebal, Shepho, and
Onam. The following are the sons of
Zibeon: Aiah and Anah (he is the 24
Anah who found the hot springs in
the desert while he was pasturing the
asses of his father Zibeon). The follow- 25
ing are the sons of Anah: Dishon and
Oholibamah, the daughter of Anah.
The following are the sons of Dishon: 26
Hemdan, Eshban, Ithran, and Cheran.
The following are the sons of Ezer: Bil- 27
han, Zaavan, and Akan. The following 28
are the sons of Dishan: Uz and Aran.

The following are the chieftains of 29
the Horites: the chieftains of Lotan,
Shobal, Zibeon, Anah, Dishon, Ezer, 30
and Dishan. These were the chieftains
of the Horites in the land of Seir, chieftain by chieftain.

The following are the kings who 31
reigned in the land of Edom before the
Israelites had a king. Bela, the son of 32
Beor, reigned in Edom, the name of his
capital being Dinhabah. After the 33
death of Bela, Jobab, the son of Zerah
of Bozrah, succeeded to the throne.
After the death of Jobab, Husham from 34
the land of the Temanites succeeded to
the throne. After the death of Husham, 35
Hadad, the son of Bedad, who defeated
the Midianites in the country of Moab,
succeeded to the throne, the name of
his capital being Avith. After the death 36
of Hadad, Samlah of Masrekah succeeded to the throne. After the death 37
of Samlah, Shaul of Rehoboth-nahar
succeeded to the throne. After the 38
death of Shaul, Baal-hanan, the son of
Achbor, succeeded to the throne. After 39
the death of Baal-hanan, the son of
Achbor, Hadar succeeded to the throne,
the name of his capital being Peor, and
his wife's name Mehetabel, the daughter of Matred, the son of Me-zahab.

The following are the names of the 40
chieftains of Esau, arranged according
to their clans and places of residence, in
the order of their names: the chieftains

41 of Timna, Alvah, Jetheth, Oholibamah,
42 Elah, Pinon, Kenaz, Teman, Mibzar,
43 Magdiel, and Iram. These were the
chieftains of Edom (that is Esau, the
ancestor of Edom), arranged according
to their places of residence in the regions that they held.

37 Jacob, however, made his home in
the land where his father had lived as
an immigrant, the land of Canaan.

THE STORY OF JOSEPH, 37:2—48:22

2 The following are the descendants of
Jacob.
At the age of seventeen Joseph used
to accompany his brothers in looking
after the flocks, being a mere lad alongside the sons of Bilhah and Zilpah, his
father's wives; and Joseph brought a
bad report of them to their father.
3 Now Israel loved Joseph more than
any of his other sons, because he was
the son of his old age; so he made a long
4 cloak for him. When his brothers saw
that their father loved him more than
any of his brothers, they hated him,
and could not say a good word about
him.
5 Joseph had a dream, which he told to
his brothers, so that they hated him all
6 the more. He said to them,
"Listen to this dream that I have
7 had. While we were binding sheaves in
the field, my sheaf rose up and remained standing, while your sheaves
gathered round it, and made obeisance
to my sheaf!"
8 His brothers said to him,
"Are you indeed to be king over us;
would you actually rule us?"
So they hated him all the more for his
dreams and for his words.
9 Then he had another dream which he
recounted to his brothers.
"I have just had another dream," he
said, "and the sun, moon, and eleven
stars made obeisance to me!"
10 When he recounted it to his father
and his brothers, his father reproved
him, saying to him,
"What is this dream that you have
had? Am I actually to come with your
mother and your brothers, and make
obeisance to the earth to you?"
11 But while his brothers became jealous of him, his father kept the matter
in mind.

After his brothers had gone off to 12
pasture their father's flocks at Shechem,
Israel said to Joseph, 13
"Are not your brothers pasturing the
flocks at Shechem? Come, let me send
you to them."
"I am ready," he replied.
So he said to him, 14
"Go and see how your brothers are,
and the flocks; and bring me back
word."
So he despatched him from the valley
of Hebron; and he arrived at Shechem.
But a man found him wandering about 15
the country; so the man asked him,
"What are you looking for?"
"I am looking for my brothers," he 16
said; "do tell me where they are pasturing the flocks."
The man said, 17
"They have moved from here; for I
heard them say, 'Let us go to Dothan.'"
So Joseph followed his brothers, and
found them at Dothan. But they saw 18
him in the distance, and before he could
reach them, they plotted against him
to kill him.
"There comes the dreamer yonder!" 19
they said to one another. "Come now, 20
let us kill him, and throw him into one
of the pits. We can say that a wild
beast devoured him. Then we shall see
what his dreams will come to."
But when Reuben heard this, he tried 21
to save him from their hands; so he
said,
"Let us not take his life."
"Do not shed any blood," Reuben 22
said to them; "throw him into the pit
here in the wilderness, but do not lay
hands on him" (his idea being to save
him from their hands, and restore him
to his father).
As soon as Joseph reached his broth- 23
ers, they stripped him of his cloak (the
long cloak that he was wearing), and 24
seizing him, they threw him into the
pit. The pit, however, was empty, with
no water in it.
Then they sat down to eat a meal; 25
but raising their eyes, they saw a caravan of Ishmaelites coming from Gilead,
with their camels carrying gum, balm,
and laudanum, which they were engaged in taking down to Egypt. There- 26
upon Judah said to his brothers,
"What is the good of killing our
brother and covering up his blood?

27 Come, let us sell him to the Ishmaelites, and not lay hands on him; for after
all he is our brother, our own flesh."
28 His brothers agreed. Some Midianite
traders passed by, so pulling Joseph up,
they lifted him out of the pit. They sold
Joseph to the Ishmaelites for twenty
shekels of silver; and they took him to
Egypt.
29 So when Reuben went back to the
pit, there was no Joseph in the pit.
30 Then he tore his clothes, and returning
to his brothers, said,

"The boy is gone! And I, how can I
go home?"
31 Then they took Joseph's cloak, and
killing a goat, they dipped the cloak in
32 the blood. So they soiled the long cloak,
and then they brought it to their father,
saying,

"We found this; see whether it is your
son's cloak or not."
33 Examining it, he said,

"It is my son's cloak! Some wild
beast has devoured him; Joseph must
be torn to pieces."
34 Then Jacob tore his clothes, and
girded himself with sackcloth, and
35 mourned for his son for a long time. His
sons and daughters all tried to console
him, but he would not be consoled.

"No," he said, "I will go down
mourning to Sheol to my son."

Thus did his father weep for him.
36 Meanwhile the Midianites had sold
him in Egypt to Potiphar, an officer of
Pharaoh, his head steward.

38 It was at that time that Judah separated from his family, and joined an
Adullamite whose name was Hirah.
2 There Judah saw the daughter of a Canaanite whose name was Shua. Marrying her, he had intercourse with her,
3 and she conceived and bore a son,
4 whom he named Er. Again she conceived and bore a son, whom she named
5 Onan. She bore still another son whom
she named Shelah. It was at Chezib
that she bore him.
6 For Er, his first-born, Judah chose a
7 wife whose name was Tamar; but Er,
Judah's first-born, was so displeasing to
the LORD that the LORD killed him.
8 Then Judah said to Onan,

"Marry your brother's widow; do
the duty of a brother-in-law to her, and
rear a family for your brother."
9 But Onan, knowing that the family
would not be his, wasted his semen on
the ground whenever he had intercourse with his brother's widow, so as
not to give his brother a family. What 10
he did was so displeasing to the LORD
that he killed him too. So Judah said to 11
his daughter-in-law Tamar,

"Remain a widow in your father's
house until my son Shelah grows up."
"Lest," thought he, "he too should perish like his brothers."

So Tamar went away, and lived in
her father's house.

In the course of time Judah's wife, 12
the daughter of Shua, died. After completing the mourning ceremonies, Judah went up to Timnah with his friend
Hirah, the Adullamite, to look after the
shearing of his sheep; and news of it 13
was brought to Tamar, "Your father-
in-law is going up to Timnah to shear
his sheep." So she took off her widow's 14
dress, and covered herself with a veil;
and thus veiled, she sat down at the
gateway of Enaim, which was on the
road to Timnah; for she realized that
although Shelah had grown up she
would not be given to him in marriage.
When Judah saw her, he took her for 15
a harlot, because she had veiled her
face. So he stepped over to her at the 16
roadside, and said,

"Here, let me have intercourse with
you" (for he did not know that she
was his daughter-in-law).

"What will you give me," she said,
"for having intercourse with me?"

"I will send you a kid from the 17
flock," he said.

"Will you give me a pledge until you
send it?" she asked.

"What pledge shall I give you?" he 18
said.

"Your signet-ring," she said, "your
cord for it, and the staff that is in your
hand."

So he gave them to her, and then had
intercourse with her, and she conceived
by him. Then she rose and went away, 19
and taking off her veil, she put on her
widow's dress.

When Judah sent the kid by his 20
friend, the Adullamite, to recover the
pledge from the woman, he could not
find her. So he asked the men of the 21
place,

"Where is the temple-prostitute who
was by the roadside at Enaim?"

"No temple-prostitute has been
here," they said.

22 He then went back to Judah, and
said,
"I could not find her, and further, the
men of the place say, 'No temple-prostitute has been here.'"
23 So Judah said,
"Let her keep the things, lest we incur a scandal; anyway I sent the kid,
but you could not find her."
24 It was some three months later that
Judah was told, "Tamar, your daughter-in-law, has played the harlot, and
further, she is with child as a result of
the harlotry."
"Bring her out, and let her be
burned," said Judah.
25 But as she was being brought out,
she sent word to her father-in-law,
"By the man to whom these things
belong, I am with child." "Please note
whose they are," she said, "this signet-ring and cord and staff."
26 Judah acknowledged them, and said,
"She is more in the right than I, inasmuch as I did not marry her to my
son Shelah."
But never again did he have intercourse with her.
27 When the time of her delivery came,
28 there were twins in her womb! In the
course of her delivery one put out his
hand, whereupon the midwife took a
scarlet thread and tied it on his hand,
saying,
"This one should be born first."
29 But just as he drew back his hand, his
brother was born.
"How you have forged your way
through!" she said.
So he was named Perez [a forging
through].
30 Afterward his brother was born,
who had the scarlet thread on his hand;
so he was named Zerah [scarlet].
39 When Joseph was taken down to
Egypt, Potiphar, an Egyptian, an officer of Pharaoh, his head steward,
bought him from the Ishmaelites who
2 had taken him down there. The LORD
was with Joseph, so that he became a
prosperous man. He lived in the house
3 of his master, the Egyptian; and his
master noticed that the LORD was with
him and that the LORD made everything prosper with him that he under-
4 took; so Joseph found favor with him,
and was made his personal attendant;
then he made him superintendent of
his household, and put him in charge of
all his property. From the time that he 5
made him superintendent of his household and all his property, the LORD
blessed the house of the Egyptian for
Joseph's sake, the LORD'S blessing resting on everything that belonged to him,
both indoors and outdoors. So he left 6
everything that he had to Joseph's
charge, and having him, gave no concern to anything, except the food that
he ate.
Now Joseph was so handsome and 7
good-looking that some time later the
wife of his master took a fancy to
Joseph, and said,
"Lie with me."
But he refused, saying to his mas- 8
ter's wife,
"Having me, my master is giving no
concern to anything in the house, but
has committed all his property to my
charge; there is no one in this house 9
greater than I; he has kept nothing
from me except yourself, and that because you are his wife. How then can I
commit this great crime, and sin against
God?"
Though she spoke to Joseph day after 10
day, he would not listen to her solicitations to lie with her, or be with her.
One day, however, when he went into 11
the house to do his work, none of the
household servants being anywhere in
the house, she caught hold of his coat, 12
saying,
"Lie with me."
But he fled, leaving the coat in her
hands, and went outdoors. When she 13
saw that he had fled outdoors, leaving
his coat in her hands, she called her 14
household servants, and said to them,
"See how he has brought this Hebrew
fellow into our house to violate us! He
came into my room to lie with me, but
I screamed; and as soon as he heard me 15
scream and call, he fled, leaving his coat
beside me, and went outdoors."
So she left the coat beside her until 16
his master came home, and then told 17
him this same story,
"The Hebrew slave whom you
brought into our house came into my
room to violate me, but as soon as I 18
screamed and called, he fled outdoors,
leaving his coat beside me."
When Joseph's master heard the 19
statements of his wife who said to him,
"This is the way your slave treated
me," his anger blazed, and Joseph's 20

master took him and threw him into the
prison where state prisoners were confined. So he lay there in prison.
21 The LORD, however, was with
Joseph and was kind to him, and got
22 him into the good graces of the jailer, so
that the jailer put Joseph in charge of
all the prisoners who were in the jail,
and he looked after everything that was
23 done there. The jailer exercised no
oversight over anything in his charge,
because the LORD was with him, and
the LORD made whatever he undertook
prosper.
40 Some time after these events the
butler and the baker of the king of
Egypt offended their lord, the king of
2 Egypt, so that Pharaoh became angry
with his two officers, the chief butler
3 and the chief baker, and put them in
custody in the head steward's house, in
the prison where Joseph was confined.
4 The head steward intrusted Joseph
with them, and he waited on them.
After they had been in custody some
5 time, they both had dreams on the same
night, each having a dream of different
meaning—the butler and the baker of
the king of Egypt who were confined in
6 the prison. When Joseph came to them
in the morning, he saw that they were
7 worried, so he asked Pharaoh's officers
who were in custody with him in his
master's house,
"Why do you look so gloomy today?"
8 "We have had dreams," they replied,
"and there is no one to interpret them."
Joseph said to them,
"Does not dream interpretation belong to God? Pray recount them to
me."
9 So the chief butler recounted his
dream to Joseph.
"In my dream," he said to him,
10 "there was a vine in front of me, and on
the vine were three branches. As soon
as it budded, its blossoms shot up, its
11 clusters ripened into grapes. With
Pharaoh's cup in my hand, I took the
grapes, and squeezing them into Pharaoh's cup, I placed the cup in Pharaoh's hand."
12 Joseph said to him,
"This is its interpretation: the three
13 branches represent three days; within
three days Pharaoh shall summon you,
and restore you to your position, so that
you shall place Pharaoh's cup in his
hand as you used to do when you were
his butler; so, if you will be good enough 14
to keep me in mind when prosperity
comes to you, do me the kindness of
mentioning me to Pharaoh, and so liberate me from this house; for I was 15
really kidnapped from the land of the
Hebrews, and further, I have done
nothing here that I should be put into a
dungeon."
When the chief baker found that the 16
interpretation was favorable, he said to
Joseph,
"I too had a dream; in mine there
were three open-work baskets on my
head, and in the top basket was some of 17
every kind of baked food for Pharaoh,
but the birds were eating it out of the
basket on my head."
Joseph answered, 18
"This is its interpretation: the three
baskets represent three days; within 19
three days Pharaoh shall summon you,
and hang you on a tree, and the birds
shall eat the flesh off you."
On the third day, which was Pha- 20
raoh's birthday, he held a feast for all his
officials; and among his officials he summoned the chief butler and the chief
baker. The chief butler he restored to 21
his duties, so that he again placed the
cup in Pharaoh's hand; but the chief 22
baker he hanged, as Joseph had told
them in his interpretation. The chief 23
butler, however, did not keep Joseph in
mind, but forgot him.
Two whole years later Pharaoh 41
dreamed that he was standing beside
the Nile, when seven beautiful, fat cows 2
came up out of the Nile, and browsed
in the sedge. After them seven other 3
cows came up out of the Nile, ugly and
thin, and stood beside the other cows on
the bank of the Nile. Then the thin, 4
ugly cows ate up the seven beautiful,
fat cows, whereupon Pharaoh awoke.
When he fell asleep again, he had a sec- 5
ond dream: there were seven ears of
grain growing on a single stalk, fine and
plump, and after them there sprouted 6
seven other ears, thin and blasted by
the east wind. Then the thin ears swal- 7
lowed up the seven fine, full ears,
whereupon Pharaoh awoke, only to find
it a dream!
Next morning he was so perturbed 8
that he sent for all the magicians and
wise men of Egypt. To them Pharaoh
recounted his dreams, but no one could

9 interpret them for Pharaoh. Then the
chief butler said to Pharaoh,
"I would today recall my offense,
10 how Pharaoh became angry with his
servants, and put them in custody in
the house of the head steward, myself
11 and the chief baker. On the same night
we had dreams, he and I, each of us
having a dream of different meaning.
12 With us there was a Hebrew youth, a
slave belonging to the head steward,
and when we recounted our dreams to
him, he interpreted them for us, giving
each the proper interpretation of his
13 dream. And it fell out just as he had indicated in the interpretation; I was restored to my position, while the other
was hanged."
14 Thereupon Pharaoh sent for Joseph,
and he was brought hurriedly from the
dungeon. When he had shaved and
changed his clothes, he came into Pharaoh's presence.
15 "I have had a dream," Pharaoh said
to Joseph, "but there is no one to interpret it. However, I have heard it said
of you that you know how to interpret
dreams."
16 "Apart from God can Pharaoh be
given a favorable response?" Joseph
answered Pharaoh.
17 Then Pharaoh said to Joseph,
"I dreamed that I was standing on
18 the bank of the Nile, when seven fat
and beautiful cows came up out of the
19 Nile, and browsed in the sedge. After
them came up seven other cows, thin
and very ugly and lean—I have never
seen such poor cows in all the land of
20 Egypt. Then the lean, ugly cows ate
21 up the first seven fat cows; they passed
right into them, but no one would have
known that they had done so—they
looked just as bad as before. Then I
awoke.
22 "In another dream I saw seven ears
of grain growing on a single stalk, full
23 and plump, and after them there
sprouted seven other ears, withered,
thin, and blasted by the east wind.
24 Then the thin ears swallowed up the
seven plump ears. I told this to the
magicians, but there was no one to explain it to me."
25 Joseph said to Pharaoh,
"Pharaoh's dream is simple; God
would reveal to Pharaoh what he is
26 about to do. The seven fat cows represent seven years, and the seven plump

ears represent seven years—it is a single
dream. The seven lean and ugly cows 27
that came up after them represent sev-
en years, and so do the seven empty
ears blasted by the east wind; there are
to be seven years of famine. It is as I 28
told Pharaoh, God would show Pharaoh
what he is about to do. Seven years of 29
great plenty are coming throughout all
the land of Egypt, but following them 30
there will be seven years of famine, so
that the plenty will all be forgotten in
the land of Egypt; the famine will devastate the land, and the plenty will be- 31
come quite unknown in the land because of that famine which is to follow;
for it will be very severe. The fact that 32
the dream was sent twice to Pharaoh in
two forms means that the matter is absolutely settled by God, and that God
will soon bring it about. Now, then, 33
let Pharaoh find a shrewd and prudent
man, and put him in control of the land
of Egypt. Let Pharaoh proceed to ap- 34
point officials over the land to forearm
the land of Egypt during the seven
years of plenty; let them collect all the 35
food of these good years that are coming, and under the authority of Pharaoh
store up grain for food in the cities, and
hold it there. The food shall serve as a 36
reserve for the land against the seven
years of famine that are to befall the
land of Egypt, so that the land may not
perish from the famine."
The proposal commended itself to 37
Pharaoh and all his courtiers, and Pha- 38
raoh said to his courtiers,
"Can we find a man with the spirit of
God in him like this one?"
So Pharaoh said to Joseph, 39
"Since God has made all this known
to you, there is no one so shrewd and
prudent as you; you shall be in charge 40
of my palace, and all my people shall be
obedient to your commands; it is only
in the matter of the throne itself that I
shall be your superior."
Thereupon Pharaoh said to Joseph, 41
"I hereby put you in charge of the
whole land of Egypt."
And taking the signet ring from his 42
finger, Pharaoh put it on Joseph's
finger; he dressed him in linen robes,
put a gold chain round his neck, and 43
had him ride in the second of his chariots, with people shouting "Bow down!"
before him, thus putting him in charge
of the whole land of Egypt.

44 "Although I continue as Pharaoh,"
said Pharaoh to Joseph, "yet without
your consent shall no one stir hand or
foot in all the land of Egypt."
45 Then Pharaoh called Joseph's name
Zaphenath-paneah, and married him to
Asenath, the daughter of Potiphera,
priest of On; and Joseph's fame spread
throughout the land of Egypt.
46 Joseph was thirty years old when he
entered the service of Pharaoh, king of
Egypt.
After leaving the presence of Pharaoh, Joseph made a tour through the
47 whole land of Egypt. During the seven
years of plenty the land produced
48 abundant crops; so he collected all the
food of the seven years when there was
plenty in the land of Egypt, and thus
stored food in the cities, storing in each
city the food from the fields around it.
49 Joseph stored up grain like the sands of
the sea, in great quantities, until he
ceased to keep account of it; for it was
past measuring.
50 Before the years of famine came, two
sons were born to Joseph by Asenath,
the daughter of Potiphera, priest of On.
51 Joseph called the name of the first-born
Manasseh [forgetfulness]; "For," said
he, "God has made me forget all about
my hardships and my father's home."
52 The name of the second he called
Ephraim [fruitfulness]; "For God has
made me fruitful in the land of my misfortune."
53 When the seven years of plenty that
had prevailed in the land of Egypt
54 came to an end, the seven years of famine set in, as Joseph had said.
There was famine in all lands, but
throughout all the land of Egypt there
was food.
55 When all the land of Egypt became
famished, the people cried to Pharaoh
for food; so Pharaoh announced to all
Egypt,
"Go to Joseph, and do what he tells
you."
56 The famine spread all over the land,
so Joseph threw open all that he had
locked up, and sold grain to the Egyptians, since the famine was severe in the
57 land of Egypt. People from all lands
came to Joseph in Egypt to buy grain;
for the famine was severe all over the
earth.
42 When Jacob learned that there was
grain in Egypt, he said to his sons,
"Why do you stare at one another?"
"I have just heard," he said, "that 2
there is grain in Egypt; go down there,
and buy some for us there, that we may
live and not die."
So ten of Joseph's brothers went 3
down to buy grain in Egypt, since Ja- 4
cob would not let Joseph's brother Benjamin go with his other brothers;
"Lest," thought he, "harm should befall him." Thus the Israelites came 5
with the rest to buy grain; for the famine was in the land of Canaan.
Now Joseph was the vizier of the 6
land; it was he who sold the grain to all
the people of the land. So Joseph's
brothers came and prostrated themselves before him, with their faces to
the ground. When Joseph saw his 7
brothers, he recognized them, but he
treated them as if he were a stranger,
and spoke harshly to them.
"Where have you come from?" he
said to them.
"From the land of Canaan to buy
food," they said.
Joseph recognized his brothers, but 8
they did not recognize him. Remem- 9
bering the dreams that he had had
about them, Joseph said to them,
"You are spies; you have come to
find out the condition of the land!"
"No, my lord," they said to him, 10
"your servants have come to buy food.
We are all sons of one man; we are hon- 11
est men; your servants are not spies."
"Not so," he said to them; "but you 12
have come to find out the condition of
the land."
But they said, 13
"Your servants are brothers, twelve
in all; we are sons of a certain man in
the land of Canaan; the youngest is at
present with our father, while the other
is no more."
But Joseph said to them, 14
"It is as I told you; you are spies. By 15
this you shall be put to the proof: as
Pharaoh lives, you shall not leave this
place unless your youngest brother
comes here. Send one of your number 16
to fetch your brother, while the rest of
you remain in custody. Thus shall your
statements be put to the proof as to
whether you are truthful or not. As
Pharaoh lives, you are spies!"
So he bundled them off to prison for 17
three days, but on the third day Joseph 18
said to them,

"Since I am one who fears God, you
19 may save your lives, if you do this: if
you are honest men, let one of you
brothers remain confined in your prison
and then the rest of you, go and take
grain home to your starving house-
20 holds; but you must bring me your
youngest brother. Thus shall your
words be verified, and you shall not
die."
21 They proceeded to do so, saying to
one another,
"Unfortunately, we were to blame
about our brother, upon whose distress,
when he pleaded with us for mercy, we
gazed unmoved; that is why this distress has come to us."
22 Then Reuben spoke up and said to
them,
"Did I not say to you, 'Do not sin
against the lad'? But you paid no attention; so now comes a reckoning for
his blood!"
23 They did not know that Joseph heard
them; for the intermediary was between
24 them. He turned from them, and wept.
On coming back to them, he spoke to
them, took Simeon from them, and im-
25 prisoned him in their presence. Joseph
then ordered their receptacles to be
filled with grain, the money of each of
them to be replaced in his sack, and
provisions to be given them for the
26 journey. This was done for them. Then
they loaded their asses with their grain,
and departed.
27 At the camping-place for the night
one of them opened his sack to give his
ass some fodder, and there he saw his
money in the mouth of his sack!
28 "My money has been put back! It
is right here inside my sack!" he said to
his brothers.
Thereupon their hearts sank, and
they turned to one another in fear, saying,
"What is this that God has done to
us?"
29 On reaching their father Jacob in
the land of Canaan, they told him all
that had befallen them:
30 "The man, the lord of the land,
talked harshly to us, making us out to
31 be spies of the land. But we said to
him, 'We are honest men; we are not
32 spies. We are brothers on our father's
side, twelve in all; one is no more, and
the youngest is at present with our fa-
33 ther in the land of Canaan.' Then the
man, the lord of the land, said to us,
'By this I shall find out whether you are
honest men: leave one of your brothers
with me, and taking something for your
famishing households, be off; and then 34
bring me your youngest brother. Thus
shall I know that you are not spies, but
honest men. I will restore your brother
to you, and you will be free to trade in
the land.'"
When they came to empty their 35
sacks, there was the money-packet of
each in his sack! On seeing their mon-
ey-packets, both they and their father
were dismayed, and their father Jacob 36
said to them,
"It is I that you bereave. Joseph is
no more, Simeon is no more, and now
you would take Benjamin! It is on me
that all this falls."
Reuben said to his father, 37
"You may kill my two sons if I do not
bring him home to you! Put him in my
charge, and I will bring him back to
you."
But he said, 38
"My son shall not go down with you;
for his brother is dead, and he alone is
left. If harm were to befall him on the
journey that you make, you would
bring my gray hairs down to Sheol in
sorrow."
The famine continued severe in the 43
land, so when they had finished eating 2
all the grain which they had brought
from Egypt, their father said to them,
"Go again, and buy us a little food."
But Judah said to him, 3
"The man strictly warned us: 'You
cannot have audience with me unless
your brother is with you.' If you are 4
ready to let our brother go with us, we
will go down and buy food for you; but 5
if you are not ready to let him go, we
cannot go down; for the man said to us,
'You cannot have audience with me unless your brother is with you.'"
"Why did you bring this trouble on 6
me," said Israel, "by telling the man
that you had another brother?"
They said, 7
"The man persisted in asking about
ourselves and our family—'Is your father still living? Have you another
brother?' We only gave him the information demanded by these questions of
his. How could we possibly know that
he would say, 'Bring your brother
down'?"

8 "Let the lad go with me," said Judah
to his father Israel; "but we must go at
once, if we would save our lives and not
die, both we, you, and our dependents.
9 I will be surety for him; you may hold
me responsible for him. If I do not
bring him back to you and set him before you, you may blame me for it all
10 my life; in fact if we had not wasted so
much time, we could have made a second trip by now."
11 Then their father Israel said to them,
"If it must be so, then do this: take
some of the country's best in your receptacles, and take it down to the man
as a present—a little balm, a little honey, gum, laudanum, pistachio nuts, and
12 almonds. Also take double the money
with you, and so take back with you the
money that was replaced in the mouths
of your sacks—perhaps there was a mis-
13 take. Take your brother too, and go,
14 return to the man. May God Almighty
grant you such kindness with the man
that he will release your other brother
for you, as well as Benjamin. As for me,
as I am bereaved, I am bereaved.
15 So the men took this present, and
taking double the money with them, as
well as Benjamin, they started off, went
down to Egypt, and stood in the pres-
16 ence of Joseph. When Joseph saw Benjamin with them, he said to his house-
steward,
"Take the men home, kill an animal,
and get it ready; for the men are to dine
with me at noon."
17 The man did as Joseph said, and
18 brought the men to Joseph's house. On
being brought to Joseph's house, the
men became frightened, saying,
"It is because of the money which reappeared in our sacks the first time that
we are being brought in, so that he may
devise some pretext against us, and falling upon us, take us into slavery, together with our asses."
19 So they went up to Joseph's house-
steward, and spoke to him at the doorway of the house.
20 "If you please sir," they said, "we
came down the first time specially to
21 buy food, but when we reached the
camping-place for the night, and
opened our sacks, there was each man's
money in the mouth of his sack—our
money in full. Accordingly we have
22 brought it back with us, and we have
brought other money down with us to
buy food. We do not know who put our
money in our sacks."
"Be at ease," he said, "do not be 23
afraid! It must have been your God,
the God of your fathers, who put treasure in your sacks for you. I received
your money."
Then he brought Simeon out to them.
After bringing the men into Joseph's 24
house, the man gave them water to
wash their feet, and he gave them fodder for their asses. Then they set out 25
the present in anticipation of Joseph's
arrival at noon; for they had heard that
they were to dine there. When Joseph 26
came home, they brought him the present that they had carried into the
house, and bowed to the ground before
him. He asked after their health. 27
"Is your father well," he said, "the
old man of whom you spoke? Is he still
living?"
"Your servant, our father, is well; he 28
is still living," they said, bowing in
homage to him.
Raising his eyes, he saw his brother 29
Benjamin, the son of his own mother,
and said,
"Is this your youngest brother, of
whom you told me?"
"May God be gracious to you, my
son!" he said.
Thereupon Joseph hastily sought a 30
place to weep; for his heart was deeply
stirred at sight of his brother; he retired to his room, and wept there. Then 31
he bathed his face, and came out, and
controlling himself, said,
"Serve the meal."
The meal was served, separately for 32
him, for them, and for the Egyptians
that were dining with him; for the
Egyptians could not eat with the Hebrews, because that would be abhorrent
to the Egyptians. They were seated 33
in his presence in order of age, from the
oldest to the youngest, so that the men
stared at one another in amazement.
Portions were carried from his own ta- 34
ble to them, but Benjamin's portion
was five times as much as any other's.
So they feasted, and drank with him.
He then gave orders to his house- 44
steward,
"Fill the men's sacks as full as they
will hold with food, and put each man's
money in the mouth of his sack; in the 2
mouth of the sack belonging to the

youngest put my cup, the silver cup,
along with his money for the grain."
He followed the instructions which
Joseph gave.
3 With the dawn of morning the men
with their asses were sent on their way.
4 Although they had left the city, they
had not gone far, when Joseph said to
his house-steward,
"Run at once after the men, and
when you overtake them, say to them,
'Why have you returned evil for good?
Why have you stolen my silver cup?
5 Is not this the one from which my lord
drinks, which in fact he uses for divination?
It is a wicked thing that you have
done.'"
6 So he overtook them, and addressed
7 these words to them; but they said to
him,
"Why should my lord speak like this?
Your servants would never think of do-
8 ing such a thing! Why, we even
brought you back from the land of
Canaan the money that we found in the
mouths of our sacks. How then could
we steal silver or gold from your mas-
9 ter's house? That one of your servants
in whose possession it is found shall die,
and the rest of us will become slaves to
my lord."
10 "Although it may indeed be just as
you say," he said, "yet the one in whose
possession it is found shall become my
slave, but the rest of you shall be held
blameless."
11 Then each of them quickly lowered
his sack to the ground, and opened it,
12 and search being made, beginning with
the oldest and ending with the youngest, the cup was found in Benjamin's
13 sack. Thereupon they tore their clothes,
and each having reloaded his ass, they
returned to the city.
14 Judah and his brothers arrived at the
house of Joseph, while he was still there,
so they flung themselves on the ground
before him.
15 "What is this that you have done?"
Joseph said to them. "Did you not
know that a man like me would be sure
to use divination?"
16 Judah said,
"What can we say to my lord? What
can we urge? How can we prove our
innocence? God has discovered the
crime of your servants; here we are, the
slaves of my lord, both we and he in
whose possession the cup has been
found."
"I could not think of doing such a 17
thing," he said; "only the man in whose
possession the cup has been found shall
be my slave; the rest of you are free to
go back to your father."
Then Judah went up to him, and 18
said,
"If you please, my lord, let your servant speak a word in the ear of my lord,
and your anger not blaze against your
servant; for you are the equal of Pharaoh himself. My lord asked his serv- 19
ants, 'Have you a father or a brother?'
And we said to my lord, 'We have an 20
aged father, and a young brother, the
child of his old age; his brother is dead,
so that he alone is left of his mother's
children, and his father loves him.'
Then you said to your servants, 'Bring 21
him down to me that I may see him.'
But we told my lord, 'The boy cannot 22
leave his father; his father would die if
he were to leave him.' Whereupon you 23
said to your servants, 'Unless your
youngest brother comes down with you,
you cannot have audience with me
again.'
"When we went back to your serv- 24
ant, my father, we reported to him the
words of my lord. Then our father said, 25
'Go again and buy a little food for us.'
But we said, 'We cannot go down; if our 26
youngest brother accompanies us, we
can go down; for we shall not be allowed
to have audience with the man unless
our youngest brother is with us.' Then 27
your servant, my father, said to us,
'You know that my wife bore me only
two children; then one of them left me, 28
and I think he must surely have been
torn to pieces; for I have never seen him
since. If then you take this one from 29
me too, and harm befall him, you will
bring down my gray hairs to Sheol in
trouble.'
"And now, when I rejoin your serv- 30
ant, my father, and the boy not with
us, his life is so bound up with the boy's
that he will die when he sees that there 31
is no boy, and your servants will bring
down the gray hairs of your servant,
our father, to Sheol in sorrow; for your 32
servant went surety for the boy to my
father, saying, 'If I do not bring him
back to you, let my father blame me for
it all my life.' Now then, pray let your 33
servant remain in the boy's place as my

lord's slave, but let the boy go back
34 with his brothers; for how can I go back
to my father unless the boy is with me,
and witness the agony that would come
to my father?"
45 Joseph could no longer control himself before all his attendants, so he cried
out,
"Have everyone withdraw from me."
So there was no one with Joseph
when he made himself known to his
2 brothers; but he wept so loudly that the
Egyptians heard it, and Pharaoh's
3 household heard it. Joseph said to his
brothers,
"I am Joseph. Is my father still living?"
But his brothers could not answer
him, because they were so dismayed at
4 being in his presence. So Joseph said
to his brothers,
"Come nearer to me."
When they came nearer, he said,
"I am your brother Joseph whom
5 you sold into Egypt. Now do not be
distressed nor angry with yourselves
that you sold me here; for it was to save
6 life that God sent me ahead of you; for
it is two years now that the famine has
prevailed in the land, but there are still
five years in which there will be no
7 plowing or reaping. God sent me
ahead of you to insure you a remnant
in the earth, and to be the means of a
8 remarkable escape for you. So then it
was not you, but God who sent me here,
and made me a father to Pharaoh, lord
of all his house, and ruler over all the
9 land of Egypt. Hurry back to my father and say to him, 'Thus speaks your
son Joseph: "Since God has made me
lord of all Egypt, come down to me
10 without delay. You shall live in the
land of Goshen, and be near me, you,
your sons, your grandsons, your flocks,
your herds, and all that belong to you;
11 and there I will provide for you, lest
you, your household, and all that belong to you come to want; for there are
still five years of famine to come."'
12 You can see for yourselves and my
brother Benjamin for himself that it is
13 I who speak to you. You must tell my
father all about my splendor in Egypt,
and all that you have seen; hurry and
bring my father here."
14 Then he fell on the neck of his brother Benjamin and wept, while Benjamin
15 wept on his neck. He kissed all his
brothers, and wept on their shoulders,
after which his brothers talked with
him.
When the news was received at Pha- 16
raoh's palace that Joseph's brothers had
arrived, Pharaoh was delighted, as were
also his courtiers. Pharaoh said to 17
Joseph,
"Say to your brothers, 'Do this: load
your animals, go back to the land of
Canaan, and taking your father and 18
your households, come to me, and I will
give you the best of the land of Egypt,
so that you shall eat the fat of the land.
Also, carry out this order: take wagons 19
from the land of Egypt for your little
ones and your wives; convey your father in them, and come back. Never 20
mind your goods; for the best of the
whole land of Egypt will be yours.'"
The sons of Israel did so. Joseph 21
gave them wagons in accord with the
command of Pharaoh, and he also gave
them provisions for the journey. To 22
each of them he gave a festal garment,
but to Benjamin he gave three hundred
shekels of silver and five festal garments. To his father he sent likewise 23
ten asses loaded with the best products
of Egypt, and ten she-asses loaded with
grain, bread, and provisions for his father on the journey. Then he sent his 24
brothers away; and as they left, he said
to them,
"Do not get too excited on the way."
So they went up from Egypt, and 25
came to the land of Canaan, to their father Jacob.
"Joseph is still living, and he is ruler 26
over all the land of Egypt," they told
him.
But he was so stunned that he would
not believe them. However, when they 27
told him all that Joseph had said to
them, and he saw the wagons that
Joseph had sent to convey him, their
father Jacob recovered.
"Enough!" said Israel; "my son Jo- 28
seph is still living; I will go and see him
before I die."
So Israel set out with all that be- 46
longed to him. On reaching Beersheba,
he offered sacrifices to the God of his
father Isaac. In a vision by night God 2
spoke to Israel.
"Jacob! Jacob!" he said.
"Here I am," he said.
"I am El, the God of your father," 3
he said; "do not be afraid to go down to

Egypt; for there I will make you a great
4 nation. I will myself go down to Egypt
with you—yes, and I will bring you up
again, when Joseph's hand shall close
your eyes."
5 Then Jacob set out from Beersheba;
and the sons of Israel conveyed their
father Jacob, with their little ones and
their wives, in the wagons which Pha-
6 raoh had sent to convey him. Taking
their live stock and the property which
they had acquired in the land of Canaan, Jacob and all his family migrated
7 to Egypt; his sons and his grandsons
accompanied him, as well as his daughters and his grand-daughters; he
brought all his family with him into
Egypt.
8 The following are the names of the
Israelites, Jacob and his children, who
migrated to Egypt: Reuben, Jacob's
9 first-born, and the sons of Reuben,
10 Hanoch, Pally, Hezron, and Carmi; the
sons of Simeon, Jemuel, Jamin, Ohad,
Jachin, Zohar, and Shaul, the son of a
11 Canaanite woman; the sons of Levi,
12 Gershon, Kohath, and Merari; the sons
of Judah, Er, Onan, Shelah, Perez, and
Zerah, of whom Er and Onan died in
the land of Canaan, and the sons of
13 Perez were Hezron and Hamul; the sons
of Issachar, Tola, Puvvah, Job, and
14 Shimron; the sons of Zebulun, Sered,
15 Elon, and Jahleel (these were the sons
which Leah bore to Jacob in Paddan-
aram, together with his daughter Dinah, the total number of his sons and
16 daughters being thirty-three); the sons
of Gad, Ziphion, Haggi, Shuni, Ezbon,
17 Eri, Arodi, and Areli; the sons of Asher,
Imnah, Ishvah, Ishvi, and Beriah, with
their sister Serah, and the sons of Be-
18 riah, Heber and Malchiel (these were
the sons of Zilpah, whom Laban gave to
his daughter Leah; these she bore to
19 Jacob—sixteen persons); the sons of
Jacob's wife Rachel, Joseph and Ben-
20 jamin, and to Joseph in the land of
Egypt were born Manasseh and Ephraim, whom Asenath, the daughter of
Potiphera, priest of On, bore to him;
21 the sons of Benjamin, Bela, Becher,
Ashbel, Gera, Naaman, Ehi, Rosh,
22 Muppim, Huppim, and Ard (these were
the sons of Rachel, who were born to
23 Jacob—a total of fourteen persons); the
24 son of Dan, Hushim; the sons of Naphtali, Jahzeel, Guni, Jezer, and Shillem
25 (these were the sons of Bilhah, whom
Laban gave to his daughter Rachel;
these she bore to Jacob—a total of sev-
en persons). The total number of 26
persons belonging to Jacob who came to
Egypt, his direct descendants, exclud-
ing the wives of his sons, was sixty-six;
but the sons of Joseph that were born to 27
him in Egypt were two, the total number of persons belonging to Jacob's
household who migrated to Egypt being seventy.
Israel sent Judah ahead of him to 28
Joseph in Goshen, to appear before
him. On their arrival in the land of 29
Goshen Joseph hitched the horses to his
chariot, and went up to meet his father
Israel in Goshen. When he presented
himself to him, he fell on his neck,
weeping again and again on his neck.
"Now at last I may die," Israel said 30
to Joseph, "after having seen from your
very self that you are still alive."
Then Joseph said to his brothers and 31
his father's household,
"I will go and tell Pharaoh, and say
to him, 'My brothers and my father's
household who used to live in the land
of Canaan have come to me. Since the 32
men are shepherds, having to do with
live stock, they have brought their
flocks and herds and everything that
they own.' Accordingly, when Pharaoh 33
summons you, and says to you, 'What is
your occupation?' you must say, 'Your 34
servants have been concerned with live
stock from our youth until now, both
we and our fathers'—in order that you
may settle in the land of Goshen; for
shepherds are all abhorrent to the
Egyptians."
So Joseph came and told Pharaoh. 47
"My father and brothers," he said,
"together with their flocks and herds
and everything that they own, have
come from the land of Canaan, and are
now in the land of Goshen."
Taking five of the ablest of his broth- 2
ers, he presented them to Pharaoh.
"What is your occupation?" Pha- 3
raoh said to his brothers.
"Your servants are shepherds," they
said to Pharaoh, "both we and our fathers." "We have come to settle as im- 4
migrants in the land," they said to Pharaoh; "for there is no pasture for the
flocks belonging to your servants, because the famine is so severe in the land
of Canaan. Pray let your servants settle, then, in the land of Goshen."

5 Then Pharaoh said to Joseph,
"Now that your father and brothers
6 have joined you, the land of Egypt is
at your disposal; settle your father and
brothers in the best part of the land;
let them settle in the land of Goshen,
and if you know of any competent men
among them, put them in charge of my
own live stock."
7 Then Joseph brought his father Jacob and presented him to Pharaoh, and
Jacob paid his respects to Pharaoh.
8 "How old are you?" Pharaoh said to
Jacob.
9 "The length of my life as an immigrant has been one hundred and thirty years," Jacob said to Pharaoh; "few and hard have been the years of my life; they have not equaled the number of years that my fathers lived in their lifetime as immigrants."
10 After paying his respects to Pharaoh, Jacob withdrew from the presence of Pharaoh.
11 So Joseph settled his father and brothers, giving them property in the land of Egypt in the very best part of the land, in the land of Rameses, as
12 Pharaoh had commanded. Joseph provided his father and brothers and all his father's household with food sufficient for the needs of the dependents.
13 There was now no food anywhere in the land; for the famine was very severe, so that the lands of Egypt and Canaan were languishing because of the
14 famine. Joseph had gathered up all the money that was to be found in the lands of Egypt and Canaan in payment for the grain which was bought, and had brought the money to Pharaoh's pal-
15 ace. So when the money was exhausted in the lands of Egypt and Canaan, all the Egyptians came to Joseph, saying,
"Give us food; why should we die right under your eyes, just because our money is gone?"
16 "Give me your live stock," said Joseph; "I will give you food in exchange for your live stock, if your money is gone."
17 So they brought their live stock to Joseph, and Joseph gave them food in exchange for horses, sheep, cattle, and asses; thus he supported them with food that year in exchange for all their live stock.
18 When that year was over, they came to him the next year, and said to him,

"We would hide nothing from my lord; but our money is gone, and our live stock has come into the possession of my lord; there is nothing left for my lord except our persons and our lands.
Why should we perish before your very 19
eyes, both we and our land? Buy us and our land in exchange for food, and we and our land shall become feudatory to Pharaoh; but give us seed that we may live and not die, and the land not become a waste."
So Joseph bought all the land of 20
Egypt for Pharaoh; for everyone of the Egyptians sold his field, because the famine was so severe on them. Thus the
land became Pharaoh's, and the people 21
themselves he transferred to the towns from one end of Egypt's domain to the
other. It was only the priests' land that 22
he did not buy; for the priests had a subvention from Pharaoh, and lived off the subvention which Pharaoh gave them; that was why they did not have to sell their land.
"Observe," said Joseph to the people, 23
"that I have today bought you and your land for Pharaoh. Here is seed for
you tc sow the land; a fifth of the crop 24
you shall give to Pharaoh, and four fifths shall go to yourselves as seed for the fields, and as food for yourselves and your households, and as food for your little ones."
"You have saved our lives," they 25
said, "we would thank my lord; and we will become slaves to Pharaoh."
So Joseph made it a statute for the 26
land in Egypt, which continues to this day, that a fifth of the produce should go to Pharaoh, the land of the priests alone being exempt from Pharaoh's claims.
So the Israelites settled in the land of 27
Egypt, in the land of Goshen, where they acquired property, were prolific, and became very numerous.
Jacob lived in the land of Egypt for 28
seventeen years, so that the length of Jacob's life was one hundred and forty-seven years.
When the time approached for Israel 29
to die, he summoned his son Joseph, and said to him,
"If I have found favor with you, pray put your hand under my thigh and swear that you will deal kindly and faithfully by me; please do not bury me
in Egypt, but let me sleep with my fa- 30

were born on the knees of
Joseph said to his brothers,
about to die; but God will be
ake note of you, and take you
f this land to the land which he
d on oath to Abraham, Isaac,
cob."

Joseph then made the sons of Israel 25
swear,
"When God does indeed take note of
you, you must take my bones up with
you from here."
So Joseph died at the age of one hun- 26
dred and ten years; and he was embalmed, and placed in a coffin in Egypt.

thers; take me out of Egypt, and bury
me in their burial-place."
"I will do as you say," he said.
31 "Give me your oath," he said.
So he gave him his oath, whereupon
Israel settled back on the head of his
bed.

48 Some time after this word was
brought to Joseph,
"Your father is ill."
So he took his two sons, Manasseh
and Ephraim, with him, and came to
2 see Jacob. Then Jacob was told.
"Your son Joseph has just come to
see you."
Collecting his strength, Israel sat up
in bed.
3 "God Almighty appeared to me at
Luz in the land of Canaan, and blessed
4 me," Jacob said to Joseph; "he said to
me, 'I will make you prolific and numerous, I will make you a company of
peoples, and I will give this land to your
descendants as a possession for all time.'
5 I do therefore adopt your two sons that
were born to you in the land of Egypt
before I joined you in Egypt; Ephraim
and Manasseh shall be as much mine as
6 Reuben and Simeon. But the children
that were born to you after them
are to be counted to you; upon receiving their heritage they shall be called by
7 the names of their brothers. It was
when I was coming from Paddan that
Rachel to my sorrow died in the land of
Canaan, some little distance from the
vicinity of Ephrath, and I buried her
there on the road to Ephrath (that is,
Bethlehem)."
8 When Israel saw Joseph's sons, he
said,
"Who are these?"
9 Joseph said to his father,
"They are my sons, whom God has
given me here."
"Bring them to me," he said, "that I
may bless them."
10 (Now Israel's eyes were so dim with
age that he could not see.)
So Joseph brought them up to him,
and he kissed them, and embraced
them.
11 "I never expected to see even you,"
Israel said to Joseph, "and here God
let me see your children as well!"
12 Then Joseph removed them from his
knees, and bowed on his face to the
ground.
13 Joseph took the two of them, Ephraim in his right hand at Israel's left, and
Manasseh in his left hand at Israel's
right, and he brought them up to him.
But Israel stretched out his right hand 14
and put it on the head of Ephraim, although he was the younger, and his left
hand on the head of Manasseh, confusing his hands, because Manasseh was
the first-born.
He blessed Joseph, saying, 15
"May the God in whose favor my
fathers, Abraham and Isaac, lived, the
God who has been my shepherd all my
life long until this day, the angel who 16
has delivered me from all harm—may
he bless the lads, so that my name may
be carried on through them, together
with the names of my fathers, Abraham and Isaac; may they grow into
multitudes in the earth."
When Joseph saw that his father was 17
putting his right hand on the head of
Ephraim, it distressed him; so he seized
his father's hand in order to remove it
from the head of Ephraim to that of
Manasseh.
"Not so, my father," Joseph said to 18
his father; "for this one is the first-born;
put your right hand on his head."
But his father refused, saying, 19
"I know, my son, I know; he too
shall become a people, and he too shall
be great, but his younger brother shall
be greater than he, and his descendants
shall become a multitude of nations."
So he blessed them that day, saying, 20
"The Israelites will invoke blessings
on one another through you, saying,
'May God make you like Ephraim and
Manasseh!' "—thus putting Ephraim
before Manasseh.
Then Israel said to Joseph, 21
"I am about to die, but God will be
with you, and will bring you back to the
land of your fathers. As the one above 22
your brothers, I hereby give you Shechem, which I captured from the Amorites with my sword and bow."

THE BLESSING OF JACOB, 49:1–28

Then Jacob summoned his sons, and 49
said,
"Come together that I may tell you
what is to befall you in days to come:
Gather round and listen, you sons of 2
Jacob;
Listen to Israel, your father.

3 Reuben, you are my first-born,
My strength and the first issue of my manly vigor;
Excessively proud and excessively fierce,
4 Turbulent as water—you shall no longer excel;
For you went up to your father's bed;
So I degraded him who went up to my couch.

5 Simeon and Levi are brothers;
Ruthless weapons are their daggers.
6 I will never enter their circle;
I will never join in their assembly;
For in their anger they slay men,
And in their normal mood they hamstring oxen.
7 Cursed be their anger, for it is fierce,
And their wrath, for it is cruel!
I will disperse them throughout Jacob,
And scatter them throughout Israel.

8 Your brothers shall praise you, O Judah;
With your hand on the necks of your foes,
Your father's sons shall bow down to you.
9 A lion's whelp is Judah;
On prey you have grown up, my son.
He crouches, he couches like a lion,
Like an old lion; who dare disturb him?
10 The scepter shall never depart from Judah,
Nor the staff from between his feet,
Until his ruler comes,
To whom the peoples shall be obedient.
11 He tethers his ass to the vine,
And his ass's colt to the choicest vine;
He washes his garments in wine,
And his robes in the blood of grapes;
12 His eyes are darker than wine,
And his teeth whiter than milk.

13 Zebulun shall dwell by the seashore;
He shall be a haven for ships,
With his flank at Sidon.

14 Issachar is a sturdy ass,
Lounging among the ravines;
15 He saw that settled life was good,
And that the land was pleasant;
So he offered his shoulder to bear burdens,
And became a gang-slave.

Dan shall judge his people, 16
As any other of the tribes of Israel.
May Dan be a serpent by the roadside, 17
A viper beside the path,
That bites the horse's hoofs,
So that its rider tumbles backward.

For succor from thee, O LORD, I wait! 18

As for Gad, raiders shall raid him, 19
But he shall raid their rear.

As for Asher, his food shall be rich, 20
And he shall yield royal dainties.

Naphtali is a free-ranging deer, 21
That bears beautiful fawns.

Joseph is a young bull, 22
A young bull at a spring,
A wild-ass at Shur.
Shooting at him in enmity, 23
The archers fiercely assailed him;
But their bow was broken by the Eternal, 24
And their arms and hands trembled,
At the might of the Mighty One of Jacob,
At the name of the Shepherd, the Rock of Israel,
At your father's God, who helps you,
And God Almighty, who blesses you 25
With the blessings of the heavens above,
The blessings of the abyss couching below;
The blessings of breast and of womb,
The blessings of fatherhood, yea of man and child; 26
The blessings of the ancient mountains,
The dainties of the eternal hills—
May these rest on the head of Joseph,
And on the brow of him who was cursed by his brothers!

Benjamin is a ravenous wolf; 27
Devouring prey in the morning,
And dividing spoil at evening."

All these constituted the twelve 28
tribes of Israel, and this was what their
father said to them. He blessed them,
bestowing on each the blessing suited to
him.

THE DEATH AND BURIAL OF JACOB, AND THE DEATH OF JOSEPH, 49:29—50:26

29 He then gave them a charge.
"I am about to be gathered to my
fathers," he said to them; "bury me
with my fathers in the cave which is in
30 the field of Ephron, the Hittite, the
cave in the field of Machpelah, which
faces Mamre, in the land of Canaan,
which along with the field Abraham
bought from Ephron, the Hittite, for
use as a burial-ground of his own. It
31 was there that Abraham and his wife
Sarah were buried; it was there that
Isaac and his wife Rebekah were
buried; and it was there that I buried
32 Leah—the field with the cave in it having been purchased from the Hittites."
33 After Jacob had finished giving his
instructions to his sons, he drew his feet
up into the bed, breathed his last, and
was gathered to his fathers.
50 Joseph fell on his father's face, weep-
2 ing over him, and kissing him. He then
ordered the physicians among his slaves
3 to embalm his father. So the physicians
embalmed Israel, spending forty days
at it; for that is the time that it takes to
embalm. There was weeping for him in
Egypt for seventy days.
4 After the days of weeping for him
were over, Joseph said to Pharaoh's
household,
"If perchance I find favor with you,
5 please tell Pharaoh this: 'My father exacted an oath of me, saying, "Here am I
at the point of death; you must bury
me in the sepulcher that I dug for myself in the land of Canaan." Now then,
let me go up and bury my father. I will
surely return.'"
6 Whereupon Pharaoh said,
"Go up and bury your father, as he
made you swear."
7 So Joseph went up to bury his father,
and with him went all of Pharaoh's
courtiers, the elders of his household,
and all the elders of the land of Egypt,
8 as well as all of Joseph's own household,
his brothers, and his father's household,
leaving only their children and their
flocks and herds in the land of Goshen.
9 Both chariotry and cavalry went up
with him, so that there was a very large
caravan.

Arriv
yond the
and sorro
Joseph ob
mourning
habitants o
saw the mou
said,
"This is a
the Egyptians
That is how
called Abel-Mizr
Egyptians], which
dan.
Jacob's sons did
had commanded the
him to the land of C
him in the cave in th
pelah, which faces Ma
Abraham had bought f
al-ground of his own fro
Hittite. After burying h
seph returned to Egypt w
ers and all who had gone u
bury his father.
Realizing that their fathe
Joseph's brothers said,
"Suppose Joseph should
aversion to us, and pay us bac
the harm that we did him!"
So they sent a message to
saying,
"Before his death your father
this command: 'Thus shall you s
Joseph: "Pray forgive the crime
sin of your brothers in doing
harm."' So now, please forgive t
crime of the servants of your father
God."
Joseph wept when they spoke to him,
so that his brothers went and fell down
before him, saying,
"Here we are, your slaves!"
But Joseph said to them, 19
"Do not be afraid; for can I take
God's place? You meant to do me 20
harm, but God accounted it good, in
order to do as he has done today: save
the lives of many people. So now, do 21
not be afraid; I myself will provide for
you and your dependents."
Thus he reassured them, speaking
kindly to them.
So Joseph and his father's household 22
lived in Egypt. Joseph lived one hundred and ten years, living to see the 23
third generation of Ephraim's children;
the sons, too, of Machir, the son of

Manasseh
Joseph.
Then J
24 "I am
sure to t
up out o
promise
and Ja

THE BOOK OF EXODUS

THE OPPRESSION OF THE HEBREWS IN EGYPT, 1:1–22

1 THE following are the names of
the sons of Israel who came to
Egypt in the company of Jacob,
2 each with his household: Reu-
3 ben, Simeon, Levi, and Judah, Issa-
4 char, Zebulun, and Benjamin, Dan and
5 Naphtali, Gad and Asher. The total
number of persons that were direct descendants of Jacob was seventy, Joseph
6 being already in Egypt. Then Joseph
died, and likewise all his brothers and
7 all that generation; but the Israelites
were fruitful and prolific; they increased
in numbers, and grew greater and
greater, so that the land was filled with
them.

8 Then a new king rose over Egypt,
9 who had no knowledge of Joseph; he
said to his people,

"See, the Israelite people have become
too numerous and too strong for us;
10 come, let us take precautions against
them lest they become so numerous
that in the case of a war they should
join forces with our enemies and fight
against us, and so escape from the
land."

11 Accordingly, gang-foremen were put
in charge of them, to oppress them with
their heavy labor; and they built Pi-
thom and Raamses as store-cities for
12 Pharaoh. But the more they oppressed
them, the more they multiplied and expanded, so that they became apprehen-
sive about the Israelites.

13 The Egyptians reduced the Israelites
14 to rigorous slavery; they made life bitter for them in hard work with mortar
and bricks, and in all kinds of work in
the fields, all the work that they exacted of them being rigorous.

15 Then the king of Egypt spoke to the
midwives attending the Hebrew wom-
en, of whom the name of one was Shiph-
rah and that of the other Puah.

16 "When you act as midwives for the
Hebrew women," he said, "you are to
look at the genitals; if it is a boy, you
must kill him, but if it is a girl, she may
live."

But the midwives stood in awe of 17
God, and so did not do as the king of
Egypt told them, but let the male children live. So the king of Egypt sum- 18
moned the midwives, and said to them,

"Why have you done this: let the
male children live?"

The midwives said to Pharaoh, 19

"Because the Hebrew women are not
like the Egyptian women; but are animals, in that they are delivered before
the midwife reaches them!"

So God was good to the midwives; 20
the people multiplied and grew very
numerous, and because the midwives 21
stood in awe of God, they established
families for them.

So Pharaoh commanded all his peo- 22
ple,

"Every boy that is born to the Hebrews, you must throw into the Nile,
but you are to let all the girls live."

MIRIAM - sister of Moses

THE RISE OF THE DELIVERER, MOSES, 2:1—7:13

Now a man belonging to the house of 2
Levi went and married a daughter of
Levi. The woman conceived and bore a 2
son, and seeing that he was robust, she
hid him for three months. When she 3
could no longer hide him, she procured
an ark of papyrus reeds for him, and
daubing it with bitumen and pitch, she
put the child in it, and placed it among
the reeds beside the bank of the Nile.
His sister posted herself some distance 4
away to see what would happen to him.

Presently Pharaoh's daughter came 5
down to bathe at the Nile, while her
maids walked on the bank of the Nile.
Then she saw the ark among the reeds
and sent her maid to get it. On opening 6
it, she saw the child, and it was a boy
crying! She took pity on him, and said,

"This is one of the Hebrews' children."

assists women at birth

7 Thereupon his sister said to Pharaoh's daughter,
"Shall I go and summon a nurse for
you from the Hebrew women, to nurse
the child for you?"
8 "Go," said Pharaoh's daughter to
her.
9 So the girl went and called the child's
mother, to whom Pharaoh's daughter
said,
"Take this child away and nurse it
for me, and I will pay the wages due
you."
So the woman took the child and
10 nursed him; and when the child grew
up, she brought him to Pharaoh's
daughter, and he became her son. She
called his name Moses [drawn out];
"For," said she, "I drew him out of the
water."
11 It was in those days that Moses, now
grown up, went out to visit his fellow-
countrymen and noted their heavy labor. He saw an Egyptian kill a He-
12 brew, one of his own countrymen; so,
looking this way and that, and seeing
that there was no one in sight, he killed
the Egyptian, and hid him in the sand.
13 Another day, when he went out, there
were two Hebrews fighting! So he said
to him that was in the wrong,
"Why do you strike your companion?"
14 He replied,
"Who made you ruler and judge over
us? Are you thinking of murdering me
as you did the Egyptian?"
Then was Moses afraid. "The incident must surely be known," he
thought.
15 When Pharaoh heard about the matter, he tried to kill Moses, but Moses
fled from Pharaoh and went to the land
of Midian, and sat down beside a well.
16 Now the priest of Midian had seven
daughters, who came to draw water,
and fill the troughs to water their fa-
17 ther's flock, but some shepherds came
and drove them off. So Moses went to
their rescue and watered their flock.
18 When they came home to their father
Reuel, he said,
"How did you come to get home so
soon today?"
19 They said,
"An Egyptian protected us against
the shepherds; he even drew water for
us, and watered the flock."
20 "Then where is he?" he said to his
daughters. "Why did you leave the
man behind? Invite him to have a
meal."
When Moses agreed to live with the 21
man, he gave Moses his daughter Zipporah in marriage; and she bore a son, 22
whom he named Gershom [immigrant];
"For," said he, "I am an immigrant in
a foreign land."
In the course of this long time the 23
king of Egypt died. The Israelites,
groaning under their bondage, cried for
help, and their cry because of their
bondage came up to God. God heard 24
their moaning, and God remembered
his covenant with Abraham, Isaac, and
Jacob; God saw the plight of Israel, and 25
took cognizance of it.
While Moses was tending the flock 3
of his father-in-law, Jethro, the priest
of Midian, he led the flock to the western side of the desert, and came to the
mountain of God, Horeb. Then the an- 2
gel of the LORD appeared to him in a
flame of fire, rising out of a bush. He
looked, and there was the bush burning
with fire without being consumed! So 3
Moses said,
"I will turn aside and see this great
sight, why the bush is not burned up."
When the LORD saw that he had 4
turned aside to look at it, God called to
him out of the bush.
"Moses, Moses!" he said.
"Here I am!" said he.
"Do not come near here," he said; 5
"take your sandals off your feet; for the
place on which you are standing is holy
ground." "I am the God of your fa- 6
ther," he said, "the God of Abraham,
Isaac, and Jacob."
Then Moses hid his face; for he was
afraid to look at God.
"I have indeed seen the plight of my 7
people who are in Egypt," the LORD
said, "and I have heard their cry under
their oppressors; for I know their sorrows, and I have come down to rescue 8
them from the Egyptians and bring
them up out of that land to a land, fine
and large, to a land flowing with milk
and honey, to the country of the Canaanites, Hittites, Amorites, Perizzites,
Hivvites, and Jebusites. Now the cry 9
of the Israelites has reached me, and I
have also seen how the Egyptians are
oppressing them; so come now, let me 10
send you to Pharaoh, that you may

thers; take me out of Egypt, and bury
me in their burial-place."
"I will do as you say," he said.
31 "Give me your oath," he said.
So he gave him his oath, whereupon
Israel settled back on the head of his
bed.

48 Some time after this word was
brought to Joseph,
"Your father is ill."
So he took his two sons, Manasseh
and Ephraim, with him, and came to
2 see Jacob. Then Jacob was told.
"Your son Joseph has just come to
see you."
Collecting his strength, Israel sat up
in bed.
3 "God Almighty appeared to me at
Luz in the land of Canaan, and blessed
4 me," Jacob said to Joseph; "he said to
me, 'I will make you prolific and numerous,
I will make you a company of
peoples, and I will give this land to your
descendants as a possession for all time.'
5 I do therefore adopt your two sons that
were born to you in the land of Egypt
before I joined you in Egypt; Ephraim
and Manasseh shall be as much mine as
6 Reuben and Simeon. But the children
that were born to you after them
are to be counted to you; upon receiving
their heritage they shall be called by
7 the names of their brothers. It was
when I was coming from Paddan that
Rachel to my sorrow died in the land of
Canaan, some little distance from the
vicinity of Ephrath, and I buried her
there on the road to Ephrath (that is,
Bethlehem)."
8 When Israel saw Joseph's sons, he
said,
"Who are these?"
9 Joseph said to his father,
"They are my sons, whom God has
given me here."
"Bring them to me," he said, "that I
may bless them."
10 (Now Israel's eyes were so dim with
age that he could not see.)
So Joseph brought them up to him,
and he kissed them, and embraced
them.
11 "I never expected to see even you,"
Israel said to Joseph, "and here God
let me see your children as well!"
12 Then Joseph removed them from his
knees, and bowed on his face to the
ground.
13 Joseph took the two of them, Ephraim
in his right hand at Israel's left, and
Manasseh in his left hand at Israel's
right, and he brought them up to him.
But Israel stretched out his right hand 14
and put it on the head of Ephraim, although
he was the younger, and his left
hand on the head of Manasseh, confusing
his hands, because Manasseh was
the first-born.
He blessed Joseph, saying, 15
"May the God in whose favor my
fathers, Abraham and Isaac, lived, the
God who has been my shepherd all my
life long until this day, the angel who 16
has delivered me from all harm—may
he bless the lads, so that my name may
be carried on through them, together
with the names of my fathers, Abraham
and Isaac; may they grow into
multitudes in the earth."
When Joseph saw that his father was 17
putting his right hand on the head of
Ephraim, it distressed him; so he seized
his father's hand in order to remove it
from the head of Ephraim to that of
Manasseh.
"Not so, my father," Joseph said to 18
his father; "for this one is the first-born;
put your right hand on his head."
But his father refused, saying, 19
"I know, my son, I know; he too
shall become a people, and he too shall
be great, but his younger brother shall
be greater than he, and his descendants
shall become a multitude of nations."
So he blessed them that day, saying, 20
"The Israelites will invoke blessings
on one another through you, saying,
'May God make you like Ephraim and
Manasseh!' "—thus putting Ephraim
before Manasseh.
Then Israel said to Joseph, 21
"I am about to die, but God will be
with you, and will bring you back to the
land of your fathers. As the one above 22
your brothers, I hereby give you Shechem,
which I captured from the Amorites
with my sword and bow."

THE BLESSING OF JACOB, 49:1–28

Then Jacob summoned his sons, and 49
said,
"Come together that I may tell you
what is to befall you in days to come:
Gather round and listen, you sons of 2
Jacob;
Listen to Israel, your father.

3 Reuben, you are my first-born,
My strength and the first issue of my manly vigor;
Excessively proud and excessively fierce,
4 Turbulent as water—you shall no longer excel;
For you went up to your father's bed;
So I degraded him who went up to my couch.

5 Simeon and Levi are brothers;
Ruthless weapons are their daggers.
6 I will never enter their circle;
I will never join in their assembly;
For in their anger they slay men,
And in their normal mood they hamstring oxen.
7 Cursed be their anger, for it is fierce,
And their wrath, for it is cruel!
I will disperse them throughout Jacob,
And scatter them throughout Israel.

8 Your brothers shall praise you, O Judah;
With your hand on the necks of your foes,
Your father's sons shall bow down to you.
9 A lion's whelp is Judah;
On prey you have grown up, my son.
He crouches, he couches like a lion,
Like an old lion; who dare disturb him?
10 The scepter shall never depart from Judah,
Nor the staff from between his feet,
Until his ruler comes,
To whom the peoples shall be obedient.
11 He tethers his ass to the vine,
And his ass's colt to the choicest vine;
He washes his garments in wine,
And his robes in the blood of grapes;
12 His eyes are darker than wine,
And his teeth whiter than milk.

13 Zebulun shall dwell by the seashore;
He shall be a haven for ships,
With his flank at Sidon.

14 Issachar is a sturdy ass,
Lounging among the ravines;
15 He saw that settled life was good,
And that the land was pleasant;
So he offered his shoulder to bear burdens,
And became a gang-slave.

Dan shall judge his people, 16
As any other of the tribes of Israel.
May Dan be a serpent by the roadside, 17
A viper beside the path,
That bites the horse's hoofs,
So that its rider tumbles backward.

For succor from thee, O LORD, I wait! 18

As for Gad, raiders shall raid him, 19
But he shall raid their rear.

As for Asher, his food shall be rich, 20
And he shall yield royal dainties.

Naphtali is a free-ranging deer, 21
That bears beautiful fawns.

Joseph is a young bull, 22
A young bull at a spring,
A wild-ass at Shur.
Shooting at him in enmity, 23
The archers fiercely assailed him;
But their bow was broken by the Eternal, 24
And their arms and hands trembled,
At the might of the Mighty One of Jacob,
At the name of the Shepherd, the Rock of Israel,
At your father's God, who helps you,
And God Almighty, who blesses you 25
With the blessings of the heavens above,
The blessings of the abyss couching below;
The blessings of breast and of womb,
The blessings of fatherhood, yea of 26
man and child;
The blessings of the ancient mountains,
The dainties of the eternal hills—
May these rest on the head of Joseph,
And on the brow of him who was cursed by his brothers!

Benjamin is a ravenous wolf; 27
Devouring prey in the morning,
And dividing spoil at evening."

All these constituted the twelve 28
tribes of Israel, and this was what their
father said to them. He blessed them,
bestowing on each the blessing suited to
him.

the knees of
brothers,
God will be
nd take you
nd which he
ham, Isaac,

Joseph then made the sons of Israel 25
swear,
"When God does indeed take note of
you, you must take my bones up with
you from here."
So Joseph died at the age of one hun- 26
dred and ten years; and he was embalmed, and placed in a coffin in Egypt.

THE DEATH AND BURIAL OF JACOB, AND THE DEATH OF JOSEPH, 49:29—50:26

29 He then gave them a charge.
"I am about to be gathered to my
fathers," he said to them; "bury me
with my fathers in the cave which is in
30 the field of Ephron, the Hittite, the
cave in the field of Machpelah, which
faces Mamre, in the land of Canaan,
which along with the field Abraham
bought from Ephron, the Hittite, for
use as a burial-ground of his own. It
31 was there that Abraham and his wife
Sarah were buried; it was there that
Isaac and his wife Rebekah were
buried; and it was there that I buried
32 Leah—the field with the cave in it having been purchased from the Hittites."
33 After Jacob had finished giving his
instructions to his sons, he drew his feet
up into the bed, breathed his last, and
was gathered to his fathers.
50 Joseph fell on his father's face, weep-
2 ing over him, and kissing him. He then
ordered the physicians among his slaves
3 to embalm his father. So the physicians
embalmed Israel, spending fort
at it; for that is the time th
embalm. There was we
Egypt for seventy d
fter the d

Arriving a
yond the Jor
and sorrowf
Joseph obse
mourning fo
habitants of
saw the mou
said,
"This is
the Egypti
That is
called Abe
Egyptians
dan.
Jacob's
had com
him to t
him in
pelah,
Abraha
al-grou
Hittit
seph
ers ar
bury
R
Jo

out to meet you, and will be overjoyed
15 at seeing you. You must speak to him,
and put the words in his mouth; I will
help both you and him to speak, and I
16 will instruct you both what to do. He
shall speak for you to the people; he
shall serve as a mouthpiece for you,
and you shall act the part of God to
17 him. You must take this staff in your
hand, with which to perform the signs."

18 Then Moses went off, and returning
to his father-in-law Jethro, said to him,

"Pray let me go back to my relatives in Egypt, to see whether they are still living."

"Go in peace," said Jethro to Moses.

19 The LORD said to Moses in Midian,

"Go, return to Egypt; for all the men who sought your life are dead."

20 So Moses took his wife and sons, and
mounted them on an ass, to return to
the land of Egypt; Moses also took the
staff of God in his hand.

21 The LORD said to Moses,

"When you return to Egypt, see that
you perform before Pharaoh all the portents which I have put in your power;
but I will make him obstinate, so that
22 he will not let the people go. Then you
are to say to Pharaoh, 'Thus says the
23 LORD: "Israel is my first-born son; so
I said to you, 'Let my son go, that he
may serve me'; but you refused to let
him go; accordingly I am going to slay
your first-born son." ' "

24 At a camping-place in the course of
the journey the LORD encountered
25 him, and tried to kill him. So Zipporah
took a flint, and cutting off her son's
foreskin, she touched his person with it,
saying,

"You are my bridegroom in blood."

26 Then he let him alone.

At that time a person when circumcised was spoken of as a bridegroom in blood.

27 The LORD said to Aaron,

"Go into the desert to meet Moses."

So he went; and he met him at the
mountain of God and kissed him.
28 Then Moses told Aaron all the words
with which the LORD had commissioned him and all the signs with which
29 he had charged him. So Moses and
Aaron went and assembled all the eld-
30 ers of the Israelites, and Aaron spoke all
the words that the LORD had spoken to
Moses, and performed the signs in the
31 sight of the people, so that the people
believed. When they heard that the
LORD had taken note of the Israelites
and had marked their plight, they
bowed their heads in homage.

Following this, Moses and Aaron 5
came and said to Pharaoh,

"Thus says the LORD, the God of Israel: 'Let my people go, that they may hold a feast for me in the desert.' "

But Pharaoh said, 2

"Who is the LORD that I should heed his plea to let Israel go? I have no knowledge of the LORD, and besides, I will not let Israel go."

They said, 3

"The God of the Hebrews has paid us a visit; pray let us make a three days' journey into the desert to offer sacrifices to the LORD our God, lest he strike us with pestilence or sword."

"Moses and Aaron," said the king of 4
Egypt to them, "why would you draw
the people from their work? Mind your
own business."

"The people of the land are lazy as it 5
is," said Pharaoh, "and yet you would
relieve them of their burdens!"

So that same day Pharaoh com- 6
manded the taskmasters in charge of
the people and their foremen,

"You must no longer provide the 7
people with straw for making bricks as
previously; let them go and gather
straw for themselves. But you must re- 8
quire of them the same quantity of
bricks that they have been making in
the past, without diminishing it at all;
for they are lazy; that is why they are
crying, 'Let us go and offer sacrifices to
our God.' Let heavier work be loaded 9
on the men, that they may give their
attention to it and not to lying words."

So the taskmasters and foremen of 10
the people departed, and said to the
people,

"Thus says Pharaoh: 'I am not going to provide you with straw; go and 11
get straw for yourselves wherever you
can find it; but there is to be no reduction in your output.' "

So the people scattered all over the 12
land of Egypt in search of stubble for
straw, while the taskmasters urged 13
them on, saying,

"Complete your daily quota of work, as when the straw was provided for you."

The Israelite foremen were beaten, 14

bring my people, the Israelites, out of
Egypt."
1 But Moses said to God,
"Who am I, to go to Pharaoh and
bring the Israelites out of Egypt?"
2 "I will be with you," he said; "and
this shall be the sign for you that I have
sent you. When you bring the people
out of Egypt, you shall serve God at
this mountain."
3 "But," said Moses to God, "in case I
go to the Israelites and say to them,
'The God of your fathers has sent me to
you,' and they say to me, 'What is his
name?' what am I to say to them?"
4 "I am who I am," God said to Moses.
Then he said, "Thus you shall say to
the Israelites: ' "I am" has sent me to
you.' "
5 God said further to Moses,
"Thus you shall say to the Israelites:
'Yahweh [the LORD], the God of
your fathers, the God of Abraham,
Isaac, and Jacob, has sent me to you.'
This has always been my name, and
this shall remain my title throughout
6 the ages. Go and assemble the elders of
Israel, and say to them, 'The LORD,
the God of your fathers, the God of
Abraham, Isaac, and Jacob, has appeared to me, saying, "I have given
careful heed to you and your treatment
7 in Egypt, and I have resolved to bring
you up out of your tribulation in Egypt
to the land of the Canaanites, Hittites,
Amorites, Perizzites, Hivvites, and
Jebusites, to a land flowing with milk
18 and honey." ' They will heed your appeal, and then you and the elders of Israel shall come to the king of Egypt and
say to him, 'The LORD, the God of the
Hebrews, has paid us a visit; so now, let
us make a three days' journey into the
desert to offer sacrifices to the LORD
19 our God.' I know, however, that the
king of Egypt will not let you go with-
20 out the use of force; so I will stretch out
my hand and smite Egypt with all the
marvels that I shall perform in it; after
21 that he will let you go. And I will
bring this people into such favor with
the Egyptians that you shall not go
away empty-handed when you do
22 leave; each woman must ask her neighbor and the guest in her home for articles of silver and gold, and for clothing,
which you are to put on your sons and
daughters. Thus shall you despoil the
Egyptians."

"But suppose they will not believe 4
me," answered Moses, "nor heed my
plea, but say, 'The LORD did not appear to you.' "
The LORD said to him, 2
"What have you in your hand?"
"A staff," he said.
"Throw it on the ground," said he. 3
He threw it on the ground, and it became a snake. Moses ran away from
it, but the LORD said to Moses, 4
"Stretch out your hand and lay hold
of its tail"—stretching out his hand, he
seized it, and it became a staff in his
hand—"in order that they may be con- 5
vinced that the LORD, the God of their
fathers, did appear to you, the God of
Abraham, Isaac, and Jacob."
The LORD said further to him, 6
"Put your hand into your bosom."
He put his hand into his bosom, and
when he took it out, there was his hand
leprous, as white as snow!
"Put your hand back into your bos- 7
om," he said.
He put his hand back into his bosom,
and when he took it out of his bosom,
there it was, like the rest of his body
again.
"If they will not believe you, nor ac- 8
cept the evidence of the first sign, they
may acknowledge the evidence of the
second. If they will not be convinced 9
by even these two signs, nor heed your
plea, you are to take some water from
the Nile and pour it on the dry ground;
and the water that you take from the
Nile shall become blood on the dry
ground."
But Moses said to the LORD, 10
"Pray, O Lord, I have been no speaker, neither in the past nor recently, nor
since thou hast spoken to thy servant;
but I am slow of speech and slow of
tongue."
The LORD said to him, 11
"Who gives man a mouth, or makes
him dumb, or deaf, or lame, or blind?
Is it not I, the LORD? Now go; I will 12
help you to speak, and will instruct you
what to say."
But he said, 13
"Pray, O Lord, commission whom
thou wilt."
Then the anger of the LORD blazed 14
against Moses, and he said,
"Is there not your brother Aaron, the
Levite? I know that he is a ready
speaker, and further, he is just coming

7 Thereupon his sister said to Pharaoh's daughter,
"Shall I go and summon a nurse for
you from the Hebrew women, to nurse
the child for you?"
8 "Go," said Pharaoh's daughter to
her.
9 So the girl went and called the child's
mother, to whom Pharaoh's daughter
said,
"Take this child away and nurse it
for me, and I will pay the wages due
you."
So the woman took the child and
10 nursed him; and when the child grew
up, she brought him to Pharaoh's
daughter, and he became her son. She
called his name Moses [drawn out];
"For," said she, "I drew him out of the
water."
11 It was in those days that Moses, now
grown up, went out to visit his fellow-
countrymen and noted their heavy labor. He saw an Egyptian kill a He-
12 brew, one of his own countrymen; so,
looking this way and that, and seeing
that there was no one in sight, he killed
the Egyptian, and hid him in the sand.
13 Another day, when he went out, there
were two Hebrews fighting! So he said
to him that was in the wrong,
"Why do you strike your companion?"
14 He replied,
"Who made you ruler and judge over
us? Are you thinking of murdering me
as you did the Egyptian?"
Then was Moses afraid. "The incident must surely be known," he
thought.
15 When Pharaoh heard about the matter, he tried to kill Moses, but Moses
fled from Pharaoh and went to the land
of Midian, and sat down beside a well.
16 Now the priest of Midian had seven
daughters, who came to draw water,
and fill the troughs to water their fa-
17 ther's flock, but some shepherds came
and drove them off. So Moses went to
their rescue and watered their flock.
18 When they came home to their father
Reuel, he said,
"How did you come to get home so
soon today?"
19 They said,
"An Egyptian protected us against
the shepherds; he even drew water for
us, and watered the flock."
20 "Then where is he?" he said to his
daughters. "Why did you leave the
man behind? Invite him to have a
meal."
When Moses agreed to live with the 21
man, he gave Moses his daughter Zipporah in marriage; and she bore a son, 22
whom he named Gershom [immigrant];
"For," said he, "I am an immigrant in
a foreign land."
In the course of this long time the 23
king of Egypt died. The Israelites,
groaning under their bondage, cried for
help, and their cry because of their
bondage came up to God. God heard 24
their moaning, and God remembered
his covenant with Abraham, Isaac, and
Jacob; God saw the plight of Israel, and 25
took cognizance of it.
While Moses was tending the flock **3**
of his father-in-law, Jethro, the priest
of Midian, he led the flock to the western side of the desert, and came to the
mountain of God, Horeb. Then the an- 2
gel of the LORD appeared to him in a
flame of fire, rising out of a bush. He
looked, and there was the bush burning
with fire without being consumed! So 3
Moses said,
"I will turn aside and see this great
sight, why the bush is not burned up."
When the LORD saw that he had 4
turned aside to look at it, God called to
him out of the bush.
"Moses, Moses!" he said.
"Here I am!" said he.
"Do not come near here," he said; 5
"take your sandals off your feet; for the
place on which you are standing is holy
ground." "I am the God of your fa- 6
ther," he said, "the God of Abraham,
Isaac, and Jacob."
Then Moses hid his face; for he was
afraid to look at God.
"I have indeed seen the plight of my 7
people who are in Egypt," the LORD
said, "and I have heard their cry under
their oppressors; for I know their sorrows, and I have come down to rescue 8
them from the Egyptians and bring
them up out of that land to a land, fine
and large, to a land flowing with milk
and honey, to the country of the Canaanites, Hittites, Amorites, Perizzites,
Hivvites, and Jebusites. Now the cry 9
of the Israelites has reached me, and I
have also seen how the Egyptians are
oppressing them; so come now, let me 10
send you to Pharaoh, that you may

THE BOOK OF EXODUS

THE OPPRESSION OF THE HEBREWS IN EGYPT, 1:1–22

1 THE following are the names of
the sons of Israel who came to
Egypt in the company of Jacob,
2 each with his household: Reu-
3 ben, Simeon, Levi, and Judah, Issa-
4 char, Zebulun, and Benjamin, Dan and
5 Naphtali, Gad and Asher. The total
number of persons that were direct descendants of Jacob was seventy, Joseph
6 being already in Egypt. Then Joseph
died, and likewise all his brothers and
7 all that generation; but the Israelites
were fruitful and prolific; they increased
in numbers, and grew greater and
greater, so that the land was filled with
them.
8 Then a new king rose over Egypt,
9 who had no knowledge of Joseph; he
said to his people,
"See, the Israelite people have become
too numerous and too strong for us;
10 come, let us take precautions against
them lest they become so numerous
that in the case of a war they should
join forces with our enemies and fight
against us, and so escape from the
land."
11 Accordingly, gang-foremen were put
in charge of them, to oppress them with
their heavy labor; and they built Pi-
thom and Raamses as store-cities for
12 Pharaoh. But the more they oppressed
them, the more they multiplied and expanded, so that they became apprehen-
sive about the Israelites.
13 The Egyptians reduced the Israelites
14 to rigorous slavery; they made life bitter for them in hard work with mortar
and bricks, and in all kinds of work in
the fields, all the work that they exacted of them being rigorous.
15 Then the king of Egypt spoke to the
midwives attending the Hebrew wom-
en, of whom the name of one was Shiph-
rah and that of the other Puah.
16 "When you act as midwives for the
Hebrew women," he said, "you are to
look at the genitals; if it is a boy, you
must kill him, but if it is a girl, she may
live."
But the midwives stood in awe of 17
God, and so did not do as the king of
Egypt told them, but let the male children live. So the king of Egypt sum- 18
moned the midwives, and said to them,
"Why have you done this: let the
male children live?"
The midwives said to Pharaoh, 19
"Because the Hebrew women are not
like the Egyptian women; but are animals, in that they are delivered before
the midwife reaches them!"
So God was good to the midwives; 20
the people multiplied and grew very
numerous, and because the midwives 21
stood in awe of God, they established
families for them.
So Pharaoh commanded all his peo- 22
ple,
"Every boy that is born to the Hebrews, you must throw into the Nile,
but you are to let all the girls live."

Miriam - sister of Moses

THE RISE OF THE DELIVERER, MOSES, 2:1—7:13

Now a man belonging to the house of 2
Levi went and married a daughter of
Levi. The woman conceived and bore a 2
son, and seeing that he was robust, she
hid him for three months. When she 3
could no longer hide him, she procured
an ark of papyrus reeds for him, and
daubing it with bitumen and pitch, she
put the child in it, and placed it among
the reeds beside the bank of the Nile.
His sister posted herself some distance 4
away to see what would happen to him.
Presently Pharaoh's daughter came 5
down to bathe at the Nile, while her
maids walked on the bank of the Nile.
Then she saw the ark among the reeds
and sent her maid to get it. On opening 6
it, she saw the child, and it was a boy
crying! She took pity on him, and said,
"This is one of the Hebrews' children."

assists women at birth

and Pharaoh's taskmasters took them
to task, saying,
"Why have you not completed your
prescribed amount of brick-making as
usual, today just as previously?"
5 Then the Israelite foreman came and
appealed to Pharaoh,
"Why do you treat your servants
6 thus? There is no straw provided for
your servants, and yet we are told to
make bricks, and your servants get
beaten, whereas the fault lies with
you."
7 But he said,
"You are lazy, lazy; that is why you
say, 'Let us go and offer sacrifices to the
8 LORD.' Be off now to your work; straw
shall not be provided for you, but you
must deliver the set quantity of
bricks."
9 Then the Israelite foreman saw that
they were in an evil plight in having to
say, "You must make no reduction in
your daily quota of bricks."
0 On leaving the presence of Pharaoh
they met Moses and Aaron, who were
1 waiting for them, and said to them,
"May the LORD turn his attention
to you, and punish you for giving us an
unsavory reputation with Pharaoh and
his courtiers, by putting a sword into
their hands to slay us!"
2 Then Moses turned again to the
LORD, and said,
"O Lord, why hast thou brought evil
on this people? Why didst thou ever
3 send me? Ever since I came to Pharaoh
to speak in thy name, he has ill-treated
this people; and thou hast done nothing
to deliver thy people!"
The LORD said to Moses,
"Now you shall see what I will do to
Pharaoh; compelled by a mighty power
he will not only let them go, but will
drive them out of his land."
2 God spoke to Moses, saying to him,
3 "I am the LORD; I appeared to
Abraham, Isaac, and Jacob as God Almighty, but did not make myself
known to them by my name Yahweh
4 [the LORD]. I also established my covenant with them, to give them the land
of Canaan, the land in which they set-
5 tled as immigrants. And it is I too, who
have heard the groaning of the Israelites whom the Egyptians have enslaved, and I remember my covenant.
6 Accordingly, say to the Israelites, 'I am
the LORD; I will free you from the burdens of the Egyptians, and will deliver
you from their bondage, and will rescue
you by an outstretched arm and by
mighty acts of judgment; I will take 7
you as my own people, and I will be
your God, and you shall know that it is
I, the LORD your God, who shall free
you from the burdens of the Egyptians.
I will bring you to the land which I 8
swore with uplifted hand to give to
Abraham, Isaac, and Jacob, and I will
give it to you as your very own, I, the
LORD.'"
Moses told this to the Israelites, but 9
they would not listen to Moses because
of their impatience and hard service.
Then the LORD said to Moses, 10
"Go in and speak to Pharaoh, king of 11
Egypt, about letting the Israelites
leave his land."
But Moses protested to the LORD, 12
"Seeing that the Israelites have not
listened to me, how will Pharaoh ever
listen to me, poor speaker that I am?"
The LORD spoke to Moses and Aar- 13
on, and gave them a commission to the
Israelites and to Pharaoh, king of
Egypt, to bring the Israelites out of the
land of Egypt.
The following were the heads of their 14
clans: the sons of Reuben, Israel's
first-born, Hanoch, Pallu, Hezron, and
Carmi, these being the families of Reuben; the sons of Simeon, Jemuel, Jamin, 15
Ohad, Jachin, Zohar, and Shaul, the
son of a Canaanite woman, these being
the families of Simeon.
The following are the names of the 16
sons of Levi in their genealogical order:
Gershon, Kohath, and Merari (the
length of Levi's life being one hundred
and thirty-seven years); the sons of 17
Gershon, arranged by families, Libni
and Shimei; the sons of Kohath, Am- 18
ram, Ishar, Hebron, and Uzziel (the
length of Kohath's life being one hundred and thirty-three years); the sons 19
of Merari, Mahli and Mushi. These
were the families of the Levites in their
genealogical order.
Now Amram married his father's sis- 20
ter Jochebed, who bore him Aaron and
Moses (the length of Amram's life being
one hundred and thirty-seven years).
The sons of Izhar were Korah, Nepheg, 21
and Zichri; and the sons of Uzziel, 22
Mishael, Elzaphan, and Sithri. Aaron 23
married Elisheba, the daughter of Amminadab and sister of Nahshon, who 24

bore him, Nadab, Abihu, Eleazar, and
Ithamar. The sons of Korah were Assir, Elkanah, and Abiasaph; these were
25 the families of the Korahites. Aaron's
son, Eleazar, married one of the daughters of Putiel, who bore him Phinehas.
These were the heads of the Levitical
clans, arranged by families.
26 Such were the Aaron and Moses, to
whom the LORD said,
"Bring the Israelites out of the land
of Egypt with their hosts."
27 It was they who spoke to Pharaoh,
king of Egypt, about bringing the Israelites out of Egypt; it was that Moses
and Aaron.
28 The day that the LORD spoke to
29 Moses in the land of Egypt, the LORD
said to Moses,
"I am the LORD; tell Pharaoh, king
of Egypt, all that I am telling you."
30 But Moses protested to the LORD,
"Seeing that I am a poor speaker,
how will Pharaoh ever listen to me?"
7 The LORD said to Moses,
"See, I make you a god to Pharaoh,
and your brother Aaron shall serve as
2 your spokesman. You must tell him all
that I command you, and then your
brother Aaron shall tell it to Pharaoh,
to the end that he may let the Israelites
3 leave his land. But I will make Pharaoh obstinate; then I will perform
many signs and portents in the land of
4 Egypt, and if Pharaoh will not listen to
you, I will lay my hand on Egypt and
will bring my hosts, my people, the Israelites, out of the land of Egypt by
5 mighty acts of judgment. Then shall the
Egyptians know that I am the LORD,
when I stretch out my hand against
Egypt and bring the Israelites from
their midst."
6 Moses and Aaron did so; they did
just as the LORD commanded them.
7 Moses was eighty years old, and Aaron
eighty-three, when they spoke to Pharaoh.
8 The LORD said to Moses and Aaron,
9 "If Pharaoh says to you, 'Produce a
portent,' you shall say to Aaron, 'Take
your staff and throw it down in front of
Pharaoh,' and it will become a reptile."
10 So Moses and Aaron obtained audience with Pharaoh and did just as the
LORD had commanded them; Aaron
threw his staff down in front of Pharaoh
and his courtiers, and it became a rep-
11 tile. Then Pharaoh on his part summoned the sages and sorcerers, and
they too, the magicians of Egypt, did
the same with their secret arts; each 1
threw down his staff, and they became
reptiles; but Aaron's staff swallowed up
theirs. Pharaoh, however, remained 1
obstinate and would not listen to them,
just as the LORD had said.

THE PLAGUES ON EGYPT, 7:14—12:28

The LORD said to Moses,
"Pharaoh is stubborn; he refuses to
let the people go. Go to Pharaoh in the 1
morning, just as he is leaving the water;
take your stand on the banks of the
Nile so as to meet him, and take in your
hand the staff that was turned into a
snake. You shall say to him, 'The
LORD, the God of the Hebrews, sent
me to you to say, "Let my people go,
that they may serve me in the desert."
Since you have not as yet obeyed, thus 1
says the LORD, "By this you shall
know that I am the LORD—I am going
to strike the water in the Nile with the
staff that is in my hand, and it will turn
into blood, so that the fish in the Nile
shall die and the Nile itself shall become foul, and the Egyptians shall
search in vain for water to drink out of
the Nile." ' "
The LORD said to Moses,
"Say to Aaron, 'Take your staff, and
stretch out your hand over the waters
of Egypt, over its rivers, streams,
ponds, and all its reservoirs, that they
may become blood, so that there may
be blood all through the land of Egypt,
in both pails and stone jars.' "
Moses and Aaron did so, just as the
LORD commanded; he raised the staff
and struck the water in the Nile in the
sight of Pharaoh and his courtiers, and
all the water in the Nile turned into
blood, while the fish in the Nile died,
and the Nile itself became so foul that
the Egyptians could not drink the
water from the Nile; there was blood all
through the land of Egypt. But the
magicians of Egypt did the same with
their secret arts, so that Pharaoh remained obstinate and would not listen
to them, just as the LORD had said.
Pharaoh turned and went home, with
no concern even for this. The Egyptians had to dig all around the Nile for

water to drink; for they could not drink
the water of the Nile itself.
25 When seven days had passed after
8 the LORD had struck the Nile, the
LORD said to Moses,
"Obtain audience with Pharaoh, and
say to him, 'Thus says the LORD:
"Let my people go, that they may
2 serve me. If you refuse to let them go,
I will smite all your country with frogs;
3 the Nile shall swarm with frogs, and
they shall come up and enter your palace, your bedroom, your bed, the
houses of your courtiers and your people, your ovens, and your kneading-
4 bowls; the frogs shall climb up on you,
your people, and all your courtiers." ' "
5 The LORD said to Moses,
"Say to Aaron, 'Stretch your hand
with your staff over the rivers, the
streams, and ponds, and make frogs
come up on the land of Egypt.' "
6 So Aaron stretched his hand over the
waters of Egypt, and frogs came up and
7 covered the land of Egypt. But the
magicians did the same with their secret arts, making frogs come up on the
land of Egypt.
8 Then Pharaoh summoned Moses and
Aaron, and said,
"Beseech the LORD to take the frogs
away from me and my people, and then
I will let the people go, to sacrifice to
the LORD."
9 So Moses said to Pharaoh,
"Make clear to me when I am to
make supplication for you, your courtiers, and your people, that the frogs be
removed from you and your houses,
and be left only in the Nile."
10 "Tomorrow," he replied.
So he said,
"It shall be as you say, that you may
know that there is no one like the
11 LORD, our God. The frogs shall leave
you, your houses, your courtiers, and
your people, being left only in the
Nile."
12 Moses and Aaron then left the presence of Pharaoh; and Moses cried to
the LORD in regard to the promise
about the frogs that he had made to
13 Pharaoh, and the LORD did as Moses
had promised; the frogs perished from
the houses, the courtyards, and the
14 fields; they were gathered into one heap
after another, so that the land had a
15 bad smell. But when Pharaoh saw that
relief had come, he became stubborn
and would not listen to them, just as
the LORD had said.
The LORD then said to Moses, 16
"Say to Aaron, 'Stretch out your
staff, and strike the dust of the ground,
that it may become mosquitoes all
through the land of Egypt.' "
They did so; Aaron stretched out his 17
hand with his staff, and struck the dust
of the ground, and mosquitoes infested
man and beast; all the dust of the
ground became mosquitoes all through
the land of Egypt.
The magicians similarly tried to pro- 18
duce mosquitoes with their secret arts,
but they could not. The mosquitoes infested man and beast; so the magicians 19
said to Pharaoh,
"This is the finger of God!"
But Pharaoh was obstinate, and
would not listen to them, just as the
LORD had said.
Then the LORD said to Moses, 20
"Rise early in the morning and present yourself before Pharaoh, just as he
leaves the water, and say to him, 'Thus
says the LORD: "Let my people go,
that they may serve me; for if you will 21
not let my people go, I will send swarms
of gnats on you, your courtiers, your
people and into your houses, so that the
houses of the Egyptians shall teem with
gnats, as well as the ground on which
they stand. At that time, however, I 22
will set apart the land of Goshen in
which my people are living, so that
there shall be no gnats there, in order
that you may know that I, the LORD,
am in the land; thus will I make a dis- 23
tinction between my people and your
people. Tomorrow shall this sign occur." ' "
The LORD did so; masses of gnats 24
entered the palace of Pharaoh, the
houses of his courtiers, and all the land
of Egypt, the land being ruined by reason of the gnats.
Then Pharaoh summoned Moses and 25
Aaron, and said,
"Go, sacrifice to your God in the
land."
But Moses said, 26
"It would not be proper to do so; for
we would have to offer to the LORD our
God sacrifices abhorrent to the Egyptians; if we were to offer sacrifices abhorrent to the Egyptians before their
very eyes, would they not stone us?
We would make a three days' journey 27

into the desert to offer sacrifices to the
LORD our God, as he tells us."
28 So Pharaoh said,
"I will let you go, that you may offer
sacrifices to the LORD your God in the
desert; only you must not go very far
away; make supplication on my behalf."
29 Moses said,
"I now leave your presence, but I will
make supplication to the LORD that
the gnats leave Pharaoh, his courtiers,
and his people tomorrow; only Pharaoh
must not again play false, by not letting the people go, to offer sacrifices to
the LORD."
30 So Moses left the presence of Pharaoh and made supplication to the
31 LORD, whereupon the LORD did as
Moses promised; he removed the gnats
from Pharaoh, his courtiers, and his
32 people, not one being left. But this time
also Pharaoh became stubborn and
would not let the people go.
9 Then the LORD said to Moses,
"Obtain audience with Pharaoh, and
say to him, 'Thus says the LORD, the
God of the Hebrews: "Let my people
2 go, that they may serve me." For if
you refuse to let them go and continue
3 to detain them, the hand of the LORD
will fall on your live stock in the fields,
on horses, asses, camels, herds, and
4 flocks, with a very severe pest. But
the LORD will make a distinction between the live stock of Israel and that
of Egypt, so that nothing shall die of all
that belongs to the Israelites.' "
5 Then the LORD fixed a time for it,
saying,
"Tomorrow the LORD will do this in
the land."
6 And next day the LORD did it; the
live stock of the Egyptians all died, but
of the live stock of the Israelites not one
7 died. Pharaoh sent and found that not
so much as a single one of the live stock
of Israel had died. But Pharaoh remained stubborn and would not let the
people go.
8 Then the LORD said to Moses and
Aaron,
"Take two handfuls of soot from a
kiln, and let Moses toss it up to the sky
9 in the sight of Pharaoh; it shall become
fine dust all over the land of Egypt, and
produce sores that break into pustules
on man and beast all through the land
of Egypt."

So they took some soot from a kiln, 10
as they stood in front of Pharaoh,
Moses tossed it up to the sky, and it
produced sores that break into pustules
on man and beast. The magicians could 11
not appear before Moses because of the
sores; for the sores attacked the magicians, as well as all the Egyptians. But 12
the LORD made Pharaoh obstinate, so
that he would not listen to them, just
as the LORD had said to Moses. 13
Then the LORD said to Moses,
"Rise early in the morning and present yourself before Pharaoh, and say
to him, 'Thus says the LORD, the God
of the Hebrews: "Let my people go,
that they may serve me; for this time I 14
am going to send all my plagues on you,
your courtiers, and your people, in order that you may know that there is no
one like me in all the earth. For by 15
now I could have stretched out my
hand and struck you and your people
with pestilence, so that you would have
been effaced from the earth; but this is 16
why I have spared you: to show you
my power, and to have my fame recounted throughout all the earth.
Since you continue still to make a toy 17
of my people by not letting them go,
about this time tomorrow I am going to 18
send down a very heavy fall of hail,
such as there has never been in Egypt
from the day that it was founded until
now. Send therefore, and bring your 19
live stock and everything that belongs
to you in the fields, to a place of safety;
for the hail shall fall on every man and
beast that is found in the fields and is
not brought indoors, and they shall
die." ' "
Then those of Pharaoh's courtiers 20
who stood in awe of the word of the
LORD made their slaves and live stock
hurry indoors, while those that disre- 21
garded the word of the LORD left their
slaves and live stock out in the fields.
The LORD said to Moses, 22
"Stretch your hand up to the sky,
that hail may fall all through the land
of Egypt on man and beast, and on all
vegetation in the fields throughout the
land of Egypt."
So Moses stretched his staff up to the 23
sky, and the LORD sent thunder and
hail, and fire descended on the earth;
the LORD rained hail on the land of
Egypt, and there was hail with fire 24
darting in the midst of the hail, very

severe, such as there had never been in
all the land of Egypt since it became a
5 nation. The hail struck down everything in the fields all through the land
of Egypt, both man and beast; the hail
struck down all the vegetation in the
fields, and shattered every tree in the
6 fields, only in the land of Goshen, where
the Israelites were, there was no hail.
7 Then Pharaoh sent for Moses and
Aaron and said to them,
"I have sinned this time; the LORD is
in the right, while I and my people are
8 in the wrong. Make supplication to the
LORD; for there has been enough of
God's thunder and hail; so I will let you
go, you need not stay any longer."
9 Moses said to him,
"As soon as I leave the city I will
spread out my hands to the LORD; the
thunder shall cease, and there shall be
no more hail, in order that you may
know that the earth belongs to the
0 LORD. But as for you and your courtiers, I know that you do not yet stand in
awe of the LORD God."
1 The flax and barley were ruined, for
the barley was in ear, and the flax in
2 bud; but the wheat and spelt were not
ruined, for they were still under ground.
3 When Moses had retired from the
presence of Pharaoh outside the city, he
spread out his hands to the LORD, and
the thunder and hail ceased, and rain
was no longer poured on the earth.
4 When Pharaoh saw that the rain, hail,
and thunder had ceased, he sinned
again and became stubborn, both he
5 and his courtiers. Pharaoh became obstinate, and would not let the Israelites
go, just as the LORD had declared
through Moses.
1 Then the LORD said to Moses,
"Obtain audience with Pharaoh; for
I have made him and his courtiers stubborn, that I may perform these signs of
2 mine among them, and that you may
tell your sons and grandsons how I
made a toy of the Egyptians and what
signs I performed among them; so that
you may know that I am the LORD."
3 So Moses and Aaron obtained audience with Pharaoh, and said to him,
"Thus says the LORD, the God of the
Hebrews: 'How long are you going to
refuse to submit to me? Let my people
4 go, that they may serve me; for if you
refuse to let my people go, then tomorrow I will bring locusts on your country; they shall cover the surface of the 5
earth, so that the earth will not be visible; they shall eat up the residue that
escaped, that was left to you from the
hail; they shall eat up all the trees that
you have growing out of the fields; and 6
your palaces, the houses of your courtiers, and the houses of all the Egyptians
shall be filled with them, as neither
your fathers nor grandfathers have
ever seen from the time that they appeared on the earth to this day.' "
Then he turned, and left the presence
of Pharaoh.
Thereupon Pharaoh's courtiers said 7
to him,
"How long is this fellow going to endanger us? Let the men go, that they
may serve the LORD their God. Are
you not yet aware that Egypt is
ruined?"
So Moses and Aaron were brought 8
back to Pharaoh, and he said to them,
"Go and serve the LORD your God.
But which ones are to go?"
Moses said, 9
"We would go with our young and
our old, with our sons and our daughters; we would go with our flocks and
our herds; for it is the LORD'S feast
that we have to celebrate."
"May the LORD be with you," he 10
said to them, "just as soon as I let you
and your dependents go! See, you have
some evil purpose in mind. Not so, but 11
you that are warriors, go and serve the
LORD; for that is what you want."
Whereupon they were driven out of
Pharaoh's presence.
Then the LORD said to Moses, 12
"Stretch out your hand over the land
of Egypt for locusts, that they may
come up on the land of Egypt, and eat
up all the vegetation of the land, all
that the hail has left."
So Moses stretched out his staff over 13
the land of Egypt, and the LORD directed an east wind on the land all that
day and night. As morning came, the
east wind brought the locusts, and the 14
locusts came up all over the land of
Egypt, and settled down on the whole
country of Egypt, a great mass of them;
never previous to them had there been
so many locusts, nor would there ever
be after them; they covered the surface 15
of the whole land, so that the land was
dark; they ate up all the vegetation of
the land, and all the fruit on the trees

that the hail had left, so that nothing
green was left on tree or shrub in the
fields all through the land of Egypt.
16 Then Pharaoh hurriedly summoned
Moses and Aaron, and said,
17 "I have sinned against the LORD
your God and against you; pray then,
forgive my sin just this once, and make
supplication to the LORD your God,
that he at least remove from me this
deadly thing."
18 When Moses had left the presence of
Pharaoh, he made supplication to the
19 LORD, and the LORD changed the wind
into a very strong west wind, which
caught up the locusts and blew them into the Red Sea, not a single locust being
20 left in all the territory of Egypt. Nevertheless, the LORD made Pharaoh obstinate, so that he would not let the Israelites go.
21 Then the LORD said to Moses,
"Stretch out your hand to the sky,
that darkness may fall on the land of
Egypt, and people grope in darkness."
22 So Moses stretched out his hand to
the sky, and there was thick darkness
all through the land of Egypt for three
23 days; people could not see one another,
nor could anyone leave his place for
three days, although the Israelites all
had light in their places of abode.
24 Then Pharaoh summoned Moses,
and said,
"Go and serve the LORD; it is only
your flocks and herds that are to be detained; your dependents may go with
you."
25 But Moses said,
"It is you then that would have to
provide us with sacrifices and burnt-
offerings to make to the LORD our God;
26 so our live stock must also go with us;
not a hoof can be left behind; for we will
have to take some of them to use in the
service of the LORD our God, and we
do not know what we shall have to use
in the service of the LORD until we arrive there."
27 But the LORD made Pharaoh obstinate, so that he would not agree to
let them go.
28 "Leave my presence," Pharaoh said
to him; "beware; never visit me again;
for the day that you visit me you die."
29 "Just as you say," said Moses; "never again will I come to see you."
11 Then the LORD said to Moses,
"One more plague will I bring on

Pharaoh and on Egypt; after that he will let you go from here; indeed when he does let you go, he will absolutely drive you out of here. So announce to the people that each man is to ask his neighbor, and each woman her neighbor, for articles of silver and gold."

Now the LORD put the people in favor with the Egyptians; besides, the man Moses came to be very greatly esteemed in the land of Egypt by Pharaoh's courtiers and by the people.

So Moses said,

"Thus says the LORD: 'At midnight I am going to go forth among the Egyptians, when all the first-born in the land of Egypt shall die, from Pharaoh's first-born who is to sit on his throne to the first-born of the slave-girl who sits behind the mill, as well as the first-born of the live stock; all through the land of Egypt there shall be loud wailing, such as there never has been and never will be again.' But against none of the Israelites, either man or beast, shall even a dog bark, in order that you may know that the LORD does make a distinction between Egypt and Israel. Then shall all these courtiers of yours come down to me and make obeisance to me, saying, 'Depart, you and all the people that are in your train.' Only after that will I leave."

Thereupon he left the presence of Pharaoh in hot anger.

Then the LORD said to Moses,

"Pharaoh does not listen to you, in order that my portents may be multiplied in the land of Egypt."

So Moses and Aaron performed all these portents before Pharaoh; but the LORD made Pharaoh stubborn, so that he would not let the Israelites leave his land.

Then the LORD said to Moses and Aaron in the land of Egypt,

" 'This month shall be the first of the months for you; it shall be the first month of the year for you,' announce to the whole community of Israel; 'on the tenth day of this month they must provide for themselves one sheep each for their several families, a sheep for each household; if any household is too small for a sheep, it shall provide one along with its neighbor who is nearest to its own household in the number of persons, charging each for the proportionate amount of the sheep that it ate.

5 Your sheep must be a perfect male, a
year old; you may take one of the
6 lambs or goats. You must keep it until
the fourteenth day of this same month,
and then the whole assembly of the
community of Israel must slaughter it
7 at twilight, and taking some of the
blood, they must apply it to the two
door-posts and the lintels for the sake of
8 the houses in which they eat it. That
same night they must eat the flesh, eating it roasted, along with unleavened
9 cakes and bitter herbs; do not eat any of
it raw, nor cooked in any way with water,
but roasted, its head along with its legs
10 and entrails; and you must not leave
any of it over until morning; any that
might be left over until morning you
11 must burn up. This is how you are to
eat it: with your loins girded, your
sandals on your feet, and your staff in
your hand; you must eat it in trepidation, since it is a passover to the LORD.
12 This very night I will pass through the
land of Egypt, striking down all the
first-born in the land of Egypt, both
man and beast, and executing judgment
on all the gods of Egypt, I, the LORD.
13 The blood will serve as a sign for you on
the houses where you live; and when I
see the blood, I will pass by you, so that
no deadly plague will fall on you when
14 I smite the land of Egypt. This day
shall be a memorial for you; so you must
keep it as a feast to the LORD; throughout your generations you must keep it
15 as a perpetual ordinance. For seven
days you must eat unleavened cakes;
on the very first day you must clear
your houses of leaven; for if anyone
eats leavened bread from the first day
to the seventh, that person shall be cut
16 off from Israel. On the first day you
must hold a religious assembly, and on
the seventh day a religious assembly;
no work at all is to be done on these
days; only what every person has to
have to eat, that alone may be prepared
17 by you. You must observe this command; for it was on this very day that I
brought your hosts out of the land of
Egypt; so you must observe this day
throughout your generations as a per-
18 petual ordinance. On the evening of
the fourteenth day of the first month
you must eat unleavened cakes, and so
on until the evening of the twenty-first
19 day of the month; for the seven days no
leaven must be found in your houses;
for if anyone eats anything leavened,
that person shall be cut off from the
community of Israel, whether he is a
proselyte or a native of the land; you 20
must not eat anything leavened; in all
your places of abode you are to eat unleavened cakes.' "
Then Moses summoned all the elders 21
of Israel, and said to them,
"Go and provide yourselves with
sheep, family by family, and kill it as a
passover-sacrifice. Then you must take 22
a bunch of hyssop, and dipping it in the
blood that is in the basin, smear the
lintel and the two door-posts with the
blood in the basin, and none of you is to
go outside his house until morning, in 23
that the LORD will be passing through
to strike down the Egyptians, and when
he sees the blood on the lintel and the
two door-posts, the LORD will pass by
that door, and not let the destroyer
enter your houses to strike you down.
You must observe this as a rite pre- 24
scribed for you and your descendants
forever. And when you enter the land 25
which the LORD shall give you, as he
promised, you must observe this service. When your children say to you, 26
'What do you mean by this service?'
you shall say, 'It is the passover-sacri- 27
fice to the LORD, who passed by the
houses of the Israelites in Egypt when
he struck down the Egyptians, but
spared our houses.' "
Then the people bowed their heads in
reverence. The Israelites went and did 28
so; they did just as the LORD had commanded Moses and Aaron.

THE EXODUS FROM EGYPT,
12:29—15:21

At midnight the LORD struck down 29
all the first-born in the land of Egypt,
from Pharaoh's first-born who was to
sit on his throne to the first-born of the
captive in the dungeon, as well as all
the first-born of the live stock. Then 30
Pharaoh rose in the night, he and all his
courtiers and all the Egyptians, and
there arose a loud cry in Egypt; for
there was not a house where there was
not someone dead. So he summoned 31
Moses and Aaron in the night, and said,
"Withdraw at once from my people,
both you and the Israelites, and go,
serve the LORD as you suggested. Take 32
both your flocks and herds as you sug-

gested, and be gone; also ask a blessing
on me."
33 The Egyptians became urgent with
the people in their hurry to get them
out of the land; "For," said they, "we
34 shall all be dead." So the people
snatched up their dough before it was
leavened, their kneading-bowls being
wrapped up in their cloaks upon their
shoulders.
35 The Israelites followed the instructions of Moses; they asked the Egyptians for articles of silver and gold and
36 for clothing, and the LORD had put the
people in such favor with the Egyptians
that they granted them their requests,
and thus they despoiled the Egyptians.
37 So the Israelites set out from Rameses for Succoth, about six hundred
thousand men on foot, besides the de-
38 pendents; a great crowd went up with
them, as well as very much live stock,
39 both flocks and herds. With the dough
that they brought out of Egypt they
baked unleavened cakes; for it was not
leavened, because they had been driven
out of Egypt and could not wait, nor
had they prepared any provisions for
themselves.
40 The length of time that the Israelites
lived in Egypt was four hundred and
41 thirty years; and at the end of the four
hundred and thirty years, on that very
day all the hosts of the LORD left the
42 land of Egypt. Since that was a night
of vigil on the part of the LORD to
bring them out of the land of Egypt,
this night must be one of vigil for the
LORD on the part of all the Israelites
throughout their generations.
43 Then the LORD said to Moses and
Aaron,
"This is the regulation for the pass-
44 over: no foreigner may eat of it, but
any slave of a man that has been purchased may eat of it when you have cir-
45 cumcised him; no serf or hired laborer
46 may eat of it. It must be eaten in one
house; you may not take any of the
flesh outside the house; nor may you
47 break a bone in it. The whole commu-
48 nity of Israel must offer it. If a proselyte
is residing with you and would offer a
passover-sacrifice to the LORD, every
male member of his family must be circumcised; then he may draw near to
offer it; he shall count as a native of the
land; but no uncircumcised person shall
49 eat of it, the same law holding for the
native born and the proselyte who resides among you."
Thus did all the Israelites; they did 50
just as the LORD commanded Moses
and Aaron. And that very day the 51
LORD brought the Israelites out of the
land of Egypt with their hosts.
Then the LORD said to Moses, 13
"Consecrate to me every first-born, 2
everything that first opens the womb
among the Israelites, both man and
beast, since it is mine."
Moses said to the people, 3
"Commemorate this day, in which
you came out of Egypt, out of a state of
slavery; for it was by a strong hand
that the LORD brought you out from
there; so no leavened bread must be
eaten. Today you are about to leave, 4
on the new moon of Abib. And when 5
the LORD brings you into the land of
the Canaanites, Hittites, Amorites,
Hivvites, and Jebusites, which he swore
to your fathers to give you, a land flowing with milk and honey, you must hold
this service on this new moon; for seven 6
days you shall eat unleavened cakes,
and on the seventh day there shall be a
feast to the LORD; unleavened cakes 7
shall be eaten throughout the seven
days; nothing leavened must be seen in
your possession, nor any leaven anywhere in your territory. And you must 8
tell your son on that day, 'It is because
of what the LORD did for me when I
left Egypt.' It shall serve you as a sign 9
on your hand and a memorial on your
forehead, in order that instruction
about the LORD may be in your mouth,
how the LORD with a strong hand
brought you out of Egypt. So you must 10
observe this institution at its proper
time from year to year.
"When the LORD brings you into the 11
land of the Canaanites, as he swore to
you and your fathers, and gives it to
you, you must make over to the LORD 12
whatever first opens the womb, and all
the firstlings of the live stock that you
have, that are males, shall go to the
LORD. Every firstling ass, however, you 13
may redeem with a sheep, but if you do
not redeem it, you must break its neck;
and every first-born son of yours you
must redeem. And if in time to come 14
your son asks you, 'What does this
mean?' you must say to him, 'By a
strong hand the LORD brought us out
of Egypt, out of a state of slavery; and 15

when Pharaoh put obstacles in the way
of letting us go, the LORD slew every
first-born in the land of Egypt, the
first-born of both man and beast; that
is why I sacrifice to the LORD all the
males that first open the womb, but
every first-born of my sons I redeem.
16 It shall serve as a sign on your hand,
and as a mark on your forehead, that
the LORD by a strong hand brought us
out of Egypt.' "

17 Now when Paraoh let the people go,
God did not lead them in the direction
of the land of the Philistines, although
that was near at hand. "Lest," thought
God, "the people be filled with regret
when they experience war, and return
18 to Egypt." So God turned the people
in the direction of the desert and the
Red Sea. And the Israelites went up
19 armed out of the land of Egypt. Moses
took the bones of Joseph with him, for
he had made the Israelites take a solemn oath, saying, "God will be sure to
take note of you, and then you must
take my bones up from here with you."

20 Setting out from Succoth, they
camped at Etham on the edge of the
21 desert. The LORD used to go in front of
them, in a column of cloud by day to
guide them along the road, and in a column of fire by night to give them light,
in order that they might travel by day
22 and night; the column of cloud by day
and the column of fire by night never
moved from the head of the people.

14 Then the LORD said to Moses,
2 "Tell the Israelites to turn back and
camp in front of Pi-hahiroth, between
Migdol and the sea, in front of Baal-
zephon; you must camp opposite it, be-
3 side the sea. Pharaoh will say of the Israelites, 'They are wandering aimlessly
in the land; the desert has shut them
4 in.' Then I will make Pharaoh obstinate, so that he will pursue them, and
thus I will gain honor through Pharaoh
and all his army, and the Egyptians
shall know that I am the LORD."

They did so.

5 When the news was brought to the
king of Egypt that the people had fled,
Pharaoh and his courtiers changed their
minds about the people.

"What ever have we done," they
said, "to let Israel leave our service?"

6 So he hitched the horses to his chari-
7 ot, and took his people with him; he
took six hundred chariots, picked from
all the chariots of Egypt, with charioteers in charge of them all. The LORD 8
made Pharaoh, king of Egypt, obstinate, so that he pursued the Israelites,
as they were going triumphantly out;
the Egyptians pursued them, all of 9
Pharaoh's horses and chariots, his
cavalry and infantry, and overtook
them, camping by the sea, near Pi-
hahiroth, in front of Baal-zephon. As 10
Pharaoh drew near, the Israelites raised
their eyes, and there were the Egyptians setting out in pursuit of them!
The Israelites were terribly afraid, and
cried to the LORD. And they said to 11
Moses,

"Was it because there were no graves
in Egypt that you have taken us away
to die in the desert? What a way to
treat us, bringing us out of Egypt!
Isn't this what we told you in Egypt 12
would happen, when we said, 'Leave us
alone and let us serve the Egyptians;
for it is better for us to serve the Egyptians than to die in the desert.' "

But Moses said to the people, 13

"Do not be afraid; stand by and see
how the LORD is going to save you today; for although you see the Egyptians today, you shall never see them
again. The LORD will fight for you, 14
while you have only to keep still."

Then the LORD said to Moses, 15

"Why do you cry to me? Tell the
Israelites to set forth; and then raise 16
your staff and stretch out your hand
over the sea, and thus divide it in two,
so that the Israelites may proceed on
dry ground right into the sea. Then I 17
will make the Egyptians obstinate, so
that they will go in after them, and thus
I will gain honor through Pharaoh and
all his infantry, chariotry, and cavalry,
so that the Egyptians may know that 18
I am the LORD, when I have gained
honor through Pharaoh, his chariotry,
and cavalry."

Then the angel of God who was ac- 19
customed to go in front of the army of
Israel left his position and went behind them; the column of cloud also
left its position in front of them and
took its place behind them, and came 20
between the army of Egypt and that of
Israel, so that the cloud was there with
its darkness, and the night passed by
without the one coming near the other
all night.

Then Moses stretched out his hand 21

over the sea, and the LORD moved the
sea away by means of a strong east
wind all night, and turned the sea into
22 dry land. The waters were divided, so
that the Israelites proceeded on dry
ground right into the sea, the waters
forming a wall for them to right and left
23 of them. Pursuing them, the Egyptians
followed them right into the sea, all of
Pharaoh's horses, his chariotry and
24 cavalry. At the morning watch the
LORD lowered himself toward the
Egyptian army in the column of fire
and cloud, and threw the Egyptian
25 army into a panic. He clogged their
chariot-wheels, and caused them to
proceed with such difficulty that the
Egyptians said,

"Let us flee from the Israelites; for the LORD is fighting for them against the Egyptians."

26 Then the LORD said to Moses,

"Stretch out your hand over the sea, that the water may flow back upon the Egyptians, upon their chariotry and cavalry."

27 So Moses stretched out his hand over
the sea, and as morning broke, the sea
returned to its steady flow; and as the
Egyptians fled before it, the LORD
shook the Egyptians right into the sea.
28 The water returned, and covered the
chariotry and cavalry belonging to
the whole army of Pharaoh that had
followed them into the sea, not so much
29 as one being left. But the Israelites
had walked through the middle of the
sea on dry ground, the water forming a
wall for them to right and left of them.
30 Thus did the LORD save Israel that
day from the power of the Egyptians.
So Israel saw the Egyptians lying dead
31 on the seashore; and when Israel saw
the mighty act which the LORD had
performed against the Egyptians, the
people stood in awe of the LORD and
trusted the LORD and his servant
Moses.

15 Then Moses and the Israelites sang this song to the LORD; they said,

"I will sing to the LORD, for he has
completely triumphed;
The horse and its rider he has hurled
into the sea.
2 The LORD is my strength and song,
for he saved me;
He is my God whom I shall praise, my
father's God whom I shall extol.
3 The LORD is a warrior, the LORD is
his name.
4 Pharaoh's chariots and his army he
cast into the sea,
And the best of his charioteers were
engulfed in the Red Sea;
5 The floods covered them, they sank
into the depths like a stone.
6 It was thy right hand, O LORD, glorious in power,
It was thy right hand, O LORD, that
shattered the foe.
7 By the greatness of thy majesty thou
didst overthrow thine adversaries;
Thou didst let loose thy wrath, it consumed them like stubble.
8 By the blast of thy nostrils the waters
were piled up;
The streams stood up like a heap, the
floods were congealed in the heart
of the sea.
9 The foe said, 'I will pursue them, I
will overtake them,
I will divide the spoil, I will work my
will on them;
I will unsheath my sword, my hand
shall conquer them.'
10 Thou didst blow with thy breath, the
sea covered them;
They sank like lead in the mighty
waters.
11 Who is there like thee among the gods,
O LORD?
Who is there like thee, so glorious in
holiness,
So awe-inspiring in renown, such a
wonder worker?
12 Thou didst stretch out thy right
hand, the earth swallowed them.
13 In thy goodness thou didst lead the
people whom thou didst redeem;
In thy strength thou didst guide them
to thy holy abode.
14 When the nations heard of it, they
trembled,
Agony seized the inhabitants of Philistia;
15 Then were the chieftains of Edom dismayed;
The lords of Moab—trembling seized
them;
All the inhabitants of Canaan melted
away,
16 Terror and dread fell upon them;
Because of the greatness of thine arm
they became as dumb as a stone,
Until thy people, O LORD, passed
over;

Until the people whom thou didst acquire passed over.
17 Thou hast brought them and planted them in the highlands of thine own,
The place of thine abode which thou, O LORD, hast made,
The sanctuary, O LORD, which thy hands have established.
18 The LORD shall reign for ever and ever!"
19 For the horses of Pharaoh, with his chariotry and cavalry, entered the sea,
and the LORD made the waters of the
sea flow back on them, while the Israelites had walked through the middle of
the sea on dry ground.
20 Then the prophetess Miriam, the sister of Aaron, took a tambourine in her
hand, and all the women went out after
her with tambourines and dancing,
21 while Miriam responded to them in song,
"Sing to the LORD, for he has completely triumphed;
The horse and its rider he has hurled into the sea."

THE JOURNEY FROM THE RED SEA TO SINAI, 15:22—18:27

22 Then Moses had Israel set out from
the Red Sea, and they proceeded to the
desert of Shur; they journeyed for three
days in the desert without finding
23 water. Then they reached Marah, but
they could not drink the water at
Marah because it was bitter. That was
how it came to be named Marah [bitter-
24 ness]. So the people grumbled against
Moses, saying,
"What are we to drink?"
25 So he cried to the LORD, and the
LORD showed him a tree, which he
threw into the water, so that the water
became sweet.
It was there that he made a statute
and ordinance for them, and put them
to the test.
26 "If you will but heed the injunction
of the LORD your God," he said, "and
do what is right in his eyes, and pay attention to his commands, and observe
all his statutes, I will inflict none of the
diseases on you which I inflicted on the
Egyptians; for I, the LORD, make you
immune to them."
27 Then they came to Elim, where there
were twelve springs of water and seventy palm-trees; and they camped there
beside the water.
Setting out from Elim, the whole 16
Israelite community came to the desert
of Sin, which is between Elim and Sinai,
on the fifteenth day of the second
month after their departure from the
land of Egypt.
Then the whole Israelite community 2
grumbled against Moses and Aaron in
the desert.
"O that we had died by the hand of 3
the LORD in the land of Egypt, when
we sat by pots of flesh and had plenty
of food to eat," the Israelites said to
them; "for you have brought us into
this desert, to make this whole crowd
die of famine."
Then the LORD said to Moses, 4
"I am going to rain food out of the
sky for you, but the people are to go out
and gather only a day's ration each day,
in order that I may test them to see
whether they will follow my instructions or not. On every sixth day, how- 5
ever, when they measure what they
bring home, it shall be twice as much as
what they gather from day to day."
So Moses and Aaron said to all the 6
Israelites,
"At evening you shall know that it
was the LORD who brought you out of
the land of Egypt; and in the morning 7
you shall see the glory of the LORD,
since he has heard your grumbling
against the LORD, for what are we that
you should grumble against us?"
"This shall be," said Moses, "when 8
the LORD gives you flesh to eat in the
evening, and plenty of bread to satisfy
you in the morning, since the LORD has
heard the grumbling that you have
muttered against him; for what are we?
Your grumbling has really not been
against us, but against the LORD."
Then Moses said to Aaron, 9
"Say to the whole Israelite community, 'Present yourselves before the
LORD; for he has heard your grumbling.'"
When Aaron said this to the whole 10
Israelite community, they looked toward the desert, whereupon the glory of
the LORD appeared in the cloud.
Then the LORD said to Moses, 11
"I have heard the grumbling of the 12
Israelites; say to them, 'At twilight you
shall have flesh to eat, and in the morn-

ing plenty of bread to satisfy you; and
thus shall you know that I am the
LORD your God.' "
13 So it came about at evening that
quails came up and covered the camp,
and in the morning there was a fall of
14 dew around the camp; when the fall of
dew evaporated, there, on the surface
of the desert, was a fine scaly substance,
as fine as hoar-frost on the ground!
15 When the Israelites saw it, they said to
one another,

"What is it?"—for they did not know
what it was.

Then Moses said to them,

"That is the bread which the LORD
16 is giving you to eat. This is the command which the LORD has given: 'Each
of you gather as much of it as he can
use, an omer apiece, according to the
number of your members, each taking
it for those in his tent.' "
17 The Israelites did so; they gathered
it, some a large amount, some a small
18 amount; but when they measured it
with an omer, he who had gathered
much did not have too much, and he
who had gathered little did not have too
little, each having gathered only as
much as he could use.
19 Then Moses said to them,

"No one is to leave any of it over until morning."
20 But they did not obey Moses; certain ones left some of it over until morning, and it bred maggots and became
foul. So Moses became angry with
them.
21 Morning after morning they gathered
it, each as much as he could use; and
22 when the sun grew hot, it melted. On
the sixth day they gathered twice as
much food, two omers apiece; and when
the leaders of the community all came
23 and told Moses, he said to them,

"That is what the LORD meant; tomorrow is to be a day of complete rest,
a sabbath sacred to the LORD; bake
what you need to bake, and boil what
you need to boil, and all that is left over
put aside as a reserve until tomorrow
morning."
24 So they put it aside until next morning, as Moses had commanded them,
and it did not become foul, nor did mag-
25 gots appear in it. Then Moses said to
them,

"Eat this today; for today is a sabbath to the LORD; you will not find any
in the fields today. It is only for six 26
days that you are to gather it; on the
seventh day, which is a sabbath, there
will be none."

On the seventh day, however, some 27
of the people did go out to gather it,
but they found none. Then the LORD 28
said to Moses,

"How long are you going to refuse to
keep my commands and instructions?
Mark this: since the LORD has given 29
you the sabbath, he will accordingly
give you enough food on the sixth day
for two days; stay everyone of you in
his place; let no one leave his home on
the seventh day."

So the people rested on the seventh 30
day.

The Israelites called it manna; it was 31
as white as coriander seed, and its taste
was like that of wafers made with honey.

"This is the command," said Moses, 32
"which the LORD has given: 'Keep an
omerful of it for your descendants, that
they may see the food with which I fed
you in the desert when I brought you
out of the land of Egypt.' "

So Moses said to Aaron, 33

"Take a jar and put an omerful of
manna in it, and deposit it before the
LORD, to be kept for your descendants."

As the LORD had commanded 34
Moses, Aaron deposited it in front of
the decrees for safe keeping.

For forty years the Israelites ate 35
manna, until they reached an inhabited
land; they ate manna until they
reached the outskirts of the land of
Canaan.

(Now an omer is the tenth of an 36
ephah.)

From the desert of Sin the whole **17**
Israelite community traveled by stages,
in accord with the command of the
LORD, and camped at Rephidim. As
there was no water for the people to
drink, the people found fault with 2
Moses.

"Give us water to drink," they said.

"Why do you find fault with me?"
Moses said to them. "Why do you put
the LORD to the test?"

The people became so thirsty for 3
water there that they grumbled against
Moses, and said,

"Why have you brought us up out

of Egypt to have us and our children
and live stock die of thirst?"
4 So Moses cried to the LORD,
"What am I to do with this people?
They are almost ready to stone me."
5 The LORD said to Moses,
"Pass on ahead of the people, taking
with you some of the elders of Israel;
take the staff in your hand with which
6 you struck the Nile, and go on. I will
station myself there before you on the
rock at Horeb, and when you strike the
rock, water will gush out of it, so that
the people may drink."
Moses did so, in sight of the elders of
Israel.
7 So he called the name of the place
Massah [testing], as well as Meribah
[finding fault], because of the fault-
finding of the Israelites, and their testing of the LORD by saying, "Is the
LORD in our midst, or not?"
8 Then came Amalek, and fought with
9 Israel at Rephidim. So Moses said to
Joshua,
"Pick out some men for us, and hurry
out to fight with Amalek, while I will
take my stand on the top of the hill,
with the staff of God in my hand."
10 Joshua did as Moses told him, and
went out to fight against Amalek, while
Moses, Aaron, and Hur ascended to the
11 top of the hill. Whenever Moses held
up his hand, Israel prevailed; and
whenever he let down his hand, Amalek
12 prevailed. When Moses' hands became
tired, they took a stone and put it under him to sit on, while Aaron and Hur
held his hands up, the one on one side,
and the other on the other side. Thus it
was that his hands were kept stationary
13 until sunset, so that Joshua put Amalek
and his people to the sword.
14 Then the LORD said to Moses,
"Write this as a memorandum in a
book, and recite it to Joshua; for I will
blot out the very memory of Amalek
from under the heavens."
15 Then Moses built an altar, and called
its name Yahweh-nissi [the LORD is
my standard].
16 "Because a hand has been raised
against the throne of the LORD," he
said, "the LORD will have war with
Amalek from generation to generation."
18 Now Jethro, the priest of Midian, the
father-in-law of Moses, heard of all that
God had done for Moses and his people
Israel, how the LORD had brought
Israel out of Egypt. Jethro, the father- 2
in-law of Moses, had taken Moses' wife,
Zipporah, after her dismissal, along 3
with her two sons, of whom the name of
the one Gershom [immigrant] ("For,"
said he, "I am an immigrant in a foreign land"), and the name of the other 4
was Eliezer [My God is a help] ("For
the God of my father has been my help,
in delivering me from the sword of Pharaoh"). Then Jethro, the father-in-law 5
of Moses, came with his sons and his
wife to Moses, to the place in the desert
where he was camped, namely, the
mountain of God. When Moses was 6
told, "Here is your father-in-law Jethro
coming to see you, accompanied by
your wife and her two sons," Moses 7
went out to meet his father-in-law; he
bowed before him, and kissed him, and
when they had asked after each other's
health, they entered the tent. Moses 8
then told his father-in-law all that the
LORD had done to Pharaoh and the
Egyptians for Israel's sake, all the
hardship that they had encountered on
the journey, and how the LORD had delivered them. Jethro rejoiced over all 9
the goodness which the LORD had
shown Israel, in delivering them from
the power of the Egyptians.
"Blessed be the LORD," said Jethro, 10
"who delivered you from the power of
the Egyptians and the power of Pharaoh, who delivered the people from
under the power of the Egyptians. Now 11
I know that the LORD is greater than
all other gods, in that his power prevailed over them."
So Jethro, the father-in-law of Moses, 12
procured a burnt-offering and sacrifices
for God, whereupon Aaron came with
all the elders of Israel to participate
with Moses' father-in-law in the meal
before God.
Next day Moses held court for the 13
people, and the people stood about
Moses from morning until evening.
When Moses' father-in-law saw all that 14
he had to do for the people, he said,
"What ever is this that you are doing
for the people? Why do you hold court
all alone, with the people all standing
about you from morning until evening?"
"Because the people come to me to 15
inquire of God," said Moses to his father-in-law. "Whenever they have a 16

dispute, they come to me, that I may
decide between one man and another,
and let them know the statutes of God
and his decisions."
17 "You are not doing right," said
18 Moses' father-in-law to him. "You will
wear yourself out, both you and the
people here with you; for the task is too
heavy for you; you cannot do it alone.
19 Now listen to me; let me advise you,
that God may be with you: You be the
people's advocate with God, and bring
20 the cases to God; instruct them in the
statutes and decisions, and let them
know the procedure that they are to fol-
21 low and what they are to do; but do
you yourself select out of all the people
some capable, God-fearing, honest men,
with an aversion to improper gain, and
set them over them as captains of divisions of a thousand, of a hundred, of
22 fifty, and of ten; let them act as judges
for the people on all ordinary occasions;
all important cases they shall bring to
you, but all ordinary cases they shall
judge themselves. Thus it will be lighter for you, since they will share the
23 burden with you. If you do this—and
God so commands you—you will be
able to endure it, and also, this whole
people can then have their cases settled
near home."
24 Moses agreed with the suggestion of
his father-in-law, and did all that he
25 said; Moses chose capable men out of
all Israel, and set them as chieftains
over the people, as captains of divisions
of a thousand, of a hundred, of fifty,
26 and of ten; they acted as judges for the
people on all ordinary occasions; the
difficult cases they brought to Moses,
but all ordinary cases they judged
27 themselves. Then Moses saw his father-
in-law off, and he betook himself to his
own land.

THE SOJOURN AT SINAI, 19:1—40:38

19 On the third new moon after leaving
the land of Egypt, on that very day the
Israelites entered the desert of Sinai.
2 Setting out from Rephidim, they entered the desert of Sinai, and camped in
the desert; Israel camped there in front
3 of the mountain, while Moses went up
to God. Then the LORD called to him
from the mountain, saying,
"Thus shall you say to the house of
Jacob, and tell the Israelites: 'You 4
have seen for yourselves what I did to
the Egyptians, and how I bore you on
eagles' wings, and brought you to myself.
Now then, if you will but heed my in- 5
junctions, and keep my covenant, you
shall be my very own out of all the peoples (for all the earth is mine), and you 6
shall be a kingdom of priests to me, and
a holy nation.' These are the words
that you are to speak to the Israelites."
So Moses came and summoned the 7
elders of the people, and set before them
all these words which the LORD had
commanded him. Then the people all 8
answered together,
"Whatever the LORD says we will
do."
And Moses reported the words of the
people to the LORD.
The LORD said to Moses, 9
"See, I am coming to you in a thick
cloud, in order that the people may
hear me speaking with you, and may
then always trust you too."
When Moses reported the words of
the people to the LORD, the LORD said 10
to Moses,
"Go to the people, and have them go
through a period of consecration today
and tomorrow; let them wash their
clothes, and be ready by the day after 11
tomorrow; for on the day after tomorrow the LORD is going to descend on
Mount Sinai in sight of all the people.
You must mark off the mountain all 12
around, saying, 'Take care not to
ascend the mountain, nor even to touch
the edge of it; whoever touches the
mountain must be put to death, having 13
no hand touch him, but being stoned or
shot; whether it is man or beast, he
shall not be allowed to live. When a
long blast is blown on the ram's horn,
they may come up to the mountain."
So Moses descended from the moun- 14
tain to the people; he consecrated the
people, and they washed their clothes.
"Be ready by the day after tomor- 15
row," he said to the people; "approach
no woman."
On the third day, when morning 16
came, there was thunder and lightning,
with a heavy cloud over the mountain,
and a very loud trumpet-blast, so that
all the people that were in the camp
trembled. Then Moses brought the 17
people out of the camp to meet God,
and they took their stand at the foot of

18 the mountain. Mount Sinai was completely enveloped in smoke, because the
LORD had descended upon it in fire; its
smoke ascended like the smoke from a
kiln, so that the people all trembled
19 violently. As the blast of the trumpet
grew louder and louder, Moses spoke,
and God answered him with a thunder-
20 peal. The LORD descended upon
Mount Sinai, to the top of the mountain; the LORD then summoned Moses
to the top of the mountain, and when
21 Moses went up, the LORD said to
Moses,
"Go down and warn the people not
to break through to the LORD to see
22 him, or else many of them will fall. The
priests, also, whose place it is to approach the LORD, are to sanctify themselves, lest the LORD break loose upon
them."
23 Moses said to the LORD,
"The people may not ascend Mount
Sinai; for thou thyself didst charge us,
saying, 'Mark off the mountain, and
make it taboo.' "
24 The LORD said to him,
"Go down, and then come up again,
accompanied by Aaron; but the
priests and the people are not to break
through to come up to the LORD, lest
he break loose upon them."
25 So Moses went down to the people,
and told them.
20 God spoke all these words, saying,
2 "Since I, the LORD, am your God,
who brought you out of the land of
3 Egypt, out of a state of slavery, you
must have no other gods beside me.
4 "You must not carve an image for
yourself in the shape of anything that
is in the heavens above, or that is on
the earth below, or that is in the waters
5 under the earth; you must not pay
homage to them, nor serve them; for I,
the LORD your God, am a jealous God,
punishing children for the sins of their
fathers, to the third or fourth genera-
6 tion of those who hate me, but showing
kindness to the thousandth generation
of those who love me and keep my commands.
7 "You must not invoke the name of
the LORD your God to evil intent; for
the LORD will not hold him guiltless
who invokes his name to evil intent.
8 "Remember to keep the sabbath day
9 holy. Six days you are to labor and do
10 all your work, but on the seventh day, a
sabbath to the LORD your God, you
must not do any work at all, neither
you, nor your son, nor your daughter,
nor your male or female slave, nor your
cattle, nor the alien in your employ residing in your community; for in six 11
days the LORD made the heavens, the
earth, and the sea, together with all
that is in them, but rested on the seventh day; that is how the LORD came
to bless the seventh day and to hallow
it.
"Honor your father and mother, that 12
you may live long in the land that the
LORD your God is giving you.
"You must not commit murder. 13
"You must not commit adultery. 14
"You must not steal. 15
"You must not bring a false charge 16
against your fellow.
"You must not covet your neighbor's 17
home; you must not covet your neighbor's wife, nor his male or female slave,
nor his ox, nor his ass, nor anything at
all that is your neighbor's."
As the people all perceived the thun- 18
der and lightning, the blast of the
trumpet, and the mountain smoking,
the people became afraid, and fell back,
standing off at a distance.
"If you yourself will speak to us," 19
they said to Moses, "we will listen; but
do not let God speak to us, lest we die."
"Fear not," said Moses to the people, 20
"for it is only to test you that God has
come, and in order that the fear of him
may be present with you so that you
may not sin."
The people, however, stood off at a 21
distance, while Moses approached the
dense darkness where God was.
Then the LORD said to Moses, 22
"Thus shall you say to the Israelites:
'You have seen for yourselves that I
have talked with you out of the heavens. Gods of silver, and gods of gold 23
you must not make for yourselves. You 24
must construct an altar of earth for me,
and sacrifice on it your burnt-offerings,
your thank-offerings, your sheep, and
your oxen; at every sanctuary where I
record my name, I will come to you and
bless you. If, however, you construct 25
an altar of stones for me, you must not
build it of dressed stones; for if you
were to use your tools on it, you would
pollute it. Further, you must never 26
ascend my altar on steps, so that your
nakedness may not be exposed on it.'

21 "The following are the ordinances
which you are to lay before them:
2 " 'When you buy a Hebrew slave, he
is to work for you for six years, but in
the seventh year he is to go free without
3 paying anything. If he came in single,
he shall go out single; if he was married,
4 his wife shall go out with him. If his
master gives him a wife, and she bears
him sons or daughters, the wife with
her children shall belong to her master,
5 while he shall go out alone. But if the
slave declares, "I am fond of my master, my wife, and my children; I will not
6 go free," his master shall bring him
up to God; he shall bring him up to the
door or the door-post, and his master
shall pierce his ear with an awl; he shall
then be his slave permanently.
7 " 'If a man sells his daughter as a
slave, she shall not go free as the male
8 slaves do. If she is displeasing to her
master, who acquired her for himself,
he shall let her be redeemed; he shall
have no right to sell her to a foreign
people, since he has treated her unfair-
9 ly. If he acquires her for his son, he
10 must treat her like a daughter. If he
marries another, he must not diminish
her food, nor her clothes, nor her con-
11 jugal rights; if he does not observe these
three duties to her, she shall go free
without any money payment whatsoever.
12 " 'Whoever strikes another, so that
13 he dies, must be put to death; if, however, he did not lie in wait for him, but
God let him fall into his hands, I will
designate a place for you to which he
14 may flee. If a man wilfully plans to
murder another treacherously, even
from my altar you must take him, that
he may be put to death.
15 " 'Whoever strikes his father or
mother must be put to death.
16 " 'Whoever kidnaps a man, and sells
him, or if he is found in his possession,
must be put to death.
17 " 'Whoever reviles his father or
mother must be put to death.
18 " 'If men get into a quarrel, and one
strikes the other with a stone or with his
fist, so that he does not die, but is laid
19 up in bed, if he gets up again, and can
go out walking on his staff, the one who
struck him shall be let off, except that
he must pay for his loss of time, and
have him thoroughly restored to
health.

" 'If a man strikes his male or female 20
slave with a stick, so that he dies under
his hand, he must be avenged. If, how- 21
ever, he survives a day or two, he is
not to be avenged; for he is his own
property.
" 'If men get into a fight, and hurt a 22
pregnant woman so that she has a miscarriage, without further harm, he
must pay such fine as the woman's husband imposes on him, and so pay for the
miscarriage; but if there is further 23
harm, you must give life for life, eye for 24
eye, tooth for tooth, hand for hand, foot
for foot, burn for burn, wound for 25
wound, lash for lash.
" 'If a man strikes the eye of his male 26
or female slave, and destroys it, he must
let him go free in compensation for his
eye; if he knocks out the tooth of his 27
male or female slave, he must let him
go free in compensation for his tooth.
" 'If an ox gores a man or woman to 28
death, the ox must be stoned to death,
but its flesh is not to be eaten; the owner of the ox is blameless. If, however, 29
the ox has been in the habit of goring,
and its owner has been warned, but still
does not keep it in, and it kills a man or
a woman, the ox must be stoned, and its
owner must also be put to death. If 30
only a fine is imposed on him, he must
pay in redemption of his life whatever
amount is imposed on him. Whether it 31
is a free man or a free woman that it
gores, he is to be dealt with in accordance with this same ordinance. If the 32
ox gores a male or a female slave, he
must pay their master thirty shekels of
silver, and the ox must be stoned.
" 'If a man opens a cistern, or if a 33
man digs a cistern and does not cover it,
and an ox or an ass falls into it, the own- 34
er of the cistern must make restitution
by reimbursing its owner with money,
but the carcass is to be his.
" 'If a man's ox hurt another's ox, so 35
that it dies, they shall sell the live ox
and divide its price between them, and
the dead animal as well. Or, if the ox is 36
known to have been in the habit of goring, and its owner has not been keeping
it in, he must make restitution with an
ox for the ox, but the dead animal is to
be his.
" 'If a man steals an ox or a sheep, 22
and kills it or sells it, he must pay an
indemnity of five oxen for the ox, and
four sheep for the sheep; he must surely 3

make restitution; if he has nothing, he
must be sold to pay for what he stole.
4 If the stolen animal is found alive in his
possession, whether it is an ox, an ass,
or a sheep, he must make two-fold restitution.
2 " 'If the thief is caught in the act of
breaking in, and is struck a fatal blow,
3[a] there is no guilt of blood in his case; if
the sun has risen on him, then there is
guilt of blood.
5 " 'If a man in burning over a field or
vineyard lets the fire spread so that it
burns in another man's field, he must
make restitution with the very best of
6 his own field or vineyard. If fire breaks
out and catches in a thorn-hedge, so
that the shocks of grain or the standing
grain or the field itself is consumed, he
who lit the fire must make restitution.
7 " 'If a man gives money or other articles to another to keep, and it is stolen
from the latter's house, if the thief is
found, he must make two-fold restitu-
8 tion; if the thief is not found, the owner
of the house must be brought into the
presence of God to determine whether
he himself has not laid hands on the
other's property.
9 " 'In every case of dispute, whether
it concerns ox, or ass, or sheep, or clothing, or any article at all that has disappeared, concerning which claim is
made, "This is it," the case of both
parties shall come before God; he whom
God convicts must make two-fold restitution to the other.
10 " 'If a man gives an ass, or an ox, or a
sheep, or any kind of animal to another
to keep, and it dies, or is injured, or is
taken as booty when no one was look-
11 ing, there must be an oath by the LORD
between the two of them as to whether
one did not lay hands on the other's
property; the owner must then accept
it, and no restitution shall be made.
12 But if it is really stolen from him, he
13 must make restitution to its owner. If
it is torn in pieces, let him bring it as
evidence; he need not make good what
has been torn.
14 " 'If a man borrows an animal from
another, and it is injured or dies, its
owner not being employed with it, he
15 must make restitution; if the owner is
employed with it, he need not make
restitution; if it was hired, the owner is
to receive the price of its hire.
16 " 'If a man seduces a virgin who is
not betrothed, and lies with her, he
must pay the marriage-price for her,
and marry her; if her father absolutely 17
refuses to give her to him, he must pay
money equivalent to the marriage-price
of virgins.
" 'You must not let a sorceress live. 18
" 'Whoever lies with an animal must 19
be put to death.
" 'He who sacrifices to any god ex- 20
cept the LORD alone must be destroyed.
" 'You must not ill-treat a resident 21
alien, nor oppress him; for you were
once resident aliens yourselves in the
land of Egypt. You must not wrong 22
any widow or orphan. If you ever 23
wrong them and they cry aloud to me,
I will be sure to hear their cry, and my 24
anger will blaze, and I will slay you
with the sword; thus shall your own
wives become widows and your children orphans.
" 'If you lend money to my people, 25
to any poor person among you, you
must not behave like a creditor toward
him; you must not charge him any interest. If you ever take another's cloak 26
in pledge, you must return it to him by
sunset; for that is his only covering; it 27
is his cloak for his body. What else
could he sleep in? And if he should cry
to me, I would respond; for I am kind.
" 'You must not revile God, nor 28
curse a ruler of your people.
" 'You must not be dilatory with 29
your offering, whether much or little.
You must give me the first-born of your
sons; you must do the same with your 30
oxen and your sheep; for seven days it
may remain with its dam; on the eighth
day you must give it to me.
" 'Since you are men sacred to me, 31
you must not eat flesh that has been
torn in the field; you must throw it to
the dogs.
" 'You must not give false, hearsay **23**
evidence; do not join hands with a
wicked person by being a malicious
witness. You must not follow the ma- 2
jority by doing wrong, nor give evidence in a suit so as to pervert justice,
by turning aside with the majority.
Neither must you favor a poor man in 3
his case.
" 'If you chance upon your enemy's 4
ox or ass going astray, you must be sure
to take it home to him.
" 'If you see the ass of one who hates 5

you lying prostrate under its load, you
must refrain from deserting him; you
must be sure to help him get it up.
6 " 'You must not pervert the justice
7 due your poor in his case. Avoid false
charges; do not have innocent and
guiltless persons put to death, nor ac-
8 quit the wicked. You must never take
a bribe; for a bribe blinds the open-
eyed, and subverts even a just case.
9 " 'You must not oppress a resident
alien, since you know the feelings of an
alien, for you were once aliens yourselves in the land of Egypt.
10 " 'For six years you may sow your
11 land and gather in its crops, but during
the seventh year you must leave it
alone and let it lie fallow, so that the
poor of your people may eat of it, and
what they leave the wild beasts may
eat. You must do the same with your
vineyards and olive groves.
12 " 'Six days you are to do your work,
but on the seventh day you must desist, in order that your ox and ass may
rest, and that your slave and the resident alien may refresh themselves.
13 " 'Give heed to all that I have told
you; never mention the names of alien
gods; do not let them be heard on your
lips.
14 " 'Three times a year you are to hold
15 a feast for me. You must keep the feast
of unleavened cakes, eating unleavened
cakes for seven days, as I commanded
you, at the appointed time, the new
moon of Abib (for it was then that you
came out of Egypt); none may visit me
16 empty-handed. There is also the harvest feast, that of the first-fruits of your
labor, of what you sowed in the field;
and the feast of ingathering at the end
of the year, when you gather in the
17 fruit of your labor from the field. Three
times a year all your males must visit
the Lord GOD.
18 " 'You must not offer the blood of a
sacrifice to me with leavened bread.
" 'The fat of my feast must not be
left over night until morning.
19 " 'The very first of the first-fruits of
your soil you must bring to the house of
the LORD your God.
" 'You must not boil a kid in its
mother's milk.
20 " 'See, I am sending an angel before
you, to guard you on the way, and to
bring you to the place that I have pre-
21 pared. Pay attention to him and heed
his injunctions; do not oppose him, because he will not pardon your offense;
for I will manifest myself in him. But 22
if you do heed his injunctions, and do
just what I say, I will be an enemy to
your enemies, and an adversary to your
adversaries. When my angel goes be- 23
fore you, and brings you to the Amorites, Hittites, Perizzites, Canaanites,
Hivvites, and Jebusites, and I exterminate them, you must not pay hom- 24
age to their gods, nor serve them, nor
make anything like them; but you
must be sure to overthrow them, and
smash their sacred pillars. You must 25
serve the LORD your God, and then I
will bless your food and water, and I
will free you from disease; there shall be 26
none in your land who miscarries or is
barren; I will bring to completion the
full number of your days. I will send 27
my terror before you, and will throw
all the peoples to whom you come into
a panic; I will make all your enemies
turn their backs to you; I will send lep- 28
rosy ahead of you to drive the Hivvites,
Canaanites, and Hittites out of your
way; I will not drive them out of your 29
way in a single year, lest the land become desolate, and the wild beasts become too numerous for you; I will drive 30
them out of your way little by little,
until you grow in numbers and can take
full possession of the land. I will make 31
your domain the region from the Red
Sea as far as the sea of the Philistines,
and from the desert as far as the Euphrates; for I will deliver the inhabitants of the land into your power, and
drive them out of your way. You must 32
make no covenant with them, nor with
their gods; they must not remain in 33
your land lest they make you sin
against me; for if you were to serve
their gods, it would endanger you.' "
"Come up to the LORD," he said to **24**
Moses, "you, and Aaron, Nadab, Abihu, and seventy of the elders of Israel,
and worship at a distance; Moses alone 2
is to come near the LORD; the others
are not to come near, nor are the people
to go up with him."
Then Moses came, and recounted to 3
the people all the regulations of the
LORD and all the ordinances; and the
people all answered with one voice.
"All the regulations that the LORD
has given we will observe."
So Moses wrote down all the regula- 4

tions of the LORD, and rising early next
morning, he built an altar at the foot of
the mountain, along with twelve sacred
pillars, one for each of the twelve tribes
5 of Israel. Then he sent the young men
of the Israelites to offer burnt-offerings
and to sacrifice oxen as thank-offerings
6 to the LORD, while Moses himself took
half of the blood, and put it in basins,
7 dashing the other half on the altar. He
then took the book of the covenant, and
read it in the hearing of the people, who
said,
"All that the LORD has directed we
will obediently do."
8 Then Moses took the blood and
dashed it on the people, saying,
"Behold the blood of the covenant
which the LORD has made with you on
the basis of all these regulations."
9 Moses then went up, with Aaron, Nadab, Abihu, and seventy of the elders of
10 Israel, and they saw the God of Israel,
with something like a sapphire pavement under his feet, as clear as the sky
11 itself. And God did not lay hands on
the leaders of the Israelites, but they
beheld God, and ate and drank.
12 The LORD said to Moses,
"Ascend the mountain to me, and be
present there, that I may give you the
stone tablets, with the instructions and
commands that I have written on them
for their instruction."
13 So Moses, with his attendant Joshua,
rose; and Moses ascended the mountain
14 of God, saying to the elders,
"Wait here for us until we come back
to you. Aaron and Hur are here with
you; whoever has a dispute may bring
it to them."
15 So Moses ascended the mountain,
while the cloud covered the mountain,
16 and the glory of the LORD rested on
Mount Sinai; for six days the cloud covered it, but on the seventh day he called
to Moses from the midst of the cloud.
17 The glory of the LORD looked to the
Israelites like a consuming fire on the
18 top of the mountain. Moses penetrated
the cloud, and ascended the mountain;
Moses remained on the mountain for
forty days and nights.
25 The LORD said to Moses,
2 "Tell the Israelites to procure a contribution for me; get the contribution
for me from everyone whose heart
3 makes him willing. And this is the contribution that you are to procure from

them: gold, silver, and bronze, violet, 4
purple, and scarlet material, fine linen,
goats' hair, tanned rams' skins, por- 5
poise skins, acacia wood, oil for the 6
lamps, spices for the anointing oil and
the fragrant incense, onyx stones, and 7
set stones for the sacred apron and
pouch.
"They must also make me a sanctu- 8
ary, that I may dwell among them; you 9
must make it exactly as I have shown
you, after the plan for the dwelling and
all its fittings.
"They must also make an ark of aca- 10
cia wood, two and a half cubits long, a
cubit and a half wide, and a cubit and
a half high; you must overlay it with 11
pure gold, overlaying it both inside and
outside, and run a molding of gold
around it. You must cast four rings of 12
gold for it, and fasten them on its four
feet, with two rings on one side of it and
two rings on the other side of it; then 13
you must make poles of acacia wood,
overlaying them with gold, and put the 14
poles through the rings on the sides of
the ark, with which to carry the ark; the 15
poles are to remain in the rings of the
ark, never to be removed from it. In- 16
side the ark you must place the decrees
which I give you. You must also make 17
a propitiatory of pure gold, two and a
half cubits long, and a cubit and a half
wide; and make two cherubim of gold 18
at the two ends of the propitiatory,
making them of beaten work, making 19
one cherub at one end and the other
cherub at the other end, and making
the cherubim of one piece with the
propitiatory at its two ends; and the 20
cherubim are to have their wings spread
out on high, overshadowing the propitiatory with their wings and facing each
other, with the faces of the cherubim
directed toward the propitiatory. You 21
must place the propitiatory on top of
the ark, and inside the ark you must
place the decrees that I give you. I 22
will meet you there; from the place
above the propitiatory, between the
two cherubim on the ark of the decrees,
I will communicate to you all the commands that I have to give you for the
Israelites.
"You must also make a table of aca- 23
cia wood, two cubits long, a cubit wide,
and a cubit and a half high; you must 24
overlay it with pure gold, and run a
molding of gold around it; you must 25

make a rail around it a handbreadth
wide, and run a molding of gold around
26 its rail; you must make four rings of
gold for it, and fasten the rings on the
27 four corners of its four feet; the rings
are to lie close to the rail as holders for
28 the poles for carrying the table. You
must make the poles of acacia wood,
overlaying them with gold, that the ta-
29 ble may be carried with them. You
must also make its plates, its cups, its
flagons, and its bowls for pouring liba-
30 tions, making them of pure gold. You
must always have Presence-bread set
out on the table before me.

31 "You must also make a lampstand of
pure gold; the base and shaft of the
lampstand are to be made of beaten
work, its cups, each with its calyx and
32 petals, to be of one piece with it; six
branches are to extend from its sides,
three branches of the lampstand from
the one side of it, and three branches of
the lampstand from the other side of it;
33 there are to be three cups, shaped like
almond-blossoms, each with calyx and
petals, on one branch, three cups,
shaped like almond-blossoms, each with
calyx and petals, on another branch,
and so for the six branches extending
34 from the lampstand; and on the lampstand itself there are to be four cups,
shaped like almond-blossoms, each with
35 its calyx and petals; there is to be a
calyx of one piece with it under two
branches, another calyx of one piece
with it under two branches, and another
calyx of one piece with it under two
branches, for the six branches extend-
36 ing from the lampstand; their calyxes
and branches are to be of one piece with
it, the whole of it forming a single piece
37 of beaten work of pure gold. You must
then make the seven lamps for it; and
its lamps are to be put up so as to shed
38 light on the space in front of it. Its
snuffers and snuffdishes are to be of
39 pure gold. A talent of pure gold is to be
used to make it, with all these fittings.
40 And see that you make them after the
model for them that was shown you on
the mountain.

26 "The dwelling itself you must make
out of ten curtains, making them of
fine twisted linen, violet, purple, and
scarlet material, with cherubim, the
2 work of artists; the length of each curtain is to be twenty-eight cubits, and
the width of each curtain four cubits,
all the curtains to have the same measurements. Five of the curtains are to 3
be joined to one another, and the other
five curtains joined to one another; and 4
on the edge of the outermost curtain in
the one set you are to make loops of
violet, and you are to make the same
on the edge of the outermost curtain in
the other set, making fifty loops on the 5
one curtain, and fifty loops on the edge
of the curtain in the other set, the loops
to be opposite each other. You must 6
then make fifty gold clasps, and join the
curtains to one another with the clasps,
so that the dwelling may be a unit.

"Further, you must make curtains of 7
goats' hair for a tent over the dwelling,
making eleven curtains in all, the length 8
of each curtain to be thirty cubits, and
the width of each curtain four cubits,
the eleven curtains to have the same
measurements. You must join five of 9
the curtains by themselves, and the
other six curtains by themselves, doubling the sixth curtain to hang in front
of the tent. Then you must make fifty 10
loops on the edge of the outermost curtain in the one set, and fifty loops on the
edge of that in the other set, and you 11
must also make fifty bronze clasps, and
put the clasps into the loops, thus join-
ing the tent together so that it becomes
a unit. The overhanging part that is 12
left over in the tent curtains, the half
curtain that is left over, is to hang over
the rear of the dwelling, while the cubit 13
left over on each side in the length of
the tent curtains is to hang over each
side of the dwelling to cover it. Also, 14
you must make a covering for the tent
of tanned rams' skins, and above that
a covering of porpoise skins.

"You must make the frames for the 15
dwelling of durable acacia wood, ten 16
cubits to be the length of the frames,
and a cubit and a half the width of each
frame; each frame is to have two arms, 17
joined to each other by cross rungs;
you are to do the same with all the
frames for the dwelling. You must 18
make the frames for the dwelling as
follows: twenty frames for the side toward the Negeb to the south, making 19
forty silver pedestals as bases for the
twenty frames, two pedestals as bases
for one frame with its two arms, and
two pedestals as bases for another
frame with its two arms; twenty frames 20
for the second side of the dwelling, the

21 northern side, with their forty silver
pedestals, two pedestals as bases for
one frame, and two pedestals as bases
22 for another frame; and you must make
six frames for the rear of the dwelling
23 to the west, as well as two frames for
the corners of the dwelling at the rear;
24 they are to be double at the bottom,
and likewise double at the top of it, up
to the first ring, and so with both of
them; they are to form the two corners;
25 thus there shall be eight frames, with
their sixteen silver pedestals, two pedestals as bases for one frame, and two
pedestals as bases for another frame.
26 You must also make bars of acacia
wood, five for the frames on the one side
27 of the dwelling, and five bars for the
frames on the other side of the dwelling,
and five bars for the frames on the side
of the dwelling at the rear to the west;
28 the middle bar in the center of the
frames is to run through from end to
29 end. You must overlay the frames with
gold, and make the rings on them of
gold as holders for the bars, and also
30 overlay the bars with gold. So you
must erect the dwelling after the plan
for it that was shown you on the mountain.
31 "You must also make a veil of violet,
purple, and scarlet material, and fine
twisted linen, and it is to be made with
32 cherubim, the work of artists; you must
fasten it on four columns of acacia wood
overlaid with gold, with their hooks of
gold, standing on four silver pedestals;
33 you must hang the veil from the clasps,
and you must bring the ark of the decrees in there, inside the veil, so that
the veil shall divide the sacred place
from the most sacred place for you.
34 You must put the propitiatory on the
ark of the decrees in the most sacred
35 place, and place the table outside the
veil, and the lampstand opposite the
table at the south side of the dwelling,
36 placing the table at the north side. You
must also make a screen for the doorway of the tent of violet, purple, and
scarlet material, and fine twisted linen,
37 in variegated work; and for the screen
you must make five columns of acacia
wood, and overlay them with gold;
their hooks are to be gold, and you must
cast five bronze pedestals for them.

27 "You must make the altar of acacia
wood, five cubits long, and five cubits
wide; the altar is to be square, and its
height three cubits; you must make the 2
horns for it on its four corners, its horns
to be of one piece with it; and you must
overlay it with bronze. You must make 3
its ash-pans, its shovels, its basins, its
forks, and its firepans, making all its
utensils of bronze. You must make a 4
bronze grating of network for it, and on
the net you must make four bronze
rings at its four corners; you must then 5
place it under the ledge around the altar, that the net may reach half-way up
the altar. You must also make poles 6
for the altar, poles of acacia wood, and
overlay them with bronze; its poles are 7
to be put through the rings, with the
poles resting on the two sides of the altar when it is carried. You are to make 8
it hollow, with boards; it is to be made
just as it was shown you on the mountain.
"Then you must make the court of 9
the dwelling: for the southern side toward the Negeb there are to be hangings for the court of fine twisted linen,
extending one hundred cubits along the
one side, with twenty columns for them, 10
and twenty bronze pedestals for these,
the hooks of the columns and their
bands to be silver. Similarly, for the 11
north side there are to be hangings, extending to a length of one hundred
cubits, and twenty columns for them,
with twenty bronze pedestals for these,
the hooks of the columns and their
bands to be silver. For the west side, 12
the width of the court, there are to be
hangings extending for fifty cubits, ten
columns for them, and ten pedestals for
these; and the width of the court at the 13
front, the east side, is to be fifty cubits,
with hangings on the one wing for fif- 14
teen cubits, three columns for them,
and three pedestals for these, and hang- 15
ings on the other wing for fifteen cubits, three columns for them, and three
pedestals for these; while the gate of 16
the court is to have a screen measuring twenty cubits, of violet, purple,
and scarlet material, and fine twisted linen, in variegated work, with four
columns for it, and four pedestals for
these. All the columns around the 17
court are to be bound with silver, their
hooks also to be silver, but their pedestals bronze. The length of the court is 18
to be one hundred cubits, the width
fifty cubits, and the height five cubits,
hung with fine twisted linen. All the 19

utensils of the dwelling, used in all its
service, as well as all its pegs, and all the
pegs for the court are to be bronze.
20 "You must order the Israelites to
provide you with pure oil from crushed
olives for the lights, so that there may
21 always be a lamp to lift in place; in the
tent of meeting, outside the veil which
screens the decrees, Aaron and his sons
are to keep it supplied from evening until morning before the LORD; it is to be
a perpetual statute with the Israelites
throughout their generations.
28 "From among the Israelites have
your brother Aaron, accompanied by
his sons, present himself to you to serve
as priest to me, Aaron and his sons,
Nadab and Abihu, Eleazar and Itha-
2 mar. You must make sacred vestments
for your brother Aaron to his honor and
3 adornment; you must tell all the skilful
persons, whom I have endowed with
skill, to make vestments for Aaron, to
consecrate him to serve as priest to me.
4 The following are the vestments that
they must make: a pouch, an apron, a
robe, a tunic in checkered work, a turban, and a sash. They must make the
sacred vestments for your brother
Aaron and his sons, that he may serve
5 as priest to me; and they must use
gold, violet, purple, and scarlet material, and fine linen.
6 "They must make the apron of gold,
violet, purple, and scarlet material, and
7 fine twisted linen, in skilled work; it
must have two shoulder-straps joined
to it at the two ends, and thus be
8 joined. The skilfully made girdle on it
must be made like it, of one piece with
it, of gold, violet, purple, and scarlet
9 material, and fine twisted linen. You
must then procure two onyx stones, and
engrave on them the names of the Isra-
10 elites, six of their names on the one
stone, and the remaining six on the
other stone, in the order of their origin;
11 with seal engravings, the work of a jeweler, you must engrave the two stones
with the various names of the Israelites,
setting them in filigree work of gold;
12 and you must fasten the two stones on
the shoulder-straps of the apron, as
memorial stones for the Israelites, and
so Aaron shall carry their names on his
shoulders in the presence of the LORD
as a memorial.
13 "You must also make filigree objects
14 of gold, and two chains of pure gold,

making them of twisted material, of
cordage-work, and you must fasten the
corded chains to the filigree objects.
"Further, you must make an oracle 15
pouch in skilled work; you must make
it in the same way as the apron, making
it of gold, violet, purple, and scarlet
material, and fine twisted linen; it is to 16
be square, and folded double, a span
long, and a span wide; and you must 17
insert in it a setting of stones, four rows
of stones, the first row to be a row of
carnelian, topaz, and emerald, the sec- 18
ond row a ruby, a sapphire, and a crystal, the third row a jacinth, an agate, 19
and an amethyst, and the fourth row 20
a chrysolite, an onyx, and a jasper; they
are to be inclosed with gold in their settings. The stones, corresponding to the 21
names of the Israelites, are to be twelve
in number, as their names are, each to
be engraved like a seal with its proper
name for the twelve tribes. On the 22
pouch you must make chains of twisted
material, of cordage-work of pure gold;
you must then make two rings of gold 23
on the pouch, fastening the two rings at
the two ends of the pouch; you must 24
fasten the two gold cords to the two
rings at the ends of the pouch, while the 25
other two ends of the two cords you
must fasten to the two filigree objects,
fastening them to the shoulder-straps
of the apron on the front of it. You 26
must make two rings of gold, and attach them to the two ends of the pouch,
on its inner edge next to the apron. You 27
must then make two rings of gold, and
fasten them to the shoulder-straps in
front of the apron, underneath, close to
the place where it is joined, above the
skilfully made girdle; and the pouch is 28
to be tied by its rings to the rings of the
apron with a violet cord, so as to lie on
the skilfully made girdle, so that the
pouch may not swing loose from the
apron. Aaron shall carry the names of 29
the Israelites on the oracle pouch over
his heart whenever he enters the sacred
place, as a memorial before the LORD
always. You must put the Urim and 30
Thummim in the oracle pouch, that
they may lie over Aaron's heart whenever he enters the presence of the
LORD, that Aaron may always carry
the oracle of the Israelites over his heart
in the presence of the LORD.
"You must make the robe belonging 31
to the apron entirely of violet material;

32 and it must have an opening at the top,
in the middle of it; its opening is to
have a binding of woven work around
it; it is to have an opening like that of a
33 corselet, so that it may not be torn. On
its skirts you must make pomegranates
of violet, purple, and scarlet material,
34 all around its skirts, with gold bells
among them all around, a gold bell alternating with a pomegranate all
35 around the skirts of the robe. Aaron
must wear it in ministering, that the
tinkling of it may be heard when he enters the sacred place in the presence of
the LORD, and when he leaves it, and
then he will not die.

36 "You must also make a diadem of
pure gold, and with seal engravings you
must engrave on it, 'Sacred to the
37 LORD'; you must attach it to a violet
cord, and it is to rest on the turban; at
38 the front of the turban shall it be; it is
to rest on Aaron's forehead, so that
Aaron himself shall bear any guilt connected with the sacred offerings which
the Israelites may ever make as their
sacred gifts; it must always be on his
forehead to win acceptance for them
before the LORD.

39 "You must weave the tunic of fine
linen; and make a turban of fine linen,
and a sash in variegated work.

40 "For Aaron's sons, too, you must
make tunics; you must make sashes
for them, and you must also make caps
for them, to their honor and adorn-
41 ment. You must dress your brother
Aaron in these, and his sons along with
him, anointing them, installing them,
and consecrating them to serve as
42 priests to me. You must also make lin-
en breeches for them, to cover their
bare flesh, reaching from the loins to
43 the thighs; and Aaron and his sons must
wear them whenever they enter the tent
of meeting, or approach the altar to
minister in the sacred place, lest they
incur guilt, and so die; it is to be a perpetual statute for him and for his descendants after him.

29 "The following is what you must do
with them in consecrating them to serve
as priests to me: take a young bullock,
2 two perfect rams, unleavened bread,
unleavened cakes mixed with oil, and
unleavened wafers smeared with oil,
3 making them of fine wheat flour; you
must put them in a basket, and present
them in the basket, along with the bullock and the two rams. Then you must 4
have Aaron and his sons come up to the
doorway of the tent of meeting, and
wash them with water; and taking the 5
vestments, you must dress Aaron in the
tunic, the robe belonging to the apron,
the apron itself, and the pouch, and
gird him with the skilfully made girdle;
you must set the turban on his head, 6
and place the sacred crown on the turban; you must then take the anointing 7
oil, and pouring it on his head, anoint
him. You must also have his sons come 8
up, and then dress them in tunics, gird 9
them with sashes, namely Aaron and
his sons, and fasten caps on them; they
are to have the priesthood by a perpetual statute. Thus shall you instal
Aaron and his sons.

"You must then bring the bullock to 10
the front of the tent of meeting; Aaron
and his sons must lay their hands on
the head of the bullock, and then you 11
must slaughter the bullock before the
LORD at the doorway of the tent of
meeting; you must take some of the 12
bullock's blood, and put it on the horns
of the altar with your finger, pouring
out all the rest of the blood at the base
of the altar; you must take all the fat 13
covering the entrails, the lobe on the
liver, and the two kidneys with the fat
that is on them, and burn them on the
altar; but the flesh of the bullock, with 14
its hide and offal, you must burn up
outside the camp; it is a sin-offering.
You must then take one of the rams; 15
Aaron and his sons must lay their
hands on the head of the ram, and then 16
you must slaughter the ram, and taking
its blood, dash it all around the altar;
you must cut the ram into pieces, and 17
washing its entrails and legs, put them
with its other pieces and its head, and 18
then burn the whole ram on the altar;
it is a burnt-offering to the LORD, a
soothing odor, a sacrifice to the LORD.
You must then take the other ram; 19
Aaron and his sons must lay their hands
on the head of the ram, and then you 20
must slaughter the ram, and taking
some of its blood, put it on the tip of
Aaron's ear, on the tips of his sons'
right ears, on the thumbs of their right
hands, and on the great toes of their
right feet, dashing the rest of the blood
all around the altar; you must then 21
take some of the blood that is on the
altar and some of the anointing oil, and

sprinkle it on Aaron and his vestments,
as well as on his sons and the vestments
of his sons with him, so that he and his
vestments may be consecrated, as well
as his sons and the vestments of his sons
22 with him. You must also take the fat
from the ram, the fat tail, the fat covering the entrails, the lobe of the liver, the
two kidneys with the fat that is on
them, and the right thigh (for it is an
23 installation ram), together with a loaf
of bread, a cake made with oil, and a
wafer from the basket of unleavened
24 cakes which lies before the LORD; you
must lay all this in the hands of Aaron
and his sons, and present them as a
25 wave-offering before the LORD; then
you must take them from their hands,
and burn them on the altar for burnt-
offerings, as a soothing odor to the
LORD; it is a sacrifice to the LORD.
26 You must take the breast of Aaron's installation ram, and wave it as a wave-
offering before the LORD, after which it
27 is to become your share. You must consecrate the waved breast of the ram
used for the installation of Aaron and
his sons, which was waved, and the
28 thigh which was contributed; it must
go to Aaron and his sons as their perpetual due from the Israelites; for it is
a contribution; it is a contribution from
the Israelites out of their thanksgiving
sacrifices, their contribution to the
LORD.
29 "The sacred vestments of Aaron shall
pass to his sons after him, that they
may be anointed and installed in them;
30 for seven days shall that one of his sons
who is to be priest in his place wear
them when he enters the tent of meeting to minister in the sacred place.
31 "Taking the installation ram, you
32 must boil its flesh at a sacred place, and
then Aaron and his sons must eat the
flesh of the ram and the bread in the
basket at the doorway of the tent of
33 meeting; they may eat these things for
whose installation and consecration
atonement was made by them, but no
layman may eat them; for they are
34 sacred. If any of the flesh used in the
installation, or any of the bread is left
over until morning, you must burn up
what is left; it is not to be eaten, because it is sacred.
35 "This, then, is what you must do
with Aaron and his sons, just as I have
commanded you. You must spend sev-
en days installing them; each day you 36
must offer a bullock as a sin-offering to
make atonement; you must make a sin-
offering on the altar when you make
atonement for it, and then anoint it to
make it sacred; you must spend seven 37
days making atonement for the altar in
order to make it sacred; the altar will
then be completely taboo, so that
everyone touching the altar will become taboo.
"This is what you are to offer on the 38
altar: two yearling lambs regularly
each day, offering one lamb in the 39
morning, and the other lamb at twilight, and with the former lamb a tenth 40
of an ephah of fine meal mixed with
a fourth of a hin of oil from crushed
olives, and a libation of a fourth of a
hin of wine; and the other lamb you 41
must offer at twilight as a soothing
odor, a sacrifice to the LORD, accompanying it with the same cereal-offering
and libation as the offering in the morning—a regular burnt-offering to be 42
made by you throughout your generations at the doorway of the tent of
meeting before the LORD, where I will
meet you to speak to you there.
"I will meet the Israelites there, and 43
it shall be consecrated by my glory; I 44
will consecrate the tent of meeting and
the altar, and I will also consecrate
Aaron and his sons to serve as priests to
me; I will dwell in the midst of the Is- 45
raelites, and will be their God; they 46
shall know that I, the LORD, am their
God, who brought them out of the land
of Egypt that I might dwell in the
midst of them, I, the LORD their God.
"You must also make an altar for 30
burning incense, making it of acacia
wood; it is to be square, a cubit long 2
and a cubit wide, while its height is to
be two cubits, with its horns of one
piece with it; you must overlay it with 3
pure gold, its top, its sides all around,
and its horns; and you must run a gold
molding around it. You must make two 4
gold rings for it underneath its molding,
on its two sides, making them on the
two opposite sides of it, as holders for
the poles by which to carry it. You 5
must make the poles of acacia wood,
and overlay them with gold. You must 6
then place it in front of the veil which
screens the ark of the decrees, in front of
the propitiatory that lies over the decrees, where I will meet you. On it 7

Aaron must burn spices as incense,
burning it from morning to morning
8 when he trims the lamps; also when
Aaron puts up the lamps at twilight, he
must burn it, as a regular incense-offer-
ing before the LORD throughout your
9 generations. You must not offer improper incense on it, nor burnt-offerings, nor cereal-offerings, nor pour liba-
10 tions on it. Once a year Aaron must
make atonement on its horns; with the
blood of the sin-offering of atonement
he must make atonement on it once a
year throughout your generations, since
it is most sacred to the LORD."
11 The LORD said to Moses,
12 "When you take a census of the Israelites, each of them must pay a ransom for himself to the LORD at the time
that they are numbered, that no plague
may fall on them when they are num-
13 bered. And this is what every one
must pay as he joins those already numbered, a half-shekel, in terms of the sacred shekel, the shekel of twenty gerahs, a half-shekel as a contribution to
14 the LORD; every one from twenty
years old and upward, as he joins those
already numbered, must make this con-
15 tribution to the LORD; the rich are not
to give more, nor the poor less than a
half-shekel in making the contribution
to the LORD to make atonement for
16 yourselves. On taking the atonement
money from the Israelites you must
use it for the service of the tent of meeting, that it may be for the Israelites a
memorial before the LORD to make
atonement for yourselves."
17 The LORD said to Moses,
18 "You must make a bronze laver with
a bronze base for washing, and place it
between the tent of meeting and the
19 altar, putting water in it, so that Aaron
and his sons may wash their hands and
20 feet from it; whenever they enter the
tent of meeting, they must wash themselves with water, that they die not; or
whenever they approach the altar to
minister, by burning a sacrifice to the
21 LORD. So they must wash their
hands and feet, that they die not, and
it is to be a perpetual statute for them,
for him and his descendants throughout their generations."
22 The LORD said to Moses,
23 "Procure the finest spices, five hundred shekels of pure myrrh, half that
amount of fragrant cinnamon, namely

two hundred and fifty shekels, two hundred and fifty shekels of fragrant calamus, five hundred shekels of cassia, in 24
terms of the sacred shekel, and a hin of
olive oil; you must then make it into a 25
sacred anointing oil, a compound made
according to the art of the compounder
of oils; it is to be a sacred anointing
oil, and with it you must anoint the tent 26
of meeting, the ark of the decrees, the 27
table and all its fittings, the lampstand
and its fittings, the incense altar, the 28
altar for burnt-offerings and all its fittings, the laver and its base, and thus 29
make them sacred, so that they become
completely taboo, with everyone touching them becoming taboo. You must 30
also anoint Aaron and his sons, consecrating them to serve as priests to me.
You must then say to the Israelites, 31
'This is to be a sacred anointing oil for
me throughout your generations; it is 32
not to be used for anointing the body of
an ordinary person, nor are you to
make anything like it in composition for
yourselves; being sacred, it is taboo to
you. Whoever compounds anything 33
like it, or puts any of it on a layman,
shall be cut off from his people.' "
The LORD said to Moses, 34
"Procure spices, stacte, onycha, galbanum, spices, and pure frank-incense,
the same amount of each, and make it 35
into incense, a compound made by the
compounder's art, clarified, pure and
sacred. You must pulverize some of it 36
very fine, and place some of it in front
of the decrees in the tent of meeting,
where I will meet you; it is to be completely taboo to you. The incense which 37
you are to make according to its formu-
la, you must never make for yourselves;
you must regard it as sacred to the
LORD; whoever makes anything like 38
it just to smell shall be cut off from his
people."
The LORD said to Moses, **31**
"See, I have specifically chosen Bez- 2
alel, the son of Uri, the son of Hur, belonging to the tribe of Judah, filling him 3
with the spirit of God, in skill, intelligence, and knowledge in every craft,
to devise ingenious things in working 4
with gold, silver, and bronze, and in the 5
cutting of stones to be set, and in wood
carving, that he may work at every
craft. However, along with him I have 6
also appointed Oholiab, the son of Ahisamach, belonging to the tribe of Dan,

and I have endowed all those of skilful
mind with skill to make all that I have
7 commanded you, the tent of meeting,
the ark of the decrees, and the propitia-
8 tory on it, all the fittings of the tent, the
table and its fittings, the lampstand of
9 pure gold and its fittings, the incense
altar, the altar for burnt-offerings and
10 all its fittings, the laver and its base, the
woven vestments, the sacred vestments
for Aaron, the priest, and the vestments for his sons, to serve as priests,
11 the anointing oil, and the incense made
of spices for the sacred place; they shall
make them just as I have commanded
you."

12 The LORD said to Moses,

13 "Say to the Israelites, 'You must be
sure to keep my sabbaths; for that will
be a sign between me and you throughout your generations, so that it may be
known that I, the LORD, am consecrat-
14 ing you. So you must keep the sabbath;
for it is to be sacred to you; anyone des-
ecrating it must be put to death; if
there is anyone who does work on it,
that person is to be cut off from his peo-
15 ple. For six days work may be done,
but on the seventh day there is to be
the sabbath of complete rest, sacred to
the LORD; anyone who does work on
the sabbath day must be put to death.
So the Israelites must keep the sabbath,
16 observing the sabbath throughout their
generations as a perpetual covenant; it
17 is a sign between me and the Israelites
forever; for in six days the LORD made
the heavens and the earth, but on the
seventh day he rested and refreshed
himself.' "

18 As soon as he had finished talking
with Moses on Mount Sinai, he gave
him the two tablets of the decrees, the
stone tablets, inscribed by God's own
finger.

32 When the people saw that Moses was
long in coming down from the mountain, the people gathered about Aaron,
and said to him,

"Come, make us a god to go ahead of
us; for this is the way it is with Moses,
the man who brought us up out of the
land of Egypt—we do not know what
has become of him."

2 So Aaron said to them,

"Tear off the gold rings which are in
the ears of your wives, your sons, and
your daughters, and bring them to
me."

So all the people tore off the gold 3
rings which were in their ears, and
brought them to Aaron, who took the 4
material from them, and pouring it into
a mold, made it into a molten bull,
whereupon they said,

"Here is your god, O Israel, who
brought you up out of the land of
Egypt!"

On seeing this, Aaron built an altar 5
in front of it, and Aaron made proclamation,

"Tomorrow a feast shall be held to
the LORD."

So next day the people rose early, and 6
offered burnt-offerings, and presented
thank-offerings; the people sat down to
eat and drink, after which they rose to
make merry.

Then the LORD said to Moses, 7

"Go down at once; for your people
whom you brought up out of the land
of Egypt have acted perniciously, in 8
that they have been quick to swerve
from the path that I appointed them,
by making themselves a molten bull,
doing homage to it, sacrificing to it, and
saying, 'This is your god, O Israel, who
brought you up out of the land of
Egypt!' "

Further, the LORD said to Moses, 9

"I have watched this people, and it is 10
indeed a stiff-necked people. Now
then, let me alone, that my anger may
blaze against them, and that I may
consume them; and then I will make a
great nation of you."

But Moses tried to mollify the LORD 11
his God.

"O LORD," he said, "why does thy
anger blaze against thy own people
whom thou didst bring out of the land
of Egypt by great power and a strong
hand? Why should the Egyptians say, 12
'It was at a bad time that he brought
them out, slaying them in the highlands
and obliterating them from the face of
the earth?' Turn from thy fierce anger,
and change thy mind about doing evil
to thy people. Remember concerning 13
Abraham, Isaac, and Israel, thy servants, that thou didst swear by thyself
to them, saying to them, 'I will make
your descendants as numerous as the
stars in the sky, and all this land that I
have spoken of, I will give to your descendants to have as their own forever.' "

So the LORD changed his mind about 14

the evil that he said he would do to his
people.
15 Moses then turned and descended
from the mountain, with the two tablets of the decrees in his hand, tablets
written on both their sides, being writ-
16 ten on one side and on the other. The
tablets were the work of God, and the
writing was the writing of God, engraved upon the tablets.
17 When Joshua heard the sound of the
people shouting, he said to Moses,
"There is the sound of war in the
camp."
18 But he said,
"It is not the sound of the cry of
might, nor is it the sound of the cry of
defeat; it is the sound of singing that I
hear."
19 As soon as he came near the camp, he
saw the bull and the dancing, whereupon Moses' anger blazed, and he flung
the tablets from his hands, and broke
20 them at the foot of the mountain; then
he took the bull which they had made,
and burned it up, and grinding it to
powder, he scattered it on the surface of
the water, and made the Israelites
21 drink it. Then Moses said to Aaron,
"What did this people do to you,
that you have let them incur such great
guilt?"
22 Aaron said,
"Let not my lord's anger blaze; you
know yourself how bad the people are.
23 They said to me, 'Make us a god to go
ahead of us; for this is the way it is
with Moses, the man who brought us
up out of the land of Egypt—we do not
24 know what has become of him.' So I
said to them, 'Whoever has any gold,
let them tear it off'; and when they gave
it to me, I threw it into the fire, and out
came this bull!"
25 When Moses saw that the people had
become unruly (for Aaron had let them
get unruly, to be a derision among their
26 assailants), Moses stood at the gate of
the camp, and said,
"To me, whoever is for the LORD!"
27 Whereupon all the Levites gathered
to him. Then he said to them,
"Thus says the LORD, the God of Israel: 'Let each fasten his sword on his
hip, and go back and forth from gate to
gate in the camp, slaying each his kinsman, his friend, and his neighbor.'"
28 The Levites followed Moses' instructions, so that about three thousand of
the people fell that day.
Then Moses said, 29
"You have installed yourselves today
as priests to the LORD, each at the cost
of his son and his kinsman, that he may
bestow a blessing on you today."
Next day Moses said to the people, 30
"You have committed a great sin; so
now I will go up to the LORD; perhaps
I may make atonement for your sin."
So Moses returned to the LORD, and 31
said,
"Alas, this people has committed a
great sin, in that they have made a god
of gold for themselves. But now, if thou 32
wilt forgive their sin, . . .; but if not,
pray blot me out of thy book which
thou hast written."
But the LORD said to Moses, 33
"Whoever sins against me, him only
I blot out of my book. Now go, lead the 34
people where I told you; see, my angel
shall go ahead of you; but on the day
that I do punish, I will punish them for
their sin."
So the LORD smote the people for 35
having had the bull made which Aaron
made.
Then the LORD said to Moses, **33**
"Depart, you and the people that
you have brought up out of the land of
Egypt, go up from here to the land
which I promised on oath to Abraham,
Isaac, and Jacob, when I said, 'To your
descendants I will give it' (I will send 2
an angel ahead of you, and I will drive
out the Canaanites, Amorites, Hittites,
Perizzites, Hivvites, and Jebusites), to 3
a land flowing with milk and honey; for
I will not go up with you myself, lest I
destroy you on the way; for you are a
stiff-necked people."
When the people heard this bad 4
news, they mourned, and none of them
wore his ornaments.
Then the LORD said to Moses, 5
"Say to the Israelites, 'You are such
a stiff-necked people that if I were to go
up with you for a single moment, I
would destroy you; take off your ornaments then, that I may know what to
do to you.'"
So the Israelites stripped off their 6
Mount Horeb ornaments.
Now Moses used to take the tent and 7
pitch it outside the camp, at a distance
from the camp. It was called the tent of
meeting. If there was anyone who

wanted to consult the LORD, he would
go out to the tent of meeting which was
8 outside the camp. Whenever Moses
went out to the tent, the people would
all rise and stand, each at the doorway
of his tent, and gaze after Moses until
9 he entered the tent; and as soon as
Moses entered the tent, the column of
cloud would descend, and stand at the
doorway of the tent while he conversed
10 with Moses; and whenever the people
saw the column of cloud standing at the
doorway of the tent, the people would
all rise, and make obeisance, each at the
11 doorway of his tent. The LORD used to
speak to Moses face to face, as one man
would speak to another; and then he
would return to the camp; but his attendant, Joshua, the son of Nun, as servant was not accustomed to leave the
tent.

12 Moses said to the LORD,

"See, thou sayest to me, 'Lead this
people up,' but thou hast not let me know
whom thou wilt send with me. Yet
thou hast said, 'I know you by name,
and you have found favor with me too.'
13 Now then, if I have really found favor
with thee, pray let me know thy ways,
and so know thee, that I may continue
to find favor with thee. Consider, too,
that this nation is thy own people."

14 "I will go along myself," he said,
"and lead you."

15 He said to him,

"If thou art not to go along thyself,
16 do not make us go up from here. For
how then could it be known that I and
thy people have found favor with thee?
Is it not by thy going with us, so that
we may be distinguished, I and thy
people, from all other people that are
on the face of the ground?"

17 So the LORD said to Moses,

"This request also, which you have
just made, I will carry out; for you have
found favor with me, and I know you
by name."

18 Then he said,

"Show me thy glory."

19 But he said,

"I will make all my goodliness pass
before your view, and will proclaim the
name of the LORD before you, and how
I am gracious to those to whom I am
gracious, and compassionate with those
20 with whom I am compassionate." "But
you may not see my face," he said; "for
man cannot see me, and live."

However, the LORD said, 21

"Here is a place by me; station yourself on the rock; and when my glory 22
passes by, I will put you in a cleft of the
rock, and cover you with my hand until
I pass by; then I will take away my 23
hand, so that you may see my back,
while my face shall not be seen."

The LORD said to Moses, 3

"Cut two stone tablets like the former ones, and I will write on the tablets
the words that were on the former tablets which you broke. Be ready by 2
morning, and in the morning ascend
Mount Sinai, and present yourself
there to me on the top of the mountain.
No one is to ascend with you, nor is 3
anyone to be seen anywhere on the
mountain, nor must the flocks and
herds graze in front of that mountain."

So Moses cut two stone tablets like 4
the former ones, and rising early next
morning, he ascended Mount Sinai, as
the LORD had commanded him, taking
the two stone tablets in his hand. Then 5
the LORD descended in a cloud, and
took up a position with him there, while
he called upon the name of the LORD.
The LORD passed in front of him, pro- 6
claiming,

"The LORD, the LORD, a God compassionate and gracious, slow to anger,
abounding in kindness and fidelity,
showing kindness to the thousandth 7
generation, forgiving iniquity, transgression, and sin, without leaving it unpunished however, but avenging the iniquity of fathers upon their children
and grandchildren down to the third or
even the fourth generation."

Then Moses quickly bowed his head 8
to the ground, and made obeisance.

"If I have really found favor with 9
thee, O Lord," he said, "pray let the
Lord go with us; for this is a stiff-
necked people; but do thou pardon our
iniquity and our sin, and make us thy
very own."

So he said, 10

"I hereby make a covenant: before
all your people I will perform such
wonders as have never occurred anywhere on the earth nor in any nation,
so that all the people among whom you
are living shall see that it is an awful
deed that I, the LORD, am going to do
along with you. Mark what I command 11
you today. I am going to drive the Amorites, Canaanites, Hittites, Perizzites,

Hivvites, and Jebusites out of your
2 way; so you must take care not to make
a covenant with the inhabitants of the
land which you are about to enter, lest
3 they become a snare among you; but
you must tear down their altars, smash
their sacred pillars, and cut down their
4 sacred poles (for you must not pay
homage to any other god, because the
LORD, being jealous by nature, is a
5 jealous God), lest in making a covenant
with the inhabitants of the land you
run wantonly after their gods, sacrificing to their gods, and whenever anyone
invites you, partaking of his sacrifice,
6 and you marry your sons to their
daughters, which daughters will run
wantonly after their gods, and make
your sons run wantonly after their
gods.
7 "You must not make any molten
gods for yourself.
8 "You must keep the feast of unleavened cakes, eating unleavened cakes for
seven days, as I commanded you, at the
appointed time, the new moon of Abib;
for it was on the new moon of Abib that
you came out of Egypt.
9 "Whatever first opens the womb belongs to me, in the case of all your live
stock that are male, the firstlings of
0 oxen and sheep; a firstling ass, however,
you may redeem with a sheep, but if
you do not redeem it, you must break
its neck; any first-born son of yours you
may redeem.
"None may visit me empty-handed.
1 "Six days you are to labor, but on the
seventh day you must rest, resting at
ploughing-time and at harvest.
2 "You must observe the feast of
weeks, that of the first-fruits of the
wheat harvest, and also the feast of in-
3 gathering at the turn of the year; three
times a year must all your males visit
the Lord GOD, the God of Israel. For
4 I will drive nations out of your way,
and enlarge your territory; and no
one shall covet your land when you go
up to visit the LORD your God three
times a year.
5 "You must not offer the blood of a
sacrifice to me with leavened bread.
"The sacrifice of the passover feast
must not be left over night until morning.
6 "The very first of the first-fruits of
your land you must bring to the house
of the LORD your God.

"You must not boil a kid in its
mother's milk."
Then the LORD said to Moses, 27
"Write down these words; for it is on
the basis of these words that I have
made a covenant with you and Israel."
So he remained there with the LORD 28
for forty days and nights, without eating bread or drinking water; and he
wrote on the tablets the terms of the
covenant, the decalogue.
When Moses descended from Mount 29
Sinai (the two tablets of the decrees being in Moses' hand as he descended
from the mountain), Moses himself did
not know that the skin of his face was
in a glow after conversing with God;
but Aaron and the Israelites all saw 30
that the skin of Moses' face was in a
glow, and they were afraid to approach
him. But Moses called to them, and 31
then Aaron and all the leaders of the
community rejoined him, and Moses
talked to them. After that all the Is- 32
raelites came up, and he enjoined on
them all the things about which the
LORD had conversed with him on
Mount Sinai. When Moses had finished 33
conversing with them, he put a veil on his
face; but whenever Moses entered the 34
presence of the LORD to converse with
him, he used to remove the veil until he
came out again; and whenever he came
out, he would tell the Israelites what he
had been commanded, and the Israel- 35
ites would see that the skin of Moses'
face was in a glow, so Moses would replace the veil on his face until he came
again to converse with him.
Then Moses assembled the whole Is- **35**
raelite community, and said to them,
"These are the things which the
LORD has commanded to be done. For 2
six days work may be done, but the seventh day you are to keep sacred as a
sabbath of complete rest to the LORD;
whoever does any work on it must be
put to death; you must not even light a 3
fire in any of. your dwellings on the
sabbath day."
Further, Moses said to the whole 4
Israelite community,
"This is the command that the LORD 5
has given: 'Procure from your company a contribution for the LORD;
everyone whose heart is willing is to
bring it, the LORD's contribution, gold,
silver, and bronze, violet, purple, and 6
scarlet material, fine linen, goats' hair, 7

tanned rams' skins, porpoise skins, aca-
8 cia wood, oil for the lights, spices for
the anointing oil and the fragrant in-
9 cense, onyx stones, and set stones for
10 the sacred apron and pouch. Also every
skilful person among you is to come,
and make all that the LORD has com-
11 manded, the dwelling with its tent, its
covering, its clasps, its frames, its bars,
12 its columns, and its pedestals, the ark
with its poles, the propitiatory, and the
13 veil for the screen, the table with its
poles and all its fittings, and the pres-
14 ence-bread, the lampstand for the
lights with its fittings, its lamps, and
15 the oil for the lights, the incense altar
with its poles, the anointing oil, the
fragrant incense, and the screen for the
16 doorway to the dwelling, the altar for
burnt-offerings with its bronze grating,
its poles, and all its fittings, the laver
17 with its base, the hangings for the
court, with its columns and pedestals,
and the screen for the gate of the court,
18 the pegs for the dwelling, the pegs for
19 the court and their ropes, the woven
vestments for ministering in the sacred
place, the sacred vestments for Aaron,
the priest, and his sons' vestments, when
they serve as priests.' "
20 The whole assembly of Israelites then
21 left the presence of Moses; and everyone who had confidence in his ability,
and everyone whose mind made him
willing came, bringing the contributions for the LORD, for the construction of the tent of meeting, for all its
service, and for the sacred vestments.
22 They came, both men and women, all
whose hearts were willing, bringing
brooches, earrings, signet-rings, necklaces, and all sorts of gold objects—
everyone who could make an offering of
23 gold to the LORD. Everyone who possessed violet, purple, or scarlet material, fine linen, goats' hair, tanned rams'
skins, or porpoise skins, brought them.
24 Everyone who could make a contribution of silver or bronze brought it as a
contribution to the LORD; and everyone who possessed acacia wood, suitable for any of the construction work,
25 brought it. All the skilled women spun
with their own hands, and brought the
material that was spun, violet, purple,
26 and scarlet material, and fine linen; and
all the women who had confidence in
27 their ability spun the goats' hair. The
rulers brought the onyx stones, and the
set stones for the sacred apron and
pouch, the spices, and the oil for the 2
lights, for the anointing oil, and for
the fragrant incense. The Israelites 2
brought voluntary offerings to the
LORD, every man and woman what his
heart prompted him to bring for all the
work which the LORD through Moses
had commanded to be done.

Then Moses said to the Israelites, 3
"See, the LORD has specifically chosen Bezalel, the son of Uri, the son of
Hur, belonging to the tribe of Judah,
filling him with the spirit of God, in 3
skill, intelligence, and knowledge in
every craft, to devise ingenious things 3
in working with gold, silver, and
bronze, and in the cutting of stones to 3
be set, and in wood carving, that he
may work at every craft; and he has 3
given him ability to instruct others.
Both him and Oholiab, the son of Ahisamach, belonging to the tribe of Dan,
he has endowed with skill to do all 3
kinds of work, that of the engraver, the
artisan, the worker in violet, purple,
and scarlet material, and fine linen, and
the weaver, makers of all kinds of
work, and devisers of ingenious things.
Bezalel and Oholiab are to do the work,
along with every skilled person whom
the LORD has endowed with skill and
intelligence to know how to carry out
all the work of construction on the
sanctuary, just as the LORD has commanded."

So Moses summoned Bezalel and
Oholiab, and every skilled person whom
the LORD had endowed with skill,
everyone who felt that he had the ability to undertake the work, to carry it
out. Under the supervision of Moses
they received all the contributions
which the Israelites had brought for the
work of construction on the sanctuary,
to carry it out, while they still continued to bring him voluntary offerings
from morning to morning; so much so
that all the craftsmen who were carrying out the construction of the sanctuary left every man the work that he
was doing, and said to Moses,

"The people are bringing much more
than is necessary for the work of construction that the LORD gave command to carry out."

So Moses issued a command which
was proclaimed throughout the camp,
"Neither man nor woman must

make anything more for the contribution to the sanctuary."
7 Thus the people were stopped from
bringing any more, since the material
in hand was sufficient to carry out all
the work; indeed there was too much.
8 All the skilled persons among those
engaged in the work made the dwelling
out of ten curtains, making them of fine
twisted linen, and violet, purple, and
scarlet material, with cherubim, the
9 work of artists. The length of each curtain was twenty-eight cubits, and the
width of each curtain four cubits, all
the curtains having the same measure-
10 ments. They joined five of the curtains
to one another, and the other five cur-
11 tains they joined to one another; and
on the edge of the outermost curtain
in the one set they made loops of violet,
and they made the same on the edge of
the outermost curtain in the other set,
12 making fifty loops on the one curtain,
and fifty loops on the edge of the curtain in the other set, the loops being op-
13 posite each other. Then they made fifty gold clasps, and joined the curtains
to one another with the clasps, so that
the dwelling was a unit.
14 Further, they made curtains of goats'
hair, for a tent over the dwelling, mak-
15 ing eleven of these curtains, the length
of each curtain being thirty cubits, and
the width of each curtain four cubits,
the eleven curtains having the same
16 measurements. They joined five of the
curtains by themselves, and the other
17 six by themselves; and they made fifty
loops on the edge of the outermost curtain in the one set, and fifty loops on
18 the edge of that in the other set; and
they made fifty bronze clasps to join
the tent together to become a unit.
19 They also made a covering for the tent
itself of tanned rams' skins, and above
that a covering of porpoise skins.
20 Then they made the frames for the
21 dwelling of durable acacia wood, ten
cubits being the length of the frames,
and a cubit and a half the width of each
22 frame; each frame had two arms, joined
to each other by cross rungs; they did
the same with all the frames for the
23 dwelling. They made the frames for the
dwelling: twenty frames for the side to-
24 ward the Negeb to the south, making
forty silver pedestals as bases for the
twenty frames, two pedestals as bases
for one frame with its two arms, and

two pedestals as bases for another
frame with its two arms; for the second 25
side of the dwelling, the northern side,
they made twenty frames, with their 26
forty silver pedestals, two pedestals as
bases for one frame, and two pedestals
as bases for another frame; and for the 27
rear of the dwelling to the west they
made six frames, and they also made 28
two frames for the corners of the dwelling at the rear; they were double at the 29
bottom, and likewise double at the top
of it, up to the first ring; they did the
same with both of them for the two
corners; thus there were eight frames, 30
and their silver pedestals were sixteen
in number, two pedestals as bases for
each frame. They also made bars of 31
acacia wood, five for the frames on the
one side of the dwelling, and five bars 32
for the frames on the other side of the
dwelling, and five bars for the frames of
the dwelling at the rear to the west; and 33
they made the middle bar in the center
of the frames run through from end to
end. They overlaid the frames with 34
gold, and they made the rings on them
of gold as holders for the bars, and also
overlaid the bars with gold.
They also made a veil of violet, pur- 35
ple, and scarlet material, and fine twisted linen, making it with cherubim, the
work of artists. They made four col- 36
umns of acacia wood for it, and overlaid them with gold, with their hooks of
gold; and they cast four silver pedestals
for them. They also made a screen for 37
the doorway of the tent of violet, purple, and scarlet material, and fine
twisted linen, in variegated work, as
well as five columns for it, with their
hooks; they overlaid their capitals and 38
bands with gold, and their five pedestals were bronze.
Bezalel made the ark of acacia wood, 37
two and a half cubits long, a cubit and a
half wide, and a cubit and a half high;
he overlaid it with pure gold inside and 2
outside, and ran a gold molding around
it. He cast four gold rings for it on its 3
four corners, two rings on one side of it,
and two rings on the other side of it. He 4
also made poles of acacia wood, and
overlaid them with gold; and he put the 5
poles through the rings on the sides of
the ark, to carry the ark. He made a 6
propitiatory of pure gold, two and a
half cubits long, and a cubit and a half
wide. He made two cherubim of gold, 7

8 making them of beaten work, at the
two ends of the propitiatory, one cherub at one end and the other cherub at
the other end; he made the cherubim
of one piece with the propitiatory at
9 the two ends of it; and the cherubim
had their wings spread out on high,
overshadowing the propitiatory with
their wings and facing each other, with
the faces of the cherubim directed toward the propitiatory.
10 Then he made the table of acacia
wood, two cubits long, a cubit wide,
11 and a cubit and a half high; he overlaid
it with pure gold, and ran a gold mold-
12 ing around it; he made a rail around it
a handbreadth wide, and ran a gold
13 molding around its rail; he cast four
gold rings for it, and fastened the rings
14 on the four corners of its four feet, with
the rings lying close to the rail as holders for the poles for carrying the table.
15 He made the poles for carrying the table of acacia wood, overlaying them
16 with gold; and he made the dishes that
were to be used on the table of pure
gold, its plates, its cups, its flagons, and
its bowls for pouring libations.
17 He also made the lampstand of pure
gold, making the lampstand itself and
its base and shaft of beaten work, with
its cups, each with calyx and petals, of
18 one piece with it; there were six branches extending from its sides, three
branches of the lampstand from the one
side of it, and three branches of the
lampstand from the other side of it;
19 there were three cups, shaped like
almond-blossoms, each with calyx
and petals, on one branch, three cups,
shaped like almond-blossoms, each
with calyx and petals, on another
branch, and so for the six branches ex-
20 tending from the lampstand; there
were four cups, shaped like almond-
blossoms, each with its calyx and pet-
21 als, on the lampstand itself; and there
was a calyx of one piece with it under
two branches, another calyx of one
piece with it under two branches, and
another calyx of one piece with it under
two branches, for the six branches ex-
22 tending from it; their calyxes and
branches were of one piece with it, the
whole of it forming a single piece of
23 beaten work of pure gold. He then
made the seven lamps for it, with its
snuffers and snuffdishes, of pure gold,

using a talent of gold to make it and all
its fittings.
He made the incense altar of acacia 25
wood, square, a cubit long and a cubit
wide, while its height was two cubits,
with its horns of one piece with it; he 26
overlaid it with pure gold, its top, its
sides all around, and its horns; and he
ran a gold molding around it. He made 27
two gold rings for it underneath its
molding, on its two sides, on the two
opposite sides of it, as holders for the
poles, with which to carry it. He made 28
the poles of acacia wood, and overlaid
them with gold. By the compounders' 29
art he made the anointing oil sacred,
and the incense of fragrant spices pure.
He made the altar for burnt-offerings 38
of acacia wood, square, five cubits long,
and five cubits wide, while its height
was three cubits; he made the horns for 2
it on its four corners, with its horns of
one piece with it; and he overlaid it
with bronze. He made all the utensils 3
for the altar, the ash-pans, the shovels,
the basins, the forks, and the firepans,
making all its utensils of bronze. He 4
made a bronze grating of network for
the altar, underneath the ledge around
it, reaching half-way up it. He cast four 5
rings for the four corners of the bronze
grating as holders for the poles. He 6
made the poles of acacia wood, and
overlaid them with bronze; and he put 7
the poles through the rings on the sides
of the altar with which to carry it,
making it hollow, with boards.
He made the laver of bronze, and its 8
base of bronze, out of the mirrors of the
serving-women who served at the door
of the tent of meeting.
He then made the court; for the 9
southern side toward the Negeb there
were hangings for the court of fine
twisted linen, extending for one hundred cubits, with twenty columns for 10
them, and twenty bronze pedestals for
these, the hooks of the columns and
their bands being of silver; so for the 11
north side, extending for one hundred
cubits, with twenty columns for them,
and twenty bronze pedestals for these,
the hooks of the columns and their
bands being of silver; for the west side 12
there were hangings, extending for fifty
cubits, ten columns for them, and ten
pedestals for these, the hooks of the
columns and their bands being of silver;
and so for the front, the east side, ex- 13

14 tending for fifty cubits, with hangings
on the one wing for fifteen cubits, three
columns for them, and three pedestals
15 for these, and so for the other wing; on
each side of the gate of the court there
were hangings extending for fifteen cubits, with three columns for them, and
16 three pedestals for these. All the hangings around the court were of fine
17 twisted linen; the pedestals for the columns were of bronze; the hooks on the
columns and their bands of silver; the
plating on the capitals of silver; and all
the columns of the court were bound
18 with silver. The screen for the gate of
the court was variegated work, in violet, purple, and scarlet material, and
fine twisted linen, twenty cubits long,
and five cubits high in its breadth, corresponding to the hangings of the
19 court; there were four columns for it,
and four bronze pedestals for these;
their hooks were silver, and the plating
on their capitals and bands silver;
20 while all the pegs for the dwelling and
the court around it were bronze.
21 The following are the reckonings for
the dwelling, the dwelling of the decrees
which were made by command of Moses as the work of the Levites under the
supervision of Ithamar, the son of
22 Aaron, the priest. (It was Bezalel, the
son of Uri, the son of Hur, belonging to
the tribe of Judah, who made all that
23 the LORD commanded Moses; and
associated with him was Oholiab, the
son of Ahisamach, belonging to the
tribe of Dan, an engraver, an artisan,
and a worker in violet, purple, and
24 scarlet material, and fine linen.) The
total amount of gold that was used for
the work in the complete construction
of the sanctuary, the gold from the contributions, was twenty-nine talents,
and seven hundred and thirty shekels,
25 in terms of the sacred shekel, while
the silver from those of the community
that were numbered amounted to one
hundred talents, and one thousand
seven hundred and seventy-five shek-
26 els, in terms of the sacred shekel, a beka
per head (that is, a half-shekel, in terms
of the sacred shekel), for all that joined
those already numbered, from twenty
years old and upward, namely, six hundred and three thousand five hundred
27 and fifty persons; the hundred talents
of silver were used for casting the pedestals of the sanctuary and the pedestals for the veil, the hundred talents for
the hundred pedestals, a talent per pedestal; and out of the thousand seven 28
hundred and seventy-five shekels the
hooks for the columns were made, the
capitals overlaid, and their bands made.
The bronze from the contributions 29
amounted to seventy talents, and two
thousand four hundred shekels, with 30
which the pedestals for the doorway of
the tent of meeting were made, the
bronze altar with its bronze grating, all
the fittings of the altar, the pedestals 31
around the court, the pedestals for the
gate of the court, all the pegs for the
dwelling, and all the pegs for the court
around it.

From the violet, purple, and scarlet **39**
material were made the woven vestments for ministering in the sanctuary,
as well as the sacred vestments for
Aaron, as the LORD had commanded
Moses.

The apron was made of gold, violet, 2
purple, and scarlet material, and fine
twisted linen; the gold was beaten into 3
thin plates, and then cut into wires, to
be worked into the violet, purple, and
scarlet material, and fine linen, the
work of artists. Shoulder-straps were 4
made for it, joined to it, being joined to
it at its two ends; and the skilfully 5
made girdle on it was of one piece with
it, and like it worked in gold, violet,
purple, and scarlet material, and fine
twisted linen, as the LORD had commanded Moses. The onyx stones were 6
made, set in filigree work of gold, engraved with seal engravings, with the
various names of the Israelites; and 7
they were fastened on the shoulder-
straps of the apron, as memorial stones
for the Israelites, as the LORD had
commanded Moses.

Then the pouch was made, the work 8
of artists, like that of the apron, in
gold, violet, purple, and scarlet material, and fine twisted linen; the pouch 9
was square, being made double, a span
long, and a span wide, folded double;
and on it were set four rows of stones, 10
the first row a row of carnelian, topaz,
and emerald, the second row a ruby, a 11
sapphire, and a crystal, the third row a 12
jacinth, an agate, and an amethyst,
and the fourth row a chrysolite, an 13
onyx, and a jasper; they were inclosed
in gold filigree in their settings. The 14
stones, corresponding to the names of

the Israelites, were twelve in number,
as their names are, each engraved like a
seal with its proper name for the
15 twelve tribes. On the pouch were made
chains of twisted material, of cordage-
16 work of pure gold. Then two gold filigree objects and two gold rings were
made; the two rings were fastened to
17 the two ends of the pouch, and the two
gold cords were fastened to the two
18 rings at the ends of the pouch, while the
other two ends of the two cords were
fastened to the two filigree objects, being fastened to the shoulder-straps of
19 the apron, on the front of it. Two gold
rings were made, and attached to the
two ends of the pouch, on its inner edge
20 next to the apron. Two gold rings were
then made, and fastened to the two
shoulder-straps in the front of the
apron, underneath, close to the place
where it was joined, above the skilfully
21 made girdle; and the pouch was tied by
its rings to the rings of the apron with a
violet cord, so as to lie on the skilfully
made girdle, so that the pouch might
not swing loose from the apron, as the
LORD had commanded Moses.
22 The robe belonging to the apron was
23 woven entirely of violet material, with
an opening in the middle of the robe
like that of a corselet, with a binding
around the opening in it, so that it
24 might not be torn. On the skirts of the
robe pomegranates were made of violet, purple, scarlet, and twisted mate-
25 rial; bells of pure gold were also made,
and the bells were placed among the
pomegranates all around the skirts of
26 the robe, a bell alternating with a pomegranate all around the skirts of the
robe, for use in ministering, as the
LORD had commanded Moses.
27 The tunics were woven of fine linen
28 for Aaron and his sons, the turban of
fine linen, the ornamental caps of fine
linen, the linen breeches of fine twisted
29 linen, and the sashes of fine twisted linen
and violet, purple, and scarlet material in variegated work, as the LORD had
commanded Moses.
30 The diadem, the sacred crown, was
made of pure gold, and with seal engravings there was engraved on it the
31 inscription, "Sacred to the LORD"; and
a violet cord was attached to it, to fast-
en it to the top of the turban, as the
LORD had commanded Moses.
32 So all the work on the dwelling of the
tent of meeting was finished, and the
Israelites did just as the LORD had
commanded Moses. They brought the 33
dwelling to Moses, the tent and all its
fittings, its clasps, its frames, it bars, its
columns, and its pedestals, the covering 34
of tanned rams' skins, the covering of
porpoise skins, the veil for the screen,
the ark of the decrees with its poles and 35
the propitiatory, the table with all its 36
dishes and the Presence-bread, the 37
lampstand of pure gold with its lamps
(the lamps all fitted out) and all its fittings and the oil for the lights, the gold 38
altar, the anointing oil, the fragrant
incense, the screen for the doorway of
the tent, the bronze altar with its 39
bronze grating, its poles, and all its fittings, the laver with its base, the hang- 40
ings for the court with its columns and
pedestals, the screen for the gate of the
court with its ropes and pegs, all the
utensils for the service of the dwelling
of the tent of meeting, the woven vest- 41
ments for ministering in the sacred
place, the sacred vestments for Aaron,
the priest, and his sons' vestments,
when serving as priests. The Israelites 42
carried out all the work, just as the
LORD had commanded Moses; and 43
when Moses saw that they had carried
out all the work, having done just as
the LORD commanded, Moses blessed
them.
Then the LORD said to Moses, 40
"On the first day of the first month 2
you must erect the dwelling of the tent
of meeting; you must put the ark of the
decrees in it, screening the ark with the
veil; you must bring the table in, and
get it ready; you must bring the lampstand in, and put up its lamps. You
must place the gold incense altar in
front of the ark of the decrees, and put
up the screen for the doorway of the
dwelling. You must place the altar for
burnt-offerings in front of the doorway
of the dwelling of the tent of meeting,
and place the laver between the tent of
meeting and the altar, and put water in
it. You must set up the court all
around, and put up the screen for the
gate of the court. You must take the
anointing oil, and anoint the dwelling
and everything in it, thereby consecrating it and all its fittings, so that it
becomes sacred; you must anoint the 10
altar for burnt-offerings and all its fittings, thus consecrating the altar, so

that the altar becomes most sacred;
11 and you must anoint the laver and its
12 base, and thus consecrate it. You must
then bring Aaron and his sons up to the
doorway of the tent of meeting, and
13 wash them with water, and then put
the sacred vestments on Aaron; you
must anoint him, and so consecrate
14 him to serve as priest to me. You must
also bring his sons up, put tunics on
15 them, and anoint them as you did their
father, to serve as priests to me; and
their anointing shall qualify them as a
perpetual priesthood throughout their
generations."
16 Moses did so; he did just as the
17 LORD had commanded him. On the
first day of the first month, in the second year, the dwelling was erected;
18 Moses erected the dwelling, putting up
its pedestals, setting up its frames, in-
serting its bars, and erecting its col-
19 umns. He spread the tent over the
dwelling, and put the covering for the
tent on top of it, as the LORD had
20 commanded Moses. Taking the decrees, he put them inside the ark,
placed the poles on the ark, and put the
21 propitiatory on top of the ark; then he
brought the ark into the dwelling, and
set up the veil for the screen, thus
screening the ark of the decrees, as the
22 LORD had commanded Moses. He put
the table in the tent of meeting, on the
northern side of the dwelling, outside
23 the veil, and set out the proper supply
of bread on it before the LORD, as the
24 LORD had commanded Moses. He
placed the lampstand in the tent of
meeting, opposite the table, on the
southern side of the dwelling, and he 25
put up the lamps before the LORD, as
the LORD had commanded Moses. He 26
placed the gold altar in the tent of
meeting in front of the veil, and burned 27
incense of fragrant spices on it, as the
LORD had commanded Moses. He set 28
up the screen for the doorway of the
dwelling, and placed the altar for 29
burnt-offerings at the doorway of the
dwelling in the tent of meeting, offering
on it the burnt-offerings and the cereal-
offerings, as the LORD had commanded
Moses. He placed the laver between 30
the tent of meeting and the altar, and
put water in it for washing. It was 31
from it that Moses and Aaron and his
sons used to wash their hands and feet,
washing whenever they entered the 32
tent of meeting, or approached the altar, as the LORD had commanded
Moses. He erected the court around 33
the dwelling and the altar, and set up
the screen for the gate of the court. So
Moses finished the work.
Then the cloud covered the tent of 34
meeting, and the glory of the LORD
filled the dwelling; Moses could not en- 35
ter the tent of meeting because the
cloud hung over it and the glory of the
LORD filled the dwelling. Whenever 36
the cloud was lifted from the dwelling,
the Israelites always used to set out on
their journey, but if the cloud was not 37
lifted, they would not set out until the
day that it was lifted; for the cloud of 38
the LORD hung over the dwelling by
day, while there was fire in it by night,
in sight of all the house of Israel
throughout all their journeys.

THE BOOK OF LEVITICUS

LAWS RELATING TO SACRIFICE, 1:1—7:38

1 THE LORD called Moses, and
from the tent of meeting said to
him,
2 "Speak to the Israelites, and
say to them, 'When any of you would
present one of your domestic animals
as an offering to the LORD, you must
present one of your herd or flock as
3 your offering. If his offering is to be a
burnt-offering from his herd, he must
offer a perfect male, offering it at the
doorway of the tent of meeting so as to
make him acceptable before the LORD.
4 He must lay his hand on the head of the
burnt-offering victim, that it may be
5 accepted as atonement for him. He
must slaughter the bullock before the
LORD, whereupon Aaron's sons, the
priests, shall present the blood, dashing
the blood all around the altar that is at
6 the doorway of the tent of meeting. He
must then flay the burnt-offering vic-
7 tim and cut it into pieces, whereupon
the sons of Aaron, the priest, shall put
fire on the altar, arrange wood on the
8 fire, and then Aaron's sons, the priests,
shall arrange the pieces, with the head
and suet, on the wood which is on the
9 fire on the altar, while its entrails and
legs are to be washed with water. The
priest shall then burn the whole of it on
the altar as a burnt-offering, a sacrifice,
a soothing odor to the LORD.

10 " 'If his offering is to come from the
flock, one of the sheep or the goats as a
burnt-offering, he must offer a perfect
11 male. He must slaughter it before the
LORD on the north side of the altar,
whereupon Aaron's sons, the priests,
shall dash its blood all around the altar.
12 He must then cut it into pieces, whereupon the priest shall arrange them,
with its head and suet, on the wood
13 which is on the fire on the altar, while
the entrails and legs are to be washed
with water. The priest shall then offer
the whole, burning it on the altar as a
burnt-offering, that is, a sacrifice, a
soothing odor to the LORD.

" 'If his offering to the LORD is to be 14
a burnt-offering from the birds, he
must present a turtle-dove or a young
pigeon as his offering. The priest shall 15
bring it to the altar, and knocking off
its head, burn it on the altar, while its
blood is to be drained off on the side of
the altar. He shall then remove its crop 16
with its feathers and throw it into the
ash-pit at the east side of the altar. He 17
shall split it open with his hands, without completely dividing it, whereupon
the priest shall burn it on the altar on
the wood which is on the fire; it is to be
a burnt-offering, a sacrifice, a soothing
odor to the LORD.

" 'When any person would present a **2**
cereal-offering to the LORD, his offering must be fine flour. He must pour oil
on it, put frankincense on it, and bring 2
it to Aaron's sons, the priests, whereupon the priest shall take from it his
handful of the fine flour and oil, with all
its frankincense, and offer it as its
memorial sacrifice on the altar, a sacrifice, a soothing odor to the LORD, while
the remainder of the cereal-offering is
to go to Aaron and his sons as being the
most sacred part of the LORD'S sacrifices.

" 'When you would present a cereal-
offering baked in the oven, it must be
unleavened cakes of fine flour mixed
with oil, or unleavened wafers smeared
with oil. If your offering is to be a
cereal-offering prepared on a griddle, it
must consist of unleavened fine flour
mixed with oil; you must break it in
pieces, and pour oil on it, as a cereal-
offering. If your offering is to be a cereal-offering prepared in a pan, it must be
made of fine flour mixed with oil. You
must bring the cereal-offering that is
made in any of these ways to the
LORD; it shall be presented to the
priest, who shall bring it to the altar.
The priest shall take some of the cereal-
offering as its memorial sacrifice, and
burn it on the altar as a sacrifice, a
soothing odor to the LORD, while the 10
remainder of the cereal-offering is to go
to Aaron and his sons as being the most

sacred part of the LORD'S sacrifices.
11 No cereal-offering which you present to
the LORD may be made with leaven;
for you must never offer any leaven or
honey at all as a sacrifice to the LORD.
12 You may present them to the LORD
as an offering of first-fruits, but they
must never be offered up on the altar as
13 a soothing odor. You must season every cereal-offering of yours with salt;
you must not omit the salt of the covenant of your God from your cereal-
offering; you must offer salt with all
your offerings.
14 " 'If you would present a cereal-offering of first-fruits to the LORD, you
must present young ears of grain
roasted with fire, crushed new grain, as
15 your cereal-offering of first-fruits. You
must add oil to it, and put frankincense
16 on it, as a cereal-offering. As its memorial sacrifice the priest shall burn some
of its crushed grain and oil, with all its
frankincense, as a sacrifice to the
LORD.
3 " 'If his offering is to be a thanksgiving sacrifice, if he is to offer one of
his herd, whether male or female, he
must offer before the LORD one that is
2 perfect. He must lay his hand on the
head of his offering, and slaughter it at
the doorway of the tent of meeting,
whereupon Aaron's sons, the priests,
shall dash the blood all around the
3 altar. He must present part of the
thanksgiving sacrifice as a sacrifice to
the LORD, the fat covering the entrails,
4 all the fat that is on the entrails, the
two kidneys with the fat that is on
them near the loins, and the lobe on the
liver which is to be removed with the
5 kidneys. Aaron's sons shall burn it on
the altar for burnt-offerings, on the
wood which is on the fire, as a sacrifice,
a soothing odor to the LORD.
6 " 'If his offering is to be one of his
flock as a thanksgiving sacrifice,
whether male or female, he must offer
7 one that is perfect. If it is a lamb that
he is to present as his offering, he must
8 present it before the LORD, lay his
hand on the head of his offering, and
slaughter it in front of the tent of meeting, whereupon Aaron's sons shall dash
9 its blood all around the altar. He must
present part of the thanksgiving sacrifice as a sacrifice to the LORD, the fat of
it, the entire fat tail which is to be removed close to the backbone, the fat
covering the entrails, all the fat that is
on the entrails, the two kidneys with 10
the fat that is on them near the loins,
and the lobe on the liver which is to be
removed with the kidneys. The priest 11
shall burn it on the altar as food, a
sacrifice to the LORD.
" 'If his offering is to be a goat, he 12
must present it before the LORD, lay 13
his hand on its head, and slaughter it in
front of the tent of meeting, whereupon
Aaron's sons shall dash its blood all
around the altar. He must offer part of 14
it as a sacrifice to the LORD, the fat
covering the entrails, all the fat that is
on the entrails, the two kidneys with 15
the fat that is on them near the loins,
and the lobe on the liver which is to be
removed with the kidneys. The priest 16
shall burn them on the altar as food, as
a sacrifice, a soothing odor, all the fat
going to the LORD. It is to be a per- 17
petual statute throughout your generations in all your places of abode that
you are never to eat any fat or blood.' "
The LORD said to Moses, 4
"Say to the Israelites, 'When any 2
person sins inadvertently in the case of
any of the things which the LORD has
forbidden to be done, and does one of
them, if it is the anointed priest who 3
sins, thus bringing guilt on the people,
he must offer to the LORD for the sin
that he has committed a perfect young
bullock as a sin-offering. He must bring 4
the bullock to the doorway of the tent
of meeting into the presence of the
LORD, lay his hand on the head of the
bullock, and slaughter the bullock before the LORD; whereupon the anoint- 5
ed priest shall take some of the blood of
the bullock, and bringing it into the
tent of meeting, the priest shall dip his 6
finger in the blood, and sprinkle some
of the blood seven times before the
LORD in front of the veil of the sanctuary. The priest must also put some 7
of the blood on the horns of the altar
for fragrant incense, which is before the
LORD in the tent of meeting, while all
the rest of the bullock's blood he must
pour out at the base of the altar for
burnt-offerings, which is at the doorway of the tent of meeting. He must 8
remove all the fat from the bullock of
the sin-offering, the fat covering the entrails, all the fat that is on the entrails,
the two kidneys with the fat that is on 9
them near the loins, and the lobe on the

liver which is to be removed with the
10 kidneys, just as these were removed
from the ox used in the thanksgiving
sacrifice; and the priest shall burn them
11 on the altar for burnt-offerings. The
hide of the bullock and all its flesh,
with its head, legs, entrails, and offal,
12 that is, all the rest of the bullock, must
be carried out to a clean place outside
the camp at the ash-dump, and burned
up on a wood-fire, being burned at the
ash-dump.
13 " 'If the whole community of Israel
makes a mistake which escapes the notice of the community, and does any of
the things which the LORD has forbid-
14 den, and so incurs guilt, when the sin
which they committed is discovered,
the community must offer a young bullock as a sin-offering. They must bring
it to the front of the tent of meeting,
15 whereupon the elders of the community
shall lay their hands on the head of the
bullock in the presence of the LORD,
and then the bullock shall be slaugh-
16 tered before the LORD. The anointed
priest shall bring some of the blood of
17 the bullock to the tent of meeting and
the priest shall dip his finger in the
blood, and sprinkle it seven times be-
18 fore the LORD in front of the veil. He
must also put some of the blood on the
horns of the altar which is before the
LORD in the tent of meeting, while all
the rest of the blood he must pour out
at the base of the altar for burnt-offerings, which is at the doorway of the
19 tent of meeting. He must remove all
the fat from it, and burn it on the altar.
20 Thus shall he do with the bullock,
treating it just as he treated the bullock of the sin-offering, and thus the
priest shall make atonement for them,
21 and they shall be forgiven. The bullock
itself must be carried outside the camp,
and burned as the first bullock was
burned. It is to be a sin-offering for the
community.
22 " 'When a ruler sins and inadvertently does any one of all the things which
the LORD his God has forbidden, he
23 shall incur guilt, provided that the sin
which he has committed has been made
known to him. So he must bring a per-
24 fect male goat as his offering. He must
lay his hand on the head of the goat,
and slaughter it at the place where the
burnt-offering victims are slaughtered
before the LORD; it is to be a sin-
offering. The priest shall take some of 25
the blood of the sin-offering with his
finger, and put it on the horns of the altar for burnt-offerings, while the rest
of the blood he shall pour out at the
base of the altar for burnt-offerings,
and burn all the fat on the altar, as in 26
the case of the fat of the thanksgiving
sacrifice. Thus shall the priest make
atonement for him for his sin, and he
shall be forgiven.
" 'If any of the common people sins 27
inadvertently by doing any of the
things which the LORD has forbidden,
he shall incur guilt, provided that the 28
sin which he has committed has been
made known to him, So he must bring
a perfect female goat as his offering for
the sin which he has committed. He 29
must lay his hand on the head of the
sin-offering victim, and slaughter the
sin-offering victim at the place where
the burnt-offering victims are slaughtered, whereupon the priest shall take 30
some of the blood with his finger, and
put it on the horns of the altar for
burnt-offerings, while all the rest of the
blood he shall pour out at the base of
the altar, and removing all the fat as 31
the fat was removed from the thanksgiving sacrifice, the priest shall burn it
on the altar as a soothing odor to the
LORD. Thus shall the priest make
atonement for him, and he shall be forgiven.
" 'If it is a lamb that he would bring 32
as his offering for sin, he must bring a
perfect female. He must lay his hand 33
on the head of the sin-offering victim,
and slaughter it as a sin-offering at the
place where the burnt-offering victims
are slaughtered, whereupon the priest 34
shall take some of the blood of the sin-
offering with his finger, and put it on
the horns of the altar for burnt-offerings, while all the rest of the blood he
shall pour out at the base of the altar,
and removing all the fat as the fat was 35
removed from the lamb in the thanksgiving sacrifice, the priest shall burn it
on the altar used for sacrifices to the
LORD. Thus shall the priest make
atonement for him for the sin that he
committed, and he shall be forgiven.
" 'If any person sins by not giving 5
information when as a witness, either
as one who has seen it or knows of it, he
hears the oath of adjuration, he must
answer for his iniquity. Or, if any per- 2

son touches any unclean thing, either the carcass of an unclean wild animal, or that of an unclean domestic animal, or that of an unclean reptile, without being aware of it, when he does come to know of it, he shall incur guilt; or if he touches any human uncleanness of whatsoever sort the uncleanness may be, without being aware of it, when he does come to know of it, he shall incur guilt. Or, if any person utters a rash oath, either to do evil or to do good, however rash the person has been in his oath, and he is unaware of its import, when he does come to know it, he shall incur guilt in any of these cases. When he does incur guilt in any one of these cases, he must confess the sin that he has committed, and bring to the LORD as his guilt-offering for the sin that he has committed a female animal from the flock, a lamb or a goat, as a sin-offering, and the priest shall make atonement for him for his sin.

"'If he cannot afford a lamb, the person who has sinned must bring as his guilt-offering to the LORD two turtle-doves or two young pigeons, the one as a sin-offering, the other as a burnt-offering. He must bring them to the priest, who shall offer the one for the sin-offering first. He shall crush its head near its neck, without dividing it into two, and sprinkle some of the blood of the sin-offering on the side of the altar, while the rest of the blood shall be drained out at the base of the altar; it is a sin-offering. Then he shall offer the other as a burnt-offering as prescribed. Thus the priest shall make atonement for him for the sin that he committed, and he shall be forgiven.

"'If he cannot afford two turtle-doves or two young pigeons, he who sinned may bring as his offering a tenth of an ephah of fine flour as a sin-offering, without pouring any oil on it or putting any frankincense on it, because it is a sin-offering. He must bring it to the priest, and the priest shall remove his handful from it as the memorial sacrifice, and burn it on the altar used for sacrifices to the LORD; it is a sin-offering. Thus the priest shall make atonement for him for the sin which he committed in any one of these ways, and he shall be forgiven. The rest shall go to the priest, as in the case of the cereal-offering.'"

The LORD said to Moses, 14
"If any person commits fraud, sin- 15
ning inadvertently in the matter of sacred gifts to the LORD, he must bring
as his guilt-offering to the LORD a perfect ram from the flock of the proper
value in silver shekels, in terms of the
sacred shekel; he must also make good 16
the sacred gift concerning which he
sinned, adding a fifth to it, and giving
it to the priest, and the priest shall
make atonement for him with the ram
of the guilt-offering, and he shall be forgiven.
"If any person sins by doing any one 17
of all the things which the LORD has
forbidden, even though he is unaware
of it, he is guilty, and must answer for
his iniquity. He must bring a perfect 18
ram from the flock of the proper value
to the priest as a guilt-offering, and the
priest shall make atonement for him
for the mistake which he made inadvertently, without being aware of it,
and he shall be forgiven. It is a guilt- 19
offering, since he is assuredly guilty before the LORD."
The LORD said to Moses, 6
"If any person sins by committing 2
fraud against the LORD, and cheating
his neighbor in the matter of some deposit or pledge, or by robbing or de-
frauding his neighbor, or by lying about
it and swearing falsely, when he has 3
found something that was lost, sinning
in any one of all the things that men
may do, then, if he sins, and feels guil- 4
ty, and would restore what he took by
robbery, or what he got by fraud, or
what was deposited with him, or the
lost article that he found, or anything 5
about which he swore falsely, he must
make restitution in full, and add a fifth
to it, giving it to the one to whom it belongs on the day of his guilt-offering;
and he must bring his guilt-offering to 6
the LORD, to the priest, a perfect ram
from the flock of the proper value as a
guilt-offering. The priest shall make 7
atonement for him before the LORD,
and he shall be forgiven for whatsoever
he may have done to incur guilt."
The LORD said to Moses, 8
"Give Aaron and his sons this com- 9
mand: 'This is the law for the burnt-
offering: the burnt-offering must remain on the hearth upon the altar all
night until morning, while the fire of
the altar must be kept burning on it.

10 The priest must put on his linen vestments, and put his linen breeches on his
body, and then remove the ashes to
which the fire has reduced the burnt-
offering on the altar, and place them be-
11 side the altar; then, taking off his garments and putting on others, he must
take the ashes to a clean place outside
12 the camp. The fire must be kept burning on the altar, it must never go out;
the priest must light wood on it every
morning, arrange the burnt-offering on
it, and burn the fat of the thank-offer-
13 ings on it. Fire must be kept burning
on the altar continually; it must never
go out.
14 " 'This is the law for the cereal-offering: the sons of Aaron must offer it be-
15 fore the LORD in front of the altar. A
handful shall be removed from it, from
the fine flour of the cereal-offering,
with its oil and all the frankincense on
the cereal-offering, and it shall be offered on the altar as a soothing odor, its
16 memorial sacrifice to the LORD. The
remainder of it Aaron and his sons shall
eat; it must be eaten as unleavened
cakes in a sacred place; in the court of
17 the tent of meeting they must eat it; it
must not be baked with leaven. I designate it as their portion of my sacrifices; it is most sacred, like the sin-
18 offering and guilt-offering. Any male
among the sons of Aaron may eat it, as
his perpetual due from the sacrifices to
the LORD throughout your generations; whatsoever touches them becomes taboo.' "
19 The LORD said to Moses,
20 "This is the offering which Aaron and
his sons must present to the LORD on
the anniversary of his anointing; a tenth
of an ephah of fine flour as a regular
cereal-offering, half of it in the morning
21 and half of it in the evening. It must
be prepared on a griddle, mixed with
oil; you must bring it in, break the cereal-offering into pieces, and offer it as
22 a soothing odor to the LORD. The
anointed priest who of his descendants
succeeds him must supply it, the whole
of it to be burned as a perpetual due to
23 the LORD. In the case of every cereal-
offering of a priest it is to be the whole;
it is not to be eaten."
24 The LORD said to Moses,
25 "Say to Aaron and his sons, 'This is
the law for the sin-offering: at the
place where the burnt-offering victims
are slaughtered the sin-offering victim must be slaughtered before the LORD; it is most sacred. The priest who offers it for sin shall eat it; in a sacred place must it be eaten, in the court of the tent of meeting. Whatsoever touches its flesh shall become taboo, and if any of its blood is sprinkled on a garment, you must wash the part that was sprinkled in a sacred place. The earthen vessel in which it was boiled must be broken; but if it was boiled in a bronze vessel, it need only be scoured and rinsed with water. Any male among the priests may eat it, since it is most sacred; but no sin-offering of which any of the blood is brought into the tent of meeting to make atonement in the sanctuary may be eaten; it must be burned up.

" 'This is the law for the guilt-offering: since it is most sacred, the guilt-offering victim must be slaughtered at the place where the burnt-offering victims are slaughtered, its blood must be dashed all around the altar, and all its fat offered, the fat tail, the fat covering the entrails, the two kidneys with the fat that is on them near the loins, and the lobe on the liver which is to be removed with the kidneys. The priest shall burn them on the altar as a sacrifice to the LORD; it is a guilt-offering. Any male among the priests may eat it; it is to be eaten only in a sacred place; it is most sacred. The guilt-offering is like the sin-offering; the same law holds for both; the priest who makes atonement with it is to receive it. The priest who offers anyone's burnt-offering, that priest is to have for himself the hide of the burnt-offering which he offered, and every cereal-offering that is baked in the oven, and whatsoever is prepared in a pan or on a griddle shall go to the priest who offers it, while every cereal-offering, mixed with oil or dry, shall go to the sons of Aaron, to all alike.

" 'This is the law for the thanksgiving sacrifice: if the one who offers it to the LORD would offer it as a praise-offering, he must offer, in addition to the sacrifice of the praise-offering, unleavened cakes mixed with oil, unleavened wafers smeared with oil, and cakes mixed with oil, of fine flour well mixed. In addition to his sacrifice in praise for prosperity he must present cakes of

leavened bread along with his offering,
14 and from each kind of offering he must
present one cake as a contribution to
the LORD, to go to the priest who
dashes the blood of the thank-offering.
15 The flesh of the victim sacrificed as his
praise-offering for prosperity must be
eaten on the day that it is offered; he
must leave none of it over until morn-
16 ing. But if the sacrifice that is offered
is a votive-offering or a voluntary offering, while it should be eaten on the day
that he offers his sacrifice, any of it left
17 over may be eaten on the next day, but
any of the flesh of the sacrifice that is
left over on the third day must be
18 burned up. If any of the flesh of his
thanksgiving sacrifice should ever be
eaten on the third day, it shall not be
accepted; it shall not count for the one
who offered it; it shall be but refuse,
and anyone eating any of it shall answer
19 for his iniquity. Also, any flesh that
touches any unclean thing may not be
eaten; it must be burned up. Other
20 flesh anyone that is clean may eat. Any
person who eats the flesh of the thanksgiving sacrifice which belongs to the
LORD, while in a state of uncleanness,
that person shall be cut off from his peo-
21 ple. If any person touches any unclean
thing, whether it is human uncleanness,
or an unclean animal, or any unclean
reptile, and then eats some of the flesh
of the thanksgiving sacrifice, which belongs to the LORD, that person shall be
cut off from his people.' "
22 The LORD said to Moses,
23 "Say to the Israelites, 'You must
never eat the fat of ox, or sheep, or goat.
24 The fat of an animal that has died a
natural death, or from being torn, may
be put to any other use, but you must
never eat it. For whosoever eats the
fat of any animal, part of which is offered as a sacrifice to the LORD, the
person so eating shall be cut off from his
26 people. Also, you must never eat blood
in any of your places of abode, either of
bird or beast; whosoever eats any blood
at all, that person shall be cut off from
his people.' "
28 The LORD said to Moses,
29 "Say to the Israelites, 'Whoever offers a thanksgiving sacrifice to the
LORD must bring part of his thanksgiving sacrifice as his offering to the LORD,
30 bringing the sacrifices for the LORD
with his own hands, bringing the fat
along with the breast, that the breast
may be waved as a wave-offering before the LORD. The priest shall burn 31
the fat on the altar, but the breast shall
go to Aaron and his sons, while you are 32
to give the right thigh to the priest as a
contribution out of your thanksgiving
sacrifices. He of the sons of Aaron who 33
offers the blood of the thank-offerings
and the fat shall receive the right thigh
as his share. For I have taken the 34
waved breast and the thigh that was
contributed from the thanksgiving sacrifices of the Israelites, and have assigned them to Aaron, the priest, and
his sons as their perpetual due from the
Israelites. This shall be the emolument 35
of Aaron and his sons from the sacrifices to the LORD, as prescribed on the
day that they were presented to serve
as priests to the LORD, which the 36
LORD commanded to be given them
from the Israelites on the day that he
had them anointed, as their perpetual
due throughout their generations.' "
This was the law for the burnt-offer- 37
ing, for the cereal-offering, for the sin-
offering, for the guilt-offering, for the
installation-offering, and for the thanksgiving sacrifice, which the LORD en- 38
joined on Moses at Mount Sinai on the
day that he commanded the Israelites
to present their offerings to the LORD
in the desert of Sinai.

THE INSTALLATION OF THE AARONIC PRIESTHOOD, 8:1—10:20

The LORD then said to Moses, 8
"Take Aaron, along with his sons, 2
the vestments, the anointing oil, the
bullock of the sin-offering, the two
rams, and the basket of unleavened
cakes, and assemble the whole commu- 3
nity at the doorway of the tent of meeting."
Moses did as the LORD commanded 4
him. When the community had been
assembled at the doorway of the tent
of meeting, Moses said to the commu- 5
nity,
"This is what the LORD has commanded to be done."
Thereupon Moses brought Aaron and 6
his sons forward, and washed them
with water. He then put the tunic on 7
him, girded him with the sash, clothed

him with the robe, put the apron on
him, girding him with the skilfully
made girdle of the apron and fastening
8 it around him with it, placed the pouch
on him, putting the Urim and Thum-
9 mim in the pouch, and set the turban
on his head, placing the gold diadem,
the sacred crown, on the front of the
turban, as the LORD had commanded
10 Moses. Then Moses took the anointing
oil and anointed the dwelling and
everything in it, and thus consecrated
11 them. He then sprinkled some of it on
the altar seven times, and anointed the
altar with all its utensils and the laver
12 with its base, to consecrate them. He
also poured some of the anointing oil
on Aaron's head, and anointed him to
13 consecrate him. Moses then brought
Aaron's sons forward, clothed them
with tunics, girded them with sashes,
and fastened caps on them, as the
14 LORD had commanded Moses. He
brought forward the bullock of the sin-
offering; Aaron and his sons laid their
hands on the head of the bullock of the
15 sin-offering, and then Moses slaughtered it, and taking the blood, put it all
around the horns of the altar with his
finger to rid the altar of sin, while the
rest of the blood he poured out at the
base of the altar, thus consecrating it by
16 making atonement for it. Taking all
the fat on the entrails, the lobe of the
liver, and the two kidneys, with their
17 fat, Moses burned it on the altar, while
the bullock itself, its hide, flesh, and
offal he burned up outside the camp, as
18 the LORD had commanded Moses. He
then brought forward the ram of the
burnt-offering; Aaron and his sons laid
19 their hands on the head of the ram, and
then Moses slaughtered it, and dashed
20 the blood all around the altar, while
the ram itself he cut into pieces, whereupon Moses burned the head along with
21 the other pieces and the suet. Having
washed the entrails and legs with water,
Moses burned the whole ram on the altar as a burnt-offering for a soothing
odor, as a sacrifice to the LORD, as the
22 LORD had commanded Moses. He then
brought forward the other ram, the installation ram; Aaron and his sons laid
23 their hands on the head of the ram, and
then Moses slaughtered it, and taking
some of its blood, he put it on the tip of
Aaron's right ear, on the thumb of his
right hand, and on the great toe of his
right foot. He then had Aaron's sons come forward, whereupon Moses put some of the blood on the tips of their right ears, on the thumbs of their right hands, and on the great toes of their right feet, and Moses dashed the rest of the blood all around the altar. Taking the fat, the fat tail, all the fat on the entrails, the lobe of the liver, the two kidneys with their fat, and the right thigh, and taking from the basket of unleavened cakes, which was before the LORD, one unleavened cake, one loaf of bread made with oil, and one wafer, he added them to the fat and right thigh, and laid the whole in the hands of Aaron and his sons, and then waved them as a wave-offering before the LORD. Then Moses took them from their hands, and burned them on the altar for burnt-offerings; they were an installation-offering for a soothing odor, a sacrifice to the LORD. Taking the breast, Moses waved it as a wave-offering before the LORD, which went to Moses as his share of the installation ram, as the LORD had commanded Moses. Moses then took some of the anointing oil and some of the blood which was on the altar and sprinkled it on Aaron and his vestments, and on his sons with him and on the vestments of his sons, thus consecrating Aaron and his vestments, as well as his sons with him and the vestments of his sons. Then Moses said to Aaron and his sons,

"Boil the flesh at the doorway of the tent of meeting, and eat it there, together with the bread in the installation basket, as I was commanded when told, 'Aaron and his sons must eat it.' The remainder of the flesh and bread you must burn up. For seven days you must not leave the doorway of the tent of meeting, not until the days for your installation are over; for it will take seven days to instal you. As has been done today, the LORD commanded to be done, that atonement might be made for you. So you must remain at the doorway of the tent of meeting day and night for seven days, and observe the behest of the LORD, that you die not—for so I was commanded."

Aaron and his sons carried out all the commands which the LORD gave through Moses.

On the eighth day Moses summoned

Aaron and his sons and the elders of
2 Israel, and said to Aaron,
"Take a bull calf for a sin-offering
and a ram for a burnt-offering, both
perfect, and offer them before the
3 LORD, while you must say to the Israelites, 'Take a he-goat for a sin-
offering, and a calf and a lamb, both
yearlings and perfect, as a burnt-offer-
4 ing, together with an ox and a ram as a
thank-offering, to sacrifice before the
LORD, as well as a cereal-offering mixed
with oil; for today the LORD is to appear to you.' "
5 So they brought what Moses commanded to the front of the tent of meeting, and the whole community came
forward and stood before the LORD,
6 whereupon Moses said,
"This is what the LORD has commanded you to do, that the glory of the
LORD may appear to you."
7 "Come up to the altar," Moses said
to Aaron, "and offer your sin-offering
and burnt-offering, and make atonement for yourself and the people, presenting the offering of the people and
making atonement for them, as the
LORD commanded."
8 So Aaron went up to the altar, and
slaughtered the sin-offering calf that
9 was for himself, whereupon the sons of
Aaron brought the blood to him, and he
dipped his finger into the blood, and put
it on the horns of the altar, pouring out
the rest of the blood at the base of the
10 altar, while the fat, the kidneys, and the
lobe of the liver of the sin-offering victim he burned on the altar, as the LORD
11 had commanded Moses, burning up the
12 flesh and hide outside the camp. He
then slaughtered the burnt-offering
victim, whereupon Aaron's sons handed
him the blood, and he dashed it all
13 around the altar. Then they handed
him the various pieces of the burnt-offering along with the head, and he
14 burned them on the altar. He washed
the entrails and legs, and burned them
on the altar with the rest of the burnt-
15 offering. He then presented the people's offering; taking the sin-offering
goat that was for the people, he slaughtered it, and offered it for sin as in the
16 case of the former. He presented the
burnt-offering, and offered it as pre-
17 scribed. He presented the cereal-offering, taking a handful from it, and burning it on the altar in addition to the
morning burnt-offering. He slaughtered 18
the ox and the ram, the thanksgiving
sacrifice that was for the people, whereupon the sons of Aaron handed him the
blood, and he dashed it all around the
altar, while the fat pieces of the ox and 19
ram, the fat tail, that covering the entrails, the kidneys, and the lobe of the
liver, these fat pieces they added to 20
the breasts, and he burned the fat
pieces on the altar, while the breasts 21
and the right thigh Aaron waved as a
wave-offering before the LORD, as Moses
commanded. Then Aaron raised his 22
hands toward the people, and blessed
them, whereupon he came down from
offering the sin-offering, burnt-offering,
and thank-offering. Moses and Aaron 23
then entered the tent of meeting, and
when they came out, they blessed the
people, whereupon the glory of the
LORD appeared to all the people. Fire 24
came forth from the presence of the
LORD, and consumed the burnt-offering and the pieces of fat on the altar.
When all the people saw it, they shouted, and fell on their faces.
Now the sons of Aaron, Nadab and **10**
Abihu, took each his fire-pan, and putting fire on them, they placed incense
on it, and offered improper fire before
the LORD, which he had not commanded them, whereupon fire came 2
forth from the presence of the LORD,
and consumed them, so that they died
at the hands of the LORD. Then Moses 3
said to Aaron,
"This must be what the LORD meant
by saying,
'By those near me I must be treated as
holy,
That I may reveal myself in glory to
the people at large.' "
But Aaron was silent. Then Moses 4
summoned Mishael and Elzaphan, the
sons of Uzziel, Aaron's uncle, and said
to them,
"Go up and carry your kinsmen away
from the front of the sanctuary outside
the camp."
So they went up and carried them 5
away in their tunics outside the camp,
as Moses said. Then said Moses to 6
Aaron and his sons, Eleazar and Ithamar,
"Do not let the hair on your heads
hang loose, nor tear your clothes, that
you die not, and wrath be brought upon
the whole community, when your kins-

men, the whole house of Israel, are
weeping over the conflagration which
the LORD himself has brought about.
7 You must not leave the doorway of the
tent of meeting, lest you die; for it is
the LORD'S anointing oil that is on
you."

They did as Moses directed.
8 The LORD said to Aaron,
9 "Drink no wine or liquor, neither you
nor your sons with you, when you enter
the tent of meeting, that you die not;
it is to be a perpetual statute through-
10 out your generations, that a distinction
may be made between the sacred and
the profane, and between the unclean
11 and the clean, and that the Israelites
may be taught all the statutes which
the LORD has communicated to them
through Moses."

12 Moses said to Aaron and his remaining sons, Eleazar and Ithamar,

"Take the cereal-offering that is left
over from the sacrifices to the LORD,
and eat it as unleavened cakes beside
13 the altar; for it is most sacred; so you
must eat it in a sacred place, because it
is the due of you and your sons from the
sacrifices to the LORD; for so was I
14 commanded. The waved breast and the
thigh that was contributed you may eat
in a clean place, along with your sons
and daughters; for they have been designated as the due of you and your sons
out of the thanksgiving sacrifices of the
15 Israelites. The thigh that is to be contributed and the breast that is to be
waved must be brought, along with the
fat pieces for the sacrifices, to be waved
as a wave-offering before the LORD;
they are to go to you and your sons with
you as a perpetual due, as the LORD
has commanded."

16 When Moses made careful search for
the goat of the sin-offering, he found
that it had been burned! So he was angry with Eleazar and Ithamar, the remaining sons of Aaron, and said,
17 "Why have you not eaten the sin-
offering at the sanctuary? For it is
most sacred and was given to you to
bear the iniquity of the community,
that atonement might be made for
18 them before the LORD. See, the blood
from it was not brought inside the sanctuary; you ought certainly to have eat-
en it in the sanctuary, as I commanded."
19 Whereupon Aaron said to Moses,

"Yes, they have offered their sin-
offering and burnt-offering before the
LORD today, but then such dreadful
things have happened to me! But even
if I had eaten the sin-offering today,
would it have been acceptable to the
LORD?"

When Moses heard that, he was satis- 20
fied.

LAWS RELATING TO UNCLEANNESS, 11:1—16:34

The LORD spoke to Moses and 1
Aaron, saying to them,

"Say to the Israelites, 'The following 2
are the creatures that you may eat, of
all the animals that are on the earth.
Any of the animals with a cloven hoof, 3
that has the hoof completely divided,
and that chews the cud, you may eat.
However, of those that chew the cud 4
or have the hoof completely cloven, you
must not eat the following: the camel,
because, though chewing the cud, it
does not have the hoof cloven—it is unclean for you; the rock-badger, because, 5
though chewing the cud, it does not
have the hoof cloven—it is unclean for
you; the hare, because, though chewing 6
the cud, it does not have the hoof
cloven—it is unclean for you; and the 7
pig, because, though having the hoof
cloven and completely divided, it does
not chew the cud—it is unclean for you.
Of their flesh you must not eat, and 8
their carcasses you must not touch,
since they are unclean for you.

" 'Of all the things that live in the 9
water you may eat the following: whatsoever has fins and scales, living in the
water, whether in sea or stream, you
may eat, but whatsoever has not 10
fins and scales, living in sea or stream,
either any kind of water reptile or any
living creature at all that lives in the
water, they are detestable for you, and 11
must be detested by you; you must not
eat of their flesh, and their carcasses you
must detest; everything in the water 12
that does not have fins and scales is detestable for you.

" 'Of birds you must detest the fol- 13
lowing; they are not to be eaten, since
they are detestable: the griffon, the 14
vulture, the eagle, the buzzard, the kite
in its several species, the raven in all its 15
species, the ostrich, the night-hawk, 16

the sea-mew, the hawk in its several
7 species, the screech-owl, the cormorant,
8 the eagle-owl, the horned owl, the jack-
9 daw, the carrion-vulture, the stork, the
heron in its several species, the bittern,
and the bat.
0 " 'All winged insects that walk on all
1 fours are detestable for you. However,
of all winged insects that walk on all
fours you may eat the following: whatever has jointed legs above its feet with
2 which to leap upon the ground, of these
you may eat the following: the common
locust in its several species, the devastating locust in its several species, the
flying locust in its several species, and
the grasshopper in its several species.
3 But all winged insects which simply
have four feet are detestable for you.
4 " 'In the case of the following
you shall become unclean; whosoever
touches any carcass of them shall remain unclean until evening, and whosoever carries any of their carcasses must
wash his clothes, remaining unclean until evening. In the case of every animal
that has the hoof cloven, but not completely divided, and does not chew the
cud, such are unclean for you; whosoever touches them shall become unclean. Whatsoever walks on its paws,
any of the animals that walk on all
fours are unclean for you; whosoever
touches their carcasses shall remain unclean until evening, and anyone carrying their carcasses must wash his
clothes, remaining unclean until evening; they are unclean for you.
" 'Among the reptiles that swarm on
the earth the following are unclean for
you: the weasel, the mouse, the lizard
in its several species, the croaking
lizard, the agama, the gecko, the cha-
meleon, and the basilisk. Among all the
reptiles these are the ones that are unclean for you; whosoever touches them
when they are dead shall remain unclean until evening, and whatsoever
any of them falls upon when dead shall
become unclean, whether it be any
wooden article, or a garment, or a skin,
or a sack, any article at all of which use
is made; it must be put into water, remaining unclean until evening, when it
shall become clean. Any earthen vessel
into which any of them falls, since
whatever is in it becomes unclean, you
must break; of all the food that was
edible, that which has had contact with
water shall be unclean, and all the liquid in any such vessel that was drink-
able shall be unclean. Whatsoever any 35
of their dead bodies falls upon shall become unclean; an oven or a fire-pot
must be broken in pieces; they are unclean and must be unclean for you.
However, a fountain or a cistern for 36
collecting water shall be clean, but he
who touches a dead body of theirs shall
be unclean. If any of their dead bodies 37
falls upon seed for sowing that is to be
sown, it shall be clean; but if water is 38
put on the seed, and any of their dead
bodies falls on it, it shall be unclean for
you.
" 'If any animal which you use for 39
food dies, whoever touches its carcass
shall remain unclean until evening;
whoever eats any of its carcass must 40
wash his clothes, remaining unclean until evening; and whoever carries its
carcass must wash his clothes, remaining unclean until evening.
" 'Every insect that swarms on the 41
earth is detestable; it must not be eat-
en. Whatsoever crawls on its belly, 42
anything that crawls upon four legs or
anything that has many legs, any kind
of insect at all that swarms on the
earth, you must not eat; for they are
detestable. You must not render your- 43
selves detestable through any swarming
insect, nor make yourselves unclean
through them, and so defile yourselves;
for I, the LORD, am your God. Conse- 44
crate yourselves, therefore, and be holy;
for I am holy; so you must not defile
yourselves with any kind of insect that
crawls on the earth. For I am the LORD 45
who brought you up out of the land of
Egypt to be your God, and so you must
be holy; for I am holy.
" 'This is the law regarding animals, 46
birds, all living creatures that move in
the water, and all creatures that swarm
on the earth, that a distinction may be 47
made between the unclean and the
clean, between animals that are to be
eaten and those that are not to be
eaten.' "

The LORD said to Moses, **12**
"Say to the Israelites, 'When a wom- 2
an is delivered and gives birth to a boy,
she shall be unclean for seven days, being unclean as at the time of menstruation. On the eighth day the flesh of his 3
foreskin shall be circumcised, while she 4
shall remain continent for thirty-three

days, the time for her purification,
touching nothing sacred, nor entering
the sanctuary, until the time for her
5 purification is over. But if she gives
birth to a girl, she shall be unclean for
two weeks as at menstruation, and she
shall remain continent for sixty-six
days, as the time for her purification.
6 When the time for her purification is
over for either son or daughter, she shall
bring to the priest at the doorway of the
tent of meeting a yearling lamb as a
burnt-offering, and a young pigeon or a
7 turtle-dove as a sin-offering, and he
shall offer it before the LORD, and thus
make atonement for her, that she may
be cleansed from her flow of blood. This
is the law for her who gives birth to a
8 child, whether male or female. If she
cannot afford a lamb, she must take
two turtle-doves or two young pigeons,
the one for a burnt-offering, and the
other for a sin-offering; the priest shall
make atonement for her, and she shall
be clean.'"

13 The LORD said to Moses and Aaron,
2 "When anyone has a swelling or an
eruption or an inflamed spot on the skin
of his body, and it develops into an attack of leprosy on the skin of his body,
he must be brought to Aaron, the priest,
3 or to one of his sons, the priests; the
priest shall look at the mark on the skin
of his body, and if the hair on the mark
has turned white, while the mark itself
has the appearance of being deeper than
the skin of his body, it is an attack of
leprosy, and the priest upon looking at
4 him, must pronounce him unclean. But
if the inflamed spot on the skin of his
body is white and has no appearance of
being deeper than the skin, while the
hair has not turned white, the priest
shall quarantine the afflicted person for
5 seven days; the priest shall look at him
on the seventh day, and if he finds that
the mark is unchanged in color, and
that the mark has not spread on the
skin, the priest shall quarantine him for
6 another seven days; on the seventh day
the priest shall look at him again, and if
he finds that the mark has grown dim,
and has not spread on the skin, the
priest shall pronounce him clean; it is
only an eruption; so the man shall wash
7 his clothes, and be clean. But if the
eruption spreads on the skin, after he
has shown himself to the priest to be
pronounced clean, he must show himself to the priest again, and the priest
shall look at him, and if he finds that
the eruption has spread on the skin, the
priest shall pronounce him unclean,
since it is leprosy.

"When anyone has an attack of leprosy, he must be brought to the priest;
the priest shall look at him, and if he
finds that there is a white swelling on
the skin, which has turned the hair
white, and that there is quick raw flesh
in the swelling, it is chronic leprosy
on the skin of his body; so the priest
must pronounce him unclean, without
quarantining him, for he is unclean. If
the leprosy breaks out all over the skin,
so that the leprosy completely covers
the skin of the afflicted person, from
head to foot, in so far as the priest can
see, the priest shall look at him, and if
he finds that the leprosy has covered his
whole body, he shall pronounce him
clean; since it has all turned white, he is
clean. But whenever raw flesh appears
on him, he shall become unclean; when
the priest sees the raw flesh, he must
pronounce him unclean, raw flesh being
unclean, indicating leprosy. On the
other hand, if the raw flesh turns white
again, he must come to the priest, and
the priest shall look at him, and if he
finds that the mark has turned white,
the priest shall pronounce the afflicted
person clean, since he is clean.

"When anyone has a boil on the skin
of his body, and it heals, leaving a white
swelling or a reddish-white inflamed
spot, it must be shown to the priest; the
priest shall look at it, and if he finds
that it has the appearance of being
deeper than the skin and that the hair
is turned white, the priest shall pronounce him unclean, since it is an attack of leprosy, which has broken out in
the boil. But if the priest, upon looking
at it, finds no white hair on it, and it is
not deeper than the skin, but has become dim, the priest shall quarantine
him for seven days; if it then spreads all
over the skin, the priest shall pronounce
him unclean, since it is an attack; but if
the inflamed spot remains where it is,
without spreading, it is only the scar of
the boil, so the priest shall pronounce
him clean.

"Or, when anyone has a burn on the
skin of his body, and the raw flesh of
the burn becomes an inflamed spot,
reddish-white or white, the priest must

look at it, and if he finds that the hair
on the inflamed spot has turned white,
and that it has the appearance of being deeper than the skin, it is leprosy
which has broken out in the burn; so
the priest shall pronounce him unclean,
26 since it is an attack of leprosy. But if
the priest, upon looking at it, finds that
there is no white hair on the inflamed
spot, and that it is no deeper than the
skin, but has become dim, the priest
27 shall quarantine him for seven days; on
the seventh day the priest shall look at
him, and if it has spread all over the
skin, the priest shall pronounce him unclean, since it is an attack of leprosy.
28 But if the inflamed spot remains where
it is, without spreading on the skin, and
has become dim, it is only the swelling
from the burn, so the priest shall pronounce him clean; for it is only the scar
of the burn.
29 "When a man or a woman has a sore
30 on the head or the beard, the priest
must look at the sore, and if he finds
that it has the appearance of being
deeper than the skin, and that there is
thin yellow hair on it, the priest shall
pronounce him unclean, since it is ringworm, a leprous disease of the head or
31 beard. If the priest, upon looking at
the sore of the ringworm, finds that it
has no appearance of being deeper than
the skin, and that there is no black hair
on it, the priest shall quarantine the
person afflicted with the ringworm for
32 seven days; on the seventh day the
priest shall look at the sore, and if he
finds that the ringworm has not spread,
that there is no yellow hair on it, and
that the ringworm has no appearance of
33 being deeper than the skin, the person
shall shave himself, but not shave the
ringworm, and then the priest shall
quarantine the person with the ring-
34 worm for another seven days; on the
seventh day the priest shall look at the
ringworm, and if he finds that the ringworm has not spread on the skin, and
that it has no appearance of being deeper than the skin, the priest shall pronounce him clean; he shall wash his
35 clothes, and be clean. But if the ringworm spreads on the skin after he has
36 been pronounced clean, the priest shall
look at him, and if he finds that the
ringworm has spread on the skin, the
priest need not look for yellow hair; he
37 is unclean. But if the ringworm is unchanged in color, and black hair has
grown on it, the ringworm is healed; he
is clean, and the priest shall pronounce
him clean.
"When a man or a woman has in- 38
flamed spots on the skin of his body,
white inflamed spots, the priest shall 39
look at them, and if he finds that the
inflamed spots on the skin of his body
are a dull white, it is only tetter, which
has broken out on the skin, so he is
clean.
"When a man loses the hair on his 40
head, he is bald, but he is clean. If he 41
loses the hair from the front of his head,
he is bald on the forehead, but he is
clean. But if there is a reddish-white 42
mark on the bald head or bald forehead, it is leprosy breaking out on his
bald head or bald forehead; so the 43
priest shall look at it, and if he finds
that the swelling from the affection on
his bald head or bald forehead is reddish-white, like the appearance of leprosy on the skin of the body, he is a 44
leprous man, he is unclean; the priest
must be sure to pronounce him unclean,
since the affection is on his head.
"In the case of any leper who has the 45
affection, his clothes must be torn, and
the hair on his head worn loose; he
must cover his mustache, and cry, 'Unclean! Unclean!' All the time that he 46
has the affection, he shall be unclean;
being unclean, he must live alone, his
domicile must be outside the camp.
"When a garment has a leprous affec- 47
tion on it, whether it is a woolen garment or a linen garment, whether it is 48
woven or knitted material of linen or
wool, whether it is skin or anything
made of skin, if the affection on the 49
garment or the skin, or the woven or
knitted material, or the article of skin
whatever it may be, is greenish or
reddish, it is a leprous affection, and
must be shown to the priest. The 50
priest shall look at the affection, and
isolate the thing affected for seven
days; on the seventh day he shall look 51
at the affection, and if the affection has
spread on the garment, or the woven or
knitted material, or the skin, whatever
may be the use to which the skin is put,
the affection is a malignant leprosy; it
is unclean; so he must burn the gar- 52
ment, or the woven or knitted material
of wool or linen, or the article of skin
whatever it may be, which has the

affection; for it is a malignant leprosy;
53 it must be burned up. But if the priest,
upon looking at it, finds that the affection has not spread on the garment, or
the woven or knitted material, or the
54 article of skin whatever it may be, the
priest shall order the thing that has the
affection to be washed, and then isolate
55 it for another seven days. After the
affected thing has been washed, the
priest shall look at it, and if he finds
that the affection has not changed its
color, nor the affection itself spread, it
is unclean; you must burn it up, whether the virus has produced bareness on
56 the back or the front. If the priest,
upon looking at it, finds that the affection has become dim after being
washed, he shall tear it out of the garment, or the skin, or the woven or knit-
57 ted material; and if it still appears on
the garment, or the woven or knitted
material, or the article of skin whatever
it may be, it is breaking out again; you
must burn up the thing that has the
58 affection on it. But if the affection disappears from the garment, or the woven or knitted material, or the article of
skin whatever it may be, which has
been washed, it shall be washed a second time, and then it shall be clean.

59 "This is the law for leprous affections
on any garment of wool or linen, or on
woven or knitted material, or on any
article of skin whatsoever, having to do
with its pronouncement as clean or unclean."

14 The LORD said to Moses,
2 "This is the law for the leper at the
3 time that he is pronounced clean. His
case must be brought to the priest, and
the priest shall go outside the camp,
and the priest shall look at him, and if
he finds that the attack of leprosy has
4 been healed in the leper, the priest shall
order two clean live birds, some cedar
wood, scarlet string, and hyssop to be
procured for the one who is to be
5 cleansed, and then the priest shall order
one of the birds to be killed over fresh
6 water in an earthen vessel. He shall
then take the live bird, with the cedar
wood, scarlet string, and hyssop, and
dip them and the live bird in the blood
of the bird that was killed over the
7 fresh water, and sprinkling it seven
times upon the one who is to be
cleansed from leprosy, he shall pronounce him clean, and set the live bird
free in the open country. He that is to 8
be cleansed must then wash his clothes,
shave off all his hair, and bathe himself
in water, and so become clean. After
that he may re-enter the camp, but
must stay outside his tent for seven
days; on the seventh day he shall shave 9
off all the hair on his head, his beard,
and his eyebrows; and when he has
shaved off all his hair, he shall wash his
clothes, and bathe his body in water,
and so become clean. On the eighth day 10
he shall take two perfect male lambs
and one perfect yearling ewe-lamb,
along with three-tenths of an ephah of
fine flour mixed with oil as a cereal-offering, and one log of oil. Then the 11
priest who is to do the cleansing shall
set the man to be cleansed and the other
things before the LORD at the doorway
of the tent of meeting. Taking one male 12
lamb, the priest shall offer it as a guilt-offering, along with the log of oil, and
wave them as a wave-offering before the
LORD, slaughtering the lamb at the 13
place where the sin-offering and burnt-offering victims are slaughtered, at the
place where the sanctuary is; for the
guilt-offering like the sin-offering shall
go to the priest, since it is most sacred.
Taking some of the blood of the guilt- 14
offering, the priest shall put it on the
tip of the right ear of the one to be
cleansed, on the thumb of his right
hand, and the great toe of his right foot.
Taking some of the log of oil, the priest 15
shall pour it into the palm of his own
left hand, whereupon the priest shall 16
dip his right finger in the oil that is in
the palm of his left hand, and sprinkle
some of the oil with his finger seven
times before the LORD; of the rest of 17
the oil that is in his palm the priest shall
put some on the tip of the right ear of
the one to be cleansed, on the thumb of
his right hand, and the great toe of his
right foot, on top of the blood of the
guilt-offering, while the remainder of 18
the oil that is in his palm, the priest
shall put on the head of the one to be
cleansed. Thus shall the priest make
atonement for him before the LORD.
The priest shall then offer the sin-offer- 19
ing, and make atonement for the one
to be cleansed because of his uncleanness, after which he shall slaughter the
burnt-offering victim, and the priest 20
shall offer up the burnt-offering and the
cereal-offering on the altar. Thus shall

the priest make atonement for him, and
he shall become clean.
21 "If, however, he is poor, and cannot
afford so much, he may take one male
lamb as a guilt-offering to be waved in
atonement for him, and one-tenth of an
ephah of fine flour mixed with oil as a
22 cereal-offering, and a log of oil, together
with two turtle-doves or two young
pigeons, such as he can afford, the one
to be a sin-offering, and the other a
23 burnt-offering. On the eighth day he
shall bring them for his cleansing to the
priest at the doorway of the tent of
24 meeting, before the LORD, whereupon
the priest shall take the lamb of the
guilt-offering and the log of oil, and the
priest shall wave them as a wave-offer-
25 ing before the LORD. He shall then
slaughter the lamb of the guilt-offering,
and taking some of the blood of the
guilt-offering, the priest shall put it on
the tip of the right ear of the one to be
cleansed, on the thumb of his right
hand, and the great toe of his right foot,
26 while the priest shall pour some of the
oil into the palm of his own left hand,
27 and the priest shall then sprinkle with
his right finger some of the oil that is in
the palm of his left hand seven times
28 before the LORD. The priest shall put
some of the oil that remains in his palm
on the tip of the right ear of the one to
be cleansed, on the thumb of his right
hand, and the great toe of his right foot,
on the place where the blood of the
29 guilt-offering is, while the remainder of
the oil that is in his palm the priest shall
put on the head of the one to be cleansed,
to make atonement for him before the
30 LORD. Of the turtle-doves or young
31 pigeons, such as he can afford, he shall
offer the one as a sin-offering and the
other as a burnt-offering, along with
the cereal-offering. Thus shall the priest
make atonement before the LORD for
32 the one to be cleansed. This is the law
for him who has an attack of leprosy,
who cannot afford the regular offerings
for his cleansing."
33 The LORD said to Moses and Aaron,
34 "When you enter the land of Canaan
which I am giving you as your own, if I
bring a leprous affection on a house in
35 the land that you hold, the owner of
the house shall come and inform the
priest, saying, 'There appears to me to
be some kind of affection in my house';
36 whereupon the priest shall order the
house to be emptied before he goes in to
look at the affection, so that everything
that is in the house may not be made
unclean, after which the priest shall go
in to look at the house. If, upon look- 37
ing at the affection, he finds that the
affection on the walls of the house is in
greenish or reddish patches, and that
they have the appearance of being
deeper than the surface of the wall, the 38
priest shall come out of the house to the
doorway of the house, and quarantine
the house for seven days. On the sev- 39
enth day the priest shall come back,
and look at it, and if he finds that the
affection has spread on the walls of the
house, the priest shall order the stones 40
which have the affection on them to be
pulled out and thrown into an unclean
place outside the city, while he shall 41
have the inside of the house itself
scraped all around, and the mortar that
is scraped off is to be dumped into an
unclean place outside the city; fresh 42
stones shall be procured and the other
stones be replaced with them, and fresh
mortar shall be procured and the house
replastered. If the affection breaks 43
out again in the house, after the stones
have been pulled out, and the house has
been scraped and replastered, the priest 44
shall go in and look at it, and if he finds
that the affection has spread in the
house, it is malignant leprosy in the
house; it is unclean. So he must pull 45
down the house, its stones, its timbers,
and all the mortar of the house, and
take them to an unclean place outside
the city. Moreover, anyone who en- 46
ters the house while it is quarantined
shall be unclean until evening; anyone 47
who sleeps in the house must wash his
clothes, and anyone who eats in the
house must wash his clothes. If, how- 48
ever, the priest should come in, and
upon looking at it, find that the affection has not spread in the house, after
the house has been replastered, the
priest shall pronounce the house clean,
since the affection has been remedied.
To cleanse the house he shall take two 49
birds, along with some cedar wood,
scarlet string, and hyssop, and killing 50
one bird over fresh water in an earthen
vessel, he shall take the cedar wood, 51
hyssop, and scarlet string, along with the
live bird, and dipping them in the blood
of the bird that was killed and in the
fresh water, he shall sprinkle the house

52 seven times; he shall cleanse the house
with the blood of the bird and the fresh
water, along with the live bird, the
cedar wood, hyssop, and scarlet string,
53 and then he shall set the live bird free
outside the city in the open country.
Thus he shall make atonement for the
house, and it shall become clean.
54 "That is the law for every kind of
55 leprous affection, for ringworm, for
56 leprosy on a garment or in a house, for
a swelling, for an eruption, and for in-
57 flamed spots, to indicate when it is unclean and when it is clean; this is the
law for leprosy."

15 The LORD said to Moses and Aaron,
2 "Speak to the Israelites, and say to
them, 'When any man has a discharge
from his body, the discharge is unclean,
3 and such shall be the uncleanness from
his discharge that he shall be unclean
whether his body runs with the discharge, or is stopped up to prevent the
4 discharge. Every bed on which he who
has the discharge lies shall be unclean,
and every chair on which he sits shall be
5 unclean. Anyone who touches his bed
must wash his clothes, and bathe himself in water, remaining unclean until
6 evening. Whoever sits on the chair on
which he who has the discharge may
have sat must wash his clothes, and
bathe himself in water, remaining un-
7 clean until evening. Whoever touches
the body of him who has the discharge
must wash his clothes, and bathe himself in water, remaining unclean until
8 evening. If he who has the discharge
spits on one who is clean, he must wash
his clothes and bathe himself in water,
9 remaining unclean until evening. Every
seat on which he who has the discharge
10 rides shall be unclean. Whoever touches
anything at all that has been under him
shall be unclean until evening; whoever
carries such things must wash his
clothes, and bathe himself in water, re-
11 maining unclean until evening. Anyone whom he who has the discharge
touches, without having rinsed his
hands in water, must wash his clothes,
and bathe himself in water, remaining
12 unclean until evening. Any earthen pot
which he who has the discharge touches
must be broken, and every wooden article must be rinsed with water.
13 " 'When he who has the discharge is
to be cleansed of his discharge, he must
allow seven days for his cleansing; he
must wash his clothes, and bathe his
body in fresh water, and so become
clean. On the eighth day he shall pro- 14
cure two turtle-doves or two young
pigeons, and appear before the LORD at
the doorway of the tent of meeting, and
give them to the priest, whereupon the 15
priest shall offer them, one as a sin-offering and the other as a burnt-offering.
Thus shall the priest make atonement
before the LORD for him because of his
discharge.
" 'If a man has an emission of semen, 16
he must bathe his whole body in water,
remaining unclean until evening; and 17
every garment and every skin that has
the semen on it must be washed with
water, remaining unclean until evening.
If a man lies with a woman and has an 18
emission of semen, they must bathe
themselves in water, remaining unclean
until evening.
" 'If a woman has a discharge, her 19
discharge being menstruation, she shall
continue for seven days in her impurity;
and whosoever touches her shall be unclean until evening. Everything on 20
which she lies while in her impurity
shall be unclean, and every chair on
which she sits shall be unclean. Who- 21
ever touches her bed must wash his
clothes, and bathe himself in water, remaining unclean until evening. Who- 22
ever touches any chair on which she sits
must wash his clothes, and bathe himself in water, remaining unclean until
evening. If she herself is on the bed or 23
the chair, when he touches it, he shall
be unclean until evening. If a man 24
should ever lie with her, her impurity
shall be transmitted to him; he shall be
unclean for seven days; and every bed
on which he lies shall be unclean.
" 'If a woman has a discharge of 25
blood for a long time, when it is not her
menstruation period, or if she has a discharge beyond her period, she shall be
unclean during all the time of her unclean discharge, as she is during the
time of her menstruation. Every bed 26
on which she lies during all the time of
her discharge shall be affected by her in
the same way as a bed in her period, and
every chair on which she sits shall be
unclean as it is unclean in her period.
Whoever touches them shall become 27
unclean; he must wash his clothes, and
bathe himself in water, remaining unclean until evening. If she is to be 28

cleansed of her discharge, she must allow seven days for it, after which she
29 shall be clean. On the eighth day she
must procure two turtle-doves or two
young pigeons, and bring them to the
priest at the doorway of the tent of
30 meeting, whereupon the priest shall
offer one as a sin-offering and the other
as a burnt-offering. Thus shall the
priest make atonement before the
LORD for her because of her unclean
discharge.
31 "'Thus shall you rid the Israelites of
their uncleanness, lest they die for their
uncleanness, by defiling my dwelling
that is in their midst.
32 "'That is the law for one having a
discharge, or for one who has an emission of semen and is made unclean by
33 it, for her who is suffering from menstruation, for anyone who has a discharge, whether man or woman, and for
any man who lies with an unclean
woman.'"
16 After the death of Aaron's two sons,
when they approached the presence of
the LORD and died, the LORD spoke to
Moses,
2 "Tell your brother Aaron," the
LORD said to Moses, "that he must under no circumstances enter the sacred
place inside the veil in front of the propitiatory which is on the ark, that he
die not; for I manifest myself in the
3 cloud on the propitiatory; it is only
with this that Aaron may enter the
sacred place: with a young bullock as
a sin-offering and a ram as a burnt-
4 offering. He must put on the sacred
linen tunic, wear the linen breeches on
his body, be girded with the linen sash,
and wind on the linen turban, these
being the sacred vestments; when he
has bathed his body in water he shall
5 put them on. From the Israelite community he shall procure two he-goats
as a sin-offering and one ram as a burnt-
6 offering. Aaron shall offer the sin-offering bullock which is for himself, and so
make atonement for himself and his
household. He shall then take the two
goats, and set them before the LORD at
the doorway of the tent of meeting,
8 whereupon Aaron shall place lots on
the two goats, one lot for the LORD and
9 the other for Azazel. Aaron shall then
bring forward the goat which has the
lot of the LORD on it, and offer it as a
10 sin-offering, while the goat that has the
lot of Azazel on it shall be set alive before the LORD, that atonement may be
made through it by sending it off to
Azazel in the desert. Aaron shall offer 11
the sin-offering bullock which is for
himself, and so make atonement for
himself and his household. He must
slaughter the sin-offering bullock which
is for himself, and taking a pan full of 12
coals of fire from the altar before the
LORD and with his hands full of finely
ground, fragrant incense, he must bring
them inside the veil, and put the in- 13
cense on the fire before the LORD, that
the cloud of incense may cover the propitiatory which is over the decrees, that
he die not. Taking some of the blood of 14
the bullock, he must sprinkle it with his
finger on the east side of the propitiatory, and then sprinkle some of the
blood with his finger seven times in
front of the propitiatory. He must 15
then slaughter the sin-offering goat
which is for the people, and bring its
blood inside the veil; he must do with
its blood as he did in the case of the bullock's blood, sprinkling it on the propitiatory and in front of the propitiatory.
Thus he shall make atonement for the 16
sanctuary because of the uncleanness of
the Israelites and their transgressions in
all their sins. And he shall do the same
for the tent of meeting that has its
abode with them in the midst of their
uncleanness. When he goes in to make 17
atonement in the sacred place, there
must be no one present in the tent of
meeting until he comes out, that he
may make atonement for himself, his
own household, and the whole community of Israel. He must then go outside 18
to the altar which is before the LORD,
and make atonement for it; taking some
of the bullock's blood and some of the
goat's blood, he must put it all around
the horns of the altar, and sprinkle 19
some of the blood on it with his finger
seven times, to cleanse and sanctify it
from the uncleanness of the Israelites.
When he has finished making atone- 20
ment for the sacred place, the tent of
meeting, and the altar, he shall bring
forward the live goat, and laying both 21
his hands on the head of the live goat,
Aaron shall confess over it all the iniquities of the Israelites and all their
transgressions in all their sins, and laying them on the head of the goat, send it
off to the desert by a man standing in

22 readiness. Thus the goat shall carry all
their iniquities away with it into a desolate region; and he shall set the goat
23 free in the desert. Then Aaron shall re-
enter the tent of meeting, and removing
the linen vestments which he put on
when he entered the sacred place, he
24 shall leave them there; he shall bathe
his body in water at a sacred place, put
on his other clothes, and then come out
and offer his own burnt-offering and the
people's burnt-offering, making atone-
25 ment for himself and the people, while
the fat of the sin-offering he shall burn
26 on the altar. The one who lets the goat
go for Azazel must wash his clothes,
and bathe his body in water, after
27 which he may re-enter the camp. The
sin-offering bullock and the sin-offering
goat, whose blood was brought in to
make atonement in the sacred place,
must be taken outside the camp, and
their hides, flesh, and offal burned up;
28 while the one who burns them must
wash his clothes and bathe his body in
water, after which he may re-enter the
camp.
29 "It shall be a perpetual statute for
you that on the tenth day of the seventh month you shall mortify yourselves and not do any work at all, neither the native born nor the proselyte
30 who resides among you; for on this day
shall atonement be made for you to
cleanse you, that you may be cleansed
31 from all your sins before the LORD. It
shall be a sabbath of complete rest for
you, and you must mortify yourselves;
32 it is to be a perpetual statute. The
priest who shall be anointed and installed as priest in his father's place
shall make the atonement; he shall put
on the linen vestments, the sacred
33 vestments, and make atonement for
the most sacred place, make atonement
for the tent of meeting and the altar,
and make atonement for the priests and
34 all the people of the community. This
is to be a perpetual statute for you, for
making atonement once a year for the
Israelites because of all their sins."

It was done as the LORD commanded Moses.

LAWS RELATING TO HOLINESS, 17:1—26:46

17 The LORD said to Moses,
2 "Speak to Aaron and his sons and all
the Israelites, and say to them, 'This is
the command that the LORD has given:
"Anyone at all belonging to the house of
Israel who slaughters an ox or a lamb
or a goat in the camp, or slaughters it
outside the camp, and does not bring it
to the doorway of the tent of meeting,
to present it as an offering to the LORD
in front of the LORD'S dwelling, that
man shall be held guilty of bloodshed,
since he has shed blood; hence that man
shall be cut off from his people, to the
end that the Israelites may bring in
their sacrifices, which they have been
accustomed to sacrifice in the country
at large, and bring them to the LORD
at the doorway of the tent of meeting,
to the priest, and sacrifice them as
thanksgiving sacrifices to the LORD;
whereupon the priest shall dash the
blood upon the altar of the LORD at the
doorway of the tent of meeting, and
burn the fat as a soothing odor to the
LORD. They must no longer offer their
sacrifices to the satyrs after whom they
have been running in wanton fashion.
This shall be a perpetual statute for
them throughout their generations." '

"You must also say to them, 'Anyone
at all belonging to the house of Israel,
or the proselytes who reside among
them, who offers a burnt-offering or a
sacrifice, and does not bring it to the
doorway of the tent of meeting to offer
it to the LORD, that man shall be cut
off from his people.

" 'If anyone at all belonging to the
house of Israel or the proselytes who reside among them eats any blood at all,
against the person who eats blood I will
set my face, and will cut him off from
his people; for the life of the creature
is in the blood, and I direct you to place
it upon the altar, to make atonement
for you; for it is the blood which as the
life makes atonement. That is why I
say to the Israelites, "No person among
you may eat blood, nor may the proselyte who resides among you eat blood."

" 'Anyone at all of the Israelites, or
the proselytes who reside among them,
who in hunting catches an animal or a
bird that may be eaten, must pour out
its blood, and cover it with dust; for the
life of every creature is identical with its
blood; hence I say to the Israelites,
"You may not eat the blood of any creature at all"; for the life of every creature
is its blood; whosoever eats it shall be

15 cut off. Every person who eats anything
that has died a natural death or from
being torn, whether he is a native born
or a proselyte, must wash his clothes,
and bathe himself in water, remaining
unclean until evening, when he shall be-
16 come clean. If he does not wash them,
nor bathe his body, he shall answer for
his iniquity.' "

.8 The LORD said to Moses,
2 "Speak to the Israelites, and say to
3 them, 'I, the LORD, am your God. You
must not imitate the practices of the
land of Egypt in which you lived, nor
imitate the practices of the land of Canaan to which I am about to bring you,
4 nor walk in their statutes. It is my ordinances that you must observe, and my
statutes that you must keep, by walking in them, since I, the LORD, am your
5 God. So you must keep my statutes
and ordinances, by the observance of
which man shall live, since I am the
LORD.

6 " 'None of you shall approach anyone closely related to him, to have intercourse with her; since I am the
7 LORD. You must not have intercourse
with her who belongs to your father,
namely, your mother; since she is your
mother, you must not have intercourse
8 with her. You must not have intercourse with a wife of your father, since
9 she belongs to your father. You must
not have intercourse with your sister,
whether full sister or half-sister, legiti-
0 mate or illegitimate. You must not
have intercourse with your son's
daughter nor your daughter's daughter;
1 for they are your own flesh. You must
not have intercourse with your father's
wife's daughter, begotten by your fa-
2 ther, since she is your sister. You must
not have intercourse with your father's
sister, since she is your father's relative.
3 You must not have intercourse with
your mother's sister, for she is your
4 mother's relative. You must not have
intercourse with her who belongs to
your father's brother; you must not approach his wife, since she is your aunt.
5 You must not have intercourse with
your daughter-in-law; since she is your
son's wife, you must not have inter-
6 course with her. You must not have
intercourse with your brother's wife,
7 since she belongs to your brother. You
must not have intercourse with a woman and her daughter as well; you must
not take her son's daughter and her
daughter's daughter to have intercourse
with them; since they are relatives, it
would be lewdness. You must not mar- 18
ry a woman in addition to her sister as
a rival wife, having intercourse with her
as well as with the other, while she is
alive. You must not approach a woman 19
while she is unclean from menstruation,
to have intercourse with her. You must 20
not have sexual intercourse with your
neighbor's wife, defiling yourself with
her. You must not dedicate any of 21
your children to the service of Molech;
you must not profane the name of your
God, of me, the LORD. You must not 22
lie with a male as with a woman, since
that would be abominable. You must 23
not have sexual intercourse with any
animal at all, defiling yourself with it;
nor must a woman stand in front of an
animal, to lie down for it, since that
would be bestial. Do not defile your- 24
selves in any of these ways; for it was in
all these ways that the nations whom I
am driving out of your way defiled
themselves, so that the land became de- 25
filed, and I punished it for its iniquity
and the land vomited out its inhabitants. So keep my statutes and ordi- 26
nances, and do not follow any of these
abominable practices, neither the native born nor the proselytes who reside
among you (for it was all these abomi- 27
nable practices that the natives of the
land who preceded you followed, so that
the land became defiled), lest the land 28
vomit you out when you defile it, as it
vomited out the nations who preceded
you. For whoever follows any of these 29
abominable practices—the persons who
do so shall be cut off from their people.
So keep my charge by not observing 30
any of the abominable customs which
were observed before you, and do not
defile yourselves with them, since I,
the LORD, am your God.' "

The LORD said to Moses, 19
"Speak to the whole Israelite com- 2
munity, and say to them, 'You must be
holy; for I, the LORD your God, am
holy. You must each revere his father 3
and mother, and you must keep my
sabbaths, since I, the LORD, am your
God. Do not turn to unreal gods, nor 4
make yourselves molten gods, since I,
the LORD, am your God.
" 'When you offer a thanksgiving 5
sacrifice to the LORD, sacrificing it so

6 as to make you acceptable, you must
eat it on the day that you sacrifice it,
or on the next day; any left over until
7 the third day must be burned up. If
it should ever be eaten on the third day,
it would be mere refuse; it would not be
8 acceptable; anyone eating it shall answer for his iniquity, because he has
profaned what is sacred to the LORD;
so that person shall be cut off from his
people.
9 " 'When you reap the harvest of your
land, you must not reap your field to
the very corners, nor gather the glean-
10 ings of your harvest; you must not
glean your vineyards bare, nor gather
the fallen fruit of your vineyard; you
must leave them for the poor and the
resident alien, since I, the LORD, am
your God.
11 " 'You must not steal, nor cheat, nor
12 lie to one another. You must not take
a false oath in my name, and so profane
the name of your God, of me, the
LORD.
13 " 'You must not defraud your fellow,
nor rob him; the wages of a hired laborer are not to remain all night with
you until morning.
14 " 'You must not curse a deaf person,
nor place an obstacle in the way of a
blind person; you must stand in awe of
your God, of me, the LORD.
15 " 'You must do no injustice in a case,
neither showing partiality to the poor,
nor deferring to the powerful, but judging your fellow fairly.
16 " 'You must not play the part of a
talebearer against your people; you
must not secure yourself by the life of
another, since I am the LORD.
17 " 'You must not cherish hate against
your fellow-countryman; you must be
sure to reprove your fellow, but not
18 incur sin because of him. You must not
avenge yourself, nor bear a grudge
against the members of your own race,
but you must love your fellow as one of
your own, since I am the LORD.
19 " 'You must keep my statutes; you
must not let your cattle breed with a
different species; you must not sow
your field with two kinds of seed, nor
put on a garment made of two kinds of
material.
20 " 'If a man has sexual intercourse
with a woman, who is a slave, betrothed to another man, but who has
never been redeemed, nor given her
freedom, there shall be an investigation; they shall not be put to death, because she was not free, but he must 2
bring his guilt-offering to the LORD at
the doorway of the tent of meeting, a
ram as a guilt-offering, whereupon the 2
priest shall make atonement for him
with the guilt-offering ram before the
LORD for the sin that he committed,
and he shall be forgiven for the sin that
he committed.
" 'When you enter the land, and 2
plant all kinds of trees for food, you
must treat their fruit as uncircumcised,
to be held by you as uncircumcised for
three years and not to be eaten; and in 2
the fourth year all their fruit is to be
sacred, a praise-offering to the LORD;
it is only in the fifth year that you may 2
eat their fruit, that their produce may
enrich you, since I, the LORD, am your
God.
" 'You must not eat anything with 2
the blood.
" 'You must not practice augury or
soothsaying.
" 'You must not shave around your 2
temples, nor do away with the corners
of your beard; you must not make in- 2
cisions in your body for the dead, nor
tattoo any marks on yourselves, since
I am the LORD.
" 'Do not degrade your daughter by 2
making a harlot of her, lest the land
fall into harlotry, and become full of
lewdness.
" 'You must keep my sabbaths, and 3
stand in awe of my sanctuary, since I
am the LORD.
" 'Do not turn to mediums or magi- 3
cians; do not defile yourselves with
them by consulting them, since I, the
LORD, am your God.
" 'You must rise in the presence of 3
the hoary-headed, and defer to the
aged, and so stand in awe of your God,
of me, the LORD.
" 'If a proselyte is residing with you 3
in your land, you must not mistreat
him; you must treat the proselyte who 3
resides with you like the native born
among you, and love him as one of your
own, since I, the LORD, am your God;
for you were once aliens yourselves in
the land of Egypt.
" 'You must do no injustice in a case, 3
with rule, or weight, or measure; you 3
must have just balances, just weights, a
just ephah, and a just hin, since it was

I, the LORD your God, who brought
37 you out of the land of Egypt. So you
must be careful to observe all my statutes and ordinances, since I am the
LORD.' "
The LORD said to Moses,
2 "Say to the Israelites, 'Anyone at all
of the Israelites or the proselytes who
reside in Israel, who dedicates any of his
children to Molech, must be put to
death; the people of the land must
3 stone him. I, too, will set my face
against that man, and cut him off from
his people, because he has dedicated
some of his children to Molech, defiling
my sanctuary and profaning my holy
4 name. If the people of the land should
ever shut their eyes to such a man when
he dedicates some of his children to
5 Molech by not putting him to death, I
myself will set my face against that
man and his family, and cut him off
from his people, as well as all those who
run wantonly after him by running
wantonly after Molech.
6 " 'If any person turns to mediums
and magicians by running wantonly
after them, I will set my face against
that person, and cut him off from his
people.
7 " 'Sanctify yourselves therefore, and
be holy; for I, the LORD, am your God;
8 be careful to observe my statutes, since
9 it is I, the LORD, who sanctify you. For
anyone at all who curses his father or
mother must be put to death; since he
has cursed his father or mother, his
blood shall be on his head.
10 " 'In the case of any man who commits adultery with another man's wife,
who commits adultery with his neighbor's wife, both the adulterer and the
11 adulteress must be put to death. In
the case of any man who lies with his
father's wife, having intercourse with
her who belongs to his father, both of
them must be put to death; their blood
12 shall be on their heads. In the case of
any man who lies with his daughter-in-
law, both of them must be put to death;
since they have committed a bestial
act, their blood shall be on their heads.
13 If any man lies with a male as with a
woman, since they have both committed an abominable act, they must be
put to death; their blood shall be on
14 their heads. In the case of a man who
marries a woman and her mother as
well, it is lewdness; both he and they
must be burned up, that there may be
no lewdness in your midst. Any man 15
who has sexual intercourse with an animal must be put to death, and the animal must be slain. If a woman goes up 16
to any animal to lie down for it, you
must slay both the woman and the animal; they must be put to death; their
blood shall be on their heads. If a man 17
takes his sister, either his full sister or
his half-sister, and they have intercourse with each other, it is a shameful
deed; so they must be cut off in sight of
the members of their own race; since he
has had intercourse with his sister, he
must answer for his iniquity. If a man 18
lies with a woman while she is menstru-
ating, and has intercourse with her, he
has bared her fountain, and she has let
the fountain of her blood be uncovered,
so they must both be cut off from their
people. You must not have intercourse 19
with your mother's sister nor your father's sister; for such a one would have
made his relative bare; they must answer for their iniquity. In the case of a 20
man who lies with his aunt, he has had
intercourse with her who belongs to his
uncle; they shall answer for their sin by
dying childless. If a man takes his 21
brother's wife, it is an impure deed;
since he has had intercourse with her
who belongs to his brother, they shall
be childless.
" 'Be careful, then, to observe all my 22
statutes and ordinances, lest the land,
into which I am about to bring you to
live, vomit you out. You must not fol- 23
low the customs of the nations whom I
am driving out of your way; it was
because they did all of these things that
I abhor them, and say to you, "You 24
shall take possession of their land; I
give it to you to possess, a land abounding in milk and honey." I, the LORD,
am your God, who have separated you
from other peoples, so you must make a 25
distinction between clean and unclean
animals, between unclean and clean
birds; you must not make yourselves
detestable by animal or bird or any land
reptile, which I have set apart for you
to hold as unclean. You must be holy 26
to me; for I, the LORD, am holy, and
have separated you from other peoples
to be mine.
" 'If there is a man or woman who is 27
a medium or a magician, they must be

put to death by being stoned; their
blood shall be on their heads.' "
21 The LORD said to Moses,
"Speak to the priests, the sons of
Aaron, and say to them, 'No one is to
defile himself for a dead person among
2 his relatives, except for his nearest kin,
his mother, his father, his son, his
3 daughter, his brother, his sister if she
is an unmarried virgin and hence still
related to him; for such he may defile
4 himself; he must not defile himself for
those related to him by marriage by
5 profaning himself. They must not shave
part of their heads bald, nor shave off
the corners of their beards, nor make
6 incisions in their bodies. They must be
holy to their God, and not profane the
name of their God; for it is the LORD'S
sacrifices, their God's food, that they
7 offer, so they must be holy. They must
not marry a harlot or a woman who has
been violated; they must not marry a
woman who has been divorced from her
husband; for he is to be holy to his God.
8 Consecrate him therefore; for it is your
God's food that he offers; you must
treat him as holy; for I, the LORD, who
9 consecrate them, am holy. If a priest's
daughter degrades herself by playing
the harlot, she degrades her father; she
must be burned up.
10 " 'The priest who is the highest of
his fellows, on whose head the anointing oil has been poured, and who has
been installed to wear the vestments,
must not let his hair hang loose, nor
11 tear his clothes; he must never approach any corpse, defiling himself for
12 neither his father nor his mother; he
must not leave the sanctuary, nor profane the sanctuary of his God; for it is
the consecration of his God's anointing
oil that is on him; I am the LORD.
13 " 'He must marry a virgin; a widow,
14 or a divorced woman, or a woman who
has been violated, or a harlot, such he
may not marry, but a virgin of his own
15 class he must marry, that he may not
degrade his children among his clansmen; for it is I, the LORD, who consecrate him.' "
16 The LORD said to Moses,
17 "Say to Aaron, 'None of your descendants, from generation to generation, who has a defect, may draw near
18 to offer his God's food; for no one who
has a defect may come near, no one who
is blind, or lame, or has any perfora-
tions, or has a limb too long; no one
who has a fractured foot, or a fractured
hand, or is a hunchback, or has a cata-
ract, or a defect of eyesight, or scurvy,
or scabs, or crushed testicles—no one
of the descendants of Aaron, the priest,
who has a defect, may come near to
offer the LORD'S sacrifices; since he has
a defect, he may not come near to offer
his God's food. He may eat his God's
food, some of the most sacred as well as
the sacred; only he must not approach
the veil, nor come near the altar, because he has a defect in him, lest he profane my sanctuaries; for it is I, the
LORD, who consecrate them.' "
So Moses spoke to Aaron and his sons
and all the Israelites.
The LORD said to Moses,
"Tell Aaron and his sons to be careful about the sacred gifts of the Israelites, which they consecrate to me, and
not to profane my holy name, since I
am the LORD. Say to them, 'Anyone
at all out of all your descendants
throughout your generations who approaches the sacred gifts which the Israelites consecrate to the LORD, while
he is unclean, that person shall be cut
off from my presence, since I am the
LORD. No one at all of the descendants of Aaron, who is a leper, or has a
discharge, may eat any of the sacred
gifts until he is clean. Whoever touches
anyone who has been made unclean
through contact with a corpse, or anyone who has had an emission of semen,
or anyone who touches any insect
through which he may contract uncleanness, or any person through whom
he may contract whatever unlceanness
he has—the person who touches such
shall be unclean until evening, and
must not eat of the sacred gifts unless
he has bathed his body in water. When
the sun sets, he shall be clean, after
which he may eat of the sacred gifts;
for these are his food. Anything that
has died a natural death or from being
torn, he must not eat to be defiled by
it, since I am the LORD. So they must
keep my charge, that they may not
incur sin in the matter, and die because
of it, for profaning it, since it is I, the
LORD, who consecrate them. No layman may ever eat a sacred gift; a
priest's serf or hired servant may not
eat a sacred gift; but if a priest buys a
slave, he may eat of it, and those that

are born in his house may eat of his food. If a priest's daughter is married to a layman, she must not eat of the sacred contributions; but if a priest's daughter is a widow or is divorced, and having no child, has returned to her father's home as in her youth, she may eat of her father's food; but no layman may ever eat of it. If anyone eats a sacred gift inadvertently, he must add a fifth to it, and give the sacred gift to the priest. They must not profane the sacred gifts of the Israelites, which they contribute to the LORD, and so make them incur iniquity requiring a guilt-offering by eating their sacred gifts; for it is I, the LORD, who consecrate them.' "

The LORD said to Moses,

"Speak to Aaron and his sons and all the Israelites, and say to them, 'If anyone at all belonging to the house of Israel or the proselytes in Israel presents his offering, any votive offering or voluntary offering at all of theirs, which they present as a burnt-offering to the LORD—in order that you may be accepted, it must be a perfect male, in the case of either oxen, or lambs, or goats; you must not offer anything that has a blemish on it; for it would not be accepted for you. If anyone offers a thanksgiving sacrifice to the LORD as a special votive offering or voluntary offering, either in oxen or sheep, it must be perfect to be accepted, with no blemish on it at all. Anything blind, or maimed, or mutilated, or suppurating, or scurvy, or scabbed, such you must not offer to the LORD, nor offer any of them on the altar as a sacrifice to the LORD. An ox or a sheep, however, which has a limb too long or too short, you may offer as a voluntary offering, but as a votive offering it will not be accepted. Anything that has its testicles bruised or crushed or torn off or cut off, you must not offer to the LORD: you must not do such things in your land. Neither may you offer any such as food for your God when received from a foreigner; for they are marred; since they have blemishes on them, they will not be accepted for you.' "

The LORD said to Moses,

"When an ox, or a sheep, or a goat, is born, it must remain seven days with its mother, and only from the eighth
day onward will it be acceptable as a
sacrificial offering to the LORD; and in 28
the case of a cow or ewe, you must not
slaughter it and its young on the same
day.
"When you make a praise-offering 29
sacrifice to the LORD, you must sacrifice it so as to win acceptance for you;
you must eat it that very day, leaving 30
none of it over until morning, since I
am the LORD.
"So you must be careful to observe 31
my commands, since I am the LORD.
You must not profane my holy name; 32
but I must be hallowed among the Israelites, since it is I, the LORD, who
hallow you, who brought you out of the 33
land of Egypt to be your God, I, the
LORD."

The LORD said to Moses, 23
"Speak to the Israelites, and say to 2
them, 'The fixed festivals of the LORD
which you must proclaim as religious
assemblies—the following are my fixed
festivals. For six days work may be 3
done, but on the seventh day there is
to be a sabbath of complete rest, a religious assembly, when you must not do
any work at all; it is to be a sabbath for
the LORD in all your places of abode.
" 'The following are the fixed festi- 4
vals of the LORD, the religious assemblies which you must proclaim at their
proper season. On the fourteenth day 5
of the first month at twilight is the passover to the LORD. On the fifteenth day 6
of the same month is the feast of unleavened cakes to the LORD; for seven
days you must eat unleavened cakes.
On the first day you must hold a reli- 7
gious assembly, doing no hard work at
all; and for seven days you must offer 8
sacrifices to the LORD; on the seventh
day there is to be a religious assembly,
when you must do no hard work at
all.' "
The LORD said to Moses, 9
"Speak to the Israelites, and say to 10
them, 'When you enter the land which I
am about to give you, and reap its harvest, you must bring the sheaf of the
first-fruits of your harvest to the
priest, who shall wave the sheaf before 11
the LORD that you may be accepted; it
is on the day following the sabbath that
the priest shall wave it. On the day 12
when you wave the sheaf, you must
offer a perfect yearling male lamb as a
burnt-offering to the LORD, while its 13

cereal-offering shall be two-tenths of an
ephah of fine flour mixed with oil, as a
sacrifice to the LORD, a soothing odor,
and its libation shall be a fourth of a
14 hin of wine. You must eat neither bread
nor parched grain nor new grain until
this same day, until you have brought
your God's offering; it is to be a perpetual statute throughout your generations in all your places of abode.
15 " 'From the day following the sabbath, from the day that you brought
the sheaf of the wave-offering, you must
16 count seven full weeks, counting fifty
days to the day following the seventh
sabbath, and then you must offer a
cereal-offering of new grain to the
17 LORD. From your dwellings you must
bring two loaves of bread as a wave-
offering, made of two-tenths of an
ephah of fine flour, baked with leaven,
18 as first-fruits for the LORD. With the
bread you must offer seven perfect yearling male lambs, one young bullock, and
two rams; they are to be a burnt-offering to the LORD, along with their
cereal-offering and libations, a sacri-
19 fice, a soothing odor to the LORD. You
must also offer one he-goat as a sin-
offering, and two yearling male lambs
20 as a thanksgiving sacrifice; the priest
shall wave them along with the bread
of the first-fruits as a wave-offering before the LORD, in addition to the two
lambs; they are to be sacred to the
21 LORD, to the priest. On that same day
you must proclaim and hold a religious
assembly, when you must do no hard
work at all; it is to be a perpetual statute in all your places of abode throughout your generations.
22 " 'When you reap the harvest of your
land, you must not reap your field to
the very corners, nor gather the gleanings of your harvest; you must leave
them for the poor and the resident
alien, since I, the LORD, am your
God.' "
23 The LORD said to Moses,
24 "Say to the Israelites, 'On the first
day of the seventh month you must observe a memorial day of complete rest,
celebrated by the blowing of trumpets,
a religious assembly, when you must do
25 no hard work at all, but offer a sacrifice to the LORD.' "
26 The LORD said to Moses,
27 "On exactly the tenth day of this
seventh month is the day of atone-
ment, when you must hold a religious assembly, and mortify yourselves, and offer a sacrifice to the LORD. You must do no work at all on that same day; for it's a day of atonement, on which to make atonement for you before the LORD your God. For every person who will not mortify himself on that same day shall be cut off from his people, and any person who does any work at all on that same day, that person I will destroy from the midst of his people, since you must do no work at all; it is to be a perpetual statute throughout your generations in all your places of abode. You must observe it as a sabbath of complete rest, and you must mortify yourselves; on the ninth day of the month at evening, from one evening to the next, you must keep your sabbath."

The LORD said to Moses,

"Say to the Israelites, 'On the fifteenth day of this seventh month is the seven-day feast of booths for the LORD. On the first day there is to be a religious assembly, when you must do no hard work at all. For seven days you must offer sacrifices to the LORD; on the eighth day you must hold a religious assembly, and offer a sacrifice to the LORD; since it is a sacred assembly, you must do no hard work at all.

" 'These are the fixed festivals of the LORD, which you must proclaim as religious assemblies to make offerings to the LORD, a burnt-offering, a cereal-offering, a sacrifice, and libations, each on its proper day, in addition to the sabbaths of the LORD, and the gifts, votive-offerings, and voluntary offerings, which you give to the LORD.

" 'On exactly the fifteenth day of the seventh month, when you have gathered in the produce of your land, you must observe the feast of the LORD for seven days. On the first day there is to be a sabbath of complete rest, and on the eighth day there is to be a sabbath of complete rest. On the first day you must procure boughs of beautiful trees, branches of palm trees, limbs of leafy trees, and water-willows, and rejoice before the LORD your God for seven days. You must observe it as a feast to the LORD for seven days a year (a perpetual statute throughout your generations), observing it in the seventh month. For seven days you must live

in booths; all the native-born in Israel
43 must live in booths, that your descendants may know that it was in booths
that I made the Israelites live when I
brought them out of the land of Egypt,
I, the LORD your God.' "
44 So Moses announced to the Israelites
the fixed festivals of the LORD.
24 The LORD said to Moses,
2 "Order the Israelites to provide you
with pure oil from crushed olives for the
light, so that there may always be a
lamp to lift in place; in the tent of meet-
3 ing, outside the veil which screens the
decrees, Aaron must keep it continually
supplied from evening until morning
before the LORD; it is to be a perpetual statute throughout your generations;
4 he must keep the lamps on the lampstand of pure gold continually supplied
before the LORD.
5 "Taking fine flour, you must bake
twelve cakes of it, with two-tenths of an
6 ephah to each cake. You must place
them in two lots, six in each lot, on the
7 table of pure gold before the LORD, and
put pure frankincense on each lot, to
serve as memorial bread, a sacrifice to
8 the LORD. Regularly on every sabbath
day it must be set out before the LORD
—a perpetual covenant on the part of
9 the Israelites. It shall go to Aaron and
his sons, who shall eat it in a sacred
place; for it is the most sacred part of
the LORD's sacrifices for him, a perpetual due."
10 The son of an Israelite woman, whose
father was an Egyptian, had come out
with the Israelites; the son of the Israelite woman and an Israelite had a quar-
11 rel in the camp, and the son of the Israelite woman blasphemed the Name,
and cursed, so they brought him to
Moses. His mother's name was Shelomith, the daughter of Dibri, belonging
12 to the tribe of Dan. He was put in custody, so that the LORD'S will might be
13 made clear for them. So the LORD said
to Moses,
14 "Take the one who has cursed outside the camp, and let all who heard
him lay their hands on his head, and
then let the whole community stone
15 him. To the Israelites themselves say,
'When anyone at all curses his God, he
16 must answer for his sin; whoever blasphemes the name of the LORD must be
put to death by having the whole community stone him; the proselyte like
the native-born must be put to death
when he blasphemes the Name. If any- 17
one takes any other person's life, he
must be put to death. Whoever takes 18
an animal's life must make it good—a
life for a life. If anyone disfigures an- 19
other, as he did, so it shall be done to
him, fracture for fracture, eye for eye, 20
tooth for tooth; as he disfigured the
other, so shall he be disfigured. Who- 21
ever kills an animal must make it good,
but whoever kills a man must be put to
death. You shall have the one ordi- 22
nance, with proselyte and native-born
to be treated alike; for I, the LORD, am
your God.' "
Moses told the Israelites, so they 23
took the one who had cursed outside the
camp, and stoned him; the Israelites
did as the LORD had commanded
Moses.
The LORD said to Moses at Mount 25
Sinai,
"Speak to the Israelites, and say to 2
them, 'When you enter the land which
I am about to give you, the land shall
enjoy a sabbath to the LORD. For six 3
years you may sow your field, and for
six years prune your vineyard and
gather in its produce; but during the 4
seventh year there is to be a sabbath of
complete rest for the land, a sabbath to
the LORD, when you must not sow
your field nor prune your vineyard, not 5
even reaping the aftergrowth of your
harvest, nor gathering the grapes of
your undressed vines, since it is to be a
year of complete rest for the land. The 6
sabbath of the land, in the matter of
working it, shall be incumbent on you
yourself, your male and female slaves,
your hired laborer and your serf, who
live with you, and your live stock, while 7
all its produce shall serve as food for the
wild beasts that are in your land.
" 'You must count seven weeks of 8
years, seven times seven years; you
must have a full seven weeks of years,
forty-nine years. Then, on the tenth 9
day of the seventh month, you must
sound a loud trumpet blast everywhere,
sounding the trumpet blast everywhere
throughout your whole land on the day
of atonement. You must hallow the fif- 10
tieth year, and proclaim liberty throughout the land to all its inhabitants; it is
to be a jubilee for you, when each of
you shall return to his own possessions,
and each of you shall return to his own

11 family. The fiftieth year shall be a jubilee for you, when you must not sow, nor
reap any aftergrowth in it, nor gather
grapes from the undressed vines in it;
12 for, being a jubilee, it is to be sacred for
you; you must eat its produce out of the
13 field. In this year of jubilee each of you
shall return to his own possessions.
14 When you make a sale to your neighbor
or a purchase from your neighbor, you
15 must not cheat each other; you must
buy from your neighbor on the basis of
the number of years that are to follow
the jubilee, while he must sell to you on
the basis of the number of years for
16 crops; if the years are many, the price
shall be proportionately high; if the
years are few, the price shall be proportionately low; for it is the number of
17 crops that is to be sold to you. So you
must not cheat each other, but stand in
awe of your God; for I, the LORD, am
your God.

18 “ ‘You must observe my statutes,
and be careful to observe my ordinances, that you may live in security
19 upon the earth; then shall the earth
yield its fruitage, and you shall eat your
20 fill, and live in security upon it. If you
should say, “What are we going to eat
in the seventh year, seeing that we may
21 not sow, nor gather in our crops?” I
will command such a blessing for you in
the sixth year that a three years' crop
22 will be produced; then in the eighth
year you shall sow, but live on the old
crop, eating the old crop until the ninth
23 year's crop comes in. The land must
not be sold in perpetuity; for the land
is mine, since you are only resident
24 aliens and serfs under me. Hence,
throughout all the land that you hold
you must allow redemption for the
land.

25 “ ‘If a fellow-countryman of yours
becomes poor, and sells some of his
property, his next-of-kin must come
and redeem what his countryman sold.
26 If a man has no one to redeem it, but
becomes rich enough to find the means
27 to redeem it himself, he must count up
the years since its sale, and make a refund for the remainder to the man to
whom he sold it, whereupon he may re-
28 turn to his property. But if he does not
have sufficient means to recover it,
what he sold shall remain in the hands
of the purchaser until the year of jubilee; at the jubilee it shall be released,
and he shall return to his property.

“ ‘If anyone sells a dwelling-house in 29
a walled city, the right to redeem it
shall hold until the completion of the
year following its sale; the right to redeem it shall hold throughout that
time. If it is not redeemed, however, 30
by the completion of a full year, the
house in the walled city shall be made
over in perpetuity to its purchaser and
his descendants, not to be released at
the jubilee. But the houses of villages 31
which have no walls around them shall
be reckoned as belonging to the coun-
try-fields; the right of redemption shall
hold for such, and at the jubilee they
shall be released. In the case of the 32
cities of the Levites, however, in the
case of the houses of the cities in their
possession, the Levites shall have a perpetual right of redemption; anything 33
belonging to the Levites may be redeemed, while any houses sold in a city
in their possession must be released at
the jubilee; for the houses in the cities
of the Levites are their property among
the Israelites. But the fields in the pas- 34
ture-lands of their cities may not be
sold; for that is their inalienable possession.

“ ‘If a fellow-countryman of yours 35
becomes poor, so that his ability to
meet his obligation with you fails, and
you force on him the status of a resident alien or a serf, and he lives under
you, take no interest from him in mon- 36
ey or in kind, but stand in awe of your
God, while your countryman lives under you. You must not lend him your 37
money at interest, nor give him your
food for a return, since I, the LORD, am 38
your God, who brought you out of the
land of Egypt to give you the land of
Canaan, and be your God.

“ ‘If a fellow-countryman of yours 39
under obligation to you becomes poor,
and sells himself to you, you must not
make him serve as a slave; he shall have 40
the status of a hired laborer or a serf
with you, working for you until the
year of jubilee, when he shall be re- 41
leased from your service, along with his
children, and return to his own family,
and return to his ancestral property;
because they are my slaves, whom I 42
brought out of the land of Egypt, they
must not be sold as slaves. You must 43
not exert your authority over him

harshly, but stand in awe of your God.
44 As for the male and female slaves that
you may have, it is only from the nations that surround you that you may
45 buy male and female slaves; although
you may also buy them from the children of the serfs who may be living
under you, and from their descendants
in your employ who may have been
46 born in your land. They may become
your property, and you may bequeath
them to your children after you to hold
as property; you may make permanent
slaves of them; but over your fellow-
Israelites you must not exert your authority harshly, the one over the other.
47 " 'If an alien or a serf under you becomes rich, and a fellow-countryman of
yours under obligation to him becomes
poor, and sells himself to the alien or
serf under you, or to a member of the
48 alien's family, even after he has sold
himself, the right of redemption shall
hold for him; one of his brothers may re-
49 deem him, or his uncle or his uncle's son
may redeem him, or any of his near relatives belonging to his family may redeem him, or if he becomes rich enough,
50 he may redeem himself. He shall reckon
with his purchaser from the year that he
sold himself to him down to the year of
jubilee, and the price for his release
shall be based on the number of years;
he is to have the status of a hired labor-
51 er with him. If there are still many
years to run, he must refund as redemption for himself a proportionate
52 amount of his purchase price; if there
are only a few years left until the year of
jubilee, he must make a reckoning with
him, refunding as redemption for himself an amount proportionate to the
53 years left him. He shall have the same
status with him as that of a laborer
hired year by year; he must not exert
his authority over him harshly, while
54 you see it. If he is not redeemed in any
of these ways, he shall go free at the
year of jubilee, along with his children.
55 For it is to me that the Israelites are
slaves, being my slaves whom I brought
out of the land of Egypt, I, the LORD,
your God.
26 " 'You must make no idols for yourselves, nor erect a carved image or sacred pillar for yourselves, nor locate a
figured stone in your land to pay homage to it; for I, the LORD, am your
2 God. You must keep my sabbaths, and
stand in awe of my sanctuary, since I
am the LORD.
" 'If you walk in my statutes, and 3
are careful to observe my commands,
I will give rain for you in due season, 4
the land shall yield its crops, and the
trees of the field shall yield their fruit;
threshing shall last for you until the 5
time of vintage, and the time of vintage
shall last until sowing time, so that you
shall eat all that you want of your food,
and live securely in your land. I will 6
establish peace in the land, so that you
shall lie down with none to frighten
you; I will clear the land of wild beasts,
and no sword shall pass through your
land; you shall chase your enemies, and 7
they shall fall by the sword before you;
five of you shall chase a hundred, and a 8
hundred of you shall chase a myriad, so
that your enemies shall fall by the
sword before you. I will give my atten- 9
tion to you, and make you fruitful, and
multiply you; I will establish my covenant with you. You shall have so 10
much of old stores to eat, that you shall
cast out the old to make way for the
new. I will set my dwelling in your 11
midst, and will not hold you in contempt, but will move about among you, 12
and be your God, while you shall be my
people, since I, the LORD, am your 13
God, who brought you out of the land
of Egypt, out of a state of slavery to
them, and broke the bars of your yoke,
and made you walk upright.
" 'But if you will not listen to me, 14
nor observe all these commands; if you 15
reject my statutes, and treat my ordinances as abhorrent by not observing
all my commands, by breaking my covenant, I on my part will do this to you: 16
I will inflict consumption and fever
upon you as terrors, exhausting your
eyes and depressing your spirits; you
shall sow your seed in vain, since your
enemies shall consume it. I will set my 17
face against you, so that you shall be
laid low before your enemies, and your
foes shall rule over you, and you shall
flee when no one is pursuing you. If you 18
will not listen to me even for these
things, I will punish you seven more
times for your sins; I will shatter your 19
vaunted power; I will make your sky
like iron, and your earth like bronze, so 20
that your strength shall be spent in
vain, since your land shall not yield its
crops, nor the trees of the land yield

21 their fruit. If you live at enmity with
me, and will not listen to me, I will
bring seven more afflictions upon you,
22 as your sins deserve; I will let wild
beasts loose among you, that shall rob
you of your children, destroy your cattle, and reduce you in numbers, so that
23 your roads shall be desolate. And if by
this discipline you are not turned to me,
24 but live at enmity with me, then I in
turn will live at enmity with you, and I
will afflict you seven times for your
25 sins; I will bring a sword upon you that
shall wreak vengeance for the covenant,
so that you shall huddle together in
your cities; I will send pestilence
among you, and you shall be delivered
26 into the power of the enemy. When I
deprive you of the sustenance of bread,
there will be ten women to bake your
bread in a single oven, and your bread
shall be doled out in rations, and you
shall not have enough to eat to satisfy
27 you. And if you will not listen to me for
28 all this, but live at enmity with me, I
will live at fierce enmity with you, and
I on my part will punish you seven
29 times for your sins; you will have to eat
the flesh of your sons, and the flesh of
your daughters, too, you will have to
30 eat; I will destroy your high places, cut
down your incense altars, and cast your
carcasses on the ruins of your idols; I
31 will abhor you; I will make your cities
a waste, and desolating your sanctuaries, I will not smell your soothing
32 odors; I will also desolate the land, so
that your enemies who come to live in
33 it shall be amazed at it; while you yourselves I will scatter among the nations,
and unsheathe the sword on you, so
that your land shall become a desola-
34 tion and your cities a waste. Then shall
the land enjoy its sabbaths, as long as it
lies desolate, and you remain in your
enemies' land; then shall the land have
35 rest, and enjoy its sabbaths; as long as
it lies desolate, it shall have rest, which
it did not have on the sabbaths when you
36 lived in it. As for those of you that may
be left, I will inject faintness into their
hearts in the lands of their enemies, so
that the sound of a driven leaf shall
chase them, and they shall flee as from
the sword, and fall when there is no one
37 in pursuit; they shall trip over one another, as if in flight from the sword, although there is no one in pursuit. You
shall have no power to stand before
your enemies; you shall perish among 38
the nations; and the land of your enemies shall consume you. Those of you 39
that may be left shall pine away in
their enemies' lands because of their
iniquity, and also because of their father's iniquities shall they pine away.
But if they confess their iniquity and 40
the iniquity of their fathers through the
perfidy which they committed against
me, and also through living at enmity
with me, so that I in turn had to live at 41
enmity with them, and bring them into
the land of their enemies, or if their uncircumcised heart shall then be humbled, and they shall then make amends
for their iniquity, I will remember my 42
covenant with Jacob, my covenant
with Isaac too, and my covenant with
Abraham also, I will remember, and I
will remember the land. But the land 43
shall be deserted by them, and shall enjoy its sabbaths, while it lies desolate
without them, and they themselves
shall make amends for their iniquity
for the reason, for the very reason that
they rejected my ordinances, and abhorred my statutes. And yet even so, 44
when they are in the land of their enemies, I will not reject them, nor abhor
them, so as to put an end to them by
breaking my covenant with them; for I,
the LORD, am their God; but in their 45
favor I will remember the covenant
with their ancestors, whom I brought
out of the land of Egypt in sight of the
nations, that I might be their God, I,
the LORD.' "
Those were the statutes, ordinances, 46
and laws which the LORD established
between himself and the Israelites
through Moses at Mount Sinai.

THE COMMUTATION OF VOTIVE OFFERINGS AND DUES, 27:1–34

The LORD said to Moses, 27
"Speak to the Israelites, and say to 2
them, 'When anyone makes a special
votive offering to the LORD with the
money value of the persons, the valua- 3
tion of males from twenty years old up
to sixty years old shall be, the valuation shall be fifty shekels of silver, in
terms of the sacred shekel; if it is a fe- 4
male, the valuation shall be thirty
shekels. If they run from five years old 5

up to twenty years old, the valuation
of males shall be twenty shekels, and
6 for females ten shekels. If they run
from a month old up to five years old,
the valuation of males shall be five
shekels of silver, and for females the
valuation shall be three shekels of sil-
7 ver. If they run from sixty years old
and upward, if a male, the valuation
shall be fifteen shekels, and for a female
8 ten shekels. But if he is too poor to pay
the valuation, he must be set before the
priest, and the priest shall value him;
the priest shall value him proportionately to what the maker of the vow
can afford.
9 " 'If it is an animal, of a kind which
may be presented as an offering to the
LORD, whatsoever anyone gives of such
10 to the LORD shall be taboo; he must
not substitute something else for it, nor
exchange it, a good one for a bad one,
or a bad one for a good one; if he should
ever exchange the one animal for another, then both it and the one ex-
11 changed for it shall become taboo. If it
is any unclean animal at all, of a kind
which may not be presented as an offering to the LORD, he shall set the animal
12 before the priest, and the priest shall
value it midway between high and low;
13 as the priest values it, so shall it be. If
he should ever wish to redeem it, he
must add a fifth to the valuation.
14 " 'When anyone consecrates his
house as sacred to the LORD, the priest
shall value it midway between high and
low; as the priest values it, so shall it
15 stand. If the one who dedicated his
house would redeem it, he must add a
fifth of the money value to it, and it
shall be his.
16 " 'If anyone consecrates to the LORD
part of the field that he owns, the valuation shall be proportionate to the seed
for it, fifty shekels of silver in the case
17 of a homer of barley seed. If he consecrates his field from the year of jubilee
18 on, it shall stand as valued; but if he
consecrates his field after the jubilee,
the priest shall reckon for it money proportionate to the years remaining until
the next year of jubilee, and a reduc-
19 tion shall be made in the valuation. If
the person who consecrated the field
should ever wish to redeem it, he must
add a fifth of its money value to it, and
it shall pass to him. If, instead of re- 20
deeming the field, he has sold the field
to another man, it may not be redeemed any more; but the field, when 21
released at the jubilee, shall be sacred
to the LORD, like a field that has been
devoted; the possession of it shall go to
the priest. If one consecrates to the 22
LORD a field that he has bought, which
was not a part of his hereditary estate,
the priest shall reckon for it the amount 23
of the valuation up to the year of jubilee, and he shall give the valuation on
that day as a sacred gift to the LORD.
At the year of jubilee the field shall re- 24
vert to him from whom it was bought,
to whom it belonged as hereditary land.
Every valuation must be in terms of the 25
sacred shekel, the shekel of twenty
gerahs.
" 'However, a firstling among the 26
animals, which as such belongs to the
LORD, no one may consecrate; whether
it is ox or sheep, it belongs to the LORD.
If it belongs to the unclean animals, it 27
must be bought in at its valuation, with
a fifth added to it; and if it is not redeemed, it must be sold at its valuation.
" 'However, nothing at all which 28
anyone devotes to the LORD out of all
his possessions, whether of man or
beast, or of field in his heritage, may be
sold, or redeemed, since everything devoted is most sacred to the LORD. No 29
one at all of men who becomes devoted
may be ransomed; he must be put to
death.
" 'All the dues of the land, whether 30
from the grain of the land or the fruit of
the trees, belong to the LORD; they are
sacred to the LORD. If anyone should 31
ever wish to redeem any of his dues, he
must add a fifth to it. As for all the 32
dues of the herd and flock, all that pass
under the staff, the tenth is sacred to
the LORD. One must not inquire 33
whether it is good or bad, nor exchange
it; if he should ever exchange it, then
both it and the one exchanged for
it shall be taboo, it cannot be redeemed.' "

These were the commands which the 34
LORD gave Moses for the Israelites at
Mount Sinai.

THE BOOK OF NUMBERS

THE CENSUS OF THE ISRAELITES AT SINAI, 1:1—4:49

1 ON the first day of the second
month, in the second year after the exodus from the land
of Egypt, the LORD said to
Moses in the tent of meeting in the
desert of Sinai,
2 "Take a census of the whole Israelite
community, clan by clan, family by
family, counting the various individuals, that is, all the males, a head at a
3 time; all in Israel from twenty years old
and upward who can go out to war, you
and Aaron must number, company by
4 company. One man from each tribe is
to accompany you, each one the head
5 of his family, and the following are the
names of the men who are to stand
with you: from Reuben, Elizur, the son
6 of Shedeur; from Simeon, Shelumiel,
7 the son of Zurishaddai; from Judah,
8 Nahshon, the son of Amminadab; from
Issacher, Nethanel, the son of Zuar;
9 from Zebulun, Eliab, the son of Helon;
10 from the Josephites—from Ephraim,
Elishama, the son of Ammihud, and
from Manasseh, Gamaliel, the son of
11 Pedahzur; from Benjamin, Abidan, the
12 son of Gideoni; from Dan, Ahiezer, the
13 son of Ammishaddai; from Asher, Pa-
14 giel, the son of Ochran; from Gad, Elia-
15 saph, the son of Deuel; from Naphtali,
Ahira, the son of Enan."
16 These were the select men of the community, the leaders of their ancestral
tribes, who were the heads of the clans
17 of Israel. Moses and Aaron took these
men who have been indicated by name,
18 and assembled the whole community
on the first day of the second month,
when they had themselves registered
by clans, family by family, with the
various individuals counted from twenty years old and upward, a head at a
19 time. Moses numbered them in the desert of Sinai, as the LORD had commanded him.
20 The descendants of Reuben, Israel's
first-born, their registration clan by
clan, family by family, as counted by
individuals, a head at a time, that is, all
the males from twenty years old and
upward, all who could go out to war,
those of the tribe of Reuben that were 21
numbered by them were forty-six
thousand five hundred. Of the descend- 22
ants of Simeon, their registration clan
by clan, family by family, as counted
by individuals, a head at a time, that is,
all the males from twenty years old and
upward, all who could go out to war,
those of the tribe of Simeon that were 23
numbered by them were fifty-nine
thousand three hundred. Of the de- 24
scendants of Gad, their registration
clan by clan, family by family, as
counted by individuals, from twenty
years old and upward, all who could go
out to war, those of the tribe of Gad 25
that were numbered by them were
forty-five thousand six hundred and
fifty. Of the descendants of Judah, 26
their registration clan by clan, family
by family, as counted by individuals,
from twenty years old and upward, all
who could go out to war, those of the 27
tribe of Judah that were numbered by
them were seventy-four thousand six
hundred. Of the descendants of Issa- 28
char, their registration clan by clan,
family by family, as counted by individuals, from twenty years old and upward, all who could go out to war, those 29
of the tribe of Issachar that were numbered by them were fifty-four thousand
four hundred. Of the descendants of 30
Zebulun, their registration clan by
clan, family by family, as counted by
individuals, from twenty years old and
upward, all who could go out to war,
those of the tribe of Zebulun that were 31
numbered by them were fifty-seven
thousand four hundred. Of the de- 32
scendants of Joseph—of the descendants of Ephraim, their registration clan
by clan, family by family, as counted
by individuals, from twenty years old
and upward, all who could go out to
war, those of the tribe of Ephraim that 33

were numbered by them were forty
34 thousand five hundred; and of the descendants of Manasseh, their registration clan by clan, family by family, as
counted by individuals, from twenty
years old and upward, all who could go
35 out to war, those of the tribe of Manasseh that were numbered by them were
36 thirty-two thousand two hundred. Of
the descendants of Benjamin, their registration clan by clan, family by family,
as counted by individuals from twenty
37 years old and upward, all who could go
out to war, those of the tribe of Benjamin that were numbered by them were
38 thirty-five thousand four hundred. Of
the descendants of Dan, their registration clan by clan, family by family, as
counted by individuals, from twenty
years old and upward, all who could go
39 out to war, those of the tribe of Dan
that were numbered by them were six-
40 ty-two thousand seven hundred. Of the
descendants of Asher, their registration
clan by clan, family by family, as
counted by individuals, from twenty
years old and upward, all who could go
41 out to war, those of the tribe of Asher
that were numbered by them were for-
42 ty-one thousand five hundred. Of the
descendants of Naphtali, their registration clan by clan, family by family, as
counted by individuals, from twenty
years old and upward, all who could go
43 out to war, those of the tribe of Naphtali that were numbered by them were
fifty-three thousand four hundred.

44 These were the ones numbered,
whom Moses numbered, along with
Aaron and the twelve leaders of Israel,
there being one from each tribe, to rep-
45 resent his family. All the Israelites that
were numbered family by family, from
twenty years old and upward, all in Is-
46 rael who could go out to war, all that
were numbered were six hundred and
three thousand five hundred and fifty.

47 The Levites, however, were not
numbered by their ancestral tribes
48 along with the others, since the LORD
had said to Moses,

49 "Under no circumstances must you
number the tribe of Levi, nor take a
census of it with the other Israelites;
50 but you must put the Levites in charge
of the dwelling of the decrees and all its
equipment and all its belongings; they
are to carry the dwelling and all its
equipment, and take care of it, encamping around the dwelling; when- 51
ever the dwelling has to move on, the
Levites must take it down, and whenever the dwelling has to be pitched, the
Levites must put it up; any layman
who approaches it must be put to
death. The Israelites must encamp by 52
companies, each on his own camping-
ground and with his own standard,
while the Levites must encamp around 53
the dwelling of the decrees, that there
may be no outburst of wrath against
the Israelite community; and the Levites must take charge of the dwelling
of the decrees."

The Israelites did so; they did just as 54
the LORD commanded Moses.

The LORD said to Moses and Aaron, **2**
"The Israelites must encamp, each 2
by his own standard, marked with the
family device, encamping around the
tent of meeting facing it. Those who 3
are to encamp on the east side, toward
the dawn, are the standard of the camp
of Judah, arranged by companies, with
Nahshon, the son of Amminadab, as
leader of the Judeans, whose host, that 4
is, those of them that were numbered,
amounted to seventy-four thousand six
hundred. Those who are to encamp 5
next to him are the tribe of Issachar,
with Nethanel, the son of Zuar, as leader of the Issacharites, whose host, that 6
is, those in it that were numbered,
amounted to fifty-four thousand four
hundred. Then the tribe of Zebulun, 7
with Eliab, the son of Helon, as leader
of the Zebulunites, whose host, that is, 8
those in it that were numbered,
amounted to fifty-seven thousand four
hundred. The total number of those 9
belonging to the camp of Judah is one
hundred and eighty-six thousand four
hundred, arranged by companies; they
are always to be the first to set out.

"To the south is to be the standard 10
of the camp of Reuben arranged
by companies, with Elizur, the son of
Shedeur, as leader of the Reubenites,
whose host, that is, those in it that 11
were numbered, amounted to forty-six
thousand five hundred. Those who are 12
to encamp next to him are the tribe of
Simeon, with Shelumiel, the son of Zurishaddai, as leader of the Simeonites,
whose host, that is those of them that 13
were numbered, amounted to fifty-nine
thousand three hundred. Then the 14
tribe of Gad with Eliasaph, the son of

15 Deuel, as leader of the Gadites, whose
host, that is, those of them that were
numbered, amounted to forty-five
16 thousand six hundred and fifty. The total number of those belonging to the
camp of Reuben is one hundred and fif-
ty-one thousand four hundred and fifty,
17 arranged by companies; they are always to be the second to set out, after
which the tent of meeting is to move
forward, with the army of the Levites,
in the middle of the other armies; they
are to set out exactly as they encamp,
each in his place, one standard after another.
18 "To the west is to be the standard of
the camp of Ephraim, arranged by
companies, with Elishama, the son of
Ammihud, as leader of the Ephraimites,
19 whose host, that is, those of them that
were numbered, amounted to forty
20 thousand five hundred. Next to him is
to be the tribe of Manasseh, with Gamaliel, the son of Pedahzur, as leader
21 of the Manassites, whose host, that is,
those of them that were numbered,
amounted to thirty-two thousand two
22 hundred. Then the tribe of Benjamin,
with Abidan, the son of Gideoni, as
23 leader of the Benjaminites, whose host,
that is, those of them that were numbered, amounted to thirty-five thou-
24 sand four hundred. The total number
of those belonging to the camp of
Ephraim is one hundred and eight
thousand one hundred, arranged by
companies; they are always to be the
third to set out.
25 "To the north is to be the standard of
the camp of Dan, arranged by companies, with Ahiezer, the son of Ammishaddai, as leader of the Danites,
26 whose host, that is, those of them that
were numbered, amounted to sixty-two
27 thousand seven hundred. Those who
are to encamp next to him are the tribe
of Asher, with Pagiel, the son of Ochran,
28 as leader of the Asherites, whose host,
that is, those of them that were numbered, amounted to forty-one thousand
29 five hundred. Then the tribe of Naphtali, with Ahira, the son of Enan, as
30 leader of the Naphtalites, whose host,
that is, those of them that were numbered, amounted to fifty-three thou-
31 sand four hundred. The total number
of those belonging to the camp of Dan
is one hundred and fifty-seven thousand six hundred; they are always to set
out in the rear, one standard after another."
(Such were the Israelites as num- 32
bered by families; the total of the
armies as numbered by companies
amounted to six hundred and three
thousand five hundred and fifty. The 33
Levites, however, were not numbered
with the other Israelites, as the LORD
had commanded Moses.)
The Israelites did so: just as the 34
LORD had commanded Moses, they encamped by standards, and they set out
clan by clan, family by family.
The following are the descendants of 3
Aaron and Moses at the time that the
LORD spoke to Moses on Mount Sinai.
These are the names of the sons of Aar- 2
on: Nadab, the first-born, Abihu, Eleazar, and Ithamar. These were the 3
names of the sons of Aaron, the priests
that were anointed, who were installed
to serve as priests. Nadab and Abihu 4
met death at the hands of the LORD,
because they offered improper fire before the LORD in the desert of Sinai;
they had no children. Eleazar and Ithamar served as priests during the lifetime of their father Aaron.
The LORD said to Moses, 5
"Have the tribe of Levi come for- 6
ward and take their stand before Aaron, the priest, to minister to him; they 7
shall do duty for him and for the whole
community before the tent of meeting,
to look after the dwelling, taking 8
charge of all the equipment of the tent
of meeting, as well as the duties for the
Israelites, to look after the dwelling.
You must assign the Levites to Aaron 9
and his sons; they are to be assigned to
him from the rest of the Israelites as
servants. Aaron and his sons you are 10
to appoint to take charge of their
priestly duties; any layman who dares
to approach must be put to death."
The LORD said to Moses, 11
"See, I am taking the Levites from 12
among the Israelites instead of all the
first-born of the Israelites, those who
first open the womb; the Levites belong
to me, because all the first-born belong 13
to me; at the time that I slew all the
first-born in the land of Egypt, I consecrated to myself all the first-born in
Israel, both man and beast; they belong
to me, to myself, the LORD."
In the desert of Sinai, the LORD said 14
to Moses,

15 "Number the descendants of Levi
family by family, clan by clan, numbering every male from a month old and
upward."
16 So Moses numbered them by command of the LORD, as he was com-
17 manded. The following were the sons
of Levi in the order of their names:
18 Gershon, Kohath, and Merari; while
these were the names of the sons of
Gershon arranged by clans: Libni and
19 Shimei; the sons of Kohath arranged
by clans were Amram, Izhar, Hebron,
20 the Uzziel; and the sons of Merari arranged by clans were Mahli and Mushi.
These were the clans of the Levites,
family by family.
21 To Gershon belonged the clan of the
Libnites, and the clan of the Shimeites;
these were the clans of the Gershonites.
22 Those of them that were numbered in
the census of all the males, from a
month old and upward, those of them
that were numbered amounted to seven
23 thousand five hundred. The clans of
the Gershonites were to encamp behind
24 the dwelling to the west, with Eliasaph,
the son of Lael, as leader of the families
25 belonging to the Gershonites, and in the
tent of meeting the sons of Gershon had
to take charge of the dwelling, the tent
with its covering, the screen for the
26 doorway of the tent of meeting, the
hangings of the court, the screen for the
doorway into the court inclosing the
dwelling and the altar, and the ropes
for it, in short all its appurtenances.
27 To Kohath belonged the clan of the
Amramites, the clan of the Izharites,
the clan of the Hebronites, and the clan
of the Uzzielites; these were the clans of
28 the Kohathites. Those of them that
were numbered in the census of all the
males, from a month old and upward,
amounted to eight thousand six hundred, who had charge of the sacred ob-
29 jects. The clans of the sons of Kohath
were to encamp on the south side of the
30 dwelling, with Elizaphan, the son of
Uzziel, as leader of the families belong-
31 ing to the clans of the Kohathites, and
they had to take charge of the ark, the
table, the lampstand, the altars, the
utensils of the sanctuary that were used
for ministering, and the screen, in short
32 all their appurtenances, with Eleazar,
the son of Aaron, the priest, as chief
leader of the Levites and supervisor of
those having charge of the sacred objects.
To Merari belonged the clan of the 33
Mahlites and the clan of the Mushites;
these were the clans of Merari. Those 34
of them that were numbered in the census of all the males, from a month old
and upward, amounted to six thousand
two hundred, with Zuriel, the son of 35
Abihail, as leader of the families belonging to the clans of Merari. They 36
were to encamp on the north side of the
dwelling, and the sons of Merari were
given charge of the frames of the dwelling, its bars, its columns, its pedestals,
and all its fittings, in short all its appurtenances, as well as the columns 37
around the court, their pedestals, pegs,
and ropes.
Those that were to encamp in front 38
of the dwelling, to the east, in front of
the tent of meeting toward the dawn,
were Moses and Aaron with his sons,
who had charge of the sanctuary in the
matter of duties for the Israelites; any
layman who dared to approach was to
be put to death.
The total of the Levites numbered, 39
whom Moses and Aaron numbered by
command of the LORD, clan by clan,
all the males from a month old and upward, amounted to twenty-two thousand.
The LORD said to Moses, 40
"Number all the first-born males of
the Israelites from a month old and upward, and take a census of them by individuals. But you are to take the Le- 41
vites for me, myself, the LORD, instead
of all the first-born among the Israelites, and the cattle of the Levites instead of all the first-born among the
cattle of the Israelites."
So Moses numbered all the first-born 42
among the Israelites, as the LORD
commanded him; and all the first-born 43
males of those that were numbered, as
counted by individuals, from a month
old and upward, amounted to twenty-
two thousand two hundred and seventy-three.
Then the LORD said to Moses, 44
"Take the Levites instead of all the 45
first-born among the Israelites, and the
cattle of the Levites instead of their
cattle, and the Levites shall belong to
me, to myself, the LORD. As redemp- 46
tion for the two hundred and seventy-
three of the first-born of the Israelites

that exceed the number of the Levites,
47 you must take five shekels each per
head, taking it in sacred shekels, the
48 shekel of twenty gerahs, and you must
give the money for the redemption of
those in excess among them to Aaron
and his sons."
49 So Moses took the redemption-
money from those that were left over
from the number redeemed by the Le-
50 vites, taking from the first-born of the
Israelites the sum of one thousand
three hundred and sixty-five shekels in
51 sacred shekels, and Moses gave the re-
demption-money to Aaron and his sons
at the command of the LORD, as the
LORD had commanded Moses.
4 Then the LORD said to Moses and
Aaron,
2 "Take a census of the Kohathite division of the Levites, clan by clan,
3 family by family, from thirty years old
up to fifty, all who entered the service
4 to do work in the tent of meeting. The
following are to be the duties of the
Kohathites in the tent of meeting with
5 regard to the most sacred object: when
the camp is about to break up, Aaron
and his sons must go in and take down
the veil of the screen and cover the ark
6 of the decrees with it; they must then
place a covering of porpoise skin over it,
and on top of that spread a cloth made
entirely of violet material, and put its
7 poles in place. Over the table of Presence-bread they must spread a cloth of
violet material, putting the plates on it,
the cups, the flagons, and the libation-
bowls, with the ever present bread re-
8 maining on it; they must then spread a
cloth of scarlet material over them, and
cover this with a covering of porpoise
9 skin, and put its poles in place. Taking
a cloth of violet material, they must
cover the lampstand for the lights,
along with its lamps, snuffers, snuffdishes, and all its oil containers from
10 which it is supplied; they must then
put it and all its fittings into a covering
of porpoise skin, and place it on a
11 stretcher. Over the gold altar they
must spread a cloth of violet material,
and then cover it with a covering of
porpoise skin, and put its poles in place.
12 Taking all the service utensils that were
used in the service in the sanctuary,
they must put them in a cloth of violet
material, and cover them with a covering of porpoise skin, and place them on
a stretcher. They must remove the 13
ashes from the other altar, and spread
a purple cloth over it, placing on it all 14
its utensils that were used in the service
connected with it, the fire-pans, forks,
shovels, and basins, all the utensils of
the altar; they must then spread a covering of porpoise skin over it, and put
its poles in place. When Aaron and his 15
sons have finished packing up the sacred objects and all the fittings of the
sacred objects when the camp breaks up,
after that the Kohathites must come to
carry them, but without touching the
sacred objects themselves, in which
case they would die. These are to be
the duties of the Kohathites in the tent
of meeting. Eleazar, the son of Aaron, 16
the priest, is to have charge of the oil
for the lights, the fragrant incense, the
ever present cereal-offering, and the
anointing oil; he is to have charge of
the whole dwelling and of all that is in
it, whether it pertains to the sanctuary
itself or its fittings."
The LORD said to Moses and Aaron, 17
"Do not cut the tribe of Kohathite 18
families off from the Levites; but that 19
they may live, and not die, when they
approach the most sacred objects, deal
with them as follows: Aaron and his
sons are to go in, assigning to each of
them his task and his load; but they 20
themselves must not go in to look on
while the sacred objects are being
packed, in which case they would die."
The LORD said to Moses, 21
"Take a census of the Gershonites 22
also, family by family, clan by clan,
numbering those from thirty years old 23
up to fifty, all who undertook to engage
in service to do work in the tent of
meeting. The following are to be the 24
duties of the Gershonite clans in serving and carrying: they must carry the 25
curtains of the dwelling, the tent of
meeting with its covering and the covering of porpoise skin that is on top of it,
the screen for the doorway of the tent
of meeting, the hangings of the court, 26
the screen for the doorway of the gate
of the court which incloses the dwelling
and the altar, with the ropes for them
and all the appurtenances connected
with their service; whatever needs to be
done with these things, they must do.
All the duties of the Gershonites, in all 27
that they have to carry and in all that
they have to do, are to be under the

direction of Aaron and his sons, and
you are to appoint the latter over them
to look out for what they are to carry.
28 These are to be the duties of the Gershonite clans in the tent of meeting,
and their work is to be under the supervision of Ithamar, the son of Aaron, the
priest."
29 "As for the Merarites, you must
number them, clan by clan, family by
30 family, numbering those from thirty
years old up to fifty, all who entered the
service to do the work of the tent of
31 meeting. In the course of all their duties in the tent of meeting the following
are to be their responsibility for transport: the frames of the dwelling, with
32 its bars, columns, and pedestals, the
columns of the surrounding court, with
their pedestals, pegs, and ropes, in short
all their fittings and all their appurtenances; you must tell them off individually to the objects that are to be
33 their responsibility for transport. These
are to be the duties of the Merarite
clans in the course of all their duties in
the tent of meeting, under the supervision of Ithamar, the son of Aaron, the
priest."
34 So Moses and Aaron and the leaders
of the community numbered the Kohathites clan by clan and family by
35 family, from thirty years old up to fifty,
all who entered the service for work in
36 the tent of meeting; and those that
were numbered by them, clan by clan,
amounted to two thousand seven hun-
37 dred and fifty. These were the Kohathite clans that were numbered, all who
served in the tent of meeting, whom
Moses and Aaron numbered by the
command of the LORD through
Moses.
38 The Gershonites that were numbered, clan by clan, and family by fam-
39 ily, from thirty years old up to fifty, all
who entered the service for work in the
40 tent of meeting—those of them that
were numbered, clan by clan, family
by family, amounted to two thousand
41 six hundred and thirty. These were the
Gershonite clans that were numbered,
all who served in the tent of meeting,
whom Moses and Aaron numbered at
the command of the LORD.
42 The Merarite clans that were numbered, clan by clan, family by family,
43 from thirty years old up to fifty, all
who entered the service for work in the
tent of meeting—those of them that 44
were numbered, clan by clan, amounted
to three thousand two hundred. These 45
were the Merarite clans that were
numbered, whom Moses and Aaron
numbered at the command of the
LORD through Moses.
All the Levites that were numbered, 46
whom Moses and Aaron and the leaders
of Israel numbered, clan by clan, family
by family, from thirty years old up to 47
fifty, all who undertook to do the work
of serving and the work of transport in
the tent of meeting—those of them 48
that were numbered amounted to eight
thousand five hundred and eighty. At 49
the command of the LORD through
Moses, they were appointed each to his
proper task of serving or carrying,
those namely that were numbered by
him, as the LORD had commanded
Moses

VARIOUS LAWS AND REGULATIONS, 5:1—6:27

The LORD said to Moses, 5
"Command the Israelites to drive 2
from the camp every leper, everyone
who has a discharge, and everyone unclean through contact with a corpse;
you must drive out both male and fe- 3
male, driving them outside the camp,
that they may not defile the camp of
those in whose midst I myself dwell."
The Israelites did so; they drove 4
them outside the camp; the Israelites
did just as the LORD had told Moses.
The LORD said to Moses, 5
"Say to the Israelites, 'If a man or 6
woman commits any of the sins of mankind, by breaking faith with the LORD,
and that person becomes conscious of
guilt, he must confess the sin that he 7
has committed, and restore his ill-gotten gains in its original amount, adding
a fifth to it and giving it to him whom
he wronged. But if the man has no 8
next-of-kin to whom the property
wrongfully held may be restored, the
property wrongfully held that is to be
restored must go to the LORD, to the
priest, in addition to the atonement
ram with which atonement is to be
made for him. And every contribu- 9
tion, indeed all the sacred gifts that the
Israelites present to the priest shall become his property; anyone's sacred 10

offerings shall become his; whatever
anyone gives to the priest becomes
his.' "
11 The LORD said to Moses,
12 "Speak to the Israelites, and say to
them, 'If any man's wife goes wrong
13 and proves unfaithful to him, and another
man lies with her in sexual intercourse,
and it is hidden from the eyes of
her husband, and she is undetected, although
she has defiled herself, and there
are no witnesses against her, since she
14 was not caught in the act, and a fit of
suspicion comes over him and he becomes
suspicious of his wife, since she
has defiled herself, or a fit of suspicion
comes over him and he becomes suspicious
of his wife, although she may not
15 have defiled herself, the man must
bring his wife to the priest, and bring
her offering for her, a tenth of an ephah
of barley meal, without pouring oil on
it or adding frankincense to it, since it
is a cereal-offering having to do with
suspicion, a memorial cereal-offering,
16 intended to recall iniquity; the priest
must then have her come up and take
17 her stand before the LORD, whereupon
the priest must take holy water in an
earthen jar, and taking some of the dust
that is on the floor of the dwelling, the
18 priest must put it in the water; the
priest must then have the woman stand
before the LORD, loosening the hair of
the woman's head, and putting the
memorial cereal-offering in her hands
(that is, the cereal-offering having to do
with suspicion), with the priest himself
holding the water that produces pain,
19 that brings a curse; the priest must
then have her take an oath, saying to
the woman, "If no man has lain with
you, and if you have not turned aside to
indecent acts while married to your
husband, be immune to this water that
20 produces pain, that brings a curse; but
if you have gone wrong while married
to your husband, and if you have defiled
yourself, and some man besides
your husband has lain with you"—
21 then the priest must have the woman
take the oath of execration, and the
priest must say to the woman—"may
the LORD make you an execration and
an oath among your people by making
you have miscarriages, along with a
22 womb easily fertilized; may this water
that brings a curse enter your bowels,
causing your womb to be easily fertilized,
but making you have miscarriages";
and the woman must say, "So
be it; so be it." The priest must write 23
these curses in a book, and then wash
them off into the water that produces
pain; he must make the woman drink 24
the water that produces pain, that
brings a curse, so that the water that
brings a curse may enter into her and
cause pain. The priest must then take 25
the cereal-offering having to do with
suspicion from the woman's hand, and
wave the cereal-offering before the
LORD, and bringing it up to the altar,
the priest must take a handful of the 26
cereal-offering as the memorial part of
it, and burn it on the altar, after which
he must make the woman drink the water.
When he has made her drink the 27
water, if she has defiled herself and has
been unfaithful to her husband, then the
water that brings a curse, on entering
into her, shall cause pain, her womb
shall become easily fertilized, but she
shall have miscarriages, so that the
woman shall become an execration
among her people. But if the woman 28
is not defiled, but pure, she shall be immune,
and shall bear children. This is 29
the law in cases of suspicion, when a woman
while married to her husband goes
wrong and defiles herself, or when a fit 30
of suspicion comes over a man and he
becomes suspicious of his wife, in which
case he shall have the woman stand before
the LORD, and the priest shall deal
with her in strict accord with this law.
The man shall be free from guilt, but 31
that woman must answer for her
guilt.' "

The LORD said to Moses, 6
"Speak to the Israelites, and say to 2
them, 'If a man or woman makes a special
vow, the vow of a Nazirite, to set
himself apart to the LORD, he must abstain 3
from wine and liquor, drinking no
fermented wine, nor hard liquor, and
drinking no grape-juice at all, nor eating
fresh grapes or dried; as long as he 4
remains a Nazirite, he must eat nothing
that is borne by the grape-vine, neither
unripe grapes nor tendrils. As long as 5
his vow to be a Nazirite holds, no razor
is to be used on his head; until the time
is completed for which he set himself
apart to the LORD, he is to be consecrated;
he must let the locks of hair on
his head hang loose. For all the time 6
that he set himself apart to the LORD

7 he must not come near a dead body; he
must not defile himself for his father or
mother, for his brother or sister, when
they die; for a crown to his God rests on
8 his head. As long as he remains a
Nazirite, he remains consecrated to the
9 LORD. If someone should die very suddenly beside him, and he defiles his
head with its crown, he must shave his
head on the day of his cleansing, shav-
10 ing it on the seventh day, and on the
eighth day he must bring two turtle-
doves or two young pigeons to the
priest at the doorway of the tent of
11 meeting; the priest shall offer one as a
sin-offering and the other as a burnt-
offering, and so make atonement for
him, because he incurred sin through
the corpse. That same day he must re-
12 consecrate his head, and set apart to
the LORD the period that he was to be
a Nazirite, bringing a yearling male
lamb as a guilt-offering; the previous
period becomes void, since his crown
was defiled.
13 "The following is the law for the
Nazirite when the period is completed
for which he was to be a Nazirite: he
must be brought to the doorway of the
14 tent of meeting, and then he must present his offering to the LORD, one perfect yearling male lamb as a burnt-
offering, one perfect yearling ewe-lamb
as a sin-offering, one perfect ram as a
15 thank-offering, a basket of unleavened
bread, cakes of fine flour mixed with
oil, and unleavened wafers smeared
with oil, along with their cereal-offering
16 and libations. The priest must then
bring them into the presence of the
LORD, offering his sin-offering and his
17 burnt-offering, and offering the ram as
a thanksgiving sacrifice to the LORD,
with the basket of unleavened cakes, as
well as its cereal-offering and libation.
18 Then the Nazirite must shave off the
crown of his head at the doorway of the
tent of meeting, and taking his crown,
the hair of his head, lay it on the fire
which is under the thanksgiving sacri-
19 fice. The priest must take the shoulder
of the ram when it is cooked, one unleavened cake from the basket, and one
unleavened wafer, and place them in
the hands of the Nazirite after he has
20 shaved off his crown; then the priest
must wave them as a wave-offering before the LORD, these being consecrated
to the priest, along with the waved
breast and the thigh of the contribution. Thereafter the Nazirite may drink
wine. This is the law for the Nazirite 21
who takes a vow—his offering to the
LORD as a Nazirite, besides anything
else that he can afford; he must carry
out the terms of the vow that he took
in accord with the law pertaining to
his position as a Nazarite.' "
The LORD said to Moses, 22
"Say to Aaron and his sons, 'This is 23
the way that you are to bless the Israelites; say to them,
"The LORD bless you, and guard you; 24
The LORD make his face to shine 25
upon you, and be gracious unto
you;
The LORD lift up his countenance 26
upon you, and make you prosper!" '
"So shall they invoke my name in be- 27
half of the Israelites, and I will bless
them."

THE OFFERINGS OF THE TRIBAL LEADERS,

7:1–89

On the day that Moses had finished 7
the erection of the dwelling, and had
anointed and consecrated it and all its
equipment, along with the altar and all
its equipment, having anointed and
consecrated them, the leaders of Israel, 2
the heads of their families (that is, the
leaders of the tribes, those that were at
the head of those numbered), made
offerings, bringing their offerings into 3
the presence of the LORD, six draught
wagons and twelve oxen, a wagon for
every two leaders and an ox for each of
them; and they presented them in front
of the dwelling. Then the LORD said 4
to Moses,
"Take the things from them, that 5
they may be used to do the work of the
tent of meeting, and give them to the
Levites, to each in proportion to the
amount of his work."
So Moses took the wagons and oxen, 6
and gave them to the Levites; two 7
wagons and four oxen he gave to the
Gershonites in proportion to the
amount of their work, and four wagons 8
and eight oxen he gave to the Merarites
in proportion to the amount of their
work, under the direction of Ithamar,
the son of Aaron, the priest; but to the 9
Kohathites he gave nothing, because

the care of the sacred objects devolved
upon them, and they had to carry them
on their shoulders.
10 The leaders also presented dedication
gifts for the altar on the day that it was
anointed, making their offerings before
11 the altar, whereupon the LORD said to
Moses,

"They must present their offerings,
one leader each day, for the dedication
of the altar."
12 The one who presented his offering
on the first day was Nahshon, the son of
Amminadab, belonging to the tribe of
13 Judah; his offering was one silver plate,
weighing one hundred and thirty shekels, one silver basin of seventy shekels,
in terms of the sacred shekel, both of
them full of fine flour mixed with oil as
14 a cereal-offering; one gold cup of ten
15 shekels, full of incense; one young bullock, one ram, and one yearling male
16 lamb, as a burnt-offering; one male
17 goat as a sin-offering; and as a thanksgiving sacrifice, two oxen, five rams,
five he-goats, and five yearling male
lambs. This was the offering of Nahshon, the son of Amminadab.
18 On the second day Nethanel, the son
of Zuar, the leader of Issachar, made an
19 offering, presenting as his offering one
silver plate, weighing one hundred and
thirty shekels, one silver basin of seventy shekels, in terms of the sacred
shekel, both of them full of fine flour
20 mixed with oil as a cereal-offering; one
gold cup of ten shekels, full of incense;
21 one young bullock, one ram, and one
yearling male lamb, as a burnt-offering;
22 23 one male goat as a sin-offering; and as a
thanksgiving sacrifice, two oxen, five
rams, five he-goats, and five yearling
male lambs. This was the offering of
Nethanel, the son of Zuar.
24 On the third day came the leader of
the Zebulunites, Eliab, the son of He-
25 lon, with his offering, one silver plate
weighing one hundred and thirty shekels, one silver basin of seventy shekels,
in terms of the sacred shekel, both of
them full of fine flour mixed with oil as
26 a cereal-offering; one gold cup of ten
27 shekels, full of incense; one young bullock, one ram, and one yearling male
28 lamb, as a burnt-offering; one male goat
29 as a sin-offering; and as a thanksgiving
sacrifice, two oxen, five rams, five he-
goats, and five yearling male lambs.
This was the offering of Eliab, the son
of Helon.

On the fourth day came the leader of 30
the Reubenites, Elizur, the son of Shedeur, with his offering, one silver plate, 31
weighing one hundred and thirty shekels, one silver basin of seventy shekels,
in terms of the sacred shekel, both of
them full of fine flour mixed with oil as
a cereal-offering; one gold cup of ten 32
shekels, full of incense; one young bul- 33
lock, one ram, and one yearling male
lamb, as a burnt-offering; one male 34
goat as a sin-offering; and as a thanks- 35
giving sacrifice, two oxen, five rams,
five he-goats, and five yearling male
lambs. This was the offering of Elizur,
the son of Shedeur.

On the fifth day came the leader of 36
the Simeonites, Shelumiel, the son of
Zurishaddai, with his offering, one sil- 37
ver plate, weighing one hundred and
thirty shekels, one silver basin of seventy shekels, in terms of the sacred
shekel, both of them full of fine flour
mixed with oil as a cereal-offering; one 38
gold cup of ten shekels, full of incense;
one young bullock, one ram, and one 39
yearling male lamb, as a burnt-offering;
one male goat as a sin-offering; and 40 41
as a thanksgiving sacrifice, two oxen,
five rams, five he-goats, and five yearling male lambs. This was the offering
of Shelumiel, the son of Zurishaddai

On the sixth day came the leader of 42
the Gadites, Eliasaph, the son of Deuel,
with his offering, one silver plate, 43
weighing one hundred and thirty shekels, one silver basin of seventy shekels,
in terms of the sacred shekel, both of
them full of fine flour mixed with oil as
a cereal-offering; one gold cup of ten 44
shekels, full of incense; one young bul- 45
lock, one ram, and one yearling male
lamb, as a burnt-offering; one male 46
goat as a sin-offering; and as a thanks- 47
giving sacrifice, two oxen, five rams,
five he-goats, and five yearling male
lambs. This was the offering of Eliasaph, the son of Deuel.

On the seventh day came the leader 48
of the Ephraimites, Elishama, the son
of Ammihud, with his offering, one sil- 49
ver plate, weighing one hundred and
thirty shekels, one silver basin of seventy shekels, in terms of the sacred shekel,
both of them full of fine flour mixed
with oil as a cereal-offering; one gold 50
cup of ten shekels, full of incense; one 51

young bullock, one ram, and one yearling
52 male lamb, as a burnt-offering; one male
53 goat as a sin-offering; and as a thanksgiving sacrifice, two oxen, five rams,
five he-goats, and five yearling male
lambs. This was the offering of Elishama, the son of Ammihud.
54 On the eighth day came the leader of
the Manassites, Gamaliel, the son of
55 Pedahzur, with his offering, one silver
plate, weighing one hundred and thirty
shekels, one silver basin of seventy
shekels, in terms of the sacred shekel,
both of them full of fine flour mixed
56 with oil as a cereal-offering; one gold
57 cup of ten shekels, full of incense; one
young bullock, one ram, and one year-
58 ling male lamb, as a burnt-offering; one
59 male goat as a sin-offering; and as a
thanksgiving sacrifice, two oxen, five
rams, five he-goats, and five yearling
male lambs. This was the offering of
Gamaliel, the son of Pedahzur.
60 On the ninth day came the leader of
the Benjaminites, Abidan, the son of
61 Gideoni, with his offering, one silver
plate, weighing one hundred and thirty
shekels, one silver basin of seventy
shekels, in terms of the sacred shekel,
both of them full of fine flour mixed
62 with oil as a cereal-offering; one gold
63 cup of ten shekels, full of incense; one
young bullock, one ram, and one year-
64 ling male lamb, as a burnt-offering; one
65 male goat as a sin-offering; and as a
thanksgiving sacrifice, two oxen, five
rams, five he-goats, and five yearling
male lambs. This was the offering of
Abidan, the son of Gideoni.
66 On the tenth day came the leader of
the Danites, Ahiezer, the son of Ammi-
67 shaddai, with his offering, one silver
plate, weighing one hundred and thirty
shekels, one silver basin of seventy
shekels, in terms of the sacred shekel,
both of them full of fine flour mixed
68 with oil as a cereal-offering; one gold
69 cup of ten shekels, full of incense; one
young bullock, one ram, and one year-
70 ling male lamb, as a burnt-offering; one
71 male goat as a sin-offering; and as a
thanksgiving sacrifice, two oxen, five
rams, five he-goats, and five yearling
male lambs. This was the offering of
Ahiezer, the son of Ammishaddai.
72 On the eleventh day came the leader
of the Asherites, Pagiel, the son of
73 Ochran, with his offering, one silver
plate, weighing one hundred and thirty
shekels, one silver basin of seventy
shekels, in terms of the sacred shekel,
both of them full of fine flour mixed
with oil as a cereal-offering; one gold 74
cup of ten shekels, full of incense; one 75
young bullock, one ram, and one yearling male lamb, as a burnt-offering; one 76
male goat as a sin-offering; and as a 77
thanksgiving sacrifice, two oxen, five
rams, five he-goats, and five yearling
male lambs. This was the offering of
Pagiel, the son of Ochran.
On the twelfth day came the leader 78
of the Naphtalites, Ahira, the son of
Enan, with his offering, one silver plate, 79
weighing one hundred and thirty shekels, one silver basin of seventy shekels,
in terms of the sacred shekel, both of
them full of fine flour mixed with oil as
a cereal-offering; one gold cup of ten 80
shekels, full of incense; one young bul- 81
lock, one ram, and one yearling male
lamb, as a burnt-offering; one male goat 82
as a sin-offering; and as a thanksgiving 83
sacrifice, two oxen, five rams, five he-
goats, and five yearling male lambs.
This was the offering of Ahira, the son
of Enan.
This was the dedication-gift from the 84
leaders of Israel for the altar on the day
that it was anointed, twelve silver
plates, twelve silver basins, twelve gold
cups, each silver plate weighing one 85
hundred and thirty shekels, and each
basin seventy, the total amount of silver in the vessels being two thousand
four hundred shekels, in terms of the
sacred shekel; twelve gold cups, full of 86
incense, weighing ten shekels per cup,
in terms of the sacred shekel, the total
amount of gold in the cups being one
hundred and twenty shekels; all the 87
animals for burnt-offerings, twelve bullocks, twelve rams, and twelve yearling
male lambs, with their cereal-offerings;
twelve male goats as sin-offerings; all 88
the animals for thanksgiving sacrifices,
twenty-four bullocks, sixty rams, sixty
he-goats, and sixty yearling male
lambs. This was the dedication-gift for
the altar after it was anointed.
When Moses went into the tent of 89
meeting to converse with him, he heard
the voice speaking to him from above
the propitiatory that was on the ark of
the decrees, from between the two cherubim; and he spoke to him.

VARIOUS INSTRUCTIONS,
8:1—10:10

8 The LORD said to Moses,
2 "Speak to Aaron, and say to him,
'When you put up the lamps, the seven
lamps are to shed light on the space in
front of the lampstand.' "
3 Aaron did so; he put up the lamps of
the lampstand so as to shed light on the
space in front of it, as the LORD had
4 commanded Moses. And this was the
material of the lampstand, gold beaten
work, being beaten work in both its
base and its calyxes; Moses had made
the lampstand in strict accord with the
pattern that the LORD had shown him.
5 The LORD said to Moses,
6 "Separate the Levites from the Is-
7 raelites, and cleanse them; and this is
what you are to do to them in cleansing
them: the water for use in case of sin
is to be sprinkled on them; they are to
use a razor all over their bodies, and
wash their clothes, and cleanse them-
8 selves; they must then take a young
bullock, with its cereal-offering consisting of fine flour mixed with oil, while
you take another young bullock as a
9 sin-offering; you must present the Levites before the tent of meeting; assembling the whole Israelite communi-
10 ty, you must present the Levites before the LORD; the Israelites shall lay
11 their hands on the Levites, and Aaron
shall present the Levites before the
LORD as a wave-offering from the Israelites, that they may be qualified to
12 perform the service of the LORD; the
Levites shall lay their hands on the
heads of the bullocks; then sacrifice the
one as a sin-offering, and the other as a
burnt-offering, to the LORD, to make
13 atonement for the Levites. You must
then have the Levites stand before
Aaron and his sons, who shall present
them as a wave-offering to the LORD.
14 Thus shall you separate the Levites
from the rest of the Israelites that the
15 Levites may become mine. Thereafter
the Levites may enter upon their duties
in the tent of meeting, when you have
cleansed them, and presented them as a
16 wave-offering; for they have been assigned to me from the rest of the Israelites as servants; I have taken them for
myself instead of all who first open the
womb, the first-born of all of the Is-
17 raelites; for all the first-born among the
Israelites belong to me, both man and
beast; it was on the day that I slew all
the first-born in the land of Egypt that
I consecrated them to myself; so I have 18
taken the Levites instead of all the first-
born among the Israelites, assigning the 19
Levites from among the Israelites as
servants to Aaron and his sons to perform the service for the Israelites in the
tent of meeting and to make atonement
for the Israelites, so that there may be
no plague among the Israelites when
the Israelites approach the sanctuary."
Thus did Moses and Aaron and the 20
whole Israelite community to the Levites; the Israelites did to the Levites
just as the LORD had given Moses command concerning them. The Levites 21
purified themselves, and washed their
clothes; then Aaron presented them as a
wave-offering before the LORD, and
Aaron also made atonement for them to
cleanse them, after which the Levites 22
entered upon the performance of their
duties in the tent of meeting as assistants to Aaron and his sons; they did to
the Levites just as the LORD had given
Moses command concerning them.
The LORD said to Moses, 23
"This is the law which pertains to 24
the Levites: from twenty-five years
old and upward he shall enter upon the
service connected with the care of the
tent of meeting, but after fifty years of 25
age he must retire from active service,
and not work any more; he may help his 26
fellows in the tent of meeting in the performance of their duties, but he must do
no menial work. This is what you are
to do with Levites in the matter of their
duties."
At the first new moon of the second 9
year after the exodus from the land of
Egypt the LORD said to Moses in the
desert of Sinai,
"The Israelites must observe the 2
passover at its proper time; you must 3
observe it at its proper time, on the
fourteenth day of this month, at twilight, observing it in conformity with
all the statutes and ordinances for it."
So Moses told the Israelites to ob- 4
serve the passover; and they according- 5
ly observed the passover on the fourteenth day of the first month, at twilight, in the desert of Sinai; the Israelites did just as the LORD had commanded Moses.
There were some, however, who were 6

unclean through contact with a corpse,
and so could not observe the passover
on that day. So these men presented
themselves to Moses and Aaron that
7 day, and said to him,
"We are unclean through contact
with a corpse, why should we be prevented
from presenting the offering of
the LORD at its proper time along with
the other Israelites?"
8 Moses said to them,
"Wait until I hear what command
the LORD has to give concerning you."
9 So the LORD said to Moses,
10 "Say to the Israelites, 'If anyone of
you or your descendants is unclean
through contact with a dead body, or
is absent on a journey, he may still
offer the passover-sacrifice to the
11 LORD. Such persons are to offer it on
the fourteenth day of the second
month, at twilight; they must eat it
with unleavened cakes and bitter herbs,
12 without leaving any of it over until
morning, nor breaking a bone in it,
offering it in strict accord with the stat-
13 ute for the passover. Any man, however, who is clean and is not on a journey, and yet fails to offer the passover-
sacrifice, that person must be cut off
from his people, because he did not present the offering to the LORD at its
proper time; that person must answer
for his sin.
14 " 'If a proselyte is residing with you,
and would observe the passover to the
LORD, he must follow the statute for
the passover and its ordinance; you
must have the same statute for the
proselyte as for the native born of the
land.' "
15 On the day that the dwelling was
erected the cloud covered the dwelling,
that is, the tent of meeting, while at
evening it had the form of fire over the
16 dwelling until morning. It was always
so; the cloud used to cover it by day,
17 but in the form of fire by night. Whenever the cloud was lifted from the tent,
after that the Israelites would set out,
and at the place where it stopped, there
18 the Israelites would camp; it was at the
bidding of the LORD that the Israelites
set out, and it was at the bidding of the
LORD that they camped, remaining in
camp all the time that the cloud stayed
19 over the dwelling. Even when the cloud
stayed over the dwelling for many days,
the Israelites would keep the instructions
of the LORD, and not set out. Some- 20
times the cloud would remain a few days
over the dwelling. It was at the bidding
of the LORD that they camped, and it
was at the bidding of the LORD that
they set out. Sometimes the cloud would 21
remain from evening until morning, and
then the cloud would be lifted in the
morning, and they would set out; or it 22
would remain during the daytime, and
then at night the cloud would be lifted,
and they would set out; or it would remain two days, or a whole month. As
long as the cloud stayed over the
dwelling, the Israelites would remain in
camp, and not set out; but when it was
lifted, they would set out. It was at the 23
bidding of the LORD that they camped,
and it was at the bidding of the LORD
that they set out; they kept the instructions of the LORD in accordance
with the LORD'S command through
Moses.

The LORD said to Moses, 10
"Make two silver trumpets, making 2
them of beaten work. You are to use
them to summon the community and
to start the camps on the march. When 3
both are blown, the whole community
shall gather to you at the doorway of
the tent of meeting; but if only one is 4
blown, the chieftains, the heads of the
clans of Israel, shall gather to you.
When you blow an alarm, those en- 5
camped on the east side shall set out; 6
when you blow a second alarm, those
encamped on the south side shall set
out; an alarm is to be blown for them
to set out. When convoking the assem- 7
bly, however, you are to blow without
sounding an alarm. The sons of Aaron, 8
the priests, shall blow the trumpets,
and your use of them shall be a perpetual statute for you throughout
your generations. When you engage in 9
war in your own land against an adversary that is oppressing you, you
must sound an alarm with the trumpets, so that you may be remembered before the LORD your God, and be saved
from your enemies. Also on your days 10
of celebration, on your fixed festivals,
and on the first day of the month you
must blow the trumpets over your
burnt-offerings and thanksgiving sacrifices; they will serve as a reminder for
you before your God, since I, the
LORD, am your God."

THE JOURNEY FROM SINAI TO PARAN, 10:11—12:16

11 On the twentieth day of the second
month of the second year the cloud was
lifted from the dwelling of the decrees;
12 so the Israelites set out from the desert
of Sinai in successive stages, until the
13 cloud stopped at the desert of Paran. It
was the first time that they ever set out
at the bidding of the LORD through
14 Moses. The standard of the camp of
the Judeans, arranged by companies,
was the first to set out, with Nahshon,
the son of Amminadab, in charge of
15 their host, while Nethanel, the son of
Zuar, was in charge of the host of the
16 tribe of Issacharites, and Eliab, the son
of Helon, was in charge of the host of
17 the tribe of Zebulunites. Whenever the
dwelling was taken down, the Gershonites and Merarites, who carried the
18 dwelling, would set out; and then the
standard of the camp of Reuben, arranged by companies, would set out,
with Elizur, the son of Shedeur, in
19 charge of his host, while Shelumiel, the
son of Zurishaddai, was in charge of the
20 host of the tribe of Simeonites, and
Eliasaph, the son of Deuel, was in
charge of the host of the tribe of Gad-
21 ites. Then the Kohathites, who carried
the sacred objects, would set out, and
the dwelling would be erected in antici-
22 pation of their arrival. Then the standard of the camp of the Ephraimites, arranged by companies, would set out,
with Elishama, the son of Ammihud, in
23 charge of their host, while Gamaliel, the
son of Pedahzur, was in charge of the
24 host of the tribe of Manassites, and
Abidan, the son of Gideoni, was in
charge of the host of the tribe of Ben-
25 jaminites. Then the standard of the
camp of the Danites, arranged by companies, would set out as the rearguard
for all the other camps, with Ahiezer,
the son of Ammishaddai, in charge of
26 their host, while Pagiel, the son of
Ochran, was in charge of the host of the
27 tribe of Asherites, and Ahira, the son of
Enan was in charge of the host of the
28 tribe of Naphtalites. This was the order of march for the Israelites when
they set out, arranged by companies.
29 Moses said to Hobab, the son of
Reuel, the Midianite, the father-in-law
of Moses,
"We are setting out for the region of
which the LORD said, 'I will give it to
you'; come along with us, and we will
do well by you; for the LORD has promised Israel prosperity."
But he said to him, 30
"I will not go; since I must go to my
own land and kindred."
"Please do not leave us," he said. 31
"Inasmuch as you know the camping-
places for us in the desert, you will serve
as eyes for us. And then, if you go with 32
us, when that prosperity comes which
the LORD will bring to us, we will do
well by you."
Leaving the mountain of the LORD, 33
they journeyed for three days, while the
ark of the covenant of the LORD journeyed in front of them for the three
days, to look for a resting-place for
them, and the cloud of the LORD was 34
over them by day, whenever they set
out from the camp.
Whenever the ark would start, Moses 35
would say,
"Arise, O LORD, that thy foes may be
scattered,
That those who hate thee may flee be- 36
fore thee."
And whenever it would halt, he
would say,
"Halt, O LORD, and bless the clans
of Israel."
Now the people were complaining of 11
misfortune in the hearing of the LORD;
and when the LORD heard it, his anger
blazed, so that the fire of the LORD
burned among them, and consumed
some of the best parts of the camp.
Then the people cried to Moses; so 2
Moses prayed to the LORD, and the
fire abated. Hence the name of that 3
place came to be called Taberah [burn-
ing], because the fire of the LORD had
burned among them.
Now the rabble among them had a 4
craving for flesh, and the Israelites also
wept, and said,
"O that we had flesh to eat! We re- 5
member the fish that we used to eat for
nothing in Egypt, the cucumbers, the
melons, the leeks, the onions, and the
garlic; but now we are hungry, and there 6
is not a thing, except that we have the
manna to look at."
Now the manna was like coriander 7
seed, and its color was like that of resin-
ous gum. The people used to go about 8
and gather it, then grind it between
millstones or pound it in a mortar, boil

it in a pot, and make cakes of it; its
taste was like that of a cake baked with
9 oil. Whenever the dew fell on the camp
at night, the manna used to fall with it.
10 Moses heard the people weeping,
family by family, each at the doorway
of his tent; the anger of the LORD
blazed exceedingly, and Moses was displeased.
11 "Why hast thou been so hard on thy
servant?" said Moses to the LORD.
"Why have I not found favor with thee,
that thou shouldst put the burden of all
12 this people on me? Was it I who conceived all this people? Or was it I who
gave them birth, that thou shouldst say
to me, 'Carry them in your bosom, as a
nurse would carry a sucking child, to
the land which thou didst promise on
13 oath to their fathers'? Where can I get
flesh to give to all this people? For they
weep on my shoulder, saying, 'Give us
14 flesh to eat.' I am not able to carry all
this people by myself, because they are
15 too heavy for me. If this is the way
thou art going to deal with me, pray
kill me at once, if I find any favor with
thee, and let me see no more of my
trouble."
16 The LORD said to Moses,
"Gather to me seventy of the elders
of Israel, whom you know to be elders
and officers of the people; and bring
them to the tent of meeting that they
17 may take their stand there with you. I
will come down and speak with you
there, and I will withdraw some of the
spirit that is upon you and put it upon
them, that they may share the burden
of the people with you, and you not
18 bear it by yourself. Say to the people,
'Sanctify yourselves in readiness for tomorrow, that you may eat flesh; for you
have wept in the hearing of the LORD,
saying, "O that we had flesh to eat! For
we were prosperous in Egypt." So the
19 LORD will give you flesh to eat; you
shall eat, not one day, nor two days, nor
five days, nor ten days, nor twenty
20 days, but a whole month, until it comes
out of your very nostrils and becomes
loathesome to you—because you have
spurned the LORD who is in your midst,
and have wept before him, saying,
"Why did we ever leave Egypt?" ' "
21 But Moses said,
"The people, among whom I am, are
six hundred thousand men on foot, and
yet thou sayest, 'I will give them flesh
to eat for a whole month.' Can enough 22
flocks and herds be slaughtered for
them to be sufficient for them? Or if all
the fish of the sea are caught for them,
will it be sufficient for them?"
The LORD said to Moses, 23
"Is the LORD's power so limited?
You shall see now whether my word will
come true for you or not."
So Moses went out and told the peo- 24
ple the words of the LORD. He gathered
seventy elders of the people, and had
them stand around the tent. Then the 25
LORD came down in the cloud and
spoke to him; he withdrew some of the
spirit that was upon him and put it
upon the seventy elders, and as soon
as the spirit came upon them, they
prophesied—but never again. Now two 26
men had been left in the camp, the
name of the one being Eldad, and the
name of the other Medad. The spirit
rested upon them too (they were among
those recorded, but had not gone out
to the tent), and they prophesied in the
camp. Whereupon a youth ran and 27
told Moses.
"Eldad and Medad," he said, "are
prophesying in the camp."
So Joshua, the son of Nun, the at- 28
tendant of Moses from his youth up,
spoke up and said,
"My lord Moses, put a stop to
them!"
But Moses said to him, 29
"Are you jealous on my account? O
that all the LORD'S people were
prophets, that the LORD might put his
spirit upon them!"
Then Moses withdrew to the camp, 30
along with the elders of Israel.
There went forth a wind from the 31
LORD, and bringing quails across from
the sea, it dropped them near the camp,
about a day's journey on each side all
around the camp, and about two cubits
thick upon the surface of the ground.
All that day and night, and all the next 32
day, the people spent in gathering the
quails, the one who got the least gathering ten homers; then they spread them
out all around the camp. While the 33
meat was still between their teeth, before it was exhausted, the anger of the
LORD blazed against the people, and
the LORD smote them with a very great
plague. Hence the name of that place 34
came to be called Kibroth-hattaavah
[the graves of craving], because it was

there that they buried the people who
had the craving.
35 From Kibroth-hattaavah the people
set out for Hazeroth, and stayed at
Hazeroth.
12 Then Miriam and Aaron spoke
against Moses because of the Ethiopian
woman whom he had married; for he
had married an Ethiopian woman.
2 "Is it only through Moses alone that
the LORD has spoken?" they said. "Has
he not spoken through us as well?"
And the LORD heard it.
3 Now the man Moses was very modest, more so than all men upon the face
of the earth.
4 Suddenly the LORD said to Moses,
Aaron, and Miriam,
"Come out, you three, to the tent of
meeting."
5 So the three of them went out, and
the LORD came down in a column of
cloud, and stood at the doorway of the
tent.
"Aaron and Miriam!" he called.
6 Whereupon both of them went forward, and then he said,
"Hear my words!
If either of you were a prophet of the
LORD,
In visions would I make myself known
to him,
In dreams would I speak through him.
7 Not so with my servant Moses;
With all my house he has been entrusted;
8 Mouth to mouth do I speak with him,
Plainly, and not in riddles,
And the very form of the LORD does
he behold.
Why then were you not afraid
To speak against my servant Moses?"
9 So the anger of the LORD blazed
against them; and when he departed,
10 and the cloud withdrew from the tent,
there was Miriam leprous, as white as
snow! When Aaron turned to look at
Miriam, there she was leprous!
11 "O my lord!" Aaron said to Moses,
"do not punish us for the folly that we
have done and the sin that we have
12 committed. Do not let her become like
one dead, who when coming forth from
his mother's womb has half his flesh
consumed."
13 So Moses cried to the LORD,
"Pray, O God, heal her!"
14 But the LORD said to Moses,
"If her father had but spit in her
face, would she not hide in shame for
seven days? Let her be shut up for sev-
en days outside the camp, and after
that she may be taken back."
So Miriam was shut up for seven 15
days outside the camp, and the people
did not start again until Miriam was
taken back. After that, however, the 16
people set out from Hazeroth, and
camped in the desert of Paran.

THE STORY OF THE SPIES, 13:1—14:45

Then the LORD said to Moses, 13
"Send men to spy out the land of 2
Canaan, which I am going to give the
Israelites; you must send a man from
each of their ancestral tribes, everyone
a chieftain among them."
So Moses despatched them from the 3
desert of Paran in accordance with the
command of the LORD, all of them being head men of the Israelites. The fol- 4
lowing were their names: from the tribe
of Reuben, Shammua, the son of Zaccur; from the tribe of Simeon, Shaphat, 5
the son of Hori; from the tribe of Judah, 6
Caleb, the son of Jephunneh; from the 7
tribe of Issachar, Igal, the son of Joseph; from the tribe of Ephraim, Ho- 8
shea, the son of Nun; from the tribe of 9
Benjamin, Palti, the son of Raphu;
from the tribe of Zebulun, Gaddiel, the 10
son of Sodi; from the tribe of Joseph 11
(that is, from the tribe of Manasseh),
Gaddi, the son of Susi; from the tribe of 12
Dan, Ammiel, the son of Gemalli; from 13
the tribe of Asher, Sethur, the son of
Michael; from the tribe of Naphtali, 14
Nahbi, the son of Vophsi; from the tribe 15
of Gad, Geuel, the son of Machi. These 16
were the names of the men whom Moses
sent to spy out the land, but Moses
called Hoshea, the son of Nun, Joshua.
When Moses sent them to spy out the 17
land of Canaan, he said to them,
"Go up now into the Negeb; go up
into the highlands, and see what the 18
land is like, and whether the people
who are living in it are strong or weak,
whether they are few or many; and 19
what the land is like in which they are
living, whether it is good or bad; and
what the cities are like in which they
are living, whether it is in camps or in
strongholds; and what the land is like, 20
whether it is rich or poor, whether

there is wood in it or not. Do your best
to get some of the fruit of the land."
(Now the season was that of the first
ripe grapes.)
21 So they went up, and spied out the
land from the desert of Zin as far as
Rehob, toward the approach to Ham-
22 ath. They went up into the Negeb, and
reached Hebron, where Ahiman, Sheshai, and Talmai, the sons of Anak,
lived. (Now Hebron was built seven
23 years before Zoan in Egypt.) Reaching the valley of Eshcol, they cut a
branch from there with a single cluster
of grapes, and it took two of them to
carry it on a stretcher, along with some
24 pomegranates and some figs. That
place came to be called the valley of
Eshcol [cluster] because of the cluster
which the Israelites cut from there.
25 At the end of forty days they came
26 back from spying out the land. They
left and came to Moses and Aaron and
the whole Israelite community in the
desert of Paran, at Kadesh; they
brought back a report to them and the
whole community, and showed them
the fruit of the land.
27 "We reached the land to which you
sent us," they told him, "and it surely
does flow with milk and honey, and
28 here is its fruit. The people, however,
who live in the land are strong, and the
cities are fortified and very large; and
besides, we saw the Anakim [giants]
29 there. Amalek is living in the land of
the Negeb, and the Hittites, Jebusites,
and Amorites are living in the highlands, while the Canaanites are living
along the sea and the banks of the Jordan."
30 Caleb, however, broke through the
people to Moses, and said,
"We ought to go up and seize it; for
we are quite able to do so."
31 But the men who went up with him
said,
"We are not able to go up against the
people; for they are too strong for us."
32 So they gave the Israelites a bad report of the land that they had spied
out; saying,
"The land through which we passed
in spying it out is a land that destroys
its inhabitants, and all the people that
we saw in it are men of great stature.
33 We saw the Nephilim [titans] there (the
Anakim belong to the Nephilim); to
ourselves we looked like grasshoppers,
and we must have looked the same to
them."
Then the whole community lifted up 14
their voices and cried; the people wept
that night; the Israelites all grumbled 2
against Moses and Aaron.
"Would that we had died in the land
of Egypt!" the whole community said
to them. "Or would that we had died in
this desert! Why is the LORD bringing 3
us into this land, only to fall by the
sword? Our wives and little ones will
become a prey. Would it not be better
for us to return to Egypt?" "Let us take 4
our own course and return to Egypt,"
they said to one another.
Then Moses and Aaron fell on their 5
faces before the whole assembly of the
Israelite community, while Joshua, 6
the son of Nun, and Caleb, the son of
Jephunneh, who belonged to those who
had spied out the land, tore their
clothes, and said to the whole Israelite 7
community,
"The land through which we passed
in spying it out is a very, very fine land.
If the LORD is pleased with us, he will 8
bring us into this land, and give it to us
—a land which flows with milk and
honey. Only do not rebel against the 9
LORD; and do not be afraid of the people of the land; for they will simply be
food for us; their protection has left
them, while the LORD is with us; do not
be afraid of them."
But the whole community had deter- 10
mined to stone them, when the glory of
the LORD appeared to all the Israelites
at the tent of meeting.
"How long are this people going to 11
despise me?" the LORD said to Moses.
"How long is it that they are not going
to trust me, in spite of all the signs that
I performed in their midst? I will smite 12
them with pestilence, and disinherit
them, and I will make you into a nation
greater and stronger than they."
But Moses said to the LORD, 13
"When the Egyptians hear of it (for
thou didst bring this people out of their
midst by thy might), they will say— 14
when all the inhabitants of this land
have heard that thou, LORD, art in the
midst of this people, thou, LORD, being
one who is seen eye to eye, while thy
cloud stands over them, and thou thyself goest before them in a column of
cloud by day and a column of fire by
night—indeed, if thou slayest this peo- 15

ple to a man, the nations who have
16 heard about thee will say, 'It was because the LORD could not bring this
people into the land which he promised on oath to them that he slaugh-
17 tered them in the desert.' But now,
pray let the forbearance of the Lord be
as great as thou didst declare in saying,
18 'The LORD is slow to anger, abounding
in kindness, forgiving iniquity and
transgression, without leaving it completely unpunished, however, but
avenging the iniquity of fathers upon
their children down to the third or even
19 the fourth generation.' Pray pardon the
sin of this people in accordance with
thine abundant kindness, even as thou
hast forgiven this people from Egypt
until now."

20 So the LORD said,

"I will pardon them in accordance
21 with your request; but as surely as I
live and the whole earth is full of the
22 glory of the LORD, none of the men who
have seen my glory and my signs which
I performed in Egypt and the desert,
and yet have put me to the test for ten
times now, and have not heeded my in-
23 junctions, shall see the land which I
promised on oath to their fathers, and
none of those who despised me shall see
24 it. But my servant Caleb, because he
is of a different spirit, and has corroborated me, I will bring into the land
which he entered, and he shall pass it
on as a heritage to his descendants.
25 Since, however, the Amalekites and
Canaanites are living in the valleys,
turn tomorrow, and set out for the desert in the direction of the Red Sea."

26 The LORD said to Moses and Aaron,
27 "How long is this wicked community
going to keep up their grumbling
against me? I have heard the grumbling of the Israelites which they have
28 been muttering against me. Say to
them, 'As I live'—it is the oracle of the
LORD—'I will do to you just as I have
29 heard you say: your corpses shall fall
in this desert, and none of you that were
numbered, none of you that were counted from twenty years old and upward,
30 who have grumbled against me, shall
enter the land in which I swore by uplifted hand to settle you, except Caleb,
the son of Jephunneh, and Joshua, the
31 son of Nun. Your little ones, however,
who you said would become a prey, I
will bring in, and they shall come to
know the land that you have despised.
But as for yourselves, your corpses 3
shall fall in this desert, while your chil- 3
dren shall be shepherds for forty years
in the desert, and shall suffer for your
wantonness, until the last of your
corpses lies in the desert. According to 3
the number of the days that you took to
spy out the land, forty days, one year
for each day shall you suffer for your
iniquities, that is, forty years, and you
shall experience opposition from me. I, 3
the LORD, declare that this is what I
will do to all this wicked community
that are gathered against me: in this
desert they shall die to the last man.' "

So the men whom Moses had sent to 3
spy out the land, and who on their return made the whole community grumble against him by giving out a bad report concerning the land, the men who 3
gave out a bad report of the land died
by a plague at the hands of the LORD;
but Joshua, the son of Nun, and Caleb, 3
the son of Jephunneh, remained alive
out of those men who went to spy out
the land.

When Moses told these things to all 3
the Israelites, the people mourned
greatly. Next morning they rose early, 4
and proceeded up to the mountain
headlands, saying,

"Here we are, ready to go up to the
place of which the LORD spoke; for we
have indeed sinned."

But Moses said, 4

"Why is it that you go on violating
the injunctions of the LORD, when that
cannot succeed? Do not go up, lest you 4
be struck down in front of your enemies; for the LORD will not be in the
midst of you. For the Amalekites and 4
Canaanites will face you there, and you
will fall by the sword, inasmuch as you
have turned from following the LORD,
so that the LORD will not be with you."

But they presumptuously went up to 4
the mountain headlands, although
neither the ark of the covenant of the
LORD nor Moses left the camp. Then 4
the Amalekites and Canaanites who
were living in those highlands came
down and attacked them, and harried
them all the way to Hormah.

MISCELLANEOUS LAWS AND NARRATIVES, 15:1—19:22

15 The LORD said to Moses,
2 "Speak to the Israelites, and say to
them, 'When you come into your home-
3 land which I am giving you, and would
make an offering to the LORD, a burnt-
offering, or a sacrifice as a special votive
offering or as a voluntary offering, or
an offering at your stated festivals, to
make a soothing odor to the LORD with
4 an ox or a sheep, the person making the
offering must present as a cereal-offering to the LORD a tenth of an ephah of
fine flour mixed with a fourth of a hin
5 of oil, and as wine for the libation, you
must supply a fourth of a hin with the
burnt-offering or sacrifice for each
6 lamb. Or in the case of a ram, you must
supply as a cereal-offering two tenths
of an ephah of fine flour mixed with a
7 third of a hin of oil, and as wine for the
libation you must present a third of a
hin as a soothing odor to the LORD.
8 When you provide a bullock as a burnt-
offering, or as a sacrifice as a special
votive offering, or as a thank-offering
9 to the LORD, there must be presented
as a cereal-offering with the bullock
three tenths of an ephah of fine flour
10 mixed with half a hin of oil, and as wine
for the libation you must present half
a hin as a sacrifice, a soothing odor to
11 the LORD. This is what is to be done in
the case of each bullock or ram or
12 lamb or kid; according to the number
that you provide, this is what you are
to do in the case of each, whatever their
13 number. Every native born is to do
these things in this way, in presenting
a sacrifice as a soothing odor to the
14 LORD; and if there is a proselyte who
resides with you, or one living permanently in your midst, and he wishes to
make a sacrifice as a soothing odor to
the LORD, he must do just as you do.
15 As for the community, there shall be
the one statute for you and the proselyte, a perpetual statute throughout
your generations; the proselyte and
you shall be alike before the LORD;
16 there shall be one law and one ordinance for you and the proselyte residing
with you.' "
17 The LORD said to Moses,
18 "Speak to the Israelites, and say to
them, 'When you come into the land
19 to which I am bringing you, then, when
you eat of the food of the land, you
must set aside a portion for the LORD;
in the case of the first batch of baking 20
you must set aside a cake as a contribution, setting it aside as a contribution
from the threshing-floor; out of your 21
first batch of baking you must give a
portion to the LORD throughout your
generations.

" 'If you should make a mistake and 22
not carry out all these commands that
the LORD has communicated to Moses,
all that the LORD commanded you 23
through Moses, from the day that the
LORD first gave you a command,
down through your various generations,
then, if it was done inadvertently, 24
through lack of knowledge on the part
of the community, the whole community must offer one bullock as a burnt-
offering, as a soothing odor to the
LORD, along with the cereal-offering
and libation as prescribed for it, and
one he-goat as a sin-offering. Then the 25
priest shall make atonement for the
whole Israelite community, and they
shall be forgiven; for it was a mistake,
and they have brought their offering as
a sacrifice to the LORD, and their sin-
offering into the presence of the LORD
for their mistake. So the whole Israelite 26
community shall be forgiven, including
the proselyte who resides among them;
for in the case of a mistake he is included in the sum total of the people.

" 'If an individual sins inadvertently, 27
he must offer a yearling she-goat as a
sin-offering, and the priest shall make 28
atonement before the LORD for the person that made a mistake, in sinning inadvertently, making atonement for
him that he may be forgiven. In the 29
case of either the native born among the
Israelites or the proselyte who resides
among them, you must have the one
law for him who does anything inadvertently. But the person who sins wil- 30
fully, whether he belongs to the native
born or the proselytes, is reviling the
LORD, so that person must be cut
off from his people. Because it is the 31
word of the LORD that he has despised,
and his command that he has broken,
that person must be completely cut off,
his iniquity being on his own head.' "

When the Israelites were in the des- 32
ert, they found a man gathering wood
on the sabbath day. Those who found 33
him gathering wood brought him to

Moses and Aaron and the whole com-
34 munity, and they put him in custody,
because it had not been clearly explained what should be done to him.
35 Then the LORD said to Moses,
"The man must be put to death by
having the whole community stone him
outside the camp."
36 So the whole community took him
outside the camp, and stoned him to
death, as the LORD had commanded
Moses.
37 The LORD said to Moses,
38 "Speak to the Israelites and tell
them that throughout their generations
they must make tassels for themselves
on the corners of their garments, fastening the tassel to each corner with a vio-
39 let string. They shall serve you as tassels to look at and by which to be re-
minded to carry out all the commands
of the LORD and not to follow your
own desires and fancies, which you
40 used to follow so wantonly, in order
that you may remember to carry out all
my commands, and be consecrated to
41 your God, since I, the LORD, am your
God, who brought you out of the land
of Egypt to become your God, I, the
LORD, your God."

16 Now Korah, the son of Izhar, the son
of Kohath, the son of Levi, along with
Dathan and Abiram, the sons of Eliab,
and On, the son of Peleth, the son of
2 Reuben, became arrogant and took
their stand before Moses, along with
two hundred and fifty of the Israelites,
leaders of the community, picked men
3 of the assembly, men of note, They
gathered in a body against Moses and
Aaron, and said to them,
"Enough of you; for all the community are holy, every one of them, since
the LORD is in their midst; why then do
you exalt yourselves above the LORD'S
assembly?"
4 When Moses heard this, he fell on his
5 face; then he said to Korah and all his
company,
"In the morning the LORD will show
who belongs to him and who is holy,
that he may have him come near him;
and whomsoever he chooses he will
6 have come near him. Do this: take
fire-pans (that is, Korah and all his
7 company), and putting fire in them,
place incense upon them in the presence of the LORD tomorrow; and then
the man whom the LORD chooses shall
be the holy one. Enough of you, you
Levites!"
"Listen, you Levites," said Moses to 8
Korah, "is it too little for you that the 9
God of Israel has singled you out from
the community of Israel to have you
come near him to look after the LORD'S
dwelling, and to stand before the community to serve them, and that he has 10
had you come near him, and all your
fellow-Levites with you, that you
should seek the priesthood as well? It 11
is accordingly against the LORD that
you and all your company are gathered; for what is there about Aaron that
you should grumble against him?"
Moses sent for Dathan and Abiram, 12
the sons of Eliab, but they said,
"We will not go up. Is it such a trifle 13
that you have brought us up from a
land flowing with milk and honey to
kill us in the desert, that you should
also play the prince over us? Moreover, 14
you have not brought us into a land
flowing with milk and honey, nor given
us a heritage of fields and vineyards.
Are you trying to blind the eyes of these
men? We will not go up."
Then Moses became very angry, and 15
said to the LORD,
"Pay no attention to an offering from
them. Not a single ass have I taken
from them, nor done any harm to any of
them."
Moses said to Korah, 16
"Tomorrow you and all your company are to appear before the LORD—
you, and they, and Aaron; each of you 17
take his fire-pan, and putting incense
on it, each of you is to bring his fire-
pan before the LORD, that is, two hundred and fifty fire-pans; you also, and
Aaron, each with his fire-pan."
So each of them took his fire-pan, 18
and putting fire on them, they placed
incense on them, and then took their
stand at the doorway of the tent of
meeting, along with Moses and Aaron.
Korah had gathered the whole commu- 19
nity against them at the doorway of the
tent of meeting, whereupon the glory
of the LORD appeared to the whole
community. Then the LORD said to 20
Moses and Aaron,
"Separate yourselves from this com- 21
munity that I may consume them instantly."
But they fell on their faces, and said, 22
"O God, the God of the spirits of all

mankind, when only one man sins,
shouldst thou become angry with the
whole community?"
23 So the LORD said to Moses,
24 "Say to the community, 'Withdraw
from the neighborhood of the dwelling
where Korah, Dathan, and Abiram
are.'"
25 Moses rose and went to Dathan and
Abiram, and the elders of Israel fol-
26 lowed him. Then he said to the community,
"Move away from the tents of these
wicked men, and do not touch anything at all that belongs to them, lest
you be swept away with all their sins."
27 So they withdrew from the neighborhood of the dwelling where Korah,
Dathan, and Abiram were.
As Dathan and Abiram came out and
stood at the doorways of their tents,
with their wives and sons and little
28 ones, Moses said,
"Hereby shall you know that the
LORD has sent me to do all these deeds,
and that it has not been of my own
29 choice: if these men die as all men die,
and suffer the fate of all men, it is not
30 the LORD who has sent me; but if the
LORD does something new, and the
ground opens its mouth, and swallows
them up, with all that belongs to them,
and they descend into Sheol alive, then
you shall know that these men have
despised the LORD."
31 And then, just as he finished saying
these words, the ground under them
32 split open; the earth opened its mouth
and swallowed them up, with all their
households, and all the men who be-
33 longed to Korah and all their goods. So
they and all that belonged to them descended into Sheol alive; and the earth
closed over them, and they perished
34 from the community. Then all the Israelites that were in their neighborhood fled at their cries; "Lest," said
they, "the earth swallow us up."
35 Fire having come forth from the
LORD, it consumed the two hundred
and fifty men offering the incense.
36 Then the LORD said to Moses,
37 "Tell Eleazar, the son of Aaron, the
priest, to pick up the fire-pans out of
the conflagration, and then you must
scatter the fire far and wide; for these
sinners have made the fire-pans taboo
at the cost of their lives. So they must
be made into beaten plates as a covering for the altar, that they may become
a sign to the Israelites; for they were
presented before the LORD, and so have
become taboo."
So Eleazar, the priest, took the 39
bronze fire-pans which those who had
been burned had presented, and they
were beaten out as a covering for the
altar, a reminder to the Israelites, so 40
that no layman, who was not one of the
descendants of Aaron, might draw near
to burn incense before the LORD, lest
he fare like Korah and his company—
just as the LORD had directed him
through Moses.
But next day the whole Israelite com- 41
munity grumbled against Moses and
Aaron, saying,
"It is you who have slain the LORD'S
people."
But when the community gathered 42
against Moses and Aaron, they turned
toward the tent of meeting, and there
was the cloud covering it and the glory
of the LORD visible! Then Moses and 43
Aaron came to the front of the tent of
meeting, whereupon the LORD said to 44
Moses,
"Withdraw from this community, 45
that I may instantly consume them."
But they fell on their faces, and 46
Moses said to Aaron,
"Take your fire-pan, put fire from the
altar on it, place incense on it, and then
carry it quickly to the community, and
make atonement for them; for wrath
has gone forth from the LORD; the
plague has begun."
So Aaron took it, as Moses had said, 47
and ran into the midst of the community, but the plague had already begun among the people; he put on the
incense, and making atonement for the
people, he stood between the living and 48
the dead, so that the plague was
checked. But those who died from the 49
plague amounted to fourteen thousand
seven hundred, in addition to those who
died in the affair of Korah. Then Aaron 50
returned to Moses at the doorway of
the tent of meeting, now that the
plague had been checked.
The LORD said to Moses, 17
"Speak to the Israelites, and take 2
from them one staff for each clan, in all
twelve staffs from the leaders of their
clans, writing the name of each upon
his staff, and Aaron's name upon the 3
staff of Levi (for there is to be a special

4 staff for the head of their clan); you
must then deposit them in the tent of
meeting in front of the decrees, where I
5 am accustomed to meet you; and then
the staff of the man whom I choose shall
sprout. Thus will I rid myself of the
grumbling of the Israelites, which they
have been muttering against you."
6 So Moses spoke to the Israelites, and
they gave him one staff for every one of
the leaders of their clans, twelve staffs
in all, with Aaron's staff among theirs.
7 Then Moses deposited the staffs before
the LORD in the tent of the decrees;
8 and next day, when Moses entered the
tent of the decrees, he found that the
staff of Aaron, representing the clan of
Levi, had sprouted, it had put forth
sprouts, it had produced blossoms and
9 borne ripe almonds. Moses then
brought out all the staffs from the presence of the LORD to all the Israelites,
and having inspected them, each of
them took his staff.
10 Then the LORD said to Moses,
"Put Aaron's staff back in front of
the decrees, to be kept as a sign for the
rebels; and you must rid me of their
grumbling, that they die not."
11 Moses did so; he did just as the
LORD commanded him.
12 The Israelites said to Moses,
"We perish! We are lost, we are all
13 lost! If everyone who dares to approach the dwelling of the LORD is to
die, shall we ever cease dying?"
18 So the LORD said to Aaron,
"You and your sons, along with your
clan, shall answer for any guilt in connection with the sanctuary, and you
and your sons with you shall answer for
any guilt in connection with your
2 priesthood. Have your fellows too, the
tribe of Levi, your ancestral tribe, present themselves with you, that they
may be associated with you, and minister to you, while you and your sons
with you are in front of the tent of the
decrees; they shall attend to you and
3 all the tent; only they must not come
near the sacred vessels or the altar, that
4 neither they nor you die. They shall be
associated with you, and take charge of
the tent of meeting in all the work connected with the tent, since no layman
5 may come near you. You are to take
charge of the sanctuary and the altar,
that wrath may never again fall on the
6 Israelites. For my part, see, I have se-
lected your fellow-Levites from the Israelites as a gift for you, made over to the LORD to look after the tent of meeting, while you and your sons with you must reserve your priestly functions for everything connected with the altar and inside the veil, and look after them. It is a lucrative office that I am making your priesthood, while any layman who draws near shall be put to death."

Then the LORD said to Aaron,

"For my part, see, I give you the office connected with the contributions to me; in the case of all the sacred gifts of the Israelites, I give them to you as your share, and to your sons as their perpetual due. The following is to go to you from the most sacred offerings, from the sacrifices: in the case of every offering of theirs, that is, every cereal-offering of theirs, in the case of every sin-offering of theirs, and every guilt-offering of theirs with which they make restitution to me, it shall be most sacred to you and your sons; as a most sacred thing shall you eat it, that is, every male eating it, since it is sacred to you. This also shall be yours, the contributions from their gift in the case of every wave-offering of the Israelites; I give it to you, and to your sons and daughters with you, as your perpetual due, to be eaten by everyone in your family who is clean. All the best of the oil, all the best of the wine and grain. The first-fruits which they give to the LORD, I give to you. The first-ripe fruits of all that is in their land which they bring to the LORD shall be yours, to be eaten by everyone in your family who is clean. Every devoted thing in Israel is to go to you. Everything that first opens the womb, in the case of every creature that they offer to the LORD, whether man or beast, shall be yours; only you must be sure to have the first-born of man redeemed, and the first-born of unclean animals you must have redeemed. The redemption-price of the former (you must have them redeemed at a month old) shall be fixed by you at five shekels of silver in terms of the sacred shekel, which is twenty gerahs. The firstling of a cow, however, or the firstling of a sheep, or that of a goat, you must not have redeemed, since they are sacred; you must dash their blood upon the altar, and burn their fat in sacrifice as a soothing odor to the

8 LORD; but their flesh shall be yours,
becoming yours like the waved breast
9 and the right thigh. All the contributions from the sacred gifts which the Israelites contribute to the LORD, I give
to you, and to your sons and daughters
with you, as your perpetual due, to be
an inviolable covenant forever before
the LORD for you and your family
with you."
0 The LORD said to Aaron,
"You are to have no heritage in their
land, nor own any property among
them; I am to be your property and
1 heritage among the Israelites. To the
Levites, however, I give all the dues in
Israel as their heritage, in return for the
service that they perform in connec-
2 tion with the tent of meeting. The Israelites must never again come near the
tent of meeting, to answer for their sin
3 by death, but the Levites alone shall
look after the tent of meeting, while the
rest shall answer for their iniquity. It
is to be a perpetual statute throughout
your generations that they are to have
4 no heritage among the Israelites; for
the dues which the Israelites contribute
to the LORD I give to the Levites as a
heritage; that is why I have told them
that they are not to have any heritage
among the Israelites."
5 The LORD said to Moses,
6 "You must speak to the Levites, and
say to them, 'When you take from the
Israelites the dues that I have given
you from them as your heritage, you
must set apart some of it as a contribution to the LORD, a due from the dues.
7 The contribution made to you is to be
credited to you like the grain from the
threshing-floor, or the produce of the
8 winepress; in the same way you, too,
must set apart some of all the dues that
you receive from the Israelites as a contribution to the LORD, and give the
LORD's contribution from it to Aaron,
9 the priest. From all the gifts made to
you, from the best of them, you must
set apart the LORD's full contribution,
0 the most sacred of them.' Also say to
them, 'When you have contributed the
best of them, the rest is to be credited
to the Levites as in the case of the produce of the threshing-floor and that of
1 the winepress; you may eat it anywhere, you and your households; for it
is your reward in return for your serv-
2 ices at the tent of meeting. You will
not have to answer for any sin through
it when you set apart the best of it; but
you must not profane the sacred gifts
of the Israelites, that you die not.'"
The LORD said to Moses and Aaron, 19
"This is the statute of the law which 2
the LORD has commanded: 'Tell the
Israelites to bring you a red cow, sound,
in which there is no defect, and upon
which a yoke has never come; you must 3
then give it to Eleazar, the priest, to be
taken outside the camp, and slain in his
presence. Eleazar, the priest, shall take 4
some of its blood with his finger, and
sprinkle some of its blood toward the
front of the tent of meeting seven
times. The cow is then to be burned in 5
his sight; its hide, flesh, and blood, as
well as its offal, are to be burned, and 6
the priest is to take cedar wood, hyssop,
and scarlet string, and throw them
into the burning body of the cow. Then 7
the priest is to wash his clothes, and
bathe his body in water, after which he
may re-enter the camp, but the priest
shall remain unclean until evening. He 8
who burns it must also wash his clothes
in water, and bathe his body in water,
and shall remain unclean until evening.
A man that is clean shall gather up the 9
ashes of the cow, and deposit them in a
clean place outside the camp, to do
duty for the Israelite community as
water for impurity, to be used in the
case of sin. He who gathers the ashes of 10
the cow must wash his clothes, and
shall remain unclean until evening.
This is to be a perpetual statute for the
Israelites and the proselytes who reside
among them. Anyone who touches a 11
dead body, that is, any human body,
shall remain unclean for seven days; on 12
the third day and the seventh day he
must cleanse himself from sin with it,
and so become clean; if he does not
cleanse himself from sin on the third
day and the seventh day, he will not
become clean. Whoever touches a dead 13
body, the corpse of a man who may
have died, and does not cleanse himself
from sin, since he has polluted the
dwelling of the LORD, that person must
be cut off from Israel; because the water used for impurity was not thrown
over him, he remains unclean, his uncleanness being still with him.
" 'This is to be the law when a man 14
dies in a tent: everyone entering the
tent and everyone in the tent shall be

15 unclean for seven days; and every open
vessel which has no cover tied down on
16 it shall be unclean. Also, whoever in the
open fields touches a person slain by the
sword, or one who has died a natural
death, or a human bone, or a grave,
17 shall be unclean for seven days. Then
some of the ashes prepared for use in
case of sin are to be taken, and fresh
water is to be added to them in a vessel;
18 a man that is clean must then take hyssop, dip it into the water, and sprinkle it
upon the tent, upon all the furniture,
and upon the persons that were present,
and him who touched the bone, or the
person slain, or the person dead from
19 natural causes, or the grave; the clean
person must sprinkle it upon the unclean person on the third day and the
seventh day, thus cleansing him from
sin on the seventh day; he must then
wash his clothes, and bathe himself in
water, and at evening he shall be clean.
20 But the man who becomes unclean and
does not cleanse himself from sin, that
person shall be cut off from the community, because he has polluted the
sanctuary of the LORD; since the water
for use in case of impurity was not
thrown over him, he remains unclean.
21 This shall be a perpetual statute for
them. He who sprinkles the water for
use in case of impurity must wash his
clothes, while he who touches the water
for use in case of impurity shall remain
22 unclean until evening; whatever the unclean person touches shall become unclean, and the person who touches it
shall remain unclean until evening.' "

THE LATER YEARS OF THE DESERT JOURNEY,

20:1—27:23

20 In the first month the Israelites, the
whole community of them, arrived at
the desert of Zin, and the people established themselves at Kadesh. Miriam
2 died there, and was buried there. Since
there was no water for the community,
they gathered in a body against Moses
3 and Aaron; and the people found fault
with Moses.
"Would that we had perished when
our fellows perished at the hands of the
4 LORD!" they said. "Why have you
brought the LORD's community into
this desert, to die there, both we and
5 our cattle? Why have you brought us
up out of Egypt, to bring us to this
wretched place, since it is no place for
grain, or figs, or vines, or pomegranates, nor is there any water to drink?"
Then Moses and Aaron came away
from the presence of the assembly to
the doorway of the tent of meeting, and
fell on their faces, whereupon the glory
of the LORD appeared to them, and the
LORD said to Moses,
"Take the staff, and assemble the
community, you and your brother Aaron; and then in their presence tell the
rock to yield its waters; you shall produce water from the rock for them, and
thus give the community and their cattle a drink."
So Moses took the staff from its place
before the LORD, as he had commanded him. Then Moses and Aaron gath- 10
ered the assembly in front of the rock,
and he said to them,
"Listen, you rebels; is it from this
rock that we have to produce water for
you?"
And raising his hand, Moses struck 11
the rock with his staff twice, whereupon
water in abundance gushed out, and the
community and their cattle drank.
But the LORD said to Moses and 12
Aaron,
"Because you did not trust me by
paying me due honor in the presence of
the Israelites, that is why you shall not
bring this community into the land
which I have given them."
These are the waters of Meribah 13
[finding fault], where the Israelites
found fault with the LORD, but where
he vindicated himself among them.
From Kadesh Moses sent messengers 14
to the king of Edom:
"Thus says your brother Israel:
'You know all the hardships that have
befallen us, how our fathers went down 15
to Egypt, how we remained a long time
in Egypt, how badly the Egyptians
treated us and our fathers, and how,
when we cried to the LORD, he heeded 16
our cry, and sent an angel to bring us
out of Egypt. So here we are at Kadesh, a city on the edge of your territory. Pray let us pass through your 17
land; we will not pass through field or
vineyard, nor drink the water of the
wells; we will go only by the royal road,
turning neither to the right nor to the
left, until we cross your territory.' "
But Edom said to him, 18

"You must not pass through my territory, lest I come out with the sword against you."
19 "We will go up only by the road," the Israelites said to him; "and if we drink any of your water, we and our live stock, we will pay for it; let us just walk through, a matter of no consequence."
20 But he said,
"You shall not pass through."
So Edom came out against them with
21 a large army and a strong force. Thus Edom refused to grant Israel passage through his territory; so Israel turned aside from him.
22 The Israelites then set out from Kadesh, the whole community of them,
23 and came to Mount Hor. At Mount Hor, near the frontier of the land of Edom, the LORD said to Moses and Aaron,
24 "Aaron is to be gathered to his fathers; for he is not to enter the land which I have given the Israelites, because you rebelled against my instructions in connection with the waters of
25 Meribah. Take Aaron and his son Eleazar, and bring them up Mount Hor;
26 then strip Aaron of his robes, and put them on his son Eleazar, whereupon Aaron shall be gathered in death there."
27 Moses did as the LORD commanded; they ascended Mount Hor in view of
28 the whole community, and when Moses had stripped Aaron of his robes, and put them on his son Eleazar, Aaron died there on the top of the mountain. Then Moses and Eleazar descended the
29 mountain, and when the whole community saw that Aaron was dead, the whole house of Israel wept for Aaron thirty days.
21 When the Canaanite king of Arad, who lived in the Negeb, heard that Israel was coming toward Atharim, he fought against Israel, and took some of
2 them captive. Then Israel made a vow to the LORD, and said,
"If thou wilt but deliver this people into my power, I will annihilate their cities."
3 The LORD acceded to Israel's request, and delivered up the Canaanites; so they annihilated them and their cities. Hence the name of the place came to be called Hormah [annihilation].

From Mount Hor they set out in the 4
direction of the Red Sea to make a circuit of the land of Edom, and the people grew impatient over the journey; so 5
the people reproached God and Moses,
"Why have you brought us up out of Egypt to die in the desert? For there is neither food nor water, and we loathe this wretched food."
Then the LORD sent stinging ser- 6
pents among the people, and they bit the people, so that many of Israel died.
So the people came to Moses, and said, 7
"We have sinned, in that we have reproached the LORD and you; pray to the LORD that he remove the serpents from us."
So Moses prayed for the people, 8
whereupon the LORD said to Moses,
"Make a serpent, and mount it on a pole, and then everyone that is bitten shall live if he looks at it."
So Moses made a bronze serpent, and 9
mounted it on a pole; accordingly, if a serpent bit anyone, he looked at the bronze serpent, and lived.
The Israelites set out, and then 10
camped at Oboth. Setting out from 11
Oboth, they camped at Ije-abarim, in the desert opposite Moab, to the east.
Setting out from there, they camped in 12
the valley of Zered. Setting out from 13
there, they camped on the other side of the Arnon, which is in the desert extending from the frontier of the Amorites; for the Arnon constitutes the frontier of Moab between Moab and the Amorites. That is why it is said in 14
the Book of the Wars of the LORD,
" . . . . Waheb in Suphah, and the
Arnon valleys; the slope of the valleys, 15
which extends to the site of Ar, and leans toward the frontier of Moab . . . ."
From there they proceeded to Beer 16
[well], which is the well where the LORD said to Moses, "Collect the people that I may give them water." It 17
was then that Israel sang this song:
"Spring up, O well! Sing to it;
The well which the princes dug, 18
Which the nobles of the people sunk,
With the scepter, with their staffs."
From the desert they proceeded to 19
Mattanah, from Mattanah to Nahaliel,
from Nahaliel to Bamoth, and from 20
Bamoth to the valley which is in the country of Moab, at the headland of Pisgah, which overlooks Jeshimon.

21 Then Israel sent messengers to Sihon,
king of the Amorites, saying,
22 “Let us pass through your land; we
will not turn off into field or vineyard;
we will not drink the water from the
wells; we will go only by the royal road,
until we pass through your territory.”
23 But Sihon would not let Israel pass
through his territory; Sihon collected
all his forces, and sallied forth against
Israel in the desert. Arriving at Jahaz,
24 he fought against Israel, but Israel put
him to the sword, and seized his land
from the Arnon as far as the Jabbok,
that is, as far as the Ammonites; for
Jazar was the frontier of the Ammon-
25 ites. Israel captured all the cities here,
and Israel settled in all the cities of the
Amorites, in Heshbon and all its de-
26 pendencies. For Heshbon was the capital of Sihon, king of the Amorites, who
had fought against the former king of
Moab and had wrested from him all his
27 land as far as the Arnon. That is how
the bards came to say,
“Come to Heshbon! Let it be built!
Let the capital of Sihon be established!
28 For fire issued from Heshbon,
Flame from Sihon's city;
It consumed Ar of Moab,
It extended up to the heights of the
Arnon.
29 Woe to you, O Moab!
You are undone, O people of Chemosh!
He has made his sons fugitives,
And his daughters captives,
To an Amorite king, Sihon;
30 So their children perished from Heshbon as far as Dibon,
And their wives as far as Nophah,
which is near Medeba.”
31 So Israel settled in the land of the
32 Amorites. After Moses had sent the
men to spy out Jazer, they captured
its dependencies, and evicted the Amo-
33 rites that were there. Then they moved
on, and proceeded up the road to Bashan, whereupon Og, king of Bashan,
together with all his people, sallied
forth for battle against them at Edrei,
34 but the LORD said to Moses,
“Do not be afraid of him; for I am
delivering him, all his people, and his
land into your power, so that you shall
do to him as you did to Sihon, king of
the Amorites, who lived at Heshbon.”
35 So they harried him and his sons and
all his people until not a survivor was
left to him, and took possession of his
land. The Israelites then moved on, 22
and camped in the steppes of Moab on
the other side of the Jordan at Jericho.
Now Balak, the son of Zippor, saw all 2
that Israel did to the Amorites, so that 3
Moab stood in great fear of the people,
because they were so many; Moab
stood in dread of the Israelites.
“Now this horde will lick up all the 4
pasture around us, as an ox licks up the
grass of a field,” said Moab to the elders
of Midian.
Balak, the son of Zippor, was king of 5
Moab at that time; so he sent messengers to Balaam, the son of Beor, at Pethor, which is near the Euphrates, to
the land of the Ammonites, to summon
him, saying,
“Here is a people come out of Egypt!
They cover the whole face of the earth,
and are settled opposite me. Now then, 6
come and curse this people for me; for
they are too strong for me; perhaps I
may be able to defeat them and drive
them out of the land; for I know that he
whom you bless is blessed, and he
whom you curse is cursed.”
So the elders of Moab and of Midian 7
departed, they themselves being skilled
in enchantment, and coming to Balaam, they gave Balak's message to him.
“Stay here tonight,” he said to them, 8
“and I will bring you back such word as
the LORD delivers to me.”
So the chieftains of Moab stayed 9
with Balaam. Then God came to Balaam, and said,
“What business have these men with
you?”
Balaam said to God, 10
“Balak, the son of Zippor, king of
Moab, has sent word to me, ‘Here is the 11
people that came out of Egypt covering
the face of the earth! Come now, and
curse them for me; perhaps I may be
able to fight against them and drive
them out.’”
God said to Balaam, 12
“You must not go with them; you
must not curse the people; for they are
to be blessed.”
So, when Balaam rose next morning, 13
he said to Balak's chieftains,
“Go home to your own land; for the
LORD has refused to let me go with
you.”
So the chieftains of Moab started off, 14
and coming to Balak, said,

"Balaam refused to leave with us."
15 Then Balak again sent chieftains,
more in number and more distinguished
16 than the others, and coming to Balaam,
they said to him,
"Thus says Balak, the son of Zippor:
'Pray let nothing hinder you from com-
17 ing to me; for I will reward you hand-
somely, and do for you whatever you
indicate to me; pray come then and
curse this people for me.' "
18 But Balaam in reply said to Balak's
ministers,
"Though Balak were to give me his
house full of silver and gold, I could not
violate the instructions of the LORD
my God to do anything, either small or
19 great. But do you also remain here tonight, and I will ascertain what else the
LORD may have to say to me."
20 Then God came to Balaam in the
night, and said to him,
"If it is to summon you that the men
have come, be off and go with them;
but it is only the message that I give
you that you are to give."
21 So, when Balaam rose next morning,
he saddled his ass, and went off with
the chieftains of Moab.
22 The anger of God blazed at his going,
and the angel of the LORD stationed
himself on the road to obstruct him, as
he rode on his ass, accompanied by his
23 two slaves. When the ass saw the angel
of the LORD standing on the road with
his drawn sword in his hand, the ass
turned out of the road, and went into
the fields; but Balaam struck the ass to
24 turn her back into the road. Then the
angel of the LORD took his stand on a
lane between vineyards, with a wall on
25 either side; and when the ass saw the
angel of the LORD, she pressed herself
against the wall, and crushed Balaam's
foot against the wall, so that he struck
26 her again. Then the angel of the LORD
passed on further, and took his stand
at a narrow place where there was no
room to turn either to the right or to
27 the left; and when the ass saw the angel
of the LORD, she lay down under Balaam, so that Balaam's anger blazed,
and he struck the ass with his staff.
28 Then the LORD opened the mouth of
the ass, and she said to Balaam,
"What have I done to you that you
should have struck me these three
times?"
29 "Because you have made a toy of
me," said Balaam to the ass. "Would
that there had been a sword in my
hand, for then I would have killed you."
The ass said to Balaam, 30
"Am I not your own ass, upon which
you have ridden all your life long until
this day? Have I ever been accustomed
to deal thus with you?"
"No," he said.
Then the LORD opened Balaam's 31
eyes, and he saw the angel of the LORD
standing on the road, with his drawn
sword in his hand, whereupon he
bowed his head, and fell on his face.
"Why have you struck your ass these 32
three times?" the angel of the LORD
said to him. "See, it was I who came
forth to obstruct you; for your errand
is displeasing to me. The ass saw me, 33
and swerved from me these three times;
unless she had swerved from me, I
would surely have slain you just now,
but would have spared her."
"I have sinned," said Balaam to the 34
angel of the LORD; "for I did not know
that it was you who stationed yourself
on the road against me. Now then, if it
is displeasing to you, I will go back."
But the angel of the LORD said to 35
Balaam,
"Go with the men; but it is only the
message that I give you that you are to
give."
So Balaam went along with Balak's
chieftains.
When Balak heard that Balaam was 36
coming, he went out to meet him at Ir-
Moab, which is on the Arnon frontier,
at the end of the frontier.
"Did I not send urgently for you?" 37
Balak said to Balaam. "Why did you
not come to me? Am I really unable
to honor you?"
Whereupon Balaam said to Balak, 38
"See, I have come to you! Have I
now any power of myself to say anything at all to you? It is only the message that God puts in my mouth that I
can speak."
Then Balaam went along with Balak, 39
and when they came to Kirjath-huzoth,
Balak sacrificed oxen and sheep, and 40
sent some to Balaam and the chieftains
who were with him.
Next morning Balak took Balaam 41
and brought him up to Bamoth-baal,
from which he could see the nearest of
the people.
Then Balaam said to Balak, 23

"Build seven altars for me here, and offer seven bullocks and seven rams for me here."
2 Balak did as Balaam had indicated, and offered a bullock and a ram on each
3 altar. Then Balaam said to Balak,
"Stay beside your burnt-offering, while I go aside; perhaps the LORD will come to meet me; whatever message he reveals to me I will tell you."
4 So he went off by himself. Then God came to meet Balaam, whereupon he said to him,
"I have arranged the seven altars, and offered a bullock and a ram on each altar."
5 Then the LORD put a message in Balaam's mouth.
"Return to Balak," he said, "and thus shall you speak."
6 So he returned to him, and found him standing beside his burnt-offering, together with all the chieftains of Mo-
7 ab. Then he gave utterance to his oracle, saying,

"From Aram has Balak brought me,
The king of Moab, from the mountains of the east:
'Come, curse Jacob for me,
Come, execrate Israel.'
8 How can I curse one whom God has not cursed?
How can I execrate one whom the LORD has not execrated?
9 For from the top of the rocks I see them,
From the hills I behold them—
Lo, a people living by themselves,
Not accounting themselves as one of the nations.
10 Who can count Jacob's masses,
Or number Israel's myriads?
Let me die the death of the righteous,
Let my end be like theirs!"

11 "How have you treated me?" Balak said to Balaam. "It was to curse my enemies that I took you, and here you have actually blessed them."
12 "Is it not what the LORD puts in my mouth that I must be careful to speak?" he answered.
13 Then Balak said to him,
"Pray come with me to another place, from which you may see them, although it will be only the nearest of them that you shall see, and not all of them; curse them for me from there."
14 So he took him to the field of Zophim, to the top of Pisgah, where he built seven altars and offered up a bullock and a ram on each altar.
"Stay here beside your burnt-offer- 15
ing," he said to Balak, "while I go to meet him yonder."
Then the LORD came to meet Ba- 16
laam, and putting a message in his mouth, said,
"Return to Balak, and thus shall you speak."
So he came back to him, and found 17
him standing beside his burnt-offering, together with the chieftains of Moab.
"What has the LORD said?" Balak said to him.
Whereupon he gave utterance to his 18
oracle, saying,

"Come, Balak, and hear;
Give ear unto me, son of Zippor!
God is not a man that he should break 19
his word,
Nor a human being that he should change his mind.
When he has said something, will he not do it?
When he has asserted something, will he not make it good?
See, it is a blessing that I have re- 20
ceived;
He has given a blessing, so I cannot change it.
No misfortune is to be observed in 21
Jacob,
No trouble is to be seen in Israel;
The LORD their God is with them,
The King is pleased with them.
God who brought them out of Egypt 22
Is like the horns of a wild-ox for them;
For there can be no enchantment 23
against Jacob,
And no divination against Israel,
Since the times are declared to Jacob,
And what God shall do, to Israel.
Here is a people that rises like an old 24
lion,
That rears itself like a lion;
It never lies down until it devours prey,
And drinks slain creatures' blood."

"Then," said Balak to Balaam, "nei- 25
ther curse nor bless them at all!"
But Balaam in reply said to Balak, 26
"Did I not say to you, 'Whatsoever the LORD declares, that I must do'?"
Then Balak said to Balaam, 27
"Come, let me take you to another place; perhaps God will see fit to have you curse them for me from there."

8 So Balak took Balaam to the top of
Peor, which overlooks Jeshimon.
9 "Build seven altars for me here," said
Balaam to Balak, "and offer seven bullocks and seven rams for me here."
0 Balak did as Balaam said; he offered
up a bullock and a ram on each altar.
1 When Balaam saw that the LORD saw
fit to bless Israel, he did not go in search
of oracles as usual, but directed his gaze
2 toward the desert. Raising his eyes,
Balaam saw Israel grouped into their
several tribes, whereupon the spirit of
3 God came upon him, and he gave utterance to his oracle, saying,
"The oracle of Balaam, the son of Beor,
The oracle of the man who had evil
designs,
4 The oracle of him who hears the words
of God,
Who has a vision of the Almighty,
Prostrate, but with eyes open:
5 How fine your tents are, O Jacob,
Your dwellings, O Israel!
6 Like far-stretching valleys,
Like gardens beside a river,
Like aloes planted by the LORD,
Like cedars beside a stream.
7 Water shall flow from their buckets,
And their seed shall have abundant
water;
Their king shall be taller than Agag,
And their kingdom shall be exalted.
8 God who brought them out of Egypt
Is like the horns of a wild-ox for them.
They shall devour nations that are
their adversaries,
And break their bones in pieces,
And shatter their loins;
9 They crouch, they lurk like a lion,
Like an old lion; who dare disturb
them?
Blessed are they who bless you,
And cursed are they who curse you."
0 Then Balak's anger blazed against
Balaam, and he struck his fists together.
"It was to curse my enemies that I
summoned you," said Balak to Balaam; "and here you have actually
1 blessed them these three times. So
then, hurry back to your home! I intended to honor you greatly, but, as it
is, the LORD has held you back from
honor."
2 But Balaam said to Balak,
"Was it not indeed to the messengers
3 whom you sent to me that I said, 'If
Balak were to give me his house full of
silver and gold, I could not violate the
instructions of the LORD to do either
good or bad of my own accord'? It is
only what the LORD tells me that I can
say. Now then, I leave at once for my 14
own people; come, let me advise you
what this people will do to your people
in days to come."
Whereupon he gave utterance to his 15
oracle, saying,
"The oracle of Balaam, the son of Beor,
The oracle of the man who had evil de-
signs,
The oracle of him who hears the 16
words of God,
And is acquainted with the knowledge
of the Most High,
Who has a vision of the Almighty,
Prostrate, but with eyes open:
I see them, but not as they are now, 17
I behold them, but not as they are at
present;
A star has come forth from Jacob,
A comet has risen from Israel,
And has shattered the temples of
Moab,
And the skulls of all the sons of Seth;
Edom has become a possession, 18
Seir has become a possession;
Israel has performed valiantly,
Jacob has conquered his enemies, 19
And has exterminated any survivors
from Ar."
Then he looked at Amalek, and gave 20
utterance to his oracle, saying,
"The first of the nations was Amalek,
But in the end he shall perish forever."
Then he looked at the Kenites, and 21
gave utterance to his oracle, saying,
"Though your dwelling-place is endur-
ing,
And your nest set on a rock,
Nevertheless it shall be annihilated, 22
O Kain;
How long will Ashur make captives of
you?"
Then he gave utterance to his oracle, 23
saying,
"Alas, who can live longer than God has
appointed him?
Ships shall come from the coast of 24
Kittim,
They shall harass Ashur, they shall
harass Eber,
So that he in turn shall perish for-
ever."
Then Balaam rose, and departing, 25
returned home; while Balak also went
his way.

25 When Israel settled down at Shittim,
the people began to have illicit relations
2 with the women of Moab, who invited
the people to the sacrifices to their
gods, so that the people ate them, and
3 paid homage to their gods. Israel
paired themselves off in honor of the
Baal of Peor, so that the anger of the
LORD blazed against Israel.
4 "Take all the ringleaders of the people," said the LORD to Moses, "and execute them for the LORD in broad daylight, so that the fierce anger of the
LORD may be averted from Israel."
5 So Moses said to the tribes of Israel,
"Slay each of you those of your
members who paired themselves off in
honor of the Baal of Peor."
6 Now one of the Israelites came and
introduced a Midianite woman into his
family in plain sight of Moses and the
whole assembly of the Israelites, while
they were weeping at the doorway of
7 the tent of meeting. When Phinehas,
the son of Eleazar, the son of Aaron, the
priest, saw it, he withdrew from the assembly, and taking a spear in his hand,
8 followed the Israelite into the room,
and stabbed both of them, the Israelite
and the woman in her abdomen. Thus
the plague was stopped in its attack on
9 the Israelites, but those who died from
the plague amounted to twenty-four
thousand.
10 Then the LORD said to Moses,
11 "Phinehas, the son of Eleazar, the
son of Aaron, the priest, has averted my
wrath from the Israelites by showing the
same jealousy among them as I would,
and so I did not put an end to the Is-
12 raelites in my jealousy. Announce
therefore, 'I hereby give him my pledge
13 of friendship, which shall serve him and
his descendants after him as the pledge
of a perpetual priesthood, because he
was jealous for his God, and made
atonement for the Israelites.' "
14 Now the name of the slain Israelite,
who was killed with the Midianite
woman, was Zimri, the son of Salu, the
15 leader of a Simeonite clan, while the
name of the Midianite woman who was
killed was Cozbi, the daughter of Zur,
who was the head of a clan division in
Midian.
16 The LORD said to Moses,
17 "Open hostilites with the Midianites,
18 and attack them; for they have been
showing hostility toward you by their
tricks which they have played against
you in the affair of Peor and that of
their country-woman Cozbi, the daughter of a Midianite chieftain, who was
killed on the day of the plague, in the
affair of Peor."
After the plague the LORD said to 19
Moses and Eleazar, the son of Aaron, 26
the priest,
"Take a census of the whole Israelite 2
community from twenty years old and
upward, clan by clan, all who can go
out to war in Israel."
So Moses and Eleazar, the priest, had 3
them pass in review on the steppes of
Moab, beside the Jordan at Jericho,
those from twenty years old and up- 4
ward, as the LORD had commanded
Moses—that is, the Israelites who came
out of the land of Egypt: Reuben, Is- 5
rael's first-born, and the descendants of
Reuben, Hanoch, of the Hanochite
family, the Palluite family of Pallu, the 6
Hezronite family of Hezron, and the
Carmite family of Carmi. These con- 7
stituted the families of the Reubenites,
whose numbers amounted to forty-three
thousand seven hundred and thirty.
The son of Pallu, Eliab, and the sons 8
of Eliab, Nemuel, Dathan, and Abi- 9
ram, the latter being the Dathan and
Abiram, the select men of the community, who took their stand with Korah's
company against Moses and Aaron
when they ranged themselves against
the LORD, and whom the earth, open- 10
ing its mouth, swallowed up, along
with Korah, when his company died,
when the fire consumed two hundred
and fifty men, so that they became a
warning. (The sons of Korah, however, 11
did not die.)
The descendants of Simeon, arranged 12
by families: the Nemuelite family of
Nemuel, the Jaminite family of Jamin,
the Jachinite family of Jachin, the Ze- 13
rahite family of Zerah, and the Shaulite
family of Shaul. These constituted the 14
families of the Simeonites, twenty-two
thousand two hundred.
The descendants of Gad, arranged by 15
families: the Zephonite family of Zephon, the Haggite family of Haggi, the
Shunite family of Shuni, the Oznite 16
family of Ozni, the Erite family of Eri,
the Arodite family of Arod, and the 17
Arelite family of Areli. These consti- 18
stituted the families of the descendants

of Gad that were numbered, forty thousand five hundred.
9 The sons of Judah, Er and Onan, but
Er and Onan died in the land of Ca-
0 naan, so the descendants of Judah as
arranged by families were the Shelahite
family of Shelah, the Perezite family of
Perez, and the Zerahite family of Zerah,
1 while the descendants of Perez were the
Hezronite family of Hezron and the
2 Hamulite family of Hamul. These constituted the families of Judah that were
numbered, seventy-six thousand five
hundred.
3 The descendants of Issachar, arranged by families: the Tolaite family
of Tola, the Puvite family of Puvah,
4 the Jashubite family of Jashub, and the
5 Shimronite family of Shimron. These
constituted the families of Issachar
that were numbered, sixty-four thousand three hundred.
6 The descendants of Zebulun, arranged by families: the Seredite family
of Sered, the Elonite family of Elon,
and the Jahleelite family of Jahleel.
7 These constituted the families of the
Zebulunites that were numbered, sixty
thousand five hundred.
8 The descendants of Joseph, arranged
by families: Manasseh and Ephraim;
9 the descendants of Manasseh: the Ma-
chirite family of Machir and the Gileadite family of Gilead, Machir having
0 also been the father of Gilead. The following are the descendants of Gilead:
the Iezerite family of Iezer, the Helek-
1 ite family of Helek, the Asrielite family
2 of Asriel, the Shechemite family of
Shechem, the Shemidaite family of
Shemida, and the Hepherite family of
3 Hepher. Zelophehad, the son of Hepher, had no sons, but only daughters,
the names of the daughters of Zelophehad being Mahlah, Noah, Hoglah, Mil-
4 cah, and Tirzah. These constituted the
families of Manasseh, whose numbers
amounted to fifty-two thousand seven
hundred.
5 The following are the descendants of
Ephraim, arranged by families: the
Shuthelahite family of Shuthelah, the
Becherite family of Becher, and the Ta-
6 hanite family of Tahan, while the following are the descendants of Shuthe-
7 lah: the Eranite family of Eran. These
constituted the families of the descendants of Ephraim that were numbered,
thirty-two thousand five hundred.

These constituted the descendants of
Joseph as arranged by families.
The descendants of Benjamin, ar- 38
ranged by families: the Belaite family
of Bela, the Ashbelite family of Ashbel,
the Ahiramite family of Ahiram, the 39
Shuphamite family of Shupham, and
the Huphamite family of Hupham,
while the descendants of Bela were Ard 40
and Naaman, the Ardite family and
the Naamite family of Naaman. These 41
constituted the descendants of Benjamin as arranged by families, whose
numbers amounted to forty-five thousand six hundred.
The following are the descendants of 42
Dan, arranged by families: the Shu-
hamite family of Shuham. This constituted the families of Dan as arranged
by families. The total of the Shuham- 43
ite families that were numbered was
sixty-four thousand four hundred.
The descendants of Asher, arranged 44
by families: the Imnite family of Imnah, the Ishvite family of Ishvi, and
the Beriite family of Beriah, while to 45
the descendants of Beriah belong the
the Heberite family of Heber and the
Malchielite family of Malchiel, and the 46
name of Asher's daughter was Serah.
These constituted the families of the 47
descendants of Asher that were numbered, fifty-three thousand four hundred.
The descendants of Naphtali, ar- 48
ranged by families: the Jahzeelite family of Jahzeel, the Gunite family of
Guni, the Jezerite family of Jezer, and 49
the Shillemite family of Shillem. These 50
constituted the families of Naphtali as
arranged by families, whose numbers
amounted to forty-five thousand four
hundred.
These constituted the Israelites that 51
were numbered, six hundred and one
thousand seven hundred and thirty.
Then the LORD said to Moses, 52
"Among these the land is to be ap- 53
portioned as a heritage, according to
their respective numbers; for the large 54
group you must make the heritage
large, and for the small group you must
make the heritage small, to each being
given a heritage proportionate to its
numbers. However, the land is to be 55
divided by lot; they are to receive their
heritage according to the numbers in
their respective ancestral tribes; as de- 56
termined by lot their heritage is to be

divided proportionately between the
larger groups and the smaller groups."
57 The following are the Levites that
were numbered, arranged by families:
the Gershonite family of Gershon, the
Kohathite family of Kohath, and the
58 Merarite family of Merari. The following are the families of Levi: the Lib-
nite family, the Hebronite family, the
Mahlite family, the Mushite family,
and the Korahite family. Kohath was
59 the father of Amram, while the name of
Amram's wife was Jochebed, the
daughter of Levi, who was born to Levi
in Egypt; she bore Aaron and Moses to
Amram, as well as their sister Miriam.
60 To Aaron were born Nadab, Abihu,
61 Eleazar, and Ithamar, but Nadab and
Abihu died when they offered improper
62 fire before the LORD. Those of them
that were numbered amounted to twenty-three thousand, all the males from a
month old and upward; for they were
not numbered among the other Israelites, because no heritage was given
them among the Israelites.
63 These constituted those that were
numbered by Moses and Eleazar, the
priest, who numbered the Israelites on
the steppes of Moab, beside the Jordan
64 at Jericho, and among these there was
no one belonging to those who had been
numbered by Moses and Aaron, the
priest, who numbered the Israelites in
65 the desert of Sinai; for the LORD had
said of them that they would be sure to
die in the desert, and so not one of
them was left except Caleb, the son of
Jephunneh, and Joshua, the son of
Nun.

27 Then came forward the daughters of
Zelophehad, the son of Hepher, the son
of Gilead, the son of Machir, the son of
Manasseh, members of the families of
Manasseh, the son of Joseph; the following were the names of his daughters: Mahlah, Noah, Hoglah, Milcah,
2 and Tirzah. They took their stand before Moses, and Eleazar, the priest, and
before the chieftains and the whole assembly, at the doorway of the tent of
meeting, saying,
3 "Our father died in the desert,
though he did not participate with
those who gathered against the LORD
in Korah's company, but he died simply for his own sin, leaving no sons.
4 Why should our father's name be lost
to his family, just because he had no
son? Give us property along with our
father's kinsmen."

So Moses laid their case before the
LORD, and the LORD said to Moses,

"The daughters of Zelophehad are
right in their statements; you must certainly give them the possession of a
heritage along with their father's kinsmen, transferring their father's heritage
to them. Further, you must say to the
Israelites, 'If a man dies, leaving no
son, you must transfer his heritage to
his daughter. If he has no daughter,
you must give his heritage to his brothers. If he has no brothers, you must
give his heritage to his father's brothers. If his father has no brothers, you
must give his heritage to the nearest
relative in his family, and he shall take
it over.' This is to be a fixed ordinance
for the Israelites, as the LORD has commanded Moses."

Then the LORD said to Moses,

"Ascend this mountain of the Abarim, and view the land which I am giving the Israelites. When you have
viewed it, you, too, shall be gathered to
your fathers, as your brother Aaron
was, since you rebelled against my instructions when the community rebelled in the desert of Zin, in the matter
of paying me due honor in their presence at the waters" (these being the
waters of Meribath-Kadesh in the desert of Zin).

Then Moses said to the LORD,

"Let the LORD, the God of the spirits of all mankind, appoint someone
over the community, who shall come
and go before them, and lead them out
and bring them in, so that the LORD'S
community may not be like sheep without a shepherd."

So the LORD said to Moses,

"Take Joshua, the son of Nun, a man
of capacity, and lay your hand upon
him; have him stand before Eleazar,
the priest, and the whole community,
and commission him in their sight. Invest him with some of your own majesty, that the whole Israelite community
may heed him. He is to take his stand
before Eleazar, the priest, who shall
make inquiry before the LORD for him
by decision of the Urim, and at whose
bidding both he and all the Israelites
with him, the whole community, are to
come and go."

Moses did as the LORD commanded

him; he took Joshua and had him stand
before Eleazar, the priest, and the
23 whole community; he laid his hands
upon him, and commissioned him, as
the LORD had indicated through
Moses.

VARIOUS REGULATIONS, 28:1—36:13

28 The LORD said to Moses,
2 "Command the Israelites, and say to
them, 'The offering of food made to me
as a sacrifice, a soothing odor to me,
you must be careful to offer to me at the
3 proper time for it.' You must also say
to them, 'This is the sacrifice that you
are to offer to the LORD: two perfect
yearling male lambs as a regular burnt-
4 offering each day, offering the one lamb
in the morning, and the other lamb at
5 twilight, together with a tenth of an
ephah of fine flour mixed with a fourth
of a hin of oil from crushed olives, as a
6 cereal-offering—a regular burnt-offering, such as was instituted at Mount
Sinai, as a soothing odor, a sacrifice to
7 the LORD. Its libation is to be a fourth
of a hin for the one lamb, a libation of
liquor to the LORD, to be poured out in
8 the sanctuary; the other lamb you
must offer at twilight as a sacrifice, a
soothing odor to the LORD, offering it
with the same cereal-offering and libation as in the morning.
9 " 'On the sabbath day, two perfect
yearling male lambs and two-tenths of
an ephah of fine flour mixed with oil as
a cereal-offering, along with its liba-
10 tion, as the sabbath burnt-offering each
sabbath, in addition to the regular
burnt-offering and its libation.
11 " 'On your new moons you must offer
as a burnt-offering to the LORD two
young bullocks, one ram, and seven
12 perfect yearling male lambs, along with
three tenths of an ephah of fine flour
mixed with oil as a cereal-offering for
each bullock, and two tenths of an ephah
of fine flour mixed with oil as a cereal-
13 offering for the one ram, and a tenth of
an ephah of fine flour mixed with oil as a
cereal-offering for each lamb—a burnt-
offering, a soothing odor, a sacrifice to
14 the LORD. Their libations are to be
half a hin of wine per bullock, a third of
a hin for the ram, and a fourth of a hin
per lamb. This is to be the burnt-offering of the new moon, each new moon
throughout the new moons of the year.
Moreover, one he-goat is to be offered 15
as a sin-offering to the LORD, in addition to the regular burnt-offering and
its libation.
" 'On the fourteenth day of the first 16
month is the passover to the LORD,
and on the fifteenth day of this month 17
there is to be a feast. For seven days
unleavened cakes are to be eaten. On 18
the first day there is to be a religious
assembly; you must do no hard work at
all, but offer as a sacrifice, a burnt- 19
offering to the LORD, two young bullocks, one ram, and seven yearling male
lambs, having them perfect; and for 20
their cereal-offerings you must offer
fine flour mixed with oil, three tenths
of an ephah per bullock and two tenths
for the ram, offering a tenth for each of 21
the seven lambs, together with one he- 22
goat as a sin-offering, to make atonement for you. You are to offer these in 23
addition to the morning burnt-offering
which is the regular burnt-offering.
Offerings like these you must make 24
daily, for the seven days, as food, as a
sacrifice, a soothing odor to the LORD,
to be made in addition to the regular
burnt-offering and its libation; and on 25
the seventh day you must hold a religious assembly, doing no hard work at
all.
" 'On the day of first-fruits, when 26
you offer a cereal-offering of new grain
to the LORD in your festival of weeks,
you must hold a religious assembly; you
must do no hard work at all, but offer 27
as a burnt-offering, as a soothing odor
to the LORD, two young bullocks, one
ram, and seven yearling male lambs,
together with their cereal-offering, fine 28
flour mixed with oil, three tenths of an
ephah per bullock, two tenths for the 29
one ram, and a tenth for each of the
seven lambs, as well as one he-goat to 30
make atonement for you. In addition 31
to the regular burnt-offering and its
cereal-offering you are to offer these
and their libations, having them perfect.
" 'On the first day of the seventh 29
month you must hold a religious assembly, doing no hard work at all, but observing it as a day of festivity; you 2
must offer as a burnt-offering, a soothing odor to the LORD, one young bullock, one ram, and seven perfect year-

3 ling male lambs, together with their
cereal-offering, fine flour mixed with
oil, three tenths of an ephah per bul-
4 lock, two tenths for the ram, and a
5 tenth for each of the seven lambs, as
well as one he-goat as a sin-offering to
6 make atonement for you—in addition
to the burnt-offering of the new moon
with its cereal-offering, and the regular
burnt-offering with its cereal-offering,
and the libations as prescribed for
them, as a soothing odor, a sacrifice to
the LORD.

7 " 'On the tenth day of this same seventh month, you must hold a religious
assembly, and mortify yourselves; you
8 must do no work at all, but offer as a
burnt-offering to the LORD, a soothing
odor, one young bullock, one ram, and
seven yearling male lambs, having
9 them perfect, together with their cereal-offering, fine flour mixed with oil,
three-tenths of an ephah per bullock,
10 two tenths for the one ram, and a
11 tenth for each of the seven lambs, as
well as one he-goat as a sin-offering, in
addition to the atonement sin-offering
and the regular burnt-offering and its
cereal-offering, along with their libations.

12 " 'On the fifteenth day of the seventh month you must hold a religious
assembly, doing no hard work at all,
but holding a feast for the LORD for
13 seven days; you must offer as a burnt-
offering, a sacrifice, a soothing odor to
the LORD, thirteen young bullocks,
two rams, and fourteen yearling male
14 lambs that are perfect, together with
their cereal-offering, fine flour mixed
with oil, three tenths of an ephah for
each of the thirteen bullocks, two
15 tenths for each of the two rams, and a
16 tenth for each of the fourteen lambs, as
well as one he-goat as a sin-offering, in
addition to the regular burnt-offering,
its cereal-offering and libation.

17 " 'On the second day, twelve young
bullocks, two rams, and fourteen per-
18 fect yearling male lambs, together with
the cereal-offerings and libations for the
bullocks, rams, and lambs, in propor-
19 tion to their numbers, as prescribed, as
well as one he-goat as a sin-offering, in
addition to the regular burnt-offering
and its cereal-offering, along with their
libations.

20 " 'On the third day, eleven bullocks,
two rams, and fourteen perfect yearling
male lambs, together with the cereal- 21
offering and libations for the bullocks,
rams, and lambs, in proportion to their
numbers, as prescribed, as well as one 22
he-goat as a sin-offering, in addition to
the regular burnt-offering with its cereal-offering and libation.

" 'On the fourth day, ten bullocks, 23
two rams, and fourteen perfect yearling
male lambs, together with the cereal- 24
offerings and libations for the bullocks, rams, and lambs, in proportion
to their numbers, as prescribed, as well 25
as one he-goat as a sin-offering, in addition to the regular burnt-offering, its
cereal-offering and libation.

" 'On the fifth day, nine bullocks, 26
two rams, and fourteen perfect yearling
male lambs, together with the cereal- 27
offerings and libations for the bullocks,
rams, and lambs, in proportion to their
numbers, as prescribed, as well as one 28
he-goat as a sin-offering, in addition to
the regular burnt-offering, its cereal-
offering and libation.

" 'On the sixth day, eight bullocks, 29
two rams, and fourteen perfect yearling
male lambs, together with the cereal- 30
offerings and libations for the bullocks,
rams, and lambs, in accordance with
their numbers, as prescribed, as well as 31
one he-goat as a sin-offering, in addition to the regular burnt-offering, its
cereal-offering and libation.

" 'On the seventh day, seven bul- 32
locks, two rams, and fourteen perfect
yearling male lambs, together with the 33
cereal-offerings and libations for the
bullocks, rams, and lambs, in accordance with their numbers, as prescribed,
as well as one he-goat as a sin-offering, 34
in addition to the regular burnt-offering, its cereal-offering and libation.

" 'On the eighth day you must hold a 35
sacred assembly; you must do no hard
work at all, but offer as a burnt-offer- 36
ing, a sacrifice, a soothing odor to the
LORD, one bullock, one ram, and seven
perfect yearling male lambs, together 37
with the cereal-offerings and libations
for the bullock, ram, and lambs, in accordance with their numbers, as prescribed, as well as one he-goat as a sin- 38
offering, in addition to the regular
burnt-offering with its cereal-offering
and libation.

" 'These you must offer to the LORD 39
at your fixed festivals, in addition to
your votive offerings and voluntary

offerings, as your burnt-offerings, cereal-offerings, libations, and thank-offerings.' "
40 So Moses instructed the Israelites
just as the LORD commanded Moses.
30 Then Moses said to the heads of the
Israelite tribes,
"This is the command that the
2 LORD has given: 'When a man makes
a vow to the LORD or on oath binds
himself with a pledge, he must not
break his word; he must do just as he
3 declared. Also, when a woman makes a
vow to the LORD, or binds herself with
a pledge, while she is still in her youth
4 in her father's house, if her father
should hear of her vow and her pledge
with which she bound herself, and her
father gives her his tacit approval, all
her vows shall stand, and every pledge
with which she bound herself shall
5 stand. But if her father does raise objections with her, when he hears of it,
none of her vows or her pledges with
which she bound herself shall stand,
and the LORD will absolve her, because
her father raised objections with her.
6 If she should ever marry while bound
by her vows or some rash utterance
7 with which she bound herself, and her
husband should hear of it, but gives her
his tacit approval when he does hear of
it, her vows shall stand, and her pledges
with which she bound herself shall
8 stand. But if her husband raises objections with her when he hears of it, he
shall nullify the vow by which she is
bound and the rash utterance with
which she bound herself, and the
9 LORD will absolve her. In the case of
the vow of a widow, however, or a divorced woman, everything with which
she has bound herself shall be binding
10 on her. If a woman has made a vow or
bound herself with a pledge by an oath
11 while in the house of her husband, and
her husband should hear of it, but gives
her his tacit approval, by not raising
objections with her, all her vows shall
stand, and every pledge with which she
12 bound herself shall stand. But if her
husband should make them null and
void when he hears of them, nothing to
which she gave utterance by way of
vow or pledge shall stand; since her
husband nullified them, the LORD will
13 absolve her. Any vow and any oath as
a pledge to self-mortification, her hus-
14 band can validate or nullify. But if her
husband from day to day does give her
his tacit approval, he shall validate all
her vows or pledges by which she is
bound; he has validated them, because
he gave her his tacit approval when he
heard of them. But if he should at- 15
tempt to nullify them after he has
heard of them, he shall answer for her
iniquity himself.' "
These were the statutes with which 16
the LORD charged Moses, in a situation involving a man and his wife, and
a father and his daughter while she is
still in her youth in her father's house.
Then the LORD said to Moses, 31
"Avenge the Israelites on the Midi- 2
anites, after which you shall be gathered to your fathers."
So Moses commanded the people, 3
"Choose the best of your number as
an army to serve against Midian, to
execute the LORD's vengeance on Midian, selecting for the army a thousand 4
from each of all the tribes of Israel."
So a thousand per tribe were fur- 5
nished from the clans of Israel, twelve
thousand picked troops. Then Moses 6
sent them to the war, a thousand from
each tribe, together with Phinehas, the
son of Eleazar, as priest for the army,
with the sacred objects and the alarm
trumpets in his hand. They made war 7
on Midian, as the LORD had commanded Moses, and slew every male; 8
they slew the kings of Midian with the
rest of them that were slain, namely,
Evi, Rekem, Zur, Hur, and Reba, the
five kings of Midian; and they also
slew Balaam, the son of Beor, with the
sword. The Israelites took the women 9
and children of Midian captive, while
all their cattle, and flocks, and goods
they took as booty, and burned up all 10
the cities where they lived and all their
encampments. Then they took all the 11
spoil and all the booty of man and
beast, and brought the captives, booty, 12
and spoil to Moses and Eleazar, the
priest, and the Israelite community at
the camp in the steppes of Moab beside
the Jordan at Jericho.
When Moses with Eleazar, the priest, 13
and all the leaders of the community
went outside the camp to meet them,
Moses became angry with the officers 14
of the army, the captains of divisions
of a thousand and those of a hundred,
who had come from service in the war.
"And so you have let all the women 15

16 live?" Moses said to them. "Why, it
was these who led the Israelites
through the counsel of Balaam to forsake the LORD in the affair of Peor, so
that the plague appeared among the
17 LORD'S community. Now then, slay
every male among the little ones, and
slay every woman who has had intercourse with a man by lying with a male;
18 but all the girls who have not had intercourse with a man by lying with a male,
19 keep alive for yourselves. Now as for
yourselves, remain outside the camp for
seven days; all of you who have slain
anyone and all of you who have touched
a slain person, purify yourselves on the
third day and the seventh, you and
20 your captives. Also, every garment,
every article made of skin, everything
made of goat's hair, and every wooden
article, you must purify."
21 Eleazar, the priest, said to the warriors who engaged in the battle,

"This is the statute of the law which
the LORD has commanded Moses:
22 'However, the gold, silver, bronze, iron,
23 tin, and lead—everything that can
stand fire, you must put through fire,
that it may become clean, being purified, however, by the water used for impurity; whatever cannot stand fire you
24 must pass through the water. You must
wash your clothes on the seventh day,
and so become clean, after which you
may re-enter the camp.'"
25 Then the LORD said to Moses,
26 "Take a count of the booty that was
captured, both of man and beast, you,
Eleazar, the priest, and the heads of
27 families in the community, and then
divide the booty in two between the
warriors who went out to the battle and
28 all the rest of the community, levying a
tax for the LORD on the warriors who
went out to the battle, one in five hundred, of the men, the cattle, the asses,
29 and the flocks, taking it from their half,
and giving it to Eleazar, the priest, as
30 a contribution to the LORD. From the
Israelites' half you must take one
drawn from every fifty, of the men, the
cattle, the asses, and the flocks, of all
the live stock, and give them to the
Levites who have charge of the dwelling of the LORD."
31 Moses and Eleazar, the priest, did as
32 the LORD commanded Moses. Now
the plunder, what was left of the booty
that the warriors took, consisted of six
hundred and seventy-five thousand
sheep, seventy-two thousand oxen, 33
sixty-one thousand asses, and a total of 34
thirty-two thousand girls, who had 35
never had intercourse with a man by lying with a male. The half which con- 36
stituted the share of those who went
out to the battle amounted to three
hundred and thirty-seven thousand
five hundred sheep, the LORD'S tax 37
from the sheep being six hundred and
seventy-five, thirty-six thousand oxen, 38
from which the LORD'S tax was seventy-two, thirty thousand five hundred 39
asses, from which the LORD'S tax was
sixty-one, and sixteen thousand per- 40
sons, from whom the LORD'S tax was
thirty-two persons. Moses gave the tax 41
to Eleazar, the priest, as a contribution
to the LORD, as the LORD had commanded Moses. From the Israelites' 42
half which Moses divided from that of
the warriors (now the community's half 43
was three hundred and thirty-seven
thousand five hundred sheep, thirty- 44
six thousand oxen, thirty thousand five 45
hundred asses, and sixteen thousand 46
persons), from the Israelites' half 47
Moses took one drawn out of every
fifty, both of man and beast, and gave
them to the Levites who had charge of
the LORD'S dwelling, as the LORD had
commanded Moses.

Then the officers who were attached 48
to the divisions of a thousand in the
army, the captains of divisions of a
thousand and those of a hundred, came
up to Moses, and said to Moses, 49

"Your servants have taken a census
of the warriors who have been in our
charge, and not one of us is missing. So 50
we have brought as an offering to the
LORD what each had acquired, articles
of gold, armlets, bracelets, signet-rings,
earrings, and necklaces, to make atonement for ourselves before the LORD."

So Moses and Eleazar, the priest, 51
took the gold from them, all serviceable
articles, and the total amount of the 52
gold in the contribution which they
made to the LORD from the captains of
divisions of a thousand and those of a
hundred was sixteen thousand seven
hundred and fifty shekels. (The war- 53
riors, too, had taken booty, each keeping it for himself.) When Moses and 54
Eleazar, the priest, took the gold from
the captains of divisions of a thousand
and those of a hundred, they brought

it to the tent of meeting as a memorial
for the Israelites before the LORD.
32 Now the Reubenites and Gadites had
much live stock, a very great amount.
So, when they saw that the land of
Jazer and the land of Gilead was a dis-
2 trict suitable for live stock, the Gadites
and Reubenites came and said to
Moses, and Eleazar, the priest, and the
leaders of the community,
3 "Ataroth, Dibon, Jazer, Nimrah,
Heshbon, Elealeh, Sebam, Nebo, and
4 Beon, the land which the LORD laid
low before the community of Israel, is a
land suitable for live stock, and your
5 servants have live stock." "If we have
found favor with you," they said, "let
this land be given to your servants as
their property. Do not take us across
the Jordan."
6 But Moses said to the Gadites and
Reubenites,
"Ought your fellow-tribesmen to engage in war while you remain here?
7 Why should you discourage the Israelites from crossing to the land which the
8 LORD has given them? That is what
your fathers did when I sent them from
9 Kadesh-barnea to view the land. When
they went up to the valley of Eshcol
and saw the land, they discouraged the
Israelites from entering the land which
10 the LORD had given them, so that the
LORD'S anger blazed that day, and he
11 swore, saying, 'None of the men who
came up from Egypt, from twenty
years old and upward, shall ever see the
land which I promised on oath to Abraham, Isaac, and Jacob, because they
12 have not corroborated me, with the exception of Caleb, the son of Jephunneh,
the Kenizzite, and Joshua, the son of
Nun, because they have corroborated
13 the LORD.' So the LORD'S anger blazed
against Israel, and he made them wander up and down the desert for forty
years, until all the generation that had
done evil in the sight of the LORD had
14 perished. And here you have risen in
your father's place, a brood of sinners,
to augment still more the fierce anger of
15 the LORD against Israel! If you turn
from following him, he will again abandon them in the desert, and you will
bring harm to this whole people."
16 Then they came up to him, and said,
"We will but build folds here for our
live stock and cities for our dependents,
17 while we ourselves will form the picked
troops to go as special troops ahead of
the Israelites until we have brought
them to their home, and our dependents shall live in the fortified cities because of the inhabitants of the land.
We will not return to our own houses 18
until the Israelites have each come into
possession of his heritage; for we will 19
not seek any heritage with them across
and beyond the Jordan, because our
heritage has fallen to us on the other
side of the Jordan, to the east."
So Moses said to them, 20
"If you will do this, if you will form
the picked troops to go before the
LORD into battle, and all your picked 21
troops cross the Jordan in sight of the
LORD until he drives his enemies out of
his way, and the land is subdued be- 22
fore the LORD, after that you may return, quit of all obligation to the LORD
and Israel, and this land shall be yours
to hold before the LORD. But if you 23
will not do so, then you will have sinned
against the LORD, and be assured that
your sin will find you out. Build cities 24
for your dependents and folds for your
sheep, and do what you have promised."
The Gadites and Reubenites said to 25
Moses,
"Your servants shall do as my lord
commands. Our little ones, wives, 26
flocks, and all our cattle shall remain
there in the cities of Gilead; but your 27
servants, all picked troops, shall cross
over to battle in sight of the LORD, as
my lord indicates."
So Moses gave instructions concern- 28
ing them to Eleazar, the priest, to Joshua, the son of Nun, and to the heads of
families in the Israelite tribes.
"If the Gadites and Reubenites, all 29
picked troops," Moses said to them,
"cross the Jordan with you for battle
in sight of the LORD, and the land is
subdued before you, then you must give
them the land of Gilead as their property; but if they do not cross over as 30
picked troops with you, they shall receive property with you in the land of
Canaan."
Whereupon the Gadites and Reuben- 31
ites responded,
"We will do just what the LORD has
told your servants. We will cross over 32
as picked troops in sight of the LORD to
the land of Canaan, but the property
constituting our heritage shall fall to
us on the other side of the Jordan."

33 So Moses gave them, the Gadites,
Reubenites, and half-tribe of Manasseh, the son of Joseph, the kingdom of
Sihon, king of the Amorites, and the
kingdom of Og, king of Bashan, the
land with its cities in the various districts, the cities throughout the land.
34 The Gadites built Dibon, Ataroth,
35 Aroer, Atroth-shophan, Jazer, Jogbe-
36 hah, Beth-nimrah, and Beth-haran, as
fortified cities, as well as sheepfolds.
37 The Reubenites built Heshbon, Elea-
38 leh, Kirjathaim, Nebo, Baal-meon
(names to be changed), and Sibmah,
and renamed the cities that they rebuilt.
39 The descendants of Machir, the son
of Manasseh, went to Gilead, and capturing it, evicted the Amorites who
40 were in it. So Moses gave Gilead to
Machir, the son of Manasseh, and he
41 settled in it. Then Jair, the son of Manasseh, went and captured their villages, calling them Havvoth-jair [the
42 villages of Jair], while Nobah went and
captured Kenath and its dependencies,
calling it Nobah after his own name.

33 The following are the stages by which
the Israelites came from Egypt in companies, under the direction of Moses
2 and Aaron. Moses wrote down the
starting-places as commanded by the
LORD for them on their several stages,
and the following are the stages as ar-
3 ranged by their starting-places. In the
first month, on the fifteenth day of the
first month, they set out from Rameses;
on the day after the passover the Israelites went triumphantly out in sight
4 of all the Egyptians, while the Egyptians were burying all their first-born
whom the LORD had struck down
among them. The LORD had also exe-
5 cuted judgment upon their gods. The
Israelites set out from Rameses, and
6 camped at Succoth. Setting out from
Succoth, they camped at Etham, which
7 is on the edge of the desert. Setting out
from Etham, they turned back to Pi-
hahiroth, which is east of Baal-zephon,
8 and camped to the east of Migdol. Setting out from Pi-hahiroth, they passed
through the sea into the desert, and
marching for three days in the desert
9 of Etham, they camped at Marah. Setting out from Marah, they came to
Elim, where there were twelve springs
of water and seventy palm trees, so
10 they camped there. Setting out from
Elim, they camped beside the Red Sea.
Setting out from the Red Sea, they 11
camped in the desert of Sin. Setting 12
out from the desert of Sin, they camped
at Dophkah. Setting out from Doph- 13
kah, they camped at Alush. Setting 14
out from Alush, they camped at Rephidim, where there was no water for the
people to drink. Setting out from 15
Rephidim, they camped in the desert
of Sinai. Setting out from the desert of 16
Sinai, they camped at Kibroth-hattaavah. Setting out from Kibroth- 17
hattaavah, they camped at Hazeroth.
Setting out from Hazeroth, they 18
camped at Rithmah. Setting out from 19
Rithmah, they camped at Rimmon-
perez. Setting out from Rimmon- 20
perez, they camped at Libnah. Setting 21
out from Libnah, they camped at Rissah. Setting out from Rissah, they 22
camped at Kehelah. Setting out from 23
Kehelah, they camped at Mount
Shepher. Setting out from Mount 24
Shepher, they camped at Haradah. Set- 25
ting out from Haradah, they camped at
Makheloth. Setting out from Mak- 26
heloth, they camped at Tahath. Set- 27
ting out from Tahath, they camped at
Terah. Setting out from Terah, they 28
camped at Mithkah. Setting out from 29
Mithkah, they camped at Hashmonah.
Setting out from Hashmonah, they 30
camped at Moseroth. Setting out from 31
Moseroth, they camped at Bene-
jaakan. Setting out from Bene-jaakan, 32
they camped at Hor-haggidgad. Set- 33
ting out from Hor-haggidgad, they
camped at Jotbah. Setting out from 34
Jotbah, they camped at Abronah. Set- 35
ting out from Abronah, they camped at
Ezion-geber. Setting out from Ezion- 36
geber, they camped in the desert of
Zin, that is, at Kadesh. Setting out 37
from Kadesh, they camped at Mount
Hor, on the edge of the land of Edom.
(By command of the LORD, Aaron, the 38
priest, ascended Mount Hor, and died
there, in the fortieth year after the Israelites had come out of the land of
Egypt, on the first day of the fifth
month, Aaron being one hundred and 39
twenty-three years old when he died on
Mount Hor. The Canaanite king of 40
Arad, who lived in the Negeb in the
land of Canaan, heard of the coming of
the Israelites.) Setting out from Mount 41
Hor, they camped at Zalmonah. Set- 42
ting out from Zalmonah, they camped

43 at Punon. Setting out from Punon,
44 they camped at Oboth. Setting out
from Oboth, they camped at Ijeabarim,
45 on the frontier of Moab. Setting out
from Ijim, they camped at Dibon-gad.
46 Setting out from Dibon-gad, they
47 camped at Almon-diblathaim. Setting
out from Almon-diblathaim, they
camped at the Abarim mountains, east
of Nebo.
48 Setting out from the Abarim mountains, they camped on the steppes of
Moab beside the Jordan at Jericho;
49 their camp lay along the Jordan, from
Beth-jeshimoth as far as Abel-shittim,
on the steppes of Moab.
50 On the steppes of Moab beside the
Jordan at Jericho the LORD said to
Moses,
51 "Speak to the Israelites, and say to
them, 'When you cross the Jordan into
52 the land of Canaan, you must drive all
the inhabitants of the land out of your
way, destroy all their figured stones,
destroy all their molten images, and de-
53 molish all their high places. When you
have conquered the land, you are to settle in it; for it is to you that I have giv-
en the land, to take possession of it.
54 You are to apportion the land as a
heritage among yourselves by lot, clan
by clan, making the heritage large for
the large group, and making the heritage small for the small group; to whomsoever the lot gives it, his shall it be;
you are to make the apportionments
55 among you by ancestral tribes. But if
you do not drive the inhabitants of the
land out of your way, those of them
whom you allow to remain shall become
pricks in your eyes and thorns in your
sides, and they will harass you in the
56 land in which you live, and so I will
treat you as I intended to treat them.' "
34 The LORD said to Moses,
2 "Command the Israelites, and say to
them, 'When you enter the land of Canaan (this is the land that is to fall to
you as a heritage, the land of Canaan
3 throughout its extent), your southern
boundary shall run from the desert of
Zin along the side of Edom; your southern frontier shall run from the lower end
4 of the Salt Sea eastward; your frontier
shall then turn south of the slope of
Akrabbim, pass along to Zin, and end
south of Kadesh-barnea; it shall proceed to Hazar-addar, and continue to
5 Azmon; at Azmon the frontier shall
turn to the River of Egypt, and end at
the Sea. As a western frontier you shall 6
have the Great Sea with its coastland;
this shall be your western frontier. The 7
following shall be your northern frontier: from the Great Sea you shall draw
your line to Mount Hor; from Mount 8
Hor you shall draw your line to the approach to Hamath, and the frontier
shall end at Zedad; the frontier shall 9
then proceed to Ziphron, and end at
Hazar-enan. This shall be your northern frontier. For the eastern frontier 10
you shall draw your line from Hazar-
enan to Shepham; from Shepham the 11
frontier shall run down to Riblah, east
of Ain; the frontier shall then go down
and strike the spur at the sea of Chinnereth to the east; the frontier shall run 12
down to the Jordan, and end at the Salt
Sea. This is the land that you are to
have, as bounded by its various frontiers.' "
So Moses instructed the Israelites as 13
follows:
"This is the land which you are to
apportion among yourselves by lot,
which the LORD has commanded to be
given to the nine and a half tribes; for 14
the Reubenite tribe, family by family,
the Gadite tribe, family by family, and
the half-tribe of Manasseh have received their heritages; the two and a 15
half tribes have received their heritages
on the other side of the Jordan at Jericho to the east, toward the dawn."
Then the LORD said to Moses, 16
"The following are the names of the 17
men who are to apportion the land for
you: Eleazar, the priest, and Joshua,
the son of Nun. You must also take one 18
chieftain from each tribe to apportion
the land, and the following are the 19
names of the men: from the tribe of
Judah, Caleb, the son of Jephunneh;
from the Simeonite tribe, Shemuel, the 20
son of Ammihud; from the tribe of Ben- 21
jamin, Elidad, the son of Chislon; from 22
the Danite tribe, a chieftain, Bukki, the
son of Jogli; from the Josephites: from 23
the Manassite tribe, a chieftain, Hanniel, the son of Ephod, and from the 24
Ephraimite tribe, a chieftain, Kemuel,
the son of Shiphtan; from the Zebulun- 25
ite tribe, a chieftain, Elizaphan, the son
of Parnach; from the Issacharite tribe, 26
a chieftain, Paltiel, the son of Azzan;
from the Asherite tribe, a chieftain, 27
Ahihud, the son of Shelomi; and from 28

the Naphtalite tribe, a chieftain, Peda-
hel, the son of Ammihud."
29 These were those whom the LORD
commanded to apportion the heritages
to the Israelites in the land of Canaan.
35 On the steppes of Moab beside the
Jordan at Jericho the LORD said to
Moses,
2 "Command the Israelites that they
give the Levites cities to live in out of
the heritages that they hold; you must
also give the Levites the pasture-lands
3 adjacent to the cities. The cities shall
serve them to live in, while the pasture-
lands shall serve their cattle and live
4 stock, all their animals. The pasture-
lands of the cities that you give the Levites are to extend for a radius of one
thousand cubits outside the wall of the
5 city; you must make the measurements
of the east side outside the city two
thousand cubits, those of the south side
two thousand cubits, those of the west
side two thousand cubits, and those of
the north side two thousand cubits,
with the city lying in the center. This
shall be the pasture-lands of their cities.
6 The cities that you give the Levites
shall be the six cities of refuge to which
you must let the homicide flee, and in
addition to them you must designate
7 forty-two other cities. The total number of cities that you give the Levites is
to be forty-eight, together with their
8 pasture-lands. In the case of the cities
that you give them from the holdings
of the Israelites, you shall take many
from the large group, and few from the
small group; each in proportion to the
heritage that it receives shall give of its
cities to the Levites."
9 The LORD said to Moses,
10 "Speak to the Israelites, and say to
them, 'When you cross the Jordan into
11 the land of Canaan, you must select
suitable cities to serve as cities of refuge
for you, that the homicide who kills
anyone inadvertently may flee there.
12 The cities shall serve you as places of
refuge from the avenger, that the homicide may not die until he has taken his
stand before the community for trial.
13 As for the cities that you are to designate, you must have six cities of refuge,
14 designating three cities on the other
side of the Jordan and three cities in the
land of Canaan, to be cities of refuge.
15 These six cities shall serve the Israelites. as well as the resident aliens and
the serfs among them, as places of refuge, so that anyone who kills another
inadvertently may flee there. But if he 16
struck him with an iron tool, so that he
died, he is a murderer; the murderer
must be put to death. If he struck him 17
with a stone in the hand, from which
death may result, so that he died, he
is a murderer; the murderer must be
put to death. Or, if he struck him with 18
a wooden object in the hand, from
which death may result, so that he died,
he is a murderer; the murderer must be
put to death. The avenger of blood 19
shall himself put the murderer to death,
putting him to death when he encoun-
ters him. Also, if he gave him a push 20
through hatred, or threw something at
him intentionally, so that he died, or in 21
enmity struck him with his hand, so
that he died, the one who struck the
blow must be put to death, since he is a
murderer; the avenger of blood shall
put the murderer to death when he en-
counters him. But if he pushed him 22
inadvertently and not out of enmity, or
threw anything at all at him unintentionally, or without seeing him let a 23
stone of any kind fall on him from
which death might result, so that he
died, when he was not his enemy, nor
sought his harm, then the community 24
must decide between the one who
struck the blow and the avenger of
blood in accordance with these regulations; the community shall release the 25
homicide from the power of the avenger
of blood, and the community shall return him to the city of refuge to which
he fled, to live there until the death of
the high priest who was anointed with
the sacred oil. But if the homicide ever 26
goes outside the bounds of the city of
refuge to which he fled, and the avenger 27
of blood finds him outside the bounds
of his city of refuge, the avenger of
blood may slay the homicide without
incurring any guilt, because he must re- 28
main in his city of refuge until the death
of the high priest; but after the death of
the high priest the homicide may return
to his own land. These, then, are to 29
serve as a fixed ordinance for you
throughout your generations in all your
places of abode.
"In every case of murder the murder- 30
er is to be put to death only on the evidence of witnesses, the evidence of one
witness being insufficient to condemn

anyone to death. You must not accept a ransom for the life of a murderer who is guilty of death, but he must be put to death. You must not accept a ransom in place of having the person flee to his city of refuge, that he may live in the land again before the death of the high priest. Thus you will not pollute the land in which you are living; for it is blood that pollutes a land, and no atonement can be made for the blood that has been shed in a land, except by the blood of him who shed it. So you must not defile the land in which you are living, in the midst of which I dwell; for I, the LORD, am dwelling in the midst of the Israelites.' "

Then the heads of families in the clan constituting the descendants of Gilead, the son of Machir, the son of Manasseh, part of the Josephite clan, came up and addressed Moses and the chieftains, the heads of families among the Israelites.

"The LORD," they said, "commanded my lord to give the land to the Israelites as a heritage by lot, and my lord was commanded by the LORD to give the heritage of our kinsman Zelophehad to his daughters. Now if they are married into one of the other Israelite tribes, their heritage will be lost to our ancestral heritage, and will be added to the heritage of the tribe which they join, and thus be lost to our allotted heritage; when the Israelites hold the jubilee, their heritage will be added to the heritage of the tribe which they join, and thus their heritage will be lost to the heritage of our ancestral tribe."

So Moses at the bidding of the LORD 5
gave this command:
"The Josephite tribe speaks the
truth. This is the command that the 6
LORD has given concerning the daughters of Zelophehad: 'Let them be married to whom they like; only it must be into a family of their own ancestral
tribe that they are married, so that no 7
heritage of the Israelites may pass from one tribe to another; for the Israelites must keep each the heritage of his ancestral tribe. Any girl belonging to the 8
Israelite tribes who comes into possession of a heritage must be married to someone in a family belonging to her ancestral tribe, so that the Israelites may hold each his own ancestral heritage. No heritage may pass from one 9
tribe to another; for the Israelite tribes must keep each its own heritage.' "
The daughters of Zelophehad did 10
just as the LORD commanded Moses;
Mahlah, Tirzah, Hoglah, Milcah, and 11
Noah, the daughters of Zelophehad, were married to their kinsmens' sons,
being married into families of the de- 12
scendants of Manasseh, the son of Joseph, so that their heritage remained in the tribe of their ancestral family.
These were the commands and ordi- 13
nances which the LORD through Moses enjoined on the Israelites on the steppes of Moab beside the Jordan at Jericho.

THE BOOK OF DEUTERONOMY

THE FIRST DISCOURSE OF MOSES: HISTORICAL RETROSPECT, 1:1—4:43

1 THE following are the events,
concerning which Moses spoke
to all Israel beyond the Jordan,
in the wilderness, in the Arabah,
opposite Suph, between Paran, and
Tophel, Laban, Hazeroth and Di-
2 zahab, which occurred on the eleven
days of the journey from Horeb to the
highlands of Seir as far as Kadesh-
3 barnea. It was in the fortieth year, on
the first day of the eleventh month,
that Moses spoke to the Israelites, just
what the LORD commanded him to
4 say to them, after he had defeated
Sihon, king of the Amorites, who lived
at Heshbon, and at Edrei Og, king of
5 Bashan, who lived at Ashtaroth; beyond the Jordan, in the land of Moab,
Moses undertook to expound this code,
saying,
6 "The LORD our God said to us at
Horeb, 'You have remained long
7 enough at this mountain; move on, and
set out on your journey to the highlands
of the Amorites and all the surrounding
regions in the Arabah, in the highlands
and lowlands, in the steppes, and on the
seashore, the land of the Canaanites;
also to the Lebanon, as far as the Great
8 River, the river Euphrates. See, I have
put the land at your mercy; go in and
occupy the land which the LORD swore
to your fathers, Abraham, Isaac, and
Jacob, to give to them and their descendants after them.'
9 "Then I said to you at that time, 'I
am not able to bear the burden of you
10 by myself. The LORD your God has so
multiplied you that you are today like
the stars of the heavens for number.
11 (May the LORD, the God of your fathers, increase you a thousand-fold
more than you are, and bless you, as he
12 promised you!) How can I bear by
myself the load and burden of you, and
13 your discontent? Choose capable,
intelligent, and experienced men from
each of your tribes, and I will make them your chieftains.'

"Replying to me, you said, 'The action that you suggest taking is excellent.'

"So I took your capable and experienced men, and I set them as chieftains over you, as captains of divisions of a thousand, of a hundred, of fifty, and of ten, and as judges for your various tribes.

"Then I charged your judges at that time, saying, 'Hear the cases between your fellow-countrymen, and judge aright between a man and his fellow, or the resident alien in his employ. You must never show partiality in a case; you must hear high and low alike, standing in fear of no man; for the judgment is God's. Any case that is too hard for you, you must bring to me, and I will hear it.' I also enjoined on you at that time all the things that you were to do.

"Then we set out from Horeb, and traversed all that great and terrible desert, as you know, on the way to the highlands of the Amorites, as the LORD our God had commanded us. When we reached Kadesh-barnea, I said to you, 'You have reached the highlands of the Amorites, which the LORD our God is about to give us. See, the LORD your God has put the land at your mercy; go up and occupy it, as the LORD, the God of your fathers, told you; do not be afraid or dismayed.'

"Then you all came up to me, and said, 'Let us send men ahead of us to reconnoiter the land for us, and bring us back a report about the route that we should follow, and the cities that we shall reach.'

"The proposal was agreeable to me; so I chose twelve men from you, one from each tribe, and they set out on their journey up to the highlands. When they reached the valley of Eshcol, they spied it out, and taking some fruit of the land in their hands, they brought it down to us. Also they brought us back a report, and said, 'The land is fine, which the LORD our God is about to give us.'

"However, you would not go up, but scorned the injunction of the LORD your God, and grumbled in your tents, and said, 'It is because the LORD hates us that he has brought us out of the land of Egypt, to deliver us into the power of the Amorites, that they may destroy us. Our fellow-countrymen have made us lose heart by saying, "Where we are going there is a people stronger and more numerous than we; there are cities large and fortified up to the sky; and besides we saw the Anakim [giants] there." '

"Then I said to you, 'Have no dread; do not be afraid of them. The LORD your God who is going ahead of you, will himself fight for you, just as you saw him do for you in Egypt, and in the desert, as you know, where the LORD your God carried you, as a man carries his son, all the way of your journey, until you reached this place.' But in this matter you would not trust the LORD your God, who had gone ahead of you on the road, to look for a place for you to pitch your tents; in fire by night, so that you might make out the road that you should follow, and in a cloud by day.

"When the LORD heard your protestations, he was angry, and swore, saying, 'Not one of these men shall ever see the fine land that I swore to give to your fathers, except Caleb, the son of Jephunneh; he shall see it, and to him will I give the land on which he has set foot, and to his children, because he corroborated the LORD.'

"With me, too, the LORD was angry on your account, saying, 'Neither shall you enter there. Joshua, the son of Nun, your attendant, shall enter there; encourage him; for he is to put Israel in possession of it. Also your babes who you said would become a prey, and your children who as yet do not know good from evil, they shall enter there; to them I will give it, and they shall occupy it. But do you turn back, and set out for the desert in the direction of the Red Sea.'

"In reply you said to me, 'We have sinned against the LORD; we will ourselves go up and fight, just as the LORD our God commanded us.'

"Then each of you buckled on his
weapons of war, and made light of going up into the highlands. But the 42
LORD said to me, 'Say to them, "You
must not go up, nor fight, lest you be
routed before your enemies; for I will
not be with you ." ' So I spoke to you, 43
but you would not listen; you scorned
the injunction of the LORD, and in your
presumption you went up into the
highlands. Then the Amorites, who 44
lived in those highlands, came out
against you, and chased you, as a
swarm of bees would, and harried you
all the way from Seir to Hormah. Then 45
you came back, and wept before the
LORD, but the LORD would not heed
your cry, nor listen to you. So you re- 46
mained at Kadesh the long time that
you did.

"Then we turned back, and set out 2
for the desert in the direction of the
Red Sea, as the LORD had told me. For
a long time we circled round the highlands of Seir. Then the LORD said to 2
me, 'You have circled round these high- 3
lands long enough; turn northward.
Instruct the people as follows: "You 4
are about to cross the territory of your
kinsfolk, the sons of Esau, who live in
Seir. They will be afraid of you, but
you must be very careful not to pro- 5
voke them; for I am not going to give
you so much as a foot of their land, because I have given Esau the possession
of the highlands of Seir. You may pur- 6
chase food from them to eat, and you
may also buy water from them to drink;
for the LORD your God has blessed you 7
in all your undertakings; he has looked
after you in your journey in this great
desert; for forty years now the LORD
your God has been with you; you have
lacked nothing." '

"So we moved on, away from our 8
kinsfolk, the sons of Esau, who live in
Seir, away from the Arabah route, from
Elath and Ezion-geber. We turned, and
moved on toward the wilderness of
Moab. Then the LORD said to me, 'Do 9
not take a hostile attitude toward Moab, nor provoke them to battle; for I
am not going to give you possession of
any of their land, because I have given
the sons of Lot possession of Ar. (The 10
Emim used to live in it, a people as
great, numerous, and tall as the Anakim; like the Anakim they also were 11
known as Rephaim [titans], but the

12 Moabites call them Emim; and in Seir
the Horites used to live, but the sons of
Esau conquered them, and exterminated them from their way, and settled
in their place, as Israel did with the
land of their possession, which the
13 LORD gave them.) Up then, and cross
the brook Zered.'
14 "So we crossed the brook Zered. The
time that we took to journey from
Kadesh-barnea until we crossed the
brook Zered was thirty-eight years; until all that generation, that is, the warriors, had perished from the camp, as
15 the LORD had sworn to them; since the
hand of the LORD had been against
them, to exterminate them from the
camp, until they came to an end.
16 "When all the warriors had finally
17 perished from the people, the Lord
18 said to me, 'Today you are going to
19 cross Ar, the territory of Moab. When
you approach the frontier of the Ammonites, do not take a hostile attitude
toward them, nor provoke them; for I
am not going to give you possession of
any of the land of the Ammonites, because I gave the sons of Lot possession
20 of it. (It also was known as a land of
Rephaim, since Rephaim used to live
in it; but the Ammonites call them
21 Zamzummim, a people as great, numerous, and tall as the Anakim. The LORD
exterminated them from their way, so
that they conquered them, and settled
22 in their place, as he did for the sons of
Esau, who live in Seir, when he exterminated the Horites from their way, so
that they conquered them, and settled
23 in their place, as to this day. Likewise
the Avvim, who lived in villages as far
as Gaza, the Cretans, who came from
Crete, exterminated, and settled in
24 their place.) Up, move on, and cross
the river Arnon. Here I am delivering
Sihon, king of Heshbon, the Amorite,
and his land into your power. Begin
the conquest, and provoke him to bat-
25 tle. This very day I will begin to put
the dread and fear of you upon the peoples everywhere under the heavens,
who, when they hear news of you, will
tremble and quail before you.'
26 "So I sent messengers from the desert
of Kedemoth to Sihon, king of Heshbon, with a peaceful message, as fol-
27 lows: 'Let me pass through your land;
I will go only by the road, turning
28 neither to the right nor to the left. You
shall sell me food to eat, and sell me
water to drink; let me walk through,
as the sons of Esau, who live in Seir,
did for me, and the Moabites, who live
in Ar; until I cross the Jordan into the
land which the LORD our God is going
to give us.'
"But Sihon, king of Heshbon, would
not let us pass through his land; for the
LORD your God made him stubborn
and defiant, that he might deliver him
into your power, as is the case today.
"Then the LORD said to me, 'See, I
have begun by putting Sihon and his
land at your mercy; begin the conquest
by occupying his land.'
"When Sihon came out to engage us
in battle at Jahaz, with all his people,
the LORD our God put him at our
mercy, so that we defeated him and his
sons and all his people. At that time we
captured all his cities, and in every city
we massacred its men, women, and children, sparing none; only we took the
cattle as our booty, along with the spoil
of the cities that we had captured.
From Aroer which is on the edge of the
Arnon valley, and the city that is in the
valley, as far as Gilead, there was no
city that was too strong for us; the
LORD our God put all at our mercy;
only you did not go near the land of the
Ammonites, all the land along the river
Jabbok and the cities of the highlands,
just as the LORD our God had commanded us.
"When we moved on, and proceeded
up the road to Bashan, Og, king of
Bashan, together with all his people,
came out to engage us in battle at
Edrei, but the LORD said to me, 'Do
not be afraid of him; for I am delivering him and all his people and his land
into your power, so that you shall do to
him as you did to Sihon, king of the
Amorites, who lived at Heshbon.'
"So the LORD our God delivered Og
also, king of Bashan, and all his people
into our power, and we harried him
until not a survivor was left to him. At
that time we captured all his cities
(there was not a city of them that we
did not take), the sixty cities in all the
region of Argob, the kingdom of Og in
Bashan (all of these being cities fortified with high walls, gates, and bars),
besides very many unwalled towns.
We annihilated them, as we did in the
case of Sihon, king of Heshbon, in every

city massacring its men, women, and
7 children; but all the cattle and the spoil
of the cities we took as our booty.
8 "Thus we conquered at that time
from the two Amorite kings beyond the
Jordan the land from the river Arnon
9 as far as Mount Hermon (the Sidonians
call Hermon Sirion, while the Amorites
0 call it Senir), all the cities of the table-
land, the whole of Gilead, and the whole
of Bashan as far as Salecah and Edrei,
cities of the kingdom of Og in Bashan.
1 (For Og, king of Bashan, was the last
survivor of the remnant of the Rephaim; his sarcophagus was an iron sarcophagus; is it not still at the Ammonite city of Rabbah? It was nine cubits
long, and four cubits broad, according
2 to the ordinary cubit.) So we occupied
this land at that time.
"The territory beginning at Aroer,
which is on the edge of the Arnon valley, and half of the highlands of Gilead,
with its cities, I gave to the Reubenites
3 and Gadites; while the rest of Gilead
and the whole of Bashan, the kingdom
of Og, I gave to the half-tribe of Manasseh, namely, the whole region of Argob.
(That Bashan is all called a land of Re-
4 phaim. It was Jair, a Manassite, who
captured the whole region of Argob, as
far as the frontier of the Geshurites and
the Maacathites, and called it, namely,
Bashan, after his own name, Havvoth-
5 jair, as it is to this day.) To Machir,
6 then, I gave Gilead, and to the Reubenites and Gadites I gave the territory
from Gilead as far as the river Arnon,
the stream itself and its banks, and as
far as the Jabbok river, the frontier of
7 the Ammonites; along with the Arabah
and the Jordan with its banks, from
Chinnereth as far as the Sea of the
Arabah, the Salt Sea, at the foot of the
slopes of Pisgah eastward.
8 "At that time I charged you, saying,
'Since the LORD your God has given
you this land to occupy, all of you who
are stout-hearted shall cross over as
picked troops ahead of your fellow-
9 Israelites; but your wives, your little
ones, and your cattle (I know that you
have many cattle) shall remain in the
0 cities which I have given you, until the
LORD provides your kinsmen with a
home, as he has you, and they also occupy the land which the LORD your
God is giving them beyond the Jordan.
Then each of you may return to his own
property, which I have given you.'
"I charged Joshua also at that time, 21
saying, 'You have seen with your own
eyes all that the LORD your God has
done to these two kings; so shall the
LORD do to all the kingdoms into which
you are about to cross. Do not be 22
afraid of them; for it is the LORD your
God who fights for you.'
"I also entreated the LORD at that 23
time, saying, 'O Lord GOD, thou hast 24
only begun to show thy servant thy
greatness and thy mighty power; for
what god is there in the heavens or on
the earth who can do such deeds and
mighty acts as thine? Pray let me 25
go over, and see the fine land which is
beyond the Jordan, those magnificent
highlands, and the Lebanon.'
"But the LORD was angry with me 26
on your account, and would not listen
to me. The LORD said to me, 'Enough,
say not another word to me about this
matter. Climb to the top of Pisgah, and 27
look out, west, north, south, and east;
look well; for you shall not cross this
Jordan. But commission Joshua, en- 28
courage and strengthen him; for he
shall lead this people across, and he
shall put them in possession of the land
on which you look.'
"So we remained in the valley oppo- 29
site Beth-peor.
"And now, O Israel, heed the statutes **4**
and ordinances which I am teaching
you to observe, that you may live, and
go in and occupy the land which the
LORD, the God of your fathers, is giving you. You must not add anything to 2
the charge that I am enjoining on you,
nor take anything from it, that you
may keep the commands of the LORD
your God which I am giving you. You 3
saw with your own eyes what the LORD
did in the matter of the Baal of Peor;
for everyone that followed the Baal of
Peor, the LORD your God destroyed
from your midst; whereas you who held 4
fast to the LORD your God are all alive
today. Here I am teaching you, as the 5
LORD my God commanded me, to observe statutes and ordinances in the
land which you are invading for conquest. Be careful, then, that you ob- 6
serve them; for that will demonstrate
your wisdom and intelligence to the nations, who, when they hear of all these
statutes, will say, 'This great nation is

indeed a wise and intelligent people!'
7 For what great nation is there that has
a god so near it as is the LORD our God
8 whenever we call on him? And what
great nation is there that has statutes
and ordinances so just as all this code
that I am putting before you today?
9 Only take care, and watch yourselves
well that you do not forget the things
that you saw with your own eyes, and
that they do not slip from your mind
as long as you live; but that you impart them to your children and your
10 children's children—the day that you
stood before the LORD your God at
Horeb, when the LORD said to me,
'Gather the people to me, that I may let
them hear my words, so that they may
learn to stand in awe of me all the days
of their life on the earth, and so instruct
11 their children.' You came near, and
stood at the foot of the mountain,
while the mountain flamed with fire up
to the very heart of the heavens,
shrouded in darkness, cloud, and gloom.
12 The LORD spoke to you out of the fire,
when you heard the sound of words, but
saw no form, there being only a voice.
13 He made his covenant known to you,
which he commanded you to observe,
namely, the decalogue, and he wrote
14 it on two stone tablets. As for myself,
the LORD commanded me at that time
to teach you to observe statutes and
ordinances in the land into which you
15 are crossing for conquest. So watch
yourselves well (since you saw no form
at all when the LORD spoke to you at
16 Horeb out of the fire), that you do not
act perniciously by carving an image for
yourselves in the shape of any statue,
17 like male or female, like any animal that
is on the earth, or any bird that flies in
18 the air, or any reptile on the ground,
or any fish that is in the waters under
19 the earth; beware, when you look up
into the heavens and see all the host of
the heavens, the sun, moon, and stars,
that you do not let yourselves be allured into paying homage to them, and
serving them, which things the LORD
your God has allotted to all the peoples
20 everywhere under the heavens; whereas the LORD took you and brought you
out of the iron furnace, out of Egypt,
to become a people of his very own, as is
21 the case today. Although the LORD
was angry with me on your account,
and swore that I was not to cross the
Jordan, nor enter the fine land which
the LORD your God is giving you as a
heritage, but that I was to die in this
land instead of crossing the Jordan, yet
you are going to go over and occupy
that fine land. Take care that you do
not forget the covenant of the LORD
your God which he made with you and
carve an image for yourselves in the
shape of anything about which the
LORD your God gave you instructions;
for the LORD your God is a consuming
fire, a jealous God.

"When you have children and grandchildren, and grow old in the land, if
you act perniciously by carving an image in the shape of anything at all, and
do what is evil in the sight of the LORD
your God, thus provoking him to jealousy, I call heaven and earth to witness
against you today, that you shall soon
perish completely from the land which
you are about to cross the Jordan to occupy. You shall not live long upon it,
but shall be completely wiped out.
The LORD shall scatter you among the
peoples, and you shall be left a paltry
few among the nations where the LORD
drives you. There you will have to
serve man-made gods of wood and
stone, that neither see, nor hear, nor
eat, nor smell. Nevertheless you shall
seek the LORD your God there, and you
shall find him, if you search for him
with all your mind and heart. When
you are in distress, and all these things
happen to you, in the end you shall
come back to the LORD your God, and
heed his injunctions; for the LORD
your God is a merciful God; he will not
fail you, nor destroy you, nor forget the
covenant which he swore to your fathers. For inquire now of the early
times which preceded you, since the day
that God created man on the earth, and
from one end of the heavens to the
other, if anything as great as this has
ever happened, or if anything like it has
ever been heard of: did any people ever
hear the voice of a god speaking out of
fire, as you have, and still live? Or has
any god ventured to go and take a nation for himself out of another nation
by tests, signs, and portents, by war,
by a strong hand and an outstretched
arm, and by great terrors, just as you
saw the LORD your God do for you in
Egypt? You have learned to know that
the LORD is God, there being no other

5 but he. Out of the heavens he let you
hear his voice, to discipline you, and on
earth he let you see his mighty fire,
when you heard his words out of the
7 fire. Because he loved your fathers, and
chose their descendants after them, and
in his own person brought you out of
Egypt by his great power, by driving
out of your way nations greater and
stronger than you, that he might bring
you into a position to give you their
land for a heritage, as it is today; therefore be assured this day, and keep in
mind that the LORD is God in the heavens above and on the earth below, there
being no other. You must keep his
statutes and commands, which I am
giving you today, that you may prosper, and your children after you, and
that you may live long upon the land
which the LORD your God is giving you
for life."

Then Moses proceeded to set apart
three cities beyond the Jordan to the
east, that a homicide who had killed his
fellow unintentionally, without having
any standing feud with him, might flee
there, and by fleeing to one of the following cities might save his life: Bezer
in the wilderness on the table-land, for
the Reubenites; Ramoth in Gilead, for
the Gadites; and Golan in Bashan, for
the Manassites.

THE SECOND DISCOURSE OF MOSES: THE CODE OF LAWS, 4:44—26:19

This is the code which Moses put before the Israelites; these are the decrees,
statutes, and ordinances which Moses
communicated to the Israelites when
they had come out of Egypt, beyond
the Jordan, in the valley opposite
Beth-peor, in the land of Sihon, king of
the Amorites, who lived at Heshbon,
whom Moses and the Israelites defeated when they came out of Egypt, occupying his land and also the land of
Og, king of Bashan, the two Amorite
kings who lived beyond the Jordan to
the east, from Aroer, which is on the
edge of the Arnon valley, as far as
Mount Sion (that is, Hermon), along
with all the Arabah beyond the Jordan
to the east as far as the Sea of the Arabah, at the foot of the slopes of Pisgah.

Moses summoned all Israel, and said
to them,

"Hear, O Israel, the statutes and ordinances which I am delivering in your
hearing today, and you must learn them
and be careful to observe them. The 2
LORD our God made a covenant with
us at Horeb; it was not with our fore- 3
fathers that the LORD made this covenant, but with ourselves, with those of
us who are all here alive today. The 4
LORD talked with you face to face out
of the fire at the mountain, myself 5
standing between the LORD and you at
the time, to communicate to you the
words of the LORD; for you stood in
fear of the fire, and did not ascend the
mountain. He said,

" 'Since I, the LORD, am your God, 6
who brought you out of the land of
Egypt, out of a state of slavery, you 7
must have no other gods beside me.

" 'You must not carve an image for 8
yourself in the shape of anything that
is in the heavens above, or that is on the
earth below, or that is in the waters
under the earth; you must not pay 9
homage to them, nor serve them; for I,
the LORD your God, am a jealous God,
punishing children for the sins of their
fathers, to the third or fourth generation of those who hate me, but showing 10
kindness to the thousandth generation
of those who love me and keep my commands.

" 'You must not invoke the name of 11
the LORD your God to evil intent; for
the LORD will not hold him guiltless
who invokes his name to evil intent.

" 'Be careful to keep the sabbath day 12
holy, as the LORD your God commanded you. Six days you are to labor and 13
do all your work, but on the seventh 14
day, a sabbath to the LORD your God,
you must not do any work at all,
neither you, nor your son, nor your
daughter, nor your male or female
slave, nor your ox, nor your ass, nor any
of your cattle, nor the alien in your employ residing in your community, that
your male and female slaves may rest
as well as you. You must remember 15
that you were once a slave yourself in
the land of Egypt, and that the LORD
your God brought you out from there
by a strong hand and an outstretched
arm; that is why the LORD your God
has commanded you to observe the sabbath day.

" 'Honor your father and mother, as 16
the LORD your God has commanded

you, that you may live long and prosper
in the land that the LORD your God is
giving you.
17 " 'You must not commit murder.
18 " 'You must not commit adultery.
19 " 'You must not steal.
20 " 'You must not bring a false charge
against your fellow.
21 " 'You must not lust after your
neighbor's wife, nor covet your neighbor's home, his fields, his male or female slave, his ox, his ass, or anything
at all that is your neighbor's.'
22 "These words, and nothing more, the
LORD spoke to all your assemblage at
the mountain with a loud voice out of
the midst of the fire, cloud, and gloom;
and he wrote them on two stone tablets,
23 which he gave to me. When you heard
the voice out of the darkness, the mountain being aflame with fire, you came
up to me, that is, all the heads of your
24 tribes and your elders, and said, 'Seeing
that the LORD our God has let us see
his glory and his greatness, and that it
is his voice which we have heard out of
the fire, we know now that God can
25 speak with man, and he still live. Why
then should we die? For this great fire
is going to consume us! If we continue
to hear the voice of the LORD our God
26 any longer, we shall die! For what
mortal at all is there that has ever
heard the voice of the living God speak
out of fire, as we have, and has still
27 lived? Do you go near, and hear all
that the LORD our God has to say, and
then tell us whatever the LORD our
God tells you; when we hear it, we will
observe it.'
28 "When the LORD heard your protestations when you spoke to me, the
LORD said to me, 'I have heard the
protestations which this people have
made to you. They have spoken well.
29 O that their present attitude might
lead them always to stand in awe of me
and keep all my commands, that it
might go well with them and with their
30 children for all time! Go and say to
31 them, "Go home to your tents"; but do
you stand here beside me, that I may
tell you the whole charge, the statutes
and ordinances, that you are to teach
them to observe in the land which I am
about to give them to occupy.'
32 "Be careful, then, to do as the LORD
your God has commanded you, swerving neither to the right nor to the left.

You must walk in all the way that the 3
LORD your God has appointed you,
that you may live, and prosper, and
live long in the land that you are to
occupy.
"Now this is the charge, the statutes
and ordinances, which the LORD your
God commanded that you be taught
to observe in the land into which you
are crossing for conquest, a land flowing
with milk and honey, that you, with
your son and your grandson, may
stand in awe of the LORD your God all
your life by observing all his statutes
and commands which I am giving you,
and that you may live long. Therefore
heed them, O Israel, and be careful to
observe them, that you may prosper,
and multiply greatly, as the LORD, the
God of your fathers, promised you.
"Listen, O Israel; the LORD is our
God, the LORD alone; so you must
love the LORD your God with all your
mind and all your heart and all your
strength. These instructions that I am
giving you today are to be fixed in your
mind; you must impress them on your
children, and talk about them when you
are sitting at home, and when you go
off on a journey, when you lie down and
when you get up; you must bind them
on your hand as a sign, and they must
be worn on your forehead as a mark;
you must inscribe them on the door-
posts of your house and on your gates.
"When the LORD your God brings 1
you into the land which he promised
on oath to your fathers, Abraham,
Isaac, and Jacob, to give you great and
splendid cities which you did not build,
houses full of all kinds of goods with 1
which you did not fill them, cisterns already hewn out, which you did not hew
out, and vineyards and olive groves
which you did not plant, but from
which you may eat your fill, then take 1
care not to forget the LORD who
brought you out of the land of Egypt,
out of a state of slavery. You must 1
stand in awe of the LORD your God;
him you must serve; and by his name
you must swear. You must not run
after alien gods, any of the gods of the
nations that surround you, lest the an- 1
ger of the LORD your God blaze against
you, and he wipe you off the face of the
earth; for the LORD your God in your
midst is a jealous God.
"You must not put the LORD your 1

God to the test, as you did at Massah. You must be sure to keep the commands of the LORD your God, as well as his decrees and statutes which he commanded you. You must do what is right and good in the sight of the LORD, that you may prosper, and go in and occupy the fine land concerning which the LORD swore to your fathers that he would drive all your enemies out of your way, as the LORD promised.

"When your son asks you in time to come, 'What is the significance of the decrees, statutes, and ordinances which the LORD our God has commanded you?' you must say to your son, 'When we were Pharaoh's slaves in Egypt, the LORD brought us out of Egypt by a strong hand. The LORD displayed before our eyes great and ominous signs and portents against Egypt, against Pharaoh and all his court, but he brought us out from there that he might bring us into a position to give us the land which he promised on oath to our fathers. So the LORD commanded us to observe all these statutes, by standing in awe of the LORD our God for our good always, that he might keep us alive, as at this day. Hence it will stand to our credit with the LORD our God to be careful to observe all this charge, as he commanded us.'

"When the LORD your God brings you into the land which you are invading for conquest, and clears out of your way great nations like the Hittites, Girgashites, Amorites, Canaanites, Perizzites, Hivvites, and Jebusites, seven nations greater and stronger than yourselves; when the LORD your God puts them at your mercy, and you defeat them, you must be sure to exterminate them, without making a covenant with them, or giving them any quarter; you must not intermarry with them, neither giving your daughters in marriage to their sons, nor receiving their daughters for your sons; for they would turn your sons from following me to serving alien gods, and then the anger of the LORD would blaze against you, and he would quickly destroy you. But this is how you are to treat them: you must tear down their altars, smash their sacred pillars, cut down their sacred poles, and burn up their carved images. For you are a people consecrated to the
LORD your God, the LORD your God
having chosen you out of all the peoples
that are on the face of the earth to be a
people of his very own. It was not be- 7
cause you were the greatest of all peoples that the LORD set his heart on you
and chose you (for you were the smallest of all peoples), but it was because 8
the LORD loved you, and would keep
the oath that he swore to your fathers,
that the LORD brought you out by a
strong hand, and rescued you from a
state of slavery, from the power of Pharaoh, king of Egypt. Be assured, then, 9
that the LORD your God is God, a
trustworthy God, who to a thousand
generations keeps loving faith with
those that love him and keep his commands, but one who immediately re- 10
quites anyone who hates him, by destroying him, never delaying with anyone who hates him, but requiting him
immediately. So be careful to observe 11
the charge, the statutes and ordinances,
that I am enjoining on you today.

"It will be because you heed these 12
ordinances, and are careful to observe
them, that the LORD your God will
keep loving faith with you, as he swore
to your fathers; he will love you, bless 13
you, and multiply you; he will bless the
offspring of your body and the produce
of your soil, your grain and wine and
oil, the issue of your cattle, and the
progeny of your flock, in the land
which he swore to your fathers to give
you. Blessed shall you be above all peo- 14
ples, not a male or female being barren
among you or your cattle. The LORD 15
will also free you from all sickness, and
none of the malignant diseases of
Egypt, with which you are acquainted,
will he inflict on you; but he will inflict
them on all who hate you. You must 16
annihilate all the peoples whom the
LORD your God is about to surrender
to you, without giving them any quarter, so that you may not serve their
gods; for that would be dangerous for
you.

"Though you say to yourselves, 17
'These nations are greater than I; how
can I conquer them?' you must not be 18
afraid of them, remembering rather
what the LORD your God did to Pharaoh and all Egypt: the great tests 19
which you saw with your own eyes, the
signs and portents, the strong hand and
outstretched arm, by means of which

the LORD your God brought you out.
So shall the LORD your God do to all
the peoples of whom you stand in fear.
20 In fact, the LORD your God will send
leprosy among them, until any that are
left or hidden perish from your way.
21 You must not stand in terror of them;
for the LORD your God is in your
22 midst, a great and awful God. The
LORD your God, however, will only
clear these nations out of your way little by little, in that you are not to be
allowed to put an end to them all at
once, lest the wild beasts grow too nu-
23 merous for you. But the LORD your
God will put them at your mercy, and
will throw them into great confusion,
24 until they are destroyed. He will deliver their kings into your power, so
that you shall obliterate their very
name from under the heavens, not one
being able to hold his own against you,
25 until you have destroyed them. The
carved images of their gods you must
burn up; you must not covet the silver
or the gold on them, nor appropriate it
for yourselves, lest you be ensnared by
it; for it is abominable to the LORD
26 your God, and you must not bring anything abominable into your house, and
so become a doomed thing like it; you
must rather loathe it and abhor it; for
it is a doomed thing.

8 "All the charge that I am enjoining
on you today, you must be careful to
observe, that you may live and multiply, and go in and occupy the land
which the LORD promised on oath to
2 your fathers. You must remember all
the experiences through which the
LORD your God has led you for the
past forty years in the desert, that he
might bring afflictions on you to test
you, to find out whether it was your intention to keep his commands or not.
3 So he brought afflictions on you, and
let you hunger, and then fed you with
manna, with which you were not acquainted, nor were your fathers, that
he might make you understand that it
is not on bread alone that man lives,
but it is on everything produced by
command of the LORD that man lives.
4 Your clothing did not become too worn
for you to wear, nor did your feet swell
5 during the past forty years. Be assured,
then, in your mind that the LORD your
God has been disciplining you as a man
6 disciplines his son. You must keep the

commands of the LORD your God by walking in his ways and by standing in awe of him; for the LORD your God is bringing you into a fine land, a land with streams of water, with springs and pools welling up in the valleys and on the hills; a land of wheat and barley, of vines, fig-trees, and pomegranates; a land of oil-producing olives and honey; a land where you may eat food without stint, lacking nothing in it; a land whose stones contain iron, and out of whose hills you can dig copper. When you have eaten your fill, you must thank the LORD your God for the fine land that he has given you. Take care not to forget the LORD your God by not keeping his commands, ordinances, and statutes, which I am commanding you today; and when you have eaten your fill, and have built fine houses to live in, and your herds and flocks multiply, and your silver and gold increase, and all that you have increases, not to become haughty, and forget the LORD your God who brought you out of the land of Egypt, out of a state of slavery, who led you through the great and terrible desert with its venomous serpents and scorpions and thirsty waterless ground, who brought water for you out of the flinty rock, who fed you in the desert with manna, with which your fathers were not acquainted, that he might bring afflictions on you and test you, in order to make you prosper in the end; and then say to yourselves, 'My own power and the strength of my own hand have gained this wealth for me.' You must remember that it is the LORD your God who has been giving you power to gain wealth, that he might carry out his covenant which he swore to your fathers, as is the case today.

"If you ever forget the LORD your God, and run after alien gods, and serve them and pay homage to them, I warn you today that you shall most certainly perish. Like the nations that the LORD is to wipe out of your way, so shall you perish, since you would not listen to the injunctions of the LORD your God.

"Listen, O Israel; today you are about to cross the Jordan, to undertake the conquest of nations greater and stronger than yourselves, cities great and fortified up to the heavens, a people great and tall, the Anakim people, whom you yourselves know, and of whom you have heard it said, 'Who can hold his own against the Anakim?' Be assured, then, today that the LORD your God will be the one to go over ahead of you as a consuming fire; it is he who will destroy them and subdue them before you, so that you shall conquer them and kill them off easily, as the LORD promised you. After the LORD your God has driven them out of your way, never say to yourselves, 'It is because of my goodness that the LORD brought me into possession of this land'; whereas it is because of the wickedness of these nations that the LORD is about to drive them out of your way. It is not because of your goodness or integrity of mind that you are coming into possession of their land, but it is because of the wickedness of these nations that the LORD your God is about to drive them out of your way, and in order to carry out the oath that the LORD swore to your fathers, Abraham, Isaac, and Jacob. Be assured, then, that it is not because of your goodness that the LORD your God is giving you this fine land to occupy; for you are a stiff-necked people.

"Remember, never forget, how you provoked the LORD your God to anger in the desert; from the time that you left the land of Egypt until you reached this place you have been in a state of contention with the LORD. Even at Horeb you provoked the LORD to anger; indeed the LORD was angry enough with you to destroy you. When I climbed the mountain to receive the stone tablets, the tablets of the covenant which the LORD had made with you, I remained on the mountain forty days and nights, without eating food or drinking water. Then the LORD gave me the two stone tablets, inscribed by the finger of God, and on them a copy of all the words that the LORD had spoken to you at the mountain out of the fire on the day of the assemblage. At the end of forty days and nights, the LORD gave me the two stone tablets, the tablets of the covenant, and the LORD said to me, 'Rise, hurry down from here; for your people whom you brought out of Egypt have acted perniciously, in that they have been quick to swerve from the path that I appointed them, by making themselves a molten image.'

"The LORD said to me further, 'I see 13
that this people is indeed a stiff-necked
people. Let me alone, that I may de- 14
stroy them, and blot out their very
name from under the heavens, and
make you into a nation stronger and
greater than they.'

"So I turned and descended from the 15
mountain, the mountain flaming with
fire, and the two tablets of the covenant
in my two hands. I found that you had 16
indeed sinned against the LORD your
God by making yourselves a molten
bull, having quickly swerved from the
path that the LORD had appointed you.
So I seized the two tablets, and flung 17
them from my hands, and broke them
before your eyes. Then I prostrated 18
myself before the LORD, as I did before, for forty days and nights, without
eating food or drinking water, because
of all the sin that you had committed,
in doing what was evil in the sight of
the LORD, thus provoking him to jealousy. For I stood in dread of the anger 19
and wrath which the LORD had against
you to your destruction. But the
LORD listened to me on that occasion
also. With Aaron, too, the LORD was 20
angry enough to destroy him, but I
prayed for Aaron also at that time.
Then, taking the wicked thing that you 21
had made, the bull, I burned it up, and
crushed it, grinding it thoroughly until
it was as fine as dust, and then I threw
the dust of it into the stream that
flowed down from the mountain. (At 22
Taberah also, at Massah, and at Kibroth-hattaavah you continued to provoke the LORD to anger; and when the 23
LORD sent you away from Kadesh-
barnea, saying, 'Go up and occupy the
land that I am giving you,' you scorned
the command of the LORD your God;
you would not trust him, nor heed his
instructions. You have been in a state 24
of contention with the LORD ever since
I knew you.) So I lay prostrate before 25
the LORD for the forty days and nights
that I did, because the LORD had
threatened to destroy you, and I 26
prayed to the LORD, saying, 'O Lord
GOD, do not destroy thy people, thy
very own, whom thou hast rescued by
thy might, whom thou hast brought out
of Egypt by a strong hand. Remember 27
thy servants, Abraham, Isaac, and Ja-

cob; pay no attention to the obstinacy
of this people, nor their wickedness, nor
28 their sin, lest the land out of which thou
hast brought us say, "Because the
LORD could not bring them into the
land that he promised them, and because he hated them, he has brought
them out to slay them in the desert!"
29 And yet they are thy people, thy very
own, whom thou hast brought out by
thy great power and outstretched arm.'
10 "At that time the LORD said to me,
'Cut two tablets of stone like the former
ones, and ascend the mountain to me;
2 also make an ark of wood; that I may
write on the tablets the words that were
on the former tablets which you broke;
and then you are to put them in the
ark.'
3 "So I made an ark of acacia wood,
cut two tablets of stone like the former
ones, and ascended the mountain, with
4 the two tablets in my hand. When the
LORD had reproduced the former inscription on the tablets, the decalogue
which he spoke to you at the mountain
out of the fire on the day of the assemblage, the LORD gave them to me.
5 Then I turned, and descending from the
mountain, I put the tablets in the ark
that I had made, as the LORD had commanded me, and there they are."
6 (The Israelites set out from Beeroth-
bene-jaakan for Moserah, where Aaron
died, and was buried, Eleazar, his son,
7 succeeding him in the priesthood. From
there they set out for Gudgod, and
from Gudgod for Jotbah, a land with
streams of water.)
8 "At that time the LORD set apart
the tribe of Levi to carry the ark of the
covenant of the LORD, to be in attendance on the LORD as his ministers, and
to pronounce blessings in his name, as
9 they do to this day. That is why Levi
has had no property or heritage with
his fellows, the LORD being his heritage, as the LORD your God promised
him.
10 "So I remained on the mountain as
before, for forty days and nights, and
the LORD listened to me on that occasion also, in that the LORD agreed not
11 to destroy you. Then the LORD said to
me, 'Proceed at once to set out at the
head of the people, so that they may go
in and occupy the land which I swore to
their fathers to give them.'
12 "And now, O Israel, what does the
LORD your God require of you but to
fear the LORD your God, walk in all
his ways, love him, serve the LORD
your God with all your mind and heart,
by keeping the commands of the LORD
and his statutes that I am commanding you today, for your good? Even
though the heavens to the highest
heavens belong to the LORD your God,
and the earth with all that is in it, yet
the LORD set his heart on your fathers
to love them, and chose their descendants after them, even you, in preference
to all peoples, as is the case today. Be
circumcised in heart, then, and do not
be stiff-necked any more; for the LORD
your God is the God of gods, and the
Lord of lords, the great, mighty, and
awful God, who is never partial, and
never takes a bribe, who secures justice
for the orphan and the widow, and loves
the resident alien in giving him food
and clothing. So you should love the
resident alien; for you were once resident aliens yourselves in the land of
Egypt. You must stand in awe of the
LORD your God; him you must serve;
to him you must hold fast; and by his
name you must swear. He is to be your
praise, and he your God, who has performed with you these great and awful
deeds that you have seen with your
own eyes. Your fathers went down to
Egypt, seventy in number; and now the
LORD your God has made you like the
stars of the heavens for multitude.
"So you must love the LORD your
God, and always keep his charge, his
statutes, ordinances, and commands.
You must teach them to your children
who have not known or experienced the
discipline of the LORD your God, his
greatness, his strong hand and outstretched arm, his signs, and his deeds
that he did in Egypt to Pharaoh, king
of Egypt, and to all his land; and what
he did to the army of the Egyptians, to
their horses and chariots, how he made
the waters of the Red Sea engulf them
as they pursued you, and how the
LORD destroyed them, as it is to this
day; and what he did to you in the
desert until you reached this place; and
what he did to Dathan and Abiram, the
sons of Eliab, Reuben's son, how the
earth opened its mouth, and in the
midst of all Israel swallowed them up,
with their households, their tents, and
every living thing that was in their

train; for it is your eyes that saw all the great deeds which the LORD performed. Accordingly, you must keep all the charge which I am enjoining on you today, that you may be strong, and go in and occupy the land into which you are crossing for conquest, and that you may live long upon the land which the LORD swore to your fathers to give to them and their descendants, a land flowing with milk and honey. For the land which you are invading for conquest is not like the land of Egypt from which you came, where you used to sow your seed and water it by hand like a vegetable garden. On the contrary, the land into which you are crossing for conquest is a land of hills and valleys, watered by rain from the sky, a land for which the LORD your God cares, the eyes of the LORD your God being continually on it, from the beginning to the end of the year.

"If you will but heed the commands that I am giving you today, to love the LORD your God, and serve him with all your mind and heart, he will give you rain for your land in due season, the winter rain and the spring rain, so that you will gather in your grain and wine and oil, and he will produce grass in your fields for your cattle, and you will eat your fill.

"Take care lest you be deceived into turning aside to serve alien gods and to pay homage to them, and the anger of the LORD blaze against you, and he shut up the skies so that there be no rain, and the land yield no produce, and you quickly perish off the fine land that the LORD is about to give you. Accordingly, you must keep these words of mine in mind and heart; you must bind them on your hand as a sign, and they must be worn on your forehead as a mark; you must teach them to your children, talking about them when you are sitting at home and when you go off on a journey, when you lie down and when you get up; you must inscribe them on the door-posts of your house and on your gates, so that your life and the life of your children may be long in the land which the LORD swore to your fathers to give them for as long as the sky remains over the earth.

"If you are but careful to observe all this charge that I am enjoining on you,
loving the LORD your God, walking in
all his ways, and holding fast to him,
the LORD shall drive all these nations 23
out of your way, and you shall conquer
nations greater and stronger than you.
Every place on which the sole of your 24
foot treads shall be yours; the region
from the desert as far as Lebanon,
from the River, the river Euphrates, as
far as the Western Sea shall be your
domain. No one shall hold his own 25
against you, in that the LORD your
God shall put the dread and fear of you
on all the land on which you shall
tread, as he promised you.

"See, I am putting before you today 26
a blessing and a curse: a blessing, if you 27
heed the commands of the LORD your
God which I am giving you today; and 28
a curse, if you do not heed the commands
of the LORD your God, but
swerve from the way that I am appointing
you today, by running after
alien gods of whom you have had no
experience. When the LORD your God 29
brings you into the land which you
are invading for conquest, you are to
place the blessing on Mount Gerizim
and the curse on Mount Ebal. (Are 30
they not beyond the Jordan, west of it,
toward the sunset, in the land of the
Canaanites who live in the Arabah, opposite
Gilgal, beside the terebinth of
Moreh?) For you are about to cross the 31
Jordan to enter into possession of the
land which the LORD your God is giving
you. When you have conquered it,
and settled down in it, you must be 32
careful to observe all the statutes and
ordinances that I am putting before
you today.

"The following are the statutes and 12
ordinances which you must be careful
to observe in the land which the LORD,
the God of your fathers, shall give you
to hold as long as you live on the earth.

"You must be sure to destroy all the 2
sanctuaries where the nations whom
you are to dispossess served their gods,
on high mountains, on hills, and under
every spreading tree; you must tear 3
down their altars, smash their sacred
pillars, burn up their sacred poles, and
cut down the carved images of their
gods, obliterating the very name of
them from that sanctuary. You must 4
not act like this toward the LORD your
God, but to the sanctuary which the 5
LORD your God chooses out of all your

tribes as the seat of his presence, to
his habitation you must resort; there
6 you must go, and there bring your
burnt-offerings, your sacrifices, your
dues, your personal contributions, your
votive offerings, your voluntary offerings, and the firstlings of your herd and
7 flock; and there you must eat before
the LORD your God, and with your
households rejoice over all your undertakings, in which the LORD your God
has blessed you.

8 "You must not do just as we are
doing here today, each whatever he
9 pleases; for you have not as yet reached
the home and heritage which the
LORD your God is about to give you.
10 But when you cross the Jordan, and
settle down in the land which the LORD
your God is giving you as a heritage,
and when he gives you rest from all
your enemies around you, so that you
11 live in security, then to the sanctuary
that the LORD your God chooses as
the abiding-place of his presence, there
you must bring all that I am commanding you, your burnt-offerings,
your sacrifices, your dues, your personal contributions, and all your choice
votive offerings which you vow to
12 the LORD; and you are to rejoice before
the LORD your God, you, your sons
and daughters, your male and female
slaves, and the Levite living in your
community; for he has no property or
heritage with you.

13 "Take care not to offer your burnt-
offerings at any sanctuary that you see;
14 but at the sanctuary which the LORD
your God chooses in one of your tribes,
there you must sacrifice your burnt-
offerings, and there do all that I am
15 commanding you. However, whenever
you wish you may slaughter anything
for food purposes in any of your communities to the extent of the blessing
that the LORD your God accords you,
the unclean along with the clean eating
it, as though it were a gazelle or a deer;
16 only you must not partake of the
blood; you must pour it out on the
ground like water.

17 "You may not eat in your home
town the dues of your grain or wine or
oil, nor the firstlings of your herd or
flock, nor any votive-offering that you
vow, nor your voluntary offerings, nor
18 your personal contributions, but you
must eat them before the LORD your
God at the sanctuary which the LORD your God chooses, you, your son, your daughter, your male and female slaves, and the Levite living in your community, rejoicing before the LORD your God over all your undertakings. Take care not to neglect the Levite as long as you live in your land.

"When the LORD your God enlarges your territory, as he has promised you, and you say, 'I would eat meat' (seeing that you have a longing to eat meat), you may do so whenever you wish. If the sanctuary which the LORD your God chooses as the seat of his presence is far away from you, as I have instructed you, you may slaughter for food purposes in your own communities whenever you wish any of your herd or flock which the LORD has given you. You are to eat it just as you would a gazelle or a deer, the unclean and the clean eating it together; only be sure never to partake of the blood; for the blood is the life, and you must not eat the life along with the flesh; you must not eat it; you must pour it out on the ground like water. You must not eat it, that you may prosper, and your children after you; for then you will be doing what is right in the sight of the LORD. However, what consecrated gifts you have and your votive offerings, you must take, and go to the sanctuary that the LORD chooses, and offer your burnt-offerings, the flesh along with the blood, on the altar of the LORD your God; the blood of your sacrifices is to be poured out on the altar of the LORD your God, but the flesh you are to eat yourselves.

"Be careful to heed all these things that I am commanding you, that it may go well with you, and with your children after you for all time; for then you will be doing what is good and right in the sight of the LORD your God.

"When the LORD your God exterminates from your way the nations to conquer whom you are going there, and you conquer them, and settle down in their land, take care not to be beguiled into copying them, after they have been exterminated from your way; and not to resort to their gods, saying, 'How did these nations worship their gods?—that I in turn may do the same.' You must not act like this toward the LORD your God; for every kind of practice that is abominable to the LORD, what he hates, they carried on for their gods; for even their sons and daughters they used to burn to their gods.

"Everything that I am commanding you, that you must be careful to observe, without adding anything to it, or taking anything from it.

"If a prophet or a dreamer of dreams appears among you, offering you a sign or portent, and the sign or portent comes true, in connection with which he said to you, 'Let us follow alien gods! (of whom you have had no experience), and let us serve them,' you must not heed the words of that prophet or that dreamer of dreams; for the LORD your God is testing you to find out whether you really love the LORD your God with all your mind and heart. It is the LORD your God that you must follow; of him you must stand in awe; his commands you must keep; his injunctions you must heed; him you must serve; and to him you must hold fast. But that prophet or that dreamer of dreams must be put to death, because he spoke falsely against the LORD your God, who brought you out of the land of Egypt, and rescued you from a state of slavery, in order to allure you from the path in which the LORD your God commanded you to walk. Thus shall you eradicate the wicked person from your midst.

"If your brother, the son of your mother, or your son, or your daughter, or the wife of your bosom, or your friend who is as precious as your own life, entices you in secret, saying, 'Let us go and serve alien gods!' (of whom you have had no experience, nor have your fathers, namely, any of the gods of the peoples who surround you, either near you or far away from you, from one end of the earth to the other), you must not yield to him, nor heed him; you must not show him any mercy, nor spare him, nor shield him; but you must be sure to kill him; your own hand to be the first against him to put him to death, and then the hands of all the people. You must stone him to death, because he tried to allure you away from the LORD your God, who brought you out of the land of Egypt, out of a state of slavery; and when all Israel hears of it, they will be afraid, and never again do such a wicked thing as this
in your midst.
"If you hear it said that in one of 12
your cities, which the LORD your God
is giving you to live in, certain scoun- 13
drels from among you have gone out
and enticed their fellow-citizens, saying, 'Let us go and serve alien gods!'
(of whom you have had no experience),
you must examine and investigate, and 14
make a thorough inquiry; and if it
proves true and is established that this
abominable thing has been done in your
midst, you must be sure to put the in- 15
habitants of that city to the sword, ex-
terminating it and all that is in it; and 16
all its spoil you must gather into the
middle of the open square, and then
burn up the city with all its spoil as a
holocaust to the LORD your God, to lie
in ruins forever, never to be rebuilt.
Nothing of the things doomed is to be 17
appropriated by you, that the LORD
may turn from his fierce anger, and
show you mercy, and in his mercy multiply you, as he swore to your fathers;
for then you will be heeding the injunc- 18
tion of the LORD your God by keeping
all his commands which I am giving
you today, by doing what is right in the
sight of the LORD your God.

"As children of the LORD your God, **14**
you must not cut yourselves nor shave
your foreheads for the dead; for you are 2
a people consecrated to the LORD your
God, and out of all the peoples that are
on the face of the earth the LORD has
chosen you to be a people of his very
own.

"You must not eat anything abomi- 3
nable. The following are animals that 4
you may eat: the ox, the sheep, the goat, 5
the deer, the gazelle, the roebuck, the
wild-goat, the ibex, the antelope, and
the mountain-sheep. Also, you may 6
eat any animal with a cloven hoof, that
has the hoof divided completely in two,
and that chews the cud. However, of 7
those that chew the cud or have the
hoof completely cloven, you must not
eat the following: the camel, the hare,
and the rock-badger, because, though
chewing the cud, they do not have the
hoof cloven—they are unclean for you;
also the pig, because, though having 8
the hoof cloven, it does not chew the
cud—it is unclean for you. Of their
flesh you must not eat, and their carcasses you must not touch.

9 "Of all things that live in the water
10 you may eat the following: whatever
has fins and scales you may eat; but
whatever has not fins and scales you
must not eat; it is unclean for you.
11
12 "You may eat any clean bird; but the
following are the ones of which you
must not eat: the griffon, the vulture,
13 the eagle, the buzzard, the kite in its
14 several species, the raven in all its spe-
15 cies, the ostrich, the night-hawk, the
sea-mew, the hawk in its several spe-
16 cies, the screech-owl, the eagle-owl, the
17 horned owl, the jackdaw, the carrion-
18 vulture, the cormorant, the stork, the
heron in its several species, the bittern,
19 and the bat. Also, all winged insects
are unclean for you; they must not be
20 eaten. Any winged thing that is clean
you may eat.
21 "You must not eat anything that has
died a natural death; for you are a people consecrated to the LORD your God;
you may give it to any alien residing in
your community to eat, or sell it to a
foreigner.
"You must not boil a kid in its
mother's milk.
22 "Every year you must be sure to
take out the dues of all the produce of
23 your seed, that has left the field, and
before the LORD your God, at the
sanctuary which he chooses as the
abiding-place of his presence, you must
eat the dues of your grain, wine, and oil,
and the firstlings of your herd and
flock, that you may learn to stand in
24 awe of the LORD your God always. If
the road is too long for you, so that you
cannot transport it, because the sanctuary which the LORD your God
chooses as the seat of his presence is too
far away from you, then, when the
25 LORD your God blesses you, you must
give it in money, securing the money in
your hand, and going to the sanctuary
which the LORD your God chooses
26 (you may spend the money for whatever you wish, for oxen, sheep, wine, or
liquor, or for anything that you have a
craving for), and there you must feast
in joy before the LORD your God, you
27 and your household. Also, you must
not neglect the Levite living in your
community; for he has no property or
heritage with you.
28 "Every third year you must take out
all the dues of your produce for that
year, and deposit it in your community,
so that the Levite (since he has no
property or heritage with you), the
resident alien, the orphan, and the
widow, who are in your community,
may come and eat their fill, in order
that the LORD your God may bless you
in every enterprise that you undertake.

"Every seventh year you must observe a remission; and the operation of the remission is to be as follows: every creditor who has a claim against his fellow-countryman is to remit it; he is not to press it against his fellow-countryman or kinsman; for a remission has been proclaimed by the LORD. Against an alien you may press it; but anything of yours that is in the possession of your kinsman you must remit. However, there shall be no poor among you; for the LORD will be sure to bless you in the land which the LORD your God is giving you as a heritage to occupy, if you but heed the injunctions of the LORD your God by being careful to observe all this charge which I am enjoining on you today. When the LORD your God blesses you, as he has promised you, you shall have many nations obligated to you, but you shall never be obligated to them; you shall rule over many nations, but they shall never rule over you.

"If there is a needy person among you, any of your fellow-countrymen in any of your communities in the land which the LORD your God is giving you, you must not steel your heart, nor shut your hand against your needy countryman; but you must open wide your hand to him, and freely lend him sufficient for the needs that he has. Take care lest a base thought enter your head like this: 'The seventh year, the year of remission, is near!' and you behave meanly to your needy countryman by not giving him anything, and he cries to the LORD against you, and you incur guilt. You must give to him freely; and you are not to begrudge it when you give him something, because the LORD your God for this very thing will bless you in all your work and all your undertakings. For the poor will never cease to be in your land; that is why I am commanding you to open wide your hand to your poor and needy fellow-countryman in your land.

"If a countryman of yours, a Hebrew man or woman, is sold to you, he is to work six years for you, but in the seventh year you must set him free from your service. And when you set him free from your service, you must not send him away empty-handed; you must provision him liberally out of your flock, threshing-floor, and wine-press, supplying him as the LORD your God has blessed you. You must remember that you were once a slave yourself in the land of Egypt, and that the LORD your God rescued you; that is why I am giving you this command today. If, however, he says to you, 'I will not leave your service'—because he is fond of you and your household, and has fared well with you—then you must take an awl, and drive it through his ear into the door; he shall then be your slave permanently. You shall do the same with your female slave. You must not begrudge it when you set him free from your service; for he has worked six years for you at half the cost of a hired laborer. Then shall the LORD your God bless you in all that you undertake.

"You must consecrate to the LORD your God all the male firstlings of your herd and flock; you must do no work with a firstling ox, nor shear a firstling sheep. You must eat it each year with your household before the LORD your God at the sanctuary which the LORD chooses. If, however, it has any blemish, such as lameness, or blindness, or any bad blemish at all, you must not sacrifice it to the LORD your God. You must eat it in your own community, the unclean and the clean together, as though it were a gazelle or a deer; only you must not partake of the blood; you must pour it out on the ground like water.

"Observe the new moon of Abib by holding the passover for the LORD your God; for on the new moon of Abib the LORD your God brought you out of Egypt by night. You must sacrifice the passover-victim, a sheep or an ox, to the LORD your God at the sanctuary which the LORD chooses as the abiding-place of his presence. You must not eat leavened bread with it; for seven days you must eat unleavened cakes with it, the bread of distress (for in trepidation you left the land of Egypt) that you may remember the day that you left the land of Egypt all through your life.
For seven days no leaven must be seen 4
in your possession anywhere in your
territory, and none of the flesh which
you sacrifice on the evening of the first
day is to be left over until morning.
You may not offer the passover-sacri- 5
fice in any of the communities which
the LORD your God is giving you; but 6
at the sanctuary which the LORD your
God chooses as the abiding-place of his
presence, there you must offer the passover-sacrifice in the evening at sunset,
at the time that you left Egypt. You 7
must cook and eat it at the sanctuary
which the LORD your God chooses; and
in the morning you are to return to
your tents. For six days you are to eat 8
unleavened cakes; and on the seventh
day there is to be a sacred assembly for
the LORD your God, when you must do
no work.
"You must count seven weeks, be- 9
ginning your count of the seven weeks
from the time that the sickle is first put
to the grain; and then you must hold 10
the feast of weeks for the LORD your
God, as a voluntary personal gift, giving as the LORD your God blesses you;
and with your son, your daughter, your 11
male and female slaves, the Levite living in your community, the resident
alien, the orphan, and the widow, who
are among you, you are to rejoice before the LORD your God at the sanctuary which the LORD your God chooses
as the abiding-place of his presence.
You must remember that you were 12
once a slave yourself in Egypt; so you
must be careful to observe these
statutes.
"You must hold the feast of booths 13
for seven days after the ingathering
from your threshing-floor and wine-
press, rejoicing at your feast, along with 14
your son, your daughter, your male and
female slaves, the Levite, the resident
alien, the orphan, and the widow, who
are in your community. For seven days 15
you must hold a feast to the LORD your
God at the sanctuary that the LORD
chooses; for the LORD your God will
bless you in all your produce and in all
your undertakings, so that you can
only be happy.
"Three times a year all your males 16
must visit the LORD your God at the
sanctuary which he chooses; at the
feast of unleavened cakes, the feast of
weeks, and the feast of booths. And

they must not visit the LORD empty-
17 handed, but each with a personal gift
befitting the blessing which the LORD
your God has bestowed on you.
18 "In all the communities which the
LORD your God is giving you, you are
to appoint judges and officials for your
various tribes, to judge the people
19 aright. You must not pervert justice;
you must not show partiality, nor take
a bribe; for a bribe blinds the eyes of the
learned, and subverts even a just case.
20 Justice, and justice only, you must
strive for, in order that you may live,
and take possession of the land which
the LORD your God is giving you.
21 "You must plant no sacred pole, no
wooden object whatsoever, beside the
altar of the LORD your God that you
22 make, nor set up a sacred pillar, which
is hateful to the LORD your God.
17 "You must not sacrifice to the LORD
your God an ox or sheep that has a
blemish or any defect; for that would
be abominable to the LORD your God.
2 "If there is found among you in any
of your communities which the LORD
your God is giving you, a man or a
woman, who does what is evil in the
sight of the LORD your God, by violat-
3 ing his covenant, and has gone and
served alien gods, and paid homage to
them, namely, the sun, or the moon, or
the whole host of the heavens, which I
4 prohibited; if it is reported to you, and
you hear of it, you must make a thorough investigation; and if it proves
true and is established that such an
abominable thing has been done in Is-
5 rael, you must bring the man or woman
who did this evil deed out to your gates,
6 and stone him to death. On the evidence of two or three witnesses shall the
condemned person be put to death; he
must not be put to death on the evi-
7 dence of one witness; the hands of the
witnesses to be the first against him to
put him to death, and then the hands of
all the people. Thus shall you eradicate
the wicked person from your midst.
8 "If a case in law should arise in your
local community for which you have no
precedent, a case of bloodshed, or a
law-suit, or an assault, doubtful cases,
you must set out and go up to the sanctuary which the LORD your God
9 chooses, and coming to the Levitical
priests and the judge who is in office at
that time, you must inquire of them,

and they will let you know the decision
for the case. You must then comply
with the terms of the decision which
they render you from that sanctuary
which the LORD chooses, and you must
be careful to do just as they direct you,
complying with the terms of the verdict
which they give you and the judgment
which they deliver to you, swerving
neither to the right nor to the left from
the decision which they render you.
The man who acts presumptuously, in
not heeding the priest standing in attendance there on the LORD your God
or the judge, that man must be put to
death. Thus shall you eradicate the
wicked person from Israel; and when all
the people hear of it, they will be
afraid, and never act presumptuously
again.
"When you reach the land that the
LORD your God is giving you, and occupy it, and settle down in it, and then
declare, 'I must place a king over me
like all the nations surrounding me,'
you must be sure to make him king
over you whom the LORD your God
chooses. You must make one of your
own countrymen king over you; you
may not put a foreigner over you, who
is not a countryman of yours. However, he must not provide himself with
many horses, nor have the people enter
into relations with Egypt again, to provide himself with many horses, since
the LORD means that you are never
again to go back that way. Neither
must he provide himself with many
wives, so that his heart may not be
estranged; nor must he provide himself
with great quantities of silver and gold.
As soon as he has taken his seat on his
royal throne, he must write for himself in a book a copy of this code as approved by the Levitical priests; he must
keep it with him, and peruse it all the
days of his life, that he may learn to
stand in awe of the LORD his God, by
being careful to observe all the provisions of this code and these statutes,
that he may not consider himself more
exempt than his fellow-countrymen,
and that he may not swerve from the
charge to the right or to the left, in
order that he with his descendants may
continue long on the throne in Israel.
"The Levitical priests, that is, the
whole tribe of Levi, shall have no
property or heritage like the rest of Is-

rael; they shall live on the sacrifices made to the LORD and the dues made over to him. Levi shall have no heritage among his fellows, the LORD being his heritage, as he promised him. This shall be the priests' due from the people, from those sacrificing either an ox or a sheep: the shoulder, the two cheeks, and the stomach are to be given to the priest. Also, you must give him the first of your grain, wine, and oil, with the first of the fleece of your sheep. For the LORD your God has chosen him out of all your tribes, that he and his descendants for all time should be in attendance on the LORD your God to minister to him and pronounce blessings in his name.

"If a Levite leaves one of your local communities anywhere in Israel where he is a resident, he may come whenever he wishes to the sanctuary which the LORD chooses, and minister in the name of the LORD his God like all his fellow-Levites, who are in attendance there on the LORD, having an equal share with them in the living, besides his gratuities."

Concerning sorcery.—"When you enter the land which the LORD your God is giving you, you must not learn to imitate the abominable practices of these nations. There must not be found among you anyone who makes his son or his daughter pass through fire, a diviner, a soothsayer, an augur, a sorcerer, a charmer, a medium, a magician, or a necromancer. For anyone given to these practices is abominable to the LORD; indeed, it is because of these abominable practices that the LORD your God is driving them out of your way. You must be absolutely true to the LORD your God; for while these nations whom you are to conquer give heed to soothsayers and diviners, the LORD your God has not intended you to do so. Instead, the LORD your God will raise up a prophet for you from among yourselves, one of your fellow-countrymen like me (it is he that you must heed), just as you asked of the LORD your God at Horeb on the day of the assemblage, when you said, 'I must not hear the voice of the LORD my God any longer, nor see this great fire any more, that I die not.' The LORD said to me, 'They have spoken aright; from time to time I will raise up for them someone
like you from among their fellow-countrymen to be a prophet; I will put my
oracles in his mouth, and he shall tell
them everything that I command him.
If there is anyone who will not heed the 19
oracle that he delivers in my name, I
will make him answer for it myself.
But the prophet who presumes to de- 20
liver an oracle in my name which I did
not command him to deliver, or who delivers oracles in the name of alien gods,
that prophet must die.' And if you say 21
to yourselves, 'How are we to recognize
an oracle that the LORD has not given?'
—if the oracle that the prophet de- 22
livers in the name of the LORD does not
come to pass or come true, that is an
oracle which the LORD did not give,
the prophet having spoken it presumptuously; you are not to be afraid of him.

"When the LORD your God exter- **19**
minates the nations whose land the
LORD your God is giving you, and you
conquer them, and settle down in their
cities and houses, you must set apart 2
three cities in the land which the LORD
your God is giving you to occupy. You 3
must so fix the distances that you divide the area of the land which the
LORD your God is giving you for your
own into three parts, in such a way
that any homicide may flee there, so 6
that the avenger of blood may not pursue the homicide in the heat of his
anger, and overtake him, because the
way is long, and take his life, when he
did not deserve to die, since he had no
standing feud with him. The procedure 4
in the case of a homicide who flees there
to save his life is to be as follows: anyone who kills another unintentionally,
having no standing feud with him, like 5
the case of someone who goes into the
woods with another to cut wood, and
when he lets drive with the ax to fell a
tree, the head slips from the helve, and
alights upon the other so that he dies,
that person may flee to one of these
cities, and save his life. That is why 7
I am commanding you to set apart
three cities. And if the LORD your 8
God enlarges your territory, as he
swore to your fathers, and gives you all
the land which he promised your fathers to give you, provided that you 9
were careful to observe all this charge
which I am enjoining on you today, by
loving the LORD your God, and by
walking always in his ways, then you

must add three more cities to these
10 three, so that innocent blood may not
be shed in the land which the LORD
your God is giving you as a heritage, in
which case you would incur guilt of
11 blood. However, if someone has a feud
with another, and lies in wait for him,
attacking him and beating him to
death, and then flees to one of these
12 cities, the elders of his city must send
and take him from there, and hand him
over to the avenger of blood to be slain.
13 You must have no mercy on him, but
purge the guilt of innocent blood from
Israel, that you may prosper.
14 "On the property which you inherit
in the land which the LORD your God
is giving you to occupy, you must not
move your neighbor's landmark, which
the early inhabitants put in place.
15 "A single witness shall not convict a
man in the case of any crime or offense
of any kind whatsoever that he has
committed; it is only on the evidence of
two or three witnesses that a charge can
be sustained.
16 "If a plaintiff with a grudge appears
17 against a man to accuse him falsely, the
two parties who have the dispute must
appear before the LORD, that is, before
the priests, and the judges that are in
18 office at that time; the judges shall
make a thorough investigation, and if
it turns out that the plaintiff is false,
having falsely accused his fellow, you
19 must do to him as he meant to do to his
fellow. Thus shall you eradicate the
20 wicked person from your midst; and
when those that are left hear of it, they
will be afraid, and never again do such
a wicked thing as this in your midst.
21 So you must show no mercy—life for
life, eye for eye, tooth for tooth, hand
for hand, foot for foot.

20 "When you go out to battle against
your enemies, and see horses, and chariots, forces greater than your own, you
must not be afraid of them; for the
LORD your God who brought you up
from the land of Egypt is on your side.
2 When you are on the eve of a battle, a
priest must come up and speak to the
3 people. He shall say to them, 'Listen,
O Israel; today you are on the eve of a
battle against your enemies; do not be
faint-hearted, nor afraid, nor alarmed,
4 nor stand in dread of them; for the
LORD your God is going with you, to
fight for you against your enemies and
give you the victory.' Then the officers shall say to the people, 'Whoever has built a new house, but has not dedicated it, may leave and return home, lest he die in the battle, and another dedicate it. Whoever has planted a vineyard, but has not had the use of it, may leave and return home, lest he die in the battle, and another get the use of it. Whoever has betrothed a wife, but has not married her, may leave and return home, lest he die in the battle and another marry her.' The officers shall say further to the people, 'Whoever is afraid and faint-hearted must leave and return home, so that his fellows may not become faint-hearted like him.' As soon as the officers have finished addressing the people, the army commanders shall place themselves at the head of the people.

"When you invest a city, you must offer it terms of peace. If it agrees to make peace with you, and surrenders to you, then all the people to be found in it shall become forced laborers for you, and serve you. But if it will not make peace with you, but wages war with you, you are to besiege it, and when the LORD your God delivers it up to you, you must put every male in it to the sword; but the women and children and live stock and everything that is in the city, that is, all its spoil, you may take as your booty, and yourselves use the spoil of your enemies which the LORD your God gives you. So shall you treat all the cities that are very far away from you, that do not belong to the cities of the nations here. However, in the cities of the peoples here, which the LORD your God is giving you as a heritage, you must not spare a living soul; but you must be sure to exterminate them, Hittites, Amorites, Canaanites, Perizzites, Hivvites, and Jebusites, as the LORD your God commanded you, so that they may not teach you to imitate all the abominable practices that they have carried on for their gods, and so sin against the LORD your God.

"When you have to besiege a city a long time in your war on it in order to capture it, you must not destroy its trees by taking an ax to them, because you can eat their fruit; you must not cut them down; for are trees in the field men to be besieged by you? It is only trees which you know are not fruit trees that you may destroy and cut down for the construction of siege-works against the city that is waging war with you, until it is razed.

"If anyone is found slain in the land which the LORD your God is giving you to occupy, lying in the open, and it is not known who struck him, your elders and judges must go out and measure the distances to the cities that are in the neighborhood of the dead body, and the elders of the city that is nearest to the dead body must take a heifer that has never been worked, nor has pulled in a yoke; and the elders of that city must bring the heifer down to a valley with running water, which has never been ploughed or sown, and break the heifer's neck there in the valley. Then the priests, the sons of Levi, shall approach (for the LORD your God has chosen them to minister to him, and pronounce blessings in the name of the LORD, and so every case of dispute or assault is to be settled by them), and all the elders of that city, those living nearest the dead body, shall wash their hands over the heifer whose neck has been broken in the valley. Then they shall make affirmation as follows: 'Our hands did not shed this blood, nor did our eyes see it done; clear thy people Israel whom thou hast rescued, O LORD, and do not hold thy people Israel responsible for innocent blood.' Thus shall the guilt of blood be cleared from them. Because you do what the LORD regards as right, you shall purge the guilt of innocent blood from your midst.

"When you go out to battle against your enemies, and the LORD your God delivers them up to you, and you make them prisoners, if you see among the prisoners a beautiful woman upon whom you set your heart, you may take her for a wife. When you bring her into your home, she shall uncover her head, and pare her nails, and throw off her prisoner's garb. She shall remain in your house, and bewail her father and mother for a whole month. After that you may have intercourse with her. You shall be her husband, and she shall be your wife. If you lose interest in her, you must let her go absolutely free; you must not sell her, nor
mistreat her, because you have humiliated her.

"If a man has two wives, the one 15
loved and the other slighted, and both
the loved and the slighted have borne
him children, and the first-born son belongs to her that is slighted, when he 16
comes to will his property to his sons,
he may not give the right of the first-
born to the son of the loved one to the
disadvantage of the son of the slighted
wife, who is the first-born; but he must 17
give the right of the first-born to the
first-born, the son of the slighted wife,
by giving him two-thirds of all that he
owns; for he was the first issue of his
manly vigor, and the right of the first-
born belongs to him.

"If a man has a stubborn and refrac- 18
tory son, who will not obey his father
or mother, nor heed them, even when
they chastise him, his father and moth- 19
er must take hold of him, and bring
him before the elders of his city at the
gateway of his home town, and say to 20
the elders of his city, 'This son of ours is
a stubborn and refractory fellow who
will not obey us, a ne'er-do-well, and a
drunkard.' Then all his fellow-citizens 21
shall stone him to death. Thus shall
you eradicate the wicked person from
your midst, and when all Israel hears of
it, they will be afraid.

"If anyone has committed a crime 22
punishable by death, and has been put
to death, and you have impaled him on
a stake, his corpse must not remain all 23
night on the stake; but you must be
sure to bury him the same day; for an
impaled man is a terrible disgrace, and
you must not pollute the land which the
LORD your God is giving you as a heritage.

"You must not see your fellow- 22
countryman's ox or sheep go astray
without showing concern for it; you
must be sure to take it home to your
fellow-countryman. If, however, your 2
fellow-countryman is not a tribesman
of yours and you do not know him, you
must take it home with you, and keep
it until your fellow-countryman claims
it; then you must give it back to him.
You must do the same with his ass, 3
with his garment, and with anything
lost by a fellow-countryman of yours,
which he has lost and you have found;
you are not to be without concern for
it.

4 "You must not see your fellow-countryman's ass or ox foundered on the
road without showing concern for it;
you must be sure to help him to raise it
up.
5 "A woman must never wear any article belonging to a man, nor must a man
put on a woman's garment; for whosoever does such things is abominable to
the LORD your God.
6 "If you should happen to come upon
a bird's nest in any tree, or on the
ground, with young ones or eggs, and
the mother sitting on the young or the
eggs, you must not take the mother
7 with the young. You must rather let
the mother go, and only take the
young, that you may prosper, and live
long.
8 "When you build a new house, you
must make a parapet for your roof,
that you may not bring the guilt of
blood upon your house, in case anyone
should fall from it.
9 "You must not sow your vineyard
with two kinds of seed, lest the whole
produce become taboo, the crop that
you sowed as well as the harvest from
your vineyard.
10 "You must not plough with an ox
and an ass yoked together.
11 "You must not wear material blend-
ed of wool and linen.
12 "You must plait tassels on the four
corners of the cloak with which you
cover yourself.
13 "If a man marries a wife, and has intercourse with her, and then turns
14 against her, and frames wanton charges
against her, and slanders her by saying,
'I married this woman, but when I had
intercourse with her, I did not find the
15 evidence of virginity in her,' the girl's father and mother shall take the evidence
of the girl's virginity and bring it to the
16 elders of the city at the gate, and the
girl's father shall say to the elders, 'I
gave my daughter to this man in mar-
17 riage, but he turned against her, and
here he is framing wanton charges
against her, saying, "I did not find the
evidence of virginity in your daughter."
Here is the evidence of my daughter's
virginity!' Whereupon they shall spread
out the cloth before the elders of the
18 city. Then the elders of that city shall
take the man and punish him, fining
19 him one hundred shekels of silver, and
giving it to the girl's father, because he
slandered a virgin of Israel. She shall be his wife as long as he lives, without his being able to divorce her. If, however, the charge proves true, that the evidence of virginity was not to be found in the girl, the girl shall be brought out to the door of her father's house, and the men of her city shall stone her to death, because she committed a shameless act in Israel by playing the harlot in her father's house. Thus shall you eradicate the wicked person from your midst.

"If a man is caught lying with a married woman, both of them shall die, the man who lay with the woman and the woman herself; thus shall you eradicate the wicked person from Israel.

"If there should be a girl who is a virgin betrothed to a husband, and a man chances upon her in the city and lies with her, you must take them both out to the gate of that city, and stone them to death; the girl, because she did not call for help although in the city, and the man, because he seduced another's wife. Thus shall you eradicate the wicked person from your midst. If, however, it is in the open country that the man chances upon the betrothed girl, and the man seizes her, and lies with her, then simply the man who lay with her shall die; you must do nothing to the girl, since no sin deserving of death attaches to the girl; for this case is like that of a man attacking his neighbor and murdering him; because it was in the open country that he chanced upon her; the betrothed girl may have called for help, but there was no one to save her.

"If a man chances upon a girl, a virgin who is not betrothed, and seizes her, and lies with her, and they are caught, the man who lay with her must pay the girl's father fifty shekels of silver, and she shall be his wife as long as he lives, without his being able to divorce her, because he violated her.

"A man must not marry his father's wife, nor have intercourse with her who belongs to his father.

"No one who has his testicles crushed or his penis cut off shall marry into the LORD'S community. No bastard shall marry into the LORD'S community; likewise, none of his descendants to the tenth generation shall marry into the LORD'S community. No Ammonite or

Moabite shall marry into the LORD'S
community; likewise, none of their descendants to the tenth generation shall
ever marry into the LORD'S commu-
4 nity; because the one did not meet you
with food and water on the road after
you came out of Egypt, and the other
hired Balaam, the son of Beor, from
Pethor in Aram-naharaim against you,
5 to curse you. (Nevertheless the LORD
your God would not heed Balaam; but
the LORD your God turned the curse
into a blessing for you, because the
6 LORD your God loved you.) Never in
all your life are you to seek their welfare
or prosperity.
7 "You must not abhor an Edomite,
because he is your kinsman. You must
not abhor an Egyptian, because you
were once a resident alien in his land.
8 Children born to them in the third generation may marry into the LORD'S
community.
9 "When you go out against your enemies and are in camp, you must keep
yourselves clear of everything offensive.
0 If there happens to be any of you who
is not clean because of an emission at
night, he must go outside the camp; he
1 must not come inside the camp; then at
the approach of evening he must bathe
himself in water, and at sundown he
2 may come inside the camp. Also, you
must have a latrine outside the camp,
3 and you must go outside to it; you must
have a stick along with your weapons,
and when you relieve yourself outside,
you must dig a hole with it, and then
fill it up, and cover your excrement.
4 Because the LORD your God moves
within your camp to rescue you and to
put your enemies at your mercy, your
camp must be clean, so that he may not
see anything indecent with you, and
turn away from you.
5 "You must not turn a slave over to
his master when he has escaped from his
6 master to you; he shall live right in
your midst with you, in any place that
he chooses in one of your communities
as being advantageous to him; you
must not mistreat him.
7 "None of the Israelite women shall
become a temple-prostitute, nor shall
any of the Israelite men become a tem-
8 ple-prostitute. You must never bring
the gains of a harlot or the earnings of
a male prostitute as a votive offering to
the temple of the LORD your God; for
both are abominable to the LORD your
God.
"You must not exact interest on 19
loans to a fellow-countryman of yours,
interest in money, food, or anything
else that might be exacted as interest.
On loans to a foreigner you may exact 20
interest, but on loans to a fellow-countryman you must not, that the LORD
your God may bless you in all your undertakings in the land which you are
invading for conquest.
"When you make a vow to the LORD 21
your God, you must pay it without delay; for the LORD your God definitely
requires it of you, and you would incur
guilt. However, if you refrain from 22
making a vow, you will incur no guilt.
A spoken promise you must be careful 23
to observe, in the way that you promised the LORD your God, seeing that it
was a voluntary promise that you
made.
"When you enter your neighbor's 24
vineyard, you may eat your fill of the
grapes, as much as you wish; but you
must not put any in your bag.
"When you enter your neighbor's 25
grain, you may pull off some heads with
your hand; but you must not put a
sickle to your neighbor's grain.
"When a man takes a wife and mar- **24**
ries her, if it turns out that she does not
please him, because he has found some
indecency in her, and he writes her a
bill of divorce, and putting it into her
hand, dismisses her from his house, if, 2
on leaving his house, she goes and marries another man, and then the latter 3
husband turns against her, and writes
her a bill of divorce, and putting it into
her hand, dismisses her from his house,
or if the latter husband who married
her dies, her former husband who di- 4
vorced her may not marry her again,
after she has been defiled; for that is
abominable to the LORD, and you must
not bring guilt on the land which the
LORD your God is giving you as a heritage.
"When a man is newly married, he is 5
not to go out with the army, nor be
counted with it for any duty; he is to
be free at home for one year, to enjoy
himself with his wife whom he has married.
"No one is to take a handmill or an 6
upper millstone in pledge; for he would
be taking a life in pledge.

7 "If a man is caught kidnaping any
of his fellow-Israelites, to hurt him, or
to sell him, that thief shall die. Thus
shall you eradicate the wicked person
from your midst.
8 "Take care in an attack of leprosy to
be very careful to do just as the Levitical priests direct you, being careful to
follow the instructions that I gave
9 them. Remember what the LORD your
God did for Miriam during the journey
after you came out of Egypt.
10 "When you make your neighbor a
loan of any sort, you must not go into
11 his house to take his pledge; you must
wait outside, and the man to whom you
are making the loan shall bring the
12 pledge outside to you. If he is a poor
man, you must not sleep in the article
13 that he has pledged; you must be sure
to return it to him at sunset, that he
may sleep in his cloak, and so be grateful to you. It will stand to your credit
with the LORD your God.
14 "You must not defraud a hired laborer who is poor and needy, whether
he is one of your fellow-countrymen, or
one of the aliens residing in your land,
15 in your community. You must pay him
his wages by the day, before the sun
sets (for he is poor, and is expecting it),
so that he may not cry to the LORD
against you, and you incur guilt.
16 "Fathers are not to be put to death
with their children, nor are children to
be put to death with their fathers.
Everyone is to be put to death for his
own sin.
17 "You must not pervert the justice
due the resident alien, or the orphan,
nor take a widow's garment in pledge.
18 You must remember that you were once
a slave yourself in Egypt, and the
LORD your God rescued you from
there; that is why I am commanding
you to do this.
19 "When you reap your harvest in your
field, and forget a sheaf in the field, you
must not go back to get it; it is to go to
the resident alien, the orphan, and the
widow, that the LORD your God may
20 bless you in all your enterprises. When
you beat your olive trees, you must not
go over them a second time; that is to
go to the resident alien, the orphan, and
21 the widow. When you pick the grapes
of your vineyard, you must not go over
it a second time; that is to go to the
resident alien, the orphan, and the widow. You must remember that you were 22
once a slave yourself in the land of
Egypt; that is why I am commanding
you to do this.
"If two men go to law with each **2**
other, and come into court, and have
the case decided for them, so that the
innocent is acquitted and the guilty
convicted, if the guilty man deserves a 2
flogging, the judge shall make him lie
down, and have him flogged in his presence, with the number of lashes war-
ranted by his crime. He may be given 3
forty lashes, but not more, lest in being
given more than that number your fellow-countryman should be cut to rib-
bons before your eyes.
"You must not muzzle an ox when he
is treading out grain.
"If there are brothers living on a 5
joint estate, and one of them dies, leaving no son, the wife of the deceased
must not be married to a stranger; her
brother-in-law must go to her, and marry her, doing the duty of a brother-in-
law to her; and the first son that she
bears shall succeed to the name of the
deceased brother, so that his name may
not be blotted out of Israel. But if the
man does not want to marry his sister
in-law, then his sister-in-law shall go to
the elders at the city gate, and say, 'My
brother-in-law refuses to carry on his
brother's name in Israel; he will not do
the duty of a brother-in-law to me';
whereupon the elders of his city shali
summon him, and speak to him, and if
he maintains his position, and says, 'I
do not want to marry her,' his sister-in-
law shall go up to him in the presence of
the elders, and pull his sandal off his
foot, and spit in his face, and solemnly
declare, 'So shall it be done to the man
who will not build up his brother's
house'; and it shall be called in Israel, 1
'the house for which the sandal was
pulled off.'
"If two men get into a fight with each 1
other, a man and his fellow-countryman, and the wife of one comes up to
rescue her husband from his assailant,
and puts out her hand, and seizes him
by his private parts, you must cut off 1
her hand, without showing any mercy.
"You must not have weights of dif- 1
ferent sizes in your bag, a large one and
a small one; you must not have differ- 1
ent sized ephahs in your house, a large
one and a small one; you must have a 1

full, just weight; you must have a full, just ephah, that you may live long in the land which the LORD your God is giving you; for everyone given to these practices, everyone given to dishonesty, is abominable to the LORD your God.

"Remember what Amalek did to you during the journey after you came out of Egypt, how with no fear of God he fell upon you on the way, when you were tired and faint, and cut off all the stragglers in your rear. Therefore, when the LORD your God gives you rest from all your enemies around you, in the land which the LORD your God is giving you as a heritage to occupy, you must blot out the very memory of Amalek from under the heavens, being sure not to forget.

"When you enter the land which the LORD your God is giving you as a heritage, and conquer it, and settle down in it, you must take some of all the first produce of the soil that you harvest from the land which the LORD your God is giving you, and putting it in a basket, you must go to the sanctuary which the LORD your God chooses as the abiding-place of his presence. You must go to the priest who is officiating at that time, and say to him, 'I give thanks today to the LORD my God that I have entered the land which the LORD swore to our fathers to give us.' Then the priest shall take the basket from your hand, and place it in front of the altar of the LORD your God; and you shall solemnly declare before the LORD your God, 'A nomad Aramean was my father; he went down to Egypt to reside there, with a small company, and there he became a nation, great, mighty, and numerous; the Egyptians treated us harshly, oppressed us, and imposed hard servitude upon us; but we cried to the LORD, the God of our fathers, and the LORD heard our cry, and seeing our affliction, our toil, and our oppression, the LORD brought us out of Egypt, with a strong hand and an outstretched arm, with great terrors, signs, and portents; and bringing us to this place, he gave us this land, a land flowing with milk and honey. And now see, I have brought the first of the produce of the soil, which thou, O LORD, hast given me!' You must then place it before the LORD your God, and do homage before the

LORD your God, and rejoice over all 11
the good fortune which the LORD your
God has accorded you and your household, along with the Levite and the
alien residing in your midst.
"When you have finished taking out 12
all the dues of your produce in the
third year, the year for the taking out of
dues, you must give them to the Levite,
the resident alien, the orphan, and the
widow, that they may eat their fill in
your community; and then you must 13
declare before the LORD your God, 'I
have cleared the consecrated material
from my house, and furthermore, I
have given it to the Levite, the resident
alien, the orphan, and the widow, just
as thou didst command me, breaking
none of thy commands nor forgetting
them; I have not eaten any of it through 14
want; I have not disposed of any of it
improperly; I have not offered any of it
to the dead; I have heeded the injunction of the LORD my God by doing just
as thou didst command me. Look down 15
from the heavens, thy sacred dwelling-
place, and bless thy people Israel, and
the soil which thou hast given us, as
thou didst swear to our fathers—a land
flowing with milk and honey.'
"This day the LORD your God is 16
commanding you to observe these statutes and ordinances; you must be careful then to observe them with all your
mind and heart. Concerning the LORD 17
you have today avowed that he is your
God, and that you would walk in his
ways, and keep his statutes, commands,
and ordinances, and heed his injunctions; and the LORD has today avowed 18
concerning you that you are a people of
his very own, as he promised you, and
so you are to keep all his commands,
and then he will place you high above 19
all other nations whom he has made, in
praise, renown, and honor, that you
may be a people consecrated to the
LORD your God, as he promised."

CLOSING INJUNCTIONS OF MOSES, 27:1—31:13

Moses and the elders of Israel com- 27
manded the people as follows:
"Keep in mind all the charge that I
am enjoining on you today. On the 2
very day that you cross the Jordan into
the land which the LORD your God is

giving you, you must set up some large
stones, and whitewashing them with
3 lime, you must inscribe on them all the
words of this code as soon as you have
crossed, in order that you may enter the
land which the LORD your God is giving you, a land flowing with milk and
honey, as the LORD, the God of your
4 fathers, promised you. As soon as
you cross the Jordan, you must set up
these stones, concerning which I am
giving you instructions today, on
Mount Gerizim, and whitewashing
8 them with lime, you must inscribe all
the words of his code on the stones very
distinctly.
5 "You must build there an altar to the
LORD your God, an altar of stones on
6 which you must not use any iron tool; it
is with undressed stones that you must
build the altar of the LORD your God;
7 you shall offer burnt-offerings to the
LORD your God on it, and sacrifice
thank-offerings, and feast there in joy
before the LORD your God."
9 Then Moses and the Levitical priests
said to all Israel,

"Be silent and listen, O Israel; today
you have become the people of the
10 LORD your God; you must therefore
heed the injunctions of the LORD your
God, and observe his commands and
statutes, which I am commanding you
today."
11 Moses charged the people that same
day as follows:
12 "When you cross the Jordan, the following shall face Mount Gerizim for the
blessing of the people: Simeon, Levi,
Judah, Issachar, Joseph, and Benja-
13 min; and the following shall face those
pronouncing the curse on Mount Ebal:
Reuben, Gad, Asher, Zebulun, Dan,
14 Naphtali. Then the Levites with a
loud voice shall solemnly declare to all
the men of Israel:
15 " 'Cursed be he who makes a carved
or molten image, so abominable to the
LORD, the handiwork of a craftsman,
setting it up in secret!'

"And all the people in response shall
say,

" 'So be it.'
16 " 'Cursed be he who dishonors his
father or mother!'

"And all the people shall say,

" 'So be it.'
17 " 'Cursed be he who moves his neighbor's landmark!'

"And all the people shall say,

" 'So be it.'

" 'Cursed be he who misleads a blind man on the road!'

"And all the people shall say,

" 'So be it.'

" 'Cursed be he who perverts the justice due the resident alien, the orphan, and the widow!'

"And all the people shall say,

" 'So be it.'

" 'Cursed be he who lies with his father's wife; for he would have had intercourse with her who belongs to his father!'

"And all the people shall say,

" 'So be it.'

" 'Cursed be he who lies with any animal!'

"And all the people shall say,

" 'So be it.'

" 'Cursed be he who lies with his sister, whether she is his full sister or half-sister!'

"And all the people shall say,

" 'So be it.'

" 'Cursed be he who lies with his mother-in-law!'

"And all the people shall say,

" 'So be it.'

" 'Cursed be he who murders his neighbor secretly!'

"And all the people shall say,

" 'So be it.'

" 'Cursed be he who accepts a bribe to permit the murder of an innocent person!'

"And all the people shall say,

" 'So be it.'

" 'Cursed be he who does not give effect to the provisions of this code by observing them!'

"And all the people shall say,

" 'So be it.'

"If you will but heed the injunctions of the LORD your God by being careful to observe all his commands which I am giving you today, the LORD your God shall place you high above all the nations of the earth, and all the following blessings shall come upon you and overtake you; for you will be heeding the injunctions of the LORD your God.

"Blessed shall you be in the city,
And blessed shall you be in the country;
Blessed shall be the offspring of your body,

The produce of your soil, the offspring
of your live stock,
The issue of your cattle, and the progeny
of your flock;
Blessed shall be the contents of your
basket and kneading-trough;
Blessed shall you be in your coming,
And blessed shall you be in your going.

"The LORD shall cause your enemies
who attack you to be routed before you;
they may come out against you by a
single road, but they shall fly before
you by seven different roads. The
LORD shall order blessings upon you
in your barns, and in all your undertakings;
and he shall bless you in the land
which the LORD your God is giving you.
The LORD shall make you a people consecrated
to himself, as he swore to you;
for you will be keeping the commands of
the LORD your God, and will be walking
in his ways, so that all the peoples
of the earth will see that you bear
the name of the LORD, and will stand in
fear of you. The LORD shall give you
abounding prosperity in the offspring of
your body, the progeny of your cattle,
and the produce of your soil, in the land
which the LORD swore to your fathers
to give you. The LORD shall open for
you his rich treasury in the heavens, to
give rain to your land in due season and
to bless all your labor, so that you shall
have many nations under obligations to
you, but you shall never be obligated to
them. The LORD shall make you the
head, not the tail, and you shall tend
upward only, and not downward; for
you will be heeding the commands of
the LORD your God which I am giving
you today, by being careful to observe
them, swerving neither to the right nor
to the left from any of the commands
that I am giving you today, by running
after alien gods to serve them.

"If, however, you will not heed the
injunctions of the LORD your God by
being careful to observe all his commands
and statutes which I am commanding
you today, then all the following
curses shall come upon you and
overtake you.

"Cursed shall you be in the city,
And cursed shall you be in the country;
Cursed shall be the contents of your
basket and kneading-trough;
Cursed shall be the offspring of your
body, and the produce of your
soil,
The issue of your cattle, and the progeny
of your flock;
Cursed shall you be in your coming, 19
And cursed shall you be in your going.

"The LORD shall send curses on you, 20
trouble and distress in every enterprise
of yours that you undertake, until you
are destroyed, and perish quickly for
your evil doing in forsaking me. The 21
LORD shall fasten plagues on you until
he exterminates you from the land
which you are invading for conquest;
the LORD shall smite you with con- 22
sumption, fever, inflammation, and
sunstroke, with drought, blasting, and
mildew, which shall pursue you until
you perish. For you the sky overhead 23
shall be bronze, and the earth underfoot shall be iron; the LORD shall turn 24
the rain of your land into powder and
dust; it shall descend from the sky upon
you until you are destroyed. The 25
LORD shall cause you to be routed before your enemies; you may go out
against them by a single road, but you
shall fly before them by seven different
roads. You shall become a terrifying
example to all the kingdoms of the
earth. Your carcasses shall become food 26
for all the birds of the air and the beasts
of the earth, with no one to scare them
away. The LORD shall smite you with 27
Egyptian sores, with ulcers, scurvy,
and itch, of which you cannot be cured.
The LORD shall strike your minds with 28
madness, blindness, and dismay, so 29
that you shall go groping at noon as the
blind grope in the dark, and shall not
make a success of your life, but shall
simply be wronged and robbed continually, with no one to rescue you. You 30
may betroth a wife, but another man
shall ravish her; you may build a house,
but you shall not live in it; you may
plant a vineyard, but you shall not get
the use of it; your ox may be slaugh- 31
tered under your inspection, but you
shall not eat any of it; your ass shall be
snatched from under your nose, and not
be returned to you; your flock shall be
given to your enemies, with no one to
rescue it for you; your sons and daugh- 32
ters shall be handed over to an alien
people, while your eyes gaze, ever
straining after them, with nothing that
you can do; the produce of your soil 33
and all the fruits of your labor shall a
nation that is strange to you eat up,
and you shall simply be wronged and

34 oppressed continually, until you are
driven mad by the sight of what you
35 see. The LORD shall smite you on the
knees and legs, from the sole of your
foot to the crown of your head, with
malignant sores, of which you cannot
36 be cured. The LORD shall dispatch you
and the king that you place over you to
a nation that you do not know, nor did
your fathers, and there you shall serve
37 alien gods of wood and stone; you shall
become a horror, a taunt, and a byword
among all the peoples where the LORD
38 shall drive you. You may take out
much seed to the field, but you shall
harvest little; for the locust shall con-
39 sume it. You may plant vineyards,
and work them, but you shall not
drink wine, nor store it; for grubs shall
40 eat them up. You may have olive trees
all through your country, but you shall
not anoint yourselves with oil; for your
41 olives shall drop off. You may have
sons and daughters born to you, but
they shall not remain yours; for they
42 shall go into captivity. Locusts shall
infest all your trees and the produce of
43 your soil. The alien who is residing in
your midst shall rise higher and higher
above you, while you shall sink lower
44 and lower; he shall lend to you, but you
shall never lend to him; he shall be the
head, and you the tail.
45 "All these curses shall come upon
you, pursuing you and overtaking you
until you are destroyed, because you
would not heed the injunctions of the
LORD your God, by keeping his commands and statutes which he com-
46 manded you. They shall be signs and
portents against you and your descendants for all time.
47 "Because you would not serve the
LORD your God in the joy and happiness of mind that came from the abun-
48 dance of everything, you shall serve
your enemies, whom the LORD sends
against you, in hunger, thirst, nakedness, and want of everything; and he
shall put an iron yoke on your neck,
49 until he has destroyed you. The LORD
shall bring a nation against you from
afar, from the ends of the earth, swooping down like a vulture, a nation whose
50 language you do not understand, a nation, stern of face, that shall have no regard for the old, nor mercy for the
51 young, and that shall eat up the offspring of your cattle and the produce of
your soil, until you are destroyed, leaving you neither grain, nor wine, nor oil,
nor the issue of your cattle, nor the
progeny of your flock, until they exterminate you. They shall besiege you 5
in all your towns until your high, fortified walls on which you relied are razed
all through your land; they shall besiege you in all your towns all through
the land which the LORD your God has
given you, so that you shall have to 5
eat your own offspring, the flesh of the
sons and daughters whom the LORD
your God has given you in the stress of
the siege with which your enemies shall
press you. The man that is most tender 5
among you, and quite the most dainty,
will act so meanly toward his brother,
the wife of his bosom, and the remaining children that may be left to him,
that he will not give any of them any
of the flesh of his children which he has
to eat, since there is nothing else left to
him in the stress of the siege with which
your enemies shall press you in all your
towns. She that is most tender and
dainty among you, who would not venture to set the sole of her foot upon the
ground, since she is so dainty and tender, will act meanly toward the husband of her bosom, her son, and her
daughter, both in the case of the after-
birth that may come from her womb,
and the children that she may bear; for
she shall secretly eat these for want of
everything in the stress of the siege with
which your enemies shall press you in
your towns.
"If you are not careful to observe all
the provisions of this code, written in
this book, by standing in awe of this
glorious and awful name, the LORD
your God, then the LORD shall bring
extraordinary plagues on you and your
descendants, severe and prolonged
plagues, and severe and prolonged diseases; he shall bring back upon you all
the diseases of Egypt of which you
stood in dread, and they will fasten
themselves on you; indeed every kind
of sickness and plague that is not recorded in this book of the law the LORD
shall inflict on you until you are destroyed. You shall be left a paltry few,
instead of being like the stars of the
heavens for number, because you would
not heed the injunctions of the LORD
your God. As the LORD took delight in
making you prosperous and numerous,

so the LORD shall take delight in ex-
terminating and destroying you, and
you shall be torn from the land which
4 you are invading for conquest; the
LORD shall scatter you among all peoples from one end of the earth to the
other, and there you shall serve alien
gods of wood and stone, of whom you
have had no experience, nor had your
5 fathers. Among these nations you shall
have no ease, nor shall there be a resting-place for the sole of your foot, but
the LORD shall give you there an anxious mind, spent eyes, and a despondent
6 spirit; your life shall be lived in suspense; you shall live in fear day and
night, and never be certain about your
7 life; in the morning you shall say, 'O
that it were evening!' and in the evening you shall say, 'O that it were
morning!'—because of the terror of
mind which frightens you, and the
8 sights that you see. The LORD shall
take you back to Egypt in ships, which
journey I meant you never again to
make, and there you shall offer yourselves for sale to your enemies as male
and female slaves, with none to buy
you."

These were the terms of the covenant
which the LORD commanded Moses to
make with the Israelites in the land of
Moab, besides the covenant which he
had made with them at Horeb.

Moses then summoned all Israel, and
said to them,

"Although you have seen all that the
LORD did before your eyes in the land
of Egypt to Pharaoh and all his courtiers and all his land, the great tests
which you saw with your own eyes, the
signs, and those great portents, yet to
this day the LORD has not given you a
mind to understand, nor eyes to discern, nor ears to hear. For forty years I
have led you through the desert, your
clothes never getting too worn for you
to wear, nor your sandals too worn for
your feet, without bread to eat, or wine
or liquor to drink, in order that you
might come to know that I, the LORD,
am your God. When you reached this
place, Sihon, king of Heshbon, and Og,
king of Bashan, came out to engage us
in battle; but we defeated them, and
capturing their land, we gave it as a
heritage to the Reubenites, Gadites,
and half-tribe of Manassites. Be careful then to observe the terms of this
covenant, that you may succeed in
everything that you undertake.

"You are all taking your stand today 10
before the LORD your God, the heads of
your tribes, your elders, and your officers, even all the men of Israel, together 11
with your children, your wives, and the
aliens in your employ who are living in
your camps, both your wood-gatherers
and your water-drawers, that you may 12
enter into the covenant of the LORD
your God and the solemn compact
which the LORD your God is making
with you today, that he may today 13
make you his own people, and that he
may be your God, as he promised you,
and as he swore to your fathers, Abraham, Isaac, and Jacob. It is not with 14
you alone that I am making this covenant and solemn compact, but with 15
those who are here with us today,
standing before the LORD our God, and
with those who are not here with us today (for you yourselves know how we 16
once lived in the land of Egypt, and
how we passed through the territory of
the nations that you did; and so you 17
saw the detestable and horrid things of
wood and stone, of silver and gold, that
were in their possession), lest there 18
should be among you man, woman,
family, or tribe, whose heart after all
might turn from the LORD our God to
go and serve the gods of those nations;
lest there should be among you a root
bearing poison and wormwood, and 19
then upon hearing the terms of this sacred compact he should flatter himself
by saying, 'I shall be safe, even though
I persist in my stubbornness of mind,'
to the destruction of moist and dry
alike. The LORD would never consent 20
to forgive him, but instead, the anger
and resentment of the LORD would
burn against such a man; every curse
recorded in this book would settle on
him; the LORD would blot out his very
name from under the heavens; and the 21
LORD would single him out from all the
tribes of Israel for doom, by all the
curses of the covenant recorded in this
book of the law. Then the next genera- 22
tion, your children who take your place,
and the foreigners who come from a distant land, will say, when they see the
plagues of that land and the diseases
with which the LORD has afflicted it—
all its soil being brimstone and salt, 23
a burning waste, unsown and unproduc-

tive, no herbage of any kind growing in
it, like the devastation of Sodom and
Gomorrah, Admah and Zeboiim, which
the LORD devastated in his anger and
24 fury—indeed all nations will say, 'Why
has the LORD done thus to this land?
25 Why this great heat of anger?' And the
answer will be, 'Because they forsook
the covenant, which the LORD, the God
of their fathers, made with them, when
he brought them out of the land of
26 Egypt, and went and served alien gods,
and paid homage to them, gods of
whom they had no experience, and
27 whom he did not assign to them; hence
the anger of the LORD blazed against
this land, bringing it every curse re-
28 corded in this book; and the LORD uprooted them from their land in anger,
fury, and great wrath, and flung them
into an alien land, as at this day.'
29 "What is hidden is in the keeping of
the LORD our God, but what is revealed concerns us and our children forever, that we should observe all the provisions of this code.

30 "When all these things have befallen
you, the blessing as well as the curse
which I have put before you, and you
call them to mind among all the nations
where the LORD your God has driven
2 you, if you return to the LORD your
God, you and your children, and heed
his injunctions, just as I am commanding you today, with all your mind and
3 heart, then the LORD your God will restore your fortune, taking pity on you,
and gathering you again out of all the
peoples where the LORD your God
4 scattered you. Even though your outcasts are at the ends of the world, the
LORD your God will gather you from
5 there, and take you away. The LORD
your God will bring you into the land
which your fathers occupied, that you
may occupy it; and he will prosper you,
and make you more numerous than
6 your fathers. The LORD your God will
circumcise you and your descendants
in heart, to love the LORD your God
with all your mind and heart, that you
7 may live. The LORD your God will inflict all these curses on your enemies
and your antagonists who persecuted
8 you; but you yourselves shall once more
heed the injunctions of the LORD, and
observe all his commands which I am
9 giving you today; and the LORD your
God will give you abounding prosperity
in all your labor, in the offspring of your
body, the offspring of your cattle, and
the produce of your soil; for the LORD
will again take delight in prospering
you, as he did your fathers; for you will 1
be heeding the injunctions of the LORD
your God by keeping his commands
and statutes, recorded in this book of
the law; for you will be returning to the
LORD your God with all your mind and
heart.
"For this charge which I am enjoining 1
on you today is not beyond your power, nor is it out of reach; it is not in the 1
heavens, that you should say, 'O that
someone would ascend to the heavens
for us, and get to know it for us, and
then communicate it to us, so that we
may observe it!' Nor is it beyond 1
the sea, that you should say, 'O that
someone would cross the sea for us,
and get to know it for us, and then
communicate it to us, so that we may
observe it!' No, the matter is very near 1
you, in your mouth and in your mind,
for you to observe.
"See, I put before you today life and 1
prosperity, along with death and misfortune. If you heed the commands of 1
the LORD your God which I am giving
you today, by loving the LORD your
God, by walking in his ways, and by
keeping his commands, statutes, and
ordinances, then you shall live, and
multiply, and the LORD your God will
bless you in the land which you are invading for conquest. If, however, your 1
heart turns away, and you give no
heed, but are enticed to pay homage to
alien gods and serve them, I tell you today that you shall most certainly perish, without living long on the land
which you are crossing the Jordan to
invade for conquest. I call heaven and
earth to witness against you today that
I have put life and death before you,
the blessing and the curse; therefore
choose life, that you as well as your descendants may live, by loving the
LORD your God, by heeding his injunctions, and by holding fast to him; for
that will mean life to you, and a long
time to live upon the land which the
LORD swore to your fathers, Abraham,
Isaac, and Jacob, to give them."
Then Moses proceeded to speak these
words to all Israel. He said to them,
"I am one hundred and twenty years
old today; I am no longer able to come

and go, and the LORD has said to me, 'You are not to cross this Jordan.' The LORD your God will be the one to go over ahead of you; it is he who will exterminate these nations from your way so that you may dispossess them; Joshua will be the one to go over ahead of you, as the LORD promised. The LORD will do to them as he did to Sihon and Og, kings of the Amorites, and to their land, in his destruction of them; the LORD will put them at your mercy, and you must do to them just as I commanded you. Be strong, be brave, have no fear, do not stand in dread of them; for the LORD your God will be going with you, never failing you nor forsaking you."

Then Moses summoned Joshua, and said to him in the presence of all Israel,

"Be strong, be brave; for you are to bring this people into the land which the LORD swore to your fathers to give them; you are to put them in possession of it. The LORD will be the one to go ahead of you; it is he who will be with you, never failing you nor forsaking you; do not be afraid or dismayed."

When Moses had written this code, he committed it to the priests, the descendants of Levi, who carried the ark of the covenant of the LORD, and to all the elders of Israel. Then Moses commanded them as follows:

"At the end of every seven years, in the time of the year of remission, at the feast of booths, when all Israel comes to visit the LORD your God at the sanctuary which he chooses, you must read this code in the hearing of all Israel, assembling the people, men, women, and children, and any aliens in your employ that are in your community, that they may hear it, and learn to stand in awe of the LORD your God, and be careful to observe all the provisions of this code; and that their children who do not know it may hear it, and learn to stand in awe of the LORD your God; as long as you live upon the land into which you are crossing the Jordan for conquest."

THE COMMISSION OF JOSHUA AND THE SONG OF MOSES,
31:14—32:52

Then the LORD said to Moses,

"The time for you to die is indeed drawing near; call Joshua, and present yourselves at the tent of meeting, that I may commission him."

So Moses and Joshua went and presented themselves at the tent of meeting. Then the LORD appeared at the 15
tent in a column of cloud; the column
of cloud came to a stand at the doorway of the tent, and he commissioned 23
Joshua, the son of Nun, and said,

"Be strong, be brave, for you are to bring the Israelites into the land which I promised on oath to them; I will be with you."

Then the LORD said to Moses, 16

"You will soon now be sleeping with your fathers; and then this people will decide to run wantonly after the foreign gods of the land which they are soon to invade, and they will forsake me, and thus break the covenant that I made
with them. In that case my anger shall 17
blaze against them, and I will forsake them, and withhold my favor from them; they shall become a thing to be consumed, and many evils and troubles shall befall them, so that they will say at that time, 'Is it not because God is not in our midst that these evils have
befallen us?' I will certainly withhold 18
my favor at such a time, because of all the evil that they have done in turning
to alien gods. Write this song then, and 19
teach it to the Israelites, having them repeat it, that this song may be a witness for me against the Israelites. When 20
I bring them into the land which I swore to their fathers to give them, a land flowing with milk and honey, and they eat their fill, and become prosperous, and turn to alien gods, and serve them, despising me, and breaking my
covenant, then, when many evils and 21
troubles befall them, this song shall confront them as a witness (for it will never be forgotten by their descendants) that I know what their temperament will lead to, even now, before I bring them into the land, which I promised them on oath."

So Moses wrote the following song 22
that very day, and taught it to the Israelites.

When Moses had finished writing the 24
provisions of this code in a book, until
they were complete, Moses gave this 25
charge to the Levites who carried the ark of the covenant of the LORD:

"Take this book of the law, and place 26

it beside the ark of the covenant of the
LORD your God, so that it may remain
27 there as a witness against you; for I
know how contentious and stiff-necked
you are; even now while I am still living
with you, you continue in a state of
contention with the LORD; and how
28 much more after my death! Assemble
to me all the elders of your tribes and
your officers, that I may recite these
words to them, and call heaven and
29 earth to witness against them; for I
know that after my death you will be
sure to act perniciously, and swerve
from the way that I appointed you; and
in after days evil will befall you, because you will be doing what is evil in
the sight of the LORD, thus provoking
him to jealousy with your practices."

30 So Moses recited the words of this
song to its end, in the hearing of all the
assembly of Israel:

32 "Hearken, O heavens, that I may speak;
And let the earth hear the words of my mouth.
2 May my message drop as the rain,
My speech distil as the dew,
As the mist on the fresh grass,
And as showers on the vegetation.
3 For I proclaim the name of the LORD:
Give glory to our God!
4 He is a rock; what he does is right;
For all his ways are just;
A trustworthy and never deceiving God;
True and upright is he.
5 Their imperfection has been the undoing of those undutiful to him,
A twisted and crooked generation.
6 Is this the way to treat the LORD,
You foolish and senseless people?
Is he not your father who created you,
Who made you and fashioned you?
7 Remember the days of old,
Review the years, age after age;
Ask your father to inform you,
Your elders to tell you.
8 When the Most High gave heritages to the nations,
When he made divisions among mankind,
He assigned the realms of the nations
To the various deities;
9 While the LORD'S apportionment was his own people;
Jacob was the allotment for him to hold.
10 He found them in a desert land,
In the howling waste of a wilderness;
He encircled them, he cared for them;
He guarded them like the pupil of his eye.
11 Like an eagle stirring up its nestlings,
Dashing against its brood,
Spreading its wings to catch them,
And carrying them on its pinions,
12 The LORD alone was their leader,
And no foreign god was with him.
13 He made them mount the heights of the earth,
And they ate the products of the field;
He had them suck honey from crags,
And oil from flinty rocks.
14 Curds from cows and milk from sheep,
With the fat of lambs and rams,
Herds of Bashan and goats,
With the very choicest wheat,
And the blood of the grapes, a foaming draught,
Jacob ate to the fill;
15 Jeshurun grew fat, and kicked—
Gorge yourself, and you do become fat and corpulent—
So they forsook the God who made them,
And scoffed at the Rock of their salvation;
16 They provoked him to jealousy with alien gods,
They vexed him with abominable practices;
17 They sacrificed to demons that were not at all God,
Gods of whom they had had no experience;
New ones, but lately arrived,
Whom your fathers never revered.
18 You neglected the very Rock who bore you,
And forgot the God who gave you birth.
19 When the LORD saw it, he spurned them,
Because he was vexed with their sons and daughters;
20 And he said, 'I will hide my face from them;
I will see what will become of them;
For a fickle race are they,
Children in whom there is no sense of honor.
21 They provoked me to jealousy with what is no god;
They vexed me with their vanities;
So I will provoke them to jealousy with what is no nation,

With an impious people I will vex
them;
2 For a fire shall blaze within me,
And burn to the very depths of Sheol:
So that it shall consume the earth and
its produce,
And set the bases of the mountains on
fire.
3 I will exhaust calamities upon them;
I will use up my arrows on them.
4 The devastation of famine, and the
ravages of fever,
And malignant pestilence,
And ferocious beasts I will send on
them,
Along with poisonous reptiles.
5 On the street the sword shall cause
bereavement,
And terror at home,
For youth and maiden alike,
For the babe as well as the man of
gray hairs.
6 I would have said, "I will cut them in
pieces;
I will extinguish the memory of them
from men,"
7 Except that I dreaded irritation from
the enemy,
Lest their foes should misinterpret it;
Lest they should say, "It is our might
that has triumphed,
And not at all the LORD who did this";
8 For a people lacking in sense are they,
With no intelligence among them;
9 If they had any sense, they would per-
ceive this;
They would see through to their own
end.'
0 How could one person chase a
thousand,
Or two put ten thousand to flight,
Unless their Rock had sold them,
And the LORD had given them up?
1 For their rock is not like our Rock,
Nor is our God a thing of nought;
2 For their vine comes from the stock of
Sodom,
And from the fields of Gomorrah;
Their grapes are poisonous grapes;
Bitter clusters are theirs;
3 Their wine is the venom of dragons,
And the pitiless poison of cobras,
4 'Is it not stored up with me,
Sealed up in my treasuries,
5 Against the day of revenge and re-
quital,
Against the time that their foot slips?
For their day of calamity is at hand,
And their doom is coming apace.'

For the LORD will vindicate his 36
people,
And take compassion on his servants,
When he sees that their power is gone,
With neither bound nor free remain-
ing,
And that it is being said, 'Where is 37
their God,
The Rock in whom they sought refuge,
He who ate the fat of their sacrifices, 38
And drank the wine of their libations?
Let him come to your help;
Let him be a shelter over you!'
'Know now that I, I am he, 39
And that there is no god beside me;
It is I who slay, and bring to life;
When I have inflicted wounds, it is I
who heal them,
With none to give deliverance from
my power;
For I lift my hand to the heavens, 40
And declare, "As I live forever,
I will whet my flashing sword, 41
And my hand shall lay hold on justice;
I will wreak vengeance on my foes,
And punish those who hate me;
I will drench my arrows with blood, 42
With the blood of captives slain;
And my sword shall devour flesh
From the shaggy heads of the ene-
my." '
Shout among the nations, O you, his 43
people,
That he shall avenge the blood of his
servants,
And wreak vengeance on his adver-
saries,
And purge his people's land of guilt."

So Moses went and recited all the 44
words of this song to the people, along
with Hoshea, the son of Nun.

When Moses had finished reciting all 45
these words to all Israel, he said to 46
them,

"Take to heart all the things of which
I am warning you today that you may
lay them as a charge on your children,
that they may be careful to observe all
the provisions of this code; for this is by 47
no means too trivial a thing for you to
do; on the contrary it means your life,
and for this very reason you shall live
long in the land into which you are
crossing the Jordan for conquest."

That very same day the LORD said 48
to Moses,

"Ascend this mountain of the Aba- 49
rim, namely Mount Nebo, which is in
the land of Moab, facing Jericho, and

view the land of Canaan which I am giving to the Israelites as their own;
50 and then die on the mountain that you ascend, and be gathered to your fathers; as your brother Aaron died on Mount Hor and was gathered to his fa-
51 thers—because you broke faith with me among the Israelites at the waters of Meribath-Kadesh in the desert of Zin; because you did not pay me due honor
52 among the Israelites. Accordingly you shall view the land from a point of vantage; but you shall not enter the land which I am giving to the Israelites."

THE BLESSING OF MOSES, 33:1–29

33 This is the blessing which Moses, the man of God, pronounced upon the Is-
2 raelites before his death. He said:

"The LORD came from Sinai,
And dawned on us from Seir;
He shone forth from the mountains of Paran,
And advanced from Meribath-Kadesh,
With his lightning-bolts at his right hand.
3 Yea, he loves his people;
All those consecrated to him he blesses.
So they recline at thy feet,
Partaking of thine instruction,
4 Moses having charged us with a law.
His domain is Jacob's assembly,
5 And he became king in Jeshurun,
When the people's chieftains were assembled,
And all the tribes of Israel came together."

6 "May Reuben live and not die,
Though his men are few."

7 And this of Judah; he said,
"Hear, O LORD, the cry of Judah,
And bring him to his people!
As his strength, contend for him,
And be thou a help from his adversaries!"

8 And of Levi he said,
"Give thy thummim to Levi,
And thy urim to the man devoted to thee;
Whom thou didst test at Massah,
With whom thou didst contend at the waters of Meribah:
Who said of his father and mother,
'I no longer recognize them';
And disowned his brothers,
And disavowed his own children;
But he has kept thine injunctions,
And guarded thy covenant.
He communicates thine ordinances to Jacob,
And thy law to Israel;
He provides the odor of sacrifices for thy nostrils,
And holocausts on thine altars."

"O LORD, bless his might,
And graciously accept the work of his hands!
Shatter his opponents' loins,
And his adversaries beyond recovery!"

Of Benjamin he said,
"He is the beloved of the LORD;
With him he dwells securely;
He ever encircles him,
And has established his abode between his shoulders."

And of Joseph he said,
"Blessed of the LORD be his land,
With the wealth of the heavens above,
And that of the abyss couching below;
With lavish crops from the sun,
And the lavish yield of the months;
With the finest produce of the ancient mountains,
And the wealth of the eternal hills;
With the wealth of the earth and its abundance,
And the favor of him who dwelt in the bush—
May it descend on the head of Joseph,
And on the brow of him who was cursed by his brothers!
As his firstling bull may majesty be his,
And may his horns be the horns of a wild-ox,
To butt the nations with them,
And drive them to the ends of the earth!
So may these be the myriads for Ephraim,
And these the thousands for Manasseh!"

And of Zebulun he said,
"Rejoice, Zebulun, in your enterprises abroad,
And you, Issachar, in your tents at home!

They call peoples to their mountain
shrines,
There they offer the prescribed sacrifices;
For they suck up the affluence of the
seas,
And the hidden treasures of the sand."

And of Gad he said,
"Blessed be he who made Gad so great!
He lurks like a lion,
That he may tear the arm, and the
scalp as well.
He picked out the first for himself,
(For a leader's portion was reserved
there),
And he entered as the forerunner of
the people;
He carried out the just will of the
LORD,
And his ordinances for Israel."

And of Dan he said,
"Dan is a lion's whelp,
That leaps from Bashan."

And of Naphtali he said,
"O Naphtali, loaded with favors,
And filled with the blessings of the
LORD,
Take possession of the lake and the
south!"

And of Asher he said,
"Most blessed of sons may Asher be;
May he be the favorite among his
brothers,
With his foot immersed in oil!
May your bars be iron and bronze,
And your strength like your days!"

"There is none like the God of Jeshurun,
Throned in the heavens as your help,
And in the skies as the one to bring
you victory.
The eternal God is a refuge,
And underneath are the everlasting
arms;
So he drove the enemy out of your
way,
And he destroyed the Amorites,
And settled Israel in security,
The fountain of Jacob undisturbed,
In a land of grain and wine,
With his heavens, too, dropping dew.

Fortunate are you, O Israel; who is 29
there like you?
A people saved by the LORD,
The shield of your help,
And he that is the sword of your
victory;
So that your foes shall come cringing
to you,
As you march over their heights."

THE DEATH AND BURIAL OF MOSES, 34:1–12

From the steppes of Moab Moses **34**
ascended Mount Nebo, the headland of
Pisgah, which faces Jericho, and the
LORD showed him all the land—Gilead
as far as Dan, all Naphtali, the terri- 2
tory of Ephraim and Manasseh, all the
territory of Judah as far as the Western
Sea, the Negeb, and the basin or valley 3
of Jericho (the city of palms) as far as
Zoar. The LORD said to him, 4
"This is the land concerning which I
swore to Abraham, Isaac, and Jacob, as
follows: 'To your descendants I will
give it'; I have let you look upon it, but
you shall not go over there."
So Moses, the servant of the LORD, 5
died there in the land of Moab by command of the LORD; and he was buried 6
in the valley in the land of Moab opposite Beth-peor; but to this day no one
knows his burial-place.
Moses was one hundred and twenty 7
years old when he died, his eyes un-
dimmed, and his virility unabated. For 8
thirty days the Israelites wept for Moses in the steppes of Moab. When the
days of weeping in lamentation over
Moses had come to an end, since Josh- 9
ua, the son of Nun, was full of sagacity
(for Moses had laid his hands upon
him), the Israelites gave their allegiance to him, doing as the LORD had
commanded Moses.
Since then no prophet has ever ap- 10
peared in Israel like Moses, with whom
the LORD held converse face to face—
as regards all the signs and portents 11
which the LORD sent him to perform in
the land of Egypt against Pharaoh and
all his courtiers and all his land, as well 12
as all the mighty power and all the
great wonders which Moses performed
in the sight of all Israel.

They call peoples to their mountain
  shrines,
There they offer the prescribed sacrifices;
For they suck up the affluence of the
  seas,
And the hidden treasures of the sand."

And of Gad he said,
"Blessed be he who made Gad so great!
He lurks like a lion,
That he may tear the arm, and the
  scalp as well.
He picked out the first for himself,
(For a leader's portion was reserved
  there)
And he entered as the forerunner of
  the people;
He carried out the just will of the
  LORD,
And his ordinances for Israel."

And of Dan he said,
"Dan is a lion's whelp,
That leaps from Bashan."

And of Naphtali he said,
"O Naphtali, loaded with favors,
And filled with the blessings of the
  LORD,
Take possession of the lake and the
  south!"

And of Asher he said,
"Most blessed of sons may Asher be;
May he be the favorite among his
  brothers,
With his foot immersed in oil.
May your bars be iron and bronze,
And your strength like your days!"

"There is none like the God of Jeshurun,
Throned in the heavens as your help,
And in the skies as the one to bring
  you victory.
The eternal God is a refuge,
And underneath are the everlasting
  arms.
So he drove the enemy out of your
  way,
And he destroyed the Amorites,
And settled Israel in security,
The fountain of Jacob undisturbed,
In a land of grain and wine,
With his heavens, too, dropping dew.

Fortunate are you, O Israel; who is 29
  there like you?
A people saved by the LORD,
The shield of your help,
And he that is the sword of your
  victory,
So that your foes shall come cringing
  to you,
As you march over their heights."

THE DEATH AND BURIAL OF MOSES, 34:1-12

From the steppes of Moab Moses 34
ascended Mount Nebo, the headland of
Pisgah, which faces Jericho, and the
LORD showed him all the land—Gilead
as far as Dan, all Naphtali, the terri- 2
tory of Ephraim and Manasseh, all the
territory of Judah as far as the Western
Sea, the Negeb, and the basin or valley 3
of Jericho (the city of palms) as far as
Zoar. The LORD said to him, 4
"This is the land concerning which I
swore to Abraham, Isaac, and Jacob, as
follows: 'To your descendants I will
give it'; I have let you look upon it, but
you shall not go over there."
So Moses, the servant of the LORD, 5
died there in the land of Moab by command of the LORD; and he was buried 6
in the valley in the land of Moab opposite Beth-peor; but to this day no one
knows his burial-place.
Moses was one hundred and twenty 7
years old when he died, his eyes un-
dimmed, and his virility unabated. For 8
thirty days the Israelites wept for Moses in the steppes of Moab. When the
days of weeping in lamentation over
Moses had come to an end, since Josh- 9
ua, the son of Nun, was full of sagacity
(for Moses had laid his hands upon
him), the Israelites gave their allegiance to him, doing as the LORD had
commanded Moses.
Since then no prophet has ever ap- 10
peared in Israel like Moses, with whom
the LORD held converse face to face—
as regards all the signs and portents 11
which the LORD sent him to perform in
the land of Egypt against Pharaoh and
all his courtiers and all his land, as well 12
as all the mighty power and all the
great wonders which Moses performed
in the sight of all Israel.

PART II

THE HISTORICAL BOOKS

JOSHUA, JUDGES, AND RUTH; Translated by Theophile J. Meek

SAMUEL I AND II, KINGS I AND II, CHRONICLES I AND II, EZRA NEHEMIAH, AND ESTHER; Translated by Leroy Waterman

THE BOOK OF JOSHUA

THE ISRAELITE CONQUEST OF CANAAN, 1:1—12:24

NOW after the death of Moses, the servant of the LORD, the LORD said to Joshua, the son of Nun, the attendant of Moses,

"My servant Moses is dead; proceed then, to cross the Jordan here, you and all this people, into the land which I am giving them. Every place on which the sole of your foot treads I have given to you, as I promised Moses; the region from the desert as far as the Lebanon yonder, and from the Great River, the river Euphrates, as far as the Great Western Sea, all the land of the Hittites, shall be your domain. No one shall be able to hold his own against you as long as you live, in that I will be with you, as I was with Moses, never failing you nor forsaking you. Be strong and brave; for you shall put this people in possession of the land which I swore to their fathers to give them. Only be very strong and resolute to be careful to do just as my servant Moses commanded you, swerving therefrom neither to the right nor to the left, so that you may succeed in everything that you undertake. This book of the law must never be off your lips, but you must muse over it day and night, that you may be careful to comply with all that is written in it; for then you shall make your life prosperous, and you shall succeed. Have I not commanded you to be strong and brave? Do not be frightened or dismayed; for the LORD your God is with you in whatever you undertake."

Then Joshua commanded the officers of the people,

"Go through the camp, and command the people as follows: 'Provide yourselves with supplies; for within three days you are going to cross the Jordan here to enter into possession of the land which the LORD your God is giving you to conquer.' "

Also to the Reubenites, Gadites, and 12
half-tribe of Manasseh Joshua said,
"Remember the command which 13
Moses, the servant of the LORD, gave
you, when he said, 'The LORD your
God is providing you with a home, and
is giving you this land.' Your wives, 14
your little ones, and your cattle are to
remain in the land which Moses gave
you beyond the Jordan, but all of you
who are valiant warriors are to cross
over as special troops ahead of your
kinsmen, and help them, until the 15
LORD provides your kinsmen with a
home, as he has you, and they also occupy
the land which the LORD your
God is giving them. Then you may return
to the land of your own, which
Moses, the servant of the LORD, gave
you beyond the Jordan to the east."
They answered Joshua, 16
"Everything that you have commanded
us we will do, and wherever
you send us we will go. Just as we 17
obeyed Moses in everything, so will we
obey you; only may the LORD your
God be with you as he was with Moses!
Anyone who scorns your orders and 18
does not obey you in all that you command
him, shall be put to death; only
be strong and brave."
From Shittim Joshua, the son of 2
Nun, sent two men as spies, saying,
"Go, view the land, especially Jericho."
So they went off. They entered the
house of a harlot whose name was Rahab,
and lay down there. Then the 2
king of Jericho was told, "Some men
came here tonight from the Israelites to
reconnoiter the land!" So the king of 3
Jericho sent word to Rahab,
"Bring out the men who have come
to you, who have entered your house;
for they have come to reconnoiter the
whole land."
The woman, however, had taken the 4
two men and hidden them; so she said,
"Yes, the men did come to me, but I
did not know where they came from.
When it came time for the gate to be 5

closed at dark, the men went out. I do
not know where the men went. Hurry
and pursue them; for you can overtake
them."
6 She had, however, brought them up
to the roof, and had hidden them with
the stalks of flax which she had spread
out on the roof.
7 As for the men themselves, pursuers
went after them in the direction of the
Jordan as far as the fords; and the gate
was shut as soon as those in pursuit of
8 them went out. Before they had lain
down, she came up to them on the roof,
9 and said to the men,
"I know that the LORD has given
you the land, and that the terror of you
has fallen on us, and that all the inhabitants of the land are losing heart
10 because of you; for we have heard how
the LORD dried up the waters of the
Red Sea before you when you came out
of Egypt, and what you did to the two
Amorite kings who lived on the other
side of the Jordan, Sihon and Og, whom
11 you exterminated. When we heard of
it, our hearts failed, and no courage
was left in anyone because of you; for
the LORD your God is God in the heav-
12 ens above and on the earth below. Now
then, since I have dealt kindly with
you, swear to me by the LORD that you
in turn will deal kindly with my father's household, giving me a sure sign,
13 and that you will spare the lives of my
father, my mother, my brothers, and
my sisters, together with all that belong to them, and thus save us from
death."
14 The men said to her,
"We pledge our lives for yours that, if
you say nothing about this errand of
ours, we will deal kindly and honestly
with you when the LORD gives us the
land."
15 Then she let them down by a rope
through the window (for her house
was built into the city-wall, so that she
was living right in the wall).
16 "Get away to the hills," she said to
them, "lest the pursuers chance upon
you; hide yourselves there for three
days until the pursuers return, and
then you may proceed on your way."
17 The men said to her,
18 "See, when we invade the land, you
must tie this cord of scarlet string in the
window through which you let us down.
Gather your father, your mother, your
brothers, and all your father's household inside your house; in the case of 1
anyone who leaves the door of your
house for the street, his blood shall be
on his own head; we will not be to
blame; but in the case of everyone who
is with you in the house, his blood shall
be on our heads, if a hand is laid on him.
If, however, you divulge this errand of 2
ours, we shall be released from the oath
to you which you made us take."
"Let it be as you say," she said. 2
Then she saw them off; and when
they had gone, she tied the scarlet cord
in the window. So they went off and 2
entered the hills, and stayed there for
three days, until the pursuers returned.
The pursuers looked for them all along
the road, but did not find them. Then 2
the two men returned; coming down
from the hills, they crossed over and
came to Joshua, the son of Nun, and
told him all that had befallen them.
"The LORD is delivering the whole 2
land into our power," they said to
Joshua; "moreover, the inhabitants of
the land are all losing heart because of
us."
So Joshua rose early next morning,
and he and all the Israelites set out
from Shittim, and reaching the Jordan,
they passed the night there, before
crossing over. Three days afterward
the officers went through the camp, and
commanded the people as follows:
"As soon as you see the Levitical
priests taking up the ark of the covenant of the LORD your God, you must
leave your position and follow it (there
must be, however, between you and it a
space of some two thousand cubits;
you must not come any nearer to it), in
order that you may know what road to
follow; for you have never gone over
this road before."
Then Joshua said to the people,
"Consecrate yourselves; for tomorrow the LORD is going to perform
wonders among you."
To the priests Joshua said,
"Take up the ark of the covenant,
and pass over ahead of the people."
So they took up the ark of the covenant, and went ahead of the people.
Then the LORD said to Joshua,
"This day I begin to exalt you in the
sight of all Israel, that they may know
that I am with you, as I was with Moses. Now, you are to command the

priests who are carrying the ark of the
covenant as follows: 'As soon as you
reach the brink of the water of the Jordan, you must come to a halt in the
Jordan.'"
9 Then Joshua said to the Israelites,
"Come here and hear the words of
the LORD your God."
10 Joshua said,
"By this you shall know that the living God is in your midst, and that he is
surely going to drive out of your way
the Canaanites, Hittites, Hivvites,
Perizzites, Girgashites, Amorites, and
11 Jebusites. See, the ark of the covenant
of the Lord of the whole earth is to
12 cross the Jordan ahead of you. Now
then, choose twelve men from the tribes
13 of Israel, one man from each tribe. As
soon as the soles of the feet of the
priests carrying the ark of the LORD,
the Lord of the whole earth, rest in the
waters of the Jordan, the waters of the
Jordan shall be cut off, namely, the
waters flowing down from above, and
they shall come to a stop in a single
heap."
14 When the people left their tents to
cross the Jordan, with the priests carrying the ark of the covenant preceding
15 the people, then, as soon as the bearers
of the ark reached the Jordan, and the
feet of the priests carrying the ark
dipped in the brink of the water (the
Jordan being flooded above all its
banks during all the time of harvest),
16 the waters flowing down from above
came to a stop, rising up in a single
heap, and extending for a long distance
from Adamah, a city that is in the vicinity of Zarethan; while those flowing
down toward the Sea of the Arabah, the
Salt Sea, were completely cut off, so that
the people crossed over, opposite Jeri-
17 cho. The priests carrying the ark of the
covenant of the LORD took their stand
on dry ground, right in the middle of
the Jordan, while all Israel crossed over
on dry ground, until the whole nation
had finished crossing the Jordan.

4 As soon as the whole nation had finished crossing the Jordan, the LORD
said to Joshua,
2 "Choose twelve men from the people,
3 one from each tribe, and command
them as follows: 'Take up twelve
stones from here, right out of the middle of the Jordan, from the place where
the feet of the priests stood, and carrying them over with you, lay them down
at the place where you are going to
camp tonight.'"
So Joshua summoned the twelve 4
men whom he had selected from the Israelites, one from each tribe, and Josh- 5
ua said to them,
"Go over to where the ark of the
LORD your God is in the middle of the
Jordan, and each of you lift a stone
upon his shoulder, to the number of the
tribes of the Israelites, that this may be 6
a sign among you; for later your children will be asking you, 'What is the
significance of these stones to you?' and 7
then you must tell them how the waters
of the Jordan were cut off in front of
the ark of the covenant of the LORD;
when it passed into the Jordan, the
waters of the Jordan were cut off; so
these stones serve as a memorial for the
Israelites forever."
The Israelites did as Joshua com- 8
manded; they took up twelve stones
out of the middle of the Jordan, as the
LORD had told Joshua, to the number
of the tribes of the Israelites, and carrying them over with them to the camping-place, they laid them down there
(Joshua having piled up the twelve 9
stones in the middle of the Jordan at
the place where the feet of the priests
carrying the ark of the covenant stood),
and there they are to this day. The 10
priests carrying the ark remained
standing in the middle of the Jordan
until everything had been finished that
the LORD had commanded Joshua to
tell the people to do. The people hurried over, and as soon as the people had 11
all finished crossing, the ark of the
LORD, with the priests, passed over to
the van of the people. The Reubenites, 12
Gadites, and half-tribe of Manasseh
passed over as special troops ahead of
the Israelites, as Moses had told them,
some forty thousand picked troops 13
passing over in sight of the LORD to the
steppes of Jericho for battle. That day 14
the LORD exalted Joshua in the sight
of all Israel, so that they revered him as
they had revered Moses, as long as he
lived.
Then the LORD said to Joshua, 15
"Command the priests carrying the 16
ark of the decrees to come up out of the
Jordan."
So Joshua commanded the priests, 17
"Come up out of the Jordan."

18 When the priests carrying the ark of
the covenant of the LORD came up
from the middle of the Jordan, and the
soles of the feet of the priests were
lifted on to the dry ground, the waters
of the Jordan resumed their course, and
flowed as before above all its banks.
19 It was on the tenth day of the first
month that the people came up from
the Jordan, and camped at Gilgal at
20 the eastern outskirts of Jericho; and
these twelve stones which they took out
of the Jordan, Joshua set up at Gilgal.
21 Then he said to the Israelites,
"When your children in time to come
ask their fathers, 'What is the signifi-
22 cance of these stones?' you must inform your children as follows: 'Right
on dry ground Israel crossed this Jor-
23 dan.' For the LORD your God dried up
the waters of the Jordan in front of you,
until you had passed over, as the LORD
your God did to the Red Sea which he
dried up in front of us, until we had
24 passed over, that all the peoples of the
earth may know that the hand of the
LORD is strong, so that you may stand
in awe of the LORD your God always."

5 Now when all the Amorite kings who
were beyond the Jordan to the west,
and all the Canaanite kings who were
by the Sea heard how the LORD had
dried up the waters of the Jordan in
front of the Israelites, until they had
passed over, their hearts failed, and
there was no courage left in them because of the Israelites.
2 At that time the LORD said to Joshua,
"Make flint knives, and have another circumcision for the Israelites."
3 So Joshua made flint knives, and circumcised the Israelites at Gibeath-
4 araloth [the hill of the foreskins]. Now
this is the reason why Joshua had the
circumcision: all the people who had
come out of Egypt, that is, the males,
all the warriors, had died during the
journey through the desert after com-
5 ing out of Egypt; for all the people who
came out were circumcised, but none of
the people who had been born during
the journey through the desert after
coming out of Egypt had been circum-
6 cised; for the Israelites had journeyed
for forty years in the desert until the
whole generation, that is, the warriors
who came out of Egypt, had perished,
since they would not heed the injunctions of the LORD, and the LORD had
sworn to them that he would not let
them see the land which the LORD had
sworn to their fathers to give us, a land
flowing with milk and honey. So it was 7
their children who replaced them that
Joshua circumcised; for they were uncircumcised, because they had not been
circumcised on the journey. After the 8
circumcision had been completed for
the whole nation, they remained at
home in the camp until they had recovered.
Then the LORD said to Joshua, 9
"Today I have rolled the odium of
Egypt off you."
Hence the name of that place came
to be called Gilgal [rolling], as it is to
this day.
When the Israelites were camped at 10
Gilgal, they observed the passover on
the evening of the fourteenth day of the
month, on the steppes of Jericho. The 11
day after the passover they ate some of
the products of the land, unleavened
cakes and parched grain; that very 12
same day the manna ceased, when they
ate some of the products of the land, so
that the Israelites had manna no longer, but lived that year on the produce
of the land of Canaan.
When Joshua was near Jericho, he 13
raised his eyes and saw a man standing
opposite him with his drawn sword in
his hand. So Joshua approached him,
and said to him,
"Are you for us, or for our adversaries?"
"No," said he; "I come rather as 14
captain of the host of the LORD."
Then Joshua fell on his face to the
earth, and bowing down, said to him,
"What has my lord to say to his
servant?"
"Take your sandals off your feet," 15
the captain of the host of the LORD
said to Joshua; "for the place on which
you are standing is holy."
Joshua did so. (Now Jericho was 6
shut up tight because of the Israelites,
with no one going out or coming in.)
Then the LORD said to Joshua,
"See, I am delivering Jericho into
your power, along with its king. Take
the most valiant warriors, and march
around the city, all the warriors going
around the city once. Thus shall you
do for six days, while seven priests
carry seven rams' horns in front of the

ark. On the seventh day you shall
march around the city seven times,
5 while the priests blow the horns. When
they blow a long blast on the rams'
horns, as soon as you hear the sound of
the horns, all the people must raise a
mighty shout, and then the wall of the
city shall fall down flat, so that the
people can go up, each straight in front
of him."
6 So Joshua, the son of Nun, summoned the priests, and said to them,
"Take up the ark of the covenant,
and let seven priests carry seven rams'
horns in front of the ark of the LORD."
7 Then he said to the people,
"Pass on, and march around the city,
while the picked troops pass on in front
of the ark of the LORD."
8 As soon as Joshua spoke to the people, the seven priests carrying the seven
rams' horns in front of the LORD
passed on, and blew the horns, while
the ark of the covenant of the LORD
9 followed them, and the picked troops
marched in front of the priests who
were blowing the horns, and the rearguard followed the ark, blowing the
horns as they went.
10 Then Joshua commanded the people,
"You must not shout, nor let your
voices be heard, nor let a word escape
your lips, until the day that I tell you
to shout; then shout."
11 So he had the ark of the LORD taken
around the city, going around it once;
then they retired to the camp, and
spent the night in the camp.
12 Next morning Joshua rose early; the
priests took up the ark of the LORD,
13 while the seven priests carrying the
seven rams' horns in front of the ark of
the LORD went along, blowing the
horns as they went, and the picked
troops went ahead of them, and the
rearguard followed the ark of the
LORD, blowing the horns as they went.
14 So they marched once around the city
on the second day, and then returned to
the camp. Thus they did for six days.
15 Then on the seventh day they rose
early at daybreak, and marched around
the city in the same manner seven
times; it was on that day only that they
marched around the city seven times.
16 The seventh time the priests blew the
horns, and then Joshua said to the
people,
"Shout; for the LORD is giving you
the city. The city with all that is in it 17
is to be immolated to the LORD; only
Rahab, the harlot, is to be spared, she
and all who are with her in her house,
because she hid the messengers whom
we sent. As for yourselves, you are to 18
keep absolutely clear of the doomed
things, lest you covet them, and take
some of the doomed things, and so put
the camp of Israel under the ban, and
bring trouble to it. But all the silver 19
and gold, and the articles of bronze and
iron are sacred to the LORD; they are
to go into the treasury of the LORD."
So the people shouted, when the 20
horns were blown. As soon as the people heard the sound of the horns, the
people raised a mighty shout, and the
wall fell flat, so that the people went
up into the city, each straight in front
of him, and they captured the city.
They massacred all that were in the 21
city, both men and women, old and
young alike, as well as the oxen, sheep,
and asses, putting them to the sword.
But Joshua said to the two men who 22
had spied out the land,
"Go into the harlot's house, and
bring the woman out of it, with all that
belong to her, as you swore to her."
So the spies went in, and brought 23
Rahab out, with her father, her mother,
her brothers, and all that belonged to
her; they brought all her family out,
and placed them outside the camp of
Israel. The city itself they burned up, 24
with all that was in it; only the silver
and gold and articles of bronze and
iron, they put into the treasury of the
LORD. But Rahab, the harlot, and her 25
father's household, and all that belonged to her, Joshua spared; and she
lived among the Israelites, as do her descendants to this day; for she hid the
messengers that Joshua sent to spy out
Jericho.
At that time Joshua had an oath 26
taken as follows:

"Cursed be the man before the LORD,
Who undertakes to rebuild this city,
Jericho;
At the cost of his first-born shall he
lay its foundation,
And at the cost of his youngest son
shall he erect its gates."

The LORD was with Joshua, so that 27
his fame spread all through the land.
But the Israelites broke faith in the 7
case of the doomed things, in that

Achan, the son of Carmi, the son of
Zabdi, the son of Zerah, who belonged
to the tribe of Judah, took some of the
doomed things, so that the anger of the
LORD blazed against the Israelites.
2 Joshua sent men from Jericho to Ai,
which is near Bethaven, east of Bethel,
and said to them,
"Go up and spy out the land."
So the men went up and spied out Ai.
3 Then they returned to Joshua, and said
to him,
"All the people need not go up; only
two or three thousand men need go up
to attack Ai; do not make all the people toil up there; for they are few."
4 So about three thousand of the people went up there; but they fled from
5 the men of Ai. The men of Ai killed
about thirty-six of them, and pursued
them out from the city gate as far as
Shebarim, and killed them at the descent, so that the hearts of the people
failed, and turned to water.
6 Then Joshua tore his clothes, and
falling on his face to the earth before
the ark of the LORD, he lay there until
evening, together with the elders of Israel; and they threw dust on their
heads.
7 "Alas, O Lord GOD," said Joshua,
"why didst thou ever bring this people
across the Jordan, only to deliver us
into the power of the Amorites, to destroy us? Would that we had been
content to remain on the other side of
8 the Jordan! Pray, O Lord, what can I
say after Israel has turned his back on
9 his enemies? When the Canaanites and
all the inhabitants of the land hear of
it, they will surround us, and wipe us off
the earth; and what wilt thou do then
for thy great name?"
10 "Rise!" the LORD said to Joshua.
"What use is it to fall on your face?
11 Israel has sinned; they have violated
the covenant with me, which I enjoined
on them; they have taken some of the
doomed things; they have stolen them,
dissimulated about them, and put them
12 among their own things. The Israelites,
accordingly, cannot stand up against
their enemies, but turn their backs on
their enemies; for they have become
doomed themselves. I will not be with
you any more, unless you get rid of the
13 doomed things. Rise, consecrate the
people, and say, 'Consecrate yourselves
for tomorrow; for thus says the LORD,
the God of Israel: "Doomed things are
among you, O Israel; you cannot stand
up against your enemies until you remove the doomed things from your
midst." In the morning then, you shall 14
present yourselves by tribes; and the
tribe which the LORD indicates shall
come forward by clans; and the clan
which the LORD indicates shall come
forward by families; and the family
which the LORD indicates shall come
forward by individuals. Then he that is 15
indicated as having the doomed things
shall be burned, together with all that
belong to him; because he violated the
covenant of the LORD, and because he
committed an infamous act in Israel.' "
So Joshua rose early next morning, 16
and had Israel come forward by tribes,
and the tribe of Judah was indicated.
Then he had the clans of Judah come 17
forward, and the clan of the Zerahites
was indicated. Then he had the clan of
the Zerahites come forward by families,
and Zabdi was indicated. Finally he 18
had his family come forward by individuals, and Achan, the son of Carmi,
the son of Zabdi, the son of Zerah, belonging to the tribe of Judah, was indicated. Then Joshua said to Achan, 19
"My son, render homage to the
LORD, the God of Israel, and give
praise to him; but do tell me what you
did; do not hide it from me."
Achan answered Joshua, 20
"Yes, it was I who sinned against the
LORD, the God of Israel; this briefly is
what I did: when I saw among the spoil 21
a beautiful mantle from Shinar, and
two hundred shekels of silver, and a bar
of gold fifty shekels in weight, I coveted
them, and took them; they are hidden
in the ground inside my tent, with the
money underneath the mantle."
So Joshua sent messengers, who ran 22
to the tent, and there it was hidden in
his tent, with the money underneath
it! They took the things from the tent, 23
and brought them to Joshua and all the
Israelites; and they laid them before
the LORD. Then Joshua, accompanied 24
by all Israel, took Achan, the descendant of Zerah, and the silver, the mantle,
the bar of gold, his sons, his daughters,
his oxen, his asses, his sheep, his household, and all that belonged to him, and
they brought them to the valley of
Achor.
"Why have you brought trouble on 25

us?" said Joshua. "May the LORD
bring trouble on you today!"
So all Israel stoned him; they burned
26 them all up and stoned them. They
erected a great cairn of stones over
him, which remains to this day. Then
the LORD relented from his fierce anger. That is how the name of that place
came to be called the Valley of Achor
[trouble], as it is to this day.

8 Then the LORD said to Joshua,
"Do not be afraid or dismayed; take
all the warriors with you, and go, march
against Ai. See, I am delivering the
king of Ai into your power, together
with his people, his city, and his land.
2 You shall do to Ai and its king as you
did to Jericho and its king, except that
you may take its spoil and cattle as
your booty. Set an ambush for the city
west of it."
3 So Joshua, with all the warriors, prepared to march against Ai. Joshua
picked out thirty thousand of the most
valiant warriors, and sent them off by
4 night, commanding them as follows:
"See, you are to lie in ambush against
the city, to the west of it; do not go
very far from the city, but all of you be
5 ready. I and all the troops with me will
draw near to the city, and then, when
they come out against us, we shall flee
6 from them as we did the first time, and
they will come out after us, until we
draw them away from the city; for they
will say, 'They are fleeing from us as
they did the first time.' Thus we shall
7 flee from them, and then you must rise
from your ambush, and take possession
of the city. The LORD your God will
8 deliver it into your power. As soon as
you have seized the city, set the city on
fire, doing as the LORD directed. See, I
have given you your commands."
9 Then Joshua sent them off, and they
went to the place of ambush, establishing themselves between Bethel and Ai,
west of Ai; but Joshua himself spent
that night with the people.
10 Next morning Joshua rose early, and
mustered the people, and with the elders of Israel marched at the head of the
11 people to Ai. Then all the people, that
is, the warriors that were with him,
marched up until they came near it.
Arriving in front of the city, they encamped north of Ai, with the valley be-
12 tween them and Ai. Joshua took about
five thousand men, and set them in ambush between Bethel and Ai, west of
the city. So the people were given their 13
stations, the main body north of the
city, and the rearguard west of the
city: but Joshua himself spent that
night in the valley.
As soon as the king of Ai became 14
aware of it, he hurried out with all his
people to meet Israel in battle, without
knowing that there was an ambush for
him west of the city. Joshua and all Israel 15
pretended to be beaten by them, and
fled in the direction of the desert. Then 16
all the people that were in the city were
called out to pursue them; and in pursuing Joshua, they were drawn away
from the city. Not a man was left in Ai 17
or Bethel that did not go out in pursuit
of Israel; they left the city unguarded,
and pursued Israel. Then the LORD 18
said to Joshua,
"Stretch out the javelin that is in
your hand toward Ai; for I will deliver
it into your power."
So Joshua stretched out the javelin
that was in his hand toward the city;
whereupon the men in ambush rose 19
quickly from their position; as soon as
he stretched out his hand, they ran, and
entered the city, and captured it; then
they hurriedly set the city on fire.
When the men of Ai looked back, they 20
saw the smoke of the city rising to the
heavens! They had no chance to flee
this way or that; for the people who had
been fleeing to the desert turned on
their pursuers. When Joshua and the 21
main body of Israel saw that the men
in ambush had captured the city, and
that smoke was rising from the city,
they turned back and attacked the
men of Ai. Then the others came out 22
of the city against them, and thus they
were between two bodies of Israelites,
some on one side and some on the other.
They slew them until not one remained
or escaped. The king of Ai they took 23
alive, and brought him to Joshua.
When Israel had finished slaying all 24
the inhabitants of Ai in the open desert
where they had pursued them, and all
of them had fallen by the sword until
they were at an end, all Israel turned
back to Ai, and put it to the sword.
The total number of those that fell that 25
day, including men and women, was
twelve thousand, namely, all the people
of Ai; Joshua did not withdraw his 26
hand, with which he was holding out

the javelin, until he had massacred all
27 the inhabitants of Ai. The cattle, however, and the spoil of that city the Israelites took as their booty, in accordance with the command which the
28 LORD had given Joshua. So Joshua
burned Ai, and turned it permanently
into a heap of ruins, as it is to this day.
29 The king of Ai he hanged on a tree and
left until evening, but at sunset Joshua
ordered his body to be taken down
from the tree, and thrown down at the
entrance to the city's gate. A great
cairn of stones was erected over it,
which remains to this day.
30 Then Joshua built an altar to the
LORD, the God of Israel, on Mount
31 Gerizim, as Moses, the servant of the
LORD, had commanded the Israelites,
an altar of undressed stones, on which
no iron tool had been used, as it is
written in the lawbook of Moses.
Burnt-offerings to the LORD were made
on it, and thank-offerings were sacri-
32 ficed. Then he wrote there on the
stones a copy of the law of Moses
which he had written for the Israelites.
33 First all Israel, with their elders, officers, and judges, took their stand on
each side of the ark, opposite the Levitical priests who carried the ark of the
covenant of the LORD—the resident
aliens as well as the native born—half
of them in front of Mount Gerizim, and
half of them in front of Mount Ebal for
the blessing of the people of Israel, as
Moses, the servant of the LORD, had
34 instructed; and then he read all the
provisions of the law, the blessing and
the curse, just as it was written in the
35 lawbook; there was not a word of all
that Moses commanded that Joshua
did not read in the presence of all the
assemblage of Israel, with the women,
the children, and the resident aliens
who were residing with them.

9 When all the kings heard of it, who
were beyond the Jordan, in the highlands and lowlands, and all along the
coast of the Great Sea in front of Lebanon, the Hittites, Amorites, Canaanites, Perizzites, Hivvites, and Jebu-
2 sites, they formed a coalition to fight as
a single body with Joshua and Israel.
3 When the inhabitants of Gibeon
heard what Joshua had done to Jericho
4 and Ai, they on their part resorted to a
ruse; they proceeded to disguise themselves: they took old sacks to load on
their asses, and old torn, patched wine-
skins, with old, patched sandals on 5
their feet, and old garments on their
backs, and the bread for their provisions was all dry and crumbled. Then 6
they went to Joshua at the camp at
Gilgal, and said to him and the men of
Israel,

"We have come from a far country;
now then, make an alliance with us."

The men of Israel said to the Hiv- 7
vites,

"Perhaps you are living among us; so
how can we make an alliance with
you?"

"We are your servants," they said to 8
Joshua.

But Joshua said to them,

"Who are you, and where do you
come from?"

They said to him, 9

"Your servants have come from a
very far country on account of the
fame of the LORD your God; for we
have heard the report of him, and all
that he did in Egypt and all that he did 10
to the two Amorite kings who were beyond the Jordan, Sihon, king of Heshbon, and Og, king of Bashan, who lived
at Ashtaroth. Our elders and all the in- 11
habitants of our land said to us, 'Take
with you provisions for a journey, and
go to meet them, and say to them, "We
are your servants; now then, make an
alliance with us." ' This is our bread; 12
we took it fresh for our provision out of
our houses on the day that we left to
come to you, and now look; it is dry
and crumbled. These are our wine- 13
skins, which were new when we filled
them, and now look; they are torn.
These are our clothes and sandals; they
are worn out from the very long journey."

Then the men partook of their provi- 14
sions, without asking the advice of the
LORD; and Joshua came to terms with 15
them, and made a covenant with them
to let them live, and the leaders of the
community swore an oath to them.

However, three days after they had 16
made the covenant with them, they
learned that they were their neighbors,
and were living among them. So the 17
Israelites set out, and reached their
cities on the third day, their cities being
Gibeon, Chephirah, Beeroth, and Kirjath-jearim. The Israelites, however, 18
did not kill them, because the leaders of

the community had sworn an oath to
them by the LORD, the God of Israel.
The whole community grumbled at the
leaders, but the leaders all said to the
whole community,
"We have sworn an oath to them by
the LORD, the God of Israel; so now we
20 cannot touch them. This is what we
will do to them; we will let them live,
so that no wrath may come upon us for
the oath which we swore to them."
21 "They shall live," the leaders said to
them; "but they shall become hewers
of wood and drawers of water for the
whole community, as the leaders told
them."
22 Then Joshua summoned them, and
said to them,
"Why have you deceived us by saying, 'We live very far from you,' when
23 you are really living among us? Cursed
then shall you be; never shall you cease
providing slaves, hewers of wood and
drawers of water, for the temple of my
God!"
24 They answered Joshua,
"Your servants were assured that the
LORD your God had commanded his
servant Moses to give you the whole
land, and to exterminate all the inhabitants of the land from your way, so we
stood in great fear of our lives through
you, and accordingly have done this.
25 Here we are, then, in your power; do
whatever you think it right and proper
to do to us."
26 And that was what Joshua did to
them; he saved them from the Israelites, so that they did not slay them;
27 but he made them that day hewers of
wood and drawers of water for the community, and for the altar of the LORD,
for the sanctuary that he should choose,
as they are to this day.
10 When Adoni-zedek, king of Jerusalem, heard that Joshua had captured
Ai, and had annihilated it (having done
to Ai and its king as he did to Jericho
and its king), and that the inhabitants
of Gibeon had made peace with Israel,
2 and had joined them, he was in great
terror; for Gibeon was a large city,
quite like a royal city, and was larger
than Ai, and its men were all fighters.
3 So Adoni-zedek, king of Jerusalem, sent
this message to Hoham, king of Hebron,
to Piram, king of Jarmuth, to Japhia,
king of Lachish, and to Debir, king of
Eglon:
"Join me, and give me your help, 4
that we may chastise Gibeon; for it has
made peace with Joshua and the Israelites."
So the five Amorite kings, the king of 5
Jerusalem, the king of Hebron, the
king of Jarmuth, the king of Lachish,
and the king of Eglon, mustered their
forces, and coming up with all their
armies, they invested Gibeon, and
attacked it. Then the Gibeonites sent 6
this message to Joshua at the camp at
Gilgal:
"Do not abandon your servants;
come up quickly to our rescue, and
help us; for all the Amorite kings inhabiting the highlands have gathered
against us."
So Joshua went up from Gilgal, ac- 7
companied by all the warriors, as well
as all the seasoned troops.
"Do not be afraid of them," the 8
LORD said to Joshua; "for I am delivering them into your power; not one of
them shall hold his own against you."
So Joshua made a surprise attack 9
upon them, by marching all night from
Gilgal; and the LORD threw them into a 10
panic before Israel, so that they inflicted great slaughter on them at Gibeon,
and pursuing them in the direction of
the slope of Beth-horon, they harried
them all the way to Azekah and Makkedah. After they had fled from the Is- 11
raelites, while they were at the descent
of Beth-horon, the LORD cast great
stones from the sky upon them all the
way to Azekah, so that they died,
more dying from the hailstones than
the Israelites slew with the sword.
It was on the day that the LORD put 12
the Amorites at the mercy of the Israelites that Joshua spoke to the LORD,
and in the presence of Israel said,
"O sun, stop at Gibeon;
And thou moon, at the valley of
Aijalon!"
So the sun came to a stop, and the 13
moon stood still, until the nation took
vengeance on their foes. (Is this not
written in the Book of Jashar?) The
sun stood still at the zenith, and delayed its setting for about a whole day.
Never before or since has there been a 14
day like that, when the LORD heeded
the cry of a man; for the LORD fought
for Israel. Then Joshua, accompanied 15
by all Israel, returned to the camp at
Gilgal.

16 The five kings fled, and hid them-
17 selves in the cave at Makkedah; and
Joshua was told,
"The five kings have been discovered, hidden in the cave at Makkedah."
18 So Joshua said,
"Roll large stones up to the mouth of
the cave, and post men over it to guard
19 them; but do not stay there yourselves;
pursue your enemies, and attack them
in the rear; do not let them get into
their cities; for the LORD your God has
delivered them into your power."
20 When Joshua and the Israelites had
finished inflicting a very great slaughter on them until they were at an end,
and the survivors who were left of
21 them had gained the fortified cities, the
people all returned unmolested to
Joshua at the camp at Makkedah, not
a man flinging a word at the Israelites.
22 Then Joshua said,
"Open the mouth of the cave, and
bring me those five kings out of the
cave."
23 They did so; they brought him these
five kings out of the cave: the king of
Jerusalem, the king of Hebron, the
king of Jarmuth, the king of Lachish,
24 and the king of Eglon. When they had
brought these kings out to Joshua,
Joshua summoned all the men of Israel, and said to the army commanders
who had accompanied him,
"Come forward, and put your feet on
the necks of these kings."
So they came forward, and put their
25 feet on their necks. Then Joshua said
to them,
"Do not be afraid or dismayed; be
strong and brave; for thus shall the
LORD do to all your enemies with
whom you fight."
26 Joshua then felled them, and killed
them; he hanged them on five trees,
and they remained hanging on the
27 trees until evening. At sunset, on command of Joshua, they were taken down
from the trees, and thrown into the
cave where they had hidden themselves, and large stones were placed on
the mouth of the cave, which remain to
this very day.
28 That day Joshua captured Makkedah, and put it and its king to the
sword, annihilating it and every person
in it, sparing no one. He did to the king
of Makkedah as he had done to the king
of Jericho.

Then Joshua, accompanied by all Is- 29
rael, passed on from Makkedah to Libnah. He attacked Libnah, and the 30
LORD delivered it also, with its king,
into the power of Israel. He put it to
the sword, with every person that was
in it, sparing no one in it, and did to its
king as he had done to the king of Jericho.
Then Joshua, accompanied by all Is- 31
rael, passed on from Libnah to Lachish.
He invested it, and attacked it; and the 32
LORD delivered Lachish into the power
of Israel. He captured it on the second
day, and put it to the sword, with every
person that was in it, just as he had
done to Libnah. Then Horam, king of 33
Gezer, came up to help Lachish, but
Joshua harried him and his army until
not a survivor was left to him.
Then Joshua, accompanied by all Is- 34
rael, passed on from Lachish to Eglon.
They invested it, and attacked it.
They captured it that same day, and 35
put it to the sword, massacring that
day every person that was in it, just
as had been done to Lachish
Then Joshua, accompanied by all 36
Israel, marched up from Eglon to Hebron. They attacked it, and captured 37
it, and put it to the sword, with its
king, all its towns, and every person
that was in it, sparing no one, just as
had been done to Eglon. He annihilated it and every person in it.
Then Joshua, accompanied by all 38
Israel, turned back to Debir, and attacked it. He captured it and its king 39
and all its towns. He put them to the
sword, and massacred every person
that was in it, sparing no one. As he
had done to Hebron, so he did to Debir
and its king, as also he had done to Libnah and its king.
Thus Joshua conquered the whole 40
land, the highlands, the steppes, the
lowlands, and the slopes, with all their
kings, sparing no one, but massacring
every living soul, as the LORD, the God
of Israel, had directed, Joshua con- 41
quered them from Kadesh-barnea as
far as Gaza, and all the land of Goshen
as far as Gibeon. All these kings and 42
their country Joshua captured in a single campaign; for the LORD, the God
of Israel, fought for Israel. Then Josh- 43
ua, accompanied by all Israel, returned
to the camp at Gilgal.
When Jabin, king of Hazor, heard 11

about it, he sent to Jobab, king of Madon, to the king of Shimran, to the king
2 of Achshaph, to the kings that were in
the highlands to the north, in the Arabah south of Chinneroth, in the lowlands, and in the uplands of Dor to the
3 west—the Canaanites to the east and
west, the Amorites, the Hittites, the
Perizzites, the Jebusites in the highlands, and the Hivvites at the foot of
4 Hermon in the land of Mizpeh. These,
accompanied by all their troops, sallied
forth, a great host, as numerous as the
sands on the seashore, with very many
5 horses and chariots. All these kings
joined forces, and went and encamped
together at the waters of Merom, to
fight with Israel.
6 Then the LORD said to Joshua,
"Do not stand in fear of them; for tomorrow about this time I will deliver
them up to Israel all slain; you must
hamstring their horses and burn up
their chariots."
7 So Joshua, accompanied by all the
warriors, made a surprise attack upon
them at the waters of Merom, and fell
8 upon them. The LORD delivered them
into the power of Israel, so that they
defeated them, and pursued them as
far as Sidon the Great and Misrephoth-
maim and the valley of Mizpeh eastward. They harried them until not a
9 survivor was left of them. Joshua did
to them as the LORD had told him,
hamstringing their horses, and burning
up their chariots.
10 It was at that time also that Joshua
captured Hazor, and put its king to the
sword (for Hazor used to be the head of
11 all those kingdoms). They put every
person that was in it to the sword, massacring them, not a living soul being
left. Then Hazor was burned.
12 So Joshua captured all the cities of
those kings, as well as all the kings
themselves, and put them to the sword,
massacring them, as Moses, the servant
13 of the LORD, had commanded. None
of the cities, however, that stood on
mounds did Israel burn, except Hazor
14 alone, Joshua having burned it. All the
spoil of these cities and the cattle, the
Israelites took as their booty; but they
put all the men to the sword until they
had destroyed them, sparing not a liv-
15 ing soul. As the LORD had commanded
his servant Moses, so did Moses command Joshua; and thus Joshua did, neglecting nothing of all that the LORD
had commanded Moses.
So Joshua took all that land (the 16
highlands, all the steppes, all the land
of Goshen, the lowlands, the Arabah,
the highlands of Israel, and its lowlands), from Mount Halak, that rises 17
toward Seir, as far as Baal-gad in the
valley of Lebanon at the foot of Mount
Hermon. He captured all their kings,
and after scourging them, he put them
to death. For a long time Joshua car- 18
ried on war with all those kings. There 19
was no city that made peace with the
Israelites, except the Hivvites, inhabiting Gibeon; they all had to be taken
in battle. For it was at the instigation 20
of the LORD that they had been encouraged to engage Israel in battle,
that they might be annihilated, without being given any quarter, but annihilated, as the LORD had commanded
Moses.
At that same time Joshua went and 21
exterminated the Anakim from the
highlands; from Hebron, Debir, and
Anab, from all the highlands of Judah,
and all the highlands of Israel; Joshua
annihilated them, along with their
cities. No Anakim were left in the land 22
of the Israelites; it was only in Gaza,
Gath, and Ashdod that some remained.
Joshua captured the whole land, just as 23
the LORD had promised Moses. Joshua then distributed it as a heritage
among the various tribes of Israel. So
the land had rest from war.
The following are the kings of the 12
land whom the Israelites had already
vanquished, and whose land beyond the
Jordan to the east they had occupied,
from the river Arnon as far as Mount
Hermon, with all the Arabah eastward: Sihon, king of the Amorites, 2
who lived at Heshbon, and whose rule
extended from Aroer, which is on the
edge of the Arnon valley, from the
middle of the valley as far as the Jabbok river, the frontier of the Ammonites, that is, half of Gilead, along with 3
the Arabah as far as the Sea of Chinneroth to the east, and as far as the Sea
of the Arabah, the Salt Sea, to the east,
in the direction of Beth-jeshimoth, and
southward to the foot of the slopes of
Pisgah; also Og, king of Bashan, one of 4
the survivors of the Rephaim, who
lived at Ashtaroth, and Edrei, and who 5
ruled over Mount Hermon, Salecah

and the whole of Bashan, as far as the
frontier of the Geshurites and Maacathites, along with half of Gilead, as far
as the frontier of Sihon, king of Hesh-
6 bon. Moses, the servant of the LORD,
and the Israelites had vanquished
them, and Moses, the servant of the
LORD, had given the Reubenites, Gadites, and half-tribe of Manasseh possession of their land.
7 The following are the kings of the
land whom Joshua and the Israelites
vanquished beyond the Jordan to the
west, from Baal-gad in the valley of
Lebanon as far as Mount Halak which
rises toward Seir (Joshua distributed
the land among the various tribes of
8 Israel as their possession), in the highlands, the lowlands, the Arabah, the
slopes, the desert, and the steppes:
Hittites, Amorites, Canaanites, Perizzites, Hivvites, and Jebusites:

9 the king of Jericho 1
the king of Ai which is near Bethel 1
10 the king of Jerusalem . . . 1
the king of Hebron 1
11 the king of Jarmuth 1
the king of Lachish 1
12 the king of Eglon 1
the king of Gezer 1
13 the king of Debir 1
the king of Geder 1
14 the king of Hormah 1
the king of Arad 1
15 the king of Libnah 1
the king of Adullam 1
16 the king of Makkedah . . . 1
the king of Bethel 1
17 the king of Tappuah . . . 1
the king of Hepher 1
18 the king of Aphek 1
the king of Aphek in Sharon . 1
19 the king of Madon 1
the king of Hazor 1
20 the king of Shimron . . . 1
the king of Achshaph . . . 1
21 the king of Taanach . . . 1
the king of Megiddo . . . 1
22 the king of Kedesh . . . 1
the king of Jokneam in Carmel 1
the king of Dor in the uplands of
23 Dor 1
the king of the peoples in Galilee 1
24 the king of Tirzah 1

A total of 31 kings

THE ALLOTMENT OF THE LAND AMONG THE HEBREW TRIBES, 13:1—21:45

When Joshua was old, being well 1
advanced in life, the LORD said to
him,
"You are old, being well advanced in
life, but very much of the land remains
still to be conquered. The following 2
is the territory that still remains: all
the Philistine states, and all those of the
Geshurites, from the Shihor which is 3
east of Egypt as far as the frontier of
Ekron to the north (which is regarded
as Canaanite), the five principalities of
the Philistines, the Gazite, Ashdodite,
Ashkelonite, Gittite, and Ekronite;
also the territory of the Avvim to the
south, all the land of the Canaanites 4
from Mearah which belongs to the Sidonians as far as Aphek, as far as the
frontier of the Amorites; and the terri- 5
tory of the Gebalites, along with the
whole of Lebanon to the east, from
Baal-gad at the foot of Mount Hermon as far as the approach to Hamath.
All the inhabitants of the highlands 6
from Lebanon as far as Misrephoth-
maim, all the Sidonians, I will drive out
of the way of the Israelites; meanwhile,
however, allot the land to Israel as a
heritage, as I commanded you. Now 7
then, divide this land as a heritage
among the nine tribes and the half-
tribe of Manasseh."
Along with the other half-tribe, the 8
Reubenites and Gadites had received
their heritage, which Moses had given
them beyond the Jordan to the east, as
Moses, the servant of the LORD, had
assigned it to them, extending from 9
Aroer which is on the edge of the Arnon
valley, together with the city that is in
the valley, and all the table-land from
Medeba as far as Dibon, and all the 10
cities of Sihon, king of the Amorites,
who reigned in Heshbon, as far as the
frontier of the Ammonites; as well as 11
Gilead, and the territory of the Geshurites and Maacathites, and the whole
of Mount Hermon, and the whole of
Bashan as far as Salecah, the whole 12
kingdom of Og in Bashan who reigned
at Ashtaroth and Edrei (he was the
last survivor of the Rephaim)—Moses
had defeated these, and dispossessed

them. The Israelites, however, did not
evict the Geshurites or Maacathites;
but Geshur and Maacath live in the
midst of Israel to this day. To the
tribe of Levi alone was no heritage giv-
en, the LORD, the God of Israel, being
their heritage, as he had promised
them.
Moses had made assignments to the
various clans of the tribe of Reubenites. To them went the territory extending from Aroer which is on the
edge of the Arnon valley, together with
the city that is in the valley, and all
the table-land at Madeba, Heshbon and
all its towns on the table-land, Dibon,
Bamoth-baal, Beth-baal-meon, Jahaz,
Kedemoth, Mephaath, Kirjathaim,
Sibmah, Zereth-shahar on the hill in the
valley, Beth-peor, the slopes of Pisgah,
Beth-jeshimoth, all the cities on the
table-land, and the whole kingdom of
Sihon, king of the Amorites, who
reigned in Heshbon, whom Moses defeated, along with the Midianite chiefs,
Evi, Rekem, Zur, Hur, and Reba, who
as vassals of Sihon were living in the
land. Besides these victims the Israelites also slew the soothsayer Balaam,
the son of Beor, with the sword. The
territory of the Reubenites was the
Jordan and its banks; this was the heritage of the various clans of the Reubenites, the cities and their villages.
Moses had also made assignments to
the various clans of the tribe of Gad,
the Gadites. To them went the territory, Jazer, all the cities of Gilead, half
the land of the Ammonites as far as
Aroer, which is east of Rabbah, the region from Heshbon as far as Ramath-
mizpeh and Betonim, and from Mahanaim as far as the outskirts of Debir,
along with Beth-haram, Beth-nimrah,
Succoth, and Zaphon, in the valley, the
rest of the kingdom of Sihon, king of
Heshbon—the Jordan and its banks as
far as the lower end of the Sea of Chinnereth beyond the Jordan to the east.
This was the heritage of the various
clans of the Gadites, the cities and their
villages.
9 Moses had also made assignments to
the half-tribe of Manasseh, and in the
case of the half-tribe of Manassites it
0 was by clans. Their territory was that
extending from Mahanaim, the whole
of Bashan, the whole kingdom of Og,
king of Bashan, the whole of Havvoth-
jair which is in Bashan (sixty towns);
also half of Gilead, with Ashtaroth and 31
Edrei (cities belonging to the kingdom
of Og in Bashan), went to the various
clans of the descendants of Machir, the
son of Manasseh, that is, half the
Machirites.
These were the assignments which 32
Moses had made in the steppes of
Moab, beyond the Jordan, east of Jericho. To the tribe of Levi, however, 33
Moses had assigned no heritage, the
LORD, the God of Israel, being their
heritage, as he had promised them.
The following are the heritages which **14**
the Israelites received in the land of
Canaan, which Eleazar, the priest, and
Joshua, the son of Nun, and the heads
of families in the tribes of Israelites assigned to them, the assignments to 2
them being made by lot, as the LORD
through Moses had commanded for the
nine and a half tribes; for Moses had 3
already made the assignments to the
other two and a half tribes beyond the
Jordan, but to the Levites he had made
no assignment with the others. (As a 4
matter of fact the descendants of Joseph formed two tribes, Manasseh and
Ephraim.) No share of the land was
given to the Levites, except some cities
to live in, with the pasture-lands
around them for their cattle and other
live stock. As the LORD commanded 5
Moses, so did the Israelites in their allotment of the land.
The Judeans came up to Joshua at 6
Gilgal, and Caleb, the son of Jephunneh, the Kenizzite, said to him,
"You know what the LORD said to
Moses, the man of God, about you and
myself at Kadesh-barnea. I was forty 7
years old when Moses, the servant of
the LORD, sent me from Kadesh-
barnea to spy out the land. I brought
him back as conscientious a report as I
could. My kinsmen, however, who went 8
up with me, made the people lose heart,
whereas I corroborated the LORD my
God. So Moses made this oath to me 9
that day: 'The land on which your foot
has trodden is to be a heritage for you
and your descendants forever, because
you have corroborated the LORD, my
God.' Now then, seeing that the LORD 10
has let me live, as he promised, for the
past forty-five years, that is, ever since
the LORD spoke this word to Moses,
while Israel was journeying through the

desert, here I am today eighty-five
11 years old; but I am still as strong today
as I was when Moses sent me off, my
strength now being the equal of my
strength then, for war, and for going
12 and coming. Give me, then, these highlands of which the LORD spoke that
day. By the way, you heard that same
day that the Anakim were there, with
great fortified cities; but perhaps the
LORD will enable me to evict them, as
the LORD in fact promised."

13 So Joshua blessed him, and gave
Hebron to Caleb, the son of Jephunneh,
14 as a heritage. That is how Hebron became the heritage of Caleb, the son of
Jephunneh, the Kenizzite, as it is to
this day, because he corroborated the
15 LORD, the God of Israel. (The name of
Hebron used to be Kirjath-arba, Arba
having been the head man among the
Anakim.) Then the land had rest
from war.

15 The territory allotted to the various
clans of the tribe of Judeans extended
to the frontier of Edom, southward to
the desert of Zin in the extreme south.
2 Their southern frontier ran from the
lower end of the Salt Sea, from the bay
3 facing south, and continued south of
the slope of Akrabbim, passing along to
Zin, then it proceeded upward south of
Kadesh-barnea, along to Hezron, up to
4 Addar, around to Karka, on to Azmon,
and came out at the River of Egypt, so
that the frontier ended at the sea; this
5 was their southern frontier. The eastern frontier was the Salt Sea, as far as
the mouth of the Jordan. The northern
frontier ran from the bay of the Sea at
6 the mouth of the Jordan, and then the
frontier continued up to Beth-hoglah,
and passed north of Beth-arabah; the
frontier continued up to the stone of
7 Bohan, the son of Reuben; the frontier
then went up to Debir from the valley
of Achor, and turned north to Gilgal
which is opposite the slope of Adum-
min, south of the river; then the frontier continued to the waters of En-
8 shemesh, and ended at En-rogel; the
frontier then continued up the valley of
Ben-Hinnom to the southern side of the
Jebusite spur (that is, Jerusalem); then
the frontier ran to the top of the hill
which overlooks the valley of Hinnom,
to the west, at the northern end of the
9 valley of Rephaim; from the top of the
hill the frontier ran to the fountain of
Merneptah, and continued to the spur
of Mount Ephron; then the frontier ran
to Baalah (that is, Kirjath-jearim); at
Baalah the frontier turned westward to
the mountain range of Seir, continuing
to the northern spur of Mount Jearim
(that is, Chesalon), down to Beth-
shemesh, and on to Timnah; the frontier then continued north to the spur of
Ekron; the frontier ran to Shikkeron,
on to Mount Baalah, and came out at
Jabneel, and the frontier ended at the
sea. The western frontier was the Great
Sea with its coastland. This was the
frontier encircling the various clans of
the Judeans.

In accord with the command of the
LORD to Joshua, he allotted a share to
Caleb, the son of Jephunneh, among
the Judeans, namely, Kirjath-arba (Arba being the father of Anak), that is,
Hebron. Caleb evicted from there the
three sons of Anak, Sheshai, Ahiman,
and Talmai, the children of Anak.
From there he marched against the inhabitants of Debir (the name of Debir
used to be Kirjath-sepher).

"Whoever attacks Kirjath-sepher
and captures it," said Caleb, "I will
give him my daughter, Achsah, in marriage."

Othniel, the son of Caleb's brother,
Kenaz, captured it; so he gave him his
daughter, Achsah, in marriage. When
she arrived, he induced her to ask her
father for the necessary fields; so she
alighted from her ass, and when Caleb
said to her, "What do you want?" she
said,

"Give me a pool; since you have assigned me to the region of the steppes,
give me Gullath-maim."

So he gave her Upper Gullath and
Lower Gullath.

The following is the heritage assigned
to the various clans of the tribe of Judeans; the cities in their totality belonging to the tribe of Judeans toward
the frontier of Edom were, in the
steppes, Kabzeel, Eder, Jagur, Kinah,
Dimonah, Adadah, Kedesh, Hazor,
Ithnan, Ziph, Telem, Bealoth, Hazor-
haddatah, Kerioth-hezron (that is,
Hazor), Amam, Shema, Moladah,
Hazar-gaddah, Heshmon, Beth-pelet,
Hazar-shual, Beersheba with its dependencies, Baalah, Iim, Ezem, Eltolad, Chesil, Hormah, Ziklag, Madmannah, Sansannah, Lebaoth, Shilhim, and

En-rimmon—a total of twenty-nine
cities with their villages.
33 In the lowlands, Eshtaol, Zorah,
34 Ashnah, Zanoah, En-gannim, Tappuah,
35 Enam, Jarmuth, Adullam, Socoh, Aze-
36 kah, Shaaraim, Adithaim, and Gederah
—fourteen cities with their villages;
37 Zenan, Hadashah, Migdal-gad, Dilan,
38 39 Mizpeh, Joktheel, Lachish, Bozkath,
40 Eglon, Cabbon, Lahmas, Chithlish,
41 Gederoth, Beth-dagon, Naamah, and
Makkedah—sixteen cities with their
42 villages; Libnah, Ether, Ashan, Iphtah,
43 44 Ashnah, Nezib, Keilah, Achzib, and
Mareshah—nine cities with their vil-
45 lages; Ekron with its towns and vil-
46 lages; from Ekron to the sea, all that
lay alongside of Ashdod with their vil-
47 lages; Ashdod with its towns and villages, Gaza with its towns and villages,
as far as the River of Egypt, and the
Great Sea with its coastland.
48 In the highlands, Shamir, Jattir, So-
49 coh, Dannah, Kirjath-sannah (that is,
50 51 Debir), Anab, Eshtemoh, Anim, Goshen, Holon, and Giloh—eleven cities
52 with their villages; Arab, Rumah,
53 Eshan, Janum, Beth-tappuah, Aphe-
54 kah, Humtah, Kirjath-arba (that is,
Hebron), and Zior—nine cities with
55 their villages; Maon, Carmel, Ziph,
56 Juttah, Jezreel, Jokdeam, Zanoah,
57 Kain, Gibeah, and Timnah—ten cities
58 with their villages; Halhul, Beth-zur,
59 Gedor, Maarath, Beth-anoth, and El-
tekon—six cities with their villages;
60 Kirjath-baal (that is, Kirjath-jearim)
and Rabbah—two cities with their villages.
61 In the desert, Beth-arabah, Middin,
62 Secacah, Nibshan, Salt City, and Engedi—six cities with their villages.
63 The Judeans, however, could not
evict the Jebusites inhabiting Jerusalem; but the Jebusites live with the
Judeans in Jerusalem to this day.
16 The frontier of the Josephites extended from the Jordan at Jericho,
east of the waters of Jericho, up
from Jericho through the highlands to
2 the wilderness at Bethel, then leaving
Bethel (that is, Luz), it continued to
Ataroth, the domain of the Archites,
3 then to the west, down to the territory
of the Japhletites as far as the outskirts of Lower Beth-horon and Gezer,
and ended at the sea.
4 The Josephites, Manasseh and Ephra-
5 im, received their heritage. The territory of the Ephraimites was assigned to
their various clans. The eastern frontier of their heritage ran from Ataroth-
addar as far as Upper Beth-horon, then 6
the frontier continued westward to
Michmethath in the north; the frontier then turned east to Taanath-
shiloh, and continued to Otho, east of
Janoah; from Janoah it proceeded 7
down to Ataroth and Naarah, then
reached to Jericho, and came out at the
Jordan. The western frontier ran from 8
Tappuah to the brook Kanah, and ended at the sea. This was the heritage assigned to the various clans of the tribe
of Ephraimites, together with the cities 9
set aside for the Ephraimites in the
heritage of the Manassites, all the cities
with their villages. They did not evict 10
the Canaanites who were living in
Gezer; the Canaanites lived with
Ephraim, as they do to this day, but
they became forced laborers.
Then there was the allotment made **17**
to the tribe of Manasseh (Manasseh being the first-born of Joseph). To
Machir, the first-born of Manasseh,
the father of Gilead, went Gilead,
and Bashan, since he was a man
of war. Allotments were then made to 2
the various other clans of the Manassites, the Abiezrites, the Helekites, the
Asrielites, the Shechemites, the Heph-
erites, and the Shemidaites (these being
the various clans of the male descendants of Manasseh, the son of Joseph).
Zelophehad, however, the son of 3
Hepher, the son of Gilead, the son of
Machir, the son of Manasseh, had no
sons, only daughters, these being the
names of his daughters: Mahlah, Noah,
Hoglah, Milcah, and Tirzah. They ap- 4
peared before Eleazar, the priest, and
Joshua, the son of Nun, and the leaders,
saying,
"The LORD commanded Moses to
give us a heritage along with our kinsmen."
So, in accord with the command of
the LORD, they were given a heritage
along with their father's kinsmen. Ten 5
shares fell to Manasseh, apart from
the land of Gilead and Bashan, which is
on the other side of the Jordan (for the 6
daughters of Manasseh received a heritage along with his sons), while the land
of Gilead went to the rest of the Manassites.
The frontier of Manasseh ran from 7

Asher to Michmethath, which is east of
Shechem; the frontier then went south
8 to En-tappuah (the land of Tappuah
belonged to Manasseh, but Tappuah
near the frontier of Manasseh belonged
9 to the Ephraimites); the frontier then
went down to the brook Kanah, to the
south of the brook (the cities here belonged to Ephraim, although among
cities of Manasseh); the frontier of
Manasseh then ran north of the brook,
10 and ended at the sea, the land to the
south being Ephraim's, and that to the
north Manasseh's, with the sea as their
frontier. They reached to Asher on the
north, and to Issachar on the east.
11 Moreover, in Issachar and Asher there
went to Manasseh, Beth-shean with
its dependencies and Ibleam with its
dependencies, along with the inhabitants of Dor and its dependencies,
the inhabitants of En-dor and its dependencies, the inhabitants of Taanach and its dependencies, the inhabitants of Megiddo and its dependencies.
12 The Manassites, however, were not able
to evict the inhabitants of these cities;
the Canaanites clung to the habitation
13 of this region, but when the Israelites
became strong enough, they made the
Canaanites forced laborers; they never
completely evicted them.
14 Then the Josephites said to Joshua,
"Why have you allotted to us only
one share as our heritage, when we are
a numerous people, whom the LORD
has blessed thus bountifully?"
15 Joshua said to them,
"If you are such a numerous people,
go up to the forest, and there clear
ground for yourselves in the land of the
Perizzites and Rephaim; for the highlands of Ephraim are near you."
16 "The highlands are not enough for
us," said the Josephites; "and all the
Canaanites who live in the valley lands
have iron chariots, both those in Beth-
shean and its dependencies, and those
in the valley of Jezreel."
17 Then Joshua said to the clan of Joseph, Ephraim and Manasseh,
"You are a numerous people, and
have great power. One share alone shall
18 not go to you, but the highlands as well
shall be yours; for though they are
wooded, you can clear them, and their
products shall be yours. For you shall
evict the Canaanites, even though they
have iron chariots and are strong."

Then the whole Israelite community 18
assembled at Shiloh, and set up the
tent of meeting there, the region having
been brought into subjection to them.
There still remained seven tribes 2
among the Israelites, who had not yet
been allotted their heritage; so Joshua 3
said to the Israelites,
"How long are you going to put off
entering into possession of the land
which the LORD, the God of your fathers, has given you? Select three men 4
from each tribe, and I will send them
forth that they may explore the land.
They shall map it out with a view to the
heritage of each, and then report to me.
They shall divide it into seven parts, 5
Judah remaining in their territory in
the south, and the clan of Joseph in
their territory in the north. You shall 6
map out the land into seven parts, and
then report to me here. I will cast lots
for you here before the LORD our God.
The Levites, however, are to have no 7
share with you; for the priesthood of
the LORD is to be their heritage; while
Gad, Reuben, and the half-tribe of
Manasseh have already received their
heritage beyond the Jordan to the east,
which Moses, the servant of the LORD,
gave them."
So the men prepared to go; then 8
Joshua gave this command to those
that were leaving to map out the land:
"Go and explore the land, and map
it out, and come back to me. Then I
will cast lots for you here before the
LORD at Shiloh."
The men went forth, and traversed 9
the land, and mapped out its various
cities in a book into seven parts; then
they reported to Joshua at the camp at
Shiloh. So Joshua cast lots for them at 10
Shiloh before the LORD; and there
Joshua distributed the land among the
Israelites, to each his share.
The lot was drawn for the various 11
clans of the tribe of Benjaminites. The
territory allotted to them lay between
the Judeans and Josephites. Their fron- 12
tier on the north ran from the Jordan;
then the frontier went up to the northern spur of Jericho, up through the
highlands westward, and ended at the
wilderness of Bethaven; from there the 13
frontier continued to Luz, toward the
southern spur of Luz (that is, Bethel);
then the frontier ran down to Ataroth-
addar, near the hill which lies south of

14 Lower Beth-horon. The frontier continued, and for the western boundary
turned southward from the hill which
lies south of Beth-horon, and ended at
Kirjath-baal (that is, Kirjath-jearim),
a city of the Judeans. This was the
15 western boundary. The southern boundary ran from the outskirts of Kirjath-
jearim; the frontier then ran westward,
running to the fountain of Merneptah;
16 then the frontier went down to the
foot of the hill which overlooks the valley of Ben-Hinnom, which is north of
the valley of Rephaim; then down the
valley of Hinnom, to the southern side
of the Jebusite spur; then down to En-
17 rogel. It continued northward, and
ran to En-shemesh, then to Gilgal,
which is opposite the slope of Adum-
mim, then down to the stone of Bohan,
the son of Reuben, on to the spur north
18 of Beth-arabah, and then down to the
19 Arabah; the frontier then passed on to
the northern spur of Beth-hoglah, and
the frontier ended at the northern bay
of the Salt Sea, at the southern end of
the Jordan. This was the southern
20 frontier; while the Jordan bounded it
on the east. This was the heritage of
the various clans of the Benjaminites,
as bounded by its frontiers.
21 The cities assigned to the various
clans of the tribe of Benjaminites were
22 Jericho, Beth-hoglah, Emek-keziz, Beth-
23 arabah, Zemaraim, Bethel, Avvim,
24 Parah, Ophrah, Chephar-ammoni, Oph-
ni, and Geba—twelve cities with their
25 villages; Gibeon, Ramah, Beeroth,
26 27 Mizpeh, Chephirah, Mozah, Rekem,
28 Irpeel, Taralah, Zelah, Eleph, the Jebusite city (that is, Jerusalem), Gibeath,
and Kirjath-jearim—fourteen cities
with their villages. This was the heritage of the various clans of the Benjaminites.
1 The second lot fell to Simeon, to the
various clans of the tribe of Simeonites.
Their heritage lay inside that of the Ju-
2 deans. They received as their heritage
3 Beersheba, Shema, Moladah, Hazar-
4 shual, Balah, Ezem, Eltolad, Bethul,
5 Hormah, Ziklag, Beth-marcaboth, Ha-
6 zar-susah, Beth-lebaoth, and Sharuhen
—thirteen cities with their villages;
7 En-rimmon, Ether, Ashan, and Tochen
8 —four cities with their villages; together
with all the villages that surrounded
these cities, as far as Baalath-beer and
Ramah of the South. This was the her-

itage of the various clans of the Simeonites, the heritage of the Simeonites be- 9
ing taken from the territory of the
Judeans. Since the Judeans' portion
was too large for them, the Simeonites
received their heritage inside theirs.
The third lot was drawn for the vari- 10
ous clans of the Zebulunites. The frontier of their heritage reached to Sarid;
then their frontier went westward, up 11
to Maralah; it then reached to Dabbe-
sheth, and to the brook which is east of
Jokneam; from Sarid it turned east- 12
ward toward the dawn, toward the outskirts of Chisloth-tabor, on to Daberath, and up to Japhia; from there it 13
continued eastward toward the dawn,
to Gath-hepher and Eth-kazin, then to
Rimmonah, and on to Neah; the fron- 14
tier then turned north to Hannathon,
and ended at the valley of Iphtah-el.
. . . . Kattath, Nahalal, Shimron, Ida- 15
lah, and Bethlehem—twelve cities with
their villages. This was the heritage of 16
the various clans of the Zebulunites,
these cities with their villages.
The fourth lot fell to Issachar, to the 17
various clans of the Issacharites. Their 18
territory included Jezreel, Chesulloth,
Shunem, Hapharaim, Shion, Anaha- 19
rath, Rabbith, Kishion, Ebez, Remeth, 20
En-gannim, En-haddah, and Beth- 21
pazzez. The frontier reached to Tabor, 22
then to Shahazumah, and Beth-shemesh; and their frontier ended at the
Jordan. There were sixteen cities with
their villages. This was the heritage of 23
the various clans of the tribe of Issacharites, the cities with their villages.
The fifth lot fell to the various clans 24
of the tribe of Asherites. Their territory 25
included Helkath, Hali, Beten, Achshaph, Allammelech, Amad, and Mish- 26
al; it reached west to Carmel and Shi-
hor-libnath; then it turned east to 27
Beth-dagon; it reached to Zebulun and
the valley of Iphtah-el, to the north,
then to Beth-emek, and Neiel; it continued north to Cabul, then to Ebron, 28
Rehob, Hammon, and Kanah, as far as
Sidon the Great; the frontier then 29
turned to Ramah, reaching the fortified
city of Tyre; the frontier then turned to
Hosah, and ended at the sea . . . . Ma-
halab, Achzib, Acco, Aphek, and Rehob 30
—twenty-two cities with their villages.
This was the heritage of the various 31
clans of the tribe of Asherites, these
cities with their villages.

32 The sixth lot fell to the Naphtalites,
to the various clans of the Naphtalites.
33 Their frontier ran from Heleph, Elon-
bezaanannim, Adami-nekeb, and Jabneel as far as Lakkum, and ended at the
34 Jordan; the frontier then turned westward to Aznoth-tabor; from there it
continued to Hukkok, and reached to
Zebulun on the south, to Asher on the
west, and to Judah at the Jordan on the
35 east. The fortified cities were Ziddim,
Zer, Hammath, Rakkath, Chinnereth,
36 37 Adamah, Ramah, Hazor, Kedesh,
38 Edrei, En-hazor, Iron, Migdal-el, Hor-
em, Beth-anath, and Beth-shemesh—
39 nineteen cities with their villages. This
was the heritage of the various clans of
the tribe of Naphtalites, the cities with
their villages.

40 The seventh lot fell to the various
41 clans of the tribe of Danites. The territory comprising their heritage included
42 Zorah, Eshtaol, Ir-shemesh, Shaalab-
43 bin, Aijalon, Ithlah, Elon, Timnah,
44 Ekron, Eltekeh, Gibbethon, Baalath,
45 46 Jehud, Bene-berak, Gath-rimmon, Me-
jarkon, and Rakkon, with the coast-
47 line in front of Joppa. The territory of
the Danites, however, was too small for
them; so the Danites went up and attacked Leshem. They captured it, and
putting it to the sword, they took possession of it, and settled down in it,
calling Leshem Dan, after the name of
48 their ancestor Dan. This was the heritage of the various clans of the tribe of
Danites, these cities with their villages.

49 When the distribution of the various
divisions of the land had been completed, the Israelites gave Joshua, the son
of Nun, a heritage amongst themselves;
50 in accordance with the command of the
LORD they gave him the city for which
he asked, namely, Timnath-heres in the
highlands of Ephraim. He rebuilt the
city, and settled down in it.

51 These were the heritages which Eleazar, the priest, and Joshua, the son of
Nun, and the heads of families in the
Israelite tribes distributed by lot at
Shiloh before the LORD, at the doorway of the tent of meeting. Thus they
completed the division of the land.

20 Then the LORD said to Joshua,
2 "Speak to the Israelites as follows:
'Select the cities of refuge, concerning
3 which I spoke to you through Moses, so
that a homicide who kills anyone inadvertently, unintentionally, may flee
there; they shall serve you as places of refuge from the avenger of blood. When anyone flees to one of these cities, he shall stand at the entrance of the city gate, and explain his case to the elders of that city; then they shall receive him into their city, and give him a home, and he shall live with them. If the avenger of blood should pursue him, they are not to deliver the homicide into his power; for he killed his fellow unintentionally, having no standing feud with him. He shall live in that city until he appears before the community for trial, or until the death of the high priest who is in office at that time. After that the homicide may return to his own city and his own home, to the city from which he fled.' "

So they set apart Kedesh in Galilee, in the highlands of Naphtali, Shechem in the highlands of Ephraim, and Kir-jath-arba (that is, Hebron) in the highlands of Judah; and beyond the Jordan, east of Jericho, they selected Bezer in the desert, on the table-land, from the tribe of Reuben; Ramoth in Gilead, from the tribe of Gad; and Golan in Bashan, from the tribe of Manasseh. These were the cities which were designated for all the Israelites, and also for the aliens residing among them, so that anyone who killed a person inadvertently might flee there, and not die by the hand of the avenger of blood, until he had appeared before the community.

Then the heads of families among the Levites went up to Eleazar, the priest, and Joshua, the son of Nun, and the heads of families in the Israelite tribes, and said to them at Shiloh in the land of Canaan,

"The LORD gave command by Moses that we were to be given cities to live in, along with their pasture-lands for our cattle."

So the Israelites, in accordance with the command of the LORD, gave the Levites some of their own heritage, namely, the following cities with their pasture-lands.

The lot was drawn for the Kohathite clans. Thirteen cities from the tribes of Judah, Simeon, and Benjamin fell by lot to the descendants of Aaron, the priest, part of the Levites. To the rest of the Kohathites ten cities from the clans of the tribe of Ephraim, the tribe

of Dan, and the half-tribe of Manasseh
fell by lot.
6 To the Gershonites thirteen cities
from the clans of the tribe of Issachar,
the tribes of Asher and Naphtali, and
the half-tribe of Manasseh in Bashan
fell by lot.
7 To the various clans of the Merarites
fell twelve cities from the tribes of
Reuben, Gad, and Zebulun.
8 The Israelites allotted these cities
with their pasture-lands to the Levites,
as the LORD had commanded through
Moses.
9 From the tribes of Judeans and Simeonites they gave the following named
10 cities (they went to the descendants of
Aaron, one of the clans of the Kohathites, belonging to the Levites; for the
11 lot fell to them first). They gave them
Kirjath-arba (Arba being the father of
Anak), that is, Hebron, in the highlands of Judah, with its adjacent pas-
12 ture-lands; but the fields of the city and
its villages they gave to Caleb, the son
13 of Jephunneh, as his property. To the
descendants of Aaron, the priest, then,
they gave the city of refuge for the
homicide, namely, Hebron, along with
its pasture-lands, as well as Libnah with
14 its pasture-lands, Jattir with its pasture-lands, Eshtemoa with its pasture-
15 lands, Holon with its pasture-lands,
Debir with its pasture-lands, Ain with
its pasture-lands, Juttah with its pasture-lands, and Beth-shemesh with its
pasture-lands—nine cities out of those
two tribes; and out of the tribe of Benjamin, Gibeon with its pasture-lands,
Geba with its pasture-lands, Anathoth
with its pasture-lands, and Almon with
19 its pasture-lands—four cities; the total
of the cities for the descendants of
Aaron, the priests, being thirteen cities
with their pasture-lands.
20 For the clans of the Kohathites that
were Levites, that is, those that were
left of the Kohathites, the cities indicated by their lot came from the tribe of
Ephraim; so they were given the city of
refuge for the homicide, namely, Shechem in the highlands of Ephraim,
along with its pasture-lands, Gezer with
22 its pasture-lands, Kibzaim with its pasture-lands, and Beth-horon with its
pasture-lands—four cities; and out of
the tribe of Dan, Eltekeh with its pasture-lands, Gibbethon with its pasture-
lands, Aijalon with its pasture-lands,
and Gath-rimmon with its pasture-lands
—four cities; and out of the half-tribe 25
of Manasseh, Taanach with its pasture-
lands, and Ibleam with its pasture-
lands—two cities; a total of ten cities 26
with their pasture-lands for the remaining clans of the Kohathites.
To the Gershonites, one of the clans 27
of the Levites, from the half-tribe of
Manasseh went the city of refuge for
the homicide, namely, Golan in Bashan,
with its pasture-lands, and Beesh-terah
with its pasture-lands—two cities; and 28
out of the tribe of Issachar, Kishion
with its pasture-lands, Daberath with
its pasture-lands, Jarmuth with its pas- 29
ture-lands, and En-gannim with its
pasture-lands—four cities; and out of 30
the tribe of Asher, Mishal with its pasture-lands, Abdon with its pasture-
lands, Helkath with its pasture-lands, 31
and Rehob with its pasture-lands—
four cities; and out of the tribe of 32
Naphtali, the city of refuge for the
homicide, namely, Kedesh in Galilee,
with its pasture-lands, Hammoth-dor
with its pasture-lands, and Kartan with
its pasture-lands—three cities; the total 33
of the cities for the various clans of the
Gershonites being thirteen cities with
their pasture-lands.
To the clans of the Merarites, the rest 34
of the Levites, from the clan of Zebulun
went Jokneam with its pasture-lands,
Kartah with its pasture-lands, Dimnah 35
with its pasture-lands, and Nahalal
with its pasture-lands—four cities; and 36
out of the tribe of Reuben, Bezer with
its pasture-lands, Jahaz with its pasture-lands, Kedemoth with its pasture- 37
lands, and Mephaath with its pasture-
lands—four cities; and out of the tribe 38
of Gad, the city of refuge for the homicide, namely, Ramoth in Gilead, with
its pasture-lands, Mahanaim with its
pasture-lands, Heshbon with its pas- 39
ture-lands, and Jazer with its pasture-
lands—four cities in all. All these cities 40
went to the various clans of the Merarites, the rest of the Levite clans, their
allotment being twelve cities.
The total number of cities of the Le- 41
vites within the holdings of the Israelites was forty-eight cities, with their
pasture-lands, each of these cities hav- 42
ing its own pasture-lands adjacent to it,
this being the case with all of these
cities.
So the LORD gave Israel all the land 43

which he had sworn to their fathers to
give them; they occupied it, and settled
44 down in it, and the LORD gave them
peace on every side, just as he had
sworn to their fathers; not one of all
their enemies could withstand them,
the LORD having delivered all their
45 enemies into their power. Not one of
the good promises which the LORD
made to the house of Israel failed, all
being fulfilled.

THE DISMISSAL OF THE EASTERN TRIBES, AND THE DISPUTE ABOUT THEIR ALTAR, 22:1–34

22 Then Joshua summoned the Reubenites, Gadites, and half-tribe of Manas-
2 seh, and said to them,
"You have observed all that Moses,
the servant of the LORD, commanded
you, and have heeded my injunctions
3 in all that I have commanded you; you
have not deserted your kinsmen during
this long time, but down to this day you
have faithfully observed the charge of
4 the LORD your God. Now, however,
the LORD your God has given peace to
your kinsmen, as he promised them; return then, and go home to your tents
in the land of your own, which Moses,
the servant of the LORD, gave you be-
5 yond the Jordan. Only be very careful to observe the charge and law
which Moses, the servant of the LORD,
enjoined on you, loving the LORD your
God, walking in all his ways, keeping
his commands, holding fast to him, and
serving him with all your mind and
heart."
6 Then Joshua blessed them, and let
them go; and they went home to their
tents.
7 (To the one half-tribe of Manasseh
Moses had assigned territory in Bashan, and to the other half-tribe Joshua had assigned territory with their
kinsmen beyond the Jordan to the
west.)
Furthermore, when Joshua sent them
home, he blessed them.
8 "Return home with great wealth," he
said to them, "with very many cattle,
with silver, gold, bronze, and iron,
and with a great quantity of clothing;
divide the spoil of your enemies with
your kinsmen."

So the Reubenites, Gadites, and half-tribe of Manasseh went home, parting from the Israelites at Shiloh, which is in the land of Canaan, to go to the land of Gilead, the land of their own, which they had seized by command of the LORD through Moses. When they reached the region of the Jordan, which is within the land of Canaan, the Reubenites, Gadites, and half-tribe of Manasseh built an altar there beside the Jordan, a large altar for display. The Israelites heard it reported that the Reubenites, Gadites, and half-tribe of Manasseh had built an altar at the frontier of the land of Canaan, in the region of the Jordan, on the side belonging to the Israelites. When the Israelites heard of it, the whole Israelite community assembled at Shiloh to march against them in war. To the Reubenites, Gadites, and half-tribe of Manasseh in the land of Gilead, the Israelites sent Phinehas, the son of Eleazar, the priest, and with him ten chieftains, one chieftain of a household from each of the tribes of Israel, each one of them being the head of his household among the clans of Israel. They came to the Reubenites, Gadites, and half-tribe of Manasseh in the land of Gilead, and said to them,

"Thus says the whole community of the LORD: 'Why this perfidy that you have committed against the God of Israel in turning now from following the LORD by building yourselves an altar in rebellion against the LORD? Did the sin at Peor, from which we have not even yet cleansed ourselves, and for which a plague came upon the LORD'S community, mean so little to us, that you must today turn from following the LORD? If you rebel against the LORD today, he will be angry with the whole community of Israel tomorrow! If, however, the land which you hold is unclean, cross over to the land which the LORD himself holds, where the dwelling of the LORD stands, and settle among us; but do not rebel against the LORD, nor implicate us, by building another altar besides the altar of the LORD our God. Was it not Achan, the son of Zerah, who broke faith in the case of the doomed things, so that wrath fell upon the whole community of Israel? And he did not perish alone for his iniquity.' "

The Reubenites, Gadites, and half-tribe of Manasseh in reply said to the heads of the clans of Israel,

"By the LORD, the God of gods (the LORD, the God of gods, knows it, and Israel should know it), it was not in a spirit of rebellion or infidelity toward the LORD (otherwise spare us not today!) that we built an altar to turn from following the LORD, nor did we offer burnt-offerings or cereal-offerings on it, nor did we sacrifice thank-offerings on it (otherwise let the LORD himself requite us!); but we did it rather out of fear of this, namely, that in time to come your children might say to our children, 'What have you to do with the LORD, the God of Israel? The LORD made the Jordan a boundary between us and you, you Reubenites and Gadites. You have no share in the LORD.' Thus your children might make our children cease to stand in awe of the LORD. So we said, 'Let us protect ourselves by building an altar—not for burnt-offerings, nor for sacrifices, but that it might serve as a witness between you and us, and between your descendants and ours, that we do perform the service of the LORD before him with our burnt-offerings, sacrifices, and thank-offerings, so that your children may never say to our children in time to come, "You have no share in the LORD." We calculated that if in time to come this was ever said to us or to our descendants, we could say, 'Look at the copy of the altar of the LORD which our fathers made, not for burnt-offerings nor for sacrifices, but that it might serve as a witness between you and us.' Far be it from us to rebel against the LORD, or turn now from following the LORD, by building an altar for burnt-offerings, cereal-offerings, or sacrifices, besides the altar of the LORD our God which stands in front of his dwelling!"

When Phinehas, the priest, and the chieftains of the community, the heads of the clans of Israel who were with him, heard what the Reubenites, Gadites, and Manassites said, they were satisfied; and Phinehas, the son of Eleazar, the priest, said to the Reubenites, Gadites, and Manassites,

"Now we know that the LORD is in our midst, since you have not committed this act of perfidy against the LORD; thus you have saved the Israelites from the hand of the LORD."

Then Phinehas, the son of Eleazar 32
the priest, and the chieftains returned
from the Reubenites and Gadites in the
land of Gilead to the land of Canaan, to
the Israelites, and made a report to
them. The Israelites were satisfied; the 33
Israelites blessed God, and said nothing
more about marching against the Reubenites and Gadites in war, to ravage
the land in which they lived. The Reu- 34
benites and Gadites called the altar Ed
[witness]; "For," said they, "it is a witness between us that the LORD is God."

JOSHUA'S FAREWELL AND DEATH, 23:1—24:33

A long time afterward, when the 23
LORD had given Israel rest from all
their enemies around them, and Joshua
was old, being well advanced in life,
Joshua summoned all Israel, their 2
elders, leaders, judges, and officers, and
said to them,
"I am an old man, being well advanced in life; but you have seen all 3
that the LORD your God has done for
you to all these nations; for it is the
LORD your God who has been fighting
for you. See, I have allotted to you as a 4
heritage for your various tribes the territory of all the nations whom I exterminated, from the Jordan as far as the
Great Western Sea; and in the case of
those nations that are left, the LORD 5
your God will himself sweep them before you, and drive them out of your
way, and you shall occupy their land, as
the LORD your God promised you. Be 6
very resolute, then, to observe and
carry out all that is written in the lawbook of Moses, without swerving from
it to the right or to the left, never min- 7
gling with these nations, those that are
still left with you; you must not invoke
the names of their gods, nor swear by
them, nor serve them, nor pay homage
to them; but you must hold fast to the 8
LORD your God, as you have done up
to this day. The LORD has driven out 9
of your way great and strong nations,
so that no one has been able to withstand you to this day. One of you alone 10
could put a thousand to flight, because
it is the LORD your God who has been
fighting for you, as he promised you.

11 Take great care, therefore, to love the
12 LORD your God. For if you ever back-
slide, and ally yourselves with the remnant of these nations, those that are
still left with you, and intermarry with
them, and have intercourse with them
13 and they with you, be very certain that
the LORD your God will no longer drive
these nations out of your way; but they
shall be a snare and a trap for you, a
scourge in your sides, and thorns in
your eyes, until you perish from off
this fine land which the LORD your
14 God has given you. Here I am, right
now about to go the way of all the
earth; but you know with all your
minds and hearts that not one of the
good promises which the LORD your
God made concerning you has failed; all
have been realized for you, not one of
them having failed. Hence, as every good
15 promise which the LORD your God
made concerning you has come to pass
for you, so shall the LORD bring on you
every threat, until he has destroyed
you from off this fine land which the
16 LORD your God has given you. Whenever you violate the covenant of the
LORD your God which he enjoined on
you, and go and serve alien gods, and
pay homage to them, then shall the anger of the LORD blaze against you, and
you shall perish quickly from off the
fine land which he gave you."

24 Joshua assembled all the tribes of
Israel at Shechem, summoning the elders of Israel, their leaders, judges, and
officers. When they had presented
2 themselves before God, Joshua said to
all the people,

"Thus says the LORD, the God of
Israel: 'In days of old your fathers lived
beyond the River, namely, Terah, the
father of Abraham and Nahor, and
3 served alien gods; but I took your father Abraham from beyond the River,
and I had him range the whole land of
Canaan, and made his descendants nu-
4 merous. I gave him Isaac, and to Isaac
I gave Jacob and Esau. I gave the highlands of Seir to Esau to occupy, whereas Jacob and his children went down to
5 Egypt. Then I sent Moses and Aaron,
and I smote Egypt with what I did in
her midst. After that I brought you
6 out; I brought your fathers out of
Egypt, and when you reached the sea,
the Egyptians pursued your fathers
with chariotry and cavalry to the Red
Sea; but when they cried to the LORD,
he put darkness between you and the
Egyptians, and brought the sea over
them, and engulfed them. You saw
with your own eyes what I did in
Egypt. You lived for a long time in the
desert, and then I brought you to the
land of the Amorites who lived beyond
the Jordan. They fought with you, but
I delivered them into your power, so
that you took possession of their land,
since I exterminated them from your
way. Then Balak, the son of Zippor,
king of Moab, appeared, and fought
against Israel. He sent for Balaam, the
son of Beor, to curse you; but I would
not listen to Balaam, so he had to bless
you, and thus I saved you from his
power. Crossing the Jordan, you arrived at Jericho, and the citizens of
Jericho fought against you, as well as
the Amorites, Perizzites, Canaanites,
Hittites, Girgashites, Hivvites, and Jebusites; but I delivered them into your
power. I sent leprosy ahead of you to
drive the two Amorite kings out of your
way; it was not done by your sword nor
your bow. I gave you a land on which
you had never labored, and cities in
which you settled without having built
them, vineyards and olive groves from
which you eat without having planted
them.' Therefore, stand in awe of the
LORD, and serve him faithfully and
loyally; remove the gods whom your fathers served beyond the River, and in
Egypt, and serve the LORD. However,
if you find it obnoxious to serve the
LORD, choose today whom you will
serve, either the gods whom your fathers served who are beyond the River,
or the gods of the Amorites in whose
land you are living; but as for me and
my house, we will serve the LORD."

The people in reply said,

"Far be it from us that we should forsake the LORD to serve alien gods; for
it is the LORD our God who brought us
and our fathers up out of the land of
Egypt, out of a state of slavery, and
performed those great signs before our
eyes, and took care of us all through the
journey that we made, and among all
the peoples through whom we passed;
the LORD also drove out of our way all
the peoples, namely, the Amorites, who
inhabited the land, so we too will serve
the LORD; for he is our God."

Then Joshua said to the people,
"You may not serve the LORD and foreign gods as well; for being a holy God and a jealous God, he will not forgive your transgression nor your sins. If you forsake the LORD, and serve foreign gods, he will turn and do evil to you, and annihilate you, after having done you good."

"No," the people said to Joshua; "it is the LORD that we would serve."

So Joshua said to the people,
"You are witnesses against yourselves that you have chosen the LORD as the one to serve."

"We are witnesses," they said.

"Remove, then, the foreign gods that are in your midst, and turn your hearts to the LORD, the God of Israel."

The people said to Joshua,
"The LORD our God we will serve, and his injunctions we will heed."

So Joshua made a covenant with the people that day; he made statutes and ordinances for them at Shechem, and Joshua wrote these regulations in the book of the law of God; and taking a large stone, he set it up there under the oak that was in the sanctuary of the LORD. Then Joshua said to all the people,

"See, this stone shall be a witness against us; for it has heard all the words that the LORD has said to us; so it shall be a witness against you, lest you deny your God."

Then Joshua dismissed the people, 28
each to his heritage.

After these events Joshua, the son of 29
Nun, the servant of the LORD, died at
the age of one hundred and ten years;
and he was buried in the grounds of his 30
heritage, in Timnath-heres which is in
the highlands of Ephraim, north of
Mount Gaash.

Israel served the LORD during all the 31
lifetime of Joshua, and all the lifetime
of the elders who survived Joshua and
had seen all the deeds which the
LORD did for Israel.

The bones of Joseph, which the Is- 32
raelites had brought up from Egypt,
were buried at Shechem, in the piece
of ground which Jacob had bought for
one hundred kesitas from the sons of
Hamor, the ancestor of Shechem, and
had presented to the Josephites as a
heritage.

Likewise Eleazar, the son of Aaron, 33
died, and was buried at Gibeah of
Phinehas, his son, to whom it had been
given, in the highlands of Ephraim.

THE BOOK OF JUDGES

THE HEBREW TRIBES IN THEIR INVASION OF PALESTINE, 1:1–36

1 AFTER the death of Joshua the
Israelites inquired of the
LORD, saying,
"Which of us is to be the
first to go up against the Canaanites to
attack them?"
2 "Judah is to go up," said the LORD.
"See, I am delivering the land into his
power."
3 So Judah said to his brother Simeon,
"Invade with me the territory allotted to me that we may attack the
Canaanites, and I in turn will invade
with you the territory allotted to you."
4 So Simeon went with him. Then
Judah went up; and the LORD delivered the Canaanites and Perizzites into
their power, so that they defeated ten
5 thousand of them at Bezek. At Bezek
they came upon Adoni-bezek, and attacked him, and defeated the Canaan-
6 ites and Perizzites. Adoni-bezek fled;
but they pursued him, and capturing
him, they cut off his thumbs and great
7 toes; whereupon Adoni-bezek said,
"Seventy kings with their thumbs
and great toes cut off used to pick up
crumbs under my table; as I did, so has
God requited me."

Then he was brought to Jerusalem,
and died there.
8 The Judeans attacked Jerusalem,
and capturing it, they put it to the
9 sword, and set the city on fire. Afterwards the Judeans went down to attack the Canaanites inhabiting the
highlands, the steppes, and the low-
10 lands. So Judah marched against the
Canaanites who lived in Hebron (the
name of Hebron used to be Kirjath-
arba), and they defeated Sheshai,
11 Ahiman, and Talmai. Then they
marched from there against the inhabitants of Debir (the name of Debir
used to be Kirjath-sepher).
12 "Whoever attacks Kirjath-sepher
and captures it," said Caleb, "I will
give him my daughter, Achsah, in marriage."

Othniel, the son of Caleb's younger
brother, Kenaz, captured it; so he gave
him his daughter, Achsah, in marriage.
When she arrived, he induced her to
ask her father for the necessary fields;
so she alighted from her ass, and when
Caleb said to her, "What do you
want?" she said to him,

"Grant me a pool; since you have assigned me to the region of the steppes,
give me Gullath-maim."

So Caleb gave her Upper Gullath
and Lower Gullath.

The descendants of Hobab, the Kenite, the father-in-law of Moses, came
up from the City of Palms with the Judeans into the wilderness of Judah,
which is in the steppes of Arad; then
they went off to live with the Amalekites. But Judah went with his brother
Simeon, and they defeated the Canaanites inhabiting Zephath, and annihilated it; so the city came to be called
Hormah [annihilation]. Judah also captured Gaza with its territory, Askelon
with its territory, and Ekron with its
territory. The LORD was with Judah,
so that he conquered the highlands, although he was not able to conquer the
inhabitants of the plain, because they
had iron chariots. Hebron was given to
Caleb, as Moses had directed, and he
evicted from there the three sons of
Anak. The Benjaminites, however,
did not evict the Jebusites inhabiting
Jerusalem, but the Jebusites live with
the Benjaminites in Jerusalem to this
day.

Likewise the clan of Joseph marched
against Bethel, and the LORD was with
them. The clan of Joseph made a re-
connaissance at Bethel (the name of the
city used to be Luz), and when the
scouts saw a man leaving the city, they
said to him,

"Come, show us the way to get into
the city, and we will treat you kindly."

So he showed them the way to get
into the city, and they put the city to

the sword; but they let the man and all his family go free; and the man went to the land of the Hittites, and built a city, calling its name Luz, which is its name to this day.

Manasseh did not conquer Beth-shean and its dependencies, nor Taanach and its dependencies, nor the inhabitants of Dor and its dependencies, nor the inhabitants of Ibleam and its dependencies, nor the inhabitants of Megiddo and its dependencies; but the Canaanites clung to the habitation of this region. However, when Israel became strong enough, they made the Canaanites forced laborers, but they never completely evicted them.

Neither did Ephraim evict the Canaanites who lived in Gezer; but the Canaanites lived among them in Gezer.

Zebulun did not evict the inhabitants of Kitron, nor the inhabitants of Nahalol; but the Canaanites lived among them, becoming, however, forced laborers.

Asher did not evict the inhabitants of Acco, nor the inhabitants of Sidon, nor those of Ahlab, nor those of Achzib, nor those of Helbah, nor those of Aphik, nor those of Rehob; but the Asherites settled among the Canaanites inhabiting the land; for they could not evict them.

Naphtali did not evict the inhabitants of Beth-shemesh, nor the inhabitants of Beth-anath, but settled among the Canaanites inhabiting the land; nevertheless the inhabitants of Beth-shemesh and Beth-anath became forced laborers for them.

The Amorites pressed the Danites into the highlands; for they would not let them come down into the plain. The Amorites clung to the habitation of Harheres, Aijalon, and Shaalbim; but when the power of the clan of Joseph grew strong enough, they became forced laborers.

The frontier of the Edomites ran from the slope of Akrabbim, from Sela upward.

THE ORIGIN OF THE NAME BOCHIM, 2:1–5

An angel of the LORD went up from Gilgal to Bochim, and said,

"... I have brought you up out of Egypt, and have brought you into the
land which I promised on oath to your
fathers, when I said, 'I will never break
my covenant with you, but you on your 2
part must make no covenant with the
inhabitants of this land; you must tear
down their altars.' But you have not
heeded my injunction: what a way for
you to behave! So now I add, 'I will 3
not drive them out of your way; but
they shall become your adversaries,
and their gods shall become a trap for
you.'"

When the angel of the LORD spoke 4
these words to all the Israelites, the
people lifted up their voices in weeping;
so the name of that place came to be 5
called Bochim [weepers]; and sacrifices
were made there to the LORD.

INTRODUCTION TO THE STORIES OF THE JUDGES, 2:6—3:6

When Joshua had dismissed the peo- 6
ple, the Israelites went each to his heritage to occupy the land; and the peo- 7
ple served the LORD during all the lifetime of Joshua, and all the lifetime of
the elders who survived Joshua, who
had seen all the great work which the
LORD had done for Israel. Then 8
Joshua, the son of Nun, the servant of
the LORD, died at the age of one hundred and ten years, and he was buried 9
in the grounds of his heritage at Timnath-heres, in the highlands of Ephraim, north of Mount Gaash. Also all 10
that generation were gathered to their
fathers, and another generation succeeded them who had no knowledge of
the LORD, nor the work that he had
done for Israel.

Then the Israelites did what was 11
evil in the sight of the LORD, by serving the Baals and forsaking the LORD, 12
the God of their fathers, who had
brought them out of the land of Egypt,
and by running after alien gods, from
among the gods of the peoples that
surrounded them, and by paying homage to them, so that they provoked the
LORD to jealousy. Thus they forsook 13
the LORD, and served the Baals and
Ashtarts. Then the anger of the LORD 14
blazed against Israel, so that he delivered them into the power of plunderers
who plundered them, and he sold them
into the power of their enemies around
them, so that they were no longer able

15 to withstand their enemies. In every
campaign the hand of the LORD was
against them for evil, as the LORD had
declared, and as the LORD had sworn
to them, so that they were in sore
16 straits. Then the LORD raised up
champions to deliver them out of the
17 power of their plunderers; but even
their champions they did not heed; for
they ran wantonly after alien gods, and
paid homage to them, swerving quickly from the path which their fathers
had trod in obedience to the commands
of the LORD; not so did they.
18 Now when the LORD raised up
champions for them, the LORD would
be with the champion, and would deliver them out of the power of their
enemies during all the lifetime of the
champion; for the LORD would be
moved to pity by their groans under
19 their tyrants and oppressors. But
whenever the champion died, they
would relapse, and behave worse than
their fathers, by running after alien
gods to serve them and pay homage to
them; they would not abandon any of
20 their practices or stubborn ways. So
the anger of the LORD blazed against
Israel, and he said,
"Since this nation has violated the
covenant with me which I enjoined on
their fathers, and has not heeded my
21 injunctions, I on my part will no longer drive out of their way any of the nations that Joshua left when he died"
22 (his purpose being to test Israel by
them as to whether or not they would
keep to the way of the LORD by walking in it, as their fathers had).
23 So the LORD left these nations instead of driving them out at once, and
did not deliver them into the power of
3 Joshua. Now these are the nations
whom the LORD left as a means to test
Israel (that is, all who had had no experience of all the wars with Canaan
2 —merely for the sake of succeeding
Israelites, to teach them war; such only
as had had no previous experience of
3 them): namely, the five tyrants of the
Philistines, all the Canaanites, the
Sidonians, and the Hittites inhabiting
Mount Lebanon from Mount Baal-
Hermon as far as the approach to
4 Hamath. They served as a means to
test Israel to see whether they would
obey the commands which the LORD
had enjoined on their fathers through
Moses. So the Israelites settled among
the Canaanites, Hittites, Amorites,
Perizzites, Hivvites, and Jebusites;
they married their daughters, and their
own daughters they married to their
sons, and they served their gods.

CONQUEST BY CUSHAN-RISHATHAIM AND DELIVERANCE THROUGH OTHNIEL, 3:7–11*a*

So the Israelites did what was evil in
the sight of the LORD in that they forgot the LORD their God, and served
the Baals and Ashtarts. Then the anger of the LORD blazed against Israel,
so that he sold them into the power of
Cushan-rishathaim, king of Aram-
naharaim, and the Israelites were subject to Cushan-rishathaim for eight
years. Then the Israelites cried to the
LORD, and the LORD raised up a savior
for the Israelites to save them, namely
Othniel, the son of Kenaz, Caleb's
younger brother. The spirit of the 10
LORD inspired him to champion Israel; so he went forth to battle, and the
LORD delivered Cushan-rishathaim,
king of Aram, into his power, so that
his might prevailed over Cushan-
rishathaim, and the land enjoyed se- 11
curity for forty years.

CONQUEST BY THE MOABITES AND DELIVERANCE THROUGH EHUD, 3:11*b*–30

When Othniel, the son of Kenaz, had
died, the Israelites again did what was 12
evil in the sight of the LORD. So the
LORD made Eglon, king of Moab,
prevail over Israel, because they had
done what was evil in the sight of the
LORD. He allied with himself the 13
Ammonites and Amelekites, and went
and defeated Israel, and occupied the
City of Palms; and the Israelites were 14
subject to Eglon, king of Moab, for
eighteen years. Then the Israelites 15
cried to the LORD, and the LORD
raised up a savior for them, namely,
Ehud, the son of Gera, the Benjaminite, a left-handed man. The Israelites
sent tribute by him to Eglon, king of
Moab; so Ehud made himself a two- 16
edged dagger, a gomed long, and hanging it under his cloak upon his right

17 hip, he brought the tribute to Eglon,
king of Moab (Eglon being a very fat
18 man). When he had finished delivering
the tribute, he dismissed the tribute-
19 bearers; but he himself turned back at
Pesilim, which is near Gilgal, to say,

"I have a private message for you, O king."

So he said, "Begone!" whereupon all his attendants left him.

20 Then Ehud went in to him, as he sat alone in his cool roof-chamber.

"I have a message from God for you," said Ehud.

21 As he rose from his chair, Ehud
stretched out his left hand, and drawing the dagger from his right hip, he
22 plunged it into his abdomen, so that the
hilt also went in after the blade, and the
fat closed over the blade; for he did
not draw the dagger out of his abdo-
23 men, but let it go into the hole. Then
Ehud went out into the vestibule, shutting the doors of the roof-chamber on
24 him, and locking them. When he had
gone out, his servants came, and discovered that the doors of the roof-
chamber were locked; but they said,

"He is only relieving himself in the closet of the cool chamber."

25 So they waited until they became
uneasy; and then, seeing that he did not
open the doors of the roof-chamber,
they took the key and opened them,
and there was their master fallen to the
26 ground, dead! But Ehud had escaped
while they were delaying, having
passed Pesilim, and he escaped to
27 Seirah. Upon his arrival he sounded
the alarm through the highlands of
Ephraim, and the Israelites went down
with him from the highlands, with him
at their head.

28 "Follow close after me," he said to
them; "for the LORD is delivering your
enemies, the Moabites, into your power."

So they followed him down, and they
seized the fords of the Jordan against
the Moabites, and would not allow any-
29 one to cross. They slew on that occasion about ten thousand Moabites, all
stout and valiant fellows, so that not
30 one escaped. Thus was Moab brought
into subjection that day to the power of
Israel, and the land enjoyed security for
eighty years.

THE MINOR JUDGE, SHAMGAR, 3:31

After him came Shamgar, the son of 31
Anath, who slew six hundred Philis-
tines with an ox-goad; he, too, saved
Israel.

CONQUEST BY THE CANAANITES AND DELIVERANCE THROUGH DEBORAH AND BARAK, 4:1–24

Then the Israelites again did what 4
was evil in the sight of the LORD, now
that Ehud was dead. So the LORD 2
sold them into the power of Jabin, king
of Canaan, who reigned at Hazor, the
general of whose army was Sisera, who
lived in Harosheth-goiim. Then the 3
Israelites cried to the LORD; for he had
nine hundred iron chariots, and he oppressed the Israelites most severely for
twenty years. It was a prophetess, 4
Deborah, the wife of Lappidoth, who
was governing Israel at that time. She 5
lived below Tomer-Deborah, between
Ramah and Bethel, in the highlands of
Ephraim. The Israelites came to her
for direction; so she sent and sum- 6
moned Barak, the son of Abinoam,
from Kedesh in Naphtali, and said to
him,

"Does not the LORD, the God of
Israel, command, 'Go and dispose
yourself at Mount Tabor, taking with
you ten thousand men from the Naphtalites and the Zebulunites? I will lure 7
Sisera, the general of Jabin's army, out
to you at the river Kishon, together
with his chariots and his troops; and I
will deliver him into your power.'"

Then Barak said to her, 8

"If you will go along with me, I will go; but if you will not go along with me, I will not go."

"Of course I will go along with you," 9
she said; "however, you will have no
glory for the course that you are pursuing; for it is into the power of a woman that the LORD is going to sell
Sisera."

Then Deborah rose and went with
Barak to Kedesh, and Barak mustered 10
Zebulun and Naphtali at Kedesh, and
ten thousand men marched out at his
heels. Deborah also went up with him.

Now Heber, the Kenite, had parted 11

from the Kenites, the descendants of
Hobab, the father-in-law of Moses, and
had pitched his tent as far away as
Elon-bezaanim, which was near Kedesh.
12 When Sisera learned that Barak, the
son of Abinoam, had gone up to Mount
13 Tabor, Sisera collected all his chariots,
nine hundred iron chariots, and all the
people that were with him, out of Haro-
14 sheth-goiim to the river Kishon. Then
Deborah said to Barak,

"Up! for this is the day in which the
LORD is to deliver Sisera into your
power. Is it not the LORD who has
gone forth in front of you?"

So Barak went down from Mount
Tabor with ten thousand men following
15 him, and the LORD routed Sisera, all
his chariots, and all his army before
Barak at the edge of the sword, so that
Sisera alighted from his chariot, and
16 fled on foot. But Barak pursued the
chariots and army as far as Harosheth-
goiim, so that the whole army of Sisera
fell before the sword, not so much as
17 one being left. Sisera, however, fled on
foot to the tent of Jael, the wife of
Heber, the Kenite; for there were
friendly relations between Jabin, king
of Hazor, and the clan of Heber, the
18 Kenite. So Jael went out to meet Sisera, and said to him,

"Turn in, my lord; turn in with me;
do not be afraid."

So he turned in to her tent, and she
covered him with a robe.

19 "Please give me a little water," he
said to her; "for I am thirsty."

So she opened the milk-skin, and
gave him a drink, and covered him up.
20 "Stand at the doorway of the tent,"
he said to her, "and then, if anyone
comes and asks you, 'Is anyone here?'
say, 'No.'"

21 But Jael, the wife of Heber, seized a
tent-pin, and taking a hammer in her
hand, she approached him stealthily,
and drove the pin through his temple
into the ground, while he was sound
asleep from exhaustion, so that he died.
22 Just then Barak arrived in pursuit of
Sisera, and Jael went out to meet him.

"Come," she said to him, "and I
will show you the man for whom you
are looking."

So he went inside with her, and there
was Sisera fallen down dead, with the
23 tent-pin in his temple! Thus did God
that day subdue Jabin, king of Canaan,
24 before the Israelites; and the power of
the Israelites bore harder and harder
on Jabin, king of Canaan, until they
finally destroyed Jabin, king of Canaan.

THE VICTORY OF DEBORAH AND BARAK OVER THE CANAANITES, 5:1–31

5 Then sang Deborah and Barak, the
son of Abinoam, on that day, saying:

2 "When locks were worn loose in Israel,
When the people volunteered;
bless the LORD!
3 Hear, O kings; give ear, O princes!
I—to the LORD I will sing,
I will praise the LORD, the God of
Israel.

4 "O LORD, when thou camest forth
from Seir,
When thou marchedst from the land
of Edom,
The earth quaked, the heavens also
shook,
The clouds, too, dripped water,
5 The mountains rocked at the presence
of the LORD (that is, Sinai),
At the presence of the LORD, the God
of Israel.

6 "In the time of Shamgar, the son of
Anath,
In the time of Jael, caravans had disappeared,
And travelers kept to the by-roads;
7 The peasantry had disappeared, they
had disappeared in Israel,
Until you arose, O Deborah, arose as
a mother in Israel.

8 "Armorers had they none;
Armed men failed from the city.
Was shield to be seen or lance,
Among forty thousand in Israel?
9 My heart is with the commanders of
Israel,
Who volunteered among the people;
bless the LORD!

10 "O riders on tawny asses, sitting on
robes;
And you who travel on the road, attend!
11 To the noise of musicians at the
watering-places,

There the triumphs of the LORD will
be recounted,
The triumphs of his peasantry in
Israel."

Then the people of the LORD went down to the gates.

12 "Awake, awake, Deborah;
Awake, awake, strike up the song!
Up, Barak, and take your captives,
O son of Abinoam!

13 "Then the remnant went down like
nobles;
The people of the LORD went down
like heroes.
14 Ephraim surged into the valley;
Following you came Benjamin among
your clansmen.
From Machir came down commanders,
And from Zebulun those who carry the
marshal's staff.
15 The chieftains of Issachar were with
Deborah and Barak;
In like manner Barak rushed into the
valley among his foot-soldiers.

"In the clans of Reuben great were the
debates.
16 Why did you lounge among the ravines,
Listening to the bleating of the flocks?
In the clans of Reuben great were the
debates.

17 "Gilead remained beyond the Jordan;
And Dan, why did he take service on
alien ships?
Asher stayed by the sea-coast,
And remained by his creeks.

18 "Zebulun was a people who exposed
themselves to death,
And Naphtali, on the heights of the
field.
19 The kings came, they fought,
Then fought the kings of Canaan;
At Taanach, by the brooks of Megid-
do,
They won no booty of silver.
20 From the heavens fought the stars;
From their courses they fought with
Sisera.

21 "The river Kishon swept them away;
A river barring the way was the river
Kishon.
Bless thou, my soul, the might of the
LORD!
22 Then the hoofs of the horses struck
down
Their warriors by their furious plung-
ing.
23 'Curse Meroz,' said the angel of the
LORD,
'Curse utterly its inhabitants;
For they came not to the help of the
LORD,
To the help of the LORD like heroes.'
24 Most blessed of women may Jael be,
The wife of Heber, the Kenite;
Of bedouin women most blessed!
25 Water he asked; milk she gave;
In a lordly bowl she brought him curds.
26 She put her hand to the tent-pin,
And her right hand to the workman's
mallet;
And she struck down Sisera, she
crushed his head;
She shattered and smashed his temple.
27 At her feet he sank, he fell, he lay
prone;
At her feet he sank, he fell;
Where he sank, there he fell slain.

28 "Out of the window she peered, and ex-
claimed,
The mother of Sisera, out of the lat-
tice:
'Why is his chariot so long in coming?
Why is the clatter of his chariots so
delayed?'
29 The wisest of her princesses replies;
She it is who makes answer to her:
30 'Are they not finding, dividing booty?
A maid or two for each warrior;
Booty of dyed stuffs for Sisera,
Booty of dyed stuffs embroidered;
A couple of pieces of dyed embroidery
for his neck as booty.'

31 "Thus may all thine enemies perish, O
LORD;
But let thy friends be like the rising of
the sun in his might."

So the land enjoyed security for forty years.

CONQUEST BY THE MIDIANITES AND DELIVERANCE THROUGH GIDEON, 6:1—8:28

6 Then the Israelites did what was evil
in the sight of the LORD, so that the
LORD delivered them into the power of

2 Midian for seven years, and the power
of Midian prevailed over Israel. It was
because of Midian that the Israelites
made for themselves the dens which
are in the mountains, and the caves and
3 strongholds. Whenever the Israelites
put in seed, the Midianites, Amalekites, and Kedemites used to come up,
4 and attack them. They encamped
against them, and destroyed the produce of the land as far as the vicinity of
Gaza. They would leave nothing in
Israel for the sheep, oxen, and asses to
5 live on; for they used to come up with
their cattle and tents; they used to
come like locusts for number, both
they and their camels being innumerable. They came into the land to ruin
6 it. So Israel was brought very low
through Midian; and the Israelites
7 cried to the LORD. Then, when the
Israelites cried to the LORD on ac-
8 count of Midian, the LORD sent a
prophet to the Israelites, who said to
them,
"Thus says the LORD, the God of
Israel, 'It was I who brought you up
out of Egypt, and brought you out of a
9 state of slavery; I rescued you from the
power of Egypt, and from the power of
all your oppressors; I drove them out of
10 your way, and gave you their land. So
I said to you, "I, the LORD, am your
God; you must not stand in awe of the
gods of the Amorites in whose land you
are living." But you have not heeded
my injunction.' "
11 The angel of the LORD came and sat
down under the terebinth at Ophrah,
which belonged to Joash, the Abiezrite,
whose son Gideon was beating out
wheat in a wine-press, to keep it safe
12 from Midian. The angel of the LORD
appeared to him, and said to him,
"The LORD is with you, valiant warrior!"
13 "Pray, sir," Gideon said to him, "if
the LORD is with us, why, then, has all
this happened to us? Where are all his
wonderful deeds, which our fathers recounted to us, saying, 'Was it not out of
Egypt that the LORD brought us?'
But now the LORD has cast us off, and
has delivered us into the power of
Midian."
14 Then the LORD turned to him, and
said,
"Go in this strength of yours, and
save Israel from the power of Midian.
Am I not sending you?"
But he said to him, 15
"Pray, O Lord, how can I save Israel, seeing that my clan is the weakest
in Manasseh, and that I am the lowliest
in my father's family?"
But the LORD said to him, 16
"I will be with you, and you shall destroy Midian to a man."
Then he said to him, 17
"If I have really found favor with
thee, pray show me a sign that it is
thou who speakest with me. Do not 18
leave here, I pray, until I come back to
thee, and bring out my offering, and
place it before thee."
"I will wait until you return," he
said.
So Gideon went inside, and prepared 19
a kid and unleavened cakes from an
ephah of flour; he put the meat in a
basket, and put the broth in a pot, and
bringing them out to him under the
terebinth, he presented them. But the 20
angel of God said to him,
"Take the meat and the unleavened
cakes, and place them on the rock
yonder; but pour out the broth."
He did so. Then the angel of the 21
LORD stretched out the end of the staff
that was in his hand, and touched the
meat and unleavened cakes, whereupon fire burst forth from the rock, and
consumed the meat and unleavened
cakes. Then the angel of the LORD
vanished from his sight. So Gideon 22
perceived that it was the angel of the
LORD.
"Alas, O Lord GOD," said Gideon;
"inasmuch as I have seen the angel of
the LORD face to face!"
But the LORD said to him, 23
"You are safe; have no fear, you are
not to die."
So Gideon built there an altar to the 24
LORD, and called it Yahweh-shalom.
To this day it still stands in the Abiezrite city of Ophrah.
That very night the LORD said to 25
him,
"Take the choicest of the bulls that
your father has (it has been the choice
bull for seven years), and tear down the
altar of the Baal that your father has,
and cut down the sacred pole that is
beside it. Then build an altar to the 26
LORD your God on the top of this
stronghold with the material, and take

the choice bull, and offer it up as a
burnt-offering with the wood of the
sacred pole which you are to cut down."
27 So Gideon took ten of his slaves, and
did as the LORD told him; but since he
was too afraid of his father's household
and the townsmen to do it by day, he
28 did it by night. When the townsmen
rose early next morning, there was the
altar of the Baal torn down, and the
sacred pole which was beside it cut
down, and the choice bull offered up on
29 the altar which had been built! Then
they said to one another,
"Who has done this deed?"
When they had inquired and investigated, they declared,
"Gideon, the son of Joash, has done
this deed."
30 So the townsmen said to Joash,
"Bring out your son that he may die;
for he has torn down the altar of the
Baal, and has cut down the sacred pole
which was beside it."
31 But Joash said to all his opponents,
"Will you take the Baal's part, or
will you champion him? Whoever
takes his part will be put to death by
morning. If he is a god, let him take his
own part; for his altar has been torn
down!"
32 So Gideon was named Jerubbaal that
day, meaning, "Let the Baal take his
own part against him; for he tore down
his altar."
33 Then all the Midianites, Amalekites,
and Kedemites joined their forces, and
crossing over, encamped in the valley of
34 Jezreel. So the spirit of the LORD took
possession of Gideon, and he sounded
the alarm, and the Abiezrites were mus-
35 tered in his following. Then he sent
messengers all through Manasseh, and
they also were mustered in his following. He sent messengers through Asher, Zebulun, and Naphtali, and they
36 marched out to meet them. Then
Gideon said to God,
"If thou art really going to save Israel by my power, as thou hast de-
37 clared—see, I will put a fleece of wool
on the threshing-floor; if there is dew
on the fleece only, while it is dry on all
the ground, I will know that thou wilt
save Israel by my power, as thou hast
declared."
38 And so it happened. When he rose
early next morning, and wrung the
fleece, he squeezed in dew out of the
fleece a bowlful of water. Then Gideon 39
said to God,
"Let not thy anger blaze against me,
that I may speak just once more. Pray
let me make only one more test with
the fleece; pray let it be dry on the
fleece only, but on all the ground let
there be dew."
And God did so that night; it was dry 40
on the fleece only, but on all the ground
there was dew.
So Jerubbaal (that is, Gideon) and all 7
the people that were with him rose
early, and encamped near En-harod,
while the camp of Midian was north of
Gibeah-moreh in the valley. Then the 2
LORD said to Gideon,
"The people that are with you are
too many for me to deliver Midian into
their power, lest Israel should glory
over me, saying, 'My own power has
saved me.' Now then, proclaim in the 3
hearing of the people, 'Whoever is
afraid and timid must go home.'"
So Gideon put them to the test, and
twenty-two thousand of the people
went home, but ten thousand were
left. Then the LORD said to Gideon, 4
"The people are still too many.
Bring them down to the water, and let
me test them there for you; he of whom
I say to you, 'This one is to go with
you,' shall go with you; but everyone
of whom I say to you, 'This one is not
to go with you,' must not go."
So he brought the people down to the 5
water, and the LORD said to Gideon,
"Everyone who laps up the water
with his tongue as a dog laps, put off by
himself; and likewise everyone who
kneels down to drink."
The number of those who lapped 6
with their tongues was three hundred,
while all the rest of the people knelt
down to drink water. Then the LORD 7
said to Gideon,
"With the three hundred men who
lapped I will save you, and will deliver
Midian into your power; but let all the
rest of the people go each to his home."
Then they took the pitchers of the 8
people in their hands, together with
their trumpets; and he sent all the rest
of the Israelites home, each to his tent,
keeping only the three hundred men.
Now the camp of Midian was beneath
him in the valley.
That very night the LORD said to 9
him,

"Rise, descend on the camp; for I am
10 delivering it into your power. But if
you are afraid to go down alone, go
down with your servant Purah to the
11 camp, and hear what they are saying;
and after that you will have the courage
to descend on the camp."

So he went down with his servant
Purah to the outposts of the warriors
12 that were in the camp. Now the Midianites, Amalekites, and all the Kedemites were lying along the valley like
locusts for number, and their camels
were innumerable, being like the sands
13 on the seashore for number. Just as
Gideon came, a man was telling his
comrade a dream.

"I just had a dream," he said, "that a
crust of barley bread came tumbling
into the camp of Midian, and coming
to a tent, struck it so that it fell, and
turned it upside down, so that the tent
lay flat."

14 "That," his comrade responded, "is
nothing other than the sword of Gideon,
the son of Joash, an Israelite. God is
delivering Midian and all the camp into
his power."

15 As soon as Gideon heard the telling
of the dream and its interpretation, he
bowed in reverence; and returning to
the camp of Israel, he said,

"Up! for the LORD is delivering the
camp of Midian into your power."

16 Then he divided the three hundred
men into three companies, and put
trumpets into the hands of all of them,
and empty pitchers, with torches inside
the pitchers.

17 "Watch me," he said to them, "and
do likewise; as I reach the outskirts of
the camp, see that you do just as I do;
18 when I blow the trumpet, I and all
those accompanying me, you also must
blow your trumpets all around the
camp, and say, 'For the LORD and for
Gideon!'"

19 When Gideon and the hundred men
that accompanied him reached the outskirts of the camp at the beginning of
the middle watch, the guards having
just been posted, they blew their
trumpets, and smashed the pitchers
20 that were in their hands; whereupon
the three companies blew their trumpets, and shattered their pitchers, holding the torches in their left hands and
the trumpets in their right to blow
them, and they cried, "For the LORD
and for Gideon!" Then they stood each 21
in his place around the camp, and all
the camp ran; they cried out, and fled.
When the three hundred trumpets 22
were blown, the LORD set them to
fighting with one another all through
the camp; and the camp fled as far as
Bethshittah in the direction of Zererah,
as far as the edge of Abel-meholah,
near Tabbath. Israelites were mustered 23
from Naphtali, Asher, and all Manasseh to pursue Midian; and Gideon sent 24
messengers all through the highlands of
Ephraim, saying,

"Come down against Midian, and
seize the streams against them as far as
Bethbarah, and also the Jordan."

So all the Ephraimites were mustered, and seized the streams as far as
Bethbarah, and also the Jordan. Cap- 25
turing Midian's two chieftains, Oreb
and Zeeb, they killed Oreb at Zur-
Oreb, and Zeeb they killed at Jekeb-
Zeeb. They pursued Midian, and the
heads of Oreb and Zeeb they brought
to Gideon on the other side of the Jordan.

Then the Ephraimites said to him, 8

"What trick is this that you have
played us in not calling us when you
went to fight against Midian?"

They vigorously upbraided him, but 2
he said to them,

"What after all have I done as com-
pared with you? Is not the gleaning of
Ephraim better than the vintage of
Abiezer? It was into your power that 3
God delivered Midian's chieftains,
Oreb and Zeeb; so what have I been
able to do as compared with you?"

Then their anger relented against
him when he said that.

When Gideon reached the Jordan, 4
and crossed it, with the three hundred
men who accompanied him, they became exhausted in their pursuit. So he 5
said to the men of Succoth,

"Pray give some loaves of bread to
my followers, because they are exhausted in my pursuit of Zebah and Zalmunna, the kings of Midian."

But the officials of Succoth said, 6

"Are the persons of Zebah and Zalmunna already in your hands that we
should give bread to your host?"

"Accordingly," said Gideon, "when 7
the LORD delivers Zebah and Zalmunna into my hands, I will trample your

bodies among desert thorns and
briers!"
8 From there he went up to Penuel,
and spoke similarly to them; but the
men of Penuel answered him as the men
9 of Succoth had. So he said also to the
men of Penuel,
"When I come back in triumph, I
will tear down this tower."
0 Now Zebah and Zalmunna were at
Karkor, and their army with them,
about fifteen thousand men, all that remained of all the Kedemite army, since
the fallen numbered one hundred and
1 twenty thousand swordsmen. So Gideon went up the caravan route, east of
Nobah and Jogbehah, and attacked the
2 camp as it lay off its guard. Zebah and
Zalmunna fled, but he pursued them,
and captured Midian's two kings, Zebah and Zalmunna, and struck panic
3 into the whole army. Then Gideon,
the son of Joash, returned from the bat-
4 tle at the slope of Heres. He captured
a youth belonging to Succoth, and
questioned him, so that he wrote down
for him a list of the officials and elders
of Succoth, seventy-seven of them.
5 Coming to the men of Succoth, he said,
"Here are Zebah and Zalmunna,
concerning whom you taunted me, saying, 'Are the persons of Zebah and
Zalmunna already in your hands that
we should give bread to your exhausted
men?' "
6 Then he took the elders of the city
along with desert thorns and briers,
and he trampled the men of Succoth
7 into them. Also the tower of Penuel he
tore down, and slew the men of the city.
8 Then he said to Zebah and Zalmunna,
"Where are the men whom you slew
at Tabor?"
"They were like yourself," said they,
"just like the sons of a king in stature."
9 "They were my brothers," said he,
"the sons of my mother. As the LORD
lives, if you had let them live, I would
not be slaying you."
0 Then he said to Jether, his first-born,
"Go and slay them!"
But the boy would not draw his
sword, because he was afraid; for he was
1 still only a boy. Then Zebah and Zalmunna said,
"Come and fall upon us yourself; for
a man has a man's courage."
So Gideon went and slew Zebah and
Zalmunna, and he took the crescents
which were on the necks of their camels.
Then the Israelites said to Gideon, 22
"Rule over us, you, then your son,
and then your grandson; for you have
saved us from the power of Midian."
But Gideon said to them, 23
"I will not rule over you, nor shall my
son rule over you, since the LORD rules
over you."
"But let me make a request of you," 24
Gideon said to them; "each of you give
me the earrings of his captives." (For
they had gold earrings, since they were
Ishmaelites.)
"We surely will," said they. 25
So they spread out a mantle, and
each of them threw the earrings of his
captives into it, so that the weight of 26
the gold earrings for which he had asked
was one thousand seven hundred shekels in gold, exclusive of the crescents,
pendants, and purple robes worn by the
kings of Midian, and the collars which
were on the necks of their camels. Then 27
Gideon made it into an ephod, and deposited it in his city Ophrah, and all
Israel ran wantonly after it there, so
that it became a snare for Gideon and
his family. Thus were the Midianites 28
brought into subjection to the Israelites, so that they never raised their
heads again; and the land enjoyed security for forty years, during the lifetime of Gideon.

THE KINGDOM OF ABIMELECH: ITS RISE AND FALL, 8:29—9:57

Then Jerubbaal, the son of Joash, 29
went to live at home. Gideon had sev- 30
enty sons, who were his own offspring;
for he had many wives. His consort 31
who lived in Shechem had also borne
him a son, to whom he had given the
name of Abimelech. Then Gideon, the 32
son of Joash, died at a ripe old age, and
was buried in the tomb of his father
Joash, in the Abiezrite city of Ophrah.
Just as soon as Gideon died, the Israel- 33
ites again ran wantonly after the Baals,
and made Baal-berith their god. The 34
Israelites paid no attention to the
LORD their God, who had rescued them
from the power of all their enemies
around them, nor were they kind to the 35
family of Jerubbaal (that is, Gideon) in
return for all the good that he had rendered Israel.

9 Then Abimelech, the son of Jerubbaal, went to Shechem to his mother's
kinsmen, and spoke to them and to all
the clan of his mother's family, saying,
"Say in the hearing of all the citizens
2 of Shechem, 'Which is better for you,
to have seventy men rule over you, all
the sons of Jerubbaal, or to have one
man rule over you? Also remember
that I am your own flesh and blood.' "
3 So his mother's kinsmen spoke all
these words in his behalf in the hearing
of all the citizens of Shechem, so that
their sympathies turned toward Abimelech; "For," said they, "he is our kinsman."
4 So they gave him seventy shekels of
silver from the temple of Baal-berith,
and with them Abimelech hired vagabonds and reckless fellows to follow
5 him. Then he came to his father's
house at Ophrah, and slew his brothers,
the sons of Jerubbaal, seventy of them,
on a single stone; but Jotham, the
youngest son of Jerubbaal, escaped, because he hid himself.
6 Then all the citizens of Shechem and
all Beth-millo assembled, and went and
made Abimelech king, beside the terebinth connected with the sacred pillar
7 which was at Shechem. When the news
was brought to Jotham, he went and
stood on the top of Mount Gerizim, and
lifting up his voice, he called out, and
said to them,
"Listen to me, O citizens of Shechem,
8 so that God may listen to you! Once
upon a time the trees set out to anoint
a king over themselves; so they said to
the olive tree,
" 'Reign over us.'
9 "But the olive tree said to them,
" 'Do I lack my rich oil, with which
gods and men are honored, that I
should go begging to the trees?'
10 "Then the trees said to the fig tree,
" 'Do you come and reign over us!'
11 "But the fig tree said to them,
" 'Do I lack my sweetness and good
fruit that I should go begging to the
trees?'
12 "Then the trees said to the vine,
" 'Do you come and reign over us!'
13 "But the vine said to them,
" 'Do I lack my wine, which cheers
gods and men, that I should go begging
to the trees?'
14 "Finally the trees said to the thorn,
" 'Do you come and reign over us!'

"But the thorn said to the trees, 15
" 'If in good faith you are anointing
me as king over you, come and take
shelter in my shade; but if not, fire
shall burst forth from the thorn, and
consume the cedars of Lebanon.'
"So now, if you have acted in good 16
faith and integrity in making Abimelech king, and if you have acted fairly
by Jerubbaal and his family, and
treated him as he deserved—seeing 17
that my father fought for you, and
risked his life, and rescued you from the
power of Midian, whereas you have to- 18
day risen against my father's family,
and have slain his sons, seventy of
them, on a single stone, and have made
Abimelech, the son of his slave girl,
king over the citizens of Shechem, because he is your kinsman—if, I say, you 19
have acted in good faith and integrity
by Jerubbaal and his family this day,
have joy in Abimelech, and may he also
have joy in you! But if not, fire shall 20
burst forth from Abimelech, and consume all the citizens of Shechem and
Beth-millo, and fire shall burst forth
from the citizens of Shechem and Beth-
millo and consume Abimelech."
Then Jotham ran away, and fleeing, 21
went to Beer, and settled there, on account of his brother Abimelech.
For three years Abimelech held sway 22
over Israel. Then God sent an evil 23
spirit between Abimelech and the citizens of Shechem, so that the citizens of
Shechem played false by Abimelech, in 24
order that the murder of the seventy
sons of Jerubbaal and their blood
might be requited on their brother
Abimelech, who had slain them, and on
the citizens of Shechem, who had abet-
ted him in slaying his brothers. The 25
citizens of Shechem to his hurt set men
in ambush on the mountain-tops, and
robbed all who passed by them on the
road; and it was reported to Abimelech.
Now Gaal, the son of Obed, came 26
with his kinsmen, and moved into Shechem; and the citizens of Shechem put
their trust in him. They went out into 27
the fields, and cut their grapes and
trod them out. Then they held a festival, and entering the house of their god,
they ate and drank, and reviled Abimelech. Then Gaal, the son of Obed, said, 28
"What claim has Abimelech on Shechem, that we should serve him? Did
not Jerubbaal's son, and his lieutenant

Zebul, once serve the men of Hamor,
the ancestor of Shechem; so why should
9 we serve him? O that this people were
under my authority! Then would I de-
pose Abimelech, and I would say to
Abimelech, 'Your tenure of office has
been long enough; so get out!' "
0 When Zebul, the governor of the city,
heard the words of Gaal, the son of
1 Obed, his anger blazed; and he sent
messengers to Abimelech at Arumah,
saying,
"Gaal, the son of Obed, and his kinsmen have come to Shechem, and here
they are, turning the city against you!
2 Now then, start out at night, you and
the people that are with you, and lie in
3 ambush in the fields; and then rise early
next morning, just at sunrise, and make
a dash against the city. Then, just as
he and the people that are with him
come out against you, do to him as opportunity offers."
4 So Abimelech and all the people that
were with him started out at night, and
lay in ambush against Shechem, in four
5 companies. When Gaal, the son of
Obed, came out, and stood at the entrance of the city gate, Abimelech and
the people that were with him rose
6 from the ambuscade; and when Gaal
saw the people, he said to Zebul,
"See, there are people coming down
from the mountain tops."
"It is the mountain shadows," Zebul
said to him, "which look to you like
men!"
7 But Gaal said again,
"See, there are people coming down
from the vicinity of Tabburerez, and
one company is advancing from the direction of Elon-meonenim!"
8 Then Zebul said to him,
"Where is your boast now, which you
made, 'Who is Abimelech, that we
should serve him?' Are these not the
people that you despised? Come out
then, and fight against them!"
9 So Gaal led out the citizens of Shechem, and fought against Abimelech;
0 but Abimelech pursued him, and he
fled from him, while many fell wounded, right up to the entrance of the gate.
1 Abimelech, however, continued to live
at Arumah; while Zebul banished Gaal
and his kinsmen from Shechem.
2 Next day, when the people went out
into the fields, the news was brought to
3 Abimelech. So he took his men, and
dividing them into three companies,
lay in ambush in the fields. When he
saw the people coming out of the city,
he rose against them, and attacked
them. Abimelech and the company 44
that was with him made a dash, and occupied the entrance to the city gate;
while the other two companies made a
dash against all who were in the fields,
and attacked them. Abimelech fought 45
against the city all that day; and when
he captured the city, he slew the people that were in it, razed the city itself,
and sowed it with salt.
When all the citizens of Migdal-She- 46
chem heard of it, they entered the
crypt of the temple of El-berith. When 47
the news was brought to Abimelech
that all the citizens of Migdal-Shechem
were gathered there, Abimelech went 48
up to Mount Zalmon, he and all the
people that were with him; and taking
an ax in his hand, Abimelech cut down
brushwood, and lifting it up, put it on
his shoulder. Then he said to the people that were with him,
"Hurry, and do just what you saw
me do."
So all the people likewise cut down 49
brush, and following Abimelech, placed
it on the crypt, and then set the crypt
on fire over them; so that all the citizens
of Migdal-Shechem also died, about a
thousand men and women.
Then Abimelech went to Thebez, in- 50
vested Thebez, and captured it. But 51
there was a strong tower inside the city,
and thither fled all the men and women,
all the citizens of the city, and shut
themselves in, and went up on the roof
of the tower. When Abimelech reached 52
the tower, he attacked it; but as he approached the doorway of the tower to
burn it down, a woman threw an upper 53
millstone on Abimelech's head, and
crushed his skull, whereupon he called 54
quickly to his armorbearer, and said to
him,
"Draw your sword, and despatch me,
lest it be said of me, 'A woman killed
him!' "
So his servant ran him through, and
he died. When the Israelites saw that 55
Abimelech was dead, they went each to
his home. Thus did God requite the 56
crime of Abimelech which he committed against his father, in slaying seventy brothers. Also all the wickedness of 57
the men of Shechem did God requite

upon their heads, so that the curse of
Jotham, the son of Jerubbaal, came
upon them.

THE MINOR JUDGES, TOLA AND JAIR, 10:1–5

10 After Abimelech, there rose to save
Israel Tola, the son of Puah, the son of
Dodo, an Issacharite. He lived at Sha-
2 mir, in the highlands of Ephraim. He
governed Israel for twenty-three years.
Then he died, and was buried at
Shamir.
3 After him rose Jair, the Gileadite.
He governed Israel for twenty-two
4 years. He had thirty sons who rode on
thirty saddle-asses and possessed thirty
cities (they are called Havvoth-jair to
this day), which are in the land of
5 Gilead. Then Jair died, and was buried
at Kamon.

CONQUEST BY THE AMMONITES AND DELIVERANCE THROUGH JEPHTHAH, 10:6—12:7

6 Then the Israelites again did what
was evil in the sight of the LORD by
serving the Baals and Ashtarts, the
gods of Syria, the gods of Sidon, the
gods of Moab, the gods of the Ammonites, and the gods of the Philistines;
they forsook the LORD and did not
7 serve him. Then the anger of the
LORD blazed against Israel, so that he
sold them into the power of the Philistines, and into the power of the Am-
8 monites. They crushed and oppressed
the Israelites for eighteen years, that is,
all the Israelites who were beyond the
Jordan in the land of the Amorites,
9 which is in Gilead. The Ammonites
crossed the Jordan to fight also against
Judah, Benjamin, and the clan of
Ephraim, so that Israel was in sore
10 straits. Then the Israelites cried to the
LORD, saying,
"We have sinned against thee; for we
have forsaken our God and served the
Baals."
11 Then the LORD said to the Israelites,
"Is it not as easy to save from the
Ammonites and Philistines as from the
12 Egyptians and Amorites? When the
Sidonians, Amalekites, and Midianites
oppressed you, and you cried to me, I
saved you from their power. Yet you 13
have forsaken me, and served alien
gods. Accordingly, I will not save you
any more. Go and cry to the gods 14
whom you have chosen! Let them save
you in your time of distress!"
Then the Israelites said to the LORD, 15
"We have sinned; do to us just as
thou seest fit; only do rescue us this
day!"
Then they removed the foreign gods 16
from their midst, and served the LORD,
so that he had to yield to the grievances
of Israel.
The Ammonites were mustered, and 17
camped in Gilead; while the Israelites
were assembled, and camped at Mizpeh. Then the people throughout the 18
cities of Gilead said to one another,
"Whoever will take the lead in fighting
against the Ammonites, shall become
chief over the inhabitants of Gilead."
Now Jephthah, the Gileadite, was a 1
valiant warrior; but he was the son of a
harlot. Gilead was the father of Jephthah, but Gilead's wife had borne him 2
other sons, and when his wife's sons had
grown up, they had driven Jephthah
out, and had said to him,
"You shall have no inheritance in
our father's estate; for you are the son
of another woman."
So Jephthah had fled from his broth- 3
ers, and was living in the land of Tob.
Vagabonds gathered about Jephthah,
and went raiding with him. After a 4
while the Ammonites went to war with
Israel. When the Ammonites went to 5
war with Israel, the elders of Gilead
went to bring Jephthah from the land
of Tob.
"Come and be our commander," 6
they said to Jephthah, "that we may
fight against the Ammonites."
But Jephthah said to the elders of 7
Gilead,
"Are you not the men who hated me,
and drove me out of my father's house?
Why then have you come to me now,
when you are in trouble?"
"That is just why we have come back 8
to you," the elders of Gilead said to
Jephthah; "so come with us, and fight
against the Ammonites, and be chief
over us, over all the inhabitants of
Gilead."

Whereupon Jephthah said to the elders of Gilead,

"If you take me back to fight against the Ammonites, and the LORD puts them at my mercy, shall I really become your chief?"

The elders of Gilead said to Jephthah,

"The LORD shall be witness between us that we will do just as you say."

So Jephthah went with the elders of Gilead, and the people made him chief and commander over them, and Jephthah repeated all his words in the presence of the LORD at Mizpeh.

Then Jephthah sent messengers to the king of the Ammonites, saying,

"What have you against me that you have come against me to wage war on my country?"

The king of the Ammonites said to the messengers of Jephthah,

"Israel took away my lands when they came up out of Egypt, from the Arnon as far as the Jabbok and the Jordan; so now restore them peaceably."

Then Jephthah again sent messengers to the king of the Ammonites, to say to him,

"Thus says Jephthah: 'Israel did not take away the land of Moab, nor the land of the Ammonites. When they came up out of Egypt, Israel journeyed through the desert as far as the Red Sea, and then came to Kadesh. Israel then sent messengers to the king of Edom, saying, "Pray let us pass through your land"; but the king of Edom would not agree. Likewise they sent to the king of Moab, but he would not consent. So Israel remained at Kadesh. Then they journeyed through the desert, and making a circuit around the land of Edom and the land of Moab, they kept to the east of the land of Moab, and camped beyond the Arnon. They did not enter the territory of Moab; for the Arnon was the frontier of Moab. Then Israel sent messengers to Sihon, king of the Amorites, king of Heshbon. "Pray let us pass through your land to our destination," Israel said to him. But Sihon refused to let Israel pass through his territory; Sihon collected all his people, and encamped at Jahaz, and fought with Israel. Then the LORD, the God of Israel, delivered Sihon and all his people into the power
of Israel, so that they defeated them;
and Israel occupied all the land of the
Amorites inhabiting that region. They 22
occupied all the territory of the Amorites, from the Arnon as far as the Jabbok, and from the desert as far as the
Jordan. So, now that the LORD, the 23
God of Israel, has driven the Amorites
out of the way of his people Israel, are
you to occupy the territory? Should 24
you not occupy the territory of those
whom Chemosh, your own god, drives
out, while we occupy that of all those
whom the LORD, our God, has driven
out of our way? Are you then any 25
stronger than Balak, the son of Zippor,
king of Moab? Did he ever quarrel
with the Israelites, or fight with them?
While Israel lived in Heshbon and its 26
dependencies, and in Aroer and its dependencies, and in all the cities which
are on the banks of the Arnon, for three
hundred years, why did you not recover
them within that time? I have com- 27
mitted no wrong against you, but you
are doing me wrong in making war on
me. Let the LORD, as judge today,
decide the issue between the Israelites
and Ammonites!' "

But the king of the Ammonites would 28
not agree to the proposal which Jephthah sent him.

Then the spirit of the LORD inspired 29
Jephthah, so that he crossed to Gilead
and Manasseh; then he passed on to
Mizpeh of Gilead, and from Mizpeh of
Gilead he passed on to the Ammonites.
Jephthah made a vow to the LORD, 30
saying,

"If thou wilt but deliver the Ammonites into my power, whosoever 31
comes out of the door of my house to
meet me, when I return in triumph
from the Ammonites, shall be the
LORD'S; I will offer him up as a burnt-
offering!"

Then Jephthah crossed over to the 32
Ammonites, to fight against them; and
the LORD delivered them into his power. He routed them with very great 33
slaughter, from Aroer as far as the vicinity of Minnith, through twenty
cities, and as far as Abel-cheramim.
Thus were the Ammonites brought into
subjection to the Israelites.

Then Jephthah went home to Miz- 34
peh, and there was his daughter coming
out to meet him with tambourines and
dancing! She was his one and only

child; besides her he had neither son nor
35 daughter. Upon seeing her, he tore his
clothes, and said,
"Alas, my daughter, you have
stricken me low! You have indeed
brought calamity on me! For I made a
vow to the LORD, and I cannot repudiate it."
36 "My father," she said to him, "since
you have made a vow to the LORD, do
to me as you declared, now that the
LORD has wreaked vengeance for you
on your enemies, the Ammonites."
37 "But let this privilege be granted
me," she said to her father; "spare me
for two months, that I may go and
roam at large on the mountains, and bewail my maidenhood, I and my companions."
38 "Go!" he said.
So he let her go for two months, and
she went, she and her companions, to
bewail her maidenhood on the moun-
39 tains. Then, at the end of two months
she returned to her father, who did to
her what he had vowed, and she one
who had never had intercourse with a
man. Thus it became a custom in Is-
40 rael for the Israelite maidens to go annually to commemorate the daughter of
Jephthah, the Gileadite, for four days
in the year.
12 When the Ephraimites were mustered, they crossed to Zaphon, and said
to Jephthah,
"Why did you cross over to fight
against the Ammonites without inviting us to go with you? We will burn
your house over your head."
2 But Jephthah said to them,
"I had a quarrel with my people.
Then the Ammonites oppressed them
severely, and they called on you, but
you would not save them from their
3 power. When I saw that you would
not help, I took my life in my hands,
and crossed over to the Ammonites;
and the LORD delivered them into my
power. Why then have you come
against me today to fight with me?"
4 Then Jephthah collected all the
Gileadites, and fought with Ephraim;
and the Gileadites defeated Ephraim.
5 Gilead seized the fords of the Jordan
against Ephraim, and whenever a fugitive from Ephraim would say, "Let me
cross," the Gileadites would say to
him, "Are you an Ephraimite?" If he
6 said, "No," they would say to him,

"Then say 'Shibboleth.'" If he said "Sibboleth," seeing that it is not proper so to pronounce it, they would seize him, and slay him at the fords of the Jordan. Thus there fell at that time forty-two thousand of the Ephraimites.

Jephthah governed Israel for six years. Then Jephthah, the Gileadite, died, and was buried in his city in Gilead.

THE MINOR JUDGES: IBZAN, ELON, AND ABDON, 12:8–15

After him Ibzan of Bethlehem governed Israel. He had thirty sons. He married thirty daughters outside his family, and thirty daughters he brought in for his sons from outside. He governed Israel for seven years. Then Ibzan died, and was buried at Bethlehem.

After him Elon, the Zebulunite, governed Israel; he governed Israel for ten years. Then Elon, the Zebulunite, died, and was buried at Aijalon in the land of Zebulun.

After him Abdon, the son of Hillel, the Pirathonite, governed Israel. He had forty sons and thirty grandsons, who rode on seventy saddle-asses. He governed Israel for eight years. Then Abdon, the son of Hillel, the Pirathonite, died, and was buried at Pirathon in the land of Ephraim, in the highlands of the Amalekites.

THE STORY OF SAMSON, 13:1—16:31

Then the Israelites again did what was evil in the sight of the LORD; so that the LORD delivered them into the power of the Philistines for forty years.

Now there was a certain man of Zorah, belonging to the Danite clan, whose name was Manoah. His wife was barren and childless; but the angel of the LORD appeared to the woman, and said to her,

"See now, although you have been barren and childless, you are going to conceive, and bear a son. Now then, take care not to drink wine or liquor, nor to eat anything unclean; for you are going to conceive, and bear a son. A razor is not to be used on his head; for the boy is to be a Nazirite to God from conception. He it is who will take the lead in saving Israel from the power of the Philistines."

Then the woman came and told her husband, saying,

"A man of God came to me, whose appearance was like that of an angel of God, very awe-inspiring. I did not ask him where he came from, nor did he tell me his name; but he said to me, 'You are going to conceive, and bear a son; now then, do not drink wine or liquor, nor eat anything unclean; for the boy is to be a Nazirite to God from conception to the day of his death.' "

Then Manoah besought the LORD, and said,

"Pray, O Lord, let the man of God whom thou didst send come back to us, and teach us what to do for the boy that is to be born."

So God acceded to Manoah's request, and the angel of God came back to the woman while she was sitting in the field, her husband Manoah not being with her. Then the woman ran quickly to tell her husband.

"The man who came to me the other day has just appeared to me!" she said to him.

So Manoah rose and followed his wife, and coming to the man, said to him,

"Are you the man who spoke to my wife?"

"I am," he said.

"In case your promise comes true," said Manoah, "what is to be the boy's training and his vocation?"

The angel of the LORD said to Manoah,

"The woman must abstain from everything of which I spoke to her. She must not eat any of the products of the grapevine, nor drink wine or liquor, nor eat anything unclean. All that I commanded her she must observe."

Then Manoah said to the angel of the LORD,

"Pray allow us to detain you, that we may prepare a kid for you."

But the angel of the LORD said to Manoah,

"Though you detain me, I will not taste your food; but if you are going to make a burnt-offering, offer it up to the LORD." (For Manoah did not know that he was the angel of the LORD.)

Then Manoah said to the angel of the 17
LORD,
"What is your name, that we may
properly honor you when your promise
comes true?"
"Why do you ask for my name," 18
the angel of the LORD said to him,
"seeing that it is ineffable."
Then Manoah took the kid, along 19
with the cereal-offering, and offered it
up on the rock to the LORD, who performed wonders while Manoah and his
wife looked on; when the flame ascend- 20
ed from the altar heavenward, the angel of the LORD ascended in the flame
of the altar, while Manoah and his wife
looked on, and fell on their faces to the
ground. (The angel of the LORD never 21
again appeared to Manoah and his
wife.) Then Manoah knew that he was
the angel of the LORD; so Manoah said 22
to his wife,
"We shall certainly die; for we have
seen God!"
But his wife said to him, 23
"If the LORD had meant to kill us, he
would not have accepted a burnt-offering and a cereal-offering from us, nor
would he have showed us all these
things, nor would he have told us such
a thing as he did just now."
So the woman bore a son, and called 24
his name Samson. The boy grew up,
and the LORD blessed him; but the 25
spirit of the LORD first stirred him up
at Mahaneh-dan, between Zorah and
Eshtaol.

Samson went down to Timnah, and 14
saw a woman at Timnah, one of the
Philistine women. When he came back, 2
he told his father and mother.
"I saw a woman at Timnah," he said,
"one of the Philistine women; now
then, get her for me in marriage."
But his father and mother said to 3
him,
"Is there no woman among the girls
of your own kinsmen or among all my
people, that you must go and get a wife
from the uncircumcised Philistines?"
But Samson said to his father,
"Get her for me; for she is the one
that suits me."
His father and mother did not know, 4
however, that it was at the instigation
of the LORD that he was picking a
quarrel with the Philistines; for at that
time the Philistines held sway over
Israel.

5 Then Samson went down with his
father and mother to Timnah, and just
as they reached the vineyards of Timnah, a young lion came roaring at him.
6 Then the spirit of the LORD came rushing upon him, so that he split it open as
one might split a kid, although he had
nothing at all in his hands. However,
he did not tell his father and mother
7 what he had done. So he went down,
and talked to the woman, and she suit-
8 ed Samson. When he returned after a
while to marry her, he turned aside to
look at the remains of the lion, and
there was a swarm of bees in the carcass
9 of the lion, and honey! So he scraped it
out into his hands, and ate it as he went
along. When he returned to his father
and mother, he gave them some to eat,
but he did not tell them that it was out
of the carcass of the lion that he had
scraped the honey.

10 When his father went down to the
woman, Samson made a feast there; for
so bridegrooms were accustomed to do.
11 As soon as they saw him, they selected
thirty companions to accompany him.
12 To them Samson said,

"Let me propound you a riddle; if
you can but solve it for me in the seven
days of the feast, and find it out, I will
give you thirty linen robes and thirty
13 festal garments; but if you are unable to
tell me the solution, then you must give
me thirty-linen robes and thirty festal
garments."

"Propound your riddle," they said
to him, "let us hear it!"

14 So he said to them,

"Out of the eater came something to
eat,
And out of the strong came something
sweet."

When they could not solve the riddle
15 after three days, they said to Samson's
wife on the fourth day,

"Coax your husband to solve the riddle for us, lest we burn up you and your
father's house. Was it to impoverish
us that you invited us here?"

16 So Samson's wife wept on his shoulder, and said,

"You simply hate me and do not
love me at all. You have propounded
a riddle to my countrymen without
telling me the solution."

He said to her,

"Why I haven't told my father or
mother; so should I tell you?"

But she wept on his shoulder through the seven days that they kept the feast, until finally on the seventh day he told her, since she pressed him so hard. Then she told the riddle to her countrymen; and on the seventh day, as he was about to enter the bridal chamber, the men of the city said to him,

"What is sweeter than honey,
And what is stronger than a lion?"

He said to them,

"If you had not ploughed with this
heifer of mine,
You would not have found out this
riddle of mine."

Then the spirit of the LORD came rushing upon him, so that he went down to Askelon, and killing thirty of them, he despoiled them, and gave the festal garments to those who had solved the riddle. Then, blazing with anger, he went up to his father's house, and Samson's wife went to his rival, who had been a rival to him.

After a while, however, in the time of wheat harvest, Samson paid a visit to his wife with a kid.

"I am going into the bridal chamber to my wife," he said.

But her father would not let him go in.

"I thought of course that you must simply hate her," her father said, "so I gave her to your rival. Is her younger sister not better than she? Take her instead."

Then Samson said of them,

"This time I am going to get even with the Philistines; for I am going to do them harm."

So Samson went and caught three hundred foxes; he then procured torches, and turning tail to tail, he put a torch between each pair of tails. Then, setting the torches on fire, he turned the foxes loose in the standing grain of the Philistines, and burnt up both the shocks and the standing grain, and also the vineyards and olive groves.

"Who has done this?" said the Philistines.

"Samson, the son-in-law of the Timnite," it was said, "because his wife was taken away and given to his rival."

So the Philistines went up, and burned up her and her father's house.

Then Samson said to them,

"You can never do such a thing as

this without my taking revenge on you; but after this I will quit."

So he smote them hip and thigh with great slaughter; then he went down, and lived in a cleft of the crag Etam.

Then the Philistines came up, and encamped in Judah, and made a raid on Lehi.

"Why have you come up against us?" said the Judeans.

"We have come up to take Samson prisoner," they said, "that we may do to him as he did to us."

So three thousand of the Judeans went down to the cleft of the crag Etam, and said to Samson,

"Do you not know that the Philistines hold sway over us? What ever have you done to us?"

"As they did to me," he replied, "so have I done to them."

"We have come down to take you prisoner," they said to him, "to turn you over to the Philistines."

"Swear to me that you will not fall upon me yourselves," Samson said to them.

"No," they responded, "we will but take you prisoner, and turn you over to them, but we will not kill you."

So they bound him with two new ropes, and brought him up from the crag. As he reached Lehi, the Philistines came shouting to meet him. Then the spirit of the LORD came rushing upon him, so that the ropes on his arms became like flax that has caught on fire, and his bonds melted off his hands; and finding a fresh jawbone of an ass, he put out his hand, and seizing it, felled a thousand men with it. Then Samson said,

"With the red ass's jawbone I have
dyed them red;
With the red ass's jawbone I have
felled a thousand men."

As he finished speaking, he threw the jawbone away; hence that place came to be called Ramath-lehi [the hill of the jawbone]. Then he became very thirsty, so he called to the LORD, saying,

"Thou hast vouchsafed this great victory by thy servant, and am I now to die of thirst, and fall by the hands of the uncircumcised?"

Then God split open the mortar that is at Lehi, and water gushed out of it; and when he drank, his spirits rose, and he revived. That is how its name came
to be called En-hakkor [the spring of
the caller], which is at Lehi to this day.
So he governed Israel in the time of the 20
Philistines for twenty years.

Samson went to Gaza, and seeing a 16
harlot there, had intercourse with her.
When the Gazaites were told, "Samson 2
has come here," they came around, and
lay in wait for him all night at the gate
of the city. They kept quiet all night,
saying, "As soon as morning dawns, we
will kill him." Samson lay until mid- 3
night; but at midnight he rose, and
taking hold of the doors of the city gate
and the two gateposts, he pulled them
up, together with the bar, and putting
them on his shoulder, he carried them
to the top of the hill that faces Hebron.

Afterwards he fell in love with a 4
woman in the valley of Sorek, whose
name was Delilah. Then the Philistine 5
tyrants came to her, and said to her,

"Coax him, and find out why his
strength is so great, and how we can
overpower him and bind him helpless,
and we will each give you eleven hundred shekels of silver."

So Delilah said to Samson, 6

"Do tell me why your strength is so
great, and how you can be bound helpless?"

Samson said to her, 7

"If I were to be bound with seven
fresh bowstrings that have not been
dried, I should become weak, and be
like any other man."

Then the Philistine tyrants brought 8
her seven fresh bowstrings that had not
been dried, and she bound him with
them. Then, having men lie in wait in 9
the inner room, she said to him,

"The Philistines are on you, Samson!"

But he snapped the bowstrings, as a
strand of tow is snapped when it comes
near fire. So the source of his strength
was not discovered.

Then Delilah said to Samson, 10

"There, you have trifled with me,
and told me lies! Do tell me now how
you can be bound."

So he said to her, 11

"If I were but bound with new ropes
that have not been used, I should become weak, and be like any other
man."

So Delilah took new ropes, and 12
bound him with them. Then she said to
him,

"The Philistines are on you, Samson!"
(Meanwhile men were lying in wait in the inner room.)
But he snapped them off his arms like thread.
13 Then Delilah said to Samson,
"Up to now you have trifled with me, and told me lies. Tell me how you can be bound."
So he said to her,
"If you were to weave the seven locks of my head into the web, and beat them in with the pin, I should become weak, and be like any other man."
So, when he was asleep, Delilah took
the seven locks of his head and wove
14 them into the web, and beat them in
with the pin. Then she said to him,
"The Philistines are on you, Samson!"
But he awoke from his sleep, and pulled up both the loom and the web.
15 Then she said to him,
"How can you say, 'I love you,' when you do not confide in me? Three times already you have trifled with me, and have not told me why your strength is so great."
16 At last, after she had pressed him
with her words continually, and urged
17 him, he got tired to death of it, and told
her his whole secret.
"A razor has never been used on my head," he said to her; "for I have been a Nazirite to God from conception. If I were to be shaved, my strength would leave me; I should become weak, and be like any other man."
18 When Delilah saw that he had told her his whole secret, she sent for the Philistine tyrants, saying,
"Come up this once; for he has told me his whole secret."
So the Philistine tyrants came to
her, and brought the money in their
19 hands. Then she put him to sleep on
her knees, and summoning a man, she
had him shave off the seven locks of his
head, so that he became quite helpless,
20 and his strength left him. Then she
said,
"The Philistines are on you Samson!"
He awoke from his sleep, and
thought, "I shall get off as I have done
over and over again, and shake myself
free"—not knowing that the LORD
21 had left him. Then the Philistines
seized him, and gouged out his eyes, and bringing him down to Gaza, they bound him with bronze shackles, and he spent his time grinding in the prison. But the hair of his head began to grow again as soon as it had been shaved off.
Now the Philistine tyrants gathered to offer a great sacrifice to their god Dagon, and for merry-making, saying,
"Our god has delivered our enemy Samson into our power!"
When the people saw him, they praised their god; "For," said they, "our god has delivered our enemy into our hands, the devastator of our lands, and him who slew us in bands."
When they were in high spirits, they said,
"Summon Samson, that he may make sport for us!"
So Samson was summoned from the prison, and made sport before them. When they had stationed him between the pillars, Samson said to the attendant who was holding his hand,
"Put me so that I can feel the pillars on which the building is supported, that I may lean against them."
Now the building was full of men and women, and all the Philistine tyrants were there; and on the roof there were about three thousand men and women, looking on while Samson made sport. Then Samson cried to the LORD, saying,
"O Lord GOD, pray remember me, and give me strength just this one time, O God, to wreak vengeance but once upon the Philistines for my two eyes!"
Then Samson grasped the two middle pillars on which the building was supported, one with his right hand and the other with his left, and braced himself against them.
"Let me die with the Philistines!" said Samson.
Then he pulled with all his might, so that the building fell in upon the tyrants and all the people that were in it. So those that he killed at his death were more than those that he had killed during his life.
Then his kinsmen and all his father's household came down, and took him up; and bringing him away, they buried him between Zorah and Eshtaol, in the tomb of his father Manoah. He had governed Israel for twenty years.

THE STORY OF MICAH AND THE DANITES, 17:1—18:31

There was a man of the highlands of Ephraim, whose name was Micah. He said to his mother,

"The eleven hundred shekels of silver which were stolen from you, and concerning which you uttered a curse, and further, said it in my hearing, here is the silver in my possession; it was I who stole it; so now I return it to you."

His mother said,

"Blessed be my son of the LORD!"

When he returned the eleven hundred shekels of silver to his mother, his mother said,

"I do solemnly consecrate the silver to the LORD from me for my son, to make a carved image and a molten image."

So he returned the silver to his mother, and his mother took two hundred shekels of it, and gave it to a silversmith, who made it into a carved image and a molten image, to stand in Micah's house. The man Micah had a shrine; he had made an ephod and teraphim, and had installed one of his sons to be priest for him. In those days there was no king in Israel; everyone used to do as he pleased.

Now there was a young man from Bethlehem in Judah, belonging to the clan of Judah; he was a Levite, and was an immigrant there. The man had left the city, Bethlehem in Judah, to settle as an immigrant wherever he might find a place; so he came to the highlands of Ephraim to the house of Micah in the accomplishment of his errand.

"Where do you come from?" Micah said to him.

"I am a Levite from Bethlehem in Judah," he replied; "I am traveling to settle as an immigrant wherever I can find a place."

"Live with me," Micah said to him; "be father and priest to me, and I will give you ten shekels of silver a year, the necessary clothes, and your living."

So the Levite agreed to live with the man, and the young man was treated by him like one of his own sons. Micah installed the Levite, and the young man became his priest, and lived in Micah's house.

"Now," said Micah, "I know that the LORD will prosper me, seeing that the Levite has become my priest."

In those days there was no king in 18
Israel.
In those days the Danite tribe were
looking for a heritage to settle in, since
nothing in the way of a heritage had
fallen to them up to that time among
the tribes of Israel. So the Danites sent 2
from their clan five of their ablest men,
valiant fellows, from Zorah and Eshtaol, to spy out the land and explore it.
"Go and explore the land," they said
to them.
So they came into the highlands of
Ephraim to the house of Micah, to
spend the night there. As they came 3
near the house of Micah, they recognized the accent of the young Levite.
So they turned aside there, and said to
him,
"Who brought you here; what are
you doing in this place; what is your
business here?"
He said to them, 4
"So and so did Micah do for me. He
hired me, and I became his priest."
"Pray inquire of God," they said to 5
him, "so that we may know whether
the errand on which we are going will
be successful."
The priest said to them, 6
"Go forth to victory; the errand on
which you are going has the LORD'S
approval."
So the five men departed, and com- 7
ing to Laish, they found the people who
were in it living in security, after the
manner of the Sidonians, quiet and unsuspecting; there was no lack of anything in the earth; they were far from
the Sidonians and had no dealings with
Syria.
When the spies came back to their 8
clansmen at Zorah and Eshtaol, their
clansmen said to them,
"How did you get along?"
"Rise," they said, "let us go up 9
against them; for we have seen the land,
and it is surely very fine. And you sit
idle! Do not delay in setting out to go
in and occupy the land; for God is delivering it into your power. When you 10
arrive, you will come upon an unsuspecting people, while the land is extensive, a place where there is no lack of
anything at all that is in the earth."
So there set forth from there, from 11
Zorah and Eshtaol, six hundred men of
the Danite clan, armed with weapons of
war. They went up and encamped at 12

Kirjath-jearim in Judah. That is why
that place is called Mahaneh-dan [the
camp of Dan] to this day; it lies west
13 of Kirjath-jearim. From there they
passed on to the highlands of Ephraim,
and arrived at the house of Micah.
14 Then the five men who had gone to spy
out the land, Laish, spoke up, and said
to their clansmen,

"Do you know that there is an ephod
in these buildings, and teraphim and a
carved image and a molten image? Decide then what you are going to do."

15 So they turned aside there, and came
to the house of the young Levite, Mi-
16 cah's house, and greeted him. While
the six hundred men belonging to the
Danites, armed with their weapons of
war, stood at the entrance of the gate,
17 the five men that had gone to spy out
the land went up; they went inside to
take the carved image, ephod, teraphim, molten image, and priest, while
the six hundred men armed with weapons of war stood at the entrance of the
18 gate. When these went into Micah's
house, and took the carved image,
ephod, teraphim, and molten image,
the priest said to them.

"What are you doing?"

19 "Keep quiet!" they said to him.
"Clap your hand on your mouth, and
go along with us; be father and priest
to us! Is it better for you to be priest
for one man's household, or to be priest
for a whole tribe and clan in Israel?"

20 The priest was elated, and taking
the ephod, teraphim, and carved image, he went along with the people.
21 So they turned and went off, putting
the children, cattle, and goods in front
of them.

22 When they had gone some distance
from Micah's house, the men that were
in the houses near Micah's house were
mustered, and overtook the Danites.
23 They called out to the Danites, who
turned their heads, and said to Micah,

"What ails you, that you are up in
arms?"

24 "You have taken my gods, that I
made," he said, "and the priest, and
have made off! So what have I left?
What a thing to say to me, 'What ails
you?' "

25 The Danites said to him,

"Do not let your voice be heard
among us, lest some hot-tempered fellows fall upon you, and you lose your
life, with the lives of your household."

So the Danites went on their way, 26
and when Micah saw that they were
stronger than he, he turned and went
home.

Thus they took what Micah had 27
made, and the priest that he had,
and coming to Laish, to a people living
quiet and unsuspecting, they put them
to the sword, and burned the city.
There was no one to give any succor; 28
for it was far from Sidon, and they had
no dealings with Syria. It lay in the
valley belonging to Beth-rehob. Then
they rebuilt the city, and settled in it,
calling the name of the city Dan after 29
the name of their ancestor Dan, who
was born to Israel; but Laish was the
name of the city originally. The Dan- 30
ites set up the carved image for themselves, while Jonathan, the son of Gershom, the son of Moses, he and his descendants, were priests to the Danite
tribe down to the time that the ark was
carried off. So they used the carved 31
image, which Micah had made, all the
time that the temple of God stood at
Shiloh.

THE CRIME OF GIBEAH AND ITS CONSEQUENCES TO THE BENJAMINITES, 19:1—21:25

In those days, when there was no
king in Israel, there was a certain Levite, residing as an immigrant in the
distant parts of the highlands of Ephraim, who took to himself a woman from
Bethlehem in Judah as consort. But
his consort became angry with him, and
left him for her father's home at Bethlehem in Judah. When she had been
there some four months, her husband
rose and went after her, to woo her
back, taking with him his servant and
a pair of asses. So she brought him into
her father's house, and when the girl's
father saw him, he greeted him warmly. His father-in-law, the girl's father,
detained him; so he remained with him
three days. Eating and drinking, they
spent their nights there. Then on the
fourth day, when they had risen early
in the morning, he got up to go; but the
girl's father said to his son-in-law,

"Refresh yourself with a bit of food,
after which you may go."

So the two of them again ate and drank together. Then the girl's father said to the man,

"Do consent to stay the night, and enjoy yourself."

The man, however, got up to go; but his father-in-law urged him so strongly that he stayed another night there. On the morning of the fifth day he rose early to go; but the girl's father said,

"Do take some refreshment."

So they passed the time until afternoon, the two of them eating. Then the man got up to go, with his consort and servant; but his father-in-law, the girl's father, said to him,

"See, the day has drawn to its close; do stay the night. Here it is the close of the day; stay the night here, and enjoy yourself. You may rise early tomorrow for your journey, and go home."

However, the man would not stay the night, but got up and left, and reached a point opposite Jebus (that is, Jerusalem), having with him a pair of saddled asses, and his consort as well. As they were near Jebus, with the day far spent, the servant said to his master,

"Come, now, let us turn aside to this city of the Jebusites, and spend the night in it."

But his master said to him,

"We will not turn aside to a city of foreigners, who do not belong to the Israelites; we will go on to Gibeah."

"Come," he said to his servant, "let us reach one of the places, and spend the night in Gibeah or Ramah."

So they passed on and went their way; and the sun went down on them close to Gibeah, which belongs to Benjamin. So they turned aside there to enter and spend the night in Gibeah. When he entered, he sat down in the open square of the city, since no one offered to take them into the house to spend the night. But just then an old man was coming in from his work in the field at evening (now the man belonged to the highlands of Ephraim, and had settled as an immigrant in Gibeah, whereas the men of the place were Benjaminites). When he raised his eyes, he saw the traveler in the open square of the city; so the old man said,

"Where are you going, and where did you come from?"

He said to him, 18
"We are passing from Bethlehem in
Judah to the distant parts of the highlands of Ephraim, where I belong. I
went to Bethlehem in Judah, and I am
now on my way home, but no one offers
to take me into the house, although 19
there is both straw and fodder for our
asses, and also bread and wine for myself and your maidservant and the boy
with your servants, there being no lack
of anything."
"Be at ease!" the old man said. "All 20
your needs shall be solely my care; only
you must not spend the night in the
open."
So he took him home, and gave the 21
asses fodder; and after they had washed
their feet, they ate and drank.
While they were enjoying them- 22
selves, the men of the city, perverted
fellows, surrounded the house; they
kept pounding on the door, and said to
the master of the house, the old man,
"Bring out the man who has come to
your house, that we may have intercourse with him."
But the master of the house went out 23
to them, and said to them,
"No, my friends; please do not be so
depraved. Now that this man has entered my house, do not commit this
carnal deed. Here is my virgin daugh- 24
ter, and his consort; let me bring them
out that you may ravish them, and do
what you like to them; but against this
man you must not commit a deed so
carnal."
The men, however, would not listen 25
to him; so the man seized his consort,
and turned her outdoors to them; and
they had intercourse with her, and
used her wantonly all night until morning, but let her go at the approach of
dawn. As morning broke, the woman 26
came and lay prostrate until daylight
at the doorway of the man's house,
where her master was. When her mas- 27
ter rose in the morning, and opened the
doors of the house to go out and proceed on his way, there was the woman,
his consort, lying at the doorway of the
house with her hands on the threshold!
"Get up," he said to her, "and let 28
us be off!"
But there was none to answer. So
he took her on the ass, and the man
started on his way home. When he 29

reached home he took his knife, and
taking hold of his consort, he cut her
up, limb by limb, into twelve pieces,
and distributed them through all the
30 territory of Israel. He commanded the
men whom he sent, as follows:
"Thus shall you say to all the Israelites: 'Has there ever been such a deed
as this since the time that the Israelites
came up out of Egypt until this day?
Think it over, and speak out.' "

20 Then all the Israelites marched forth,
and the community to a man, from
Dan to Beersheba, along with the land
of Gilead, gathered to the LORD at
2 Mizpeh; and the leaders of all the nation, all the tribes of Israel, took their
stand in the assembly of God's people,
four hundred thousand foot-soldiers,
3 armed with swords. (The Benjaminites
heard that the Israelites had gone up to
Mizpeh.)
"Speak out," said the Israelites;
"how did this crime happen?"
4 The Levite, the husband of the murdered woman, in reply said,
"To Gibeah, which belongs to Benjamin, I came with my consort to spend
5 the night; but the citizens of Gibeah
rose against me, and at night surrounded the house against me. Me they
intended to kill, and my consort they
6 ravished, so that she died. Then I took
hold of my consort, and cutting her in
pieces, I distributed them through all
the country in the possession of Israel;
for they had committed a foul and
7 carnal deed in Israel. Here you all are,
O Israelites; come forward with your
advice and counsel in the matter."
8 Then all the people to a man rose,
saying,
"Not one of us will go home; not one
9 of us will return home; but on the contrary this is what we will do to Gibeah:
we will march against it according to
10 lot; and we will choose ten men from
every hundred belonging to all the
tribes of Israel, and a hundred from
every thousand, and a thousand from
every myriad, to procure provisions for
the army, for those setting forth to requite Gibeah in Benjamin for all the
wantonness which they committed in
Israel."
11 So all the Israelites to a man gathered
to the city in alliance.
12 Then the tribes of Israel sent messengers all through the tribe of Benjamin, saying,
"What a crime is this that has happened among you! Now then, hand
over the perverts in Gibeah that we
may put them to death; and so extir-
pate the crime from Israel."
But the Benjaminites would not accede to the request of their fellow-
Israelites. The Benjaminites gathered
from the cities to Gibeah, to engage in
battle with the Israelites. The Benjaminites mustered at that time from the
cities twenty-six thousand swordsmen,
exclusive of the inhabitants of Gibeah,
seven hundred picked men, that were
left-handed, all of them accustomed to
slinging a stone at a hair without
missing.
The Israelites, exclusive of Benjamin, mustered four hundred thousand
swordsmen, all of them warriors. Then
they proceeded to go up to Bethel to inquire of God.
"Which of us is to be the first to engage in battle with the Benjaminites?"
said the Israelites.
"Judah is to be the first," said the
LORD.
So, when the Israelites rose next
morning, they invested Gibeah. The
Israelites marched out to battle against
the Benjaminites, and the Israelites
drew up in battle array against them
at Gibeah. Then the Benjaminites
marched forth from Gibeah, and felled
to the ground that day twenty-two
thousand of the Israelites. But the
Israelite forces rallied, and again drew
up in battle array at the place where
they had drawn up on the first day.
Then the Israelites went up to Bethel, and wept before the LORD until evening, and inquired of the LORD, saying,
"Shall we again engage in battle with
our kinsmen, the Benjaminites?"
"Attack them," said the LORD.
So the Israelites advanced against
the Benjaminites on the second day;
and Benjamin marched forth from
Gibeah to meet them on the second
day, and again felled to the ground
eighteen thousand of the Israelites, all
of them swordsmen. Then all the Israelites, that is, all the army, went up
and came to Bethel, and weeping, sat
there before the LORD; they fasted
that day until evening, and offered
burnt-offerings and thank-offerings be-

7 fore the LORD. Then the Israelites inquired of the LORD (for the ark of the
covenant of God was there at that time,
8 and Phinehas, the son of Eleazar, the
son of Aaron, was minister to it at that
time), saying,

"Shall we again engage in battle with
our kinsmen, the Benjaminites, or shall
we desist?"

"Attack," said the LORD; "for tomorrow I will deliver them into your
power."

So Israel set men in ambush all
around Gibeah; and the Israelites
marched against the Benjaminites on
the third day, and drew up against
Gibeah as before. Then the Benjaminites sallied forth to meet the army, and
were drawn away from the city. As before, they started out by killing some
of the army on the roads, one of which
runs to Bethel and the other to Gibeah,
about thirty of the Israelites in the
open. So the Benjaminites thought,
"They are being routed before us as at
first"; but the Israelites said,

"Let us flee, and draw them away
from the city to the roads."

Then the main body of the Israelites
moved from their position, and drew up
at Baal-tamar, while the Israelites in
ambush rushed forth from their position, the clearing of Geba. The ten
thousand men, picked from all Israel,
reached a point opposite Gibeah. Then
the battle became furious. Before they
realized that disaster was overtaking
them, the LORD had routed Benjamin
before Israel, so that the Israelites felled
that day twenty-five thousand one hundred of the Benjaminites, all of them
swordsmen. So the Benjaminites saw
that they were defeated. Then the Israelites yielded ground to the Benjaminites; for they relied on the ambuscade that they had set against Gibeah.
The men in ambush rushed headlong
against Gibeah; the men in ambush de-
ployed, and put the whole city to the
sword. The Israelites had an arrangement with the men in ambush that they
should send up a smoke signal from the
city, whereupon the Israelites would
wheel round in the battle. Benjamin
started out by killing about thirty of
the Israelites, so that they thought,
"They are completely routed before us
as in the first battle." As the signal began to rise from the city in a column of
smoke, the Benjaminites looked back,
and there was the whole city going up
to the sky in flames! Then the Israel- 41
ites wheeled round, and the Benjaminites became panic-stricken; for they
saw that disaster had overtaken them.
So they retreated before the Israelites 42
in the direction of the desert; but the
battle pressed them close, and those
from the city were in their midst killing them. They defeated the Benja- 43
minites, and pursued them from Nohah
to a point opposite Geba toward the
east, so that eighteen thousand of the 44
Benjaminites fell, all of them men of
valor. When they retreated, they fled 45
toward the desert to the cliff of Rimmon; but they picked up five thousand
of them on the roads, and followed
hard after them as far as Gidom, killing
two thousand of them. So the total 46
number of Benjaminites who fell that
day was twenty-five thousand swordsmen, all of them men of valor. Six hun- 47
dred men, however, turned, and fled
toward the desert to the cliff of Rimmon, and remained at the cliff of Rimmon for four months. Then the Israel- 48
ites turned their attention to the other
Benjaminites, and put to the sword
both man and beast, and everything
that was to be found; all the cities, too,
that were to be found, they set on fire.

Now the Israelites had sworn at 21
Mizpeh, saying,

"None of us shall give his daughter
in marriage to Benjamin."

The people went to Bethel, and sat 2
there until evening before God, and
lifting up their voices, they wept bitterly, and said,

"Why, O LORD, God of Israel, has 3
this happened in Israel, so that one
tribe today is missing from Israel?"

Next day the people rose early, and 4
building an altar there, they offered
burnt-offerings and thank-offerings.
Then the Israelites said, 5

"Who is there out of all the tribes of
Israel that did not come up in the assembly to the LORD?"

(For a solemn oath had been taken
concerning him who did not come up
to the LORD at Mizpeh, as follows: "He
shall be put to death.")

But the Israelites changed their 6
minds concerning their brother Benjamin, and said,

"One tribe today is cut off from Is-

7 rael. What are we to do about wives for
them, the survivors, seeing that we have
sworn by the LORD not to give them
any of our daughters in marriage?"
8 Then they said,
"What one is there of the tribes of
Israel that did not come up to the
LORD at Mizpeh?"
Now, not one had come to the camp
from Jabesh-gilead, to the assembly.
9 The people were mustered, but not one
of the inhabitants of Jabesh-gilead was
10 there. So the assembly sent twelve
thousand of the bravest men there,
and commanded them, saying,
"Go and put the inhabitants of
Jabesh-gilead to the sword, along with
11 the women and children. This is what
you are to do: every male and every
woman that has had intercourse by lying with a male, you are to destroy, but
you are to spare the virgins."
12 They did so. They found among the
inhabitants of Jabesh-gilead four hundred virgin girls who had not had intercourse with a man by lying with a male;
and they brought them to the camp at
Shiloh, which is in the land of Canaan.
13 Then the whole assembly sent word
to the Benjaminites, that were at the
cliff of Rimmon, proclaiming peace to
14 them. So Benjamin returned at that
time, and they gave them the women
that they had saved alive from the
women of Jabesh-gilead; but even so
there were not enough for them.
15 The people changed their minds concerning Benjamin; for the LORD had
made a breach in the tribes of Israel.
16 The elders of the community said,
"What are we to do about wives for
the survivors; for there are no women
for Benjamin?"
"There must be heirs for the remnant 1
of Benjamin," they said, "that a tribe
may not be blotted out of Israel; and 1
yet we cannot give them wives from our
daughters."
(For the Israelites had sworn, saying,
"Cursed be he who gives a wife to Benjamin.")
So they said, 1
"There is the feast of the LORD held
annually at Shiloh!" (which is north of
Bethel, east of the road running from
Bethel to Shechem, and south of
Lebonah.)
Then they instructed the Benjamin- 2
ites as follows:
"Go and lie in wait in the vineyards,
and watch. Then, when the girls of 2
Shiloh come out to participate in the
dances, rush out of the vineyards and,
each of you catch his wife from the girls
of Shiloh, and be off to the land of Benjamin. If their fathers or kinsmen come 2
to make complaint to us, we will say to
them, 'Forgive them on our account;
for we did not get each of them a wife in
the battle, nor did you give them any;
for then you would be doing wrong.'"
The Benjaminites did so, and took as
many wives as they themselves numbered from the dancers that they carried off. Then they made off, and returning to their own territory, they
built cities, and settled in them. At
that time the Israelites grouped themselves there into their respective tribes
and clans, and then they all left there,
each for his own heritage.
In those days there was no king in Israel; everyone used to do as he pleased.

THE BOOK OF RUTH

THE ANTECEDENTS OF RUTH, 1:1–22

1 IN THE time when the judges were
in power a famine occurred in the
land; so a certain man from Bethlehem in Judah emigrated to the
country of Moab, along with his wife
2 and two sons. The man's name was
Elimelech, his wife's Naomi, and the
names of his two sons Mahlon and Chilion—Ephrathites from Bethlehem in
Judah. So they came to the country of
3 Moab, and remained there. Then Elimelech, the husband of Naomi, died; and
she was left a widow, with her two sons.
4 These married Moabite women, the
name of one being Orpah, and the name
of the other Ruth. They lived there for
about ten years, and then both Mahlon
5 and Chilion died. Then, being bereft of
her two children as well as of her hus-
6 band, the woman, with her daughters-
in-law, prepared to return from the
country of Moab; for she had heard in
the country of Moab that the LORD
had taken note of his people by giving
7 them food. So she left the place where
she was, accompanied by her two daugh-
ters-in-law, and they set out on the
road to return to the land of Judah.
8 But Naomi said to her two daughters-
in-law,

"Go, return each of you to her
mother's house. May the LORD deal as
kindly with you as you have dealt with
the dead and with me! May the LORD
enable you to find a home, each of you,
in the house of her husband!"

Then she kissed them good-bye; but
they lifted up their voices in weeping,
and said to her,

"No, we will go back with you to
your people."

But Naomi said,

"Turn back, my daughters. Why
should you go with me? Have I any
more sons in my womb to become husbands for you? Turn back, my daughters; go your way; for I am too old to
get married. If I should say that I have
hopes both of getting married tonight
and of bearing sons, would you wait for 13
them until they were grown up? Would
you forego marriage for them? No, my
daughters; but I am very sorry for your
sakes that the hand of the LORD has
been raised against me."

Then they lifted up their voices again 14
in weeping, and Orpah kissed her
mother-in-law good-bye, but Ruth
clung to her.

"See," she said, "your sister-in-law 15
has turned back to her own people and
her own gods; turn back after your
sister-in-law."

But Ruth said, 16

"Do not press me to leave you, to
turn back from following you; for
wherever you go, I will go; and wherever
you lodge, I will lodge; your people
shall be my people, and your god my
god; wherever you die, I will die, and 17
there will I be buried. May the LORD
requite me and worse, if even death
separates me from you."

When she saw that she was deter- 18
mined to go with her, she ceased arguing
with her. So the two of them went on 19
until they came to Bethlehem. Upon
their arrival in Bethlehem the whole
city became agitated over them, and
the women said,

"Is this Naomi?"

But she said to them, 20

"Do not call me Naomi [pleasant];
call me Mara [bitter]; for the Almighty
has dealt very bitterly with me. I went 21
away full, but the LORD has brought
me back destitute. Why should you
call me Naomi, seeing that the LORD
has afflicted me, and the Almighty has
brought evil upon me?"

So Naomi returned from the country 22
of Moab, accompanied by her daughter-
in-law, Ruth, the Moabitess. They
reached Bethlehem at the beginning of
the barley harvest.

THE MEETING OF RUTH AND BOAZ, 2:1–23

2 Now Naomi had a kinsman of her
husband, a man of great wealth, belonging to the family of Elimelech,
whose name was Boaz.
2 One day Ruth, the Moabitess, said
to Naomi,
"Let me go to the fields and glean
among the ears of grain after him with
whom I may find favor."
"Go, my daughter," she said to her.
3 So off she went, and came and
gleaned in the fields after the harvesters; and it was her fortune to come
upon the part of the field belonging to
Boaz, who belonged to the family of
4 Elimelech. Just then Boaz himself
came from Bethlehem.
"The LORD be with you!" he said to
the harvesters.
"The LORD bless you!" they replied.
5 "Whose girl is this?" said Boaz to
his overseer in charge of the harvesters.
6 "It is a Moabite girl who came back
with Naomi from the country of
Moab," the overseer in charge of the
7 harvesters answered. "She said, 'Let
me glean, if you please, and gather
among the sheaves after the harvesters.'
So she came, and has remained since
morning until now, without resting
even a little."
8 Then Boaz said to Ruth,
"Now listen, my girl. Do not go to
glean in another field, nor leave this
one, but stay here close by my women.
9 Note the field that they are reaping,
and follow them. Have I not charged
the servants not to molest you? And
when you are thirsty, go to the water
jars, and drink some of what the servants draw."
10 Then she fell on her face, bowing to
the ground, and said to him,
"Why have I found such favor with
you that you should take notice of me,
when I am a foreigner?"
11 Boaz in reply said to her,
"I have been fully informed of all
that you have done for your mother-in-
law since the death of your husband,
and of how you left your father and
mother, and the land of your birth, and
came to a people that you did not know
12 before. May the LORD reward your
conduct, and may you receive full recompense from the LORD, the God of
Israel, under whose wings you have
come for shelter!"
"I thank you, sir," she said; "for you 13
have cheered me, and have spoken com-
fortingly to your maidservant, even
though I do not belong to your maid-
servants."
At mealtime Boaz said to her, 14
"Come here, and eat some of the
bread, and dip your piece in the sour
wine."
So she seated herself beside the
harvesters, and he handed her roasted
grain. She ate until she was satisfied, 15
and had some left over. When she got
up to glean, Boaz gave orders to his
servants,
"Let her glean right among the
sheaves, and do not be rude to her. In- 16
deed pull out some bunches for her, and
leave them for her to glean, and do not
hinder her."
So she gleaned in the field until even- 17
ing; then she beat out what she had
gleaned, and it amounted to about an
ephah of barley. She took it up, and 18
coming into the city, showed her
mother-in-law what she had gleaned.
Then she brought out and gave her what
she had left over after being satisfied.
"Where did you glean today," her 19
mother-in-law said to her. "Where did
you work? Blessed be he who took such
notice of you!"
So she told her mother-in-law with
whom she had worked.
"Boaz is the name of the man with
whom I worked today," she said.
Then Naomi said tc her daughter-in- 20
law,
"Blessed be he of the LORD, whose
goodness has failed neither the living
nor the dead!"
"The man is a relative of ours," Naomi said to her; "he is next after our
next-of-kin."
"Furthermore," said Ruth, the Mo- 21
abitess, "he said to me, 'You must stay
close by my servants until they have
finished all my harvest.'"
"It is best, my daughter," Naomi 22
said to her daughter-in-law, Ruth, "that
you should go out with his women, so
as not to be molested in another field."
So she stayed close by the women 23
working for Boaz, gleaning until the
end of both the barley and wheat harvests; then she returned to her mother-
in-law.

RUTH'S APPEAL TO BOAZ, 3:1–18

3 Then her mother-in-law Naomi said
to her,
"Should I not be seeking a home for
you, my daughter, where you may be
2 comfortable? Now then, what about
our relative Boaz, with whose women
you have been? See, he is going to winnow barley at the threshing-floor to-
3 night. Wash and anoint yourself therefore, put on your best clothes, and go
down to the threshing-floor; but do not
let your presence be known to the man
until he has finished eating and drink-
4 ing. See to it, however, when he lies
down, that you note the place where he
lies; then go in, uncover his feet, and
lie down yourself; he will let you know
what to do."
5 "I will do just as you say," she responded.
6 So she went down to the threshing-
floor, and did just as her mother-in-law
7 had instructed her. Boaz, having eaten
and drunk, had a sense of well-being
and went to lie down at the end of the
straw stack. Then she came in stealthily, uncovered his feet, and lay down.
8 At midnight the man started up, and
turning over, discovered a woman lying
at his feet!
9 "Who are you?" he said.
"I am Ruth, your maidservant," she
said. "Take your maidservant in marriage; for you are next-of-kin."
10 "Blessed be you of the LORD, my
girl!" he said. "This last kindness of
yours is lovelier than the first, in that
you have not run after the young men,
11 either poor or rich. And now, my girl,
have no fear; I will do for you all you
ask; for all the council of my people
know that you are a woman of worth.
12 But now, as matter of fact, I am really
not next-of-kin, since there is another
13 nearer than I who is next-of-kin. Stay
here tonight, and then, in the morning,
if he will do the duty of next-of-kin for
you, good; let him do so; but if he does
not wish to do the duty of next-of-kin
for you, then, as the LORD lives, I will
do so for you. Lie down until morning."
14 So she lay at his feet until morning,
but got up before one could recognize
another; for he said, "It must not be
known that the woman came to the
threshing-floor."
"Bring the mantle which you have 15
on," he said, "and hold it out."
So she held it out, and he poured out
six homers of barley, and put it on her
shoulder; then she went back to the
city, and came to her mother-in-law. 16
"How did you get along, my daughter?" she said.
Then she told her all that the man
had done for her.
"These six homers of barley he gave 17
to me," she said; " 'For,' said he, 'you
must not go back empty-handed to
your mother-in-law.' "
"Wait, my daughter," she said, "until 18
you learn how the matter turns out; for
the man will not rest unless he settles
the matter today."

RUTH'S MARRIAGE TO BOAZ AND THEIR DESCENDANTS, 4:1–22

Meanwhile Boaz went up to the city 4
gate, and sat down there just as the
next-of-kin was passing, of whom Boaz
had spoken.
"Come over and sit down here somewhere," he said.
So he came over and sat down. Then 2
Boaz got ten of the elders of the city,
and said,
"Sit down here."
When they had seated themselves, he 3
said to the next-of-kin,
"Naomi, who has come back from the
country of Moab, is selling the piece of
land which belonged to our relative,
Elimelech; so I thought that I would 4
tell you about it, suggesting that you
buy it in the presence of those who are
sitting here, and in the presence of the
elders of my people. If you will redeem
it, do so; but if you will not redeem it,
then tell me, so that I may know; for
there is no one but you to redeem it,
and I come after you."
"I will redeem it," he said.
Then Boaz said, 5
"At the time that you buy the field
from Naomi, you must also buy Ruth,
the Moabitess, the widow of the deceased, in order to restore the name of
the deceased to his estate."
Then the next-of-kin said, 6
"I cannot redeem it for myself, lest

I ruin my own estate. Use my right of redemption for yourself; for I cannot do so."

7 Now this was the ancient custom in Israel: to validate any transaction in the matter of the right of redemption and its conveyance, the one pulled off his sandal, and gave it to the other; this was the manner of attesting in Israel.
8 Accordingly, when the next-of-kin said
to Boaz, "Buy it for yourself," he drew
9 off his sandal. Then Boaz said to the
elders and all the people,

"You are witnesses today that I am buying from Naomi all that belonged to Elimelech and all that belonged to
10 Chilion and Mahlon. Also Ruth, the
Moabitess, the widow of Mahlon, I am buying to be my wife, in order to restore the name of the dead to his estate, so that the name of the dead may not be cut off from among his relatives nor from the council of his home; you are witnesses today."

11 Whereupon all the people at the gate and the elders said,

"We are witnesses. May the LORD make the woman who is coming into your home like Rachel and Leah, both of whom built up the house of Israel; may you achieve wealth in Ephrath, and gain fame in Bethlehem; and from the offspring that the LORD gives you by this young woman, may you have a house like the house of Perez, whom Tamar bore to Judah!"

So Boaz took Ruth, and she became his wife; he had intercourse with her, and the LORD made her conceive, and she bore a son. Then the women said to Naomi,

"Blessed be the LORD, who has not left you this day without a next-of-kin! May the boy's name become famous in Israel! He shall renew your youth, and be the stay of your old age; for your daughter-in-law, who loves you, has borne him, who herself is more to you than seven sons."

Then Naomi took the child, and laid him in her bosom, and became his nurse; and the women of the neighborhood gave him a name, saying, "A son has been born to Naomi!" So they called his name Obed. He was the father of Jesse, the father of David.

Now this is the genealogy of Perez: Perez was the father of Hezron, Hezron of Ram, Ram of Amminadab, Amminadab of Nahshon, Nahshon of Salmon, Salmon of Boaz, Boaz of Obed, Obed of Jesse, and Jesse of David.

THE FIRST BOOK OF SAMUEL

THE BIRTH AND DEDICATION OF SAMUEL, 1:1–28

NOW there was a certain man of Ramah, a Zuphite of the highlands of Ephraim, whose name was Elkanah, the son of Jeroham, the son of Elihu, the son of Tohu, the son of Zuph, an Ephraimite, and he had two wives; the name of the one was Hannah, and that of the other Peninnah. Peninnah had children, but Hannah went childless.

This man used to go up from his city annually to worship and sacrifice to the LORD of hosts in Shiloh. Now the priests of the LORD there were Eli and his two sons, Hophni and Phinehas. When therefore the accustomed day arrived that Elkanah sacrificed, he used to give portions to Peninnah his wife and to all her sons and daughters, while to Hannah he would give but one portion; however he loved Hannah; but the Lord had made her childless. Her fellow-wife also used to vex her bitterly on account of her misfortune, because the LORD had made her childless. So she did year by year; as often as they went up to the house of the LORD, she used to vex her; therefore she wept and could not eat. Accordingly Elkanah her husband said to her,

"Hannah, why do you weep? Why do you not eat, and why is your heart sad? Am I not dearer to you than ten sons?"

Now Hannah rose up, after they had eaten in Shiloh, and took her stand before the LORD. Meanwhile Eli the priest was sitting upon the seat beside the door-post of the temple of the LORD. She was very wretched and prayed to the LORD, and weeping bitterly, she vowed a vow and said,

"O LORD of hosts, if thou wilt indeed look on the affliction of thy maidservant, and remember me, and not forget thy maidservant, but will give unto thy maidservant a son, then will I give
him to the LORD all the days of his life,
and a razor shall never touch his head."
Now it happened, as she kept on 12
praying for a long time before the
LORD, that Eli's attention was called
to her mouth. But Hannah herself was 13
speaking inwardly; only her lips moved,
while her voice was not heard; accordingly Eli took her to be a drunken
woman. So Eli said to her, 14
"How long will you make yourself a
drunken spectacle? Throw off your
wine from you."
But Hannah answered and said, 15
"Not so, sir. I am an unfortunate
woman, I have drunk neither wine nor
strong drink, but have been pouring out
my heart before the LORD. Count not 16
your maidservant for a base woman;
for out of the abundance of my despair
and vexation have I spoken thus far."
Then Eli answered and said, 17
"Go in peace; and the God of Israel
grant your petition that you have asked
of him."
"Let your maidservant find favor in 18
your eyes," she said.
Then the woman went her way to the
sacrificial chamber, and she ate and
drank with her husband, and her countenance was no more sad.
So they rose up early in the morning, 19
and having prostrated themselves before the LORD, they returned, and came
to their house at Ramah. Then Elkanah sought offspring of Hannah his
wife, and the LORD remembered her,
so that Hannah conceived; and when 20
the time came around, Hannah bore a
son, and called his name Samuel; for
she said,
"I have asked him of the LORD."
Again the man Elkanah and all his 21
house went up to sacrifice the annual
sacrifice to the LORD in Shiloh, and to
keep his vow. But Hannah did not go 22
up; for she said to her husband,
"When the child is weaned, then I
shall bring him, that he may appear in 23
the presence of the LORD, and there
abide forever."

Thereupon Elkanah her husband said
to her,

"Do what seems best to you; remain
until you have weaned him; only the
LORD establish your words."

So the woman remained and nursed
24 her son, until he was weaned; and when
she had weaned him, she took him up
with her, along with a three-year-old
bull and an ephah of meal and a skin of
wine. Thus she came to the house of
the LORD in Shiloh, accompanied by
25 the child; and they slew the bull and
26 Hannah brought the child to Eli, and
said,

"O sir! as surely as you live, sir, I am
the woman that was standing here in
your presence, engaged in prayer unto
27 the LORD. I prayed earnestly for this
boy; and the LORD has given me my re-
28 quest which I asked of him. Therefore
I have dedicated him to the LORD; as
long as he lives he is set apart to the
LORD."

And he worshiped the LORD there.

HANNAH'S SONG OF PRAISE, 2:1–10

2 Then Hannah prayed and said:

"My heart exults in the LORD;
My strength is exalted through my God.
My mouth is enlarged against my foes,
Because I rejoice in thy salvation.

2 "There is none holy like the LORD;
(there is none beside thee);
There is none righteous like our God.

3 "Boast no more so very proudly;
Let not arrogance go forth from your mouth;
For the LORD is a God of knowledge,
And by him actions are accounted.

4 "The bows of the heroes are shattered;
While they that are feeble gird on might.
5 They that were replete have hired out for bread;
While the hungry have ceased to toil.
The barren has borne seven;
While the one rich in children languishes alone.

6 "The LORD slays and makes alive;
He brings down to Sheol and raises up.
The LORD impoverishes, and he makes rich;
He brings low, he also exalts.

"He raises up the poor from the dust;
He exalts the needy from the refuse heap,
To make them sit with the noble,
And inherit a seat of honor;
For the pillars of the earth are the LORD'S,
And he has set the world upon them.

"He will guard the feet of his pious ones;
But the wicked shall be cut off in darkness;
For not by might shall a man prevail.

"The adversaries of the LORD will be dismayed;
Against them will he thunder in heaven.
The LORD will judge the ends of the earth;
And he will give strength to his king,
And exalt the power of his anointed."

So she left him there before the
LORD, and went back to Ramah. Thus
the child began to minister to the LORD
in the presence of Eli the priest.

THE SIN AND DOOM OF THE HOUSE OF ELI, 2:12–36

Now the sons of Eli were unscrupulous men. They did not regard the LORD, nor the rightful dues of the priest from the people. Whenever any man was about to make a sacrifice, an attendant of the priest would come, while the meat was still boiling, and with a three-pronged fork in his hand, he would thrust into the pot, or kettle, or cauldron, or vessel; all that the fork brought up the priest would take for himself. So they used to do to all the Israelites who came there to sacrifice to the LORD in Shiloh. Also, before they burned the fat, the attendant of the priest would come, and say to the man about to sacrifice,

"Give meat to roast for the priest; for he will not accept boiled meat from you, but raw."

Should the man, however, say to him, "They will surely burn the fat first of

all, and then take to your heart's content."
"No, but you shall give it now," he
would say, "and if not, I will surely
take it by force."
17 Thus the sin of the young men was
exceedingly great in the sight of the
LORD; for the men despised the offering of the LORD.
18 Meanwhile Samuel continued to minister in the presence of the LORD, as a
19 lad, girt with a linen apron. Moreover
his mother used to make for him a little
outer garment, and bring it up to him
each year, when she went up with her
husband to offer the annual sacrifice.
20 And Eli would bless Elkanah and his
wife, and would say,
"The LORD reward you with offspring from this woman, because of the
object of her petition which she dedicated to the LORD."
Then they would go to their own
21 home. So the LORD visited Hannah,
and she conceived and bore three sons
and two daughters. Meanwhile the lad
Samuel grew up in the service of the
LORD.
22 Now Eli was exceedingly old; and
when he kept hearing all that his sons
were habitually doing to all Israel, how
they lay with the women who served at
23 the door of the tent of meeting, he said
to them,
"Why do you do according to these
evil rumors which I am constantly hear-
24 ing from all the people? No, my sons;
for the report is not a good one which
I hear the people of the LORD are
25 spreading abroad. If a man sin against
a man, God will mediate for him; but if
a man sin against the LORD, who will
intercede for him?"
But they would not listen to the
voice of their father; for it was the
pleasure of the LORD to destroy them.
26 Now as the child Samuel grew older,
more and more he won the approval
both of the LORD and of men.
27 Now there came a man of God to Eli,
and said to him,
"Thus says the LORD: 'I did indeed
reveal myself to the house of your
father, when they were in Egypt sub-
28 ject to the house of Pharaoh; and I
chose him out of all the tribes of Israel
to be my priest, to go up to my altar, to
burn incense, to wear a priestly apron
before me; and I gave to the house of
your father all the fire offerings of the
Israelites. Why do you look with an 29
envious eye upon my sacrifice and my
offering which I commanded, and honor
your sons above me, by feeding greedily
in my presence upon the choicest of all
the offerings of Israel?' Therefore it is 30
the oracle of the LORD, the God of
Israel, 'I did indeed say that your house
and the house of your father should
prosper before me forever'; but now it
is the oracle of the LORD, 'Far be it
from me; for them that honor me I will
honor, and they that despise me shall
be lightly esteemed. Behold, the days 31
are about to come, when I will cut off
your strength, and the strength of your
father's house, that there shall not be
an old man in your house. You shall 32
also look upon distress, eyeing envious-
ly all the prosperity which I will bestow
on Israel; and there shall not be an old
man in your house forever. That man 33
of you whom I shall not cut off from my
altar shall be left to weep out his eyes,
and to eat out his heart; and all the increase of your house shall die by the
sword of men. This then is to be the 34
sign to you, that shall come upon your
two sons, Hophni and Phinehas: both
of them shall die on the same day. But 35
I will raise up for myself a faithful
priest, who will do according to that
which is in my mind and in my heart;
and I will build for him a sure house,
and he shall continue before my
anointed forever. The time shall also 36
come, when everyone that is left in your
house shall come to supplicate him for a
piece of money or a loaf of bread, and
shall say, "Attach me, I pray, to one of
the priestly offices, that I may not lack
a morsel of bread." ' "

THE CALL OF SAMUEL, 3:1—4:1*a*

The child Samuel was ministering in 3
the presence of the LORD before Eli.
And the word of the LORD was rare in
those days; there was no frequent vision. Now it happened at that time, as 2
Eli was lying down in his place (his eyesight had begun to fail, so that he could
not see), and the lamp of God had not 3
yet gone out, and Samuel was lying
down in the temple of the LORD, where
the ark of God was, that the LORD 4
called,
"Samuel! Samuel!"

"Here I am!" he said.
5 So he ran to Eli, and said,
"Here I am; for you called me."
"I did not call," he said, "go back
and lie down."
6 So he went and lay down. Then the
LORD called once again,
"Samuel! Samuel!"
Again Samuel arose and went to Eli,
and said,
"Here I am; for you called me."
"I did not call, my son," he said, "go
back and lie down."
7 Now Samuel did not yet know the
LORD, neither was the word of the
8 LORD yet revealed to him. So when the
LORD called Samuel again the third
time, he arose and went to Eli, and
said,
"Here I am; for you called me."
9 Then Eli perceived that the LORD
was calling the lad. Therefore Eli said
to Samuel,
"Go, lie down: and it shall be, if he
calls you, you shall say, 'Speak, LORD;
for thy servant hears.'"
So Samuel went and lay down in his
10 place. Then the LORD came, and took
his stand, and called as at other times,
"Samuel! Samuel!"
So Samuel said,
"Speak, for thy servant hears."
11 Then the LORD said to Samuel,
"Behold, I am about to do a thing
in Israel, at which both ears of every-
12 one that hears it will tingle. At that
time I will execute against Eli all that I
have spoken concerning his house, from
13 beginning to end. You shall tell him
that I am about to judge his house forever, for the wrong-doing which he
knew, because his sons were blaspheming God, and he did not rebuke them.
14 Therefore I have sworn to the house of
Eli, that the wrong-doing of Eli's house
shall not be expiated by sacrifice or offering forever."
15 So Samuel lay until morning; then he
rose early in the morning, and opened
the double doors of the house of the
LORD. But Samuel feared to show Eli
16 the vision. Then Eli called Samuel, and
said,
"Samuel, my son."
"Here I am," he said.
17 "What is the thing that he spoke to
you?" he said. "Do not, I beg of you,
hide it from me. May God requite you
and worse, if you hide anything from
me of the whole matter which he spoke
to you."
Then Samuel told him everything, 18
and concealed nothing from him.
"It was the LORD," he said, "let him
do what is good in his sight."
Thus Samuel grew, and the LORD 19
was with him, and he let none of his
words fall to the ground. All Israel 20
from Dan even to Beersheba knew that
Samuel was one accredited as a prophet
of the LORD, since the LORD continued 21
to reveal himself in Shiloh; for the
LORD revealed himself to Samuel. But
Eli was exceedingly old, and his sons
kept right on making their conduct
hateful before the LORD. Thus the 4
word of Samuel came to all Israel.

WARS WITH THE PHILISTINES, 4:1b—7:14

Now it happened in those days, that 1b
the Philistines mustered against Israel
for war; and Israel went out to meet the
Philistines in battle, and encamped at
Ebenezer, while the Philistines encamped in Aphek. Then the Philistines 2
drew up in line of battle to meet Israel;
and when the battle became general
Israel was beaten by the Philistines,
about four thousand men being slain on
the field of battle. So when the people
reached the camp, the older men of
Israel said,
"Why has the LORD put us to rout
today before the Philistines? Let us
take the ark of the covenant of our God
from Shiloh, that it may come into our
midst, and deliver us from the power of
our enemies."
So the people sent to Shiloh; and they
brought from there the ark of the covenant of the LORD of hosts who is seated
upon the cherubim; and the two sons of
Eli, Hophni and Phinehas, were there
with the ark of the covenant of God.
Now when the ark of the covenant of
the LORD reached the camp, all Israel
gave a great cheer, so that the earth re-
echoed. But when the Philistines heard
the noise of the cheering, they said,
"What is the meaning of this great
sound of cheering in the camp of the
Hebrews?"
Then they learned that the ark of the
LORD had arrived at the camp. And
the Philistines were afraid, for they
said,

"The gods have come to them to the
camp."
8 "Alas for us!" they said, "for nothing
like this has happened before. Alas for
us! who shall deliver us from the power
of these majestic gods? These are the
gods that struck down the Egyptians
with every sort of calamity and plague.
9 Strengthen yourselves, and be real men,
O Philistines, lest you become slaves to
the Hebrews, as they have been to you;
be real men and fight."
10 So the Philistines fought, and Israel
was defeated, and they fled in confusion, every man for himself; and the
number killed was very great indeed,
for there fell of Israel thirty thousand
11 footmen. And the ark of God was
taken; and the two sons of Eli, Hophni
and Phinehas, perished.
12 Now a man of Benjamin ran from the
battle line, and came to Shiloh the same
day, with his clothes torn, and with
13 earth upon his head. Just as he arrived,
Eli was sitting on the seat beside the
gate, anxiously watching the road, because he was deeply stirred regarding
the ark of God. Then as the man came
to tell it in the city, all the city was in
14 uproar; and when Eli heard the noise of
the outcry, he said,
"What is this confused noise?"
Then the man came in haste and told
15 Eli. (Now Eli was ninety-eight years
old, and his eyes were set, so that he
16 could not see.) The man said to Eli,
"I am he who came from the camp,
for I fled today from the battle line."
"What has happened, my son?" he
said.
17 He that brought the tidings answered
and said,
"Israel has fled before the Philistines,
and likewise there has been a great
slaughter among the people, and your
two sons also, Hophni and Phinehas,
are dead, and the ark of God has been
taken."
18 Then it was, as he mentioned the ark
of God, that Eli fell from his seat backward through the gate opening; and his
neck was broken and he expired, for the
man was old and heavy. He had judged
Israel forty years.
19 Moreover, his daughter-in-law, the
wife of Phinehas, was about to become
a mother. When she heard the report
in regard to the capture of the ark of
God, and that her father-in-law and her
husband were dead, she reclined and
gave birth; for she was in travail. At 20
about the time of her death the attending women said to her,
"Fear not; for you have borne a son."
Yet she neither answered nor gave
heed. But she named the child Ichabod, 21
saying,
"The glory is departed from Israel."
Because the ark of God was captured
and because of her father-in-law and
her husband, she said, 22
"The glory is departed from Israel;
For the ark of God is taken."
Now the Philistines had captured the 5
ark of God, and taken it from Ebenezer
to Ashdod. The Philistines also took 2
the ark of God, and brought it to the
house of Dagon and set it up by the side
of Dagon. But when the people of Ash- 3
dod arose early the next day and went
to the house of Dagon, they looked and
there was Dagon fallen face downward
upon the ground before the ark of the
LORD. So they lifted up Dagon and restored him to his place. But when they 4
arose early on the morning following,
there was Dagon fallen face downward
upon the ground before the ark of the
LORD; and the head of Dagon and both
the palms of his hands were cut off upon
the threshold, only his body being left.
Therefore neither the priests of Dagon 5
nor any who enter Dagon's house tread
on the threshold of Dagon in Ashdod to
this day, but leap over it.
The hand of the LORD also was heavy 6
upon the Ashdodites, and he ravaged
them, and brought upon them plague-
boils, both upon Ashdod and its borders.
When the men of Ashdod saw that it 7
was so, they said,
"The ark of the God of Israel shall
not remain with us; for his hand is
severe upon us, and upon Dagon our
god."
Accordingly they sent and brought 8
together all the city rulers of the Philistines, and said,
"What shall we do with the ark of the
God of Israel?"
"Let the ark of the God of Israel be
brought around to Gath," they said.
So they brought the ark of the God of 9
Israel around. But after they had
brought it around, the hand of the
LORD was against the city—there was
a very great panic—and he smote the
men of the city, both young and old, so

that plague-boils broke out upon them.
10 Therefore they sent the ark of God to
Ekron. But as soon as the ark of God
came to Ekron, the Ekronites cried out,
saying,
"They have brought around the ark
of the God of Israel to us, to slay us and
our people."
11 They sent therefore and gathered
together all the city rulers of the Philistines, and said,
"Send away the ark of the God of
Israel, and let it return to its own place
and not kill us and our people."
For a deadly panic raged throughout
the entire city; the hand of God was
12 very heavy there. The men who did not
die were stricken with plague-boils; and
the cry of the city for help arose to
heaven.
6 Now the ark of the LORD had been
in the territory of the Philistines seven
2 months, when the Philistines called for
the priests and the diviners, saying,
"What shall we do with the ark of
the LORD? Show us how we shall send
it to its place."
3 "If you are going to send away the
ark of the God of Israel," they said, "do
not send it away empty, but be sure to
return to him a guilt-offering. Then you
will be healed and it shall be made
known to you why his hand is not removed from you."
4 "What should be the guilt-offering
which we should return to him?" they
said.
"Five plague-boils of gold," they
said, "and five golden mice, according
to the number of the city rulers of the
Philistines; for one plague was upon
5 you and upon your city rulers. Therefore you should make images of your
plague-boils and images of your mice
that ravage the land; and give glory to
the God of Israel; perhaps he will relax
the grip of his hand from you and from
6 your gods and from your land. Why
then should you make your minds stubborn, as the Egyptians and Pharaoh
made their minds stubborn? Was it not
after he had flouted them that they let
7 them go, and they departed? Now
therefore take and make ready a new
cart, and two milch cows upon which
there has never been a yoke; and hitch
the cows to the cart, but keep their
8 calves behind them at home. Take the
ark of the LORD and place it in the cart
and put in a box at its side the objects
of gold which you must surely return to
him as a guilt-offering. Then send it off
that it may be on its way. But observe,
if it goes up on the way to its own territory to Bethshemesh, it is he who has
done us this great harm; but if not, then
we shall know that his hand did not
touch us; we simply met with an accident."
Accordingly the men did so, and took
two milch cows and hitched them to the
cart, and shut up their calves in the
house. They put the ark of the LORD
in the cart, and the box with the golden
mice and the images of their plague-
boils. The cows went straight in the
direction of Bethshemesh, keeping to
one highway, and lowing as they went
along. They turned neither to the right
nor the left; and the city rulers of the
Philistines were proceeding along after
them as far as the border of Bethshemesh. Now the inhabitants of Bethshemesh were reaping their wheat harvest in
the valley; and they lifted up their eyes
and saw the ark, and came with rejoicing to meet it. But when the cart came
into the field of Joshua the Bethshemeshite, there it stopped, where there
was a huge stone. So they broke up the
wood of the cart and offered the cows as
a burnt-offering to the LORD. Also the
Levites took down the ark of the LORD
and the box that was beside it, in which
were the golden objects, and set them
upon the great stone; and the men of
Bethshemesh offered burnt-offerings
and sacrificed sacrifices on that day to
the LORD. When the five city rulers of 1
the Philistines saw it, they returned
that day to Ekron.
These are the golden plague-boils
which the Philistines returned as a
guilt-offering to the LORD: one for
Ashdod, one for Gaza, one for Askelon,
one for Gath, one for Ekron. But the
golden mice corresponded to the number of all the cities of the Philistines belonging to the five city rulers, including
both fortified cities and country villages. The great stone also is a witness,
beside which they caused the ark of the
LORD to rest. To this day it is in the
field of Joshua the Bethshemeshite.
The sons of Jechoniah, however, did
not rejoice with the men of Bethshemesh, when they looked upon the ark of
the LORD. Therefore he smote among

them seventy men (fifty thousand men)
and the people mourned because the
LORD had made a great slaughter
20 among the people. Therefore the men
of Bethshemesh said,
"Who is able to stand before the
LORD, this holy God? And to whom
shall he go up from us?"
21 Then they sent messengers to the inhabitants of Kirjath-jearim, saying,
"The Philistines have brought back
the ark of the LORD. Come down and
take it up to you."
7 Accordingly the men of Kirjath-
jearim came and took up the ark of the
LORD, and brought it into the house of
Abinadab on the hill, and he consecrated Eleazar his son to have charge
2 of the ark of the LORD. So from the
day that the ark found lodgment in
Kirjath-jearim, the time ran on, and it
was twenty years.
Moreover all the house of Israel
3 sought after the LORD. Then Samuel
spoke to all the house of Israel, saying,
"If with all your heart you are turning to the LORD, put away the foreign
gods and the Ashtarts from your midst,
and direct your attention toward the
LORD and serve him alone that he may
deliver you out of the hand of the Philistines."
4 So the Israelites put away the Baals
and the Ashtarts, and served the LORD
alone.
5 Accordingly Samuel said,
"Assemble all Israel at Mizpeh that
I may intercede on your behalf with the
LORD."
6 So they assembled at Mizpeh, and
drew water and poured it out before the
LORD, and fasted on that day, saying,
"We have sinned against the LORD."
Samuel also judged the Israelites in
7 Mizpeh; and when the Philistines heard
that the Israelites were assembled together at Mizpeh, the city rulers of the
Philistines went up against Israel. But
when the Israelites heard of it, they
were afraid of the Philistines.
8 Then the Israelites said to Samuel,
"Cease not to cry out to the LORD
our God for us, that he may save us
from the power of the Philistines."
9 Accordingly Samuel took a sucking
lamb and offered it as a burnt-offering
to the LORD. Samuel also cried out to
the LORD in behalf of Israel, and the
10 LORD answered him; for just as Samuel
was offering the burnt-offering, the Philistines came on for an attack upon
Israel; but the LORD thundered with a
mighty voice that day against the Philistines, and threw them into confusion
and they were overcome before Israel.
Whereupon the men of Israel went forth 11
from Mizpeh and pursued the Philistines and harassed them until they
were below Bethcar.
Then Samuel took a stone and set it 12
between Mizpeh and Yeshana and
called its name Ebenezer, for he said,
"Hitherto the LORD has helped us."
Thus the Philistines were humbled 13
and came no more into the territory of
Israel. The hand of the LORD was
against the Philistines all the days of
Samuel. Also the cities which the Phi- 14
listines had taken from Israel were restored to Israel, from Ekron even to
Gath; and Israel rescued their territory
from the power of the Philistines. Thus
there was peace between Israel and the
Amorites.

THE CHOICE OF SAUL AS KING, 7:15—12:25

Now Samuel judged Israel all the 15
days of his life. He used to go around 16
as often as once a year in succession to
Bethel, Gilgal, and Mizpeh; and he
used to judge Israel in all these places.
The end of his circuit was Ramah, for 17
there was his home; there too he judged
Israel; and he built there an altar for
the LORD.
But as Samuel grew old, he estab- 8
lished his sons as judges over Israel.
The name of his eldest son was Joel, 2
and that of his second, Abijah; they
were judges in Beersheba. However, 3
his sons did not follow his example, but
became grasping for gain by methods
of violence and received bribes and perverted justice.
Then all the elders of Israel gathered 4
together and came to Samuel at Ramah,
and they said to him, 5
"Consider, you have become old and
your sons do not follow in your footsteps. Now set up for us a king to judge
us like all the nations."
But the thing was evil in the sight of 6
Samuel, when they said,
"Give us a king to judge us."
Nevertheless Samuel prayed earnest-

7 ly unto the LORD; and the LORD said
to Samuel,
"Listen to the voice of the people according to all that they say to you; for
they have not rejected you, but they
have rejected me from being king over
8 them. Like all the deeds which they
have done to me from the day I brought
them up from Egypt even to this day,
inasmuch as they have forsaken me and
served other gods, so they are also doing
9 to you. Now therefore listen to their
utterance, except that you shall certainly warn them, and show them the
procedure of the king who shall reign
over them."
10 Then Samuel told all the words of the
LORD to the people who were asking of
11 him a king; and he said,
"This will be the procedure of the
king who shall reign over you: he will
take your sons and appoint them for
himself for his chariots and for his
horsemen; and they shall run before his
12 chariots; and he will appoint for himself commanders of thousands and commanders of hundreds, and some to do
his plowing and to reap his harvests and
make his implements of war and the
13 equipment for his chariots. He will
take your daughters for perfumers, for
14 cooks, and for bakers. He will take the
best of your fields and your vineyards
and your olive orchards, and give them
15 to his servants. He will take the tenth
of your grain crops and of your vineyards and give it to his eunuchs and to
16 his servants. He will take your male
and female slaves, and the best of your
cattle and your asses, and make use of
17 them for his work. He will take a tenth
of your flocks; and you yourselves will
18 become his slaves. Then you will cry
out on that day because of your king
whom you will have chosen for yourselves; but the LORD will not answer
you on that day."
19 But the people refused to listen to the
voice of Samuel, and said,
20 "No but there shall be a king over
us, that we also may be like all the nations, and that our king may judge us
and go forth before us and fight our
battles."
21 When Samuel had heard all the words
of the people, he repeated them in the
22 presence of the LORD. Then the LORD
said to Samuel,

"Listen to their appeal and make
them a king."
Samuel then said to the men of Israel,
"Go every man to his city."
Now there was a man of Benjamin, 9
whose name was Kish, the son of Abiel,
the son of Zeror, the son of Becorath,
the son of Aphiah, a Benjaminite, a
well-to-do person; and he had a son 2
whose name was Saul, a handsome
young man; and there was not a man
among the Israelites more handsome
than he. From his shoulders and up-
wards, he was taller than any of the
people.
Now the she-asses of Kish, Saul's 3
father, were lost. Accordingly Kish
said to Saul his son,
"Take now one of the lads with you
and arise, go and seek the she-asses."
So they passed through the highlands 4
of Ephraim and the land of Shalisha,
but they did not find them. Then they
passed through the land of Shaalim, but
they were not there. They also passed
through the land of the South, but did
not find them. As they came into the 5
land of Zuph, Saul said to his servant
who was with him,
"Come, let us go back, lest my father
cease to be concerned for the asses and
become anxious for us."
But he said to him,
"See now, there is a man of God in 6
this city, and the man is held in honor;
all that he speaks is sure to prove true.
Now let us go there; perhaps he can tell
us of our mission on which we have
started."
Then Saul said to his servant, 7
"Very well, suppose we go, but what
shall we offer to the man? for the provisions are used up from our sacks, and
there is no present to offer to the man
of God. What have we?"
The lad answered Saul again, and 8
said,
"See, there is in my possession a
fourth of a shekel of silver, and you
shall give it to the man of God that he
may inform us regarding our mission."
(Formerly, in Israel, when a man 9
went to inquire of God, thus he said,
"Come, let us go to the seer";
for he who is now called a prophet was
earlier called a seer.)
Then Saul said to his servant, 10
"Your advice is good; come, let us
go."

So they went to the city where the
man of God was.
11 As they were going up the ascent to
the city, they met maidens going forth
to draw water and said to them,
"Is there a seer here?"
12 They answered them and said,
"There is; he is directly before you.
He has just now come to the city; for
the people have a sacrifice today on the
13 high place. As you come to the city,
you may find him at once before he goes
up to the high place to eat; for the
people will not eat until he arrives, for
he is accustomed to bless the sacrifice;
afterward the invited guests eat. Now
therefore go up; for you may immediately meet him."
14 So they went up to the city. They
were just about to enter the city, when,
behold, Samuel was already coming out
toward them, to go up to the high place.
15 Now the day before Saul came, the
LORD had communicated to Samuel
the following message:
16 "About this time tomorrow I will
send you a man out of the land of
Benjamin and you shall anoint him to
be a leader of my people Israel. He
shall deliver my people from the power
of the Philistines; for I have seen the
affliction of my people and their cry has
come to me."
17 Thus when Samuel saw Saul, the
LORD indicated to him,
"Behold the man of whom I spoke to
you! He it is who shall bear rule over
my people."
18 Then Saul approached Samuel in the
gate, and said,
"Pray tell me, where is the house of
the seer?"
19 Samuel answered Saul and said,
"I am the seer; go up before me to
the high place, for you shall eat with
me today; and in the morning I will
gladly further your journey, and tell
20 you all that is on your mind. As for
your asses that were lost three days ago,
dismiss them from your mind, for they
have been found. For whom is all that
is desirable in Israel reserved? Is it not
for you and for your father's house?"
21 But Saul answered and said,
"Am I not a Benjaminite, from the
smallest of the tribes of Israel, and is
not my family the least of all the families of the tribe of Benjamin? Why
then have you spoken to me after this
manner?"
But Samuel took Saul and his servant 22
and brought them to the sacred hall and
gave them a place at the head of the
guests, who were about thirty persons.
Samuel also said to the cook, 23
"Bring the portion I gave you, which
I told you to put aside."
Accordingly the cook took up the leg 24
and the fat tail and set them before
Saul. Then Samuel said,
"Behold that which was reserved to
set before you! Eat! for it was being
kept for you until the appointed time,
before I invited the people."
So Saul ate with Samuel that day.
Now after they came down from the 25
high place into the city, they spread a
bed for Saul upon the roof, and he retired. Then at dawn Samuel called to 26
Saul on the roof, saying,
"Up, that I may further your journey."
So Saul arose, and he and Samuel
went out into the street. As they were 27
going down near the city limits, Samuel
said to Saul,
"Tell the servant to pass on before
us (and he passed on), but do you halt
at this point that I may make known to
you the word of God."
Then Samuel took a vial of oil, and 10
poured it on his head, and kissed him
and said,
"Has not the LORD anointed you to
be a leader over his people Israel? You
shall rule over the people of the LORD
and deliver them from the power of
their enemies round about; and this
shall be the sign that the LORD has
anointed you to be a leader over his
heritage: when you go from me today 2
you will find two men at Rachel's tomb,
in the territory of Benjamin at Zelzah;
and they will say to you, 'The asses
which you went to seek are found, and
now your father has dismissed the matter of the asses only to become anxious
about you, saying, "What shall I do regarding my son?"' Then you shall 3
hasten on from there until you come to
the oak of Tabor; and there three men
going up to God to Bethel will meet
you, one carrying three kids, and
another carrying three loaves of bread,
and another carrying a skin of wine.
They will greet you and give you two 4
loaves of bread which you shall take

5 from their hands. Afterward you will
come to the hill of God, where there is a
Philistine post; and furthermore when
you come there to the city, you will
meet a band of prophets coming down
from the high place with a lyre, a tambourine, a flute, and a harp before
them; and they will be prophesying
6 ecstatically. Then the spirit of the
LORD shall suddenly seize upon you,
and you shall prophesy ecstatically
with them and you shall be changed
7 into another man. When these signs
come to you, do as the occasion de-
8 mands; for God is with you. You shall
go down before me to Gilgal; and behold, I shall be coming down to you, to
offer burnt-offerings and to sacrifice
thank-offerings. Wait seven days until
I come to you and show you what you
shall do."

9 Accordingly when he turned about to
leave Samuel, God gave him another
heart, and all these signs took place
10 that day. When they came there to the
hill, behold, a band of prophets met
him; and the spirit of God suddenly
seized upon him, and he prophesied
11 ecstatically among them. When all his
former acquaintances saw that he really
prophesied with the prophets, the
people said to one another,

"What is this that has happened to
the son of Kish? Is Saul also among the
prophets?"

12 A bystander answered and said,
"But who is their father?"
Therefore it became a proverb,
"Is Saul also among the prophets?"

13 Now when he had finished prophesying, he went home.

14 Saul's uncle also said to him and to
his servant,

"Where have you been?"

"To seek the asses," he said, "and
when we saw that they were not to be
found, we went to Samuel."

15 Then Saul's uncle said,

"Tell me, I pray, what Samuel said
to you."

16 So Saul said to his uncle,

"He told us emphatically that the
asses were found."

But the matter of the kingdom, of
which Samuel had spoken, he did not
mention to him.

17 Thereafter Samuel summoned the
18 people unto the LORD to Mizpeh; and
he said to the Israelites,

"Thus says the LORD the God of
Israel: 'I brought up Israel out of
Egypt, and I delivered you from the
power of the Egyptians, and from the
power of all the kingdoms that were oppressing you. But you yourselves have 1
this day despised your God, who himself is your savior from all your calamities and your distresses, and you
have said, "No, but a king you shall set
over us." Now therefore take your
stand before the LORD by your tribes
and by your thousands.'"

Then Samuel caused all the tribes of 2
Israel to approach, and the tribe of
Benjamin was taken. He caused the 2
tribe of Benjamin to approach by its
clans, and the clan of the Matrites was
taken; and he caused the clan of the
Matrites to approach man by man, and
Saul, the son of Kish, was taken; but
when they sought him, he could not be
found. Therefore they asked of the 2
LORD further,

"Did the man come hither?"

And the Lord said,

"Behold, he has hidden himself
among the baggage."

So they ran and brought him from 2
there; and as he took his stand in the
midst of the people, he was taller than
any of the people from his shoulders
upward. So Samuel said to all the 2
people,

"Do you see him whom the LORD
has chosen? for there is not his peer
among all the people."

Then all the people gave a mighty
shout and said,

"Long live the king!"

Samuel also described to the people 2
the nature of the kingdom; and wrote
it in a book, and laid it up before the
LORD. Thereupon Samuel sent all the
people away, each one to his own home.
Saul also went to his home at Gibeah; 2
and there went with him some brave
men whose hearts the LORD had
touched. But there were some worth- 2
less individuals who said,

"How shall this man save us?"

Thus they despised him, and brought
him no present.

Now it happened after about a
month that Nahash the Ammonite
went up and besieged Jabesh-gilead;
and all the men of Jabesh said to Nahash,

"Make a treaty with us and we will serve you."

But Nahash the Ammonite said to them,

"On this condition will I make terms with you: that I gouge out the right eye of every one of you, thereby making it a reproach against all Israel."

But the elders of Jabesh said to him,

"Give us seven days respite, that we may send messengers through all the territory of Israel. Then if there should be none to save us we will come out to you."

Thus the messengers came to Gibeah of Saul and stated these things in the hearing of the people, and all the people raised a cry of lamentation, just as Saul was coming from the field behind the oxen; and Saul said,

"What is the trouble with the people that they are weeping?"

Then they related to him the words of the men of Jabesh; and the spirit of the LORD suddenly seized upon Saul when he heard these words, and he became violently enraged. So he took a yoke of oxen, and cut them in pieces, and dispatched them throughout all the territory of Israel by the hand of messengers, saying,

"Whoever does not come forth after Saul and after Samuel, so shall it be done to his oxen."

Then a terror from the LORD fell upon the people, and they rallied with one accord. Thus he mustered them in Bezek; and the Israelites were three hundred thousand, and the men of Judah thirty thousand. Then he said to the messengers who came,

"Thus shall you say to the men of Jabesh-gilead: 'Tomorrow, by the time the sun is hot, deliverance shall come to you.' "

So the messengers went and told the men of Jabesh, and they were glad. Therefore the men of Jabesh said,

"Tomorrow we will come out to you, and you may do to us whatever you please."

Accordingly on the day following, Saul divided the people into three contingents; and they came into the midst of the camp at the morning watch, and they fought the Ammonites until the heat of the day, even until those who remained scattered, so that no two of them were left together.

Then the people said to Samuel, 12
"Who is he that says, 'Saul shall not
reign over us?' Bring the men that
we may put them to death."
"There shall not a man be put to 13
death today," said Saul, "for today the
LORD has brought about deliverance
in Israel."
Then Samuel said to the people, 14
"Come, and let us go to Gilgal and
renew there the kingdom."
So all the people went to Gilgal, and 15
there Samuel anointed Saul king before
the LORD in Gilgal; and there they
sacrificed thank-offerings before the
LORD; and there Samuel and all the
men of Israel held a great celebration.
Then Samuel said to all Israel, **12**
"See, I have yielded to your plea in
all that you have said to me and have
appointed a king over you. Behold 2
now the king who is to go out and in
before you; but as for me, I am old and
gray, and my sons are here with you;
and I have conducted myself before
you from my youth unto this day. Here 3
I stand; testify against me before the
LORD, and before his anointed: whose
ox have I taken, or whose ass have I
taken, or whom have I oppressed?
Whom have I defrauded, or from whose
hand have I taken a ransom, or a pair
of sandals? Testify against me and I
will restore it to you."
"You have not oppressed us," they 4
said, "or defrauded us, nor have you
taken anything from anyone's hand."
Therefore he said to them, 5
"The LORD is witness against you,
and his anointed is witness this day,
that you have found nothing in my
hand."
"He is witness," they said.
Then Samuel said to the people, 6
"The LORD is witness, who appointed Moses and Aaron and who brought
your fathers up out of the land of
Egypt. Now therefore take your stand 7
that I may enter into court with you
before the LORD and let me declare to
you all the righteous acts of the LORD,
which he did to you and to your fathers. When Jacob went to Egypt, and 8
the Egyptians afflicted them, your fathers cried to the LORD, and the LORD
sent Moses and Aaron, and they
brought your fathers out of Egypt, and
he made them dwell in this place. But 9
they forgot the LORD their God, and he

sold them into the hand of Sisera, commander of the army of Hazor, and into
the hand of the Philistines, and into the
hand of the king of Moab; and they
10 fought against them. Then they cried
to the LORD and said, 'We have sinned
because we have forsaken the Lord and
served the Baals and the Ashtarts.
But now deliver us out of the hand of
our enemies, and we will serve thee.'
11 So the LORD sent Jerubbaal, and Barak, and Jephthah, and Samson, and
delivered you out of the hand of your
enemies round about you so that you
12 dwelt in safety. And you saw that
Nahash, king of the Ammonites, came
against you. Accordingly you said to
me, 'No, but a king shall reign over us,'
although the LORD your God was your
king.
13 "Now therefore see the king whom
you have chosen and whom you have
requested; for the LORD has now set a
14 king over you. If you will fear the
LORD and serve him and listen to his
voice, and not rebel against the command of the LORD, and both you and
the king who reigns over you follow the
15 LORD your God, it is well. But if you
will not listen to the voice of the LORD,
but rebel against the command of the
LORD, then shall the hand of the
LORD be against you and your king to
16 destroy you. Now therefore take your
stand and see this great thing which
the LORD is about to do before your
17 eyes. Is it not wheat harvest today? I
will call upon the LORD to send thunder and rain; and you shall know and
see that your wickedness is great,
which you have done in the sight of the
LORD in asking for yourselves a king."
18 So Samuel called upon the LORD,
and the LORD sent thunder and rain
that day; and all the people were greatly afraid of the LORD and Samuel.
19 Then all the people said to Samuel,
"Intercede with the LORD your God
in behalf of your servants that we die
not; for we have added to all our sins
the wickedness of asking for ourselves
a king."
20 But Samuel said to the people,
"Fear not; you have indeed done all
this evil, yet do not turn aside from following the LORD, but serve the LORD
21 with all your heart; and do not turn
aside after vain things which cannot
22 profit or deliver; for they are vain. For
the LORD because of his great name will not cast away his people; for the LORD has undertaken to make you a people for himself. Moreover, as for me, far be it from me that I should sin against the LORD in ceasing to intercede on your behalf; but I will instruct you in the good and the right way. Only fear the LORD and serve him in truth with all your heart, for see what a great thing he has done in your presence. But if you persist in wrong-doing, both you and your king shall be swept away."

THE REJECTION OF KING SAUL, 13:1–18

Saul was . . . . . years old when he began to reign; and he reigned . . . . . years over Israel. Now Saul chose for himself three thousand men of Israel: two thousand were with Saul in Michmash and on the mountain of Bethel, and a thousand were with Jonathan his son in Gibeah of Benjamin. But the rest of the people he had sent away, each to his home. Now Jonathan overcame the garrison of the Philistines that was in Gibeah. Thus the Philistines heard the report: the Hebrews have revolted. But Saul had meantime sent the trumpet call throughout all the land; and all Israel heard the report that Saul had smitten the garrison of the Philistines, and also that Israel was now in bad odor with the Philistines. Accordingly the people were summoned after Saul to Gilgal. Likewise the Philistines were gathered together to fight with Israel, three thousand chariots and six thousand horsemen, and people as numerous as the sand which is on the seashore; and they came up, and encamped in Michmash, on the east side of Bethaven. When the men of Israel saw that they were in jeopardy (for the people were at their wits' end), the people hid themselves in caves, in thickets, in rocky crags, in caverns, and in pits. They also crossed the fords of the Jordan to the land of Gad and Gilead; but Saul was still in Gilgal, and all the people were on the point of desertion. Thus he waited seven days according to the appointed time which Samuel had said; but Samuel did not come to Gilgal, and the peo-

ple were scattering from him. Therefore Saul said,
"Bring here to me the burnt-offering
and the thank-offerings."
So he offered the burnt-offering. Then
just as he finished offering the burnt-
offering, Samuel came; and Saul went
out to welcome him. But Samuel said,
"What have you done?"
Then Saul said,
"Because I saw that the people were
scattering from me and you did not
come within the appointed time, and
the Philistines were gathering at
Michmash, I said, 'Now the Philistines
will come down against me at Gilgal,
and I shall not have appeased the
LORD.' So I forced myself and offered
the burnt-offering."
Then Samuel said to Saul,
"You have acted foolishly, in that
you have not kept the command of the
LORD your God, which he commanded
you; for now would the LORD have
established your kingdom over Israel
forever. But now your kingdom shall
not continue. The LORD has sought
out a man after his own heart, and the
LORD has appointed him a leader over
his people, because you have not kept
that which the LORD commanded you."
Then Samuel arose and went up
from Gilgal and proceeded on his way;
and the rest of the people went up after
Saul to meet the men of war, and they
went from Gilgal to Gibeah of Benjamin. Saul also numbered the people
that were left with him, about six hundred men. Thus Saul and Jonathan his
son, together with the people that remained with them, were staying in
Gibeah of Benjamin, while the Philistines encamped in Michmash. Meanwhile raiders went out of the camp of
the Philistines in three detachments, one
detachment turning in the direction of
Ophrah in the land of Shual, and another detachment turning in the direction of Beth-horon, and another detachment turning in the direction of the
hill that looks down over the valley of
Zeboim toward the desert.

WAR WITH THE PHILISTINES, 13:19—14:52

Now there was no smith found
throughout all the land of Israel, for
the Philistines said,
"Lest the Hebrews make sword or
spear."
But all the Israelites went down to 20
the Philistines to sharpen each his
plowpoint and his coulter and his ax
and his mattock; and the price for the 21
plowpoints and the coulters was a pim
and a third of a shekel for the axes and
for setting the goads. Accordingly on 22
the day of Michmash neither sword nor
spear was found in the possession of all
the people who were with Saul and
Jonathan; but Saul and Jonathan his
son had them.
Now an outpost of the Philistines 23
was advanced to the pass of Michmash.
Thus it happened one day that Jona- 14
than, the son of Saul, said to the youth
who bore his armor,
"Come, let us go over to the post
of the Philistines, that is on the other
side yonder."
But he did not tell his father. Now 2
Saul was tarrying in the outskirts of
Gibeah, under the pomegranate tree
which is by the threshing-floor, and the
people who were with him were about
six hundred men; and Ahijah, the son 3
of Ahitub, Ichabod's brother, the son
of Phinehas, and son of Eli, the priest
of the LORD at Shiloh, was in charge of
an ephod. The people also did not
know that Jonathan had gone. Now 4
between the passes by which Jonathan
sought to go over to the Philistine post
there was a sharp crag on the one side,
and a sharp crag on the other side; and
the name of the one was Bozez and the
name of the other Seneh. The one crag 5
was on the north in front of Michmash,
and the other on the south in front of
Geba. Then Jonathan said to the 6
young man who bore his armor,
"Come, let us go over to the post of
these uncircumcised Philistines; perchance the LORD will act on our behalf, for with the LORD there is no
limitation to deliver by many or by
few."
Accordingly his armor-bearer said 7
to him,
"Do whatever your judgment determines; see, I am with you; your in-
clination is mine."
Then Jonathan said, 8
"See, we are going to pass over to the
men and show ourselves to them. If 9
they say to us, 'Halt, until we can

reach you,' then we will remain where
we are, and will not go up to them.
10 But if they say thus, 'Come up to us,'
then we will go up; for the LORD has
given them into our hand; and this
shall be the sign to us."
11 Now when they both showed themselves to the Philistine post, the Philistines said,
"Look! Hebrews are coming out of
the holes where they have hidden themselves."
12 So the men of the post hailed Jonathan and his armor-bearer, saying,
"Come up to us, we have something
to tell you."
Then Jonathan said to his armor-
bearer,
"Come up after me; for the LORD
has given them into the hand of
Israel."
13 Thereupcn Jonathan scrambled up
on his hands and feet, and his armor-
bearer after him. But they turned back
at the approach of Jonathan and he
attacked them, and his armor-bearer
was despatching the wounded after
him, with arrows, with slingstones, and
14 with stones of the field. That first
slaughter, which Jonathan and his
armor-bearer made, amounted to about
twenty men, part from the post and
15 part from the field. There was also terror in the camp, in the field, and
among all the people; the garrison and
even the raiders trembled; and the
earth quaked so that it became a terror
inspired of God.
16 The watchmen of Saul in Gibeah of
Benjamin looked and behold the camp
17 melted away hither and thither. Then
Saul said to the people who were with
him,
"Investigate now and see who is
gone from among us."
When they had investigated, behold,
Jonathan and his armor-bearer were
18 not there. Then Saul said to Ahijah,
"Bring the ephod here."
For at that time he was intrusted
with the ephod before the Israelites.
19 But while Saul was still speaking to the
priest, the tumult in the camp of the
Philistines kept on increasing. Therefore Saul said to the priest,
"Withdraw your hand."
20 Thereupon Saul and all the people
who were with him rallied, and came to
the battle, and now every man's sword
was against his fellow in wild confusion. Those Hebrews too who had thus
far been with the Philistines, who had
gone up with them into the camp, even
these turned to be with the Israelites
who were with Saul and Jonathan.
Likewise all the men of Israel who were
in hiding in the highlands of Ephraim,
when they heard that the Philistines
had fled, also pursued after them in the
battle. So the LORD saved Israel that
day, and the battle passed beyond
Beth-horon. All the people with Saul
were about ten thousand men; and the
fighting was scattered over the entire
highlands of Ephraim. But Saul committed a grave error that day, for he
put the people under oath, saying,
"Cursed be the man who shall eat
food until evening and I avenge myself
on my enemies."
So none of the people tasted food.
Now there was comb honey in the
fields; and when the people came to
the honeycomb, the bees had just
flown away; but no one put his hand to
his mouth, for the people feared the
oath. But Jonathan had not heard
when his father adjured the people;
therefore he put forth the end of the
staff that was in his hand and dipped it
in the honeycomb and put his hand to
his mouth, and his eyes brightened.
Then up spoke one of the people, and
said,
"Your father strictly adjured the
people saying, 'Cursed be the man who
eats food today.' "
But the people were faint. Then said
Jonathan, "My father has perturbed
the land. See, now, how my eyes brightened because I tasted a little of this
honey. The more, then, if the people
had eaten freely today of the spoil of
their enemies which they found, would
there have been a great slaughter among
the Philistines."
Nevertheless they fought the Philistines that day from Michmash to Aijalon, and the people were exceedingly
faint. Then the people flung themselves upon the spoil, and took sheep
and oxen and calves, and slew them on
the ground, and the people were eating
them with the blood. When they told
Saul, saying,
"See, the people are sinning against
the LORD in eating with the blood,"
he said,

"You have dealt treacherously; roll hither to me a great stone."

Saul also said,

"Disperse yourselves among the people and say to them, 'Let each man bring to me his ox and his sheep, and slay it here and eat; but do not sin against the LORD by eating the flesh together with the blood.' "

Accordingly all the people brought that night, each what he had in his possession, and slew them there. So Saul built an altar unto the LORD: that marked the beginning of his building of altars to the LORD.

"Let us go down after the Philistines by night," said Saul, "and plunder among them until dawn, and let us not leave a man of them."

"Do whatever you deem best," they said.

But the priest said,

"Let us here draw near to God."

So Saul asked of God,

"Shall I go down after the Philistines? Wilt thou deliver them into the hand of Israel?"

But he did not answer him that day. Then Saul said,

"Draw near here, all you chiefs of the people, and find out and see wherein was this sin today. For as the LORD lives, who delivers Israel, though it be in Jonathan my son, he shall surely die."

But no one of all the people answerd him. Then he said to all Israel,

"You shall be on one side, and I and Jonathan my son will be on the other side."

Then the people said to Saul,

"Do as it seems good to you."

Therefore Saul said,

"O LORD, God of Israel, why hast thou not answered thy servant this day? If the guilt be in me or in Jonathan my son, O LORD, God of Israel, give Urim: but if it be in thy people Israel, give Thummim."

Then Jonathan and Saul were taken and the people escaped.

"Cast the lot between me and Jonathan my son," said Saul. "He whom the LORD shall take, must die."

"It shall not be so!" the people said.

But Saul overruled the people and they cast the lot between him and Jonathan his son; and Jonathan was taken.

Then Saul said to Jonathan, 43
"Tell me what you have done."
So Jonathan told him, saying,
"I did indeed taste a little honey
with the end of the staff that was in my
hand; here I am, ready to die."
"May God requite me and worse; 44
you shall surely die, Jonathan," said
Saul.
But the people said to Saul, 45
"Shall Jonathan die who has brought
about this great deliverance in Israel?
Far from it! As the LORD lives, there
shall not a hair of his head fall to the
ground; for he has worked with God
this day."
Therefore the people ransomed Jonathan, so that he did not die. Then 46
Saul went up from pursuing the Philistines; and the Philistines went to their
own place.
Now when Saul had taken the king- 47
dom over Israel, he fought against all
his enemies on every side: against
Moab and the Ammonites, and Edom
and Beth-rehob, the king of Zobah, and
the Philistines; and wherever he
turned he was successful. He acted 48
vigorously and conquered the Amalekites and delivered Israel out of the
hands of its plunderers.
Now the sons of Saul were Jona- 49
than, Ishbaal, and Malchishua; and
these were the names of his two daughters: the name of the eldest was Merab,
and that of the youngest, Michal. The 50
name of Saul's wife was Ahinoam, the
daughter of Ahimaaz. The name of the
commander of his army was Abner, the
son of Ner, Saul's cousin; and Kish, the 51
father of Saul, and Ner, the father of
Abner, were the sons of Abiel.
But the war against the Philistines 52
was severe all the days of Saul. Therefore whenever Saul saw any valiant or
outstanding man, he would attach him
to himself.

A RAID UPON THE AMALEKITES, 15:1–35

Now Samuel said to Saul, 15
"The LORD sent me to anoint you to
be king over his people Israel. Now
then listen to the words of the LORD.
Thus says the LORD of hosts: 'I will 2
punish Amalek for what he did to Israel, in that he opposed him on the

way, when he came up out of Egypt.
3 Now go and attack Amalek and utterly
destroy him and all that he has, and
spare him not, but slaughter both man
and woman, child and infant, ox and
sheep, camel and ass.' "
4 So Saul summoned the people and
mustered them in Telaim, two hundred
thousand footmen and ten thousand
5 men of Judah. Accordingly when Saul
came to the city of Amalek, he laid an
6 ambush in the valley. But Saul said to
the Kenites,
"Come, withdraw, come down from
among the Amalekites, lest I destroy
you with them; for you showed kindness to the Israelites when they came
up from Egypt."
So the Kenites departed from among
7 the Amalekites. Then Saul overcame
the Amalekites from Havilah as far as
Shur, which is contiguous to Egypt;
8 and he took Agag, the king of Amalek,
alive and completely destroyed all the
9 people with the sword. But Saul and
the people spared Agag and the best of
the sheep, the oxen, the fatlings, the
lambs, and all that was good, and were
not willing utterly to destroy them;
but everything that was vile and despised, that they completely destroyed.
10 Then the word of the LORD came to
Samuel, saying,
11 "I repent that I have made Saul
king; for he has turned from following
me and has not carried out my commands."
12 Thereupon Samuel was angry and
cried to the LORD all night. In the
morning Samuel rose early to meet
Saul; and it was told Samuel, saying,
"Saul came to Carmel and behold,
he has set up a trophy for himself, and
has turned and passed on and gone
down to Gilgal."
13 When Samuel came to Saul, Saul
said to him,
"Blessed be you of the LORD! I
have fulfilled the command of the
LORD."
14 "What then is this bleating of sheep
in my ears and the lowing of cattle
which I hear?" said Samuel.
15 "They have brought them from the
Amalekites," said Saul, "for the people
spared the best of the sheep and the
oxen to sacrifice to the LORD your
God; and the rest we have completely
destroyed."

"Desist! and let me tell you what the LORD spoke to me last night," said Samuel to Saul.

"Declare it," he said to him.

"Though you are insignificant in your own eyes," said Samuel, "are you not the head of the tribes of Israel? The LORD anointed you king over Israel, and the LORD sent you on a mission and said, 'Go and completely wipe out the sinners, the Amalekites, and fight against them until you have consumed them.' Why then did you not obey the voice of the LORD and why did you fling yourselves upon the spoil and do that which was evil in the sight of the LORD?"

"I have obeyed the voice of the LORD," said Saul to Samuel, "and have gone on the mission upon which the LORD sent me and have brought back Agag, king of the Amalekites, and have completely destroyed the Amalekites. But the people took some of the spoil, sheep and cattle, the best of that which was put under the ban, to sacrifice to the LORD your God in Gilgal."

But Samuel said,

"Does the LORD delight in burnt-offerings and sacrifices
As much as in obedience to the voice of the LORD?
Behold, to obey is better than sacrifice,
And to hearken, than the fat of rams.
For the sin of divination is rebellion,
And the iniquity of the teraphim is arrogance.
Because you have rejected the word of the LORD,
He has rejected you from being king."

Then Saul said to Samuel,

"I have sinned; for I have transgressed the command of the LORD and your words, because I feared the people and listened to their voice. Now therefore pardon my sin and turn back with me, that I may worship the LORD."

But Samuel said to Saul,

"I will not turn back with you; for you have rejected the word of the LORD and the LORD has rejected you from being king over Israel."

As Samuel turned to go, Saul seized the skirt of his outer garment, and it tore. Then Samuel said to him,

"Today the LORD has torn the kingdom of Israel from you and given it to your neighbor who is better than you. Moreover the Glory of Israel will not lie nor repent; for he is not a man that he should repent."

"I have sinned," he said, "yet honor me now before the elders of my people and before Israel, and return with me, that I may worship the LORD your God."

So Samuel turned back after Saul, while Saul worshiped the LORD.

"Bring to me here Agag, the king of the Amalekites," said Samuel.

Then Agag came to him trembling; and Agag said,

"Surely death is bitter."

"As your sword has bereaved women," said Samuel, "so shall your mother be the most bereaved of women."

Thereupon Samuel hewed Agag in pieces before the LORD in Gilgal. Then Samuel went to Ramah, but Saul went up to his house to Gibeah of Saul. So Samuel saw Saul no more until the day of his death, for Samuel grieved over Saul. Moreover the LORD repented that he had made Saul king over Israel.

THE ANOINTING OF DAVID AS KING, 16:1–13

Now the LORD said to Samuel,

"How long will you grieve over Saul, since I have rejected him from being king over Israel? Fill your horn with oil and go. I will send you to Jesse the Bethlehemite; for I have discovered for myself a king among his sons."

"How can I go," said Samuel, "since Saul will hear of it and kill me?"

Accordingly the LORD said,

"You shall take a young heifer with you and say, 'I have come to sacrifice to the LORD.' You shall invite Jesse to the sacrifice, and I will show you what you shall do, and you shall anoint for me him whom I indicate to you."

Samuel did that which the LORD had commanded; and when he came to Bethlehem, the elders of the city came trembling to meet him and said,

"Is your coming peaceable?"

"Yes, I have come to sacrifice to the LORD," he said. "Purify yourselves and rejoice with me today."

Then he purified Jesse and his sons and invited them to the sacrifice.
When they came and he saw Eliab, he 6
said,

"Surely the LORD's anointed is before him."

But the LORD said to Samuel, 7
"Do not look at his appearance or the height of his stature, since I have rejected him; for the LORD does not see as man sees, for man looks on the outward appearance, but the LORD looks at the heart."

Then Jesse called Abinadab, and 8
presented him before Samuel.

"Neither has the LORD chosen this one," he said.

Then Jesse presented Shammah. 9
But he said,

"Neither has the LORD chosen this one."

Then Jesse presented his seven sons 10
before Samuel. But Samuel said to Jesse,

"The LORD has not chosen these."

"Are these all the young men?" 11
Samuel said to Jesse.

"There is still the youngest," he said, "but just now he is shepherding the flock."

"Send and bring him," said Samuel, "for we will not sit down until he arrives."

So he sent and brought him in. Now 12
he was ruddy, a youth with beautiful eyes and attractive appearance. Then the LORD said,

"Arise, anoint him, for this is he."

Then Samuel took the horn of oil and 13
anointed him in the midst of his brothers, and the spirit of the LORD seized upon David from that day forward. Then Samuel arose and went to Ramah.

DAVID AS SAUL'S MUSICIAN, 16:14–23

Now the spirit of the LORD had de- 14
parted from Saul and an evil spirit
from the LORD terrified him. So the 15
servants of Saul said to him,

"See now, an evil spirit from the
LORD is terrorizing you. Let now 16
your servants who are before you speak: let them seek for our lord a man skilful in playing the lyre. Then whenever the evil spirit comes upon you he will play with his hand, and you will be well."

17 Accordingly Saul said to his servants,
"Provide me now with a man who
plays well, and bring him to me."
18 Thereupon one of the young men answered and said,
"Behold, I have seen a son of Jesse the Bethlehemite who is skilful in playing and a man of unusual power, a warrior, judicious in speech, a distinguished looking man, and the LORD is with him."
19 Therefore Saul sent messengers to Jesse and said,
"Send me David your son, who is with the flock."
20 Then Jesse took ten loaves of bread,
a skin of wine, and a kid, and sent them
21 to Saul by David his son. So David
came to Saul and became his personal
attendant; and he greatly loved him, so
much so that he became one of his
22 armor-bearers. Wherefore Saul sent to
Jesse, saying,
"Let David now stand in my presence, for he has found favor in my sight."
23 So whenever the evil spirit from God came upon Saul, David would take the lyre and play with his hand, and Saul would be relieved and feel restored and the evil spirit would depart from him.

DAVID SLAYS GOLIATH, 17:1–58

17 Now the Philistines mustered their
armed forces for war, and they were
gathered together at Socoh, which belongs to Judah, and they encamped
between Socoh and Azekah, in Ephes-
2 dammim. Saul and the men of Israel
were gathered together and encamped
in the valley of Elah; and they drew up
in line of battle facing the Philistines.
3 The Philistines were stationed on the
mountain on one side, and the Israelites were stationed on the mountain on
the other side, and the valley was be-
4 tween them. Then there came out a
champion from the camp of the Philistines, named Goliath of Gath, whose
5 height was six cubits and a span. He
had a helmet of bronze upon his head,
and he was clad with a coat of mail of
bronze scales, whose weight was about
6 five thousand shekels. He had greaves
of bronze upon his legs and a javelin of
7 bronze between his shoulders. The
shaft of his spear was like a weaver's beam, and the head of his iron spear weighed six hundred shekels; and his shield-bearer went before him.

He stood and shouted to the battle-line of Israel and said to them,

"Why have you come out to draw up the line of battle? Am I not a Philistine and you the servants of Saul? Choose for yourselves a man and let him come down to me. If he is able to fight with me and can kill me, then we will be your servants; but if I overcome him and kill him, then you shall be our servants and serve us."

"I challenge the ranks of Israel this day," said the Philistine, "give me a man that we may fight together."

When Saul and all Israel heard the words of the Philistine, they were terrified and panic-stricken.

Now David was the son of an Ephrathite of Bethlehem in Judah, whose name was Jesse, who had eight sons. The man was old in the days of Saul, well advanced in years. The three eldest sons of Jesse had gone after Saul to the war; and the names of these three sons who went to the war were Eliab the eldest, the second Abinadab, and the third Shammah. But David was the youngest. The three eldest had followed Saul; but David went to and fro from Saul to feed his father's sheep at Bethlehem.

So the Philistine drew near morning and evening and took his stand for forty days. Then Jesse said to David his son,

"Take now for your brothers an ephah of this parched grain and these ten loaves and take them quickly to the camp to your brothers. But bring these ten cheeses to the captain of the thousand, and look into the welfare of your brothers and take assurance of them."

Now Saul and they and all the men of Israel were in the valley of Elah fighting with the Philistines.

So David rose up early in the morning and left the flock with a keeper and took and went, as Jesse had commanded him. He came to the intrenchment just as the army was going forth to the battle-line, raising the shout of battle. Israel and the Philistines drew up the battle-lines facing each other. Then David left his supplies in care of the keeper of the baggage and ran to the battle-line and came and greeted his brothers. While he was talking with them, the champion, the Philistine of Gath, Goliath by name, was seen coming up from the Philistine lines and he spoke the same words as before; and David heard them. Then all the men of Israel, when they saw the man, fled from him and were panic-stricken. The men of Israel said,

"Have you seen this man who comes up? Surely to taunt Israel he comes up. Whoever overcomes him, the king will make very rich and will give him his daughter and make his father's house free in Israel."

Then said David to the men standing by him,

"What shall be done for the man who overcomes yonder Philistine and takes away the reproach of Israel? For who is this uncircumcised Philistine, that he should taunt the battle-lines of the living God?"

The people replied to him according to the above words, saying,

"Thus shall it be done to the man who overcomes him."

Now Eliab, his eldest brother, heard when he spoke to the men; and Eliab's anger blazed against David, and he said,

"Why now have you come down? With whom have you left those few sheep in the desert? I know your insolence, and the wickedness of your heart; for you have come down to look at the battle."

"What have I now done?" said David. "Is there not a cause?"

And turning away from him to another, he spoke as before; and the people returned answer as at the first. Now when the words which David spoke were heard, they reported them to Saul; and they took him and brought him before Saul.

Then David said to Saul,

"Let not my lord's courage fail him; your servant will go and fight with this Philistine."

"You are not able to go against this Philistine to fight with him," said Saul to David, "for you are but a youth and he has been a warrior from his youth."

But David said to Saul,

"Your servant has been a shepherd with his father's flock; and when a lion
or a bear would come and take a sheep
out of the flock, I would go out after 35
him and attack him and deliver it from
his mouth; and if he rose up against
me, I would seize him by his beard and
wound him and kill him. Your servant 36
has slain both lion and bear; and this
uncircumcised Philistine shall be as one
of them, since he has taunted the battle-lines of the living God."

"The LORD who delivered me from 37
the paw of the lion, and from the paw
of the bear, will deliver me from the
hand of this Philistine," said David.

So Saul said to David,

"Go, and may the LORD be with you."

Saul clothed David with his gar- 38
ments, and put a helmet of bronze on
his head, and equipped him with a coat
of mail. He also girded David with his 39
sword over his outer garments; and he
struggled in vain to go, for he had not
tried them.

"I cannot go with these, for I have not tried them," said David to Saul.

So David put them off him.

But he took his stick in his hand, and 40
chose five smooth stones out of the
brook and put them in his bag, and
with his sling in his hand he advanced
toward the Philistine. The Philistine 41
began cautiously to approach David,
having the bearer of his shield directly
in front of him; and when the Philistine 42
looked about and saw David, he
scorned him; for he was youthful and
ruddy, and of attractive appearance.

"Am I a dog that you come to me 43
with sticks?" said the Philistine to
David.

The Philistine also cursed David by 44
his gods; and the Philistine said to
David,

"Come to me and I will give your flesh to the birds of the air and to the beasts of the field."

Then David said to the Philistine, 45

"You come to me with a sword and a
spear and a javelin,
But I come to you in the name of the
LORD of hosts,
The God of the battle-lines of Israel
whom you have taunted.
This day the LORD will deliver you 46
into my hand,
That I may slay you and sever your
head from your body;

And I will this day give your dead body and the dead of the camp of the Philistines
To the birds of the air and to the wild beasts of the earth,
That all the earth may know that there is a God in Israel,
47 And that all this assembly may know
That not with sword and spear does the LORD deliver;
For the battle is the LORD'S and he will give you into our hands."

48 Now when the Philistine arose and
came and drew near to meet David,
David also hastened and ran toward
49 the line to meet the Philistine. David
put his hand in his bag and took from
it a stone and slung it and it struck the
Philistine on his forehead; and the
stone sank into his forehead, so that he
50 fell on his face to the earth. So David
overpowered the Philistine with a sling
and a stone, and he struck the Philistine, and slew him, although there was
51 no sword in David's hand. Then David
ran and stood over the Philistine, and
took his sword, and drew it out of its
sheath, and slew him, and cut off his
head with it.

Now when the Philistines saw that
their champion was dead, they fled;
52 and the men of Israel and Judah arose
and raised a shout and pursued the
Philistines to the entrance to Gath and
the gates of Ekron, so that the wounded
of the Philistines fell down on the way
from Shaaraim, even to Gath and
53 Ekron. When the Israelites returned
from pursuing the Philistines, they
54 plundered their camp, but David took
the head of the Philistine and brought
it to Jerusalem; and he put his armor
in his tent.

55 When Saul saw David going out
against the Philistine, he said to Abner,
the commander of the army,

"Whose son is this lad, Abner?"

56 "As you live, O king, I do not
know," said Abner.

"Inquire whose son the youth is,"
said the king.

57 When David returned from slaying
the Philistine, Abner took him, and
brought him before Saul with the Philis-
58 tine's head in his hand; and Saul said
to him,

"Whose son are you, my lad?"

"The son of your servant Jesse, the
Bethlehemite," said David.

SAUL'S JEALOUSY OF DAVID, 18:1—20:42

Now when he had finished speaking with Saul, the soul of Jonathan was knit to the soul of David, and Jonathan loved him as himself. Saul took him at that time and would not allow him to return to his father's house; and Jonathan made a covenant with David, because he loved him as his own life. Jonathan also stripped off the cloak which he had on and gave it to David and his equipment, even to his sword, his bow, and his girdle. So David went out; wherever Saul sent him he had good success, so that Saul appointed him over the fighting forces. He was well pleasing in the estimation of all the people and in the estimation of the servants of Saul.

Accordingly when they came back, as David returned from fighting the Philistine, the women came dancing out of all the cities of Israel, to meet David, with tambourines, with rejoicing, and with sistrums. The women sang as they played, and said,

"Saul has slain his thousands,
But David his ten thousands."

Then Saul was very angry, and this saying displeased him and he said,

"They have ascribed to David the ten thousands, while to me they have ascribed but the thousands, and what more can he have but the kingdom?"

So Saul kept his eye on David from that day forward.

On the next day the evil spirit from God seized upon Saul, and he was filled with prophetic frenzy within the house, while David was playing with his hand as he did each day. Now Saul had his spear in his hand; and Saul lifted up his spear, saying,

"I will pin David to the wall."

But David escaped from his presence twice.

Saul was afraid of David because the LORD was with him and had departed from Saul. Therefore Saul removed him from him, and made him his commander of a thousand; and he went out and came in before the people. David had good success in all his undertakings, for the LORD was with him. So when Saul saw that he exercised very good judgment, he stood in dread of him. But all Israel and Judah loved

David; for he went out and came in before the people.
Then Saul said to David,
"Here is my eldest daughter, Merab,
I am ready to give her to you in marriage; only be zealous for me and fight
the battles of the LORD."
For Saul said,
"Let not my hand be upon him, but
let the hand of the Philistines be upon
him."
18 David said to Saul,
"Who am I, and who are my kinsfolk
in Israel, that I should be the king's
son-in-law?"
19 But when the time came that Merab,
Saul's daughter, should have been giv-
en to David, she was given as wife to
Adriel, the Meholathite.
20 However, Michal, Saul's daughter,
loved David; and when they told Saul,
the thing was agreeable to him.
21 "I will give her to him, that she may
be a snare to him and that the hand of
the Philistines may be upon him," said
Saul.
Therefore Saul said to David,
"You shall this day be my son-in-
law."
22 So Saul commanded his servants as
follows:
"Communicate with David secretly
and say, 'You see, the king is pleased
with you and all his servants love you;
now therefore make yourself the king's
son-in-law.'"
23 The servants of Saul spoke these
words in the ears of David.
"Is it an easy thing in your estimation to make one's self the king's son-in-
law, and I a poor man and of humble
station?" said David.
24 So Saul's servants told him, saying,
"David spoke according to these
words."
25 Then Saul said,
"Thus shall you say to David: 'The
king desires no dowry, but a hundred
foreskins of the Philistines, in order to
take vengeance on the king's enemies.'"
Now Saul thought to make David
fall by the hand of the Philistines.
26 When his servants told David these
words, David was well pleased to become the king's son-in-law. The days
27 had not expired; so David arose and
went, and he together with his men
slew of the Philistines one hundred
men; and David brought their foreskins and gave them in full to the king,
in order to make himself the king's son-
in-law. Accordingly Saul gave him Michal, his daughter, as wife. But when 28
Saul saw and realized that the LORD
was with David and that all Israel
loved him, Saul was still more afraid of 29
David. Thus Saul remained permanently hostile to David. At times the 30
princes of the Philistines went forth;
and as often as they went forth, David
had better success than all the servants
of Saul, so that his name was very
highly esteemed.
Saul spoke to Jonathan his son and 19
to all his servants that they should put
David to death. But Jonathan, Saul's 2
son, was exceedingly fond of David. So
Jonathan told David, saying,
"Saul my father is plotting to kill
you; now therefore, I pray you, be on
your guard in the morning and remain
out of sight and keep yourself hidden.
I will go out and stand beside my fa- 3
ther in the field where you are, and I
will speak about you to my father, and
whatever I discover I will tell you."
Accordingly Jonathan spoke well of 4
David to Saul his father, and said to
him,
"Let not the king sin against his servant David, because he has not sinned
against you and his behavior toward
you has been very praiseworthy; for he 5
took his life in his hand and overcame
the Philistine, and the LORD brought
about a great deliverance for all Israel.
You saw it and rejoiced. Why then will
you sin against innocent blood, by slaying David without a cause?"
So Saul listened to the appeal of 6
Jonathan; and Saul took oath,
"As the LORD lives, he shall not be
put to death."
Then Jonathan called David, and 7
Jonathan told him all these words; and
Jonathan brought David to Saul, so
that he was again in his presence as
formerly. Thus when there was again 8
war, David went out and fought
against the Philistines, and overcame
them with great slaughter, so that they
fled before him. Then an evil spirit 9
from the LORD was upon Saul, while he
was sitting in his house with his spear
in his hand, and David was playing
with his hand; and Saul tried to pin 10
David to the wall with his spear, but he

slipped away out of Saul's presence, so
that he drove the spear into the wall,
and David fled and escaped.
11 That night Saul sent messengers to
David's house to watch him, in order to
slay him in the morning. But Michal,
his wife, informed David saying,
"If you do not make your escape tonight, tomorrow you will be a corpse."
12 So Michal let David down through a
window; and he stole away and es-
13 caped. Michal then took the teraphim
and laid it in the bed, and put a quilt
of goat's hair at its head and covered
14 it with a garment. And when Saul sent
messengers to take David, she said,
"He is sick."
15 Then Saul sent the messengers to see
David, saying,
"Bring him up to me in the bed, that
I may put him to death."
16 But when the messengers entered, behold, there was the teraphim in the bed,
with a quilt of goat's hair at its head.
17 So Saul said to Michal,
"Why have you deceived me thus,
and let my enemy go, so that he has
escaped?"
Michal said to Saul,
"He said to me, 'Let me go; why
should I kill you?' "
18 Now David fled and escaped and
came to Samuel at Ramah and told him
all that Saul had done to him. Then he
and Samuel went and stayed in Naioth.
19 Accordingly when it was told Saul,
saying,
"David is there at Naioth in Ramah,"
20 Saul sent messengers to take David.
But when they saw an assemblage of
prophets prophesying with Samuel
standing as head over them, the spirit
of God came upon the messengers of
Saul, so that they also prophesied.
21 When they told Saul, he sent other
messengers, and they also prophesied
ecstatically. Saul sent messengers
again the third time, and they also
22 prophesied ecstatically. Then Saul's
anger was aroused and he himself went
to Ramah. When he came to the cistern of the threshing floor, which is on
the bare height, he asked and said,
"Where are Samuel and David?"
"You will find him at Naioth in Ramah," they said.
23 But when he went from there to
Naioth in Ramah, the spirit of God
came upon him also, and as he went
along he prophesied ecstatically, until
he came to Naioth in Ramah. He even
stripped off his clothes, and he also
prophesied ecstatically before Samuel,
and fell down and lay naked all that
day and all night. Therefore they say,
"Is Saul also among the prophets?"
Then David fled from Naioth in
Ramah.
Moreover he came and said before
Jonathan,
"What have I done; what is my guilt;
and what is my sin before your father,
that he is seeking my life?"
He said to him,
"Far from it! You shall not die. Now
my father does nothing great or small,
but that he discloses it to me; and why
should my father hide this thing from
me? Not so."
David replied and said,
"Your father well knows that I have
found favor in your eyes, and he has
said to himself, 'Let not Jonathan know
this lest he be pained.' Nevertheless as
surely as the LORD lives, and as you
live, there is but a step between me and
death."
Then Jonathan said to David,
"What do you desire that I do for
you?"
So David said to Jonathan,
"Behold, tomorrow is the new moon
and I should indeed sit at table with the
king; but let me go and I will hide myself in the field until evening. If your
father does indeed miss me, then say,
'David urgently asked leave of me to
run to his city Bethlehem; for the annual sacrifice is there for the whole
family.' If he says, 'Good,' then it is
well with your servant, but if it really
stirs up his anger, then know that evil is
determined upon by him. Now deal
kindly with your servant, for you have
brought your servant into a covenant
of the LORD with yourself; but if there
be guilt in me, slay me yourself, for why
should you bring me thus to your
father?"
"Far be it from you!" said Jonathan,
"for if I should indeed learn that my
father had determined that evil should
come upon you, would I not tell you
that?"
Then David said to Jonathan,
"Who will tell me, if your father answers you harshly?"
So Jonathan said to David,

"Come, and let us go out to the
field."
So the two of them went out to the
field.
12 Then Jonathan said to David,
"The LORD, the God of Israel be witness, that I will sound my father at this
time tomorrow [or the third day], and
if he be well disposed to David, then
will I not send to you and disclose it to
13 you? May the LORD requite Jonathan
and worse, if my father be pleased to
do you harm and I disclose it not to
you, and send you away that you may
go in peace. May the LORD be with
14 you as he has been with my father. But
O may you, if I am still alive, O may
you show me the kindness of the LORD!
15 But if I should die, may you never cut
off your kindness from my house. When
the LORD cuts off the enemies of
David, everyone from the face of the
16 ground, the name of Jonathan shall not
be cut off from the house of David, and
may the LORD require it at the hand of
David's enemies."
17 So Jonathan took oath again to
David because of his love to him; for
he loved him as his own life.
18 Then Jonathan said to him,
"Tomorrow is the new moon and you
will be missed, because your seat will be
19 empty; and on the third day you will
be greatly missed. Then you shall come
to the place where you hid yourself on
the day of the affair, and you shall sit
20 down there beside that stone heap. On
the third day I will shoot to its side with
arrows, as though I shot at a mark.
21 Then I will send a lad, (saying), 'Go,
find the arrows.' If I say explicitly to
the lad, 'See, the arrows are on this side
of you; get them!'—then come; for it is
well for you, and, as the LORD lives,
22 there is nothing the matter. But if I
say thus to the youth, 'See, the arrows
are beyond you,' go, for the LORD has
23 sent you away. As for the word which
we have spoken, you and I, behold, the
LORD is between you and me forever."
24 So David hid himself in the field; and
when it was new moon, the king sat at
25 table to eat. The king sat upon his seat
as usual, even on the seat by the wall,
and Jonathan sat opposite, and Abner
sat by Saul's side; but David's place
26 was empty. Nevertheless Saul did not
remark anything that day, for he
thought,

"It is an accident; he is not ceremonially clean, for he has not been cleansed."
But when on the morrow of the new 27
moon, even on the second day, David's
place was empty, Saul said to Jonathan
his son,
"Why has not the son of Jesse come
to the meal, either yesterday or today?"
So Jonathan answered Saul, 28
"David urgently asked leave of me
to go to Bethlehem, for he said, 'Let me 29
go, I pray you, since our family has a
sacrifice in the city; and my brothers
have commanded me. Now if I have
found favor in your sight, let me slip
away, I pray you, and see my brothers.'
Therefore he has not come to the king's
table."
Then Saul's anger blazed against 30
Jonathan, and he said to him,
"Son of a renegade girl! Do I not
know that you are attached to the son
of Jesse to your own shame and to the
shame of your mother's nakedness?
For as long as the son of Jesse lives on 31
the ground, neither you nor your kingdom will be established. Therefore now
send and bring him to me, for he is condemned to die."
Then Jonathan answered Saul his 32
father and said to him,
"Why should he be put to death?
What has he done?"
But Saul lifted up his spear at him to 33
strike him. So Jonathan knew that his
father had determined to put David to
death. Therefore Jonathan rose from 34
the table in fierce anger and ate no food
on the second day of the month, for he
was grieved for David, because his
father had vilified him. But in the 35
morning Jonathan went out to the field
at the time agreed with David, accompanied by a small boy. He said to 36
his lad,
"Run, find now the arrows that I am
about to shoot."
Then as the lad ran, he shot an arrow
beyond him; and when the boy came to 37
the location of the arrow which Jonathan had shot, Jonathan called after
the lad, and said,
"Is not the arrow beyond you?"
Again Jonathan called after the boy, 38
"Make haste, be quick, do not stand
still!"
So Jonathan's lad gathered up the
arrows, and brought them to his mas-

39 ter. But the lad did not perceive anything; only David and Jonathan under-
40 stood the matter. Then Jonathan gave
his weapons to the lad who was with
him, and said to him,
"Go, take them to the city."
41 The lad departed, whereupon David
arose from beside the stone heap, and
fell on his face to the ground and prostrated himself three times; and they
kissed each other and wept together
42 profusely. Then Jonathan said to David,
"Go in peace! inasmuch as we two
have sworn in the name of the LORD, saying, 'The LORD will be between me and you and between my descendants and your descendants forever.' "

Then David rose and departed, while Jonathan went into the city.

DAVID IN FLIGHT FROM SAUL, 21:1—24:22

21 Thereupon David came to Nob, to
Ahimelech the priest. But Ahimelech came trembling to meet David and said to him,
"Why are you alone and no one with you?"
2 Then David said to Ahimelech the
priest,
"The king has charged me with a matter and has said to me, 'Let no one know anything about the mission upon which I am sending you and which I have commanded you; and I have appointed the young men to such and
3 such a place.' Now what is there in
your possession? Five loaves of bread? Give them, or whatever can be found, into my hand."
4 The priest answered David and said,
"There is no ordinary bread in my possession, but there is holy bread, if only the young men have kept them-selves from women."
5 David answered the priest and said,
"Of a truth women have been kept from us; as usual when I set out, the weapons of the young men are ceremonially cleansed, even though it be an ordinary journey; how much more then today shall their weapons be holy!"
6 So the priest gave him holy bread; for
there was no bread there but the Presence-bread, that was taken from before the LORD in order to put hot bread there the day it was taken away. Now one of the servants of Saul was there that day, detained before the LORD, whose name was Doeg, an Edomite, the chief of Saul's shepherds. David then said to Ahimelech,

"Is there not here in your possession a spear or a sword? for I brought neither my sword nor my equipment with me, because the king's business required haste."

"The sword of Goliath the Philistine, whom you slew in the valley of Elah, see, it is wrapped in a garment behind the ephod," said the priest. "If you wish to take that, take it, for there is no other except that here."

"There is none like it, give it to me," said David.

Then David arose and fled that day 1
from before Saul, and went to Achish,
the king of Gath. Whereupon the serv- 1
ants of Achish said to him,
"Is not this David, the king of the land? Was it not of him that they used to sing responsively in the dances, saying,
'Saul has slain his thousands,
But David his ten thousands?' "
Now David took these words to heart 1
and was greatly afraid of Achish, the
king of Gath. So he disguised his sanity 1
before them, and pretended to be mad in their hands and drummed on the doors of the gate and let his spittle run
down on his beard. Then Achish said 1
to his servants,
"Truly you look upon a man de-
mented; why do you bring him to me?
Do I lack madmen that you have 1
brought this wretch to act the madman in my presence? Should this fellow come to my house?"
So David departed from there and 2
escaped to the cave of Adullam. Now when his brothers and all his father's clan heard it, they went down there to
him. There were also drawn together 2
to him everyone that was in distress, and everyone who was in debt, and everyone who was embittered, and he became their leader. There were thus with him about four hundred men.
David then went forth from there to 3
Mizpeh of Moab; and he said to the king of Moab,
"I pray you, let my father and my mother dwell with you, until I know what God will do for me."

So he left them in the presence of the king of Moab; and they remained with him all the time that David was in the stronghold. Then Gad the prophet said to David,

"Do not remain in Mizpeh; but go and enter the land of Judah."

So David went and entered the forest of Hereth.

Now when Saul heard that David and the men who were with him were discovered (Saul was sitting in Gibeah under a tamarisk tree on the high place, with his spear in his hand, and all his servants were standing about him), Saul said to his servants who were standing about him,

"Hear now O Benjaminites! Will the son of Jesse also give to everyone of you fields and vineyards? Will he make you all commanders of thousands and commanders of hundreds, that all of you have conspired against me, and there is no one that discloses to me when my son makes a covenant with the son of Jesse, and none of you sympathizes with me, or discloses to me that my son has incited my servant against me as an enemy, as it is this day?"

Then Doeg the Edomite, who was appointed over the servants of Saul, answered and said,

"I saw the son of Jesse as he came to Nob, to Ahimelech, the son of Ahitub. He inquired of God for him and gave him provisions and the sword of Goliath the Philistine."

Then the king sent a summons to Ahimelech, the son of Ahitub the priest, and to all his father's house, the priests who were in Nob, and all of them came to the king. Saul said,

"Hear now, O son of Ahitub!"

"I am here, my lord!" he said.

Then Saul said to him,

"Why have you and the son of Jesse conspired against me, in that you have given him bread and a sword and have inquired of God for him, that he should rise against me as an enemy, as it is this day?"

Ahimelech answered the king and said,

"But who among all your servants is trusted as is David, being both the king's son-in-law and commander of your body-guard and honored in your house? Have I begun today to inquire of God for him? Far be it from me! Let
not the king impute anything to his
servant nor to anyone of my father's
house, for your servant knew nothing
at all about all this."
"You shall surely die, Ahimelech, 16
you and your entire house," said the
king.
Then the king said to the runners 17
that were standing by him,
"Turn and slay the priests of the
LORD, for their hand also was with
David, and because they knew that he
was a fugitive, but would not disclose
it to me."
But the servants of the king would
not put forth their hands to slay the
priests of the LORD. Then the king 18
said to Doeg,
"Doeg, turn about and fall upon the
priests."
Accordingly Doeg the Edomite turned
and fell upon the priests, and he slew
that day eighty-five men who wore the
linen apron. Also Nob, the city of the 19
priests, he put to the sword, both
men and women, children and infants,
oxen and asses and sheep.
But one son of Ahimelech, the son of 20
Ahitub, named Abiathar, escaped and
fled after David. And Abiathar told 21
David that Saul had slain the priests of
the LORD. Then David said to Abiath- 22
ar,
"I knew that day, because Doeg the
Edomite was there, that he would
surely tell Saul. I myself am responsible for all the lives of your father's
house. Remain with me, fear not; for 23
he that seeks my life seeks your life, for
you shall be a charge to me."
Now when they told David, saying, **23**
"Behold, the Philistines are fighting
against Keilah, and are robbing the
threshing-floors,"
David inquired of the LORD, saying, 2
"Shall I go and attack these Philistines?"
So the LORD said to David,
"Go and attack the Philistines, and
save Keilah."
But David's men said to him, 3
"We are afraid here in Judah; how
much more if we go to Keilah against
the forces of the Philistines."
Then David inquired once again of 4
the LORD; and the LORD answered
him and said,
"Arise, go down to Keilah, for I am

about to deliver the Philistines into
your hand."
5 So David and his men went to Keilah
and fought with the Philistines and
drove off their cattle and caused them
heavy loss of life. Thus David relieved
6 the inhabitants of Keilah. Now when
Abiathar, the son of Ahimelech, fled to
Keilah to David, he went down with an
7 ephod in his hand. When it was told
Saul that David had gone to Keilah,
Saul said,
"God has sold him into my hand; for
he has entrapped himself by going into
a town that has double doors and bars."
8 Accordingly Saul summoned all the
people for war, to go down to Keilah,
9 and besiege David and his men. When
therefore David learned that Saul was
devising evil against him, he said to
Abiathar the priest,
"Bring the ephod here."
10 "O LORD, God of Israel," said David,
"thy servant has indeed heard that
Saul is seeking to come to Keilah, to
11 destroy the city because of me. Will
the citizens of Keilah deliver me into
his hand? Will Saul come down, as thy
servant has heard? O LORD, God of
Israel, I beseech thee, tell thy servant."
Then the LORD said,
"He will come down."
12 "Will the citizens of Keilah deliver
me and my men into the hand of Saul?"
said David.
The LORD said,
"They will deliver you up."
13 Then David and his men, who were
about six hundred, arose and departed
from Keilah, and they went on their
wanderings as they used to go. When
it was told Saul that David had escaped
from Keilah, he gave up the campaign.
14 So David dwelt in the desert in the
strongholds, and in the hilly country in
the Desert of Ziph. Saul was always
seeking him, but the LORD did not deliver
him into his hand.
15 Now David was afraid because Saul
had come out to seek his life; and David
was in the Desert of Ziph in Horesha.
16 Jonathan, Saul's son, arose and went to
David in Horesha and strengthened his
17 hand in God; and he said to him,
"Fear not, for the hand of Saul my
father shall not find you, and you shall
be king over Israel and I shall be next
to you; and that too my father Saul
well knows."

So they two made a covenant before the LORD; and David remained in Horesha, while Jonathan went to his home.

Then the Ziphites went up to Saul to Gibeah, saying,

"Is not David stealing from one hiding place to another among us in the strongholds in Horesha, in the hill of Hachilah, which is to the south of the Desolate Waste? Now therefore, O king, according to all your heart's desire, come down, and it shall be our part to deliver him into the hand of the king."

Then Saul said,

"Blessed be you of the LORD; for you have had compassion on me. Go now, make still more sure, and know and see the place where his haunt is and who has seen him there; for I am told that he is very cunning. Therefore know and see and learn all the secret places where he is accustomed to conceal himself, and return to me with evidence, and I will go with you, and if he be in the land, I will search him out of all the thousands of Judah."

So they arose and went to Ziph before Saul. But David and his men were in the Desert of Maon, in the Arabah to the south of the Desolate Waste. When Saul and his men went to seek him, they told David, and he went down to the crag which is in the Desert of Maon. When Saul heard it, he pursued David to the Desert of Maon. Saul went on one side of the mountain, and David and his men on the other side of the mountain; and David was in desperate straits to escape from Saul, for Saul and his men were at the point of surrounding David and his men, to seize them, when a messenger came to Saul, saying,

"Come quickly, for the Philistines have made a raid upon the land."

So Saul returned from pursuing David and went to meet the Philistines; therefore they called that place the Crag of the Divisions. Then David went up from there, and dwelt in the strongholds of Engedi.

Now when Saul returned from following the Philistines, it was told him, saying,

"Behold, David is in the Desert of Engedi."

Then Saul took three thousand men

chosen from all Israel and went to seek
David and his men upon the Rocks of
3 the Wild Goats; and he came to the
sheepfolds by the way, and there was a
cave. So Saul went in to cover his feet,
while David and his men were lodging
in the inner recesses of the cave.
4 Then David's men said to him,
"Behold the day of which the LORD
said to you, 'Truly I am about to give
your enemy into your hand and you
shall do to him as it shall seem good in
your sight.' "
David then arose and secretly cut off
5 the skirt of Saul's mantle. But afterward David was conscience-stricken because he had cut off the skirt of Saul's
6 mantle. Therefore he said to his men,
"The LORD forbid that I should do
this thing to my lord, the LORD'S
anointed, to put forth my hand against
him, since he is the LORD'S anointed."
7 So David persuaded his men with
these words, and did not permit them
to rise up against Saul.
But when Saul arose from the cave
8 and went on his way, David also arose
after him and went from the cave and
called after Saul, saying,
"My lord the king!"
Then when Saul looked behind him,
David bowed his face to the earth, and
9 did obeisance; and David said to Saul,
"Why did you listen to the words of
the men who said, 'See, David seeks
10 your hurt?' Behold, this day your eyes
see that the LORD gave you into my
hand in the cave, but I refused to kill
you and had pity on you, and I said, 'I
will not put forth my hand against my
lord, for he is the LORD'S anointed.'
11 Moreover, my father, see indeed the
skirt of your mantle in my hand; in that
I cut off the skirt of your mantle and
did not kill you, know and see that
there is neither wrong nor crime in my
hands, and I have not sinned against
you, though you are lying in wait to
12 take my life. The LORD judge between
me and you, and the LORD avenge me
of you; but my hand shall not be upon
13 you. As runs the old saying, 'Out of the
wicked comes wickedness.' But my
14 hand shall not be against you. After
whom has the king of Israel come forth?
Whom are you pursuing? A dead dog?
15 A single flea? The LORD therefore be
judge and execute justice between me
and you and see and plead my cause
and acquit me from your hand."
Now as David finished speaking these 16
words to Saul, Saul said,
"Is this your voice, my son David?"
Then Saul lifted up his voice and
wept, and he said to David, 17
"You are more righteous than I, for
you have shown me kindness, while I
have shown you evil. You have shown 18
exceptional kindness in what you have
done to me, in that today, when the
LORD had shut me up in your hand,
you did not kill me. For when a man 19
finds his enemy, does he send him away
safely? Therefore may the LORD reward you richly in return for what you
have done to me this day. Now indeed 20
I know that you shall surely be king,
and that by your hand the kingdom of
Israel shall be established. So now 21
swear to me by the LORD, that you will
not cut off my descendants after me
and that you will not destroy my name
from my father's house."
So David swore to Saul. Then Saul 22
went home, while David and his men
went up to the stronghold.

DAVID'S RAID UPON NABAL, 25:1–43

Now Samuel had died and all Israel 25
gathered themselves together and lamented for him and buried him in his
own house in Ramah. Then David
arose and went down to the Desert of
Maon. Now there was a man in Maon, 2
whose business was in Carmel. The
man was very prosperous, and he had
three thousand sheep and a thousand
goats, and he was shearing his sheep in
Carmel. Now the man's name was Na- 3
bal; and the name of his wife was Abigail; and the woman had good sense
and was fair to look upon, but the man
was rough and uncouth; and he was a
Calebite.
David heard in the desert that Nabal 4
was shearing his sheep. So David sent 5
ten young men, and David said to the
young men,
"Go up to Carmel and visit Nabal
and greet him in my name; and you 6
shall say thus to my brother, 'Peace be
to you and your house and all that you
have. I have heard that you have 7
shearers. Now your shepherds were

with us, and we did not insult them,
and nothing of theirs was missing all the
8 time they were in Carmel. Ask your
young men and let them tell you.
Therefore let the young men find favor
in your eyes, for we have come on a
propitious day. Give therefore whatever you have at hand to your servants
and to your son David.' "
9 So when David's young men came,
they spoke to Nabal in accordance
with all these words in the name of
David, and then they waited.
10 But Nabal answered David's servants, and said,
"Who is David, and who is the son of
Jesse? There are many slaves today
who connivingly break away, each from
11 his master! Should I then take my
bread and my water and my meat that
I have slaughtered for my shearers, and
give it to men whose origin I do not
know?"
12 So David's young men retraced their
steps, and returned and came and reported to him in accordance with all
13 these words. So David said to his men,
"Let every man gird on his sword."
And they girded on each man his
sword. David also girded on his sword;
and there went up after David about
four hundred men, while two hundred
remained with the baggage.
14 But one of the young men told Abigail, Nabal's wife, saying,
"David has just sent messengers from
the desert to salute our master, and he
15 railed at them. But the men have been
very kind to us and we have not been
insulted nor have we missed anything,
as long as we were associated with
16 them, while we were in the field. They
were a wall about us both by night and
by day, all the time we were with them
17 keeping the sheep. Now therefore know
and consider what you will do, for evil
is determined against our master and
against all his house, for he is such a
base rascal that no one can speak to
him."
18 Then Abigail hastened and took two
hundred loaves of bread and two skins
of wine and five dressed sheep and five
homers of parched grain and a hundred
bunches of raisins and two hundred
cakes of figs, and loaded them on asses;
19 and she said to her young men,
"Go on before me; see, I am coming
after you."

But she did not tell Nabal, her husband. As she was riding on the ass and 20
coming down through a defile of the
mountain, David and his men were also
coming down in her direction, so that
she met them. Now David had said, 21
"Surely in vain have I guarded all
that this fellow has in the desert, so that
nothing was missing of all that belongs
to him, and he has returned me evil for
good. May God requite David and 22
worse, if I leave of all that belongs to
him until tomorrow as much as a single
male person."
Therefore when Abigail saw David, 23
she hastened and dismounted from her
ass and fell on her face before David
and bowed herself to the ground. She 24
fell at his feet, and said,
"Upon me, my lord, even me, be the
blame. Only, I pray you, let your maidservant speak in your ears, and give
heed to the words of your maidservant.
Let not my lord, I pray you, take seri- 25
ously this worthless individual, Nabal,
for as his name is, so is he; 'Fool' is his
name, and folly his boon companion;
but as for myself your maidservant, I
did not see the young men of my lord,
whom you sent. Now therefore, my 26
lord, as the LORD lives and as you live,
since the LORD has restrained you
from shedding blood and from finding
redress for yourself by your own hand—
and now may your enemies and those
who seek to harm my lord be as Nabal
—let now this gift, which your humble 27
servant has brought to my lord, be
given to the young men who accompany my lord. Forgive, I pray, the 28
transgression of your maidservant, for
the LORD will surely make for my lord
a secure house, for my lord is fighting
the wars of the LORD, and evil shall not
be found in you all your days. Should 29
man rise up to pursue you and seek
your life, the life of my lord shall be
bound in the bundle of the living along
with the LORD your God, but he will
sling out the life of your enemies as
from the hollow of a sling. When the 30
LORD shall do to my lord in accordance
with all the good which he spoke concerning you and shall appoint you
prince over Israel, then this shall not 31
be a qualm of conscience or a burden of
remorse to my lord, that you have
shed blood without cause or that my
lord has found redress for himself by

his own hand. When therefore the LORD shall prosper my lord, then remember your maidservant."
32 Then David said to Abigail,
"Blessed be the LORD, the God of Israel, who sent you this day to meet
33 me, and blessed be your discernment, and blessed be you yourself, who have restrained me this day from bloodshed and from finding redress for myself by
34 my own hand. For in very deed as the LORD, the God of Israel, lives, who has restrained me from doing you harm, except you had made haste and come to meet me, surely there would not have been left to Nabal by the morning light so much as one male person."
35 So David received from her hand that which she had brought him; and he said to her,
"Go up to your house in peace. See, I have listened to your plea, and shown you favor."
36 But when Abigail came to Nabal, he was just holding a drinking bout in his house, like the drinking bout of a king. Nabal's heart was merry within him, for he was very drunk, so that she could not tell him anything at all until the
37 morning light. But in the morning, when the effects of the wine upon Nabal were passing off, his wife told him these things, and his heart died within him
38 and he became like a stone. And about ten days later the LORD inflicted a stroke upon Nabal, so that he died.
Accordingly when David heard that Nabal was dead, he said,
"Blessed be the LORD, who has vindicated my charge of reproach at the hand of Nabal and has kept back his servant from evil; and the LORD has returned the evil-doing of Nabal upon his own head."
Then David sent and made his proposal to Abigail to take her to him to be his wife. And when the servants of David came to Abigail at Carmel and said to her,
"David has sent us to you to take you to him to be his wife," she arose and bowed her face to the earth and said,
"Behold your female slave, a maidservant to wash the feet of my lord's servants."
Then Abigail hastily arose and mounted an ass, and five of her maidens followed in her train. So she went after the messengers of David and became his wife.
David also took Ahinoam of Jezreel 43
and they both became his wives. Now Saul had given Michal his daughter, David's wife, to Paltai, the son of Laish of Gallim.

DAVID SPARES SAUL'S LIFE, 26:1–25

Now the Ziphites came to Saul at 26
Gibeah, saying,
"Is not David in hiding in the hill of Hachilah, which is east of the Desolate Waste?"
Accordingly Saul arose and went 2
down to the Desert of Ziph, having three thousand chosen men of Israel with him, to seek David in the Desert
of Ziph; and Saul encamped in the hill 3
of Hachilah, which is east of the Desolate Waste, by the way. But David was staying in the desert. And when he saw that Saul had come to the desert in pursuit of him, David sent out spies, and 4
when he learned that Saul was coming
straight on, David arose and came to 5
the place where Saul was encamped. So David saw the place where lay Saul and Abner the son of Ner, the commander of his army; and Saul lay within the barricade, and the people were encamped round about him.
Then David spoke up and said to 6
Ahimelech the Hittite and to Abishai, the son of Zeruiah, Joab's brother, saying,
"Who will go down with me to Saul to the camp?"
"I will go down with you," said Abishai.
So David and Abishai came to the 7
people by night; and there was Saul lying asleep within the barricade, with his spear thrust into the earth at his head; and Abner and the people were lying round about him.
"God has today delivered up your 8
enemy into your hand," said Abishai to David. "Now therefore, I pray you, let me pin him to the earth with but one thrust of his own spear, and I shall have no occasion to repeat the blow, so far as he is concerned."
But David said to Abishai, 9
"Destroy him not; for who can lay his hand upon the LORD'S anointed and be innocent?"

10 "As the LORD lives," said David,
"either the LORD shall smite him, or
his day shall come to die, or he shall go
11 down into the battle and perish. The
LORD forbid that I should put forth my
hand against the LORD'S anointed; but
take now, I pray you, the spear that is
at his head and the jug of water and let
us go."
12 So David took the spear and the jug
of water from Saul's head and they
withdrew. No one saw it or knew it,
neither did any awake; for they were all
asleep because a deep sleep from the
LORD had fallen upon them.
13 Thereupon David went over to the
other side and stood on the top of a
mountain at a safe distance, a great
14 space being between them. Then David
called to the people and to Abner, the
son of Ner, saying,
"Will you not answer, Abner?"
Abner answered and said,
"Who are you that calls?"
15 So David said to Abner,
"Are you not a man? Who is like you
in Israel? Why then have you not
guarded your lord the king? For one of
the people came to destroy the king
16 your lord. This thing that you have
done is not good. As the LORD lives,
you are worthy of death, because you
did not keep watch over your master,
the LORD'S anointed. See now where
the king's spear is and the jug of water
that was at his head."
17 Then Saul recognized David's voice
and said,
"Is that your voice, my son David?"
"It is my voice, my lord, O king,"
said David.
18 "Why is my lord pursuing his servant," he said, "for what have I done,
19 or of what evil am I guilty? Now therefore, I pray, let my lord the king listen
to the words of his servant. If the
LORD has stirred you up against me,
let him be appeased by an offering; but
if they be the sons of men, cursed be
they before the LORD; for they have
driven me out today, so that I have no
share in the heritage of the LORD, say-
20 ing, 'Go serve other gods.' Now therefore, may my blood not fall to the
earth far removed from the presence of
the LORD; for the king of Israel has
come forth to seek my life, as one hunts
a partridge in the mountains."
21 "I have sinned," Saul said, "return,
my son David, for I will do you no more
harm, because my life was held sacred
by you this day. I have acted foolishly 2
indeed and have erred exceedingly."
Then David answered and said,
"Here is the king's spear! Now let
one of the young men come over and
get it. The LORD will recompense 2
every man's righteousness and fidelity;
for the LORD delivered you into my
hand today, but I refused to stretch
forth my hand against the LORD'S
anointed. Just as your life was highly
valued in my sight today, so may my
life be highly valued in the sight of the
LORD, and may he deliver me out of
every distress."
Then Saul said to David,
"Blessed are you my son David; you
will certainly succeed in whatever you
undertake."
So David went his way, while Saul
returned to his home.

DAVID'S RESIDENCE AMONG THE PHILISTINES, 27:1—28:2

Thereupon David said to himself,
"I shall be captured some day by the
hand of Saul. There is nothing better
for me than that I should make good
my escape to the land of the Philistines;
then Saul will despair of seeking me
further in all the territory of Israel, and
I shall escape from his hand."
So David arose and went over, accompanied by the six hundred men who
were with him, to Achish, the son of
Maoch, king of Gath. David with his
men remained with Achish at Gath,
each with his household, David with his
two wives, Ahinoam the Jezreelitess
and Abigail the Carmelitess, Nabal's
widow. Now when it was told Saul that
David had fled to Gath, he gave up entirely his search for him.
"If now I have found favor in your
sight," David said to Achish, "let a
place be given me in one of the country
towns, that I may dwell there; for why
should your servant dwell in the royal
city with you?"
Then Achish gave him Ziklag at that
time; therefore Ziklag has belonged to
the kings of Judah to this day. The
length of time that David dwelt in the
country of the Philistines was a year

and four months. David and his men went up and made raids upon the Geshurites, the Girzites, and the Amalekites; for these tribes dwell in the land which extends from Telem as one goes to Shur, even to the land of Egypt. And whenever David attacked the land, he would not leave alive either man or woman, but he would take the sheep and cattle, the asses and camels, and clothing; and when he returned and came to Achish, and Achish said,

"Against whom have you made a raid today?"

David would say,

"Against the Negeb of Judah, or against the Negeb of the Jerahmeelites, or against the Negeb of the Kenites."

But David would never leave alive man or woman, to bring them to Gath, "Lest," said he, "they should report concerning us and say, 'Thus David has done.' "

Such was his custom as long as he remained in the country of the Philistines; and Achish believed in David, saying,

"He has surely made himself abhorrent to his people Israel; therefore he shall be my servant permanently."

Now in those days the Philistines assembled their armed camps in order to make war upon Israel. Achish said to David,

"Know for a certainty that you shall go forth with me into the camp, you and your men."

David said to Achish,

"Then you shall now know what your servant is capable of."

So Achish said to David,

"Then I make you my body-guard from this time forth."

SAUL AND THE WITCH OF ENDOR, 28:3–25

Now Samuel had died and all Israel had lamented for him and buried him in Ramah, his own city. And Saul had put the mediums and the wizards out of the land. Then when the Philistines gathered together and came and encamped in Shunem, Saul assembled all Israel, and encamped in Gilboa. But when Saul saw the camp of the Philistines, he was afraid and his mind was filled with misgivings. Consequently Saul inquired of the LORD, but the
LORD did not answer him either by
dreams or by Urim or by prophets.
Then Saul said to his servants, 7
"Seek for me a woman who has a divining talisman that I may go to her
and inquire of her."
So his servants said to him,
"Behold, there is a woman at Endor
who has a divining talisman."
Then Saul disguised himself by put- 8
ting on other garments and went, accompanied by two men, and they came
to the woman by night.
"Divine now for me by the talisman,"
he said, "and bring up for me the one
whom I shall indicate to you."
But the woman said to him, 9
"Surely you know what Saul has
done, how he has cut off the mediums
and the wizards from the land. Why
then are you laying a snare for my life,
to bring about my death?"
Then Saul swore to her by the LORD, 10
saying,
"As the LORD lives, no guilt shall 11
come upon you from this matter."
"Whom shall I bring up to you?"
said the woman.
"Bring Samuel up for me," said he.
Now when the woman saw Samuel, 12
she gave a great shriek; and the woman
said to Saul,
"Why have you deceived me, for you
are Saul?"
So the king said to her, 13
"Do not be alarmed. What have you
seen?"
The woman said to Saul,
"I have seen a divine being coming
up out of the earth."
"What was his appearance?" said he 14
to her.
"An old man is coming up," she said,
"and he is wrapped in a mantle."
Then Saul knew that it was Samuel,
and he bowed with his face to the earth
and did obeisance.
Then Samuel said to Saul, 15
"Why have you disturbed me by
bringing me up?"
"I am in great distress," said Saul,
"for the Philistines are waging war
against me, and God has turned from
me and answers me no more, either by
prophets or by dreams; therefore I have
called you to tell me what I should do."
"Why do you ask me when the LORD 16
has turned from you and become your
adversary?" said Samuel. "The LORD 17

has done to you as he spoke by me; for
the LORD has wrenched the kingdom
from your hand, and given it to your
18 neighbor—to David. Because you did
not listen to the voice of the LORD, and
did not execute the fierceness of his
wrath against Amalek, the LORD has
done this thing to you today. Moreover the LORD will give Israel along
with you into the hand of the Philistines; and tomorrow you and your
19 sons with you will fall; the LORD will
also deliver the camp of Israel into the
hand of the Philistines."

20 Immediately Saul fell at full length
upon the earth and was exceedingly
fearful because of the words of Samuel;
besides he had no strength in him, for
he had not eaten food during a whole
21 day and that whole night. Accordingly
when the woman came to Saul and saw
that he was panic-stricken, she said to
him,

"You see, your maidservant has
heeded your voice, and I have taken my
life in my hand and have listened to
your words which you spoke to me.
22 Now therefore, listen, I beg of you, even
you yourself to the voice of your maidservant; and let me set before you a bit
of food, and eat that you may have
strength when you go on your way."

23 But he refused and said,

"I cannot eat."

However, his servants together with
the woman proceeded to urge him, until
he yielded to their entreaty. So he
arose from the earth and sat upon a
24 couch. Now the woman had a fatted
calf in the house; and she speedily slew
it, and took flour and kneaded it and
25 baked from it unleavened cakes. She
set it before Saul and his servants, and
they ate. Then they arose and went
away that night.

DAVID WITH THE PHILISTINES
29:1—30:31

29 Now the Philistines had assembled
all their forces at Aphek; and the
Israelites were encamped by the foun-
2 tain which is in Jezreel. The princes of
the Philistines were pressing forward
(with their forces) by companies and by
regiments; and David and his men were
3 bringing up the rear with Achish. Then
the commanders of the Philistines said,

"What are these Hebrews?"

So Achish said to the commanders of the Philistines,

"Is not this David, the servant of Saul king of Israel, who has been with me two years? and I have found no fault in him from the day of his desertion to me until now."

But the commanders of the Philistines were enraged against him, and the commanders of the Philistines said to him,

"Send the man back that he may return to the place where you have assigned him residence; he shall not go down with us to battle, that he may not be an adversary to us in the fray; for with what could this fellow reconcile himself to his lord? Might it not be with the heads of these men? Is not this David of whom they sang in the dances, saying,

'Saul has slain his thousands,
But David his ten thousands?' "

Then Achish called to David and said to him,

"As the LORD lives, you are reliable, and your going out and coming in with me in the camp is pleasing in my sight; for I have found no evil in you from the day that you came to me until this day, but you are not acceptable in the eyes of the princes. Now therefore return and go away quietly, that you may do nothing offensive in the sight of the princes of the Philistines."

"But what have I done?" David said to Achish, "and what have you found in your servant from the day that I came into your presence to this day, that I may not go and fight against the enemies of my lord the king?"

Achish answered and said to David,

"I acknowledge that you are as acceptable in my sight as a messenger of God; nevertheless the commanders of the Philistines have said, 'He shall not go up with us to the battle.' Now therefore rise early in the morning, together with the servants of your master who came with you, and go to the place where I have assigned you residence, and allow no base thought to enter your mind, for you are upright in my sight; but rise early in the morning, and as soon as you can see, depart."

So David rose up early, together with his men, to go in the morning to return to the land of the Philistines; and the Philistines went up to Jezreel.

1 Now when David and his men arrived at Ziklag on the third day, the
Amalekites had made a raid on the
Negeb and upon Ziklag, and had over-
2 come Ziklag and burned it, and they
took captive the women and all who
were in it, from the least to the greatest, but without slaying any, and car-
3 ried them off and went their way. And
when David and his men came to the
city, there were only the burnt ruins;
for their wives and their sons and their
4 daughters were carried off. Then David
and the people who were with him
raised a cry and wept until they were
5 without strength even to weep. Also
David's two wives were taken captive,
Ahinoam the Jezreelitess, and Abigail,
the widow of Nabal the Carmelite.
6 Moreover David was in a serious pre-
dicament; for the people threatened to
stone him, for the spirit of all the people
was embittered, each for his sons and
for his daughters; but David strength-
7 ened himself in the LORD his God; and
David said to Abiathar the priest, the
son of Ahimelech,
"Now bring to me the ephod."
8 So Abiathar brought the ephod to
David; and David inquired of the
LORD, saying,
"Shall I pursue this band?
Shall I overtake them?"
Then he said to him,
"Pursue, for you shall assuredly overtake,
And as certainly, rescue."
9 So David set out, together with the
six hundred men who were with him,
and they came to the Brook Besor, and
10 the ones left behind remained. But
David together with four hundred men
kept up the pursuit; while two hundred
men remained behind, who were too
11 faint to cross the Brook Besor. Then
they found an Egyptian in a field and
they brought him to David, and gave
him food and he ate, and they provided
12 him with water to drink; and what they
gave him was a piece of a cake of figs,
and two clusters of raisins. When he
had eaten, his energy came back to him;
for he had not tasted food or drunk
water for three days and three nights.
13 Then David said to him,
"To whom do you belong? And
whence are you?"
"I am an Egyptian youth, a slave of
an Amalekite," he said, "and my master left me when I fell sick three days
ago. We had been making a raid upon 14
the Negeb of the Cherethites and upon
that which belongs to Judah and upon
the Negeb of Caleb, and had burned
Ziklag."
"Will you bring me down to this 15
band?" said David to him.
"Swear to me by God," he said, "that
you will neither kill me nor deliver me
over to my master, and I will bring you
down to this band."
So when he had brought him down, 16
they were there scattered over the face
of the whole landscape, eating and
drinking and dancing, because of all
the vast booty which they had taken
from the land of the Philistines and
from the land of Judah. But David 17
slaughtered them from dawn until
evening in order to exterminate them.
Not a man escaped except four hundred
young men who rode upon camels and
fled. So David rescued all whom the 18
Amalekites had taken; and likewise
David rescued his two wives. Nothing 19
belonging to them was missing, whether
much or little, sons or daughters, booty
or anything that they had taken for
themselves—David recovered everything. So they took all the sheep and 20
cattle and drove them before him and
said,
"This is David's spoil."
But when David came to the two 21
hundred men who had been too faint to
follow David, so that he had halted
them at the Brook Besor, they went out
to meet David and the people who were
with him, and when they drew near to
the people, they saluted them. Then 22
every base and worthless rascal among
the men who went with David spoke up
and said,
"Because they did not go with us, we
will not give them any share of the spoil
which we have recovered, except to
each his wife and his children, that he
may take them away and be gone."
But David said, 23
"Do not do so after what the LORD
has given us and the way in which he
has kept us and delivered the band that
came against us into our hand. Who 24
will listen to you in this matter? For:
As is the share of him who goes down
into the battle,

Even so is his portion who remains with
the baggage;
They shall share alike."
25 Accordingly he made it a statute and
an ordinance in Israel from that day
forward to this day.
26 Now when David came to Ziklag, he
sent some of the spoil to the elders of
Judah, his friends, saying, "Here is a
gift for you from the booty of the
27 enemies of the LORD": to those who
were in Bethel, to those who were in
Ramoth of the Negeb, and to those in
28 Jattir, to those who were in Aroer, in
29 Siphmoth and in Eshtemoa, to those
who were in Carmel, and in the cities
of the Jerahmeelites, and in the cities
30 of the Kenites, to those who were in
Hormah, and in Beersheba, and in
31 Athach, and to those who were in Hebron, and to all the places which David
and his men had frequented.

THE DEATH OF SAUL, 31:1–13

31 Now the Philistines fought against
Israel, and the men of Israel fled before
the Philistines, and the wounded fell on
2 Mount Gilboa. The Philistines overtook Saul and his sons; and the Philistines slew Jonathan and Abinadab and
3 Malchishua, the sons of Saul. Thus the
battle raged about Saul, and the archers
found their mark, and he was seriously
4 wounded in the abdomen. Then Saul
said to his armor-bearer,
"Draw your sword and run me
through with it, lest these uncircumcised men come and run me through
and make sport of me."
But his armor-bearer would not, for
he was terrified. Therefore Saul took
his sword and fell upon it. So when his
armor-bearer saw that Saul was dead,
then he also fell upon his sword and
died with him. Thus Saul and his three
sons and his armor-bearer and all his
men died together on the same day.
Likewise when the men of Israel who
were across the valley and beyond the
Jordan saw that the Israelites had fled
and that Saul and his sons were dead,
they abandoned their cities and fled,
and the Philistines came and occupied
them. Then on the morrow when the
Philistines came to strip the slain, they
found Saul and his three sons fallen on
Mount Gilboa. They cut off his head
and stripped off his armor and dispatched them throughout the land of
the Philistines to bring good tidings to
their idols and to the people. They also
put his armor in the temple of Ashtart,
and they impaled his body on the wall
of Beth-shan. Now when the inhabitants of Jabesh-gilead heard of it, namely, what the Philistines had done to
Saul, all the valiant men arose and
marched all night and took the bodies
of Saul and his sons from the wall of
Beth-shan; and they came to Jabesh
and burned them there. Then they
took their bones and buried them under
the tamarisk tree at Jabesh, and they
fasted seven days.

THE SECOND BOOK OF SAMUEL

DAVID AVENGES THE DEATH OF SAUL, 1:1–16

1 NOW after Saul's death, when
David had returned from
overcoming the Amalekites,
David remained two days in
2 Ziklag. Then on the third day, behold,
a man came from the camp from Saul,
with his garments rent and with earth
upon his head. When he came to David, he fell to the earth and did obei-
3 sance; and David said to him,
"From where do you come?"
"From the camp of Israel I have escaped," he said to him.
4 "What is the situation? I pray you,
tell me," said David to him.
"The people," he said, "fled from the
battle, and many of the people have
fallen, and also Saul and Jonathan his
son are dead."
5 Then David said to the young man
who told him,
"How do you know that Saul and
Jonathan his son are dead?"
6 The young man who told him said,
"By chance I happened to be on
Mount Gilboa, and right there was Saul
leaning upon his spear, and at the same
time the chariotry and the leaders of
the horsemen were sweeping toward
7 him. When he looked behind him, he
saw me and called to me; and I said,
8 'Here I am.' He said to me, 'Who are
you?' So I said to him, 'I am an
9 Amalekite.' Then he said to me, 'Stand,
I pray you, beside me and despatch me;
for confusion has seized me, because my
10 life is still in me.' So I stood beside him
and despatched him, because I was convinced that he could not live after he
had fallen; and I took the crown that
was upon his head, and the armlet that
was on his arm, and I have brought
them here to my lord."
11 Then David grasped his garments
and tore them; as did likewise all
12 the men who were with him. They
mourned and lamented and fasted until
evening over Saul and over Jonathan
his son and over the people of the LORD
and over the house of Israel, because
they had fallen by the sword.
Then David said to the young man 13
who had reported to him,
"Whence are you?"
"I am the son of an Amalekite sojourner," he said.
"Why were you not afraid to stretch 14
forth your hand to destroy the LORD'S
anointed?" said David to him.
David also said to him, 16
"Your blood be upon your head; for
your own mouth has testified against
you, by saying, 'I have slain the
LORD'S anointed.' "
Then David called to one of the 15
young men, and said,
"Here! Cut him down."
So he struck him a blow, and he died.

DAVID'S DIRGE OVER SAUL AND JONATHAN, 1:17–27

Then David sang this dirge over 17
Saul and Jonathan his son (behold, it is 18
written in the Book of Jashar to instruct the Judeans), and he said,

"Your beauty, O Israel, 19
Upon your heights is slain.
How have the heroes fallen!

"Tell it not in Gath, 20
Announce it not in the streets of Askelon;
Lest the daughters of the Philistines
rejoice,
Lest the daughters of the uncircumcised exult.

"O mountains of Gilboa, let neither 21
dew fall,
Nor rain be upon you, O fields of
death!
For there was the shield of the mighty
thrown aside,
The shield of Saul, not anointed with
oil.

22 "From the blood of the slain,
From the fat of the mighty,
The bow of Jonathan turned not back,
Nor empty returned the sword of Saul.

23 "Saul and Jonathan, beloved and lovely!
In life and in death they were not divided;
Swifter than eagles were they,
They were stronger than lions.

24 "O daughters of Israel, weep over Saul,
Who clothed you in scarlet daintily,
Who adorned your garments with gold and jewels;
25 How are the mighty fallen in the midst of battle!

"O Jonathan! by your death am I mortally wounded,
26 I am distressed for you, my brother Jonathan!
You were exceedingly dear to me,
Your love was more marvelous to me than the love of women.

27 "How have the mighty fallen,
And the weapons of war perished!"

WARS BETWEEN DAVID AND THE FORCES OF SAUL,

2:1—3:39

2 Now after that David inquired of the LORD, saying,

"Shall I go up to one of the cities of Judah?"

The LORD said to him,

"Go up."

And when David said,

"Whither shall I go up?"

He said,

"To Hebron."

2 So David went up there with his two
wives, Ahinoam the Jezreelitess, and
Abigail, the widow of Nabal the Car-
3 melite. David also brought up the men
who were with him, each with his
household, and they dwelt in the towns
4 of Hebron. Then the men of Judah
came and there anointed David king
over the house of Judah.

Now when they told David, saying
that the men of Jabesh-gilead had
5 buried Saul, David sent messengers to
the men of Jabesh-gilead, and said to
them,

"Blessed are you of the LORD, because you have shown this kindness to your lord, even to Saul, and have buried him. Now may the LORD show kindness and truth to you; and I also will do well by you, because you have done this thing. Therefore let your hands be strong and be valiant; for Saul your lord is dead, and the house of Judah has anointed me king over them."

Now Abner, the son of Ner, commander of Saul's army, had taken Ishbaal, the son of Saul, and brought him
over to Mahanaim. He had him made
king over Gilead and the Ashurites and
Jezreel and Ephraim and Benjamin and
all Israel. Ishbaal, Saul's son, was for- 1
ty years old when he became king over
Israel, and he reigned two years. But
the house of Judah followed David; and 1
the length of time that David was king
in Hebron over the house of Judah was
seven years and six months.

Now Abner, the son of Ner, and the
servants of Ishbaal, the son of Saul,
went out from Mahanaim to Gibeon;
and Joab, the son of Zeruiah, and the
servants of David went out from Hebron and met them at the pool of Gibeon. They sat down, the one on the one
side of the pool and the other on the
other side of the pool. Then Abner said 1
to Joab,

"I pray you, let the young men arise and make sport before us."

"Let them arise," said Joab. 1

Then they arose and were numbered
off: twelve for Benjamin, and Ishbaal
the son of Saul, and twelve for the servants of David. Thereupon they seized
each his adversary by the head and his
sword transfixed his side, so they fell
down together. So they called that
place the Portion of Ground of the
Sides, which is in Gibeon. The battle 1
was very bitterly fought that day, and
Abner and the men of Israel were put
to rout before the servants of David.

There were three sons of Zeruiah 1
there, Joab, Abishai, and Asahel; and
Asahel was as swift of foot as one of the
gazelles which are in the field. Now 1
Asahel pursued Abner; and he turned
not in his course to the right or to the
left from his pursuit of Abner. So Ab- 2
ner turned about and said,

"Is that you, Asahel?"

"It is I," he said.

1 So Abner said to him,
"Turn aside to your right or to your
left and seize one of the young men and
take for yourself his spoil."
But Asahel would not turn from pur-
2 suing him. Therefore Abner said again
to Asahel,
"Turn aside from following me. Why
should I fell you to the earth? How
then could I look your brother Joab in
the face?"
3 But he refused to turn aside. Therefore Abner struck him with a backward
thrust of the spear in the abdomen, so
that the spear came out at his back, and
he fell there and died in his tracks. So
all who came to the place where Asahel
had fallen and died, stood still.
4 Then Joab and Abishai took up the
pursuit of Abner; and as the sun was
setting, they came to the hill of Am-
mah, which is in front of Giah on the
5 way to the Desert of Gibeon. The Benjaminites rallied their forces around
Abner and formed into line, and halted
6 on a hilltop. Then Abner called to Joab
and said,
"Shall the sword devour forever?
Do you not know that it will be bitter
in the end? How long then before you
are going to tell the people to give up
the pursuit of their brothers?"
7 "As the LORD lives," said Joab, "unless you had spoken, then only after the
morning would the people have given
8 up, each from pursuing his brother. So
Joab blew the trumpet and all the people halted and pursued Israel no more,
9 nor was there any more fighting. Then
Abner and his men marched all that
night through the Arabah and crossed
the Jordan and traversed the whole of
Bithron and arrived at Mahanaim.
0 So Joab returned from pursuing Abner. But when he had assembled all the
people, nineteen of David's servants
1 were missing, besides Asahel; while the
servants of David had slain from Benjamin and among Abner's men three
2 hundred and sixty. Moreover they
took up Asahel and buried him in his
father's grave, which was in Bethlehem. Then Joab and his men marched
all night, and the light broke upon
them at Hebron.
3 Moreover the war between the house
of Saul and the house of David grew
more strenuous; and David kept growing stronger, while the house of Saul
became gradually weaker.
Also sons were born to David in He- 2
bron; his first-born was Amnon, the son
of Ahinoam the Jezreelitess; and his 3
second, Chileab, the son of Abigail, the
widow of Nabal the Carmelite; and the
third, Absalom, the son of Maacah, the
daughter of Talmai, king of Geshur;
and the fourth, Adonijah, the son of 4
Haggith; and the fifth, Shephetaiah,
the son of Abital; and the sixth, Ith- 5
ream, belonged to Eglah, David's wife.
These were born to David in Hebron.
Now, while there was war between 6
the house of Saul and the house of David, Abner was strengthening himself in
the house of Saul. Saul had a concu- 7
bine, whose name was Rizpah, the
daughter of Aiah, and Ishbaal, the son
of Saul, said to Abner,
"Why do you go in unto my father's
concubine?"
Then Abner was very angry at the 8
words of Ishbaal and said,
"Am I a dog's head, that today I am
showing kindness to the house of Saul
your father, to his brothers, and to his
friends, and have not delivered you
into the hand of David, that you now
charge me with guilt in relation to a
woman? May God requite Abner and 9
worse, if, as the LORD has sworn to
David, I do not even so to him, by 10
transferring the kingdom from the
house of Saul and by establishing the
throne of David over Israel and Judah
from Dan to Beersheba."
But he could not answer Abner a 11
single word, because of his fear of him.
Accordingly Abner sent messengers 12
to David to Hebron, saying,
"Make your covenant with me; then
my hand shall be with you to bring all
Israel to you."
"It is well," he said; "I will make a 13
covenant with you, but one thing I demand of you, namely, you shall not see
my face unless you bring Michal, Saul's
daughter, when you come to see me."
Then David sent messengers to Ish- 14
baal, Saul's son, saying,
"Give me my wife Michal, whom I
acquired for a hundred foreskins of the
Philistines."
So Ishbaal sent and took her from her 15
husband, Paltiel, the son of Laish. But 16
her husband accompanied her, weeping

as he followed her as far as Bahurim.
Then Abner said to him,
"Go, return."
So he returned.
17 Now Abner had communicated with
the elders of Israel, saying,
"Already some considerable time ago
you were seeking to have David king
18 over you. Now then do it; for the
LORD has said of David, 'By the hand
of my servant David I will save my
people Israel from the hand of the
Philistines and from the power of all
their enemies.'"
19 Abner also spoke in the ears of Benjamin, and Abner went also to speak to
David personally in Hebron all that
seemed good in the sight of Israel and
in the sight of the whole house of Benjamin.
20 So when Abner came to David at
Hebron, accompanied by twenty men,
David made Abner and the men who
21 were with him a feast. Then Abner said
to David,
"I will arise and assemble all Israel
to my lord the king, that they may
make a covenant with you and that you
may be king over all, as you personally
desire."
Then David sent Abner away, and
he went in peace.
22 Just then the servants of David and
Joab arrived from a raid, and they
brought a large amount of plunder
with them; but Abner was not with
David in Hebron, because David had
sent him away, and he had gone in
23 peace. But when Joab and all the force
that was with him came in, they told
Joab, saying,
"Abner, the son of Ner, has been
with the king, but he has sent him
away, and he has gone in peace."
24 Then Joab went to the king and said,
"What have you done? I understand
that Abner has been to see you; why
have you now sent him away, so that he
25 is gone? Do you not know Abner, the
son of Ner, that he has come to deceive
you and to learn of your going out and
your coming in and to know all that
you are doing?"
26 Therefore when Joab came out from
David's presence, he sent messengers
after Abner and they brought him back
from the Well of Sirah without David's
27 knowledge. Then when Abner returned

to Hebron, Joab beckoned him to the
side of the gate to speak with him privately and stabbed him there in the abdomen. So he died for the blood of
Asahel Joab's brother.
Now when David heard of it, he said, 2
"I and my kingdom are forever innocent before the LORD of the blood of
Abner, the son of Ner. May it fall tem- 2
pestuously upon the head of Joab and
upon all his father's house, and may
there not be lacking from the house of
Joab one who has an issue, or who is
leprous, or who holds the distaff, or
who falls by the sword, or who lacks
bread."
But Joab and Abishai his brother 3
slew Abner because he had killed Asahel their brother in the battle at Gibeon.
Then David said to Joab, and to all 3
the people who were with him,
"Rend your garments and gird on
sackcloth, and lament before Abner!"
Also King David followed the bier;
and when they buried Abner in Hebron,
the king raised a loud wailing at the
grave of Abner, and all the people
wept. David also chanted a dirge for 3
Abner and said,

"Should Abner die as dies the wanton
fool?
Your hands were not bound, 3
Nor your feet cramped in fetters;
As one falls before bandits, you have
fallen."

Then all the people wept afresh for
him. Afterward all the people came to 3
persuade David to eat food while it was
still day; but David swore, saying,
"May God requite me and worse, if I
taste bread or anything else before the
sun sets."
Now when all the people took notice, 3
it was pleasing in their eyes; for everything which the king did was pleasing
in the sight of all the people. So all the 3
people and all Israel perceived that day
that it was not the intention of David
to slay Abner, the son of Ner. Then 38
the king said to his servants,
"Do you not know that a prince and
a great man has fallen this day in Israel? I am today weak, though anoint- 39
ed king; for these men, the sons of
Zeruiah, are too difficult for me May
the LORD requite the evil-doer according to his guilt!"

THE END OF SAUL'S HOUSE, 4:1–12

4 Accordingly when Ishbaal, Saul's
son, heard that Abner was dead in Hebron, his hands became listless and all
2 Israel was dismayed. Ishbaal, Saul's
son, had two men who were captains of
guerilla bands: the name of one was
Baanah, and the name of the other was
Rechab, sons of Rimmon the Beerothite, of the Benjaminites (for Beeroth is
3 also reckoned to Benjamin, and the
Beerothites fled to Gittaim and have
been sojourners there until this day).
4 Also Jonathan, Saul's son, had a son
who was crippled in his feet. He was
five years old when the news of Saul
and Jonathan came from Jezreel; and
his nurse took him up and fled, and as
she fled in haste, he fell and was made
5 lame. His name was Meribaal. Then
the sons of Rimmon the Beerothite,
Rechab and Baanah, went forth and
came to the house of Ishbaal about the
heat of the day as he was taking his
6 mid-day siesta. At that particular time
the doorkeeper of the house was clean-
ing wheat, but she had become drowsy
7 and slept. So Rechab and Baanah his
brother slipped through and thus entered the house, as he was lying on his
couch in his sleeping room, and they
struck him and killed him and cut off
his head.
Then they took his head and journeyed all night by the way of the Ara-
8 bah, and they brought the head of Ishbaal to David at Hebron and said to
the king,
"Here is the head of Ishbaal, the son
of Saul your enemy, who sought your
life. Thus the LORD has granted vengeance to my lord the king this day on
Saul and his descendants."
9 Then David answered Rechab and
Baanah his brother, the sons of Rimmon the Beerothite, and said to them,
"As the LORD lives, who has delivered my life out of every distress,
10 when one told me, saying, 'Behold, Saul
is dead,' considering himself a messenger of good tidings, I seized him and
killed him in Ziklag, to give him a re-
11 ward for his tidings. How much more,
when wicked men have slain a righteous
man in his own house upon his bed,
shall I not hold you responsible for his
blood, and destroy you from the
earth?"
Then David gave a command to his 12
young men and they slew them and
cut off their hands and their feet and
hanged them up beside the pool in Hebron. But the head of Ishbaal they
took and buried in the grave of Abner
in Hebron.

DAVID, KING OF ISRAEL, 5:1–16

Then all the tribes of Israel came to 5
David to Hebron and said as follows:
"Behold, we are your bone and your
flesh. Also formerly when Saul was 2
king over us, it was you who led out and
brought in Israel, and the LORD said to
you, 'You shall shepherd my people Israel, and you shall be a leader over Israel.'"
So all the elders of Israel came to the 3
king at Hebron, and King David made
a covenant with them in Hebron before
the LORD, and they anointed David
king over Israel.
David was thirty years old when he 4
became king, and he reigned forty
years. In Hebron he reigned over Ju- 5
dah seven years and six months, and in
Jerusalem he reigned thirty-three years
over all Israel and Judah.
The king and his men went to Jeru- 6
salem against the Jebusites, the inhabitants of the land, who spoke to
David, saying, "You shall not come in
here, but the blind and the lame shall
prevent you," thinking David could
not enter there.
Nevertheless David took the citadel 7
of Zion (that is the city of David).
David said on that day, 8
"He who would smite the Jebusites,
let him gain the water shaft, and all
will be as the lame and blind who hate
David's life."
Therefore it is said,
"The blind and the lame cannot
come into the house."
So David dwelt in the citadel, and 9
called it the City of David.
David also built an encircling wall
from the Millo and inward.
Thus David kept on increasing in 10
power, for the LORD of hosts was with
him. Therefore Hiram, king of Tyre, 11
sent messengers to David, also cedar

trees and carpenters and stone-cutters
12 and they built David a house; and David realized that the LORD had established him king over Israel; for his
kingdom had been exalted for the sake
of his people Israel.
13 David also took more concubines
and wives from Jerusalem, after he
14 came from Hebron; and there were
other sons and daughters born to David. These are the names of those who
were born to him in Jerusalem: Sham-
15 mua, Shobab, Nathan, Solomon, Ibhar,
16 Elishua, Nepheg, Japhia, Elishama,
Baaliada, and Eliphelet.

WAR WITH THE PHILISTINES, 5:17–25

17 Accordingly when the Philistines
heard that they had anointed David
king over Israel, all the Philistines went
up to seek David; and when David
heard of this he went down to the
stronghold.
18 Now the Philistines had come and
spread themselves out in the valley of
19 Rephaim. Therefore David inquired of
the LORD, saying,

"Shall I go up against the Philistines? Wilt thou deliver them into my
hand?"

Then the LORD said to David,

"Go up; for I will certainly deliver
the Philistines into your hand."
20 So David came to Baal-perazim, and
David defeated them there; and he
said,

"The LORD has burst forth upon my
enemies before me, like the bursting of
a dam."

Therefore he called the name of that
21 place Baal-perazim. Moreover they left
their gods there, and David and his
men carried them away.
22 The Philistines came up once again
and spread themselves out in the valley
23 of Rephaim; and when David inquired
of the LORD, he said,

"You shall not go up; go around to
their rear and come upon them oppo-
24 site the balsam trees. Then when you
hear the sound of marching in the tops
of the balsam trees, make haste, for at
that moment the LORD has gone forth
before you to fall upon the camp of the
Philistines."
25 So David did as the LORD com-
manded him, and he joined battle with the Philistines from Gibeon as far as Gezer.

THE RETURN OF THE ARK TO JERUSALEM, 6:1–23

David again mustered all the chosen men of Israel, thirty thousand. Then David and all the people who were with him arose and went to Baal-Judah, to bring up from there the ark of God which is called by the name of the LORD of hosts who is seated upon the cherubim. Also they conveyed the ark of God upon a new cart, and they brought it up from the house of Abinadab which was on the hill, and Uzzah and Ahio, the sons of Abinadab, were guiding the cart: Uzzah was walking beside the ark of God, while Ahio was walking in front of the ark. At the same time David and all the house of Israel were reveling before the LORD with all their might with songs and harps and lyres and with tambourines and castanets and cymbals. But when they came to the threshing floor of Nacon, Uzzah put out his hand to the ark of God and grasped hold of it, for the oxen jostled it. Then the anger of the LORD blazed against Uzzah and God struck him down there because he put his hand to the ark and there he died beside the ark of God. Whereupon David was angry because the LORD had broken forth upon Uzzah. Therefore that place is called Perez-uzzah [Breach of Uzzah] to this day. Moreover David was afraid of the LORD that day and he said,

"How can the ark of the LORD come to me?"

So David was unwilling to remove the ark of the LORD unto him into the city of David, but took it aside into the house of Obed-edom the Gittite. Thus the ark of the LORD remained in the house of Obed-edom the Gittite three months. But the LORD blessed Obed-edom and all his house.

Now when it was told King David that the LORD had blessed the house of Obed-edom and all that belonged to him, because of the ark of God, David went and brought up the ark of God with joy from the house of Obed-edom to the city of David. Accordingly

when the bearers of the ark of the
LORD had advanced six paces, he sac-
4 rificed an ox and a fatling. David was
also whirling in a dance with all his
might, and David was girded with a
5 linen apron. So David and all the
house of Israel brought up the ark of
the LORD with shouting and the sound
of the trumpet.
6 Then as the ark of the LORD was
coming to the city of David, and Michal, the daughter of Saul, was looking
out of the window, she saw King David
whirling and leaping before the LORD,
7 and despised him in her heart. Now
when they brought in the ark of the
LORD and set it in its place within the
tent that David had pitched for it,
David offered burnt-offerings and
8 thank-offerings before the LORD; and
when David finished offering the burnt-
offerings and the thank-offerings, he
blessed the people in the name of the
9 LORD of hosts. He also distributed to all
the people, even the whole multitude
of Israel, both men and women, to each
a loaf of bread and a portion of meat
and a raisin cake. Then all the people
departed each to his home.
0 But when David returned to bless his
family, Michal the daughter of Saul
came out to meet David and said,
"How dignified was the king of Israel
today as he stripped himself in the
sight of the maidservants of his retainers, as a common rake exposes himself!"
1 "It is before the LORD that I dance,"
said David to Michal. "Blessed be the
LORD, who chose me rather than your
father or any of his house to appoint
me as a leader over the people of the
LORD, over Israel. Therefore I will dis-
2 port myself before the LORD and I will
be still more abandoned than that, and
I will be vile in your eyes. But with the
maid-servants to whom you have referred I shall indeed be held in honor."
3 Michal the daughter of Saul had no
child to the day of her death.

DAVID'S DESIRE TO BUILD A TEMPLE, 7:1–29

Now when the king dwelt in his
house, and the LORD had given him
rest from all his enemies on every side,
2 the king said to Nathan the prophet,
"See here, I dwell in a house of cedar,
but the ark of God dwells under tent
curtains."
Then Nathan said to the king, 3
"Go, do all that is in your mind, for
the LORD is with you."
But that very night the word of the 4
LORD came to Nathan, saying,
"Go and say to my servant David, 5
'Thus says the LORD: "Should you
build me a house to dwell in? for I have 6
not dwelt in a house since the day I
brought up the Israelites out of Egypt,
even to this day, but I have been making my abode in a tent as a dwelling.
In all the places where I have made my 7
abode with all the Israelites, did I
speak a word with one of the judges of
Israel whom I commanded to shepherd
my people Israel, saying, 'Why have
you not built me a house of cedar?' " '
Now therefore thus you shall say to my 8
servant David, 'Thus says the LORD of
hosts: "I took you from the pasture,
from following the sheep, that you
should be a leader over my people, over
Israel; and I have been with you wher- 9
ever you have gone, and I have cut off
all your enemies from before you, and I
will make for you a great name, like the
name of the great who are in the earth.
I will also appoint a place for my people 10
Israel and will plant them that they
may dwell in their own place, and be
disturbed no more. The wicked shall no
more afflict them as formerly, even from 11
the day that I commanded judges to be
over my people Israel.

"Thus I will give you respite from all
your foes.
The LORD also declares to you
That he will make you a house;
And when your days are finished, 12
And you are laid with your fathers,
I will raise up your heir after you,
Who shall be born of your body;
And I will establish his kingdom.
He shall build a house for my name, 13
And I will establish the throne of his
kingdom forever.

"I will be a father to him, 14
And he shall be a son to me;
When he goes astray,
I will chasten him with the rod of men,
And with the stripes of the sons of
Adam.
But my kindness shall not depart from 15
him,

As I withdrew it from him who was
before you.
16 Your house and your kingdom shall
be confirmed before me forever;
Your throne shall be established forever.' ' "
17 In accordance with all these words
and all this vision, so did Nathan speak
to David.
18 Then King David went in and sat
down before the LORD and said,
"Who am I, my lord GOD, and what
is my house, that thou hast brought me
19 thus far? As though this were too small
a thing in thine eyes, O my lord GOD,
thou hast gone on to speak concerning
the house of thy servant for a long time
to come, and hast made me see the coming generations of men, O my lord
20 GOD! Now what more can David say
to thee? for thou knowest thy servant,
21 O my lord GOD. For thy word's sake,
and according to thine own heart hast
thou brought about all this greatness to
22 show it to thy servant. Therefore thou
art great, O LORD God, for there is
none like thee, and there is no God beside thee, according to all that we have
23 heard with our ears. What other nation
in the earth is like thy people Israel,
whom God went to redeem for himself
as a people, to make himself a name by
doing great and terrible things for them
(for thy land) in driving out from before his people, whom thou didst redeem for thyself from Egypt, a nation
24 and its gods? And thou didst establish
for thyself thy people Israel for thine
own people forever, and thou, O LORD,
25 didst become their God. Now, therefore, O LORD God, confirm forever the
word which thou hast spoken concerning thy servant and concerning his
26 house, and do as thou hast spoken, that
thy name may be magnified forever, in
saying, 'The LORD of hosts is God over
Israel; and the house of thy servant
David shall be established before thee.'
27 For thou, O LORD of hosts, God of Israel, hast revealed to thy servant, saying, 'I will build you a house'; therefore
thy servant has found his courage to
28 pray unto thee this prayer. And now,
O my lord GOD, thou art God, and thy
words are truth, and thou hast spoken
29 this good word to thy servant; now
therefore may it please thee to bless the
house of thy servant that it may continue before thee forever; for thou, O
my lord GOD, hast spoken; and with
thy blessing the house of thy servant
shall be forever blest."

DAVID'S WARS, 8:1–18

Now after this David defeated the Philistines and subdued them; and David took the control of the metropolis out of the hand of the Philistines. He also defeated the Moabites and measured them off with a line, making them lie down on the ground; and he measured two lines to put to death and one line to save alive. Thus the Moabites became subject to David and brought tribute. Then David defeated Hadadezer, the son of Rehob, the king of Zobah, as he went to establish his power at the River; and David took from him a thousand chariots, seven thousand cavalry, and twenty thousand infantry; and David hamstrung all the chariot horses, but reserved enough of them for one hundred chariots.

Likewise when the Syrians of Damascus came to help Hadadezer, king of Zobah, David slew of the Syrians twenty-two thousand men. Then David put garrisons in Damascene Syria, and the Syrians became subject to David and brought tribute. Thus the LORD gave victory to David wherever he went. David also took the shields of gold that were on the servants of Hadadezer, and brought them to Jerusalem; and from Tabah and Berothai, cities of Hadadezer, King David took a very large amount of bronze.

Now when Toi, king of Hamath, heard that David had defeated all the army of Hadadezer, Toi sent Hadoram his son to King David, to greet him and congratulate him because he had fought against Hadadezer and defeated him; for Hadadezer had been Toi's opponent in war; and he brought with him articles of silver, gold, and bronze. These also King David dedicated to the LORD, along with the silver and gold that he dedicated from all the nations that he had subdued—from Edom, Moab, the Ammonites, the Philistines, and Amalek, and from the spoil of Hadadezer, son of Rehob, king of Zobah. So David won fame. On his return, he overcame eighteen thousand

Edomites in the Valley of Salt; and he put garrisons throughout all Edom; and all the Edomites became David's servants. Thus the LORD gave David victory wherever he went.

David was king over all Israel; and David administered justice and righteousness for all his people. Joab, the son of Zeruiah, was in command of the army, and Jehoshaphat, the son of Ahilud, was recorder, and Zadok, the son of Ahitub, and Abiathar, the son of Ahimelech, were priests, and Seraiah was scribe, and Benaiah, the son of Jehoiada, was in command of the Cherethites and Pelethites, and David's sons were priests.

DAVID'S KINDNESS TO JONATHAN'S SON, 9:1-13

"Is there anyone left of the family of Saul to whom I may show kindness for Jonathan's sake?" said David.

Now there was a retainer of Saul's house whose name was Ziba, and they called him to David; and the king said to him,

"Are you Ziba?"

"Your servant," he said.

"Is there not still someone belonging to the house of Saul to whom I may show the kindness of God?" said the king.

"There is a son of Jonathan still living, who is crippled in his feet," said Ziba to the king.

"Where is he?" said the king to him.

"Behold, he is in the house of Machir, the son of Ammiel, in Lodebar," Ziba said to the king.

Then King David sent and took him from the house of Machir, the son of Ammiel, from Lodebar. When Meribaal, the son of Jonathan, the son of Saul, came to David, he fell on his face and did obeisance; and David said,

"Meribaal!"

"Behold your servant," he said.

"Fear not," said David to him, "for I will surely show you kindness for the sake of Jonathan your father and I will restore to you the entire estate of Saul your grandfather, and you shall always eat bread at my table."

Again he did obeisance and said,

"What is your servant that you should regard such a dead dog as I am?"

Then the king called to Ziba, Saul's 9
domestic, and said to him,
"All that belonged to Saul and to all
his house I give to your master's son;
and you together with your sons and 10
your servants shall cultivate the soil for
him, and bring in the harvest that your
master's son may have food to eat; but
Meribaal, your master's son, shall always eat bread at my table."
Now Ziba had fifteen sons and twenty servants. Then Ziba said to the king, 11
"Your servant will do just as my
lord the king commands his servant."
So Meribaal ate at David's table like
one of the king's sons. And Meribaal 12
had a little son and his name was Mica;
and all who dwelt in Ziba's house were
Meribaal's servants. So Meribaal 13
dwelt in Jerusalem; for he ate regularly
at the king's table, being crippled in
both feet.

DAVID'S VICTORY OVER AMMON, 10:1-19

Now after this, the king of the Am- **10**
monites died and Hanun his son became king in his stead. Then David 2
said,
"I will show kindness to Hanun, the
son of Nahash, as his father showed
kindness to me."
So David sent by his servants to condole with him concerning his father.
But when the servants of David came
to the land of the Ammonites, the 3
princes of the Ammonites said to Hanun their lord,
"Do you imagine that David is honoring your father in sending you comforters? Is it not to inspect the city and
to spy it out and to overthrow it, that
David has sent his servants to you?"
Whereupon Hanun took David's 4
servants, and shaved off one side of
their beards, cut their garments off at
the hips, and sent them away. When 5
they told David about the men, he sent
to meet them, for the men were deeply
ashamed. So the king said,
"Remain at Jericho until your
beards are grown and then return."
Now when the Ammonites saw that 6
they were in bad odor with David, the
Ammonites sent and hired the Arameans of Beth-Rehob, and the Arameans
of Zobah, twenty thousand infantry,
and the king of Maacah with a thou-

sand men, and Ishtob with twelve
7 thousand men. When David heard of
it, he sent Joab and all the army of sea-
8 soned troops. Then the Ammonites
came out and drew up in line of battle
at the entrance of the city; and the
Arameans of Zobah and Rehob, and
Ishtob and Maacah, were by themselves in the open country.
9 Now when Joab saw that he had to
meet both a frontal and rear attack, he
made a selection from all the picked
men of Israel, and drew them up in line
10 against the Arameans. The rest of the
people he placed in command of Abishai his brother; and he drew them up
11 in line against the Ammonites. Then
he said,

"If the Arameans prove too strong
for me, then you shall be my help, but
if the Ammonites prove too strong for
12 you, then I will come to your aid. Be
courageous, and let us show ourselves
strong for the sake of our people and for
the cities of our God; and may the LORD
do that which is good in his sight."

13 Now when Joab and the people who
were with him drew near to join battle
with the Arameans, they fled before
14 him; and when the Ammonites saw
that the Arameans had fled, they likewise fled before Abishai, and entered
the city. Then Joab returned from his
attack upon the Ammonites, and came
to Jerusalem.
15 But when the Arameans saw that
they had been defeated by Israel, they
16 gathered themselves together. Moreover Hadadezer sent, and brought the
Arameans who were beyond the River,
and they came to Helam, with Shobach, the commander of Hadadezer's
17 army, at their head. Now when it was
told David, he gathered all Israel together and crossed the Jordan and
came to Helam. Thereupon the Arameans drew up their lines to meet Da-
18 vid and fought with him. But the Arameans fled before Israel; and David destroyed seven hundred chariots and
forty thousand horsemen and he mortally wounded Shobach, the commander of their army, so that he died there.
19 When all the kings who were servants
of Hadadezer, saw that they were defeated by Israel, they made peace with
Israel and became subject to them. So
the Arameans feared to help the Ammonites any more.

DAVID'S SIN WITH BATH-SHEBA, 11:1—12:25

Now at the return of spring, at the time when kings go forth, David sent Joab and his servants with him, even all Israel, and they ravaged the Ammonites, and besieged Rabbah. But David remained in Jerusalem. Then one day at sunset, David got up from his couch, and walked to and fro upon the roof of the king's house; and from the roof he saw a woman bathing. The woman was very beautiful. Therefore David sent and sought for the woman, and said,

"Is not this Bathsheba, the daughter of Eliam, the wife of Uriah the Hittite?"

So David sent messengers and took her; and she came to him, and he lay with her at the time she was cleansing herself from her impurity; then she returned to her house. So the woman conceived; and she sent and informed David, and she said,

"I am with child."

Then David sent to Joab,

"Send me Uriah the Hittite."

Accordingly Joab sent Uriah the Hittite to David; and when Uriah came to him, David asked concerning the welfare of Joab and the condition of the people and the course of the war. Then David said to Uriah,

"Go down to your house and wash your feet."

So Uriah went out of the king's house, and there followed him a present from the king. But Uriah slept at the entrance of the king's house, along with all the servants of his lord, and did not go down to his house. Now when they told David that Uriah did not go down to his house, David said to Uriah,

"Have you not come from a journey? Why have you not gone down to your house?"

Then Uriah said to David,

"The ark and Israel and Judah dwell in booths, and my master Joab and the servants of my lord are camping in the open field; and should I enter my house to eat and drink and to lie with my wife? As the LORD lives and as you yourself live, I could not do this thing."

So David said to Uriah,

"Remain here today also, and tomorrow I will send you away."

Accordingly Uriah remained in Jeru-

3 salem that day. But on the morrow
David summoned him and he ate and
drank before him, so that he made him
drunk; and in the evening he went out to
lie on his bed with the servants of his
lord, but he did not go down to his
house.
4 Then in the morning, David wrote a
letter to Joab, and sent it by the hand
5 of Uriah; and he wrote in the letter,
saying,
"Put Uriah in the forefront of the
hottest fighting, then draw back from
him, that he may be struck down and
die."
6 Therefore as Joab pressed the siege
against the city, he put Uriah at a point
where he knew the best opposing troops
7 were; and when the men of the city
sallied out and fought with Joab, some
of the men of David's forces fell, and
Uriah the Hittite was also among the
8 slain. Then Joab sent and reported to
David the full details of the fighting.
9 He also gave instructions to the messenger, saying,
"When you have finished telling all
the details of the fighting to the king,
0 then if the king's anger is aroused, and
he say to you, 'Why did you go so near
the city to fight? Did you not know
that they would shoot from the wall?
Who killed Abimelech, the son of Jerubbaal? Did not a woman drop an
upper millstone upon him from the
wall, so that he died in Thebez? Why
did you go near the wall?' Then you
shall say, 'Your servant Uriah the Hittite is dead also.'"
So the messenger of Joab set out and
came and when he told David all that
with which Joab had charged him, even
all the details of the fighting, then David was enraged at Joab, and he said to
the messenger,
"Why did you go near the city to
fight? Did you not realize that you
would be attacked from the wall? Who
killed Abimelech, the son of Jerubbaal?
Did not a woman drop an upper millstone upon him from the wall, so that
he died in Thebez? Why did you go
near the wall?"
3 Then the messenger said to David,
"Because the men gained an advantage over us and came out to fight
us in the open field, but we fought them
back to the very entrance of the gate,
and then the archers shot from the
wall at your servants; and some of the
king's servants are dead, and your
servant Uriah the Hittite is dead also."
Thereupon David said to the messenger, 25
"Thus shall you say to Joab: 'Let
not this affair depress you, for the
sword devours one as well as another;
strengthen your attack upon the city
and overthrow it,' and do you encourage him."
Now when the wife of Uriah heard 26
that Uriah her husband was dead, she
made lamentation for her husband.
But when the mourning was over, Da- 27
vid sent and removed her to his house,
and she became his wife and bore him a
son. But the thing that David had
done displeased the LORD.
Accordingly, the LORD sent the **12**
prophet Nathan to David; and he came
to him, and said to him,
"There were two men in a certain
city, the one rich, and the other poor.
The rich man owned very many flocks 2
and herds. But the poor man had 3
nothing but a single little ewe lamb,
which he had bought. He reared it and
it grew up with him and with his children. It would eat from his food and
drink from his cup, and it lay in his
bosom, and it was like a daughter to
him. Now there came a traveler to the 4
rich man, and he refused to take from
his own flock or his own herd to make
ready for the wayfarer who had come
to him, but he took the poor man's
lamb and prepared it for the man who
had come to him."
Then David's anger became furious 5
against the man, and he said to Nathan,
"As the LORD lives, the man that
does this is worthy of death; he shall re- 6
store the lamb sevenfold, because he
did this and because he showed no
pity."
"You are the man!" said Nathan to 7
David. "Thus says the LORD God of
Israel: 'I anointed you king over Israel
and I delivered you out of the hand of
Saul, and I gave you your master's 8
house and your master's wives into
your bosom; I also gave you the house
of Israel and of Judah, and if that were
too little, I would add in this or that
way. Why have you despised the 9
LORD by doing that which is evil in
my sight? You have slain Uriah the

Hittite with the sword, and you have
taken his wife to be your wife, having
slain him with the sword of the Am-
10 monites. Now therefore the sword shall
never depart from your house, because
you have despised me and have taken
the wife of Uriah the Hittite to be your
11 wife.' Thus says the LORD: 'Behold,
I will raise up evil against you out of
your own house, and I will take your
wives from before your eyes and give
them to your neighbor, and he shall lie
with your wives in the sight of this sun,
12 for you did it secretly; but I will do this
thing before all Israel in the open light
of day.'"
13 Then David said to Nathan,
"I have sinned against the LORD."
"The LORD has also taken away
your sin; you shall not die," said Nathan
14 to David. "Nevertheless, because you
have openly spurned the LORD by this
deed, the child that is born to you shall
surely die."
15 Then Nathan went to his house.
And the LORD struck the child that
the wife of Uriah bore to David, so that
16 it was taken ill; and David besought
the LORD in behalf of the child, and he
kept a fast and went in and lay in sack-
17 cloth upon the earth. Then the older
men of his household arose and stood
beside him in order to raise him up
from the earth, but he would not,
neither would he eat food with them.
18 Now on the seventh day the child
died; and the servants of David feared
to tell him that the child was dead, for
they said,
"Behold, while the child was still
alive, we spoke to him, and he heeded
not our voice; how can we say to him,
the child is dead? How desperate it
will make him!"
19 But when David saw that his servants were whispering to one another,
David perceived that the child was
dead, and David said to his servants,
"Is the child dead?"
"He is dead," they said.
20 Thereupon David arose from the
earth, and bathed and anointed himself, and changed his garments; and he
went into the house of the LORD and
worshiped. Then he went to his own
house; and he asked for food and they
21 set it before him and he ate. However,
his servants said to him,
"What is the meaning of this thing
that you have done? You have fasted
and wept for the child, while it was
alive, but when the child died, you have
arisen and eaten food!"
"While the child was still alive," he
said, "I fasted and wept; for I said,
'Who knows whether the LORD will
show himself merciful to me and let the
child live?' But now he is dead; why
should I fast? Can I bring him back
again? I expect to go to him, but he
will never come back to me."
Then David comforted Bathsheba
his wife, and went in to her and lay
with her and she conceived and bore a
son, and he called his name Solomon.
The LORD loved him, and sent a message through Nathan the prophet; so he
called his name Jedidiah, according to
the command of the LORD.

DAVID'S CAPTURE OF RABBAH OF AMMON, 12:26-31

Joab fought against Rabbah of the
Ammonites and took the City of the
Waters. Then Joab sent messengers to
David, and said,
"I have fought against Rabbah; I
have also taken the City of the Waters.
Now therefore muster the rest of the
people, and encamp against the city,
and take it, lest I take it and my name
be proclaimed over it."
So David mustered all the people and
went to Rabbah and fought against it
and took it. He also took the crown of
Milcom from his head; and its weight
was about a talent of gold, and in it was
a precious stone; and it was placed on
David's head. And he brought away
the very great amount of the city's
spoil. He also brought forth the people
who were in it, and set them to the
saws and to cutting instruments of iron
and to axes of iron, and on occasion he
made them labor at the brick-molds.
Even thus he did in turn to all the cities
of the Ammonites. Then David and all
the people returned to Jerusalem.

DAVID'S FAMILY TROUBLES, 13:1—14:33

Now Absalom, a son of David, had a
beautiful sister, whose name was Tamar; and it happened after this that

Amnon, a son of David, loved her. Amnon was so distressed that he made himself sick because of his sister Tamar—for she was a virgin—and it seemed impossible to Amnon to get any approach to her.

But Amnon had a friend whose name was Jonadab, the son of Shimeah, David's brother, and Jonadab was a very shrewd man.

"Why, O prince, are you so depressed morning after morning?" he said to him. "Will you not tell me?"

"I love Tamar, my brother Absalom's sister," said Amnon to him.

"Lie down on your bed, and pretend to be ill," Jonadab said to him. "Then when your father comes to see you, say to him, 'Let now my sister Tamar come and serve me some food, and let her prepare the food in my sight, that I may see it and eat from her hand.' "

So Amnon lay down and pretended to be ill. And when the king came to see him, Amnon said to the king,

"Let now my sister Tamar come and make a couple of cakes in my sight, that I may eat from her hand."

So David sent to the house for Tamar, saying,

"Go now to your brother Amnon's house, and prepare food for him."

Then Tamar went to her brother Amnon's house while he was there in bed. She took dough and kneaded it and make cakes before him, and fried the cakes; and she took the pan and poured them out before him, but he refused to eat. Amnon then said,

"Put out everybody from attending me."

So they all withdrew from him. Then Amnon said to Tamar,

"Bring the food into the chamber, that I may eat from your hand."

So Tamar took the cakes that she had made, and brought them into the chamber to Amnon her brother. But when she had brought them near to him to eat, he took hold of her and said to her,

"Come, lie with me, my sister."

"No, my brother," she said to him, "do not humiliate me, for it is not so done in Israel; do not this disgraceful folly. As for me, whither could I carry my shame? and as for you, you would become as one of the impious profligates in Israel. Now therefore, I pray
you, speak to the king; for he will not
withold me from marrying you."
But he would not listen to her voice, 14
and being stronger than she, he overpowered her and lay with her.
Then Amnon hated her with unut- 15
terable hatred, for the hatred with
which he hated her was greater than
the love with which he had loved her.
"Arise be gone!" said Amnon to her.
But she said to him, 16
"No, my brother; for greater would
be this wrong, to send me away, than
the first that you have done to me."
However, he would not listen to her,
but called his servant, who ministered 17
to him, and said,
"Put out now this female from my
presence, and bolt the door after her."
Now she wore a long-sleeved tunic 18
reaching to the ankles, for thus the virgin
princesses were formerly accustomed
to be clad. So his servant put her out
and bolted the door after her. Then Ta- 19
mar put ashes on her head, and rent the
long-sleeved tunic which she wore; and
putting her hand on her head, she departed, crying aloud as she went along.
Accordingly Absalom her own broth- 20
er said to her,
"Has Amnon your brother been with
you? But now, my sister, be quiet, he
is your brother; do not take this matter
to heart."
So Tamar remained desolate in the
house of Absalom her brother. More- 21
over when king David heard all these
things, he was very angry, but he did
not reprove Amnon his son, for he loved
him, because he was his first-born. But 22
Absalom spoke to Amnon neither good
nor bad; for Absalom hated Amnon,
because he had violated his sister Tamar.
Now it happened just two years lat- 23
er, that Absalom had sheep-shearers in
Baal-hazor near Ephraim, and Absalom invited all the king's sons. Like- 24
wise Absalom went to the king and
said,
"See now, your servant has sheep-
shearers, let the king and his servants,
I pray you, go with your servant."
But the king said to Absalom, 25
"No, my son, let us not all go now,
lest we be a burden to you."
He pressed him, but he would not go,
but he added his blessing.
"If not, then I pray you, let my 26

brother Amnon go with us," said Absalom.
"Why should he go with you?" said the king to him.
27 But when Absalom pressed him, he let Amnon and all the king's sons go with him. So Absalom made a feast
28 like a royal feast. Then Absalom commanded his servants, saying,
"See now, when Amnon's heart is merry with wine, and when I say to you, 'Strike down Amnon,' then kill him. Fear not; have I not given you your orders? Be courageous and show yourselves valiant."
29 So the retainers of Absalom did to Amnon as Absalom commanded. Then all the king's sons arose and each mounted his mule and fled.
30 While they were on the way, the report came to David that Absalom had murdered all the king's sons so that
31 there was not one of them left. Then the king arose and tore his garments and lay on the earth; and all his servants who were standing by him tore their
32 garments. But Jonadab, the son of Shimeah, David's brother, answered and said,
"Let not my lord suppose that they have killed all the young men, the king's sons, for Amnon alone is dead, since by the mouth of Absalom this has been determined ever since he violated
33 his sister Tamar. Now therefore let not my lord the king take the report so seriously to heart as to imagine that all the king's sons are dead; but Amnon alone is dead."
34 When the youth who kept the watch lifted up his eyes and looked, behold many people were coming on the Horonaim road; and the watchman came and told the king, saying,
"I have seen men coming down from the Horonaim road by the side of the mountain."
35 So Jonadab said to the king,
"There, the king's sons have come; according to the word of your servant, so it has come about."
36 As soon as he had finished speaking, behold, the king's sons arrived, and they lifted up their voice and wept; and the king also and all his servants wept very bitterly.
37 But Absalom fled and went to Talmai, son of Ammihud, king of Geshur, and David kept on mourning for his son

day after day. So Absalom fled and went to Geshur, and he was there three years. But the spirit of King David pined for Absalom, for he was comforted concerning Amnon, seeing that he was dead.

Now when Joab, the son of Zeruiah, perceived that the king's heart was inclined toward Absalom, Joab sent to Tekoa and brought from there a wise woman and said to her,

"Pretend now to be a mourner and put on mourning garments, I pray you, and do not anoint yourself with oil, but become as a woman who has been mourning many days for the dead; and go to the king and speak thus to him."

So Joab put the words into her mouth.

Accordingly when the woman of Tekoa came to the king, she fell on her face to the earth and did obeisance, and said,

"Help, O king!"

"What is your trouble?" said the king to her.

"Of a truth I am a widow," she said, "and my husband is dead. Your maidservant had two sons, and the two of them struggled together in the field, and there being no one to part them, the one struck the other and killed him. Now the whole clan has risen up against your maidservant and they say, 'Deliver up the slayer of his brother, that we may kill him for the life of his brother whom he slew,' that they may destroy the heir also. Thus they will quench my remaining hope, so as to leave to my husband neither name nor remnant on the face of the ground."

Then the king said to the woman,

"Go to your house and I will give orders concerning you."

But the woman of Tekoa said to the king,

"Upon me, my lord, O king, be the guilt and on my father's house; and the king and his throne be innocent."

"Whoever speaks to you, bring him to me and he shall not touch you again," said the king.

"I pray you," she said, "let the king remember the LORD your God, not to allow the avenger of blood to destroy and not to let them murder my son."

"As the LORD lives," he said, "not one hair of your son shall fall to the earth."

"I pray you," said the woman, "let your maidservant speak a word to my lord the king."

"Speak," he said.

"Why then," said the woman, "have you devised such a thing against the people of God? For in speaking this word the king is as one that is guilty, in that the king does not bring back his banished one. For we must indeed die and are as water poured upon the earth, that cannot be gathered up again; nor can God take it up. Therefore a person should devise plans not to keep in banishment the one who is banished. Now the reason why I have come to speak this word to the king my lord is because the people frightened me, and your maidservant said, 'I will now speak to the king; it may be that the king will perform the request of his handmaid.' For the king will hearken, to deliver his handmaid from the hand of the man who seeks to destroy me and my son from the heritage of the LORD. Then your maidservant said, 'Let the word of my lord the king be a comfort,' for as the angel of God, so is my lord the king to hear good and evil; and the LORD your God be with you."

Then the king answered and said to the woman,

"Do not, I pray you, conceal from me anything that I ask you."

The woman said,

"Let now my lord the king speak."

"Is the hand of Joab with you in all this?" said the king.

The woman answered and said,

"As sure as you are alive, my lord the king, one cannot turn to the right hand or to the left hand from all that my lord the king has spoken; for your servant Joab, he it was that commanded me, and he put all these words in the mouth of your maidservant; in order to change the face of the matter your servant Joab did this thing. But my lord is wise, according to the wisdom of the angel of God, so that he knows all things that are in the earth."

Therefore the king said to Joab,

"See now, you have accomplished this thing; go therefore, bring the young man Absalom back."

Then Joab fell on his face to the earth and did obeisance and blessed the king; and Joab said,

"Today your servant knows that I
have found favor in your sight, my lord,
O king, in that the king has performed
the request of his servant."
So Joab arose and went to Geshur, 23
and brought Absalom back to Jerusalem. However the king said, 24
"Let him live apart in his own house,
since he is not to visit me."
So Absalom lived apart in his own
house, and did not visit the king.
Now in all Israel there was no man so 25
much to be praised for his beauty as
Absalom; from the sole of his foot to
the crown of his head there was no
blemish in him. When he shaved his 26
head—now at the end of every year he
used to cut his hair, because it was
heavy on him, therefore he cut it—he
used to weigh his hair, two hundred
shekels by the royal standard of weight.
There were born to Absalom three sons 27
and one daughter, whose name was
Tamar—she was a beautiful woman.
Absalom dwelt two full years in Je- 28
rusalem, without visiting the king.
Then Absalom sent for Joab to send 29
him to the king; but he would not come
to him. So he sent a second time, but 30
he refused to come. Therefore he said
to his servants,
"See, Joab's field borders mine, where
he has barley; go and set it on fire."
Later Joab's servants came to him
with torn garments, and said,
"The servants of Absalom have set
the field on fire."
Then Joab arose, and went to Ab- 31
salom at his house and said to him,
"Why have your servants set my
field on fire?"
Accordingly Absalom said to Joab, 32
"Behold, I sent to you saying, 'Come
here that I may send you to the king, to
say, "Why have I come from Geshur?
It were better that I were still there."
Now therefore let me visit the king, and
if there is guilt in me, let him kill me.' "
Therefore when Joab went to the 33
king and told him, he summoned Absalom. So he went to the king and did
obeisance and fell upon his face to the
earth before the king. Then the king
kissed Absalom.

ABSALOM'S REVOLT, 15:1—19:42

Now afterward Absalom provided 15
for himself a chariot and horses and

2 fifty men to run before him. Also Absalom used to rise early and stand beside the way of the gate, and whenever
any man had a suit to come to the king
for judgment, Absalom would take occasion to call to him and say
"Of what city are you?"
And when he said,
"Your servant is of some one of the
tribes of Israel,"
3 Absalom would say to him,
"It is evident your claims are valid
and legitimate; but there is no one
deputed by the king to hear you."
4 Absalom said moreover,
"O that someone would make me a
judge in the land, that any man who
had a suit or cause might come to me,
that I might give him justice!"
5 Whenever a man came near to do
obeisance to him, he would put out his
hand and take hold of him and kiss him.
6 After this manner Absalom dealt with
all the Israelites who came to the king
for judgment. So Absalom alienated
the hearts of the men of Israel.
7 Now at the end of four years, Absalom said to the king,
"Let me go, I pray you, and pay my
vow, which I vowed to the LORD, in
8 Hebron. For your servant vowed a vow,
while I abode at Geshur in Syria, as
follows: 'If the LORD will indeed bring
me back to Jerusalem, then I will serve
the LORD in Hebron.' "
9 "Go in peace," said the king to him.
10 So he arose and went to Hebron. But
Absalom sent emissaries throughout all
the tribes of Israel, saying,
"As soon as you hear the sound of
the trumpet, then say, 'Absalom is king
in Hebron.' "
11 Also with Absalom went two hundred
men from Jerusalem, who went in all
innocence as invited guests, and were
not aware of any plot.
12 Moreover Absalom sent and called
Ahithophel the Gilonite, David's counselor, from his city Giloh, where he was
offering sacrifices; and the conspiracy
was strong, for the people with Absalom kept on increasing.
13 Therefore when a messenger came to
David, saying,
"The heart of the men of Israel has
gone after Absalom,"
14 David said to all his servants who
were with him at Jerusalem,
"Up and away; for otherwise there
will be for us no escape from Absalom.
Make haste to be off, lest he quickly
overtake us and set evil in motion
against us and put the city to the
sword."
Then the king's servants said to the
king,
"In accordance with all that my lord
the king decides, your servants are
ready."
So the king went out and all his
household after him. But the king left
behind ten concubines to keep the
palace. The king and all his attendants
who followed after him went forth and
halted at the last house, while all the
people marched past him; and all the
Cherethites and all the Pelethites and
all the men of Ittai the Gittite, six hundred men who had followed him from
Gath, passed on before the king.
Then the king said to Ittai the Gittite,
"Why will you also go with us? Return and remain with the king; for you
are a foreigner and an exile from your
own home. You came but yesterday
and shall I today cause you to wander
with us, while I go wherever I may?
Return and lead back your fellow-countrymen with you; and the LORD will
show you kindness and faithfulness."
But Ittai answered the king and said,
"As the LORD lives and as my lord
the king lives, wherever my lord the
king shall be—whether for death or for
life—there will your servant be."
Wherefore David said to Ittai,
"Go and pass on."
So Ittai the Gittite passed on with all
his men and all the children that were
with him.
Moreover all the countryside was in
loud lamentation as all the people were
passing by. While the king stood in the
Kidron valley, all the people were passing on before him by way of the olive
tree which is in the desert. There too
were both Zadok and Abiathar with
him, bearing the ark of the covenant of
God, and they halted the ark of God
until all the people had entirely passed
out of the city. Then the king said to
Zadok and Abiathar,
"Carry back the ark of God into the
city and let it remain in its place. If I
shall find favor in the eyes of the LORD,
he will bring me back, and show me
both it and his abode. But if he say, 'I

have no delight in you,' then here I am, let him do to me as seems good in his sight."

The king also said to Zadok and Abiathar the priests,

"Return to the city in peace and your two sons with you, Ahimaaz your son and Jonathan, the son of Abiathar. See, I am going to wait at the fords of the desert, until word comes from you to inform me."

Therefore Zadok and Abiathar carried the ark of God back to Jerusalem, and they remained there.

But David went up the ascent of Olivet, weeping as he went, with his head covered and walking barefoot, and all the people who were with him covered each his head, and they went up, weeping as they ascended; and when it was told David, saying,

"Ahithophel is among the conspirators with Absalom,"

David said,

"O LORD, I pray, turn the counsel of Ahithophel to foolishness."

When David came to the top where one worships God, there was Hushai the Archite to meet him with his tunic torn and earth upon his head; and David said to him,

"If you accompany me you will be a burden to me. But if you return to the city, and say to Absalom, 'O king, I will be your servant; and as I have been your father's servant in time past, so now I will be your servant,' thus you can defeat for me the counsel of Ahithophel. Are there not there with you Zadok and Abiathar the priests? It shall be that, everything which you shall hear from the house of the king, you shall make known to Zadok and Abiathar the priests. Behold, there are with them their two sons, Ahimaaz, Zadok's son, and Jonathan, Abiathar's son; and you shall send to me by them everything that you shall hear."

So Hushai, David's friend, came to the city just as Absalom was entering Jerusalem.

Now when David had passed a little beyond the summit, Ziba, the servant of Meribaal, met him with a couple of asses saddled, loaded with two hundred loaves of bread, a hundred bunches of raisins, a hundred of summer fruits, and a skin of wine.

"Why have you these?" said the king 2
to Ziba.
"The asses," said Ziba, "are for the
king's household to ride on, and the
bread and the summer fruit for the
young men to eat, and the wine, that
those who become faint in the desert
may drink."
"And where is your master's son?" 3
said the king.
"He remains yonder at Jerusalem,"
Ziba said to the king, "for he has said,
'Today will the house of Israel give
back to me the kingdom of my father.' "
Then the king said to Ziba, 4
"See, all is now yours that belonged
to Meribaal."
"I do obeisance," said Ziba. "Let me
continue to find favor in your sight, my
lord, O king!"
When King David came to Bahurim, 5
there was a man coming out from there
of the family of the house of Saul, whose
name was Shimei, the son of Gera, uttering
a stream of curses as he came
along. Also he threw stones at David 6
and all the attendants of King David
and at all the people and all the famous
warriors on his right hand and on his
left; and thus he said as he cursed: 7
"Begone, begone, man of blood and
vile scoundrel! The LORD has brought 8
back upon you all the blood of the
house of Saul, in whose stead you have
ruled; and the LORD has delivered the
kingdom into the hand of Absalom your
son; and here you are undone; for you
are a man of blood!"
Then Abishai, the son of Zeruiah, 9
said to the king,
"Why should this dead dog curse my
lord the king? Let me go over now and
take off his head."
But the king said, 10
"What have I in common with you,
O sons of Zeruiah? If he curses when
the LORD has said to him, 'Curse
David!' then who shall say, 'Why have
you done so?' "
David also said to Abishai and to all 11
his attendants,
"See, my own son who came forth
from my body seeks my life; how much
more now a Benjaminite! Let him
alone and let him curse, for the LORD
has commanded him. Perhaps the 12
LORD will look on my affliction, and
the LORD may requite good to me instead
of his cursing today."

13 So David and his men kept on the
road; but Shimei, proceeding along the
hillside opposite him and cursing as he
went along, continued to throw stones
14 and fling dust at him. Finally the king
and all the people who were with him
arrived weary at the Jordan, and he refreshed himself there.

15 Then Absalom and all the men of
Israel came to Jerusalem, and Ahitho-
16 phel with him. Now when Hushai the
Archite, David's friend, came to Absalom, Hushai said to Absalom,

"Long live the king, long live the
king!"

17 "Is this your loyalty for your friend?"
said Absalom to Hushai. "Why did you
not go with your friend?"

18 Then Hushai said to Absalom,

"No! for whom the LORD and this
people and all the men of Israel have
chosen, his will I be and with him will
19 I remain; and secondly, whom should
I serve? Should it not be his son? As I
served your father, so will I serve you."

20 "Give your counsel," said Absalom
to Ahithophel. "What shall we do?"

21 "Go in to your father's concubines,
whom he has left to keep the house,"
said Ahithophel to Absalom; "and all
Israel will hear that you are in bad odor
with your father and the hands of all
who are with you will be strengthened."

22 So they pitched a tent for Absalom
upon the roof; and Absalom went in to
the concubines of his father in the sight
23 of all Israel. The counsel of Ahithophel,
which he gave in those days, was as if
one consulted an oracle of God—so was
all the counsel of Ahithophel regarded
both by David and by Absalom.

17 Later Ahithophel said to Absalom,

"Let me, I pray you, choose twelve
thousand man, and let me arise and
2 pursue David tonight; thus I will come
upon him when he is weary and exhausted and I will throw him and all the
people who are with him into a panic;
3 and I will strike down the king alone. I
will then bring back all the people to
you as the bride returns to her husband.
You seek only the life of one man, and
all the people shall be at peace."

4 Now the plan pleased Absalom, and
all the elders of Israel.

5 "Call now Hushai the Archite also,"
said Absalom, "and let us hear likewise
what he has to offer."

Accordingly when Hushai came to Absalom, Absalom said to him,

"Thus Ahithophel has spoken; shall we carry out his plan? If not, speak out."

Then Hushai said to Absalom,

"This time the counsel that Ahithophel has given is not good."

"You know your father and his men," said Hushai, "that they are tried warriors and thoroughly aroused, like a bear in the open robbed of her cubs. Furthermore your father is an expert campaigner and will not spend the night with the people. Even now he has hidden himself in one of the caves or in some other place. In case he falls upon the people at the first, whoever hears the report will say, 'There has been a slaughter among the people who follow Absalom.' Then even the valiant man whose heart is like the heart of a lion, will utterly lose courage; for all Israel knows that your father is a skilled warrior, and those who are with him are valiant men. But I counsel that all Israel be surely gathered together to you, from Dan to Beersheba, as many as the sand that is by the sea, with you yourself marching in their midst. Thus we will come upon him in some place where he has been located, and we will light upon him as the dew falls upon the ground; and of him and of all the men who are with him there shall not be left even one. But if he withdraws into a city, then all Israel will bring ropes to that city and we will drag it into the valley, until not even a pebble can be found there."

Then Absalom and all the men of Israel said,

"The counsel of Hushai the Archite is better than the counsel of Ahithophel."

For the LORD had ordained the good counsel of Ahithophel to be frustrated, in order that the LORD might bring evil upon Absalom.

Then Hushai said to Zadok and Abiathar the priests,

"Thus and so did Ahithophel counsel Absalom and the elders of Israel; and thus and so have I counselled. Now therefore send quickly and tell David, saying, 'Do not camp tonight at the fords of the desert, but cross over without fail, lest the king and all the people with him be swallowed up.' "

Now Jonathan and Ahimaaz were

stationed at En-rogel; and a maidservant used to go and keep them informed, and they would go and tell king David, for they dared not be seen to enter the city. But a lad saw them, and told Absalom. Then they both went away in haste and entered into the house of a man in Bahurim, who had a well in his courtyard into which they descended; and a woman took and spread a covering over the well, and strewed dried fruit upon it, so that nothing was known. And when the servants of Absalom came to the woman to the house and said,

"Where are Ahimaaz and Jonathan?"

The woman said to them,

"They have crossed the source of the watercourses."

So when they had sought and could find no trace, they returned to Jerusalem. Now as soon as they had gone away, the two came up out of the well, and went and told King David and said to David,

"Arise, cross quickly over the water, for thus has Ahithophel counselled against you."

Then David and all the people who were with him arose and crossed the Jordan. By daybreak there was not one left behind who had not passed over the Jordan.

Now when Ahithophel saw that his counsel had not been carried out, he saddled his ass and arose, and went home to his own city. And after giving orders concerning his household, he strangled himself, and died and was buried in his father's grave.

Then David came to Mahanaim; and Absalom crossed the Jordan, together with all the men of Israel. And Absalom put Amasa in command of the army in place of Joab. Now Amasa was the son of an Ishmaelite by the name of Jether, who married Abigail the daughter of Jesse, the sister of Zeruiah, Joab's mother. Israel and Absalom encamped in the land of Gilead. When David arrived at Mahanaim, Shobi, the son of Nahash of the Ammonite Rabbah, and Machir, the son of Ammiel of Lodebar, and Barzillai, the Gileadite of Rogelim, brought couches and rugs and bowls, and earthen vessels, and wheat, barley, meal, parched grain, beans, lentils, honey, curds, sheep and calves for David, and for the people who were with
him, to eat; for they thought,
"The people must have been hungry
and weary and thirsty in the desert."
Then David mustered the people who 18
were with him, and appointed over
them commanders of thousands and
commanders of hundreds; and David 2
divided the people into three divisions,
one-third being under the command of
Joab, another third under Abishai, the
son of Zeruiah, Joab's brother, and
another third under the command of
Ittai the Gittite. And the king said to
the people,
"I will surely go with you myself."
But the people said, 3
"You shall not go out; for if we do
indeed run away, no one will trouble
about us; or if half of us die, no one will
trouble about us; but you are equal to
ten thousand of us; and now the important thing is for you to be ready to
help us from the city."
Then the king said to them, 4
"Whatever seems good in your eyes I
will do."
So the king stood at the side of the
gate, while all the people marched out
by hundreds and by thousands. But the 5
king commanded Joab, and Abishai,
and Ittai, saying,
"Deal gently for my sake with the
young man, with Absalom!"
And all the people heard when the
king gave orders to all the commanders
regarding Absalom. Then the people 6
took the field against Israel; and the
battle was in the forest of Ephraim.
The people of Israel were defeated there 7
by the servants of David; and the
slaughter on that day was great—twenty thousand men. Also the battle was 8
there spread out over the whole landscape; and the forest devoured more
people that day than the sword.
But Absalom happened to meet the 9
servants of David. Absalom was riding
upon a mule, and the mule went under
the thick branches of a great oak and
his head caught fast in the oak, and he
was left hanging between heaven and
earth, while the mule that was under
him passed on. Now when a certain 10
man saw it, he told Joab and said,
"Behold, I saw Absalom hanging in
an oak."
Then Joab said to the man who had 11
told him,

"You mean to say that you saw him! Why then did you not fell him to the ground at once? Then it would have been my part to have given you ten shekels of silver and a girdle."
12 "Though I were to feel the pressure of a thousand shekels of silver in my hand," said the man to Joab, "I would not put forth my hand against the king's son; for in our hearing the king charged you and Abishai and Ittai, saying, 'Spare for my sake the young man
13 Absalom.' Or if I had treacherously made away with him, nothing would have been hidden from the king, and you yourself would have stood aloof."
14 "Not so," said Joab; "I would have assuaged his wrath."

Then he took three weapons in his hand, and thrust them into Absalom's vitals, while he was still alive in the
15 midst of the oak; and ten young men who bore Joab's armor gathered around and smote Absalom until he was dead.
16 Then Joab blew the trumpet, and the people returned from pursuing Israel;
17 for Joab held back the people. Thereupon they took Absalom and cast him into a great pit in the forest, and raised over him a great heap of stones. Meanwhile all Israel fled each to his own
18 home. Now Absalom already in his lifetime had taken and set up for himself a pillar which is in the king's valley; for he said,

"I have no son to keep my name in remembrance."

And he named the pillar after his own name; and it is called Absalom's Monument to this day.
19 Now when Ahimaaz, the son of Zadok, said to Joab,

"Let me run now and bring the news to the king that the LORD has freed him from the power of his enemies,"
20 Joab said to him,

"You are not the man to carry tidings today. On another day you may carry news, but you shall not do so today, for the king's son is dead."
21 Then Joab said to the Cushite,

"Go, tell the king what you have seen."

So the Cushite did obeisance to Joab
22 and proceeded to run. But Ahimaaz the son of Zadok said again to Joab,

"Whatever happens, I should still very much like to run even after the Cushite."

"Why is it that you would run, my son," said Joab, "since you will have no reward for news as a result of going."

"However it may be, I would run," he said.

So he said to him,

"Run."

And Ahimaaz ran by way of the plain of the Jordan; and he passed the Cushite.

Now David was sitting between the two gates; and the watchman had gone up to the roof of the gate by the wall; and when he lifted up his eyes and looked, there was a man running alone. Then the watchman called and told the king; and the king said,

"If he be alone, there are good tidings in his mouth."

Meantime he kept on drawing nearer. Whereupon the watchman saw another man running; and the watchman called toward the gate, and said,

"See, another man running alone!"

"He also is bringing good news," said the king.

"I see that the running of the first is like the running of Ahimaaz, the son of Zadok," said the watchman.

"He is a good man," said the king, "and comes with good news."

Then Ahimaaz drew near and said to the king,

"All is well."

He bowed with his face to the earth, and said,

"Blessed be the LORD your God, who has delivered up the men who lifted up their hand against my lord the king."

"Is it well with the young man Absalom?" said the king.

"When Joab sent your servant I saw a great tumult, but I did not learn what it was," said Ahimaaz.

"Turn aside and take your stand here," said the king.

So he turned aside and stood still. At that moment the Cushite entered; and the Cushite said,

"Let my lord the king receive the good news that the LORD has freed you this day from all those that rose up against you."

Then the king said to the Cushite,

"Is it well with the young man Absalom?"

"Let the enemies of my lord the king and all who rise up against you for evil

be as this young man!" said the Cushite.
Then the king was deeply moved and
went up to the chamber over the gate
and wept. Thus he said, as he wept,
9 "My son Absalom, my son, my son
Absalom! O that I, even I, had died
instead of you, Absalom, my son, my
son!"
Then it was told Joab,
"Behold, the king is weeping and
lamenting over Absalom."
2 And the victory that day was turned
to mourning for all the people, since the
people heard that day, saying,
"The king is grieved over his son."
3 Therefore the people stole away
furtively into the city, as people who
are put to shame when they have fled
4 in battle steal away. But the king covered his face, and cried with a loud
voice,
"My son Absalom, Absalom, my son,
my son!"
5 So Joab went to the king in the house
and said,
"You have covered with shame today
the faces of all your servants, who have
preserved your life today, and the lives
of your sons and your daughters, and
the lives of your wives and your con-
6 cubines, by loving them who hate you
and hating them who love you. For you
have shown today that commanders
and servants are nothing to you; for
now I know that if Absalom were alive
and all of us dead today, then you would
7 be well pleased. Now therefore arise,
go forth, and speak reassuringly to your
subjects; for I swear by the LORD, if
you do not go forth, not a man will be
with you tonight, and this will be worse
for you than all the misfortune that has
befallen you from your youth until
now."
8 Then the king arose and sat at the
gate; and when the word passed to all
the people, saying, "See, the king is
sitting at the gate," all the people came
before the king.
Now Israel had fled every man to his
9 home; and all the people murmured
throughout all the tribes of Israel, saying,
"The king delivered us from the hand
of our enemies, and he has freed us out
of the hand of the Philistines, but now
he has fled from the land on account of
10 Absalom. As for Absalom, whom we
anointed over us, he has died in battle.
Now therefore why do you remain
silent about bringing the king back?"
Thus the word of all Israel came to
the king.
Then King David sent to Zadok and 11
Abiathar the priests, saying,
"Speak to the elders of Judah, saying, 'Why are you the last to bring the
king back to his house? You are my 12
kinsmen, my bone and my flesh, why
then are you the last to bring the king
back?' Say to Amasa, 'Are you not 13
my bone and my flesh? May God requite me and worse, if you shall not
become commander of the army henceforth instead of Joab.' "
Accordingly Amasa swayed the hearts 14
of all the men of Judah as one man, so
that they sent word to the king:
"Return, both you and all your followers."
So the king returned and came to the 15
Jordan; and Judah came to Gilgal in
order to go and meet the king and bring
him across the Jordan.
Moreover Shimei, the son of Gera the 16
Benjaminite, who was of Bahurim,
made haste and went down with the
men of Judah to meet King David, with 17
a thousand men of Benjamin; and with
him was Ziba, the servant of the house
of Saul, with his fifteen sons and his
twenty servants; and they hurried
down to the Jordan before the king,
and crossed over the ford to bring over 18
the king's household and to do whatever was pleasing in his sight. As he
was about to cross the Jordan, Shimei,
the son of Gera, fell down before the
king, and he said to the king, 19
"Let not my lord hold me guilty nor
remember that which your servant did
perversely the day that my lord the
king went out of Jerusalem, that the
king should take it to heart. For your 20
servant knows that I have sinned;
therefore, see, I have come today the
first of all the house of Joseph to come
down to meet my lord the king."
But Abishai, the son of Zeruiah, an- 21
swered and said,
"Shall not Shimei be put to death for
this, because he cursed the LORD'S
anointed?"
"What have I to do with you, you 22
sons of Zeruiah, that you should be
as an adversary to me this day?"
said David. "Should anyone be put to

death in Israel today? For do you not
know that I am today king over Israel?"
23 "You shall not die," said the king
to Shimei.
And the king swore to him.
24 Also Meribaal, the son of Saul, came
down to meet the king; and he had
neither dressed his feet nor trimmed his
moustache nor washed his clothes from
the day the king departed until the day
he came back in safety.
25 And when he came from Jerusalem to
meet the king, the king said to him,
"Why did you not go with me, Meribaal?"
26 "My lord, O king," said he, "my
servant deceived me; for your servant
said to him, 'Saddle for me an ass, on
which I may ride and go with the king,'
27 because your servant is lame; but he
slandered your servant to my lord the
king. My lord the king is as the angel
of God; do therefore what is good in
28 your eyes. For though all the house of
my father were naught but men deserving of death in the sight of my lord
the king, nevertheless you have set your
servant among those who eat at your
table. From whose hand shall I receive
justice?"
And he cried out again to the king;
29 and the king said to him,
"Why do you continue to amplify
your words? I have settled it; you and
Ziba shall divide the estate."
30 Meribaal then said to the king,
"Rather let him take the whole, inasmuch as my lord the king has come
home in safety."
31 Now Barzillai the Gileadite had come
down from Rogelim, and passed on with
the king to the Jordan to bid him fare-
32 well at the Jordan. Barzillai was very
aged, being eighty years old, and he had
provisioned the king while he waited at
Mahanaim; for he was a very great
33 man. And the king said to Barzillai,
"Cross over with me, and I will provide for your old age with me in Jerusalem."
34 But Barzillai said to the king,
"How many years is my life, that I
should go up with the king to Jerusa-
35 lem? I am today eighty years old. Can
I distinguish between good and bad?
Can your servant relish what he eats or
what he drinks? Can I hear any more
the voice of singing men and singing
women? Why then should your servant
be an added burden to my lord the
king? For your servant would only
pass over the Jordan a little way with
the king, and why should the king bestow upon me this boon? Let your
servant return, I pray you, that I may
die in my native city, by the grave of
my father and mother. But here is your
servant Chimham; let him cross over
with my lord the king; and deal with
him as seems good in your sight."
"Chimham shall cross over with me,"
said the king, "and I will deal with him
as it would please you; and whatever
you shall wish of me, that will I do for
you."
Then all the people crossed the Jordan. But the king stood still. And the
king kissed Barzillai, and blessed him,
and he returned to his home.
Then the king crossed over to Gilgal,
Chimham being with him; and all the
people of Judah and also half the people
of Israel brought the king back; and all
the men of Israel approaching the king,
said to the king,
"Why have our kinsmen, the men of
Judah, stolen you away, and brought
from over the Jordan the king and his
household, and all the men of David
with him?"
Then all the men of Judah retorted to
the men of Israel,
"Because the king is near of kin to us.
Why then are you angry over this matter? Have we eaten at all at the king's
expense? or has anything been carried
away by us?"
But the men of Israel answered the
men of Judah, and said,
"We have ten shares in the king;
moreover we are the first-born rather
than you; why then did you despise us?
Was it not our advice first to bring back
our king?"
But the words of the men of Judah
were fiercer than the words of the men
of Israel.
Now there happened to be there a
base rascal, whose name was Sheba,
the son of Bichri, a Benjaminite; and he
blew a trumpet and said,
"We have no portion in David,
And we have no share in Jesse's son!
Each man to his tents, O Israel!"
Then all the men of Israel withdrew
from David, and followed Sheba, the

son of Bichri; but the men of Judah remained steadfast to their king, from the
Jordan even to Jerusalem.
3 Now when David came to his house
at Jerusalem, the king took the ten
concubines, whom he had left to look
after the house, and put them in the
palace keep and supported them, but
did not go in to them. So they were
shut up until the day of their death,
living as widows.
4 "Summon for me the men of Judah
within three days, and report here in
person," said the king to Amasa.
5 So Amasa went to summon Judah.
But when he delayed beyond the set
time which he had appointed him,
6 David said,
"Now will Sheba, the son of Bichri,
do us more damage than did Absalom;
take your lord's servants and pursue
him, lest he find for himself fortified
cities and escape from us."
So there went out after Abishai, Joab
and the Cherethites and the Pelethites,
and all the seasoned warriors; and they
set out from Jerusalem to pursue Sheba,
the son of Bichri. When they were at
the great stone which is in Gibeon,
Amasa came to meet them. Now Joab
was girt with a sword under his cloak,
and outside his clothing he was girt with
another sword in its sheath, bound
upon his loins, and this came out and
fell. And Joab said to Amasa,
"Is it well with you, my brother?"
Then Joab took Amasa by the beard
with his right hand to kiss him. But as
Amasa was not on his guard against the
sword that was in Joab's hand, he
stabbed him in the body, and shed his
bowels to the ground, with a single
thrust; and he died. Thereafter Joab
and Abishai his brother pursued after
Sheba, the son of Bichri; and one of
Joab's young men stood by him and
said,
"Whoever favors Joab, and whoever
is for David, let him follow Joab."
But Amasa lay wallowing in blood in
the middle of the highway. And when
the man saw that all the people stopped,
he carried Amasa out of the highway into
a field, and threw a garment over him,
inasmuch as he saw that everyone who
came to him halted. When he was removed out of the highway, every man
passed on after Joab, to pursue Sheba,
the son of Bichri.

Now he passed on through all the 14
tribes of Israel to Abel-beth-maacah;
and all the Bichrites assembled and entered after him. Then they came and 15
besieged him in Abel-beth-maacah; and
they threw up a mound against the city,
for it stood even with the rampart; and
all the people with Joab were contriving
how to throw down the wall. Now a 16
wise woman out of the city called,
"Hear, hear! Say, I pray you, to
Joab, 'Come here that I may speak to
you.'"
So he came near her; and the woman 17
said,
"Are you Joab?"
"I am," said he.
"Listen to the words of your maidservant," said she to him.
"I am listening," said he.
Then she said, 18
"They used to speak formerly, saying, 'Let them but inquire at Abel,' and
so a matter was settled. I am of those 19
who are peaceable and faithful in Israel.
You seek to destroy a city and a mother
in Israel; why will you destroy the
heritage of the LORD?"
Then Joab answered and said, 20
"Far be it, far be it from me that I
should destroy or devastate! That is 21
not the case. But a man of the highlands of Ephraim, Sheba, the son of
Bichri, by name, has lifted up his hand
against King David; only deliver him
up, and I will withdraw from the city."
"Behold, his head shall be thrown to
you from the wall," said the woman to
Joab.
Then she went and advised all the 22
people in her wisdom; and they cut off
the head of Sheba, the son of Bichri,
and threw it down to Joab. Therefore
he blew the trumpet and they were dispersed from the city, each to his home;
and Joab returned to Jerusalem, to the
king.
Joab was commander-in-chief of the 23
whole army of Israel, and Benaiah, the
son of Jehoiada, was in command of the
Cherethites and the Pelethites; and 24
Adoram was in charge of the forced
labor; and Jehoshaphat, the son of
Ahilud, was the recorder; and Shiva 25
was scribe; and Zadok and Abiathar
were priests; and also Ira the Jairite 26
was a priest to David.

A FAMINE—ITS CAUSE AND CURE, 21:1–14

21 Now there was a famine in the days
of David for three years in succession;
and when David sought the face of the
LORD, the LORD said,
"It is because of Saul and his bloody
house, because he put to death the
Gibeonites."
2 So David called the Gibeonites and
said to them (now the Gibeonites were
not of the Israelites, but of the remnant
of the Amorites; however the Israelites
had taken oath with them; and Saul
had sought to slay them in his zeal for
the Israelites and the Judeans),
3 "What can I do for you? Wherewith
can I make expiation, so that you may
bless the heritage of the LORD?"
4 "It is not a matter of silver or gold
between us and Saul or his house;
neither is it for us to put to death any
man in Israel," said the Gibeonites to
him.
"What do you say that I shall do for
you?" he repeated.
5 Then they said to the king,
"As for the man who consumed us,
and who planned to destroy us that we
should find no place in any of the bor-
6 ders of Israel—let seven of his sons be
given to us, that we may hang them up
to the LORD in Gibeon, the mountain
of the LORD."
"I will give them," said the king.
7 But the king spared Meribaal, the
son of Jonathan, the son of Saul, because of the oath of the LORD which
was between them, between David and
8 Jonathan, the son of Saul. The king
took the two sons of Rizpah, the daughter of Aiah, whom she bore to Saul,
Armoni and Meribaal, and the five sons
of Merab, the daughter of Saul, whom
she bore to Adriel, the son of Barzillai,
9 the Meholathite; and he gave them into
the hand of the Gibeonites, and they
hanged them in the mountain before
the LORD, so that the seven of them
fell together; and they were put to
death in the first days of harvest, at the
beginning of the barley harvest.
10 Then Rizpah, the daughter of Aiah,
took sackcloth and spread it for her on
the rock, from the beginning of barley
harvest until water was poured upon
them from the heavens; and she did not
permit the birds of the air to light upon
them by day nor the beasts of the field
by night. When it was told David what
Rizpah, the daughter of Aiah, the concubine of Saul had done, David went
and took the bones of Saul and the
bones of Jonathan his son from the men
of Jabesh in Gilead, who had stolen
them from the open square of Beth-
shan, where the Philistines had hanged
them, on the day that the Philistines
overcame Saul at Gilboa. He brought
up from there the bones of Saul and the
bones of Jonathan his son and they
gathered up the bones of those who
were hanged; and they buried the bones
of Saul and the bones of Jonathan his
son in the land of Benjamin, by the side
of the grave of Kish his father, and they
did all that the king commanded. After
that God was propitiated toward the
land.

DAVID'S MIGHTY MEN, 21:15–22

Now when the Philistines were again
at war with Israel, David went down
together with his servants and encamped in Gob and fought against the
Philistines. Then arose Dodo, who was
one of the descendants of the giants, the
weight of whose spear was three hundred shekels of bronze, and he had a
new girdle; and he thought to slay David. But Abishai, the son of Zeruiah,
succored him and attacked the Philistine and killed him. Then the men of
David swore to him, saying,
"You shall go out no more with us to
battle, that you may not quench the
lamp of Israel."
Now when afterward there was again
war with the Philistines at Gob, Sibbecai the Shuhite slew Saph, who was
one of the descendants of the giants.
When there was again war with the
Philistines in Gob, Elhanan, the son of
Jaareoregim the Bethlehemite, slew
Goliath the Gittite, the shaft of whose
spear was like a weaver's beam.
There was again war at Gath, where
there was a man of great stature, who
had six fingers on each hand and six
toes on each foot, twenty-four in number; and he also was of the race of
giants; and when he defied Israel, Jonathan, the son of Shimei, David's
brother, slew him. These four were de-

scended from the giants in Gath; and they fell by the hand of David and by the hand of his servants.

A VICTOR'S HYMN OF PRAISE, 22:1–51

David spoke to the LORD the words of this song, on the day that the LORD delivered him from the hand of all his enemies, and from the hand of Saul;
2 and he said,

"The LORD is my rock, my fortress,
and my deliverer;
3 My God, my rock in whom I take refuge;
My shield, the weapon of my deliverance, my tower, and my refuge;
My savior, thou savest me from violence.
4 I call upon the LORD, who is worthy
to be praised,
That I may be rescued from my enemies.

5 "The breakers of death engulfed me,
Torrents of ruin terrified me;
6 The cords of Sheol surrounded me,
Snares of death confronted me.

7 "In my distress I called upon the LORD,
And unto my God I cried for help;
He heard my voice from his palace,
And my cry reached his ears.

8 "Then the earth quaked and rocked;
The foundations of the heavens trembled
And rocked, when he was angry.
9 Smoke rose from his nostrils,
And fire from his mouth devoured;
Coals were kindled by it.

"He bowed the heavens and came down;
Thick darkness was under his feet.
He rode upon a cherub and flew,
And he sped on with the wings of the wind.

"He made darkness his encircling pavilions,
His covert was the darkness of the heavens,
Thick clouds without brightness;
Before him coals of fire were kindled.

The LORD thundered from the heavens, 14
The Most High uttered his voice.

"He let fly his arrows and scattered them, 15
Lightning, and discomfited them.
Then the floor of the sea was revealed, 16
And the foundations of the world were bared
At the rebuke of the LORD,
At the fierce breath of his wrath.
He sent from on high, he took me, 17
He drew me out of many waters.
He delivered me from my strong enemy, 18
From my foes; for they were too strong for me.

"They confronted me on the day of my calamity, 19
But the LORD became my stay.
He led me forth into a broad place; 20
He set me free, for he was pleased with me.
The LORD rewarded me in accordance
with my righteousness; 21
He requited me in accordance with the cleanness of my hands.
For I have kept the ways of the LORD, 22
And have not transgressed against my God.
For all his ordinances are before me, 23
And from his statutes I do not turn aside.
I was blameless with him, 24
And guarded myself from my guilt.

"So the LORD requited me in accordance with my righteousness, 25
In accordance with my cleanness in his sight.

"Toward the godly thou dost act graciously; 26
Toward the blameless thou dost act blamelessly;
Toward the pure thou dost act purely; 27
And toward the crooked thou dost act craftily.
For thou wilt deliver a humble people, 28
But thine eyes are upon the haughty, to bring them low.
For thou, O LORD, art my lamp, 29
And the LORD lightens my darkness.
For through thee I can break down a rampart, 30
Through my God I can scale a wall.

31 "The way of God is blameless,
The speech of the LORD is sincere;
A shield is he to all who take refuge in him.
32 For who is God but the LORD?
And who is a rock save our God?

33 "God is my stronghold;
He makes my way blameless,
34 Making my feet like the doe's,
And making me stand securely on my heights;
35 The one who trains my hands for battle,
So that my arms can bend a bow of bronze.
36 And thou hast given me thy saving shield,
And thy help makes me great.
37 Thou dost enlarge the range of my steps,
And my ankles do not give way.

38 "I pursue my foes and destroy them,
And do not turn back until they are consumed.
39 And I consume them and thrust them through,
So that they cannot rise;
Beneath my feet they fall.

40 "And thou dost gird me with strength for the battle;
Thou dost subdue my opponents under me.
41 And thou dost make my foes show me the back;
And those that hate me I destroy.
42 They cry for help, but there is none to deliver,
To the LORD, but he does not answer them.
43 Then I grind them to powder like the dust of the earth,
I crush them like the dirt of the streets, by stamping upon them.
44 Thou dost deliver me from the feuds of the people;
Thou dost keep me as head of the nations;
People that I have not known serve me;
45 Foreigners fawn upon me;
As soon as they hear of me, they submit to me;
46 Foreigners fade away,
And come trembling from their fortresses.

"All hail to the LORD! And blessed be my Rock!
And may the God of my deliverance be exalted!
The God who gives me vengeance,
And puts peoples in subjection under me;
Who frees me from my foes.
Yea, thou dost exalt me above my adversaries;
From violent men thou dost rescue me.

"Therefore I shall praise thee among the nations, O LORD,
And sing praises to thy name;
To him who gives great victories to his king,
And shows kindness to his anointed,
To David and his descendants forever."

THE LAST WORDS OF DAVID, 23:1–7

Now these are the last words of David:
"The oracle of David, the son of Jesse,
The oracle of the man who was raised on high,
The anointed of the God of Jacob,
And the pleasant theme of the songs of Israel.
By me the spirit of the LORD has spoken,
And his word is upon my tongue.
The God of Israel said,
The Rock of Israel spoke to me:
'When one rules over men, as a righteous one,
When one rules in the fear of God,
Then it is as the light of the morning
When the sun rises,
A morning cloudless clear, after rain
Upon the tender grass.
For should not my house be so with God?
For he has decreed for me an eternal covenant,
Set in order in all things and secured;
For all my security and all my desire,
Will he not bring into being?
But the ungodly!—as thorns to be thrust away are all of them;
For with the hand they cannot be taken.
But the man who touches them

Arms himself with iron and spear-
shaft,
And they are utterly burned forthwith."

A LIST OF DAVID'S HEROES, 23:8–39

8 These are the names of David's heroic followers: Ishbaal the Hachmonite,
who was the leader of the Three; he
raised aloft his spear over eight hun-
9 dred slain at one time. Next to him
among the three heroes was Eleazar,
the son of Dodi, the son of the Ahohite.
He was with David at Pasdammim
when the Philistines were gathered
there for battle. But when the Israel-
10 ites withdrew, he arose and attacked
the Philistines until his hand was
weary and was as if grown fast to the
sword. So the LORD brought about a
great victory that day; and the people
returned after him only to strip the
11 slain. Next to him was Shammah, the
son of Agee, a Hararite. The Philistines were gathered together at Lehi;
and there was a plot of ground full of
lentiles. But when the people fled from
12 the Philistines, he took his stand in the
midst of the plot and defended it and
slew the Philistines. So the LORD
brought about a great victory.
13 Now three of the Thirty went down
to the rock to David to the cave of
Adullam, while the camp of the Philistines was pitched in the Valley of Re-
14 phaim. David was then in the stronghold, and the garrison of the Philistines
was at the same time in Bethlehem.
15 Moreover David longed earnestly and
said,

"Oh that someone would give me a
drink of water from the well of Bethlehem that is at the gate!"

16 So the three heroes broke through
the camp of the Philistines and drew
water out of the well of Bethlehem that
was at the gate, and took it and
brought it to David. But he would not
drink of it, but poured it out to the
17 LORD. And David said,

"Far be it from me, O LORD, that I
should do this! It is the blood of men
who went at the risk of their lives."

Therefore he would not drink it.
These things did the three heroes.
18 Now Abishai, the brother of Joab,
the son of Zeruiah, was chief of the
Thirty; and he wielded his spear over
three hundred slain, and so won a name
among the Thirty. He was indeed the 19
most honorable of the Thirty, so that
he became their commander, but he did
not attain to the Three.
Benaiah, the son of Jehoiada, was a 20
valiant man of Kabzeel, a man of great
prowess; he slew two sons of Ariel of
Moab. He also went down and slew a
lion in the midst of a pit on a snowy
day. He slew besides an Egyptian, a 21
formidable looking man, armed with a
spear, but he went down to him with a
club, and wrenched the spear out of the
Egyptian's hand and slew him with his
own spear. These things did Benaiah, 22
the son of Jehoiada, and won for himself
a name among the thirty heroes. He 23
was very honorable among the Thirty,
but he did not attain to the Three.
Nevertheless David set him over his
guard.
Asahel, the brother of Joab, was 24
among the Thirty; Elhanan, the son of
Dodo of Bethlehem, Shammah the 25
Harodite, Elika the Harodite, Helez the 26
Paltite, Ira, the son of Ikkesh, the Tekoite, Abiezer the Anathothite, Sibbe- 27
cai the Hushathite, Zalmon the Aho- 28
hite, Maharai the Netophathite, Heled, 29
the son of Baanah, the Netophathite,
Ittai, the son of Ribai of Gibeah of the
Benjaminites, Benaiah a Pirathonite, 30
Hiddai of the brooks of Gaash, Abiel 31
the Arbathite, Azmaveth the Barhum-
ite, Eliahba, the Shaalbonite, Jashen 32
the Gunite, Jonathan, the son of Shammah, the Hararite, Ahiam, the son of 33
the Ararite, Eliphelet, the son of Ahas- 34
bai, the Maacathite, Eliam, the son of
Ahithophel, the Gilonite, Hezro the 35
Carmelite, Paarai, the Arbite, Igal the 36
son of Nathan of Zobah, Bani the
Gadite, Zelek the Ammonite, Naharai 37
the Beerothite, the armor bearers of
Joab, the son of Zeruiah, Ira the 38
Ithrite, Gareb the Ithrite, Uriah the 39
Hittite—a total of thirty-seven.

DAVID'S CENSUS, 24:1–25

Now the LORD was again angered 24
against Israel, and he incited David
against them, saying,
"Go number Israel and Judah!"
So the king said to Joab and the 2

commanders of the army which was
with him,
"Go about now throughout all the
tribes of Israel, from Dan even to
Beersheba, and take a census of the
people that I may know the number of
the people."
3 Joab said to the king,
"May the LORD your God add to the
people a hundred times as many as
they are, while the eyes of my lord the
king look on! But why does my lord
the king take delight in this thing?"
4 But the word of the king prevailed
over Joab and the commanders of the
army. Therefore Joab and the commanders of the army went out from the
king's presence to take the census of the
5 people of Israel. They crossed the Jordan and started from Aroer, and from
the city that is in the midst of the torrent valley, toward Gad and on to
6 Jazer. Then they came to Gilead and
to the land of the Hittites, to Kadesh;
and they came to Dan, and from Dan
7 they went around to Sidon, and came
to the fortress of Tyre and all the cities
of the Hivvites, and of the Canaanites;
and they went forth to the Negeb of
8 Judah at Beersheba. When they had
gone about through the whole land,
they came to Jerusalem at the end of
9 nine months and twenty days; and
Joab gave the number of the census of
the people to the king, and Israel consisted of eight hundred thousand able-
bodied men who drew sword, and the
men of Judah were five hundred thousand.
10 But David's conscience smote him
after he had numbered the people.
Then David said to the LORD,
"I have sinned exceedingly in what
I have done. But now, O LORD, take
away, I pray thee, the iniquity of thy
servant, for I have done very foolishly."
11 When David arose in the morning,
the word of the LORD came to Gad the
prophet, David's seer, saying,
12 "Go and speak to David, 'Thus says
the LORD: "Three things I offer you;
choose one of them that I may do it to
you." ' "
13 So Gad came to David and told him;
and said to him,
"Shall there come for you three years
of famine upon your land? or shall
there be three months of flight before
your adversary, while he pursues you?
or shall there be a three days' pestilence
in your land? Now find out and consider what answer I shall return to him
who sent me."
Then David said to Gad,
"I am in great distress. Let us fall
now into the hand of the LORD, for his
mercy is great, but let me not fall into
the hand of man."
So the LORD sent a pestilence, and
the days when the plague began were
the days of wheat harvest, and it slew
of the people from Dan to Beersheba
seventy thousand men. Now when the
angel of the LORD stretched forth his
hand toward Jerusalem to destroy it,
the LORD repented of the evil, and said
to the angel who was destroying among
the people,
"It is enough; now stay your hand."
Now the angel of the LORD was by
the threshing-floor of Araunah the
Jebusite. Then David spoke to the
LORD, when he saw the angel who was
smiting the people, and he said,
"Behold, I myself have sinned and
have done wickedly; but these are
sheep, what have they done? I pray
thee, let thy hand be against me and
my father's house."
Gad came to David that day, and
said to him,
"Go up, rear an altar to the LORD on
the threshing-floor of Araunah the
Jebusite."
So David went up according to the
word of Gad, as the LORD commanded.
When Araunah looked down and saw 2
the king and his servants crossing over
to him, Araunah went forth and did
obeisance to the king with his face to
the earth, and Araunah said, 2
"Why has my lord the king come to
his servant?"
"To purchase of you the threshing-
floor," said David, "to build an altar
to the LORD, that the plague may be
stayed from the people."
Then Araunah said to David, 2
"Let my lord the king take and offer
up what is good in his sight. Here are
the cattle for a burnt-offering and the
threshing-sledges and the implements
of the cattle for the wood. The servant 2
of my lord the king gives it all to the
king."
Araunah said to the king,
"The LORD your God accept you!"

24 But the king said to Araunah,
"No, but I will surely buy it of you
for a price. I cannot offer burnt-offerings to the LORD my God that cost me
nothing."
So David bought the threshing-floor
and the cattle for fifty shekels of silver.
Then David built there an altar to the 25
LORD, and offered burnt-offerings and
thank-offerings. So the LORD was entreated for the land and the plague was
stayed from Israel.

THE FIRST BOOK OF KINGS

THE LAST DAYS OF DAVID, 1:1—2:11

1 NOW King David was getting
old and well advanced in
years, and although they
wrapped him in garments he
2 could not keep warm. Therefore his
servants said to him,
"Let them seek for my lord the king
a young maiden and let her attend the
king and act as his nurse; and let her
lie in your bosom, that my lord the
king may be warm."
3 So they sought for a beautiful maid-
en throughout all the territory of Israel, and they found Abishag the Shunammite and they brought her to the
4 king. The maiden was exquisitely
beautiful; and she became the king's
nurse, and ministered to him; but the
king had no intercourse with her.
5 Then Adonijah, the son of Haggith,
began making his boast, saying,
"I will be king."
Therefore he provided for himself a
chariot and horsemen and fifty men as
6 runners to go before him. Now his father had never in his life restrained
him by saying,
"Why do you do thus and so?"
He was besides a very handsome
man, and he was born next after Ab-
7 salom. Accordingly he negotiated with
Joab, the son of Zeruiah, and with Abiathar the priest, so that they became
8 Adonijah's helpers. But Zadok the
priest and Benaiah, the son of Jehoiada, and Nathan the prophet and Shimei and Rei and David's trained war-
9 riors were not with Adonijah. Now
Adonijah sacrificed sheep and oxen and
fat cattle by the Serpent's Stone, which
is beside En-rogel, and he invited all his
brothers, the king's sons, together with
10 all the royal officials of Judah; but he
did not invite Nathan the prophet, nor
Benaiah, nor the trained warriors, nor
Solomon his brother.
11 Then Nathan said to Bathsheba, the
mother of Solomon,

"Have you not heard that Adonijah,
the son of Haggith, has been made king
and our lord David does not know it?
Now therefore let me, I pray you, ad- 12
vise you, that you may save your own
life and the life of your son Solomon.
Go in to King David and say to him, 13
'Have you not, my lord, O king, sworn
to your maidservant, saying, "Solomon
your son shall be king after me, and he
shall sit on my throne?" Why then has
Adonijah been made king?' Now while 14
you are still speaking there with the
king, I also will come in after you and
confirm your words."
So Bathsheba went in to the king to 15
his chamber; (now the king was exceedingly old and Abishag the Shunammite was ministering to the king).
Bathsheba then bowed and did obei- 16
sance to the king; and the king said,
"What do you want?"
"My lord," she said to him, "you 17
yourself swore to your maidservant by
the LORD your God, 'Solomon your
son shall be king after me and he shall
sit on my throne.' Now, behold, Adoni- 18
jah is king and you, my lord, O king, do
not know it. He has sacrificed oxen and 19
fat cattle and sheep in abundance, and
has invited all the sons of the king, and
Abiathar the priest, and Joab, the commander of the army; but he has not invited Solomon your servant. Now, my 20
lord, O king, the eyes of all Israel are
upon you, that you should tell them
who shall sit on the throne of my lord
the king after him. As it stands, the re- 21
sult will be that when my lord the king
shall sleep with his fathers, I and my
son Solomon will be regarded as rebels."
But while she was still speaking with 22
the king, Nathan the prophet entered;
and they told the king, 23
"Nathan the prophet is here."
So he came before the king and did
obeisance to the king with his face to
the earth; and Nathan said, 24
"My lord, O king, have you said,
'Adonijah shall be king after me, and he
shall sit on my throne?' For he has gone 25

down today and sacrificed oxen and fat
cattle and sheep in abundance, and invited all the king's sons, and Joab, the
commander of the army, and Abiathar
the priest, and behold, they are eating
and drinking before him, and have said,
26 'Long live King Adonijah!' But as for
me, even me your servant, and Zadok
the priest, and Benaiah, the son of Jehoiada, and Solomon your servant he
27 has not invited. Has this thing been
brought about by my lord the king, and
you have not told your servants who
should sit upon the throne of my lord
the king after him?"
28 Then King David spoke up and said,
"Call Bathsheba to me."
So she came into the presence of the
29 king and stood before him; and the
king swore, saying,
"As the LORD lives, who has ran-
30 somed my life out of all adversity, as
I swore to you by the LORD, the God of
Israel, saying 'Solomon your son shall
be king after me and he shall sit on my
throne in my stead'; so will I do this
day."
31 Then Bathsheba bowed with her face
to the earth, and did obeisance to the
king and said,
"My lord King David live forever!"
32 "Call Zadok the priest for me, and
Nathan the prophet, and Benaiah, the
son of Jehoiada," said King David.
And when they came before the
33 king, the king said to them,
"Take with you the servants of your
lord and cause Solomon my son to ride
upon my own mule, and bring him
34 down to Gihon; and let Zadok the
priest and Nathan the prophet anoint
him there king over Israel; then blow
the trumpet and say, 'Long live King
35 Solomon!' You also shall go up behind
him and he shall come in and sit upon
my throne and he shall be king in my
stead; him have I commanded to be
leader over Israel and Judah."
36 Then Benaiah, the son of Jehoiada,
answered the king and said,
"So be it! So may the LORD confirm
37 the words of my lord the king. As the
LORD has been with my lord the king,
so may he be with Solomon, and make
his throne greater than the throne of
my lord King David!"
38 Accordingly Zadok the priest, and
Nathan the prophet, and Benaiah, the
son of Jehoiada, together with the
Cherethites and the Pelethites, caused
Solomon to ride on the mule of King
David, and brought him to Gihon.
Then Zadok the priest took a horn of 39
oil from the tent and anointed Solomon. Whereupon they blew the trumpet and all the people said,
"Long live King Solomon!"
Then all the people went up after 40
him playing upon flutes and rejoicing
with such great outburst that the earth
was rent with their noise.
Now Adonijah and all the guests who 41
were with him heard it just as they
finished feasting; and when Joab heard
the sound of the trumpet, he said,
"Why this noise of the town in uproar?"
While he was still speaking, there 42
came Jonathan, the son of Abiathar the
priest; and Adonijah said,
"Enter, for you are a valiant man
and bring good news."
Jonathan answered and said to 43
Adonijah,
"No, rather our lord King David has
made Solomon king. Moreover the king 44
has sent with him Zadok the priest, and
Nathan the prophet, and Benaiah, the
son of Jehoiada, together with the
Cherethites and the Pelethites, and
they have caused him to ride on the
king's mule. Zadok the priest and Na- 45
than the prophet have anointed him
king in Gihon, and they have gone up
from there rejoicing, so that the town is
in uproar. That was the noise which
you heard. So Solomon has actually 46
taken his seat on the throne of the kingdom. Moreover the servants of the king 47
have already come to congratulate our
lord King David, saying, 'May your
God make the name of Solomon better
than your name and his throne greater
than your throne!' Then the king
bowed himself on his bed. Furthermore, 48
thus the king has said, 'Blessed be the
LORD, the God of Israel, who has today
granted one of my offspring to sit on
my throne, my own eyes beholding it.'"
Then all the guests whom Adonijah 49
had were terrified and arose and each
went his way. But Adonijah was in 50
such fear of Solomon that he arose and
went and caught hold of the horns of
the altar. And it was told Solomon, 51
saying,
"See, Adonijah fears King Solomon,
and now he has laid hold of the horns

of the altar, saying, 'Let King Solomon
swear to me first that he will not slay
his servant with the sword.'"
52 "If he be a worthy man," said Solomon, "not a hair of him shall fall to the
earth, but if evil be found in him then
he shall die."
53 So King Solomon sent and they
brought him down from the altar, and
he came and did obeisance to King
Solomon.

"Go to your house," said Solomon to
him.
2 When David's time to die drew near,
he charged Solomon his son, saying,
2 "I am about to go the way of all the
earth. Be strong then and show your-
3 self a man, and keep the charge of the
LORD your God, by walking in his
ways, by keeping his statutes, his commands, his ordinances, and his decrees,
as it is written in the law of Moses, that
you may have success in all that you
4 do and in all that you undertake; that
the LORD may establish his word that
he spoke to me, saying, 'If your sons
guard their steps by walking before me
in truth with all their mind and with all
their heart, there shall not fail you a
man on the throne of Israel.'
5 "Now furthermore, you know what
Joab, the son of Zeruiah, did to me, how
he treated the two commanders of the
armies of Israel, Abner, the son of Ner,
and Amasa, the son of Jether, how he
slew them and avenged blood shed in
war in time of peace, and put innocent
blood upon his girdle that was about his
loins and upon his sandals that were on
6 his feet. Act therefore according to
your wisdom, so that you do not allow his hoary head to go down in peace
7 to Sheol. But show kindness to the sons
of Barzillai the Gileadite, and let them
be among those who eat at your table;
for so they presented themselves to me
when I fled from Absalom your broth-
8 er. There is also with you Shimei, the
son of Gera, the Benjaminite of Bahurim, who cursed me with a grievous
curse on the day when I went to Mahanaim. But when he came down to meet
me at the Jordan, I swore to him by the
LORD, saying, 'I will not slay you with
9 the sword.' But do you yourself not
hold him guiltless; you are a wise man
and know what you should do to him,
and you shall bring down his old age
with blood to Sheol."

So David slept with his fathers and 10
was buried in the city of David. The 11
time that David was king over Israel
was forty years: seven years he was
king in Hebron, and thirty-three years
he was king in Jerusalem.

SOLOMON'S EXECUTION OF DAVID'S WILL, 2:12–46

Thus Solomon sat upon the throne of 12
David his father and his rule was thoroughly established. Now Adonijah, the 13
son of Haggith, came to Bathsheba, the
mother of Solomon, and did obeisance
to her.

"Is your coming friendly?" she said.

"Friendly," he said.

"I would have a word with you," he 14
went on to say.

"Speak," she said.

"You know," he said, "that the king- 15
dom belonged to me and that all Israel
openly expected me to reign, but now
the kingdom has been changed and has
become my brother's, for it was his from
the LORD. Now, however, I am about 16
to make one request of you; do not refuse me."

"Speak on," she said to him.

Then he said, 17

"Suggest, I pray you, to Solomon
the king, for he will not refuse you, that
he give me Abishag the Shunammite as
wife."

"Very well, I will speak for you to 18
the king," said Bathsheba.

Accordingly Bathsheba went in to 19
King Solomon to speak to him concerning Adonijah; and the king arose to
meet her and did obeisance to her, and
sat down on his throne, and a seat was
placed for the mother of the king, and
she sat on his right. Then she said, 20

"A small request I am about to make
of you; do not refuse me."

"Ask, my mother, for I will not refuse you," the king said to her.

Then she said, 21

"Let Abishag the Shunammite be
given to Adonijah your brother as
wife."

But King Solomon answered and said 22
to his mother,

"Why then do you ask Abishag the
Shunammite for Adonijah? Ask for
him the kingdom also! for he is my elder

brother, and on his side are Abiathar
the priest and Joab, the son of Zeruiah."
23 Then King Solomon swore by the
LORD, saying,
"May God requite me and worse, if
Adonijah has not spoken this word
24 against his own life. Now therefore, as
the LORD lives, who has established me
and caused me to sit upon the throne
of David my father, and who has made
me a house as he promised, Adonijah
shall today be put to death."
25 So King Solomon sent by the hand of
Benaiah, the son of Jehoiada, who
struck him down, so that he died.
26 Then the king said to Abiathar the
priest,
"Go to Anathoth to your estate, for
you are worthy of death, but I will not
put you to death at this time, because
you bore the ark of the LORD before
David my father, and because you suffered affliction in all that my father endured."
27 So Solomon ousted Abiathar from
being priest to the LORD, in fulfilment
of the word of the LORD which he
spoke concerning the house of Eli in
Shiloh.
28 Now when the report came to Joab—
for Joab had followed Adonijah but he
had not followed Absalom—Joab fled
to the tent of the LORD and laid hold of
29 the horns of the altar. When it was
told King Solomon that Joab had fled
to the tent of the LORD and was there
beside the altar, Solomon sent to Joab,
saying,
"How does it happen that you have
fled to the altar?"
"I was afraid of you and so I fled to
the LORD," said Joab.
Then Solomon sent Benaiah, the son
of Jehoiada, saying,
"Go, strike him down."
30 So Benaiah went into the tent of the
LORD and said to him,
"Thus the king has said, 'Come
out.'"
But he said,
"No, for I prefer to die here."
Then Benaiah brought the king
word again, saying,
"Thus Joab spoke and thus he answered me."
31 Then the king said to him,
"Do as he has spoken; strike him
down and bury him, that you may take
away from me and from my father's
house the innocent blood which Joab
shed. The LORD will also requite his 32
bloody deeds upon his own head, because he fell upon two men more righteous and honorable than he, and slew
them with the sword, without the
knowledge of my father David: Abner,
the son of Ner, commander of the army
of Israel, and Amasa, the son of Jether,
commander of the army of Judah. So 33
shall their blood return upon the head
of Joab and upon the head of his descendants forever; but to David, and
to his descendants, and to his house,
and to his throne, may there be peace
from the LORD for evermore."
Then Benaiah, the son of Jehoiada, 34
went up and fell upon him and slew
him; and he was buried in his own
house in the desert. Thereupon the 35
king put Benaiah, the son of Jehoiada,
over the army in his stead, and the king
put Zadok the priest in the place of
Abiathar.
Then the king called Shimei and said 36
to him,
"Build for yourself a house in Jerusalem and dwell there, and do not go
forth from there to any place whatever. For the day you go forth and 37
cross the Brook Kidron, know for a certainty that you shall surely die; your
blood shall be upon your own head."
"The stipulation is fair," said Shimei 38
to the king; "as my lord the king has
spoken so will your servant do."
So Shimei lived in Jerusalem many
days.
But at the end of three years, two of 39
Shimei's slaves ran away to Achish, the
son of Maachah, king of Gath. So when
they told Shimei, saying, "Behold, your
slaves are in Gath," Shimei arose and 40
saddled his ass and went to Gath to
Achish to seek his slaves. Thus Shimei 41
went and brought his slaves from
Gath. Accordingly when it was told
Solomon that Shimei had gone from
Jerusalem to Gath and returned, the 42
king sent and called Shimei, and said to
him,
"Did I not cause you to swear by the
LORD and solemnly admonish you,
saying, 'On the day that you go forth
and go to any place whatever, know of
a certainty that you shall surely die?'
And you said to me, 'The stipulation is
fair, I have heard it.' Why then have 43

you not kept the oath of the LORD and
the command which I laid upon you?"
44 The king also said to Shimei,
"You are conscious of all the evil
which you yourself know, that you did
to David my father; now the LORD is
bringing your iniquity upon your own
45 head. But King Solomon shall be
blessed and the throne of David shall
be established before the LORD forever."
46 So the king commanded Benaiah, the
son of Jehoiada, and he went forth and
struck him down, so that he died. Thus
the kingdom was completely established in the hand of Solomon.

SOLOMON'S DREAM AND HIS ANSWERED PRAYER, 3:1–28

3 Solomon formed a marriage alliance
with Pharaoh, king of Egypt, and he
took Pharaoh's daughter, and brought
her into the city of David, until he had
finished the building of his house and
the house of the LORD and the wall
2 around Jerusalem. However the people
sacrificed on the high places because
there was no house built for the name of
the LORD until those days.
3 Now Solomon loved the LORD so
that he walked in the statutes of David
his father; only he sacrificed and
burned incense on the high places.
4 Moreover the king went to Gibeon to
sacrifice there; for that was the great
high place; and Solomon used to offer
a thousand burnt-offerings on that
altar.
5 In Gibeon the LORD appeared to
Solomon in a dream by night; and God
said,
"Ask what I shall give you."
6 Then Solomon said,
"Thou hast shown great kindness to
thy servant David my father, according as he walked before thee in truth,
in righteousness, and in uprightness of
heart with thee; and thou hast kept in
store for him this great kindness, in
that thou hast given him a son who sits
7 on his throne this day. Now therefore,
O LORD my God, thou hast made thy
servant king in the place of David my
father, while I am a little child in comparison. I know not how to go out or
8 come in. Thy servant also is in the
midst of thy people whom thou hast
chosen, a vast people, who cannot be
numbered or counted for multitude.
Give thy servant therefore an attentive 9
mind to judge thy people in righteousness and to discern between good and
evil; for who is able to judge this great
people of thine?"
It was pleasing in the eyes of the 10
LORD that Solomon had asked this
thing; so God said to him, 11
"Because you have asked this thing
and have not asked for yourself long
life nor riches nor the life of your enemies, but have asked for yourself understanding to perceive justice; behold, 12
I have done according to your word:
see, I give you a wise and discerning
mind, so that there has been none like
you before you, and none like you shall
arise after you. I give also what you
did not ask, both riches and honor, so 13
that, all your days, there shall not be
any like you among the kings. If you 14
walk in my ways so that you keep my
statutes and my commands as did your
father David, then I will prolong your
days."
Now when Solomon awoke, behold, it 15
was a dream. Then he came to Jerusalem and stood before the ark of the
covenant of the LORD and offered
burnt-offerings and made thank-offerings and made a feast for all his servants.
Then two women of ill fame came to 16
the king and stood before him, and the 17
one woman said,
"O, my lord, this woman and I dwell
in the same house; and I gave birth to 18
a child while she was in the house.
Then on the third day after I was delivered, this woman also gave birth to a
child and we were together, there being
no stranger with us in the house besides
us two in the house. But the child of 19
this woman died in the night, because
she lay upon it. Then she arose in the 20
middle of the night and took my child
from my side while your maidservant
slept, and laid it in her bosom and laid
her dead child in my bosom. Thus when 21
I arose toward morning to nurse my
child, behold, it was dead; but when I
was able to examine it closely in the
morning, behold, it was not my child
which I had borne."
"No; but the living child is mine and 22
the dead child is your child," the other
woman said.

But the first woman was saying at
the same time,
"No; but the living child is mine and
the dead child is your child."
Thus they spoke before the king.
23 Then the king said,
"This one declares, 'This is my child,
the living one, and your child is dead.'
And the other declares, 'No; but your
son is the dead and my son is the
living!' "
24 "Get me a sword," said the king.
So they brought in a sword before the
25 king. The king then said,
"Cut the living child in two and give
half to one and half to the other."
26 But the woman to whom the living
child belonged spoke to the king—for
her motherly tenderness was aroused
for her son—and she said,
"O, my lord, give her the living child,
and by no means slay it."
But the other interrupted,
"It shall be neither mine nor yours!
Divide it!"
27 Then the king answered and said,
"Give her the living child, and by no
means slay it, for she is its mother."
28 Now when all Israel heard of the
judgment that the king had rendered,
they stood in awe of the king; for they
perceived that the wisdom of God was
in him to administer justice.

THE ORGANIZATION OF SOLOMON'S KINGDOM, 4:1–28

4 Now King Solomon was king over all
2 Israel; and these were the princes
whom he had: Azariah, the son of
3 Zadok, was the priest; Elihoreph and
Ahijah, the sons of Shisha, were
scribes; Jehoshaphat, the son of Ahi-
4 lud, was the recorder; and Benaiah, the
son of Jehoiada, was in command of the
army; and Zadok and Abiathar were
5 priests; and Azariah, the son of Nathan,
was in charge of the officers; and Za-
bud, the son of Nathan, was priest and
6 the king's friend; and Ahishar was in
charge of the house; and Adoniram, the
son of Abda, was in charge of the forced
labor.
7 Solomon also had twelve officers over
all Israel, and they used to provide food
for the king and his household; each
man had to make provision for one
month in the year.

These were their names: Ben-hur, in 8
the highlands of Ephraim; Ben-deker, 9
in Makaz, and in Shaalbaim, and Beth-
Shemesh, and Elonbethhanan; Ben- 10
hesed, in Arubboth; he had Socoh and
all the land of Hepher; Ben-abinadab, 11
in all the highland of Dor (he had
Taphath the daughter of Solomon as
wife); Baanah, the son of Ahilud, in 12
Taanach and Megiddo and all of Beth-
shean, which is beside Zarethan, beneath Jezreel, from Beth-shean to Abel-
meholah, as far as the other side of
Jokneam; Ben-geber in Ramoth-Gil- 13
ead; he had the villages of Jair, the son
of Manasseh, which are in Gilead; he
had the region of Argob, which is in
Bashan, sixty great cities with walls
and bronze bars; Ahinadab, the son of 14
Iddo, at Mahanaim; Ahimaaz in 15
Naphtali (he also took Basemath, the
daughter of Solomon, to wife); Baanah, 16
the son of Hushai, in Asher in Bealoth;
Jehoshaphat, the son of Paruah, in 17
Issachar; Shimei, the son of Ela, in Ben- 18
jamin; Geber, the son of Uri, in the land 19
of Gilead, the land of Sihon, king of the
Amorites, and of Og, king of Bashan;
and one officer was over all the officials
who were in the land.
Judah and Israel were as the sand 20
which is by the sea for multitude; they
were continually eating and drinking
and making merry. Solomon was the 21
ruler over all the kingdoms from the
River even to the land of the Philistines
and to the border of Egypt. They
brought tribute and continued to serve
Solomon all the days of his life.
Solomon's provision for one day was 22
thirty kors of fine flour, and sixty kors
of meal, ten fat cattle and twenty pas- 23
ture fed cattle and a hundred sheep, besides harts and gazelles and roebucks
and fatted fowls. For he had dominion 24
over everything beyond the River,
from Tiphsah even to Gaza, over all the
kings beyond the River. And he had
peace on all sides round about him, so 25
that Judah and Israel dwelt in safety
from Dan even to Beersheba, every
man under his own vine and fig tree, all
the days of Solomon. Now Solomon 26
had forty thousand stalls of horses for
his chariots, and twelve thousand
horsemen.
These officers supplied provisions for 27
King Solomon and for all who came to
King Solomon's table, each in his

month. They fell short in nothing.
28 Also barley and straw for the horses
and the swift steeds they brought to the
place where it should be, each according
to his assignment.

THE WISDOM OF SOLOMON, 4:29–34

29 God gave Solomon wisdom and understanding
in very exceptional measure,
and breadth of mind, like the sand
30 that is on the seashore, so that Solomon's
wisdom surpassed the wisdom of
all the eastern Arabs and all the wis-
31 dom of Egypt. For he was wiser than
all men: than Ethan the Ezrahite, and
Heman, and Chalcol, and Darda, the
sons of Mahol; and his fame was in all
32 the neighboring nations. He also spoke
three thousand proverbs and his songs
33 were five thousand. He spoke concerning
trees, from the cedar which is in
Lebanon even to the hyssop that
springs out of the wall; he spoke also of
beasts, of birds, of reptiles, and of fish;
34 and men came from all peoples to hear
the wisdom of Solomon, sent from all
the kings of the earth who had heard of
his wisdom.

SOLOMON'S PREPARATIONS FOR THE TEMPLE, 5:1–18

5 Now Hiram, king of Tyre, had sent
his servants to Solomon when he heard
that they had anointed him king in
place of his father; for Hiram had always
been fond of David.
2 And Solomon sent to Hiram, saying,
3 "You yourself knew David my father,
how he was unable to build a
house for the name of the LORD his
God because of the hostile forces that
surrounded him until the LORD put
4 them under the soles of his feet. But
now the LORD my God has given me
rest on all sides, in that there is no ad-
5 versary and no untoward event. So
now I am planning to build a house for
the name of the LORD my God, as the
LORD spoke to David my father, saying,
'Your son whom I will put in your
place upon your throne, he shall build
6 the house for my name.' Now therefore
command that they cut for me
cedars of Lebanon; and my servants
will accompany your servants, and I
will pay you wages for your servants
exactly as you say; for you know that
there is no one among us who knows
how to cut timber like the Sidonians."
When Hiram heard the words of 7
Solomon, he was very greatly pleased
and said,
"Blessed be the LORD today, who
has given David a wise son to be over
this great people."
So Hiram sent to Solomon, saying, 8
"I have heard what you have requested
of me; I stand ready to perform
all your pleasure in the matter of
cedar and cypress timbers. My serv- 9
ants shall bring them down to the sea
from Lebanon, and I will make them
into rafts to go by sea to the place that
you shall direct me, and I will have
them broken up there, and you shall
take them up. You shall also accomplish
my desire by providing food for
my household."
So Hiram kept Solomon supplied 10
with cedar and cypress timber to his
entire satisfaction. Solomon gave Hi- 11
ram twenty thousand kors of wheat
as food for his household, and twenty
baths of oil from crushed olives. This
much Solomon used to give Hiram annually.
And the LORD gave Solomon 12
wisdom as he promised him; and there
was peace between Hiram and Solomon,
and the two of them ratified a
treaty.
King Solomon raised a levy of forced 13
laborers out of all Israel, and the levy
consisted of thirty thousand men. He 14
sent them to Lebanon, ten thousand a
month in relays; a month they were in
Lebanon and two months at home; and
Adoniram was in command of the levy.
Solomon also had seventy thousand 15
burden bearers and eighty thousand
hewers of stone in the mountains, be- 16
side Solomon's superior officers who
were set over the work, three thousand
three hundred, who had charge of the
people who were doing the work. And 17
the king commanded that they should
hew out great, costly stones, to lay the
foundation of the house with cut stone.
So Solomon's builders and Hiram's 18
builders and the Gebalites did the hewing
and prepared the timbers and the
stones to build the house.

THE BUILDING PLANS OF THE TEMPLE, 6:1–38

1 Now in the four hundred and eight-
ieth year after the exodus of the Israelites from the land of Egypt, in the
fourth year of Solomon's reign over
Israel, in the month of Ziv, which is the
second month, he built the house of the
2 LORD. As for the house which King
Solomon built for the LORD, its length
was sixty cubits, its breadth twenty
3 cubits, and its height thirty. The
porch in front of the temple was twenty
cubits in length, corresponding to the
breadth of the house, and it was ten
cubits wide at the front of the house.
4 He made for the house windows with
narrow frames.
5 He also built inclosed galleries
against the wall of the house round
about in conformity with the walls of
the house round about, both around the
temple proper and the inner room, and
he made side chambers round about.
6 The lower side chamber was five cubits
broad and the middle six cubits broad
and the third seven cubits broad; on the
outside of the house round about he
made offsets in order that the supports
should not be inserted into the walls
7 of the house. When the house was built,
it was done with stone prepared at the
quarry; and neither hammer nor ax nor
any iron tool was heard in the temple
8 while it was being built. The entrance
into the lower side chamber was on the
right side of the house; and by means
of a circular trap door they could go up
into the middle chamber and from the
9 middle into the third. So he built the
house and finished it; and he covered
10 the house with cedar. He also built the
inclosed galleries against the whole
house, five cubits being the height of
each; and they were joined to the house
with timbers of cedar.
11 Now the word of the Lord came to
Solomon, saying,
12 "With regard to this house you are
building, if you will walk in my statutes, and carry out my ordinances, and
keep all my commands by conforming
your conduct to them; then I will confirm my word with you which I spoke
13 to David your father; and I will dwell
in the midst of the Israelites and will
not forsake my people Israel."

So Solomon built the house and fin- 14
ished it.
He built the walls of the house on the 15
inside with boards of cedar; from the
floor of the house to the rafters of the
ceiling he covered them on the inside
with wood, and he covered the floor of
the house with boards of cypress. He 16
built off twenty cubits from the back of
the house with boards of cedar from the
floor to the rafters; and he built for
himself within, an inner room, for the
most sacred place. The house, that is, 17
the temple proper, in front of the inner
room, was forty cubits long. There was 18
also cedar within the interior of the
house carved in the form of gourds and
open flowers; the whole was cedar,
there was no stone seen. Then he pre- 19
pared an inner room within the interior
of the house to place there the ark of
the covenant of the LORD. The inner 20
room was twenty cubits long, twenty
cubits wide, and twenty cubits high;
and he overlaid it with rare gold. He
also made an altar of cedar in front of 21
the inner room and covered it with
gold. Then he overlaid the entire house 22
with gold, until the whole house was
finished.
He made in the inner room two cher- 23
ubim of olive wood, ten cubits in
height. One wing of the cherub was 24
five cubits and the other wing of the
cherub was five cubits—it was ten cu
bits from the tip of one wing to the tip
of the other. The other cherub also
measured ten cubits; both cherubim 25
had the same measurement and form.
The height of the one cherub was ten 26
cubits, even so was the other cherub.
Thus he put the cherubim within the 27
inner part of the house, and they
spread out the wings of the cherubim,
so that the wing of the one touched the
wall, while the wing of the other cherub
reached the other wall, and their wings
touched each other in the middle of the
house. He also overlaid the cherubim 28
with gold.
He carved all the walls of the house 29
round about with carved figures of
cherubim and palm trees and open
flowers, within and without. The floor
of the house he overlaid with gold within and without.
For the entrance of the inner room he 31
made folding doors of olive wood: the
pilasters and doorposts formed a pentag-

32 onal. The two doors of olive wood he
decorated with carvings of cherubim
and palm trees and open flowers, and
he overlaid them with gold; and he
spread the gold upon the cherubim and
the palm trees.
33 So also he made for the entrance of
the temple proper, doorposts of olive
wood four square; and two doors of
34 cypress wood; the two leaves of the one
door were folding, and the two leaves of
35 the other door were folding. He carved
cherubim and palm trees and open
flowers, and overlaid them with gold
36 evenly applied to the carved work; and
he built the inner court with three
courses of hewn stone, and a course of
hewn cedar beams.
37 In the fourth year was the foundation
of the house of the LORD laid, in the
38 month Ziv. In the eleventh year, in
the month Bul, which is the eighth
month, the house was finished in all its
details and according to all its specifica-
tions. Thus he was seven years in
building it.

DETAILS OF SOLOMON'S BUILDINGS, 7:1–51

7 But Solomon was thirteen years
building his own house until he had
2 finished his entire house. Thus he
built the Forest of Lebanon House; its
length was one hundred cubits, and its
breadth fifty cubits, and its height
thirty cubits, upon three rows of cedar
columns, with cedar beams upon the
3 columns. Above it was covered with
cedar over the forty-five beams that
were upon the columns, and the number of the columns was fifteen in a row.
4 There were also window-frames in three
rows, and window was over against win-
5 dow, in three tiers. All the doorways
and windows had square frames; and
door was over against door in three
6 tiers. He also made the pillared porch
fifty cubits long and thirty cubits
7 broad, and a porch in front of them and
columns and a cornice in front of them.
And he made the porch of the throne
where he might pronounce judgment,
even the Porch of Judgment; and it was
covered with cedar from floor to rafters.
8 His own house, where he was to
dwell, belonging to another court farther back from the Porch of Judgment,
was of like workmanship. He also made
a house for Pharaoh's daughter (whom
Solomon had taken to wife) like this
porch.
All these were of costly stones, hewn 9
according to measurements, sawed with
saws, within and without, even from
the foundation to the coping, and from
the outside to the great court. The 10
foundation also was of costly, great
stones—stones of ten cubits and stones
of eight cubits; likewise above were 11
costly stones, hewn according to measurement, as well as cedar; also the great 12
encircling court had three courses of
hewn stone and a course of cedar
beams, as in the case of the inner court
of the house of the LORD and the court
of the porch of the house.
Then King Solomon sent and 13
brought Hiram from Tyre. He was the 14
son of a widow of the tribe of Naphtali;
and his father was a man of Tyre, a
worker in bronze; and he was equipped
with skill, understanding, and knowledge to execute any work in bronze. So
he came to King Solomon and did all
his work. Thus he cast the two columns 15
of bronze for the porch of the temple.
Eighteen cubits was the height of one
column, and a cord of twelve cubits
measured its circumference; the thickness of the column was four fingers; it
was hollow, and the second column was
similar. He also made two capitals of 16
molten bronze, to set upon the tops of
the columns, the height of the one
capital being five cubits, and five cubits
being the height of the other capital.
Then he made two nets (woven work, 17
festoons, chain work) for the capitals
which were upon the top of the columns; a net for the one capital, and a
net for the other capital. He likewise 18
made the pomegranates; and two rows
of bronze pomegranates were upon the
one to cover the capitals that were upon
the top of the columns; he also treated
the other capital in the same manner.
Now the capitals that were upon the 19
tops of the columns in the porch were
of lily work—four cubits. There were 20
also capitals above upon the two columns close to the rounded projection of
the column which was beside the network; and the pomegranates were two
hundred, in two rows around the second capital. Thus he set up the col- 21
umns of the porch of the temple; and he

set up the right hand column and called
its name Jachin; and he set up the left
hand column and called its name Boaz.
22 Now upon the top of the columns was
lily work. So he finished the work of
the columns.
23 Then he made the molten sea, ten
cubits in diameter from brim to brim,
round in form, five cubits high, and
24 thirty cubits in circumference; and under
its brim were gourds encircling it for
ten cubits, completely surrounding the
sea. The gourds were in two rows, cast
26 when it was cast. Now its thickness
was a handbreadth, and its brim was in
workmanship like the brim of a cup,
similar to the flower of a lily. It held
25 two thousand baths. It stood on
twelve oxen, three facing north, three
facing west, three facing south, and
three facing east; and the sea was superimposed
upon them, while their
haunches were all directed inward.
27 He made also ten stands of bronze,
each stand being four cubits long, four
28 cubits wide and three cubits high. The
construction of the stands was as follows:
they had border-frames and the
border-frames were between the sup-
29 ports; and on the border-frames that
were between the supports were lions,
oxen, and cherubim; and upon the supports
likewise, above and below the
lions, oxen, and wreaths, was bevelled
30 work. Moreover each stand had four
bronze wheels, and axles of bronze, and
the four corners had shoulder-pieces:
beneath the bowl the shoulder-pieces
were cast, with wreaths at the sides of
31 each. Its mouth within the shoulder-piece
was a cubit, and its mouth was
round after the work of a pedestal, a
cubit and a half, and also upon its
mouth were gravings, and its border-
32 frames were square, not round. Also
the four wheels were underneath the
border-frames; and the axletrees of the
33 wheels were in the stand. The construction
of the wheels was like the construction
of a chariot wheel: their supports,
their felloes, their spokes, and their
34 hubs, were all cast. There were four
shoulder-pieces at the four corners of
each stand; the shoulder-pieces were a
part of the stand.
35 Now in the top of the stand there
was a round opening half a cubit high,
and upon the top of the stand were its
36 supports and its border-frames. And
on the smooth surface of the supports
and border-frames he carved cherubim,
lions, and palm trees, according to the
clear space on each, with wreaths round
about. After this manner he made the 37
ten stands: all of them were of one casting
and of one measure and form.
He also made ten lavers of bronze: 38
one laver held forty baths, and one
laver measured four cubits; and on each
one of the ten stands was a laver. Then 39
he put the stands, five on the right side
of the house, and five on the left side of
the house; and he put the sea on the
right side of the house toward the
south.
Hiram also made the pots, the shov- 40
els, and the basins. So Hiram finished
all the work that he did for King Solomon
on the house of the LORD: the two 41
columns, the two bowl-shaped capitals
that were on the top of the columns,
the two networks to cover the two bowls
of the capitals that were on the top of
the columns, and the four hundred 42
pomegranates for the two networks,
two rows of pomegranates for each network,
to cover the two bowl-shaped
capitals that were on the tops of the columns,
and the ten stands and the ten 43
lavers upon the stands, and the one 44
sea and the twelve oxen underneath the
sea.
Now the pots, and the shovels, and 45
the basins, even all these utensils which
Hiram made for King Solomon in the
house of the LORD, were of burnished
bronze. There was no weighing of the 47
bronze from which he made all these
utensils because it was so very much;
the weight of the bronze could not be
determined. In the plain of the Jordan 46
he cast them, in the clay ground between
Succoth and Zarethan. So Solo- 48
mon placed all the utensils which he had
made in the house of the LORD: the
golden altar, and the golden table upon
which was the Presence-bread; and the 49
lampstands, five on the right side, and
five on the left in front of the inner
room, of rare gold; and the flowers, the 50
lamps, and the tongs of gold; and the
cups, snuffers, basins, saucers, and firepans
of rare gold; and the golden
hinges, both for the folding doors of the
inner house (the most sacred place)
and for the folding doors of the temple
proper.
Thus all the work was completed that 51

King Solomon performed on the house
of the LORD. Solomon also brought in
the things which David his father had
dedicated, the silver, the gold, and the
utensils, placing them in the treasuries
of the house of the LORD.

THE DEDICATION OF THE TEMPLE, 8:1–66

8 Then Solomon assembled the elders
of Israel and all the heads of the tribes,
the princes of families of the Israelites,
to King Solomon in Jerusalem, to bring
up the ark of the covenant of the LORD
from the city of David, that is Zion.
2 So all the men of Israel assembled to
King Solomon at the feast in the
month Ethanim, which is the seventh
3 month. Likewise all the elders of Israel
came, and the priests took up the ark;
4 and they brought up the ark of the
LORD, and the tent of meeting, and all
the holy vessels that were in the tent;
the priests and Levites brought them
5 up. Then King Solomon and all the assembly of Israel, that were assembled
to him, were with him before the ark,
sacrificing so many sheep and oxen that
they could not be counted or numbered.
6 Then the priests brought the ark of the
covenant of the LORD to its place in
the inner room of the house, in the
most sacred place, underneath the
7 wings of the cherubim; for the cherubim
had their wings spread over the place
of the ark, so that the cherubim made a
covering above the ark and its poles.
8 But the poles were so long that the ends
of the poles were seen from the holy
place in front of the inner room, yet
they were not seen outside, and there
9 they are to this day. There was nothing
in the ark except the two tablets of
stone which Moses had placed there at
Horeb, when the LORD made a covenant with the Israelites at the time they
10 came out of the land of Egypt. Now
when the priests came out of the sanctuary, a cloud filled the house of the
11 LORD, so that the priests could not
stand to minister because of the cloud;
for the glory of the LORD filled the
house of the LORD.

12 Then Solomon said,

"The LORD established the sun in the
heavens,
But he himself said that he would
dwell in thick darkness;
"'Build my house, a house of habitation for me,
That I may dwell therein forever.'
Is it not written in the Book of
Jashar?"

Then the king faced about and
blessed all the assembly of Israel, and
all the assembly of Israel stood up; and
he said,
"Blessed be the LORD, the God of
Israel, who with his own mouth spoke
to David my father, and with his own
hand has fulfilled it, saying, 'Since the
day that I brought forth my people
Israel out of Egypt, I chose no city out
of all the tribes of Israel in which to
build a house that my name might be
there, but I have chosen David to be
over my people Israel.' Now it was in
the mind of David my father to build a
house for the name of the LORD, the
God of Israel. But the LORD said to 1
David my father, 'Because it was in
your mind to build a house for my
name, you did well that it was in your
mind; nevertheless you yourself shall
not build the house; but your son, who
shall come forth from your loins, he
shall build the house for my name.'
Now the LORD has made good his word 2
which he spoke; for I have risen up in
the place of David my father and sit on
the throne of Israel, as the LORD promised, and I have built the house for the
name of the LORD, the God of Israel;
and there I have provided a place for 2
the ark in which is the covenant of the
LORD, which he made with our fathers,
when he brought them out of the land
of Egypt."
Then Solomon stood up before the 2
altar of the LORD in the presence of
the whole assembly of Israel and spread
forth his hands toward the heavens, and 2
said,
"O LORD, the God of Israel, there is
no God like thee in the heavens above
nor upon the earth beneath, who keepest loving faith with thy servants who
walk before thee with all their heart,
who hast kept with thy servant David, 2
my father, that which thou didst promise him; for thou didst speak with thy
lips, and with thy hand thou hast fulfilled it, as it is this day. Now there- 2
fore, O LORD, the God of Israel, keep
with thy servant David, my father,
that which thou didst promise him,

saying, 'You shall never lack a man in my sight to sit on the throne of Israel, if only your sons take heed to their way, to walk before me as you have walked before me.' Now therefore, O God of Israel, let thy word be confirmed, I pray thee, which thou hast spoken to thy servant David, my father.

"But can God really dwell with men on the earth? Behold, the heavens and the highest heaven cannot contain thee; how much less this house which I have built! Yet turn thou to the prayer of thy servant and to his supplication, O LORD my God, to listen to the cry and to the prayer which thy servant offers before thee this day, that thine eyes may be open toward this house night and day, even toward the place of which thou hast said, 'My name shall be there,' to listen to the prayer which thy servant shall pray toward this place; and listen thou to the supplication of thy servant and of thy people Israel, when they shall pray toward this place; yea, hear thou in the heavens, thy dwelling place, and when thou hearest, forgive.

"If a man sin against his neighbor, and an oath be laid upon him compelling him to swear, and he come and swear before thine altar in this house, then hear thou in the heavens; take action and judge thy servants, punishing the wicked by bringing his course of action upon his own head, and vindicating the righteous by rewarding him according to his righteousness.

"When thy people Israel are defeated before the enemy because they have sinned against thee, if they turn again to thee and praise thy name and pray and make supplication to thee in this house, then hear thou in the heavens and forgive the sin of thy people Israel and restore them to the land which thou gavest to their fathers.

"When the heavens are shut up and there is no rain because they have sinned against thee, if they pray toward this place and confess thy name and turn from their sin, when thou dost afflict them, then hear thou in the heavens and forgive the sin of thy servants and thy people Israel, when thou teachest them the good way in which they should walk, and send rain upon thy land, which thou hast given to thy people as a heritage.

"If there be in the land famine, if
there be pestilence, blasting, mildew,
locusts, or caterpillars, if their enemy
besiege them in any of their gates,
whatever be the plague, whatever be
the sickness—whatever prayer, what- 38
ever supplication be made by any man,
or by all thy people Israel, who knows
each his own personal affliction, and
stretches out his hand toward this
house, then hear thou in the heavens 39
thy dwelling-place and forgive and act
and render to each according to all his
ways, whose heart thou knowest (for
thou, even thou alone, knowest the
hearts of all the sons of men), that they 40
may fear thee all the days that they
live on the face of the land which thou
gavest to our fathers.

"Moreover concerning the resident 41
alien, who is not of thy people Israel,
but comes from a far country for thy
name's sake (for they shall hear of thy 42
great name and thy mighty hand and
thine outstretched arm), when he shall
come and pray toward this house, then 43
hear thou in the heavens thy dwelling-
place and do just as the alien petitions
of thee, that all the peoples of the earth
may know thy name, to fear thee, as
do thy people Israel, and that they may
know that this house which I have built
is called by thy name.

"If thy people go out to battle 44
against their enemy, by whatever way
thou shalt send them, and they pray to
the LORD in the direction of the city
which thou hast chosen and the house
which I have built for thy name, then 45
hear thou in the heavens their prayer
and their supplication, and uphold their
cause.

"If they sin against thee (for there is 46
no man who does not sin), and thou be
angry with them and deliver them to
the enemy, so that they carry them
away captive to the land of the enemy,
far off or near; yet if they take thought 47
in the land to which they have been
carried captive and turn again and
make supplication to thee in the land of
their captivity, saying, 'We have sinned
and have acted perversely and wickedly,' if they return to thee with all their 48
mind and heart in the land of their enemies, who carried them captive, and
pray to thee in the direction of their
land, which thou gavest to their fathers, and the city which thou has
chosen, and the house which I have

49 built for thy name, then hear thou in
the heavens thy dwelling-place their
prayer and their supplication, and up-
50 hold their cause, and forgive thy people
who have sinned against thee, and all
their transgressions which they have
transgressed against thee, and grant
them compassion in the sight of those
who carried them captive, that they
51 may have compassion on them (for they
are thy people and thy heritage, that
thou didst bring forth out of Egypt,
52 from the midst of the iron furnace),
that thine eyes may be open to the supplication of thy servant and to the supplication of thy people Israel, to give
ear to them whenever they cry to thee.
53 For thou didst separate them from all
the peoples of the earth to be thy heritage, as thou didst promise through
Moses thy servant, when thou didst
bring our fathers out of Egypt, O Lord
GOD."

54 Now when Solomon had finished
praying all this prayer and supplication
to the LORD, he arose from kneeling
on his knees before the altar of the
LORD with his hands stretched out to-
55 ward the heavens, and stood, and
blessed all the assembly of Israel with
a loud voice, saying,

56 "Blessed be the LORD who has given
rest to his people Israel, just as he
promised. Not one word has failed of
all his good promise which he spoke by
57 Moses his servant. The LORD our God
be with us, as he was with our fathers;
58 let him not leave us or forsake us, that
he may incline our hearts to him, to
walk in all his ways and to keep his
commands, his statutes, and his ordinances, which he commanded our fa-
59 thers. Let these words of mine, with
which I have made supplication before
the LORD, be near to the LORD, our
God, day and night, that he maintain
the right of his servant and the right of
his people Israel, as each day requires;
60 that all the peoples of the earth may
know that the LORD is God; there is no
61 other. Let your heart therefore be perfect with the LORD our God, to walk in
his statutes and to keep his commands,
as at this day."

62 The king and all Israel with him of-
63 fered sacrifices before the LORD. Solomon moreover offered as the sacrifice
of thank-offerings, which he offered to
the LORD, twenty-two thousand oxen,
and a hundred and twenty thousand
sheep. Thus the king and all the Israelites dedicated the house of the LORD.
The same day the king consecrated the
interior of the court that was in front of
the house of the LORD; for there he
offered the burnt-offering, and the
cereal-offering, and the fat pieces of the
thank-offerings, because the bronze
altar that was before the LORD was too
small to receive the burnt-offering and
the cereal-offering and the fat pieces of
the thank-offerings. So Solomon made
a feast at that time and all Israel with
him—a great assembly, from the entrance of Hamath to the Brook of
Egypt—before the LORD our God,
seven days. But on the eighth day he
sent the people away; and with a blessing upon the king they went to their
homes, joyful and glad of heart for all
the goodness that the LORD had shown
to David his servant, and to Israel his
people.

SOLOMON'S VISION, 9:1–9

Now when Solomon had finished building the house of the LORD and the king's house and all the work of Solomon which he was pleased to do, the LORD appeared to Solomon a second time, as he had appeared to him in Gibeon. The LORD said to him,

"I have heard your prayer and your supplication, which you have made before me. I have sanctified this house which you have built in which to put my name forever; and my eyes and my heart shall be there for all time. If you will indeed walk before me, as David your father walked, in integrity of heart and in uprightness, doing just as I have commanded you, and will keep my statutes and my ordinances, then I will establish the throne of your kingdom over Israel forever, as I promised David your father, saying, 'You shall never lack a man upon the throne of Israel.' But if you shall indeed turn aside from following me, you or your children, and shall not keep my commands and my statutes which I have set before you, but go and serve other gods, and worship them, then I will cut off Israel from the land which I have given them; and the house, which I have sanctified for my name, will I cast away from me, and Israel shall be a proverb and a byword among all peoples. Moreover, this house shall become ruins; every passer-by shall be amazed and shall hiss, and they shall say, 'Why has the LORD done thus to this land and to this house?' Then they shall say, 'Because they forsook the LORD their God, who brought forth their fathers out of the land of Egypt, and took up with other gods and worshiped them and served them; therefore the LORD has brought upon them all this evil.' "

THE ORIGIN OF THE NAME CABUL, 9:10–14

Now at the end of twenty years, during which Solomon had built the two houses, the house of the LORD and the king's house, Hiram king of Tyre having supplied Solomon with cedar and cypress timber and with gold as much as he required, King Solomon at that time proceeded to give to Hiram twenty cities in the land of Galilee. But when Hiram came out from Tyre to see the cities which Solomon had given him, they were not acceptable in his sight. Therefore he said,

"What are these cities which you have given me, my brother?"

So they are called the land of Cabul even to this day. However, Hiram sent to the king one hundred and twenty talents of gold.

SOLOMON'S VARIED INTERESTS, 9:15—10:29

Now this is the account of the levy of forced service which King Solomon raised to build the house of the LORD, his own house, Millo, the wall of Jerusalem, Hazor, Megiddo, and Gezer (Pharaoh king of Egypt had gone up, and captured Gezer, and burned it, and slain the Canaanites who dwelt in the city, and had given it as a dowry to his daughter, Solomon's wife. So Solomon rebuilt Gezer), lower Beth-horon, Baalath, and Tamar in the desert in the land of Judah, and all the store-cities that Solomon had, and cities for his chariots, and the cities for his horsemen, and whatsoever Solomon desired to build in Jerusalem, in Lebanon, and in all the
land under his rule. All the people 20
who were left of the Amorites, the Hittites, the Perizzites, the Hivvites, and
the Jebusites, who were not of the Israelites, their descendants who were 21
left after them in the land, whom the
Israelites were unable to destroy utterly, of them Solomon raised a forced
levy of slaves, as it is to this day. But 22
Solomon made no slave of the Israelites; for they were the soldiers and his
attendants, his commanders, his officers
of third rank, his chariot commanders,
and his horsemen.

These were the chief officers who 23
were over Solomon's work, five hundred
and fifty, who had charge of the people
who did the work.

But Pharaoh's daughter went up 24
from the city of David to her own house
which he had built for her; then he built
Millo.

Now Solomon used to offer burnt- 25
offerings and thank-offerings three
times a year upon the altar which he
built to the LORD, and he used to burn
incense before the LORD. So he completed the house.

King Solomon also made a fleet of 26
ships at Ezion-geber, which is near
Eloth on the shore of the Red Sea in the
land of Edom; and Hiram sent with the 27
fleet his servants—seamen, who were
familiar with the sea—together with
the servants of Solomon. Now they 28
went to Ophir and took from there gold,
to the amount of four hundred and
twenty talents, and brought it to Solomon.

Now when the queen of Sheba heard 10
of the fame of Solomon through the
name of the LORD, she came to test
him with hard questions. So she came 2
to Jerusalem with a very large retinue,
with camels bearing spices and very
much gold and precious stones; and
when she came to Solomon, she conversed with him about all that was in
her mind; and Solomon answered all her 3
questions; there was nothing hidden
from the king which he could not explain to her. Then when the queen of 4
Sheba had observed all the wisdom of
Solomon, the house that he had built,
the viands of his table, the appoint- 5
ment of his servants, the attendance of
his waiters, their clothing, his cupbearers, and his burnt-offerings which he
used to offer at the house of the LORD,

6 there was no more spirit in her. So she
said to the king,
"The report which I heard in my own
land of your affairs and your wisdom
7 was true; but I would not believe the
words until I came and saw with my
own eyes, and behold, the half was not
told me; you surpass in wisdom and
prosperity the report which I heard.
8 Happy are your wives; happy are these
servants of yours who stand before you
continually and hear your wisdom!
9 Blessed be the LORD your God who has
delighted in you, to set you on the
throne of Israel! Because the LORD
loved Israel forever, he has made you
king, to administer justice and righteousness."
10 Then she gave the king one hundred
and twenty talents of gold and a very
great amount of spices and precious
stones; never did such a multitude of
spices come, as that which the queen of
11 Sheba gave to King Solomon. In addition Hiram's fleet, that brought gold
from Ophir, also brought a very great
amount of sandalwood and precious
12 stones. Accordingly the king made of
the sandalwood pilasters for the house
of the LORD and for the king's house,
and harps and lyres for the singers.
There never had come such sandalwood, nor has it been seen to this day.
13 Now King Solomon gave to the
queen of Sheba all that it pleased her to
ask for, besides what he gave her according to his royal bounty. Then she
turned and went to her own land, together with her servants.
14 The weight of gold that came to Solomon in one year was six hundred and
15 sixty-six talents of gold, besides what
came from the traffic of the merchants
and from all the kings of the Arabs and
from the governors of the land.
16 Now King Solomon made two hundred large shields of beaten gold (six
hundred shekels of gold going to each
17 shield) and three hundred shields of
beaten gold (three manas of gold going
to each shield), and the king put them
in the House of the Forest of Lebanon.
18 The king also made a great throne of
ivory and overlaid it with the finest
19 gold. The throne had six steps and at
the back of the throne were calves'
heads, and on both sides of the seat
were arms, and two lions stood beside
20 the arms, while twelve lions stood there

on the six steps on each side. The like was never made in any kingdom.

All the drinking vessels of King Solomon were of gold, and all the vessels of the House of the Forest of Lebanon were of rare gold; none were of silver, since it was thought nothing of in the days of Solomon. For the king had at sea a fleet of Tarshish ships with the fleet of Hiram. Once every three years the fleet of Tarshish ships used to come bringing gold, silver, ivory, apes, and peacocks. King Solomon excelled all the kings of the earth in riches and wisdom; and the whole earth sought the presence of Solomon to hear the wisdom which God had put into his mind. They brought each his present: articles of silver and gold, clothing, equipment, spices, horses, and mules, so much year by year.

Moreover Solomon gathered together chariots and horsemen; and he had fourteen hundred chariots and twelve thousand horsemen, that he stationed in the chariot cities and with the king in Jerusalem. The king made silver in Jerusalem as common as stone, and he made cedars as plentiful as the sycamore trees that are in the lowland. Solomon's transport of horses was between Egypt and Kuë; the king's traders received them from Kuë at a price, and a chariot could be imported from Egypt for six hundred shekels of silver and a horse for a hundred and fifty. In this manner they carried on trade with all the kings of the Hittites and the kings of the Arameans.

SOLOMON'S SINS AND THEIR PENALTIES, 11:1–43

Now King Solomon was a lover of women; and he married many foreign wives—Moabites, Ammonites, Edomites, Sidonians, and Hittites, from the nations concerning which the LORD had said to the Israelites, "You shall not go among them, neither shall they come among you; for surely they will turn away your heart after their gods"; Solomon clung to these in love.

And he had seven hundred wives, princesses, and three hundred concubines; and his wives turned away his heart. Now when Solomon was old, his heart was not perfect with the LORD

his God, as was the heart of David his
5 father; and his wives turned away his
heart after their gods. Solomon also
went after Ashtart, the goddess of the
Sidonians, and after Milcom, the abom-
6 ination of the Ammonites. Thus Solomon did that which was evil in the sight
of the LORD, and went not fully after
the LORD as David his father had done.
7 Then Solomon built a high place for
Chemosh, the god of the Moabites, in
the mountain over against Jerusalem,
and for Milcom, the god of the Am-
8 monites. Even so he did for all his foreign wives, burning incense and sacri-
9 ficing to their gods. Thus the LORD
was angry with Solomon, because his
heart was turned away from the LORD,
the God of Israel, who had appeared to
10 him twice, and had commanded him
concerning this thing, that he should
not go after other gods; but he did not
heed that which the LORD had commanded.

11 Therefore the LORD said to Solomon,

"Inasmuch as this is your attitude
and you have not kept my covenant
and my statutes, which I have commanded you, I will surely rend the kingdom from you, and will give it to your
12 servant. Nevertheless I will not do it
in your days, for David your father's
sake; but I will rend it out of the hand
13 of your son. However I will not tear
away the whole kingdom; but I will
give one tribe to your son, for David
my servant's sake and for the sake of
Jerusalem which I have chosen."

14 Accordingly the LORD raised up
against Solomon an adversary, Hadad
the Edomite, of the royal house that
15 was in Edom; for when David was in
Edom, also when Joab, the commander
of the army, went up to bury the slain,
16 he slew every male in Edom (for Joab
and all Israel remained there six months
until he had cut off every male in
17 Edom). Hadad and certain Edomites
from the servants of his father fled with
him, to go into Egypt, Hadad being a
18 little child. They set out from Midian
and came to Paran and took men with
them from Paran and came to Egypt to
Pharaoh, king of Egypt, who gave him
a house and appointed him food and
19 gave him land. Thus Hadad found
great favor in the sight of Pharaoh, so
that he gave him to wife the sister of
his own wife, the sister of Tahpenes the
queen. Also the sister of Tahpenes 20
bore him Genubath his son, whom Tahpenes weaned in Pharaoh's house; and
Genubath was in Pharaoh's house
among the sons of Pharaoh. Now 21
when Hadad heard in Egypt that David slept with his fathers, and that
Joab, the commander of the army, was
dead, Hadad said to Pharaoh,

"Send me away and let me go to my
own country."

But Pharaoh said to him, 22
"What have you lacked with me that
you are now seeking to go to your own
country?"

"Do let me go" he said to him.

God also raised up as an adversary to 23
him, Rezon, the son of Eliada, who had
fled from his master, Hadadezer, king
of Zobah. So he gathered men about 24
him and became leader of a marauding
band, and they went to Damascus and
dwelt there and reigned in Damascus.
He was an adversary of Israel all the 25
days of Solomon besides the evil which
Hadad did; and he abhorred Israel and
ruled over Edom.

Jeroboam, the son of Nebat, an 26
Ephraimite of Zeredah, a servant of
Solomon, whose mother's name was
Zeruiah, a widow, also lifted up his
hand against the king. Now this was 27
the reason why he lifted up his hand
against the king: Solomon built Millo
and closed up the breach of the city of
David his father. Now the man Jero- 28
boam was very able and when Solomon
saw that the young man was industrious, he gave him charge of all the forced
labor of the house of Joseph.

Thus it happened at that time, when 29
Jeroboam went out of Jerusalem, that
the prophet Ahijah the Shilonite found
him on the road and he turned him
aside from the road. Now Ahijah had
clad himself with a new garment; and
the two of them were alone in the field.
Then Ahijah laid hold of the new gar- 30
ment that was on him and tore it into
twelve pieces; and he said to Jero- 31
boam,

"Take for yourself ten pieces; for
thus says the LORD, the God of Israel:
'Behold, I am about to tear the kingdom from the hand of Solomon and will
give you ten tribes; but he shall have 32
one tribe, for my servant David's sake
and for the sake of Jerusalem, the city

which I have chosen out of all the tribes
33 of Israel, because he has forsaken me
and worshiped Ashtart, the goddess of
the Sidonians, Chemosh, the god of
Moab, and Milcom, the god of the Ammonites,
and has not walked in my
ways to do that which is right in my
sight, and to keep my statutes and my
ordinances, as David his father did.
34 Nevertheless I will not take the whole
kingdom out of his hand; but I will certainly
establish him as ruler during his
lifetime, for David my servant's sake
whom I chose, who kept my com-
35 mands and my statutes. I will take the
kingdom out of his son's hand, and will
36 give to you, even ten tribes. Yet to his
son I will give one tribe, that David my
servant may always have a lamp before
me in Jerusalem, my city, where I
37 have chosen to put my name. But I
will take you and you shall reign over
all that you yourself desire, and you
38 shall be king over Israel; and if you will
hearken to all that I command you, and
will walk in my ways and do that which
is right in my sight, by keeping my statutes
and my commands, as David my
servant did, then I will be with you and
build you a lasting house, as I built for
David, and I will give Israel to you.
39 Thus I will afflict the descendants of
David for this, but not forever.' "
40 Solomon therefore sought to kill
Jeroboam, but Jeroboam arose and fled
to Egypt, to Shishak king of Egypt,
and was in Egypt till the death of Solomon.
41 Now the rest of the records of Solomon,
and all that he did, and his wisdom,
are they not written in the Book of
42 the Records of Solomon? The time that
Solomon reigned in Jerusalem over all
43 Israel was forty years. Then Solomon
slept with his fathers and was buried in
the city of David his father; and Rehoboam
his son reigned in his stead.

THE DISRUPTION OF THE KINGDOM, 12:1–20

12 Then Rehoboam went to Shechem,
for all Israel had come to Shechem to
2 make him king. But as soon as Jeroboam,
the son of Nebat, heard of it (for
he was still in Egypt, where he had fled
from the presence of Solomon the king,
and he was living in Egypt), he returned
to his native city of Zeredah in
the highlands of Ephraim. So they 3
sent and called Jeroboam, and he, with
all the assembly of Israel, came; and
they spoke to Rehoboam, saying,
"Your father made our yoke galling. 4
Now then lighten the galling service of
your father and his heavy yoke which
he laid upon us, and we will serve you."
Then he said to them, 5
"Go away for three days, then return
to me."
So the people went away.
Then King Rehoboam took counsel 6
with the old men who had stood before
Solomon his father, while he was still
alive, saying,
"How do you advise me to reply to
this people?"
They spoke to him, saying, 7
"If you will be a servant to this people
today and will serve them, and
when you answer them, speak kindly
to them, then they will be your servants
forever."
But he rejected the counsel of the 8
old men which they had given him, and
took counsel with the young men, who
had grown up with him and who were
his companions. So he said to them, 9
"What do you advise that we reply
to this people, who have spoken to me
saying, 'Lighten the yoke that your
father laid upon us'?"
Then the young men who had grown 10
up with him spoke to him, saying,
"Thus shall you say to this people
who have said to you, 'Your father
made our yoke heavy, but do you lighten
our yoke'; thus shall you say to
them: 'My little finger is thicker than
my father's loins! And now, whereas 11
my father loaded you with a heavy
yoke, I will add to your yoke; my father
chastised you with whips, but I will
chastise you with scorpions!' "
So when Jeroboam and all the people 12
came to Rehoboam the third day, as
the king commanded, saying, "Return
to me the third day," the king an- 13
swered them harshly, and rejected the
counsel of the old men which they offered
him. So he spoke to them accord- 14
ing to the counsel of the young men,
saying,
"My father made your yoke heavy,
but I will add to your yoke; my father
chastised you with whips, but I will
chastise you with scorpions."

15 So the king did not listen to the people, for it was a thing brought about by
the LORD to establish his word which
the LORD spoke by Ahijah the Shilonite to Jeroboam, the son of Nebat.
16 Now when all Israel saw that the
king had not listened to them, the people replied to the king, saying,
“What portion have we in David?
Yea, we have no heritage in the son of
Jesse. To your tents, O Israel! see now
to your own house, O David!”
So the Israelites went to their tents.
17 But Rehoboam reigned over the
Israelites who dwelt in the cities of
18 Judah. Then King Rehoboam sent
Adoram, who was over the forced labor, but all Israel stoned him to death;
whereupon King Rehoboam leaped into
19 his chariot, to flee to Jerusalem. So
Israel has been in rebellion against the
house of David down to this day.
20 Now as soon as all Israel heard that
Jeroboam had returned, they sent and
called him to the assembly and made
him king over all Israel. None, except
the tribe of Judah alone, remained loyal
to the house of David.

SHEMAIAH'S PROPHECY, 12:21–24

21 When Rehoboam reached Jerusalem,
he assembled all the house of Judah
and the tribe of Benjamin, a hundred
and eighty thousand seasoned troops,
to fight against the house of Israel to
bring back the kingdom to Rehoboam,
22 the son of Solomon. But the word of
God came to Shemaiah, a man of God,
saying,
23 “Speak to Rehoboam, son of Solomon, king of Judah, and to all the house
of Judah and Benjamin, and to the rest
24 of the people, saying, ‘Thus says the
LORD: “You shall not go up to fight
against your brothers, the Israelites;
return every man to his house, for this
thing is from me.” ’ ”
So they listened to the word of the
LORD, and turned and went away according to the word of the LORD.

THE MAKING OF THE GOLDEN CALVES, 12:25—13:34

25 Then Jeroboam built Shechem in the
highlands of Ephraim and dwelt there.
He also went out from there and built
Penuel.
Moreover Jeroboam said to himself, 26
“Now the kingdom will revert to the
house of David. If this people go up to 27
make sacrifices in the temple of the
LORD in Jerusalem, then will the heart
of this people return to their lord, even
to Rehoboam, king of Judah; and they
will slay me, and return to Rehoboam,
king of Judah.”
So the king took counsel and made 28
two calves of gold, and said to the people,
“You have gone up to Jerusalem
long enough. Behold your gods, O Israel, who brought you up from the land
of Egypt!”
So he set up the one in Bethel, and 29
the other he put in Dan; and this thing 30
became a sin to Israel, for the people
went to seek the one, even to Dan. He 31
also made sanctuaries at high places,
and made priests from among all sorts
of people, who were not of the sons of
Levi. Jeroboam established a feast in 32
the eighth month, on the fifteenth day
of the month, like the feast that is in
Judah, and he went up to the altar; so
he did in Bethel, sacrificing to the
calves that he had made; and he stationed in Bethel the priests of the high
places that he had made. And Jero- 33
boam went up on the fifteenth day of
the eighth month to the altar which he
had made in Bethel, which he had devised of his own accord; and he established a feast for the Israelites and went 13
up to the altar to burn incense. Now
at the command of the LORD there
came a man of God from Judah to
Bethel, just as Jeroboam was standing
by the altar to burn incense. The man 2
cried out against the altar at the command of the LORD and said,
“O Altar, altar, thus says the LORD:
‘Behold, a son shall be born to the house
of David, Josiah by name, and upon
you he shall sacrifice the priests of the
high places who burn incense upon you,
and he shall burn men's bones on
you.’ ”
He also gave a sign the same day, 3
saying,
“This is the sign which the LORD has
spoken, ‘Behold, the altar shall be rent,
and the ashes which are upon it shall be
poured out.’ ”
Now when the king heard the word of 4

the man of God which he cried against
the altar in Bethel, Jeroboam put forth
his hand from the altar, saying,
"Arrest him."
But his hand which he put forth
against him, withered up, so that he
5 could not draw it back to himself. The
altar also was rent, and the ashes
poured out from the altar in accordance
with the sign which the man of God
had given at the command of the
6 LORD. Then the king answered and
said to the man of God,
"Entreat now the favor of the LORD
your God, and pray for me that my
hand may be restored to me."
So the man of God entreated the
favor of the LORD, and the king's
hand was restored to him again and be-
7 came as it was before. Thereupon the
king spoke to the man of God,
"Come home with me and take refreshment and I will give you a reward."
8 But the man of God said to the
king,
"If you were to give me half of your
house, I would not go with you, nor
would I eat bread or drink water in this
9 place! For so it was charged me by the
word of the LORD, saying, 'You shall
neither eat bread nor drink water, nor
return by the way that you came.'"
10 So he went another way and did not
return by the way that he came to
Bethel.
11 Now a certain aged prophet lived in
Bethel; and his sons came and told him
all the deeds that the man of God had
done that day in Bethel; they also related to their father the words that he
12 had spoken to the king; and their father
spoke to them,
"Which way did he go?"
So his sons pointed out which way
the man of God who came from Judah
13 had gone. Then he said to his sons,
"Saddle the ass for me."
So they saddled the ass for him and
14 he rode off upon it. Now he went after
the man of God, and found him
sitting under an oak; and he said to
him,
"Are you the man of God who came
from Judah?"
"I am" he said.
15 "Come home with me and eat bread"
he said to him.
16 "I am not permitted to return with
you," he said, "nor go in with you, nor
may I eat bread or drink water with
you in this place; for it was declared 17
unto me by the word of the LORD, 'You
shall neither eat bread nor drink water
there, nor depart by the way you
came.'"
Then he said to him, 18
"I too am a prophet as you are; and
an angel spoke to me at the command
of the Lord, saying, 'Bring him back
with you to your house, that he may
eat bread and drink water.'"
But he lied to him. So he returned 19
with him, and ate bread in his house
and drank water.
But while they were sitting at the 20
table, the word of the LORD came to
the prophet who brought him back; and 21
he cried to the man of God who came
from Judah, saying,
"Thus says the LORD: 'Since you
have disobeyed the word of the LORD,
and have not kept the command which
the LORD your God commanded you,
but have returned and eaten bread and 22
drunk water in the place of which he
told you, "Eat no bread, and drink no
water," your body shall not come to
the grave of your fathers.'"
Now after he had eaten bread and 23
drunk, he saddled the ass for him and
once more he departed. But a lion met 24
him on the way and slew him, and his
body was cast upon the road, and the
ass stood beside it; the lion also was
standing by the body; and thus as men 25
were passing by they saw the body
cast upon the road, and the lion standing beside the body; and they came and
reported it in the city where the aged
prophet dwelt.
So when the prophet who brought 26
him back from the way heard of it, he
said,
"It is the man of God who rebelled
against the word of the LORD; therefore the LORD gave him to the lion,
which has mangled him and slain him,
according to the word of the LORD,
which he spoke to him."
Then he spoke to his sons, saying, 27
"Saddle the ass for me."
So they saddled it. Thus he went 28
and found his body cast upon the road
and the ass and the lion standing beside the body; the lion had not eaten
the body nor torn the ass. Then the 29
aged prophet took up the body of the

man of God, and laid it upon the ass,
and brought it back to the city that he
30 might mourn and bury him; and he
laid his body in his own grave; and they
mourned over him,
"Alas, my brother!"
31 After he had buried him, he said to
his sons,
"When I die, bury me in the grave
in which the man of God is buried; lay
32 my bones beside his bones; for the saying which he cried at the command of
the LORD against the altar which is in
Bethel, and against all the shrines of the
high places which are in the cities of
Samaria shall surely come to pass."
33 After this episode Jeroboam did not
turn from his evil way, but made again
from among all sorts of people priests
of the high places. Whomsoever he
would, he installed to be priests of the
34 high places; and this thing became a
sin to the house of Jeroboam, even to
cut it off and to destroy it from the face
of the ground.

JEROBOAM DENOUNCED BY AHIJAH, 14:1–20

4 At that time Abijah, the son of
2 Jeroboam, fell sick. Then Jeroboam
said to his wife,
"Arise, I pray you, and disguise
yourself, that you may not be known
to be the wife of Jeroboam, and go to
Shiloh. There is Ahijah the prophet,
who declared to me that I should be
3 king over this people. Take with you
ten loaves of bread and cakes and a
jar of honey, and go to him; he will tell
you what shall become of the child."
4 Then Jeroboam's wife did so; she
arose and went to Shiloh and came to
the house of Ahijah. Now Ahijah was
unable to see, for his eyes had become
5 dim because of his age; but the LORD
had said to Ahijah,
"Behold the wife of Jeroboam is coming to seek a word from you concerning
her son, for he is sick; thus and thus
shall you speak to her."
When she came in she pretended to
be a strange woman.
6 Now when Ahijah heard the sound of
her feet, as she came in at the doorway,
he said,
"Come in, wife of Jeroboam, why do
you pretend to be another, seeing that
I am sent to you with a harsh message?
Go, say to Jeroboam, 'Thus says the 7
LORD, the God of Israel: "Because I
exalted you from the midst of the people and made you a leader over my people Israel, and rent the kingdom away 8
from the house of David and gave it to
you, and you have not been like my
servant David, who kept my command,
and followed me with all his heart to
do only that which was right in my
sight, and you have done worse than 9
any that were before you, and have
gone and made for yourself other gods
and molten images, thus provoking me
to jealousy, and have cast me behind
your back; therefore, behold, I am about 10
to bring evil upon the house of Jeroboam
and I will cut off from Jeroboam every
male—him that is shut up and him that
is left at large in Israel—and I will
utterly consume the house of Jeroboam, as a man consumes refuse, until
it is gone. Him that dies of Jeroboam 11
in the city shall the dogs eat, and him
that dies in the field shall the birds of the
air eat; for the LORD has spoken it." '
But do you arise, go to your home; when 12
your feet enter the city, the child shall
die; and all Israel shall mourn for him 13
and bury him; for he only of Jeroboam
shall come to the grave, because in him
there is found some good thing toward
the LORD, the God of Israel, in the
house of Jeroboam. Moreover the 14
LORD will raise up for himself a king
over Israel, who shall cut off this house
of Jeroboam. Today and from now on 15
the LORD will smite Israel, as a reed is
shaken in the water, and he will root up
Israel from this good land which he
gave to your fathers, and will scatter
them beyond the river, because they
have made their Ashtarts, provoking
the LORD to anger. He will also give 16
up Israel because of the sins which Jeroboam has committed, and with which
he has made Israel sin."
Then Jeroboam's wife arose and de- 17
parted and came to Tirzah—she was
just entering over the threshold of the
house when the child died; and all 18
Israel buried him and mourned for him
according to the word of the LORD
which he spoke by his servant Ahijah,
the prophet.
Now the rest of the records of Jero- 19

boam, how he made war and how he
ruled, they are written in the Book of
the Chronicles of the Kings of Israel.
20 The time that Jeroboam reigned was
twenty-two years; then he slept with
his fathers, and Nadab his son became
king in his stead.

THE REIGN OF REHOBOAM IN JUDAH, 14:21–31

21 Now Rehoboam, the son of Solomon,
reigned in Judah. Rehoboam was forty-
one years old when he became king, and
he reigned seventeen years in Jerusalem, the city in which the LORD had
chosen out of all the tribes of Israel to
put his name; and his mother's name
was Naamah, the Ammonitess.
22 Judah did that which was evil in the
sight of the LORD, and they aroused
him to jealous anger with the sins
which they committed, more than all
23 their fathers had done. They also built
for themselves high places, sacred pillars, and sacred poles, on every high
hill and under every spreading tree;
24 there were also male devotees of the
fertility cult in the land. They did according to all the abominations of the
nations which the LORD drove out before the Israelites.
25 Now in the fifth year of King Rehoboam, Shishak, king of Egypt, came up
26 against Jerusalem; and he took away
the treasures of the house of the LORD
and the treasures of the king's house;
he took all away. He also took away
all the shields of gold which Solomon
27 had made. King Rehoboam made
shields of bronze in their stead and intrusted them to the commanders of the
guards, who guarded the door of the
28 king's house. Then, as often as the king
went into the house of the LORD, the
guards would take them up and bring
them back to the guard-room.
29 Now the rest of the records of Rehoboam and all that he did, are they not
written in the Book of the Chronicles
30 of the Kings of Judah? There was war
continually between Rehoboam and
31 Jeroboam. So Rehoboam slept with his
fathers, and he was buried with his fathers in the city of David; and his
mother's name was Naamah, the Ammonitess; and Abijam his son became
king in his stead.

THE REIGN OF ABIJAM IN JUDAH, 15:1–8

Now in the eighteenth year of King 1
Jeroboam, the son of Nebat, Abijam became king over Judah. He reigned 2
three years in Jerusalem; and his
mother's name was Maacah, the
daughter of Abishalom. But he walked 3
in all the sins of his father, which he
had committed before him; and his
heart was not perfect with the LORD
his God like the heart of David his father. Nevertheless, for David's sake, 4
the LORD his God gave him a lamp in
Jerusalem, in that he raised up his son
after him and established Jerusalem,
because David did that which was right 5
in the sight of the LORD and did not
turn aside from anything that he commanded him all the days of his life, except in the matter of Uriah the Hittite.
There was war between Rehoboam and 6
Jeroboam all the days of his life.
Now the rest of the records of Abi- 7
jam and all that he did, are they not
written in the Book of the Chronicles
of the Kings of Judah? There was war
between Abijam and Jeroboam. So 8
Abijam slept with his fathers, and they
buried him in the city of David; and
Asa his son became king in his stead.

ASA OF JUDAH AND NADAB OF ISRAEL, 15:9–32

Now in the twentieth year of Jero- 9
boam, king of Israel, Asa became king
of Judah, and he reigned forty-one 10
years in Jerusalem; and his mother's
name was Maacah, the daughter of
Abishalom. Asa did that which was 11
right in the sight of the LORD, as did
David his father. He put away the 12
male devotees of the fertility cult out
of the land, and removed all the idols
that his fathers had made. He also re- 13
moved Maacah his mother from being
queen-mother, because she made an
obscene image as an Asherah; and Asa
cut down her obscene image, and
burned it in the Kidron Valley. But 14
the high places were not removed;
nevertheless the heart of Asa was perfect with the LORD all his days. He 15
brought into the house of the LORD the
dedicated things of his father and his
own dedicated things, silver and gold
and utensils.

16 Now there was war between Asa and
Baasha, king of Israel, all their days.
17 Baasha, king of Israel, went up against
Judah and built Ramah, to prevent
anyone from going out or coming in to
18 Asa, king of Judah. Then Asa took all
the silver and gold that were left in the
treasuries of the house of the LORD and
the treasuries of the king's house, and
put them in charge of his servants; and
King Asa sent them to Ben-hadad, the
son of Tabrimmon, the son of Hezion,
king of Syria, who dwelt in Damascus,
saying,
19 "There is a league between me and
you and between my father and your
father. See, I send you a present of silver and gold. Go, break your alliance
with Baasha, king of Israel, that he
may withdraw from me."
20 Ben-hadad therefore listened to
King Asa and sent the commanders of
his forces against the cities of Israel,
and conquered Ijon, Dan, Abel-beth-
Maacah, and all Chinneroth, with all
21 the land of Naphtali. Now when Baasha heard of it, he stopped building
22 Ramah and dwelt in Tirzah. Thereupon King Asa made a proclamation
to all Judah—none were exempted—
and they carried away the stones of
Ramah and its timbers with which
Baasha had built. Then King Asa built
with them Geba of Benjamin and
23 Mizpeh. Now the rest of all the records of Asa and all his prowess and all
that he did, and the cities that he built,
are they not written in the Book of the
Chronicles of the Kings of Judah? In
the time of his old age he was diseased
24 in his feet. So Asa slept with his fathers, and was buried with his fathers
in the city of David his father; and
Jehoshaphat his son became king in his
stead.
25 Now Nadab, the son of Jeroboam,
became king over Israel in the second
year of Asa, king of Judah, and he
26 reigned over Israel two years. He did
that which was evil in the sight of the
LORD, and walked in the way of his
father, and in his sin with which he
27 made Israel sin. Then Baasha, the son
of Ahijah of the house of Issachar, conspired against him, and Baasha struck
him down at Gibbethon, which belonged to the Philistines, while Nadab
and all Israel were besieging Gibbeth-
28 on. So Baasha slew him in the third
year of Asa, king of Judah, and reigned
in his stead; also as soon as he became 29
king, he struck down all the house of
Jeroboam. He did not leave a single
person alive to Jeroboam until he had
destroyed him, according to the word of
the LORD which he spoke by his servant Ahijah the Shilonite, because of the 30
sins of Jeroboam which he committed
and with which he made Israel sin, and
by his provocation with which he provoked the LORD, the God of Israel, to
jealousy. Now the rest of the records of 31
Nadab and all that he did, are they not
written in the Book of the Chronicles
of the Kings of Israel? There was war 32
between Asa and Baasha, king of Israel,
all their days.

THE REIGN OF BAASHA OF ISRAEL, 15:33—16:7

In the third year of Asa, king of Ju- 33
dah, Baasha, the son of Ahijah, became
king over all Israel in Tirzah, and
reigned for twenty-four years. He did 34
that which was evil in the sight of the
LORD, and walked in the way of Jeroboam and in his sin with which he made
Israel sin.
Accordingly the word of the LORD 16
came to Jehu, the son of Hanani,
against Baasha, saying,
"Inasmuch as I exalted you out of 2
the dust, and made you prince over my
people Israel, and you have walked in
the way of Jeroboam and have made
my people Israel sin, thus provoking
me to jealousy with their sins, behold, 3
I will utterly sweep away Baasha and
his house, and I will make your house
like the house of Jeroboam, the son of
Nebat. Whoever belonging to Baasha 4
dies in the city, him shall the dogs eat,
and whoever belonging to him dies in
the field the birds of the air shall eat."
Now the rest of the records of Baa- 5
sha, and what he did and his prowess,
are they not written in the Book of the
Chronicles of the Kings of Israel? So 6
Baasha slept with his fathers and was
buried in Tirzah, and Elah his son became king in his stead. By the prophet 7
Jehu, the son of Hanani, the word of
the LORD came against Baasha and his
house, both on account of the evil that
he did in the sight of the LORD by provoking him to jealousy with the work of

hands, in being like the house of Jeroboam, and also because he smote it.

CIVIL STRIFE IN ISRAEL, 16:8–22

8 In the twenty-sixth year of Asa, king
of Judah, Elah, the son of Baasha, became king over Israel in Tirzah, and he
9 reigned for two years. Then his servant
Zimri, captain of half his chariots, conspired against him. He was in Tirzah
drinking himself drunk in the house of
Arzah, who was over the household in
10 Tirzah; and Zimri went in and struck
him down and killed him in the twenty-seventh year of Asa, king of Judah,
11 and reigned in his stead. But when he
became king, as soon as he had seated
himself upon his throne, he slew all the
house of Baasha; he left him not a
single male, neither next-of-kin nor
12 friend. Thus Zimri destroyed all the
house of Baasha, according to the word
of the LORD which he spoke against
13 Baasha by Jehu the prophet, for all the
sins of Baasha and the sins of Elah, his
son, which they committed and with
which they made Israel sin, thus provoking the jealousy of the LORD, the
14 God of Israel, with their vanities. Now
the rest of the records of Elah and all
that he did, are they not written in the
Book of the Chronicles of the Kings of
Israel?

15 In the twenty-seventh year of Asa,
king of Judah, Zimri reigned seven days
in Tirzah. Now the people were encamped against Gibbethon, which be-
16 longed to the Philistines. When the
people who were encamped heard the
report, "Zimri has conspired and also
slain the king," then all Israel made
Omri, the commander of the army,
king over Israel that day in the camp.
17 So Omri went up and all Israel with
him from Gibbethon, and they be-
18 sieged Tirzah. But as soon as Zimri
saw that the city was taken, he went
into the castle of the king's house, and
burned the king's house over him, and
19 so died, because of his sins which he
committed, by doing that which was
evil in the sight of the LORD, by walking in the way of Jeroboam and by his
sins which he did to make Israel sin.
20 Now the rest of the records of Zimri,
and his conspiracy which he carried out,
are they not written in the Book of the
Chronicles of the Kings of Israel?

THE REIGN OF OMRI OF ISRAEL, 16:21–28

Then the people of Israel were divided. 21
Half of the people followed Tibni, the
son of Ginath, to make him king, and
the other half followed Omri. However, 22
the people who followed Omri were
stronger than the people who followed
Tibni, the son of Ginath. As a result
Tibni died and Omri became king. In 23
the thirty-first year of Asa, king of
Judah, Omri became king over Israel,
and continued twelve years; he reigned
six years in Tirzah.

Then he bought the mountain of 24
Samaria from Shemer for two talents of
silver; and he built on the hill and
named the city which he built Samaria
after the name of Shemer, the owner of
the hill. But Omri did that which was
evil in the sight of the LORD, and did 25
more wickedly than all those who were
before him. For he walked in all the 26
way of Jeroboam, the son of Nebat, and
in his sins with which he made Israel
sin, thus provoking the jealousy of the
LORD, the God of Israel, with their
vanities. Now the rest of the acts of 27
Omri that he did, and his prowess that
he showed, are they not written in the
Book of the Chronicles of the Kings of
Israel? So Omri slept with his fathers 28
and was buried in Samaria; and Ahab
his son became king in his stead.

THE REIGN OF AHAB OF ISRAEL, 16:29–34

Ahab, the son of Omri, became king 29
over Israel in the thirty-eighth year of
Asa, king of Judah, and Ahab, the son
of Omri, reigned over Israel in Samaria
twenty-two years. But Ahab, the son 30
of Omri, did that which was evil in the
sight of the LORD above all who were
before him. Moreover as though it had 31
been a slight thing for him to walk in
the sins of Jeroboam, the son of Nebat,
he took as wife Jezebel, the daughter of
Ethbaal, king of the Sidonians, and
went and served the Baal and worshiped him. Thus he erected an altar 32
for the Baal in the house of the Baal,

which he built in Samaria. Ahab also made a sacred pole, and Ahab did more to provoke the jealousy of the LORD, the God of Israel, than all the kings of Israel who were before him. In his days Hiel the Bethelite rebuilt Jericho. He laid its foundations upon Abiram his first-born, and he set up its gates upon Segub his youngest son, according to the word of the LORD which he spoke by Joshua, the son of Nun.

ELIJAH AND THE DROUGHT, 17:1—18:46

Now Elijah the Tishbite, of Tishbe in Gilead, said to Ahab,

"As the LORD, the God of Israel, lives, before whom I stand, there shall be neither dew nor rain these years, except by my word."

Furthermore, the word of the LORD came to him, saying,

"Depart from here and turn eastward, and hide yourself by the Brook Cherith, that is east of the Jordan, and you shall drink from the brook; and I have commanded the ravens to feed you there."

So he went and did according to the word of the LORD and went and dwelt by the Brook Cherith that is east of Jordan; and the ravens brought him bread and flesh in the morning and bread and flesh in the evening, and he used to drink from the brook. But after a time the brook dried up because there was no rain in the land.

Then the word of the LORD came to him, saying,

"Arise, go to Zarephath, which belongs to Sidon, and dwell there; see, I have commanded a widow there to provide for you."

So he arose and went to Zarephath; and as he came to the gate of the city, there was a widow there gathering sticks, and calling to her, he said,

"Bring me, I pray you, a little water in a vessel that I may drink."

But as she was going to bring it, he called to her and said,

"Bring me, I pray you, a morsel of food in your hand."

"As the LORD your God lives," she said, "I have nothing but a handful of meal in the jar and a little oil in a cruse; and now I am gathering a few sticks

that I may go in and prepare it for myself and my son, that we may eat it and
die."
But Elijah said to her, 13
"Fear not; go and do as you have
said; but first make me from it a little
cake, and bring it to me, and afterward make one for yourself and for
your son. For thus says the LORD, the 14
God of Israel: 'The jar of meal shall
not be exhausted nor the cruse of oil
spent until the day that the LORD
sends rain upon the ground.' "
So she went and did according to the 15
word of Elijah; and she and he and her
household did eat day after day. The 16
jar of meal was not exhausted, neither
did the cruse of oil fail, according to
the word of the LORD which he spoke
by Elijah.
Now after these things, the son of the 17
mistress of the house fell sick; and his
illness was so severe that there was no
breath left in him. Then she said to 18
Elijah,
"What have I to do with you, O man
of God? You have come to me to remind me of my iniquity and to kill my
son!"
"Give me your son," he said to her. 19
Then he took him from her bosom
and carried him into the upper chamber, where he was staying, and laid him
upon his own bed; and he cried to the 20
LORD and said,
"O LORD, my God, hast thou also
brought evil upon this widow, with
whom I am staying, by slaying her
son?"
Then he stretched himself upon the 21
child three times, and cried to the
LORD and said,
"I pray thee, may this child's life
return into him again."
So the LORD hearkened to the voice 22
of Elijah; and the life of the child came
back to him again, so that he lived.
Then Elijah took the child and brought 23
him down from the upper chamber into
the house and gave him to his mother.
"See, your son is alive," said Elijah.
Then the woman said to Elijah, 24
"Now indeed I know that you are a
man of God, and that the word of the
LORD is in your mouth."
Now after many days the word of the 18
LORD came to Elijah, in the third year,
saying,
"Go, show yourself to Ahab; and I

will bring rain upon the face of the
ground."
2 So Elijah went to show himself to
Ahab. The famine was severe in
3 Samaria; and Ahab had called Obadiah
who was in charge of the household
(now Obadiah deeply revered the
4 LORD; for when Jezebel ordered the
prophets of the LORD exterminated,
Obadiah had taken a hundred prophets
and hidden them by fifties in a cave
and supplied them with bread and
5 water); and Ahab said to Obadiah,
"Come, let us go through the land to
all the springs of water and to all the
brooks; perhaps we shall find grass and
so save the horses and mules alive, that
we may not lose the beasts."
6 So they divided the land between
them to pass through it: Ahab went in
one direction by himself, and Obadiah
went in another direction by himself.
7 Now while Obadiah was on the way,
suddenly Elijah met him, and when he
recognized him, he fell on his face and
said,
"Is it you, my lord Elijah?"
8 "It is I," he said to him, "go, tell
your master, 'Elijah is here.'"
9 "Wherein have I sinned," he said,
"that you should deliver your servant
10 into the hand of Ahab, to slay me? As
the LORD your God lives, there is no
nation or kingdom where my lord has
not sent to seek you; and when they
said, 'He is not here,' he would put the
kingdom and nation under oath that no
11 one could find you; and now you say,
'Go, say to your lord, "Elijah is here."'
12 But when I go from you the spirit of
the LORD will carry you where I know
not; accordingly, when I come and tell
Ahab, and he cannot find you, he will
slay me, although I, your servant, have
13 feared the LORD from my youth. Has
it not been told my lord what I did
when Jezebel slew the prophets of the
LORD, how I hid a hundred prophets
of the LORD by fifties in a cave and
supplied them with food and water?
14 Yet now you say, 'Go, tell your lord,
"Elijah is here,"' that he may slay
me!"
15 "As the LORD of hosts lives, before
whom I stand," said Elijah, "I will
show myself to him today."
16 So Obadiah went to meet Ahab, and
told him, and Ahab went to meet Elijah. Now as soon as Ahab saw Elijah, Ahab said to him,

"Is it you, you troubler of Israel?"

"I have not troubled Israel," he said, "but you and your father's house, in that you have forsaken the commands of the LORD and have gone after the Baal. Now therefore send and gather to me all Israel, to Mount Carmel, together with the four hundred and fifty prophets of the Baal and the four hundred prophets of the Asherah, who eat at Jezebel's table."

So Ahab sent to all the Israelites and gathered the prophets together to Mount Carmel. Then Elijah came near to all the people and said,

"How long are you going to limp upon two diverse opinions? If the LORD be God, follow him, but if the Baal, follow him."

But the people gave him no answer. Then Elijah said to the people,

"I, even I only, am left as a prophet of the LORD, but the prophets of the Baal are four hundred and fifty men. Let them therefore give us two bulls, and let them choose one bull for themselves and cut it in pieces and lay it on the wood but make no fire, and I will prepare the other bull and place it on the wood, but I will make no fire. Then call you on the name of your god and I will call on the name of the LORD; and the god who answers by fire, he is God."

Thereupon all the people answered and said,

"It is a fair test!"

So Elijah said to the prophets of the Baal,

"Choose for yourselves a bull and prepare it first, for you are many, and call on the name of your god, but make no fire."

Then they took the bull which he gave them and prepared it, and called on the name of the Baal from morning until noon, saying,

"O Baal, answer us."

But there was no voice and none answered. Then they performed a limping dance around the altar which they had made. But at noon Elijah mocked them, and said,

"Cry with a loud voice, for he is a god; either he is meditating, or he has gone aside, or he is on a journey, or perhaps he is asleep and needs to be awakened!"

So they cried with a loud voice, and proceeded to slash one another according to their custom, with swords and with lances until the blood gushed out upon them; and when midday had passed they worked themselves into a prophetic frenzy until the offering of the oblation; but there was no voice, nor answer, and none regarded. Then Elijah said to all the people,

"Come near to me."

So all the people drew near to him; and he repaired the altar of the LORD which had been torn down. Accordingly Elijah took twelve stones, corresponding to the number of the tribes of the sons of Jacob to whom the word of the LORD came, saying,

"Israel shall be your name."

With the stones he made an altar in the name of the LORD. Then he made a trench around the altar of the capacity of two homers of seed. He also laid the pieces of wood in order, cut up the bull, and laid it upon the wood; and he said,

"Fill four jars with water and pour it on the burnt-offering and on the wood."

"Do it a second time," he said.

So they did it a second time.

"Do it a third time," he said.

So they did it a third time, so that the water ran around the altar; and he also filled the trench with water.

Then when it was time to offer the oblation, Elijah the prophet came near and said,

"O LORD, God of Abraham, Isaac, and Israel, let it be known today that thou art God in Israel and that I am thy servant, and that at thy command I have done all these things. Answer me, O LORD, answer me, that this people may know that thou, O LORD, art God, and that thou hast turned their heart back again."

Then the fire of the LORD fell and consumed the burnt-offering and the wood, the stones and the dust, and licked up the water that was in the trench. So when all the people saw it, they fell upon their faces and said,

"The LORD, he is God; the LORD, he is God."

But Elijah said to them,

"Seize the prophets of the Baal; let not a man of them escape."

So they seized them, and Elijah brought them down to the Brook Kishon and slew them there.

Then Elijah said to Ahab, 41
"Go up, eat and drink; for there is
the rushing sound of rain."
So Ahab went up to eat and drink, 42
but Elijah went up to the top of Carmel, and crouched down upon the
earth, with his face between his knees;
and he said to his servant, 43
"Go up now, look toward the sea."
So he went up, and looked and said,
"There is nothing."
"Go back seven times," he said.
So the servant went back seven 44
times. However, the seventh time he
said,
"There is a cloud the size of a man's
hand, rising out of the sea."
"Go up," he said, "say to Ahab,
'Harness your steeds and go down, so
that the rain may not stop you.'"
Moreover, in a very short time the 45
heavens grew black with clouds and
wind, and there was a great downpour.
But Ahab rode on and arrived at Jezreel. The hand of the LORD also was on 46
Elijah so that he girded up his loins and
ran before Ahab to the entrance of
Jezreel.

ELIJAH ON MOUNT HOREB, 19:1–18

Now when Ahab told Jezebel all that 19
Elijah had done, and how he had slain
all the prophets with the sword, Jezebel 2
sent a messenger to Elijah, saying,
"As surely as you are Elijah and I am
Jezebel, so may God requite me and
worse, if I do not make your life as the
life of one of them by tomorrow about
this time."
Then he was afraid and arose and 3
went for his life, and came to Beersheba
that belongs to Judah; and there he
left his servant. But he himself went 4
into the desert a day's journey, and
came and sat down under a broom tree,
and he requested for himself that he
might die, and he said,
"It is enough; now, O LORD, take
away my life, for I am no better than
my fathers."
Then he lay down and slept under a 5

broom tree. Suddenly an angel was
touching him, and he said to him,
"Arise, eat."
6 And when he looked, behold there
was at his head a cake baked on hot
stones, and a cruse of water. So he ate
7 and drank and lay down again. But the
angel of the LORD returned a second
time and touched him and said,
"Arise, eat, for the journey is too
great for you."
8 So he arose and ate and drank and
went in the strength of that food forty
days and forty nights to Horeb, the
9 Mount of God; and he came there to a
cave and lodged there.
But the word of the LORD came to
him, and he said to him,
"What are you doing here, Elijah?"
"I have been very jealous for the
10 LORD, the God of hosts," he said, "for
the Israelites have forsaken the covenant with thee, thrown down thine altars, and slain thy prophets with the
sword; and I, even I only, am left, and
they are seeking to take away my life."
11 "Go forth," he said, "and stand upon
the mount before the LORD."
Now behold, the LORD was passing
by, and a great and mighty wind was
rending the mountain and shattering
the rocks before the LORD; but the
LORD was not in the wind. After the
wind came an earthquake, but the
12 LORD was not in the earthquake. After
the earthquake a fire; but the LORD
was not in the fire, and after the fire
13 the sound of a gentle whisper. Now as
soon as Elijah perceived it, he wrapped
his face in his mantle and went out and
stood at the entrance of the cave. Then
there came a voice to him and said,
"What are you doing here, Elijah?"
"I have been very jealous for the
14 LORD, the God of hosts," he said, "because the Israelites have forsaken the
covenant with thee, thrown down thine
altars, and slain thy prophets with the
sword, and I, even I only, am left, and
they are seeking to take away my life."
15 But the LORD said to him,
"Go, return on your way to the desert of Damascus, and when you arrive,
anoint Hazael to be king over Syria;
16 and Jehu, the son of Nimshi, you shall
anoint to be king over Israel; and Elisha, the son of Shaphat of Abel-meholah, you shall anoint to be prophet in
17 your place. It shall be that whoever
escapes the sword of Hazael shall Jehu
slay; and whoever escapes the sword of
Jehu, shall Elisha slay. Yet will I
spare seven thousand in Israel—all the
knees that have not bowed to the Baal
and every mouth that has not kissed
him."

THE CALL OF ELISHA, 19:19–21

Now when he departed from there he
found Elisha, the son of Shaphat, as he
was plowing behind twelve yoke of
oxen, he being with the twelfth. Then
Elijah came over to him and threw his
mantle upon him. Thereupon he left
the oxen and ran after Elijah, and he
said,
"Let me, I pray you, kiss my father
and my mother, and then I will follow
you."
"Go back again," he said to him, "for
what have I done to you?"
So he returned from following him
and took a yoke of oxen and sacrificed
them, and using the ox-yoke to boil
their flesh, he gave it to the people and
made them a feast; then he arose and
went after Elijah and became his attendant.

ISRAEL'S WARS WITH SYRIA, 20:1–43

Now Ben-hadad, king of Syria, assembled all his army, and there were
thirty-two kings with him, together
with horses and chariots. Thereupon he
went up and besieged Samaria and
fought against it. Moreover, he sent
messengers into the city to Ahab, king
of Israel and said to him,
"Thus says Ben-hadad: 'Your silver
and your gold are mine; your wives also
and your children are mine.'"
The king of Israel then answered and
said,
"According to your statement, my
lord, O king, I am yours, together with
all that I possess."
Presently the messengers came again
and said,
"Thus says Ben-hadad: 'I sent to
you, saying, "You shall deliver to me
your silver and your gold, your wives
and your children; but about this time

tomorrow, I shall send my servants to
you and they shall ransack your house
and the houses of your servants; and
whatever pleases them they shall take
in their hands and carry it away.' ' "
7 Then the king of Israel called to all
the elders of the land, and said,
"Mark, I pray you, and take note
how this man is looking for trouble;
for he sent to me for my wives and my
children, my silver and gold, and I did
not deny him."
8 But all the elders and all the people
said to him,
"Obey not, nor consent!"
9 So he said to the messengers of Ben-hadad,
"Say to my lord the king, 'All that
you demanded of your servant at the
first I was ready to do, but this thing I
cannot do.' "
10 So the messengers went away and
brought him word again. Thus Ben-hadad sent to him and said,
"May the gods requite me and worse,
if the dust of Samaria suffice for handfuls for all the people who follow me."
11 But the king of Israel answered and
said,
"Tell him, 'Let not him who is girding on his weapon boast himself as he
who is ungirding.' "
12 Now at the time when he heard this
message—he was drinking with the
kings in the pavilions—he said to his
servants,
"Form in line."
So they formed in line against the
city.
13 At this juncture a certain prophet
drew near to Ahab, king of Israel, and
said,
"Thus says the LORD: 'Do you see
all this great multitude? Behold, I am
about to deliver them into your hand
today, and you shall know that I am
the LORD.' "
14 But Ahab said,
"By whom?"
"Thus says the LORD: By the young
men under the commanders of the
provinces," he said,
"Who shall begin the battle?" he
said.
"You," he answered.
15 Then he mustered the young men
under the commanders of the provinces, and they were two hundred and
thirty-two; and after them he mustered
all the people, even all the Israelites,
seven thousand. And at noon they 16
made the attack, while Ben-hadad was
drinking himself drunk in the pavilions,
together with the thirty-two kings, his
allies. Moreover the young men under 17
the commanders of the provinces went
out first. Then they sent to Ben-hadad
and reported to him, saying,
"Men have come out from Samaria."
"Whether they have come out for 18
peace, take them alive; or whether they
have come out for war, take them
alive," he said.
So these (the young men under the 19
commanders of the provinces) and the
force which followed them went out of
the city. Then they slew each his man, 20
so that the Syrians fled; and Israel pursued them, but Ben-hadad, the king of
Syria, escaped on a horse with horsemen. Then the king of Israel went out 21
and captured horses and chariots, and
made a great slaughter among the
Syrians.
Moreover a prophet approached the 22
king of Israel and said to him,
"Go, strengthen yourself, and mark
and see what you will do, for at the return of spring the king of Syria will be
coming up against you."
Now the servants of the king of Syria 23
said to him,
"Their gods are mountain gods,
therefore they were too strong for us;
but let us fight against them in the
plain, and surely we shall be stronger
than they. Also do this thing: take the 24
kings away, each from his place and put
captains in their stead, and do you 25
yourself muster a force like the force
you have lost, horse for horse and
chariot for chariot; then we shall fight
them in the plain, and surely we shall
be stronger than they."
So he hearkened to their voice and
did accordingly.
It was at the return of spring that 26
Ben-hadad mustered the Syrians and
went up to Aphek to fight against Israel. Also the Israelites were mustered 27
and provisioned, and went against
them; but the Israelites encamped before them like two small flocks of goats,
while the Syrians filled the country.
Then a man of God came near and said 28
to the king of Israel,
"Thus says the LORD, 'Because the

Syrians say, "The LORD is a god of the
mountains and not a god of the valleys," therefore I will deliver all this
great multitude into your hand, that
you may know that I am the LORD.'"
29 So they encamped facing each other
seven days. But on the seventh day the
battle was joined; and the Israelites
slew of the Syrians a hundred thousand
30 footmen in one day; and the rest fled
to Aphek into the city; and the wall fell
upon twenty-seven thousand of the
men who were left. Ben-hadad also
fled, and came into an inner chamber.
31 Then his servants said to him,
"Behold now, we have heard that the
kings of the house of Israel are merciful
kings; let us therefore, I pray you, put
sackcloth on our loins, and ropes about
our heads, and go out to the king of
Israel; perhaps he will spare your
life."
32 So they girded sackcloth on their
loins and put ropes about their heads,
and went to the king of Israel and said,
"Your servant Ben-hadad says, 'I
pray you, let me live.'"
"Is he still alive? He is my brother,"
he said.
33 Now the men were trying to divine
his meaning, and they quickly caught it
from him and said,
"Ben-hadad is your brother."
"Go, bring him!" he said.
Accordingly when Ben-hadad came
to him, he took him up into his chariot.
34 "The cities which my father took
from your father I will restore," he said
to him, "and you may maintain bazaars
of your own in Damascus as my father
did in Samaria."
"And I," said Ahab, "will let you go
with this understanding."
So he made a covenant with him and
he let him go.
35 Now a certain man of the prophetic
order said to his neighbor through the
word of the LORD,
"I pray you, strike me."
But the man refused to strike him.
36 Then he said to him,
"Because you have not listened to
the voice of the LORD, behold, as soon
as you take leave of me a lion shall slay
you."
So when he departed from him, a
lion found him and slew him.
37 Then he found another man and said,
"I pray you, strike me."
Accordingly the man struck him so as
to wound him. The prophet then went 38
and waited for the king by the way, dis-
guising himself with a bandage over his
eyes; and as the king was passing by, he 39
cried to the king, and said,
"Your servant had gone out into the
midst of the battle, when suddenly a
man turned and brought a man to me
and said, 'Keep this man; if by any
means he be missing, then your life
shall be for his life, or else you shall pay
a talent of silver.' But as your servant 40
was turning to look here and there, he
was gone."
Wherefore the king of Israel said to
him
"Such is your verdict: you yourself
have decided it."
Then he hastily took the bandage 41
away from his eyes, and the king of
Israel recognized him as one of the
prophets. So he said to him, 42
"Thus says the LORD: 'Because you
have let go out of your hand the man
under my ban of destruction, therefore
your life shall go for his life and your
people for his people.'"
Then the king of Israel went to his 43
house vexed and sullen, and entered
Samaria.

AHAB SEIZES NABOTH'S VINEYARD, 21:1–29

Now Naboth the Jezreelite had a 21
vineyard in Jezreel beside the palace of
Ahab, king of Samaria; and Ahab spoke 2
to Naboth, saying,
"Give me your vineyard that I may
have it for a vegetable garden, because
it is close beside my house; and I will
give you a better vineyard than it, in
its stead; or if you prefer, I will gladly
give you its value in money."
But Naboth said to Ahab, 3
"The LORD forbid, that I should
give you the inheritance of my fathers."
Whereupon Ahab came into his house 4
vexed and sullen, because of the word
which Naboth the Jezreelite had spoken
to him; for he had said,
"I will not give you the inheritance
of my fathers."
And he lay on his bed and covered his
face and refused food. But Jezebel his 5
wife came to him and spoke to him,
"Why is your spirit so vexed that you
eat no food?"

6 Accordingly he spoke to her,
"Because I spoke to Naboth the
Jezreelite and said to him, 'Give me
your vineyard for money; or if you prefer, I will gladly give you a vineyard
in its stead'; but he said, 'I will not give
you my vineyard.' "
7 Then Jezebel his wife said to him,
"Do you now hold sway in Israel?
Arise, eat bread, and let your heart be
of good cheer. I will get the vineyard
of Naboth the Jezreelite for you."
8 So she wrote letters in Ahab's name
and sealed them with his seal, and sent
them to the elders and to the nobles
who were in his city, who presided with
Naboth.
9 Now she had written in the letters,
saying,
"Proclaim a fast and seat Naboth in
a conspicuous place among the people.
10 Then seat two unscrupulous men before him and let them bear witness, saying, 'You have cursed God and the
king.' Then take him out and stone
him to death."
11 So the men of his city, the elders and
the nobles who presided in his city, did
as Jezebel had sent to them. As it was
written in the letters which she had
12 sent to them, they proclaimed a fast,
and gave Naboth a seat in a conspicu-
13 ous place among the people. Also two
unscrupulous men came in and sat before him, and the rascals bore witness
against Naboth in the presence of the
people, saying,
"Naboth cursed God and the king."
So they took him outside of the city
14 and stoned him to death. Then they
sent to Jezebel, saying,
"Naboth has been stoned and is
dead."
15 Accordingly, as soon as Jezebel heard
that Naboth had been stoned and was
dead, Jezebel said to Ahab,
"Arise, take possession of the vineyard of Naboth the Jezreelite, which he
refused to sell for money; for Naboth is
not alive but dead."
16 Now as soon as Ahab heard that Naboth was dead, Ahab arose to go down
to the vineyard of Naboth the Jezreelite to take possession of it.
17 But the word of the LORD came to
Elijah the Tishbite, saying,
18 "Arise, go down to meet Ahab, king
of Israel, who is in Samaria. See, he is
in the vineyard of Naboth, where he
has gone down to take possession. Do 19
you speak to him, saying, 'Thus says
the LORD: "Have you killed, and also
taken possession?" ' And you shall say
to him, 'Thus says the LORD: "In the
place where the dogs licked up the
blood of Naboth will the dogs lick up
your own blood." ' "
"Have you found me, O my enemy?" 20
said Ahab to Elijah.
"I have," he said. "Because you have
sold yourself to no purpose by doing
that which is evil in the sight of the
LORD, behold, I am about to bring evil 21
upon you, and I will utterly sweep you
away and will cut off from Ahab every
male, both him that is shut up and him
that is left at large in Israel. I will also 22
make your house like the house of Jeroboam, the son of Nebat, and like the
house of Baasha, the son of Ahijah, because of the indignation which you have
aroused and because you have caused
Israel to sin. Also concerning Jezebel 23
the LORD has spoken, saying, 'The
dogs shall eat Jezebel in the district of
Jezreel.' Whoever belonging to Ahab 24
dies in the city the dogs shall eat; and
whoever dies in the field, the birds of
the air shall eat."
There was absolutely no one who 25
sold himself to do evil in the sight of the
LORD, as did Ahab, because Jezebel
his wife incited him. For he did very 26
abominably in following idols, just as
all the Amorites had done whom the
LORD dispossessed before the Israelites.
Now as soon as Ahab heard these 27
words he tore his garments and put
sackcloth on his flesh and fasted, he also
lay in sackcloth, and went about quietly. Then the word of the LORD came to 28
Elijah the Tishbite, saying,
"Have you seen how Ahab has 29
humbled himself before me? Because
he has humbled himself before me, I
will not bring the evil in his days; in his
son's days I will bring the evil upon his
house."

AHAB ATTACKS RAMOTH-GILEAD AND IS SLAIN, 22:1–40

Now for three years Syria and Israel 22
continued without war. But in the 2
third year Jehoshaphat, king of Judah,

3 came down to the king of Israel, and
the king of Israel said to his servants,
"Do you know that Ramoth-gilead
belongs to us, yet we are inactive instead of taking it from the hand of the
king of Syria?"
4 Then he said to Jehoshaphat,
"Will you go with me to fight against
Ramoth-gilead?"
"I am as you are, my people as your
people, my horses as your horses," said
Jehoshaphat to the king of Israel.
5 Jehoshaphat said further to the king
of Israel,
"Inquire today, I pray, for the word
of the LORD."
6 Then the king of Israel assembled the
prophets, about four hundred men, and
said to them,
"Shall I go to battle against Ramoth-
gilead, or shall I forbear?"
"Go up," they said; "for the LORD
will deliver it into the hand of the
king."
7 But Jehoshaphat said,
"Is there not here another prophet of
the LORD through whom we may inquire?"
8 Then the king of Israel said to
Jehoshaphat,
"There is another man through
whom we might inquire of the LORD,
Micaiah, the son of Imlah, but I hate
him; for he never prophesies good concerning me, but only evil."
"Let not the king say so," said
Jehoshaphat.
9 So the king of Israel called a eunuch
and said,
"Bring quickly Micaiah, the son of
Imlah."
10 Now the king of Israel and Jehoshaphat, the king of Judah, were sitting
each on his throne, arrayed in their
robes, at the entrance of the gate of
Samaria, and all the prophets were engaged in ecstatic prophecy before them.
11 Then Zedekiah, the son of Chenanaiah,
made for himself horns of iron and he
said,
"Thus says the LORD: 'With these
you shall gore the Syrians until they are
destroyed.'"
12 So all the prophets prophesied, saying,
"Go up to Ramoth-gilead and prosper; for the LORD will deliver it into
the hand of the king."

Now the messenger who went to call 13
Micaiah spoke to him, saying,
"See, now, the prophets with one
accord have spoken good to the king;
let your word, I pray you, be like the
word of one of them and speak good."
"As the LORD lives," said Micaiah, 14
"what the LORD says to me, that will
I speak."
Now when he came to the king, the 15
king said to him,
"Micaiah, shall we go to Ramoth-
gilead to battle, or shall we forbear?"
"Go up and prosper," he said to him;
"for the LORD will deliver it into the
hand of the king!"
But the king said to him, 16
"How many times must I adjure you
that you speak to me nothing but the
truth in the name of the LORD?"
"I saw all Israel scattered on the 17
mountains," he said, "like sheep without a shepherd; and the LORD said,
'These have no master; let them return
each to his home in peace.'"
Then the king of Israel said to 18
Jehoshaphat,
"Did I not say to you that he would
not prophesy good concerning me, but
only evil?"
But Micaiah said, 19
"Therefore hear the word of the
LORD: I saw the LORD sitting on his
throne and all the army of the heavens
standing by him on his right hand and
on his left; and the LORD said, 'Who 20
will deceive Ahab so that he may go up
and fall at Ramoth-gilead?' Then one
said one thing and another another,
until a spirit came forth and stood be- 21
fore the LORD and said, 'I will deceive
him'; and the LORD said to him, 'By 22
what means?' He said, 'I will go forth
and become a lying spirit in the mouth
of all his prophets.' Thereupon he said,
'You shall deceive him and also succeed! Go forth and do so.' Now there- 23
fore, behold, the LORD has put a lying
spirit in the mouth of all these prophets
of yours, since the LORD has spoken
evil concerning you."
Then Zedekiah, the son of Chena- 24
naiah, approached and struck Micaiah
upon the cheek, and said,
"Which way did the Spirit of the
LORD go from me to speak with you?"
"Indeed, you shall see on that day 25
when you go into an inner chamber to
hide yourself," said Micaiah.

Then the king of Israel said,
"Seize Micaiah and take him back to
mon, the governor of the city, and to
oash, the king's son, and say, 'Thus
ays the king: "Put this fellow in the
rison and feed him with bread and
ater scantily until I return vic-
orious."'"
Whereupon Micaiah said,
"If you do indeed return victorious,
he LORD has not spoken by me."
Hear, all you peoples!"
So the king of Israel and Jehosha-
hat, the king of Judah, went up to
Ramoth-gilead. Then the king of Israel
aid to Jehoshaphat,
"I will disguise myself and go into
attle, but do you put on your own
obes."
So the king of Israel disguised him-
elf and went into the battle.
Now the king of Syria had charged
is thirty-two chariot commanders,
aying,
"Fight with neither small nor great,
xcept only with the king of Israel."
Accordingly when the chariot com-
nanders saw Jehoshaphat, they said,
"Surely it is the king of Israel."
So they surrounded him to fight
gainst him, but Jehoshaphat cried out.
When the chariot commanders saw that
t was not the king of Israel, they
urned back from pursuing him. But a
nan drew a bow at a venture and shot
he king of Israel between the jointed
ieces and the breast-plate. Therefore
e said to his charioteer,
"Wheel about and take me out of the
ight; for I am badly wounded."
Now the battle grew fiercer that day,
while the king held himself upright in
is chariot facing the Syrians until
vening, and the blood from the wound
an out into the bottom of the chariot.
But at evening he died; and about sun-
et the cry passed through the army,
"Each to his city and each to his
and, for the king is dead!"
So they came to Samaria and buried
he king in Samaria; and when they
washed off the chariot by the pool of
Samaria, the dogs licked up his blood,
nd the harlots washed in it according
o the word which the LORD had spo-
en. Now the rest of the records of Ahab
nd all that he did and the ivory house
which he built and all the cities that he
uilt, are they not written in the Book
of the Chronicles of the Kings of Israel?
So Ahab slept with his fathers, and 40
Ahaziah his son became king in his
stead.

THE REIGNS OF JEHOSHAPHAT AND AHAZIAH, 22:41–53

Jehoshaphat, the son of Asa, became 41
king over Judah in the fourth year of
Ahab, king of Israel. Jehoshaphat was 42
thirty-five years old when he became
king, and he reigned twenty-five years
in Jerusalem; and the name of his
mother was Azubah, the daughter of
Shilhi. He walked in all the way of Asa 43
his father; he did not turn aside from it,
doing that which was right in the sight
of the LORD. Only the high places
were not taken away, but the people
still continued to sacrifice and burn incense on the high places. Jehoshaphat 44
also made peace with the king of Israel.
Now the rest of the records of 45
Jehoshaphat and his prowess that he
showed, and how he made war, are
they not written in the Book of the
Chronicles of the Kings of Judah? The 46
rest of the male devotees of the fertility
cult who remained in the days of his
father Asa, he eradicated from the land.
Now there was no king in Edom. 47
But the deputy of King Jehoshaphat 48
made ships of Tarshish to go to Ophir
for gold. However they did not go; for
the ships were wrecked at Ezion-geber.
Then Ahaziah, the son of Ahab, said to 49
Jehoshaphat,
"Let my servants go with your servants in the ships."
But Jehoshaphat refused. Then Je- 50
hoshaphat slept with his fathers, and
was buried with his fathers in the city
of David his father; and Jehoram his
son became king in his stead.
Ahaziah, the son of Ahab, became 51
king over Israel in Samaria in the seventeenth year of Jehoshaphat, king of
Judah, and he reigned over Israel two
years. He did that which was evil in 52
the sight of the LORD, and walked in
the way of his father and in the way of
his mother and in the way of Jeroboam,
the son of Nebat, who had caused Israel to sin. Moreover he served the 53
Baal and worshiped him, and aroused
the jealous anger of the LORD, the God
of Israel, just as his father had done.

THE SECOND BOOK OF KINGS

ELIJAH AND THE DEATH OF AHAZIAH, 1:1–18

1 MOAB rebelled against Israel
after the death of Ahab.
2 Now Ahaziah had fallen
through the lattice in his upper chamber in Samaria, and lay sick.
So he sent messengers, and said to
them,
"Go, inquire of Baal-zebub, the god
of Ekron, whether I shall recover from
this illness."
3 But the angel of the LORD spoke to
Elijah the Tishbite,
"Arise, go up to meet the messengers
of the king of Samaria and say to them,
'Is it because there is no God in Israel,
that you are on your way to inquire of
4 Baal-zebub, the god of Ekron?' Now
therefore thus says the LORD: 'You
shall not come down from the bed
whither you have gone up, but you
shall certainly die.'"
Then Elijah passed on.
5 When the messengers returned to
him, he said to them,
"Now why have you returned?"
6 "A man came up to meet us," they
said to him, "and said to us, 'Go, return to the king who sent you and declare to him, "Thus says the LORD: 'Is
it because there is no God in Israel that
you are sending to inquire of Baal-
zebub, the god of Ekron? Therefore
you shall not come down from the bed
whither you have gone up, but you
shall certainly die.'"'"
7 Then he said to them,
"What sort of man was he who came
up to meet you, and spoke to you these
words?"
8 "He was a hairy man and girt with a
leathern girdle about his loins," they
said to him.
"It was Elijah the Tishbite," he said.
9 Thereupon he sent to him a commander of fifty with his fifty. And
when he went up to him—for there he
sat on the top of the hill—he said to
him.

"O man of God, the king has give
the order, 'Come down.'"
Then Elijah answered and said to th
captain of fifty,
"If I be a man of God, let fire fron
heaven come down and consume yo
and your fifty."
Then fire came down from heave
and consumed him and his fifty. Agai
he sent to him another commander o
fifty with his fifty; and he answered an
said to him,
"O man of God, thus says the king
'Come down quickly.'"
But Elijah answered and said to then
"If I be a man of God, let fire com
down from heaven and consume yo
and your fifty."
Then the fire of God came dow
from heaven and consumed him and hi
fifty. Again he sent a commander of
third fifty with his fifty. But when th
commander of the third fifty went up
he came and fell on his knees befor
Elijah and besought him and said t
him,
"O man of God, I pray you, let m
life and the lives of these fifty servant
of yours be precious in your sight. Be
hold, fire has already come down fron
heaven and consumed the two forme
commanders of fifty with their fiftie
but now let my life be precious in you
sight."
Then the angel of the LORD said t
Elijah,
"Go down with him; do not be afrai
of him."
So he arose and went down with hir
to the king. Thereupon he said to hir
"Thus says the LORD: 'Becaus
you have sent messengers to inquire c
Baal-zebub, the god of Ekron—is it be
cause there is no God in Israel to in
quire of his word?—therefore you sha
not come down from the bed whithe
you have gone up, but you shall cer
tainly die."
So he died according to the word c
the LORD which Elijah had spoker
and Jehoram became king in his stea

n the second year of Jehoram, the son
of Jehoshaphat, king of Judah, because
ıe had no son. Now the rest of the acts
of Ahaziah which he did, are they not
vritten in the Book of the Chronicles of
:he Kings of Israel?

THE TRANSLATION OF ELIJAH, 2:1–18

Now when the LORD took up Elijah
oy a whirlwind into the heavens, Elijah
and Elisha were on their way from Gil-
;al, and Elijah said to Elisha,

"I pray you, remain here, for the
ORD has sent me to Bethel."

"As the LORD lives," said Elisha,
'and as you yourself are alive, I will not
eave you."

So they went down to Bethel. Then
he members of the prophetic order
vho were at Bethel came out to Elisha
and said to him,

"Do you know that today the LORD
s about to take away your master
rom being your leader?"

"Yes, I know it; hold your peace,"
ıe said.

Again Elijah said to him,

"Elisha, remain here, I pray you, for
he LORD has sent me to Jericho."

"As the LORD lives and as you your-
elf are alive, I will not leave you," he
aid.

So they entered Jericho; and the
nembers of the prophetic order who
vere in Jericho approached Elisha and
aid to him,

"Do you know that the LORD is
about to take away your master from
oeing your leader today?"

"Yes, I know it. Hold your peace,"
ıe said.

Elijah again said to him,

"Remain here, I pray you, for the
ORD has sent me to the Jordan."

"As the LORD lives and as you your-
elf are alive, I will not leave you," he
aid.

So the two of them went on.

Now fifty men of the prophetic order
went and stood opposite them at a
distance, while they two stood by the
Jordan. Then Elijah took his mantle
and rolled it up and struck the waters;
and they were divided on either side so
that the two of them passed over on dry
ground. Now as soon as they had
crossed over, Elijah said to Elisha,

"Ask what I shall do for you, before
I am taken from you."

"Let there be now a twofold share of
your spirit upon me!" said Elisha.

"You have asked a hard thing," he 10
said, "still, if you see me as I am being
taken from you, so shall it be with you;
but if not, it shall not be so."

Now as they were going along con- 11
versing, suddenly a chariot of fire and
horses of fire separated the two of them;
and Elijah went up by a whirlwind into
the heavens.

As Elisha looked, he cried out, 12

"My father, my father! the chariots
of Israel and its horsemen!"

But he saw him no more, and he took
hold of his own garments and tore
them in two pieces. He also took up the 13
mantle of Elijah that had fallen from
him and returned and stood by the
brink of the Jordan. Then he took the 14
mantle of Elijah that had fallen from
him and struck the waters and said,

"Where now is the LORD, the God of
Elijah?"

And when he had struck the waters
they were divided on either side so that
Elisha passed over; and when the mem- 15
bers of the prophetic order who were at
Jericho opposite him saw him, they
said,

"The spirit of Elijah is upon Elisha."

Then they came to meet him and
bowed before him to the earth, and
said to him, 16

"Behold now, there are with your
servants fifty able-bodied men; let
them go, we pray, and let them seek
your master, lest the wind of the LORD
has taken him up and cast him upon
some mountain or into some valley."

"You shall not send," he said.

Yet when they pressed him, until he 17
was ashamed, he said,

"Send."

Accordingly, they sent fifty men;
and they searched three days but did
not find him. Therefore when they re- 18
turned to him, while he was staying at
Jericho, he said to them,

"Did I not say to you, 'Do not go?' "

ELISHA'S COMMISSION MIRACULOUSLY ATTESTED, 2:19—3:31

Then the men of the city said to 19
Elisha,

"See now, the site of the city is pleasant as my lord sees; but the water is bad, and the land is unfruitful."
20 "Bring me a new jar," he said, "and put salt in it."
21 So they brought it to him. Then he went out to the spring of the water supply and cast salt in it and said,

"Thus says the LORD: 'I have rendered these waters pure; neither death nor untimely birth shall be due to them any more.'"
22 So the waters have continued pure down to this day, in accordance with the word of Elisha which he spoke.
23 Later he went up from there to Bethel. But while he was going up on the way, some little boys came out of a city and jeered at him, and said,

"Go up, you baldhead; go up, baldhead."
24 When he turned around and saw them, he cursed them in the name of the LORD. Then two she-bears came out of a wood and mangled forty-two of
25 the boys. But he kept on from there to Mount Carmel, and from there returned to Samaria.
3 Now Jehoram, the son of Ahab, became king over Israel in Samaria in the eighteenth year of Jehoshaphat, king of Judah, and he reigned twelve years.
2 But he did that which was evil in the sight of the LORD, but not as his father and mother, for he put away the sacred pillar of the Baal which his father had
3 made. Nevertheless he clung to the sins of Jeroboam, the son of Nebat, with which he made Israel sin. He did not turn from them.

WAR BETWEEN ISRAEL AND MOAB, 3:4–27

4 Now Mesha, king of Moab, was a sheep-breeder. He used to pay to the king of Israel a hundred thousand lambs and the wool of a hundred thou-
5 sand rams, but as soon as Ahab died, the king of Moab rebelled against the king of Israel.
6 Accordingly King Jehoram went out of Samaria at that time and mustered
7 all Israel. He then proceeded to send to Jehoshaphat, king of Judah, saying,

"The king of Moab has rebelled against me; will you go with me to fight against Moab?"

"I will go up," he said, "I am as you, my people as your people, my horses as your horses."

"Which way shall we go up?" he said.

"By the way of the desert of Edom," he said.

So the king of Israel went with the king of Judah and the king of Edom. But when they had made a circuitous journey of seven days, there was no water for the army nor for the cattle that followed them. Then the king of Israel said,

"Alas! for the LORD has summoned these three kings to give them into the hand of the king of Moab!"

But Jehoshaphat said,

"Is there not here a prophet of the LORD, that through him we may seek the LORD?"

Then one of the servants of the king of Israel answered and said,

"Elisha, the son of Shaphat, is here, who poured water on the hands of Elijah."

"The word of the LORD is with him," said Jehoshaphat.

So the king of Israel, and Jehoshaphat, and the king of Edom went down to him.

"What have I to do with you?" said Elisha to the king of Israel. "Go to the prophets of your father, and the prophets of your mother."

But the king of Israel said to him,

"No; for the LORD has summoned these three kings to give them into the hand of Moab."

"As the LORD of hosts lives, whom I serve," said Elisha, "were it not that I respect Jehoshaphat, the king of Judah, I would neither look at you nor notice you. Now therefore, bring me a minstrel."

When the minstrel played, the power of the LORD came upon him, and he said,

"Thus says the LORD: 'I will certainly make this dry brook a series of pools.' For thus says the LORD: 'You shall not see wind, neither shall you see rain; yet that dry brook shall be filled with water, so that you yourselves shall drink, together with your army and your cattle. This being a light thing in the sight of the LORD, he shall also give Moab into your hand. You shall conquer every fortified city and every choice city and fell every good tree and stop up all the springs of water and ruin every good piece of land with stones.' "

Accordingly, in the morning at the time of presenting the offering, suddenly water came from the direction of Edom, so that the land was filled with the water.

Now when all the Moabites had heard that the kings had come up to fight against them, all who were old enough to put on a girdle were called out and drawn up at the frontier. But when they arose early in the morning, and the sun had risen over the water, the Moabites saw the water opposite them as red as blood. Therefore they said,

"This is blood! The kings have surely fought together and have slain one another. Now therefore, Moab to the spoil!"

However, when they came to the camp of Israel, the Israelites arose and attacked the Moabites, so that they fled before them; and they went forward slaughtering the Moabites as they went. Thus they kept on overthrowing the cities and on every good piece of land they cast each his stone, until they filled it, every spring of water also they stopped up, and felled every good tree, and they harried Moab until only the men in Kir-hareseth were left, and the slingers surrounded and attacked it.

Now when the king of Moab saw that the battle was too fierce for him, he took with him seven hundred men, that drew sword, to break through against the king of Edom, but they could not. Then he took his oldest son, who was to reign in his stead, and offered him as a burnt-offering upon the wall. Then there came great wrath upon Israel, so that they departed from him and returned to their own land.

THE MIRACULOUS DEEDS OF ELISHA, 4:1—8:15

Now the wife of one of the members of the prophetic order cried out to Elisha, saying,

"My husband your servant is dead, and you know that your servant feared the LORD; but the creditor has come to take my two children to be his slaves."
"What shall I do for you?" Elisha 2
said to her. "Tell me; what have you in the house?"

"Your maidservant has nothing in the house," she said, "except a flask of oil."

"Go," said he, "borrow vessels 3
abroad of all your neighbors, even empty vessels not a few. Then go in and 4
shut the door upon yourself and your sons, and pour out into all these vessels, and when one is full set it aside."

So she went from him and shut 5
the door upon herself and her sons; they kept bringing the vessels to her while she was pouring out. As soon as 6
the vessels were full, she said to her son,

"Bring me another."

"There is not another vessel!" he said to her.

Then the oil stopped. Whereupon 7
she came and told the man of God.

"Go", said he, "sell the oil and pay your debts, and you and your sons can live on what is left."

Now there came a day when Elisha 8
passed over to Shunem, where there was an influential woman and she persuaded him to eat food, so that afterward as often as he passed by, he would turn aside there to eat food. Accord- 9
ingly, she said to her husband,

"See here, I am sure that this is a holy man of God who is continually passing by us. Let us make now a little 10
inclosed roof chamber, and let us put a bed for him there, a table, a chair, and a lamp, so that whenever he comes to us, he can go in there."

Now one day he came there and 11
turned aside into the chamber and rested there. Then he said to Gehazi 12
his servant,

"Call this Shunammite woman."

When he had called her she stood be- 13
fore him, and he said to him,

"Say now to her, 'Here you have shown all this anxious care for our comfort; what is to be done for you? Would you be commended to the king or the commander of the army?' "

"I dwell among my own people," she said.

"What then is to be done for her?" 14
said he.

"Verily, she has no son and her husband is old," said Gehazi.

15 "Call her," he said.
16 When he had called her, she stood in
the doorway, and he said,
"At this season, next spring, you
shall embrace a son."
"No! my lord!" she said. "O man of
God, do not deceive your maidservant."
17 But the woman conceived and bore a
son about the same time the next
spring as Elisha had spoken to her.
18 Now when the child was grown, he
went out one day to his father to the
19 reapers, and he said to his father,
"My head, my head!"
20 "Carry him to his mother," he said to
a servant. When he had taken him up
and brought him to his mother, he sat
upon her lap till noon, and then died.
21 Thereupon she took him up and laid
him on the bed of the man of God, and
she closed the door after him and went
out.
22 Then she called to her husband and
said,
"Send me, now, one of the servants
and one of the asses that I may speed to
the man of God and return."
23 "Why are you about to go to him today," he said, "since it is neither new
moon nor sabbath?"
"It is for the best," she said.
24 Then she saddled the ass and said to
her servant,
"Drive fast; do not slacken the riding for me unless I tell you."
25 So she set out and came to Mount
Carmel, to the man of God. Now as
soon as the man of God saw her at a
distance he said to Gehazi his servant,
"Look, there is the Shunammite
26 yonder! Now run, I pray you, to meet
her and say to her, 'Is it well with you?
Is it well with your husband? Is it well
with the child?' "
"It is well," she said.
27 But when she came to the Mount, to
the man of God, she caught hold of his
feet. When Gehazi came near to thrust
her away, the man of God said,
"Let her alone, for she has had a bitter experience and the LORD has hidden it from me and has not told me."
28 "Did I ask a son of my lord?" she
said. "Did I not say, 'Do not deceive
me?' "
29 At once Elisha said to Gehazi,
"Gird up your loins, and take my
staff in your hands, and go! If you

meet a man, do not salute him, and if a man salute you, do not reply to him, but lay my staff on the face of the child."

But the child's mother said,

"As the Lord lives, and as you yourself are alive, I will not leave you."

So he arose and went after her. Now Gehazi had gone on before them and laid the staff upon the child's face, but there was neither sound nor response. Therefore he returned to meet him and told him, saying,

"The child has not awakened."

When Elisha came to the house, behold, the boy was lying dead on his bed. He went in, therefore, and closed the door upon the two of them, and prayed to the LORD. Then he went up and lay upon the child and put his mouth upon his mouth and his eyes upon his eyes and his hands upon his hands, and as he crouched upon him, the flesh of the child became warm. Whereupon he withdrew and paced back and forth in the house; then he went up again and crouched upon him, and at this the boy sneezed seven times; and the boy opened his eyes. At once he called to Gehazi and said,

"Call this Shunammite."

So he called her and when she came to him, he said,

"Take up your son."

Then she entered, fell at his feet, and bowed herself to the earth; presently she took up her son and went out.

Now Elisha returned to Gilgal while there was a famine in the land. When the members of the prophetic order were sitting before him, he said to his servant,

"Set on the great pot and make a vegetable stew for the prophets."

Then one of them went out into the field to gather herbs and found a wild vine and gathered from it his lap full of wild gourds, and came and cut them up for the pot of vegetable stew, for they did not know what they were. So they poured out for the men to eat. But while they were still eating of the stew, they cried out and said,

"O man of God, there is death in the pot."

So they could not eat of it.

"Bring meal," he said.

Then he cast it into the pot and said,

"Pour out for the people that they nay eat."

There was now no harm in the pot.

Then a man came from Baal-shalish-h and brought the man of God bread of the first fruits, twenty loaves of barey, and fresh vegetables in his sack.

"Give them to the people that they nay eat," he said.

"What, shall I set this before a hunlred men?" said his attendant.

So he repeated,

"Give them to the people that they nay eat; for thus says the LORD: They shall eat and have some left.' "

Then he set it before them, and they ite and left some over according to the vord of the LORD.

Now Naaman, the commander of the army of the king of Syria, was a great nan with his master and highly eseemed, because through him the ORD had given victory to Syria. But, although a valiant man, he was a eper. The Syrians had gone out as narauding bands and had carried off a ittle girl from the land of Israel, and he waited on Naaman's wife.

"Would that my master were with he prophet who is in Samaria!" she aid to her mistress. "Then he would ure him of his leprosy."

So he went in and told his lord, sayng,

"Thus and so spoke the maiden who s from the land of Israel."

Then the king of Syria said,

"Go now, and I will send along a leter to the king of Israel."

So he set out, taking with him ten alents of silver and six thousand shekels of gold and ten festal garments; and e brought to the king of Israel the leter which read,

"Now when this letter reaches you, e informed that I have sent to you my ervant Naaman, that you may cure im of his leprosy."

When, however, the king of Israel ead the letter he tore his garments and aid,

"Am I a god to kill and to make alive, that this man is sending to me to ure a man of his leprosy? Take note and observe how he is seeking occasion against me."

But as soon as Elisha the man of God heard that the king of Israel had
torn his garments, he sent to the king,
saying,
"Why have you torn your garments?
I pray you, let him come to me, that he
may know that there is a prophet in
Israel."
So Naaman came with his horses and 9
with his chariots and halted at the door
of Elisha's house. Whereupon Elisha 10
sent a messenger to him, saying,
"Go and wash in the Jordan seven
times, and your flesh shall be restored
and you shall be clean."
But Naaman was enraged and left, 11
and he said,
"Here I have been saying to myself,
'He will surely come out and stand and
call on the name of the LORD his God,
and wave his hand toward the place
and cure the leper.' Are not Amana 12
and Pharpar, the rivers of Damascus,
better than all the waters of Israel?
Could I not wash in them and be
clean?"
So he turned and went away in a 13
rage. Then his servants came near and
spoke to him, saying,
"My father, if the prophet had demanded of you some great thing, would
you not have done it? How much rather then, when he has said to you, 'Wash
and be clean?' "
So finally he went down and dipped 14
himself seven times in the Jordan, according to the word of the man of God,
and his flesh was restored like the flesh
of a little child, and he was clean.
Then he returned to the man of God, 15
with all his retinue, and came and stood
before him and said,
"Verily, now I know that there is no
God in all the earth, but in Israel; now
therefore, I pray you, accept a present
from your servant."
"As the LORD lives whom I serve I 16
will take nothing," he said.
And although he pressed him to take
it, he refused.
"If not," said Naaman, "at any rate 17
let there be given to your servant two
mules' burden of earth; for your servant will henceforth offer neither burnt-offering nor sacrifice to other gods, but
to the LORD. In this matter may the 18
LORD pardon your servant—when my
master goes into the house of Rimmon
to worship there, leaning on my arm,
and I bow myself in the house of Rimmon, when I bow myself in the house of

Rimmon, then may the LORD pardon
your servant in this matter."
19 "Go in peace," he said to him.
20 But when he had gone from him a
short distance, Gehazi, the servant of
Elisha the man of God, said,
"See, my master has spared this
Syrian, Naaman, without accepting
from his hand what he brought! As the
LORD lives, I will certainly run after
him and get something from him."
21 So Gehazi ran after Naaman, and
when Naaman saw someone running
after him, he alighted from his chariot
to meet him, and said,
"Is it well?"
22 "All is well," he said. "My master
sent me saying, 'There have just now
come to me two young men of the
prophetic order from the highlands of
Ephraim. I pray you, give them a talent of silver and two festal garments.' "
23 "Consent to accept two talents,"
said Naaman.
So he urged him, and tied up two
talents of silver in two bags, with two
festal garments, and he gave them to
two of his servants, and they carried
24 them before him. But when he came to
the hill, he took them from their hand
and deposited them in the house, and
sent the men away and they departed.
25 When he went in and stood before
his master, Elisha said to him,
"Where have you been, Gehazi?"
"Your servant has not been away
anywhere," he said.
26 "Was I not present in spirit when the
man turned from his chariot to meet
you?" he said. "Is it a time to accept
money, and garments, and olive orchards and vineyards, and sheep and
oxen, and menservants and maidserv-
27 ants? The leprosy of Naaman shall fasten upon you and upon your descendants forever."
So he went out from his presence, a
leper as white as snow.
6 Now the members of the prophetic
order said to Elisha,
"See now, the place before you where
2 we dwell is too limited for us. Let us go
now to the Jordan and each take from
there a beam and let us make a place
for us there, where we may dwell."
"Go," he said.
3 Then a certain one said,
"Be pleased, now, to go with your
servants."

"I will go," he said.
So he went with them, and when
they came to the Jordan, they cut down
the trees, but as one was felling a beam
his iron ax fell into the water. At that
he cried out, and said,
"Alas, my master! for it was borrowed."
"Where did it fall?" said the man of
God.
When he showed him the place, he
cut off a stick and threw it in there, and
made the iron float.
"Take it up," he said.
So he reached out his hand and took
it.
Once when the king of Syria was at
war with Israel, he took counsel with
his servants, saying,
"In such and such a place let us make
an ambush and conceal ourselves."
But the man of God sent to the king
of Israel, saying,
"Beware that you do not pass this
place, for Syrians have concealed
themselves there."
So the king of Israel sent to the place
of which the man of God had told him.
Thus he used to warn him, so that he
could guard himself there, not once or
twice.
Therefore the mind of the king of
Syria was agitated because of this fact
and he called his servants and said to
them,
"Will you not tell me, who of us is for
the king of Israel?"
"There is no one, my lord, O king!"
said one of his servants, "but Elisha,
the prophet who is in Israel, tells the
king of Israel the words that you speak
in your bedroom."
"Go and see where he is," he said,
"that I may send and take him."
Then it was told him, saying,
"Behold he is in Dothan."
Accordingly he sent there horses and
chariots and a large force; and they
came by night, and surrounded the
city. So on the morrow when the man
of God arose early in the morning and
went out, there was an army of horses
and chariots surrounding the city, so
that his servant said to him,
"Alas, my master! What shall we
do?"
"Fear not," he said, "for they who
are with us are more than they who
are with them."

17 Then Elisha prayed and said,
"O LORD, open now his eyes that he
may see."
The LORD opened the eyes of the
lad, and he saw, and behold the mountain was full of horses and chariots of
18 fire around Elisha. When they came
down to him, Elisha prayed to the
LORD and said,
"Smite now this people with blindness."
So he smote them with blindness according to the word of Elisha.
19 Then Elisha said to them,
"This is neither the way nor the city.
Follow me and I will bring you to the
man whom you seek!"
So he brought them to Samaria.
20 But as soon as they came to Samaria, Elisha said,
"O LORD, open the eyes of these
men, that they may see."
So the LORD opened their eyes and
they saw, and behold, they were in the
21 midst of Samaria. Thereupon the king
of Israel said to Elisha when he saw
them,
"My father, shall I slay them? Shall
I slay them?"
22 "You shall not slay," he said; "would
you slay those whom you have not tak-
en prisoner with your sword and with
your bow? Set bread and water before
them, that they may eat and drink and
go to their master."
So he prepared for them a great
23 feast; and when they had eaten and
drunk he sent them away, and they
went to their master. Then the marauding Syrian bands came no more into
the land of Israel.
24 It was after this that Ben-hadad king
of Syria assembled all his army and
25 went up and besieged Samaria. Consequently there was a great famine in
Samaria, and there the besiegers continued until an ass's head was sold for
eighty shekels of silver, and a pint of
dove's dung for five shekels of silver.
26 Now as the king of Israel was passing
along upon the wall, a woman cried out
to him saying,
"Help, my lord, O king!"
27 "Let the LORD help you!" he said to
her. "Out of what can I help you? Out
of the threshing floor or out of the
winepress?"
28 However, the king said to her,
"What is your trouble?"
Then the woman said,
"This woman said to me, 'Give your
son, that we may eat him today, and
we will eat my son tomorrow.' So we 29
boiled my son, and ate him, and I said
to her on the next day, 'Give your son,
that we may eat him'; but she has hidden her son."
Now when the king heard the words 30
of the woman, he tore his garments—
and as he was passing along upon the
wall, the people saw, and behold, he
had sackcloth within on his flesh—and 31
he said,
"May God requite me and worse, if
the head of Elisha, the son of Shaphat,
remain in his possession today."
Now Elisha was sitting in his house 32
with the elders sitting beside him. And
the king sent a man from his presence.
But before the messenger came to him,
he said to the elders,
"You see how this son of a murderer
has sent to remove my head. Look.
When the messenger comes, close the
door, and hold the door fast against
him. Is not the sound of his master's
feet behind him?"
While he was still speaking with 33
them, behold, the king came down to
him and said,
"See, this is the evil from the LORD!
Why should I wait for the LORD any
longer?"
"Hear the word of the LORD," said 7
Elisha. "Thus says the LORD: "Tomorrow about this time shall a measure
of fine meal be sold for a shekel, and
two measures of barley for a shekel at
the gate of Samaria." ' "
Then the third officer of the king on 2
whose hand the king leaned, answered
the man of God and said,
"If the LORD himself should make
windows in the heavens, could this
thing be?"
"You, yourself," he said, "shall see it
with your own eyes, but you shall not
eat of it."
Now there were four men who were 3
lepers at the entrance of the gate; and
they said to one another,
"Why do we remain here until we
die? If we say, 'Let us enter the city,' 4
the famine is in the city and we shall
die there; but if we remain here, we die
also. Now therefore come and let us
desert to the army of the Syrians. If

they save us alive, we shall live; and if
they kill us, we shall but die."
5 So they arose at twilight to go to
the army of the Syrians. But when
they came to the confines of the camp
of the Syrians, there was no one there;
6 for the LORD had caused the army of
the Syrians to hear a sound of chariots
and of horses and of a great army, so
that they said one to another,

"Surely the king of Israel has hired against us the kings of the Hittites and the kings of Egypt to come upon us."

7 Therefore they arose and fled in the
twilight and forsook their tents, their
horses, and their asses, even the camp
8 as it was, and fled for their lives. When
these lepers came to the confines of the
camp, they entered into a tent and ate
and drank and carried away silver and
gold and clothing and went and hid
them. Then they returned and entered
another tent and carried away what
was there and went and hid it.
9 Then they said to one another,

"We are not doing right; this is a day of good news, but we are keeping still. If we wait until the morning light, punishment will overtake us. Now therefore, come, let us go and inform the house of the king."

10 So they came and called the gatekeepers of the city and told them, saying,

"We came to the camp of the Syrians, and behold, there was no one there and no sound of man, but the horses were tied and the asses tied, and the tents were as they had been."

11 Then the gate-keepers called out and
informed the house of the king within.
12 So the king arose in the night and said
to his servants,

"Let me tell you now what the Syrians have done to us. They know that we are hungry; therefore they have gone from the camp to hide themselves in the field, thinking, 'When they come out of the city we shall capture them alive and we shall get into the city.'"

13 But one of his servants answered and said,

"Send men and let them take five of the remaining horses; if they live, behold, they are like all the multitude of Israel that survive here, but if they perish, behold, they are like all the multitude of Israel that are consumed. Therefore let us send and see."

However, they took two mounted 14
men, and the king sent them after the army of the Syrians, saying,

"Go and see."

Accordingly they went after them to 15
the Jordan and behold, all the way was full of garments and equipment which the Syrians had thrown away in their haste, and the messengers returned and told the king.

Then the people went out and plun- 16
dered the camp of the Syrians. So a
homer of fine meal sold for a shekel and
two measures of barley for a shekel, according to the word of the LORD. Now 17
the king had appointed the third officer
on whose hand he leaned to take charge
of the gate; but the people trampled
upon him at the gate so that he died,
just as the man of God had said when
the king came down to him. It also 18
happened just as the man of God had
spoken to the king, saying,

"Two measures of barley shall be sold for a shekel, and a measure of fine flour for a shekel, about this time tomorrow at the gate of Samaria."

The third officer had answered the 19
man of God and said,

"If the LORD himself should make windows in the heavens, could this thing be?"

And he had said,

"You yourself shall see it with your own eyes, but you shall not eat of it."

So it happened to him, for the people 20
trampled upon him at the gate so that he died.

Now Elisha spoke to the woman, 8
whose son he restored to life, saying,

"Arise, and depart with your household, and sojourn wherever you are able, for the LORD has called for a famine; and furthermore, it shall come upon the land for seven years."

So the woman arose and did according to the word of the man of God: she went with her household and sojourned in the land of the Philistines seven years; and at the end of seven years when the woman returned from the land of the Philistines, she went forth to appeal to the king for her house and her field.

Now at the time, the king was speaking to Gehazi, the servant of the man of God, saying,

"Relate to me now all the great things that Elisha has done."

5 While he was still relating to the king
how he had restored to life the dead,
just then the woman whose son he had
restored to life began her appeal to the
king about her house and her field.
"My lord, O king," said Gehazi,
"this is the woman and this is her son,
whom Elisha restored to life."
6 Then when the king asked the woman, she related it to him. So the king
put at her disposal an official, saying,
"Restore all that was hers together
with all the produce of the field from
the day that she left the land until
now."
7 Now Elisha came to Damascus; and
Ben-hadad, the king of Syria, was sick.
So when it was told him, saying,
"The man of God has come here,"
8 the king said to Hazael,
"Take with you a present and go to
meet the man of God, and inquire of
the LORD through him, saying, 'Shall I
recover from this sickness?' "
9 So Hazael went to meet him and took
a present with him, even all kinds of
goods of Damascus, forty camel loads.
When he came he stood before him and
said,
"Your son Ben-hadad, king of Syria,
has sent me to you, saying, 'Shall I recover from this sickness?' "
10 Then Elisha said to him,
"Go, say to him, 'You shall surely
recover,' but the LORD has shown me
that he shall certainly die."
11 And he fixed his gaze and stared at
him until he was ashamed; but the man
of God wept.
12 "Why does my lord weep?" said Hazael.
"Because," he said, "I know the evil
that you will do to the Israelites: Their
fortresses you will set on fire, their
choice young men you will slay with the
sword, their little children you will dash
in pieces, and their women with child
you will disembowel."
13 "But what is your servant—a dead
dog—that he should do this great
thing?" said Hazael.
"The LORD has shown me that you
are to be king over Syria," said Elisha.
14 When he left Elisha and came to his
master, he said to him,
"What did Elisha say to you?"
Then he said,
"He said to me that you would certainly live."

But on the morrow he took the cov- 15
erlet and dipped it in water and spread
it over his face, so that he died. And
Hazael became king in his stead.

JEHORAM AND AHAZIAH OF JUDAH, 8:16–29a

Now in the fifth year of Joram, the 16
son of Ahab, king of Israel, Jehoram,
the son of Jehoshaphat, king of Judah,
became king. He was thirty-two years 17
old when he became king, and he
reigned eight years in Jerusalem. He 18
walked in the way of the kings of Israel,
as the house of Ahab had done, for the
daughter of Ahab became his wife, and
he did that which was evil in the sight
of the LORD. However, the LORD 19
would not destroy Judah because of
David his servant, since he had said to
him that he would give him a lamp before him always.
In his days Edom revolted from the 20
rule of Judah and established a king of
its own. Then Joram passed over to 21
Zair, and all his chariots with him; and
he, together with his chariot commanders, rose by night and broke through
the Edomites who had surrounded him.
So Edom has been in revolt from the 22
rule of Judah to this day. Libnah likewise revolted at the same time. Now 23
the rest of the records of Joram and all
that he did, are they not written in the
Book of the Chronicles of the Kings of
Judah? So Joram slept with his fathers 24
and was buried with his fathers in the
city of David; and Ahaziah his son became king in his stead.
In the twelfth year of Joram, the son 25
of Ahab, king of Israel, Ahaziah, the
son of Jehoram, king of Judah, became
king. Ahaziah was twenty-two years 26
old when he became king, and he
reigned one year in Jerusalem; and his
mother's name was Athaliah, the
granddaughter of Omri, king of Israel.
He walked in the way of the house of 27
Ahab and did that which was evil in the
sight of the LORD as did the house of
Ahab, for he was son-in-law to the
house of Ahab. Moreover he went with 28
Joram, the son of Ahab, to make war
against Hazael, king of Syria, at Ramoth-gilead. But the Syrians wounded
Joram. Therefore King Joram returned 29
to be healed in Jezreel of the wounds

which the Syrians had given him at
Ramah, when he fought with Hazael,
king of Syria.

THE REVOLT OF JEHU, 8:29*b*—10:36

Now Ahaziah, the son of Joram, king
9 of Judah, went down to see Joram, the
son of Ahab, in Jezreel, because he was
sick. Then Elisha the prophet called to
one of the members of the prophetic order and said to him,
"Gird up your loins and take this
flask of oil in your hand and go to
2 Ramoth-gilead. And when you come
there, look there for Jehu, the son of
Jehoshaphat, the son of Nimshi, and
go in and make him rise up from among
his brothers and bring him into an inner
3 chamber. Then take the flask of oil and
pour it on his head and say, 'Thus says
the LORD: "I have anointed you king
over Israel." ' Then open the door and
flee, and do not wait."
4 So the young man (the servant of the
5 prophet) went to Ramoth-gilead; and
just as he came, the commanders of the
army were in session.
"I have a word for you, O commander," he said.
"For which one of us all?" said Jehu.
"For you, O commander," he said.
6 Then he arose and went into the
house; and the servant poured the oil
on his head and said to him,
"Thus says the LORD, the God of
Israel: 'I have anointed you king over
the people of the LORD, even over
7 Israel. And you shall cut off the house
of Ahab, your master, that I may
avenge the blood of my servants, the
prophets, and the blood of all the
servants of the LORD at the hands of
8 Jezebel. For the whole house of Ahab
shall perish and I will cut off from Ahab
every male, him who is shut up and him
9 who is at large in Israel. I will make the
house of Ahab like the house of Jeroboam, the son of Nebat, and like the
10 house of Baasha, the son of Ahijah; and
the dogs shall eat Jezebel in the territory of Jezreel and none shall bury
her.' "
Then he opened the door and fled.
11 Now when Jehu came out to the
servants of his master, they said to him,
"Is all well? Why did this mad man
come to you?"
"You know the man and his talk,"
he said to them.
"It is false! Tell us now," they said. 12
So he said,
"Thus and thus he said to me, saying, 'Thus says the LORD: "I have a-
nointed you king over Israel." ' "
Then they quickly took each his gar- 13
ment, and put it under him on the stairway, and blew the trumpet and said,
"Jehu is king!"
Thus Jehu, the son of Jehoshaphat, 14
the son of Nimshi, conspired against
Joram, while Joram, together with all
Israel, was holding Ramoth-gilead
against Hazael, king of Syria; but King 15
Joram had returned to Jezreel to be
healed of the wounds which the Syrians
had inflicted upon him, when he fought
with Hazael, king of Syria. So Jehu said,
"If it be your mind, let no one make
his escape from the city to go and tell it
in Jezreel."
Then Jehu mounted his chariot and 16
went to Jezreel, for Joram was lying
there; and Ahaziah, king of Judah, had
gone down to see Joram. Now as the 17
watchman was standing on the tower
in Jezreel, he saw the dust cloud raised
by Jehu, as he came on, and he said,
"I see a dust cloud."
"Take a horseman and send him to
meet them that he may say, 'Is it
peace?' " said Joram.
Accordingly the rider of the horse 18
went to meet him and said,
"Thus says the king: 'Is it peace?' "
"What have you to do with peace?"
said Jehu. "Rein in behind me."
So the watchman reported, saying,
"The messenger came to them, but
he does not return."
Then he sent out a second horseman 19
who came to them and said,
"Thus says the king: 'Is it peace?' "
"What have you to do with peace?"
said Jehu. "Rein in behind me."
Again the watchman reported, say- 20
ing,
"He came to them, but he does not
return; also the driving is like the driv-
ing of Jehu, the son of Nimshi, for he is
accustomed to drive furiously."
"Make ready," said Joram. 21
As soon as they had made ready his
chariot, Joram, king of Israel, and
Ahaziah, king of Judah, set out each in
his chariot. Thus they went to meet
Jehu, and they reached him in the field

22 of Naboth the Jezreelite; and when
Joram saw Jehu he said,
"Is it peace, Jehu?"
"How can there be peace," he said,
"as long as the harlotries of Jezebel
your mother and her witchcrafts are so
many?"
23 Then Joram reined about and fled,
and said to Ahaziah,
"Treachery, Ahaziah!"
24 But Jehu drew his bow and shot Joram between his shoulders, so that the
arrow went clear through his body; and
25 he collapsed in his chariot. Then Jehu
said to Bidkar, his third officer,
"Take him up and cast him into that
portion of field belonging to Naboth the
Jezreelite; for I remember how when
you and I were riding side by side after
Ahab his father, the LORD took up this
26 oracle against him: 'Surely I saw
yesterday the blood of Naboth and the
blood of his sons,' is the oracle of the
LORD; 'and I will requite you in this
very field,' is the oracle of the LORD.
Now therefore, take him up and cast
him into the plot of ground, according
to the word of the LORD."
27 Now when Ahaziah, king of Judah,
saw this, he fled in the direction of
Beth-haggan. But Jehu pursued him,
and said,
"Him also! Pin him to the chariot."
So they wounded him at the ascent
of Gur, which is by Ibleam. Nevertheless he kept on to Megiddo where he
28 died. Then his servants took him by
chariot to Jerusalem, and buried him in
his own sepulcher with his fathers in the
29 city of David. Now in the eleventh
year of Joram, the son of Ahab, Ahaziah
30 became king over Judah. When Jehu
came to Jezreel, Jezebel heard of it, and
she painted her eyelashes and adorned
her head and peered out at the window.
31 As Jehu was entering the gate, she said,
"Is it well, you Zimri, your master's
murderer?"
32 But he raised his eyes to the window
and said,
"Who is on my side? Who?"
33 At that two or three eunuchs peered
out at him.
"Let her drop," he said.
So they let her drop, so that some of
her blood spattered on the wall and on
34 the horses, and he drove over her. Then
he went in and ate and drank.
"Take charge now of this cursed
woman, and bury her; for she is a king's
daughter," he said.
But when they went to bury her, 35
they found no more of her than the
skull, the feet, and the palms of the
hands.
When, therefore, they returned and 36
told him, he said,
"This is the word of the LORD, which
he spoke by his servant, Elijah the
Tishbite, saying, 'In the territory of
Jezreel shall the dogs eat the flesh of
Jezebel. And the corpse of Jezebel shall 37
be as dung on the face of the field in the
territory of Jezreel, so that they cannot say, "This is Jezebel." ' "
Now Ahab had seventy descendants **10**
in Samaria. So Jehu wrote letters and
sent to Samaria to the rulers of the city,
to the elders, and those who had charge
of the descendants of Ahab, saying,
"Now therefore, as soon as this letter 2
comes to you, since your master's sons
are with you, as well as chariots and
horses, fortified cities and weapons,
select the best and fittest of your mas- 3
ter's sons, and set him on the throne of
his father and fight for your master's
house."
But they were panic-stricken and 4
said,
"Behold, the two kings could not
stand before him; how then shall we
ourselves stand?"
So he who was over the palace and he 5
who was over the city, together with
the elders and the guardians, sent to
Jehu, saying,
"We are your servants, and all that
you tell us we will do; we will make no
one king; do whatever is good in your
eyes."
So he wrote to them a second letter, 6
saying,
"If you are on my side and if you are
ready to obey me, then take the heads
of the men, the sons of your master, and
come to me to Jezreel tomorrow at this
time."
Now the royal princes, seventy in
number, were with the great men of the
city, who were bringing them up. Ac- 7
cordingly, as soon as the letter came to
them, they took the royal princes and
slew them, seventy persons, and put
their heads in baskets and sent them to
him to Jezreel. When the messenger 8
came and told him, saying,

"They have brought the heads of the
royal princes,"
he said,
"Put them in two heaps at the entrance of the gate until the morning."
9 Then in the morning when he went
out, he stood and said to all the people,
"You are upright; it is true I conspired against my master and slew him,
10 but who killed all these? Know then
that there shall fall to the earth nothing
of the word of the LORD, which the
LORD spoke against the house of Ahab;
for the LORD has done what he spoke
by his servant Elijah."
11 Thereupon Jehu slew all that were
left of the house of Ahab in Jezreel, together with all his kinsmen, and his
familiar friends, and his priests, until
12 he left him none remaining. Then he
arose and departed for Samaria; and as
he was at Beth-eked of the shepherds
13 on the way, Jehu met with the kinsmen
of Ahaziah, king of Judah, and said,
"Who are you?"
"We are the kinsmen of Ahaziah,"
they said, "and we have come down to
greet the household of the king and the
household of the queen mother."
14 "Take them alive," he said.
Then they took them alive and slew
them at the pit of Beth-eked, forty-two
persons, so that he spared none of them;
15 and when he set out from there he met
with Jonadab, the son of Rechab, coming to meet him. He greeted him and
said to him,
"Is your heart in accord with my
heart, as mine is with yours?"
"It is," said Jonadab.
"If it be, give me your hand," said
Jehu.
So he gave him his hand and he took
him up to him into the chariot.
16 "Come with me, and see my zeal for
the LORD," he said.
So he induced him to ride in his
17 chariot, and when he came to Samaria,
he slew all who remained to Ahab in
Samaria, until he had exterminated
them according to the word of the
18 LORD which he spoke to Elijah. Then
Jehu assembled all the people and said
to them,
"Ahab served the Baal a little; Jehu
19 will serve him much. Now therefore,
summon to me all the prophets of the
Baal, all who serve him, and all his
priests; let none be absent; for I have a
great sacrifice for the Baal; whoever is
absent shall not live."
But Jehu did it with deliberate cunning in order to wipe out the worshipers of the Baal.
"Sanctify a solemn assembly for the 20
Baal," said Jehu.
So they proclaimed it. Moreover Je- 21
hu sent through all Israel, and all the
worshipers of the Baal came so that
there was not a man left who did not
come; and when they had entered the
house of the Baal, the house of the Baal
was filled from one end to the other.
Then he said to the one in charge of the 22
wardrobe,
"Bring out garments for all the worshipers of the Baal."
So he brought out the garments for
them. Then Jehu together with Jo- 23
nadab, the son of Rechab, went into the
house of the Baal, and said to the worshipers of the Baal,
"Search and see that there may not
be here with you any of the servants of
the LORD, but only worshipers of the
Baal."
Thereupon he proceeded to offer the 24
sacrifices and the burnt-offerings. Now
Jehu had stationed eighty men outside
and he had said,
"The man who allows any of the men
whom I put in your charge to escape,
his life shall be for that one's life."
Now as soon as he had made the of- 25
fering Jehu said to the guards and to
the third officers,
"Go in, slay them, let not a man escape."
So they put them to the sword, and
the guards and the third officers cast
them out, and went into the inner room
of the house of the Baal, and brought 26
out the sacred pole from the house of
the Baal and burned it. They also de- 27
molished the sacred pillar of the Baal
and demolished the house of the Baal
and made it a lavatory, as it is to this
day. Thus Jehu eradicated the Baal 28
from Israel. Nevertheless from the sins 29
of Jeroboam the son of Nebat, with
which he made Israel sin, from these,
the golden calves that were in Bethel
and in Dan, Jehu turned not aside. But 30
the LORD said to Jehu,
"Because you have done well in performing that which was right in my
sight, and have done to the house of
Ahab according to all that was in my

heart, your sons to the fourth generation shall sit on the throne of Israel."
31 Yet Jehu took no heed to walk in the
law of the LORD, the God of Israel, with
all his heart: he did not turn from the
sins of Jeroboam with which he made
32 Israel sin. In those days the LORD began to be angry with Israel, and Hazael
defeated them throughout the territory
33 of Israel, from the Jordan eastward, all
the land of Gilead, the Gadites, the
Reubenites, and the Manassites, from
Aroer which is by the valley of the Ar-
34 non, both Gilead and Bashan. Now the
rest of the records of Jehu and all that
he did and all his prowess, are they not
written in the Book of the Chronicles
35 of the Kings of Israel? So Jehu slept
with his fathers, and they buried him in
Samaria; and Jehoahaz his son became
36 king in his stead. The time that Jehu
reigned over Israel in Samaria was
twenty-eight years.

THE REGENCY OF ATHALIAH, 11:1–20

1 Now when Athaliah, the mother of
Ahaziah, saw that her son was dead, she
arose and destroyed all the royal family.
2 But Jehosheba, the daughter of King
Joram, the sister of Ahaziah, took Joash, the son of Ahaziah, and stole him
away from the king's sons, that were
about to be slain, and put him and his
nurse in a bed-chamber. Thus she hid
him from Athaliah, so that he was not
3 slain. So he was with her, hidden in the
house of the LORD six years, while
4 Athaliah reigned over the land. But in
the seventh year Jehoiada sent and
brought the commanders of hundreds
of the Carites and the guards and
brought them to him in the house of the
LORD. Thereupon he made a covenant
with them and made them swear in the
house of the LORD, and showed them
5 the king's son. Then he commanded
them saying,
"This is the thing that you shall do:
one third of you, who enter on the Sabbath and keep guard over the house of
6 the king—a third shall be at the gate
Sur, and another third at the gate behind the guards—shall keep watch over
7 the house of the king; and two divisions
of you, even all who go forth on the
Sabbath to keep watch over the house
of the LORD about the king, shall sur- 8
round the king each with drawn weapons. Whoever comes up to the ranks
shall be slain. So be with the king when
he goes out and when he comes in."
So the commanders of hundreds did 9
just as Jehoiada the priest had commanded: they brought each his men
who were to enter upon the Sabbath,
with those who were to go out on the
Sabbath, and came to Jehoiada the
priest. Then the priest delivered to the 10
commanders of hundreds the spears and
shields that had been King David's,
which were in the house of the LORD.
Accordingly the guards stood each with 11
his weapons in his hand, from the right
side of the house to the left side of the
house, before the altar and before the
temple, by the king round about. Then 12
he brought out the king's son and put
the crown and the armlet upon him,
and they proclaimed him king and
anointed him, and clapped their hands
and said,
"Long live the king!"
But when Athaliah heard the noise of 13
the people, she came to the people into
the house of the LORD; and when she 14
looked, there was the king standing by
the column, as was the custom, and the
commanders and the trumpeters beside
the king, and all the people of the land
rejoicing and blowing trumpets. Then
Athaliah tore her garments and cried,
"Treason! Treason!"
Then Jehoiada the priest gave orders 15
to the commanders of hundreds who
were appointed over the army, and said
to them,
"Bring her out between the ranks;
and whoever follows her slay with the
sword!"
For the priest had said,
"Let her not be slain in the house of
the LORD."
So they laid hands on her, and as she 16
went through the horses' entrance to
the king's house, there she was slain.
Then Jehoiada made a covenant be- 17
tween the LORD and the king and the
people, that they should be the LORD'S
people; likewise between the king and
the people. Then all the people of the 18
land went to the house of the Baal and
destroyed it; his altar and his images
they completely shattered, and Mattan, the priest of the Baal, they slew
before the altars. Then the priest ap-

pointed watchmen over the house of the
19 LORD; and he took the commanders of
hundreds and the Carites, and the
guards and all the people of the land,
and they brought down the king from
the house of the LORD and entered by
way of the gate of the guards to the
20 king's house; and he sat on the throne
of the kings. So all the people of the
land rejoiced and the city was quiet.
Thus they slew Athaliah with the sword
in the king's house.

JEHOASH OF JUDAH, 11:21—12:21

21 Jehoash was seven years old when he
12 became king. In the seventh year of
Jehu, Jehoash became king, and he
reigned forty years in Jerusalem; and
his mother's name was Zibiah of Beer-
2 sheba. Jehoash did that which was
right in the sight of the LORD all his
days. It was he whom Jehoiada the
3 priest instructed. Nevertheless the high
places were not taken away; the people
still continued to sacrifice and burn incense on the high places.
4 Then Jehoash said to the priests,
"All the money of sacred gifts which
is brought into the house of the LORD,
the money from each man's property
assessment, the money from the assessment of persons, and all the money
which a man's heart prompts him to
5 bring to the house of the LORD, let the
priests take that for themselves, each
from his acquaintance. However they
shall make the repairs on the house
wherever any need of repairs is discovered."
6 Nevertheless in the twenty-third year
of King Jehoash, the priests had not
7 made the repairs on the house. Therefore King Jehoash summoned Jehoiada
the priest and the other priests, and
said to them,
"Why have you not been keeping up
the repairs on the house? Now therefore, take no more money from your acquaintances, but pay it directly for the
repairs of the house."
8 So the priests agreed that they should
neither take more money from the
people nor make the repairs on the
house.
9 Then Jehoiada the priest took a
chest, bored a hole in its lid and put it
beside the doorpost at the right side as
one entered the house of the LORD;
and the priests, who guarded the
threshold, used to put in it all the
money that was brought into the house
of the LORD. As soon as they saw that
there was much money in the chest, the
king's scribe and the high priest came
up, and counted and tied up in bags the
money that was found in the house of
the LORD. Then they used to give the
money that was weighed out into the
hands of those who were doing the
work, who had the oversight of the
house of the LORD; and they paid it
out to the carpenters and to the builders, who worked on the house of the
LORD, and to the masons and the
stone-cutters, and for buying timber
and hewn stone for making the repairs
on the house of the LORD, and for all
that continued to go into the repairs of
the house. However, there were not
made for the house of the LORD silver
cups, snuffers, basins, trumpets, or any
vessels of gold or vessels of silver from
the money brought into the house of
the LORD, but they gave it to those
who did the work, and thereby proceeded with the repair of the house of
the LORD. Moreover they reckoned
not with the men, into whose hand they
delivered the money to pay out to those
who were doing the work, for they dealt
faithfully. The money from the guilt-
offering and from the sin-offerings was
not brought into the house of the LORD;
it belonged to the priests.
Then Hazael, king of Syria, went up
and fought against Gath, and took it.
But when Hazael set his course to go up
to Jerusalem, Jehoash, the king of
Judah, took all the consecrated things
that Jehoshaphat and Jehoram and
Ahaziah, his forbears, the kings of Judah, had dedicated, and his own consecrated gifts and all the gold that was
found in the treasuries of the house of
the LORD and the house of the king,
and sent it to Hazael, king of Syria.
Then he went away from Jerusalem.
Now the rest of the records of Joash
and all that he did, are they not written
in the Book of the Chronicles of the
Kings of Judah? His servants arose
and made a conspiracy and slew Joash
in the house of Millo that goes down to
Silla; for Jozacar, the son of Shimeath,
and Jehozabad, the son of Shomer, his

servants, brought about his death; and they buried him with his fathers in the city of David; and Amaziah his son became king in his stead.

JEHOAHAZ AND JEHOASH OF ISRAEL, 13:1–13

In the twenty-third year of Joash, the son of Ahaziah, king of Judah, Jehoahaz, the son of Jehu, became king over Israel in Samaria, and he reigned seventeen years. He did that which was evil in the sight of the LORD, and went after the sins of Jeroboam, the son of Nebat, with which he made Israel sin—he did not turn from them. So the anger of the LORD blazed against Israel and he delivered them continually into the hand of Hazael, king of Syria, and into the hand of Ben-hadad, the son of Hazael. Then Jehoahaz entreated the favor of the LORD, and the LORD listened to him; for he saw the oppression of Israel, how the king of Syria oppressed them. Therefore the LORD gave Israel a deliverer, so that they escaped from the hand of Syria, and the Israelites dwelt in their habitations as formerly. Nevertheless they did not turn away from the sins of the house of Jeroboam, with which he made Israel sin, but walked therein. Also the sacred pole continued to stand in Samaria. For there was not left to Jehoahaz of the people more than fifty horsemen, ten chariots, and ten thousand footmen, for the king of Syria destroyed them and made them like the dust of the threshing. Now the rest of the records of Jehoahaz and all that he did and his prowess, are they not written in the Book of the Chronicles of the Kings of Israel? So Jehoahaz slept with his fathers, and they buried him in Samaria; and Jehoash his son became king in his stead.

In the thirty-seventh year of Joash, king of Judah, Jehoash, the son of Jehoahaz, became king over Israel in Samaria, and reigned sixteen years. He did that which was evil in the sight of the LORD: he did not turn away from all the sins of Jeroboam, the son of Nebat, with which he made Israel sin, but he walked therein. Now the rest of the records of Jehoash and all that he did, and his prowess with which he fought against Amaziah king of Judah,
are they not written in the Book of the
Chronicles of the Kings of Israel? So 13
Jehoash slept with his fathers, and Jeroboam sat upon his throne; and Joash was buried in Samaria with the kings of Israel.

ELISHA'S DEATH, 13:14–21

Now when Elisha became sick of the 14
illness of which he was to die, Joash, king of Israel, went down to him, and wept over him and said,

"My father, my father! the chariots of Israel and its horsemen!"

"Take bow and arrows," Elisha said 15
to him.

So he took bow and arrows, and he 16
said to the king of Israel,

"Lay your hand upon the bow."

When he had done so, Elisha put his hands upon the king's hands.

"Open the window toward the east," 17
he said.

And when he opened it, Elisha said,

"Shoot."

So he shot.

"The LORD'S arrow of victory and the arrow of victory over Syria," he said, "for you are to fight Syria in Aphek to a finish."

"Take the arrows," he said. 18

When he had taken them, he said to the king of Israel,

"Strike on the ground."

He struck three times and stopped.
Then the man of God was enraged at 19
him and said,

"You should have struck five or six times; then you would have fought Syria to a finish. But now you will defeat Syria only three times."

So Elisha died and they buried him. 20
Now bands of Moabites were in the
habit of raiding the land at the coming
in of the year; and while they were 21
burying a man, suddenly they saw a marauding band. So they cast the man into the grave of Elisha and went on. But when the man touched the bones of Elisha, he revived and arose and stood on his feet.

JEHOASH OF ISRAEL AND AMAZIAH OF JUDAH, 13:22—14:22

Now Hazael, king of Syria, oppressed 22
Israel all the days of Jehoahaz. But the 23

LORD was gracious to them and had
compassion on them and turned toward
them because of his covenant with
Abraham, Isaac, and Jacob, and would
not destroy them, nor has he cast them
from his presence even until now.
24 But when Hazael, king of Syria, died,
Ben-hadad, his son, became king in his
25 stead. Then Jehoash, the son of Jehoahaz, took again from Ben-hadad,
the son of Hazael, the cities which he
had taken in the war from Jehoahaz,
his father. Three times Jehoash defeated him and recovered the cities of
Israel.
14 In the second year of Joash, the son
of Jehoahaz, king of Israel, Amaziah,
the son of Joash, king of Judah, became
2 king. He was twenty-five years old
when he became king, and he reigned
twenty-nine years in Jerusalem; and the
name of his mother was Jehoaddin of
3 Jerusalem. He did that which was right
in the sight of the LORD, yet not like
David his ancestor; he did just as Joash
4 his father had done. However, the high
places were not removed; the people
still continued to sacrifice and burn incense on the high places.
5 Now when the kingdom was firmly in
his grasp, he slew his servants who had
6 murdered the king his father. But the
children of the murderers he did not
kill according to that which is written
in the book of the law of Moses, as the
LORD commanded, saying,
"The fathers shall not be put to
death for the children, nor the children
be put to death for the fathers, but
everyone shall be put to death for his
own sin."
7 He slew of Edom in the Valley of Salt
ten thousand men, and took Sela by
storm, which has been named Joktheel
down to this day.
8 Then Amaziah sent messengers to
Jehoash, the son of Jehoahaz, the son
of Jehu, king of Israel, saying,
"Come, let us face each other."
9 But Jehoash, king of Israel, sent to
Amaziah, king of Judah, saying,
"The thistle that was in Lebanon
sent to the cedar which was in Lebanon,
saying, 'Give your daughter to my son
as wife.' But a wild beast that was in
Lebanon passed by and trampled down
10 the thistle. You have indeed conquered
Edom and it has turned your head.
Adorn yourself, but remain at home;

for why should you court trouble, so that you and Judah with you should fall?"

But Amaziah would not listen. So Jehoash, king of Israel, went up and they faced each other, he and Amaziah, king of Judah, at Beth-shemesh, which belongs to Judah. Judah, however, was defeated by Israel, so that they fled each to his home. Jehoash, king of Israel, captured Amaziah, king of Judah, the son of Jehoash, the son of Ahaziah, at Beth-shemesh; and he came to Jerusalem and tore down the wall of Jerusalem from the Gate of Ephraim to the Corner Gate, a distance of four hundred cubits. He also took all the gold and silver and all the utensils that were found in the house of the LORD and in the treasuries of the king's house and likewise hostages, and returned to Samaria.

Now the rest of the acts of Jehoash that he did and his prowess and how he fought with Amaziah, king of Judah, are they not written in the Book of the Chronicles of the Kings of Israel? So Jehoash slept with his fathers, and was buried in Samaria with the kings of Israel; and Jeroboam his son became king in his stead.

Now Amaziah, the son of Joash, king of Judah, lived after the death of Jehoash, the son of Jehoahaz, king of Israel, fifteen years. As for the rest of the records of Amaziah, are they not written in the Book of the Chronicles of the Kings of Judah? They made a conspiracy against him in Jerusalem; and he fled to Lachish, but they sent after him to Lachish and slew him there. Then they brought him upon horses and he was buried in Jerusalem with his fathers in the city of David. Then all the people of Judah took Azariah, who was sixteen years old, and made him king in the place of Amaziah his father. He built Elath and restored it to Judah after the king slept with his fathers.

JEROBOAM OF ISRAEL, 14:23–29

In the fifteenth year of Amaziah, the son of Joash, king of Judah, Jeroboam the son of Joash, king of Israel, became king in Samaria and reigned forty-one years. He did that which was evil in the sight of the LORD; he did not turn away from all the sins of Jeroboam, the son of Nebat, with which he made Israel sin. He restored the territory of Israel from the entrance of Hamath to the sea of the Arabah, according to the word of the LORD, the God of Israel, which he spoke by his servant Jonah, the son of Amittai, the prophet who was of Gath-hepher. For the LORD saw the very bitter affliction of Israel, that none was shut up nor left at large, and that there was no helper for Israel. But the LORD promised not to blot out the name of Israel from under the heavens; so he saved them by the hand of Jeroboam, the son of Joash.

Now the rest of the records of Jeroboam and all that he did and his prowess, how he fought with Damascus and how he turned away the wrath of the LORD against Israel, are they not written in the Book of the Chronicles of the Kings of Israel? So Jeroboam slept with his fathers, even with the kings of Israel, and Zechariah his son became king in his stead.

AZARIAH AND JOTHAM OF JUDAH, 15:1–7

In the twenty-seventh year of Jeroboam, king of Israel, Azariah, the son of Amaziah, king of Judah, became king. He was sixteen years old when he became king, and he reigned fifty-two years in Jerusalem; and his mother's name was Jecoliah of Jerusalem. He did that which was right in the sight of the LORD, just as Amaziah his father had done. Nevertheless, the high places were not taken away; the people still continued to sacrifice and burn incense on the high places. Therefore the LORD afflicted the king, so that he was a leper to the day of his death; and he dwelt in a separate house, while Jotham, the crown prince, was over the household, judging the people of the land. Now the rest of the records of Azariah and all that he did, are they not written in the Book of the Chronicles of the Kings of Judah? So Azariah slept with his fathers, and they buried him with his fathers in the city of David; and Jotham his son became king in his stead.

REVOLT AND COUNTER-REVOLT, 15:8–31

In the thirty-eighth year of Azariah, 8
king of Judah, Zechariah, the son of
Jeroboam, became king over Israel in
Samaria, and he reigned six months.
He did that which was evil in the sight 9
of the LORD, as his fathers had done;
he did not turn away from the sins of
Jeroboam, the son of Nebat, with which
he made Israel sin. Shallum, the son of 10
Jabesh, conspired against him, and attacked him in Ibleam and killed him
and became king in his stead.

Now the rest of the records of Zech- 11
ariah, behold, they are written in the
Book of the Chronicles of the Kings of
Israel.

This was the word of the LORD which 12
he spoke to Jehu, saying,
"Thy sons to the fourth generation
shall sit upon the throne of Israel."
And so it came about.

Shallum, the son of Jabesh, became 13
king in the thirty-ninth year of Uzziah,
king of Judah; and he reigned one
month in Samaria. Then Menahem, 14
the son of Gadi, went up from Tirzah,
and came to Samaria, and defeated
Shallum, the son of Jabesh, in Samaria,
and slew him and became king in his
stead. Now the rest of the records of 15
Shallum and his conspiracy which he
made, behold, they are written in the
Book of the Chronicles of the Kings of
Israel.

Then Menahem destroyed Tappuah 16
and all who were in it and its territory
from Tirzah on; because they did not
open it to him, therefore he destroyed
it, and all the women in it with child,
he disemboweled.

In the thirty-ninth year of Azariah, 17
king of Judah, Menahem, the son of
Gadi, became king over Israel, and
reigned ten years in Samaria. He did 18
that which was evil in the sight of the
LORD; he did not turn away from the
sins of Jeroboam, the son of Nebat,
with which he made Israel sin.

In his days Pul, king of Assyria, came 19
against the land. And Menahem gave
Pul a thousand talents of silver, that
his hand might be with him to establish
the kingdom under his rule. So Mena- 20
hem commanded Israel, even all the
men of wealth, to give to the king of
Assyria, fifty shekels of silver each. So

the king of Assyria withdrew, staying
no longer there in the land.
21 Now the rest of the records of Menahem and all that he did, are they not
written in the Book of the Chronicles of
22 the Kings of Israel? So Menahem slept
with his fathers, and Pekahiah his son
became king in his stead.
23 In the fiftieth year of Azariah, king
of Judah, Pekahiah, the son of Menahem, became king over Israel in Sa-
24 maria, and reigned two years. He did
that which was evil in the sight of the
LORD; he did not turn away from the
sins of Jeroboam, the son of Nebat,
25 with which he made Israel sin. Pekah,
the son of Remaliah, his third officer,
conspired against him and slew him in
Samaria in the castle of the king's
house; and with him were fifty Gileadites; and he slew him and became king
26 in his stead. Now the rest of the records
of Pekahiah and all that he did, behold,
they are written in the Book of the
Chronicles of the Kings of Israel.
27 In the fifty-second year of Azariah
king of Judah, Pekah, the son of Remaliah, became king over Israel in Sa-
28 maria, and reigned twenty years. He
did that which was evil in the sight of
the LORD; he did not turn away from
the sins of Jeroboam, the son of Nebat,
with which he made Israel sin.
29 In the days of Pekah, king of Israel,
Tiglath-pileser, king of Assyria, came
and captured Ijon, Abel-beth-maacah,
Janoah, Kedesh, Hazor, Gilead, and
Galilee, all the land of Naphtali, and
carried the inhabitants captive to Assyria.
30 Then Hoshea, the son of Elah, made
a conspiracy against Pekah, the son of
Remaliah, and overcame him and slew
him and became king in his stead in the
twentieth year of Jotham, the son of
31 Uzziah. Now the rest of the records of
Pekah and all that he did, behold, they
are written in the Book of the Chronicles of the Kings of Israel.

JOTHAM OF JUDAH, 15:32–38

32 In the second year of Pekah, the son
of Remaliah, king of Israel, Jotham, the
son of Uzziah, king of Judah, became
33 king. He was twenty-five years old
when he became king, and he reigned
sixteen years in Jerusalem; and his mother's name was Jerusha, the daughter of Zadok. He did that which was right in the sight of the LORD, just as Uzziah his father had done. Nevertheless the high places were not removed; the people still continued to sacrifice and burn incense on the high places. He built the upper gate of the house of the LORD. Now the rest of the records of Jotham and all that he did, are they not written in the Book of the Chronicles of the Kings of Judah?

In those days the LORD began to send against Judah Rezin, the king of Syria, and Pekah, the son of Remaliah. So Jotham slept with his fathers and was buried with his fathers in the city of David, his ancestor; and Ahaz his son became king in his stead.

AHAZ OF JUDAH AND THE SYRO-EPHRAIMITISH WAR, 16:1–20

In the seventeenth year of Pekah, the son of Remaliah, Ahaz, the son of Jotham, king of Judah, became king. Ahaz was twenty years old when he became king, and he reigned sixteen years in Jerusalem. He did not do that which was right in the sight of the LORD his God, as David his ancestor had done, but walked in the way of the kings of Israel. He also made his son to pass through the fire according to the abominations of the nations, whom the LORD had dispossessed before the Israelites. Moreover he sacrificed and burned incense on the high places and under every spreading tree.

Then Rezin, king of Syria, and Pekah, the son of Remaliah, king of Israel, came up to attack Jerusalem; and they besieged Ahaz, but were not able to come to blows with him. At that time the king of Edom recovered Elath for Edom and drove out the Judeans from Elath; and the Edomites came to Elath and have dwelt there to this day.

Now Ahaz had sent messengers to Tiglath-pileser, king of Assyria, saying, "I am your servant and your son; come up and deliver me from the hand of the king of Syria and from the hand of the king of Israel, who are besieging me."

Ahaz also took the silver and the gold

that were found in the house of the LORD and in the treasuries of the king's house, and sent them as a present to the king of Assyria. So the king of Assyria listened to him; and the king of Assyria went up to Damascus and captured it, and carried its inhabitants captive to Kir, and killed Rezin.

Now when King Ahaz went to meet Tiglath-pileser, king of Assyria, at Damascus, he saw the altar which was in Damascus. Then King Ahaz sent to Urijah the priest a model of the altar and its pattern according to all its workmanship. So Urijah the priest built an altar; according to all the directions that King Ahaz had sent from Damascus, even so did Urijah the priest make it, before King Ahaz came from Damascus. Therefore when the king came from Damascus and saw the altar, the king drew near to the altar and went up on it, and burned his burnt-offering and his cereal-offering, and poured his libation and dashed the blood of his thank-offerings against the altar. But the bronze altar that was before the LORD, he brought from the front of the temple, from between his altar and the house of the LORD, and put it on the north side of his altar. Then King Ahaz commanded Urijah the priest, saying,

"On the great altar burn the morning burnt-offering and the evening cereal-offering and the burnt-offering of the king and his cereal-offering, with the burnt-offerings of all the people of the land, and their cereal-offerings and their libations, and all the blood of the burnt-offering and all the blood of the sacrifice you shall dash against it; but the bronze altar shall be for me to inquire by."

Thus did Urijah the priest, just as King Ahaz commanded.

King Ahaz also cut off the border-frames of the stands and removed the lavers from them; he also took down the sea from the bronze oxen that were under it, and put it upon a stone pediment. And the foundation of the seat that they had built in the temple, and the outer entrance for the king he caused to turn from the house of the LORD on account of the king of Assyria.

Now the rest of the acts of Ahaz that he did, are they not written in the Book of the Chronicles of the Kings of Judah? So Ahaz slept with his fathers, and was buried with his fathers in the city of David; and Hezekiah his son became king in his stead.

THE FALL OF SAMARIA, 17:1–41

17 In the twelfth year of Ahaz, king of
Judah, Hoshea, the son of Elah, became
king over Israel in Samaria, and reigned
nine years. 2 He did that which was evil
in the sight of the LORD, yet not as the
kings of Israel who were before him.
3 Against him came up Shalmanezer,
king of Assyria; and Hoshea became his
servant and paid him tribute.
4 But when the king of Assyria found
Hoshea guilty of conspiracy—for he
had sent messengers to Sewe, king of
Egypt, and did not bring up tribute to
the king of Assyria, as he had done
year by year—the king of Assyria arrested
him and shut him up in prison.
5 Then the king of Assyria came up
against the whole land, and went up to
Samaria and besieged it three years. 6 In
the ninth year of Hoshea, the king of
Assyria took Samaria and carried Israel
away captive to Assyria and settled
them in Halah and on the Habor and
the river Gozan, and in the cities of the
Medes.
7 Now this came about because the
Israelites had sinned against the LORD
their God, who had brought them up
from the land of Egypt from the control
of Pharaoh, king of Egypt, and had
8 feared other gods, and walked in the
statutes of the nations whom the LORD
dispossessed before the Israelites. 9 The
Israelites uttered things that were not
right against the LORD their God and
built for themselves high places in all
their cities, from the watchtower even
10 to the fortified city, and set up for
themselves sacred pillars and sacred
poles on every high hill and under every
11 spreading tree, and offered sacrifices
there on all the high places, as did all
the nations whom the LORD had carried
away captive before them, and
they did evil things, thus provoking the
12 LORD to jealousy. They also served
idols in regard to which the LORD had
said to them,

"You shall not do this thing."

13 Yet the LORD warned Israel and Judah
by all his prophets and seers, saying,

"Turn from your evil ways and keep
my commands and my statutes in accordance with all the law which I commanded your fathers and which I sent
to you by my servants, the prophets."
14 However, they would not listen, but
were wilful, as were their fathers, who
did not believe in the LORD their God.
15 Moreover they rejected his statutes and
his covenant which he made with their
fathers, and his decrees which he decreed for them, and followed vanity and
became vain in accordance with the
nations who were round about them,
concerning whom the LORD had commanded them that they should not do
16 as they did. They forsook all the commands of the LORD their God and made
for themselves molten images, even two
calves, and made a sacred pole, and
worshiped all the host of the heavens
17 and served the Baal. They also made
their sons and their daughters pass
through the fire, and used divination
and sorcery, and sold themselves to do
evil in the sight of the LORD, thus pro-
18 voking him to jealousy. Therefore the
LORD was exceedingly angry with Israel and removed them out of his sight;
there was nothing left but the tribe of
Judah only.
19 Also Judah did not keep the commands of the LORD their God, but
walked in the statutes of Israel which
20 they made, so that the LORD rejected
the whole race of Israel and afflicted
them and gave them over to plunderers
until he had cast them out of his sight.
21 When he had torn Israel from the
house of David and they had made Jeroboam, the son of Nebat, king, Jeroboam drove Israel from following the
LORD and caused them to commit great
22 sin. So the Israelites walked in all the
sins of Jeroboam which he had committed; they departed not from them,
23 until the LORD removed Israel out of
his sight, as he spoke by all his servants
the prophets. So Israel was carried
away out of their own land to Assyria,
as it is to this day.
24 Moreover the king of Assyria brought
people from Babylon, Cuthah, Avva,
Hamath, and Sepharvaim and settled
them in the cities of Samaria in place of
the Israelites. So they took possession
of Samaria and dwelt in its cities.
25 Now at the beginning of their settling
there, they did not fear the LORD.

Therefore the LORD sent lions among them which were constantly killing some of them.

So they told the king of Assyria, saying,

"The nations which you have carried away and settled in the cities of Samaria do not know the custom of the god of the land; therefore he has sent lions among them and behold, they are constantly killing them, because they are not acquainted with the custom of the god of the land."

Then the king of Assyria gave command, saying,

"Send there one of the priests whom I carried away from there; and let him go and dwell there, and let him teach them the custom of the god of the land."

So one of the priests whom they carried away from Samaria came and dwelt in Bethel and taught them how they should fear the LORD. But each of the nations had made gods of their own and had placed them in the temples of the high places which the Samaritans had made, each people in their cities in which they dwelt. The men of Babylon had made Succoth-benoth, and the men of Cuth had made Nergal, and the men of Hamath had made Ashima, and the Avvites had made Nibhaz and Tartak and the Sepharvites burned their children in the fire to Adrammelech and Anammelech, the gods of Sepharvaim. But when they came to fear the LORD they made for themselves from their own number priests of the high places who acted for them in the temples of the high places. Thus they came to fear the LORD, but they also continued to serve their own gods, according to the custom of the nations from which they had been carried away. To this day they continue to do according to the earlier custom. They certainly do fear the LORD, but they do not follow his statutes and ordinances, nor the law nor the commands which the LORD commanded the descendants of Jacob whom he named Israel, with whom the LORD made a covenant and commanded them, saying,

"You shall not fear other gods, nor worship them, nor serve them, nor sacrifice to them; but the LORD who brought you up from the land of Egypt with great power and with an out tretched arm, him you shall fear, and ıim shall you worship and to him shall ʼou sacrifice; and the statutes and the ›rdinances and the law and the com- nand which he wrote for you, you shall ›e careful to observe forever, but you hall not fear other gods; and the cove- ıant that I have made with you, you hall not forget, neither shall you fear ›ther gods. But the LORD your God ʼou shall fear; and he will deliver you rom the hand of all your enemies."

However, they would not listen, but ontinued to do according to their earlier ustom. So while these peoples came to ear the LORD, they were also serving heir carved images; moreover their hildren and their children's children— s their fathers did, so do they continue o do to this day.

HEZEKIAH OF JUDAH AND SENNACHERIB'S INVASION, 18:1—19:37

Now in the third year of Hoshea, the on of Elah, king of Israel, Hezekiah, he son of Ahaz, king of Judah, became ing. He was twenty-five years old vhen he became king, and he reigned wenty-nine years in Jerusalem; and ıis mother's name was Abi, the daugh- er of Zechariah. He did that which vas right in the sight of the LORD just s David his ancestor had done.

He removed the high places and ›roke down the sacred pillars and cut lown the sacred poles. He also broke in ›ieces the bronze serpent that Moses ıad made; for as late as those days the sraelites offered sacrifices to it; and hey called it Nehushtan. He trusted n the LORD, the God of Israel; so that fter him there was none like him among ll the kings of Judah, nor among those vho were before him. For he was loyal o the LORD, he turned not away from ollowing him, but kept his commands vhich the LORD had commanded Moses.

Moreover the LORD was with him; n all his ventures he prospered, and he ebelled against the king of Assyria, and ıo longer served him. He conquered he Philistines as far as Gaza and its erritory from the watchtower to the ortified city.

Now in the fourth year of King Hezekiah—that is, the seventh year of
Hoshea, the son of Elah—Shalmaneser,
king of Assyria, came up against Samaria and besieged it. They took it at 10
the end of three years, in the sixth year
of Hezekiah—that is, in the ninth year
of Hoshea, king of Israel, was Samaria
taken. Then the king of Assyria carried 11
Israel away to Assyria and settled them
in Halah and on the Habor and the
river Gozan, and in the cities of the
Medes, because they did not listen to 12
the voice of the LORD their God, but
transgressed his covenant, even all that
Moses the servant of the LORD had
commanded, and would neither listen
nor keep it.

Now in the fourteenth year of King 13
Hezekiah, Sennacherib, king of Assyria,
came up against all the fortified cities
of Judah and captured them. Then 14
Hezekiah, king of Judah, sent to the
king of Assyria to Lachish, saying,
"I have offended; withdraw from me;
whatever you lay on me I will bear."
So the king of Assyria made Hezekiah,
king of Judah, pay three hundred talents of silver and thirty talents of gold.
So Hezekiah gave him all the silver that 15
was found in the house of the LORD,
and in the treasuries of the king's house.
At that time Hezekiah stripped the 16
doors of the temple of the LORD and
the columns, which Hezekiah, king of
Judah, had overlaid, and gave the gold
to the king of Assyria.

Then the king of Assyria sent the 17
commander-in-chief, and the chief of
the eunuchs and the field marshal from
Lachish with a large army against King
Hezekiah at Jerusalem. So they went
up, and when they came to Jerusalem,
they came and took up their position
by the conduit of the upper pool, which
is on the highway to the laundrymen's
field.

Now when they called for the king, 18
Eliakim, the son of Hilkiah, who was
the steward of the palace, and Shebna,
the scribe, and Joah, the son of Asaph,
the recorder, went out to them. Then 19
the field marshal said to them,

"Say now to Hezekiah, 'Thus says
the great king, the king of Assyria:
"What confidence is this in which you
trust? Do you think that a mere word 20
of the lips is counsel and strength for
war? Now in whom do you trust that
you have rebelled against me? You 21

have put your trust evidently in the
staff of this broken reed, Egypt, on
which if a man lean, it will run into his
hand and pierce it. So is Pharaoh, king
22 of Egypt, to all who trust in him. But
if you say to me, 'We trust in the LORD
our God,' is not he the one whose high
places and altars Hezekiah has taken
away, saying to Judah and Jerusalem,
'You shall worship before this altar in
23 Jerusalem?' And now, pray make a
wager with my master, the king of Assyria: I will give you two thousand
horses, if you are able on your part to
24 set riders upon them. How then can you
repulse the attack of one of the least of
my master's servants? Yet you trust
in Egypt for chariots and horsemen.
25 Now have I come up against this place
to destroy it without the LORD'S approval? The LORD himself said to me,
'Go up against this land and destroy
it.' " '"
26 Then Elkanah, the son of Hilkiah,
and Shebna and Joah said to the field
marshal,
"Speak now to your servants in Aramaic, for we understand it; but do not
speak to us in Judean in the hearing of
the people who are on the wall."
27 But the field marshal said to them,
"Was it to your master and you that
my master sent me to speak these
words? Was it not rather to the men
who are sitting on the wall, doomed
with you to eat their own excrement
and drink their own urine?"
28 Then the field marshal stood up and
cried with a loud voice in Judean and
spoke, saying,
"Hear the word of the great king, the
29 king of Assyria! Thus says the king:
'Do not let Hezekiah deceive you; for
he will not be able to deliver you from
30 his hand. Neither let Hezekiah cause
you to trust in the LORD by saying,
"The LORD will surely deliver us; this
city shall not be given into the hand of
31 the king of Assyria." Do not listen to
Hezekiah; for thus says the king of Assyria: "Make peace with me and surrender to me; and eat each of you from
his own vine and his own fig tree and
32 drink the water of his own cistern, until
I come and take you away to a land like
your own, a land of grain and wine, a
land of bread and vineyards, a land of
olive trees and honey, that you may
live and not die." But do not listen to

Hezekiah, when he would lure you or
by saying, "The LORD will deliver us.'
Has any of the gods of the nations delivered his land from the hand of the
king of Assyria? Where are the gods of
Hamath and Arpad? Where are the
gods of Sepharvaim, Hena, and Ivvah?
Where are the gods of Samaria? Did
they deliver Samaria from my hand?
Who were there among all the gods of
the lands that delivered their land from
my hand, that the LORD should deliver
Jerusalem from my hand?' "

Then the people were silent and answered him not a word; for the king's
command was, "Do not answer him."

Then Eliakim, the son of Hilkiah
who was steward of the palace, and
Shebna, the scribe, and Joah, the son of
Asaph, the recorder, came to Hezekiah
with their garments torn, and told him
the words of the field marshal.

As soon as King Hezekiah heard it
he tore his garments, covered himself
with sackcloth, and went into the house
of the LORD. He also sent Eliakim who
was steward of the palace and Shebna
the scribe, and the oldest of the priests
covered with sackcloth, to the prophet
Isaiah, the son of Amoz. They said to
him,

"Thus says Hezekiah: 'This is a day
of distress, rebuke, and disgrace; for
children have come to the birth, and
there is no strength to bear them. It
may be that the LORD your God will
hear all the words of the field marshal
whom his master, the king of Assyria
has sent to insult the living God, and
will rebuke the words which the LORD
your God has heard. Therefore lift up a
prayer for the remnant that is left.' "

But when the servants of King Hezekiah came to Isaiah, Isaiah said to them

"Thus shall you say to your master
'Thus says the LORD: "Do not be
afraid of the words that you have heard
with which the menials of the king of
Assyria have blasphemed me. Behold
I will put a spirit in him, so that when
he hears a certain rumor he shall return
to his own land, and I will cause him to
fall by the sword in his own land." ' "

Then the field marshal returned, and
found the king of Assyria warring
against Libnah; for he had heard that
he had left Lachish. But when he heard
concerning Tirhakah, king of Ethiopia
"Behold, he has come out to fight

against you," he sent messengers again
to Hezekiah, saying,
0 "Thus shall you say to Hezekiah,
king of Judah: 'Do not let your God in
whom you trust deceive you, saying,
"Jerusalem shall not be given into the
1 hand of the king of Assyria." You have
surely heard what the kings of Assyria
have done to all the lands in completely
destroying them, and will you be de-
2 livered? Did the gods of the nations
which my fathers destroyed deliver
them—Gozan, Haran, Rezeph, and the
3 Edenites who were in Telassar? Where
is the king of Hamath, the king of Arpad, and the king of the city of Sepharvaim, of Hena, and of Ivvah?'"
4 So Hezekiah received the letter from
the hand of the messengers and read it.
Then Hezekiah went up to the house of
the LORD and spread it out before the
5 LORD; and Hezekiah prayed before the
LORD and said,
"O LORD, the God of Israel, who art
seated upon the cherubim, thou art
God, even thou alone, over all the kingdoms of the earth; thou hast made the
6 heavens and the earth. Incline thine
ear, O LORD, and hear; open thine eyes,
O LORD, and see, and hear all the
words of Sennacherib, which he has
7 sent to insult the living God. Of a
truth, O LORD, the kings of Assyria
have laid waste the nations and their
8 land, and have cast their gods into the
fire, for they were no gods, but the work
of men's hands, wood and stone; and so
9 they have destroyed them. But now, O
LORD our God, deliver us from his
hand, that all the kingdoms of the earth
may know that thou, O LORD, art God
alone."
0 Then Isaiah, the son of Amoz, sent to
Hezekiah, saying,
"Thus says the LORD, the God of
Israel: 'What you have prayed to me
concerning Sennacherib, king of As-
1 syria, I have heard.' This is the word
that the LORD has spoken against him:
'She despises you, laughs at you—
the virgin daughter of Zion!
Behind you she wags the head—
the daughter of Jerusalem!
2 Whom have you insulted and blasphemed?
Against whom have you raised your
voice,
And lifted up your eyes on high?
against the Holy one of Israel!
By the hand of your messengers 23
you have insulted the Lord and
have said,
"With the multitude of my chariots
I ascended the mountain heights,
the recesses of Lebanon;
And I felled its tallest cedars,
its choicest cypresses;
And I entered its remotest retreat,
its densest thicket.
I dug down, 24
and drank foreign waters;
And with the soles of my feet I dried
up
all the streams of Egypt."
Have you not heard 25
how I prepared it long ago,
How I planned it in days of old,
and now have brought it to
pass—
That you should turn fortified cities
into ruin heaps,
While their inhabitants, shorn of their 26
strength,
are dismayed and confounded,
Are become like grass of the field,
like tender green grass,
Like grass on the housetops,
blasted before it is grown up.
I know your rising and sitting, 27
your going and coming,
and your raging against me.
Because you have raged against me
and your arrogance has come 28
up to my ears,
Therefore I will put my hook in your
nose
and my bridle in your lips,
And I will cause you to return by the
way
by which you came.'"
"'And this shall be a sign for you: 29
You shall eat this year that which grows
of itself, and in the second year that
which springs from the same; but in the
third year sow and reap, plant vineyards and eat their fruit. The remnant 30
that survives of the house of Judah
shall again take root downward and
bear fruit upward; for out of Jerusalem 31
shall go forth a remnant and from
Mount Zion an escaped band. The zeal
of the LORD shall accomplish this.'
"Therefore thus says the LORD con- 32
cerning the king of Assyria: 'He shall
not enter this city, or shoot an arrow
there; neither shall he come before it
with shield, or cast up a mound against
it. By the way that he came, by the 33

same shall he return; but he shall not
enter this city,' is the LORD'S oracle.
34 'For I will defend and save this city
for my own sake and for the sake of my
servant David.' "
35 Now that night the angel of the
LORD went forth and slew in the camp
of the Assyrians one hundred and
eighty-five thousand; and when men
rose early next morning, they were all
dead bodies.
36 Then Sennacherib, king of Assyria,
set out and went and returned, and
37 dwelt at Nineveh. But as he was worshiping in the temple of Nisroch his
god, Adrammelech and Sarezer slew
him with the sword, and they escaped
into the land of Ararat; and Esarhaddon
his son became king in his stead.

HEZEKIAH'S SICKNESS AND ISAIAH'S PREDICTION, 20:1–11

20 In those days Hezekiah became dan-
gerously ill; and Isaiah the prophet, the
son of Amoz, came to him and said,
"Thus says the LORD: 'Set your
house in order for you shall die and not
live.' "
2 Then he turned his face to the wall,
and prayed to the LORD, saying,
3 "Remember now, O LORD, I pray
thee, how I have walked before thee in
truth and sincerity of heart, and have
done that which was good in thy sight."
4 Hezekiah also wept profusely. Now
before Isaiah had gone out of the middle courtyard, the word of the LORD
came to him saying,
5 "Return and say to Hezekiah, the
prince of my people, 'Thus says the
LORD, the God of David your father:
"I have heard your prayer, I have seen
your tears; see, I will heal you; on the
third day you shall go up to the house
6 of the LORD. I will also add fifteen
more years to your life, and I will deliver you and this city from the hand of
the king of Assyria, and I will defend
this city for my own sake and for the
sake of my servant David." ' "
7 Isaiah also said,
"Let them take a cake of figs, and
place it upon the boil that he may recover."
8 Then Hezekiah said to Isaiah,
"What will be the sign that the
LORD will heal me, and that I shall go
up to the house of the LORD the third
day?"
So Isaiah said,
"This will be the sign to you from the
LORD, that the LORD will do the thing
that he has promised: shall the shadow
go forward ten steps, or back ten
steps?"
Hezekiah said, 10
"It is easy for the shadow to go forward ten steps; rather let the shadow
turn back ten steps."
So Isaiah the prophet cried to the 11
LORD; and he brought back the shadow
the ten steps which it had gone down
on the sundial of Ahaz.

THE BABYLONIAN MISSION AND ISAIAH'S DISAPPROVAL, 20:12–21

At that time Merodach-baladan, the 12
son of Baladan, king of Babylon, sent
ambassadors with a present to Hezekiah; for he had heard that Hezekiah
had been sick. Hezekiah was pleased 13
with them, and showed them all his
treasure-house, the silver, the gold, the
spices, the fine oil, and his armory—all
that was found among his treasures;
there was nothing in his house or in all
his kingdom that Hezekiah did not
show them.
Then Isaiah the prophet came to 14
King Hezekiah and said to him,
"What did these men say, and from
where have they come to you?"
"They have come from a distant
land, from Babylon," said Hezekiah.
"What did they see in your house?" 15
he said.
"They have seen all that is in my
house," said Hezekiah; "there was
nothing among my treasures that I did
not show them."
Then Isaiah said to Hezekiah, 16
"Hear the word of the LORD, 'Behold, 17
days are coming when all that is in your
house and that which your fathers have
stored up to this day shall be carried
away to Babylon; nothing shall be left,'
says the LORD. 'Also some of your sons 18
who shall be your issue, whom you shall
beget, they shall take, and they shall
become eunuchs in the palace of the
king of Babylon.' "
Then Hezekiah said to Isaiah, 19

"Good is the word of the LORD which
you have spoken."
For he thought,
"Shall it not be so, if there be peace
and security in my time?"
20 Now the rest of the records of Hezekiah and all of his prowess and how he
made the pool and the conduit and
brought water into the city, are they
not written in the Book of the Chronicles of the Kings of Judah? So Hezekiah slept with his fathers, and Manasseh his son became king in his stead.

REACTION UNDER MANASSEH AND AMON, 21:1–26

Manasseh was twelve years old when
he became king, and he reigned fifty-
five years in Jerusalem; and his mother's
2 name was Hephzibah. He did that
which was evil in the sight of the LORD,
according to the abominations of the
nations which the LORD dispossessed
3 before the Israelites. For he built again
the high places which Hezekiah his
father had destroyed, and he erected
altars for the Baal, and made a sacred
pole as Ahab, king of Israel, had done,
and worshiped all the host of the
4 heavens and served them. He also built
altars in the house of the LORD of
which the LORD had said,
"In Jerusalem will I put my name."
5 Moreover he built altars for all the
host of the heavens in the two courts of
6 the house of the LORD. Likewise he
caused his son to pass through the fire
and practiced augury and witchcraft
and he used to appoint necromancers
and wizards. He did much evil in the
sight of the LORD, thus provoking him
to jealousy.
7 He also set up the carved image of an
Asherah that he had made, in the
temple of which the LORD had said to
David and to Solomon his son,
"In this house and in Jerusalem,
which I have chosen out of all the tribes
of Israel, I will put my name forever,
8 and I will not cause the feet of Israel to
wander any more out of the land which
I gave to their fathers, if only they will
be careful to do just as I have commanded them, and according to all the
law that my servant Moses commanded
them."
9 But they did not listen, and Manasseh seduced them to do evil more than
did the nations which the LORD destroyed before the Israelites. Then the 10
LORD spoke by his servants the
prophets, saying,
"Because Manasseh, king of Judah, 11
has done these abominations and has
done more wickedly than all that the
Amorites did who were before him, and
has made Judah also sin with his idols,
therefore, thus says the LORD, the God 12
of Israel: 'Behold I am about to bring
such evil on Jerusalem and Judah, that
both ears of him who hears of it shall
tingle. I will also stretch over Jerusalem 13
the measuring line of Samaria, and the
plummet of the house of Ahab; and I
will wipe Jerusalem as one wipes a dish,
wiping and turning it upside down.
Moreover I will cast off the remnant of 14
my inheritance and deliver them into
the hand of their enemies, that they
may become a prey and a spoil to all
their enemies, because they have done 15
that which was evil in my sight and
have aroused me to anger, since the day
their fathers came forth from Egypt,
even to this day.' "
Furthermore Manasseh shed very 16
much innocent blood until he had filled
Jerusalem from one end to the other,
besides his sin with which he caused
Judah to sin, in doing that which was
evil in the sight of the LORD.
Now the rest of the records of Manas- 17
seh and all that he did, and his sin
which he committed, are they not
written in the Book of the Chronicles
of the Kings of Judah? So Manasseh 18
slept with his fathers and was buried in
the garden of his house, in the garden
of Uzzah; and Amon his son became
king in his stead.
Amon was twenty-two years old 19
when he became king, and he reigned
two years in Jerusalem; and his mother's
name was Meshullemeth, the daughter
of Haruz of Jotbah. He did that which 20
was evil in the sight of the LORD, as
Manasseh his father had done. He 21
walked in all the way wherein his father
had walked, and served the idols which
his father served, and worshiped them.
He forsook the LORD, the God of his 22
fathers, and walked not in the way of
the LORD.
At length the servants of Amon con- 23
spired against him and slew the king in
his house. But the people of the land 24

slew all the conspirators against King
Amon; and the people of the land made
25 Josiah his son king in his stead. Now
the rest of the acts of Amon which he
did, are they not written in the Book of
the Chronicles of the Kings of Judah?
26 So they buried him in the grave of his
father in the garden of Uzzah; and
Josiah his son became king in his stead.

JOSIAH'S REFORM, 22:1—23:30

22 Josiah was eight years old when he
became king, and he reigned thirty-one
years in Jerusalem; and the name of his
mother was Jedidah, the daughter of
2 Adaiah of Bozkath. He did that which
was right in the sight of the LORD and
walked in all the way of David his ancestor, turning neither to the right nor
the left.
3 Now in the eighteenth year of King
Josiah, the king sent Shaphan, the son
of Azaliah, the son of Meshullam the
scribe, to the house of the LORD, saying,
4 "Go up to Hilkiah the high priest,
that he may take the sum of the money
which has been brought into the house
of the LORD, which the keepers of the
threshold have collected from the
5 people. Let them deliver it into the
hands of the workmen who have the
oversight of the house of the LORD,
that they may give it to the workmen
who are in the house of the LORD, to
6 make the repairs on the temple—to the
carpenters and the builders and the
masons, also for buying timber and
hewn stone to repair the temple."
7 However, there was no reckoning
made with them regarding the money
delivered to them, for they dealt faithfully.
8 At that time Hilkiah the high priest
said to Shaphan the scribe,
"I have found a book of law in the
house of the LORD."
So Hilkiah gave the book to Shaphan,
9 and he read it. Then Shaphan the
scribe went to the king and reported to
the king, saying,
"Your servants have emptied out the
money found in the temple and have
delivered it into the charge of the workmen who have charge of the house of
the LORD."
10 Shaphan the scribe also told the king,
saying,

"Hilkiah the priest gave me a book."
Then Shaphan read it before the
king.
Now when the king heard the words 11
of the book of law, he tore his garments.
Then the king commanded Hilkiah the 12
priest, and Ahikam, the son of Shaphan,
and Achbor, the son of Michaiah, and
Shaphan the scribe, and Asaiah, the
king's servant, saying,
"Go, inquire of the LORD for me and 13
for the people and for all Judah, concerning the words of this book that has
been found; for great is the wrath of the
LORD that is kindled against us, because our fathers have not listened to
the words of this book, to conform to
all that is written in it concerning us."
So Hilkiah the priest and Ahikam 14
and Achbor and Shaphan and Asaiah
went to Huldah the prophetess, the
wife of Shallum, the son of Tikvah, the
son of Harhas, keeper of the wardrobe,
who dwelt in Jerusalem in the second
quarter, and they spoke to her. So she 15
said to them,
"Thus says the LORD, the God of
Israel: 'Say to the man who sent you to
me, "Thus says the LORD: 'Behold, I 16
am about to bring evil upon this place
and upon its inhabitants, namely, all
the words of the book which the king of
Judah has read. Because they have 17
forsaken me and have sacrificed to
other gods, thus provoking me to
jealousy with all the work of their
hands, therefore my wrath shall be kindled against this place and it shall not
be quenched.' " ' But to the king of 18
Judah who sent you to inquire of the
LORD, thus shall you say to him:
'Thus says the LORD, the God of Israel:
"Regarding the words which you have
heard—because your heart was peni- 19
tent and you humbled yourself before
the LORD, when you heard what I
spoke against this place and against
its inhabitants, that they should become
a desolation and a curse, and tore your
garments and wept before me, I also
have heard you," is the oracle of the
LORD. "Therefore behold, I will gather 20
you to your fathers and you shall be
gathered to your grave in peace; neither
shall your eyes see all the evil which I
am about to bring upon this place." ' "
So they brought back word to the
king.
Then the king sent, and they

gathered to him all the elders of Judah
and Jerusalem. Thereupon the king
went up to the house of the LORD together with all the men of Judah and
all the inhabitants of Jerusalem, and
the priests and the prophets, and all
the people, both small and great; and
he read in their hearing all the words of
the book of the covenant which was
3 found in the house of the LORD. Then
the king stood by the column and made
a covenant before the LORD, to walk
after the LORD and to keep his commands, his decrees, and his statutes
with all his mind and heart, to establish
the words of this covenant that were
written in this book. And all the people
confirmed the covenant.

4 Then the king commanded Hilkiah,
the high priest, and the second priest
and the keepers of the threshold to
bring out of the temple of the LORD all
the vessels that were made for the Baal
and the Asherah and for all the host of
the heavens; and he burned them outside Jerusalem in the limekilns by the
Kidron, and carried their ashes to
5 Bethel. He also did away with the
idolatrous priests, whom the kings of
Judah had ordained to offer sacrifices
in the high places in the cities of Judah
and in the sanctuaries around Jerusalem; and those who offered sacrifices to
the Baal, to the sun, the moon, and the
constellations, and all the host of the
6 heavens. Moreover he brought the
Asherah from the house of the LORD
outside Jerusalem to the Brook Kidron
and burned it at the Brook Kidron, and
ground it to powder, and cast the powder of it upon the graves of the common
7 people. Furthermore he tore down the
houses of the devotees of the fertility
cult which were in the house of the
LORD, where the women wove tunics
8 for the Asherah. Then he brought all
the priests from the cities of Judah and
defiled the high places, where the
priests offered sacrifices, from Geba to
Beersheba. He also tore down the high
places of the Satyrs, which stood at the
entrance of the gate of Joshua, the governor of the city, which were on the
9 left as one enters the city gate. However, the priests of the high places did
not come up to the altar of the LORD in
Jerusalem, but ate unleavened cakes
10 among their kinsmen. He also defiled
Topheth, which is in the valley of Ben-
Hinnom, that no man might make his
son or his daughter pass through the
fire to Molech. He took away the 11
horses which the kings of Judah had
given to the sun, at the entrance of the
house of the LORD, by the chamber of
Nathan-melech, the eunuch, which was
among the summer houses, and he
burned the chariots of the sun. The 12
altars which were on the roof, the upper
chamber of Ahaz which the kings of
Judah had made, and the altars which
Manasseh had made in the two courts
of the house of the LORD, the king demolished and beat them down there,
and cast the dust into the Brook Kidron. Moreover the high places that 13
were east of Jerusalem, to the south of
the hill of destruction, which Solomon,
the king of Israel, had built for Ashtart,
the abomination of the Sidonians, and
for Chemosh, the abomination of Moab,
and for Milcom, the abomination of the
Ammonites, the king defiled. He shat- 14
tered the sacred pillars, and cut down
the sacred poles, and filled their places
with the bones of men.

Likewise the altar that was at Bethel, 15
and the high place which Jeroboam, the
son of Nebat, had made, who caused
Israel to sin, even that altar and the
high place he demolished and shattered
its stones, grinding them to powder,
and burned the sacred pole.

Now when Josiah turned and saw the 16
graves that were there on the mount,
he sent and took the bones out of the
graves and burned them on the altar
and defiled it according to the word of
the LORD which the man of God proclaimed, who proclaimed these things.

"What is yonder tombstone that I 17
see?" he said.

Then the men of the city said to him,
"It is the grave of the man of God,
who came from Judah and proclaimed
that which you have done against the
altar of Bethel."

"Let him be," he said; "let no one 18
move his bones."

So his bones rescued the bones of the
prophet who came from Samaria.

Also all the temples of the high places 19
that were in the cities of Samaria, which
the kings of Israel had made, thus provoking the LORD to jealousy, Josiah
took away and did to them just as he
had done to Bethel. Moreover all the 20
priests of the high places, who were

there, he slew upon the altars and
burned men's bones upon them. Then
he returned to Jerusalem.
21 Thereupon the king commanded all
the people, saying,
"Keep the passover to the LORD
your God, as it is written in this book of
the covenant."
22 For such a passover as this had not
been kept from the days of the judges
who judged Israel, and during all the
days of the kings of Israel and the kings
23 of Judah; but in the eighteenth year of
King Josiah this passover was kept to
24 the LORD in Jerusalem. Moreover the
necromancers and the wizards and the
teraphim, the idols and all the abominations that were seen in the land of
Judah and in Jerusalem Josiah put
away, that he might establish the words
of the law which were written in the
book which Hilkiah the priest found in
25 the house of the LORD. There was no
king like him before him, who turned to
the LORD with all his mind and all his
heart and with all his strength in accordance with all the law of Moses;
neither did there arise after him any
26 like him. However the LORD did not
turn from the fierceness of his great
anger, since his anger was kindled
against Judah because of all the provo-
cations with which Manasseh had pro-
27 voked him. So the LORD said,
"Judah also I will remove from my
sight, as I removed Israel, and I will
cast off this city which I have chosen,
even Jerusalem, and the temple of
which I said, 'My name shall be
there.'"
28 Now the rest of the records of Josiah
and all that he did, are they not written
in the Book of the Chronicles of the
Kings of Judah?
29 In his days Pharaoh-necho, king of
Egypt, went up unto the king of Assyria to the River Euphrates; and King
Josiah went to meet him; and Pharaoh-
necho slew him at Megiddo, as soon as
30 he saw him. Then his servants transported his dead body in a chariot from
Megiddo and brought him to Jerusalem,
and buried him in his own grave. Thereupon the people of the land took Jehoahaz, the son of Josiah, and anointed
him and made him king in place of his
father.

THE LAST DAYS OF JUDAH, 23:31—25:30

Jehoahaz was twenty-three years old when he became king and he reigned three months in Jerusalem, and the name of his mother was Hamutal, the daughter of Jeremiah of Libnah. He did that which was evil in the sight of the LORD, just as his fathers had done. Then Pharaoh-necho imprisoned him in Riblah in the land of Hamath, that he might not reign in Jerusalem, and he put the land under an indemnity of a hundred talents of silver and a talent of gold. Pharaoh-necho then made Eliakim, the son of Josiah, king in place of Josiah his father, and changed his name to Jehoiakim. But he took Jehoahaz and brought him to Egypt, where he died. So Jehoiakim gave the silver and the gold to Pharaoh, but he had to lay a forced levy on the land in order to give the money according to the demand of Pharaoh. From each according to his ability he exacted the silver and the gold of the people of the land to give it to Pharaoh-necho.

Jehoiakim was twenty-five years old when he became king and he reigned eleven years in Jerusalem; and his mother's name was Zebidah, the daughter of Pedaiah of Rumah. He did that which was evil in the sight of the LORD, just as his fathers had done.

In his days Nebuchadnezzar, king of Babylon, came up, and Jehoiakim became subject to him for three years; then he turned and rebelled against him. The LORD sent against him marauding bands of Chaldeans, Syrians, Moabites, and Ammonites; thus he sent them against Judah to destroy it, according to the word of the LORD, which he had spoken by his servants the prophets. Surely at the command of the LORD this came upon Judah to remove it out of his sight, because of the sins of Manasseh, in accordance with all that he had done, and also because of the innocent blood which he had shed, for he filled Jerusalem with innocent blood; therefore the LORD would not pardon. Now the rest of the records of Jehoiakim and all that he did, are they not written in the Book of the Chronicles of the Kings of Judah? So Jehoiakim slept with his fathers, and Jehoiachin his son became king in his

stead. The king of Egypt came up no
more out of his land; for the king of
Babylon had taken all that had belonged to the king of Egypt from the
Brook of Egypt to the River Euphrates.
8 Jehoiachin was eighteen years old
when he became king and he reigned
three months in Jerusalem; and his
mother's name was Nehushta, the
daughter of Elnathan of Jerusalem. He
did that which was evil in the sight of
the LORD, just as his fathers had done.
10 At that time the servants of Nebuchadnezzar, king of Babylon, came up
against Jerusalem, and the city was
besieged. Nebuchadnezzar, king of
Babylon, also came to the city while his
12 servants were besieging it; and Jehoiachin, king of Judah, went out to the
king of Babylon, he and his mother, his
servants, and his nobles and his eunuchs. The king of Babylon took him
captive in the eighth year of his reign.
13 He also took forth from there all the
treasures of the house of the LORD and
the treasures of the king's house and he
broke up all the vessels of gold which
Solomon, king of Israel, had made in
the temple of the LORD, as the LORD
14 had said. Moreover he carried away
captive all of Jerusalem and all the
nobles and all the renowned warriors,
even ten thousand captives, and all the
craftsmen and the smiths: none were
left, except the poorest people of the
15 land. Thus he carried away Jehoiachin
to Babylon; and the king's mother and
the king's wives, and his eunuchs, and
the chief men of the land, he caused to
go into captivity from Jerusalem to
16 Babylon. Also all the men of ability,
even seven thousand, and the craftsmen and the smiths a thousand, all the
strong men fit for war, them the king of
17 Babylon took captive to Babylon. Then
the king of Babylon made Mattaniah,
Jehoiachin's uncle, king in his stead,
and changed his name to Zedekiah.
18 Zedekiah was twenty-one years old
when he became king, and he reigned
eleven years in Jerusalem; and his
mother's name was Hamutal, the
19 daughter of Jeremiah of Libnah. He
did that which was evil in the sight of
the LORD, just as Jehoiachin had done.
20 For, in accordance with the anger of the
LORD, it continued against Jerusalem
and Judah until he had cast them out of
25 his presence. Then Zedekiah rebelled
against the king of Babylon. Thereupon in the ninth year of his reign, on
the tenth day of the tenth month,
Nebuchadnezzar king of Babylon came,
he and all his army, against Jerusalem,
encamped against it, and built a siege
wall around it; and the city remained 2
under siege until the eleventh year of
King Zedekiah. On the ninth day of the 3
fourth month, when the famine was so
severe in the city that there was no
bread for the common people, the city 4
was breached, and the king and all the
soldiers fled by night by way of the
gate between the two walls, which was
by the king's garden, while the Chaldeans were beleaguering the city, and
went in the direction of the Arabah.
But the army of the Chaldeans pursued 5
the king and overtook him in the
steppes of Jericho, all his army having
scattered from him. Then they took the
king and brought him up to the king of 6
Babylon at Riblah; and they pronounced judgment against him. They 7
also slew the sons of Zedekiah before his
eyes and put out his eyes and bound
him in fetters and carried him to Babylon.

In the fifth month, on the seventh 8
day of the month—this was in the
nineteenth year of King Nebuchadnezzar, king of Babylon—Nebuzaradan,
the commander of the guard, a servant
of the king of Babylon, came to Jerusalem and burned the house of the 9
LORD and the king's house; and all the
houses of Jerusalem, even every great
house he burned. All the army of the 10
Chaldeans, who were with the commander of the guard, broke down
the walls of Jerusalem round about.
Also the rest of the people who were left 11
in the city and the deserters who had
deserted to the king of Babylon and the
rest of the rabble, Nebuzaradan, the
commander of the guard, carried away
captive. But the commander of the 12
guard left some of the poorest of
the land as vinedressers and plowmen.
Moreover, the bronze pillars of the 13
house of the LORD, the stands, and the
bronze sea that were in the house of the
LORD, the Chaldeans broke up and
carried the bronze from them to Babylon. Also the pots, the shovels, the 14
snuffers, the bowls, and all the vessels
of bronze with which the service was
conducted, they took away. Likewise 15

the firepans and the basins, what was
of gold, the commander of the guard
took away as gold, and what was of
16 silver as silver—besides the two columns, the one sea, and the stands which
Solomon had made for the house of the
LORD, the bronze of all these vessels
17 being beyond weight. The height of
each column was eighteen cubits, and a
bronze capital surmounted it; and the
height of the capital was three cubits,
with network and pomegranates round
about the capital, all of bronze; and the
second column had the same, with network.
18 Then the commander of the guard
took Seraiah, the chief priest, and
Zephaniah, the second priest, with the
19 three keepers of the threshold. And
from the city he took a eunuch who had
charge of the soldiers, and five of the
personal companions of the king who
were found in the city, the scribe of the
commander of the army who mustered
the people of the land, and sixty men
of the people of the land who were
20 found in the city. Having taken them,
Nebuzaradan, the commander of the
guard, brought them to the king of
21 Babylon at Riblah. Then the king of
Babylon struck them down and put
them to death at Riblah in the land of
Hamath. Thus was Judah carried captive from its land.
22 Now over the people who were left in
the land of Judah whom Nebuchadnezzar, king of Babylon, had left, he appointed Gedaliah, the son of Ahikam,
23 the son of Shaphan. When all the commanders of the forces together with
their men heard that the king of Babylon had appointed Gedaliah, they came
to Gedaliah, to Mizpeh, namely, Ishmael, the son of Nethaniah, Johanan,
the son of Kareah, Seraiah, the son of
Tanhumeth the Netophathite, and Ja-
zaniah, the son of the Maacathite, together with their men. Thereupon Gedaliah swore to them and to their men,
and said to them,

"Fear not because of the servants of
the Chaldeans; settle in the land and
serve the king of Babylon, and it will
be well with you."

But in the seventh month, Ishmael,
the son of Nethaniah, the son of Elishama, of the royal family, came with ten
men, and struck down Gedaliah so that
he died, and the Jews and the Chaldeans
who were with him at Mizpeh. Then
all the people, both small and great,
and the commanders of the forces arose
and came to Egypt; for they were afraid
of the Chaldeans.

In the thirty-seventh year of the captivity of Jehoiachin, king of Judah, in
the twelfth month, on the twenty-
seventh day of the month, Evil-merodach, in the year that he became king,
summoned Jehoiachin, king of Judah,
from prison. He spoke kindly to him,
and set his throne above the throne of
the kings who were with him in Babylon. So he changed his prison garb, and
Jehoiachin dined in his presence regularly all the days of his life; and for his
provision, a regular allowance was given
him from the king, a portion for each
day, all the days of his life.

THE FIRST BOOK OF CHRONICLES

ADAM'S DESCENDANTS,
1:1–42

1 2 ADAM, Seth, Enosh; Kenan,
3 Mahalalel, Jared, Enoch, Me-
4 thuselah, Lamech; Noah,
Shem, Ham, and Japheth.
5 The descendants of Japheth were
Gomer, Magog, Madai, Javan, Tubal,
6 Meshech, and Tiras; and the descendants of Gomer were Ashkenaz, Di-
7 phath, and Togarmah; and the descendants of Javan were Elishah, Tar-
shishah, Kittim, and Rhodanim.
8 The descendants of Ham were Cush
9 and Egypt, Put and Canaan. The descendants of Cush were Seba, Havilah,
Sabta, Raama, and Sabteca; and the
descendants of Raama were Sheba and
10 Dedan. Cush was the father of Nimrod. He began to be an outstanding
11 man in the earth. Egypt also became
the father of Ludim, Anamim, Laha-
12 bim, Naphtuhim, Pathrusim, and Casluhim—from whom came the Philis-
13 tines—and Caphtorim. Canaan was
the father of Sidon, his first-born, then
14 Heth, the Jebusite, the Amorite, and
15 the Girgashite, the Hivvite, the Arkite,
16 and the Sinite, the Arvadite, Zemarite,
and the Hamathite.
17 The descendants of Shem were Elam,
Assyria, Arphachshad, Lud, Aram, Uz,
18 Hul, Gether, and Meshech. Arphachshad was the father of Shelah, and She-
19 lah was the father of Eber. And to Eber
were born two sons; the name of the
one was Peleg, because in his days the
earth was divided, and the name of his
20 brother was Joktan. Joktan was the
father of Almodad, Sheleph, Hazarma-
21 veth, and Jerah, Hadoram, Uzal, and
22 Diklah, Ebal, Abimael and Sheba,
23 Ophir, Havilah, and Jobab. All these
were the descendants of Joktan.
24 25 Shem, Arphachshad, Shelah, Eber,
26 Peleg, Reu, Serug, Nahor, Terah,
27 Abram, that is Abraham.
28 The descendants of Abraham were
29 Isaac and Ishmael. These are their
generations: Ishmael's first-born was
Nebaioth, then Kedar, Adbeel, Mibsam, Mishma, Dumah, Massa, Hadad, 30
and Tema, Jetur, Naphish and Kede- 31
mah. These are the descendants of
Ishmael. The descendants of Keturah, 32
the concubine of Abraham: she bore
Zimran, Jokshan, Midian, Ishbak, and
Shuah. The sons of Jokshan were She-
ba and Dedan; the sons of Midian were 33
Ephah, Epher, Hanoch, Abida, and
Eldah. All these were the descendants
of Keturah.
Abraham was the father of Isaac, and 34
Isaac's sons were Esau and Israel. The 35
sons of Esau were Eliphaz, Reuel, Je-
ush, Jalam, and Korah. The sons of 36
Eliphaz were Teman, Omar, Jephi,
Gatam, Kenaz, Timua, and Amalek.
The sons of Reuel were Nahath, Zerah, 37
Shammah, and Mizzah.
The sons of Seir were Lotan, Shobal, 38
Zibeon, Anah, Dishon, Ezer, and
Dishan. The sons of Lotan were Hori 39
and Homam; and Timna was Lotan's
sister. The sons of Shobal were Alian, 40
Manahath, Ebal, Shephi, and Onam;
and the sons of Zibeon were Aiiah and
Anah. The descendants of Anah were 41
Dishon, and Dishon's sons were Ham-
ran, Eshban, Ithran, and Cheran. The 42
sons of Ezer were Belhan, Zaavan, and
Jaakan. The sons of Dishon were Uz
and Aran.

THE KINGS OF EDOM,
1:43–54

Now these are the kings that reigned 43
in the land of Edom before any king
reigned over the Israelites. Bela was
the son of Beor, the name of whose city
was Dinhabah. When Bela died, Jo- 44
bab, the son of Zerah of Bozrah, became king in his stead. When Jobab 45
died, Husham of the land of the Temanites became king in his stead.
When Husham died, Hadad, the son of 46
Bedad, who conquered Midian in the
country of Moab, became king in his
stead, and the name of his city was

47 Avith. When Hadad died, Samlah of
Masrekah became king in his stead.
48 When Samlah died, Shaul of Rehoboth
on the River became king in his stead.
49 When Shaul died, Baalhanan, the son
of Achbor, became king in his stead.
50 When Baalhanan died, Hadad became
king in his stead; the name of his city
was Pai, and his wife's name was
Mehetabel, the daughter of Matred,
51 the daughter of Mezahab. Then Hadad
died.
Now the chiefs of Edom were chief
52 Timna, chief Aliah, chief Jetheth, chief
Aholibamah, chief Elah, chief Pinon,
53 chief Kenaz, chief Teman, chief Mib-
54 zar, chief Magdiel, chief Iram. These
were the chiefs of Edom.

THE GENEALOGY OF ISRAEL, 2:1–55

2 These are the sons of Israel: Reuben,
Simeon, Levi, and Judah, Issachar, and
2 Zebulun, Dan, Joseph, Benjamin,
3 Naphtali, Gad, and Asher. The sons of
Judah were Er, Onan, and Shelah,
which three were born to him from
Bathshua the Canaanitess. Now Er,
Judah's first-born, was wicked in the
4 sight of the LORD, so he slew him. His
daughter-in-law Tamar also bore him
Perez and Zerah—Judah had five sons
5 in all. The sons of Perez were Hezron
6 and Hamul; and the sons of Zerah were
Zimri, Ethan, Heman, Chalcol, Darda,
7 a total of five. Karmi's son was Achan,
the troubler of Israel who dealt treacherously in the matter of the devoted
8 thing; and Ethan's son was Azariah.
9 The sons of Hezron, that were born
to him were Jerahmeel, Ram, Chelubai.
10 Ram was the father of Amminadab,
and Amminadab was the father of Nah-
11 shon, a chieftain of the Judeans. Nahshon was the father of Salma, and Sal-
12 ma of Boaz, Boaz of Obed, Obed of
13 Jesse; Jesse was the father of Eliab, his
first-born, Abinadab his second, and
14 Shimei his third, Nathanel the fourth,
15 Raddai the fifth, Ozem the sixth, David
16 the seventh; and their sisters were Zeruiah and Abigail. And the sons of Zeruiah were Abishai, Joab, and Asahel,
17 three; and Abigail bore Amasa, and the
father of Amasa was Jether the Ishmaelite.
18 Now Caleb, the son of Hezron, had
children by his wife Azubah, the daughter of Jerioth; and these were her sons,
Jesher, Shobab, and Ardon. When 19
Azubah died, Caleb married Ephrath,
who bore him Hur. Hur was the father 20
of Uri, and Uri was the father of Bezalel. Afterward Hezron sought offspring 21
from the daughter of Machir the father
of Gilead, whom he married when he
was sixty years old; and she bore him
Segub; and Segub was the father of 22
Jair, who had twenty-three cities in the
land of Gilead. Moreover Geshur and 23
Aram took the towns of Jair from them,
and Kenath, with its sixty villages. All
these were descendants of Machir, the
father of Gilead. Now after the death 24
of Hezron, Caleb sought offspring from
Ephratha, the wife of Hezron his father, and she bore him Ashbur, the
father of Tekoa.
The sons of Jerahmeel, the first-born 25
of Hezron, were Ram, his first-born,
then Bunah, Oren, Ozem, and Ahijah.
Jerahmeel also had another wife 26
whose name was Atarah; she was the
mother of Onam. The sons of Ram, the 27
first-born of Jerahmeel, were Maaz,
Jamin and Eker. Likewise the sons of 28
Onam were Shammai, and Jada; and
the sons of Shammai were Nadab and
Abishur. The name of Abishur's wife 29
was Abihail, and she bore him Ahban
and Molid. Nadab's sons were Seled 30
and Appaim; and Seled died childless.
But the son of Appaim was Ishi, and 31
the son of Ishi, Sheshan, and the son of
Sheshan, Ahlai. The sons also of Jada, 32
Shammai's brother, were Jether and
Jonathan; and Jether died childless,
but the sons of Jonathan were Peleth 33
and Zaza. These were the descendants
of Jerahmeel. Now Sheshan had no 34
sons, only daughters; but Sheshan had
an Egyptian slave, whose name was
Jarha. Accordingly Sheshan gave his 35
daughter to Jarha his slave in marriage;
and she bore him Attai. Attai was the 36
father of Nathan, and Nathan of Zabad. Zabad was the father of Ephlal, 37
and Ephlal of Obed. Obed was the fa- 38
ther of Jehu, and Jehu of Azariah. Aza- 39
riah was the father of Halez, and Halez
of Eleasah. Eleasah was the father of 40
Sismai, and Sismai of Shallum. Shal- 41
lum was the father of Jekamiah, and
Jekamiah of Elishama.
The sons of Caleb, the brother of 42
Jerahmeel, were Mareshah his first-

born, who was the father of Ziph, and
43 the father of Hebron. The sons of Hebron were Korah, Tappuah, Rekem,
44 and Shema; and Shema was the father
of Raham, the father of Jorkeam; and
Rekem was the father of Shammai.
45 The son of Shammai was Maon, and
Maon was the father of Bethzur.
46 Ephah also, Caleb's concubine, bore
Haran, Moza, and Gazez; and Haran
47 was the father of Gazez. The sons of
Jahdai were Regem, Jotham, Geshan,
48 Pelet, Ephah, and Shaaph. Maacah,
Caleb's concubine, bore Sheber and
49 Tirhanah. She also bore Shaaph, the
father of Madmannah, Sheva, the father of Machbenah and the father of
Gibea; and the daughter of Caleb was
50 Achsah. These were the children of
Caleb.
The sons of Hur, the first-born of
Ephrathah, were Shobal, the father of
51 Kirjath-jearim, Salma, the father of
Bethlehem, and Hareph, the father of
52 Bethgader; Shobal, the father of Kirjath-jearim, had other sons, namely,
53 Haroeh and half of the Menuhites, and
of the families of Kirjah-jearim, the
Ithrites, the Puthites, the Shumathites,
and the Mishraites; from these came
the Zorathites and the Eshtaolites.
54 The sons of Salma were Bethlehem, and
the Netophathites, Atroth-bethjoab,
and half of the Manahathites, the Zo-
55 rites. The families also of the scribes
that dwelt at Jabez were the Tirathites,
the Shimeathites, and the Sucathites.
These are the Kenites who came from
Hammath, the father of the house of
Rechab.

THE FAMILY OF DAVID,
3:1–24

3 Now these are the sons of David,
that were born to him at Hebron: the
first-born was Amnon by Ahinoam the
Jezreelitess; the second was Daniel by
2 Abigail the Carmelitess; the third was
Absalom, whose mother was Maacah,
the daughter of Talmai, king of Geshur;
the fourth was Adonijah whose mother
3 was Haggith; the fifth was Shephatiah
by Abital; the sixth was Ithream by
4 his wife Eglah; six were born to him in
Hebron, where he reigned for seven
years and six months. At Jerusalem he
5 reigned thirty-three years. There also
were born to him in Jerusalem, Shimea,
Shobab, Nathan, and Solomon, four by
Bathshua, the daughter of Ammiel; 6
then Ibhar, Elishama, Eliphelet, No- 7
gah, Nepheg, Japhia, Elishama, Eliada, 8
and Eliphelet, nine. All these were Da- 9
vid's sons, besides the sons of the concubines; and Tamar was their sister.
The descendants of Solomon were 10
Rehoboam, Abijah his son, Asa his son,
Jehoshaphat his son, Joram his son, 11
Ahaziah his son, Joash his son, Ama- 12
ziah his son, Aziariah his son, Jotham
his son, Ahaz his son, Hezekiah his son, 13
Manasseh his son, Amon his son, Josiah 14
his son. The sons of Josiah were Johan- 15
an, his first-born, the second, Jehoiakim, the third, Zedekiah, the fourth,
Shallum. The descendants of Jehoia- 16
kim were Jeconiah his son, Zedekiah his
son; and the sons of Jeconiah, who was 17
taken captive, were Shealtiel, Malchir- 18
am, Pedaiah, Shenazzar, Jekamiah,
Hoshama and Nedabiah; and the sons 19
of Pedaiah were Zerubbabel, and
Shimei; and the sons of Zerubbabel
were Meshullam, and Hananiah; and
Shelomith was their sister; there were 20
also Hashubah, Ohel, Berachiah, Hasadiah, and Jushabhesed, five. The son of 21
Hananiah was Pelatiah, and Jeshaiah
was his son, and Rephaiah was his son,
Arnan his son, Obadiah his son, and
Shecaniah his son. The son of Shecani- 22
ah was Shemaiah, and the sons of
Shemaiah were Hattush, Igal, Bariah,
Neariah, and Shaphat, six. The sons of 23
Neariah were Elioenai, Hezekiah, and
Azrikam, three. And the sons of Elio- 24
enai were Hodaviah, Eliashib, Pelaiah,
Akkub, Johanan, Dalaiah, and Anani,
seven.

THE FAMILY OF JUDAH,
4:1–23

The sons of Judah were Perez, Hez- 4
ron, Carmi, Hur, and Shobal. Also 2
Reaiah, the son of Shobal, was the father of Jahath, and Jahath was the
father of Ahumai and Lahad. These
are the families of the Zorathites.
These are the sons of Etam, Jezreel, 3
Ishma, and Idbash; and the name of
their sister was Hazelel-poni; and Pen- 4
uel was the father of Gedor, and Ezer
the father of Hushah. These are the
sons of Hur, the first-born of Ephrathah, the father of Bethlehem.
Now Ashur, the father of Tekoa, had 5

6 two wives, Helah and Naarah; Naarah
bore him Ahuzzam, Hepher, Temeni,
and Haahashtari. These were the sons
7 of Naarah. The sons of Helah were
8 Zereth, Izhar, and Ethnan. Koz was
the father of Anub, Zobebah, and the
families of Aharhel, the son of Harum.
9 Jabez was more honorable than his
brothers, and his mother called his
name Jabez, saying,
"Because I bore him in pain."
10 Now Jabez called on the God of Israel, saying,
"Oh that thou wouldst surely bless
me and enlarge my border, and that
thy hand might be with me, and that
thou wouldst keep me from evil, so that
it should not harm me!"
Accordingly God granted what he
11 asked. Chelub, the brother of Shuhah,
was the father of Mehir, and the latter
12 was the father of Eshton. Eshton was
the father of Bethrapha, Paseah, and
Tehinnah, the father of Irnahash.
13 These are the men of Recah. The sons
of Kenaz were Othniel and Seraiah, and
14 the son of Othniel was Hathath. Me-
onothai was the father of Ophrah, and
Seraiah was the father of Joab, the
father of Ge-harashim [the valley of the
craftsmen], for they were craftsmen.
15 The sons of Caleb, the son of Jephunneh, were Iru, Elah, and Naam; and the
16 son of Elah was Kenaz. The sons of
Jehalelel were Ziph, Ziphah, Tiria, and
17 Asarel. The sons of Ezrah were Jether,
Mered, Epher, and Jalon. These are
the sons of Bithia, the daughter of
Pharaoh, whom Mered married; and
Jether was the father of Miriam and
Shammai, and Jishbah the father of
18 Eshtemoa. And his Jewish wife bore
Jered, the father of Gedor, Heber, the
father of Socoh, and Jekuthiel, the fa-
19 ther of Zenoah. The sons of the wife
of Hodiah, the sister of Naham, were
the fathers of Keilah, the Garmite, and
20 Eshtemoa, the Maacathite. The sons
of Shimon were Amnon, Rinnah, Ben-
hanan, and Tilon; and the sons of Ishi
21 were Zoheth, and Benzoheth. The sons
of Shelah, Judah's son, were Er, the father of Lecah, Laadah, the father of
Mareshah, and the families of the house
22 of linen workers at Beth-Ashbea; also
Jokim, and the men of Cozeba, Joash,
and Saraph who ruled in Moab and returned to Bethlehem, and the records
23 are ancient. These were the potters and
inhabitants of Netaim and Gederah;
they resided there with the king for his
work.

THE DESCENDANTS OF SIMEON, 4:24-43

The sons of Simeon were Nemuel, 24
Jamin, Jarib, Zerah, and Shaul; Shal- 25
lum was his son, Mibsam his son, and
Mishma his son. Mishma's son was 26
Hammuel, Zaccur his son, Shimei his
son. Now Shimei had sixteen sons and 27
six daughters; but his brothers had not
many sons, nor did all their family multiply as did the Judeans. They lived at 28
Beersheba, Moladah, and Hazarshual,
at Bilhah, Ezem, and Tolad, at Bethu- 29 30
el, Hormah, and Ziglag, at Bethmarca- 31
both, Hazarsusim, Beth-biri, and Shaaraim. These were their cities until
David reigned. Their villages were 32
Etam, Ain, Rimmon, Tochen, and
Ashan, five cities, along with all their 33
villages that were round about these
cities as far as Baal. These were their
settlements, and they kept a genealogical enrolment.
Meshobab, Jamlech, Joshah, the son 34
of Amaziah, Joel, Jehu, the son of Josh- 35
ibiah, the son of Seraiah, the son of
Asiel, Elioenai, Jaakobah, Jeshohaiah, 36
Asaiah, Adiel, Jesimiel, Benaiah, Ziza, 37
the son of Shiphi, the son of Allon, the
son of Jedaiah, the son of Shimri, the
son of Shemaiah—these enumerated by 38
name were leaders in their families, and
their families increased greatly. They 39
went to the entrance of Gedor, even to
the east side of the valley to seek pasture for their flocks, where they found 40
rich, luscious pasture, and the land was
broad, quiet, and peaceable; for the inhabitants there formerly belonged to
Ham. Also these written by name came 41
in the days of Hezekiah, king of Judah,
and destroyed their tents and the Me-
unim who were found there, and exterminated them, as it is to this day, and
settled in their place, because there was
pasture there for their flocks. More- 42
over from these Simeonites five hundred men went to Mount Seir, having
as their leaders, Pelatiah, Neariah,
Rephaiah, and Uzziel, the sons of Ishi;
and they overcame the remnant of the 43
Amalekites that had escaped, and they
have dwelt there to this day.

THE DESCENDANTS OF REUBEN, 5:1–26

5 Now the sons of Reuben, the first-
born of Israel—for he was the eldest,
but because he polluted his father's
marriage bed, his birthright was given
to the sons of Joseph, the son of Israel,
so that he is not enrolled in the genealo-
2 gy according to the birthright, and
though Judah grew strong among his
brothers, and became prince over him,
yet the birthright belonged to Joseph—
3 the sons of Reuben, the first-born of
Israel, were Enoch, Pallu, Hezron, and
4 Carmi. The descendants of Joel were
Shemaiah his son, Gog his son, Shimei
5 his son, Micah his son, Reaiah his son,
6 Baal his son, Beerah his son, whom
Tiglath-pileser king of Assyria, carried
away captive—he was a chieftain of the
7 Reubenites, and his kinsmen, according to their families, when the genealogy of their generations was reckoned,
8 were chief Jeiel, Zechariah, Bela, the
son of Azaz, the son of Shema, the son
of Joel, who dwelt in Aroer, even to
9 Nebo and Baalmeon. Also eastward he
dwelt to the entrance of the desert as
far as the Euphrates, because their cattle were so many in the land of Gilead.
10 Moreover in the days of Saul they made
war upon the Hagrites, who fell by
their hand so that they dwelt in their
tents throughout the territory east of
Gilead.
11 Now the Gadites dwelt opposite
them in the land of Bashan as far as
12 Salcah. Joel was the chief, Shapham
next, then Janai, and Shaphat in Bash-
13 an, together with their kinsmen according to their families, Michael, Meshullam, Sheba, Jorai, Jacan, Zia, and Eber,
14 seven. These were the sons of Abihail,
the son of Huri, the son of Jaroah, the
son of Gilead, the son of Michael, the
son of Jeshishai, the son of Jahdo, the
15 son of Buz, Ahi, the son of Abdiel, the
16 son of Guni, chiefs in their families; and
they dwelt in Gilead, in Bashan, in its
towns, and in all the pasture-lands of
17 Sirion to their limits. All of these were
enrolled in the genealogical records in
the days of Jotham, king of Judah and
in the days of Jeroboam, king of Israel.
18 The Reubenites, the Gadites and the
half-tribe of Manasseh, consisting of
valiant men, able to carry shield and
sword, skilled bowmen, expert in war,
amounted to forty-four thousand seven
hundred and sixty in active service.
They also made war upon the Hagrites, 19
also Jetur, Naphish, and Nodab, and 20
they were helped against them, and the
Hagrites and all who were with them
were delivered into their hands. They
cried to God in the battle, and he was
entreated for them because they trusted in him. Moreover they carried off 21
their cattle, fifty thousand of their
camels, two hundred and fifty thousand sheep, two thousand asses, and a
hundred thousand men alive. For 22
many fell slain, because the war was
God's; and they dwelt in their stead
until the exile.
The members of the half-tribe of 23
Manasseh dwelt in the land; they increased from Bashan to Baalhamon and
Senir and Mount Hermon. These were 24
the heads of their families, Epher, Ishi,
Eliel, Azriel, Jeremiah, Hodaviah, and
Jahdiel, valiant fighters, famous men,
heads of their families. But they acted 25
treacherously toward the God of their
fathers, and ran wantonly after the
alien gods of the peoples of the land
whom God had destroyed before them.
So the God of Israel stirred up the spirit 26
of Pul, king of Assyria, and the spirit of
Tiglath-pileser, king of Assyria, and he
carried them away, even the Reubenites, the Gadites, and the half-tribe of
Manasseh, and brought them to Halah,
Habor, Hara, and the river Gozan, as
it is to this day.

THE DESCENDANTS OF LEVI, 6:1–48

The sons of Levi were Gershom, Ko- 6
hath, and Merari. The sons of Kohath 2
were Amram, Izhar, Hebron, and Uzziel; and the children of Amram were 3
Aaron, Moses, and Miriam; and the
sons of Aaron were Nadab, Abihu, Eleazar, and Ithamar. Eleazar was the fa- 4
ther of Phinehas, Phinehas of Abishua,
Abishua of Bukki, Bukki of Uzzi, 5
Uzzi of Zerahiah, Zerahiah of Meraioth, 6
Meraioth of Amariah, Amariah of 7
Ahitub, Ahitub of Zadok, Zadok of Ahi- 8
maaz, Ahimaaz of Azariah, Azariah of 9
Johanan, and Johanan of Azariah (it 10
was he who served as priest in the house
which Solomon built in Jerusalem). Az- 11
ariah was the father of Amariah, Ama-

12 riah of Ahitub, Ahitub of Zadok, Zadok
13 of Shallum, Shallum of Hilkiah, Hilkiah
14 of Azariah, Azariah of Seraiah, and
15 Seraiah of Jehozadak; and Jehozadak
went along when the LORD caused Judah and Jerusalem to go into captivity by the hand of Nebuchadnezzar.

16 The sons of Levi were Gershom, Ko-
17 hath, and Merari; and these are the
names of the sons of Gershom: Libni and
18 Shimei; the sons of Kohath were Am-
19 ram, Izhar, Hebron, and Uzziel. The
sons of Merari were Mahli and Mushi.
These are the families of the Levites ac-
20 cording to their parentage. From Gershom was his son Libni, Jahath was his
21 son, Zimmah his son, Joah his son, Iddo
his son, Zerah his son, Jeatherai his son.
22 The descendants of Kohath were Amminadab his son, Korah his son, Assir
23 his son, Elkanah his son, Ebiasaph his
24 son, and Assir his son, Tahath his son,
Uriel his son, Uzziah his son, and Shaul
25 his son. The sons of Elkanah were
26 Amasai and Ahimoth. As for Elkanah,
the descendants of Elkanah were Zo-
27 phai his son, and Nahath his son, Eliab
his son, Jeroham his son, Elkanah his
28 son; and the sons of Samuel were Joel
29 the first-born, then Abiah. The sons of
Merari were Mahli, Libni his son,
30 Shimei his son, Uzzah his son, Shimea
his son, Haggiah his son, Asaiah his son.
31 Now these are those whom David
put in charge of the service of song in
the house of the LORD, after the ark
32 rested there. They ministered with
song before the dwelling of the tent of
meeting, until Solomon built the house
of the LORD in Jerusalem; and they ful-
33 filled their service in due order. Now
these are they that served, and their
sons. From the sons of the Kohathites
was Heman the singer, the son of Joel,
34 the son of Samuel, the son of Elkanah,
the son of Jeroham, the son of Eliel,
35 the son of Toah, the son of Ziph, the
son of Elkanah, the son of Mahath,
the son of Amasai, the son of Elkanah, the son of Joel, the son of Aza-
37 riah, the son of Zephaniah, the son
of Tahath, the son of Assir, the son of
38 Ebiasaph, the son of Korah, the son of
Izhar, the son of Kohath, the son of
39 Levi, the son of Israel; and his brother
40 the son of Shimea, the son of Michael,
the son of Baaseriah, the son of Malchi-
41 jah, the son of Ethni, the son of Zerah,
42 the son of Adaiah, the son of Ethan, the
son of Zimmah, the son of Shimei, the 43
son of Jahath, the son of Gershom, the
son of Levi. While on their left were 44
their kinsmen the sons of Merari:
Ethan, the son of Kishi, the son of Abdi, the son of Malluch, the son of Hash- 45
abiah, the son of Amaziah, the son of
Hilkiah, the son of Amzi, the son of 46
Shemer, the son of Mahli, the son of 47
Mushi, the son of Merari, the son of
Levi; and their kinsmen the Levites 48
were appointed for all the service of the
dwelling of the house of God.

THE DESCENDANTS OF AARON, 6:49–81

But Aaron and his sons officiated at 49
the altar of burnt-offering and at the
altar of incense for all the work of the
most sacred place, and to make atonement for Israel, just as Moses the
servant of God had commanded. Now 50
these are the descendants of Aaron,
Eleazar his son, Phinehas his son,
Abishua his son, Bukki his son, Uzzi his 51
son, Zerahiah his son, Meraioth his son, 52
Amariah his son, Ahitub his son,
Zadok his son, Ahimaaz his son. 53

These also are their dwelling-places 54
according to their encampments within
their boundaries. To the descendants
of Aaron of the families of the Kohathites—for theirs was the first lot—and 55
they gave to them Hebron in the land
of Judah and its commons round about
it, but the fields of the city and its vil- 56
lages they gave to Caleb, the son of
Jephunneh. To the descendants of Aar- 57
on they gave the cities of asylum,
Hebron, Libnah with its commons, Jattir, Eshtemoa with its commons, Hilen 58
with its commons, Debir with its commons, Ashan with its commons, Beth- 59
shemesh with its commons; and from 60
the tribe of Benjamin, Geba with its
commons, Allemeth with its commons,
and Anathoth with its commons. All
their cities among their families were
thirteen.

The rest of the Kohathites had by lot 61
out of the families of the tribe of
Ephraim and of Dan and the half-tribe
of Manasseh, ten cities. The Gershom- 62
ites according to their families were allotted thirteen cities out of the tribes of
Issachar, Asher, Naphtali, and Manasseh in Bashan. The Merarites ac- 63

cording to their families were allotted
twelve cities out of the tribes of Reu-
64 ben, Gad, and Zebulon. So the Israelites gave the Levites the cities with
65 their common lands. They also gave
them by lot out of the tribe of the Judeans, Simeonites, and Benjaminites
these cities which are mentioned by
name.
66 Also some of the families of the Kohathites had cities allotted them from
67 the tribe of Ephraim. They gave them
the cities of asylum, Shechem, with its
commons in the highlands of Ephraim,
68 Gezer with its commons, Jokmeam
with its commons, Beth-horon with its
69 commons, Aijalon with its commons,
70 Gath-rimmon with its commons, and
out of the half-tribe of Manasseh—
Aner with its commons, Bileam with its
commons, for the rest of the families of
71 the Kohathites; to the Gershomites out
of the families of the half-tribe of Manasseh, Golan in Bashan with its commons, and Ashtaroth with its com-
72 mons; and out of the tribe of Issachar,
Kedesh with its commons, Daberath
73 with its commons, Ramoth with its
commons, Anem with its commons;
74 out of the tribe of Asher, Mashal with
its commons; Abdon with its commons,
75 Hukak with its commons, and Rehob
76 with its commons; out of the tribe of
Naphtali, Kedesh in Galilee with its
commons, Hammon with its commons,
77 Kiriathaim with its commons. To the
Merarites that were left were allotted
out of the tribe of Zebulon, Rimmono
with its commons, Tabor with its com-
78 mons, and beyond the Jordan, Jericho,
on the east side of the Jordan out of the
tribe of Reuben, Bezer in the desert
with its commons, Jahzah with its
79 commons, Kedemoth with its commons and Mephaath, with its com-
80 mons; and out of the tribe of Gad,
Ramoth in Gilead with its commons,
81 Mahanaim with its commons, Heshbon
with its commons, and Jazer with its
commons.

THE DESCENDANTS OF ISSACHAR, BENJAMIN AND NAPHTALI, 7:1–19

7 The sons of Issachar were four, Tola,
2 Puah, Jashib, and Shimron; the sons of
Tola were Uzzi, Rephaiah, Jeriel, Jah-
mai, Jibsam, and Samuel, chiefs of
their families, namely, of Tola, distinguished warriors of their generations,
their number in the days of David being twenty-two thousand six hundred.
The son of Uzzi was Izrahiah, and the 3
sons of Izrahiah were Michael, Obadiah, Joel, Isshiah, all five of them being
chief men; and along with them, by 4
their generations according to their
families, were units of the army for war,
thirty-six thousand; for they had many
wives and sons. Also their kinsmen be- 5
longing to all the families of Issachar
were a total of eighty-seven thousand
distinguished warriors, reckoned by
genealogy.
Likewise the sons of Benjamin were 6
three, Bela, Becher, and Jediael; Bela's 7
sons were five, Ezbon, Uzzi, Uzziel,
Jerimoth, and Iri, heads of their families, distinguished warriors; and their
reckoning by genealogies was twenty-
two thousand and thirty-four. The 8
sons of Becher were Zemirah, Joash,
Eliezer, Elioenai, Omri, Jeremoth, Abijah, Anathoth, and Alemeth; all these
were the sons of Becher; and their en- 9
rolment by genealogies, according to
their generations, as heads of their
families, distinguished warriors, was
twenty thousand and two hundred.
The son of Jediael was Bilhan, and the 10
sons of Bilhan were Jeush, Benjamin,
Ehud, Chenaanah, Zethan, Tarshish,
and Ahishahar. All these were the sons 11
of Jediael according to the heads of
their families, distinguished warriors,
seventeen thousand two hundred on active service for war. (Also Shuppim and 12
Huppim were sons of Ir, Hushim the
son of Aher.)
The sons of Naphtali were Jahziel, 13
Guni, Jezer, and Shallum whose mother
was Bilhah. The sons of Manasseh 14
were Asriel, whom his concubine the
Aramitess bore; she bore Machir the
father of Gilead; and Gilead took a 15
wife whose name was Maacah, and the
name of his sister was Hammolecheth
and the name of his brother Zelophad,
and Zelophad had daughters. Now 16
Maacah, the wife of Machir, bore a son,
and she called his name Peresh, and the
name of his brother was Sheresh; and 17
his sons were Ulam and Rekem. The
son of Ulam was Bedan. These are the
descendants of Gilead, the son of Machir, the son of Manasseh. Also his sis- 18

ter Hammolecheth bore Ishbod, Abi-
19 ezer, and Mahlah. The sons of Shemida
were Ahian, Shechem, Likhi, and
Aniam.

THE DESCENDANTS OF EPHRAIM, ASHER AND BENJAMIN, 7:20—8:40

20 Now the descendants of Ephraim
were Shuthelah, and Bered his son,
Tahath his son, Eleada his son, Tahath
21 his son, Zabad his son, Shuthelah his
son, and Ezer, and Elead, whom the
men of Gath who were born in the land
slew, because they came down to raid
22 their cattle. Therefore Ephraim their
father mourned many days, and his
23 brothers came to comfort him. Then
he had intercourse with his wife, and
she conceived and gave birth to a son;
and he called his name Beriah, because
24 evil had befallen his house. Now his
daughter was Sheerah, who built both
upper and lower Beth-horon, and Uz-
25 zen-sheerah. Rephah was his son, and
Resheph, Telah his son, and Tahan his
26 son, Ladan his son, Ammihud his son,
27 Elishama his son, Nun his son, Joshua
28 his son. Their possessions and settlements were Bethel and its towns, and
eastward Naaran, and westward Gezer
and its towns, Shechem and its towns,
29 and Azzah and its towns; also along the
borders of the Manassites, Beth-shean
and its towns, Taanach and its towns,
Megiddo and its towns, Dor and its
towns. In these dwelt the descendants
of Joseph, the son of Israel.
30 The sons of Asher were Imnah, Ishvah, Ishvi, Beriah, and their sister
31 Serah; and the sons of Beriah were Heber and Malchiel, who was the father of
32 Birzaith; also Heber was the father of
Japhlet, Shomer, Hotham, and Shua
33 their sister; the sons of Japhlet were
Pasach, Bimhal, and Ashvath. These
34 are the sons of Japhlet: the sons of
Shemer, his brother, were Rohgah,
35 Jehubbah, and Aram; and the sons of
Helem were Zophah, Imna, Shelesh,
36 and Amal. The sons of Zophah were
Suah, Harnepher, Shual, Beri, Imrah,
37 Bezer, Hur, Shamma, Shilshah, Ithran,
38 and Beera; and the sons of Jether were
39 Jephunneh, Pispah, and Ara. The sons
of Ulla were Arah, Hanniel, and Rizia.
40 All these were Asherite heads of the
families, select, distinguished warriors,
foremost of the chieftains. Their number reckoned by genealogies, for active
service in war, was twenty-six thousand
men.

Benjamin was the father of Bela his 8
first-born, Ashbel the second, and
Aharah the third, Nohah the fourth, 2
and Rapha the fifth. The sons of Bela 3
were Addar, Gera, Abihud, Abishua, 4
Naaman, Ahoah, Gera, Shephuphan, 5
and Huram. These are the sons of 6
Ehud, heads of families of the inhabitants of Geba, and they carried them
captive to Manahath, Naaman, and 7
Ahijah; and Gera was the one who carried them captive; he was the father of
Uzza and Ahihud. Also Shaharaim had 8
sons in the country of Moab after he
had sent away Hushim and Baarah his
wives. He had offspring by Hodesh his 9
wife, Jobab, Zibia, Mesha, Malcam,
Jeuz, Sachia, and Mirmah. These were 10
his sons, heads of families; and he had 11
offspring by Hushim, Abitub and Elpaal. The sons of Elpaal were Eber, 12
Misham, and Shemed, who built Ono
and Lod with its towns, and Beriah and 13
Shema (who were heads of families of
the inhabitants of Aijalon, who put to
flight the inhabitants of Gath); and 14
their brothers were Shashak and Jeremoth, while Zebadiah, Arad, Eder, 15
Michael, Ishpah, and Joha were the 16
sons of Beriah. Zebadiah, Meshullam, 17
Hizki, Heber, Ishmerai, Izliah, and Jo- 18
bab were the sons of Elpaal. Jakim, 19
Zichri, Zabdi, Elienai, Zillethai, Eliel, 20
Adaiah, Beriah, and Shimrath were the 21
sons of Shimei. Ishpan, Eber, Eliel, 22 23
Abdon, Zichri, Hanan, Hananiah, 24
Elam, Anathothijah, Iphdeiah, and 25
Penuel were the sons of Shashak.
Shamsherai, Shehariah, Athaliah, Jaar- 26 27
ishiah, Elijah, and Zichri were the sons 28
of Jeroham. These were the heads of
the families, according to their genera-
tions, leaders, who lived at Jerusalem.

At Gibeon there dwelt the father of 29
Gibeon, Jeuel, whose wife's name was
Maacah. His first-born son was Abdon, 30
then Zur, Kish, Baal, Ner, Nadab, Ge- 31
dor, Ahio, Zecher, and Mikloth (he was 32
the father of Shimeah). Now these also
dwelt together opposite their kinsmen
in Jerusalem.

Ner was the father of Abner, Kish of 33
Saul, Saul of Jonathan, Malchishua,
Abinadab, and Eshbaal; and the son of 34

Jonathan was Meribaal, and Meri-
35 baal was the father of Micah. The sons
of Micah were Pithon, Melech, Tarea,
36 and Ahaz; and Ahaz was the father of
Jehoaddah, and Jehoaddah was the father of Alemeth, Azmaveth, and Zimri;
37 Zimri was the father of Moza. Moza
was the father of Binea, Rapha was his
38 son, Eleasah his son, Azel his son. Azel
had six sons, whose names were Azrikam, Bocheru, Ishmael, Sheariah, Obadiah, and Hanan. All these were the
39 sons of Azel. The sons of Eshek his
brother were Ulam his first-born, Jeush
40 the second, Eliphelet the third. The
sons of Ulam were men who were distinguished warriors, expert bowmen,
having many sons and grandsons, a
hundred and fifty. All these were Benjaminites.

A LIST OF EXILES RETURNED FROM BABYLON, 9:1–44

1 So all Israel was registered by genealogies; they are written there in the
Book of the Kings of Israel. And Judah
was carried captive to Babylon because
2 of their unfaithfulness. Now the first to
dwell again in their possessions in their
cities, were Israelite laymen, the
3 priests, and the temple servants, while
some Judeans, Benjaminites, Ephraimites, and Manassites dwelt in Jerusa-
4 lem, namely, Uthai, the son of Ammihud, the son of Omri, the son of Imri,
the son of Bani, belonging to the descendants of Perez the son of Judah;
5 and of the Shilonites, Asaiah, the oldest
6 member and his sons; of the descendants of Zerah, Jeuel and their kinsmen,
7 six hundred and ninety; of the Benjaminites, Sallu, the son of Meshullam,
the son of Hodaviah, the son of Has-
8 senuah, Ibneiah, the son of Jeroham,
Elah, the son of Uzzi, the son of Michri,
and Meshullam, the son of Shephatiah,
the son of Reuel, the son of Ibnijah;
9 and their kinsmen according to their
generations, nine hundred and fifty-six.
All these men were heads of families according to their fathers' houses.
10 Also of the priests there were Jedai-
11 ah, Jehoiarib, Jachin, and Azariah, the
son of Hilkiah, the son of Meshullam,
the son of Zadok, the son of Meraioth,
the son of Ahitub, the ruler of the house
12 of God; and Adaiah, the son of Jeroham, the son of Pashhur, the son of
Malchijah, and Maasai the son of Adiel, the son of Jahzerah, the son of
Meshullam, the son of Meshillemith,
the son of Immer; besides their kins- 13
men, heads of their fathers' houses, one
thousand seven hundred and sixty, men
of distinguished capabilities, for the
work of the service of the house of God.
Of the Levites there were Shemaiah, 14
the son of Hasshub, the son of Azrikam,
the son of Hashabiah, of the Merarites;
with Bakbakkar, Heresh, Galal, and 15
Mattaniah, the son of Mica, the son of
Zichri, the son of Asaph; also Obadiah, 16
the son of Shemaiah, the son of Galal,
the son of Jeduthun, and Berachiah,
the son of Asa, the son of Elkanah, who
dwelt in the villages of the Netophathites.
The gatekeepers were Shallum, Ak- 17
kub, Talmon, Ahiman, and their kinsmen (Shallum being the chief), sta- 18
tioned till now in the king's gate on the
east side. These were the gatekeepers
of the camp of the Levites. Shallum, 19
the son of Kore, the son of Ebiasaph,
the son of Korah, and his kinsmen of
his father's house, the Korahites, were
over the service, keepers of the thresholds of the tent, as their fathers had
been over the camp of the LORD, keepers of the entrance. And Phinehas, the 20
son of Eleazar, was the ruler over them
in time past (may the Lord be with
him!). Zechariah, the son of Meshel- 21
emiah, was gatekeeper at the entrance
of the tent of meeting. All these that 22
were chosen as gatekeepers at the
thresholds were two hundred and
twelve. They were reckoned by their
genealogies in their villages, whom David and Samuel the seer appointed to
their office of responsibility. So they 23
and their sons had charge of the gates of
the house of the LORD, even the house
of the Tent, as guards. The gatekeep- 24
ers were on the four sides, on the east,
the west, the north, and the south; and 25
their kinsmen who were in their villages
were obliged to come in every seven
days, from time to time, to be with 26
these; for the four most distinguished
gatekeepers, who were Levites, were
constantly on duty in charge of the
chambers and the treasuries of the
house of God. They also used to lodge 27
round about the house of God; for upon
them rested the duty of watching, and

they had charge of opening it every
morning.
28 Moreover some of them had charge
of the utensils of the service, for they
were required to count them when they
29 were brought in and taken out. Others
of them were appointed over the furniture, and over all the sacred utensils, as
well as over the fine flour, the wine, the
30 oil the incense, and the spices. Others,
of the sons of the priests, prepared the
31 mixing of the spices, while Mattethiah
a Levite, the first-born of Shallum the
Korahite, was responsible for the pas-
32 try of flatcakes. And some of their
kinsmen of the Kohathites had charge
of the bread that is arranged in layers,
to prepare it every sabbath.
33 Now these are the singers, the heads
of families of the Levites, dwelling in
the chambers of the temple free from
other service, for they were on duty
34 day and night. These were heads of
families of the Levites, according to
their generations, leaders, who lived at
Jerusalem.
35 At Gibeon dwelt the father of Gibeon, Jeiel, whose wife's name was Maa-
36 cah; and his first-born son was Abdon,
then Zur, Kish, Baal, Ner, Nadab,
37 Gedor, Ahio, Zechariah, and Mikloth,
38 while Mikloth was the father of Shime-
am; and they also dwelt together oppo-
39 site their kinsmen in Jerusalem. Ner
was the father of Kish, Kish of Saul,
Saul of Jonathan, Malchishua, Abina-
40 dab, and Eshbaal; and the son of Jonathan was Meribaal, and Meribaal was
41 the father of Micah. The sons of Micah were Pithon, Melech, and Tahrea;
42 and Ahaz was the father of Jarah, and
Jarah of Alemeth, Azmaveth, and
Zimri; and Zimri was the father of Mo-
43 za. Moza was the father of Binea, and
Rephaiah was his son, Eleasah his son,
44 Azel his son. Also Azel had six sons,
whose names are Azrikam, Bocheru,
Ishmael, Sheariah, Obadiah, and Hanan; these were the sons of Azel.

SAUL'S DEATH AND BURIAL, 10:1–14

10 Now the Philistines fought against
Israel, and the men of Israel fled before the Philistines, and the wounded
2 fell on Mount Gilboa. Moreover the
Philistines overtook Saul and his sons;
and the Philistines slew Jonathan and
Abinadab and Malchishua, the sons of
Saul. The battle raged about Saul, and
the archers found their mark, and he
was wounded by the archers. Then
Saul said to his armor-bearer,
"Draw your sword and run me
through with it, lest these uncircumcised men come and make sport of me."
But his armor-bearer would not, for
he was terrified. Therefore Saul took
his sword and fell upon it; and when his
armor-bearer saw that Saul was dead,
then he also fell upon his sword and
died. Thus Saul and his three sons and
all his house died together.
Now when all the men of Israel who
were in the valley saw that Israel had
fled, and that Saul and his sons were
dead, they abandoned their cities and
fled, and the Philistines came and occupied them. Then on the morrow when
the Philistines came to strip the slain,
they found Saul and his three sons fall-
en on Mount Gilboa; and they stripped
him and took away his head and his
armor and dispatched them throughout
the land of the Philistines to bring good
tidings to their idols and to the people.
They also put his armor in the house of 1
their gods and his body they impaled on
the wall of the temple of Dagon. Now 1
when all the inhabitants of Jabesh-
gilead heard all that the Philistines had
done to Saul, all the valiant men arose 1
and took the body of Saul and the
bodies of his sons and brought them to
Jabesh, and buried their bones under
the oak in Jabesh, and they fasted sev-
en days.
Thus Saul died for his faithlessness 1
wherein he was faithless toward the
LORD because of the word of the LORD
which he did not observe, and also because he consulted a medium, resorting
to it and not to the LORD. Therefore 1
he killed him and turned the kingdom
over to David, the son of Jesse.

DAVID BECOMES KING AND CAPTURES JERUSALEM, 11:1–9

Then all Israel assembled to David 1
to Hebron, saying,
"See, we are your bone and your
flesh. In times past when Saul was
king over us, it was you who led out and

brought in Israel, and the LORD your God said to you, 'You shall shepherd my people Israel, and you shall be prince over my people Israel.' "

So all the elders of Israel came to the king to Hebron, and David made a covenant with them in Hebron before the LORD, and they anointed David king over Israel according to the word of the LORD by Samuel.

Then David and all Israel went to Jerusalem (that is Jebus); and the Jebusites, the inhabitants of the land, were there. Then the inhabitants of Jebus said to David,

"You shall not come here."

David nevertheless took the stronghold of Zion (that is, the city of David).

"Whoever slays the Jebusites first shall be chief and commander," said David.

Then Joab, the son of Zeruiah, went up first and so became chief. Accordingly David dwelt in the stronghold; therefore they called it the city of David. He also built the city round about from Millo, even round about, and Joab restored the rest of the city. So David kept on becoming greater, for the LORD of hosts was with him.

DAVID'S HEROES, 11:10–47

Now these are the chiefs of the heroic men whom David had, who showed themselves strong with him in his kingdom, together with all Israel, to make him king, according to the word of the LORD concerning all Israel. This is the number of the heroes whom David had: Jashobeam, the son of a Hachmonite, the chief of the Thirty who wielded his spear against three hundred whom he slew at one time. After him was Eleazar, the son of Dodo the Ahohite, who was one of the three heroes. He was with David at Pasdammim, when the Philistines were gathered together there for battle, and there was a plot of land full of barley; and when the people fled before the Philistines, they held their ground in the midst of the plot and defended it, and slew the Philistines; so the LORD saved them by a great victory. Now three of the thirty chiefs went down to the rock to David, to the cave of Adullam, while the camp of the Philistines was pitched in the valley of Rephaim. David at the time was in the
stronghold, and a garrison of the Phi-
listines was then in Bethlehem. Then 17
David longed and said,
"Oh that someone would give me a
drink of water from the well of Bethlehem, that is at the gate!"
So the Three broke through the Phi- 18
listine lines and drew water from the
well of Bethlehem that was at the gate,
and took it and brought it to David.
But David would not drink of it, but
poured it out to the LORD, and said, 19
"God forbid that I should do this!
Am I to drink the blood of these men
who went at the risk of their lives? for
at the risk of their lives they have
brought it."
Therefore he would not drink it.
These things did the three heroes.
Abishai also, the brother of Joab, was 20
chief of the Thirty, for he wielded his
spear against three hundred whom he
slew and won a name among the Thirty. He was the most distinguished of 21
the Thirty and became their chief, but
he did not attain to the Three. Benaiah 22
was the son of Jehoiada, the son of a
valiant man from Kabzeel, mighty in
deeds; he slew the two sons of Ariel of
Moab. He also went down and slew a
lion in the midst of a pit upon a snowy
day. Moreover, he slew an Egyptian, a 23
man of great stature five cubits tall,
who had a spear in his hand like a weaver's beam, but he went down to him
with a club and wrenched the spear out
of the Egyptian's hand, and slew him
with his own spear. These things did 24
Benaiah, the son of Jehoiada, and won
a name like the three heroes. He was 25
indeed renowned above the Thirty, but
he did not attain to the Three, and
David set him over his body-guard.
Now the heroes of the army were 26
Asahel, the brother of Joab; Elhanan,
the son of Dodo of Bethlehem, Sham- 27
moth the Harorite, Helez the Pelonite,
Ira, the son of Ikkesh the Tekoite, 28
Abiezer the Anathothite, Sibbecai the 29
Hushathite, Ilai the Ahohite, Maharai 30
the Netophathite, Heled, the son of
Baanah the Netophathite, Ithai, the 31
son of Ribai of Gibeah of the Benjaminites, Benaiah the Pirathonite, Hurai 32
of the brooks of Gaash, Abiel the Ar-
bathite, Azmaveth the Baharumite, 33
Eliahba the Shaalbonite; the sons of Ha- 34
shem the Gizonite, Jonathan, the son of
Shagee the Hararite, Ahiam, the son of 35

Sacar the Hararite, Eliphal, the son of
36 Ur, Hepher the Mecherathite, Ahijah
37 the Pelonite, Hezro the Carmelite, Naar-
38 ai the son of Ezbai, Joel, the brother
of Nathan, Mibhar, the son of Hagri,
39 Zelek the Ammonite, Naharai the Bero-
thite, the armor-bearer of Joab, the son
40 of Zeruiah, Ira the Ithrite, Gareb the
41 Ithrite, Uriah the Hittite, Zabad, the
42 son of Ahlai, Adina, the son of Shiza the
Reubenite, a chief of the Reubenites,
43 and thirty with him, Hanan, the son of
44 Maacah, Joshaphat the Mithnite, Uz-
zia the Ashterathite, Shama and Jeiel,
the sons of Hotham the Aroerite,
45 Jediael the son of Shimri, and Joha, his
46 brother, the Tizite, Eliel the Mahavite,
Jeribai and Joshaviah, the sons of
47 Elnaam, Ithmah the Moabite, Eliel,
Obed, and Jaasiel the Mezobaite.

DAVID'S ARMY, 12:1–40

12 Now these are they who came to
David at Ziklag, while he was still holding himself aloof from Saul, the son of
Kish; and they were among the heroes,
2 his helpers in war. They were expert
with the bow and could use both the
right hand and the left hand in hurling
stones and in shooting arrows from the
bow; they were of Saul's kinsmen of Ben-
3 jamin. The chief was Ahiezer; then Joash, the sons of Shemaah the Gibea-
thite, Jeziel and Pelet, the sons of Azmaveth, Beracah, Jehu the Anatho-
4 thite, Ishmaiah the Gibeonite, a hero
among the Thirty and over the Thirty,
Jeremiah, Jahaziel, Johanan, Jozabad
5 the Gederathite, Eluzai, Jerimoth,
Bealiah, Shemariah, Shephatiah the
6 Haruphite, Elkanah, Isshiah, Azarel,
Joezer, and Jashobeam, the Korahites,
7 Joelah and Zebadiah, the sons of Jeroham of Gedor.
8 From the Gadites there withdrew to
David, to the stronghold in the desert,
intrepid warriors, men trained for war,
who could handle shield and spear,
whose faces were like the faces of lions,
who were like the gazelles on the moun-
9 tains for swiftness: Ezer the first, Oba-
10 diah the second, Eliab the third, Mish-
mannah the fourth, Jeremiah the fifth,
11 12 Attai the sixth, Eliel the seventh, Johanan the eighth, Elzabad the ninth,
13 Jeremiah the tenth, Machbannai the
14 eleventh. These from the Gadites were
commanders of the army. The least
was equal to a hundred, and the greatest to a thousand. These are they who crossed the Jordan in the first month, when it had overflowed all its banks, and they put to flight all the inhabitants of the valleys both toward the east and toward the west.

There also came some of the Benjaminites and Judeans to the stronghold to David; and David went out to meet them, and answered and said to them, "If you come peaceably to me to help me, my heart shall be ready to become one with yours; but if to betray me to my adversaries, since there is no wrong in my hands, the God of our fathers look thereon and rebuke it."

Then the spirit came upon Amasai, the chief of the Thirty:

"Yours are we, O David,
And with you, O son of Jesse!
Peace, peace to you,
And peace to your helpers,
For your God helps you."

Then David received them and made them chiefs of the raiders.

From Manasseh also some deserted to David, when he came with the Philistines against Saul to battle, but they did not help them, for the city rulers of the Philistines after consultation forced him to go away, saying,

"He will desert to his master Saul to the jeopardy of our heads."

As he went to Ziklag there went over to him from Manasseh, Adnah, Jozabad, Jediael, Michael, Jozabad, Elihu, and Zillethai, commanders of thousands, who belonged to Manasseh. They also helped David against the raiders; for they were all valiant warriors and commanders in the army. Thus from day to day they came to David to help him, until there was a great army, like the army of God. Now these are the numbers of the heads of those equipped for war, who came to David to Hebron, to turn over to him the kingdom of Saul, according to the word of the LORD. The Judeans who bore shield and spear were six thousand eight hundred, equipped for war. Of the Simeonites, valiant men for war, there were seven thousand one hundred. Of the Levites there were four thousand six hundred. Now Jehoiada was the prince of the house of Aaron, and with him were three thousand seven hundred, also Zadok, a youth of unusual ability, together with his father's house: twenty-two commanders. Of the Benjaminites, the kinsmen of Saul, there were three thousand; for hitherto the majority of them had remained loyal to the house of Saul. Of the Ephraimites there were twenty thousand eight hundred, valiant warriors, famous men in their fathers' houses. Of the half-tribe of Manasseh there were eighteen thousand, who were mentioned by name to come and make David king. Of the Issacharites, men who had understanding of the times so that they knew what Israel ought to do, their two hundred chiefs, and all their kinsmen were under their command. Of Zebulon there were fifty thousand fit to join the army and take the field with all the weapons of war, prepared to give assistance with singleness of purpose. Of Naphtali there were a thousand commanders, and with them thirty-seven thousand with shield and spear. Of the Danites, ready to take the field, there were twenty-eight thousand six hundred. Of Asher, fit to join the army and render assistance in battle, there were forty thousand. Also from beyond the Jordan, of the Reubenites, the Gadites, and the half-tribe of Manasseh, there were a hundred and twenty thousand fully equipped for battle with all arms of the service. All these warriors, ready to take the field, moved by a single purpose came to Hebron to make David king over all Israel. All the rest of Israel also had the one purpose of making David king.

They were there with David three days, eating and drinking; for their kinsmen had made preparation for them. Also those who were near them as far as Issachar, Zebulon, and Naphtali brought food on asses, camels, mules, and oxen—provisions such as meal, cakes of figs, bunches of raisins, wine, oil, oxen, and sheep in abundance; for gladness reigned in Israel.

DAVID'S ATTEMPT TO BRING THE ARK OF GOD TO JERUSALEM, 13:1–14

3 Then David consulted with the commanders of thousands and of hundreds,
even with every leader; and David said
to all the assembly of Israel,
"If it seem good to you and acceptable to the LORD our God, let us send to all our remaining kinsmen in all the land of Israel, since the priests and Levites are with them in their cities which have common pasture-lands, that they
may be gathered together to us, in order 3
that we may bring back the ark of our God to us, for we did not seek it during the days of Saul."
Then all the assembly voted to do so, 4
for the thing seemed right in the eyes of
all the people. So David assembled all 5
Israel from the River of Egypt to the entrance of Hamath, to bring the ark of
God from Kirjath-jearim. Then David 6
went up together with all Israel to Baalah, that is, to Kirjath-jearim, which belongs to Judah, to bring up from there the ark of God, the LORD who is seated upon the cherubim, that is called by the
Name; and they caused the ark of God 7
to ride in a new cart from the house of Abinadab, with Uzza and Ahio guiding
the cart, while David and all Israel 8
played before God with all their might, with songs and harps and lyres and tambourines and cymbals and trumpets.
But when they came to the threshing- 9
floor of Chidon, Uzza put out his hand to hold the ark, for the oxen jostled it.
Then the anger of the LORD blazed 10
against Uzza and he struck him down because he put out his hand to the ark;
and he died there before God. David 11
was angry because the LORD had brok-
en forth upon Uzza, therefore that place 12
is called Perez-uzza [Breach of Uzza] to this day. And David was afraid of God that day, saying,
"How can I bring the ark of God home to me?"
So David did not remove the ark to 13
him to the city of David, but carried it aside into the house of Obed-edom, the
Gittite. Therefore the ark of God re- 14
mained with the family of Obed-edom at his house three months, and the LORD blessed the house of Obed-edom and all that he had.

DAVID'S WIVES, AND HIS WARS WITH THE PHILISTINES, 14:1–17

Now Hiram, king of Tyre, sent mes- 14
sengers to David, and cedar timbers

and masons and carpenters to build
2 a house for him. Accordingly David
perceived that the LORD had established him as king over Israel, for his kingdom had been exalted for the sake of his people Israel.
3 Then David took more wives in Jerusalem, and David became the father of
4 more sons and daughters. These are the names of those who were born to him in Jerusalem: Shammua, Shobab,
5 Nathan, Solomon, Ibhar, Elishua,
6 Eliphelet, Nogah, Nepheg, Japhia,
7 Elishama, Beeliada, and Eliphelet.
8 Now when the Philistines heard that David had been anointed king over all Israel, all the Philistines came up in search of David; and when David heard
9 of it he withdrew before them; so the Philistines came on and made a raid in
10 the valley of Rephaim. Therefore David inquired of God, saying,

"Shall I go up against the Philistines, and wilt thou deliver them into my hand?"

Then the LORD said to him,

"Go up, for I will deliver them into your hand."

11 So they came up to Baal-perazim and there David defeated them; and David said,

"God has broken through my enemies by my hand, like the bursting of water through a dam."

Therefore they called the name of
12 that place Baal-perazim. They also left their gods there, and David gave the command and they were burned.
13 Then the Philistines made another
14 raid in the valley. Accordingly when David inquired again of God, God said to him,

"Do not go up after them; go around to their rear and come at them oppo-
15 site the balsam trees; and when you hear the sound of marching in the tops of the balsam trees, then go out to battle, for God has gone forth before you to overcome the camp of the Philistines."

16 So David did as God commanded him, and they put to rout the camp of the Philistines from Gibeon as far as
17 Gezer. Thus David's fame went out into all the lands, and the LORD brought the fear of him on all the nations.

DAVID BRINGS THE ARK TO JERUSALEM IN STATE, 15:1—16:43

Thereupon David made for himself houses in the city of David, and prepared a place for the ark of God, and pitched a tent for it. Then David said, "None ought to carry the ark of God but the Levites; for the LORD chose them to carry the ark of God and to minister to him forever."

So David assembled all Israel to Jerusalem, to bring up the ark of the LORD to its place, which he had prepared for it; and David gathered together the sons of Aaron, as well as the Levites; of the Kohathites, Uriel the chief, with his kinsmen, a hundred and twenty; of the Merarites, Asaiah the chief, with his kinsmen, two hundred and twenty; of the Gershomites, Joel the chief, with his kinsmen, a hundred and thirty; of the Elizaphanites, Shemaiah the chief, with his kinsmen, two hundred; of the Hebronites, Eliel the chief, with his kinsmen, eighty; of the Uzzielites, Amminadab the chief, with his kinsmen, a hundred and twelve. Then David called for Zadok and Abiathar the priests and for the Levites, Uriel, Asaiah, Joel, Shemaiah, Eliel, and Amminadab, and said to them,

"You are the heads of the families of the Levites; sanctify yourselves, both you and your kinsmen, that you may bring up the ark of the LORD, the God of Israel, to the place that I have prepared for it. Because you were not ready at the first, the LORD our God broke out upon us, for we did not seek him in the proper way."

So the priests and Levites sanctified themselves to bring up the ark of the LORD, the God of Israel; and the members of the Levitical order carried the ark of God on their shoulders, with the poles, as Moses commanded according to the word of the LORD.

Then David ordered the chiefs of the Levites to appoint their kinsmen the singers, with instruments of music, lyres, harps, and cymbals who should sound aloud and lift up the voice with gladness. So the Levites appointed Heman, the son of Joel; and of his kinsmen, Asaph, the son of Berechiah; and of the Merarites their kinsmen, Ethan, the son of Kushaiah; and with them their kinsmen of the second rank, Zechariah, Jaaziel, Shemiramoth, Jehiel, Unni, Eliab, Benaiah, Maaseiah, Mattithiah, Eliphelehu, Mikneiah, Obed-edom, and Jeiel, the doorkeepers. So the singers Heman, Asaph, and Ethan were to sound aloud on bronze cymbals; while Zechariah, Uzziel, Shemiramoth, Jehiel, Unni, Eliab, Maaseiah, and Benaiah played with lyres set to Alamoth, and Mattithiah, Eliphelehu, Mikneiah, Obed-edom, Jeiel, and Azaziah, with harps set to the octave to lead. Moreover Chenaniah, chief of the Levites in carrying, controlled the carrying because he was skilful. And Berechiah and Elkanah were doorkeepers for the ark. Shebanaiah, Joshaphat, Nathanel, Amasai, Zechariah, Benaiah, and Eliezer, the priests, blew the trumpets before the ark of God; Obed-edom and Jehiah were also doorkeepers for the ark. So David, with the elders of Israel and the commanders of thousands, went to bring up with gladness the ark from the house of Obed-edom; and as God helped the Levites who bore the ark of the covenant of the LORD, they sacrificed seven bulls and seven rams. Now David was clothed with a robe of fine linen, and all the Levites who bore the ark, and the singers, and Chenaniah who was in charge of the transport; David also had on a linen apron. Thus all Israel was bringing up the ark of the covenant of the LORD, with shouting and with the sound of the cornet and trumpets and cymbals sounding aloud, with lyres and harps.

But while the ark of the covenant of the LORD was coming to the city of David, Michal, the daughter of Saul, looked out at the window and saw King David leaping and playing and she despised him in her heart.

When they brought in the ark of God, they set it within the tent that David had pitched for it, and they offered burnt-offerings and thank-offerings before God; and when David had finished offering the burnt-offerings and the thank-offerings, he blessed the people in the name of the LORD. He also distributed to every Israelite, both man and woman, a loaf of bread, and a portion of meat, and a bunch of raisins. Moreover he appointed some of the Levites to minister before the ark of the LORD and to celebrate, thank, and
praise the LORD, the God of Israel:
Asaph the chief, and second to him 5
Zechariah, then Uzziel, Shemiramoth,
Jehiel, Mattithiah, Eliab, Benaiah,
Obed-edom, and Jeiel, with lyres and
harps; while Asaph played loudly with
cymbals, and Benaiah and Jahaziel, the 6
priests, with trumpets continually before the ark of the covenant of God.
Then on that day David for the first 7
time entrusted to Asaph and his kinsmen the giving of thanks to the LORD.

Give thanks to the LORD; call upon 8
his name;
Make known his deeds among the
peoples!
Sing to him; sing praises to him; 9
Tell of all his wonders!
Glory in his holy name! 10
May the heart of those who seek the
LORD rejoice!
Inquire of the LORD and his might; 11
Seek his face continually!

Remember his wonders that he has 12
done,
His portents, and the judgments of
his mouth,
O descendants of Israel, his servant, 13
Children of Jacob, his chosen!
He is the LORD, our God; 14
His judgments are in all the earth.
He remembers his covenant forever, 15
The word he has commanded, to a
thousand generations;
The covenant he made with Abraham, 16
And his oath to Isaac.

For he confirmed it to Jacob as a stat- 17
ute,
To Israel as an eternal covenant;
Saying, "To you I give the land of 18
Canaan
As your portion and your inheritance."
While you were but few in number, 19
Of slight importance and but strangers therein,
When they went back and forth from 20
one nation to another,
And from one kingdom to another
people,
He permitted no man to oppress them, 21
And warned kings concerning them,
"Touch not my anointed, 22
And do my prophets no harm!"

23 Sing to the LORD, all the earth,
Publish his deliverance abroad from day to day.
24 Tell among the nations his glory,
Among all the peoples, his wonders.
25 For great is the LORD and greatly to be praised;
Fearful is he above all gods;
26 For all the gods of the peoples are nonentities,
But the LORD made the heavens.
27 Honor and majesty are before him;
Strength and beauty are in his sanctuary.

28 Ascribe to the LORD, O families of peoples,
Ascribe to the LORD glory and strength.
29 Ascribe to the LORD the glory of his name;
Bring an offering and come into his courts.
Worship the LORD in holy array;
30 Tremble before him all the earth;
The world also is established that it cannot be moved.
31 Let the heavens rejoice, and let the earth exult;
And let them say among the nations that the LORD is king.

32 Let the sea roar, and its fulness;
Let the field exult and all that is therein.
33 Then let all the trees of the wood shout for joy before the LORD,
For he comes to judge the earth.
34 Praise the LORD, for he is good;
For his kindness is everlasting.

35 Then say, "Save us, O God of our salvation,
Assemble us and deliver us from the nations,
To give thanks to thy holy name,
To triumph in thy praise."
36 Blessed be the LORD, the God of Israel,
From everlasting even to everlasting.

Then all the people said, "Amen,"
and praised the LORD.
37 So he left there, before the ark of the
covenant of the LORD, Asaph and his
kinsmen to minister before the ark continually, as each day's work required;
38 namely, Obed-edom with their kinsmen, sixty-eight; Obed-edom also, the
son of Jeduthun, and Hosah to be doorkeepers; Zadok the priest and his kinsmen the priests, before the dwelling of the LORD in the high place that was in Gibeon, to offer burnt-offerings to the LORD upon the altar of burnt-offering continually morning and evening, according to all that is written in the law of the LORD, which he commanded Israel; and with them Heman and Jeduthun, and the rest of those selected, who were mentioned by name to give thanks to the LORD, because his kindness is everlasting; and with them Heman and Jeduthun, trumpets and cymbals, to make music, and instruments for the songs of God, and the sons of Jeduthun for the gate. Then all the people went each to his house, and David returned to greet his family.

DAVID'S DESIRE TO BUILD A TEMPLE, 17:1–27

Now when David dwelt in his house, David said to Nathan the prophet,

"See, I dwell in a house of cedar, while the ark of the covenant of God dwells under tent curtains."

Then Nathan said to David,

"Do all that is in your mind, for God is with you."

But that very night the word of God came to Nathan, saying,

"Go and say to my servant David, Thus says the LORD: 'You shall not build me a house to dwell in; for I have not dwelt in a house since the day I brought up Israel even to this day, but I have gone from tent to tent and from dwelling to dwelling. During all the time that I have gone to and fro with all Israel, did I speak a word to one of the judges of Israel whom I commanded to shepherd my people, saying, "Why have you not built me a house of cedar?" Now therefore thus shall you say to my servant David: "Thus the LORD of hosts has said, 'I took you from the pasture, from following the flock, that you should be a leader over my people Israel; and I have been with you wherever you have gone, and have cut off all your enemies from before you; and I will make for you a name, like the name of the great who are in the earth. I will also appoint a place for my people Israel and will plant them

that they may dwell in their own place,
and be disturbed no more. The wicked
shall no more consume them as former-
10 ly, even from the day that I commanded judges to be over my people Israel.
I will also subdue all your enemies.
Moreover I tell you that the LORD will
11 build for you a house; and when your
days are finished, to go with your fathers, then I will establish your heir
after you, who shall be one of your
sons, and I will establish his kingdom.
12 He shall build me a house, and I will
establish his throne forever.
13 "I will be a father to him,
And he shall be a son to me;
And I will not withdraw my kindness
from him,
As I withdrew it from him who was
before you.
14 But I will appoint him in my house
and my kingdom forever;
And his throne shall be established
forever.' " ' "
15 In accordance with all these words
and all this vision, so did Nathan speak
to David.
16 Then King David went in and sat
down before the LORD and said,
"Who am I, O LORD God, and what
is my house, that thou hast brought me
17 thus far? As though this was too small
a thing in thy sight, O God, thou hast
gone on to speak concerning the house
of thy servant for a long time to come.
Thou regardest me after the manner of
a man, thou who exaltest me, O LORD
18 God! What more can David say to
thee concerning the honor done thy
servant? for thou knowest thy servant.
19 O LORD, for thy servant's sake, and according to thine own heart hast thou
wrought all this greatness, to make
20 known all great things. O LORD, there
is none like thee, and there is no God
beside thee, according to all that we
21 have heard with our ears. What other
nation in the earth is like thy people
Israel, whom God went to redeem for
himself as a people, to make for thee a
name by great and terrible things, in
driving out nations before thy people,
whom thou didst redeem out of Egypt?
22 For thy people Israel thou didst make
thine own people forever, and thou, O
23 LORD, didst become their God. Now
therefore, O LORD, let the word that
thou hast spoken concerning thy servant and concerning his house be confirmed forever, and do as thou hast
spoken, that thy name may be estab- 24
lished and magnified forever, in saying,
'The LORD of hosts is the God of Israel,
a God to Israel, and the house of David thy servant shall be established before thee.' For thou, O my God, hast re- 25
vealed to thy servant, that thou wilt
build for him a house; therefore thy
servant has found courage to pray before thee. And now, O LORD, thou art 26
God, and thou hast spoken this good
word to thy servant. Now therefore, it 27
has pleased thee to bless the house of
thy servant that it may continue before thee forever! For thou, O LORD,
hast blessed, and it is blessed forever."

DAVID'S CONQUESTS, 18:1–17

Now after this David defeated the 18
Philistines and subdued them, and took
Gath and its towns from the Philistines. He also defeated Moab, and the 2
Moabites became subject to David and
brought tribute. Then David defeated 3
Hadadezer, king of Zobah, at Hamath,
as he went to establish his power at the
Euphrates river; and David took from 4
him a thousand chariots, seven thousand horsemen, and twenty thousand
footmen; and David hamstrung all the
chariot horses, but reserved enough of
them for one hundred chariots.
Likewise when the Syrians of Damas- 5
cus came to help Hadadezer, king of
Zobah, David slew of the Syrians twenty-two thousand men. Then David put 6
garrisons in Damascene Syria, and the
Syrians became subject to David and
brought tribute. Thus the LORD gave
victory to David wherever he went.
David also took the shields of gold that 7
were on the servants of Hadadezer, and
brought them to Jerusalem; and from 8
Tibhath and Cun, cities of Hadadezer,
David took a very large amount of
bronze, with which Solomon made the
bronze sea and the columns and the
utensils of bronze.
Now when Tou, king of Hamath, 9
heard that David had defeated all the
army of Hadadezer, king of Zobah, he 10
sent Hadoram his son to King David to
greet him and congratulate him, because he had fought against Hadadezer
and defeated him; for Hadadezer had
been Tou's opponent in war; and he had

with him all sorts of vessels of gold, sil-
11 ver, and bronze. These also did King
David dedicate to the LORD, together
with the silver and gold that he carried
away from all the nations—from Edom,
Moab, the Ammonites, the Philistines,
and Amalek.
12 Moreover Abishai, the son of Zeruiah, slew of the Edomites in the Valley
13 of Salt, eighteen thousand men. Then
he put garrisons in Edom, and all Edom
became subject to David. Thus the
LORD gave victory to David wherever
he went.
14 So David became king over all Israel,
and he administered justice and right-
15 eousness to all the people. Now Joab,
the son of Zeruiah, was in command of
the army, and Jehoshaphat, the son of
16 Ahilud, was recorder, and Zadok, the
son of Ahitub, and Abimelech, the son
of Abiathar, were priests, and Shawsha
17 was scribe; Benaiah, the son of Jehoiada, was in command of the Cherethites
and the Pelethites, and David's sons
were chiefs at the side of the king.

DAVID'S VICTORIES, 19:1—20:8

19 Now after this, Nahash, the king of
the Ammonites, died and his son be-
2 came king in his stead. Then David
said,
"I will show kindness to Hanun, the
son of Nahash, because his father
showed kindness to me."
So David sent messengers to condole
with him concerning his father. But
when David's servants came to the land
of the Ammonites to Hanun to condole
3 with him, the princes of the Ammonites said to Hanun,
"Do you imagine that David is honoring your father in sending you comforters? Have not his servants come to
inspect and to overthrow and to spy
out the land?"
4 So Hanun took David's servants, and
shaved them, cut their garments off at
5 the hips, and sent them away. Then
certain ones went and told David concerning the men, and he sent to meet
them, for they were greatly ashamed.
So the king said,
"Remain at Jericho until your beards
are grown and then return."
6 Now when the Ammonites saw that
they were in bad odor with David,
Hanun and the Ammonites sent a
thousand talents of silver to hire chariots and horsemen from Aram-of-the-
two-rivers, and Aram-Maacah, and
from Zobah. So they hired thirty-two 7
thousand chariots, and the king of
Maacah and his people, who came and
encamped before Medeba. Then the
Ammonites gathered themselves together from their cities and came for
battle. When David heard of it, he sent 8
Joab and all the army of seasoned
troops. Then the Ammonites came out 9
and drew up in line of battle at the entrance of the city, but the kings who
came were by themselves in the open
country.
Now when Joab saw that he had to 10
meet both a frontal and rear attack, he
made a selection from all the picked
men of Israel, and drew them up in
line against the Arameans. Then the 11
rest of the people he placed in command
of Abishai his brother; and he drew
them up in line against the Ammonites.
Then he said, 12
"If the Arameans prove too strong
for me, then you shall be my help, but
if the Ammonites prove too strong for
you, then I will assist you. Be coura- 13
geous, and let us show ourselves
strong for the sake of our people and for
the cities of our God; and may the
LORD do that which is good in his
sight."
Now when Joab and the people who 14
were with him drew near to join battle
with the Arameans, they fled before
him; and when the Ammonites saw that 15
the Arameans had fled, they likewise
fled before Abishai his brother, and entered the city. Then Joab came to
Jerusalem.
But when the Arameans saw that 16
they had been defeated by the Israelites, they sent messengers and brought
the Arameans who were beyond the
river, with Shophach, the commander
of the army of Hadadezer, at their head.
Now when it was told David, he gath- 17
ered together all Israel and crossed the
Jordan and came upon them; and David drew up the battle line facing the
Arameans, and they fought with him.
But the Arameans fled before Israel, 18
and David slew of the Arameans seven
thousand horsemen and forty thousand
footmen. He also slew Shophach, the
commander of the army. When the 19
servants of Hadadezer saw that they

had been defeated by Israel, they made
peace with David and served him. So
the Arameans were not willing to succor the Ammonites any more.
20 Now at the return of spring, at the
time when kings go forth, Joab led out
the main force of the army and laid
waste the land of the Ammonites, and
came and besieged Rabbah. But David
remained at Jerusalem; and Joab at-
2 tacked Rabbah and destroyed it. Then
David took the crown of their king from
his head, and found its weight to be a
talent of gold, and in it was a precious
stone; and it found a place on David's
head. And he brought away a very
3 large amount of spoil of the city. He
also brought forth the people who were
in it and put them to saws and to iron
picks and axes. Thus David did to all
the cities of the Ammonites; and David
returned with all the people to Jerusalem.
4 After this a war broke out with the
Philistines at Gezer; then Sibbecai the
Hushathite slew Sippai of the descendants of the giant, and they were sub-
5 dued. Again there was war with the
Philistines, and Elhanan, the son of
Jair, slew Lahmi, the brother of Goliath
the Gittite, the staff of whose spear was
6 like a weaver's beam. There was still
another war at Gath, where a huge man
with six fingers on each hand and six
toes on each foot, also a descendant of
7 the giant, defied Israel; but Jonathan,
the son of Shimea, David's brother,
8 slew him. These were born to the giant
in Gath, and they fell by the hand of
David and by the hand of his servants.

DAVID'S CENSUS AND THE PLAGUE, 21:1–30

21 Then Satan stood up against Israel
2 and moved David to number Israel. So
David said to Joab and to the commanders of the people,

"Go number Israel from Beersheba
even to Dan; and bring me word that I
may know their number."
3 Then Joab said,

"May the LORD add to his people a
hundred times as many as they are!
But, my lord, O king, are they not all
my lord's servants? Why does my lord
seek this thing? Why should he be a
cause of guilt to Israel?"

But the king's word prevailed over 4
Joab. Therefore Joab went forth, and
went to and fro throughout all Israel
and came to Jerusalem. So Joab gave 5
to David the number of the people mustered. All Israel were one million one
hundred thousand men that drew
sword; and Judah was four hundred
and seventy thousand men that drew
sword. But Levi and Benjamin he did 6
not count among them, for the king's
order was abominable to Joab.
Now this thing was evil in the sight of 7
God, so that he attacked Israel. There- 8
fore David said to God,

"I have sinned greatly, in that I have
done this thing. But now, take away, I
pray thee, the iniquity of thy servant,
for I have done very foolishly."
Then the LORD spoke to Gad, Da- 9
vid's seer, saying,

"Go and speak to David saying, 10
'Thus says the LORD: "Three things
I offer you; choose one of them that I
may do it to you." ' "
So Gad came to David and said to
him, 11

"Thus says the LORD: 'Choose either 12
three years of famine or three months of
sweeping defeat at the hands of your
foes with the sword of your enemies
overtaking you; or else that for three
days the sword of the LORD and pestilence be in the land, and the angel of
the LORD act as a destroyer throughout all the territory of Israel.' Now
therefore consider what answer I shall
return to him who sent me."
Then David said to Gad, 13

"I am in great distress. I would
rather fall into the hand of the LORD,
for his mercy is very great; but let me
not fall into the hand of man."
So the LORD sent a pestilence upon 14
Israel; and there fell of Israel seventy
thousand men. And God sent an angel 15
to Jerusalem to destroy it; but as he was
about to destroy it, the LORD saw it
and repented of the evil, so that he said
to the destroying angel,

"It is enough; now stay your hand."
Now the angel of the LORD was standing by the threshing-floor of Ornan the
Jebusite.
So when David lifted up his eyes and 16
saw the angel of the LORD standing between the earth and the heavens, with
a drawn sword in his hand stretched out
over Jerusalem, then David and the

elders, covered with sackcloth, fell upon
17 their faces; and David said to God,
"Is it not I who gave orders to number the people? I am the one who has
sinned and done very wickedly; but
these sheep, what have they done? O
LORD, my God, let thy hand, I pray
thee, be against me and against my
father's house; but not against thy people that they should be plague-strick-
en."
18 Then the angel of the LORD told Gad
to say to David, that David should go
up and rear an altar to the LORD in the
threshing-floor of Ornan the Jebusite.
19 So David went up at the word of Gad,
which he spoke in the name of the
20 LORD; and when Ornan turned and saw
the angel, his four sons who were with
him hid themselves. Now Ornan was
21 threshing wheat and when David came
to Ornan, Ornan looked up and saw
David, and came out of the threshing-
floor and did obeisance to David with
22 his face to the earth. Then David said
to Ornan,
"Give me the place of the threshing-
floor that I may build on it an altar to
the LORD; for the full price you shall
give it to me, that the plague may be
stayed from the people."
23 "Take it as your own," said Ornan to
David, "and let my lord the king do
what is good in his sight. See, I give the
oxen for a burnt-offering and the
threshing-sledges for wood and the
wheat for the cereal-offering—I give it
all."
24 But King David said to Ornan,
"No, but I will surely buy it for the
full price; for I will not take that which
is yours for the LORD, or offer a burnt-
offering which costs me nothing."
25 So David gave to Ornan for the place
six hundred shekels of gold by weight.
26 Then David built there an altar to the
LORD and offered burnt-offerings and
thank-offerings. Accordingly when he
called to the LORD, he answered him
with fire from heaven upon the altar
27 of burnt-offering. Then the LORD
spoke to the angel, and he put his sword
again in its sheath.
28 At that time, when David saw that
the LORD had answered him in the
threshing-floor of Ornan the Jebusite,
29 he sacrificed there. Now the dwelling
of the LORD, which Moses had made in
the desert, and the altar of burnt-offering were at that time in the high place
at Gibeon; and David was not able to 30
go before it to inquire of God, for he was
afraid because of the sword of the angel
of the LORD.

DAVID'S PREPARATIONS FOR THE TEMPLE AND ITS WORSHIP, 22:1—23:32

Then David said, 22
"This is the house of the LORD God,
and this is the altar of burnt-offering for
Israel."
Therefore David gave orders to gath- 2
er together the foreigners who were in
the land of Israel, and he set masons to
hewing out cut stones to build the house
of God. David also prepared iron in 3
abundance for the nails for the doors of
the gates and for the clamps, likewise
bronze in abundance beyond weight;
and innumerable cedar timbers, for the 4
Sidonians and the Tyrians brought
cedar timbers in abundance to David.
Then David said, 5
"Solomon my son is young and inexperienced, and the house that is to be
built for the LORD must be exceedingly
magnificent, far-famed, and glorious
throughout all lands. I will therefore
prepare for it."
So David made extensive preparations before his death.
Then he called for Solomon his son 6
and commanded him to build a house
for the LORD, the God of Israel. Ac- 7
cordingly David said to Solomon his
son,
"I myself had in mind to build a
house to the name of the LORD my
God. But the word of the LORD came 8
to me saying, 'You have shed much
blood, and have carried on great wars;
you shall not build a house to my name,
because you have shed much blood before me upon the earth. Behold, a son 9
shall be born to you, who shall be a man
of rest, and I will give him rest from all
his enemies round about, for his name
shall be Solomon [the peaceful one], and
I will give peace and quietness to Israel in his days. He shall build a house 10
to my name, and he shall be my son and
I will be his father; and I will establish
the throne of his kingdom over Israel
forever.' Now, my son, the LORD be 11
with you, that you may prosper and
build the house of the LORD your God,

12 as he has spoken concerning you. Only
the LORD give you discretion and insight when he gives you charge of Israel, that thus you may keep the law of
13 the LORD your God. Then you will
prosper, if you are careful to observe
the statutes and the ordinances which
the LORD commanded Moses concerning Israel. Be strong and courageous,
14 fear not, neither be dismayed. Now,
behold, in my poverty, I have prepared
for the house of the LORD a hundred
thousand talents of gold, a million
talents of silver, and bronze and iron
so abundant that it cannot be weighed;
timber also and stone I have prepared,
15 and you may add thereto. Moreover
there are with you workmen in abundance, hewers and workers of stone and
timber and all who are skilful in every
16 kind of work. Of the gold, the silver,
the bronze, and the iron, there is no
end. Arise and be doing, and the LORD
be with you."

17 David also commanded all the
princes of Israel to help Solomon his
son:

18 "Is not the LORD your God with
you, and has he not given you rest on
every side? For he has delivered into
my hand the inhabitants of the land,
and the land is subdued before the
19 LORD and before his people. Now set
your heart and your mind to seek the
LORD your God; arise therefore, and
build the sanctuary of the LORD God,
that you may bring the ark of the covenant of the LORD and the holy vessels
of God into the house that is to be built
to the name of the LORD."

23 Accordingly when David had reached
a ripe old age, he made Solomon his son
2 king over Israel. Then he gathered together all the princes of Israel, with the
3 priests and the Levites. Now the Levites were numbered from thirty years
old and upward, and their number according to the polls of their males was
4 thirty-eight thousand. Of these twenty-four thousand were to oversee the
work of the house of the LORD, and six
thousand were recorders and judges,
5 and four thousand were doorkeepers,
while four thousand were praising the
LORD with instruments which were
6 made, to praise therewith; and David
arranged them in divisions, according
to the sons of Levi: Gershom, Kohath,
and Merari.

Of the Gershonites, Ladan and 7
Shimei. Ladan's three sons were Jehiel 8
the chief, Zetham, and Joel. The three 9
sons of Shimei were Shelomoth, Haziel,
and Haran; these were the heads of the
families of Ladan. And the sons of 10
Shimei were Jahath, Ziza, Jeush, and
Beriah. These four were the sons of
Shimei. Jahath was the first and Zizah 11
the second; but Jeush and Beriah did
not have many sons; they were therefore regarded as a family for one appointment.

The four sons of Kohath were Am- 12
ram, Izhar, Hebron, and Uzziel. The 13
sons of Amram were Aaron and Moses;
and Aaron was set apart to be sanctified as most sacred, that he and his
sons should burn incense before the
LORD forever, to minister and to bless
in his name for all time. As for Moses 14
the man of God, his sons were reckoned
among the tribe of Levi. The sons of 15
Moses were Gershom and Eliezer. The 16
sons of Gershom were Shebuel the first;
and the son of Eliezer was Rehabiah the 17
first; for Eliezer had no other sons, but
the sons of Rehabiah were very many.
Izhar's son was Shelomith the first. 18
The sons of Hebron were Jeriah, the 19
first, Amariah the second, Jahaziel the
third, and Jekameam the fourth. The 20
sons of Uzziel were Micah the first and
Isshiah the second. The sons of Merari 21
were Mahli and Mushi, the sons of
Mahli, Eleazer and Kish. Now Eleazar 22
died and had no sons, but daughters
only; and their kinsmen, the sons of
Kish, took them in marriage. The sons 23
of Mushi were three, Mahli, Eder, and
Jeremoth.

These were the Levites according to 24
their father's houses, heads of families,
according to their registration, by the
number of names according to their
polls, who did the work for the service
of the house of the LORD, from twenty
years old and upward. For David said, 25
"The LORD, the God of Israel, has
given rest to his people, and he now
dwells in Jerusalem for all time. So 26
the Levites shall no more be required to
carry the dwelling or any of the utensils for its service."

For by the last words of David, the 27
number of the Levites was from twenty
years old and upward. Likewise their 28
function was to attend the sons of
Aaron for the service of the house of the

LORD, about the courts and chambers,
and in the purifying of all the holy
things, even the work of the service of
29 the house of God; for the bread that is
arranged in layers, also, and for the fine
flour for the cereal-offering, whether for
unleavened cakes or that which is for
the baking pan or what is mixed, and
for all measures of capacity and meas-
30 ures of length; and to stand every
morning to thank and praise the LORD
31 and likewise at evening; and to offer all
burnt-offerings to the LORD on the sabbaths and at the new moons, and at the
fixed festivals, in number according to
the ordinance concerning them, con-
32 tinually before the LORD; and that
they should have charge of the tent of
meeting, and the charge of the sanctuary, and the charge of the sons of
Aaron their kinsmen, for the service of
the house of the LORD.

DAVID'S ORGANIZATION OF THE TEMPLE STAFF, 24:1—26:32

24 Now the sons of Aaron were in divisions. The sons of Aaron were Nadab
2 and Abihu, Eleazar and Ithamar. But
Nadab and Abihu died before their
father and had no children; so Eleazar
3 and Ithamar served as priests. Then
David, with the aid of Zadok of the
sons of Eleazar and Ahimelech of the
sons of Ithamar, divided them according to their appointment in their serv-
4 ice. Now there were found to be more
chief men of the sons of Eleazar than of
the sons of Ithamar; therefore they assigned them thus: of the sons of Eleazar, sixteen heads of families and of the
sons of Ithamar, eight according to
5 families. Thus they divided them by
lot, one like the other; for there were
princes of the sanctuary and of God,
both of the sons of Eleazar and of the
6 sons of Ithamar. Moreover Shemaiah,
the son of Nethanel the scribe, who was
of the Levites, recorded them in the
presence of the king and the princes,
and Zadok the priest, and Ahimelech,
the son of Abiathar, and the heads of
families of the priests and of the Levites, one family being taken for Eleazar, and one taken for Ithamar.
7 Now the first lot came forth to Je-
8 hoiarib, the second to Jedaiah, the
third to Harim, the fourth to Seorim,
the fifth to Malchijah, the sixth to
Mijamin, the seventh to Hakkoz, the 1
eighth to Abijah, the ninth to Jeshua, 1
the tenth to Shecaniah, the eleventh to 1
Eliashib, the twelfth to Jakim, the thir- 1
teenth to Huppah, the fourteenth to
Jeshebeah, the fifteenth to Bilgah, the 1
sixteenth to Immer, the seventeenth to 1
Hezir, the eighteenth to Happizzez, the 1
nineteenth to Pethahiah, the twentieth
to Jehezkel, the twenty-first to Jachin, 1
the twenty-second to Gamul, the twen- 1
ty-third to Delaiah, the twenty-fourth
to Maaziah. Such was their appoint- 1
ment for their service to come into the
house of the LORD according to the
ordinance given them by Aaron their
father, as the LORD, the God of Israel,
had commanded him.

Also of the rest of the Levites, of the 2
sons of Amram there was Shubael; of
the sons of Shubael, Jehdeiah; of Reha- 2
biah, of the sons of Rehabiah, Isshiah
the chief; of the Izharites, Shelomoth, 2
of the sons of Shelomoth, Jahath; and 2
of the sons of Hebron, Jeriah the first,
Amariah the second, Jahaziel the third,
Jekameam the fourth. The son of Uz- 2
ziel was Micah, of the sons of Micah,
Shamir; the brother of Micah, Isshiah; 2
of the sons of Isshiah, Zechariah. The 2
sons of Merari were Mahli and Mushi;
the son of Jaaziah, Beno. The sons of 2
Merari, of Jaaziah, Beno, Shoham,
Zaccur, and Ibri; of Mahli, Eleazar, 2
who had no sons; of Kish, the sons of 2
Kish, Jerahmeel; and the sons of Mushi 3
were Mahli, Eder, and Jerimoth. These
were the Levites according to their
families. They likewise cast lots, even 3
as did their kinsmen the Aaronites before David the king, Zadok, Ahimelech,
and the heads of families of the priests
and of the Levites; the fathers of the
chief, even as those of his younger
brother.

David and the commanders of the **2**
army also set apart for the service certain of the sons of Asaph, Heman, and
Jeduthun, who should prophesy with
lyres, harps, and cymbals; and the
numbers of the men who did the work
according to their service were: of the 2
sons of Asaph, Zaccur, Joseph, Nethaniah, and Asharelah, the son of Asaph,
under the direction of Asaph, who
prophesied at the bidding of the king;
of Jeduthun, the sons of Jeduthun, 3

Gedaliah, Zeri, Jeshaiah, Hashabiah,
and Mattithiah, six under the direction
of their father Jeduthun with the lyre,
who prophesied, thanking and praising
4 the LORD; of Heman, the sons of Heman, Bukkiah, Mattaniah, Uzziel, Shebuel, Jerimoth, Hananiah, Hanani,
Eliathah, Giddalti, Romamtiezer, Joshbekashah, Mallothi, Hothir, Mahazi-
5 oth. All these were the sons of Heman,
the king's seer in the affairs of God, to
lift up the horn. Moreover God gave to
Heman fourteen sons and three daugh-
6 ters. All these were under the direction
of their father for song in the house of
the LORD, with cymbals, harps, and
lyres for the service of the house of God,
while Asaph, Jeduthun, and Heman
7 were at the command of the king. Also
the number of them together with their
kinsmen instructed in singing to the
LORD, including all that were skilful,
was two hundred and eighty-eight.
8 They cast lots for their duties, the small
as well as the great, the teacher as the
pupil.

9 Now the first lot came forth for
Asaph to Joseph, the second to Gedaliah, he and his kinsmen and his sons
10 being twelve; the third to Zaccur, his
11 sons and his kinsmen being twelve; the
fourth to Izri, his sons and his kins-
12 men being twelve; the fifth to Nethaniah, his sons and his kinsmen being
13 twelve; the sixth to Bukkiah, his sons
14 and his kinsmen being twelve; the seventh to Jesharelah, his sons and his
15 kinsmen being twelve; the eighth to
Jeshaiah, his sons and his kinsmen be-
16 ing twelve; the ninth to Mattaniah,
his sons and his kinsmen being twelve;
17 the tenth to Shimei, his sons and his
18 kinsmen being twelve; the eleventh to
Azarel, his sons and his kinsmen being
19 twelve; the twelfth to Hashabiah, his
20 sons and his kinsmen being twelve; for
the thirteenth Shubael, his sons and his
21 kinsmen being twelve; for the fourteenth Mattithiah, his sons and his
22 kinsmen being twelve; for the fifteenth
Jeremoth, his sons and his kinsmen be-
23 ing twelve; for the sixteenth Hananiah,
his sons and his kinsmen being twelve;
24 for the seventeenth Joshbekashah, his
25 sons and his kinsmen being twelve; for
the eighteenth Hanani, his sons and his
26 kinsmen being twelve; for the nineteenth Mallothi, his sons and his kins-
27 men being twelve; for the twentieth
Eliathah, his sons and his kinsmen being twelve; for the twenty-first Hothir, 28
his sons and his kinsmen being twelve;
for the twenty-second Giddalti, his 29
sons and his kinsmen being twelve; for 30
the twenty-third Mahazioth, his sons
and his kinsmen being twelve; for the 31
twenty-fourth Romamti-ezer, his sons
and his kinsmen being twelve.

For the divisions of the doorkeepers 26
there was of the Korahites, Meshelemiah, the son of Kore, of the sons of
Asaph. Meshelemiah also had sons, 2
Zechariah the first-born, Jediael the
second, Zebadiah the third, Jathniel the
fourth, Elam the fifth, Jehohanan the 3
sixth, Eliehoenai the seventh. Obed- 4
edom had sons, Shemaiah the first-
born, Jehozabad the second, Joah the
third, Sacar the fourth, Nathanel the
fifth, Ammiel the sixth, Issachar the 5
seventh, Peullethai the eighth; for God
blessed him. Also to Shemaiah his son 6
were sons born, who ruled over the
house of their father; for they were
men of ability. The sons of Shemaiah 7
were Othni, Rephael, Obed, and Elzabad, whose kinsmen were men of ability, Elihu and Semachiah. All these 8
were of the sons of Obed-edom: they
and their sons and their kinsmen were
able men in strength for the service,
sixty-two of Obed-edom. And Meshele- 9
miah had sons and kinsmen, men of
ability, eighteen in all. Also Hosah of 10
the Merarites had sons, Shimri the
chief; for though he was not the first-
born, his father made him chief, Hilkiah 11
the second, Tebaliah the third, Zechariah the fourth; all the sons and kinsmen of Hosah were thirteen.

Of these were the divisions of door- 12
keepers, even of the chief men, having
functions like their kinsmen, to minister in the house of the LORD. They 13
also cast lots, the small as well as the
great, according to their families, for
each gate. Thus the lot eastward fell 14
to Shelemiah. Then for Zechariah his
son, a discreet counselor, they cast lots
and his lot came out northward; to 15
Obed-edom southward, and to his sons
the storehouse; to Hosah westward, by 16
the gate that goes into the ascending
highway, watch against watch. East- 17
ward were six Levites, northward four
a day, southward four a day, and for
the storehouse two by two, for the 18
colonnade westward, four at the high-

19 way and two at the colonnade. These
were the divisions of the doorkeepers
of the Korahites and the Merarites.
20 Also of the Levites, Ahijah was in
charge of the treasures of the house of
God, and the treasures of the dedicated
21 things. The sons of Ladan, the descendants of Gershon through Ladan,
the heads of families of Ladan the Ger-
22 shonite, Jehieli and his kinsmen, Zetham and Joel, were in charge of the
23 treasures of the house of God. Of the
Amramites, Izharites, Hebronites, and
24 Uzzielites was Shebuel, son of Gershom, son of Moses, ruler over the
25 treasures, and his kinsmen through
Eliezer were Rehabiah his son, Jeshaiah
his son, Joram his son, Zichri his son,
26 and Shelomoth his son. This Shelomoth
and his kinsmen were in charge of all
the treasures of dedicated things which
David the king and the heads of families, the commanders of thousands and
hundreds, and the commanders of the
27 army, had dedicated. From wars and
from the spoil they dedicated them for
the repair of the house of the LORD.
28 Thus all that Samuel the seer had dedicated as well as Saul, the son of Kish,
Abner, the son of Ner, and Joab, the
son of Zeruiah—whoever dedicated
anything, it was under the charge of
29 Shelomoth and his kinsmen. Of the
Izharites, Chenaniah and his sons were
for the outward business over Israel, as
30 scribes and judges. Of the Hebronites,
Hashabiah and his kinsmen, one thousand seven hundred able men, were in
charge of Israel beyond the Jordan
westward for all the work of the LORD
31 and the service of the king. Jerijah
was chief of the Hebronites, even the
Hebronites, according to their generations by families. In the fortieth year
of the reign of David there were sought
out and found among them valiant
32 men, Jazer of Gilead and his kinsmen,
men of valor, two thousand seven hundred heads of families; and David the
king appointed them over the Reubenites, the Gadites, and the half-tribe of
Manasseh for every affair of God and
every affair of the king.

DAVID'S ADMINISTRATIVE OFFICERS, 27:1–34

27 Now the Israelites according to their
number, heads of families, commanders of thousands and of hundreds, and
their scribes that served the king in
every matter of the divisions that came
in and went out month by month
throughout all the months of the year,
of every division there were twenty-
four thousand. Over the first division 2
for the first month was Jashobeam, the
son of Zabdiel, and in his division were
twenty-four thousand; he was one of 3
the sons of the descendants of Perez,
the chief of all the commanders of the
army for the first month. Over the divi- 4
sion of the second month, Dodai the
Ahohite and his division, and Mikloth
the leader; and in his division were
twenty-four thousand. The third com- 5
mander of the army of the third month
was Benaiah, the son of Jehoiada the
priest, chief; and in his division were
twenty-four thousand. The same was 6
Benaiah, a hero of the Thirty, and in
charge of the Thirty; and of his division was Ammizabad his son. The 7
fourth for the fourth month was Asahel,
the brother of Joab, and Zebadiah his
son after him, and in his division were
twenty-four thousand. The fifth com- 8
mander for the fifth month was Sham-
huth the Izrahite, and in his division
were twenty-four thousand. The sixth 9
for the sixth month was Ira, the son of
Ikkesh the Tekoite, and in his division
were twenty-four thousand. The sev- 10
enth for the seventh month was Helez
the Pelonite of the Ephraimites, and in
his division were twenty-four thousand. The eighth for the eighth month 11
was Sibbecai the Hushathite of the
Zerahites, and in his division were
twenty-four thousand. The ninth for 12
the ninth month was Abiezer the
Anathothite of the Benjaminites, and in
his division there were twenty-four
thousand. The tenth for the tenth 13
month was Maharai the Netophathite
of the Zerahites, and in his division
were twenty-four thousand. The elev- 14
enth for the eleventh month was Benaiah the Pirathonite of the Ephraimites,
and in his division were twenty-four
thousand. The twelfth for the twelfth 15
month was Heldai the Netophathite of
Othniel, and in his division were twenty-four thousand.

Furthermore in command of the 16
tribes of Israel there were Eliezer, the
son of Zichri, ruler of the Reubenites,

Shephatiah, the son of Maacah of the Simeonites, Hashabiah, the son of Kemuel of the Levites, Zadok of Aaron, Elihu, one of the brothers of David of Judah, Omri, the son of Michael of Issachar, Ishmaiah, the son of Obadiah of Zebulon, Jeremoth, the son of Azriel of Naphtali, Hoshea, the son of Azaziah of the Ephraimites, Joel, the son of Pedaiah of the half-tribe of Manasseh in Gilead, Iddo, the son of Zechariah of the half-tribe of Manasseh, Jaasiel, the son of Abner of Benjamin, Azarel, the son of Jeroham of Dan. These were in command of the tribes of Israel. Now David did not take the census of those under twenty years of age, because the LORD had said that he would increase Israel like the stars of the heavens. Joab, the son of Zeruiah, began the census but he did not complete it; and since this brought wrath upon Israel, the census was not entered in the records of the Chronicles of King David.

Now over the king's stores was Azmaveth, the son of Adiel, and over the stores in the fields, in the cities, in the villages and watchtowers, was Jonathan, the son of Uzziah. Ezri, the son of Chelub, was overseer of the field workers for tilling the soil. Over the vineyards was Shimei the Ramathite; and over the increase of the vineyards was Zabdi the Shiphmite; over the olive trees and sycamores which were in the lowlands was Baal-hanan the Gederite, and over the stores of oil Joash; and over the herds that pastured in Sharon was Shitrai the Sharonite, and over the herds that pastured in the valleys was Shaphat, the son of Adlai; over the camels was Obil the Ishmaelite, and over the asses was Jehdeiah the Meronothite; over the flocks was Jaziz the Hagrite. All these were overseers of the property of King David.

Also Jonathan, David's uncle, was a counselor, a man of understanding and a scribe; and Jehiel, the son of Hachmoni, was a companion of the king's sons. Ahithophel was also the king's counselor; and Hushai the Archite was the king's friend, and after Ahithophel was Jehoiada, the son of Benaiah, and Abiathar; and Joab was commander of the king's army.

DAVID ENTRUSTS TO SOLOMON THE PLANS FOR THE TEMPLE, 28:1–21

Then David assembled at Jerusalem 28
all the commanding officers of Israel,
the chiefs of the tribes, the heads of the
divisions that ministered to the king,
the commanders of thousands and the
commanders of hundreds, and the overseers of all the property and possessions
of the king and of his sons, together
with the eunuchs and the heroes, even
all the valiant men. Thereupon David 2
rose to his feet and said,
"Hear me, my kinsmen and my people; I had in mind to build a house of
rest for the ark of the covenant of the
LORD and for a footstool of the feet of
our God; and I had prepared to build
it, but God said to me, 'You shall not 3
build a house for my name, for you are
a man of wars and have shed blood.'
However, the LORD, the God of Israel, 4
chose me out of all my father's house to
be king over Israel forever, for he has
chosen Judah to be prince; and from the
house of Judah, my father's house, and
from my father's sons, he took pleasure
in me to make me king over all Israel.
Now of all my sons—for the LORD has 5
given me many—he has chosen Solomon my son to sit upon the throne of
the LORD'S kingdom over Israel, and 6
he has said to me, 'Solomon your son
shall build my house and my courts for
I have chosen him to be a son to me,
and I will be a father to him; I will 7
establish his kingdom even forever, if
he be strong to perform my commands,
and my ordinances as at this day.'
Now therefore in the sight of all Israel, 8
the assembly of the LORD, and in the
hearing of our God be careful to seek
after all the commands of the LORD
your God, in order that you may continue to possess this good land, and
leave it as an inheritance to your children after you for all time. As for you, 9
Solomon my son, learn to know the
God of your father and serve him with
a perfect heart and a willing mind; for
the LORD searches all hearts and understands all the imagination of the
thoughts. If you seek him, he will be
found of you; but if you forsake him,
he will reject you forever. Take heed 10
now, for the LORD has chosen you to

build a house for the sanctuary; be
strong and do it."
11 Then David gave to Solomon his son
the pattern of the porch, its houses, its
treasuries, its upper chambers, and its
rooms within, and the house of propitia-
12 tion; and the pattern of all that he had
by the spirit for the courts of the house
of the LORD and for all the chambers
round about, for the treasuries of the
house of God, and for the treasuries of
13 the dedicated things; also for the divisions of the priests and the Levites and
for all the work of the service of the
house of the LORD and for all the utensils of the service of the house of the
14 LORD; and of gold by weight for the
gold of the utensils of service of every
sort, and for all the utensils of silver by
weight for all the vessels of service of
15 every sort; and the weight for the gold-
en lampstands, and their lamps of gold
by weight for every lampstand and
their lamps; and for the silver lampstands by weight for every lampstand
according to the service of every lamp-
16 stand; and the gold by weight for the
tables of the bread that is arranged in
layers, for every table; and silver for
17 the tables of silver; and for the forks,
basins, and jars of pure gold, and for
the golden bowls by weight for every
bowl, and of the silver bowls by weight
18 for every bowl; and for the altar of incense of refined gold by weight, and gold
for the pattern of the chariot of the
cherubim, flying and covering the ark
of the covenant of the LORD.
19 "The whole in writing is from the
hand of the LORD to me, causing me to
understand, even all the works of the
pattern."
20 David also said to Solomon his son,
"Be strong and courageous, and do
it; fear not, nor be dismayed, for the
LORD God, even my God, is with you;
he will not fail you nor forsake you until
all the work of the service of the house
21 of the LORD is finished. Now behold
the pattern of the porch and its houses,
its treasuries, its upper rooms, and its
inner chambers, and of the house of
propitiation, even the pattern of the
house of the LORD. Behold also the
divisions of the priests and the Levites
for all the service of the house of God;
and there shall be with you for all manner of work every willing man that has
skill for all manner of service; also the
overseers and all the people will be entirely at your command."

THE CLOSING SCENES OF DAVID'S LIFE, 29:1-30

Then David, the king, said to all the assembly,

"Solomon my son, whom alone God has chosen, is still young and inexperienced, and the work is great; for the palace is not for man but for the LORD God. Now I have prepared with all my vigor for the house of my God the gold for the things to be of gold, silver for the silver, bronze for the bronze, iron for the iron, wood for the uses of wood, stones of onyx, and stones to be set, stones of antimony, stones of various colors, and all sorts of precious stones and marble plentifully. Furthermore in my devotion to the house of my God, as I have a private treasure of gold and silver, I give it for the house of my God over and above all that I have prepared for the sanctuary, namely, three thousand talents of gold, of the gold of Ophir, and seven thousand talents of refined silver, for overlaying the walls of the buildings, gold for the uses of gold, silver for the silver, even for every work by the hands of workmen. Now who will make a voluntary offering today like one consecrating himself to the priesthood?"

Then the heads of families and the princes of the tribes of Israel, the commanders of thousands, the commanders of hundreds, and the overseers of the work of the king made a voluntary offering; they thus gave for the service of the house of God five thousand talents of gold, beside ten thousand darics, ten thousand talents of silver, eighteen thousand talents of bronze, and a hundred thousand talents of iron. Those in possession of stones gave them to the treasure of the house of the LORD, in charge of Jehiel the Gershonite. Then the people rejoiced for they offered willingly, because with a perfect heart they offered voluntary offerings to the LORD; and David the king also rejoiced greatly.

So David blessed the LORD in the sight of all the assembly, and David said,

"Blessed art thou, O LORD God of Israel, our father forever and ever.

Thine, O LORD, is the greatness and the power and the glory and the preeminence and the majesty, for all that is in the heavens and on the earth is thine; thine is the dominion O LORD, and thou are exalted as the supreme head. Riches and honor come from thee, since thou rulest over all; in thy hand are power and might, and it lies in thy hand to make all great and strong. Now therefore our God we thank thee and praise thy glorious name. Yet who am I and what is my people that we should be able to offer such voluntary offerings? for all things come from thee, and we give thee only what is thine. For we are strangers before thee and passing guests as all our fathers were; our days upon earth are like a shadow and without hope. O LORD our God, all these materials that we have prepared to build thee a house for thy holy name came from thy hand and are all thine own. I know also, O my God, that thou triest the heart and delightest in uprightness. As for me, in the uprightness of my heart I have freely offered all these things, and now I have seen with joy thy people that are present here make a voluntary offering to thee. O LORD, the God of Abraham, Isaac, and Israel, our fathers, keep this forever as the imagination of the thoughts of the heart of thy people, and direct their hearts toward thee; and grant to Solomon my son a perfect heart to keep thy commands, thy decrees, and thy statutes, and to do all these things and to build the palace for which I have made provision."

Then David said to all the assembly, "Bless now the LORD your God."

Thereupon all the assembly blessed
the LORD, the God of their fathers, and
bowed down and did obeisance before
the LORD and before the king. On the 21
next day they also sacrificed sacrifices
and offered burnt-offerings to the
LORD, a thousand bulls, a thousand
rams, and a thousand lambs with their
libations, and sacrifices in abundance
for all Israel, and ate and drank before 22
the LORD that day with great rejoicing.

Then they made Solomon, the son of
David, king the second time, and
anointed him to be the prince of the
LORD, and Zadok to be priest. So 23
Solomon sat on the throne of the LORD
as king in place of David his father, and
prospered; and all Israel obeyed him.
Accordingly all the princes and heroes, 24
as well as all the sons of King David,
submitted to Solomon the king. More- 25
over the LORD exalted Solomon greatly in the sight of all Israel, bestowing
upon him such royal majesty as no king
before him in Israel had enjoyed.

Now David, the son of Jesse, ruled 26
over all Israel. The time that he ruled 27
over Israel was forty years; he reigned
seven years in Hebron, and thirty-three
years in Jerusalem. At length he died 28
at a ripe old age, wealthy and honored,
and Solomon his son became king in his
stead. Now the records of David the 29
king from first to last, behold, they are
written in the Records of Samuel the
seer and the Records of Nathan the
prophet and the Records of Gad the
seer, with all his reign and his prowess 30
and the times through which he and
Israel passed, and likewise all the kingdoms of the other countries.

THE SECOND BOOK OF CHRONICLES

SOLOMON'S PRAYER AND ITS ANSWER, 1:1–17

1 NOW Solomon, the son of David, established himself over
his kingdom, and the LORD
his God was with him and
2 greatly exalted him. Accordingly Solomon spoke to all Israel, to the commanders of thousands and of hundreds,
to the judges and to every prince in all
3 Israel, heads of families. Then Solomon
accompanied by the whole assembly
went to the high place that was at
Gibeon, for there was the tent of meeting of God, which Moses, the servant
of the LORD, had made in the desert.
4 But David had brought up the ark of
God from Kirjathjearim to the place
that David had prepared for it, for he
had pitched a tent for it at Jerusalem.
5 Moreover the bronze altar, that Bezalel, the son of Uri, the son of Hur,
had made, was there before the dwelling
6 of the LORD, and Solomon and the assembly resorted to it. Solomon accordingly made an offering there on the
bronze altar before the LORD which
was at the tent of meeting, and offered
upon it a thousand burnt-offerings.
7 The following night God appeared to
Solomon, and said to him, "Ask what I
shall do for you."
8 Then Solomon said to God,
"Thou hast shown great kindness to
David my father and hast made me
9 king in his stead. Now O LORD God,
let thy promise to David my father be
established; for thou hast made me
king over a people as numerous as the
10 dust of the earth. Give me now wisdom
and knowledge, that I may go out and
come in before this people; for who can
judge this great people of thine?"
11 Then God said to Solomon,
"Because this was in your mind and
you have not asked for riches, wealth,
or honor, nor the life of those who hate
you, and have not asked for long life,
but have asked wisdom and knowledge
for yourself, that you may judge my
people over whom I have made you
king, wisdom and knowledge are
granted to you, and I will give you
riches and wealth and honor, such as
none of the kings have had who have
been before you, nor shall any after you
have the like."

So Solomon came from the high place which was at Gibeon from before the tent of meeting to Jerusalem; and he reigned over Israel.

Now Solomon gathered together chariots and horsemen until he had fourteen hundred chariots and twelve thousand horsemen that he placed in the chariot cities and with the king at Jerusalem. Likewise the king made silver and gold as common in Jerusalem as stones, and cedar as plentiful as sycamores in the lowland. Now Solomon's import of horses was from Egypt and from Kue, the king's dealers being accustomed to receive them for a price. Also they brought up and took from Egypt a chariot for six hundred shekels of silver and a horse for a hundred and fifty; and so for all the kings of the Hittites and the kings of Aram, they were brought out through their agency.

SOLOMON PREPARES TO BUILD THE TEMPLE, 2:1–18

Now Solomon directed that a house be built for the name of the LORD, and a house for his kingdom. So Solomon told off seventy thousand men as forced laborers, and eighty thousand woodcutters in the mountains, besides three thousand six hundred to oversee them. Moreover Solomon sent to Hiram, king of Tyre, saying,

"As you dealt with David my father when you sent him cedars to build himself a house for his residence, so now I am about to build a house for the name of the LORD my God, to dedicate it to him, and to burn before him incense of sweet spices, and for the continual array of layers of bread and for the burnt-

offering morning and evening, on the
sabbaths and at the new moons, and
fixed festivals of the LORD our God
(which are perpetually binding upon
5 Israel). Moreover the house which I
am about to build is to be great, for our
6 God is greater than all gods. But who
is able to build him a house, since the
heavens and the very highest heavens
cannot contain him? Who am I then,
that I should build him a house, to burn
7 incense before it? Now therefore, send
me a man skilled to work in gold and
silver, in bronze and iron, in purple,
crimson, and violet stuffs, and who
knows how to engrave engravings in
conjunction with the skilled men who
are with me in Judah and Jerusalem,
8 whom David my father provided. Send
me also cedars, firs, and sandalwood
from Lebanon, for I know that your
servants understand how to cut timber
in Lebanon, and, behold, my servants
9 will join with your servants to prepare
the timber in abundance, for the house
which I am about to build is to be great
10 and wonderful. See now, I will indeed
give your servants the cutters that cut
the timber twenty thousand kors of
crushed wheat, twenty thousand kors
of barley, twenty thousand baths of
wine, and twenty thousand baths of oil."
11 Then Hiram, king of Tyre, answered
in writing and sent it to Solomon,
"Because the LORD loves his people
he has made you king over them."
12 Moreover Hiram said,
"Blessed be the LORD, the God of
Israel, who made the heavens and the
earth, who has given to David the
king a wise son, endued with discretion
and understanding, who should build a
house for the LORD and a house for his
13 kingdom. Now then I have sent a skilful man, endued with understanding,
14 Huram-abi, the son of a Danite woman,
but his father was a Tyrian, who knows
how to work in gold, silver, bronze,
iron, stone, and wood, in purple, violet,
and fine linen, and in crimson, also to
perform all manner of engraving and to
sketch any artistic device that may be
assigned to him, together with your
skilled workmen and the skilled workmen of my lord David, your father.
15 Therefore the wheat and the barley, the
oil and the wine, of which my lord has
spoken, let him send to his servants,
16 and we will cut the timber out of Lebanon according to all your requirement, and we will bring it to you by sea
to Joppa, and you shall take it up to
Jerusalem."
Then Solomon took a census of all 17
the resident aliens who were in the land
of Israel, according to the census which
David his father had made; and there
were found a hundred and fifty-three
thousand six hundred. Accordingly he 18
made seventy thousand of them laborers, and eighty thousand hewers in the
mountains, and three thousand six hundred overseers to see that the people
worked.

PLANS AND SPECIFICATIONS FOR THE TEMPLE, 3:1–17

Then Solomon began to build the 3
house of the LORD at Jerusalem on
Mount Moriah where the LORD had
appeared to David his father, in the
place which David had prepared, on
the threshing-floor of Ornan the Jebusite. He began to build on the second 2
day of the second month in the fourth
year of his reign. Now these are the 3
foundations which Solomon laid for the
building of the house of God. The
length according to the old measure was
sixty cubits and the breadth twenty
cubits. Also the porch that was in 4
front—its length, corresponding to the
breadth of the house, was twenty cubits,
and the height one hundred and twenty;
and he overlaid it within with pure
gold. And the large room he ceiled with 5
cypress wood which he overlaid with
fine gold and worked on it palm trees
and chains. He adorned the house with 6
exquisite precious stones, and the gold
was gold of Parvaim. He also covered 7
the house, the beams, the thresholds,
the walls, and the doors with gold, and
engraved cherubim on the walls. Like- 8
wise he made the most sacred room: its
length, corresponding to the breadth of
the house, was twenty cubits and its
breadth twenty cubits, and he covered
it with fine gold, amounting to six hundred talents. Moreover the weight of 9
the nails was fifty shekels of gold each,
and he covered the upper chambers
with gold. In the most sacred room he 10
made two cherubim of image work and
they overlaid them with gold. The 11
wings of the cherubim were twenty cu-

bits in length; the wing of the one
cherub extended five cubits to the wall
of the house, and the other wing likewise extended five cubits to the wing of
12 the other cherub; and the one wing of
the other cherub extended five cubits to
the wall of the house, while the other
wing joined the wing of the other
13 cherub. The wings of these cherubim
as they flew were twenty cubits, though
they stood on their feet with their faces
toward the house.
14 He also made a veil of violet, purple,
crimson, and fine linen, and worked
cherubim on it.
15 Moreover he made in front of the
house two columns thirty-four and two
thirds cubits high, with a capital five
16 cubits in height on the top of each. He
also made chains in the inner room and
put them on the top of the columns;
and he made a hundred pomegranates
17 and put them on the chains. So he set
up the columns in front of the temple,
one on the right hand and the other on
the left; and he called the name of the
one on the right hand Jachin, and the
name of the one on the left Boaz.

THE EQUIPMENT OF THE TEMPLE, 4:1–22

4 Moreover he made an altar of bronze
twenty cubits long, twenty cubits
broad, and ten cubits high. He also
made the molten sea, ten cubits in diameter from brim to brim, round in
form, five cubits high, and thirty cubits
3 in circumference; and underneath it
were the figures of bulls encircling it
for ten cubits, completely surrounding
the sea. The bulls were in two rows,
4 cast when it was cast. It stood on
twelve bulls, three facing north, three
facing west, three facing south, and
three facing east; and the sea was superimposed upon them, while their
5 haunches were all directed inward. It
was about four inches thick and the
brim was made like the brim of a cup,
like a lily bud, and it had a capacity of
6 three thousand baths. He also made
ten lavers, and put five on the right side
and five on the left, for use in washing;
such things as the burnt-offering they
washed in them; but the sea was for the
7 priests to wash in. He made ten lampstands of gold according to their pattern and he placed them in the temple,
five on the right side and five on the
left. He also made ten tables and set 8
them in the temple, five on the right
side and five on the left; and he made a
hundred basins of gold. Furthermore 9
he made the court of the priests, and
the great court, and the doors for the
court, and he overlaid the doors with
bronze. He put the sea on the right side 10
of the house facing the southeast.
Hiram also made the pots, the shovels, 11
and the basins. So Hiram completed
the work which he did for King Solomon in the house of God: two columns, 12
the two bowl-shaped capitals that were
on the top of the columns, the two networks to cover the two bowls of the
capitals that were on the top of the
columns, and the four hundred pome- 13
granates for the two networks, two rows
of pomegranates for each network, to
cover the two bowl-shaped capitals that
were on the top of the columns. He also 14
made stands and he made lavers upon
the stands; the one sea, with the twelve 15
bulls under it, the pots, the shovels, the 16
forks, and all their utensils did Hiram
his father make for King Solomon, for
the house of the LORD, of burnished
bronze.
The king cast them in the plain of the 17
Jordan, in the clay ground between
Succoth and Zeredah. Thus Solomon 18
made an enormous amount of these
utensils, for the weight of the bronze
was beyond reckoning. Likewise Solo- 19
mon made all the utensils that were in
the house of God, also the golden altar,
the tables, upon which was the Presence-bread, the lampstands with their 20
lamps to burn according to the prescription before the inner room, of rare
gold, the flowers, the lamps, and the 21
tongs of gold, and that purest gold, the 22
snuffers, basins, cups, and the fire pans
of rare gold. Even the entrance of the
house and its doors in front of the
sacred place and the doors of the house,
that is, for the temple, were of gold.

THE DEDICATION OF THE TEMPLE, 5:1—7:10

Thus all the work which Solomon 5
performed for the house of the LORD
was completed, and Solomon brought
in the things which David his father

had dedicated; and the silver and gold
and all the utensils he put in the treasur-
2 ies of the house of God. Then Solomon
assembled the elders of Israel and all
the heads of the tribes, the princes of
families of the Israelites, to Jerusalem,
to bring up the ark of the covenant of
the LORD from the city of David, that
3 is *Zion*. So all the men of Israel assembled to the king at the feast in the
4 seventh month. Likewise all the elders
of Israel came, and the Levites took up
5 the ark; and they brought up the ark of
meeting and all the holy utensils that
were in the ark; the priests and the
6 Levites brought these up. Then King
Solomon and all the assembly of Israel,
that were assembled to him, were before
the ark sacrificing so many sheep and
oxen that they could not be counted or
7 numbered. Then the priests brought
the ark of the covenant of the LORD to
its place in the inner room of the house,
in the most holy place, beneath the
8 wings of the cherubim, for the cherubim
had their wings spread over the place of
the ark, so that the cherubim made a
covering above the ark and its poles.
9 But the poles were so long that the ends
of the poles were seen from the ark in
front of the inner room, yet they were
not seen outside, and there they are to
10 this day. There was nothing in the ark
except the two tablets which Moses had
placed there at Horeb, when the LORD
made a covenant with the Israelites at
the time they came out of Egypt.
11 Now when the priests came out of the
sanctuary (for all the priests who were
present sanctified themselves), there
was no attempt to keep their divisions.
12 The Levites who were singers, all of
of them, Asaph, Heman, Jeduthun,
their sons, and their kinsmen, clothed
in fine linen, with cymbals, lyres, and
harps, stood at the east side of the altar
and with them a hundred and twenty
13 priests blowing upon trumpets. Now
when the trumpeters and singers joined
in unison to make a great volume of
sound in praising and thanking the
LORD, and when they raised a sound
with trumpets and with cymbals and
with instruments of song, and when
they praised the LORD, saying,
"For he is good;
For his kindness is everlasting,"
then the house was filled with a cloud,
14 even the house of the LORD; so that the
priests were not able to stand to minister because of the cloud; for the glory
of the LORD filled the house of the
LORD.
Then Solomon said, 6
"The LORD has said that he would
dwell in thick darkness, but I have 2
built thee a house of lofty abode and a
fixed place for thee to dwell in forever."
Then the king faced about and 3
blessed all the assembly of Israel, and
all the assembly of Israel stood up; and 4
he said,
"Blessed be the LORD, the God of
Israel, who spoke with his own mouth
to David my father, and with his own
hands has fulfilled it, saying, 'Since the 5
day that I brought forth my people out
of the land of Egypt, I chose no city out
of all the tribes of Israel in which to
build a house that my name might be
there, neither did I choose any man to
be a ruler over my people Israel; but I 6
have chosen Jerusalem that my name
might be there, and I chose David to be
over my people Israel.' Now it was in 7
the mind of David my father to build a
house for the name of the LORD, the
God of Israel, but the LORD said to 8
David my father, 'Because it was in
your mind to build a house for my
name, you did well that it was in your
mind; nevertheless you yourself shall 9
not build the house but your son, who
shall come forth from your loins, he
shall build the house for my name.'
Now the LORD has made good his word 10
that he spoke; for I have risen up in the
place of David my father and sit upon
the throne of Israel, as the LORD
promised, and I have built the house
for the name of the LORD, the God of
Israel; and there I have put the ark in 11
which is the covenant of the LORD,
which he made with the Israelites."
Then he stood up before the altar of 12
the LORD in the presence of the whole
assembly of Israel and spread forth his
hands. For Solomon had made a bronze 13
platform five cubits long, five cubits
wide, and three cubits high, and had
set it in the midst of the court; and he
stood upon it, and kneeled upon his
knees before all the assembly of Israel,
and stretched out his hands toward the
heavens, and said, 14
"O LORD, the God of Israel, there is
no God like thee in the heavens or on
the earth, who keepest loving faith

with thy servants who walk before thee
15 with all their heart, who hast kept with
thy servant David my father that
which thou didst promise him; for thou
didst speak with thy mouth and with
thy hand thou hast fulfilled it, as it is
16 this day. Now therefore, O LORD, the
God of Israel, keep with thy servant
David my father that which thou didst
promise him, saying, 'You shall never
lack a man in my sight to sit upon the
throne of Israel, if only your sons take
heed to their way, to walk in my law as
17 you have walked before me.' Now
therefore, O LORD, the God of Israel,
let thy word be confirmed which thou
hast spoken to thy servant David.
18 "But can God really dwell with man
upon the earth? Behold, the heavens
and the highest heavens cannot contain
thee; how much less this house which I
19 have built! Yet turn thou to the prayer
of thy servant and to his supplication,
O LORD my God, to listen to the cry
and to the prayer which thy servant
20 offers before thee, that thine eyes may
be open toward this house day and
night, even toward the place of which
thou hast said thou wouldst put thy
name there; to listen to the prayer
which thy servant shall pray toward
21 this place; and listen thou to the supplications of thy servant and thy people
Israel, when they shall pray toward this
place; yea, hear thou from thy dwelling-place, even from the heavens, and when
thou hearest forgive.
22 "If a man sin against his neighbor,
and an oath be laid on him compelling
him to swear, and he come and swear
23 before thine altar in this house, then do
thou hear from the heavens; take action
and judge thy servants, punishing the
wicked by bringing his course of action
upon his own head, and vindicating the
righteous by rewarding him according
to his righteousness.
24 "Moreover if thy people Israel be
defeated before the enemy because they
have sinned against thee, if they turn
and confess thy name and pray and
make supplication before thee in this
25 house, then hear thou from the heavens
and forgive the sin of thy people Israel
and restore them to the land which
thou gavest to them and to their
fathers.
26 "When the heavens are shut up and
there is no rain because they have
sinned against thee, if they pray toward
this place and confess thy name and
turn from their sin, when thou dost
afflict them, then hear thou from the 27
heavens and forgive the sin of thy
servants and thy people Israel, when
thou teachest them the good way in
which they should walk, and send rain
upon thy land, which thou hast given
to thy people as a heritage.
"If there be in the land a famine, if 28
there be pestilence, blasting, mildew,
locusts, or caterpillars, if their enemies
besiege them in any of their gates,
whatever be the plague, whatever be
the sickness—whatever prayer, what- 29
ever supplication be made by any man,
or by all thy people Israel, who knows
each his own affliction and his own sorrow, and stretches out his hands toward
this house, then hear thou from the 30
heavens thy dwelling-place and forgive
and render to every man according to
all his ways, whose heart thou knowest (for thou, even thou alone, knowest
the hearts of the sons of men), that in 31
fear of thee they may walk in thy ways
as long as they live in the land which
thou gavest to our fathers.
"Moreover concerning the resident 32
alien, who is not of thy people Israel,
but comes from a far country for thy
great name's sake and thy mighty hand
and thy outstretched arm, when they
shall come and pray toward this house,
then hear thou from the heavens thy 33
dwelling-place and do in accordance
with all that the alien petitions of thee,
that all the peoples of the earth may
know thy name and fear thee, as do thy
people Israel, and that they may know
that this house which I have built is
called by thy name.
"If thy people go out to battle against 34
their enemies, by whatever way thou
shalt send them, and they pray to thee
in the direction of this city which thou
hast chosen and the house which I have
built for thy name, then hear thou from 35
the heavens their prayer and their supplication, and uphold their cause.
"If they sin against thee (for there is 36
no man who does not sin), and thou be
angry with them and deliver them to
the enemy, so that they carry them
away captive to a land far off or near;
yet if they take thought in the land to 37
which they have been carried captive,
and turn again and make supplication

to thee in the land of their captivity, saying, 'We have sinned, we have acted perversely and wickedly,' if they return to thee with all their mind and heart, in the land of their captivity to which they have been carried captive, and pray in the direction of their land, which thou gavest to their fathers, and the city which thou hast chosen, and the house which I have built for thy name, then hear thou from the heavens thy dwelling-place their prayer and their supplication, and uphold their cause and forgive thy people who have sinned against thee.

"Now O my God, let, I pray thee, thine eyes be open and thine ears attentive to the prayer made in this place. Now therefore O LORD God, arise to thy resting place, thou and the ark of thy strength; let thy priests O LORD God, be clothed with salvation and let thy pious ones rejoice in prosperity. O LORD God, turn not away the face of thine anointed; remember thy kindness toward David thy servant."

Now when Solomon had finished praying, the fire came down from the heavens and consumed the burnt-offering and the sacrifices, and the glory of the Lord filled the temple, so that the priests could not enter the house of the LORD, for the glory of the LORD filled the house of the LORD; and all the Israelites looked on, when the fire came down and the glory of the LORD was upon the temple; then they bowed down with their faces to the earth upon the pavement, and worshiped and gave thanks to the LORD:

"For he is good;
For his kindness is everlasting."

Then the king and all the people offered sacrifices before the LORD. King Solomon made a sacrifice of twenty-two thousand cattle and a hundred and twenty thousand sheep. So the king and all the people dedicated the house of God. Moreover the priests stood according to their appointed stations, the Levites also with instruments for the song of the LORD, which David the king had made to give thanks to the LORD (for his kindness is everlasting), when David offered praise by their aid; and the priests blew the trumpets before them, and all Israel stood up. Solomon also sanctified the interior of the court that was before the house of the
LORD; for there he offered the burnt-
offerings and the fat pieces of the thank-
offerings, because the bronze altar which
Solomon had made was unable to contain the burnt-offering, the cereal-
offering, and the fat pieces.
Thus Solomon held the feast at that 8
time seven days, and all Israel with
him, a very great assembly from the
Pass of Hamath to the Brook of Egypt.
Then on the eighth day they held a 9
closing celebration; for they gave seven
days to the dedication of the altar and
seven days to the feast. So on the 10
twenty-third day of the seventh month
he sent the people away to their homes,
rejoicing and glad of heart, because of
the goodness which the LORD had
shown to David and Solomon, and to
Israel his people.

SOLOMON'S VISION, 7:11–22

Thus Solomon finished the house of 11
the LORD and the king's house, and all
that came into Solomon's mind to make
in the house of the LORD and in his own
house he carried out successfully. Then 12
the LORD appeared to Solomon by
night and said to him,
"I have heard your prayer and have
chosen this place as my house of sacrifice. If I shut up the heavens so that 13
there is no rain, if I command the locust
to devour the land, and if I send a pestilence among my people, then if my 14
people who are called by my name
humble themselves and pray and seek
my face and turn from their wicked
ways, I also will hear from the heavens
and will forgive their sins and heal their
land. Now my eyes shall be open and 15
my ears attentive to the prayer offered
in this place. Therefore I have chosen 16
and sanctified this house that my name
may be there forever, and my eyes and
my heart shall be there always. As for 17
you, if you will conduct yourself before
me as did David your father and do just
as I have commanded you and keep my
statutes and my ordinances, then will 18
I establish the throne of your kingdom
as I covenanted with David your
father, saying, 'You shall never lack a
man to rule over Israel.' But if you 19
turn and forsake my statutes and my
commands which I have set before you
and go and serve other gods and worship them, then will I uproot them out 20

of my land which I gave to them, and
this house which I have sanctified for
myself I will cast out of my sight, and
I will make it a proverb and a byword
21 among all peoples. And as for this
house which is so exalted, every passer-
by shall be amazed and say, 'Why has
the LORD done thus to this land and to
22 this house?' Then they shall say, 'Because they forsook the LORD, the God
of their fathers, who brought them out
of the land of Egypt, and took up with
other gods and worshiped them and
served them; therefore he has brought
upon them all this evil.' "

SOLOMON'S ADMINISTRATION, 8:1–18

8 Now at the end of twenty years, during which Solomon had built the house
2 of the LORD and his own house, Solomon built up the cities which Huram
had given to Solomon and caused the
Israelites to dwell there.
3 Then Solomon went against Hamath-
4 zobah and conquered it. He also built
Tadmor in the desert and all the store-
5 cities which he built in Hamath. Moreover he built Beth-horon the upper and
Beth-horon the lower, fortified cities
6 with walls, double gates, and bars, and
Baalath and all the store-cities that
Solomon had and all the cities for
chariots and the cities for horsemen,
and all that Solomon was pleased to
build in Jerusalem, in Lebanon, and
throughout all his realm.
7 As for all the people who were left of
the Hittites, the Amorites, the Perizzites, the Hivvites, and the Jebusites,
8 who were not of Israel, of their descendants who were left after them in the
land, whom the Israelites did not wipe
out, Solomon raised a forced levy of
9 slaves, as it is to this day. But of the
Israelites Solomon made no slaves for
his work, but they were his soldiers, the
commanders of his officers, and the
commanders of his chariots and his
10 horsemen. Now these were the garrison
commanders whom King Solomon had,
even two hundred and fifty who exer-
11 cised authority over the people. Solomon brought up the daughter of Pharaoh from the city of David to the
house which he had built for her, for he
said,
"My wife shall not dwell in the house
of David, king of Israel, because the places are holy wherever the ark of God has come."

Then Solomon offered burnt-offerings to the LORD upon the altar of the LORD, which he had built in front of the porch, according to the prescription for each day, offering according to the command of Moses, on the sabbath, at the new moons, and the fixed festivals, three times a year, the feast of unleavened cakes, the feast of weeks, and the feast of booths. According to the ordinance of David his father he appointed the divisions of the priests for their service, and the Levites to their functions, to praise and to minister before the priests according to the requirement of each day, and the doorkeepers by their divisions at each gate, for such was the command of David, the man of God; and they did not turn from the commands of the king concerning the priests and the Levites in any respect nor concerning the treasures. Thus all the work of Solomon was accomplished from the day of the foundation of the house of the LORD to the completion of the house of the LORD by Solomon.

Then Solomon went to Ezion-geber, and to Eloth on the seashore in the land of Elam; and Huram sent him by the hands of his servants ships and servants that had knowledge of the sea; and they came with the servants of Solomon to Ophir, and brought from there four hundred and fifty talents of gold, and brought them to King Solomon.

THE VISIT OF THE QUEEN OF SHEBA, 9:1–12

Now when the queen of Sheba heard of the fame of Solomon, she came to test him with hard questions at Jerusalem, accompanied by a very large retinue, with camels bearing spices and very much gold and precious stones, and when she came to Solomon, she conversed with him about all that was in her mind; and Solomon answered all her questions; there was nothing hidden from Solomon which he could not explain to her. Then when the queen of Sheba had seen the wisdom of Solomon, the house that he had built, the viands of his table, the appointment of his servants, the attendance of his waiters their clothing, his cupbearers, their clothing, and the burnt-offerings which he used to offer at the house of the LORD, there was no more spirit in her. So she said to the king,

"The report which I heard in my own land of your affairs and your wisdom was true; but I would not believe their words until I came and saw with my own eyes, and behold, the half was not told me about your great wisdom; you surpass the report which I heard. Happy are your wives, and happy are these servants of yours who stand before you continually and hear your wisdom! Blessed be the LORD your God who delighted in you, to set you on his throne to be king for the LORD your God. Because your God loved Israel to establish them forever, he has made you king over them, to administer justice and righteousness."

Then she gave the king five and a half talents of gold, a very great amount of spices and precious stones; there never were such spices as the queen of Sheba gave to Solomon. Also the servants of Huram, and the servants of Solomon who brought gold from Ophir, brought sandalwood and precious stones. Accordingly the king made of the sandalwood raised platforms for the house of the LORD and for the house of the king, and lyres and harps for the singers, the like of which were not seen before in the land of Judah.

Now King Solomon gave to the queen of Sheba all that it pleased her to ask for, besides the value of what she had brought to the king. Then she turned and went to her own land, together with her servants.

SOLOMON'S WEALTH, 9:13–31

The weight of gold that came to Solomon in one year was six hundred and sixty-six talents, besides what came from the traffic of the merchants and from all the kings of Arabia and from the governors of the land, who brought gold and silver to Solomon.

Now King Solomon made two hundred large shields of beaten gold (six hundred shekels of gold going to each shield), and three hundred shields of beaten gold (three hundred shekels of gold going to each shield), and the king put them in the House of the Forest of
Lebanon. The king also made a great 17
throne of ivory and overlaid it with
pure gold. The throne had six steps and 18
a footstool of gold fixed to the throne,
with arms on each side of the place of
the seat and two lions standing beside
the arms, while twelve lions stood there 19
on the six steps on each side. The like
was never made in any kingdom.

All King Solomon's drinking vessels 20
were of gold, and all the vessels of the
House of the Forest of Lebanon were
of rare gold. Silver was thought nothing
of in the days of Solomon. For the king 21
had ships that went to Tarshish with
the servants of Huram. Once every
three years the ships of Tarshish used
to come bringing gold, silver, ivory,
apes, and peacocks. So King Solomon 22
excelled all the kings of the earth in
riches and wisdom; and all the kings of 23
the earth sought the presence of Solomon to hear his wisdom, which God had
put into his mind. They brought each 24
his present: articles of silver and gold,
clothing, equipment, spices, horses, and
mules, so much year by year.

Moreover Solomon had four thousand 25
stalls for horses and chariots, and
twelve thousand horsemen, that he
stationed in the chariot cities and
with the king in Jerusalem; and he 26
ruled over all the kings from the River
to the land of the Philistines and as far
as the border of Egypt. The king made 27
silver as common in Jerusalem as stone,
and he made cedars as plentiful as sycamore trees that are in the lowland.
Horses were brought to Solomon from 28
Egypt and from all lands.

Now the rest of the records of Solo- 29
mon from first to last are they not
written in the Records of Nathan the
prophet, and in the Prophecy of Ahijah
the Shilonite, and in the Visions of Iddo
the seer regarding Jeroboam, the son of
Nebat? Thus Solomon reigned in Je- 30
rusalem over all Israel forty years.
Then Solomon slept with his fathers, 31
and they buried him in the city of
David his father, and Rehoboam his
son became king in his stead.

THE DISRUPTION OF THE KINGDOM, 10:1–19

Then Rehoboam went to Shechem, 10
for all Israel had come to Shechem to
make him king. But as soon as Jero- 2

boam, the son of Nebat, heard of it (for
he was in Egypt where he had fled from
the presence of Solomon the king),
3 Jeroboam returned from Egypt. So
they sent and called him, and Jeroboam
and all Israel came; and they spoke to
Rehoboam, saying,
4 "Your father made our yoke galling.
Now then lighten the galling service of
your father and his heavy yoke which
he laid upon us, and we will serve you."
5 Then he said to them,
"Go away and after three days return to me."
So the people went away.
6 Then King Rehoboam took council
with the old men who had stood before
Solomon his father, while he was still
alive, saying,
"How do you advise me to reply to
this people?"
7 They spoke to him, saying,
"If you will be kind to this people
and please them and speak kind words
to them, then they will be your servants
forever."
8 But he rejected the counsel of the old
men which they had given him, and
took counsel with the young men, who
had grown up with him and who were
9 his companions. So he said to them,
"What do you advise that we reply
to this people, who have spoken to me,
saying, 'Lighten the yoke which your
father laid upon us'?"
10 Then the young men who had grown
up with him spoke to him, saying,
"Thus you shall say to the people
who have spoken to you, saying, 'Your
father made our yoke heavy, now do
you lighten our yoke'; thus shall you
say to them: 'My little finger is thicker
11 than my father's loins! And now,
whereas my father loaded you with a
heavy yoke, I will add to your yoke;
my father chastised you with whips,
but I will chastise you with scorpions!'"
12 So when Jeroboam and all Israel
came to Rehoboam on the third day as
the king commanded, saying, "Return
13 to me the third day," the king answered them harshly, and King Rehoboam rejected the counsel of the old
14 men. So he spoke to them according to
the counsel of the young men, saying,
"My father made your yoke heavy,
but I will add to it. My father chastised
you with whips, but I will chastise you
with scorpions."

So the king did not listen to the people, for it was brought about by God, that the LORD might establish his word which he spoke by Ahijah the Shilonite to Jeroboam, the son of Nebat.

Now when all Israel saw that the king had not listened to them, the people replied to the king, saying,

"What portion have we in David? Yea, we have no heritage in the son of Jesse. All to your tents, O Israel! See now to your own house, O David!"

So all Israel departed to their tents.

But as for the Israelites who dwelt in the cities of Judah, Rehoboam reigned over them. Then King Rehoboam sent Hadoram who was in charge of the forced labor, but the Israelites stoned him to death with stones; whereupon King Rehoboam hastily leaped into his chariot, to flee to Jerusalem. So Israel has been in rebellion against the house of David down to this day.

THE ADMINISTRATION OF REHOBOAM, 11:1–23

When Rehoboam reached Jerusalem, he assembled the house of Judah and Benjamin, a hundred and eighty thousand picked warriors, to fight against Israel to bring back the kingdom to Rehoboam. But the word of the LORD came to Shemaiah, a man of God, saying,

"Speak to Rehoboam, the son of Solomon, king of Judah, and to all Israel in Judah and in Benjamin, saying, 'Thus says the LORD: "You shall not go up or fight against your kinsmen. Return every man to his house, for this thing is from me." ' "

So they listened to the words of the LORD and gave up the expedition against Jeroboam.

Accordingly Rehoboam dwelt in Jerusalem, and built cities for defense in Judah. Thus he built Bethlehem, Etam, Tekoa, Beth-zur, Soco, Adullam, Gath, Mareshah, Ziph, Adoraim, Lachish, Azekah, Zorah, Aijalon, and Hebron, which are in Judah and Benjamin, fortified cities. He also strengthened the fortresses and put commanders in them and stores of provisions, oil and wine. Also in each city he put shields and spears, and thus he made them very strong indeed. So he retained Judah and Benjamin.

Moreover the priests and the Levites who were in all Israel resorted to him from all their localities. For the Levites left their common lands and their possessions and went to Judah and to Jerusalem, because Jeroboam and his descendants had barred them from acting as priests to the LORD. But he appointed for himself priests for the high places, for the satyrs, and for the calves which he had made. And after them there came to Jerusalem from all the tribes of Israel those who had set their minds to seek the LORD, the God of Israel, and to sacrifice to the LORD, the God of their fathers. So they strengthened the kingdom of Judah, and made Rehoboam, the son of Solomon, strong for three years; for they walked three years in the way of David and Solomon.

Now Rehoboam took as wife Mahalath, the daughter of Jerimoth, the son of David, and of Abihail, the daughter of Eliab, the son of Jesse. She bore him sons: Jeush, Shemariah, and Zaham. Then after her he married Maacah, the daughter of Absalom, and she bore him Abijah, Attai, Ziza, and Shelomith. But Rehoboam loved Maacah, the daughter of Absalom, more than all his wives and concubines (for he took eighteen wives and sixty concubines, and he became the father of twenty-eight sons and sixty daughters). Moreover Rehoboam appointed Abijah, the son of Maacah, at the head as the crown prince among his brothers, for his purpose was to make him king. He also had the wisdom to distribute all his sons throughout all the districts of Judah and Benjamin and to all the fortified cities, and he gave them abundant provisions and sought for them a great number of wives.

THE INVASION OF JUDAH BY SHISHAK OF EGYPT, 12:1–16

Now when the kingdom of Rehoboam was established and he was strong, he forsook the law of the LORD and all Israel with him. In the fifth year of King Rehoboam, Shishak, king of Egypt, came up against Jerusalem, because they had acted treacherously toward the LORD, with twelve hundred chariots, and sixty thousand horsemen,
and the people who came with him out
of Egypt were without number: Lubians, Sukkiites, and Ethiopians. More- 4
over he took the fortified cities which
belonged to Judah and came to Jerusalem.
Then Shemaiah the prophet came to 5
Rehoboam and the princes of Judah
who were gathered together to Jerusalem because of Shishak, and said to
them,
"Thus says the LORD: 'You have
abandoned me, therefore I also have
abandoned you to Shishak.'"
Then the princes of Israel and the 6
king humbled themselves and said,
"The LORD is righteous."
But when the LORD saw that they 7
humbled themselves, the word of the
LORD came to Shemaiah, saying,
"They have humbled themselves. I
will not destroy them, but I will give
them some deliverance and my wrath
shall not be poured out upon Jerusalem
by Shishak. Nevertheless they shall be 8
his servants that they may know my
service from the service of the kingdoms of the lands."
So Shishak, king of Egypt, came up 9
against Jerusalem and took away the
treasures of the house of the LORD and
the treasures of the king's house, taking
all away. He also took away the shields
of gold which Solomon had made. Then 10
King Rehoboam made in their stead
shields of bronze and intrusted them to
the commanders of the guard, who
guarded the door of the king's house.
Then as often as the king came to the 11
house of the LORD, the guards would
come and take them up and bring them
back into the guard-room. But because 12
he humbled himself, the wrath of the
LORD turned from him, so as not to destroy him completely, and besides in
Judah good conditions persisted. So 13
King Rehoboam strengthened himself
in Jerusalem and reigned; for Rehoboam was forty-one years old when be became king and he reigned seventeen
years in Jerusalem, the city which the
LORD chose out of all the tribes of Israel to put his name there; and his
mother's name was Naamah the Ammonitess. But he did that which was 14
evil, for he did not set his mind to seek
the LORD.
Now the records of Rehoboam from 15
first to last are they not written in the

Records of Shemaiah the prophet and
Iddo the seer, according to genealogical enrolment? There were wars continually between Rehoboam and Jero-
16 boam. So Rehoboam slept with his
fathers, and he was buried in the city of
David; and Abijah his son became king
in his stead.

THE REIGN OF ABIJAH OF JUDAH, 13: 1–22

13 In the eighteenth year of King Jeroboam Abijah became king over Judah.
2 He reigned three years in Jerusalem,
and his mother's name was Micaiah,
the daughter of Uriel of Gibeah. There
was war between Abijah and Jeroboam;
3 and Abijah joined battle with an army
of distinguished warriors, composed of
four hundred thousand picked men,
and Jeroboam drew up the battle line
against him with eight hundred thousand picked men who were of distinguished prowess.
4 Then Abijah drew up on Mount
Zemaraim, which is in the highlands of
Ephraim, and said,
"Hear me, O Jeroboam and all Is-
5 rael: Ought you not to know that the
LORD, the God of Israel, gave the kingdom over Israel to David forever, even
to him and his sons by a covenant of
6 salt? Yet Jeroboam, the son of Nebat,
the servant of Solomon, the son of David, rose up and rebelled against his
7 lord, and there were gathered to him
worthless men, base scoundrels, who
strengthened themselves against Rehoboam, the son of Solomon, when Rehoboam was a youth and inexperienced,
8 and could not withstand them. Now
you think to withstand the kingdom of
the LORD under the sons of David; and
you are a great multitude, and with you
are the golden bulls which Jeroboam
9 made for you as gods. Have you not
driven out the priests of the LORD, the
sons of Aaron, and the Levites, and
made for yourselves priests like the
peoples of other lands? Whoever comes
to consecrate himself with a young bull
and seven rams, even he may become a
10 priest of the no-gods. But as for us, the
LORD is our God, and we have not forsaken him; the sons of Aaron minister
to the LORD as priests, and the Levites
11 with their work; and they burn to the
LORD every morning and every evening burnt-offerings and sweet incense
and bread is set in layers upon a clean
table and the golden lampstand with
its lamps to burn every evening, for we
keep the charge of the LORD our God
but you have forsaken him. See, God is
with us at our head, and his priests
with the trumpets of alarm to sound the
alarm against you. O Israelites, do not
fight against the LORD, the God of
your fathers; for you will not succeed."
However, Jeroboam laid an ambush
to come at their rear, so that they were
in front of Judah and the ambush was
behind them. Therefore when Judah
faced them, behold, the battle was in
front and rear. Then they cried out to
the LORD and the priests sounded with
the trumpets, and the men of Judah
gave a shout. Now when the men of
Judah shouted, God routed Jeroboam
and all Israel before Abijah and Judah;
and when the Israelites fled before Judah, God delivered them into their
hand, so that Abijah and his people
made a great slaughter among them,
and the slain of Israel who fell were five
hundred thousand picked men. Thus
the Israelites were humbled at that
time, and the Judeans prevailed, because they relied on the LORD, the God
of their fathers. Then Abijah pursued
Jeroboam, and took certain cities from
him, Bethel with its towns, Jeshanah
with its towns, and Ephron with its
towns. Jeroboam did not recover
strength again in the days of Abijah,
but the LORD struck him down and he
died.
But Abijah made himself strong and
took for himself fourteen wives and became the father of twenty-two sons and
sixteen daughters. Now the rest of the
records of Abijah, his ways and his
words, are written in the Midrash of the
Prophet Iddo.

THE REIGN OF ASA OF JUDAH, 14:1—16:14

So Abijah slept with his fathers, and
they buried him in the city of David,
and Asa his son became king in his
stead. In his days the land was quiet
for ten years. Asa did that which was
right in the sight of the LORD his God;
for he removed the foreign altars and
the high places, and broke down the

sacred pillars and cut down the sacred
poles; and he told Judah to seek the
LORD, the God of their fathers, and to
obey the law and the command. He also removed out of all the cities of Judah
the high places and the incense altars;
and the kingdom was quiet under him.
Furthermore he built fortified cities in
Judah, for the land was quiet, and he
had no war in those years, for the LORD
had granted him rest; and he said to
Judah,
"Let us build these cities and surround them with walls and towers,
gates and bars; the land is still at our
disposal because we have sought the
LORD our God; we have sought him,
and he has given us rest on every side."
So they built and prospered.
Now Asa had an army equipped with
shields and spears: out of Judah three
hundred thousand, and out of Benjamin, that carried shields and drew
bows, two hundred and eighty thousand—all of them distinguished warriors. Now Zerah, the Ethiopian, came
out against them with an army of a
million men and three hundred chariots, and advanced to Mareshah. Then
Asa went out to meet him, and they
drew up the battle line in the valley of
Zephathah at Mareshah. Asa cried to
the LORD his god and said,

"O LORD there is none besides thee to
help,
As between the mighty and him that
is without strength.
Help us, O LORD, our God;
For we rely on thee,
And in thy name we have come
against this multitude.
O LORD thou art our God;
Let not man prevail against thee."

Then the LORD routed the Ethiopians before Asa and before Judah, so
that the Ethiopians fled. Thereupon
Asa and the people who were with him
pursued them to Gerar; so that there
fell of the Ethiopians so many that
there were none left alive, for they were
shattered before the LORD and before
his army. They took a very large
amount of booty; they also conquered
all the cities in the neighborhood of
Gerar, for a panic from the LORD was
upon them, and they plundered all the
cities, for there was rich plunder in
them. In addition they captured the
tents of cattle and drove away a very
great number of sheep and camels;
then they returned to Jerusalem.
At that time the spirit of God came 15
upon Azariah, the son of Oded, so that 2
he went out to meet Asa, and said to
him,
"Listen to me, Asa, and all Judah
and Benjamin. The LORD has been
with you, because you have been true
to him; and if you seek him, he will be
found by you; but if you forsake him,
he will forsake you. Now for a long 3
time Israel has been without the true
God and without priestly instruction
and without law; but when in their dis- 4
tress they turned to the LORD, the God
of Israel, and sought him, he was found
by them. Now in those times there was 5
no peace to him that went out or to him
that came in, but great turmoils came
upon all the inhabitants of the lands;
and they were dashed in pieces, nation 6
against nation, and city against city,
for God discomfited them with all kinds
of distress. But be strong and let not 7
your hands slacken, for your work shall
be rewarded."
Now when Asa heard these words 8
and the prophecy of Oded the prophet,
he took courage and put away the
abominations from all the land of Judah and Benjamin and from the cities
which he had taken from the highlands
of Ephraim, and he repaired the altar
of the LORD that was in front of the
porch of the LORD. Then he assembled 9
all Judah and Benjamin together
with those who sojourned with them
out of Ephraim, Manasseh, and Simeon; for a very great number came over
to him from Israel, when they saw that
the LORD his God was with him. So 10
they assembled at Jerusalem in the
third month in the fifteenth year of the
reign of Asa; and they sacrificed to the 11
LORD on that day, of the booty which
they had brought, seven hundred cattle and seven thousand sheep. Then 12
they entered into a covenant to seek
the LORD, the God of their fathers,
with all their mind and with full determination, and that whoever would not 13
seek the LORD, the God of Israel,
should be put to death, whether small
or great, whether man or woman. They 14
also took oath to the LORD with a loud
voice and with shouting and the blasts
of trumpets, and rams' horns. Thus all 15
Judah rejoiced at the oath, for they had

sworn with all their heart and with all
their will, so that he was found by
them; and the LORD gave them rest on
every side.
16 Moreover Maacah, the mother of
Asa the king, he deposed from being
queen-mother, because she had made
an obscene image as an Asherah; and
Asa cut down her obscene image and
ground it to powder and burned it in
17 the Kidron valley. But the high places
were not removed from Israel; however
18 Asa's heart was perfect all his days. He
brought into the house of God the dedicated things of his father and his own
dedicated things, silver and gold and
19 utensils; and there was no more war
until the thirty-fifth year of the reign
of Asa.
16 In the thirty-sixth year of Asa's
reign, Baasha, king of Israel, came up
against Judah and built Ramah, to prevent anyone from going out or coming
2 in to Asa king of Judah. Then Asa
brought out silver and gold from the
treasuries of the house of the LORD and
the king's house and sent them to Ben-
hadad, king of Syria, who dwelt in
Damascus, saying,
3 "There is an alliance between me and
you, as there was between my father
and your father. See, I send you silver
and gold. Go, break your alliance with
Baasha, king of Israel, that he may
withdraw from me."
4 Accordingly Ben-hadad listened to
King Asa, and sent the commanders of
his forces against the cities of Israel,
and they conquered Ijon, Dan, and
Abel-maim, and all the store-cities of
5 Naphtali. Now when Baasha heard of
it, he stopped building Ramah, and
6 brought his work to an end. Then Asa
the king took all Judah and they carried away the stones of Ramah and its
timber with which Baasha had built,
and with them he built Geba and Mizpeh.
7 At that time Hanani the seer came to
Asa, king of Judah, and said to him,
"Because you have relied on the king
of Syria, and have not relied on the
LORD your God, therefore the army of
the king of Syria has escaped out of
8 your hand. Were not the Ethiopians
and the Lubians a vast army with an
enormous number of chariots and
horsemen? Yet because you relied on
the LORD he delivered them into your
hand. For the eyes of the LORD rang
the whole earth to exert his strength i
behalf of those who are devoted to hir
You have acted foolishly in this mat
ter, for from now on you shall hav
wars."
Then Asa was vexed at the seer an
put him in the prison-house, for he wa
in a rage with him because of this thing
Asa also tortured some of the people a
the same time.
Now the records of Asa from first t
last, behold, they are written in th
Book of the Kings of Judah and Israe
In the thirty-ninth year of his reign
Asa became diseased in his feet; the dis
ease was exceedingly painful; neverthe
less in his disease he did not seek th
LORD, but the physicians. So Asa slep
with his fathers, having died in th
forty-first year of his reign; and the
buried him in his own tomb which h
had cut out for himself in the city o
David, and they laid him in the be
which had been filled with all kinds o
spices, skilfully mixed; and they burne
for him a very great sacrifice.

THE PROSPERITY OF JEHOSH-APHAT, 17:1–19

Now Jehoshaphat his son becam
king in his stead and strengthened himself against Israel; and he placed troop
in all the fortified cities of Judah and
put garrisons in the land of Judah and
in the cities of Ephraim, which Asa his
father had taken. Moreover the LORD
was with Jehoshaphat because he
walked in the earlier ways of David his
ancestor and did not seek the Baals, but
sought the God of his ancestor, and
walked in his commands, and not according to the works of Israel. Therefore the LORD established the kingdom
in his hand, and all Judah brought gifts
to Jehoshaphat so that he had abundant wealth and honor. Then his heart
was exalted in the ways of the LORD,
and besides he put away the high places
and the sacred poles out of Judah.
Also in the third year of his reign, he
sent his princes Ben-hail, Obadiah,
Zechariah, Nethanel, and Micaiah to
teach in the cities of Judah; and with
them the Levites, Shemaiah, Nethaniah, Zebadiah, Asahel, Shemiramoth,
Jehonathan, Adonijah, Tobijah, and

Tobadonijah, the Levites; together
with Elishama and Jehoram, the
9 priests. Thus they taught in Judah,
having with them the book of the law
of the LORD; and they went about
throughout all the cities of Judah and
taught among the people.
10 Now the terror of the LORD was on
all the kingdoms of the lands that were
round about Judah, so that they did
11 not make war on Jehoshaphat. Also
some of the Philistines brought Jehoshaphat tribute, even a mass of silver;
likewise the Arabs brought him flocks:
seven thousand seven hundred rams,
and seven thousand seven hundred he-
12 goats. Thus Jehoshaphat kept on becoming more and more powerful, so
that he built in Judah castles and store-
13 cities. Moreover he had a large amount
of stores in the cities of Judah, and soldiers, distinguished warriors, in Jerusa-
14 lem. This was their roster according to
their families: of Judah, the commanders of thousands, Adnah the commander, and with him three hundred
15 thousand distinguished warriors; and
next to him Jehohanan the commander,
and with him two hundred and eighty
16 thousand; and next to him Amasiah,
the son of Zichri, who had volunteered
for the service of the LORD, and with
him two hundred thousand distin-
17 guished warriors. Also of Benjamin:
Eliada a distinguished warrior, and
with him two hundred thousand fur-
18 nished with bow and shield, and next to
him Jehozabad, and with him a hundred and eighty thousand, equipped for
19 war. These were those who served the
king, besides those whom the king
placed in the fortified cities throughout
Judah.

THE CAMPAIGN OF JEHOSHAPHAT AND AHAB AGAINST RAMOTH-GILEAD, 18:1–34

18 Now when Jehoshaphat had attained
very great riches and honor, he made a
2 marriage alliance with Ahab; and after
some years he went down to Ahab to
Samaria. Ahab killed a great number
of sheep and cattle for him and those
who accompanied him, and he induced
him to go up with him to Ramoth-
3 gilead. Accordingly Ahab, king of Israel, said to Jehoshaphat, king of Judah,
"Will you go with me to Ramoth-
gilead?"
"I am as you are, and my people as
your people; I will join you in the
war," he said to him.
Jehoshaphat said further to the king 4
of Israel,
"Inquire today, I pray, for the word
of the LORD."
Then the king of Israel assembled the 5
prophets, four hundred men, and said
to them,
"Shall I go to Ramoth-gilead to battle, or shall I forbear?"
"Go up," they said; "for God will deliver it into the hand of the king."
But Jehoshaphat said, 6
"Is there not here another prophet of
the LORD through whom we may inquire of him?"
Then the king of Israel said to Je- 7
hoshaphat,
"There is another man through
whom we might inquire of the LORD,
but I hate him; for he never prophesies
good concerning me, but always evil:
that is Micaiah, the son of Imla."
"Let not the king say so," said Jehoshaphat.
So the king of Israel called one of the 8
eunuchs and said,
"Bring quickly Micaiah, the son of
Imla."
Now the king of Israel and Jehosha- 9
phat, the king of Judah, were sitting
each on his throne, arrayed in their
robes, and they were sitting at the entrance of the gate of Samaria, and all
the prophets were engaged in ecstatic
prophecy before them. Then Zedekiah, 10
the son of Chenaanah, made for himself horns of iron and he said,
"Thus says the LORD: 'With these
you shall gore the Syrians until they
are destroyed.' "
So all the prophets prophesied, say- 11
ing,
"Go up to Ramoth-gilead and prosper; for the LORD will deliver it into
the hand of the king."
Now the messenger who went to call 12
Micaiah spoke to him, saying,
"See, the prophets with one accord
have spoken good to the king. Now, I
pray you, let your word be like one of
theirs and speak good."
"As the LORD lives," said Micaiah, 13
"what my God says, that will I speak."

14 Now when he came to the king, the
king said to him,
"Micaiah, shall I go to Ramoth-
gilead to battle, or shall I forbear?"
"Go up and prosper," he said; "for
the LORD will give it into your hand."
15 But the king said to him,
"How many times must I adjure you
that you speak to me nothing but the
truth in the name of the LORD?"
16 "I saw all Israel scattered on the
mountains," said he, "like sheep without a shepherd; and the LORD said,
'These have no master; let them return
each to his house in peace.' "
17 Then the king of Israel said to Jehoshaphat,
"Did I not say to you that he would
not prophesy good concerning me, but
only evil?"
18 But Micaiah said,
"Therefore hear the word of the
LORD: I saw the LORD sitting upon
his throne and all the army of the heavens standing on his right hand and on
19 his left; and the LORD said, 'Who will
deceive Ahab, king of Israel, so that he
may go up and fall at Ramoth-gilead?'
Then one said one thing and another
20 another, until a spirit came forth and
stood before the LORD and said, 'I will
deceive him,' and the LORD said to
21 him, 'By what means?' He said, 'I will
go forth and become a lying spirit in the
22 mouth of all his prophets.' Now therefore, behold, the LORD has put a lying
spirit in the mouth of these prophets of
yours, since the LORD has spoken evil
concerning you."
23 Then Zedekiah, the son of Chenaanah, approached and struck Micaiah on
the cheek, and said,
"Which way did the spirit of the
LORD go from me to speak to you?"
24 "Indeed, you shall see on the day
when you go into an inner chamber to
hide yourself," said Micaiah.
25 Then the king of Israel said,
"Seize Micaiah and take him back to
Amon, the governor of the city, and to
26 Joash, the king's son, and say, 'Thus
says the king: "Put this fellow in the
prison and feed him on bread and
water scantily until I return victorious." ' "
27 Whereupon Micaiah said,
"If you do indeed return victorious,
the LORD has not spoken by me. Hear,
all you peoples!" he said.

So the king of Israel and Jehosha- 28
phat, the king of Judah, went up to
Ramoth-gilead. Then the king of Is- 29
rael said to Jehoshaphat,
"I will disguise myself and go into
the battle, but do you put on your own
robes."
So the king of Israel disguised himself and went into the battle. Now the 30
king of Syria had charged his chariot
commanders, saying,
"Fight neither with small nor great,
except only with the king of Israel."
Accordingly when the chariot com- 31
manders saw Jehoshaphat, they said,
"It is the king of Israel."
So they surrounded him to fight
against him, but Jehoshaphat cried out,
and the LORD helped him, in that God
diverted them from him. When the 32
chariot commanders saw that it was
not the king of Israel, they turned back
from pursuing him. But a man drew 33
his bow at a venture and shot the king
of Israel between the jointed pieces and
the breastplate; then he said to the
charioteer,
"Wheel about and take me out of the
army; for I am badly wounded."
Now the battle grew fiercer that day, 34
while the king of Israel held himself upright in his chariot facing the Syrians
until evening; but about sunset he died.

JEHOSHAPHAT'S PIETY AND ITS VINDICATION,

19:1—21:1

Then Jehoshaphat, king of Judah, re- 1
turned to his house in Jerusalem in
peace. Whereupon Jehu, the son of 2
Hanani, the seer, went out to meet him
and said to King Jehoshaphat,
"Should you help the wicked, and
love those who hate the LORD? For
this reason wrath has come upon you
from the LORD. Nevertheless there is
still some good in you, in that you have
put away the sacred poles from the land
and have made up your mind to seek
God."
Now Jehoshaphat dwelt at Jerusa- 4
lem and again he went forth among the
people from Beersheba to the highlands
of Ephraim and brought them back to
the LORD, the God of their fathers. He 5
also appointed judges in the land in all
the fortified cities of Judah, city by
city; and he said to the judges, 6

"Consider what you do; for you do
not judge for man but for the LORD,
who is with you in the pronouncing of
7 judgment. Now therefore let the fear of
the LORD be upon you; take heed and
act; for there is no injustice with the
LORD our God, nor respect of persons,
nor taking of bribes."
8 Moreover Jehoshaphat established in
Jerusalem some of the Levites, priests,
and heads of families of Israel for the
judgment of the LORD, and for civil
disputes. Then they returned to Jeru-
9 salem, and he commanded them, saying,
"Thus you shall act in the fear of the
LORD, in faithfulness and with single-
10 ness of mind. Every case which comes
to you from your kinsmen who dwell in
their cities, between law and command,
statutes and ordinances, you shall warn
them that they be not guilty towards
the LORD, and thus wrath come upon
you and upon your kinsmen; do thus
11 and you shall not be guilty. Behold,
Amariah the priest is in authority over
you in every matter of the LORD, and
Zebadiah, the son of Ishmael, is the
prince of the house of Judah in all the
king's matters; the Levites are notaries
before you. Be strong and act, and the
LORD be with the upright."
0 Now afterwards when the Moabites
and the Ammonites and some of the
Meunites came against Jehoshaphat to
2 battle, some came and told Jehoshaphat, saying,
"A great multitude is coming against
you from beyond the sea from Edom;
and behold they are in Hazazon-tamar
(that is, Engedi)."
3 Then Jehoshaphat was afraid and set
himself to seek the LORD and proclaimed a fast throughout all Judah.
4 Accordingly Judah assembled to seek
the LORD; out of all the cities of Judah
they came to seek the LORD.
5 Thereupon Jehoshaphat stood up in
the assembly of Judah and Jerusalem
in the house of the LORD, in front of
6 the new court, and said,
"O LORD, the God of our fathers, art
thou not God in the heavens? and thou
art ruler over all the kingdoms of the
nations, and in thy hand is power and
might, so that none is able to withstand
7 thee. Didst not thou, O our God, dispossess the inhabitants of this land before thy people Israel, and give it to the
descendants of Abraham thy friend
forever? So they have dwelt in it and 8
built for thee a sanctuary in it for thy
name, saying, 'If evil come upon us, the 9
sword in judgment, pestilence, or famine, we will stand before this house and
before thee (for thy name is in this
house), and cry out to thee in our affliction, and thou wilt hear and save.'
Now, behold, the Ammonites, the 10
Moabites, and the people of Mount
Seir, whom thou wouldst not let Israel
invade when they came out of the land
of Egypt, for they turned aside from
them and did not destroy them; see 11
now, how they reward us, by coming to
drive us out of thy possessions, which
thou hast caused us to possess. O our 12
God, wilt thou not judge them? For
we have no strength before this vast
multitude that is coming against us,
nor do we know what to do, but our
eyes are upon thee!"
Meanwhile all Judah stood before the 13
LORD with their infants, their wives,
and their children.
Then upon Jahaziel, the son of Zech- 14
ariah, the son of Benaiah, the son of
Jeiel, the son of Mattaniah, the Levite
of the descendants of Asaph, came the
spirit of the LORD in the midst of the
assembly, and he said, 15
"Give attention, all Judah and the
inhabitants of Jerusalem and you King
Jehoshaphat; 'Thus says the LORD to
you: "Fear not, nor be dismayed before this vast multitude; for the battle
is not yours, but God's. Tomorrow go 16
down against them. See, they are coming up by the ascent; and you shall find
them at the end of the valley in front of
the desert of Jeruel. It is not for you to 17
fight in this battle; take up your position, stand still and see the deliverance
of the LORD, who is on your side, O
Judah and Jerusalem. Fear not, neither be dismayed; tomorrow go forth
against them, for the LORD is with
you." ' "
Then Jehoshaphat bowed his face to 18
the earth, and all Judah and the inhabitants of Jerusalem fell down before
the LORD to worship the LORD.
Thereupon the Levites, of the descend- 19
ants of the Kohathites, and of the descendants of the Korahites, stood up to
praise the LORD, the God of Israel,
with an exceedingly loud voice.
So they rose up early the next morn- 20
ing and went forth to the desert of Te-

koa; and as they went forth, Jehoshaphat halted and said,
"Hear me, O Judah and you inhabitants of Jerusalem; believe in the
LORD your God, and then you shall be
established. Believe in his prophets,
and then you shall prosper."
21 When he had taken counsel with the
people, he appointed singers to praise
the LORD in holy array, as they went
before the troops, and to say,
"Give thanks to the LORD;
For his kindness is everlasting."
22 Now when they began to sing and
praise, the LORD set an ambush against
the Ammonites, Moabites, and the people of Mount Seir, who had come
against Judah, so that they destroyed
23 themselves. For the Ammonites and
Moabites took up a position against the
inhabitants of Mount Seir to wipe out
and completely destroy them; and
when they had made an end of the inhabitants of Seir, each helped to destroy his neighbor.
24 So when Judah came to the Watch
Tower of the Desert and looked for the
multitude, there were only dead bodies
fallen to the earth, and none had
25 escaped. Accordingly when Jehoshaphat and his people came to carry off
the spoil they found a very large number of cattle, goods, garments, and
precious jewels, which they stripped off
for themselves, more than they could
carry; and they were three days taking
away the spoil, it was so much.
26 At length on the fourth day they
assembled in the Valley of Beracah, for
there they blessed the LORD; therefore
the name of that place has been called
the Valley of Beracah [blessing] to this
27 day. Then all the men of Judah and
Jerusalem, with Jehoshaphat at their
head, returned to re-enter Jerusalem
with joy; for the LORD had made them
28 rejoice over their enemies. So they
came to Jerusalem with harps, lyres,
and trumpets, to the house of the
29 LORD. Then a terror from God came
upon all the kingdoms of the countries,
when they heard that the LORD fought
30 against the enemies of Israel. So the
realm of Jehoshaphat was quiet, for his
God gave him rest on all sides.
31 Now Jehoshaphat reigned over Judah. He was thirty-five years old when
he became king, and he reigned twenty-
five years in Jerusalem; and his mother's name was Azubah, the daughter of
Shilhi. He walked in the way of his fa- 32
ther Asa, and did not turn from it, doing that which was right in the sight of
the LORD. However, the high places 33
were not removed nor had the people
as yet directed their hearts to the God
of their fathers. Now the rest of the 34
records of Jehoshaphat from first to
last, behold, they are written in the
Records of Jehu, the son of Hanani,
which are inserted in the Book of the
Kings of Israel.
Now later Jehoshaphat, king of Ju- 35
dah, allied himself with Ahaziah, king
of Israel, who did very wickedly. For 36
he united with him to make ships to go
to Tarshish, and they made the ships in
Ezion-geber. But Eliezer, the son of 37
Dodavahu of Mareshah, prophesied
against Jehoshaphat, saying,
"Because you have allied yourself
with Ahaziah, the LORD will surely
break up your enterprise."
Accordingly the ships were wrecked
so that they were not able to go to
Tarshish.
Then Jehoshaphat slept with his fa- 2
thers and he was buried with his fathers
in the city of David, and Jehoram his
son became king in his stead.

THE MISFORTUNES OF JEHORAM, 21:2–20

Now Jehoram had brothers, the sons 2
of Jehoshaphat: Azariah, Jehiel, Zechariah, Michael, and Shephatiah; all
these were sons of Jehoshaphat, king of
Israel. Moreover their father gave 3
them rich gifts of silver, gold, and
precious things, with fortified cities in
Judah, but the kingdom he gave to
Jehoram, because he was the first-born.
Now when Jehoram had become estab- 4
lished over the kingdom of his father,
and had made himself strong, he put all
his brothers to the sword, together with
certain of the nobles of Israel. Jehoram 5
was thirty-two years old when he became king, and he reigned eight years
in Jerusalem. He walked in the way of 6
the kings of Israel, as the house of Ahab
had done, for his wife was Ahab's
daughter; accordingly he did that
which was evil in the sight of the LORD.
However the LORD would not destroy 7
the house of David, because of the cov-

enant that he made with David, and
because he promised to give a lamp to
him and to his sons for all time.
8 In his days Edom revolted from the
rule of Judah, and set up a king of its
9 own. Then Jehoram passed over with
his commanders, and all his chariots
with him; and he, together with the
chariot commanders, rose by night and
defeated the Edomites that surrounded
10 him. So Edom has been in revolt from
the rule of Judah to this day. Likewise
Libnah revolted at the same time from
his rule, because he had forsaken the
LORD, the God of his fathers.
11 He also made high places in the
mountains of Judah, and led the inhabitants of Jerusalem into unfaithful-
12 ness, and led Judah astray. Then there
came to him a writing from Elijah the
prophet, saying,
"Thus says the LORD, the God of
David your ancestor: 'Because you
have not walked in the ways of Jehoshaphat your father, nor in the ways of
13 Asa, king of Judah, but have walked in
the way of the kings of Israel and have
led Judah and the inhabitants of Jerusalem into unfaithfulness, as did the
house of Ahab, and also have slain your
brothers of your father's house who
14 were better than yourself, now the
LORD will strike down with a great
plague your people, your children, your
15 wives, and all your property; and you
yourself shall suffer severely from a disease of your bowels, until your bowels
shall waste away from day to day because of the disease.'"
16 Then the LORD stirred up against
Jehoram the spirit of the Philistines
and the Arabs, who live beside the
17 Ethiopians, so that they came up
against Judah, and invaded it, and
carried away all the possessions that
were found in the house of the king, together with his sons and his wives, so
that no son was left to him, except
18 Jehoahaz his youngest. Then after all
this the LORD afflicted him with an in-
19 curable disease of the bowels, so that
gradually as time went on, at the end
of two years, his bowels had wasted
away because of his disease and he died
in great pain. His people burned for
him no sacrifice to compare with the
20 sacrifice for his fathers. He was thirty-two years old when he became king,
and he reigned eight years in Jerusalem.
He departed without being lamented,
and they buried him in the city of David, but not in the sepulcher of the
kings.

AHAZIAH AND ATHALIAH, 22:1-12

Then the inhabitants of Jerusalem 22
made Ahaziah, his youngest son, king
in his stead; for the marauding band
that came with the Arabs to the camp
had slain all the older sons. So Ahaziah,
the son of Jehoram, became king of Judah. Forty-two years old was Ahaziah 2
when he became king, and he reigned
one year in Jerusalem; and his mother's
name was Athaliah, the daughter of
Omri. He walked in the ways of the
house of Ahab, for his mother was his 3
counsellor in doing wickedness. More- 4
over he did that which was evil in the
sight of the LORD as did the house of
Ahab, for they were his counsellors,
after the death of his father, to his destruction. He also followed their coun- 5
sel and went with Jehoram, the son of
Ahab, king of Israel, to make war on
Hazael, king of Syria, at Ramoth-gilead. But the Syrians wounded Joram.
Accordingly he returned to be healed in 6
Jezreel of the wounds which they had
given him at Ramah, when he fought
against Hazael, king of Syria; and
Ahaziah, the son of Jehoram, king of
Judah, went down to see Jehoram, the
son of Ahab, in Jezreel, because he was
sick. Now the destruction of Ahaziah 7
was purposed by God, in that he went
to Joram, and after his arrival he went
out with Jehoram to meet Jehu, the son
of Nimshi, whom the LORD had
anointed to cut off the house of Ahab.
Now when Jehu was executing judg- 8
ment on the house of Ahab, he found
the princes of Judah and the sons of the
kinsmen of Ahaziah ministering to Ahaziah and slew them. Then he sought 9
Ahaziah. They caught him, while he
was hiding himself in Samaria, and they
brought him to Jehu and slew him and
buried him; for they said,
"He was the son of Jehoshaphat who
sought the LORD with all his heart."
So the house of Ahaziah had no one
who had sufficient strength to rule.
Now when Athaliah, the mother of 10
Ahaziah, saw that her son was dead she

arose and drove out all the royal family
11 of the house of Judah. But Jehoshabeath, the daughter of the king, took
Joash, the son of Ahaziah, and stole
him away from among the sons of the
king who were about to be slain, and
put him and his nurse in a bedchamber.
Thus Jehoshabeath, the daughter of
King Jehoram, the wife of Jehoiada the
priest (for she was the sister of Ahaziah), hid him from Athaliah, so that she
12 did not slay him. Accordingly he was
with them in the house of God six years,
while Athaliah reigned over the land.

JEHOIADA'S REVOLT AGAINST ATHALIAH, 23:1–21

23 But in the seventh year, when Jehoiada felt himself strong enough, he took
the commanders of hundreds, Azariah,
the son of Jeroham, Ishmael, the son of
Jehohanan, Azariah, the son of Obed,
Maaseiah, the son of Adaiah, and
2 Elishaphat, the son of Zichri; and they
went about Judah, and assembled the
Levites from all the cities of Judah, and
the heads of the Israelite families, and
3 came to Jerusalem. Then all the assembly made a covenant with the king in
the house of God, and he said to them,
"Behold, the king's son shall reign, as
the LORD spoke concerning the sons of
4 David. This is the thing that you shall
do: a third of you, the priests and
Levites, who come in on the sabbath
shall be keepers of the thresholds, and a
5 third shall be in the king's house, and a
third at the Gate Jesod; and all the
people shall be in the courts of the
6 house of the LORD. But let none enter
the house of the LORD except the
priests and the ministering Levites;
they shall enter, for they are holy; but
all the people shall keep the charge of
7 the LORD. Moreover the Levites shall
surround the king, each with his weapons
in his hand; and whoever enters the
house let him be slain. Thus they shall
be with the king when he comes in and
when he goes out."
8 So the Levites and all Judah did just
as Jehoiada the priest commanded; each
brought his men, both those who were
to enter on the sabbath, and those who
were to go out on the sabbath; for Jehoiada the priest did not dismiss the
9 divisions. Then Jehoiada the priest delivered to the commanders of hundreds
the spears, bucklers, and shields that
had belonged to King David, which
were in the house of God. Moreover he 10
stationed all the people, each with his
weapon in his hand from the right side
of the house to the left side of the house,
by the altar and by the house around
the king. Then they brought out the 11
king's son and put the crown and the
armlet upon him and declared him
king, and Jehoiada and his sons anointed
him and said,
"Long live the king!"
But when Athaliah heard the noise of 12
the people running and praising the
king, she came to the people to the
house of the LORD; and when she 13
looked, there was the king standing by
his column at the entrance, and the
commanders and the trumpeters beside
the king, and all the people of the land
rejoicing and blowing trumpets, and
the singers with musical instruments,
leading the praise. Then Athaliah tore
her garments and said,
"Treason! Treason!"
Then Jehoiada the priest brought out 14
the commanders of hundreds who were
over the army and said to them,
"Bring her out between the ranks;
and whoever follows her, let him be
slain with the sword."
For the priest had said,
"Do not slay her in the house of the
LORD."
So they laid hands on her, and as she 15
came to the entrance of the horse-gate
to the king's house, they slew her there.
Then Jehoiada made a covenant be- 16
tween himself and all the people and
the king, that they should be the
LORD'S people. Accordingly all the 17
people went to the house of the Baal
and destroyed it; his altars and his
images they completely shattered, and
Mattan, the priest of the Baal, they
slew before the altars.
Then Jehoiada appointed watchmen 18
over the house of the LORD under the
authority of the priests and the Levites
whom David had apportioned over the
house of the LORD, to offer the burnt-
offerings of the LORD, as it is written
in the law of Moses, with gladness and
with song, according to the direction of
David. Moreover he stationed the 19
gatekeepers over the gates of the house
of the LORD, that no one who was un-

clean in any respect should enter.
0 Then he took the commanders of hundreds and the nobles and those who
ruled the people and all the people of
the land, and brought down the king
from the house of the LORD. When
they had come through the upper gate
to the house of the king, they placed the
king upon the throne of the kingdom.
1 Then all the people of the land rejoiced
and the city was quiet. Thus they slew
Athaliah with the sword.

JOASH GUIDED ARIGHT BY JEHOIADA, 24:1–16

4 Joash was seven years old when he
became king, and he reigned forty
years in Jerusalem; and his mother's
2 name was Zibiah, of Beersheba. Joash
did that which was right in the sight of
the LORD all the days of Jehoiada the
3 priest. Jehoiada took for himself two
wives, and he became the father of sons
and daughters.
4 Now after this it occurred to Joash to
5 restore the house of the LORD. Accordingly he assembled the priests and
the Levites, and said to them,
"Go out to the cities of Judah and
collect from all Israel money to repair
the house of your God from year to
year; but do you hasten the matter."
6 However, the Levites did not hasten.
Then the king summoned Jehoiada the
chief and said to him,
"Why have you not required the
Levites to bring in from Judah and Jerusalem the tax of Moses the servant of
the LORD, and of the assembly of Israel for the tent of the decrees?"
7 For the wicked Athaliah and her sons
had wrought havoc in the house of God,
and had made use of all the consecrated things of the house of the LORD for
8 the Baals. So the king gave command
and they made a chest and set it outside at the gate of the house of the
9 LORD. Then they made a proclamation throughout Judah and Jerusalem
that they should bring in for the LORD
the tax that Moses the servant of God
10 laid upon Israel in the desert. Accordingly all the princes and all the people
were glad and brought in and cast into
11 the chest until it was full. Moreover at
whatever time the chest was brought to
the appointed officials of the king by
the Levites and they saw that there
was much money, the king's scribe
came and the deputy of the chief priest
and emptied the chest and took it up
and returned it to its place. Thus they
did day by day and took in a very large
amount of money. Then the king and 12
Jehoiada gave it to those who carried
out the work of construction on the
house of the LORD, and they hired masons and carpenters to restore the house
of the LORD and also workers in iron
and bronze to repair the house of the
LORD. So the workmen toiled and 13
thus the work of restoration went forward in their hands; and they set up
the house of God according to its design, and strengthened it. Then when 14
they had finished, they brought the rest
of the money before the king and Jehoiada, who used it to make utensils for
the house of the LORD, utensils for the
service and for making the offerings,
and spoons and vessels of gold and silver. So they offered burnt-offerings in
the house of the LORD continually all
the days of Jehoiada.
But when Jehoiada became old after 15
a long life, he died. A hundred and
thirty years old was he when he died;
and they buried him in the city of Da- 16
vid with the kings, because he had done
good to Israel and toward God and his
house.

THE WICKEDNESS OF JOASH, 24:17–27

Now after the death of Jehoiada, the 17
princes of Judah came in and did obeisance to the king, and the king listened
to them. Then they forsook the house 18
of the LORD, the God of their fathers,
and served the sacred poles and the
idols, and wrath came upon Judah and
Jerusalem for this guilt of theirs. Yet 19
he sent prophets to them to bring them
back to the LORD, who testified against
them; but they would not listen.
Then the spirit of God took posses- 20
sion of Zechariah, the son of Jehoiada
the priest, so that he stood above the
people and said to them,
"Thus says God: 'Why have you
transgressed the commands of the
LORD, so that you cannot prosper?
Because you have forsaken the LORD,
he has also forsaken you.' "

21 But they conspired against him, and
at the command of the king they stoned
him to death in the court of the house
22 of the LORD. Thus Joash the king did
not remember the kindness which Jehoiada his father had done him, but
slew his son! And when he died, he
said,
"May the LORD see and punish!"
23 It was a year later that the army of
the Syrians came up against him and
penetrated Judah and Jerusalem and
destroyed all the princes of the people
from among the people, and all their
spoil they sent to the king of Damascus.
24 For with few men the army of the Syrians came, but the Lord delivered a very
great army into their hands, because
they had forsaken the LORD, the God
of their fathers. So they executed judg-
25 ment upon Joash. Accordingly when
they departed from him (for they left
him in very great suffering), his own
servants conspired against him, because
of the murder of the son of Jehoiada the
priest, and slew him on his bed. Thus
he died, and they buried him in the city
of David, but they did not bury him in
26 the sepulchers of the kings. These were
the conspirators against him: Zabad,
the son of Shimeath, the Ammonitess,
and Jehozabad, the son of Shimrith, the
27 Moabitess. Now about his sons and the
many oracles against him, and the rebuilding of the house of God, behold, it
is written in the Midrash of the Book of
Kings. Then Amaziah, his son, became
king in his stead.

AMAZIAH'S MISDEEDS, 25:1–28

25 Amaziah was twenty-five years old
when he became king, and he reigned
twenty-nine years in Jerusalem; and his
mother's name was Jehoaddan of Jeru-
2 salem. He did that which was right in
the sight of the LORD, yet not with a
3 perfect heart. Now when the kingdom
was firmly in his grasp, he slew his
servants who had murdered the king
4 his father. However, he did not kill
their children, but did according to that
which is written in the law of the books
of Moses, as the LORD commanded,
saying,
"The fathers shall not be put to
death for the children, nor the children
be put to death for the fathers, but
everyone shall be put to death for his
own sin."
Then Amaziah assembled Judah, and
appointed them according to their
families under commanders of thousands and commanders of hundreds,
even all Judah and Benjamin, and
numbered them from twenty years old
and upward, and found them to be
three hundred thousand picked men fit
for the army, able to handle spear and
shield. He also hired a hundred thousand seasoned warriors from Israel for
one hundred talents of silver. But a
man of God came to him, saying,
"O king, let not the army of Israel go
with you; for the LORD is not with Israel, even all the Ephraimites. But go
by yourself, take the initiative, be courageous for battle; for God will not allow you to fall before the enemy, for
God has power to help and to cast
down."
Then Amaziah said to the man of
God,
"But what shall I do about the hundred talents I have given to the armed
band of Israel?"
"The LORD is able to give you much
more than this," said the man of God.
Then Amaziah separated them, 10
namely, the armed band that came to
him out of Ephraim, that they might
return home. But their anger burned
fiercely against Judah, and they returned home in hot anger. Amaziah, 11
however, strengthened himself and led
forth his people to the Valley of Salt
and slew ten thousand of the men of
Seir.
And ten thousand others did the Ju- 12
deans carry away alive, and they
brought them to the top of a crag, and
cast them down from the top of the
crag, so that all of them were dashed to
pieces. But the men of the band whom 13
Amaziah had sent back without allowing them to go with him to battle fell
upon the cities of Judah from Samaria
to Bethhoron, and slew of them three
thousand and took a large amount of
spoil.
Now after Amaziah returned from 14
the slaughter of the Edomites, he
brought the gods of the people of Seir
and set them up to be his gods, and
bowed down to them and sacrificed to
them. Therefore the anger of the LORD 15

was kindled against Amaziah and he
sent to him a prophet, who said to him,
"Why have you sought after the gods
of the people who have not delivered
their own people out of your hand?"
Now as he spoke to him, he said to
him,
"Have we made you the king's counsellor? Desist; why should they strike
you down?"
Then the prophet desisted and said,
"I know that God has determined to
destroy you, because you have done
this and have not listened to my counsel."
Then Amaziah, king of Judah, took
advice and sent to Joash, the son of
Jehoahaz, the son of Jehu, the king of
Israel, saying,
"Come, let us face each other."
But Joash, king of Israel, sent to
Amaziah, king of Judah, saying,
"The thistle that was in Lebanon
sent to the cedar that was in Lebanon,
saying, 'Give your daughter to my son
as wife.' But a wild beast that was in
Lebanon passed by and trampled down
the thistle. You say to yourself, you
have indeed conquered Edom; and now
your heart has stirred you up to seek
renown. Remain at home; why should
you court disaster, so that you should
fall and Judah with you?"
But Amaziah would not listen, for it
was purposed by God to deliver them
into the hand of the enemy, because
they had sought after the gods of
Edom. Then Joash, king of Israel,
went up and they faced each other at
Beth-shemesh, which belongs to Judah.
Judah, however, was defeated by Israel, so that they fled each to his home.
Joash, king of Israel, captured Amaziah, king of Judah, the son of Joash, the
son of Jehoahaz, at Beth-shemesh, and
brought him to Jerusalem; and tore
down the wall of Jerusalem from the
Gate of Ephraim to the Corner Gate, a
distance of four hundred cubits. He also took all the gold and silver and all
the utensils that were found in the
house of God with Obed-edom, together
with the treasures of the king's house
and the hostages, and returned to
Samaria.
Amaziah, the son of Joash, king of
Judah, lived after the death of Joash,
the son of Jehoahaz, king of Israel, fifteen years. Now the rest of the records
of Amaziah from first to last are they
not written in the Book of the Kings of
Judah and Israel? Also from the time 27
that Amaziah turned away from following the LORD, they made a conspiracy against him in Jerusalem, and he
fled to Lachish; but they sent after him
to Lachish and slew him there. Then 28
they brought his body upon horseback
and buried him with his fathers in the
city of Judah.

UZZIAH'S VICTORIES, 26:1–15

Then all the people of Judah took **26**
Uzziah who was sixteen years old and
made him king in the place of his father
Amaziah. He built Eloth and restored 2
it to Judah after the king slept with his
fathers. Uzziah was sixteen years old 3
when he became king, and he reigned
fifty-two years in Jerusalem; and the
name of his mother was Jechiliah of Jerusalem. He did that which was right 4
in the sight of the LORD, just as Amaziah his father did. He proceeded to seek 5
God in the days of Zechariah who instructed him in the fear of God; and in
the days that he sought the LORD, God
prospered him.
Moreover he went out and fought 6
against the Philistines, and broke down
the wall of Gath and the wall of Jabneh
and the wall of Ashdod and built cities
among the Philistines; for God helped 7
him against the Philistines and against
the Arabs who dwelt in Gurbaal, and
the Meunites. The Ammonites also 8
gave tribute to Uzziah; and his fame
extended even to the entrance to
Egypt; for he became increasingly
strong.
Moreover Uzziah built towers in Je- 9
rusalem at the Corner Gate and at the
Valley Gate and at the angles of the
wall and fortified them. He also built 10
towers in the desert and hewed out
many cisterns; for he had large herds,
both in the lowland and in the plain,
and he had farmers and vinedressers in
the hills and in the fruitful fields, for he
was a lover of the soil.
Furthermore Uzziah had a force of 11
fighting men trained in the army by detachments according to the number of
their reckoning made by Jeiel the scribe
and Maaseiah the notary, under the
direction of Hananiah, one of the king's
commanders. The entire number of 12

heads of families, seasoned warriors,
13 was two thousand six hundred, and
under their command was a powerful army of three hundred and seven
thousand five hundred fighting men of
great strength, to help the king against
14 the enemy. Moreover Uzziah equipped
them, even the entire army, with
shields, spears, helmets, coats of mail,
15 bows, and stones for slinging. Also he
made in Jerusalem machines skilfully
devised, which were placed upon the
towers and on the corners, with which
to shoot arrows and great stones; and
his fame spread far and wide, for he
was marvelously helped until he became strong.

UZZIAH'S SIN, 26:16–23

16 But as soon as he was strong, he became so puffed up that it ruined him.
And he trespassed against the LORD
his God, for he went into the temple of
the LORD to burn incense on the altar
17 of incense. Then Azariah the priest
went in after him with eighty priests of
18 the LORD, men of courage, who opposed Uzziah the king and said to him,
"It is not for you Uzziah, to burn incense of the LORD, but for the priests,
the sons of Aaron, who have been consecrated to burn incense. Withdraw
from the sanctuary, for you have trespassed and that shall not be to your
honor before the LORD God."
19 Then Uzziah was enraged, and he
had a censer in his hand to burn incense. And while he was enraged with
the priests, the leprosy broke out on his
forehead before the priests in the house
of the LORD beside the altar of incense.
20 When Azariah the high priest together
with all the priests faced him, behold,
he was leprous on his forehead. So they
hurried him from there, as he also made
haste to go out, because the LORD had
21 smitten him. So Uzziah the king was a
leper to the day of his death and dwelt
in a house apart, being a leper, for he
was cut off from the house of the
LORD, while Jotham his son took
charge of the king's household, ruling
22 the people of the land. Now the rest of
the records of Uzziah, from first to last,
Isaiah the prophet, the son of Amoz,
23 has written. So Uzziah slept with his
fathers, and they buried him with his
fathers in the cemetery which belonged
to the kings, for they said,
"He is a leper."
Then Jotham his son became king in
his stead.

THE REIGN OF JOTHAM, 27:1–9

Jotham was twenty-five years old when he became king and he reigned sixteen years in Jerusalem; and his mother's name was Jerushah, the daughter of Zadok. He did that which was right in the sight of the LORD, just as Uzziah his father had done. However, he did not enter into the temple of the LORD; and the people were still perverse. He built the upper gate of the house of the LORD; also on the wall of Ophel he built extensively. Moreover he built cities in the highlands of Judah and in the forests he built castles and towers. He fought also with the king of the Ammonites and conquered them and the Ammonites gave him that year a hundred talents of silver and ten thousand kors of wheat and ten thousand kors of barley. The Ammonites rendered to him the same amount the second year and the third year. So Jotham became powerful, because he established his ways in the sight of the LORD his God. Now the rest of the records of Jotham and all his wars and his doings, behold, they are written in the Book of the Kings of Israel and Judah. He was twenty-five years old when he became king and he reigned sixteen years in Jerusalem. So Jotham slept with his fathers, and they buried him in the city of David, and Ahaz his son became king in his stead.

THE REIGN OF AHAZ, 28:1–27

Ahaz was twenty years old when he became king and he reigned sixteen years in Jerusalem. However, he did not do that which was right in the sight of the LORD, like David his ancestor, but he walked in the ways of the kings of Israel, and also made molten images for the Baals. Moreover he burned incense in the valley of Ben-Hinnom and burned his sons in the fire according to the abominable practices of the nations whom the LORD had dispossessed before the Israelites. He sacrificed and burned incense on the high places and on the hill-tops and under every spreading tree.

Therefore the LORD his God delivered him into the hand of the king of Syria, and he defeated him and carried away a great multitude of his people as captives, and brought them to Damascus. He was also delivered into the hand of the king of Israel, who defeated him with great slaughter; for Pekah, the son of Remaliah, slew in Judah a hundred and twenty thousand in one day, all of them valiant men, because they had forsaken the LORD, the God of their fathers. Moreover Zichri, an Ephraimite hero, slew Maaseiah, the king's son, and Azrikam, the commander of the palace, and Elkanah, who was next to the king.

Now the Israelites carried away captive of their kinsmen two hundred thousand, women, sons, and daughters; they also took from them an immense amount of spoil, and brought the spoil to Samaria. But a prophet of the LORD was there, Obed by name; and he went out to meet the army that was coming to Samaria, and he said to them,

"See, because of the wrath of the LORD, the God of your fathers, against Judah, he has delivered them into your hand; and you have slain them with a fury that has reached up to the heavens. But now you think to subdue the Judeans and Jerusalem to be bondmen and bondwomen to you; but are not you yourselves guilty of crimes against the LORD your God? Now therefore, listen to me and restore the captives whom you have taken of your kinsmen; for the fierce wrath of the LORD is upon you."

Then some of the chiefs of the Ephramites, Azariah, the son of Johanan, Berechiah, the son of Meshillemoth, Jehizkiah, the son of Shallum, Amasa, the son of Hadlai, stood up to oppose those who came from the war. They said to them,

"You shall not bring the captives here; for what you purpose will bring upon us guilt against the LORD, to add to our sins and our guilt, for our guilt is very great, and there is fierce wrath against Israel."

So the armed men left the captives 14
and the spoil before the princes and the
whole assembly. Then the men already 15
mentioned by name arose and took the
captives and clothed all the naked from
the spoil, and having clothed them,
provided them with sandals, gave them
something to eat and drink, anointed
them, and carried all of them who were
feeble on asses, and brought them to
Jericho, the city of palm trees, to their
kinsmen, and then they returned to
Samaria.

At that time King Ahaz sent for the 16
king of Assyria to help him, for the 17
Edomites had come again and attacked
Judah and carried away captives. The 18
Philistines also had raided the cities of
the lowland and the South of Judah and
had captured Beth-shemesh, Aijalon,
Gederoth, Soco with its towns, Timnah
with its towns, and Gimzo with its
towns, and were living there. For the 19
LORD brought Judah low because of
Ahaz, king of Israel, because he had
acted wantonly with Judah and had behaved very treacherously toward the
LORD. So Tiglath-pileser, king of As- 20
syria, came to him, but he proved a
burden to him instead of giving him
strength; for Ahaz plundered the house 21
of the LORD and the house of the king
and the princes and gave it to the king
of Assyria, but it failed to help him. In 22
the time of his distress he acted still
more treacherously against the LORD
—this same King Ahaz, for he sacri- 23
ficed to the gods of Damascus who
overcame him, and he said,

"Because the gods of the kings of
Syria helped them, I will sacrifice to
them, that they may help me."

But they were the ruin of him and of
all Israel. Ahaz gathered up all the 24
utensils of the house of God and cut
them in pieces and closed the doors of
the house of the LORD and made for
himself altars in every corner of Jerusalem. In every city of Judah he made 25
high places to burn incense to alien
gods and provoked the anger of the
LORD, the God of their fathers. Now 26
the rest of his records, and all his doings
from first to last, behold, they are
written in the Book of the Kings of
Judah and Israel. So Ahaz slept with 27
his fathers and they buried him in the

city, in Jerusalem, for they did not
bring him to the sepulchers of the kings
of Israel; and Hezekiah, his son, became king in his stead.

HEZEKIAH'S CLEANSING OF THE TEMPLE, 29:1–36

29 Hezekiah became king at twenty-five
years of age and reigned twenty-nine
years in Jerusalem, and his mother's
name was Abijah, the daughter of
2 Zechariah. He did that which was right
in the sight of the LORD, just as David
3 his ancestor had done. In the first year
of his reign in the first month, he
opened the doors of the house of the
4 LORD and repaired them. He also
brought in the priests and the Levites,
and assembled them in the open square
5 on the east. Then he said to them,
"Listen to me, O Levites; sanctify
yourselves and reconsecrate the house
of the LORD, the God of your fathers,
and carry out the filth from the holy
6 place. For our fathers acted treacherously and did that which was evil in the
sight of the LORD our God, and forsook
him and turned away their faces from
the habitation of the LORD and turned
7 their backs. They have also closed the
doors of the porch and put out the
lamps, and have not burned incense or
offered burnt-offerings in the sanctuary
8 of the God of Israel. Therefore the
wrath of the LORD was against Judah
and Jerusalem, and he has delivered
them to be an object of terror, astonishment, and derision, as you see with
9 your own eyes. For now our fathers
have fallen by the sword; our sons, our
daughters, and our wives are in cap-
10 tivity for this. Now it is in my heart
to make a covenant with the LORD, the
God of Israel, that his fierce anger may
11 turn away from us. My sons, do not
now be negligent; for the LORD has
chosen you to stand before him to minister to him, and that you should be his
ministers and burn incense."
12 Then the Levites arose, Mahath, the
son of Amasai, and Joel, the son of
Azariah, of the sons of the Kohathites
and of the Merarites, Kish, the son of
Abdi, and Azariah, the son of Jehallelel,
and of the Gershonites Joah, the son of
Zimmah, and Eden, the son of Joah;
13 also of the sons of Elizaphan, Shimri
and Jeuel; and of the sons of Asaph,
Zechariah and Mattaniah; and of the
sons of Heman, Jehuel and Shimei; and
of the sons of Jeduthun, Shemaiah and
Uzziel. Then they assembled their
kinsmen and sanctified themselves and
went in according to the command of
the king by the words of the LORD to
cleanse the house of the LORD. The
priests also went into the inner court of
the house of the LORD to cleanse it and
brought out all the uncleanness that
they found in the temple of the LORD
into the court of the house of the LORD;
and the Levites took it up to carry it
outside to the Brook Kidron. Now they
began on the first day of the first month
the work of sanctifying, and on the
eighth day of the month they came to
the porch of the LORD, and they sanctified the house of the LORD in eight
days; and on the sixteenth day of the
first month they completed the work.
Then they came to Hezekiah, the king,
within the palace and said,
"We have cleansed the entire house
of the LORD, and the altar of burnt-
offering with all its utensils, and the
table for the bread that is arranged in
layers, with all its utensils. Moreover
all the utensils, which King Ahaz in his
reign had cast aside when he acted
faithlessly, we have restored and sanctified, and they are now before the altar
of the LORD."
Thereupon Hezekiah the king rose up
early in the morning and assembled the
princes of the city, and went up to the
house of the LORD. Then they brought
seven bulls, seven rams, seven lambs,
and seven he-goats for a sin-offering on
behalf of the kingdom and the sanctuary and Judah; and he ordered the
sons of Aaron the priests to offer them
on the altar of the LORD. So they
slaughtered the bulls, and the priests
received the blood and dashed it against
the altar, and they slaughtered the
rams and dashed the blood against the
altar; they also slaughtered the lambs
and dashed the blood against the altar.
Moreover they brought up the he-goats
for the sin-offering before the king and
the assembly, and they laid their hands
upon them. Then the priests slaughtered them and made a sin-offering
with their blood on the altar to make
atonement for all Israel; for the king
ordered the burnt-offering and the sin-
offering for all Israel.

He stationed the Levites in the house of the LORD, with cymbals, harps, and lyres, according to the command of David and Gad, the king's seer, and of Nathan the prophet; for the command was from the LORD by his prophets. Thus the Levites stood with the instruments of David, and the priests with the trumpets. Thereupon Hezekiah commanded them to offer the burnt-offering upon the altar; and when the burnt-offering began, the song in honor of the LORD began also, and the trumpets, accompanied by the instruments of David, king of Israel. Then all the assembly bowed themselves, and the singers sang, and the trumpeters sounded; all this continued until the burnt-offering was finished; and when they had made an end of offering, the king and all who were present with him bowed themselves and worshiped. Then, Hezekiah the king and the princes commanded the Levites to praise the LORD with the words of David and Asaph the seer. So they sang praises with gladness and bowed their heads and worshiped.

Then Hezekiah spoke up and said, "Now that you have consecrated yourselves to the LORD, come near and bring sacrifices and thank-offerings, and every generous-minded man burnt-offerings."

And the number of burnt-offerings which the assembly brought in was seventy bulls, a hundred rams, two hundred lambs; all these were for a burnt-offering to the LORD. The consecrated things were six hundred bulls and three thousand sheep. But the priests were too few to prepare all the burnt-offerings. Therefore their kinsmen, the Levites, helped them till the work was completed and the priests had sanctified themselves; for the Levites were more upright in heart to sanctify themselves than the priests. There were also burnt-offerings in abundance, together with the fat of the thank-offerings and the libations for every burnt-offering. So the service of the house of the LORD was set in order. Thus Hezekiah and all the people rejoiced, because of that which God had prepared for the people; for the thing was done suddenly.

HEZEKIAH'S PASSOVER, 30:1–27

Then Hezekiah sent to all Israel and 30
Judah and also wrote letters to Ephraim
and Manasseh, that they should come
to the house of the LORD at Jerusalem,
to keep the passover of the LORD, the
God of Israel; for the king and his 2
princes and all the assembly in Jerusalem had decided to keep the passover
in the second month, since they could 3
not keep it at that time because the
priests had not sanctified themselves in
sufficient numbers, neither had the
people gathered themselves together to
Jerusalem. Accordingly the thing 4
seemed good in the eyes of the king and
all the assembly. So they passed a de- 5
cree to send a proclamation throughout
all Israel, from Beersheba even to Dan,
that they should come and keep the
passover in honor of the LORD, the God
of Israel in Jerusalem; for they had not
kept it in such great numbers, according to the record. So the couriers went 6
with the letters from the king and his
princes through all Israel and Judah,
according to the command of the king,
saying,
"O Israelites! turn again to the
LORD, the God of Abraham, Isaac, and
Israel, that he may turn to the remnant
which is left of you from the hand of
the kings of Assyria. Also be not like 7
your ancestors and your kinsmen who
acted unfaithfully toward the LORD,
the God of their fathers, so that he gave
them over to devastations, as you see.
Now be not stubborn, as were your 8
fathers, but yield yourselves to the
LORD, and enter into his sanctuary
which he has sanctified forever, and
serve the LORD your God, that he may
turn his fierce anger from you. For by 9
your returning to the LORD, your kinsmen and your sons shall find compassion in the presence of their captors so
that they shall be allowed to return to
this land; for the LORD your God is
gracious and merciful, and will not turn
away his face from you if you return to
him."
So the couriers passed from city to 10
city through the land of Ephraim and
Manasseh, even to Zebulun, but they
laughed them to scorn and mocked
them. Nevertheless some men from 11
Asher and Manasseh and Zebulun

humbled themselves and came to Jeru-
12 salem. Also the hand of God was upon
Judah to give them one heart, to do the
bidding of the king and the princes by
the word of the LORD.
13 So a great crowd of people assembled
at Jerusalem to keep the feast of unleavened cakes in the second month—
14 a very great assembly. Then they rose
up and took away the altars that were
in Jerusalem, and all the altars for incense they took away and cast into the
15 Brook Kidron. They slaughtered the
passover on the fourteenth day of the
second month; and the priests and the
Levites were ashamed and sanctified
themselves, and brought burnt-offerings
16 into the house of the LORD. Moreover
they stood in their place as was their
custom, according to the law of Moses
the man of God; the priests dashed the
blood received from the hand of the
17 Levites, for there was a large number
in the assembly who had not sanctified
themselves; therefore the Levites had
charge of the slaughtering of the passover lambs for everyone who was not
clean in order to consecrate them to the
18 LORD. For a great number of people,
chiefly from Ephraim, Manasseh, Issachar, and Zebulun, had not purified
themselves, yet they ate the passover
otherwise than it is written, for Hezekiah had prayed for them, saying,
19 "The kind LORD pardon everyone
who has set his heart to seek God, the
LORD, the God of his fathers, though
he be not clean according to the purification of the sanctuary."
20 Now the LORD listened to Hezekiah
21 and healed the people, so the Israelites
that were found in Jerusalem kept the
feast of unleavened cakes seven days
with great gladness; and the Levites
and the priests praised the LORD day
22 by day, with all their might. Accordingly Hezekiah spoke encouragingly to
all the Levites who had shown good
skill in the service of the LORD; and
they ate the offerings of the sacred season seven days, offering sacrifices of
thank-offerings, and giving thanks to
the LORD, the God of their fathers.
23 Then the whole assembly decided to
keep another seven days, and so they
kept seven days more with gladness;
24 for Hezekiah, king of Judah, presented
to the assembly a thousand bulls and
seven thousand sheep, and the princes
presented to the assembly a thousand
bulls and ten thousand sheep; and a
great number of priests sanctified themselves. Then all the assembly of Judah
together with the priests and the
Levites and all the assembly, that came
out of Israel, and the resident aliens,
who came out of Israel, and who dwelt
in Judah, rejoiced. So there was great
joy in Jerusalem; for since the time of
Solomon, the son of David, king of
Israel, there had been nothing like this
in Jerusalem. Then the priests and the
Levites arose and blessed the people;
and their voice was heard and their
prayer came up to his holy habitation,
even to the heavens.

HEZEKIAH'S WORK OF REFORM, 31:1–21

Now when all this was finished, all Israel who were present went out to the cities of Judah and broke in pieces the sacred pillars and cut down the sacred poles and broke down the high places and the altars throughout all Judah and Benjamin, also in Ephraim and Manasseh, until they had made an end of them. Then all the Israelites returned to their cities, each to his own possession.

Hezekiah appointed the divisions of the priests and the Levites according to their divisions—each of the priests and the Levites according to his service—for burnt-offering and for thank-offerings, to minister and to give thanks and praise in the gates of the camp of the LORD. The king's portion from his possessions was for burnt-offerings, for the morning and evening burnt-offerings, as well as for the burnt-offerings of the sabbaths, the new moons, and the fixed festivals, as it is written in the law of the LORD. Moreover he charged the people who dwelt in Jerusalem to provide the portion of the priests and the Levites, that they might devote themselves to the law of the LORD. Now as soon as the order was known, the Israelites gave generously the first-fruits of grain, wine, oil, honey, and all the produce of the field; and the tithe of everything they brought in abundantly. The Israelites and Judeans who dwelt in the cities of Judah, they also brought in the tithe of cattle and sheep, and the tithe of the dedicated things, which were consecrated to the LORD their God, and laid them in heaps. In the third month they began the foundations of the heaps and finished them in the seventh month; and when Hezekiah and the princes came and saw the heaps, they blessed the LORD and his people Israel. Then Hezekiah questioned the priests and the Levites concerning the heaps. So Azariah, the chief priest of the house of Zadok, answered him and said,

"Since they began to bring the contribution to the house of the LORD, there has been sufficient and there has been a large amount left, for the LORD has blessed his people; and there has been left this great store."

Then Hezekiah gave orders to prepare chambers in the house of the LORD; and they prepared them. Then they faithfully brought in the contribution and the tithe and the dedicated things, and Conaniah the Levite was the overseer in charge of them, and Shimei his brother was next to him in authority. Jehiel, Azaziah, Nahath, Asahel, Jerimoth, Jozabad, Eliel, Ismachiah, Mahath, and Benaiah, were overseers under the authority of Conaniah and Shimei his brother, by the appointment of Hezekiah the king and Azariah, the ruler of the house of God. Kore, the son of Imnah, the Levite, the keeper of the east gate, was in charge of the voluntary contributions to God, to distribute the oblations of the LORD and the most sacred things. Also under him were Eden, Miniamin, Jeshua, Shemaiah, Amariah, Shecaniah, in the cities of the priests, faithfully to distribute to their kinsmen by divisions to great and small alike, with the exception of those males registered from three years old and upward—that is, to everyone who entered the house of the LORD for his daily portion of their service in their offices according to their divisions. Now in regard to the registration of the priests, it was according to their families; moreover the Levites from twenty years old and upward were registered in their offices by their divisions. There was also the purpose of registering all their children, their wives, their sons, and daughters throughout all the assembly, for they devoted themselves faithfully to the

holy things. But for the sons of Aaron 19
the priests, who were in the territory of
the common lands of their cities—in
every city there were men who were
designated by name to distribute portions to every male among the priests
and to everyone registered among the
Levites.
Thus Hezekiah did throughout all 20
Judah; and he did that which was good
and right and true before the LORD his
God. Moreover every work that he be- 21
gan in the service of the house of God,
both in the law and the commands, in
order to seek his God, he did with all
his heart and prospered.

SENNACHERIB'S INVASION, 32:1–23

It was after these things and this 32
loyalty, that Sennacherib, king of Assyria, came and invaded Judah, and
besieged the fortified cities and expected to take them. When Hezekiah 2
saw that Sennacherib had come determined to attack Jerusalem, he de- 3
cided in council with his princes and his
leading men to stop the water of the
fountains that were outside the city,
and they helped him. Indeed a great 4
crowd of people collected and stopped
up all the fountains and the torrent
that coursed through the midst of the
land, saying,
"Why should the kings of Assyria
come and find abundant water?"
He also took courage and built up all 5
the wall that had been broken down,
raised up towers on it, and reared
another outside wall, and strengthened
Millo in the city of David, and made
weapons and shields in great quantity.
Then he set commanders of war over 6
the people and gathered them to him in
the open square at the gate of the city
and spoke reassuringly, saying,
"Be strong and courageous, fear not, 7
neither be dismayed because of the
king of Assyria, nor because of all the
multitude that is with him; for there is
greater with us than with him. With 8
him is an arm of flesh, but with us is the
LORD our God to help us and to fight
our battles." And the people were reassured by the words of Hezekiah, king
of Judah.
After this Sennacherib, the king of 9

Assyria, while he himself with all his
forces was before Lachish, sent his
servants to Jerusalem, to Hezekiah
king of Judah and to all Judah who
were at Jerusalem, saying,
10 "Thus says Sennacherib, the king of
Assyria: 'On what are you trusting that
you are awaiting the siege in Jerusalem?
11 Is not Hezekiah leading you on in order
to give you over to die by hunger and
thirst, saying, "The LORD our God will
deliver us out of the hand of the king of
12 Assyria?" Has not the same Hezekiah
taken away his high places and his
altars, and said to Judah and Jerusalem, "You shall worship before one
altar, and upon it you shall sacrifice."
13 Do you not know what I and my
fathers have done to all the peoples of
the lands? Were the gods of the nations
of the lands able to deliver their lands
14 out of my hand? Who was there among
all the gods of those nations which my
fathers put under the ban who was able
to deliver his people from my hand,
that your god should be able to deliver
15 you out of my hand? Now therefore,
let not Hezekiah deceive you nor mislead you in this way, and do not believe
him; for since no god of any nation or
kingdom has been able to deliver his
people from my hand and from the
hand of my fathers, how much less shall
your gods deliver you out of my
hand.' "
16 His servants spoke still more against
the LORD God, and against his servant
17 Hezekiah, while he wrote letters insult-
ing the LORD, the God of Israel, and
inveighing against him as follows:
"As the gods of the nations of the
lands have not delivered their people
out of my hand, so the God of Hezekiah
shall not be able to deliver his people
out of my hand."
18 Then they shouted with a loud voice
in the Jewish language to the people of
Jerusalem who were on the wall to
frighten and terrify them, that they
19 might take the city. Moreover they
spoke of the God of Jerusalem as of the
gods of the peoples of the earth, that
are the work of men's hands.
20 Then Hezekiah the king and Isaiah
the prophet, the son of Amoz, prayed
concerning this and cried to the
21 heavens. Therefore the LORD sent an
angel who destroyed all the seasoned
warriors, together with the leaders and
commanders, in the camp of the king
of Assyria, so that he returned in disgrace to his own land; and when he
went into the house of his god, they
who were his own offspring slew him
there with the sword. Thus the LORD
saved Hezekiah and the inhabitants of
Jerusalem from the hand of Sennacherib, king of Assyria, and from the hand
of all their enemies, and gave them rest
on every side. Many brought gifts to
the LORD to Jerusalem and precious
things to Hezekiah, king of Judah, so
that from that time on he was exalted
in the eyes of all the nations.

A FINAL ESTIMATE OF HEZEKIAH, 32:24–33

In those days Hezekiah became dan-
gerously ill, and he prayed to the LORD,
and when he was entreated by him, he
gave him a sign. But Hezekiah made
no return according to the benefit bestowed on him, for his heart was lifted
up; therefore wrath came upon him and
upon Judah and Jerusalem. However,
Hezekiah humbled himself for the pride
of his heart, both he and the inhabitants
of Jerusalem, so that the wrath of the
LORD did not come upon them in the
days of Hezekiah.
Now Hezekiah had enormous wealth
and honor, and he provided himself
with treasuries for silver, gold, precious
stones, spices, shields, and all kinds of
artistic articles, storehouses also for the
increase of grain, wine, and oil, and inclosures for all kinds of cattle and for
flocks. Moreover he made for himself
cities and had vast possessions of sheep
and cattle; for God gave him very great
riches. It was Hezekiah who stopped
the upper springs of Gihon and directed
the waters straight down on the west
side of the city of David. So Hezekiah
prospered in all his works. However, in
the case of the ambassadors of the
princes of Babylon who were sent to
him to inquire about the sign that was
done in the land, God forsook him in
order to test him, that he might find
out all that was in his heart.
Now the rest of the records of Hezekiah and his good deeds, behold, they
are written in the Vision of Isaiah the
prophet, the son of Amoz, in the Book
of the Kings of Judah and Israel. So

Hezekiah slept with his fathers, and
they buried him in the ascent of the
sepulchers of the descendants of David,
and all Judah and the inhabitants of
Jerusalem paid him honor when he
died; and Manasseh his son became
king in his stead.

THE REACTION UNDER MANASSEH AND AMON, 33:1–25

3 Manasseh was twelve years old when
he became king, and he reigned fifty-
2 five years in Jerusalem. He did that
which was evil in the sight of the LORD
according to the abominations of the
nations which the LORD had dispos-
3 sessed before the Israelites. He also rebuilt the high places which Hezekiah
his father had torn down, and he set up
altars for the Baals and made sacred
poles, and worshipped all the host of
4 the heavens and served them; and he
built altars in the house of the LORD,
of which the LORD had said,
"In Jerusalem shall my name be forever."
5 He built altars to all the host of the
heavens in the two courts of the house
6 of the LORD. He also burned his children in the fire in the Valley of Ben-
Hinnom, and practiced augury and sorcery, and appointed mediums and wizards. He did great evil in the sight of
the LORD, thus provoking him to jeal-
7 ousy. Moreover he set the carved image of an idol which he had made in the
house of God, of which God had said to
David and to Solomon his son,
"In this house and in Jerusalem
which I have chosen out of all the tribes
8 of Israel I will put my name forever. I
will never again remove the feet of Israel from the land which I have appointed for your fathers, if only they
will be careful to do all that I have
commanded them by the hand of
Moses, even all the law and the statutes
and the ordinances."
But Manasseh seduced Judah and
the inhabitants of Jerusalem to do evil
more than the nations which the LORD
had destroyed before the Israelites.
The LORD spoke to Manasseh and to
his people, but they gave no heed. So
the LORD brought against them the
commanders of the army of the king of
Assyria, and they took Manasseh in
chains and bound him in fetters and
brought him to Babylon. But when he 12
was in distress, he besought the LORD
his God and humbled himself greatly
before the God of his fathers. He also 13
prayed to him, so that he was entreated
by him and heard his supplication and
restored him to his kingdom in Jerusalem. Then Manasseh knew that the
LORD was indeed God.
Now after this he built an outer wall 14
of the city of David on the west side of
Gihon in the valley, even to the entrance at the Fish Gate, so that it inclosed Ophel; and he raised it up to a
very great height. He also placed
competent commanders in all the fortified cities of Judah.
Moreover he put away the foreign 15
gods and the idol out of the house of the
LORD and all the altars which he had
built in the mount of the house of the
LORD and in Jerusalem and cast them
out of the city. Then he rebuilt the 16
altar of the LORD and sacrified upon it
sacrifices of thank-offerings and of
thanksgiving, and ordered Judah to
serve the LORD, the God of Israel.
Nevertheless the people still sacrificed 17
on the high places, but only to the
LORD their God.
Now the rest of the records of Ma- 18
nasseh and his prayer to God, as well as
the words of the seers who spoke to him
in the name of the LORD, the God of
Israel, behold, they are among the
Records of the Kings of Israel. His 19
prayer also, and how God was entreated
by him, and all his sin and his guilt, and
the sites on which he built the high
places and set up the sacred poles and
the carved images, before he humbled
himself, behold, they are written in the
Records of the Seers. So Manasseh 20
slept with his fathers, and they buried
him in the garden of his house; and
Amon his son became king in his stead.
Amon was twenty-two years old 21
when he became king, and he reigned
two years in Jerusalem. He did that 22
which was evil in the sight of the LORD
as Manasseh his father had done; for
Amon sacrificed to all the carved images
which Manasseh his father had made,
and served them. Moreover he did not 23
humble himself before the LORD as
Manasseh his father humbled himself;
but Amon multiplied offenses. There- 24

fore his servants conspired against him
and murdered him in his own house.
25 But the people of the land slew all the
conspirators against King Amon; and
the people of the land made Josiah his
son king in his stead.

THE DEUTERONOMIC REFORM, 34:1–33

34 Josiah was eight years old when he
became king and he reigned thirty-one
2 years in Jerusalem. He did that which
was right in the sight of the LORD and
walked in the ways of David his ancestor, turning neither to the right nor the
left.
3 Now in the eighth year of his reign,
while he was still a lad, he began to
seek after the God of David his ancestor, and in the twelfth year he began to
purge Judah and Jerusalem of the high
places, the sacred poles, the carved
4 images, and the molten images. Thus
at his direction they broke down the
altars of the Baals, and the incense
altars that stood high above them he
hewed down, and the sacred poles, the
carved images, and the molten images,
he demolished and ground to powder,
and scattered it on the graves of those
5 who had sacrificed to them. Also he
burned the bones of the priests upon
their altars, and purged Judah and Je-
6 rusalem. Likewise in the cities of Manasseh and Ephraim and Simeon and
as far as Naphtali, in their ruins round
7 about, he destroyed the altars and
ground the sacred poles and the carved
images to powder and hewed down all
the incense altars throughout all the
land of Israel, and then he returned to
Jerusalem.
8 Now in the eighteenth year of his
reign, in order to purge the land and the
temple, he sent Shaphan, the son of
Azaliah, and Maaseiah, the commander
of the city, and Joah, the son of Joahaz,
the recorder, to repair the house of the
9 LORD his God. So they came to Hilkiah the high priest, and gave the
money that was brought into the house
of God, which the Levites, the keepers
of the threshold, had gathered from
Manasseh and Ephraim and from all
the remnant of Israel, and from all
Judah and Benjamin, and had returned
10 to Jerusalem. They in turn gave it to
the workmen who were responsible for
the house of the LORD; and the workmen who did the actual work on the
house of the LORD dispensed it to restore and repair the temple; to the carpenters they gave it and to the builders,
that they might buy hewn stone and
timber for framing and for beams for
the structures which the kings of Judah
had destroyed. The men worked faithfully on the task; and the overseers over
them were Jahath and Obadiah, the
Levites, of the descendants of Merari,
and Zechariah and Meshullam, of the
sons of the Kohathites to direct it. The
Levites—all who were skilful with instruments of music—were over the burden-bearers, and directed all the workmen in every sort of service; and some
of the Levites were scribes, notaries,
and gate-keepers.

Now when they brought out the
money that had been brought to the
house of the LORD, Hilkiah the priest
found a book of the law of the LORD
given by Moses. Accordingly Hilkiah
spoke up and said to Shaphan the
scribe,

"I have found a book of law in the
house of the LORD."

So Hilkiah gave the book to Shaphan.
Then Shaphan brought the book to the
king and also reported to the king, saying,

"All that has been committed to your
servants, they are doing, and they have
emptied out the money that was found
in the house of the LORD and have delivered it into the charge of the overseers and the workmen."

Shaphan the scribe also told the king,
saying,

"Hilkiah the priest has given me a
book."

Then Shaphan read out of it before
the king.

Now when the king heard the words
of the law, he tore his garments. Then
the king commanded Hilkiah, and Ahikam, the son of Shaphan, and Achbor,
the son of Micaiah, and Shaphan the
scribe, and Asaiah, the king's servant,
saying,

"Go, inquire of the LORD for me and
for those who are left in Israel and Judah, concerning the words of the book
that has been found; for great is the
wrath of the LORD that is poured out
upon us, because our fathers have not

kept the word of the LORD, to conform
to all that is written in this book."
So Hilkiah and those whom the king
mentioned went to Huldah the prophetess, the wife of Shallum, the son of
Tokhath, the son of Hasrah, keeper of
the wardrobe, who dwelt in Jerusalem
in the second quarter, and they spoke
to her about this. So she said to them,
"Thus says the LORD, the God of
Israel: 'Say to the man who sent you to
me, "Thus says the LORD: 'Behold, I
am about to bring evil upon this place
and upon its inhabitants, namely, all
the curses that are written in the book
which they have read before the king of
Judah. Because they have forsaken me
and have sacrificed to other gods, thus
provoking me to jealousy with all the
work of their hands; therefore my
wrath shall be poured out upon this
place and it shall not be quenched.' " '
But to the king of Judah who sent you
to inquire of the LORD, thus shall you
say to him: 'Thus says the LORD, the
God of Israel: "Regarding the words
which you have heard—because your
heart was penitent and you humbled
yourself before the LORD, when you
heard my words against this place and
against its inhabitants, and have humbled yourself before me, and have torn
your garments and wept before me, I
also have heard you," ' " is the oracle
of the LORD. " ' "Behold, I will gather
you to your fathers and you shall be
gathered to your grave in peace, neither
shall your eyes see all the evil which I
am about to bring upon this place and
upon its inhabitants." ' "
So they brought back word to the
king.
Then the king sent and gathered together all the elders of Judah and Jerusalem. Thereupon the king went up
to the house of the LORD together with
all the men of Judah and the inhabitants of Jerusalem, and the priests and
the Levites, and all the people, both
small and great; and he read in their
hearing all the words of the book of the
covenant that was found in the house
of the LORD. Then the king stood in
his place and made a covenant before
the LORD, to walk after the LORD and
to keep his commands, his decrees, and
his statutes with all his mind and heart,
to perform the words of the covenant
that were written in this book. Then
he caused all who were found in Jerusalem and Benjamin to adhere to the
covenant; and the inhabitants of Jerusalem did according to the covenant of
God, the God of their fathers. More- 33
over Josiah put away all the abominations out of all the lands that belonged
to the Israelites, and made all who were
found in Israel to serve, even to serve
the LORD their God. All his days they
did not depart from following the
LORD, the God of their fathers.

JOSIAH'S PASSOVER, 35:1–19

Now Josiah kept a passover to the **35**
LORD in Jerusalem; and they slew the
passover on the fourteenth day of the
first month. Accordingly he set the 2
priests in their offices and encouraged
them for the service of the house of the
LORD. He said to the Levites who 3
taught all Israel, who were holy to the
LORD,
"Put the holy ark in the house which
Solomon, the son of David, king of Israel, built. It shall no more be a burden
on your shoulders. Now serve the 4
LORD your God and his people Israel,
and prepare yourselves after your
fathers' houses by your divisions, according to the prescription of David,
king of Israel, and according to the prescription of Solomon his son; and stand 5
in the holy place according to the divisions of the families of your kinsmen
the common people, and for each a part
of a Levitical family. Then slay the 6
passover and sanctify yourselves and
prepare it for your kinsmen to keep it
according to the word of the LORD by
Moses."
Then Josiah presented to the com- 7
mon people flocks, lambs, and kids—all
of them for the passover offerings to all
who were present, to the number of
thirty thousand, and three thousand
bulls, these being from the king's property. His princes also gave as a volun- 8
tary gift to the people, to the priests,
and to the Levites—Hilkiah, Zechariah, and Jehiel, the rulers of the house
of God, gave to the priests for the passover offerings—two thousand and six
hundred lambs and three hundred cattle. Conaniah also, and Shemaiah and 9
Nathanel his kinsmen, and Hashabiah,
Meiel, and Jozabad, the chiefs of the
Levites, gave to the Levites for the

passover-offerings, five thousand lambs
and five hundred cattle.
10 So the service was established and
the priests stood at their posts, and the
Levites by their divisions, according to
11 the king's command. Thus they slew
the passover, and the priests sprinkled
the blood from their hands, while the
12 Levites skinned the victims. Then they
removed the burnt-offerings that they
might distribute them according to the
divisions of the families of the common
people, to offer to the LORD as it is
prescribed in the book of Moses; and so
13 they did with the cattle. Moreover they
boiled the passover on the fire according
to the ordinance, while they boiled the
holy offerings in pots, in caldrons, and
in pans, and carried them quickly to all
14 the common people. Afterward they
prepared some for themselves and for
the priests, because the priests, the sons
of Aaron, were occupied in offering up
the burnt-offerings and the fat pieces
until night; therefore the Levites prepared it for themselves and for the
priests, the sons of Aaron.
15 The singers, the sons of Asaph, were
at their posts according to the command of David, Asaph, Heman, and
Jeduthun, the king's seer, and the gatekeepers were at each gate; they had no
need to depart from their service, for
their kinsmen the Levites prepared it
16 for them. So all the service of the LORD
was established the same day that they
kept the passover and offered burnt-
offerings upon the altar of the LORD
according to the command of King Jo-
17 siah. Thus the Israelites who were
present kept the passover at that time
and the feast of unleavened cakes seven
18 days. Indeed there was no passover like
that kept in Israel since the days of
Samuel the prophet; neither did any of
the kings of Israel keep such a passover
as did Josiah; and the priests and the
Levites and all Judah and Israel were
present, together with the inhabitants
19 of Jerusalem. In the eighteenth year of
Josiah's reign was this passover kept.

THE DEATH OF JOSIAH, 35:20–27

20 After all this, when Josiah had restored the temple, Necho king of Egypt
went up to fight at Carchemish on the
Euphrates; and Josiah went out to
intercept him. But he sent messengers
to him, saying,

"What have we to do with each other, king of Judah? I come not against you this day, but to fight with another house, and God has said to me to make haste; cease then to provoke God who is with me, that he do not destroy you."

Nevertheless Josiah refused to turn away his face from him, but presumed to wage war with him and would not listen to the words of Necho from the mouth of God. So he went to fight in the valley of Megiddo. Then the archers shot at King Josiah, and the king said to his servants,

"Take me away, for I am badly wounded."

So his servants took him out of the chariot and made him ride in the second chariot that he had and brought him to Jerusalem where he died, and he was buried in the sepulchers of his fathers, and all Judah and Jerusalem mourned for Josiah. Jeremiah also chanted a dirge for Josiah and all the singing men and women speak of Josiah in their chants down to this day; and they made them a custom in Israel; and behold, they are written in the Lamentations.

Now the rest of the records of Josiah and his good deeds, according to that which is prescribed in the law of the LORD, and his acts from first to last are written in the Book of the Kings of Israel and Judah.

THE LAST DAYS OF THE KINGDOM OF JUDAH, 36:1–23

Then the people of the land took Jehoahaz, the son of Josiah, and made him king in his father's stead in Jerusalem. Joahaz was twenty-three years old when he became king and he reigned three months in Jerusalem. Then the king of Egypt deposed him at Jerusalem, and he fined the land a hundred talents of silver and a hundred talents of gold. The king of Egypt then made Eliakim, his brother, king over Judah and Jerusalem, and changed his name to Jehoiakim. But Necho took Joahaz his brother and brought him to Egypt.

Jehoiakim was twenty-five years old

when he became king and he reigned in
Jerusalem eleven years; and he did
that which was evil in the sight of the
6 LORD his God. Against him came up
Nebuchadnezzar, king of Babylon, and
bound him in fetters to bring him to
7 Babylon. Nebuchadnezzar also carried
some of the utensils of the house of the
LORD to Babylon and put them in his
8 temple in Babylon. Now the rest of the
records of Jehoiakim and his abominations which he did and that which was
found in him, behold, they are written
in the Book of the Kings of Israel and
Judah; and Jehoiachin his son became
king in his stead.
9 Jehoiachin was eight years old when
he became king and he reigned in Jerusalem three months and ten days; and
he did that which was evil in the sight
10 the LORD. Then at the return of spring
King Nebuchadnezzar sent and brought
him to Babylon, with the choice vessels
of the house of the LORD, and he made
Zedekiah, his brother, king over Judah
and Jerusalem.
11 Zedekiah was twenty-one years old
when he became king, and he reigned
12 eleven years in Jerusalem. He did that
which was evil in the sight of the LORD
his God, and did not humble himself
before Jeremiah the prophet at the
13 word of the LORD. He also rebelled
against King Nebuchadnezzar, who had
made him swear by God. But he became obstinate and stubbornly refused
to turn to the LORD, the God of Israel.
14 Also all the chiefs of the priests and the
people proved utterly faithless, in accordance with all the abominations of
the nations, and they polluted the
house of the LORD which he had sancti-
15 fied in Jerusalem. Still the LORD, the
God of their fathers, eagerly sent to
them by his messengers, because he had
compassion on his people and on his
dwelling-place, but they mocked God's 16
messengers and despised his words and
derided his prophets, until the wrath of
the LORD arose against his people till
there was no remedy. So he brought up 17
against them the king of the Chaldeans
who slew their young men with the
sword in the house of their sanctuary,
and spared neither youths nor maidens,
neither the aged nor the decrepit. He
delivered them all into his hand. Also 18
all the utensils of the house of God both
large and small, together with the
treasures of the house of the LORD and
the treasures of the king and his princes
—all these he brought to Babylon.
Moreover they burned the house of 19
God, and broke down the wall of Jerusalem, and all its palaces they burned
with fire, and all its choice vessels were
given to destruction. Those who es- 20
caped the sword he carried captive to
Babylon, where they became slaves to
him and to his sons until the dominance
of the kingdom of Persia, in order that
the words of the LORD by the mouth of 21
Jeremiah might be fulfilled, until the
land had enjoyed its sabbaths. All the
days of the desolation it kept sabbath,
to complete the seventy years.
In the first year of Cyrus, king of 22
Persia, that the word of the LORD by
the mouth of Jeremiah might be accomplished, the LORD stirred up the
spirit of Cyrus, king of Persia, so that
he issued a proclamation throughout
his kingdom and also put it in writing,
as follows:
"Thus says Cyrus, king of Persia: 23
'The LORD, the God of the heavens,
has given me all the kingdoms of the
earth, and he has commissioned me to
build him a house in Jerusalem, which
is in Judah. Whosoever there is among
you of all his people, the LORD his God
be with him; let him go up.' "

THE BOOK OF EZRA

THE DECREE OF CYRUS AND THE RETURN, 1:1–11

1 NOW in the first year of Cyrus,
king of Persia, that the word
of the LORD by the mouth
of Jeremiah might be accomplished, the LORD stirred up the spirit
of Cyrus, king of Persia, to issue a proclamation throughout all his kingdom
and also to put it in writing, as follows:
2 "Thus says Cyrus, king of Persia:
'All the kingdoms of the earth has the
LORD, the God of the heavens, given
me, and he has commissioned me to
build him a house in Jerusalem, which
3 is in Judah. Whoever there is among
you of all his people who desires to go,
his God be with him; let him go up to
Jerusalem, which is in Judah, and build
the house of the LORD, the God of Israel, since he is the God who is in Jeru-
4 salem. Whoever is left in any place
where he resides as an alien, let the men
of his place aid him with silver and gold
and goods and beasts of burden, as well
as with voluntary offerings for the
house of God which is in Jerusalem.' "
5 Then the heads of families of Judah
and Benjamin, and the priests and the
Levites, even all whose spirit God had
roused to go up to build the house of the
6 Lord which is in Jerusalem, arose; and
all those who were about them supplied
them with utensils of silver, with gold,
with goods, and with beasts, and with
precious things, besides all that was
7 voluntarily offered. Also King Cyrus
brought forth the utensils of the house
of the LORD, which Nebuchadnezzar
had brought from Jerusalem and had
8 put in the house of his gods. So Cyrus,
king of Persia, brought them out under
the charge of Mithredath the treasurer, and counted them out to Shesh-
9 bazzar, the prince of Judah; and this is
the number of them: thirty golden
basins, a thousand silver basins, twen-
10 ty-nine censers, thirty golden bowls,
two thousand four hundred and ten
silver bowls, and a thousand other vessels. All the vessels of gold and silver
were five thousand four hundred. All
these Sheshbazzar brought up, when
the exiles were brought up from Babylon to Jerusalem.

LISTS OF THE RETURNING EXILES, 2:1–70

Now these belonged to the province,
that went up out of the captivity, who
had been carried away, whom Nebuchadnezzar, king of Babylon, had carried away to Babylon; and they returned to Jerusalem and Judah, each to
his city, those who came with Zerubbabel, Jeshua, Nehemiah, Seraiah,
Reelaiah, Mordecai, Bilshan, Mispar,
Bigvai, Rehum, Baanah.
The number of the men of the people
of Israel were: the descendants of
Parosh, two thousand one hundred and
seventy-two; the descendants of Shephatiah, three hundred and seventy-
two; the descendants of Arah, seven
hundred and seventy-five; the descendants of Pahathmoab through the
descendants of Jeshua and Joab, two
thousand eight hundred and twelve;
the descendants of Elam, a thousand
two hundred and fifty-four; the descendants of Zattu, nine hundred and
forty-five; the descendants of Zaccai,
seven hundred and sixty; the descendants of Bani, six hundred and forty-
two; the descendants of Bebar, six hundred and twenty-three; the descendants of Azgad, a thousand two hundred
and twenty-two; the descendants of
Adonikam, six hundred and sixty-six;
the descendants of Bigvai, two thousand and fifty-six; the descendants of
Adin, four hundred and fifty-four; the
descendants of Ater, of Hezekiah,
ninety-eight; the descendants of Bezai,
three hundred and twenty-three; the
descendants of Jorah, a hundred and
twelve; the descendants of Hashum,
two hundred and twenty-three; the descendants of Gibbar, ninety-five; the

descendants of Bethlehem, one hundred
2 and twenty-three; the men of Neto-
3 phah, fifty-six; the men of Anathoth,
4 one hundred and twenty-eight; the
descendants of Azmaveth, forty-two;
5 the descendants of Kirjath-jearim,
Chephirah and Beeroth, seven hundred
6 and forty-three; the descendants of
Ramah and Geba, six hundred and
7 twenty-one; the men of Michmash, one
8 hundred and twenty-two; the men of
Bethel and Ai, two hundred and twen-
9 ty-three; the descendants of Nebo,
0 fifty-two; the descendants of Magbish,
1 one hundred and fifty-six; the descendants of the other Elam, one thousand
2 two hundred and fifty-four; the descendants of Harim, three hundred and
3 twenty; the descendants of Lod, Hadid,
and Ono, seven hundred and twenty-
4 five; the descendants of Jericho, three
5 hundred and forty-five; the descendants of Senaah, three thousand six hundred and thirty.
6 The priests: the descendants of Jedaiah, of the house of Jeshua were nine
7 hundred and seventy-three; the descendants of Immer, one thousand and
8 fifty-two; the descendants of Pashhur,
one thousand two hundred and forty-
9 seven; the descendants of Harim, one
thousand and seventeen.
0 The Levites: the descendants of
Jeshua and Kadmiel, of the descend-
1 ants of Hodaviah, seventy-four; the
singers of the descendants of Asaph, one
2 hundred and twenty-eight; the descendants of the gatekeepers were: the
descendants of Shallum, the descendants of Ater, the descendants of Tala-
mon, the descendants of Akkub, the descendants of Hatita, the descendants of
Shobai, in all one hundred and thirty-
nine.
3 The temple servants were: the descendants of Ziha, the descendants of
4 Hasupha, the descendants of Tabbaoth, the descendants of Keros, the
5 descendants of Siaha, the descendants of Padon, the descendants of
Lebanah, the descendants of Haga-
6 bah, the descendants of Akkub, the descendants of Hagab, the descendants of
Shamlai, the descendants of Hanan,
7 the descendants of Giddel, the descendants of Gahar, the descendants of Rea-
8 iah, the descendants of Rezin, the descendants of Nekoda, the descendants
9 of Gazzan, the descendants of Uzza, the
descendants of Paseah, the descendants
of Besai, the descendants of Asnah, the 50
descendants of the Meunites, the descendants of Nephisim, the descendants of Bakbuk, the descendants of 51
Hakupha, the descendants of Harhur,
the descendants of Bazluth, the de- 52
scendants of Mehida, the descendants
of Harsha, the descendants of Barkos, 53
the descendants of Sisera, the descendants of Temah, the descendants of Ne- 54
ziah, the descendants of Hatipha.
The descendants of Solomon's serv- 55
ants were: the descendants of Sotai,
the descendants of Hassophereth, the
descendants of Peruda, the descendants 56
of Jaalah, the descendants of Darkon,
the descendants of Giddel, the de- 57
scendants of Shephatiah, the descendants of Hattil, the descendants of Pochereth-Hazzabaim, the descendants
of Ami, all the temple servants, and the 58
descendants of Solomon's servants,
were three hundred and ninety-two.
Now these were those who went up 59
from Telmelah, Telharsha, Cherub,
Addan, and Immer; but they could not
show their fathers' lineage nor their
descent, whether they were of Israel:
the descendants of Delaiah, the de- 60
scendants of Tobiah, the descendants
of Nekoda, six hundred and fifty-two;
also of the priests: the descendants of 61
Habaiah, the descendants of Hakkoz,
the descendants of Barzillai, who took a
wife from the daughters of Barzillai,
the Gileadite, and was called by their
name. These sought their register 62
among those reckoned by genealogy,
but it was not found; therefore they
were excluded from the priesthood as
polluted. Also the governor told them 63
that they should not eat of the most
sacred things, until there should stand
a priest with the Urim and Thummim.
The whole assembly together was 64
forty-two thousand three hundred and
sixty, besides their male and female 65
slaves, of whom there were seven thousand three hundred and thirty-seven.
Their horses were seven hundred and 66
thirty-six; their mules, two hundred
and forty-five; their camels, four hun- 67
dred and thirty-five; their asses, six
thousand seven hundred and twenty.
Now some of the heads of families, 68
when they came to the house of the
LORD which is in Jerusalem, made
voluntary gifts to the house of God to

69 set it up in its place. They gave according to their ability into the treasury of the work sixty-one thousand
darics of gold, and five thousand manas
of silver, and one hundred priests' gar-
70 ments. So the priests, the Levites,
some of the people, the porters, the
singers, and the temple servants dwelt
in their cities, and all Israel in their
cities.

THE RENEWAL OF WORSHIP AT JERUSALEM, 3:1–6

3 Now when the seventh month arrived, and the Israelites were in their
cities, the people assembled as one man
2 to Jerusalem. Then Jeshua, the son of
Jozadak, and his kinsmen the priests,
and Zerubbabel, the son of Shealtiel,
and his kinsmen arose and built the altar of the God of Israel to offer burnt-
offerings on it, as prescribed in the law
3 of Moses, the man of God. So they set
up the altar in its place, for fear was
upon them, because of the peoples of
the lands, and they offered upon it
burnt-offerings to the LORD, even
burnt-offerings morning and evening.
4 Moreover they kept the feast of booths
as it is written, and offered the fixed
number of burnt-offerings day by day
according to the direction for each day;
5 and afterward the regular burnt-offerings and the offerings at the new moons,
and those of all the fixed festivals of the
LORD, that were consecrated, and
those of everyone who offered a volun-
6 tary offering to the LORD. From the
first day of the seventh month they began to offer burnt-offerings to the
LORD, although the foundation of the
temple of the LORD was not yet laid.

THE FOUNDATION OF THE TEMPLE LAID, 3:7–13

7 They gave money to the masons and
to the carpenters, and food, and drink,
and oil to the Sidonians and the Tyrians
to bring cedar trees from Lebanon by
sea to Joppa, according to the grant
that they had from Cyrus, king of
Persia.
8 Now in the second year of their coming to the house of God at Jerusalem,
in the second month, Zerubbabel, the
son of Shealtiel, and Jeshua, the son of
Jozadak, and the rest of their kinsmen
the priests and the Levites, and all who
came from the captivity to Jerusalem,
made a beginning and appointed the
Levites from twenty years old and upward to have the oversight of the work
of the house of the LORD. Then Jesh- 9
ua stood up with his sons and his kinsmen, Kadmiel and his sons, Judeans, to
have together direction over the execution of the work in the house of God;
the sons of Henadad also, with their
sons and their kinsmen the Levites. Now 10
when the builders had laid the foundation of the temple of the LORD, they
stationed the priests in their official
robes with trumpets and the Levites,
the sons of Asaph, with cymbals to
praise the LORD according to the directions of David, king of Israel; and they 11
sang responsively in praising and giving
thanks to the LORD, saying,
"For he is good,
For his kindness over Israel is everlasting."
Then all the people raised a great
shout when they praised the LORD,
because the foundation of the house of
the LORD had been laid. But many of 12
the priests and the Levites and heads of
families and the old men, who had seen
the first house, when the foundation of
this house was laid before their eyes,
wept with a loud voice, while many
shouted aloud for joy, so that the peo- 13
ple could not distinguish the sound of
the shout of joy from the sound of the
weeping of the people, for the people
shouted with a great shout, and the
sound was heard a great distance away.

OPPOSITION TO THE REBUILDING, 4:1–24

Now when the adversaries of Judah 4
and Benjamin heard that the exiles
were building a temple for the LORD,
the God of Israel, they approached 2
Zerubbabel and the heads of families,
and said to them,
"Let us build with you; for we seek
your God, as you do, and we have been
sacrificing to him since the days of
Esarhaddon, king of Assyria, who
brought us up here."
But Zerubbabel and Jeshua and the 3
rest of the heads of families of Israel
said to them,

"You have nothing in common with
us in building a house to our God; but
we ourselves will together build to the
LORD, the God of Israel, as King
Cyrus, the king of Persia, has commanded us."
4 Then the people of the land continued to weaken the hands of the people of Judah, and terrorize them out of
5 building, and hire counselors against
them to frustrate their counsel, all the
days of Cyrus, king of Persia, even until the reign of Darius, king of Persia.
6 Moreover in the reign of Xerxes, in the
beginning of his reign, they wrote an
accusation against the inhabitants of
Judah and Jerusalem.
7 Now in the days of Artaxerxes wrote
Bishlam, Mithredath, Tabeel, and the
rest of his companions to Artaxerxes,
the king of Persia; and the script of the
letter was written in Aramaic and in-
8 terpreted in Aramaic. Rehum, the commander, and Shimshai, the scribe,
wrote a letter against Jerusalem to
9 Artaxerxes the king as follows. Then
wrote Rehum, the commander, and
Shimshai, the scribe, and the rest of
their associates, the Dinaites and the
Apharsathchites, the Tarpelites, the
Apharsites, the Archevites, the Babylonians, the people of Susa, the Deha-
10 ites, the Elamites, and the rest of the
peoples whom the great and noble Ash-
urbanipal transported and settled in the
city of Samaria and in the rest of the
province beyond the River. Now—
11 this is a copy of the letter that they sent
to Artaxerxes the king:
12 "Your servants, the men of the province beyond the River. Now be it
known to the king that the Jews who
came up from you to us have reached
Jerusalem. This rebellious and bad city
they are rebuilding and have completed
its walls and cleared the foundations.
13 Therefore be it known to the king, that
if this city be rebuilt and its walls finished, they will not pay tribute, custom,
or toll, and immediately it will injure
14 the revenue of the kings. Now because we eat the salt of the palace and
it is not fitting for us to behold the
king's dishonor, therefore we have sent
15 and informed the king, that search be
made in the book of the records of your
fathers; for you will find in the book of
the records and learn that this city is a
rebellious city and one that causes damage to kings and provinces and that the
Jews have stirred up sedition in it from
ancient times, for which cause this city
was laid waste. We make known to the 16
king that, if this city is rebuilt and its
walls finished, you will have as a result
no portion in the lands beyond the
River."

The king sent a message to Rehum, 17
the commander, and to Shimshai, the
scribe, and to the rest of their associates who dwelt in Samaria and in the
rest of the province beyond the River:
"Greeting, and as follows: The letter 18
which you sent to us has been plainly
read before me. I gave command and 19
search has been made, and it has been
found that this city from ancient times
has been rebellious against kings and
that rebellion and sedition have taken
place in it. Moreover there have been 20
mighty kings over Jerusalem who have
ruled over all the country beyond the
River and tribute, custom, and toll
were paid to them. Now give com- 21
mand that these men cease and that
this city be not rebuilt until a decree
shall be issued by me. Also be careful 22
that there be no neglect about this; why
should the damage increase to the detri-
ment of the kings?"
When the copy of King Artaxerxes' 23
letter had been read to Rehum and
Shimshai, the scribe, and their associates, they went in haste to Jerusalem to
the Jews, and by force and compulsion
made them stop. Thus the work on the 24
house of God which is in Jerusalem
came to an end, and it ceased until the
second year of the reign of Darius, king
of Persia.

THE TEMPLE REBUILT AND DEDICATED, 5:1—6:22

Now the prophets Haggai and Zecha- 5
riah, the son of Iddo, prophesied to the
Jews who were in Judah and Jerusalem,
in the name of the God of Israel who
was over them. Then Zerubbabel, the 2
son of Shealtiel, and Jeshua, the son
of Jozadak, arose and began to build
the house which is at Jerusalem; and
with them were the prophets of God
supporting them.
At that time Tattenai, the governor 3
of the province beyond the River, and
Shethar-bozenai and their associates
came to them, and spoke to them thus,

"Who gave you a permit to build this
house and finish this sanctuary? And
who are the builders who are doing this
work?"
4 Accordingly we told them what the
names of the men were, who were build-
5 ing this structure. But the eye of their
God was upon the elders of the Jews,
so that they did not make them cease
until a report should come to Darius,
and then a written reply be returned
concerning it.
6 The copy of the letter that Tattenai,
the governor beyond the River, and
Shethar-bozenai and his associates the
Apharsachites, who were beyond the
7 River, sent to Darius, the king. They
sent a dispatch to him, wherein was
written as follows:
8 "To Darius, the king, all hail! Be it
known to the king that we have gone
into the province of Judah, to the house
of the great God, which was built with
huge stones and timber laid on the
walls; this work is being thoroughly
done and is prospering in their hands.
9 Then we asked those elders, and said to
them thus, 'Who gave you a permit to
build this house and to complete this
10 building?' We also asked them their
names, in order to inform you, that we
might write the names of the men who
11 were at their head; and they returned
us answer as follows: "We are the servants of the God of the heavens and the
earth, and we are rebuilding this house
that was built many years ago, which a
great king of Israel built and finished,
12 but after our fathers had roused the
wrath of the God of the heavens, he
gave them into the hand of Nebuchadnezzar, king of Babylon, the Chaldean,
who destroyed this house and carried
13 the people away to Babylon. However
in the first year of Cyrus, king of Babylon, Cyrus, the king, made a decree that
14 this house of God be rebuilt. The gold
and silver utensils also of the house of
God, which Nebuchadnezzar took from
the temple that was at Jerusalem and
brought to the temple in Babylon, those
Cyrus, the king, took out of the temple
in Babylon, and they were delivered to
one Sheshbazzar by name, whom he
15 had made governor; and he said to him,
"Take these vessels, go, put them in the
temple that is in Jerusalem, and let the
house of God be rebuilt in its place."
16 Then this Sheshbazzar came and laid
the foundations of the house of God
which is in Jerusalem. Since that time
even until now it has been building, and
it is not yet finished.' Now therefore, if 17
it please the king, let search be made in
the king's treasure-house there at
Babylon, whether it be so, that a decree was issued by Cyrus the king to rebuild this house of God at Jerusalem;
and let the king send to us his good
pleasure concerning this matter."
Accordingly Darius, the king, issued 6
a decree, and search was made in the
house of the archives where the treasures were stored there at Babylon. And 2
at Ecbatana, in the castle that is in the
province of Media, a roll was found and
in it was written:
"A record: In the first year of Cyrus, 3
the king, Cyrus, the king, issued a decree: 'Concerning the house of God at
Jerusalem, let the house, the place
where sacrifices are offered, be rebuilt,
and let its foundations be prepared; its
height shall be sixty cubits and its
breadth sixty cubits, with three courses 4
of huge stones and a course of new timber, the expenses to be paid out of the
king's treasury. Also let the gold and 5
silver utensils of the house of God,
which Nebuchadnezzar took from the
temple at Jerusalem and brought to
Babylon, be restored and brought to
the temple which is in Jerusalem, each
to its place; and you shall put them in
the house of God.'
"Now therefore, Tattenai, governor 6
of the province beyond the River, Shethar-bozenai, and their associates the
Apharsachites, who are beyond the
River, withdraw from there. Let the 7
work of this house of God alone; let the
governor of the Jews and the elders of
the Jews rebuild this house of God in
its place. Moreover I make a decree in 8
regard to what you shall do for these
elders of the Jews for the building of
this house of God: that out of the
king's funds from the tribute of the
province beyond the River the expenses
be paid in full to these men, and that
without delay. Whatever is needed, 9
both young bulls and rams and lambs
for burnt-offerings to the God of the
heavens, wheat, salt, wine, and oil according to the word of the priests at
Jerusalem, let it be given to them day
by day without fail, that they may offer
sacrifices of a soothing odor to the God 10

of the heavens; and pray for the life of
11 the king and his sons. Also I make a
decree that any man who alters this
command, a beam shall be pulled out
from his house and he shall be impaled
upon it, and his house shall be made a
12 refuse-heap for this. The God who has
caused his name to dwell there shall
overthrow any king or people who shall
put forth his hand to alter this, or to
destroy this house of God, which is in
Jerusalem. I, Darius, have issued a
decree, let it be executed to the letter."
13 Then Tattenai, the governor of the
province beyond the River, and Shethar-bozenai, and their associates did
precisely as Darius, the king, had di-
14 rected. So the elders of the Jews built
and prospered, through the prophesying of Haggai, the prophet, and Zechariah, the son of Iddo. Thus they built
and finished it, according to the command of the God of Israel and according to the decree of Cyrus and Darius
15 and Artaxerxes, the king of Persia. So
this house was finished on the third day
of the month Adar, which was in the
sixth year of the reign of Darius the
king.
16 Then the Israelites, the priests, the
Levites, and the rest of the returned exiles, celebrated the dedication of this
17 house of God with joy. They offered at
the dedication of this house of God a
hundred bulls, two hundred rams, four
hundred lambs, and twelve he-goats as
a sin-offering for all Israel, according to
18 the number of the tribes of Israel. They
also set the priests in their divisions
and the Levites in their courses, for the
service of God at Jerusalem, as it is prescribed in the book of Moses.
19 Moreover the returned exiles kept
the passover upon the fourteenth day
20 of the first month. For the priests and
the Levites had purified themselves to
a man, all of them being ceremonially
clean. They slaughtered the passover
for all the returned exiles, both for
their kinsmen the priests and for them-
21 selves. Then the Israelites who had returned from the captivity, and everyone who separated himself from the uncleanness of the peoples of the land to
join them in order to seek the LORD,
22 the God of Israel, ate, and kept the
feast of unleavened cakes seven days
with gladness; for the LORD had made
them joyful, and had turned the heart
of the king of Persia to them, to
strengthen their hands in the work of
the house of God, the God of Israel.

EZRA'S MISSION TO JERUSALEM, 7:1–28

Now after these things, in the reign 7
of Artaxerxes, king of Persia, there
went up Ezra, the son of Seraiah, the
son of Azariah, the son of Hilkiah, the 2
son of Shallum, the son of Zadok,
the son of Ahitub, the son of Amariah, 3
the son of Azariah, the son of Meraioth,
the son of Zerahiah, the son of Uzzi, 4
the son of Bukki, the son of Abishua, 5
the son of Phineas, the son of Eleazar, the son of Aaron the chief priest.
This Ezra went up from Babylon; 6
and he was a scribe skilled in the
law of Moses, which the LORD, the
God of Israel, had given; and the king
granted him all his request, because the
hand of the Lord his God was upon
him. Moreover some of the Israelites 7
and the priests, the Levites, the singers,
the doorkeepers, and the temple servants went up to Jerusalem in the seventh year of Artaxerxes the king. He 8
came to Jerusalem in the fifth month,
which was in the seventh year of the
king; for on the first day of the first 9
month he began the journey up from
Babylon, and on the first day of the
fifth month he arrived at Jerusalem,
since the good hand of his God was
upon him. For Ezra had set his heart 10
to seek the law of the Lord, to keep it,
and to teach in Israel statutes and
ordinances.
Now this is a copy of the letter 11
which King Artaxerxes gave to Ezra
the priest, the scribe, learned in matters of the commands of the LORD and
his statutes in Israel:
"Artaxerxes, king of kings, to Ezra 12
the priest, learned in the law of the God
of the heavens, heartiest greetings. I 13
now make a decree that anyone of the
people of Israel, or their priests or Levites in my realm, who is willing to go
to Jerusalem, shall go with you. Be- 14
cause you have been sent by the king
and his seven counselors to make investigations concerning Judah and
Jerusalem in accordance with the law
of your God which is in your hand, and 15
to carry the silver and gold which the

king and his counselors have freely
offered to the God of Israel, whose
16 dwelling is in Jerusalem, with all the
silver and gold that you shall find in all
the province of Babylon, together with
the voluntary offerings of the people
and the priests, offered willingly for
the house of their God, which is in Jeru-
17 salem; accordingly with this money you
shall faithfully buy bulls, rams, lambs,
with their cereal-offerings and their
libations, and shall offer them on the
altar of the house of your God, which
18 is in Jerusalem. Moreover whatever
shall seem good to you and to your kinsmen to do with the rest of the silver and
the gold, so do according to the will of
19 your God. The utensils that have been
given you for the service of the house of
your God, deliver before the God of
20 Jerusalem; and whatever things besides are required for the house of your
God, which you shall have occasion to
bestow, you shall give it out of the
king's treasure-house.
21 "Moreover I, even I, Artaxerxes, the
king, do make a decree to all the treasurers of the province beyond the River,
that whatever Ezra the priest, learned
in the law of the God of the heavens,
shall require of you, let it be faithfully
22 done, up to a hundred talents of silver,
a thousand measures of wheat, a hundred baths of wine, a hundred baths
of oil, and salt without reckoning.
23 Whatever is commanded by the God of
the heavens, let it be faithfully done for
the house of the God of the heavens; for
why should there be wrath against the
24 realm of the king and his sons? Also be
it known to you that it is unlawful for
you to impose tax, tribute, or toll on
any priests, Levites, singers, doorkeepers, temple servants, or menials of this
25 house of God. Moreover do you Ezra,
according to the wisdom of your God
that is in your grasp, appoint governors
and judges who may judge all the people beyond the River, all such as know
the laws of your God, and instruct any
26 who do not know them. Whoever will
not obey the law of your God and the
law of the king, let strict judgment be
executed upon him, whether it be
death, or punishment, or confiscation of
goods, or imprisonment."
27 Blessed be the LORD, the God of our
fathers, who has put such a thing as this
in the king's heart, to beautify the
house of the LORD, which is in Jerusalem, and has extended grace to me 28
before the king and his counselors and
all the distinguished princes of the
king. Thus I was strengthened, since
the hand of the LORD my God was with
me, and I gathered leading men from
Israel to go up with me.

EZRA'S COMPANY AND EQUIPMENT, 8:1–36

Now these are the heads of families, 8
and this is the genealogy of those who
came up with me from Babylon in the
reign of Artaxerxes, the king: Of the 2
descendants of Phinehas, Gershom; of
the descendants of Ithamar, Daniel; of
the descendants of David, Hattush, the 3
son of Shecaniah; of the descendants of
Parosh, Zechariah, and with him were
reckoned by genealogy a hundred and
fifty males; of the descendants of Pa- 4
hath-moab, Eliohenai, the son of Zerahiah, and with him two hundred males;
of the descendants of Shecaniah, the 5
son of Jahaziel, and with him three
hundred males; and of the descendants 6
of Adin, Ebed, the son of Jonathan, and
with him fifty males; of the descendants 7
of Elam, Jeshaiah, the son of Athaliah,
and with him seventy males; of the de- 8
scendants of Shephatiah, Zebadiah, the
son of Michael, and with him eighty
males; of the descendants of Joab, Oba- 9
diah, the son of Jehiel, and with him
two hundred and eighteen males; of 10
the descendants of Bani, Shelomith, the
son of Josiphiah, and with him a hundred and sixty males; of the descend- 11
ants of Bebai, Zechariah, the son of
Bebai, and with him twenty-eight
males; of the descendants of Azgad, 12
Johanan, the son of Hakkatan, and
with him a hundred and ten males; of 13
the descendants of Adonikam, those
who came last, and these are their
names: Eliphelet, Jeuel, and Shemaiah,
and with them sixty males; and of the 14
descendants of Bigvai, Uthai and Zab-
bub, and with them seventy males.
Accordingly I gathered them to- 15
gether to the river that flows toward
Ahava, and there we encamped three
days, while I inspected the people and
the priests and found there none of the
descendants of Levi. Then I sent for 16
Eleazer, Ariel, Shemaiah, Elnathan,

Jarib, Elnathan, Nathan, Zechariah,
and Meshullam, leading men; also for
Joiarib and Elnathan, who were teach-
17 ers; and I sent them to Iddo, the chief
of the place Casiphia. I put in their
mouths the words they were to speak to
Iddo and his kinsmen the temple servants at the place Casiphia, namely,
that they should bring us ministrants
18 for the house of our God. And because
the good hand of our God was with us,
they brought us a man of discretion, of
the descendants of Mahli, the son of
Levi, the son of Israel, and Sherebiah,
with his sons and his kinsmen, eighteen;
19 and Hashabiah and Jeshaiah of the descendants of Merari, their kinsmen and
20 their sons, twenty; and of the temple
servants, whom David and the princes
had given for the service of the Levites,
two hundred and twenty temple servants; all of them were mentioned by
21 name. Then I proclaimed there a fast
at the river Ahava, that we might humble ourselves before our God to seek
from him a safe journey for us and for
our little ones and for all our posses-
22 sions. For I was ashamed to ask of the
king an armed force and horsemen to
help us against the enemy on the way,
because we had said to the king,

"The hand of our God is with all who
seek him for good, but his power and
his wrath are against all who forsake
him."

23 So we fasted and besought our God
for this; and he was entreated by us.

24 Then I set apart twelve of the chiefs
of the priests, even Sherebiah, Hashabiah, and ten of their kinsmen with
25 them, and weighed to them the silver,
and the gold, and the utensils, even the
contribution to the house of our God,
which the king and his counselors, and
his princes and all Israel there present
26 had offered. Thus I weighed into their
hands six hundred and fifty talents of
silver, and utensils of silver a hundred
talents, of gold one hundred talents;
27 and twenty bowls of gold of a thousand
darics, and two vessels of fine burnished
28 bronze, precious as gold; and I said to
them,

"You are holy to the LORD, and the
vessels are holy, and the silver and gold
are a voluntary offering to the LORD,
29 the God of your fathers. Watch and
keep them until you weigh them before
the chiefs of the priests and the Levites
and the chiefs of the families of Israel
at Jerusalem in the chambers of the
house of the LORD."

So the priests and the Levites re- 30
ceived the weight of the silver and the
gold and the utensils, to bring them to
Jerusalem to the house of our God.
Then we departed from the river 31
Ahava on the twelfth day of the first
month to go to Jerusalem.

The hand of our God was upon us
and he delivered us from the hand of
the enemy and the lier-in-wait by the
way; and when we arrived at Jeru- 32
salem, we remained there three days.
Then on the fourth day the silver, the 33
gold, and the utensils were weighed in
the house of our God into the hands of
Meremoth, the son of Uriah, the priest;
and with him was Eleazar, the son of
Phinehas, and with them were Jozabad,
the son of Jeshua, and Noadiah, the son
of Binnui, the Levites. The whole was 34
numbered and weighed, and the weight
of everything was recorded. At that 35
time those who had come from the captivity, the returned exiles, offered
burnt-offerings to the God of Israel,
twelve bulls for all Israel, ninety-six
rams, seventy-seven lambs, twelve he-
goats as a sin-offering, the whole being
a burnt-offering to the LORD. More- 36
over they delivered the king's commission to the king's satraps and to the
governors of the provinces beyond the
River; and they gave support to the
people and the house of God.

THE EXPULSION OF FOREIGN WIVES, 9:1—10:17

Now when these things had been 9
completed, the princes approached me
and said,

"The people of Israel and the priests
and the Levites have not separated
themselves from the peoples of the
lands, from their abominations, even
from the Canaanites, the Hittites, the
Perizzites, the Jebusites, the Ammonites, the Moabites, the Egyptians, and
the Amorites. For they have taken 2
wives from their daughters for themselves and their sons, so that the holy
race has mixed itself with the peoples
of the lands, and the hands of the
princes and the rulers have been foremost in this inconsistency."

3 Now when I heard this thing, I tore
my garment and my mantle, and pulled
the hair from my head and my beard,
4 and sat down appalled. Then were assembled to me all who trembled at the
words of the God of Israel because of
the inconstancy of the exiles, and I sat
appalled until the evening oblation.
5 But at the evening oblation I arose
from my self-abasement, and having
torn my garment and my mantle, I fell
upon my knees and spread out my
6 hands to the LORD my God and said,
"O my God, I am ashamed and blush
to lift up my face to thee, my God, for
our iniquities have risen higher than our
heads and our guilt has grown even to
7 the heavens. Since the days of our fathers even to this day we have been involved in great guilt, and for our iniquities we, our kings, and our priests
have been delivered into the hand of the
kings of the lands, to the sword, captivity, plunder, and confusion of face, as it
8 is this day. Now for a little while there
has been favor from the LORD our God,
in that he has left us an escaped remnant and given us a stake in his holy
place, that our God may lighten our
eyes and give us a little reinvigoration
9 in our bondage. For we are slaves; yet
in our bondage our God hast not forsaken us, but has extended to us kindness in the sight of the kings of Persia,
to give us a reinvigoration to raise up
the house of our God, to repair its ruins,
and to give us a wall in Judah and Jeru-
10 salem. Now, O our God, what shall we
say after this? For we have forsaken
11 thy commands, which thou has commanded by thy servants the prophets,
saying, 'The land to which you go for
conquest is an unclean land because of
the uncleanness of the peoples of the
lands, through their abominable rites,
which have filled it from one end to the
12 other with their uncleanness. Therefore do not give your daughters to their
sons, nor take their daughters as wives
for your sons, and never seek their
peace or prosperity, that you may be
strong and enjoy the good of the land,
and cause your children to inherit it
13 forever.' Now after all that has come
upon us for our evil deeds and our great
guilt, inasmuch as thou, O our God,
hast punished us less than our iniquities deserve, and hast given us a rem-
14 nant such as this, shall we again break
thy commands, and make marriage alli-
ances with the peoples who perform
these abominable rites? Wouldst thou
not be enraged at us until thou hadst
consumed us, until neither remnant nor
survivor was left? O LORD, the God 15
of Israel, thou art righteous; for we are
left a remnant that has escaped, as it
is this day. Behold, we are before thee
in our guilt, for none can stand before
thee because of this."

Now while Ezra was praying and 10
making confession, weeping and casting
himself down before the house of God,
there was assembled to him out of Israel a very great assembly of men, wom-
en, and children; for the people wept
bitterly. Then Shecaniah, the son of 2
Jehiel, one of the sons of Elam, spoke
up and said to Ezra,
"We have broken faith with our God
and have married foreign women of the
people of the land, yet now there is hope
for Israel concerning this matter. Now 3
therefore let us make a covenant with
our God to put away all the wives and
those born of them, according to the
counsel of my lord and of those who
tremble at the command of our God,
and let it be done according to the law.
Arise, for it is your task, and we are with 4
you; be strong and act."
Then Ezra arose and made the chiefs 5
of the priests, the Levites and all Israel
swear that they would do according to
this proposal. So they took oath.
Thereupon Ezra rose up from before 6
the house of God and went into the
chamber of Jehohanan, the son of Eliashib, and when he came there he neither
ate bread nor drank water, for he continued to mourn because of the unfaithfulness of the exiles. Then they issued 7
a proclamation throughout Judah and
Jerusalem to all the returned exiles to
assemble at Jerusalem; and that who- 8
ever did not come within three days,
according to the counsel of the princes
and the elders, all his property should
be confiscated and he himself be excluded from the assembly of the exiles.
Then all the men of Judah and Ben- 9
jamin assembled at Jerusalem within
the three days (this was in the twentieth day of the ninth month); and all the
people sat in the open square in front of
the house of God, trembling on account
of the occasion itself and also because of

10 the pouring rain. Thereupon Ezra the
priest arose and said to them,
"You have broken faith and have married foreign women to increase the guilt
11 of Israel. Now therefore make confession to the LORD, the God of your fathers, and do his will and separate
yourselves from the peoples of the land
and from the foreign wives."
12 Then all the assembly answered and
said with a loud voice,
13 "We must do as you have said. But
the people are many, and it is the rainy
season, and we cannot stand outside,
and this is not a task of one day or two
for we have lamentably transgressed
14 in this matter. Let now our princes represent the whole assembly and let all
those in our cities who have married
foreign women come at appointed
times, with the elders of each city and
its judges, in order to turn aside the
fierce wrath of our God from us because
of this matter."
15 Only Jonathan, the son of Asahel,
and Jahzeiah, the son of Tikvah, opposed this, and Meshullam and Shabbethai the Levite supported them.
16 Then the returned exiles took action
thus: Ezra the priest and certain heads
of families according to their fathers'
houses, and all of them by their names,
were selected; and they held a sitting
on the first day of the tenth month to
17 examine the matter. Accordingly they
finished dealing with all the men who
had married foreign women by the first
day of the first month.

LISTS OF MEN MARRIED TO FOREIGNERS, 10:18–44

18 Now among the descendants of the
priests who had married foreign women
were found the sons of Jeshua, the sons
of Jozadak, and his clansmen: Maaseiah, Eliezer, Jarib, and Gedaliah. They 19
gave their hand that they would divorce
their wives; and their guilt-offering was
a ram of the flock for their guilt. Also 20
the sons of Immer: Hanani and Zeba- 21
diah; of the sons of Harim: Maaseiah,
Elijah, Shemaiah, Jehiel, and Uzziah;
of the sons of Pashhur: Elioenai, Maase- 22
iah, Ishmael, Nethanel, Jozabad, and
Elasah; of the Levites: Jozabad, Shi- 23
mei, Kelaiah (the same is Kelita), Pethahiah, Judah, and Eliezer; of the 24
singers: Eliashib and Zaccur; and of
the doorkeepers, Shallum, Telem, and
Uri.
Finally of Israel: of the sons of Pa- 25
rosh: Ramiah, Izziah, Malchijah, Mijamin, Eleazer, Malchijah, and Benaiah; of the sons of Elam: Mattaniah, 26
Zechariah, Jehiel, Abdi, Jeremoth, and
Elijah; of the sons of Zattu: Elioenai, 27
Eliashib, Mattaniah, Jeremoth, Zabad,
and Aziza; of the sons of Bebai: Jeho- 28
hanan, Hananiah, Zabbai, Athlai; of 29
the sons of Bani: Meshullam, Malluch,
Adaiah, Jashub, Sheal, and Jeremoth;
of the sons of Pahath-moab: Adna, 30
Chelal, Benaiah, Maaseiah, Mattaniah,
Bezalel, Binnui, and Manasseh; of the 31
sons of Harim: Eliezer, Isshijah, Malchijah, Shemaiah, Shimeon, Benjamin, 32
Malluch, Shemariah; of the sons of 33
Hashum: Mattenai, Mattattah, Zabad, Eliphelet, Jeremai, Manasseh,
Shimei; of the sons of Bani: Maadai, 34
Amram, Joel, Benaiah, Bedeiah, Che- 35
luhi, Vaniah, Meremoth, Eliashib, 36
Mattaniah, Mattenai, Jaasu; of the 37 38
sons of Binnui: Shimei, Shelemiah, 39
Nathan, Adaiah, Machnadebai, Sha- 40
shai, Sharai, Azarel, Shelemiah, She- 41
mariah, Shallum, Amariah, Joseph; of 42 43
the sons of Nebo: Jeiel, Mattithiah,
Zabad, Zebina, Iddo, Joel, Benaiah.
All these had married foreign women; 44
and they cast off the wives and the
children.

THE BOOK OF NEHEMIAH

NEHEMIAH'S PRAYER FOR JERUSALEM, 1:1–11

1 THE account of Nehemiah, the
son of Hacaliah.
Now it happened in the
month of Chislev, in the twentieth year, as I was in the citadel of Shu-
2 shan, that Hanani, one of my kinsmen,
came, together with certain men from
Judah, and I asked them concerning
the Jews who had escaped, who were
left from the captivity, and concerning
3 Jerusalem. So they said to me,
"The survivors who are left from the
captivity there in the province are in
great misery and reproach, and the wall
of Jerusalem is broken down and its
gates have been destroyed by fire."
4 Now when I heard these words, I sat
down and wept and mourned certain
days; and I fasted and prayed before the
5 God of the heavens, and I said,
"I beseech thee, O LORD, the God of
the heavens, the great and terrible God,
who keeps loving faith with those who
6 love him and keep his commands. Let
thine ears now be attentive and thine
eyes open, to hear the prayer of thy
servant, which I am making before thee
day and night for the Israelites thy
servants, while I confess the sins of the
Israelites, which we have sinned against
thee, as I myself also and my father's
7 family have sinned. We have acted very
wickedly against thee, and have not
kept the commands, or statutes, or
ordinances, which thou didst command
8 Moses, thy servant. Remember now
the word which thou didst command
Moses, thy servant, saying, 'If you tres-
pass, I will scatter you among the
9 peoples; but if you return to me, and
keep my commands and do them,
though your outcasts be under the remotest skies, yet will I gather them
from there and bring them to the place
that I have chosen, to cause my name
10 to dwell there.' Now these are thy
servants and thy people, whom thou
hast redeemed by thy great power and
by thy mighty hand. O LORD, I be- 11
seech thee, let thine ear now be attentive to the prayer of thy servant and to
the prayer of thy servants, who delight
to fear thy name; and prosper, I pray
thee, thy servant this day, and grant
him mercy in the sight of this man."

NEHEMIAH SENT TO JERUSALEM AS ROYAL COMMISSIONER, 1:11*b*–2:10

Now I was cupbearer to the king.
Accordingly it happened in the month 2
Nisan in the twentieth year of Artaxerxes the king, when the wine was served,
that I took up the wine and gave it to
the king; and I had not formerly been
sad. So the king said to me, 2
"Why is your countenance sad, since
you are not ill? This is nothing else but
sorrow of heart."
Then I was exceedingly frightened,
and I said to the king, 3
"Let the king live forever! Why
should not my countenance be sad,
when the city, the place of my father's
sepulchers is desolate, and its gates
have been destroyed by fire."
"For what then do you make re- 4
quest?" the king said to me.
So I prayed to the God of the heavens;
and I said to the king, 5
"If it please the king, and if your
servant be acceptable in your sight,
that you would send me to Judah to the
city of my fathers' sepulchers, that I
may rebuild it."
Then the king said to me, the queen 6
also being seated beside him,
"For how long will your journey be?
And when will you return?"
However it pleased the king to let me
go; for I proposed to him a time limit.
Moreover I said to the king, 7
"If it please the king, let letters be
given me to the governors of the
provinces beyond the River, that they
may let me pass through until I come to
Judah, and a letter to Asaph, the keep- 8

er of the king's park, that he may give
me timber to furnish the beams for the
gates of the citadel, which belongs to
the temple, and for the walls of the city,
and for the house that I shall enter."
So the king granted my request, according to the good hand of my God
upon me.
9 Then I came to the governors of the
provinces beyond the River, and gave
them the king's letters. Moreover the
king had sent with me army officers and
10 horsemen. But when Sanballat the
Horonite and Tobiah the Ammonite
slave heard of it, it caused them great
irritation that a man had come to seek
the welfare of the Israelites.

NEHEMIAH BEGINS REBUILDING THE CITY WALLS, 2:11–20

11 So I came to Jerusalem and was there
12 three days. Then I arose in the night,
I and a few men with me, but I told no
man what my God had put in my heart
to do for Jerusalem, neither was there
any beast with me except the beast on
13 which I rode. Accordingly I went out
by night through the Valley Gate, even
toward the Serpent's Well and to the
Refuse Gate, and I examined in detail
the walls of Jerusalem, which were
broken down, and its gates destroyed
14 by fire. So I passed on to the Fountain
Gate and to the King's Pool, but there
was no place for the beast that was
15 under me to pass. Then I went on up
in the night along the valley, examining
the wall, whereupon I turned back and
entered by the Valley Gate, and so re-
16 turned; and the rulers did not know
where I had gone or what I had been
doing, neither had I as yet told it to the
Jews, nor to the priests, nor to the
nobles, nor to the rulers, nor to the rest
who did the work.
17 Then I said to them,
"You see the serious condition in
which we are, how Jerusalem is desolate
and its gates are destroyed by fire.
Come, let us rebuild the wall of Jerusalem, that we may no longer be an object of reproach."
18 Then I told them of the good hand of
my God that was with me, and also of
the king's words that he had spoken to
me. Whereupon they said,
"Let us arise and build."
So they took courage for the good
work. But when Sanballat the Horo- 19
nite, Tobiah the Ammonite slave, and
Geshem the Arabian heard of it, they
derided and despised us, and said,
"What is this thing that you are
doing? Are you about to rebel against
the king?"
Then I answered and said to them, 20
"The God of the heavens, he will
prosper us; therefore we his servants
will arise and build; but you have no
portion or right or memorial in Jerusalem."

THE DISTRIBUTION OF THE WORK, 3:1–32

Then Eliashib the high priest arose 3
with his kinsmen the priests and built
the Sheep Gate; they sanctified it and
set up its doors; even to the Tower of
the Hundred they sanctified it, and to
the Tower of Hananel; and next to him 2
the men of Jericho built; and next to
them Zaccur, the son of Imri, built.
The sons of Hassenaah built the Fish 3
Gate; they laid its beams and set up its
doors, its bolts, and its bars. Next to 4
them Meremoth, the son of Uriah, the
son of Hakkoz, made repairs; and next
to them Meshullam, the son of Berachiah, the son of Meshezabel, made repairs; and next to them Zadok, the son 5
of Baana, made repairs. Next to them
the Tekoites made repairs; but their
nobles did not bend their necks in the
service of their lords.
The Old Gate Joiada, the son of Pa- 6
seah, and Meshullam, the son of Be-
sodeiah, repaired. They laid its beams
and set up its doors, its bolts, and its
bars. Next to them Malatiah the Gibe- 7
onite made repairs, and Jadon the
Meronothite, the men of Gibeon and
Mizpeh belonging to the throne of the
governor beyond the River; and next to
him Hananiah, one of the perfumers,
repaired. Next to them Uzziel, the son 8
of Harhaiah, one of the goldsmiths
made repairs; and next to him Hananiah, one of the perfumers, made repairs.
Thus they fortified Jerusalem even to
the broad wall. Next to them Rephiah, 9
the son of Hur, the ruler of half the district of Jerusalem, made repairs. Next 10
to them Jedaiah, the son of Harumaph,
made repairs opposite his house; and

next to him Hattush, the son of
11 Hashabneiah, made repairs. Malchijah,
the son of Harim, and Hasshub, the son
of Pahath-moab, repaired another section even to the Tower of the Furnaces.
12 Next to him Shallum, the son of Ha-
lohesh, the ruler of half the district of
Jerusalem, together with his daughters,
13 made repairs. The Valley Gate Hanun
and the inhabitants of Zanoah repaired;
they built it and set up its doors, its
bolts, and its bars, as well as one
thousand cubits of the wall to the
14 Refuse Gate. The Refuse Gate itself
Malchijah, the son of Rechab, the ruler
of the district of Beth-cherem, repaired;
he built it and set up its gates, its bolts,
and its bars.
15 The Fountain Gate Shallum, the son
of Colhozeh, the ruler of the district of
Mizpeh repaired; he built it and covered it, and set up its doors, its bolts,
and its bars; he also built the wall of the
pool of Siloam by the King's Garden,
even to the stairs that go down from
16 the city of David. After him Nehemiah,
the son of Azbuk, the ruler of half the
district of Bethzur, repaired to the
place opposite the sepulchers of David,
even to the artificial pool and the House
17 of the Heroes. After him the Levites,
including Rehum, the son of Bani, made
repairs; next to him Hashabiah, the
ruler of half the district of Keilah, made
18 repairs for his district. After him their
kinsmen, Bennui, the son of Henadad,
the ruler of half the district of Keilah,
19 made repairs. Ezer, the son of Jeshua,
the ruler of Mizpeh, repaired next to
him another section, opposite the ascent
to the armory at the corner buttress.
20 After him Baruch, the son of Zabbai,
repaired in the direction of the hill
another section, from the corner buttress to the entrance of the house of
21 Eliashib, the high priest. After him
Meremoth, the son of Uriah, the son of
Hakkoz, repaired another section, from
the entrance of the house of Eliashib
even to the end of the house of Eliashib.
22 After him the priests, the men of the
23 Plain, made repairs. After them Benjamin and Hasshub made repairs opposite
their house; and after them Azariah,
the son of Maaseiah, the son of
Ananiah, made repairs beside his house.
24 After him Binnui, the son of Henadad,
repaired another section, from the house
of Azariah to the corner buttress and to
the corner. Palal, the son of Uzai, made 2
repairs opposite the corner buttress and
the upper tower that extends from the
king's house, which is toward the court
of the guard. After him Pedaiah, the
son of Parosh, made repairs. (Now the 2
temple servants were dwelling in Ophel
as far as the place over the Water Gate
eastward and the projecting tower.)
After him the Tekoites repaired another 2
section opposite the great projecting
tower as far as the wall of Ophel.
The priests made repairs above the 2
Horse Gate, each one opposite his own
house. After them Zadok, the son of 2
Immer, made repairs opposite his
house. After him Shemaiah, the son of
Shechaniah, the keeper of the East
Gate, made repairs. After him Hanan- 3
iah, the son of Shelemiah, and Hanun,
the sixth son of Zalaph, repaired another
section. After him Meshullam, the son
of Berachiah, made repairs opposite his
chamber. After him Malchijah, one of 3
the goldsmiths, made repairs as far as
the house of the temple servants and
the merchants, opposite the Gate of the
Muster and the ascent of the corner;
and between the ascent of the corner 3
and the Sheep Gate the goldsmiths and
the merchants made repairs.

OPPOSITION TO THE BUILDING ENTERPRISE, 4:1–9

Now when Sanballat heard that we 4
were rebuilding the wall, he was enraged and very indignant and derided
the Jews. Accordingly he spoke before
his kinsmen and the army of Samaria
and said,
"What are these feeble Jews doing?
Will they fortify themselves? Will they
sacrifice? Will they finish it in a day?
Will they revive the stones out of the
rubbish heaps, now that they are
burned?"
Now Tobiah the Ammonite was with 3
him, and he said,
"If a fox should go up he would break
down their stone wall, even that which
they are building."
"Hear, O our God—for we are de- 4
spised—and turn back their reproach
upon their own head, and make them
an object of plunder in a land of captivity; and cover not their iniquity and 5
let not their sin be blotted out from thy

sight; for they have provoked thee to
anger before the builders."
6 So we built the wall; and all the wall
was joined together to half its height,
7 for the people had a mind to work. But
when Sanballat, Tobiah, the Arabs, the
Ammonites, and the Ashdodites heard
that the restoration of the walls of Jerusalem was going forward so that the
breaches began to be stopped, they
8 were in a great rage. Accordingly, all
of them conspired together to come and
make war on Jerusalem, and make con-
9 fusion in it. But we made supplication
to our God, and set a watch as a protection against them day and night.

MEASURES OF PROTECTION, 4:10–23

10 Then Judah said,
"The strength of the burden-bearers
is overtaxed, for there is much rubbish,
so that we are not able to go on with
the wall."
11 Moreover our adversaries said,
"They shall neither know nor see,
until we come into their midst, and slay
them and cause the work to cease."
12 When the Jews came who dwelt beside them, they said to us ten times,
"From all the places where they
dwell they will come up against us."
13 Therefore I assigned some of the lowest parts of the space behind the wall
in the exposed places, and appointed
the people according to families with
their swords, their spears, and their
14 bows; and when I saw them, I arose and
said to the nobles and to the rulers and
to the rest of the people,
"Be not afraid of them. Remember
the LORD, who is great and terrible,
and fight for your kinsmen, your sons
and your daughters, your wives and
your houses."
15 Now when our enemies heard that it
was known to us, and that God had
frustrated their counsel, we all returned
16 to the wall, each to his own task. Moreover from that day forth while half of
my men went on with the work half of
them held the spears, the shields, the
bows, and the coats of mail; and the
rulers supported all the house of Judah.
17 The builders on the wall and those who
bore burdens were also armed, each
carrying on the work with one hand and
18 with the other holding his weapon; and
each of the builders had his sword
girded by his side as he built; and the 19
trumpeter was beside me. Then I said
to the nobles and to the rulers and to
the rest of the people,
"The work is great and far-extended,
and we upon the wall are separated far
from each other. In whatever place you 20
hear the sound of the trumpet, rally to
us there; our God will fight for us."
Thus we went on with the work, 21
while half of them held the spears from
the beginning of dawn until the stars
came out. Also at that time I said to 22
the people,
"Let each man with his servant lodge
within Jerusalem, that they may be a
guard to us by night and ready for the
work by day."
So neither I, nor my kinsmen, nor my 23
servants, nor the men of the guard who
escorted me, none of us took off our
clothes; each kept his weapon in his
hand.

NEHEMIAH REBUKES THE RICH OPPRESSORS BY PRECEPT AND EXAMPLE, 5:1–19

Now there arose a great outcry of the **5**
people and their wives against their
Jewish kinsmen. For there were those 2
who said,
"We are giving our sons and our
daughters in pledge to secure grain that
we may eat and live."
There were also those who were say- 3
ing,
"We are giving our fields, our vineyards, and our houses in pledge that we
may secure grain because of the
famine."
There were those too who were say- 4
ing,
"We have borrowed money for the
king's tribute. Now our flesh is as the 5
flesh of our kinsmen, our children are
as their children; but here we are bringing our sons and our daughters into
slavery, and some of our daughters are
already enslaved; neither is it in our
power to help it, for others possess our
fields and our vineyards."
I was exceedingly angry when I heard 6
their complaint and these assertions.
So after thinking it over, I contended 7
with the nobles and governors and said
to them,

"You are taking interest each of his
own kinsmen."
So I held a great assembly against
8 them; and I said to them,
"We have, according to our ability,
redeemed our Jewish kinsmen who have
been sold to the nations; and would you
yourselves nevertheless sell your kinsmen, and should they sell themselves
to us?"
Then they were silent and had nothing
9 to say. So I said,
"The thing that you are doing is not
good. Ought you not to walk in the
fear of our God, because of the reproach
10 of the nations our enemies? For I also,
my kinsmen and my servants, lend
them money and grain. Let us, I pray
11 you, leave off this interest. Restore now
to them at once their fields, their vineyards, their olive orchards, and their
houses, the hundredth part of the money,
the grain, the wine, and the oil that you
exact of them."
12 Then they said,
"We will make restitution and will
require nothing of them; we will do
precisely as you say."
Then I called the priests and made
them take oath to do according to this
13 promise. Also I shook out the bosom of
my garment, and said,
"So may God shake out every man
from his house and from the fruit of his
labor who does not keep this promise;
even thus may he be shaken out and
emptied!"
And all the assembly said,
"So be it."
And they praised the LORD, and the
people did according to this promise.
14 From the time that I was appointed
to be their governor in the land of Judah, from the twentieth year even to
the thirty-second year of Artaxerxes,
the king, that is, for twelve years,
neither I nor my kinsmen had eaten the
15 bread due the governor. But the former
governors who were before me laid a
heavy burden on the people, and took
from them bread and wine, besides
forty shekels of silver; also their
servants domineered over the people.
But I did not do so, because of the fear
16 of God. Also I was occupied with the
work of this wall, and we bought no
land; and all my servants gathered
17 there for the work. Moreover the Jews
and the rulers, a hundred and fifty men,
besides those who came to us from the surrounding nations, were at my table. Now that which was prepared for each day was one ox and six choice sheep and fowls. They were prepared for me, and once in ten days skins of wine in abundance. But even so I did not exact the bread due the governor, because the service was burdensome upon this people. Remember to my credit, O my God, all that I have done for this people.

FUTILE EFFORTS TO FRUSTRATE NEHEMIAH, 6:1–19

Now when it was reported to Sanballat and Tobiah, and to Geshem, the Arabian, and to the rest of our enemies, that I had rebuilt the wall and that there was no breach left in it—though even at that time I had not set up the doors in the gates—Sanballat and Geshem sent to me, saying,

"Come, let us meet together in one of the villages in the plain of Ono."

But they intended me harm. So I sent messengers to them, saying,

"I am doing a great work, so that I cannot come down; why should the work cease, while I leave it and come down to you?"

But they sent to me four times in this manner, and I replied in the same way. Then Sanballat sent his servant to me in the same manner a fifth time with an open letter in his hand, in which was written,

"It is reported among the nations, and Geshem affirms it, that you and the Jews are planning to rebel, and so are rebuilding the wall, and that you would be their king, and that you have also appointed prophets to preach of you at Jerusalem, saying, 'There is a king in Judah.' Now it will be reported to the king according to these words. Come now, therefore, and let us take counsel together."

Then I sent to him, saying,

"No such things as you say have been done, but you have invented them in your own mind."

For they all would terrify us, saying,

"Their hands shall be weakened from the work, that it may not be done."

But do thou strengthen my hands.

10 Moreover when I went to the house
of Shemaiah, the son of Delaiah, the
son of Mehetabel, who was confined at
home, he said,
"Let us meet together in the house of
God, within the temple, and let us shut
the doors of the temple, for they are
coming to slay you, and they are going
to slay you by night."
11 But I said,
"Should a man like me flee? How
can any one like me enter the temple to
save his life? I will not enter."
12 Then I perceived clearly that God
had not sent him; but he declared his
prophecy concerning me because Tobi-
13 ah and Sanballat had hired him, that I
might be afraid and act accordingly and
sin, so that he might furnish them an
evil report, in order that they might re-
14 proach me. Remember, O my God,
Tobiah and Sanballat according to
these works of theirs, and also the
prophetess, Noadiah, and the rest of the
prophets who would have frightened
me.
15 So the wall was finished on the twenty-fifth day of Elul, in fifty-two days.
16 When all our enemies heard of it, all the
nations round about us feared and fell
decidedly in their own esteem; for they
perceived that this work had been done
with the help of our God.
17 Moreover in those days the nobles of
Judah sent many letters to Tobiah, and
18 those of Tobiah came to them. For
many in Judah were under oath to him,
because he was the son-in-law of Shechaniah, the son of Arah, and his son Jehohanan had married the daughter of
19 Meshullam, the son of Berachiah. Also
they were praising his good deeds before me and reporting my words to him.
Then Tobiah sent letters to frighten
me.

LISTS OF THE POPULATION OF JUDEA, 7:1–73

7 Now when the wall had been rebuilt
and I had set up the doors, and the
doorkeepers and the singers and the
2 Levites had been appointed, I put Hanani my brother and Hananiah, the
commander of the castle, in charge of
Jerusalem; for he was a faithful man
3 and feared God more than many. Then
I said to them,
"Let not the gates of Jerusalem be
opened until the sun is hot, and while
they are still on guard, let them shut
the doors and bar them; and appoint
watches of the inhabitants of Jerusalem, each to his watch and each opposite
his own house."
Now the city was wide and large; the 4
people in it were few and the houses
were not built. Accordingly my God 5
put it into my mind to gather together
the nobles and the rulers and the people, in order to reckon them by genealogies. Then I found the book of the
genealogy of those who came up first;
and I found written therein:
These are the inhabitants of the 6
province, who went up out of the captivity of those who had been carried
away, whom Nebuchadnezzar, king of
Babylon, had carried away, and who
returned to Jerusalem and Judah, each
to his city, who came with Zerubbabel, 7
Jeshua, Nehemiah, Azariah, Raamiah,
Nahamani, Mordecai, Bilshan, Mispe-
reth, Bigvai, Nehum, Baanah. The
number of men of the people of Israel
was:
The descendants of Parosh, two 8
thousand one hundred and seventy-
two; the descendants of Shephetaiah, 9
three hundred and seventy-two; the de- 10
scendants of Arah, six hundred and
fifty-two; the descendants of Pahath- 11
moab, of the descendants of Jeshua and
Joab, two thousand eight hundred and
eighteen; the descendants of Elam, one 12
thousand two hundred and fifty-four;
the descendants of Zattu, eight hun- 13
dred and forty-five; the descendants of 14
Zaccai, seven hundred and sixty; the 15
descendants of Binnui, six hundred and
forty-eight; the descendants of Bebai, 16
six hundred and twenty-eight; the de- 17
scendants of Azgad, two thousand
three hundred and twenty-two; the 18
descendants of Adonikam, six hundred
and sixty-seven; the descendants of 19
Bigvai, two thousand and sixty-seven; 20
the descendants of Adin, six hundred and
fifty-five; the descendants of Ater, of 21
Hezekiah, ninety-eight; the descend- 22
ants of Hashum, three hundred and
twenty-eight; the descendants of Bezai, 23
three hundred and twenty-four; the de- 24
scendants of Hariph, one hundred and
twelve; the descendants of Gibeon, 25
ninety-five; the men of Bethlehem and 26
Netophah, one hundred and eighty-
eight; the men of Anathoth, one hun- 27

28 dred and twenty-eight; the men of
29 Beth-azmaveth, forty-two; the men of
Kirjath-jearim, Chephirah, and Beeroth, seven hundred and forty-three;
30 the men of Rama and Geba, six hun-
31 dred and twenty-one; the men of Mich-
32 mas, one hundred and twenty-two; the
men of Bethel and Ai, one hundred and
33 twenty-three; the men of the other
34 Nebo, fifty-two; the descendants of the
other Elam, one thousand two hundred
35 and fifty-four; the descendants of Ha-
36 rim, three hundred and twenty; the
men of Jericho, three hundred and for-
37 ty-five; the men of Lod, Hadid, and
Ono, seven hundred and twenty-one;
38 the descendants of Senaah, three thousand nine hundred and thirty.
39 The priests were: the descendants of
Jedaiah, of the house of Jeshua, nine
40 hundred and seventy-three; the descendants of Immer, one thousand and
41 fifty-two; the descendants of Pashhur,
one thousand two hundred and forty-
42 seven; the descendants of Harim, one
thousand and seventeen.
43 The Levites were: the descendants
of Jeshua, namely, of Kadmiel of the
descendants of Hodevah, seventy-four;
44 the singers: the descendants of Asaph,
45 one hundred and forty-eight; the doorkeepers: the descendants of Shallum,
the descendants of Ater, the descendants of Talmon, the descendants of Akkub, the descendants of Hatita, the descendants of Shobai, one hundred and
thirty-eight.
46 The temple servants were: the descendants of Ziha, the descendants of
Hasupha, the descendants of Tabba-
47 oth, the descendants of Keros, the descendants of Sia, the descendants of
48 Padon, the descendants of Lebana, the
descendants of Hagaba, the descend-
49 ants of Salmai, the descendants of Hanan, the descendants of Giddel, the de-
50 scendants of Gahar, the descendants of
Reaiah, the descendants of Rezin, the
51 descendants of Nekoda, the descendants of Gazzam, the descendants of
52 Uzza, the descendants of Paseah, the
descendants of Besai, the descendants
of the Meunites, the descendants of
53 Nephushesim, the descendants of Bakbuk, the descendants of Hakupha, the
54 descendants of Harhur, the descendants of Bazlith, the descendants of Me-
55 hida, the descendants of Harsha, the
descendants of Barkos, the descendants of Sisera, the descendants of Temah, the descendants of Neziah, the 56
descendants of Hatipha.
The descendants of Solomon's serv- 57
ants were: the descendants of Sotai,
the descendants of Sophereth, the descendants of Perida, the descendants of 58
Jaala, the descendants of Darkon, the
descendants of Giddel, the descendants 59
of Shephatiah, the descendants of Hattil, the descendants of Pochereth-
hazzebaim, the descendants of Amon.
All the temple servants and the de- 60
scendants of Solomon's servants were
three hundred and ninety-two. These 61
were they who went up from Tel-melah,
Tel-harsha, Cherub, Addon, and Immer; but they could not show their fathers' lineage nor their descent, whether they were of Israel. These were the 62
descendants of Delaiah, the descendants of Tobiah, the descendants of Nekoda, six hundred and forty-two; also 63
of the priests: the descendants of Ho-
baiah, the descendants of Hakkoz, the
descendants of Barzillai, who took a
wife from the daughters of Barzillai,
the Gileadite, and was called by their
name. These sought their register 64
among those reckoned by genealogy,
but it was not found; therefore they
were excluded from the priesthood as
polluted. Also the governor told them 65
that they should not eat of the most
sacred things, until there should stand
a priest with the Urim and Thummin.
The whole assembly together was 66
forty-two thousand three hundred and
sixty, besides their male and female 67
slaves, of whom there were seven thousand three hundred and thirty-seven.
They also had two hundred and forty-
five singing men and singing women.
Their horses were seven hundred and 68
thirty-six; their mules, two hundred
and forty-five; camels, four hundred 69
and thirty-five; asses, six thousand
seven hundred and twenty.

Now some of the heads of families 70
made gifts to the work. The governor
gave to the treasury a thousand darics
of gold, fifty basins, five hundred manas
of silver, and thirty priests' garments.
Some of the heads of families gave into 71
the treasury for the work twenty-two
thousand darics of gold and two thousand two hundred manas of silver; and 72
that which the rest of the people gave
was twenty-two thousand darics of

gold, and two thousand manas of silver,
3 and sixty-seven priests' garments. So
the priests, the Levites, the doorkeepers, the singers, some of the people, the temple servants, and all Israel dwelt in their cities.

THE JEWS BIND THEMSELVES TO THE OBSERVANCE OF EZRA'S LAW, 8:1—10:39

8 Now when the seventh month drew
near, the Israelites were in their cities,
and all the people assembled as one
man to the open square that was in
front of the Water Gate, and they told
Ezra the scribe to bring the book of the
law of Moses, which the LORD had
2 commanded Israel. Then Ezra the
priest brought the law before the assembly, both men and women, and all
that could hear discerningly, on the
3 first day of the seventh month. He read
from it before the open square that was
in front of the Water Gate from daylight until midday, in the presence of
the men and women and those who
could understand; and the ears of all
the people were attentive to the book
4 of the law. Now Ezra the scribe stood
upon a raised wooden platform which
they made for the purpose; and beside
him stood Mattithiah, Shema, Anaiah,
Uriah, Hilkiah, and Maaseiah, on his
right hand, and on his left Pedaiah,
Mishael, Malchijah, Hashum, Hashbaddanah, Zechariah, and Meshullam.
5 Then Ezra opened the book in the sight
of all the people—for he was above all
the people—and when he opened it all
6 the people stood up. Thereupon Ezra
blessed the LORD, the great God; and
all the people answered, "Amen,
Amen," with uplifted hands as they
bowed with their faces to the ground
7 and worshiped the LORD. Also Jeshua, Bani, Sherebiah, Jamin, Akkub,
Shabbethai, Hodiah, Masseiah, Kelita,
Azariah, Jozabad, Hanan, Pelaiah, and
the Levites instructed the people in the
law, and the people remained in their
8 place. Thus they read in the book of
the law of God distinctly, and gave the
sense, so that they understood the reading.
9 Then Nehemiah, who was the governor, and Ezra the priest, the scribe, and
the Levites who taught the people said
to all the people,
"This day is holy to the LORD your
God; do not mourn or weep."
For all the people wept when they
heard the words of the law. Then he 10
said to them,
"Go your way, eat the fat and drink
the sweet, and send portions to him for
whom nothing is prepared, for this day
is holy to the LORD; and do not be depressed, for the joy of the LORD is your
refuge."
So the Levites quieted all the people, 11
saying,
"Be still, for the day is holy, and do
not be depressed."
Then all the people departed to eat 12
and drink and to send portions and to
make a great celebration; for they had
understood the words which had been
made known to them.
Now on the second day the heads of 13
families of all the people, the priests,
and the Levites were assembled to Ezra
the scribe, in order to comprehend the
words of the law. They found written 14
in the law how the LORD had given
command by Moses that the Israelites
should dwell in booths at the feast of
the seventh month; and that they 15
should announce and make a proclamation throughout all their cities as well
as in Jerusalem, saying,
"Go forth to the mountain and bring
olive foliage and leafy branches of wild
olive and myrtle and palm branches
and branches of thick trees to make
booths, as it is written."
So the people went forth and brought 16
them and made for themselves booths,
each upon the roof of his house and in
their courts and in the courts of the
house of God and in the open square at
the Water Gate and in the open square
at the Gate of Ephraim. Thus all the 17
assembly of returned exiles made
booths and lived in the booths; for
since the days of Joshua, the son of
Nun, to that day the Israelites had not
done so, and there was very great gladness. Accordingly, day by day, from 18
the first to the last day, he read in the
book of the law of God. They kept the
feast seven days, and on the eighth day,
there was a sacred assembly according
to the ordinance.
Now on the twenty-fourth day of this 9
month, the Israelites were assembled
with fasting, and with sackcloth and
earth upon their heads. Moreover the 2

descendants of Israel separated themselves from all foreigners, and stood and
confessed their sins and the iniquities of
3 their fathers. They stood up in their
place and read in the book of the law of
the LORD their God a fourth part of the
day; and a fourth part they confessed
and worshiped the LORD their God.
4 Then Jeshua, Bani, Kadmiel, Shebaniah, Bunni, Sherebiah, Bani, and Chen-
ani stood on the stairs of the Levites
and cried with a loud voice to the LORD
5 their God. Also the Levites Jeshua,
Kadmiel, Bani, Hashabneiah, Sherebiah, Hodiah, Shebaniah, and Pethahiah
said,
"Arise and bless the LORD your God
from everlasting to everlasting; and
blessed be thy glorious name which is
exalted above all blessing and praise."
And Ezra said,
6 "Thou art the LORD, even thou
alone; thou hast made the heavens and
the heavens of heavens, with all their
host, the earth and all things upon it,
the seas and all that is in them, and
thou preservest them all and the host
7 of the heavens worship thee. Thou art
the LORD God, who didst choose Abraham and didst bring him out of Ur of the
Chaldees, and didst give him the name
8 of Abraham, and didst find his heart
faithful before thee and madest a covenant with him to give the land of the
Canaanites, the Hittites, the Amorites,
the Perizzites, the Jebusites, and the
Girgashites, to give it to his descendants, and hast fulfilled thy words, for
thou art righteous.
9 "Moreover thou didst see the affliction of our fathers in Egypt and didst
10 hear their cry by the Red Sea, and
didst show signs and wonders upon
Pharaoh and upon all his servants and
upon all the people of his land; for thou
knewest that they acted insolently toward them; and so thou didst get for
11 thyself a name, as it is this day. Thou
didst also divide the sea before them,
so that they passed through the sea on
the dry land; and thou didst cast their
pursuers into the depths as a stone into
the mighty waters.
12 "Furthermore by a column of cloud
by day thou leddest them, and by a
column of fire by night thou didst illumine the way in which they should
13 go. Thou camest down also upon
Mount Sinai, and spakest with them
from the heavens, and gavest them
right ordinances and true laws, good
statutes and commands, and madest 1
known to them thy holy sabbath, and
gavest them commands and statutes
and a law by Moses thy servant, and 1
gavest them bread from the heaven for
their hunger, and broughtest forth
water for them out of the rock for their
thirst, and commandest them that they
should go in to take possession of the
land which thou hadst sworn to give
them.
"But they and our fathers acted ar- 1
rogantly and stubbornly and heeded
not thy commands, and refused to lis- 1
ten; neither were they mindful of thy
wonders which thou didst among them,
but acted stubbornly, and set their
head to return to their bondage in
Egypt. But thou art a God ready to
pardon, gracious and merciful, slow to
anger, and abounding in kindness, and
thou didst not forsake them. Yea, when 1
they had made for themselves a molten
bull and said, 'This is your God who
brought you out of Egypt,' and committed great blasphemies, yet thou in 1
thy great mercy didst not forsake them
in the desert; the column of cloud did
not depart from over them by day to
lead them in the way, nor the column of
fire by night to illumine the way on
which they should go. Thou gavest also 2
thy good spirit to instruct them, and
withheldst not thy manna from their
mouth, and gavest them water for their
thirst. Yea, forty years didst thou sus- 2
tain them in the desert, and they lacked
nothing; their clothes did not wear out,
nor did their feet blister.
"Moreover thou gavest them king- 2
doms and peoples, which thou didst allot according to their territory, so they
took possession of the land of Sihon,
king of Hesbon, and the land of Og,
king of Bashan. Thou didst also in- 2
crease their children as the stars of the
heavens, and broughtest them into the
land concerning which thou didst say
to their fathers, that they should go in
to take possession of it. So the children 2
went in and took possession of the land,
and thou didst subdue before them the
inhabitants of the land, the Canaanites, and didst give them into their
hand, with their kings and the peoples
of the land, that they might do with
them as they would. Accordingly they 2

took fortified cities and a fertile land,
and took possession of houses full of all
good things, and cisterns hewn out,
vineyards, olive orchards, and fruit
trees in abundance. So they ate and
were filled, and became fat and lived
bountifully in thy great goodness.
26 Nevertheless they were disobedient and
rebelled against thee and cast thy law
behind their back and slew thy prophets, who testified against them to turn
them again to thee, and committed
27 great blasphemies. Therefore thou
didst deliver them into the hands of
their adversaries, who tormented them.
Then in the time of their distress, when
they cried to thee, thou heardest from
the heavens and according to thine
abundant mercy thou didst give them
deliverers who saved them out of the
28 hand of their adversaries. But as soon
as they had rest, they did evil again before thee; therefore thou didst leave
them in the hands of their enemies, so
that they ruled over them; yet when
they again cried to thee, thou didst hear
from the heavens, and many times
didst thou deliver them in accordance
29 with thy mercy, and didst testify
against them, in order to restore them
to thy law. Yet they acted insolently
and did not heed thy commands, but
sinned against thine ordinances—which
if a man keep he shall live—and turned
a stubborn shoulder and acted obsti-
30 nately and would not listen. For many
years thou didst bear with them, and
didst testify against them by thy spirit
through thy prophets; still they would
not listen. Therefore thou gavest them
into the hands of the peoples of the
31 lands. Nevertheless in thine abundant
mercy thou didst not annihilate them
or forsake them; for thou art a gracious
and merciful God.
32 "Now therefore, our God, the great,
the mighty, and the terrible God, who
keepest loving faith, let not all the distress seem insignificant before thee,
that has come on us, our kings, our
princes, our priests, our prophets, our
fathers, and on all thy people, since the
days of the kings of Assyria to this day.
33 However thou art just in all that has
come upon us; for thou hast exemplified
the truth, but we have done wickedly;
34 neither have our kings, our princes, our
priests, nor our fathers kept thy law or
observed thy commands and thy decrees which thou didst decree against
them. For they did not serve thee in 35
their kingdom, and in spite of thy great
goodness which thou didst bestow on
them, and the large and fat land which
thou gavest them, they have not turned
from their evil deeds. Behold, we are 36
slaves this day, and as for the land that
thou gavest to our fathers to enjoy its
fruit and its good gifts, we are only
slaves in it. But it yields a large income 37
to the kings whom thou hast set over us
because of our sins; also they have power over our bodies and over our cattle
according to their pleasure, and we are
in great distress.
"Now in view of all this we make and 38
sign a binding covenant, and our nobles, our Levites, and our priests are enrolled upon the sealed document."
Those included in the sealed docu- **10**
ment were Nehemiah, the governor,
the son of Hachaliah, and Zedekiah, 2
Seraiah, Azariah, Jeremiah, Pashhur, 3
Amariah, Malchijah, Hattush, Sheba- 4
niah, Malluch, Harim, Meremoth, Oba- 5
diah, Daniel, Ginnethon, Baruch, 6
Meshullam, Abijah, Mijamin, Maazi- 7 8
ah, Bilgai, Shemaiah; these were the
priests. And the Levites were: Jeshua 9
the son of Azaniah, Binnui of the sons
of Henadad, Kadmiel; also their kins- 10
men, Shechaniah, Hodaviah, Kelita,
Pelaiah, Hanan, Mica, Rehob, Hasha- 11
biah, Zaccur, Sherebiah, Shebaniah, 12 13
Hodijah, Bani, Beninu. The chiefs of 14
the people were: Parosh, Pahath-moab,
Elam, Zattu, Bani, Bunni, Azgad, Be- 15
bai, Adonijah, Bigvai, Adin, Ater, Hez- 16 17
ekiah, Azzur, Hodiah, Hashum, Bezai, 18
Hariph, Anathoth, Nobai, Magpiash, 19 20
Meshullam, Herzir, Meshezabel, Za- 21
dok, Jaddua, Pelatiah, Hanan, Anaiah, 22 23
Hoshea, Hananiah, Hasshub, Hallo- 24
hesh, Pilha, Shobek, Rehum, Hashab- 25
nah, Maaseiah, Ahiah, Hanan, Anan, 26
Malluch, Harim, Baanah. 27
"Moreover the rest of the people, the 28
priests, the Levites, the doorkeepers,
the singers, the temple servants, and all
those who separated themselves from
the peoples of the lands to the law of
God, their wives, their sons, and their
daughters, everyone who had knowledge and insight, are supporting their 29
kinsmen, their nobles, and take oath,
under penalty of a curse, to walk in the
law of God which was given by Moses
the servant of God, and to be careful to

observe all the commands of the LORD
our Lord, and his ordinances and his
30 statutes; and that we will not give our
daughters to the peoples of the land or
take their daughters as wives for our
31 sons; and that, if the peoples of the land
bring wares or any grain on the Sabbath day to sell, we will not buy from
them on the sabbath or on a holy day;
and that in the seventh year we will
leave the land fallow and refrain from
the exaction of any debt.
32 "We also lay upon ourselves the
charge to give the third part of a shekel
yearly for the service of the house of
33 our God, for the bread that is arranged
in layers, and for the regular burnt-offering, for the sabbaths, the new
moons, the fixed festivals, and the holy
things, and for the sin-offerings to make
atonement for Israel, and for all the
34 work of the house of our God. Moreover we will cast lots, the priests, the
Levites, and the people, concerning the
wood-offering, to bring it into the house
of our God, according to our fathers'
houses, at appointed times year by
year, to burn upon the altar of the
LORD our God, as it is written in the
35 law; and to bring the first produce of
our ground and the first of all fruit of
every kind of tree year by year to the
36 house of the LORD; also the first-born
of our sons and of our cattle, as it is
written in the law, and the firstlings of
our herds and our flocks, to bring to the
house of our God to the priests who
37 minister in the house of our God; and
to bring our first batch of baking, our
contributions, the fruit of every kind of
tree, the wine, and the oil, to the priests
in the chambers of the house of our
God; and the tithes of our ground to
the Levites, since they, the Levites,
take the tithes in all the cities depend-
38 ent on our agriculture. Now the priest,
the son of Aaron, shall be with the Levites, when the Levites tithe, and the
Levites shall bring up the tithe of the
tithes to the house of our God, to the
39 chambers into the treasure-house. For
the Israelites and the members of the
Levites shall bring the contributions of
grain, wine, and oil into the chambers,
where the vessels of the sanctuary are,
and the priests who minister, the doorkeepers, and the singers. So we will not
neglect the house of our God."

THE POPULATION OF JERUSALEM, 11:1—12:26

The princes of the people dwelt in 1
Jerusalem, and the rest of the people cast lots, to bring one out of
every ten to dwell in Jerusalem the
holy city, while nine-tenths remained
in the other cities. The people also
blessed all the men who volunteered to
dwell in Jerusalem.

Now these are the chief men of the
provinces who dwelt in Jerusalem; but
in the cities of Judah they dwelt each
on his own property in their respective
cities: Israel, the priests, the Levites,
the temple servants, and the descendants of Solomon's servants. In Jerusalem there dwelt some Judeans and some
Benjaminites. Of the Judeans: Athaiah, the son of Uzziah, the son of Zechariah, the son of Amariah, the son of
Shephatiah, the son of Mahalalel; of
the descendants of Perez, all the descendants of Perez who dwelt in Jerusalem were four hundred and sixty-eight able men; and Maaseiah, the son
of Baruch, the son of Col-hozeh, the son
of Hazaiah, the son of Adaiah, the son
of Joiarib, the son of Zechariah, the son
of the Shilonite.

These are the Benjaminites: Sallu,
the son of Meshullam, the son of Joed,
the son of Pedaiah, the son of Kolaiah,
the son of Maaseiah, the son of Ithiel,
the son of Jeshaiah. His kinsmen were
able-bodied warriors, nine hundred and
twenty-eight; and Joel, the son of Zichri, was appointed over them; and Judah, the son of Hassenuah, was second
in charge of the city.

Of the priests: Jedaiah, the son of 1
Joiarib, Jachin, and Seraiah, the son of 1
Hilkiah, the son of Zadok, the son of
Meraioth, the son of Ahitub, the ruler
of the house of God, and their kinsmen 1
who did the work of the house, eight
hundred and twenty-two; and Adaiah,
the son of Jeroham, the son of Pelaliah,
the son of Amzi, the son of Zechariah,
the son of Pashhur, the son of Malchijah,
and his kinsmen, chief men of families, 1
two hundred and forty-two; and Amasai, the son of Azarel, the son of Ahzai,
the son of Meshillemoth, the son of Im-
mer, and his kinsmen, able-bodied war- 1
riors, one hundred and twenty-eight;
and Zabdiel, the son of Haggedolim,
was appointed over them.

15 And of the Levites: Shemaiah, the son
of Hasshub, the son of Azrikam, the son
16 of Hashabiah, the son of Bunni; and
Shabbethai and Jozabad, of the chief
men of the Levites, who were in charge
of the outside work of the house of God;
17 and Mattaniah, the son of Mica, the
son of Zabdi, the son of Asaph, was the
chief who led the song of praise for the
prayer, and Bakbukiah was second
among his kinsmen; and Abda, the son
of Shammua, the son of Galal, the son
18 of Jeduthun. All the Levites in the holy
city were two hundred and eighty-four.
19 Also the doorkeepers, Akkub, Talmon, and their kinsmen, who kept the
watch at the gates, were one hundred
20 and seventy-two. And the rest of Israel, the priests, and the Levites, were
in all the cities of Judah, each man in
21 his own heritage. Moreover the temple
servants dwelt in Ophel; and Ziha and
Gishpa were over the temple servants.
22 Now the overseer of the Levites at
Jerusalem was Uzzi, the son of Bani,
the son of Hashabiah, the son of Mattaniah, the son of Mica, of the sons of
Asaph, the singers, over the work of the
23 house of God. For there was a command from the king concerning them,
and a fixed provision for the singers, as
24 each day required. Moreover Pethahiah, the son of Meshezabel, of the descendants of Zerah, the son of Judah,
was the king's agent in all matters concerning the people.
25 Now as for the villages with their
fields, some of the Judeans dwelt in Kirjath-arba and its dependencies, in Dibon
and its dependencies, in Jekabzeel and
26 its villages, in Jeshua, in Moladah, in
27 Bethpelet, in Hazar-shual, and in Beer-
28 sheba and its dependencies, and in Ziklag and in Meconah and its dependen-
29 cies, in En-rimmon, in Zorah, in Jar-
30 muth, Zanoah, Adullam and their villages, Lachish and its fields, Azekah
and its dependencies. So they encamped in the region between Beer-
31 sheba and the valley of Hinnom. The
Benjaminites dwelt at Geba, Michmash, Aija, Bethel, and its dependen-
32 33 cies, at Anathoth, Nob, Ananiah, Ha-
34 zor, Ramath, Gittaim, Hadid, Zeboim,
35 Naballat, Lod, and Ono, the valley of
36 the craftsmen. And of the Levites, certain divisions belonged to Judah and to
Benjamin.
12 Now these are the priests and the
Levites who came up with Zerubbabel,
the son of Shealtiel and Jeshua, Seraiah, Jeremiah, Ezra, Amariah, Mal- 2
luch, Hattush, Shecaniah, Rehun, 3
Meremoth, Iddo, Ginnethoi, Abijah, 4
Mijamin, Maadiah, Bilgah, Shemai- 5 6
ah and Joiarib, Zedaiah, Sallu, Amok, 7
Hilkiah, Jedaiah. These were the chief
men of the priests and of their kinsmen
in the days of Jeshua.
Moreover the Levites: Jeshua, Bin- 8
nui, Kadmiel, Sherebiah, Judah and
Mattaniah, he and his kinsmen were in
charge of the thanksgiving. Also Bak- 9
bukiah and Unno, their kinsmen, stood
opposite them in the execution of their
official duties.
Now Jeshua was the father of Joi- 10
akim, and Joiakim was the father of
Eliashib, and Eliashib was the father of
Joiada, and Joiada was the father of 11
Jonathan, and Jonathan was the father
of Jaddua.
In the days of Joiakim the priests, 12
the heads of families, were: of Seraiah,
Meraiah; of Jeremiah, Hananiah; of 13
Ezra, Meshullam; of Amariah, Jehohanan; of Malluchi, Jonathan; of Sheba- 14
niah, Joseph; of Harim, Adna; of Mer- 15
aioth, Helkai; of Iddo, Zechariah; of 16
Ginnethon, Meshullam; of Abijah, 17
Zichri; of Miniamin, of Moadiah, Pil-
tai; of Bilgah, Shammua; of Shemaiah, 18
Jehonathan; of Joiarib, Mattenai; of 19
Jedaiah, Uzzi; of Sallai, Kallai; of 20
Amok, Eber; of Hilkiah, Hashabiah; of 21
Jedaiah, Nethanel.
As for the Levites, in the days of Eli- 22
ashib, Joiada, Johanan, and Jaddua
were recorded as heads of families, also
the priests until the reign of Darius the
Persian. The descendants of Levi, 23
heads of families, were recorded in the
Book of Chronicles, even until the days
of Johanan, the son of Eliashib. Also 24
the chief men of the Levites were:
Hashabiah, Sherebiah, Jeshua, Bennui,
and Kadmiel and their kinsmen opposite them to praise and give thanks, according to the command of David, the
man of God, watch succeeding watch.
Mattaniah, and Bakbukiah, Obadiah, 25
Meshullam, Talmon, Akkub were porters keeping watch at the stores of the
gates. These were in the days of Joi- 26
akim, the son of Jeshua, the son of
Jozadak, and in the days of Nehemiah
the governor, and of Ezra the priest,
the scribe.

THE DEDICATION OF THE CITY WALL, 12:27–47

27 Now at the dedication of the wall of
Jerusalem they sought the Levites out
of all their places, to bring them to Jerusalem to celebrate the dedication with
all gladness, with thanksgiving and song,
28 with cymbals, harps, and lyres. So the
members of the guilds of singers were
assembled from the plains of the Jordan
and from the environs of Jerusalem
and from the villages of the Netophath-
29 ites, also from Beth-gilgal and from the
fields of Geba and Azmaveth; for the
singers had built for themselves vil-
30 lages round about Jerusalem. Accordingly the priests and the Levites purified themselves; and they purified the
people and the gates and the wall.
31 Then I brought up the princes of Judah upon the wall, and I appointed
two great companies that gave thanks,
and the one went to the right upon the
32 wall to the Refuse Gate; and behind
them went Hoshaiah and half of the
33 princes of Judah, and Azariah, Ezra,
34 Meshullam, Judah, Benjamin, Shema-
35 iah, Jeremiah, and certain of the
priests' sons with trumpets: Zechariah,
the son of Jonathan, the son of Shemaiah, the son of Mattaniah, the son of
Micaiah, the son of Zaccur, the son of
36 Asaph, and his kinsmen, Shemaiah,
Azarel, Milalai, Gilalai, Maai, Nethanel, Judah, and Hanani, with the musical instruments of David, the man of
God. Ezra the scribe was in front of
37 them; and by the Fountain Gate, they
went straight up the stairs of the city
of David at the ascent of the wall above
the house of David, even to the Water
Gate on the east.
38 Now the other company that gave
thanks went to the left, and I after
them, with half of the people upon the
wall, above the Tower of the Furnaces,
39 even to the Broad Wall, and above the
Gate of Ephraim and by the Old Gate
and by the Fish Gate and the Tower of
Hananel and the Tower of the Hundred, even to the Sheep Gate; and they
40 halted in the Gate of the Guard. So
both companies that gave thanks halted at the house of God, and I, and the
41 half of the officials with me; and the
priests, Eliakim, Maaseiah, Miniamin,
Micaiah, Elioenai, Zechariah, and
42 Hananiah, with trumpets; and Maaseiah, Shemaiah, Eleazar, Uzzi, Jehohanan, Malchijah, Elam, and Ezer, and
the singers raised their voices following
Jezrahiah their leader. They offered 43
great sacrifices that day and rejoiced;
for God had made them rejoice with
great joy; and the women also and the
children rejoiced, so that the joy of Jerusalem was heard far way.
Moreover on that day men were ap- 44
pointed over the chambers for the
treasures, the contributions, the first
fruits, and the tithes, to gather them
into them, for the chiefs of the cities,
the legal apportionments for the priests
and the Levites. For Judah rejoiced
in the priests and the Levites who
served; and they kept the charge of 45
their God, and the charge of the purification, as did the singers and the gatekeepers, according to the command of
David and of Solomon his son. For in 46
the days of David and Asaph of old
there was a chief of the singers, and
songs of praise and thanksgiving to
God. Moreover all Israel, in the days 47
of Zerubbabel and in the days of Nehemiah, gave the portions of the singers
and the gatekeepers, as each day required; and they set apart what was for
the Levites, and the Levites set apart
what was for the sons of Aaron.

NEHEMIAH'S REFORM MEASURES, 13:1–31

On that day they read in the book of 1
Moses in the hearing of the people, and
it was found written in it that no Ammonite or Moabite should ever marry
into the assembly of God; for they did
not meet the Israelites with bread and
water, but hired Balaam against them
to curse them; but our God turned the
curse into a blessing. Accordingly when
they heard the law they separated from
Israel all the alien mixture.
Now before this, Eliashib the priest,
who was appointed over the chambers
of the house of our God, being related to
Tobiah, had prepared for him a great
chamber, where formerly they had put
the cereal-offerings, the incense, the
vessels, the tithes of grain, the wine,
and the oil, which were given by command to the Levites, the singers, and
the gatekeepers, and the contributions
for the priests. But during all this time

I had not been at Jerusalem; for in the
thirty-second year of Artaxerxes, king
of Babylon, I went to the king. But
after some time, I asked leave of the
7 king; and I came to Jerusalem and discovered the evil that Eliashib had done
for Tobiah, in preparing for him a chamber in the court of the house of God;
8 and it greatly displeased me; so I cast
all of Tobiah's household property out
9 of the chamber. Then I spoke, and
they cleansed the chambers, and I
brought back there the vessels of the
house of God, with the cereal-offerings
and the incense.
10 I also learned that the portions of the
Levites had not been given them; so
that the Levites and the singers who
conducted the service had fled each to
11 his own field. Then I contended with
the rulers and said,
"Why is the house of God forsaken?"
So I gathered them together and re-
12 stored them to their posts. Thereupon
all Judah brought the tithe of the grain
and the wine and the oil to the treasur-
13 ies. Moreover I appointed in charge of
the treasuries: Shelemiah the priest
and Zadok the scribe, and of the Levites, Pedaiah; and next to them was
Hanan, the son of Zaccur, the son of
Mattaniah; for they were considered
faithful, and it was their task to dis-
14 tribute to their kinsmen. Remember
me, O my God, concerning this, and do
not wipe out my good deeds that I have
done for the house of my God and for
its services.
15 In these days I saw in Judah men
treading wine presses on the sabbath
and bringing in heaps of grain loaded on
asses, also wine, grapes, figs, and all
kinds of burdens which they brought
into Jerusalem on the sabbath day; and
I protested on the day when they sold
16 provisions. Tyrians also dwelt therein,
who brought in fish and all kinds of
wares, and sold them on the sabbath to
17 the Judeans and in Jerusalem. Then I
contended with the nobles of Judah and
said to them,
"What evil thing is this that you are
doing, and so profaning the sabbath
18 day? Did not your fathers do this, and
did not our God bring all this misfortune upon us and upon this city? Yet
you are bringing more wrath upon Israel by profaning the sabbath."
19 Accordingly when the gates of Jerusalem began to be in darkness, before
the sabbath, I commanded that the
gates be shut; and I gave orders that
they should not be opened until after
the sabbath. Also I put some of my
servants in charge of the gates, that
none should bring in a burden on the
sabbath day. Then the traders and sell- 20
ers of all kinds of wares lodged once or
twice outside Jerusalem. So I warned 21
them and said to them,
"Why do you lodge in front of the
wall? If you repeat it, I shall arrest you."
From that time on they came no
more on the sabbath. Then I gave or- 22
ders to the Levites that they should
purify themselves and that they should
come and guard the gates, to keep the
sabbath day holy. Remember, O my
God, this also to my account and have
compassion upon me according to thine
abundant kindness.
In those days also I saw the Jews 23
who had married women of Ashdod, of
Ammon, and of Moab, and their chil- 24
dren spoke half in the language of Ashdod, and none of them could speak in
the Jews' language, but according to
the language of each people. Therefore 25
I contended with them and cursed
them and beat some of them and pulled
out their hair and made them swear by
God, saying,
"You shall neither give your daughters to their sons nor take their daughters as wives for your sons or for yourselves. Did not Solomon, king of Isra- 26
el, sin by these means? Yet among
many nations there was no king like
him, and he was beloved by his God,
and God made him king over all Israel;
nevertheless foreign wives were the
cause of his sin; and shall it be reported 27
of you that you do all this great evil,
and break faith with our God in marrying foreign women?"
Now one of the sons of Joiada, the 28
son of Eliashib, the high priest, was the
son-in-law of Sanballat, the Horonite;
so I chased him from me. Remember 29
them, O my God, because they have defiled the priesthood and the covenant of
the priesthood and the Levites. Thus I 30
cleansed them from all foreigners and
established the duties for the priests
and the Levites, each for his own task,
and for the wood-offering at appointed 31
times, and for the firstfruits. Remember it, O my God, to my credit.

THE BOOK OF ESTHER

QUEEN VASHTI'S DISMISSAL, 1:1–22

1 NOW in the days of Xerxes—
that is, the Xerxes who
reigned from India even to
Ethiopia, over a hundred and
2 twenty-seven provinces—it happened
in those days when King Xerxes sat on
his royal throne, which was in the cas-
3 tle at Shushan, in the third year of his
reign, that he made a feast for all his
princes and his servants. The commanders of the army of Persia and
Media, the nobles and rulers of the
4 provinces were before him, while he
showed the riches of his glorious kingdom and the precious things of his
great majesty many days, even a hun-
5 dred and eighty days. When these days
were completed, the king made for all
the people who were present in the
castle at Shushan, both great and small,
a seven days' feast in the court of the
6 garden of the king's palace. There was
white stuff of cotton, and there were
blue hangings, fastened with cords of
fine linen and purple to silver rings and
columns of marble; couches of gold and
silver were upon a pavement of por-
phyry, marble, mother-of-pearl, and
7 precious stones. They served wine in
golden beakers, with no two alike, and
the royal wine was abundant according
8 to the liberality of the king. The drinking also was according to the law; none
could compel, for so the king had decreed to all the officers of his house, to
do according to each man's pleasure.
9 Also Vashti the queen made a feast
for the women in the royal palace which
10 belonged to King Xerxes. On the seventh day, when the king's heart was
joyous with wine, he commanded Me-
human, Biztha, Harbona, Bigtha, and
Abagtha, Zethar, and Carcas, the seven
eunuchs who ministered in the presence
11 of Xerxes the king, to bring Vashti the
queen before the king with the royal
crown, to show the peoples and the
princes her beauty, for she was beautiful. But Queen Vashti refused to come 12
at the king's command by the eunuchs;
therefore the king was greatly enraged
and his anger burned within him.
Then the king said to the wise men 13
who knew the times—for so the king
was accustomed to speak before all who
knew law and government; and those 14
next to him were Carshena, Sethar,
Admatha, Tarshish, Meres, Marsena,
and Memucan, the seven princes of
Persia and Media who saw the king's
face and held the first place in the
kingdom—
"What shall we do to Queen Vashti 15
according to law, because she has not
done the bidding of King Xerxes by the
eunuchs?"
Then Memucan said before the king 16
and the princes,
"Vashti the queen has not done
wrong to the king only, but also to all
the princes and to all the peoples, that
are in all the provinces of King Xerxes.
For this behavior of the queen will be 17
reported to all women, making their
husbands contemptible in their sight,
when it shall be said, 'King Xerxes
commanded that Vashti the queen be
brought before him; but she did not
come.' Even this day the princesses of 18
Persia and Media who have heard of
the queen's behavior will relate it to all
the king's princes and there will be a
surfeit of contempt and rage. If it 19
please the king, let there go forth from
him, and let it be written among the
laws of the Persians and the Medes so
that it may not be altered, that Vashti
the queen come no more before King
Xerxes, and that the king give her royal position to another who is better
than she. So when the king's decree 20
which he shall make shall be published
throughout all his kingdom—great
though it is—all the women will give
honor to their husbands, both high and
low."
The proposal pleased the king and 21
the princes, and the king did according
to the counsel of Memucan; and he sent 22

letters to all the royal provinces, into
every province according to its form of
script and to every people according to
its language, that every man should be
master in his own house and should
speak whatever seemed proper to him.

ESTHER, THE JEWESS, CHOSEN QUEEN, 2:1–18

2 After these things, when the wrath of
King Xerxes was pacified, he remembered Vashti and what she had done
and what was decreed against her.
2 Then the king's servants who ministered to him said,
"Let beautiful young maidens be
3 sought out for the king, and let the king
appoint officers in all the provinces of
his kingdom that they may gather together all the beautiful young maidens
to the castle at Shushan, to the harem
under the custody of Hegai, the king's
eunuch, keeper of the women, and let
the cosmetics for their beautifying be
4 given them. Then let the maiden who
pleases the king be queen instead of
Vashti."
The proposal pleased the king, and
he did so.
5 Now there was a certain Jew in the
castle at Shushan whose name was
Mordecai, the son of Jair, the son of
Shimei, the son of Kish, a Benjaminite,
6 who had been carried away from Jerusalem with the captives who had been
carried away with Jeconiah, king of
Judah, whom Nebuchadnezzar, king of
7 Babylon, had carried away. He had
brought up Hadassah, that is, Esther,
his uncle's daughter, for she had neither
father nor mother; and the maiden was
fair and beautiful, and when her father
and mother died, Mordecai took her as
his own daughter.
8 So when the king's command and his
decrees were reported, and when many
maidens were gathered together to the
castle at Shushan under the custody of
Hegai, Esther was also taken into the
king's palace under the custody of He-
9 gai, keeper of the women. Moreover
the maiden pleased him and she met
with kindness at his hands, and he
hastened to give her cosmetics for
beautifying herself, with her portions,
and seven picked maidens who were to
be given her from the king's palace;
and he removed her and her maidens to
the best apartments in the harem.
Esther had not made known her people 10
or her kindred; for Mordecai had
charged her that she should not make
it known. Moreover Mordecai used to 11
walk to and fro every day in front of
the court of the harem, to learn how
Esther was and how she was faring.
Now when the turn of each maiden 12
came to visit King Xerxes, after it had
been done to her according to the law
for the women twelve months—for so
long the days of their beautifying lasted, six months with oil of myrrh, and
six months with spices and with preparations for the beautifying of the
women—in this way the maiden came 13
to the king: whatever she mentioned
was given to her to go with her from the
harem to the king's palace. In the 14
evening she went in and in the morning
she returned to the second harem to the
custody of Shaashgaz, the king's eunuch, who kept the concubines. She
did not again visit the king, unless the
king delighted in her and she was summoned by name. Now when the turn of 15
Esther, the daughter of Abihail, the uncle of Mordecai, who had taken her for
his own daughter, came to visit the
king, she asked for nothing except
what Hegai, the king's eunuch, the
keeper of the women, prescribed. Thus
Esther won favor in the sight of all who
saw her.
So Esther was taken to King Xerxes 16
into his royal palace in the tenth
month, that is, the month Tebet, in the
seventh year of his reign. Then the 17
king loved Esther more than all the
women, and she won favor and kindness in his presence more than all the
maidens; so that he set the royal crown
upon her head and made her queen instead of Vashti. Then the king made a 18
great feast for all his princes and his
servants, even Esther's feast; and he
made it a holiday for the provinces and
gave gifts, according to the liberality of
the king.

MORDECAI'S OPPORTUNITY, 2:19–23

Now when the maidens were gath- 19
ered together a second time Mordecai

was sitting in the gate of the king.
20 Esther had not as yet made known her
kindred or her people, as Mordecai had
charged her; for Esther kept the command of Mordecai just as when she was
21 being reared by him. In those days, as
Mordecai was sitting at the king's gate,
two of the king's eunuchs who guarded
the threshold, Bigthan and Teresh, became enraged and sought to do violence
22 to King Xerxes, but the plot became
known to Mordecai, who revealed it to
Esther the queen; and Esther told the
23 king in Mordecai's name. Accordingly
the matter was investigated and when
it was found to be so, they were both
hanged on a tree; and it was written in
the book of the chronicles in the king's
presence.

HAMAN'S CRUEL PURPOSE, 3:1–15

3 After these things King Xerxes promoted Haman, the son of Hammedatha, the Agagite, and advanced him
and placed his seat above all the
2 princes who were with him. Thus all
the king's servants who were at the
king's gate bowed down and did obeisance to Haman; for the king had so
commanded concerning him. But Mordecai would not bow down or do obei-
3 sance. Then the king's servants who
were at the king's gate, said to Mordecai,

"Why do you transgress the king's
command?"

4 Now when they thus spoke to him
daily and he did not listen to them,
they told Haman, to see whether Mordecai's conduct would stand; for he had
5 told them that he was a Jew. So when
Haman saw that Mordecai did not bow
down or do obeisance to him, Haman
6 was filled with rage. But he thought it
beneath him to lay hands on Mordecai
alone; for they had told him Mordecai's
race. So Haman sought to destroy all
the Jews who were throughout the
whole kingdom of Xerxes, even the people of Mordecai.

7 In the first month, which is the
month Nisan, in the twelfth year of
King Xerxes, one cast Pur, that is, the
lot, before Haman from day to day and
from month to month, to the twelfth
8 month, which is the month Adar. Then
Haman said to King Xerxes,

"There is a certain people scattered
abroad and dispersed among the peoples throughout all the provinces of
your kingdom, and their laws are different from every other people; neither do
they observe the king's laws; therefore
it is not fitting to leave them alone. If 9
it please the king, let it be prescribed
that they be destroyed; and I will pay
ten thousand talents of silver into the
hands of those who do the accounting,
that they may bring it into the king's
treasuries."

Then the king took his signet ring 10
from his hand and gave it to Haman,
the son of Hammedatha, the Agagite,
the Jews' enemy. The king also said to 11
Haman,

"The silver is yours and the people
too, to do with them as seems good to
you."

Then the king's scribes were sum- 12
moned on the thirteenth day of the
first month, and it was written just as
Haman commanded to the king's satraps and to the governors who were
over every province and to the princes
of every people, to every province according to its script, and to every people according to their language. In the
name of King Xerxes it was written and
it was sealed with the king's signet.
These letters were sent by couriers into 13
all the king's provinces, to wipe out, to
slay, and to destroy all the Jews, both
young and old, infants and women in
one day, even upon the thirteenth day
of the twelfth month, which is the
month Adar, and to take the spoil of
them as plunder. A copy of the writ- 14
ings to be given out as a decree in every
province was published to all the peoples that they should be ready for that
day. The couriers went forth in haste 15
at the king's command, and the decree
was given out in the castle at Shushan.
Then the king and Haman sat down to
drink; but the city of Shushan was perplexed.

MORDECAI'S APPEAL TO ESTHER, 4:1–17

Now when Mordecai learned all that 4
had been done, Mordecai tore his garments and put on sackcloth with ashes,
and went out into the midst of the city
and cried out with a loud and bitter

2 lamentation. He even came before the
king's gate; for none might enter the
king's gate clothed with sackcloth.
3 Moreover in every province wherever
the king's command and his decree
came, there was great mourning among
the Jews, and fasting, weeping, and
wailing; and many lay in sackcloth and
4 ashes. When Esther's maidens and her
eunuchs came and told her, the queen
was exceedingly distressed, and she
sent garments to clothe Mordecai that
he might take off his sackcloth; but he
5 did not accept them. Then Esther
called for Hathach, one of the king's
eunuchs, who had been appointed to
attend her, and ordered him to go to
Mordecai, to learn what this was and
6 why it was. So Hathach went forth to
Mordecai to the open square of the
city which was in front of the king's
7 gate. Then Mordecai told him all that
had happened to him and the exact
sum of money that Haman had promised to pay to the king's treasuries for
8 the destruction of the Jews. He also
gave him a copy of the writing of the
decree that was given out in Shushan to
destroy them, that he might show it to
Esther and inform her and charge her
to go in to the king to implore him and
to make request before him for her
people.

9 So Hathach came and told Esther the
10 words of Mordecai. Then Esther spoke
to Hathach, and gave him a message to
Mordecai, saying,

11 "All the king's servants and the people of the king's provinces know that whoever, whether man or woman, comes to the king into the inner court who is not summoned, there is one law for him, that he be put to death, except those to whom the king shall hold out the golden scepter that he may live; but I have not been summoned to come to the king these thirty days."

12 So they told Mordecai Esther's words.

13 Then Mordecai told them to return answer to Esther,

"Think not to yourself that you will
escape inside the royal palace any more
14 than all the rest of the Jews. For if you
remain altogether silent at this time,
then relief and deliverance will rise up
for the Jews from another quarter, but
you and your father's house will perish;
and who knows whether you have not
come to the kingdom for such a time as
this?"

Thereupon Esther told them to return answer to Mordecai, 15

"Go, assemble all the Jews that are 16
to be found in Shushan and fast for me,
and neither eat nor drink for three days,
night or day. I also and my maidens
will likewise fast, and then I will go to
the king, which is not according to the
law; and if I perish, I perish."

So Mordecai went his way and did 17
just as Esther commanded him.

HAMAN'S RISE AND FALL, 5:1—7:10

So it came about on the third day 5
that Esther put on her royal robes, and
stood in the inner court of the king's
palace directly opposite the king's
apartment; and the king was sitting
upon his royal throne in the royal
palace opposite the entrance of the
palace. When the king saw Esther the 2
queen standing in the court, she met
with favor in his sight, and the king extended to Esther the golden scepter
that was in his hand. So Esther drew
near and touched the top of the scepter.

Then the king said to her, 3

"What is your wish, Queen Esther, and what is your request? It shall be given you even to the half of the kingdom."

"If it please the king," said Esther, 4
"let the king and Haman come today
to a banquet that I have prepared for
him."

"Bring Haman in haste that he may 5
fulfil Esther's wish," said the king.

So the king and Haman came to the banquet that Esther had prepared.

Then the king said to Esther at the 6
banquet of wine,

"Whatever your petition, it shall be granted you; and whatever your request, even to the half of the kingdom, it shall be performed."

So Esther answered and said, 7

"My petition and my request is: If 8
I have found favor in the sight of the
king, and if it please the king to grant
my petition, and to perform my request, let the king and Haman come to
my banquet that I shall prepare for
them, and tomorrow I will do as the
king has said."

9 Then Haman went out that day joyful and glad of heart. But when Haman
saw Mordecai at the king's gate, and he
neither stood up nor moved for him,
Haman was filled with wrath against
10 Mordecai. Nevertheless Haman restrained himself and returned home,
and sent and brought in his friends and
11 Zeresh his wife. Thereupon Haman recounted to them the glory of his riches
and the multitude of his children and
every instance where the king had promoted him, and how he had advanced
him above the princes and the servants
of the king.
12 "Even Esther the queen," said Haman, "has permitted no man but me to
come in with the king to the banquet
that she has prepared, and tomorrow
also I am invited by her together with
13 the king. Yet all this does not satisfy
me so long as I see Mordecai the Jew
sitting at the king's gate."
14 Then Zeresh his wife and all his
friends said to him,
"Let a gallows fifty cubits high be
erected and in the morning speak to the
king that Mordecai may be hanged on
it. Then go in merrily with the king to
the banquet."
The idea pleased Haman, and he had
the gallows made.
6 On that night sleep deserted the king,
and he gave orders to bring the book of
records of the chronicles, and they were
2 read before the king; and there was
found written what Mordecai had told
concerning Bigthana and Teresh, two
of the king's eunuchs, of those who
guarded the threshold, who had sought
3 to lay hands on King Xerxes. Whereupon the king said,
"What honor and dignity have been
bestowed on Mordecai for this?"
Then the king's servants who ministered to him said,
"Nothing has been done for him."
4 "Who is in the court?" said the king.
Now Haman had entered the outer
court of the king's house to request the
king to hang Mordecai on the gallows
5 that he had prepared for him. So the
king's servants said to him,
"Behold, Haman is standing in the
court."
"Let him enter," said the king.
6 So Haman came in, and the king said
to him,

"What shall be done to the man
whom the king delights to honor?"
Now Haman said to himself,
"Whom would the king delight to
honor more than myself?"
So Haman said to the king,
"For the man whom the king delights
to honor, let royal garments be brought,
which the king has worn, and a horse
which the king has ridden, on the head
of which a royal crown is set. Let the
garments and the horse be delivered to
one of the king's most noble princes,
and let them clothe the man whom the
king delights to honor and cause him to
ride on horseback through the open
square of the city, and proclaim before
him, 'Thus shall it be done to the man
whom the king delights to honor.' "
Then the king said to Haman, 1
"Make haste, and take the garments
and the horse, as you have said, and do
even so to Mordecai the Jew who sits at
the king's gate. Let nothing fail of all
that you have spoken."
So Haman took the garments and the 1
horse and clothed Mordecai and caused
him to ride through the open square of
the city and proclaimed before him,
"Thus shall it be done to the man
whom the king delights to honor."
Then Mordecai returned to the king's 1
gate. But Haman hurried home, mourning and with his head covered. When 1
Haman had related to Zeresh his wife
and to all his friends all that had befallen him, his wise men and Zeresh his
wife said to him,
"If Mordecai, before whom you have
begun to fall, be of the Jewish race, you
will make no headway against him, but
will surely fall before him."
While they were still speaking with 1
him, the king's eunuch arrived and hurriedly brought Haman to the banquet
that Esther had prepared.
So the king and Haman went in to 7
drink with Esther the queen; and the
king said again to Esther on the second
day of the banquet of wine,
"Whatever your petition, Queen
Esther, it shall be granted you; and
whatever your request, even to the half
of the kingdom, it shall be performed."
Then Esther the queen answered,
saying,
"If I have found favor in the sight of
the king, and if it please the king, let
my life be given me at my petition and

4 my people at my request; for we are
sold, I and my people, to be destroyed,
to be slain, and to perish. But if we had
been sold as male and female slaves, I
would have held my peace, since the
distress would not have been worth disturbing the king."
5 Then King Xerxes spoke and said to
Esther the queen,
"Who is he, and where is he who
dares presume in his heart to do so?"
6 "An adversary and an enemy, this
wicked Haman," said Esther.
7 Then Haman was terrified before the
king and queen; and when the king
arose in his wrath from the banquet of
wine and went into the palace garden,
Haman stood up to beg for his life from
Esther the queen, for he saw that evil
was determined against him by the
8 king. Accordingly when the king returned from the palace garden to the
apartment of the banquet of wine, Haman was prostrate upon the couch upon
which Esther was.
"Will he violate the queen in my
presence in the house?" said the king.
9 As the words left the mouth of the
king, they covered Haman's face. Then
Harbonah, one of the eunuchs in attendance on the king said,
"There is indeed the gallows fifty
cubits high standing in the house of
Haman, which Haman has made for
Mordecai, who spoke good in behalf of
the king."
"Hang him on it," said the king.
10 So they hanged Haman on the gallows that he had prepared for Mordecai. Then the king's wrath abated.

THE TRIUMPH OF ESTHER AND MORDECAI, 8:1–17

8 On that day King Xerxes gave the
house of Haman, the Jews' enemy, to
Esther the queen; and Mordecai came
before the king, for Esther had told
2 what he was to her. Then the king took
off his ring, which he had taken from
Haman, and gave it to Mordecai; and
Esther set Mordecai over the house of
3 Haman. Again Esther spoke before the
king, and fell at his feet and besought
him with tears to avert the evil plan of
Haman, the Agagite, and his scheme
4 which he had against the Jews. Thereupon the king held out to Esther the
golden scepter. So Esther arose, and
stood before the king; and she said, 5
"If it please the king, and if I have
found favor in his sight, and the thing
seem right before the king, and I am
pleasing in his sight, let it be written to
reverse the letters devised by Haman,
the son of Hammedatha, the Agagite,
which he wrote that the Jews who are in
all the king's provinces might be destroyed. For how can I endure to see 6
the calamity that will come upon my
people, or how can I endure to see the
destruction of my kindred?"
Then King Xerxes said to Esther the 7
queen and to Mordecai the Jew,
"Behold, I have given Esther the
house of Haman, and him they have
hanged upon the gallows, because he
laid his hands upon the Jews. Write 8
also concerning the Jews as it please
you, in the king's name and seal it with
the king's signet; for the writing which
is written in the king's name and sealed
with the king's signet, may no man reverse."
So the king's scribes were called at 9
that time in the third month, which is
the month Sivan, on the twenty-third
day; and it was written just as Mordecai
commanded to the Jews, the satraps,
the governors, and princes of the
provinces which are from India to
Ethiopia, a hundred and twenty-seven
provinces, to every province according
to its script and to every people according to its language, and to the Jews according to their script and according to
their language. He wrote in the name 10
of King Xerxes, and sealed it with the
king's signet and sent the letters by
swift couriers on horseback, riding on
steeds bred of the royal stud; wherein 11
the king allowed the Jews who were in
every city to assemble and fight for
their lives, to wipe out, to slay, and to
destroy all the armed forces of the
people and the provinces that might
attack them, their little ones and
women, and to take the spoil of them as
plunder upon one day in all the prov- 12
inces of King Xerxes, namely, on the
thirteenth day of the twelfth month,
which is the month Adar. A copy of the 13
writing, to be given out as a decree in
every province, was published to all the
peoples, that the Jews should be ready
on that day to avenge themselves on
their enemies. So the couriers riding on 14

the royal steeds went out, being hastened and pressed on by the king's command; and the decree was given out in
the castle at Shushan.
15 Then Mordecai went from the
presence of the king in royal garments
of blue and white stuff, and with a great
crown of gold, and with a robe of fine
linen and purple; and the city of Shu-
16 shan shouted and was glad. The Jews
had light and gladness and joy and
17 honor. Likewise in every province and
in every city, wherever the king's command and his decree came, there was
gladness and joy for the Jews, a feast
and a holiday, and many from among
the peoples of the land became Jews;
for the fear of the Jews had fallen upon
them.

THE JEWS TURN UPON THEIR FOES, 9:1–16

9 Now in the twelfth month, which is
the month Adar, on the thirteenth day
of the same, when the king's command
and his decree was about to be en-
forced, on the day that the enemies of
the Jews hoped to lord it over them,
whereas the contrary happened so that
the Jews themselves got the mastery
2 over those who hated them, the Jews
assembled in their cities throughout all
the provinces of King Xerxes, to lay
hands on such as sought their hurt; and
no one could stand before them; for the
fear of them had fallen upon all the
3 peoples. Moreover all the princes of the
provinces and the satraps and the governors and they who did the king's business aided the Jews, because the fear of
4 Mordecai had fallen upon them. For
Mordecai was great in the king's palace
and his fame spread throughout all the
provinces; for the man Mordecai con-
5 stantly grew more powerful. So the
Jews vanquished all their enemies with
the drawn sword and with slaughter
and destruction, and had their own way
6 with those who hated them. Likewise
in the castle at Shushan the Jews slew
7 and destroyed five hundred men. They
also slew Parshandatha, Dalphon, As-
8 patha, Poratha, Adalia, Aridatha, Par-
9 mashta, Arisai, Aridai and Vaizatha,
10 the ten sons of Haman, the son of Hammedatha, the Jews' enemy; but they
11 did not lay their hand on any spoil. On
that day the number of those that were
slain in the castle at Shushan was reported to the king; and the king said to 12
Esther the queen,
"The Jews have slain and destroyed
in the castle at Shushan five hundred
men and the ten sons of Haman; what
must they have done in the rest of the
king's provinces! Now whatever your
petition, it shall be granted you; and
whatever your request further, it shall
be performed."
Then Esther said, 13
"If it please the king, let it be allowed the Jews who are in Shushan to
act tomorrow also according to this
day's decree, and let Haman's ten sons
be hanged upon the gallows."
Accordingly the king ordered it so to
be done; and a decree was given out in 14
Shushan; and they hanged Haman's
ten sons. Likewise the Jews who were 15
in Shushan assembled on the fourteenth day of the month Adar, and slew
three hundred men in Shushan; but
they did not lay their hands on the
spoil. Also the other Jews who were in 16
the king's provinces assembled and
fought for their lives, and had relief
from their enemies, and slew of those
who hated them seventy-five thousand;
but they did not lay hands on the spoil.

THE FEAST OF PURIM, 9:17–31

On the thirteenth day of the month 17
Adar and the fourteenth day of the
same, they rested and made a day of
feasting and gladness. But the Jews 18
who were in Shushan assembled on the
thirteenth and on the fourteenth, and
on the fifteenth day of the same they
rested and made it a day of feasting and
gladness. Therefore the Jews who are 19
village dwellers, who live in the unwalled towns, make the fourteenth day
of the month Adar an occasion of gladness and feasting and holiday-making,
and a day in which they send portions
of food to one another.
Then Mordecai wrote down these 20
things and sent letters to all the Jews
who were in all the provinces of King
Xerxes, both near and far, to enjoin 21
them that they should keep the fourteenth day of the month Adar and the
fifteenth day of the same yearly, as the 22
days on which the Jews had rest from

their enemies, and the month which was
changed for them from sorrow to gladness and from mourning to a holiday,
that they should make them days of
feasting and gladness and of sending
portions to one another, and of gifts to
the poor.
23 So the Jews adopted as a custom
what they had begun to do, and what
24 Mordecai had written to them. For
Haman, the son of Hammedatha, the
Agagite, the enemy of all the Jews, had
plotted against the Jews to destroy
them, and had cast Pur, that is, the lot,
25 to consume and to destroy them. But
when the matter came before the king,
he commanded by letters that his
wicked scheme which he had devised
against the Jews should come upon his
own head, and that he and his sons
26 should be hanged on the gallows. Hence
they called these days Purim, after the
name of Pur. Therefore because of all
the words of this letter, and of that
which they had seen concerning this
matter, and that which had come to
27 them, the Jews ordained and took upon
them and upon their descendants and
upon all those who joined themselves
to them, so that it should not fail, that
they should observe these two days as
feasts according to the written command and according to the time ap-
28 pointed every year, and that these days
should be remembered and kept
throughout every generation, every
family, every province, and every city;
and that these days of Purim should
not lapse among the Jews nor the remembrance of them be cut off from
their descendants. Then Esther, the 29
queen, the daughter of Abihail, and
Mordecai, the Jew, wrote with all authority to confirm this second letter of
Purim. Also the latter sent letters to 30
all the Jews, to the hundred and twenty-
seven provinces of the kingdom of
Xerxes, containing words of peace and
truth, to confirm these days of Purim 31
in their appointed times, as Mordecai,
the Jew, and Esther, the queen, had
imposed them upon them, and as they
had ordained for themselves and for
their descendants, in the matter of the
fastings and their cry of lamentation.
The command of Esther also confirmed 32
these matters of Purim; and it was
written in a book.

THE POWER OF MORDECAI, 10:1–3

Now King Xerxes laid a tribute on **10**
the land and the coast-lands of the sea.
All the acts of his power and of his 2
might, and the full account of the
greatness of Mordecai to which the
king advanced him, are they not written in the Book of the Chronicles of the
Kings of Media and Persia? For Mor- 3
decai, the Jew, was next in rank to King
Xerxes, and great among the Jews, and
a favorite with the mass of his fellow-
countrymen; for he sought the good of
his people and voiced the welfare of his
entire race.

PART III

THE POETICAL BOOKS

JOB, PSALMS, AND ECCLESIASTES; Translated by J. M. Powis Smith

PROVERBS; Translated by Alex. R. Gordon

SONG OF SONGS; Translated by Theophile J. Meek

THE BOOK OF JOB

JOB'S CALAMITIES, 1:1—3:1

1 THERE was a man in the land of
Uz whose name was Job; and
that man was perfect and upright, and he feared God and
2 shunned wickedness. Now there were
born to him seven sons and three
3 daughters. And his property was seven
thousand sheep and three thousand
camels and five hundred yoke of oxen
and five hundred she-asses and a very
large number of slaves. So that man
was the greatest of all the people of the
4 East. His sons would go and hold a
feast in the house of each one on his
day; and they would send and invite
their three sisters to eat and drink with
5 them. When the days of feasting had
gone round, Job would send and sanctify them, and he would get up early in
the morning and offer sacrifices according to the number of them all; for Job
said,

"Perhaps my children have sinned,
And cursed God in their thoughts."

Thus would Job do always.

6 Now one day when the heavenly beings had come to stand in the presence
of the LORD, and the Satan too had
7 come among them, the LORD said to
the Satan,

"Whence do you come?"

And the Satan answered the LORD,
saying,

"From roaming in the earth and from
going to and fro therein."

8 Then the LORD said to the Satan,
"Have you noticed my servant Job,
That there is none like him in the earth,
A man perfect and upright, who fears God and shuns wickedness?"

9 But the Satan answered the LORD,
saying,
"Has Job feared God for nothing?
10 Hast thou not hedged him round about,
And his house and all that belongs to him?
Thou hast blessed the labor of his hands;
And his wealth has spread abroad in the land.
But now, put forth thy hand, 11
And touch whatsoever he has:
He will curse thee to thy face!"

So the LORD said to the Satan, 12
"Behold, all that he has is in your power;
Only upon himself you shall not lay your hand."

Then the Satan went out from the
presence of the LORD.

Now one day when his sons and 13
daughters were eating and were drinking wine in the house of their oldest
brother, a messenger came to Job, say- 14
ing,

"While the oxen were plowing,
And the she-asses grazing close by,
The Sabeans fell upon them and seized them, 15
And put the servants to the sword;
And I only have escaped alone to tell you."

While he was still speaking, another 16
came, saying,
"The fire of God fell down from the heavens,
And burned up the flocks and the servants and consumed them;
And I only have escaped alone to tell you."

While he was still speaking, another 17
came, saying,
"The Chaldeans formed three divisions,
And swooped down upon the camels and seized them,
And put the servants to the sword;
And I only have escaped alone to tell you."

While he was still speaking, another 18
came, saying,
"As your sons and your daughters were eating
And were drinking wine in the house of their oldest brother,
A mighty wind came from beyond the wilderness, 19
And smote the four corners of the house,
So that it fell upon the young folks and they died.

And I only have escaped alone to tell
you."
20 Then Job arose and tore his mantle
and shaved his head and fell to the
21 earth and worshiped; and he said,
"Naked did I come forth from my
mother's womb,
And naked shall I return thither.
The LORD gave and the LORD has
taken away;
Blessed be the name of the LORD."
22 Notwithstanding all this, Job did not
sin; nor did he charge anything un-
seemly against God.
2 One day when the heavenly beings
had come to present themselves before
the LORD, and when the Satan too had
come among them to present himself
2 before the LORD, the LORD said to the
Satan,
"Whence do you come?"
The Satan answered the LORD, saying,
"From roaming in the earth and from
going to and fro therein."
3 Then the LORD said to the Satan,
"Have you noticed my servant Job,
That there is none like him in the
earth,
A perfect and upright man, who fears
God and shuns wickedness?
He still holds fast to his integrity,
Though you incited me against him,
to ruin him without cause."
4 Then the Satan answered the LORD,
saying,
"Skin for skin!
All that a man has will he give for his
life.
5 Now, just put forth thy hand,
And touch his bone and his flesh:
He will curse thee to thy face!"
6 So the LORD said to the Satan,
"Behold, he is in your power; but
preserve his life."
7 Then the Satan went forth from the
presence of the LORD, and smote Job
with severe leprosy from the sole of his
8 foot to the crown of his head; so that he
took a potsherd with which to scrape
himself as he sat in the midst of the ash-
9 heap. So his wife said to him,
"Do you still hold fast to your integrity?
Curse God and die!"
10 But he said to her,
"You speak as one of the foolish women
might speak.
Should we, indeed, receive good from
God,
And should we not receive evil?"
Notwithstanding all this, Job did not
sin with his lips.
When the three friends of Job heard 1
all this disaster that had befallen him,
they came each from his place, Eliphaz
the Temanite, Bildad the Shuhite, and
Zophar the Naamathite; for they had
arranged together to come to condole
with him and to comfort him. When 1
they lifted up their eyes from afar, they
did not recognize him; so they raised
their voices and wept. Then they tore,
each his mantle, and they cast dust over
their heads toward the heavens. Then 1
they sat down with him upon the
ground for seven days and seven nights;
and no one spoke a word to him, for
they saw that his affliction was very
severe. Afterward Job opened his
mouth and cursed his day.

JOB'S LAMENT THAT HE WAS EVER BORN, 3:2–26

Then Job spoke, saying,
"Perish the day wherein I was born,
And the night which said, 'A man is
conceived.'
May that day be darkness;
May God on high not search for it;
May light not shine upon it;
May the blackest darkness reclaim it;
May a cloud drop down thereon;
May the blackening of the day terrify
it.
That night—may blackness seize it;
May it not rejoice among the days of
the year;
Into the number of the months may it
not come.
As for that night—may it be barren;
May no sound of joy enter it.
May they curse it who curse the day,
Who are skilled in arousing Leviathan.
May the stars of its twilight be dark-
ened;
May it wait for light and there be none;
And may it not see the eyelids of the
dawn.
Because it did not shut the doors of
my mother's womb,
And so conceal trouble from my eyes.

"Why did I not die at birth,
Come forth from the womb and expire?
Why did the knees receive me?
Or why the breasts, that I should suck?

13 For then I had lain down and been quiet,
I had slept; then were I at rest
14 With kings and counselors of the earth,
Who rebuild ruins for themselves;
15 Or with nobles who have gold,
Who fill their houses with silver.
16 Or like a hidden untimely birth I should not be,
Like babes that never saw light.
17 There the wicked cease from troubling;
There the weary are at rest.
18 The prisoners also are at ease;
They hear not the voice of the overseer.
19 The small and the great are there,
And the slave is free from his master.

20 "Why is light given to the wretched,
And life to the bitter of spirit;
21 Who long for death, but it comes not,
And hunt for it more than for buried treasures,
22 Those who would rejoice exultingly,
And would be glad, if they could find the grave?
23 To a man whose way is hidden,
Whom God has fenced in?
24 For my sighing comes in place of my food,
And my groans are poured forth like water.
25 If I entertain a fear, then it comes upon me;
And what I was afraid of befalls me.
26 I am not at ease, nor am I quiet,
Nor am I at rest; for trouble keeps coming."

THE DEBATE BETWEEN THE FRIENDS AND JOB, 4:1—31:40

THE FIRST CYCLE, 4:1—14:22

The Speech of Eliphaz, 4:1—5:27

4 Then Eliphaz, the Temanite, replied, saying,
2 "If one should venture a word with you, would you be bored?
Yet who can refrain from speech?
3 Verily, you have instructed many,
And you have strengthened drooping hands.
4 Your words have upheld the one who was falling,
And you have supported the bending knees.
But now that it comes upon you, you lose heart; 5
It touches you and you are dismayed.
Is not your religion your confidence, 6
And the integrity of your ways, your hope?
Recall now—who ever perished that was innocent? 7
Or where were the upright cut off?
As I have seen, those who plow guilt 8
And sow sorrow reap it.
Through the breath of God they perish, 9
And through his angered spirit they are destroyed.
The roar of the lion and the voice of the roarer— 10
And the teeth of the young lion are knocked out.
The lion perishes for lack of prey, 11
And the cubs of the lioness are scattered.

"Now to me there came a word stealthily, 12
So that my ear caught just a whisper from it,
In thoughts, from visions of the night, 13
When sound sleep falls upon men;
Fear fell upon me, and trembling, 14
And filled all my bones with dread,
And a breath swept over my face; 15
The hair of my flesh stood on end.
It stood; but I could not discern its appearance; 16
A form was before my eyes;
I heard a gentle voice:
'Can a mortal be righteous before God, 17
Or a man be pure before his Maker?
Even in his servants he does not trust, 18
And his angels he charges with error.
How much less them that dwell in houses of clay, 19
Whose foundation is in the dust,
Who are crushed before the moth!
Between morning and evening they are crushed; 20
Without anyone noticing it, they perish forever.
If their tent-rope is torn up within them, 21
Do they not die, and that without wisdom?'

"Call now; is there anybody to answer you? 5
Or to which of the holy ones will you turn?

2 Indeed, vexation slays the fool;
And passion kills the simpleton.
3 I have observed the fool taking root;
But I cursed his habitation suddenly.
4 His children were far from safety,
And were crushed in the gate with none to rescue them.
5 Their harvest, the hungry did eat,
And even from thorns he took it,
And snares gaped for their wealth.
6 Surely misfortune does not come forth from the dust,
Nor does trouble sprout forth from the ground;
7 But man is born for trouble,
Even as sparks fly upward.

8 "I, however, would seek for God,
And to God I would state my case,
9 Who does great things past searching out,
Wonders beyond number;
10 Who sends rain upon the surface of the earth,
And sends forth water upon the surface of the fields;
11 Setting the lowly on high,
While mourners are exalted to safety;
12 Who frustrates the plans of the crafty,
So that their hands accomplish no success;
13 Who catches the wise in their own tricks,
So that the counsel of schemers is confused;
14 In the daytime they meet with darkness,
And at noon they grope as in the night;
15 So that he saves the needy from the sword of their mouth,
And from the hand of the strong.
16 Then there is hope for the poor,
And iniquity shuts its mouth.

17 "Happy, indeed, is the man whom God reproves;
So do not reject the instruction of the Almighty.
18 For he wounds, but he binds up;
He smites, but his hands heal.
19 In six dangers he will rescue you,
And in seven, evil will not touch you.
20 In famine, he will redeem you from death;
And in war, from the power of the sword.
21 During the scourge of the tongue you will be concealed,
And you will not be afraid of destruction when it comes.
At destruction and at famine you will laugh,
And you will not fear the beasts of the earth;
For you will have a covenant with the stones of the field,
And the beasts of the field will be at peace with you.
And you will know that your tent is prosperous;
And when you inspect your homestead, you will miss nothing.
You will know also that your descendants are many,
And your progeny like the grass of the earth.
You will come to the grave in ripe old age,
As a shock of grain comes up in its season.
"There it is! We have investigated it; it is so!
Hear it, and know it for your very self!"

JOB'S REPLY TO ELIPHAZ, 6:1—7:21

Then Job replied, saying,
"O that my vexation were carefully weighed,
And that my calamity were also laid on the scales!
For then it would be heavier than the sand of the seas;
Therefore have my words been rash.
For the arrows of the Almighty are with me,
And their poison my spirit is drinking;
The terrors of God beset me.
Does the wild ass bray over grass?
Or does the ox low over his fodder?
Is a tasteless thing eaten without salt?
Or is there taste in the slime of purslain?
My appetite refuses to touch them!
They are like uncleanness in my food.

"O that my request might come to pass,
And that God would grant my hope!
O that God would consent to crush me,
That he would let loose his hand and cut me off!
Then I should still have the consolation—
And I would exult in pain unsparing—

That I had not hidden the words of
the Holy One.
11 What is my strength that I should
wait?
And what is my end that I should be
patient?
12 Is my strength the strength of stones?
Is my flesh bronze?
13 Verily, there is no help in me,
And effective aid is removed far from
me.
14 "To him who is faint there should be
kindness from his friend,
Though he forsake the fear of the Almighty.
15 My friends have been faithless like a
torrent,
Like the bed of rivers which pass away,
16 That run black because of ice,
Wherein the snow hides itself.
17 When it becomes hot, they are cut off;
When it warms up, they dry up from
their place.
18 The caravans divert their route;
They go up into the waste and perish.
19 The caravans of Tema look,
The companies of Sheba wait for them;
20 They are ashamed because they
trusted;
They come to them and they are disappointed.
21 Such now have you become to me;
You see a terror, and you are afraid.
22 Have I said, 'Give to me,'
Or 'From your substance offer a bribe
for me,'
23 Or 'Rescue me from the hand of an
enemy,'
Or 'From the hand of brigands ransom
me'?
24 Teach me, and I will be silent;
Make clear to me wherein I have erred.
25 How forceful are honest words!
But what does your reproving reprove?
26 Do you mean to reprove words?
But for wind are the words of one in
despair.
27 Even upon an orphan you would cast
lots,
And you would bargain over your
friend!

28 "Now, be pleased to look me in the face,
And to your faces, I will not lie!
29 Turn back, now; let there be no injustice.
O, turn again! My justification is in it.

Is there injustice in my tongue? 30
Or is my palate insensible to calamities?

Is there not hard labor for man upon 7
earth,
And are not his days like the days of a
hireling?
Like a slave who longs for the evening, 2
And like a hireling who waits for his
wages,
So I am made to possess months of 3
emptiness,
And nights of trouble are allotted me.
When I lie down, I say, 'When can I 4
arise?'
But the evening is prolonged;
And I am satiated with tossings until
dawn.
My flesh is clothed with worms and 5
clods of dust;
My skin hardens and then runs.
My days are swifter than a weaver's 6
shuttle,
And they come to an end without
hope.
Remember that my life is a breath; 7
My eye will not again see good.
The eye of him who looks at me will 8
not see me;
Thine eye will be upon me, but I shall
not be.
A cloud dissolves and it is gone; 9
So is the one who descends to Sheol;
he will not ascend.
He will not return again to his house; 10
Nor will his place know him again.
I, then, will not restrain my mouth; 11
I will speak in the anguish of my
spirit;
I will complain in the bitterness of my
being.
Am I the sea, or a dragon, 12
That thou appointest a watch over me?
When I think my couch may comfort 13
me,
Or my bed relieve my complaint,
Then thou dost terrify me with 14
dreams,
Thou dost startle me by nightmares;
So that I prefer strangling, 15
Death rather than my bones.
I refuse; I shall not live forever. 16
Let me alone! For my days are but a
breath.
What is man that thou shouldst magnify him, 17
And shouldst set thy mind upon him,
And shouldst inspect him every morning, 18

And test him every moment?
19 How long wilt thou not look away from me,
Nor let me alone till I swallow my saliva?
20 Have I sinned? What do I unto thee, O thou keeper of man?
Why dost thou make me a target for thyself,
So that I am become a burden to thee?
21 Why dost thou not forgive my transgression,
And make my guilt to pass away?
For soon I shall lie down in the dust;
And thou wilt search for me, but I shall not be."

THE SPEECH OF BILDAD, 8:1–22

8 Then Bildad, the Shuhite, replied, saying,
2 "How long will you utter such things,
And the words of your mouth be a strong wind?
3 Does God pervert justice?
Or the Almighty pervert the right?
4 If your sons have sinned against him,
He has but delivered them into the power of their transgression.
5 If you yourself would seek God,
And make supplication to the Almighty—
6 If you were but pure and straight,
Then, indeed, he would bestir himself in your behalf,
And he would protect your righteous dwelling;
7 And though your beginning were small,
He would make your end very great.
8 But inquire now of the previous generation,
And apply yourself to what their fathers discovered—
9 For we are of yesterday, and we know nothing;
For our days upon the earth are but a shadow—
10 Will they not teach you and speak to you,
And bring forth words from their minds?
11 "Will papyrus grow where there is no mire,
Or the rush grow tall without water?
While it is still in its greenness and not plucked, 1
Before any other herb, it withers.
So are the paths of all who forget God, 1
And the hope of the irreligious man perishes;
For his confidence breaks, 1
And the object of his trust is a spider's house.
If he leans upon his house, it will not stand; 1
If he lays hold of it, it will not endure.
Green is he before the sun; 1
And over his garden his shoots go forth;
Over the roof his roots are intertwined; 1
He penetrates between the stones;
If he be destroyed from his place, 1
Then it will repudiate him, 'I have not seen you.'
That, then, is the joy of his way! 1
And from the dust another springs forth.
Verily, God will not reject a perfect man, 2
Nor will he lay hold of the hand of evil-doers.
He will yet fill your mouth with laughter, 2
And your lips with shouting.
Those who hate you will be clothed with shame; 2
And the tent of the wicked will not be."

JOB'S REPLY TO BILDAD, 9:1—10:22

Then Job replied, saying,
"Of course, I know that it is so.
But how can a man be right with God?
If he should be willing to debate with him,
He could not answer him once in a thousand times.
The wisest of mind and stoutest in strength—
Who ever resisted him and succeeded?—
Him, who removes mountains, they know not how,
Who overturns them in his anger;
Who shakes the earth from its place,
And its pillars are shattered;
Who speaks to the sun, and it does not rise;

And he seals up the stars;
Who stretched out the heavens by
himself,
And treads upon the billows of the
sea;
Who made the Bear, Orion,
The Pleiades, and the Chambers of
the South;
Who does great things past finding
out,
And wonders without number.

"Lo, he passes by me and I see him
not,
And he glides past and I do not perceive him.
If he should break through, who
could turn him back?
Who could say to him, 'What are you
doing?'
God will not turn back his anger.
Under him the helpers of Rahab
bowed;
How much less could I answer him,
Or choose my words with him,
Whom, though I be innocent, I could
not answer?
I should be making entreaty to my
judge!
Were I to call and he to answer me,
I could not believe that he would
give ear to my voice;
For he crushes me with a tempest,
And multiplies my wounds without
cause.
He does not let me draw my breath,
But surfeits me with bitterness.
If it were a question of the strength
of the mighty, there is he!
And if of judgment, who could summon me?
Though I be innocent, my mouth
would declare me guilty;
Though I be perfect, he would declare me crooked.
I am perfect; I do not know myself;
I loathe my life.
It is all one—therefore I say,
The perfect and the wicked he destroys.
If the scourge kills instantly,
He mocks at the despair of the guiltless.
The earth is given into the hand of
the wicked;
He covers the faces of its judges.
If it is not he—who then is it?
My days are swifter than a runner;
They speed away; they see no good
thing.
They follow one another like boats 26
of papyrus,
Like a vulture swooping upon prey.
If I say, 'I will forget my complaint, 27
I will change my appearance and be
cheerful';
I fear all my pains. 28
I know that thou dost not hold me
guiltless;
I am declared guilty. 29
Why, then, should I toil in vain?
If I should wash myself in snow, 30
And clean my hands with lye,
Then thou wouldst plunge me into 31
the cesspool,
And my clothes would abhor me.
For he is not a man like myself whom 32
I could answer,
That we could come together in the
court.
O that there were an umpire between 33
us,
That he might lay his hand upon
both of us,
That he might turn aside his rod 34
from upon me,
And that fear of him might not terrify me;
That I might speak and not be afraid 35
of him.
For I am not so with myself.

"I myself loathe my life. 10
I will make complaint freely;
I will speak of my own bitterness,
I will say unto God, 'Do not condemn me; 2
Tell me why thou dost quarrel with
me.
Does it seem good to thee that thou 3
shouldst oppress,
That thou shouldst reject the work
of thine own hands,
And shine upon the counsel of the
wicked?
Hast thou eyes of flesh, 4
Or dost thou see as men see?
Are thy days like the days of a mortal, 5
Or thy years like the years of a man,
That thou seekest for my guilt, 6
And searchest for my sin,
Although thou knowest that I am 7
not guilty,
And none can deliver from thy hand?
Thy hands did form me and make 8
me;

And afterward wouldst thou turn and destroy me?
9 Recall, now, that thou didst make me like clay;
And wilt thou return me to the dust?
10 Didst thou not pour me out like milk,
And curdle me like cheese?
11 With skin and flesh thou didst clothe me,
And with bones and muscles thou didst knit me together.
12 Life and kindness hast thou exercised with me,
And thy solicitude has preserved my spirit;
13 While these things thou didst hide in thy heart.
I know that this is in thy mind:
14 If I sin, then thou wilt watch me,
And wilt not absolve me from my guilt.
15 " 'If I be guilty, woe is me;
And if I be innocent, I may not lift up my head,
Being sated with shame and drenched with misery.
16 Should it lift itself up, thou wouldst hunt me like the lion,
And thou wouldst again deal wondrously with me.
17 Thou wouldst renew thy witnesses before me.
And thou wouldst increase thine anger with me,
And new hardships for me.
18 Why didst thou bring me forth from the womb?
I should have expired and no eye have seen me;
19 I should have been as though I had not been;
From the womb to the grave I should have been carried.
20 Are not the days of my life few?'
Let him leave me alone, that I may brighten up a little,
21 Before I go, never to return,
To a land of darkness and blackness,
22 A land of shadow, like gloom,
Of blackness without order,
And when it shines, it is like gloom."

THE SPEECH OF ZOPHAR,

11:1–20

11 Then Zophar, the Naamathite, replied, saying,

"Should not one of many words be answered?
Or is a man of ready lips in the right?
Shall your boastings put men to silence?
And when you scoff, is no one to rebuke you?
For you have said, 'My teaching is pure,
And I am clean in thy sight.'
But would that God might speak,
That he might open his lips with you,
And tell you the secrets of wisdom;
For insight is a wonderful thing.
Know then that God reckons not against you all of your guilt.
Can you find out the limits of God?
Or can you attain unto the boundary of the Almighty?
It is higher than the heavens—what can you do?
Deeper than Sheol—what can you know?
Longer than the earth is its extent,
And broader than the sea.
If he glide by and deliver up,
And call an assembly, who can turn him back?
For he knows worthless men;
And he sees iniquity and gives heed to it.
But an inane man will get intelligence,
When a wild ass's colt is born a man.
"If you would only apply your mind,
And spread out your hands unto him!
If iniquity be in your hand, put it far away;
Let not perversity dwell in your tent.
Then, indeed, you might lift up your face without blemish,
And you would be steadfast, and would not fear.
For then you would forget trouble,
You would recall it like waters that have passed on.
And life would rise up brighter than the noon-day; 1
Darkness would be like the morning;
And you would trust because there was hope,
And you would search and in confidence go to rest;
You would lie down, with none to disturb. 1
Many would pay court to you.
But the eyes of the wicked will grow dim; 2
And refuge will fail them;
And their hope is an expiring breath."

JOB'S REPLY TO ZOPHAR, 12:1—14:22

12 Then Job replied, saying,
2 "No doubt but you are the people,
And wisdom will die with you!
3 But I too have a mind as well as you,
I am not inferior to you!
Who has not experienced such things as these?
4 I am become 'a laughing-stock to his friend,'
One whom God answered when he called;
A laughing-stock is the righteous, the perfect one.
5 For the unfortunate there is contempt in the thought of him who is prosperous,
Ready for those whose feet slip.
6 The households of spoilers prosper,
And those who provoke God are secure,
Those whom God brings into his power.
7 "But now ask the beasts and let them teach you,
And the birds of the air and let them tell you,
8 Or speak to the earth and let it teach you,
And let the fish of the sea recount to you.
9 Which among all these does not know
That the hand of the LORD has done this,
10 In whose hand is the life of every living thing,
And the breath of all human beings.
11 Does not the ear try words,
And the palate taste its own food?
12 'With the aged is wisdom,
And length of days is understanding.'
13 With Him are wisdom and power,
He has counsel and understanding.
14 If he destroys, it cannot be rebuilt;
When he shuts up a man, it cannot be reopened.
15 If he restrains the waters, they dry up;
If he send them forth, they overturn the earth.
16 With him are strength and sure insight;
The misled and the misleader are his;
17 Who makes counselors walk barefoot,
And renders judges foolish.
18 He looses the bond of kings,
And binds a waist-cloth on their loins.
He makes priests walk barefoot, 19
And overthrows them that are firmly established.
He deprives the self-confident of speech, 20
And takes away the discretion of elders.
He pours contempt upon nobles, 21
And he brings low the pride of the learned.
He uncovers the depths of darkness, 22
And brings forth dense darkness to the light.
He makes the nations great, and he destroys them, 23
He expands the nations, and leads them away.
He takes away the intelligence of the chiefs of the people of the earth, 24
And makes them wander in a pathless waste.
They grope in darkness with no light, 25
And he makes them wander like a drunken man.

"Lo, my eye has seen it all; 13
My ear has heard and understood it.
I too know just as much as you; 2
I am not inferior to you.
But I would speak to the Almighty, 3
And I desire to argue with God.
But you—forgers of lies, 4
Worthless physicians are you all.
O that you would keep strict silence, 5
And that it might be your wisdom!
Hear, now, my argument; 6
And listen to the pleadings of my lips.
Is it for God that you speak falsehood, 7
And for him do you speak deceit?
Will you be partial toward him? 8
Or will you strive for God?
Will it be well when he examines you? 9
Or will you deceive him as one deceives a man?
He will severely rebuke you, 10
If you are secretly partial.
Should not his majesty terrify you, 11
And awe of him fall upon you?
Your maxims are proverbs of ashes; 12
Your defenses are become defenses of clay.
Keep silent before me, that I myself may speak, 13
Whatever may befall me.
I will take my flesh in my teeth, 14
And my life I will take in my hand.
Lo, he will slay me; I have no hope; 15

Yet I will defend my ways to his face.
16 But this will be my deliverance,
That an impious man would not come before him.
17 Listen closely to my speech,
And my declaration in your hearing.
18 See, now, I draw up my case;
I know that I am innocent.
19 Who is there to contend with me?
For then I would keep silence and die.
20 Yet two things do not do to me—
Then I will not conceal myself from before thee.
21 Remove thy hand from upon me,
And let not the dread of thee terrify me!
22 But call, and I will reply;
Or I will speak, and do thou answer me.
23 How many are my iniquities and sins?
Tell me my offense and my sin.
24 Why dost thou hide thy face,
And reckon me as thy foe?
25 Wilt thou scare a driven leaf,
And chase the dry stubble,
26 That thou writest bitter charges against me,
And dost make me inherit the faults of my youth,
27 And puttest my feet in the stocks,
And watchest all my paths?
Thou drawest a line about the soles of my feet.

14 "Man, that is born of woman,
Is of few days and full of trouble.
2 Like a blossom he comes forth and is withered,
And he flees like the shadow and does not endure.
28[1] And he wastes away like a rotten thing,
Like a garment which the moth has eaten.
3 Yet upon such an one thou openest thine eye,
And bringest me into judgment with thyself.
4 O that there were a pure one among the impure! There is not one.
5 If his days are decreed,
And the number of his months is with thee;
If thou hast established his bounds so that he may not pass over,
6 Look away from him that he may cease,
Until he enjoy, like a hireling, his day.

[1] This verse does not belong in chap. 13 where it is placed in the Hebrew text.

"For there is hope for the tree;
If it be cut down, then it will sprout again,
And its shoots will not cease.
If its root becomes old in the ground,
And its trunk dies in the soil,
At the scent of water it will bud,
And put forth shoots like a young plant.
But man dies, and is powerless.
And man expires, and where is he?
Water departs from the lake,
And a stream parches and dries up;
So man lies down and does not rise.
Until the heavens are no more they will not awake,
Nor will they be roused from their sleep.
O that thou wouldst hide me in Sheol,
That thou wouldst conceal me until thy wrath turn,
That thou wouldst set me a time and remember me!
If a man dies, does he live?
All the days of my service I would wait
Until my turn should come;
Thou wouldst call and I would answer thee;
Thou wouldst yearn for the work of thy hands.
But now thou dost number my steps;
Dost thou not watch over my sin?
My transgression is sealed up in a bag,
And thou dost plaster over my guilt.
But if a mountain falls, it crumbles away;
And a rock moves from its place;
Water wears away stones;
Its torrent sweeps away the soil of the earth;
So thou destroyest the hope of man.
Thou dost overpower him forever and he passes on;
Thou dost change his looks and send him away.
His children come to honor, but he does not know it;
And they sink into insignificance, but he does not perceive them.
But he grieves over himself,
And he mourns over himself."

THE SECOND CYCLE,

15:1—21:34

The Speech of Eliphaz 15:1-35

Then Eliphaz, the Temanite, replied, saying,

2 "Should a wise man answer with windy
knowledge,
And fill his breast with the east wind?
3 Should he argue with speech that is
not profitable,
And words which are of no value?
4 Yet you destroy reverence,
And you do away with meditation before God.
5 For your guilt instructs your mouth,
And you choose the tongue of the
crafty.
6 Your own mouth condemns you, and
not I;
And your own lips witness against
you.
7 Were you the first one that was born
a man?
Were you brought forth before the
hills?
8 Do you listen in the secret council of
God?
And have you a monopoly of wisdom?
9 What do you know that we do not?
What do you understand that is not
ours?
10 The gray-headed and aged are with
us,
Older than your father in days.
11 Are the consolations of God too slight
a thing for you,
And a word that deals gently with
you?
12 Why does your heart carry you away,
And what do your eyes suggest,
13 That you turn your breath against
God,
And send forth words from your
mouth?

14 "What is man, that he should be pure,
And the child of a woman, that he
should be innocent?
15 Lo, he puts no trust in his holy ones,
And the heavens are not pure in his
eyes;
How much less one who is loathsome
and foul,
A man who drinks down wickedness
like water!
17 I will tell you; listen to me!
And this that I have seen I will relate,
18 What the wise declare,
Without hiding it, from their fathers,
19 To whom alone the land was given,
And no alien passed among them.
All the days of the wicked he writhes
in pain;
And but few years are in store for the
tyrant.
Dreadful sounds are in his ears; 21
In the midst of peace, the spoiler
comes upon him.
He does not believe that he will re- 22
turn from darkness;
And he is watched for by the sword.
He wanders about for bread; 'Where 23
is it?'
He knows that a day of darkness is
ready at hand.
Distress and anguish terrify him; 24
They overpower him like a king ready
for the fray,
Because he has stretched out his hand 25
against God,
And conducts himself arrogantly to-
ward the Almighty.
He runs upon him with a stubborn 26
neck,
With the thick bosses of his shields.
For he has covered his face with his 27
fat,
And amassed fat upon his loins.
And he has dwelt in ruined cities, 28
In houses wherein no one lives,
Which are destined for ruins.
He will not get rich, nor will his wealth 29
endure,
Nor will he strike root in the earth.
He will not turn aside from darkness; 30
The flame will shrivel his shoots,
And his blossom will be blown away
by the wind.
Let him not trust in emptiness, being 31
misled,
For his reward will be emptiness.
Before his time it will be fulfilled, 32
And his palm-branch will not be fresh.
He will mar, like a vine, his green 33
grapes,
And he will cast, like an olive, his
blossom.
For the assembly of the godless is bar- 34
ren,
And fire devours the tents of bribery.
They conceive trouble and bring forth 35
misery,
And their womb prepares deception."

JOB'S REPLY TO ELIPHAZ, 16:1—17:16

Then Job replied, saying, 16
"I have heard many things like these. 2
Troublesome comforters are you all!
Is there any end to words of wind? 3

Or what provokes you that you answer?
4 I too could speak like you,
If you were in my place.
I could compose words against you,
And I could shake my head at you.
5 I could strengthen you with my mouth,
And the comfort of my lips would assuage.
6 If I speak, my suffering is not restrained;
And if I am silent, what departs from me?
7 But now, he has tired me out.
Thou hast laid waste all my company,
8 And thou hast shrivelled me up; it has become a witness!
Yea, my leanness has risen against me; it testifies to my face.
9 His wrath has torn and attacked me;
He has gnashed upon me with his teeth.
My enemy looks daggers at me.
10 They gape upon me with their mouths;
In scorn they smite my cheeks;
They mass themselves together against me.
11 God delivers me over to the unjust,
And into the hands of the wicked he surrenders me.
12 I was at ease, but he shattered me.
And he seized me by the neck and smashed me.
He set me up as his target;
13 His arrows encircle me about;
He splits my kidneys without mercy;
He pours my gall on the ground.
14 He breaks me with breach upon breach;
He runs upon me like a warrior.
15 I have sewed sackcloth upon my sores;
And I have laid my horn in the dust.
16 My face is flushed from weeping,
And black shadows are on my eyelids;
17 Although there is no violence on my hands,
And my prayer is pure.
18 O earth, cover not my blood,
That there be no place for my cry.
19 Yet now; lo, my witness is in the heavens,
And he who testifies for me is on high.
20 My thoughts are my intercessors;
Unto God my eye weeps,
21 That one might plead for a man with God,
Even as with a man for one's friend.

For a few years will come. 2
And I shall go the way that I shall not return.
My spirit is broken, my days are snuffed out;
The grave is mine.
Surely mockery is with me,
And my eye dwells on their obstinacy.
Give surety for me, now, with thyself.
Who is there that will strike hand in mine?
Because thou hast closed their mind against reason,
Therefore thou wilt not exalt them.
He who denounces friends for a portion—
The eyes of his children will fail.
He has made me a byword of the peoples,
And one before whom men spit am I become.
My eye is dim because of grief,
And all my members are like a shadow.
The upright are amazed at this,
And the innocent bestirs himself against the godless;
But the righteous will hold to his way,
And the clean-handed will grow stronger.
But all of you, return and come now:
I shall not find a wise man among you!
My days have passed on; my plans are broken,
The desires of my heart.
They turn night into day,
And declare light near in the face of darkness.
If I wait for Sheol as my home,
If I spread out my couch in darkness,
If I address the Pit, 'You are my father,'
And say to the worm, 'My mother and my sister,'
Where then is my hope?
And who will see my prosperity?
Will they go down to Sheol with me?
Or shall we descend together to the dust?"

THE SPEECH OF BILDAD, 18:1–21

Then Bildad, the Shuhite, replied, saying,
"How long will you set snares for words?

Understand, and afterward we will speak.
3 Why are we accounted as beasts?
Why are we stupid in your eyes?
4 You who tear yourself in your anger—
Is the land to be forsaken on your account,
Or the rock to be moved from its place?

5 "Now, the light of the wicked goes out,
And the flame of his fire does not shine.
6 The light grows dark in his tent,
And his lamp goes out above him.
7 His strong steps are narrowed,
And his own counsel casts him out.
8 For he is hurled into the net by his own feet,
And he walks upon a pit-fall.
9 A trap seizes him by the heel;
A snare lays hold upon him.
10 A noose is concealed for him in the ground,
And a springe for him upon the path.
11 All around terrors startle him,
And dog his footsteps.
12 His strength is famished,
And calamity is ready at his side.
13 By sickness his skin is consumed;
The first-born of death devours his limbs.
14 He is snatched away from his tent in which he trusted,
And thou dost march him to the king of terrors.
15 There dwells in his tent nothing of his;
Brimstone is strewn upon his habitation.
16 His roots dry up under him,
And his branches are cut off from above.
17 Memory of him perishes from the land,
And he has no name upon the surface of the plain.
18 They drive him from light into darkness,
And chase him from the world.
19 He has no kith or kin among his people,
Nor is there a survivor in his haunts.
20 At his day younger men will be appalled,
And horror will seize upon older ones.
21 But such are the dwellings of the wicked,
And such is the place of him who knows not God."

JOB'S REPLY TO BILDAD, 19:1–29

Then Job replied, saying, 19
"How long will you torment me, 2
And crush me with words?
Now ten times you abuse me; 3
You wrong me shamelessly.
But suppose, indeed, I have erred; 4
With myself my error dwells.
If, indeed, you magnify yourselves against me, 5
And argue my disgrace against me,
Know, then, that God has overturned me, 6
And has inclosed me in his net.
Lo, I cry 'Murder,' but I am not answered; 7
I call for help, but there is no justice.
My way he has walled up that I may not pass on; 8
And upon my paths he sets darkness.
My glory he has stripped from upon me, 9
And has taken the crown off my head.
He has broken me down on every side, and I am gone; 10
And he has torn up my hope like a tree.
His anger burns against me, 11
And he reckons me as one of his foes.
His troops also come, 12
They cast up their way against me,
And they have encamped around my tent.
He has put my brothers far from me; 13
And my friends are wholly estranged from me.
My relatives have disappeared, 14
And my intimates have forgotten me.
The guests of my house and my maids reckon me a stranger; 15
An alien am I become in their eyes.
I call my servant, but he will not answer; 16
With my mouth I must implore him.
My breath is offensive to my wife, 17
And I am loathsome to my brothers.
Even the urchins despise me; 18
When I arise, they turn their backs upon me.
All the men of my circle abhor me; 19
And those whom I have loved have turned against me.
My bone cleaves to my skin, 20
And I am escaped with my flesh in my teeth.

"Have pity on me, have pity on me, O you, my friends, 21

For the hand of God has struck me!
22 Why do you pursue me like God,
And are not satisfied with my flesh?
23 Would, then, that my words were written!
Would that they were inscribed in a scroll!
24 That with an iron pen and lead
They were hewn in the rock forever!
25 But as for me, I know that my Vindicator lives;
And as the next-of-kin he will stand upon my dust;
26 And as the next-of-kin he will rise as my witness,
And I shall see God as my defender;
27 Whom I shall see on my side,
And my eyes will see to be no stranger.
My emotions are spent within me!
28 If you say, 'How we will persecute him,
Since the root of the matter is found in him!'
29 Tremble for yourselves before the sword;
For such things are crimes deserving the sword,
That you may know that there is judgment."

THE SPEECH OF ZOPHAR, 20:1–29

20 Then Zophar, the Naamathite, replied, saying,
2 "Therefore, my thoughts answer me;
And because of the agitation within me,
3 I hear the rebuke that would put me to shame,
And my intelligent spirit replies to me.

4 "Do you know this as from of old,
Since man was placed upon the earth,
5 That the triumph of the wicked is but short,
And the mirth of the ungodly is but for a moment?
6 If his pride mount up to the heavens,
And his head touch the clouds,
7 He will perish forever like his own dung;
Those that saw him will say, 'Where is he?'
8 Like a dream he will fly away and they will not find him,
And he will flee like a vision of the night;
9 The eye that saw him will see him no more,
Nor will his place see him again.
10 His sons will conciliate the poor,
And his own hands will give back his wealth.
11 While his bones are full of his youth,
With him it will lie down in the dust.

12 "If wickedness be sweet in his mouth,
If he hide it under his tongue;
13 If he be sparing of it and will not let it go,
But withhold it in his palate;
14 His food in his bowels is turned
Into the gall of asps within him.
15 He swallows down riches but vomits them up;
God drives them forth from his belly.
16 He sucks the poison of asps;
The tongue of the adder slays him.
17 Never shall he gaze upon rich meadows,
Upon valleys of honey and curds.
18 He gives back the product of toil and cannot consume it;
He does not rejoice in proportion to the wealth he gains by trade.
19 Because he has oppressed and forsaken the poor,
And has seized a house that he did not build;
20 Because he knew no peace of mind,
But in his greed spared none,
21 And there is nothing left of his meal;
Therefore his prosperity will not endure.
22 In the fulness of his abundance he will be in straits;
All the weight of trouble will come upon him;
23 May his belly be filled!
He will send forth upon him the heat of his anger,
And rain down his war upon him.
24 He will flee from the weapon of iron,
And the bow of bronze will pierce him;
25 He draws it forth and it comes out of his back,
And the glittering sword out of his gall.
Terror comes upon him;
26 All darkness is stored up for his treasures.
A fire that is not blown will devour him;
It will feed on what is left in his tent.
27 The heavens will disclose his guilt,
And the earth will rise up against him.

8 The increase of his house will go into exile,
Like things melting away on the day of his wrath.

29 "This is the lot of a wicked man from God,
And the inheritance allotted him from God."

JOB'S REPLY TO ZOPHAR, 21:1–34

1 Then Job replied, saying,
2 "Listen closely to my speech,
And let this be your consolation to me.
3 Suffer me while I speak,
And after I have spoken, you may jeer.

4 "Is my complaint regarding man?
Or why should I not be impatient?
5 Look at me and be dumbfounded,
And lay your hand upon your mouth.

6 "When I think of it, I am amazed;
And shuddering lays hold of my flesh.
7 Why do the wicked live,
Grow old, and amass wealth?

8 "Their descendants are established in their presence with them,
And their offspring before their very eyes.
9 Their houses are safe from terror;
And the rod of God is not upon them.

0 "His bull genders without fail,
His cow brings forth without miscarriage.
1 They send forth their little ones like a flock,
And their children skip about.

12 "They sing to the timbrel and harp,
And they make merry to the sound of the flute.
3 They complete their days in prosperity,
And in a moment they go down to Sheol.

4 "Yet they say to God, 'Depart from us;
We do not want to know thy ways.
What is the Almighty, that we should serve him? 15
And what does it profit us that we pray to him?'

"Behold, their prosperity is not in their power; 16
The counsel of the wicked is far from me.

"How often is it that the lamp of the wicked is put out, 17
Or that their calamity comes upon them?
That he apportions snares in his anger,
That they are like straw before the wind, 18
Or like chaff that the whirlwind carries away?

" 'God stores up his trouble for his sons!' 19
Let him requite it unto him himself that he may know,
That his own eyes may see his ruin, 20
And that he may drink of the wrath of the Almighty.
For what does he care about his house after him, 21
When the number of his months is reckoned up?

"Can anyone teach God knowledge? 22
He judges the highest!
One man dies at the height of his powers, 23
Wholly at ease and satisfied;
His vessels are full of milk, 24
And the marrow of his bones is moistened.
Another dies in a mood of bitterness, 25
Never having enjoyed good.
They both lie down in the dust, 26
And the worm covers them over.

"Indeed I know your plans, 27
And the purposes you meditate against me.
For you say, 'Where is the house of the noble? 28
And where is the tent in which the wicked dwell?'

"Have you not asked those that pass by on the road? 29
And do you not recognize their evidence,

30 That the wicked is spared in the day
of disaster,
That they are led away on the day
of wrath?

31 "Who declares his way to his face?
And who requites to him what he has
done?
32 He is led along to the grave,
And watch is kept over the tomb.
33 The clods of the valley are sweet to
him,
And all men follow after him,
Even as they are innumerable before
him.

34 "How then do you offer me empty
comfort?
For your answers are nothing but
pretexts."

THE THIRD CYCLE, 22:1—31:40

The Speech of Eliphaz, 22:1–30

22 Then Eliphaz, the Temanite, replied,
saying,
2 "Can man be of value to God,
That a wise man should be of value to
him?
3 Is it of any concern to the Almighty
that you are righteous?
Or is it of any gain to him that you
should make your ways perfect?
4 Is it because of your piety that he
chastens you,
And enters into judgment with you?
5 Is not your wickedness great?
There is no end to your guilt.
6 For you take pledges of your brothers
for nothing;
You strip the clothes off the naked;
7 You do not give the thirsty water to
drink;
And you withhold food from the hungry;
8 But the man of power may have the
earth,
And the favored man may dwell
therein.
9 Widows you have sent empty away,
And the arms of the orphans are
crushed.
10 Therefore snares are round about you,
And terror will suddenly overwhelm
you;
11 Or darkness so that you cannot see,
And a flood of water will cover you.
12 "Is not God as high as the heavens?
And see the topmost stars, how high
they are.
Yet you say, 'What does God know?
Can he judge through deep darkness?
Thick clouds conceal him so that he
cannot see,
And he walks upon the vault of the
heavens.'
Will you keep to the old path,
Which wicked men have trodden,
Who were snatched away before their
time,
Whose foundation was poured out
like a river;
Who said to God, 'Depart from us,'
And, 'What does the Almighty do for
us?'
Yet it was he who filled their houses
with good things.
The counsel of the wicked be far from
me!
The righteous see and are glad,
And the innocent scoffs at them:
'Surely our enemies are destroyed,
And their surplus the fire has de-
voured.'

"Acquaint yourself, now, with him and
be at peace;
Thereby will your increase be good.
Receive instruction, now, from his
mouth,
And place his words in your heart.
If you return to the Almighty and
humble yourself,
If you put injustice far from your
tent,
And lay gold in the dust,
And gold of Ophir among the stones
of the brooks;
The Almighty will be your gold,
And your shining silver.
For then you will delight yourself in
the Almighty,
And you will lift up your face unto
God.
You will pray to him and he will hear
you,
And you will fulfil your vows.
You will decide a matter, and it will
stand for you;
And light will shine upon your ways.
For God will abase the high and
proud,
And will deliver him that is lowly of
eye.
He will free the innocent man,
And he will be freed through the pur-
ity of his hands."

JOB'S REPLY TO ELIPHAZ, 23:1—24:25

Then Job replied, saying,
"Today also is my complaint defiant,
His hand is heavy upon my groaning.
O that I knew where I might find him,
That I might come to his dwelling!
I would set my case in order before him,
And I would fill my mouth with arguments.
I would know the words he would answer me,
And understand what he would say to me.
Would he contend with me in his great strength?
No; but he would pay heed to me.
Then an upright man would argue with him;
And I should deliver myself forever from my judge.
Lo, I go forward, but he is not;
And backward, but I perceive him not;
On the left I seek him, but cannot see him;
I turn to the right, and do not behold him.
When he knows my manner of life,
When he has tested me, I shall come forth like gold.
My foot has held fast to his step;
I have kept to his way, and not turned aside,
To the command of his lips, and do not recede;
I have treasured up in my breast the words of his mouth.
But he has chosen and who can turn him back?
And what he himself desires, he does.
For he will complete what he has decreed for me;
And many such things are in his mind.
Therefore I am dismayed before him;
When I consider, I am in terror of him.
But God has weakened my heart;
And the Almighty has overwhelmed me;
For I am overcome because of darkness,
And blackness has covered my face.

"Why are not times stored up by the Almighty?
And why have not those who know him seen his days?
Men remove boundaries; 2
They steal flocks and pasture them;
They lead away the ass of the orphan; 3
They take as a pledge the ox of the widow;
They turn aside the needy from the way; 4
Moreover the needy of the land hide themselves.
"Indeed, like wild-asses in the wilderness, 5
They go forth to their work, seeking for food;
The steppe furnishes them bread for the children.
They make harvest in the field by night; 6
And they glean the vineyard of the wicked.
Naked they pass the night without clothing, 7
And they have no covering against the cold.
They are drenched by the rain from the mountains, 8
And for lack of refuge they cleave to the rocks.
They snatch the orphan from the breast, 9
And they take the infant of the poor as security.
Naked they go about, without clothing, 10
And hungry, they carry sheaves.
Within walls they make oil; 11
They tread the wine-presses, but are thirsty.
From the city the dying groan, 12
And those who are wounded call for help;
But God does not hear their prayer.

"They are enemies of the light; 13
They do not know its ways;
Nor do they dwell in its paths.
At daylight the murderer arises, 14
That he may kill the poor and needy;
And in the night he is like the thief.
The eye of the adulterer watches for the twilight, 15
Saying, 'No eye shall see me';
And he puts a veil over his face.
He digs through houses in the darkness; 16
By day they shut themselves up;
They do not know light.

17 Furthermore, midnight is morning to
them,
For they are acquainted with the terrors of midnight.
18 ["They are accursed in the sight of the
heavens;
Cursed is their portion in the earth.
No treader turns toward their vineyard.
19 Drought and heat snatch away snow
water;
So does Sheol those who have sinned.
20 The womb forgets him; the worm
sucks him;
He is no longer remembered;
And untruth is broken like a tree."]

21 "He feeds on the barren woman with
no child,
And he does no good to the widow.
22 He prolongs the life of the mighty by
his power;
He arises with no hope of life;
23 But he gives him confidence and he is
sustained;
And his eyes are upon their ways.

24 ["They are exalted for a little, and then
they are not;
They are brought low and like all things they are plucked off;
And like the top of the ear of grain they are cut off.]
25 If it is not so, then who will prove me
wrong,
And show my speech to be nothing?"

THE SPEECH OF BILDAD, 25:1–6; 26:5–14

25 Then Bildad, the Shuhite, replied,
saying,
2 "Dominion and fear are with him;
He dispenses prosperity in his high places.
3 Is there any limit to his troops?
And upon whom does not his light arise?
4 How can a man be justified with
God?
Or how can he be pure that is born of a woman?
5 Verily, even the moon does not shine
brightly,
Nor are the stars bright in his eyes.
How much less man that is a maggot,
And the son of man that is a worm.

"The shades quake,
The waters and their inhabitants underneath;
Sheol lies bare before him,
And Abaddon has no covering.
He stretches out the north over the void;
He hangs the earth upon nothing.
He binds up the water in his clouds,
And the cloud is not split under its weight.
He enclosed the front of his throne,
Spreading out his cloud over it.
He inscribed a circle upon the surface of the water,
Unto the limits of light and darkness.
The pillars of the heavens tottered,
And were dazed at his rebuke.
Through his power the sea was stilled,
And by his skill he smote through Rahab.
By his wind the skies were cleared;
His hand slew the fleeing serpent.

"Behold these are the outskirts of his way;
And how slight a whisper do we hear of him!
But the thunder of his power, who could comprehend?"

JOB'S REPLY TO BILDAD, 26:1–4; 27:1–6

Then Job replied, saying,
"How you have helped him that was powerless,
And saved the arm that was not strong!
How you have counselled him that was without wisdom,
And abundantly made known sound wisdom!
Whom have you told mere words,
And whose breath issued from you?"[1]
Then Job again took up his discourse, saying,
"As God lives, who has put away my right;
And the Almighty, who has embittered my spirit—
For all my breath is still in me,

[1] For 26:5–14, see on this page after 25:6.

And the breath of God is in my nostrils—
My lips do not speak untruth,
Nor my tongue utter deceit.
Far be it from me that I should justify you;
Till I die I will not put my integrity from me.
I will hold on to my innocence and will not let it go.
My conscience does not reproach any of my days."

THE SPEECH OF ZOPHAR (?), 27:7–23

"May my enemy be like the wicked,
And my adversary like the unjust.
For what is the hope of the irreligious when he cuts off,
When God takes away his life?
Will God hear his request,
When trouble comes upon him?
Does he delight in the Almighty?
Does he call upon God at all times?
I will teach you concerning the power of God;
What is with the Almighty I will not hide.
Indeed you yourselves have all seen;
Why, then, are you altogether vain?
This is the lot of a wicked man with God,
And the heritage which tyrants receive from the Almighty.
If his sons be many, they are for the sword;
And his offspring have not enough bread.
Those who survive him are buried in death,
And there will be no widows to weep.
Though he heap up silver like dust,
And prepare clothes like the clay;
He may prepare—but the righteous will wear it;
And silver—the pure will divide it.
He has built his house like a spider's web,
And like a booth that the watchman makes.
He lies down rich, but does so no more;
He opens his eyes, and it is gone.
Terrors overtake him like water;
A storm snatches him away in the night.
The sirocco picks him up and he goes,
And it whirls him away from his place;
Yea, it hurls itself at him unsparingly; 22
From its grasp he flees precipitately.
Men clench their fists at him, 23
And hiss him from his place."

THE PRAISE OF WISDOM, 28:1–28

"Surely there is a mine for silver, 28
And a place where they refine gold.
Iron is taken from the dust, 2
And from the stone copper is smelted.
Man sets an end to darkness, 3
And to the furthest bound he searches out
The ore from the blackness and dense darkness.
He breaks open a shaft far from the traveler; 4
In places forgotten by men's feet,
They hang far from men, they swing to and fro.
The earth—bread comes forth from it, 5
But underneath it is turned into what looks like fire.
Its stones are the source of sapphires, 6
And it has dust of gold.
The path to it no bird of prey knows, 7
Nor has the vulture's eye seen it.
The beasts of prey have not trodden it, 8
Nor has the lion passed over it.
Man puts forth his hand to the rocks; 9
He turns the mountains upside down.
He cleaves rivers in the rocks; 10
And all precious things his eye sees.
He binds up the streams that they do not flow, 11
And what is hidden he brings forth to the light.

"But where can wisdom be found? 12
And where is the place of understanding?
Man knows not the way of it, 13
Nor is it found in the land of the living.
The abyss says, 'It is not in me'; 14
And the sea says, 'It is not with me.'
Pure gold cannot be given for it, 15
Nor can silver be weighed out as its price.
It cannot be bought with gold of Ophir, 16
With precious onyx and sapphires.
Gold and glass cannot equal it, 17

Nor can articles of fine gold be exchanged for it.
18 No mention may be made of coral and crystal;
The acquisition of wisdom is above that of corals.
19 The topaz of Ethiopia does not equal it;
Nor can it be valued in terms of pure gold.
20 "Whence does wisdom come?
And where is the place of understanding?
21 It is hidden from the eyes of all the living,
And from the birds of the air it is concealed.
22 Abaddon and Death say,
'With our ears we have but heard the report of it.'
23 God understands its way,
And he knows its location.
24 For he looks to the ends of the earth;
Beneath the whole heavens he sees.
25 When he made a weight for the wind,
And meted out the waters by measure;
26 When he made a law for the rain,
And a way for the thunderbolt;
27 Then did he see it and declare it;
He established it and investigated it.
28 Then he said to man:
'Behold the fear of the Lord, that is wisdom;
And to depart from evil is understanding.'"

JOB'S REPLY TO ZOPHAR, 29:1—31:40

29 Then Job again took up his discourse and said:
2 "O that I were as in months of old,
As in the days when God guarded me;
3 When his lamp shone over my head,
And by its light I walked in darkness;
4 Even as I was in the days of my prime,
When the friendship of God was over my tent;
5 When the Almighty was still with me,
And my young ones were around me;
6 When my goings were bathed in curds,
And the rock poured out for me streams of oil.
7 When I went forth from my gate up to the city,
And prepared my seat in the square;
8 Young men saw me and withdrew,
And old men arose and stood;
Princes stopped talking,
And placed their hands upon their mouths;
The voice of the nobles was silent,
And their tongues clove to their palates.
For when the ear heard, it called me happy;
And when the eye saw, it testified for me:
That I delivered the poor who cried for help,
And the orphan, and him that had no helper.
The blessing of him that was ready to perish came upon me,
And the heart of the widow I made glad.
I put on righteousness, and it clothed me;
Like a robe and a turban was my justice.
Eyes was I to the blind,
And feet was I to the lame.
I was a father to the needy,
And I investigated the cause which I did not know.
I broke the talons of the wicked,
And I drew the prey out of his teeth.
And I said, 'I shall die with my nestlings,
And make my days as many as the sand;
My root open to the water,
And dew lying on my boughs,
My glory new with me,
And my bow renewed in my hand.'
For me men listened and waited,
And kept silence for my counsel;
After my speech, they did not reply,
And my word dropped upon them.
They waited for me as for the rain,
And opened their mouths as for the spring rain.
I laughed at them when they did not believe,
And the light of my countenance they could not cast down.
I chose their way and sat as chief,
And I dwelt like a king in a host,
Like one who comforts mourners.

"But now they laugh at me,
Those who are younger than I,
Whose fathers I disdained
To set with the dogs of my flock.
The strength of their hands, too—of what use is it to me?

Among them manly vigor has perished;
With want and hunger they are spent;
They gnaw the dry ground,
The source of dearth and desolation;
They pluck salt-wort by the bushes,
And their food is the root of the broom:
From the community they are driven forth—
Men cry out against them as against the thief—
To dwell in a gully of the valleys,
In holes of the earth and rocks;
Among the bushes they howl,
Beneath the scrub they huddle together.
Worthless and nameless,
They are scourged out of the land.

"And now, I am become their song,
And I am a by-word unto them.
They loathe me, they stay far from me,
They do not refrain from spitting in my face.
Because he has loosened my bowstring and humiliated me,
They have cast off restraint in my presence.
On the right they rise up in swarms,
And they grade up against me their ways of destruction.
They break up my path,
They help on my ruin—
Men who have no helper.
As through a wide breach they advance;
Under the crash they roll on.
Terrors are turned upon me;
My honor flees like the wind,
And like a cloud my welfare has passed away.
But now my grief pours itself out upon me;
The days of my trouble lay hold of me.
The night racks my bones from upon me;
And my bare bones cannot lie down.
With great force he seizes me by the clothing;
He lays hold of me by the neck of my tunic;
He hurls me into the mire;
And I am made like dust and ashes.

"I cry to thee for help, but thou dost not answer me;
I stand, and thou dost not heed me.
Thou art turned into one that is cruel to me; 21
With the strength of thy hand thou dost attack me.
Thou dost pick me up, on the wind thou dost cause me to ride, 22
And thou dost dissolve me in the uproar.
For I know that thou wilt turn me over to Death, 23
And to the house of assembly for all living.
Yet will not a man in trouble stretch forth his hand, 24
Or in his misfortune utter a cry for help because of such things?
I have certainly wept for him whose times were hard; 25
I was grieved for the needy.
But I hoped for good, and evil came, 26
And I waited for light, but darkness came.
My bowels rumble and are not silent; 27
The days of my affliction have come to meet me.
I go about in black, without the sun; 28
I arise in the assembly, calling for help.
I have been a brother to jackals, 29
And a companion of ostriches.
My skin has grown black upon me, 30
And my bones burn from the heat.
And my harp has become mourning, 31
And my flute the voice of those who weep.

"I imposed a rule on my eyes; **31**
How, then, could I give heed to a virgin?
And what is the portion of God from above, 2
And the heritage of the Almighty from the heights?
Is it not calamity for the unrighteous, 3
And disaster for wrong-doers?
Does he not see my ways, 4
And number all my steps?
If I walk with falsehood, 5
And my foot hastens toward deceit—
Let him weigh me in just scales, 6
And may God know my integrity!—
If my step turn from the way, 7
And my heart walk after my eyes,
And a spot stick to my hands;
May I sow, but another eat; 8
And may my crops be uprooted!

"If my heart be enticed after a woman, 9
And I lie in wait at the door of my friend;

10 May my wife grind for another man,
And may others bend over her!
11 For that is a crime,
And it is a heinous sin.
12 For it is a fire that would devour unto
Abaddon;
And it would uproot all my increase.

13 "If I set at nought the cause of my
male or female slave
When they strove with me;
14 Then what shall I do when God
arises?
And when he inquires, what can I answer him?
15 Did not he who made me in the womb
make him?
And did not one prepare us in the
womb?

16 "If I withheld ought from the desire of
the poor,
And caused the eyes of the widow to
grow dim;
17 Or ate my portion alone,
And the orphan did not eat of it—
18 For from my youth he reared me like
a father,
And from my mother's body he led
me—
19 If I saw any perishing for lack of
clothing,
And there was no covering for the
needy;
20 If his loins did not bless me,
And from the fleece of my sheep he did
not keep himself warm;
21 If I shook my fist at the orphan,
Because I saw my help in the gate;
22 May my shoulder-blade drop from the
shoulder,
And my arm be broken from the
socket.
23 For calamity from God was a terror
to me,
And because of his majesty I was powerless.
24 If I made gold my confidence,
And called fine gold my trust;
25 If I rejoiced because my wealth was
great,
Or because my hand came upon great
riches;
26 If I looked upon the great light when
it shone,
Or the moon moving along majestically,
27 And my heart was secretly seduced,
And my hand kissed my mouth;

That too were a heinous crime,
For I had been false to God on high.

"If I rejoiced at the calamity of hin
who hated me,
And was elated when evil came upor
him—
I did not let my palate sin
By calling down curses upon him.
Verily the men of my household said
'Is there anyone that has not beer
satisfied with his meat?'
The stranger did not lodge in th
street;
I opened my doors to the wayfarer.

"If I covered up my transgression
from men,
Hiding my guilt in my bosom;
Because I dreaded the great crowd,
And the contempt of the clans terri
fied me,
So that I was silent, not going fortl
from the door—

"O that one would listen to me!
Here is my signature! Let the Al
mighty answer me!
And the scroll which my opponent ha
written—
Surely I would carry it upon my
shoulder;
I would wind it around me as my dia
dem.
The number of my steps I would de
clare;
Like a prince would I present it.

"If my land cried out against me,
And its furrows also wept;
If I ate its product without paying,
And snuffed out the life of its owners
Instead of wheat, let thorns grow up
And weeds instead of barley."

The words of Job are finished.

THE INTERLUDE OF ELIHU, 32:1—37:24

Then these three men ceased answer
ering Job, because he was righteous i
his own eyes. Then the anger of Elihu
the son of Barachel, the Buzite, of th
clan of Ram, blazed up; against Job hi
anger blazed, because he held himself i
the right, rather than God. An
against his three friends his wrat

blazed, because they had found no answer, and so had put God in the wrong.
Now Elihu had waited for Job while they were speaking, because they were older than he; but when Elihu saw that there was no answer in the mouth of the three men, his anger blazed up.

THE FIRST SPEECH OF ELIHU, 32:6—33:33

Then Elihu, the son of Barachel, the Buzite, replied, saying:
"I am of few days, while you are aged;
Therefore I feared and was afraid
To show you my knowledge.
I thought days should speak,
And many years should teach wisdom.
However, it is a spirit in man,
And the breath of the Almighty, that makes them intelligent;
It is not the old that are wise,
Nor the elders who understand justice.
Therefore I say 'Hear me;
I will declare my knowledge, even I.'

"Behold, I waited for your words,
I listened for your wisdom,
Until you should find words;
And unto you I gave heed.
But lo, there was not one to confute Job,
Not one of you to answer his words.
Lest you say, 'We have met with wisdom;
God may rout him, not man';
He has not arrayed words against me;
And with your arguments I will not answer him.

"They are dismayed; they answer no more;
Words have failed them.
And am I to wait, because they do not speak,
Because they stop, and answer no more?
I also will answer my share,
I too will declare my knowledge.
For I am full of words;
The spirit within me constrains me.
Behold, my bosom is like wine that has no vent;
Like skins of new wine it is ready to burst.
Let me speak, that I may get relief;
Let me open my lips, and reply.

"Let me not be partial toward anybody,
Nor flatter any man;
For I do not know how to flatter, 22
Else would my Maker soon take me away.

"But hear now, O Job, my words, 33
And listen to all my sayings.
Lo now, I have opened my mouth; 2
My tongue in my palate has spoken.
My words are straight from my heart, 3
And the knowledge of my lips they speak sincerely.
The spirit of God made me, 4
And the breath of the Almighty gave me life.
If you can, answer me; 5
Draw up before me; take your position.
Behold, I am just like you with God; 6
From clay I too was nipped off.
Lo, dread of me will not overwhelm you; 7
Nor will care of me be heavy upon you.

"Yet you have said in my hearing, 8
And I heard the sound of the words:
'I am pure, without transgression; 9
Clean am I, and without guilt.
Behold, he finds pretexts against me; 10
He holds me as his enemy.
He sets my feet in the stocks, 11
He watches all my paths.'

"But in this you are not right; I will answer you; 12
For God is greater than man.
Why do you make accusations against him, 13
That 'he answers none of my arguments'?
For God speaks in one way, 14
And in two, though one heeds it not.
In a dream, a vision of the night, 15
When sound sleep falls upon men,
In slumbers upon the bed;
Then he uncovers the ear of men, 16
And seals up their instruction,
To remove man from toil, 17
And to withhold deep grief from man;
That he may hold him back from the Pit, 18
And his life from passing into Sheol.
And he is chastened with pain upon his bed, 19
And the strife of his bones is perpetual;
So his life loathes bread, 20
And his appetite the daintiest food.
His flesh wastes away out of sight, 21
And bare are his bones past seeing.

22 And so he himself draws near to the Pit,
And his life to the destroyers.

23 "If there be by him an angel,
A mediator, one of a thousand,
To declare to man what is his right;
24 And if he be gracious to him, and say:
'Deliver him from going down into the Pit;
I have found a ransom;
25 Let his flesh become fresher than a child's,
Let him return to the days of his youth';
26 Then he prays to God and he accepts him,
And he sees his face with joy,
And he restores to a man his righteousness.
27 He sings to men and says:
'I sinned and I distorted that which was straight,
And he did not requite it to me.
28 He rescued me from going down into the Pit,
And my life gazes upon the light.'

29 "Lo, all such things does God do
Twice, three times with a man;
30 To turn him back from the Pit,
That he may see the light of life.
31 Give heed Job; listen to me,
Be silent, while I speak.
32 If you have anything to say, answer me;
Speak, for I desire to acquit you.
33 If not, then do you listen to me;
Keep silent, that I may teach you wisdom."

ELIHU'S SECOND SPEECH,
34:1–37

34 Then Elihu replied, saying:
2 "Hear, O wise men, my words,
And you learned ones, give ear to me—
3 For the ear should test words,
Even as the palate tastes food—
4 Let us choose for ourselves what is right,
Let us know among us what is good.
5 For Job says, 'I am innocent,
And God has taken away my right.
6 Against my right shall I lie?
Incurable is my wound, though I am not at fault.'
7 "What man is there like Job?
He drinks up scorn like water!
And he walks in company with doers of evil,
And goes with wicked men.
For he says, 'A man gains nothing
By being on good terms with God.'

"Therefore, O men of understanding, hear me:
Far be it from God to do wickedness,
And from the Almighty to do wrong.
But a man's work he requites to him,
And he makes it befall each according to his way.
Of a surety then God does not falsify,
And the Almighty does not distort the right.

"Who gave him authority over the earth?
And who gave him charge of the whole world?
If he were to withdraw his spirit to himself,
And to gather in his breath to himself,
All flesh would expire at once,
And man would return to the dust.

"If you have insight, hear this;
Give ear to the sound of my words.
Can one who hates right govern?
Or can you declare guilty the mighty just one;
Him who says to a king, 'You villain!'
And to nobles, 'You wicked!'
Him who is not partial to princes,
Who does not favor the prosperous above the poor;
For they are all the work of his hands?

"In a moment they die, and in the middle of the night
People are shaken violently and pass away;
The mighty are removed by an unseen hand.
For his eyes are upon the ways of a man,
And all his steps he sees.
There is no darkness and no dense blackness
Where doers of evil can hide themselves.
For he does not set a stated time for a man
To go unto God in judgment.

"He breaks down the mighty, without investigation,
And he sets others in their place.

Therefore he knows their works,
And overturns them in the night and they are crushed.
He shatters the wicked;
He smites them in the sight of the public.
Because they turned aside from following him,
And heeded none of his ways;
That they might cause the cry of the poor to come unto him,
And he might hear the cry of the needy.

"If he keep quiet, who can condemn?
And if he hide his face, who can see him?
He watches over a nation and over man alike,
Setting up a godless man as king,
Because of the stubbornness of the people.

"For unto God has he said,
'Forgive me, I will not act wickedly;
In addition to what I see, do thou teach me;
If I have done wrong, I will do so no more'?
Will he requite it according to your standard,
That you reject it?
For you must choose, and not I;
And what you know, declare.

"Men of understanding will say to me,
And a wise man who listens to me:
'Job speaks without knowledge,
And his words are without discernment.'
Would that Job might be tried unto the end,
For his answers among wicked men.
For he adds rebellion unto his sin;
He clenches his fists at us,
And he multiplies his charges against God."

ELIHU'S THIRD SPEECH, 35:1–16

Then Elihu replied, saying:
"Do you consider this to be just,
Do you say, 'It is my righteousness before God'?
That you say, 'What does it profit me?
What do I gain more than if I had sinned'?

"I will answer you with words, 4
And your friends along with you.
Look to the heavens, and see; 5
And gaze upon the clouds—they are higher than you!
If you have sinned, how does it affect him? 6
And if your offenses be many, what do you do to him?
If you are righteous, what do you give to him? 7
Or what does he take from your hand?
Your wickedness concerns a man like yourself, 8
And your righteousness, a human being.

"Because of many deeds of oppression men cry out; 9
They call for help because of the strength of the mighty.
And nobody has said, 'Where is God my Maker, 10
Who gives songs in the night,
Who teaches us more than the beasts of the earth, 11
And makes us wiser than the birds of the air?'
Then they cry, but he does not answer, 12
Because of the pride of the wicked.

"But God will not hear falsehood, 13
Nor will the Almighty look upon it.
How much less when you say you do not behold him; 14
The case is before him, and you wait for him.
And now because his anger does not punish, 15
And he does not notice folly much,
Job opens his mouth emptily, 16
He multiplies words without knowledge."

ELIHU'S FOURTH SPEECH,

36:1—37:24

Then Elihu spoke again: 36
"Wait for me a little, that I may show you 2
That there are still things to be said in God's behalf,
I will fetch my knowledge from afar, 3
And ascribe righteousness to my Maker.
For of a truth my words are not false; 4
One who is perfect in knowledge is with you.

5 "Lo, God is mighty and does not despise,
Mighty in strength of understanding.
6 He will not keep the wicked alive,
And he grants the right of the poor.
7 He does not withdraw his eyes from the righteous,
But with kings on the throne
He makes them sit forever, and they are exalted.

8 "And if they be bound in chains,
And be caught in the cords of trouble,
9 Then he makes known to them their works,
And their transgressions, that they magnify themselves.
10 And he uncovers their ear to instruction,
And commands that they turn from wrong.

11 "If they hear and serve him,
They fulfil their days in prosperity and their years in pleasure.
12 But if they do not hear, they pass away into Sheol,
And they expire without knowledge.
13 The impious in heart lay up anger;
They do not call for help when he chastises them.
14 They die in youth,
And their life ends prematurely.

15 "He rescues the poor through his poverty,
And uncovers their ear through oppression.
16 Furthermore, he enticed you from the mouth of straits,
And instead, you have unlimited room,
And your table is filled with fat.
17 And you are full of the judgment on the wicked,
Judgment and justice lay hold of you.

18 "But beware, lest he allure you with riches,
And let not a heavy bribe mislead you.
19 Will your wealth that is without stint avail,
Or all your reinforcements of strength?
20 Long not for the night,
That peoples may go up in their place.
21 Be careful that you turn not to wrong;
Because for this you were tried by suffering.

22 "Lo, God is exalted in his might;
Who is a teacher like him?
Who has ever appointed unto him his way?
Or who has said, 'Thou hast done injustice'?
Remember that you extol his work,
Whereof men have sung.
All men have beheld it,
Man looks upon it from afar.

"Lo, God is exalted, and we cannot know;
The number of his years is unsearchable.
For he draws up the drops of water;
They pour out as rain in his flood,
Which the clouds pour down;
They drop down upon many men.
Can anyone understand the spreading out of the clouds,
The crashings of his covert?

"Lo, he spreads his mist about him,
And covers the tops of the mountains.
For therewith he judges peoples;
He gives food in abundance.
He covers his two hands with lightning,
And commands it concerning the mark.
The thunder declares regarding him,
The cattle also concerning what is coming up.

"At this also my heart is disturbed,
And leaps from its place.
Listen closely to the roar of his voice,
And the rumbling that goes forth from his mouth.
Beneath the whole heavens he flashes,
And his lightning reaches the corners of the earth.
After it, a sound roars;
He thunders with his majestic voice;
And he delays them not when his voice is heard.

"God thunders with his wondrous voice,
Doing great things that we cannot understand.
For he commands the snow, 'Fall to the earth,'
The downpour and the rain, 'Be strong.'
He seals up the hand of every man,
That all men may know his work.
Then the wild beast goes into its lair,
And dwells in its dens.

"From the South comes the whirlwind;
And from the North, the ice.

10 By the breath of God ice is formed,
And the broad waters are congealed.
11 Also with moisture he loads the cloud;
He scatters abroad his lightning-cloud.
12 And they encircle and turn about by his guidance,
That they may do all that he commands them,
Upon the surface of the populous earth;
13 Whether it be for chastisement to the earth,
Or for kindness, that he causes it to find its mark.

14 "Give ear to this, O Job;
Stand still and consider the wonders of God.
15 Do you know when God does his work,
And causes the light of his cloud to shine?
16 Do you know regarding the balancings of the cloud,
The wonders of the one perfect in knowledge?
17 You whose clothes are hot,
When the earth is still because of the southwind,
18 Can you beat out with him the skies,
Hard as a molten mirror?

19 "Tell us what we shall say to him!
We cannot draw up a statement because of darkness!
20 Shall it be told him that I am speaking?
Or if a man talk will he be swallowed up?
21 And now men saw not the light;
It was obscure in the skies;
But the wind passed over and cleared them.
22 From the north golden brightness comes;
Over God splendor appears.
23 But we have not found the Almighty;
Great is he in strength and justice;
And abounding in righteousness, he will not afflict.
24 Therefore do men fear him;
He does not consider any that are wise of heart."

JOB'S INTERVIEW WITH THE LORD, 38:1—42:6

THE FIRST ADDRESS OF THE LORD, 38:1—39:30

Then the LORD answered Job from the whirlwind, saying,

"Who is this that obscures counsel 2
By words without knowledge?
Gird up, now, your loins like a man, 3
That I may question you, and do you instruct me.

"Where were you when I laid the foundations of the earth? 4
Declare, if you have insight.
Who fixed its measurements, for you should know? 5
Or who stretched a line over it?
Upon what were its bases sunk, 6
Or who laid its cornerstone,
When the morning stars sang together, 7
And all the heavenly beings shouted for joy?

"Who enclosed the sea with doors, 8
When it burst forth, issuing from the womb,
When I made the cloud its covering, 9
And dense darkness its swaddling-band;
When I imposed upon it my decree, 10
And established its barrier and doors;
And said, 'Thus far shall you come and no farther, 11
And here shall your proud waves be stayed'?

"Have you ever in your life commanded the morning? 12
Or assigned its place to the dawn,
That it should lay hold of the corners of the earth, 13
And the wicked be shaken out of it?
It changes like clay under the seal, 14
And is dyed like a garment.
Their light is withdrawn from the wicked, 15
And the arm of the proud is broken.

"Have you gone to the sources of the sea, 16
Or walked in the hollows of the deep?
Have the gates of death been revealed to you, 17
Or can you see the gates of darkness?
Have you considered the breadth of the earth? 18
Tell, if you know all this.

"Which is the way where light dwells, 19
And which is the place of darkness,
That you may take it to its border, 20
And that you may perceive the paths to its home?

21 You know, for you were born then,
And the number of your days is great!
22 "Have you been to the storehouses of snow,
Or do you see the storehouses of hail,
23 Which I have reserved against the time of distress,
Against the day of war and battle?
24 Which is the way to where light is distributed?
Where does the east wind spread itself over the earth?
25 Who cleaved its channel for the torrent,
And a way for the thunderbolts,
26 To send rain on a land without people,
On the steppe where there is no man;
27 To satisfy the waste ground and desolate,
And to cause the blade of grass to spring up?

28 "Has the rain a father?
Or who brought forth the dew drops?
29 From whose womb did the ice come forth?
And who gave birth to the hoarfrost of the skies,
30 When the waters congeal like a stone,
And the surface of the deep is frozen solid?

31 "Can you bind the chains of the Pleiades,
Or loosen the girdle of Orion?
32 Can you send forth Mazzaroth in its season,
And lead forth the Bear with its satellites?
33 Do you know the laws of the heavens?
Or do you appoint the arrangements of the earth?
34 Can you lift your voice up to the clouds,
That a flood of waters may cover you?

35 "Can you send forth the lightnings that they may go
And say to you, 'Here we are!'
36 Who put wisdom in the inner parts,
Or who gave insight to the mind?
37 Who counts the clouds by wisdom?
And who tilts the waterskins of the heavens,
38 When the dust runs into a mass,
And the clods stick together?

39 "Do you hunt prey for the lioness,
Or satisfy the hunger of young lions,
When they crouch in dens,
Or lie in wait in the thicket?
Who provides its prey for the raven,
When its young ones cry unto God,
And wander without food?

"Do you know the time when the mountain-goats bear young?
Do you watch the travail of the does?
Do you number the months that they fulfil,
And know the time that they bear,
When they kneel down, bring forth their young,
Deliver their offspring?
Their young are robust, they grow up in the open,
They go forth, and do not return to them.

"Who sent forth the wild ass free?
And who loosened the bonds of the mustang,
Whose range I made the steppe,
And his dwellings the salt-marshes?
He laughs at the roar of the city;
The shouts of the driver he does not hear.
He explores the mountains, his pasture,
And searches after everything green.

"Is the wild-ox willing to serve you?
Or will he pass the night at your crib?
Can you bind the wild-ox to the furrow with cords,
Or will he harrow the valleys after you?
Do you trust in him because his strength is great?
And do you leave your hard-won gains to him?
Do you rely on him, that he will return your grain,
And gather it to the threshing-floor?

"Is the wing of the ostrich joyful,
Or has she a kindly pinion and feathers,
That she leaves her eggs on the ground,
And warms them on the dust,
And forgets that the foot may crush them,
Or the beast of the field trample them?
She is hard on her young as though not her own;
For nothing is her labor; she has no anxiety.
For God has made her oblivious of wisdom,

And has not given her a share in understanding.
When she flaps her wings aloft,
She laughs at the horse and his rider.

"Can you give strength to the horse?
Can you clothe his neck with power?
Do you make him leap like the locust,
With majesty and terrible snorting?
They paw in the valley and exult in strength,
Going forth to meet the battle.
He laughs at terror and is not frightened;
Nor does he turn back from the sword.
Against him rattles the quiver,
The flashing spear and the javelin.
In quivering excitement he devours the ground,
And does not stand firm when there is the sound of the trumpet.
As often as the trumpet sounds he says 'Aha';
And smells the battle from afar,
The thunder of the captains and the war-cry.

"Is it by your understanding that the hawk soars,
And spreads his wings toward the south?
Or does the vulture fly high at your command,
When he sets his nest aloft?
He occupies the cliff and makes a lodging
Upon the peak of the cliff and the rocky hold.
Thence he searches for food;
His eyes look afar off.
His brood gorge themselves with blood,
And wherever the slain are, there are they."

THE SECOND ADDRESS OF THE LORD, 40:1, 2

1 Then the LORD answered Job, saying:
2 "Will the fault-finder argue with the Almighty?
He who chides God, let him answer for it."

JOB'S SUBMISSION, 40:3–5

3 Then Job replied to the LORD, saying:
"Behold, I am insignificant; what can I answer thee? 4
I put my hand over my mouth.
I have spoken once, and I will not reply; 5
Yes, twice; but not again."

THE CLOSING ADDRESS OF THE LORD, 40:6—41:34

Then the LORD answered Job from the tempest, saying: 6
"Gird up your loins, now, like a man; 7
I will ask you, and do you instruct me.
Will you, indeed, break down my right? 8
Will you make me guilty that you may be innocent?
Or have you an arm like God, 9
And can you thunder with a voice like his?
Deck yourself, now, with majesty and eminence, 10
And clothe yourself with glory and splendor.
Scatter abroad the rage of your wrath; 11
And look upon everyone that is proud and abase him.
Look upon everyone who is proud and bring him low; 12
And crush the wicked where they stand.
Bury them in the dust likewise; 13
Bind up their faces in the hidden place.
Then I indeed will praise you, 14
That your own right hand can deliver you.

"Behold, now, the hippopotamus which I made along with you; 15
He eats grass like the ox.
Behold, now, his strength in his loins, 16
And his might in the muscles of his body.
He stiffens his tail like a cedar; 17
The sinews of his thighs are knit together.
His bones are tubes of bronze; 18
His limbs are like bars of iron.
He is the chief of the ways of God; 19
Let him who made him bring near his sword!
For the mountains bring him their produce, 20
And all the beasts of the field play there.
Beneath the lotus bushes he lies down, 21

In the depths of reed and swamp.
22 The lotus bushes screen him as his shade;
The willows of the brook surround him.
23 If the river press upon him, he is not disturbed;
He is confident when the Jordan swells to his mouth.
24 Can one seize him by his eyes?
Can one pierce his nose with traps?

1 "Can you draw up the crocodile with a fish-hook,
Or can you press down his tongue with a cord?
2 Can you put a rush-line through his nose,
Or pierce his jaw with a hook?
3 Will he make many entreaties to you,
Or will he speak soft words to you?
4 Will he make a bargain with you,
That you may take him as a servant for life?
5 Can you play with him as with a bird,
And bind him for your maidens?
6 Will traders bargain over him?
Will they divide him among merchants?
7 Will you stick his hide full of darts,
Or his head full of harpoons?
8 Lay your hand upon him;
Think of the struggle; you will not do it again!
9 Behold his hope is disappointed.
At the very sight of him he is laid prostrate.
10 Is he not too fierce for one to stir him up?
Who then is he that can stand before me?
11 Who has ever come before me that I should repay him?
Whatever is under the whole heavens is mine.
12 I will not be silent about his limbs,
And the account of his power and the grace of his structure.
13 Who has stripped off his outer clothing?
Who can come within his double coat-of-mail?
14 Who has ever opened the doors of his face?
Round about his teeth there is terror.
15 His back is made of rows of shields,
Closed up like a tight seal;
16 One is so close to another
That no air can come between them;
Each sticks to his fellow;
They cling together and cannot be separated.
His sneezing flashes forth light,
And his eyes are like the eyelids of the dawn.
From his mouth flames go forth,
Sparks of fire escape.
From his nostrils smoke comes forth,
Like a pot on a blown fire and rushes.
His breath kindles live coals,
And flame goes out of his mouth.
Strength dwells in his neck,
And before him despair dances.
The flakes of his flesh cleave together,
Firm upon him and immovable.
His heart is hard like a stone,
Hard as a nether mill-stone.
When he rises up the gods fear;
Because of panic they are beside themselves.
When one approaches him with the sword it does not hold,
Nor does the spear, the javelin, or the dart.
He estimates iron as but straw,
And bronze as rotten wood.
The arrow does not put him to flight;
Sling-stones are turned to chaff for him.
The bludgeon is reckoned as but chaff,
And he laughs at the whiz of the lance.
His lower parts are like sharp potsherds;
He prints a threshing-sledge upon the mud.
He makes the deep boil like a pot;
He makes the sea like a jar of ointment.
Behind him he makes a shining path;
One would think that the deep was hoary.
There is not his like upon earth,
One made without fear.
Everything that is high fears him,
Who is king over all proud beings."

JOB'S RETRACTION, 42:1–6

Then Job replied to the LORD, saying:
"I know that thou canst do all things;
And no plan is too difficult for thee.
[Who is this who hides counsel without knowledge?]
Therefore I have declared, without understanding,
Things too wonderful for me, without knowing.

4 [Listen now, while I speak;
I will question you, and do you instruct me.]
5 I had heard of thee by the hearing of the ear;
But now my eye has seen thee.
6 Therefore I retract and repent,
In dust and ashes."

THE EPILOGUE, 42:7–16

7 After the LORD had spoken these
words to Job, then the LORD said to
Eliphaz, the Temanite,
"My anger blazes against you and
your two friends, because you have not
spoken regarding me what is true, as
8 my servant Job has. So now take for
yourselves seven bullocks and seven
rams, and go to my servant Job, and
offer up a burnt-offering for yourselves,
and my servant Job will pray for you;
for his plea will I accept, that I deal not
harshly with you, because you have not
spoken regarding me what is true, as
my servant Job has."
9 Then Eliphaz, the Temanite, and
Bildad, the Shuhite, and Zophar, the
Naamathite, went and did as the LORD
had told them; and the LORD accepted
the plea of Job.
Then the LORD restored the fortune 10
of Job when he interceded for his
friends; and the LORD doubled all Job's
possessions. And all his brothers and 11
all his sisters and all his friends came to
him as of old, and they did eat food
with him in his house; and they consoled him and comforted him for all the
misfortune that the LORD had brought
upon him. And they gave him each a
piece of gold and each a golden ring.
So the LORD blessed the end of Job 12
more than his beginning; and he came
to have fourteen thousand sheep, and
six thousand camels, and a thousand
yoke of oxen, and a thousand she-asses.
And he had seven sons and three daugh- 13
ters. He named the first Jemimah, the 14
second Kezia, and the third Keren-
happuch. There were not found women 15
as fair as the daughters of Job in all the
land. And their father gave them a
heritage among their brothers.
Thereafter Job lived one hundred 16
and forty years, so that he saw his sons
and his sons' sons, four generations. So
Job died, an old man, satisfied with life.

THE PSALMS

BOOK I, PSS. 1–41

THE PROSPERITY OF THE PIOUS

1 HOW happy is the man who has not walked in the counsel of the wicked,
Nor stood in the way of sinners,
Nor sat in the seat of scoffers!
2 But his delight is in the law of the LORD,
And in his law does he study day and night.
3 For he is like a tree planted by streams of water,
That yields its fruit in its season,
And whose leaf does not wither;
And whatever it bears comes to maturity.

4 The wicked are not so;
But are like the chaff which the wind drives away.
5 Therefore the wicked will not stand in the judgment,
Nor sinners in the assembly of the righteous.
6 For the LORD knows the way of the righteous.
But the way of the wicked will perish.

A WARNING TO THE NATIONS

2 Why do the nations rage,
And the peoples plot in vain?
2 The kings of the earth stand up,
And the princes also take counsel,
Against the LORD and against his anointed:
3 "Let us burst their bonds asunder,
And cast their cords from us."
4 He that sits in the heavens laughs;
The Lord makes sport of them.
5 Then will he speak to them in his wrath,
And terrify them in his fury:
6 "I, indeed, have anointed my king
On Zion, my holy hill."

7 Let me tell of the decree of the LORD:
He said to me, "You are my son;
Today have I begotten you.
Ask of me, and I will make the nations your inheritance,
And the ends of the earth your possession.
You shall break them with an iron rod;
You shall crush them like a potter's vessel."

Be cautious, therefore, O kings;
Take warning, O rulers of the earth.
Serve the LORD with fear,
Kiss the chosen one,
Lest he be angry and you perish in the way;
For his wrath is soon kindled.
How happy are they who take refuge in him!

AN ASSURANCE OF DIVINE DELIVERANCE

[A psalm of David when he fled from before his son Absalom]

How many are my foes, O LORD!
Many are rising up against me.
Many are saying concerning me:
"There is no help for him in God."
Selah

But thou, O LORD, art a shield about me,
My glory, and the one who raises my head.
I cry aloud to the LORD,
And he answers me from his holy hill.
Selah

I lie down and sleep;
I awake, for the LORD sustains me.
I am not afraid of the myriads of people
That have beset me round about.

Arise, O LORD; deliver me, O my God.
Verily, thou wilt smite all my foes upon the cheek;
Thou wilt break the teeth of the wicked.
Salvation belongs unto the LORD.
Upon thy people be thy blessing!
Selah

A HYMN OF FAITH

[To the director: with harps. A Psalm of David]

4 When I call, answer me, O God of my righteousness,
Thou who didst give me room when I was in distress;
Be gracious unto me and hear my prayer.
2 O sons of men, how long is my glory to be a shame,
While you love a thing of nought
And seek after lies? *Selah*

3 But know that the LORD has set apart the godly for himself;
The LORD will hear when I cry unto him.
4 Tremble, and do not sin;
Commune with your own hearts upon your bed and be still. *Selah*

5 Offer righteous sacrifices,
And trust in the LORD.
6 There are many who say, "O that we might see some good!"
Lift up upon us the light of thy countenance, O LORD.
7 Thou hast put joy in my heart,
More than in the time that their grain and wine increase.
8 In peace will I both lie down and sleep;
For thou alone, O LORD, makest me dwell in safety.

A PRAYER FOR DIVINE AID

[To the director: for the flutes. A Psalm of David]

5 Give ear to my words, O LORD;
Attend to my sighing.
2 Give heed to the sound of my cry,
My king and my God;
For unto thee do I pray, O LORD.
3 In the morning thou wilt hear my voice;
In the morning I will lay it before thee and wait.

4 For thou art not a God that takes pleasure in wickedness;
Nor may evil dwell with thee.
5 The boastful may not stand before thine eyes;
Thou hatest all that do wrong.
6 Thou destroyest those who tell lies;
The LORD abhors the man of blood and deceit.
But I shall enter thy house by thine abundant kindness; 7
I shall bow down toward thy holy temple in awe of thee.
O LORD, lead me in thy righteousness, because of my enemies; 8
Make thy way straight before me.
For there is nothing trustworthy in their mouth, their heart is treacherous. 9
Their throat is an open sepulcher; with their tongue they flatter.

Condemn them, O God, that they may fall by their own devices; 10
Because of their many transgressions cast them out because they have rebelled against thee;
That all who take refuge in thee may rejoice and shout for joy forever; 11
And do thou protect them, that those who love thy name may exult in thee.
For thou dost bless the righteous, O LORD; 12
Thou dost surround him with favor as with a shield.

A PRAYER FOR RELIEF FROM FOES

[To the director: with stringed instruments; according to the *sheminith*. A Psalm of David]

Chide me not in thine anger, O LORD, 6
Neither chasten me in thy wrath.
Pity me, O LORD, for I am faint; 2
Heal me, O LORD, for my bones are shaken,
And my spirit is greatly shaken. 3
And thou, O LORD—how long?

Return, O LORD, and deliver me, 4
Save me because of thy kindness;
For in death there is no remembrance of thee. 5
In Sheol who praises thee?
I am worn out with my moaning; 6
Every night I flood my bed with tears;
With my weeping I water my couch.
My eye is dimmed because of trouble, 7
It grows old because of all my foes.

Depart from me, all evildoers; 8
For the LORD has heard the sound of my weeping.
The LORD has heard my entreaty; 9
The LORD receives my prayer.

10 All my foes shall be ashamed and greatly terrified;
They shall turn back; they shall be suddenly ashamed.

A PLEA FOR JUSTICE

[A *dithyramb* of David which he sang to the Lord concerning Cush, a Benjaminite]

7 I have taken shelter in thee, O LORD, my God.
Save me from all who pursue me, and deliver me;
2 Lest like a lion they tear me,
Dragging me away, with none to rescue.
3 O LORD, my God, if I have done this,
If there is guilt on my hands,
4 If I have requited evil to my friend,
Or plundered him that was my enemy without cause,
5 May the enemy pursue me,
And overtake me, and trample my life to the earth;
May he lay my honor in the dust.
Selah
6 Arise, O LORD, in thine anger,
Lift up thyself in wrath against my foes,
And rise up for me at the judgment thou hast appointed.
7 And surround thyself with the assembly of the peoples,
And return thou thereon to the heights.
8 The LORD judges the peoples: do me justice, O LORD,
In accordance with my righteousness and my integrity.

9 May the evil of the wicked come to an end, and establish thou the righteous,
Since he who tries heart and mind is the righteous God.
10 My shield is with God,
Who saves the upright in heart.
11 God is a just judge,
And a God who is angry daily.

12 He will surely whet his sword again;
He has bent his bow and aimed it.
13 And he has got ready his deadly weapons;
His arrows he turns into fiery shafts.
14 Behold, he conceives wrong,
And he is pregnant with mischief and brings forth lies.
15 He digs and excavates a pit;
But falls into the hole that he makes.
His mischief recoils upon his own head; 16
And upon his own pate his villainy descends.
I will praise the LORD for his righteousness, 17
And sing praises to the name of the LORD most high.

THE DIGNITY OF MAN AND THE GLORY OF GOD

[To the director: upon *Gittith*. A Psalm of David]

O LORD, our Lord, 8
How glorious is thy name in all the earth!
Thou whose praise is sung to the heavens,
From the mouths of babes and infants. 2
Thou hast established strength because of thine enemies,
To still the enemy and the revengeful.

When I see thy heavens, the work of thy fingers, 3
The moon and the stars which thou hast formed;
What is man that thou shouldst think of him, 4
And the son of man that thou shouldst care for him?

Yet thou hast made him but little lower than God, 5
And dost crown him with glory and honor!
Thou makest him ruler over the works of thy hands, 6
Thou hast put all things under his feet:

All sheep and oxen, 7
And also the beasts of the field;
The birds of the heavens and the fish of the sea, 8
That traverse the paths of the seas.

O LORD, our Lord, 9
How glorious is thy name in all the earth.

THE WICKED SHALL BE OVERTHROWN

[To the director: upon *muth-labben*. A Psalm of David]

א

I will praise the LORD with all my heart; 9

I will tell of all thy wonders.
2 I will rejoice and exult in thee,
I will sing praises to thy name, O Most High;

ב

3 Because my enemies turn back,
They stumble and perish from before thee.
4 For thou hast maintained my just cause;
Thou hast sat upon the throne giving righteous judgment.

ג

5 Thou hast rebuked the nations, thou hast destroyed the wicked,
Their name thou hast blotted out forever and ever.
6 The foe—they are destroyed;
Perpetual ruins are the cities which thou hast rooted up;
The very memory of them has perished.

ה

7 Behold, the LORD abides forever.
He has established his throne for judgment;
8 And he judges the world in righteousness;
He passes sentence on peoples with equity.

ו

9 Thus the LORD is a stronghold for the oppressed,
A stronghold in times of need.
10 And those who know thy name trust in thee,
For thou hast not forsaken those who seek thee, O LORD.

ז

11 Sing praises to the LORD who dwells in Zion;
Make known among the peoples his deeds!
12 For as avenger of blood he has remembered them;
He has not forgotten the cry of the poor.

ח

13 Have pity on me, O LORD; see my trouble from those who hate me,
O thou my deliverer from the gates of death,
14 That I may recount all thy praises,
That in the gates of the daughter of Zion I may rejoice in thy deliverance.

ט

The nations are plunged into the pit which they have made; 15
Their foot is caught in the net which they have hidden.
The LORD is made known; he has executed judgment. 16
In his own handiwork the wicked is snared. *Higgaion. Selah*

י

The wicked will return to Sheol, 17
All the nations that forget God.

כ

For the poor shall not be always forgotten, 18
Nor shall the hope of the meek perish forever.
Arise, O LORD, let not man prevail; 19
Let the nations be judged in thy presence.
Put them in terror, O LORD, 20
That the nations may know they are but men. *Selah*

ל

Why dost thou stand afar off, O LORD, 10
And hide thyself in times of need?
The wicked in his arrogance consumes the poor; 2
May they be caught in the schemes which they have devised!

The wicked sings the praises of his own desires, 3
And the robber curses, and rejects God;
The wicked in the pride of his countenance does not seek him; 4
All his thought is, "There is no God."
His ways prosper at all times. 5
Thy judgments are on high, out of his sight
As for all his foes,—he puffs at them.
He says to himself, "I shall not be moved; 6
Throughout the ages my steps will not be in distress."
His mouth is filled with curses and deceit and violence; 7
Mischief and wrong are under his tongue.
He sits in the lurking-places of villages; 8

In hiding-places he murders the innocent;
His eyes lie in wait for the unfortunate.
9 He lurks in secret like a lion in a thicket;
He lurks that he may rob the weak;
He robs the weak when he draws him into his net.
10 And he bends over, he crouches;
And the unfortunate fall by his mighty men.
11 He says to himself, "God has forgotten;
He has hidden his face; he will never see it."

ק

12 Arise, O LORD; O God, lift up thy hand.
Do not forget the poor.
13 Why has the wicked despised God,
And said to himself, "Thou wilt not search out?"

ר

14 Thou seest; for thou dost look upon trouble and vexation,
To give them into thy power.
The unfortunate leaves himself to thee;
Thou hast been a helper to the orphan.

ש

15 Break thou the arm of the wicked and the evildoer;
Let his wickedness be sought and not found.
16 The LORD is king forever and ever;
The nations will perish from his land.

ת

17 Thou hast heard the desire of the meek, O LORD,
Thou dost set thy mind, thou dost pay close heed,
18 So as to do justice to the orphan and the oppressed,
That man who is of the earth may never again strike terror.

THE COMING JUDGMENT

[For the director: of David]

11 I have taken refuge in the LORD;
How then can you say to me:
"Flee like a bird to your mountain?"
2 For, lo, the wicked bend the bow,
They fit their arrow to the string,
To shoot in the dark at the upright in heart.
When the foundations are torn down, 3
What has the righteous done?

The LORD is in his holy temple, 4
The LORD, whose throne is in the heavens;
His eyes behold, his eyelids test the sons of men.

The LORD tests the righteous and the wicked, 5
And he hates the lover of violence.
On the wicked he will rain coals of fire; 6
Brimstone and scorching wind will be the portion of their cup.
For the LORD is righteous; he loves righteousness; 7
The upright will behold his face.

A PLEA FROM THOSE IN DISTRESS

[For the director: according to the *sheminith*. A Psalm of David]

Save, LORD, for the godly cease to be, 12
For the faithful disappear from the sons of men.
They speak lies each with his neighbor; 2
With false lip and double heart they speak.
May the LORD cut off all false lips, 3
And the tongue that makes great boasts,
Those who say, "We will make ourselves great by our tongue. 4
Our lips are with us; who is our master?"

"Because the poor are exploited, because the needy groan, 5
I will now arise," says the LORD;
"I will place him in the safety for which he longs."
The words of the LORD are pure words, 6
Silver refined in a furnace on the ground,
Purified sevenfold.

Do thou protect us, O LORD; 7
Guard us from this generation forever.
The wicked parade to and fro, 8
When baseness is exalted among the sons of men.

A PRAYER IN FAITH

[For the director: A Psalm of David]

13 How long, O LORD—wilt thou continually forget me?
How long wilt thou hide thy face from me?
2 How long am I to lay cares upon myself,
And trouble in my heart daily?
How long shall my enemy triumph over me?

3 Look upon me and answer me, O LORD, my God.
Lighten my eyes, lest I sleep in death;
4 Lest my enemy say, "I have overcome him,"
And my foes exult because I am shaken.

5 But I have trusted in thy kindness;
My heart shall rejoice in thy deliverance.
6 I will sing unto the LORD,
Because he has treated me kindly.

THE VINDICATION OF GOD

[For the director: of David]

14 The fool said in his heart, "There is no God."
They acted basely, they did abominable things;
There was none that did good.

2 The LORD looked forth from the heavens upon the sons of men,
To see if there were any that acted wisely,
That sought after God.

3 They had all gone astray and all of them had done wrong;
There was none that did good,
No, not even one.

4 Do they know nothing, all the evildoers,
Who eat up my people as they eat bread,
But do not call upon the LORD?

5 Then were they in great terror;
For God was with the righteous generation.
6 You would put to shame the plans of the poor;
But the LORD is his refuge.

O that the deliverance of Israel would come from Zion! 7
When the LORD restores the fortune of his people,
Jacob shall exult; Israel shall rejoice.

THE FRIEND OF GOD

[A Psalm of David]

Who may sojourn in thy pavilion, O LORD? 15
Who may dwell upon thy holy hill?
"He who walks blamelessly, and does right, 2
And speaks truth from his heart.
He is not hasty with his tongue. 3
He does no wrong to his fellows;
Nor does he take blame upon himself because of his neighbor.
In his eyes a bad man is despised; 4
But he honors those who fear the LORD.
He swears to his own hurt and does not retract.
He does not put out his money on interest, 5
Nor take a bribe against the innocent.
He who does such things will never be moved."

FAITH AND HOPE

[A *miktam* of David]

Preserve me, O God, for I have sought refuge in thee. 16
I have said to the LORD, "O Lord, thou art my welfare; 2
There is none besides thee."
As to the gods who are in the land 3
And the lofty ones, I have no pleasure in them.
Their images are many; others praise them; 4
But I will not pour out their libations of blood,
Nor will I take their names upon my lips.
The LORD is my portion, my share, and my cup; 5
Thou holdest my lot.
The lines have fallen for me in pleasant places; 6
My inheritance indeed pleases me.
I will bless the LORD who has counseled me; 7
In the night also my thoughts instruct me.
I have kept the LORD continually before me; 8

For, with him at my right hand, I
shall not be moved.
9 Therefore my heart is glad and my
spirit rejoices;
My flesh also dwells in security;
10 For thou wilt not abandon me to
Sheol;
Thou wilt not let thy godly one see the
Pit.
11 Thou wilt show me the path of life.
Fulness of joy is in thy presence;
Pleasures are always in thy right hand.

A PRAYER FOR VINDICATION

[A prayer of David]

17 Hear the right, O LORD;
Give heed to my cry;
Listen to my prayer,
Which is not from deceitful lips.
2 From thy presence may my judgment
proceed;
May thine eyes see the right.
3 Thou hast tried my heart; thou hast
visited me by night;
Thou hast purified me by fire;
Thou dost not find iniquity in me;
My mouth does not transgress.
4 According to the deeds of man,
through the word from thy lips
I have kept the prescribed ways.
5 My steps have held fast to thy tracks;
My footsteps have not faltered.
6 I call upon thee, for thou wilt answer
me, O God.
Incline thine ear to me; hear my
speech.
7 Show thy wonderful kindness, O savior of those who seek shelter
From their adversaries at thy right
hand.
8 Protect me like the pupil, the daughter of the eye;
Hide me in the shadow of thy wings,
9 From the wicked who despoil me,
My deadly enemies who surround me.

10 They have closed their hearts to pity;
With their mouths they speak in pride.
11 I see them; they have now encompassed me;
They set their eyes to cast me to the
ground.
12 He is like a lion that is eager for prey,
And a young lion that lurks in ambush.

Arise, O LORD, confront him, bring 13
him low;
Deliver me from the wicked by thy
sword,
From men by thy hand, O LORD, 14
From men whose lot in life is fatness,
And whose belly is filled with thy 15
treasures;
Whose children are satiated;
And who leave the rest for their babes.
But I in justification shall behold thy 16
face;
I shall be satisfied when thy form
awakes.

A VICTOR'S HYMN OF PRAISE

[For the director: of the servant of the LORD, David, who addressed the words of this song to the LORD, on the day that the LORD rescued him from the hand of all his foes and from the hand of Saul. And he said:]

I love thee, O LORD, my strength! 18
The LORD is my rock, my fortress, 2
and my deliverer;
My God, my rock in whom I take
refuge;
My shield, and the horn of my deliverance, my tower.
I call upon the LORD, who is worthy 3
to be praised,
That I may be rescued from my enemies.

The breakers of death engulfed me, 4
Torrents of ruin terrified me.
The cords of Sheol surrounded me, 5
Snares of death confronted me.

In my distress I called upon the 6
LORD,
And unto my God I cried for help;
He heard my voice from his palace,
And my cry unto him reached his
ears.

Then the earth quaked and rocked, 7
And the foundations of the hills trembled
And rocked, when he was angry.
Smoke rose from his nostrils, 8
And fire from his mouth devoured;
Coals were kindled by it.

He bowed the heavens and came 9
down;
Thick darkness was under his feet.
He rode upon a cherub and flew, 10
And he sped on with the wings of the
wind.

11 He made darkness his covert;
His encircling pavilion was the darkness of the heavens,
Thick clouds without brightness;
12 Before him passed his thick clouds,
Hailstones, and coals of fire,
13 And the LORD thundered from the heavens,
The Most High uttered his voice.
14 He let fly his arrows and scattered them;
Lightnings he hurled and routed them.
15 Then the floor of the sea was revealed,
And the foundations of the world were bared;
At thy rebuke, O LORD,
At the fierce breath of thy wrath.
16 He sent from on high, he took me,
He drew me out of many waters.
17 He delivered me from my strong enemy,
From my foes; for they were too strong for me.

18 They confronted me on the day of my calamity,
But the LORD became my stay.
19 He led me forth into a broad place;
He set me free, for he was pleased with me.
20 The LORD rewarded me in accordance with my righteousness;
He requited me in accordance with my cleanness of hands.
21 For I have kept the ways of the LORD,
And have not transgressed against my God.
22 For all his ordinances are before me,
And his statutes I do not put away from me.
23 I was blameless with him,
And guarded myself from my guilt.
24 So the LORD requited me in accordance with my righteousness,
In accordance with my cleanness of hands in his sight.

25 Toward the godly thou dost act graciously;
Toward the blameless thou dost act blamelessly;
26 Toward the pure thou dost act purely;
And toward the crooked thou dost act craftily.
27 For thou wilt deliver a humble people,
But haughty eyes thou wilt bring low.
28 For thou dost light my lamp, O LORD,
My God lightens my darkness.
For through thee I can break down a rampart, 29
And through my God I can scale a wall.

The way of God is blameless, 30
The speech of the LORD is sincere;
A shield is he to all who take refuge in him.
For who is God but the LORD? 31
And who is a rock save our God?

The God who girds me with might, 32
And makes my way blameless,
Making my feet like the doe's, 33
And making me stand securely on my heights;
The one who trains my hands for battle, 34
So that my arms can bend a bow of bronze.
And thou hast given me thy saving shield, 35
And thy right hand supports me;
And thy help makes me great.
Thou dost enlarge the range of my steps, 36
And my ankles do not give way.

I pursue my foes and overtake them, 37
And do not turn back until they are consumed.
I smite them so that they are unable to rise; 38
Beneath my feet they fall.

And thou dost gird me with strength for the battle; 39
Thou dost subdue my opponents under me;
And thou dost make my foes show me the back; 40
And those that hate me I destroy.
They cry for help, but there is none to deliver; 41
To the LORD, but he does not answer them.
Then I pulverize them like dust before the wind; 42
I crush them like the dirt of the streets.
Thou dost deliver me from the feuds of the people; 43
Thou dost establish me as head of the nations;
People that I have not known serve me;
As soon as they hear of me, they submit to me; 44

Foreigners fawn upon me;
45 Foreigners fade away,
And come trembling from their fortresses.

46 All hail to the LORD! And blessed be my Rock!
And may the God of my deliverance be exalted!
47 The God who gives me vengeance,
And puts peoples in subjection under me;
48 Who frees me from my foes.
Yea, thou dost exalt me above my adversaries;
From violent men thou dost rescue me.

49 Therefore I shall praise thee among the nations, O LORD,
And sing praises to thy name;
50 To him who gives great victories to his king,
And shows kindness to his anointed,
To David and his descendants forever.

GOD'S PRAISE IN THE PHYSICAL AND MORAL UNIVERSE

[For the director: A Psalm of David]

19 The heavens are telling the glory of God,
And the sky shows forth the work of his hands.
2 Day unto day pours forth speech,
And night unto night declares knowledge.

3 There is no speech, nor are there words;
Their voice is not heard;
4 Yet their voice goes forth through all the earth,
And their words to the ends of the world.

In them he has pitched a tent for the sun,
5 Who is like a bridegroom coming forth from his chamber,
And rejoices like a strong man to run the course;
6 From one end of the heavens is his starting-point,
And his circuit is to the other end;
And nothing is hid from the heat thereof.

The law of the LORD is perfect, renewing the life; 7
The decree of the LORD is trustworthy,
making wise the simple;
The precepts of the LORD are right, rejoicing the heart; 8
The command of the LORD is pure,
enlightening the eyes;
The fear of the LORD is clean, enduring forever. 9
The judgments of the LORD are true,
they are also right;
They are more valuable than gold, and much fine gold; 10
Also sweeter than honey,
and the droppings of the honeycomb.

Thy servant also is instructed by them, 11
In keeping them there is great reward.
Who can discern his errors? 12
Of unconscious ones, hold me guiltless!
Moreover, restrain thy servant from wilful ones, 13
May they not rule over me!
Then shall I be blameless, and be acquitted of much transgression.
May the words of my mouth and the meditation of my heart 14
Be acceptable before thee,
O LORD, my rock and my avenger!

A PRAYER FOR VICTORY

[For the director: A Psalm of David]

The LORD answer you on the day of trouble! 20
The name of the God of Jacob set you on high!
May he send you help from the holy place, 2
And give you support from Zion!
May he keep in mind all your gifts, 3
And your burnt-offerings may he accept! *Selah*

May he grant you your heart's desire, 4
And fulfil all your plans!
May we shout with joy over your victory, 5
And in the name of our God set up our standards!
May the LORD fulfil all your requests!

Now I know that the LORD will give victory to his anointed, 6

That he will answer him from his holy heavens,
Through the saving strength of his right hand.
7 Some are strong through chariots and some through horses,
But we, through the name of the LORD, our God.
8 They will bow down and fall;
But we shall arise and stand upright.
9 O LORD, give the king victory;
Do thou answer us when we call.

A HYMN OF PRAISE AND GRATITUDE

[For the director: A Psalm of David]

1 In thy strength the king rejoices, O LORD;
And in thy victory how greatly he exults!
2 Thou hast given him the desire of his heart;
And the petition of his lips thou hast not withheld. *Selah*

3 For thou dost send goodly blessings to meet him,
Thou dost place upon his head a crown of gold.
4 He asked life of thee—thou hast given it to him,
Long life, forever and ever.

5 His glory is great through thy help;
Praise and honor thou layest upon him.
6 Thou dost make him blessed forever;
Thou dost gladden him with joy in thy presence.

7 For the king trusts in the LORD;
And, through the goodness of the Most High, he will never be moved.

8 Your hand will find all your foes.
Your right hand will find those that hate you.
9 You will put them in an oven of fire,
When you show your face.

The LORD in his anger will destroy them,
And fire will consume them.
10 Their offspring you will destroy from the earth,
And their descendants from among the sons of men.
11 When they plan evil against you,
And devise malice, they shall not succeed.
12 You will make them turn their backs with your bowstrings,
You will aim at their faces.

13 Arise, O LORD, in thy strength,
That we may play and sing of thy power.

THE CRY OF A DESOLATE SPIRIT

[For the director: upon *aijeleth hash-shahar*. A Psalm of David]

22 My God, my God, why hast thou forsaken me?
And why art thou far from helping me, at the words of my wailing?
2 My God, I cry by day, but thou dost not answer;
And by night, and get no rest.

3 Yet thou art holy;
The praise of Israel will endure.
4 In thee our fathers trusted;
They trusted and thou didst deliver them.
5 Unto thee they cried and were set free;
In thee they trusted and were not disgraced.

6 But I am a worm and not a man,
A shame to mankind, and despised of the people.
7 All who see me make sport of me;
They make mouths at me and toss their heads:
8 "Let him rejoice in the LORD; let him deliver him;
Let him rescue him; for he is pleased with him."
9 Yet thou didst bring me forth from the womb;
Thou didst give me security on my mother's breast.
10 Upon thee was I cast from birth;
From my mother's womb thou hast been my God.
11 Do not stay far from me;
For trouble is near;
For there is none to help.
12 Strong bulls surround me;
Mighty ones of Bashan encircle me.
13 They open wide their mouths at me,
Like a ravening and roaring lion.

14 I am poured out like water,
And all my bones are disjointed.

My heart is like wax,
Melted in the midst of my bosom.

15 My strength is dried up like a potsherd,
And my tongue cleaves to my palate;
And they lay me in the dust of death.
16 For dogs have surrounded me,
A gang of villains encircles me.
My hands and my feet are crippled.

17 I can count all my bones;
They look, they stare at me.
18 They distribute my garments among them,
And over my robe they cast lots.

19 But, thou, O LORD, be not far off;
O my strength, hasten to my aid.
20 Deliver my life from the sword,
My only one from the power of the dog.

21 Save me from the lion's mouth,
And my afflicted self from the horns of the wild ox.
22 Then will I publish thy name to my brethren;
In the midst of the assembly I will praise thee.
23 You who fear the LORD praise him!
All you descendants of Jacob honor him!
Stand in awe of him all you descendants of Israel;
24 Because he has not despised, nor has he loathed the affliction of the afflicted;
Nor has he hidden his face from him;
But he has listened when he cried to him for aid.
25 From thee is my praise in the great assembly;
In the presence of those who fear him I will pay my vows.
26 The humble will eat and be satisfied;
Those who seek the LORD will praise him.
May your heart live forever!
27 All the ends of the earth will remember and turn unto the LORD;
All the clans of the nations will worship before him.
28 For the kingdom belongs to the LORD;
And he rules over the nations.

29 Him alone will all the fat ones of the earth worship;
Before him all those who go down to the dust will bow;
For none keeps himself alive.
The descendants will serve him, 30
May it be told of the Lord to the coming generation,
And may they tell of his righteousness 31
to the people that shall be born,
That he has wrought it.

THE GOOD SHEPHERD

[A Psalm of David]

The LORD is my shepherd; I shall not want; 23
In green pastures he makes me lie down; 2
Beside refreshing waters he leads me.
He gives me new life; 3
He guides me in paths of righteousness for his name's sake.
Even though I walk in the darkest valley, 4
I fear no harm; for thou art with me;
Thy rod and thy staff—they comfort me.
Thou layest a table before me in the presence of my enemies; 5
Thou anointest my head with oil; my cup overflows.
Surely goodness and kindness shall follow me all the days of my life; 6
And I shall dwell in the house of the LORD to an old age.

THE GLORY OF GOD AND THE GOOD MAN

[A Psalm of David]

The earth is the LORD'S and its fulness, 24
The world and those who dwell therein.
For he founded it upon the seas, 2
And established it upon the ocean-currents.

Who can ascend into the hill of the LORD? 3
And who can stand in his holy place?
He who has clean hands and a pure heart, 4
Who has had no desire for falsehood,
And has not sworn to a lie.
He will receive a blessing from the LORD, 5
And justification from the God of his deliverance.

6 This is the generation of those who
search for him,
Who seek the face of the God of Jacob.
Selah

7 Lift up your heads, O gates!
And lift yourselves up, O ancient
doors,
That the king of glory may come in!
8 Who, then, is the king of glory?
The LORD strong and mighty,
The LORD mighty in battle!
9 Lift up your heads, O gates!
And lift yourselves up, O ancient
doors,
That the king of glory may come in!
10 Who, then, is the king of glory?
The LORD of hosts,
He is the king of glory! *Selah*

A PRAYER FOR DIVINE HELP

[Of David]

א

25 Unto thee, O LORD, do I lift up my
desire.

ב

2 My God, in thee have I trusted; let
me not be put to shame;
Let not my foes exult.

ג

3 Yea, let none that wait upon thee be
put to shame;
May they be put to shame who have
been deceitful without cause.

ד

4 Thy ways, O LORD, make me know;
Teach me thy paths.

ה, ו

5 Lead me in thy truth, and teach me;
For thou art the God of my help;
For thee do I long continually.

ז

6 Remember thy mercy, O LORD, and
thy kindness,
For they have been from of old.

ח

7 The sins of my youth and my offenses
do not remember;
In accordance with thy kindness, do
thou remember me,
For thy goodness' sake, O LORD.

ט

Good and upright is the LORD, 8
Therefore he instructs sinners in the
way.

י

He leads the meek in justice, 9
And he teaches the meek his way.

כ

All the paths of the LORD are kind- 10
ness and truth,
For those who observe his covenant
and his commands.

ל

For thy name's sake, O LORD, 11
Pardon my guilt, though it is great.

מ

What man is there that fears the 12
LORD?
He will teach him in the way that he
must choose.

נ

He will dwell in good times, 13
And his descendants will possess the
land.

ס

The secret of the LORD is for those 14
who fear him,
And his covenant, that he may teach
them.

ע

My eyes are ever toward the LORD, 15
That he may bring forth my feet from
the net.

פ

Turn unto me and have mercy upon 16
me,
For I am lonely and afflicted.

צ

Enlarge the straits of my heart, 17
And lead me forth from my distresses.

ק

See my affliction and my trouble, 18
And forgive all my sins.

ר

See how many my foes are, 19
And with what violent hatred they
hate me.

ש

Preserve me and rescue me; 20
Let me not be put to shame; for I take
refuge in thee.

ת

21 Let integrity and uprightness protect me,
For I hope in thee.

22 Redeem Israel, O God,
From all its troubles.

THE CLAIMS OF THE RIGHTEOUS

[Of David]

26 Give me justice, O LORD, for I have walked in my integrity,
And I have trusted in the LORD, without wavering.
2 Try me, O LORD, and test me,
Examine my mind and my heart.

3 For thy kindness is before my eyes,
And I have walked in thy truth.
4 I do not sit with faithless men,
Nor with dissemblers do I go in.

5 I hate the company of evildoers,
And with reprobates I will not sit down.
6 I wash my hands in innocence,
And march round thy altar, O LORD,
7 To proclaim with a voice of praise,
And to recount all thy wonders.

8 O LORD, I have loved the habitation of thy house,
And the place where thy glory dwells.
9 Take me not away along with sinners,
Nor my life along with men of blood,
10 In whose hands is an evil purpose,
And whose right hand is full of bribes.

11 But as for me, I walk in my integrity;
Deliver me and be gracious to me.
12 My foot stands upon level ground;
In the congregations I bless the LORD.

A SONG OF ASSURANCE

[Of David]

27 The LORD is my light and my salvation;
whom shall I fear?
The LORD is the refuge of my life;
of whom shall I be afraid?

2 When evildoers pressed in upon me,
to eat up my flesh,
My adversaries and my foes,
they stumbled and fell.

Though a host encamp against me,
my heart will not fear;
Though war arise against me,
in this will I be confident.

One thing I ask from the LORD,
that do I seek;
That I may dwell in the house of the LORD
all the days of my life,
To behold the beauty of the LORD,
and to inquire in his temple.

For he will hide me in his pavilion,
on the day of trouble;
He will conceal me in his secret tent,
he will set me up upon a rock.

And now my head is high
above my foes on every side;
And I will sacrifice in his tent
sacrifices with shouts;
I will sing and make music to the LORD.

Hear, O my LORD, my voice with which I cry;
be gracious to me and answer me.
Concerning thee my heart says,
"Seek you my face!"
Thy face, O LORD, do I seek;
hide not thy face from me.

Turn not thy servant away in anger,
thou who hast been my help.
Cast me not off, neither forsake me,
O God of my salvation!
If my father and my mother forsake me,
then the LORD will take me up.
Teach me thy way, O LORD,
And guide me in a level path,
because of my enemies.

Yield me not to the desire of my foes;
For false witnesses have risen against me,
and such as breathe forth violence.
I believe that I shall see the goodness of the LORD
in the land of the living.

Wait thou for the LORD;
Be strong and keep a stout heart;
And wait thou for the LORD.

A PRAYER FOR THE PUNISHMENT OF THE WICKED

[Of David]

28 Unto thee, O LORD, do I call;
O my rock, be not deaf to me;
Lest, because thou payest no heed to me,
I become like those who go down to the Pit.

2 Hear the voice of my supplication,
when I cry to thee for help,
when I lift up my hands unto thy holy shrine.
3 Snatch me not away with the wicked,
and with those who do wrong,
Who offer friendly greetings to their neighbors,
while evil is in their hearts.

4 Render to them according to their work,
and according to their evil deeds.
According to the work of their hands render to them;
pay back to them what they have done.
5 Because they do not give heed to the works of the LORD,
and to the work of his hands,
he will tear them down and not build them up.

6 Blessed be the LORD! For he has heard
the voice of my supplications.
7 The LORD is my strength and my shield;
in him my heart has trusted;
And I have been helped and my heart exults,
and with my song I praise him.
8 The LORD is the strength of his people and a refuge;
the help of his anointed is he.

9 Give victory to thy people,
and bless thine inheritance;
shepherd them and carry them evermore.

THE GOD OF THE STORM

[A Psalm of David]

29 Ascribe unto the LORD, O heavenly beings,
Ascribe unto the LORD glory and strength.
Ascribe unto the LORD the glory of his name; 2
Worship the LORD in holy array.

The voice of the LORD is above the waters; 3
The God of glory thunders.
The LORD is over the great waters;
The voice of the LORD is mighty. 4
The voice of the LORD is majestic.

The voice of the LORD breaks the cedars, 5
And the LORD shatters the cedars of Lebanon.
He makes them skip like a calf, 6
Lebanon and Sirion like a young wild-ox.

The voice of the LORD hews out flames of fire; 7
The voice of the LORD makes the desert whirl; 8
The LORD whirls the desert of Kadesh.
The voice of the LORD whirls the terebinths, 9
And causes bleating kids to be born in haste,
While in his palace everything says, "Glory!"

The LORD sits over the flood; 10
The LORD sits as king forever.
The LORD gives strength to his people; 11
The LORD blesses his people with peace.

PRAISE FOR THE HELP OF THE LORD

[A Psalm; a song of the dedication of the house; of David]

I will extol thee, O LORD, for thou hast drawn me forth, 30
And hast not let my foes rejoice over me.
O LORD, my God, I cried for help unto thee, 2
And thou didst heal me.
O LORD, thou hast brought me up from Sheol, 3
Thou hast revived me from among those who go down to the Pit.

Sing praises to the LORD, O you his godly ones, 4
And praise his holy name.

5 For though there be a moment in his wrath, there is a lifetime in his favor.
Weeping may lodge with us at evening, but in the morning there is a shout of joy.

6 But I said in my security,
"I shall never be moved."
7 O LORD, by thy favor thou hast made my mountain to stand strong;
Thou didst hide thy face; I was dismayed.
8 Unto thee, O LORD, I called;
And unto the Lord I made supplication:
9 "What profit is there in my blood, when I go down to the Pit?
Will the dust praise thee? Will it declare thy faithfulness?
10 Hear, O LORD, and be gracious to me.
O LORD, be thou my helper."

11 Thou hast turned my mourning into dancing;
Thou hast put off my sackcloth and girded me with gladness;
12 In order that I may sing praises to thee and not be silent;
O LORD, my God, I will evermore praise thee.

MINGLED PRAYER AND PRAISE

[For the director: A Psalm of David]

31 In thee, O LORD, I have taken refuge;
Let me nevermore be put to shame;
Through thy justification, deliver me!
2 Incline thine ear unto me,
Quickly rescue me!
Become for me a rock of refuge,
A mountain-fort to save me!

3 For thou art my rock and my fortress;
And for thy name's sake thou wilt lead me and guide me.
4 Thou wilt bring me forth from the net which they have laid for me;
For thou art my refuge.
5 Into thy hand I commit my spirit;
Thou wilt redeem me, O LORD, thou faithful God.

6 I hate them that pay regard to false vanities;
But I myself have trusted in the LORD.

I will exult and rejoice in thy kindness,
For thou hast seen my affliction,
Thou hast taken heed of my straits.
And thou hast not delivered me into the hand of the foe;
But hast established my feet upon a broad place.

Be gracious unto me, O LORD, for I am in trouble;
Through grief my eye is weakened, myself and my body.
For my life is consumed in sorrow, and my years in groaning.
My strength has failed through my affliction, and my bones have wasted away.

I am become an object of reproach from all my foes, 1
a thing of dread to my neighbors,
A terror to my acquaintances who see me on the street;
they flee from me.
I am forgotten like a dead man; out of mind, 1
like a lost article am I;
For I hear the remark of many, 1
"Terror on every side,"
When they counsel together against me;
they plan to take my life.

But I have trusted in thee, O LORD; 1
I have said, "Thou art my God;
My times are in thy hand.
Rescue me from the hand of my foes and those who pursue me;
Let thy face shine upon thy servant;
Deliver me through thy kindness.

"O LORD, let me not be put to shame, 1
for I have called upon thee;
Let the wicked be put to shame; let them wait for Sheol.
May lying lips be made dumb, 1
Those that speak insolence against the righteous,
In pride and scorn.

"How great is thy goodness which thou hast in store for those who fear thee, 1
Which thou hast wrought for those relying upon thee, in the presence of the sons of men.
Thou dost secrete them in the secret of thy presence from the plottings of man; 2

Thou dost shelter them in thy pavilion
from the strife of tongues."
21 Blessed be the LORD!
For he showed me his wonderful kindness in a besieged city.
22 I said in my alarm,
"I am cut off from before thine eyes."
But thou didst hear the voice of my supplication,
When I cried to thee for aid.
23 Love the LORD, all you his godly ones;
The LORD preserves the faithful;
But he requites to excess him who acts haughtily.
24 Be strong, and let your heart be firm,
All you who wait for the LORD.

THE BLESSED LOT OF THE PIOUS

[Of David. A *maskil*]

32 How happy is he whose transgression is forgiven, whose sin is covered!
2 How happy is the man to whom the LORD charges no guilt,
And in whose spirit there is no guile!
3 When I kept silent my bones wasted away
Through my groaning all day long.
4 For, day and night, thy hand lay heavy upon me;
My sap was turned into the drought of summer. *Selah*

5 My sin I declared to thee, and my guilt I have not concealed;
I said, "I will confess my transgressions to the LORD."
And thou didst forgive the guilt of my sin. *Selah*

6 Therefore let every godly man pray to thee,
That in the time of distress, in the rush of great waters,
They may not reach him.
7 Thou art my hiding-place; from the foe thou guardest me;
Thou dost surround me with deliverance. *Selah*

8 I will instruct thee and show thee the way which thou must go;
I will counsel thee, with my eye upon thee.
9 Be not like a horse or a mule, without sense,
Whose temper must be restrained with bridle and bit,
That he come not near you.
10 The wicked has many sorrows,
But him who trusts in the LORD he surrounds with kindness.
11 Rejoice in the LORD and exult, O righteous,
And shout for joy, all you who are right-minded.

THE LORD OF ALL CREATION

33 Rejoice in the LORD, O righteous ones;
Praise befits the upright.
2 Praise the LORD with the harp;
Play to him on the ten-stringed lute.
3 Sing unto him a new song;
Play skilfully with glad shouts.

4 For the word of the LORD is right,
And all his work is faithful.
5 He loves righteousness and justice;
The earth is full of the goodness of the LORD.

6 By the word of the LORD the heavens were made,
And by the breath of his mouth all their host.
7 He gathers the waters of the sea as in a waterskin;
He puts the deeps in storehouses.

8 Let all the earth fear the LORD;
Let all the inhabitants of the world stand in awe of him.
9 For he spoke and it was!
He commanded and it stood fast!

10 The LORD annuls the counsel of the nations;
He frustrates the plans of the peoples.
11 But the counsel of the LORD stands forever,
The plans of his heart throughout the ages.
12 How happy is the nation whose God is the LORD,
The people that he has chosen as his heritage!

13 The LORD looks down from the heavens,
He sees all the sons of men.
14 From the place of his dwelling he looks forth
Upon all the inhabitants of the earth;

15 He who fashions the hearts of them all,
Who considers all their deeds.

16 The king is not saved by the size of his army;
A warrior is not rescued by his great strength.
17 The horse is a delusion for victory,
And he does not deliver by his great strength.

18 So the eye of the LORD is upon those who fear him,
Those who wait for his goodness,
19 To rescue them from death,
And to keep them alive in famine.

20 We wait for the LORD;
He is our help and our shield;
21 For our heart rejoices in him,
For in his holy name we trust.
22 May thy goodness, O LORD, be over us,
According as we hope in thee.

THE GOODNESS OF GOD

[Of David; when he changed his behavior before Abimelech, so that he drove him out and he departed]

א

34 I bless the LORD at all times,
His praise is constantly in my mouth.

ב

2 I glory in the LORD;
Let the godly hear and rejoice.

ג

3 Magnify the LORD with me,
And let us all exalt his name.

ד

4 I sought the LORD and he answered me,
And delivered me from all my terrors.

ה, ו

5 Look at me, and so be jubilant,
And let not your faces be abashed.

ז

6 This poor man called and the LORD heard,
And delivered him from all his troubles.

ח

7 The angel of the LORD encamps
Around those who fear him, and rescues them.

ט

Taste and see that the LORD is good;
How happy is the man who takes refuge in him!

י

Fear the LORD, you his holy ones;
For those who fear him feel no lack.

כ

Young lions do lack, and suffer hunger;
But those who seek the LORD lack no good thing.

ל

Come, children, listen to me,
And I will teach you reverence for the LORD.

מ

What man is there who desires life,
Who loves length of days that he may see good?

נ

Keep your tongue from evil,
And your lips from telling lies.

ס

Depart from evil and do good;
Seek peace, and pursue it.

פ

The face of the LORD is against those who do evil,
That he may cut off the memory of them from the earth.

ע

The eyes of the LORD are upon the righteous,
And his ears are open to their cry.

צ

They call and the LORD hears,
And he rescues them from all their troubles.

ק

The LORD is near to the broken-hearted,
And he delivers those who are crushed in spirit.

ר

Many are the ills of the righteous,
But from them all the LORD delivers him.

ש

He guards all his bones,
So that not one of them is broken.

ת

1 Evil will slay the wicked;
And those who hate the righteous will be held guilty.
2 The LORD will redeem the life of his servants,
And none who take refuge in him will be held guilty.

A PRAYER FOR VENGEANCE

[Of David]

5 Oppose, O LORD, my opponents;
Fight those who fight me.
2 Lay hold of buckler and shield,
And rise up to my help.
3 Draw the spear and battle-ax to meet my pursuers;
Say to me, "I am thy deliverance."

4 May they be put to shame and confusion who seek my life;
May they be turned back and disgraced who plan evil against me.
5 May they be like chaff before the wind,
With the angel of the LORD chasing them.
6 May their road be darkness and slipperiness,
With the angel of the LORD pursuing them.
7 For without cause they hid their net for me;
Without cause they dug a pit for me.
8 May destruction come upon him unawares;
And may the net which he has hidden catch himself;
In destruction may he fall therein!

9 But I shall exult in the LORD,
And rejoice in his deliverance.
0 All my bones will say,
"O LORD, who is like thee,
Saving the poor from him that is too strong for him,
The poor and the needy from him that would rob him?"

1 Malicious witnesses rise up,
Who ask me regarding that of which I know nothing.
2 They requite me evil for good,
To my personal bereavement.
3 As for myself, when they were sick—my clothing was sackcloth,
I afflicted myself by fasting,
And my prayer returned to my own lap.

As though it were my friend or brother I went about; 14
As in sorrow for a mother I bowed down mourning.

But at my fall they rejoice and gather together, 15
Smiters gather together against me whom I know not;
They rend without ceasing.
When I assert my friendship they jeer scornfully, 16
Gnashing at me with their teeth.
O Lord, how long wilt thou look on? 17
Draw me back from the roaring ones,
My solitary self from the young lions.
I will thank thee in the great assembly; 18
Among a mighty people will I praise thee.

Let not those who are wrongfully my foes rejoice over me, 19
Nor those who hate me without cause wink the eye.
For they do not speak peace; 20
But against those who are at ease in the land
They devise treacherous things.
And they open wide their mouths against me. 21
They say, "Aha, Aha, our eye sees it!"

Thou hast seen, O LORD; be not silent! 22
O Lord, be not far from me!
Bestir thyself and rise up to do me justice, 23
My God and my Lord, to plead my cause!
Do me justice in accordance with thy righteousness, O LORD, my God! 24
And let them not rejoice over me!

May they not say to themselves, "Aha, our desire!" 25
May they not say, "We have swallowed him up."
May they be put to shame and disgraced 26
Who rejoice over my calamity;
May they be clothed with shame and disgrace
Who magnify themselves against me.
May they shout for joy and be glad who are pleased at my vindication. 27
And may they continually say, "The LORD is great,

Who desires the welfare of his servant."
28 Then my tongue will proclaim thy righteousness,
And thy praise all the day long.

THE GOODNESS OF GOD AND THE SIN OF THE WICKED

[For the director: of the servant of the LORD, of David]

36 Rebellion is delightful to the wicked within his heart;
There is no dread of God before his eyes.
2 For it deceives him in his own eyes,
Concerning the finding out of his guilt and the hatred of it.
3 The words of his mouth are wrong and deceit;
He has ceased to be wise and to do good.
4 He plans wrongdoing while in bed;
He takes his stand on a way that is not good;
He does not despise wickedness.

5 O LORD, thy kindness extends to the heavens,
Thy faithfulness unto the clouds.
6 Thy righteousness is like the highest mountains;
Thy judgments are a great deep;
Thou savest man and beast, O LORD.

7 How precious is thy kindness, O God!
The sons of men take refuge under the shadow of thy wings.
8 They drink their fill of the fatness of thy house,
And thou givest them drink of the stream of thy pleasures.

9 For with thee is the fountain of life;
Through thy light do we see light.
10 Continue thy kindness to those that know thee,
And thy justification to the right-minded.

11 May the foot of pride not come upon me,
Nor the hand of the wicked drive me out.
12 There the workers of wrong are fallen;
They are overthrown and are not able to rise.

GOD'S CARE FOR THE PIOUS

[Of David]

א

Fret not yourself because of evildoers, 37
Be not incensed because of wrongdoers;
For they will soon wither like grass, 2
And fade away like the green herb.

ב

Trust in the LORD and do good; 3
Inhabit the land and feed in security.
Take your delight in the LORD, 4
And he will give you the desire of your heart.

ג

Commit your way unto the LORD, 5
And trust in him; and he will act.
He will bring forth your right like the light, 6
And your just cause like the noonday.

ד

Wait patiently for the LORD and hope in him; 7
Fret not yourself because of him who makes his way prosper,
Him who succeeds in his plans.

ה

Cease from anger, and forsake wrath; 8
Fret not yourself; it does nothing but harm;
For evildoers shall be cut off;
While those who wait upon the LORD shall possess the land.

ו

Yet a little while and the wicked shall be no more; 10
Though you look hard at his place, he will not be there.
But the meek shall possess the land, 11
And rejoice in abundant prosperity.

ז

Though the wicked plot against the innocent, 12
And gnash his teeth at him,
The Lord laughs at him; 13
For he sees that his day will come.

ח

The wicked draw the sword and bend their bow, 14

To bring down the poor and needy,
To slay those whose way is right.
15 Their sword shall enter their own hearts,
And their bows shall be broken.

ט

16 Better is the little of the righteous
Than the wealth of many wicked.
17 For the resources of the wicked shall be broken,
But the LORD supports the righteous.

י

18 The LORD knows the days of the innocent,
And their possession abides forever.
19 They shall not be put to shame in bad times,
And in the time of famine they shall be satisfied.

כ

20 For the wicked shall perish;
And the enemies of the LORD, like a brand in the furnace,
Shall vanish in smoke.

ל

21 If the wicked borrows, ne does not pay back;
But the righteous is generous and gives.
22 Those who bless him shall possess the land,
But those who curse him shall be cut off.

מ

23 The steps of a man are from the LORD,
And he establishes him with whose way he is pleased.
24 Though he fall, he shall not lie prostrate,
For the LORD holds his hand.

נ

25 I have been young, and now I am old;
But I have not seen the righteous forsaken,
Nor his descendants begging their bread.
26 He is always generous and ever lending,
And his descendants become a blessing.

ס

27 Shun evil and do good,
shall you abide forever.

28 For the LORD loves the right,
And he does not desert his saints.

ע

They are kept forever,
But the descendants of the wicked are cut off.
29 The upright shall possess the land,
And shall dwell therein forever.

פ

30 The mouth of the upright utters wisdom,
And his tongue speaks justice.
31 The law of his God is in his heart;
His steps do not slip.

צ

32 When the wicked spies upon the upright,
And seeks to kill him,
33 The LORD will not deliver him into his hand,
Nor will he declare him guilty when he is brought to trial.

ק

34 Wait for the LORD, and keep his way;
And he will exalt you to possess the land.
You shall gaze upon the destruction of the wicked.

ר

35 I saw the wicked triumphing,
And towering aloft like the cedar of Lebanon;
36 But I passed by and lo, he was not!
And when I sought for him he was not to be found.

ש

37 Watch integrity and look upon right;
For there is a posterity for the man of peace.
38 But lawbreakers are wholly destroyed;
The posterity of the wicked is cut off.

ת

39 The help of the innocent comes from the LORD;
Their strength is he in time of need.
40 The LORD helps them and rescues them;
He rescues them from the wicked and makes them victorious,
Because they trust in him.

A PRAYER OF ONE IN GREAT TROUBLE

[A Psalm of David. To make a memorial]

38 Do not reprove me in thy wrath, O LORD,
Nor correct me in thy fury.
2 For thine arrows have sunk deep into me,
And thy hand has come down upon me.

3 There is no soundness in my flesh because of thine anger;
There is no health in my bones because of my sin.
4 For my guilt has passed over my head;
Like a heavy load it is too heavy for me.

5 My wounds are fetid, they fester,
Because of my folly.
6 I am bent, I am bowed down exceedingly;
I go about mourning all day long.
7 For my loins are full of inflammation,
And there is no soundness in my flesh.
8 I am benumbed and badly crushed;
I groan because of the moaning of my heart.

9 O LORD, all my desire is before thee,
And my sighing is not hidden from thee.
10 My heart palpitates; my strength has left me;
Even the light of my eyes is not with me.

11 Those who love me and my friends stand back from my plague,
And my kinsmen stand afar off.
12 They that seek my life lay snares for me,
And those who desire my harm speak of ruin,
And they meditate deceit all day long.
13 But I, like a deaf man, hear not;
And I am like a dumb man who does not open his mouth.
14 I am like a man that does not hear,
And one in whose mouth there are no arguments.
15 But for thee, O LORD, do I wait;
Thou wilt answer, O Lord, my God!
16 For I think, "Else will they rejoice over me;
When my foot slips, they will magnify themselves against me."
For I am ready for a fall, 17
And my grief is ever before me.
I am in horror of my guilt; 18
I am sorry for my sin.

My foes without reason are numerous; 19
Many are those that hate me falsely,
And render me evil for good; 20
They oppose me because I follow after good.

Do not forsake me, O LORD; 21
My God, be not far from me!
Hasten to my help; 22
O Lord, to my rescue!

A PLEA FOR MERCY TOWARD A MAN OF FLEETING EXISTENCE

[For the director: for *Jeduthun*. A Psalm of David]

I said, "I will watch my ways 39
That I may not sin with my tongue;
I will put a muzzle on my mouth,
As long as the wicked is before me."
I was dumb in silence; 2
I refrained from good,
And my pain was aroused.
My heart burned within me; 3
While I meditated, a fire kindled;
I spoke with my tongue:

"O LORD, teach me my end, 4
And what is the extent of my days;
Let me know how I shall end.
Lo, thou hast fixed my days but as handbreadths, 5
And my lifetime is as nothing before thee;
As a mere breath every man stands.
Selah
As but a shadow a man walks; 6
As but a breath he bestirs himself;
He heaps up and knows not who will gather it in.

"And now for what do I wait, O LORD? 7
My hope is in thee!
From all my transgressions deliver me! 8
Make me not the scorn of the reprobate.
I am dumb; I do not open my mouth; 9
For it is thou who hast done it.
Remove thy plague from me; 10
By the blows of thy hand I perish.

11 With rebukes for guilt thou dost chastise a man,
And thou dost wipe out his desire like a cobweb.
Verily, all men are but a breath. *Selah*

12 "Hear my prayer, O LORD,
And give heed to my cry!
Be not unresponsive to my tears;
For I am a guest with thee,
A sojourner, like all my ancestors.
13 Turn thy gaze away from me, that I may be glad,
Before I go away and be no more."

A PRAYER FOR SPEEDY RELIEF FROM TROUBLE

[For the director: A Psalm of David]

40 I waited patiently for the LORD,
and he paid heed to me and heard my plea.
2 So he drew me up from the pit of ruin,
from the miry swamp;
And he set my feet upon a rock,
establishing my steps.
3 And he put a new song in my mouth,
praise to our God.
Many will see and be afraid,
and will trust in the LORD.

4 How happy is the man who has made the LORD his trust,
And has not turned to idolaters,
and lying apostates.
5 Thou hast done great things,
O LORD my God;
Wonderful are thy thoughts toward us;
there is none to compare with thee.
Were I to declare and tell them,
they would be too many to enumerate.

6 Sacrifice and offering thou dost not desire—
Thou hast opened my ears—
Burnt-offering and sin-offering thou dost not demand.
7 Then said I, "Lo, I come—
In the roll of a book which was written for me—
8 I delight to do thy will, O my God
And thy law is in my very heart.

9 "I have proclaimed thy vindication in the great assembly.
Lo, I do not close my lips;
O LORD, thou knowest.
Thy vindication I have not concealed within my heart; 10
Thy faithfulness and thy victory I have told.
I have not withheld thy kindness and thy fidelity from the great assembly.
Do thou, O LORD, not withhold thy mercy from me. 11
May thy kindness and thy fidelity always protect me.

"For sins beyond number beset me, 12
My offenses have overtaken me,
so that I cannot see.
They are more numerous than the hairs of my head;
and my heart has failed me.

"Be pleased, O LORD, to rescue me; 13
O LORD, hasten to my help.
May they be both put to shame and abashed 14
who seek to take away my life!
May they be driven back and routed
who desire my ruin!
May they be appalled by reason of their shame, 15
who say to me, 'Aha, Aha!'

"May they rejoice and be glad in thee, 16
all who seek thee!
May they continually say, 'Great is the LORD,'
who love thy deliverance.
Since I am poor and needy, 17
O Lord, hasten to me!
Thou art my help and my deliverer;
O my God, do not tarry!"

A PRAYER FOR VENGEANCE

[For the director: A Psalm of David]

How happy is he who is considerate of the weak; 41
On the day of trouble the LORD delivers him.
The LORD protects him and keeps him alive; 2
He is called happy in the land.
Thou wilt not give him over to the rage of his foes;
The LORD sustains him upon his sickbed. 3

All his bed thou hast changed in his illness.
4 I say, "Have mercy on me, O LORD!
Heal me; for I have sinned against thee!"
5 My foes say evil of me,
"How long till he die, and his name perish?"
6 If he comes to see me, he speaks lies;
His heart lays up malice;
He goes outside and talks.
7 All who hate me whisper together against me;
They devise evil against me.

8 An evil thing is devised against him,
That when he lies down, he may not rise again.
Even my friend in whom I trusted, 9
He who ate my bread, has acted deceitfully against me.
But thou, O LORD, be gracious to me and raise me up, 10
That I may repay them!
By this I shall know that thou art pleased with me, 11
In that my foe does not triumph over me.
But as for me, because of my integrity thou dost maintain me, 12
And thou dost set me before thee evermore.

Blessed be the LORD, the God of Israel, 13
From everlasting to everlasting.
Amen and amen.

BOOK II, PSS. 42–72

A SONG OF ASSURANCE

[For the director: a *maskil* of the sons of Korah]

42 As a deer longs for the water-courses,
So my whole being longs for thee, O God.
2 My whole being thirsts for God, for the living God:
How long till I come and see the face of God?
3 My tears have been my food day and night,
While men say to me all day long, "Where is your God?"

4 These things I ponder upon and pour out my very self:
How I used to pass along in the company of nobles to the house of God,
With the sound of jubilation and praise—a festal crowd.
5 Why are you downcast, O my spirit?
And why do you moan within me?
Wait for God; for I shall again praise him,
My help and my God.

6 My spirit is downcast within me;
Therefore do I think of thee from the land of the Jordan,
And the Hermons, from the hill Mizar.
7 Deep calls to deep to the sound of thy waterfalls;
All thy waves and thy billows pass over me.
By day the LORD orders his kindness, 8
And by night his song is with me,
A prayer to the God of my life.

I say to God, my rock, "Why hast thou forgotten me? 9
Why do I go mourning because of oppression by the foe?"
With piercing pain my enemies reproach me, 10
While they say unto me all day long, "Where is your God?"
Why are you downcast, O my spirit? 11
And why do you moan within me?
Wait for God; for I shall again praise him,
My help and my God.

Do me justice, O God, and plead my case! 43
From a godless people, from deceitful and wicked men do thou release me.
For thou, O God of my fortress, why hast thou cast me off? 2
Why do I walk in mourning because of the oppression of the foe?
Send forth thy light and thy faithfulness; may they guide me, 3
May they bring me to thy holy hill, and to thy dwelling-place.

4 May I go to the altar of God, to God
my highest joy;
And may I praise thee with the lute,
O God my God.
5 Why are you downcast, O my spirit?
And why do you moan within me?
Wait for God; for I shall again praise
him,
My help and my God.

AN APPEAL TO THE JUSTICE OF GOD

[For the director: of the sons of Korah; a *maskil*]

44 O God, we have heard with our ears,
Our fathers have told us,
The work that thou didst in their
days, in days of old.
2 Thou didst dispossess the nations by
thy hand, but them thou didst
plant;
Thou didst break up the peoples, but
them thou didst spread abroad.
3 For not by their sword did they seize
the land,
Nor did their own arm give them victory,
But thy right hand and thine arm,
And the light of thy countenance; for
thou wast gracious to them.

4 It is thou, my king, O God,
Who orderest victory for Jacob.
5 Through thee we push down our foes;
Through thy name we trample upon
our adversaries.
6 For not in my bow do I trust,
Nor does my sword bring me victory;
7 But thou hast saved us from our foes,
And hast put to shame those that hate
us.
8 In God we have made our boast continually,
And thy name we will praise forever.
Selah

9 Yet thou hast spurned and brought us
to shame,
And thou dost not go forth with our
armies.
10 Thou dost turn us back from the foe,
And those who hate us have taken
spoil for themselves.
11 Thou dost make us food like sheep,
And among the nations thou hast dispersed us.
12 Thou sellest thy people for nothing,
And dost not make much by their
price.
13 Thou makest us a taunt to our neighbors,
A scorn and a derision to those around
us.
14 Thou makest us a byword among the
nations,
A laughingstock among the peoples.
15 All day long my disgrace is before me,
And shamefacedness covers me,
16 Because of the voice of the scoffer and
the scorner,
Because of the enemy and the vengeful one.

17 All this has come upon us, though we
have not forgotten thee,
Nor have we been false to thy covenant.
18 Our heart has not turned back,
Nor our step swerved from thy path.
19 Yet thou hast crushed us in the region
of the jackals,
And covered us with thick darkness.
20 If we have forgotten the name of our
God,
Or have spread forth our hands to a
foreign god,
21 Does not God search this out?
For he knows the secrets of the heart.
22 But because of thee we are slain the
whole day long,
We are counted as sheep for the
slaughter.

23 Awake! Why sleepest thou, O Lord?
Arouse thyself; do not spurn us forever!
24 Why dost thou hide thy face,
Forgetting our affliction and oppression?
25 For we are sunk down to the dust;
Our body cleaves to the earth.
26 Arise to our help;
And release us because of thy kindness.

A ROYAL MARRIAGE SONG

[For the director: upon lilies; of the sons of Korah; a *maskil;* a love-song]

45 My heart is stirred by a good theme;
I say, "My work concerns a king;
My tongue is the pen of a rapid writer."

2 You are the most fair of the sons of
men;

Grace is poured out through your lips;
Therefore God has blessed you evermore.
3 Gird your sword upon your thigh, O warrior;
Success to your praise and your majesty!
4 Ride on for the cause of truth and to hear the right;
And may your right hand show you wonders!
5 May your sharp arrows be in the midst of the king's foes!
May peoples fall under you!
6 Thy throne, O God, is forever and ever!
A righteous scepter is the scepter of your kingdom.

7 You love righteousness and hate wickedness;
Therefore has God, your God, anointed you
With the oil of gladness above your companions.
8 Myrrh and aloes and cassia are on all your garments;
From ivory palaces stringed instruments delight you.
9 Kings' daughters are among your treasures;
A princess stands at your right hand with gold from Ophir.

10 Hear, O daughter, and see; and incline your ear;
And forget your people and your father's house.
11 Since the king deserves your beauty,
Because he is your lord, bow yourself before him!
12 The daughter of Tyre with an offering is before you;
The richest of the peoples court you.
13 All glorious is the king's daughter within;
Her clothing is embroidered with gold.
14 In brilliant colors she is brought to the king;
The virgins in her train, her companions, are brought to you.
15 With gladness and joy are they brought in;
They enter the palace of the king.

16 Instead of your fathers shall be your sons;
You shall make them princes throughout the land.

I will extol your name through all generations; 1
Therefore peoples shall praise you forever and ever.

THE MIGHTY GOD

[For the director: of the sons of Korah.
Upon *alamoth*. A song]

God is our refuge and strength, 4
A well-proved help in trouble.
Therefore we will not fear though the earth totter,
And the mountains topple into the heart of the sea;
Though its waters roar and foam, 3
Though the mountains quake at its uproar. *Selah*

There is a river whose streams make glad the city of God, 4
The holiest habitation of the Most High;
God is in the midst of her; she will not totter; 5
God will help her at break of dawn.
The nations roar; the kingdoms totter; 6
He utters his voice—the earth melts.
The LORD of Hosts is with us; 7
The God of Jacob is our high tower. *Selah*

Come, see the deeds of the LORD, 8
How he has wrought ruin in the earth!
He makes wars to cease to the end of the earth; 9
He breaks the bow and cuts off the lance;
He burns the chariots.
Be still, and know that I am God; 10
I am exalted among the nations, I am exalted in the earth.
The LORD of Hosts is with us; 11
The God of Jacob is our high tower. *Selah*

THE VICTORIOUS GOD

[For the director: of the sons of Korah;
a Psalm]

O all peoples, clap your hands! 4
Shout to God with a glad voice!
For the LORD, most high, is terrible, 2
A great king over all the earth.
He subjected peoples under us, 3
And put nations under our feet.
He chose our possession for us, 4
The pride of Jacob whom he loved. *Selah*

5 God went up with a shout,
The LORD with the sound of the trumpet.

6 Sing praises to God, sing praises!
Sing praises to our king, sing praises!
7 For God is king over the whole earth.
Sing praises with a *maskil*.
8 God rules over the nations;
God sits upon his holy throne.
9 The nobles of the peoples are assembled
With the people of the God of Abraham.
For the shields of the earth belong to God;
He is highly exalted.

THE FAITHFUL GOD

[A song: A Psalm of the sons of Korah]

48 Great is the LORD and greatly to be praised,
In the city of our God, his holy hill.
2 Beautiful in elevation, the joy of the whole earth
Is the hill of Zion in the far north,
The city of the great king.
3 God, in her palaces,
Has shown himself a tower of strength.

4 For lo, the kings conspired together,
And they became enraged.
5 They saw; thereupon they were amazed;
They were overwhelmed, they fled in terror.
6 Panic seized them there,
Anguish as of one in travail.
7 By an east wind
Thou didst shatter the ships of Tarshish.
8 As we have heard, so have we seen,
In the city of the LORD of Hosts,
In the city of our God—
God establishes her forever. *Selah*

9 We have pondered upon thy goodness, O God,
In the midst of thy temple.
10 As thy name, O God, so also thy praise
Reaches the ends of the earth.
Thy right hand is full of righteousness.

11 Let Mount Zion rejoice,
Let the daughters of Judah exult,
Because of thy judgments.
12 Encircle Zion and walk around her;
Count her towers;
13 Set your mind upon her wall;
Go through her palaces;
That you may tell the next generation
14 That such is God,
Our God forever and ever.
He will guide us until death.

THE END OF ALL FLESH

[For the director: of the sons of Korah; a Psalm]

49 Hear this, all you peoples;
Give heed, all you dwellers in the world,
2 Sons of men, and all mankind,
Both rich and poor.
3 My mouth speaks wisdom,
And my heart's meditation is insight.
4 I incline my ear to a proverb;
I solve my riddle on the lyre.

5 Why should I fear in days of trouble,
When the guilt of my foes surrounds me,
6 Those who trust in their wealth,
And boast of the abundance of their riches.
7 But no man can at all ransom himself,
Or give a price for himself to God;
8 Since the ransom of his person forever and ever is too costly,
9 That he should continue to live forever,
Without seeing the Pit.
10 But see if he shall! Even wise men die;
The fool and the brutish alike perish,
And leave their wealth to others.
11 Their graves are their everlasting home,
Their dwelling throughout the ages,
Though lands are named after them.
12 But man is an ox without understanding;
He is like the beasts that perish.

13 This is the fate of those who are self-sufficient,
And the end of those who are satisfied with their own words. *Selah*
14 Like sheep they are appointed to Sheol;
Death shall shepherd them;
The upright shall rule over them in the morning.
Soon their form must decay;
Sheol is their dwelling.
15 But God will ransom me
From the power of Sheol, when it seizes me. *Selah*

16 Fear not when a man gets rich,
When the splendor of his house increases;
17 For he will take nothing with him when he dies;
His splendor will not go down after him.
18 Though he counts himself happy in being alive,
And congratulates himself that things go well with him,
19 He must join the generation of his fathers;
Never more will he see the light.
20 Man is an ox without understanding,
He is like the beasts that perish.

THE ESSENCE OF WORSHIP

[A Psalm of Asaph]

50 The God of gods, the LORD, spoke,
And called the earth from the rising of the sun unto its setting.
2 From Zion, the perfection of beauty, God shone forth.
3 May our God come and not be silent!
Fire devours before him;
And round about him the storm rages terribly.
4 He called to the heavens above,
And to the earth, to judge his people.
5 "Gather to me my saints,
Who have made a covenant with me by sacrifice."
6 Then the heavens declared his righteousness,
That God was giving judgment.
Selah
7 "Hear, O my people, and let me speak,
Hear, O Israel, and let me witness against you.
I am God, your God.
8 Not because of your sacrifices do I rebuke you,
For your burnt-offerings are constantly before me.
9 I will take no yearling from your house,
Nor ram from your folds.
10 For all the beasts of the forests are mine,
The cattle upon a thousand hills.
11 I know every bird of the mountains,
And whatsoever moves in the field is mine.
12 If I were hungry I would not tell you;
For mine is the world and everything therein.
13 Will I eat the flesh of oxen,
And drink the blood of goats?
14 Sacrifice to God a thank-offering,
And fulfil your vows to the Most High;
15 And call upon me on the day of trouble;
Then I will deliver you and you will honor me!"

16 But to the wicked God says:
"What right have you to recount my statutes,
And to take my covenant upon your lips?
17 For you hate instruction,
And you cast my words behind you!
18 If you see a thief, you are friendly with him;
And you make common cause with adulterers.
19 You charge your mouth with evil,
And your tongue frames up deceit.
20 You sit down and speak against your brother,
Against the son of your mother you utter slander.
21 These things you have done—and am I to be silent?
You thought that I was just like yourself!
I will correct you and set it forth in your sight.
22 Consider this then, O you who forget God;
Lest I rend and there be no one to rescue.
23 He who offers thanksgiving honors me;
And to him who heeds the way, I will show God's deliverance."

THE PLEA OF A PENITENT

[For the director: a Psalm of David, when Nathan, the prophet, came to him, after he had visited Bathsheba]

51 Have pity on me, O God, in accordance with thy kindness;
In thine abundant mercy wipe out my transgressions.
2 Wash me thoroughly from my guilt,
And cleanse me from my sin.

3 For I know my transgressions,
And my sin is ever before me.
4 Against thee, thee only, have I sinned,
And done that which is evil in thy sight.

Inasmuch as thou art in the right
when thou speakest,
And pure when thou givest judgment;
5 So in guilt was I begotten,
And in sin did my mother conceive me.

6 Verily thou dost delight in faithfulness,
The confidence of wisdom thou dost make me know.
7 Purge me with hyssop, that I may be clean;
Wash me, that I may be whiter than snow.

8 Let me hear joy and gladness;
Let the bones which thou hast crushed rejoice.
9 Hide thy face from my sins,
And wipe out all my guilt.
10 Create for me a clean heart, O God,
And renew a steadfast spirit within me.
11 Cast me not away from thy presence,
And take not thy holy spirit from me.

12 Restore to me the joy of thy deliverance,
And sustain me with a willing spirit.
13 Let me teach transgressors thy ways,
That sinners may return unto thee.

14 Rescue me from blood-guiltiness, O God,
The God of my deliverance;
That my tongue may sing aloud thy righteousness.
15 O Lord, open thou my lips,
That my mouth may declare thy praise.

16 For thou desirest not sacrifice,
And should I give burnt-offering thou wouldst not be pleased.
17 The sacrifice of God is a broken spirit;
A broken and a contrite heart,
O God, thou wilt not despise.

18 Do good in thy good will unto Zion;
Build thou the walls of Jerusalem.
19 Then shalt thou be pleased with right offerings,
Burnt-offering and whole burnt-offering;
Then shall bullocks come up upon thine altar.

THE FATE OF THE WICKED

[For the director: a *maskil* of David, when Doeg, the Edomite, came and told Saul and said to him: "David has entered the house of Abimelech"]

Why do you boast of evil, O mighty man? 52
The kindness of God is all day long.

Your tongue contrives guile, 2
Like a sharp razor it works deceit.
You love the bad better than the good, 3
You would rather lie than tell the truth. *Selah*

You love destructive words, the deceitful tongue; 4
But God will crush you forever; 5
He will seize you and pluck you out of your tent,
And uproot you from the land of the living. *Selah*

The righteous will behold and be reverent; 6
But at him they will laugh, saying,
"See the man who would not make God his stronghold, 7
But trusted in the abundance of his riches, and was strong in his guile."

But I am like a green olive tree in God's house; 8
I trust in the kindness of God forever and ever.
I will praise thee forever because thou hast done it; 9
And in the presence of thy saints I will proclaim that thy name is good.

THE VINDICATION OF GOD

[For the director: upon *mahalath;* a *maskil* of David]

The fool said in his heart: "There is no God." 53
They acted basely; they did abominable things;
There was none that did good.

God looked forth from the heavens upon the sons of men, 2
To see if there were any that acted wisely,
That sought after God.

They had all gone astray and all of them had done wrong; 3
There was none that did good,

No, not even one!
4 "Do they know nothing, all the evil-doers,
Who eat up my people as they eat bread,
But do not call upon God?"

5 There were they in great terror,
Where no terror had been.
For God scattered the bones of him who besieged you;
You brought them to shame, for God rejected them.

6 O that the deliverance of Israel would come from Zion!
When God restores the fortune of his people,
Jacob shall exult; Israel shall rejoice.

THE TRIUMPH OF THE PIOUS

[For the director: with stringed instruments. A *maskil* of David, when the Ziphites came and said to Saul, "Surely, David is in hiding with us"]

54 O God, deliver me by thy name,
And by thy power do me justice.
2 O God, hear my prayer;
Give heed to the words of my mouth!
3 For aliens have risen against me,
And men of violence seek my life.
They do not keep God before them.
Selah
4 Behold, God is my helper;
The Lord is my supporter.
5 He will requite the evil to my foes;
In thy faithfulness, destroy them!
6 Liberally I will sacrifice to thee.
I will praise thy name, O LORD, that it is good.
7 For he has delivered me from every trouble;
My eye has gloated over my foes.

A PROTEST TO GOD AGAINST THE WICKED

[For the director: with stringed instruments. A *maskil* of David]

55 Hear my prayer, O God;
And do not hide thyself from my entreaty.
2 Give heed to me, and answer me!
I am burdened with my complaint, and I am distracted,
3 Because of the voice of the foe,
Because of the oppression of the wicked.
For they bring trouble upon me,
And they attack me with fury.
My heart is in anguish within me,
And the terrors of death have fallen upon me.
Fear and trembling come upon me,
And shudders overwhelm me.
And I say, "Oh, that I had wings like a dove,
That I might fly away and dwell in peace!"
Lo, I would flee far away;
I would lodge in the wilderness.
Selah
I would haste to my shelter
Faster than the stormy wind and the tempest.

Confuse, O Lord, and divide their tongues!
For I have seen violence and strife in the town;
Day and night they encircle her upon 10
her walls,
And trouble and toil are within her;
Ruin is within her; 11
Oppression and fraud do not depart from her market-place.
For it is not an enemy who reviles me 12
—then I could bear it;
Nor does he who hates me magnify himself against me—
Then I could hide myself from him;
But you, my equal, my intimate 13
friend.
We held sweet converse together; 14
We entered the house of God in the procession.
Destruction will come upon them! 15
They shall go down alive to Sheol!
For wickedness is in their habitation, within them.

But I shall call upon God, 16
And the LORD will deliver me.
Evening, morning, and at noon 17
I will sigh and moan; and he will hear my voice.
He will deliver me safely from my foes, 18
Though many there be against me.
God will hear me and answer them, 19
He who has been enthroned from of old,
Selah
With whom there is no change;
Yet they fear not God.
He put forth his hand with his allies, 20
But violated his treaty!
His mouth was smoother than butter, 21
While war was in his heart;

Softer than oil were his words,
But they were drawn swords.
22 Cast your burden upon the LORD,
And he will sustain you.
He will never let the righteous totter.
23 But thou, O God, wilt bring them down into the pit of destruction;
Men of blood and fraud will not live out half their days.
So I will trust in thee.

THE ALL-SUFFICIENT GOD

[For the director: according to the dove of distant terebinths; a *miktam* of David, when the Philistines seized him in Gath]

56 Pity me, O God, for man tramples upon me;
All day long the adversary oppresses me;
2 My foes are trampling upon me all day long.
For many there be fighting against me.
3 Far away is the day when I fear,
For I trust in thee.
4 In God—I praise his word—
In God I trust without fear.
What can flesh do unto me?

5 All day long they trouble my affairs;
All their purposes are against me for evil.
6 They make attacks, they lie in wait, they watch my steps,
Inasmuch as they wait for my life.
7 For their crimes recompense them;
In wrath cast down the peoples, O God!
8 My misery thou hast reckoned;
Put thou my tears in thy bottle!
Are they not in thy book?
9 Then my enemies will be turned backward,
On the day when I call.
This I know, that God is for me.
10 In God—I praise his word—
In the LORD—I praise his word—
11 In God I trust without fear.
What can man do unto me?

12 Upon me, O God, are thy vows;
I will fulfil them with praises to thee.
13 For thou hast rescued me from death;
Hast thou not saved my feet from stumbling,
So that I walk before God in the light of life?

TRUST IN THE MIDST OF TROUBLES

[For the director: "Do not destroy." A *miktam* of David, when he fled from Saul into the cave]

Have pity on me, O God; have pity on me; 57
For in thee I am taking refuge;
And in the shadow of thy wings I take refuge,
Until ruin pass over.
I shall cry unto God, Most High, 2
To the God who rewards me.
He will send forth from the heavens and deliver me; 3
He will bring to shame him who tramples upon me; *Selah*
God will send forth his kindness and his faithfulness.
In the midst of lions that devour I must dwell, 4
Men whose teeth are a spear and arrows,
And their tongue a sharp sword.
Exalt thyself above the heavens, O God; 5
Let thy glory be over all the earth.

They have spread a net for my footsteps; 6
I am bowed down:
They dug a pit before me;
They fell into the midst of it. *Selah*
My heart is steadfast, O God, 7
My heart is steadfast.
I will play and sing.
Awake, my glory! 8
Awake, lute and lyre!
I will awaken the dawn!
I will praise thee among the peoples, O Lord; 9
I will sing praises to thee among the nations.

For thy kindness is great unto the heavens, 10
And thy faithfulness unto the clouds.
Arise above the heavens, O God! 11
Let thy glory be over all the earth!

THE WICKED AND THEIR DESTRUCTION

[For the director: "Do not destroy." A *miktam* of David]

Do you really speak what is right, O gods? 58
Do you judge mankind impartially?

2 Nay, but in the heart you work wickedness,
And on earth your hands weave violence.
3 The wicked go astray from the womb;
They wander from birth, speakers of lies.
4 Their venom is like a serpent's venom,
Like a deaf adder that stops its ear,
5 So that it hears not the voice of the charmer,
The most skilful weaver of spells.

6 O God, break their teeth in their mouth!
Knock out the fangs of the lions, O LORD!
7 May they disappear like water which runs off,
Like tender grass which wilts away,
8 Like the snail which passes away in slime;
Like the untimely birth of a woman, not seen by the sun.
9 Before your pots feel the thorns,
Whether green or burning, may he blow it away.
10 The righteous shall rejoice that he has seen vengeance;
He shall wash his footsteps in the blood of the wicked.
11 And men shall say, "There certainly is a reward for the righteous;
There certainly is a God who judges on earth."

A PRAYER FOR RESCUE FROM THE WICKED

[For the director: "Do not destroy." A *miktam* of David, when Saul sent forth and they watched the house to put him to death]

59 Rescue me from my enemies, O my God!
Protect me from those who rise up against me.
2 Rescue me from malefactors,
And from bloodthirsty men deliver me.

3 For lo, they lie in wait for me,
Mighty men are making attack upon me,
For no transgression or sin of mine, O LORD;
4 For no guilt of mine, they run and get themselves ready.

Arise to meet me, and see!
5 Do thou, O LORD, God of Hosts, God of Israel,
Awake, to punish all the nations!
Have no pity upon any of the wicked deceivers. *Selah*

They keep howling like dogs in the evening; 6
And they encircle the city.
Behold, they bark with their mouths; 7
Swords are in their lips;
But who hears them?

For thou, O LORD, dost laugh at them, 8
Thou dost hold all the nations in scorn.
My Strength, for thee do I watch; 9
For God is my fortress.

My gracious God will go before me; 10
God will let me gloat over my foes.
Slay them not, lest my people forget; 11
Shake them by thy power, and bring them down,
O Lord, our shield.

By the sin of their mouth, the word of their lips, 12
May they be caught in their pride.
And for the curses and lies which they utter,
Destroy them in wrath, destroy them that they be no more, 13
That they may know that God is ruling in Jacob,
Unto the ends of the earth. *Selah*

They keep howling like dogs in the evening, 14
And they encircle the city.
They wander about to devour; 15
If they are not satisfied, they grumble.

But I will sing of thy strength; 16
I will extol thy kindness in the morning.
For thou hast been a fortress for me,
And a refuge on the day of my trouble.
My Strength, I will sing praises unto thee; 17
For God is my fortress, my gracious God.

A PRAYER FOR DELIVERANCE

[For the director: upon *shushan eduth;* a *miktam* of David, to teach; when he strove with Aram of the two rivers and Aram-Zobah, and Joab returned and smote of Edom in the Valley of Salt twelve thousand]

O God, thou hast spurned us, thou hast broken us; 60
Thou hast been angry, and hast turned against us.

2 Thou hast made the earth quake, thou hast rent it;
Heal its wounds; for it staggers.
3 Thou hast made thy people see hardship;
Thou hast made us drink intoxicating wine.

4 Thou hast given a standard to those who fear thee,
To which they may flee from before the bow, *Selah*
5 That thy loved ones may be rescued;
Give victory by thy right hand and answer us.

6 God has spoken in his sanctuary:
"I will exult; I will divide Shechem,
And measure off the valley of Succoth.
7 Gilead is mine, and Manasseh is mine,
And Ephraim is the defense of my head;
Judah is my scepter.
8 Moab is my washbowl;
Upon Edom I cast my sandal;
Over Philistia I raise the shout of victory.
9 Who will bring me to the fortified city?
Who will lead me to Edom?"

10 Hast not thou, O God, rejected us?
And thou goest not forth, O God, with our armies!
11 Give us aid against the foe,
For futile is the help of man.
12 Through God we shall do valiantly,
For he will tread down our foes.

A PRAYER OF ASSURANCE

[For the director: with stringed instruments. Of David]

61 Hear my cry, O God!
Give ear to my prayer!
2 From the end of the earth I cry unto thee,
When my heart faints.
Upon a rock that is too high for me thou wilt set me.
3 For thou hast been my refuge,
A tower of strength against the foe.
4 Let me dwell in thy tent forever;
Let me find refuge in the covert of thy wings. *Selah*
5 For thou, O God, hast heard my vows;
Thou hast granted the wish of those who fear thy name.

Thou wilt add days unto the king's days; 6
His years will be as generation on generation.
He will dwell forever before God; 7
Charge Kindness and Fidelity that they protect him.
So shall I sing praises to thy name forever, 8
Fulfilling my vows day by day.

AN UNSHAKEN FAITH

[For the director: upon *Jeduthun;* a Psalm of David]

To God alone is my spirit resigned; **62**
From him is my deliverance.
He only is my rock and my deliverance, 2
My fortress; I shall not be roughly shaken.
For how long will you set upon a man 3
That you may murder him, all of you,
Like a leaning fence, like a fallen wall?
From his height they plan but to hurl him down; 4
They delight in lies; with their mouths they bless,
But in their hearts they curse. *Selah*

To God alone be resigned, O my spirit; 5
For from him is my hope.
He alone is my rock and my deliverance, 6
My fortress; I shall not be shaken.
Upon God rests my salvation and my glory; 7
My mighty rock, my refuge is in God.
Trust in him at all times, O people; 8
Pour out your heart before him.
God is our refuge. *Selah*

A mere illusion are the sons of Adam, 9
The sons of men are untrustworthy;
If put in scales they are lighter than a mere breath.
Trust not in oppression, and put no vain hope in robbery; 10
If wealth increase, set not your heart upon it.
One thing has God said; 11
Two things are those that I have heard:
That power belongs to God;
And kindness, O Lord, is thine; 12
For thou dost requite a man according to his work.

FAITH AND FELLOWSHIP

[A Psalm of David, when he was in the wilderness of Judah]

63 O God, thou art my God; I seek for thee;
My spirit thirsts for thee; my flesh yearns for thee,
As in a dry and parched land where no water is;
2 So have I beheld thee in the sanctuary,
While seeing thy power and thy glory.
3 Because thy kindness is better than life,
My lips do praise thee.
4 So shall I bless thee as long as I live;
In thy name I shall raise my hands.
5 As with marrow and fatness my desire is satisfied,
And my mouth praises thee with jubilant lips,
6 When I remember thee upon my couch,
And meditate on thee in the night-watches.
7 For thou hast been my help,
And in the shadow of thy wings I shout for joy.
8 I have clung close to thee;
Thy right hand has sustained me.
9 And they who seek my life to destroy it,
Shall go into the lowest depths of the earth;
10 They shall be given over to the power of the sword;
They shall become the portion of jackals.
11 But the king shall rejoice in God;
Everyone who swears by him shall sing praises;
For the mouth of liars shall be closed.

THE WAYS OF THE WICKED AND THE WAY OF GOD

[For the director: a Psalm of David]

64 Hear my voice, O God, when I complain;
From terror of the foe, protect my life.
2 Hide me from the council of evildoers,
From the commotion of wrongdoers,
3 Who whet their tongue like a sword;
They fit their arrow, a bitter word,
4 To shoot, in concealment, at the innocent;
Suddenly, they shoot him and are not afraid.
They strengthen for themselves a wicked scheme; 5
They talk of laying snares secretly;
They say, "Who will see them?"
They search out wicked plans; 6
They conceal a well-laid plot;
For the inner man and the heart are deep.

Then God shoots them with his arrow; 7
Suddenly their wounds are there;
So they make their tongue a stumbling-block for themselves; 8
All who look at them wag the head;
And all men fear, 9
And tell of the deed of God,
And understand his work.
The righteous rejoices in the LORD 10
and takes refuge in him;
And all the upright in heart sing praises.

THE GOD OF THE UNIVERSE

[For the director: a Psalm of David; a Song]

Praise befits thee, O God, in Zion; 65
And unto thee is the vow fulfilled.
O thou that hearest prayer,
Unto thee do all flesh come.
If deeds of guilt are too strong for me,
Thou dost wipe out our transgressions.

How happy is he whom thou dost choose and bring near
to dwell in thy courts!
We are satisfied with the goodness of thy house,
thy holy temple.
Through terrible deeds thou dost answer us in vindication,
O God of our deliverance,
Thou confidence of all the ends of the earth,
and the faraway islands.
He who prepared the mountain by his strength
is girded with power.

O thou who dost assuage the roar of the seas,
The roar of their waves and the uproar of peoples,
Those who dwell in the far regions are afraid of thy tokens;
Thou makest the dawn and the sunset to shout with joy.
Thou visitest the land and makest it overflow;
Thou greatly enrichest it.

Through the brook of God, which is full of water,
Thou preparest their grain; for thus dost thou prepare it:
Thou dost saturate its furrows; thou dost settle its ridges;
With showers thou dost soften it;
Its young growth thou dost bless.
Thou crownest the year with thy goodness,
And thy paths drip fatness.
The meadows of the plain drip,
And the hills gird themselves with joy.
The pastures are clothed with flocks;
And the valleys are covered with grain;
They shout for joy; yea, they sing!

A HYMN OF GRATITUDE

[For the director: a Song, a Psalm]

Make a joyous shout to God, all the earth;
Praise the glory of his name;
Make his praise glorious!
Say to God: "How awful is thy work!
Because of thy great power thy foes fawn upon thee!
All the earth worships thee,
And sings praises to thee, singing the praises of thy name." *Selah*

Come and see the works of God,
Awful in deeds against mankind.
He changed the sea into dry land;
They passed through the river on foot.
There we rejoiced in him.
He rules by his power forever;
His eyes watch over the nations.
Let not the adversaries exalt themselves. *Selah*

Bless our God, O peoples;
And sound abroad the praise of him
Who has kept us among the living,
And has not suffered our feet to stumble.

For thou hast tested us, O God;
Thou hast refined us as silver is refined.

Thou didst bring us into the net;
Thou didst lay a heavy load upon our loins.
Thou didst let men ride over our heads;
We went through fire and water;
But thou hast brought us forth to a spacious place.
I will enter thy house with offerings,
I will fulfil to thee the vows,
Which my lips have expressed,
And my mouth has spoken when I was in trouble.
Burnt-offerings of fatlings I will offer to thee, 15
Together with the savory smoke of rams;
I will prepare an ox and he-goats. *Selah*

Come, listen, all you who revere God, 16
While I tell what he has done for me:
Unto him did I cry with my mouth, 17
And I was raised from under my foes.
Had I cherished deceit in my heart, 18
The Lord would not have heard.
But God did hear; 19
He gave heed to my prayerful voice.

Blessed be God, 20
Who did not reject my prayer,
Nor turn away his kindness from me.

A PRAYER FOR GOD'S BLESSING

[For the director: with stringed instruments; a Psalm, a Song]

May God be merciful unto us and bless us, **67**
And cause his face to shine upon us! *Selah*
That thy way may be known in the earth, 2
Thy salvation among all nations,
Let the peoples praise thee, O God, 3
Let all the peoples praise thee.

Let the nations be glad and sing for joy, 4
Because thou judgest the peoples justly,
And leadest the nations in the earth. *Selah*
Let the peoples praise thee, O God; 5
Let all the peoples praise thee!

Earth has yielded her increase. 6
May God, our own God, bless us!
May God bless us; 7
And may all the ends of the earth fear him!

THE MIGHT AND GLORY OF GOD

[For the director: of David; a Psalm, a Song]

Let God arise! Let his foes be scattered! **68**
And let those that hate him flee before him!

2 As smoke is driven away by the wind,
As wax melts before the fire,
So do the wicked perish from before God.
3 But the righteous rejoice;
They exult before God;
And they are jubilant with joy.

4 Sing unto God; praise his name!
Extol him who rides upon the storm-clouds,
Whose name is Yah, and exult before him!
5 A father to the fatherless and the judge of widows
Is God in his holy dwelling.
6 God brings home the desolate;
He leads prisoners forth into prosperity;
Only the rebellious dwell in a parched land.
7 O God, when thou didst go forth before thy people,
When thou didst march through the desert, *Selah*
8 The earth quaked, the heavens also poured down at the presence of God;
Even yon Sinai, at the presence of God, Israel's God.
9 A copious rain didst thou pour down, O God;
Thine exhausted and worn-out land thou didst re-establish.
10 Thy flock dwelt therein;
Thou didst prepare it in thy goodness for the poor, O God.

11 The Lord gave the command;
The messengers were a great host.
12 Kings of hosts fled, they fled!
The women divided the spoil:
13 (Did you lie among the sheepfolds?)
The wings of a dove covered with silver,
And its pinions with glittering gold.
14 When the Almighty made kings fly therein,
It was snowing in Zalmon.

15 O mighty mountain, O Mount Bashan;
O many-peaked mountain, O Mount Bashan;
16 Why, O many-peaked mountains, do you envy
The mountain that God has desired for his abode?
Yet the LORD will dwell there forever.

The chariots of God are myriads, thousands upon thousands;
The Lord came from Sinai into the sanctuary.

Thou hast ascended on high; thou hast carried away captives;
Thou hast taken tribute of men,
Yea, of rebels too, that the LORD God may dwell there.
Blessed be the Lord, who daily bears our burden;
The God who is our salvation; *Selah*
The God who is our saving God;
And unto GOD, the Lord, belong the exits to death.

God will surely crush the head of his foes,
The skull of Seir who goes on in his guilt.
The Lord said, "I will bring them back from Bashan,
I will bring them back from the depths of the sea;
That your foot may bathe in blood,
And the tongue of your dogs have its share of your foes."

Thy processions are seen, O God,
The processions of my God, my King, in the sanctuary.
Singers lead; at the rear, the stringed instruments;
In the middle, maidens playing timbrels.
In choirs, they bless God,
The Lord, those from Israel's fountain.
There is Benjamin, the youngest, ruling them;
The princes of Judah in a throng,
The princes of Zebulun, and the princes of Naphtali.

Command thy strength, O God;
Be strong, O God, thou who hast wrought for us.
From thy temple at Jerusalem,
Where kings bring gifts to thee,
Threaten the beasts of the marsh reeds,
The herd of bulls, with calves of the peoples;
Trample upon those who rejoice in spoil;
Scatter the peoples that delight in war.

31 Let envoys come from Egypt;
Let Ethiopia eagerly stretch forth her hands to God.
32 Sing to God, O kingdoms of the earth.
Sing praises to the Lord, *Selah*
33 To him who rides upon the most ancient heavens.
Lo, he utters his voice, a mighty voice!
34 Ascribe power unto God!
Over Israel is his majesty,
And his power is in the clouds.

35 Terrible art thou, O God, from thy sanctuary.
Unto Israel he gives power,
And strength to the people.
Blessed be God!

AN IMPRECATORY PSALM

[For the director: upon lilies; of David]

69 Save me, O God,
for the water mounts to my chin,
2 I am sunk in deep mire,
where there is no foothold.
I have got into deep water,
and the flood overwhelms me.

3 I am worn out by my crying,
my throat is parched.
My eyes fail
with waiting for my God.

4 More numerous than the hairs of my head
are they that hate me without cause.
Many are they that would destroy me,
my enemies wrongfully.
What I did not steal,
forsooth, I must restore!

5 O God, thou knowest my foolishness;
and my guilt is not hidden from thee.
6 May they who hope in thee be not put to shame through me,
O Lord, GOD of hosts!
May they who seek thee be not brought to disgrace through me,
O God of Israel.

7 For because of thee I bear reproach,
Dishonor covers my face.
8 I have become a stranger to my brothers,
An alien to my mother's sons.
9 For zeal for thy house has eaten me up;
And the abuse of them that abuse thee has fallen on me.
When I afflict myself by fasting, 10
It becomes my reproach.
If I assume sackcloth as my clothing, 11
I become a joke to them.
They who sit in the gate talk of me, 12
And I have become the song of the drunkards.

But my prayer unto thee, O LORD, is 13
for an acceptable time;
O God, in thine abundant kindness,
Answer me with thy saving faithfulness.
Rescue me from the mire that I sink 14
not;
Let me be delivered from my enemies
and from the deep water;
Let not the flood of water overwhelm 15
me;
Let not the depths swallow me up;
And let not the pit close its mouth upon me.

Answer me, O LORD, for thy kindness 16
is good;
In accordance with thine abundant mercy turn to me!
And do not hide thy face from thy 17
servant,
For I am in trouble; answer me quickly!
Fight for me and deliver me; 18
Because of my enemies, release me.

Thou knowest my abuse, 19
And my shame and disgrace;
All my foes are before thee.
Abuse breaks my heart and I am sick; 20
And I look for sympathy, but there is none;
And for comforters, but I find none.
Yea, they put poison in my food, 21
And give me vinegar to drink for my thirst.

May their table become a snare before 22
them,
And their peace-offerings a trap.
May their eyes be so darkened that 23
they cannot see,
And make their loins tremble constantly.
Pour out upon them thy wrath, 24
And let thy fierce anger overtake them.
May their encampment be a waste; 25
In their tents may there be no inhabitant.

26 For him whom thou hast smitten they persecute,
And unto the pain of thy victims they add.
27 Add guilt to their guilt,
And let them not enter into thy justification.
28 May they be blotted out from the book of life,
And not be inscribed among the righteous.
29 But as for me, though afflicted and in pain,
Thy salvation, O God, will set me on high.
30 I will praise the name of God in song,
And I will magnify him with thanksgiving;
31 And that will please the LORD more than an ox,
Or a bullock with horns and hoofs.
32 Behold, O you humble, and be glad!
O you who seek God, let your heart revive!
33 For the LORD listens to the needy,
And does not despise his prisoners.
34 The heavens and the earth will praise him,
The sea and all that stirs therein;
35 Because God delivers Zion,
And rebuilds the cities of Judah;
So that they dwell there and take possession;
36 And the descendants of his servants inherit it,
And those loving his name shall dwell therein.

A PRAYER FOR THE HELP OF GOD

[For the director: of David; to make a memorial]

70 Be pleased, O God, to rescue me!
O LORD, hasten to my help!
2 May they be put to shame and abashed
who seek my life!
May they be driven back and routed
who desire my ruin!
3 May they be appalled by reason of their shame,
who say, "Aha, Aha!"
4 May they rejoice and be glad in thee,
all who seek thee!
And may they continually say, "Great is God,"
who love thy deliverance.

Since I am poor and needy,
O God, hasten to me!
Thou art my help and my deliverer;
O LORD, do not tarry!

A PRAYER FOR AID AGAINST THE FOE

In thee, O LORD, have I found refuge;
May I never be put to shame!
In thy righteousness, rescue me and deliver me!
Incline thine ear unto me and save me!
Become unto me a rock of refuge,
To which I may always resort.
Thou hast given command to save me;
For thou art my rock and my fortress.

O my God, deliver me from the hand of the wicked,
From the fist of the evildoer and the violent!
For thou hast been my hope, O Lord GOD,
My confidence from my youth:
Upon thee have I leaned from birth;
From my mother's womb thou hast been my stay;
In thee is my hope continually.
Like a portent have I been to many;
But thou art my strong refuge.
My mouth is filled with thy praise,
And thy beauty all day long.

Do not cast me off in my old age;
When my strength fails, do not forsake me!
For my foes say concerning me,
And those who watch for my life make plans also,
Saying, "God has abandoned him;
Pursue and seize him; for there is no one to rescue him."
O God, be not far from me!
Hasten, O my God, to my help!

May they be put to shame and destroyed who are hostile to me;
May they be covered with abuse and shame who seek to injure me.

But I will hope continually,
And will add more to all thy praise.
My mouth will relate thy righteousness,
And thy deeds of deliverance all day long;
For were I skilled in writing,
And should I reach an advanced age,
O Lord GOD,
I could record thy righteousness only.

17 O God, thou hast taught me from my youth until now;
I declare thy wonders.
18 Yea, even to old age and gray hairs, do not forsake me, O God;
So that I may tell of thy mighty arm to the generations,
To all that are to come.

19 Thy power and thy righteousness
Extend, O God, unto the high heavens.
Thou who hast done great things,
O God, who is like thee?

20 O thou who hast made us see many dangers and disasters,
Do thou quicken us again,
And from the depths of the earth bring us up again.
21 Do thou increase my greatness,
And turn and comfort me!
22 I also will praise thee with the lyre,
I will sing of thy faithfulness, O my God, with the harp,
O thou holy one of Israel.
23 My lips shall joyfully shout when I sing praises to thee,
And my life which thou hast redeemed.
24 My tongue, too, shall tell of thy righteousness all day long;
For they shall be put to shame, they shall be disgraced, who sought to do me harm.

LONG LIVE THE KING!

[Of Solomon]

72 Give the king thy justice, O God,
And thy righteousness to the king's son,
2 That he may judge thy people with right,
And thine afflicted with justice!

3 May the mountains bring the people peace,
And the hills righteousness!
4 May he judge the afflicted of the people,
And give deliverance to the poor,
And crush the oppressor!

5 May he live as long as the sun,
And as long as the moon, throughout the ages!
May he descend like rain upon the mown grass, 6
Like showers that water the earth.

May the righteous flourish in his days, 7
And may peace abound, till the moon be no more!
May he rule from sea to sea, 8
And from the river to the ends of the earth!

Before him may foes bend low, 9
And his enemies lick the dust!
May the kings of Tarshish and the coast-lands 10
return tribute,
The kings of Sheba and Seba
bring gifts!
And may all kings do obeisance to him, 11
All nations serve him!

For he rescues the needy when he calls for help, 12
And the afflicted who has no helper.
He takes pity upon the poor and needy, 13
And saves the life of the poor.
From oppression and violence he ransoms them; 14
And precious is their blood in his eyes.

So, may he live and be given of the gold of Sheba; 15
And may men pray for him constantly;
All day long may they bless him!
May there be abundance of grain in the land; 16
On mountain tops may its fruit shake like Lebanon;
And may those from the cities blossom like the grass of the earth!

May his name endure forever! 17
As long as the sun may his name abide!
May men invoke blessings on one another through him!
May all nations call him blessed!

Blessed be the LORD God, the God of Israel, 18
Who alone does great wonders!
And blessed be his glorious name forever! 19
And may the whole earth be filled with his glory!
Amen and amen!

The prayers of David, the son of Jesse, are ended. 20

BOOK III, PSS. 73–89

FELLOWSHIP WITH GOD

[A Psalm of Asaph]

73 Surely, God is good to Israel,
To those who are pure in heart.
2 But as for me, my feet were almost gone,
My steps had well-nigh slipped.
3 For I was incensed at fools,
As I saw the prosperity of the wicked.

4 For they have no pangs;
Sound and healthy is their body.
5 In trouble, like other men, they are not;
Nor are they plagued like others.
6 Hence pride is their necklace;
A robe of violence covers them.

7 Their eye goes forth beyond the best,
They transcend the imaginations of the heart.
8 They mock and speak in wickedness;
Oppression from on high they speak.
9 They have set their mouth in the heavens,
And their tongue ranges the earth.

10 Therefore the people turn to them,
And find no fault in them.
11 And they say, "How can God know?
And is there knowledge in the Most High?"
12 Lo, such are the wicked!
And in perpetual ease they amass wealth.
13 All to no purpose have I kept my heart pure,
And washed my hands in innocence.
14 For I have been smitten all day long,
And chastened every morning.

15 If I had said, "I will speak thus,"
I should, indeed, have betrayed the generation of thy children.
16 But when I pondered how to understand this,
It was in my sight a troublesome task,
17 Until I came into the sanctuary of God;
Then I perceived their future lot.

18 Surely thou settest them in slippery places;
Thou dost hurl them down to ruin.
19 How they become a desolation as in a moment,
Are swept away, are destroyed through horrors!
As a dream when one awakes, O Lord,
So, when thou dost bestir thyself, thou wilt set at nought their fancies.

When my heart was stirred up,
And my feelings were aroused,
Then I was stupid and knew nothing;
A brute was I toward thee!

Yet I am always with thee;
Thou holdest my right hand.
By thy counsel thou leadest me;
And by the hand thou dost take me after thee.

Whom have I in the heavens but thee?
And having thee, I wish nought else on earth.
My flesh and my heart fail;
But my heart's rock and my portion is God forever.

For lo, those far from thee will perish;
Thou destroyest all who are apostates from thee.
But as for me, the nearness of God is my good;
I put my reliance upon the Lord GOD;
That I may recount all thy wonders.

AN APPEAL TO GOD AGAINST VANDALS

[A *maskil* of Asaph]

Why, O God, hast thou cast us off forever?
Why does thine anger smoke against the flock of thy pasture?
Remember thy community which thou didst obtain of old,
Which thou didst redeem as the tribe of thine inheritance,
Mount Zion wherein thou hast dwelt.

Lift up thy footsteps unto the perpetual ruins;
The enemy has destroyed everything in the sanctuary.
Thy foes roar in the midst of thine assembly;
They set up their own signs as signs.

They hew down at the upper entrance
The wooden trellis work with axes;
And now its carvings also,
With hatchet and adzes they smash.

7 They have set thy sanctuary on fire;
They have defiled to the ground the dwelling-place of thy name.
8 They said to themselves, "We will oppress them also."
They burned all the synagogues of God in the land.
9 Our signs we did not see;
There was no longer a prophet;
There was nobody among us that knew how long.
10 How long, O God, shall the foe blaspheme?
Shall the enemy revile thy name forever?
11 Why dost thou withdraw thy hand,
And restrain thy right hand within thy bosom?

12 God is my king from of old,
Who wrought victory in the midst of the earth.
13 Through thy power thou didst divide the sea;
Thou didst crush the heads of the dragons upon the waters.

14 Thou didst shatter the heads of Leviathan;
Thou didst give him as food to the desert demons.
15 Thou didst cleave out fountain and brook;
Thou didst dry up unfailing rivers.

16 Day and night are both thine;
Thou didst establish sun and moon.
17 Thou didst fix all the bounds of the earth;
Thou didst make both summer and winter.

18 Recall this: the enemy blasphemed the LORD,
And a reprobate people reviled thy name.
19 Do not give to the wild beasts the life of thy turtle-dove;
Do not forget the life of thine afflicted one forever.

20 Have regard to the covenant;
For the dark places of the land are full of the habitations of violence.
21 Let not the crushed be again put to shame;
May the poor and the needy praise thy name!

Arise, O God; plead thine own cause; 22
Remember thy reproach from the reprobate all the day long.
Do not forget the voice of thy foes, 23
The uproar of thine adversaries which continually ascends.

GOD AS JUDGE

[For the director: "Do not destroy." A Psalm of Asaph, a Song]

We give thanks to thee, O God; we give thanks, 75
And they who call upon thy name recount thy wonders.

"When I take the appointed time, 2
I shall judge with equity.
The earth with all its inhabitants will melt away, 3
Since it was I who established its pillars. *Selah*

"I say to the boasters, 'Do not boast'; 4
And to the wicked, 'Do not lift up the horn;
Do not lift up your horn on high, 5
Nor speak with an insolent neck.' "

For not from the East, nor from the West, 6
Nor yet from the steppe nor from the mountains—
But God is the judge! 7
He humbles one and exalts another.

For the cup is in the hand of the LORD, 8
With foaming wine, thoroughly mixed;
And he pours out to one and another.
Surely all the wicked of the earth
Must drink and drain its dregs.

But I will forever rejoice, 9
And sing praises to the God of Jacob.
For all the horns of the wicked he will break off, 10
That the horns of the righteous may be exalted.

THE TERRIBLE ONE

[For the director: with stringed instruments. A Psalm of Asaph, a Song]

In Judah is God known, 76
His name is great in Israel.
And his tent is in Salem, 2
His dwelling in Zion.
There did he break the fiery shafts of the bow, 3
Shield, and sword, and battle. *Selah*

4 Terrible art thou, mightier than a devouring lion;
5 Devastated are the stout-hearted,
They sleep their sleep,
And none of the men of war have found their hands.
6 At thy rebuke, O God of Jacob,
Chariots and horsemen are sunk in deep sleep.
7 Thou thyself art terrible;
And who can stand before thee, because of the intensity of thine anger?
8 From the heavens thou didst pronounce sentence;
Earth feared and was still,
9 When God arose to judgment,
To save all the humble of the earth. *Selah*
10 Surely, the most violent of men will give thanks to thee,
The most persistently violent will put on sackcloth.
11 Make vows and pay them to the LORD, your God;
Let all who are around him bring gifts to him that is terrible.
12 He cuts off the breath of princes;
He is terrible to the kings of the earth.

THE MIGHTY GOD

[For the director: upon *Jeduthun*. A Psalm of Asaph]

77 I will raise my voice to God and cry aloud;
I will raise my voice to God, that he may hear me.
2 On my day of trouble I sought the Lord;
My hand was stretched out by night without ceasing;
My mind refused consolation.
3 When I recall this, O God, I groan;
When I ponder upon it, my spirit faints. *Selah*
4 Thou holdest the lids of my eyes;
I am restless and cannot speak.
5 I have thought upon the days of old,
The years of ancient times.
6 By night I recall my song;
I commune with my heart and search my spirit:
7 "Will the Lord cast us off forever,
And never again be gracious?
8 Is his kindness at an end forever?
Has his word ceased throughout the ages?

Has God forgotten how to be gracious?
Or has he shut up his mercy in anger?" *Selah*

Then I say, "This is my disaster:
That the right hand of the Most High has changed."

I will recall the works of the LORD;
I will remember thy wonders of old,
And I will ponder upon all thy work,
And meditate upon thy doings.

O God, thy way is in holiness. 1
What deity is as great as God?
Thou art the God that does wonders; 1
Thou hast made thy strength known among the peoples.
Thou didst by thy power redeem thy 1
people,
The sons of Jacob and Joseph. *Selah*

The waters saw thee, O God; 1
The waters saw thee; they suffered pangs;
The very deeps were convulsed.
The clouds poured down water,
The skies gave forth their voice;
Thine arrows flashed hither and thither.

The sound of thy thunder was in the 1
cyclone;
Lightning lit up the world.
The land trembled and quaked.
Thy way was in the sea, 1
And thy path on the great waters;
But thy footsteps were not traced.
Thou didst lead thy people like a flock, 2
By the hand of Moses and Aaron.

A RELIGIOUS BALLAD

[A *maskil* of Asaph]

Hearken, my people, to my teaching; 7
Incline your ear to the words of my mouth!
I will open my mouth in a parable;
I will utter riddles from of old,
What we have heard and known,
And our fathers told us.
We will not conceal it from their children,
Telling to the coming generation the praises of the LORD,
And his might and his wonders which he wrought,
When he established a decree in Jacob,
And gave Israel a law,

Which he commanded our fathers
To teach unto their children,
6 That the coming generation should know,
That children yet unborn should arise,
And tell to their children,
7 That they should set their trust in God,
And not forget the works of God;
But keep his commands,
8 And not be like their fathers,
A stubborn and rebellious generation,
A generation that did not set its heart aright;
Nor was its spirit loyal to God.

9 The Ephraimites—archers, equipped with the bow—
Turned back on the day of battle.
10 They did not keep the covenant of God,
And refused to walk in accordance with his law;
11 But forgot his works,
And his wonders which he had showed them.
12 Before their fathers he did wonders
In the land of Egypt, on the fields of Zoan.
13 He cleft the sea and led them through,
And made the waters stand like a wall.
14 And he led them with a cloud by day,
And all night through by the light of a fire.
15 He split rocks in the desert,
And gave them drink abundantly as from the great depths.
16 And he brought forth streams from the rock,
And made water run down like rivers.
17 But they sinned still more against him,
Rebelling in the desert against the Most High.
18 Then they tried God in their hearts,
By demanding food according to their desire;
19 And they spoke against God and said,
"Can God spread a table in the desert?
20 He did, indeed, smite the rock, so that the water flowed,
And streams poured forth;
Can he also give bread,
Or provide meat for his people?"
21 Therefore the LORD heard and became angry,
And fire blazed forth against Jacob,
And wrath mounted against Israel;
22 Because they did not believe in God,
And put no confidence in his deliverance.
So he commanded the skies from above, 23
And opened the doors of the heavens;
And he rained manna upon them for food, 24
And gave them of the grain of the heavens.
The bread of the mighty did a man eat; 25
Provisions he furnished them in abundance.
He let loose the east wind in the heavens, 26
And in his might he guided the south wind;
And he rained flesh upon them like dust, 27
And winged birds like the sand of the seas,
And he let them fall in the midst of their camp, 28
Round about their dwellings.
So they did eat and were completely satisfied; 29
He brought them their desire.
They were not yet tired of their craving, 30
Their food was still in their mouths,
When the anger of God mounted against them, 31
And he slew the stoutest among them,
And laid low the choicest in Israel.
Notwithstanding all this, they sinned still more, 32
And believed not in his wondrous works;
So he brought their days to an end in a breath, 33
And their years in sudden ruin.
When he smote them, then they sought him, 34
And again they inquired of God.
And they remembered that God was their rock, 35
And that the most high God was their avenger.
So they beguiled him with their mouth, 36
And lied to him with their tongue;
But their heart was not steadfast with him, 37
Nor were they loyal to his covenant.
But he is merciful; 38
He pardons guilt and does not destroy.
And frequently he restrains his anger,
And does not arouse all his rage.

39 So he remembered that they were flesh,
A breath that passes and does not come back.
40 How often did they oppose him in the wilderness,
And grieve him in the desert!
41 They tried God again and again,
And vexed the holy one of Israel.
42 They did not remember his power:
The day that he delivered them from the foe;
43 How he set his wonders in Egypt,
And his portents in the fields of Zoan,
44 And turned their rivers to blood,
So that they could not drink of their streams!
45 How he sent forth among them swarms of insects which devoured them,
And frogs, which destroyed them;
46 And how he gave their produce to the caterpillar,
And the fruit of their labor to the locust;
47 How he destroyed their vines with hailstones,
And their sycamore trees with frost;
48 And how he gave their cattle over to the plague,
And their flocks to the pestilence.

49 He sent upon them his fierce anger,
Wrath and fury and trouble,
An embassy of messengers of woe.
50 He made a smooth path for his anger,
He did not restrain them from death,
But handed over their life to the plague.
51 He smote all the first-born in Egypt,
The first-fruits of virile strength in the tents of Ham;
52 And he sent forth his people like a flock,
Guided them like a herd in the wilderness,
53 And led them safely so that they were not afraid;
But their foes the sea did overwhelm.
54 So he brought them to his holy region,
To this mountain which his right hand had won.
55 And he drove out the nations from before them,
And distributed them as a possession,
And gave the tribes of Israel dwellings in their tents.

56 But they tried and vexed God, the Most High,
And did not keep his injunctions.
And they turned back and were faithless like their fathers; 5
They turned around like a treacherous bow.
They provoked him with their sanctuaries; 5
And with their idols, they aroused his hot wrath.
God heard and became furious, 5
And utterly rejected Israel,
And spurned the sanctuary at Shiloh, 6
The tent which he had occupied among men.
He surrendered his strength to captivity, 6
And his splendor into the hand of the foe.
He delivered his people to the sword, 6
And raged against his heritage.
Fire devoured his youths, 6
And his maidens had no wedding songs.
His priests fell by the sword, 6
And his widows could not weep.

Then the Lord awoke like one asleep, 6
Like a strong man overcome by wine.
And he smote his foes backward, 6
And he inflicted upon them a perpetual disgrace.
He rejected the house of Joseph, 6
And chose not the tribe of Ephraim.
But he chose the tribe of Judah, 6
Mount Zion, which he loved.
He built his sanctuary like the heights, 6
Like the earth which he has founded forever.
He chose David, his servant. 7
And took him from the sheepfolds.
From behind the ewes he brought him, 7
To be the shepherd of Jacob, his people,
And Israel, his heritage.
He tended them in accordance with the integrity of his heart, 7
And by the skill of his hands he led them.

A PRAYER FOR VENGEANCE

[A Psalm of Asaph]

O God, the nations have come into thine inheritance;
They have defiled thy holy temple;
They have laid Jerusalem in ruins.
They have given the corpses of thy servants

As food to the birds of the air;
The flesh of thy saints to the beasts of the land.
3 They have poured out their blood like water
Round about Jerusalem, and there is none to bury them.
4 We are become a taunt for our neighbors,
Derision and mockery for those around us.

5 How long, O LORD? Wilt thou be angry forever?
Will thy jealousy burn like fire?
6 Pour out thy wrath upon the nations who do not acknowledge thee,
And upon the kingdoms that do not invoke thy name;
7 For they have devoured Jacob,
And have laid waste his habitation.
8 Do not remember against us our early sins;
May thy mercies quickly meet us,
For we are brought very low.
9 Help us, O God of our salvation,
Because of the glory of thy name;
And deliver us and forgive our sins for thy name's sake.

10 Why should the nations say, "Where is their God?"
May there be known among the nations, in our sight,
Vengeance for the blood of thy servants that has been shed!
11 May the groan of the prisoner come before thee!
According to thy great power make those doomed to death survive;
12 And requite to our neighbors, sevenfold into their bosom,
The reproach wherewith they reproached thee, O Lord.
13 Then we, thy people, and the flock of thy pasture,
Will praise thee forever;
Throughout the ages we will recount thy praise.

A PRAYER FOR RESTORATION

[For the director: to the lilies; a testimony of Asaph; a Psalm]

1 O Shepherd of Israel, give ear;
Thou that leadest Joseph like a flock,
Thou that art seated upon the cherubim, shine forth.
Before Ephraim, Benjamin, and Manasseh, 2
Stir up thy might,
And come to our deliverance.
O God, restore us; 3
And let thy face shine, that we may be delivered.

O LORD, God of hosts, 4
How long thou hast been enraged at the prayer of thy people!
Thou hast fed them with the bread of tears; 5
Thou hast made them drink tears beyond reason.
Thou dost make us a butt for our neighbors, 6
And our foes make mock of us.
O God of hosts, restore us; 7
And let thy face shine that we may be delivered.

Thou didst remove a vine from Egypt; 8
Thou didst expel the nations and replant it;
Thou didst smooth the way for it, 9
So that it struck root and filled the land.
The mountains were covered with its shade, 10
And the cedars of God with its branches.
It sent forth its boughs to the sea, 11
And its tendrils to the river.
Why, then, hast thou broken down its walls, 12
So that all who pass by pluck its fruit?
The wild boar devours it, 13
And the beasts of the field feed upon it.
O God of hosts, restore us; 14
And let thy face shine that we may be delivered.

Look forth from the heavens and see, 15
And watch over this vine,
And the garden which thy right hand planted,
And the son whom thou didst raise up for thyself.
It is burned; it is cut down. 16
May they perish at the rebuke of thy presence.
May thy hand be over the man, 17
Thy right hand over the man whom thou didst raise up for thyself!
He has not turned back from thee. 18

Revive us, and upon thy name we will call.
19 O LORD, God of hosts, restore us!
Let thy face shine upon us that we may be delivered!

AN APPEAL TO EXPERIENCE

[For the director: on *Gittith;* of Asaph]

81 Sing joyously of God our strength;
Shout aloud of Jacob's God.
2 Raise the chant and beat the drum,
Both the pleasant harp and the lute.
3 Blow the trumpet at the new moon,
At the full moon on our festal day.
4 For it is a statute in Israel,
An ordinance of Jacob's God.
5 He made it a decree in Joseph,
When he went forth against the land of Egypt.
I heard an unknown tongue saying,
6 "I removed the burden from upon his shoulder;
His hands were freed from the heavy basket.
7 In trouble you called and I rescued you;
I answered you in the secret place of thunder;
I tested you by the waters of Meribah. *Selah*
8 "Listen, O my people, while I warn you;
If you would but listen to me, O Israel!
9 There would be no strange god among you;
Nor would you bow down to a foreign god.
10 I, the LORD, am your God;
He who brought you up from the land of Egypt.
Open wide your mouth that I may fill it.
11 But my people did not listen to my voice;
Israel would have none of me.
12 "So I gave them over to their own self-will,
That they might follow their own devices.
13 If my people would but listen to me,
If Israel would only walk in my ways,
14 I would quickly humble their foes,
And turn my hand against their enemies.
15 Those who hate the LORD would fawn upon him,
And terror would be upon them forever;
But he would be fed with the finest of the wheat, 16
And with honey from the rock would I satisfy you."

A HOMILY FOR "DIVINE" RULERS

[A Psalm of Asaph]

God takes his stand in the divine assembly; 82
In the midst of the gods he gives judgment.
"How long will you judge unjustly, 2
And show partiality toward the wicked? *Selah*

"Give justice to the weak and the orphan; 3
Do right by the afflicted and wretched;
Set free the weak and needy;
Rescue them from the hand of the wicked."

They have neither knowledge nor sense; 5
They wander about in darkness;
All the foundations of the earth shake.

I say, "You are gods,
And all of you sons of the Most High!
Yet you will die as men do,
And fall like any prince."

Arise, O God, judge the earth!
For thou wilt take possession of all the nations.

A PRAYER FOR THE OVERTHROW OF NATIONS

[A Song. A Psalm of Asaph]

Keep not silence, O God; 83
Be not still, and be not quiet, O God!
For lo! thine enemies roar,
And those who hate thee carry a high head.
Against thy people they make crafty plans,
And take counsel together against thy hidden ones.
They say, "Come, let us destroy them that they be no more a people,
And that the name Israel be remembered no more."

5 For they conspire with one mind;
Against thee do they make an alliance,
6 The tents of Edom and the Ishmaelites,
Moab and the Hagarenes,
7 Gebal, and Ammon, and Amalek,
Philistia, with the inhabitants of Tyre;
8 Assyria also is leagued with them;
They are the strength of the children
of Lot. *Selah*

9 Deal with them as with Midian,
As with Sisera and Jabin by the brook
Kishon,
10 Who were destroyed at Endor;
They became dung for the ground.
11 Make their chieftains like Oreb and
Zeeb,
All their princes like Zebah and Zal-
munnah,
12 Who said, "We will seize for ourselves
The very finest meadows."
13 My God, make them like a tumble-
weed,
Like chaff before the wind.
14 Like a fire that burns up a wood,
And like the flame that sets mountains
afire;
15 So do thou pursue them with thy
tempest,
And terrify them with thy hurricane.
16 Fill their faces with shame,
That they may seek thy name, O
LORD!
17 Let them be disgraced and terrified
forever,
And may they be put to shame and
perish;
18 That they may know that it is thou
alone whose name is the LORD,
That art Most High over all the earth.

THE JOY OF THE GODLY

[For the director: on *Gittith;* of the sons of Korah; a Psalm]

84 How lovely is thy dwelling-place,
O LORD of hosts!
2 My spirit longs and pines
for the courts of the LORD.
My heart and my flesh give a shout of
joy
for the living God!

3 Even the wren has found a house,
and the swallow a nest for herself,
where she may put her young,
Even thine altars, O LORD of hosts,
my king, and my God.

How happy are those who dwell in thy 4
house,
ever praising thee! *Selah*

How happy are the men whose 5
strength is in thee;
the highways are in their
minds!
Those who pass through the valley of 6
Baca
make it a region of springs;
the winter rain covers it with
blessings.
They go from strength to strength; 7
The God of gods is seen in Zion.

O LORD, God of hosts, hear my 8
prayer;
Give heed, O God of Jacob! *Selah*
O God, our shield, behold 9
And look upon the face of thine
anointed!
For better is one day in thy courts 10
than a thousand elsewhere;
I would rather stand outside the door
of the house of my God
Than dwell in the tents of wickedness.
For the LORD God is a sun and shield. 11
Favor and honor the LORD bestows;
He does not withhold prosperity from
them that walk in integrity.

O LORD of hosts, 12
How happy is the man who trusts in
thee!

A PLEA FOR GOD'S PARDON

[For the director: of the sons of Korah; a Psalm]

Thou wast favorable to thy land, O 85
LORD;
Thou didst restore the fortune of Ja-
cob;
Thou didst pardon the guilt of thy 2
people;
Thou didst cover up all their sin.
Selah
Thou didst withdraw all thy wrath; 3
Thou didst turn away from thy fierce
anger.
Restore us, O God of our deliverance, 4
And break off thy vexation against us!

Wilt thou be angry with us forever? 5
Wilt thou prolong thine anger throughout the ages?

6 Wilt thou not revive us again,
That thy people may rejoice in thee?
7 Show us thy kindness, O LORD;
And grant us thy salvation.

8 I would hear what God the LORD will speak.
Surely he will speak prosperity unto his people and his saints,
And those who turn their hearts to him.
9 For his salvation is close to them that fear him,
That honor may dwell in our land.

10 Kindness and Fidelity are met together;
Righteousness and Peace have kissed each other.
11 Fidelity springs up from the earth,
And Righteousness looks forth from the heavens.

12 The LORD will give prosperity,
And our land will yield its increase.
13 Righteousness will go before it.
And mark the way with its footsteps.

A PLEA FOR GOD'S HELP

[A Prayer of David]

86 Incline thine ear, O LORD, answer me,
For I am afflicted and needy.
2 Preserve me, for I am a godly man;
O thou, my God, deliver thy servant who trusts in thee.

3 Be gracious unto me, O Lord;
For unto thee do I call all day long.
4 Gladden the heart of thy servant,
For I lift up my heart unto thee.

5 For thou, O LORD, art good and forgiving,
And abounding in kindness to all that call upon thee.

6 Listen to my prayer, O LORD;
And heed my supplicating voice!

7 On my day of trouble I call upon thee,
For thou wilt answer me.
8 There is none like thee among the gods, O Lord;
Nor are there any works like thine.

9 All the nations which thou hast made,
Will come and bow down before thee, O Lord,
And will honor thy name;
10 For thou art great and doest wonders;
Thou alone art God.

11 Teach me thy way, O LORD,
That I may walk in fidelity to thee,
That my heart may rejoice in the fear of thy name.
12 I will thank thee, O Lord, my God, with all my heart;
And I will honor thy name forever.

13 For thy kindness toward me is great,
In that thou hast rescued me from the depths of Sheol.
14 O God, the proud have risen up against me,
And a gang of bandits seeks my life,
And does not keep thee in mind.

15 But thou, O Lord, art a merciful and gracious God,
Slow to anger and abounding in kindness and fidelity.
16 Turn to me and pity me;
Grant thy servant thy strength,
And deliver the son of thy handmaid.

17 Work in my behalf a sign for good,
That those who hate me may see it and be put to shame,
Because thou, O LORD, hast helped me and comforted me.

ZION GLORIES IN HER CHILDREN

[Of the sons of Korah; a Psalm; a Song]

87 His foundation is in the holy mountains.
2 The LORD loves the gates of Zion
More than all other dwellings of Jacob.
3 Glorious things he speaks of you,
O city of God. *Selah*

4 I may mention Rahab and Babylon on account of their famous men,
Philistia, Tyre, and also Ethiopia;
"Such a one was born there!"
5 But of Zion it will be said,
"This one and that one were born in her!"
And that will place her in the highest rank.
6 The LORD, when he lists the nations, will record,
"Such a one was born there." *Selah*

7 Those who behold will be like men
dreaming,
All who closely watch you.

LAMENTATION OF ONE IN TROUBLE

[A song; a Psalm of the sons of Korah. For the director: upon *mahalath leannoth;* a *maskil* of Heman the Ezrachite]

8 I call for help by day, O LORD, my
God;
I cry before thee at night;
2 Let my prayer come before thee;
Incline thine ear unto my call!

3 For I am surfeited with troubles,
And my life verges on Sheol.
4 I am reckoned among those that go
down to the Pit;
I am become like a man without help,
5 Separated among the dead;
Like the slain that lie in the grave,
Whom thou dost no more remember,
For they are cut off from thy hand.
6 Thou hast put me in the deepest pit,
In darkest regions, in the depths.

7 Thy wrath rests upon me,
And thou dost press down upon me
all thy breakers. *Selah*
8 Thou hast removed my acquaintances
far from me;
Thou hast made me a horror to them;
I am shut in and cannot go out.
9 My eye wastes away with sorrow;
I have called upon thee, O LORD, all
day long;
I have spread out my hands toward
thee.

10 Is it for the dead that thou wilt do
wonders?
Will the ghosts arise to thank thee?
Selah
11 Will thy kindness be recounted in the
grave?
Or thy faithfulness in Hades?
12 Will thy wonders be made known in
the darkness?
Or thy righteousness in the land of
oblivion?

13 But I, O LORD, call unto thee for
help,
And in the morning my prayer comes
before thee.
14 Why, O LORD, dost thou reject me,
And hide thy face from me?
I have been afflicted and at the point 15
of death from my youth up;
I have borne thy terrors; I am overcome.

Thy fierce anger has gone over me; 16
Thy terrors have destroyed me;
They surround me like water all day 17
long;
They encircle me completely.
Thou hast put friend and companion 18
far from me,
And my acquaintances are in the
place of darkness.

THE SORROWS OF JUDAH

[A *maskil* of Ethan the Ezrachite]

The gracious deeds of the LORD I will 89
sing forever;
Throughout the ages I will proclaim
thy faithfulness with my mouth.
For I say, "Kindness will be renewed 2
forever;
In the heavens thou dost establish thy
faithfulness."

I made an agreement with my chosen 3
one,
I swore to David, my servant,
"I will establish your posterity forever; 4
And I will build your throne thorough-
out the ages." Selah

The heavens praise thy wonders, O 5
LORD,
And thy faithfulness in the divine as-
sembly.
For who in the skies can be compared 6
to the LORD?
Who is like the LORD among the heav-
enly beings?

A God to be feared in the divine coun- 7
cil,
Great and terrible over all around
him;
O LORD, God of hosts, 8
Who is strong like thee, O LORD?
And thy faithfulness is round about
thee.

Thou rulest over the raging of the sea; 9
When its waves rise thou stillest them.
Thou hast crushed Rahab like one who 10
is slain;
With thy strong arm thou hast scat-
tered thy foes.

11 The heavens are thine, the earth also is thine;
The world and its contents thou hast founded.
12 The north and the south thou didst create;
Tabor and Hermon celebrate thy name.

13 Thine is an arm with power;
Thy hand is strong; thy right hand is high.
14 Righteousness and justice are the foundation of thy throne;
Kindness and faithfulness go before thee.

15 How happy are the people who know the festal trumpet-call!
O LORD, they walk in the light of thy face.
16 In thy name they rejoice all day long;
And through thy righteousness are they exalted.

17 For thou art the glory of their strength,
And through thy favor our horn is exalted.
18 For the LORD is our shield,
And the holy one of Israel our king.

19 Once thou didst speak in vision to thy faithful one,
And didst say, "I have placed a diadem upon a warrior;
I have raised up a chosen one from the people.
20 I have found David my servant,
With my holy oil I have anointed him,
21 Whom my hand holds firm,
And my arm strengthens.

22 "The enemy shall not overcome him;
Nor the wicked man afflict him;
23 For I will crush his foes before him,
And those who hate him I will smite.

24 "My faithfulness and my kindness shall be with him;
And through my name his honor shall be exalted.
25 I will set his hand upon the sea,
And his right hand upon the river.

26 "He shall call unto me, 'Thou art my father,
My God, and the rock of my deliverance.'

And I will make him the first-born, 27
The highest of the kings of the earth.

"I will always keep my kindness for him, 28
And my covenant shall stand firm for him;
And I will give him posterity forever, 29
And his throne shall be like the days of the heavens.

"If his sons forsake my law, 30
And do not walk in my judgments;
If they violate my decrees, 31
And observe not my commands,

"Then I will punish their offense with the rod, 32
And their guilt with blows;
But my kindness I will not withdraw from them; 33
Nor will I be false to my fidelity.

"I will not violate my covenant, 34
Nor will I alter what my lips have uttered.
Once I swore by my holiness— 35
And I would not lie to David—

"That his posterity should be forever, 36
And his throne be like the sun before me;
Like the moon it should be established forever, 37
And should stand firm as long as the skies." *Selah*

But thou hast rejected and cast off, 38
Thou hast raged against thine anointed.
Thou hast broken the covenant with thy servant; 39
Thou hast defiled his diadem in the dust.
Thou hast broken down all his walls; 40
Thou hast laid his forts in ruin.
All that pass by plunder him; 41
He has become a jest to his neighbors.

Thou hast raised up the right hand of his enemies; 42
Thou hast made all his foes glad.
Moreover, thou hast turned back the edge of his sword, 43
And hast not supported him in battle.

Thou hast put an end to his splendor, 44
And hurled his throne to the ground.
Thou hast cut off the days of his prime, 45
And covered him with shame. *Selah*

How long, O LORD? Wilt thou hide
thyself forever?
Will thy wrath burn on like a fire?
Remember, O LORD, what our span of
life is;
For what frailty thou hast created all
the sons of men.

What man can live and not see death,
Can deliver himself from the power
of Sheol? *Selah*
Where are thy former gracious deeds,
O Lord,
Which thou didst swear to David by
thy faithfulness?

Remember, O Lord, the disgrace of 50
thy servant,
How I carry in my bosom the reproach of the peoples;
How thy foes insult, O LORD, 51
How they insult the footsteps of thine
anointed!

Blessed be the LORD forever, 52
Amen and amen.

BOOK IV, PSS. 90–106

A PLEA FOR GOD'S MERCY

[A prayer of Moses, the man of God]

O LORD, thou art a dwelling-place;
Thou hast been ours throughout the
ages;
Before the mountains were born,
Or ever thou hadst brought forth the
earth and the world,
Even from everlasting to everlasting
thou art, O God.

Thou turnest man back to dust,
And sayest, "Return, O sons of men."
For a thousand years in thy sight
Are but as yesterday when it is past,
And as a watch in the night.

Thou cuttest them off; they are as a
dream;
They are like grass which shoots up in
the morning;
In the morning it flourishes and shoots
up;
At evening it is cut down and withers.

For we are destroyed by thine anger,
And by thy wrath we are ruined.
Thou dost place our crimes before
thee,
Our unconscious sins in the light of
thy face.

For all our days vanish in thy wrath;
We come to an end; our years are like
a cobweb wiped away.
The length of our life is seventy years,
Perchance through strength eighty
years;
But their whole extent is travail and
trouble;
For it is quickly cut off and we fly
away.

Who knows the power of thine anger? 11
Or thy wrath according to the fear
due thee?
So teach us to number our days 12
That we may obtain an understanding
heart.

Return, O LORD; how long? 13
And have compassion upon thy servants.
Satisfy us in the morning with thy 14
kindness,
That we may shout with joy and be
glad throughout our days.
Gladden us in proportion to the days 15
wherein thou hast afflicted us,
The years wherein we have seen disaster.

May thy work appear unto thy serv- 16
ants,
And thy splendor be upon their children.
May the favor of the Lord our God be 17
upon us,
And the work of our hands do thou
establish upon us;
Yea, the work of our hands establish
thou it.

THE FAVOR OF GOD UPON THE FAITHFUL

He who dwells under the shelter of the 91
Most High,
Who abides under the shadow of the
Almighty,

2 Says of the LORD, "My refuge and my fortress,
My God, in whom I trust."
3 For he rescues you from the snare of the fowler,
From the deadly pestilence;
4 With his pinions he covers you,
And under his wings you find refuge.
His faithfulness is a shield and buckler.

5 You will not be afraid of the terror by night,
Nor the arrow that flies by day,
6 Nor the pestilence that stalks in darkness,
Nor the plague that wastes at noonday.

7 A thousand may fall at your side,
And ten thousand at your right hand;
But it will not come near you.
8 You will but gaze upon with your eyes
And see the reward of the wicked.

9 Because you have made the LORD your refuge,
And the Most High your habitation,
10 No disaster will befall you,
Nor calamity come near your tent.

11 For he will give his angels charge over you,
To guard you in all your ways.
12 They will bear you up upon their hands,
Lest you strike your foot upon a stone.
13 Upon the lion and the adder you may tread;
Upon the young lion and the dragon you may trample.

14 Because he clings fast to me in love, I will deliver him;
I will set him on high because he knows my name.
15 When he calls upon me, I will answer him;
I will be with him in trouble;
I will set him free and honor him.
16 With long life will I satisfy him,
And show him my salvation.

A HYMN OF GRATITUDE

[A Psalm; a Song for the sabbath day]

92 It is good to give thanks to the LORD,
And to sing praises to thy name, O Most High;
To proclaim thy kindness in the morning,
And thy faithfulness every night,
Upon the ten-stringed lyre and the lute,
To a melody with the harp.

For thou hast made me glad, O LORD, by thy works;
Of the deeds of thy hands I joyfully sing.
How great are thy doings, O LORD;
How very deep thy designs!

A stupid man cannot know,
A senseless one cannot understand this.
When the wicked shoot up like grass,
And all wrongdoers flourish,
It is that they may be destroyed forever.

But thou art on high forever, O LORD!
For lo, thine enemies, O LORD;
For lo, thine enemies will perish!
All wrongdoers will be scattered.

But thou hast exalted my horn like that of the wild ox;
I am anointed with fresh oil.
And my eye looks upon them that lie in wait for me;
My ears hear the wicked that rise up against me.

The righteous will flourish like the palm tree;
He will grow high like a cedar in Lebanon.
Planted in the house of the LORD,
They will flourish in the courts of our God.

They will still yield fruit in old age;
Full of sap and green will they be;
To proclaim that the LORD is right,
My rock, in whom there is no wrong.

THE RULER OF THE UNIVERSE

The LORD is king; he is clothed with majesty;
The LORD is clothed, he is girded with strength.
Indeed, the world is established immovable.
Thy throne has been established from of old;
Thou art from remotest antiquity.

The floods have lifted up, O LORD,
The floods have lifted up their voice;
The floods lift up their roar
Above the sound of many waters.
Mightier than the breakers of the sea,
The LORD on high is mighty!

Thy decrees are very sure.
Holiness befits thy house,
O LORD, for all time.

DESTRUCTION TO THE WICKED!

O LORD, thou avenging God,
O thou avenging God, shine forth!
Rise up, O judge of the earth;
Render to the proud their deserts.
How long shall the wicked, O LORD,
How long shall the wicked exult,
Shall they bubble over speaking insolence,
Shall all wrongdoers brag?

They crush thy people, O LORD,
And they afflict thy heritage.
The widow and the stranger they slay,
And the orphan they murder.
And they say, "The LORD does not see;
The God of Jacob does not observe."

Ponder, O stupid ones among the people,
When will you become wise, O fools?
Does he who planted the ear not hear?
Or he who formed the eye not see?
Will he who instructs the nations not punish them,
He who teaches man knowledge?
The LORD knows the devices of men,
That they are but a breath.

Happy the man whom thou chastenest,
And teachest of thy law, O LORD;
That he may have relief from times of trouble,
Until the pit be dug for the wicked!
For the LORD will not spurn his people,
Nor abandon his heritage.
For judgment will return to the righteous,
And after him all the upright in heart will go.

Who rises up for me against the doers of evil?
Who takes his stand for me against the wrongdoers?
Had not the LORD been my help, 17
I should soon have lain down in silence!
If I think, "My foot is slipping," 18
Thy kindness, O LORD, sustains me!
When my cares are many within me, 19
Thy comforts give me cheer.

Can the throne of wickedness be allied with thee, 20
That frames wickedness by statute—
They who make assaults upon the life of the righteous, 21
And pronounce condemnation upon innocent blood?
But the LORD is my high tower; 22
My God is the rock of my refuge.
And he requites them for their guilt, 23
And for their wickedness destroys them;
The LORD, our God, destroys them!

A PAEAN OF PRAISE

Come, let us sing unto the LORD; **95**
Let us raise joyful shouts to the rock of our deliverance!
Let us come before his face with thanksgiving; 2
Let us raise joyful shouts to him in psalms.

For the LORD is a great God, 3
And a great king over all gods.
In his hand are the depths of the earth; 4
The summits of the hills are his also.
The sea is his, for he made it; 5
And his hands formed the dry land.

Come, let us worship and bow down; 6
Let us kneel before the LORD, our maker!
For he is our God; 7
And we are the people of his pasture, and the sheep of his hand.

Today, if you obey his voice,
Harden not your hearts as at Meribah, 8
As on the day at Massah in the wilderness,
When your fathers tried me, 9
Tested me, and saw my works.
For forty years I loathed that generation, 10
And I said, "They are a people who err in their hearts,
And do not know my ways."

11 So that I swore in my anger,
That they should not enter into my rest.

THE GLORY OF GOD

96 Sing to the LORD a new song;
Sing to the LORD, all the earth;
2 Sing to the LORD, bless his name;
Publish his deliverance abroad from day to day.
3 Tell among the nations his glory,
Among all the peoples, his wonders.
4 For great is the LORD and greatly to be praised;
Fearful is he above all gods.
5 For all the gods of the peoples are nonentities,
While the LORD made the heavens.
6 Honor and majesty are before him;
Strength and beauty are in his sanctuary.

7 Ascribe to the LORD, O families of peoples,
Ascribe to the LORD glory and strength.
8 Ascribe to the LORD the glory of his name;
Bring an offering and come into his courts.
9 Worship the LORD in holy array;
Tremble before him all the earth.

10 Tell among the nations that the LORD is king;
The world also is established that it cannot be moved.
He judges the peoples in equity.

11 Let the heavens rejoice and the earth exult,
The sea roar, and its fulness.
12 Let the field exult and all that is therein;
Then let all the trees of the wood shout for joy
13 Before the LORD, for he comes,
For he comes to judge the earth.
He will judge the world with righteousness,
And peoples with his faithfulness.

THE MAJESTY OF GOD

97 The LORD reigns; let the earth rejoice!
Let the many coast-lands be glad!
2 Clouds and darkness are around him;
Righteousness and justice are the foundation of his throne.

Fire goes before him,
And blazes around his steps.
His lightnings illuminate the world;
The earth beholds and trembles.
The mountains melt like wax before the LORD,
Before the Lord of all the earth.
The heavens proclaim his righteousness,
And all the peoples see his glory.
All who serve wrought images are put to shame,
They who prided themselves on their nonentities.
Worship him, all you gods!

Zion hears and rejoices,
And the daughters of Judah exult,
Because of thy judgments, O LORD.
For thou, O LORD, art the highest over all the earth;
Thou art exalted high above all gods.

The LORD loves those who hate evil;
He preserves the lives of his saints;
From the hand of the wicked he rescues them.
Light is sown for the righteous,
And joy for the upright in heart.
Rejoice in the LORD, O righteous,
And praise his holy name.

A SONG OF TRIUMPH

[A Psalm]

Sing to the LORD a new song,
For he has done wonderful things!
His right hand and his holy arm have brought him victory.
The LORD has made known his victory;
In the sight of the nations he has revealed his righteousness.
He has remembered his kindness and his faithfulness to the house of Israel;
All the ends of the earth have seen the triumph of our God.

Shout aloud to the LORD, all the earth;
Rejoice, be jubilant, and sing praises:
Sing praises to the LORD with the lyre,
With the lyre and the sound of song.
With trumpets and the sound of the horn,

Shout aloud before the king, the LORD!

Let the sea roar and all that is in it;
The world and those living in it!
Let the rivers clap their hands;
Let the mountains also sing,
Before the LORD, for he is coming to judge the earth!
He will judge the world with righteousness,
And the peoples with equity.

THE HOLY GOD

The LORD is king; let the peoples tremble!
He is seated upon the cherubim; let the earth quake!
The LORD is great in Zion,
And high is he over all the peoples.
Let them praise thy great and terrible name!
Holy is he and strong!

O King, who lovest justice,
Thou hast established equity;
Thou hast wrought justice and righteousness in Jacob.
Exalt the LORD, our God!
And prostrate yourselves at his footstool!
Holy is he!

Moses and Aaron were among his priests;
And Samuel was among those calling upon his name.
They called upon the LORD and he answered them;
Through the pillar of cloud he spoke to them;
They kept his decrees and the law which he gave them.

O LORD, our God, thou didst answer them!
Thou wast a forgiving God to them;
But one taking vengeance for their sins.
Exalt the LORD, our God,
And prostrate yourselves at his holy mountain!
For holy is the LORD, our God!

THE FAITHFUL GOD

[A Psalm for the thank-offering]

0 Hail the LORD joyously, all the earth!
Serve the LORD with gladness!
Come before him with joyful song!
Know that the LORD is God! 3
He made us, and his we are,
His people and the sheep of his pasture.

Come into his gates with thanksgiving, 4
And into his courts with praise!
Give thanks to him; bless his name!
For the LORD is good; his kindness is everlasting; 5
And his faithfulness endures throughout the ages.

THE MORAL CODE OF A KING

[Of David. A Psalm]

I will sing of kindness and justice; 101
to thee, O LORD, will I sing praises.
I will give heed to the path of the perfect; 2
how long till thou wilt come to me?

I will walk in the integrity of my heart,
within my own home.
I will set before my eyes 3
no base thing;
I loathe the doing of transgression;
it shall not cling to me.
A perverse heart is far from me; 4
I know no evil.
If a man slanders his neighbor in secret, 5
I destroy him.
The supercilious and high-minded
I cannot endure.
My eye is upon the faithful in the land, 6
that they may dwell with me.
If a man walks in the perfect way,
he shall serve me.

He shall not dwell within my house 7
who practices deceit.
He who tells lies shall not be established
before my eyes.
Every morning I will destroy 8
all the wicked of the land,
Cutting off from the city of the LORD
all the malefactors.

THE EVERLASTING GOD

[A prayer of the afflicted when he is overwhelmed and pours out his plaint before the LORD]

102 Hear my prayer, O LORD,
And let my cry for help come before thee!
2 Do not hide thy face from me on my day of trouble;
Incline thine ear unto me;
On the day when I call answer me speedily.
3 For my days vanish like smoke,
And my bones are charred like a hearth.
4 My heart is stricken and withered like grass;
For I forget to eat my food.
5 Because of the sound of my moaning,
My bone cleaves to my flesh.

6 I am like a jackdaw of the wilderness;
I have become like an owl of the ruins.
7 I am sleepless and I have become
Like a solitary bird upon the roof.
8 All day long my foes insult me;
Those who deride me curse by me.
9 For I eat ashes like bread;
And my drink do I mingle with tears,
10 Because of thine anger and thy wrath;
For thou hast lifted me up and cast me off.
11 My days are like a lengthened shadow,
And I am withered like grass.

12 But thou, O LORD, abidest forever,
And thy name endures throughout the ages.
13 Thou wilt arise; thou wilt have pity on Zion;
For it is time to be gracious to her; for the fixed time has come.
14 For thy servants delight in her stones,
And her dust they commiserate.
15 And the nations will fear the name of the LORD,
And all the kings of the earth thy glory,
16 When the LORD rebuilds Zion,
When he is seen in his glory,
17 When he turns himself toward the prayer of the destitute,
And does not despise their prayer.

18 Let this be written for coming generations,
That people yet unborn may praise the LORD:
That he looked forth from his holy height,
The LORD looked from the heavens toward the earth,
To hear the groans of the prisoner,
To set free those doomed to death,
That they may recount in Zion the renown of the LORD,
And his praise in Jerusalem,
When peoples gather together,
And kingdoms, to serve the LORD.

He has weakened my strength,
He has cut short my days.
I say, "O my God, take me not away in the midst of my days;
Thou whose years endure throughout the ages!
Of old thou didst lay the foundation of the earth;
And the heavens are the work of thy hands.
They may perish, but thou wilt endure;
All of them may wear out like a garment;
Thou mayest change them like clothing and they will change;
But thou art always the same,
And thy years have no end.
The children of thy servants will abide;
And their posterity will be established before thee."

THE GOODNESS OF GOD

[Of David]

Bless the LORD, O my spirit;
Let my whole being bless his holy name!
Bless the LORD, O my spirit,
And forget not all his benefits,
Who forgives all my guilt,
Who heals all my sicknesses,
Who rescues my life from the Pit,
Who crowns me with kindness and mercy,
Who satisfies my desires with good,
So that my youth renews itself like an eagle.

The LORD executes righteousness
And justice for all that are oppressed.
He made known his ways to Moses,
His deeds to the children of Israel.
The LORD is merciful and compassionate,
Slow to anger and abounding in kindness.

9 He will not always chide,
Nor hold his anger forever.
10 He has not treated us according to our sins,
Nor rewarded us according to our iniquities.

11 But high as the heavens are above the earth,
So great is his kindness toward them that revere him;
12 Far as the east is from the west,
So far has he removed our offenses from us.
13 As a father is kind to his children,
So the LORD is kind to those who revere him.

14 For he knows our frame;
He remembers that we are but dust.
15 A man's days are like the grass;
Like a flower of the field, so he blossoms;
16 For the wind passes over it, and it is not,
And its place knows it no more.
17 But the kindness of the LORD is from age to age upon those who revere him,
And his righteousness to children's children,
18 For those who keep his covenant,
And remember to observe his precepts.
19 The LORD has established his throne in the heavens,
And his kingdom rules over all.

20 Bless the LORD, O you his angels,
Mighty beings, who do his bidding,
Obeying his spoken word!
21 Bless the LORD, all his hosts,
His ministers who carry out his will!
22 Bless the LORD, all his works,
In all parts of his dominion!
Bless the LORD, O my spirit!

THE CREATOR AND SUSTAINER OF THE UNIVERSE

104 Bless the LORD, O my spirit!
O LORD, my God, thou art very great;
Thou art robed with majesty and honor;
2 Who veilest thyself in light as in a garment;
Who stretches out the heavens like a tent;

Who lays the beams of his upper chambers in the waters; 3
Who makes the clouds his chariot;
Who walks upon the wings of the wind;
Who makes the winds his messengers; 4
His ministers, flames of fire.
He founded the earth upon its pillars, 5
That it might not be moved forever and ever.

Thou didst cover it with the deep as with a garment; 6
The waters stood upon the mountains.
At thy rebuke they fled; 7
At the sound of thy thunder they fled in terror.
Thou didst set a bound which they should not cross, 8
So that they should not again cover the earth.
The mountains rose, the valleys sank down, 9
To the place which thou hadst founded for them.
He causes fountains to flow in the valleys; 10
Between mountains they run.
They furnish drink for all the beasts of the field; 11
Wild asses quench their thirst there.
Beside them the birds of the air dwell; 12
From among the branches they send forth song.
Thou waterest the mountains from thine upper chambers; 13
The earth is full of the fruit of thy works.

He makes grass grow for the cattle, 14
And fodder for the working animals of man,
So that bread may come forth from the earth;
And wine may cheer man's heart, 15
Making his face brighter than oil;
And bread to stay man's heart.

The trees of the LORD have their fill, 16
The cedars of Lebanon which he planted;
Wherein the birds build their nests, 17
And the stork, whose home is the cypress.
The high mountains are for the wild goats; 18
The rocks are a refuge for the marmots.

19 He made the moon for fixed times;
The sun knows its time of setting.
20 Thou makest darkness and it becomes night,
In which all the beasts of the forest prowl,
21 The young lions roaring after prey,
And seeking their food from God.
22 When the sun rises, they withdraw,
And crouch in their dens.
23 Man goes forth to his work,
And to his labor until evening.

24 How many are thy works, O LORD!
In wisdom hast thou made them all;
The earth is full of thy creations.
25 There is the sea, great and broad,
Where are reptiles innumerable,
Creatures small and great;
There go the sea-monsters,
26 The crocodile whom thou didst form to frolic therein.
27 They all wait upon thee,
To give them their food in due season.
28 What thou givest them, they gather up;
When thou openest thy hand, they are satisfied with good things.
29 When thou hidest thy face, they are worried;
When thou takest away their breath they die,
And turn again into dust.
30 When thou sendest forth thy breath, they are created;
And thou renewest the face of the earth.

31 May the glory of the LORD endure forever!
May the LORD rejoice in his works!
32 He looks at the earth and it quakes;
He touches the mountains and they smoke!
33 I will sing to the LORD as long as I live;
I will sing praises to my God as long as I breathe.
34 May my meditation please him!
I will rejoice in the LORD.
35 Let sinners vanish from the earth!
And may the wicked be no more!
Bless the LORD, O my spirit!
Hallelujah!

THE WONDERS OF GOD

105 Give thanks to the LORD; call upon his name;
Make known his deeds among the peoples!
Sing to him; sing praises to him;
Tell of all his wonders!
Glory in his holy name!
May the heart of those who seek the LORD rejoice!
Inquire of the LORD and his might!
Seek his face continually!

Remember the wonders that he has done,
His portents, and the judgments of his mouth,
O descendants of Abraham, his servant,
Children of Jacob, his chosen!
He is the LORD, our God;
His judgments are in all the earth.
He remembers his covenant forever,
The word he has commanded, to a thousand generations;
The covenant he made with Abraham,
And his oath to Isaac.

For he confirmed it to Jacob as a statute,
To Israel as an eternal covenant;
Saying, "To you I give the land of Canaan,
As your portion and inheritance."
When they were but few in number,
Of slight importance and but strangers therein;
When they went back and forth from one nation to another,
And from one kingdom to another people,
He permitted no man to oppress them,
And warned kings concerning them,
"Touch not my anointed,
And do my prophets no harm!"

Then he called a famine upon the land;
He broke every staff of bread.
He sent forth a man before them;
Joseph was sold as a slave.
They forced his feet into fetters;
He himself was laid in irons.
Until what he had said came about,
The word of the LORD tested him.

The king sent and released him,
The ruler of peoples, and set him free.
He made him overseer of his house,
And ruler over all his possessions;
That he might give orders to his officers as he pleased,
And might instruct his elders.

23 Then Israel went into Egypt,
And Jacob dwelt in the land of Ham.
24 And he made his people very prolific,
And made them more numerous than their foes.
25 He changed their heart so that they hated his people,
So that they dealt treacherously with his servants.
26 He sent forth Moses, his servant,
And Aaron, whom he had chosen.
27 They wrought among them wondrous signs,
And portents in the land of Ham.
28 He sent forth darkness so that it became dark;
But they rebelled against his words.
29 He turned their water into blood,
And so killed their fish.
30 Their land swarmed with frogs;
They were in the chambers of their kings.
31 He spoke and a swarm of flies came,
Mosquitoes throughout their country.
32 He gave them hail for rain;
Flaming fire was in their land.
33 He smote their vine and fig tree,
And broke down the trees of their country.
34 He spoke, and the locust came,
And insects innumerable.
35 They ate up all the fodder in their land;
They ate up all the products of their soil.
36 Then he smote all the first-born in their land,
The first-fruits of all their virile strength.
37 Then he sent them forth with silver and gold,
And there was no straggler in their ranks;
38 Egypt was glad when they went forth,
For terror had fallen upon them.
39 He spread out a cloud as a screen,
And fire to give light by night.
40 They asked, and he brought in quails;
And with bread from the heavens he satisfied them.
41 He split the rock and water flowed forth;
There ran a river in the sands.
42 For he remembered his sacred word
To Abraham, his servant.
43 And he brought forth his people with joy,
His chosen ones with joyous song.
44 And he gave them the lands of the nations;
Of the toil of the peoples they took possession.
45 That they might keep his statutes
And observe his laws.
Hallelujah!

THE LONG-SUFFERING GOD

106 Hallelujah!
O give thanks to the LORD, for he is good;
For his kindness is everlasting.
2 Who can tell the mighty deeds of the LORD?
Or publish all his praise?

3 Happy are they who observe justice,
Who do right at all times!
4 Remember me, O LORD, in thy favor toward thy people;
Visit me when thou deliverest them;
5 That I may look upon the welfare of thy chosen,
That I may rejoice in the joy of thy nation,
That I may glory with thine inheritance.

6 We have sinned like our fathers;
We have done evil; we have acted wickedly.
7 Our fathers in Egypt disregarded thy wonders;
They remembered not thine abundant kindness;
But rebelled against the Most High at the Red Sea.
8 Yet he delivered them for his name's sake,
In order to make known his might.
9 So he rebuked the Red Sea and it became dry,
And he led them through the depths as through a meadow.
10 He rescued them from hostile hands,
And delivered them from the power of the foe.
11 And the water covered their enemies;
Not one of them survived.
12 Then did they believe his word;
They sang his praise.

13 But they soon forgot his deeds;
They waited not for his advice.

14 They felt a craving in the wilderness,
And they tried God in the waste.
15 And he granted their request,
But sent disease upon them.
16 When they were envious of Moses in the camp,
And of Aaron, the holy one of the LORD,
17 The earth opened and swallowed Dathan,
And engulfed the company of Abiram.
18 Fire burned up their company;
Fire consumed the wicked.

19 They made a calf in Horeb,
And worshiped a molten image.
20 Thus they exchanged their glory
For the image of an ox that eats fodder!
21 They forgot God who had delivered them,
Who had done great things in Egypt,
22 Wonderful things in the land of Ham,
Terrible things at the Red Sea.
23 So he threatened to destroy them,
Had not Moses, his chosen one,
Stood in the breach before him
To turn back his wrath from destruction.

24 Then they rejected the pleasant land,
They did not believe his promise;
25 But grumbled in their tents;
They did not listen to the voice of the LORD.
26 So he swore to them with uplifted hand,
That he would let them perish in the desert,
27 And that he would scatter their descendants among the nations,
And strew them through the lands.
28 They allied themselves with the Baal of Peor,
And ate sacrifices offered to the dead.
29 They offended him by their deeds,
And plague broke out among them.
30 But Phinehas stood up and executed judgment,
And the plague was checked.
31 That has been credited to him as righteousness
Throughout the ages forever.

32 They stirred him to anger also at the waters of Meribah,
And it went hard with Moses on their account,
Because they embittered his spirit, 33
And he spoke rashly with his lips.
They did not destroy the peoples, 34
As the LORD had commanded them;
But mingled with the nations, 35
And learned their works.
So they served their idols, 36
Which became a snare to them.

And they sacrificed their sons 37
And their daughters to demons.
And they shed innocent blood, 38
The blood of their sons and their daughters,
Whom they sacrificed to the idols of Canaan;
And the land was polluted with bloodshed.
They became unclean through their acts, 39
And played the harlot by their deeds.

So the anger of the LORD was hot against his people, 40
And he loathed his heritage.
And he gave them over to the power of the nations, 41
And those who hated them ruled over them.
Their enemies oppressed them, 42
And they were subdued under their hand.
Many times did he deliver them, 43
But they followed their own stubborn counsel,
And were brought low by their guilt.
But he saw when they were in trouble, 44
When he heard their cry for help;
And he recalled for them his covenant, 45
And had compassion in accordance with his abundant kindness.
He made them objects of compassion, also, 46
On the part of all their captors.

Deliver us, O LORD, our God, 47
And gather us from among the nations,
That we may give thanks to thy holy name,
That we may glory in thy praise.
Blessed be the LORD, the God of Israel, 48
From age unto age;
And let all the people say, "Amen."
Hallelujah!

BOOK V, PSS. 107–150

GOD IN HISTORY

107 "O give thanks to the LORD, for he is good,
For his kindness is everlasting."
2 So may they say, whom the LORD has rescued,
Whom he has rescued from the hand of the foe;
3 Those whom he has gathered in from the lands,
From east and west,
From north and south.

4 They wandered in the wilderness, in the waste,
They found no way to an inhabited town.
5 They were hungry and thirsty,
Their courage collapsed within them,
6 When they cried to the LORD in their trouble,
He delivered them from their distress,
And guided them in a straight way,
7 So that they came to an inhabited town.
8 Let them thank the LORD for his kindness,
And his wonders toward the sons of men.
9 For he satisfied the thirsty spirit,
And the hungry heart he filled with good.

10 Those who dwelt in darkness and in deepest gloom,
Bound in misery and iron;
11 Because they opposed the orders of God,
And spurned the counsel of the Most High;
12 He bowed down their heart with labor;
They stumbled, with none to help.
13 When they cried to the LORD in their trouble,
He delivered them from their distress.
14 He brought them out of darkness and deepest gloom,
And burst their bonds asunder.
15 Let them thank the LORD for his kindness,
And his wonders toward the sons of men.
16 For he shattered bronze doors,
And broke down iron bars.

Fools, because of their wicked ways 17
And because of their guilty deeds, were afflicted.
They loathed every kind of food, 18
And they drew near to the gates of death.
When they cried to the LORD in their trouble, 19
He delivered them from their distress.
He sent forth his word to heal them, 20
And to free them from their graves.
Let them thank the LORD for his kindness, 21
And his wonders toward the sons of men.
And let them offer sacrifices of thanksgiving, 22
And tell of his works with song.

Those who go down to the sea in ships, 23
And do business in the great waters,
They saw the works of the LORD, 24
And his wonders in the deep,
For he spoke and raised up the storm-wind, 25
Which lifted its billows on high.
They mounted to the heavens, they descended to the depths. 26
They were dissolved in their distress.
They reeled and staggered like a drunken man, 27
And were at their wits' end.
When they cried to the LORD in their trouble, 28
He delivered them from their distress.
He stilled the storm to a whisper, 29
And the waves were hushed.
Then they rejoiced because they were quiet, 30
And he brought them to their desired haven.
Let them thank the LORD for his kindness, 31
And his wonders to the sons of men.
And let them exalt him in the assembly of the people, 32
And praise him in the company of the elders.

He turned rivers into a desert, 33
And springs of water into parched ground;
A fruitful land into a salt-marsh, 34
Because of the wickedness of those who dwelt therein.
He turned a desert into pools of water, 35

And dry land into springs of water;
36 And he settled the hungry there,
So that they established an inhabited town.
37 They sowed fields and planted vineyards,
Which yielded fruits for harvest.
38 Then he blessed them and they multiplied greatly,
And he suffered not their cattle to decrease.
39 When they themselves decreased and were brought low
Through oppression, adversity, and sorrow,
40 He poured contempt upon the princes,
And made them wander in the trackless waste.
41 But he exalted the needy above affliction,
And made his families like a flock.

42 Let the righteous see and rejoice,
And all wickedness shut its mouth.
43 Whoso is wise, let him heed such things,
And consider the gracious deeds of the LORD.

A PRAYER FOR GOD'S HELP

[A Song; a Psalm of David]

108 My heart is steadfast, O God;
I will play and sing.
2 Awake, then, my glory!
Awake, lute and lyre!
I will awaken the dawn!
3 I will praise thee among the peoples, O LORD,
I will sing praises to thee among the nations.
4 For thy kindness is great even unto the heavens,
And thy faithfulness unto the clouds.
5 Arise above the heavens, O God!
Let thy glory be over all the earth!

6 That thy loved ones may be rescued,
Give victory by thy right hand and answer us.
7 God has spoken in his sanctuary:
"I will exult; I will divide Shechem;
And measure off the valley of Succoth.
8 Gilead is mine; Manasseh is mine;
Ephraim is the defense of my head;
Judah is my scepter.
Moab is my washbowl; 9
Upon Edom I cast my sandal;
Over Philistia I raise the shout of victory.
Who will bring me to the fortified city? 10
Who will lead me to Edom?"

Hast not thou, O God, rejected us? 11
And thou goest not forth, O God, with our armies!
Give us aid against the foe; 12
For futile is the help of man.
Through God we shall do valiantly; 13
For he will tread down our foes.

A MALEDICTION

[For the director: of David; a Psalm]

God whom I praise, be not silent! 10
For they have opened wicked and deceitful mouths against me. 2
They talk about me with a lying tongue,
With malicious words do they encircle me, 3
And they attack me for no cause.
In return for my love, they are my enemies; 4
While I rescued them.
So they return me evil for good, 5
And hatred for my love.

Appoint thou a wicked man over him;
And may Satan stand at his right hand!
When he is put on trial may he come forth guilty;
And may his prayer become a sin!
May his days be few!
Let another take his office!
May his children become fatherless,
And his wife a widow!
May his children wander about and beg; 1
And may they be expelled from their hovels!

May his creditor levy upon all that he has, 1
And may strangers plunder his earnings!
May there be none to show him kindness, 1
Nor any to pity his fatherless children!
May his posterity be cut off; 1
In the next generation may their name be blotted out!

14 May the guilt of his fathers be remembered by the LORD;
And may the sin of his mother not be blotted out!
15 May they be before the LORD continually;
And may the memory of them be cut off from the earth!

16 Because he remembered not to show kindness,
But pursued the poor man, the needy,
And the broken-hearted to kill him;
17 Because he loved cursing and it entered into him;
Because he disliked blessing and it remained far from him;
18 And because he clothed himself with cursing as with a garment,
And it entered into him like water,
And was like oil in his bones;
19 May it be unto him like a garment which enfolds him,
And a girdle that he always wears.
20 May this be the reward of my accusers from the LORD,
And of those who speak evil against me!

21 But thou, O GOD, my Lord,
Deal with me, for thy name's sake!
Since thy kindness is good, rescue me!
22 For I am weak and needy,
And my heart is dead within me!
23 Like a lengthening shadow I am passing away;
I am shaken off like a locust.
24 My knees give way from fasting;
My flesh is wasting away and unanointed with oil.
25 And I am become a taunt to them;
All that see me wag their heads.

26 Help me, O LORD, my God!
Deliver me in accordance with thy kindness!
27 And let them know that this is thy hand;
That thou, O LORD, hast done it!
28 They may curse, but do thou bless!
Let my adversaries be ashamed, but let thy servant rejoice!
29 May my accusers be clothed with dishonor;
May they wrap themselves in their shame as a robe.
30 I will thank the LORD greatly with my mouth;
And in the midst of many I will praise him.
For he stands at the right hand of the poor, 31
To save him from those who would condemn him.

A PROMISE OF GOD'S AID TO THE KING

[Of David; a Psalm]

An oracle of the LORD to my lord: 110
"Sit at my right hand,
Till I make your enemies your footstool."
The scepter of your strength the LORD sends forth from Zion. 2
Reign in the midst of your enemies.
Your people will volunteer freely on your day of war. 3
In holy array, from the womb of dawn,
The dew of your youth is yours.
The LORD has sworn and he will not retract: 4
"You shall be a priest for life,
A Melchizedek, because of me."

The Lord is at your right hand. 5
He has shattered kings on the day of his wrath.
He will sit in judgment upon the nations; he will fill the valleys. 6
He has shattered the chief over a broad land.
From a brook by the wayside he will drink; 7
Therefore he will lift up his head.

THE WONDERFUL WORKS OF GOD

Hallelujah! 111

א

I give thanks to the LORD with all my heart,

ב

In the council of the upright and in the assembly.

ג

Great are the works of the LORD, 2

ד

To be studied by all who delight in them.

ה

Majestic and glorious is his work, 3

ו

And his righteousness stands fast forever.

ז

4 He has made his wonders an enduring memory;

ח

Gracious and merciful is the LORD.

ט

5 He has provided nourishment for those who fear him;

י

He remembers his covenant forever.

כ

6 His powerful deeds he has made known to his people,

ל

In giving them possession of the nations.

מ

7 The works of his hands are faithfulness and justice;

נ

Trustworthy are all his precepts;

ס

8 Sure are they forever and ever;

ע

Done in faithfulness and uprightness.

פ

9 He has sent forth release for his people;

צ

His covenant he has ordained forever.

ק

Holy and terrible is his name.

ר

10 The beginning of wisdom is reverence for the LORD;

ש

It is good judgment in all who practice it.

ת

His praise stands fast forever.

THE LOT OF THE PIOUS

Hallelujah! 112

א

How happy is the man who reverences the LORD,

ב

Who greatly delights in his commands!

ג

His descendants will be mighty in the land; 2

ד

The generation of the upright will be blessed.

ה

Prosperity and riches will be in his house, 3

ו

And his righteousness will endure forever.

ז

Unto the upright he arises as a light in the darkness, 4

ח

Gracious, merciful, and righteous.

ט

It is well with the man who is a gracious lender, 5

י

Who conducts his business with justice;

כ

For he will never be shaken.

ל

The righteous man will be an abiding memory.

מ

He will not be frightened by evil tidings, 7

נ

His heart is firm, trusting in the LORD,

ס

His heart is supported, he will not be afraid,

ע

Until he gaze upon his foes.

פ

9 He has scattered abroad; he has given
to the needy;

צ

His righteousness will endure forever.

ק

His horn will be exalted in honor.

ר

10 The wicked will see and be vexed.

ש

He will gnash his teeth and melt
away.

ת

The desire of the wicked will perish.

THE GENEROUS DEEDS OF GOD

113 Hallelujah!
Praise, O servants of the LORD,
Praise the name of the LORD!
2 Blessed be the name of the LORD,
From henceforth even forever.
3 From the rising of the sun unto its
setting,
Let the LORD'S name be praised.

4 High above all nations is the LORD,
Above the heavens is his glory.
5 Who is like the LORD, our God,
Seated on high,
6 Seeing far below,
In the heavens and on earth?

7 He lifts up the poor from the dust;
He raises the needy from the refuse
heap,
8 To make them sit with princes,
With the princes of his people.
9 He makes the childless woman abide
in the household
As the happy mother of its children.
Hallelujah!

THE WONDERS OF THE EXODUS

114 When Israel went forth from Egypt,
The house of Jacob from a people of
alien speech,
2 Judah became his sanctuary,
Israel his domain.
3 The sea saw it and fled;
The Jordan turned back;
The mountains skipped like rams, 4
The hills like lambs.

What ailed you, O sea, that you fled? 5
Jordan, that you turned back?
Mountains, that you skipped like 6
rams?
Hills, like lambs?

Tremble, O earth, before the Lord, 7
Before the God of Jacob;
Who turned the rock into a pool of 8
water,
The flint into a fountain of water.

GOD AND THE IDOLS

Not unto us, O LORD, not unto us, 115
But to thy name, give honor;
Because of thy kindness, because of
thy faithfulness!
Why should the nations say, 2
"Where, now, is their God?"
Verily, our God is in the heavens; 3
He does whatever he pleases.

Their idols are but silver and gold, 4
The product of men's hands.
They have mouths, but cannot speak; 5
Eyes have they, but cannot see;
Ears have they, but cannot hear; 6
Noses have they, but cannot smell;
They have hands, but they cannot 7
handle;
Feet have they, but cannot walk;
Nor can they make a sound in their
throat.
Those who make them will become 8
like them,
Everyone who trusts in them.

O Israel, trust in the LORD! 9
He is their help and their shield.
O house of Aaron, trust in the LORD! 10
He is their help and their shield.
You who reverence the LORD, trust 11
in the LORD!
He is their help and their shield.

The LORD has remembered us; he 12
will bless,
He will bless the house of Israel;
He will bless the house of Aaron;
He will bless those who reverence the 13
LORD,
Both small and great.

May the LORD give you increase, 14
Both you and your children.

15 Blessed be you of the LORD,
Who made heaven and earth.
16 The heavens are the heavens of the LORD,
But the earth has he given to mankind.

17 The dead will not praise the LORD,
Nor any who go down into silence.
18 But we, we will bless the LORD,
From this time forth and forever.
Hallelujah!

A SONG OF THANKSGIVING

116 I love the LORD, because he hears
The voice of my supplication;
2 Because he inclines his ear unto me;
And I will call upon him as long as I live.

3 The cords of death encircled me;
And the tortures of Sheol found me;
I found trouble and sorrow;
4 But I called upon the name of the LORD,
"O LORD, deliver me!"
5 Gracious is the LORD and righteous;
And our God is merciful.
6 The LORD guards the simple;
When I am brought low, he delivers me.
7 Return to your rest, O my spirit,
For the LORD has dealt well with you;
8 For thou hast delivered me from death,
My eyes from tears,
And my foot from stumbling.

9 I shall walk before the LORD
In the lands of the living.
10 I believe what I say;
I am fully responsible for it;
11 I say in my distress,
"All mankind is unreliable."

12 How can I repay the LORD
All his benefits to me?
13 I will take the cup of deliverance,
And will call upon the name of the LORD.

14 I will pay my vows to the LORD,
In the very presence of all his people.
15 Precious in the eyes of the LORD
Is the death of his saints.

Ah, LORD, because I am thy servant,
I am thy servant, the son of thy handmaid,
Thou hast loosened my bonds.
I will offer to thee the thank-offering, 1
And will call upon the name of the LORD.

My vows to the LORD I will pay, 1
In the very presence of all his people;
In the courts of the house of the LORD, 1
In the midst of you, O Jerusalem.
Hallelujah!

A SHOUT OF PRAISE

Praise the LORD, all nations; 1
Extol him, all peoples;
For great is his kindness toward us;
And the faithfulness of the LORD is everlasting.
Hallelujah!

EVERLASTING GRACE

Give thanks to the LORD; for he is good, 1
For his kindness is everlasting.
Let Israel now say,
That his kindness is everlasting.
Let the house of Aaron now say,
That his kindness is everlasting.
Let those that reverence the LORD now say,
That his kindness is everlasting.

When in straits, I called upon the LORD;
He answered me with abundant room.
With the LORD for me, I do not fear
What man may do to me.
With the LORD for me as my helper,
I shall gaze in triumph on those who hate me.
It is better to seek refuge in the LORD
Than to trust in man.
It is better to seek refuge in the LORD
Than to trust in princes.

Though all nations surround me, 1
In the name of the LORD I will ward them off.
Though they encompass, yea, surround me, 1
In the name of the LORD I will destroy them.
Though they surround me like bees, 1

Though they burn like a fire of thorns,
In the name of the LORD I will ward them off.
13 I was sore beset, about to fall,
But the LORD helped me.
14 The LORD is my strength and song,
And he is become my deliverance.
15 Hark, the joyous shout of triumph among the tents of the righteous!
The right hand of the LORD works victoriously.
16 The right hand of the LORD is exalted.
The right hand of the LORD works victoriously.

17 I shall not die, but live
To tell of the deeds of the LORD.
18 The LORD has disciplined me severely;
But he has not given me up to death.
19 Open for me the gates of victory,
That I may enter through them to give thanks to the LORD.
20 This is the gate of the LORD,
Through which the victors may enter.

21 I thank thee that thou hast answered me,
And hast become my deliverance.
22 The stone that the builders rejected
Has become the chief cornerstone.

23 From the LORD has this come,
It is wonderful in our eyes.
24 This is the day that the LORD has made;
Let us rejoice and be glad therein!

25 O LORD, deliver, I pray;
O LORD, give success, I pray!
26 Blessed be he who enters in the name of the LORD;
We will bless you from the house of the LORD!

27 The LORD is God and he has given us light.
Arrange the festal dance with branches,
Up to the horns of the altar.
28 Thou art my God, and I thank thee;
My God, I exalt thee.

29 Give thanks to the LORD, for he is good,
For his kindness is everlasting.

THE LAW OF THE LORD

א

How happy are they whose way is blameless, 119
Who walk in the law of the LORD!
How happy are they who keep his decrees, 2
Who seek him with the whole heart!
Surely they do no wrong, 3
But they walk in his ways.
Thou hast ordained thy precepts, 4
That we should keep them diligently.
O that my ways were firmly set 5
To keep thy statutes!
Then I should not be put to shame, 6
When I look upon all thy commands.
I thank thee with a right heart, 7
When I learn thy righteous ordinances.
I will observe thy statutes; 8
Do not wholly abandon me!

ב

How can a young man keep his path pure? 9
By heeding thy word.
I seek thee with my whole heart; 10
Let me not wander from thy commands!
I have stored thy message in my heart, 11
That I may not sin against thee.
Blessed be thou, O LORD; 12
Teach me thy statutes!
With my lips I recount 13
All the ordinances of thy mouth.
In the way of thy decrees I delight, 14
As much as in all wealth.
I meditate upon thy precepts, 15
And I observe thy paths.
I find joy in thy statutes; 16
I will not forget thy word.

ג

Deal generously with thy servant, that I may live, 17
And I will keep thy word.
Unveil my eyes, that I may behold 18
Wonderful things out of thy law.
I am but a guest in the land; 19
Hide not thy commands from me!
I study with eagerness 20
Upon thine ordinances all the time.
Thou dost rebuke the arrogant, the accursed, 21
Who go astray from thy commands.
Take away from me disgrace and scorn, 22

For I have kept thy decrees.
23 Though princes sit and talk with me,
Thy servant meditates upon thy statutes.
24 Thy decrees are my delight,
They are my counselors.

ד

25 My spirit clings to the dust;
Revive me according to thy word.
26 I have told of my ways and thou didst answer me;
Teach me thy statutes.
27 Make me understand the way of thy precepts,
That I may meditate upon thy wonders.
28 I am downcast because of sorrow;
Raise me up according to thy word.
29 False ways put far from me;
And graciously grant me thy law.
30 I have chosen the way of trustworthiness,
Thine ordinances I crave.
31 I have clung to thy decrees;
O LORD, put me not to shame!
32 I run in the way of thy commands,
For thou dost enlarge my heart.

ה

33 Teach me, O LORD, the way of thy statutes,
That I may keep it to the end.
34 Make me to understand, that I may keep thy law,
And observe it with my whole heart.
35 Let me walk in the path of thy commands;
For therein do I delight.
36 Incline my heart toward thy decrees,
And not toward profits.
37 Turn my eyes away from looking upon unreality;
Revive me in thy way.
38 Establish thy promise for thy servant,
Which is for those who revere thee.
39 Turn away from me the disgrace which I fear;
For thine ordinances are good.
40 Lo, I have longed for thy precepts;
Revive me through thy righteousness.

ו

41 May thy gracious deeds come to me, O LORD,
Thy deliverance according to thy promise;
42 That I may answer those who insult me;
For I have trusted in thy word.
43 Do not snatch the word of truth utterly out of my mouth;
For I have waited for thine ordinances,
44 That I may observe thy law continually,
Forever and ever.
45 May I walk at large,
Because I have sought thy precepts.
46 I will speak of thy decrees in the presence of kings,
And I shall not be put to shame.
47 I delight myself in thy commands
Which I love.
48 I raise my hands to thy commands which I love;
And I meditate upon thy statutes.

ז

49 Remember the word to thy servant,
Upon which thou hast led me to hope.
50 This is my comfort in my trouble,
That thy promise revives me.
51 The arrogant have scoffed at me bitterly,
But I have not turned away from thy law.
52 I remember thine ordinances from of old, O LORD,
And I am comforted.
53 Burning rage lays hold of me because of the wicked,
Who abandon thy law.
54 Thy statutes are my songs of praise,
In my house of pilgrimage.
55 I remember thy name in the night, O LORD,
And I observe thy law.
56 This is mine,
That I keep thy precepts.

ח

57 The LORD is my portion;
I have said that I would observe thy words.
58 I beseech thee with my whole heart:
Be gracious to me according to thy promise.
59 I have considered my ways,
And turned my feet toward thy decrees.
60 I have hastened, and not delayed
In the observance of thy commands.
61 The cords of the wicked have encircled me,
But I have not forgotten thy law.
62 At midnight I rise up to give thee thanks,

Because of thy righteous ordinances.
63 I am the companion of all who revere thee,
And observe thy precepts.
64 The earth is full of thy kindness, O LORD;
Teach me thy statutes.

ט

65 Thou hast treated thy servant well,
O LORD, according to thy word.
66 Teach me good judgment and knowledge,
For I have trusted in thy commands.
67 Before I was afflicted, I went astray;
But now I keep thy sayings.
68 Thou art good, and doest good;
Teach me thy statutes.
69 The arrogant have told lies about me;
But I keep thy precepts with all my heart.
70 Their heart is gross, like fat;
But I delight in thy law.
71 It is good for me that I was afflicted,
That I might learn thy statutes.
72 The law of thy mouth is worth more to me
Than thousands in gold and silver.

י

73 Thy hands made me and fashioned me;
Give me understanding that I may learn thy commands.
74 May they who revere thee see me and rejoice,
Because I wait upon thy word.
75 I know, O LORD, that thine ordinances are right,
And that in good faith thou hast afflicted me;
76 But now let thy kindness comfort me,
According to thy promise to thy servant.
77 Let thy mercies come to me that I may live;
For my delight is in thy law.
78 Let the arrogant be put to shame, for they have falsely traduced me;
But I will meditate upon thy precepts.
79 Let those who revere thee turn to me,
And those who know thy decrees!
80 Let my heart be blameless in thy statutes,
That I be not put to shame.

כ

I pine for thy deliverance; 81
I wait for thy word.
My eyes fail for thy promise, 82
Saying, "How long till thou comfort me?"
Though I have become like a wine skin in the smoke, 83
I have not forgotten thy statutes.
How many are thy servant's days? 84
How long till thou execute judgment upon my pursuers?
Pits have been dug for me by the arrogant, 85
Who are not in accord with thy law.
All thy commands are sure. 86
They persecute me on false charges; help me!
They have nearly destroyed me in the land; 87
But I have not forsaken thy precepts.
In accordance with thy kindness revive me, 88
That I may observe the decrees of thy mouth.

ל

Forever, O LORD, 89
Thy word stands fast in the heavens,
Thy faithfulness throughout the ages; 90
Thou didst establish the earth and it stood fast.
By thine ordinances they stand today; 91
For all things are thy servants.
Had not thy law been my delight, 92
Then I had perished in my affliction.
I shall never forget thy precepts; 93
For by them thou didst keep me alive.
I am thine, save me; 94
For I have sought after thy precepts!
The wicked lie in wait to ruin me; 95
I consider thy decrees.
I have seen a limit to all perfection; 96
Thy command is exceedingly broad.

מ

O how I love thy law! 97
It is my meditation all day long.
Thy command makes me wiser than my foes; 98
For it is always mine.
I am wiser than all my teachers; 99
For thy decrees are my meditation.
I have more discretion than the aged; 100
For I kept thy precepts.
I have withheld my feet from every wicked path, 101
That I might observe thy word.

102 I have not turned aside from thine
ordinances;
For thou thyself hast taught me.
103 How sweet are thy promises to my
palate,
Sweeter than honey to my mouth!
104 From thy precepts I get discretion;
Therefore I hate every false way.

נ

105 Thy word is a lamp to my feet,
And a light on my path.
106 I have sworn, and I will perform it,
To observe thy righteous ordinances.
107 I am sorely afflicted;
O LORD, revive me in accordance
with thy word.
108 Accept, now, O LORD, the voluntary
offerings of my mouth,
And teach me thine ordinances.
109 I carry my life in my hand continually,
But I have not forgotten thy law.
110 The wicked set a trap for me,
But I have not strayed from thy precepts.
111 I have thy decrees as a heritage forever;
For they are the joy of my heart.
112 I incline my heart to execute thy
statutes,
Henceforth forever.

ס

113 I hate dissemblers;
But I love thy law.
114 Thou art my shelter and my shield;
I wait for thy word.
115 Depart from me, O doers of evil,
That I may keep the commands of
my God.
116 Sustain me according to thy promise
that I may live;
And make me not ashamed of my
hope.
117 Strengthen me that I may be delivered;
And let me constantly contemplate
thy statutes.
118 Thou dost despise all who swerve
from thy statutes,
For their deceit is useless.
119 Like dross, thou puttest an end to all
the wicked of the earth;
Therefore I love thy decrees.
120 My flesh creeps in awe of thee,
And I revere thine ordinances.

ע

I have done what is just and right; 121
Leave me not to my oppressors.
Pledge me thy word for good; 122
Let not the arrogant oppress me.
My eyes fail with longing for thy de- 123
liverance,
And for thy righteous promise.
Deal with thy servant according to 124
thy kindness;
And teach me thy statutes.
I am thy servant; give me under- 125
standing,
That I may know thy decrees.
It is time for the LORD to act; 126
They have broken thy law.
Therefore I love thy commands, 127
More than gold or beaten gold.
Therefore I declare all thy precepts 128
to be right;
I hate every false path.

פ

Thy decrees are wonderful; 129
Therefore will I keep them.
The exposition of thy words gives 130
light,
Giving understanding to the open-
hearted.
I have opened wide my mouth and 131
panted;
For I long for thy commands.
Turn toward me and be gracious to 132
me,
As is the right of those who love thy
name.
Establish my footsteps by thy saying, 133
And let no wrong have power over
me.
Free me from man's oppression, 134
That I may observe thy precepts.
Let thy face beam upon thy servant, 135
And teach me thy statutes.
With streams of water my eyes run 136
down,
Over those who have not kept thy
law.

צ

Thou art righteous, O LORD, 137
And thine ordinances are right.
Thou hast issued thy decrees in right- 138
eousness,
And in exceeding faithfulness.
My zeal consumes me, 139
Because my foes forget thy words.
Thy promise has been tried to the ut- 140
most,
And thy servant loves it.

141 Little am I, and insignificant,
But I have not forgotten thy precepts.
142 Thy righteousness is right forever;
And thy law is truth.
143 Trouble and anguish befall me;
But thy commands are my delight.
144 Thy decrees are eternally right;
Give me understanding that I may live.

ק

145 I call with all my heart; answer me, O LORD!
I will keep thy statutes.
146 I call upon thee; deliver me,
That I may keep thy decrees.
147 I arise at dawn, and call for help;
I wait for thy word.
148 My eyes anticipate the night-watches,
In meditation upon thy promise.
149 Hear my voice according to thy kindness;
O LORD, revive me according to thy justice.
150 My pursuers are in close touch with malice;
But they are far from thy law.
151 Thou art near, O LORD;
And all thy commands are true.
152 Long ago I knew from thy decrees,
That thou hadst founded them forever.

ר

153 Behold my affliction, and rescue me;
For I have not forgotten thy law!
154 Plead thou my case, and avenge me;
Revive me in accordance with thy promise.
155 Deliverance is far from the wicked;
For they have not sought thy statutes.
156 Thy mercies are many, O LORD;
Revive me according to thy justice.
157 Many are my pursuers and my foes,
But I have not turned away from thy decrees.
158 I see apostates and loathe them,
Because they do not keep thy word.
159 See how I love thy precepts!
O LORD, revive me according to thy kindness.
160 The sum of thy word is truth;
And all thy righteous judgments are everlasting.

ש

161 Princes persecute me without cause;
But my heart is in awe of thy word.
I delight in thy promise, 162
Like one who finds abundant spoil.
Falsehood I hate and loathe; 163
Thy law do I love.
Seven times daily I praise thee, 164
Because of thy righteous ordinances.
Great prosperity have they who love thy law, 165
And no obstacles confront them.
I hope for thy deliverance, O LORD, 166
And I do thy commands.
I keep thy decrees, 167
And I love them dearly.
I observe thy precepts and thy decrees; 168
For all my ways are before thee.

ת

Let my cry come before thee, O LORD; 169
Give me understanding according to thy word.
Let my entreaty come before thee; 170
Rescue me according to thy promise.
Let my lips speak forth praise, 171
Because thou dost teach me thy statutes.
May my tongue sing of thy word, 172
For all thy commands are right.
May thy hand come to my help, 173
For I have chosen thy precepts.
I long for thy deliverance, O LORD, 174
And thy law is my delight.
May I live to praise thee, 175
And may thine ordinances help me.
I have gone astray like a lost sheep; 176
seek thy servant;
For I have not forgotten thy commands.

A WARNING TO LIARS

[A Song of Ascents]

To the LORD in my distress **120**
I call, and he answers me.
O LORD, deliver me from lying lips, 2
From the deceitful tongue.

What will he give you, and what more, 3
O deceitful tongue?
The sharpened arrows of the warrior, 4
With live broom coals!

Alas that I sojourn in Meshech, 5
That I dwell with the clans of Kedar!
Too long a time have I dwelt 6
With the haters of peace.
I am for peace, but when I speak, 7
They are for war!

THE GUARDIAN GOD

[A Song for the Ascents]

121 I raise my eyes to the hills;
whence does my help come?
2 My help is from the LORD,
who made the heavens and the earth.
3 He will not let your foot slip,
your guardian will not slumber.
4 He will neither slumber, nor sleep,
he that guards Israel.

5 The LORD is your guardian;
the LORD is your shade upon your right hand.
6 By day the sun will not smite you,
nor the moon by night.

7 The LORD will guard you from all evil;
the LORD will guard your life.
8 The LORD will guard your goings and comings
henceforth and forever.

A PRAYER FOR JERUSALEM

[A Song of Ascents. Of David]

122 I was glad when they said to me,
"Let us go to the house of the LORD."
2 Our feet are standing
Within your gates, O Jerusalem;
3 Jerusalem that is rebuilt like a city,
Which is reconsolidated;
4 Whither the tribes go up,
The tribes of the LORD—
It is a decree for Israel—
To give thanks to the name of the LORD;
5 For there were set thrones of judgment,
The thrones of the house of David.

6 Pray for the peace of Jerusalem;
They will prosper who love you.
7 Peace be within your walls,
Prosperity in your palaces!
8 For the sake of my brethren and my friends,
I will say, "Peace be within you!"
9 For the sake of the house of the LORD, our God,
I will seek your good.

A SONG OF SIGHS

[A Song of Ascents]

123 Unto thee I raise my eyes,
O thou, who dwellest in the heavens!
Lo, as the eyes of slaves are to the hand of their master, 2
As the eyes of a maid are to the hand of her mistress,
So our eyes are toward the LORD, our God,
Till he take pity upon us.

Have pity on us, O LORD, have pity on us! 3
For we are abundantly sated with contempt.
We are abundantly sated with it, 4
With the scorn of the arrogant,
The contempt of the insolent.

A SONG OF GRATITUDE

[A Song of Ascents. Of David]

"Had it not been the LORD who was on our side," 124
Let Israel say,
"Had it not been the LORD who was on our side, 2
When men rose up against us,
Then had they swallowed us up alive, 3
When their anger blazed forth against us;
Then had the waters swept us away, 4
The torrent had gone over us;
Then had gone over us 5
The seething waters.

"Blessed be the LORD, 6
Who did not yield us a prey to their teeth.
We are like a bird escaped from the fowler's snare; 7
The snare is broken and we have escaped.
Our help is in the name of the LORD, 8
Who made the heavens and the earth."

UNSHAKABLE FAITH

[A Song of Ascents]

They who trust in the LORD 125
Are like Mount Zion which cannot be moved,
But abides forever.
Even as the mountains encircle Jerusalem, 2
So the LORD encircles his people,
Henceforth and forever.

For the wicked scepter will not rest upon the lot of the righteous, 3
That the righteous may not put forth their hands unto wrong.

4 Do good, O LORD, to the good,
And to them that are upright in heart.
5 But those who make their ways crooked—
May the LORD make them go with malefactors!
Peace be upon Israel!

SHOUTS OF JOY

[A Song of Ascents]

126 When the LORD brings back captive Zion
We shall be like dreamers!
2 Then will our mouth be filled with laughter,
And our tongue with shouts of joy.
Then will they say among the nations,
"The LORD has done great things for them."
3 The LORD has done great things for us;
We are glad.

4 Restore our fortune, O LORD,
Like torrents in the southland.
5 May those who sow in tears
Reap with shouts of joy!
6 He who goes forth weeping, bearing seed for sowing,
Will indeed come back with joyful shouts, bearing his sheaves.

THE SUSTAINING GOD

[A Song of Ascents. Of Solomon]

127 Unless the LORD build the house,
Its builders toil thereon in vain.
Unless the LORD keep the city,
The watchman keeps awake in vain.
2 In vain do you rise up early,
And stay up late,
And eat hard-earned bread;
So he gives his loved ones sleep.
3 Lo, children are a heritage from the LORD;
The fruit of the womb is a reward.
4 Like arrows in the hand of a warrior,
So are the children of one's youth.
5 How happy is the man whose quiver is filled with them!
They will not be put to shame when they speak with their enemies in the gate.

THE TRULY HAPPY MAN

[A Song of Ascents]

128 How happy is everyone who reveres the LORD,
Who walks in his ways!
2 Of the toil of your hands you shall eat;
Happy and prosperous shall you be!

3 Your wife shall be like a fruitful vine,
In the interior of your house;
Your children like young olive trees,
Around your table.
4 For lo, thus shall the man be blessed,
Who reveres the LORD.

5 The LORD bless you from Zion!
And may you look upon the welfare of Jerusalem
All the days of your life!
6 And may you look upon your children's children!
Peace be upon Israel!

THE FLEETING FORTUNE OF THE WICKED

[A Song of Ascents]

129 "Grossly have they abused me from my youth up,"
May Israel, indeed, say;
2 "Grossly have they abused me from my youth up,
But they have not prevailed against me.
3 The plowers plowed upon my back,
They made their furrows long,"
4 But the LORD is righteous;
He has cut the cords of the wicked.

5 They are put to shame and turned back,
All who hate Zion.
6 They will be like the grass on the roofs,
That withers before it has shot up,
7 With which the reaper does not fill his hands,
Nor the binder of sheaves his bosom.
8 Those passing by will not say to them,
"The blessing of the LORD be upon you;
We bless you in the name of the LORD!"

DE PROFUNDIS

[A Song of Ascents]

130 Out of the depths I cry to thee, O LORD!
2 O LORD, hear my voice!
Let thine ears be attentive
To my supplicating voice.

3 If thou, O LORD, shouldst record iniquities,
O LORD, who could stand?
4 But with thee there is forgiveness,
That thou mayest be revered.

5 I wait for the LORD, my whole being waits,
And for his word I hope.
6 I wait for the LORD,
More than watchmen for the dawn,
Watchmen for the dawn.

7 Hope, O Israel, in the LORD,
For with the LORD is kindness,
And with him is plenteous redemption.
8 For he will redeem Israel
From all its guilt.

A PATIENT SAINT

[A Song of Ascents. Of David]

131 My heart is not proud, O LORD,
Nor are my eyes lofty;
Nor do I deal with things
Too great and too wonderful for me.
2 I have, indeed, calmed and stilled my spirit,
Like a weaned child with its mother;
My spirit is with me like a weaned child.

3 Wait, O Israel, for the LORD,
Henceforth and forever!

THE ANCIENT PROMISE

[A Song of Ascents]

132 Remember, O LORD, for David's sake,
All his affliction:
2 How he swore to the LORD,
And vowed to the Mighty One of Jacob:
3 "I will not enter my dwelling-house,
Nor will I mount my bed to lie down,
4 Nor permit sleep to my eyes,
Nor slumber to my eyelids,
5 Until I find a place for the LORD,
A dwelling for the Mighty One of Jacob."

6 Lo, we heard that it was in Ephrathah;
We found it in the fields of Jaar.
7 Let us go to his dwelling,
Let us worship at his footstool.
8 Arise, O LORD, to thy resting-place,
Thou and the ark of thy strength.
Let thy priests robe themselves in righteousness, 9
And thy saints shout with joy.
Because of David, thy servant, 10
Turn not away the face of thine anointed.

The LORD swore to David 11
An inviolable oath from which he will not swerve:
"Of the fruit of your body,
I will establish a dynasty for you.
If your sons keep my covenant, 12
And my decrees which I teach them,
Then their sons, forever,
Shall sit upon your throne."
For the LORD has chosen Zion; 13
He has desired it for his dwelling-place:

"This is my resting-place forever; 14
Here will I dwell, for I desired it.
I will richly bless its food supply, 15
Its needy I will satisfy with bread.
Its priests will I clothe with salvation, 16
And its saints shall shout aloud with joy.
There will I cause a horn to spring forth for David; 17
I will set in order a lamp for my anointed,
His enemies I will clothe with shame; 18
But upon him his diadem shall shine."

ZION'S PERPETUAL BLESSING

[A Song of Ascents. Of David]

Lo, how good and lovely it is 133
When brethren dwell together as one.
Like the goodly oil upon the head, 2
Which flows down upon the beard,
Aaron's beard,
That flows down upon the edge of his robes,
So is the dew of Hermon that flows down upon the mountains of Zion; 3
For there has the LORD commanded the blessing:
Life for evermore.

A CALL TO WORSHIP

[A Song of Ascents]

Lo, bless the LORD, all you servants of the LORD, 134
Who stand in the house of the LORD by night!

2 Lift up your hands toward the sanctuary,
And bless the LORD!
3 May the LORD, maker of the heavens and the earth,
Bless you from Zion.

A SONG OF PRAISE

135 Hallelujah!
Praise the name of the LORD!
Praise him, O you servants of the LORD,
2 Who stand in the house of the LORD,
In the courts of the house of our God!
3 Praise the LORD, for the LORD is good!
Sing praises to his name, for he is gracious.
4 For the LORD has chosen Jacob as his own,
And Israel as his own treasure.
I know, indeed, that the LORD is great,
That our Lord is greater than all the gods.
6 The LORD does whatsoever he pleases,
Whether in the heavens or on the earth,
In the seas and in all deeps;
7 Raising clouds from the ends of the earth.
He makes the lightning flashes for the rain,
Bringing forth the wind from his treasuries.

8 It was he who smote the first-born of Egypt,
Both of man and beast.
9 He sent forth wonders and portents
Into the midst of thee, O Egypt,
Upon Pharaoh and upon all his servants!
10 It was he who smote many nations,
And slew mighty kings,
11 Sihon, the king of the Amorites,
Og, the king of Bashan,
And all the kingdoms of Canaan.
12 And he gave their land as a possession,
A possession to his people Israel.
13 O LORD, thy name is forever;
Thy memorial, O LORD, is throughout the ages.
14 For the LORD will give his people justice,
And will have compassion upon his servants.

The idols of the nations are but silver and gold, 15
The product of men's hands.
They have mouths, but cannot speak; 16
Eyes have they, but cannot see;
Ears have they, but cannot hear; 17
Neither, indeed, is there any breath in their mouth.
Those who make them will become like them, 18
Everyone who trusts in them.

O house of Israel, bless the LORD; 19
O house of Aaron, bless the LORD;
O house of the Levites, bless the LORD; 20
You who revere the LORD, bless the LORD!
Blessed from Zion be the LORD, 21
Who dwells at Jerusalem!
Hallelujah!

THE KINDNESS OF GOD

Give thanks to the LORD, for he is good, 136
For his kindness is everlasting.
Give thanks to the God of gods, 2
For his kindness is everlasting.
Give thanks to the Lord of lords, 3
For his kindness is everlasting;
To him who did great wonders alone, 4
For his kindness is everlasting;
To him who made the heavens with skill, 5
For his kindness is everlasting;
To him who spread out the earth upon the waters, 6
For his kindness is everlasting;
To him who made the great lights, 7
For his kindness is everlasting;
The sun to rule by day, 8
For his kindness is everlasting;
The moon and the stars to rule by night, 9
For his kindness is everlasting;
To him who smote the Egyptians in their first-born, 10
For his kindness is everlasting;
And brought forth Israel from the midst of them, 11
For his kindness is everlasting;
With a strong hand and an outstretched arm, 12
For his kindness is everlasting;
To him who divided the Red Sea into two parts, 13

For his kindness is everlasting;
14 And led Israel over through the midst
of it,
For his kindness is everlasting;
15 And shook Pharaoh and his army into
the Red Sea,
For his kindness is everlasting;
16 To him who led his people through
the wilderness,
For his kindness is everlasting;
17 To him who smote great kings,
For his kindness is everlasting;
18 And slew mighty kings,
For his kindness is everlasting;
19 Sihon, the king of the Amorites,
For his kindness is everlasting;
20 And Og, the king of Bashan,
For his kindness is everlasting;
21 And gave their land as a possession,
For his kindness is everlasting;
22 A possession to Israel, his servant,
For his kindness is everlasting;
23 Who remembered us in our abase-
ment,
For his kindness is everlasting;
24 And rescued us from our foes,
For his kindness is everlasting;
25 Who gives food to all flesh,
For his kindness is everlasting.
26 Give thanks to the God of the heavens,
For his kindness is everlasting.

REVENGE UPON ISRAEL'S FOES

137 By the rivers of Babylon,
There we sat down, and wept,
When we remembered Zion.
2 Upon the poplars, in the midst of
her,
We hung up our harps.
3 For there our captors
Demanded of us songs,
And our tormentors, mirth:
"Sing us some of the songs of Zion."

4 How could we sing the songs of the
LORD
In a foreign land?
5 If I forget you, O Jerusalem,
May my right hand fail me!
6 May my tongue cleave to my palate,
If I do not remember you;
If I set not Jerusalem
Above my highest joy!

7 Remember, O LORD, against the
Edomites,
The day of Jerusalem!
They who said, "Raze it, raze it,
To its very foundations!"
O daughter of Babylon, destructive 8
one,
Blessed be he who requites to you
The treatment that you dealt out to
us!
Blessed be he who seizes your little 9
ones,
And dashes them to pieces upon a rock!

THE HELP OF GOD

[Of David]

I give thee thanks with all my heart; **138**
In the presence of the gods, I sing
praises to thee.
I prostrate myself toward thy holy 2
temple;
And give thanks to thy name for thy
kindness and thy faithfulness;
For thou hast magnified thy name
over all.
On the day when I called thou didst 3
answer me;
Thou didst increase thy power in me.

All the kings of the earth will give 4
thanks to thee, O LORD,
When they have heard the words of
thy mouth.
And they will sing of the ways of the 5
LORD,
That the glory of the LORD is great.
The LORD looks upon the high and 6
the low,
But the haughty he knows from afar.

Though I walk in the midst of hostil- 7
ity, thou dost preserve my life;
Against the wrath of my foes; thou
dost stretch forth thy hand,
And thy right hand delivers me.
The LORD rewards me. 8
O LORD, thy kindness is everlasting;
Forsake not the work of thine own
hands!

THE OMNIPRESENT AND OMNISCIENT GOD

[For the director: a Psalm of David]

Thou hast searched me and known **13**
me, O LORD;
Thou knowest when I sit down and 2
when I stand up;
Thou discernest my thought from
afar.

3 Thou dost measure out my course and
my camp,
And art intimately acquainted with
all my ways.
4 For there is not a word on my tongue,
But LORD, thou knowest it all.
5 Thou dost enfold me behind and before,
And dost put thy hand upon me;
6 Such knowledge is too wonderful for
me;
It is too lofty; I am not equal to it.

7 Whither shall I go from thy spirit?
And whither shall I flee from thy
presence?
8 If I ascend to the heavens, thou art
there!
If I make Sheol my bed, thou art
there also!
9 If I take up the wings of the dawn,
And dwell at the back of the sea,
10 Even there thy hand will guide me,
And thy right hand will hold me.
11 If I say, "Darkness will surely cover
me,"
Then the night becomes light about
me.
12 Darkness makes it not too dark for
thee;
But the night is as bright as the day;
Darkness and light are both alike to
thee.

13 For thou didst create my vitals,
Thou didst fashion me in my mother's
womb.
14 I praise thee because thou art fear-
fully wonderful;
Wondrous are thy works,
And I myself know it well.
15 My bones were not hidden from thee,
When I was made in secret,
And molded in the lowest parts of the
earth.
16 Thine eyes saw the sum total of my
days,
And in thy book they were all written;
They were formed, when there was
not one among them.
17 How precious are thy thoughts to me,
O God!
How great the sum of them!
18 Were I to count them—they would
outnumber the sands!
Were I to come to the end of them,
my life-span must be like thine!

If thou wouldst but slay the wicked, 19
O God,
And the men of blood would depart
from me,
Who oppose thee in their thoughts, 20
Who utter thy name to a lie!
Do I not hate them that hate thee, O 21
LORD?
And do I not loathe them who oppose
thee?
With the deadliest hatred, I hate 22
them;
They are my own enemies.
Search me, O God, and know my 23
heart;
Try me, and know my thoughts;
And see if there be any false way 24
in me;
And lead me in the way everlasting.

A PRAYER FOR VINDICATION

[For the director: a Psalm of David]

Free me, O LORD, from wicked men! **140**
Rescue me from violent men,
Who plan evil things in their heart, 2
Who constantly stir up wars!
They have a sharp tongue like a ser- 3
pent;
The venom of adders is under their
lips. *Selah*

Keep me, O LORD, from the hand of 4
the wicked;
Rescue me from violent men,
Who plan to trip my steps.
The arrogant have laid a snare for me, 5
and lines;
They have spread a net for me by the
wayside;
They have set traps for me. *Selah*

I say to the LORD, "Thou art my 6
God;
Listen, O God, to my supplicating
cry.
O GOD, the Lord, my strong deliv- 7
erer,
Thou hast covered my head on the
day of battle.
Grant not, O LORD, the desires of the 8
wicked;
Let not his purpose succeed! *Selah*

"Let not those who encompass me 9
raise their heads;
May the mischief of their own lips
cover them!
May coals of fire fall down upon them! 10

May they be cast into pits whence
they cannot rise again!
11 May the slanderer have no standing
in the land!
May disaster pursue the violent man
with blow upon blow!"

12 I know that the LORD will maintain
The cause of the wretched, the rights
of the poor.
13 Surely, the righteous shall give
thanks to thy name;
The upright shall dwell in thy presence.

A PRAYER FOR PROTECTION

[A Psalm of David]

141 I call upon thee, O LORD, make haste
to me;
Listen to my voice, when I call upon
thee!
2 Let my prayer rise like incense before
thee,
The lifting of my hands like the evening offering!
3 Set a guard, O LORD, over my
mouth;
Keep watch at the door of my lips.
4 Incline not my heart to any evil
thing,
To participate in wicked deeds,
With men who do wrong;
And let me not eat of their dainties.
5 If the righteous smite me—it is a
kindness,
And if he rebuke me—it is the finest
oil;
Let not my head refuse it!
Indeed, my prayer is ever for them in
trouble.
6 They will be hurled into the hands of
their chieftains,
And they will learn that the word of
the LORD is true.
7 Like a rock, split and crushed on the
land,
Their bones will lie scattered at the
jaws of Sheol.

8 But my eyes are toward thee, O Lord
GOD;
In thee I seek refuge; leave me not defenseless!
9 Keep me from the hold of the snare
which they have set for me,
And the traps of wrongdoers!
10 May the wicked fall into their own pits,
While I, indeed, pass by.

A PRAYER FOR SAFETY FROM FOES

[A *maskil* of David when he was in the cave. A prayer]

I cry aloud to the LORD; 142
I make supplications aloud to the
LORD!
I pour out my complaint before him; 2
I tell my trouble before him.
When my spirit faints, 3
Thou knowest my way.

In the path where I must walk,
They lay a snare for me.
Look to the right, and see 4
That I have no friend.
Escape is cut off from me;
Nobody cares for my life.

I cry unto thee, O LORD; 5
I say, "Thou art my refuge,
My portion in the land of the living.
Give heed unto my cry; 6
For I am brought very low.
Rescue me from my pursuers;
For they are too strong for me.
Bring me forth from prison, 7
That I may give thanks to thy name.
The righteous will throng around me,
When thou dealest well with me."

A PRAYER FOR DELIVERANCE

[A Psalm of David]

Hear my prayer, O LORD; 14
Listen to my supplications!
In thy fidelity answer me, and in thy
righteousness!
And enter not into judgment with thy 2
servant;
For in thy sight can no man living be
innocent.

For the enemy has pursued me; 3
He has crushed my life to the earth,
He has made me dwell in dark regions, like those long dead.
And my spirit faints within me; 4
My heart within me is appalled.

I recall the days of old; 5
I meditate upon all thy deeds;
I ponder the work of thy hands.
I spread forth my hands to thee; 6
I long for thee like a parched land.
Selah

Answer me quickly, O LORD; my 7
spirit fails.

Hide not thy face from me,
Lest I become like those that have
gone down to the Pit.
8 Let me hear of thy kindness in the
morning,
For I have trusted in thee!
Teach me the way that I should go,
For unto thee I lift my desire.

9 Deliver me from my enemies, O
LORD;
I seek refuge in thee.
10 Teach me to do thy will,
For thou art my God;
Let thy good spirit guide me in a
straight path.

11 For thy name's sake, O LORD, save
my life!
In the vindication of thyself bring me
out of trouble!
12 In thy kindness cut off my enemies,
And destroy all my adversaries;
For I am thy servant.

A PRAYER FOR DIVINE REINFORCEMENTS

[Of David]

144 Blessed be the LORD, my rock,
Who trains my hands for war,
My fingers for battle;
2 My refuge, and my fortress,
My precipice, and my deliverer,
My shield, and him with whom I seek
refuge;
The one who subdues the peoples under him.

3 O LORD, what is man that thou
shouldst know him,
The son of man that thou shouldst
take thought of him?
4 Man is like a breath,
His days are like a passing shadow.

5 O LORD, bow thy heavens and come
down!
Touch the mountains that they
smoke!
6 Hurl the lightning and scatter them;
Send forth thine arrows and rout
them.

7 Send forth thy hand from on high!
Deliver me and rescue me from the
mighty waters,
From the hand of aliens,
8 Whose mouths speak lies,
And whose right hand is one of falsehood!

O God, I will sing thee a new song; 9
Upon a ten-stringed lute will I play
to thee,
Who makest kings victorious, 10
Who delivered David, his servant,
from the wicked sword.
Deliver me, and rescue me from the 11
hand of aliens,
Whose mouths speak lies,
And whose right hand is one of falsehood!

A CONTENTED PEOPLE

Our sons are like plants grown large 12
in their youth;
Our daughters are like cornices
carved after the fashion of a palace.
Our garners are filled to overflowing, 13
garners of all sorts;
Our flocks increase by thousands and
tens of thousands in our fields.
Our oxen are heavily laden. 14
There is no riot and no alarm,
And no outcry in our streets.
How happy the people that are in 15
such a state!
How happy the people whose God is
the LORD!

AN ALPHABETIC DOXOLOGY

[A prayer of David]

א

I will exalt thee, my God, O King; 145
And bless thy name forever and ever.

ב

All day long will I bless thee, 2
And praise thy name forever and
ever.

ג

Great is the LORD; and highly to be 3
praised,
And his greatness is unlimited.

ד

One generation shall praise thy works 4
to another,
And shall declare thy mighty acts.

ה

They shall speak of the splendor of 5
thy glorious majesty;
And I will tell of thy wonders.

ו

6 They shall talk of thy terrible might;
And I will narrate thy greatness.

ז

7 They shall publish the memory of thy great goodness,
And they shall joyously proclaim thy righteousness.

ח

8 Gracious and merciful is the LORD,
Slow to anger and abounding in kindness.

ט

9 The LORD is good to all,
And his mercy is over all his works.

י

10 All thy works give thanks to thee, O LORD;
And thy saints bless thee.

כ

11 They declare the glory of thy kingdom,
And tell of thy might;

ל

12 To make known his mighty deeds to the sons of men,
And the glorious splendor of his kingdom.

מ

13 Thy kingdom is an everlasting kingdom,
And thy dominion endures throughout the ages.

ס

14 The LORD supports all who fall,
And raises up all who are bowed down.

ע

15 The eyes of all wait upon thee,
And thou givest them their food in due season.

פ

16 Thou openest thy hand,
And completely satisfiest every living thing.

צ

The LORD is righteous in all his ways, 17
And gracious in all his works.

ק

The LORD is near to all who call upon him, 18
To all who call upon him sincerely.

ר

He fulfils the desire of those who revere him; 19
He hears their cries for help and delivers them.

ש

The LORD preserves all those who love him; 20
But all the wicked he destroys.

ת

May my mouth speak the praise of the LORD, 21
And let all flesh bless his holy name,
Forever and ever!

THE PRAISEWORTHY GOD

Hallelujah! 1
Praise the LORD, O my spirit!
I will praise the LORD as long as I live;
I will sing praises to my God as long as I exist.
Put no trust in princes,
In a mere man, in whom is no help.
When his breath departs he returns to his earth;
On that very day his plans perish.

How happy is he whose help is the God of Jacob!
Whose hope is upon the LORD, his God,
Who made the heavens and the earth,
The sea and all that is therein;
Who preserves fidelity forever;
Who renders justice to the oppressed;
Who gives bread to the hungry.

The LORD releases the prisoners;
The LORD opens the eyes of the blind;
The LORD lifts up them that are bowed down;
The LORD loves the righteous;
The LORD watches over the strangers;

The orphan and the widow he supports;
But the way of the wicked he thwarts.
The LORD reigns forever,
Thy God, O Zion, throughout the ages!
Hallelujah!

THE WORKS OF GOD ALMIGHTY

7 Hallelujah!
For it is good to sing praises to our God;
For he is gracious; praise befits him.
The LORD restores Jerusalem;
He assembles the outcasts of Israel.
He heals the broken-hearted,
And binds up their wounds.
He determines the number of the stars;
He gives names to all of them.
Great is our Lord, and abounding in strength;
There is no limit to his understanding.
The LORD upholds the humble;
But he casts the wicked to the ground.

Sing to the LORD with thanksgiving;
Sing praises to our God upon the lute!
For he covers the heavens with clouds;
He prepares rain for the earth;
He makes grass spring forth upon the hills.
He gives to the cattle their food,
And to the young ravens when they cry.
He has no pleasure in the strength of a horse;
He has no delight in the legs of a man!
The LORD is pleased with those who revere him;
With those who wait for his kindness.

Praise the LORD, O Jerusalem!
Extol your God, O Zion!
For he strengthens the bars of your gates;
He blesses your children within you.
He makes your boundary peace;
He satisfies you with the finest of the wheat.
He sends forth his command to the earth;
His word runs with utmost speed.
He gives snow like wool, 16
He scatters hoarfrost like ashes.
He casts forth his ice like crumbs; 17
Who can stand before his cold?
He sends forth his word and melts them; 18
He makes his wind blow, the water flows.
He declares his word to Jacob, 19
His statutes and judgments to Israel.
He has not acted thus with any other nation; 20
Nor do they know his judgments.
Hallelujah!

A HALLELUJAH CHORUS

Hallelujah! 148
Praise the LORD from the heavens;
Praise him in the heights!
Praise him, all his angels; 2
Praise him, all his host!
Praise him, sun and moon; 3
Praise him, all you stars of light!
Praise him, highest heavens, 4
And waters that are above the heavens!
Let them praise the name of the LORD! 5
For he commanded and they were created.
And he fixed them fast forever and ever; 6
He gave a statute that they should not transgress.
Praise the LORD from the earth; 7
Sea-monsters and all deeps!
Fire and hail, snow and fog, 8
Stormy wind, fulfilling his word!
Mountains and all hills, 9
Fruit-trees and all cedars!
Wild beasts and all cattle, 10
Reptiles and winged birds!
Kings of the earth and all peoples, 11
Princes and all rulers of the earth!
Young men and maidens, too, 12
Old men and boys!

Let them praise the name of the LORD; 13
For his name alone is exalted;
His majesty is over the earth and the heavens,
And he has raised up a horn for his people. 14
The praise is he of all his saints,
The sons of Israel, the people near him.
Hallelujah!

PRAISE TO THE CONQUERING GOD

149 Hallelujah!
Sing to the LORD a new song,
His praise in the assembly of the pious.
2 Let Israel rejoice in his maker;
Let the sons of Zion triumph in their king.
3 Let them praise his name with dancing;
Let them play to him on drum and lute.
4 For the LORD is pleased with his people;
He adorns the humble with victory.

5 Let the pious exult in honor;
Let them shout with joy upon their beds,
6 With exaltations of God in their throats,
And double-edged swords in their hands,
7 To wreak vengeance upon the nations,
Punishment upon the peoples;
To bind their kings with chains,
And their nobles with fetters of iron;
To execute upon them the verdict that is written:
Such honor have all his saints.
Hallelujah!

THE CLOSING DOXOLOGY

Hallelujah!
Praise God in his sanctuary!
Praise him in his mighty firmament!
Praise him for his mighty deeds!
Praise him for his abundant greatness!
Praise him with the blast of the horn!
Praise him with lyre and lute!
Praise him with drum and dance!
Praise him with strings and pipe!
Praise him with clanging cymbals!
Praise him with crashing cymbals!
Let everything that breathes praise the LORD!
Hallelujah!

THE BOOK OF PROVERBS

INTRODUCTION, 1:1–6

1 THE proverbs of Solomon, the son of David, king of Israel:
2 That men may gain wisdom and instruction,
May understand words of intelligence;
3 That they may receive instruction in wise conduct,
In rectitude, justice, and honesty;
4 That sense may be imparted to the simple,
Knowledge and discretion to the inexperienced—
5 The wise man also may hear and increase his learning,
The man of intelligence acquire sound principles—
6 That they may understand proverb and parable,
The words of the wise and their epigrams.

THE FIRST PRINCIPLE OF WISDOM, 1:7

7 Reverence for the LORD is the beginning of knowledge;
Fools despise wisdom and instruction.

EXHORTATION AND WARNING, 1:8–19

8 Hear, my son, your father's instruction,
And reject not your mother's teaching;
9 For a graceful garland will they be for your head,
And a chain for your neck.

10 My son, if sinners entice you, consent not.
11 If they say, "Come with us, let us lie in wait for the honest,
Let us wantonly ambush the innocent;
12 Let us swallow them up alive and sound in health,
As Sheol swallows up those who go down to the Pit!
13 All kinds of precious wealth shall we find,
We shall fill our houses with spoil;
Cast in your lot with us, 14
We will all have one purse"—
My son, walk not in the way with them, 15
Keep your foot clear of their path;
For their feet run to evil, 16
They hasten to shed blood.
As the net is baited in vain 17
In the eyes of any bird,
While men lie in wait for their own blood, 18
And lurk for their own lives,
So is it with every one who traffics in ill-gotten gain; 19
It takes away the life of its owners.

THE APPEAL OF WISDOM, 1:20–33

Wisdom cries aloud in the streets, 20
She lifts up her voice in the squares;
At the head of noisy thoroughfares she calls, 21
At the openings of the city gates she utters her words:
"How long, you simple ones, will you love simplicity, 22
And scoffers delight in scoffing,
And fools hate knowledge?
If you but turn and pay heed to my admonition, 23
Lo! I will open my mind to you,
I will acquaint you with my thoughts.
Because I called and you refused to listen, 24
I stretched out my hand and no one paid heed;
You ignored all my counsel, 25
And would not have my admonition;
I in my turn will laugh in the hour of your doom, 26
I will mock when your terror comes;
When your terror comes like a storm, 27
And your doom descends like a whirlwind,
When distress and anguish befall you.
Then they may call me, but I will not answer; 28
They may seek me, but they shall not find me.
Because they hated knowledge, 29
And chose not reverence for the LORD;

30 They would not have my counsel,
They spurned all my admonition;
31 Now shall they eat of the fruit of their conduct,
And shall have their fill of what they purposed.
32 For the waywardness of the simple shall slay them,
And the complacency of fools shall destroy them;
33 While he who listens to me shall live in security,
And shall enjoy peace of mind without dread of evil."

THE BLESSINGS OF WISDOM, 2:1–22

2 My son, if you receive my words,
And store my commands within you,
2 Inclining your ear to wisdom,
And applying your mind to reason;
3 If you appeal to intelligence,
And lift up your voice to reason;
4 If you seek her as silver,
And search for her as for hidden treasures—
5 Then will you understand reverence for the LORD,
And will discover the knowledge of God;
6 For the LORD gives wisdom,
Out of his mouth come knowledge and reason;
7 He has help in store for the upright,
He is a shield to those who walk honestly;
8 He guards the paths of justice,
And protects the way of his pious ones;
9 Then will you understand rectitude and justice,
And will keep to every good course;
10 For when wisdom finds a welcome within you,
And knowledge becomes a pleasure to you,
11 Discretion will watch over you,
Reason will guard you—
12 Saving you from the way of evil men,
From men who use perverse speech;
13 Who leave the paths of uprightness,
To walk in ways of darkness;
14 Who delight in doing evil,
Exult in wanton wickedness;
15 Who are crooked in their ways,
And tortuous in their paths—
16 Saving you from the wife of another,
From the adulteress who plies you with smooth words,
Who forsakes the companion of her youth, 17
And forgets her pledge to her God;
For her paths lead down to death, 18
And her tracks descend to the Shades;
None who go to her come back again, 19
Or reach the paths of life—
Helping you to walk in the way of good men, 20
And to keep to the paths of the righteous;
For the upright will live in the land, 21
And the honest will remain in it;
While the wicked will be cut off from the land, 22
And the faithless will be rooted out of it.

THE FEAR OF THE LORD, 3:1–12

My son, forget not my teaching, 3
But keep my commands in mind;
For a long and happy life, 2
With abundant prosperity, will they bring to you.

Let not kindness and good faith leave you; 3
Fasten them round your neck,
Write them on the tablet of your mind;
So will you find favor and good will 4
In the eyes of God and man.

Trust in the LORD with all your heart, 5
And rely not on your own understanding;
In all your ways acknowledge him, 6
And he will make straight your paths.

Be not wise in your own eyes, 7
Revere the LORD, and withdraw from evil;
This will be health to your flesh, 8
And refreshment to your bones.

Honor the LORD with your substance, 9
With the firstfruits of all your produce;
So will your barns be filled with grain, 10
And your vats will be bursting with wine.

My son, despise not the discipline of the LORD, 11
And resent not his correction;
For whom the LORD loves he corrects, 12
Even as a father the son in whom he delights.

THE WORTH OF WISDOM, 3:13–26

13 How happy is the man who finds wisdom,
The man who gains understanding!
14 For her income is better than income of silver,
And her revenue than gold.
15 She is more precious than corals,
And none of your heart's desires can compare with her.
16 Long life is in her right hand,
In her left are riches and honor.
17 Her ways are ways of pleasantness,
And all her paths are peace.
18 She is a tree of life to those who grasp her,
And happy is every one who holds her fast.

19 The LORD by wisdom founded the earth,
By reason he established the heavens;
20 By his knowledge the depths are broken up,
And the clouds drop down dew.

21 My son, keep guard on wisdom and discretion,
Let them not slip from your eyes;
22 They will be life to you,
And an ornament round your neck.
23 Then you may go your way in security,
Without striking your foot on a stone;
24 When you rest, you will not be afraid,
When you lie down, your sleep will be sweet;
25 You will fear no sudden terror,
Nor the storm that falls on the wicked;
26 For the LORD will be your confidence,
And will keep your foot from the snare.

WISE COUNSELS, 3:27–35

27 Withhold not help from the needy,
When it is in your power to render it.
28 Say not to your neighbor, "Go, and come again;
Tomorrow I will give," when you have it beside you.
29 Plot no mischief against your neighbor,
When he lives in confidence beside you.
30 Do not idly quarrel with a man,
If he have done you no harm.
31 Envy not the lawless man,
And choose none of his ways;
For the crooked man is an abomination to the LORD, 32
While the upright enjoy his confidence.
The curse of the LORD is on the house of the wicked, 33
But the home of the righteous he blesses;
The scoffers he scoffs at, 34
But to the humble he shows favor;
Wise men come to honor, 35
But fools gain nothing but shame.

A FATHER'S INSTRUCTIONS, 4:1–27

Hear, my son, a father's instruction, 4
And attend, that you may gain understanding;
Because I give you sound learning, 2
Forsake not my teaching!
When as a boy I was tender in my father's sight, 3
And dearly beloved in the eyes of my mother,
He taught me, and said to me: 4
"Hold fast my words in your mind,
Keep my commands, and live—
Forget not, and swerve not from the words of my mouth— 5
Get wisdom, get understanding;
Forsake her not, and she will watch over you; 6
Love her, and she will safeguard you.
Above all things get wisdom; 7
Whatever else you get, get understanding.
Prize her, and she will exalt you; 8
Embrace her, and she will bring you to honor.
A graceful garland will she place upon your head; 9
A glorious crown will she bestow upon you."

Hear, my son, and receive my sayings, 10
That the years of your life may be many.
I teach you the way of wisdom; 11
I lead you in paths of uprightness.
When you walk, your steps will not be hampered, 12
And if you run you will not stumble.
Keep fast hold of instruction, let her not go; 13
Guard her, for she is your life.
Enter not the path of the wicked, 14
And walk not in the way of evil men;
Avoid it, traverse it not, 15
Shun it, and pass on.

16 For they sleep not unless they have
done mischief to someone,
Their slumber is broken unless they
have caused someone to stumble;
17 The bread they eat is won by crime,
And the wine they drink is won by
lawlessness.
19 The way of the wicked is dark as
pitch;
They know not at what they stumble.
18 But the path of the righteous is like
the light of the dawn,
That shines ever more brightly till the
day is full.

20 My son, attend to my words,
Incline your ear to my sayings;
21 Let them not slip from your eyes,
Keep them fixed in your mind;
22 For they are life to those who find
them,
Health to all their flesh.
23 Guard your heart with all vigilance,
For thence are the well-springs of life.
24 Perverse words put away from you,
And crooked speech put far from you.
25 Let your eyes look right in front,
And your eyelids be directed straight
ahead of you.
26 Keep level the track for your foot,
And let all your ways be firm.
27 Turn not to right or left,
Remove your foot from evil.

PURE AND IMPURE LOVE, 5:1–23

5 My son, attend to wisdom,
Incline your ear to reason;
2 That you may be kept from vile counsels,
And be preserved from evil lips.
3 For the lips of the adulterous woman
drop honey,
And her mouth is smoother than oil;
4 But the end of her is as bitter as wormwood,
As sharp as a two-edged sword.
5 Her feet go down to death,
Her steps lead straight to Sheol;
6 No level path of life she treads,
Her tracks wander—she knows not
whither.

7 So now, my son, listen to me,
And swerve not from the words of my
mouth.
8 Keep far away from her,
And approach not the door of her
house;
Lest you give up your wealth to others, 9
The earnings of your life to aliens;
Lest strangers have their fill of your 10
substance,
And the produce of your labors go to
an alien's house;
And then you groan when your end 11
comes,
When your flesh and blood come to an
end;
And you say, "How I hated instruc- 12
tion,
And scorned admonition,
And listened not to the voice of my 13
teachers,
Nor inclined my ear to my instructors!
I had well-nigh come to utter evil 14
In the midst of the assembled com-
munity."

Drink water from your own cistern, 15
Running water from your own well.
Why should your springs be scattered 16
abroad,
Your streams of water in the streets?
Let them be for yourself alone, 17
And not for strangers along with you.
Let your fountain be blessed to you, 18
And get your enjoyment from the wife
of your youth.
A lovely hind, a graceful doe— 19
Let her breasts intoxicate you always,
With her love be continually ravished.
Why, my son, should you be ravished 20
with the wife of another,
And embrace the bosom of an adulter-
ess?
For the ways of a man are before the 21
eyes of the LORD,
And all his paths he weighs in the
balance;
The wicked will be caught by his own 22
misdeeds,
He will be held in the toils of his own
sin;
He will die for want of instruction, 23
He will stagger to ruin through the
greatness of his folly.

WARNINGS AGAINST FOOLISH WAYS, 6:1–19

My son, if you have become surety for
your neighbor,
Have pledged yourself for another;
If you have been snared by your lips,

Have been caught by the words of your mouth;
3 Do this now, my son, and free yourself—
Since you have fallen into your neighbor's power—
Go in hot haste, and lay siege to your neighbor;
4 Give no sleep to your eyes,
Nor slumber to your eyelids;
5 Free yourself like a gazelle from the snare,
Like a bird from the hand of the fowler.

6 Go to the ant, O sluggard,
Study her ways, and learn wisdom;
7 For though she has no chief,
No officer, or ruler,
8 She secures her food in the summer,
She gathers her provisions in the harvest.
9 How long will you lie, O sluggard?
When will you rise from your sleep?
10 "A little sleep, a little slumber,
A little folding of hands to rest"—
11 So will poverty come upon you like a footpad,
And want like an armed man.

12 A knave, a villain,
Is he who deals in crooked speech,
13 Winks with his eyes, shuffles with his feet,
Signs with his fingers,
14 In whose mind is perversity,
Who plots mischief all the time,
Who sows discord.
15 Therefore his doom will come suddenly,
In an instant he will be crushed beyond recovery.

16 Six things the LORD hates,
Seven are an abomination to him:
17 Haughty eyes, a lying tongue,
And hands that shed innocent blood;
18 A mind that plots mischievous schemes,
Feet that are quick to run after evil;
19 A false witness who utters lies,
And he who sows discord among brothers.

WARNINGS AGAINST THE ADULTERESS, 6:20—7:27

20 Keep, my son, your father's charge,
And reject not your mother's instruction;
21 Fasten them forever on your mind,
Hang them round your neck.
When you walk, she will guide you; 22
When you lie down, she will watch over you;
When you awake, she will talk with you.
For the charge is a lamp, and the instruction a light; 23
The admonitions of discipline are the way of life;
Keeping you safe from the evil woman, 24
From the smooth tongue of the adulteress.
Lust not in your heart after her beauty, 25
Nor let her catch you with her eyelids!
For the price of a harlot is but a piece of bread, 26
But the adulteress hunts for the precious life.
Can a man take fire in his bosom, 27
And his clothes not be burned?
Or can a man walk on red-hot coals, 28
And his feet not be scorched?
So is it with him who goes in to his neighbor's wife; 29
None who touches her will go unpunished.
Do not men despise a thief even if he steal 30
To satisfy his appetite when he is hungry?
And if he be caught he must pay back sevenfold, 31
He must give up all the goods in his house.
But he who commits adultery with a woman is devoid of sense, 32
Only he who would bring ruin on himself does such a thing.
Ignominious blows will he get, 33
And his disgrace will not be wiped out.
For jealousy maddens a man, 34
So that he has no mercy on the day of vengeance;
He will accept no ransom, 35
Nor will he be satisfied though you bring him many gifts.

My son, keep my words, 7
And store my commands within you;
Keep my commands, and live— 2
My teaching like the pupil of your eye;
Fasten them on your fingers, 3
Write them on the tablet of your mind.
Say to Wisdom, "Thou art my sister," 4
And call Intelligence your friend,
That they may keep you from the wife of another, 5

From the adulteress who plies you
with smooth words.
6 For at the window of my house
Through my lattice I looked out;
7 I saw among the simple ones,
I observed among the youths,
A lad devoid of sense,
8 Passing through the street near her
corner,
Stepping along the way to her house,
9 In the evening twilight,
In the darkness at the dead of night;
10 And lo! the woman comes to meet him,
In harlot's dress, and with treacherous
mind—
11 She is boisterous and fickle,
Her feet cannot rest at home;
12 Now she is in the street, now in the
square,
By every corner she lies in wait.
13 So she catches him, and kisses him,
She puts on a bold face, and says to
him:
14 "I was due to hold a thanksgiving feast,
And today I am paying my vows;
15 So I came out to meet you,
To look for you, and I have found you!
16 I have spread my couch with coverlets,
With striped sheets of Egyptian yarn;
17 I have perfumed my bed with myrrh,
With aloes, and with cinnamon;
18 Come, let us take our fill of love till
morning,
Let us revel in caresses!
19 For my husband is not at home,
He has gone a far journey;
20 A bag of money he took with him,
He will not come home till full moon."
21 With her much fair speech she beguiles
him,
With her smooth lips she carries him
away;
22 He follows her bewitched,
Like an ox that goes to the slaughter,
Or a bird that speeds to the snare,
23 Or a stag that is lured to the net,
And knows not that its life is in danger,
Till an arrow pierces its liver.
24 So now, my son, listen to me,
And attend to the words of my mouth;
25 Swerve not toward her ways,
Stray not into her paths;
26 For many are the dead she has laid low,
A mighty host has she slain;
27 The ways to her house are ways to
Sheol,
Leading down to the chambers of
death.

THE INVITATION OF WISDOM, 8:1–36

Does not Wisdom call, 8
And Reason lift up her voice?
At the head of the highways, on the 2
road,
Between the streets she takes her
stand;
By the gates that enter the city, 3
At the doorways she cries aloud:
"To you, O men, I call, 4
And my appeal is to the sons of men.
You simple ones, learn sense, 5
You foolish ones, learn wisdom.
Listen! for noble things I shall speak, 6
With right things my lips will open;
My mouth will utter truth, 7
While wickedness is an abomination
to my lips;
Sincere are all the words of my mouth, 8
There is nothing tortuous or perverse
in them;
They are all of them straightforward 9
to the man of understanding,
And right to those who find knowledge.
Receive instruction instead of silver, 10
And knowledge rather than choice
gold;
For wisdom is better than corals, 11
With her no treasures can compare.

"I, Wisdom, have my home with good 12
sense,
So I obtain knowledge of evil devices.
Reverence for the LORD is hatred of 13
evil;
Pride and arrogance, evil ways,
And perverse speech I hate.
Mine are counsel and skill, 14
Mine are reason and might.
By me kings reign, 15
And rulers administer justice;
By me princes hold sway, 16
And nobles govern the earth.
I love those who love me, 17
And those who seek me will find me.
Riches and honor are with me, 18
Dazzling wealth and prosperity.
My fruit is better than gold, even the 19
finest of gold,
And my produce than choice silver.
I walk in the way of rectitude, 20
In the midst of the paths of justice,
Endowing my friends with wealth, 21
And filling their treasuries.

"The LORD formed me as the first of 22
his works,

The beginning of his deeds of old;
23 In the earliest ages was I fashioned,
At the first, when the earth began.
24 When there were no depths was I brought forth,
When there were no fountains brimming with water;
25 Before the mountains were sunk,
Before the hills was I brought forth;
26 While as yet he had not made the earth and the fields,
Nor the first clods of the world.
27 When he established the heavens I was there,
When he traced the vault over the face of the deep;
28 When he made firm the skies above,
When he fixed the fountains of the deep;
29 When he set for the sea its bound,
So that the waters should not transgress his command;
When he traced the foundations of the earth,
30 I was beside him as a ward of his;
And daily was I filled with delight,
As I sported before him all the time,
31 Sported in this world of his,
And found my delight in the sons of men.

32 "So now, O children, listen to me;
For happy are those who keep my ways.
33 Hear instruction, and be wise,
And reject it not!
34 Happy is the man who listens to me,
Watching daily at my gates,
Waiting at my door-posts;
35 For he who finds me finds life,
And wins favor from the LORD;
36 But he who misses me wrongs himself,
All who hate me love death."

WISDOM AND FOLLY, 9:1–6,[1] 13–18

9 Wisdom has built her house,
She has set up her seven pillars;
2 She has slain her beasts, she has mingled her wine,
She has spread her table.
3 She has sent out her maidens, and calls
On the heights of the city highways:
4 "He who is simple, let him turn in here,"
While to him who is senseless she says:
5 "Come, eat of my bread,
And drink of the wine I have mingled;
6 Forsake your folly, and live,
And keep straight on the path of reason."

13 Folly is boisterous and wanton,
She has no sense of shame.
14 She sits at the door of her house,
On a seat by the city highways,
15 Calling to those who pass by,
Who are keeping straight on their ways:
16 "He who is simple, let him turn in here,"
While to him who is senseless she says:
17 "Stolen water is sweet,
And bread eaten in secret is pleasant."
18 But he knows not that the Shades are there,
That her guests are in the depths of Sheol.

THE FRUITS OF WISDOM AND FOLLY, 9:7–12

7 He who corrects a scoffer draws insult on himself;
And he who reproves a wicked man—it becomes a blot to him.
8 Reprove not a scoffer, lest he hate you;
Reprove a wise man, and he will love you.
9 Instruct a wise man, and he will become still wiser;
Teach a righteous man, and he will learn the more.

10 The beginning of wisdom is reverence for the LORD,
And the knowledge of the Holy One is understanding;
11 For through me your days will be multiplied,
And the years of your life will be increased.
12 If you are wise, your wisdom will turn to your profit;
But if you are a scoffer, you must bear the consequences alone.

THE PROVERBS OF SOLOMON, 10:1—22:16

10 A wise son makes a glad father;
But a foolish son is a grief to his mother.

2 Treasures unjustly acquired are of no avail;
But honesty saves from death.

[1] For vss. 7–12 see next column.

3 The LORD will not suffer the righteous to hunger;
But he will thwart the desire of the wicked.

4 A slack hand brings poverty;
But the hand of the diligent brings wealth.

5 He who reaps in summer acts wisely;
He who sleeps in harvest acts shamefully.

6 Blessings are upon the head of the righteous;
But sorrow will cover the face of the wicked.

7 The memory of the righteous is a blessing;
But the name of the wicked will rot.

8 A wise man will take commands;
But a prating fool will fall.

9 He who walks honestly walks safely;
But he who walks crookedly will be found out.

10 He who winks with the eye makes trouble;
He who frankly reproves makes peace.

11 The mouth of the righteous is a fountain of life;
But the mouth of the wicked is filled with violence.

12 Hatred stirs up strife;
But love draws a veil over all transgressions.

13 On the lips of a sensible man wisdom is found;
But a man without sense needs a rod for his back.

14 Wise men store up knowledge;
But the mouth of a fool precipitates ruin.

15 A rich man's wealth is his fortress;
The ruin of the poor is their poverty.

16 The earnings of the righteous conduce to life;
The income of the wicked to death.

17 He who pays heed to instruction is on the way of life;
But he who rejects admonition goes astray.

Righteous lips cover up hatred; 18
But he who lets out slander is a fool.

Where words abound, sin will not be wanting; 19
But he who holds his tongue acts wisely.

The tongue of the righteous is choice silver; 20
The mind of the wicked is of little worth.

The lips of the righteous are a sustenance to many; 21
But fools die for want of sense.

The blessing of the LORD makes rich; 22
Toil yields no increase like it.

To a fool it is like sport to do wrong; 23
But it is hateful to a man of sense.

What the wicked man dreads will befall him; 24
But the desire of the righteous will be granted.

As the whirlwind passes, so the wicked man vanishes; 25
But the righteous is rooted forever.

As vinegar to the teeth, and as smoke to the eyes, 26
So is the sluggard to those who send him on an errand.

Reverence for the LORD prolongs life; 27
But the years of the wicked will be shortened.

The hope of the righteous will end in gladness; 28
But the expectation of the wicked will come to nought.

The LORD is a stronghold to him who walks honestly; 29
But ruin to those who do evil.

The righteous will never be moved; 30
But the wicked will have no foothold in the land.

The mouth of the righteous buds with wisdom; 31
But the perverse tongue will be cut off.

32 The lips of the righteous know good
will;
But the mouth of the wicked, malice.

11 False scales are an abomination to the
LORD;
But a just weight is his delight.

2 When pride comes, scorn comes;
But with the modest is wisdom.

3 Upright men are guided by their honesty;
But faithless men are ruined by their
crookedness.

4 Wealth is of no avail on the day of
wrath;
But righteousness saves from death.

5 The honest man's path is kept straight
by his righteousness;
But the wicked will fall by his wickedness.

6 The upright are saved by their righteousness;
But the faithless are caught by their
lusts.

7 When a wicked man dies, his expectation perishes;
All hope of success is lost.

8 The innocent man is rescued from
trouble;
And the guilty takes his place.

9 With his mouth would the godless
man ruin his neighbor;
But through knowledge the righteous
are saved.

10 When righteous men prosper, the city
exults;
And when wicked men perish, there is
jubilation.

11 Through the blessing of the upright
the city is exalted;
But through the mouth of the wicked
it is overthrown.

12 The senseless man pours contempt on
his neighbor;
But the intelligent man keeps silent.

13 A talebearer reveals secrets;
But a trustworthy man keeps a confidence.

For want of guidance a people will 14
fall;
But safety lies in a wealth of counselors.

He who becomes surety for a stranger 15
will suffer for it;
But he who hates giving pledges is secure.

A gracious woman wins respect; 16
And diligent men win riches.

A kindly man does good to himself; 17
But a cruel man does harm to himself.

The wicked man earns illusive wages; 18
But he who sows righteousness has a
true reward.

He who devotes himself to righteous- 19
ness takes the road to life;
But he who pursues wickedness the
road to death.

Those perverted in mind are an abom- 20
ination to the LORD;
But those who walk honestly are his
delight.

My hand upon it! the evil man will 21
not go unpunished;
But the race of the righteous will
escape.

Like a golden ring in the snout of a 22
sow
Is a beautiful woman lacking in taste.

The desire of the righteous can end 23
only in good;
The expectation of the wicked in
wrath.

One man spends, and grows still 24
richer;
Another holds back his due share, only
to bring himself to want.

The generous man will be enriched; 25
And he who waters will himself be
watered.

He who holds back grain will be 26
cursed by the people;
But blessing will be upon the head of
him who sells it.

He who seeks what is good will win 27
favor;

But he who aims at what is harmful
will bring it upon himself.

28 He who trusts in his riches will fall;
But like green leaves will the righteous
flourish.

29 He who stints his household will reap
nothing but wind;
A wise man's slave will such a fool become.

30 The fruit of righteousness is a tree of
life;
But lawlessness destroys men.

31 If the most righteous in the land are
punished,
How much more the wicked and the
sinner!

12 He who loves instruction loves knowledge;
But he who hates admonition is stupid.

2 A good man will win favor from the
LORD;
But a schemer will he condemn.

3 By wickedness no man can stand;
But the root of the righteous will never be moved.

4 A good wife is a crown to her husband;
But one who acts shamefully is like
rot in his bones.

5 The plans of the righteous are honest;
The designs of the wicked are treacherous.

6 The words of the wicked lie in wait for
blood;
But the speech of the upright saves
men.

7 When the wicked are overthrown, and
cease to be,
The house of the righteous will stand.

8 A man is praised according to his intelligence;
But one perverted in mind is despised.

9 Better a man of low rank, who works
for himself,
Than he who assumes honor, yet has
nothing to eat.

A righteous man cares for his beast; 10
But the mercy of the wicked is cruel.

He who tills his ground will have plenty of food; 11
But he who follows empty pursuits is
devoid of sense.

Evil men will be caught in the toils of 12
their wickedness;
But the root of the righteous will remain forever.

By the sin of his lips is the guilty man 13
ensnared;
While the innocent escapes from
trouble.

From the fruit of his mouth will the 14
good man enjoy good in abundance;
And the work of a man's hands will
come back to him.

The way of a fool is right in his own 15
eyes;
But a wise man listens to advice.

A fool's anger is shown at once; 16
But a sensible man ignores an affront.

He who utters the truth affirms that 17
which will stand;
But a lying witness that which will
bring disappointment.

There are those whose prating is like 18
the thrusts of a sword;
But the tongue of the wise brings
healing.

The truthful lip will endure forever; 19
But the lying tongue is only for a moment.

Disappointment comes to those who 20
plot evil;
But happiness to those who plan good.

No harm can befall the righteous; 21
But the lives of the wicked are full of
misfortune.

Lying lips are an abomination to the 22
LORD;
But those who deal truthfully are his
delight.

A man of sense conceals what he 23
knows;
But fools proclaim their folly.

4 The hand of the diligent will bear rule;
But the slack hand will be enslaved.

5 Anxiety in a man's heart makes it sink;
But a kindly word will turn it into gladness.

6 The righteous man departs from evil;
But the way of the wicked leads them astray.

7 The slothful man will not secure his prey;
But the diligent man wins precious wealth.

8 In the path of righteousness there is life;
But the way of wickedness leads to death.

3 A wise son pays heed to his father's instruction;
But a scoffer listens to no rebuke.

2 From the fruit of his mouth will the good man enjoy what is good;
But the appetite of the faithless will be fed on violence.

3 He who guards his mouth preserves his life;
He who opens wide his lips brings ruin on himself.

4 The sluggard craves, but gets nothing;
The desire of the diligent is richly supplied.

5 The righteous man hates a lie;
But the wicked acts foully and shamefully.

6 Righteousness safeguards the man of integrity;
But wickedness overthrows the sinner.

7 One man pretends to be rich, yet has nothing;
Another man pretends to be poor, yet has great wealth.

8 A man's riches provide ransom for his life;
But the poor man finds no means of redemption.

9 The light of the righteous will shine brightly;
But the lamp of the wicked will be put out.

Pride causes nothing but strife; 10
But with the modest there is wisdom.

Wealth got by scheming will diminish; 11
But he who gathers little by little will increase his store.

Hope deferred makes the heart sick; 12
But desire fulfilled is a tree of life.

He who despises the word will pay for it; 13
But he who reveres the command will be rewarded.

The teaching of the wise is a fountain of life, 14
By which to avoid the snares of death.

Good conduct wins favor; 15
But faithless conduct disfavor.

In all things the sensible man acts with intelligence; 16
But the fool displays his folly.

A faithless messenger falls into trouble; 17
But a trustworthy envoy insures success.

He who rejects instruction will have poverty and shame; 18
But he who pays heed to admonition will be honored.

Desire fulfilled is sweet; 19
But fools hate to turn from evil.

He who walks with wise men will become wise; 20
But the companion of fools will smart for it.

Ill fortune will dog sinners; 21
But good fortune will overtake the righteous.

The good man leaves an inheritance to his children's children; 22
But the wealth of the sinner is laid in store for the righteous.

The fallow land of the proud yields food in abundance; 23

But it is swept away through injustice.

24 He who spares his rod hates his son;
But he who loves him seeks to discipline him.

25 The righteous man eats to his heart's content;
But the appetite of the wicked is never satisfied.

14 The wise woman builds up her house;
But with her own hands the foolish one tears down her house.

2 He who reveres the LORD walks uprightly;
But he who despises him is crooked in his ways.

3 In the mouth of the foolish is a rod for his back;
But the lips of the wise will preserve them.

4 Where there are no oxen, there is no grain;
But abundance of produce comes through the strength of the ox.

5 A truthful witness will not lie;
But a dishonest witness breathes out lies.

6 The scoffer seeks wisdom, and finds it not;
But to the man of intelligence, knowledge is easy.

7 Leave the presence of a fool;
You will gain no knowledge from his talk.

8 The wisdom of a man of sense enables him to understand his way;
But the folly of fools misleads them.

9 Guilt has its home among fools;
Good will among the upright.

10 Every man knows his own bitterness;
And in his joy no stranger can share.

11 The house of the wicked will be destroyed;
But the tent of the upright will flourish.

12 There is a way that seems straight to a man;
But the end of it leads to death.

Even in laughter the heart may be aching;
And the end of joy may be sorrow.

The perverse man will reap the full fruit of his ways;
And the good man the full fruit of his deeds.

The simple man trusts everything;
But the sensible man pays heed to his steps.

The wise man is cautious, and keeps away from trouble;
But the fool is blustering and confident in himself.

A man of quick temper acts foolishly;
But a man of discretion is patient.

The simple gain possession of folly;
But men of sense win the crown of knowledge.

Evil men must bow before the good,
And wicked men, at the gates of the righteous.

The poor man is hated even by his neighbor;
But the rich has many friends.

He who despises his neighbor sins;
But happy is he who is kind to the poor!

Do not those go astray who plan evil,
While those who plan good meet with kindness and good faith?

In all labor there is profit;
But mere talk tends only to penury.

The crown of wise men is wisdom;
The garland of fools is folly.

A truthful witness saves lives;
But he who utters lies destroys them.

He who reveres the LORD has a strong ground of confidence,
In which his children also will find a refuge.

Reverence for the LORD is a fountain of life,
By which to avoid the snares of death.

28 In a wealth of people there is glory for
a king;
In a dearth of people there is ruin for
a prince.

29 A forbearing man shows much intelligence;
A quick-tempered man shows great
folly.

30 A tranquil mind is health for the body;
But passion is a rot in the bones.

31 He who oppresses the poor insults his
Maker;
But he who is kind to the needy hon-
ors him.

32 The wicked man is brought down by
his wrongdoing;
But the righteous man finds a refuge
in his integrity.

33 In the mind of a man of intelligence
wisdom takes up its abode;
But folly in the heart of fools.

34 Righteousness exalts a nation;
But sin is a people's ruin.

35 A capable servant will enjoy the
king's favor;
But a worthless one will incur his
wrath.

15 A gentle answer turns away wrath;
But harsh words stir up anger.

2 The tongue of the wise drops knowledge;
But the mouth of fools pours out folly.

3 The eyes of the LORD are in every
place,
Keeping watch on the evil and the
good.

4 A soothing tongue is a tree of life;
But wild words break the spirit.

5 A fool scorns his father's instruction;
But he who pays heed to admonition
shows good sense.

6 In the house of the righteous there is
ample wealth;
But the revenue of the wicked will be
cut off.

7 The lips of the wise diffuse knowledge;
Not so the mind of fools.

The sacrifice of the wicked is an abom- 8
ination to the LORD;
But the prayer of the upright is his delight.

The way of the wicked is an abomina- 9
tion to the LORD;
But he loves the man who follows after
righteousness.

Stern discipline awaits the man who 10
leaves the right way;
He who hates admonition will die.

Sheol and Abaddon lie open before the 11
LORD;
How much more the minds of men!

A scoffer loves not to be admonished; 12
To wise men he will not go.

A glad heart makes a bright face; 13
But through sadness of heart the spirit
is broken.

The mind of the intelligent man seeks 14
knowledge;
But the mouth of fools feeds on folly.

For the miserable man every day is 15
unhappy;
But the cheerful man enjoys a perpetual feast.

Better a little, with reverence for the 16
LORD,
Than much treasure, and anxiety with
it.

Better a dish of herbs, where love is, 17
Than a fatted ox, and hatred with it.

A passionate man stirs up discord; 18
But a patient man allays strife.

The way of the wicked is hedged with 19
thorns;
But the path of the upright is paved
like a highway.

A wise son makes a glad father; 20
But a foolish man despises his mother.

Folly is joy to a man without sense; 21
But a man of intelligence keeps a
straightforward course.

When no counsel is taken, plans mis- 22
carry;

But when there are many advisers,
they succeed.

23 An apt utterance is a joy to a man;
And a word in season—how good it is!

24 The wise man's path leads upward to
life,
Carrying him away from Sheol beneath.

25 The LORD will uproot the house of the
proud;
But he will establish the widow's landmark.

26 An evil man's thoughts are an abomination to the LORD;
But the words of the pure are pleasing
in his sight.

27 He who traffics in ill-gotten gain
wrecks his own household;
But he who hates a bribe will prosper.

28 The righteous man studies what he
should answer;
But the mouth of the wicked pours
out evil.

29 The LORD is far from the wicked;
But he hears the prayer of the righteous.

30 Bright eyes gladden the heart;
Good news fattens the bones.

31 He who listens to wholesome admonition
Will dwell among the wise.

32 He who rejects instruction despises
himself;
But he who listens to admonition
gains understanding.

33 Reverence for the LORD is the basis of
wisdom,
And humility leads to honor.

16 A man may arrange his thoughts;
But the utterance of the tongue is
from the LORD.

2 All the ways of a man are pure in his
own eyes;
But the LORD weighs the motives.

3 Commit your business to the LORD;
And your plans will prosper.

The LORD has made everything for its 4
own end,
Even the wicked for the day of calamity.

Every proud-minded man is an abom- 5
ination to the LORD;
My hand upon it! he will not go unpunished.

By kindness and good faith guilt is 6
atoned for;
And by reverence for the LORD one
avoids calamity.

When a man's ways are pleasing to the 7
LORD,
He makes even his enemies to be
friends with him.

Better a little, with righteousness, 8
Than great revenues, with injustice.

A man may plan his course; 9
But the LORD directs his steps.

On the lips of the king is an oracle; 10
His mouth cannot go wrong in judgment.

Balance and scales are set by the 11
LORD;
All the weights in the bag are his concern.

Wrong-doing is an abomination to 12
kings;
For a throne is established by right
eousness.

Honest lips are the delight of a king; 13
He loves the man who speaks aright.

The king's wrath is a forerunner of 14
death;
But a wise man can appease it.

In the light of the king's countenance 15
is life;
And his favor is like a spring raincloud.

How much better it is to get wisdom 16
than gold,
And more desirable to get understanding than silver!

The path of the upright avoids calam- 1
ity;

He who pays heed to his way safeguards his life.

18 Pride goes before destruction,
And a haughty spirit before a fall.

19 It is better to be humble with the lowly
Than to share spoil with the proud.

20 He who pays heed to the word will prosper;
And happy is he who trusts in the LORD!

21 The wise man is counted intelligent;
And sweetness of speech adds persuasiveness to his teaching.

22 Wisdom is a fountain of life to him who has it;
But folly brings chastisement to fools.

23 The mind of the wise man imparts intelligence to his speech,
And adds persuasiveness to the teaching of his lips.

24 Pleasant words are a honeycomb,
Sweet to the spirit, and healthful to the body.

25 There is a way that seems straight to a man;
But the end of it leads to death.

26 The laboring man's appetite labors for him;
For his hunger urges him on.

27 A depraved man digs up evil;
While the words on his lips are like a scorching fire.

28 A fickle man sows discord;
And a whisperer separates friends.

29 A lawless man entices his neighbor,
And leads him into a way that is not good.

30 He who shuts his eyes is hatching some crooked scheme;
He who tightens his lips concocts some mischief.

31 Gray hairs are a glorious crown,
Which is won by a righteous life.

32 A forbearing man is better than a warrior;
He who rules his temper than he who takes a city.

The lot is cast into the lap; 33
But the decision rests wholly with the LORD.

Better a morsel of dry bread, and 17
peace with it,
Than a house full of feasting, with strife.

A capable servant will rule over a dis- 2
solute son,
And will share the inheritance among the brothers.

Like the smelter for silver, and the 3
furnace for gold,
The LORD is a tester of hearts.

An evil man pays heed to wicked 4
words;
A false man gives ear to mischievous speech.

He who mocks the poor insults his 5
Maker;
He who rejoices at their calamity will not go unpunished.

Children's children are the crown of 6
old men;
And fathers are the pride of their children.

Lordly words are not fitting for a fool; 7
Much less are lying words for a nobleman.

A bribe is a precious gem in the eyes 8
of him who has it;
Wherever he turns, he prospers.

He who overlooks an offense promotes 9
good will;
He who repeats a matter separates friends.

A rebuke sinks deeper into a man of 10
intelligence
Than a hundred lashes into a fool.

A rebellious man is set on mischief; 11
But a ruthless messenger will be sent to him.

Better be met by a bear robbed of her 12
cubs
Than by a fool in his folly.

13 He who returns evil for good—
Evil will never depart from his house.

14 The beginning of strife is like one letting out water;
Leave off contention before a quarrel break out!

15 He who acquits the guilty, and he who condemns the innocent—
Both of them are an abomination to the LORD.

16 Of what use is money in the hand of a fool
To buy wisdom, when he has no sense?

17 A friend is friendly at all times;
But a brother is born for adversity.

18 A man devoid of sense is he who pledges himself,
And becomes security in the presence of his neighbor.

19 He loves punishment who loves strife;
He courts destruction who builds his gate high.

20 He who is perverse in mind will meet with no good;
And he who is crooked in speech will fall into trouble.

21 He who begets a fool does it to his sorrow;
And the father of a dolt will have no joy of him.

22 A happy heart is a healing medicine;
But a broken spirit dries up the bones.

23 A wicked man will accept a bribe from the bosom
To divert the course of justice.

24 The man of intelligence has his face set on wisdom;
But the eyes of a fool are on the ends of the earth.

25 A foolish son is a grief to his father,
And a bitter sorrow to her who bore him.

26 Even to fine the innocent is not right,
While to scourge the noble is beyond bearing.

27 He who spares his words has true wisdom;
And he who keeps cool in temper is a man of intelligence.

Even a fool is counted wise, if he keep silent— 28
Intelligent, if he close his lips.

The recluse seeks his own selfish interests; 18
He quarrels with every sound principle.

A fool has no pleasure in what is reasonable, 2
But only in self-display.

With wickedness comes contempt; 3
And with dishonor comes disgrace.

The words of a man's mouth are deep waters; 4
The fountain of wisdom is a bubbling brook.

It is not right to favor the guilty, 5
Nor to put the innocent in the wrong.

A fool's lips make for strife; 6
And his mouth calls for blows.

A fool's mouth is his ruin; 7
And his lips are a snare to him.

The words of a whisperer are like dainty morsels; 8
They penetrate into the innermost being.

He who is slack at his work 9
Is brother to him who destroys.

The name of the LORD is a strong tower, 10
To which the righteous man runs and is safe.

A rich man's wealth is his fortress; 11
And like a high wall are his riches.

Haughtiness goes before destruction; 12
And humility before honor.

To answer before one hears 13
Is one's folly and shame.

A brave spirit will sustain a man in his infirmity; 14
But a broken spirit who can bear?

The mind of the intelligent acquires knowledge; 15
And the ear of the wise seeks wisdom.

16 A gift from a man makes room for him,
And brings him before the great.

17 He who pleads first in a case appears to be in the right;
Then his rival comes and tests him.

18 The lot puts an end to disputes,
And decides between powerful rivals.

19 A brother helped by a brother is like a fortified city;
He holds firm as the bar of a castle.

20 Of the fruit of his mouth a man will have his fill;
With the outcome of his lips will he be satisfied.

21 Death and life are in the power of the tongue;
Those who indulge it must eat the fruit of it.

22 He who finds a wife finds good fortune;
He wins a favor from the LORD.

23 The poor man speaks entreatingly;
But the rich man answers roughly.

24 There are friends who play at friendship;
And there is a friend who sticks closer than a brother.

19 Better a poor man, who walks in his integrity,
Than one who is crooked in his ways, although he be rich.

2 To act without reflection is not good;
And to be over-hasty is to miss the mark.

3 A man's folly ruins his business;
Then he rages against the LORD.

4 Wealth adds many friends;
But the poor man is estranged from his friend.

5 A false witness will not go unpunished;
He who utters lies will not escape.

6 Many pay court to the noble;
Everyone is a friend to him who gives gifts.

A poor man's brothers all hate him; 7
How much more do his friends stand aloof from him!
When he pursues them with words, they are gone.

He who acquires wisdom is a friend to himself; 8
He who pays heed to reason will find good fortune.

A false witness will not go unpunished; 9
He who utters lies will perish.

Luxury is not fitting for a fool, 10
Much less so for a servant to rule over princes.

It is good sense in a man to be forbearing, 11
And it is his glory to pass over an offense.

A king's wrath is like a lion's roar; 12
But his favor is like dew on the grass.

A foolish son is his father's ruin; 13
And a quarrelsome wife is like a constant drip.

House and wealth are an inheritance from fathers; 14
But a sensible wife is a gift from the LORD.

Slothfulness casts into a deep sleep; 15
And an idle man will suffer hunger.

He who keeps the command keeps his life; 16
He who despises the word will die.

He who is kind to the poor lends to the LORD; 17
And he will repay him his deed.

Correct your son while there is still hope; 18
And set not your mind on destroying him.

A man who gives way to anger must pay for it; 19
And if you come to his rescue, you will only add to his anger.

Hear counsel, and accept instruction, 20
That you may be wise in the days to come.

21 A man may have many plans in his mind;
But the purpose of the LORD—that will stand.

22 Kindness is the most desirable thing for a man;
Better a poor man than a liar.

23 Reverence for the LORD conduces to life;
He who is satisfied with that will abide unvisited by misfortune.

24 The sluggard buries his hand in the dish;
He will not so much as raise it to his mouth again.

25 Smite a scoffer, and the simple will learn sense;
Admonish a man of intelligence, and he will gain knowledge.

26 He who maltreats his father, and drives away his mother,
Is a shameful and despicable son.

27 If you cease, my son, to hear instruction,
You will wander from words of knowledge.

28 An unprincipled witness scoffs at justice;
And the mouth of the wicked gulps down falsehood.

29 Punishments are prepared for scoffers;
And blows for the back of fools.

20 Wine is a mocker, strong drink a brawler;
None who reels under it is wise.

2 A king's rage is like a lion's roar;
He who provokes him to anger forfeits his life.

3 It is an honor for a man to keep aloof from strife;
But every fool is quarrelsome.

4 The sluggard will not plow in autumn;
So in harvest he looks for a crop in vain.

5 The purpose in a man's mind may be deep water;
But a man of intelligence will draw it out.

Many a man will make profession of his kindness; 6
But a faithful man who can find?

The just man who walks in his integrity— 7
Happy are his children after him!

A king seated on the judgment throne 8
Sifts every evil man with his eyes.

Who can say, "I have cleansed my heart, 9
I am pure from my sin"?

Diverse weights, diverse measures— 10
Both of them alike are an abomination to the LORD.

Even a child is known by his deeds, 11
According as his conduct is crooked or straight.

The hearing ear, and the seeing eye— 12
Both of them alike the LORD has made.

Love not sleep, lest you come to poverty; 13
Keep your eyes open, and you will have plenty of food.

"Bad, bad!" says the buyer; 14
But when he has gone, then he boasts.

Wise lips are a store of gold, 15
A wealth of corals, and precious gems.

Take a man's garment if he becomes surety for a stranger; 16
Hold him to account for the other.

Bread won by fraud tastes sweet to a man; 17
But afterward his mouth will be filled with gravel.

Form plans under advice; 18
And under wise guidance make war.

A talebearer reveals secrets; 19
So have nothing to do with a gossip.

He who curses his father or mother— 20
His light will go out in utter darkness.

An estate won hastily at the outset 21
Will in the end be unblessed.

Say not, "I will pay back evil!" 22
Wait for the LORD to help you.

3 Diverse weights are an abomination to the LORD;
And false scales are not good.

4 A man's steps are directed by the LORD;
How, then, can any man understand his way?

5 It is a snare for a man rashly to say, "This is sacred!"
And after his vows to make inquiry.

6 A wise king sifts the wicked,
And requites them for their guilt.

7 The conscience of a man is the lamp of the LORD,
Searching the whole innermost being.

8 Kindness and good faith are the safeguards of a king;
And by justice his throne is established.

9 The glory of young men is their strength;
And the beauty of old men is gray hair.

0 Sharp blows purify the wicked;
And stripes, the innermost being.

The mind of a king is like a watercourse in the hand of the LORD;
He turns it whither he will.

2 Every way of a man is right in his own eyes;
But the LORD weighs the motives.

3 The doing of right and justice
Is more acceptable to the LORD than sacrifice.

4 Haughty eyes, and an ambitious mind—
The tillage of the wicked is sin.

5 The plans of the diligent lead surely to profit;
But everyone that is over-hasty comes surely to want.

He who gains treasures by a lying tongue
Is chasing a vapor to snares of death.

The lawlessness of the wicked will sweep them away,
Because they refuse to deal justly.

The way of the vicious is crooked; 8
But the conduct of the pure is straight.

It is better to live in a corner of the housetop 9
Than to share a spacious house with a quarrelsome wife.

The wicked man is bent on doing harm; 10
His neighbor finds no pity in his eyes.

When a scoffer is punished, the simple learns wisdom; 11
When a wise man receives a lesson, he gains knowledge.

The Righteous One has regard for the household of the wicked, 12
Hurling down the wicked to ruin.

He who closes his ear against the cry of the poor 13
Will himself also call and not be answered.

A gift in secret pacifies anger, 14
And a bribe in the bosom, violent wrath.

The execution of justice is a joy to the righteous, 15
But ruin to those who do evil.

The man who wanders from the way of wisdom 16
Will rest in the assembly of the Shades.

The lover of pleasure will come to want; 17
The lover of wine and oil will not grow rich.

The wicked man becomes ransom for the righteous; 18
And the faithless man takes the place of the upright.

It is better to dwell in a desert 19
Than with a quarrelsome and nagging wife.

In the wise man's house there is precious treasure and oil; 20
But the fool will swallow it up.

He who follows after justice and kindness 21
Will find life, prosperity, and honor.

22 A wise man scales the city of the mighty,
And brings down the stronghold in which it trusted.

23 He who keeps his mouth and his tongue
Keeps himself from trouble.

24 Scoffer is he called who is haughty and arrogant,
Who acts with insolent pride.

25 The sluggard's craving for ease will slay him;
For his hands refuse to work.

26 The wicked man is greedy all day long;
But the righteous man gives without stint.

27 Sacrifice from wicked men is an abomination;
The more so when they offer it as an atonement for crime.

28 A lying witness will perish;
But a truthful witness will speak on to the end.

29 A wicked man puts on a bold face;
But an upright man pays heed to his ways.

30 No wisdom, no intelligence,
No counsel can avail against the LORD.

31 The horse may be harnessed for the day of battle;
But victory comes from the LORD.

22 A good name is more desirable than great riches,
A good reputation than silver and gold.

2 The rich and the poor meet face to face—
The LORD is the maker of them both.

3 A sensible man foresees danger, and hides from it;
But the simple pass on, and are punished.

4 The reward of humility and reverence for the LORD
Is riches, honor, and life.

Traps and snares are on the way of the crooked; 5
He who would safeguard his life will keep far from them.

Train up a child in the way he should go; 6
And even when he is old, he will not depart from it.

The rich rules over the poor; 7
And the borrower is a slave to the lender.

He who sows crime will reap calamity; 8
The result of his work will be ruin.

The man of kindly eye will be blessed; 9
For he gives of his bread to the poor.

Expel a scoffer, and discord will vanish; 10
Strife and insult will cease.

The LORD loves the pure in heart; 11
And he who is gracious in speech—the king is his friend.

The eyes of the LORD keep watch on him who has knowledge; 12
But he upsets the plans of the faithless.

The sluggard says, "There is a lion outside; 13
I shall be murdered in the streets."

The mouth of an adulterous woman is a deep pit; 14
He with whom the LORD is angry will fall into it.

Folly is bound to the mind of a child; 15
The rod of correction will remove it far from him.

He who oppresses the poor will only enrich him; 16
He who gives to the rich will come only to want.

WORDS OF THE WISE, 22:17—24:22

Incline your ear, and hear the words of the wise, 17
And apply your mind to know them;
For it is well that you should keep them within you, 18

That you should fix them firmly upon
your lips.
9 Words of life I teach you this day,
That your trust may be in the LORD.
20 Have I not written for you these
thirty sayings,
Respecting counsel and knowledge,
21 To acquaint you with the reality of
true words,
That you may bring back a true report to him who sends you?

22 Rob not the poor because he is poor,
And crush not the needy in the gate;
23 For the LORD will defend their cause,
And will rob their robbers of life.

24 Form no friendship with a hot-
tempered man,
And with a passionate man go not;
25 Lest you learn his ways,
And get yourself into a snare.

26 Be not one of those who pledge themselves,
Of those who become surety for debts;
27 For if you have nothing to pay with,
Your bed will be taken from under
you.

28 Remove not the ancient landmark,
Which your fathers set up.

29 You see a man skilled at his work?
He will stand in the presence of kings;
He will not stand in the presence of
obscure men.

23 When you sit down to dine with a
ruler,
Bear in mind who is before you;
2 And put a knife to your throat,
If you be a man of keen appetite;
3 Lust not after his dainties,
For they are larded with deceit.

4 Toil not to become rich,
Seek not superfluous wealth!
5 Scarcely have you set your eye upon
it, when it is gone;
For riches make themselves wings,
Like an eagle that flies toward the
heavens.

6 Dine not with a miserly man,
And lust not after his dainties;
7 For they will be like storm in the
throat and nausea in the gullet.
"Eat and drink," he says to you,
But in his heart he begrudges you;
You must spit out the morsel you have 8
eaten,
And lose your good things.

Speak not in the ears of a fool; 9
For he will despise your words of wisdom.

Remove not the widow's landmark, 10
Nor enter the fields of orphans;
For their Champion is strong, 11
And he will defend their cause against
you.

Apply your mind to instruction, 12
And your ear to words of knowledge.
Withhold not chastisement from a 13
child;
For if you beat him with the rod, he
will not die.
Beat him with the rod, 14
And you will save him from Sheol.

My son, if you are wise, 15
I also shall be glad;
And my heart will rejoice, 16
If your lips speak that which is right.

Be not envious of sinners, 17
But revere the LORD always;
For then will you have a future, 18
And your hope will not be cut off.

Listen, my son, and be wise, 19
And keep straight on the way.
Be not found among winebibbers, 20
Or gluttonous eaters of flesh;
For the winebibber and the glutton 21
will come to poverty,
And sottishness will clothe you in rags.

Listen to the father who begot you, 22
And despise not your mother when
she is old.
Get truth, and sell it not; 23
Get wisdom, and instruction, and
understanding.
The father of a righteous man will 24
greatly rejoice,
He who has begotten a wise son will be
glad of him.
Therefore let your father and your 25
mother be glad,
Let her who bore you rejoice.

My son, give heed to me, 26
And let your eyes take note of my
ways.

27 For the harlot is a deep pit,
And the adulteress a narrow well;
28 She lies in wait like a robber,
And increases the faithless among men.

29 Who have woe? who have pain?
Who have strifes? who have complaints?
Who have wounds without cause?
Who have redness of eyes?
30 Those who stay long over wine,
Who go often to test the mixture!
31 Look not on wine when it is red,
When it sparkles in the cup.
It may go down smoothly;
32 But at the end it bites like a serpent,
And stings like an adder.
33 You will see strange sights,
And will utter weird words;
34 You will be like a man asleep at sea,
Asleep in the midst of a violent storm.
35 "They may strike me, but I feel no pain;
They may beat me, but I know it not.
When shall I awake from my wine,
That I may seek it again?"

24 Be not envious of evil men,
Nor desire to be with them;
2 For their thoughts turn on robbery,
And their lips talk of mischief.

3 By wisdom a house is built,
By intelligence it is established;
4 And by knowledge its chambers are filled
With all precious and pleasant things.

5 A wise man is better than a strong man,
And a man of knowledge than a man of might;
6 For by wise guidance you wage war,
And victory lies in a wealth of counselors.

7 Wisdom is unattainable for a fool;
So he opens not his mouth in the gate.

8 He who plans to do evil—
Men call him a schemer.

9 The scheming of the foolish is sin;
And the scoffer is an abomination to men.

10 If you have been slack when times are hard,
Your means will be scanty.

Rescue those who are being taken away to death, 11
And hinder not the escape of those about to be executed.
If you say, "We knew nothing of this," 12
Does not he who weighs the thoughts perceive it,
And is not he who guards your life aware of it,
And will he not requite each man according to his work?

My son, eat honey, because it is good, 13
And the honeycomb, because it is sweet to your taste.
So, be assured, is wisdom to your mind— 14
If you find it, you will have a future,
And your hope will not be cut off.

Lie not in wait, O wicked man, against the home of the righteous, 15
Nor assail his dwelling-place;
For seven times will the righteous man fall and rise again, 16
While the wicked will stumble to ruin.

Rejoice not when your enemy falls, 17
Nor exult when he stumbles;
Lest the LORD see it, and be displeased, 18
And turn back his anger from him.

Fret not over evildoers, 19
Nor be envious of the wicked;
For the evil man will have no future, 20
The lamp of the wicked will be put out.

My son, reverence the LORD and the king, 21
And meddle not with those of high rank;
For suddenly comes ruin at their hands, 22
And who knows the doom that both of them bring?

THESE ALSO ARE WORDS OF THE WISE, 24:23–34 23

Partiality in judgment is not good.
He who says to the guilty man, "You are in the right"— 24
Men will curse him, people will execrate him;
But those who judge honestly will fare pleasantly, 25

On them will rest the blessing of prosperity.

26 He who gives a straight answer
Is like one who kisses the lips.

27 Set your business in order,
Arrange your work in the fields;
Afterward you may build up your house.

28 Bear not unfounded witness against your neighbor,
Nor deceive with your lips;
29 Say not, "I will do to him as he has done to me,
I will requite the man according to his work."

30 I passed by the field of the sluggard,
By the vineyard of the man without sense;
31 And lo! it was all overgrown with thistles,
Its surface was covered with nettles,
And its stone wall was broken down.
32 I looked, and reflected upon it;
I saw, and learned a lesson.
33 "A little sleep, a little slumber,
A little folding of hands to rest"—
34 So will poverty come upon you like a footpad,
And want like an armed man.

25 THESE ALSO ARE THE PROVERBS OF SOLOMON, WHICH THE MEN OF HEZEKIAH, KING OF JUDAH, EDITED, 25:1—29:27

2 It is the glory of God to conceal a matter,
But the glory of kings to fathom a matter.
3 Like the heavens for height, and the earth for depth,
The mind of kings is unfathomable.

4 Remove the dross from silver,
And it comes forth wholly pure;
5 Remove a wicked man from the presence of the king,
And his throne will be established by righteousness.

6 Claim not honor in the presence of the king,
Nor stand in the place of great men;

It is better for you to be told, "Come up hither!" 7
Than to be humbled before the noble.

What your eyes have seen
Report not hastily to the multitude; 8
Else what will you do in the outcome of the matter,
When your neighbor puts you to shame for it?
Discuss the case with your neighbor, 9
And reveal not the secret to another;
Lest he who hears it reproach you, 10
And your infamy pass not away.

Like apples of gold in a setting of 11
carved silver
Is a word that is aptly spoken.
Like an earring of gold, or a necklace 12
of fine gold,
Is a wise man's reproof on a listening ear.
Like a draught of snow-cooled water 13
in the time of harvest
Is a faithful messenger to those who send him;
He refreshes the spirit of his master.
Like clouds with wind that bring no 14
rain
Is the man who boasts of gifts that are not given.

By forbearance a ruler is pacified, 15
And a soft tongue breaks the bones.

If you find honey, eat no more than 16
you need;
Lest you be sated with it, and vomit it up.
Set your foot but sparingly in your 17
neighbor's house;
Lest he be sated with you, and give you a cool reception.

Like a club, a sword, or a sharp- 18
pointed arrow,
Is a man who bears false witness against his neighbor.
Like a crumbling tooth, or a palsied 19
foot,
Is a faithless man's ground of confidence in the time of trouble.
Like one who drops vinegar upon a 20
wound
Is he who sings songs to a sorrowful heart.

If your enemy be hungry, give him 21
bread to eat,

And if he be thirsty, give him water to drink;
22 For coals of fire will you heap on his head,
And the LORD will reward you.
23 The north wind brings forth rain,
And a slandering tongue an angry face.

24 It is better to dwell in a corner of the roof
Than to share a spacious house with a quarrelsome wife.

25 Like cold water to a weary man
Is good news from a far country.

26 Like a trampled fountain, or a polluted spring,
Is a righteous man who gives way before the wicked.

27 To eat much honey is not good;
Therefore be sparing of your compliments.

28 Like a city breached and defenseless
Is a man who has no control of his temper.

26 Like snow in summer, or rain in harvest,
Honor is unseasonable for a fool.

2 Like a sparrow flitting, a swallow fluttering,
The curse that is groundless will not reach home.

3 A whip for the horse, a bridle for the ass,
And a rod for the back of fools.

4 Answer not a fool according to his folly,
Lest you also become like him.
5 Answer a fool according to his folly,
Lest he become wise in his own eyes.

6 He cuts off his feet, drinks in disaster,
Who sends a message by a fool.

7 Like legs hanging helpless from the lame
Is a parable in the mouth of fools.

8 Like one who buries a stone in a heap
Is he who gives honor to a fool.

Like a thorn-stick brandished by a drunkard 9
Is a parable in the mouth of fools.

The master workman does everything himself; 10
But the fool hires a passer-by.

Like a dog returning to his vomit 11
Is a fool repeating his folly.

You see a man wise in his own eyes? 12
There is more hope for a fool than for him.

The sluggard says, "There is a roaring beast on the road, 13
A lion in the streets."

As a door turns on its sockets, 14
The sluggard turns on his bed.

The sluggard buries his hand in the dish; 15
He is too weary to raise it to his mouth again.

The sluggard is wiser in his own eyes 16
Than seven men who can give an apt answer.

Like a man who seizes a dog by the ears 17
Is the passer-by who meddles with a quarrel not his own.

Like a madman who hurls 18
Deadly firebrands and arrows
Is he who deceives his neighbor 19
And says, "Was I not joking?"

Where there is no wood, a fire goes out; 20
And where there is no whisperer, a quarrel dies down.

As charcoal to embers, and wood to fire, 21
Is a quarrelsome man to set strife in a blaze.

The words of a whisperer are like dainty morsels; 22
They penetrate into the innermost being.

Like a pot overlaid with glaze 23
Are flattering lips with a wicked mind.

Your enemy may dissemble with his lips, 24

But in his mind he harbors deceit;
25 When he speaks fair, believe him not,
For seven abominations are in his mind;
26 Though his hatred be craftily concealed,
His wickedness will be revealed in public assembly.

27 He who digs a pit will fall into it;
And he who rolls a stone—it will come back upon him.

28 A lying tongue brings destruction to itself;
And a flattering mouth works its own ruin.

27 Boast not of tomorrow;
For you know not what a day may bring forth.

2 Let another man praise you, and not your own mouth—
A stranger, and not your own lips.

3 A stone is heavy, and sand is weighty;
But the annoyance caused by a fool is heavier than both.

4 Wrath is ruthless, and anger a torrent;
But before jealousy who can stand?

5 Better is open rebuke
Than hidden love.

6 Sincere are the wounds of a friend;
But deceitful are the kisses of an enemy.

7 He who is sated with food disdains the honeycomb;
But to the hungry man every bitter thing is sweet.

8 Like a bird that strays from her nest
Is a man that strays from his home.

9 Oil and perfume gladden the heart;
So a man's counsel is sweet to his friend.

10 Your friend and your father's friend forsake not,
And in your time of calamity go not to your brother's house;
Better is a neighbor near at hand than a brother far away.

Be wise, my son, and gladden my heart, 11
That I may answer the man who would taunt me.

A sensible man foresees danger, and hides from it; 12
But the simple pass on, and are punished.

Take a man's garment if he become surety for a stranger, 13
And hold it in pledge for the stranger.

If a man rise early in the morning, and bless his neighbor with a loud voice, 14
It will be counted a curse to him.

A constant drip on a rainy day 15
And a quarrelsome wife are alike;
He who would restrain her would restrain the wind, 16
Or grasp oil with his right hand.

As iron sharpens iron, 17
A man sharpens the face of his friend.

He who takes care of his fig tree will eat the fruit of it; 18
And he who attends to his master will be honored.

As face reflects face in water, 19
So the mind of man reflects man.

Sheol and death are never satisfied; 20
So the eyes of man are never satisfied.

As the smelter is for silver, and the furnace for gold, 21
So a man is tested by his praise.

Though you pound a fool with a pestle, 22
Among grit in a mortar,
His folly will not leave him.

Look well to the state of your flocks, 23
And pay good heed to your herds;
For riches last not forever, 24
Nor wealth throughout the ages.
When the hay is cut, and the aftermath appears, 25
And the grass of the mountains is gathered in,
Lambs will supply you with clothing, 26
And goats with the price of a field;
Goats' milk enough will you have for your food, 27

For the food of your household,
And as maintenance for your maidens.

28 The wicked flee when no man pursues;
But the righteous are as bold as a lion.
2 When rebellion breaks out in a land, there arise many rulers;
But through men of wisdom and intelligence, order will long prevail.
3 A man who is proud and oppresses the poor
Is like a lashing rain that leaves no food.
4 Lawbreakers praise the wicked;
But the law-abiding are zealous against them.
5 Evil men have no understanding of justice;
But those who seek the LORD understand it completely.

6 Better is a poor man who walks in his integrity
Than he who is crooked in his ways, although he be rich.
7 He who pays heed to instruction is a wise son;
But the companion of profligates brings disgrace on his father.
8 He who increases his wealth by interest and usury
Gathers it for him who is kind to the poor.
9 He who turns a deaf ear to instruction—
His very prayer is an abomination.
10 He who seduces the upright into evil ways
Will himself fall into the pit he has dug;
But men of integrity will attain good fortune.
11 The rich man is wise in his own eyes;
But a poor man possessed of intelligence will test him.
12 When the righteous triumph, there is a great celebration;
But when the wicked rise to power, men hide themselves.

He who conceals his transgressions will not prosper; 13
But he who confesses and forsakes them will obtain mercy.
Happy is the man who lives always in awe; 14
But he who hardens his conscience will fall into misfortune.
Like a roaring lion, or a ravenous bear, 15
Is a wicked ruler over a poor people.
A prince who is an oppressor is devoid of intelligence; 16
But he who hates ill-gotten gain will prolong his life.
A man laden with another man's blood makes tracks for the grave; 17
None will support him.
He who walks honestly will be kept in safety; 18
But the man of crooked ways will fall into a pit.
He who tills his ground will have plenty of food; 19
But he who follows empty pursuits will have plenty of poverty.
A trustworthy man will be amply blessed; 20
But he who makes haste to be rich will not go unpunished.
To be partial in judgment is not good; 21
Even for a morsel of bread a man may fall into sin.
The avaricious man rushes after wealth, 22
Not knowing that want will befall him.
He who reproves men will get more thanks in the end 23
Than he who flatters with the tongue.
He who robs his father or his mother, 24
Saying, "There is no wrong in it,"
Is companion to him who destroys.
A greedy man stirs up strife; 25
But he who trusts in the LORD will flourish.
He who trusts in himself is a fool; 26
But he who walks wisely will be kept safe.

27 He who gives to the poor will not come
to want;
But he who shuts his eyes against them
will have many a curse.

28 When the wicked rise to power, men
hide themselves;
But when they perish, the righteous
flourish.

29 He who stiffens his neck against many
reproofs
Will suddenly be broken beyond repair.

2 When the righteous are in power, the
people rejoice;
But when the wicked bear rule, the
people groan.

3 He who loves wisdom gladdens his
father;
But he who keeps company with
harlots wastes his substance.

4 A king by justice gives stability to a
land;
But he who makes heavy exactions
brings it to ruin.

5 A man who flatters his neighbor
Is spreading a net for his steps.

6 In an evil man's sin lies a snare;
But a righteous man sings with joy.

7 A good man respects the rights of the
poor;
A wicked man knows no respect.

8 Unprincipled men set the city in a
blaze;
But wise men turn back anger.

9 If a wise man go to law with a fool,
Whether he storm or laugh, there will
be no peace.

10 Bloodthirsty men hate the innocent,
And seek the life of the upright.

11 A fool gives vent to his temper;
But a wise man restrains his anger.

12 If a ruler listen to lies,
All his servants become depraved.

13 The poor man and the oppressor meet
face to face;
The LORD gives light to the eyes of
them both.

The king who judges the poor with 14
equity—
His throne will be established forever.

The rod of correction gives wisdom; 15
But a child who is left to himself brings
disgrace on his mother.

When the wicked are in power, crime 16
increases;
But the righteous will see their downfall.

Correct your son, that he may give 17
you peace of mind,
And bring delight to your heart.

Where there is no vision, the people 18
break loose;
But those who obey the law—happy
are they!

Not by mere words can a servant be 19
trained;
For he understands, but will not pay
heed.

You see a man who is hasty in his 20
words?
There is more hope for a fool than for
him.

He who pampers his servant from 21
childhood
Will in the end gain nothing but in-
gratitude.

A man of passion stirs up discord; 22
And a hot-tempered man is the cause
of much mischief.

A man's pride will bring him low; 23
But the humble will attain to honor.

He who is partner with a thief is an 24
enemy to himself;
He hears the curse, but discloses
nothing.

The fear of man leads one into a snare; 25
But he who trusts in the LORD will be
placed in safety.

Many court the ruler's favor; 26
But a man's case is decided by the
LORD.

27 An unjust man is an abomination to
the righteous;
While an upright man is an abomination to the wicked.

30 THE WORDS OF AGUR THE SON OF JAKEH, FROM MASSA, 30:1–33

The oracle of the man: "I am wearied,
O God,
I am wearied, O God, and spent;
2 For I am but a brute beast, and no
man,
I have nought of human intelligence;
3 No wisdom have I learned,
No knowledge have I of the Holy One.
4 Who has scaled the heavens and come
down?
Who has gathered the wind in his fists?
Who has wrapped the waters in a garment?
Who has established all the bounds of
the earth?
What is his name, and what is his son's
name?
For surely you know!"

5 Every word of God is tested;
He is a shield to those who take refuge
in him.
6 Add not to his words,
Lest he call you to account, and you
be proved a liar.

7 Two things I ask of thee,
Deny them not to me before I die:
8 Put falsehood and lying far from me,
Give me neither poverty nor riches—
Provide me with food sufficient for my
needs—
9 Lest I be full, and disown thee,
Saying, "Who is the LORD?"
Or lest I be in want, and steal,
And profane the name of my God.

10 Slander not a servant to his master,
Lest he curse you, and you have to
pay for it.

11 There is a class of people who curse
their father,
And do not bless their mother.
12 There is a class of people who are pure
in their own eyes,
Yet are not cleansed of their filthiness.
13 There is a class of people with O! such
haughty eyes,
And such uplifted eyelids.
There is a class of people whose teeth 14
are swords,
And whose fangs are knives,
To devour the poor from the earth,
And the needy from among men.

The leech has two daughters: 15
"Give, give!" they cry.

There are three things that are unsated,
Four that never say, "Enough":
Sheol, and the barren womb, 16
The earth unsated with water,
And fire that never says, "Enough."

The eye that mocks a father, 17
And scorns an aged mother—
The ravens of the valley will pick it
out,
And the vultures will devour it.

There are three things too wonderful 18
for me,
Four that I cannot understand:
The way of a vulture in the air, 19
The way of a serpent on a crag,
The way of a ship in the heart of the
sea,
And the way of a man with a woman.

This is the way of an adulterous 20
woman:
She eats, and wipes her mouth,
And says, "I have done no wrong."

Under three things the earth quakes, 21
Under four it cannot bear up:
A slave when he becomes a king, 22
A fool when he is sated with food,
An unpopular woman when she is 23
married,
And a maidservant when she supplants
her mistress.

There are four things on earth that 24
are small,
And yet are exceedingly wise:
The ants—they are no strong folk, 25
Yet they lay up their food in the summer;
The marmots—they are no mighty 26
folk,
Yet they make their home in the crags;
The locusts—they have no king, 27
Yet they march all in ranks;
The lizard—she holds on by her fore- 28
feet,

Yet she finds her way into the king's
palace.
29 There are three things that are stately
in step,
Four that are stately in gait:
30 The lion, which is mightiest among
beasts,
And turns not back before any;
31 The strutting cock, and the he-goat,
And the king at the head of his people.

32 If you have been foolish in exalting
yourself,
Or if you have hatched a scheme,
Lay your hand upon your mouth!
33 For, as the pressing of milk brings
forth curds,
And the pressing of the nose brings
forth blood,
So the pressing of anger brings forth
strife.

31 THE WORDS OF LEMUEL, KING OF MASSA, WHICH HIS MOTHER TAUGHT HIM, 31:1–9

2 What, O my son? what, O son of my
womb?
What, O son of my vows?
3 Give not your strength to women,
Nor your love to those who are the
ruin of kings.
4 Nor be it for kings, O Lemuel,
For kings to drink wine,
For princes to quaff strong drink;
5 Lest, as they drink, they forget the law,
And violate the rights of any in
trouble.
6 Give strong drink to him who is perishing,
And wine to the bitter in heart;
7 That as he drinks he may forget his
poverty,
And think no more of his misery.
8 Open your mouth on behalf of the
dumb,
In defense of the rights of all who are
suffering;
9 Open your mouth on the side of justice,
And defend the rights of the poor and
the needy.

THE GOOD WIFE, 31:10–31

א

10 If one can find a good wife,
She is worth far more than corals.

ב

Her husband puts his trust in her, 11
And finds no lack of gain.

ג

She brings him good, and not harm, 12
All the days of his life.

ד

She sorts out wool and flax, 13
And works it up as she wills.

ה

She is like the ships of the merchant, 14
She brings her food from afar.

ו

She rises while it is still night, 15
And gives her household food,
With a portion for her maidens.

ז

She examines a field, and buys it; 16
With her earnings she plants a vineyard.

ח

She girds her loins with strength, 17
And she makes her arms strong.

ט

She perceives that her work is profit- 18
able,
So her lamp goes not out at night.

י

She lays her hand on the distaff, 19
Her fingers grasp the spindle.

כ

She stretches her hand to the poor, 20
She extends her arms to the needy.

ל

She is not afraid of the snow for her 21
household;
For her household are all clothed in
scarlet.

מ

She makes coverlets for herself, 22
Her clothing is linen and purple.

נ

Her husband is known at the gates, 23
As he sits among the elders of the land.

ס

She makes linen vests, and sells them, 24
She supplies the merchants with
girdles.

ע

25 She is clothed with strength and dignity,
And she laughs at the days to come.

פ

26 She opens her mouth in wisdom,
And kindly counsel is on her tongue.

צ

27 She looks well after her household,
And eats not the bread of idleness

ק

28 Her children rise up, and bless her—
Her husband also, and praises her:

ר

"Many women have done well, 29
But you have excelled them all."

ש

Charms are deceptive, and beauty is a breath; 30
But a woman who reveres the LORD—she will be praised.

ת

Give her the due reward of her work; 31
And let her deeds bring her praise at the gates.

THE BOOK OF ECCLESIASTES

THE ENDLESS ROUND OF NATURE, 1:1–11

1 THE words of Koheleth, the son
of David, who was king in Jerusalem.
2 "Vanity of vanities," says Koheleth,
"Vanity of vanities, all is vanity!
3 What does a man gain from all his
toil
At which he toils beneath the sun?
4 One generation goes, and another
comes,
While the earth endures forever.
5 The sun rises and the sun sets,
And hastens to the place where he rose.
6 The wind blows toward the south,
And returns to the north.
Turning, turning, the wind blows,
And returns upon its circuit.
7 All rivers run to the sea,
But the sea is never full;
To the place where the rivers flow,
There they continue to flow.
8 All things are wearisome;
One cannot recount them;
The eye is not satisfied with seeing,
Nor is the ear filled with hearing.
9 Whatsoever has been is that which
will be;
And whatsoever has been done is that
which will be done;
And there is nothing new under the
sun.
10 Is there a thing of which it is said, 'Lo,
this is new'?
It was already in existence in the ages
Which were before us.
11 There is no memory of earlier people;
And likewise of later people who shall
be,
There will be no memory with those
who are later still."

THE FUTILITY OF LEARNING, 1:12–18

12 "I, Koheleth, was king over Israel in
13 Jerusalem; and I set my mind to search
and to investigate through wisdom
everything that is done beneath the
heavens. It is an evil task that God has
given the sons of men with which to occupy themselves. I have seen every- 14
thing that has been done under the sun;
and lo, everything is vanity and striving for the wind.
"The crooked cannot be made straight, 15
And that which is lacking cannot be
counted.
"I thought within myself thus: I am 16
great and have increased in wisdom
above all that were before me over
Jerusalem; and my mind has seen
abundant wisdom and knowledge. So I 17
set my mind to knowing wisdom and to
knowing madness and folly. I am convinced that this too is striving for the
wind.
"For with more wisdom is more worry, 18
And increase of knowledge is increase
of sorrow."

THE FUTILITY OF ALL HUMAN EFFORT, 2:1–26

"I said to myself: 'Come now, let me 2
test you with mirth; so enjoy yourself.'
But this also was vanity. Of laughter I 2
said, 'It is mad'; and of mirth, 'What
has this done?' I searched in my mind 3
how to stimulate my flesh with wine,
and, while my mind conducted itself
with wisdom, how to lay hold upon
folly, until I might see which is better
for the sons of men to practice under
the heavens all the days of their life.
I made myself great works; I built my- 4
self houses; I planted vineyards for myself; I made myself gardens and parks, 5
and I planted therein all sorts of fruit
trees. I made myself pools of water 6
with which to irrigate a young forest.
I bought male and female slaves and 7
had a household of dependents, besides
having possessions in cattle and sheep
in far greater numbers than any who
had been in Jerusalem before me. I 8
gathered for myself silver and gold, the
treasure of kings and provinces. I
trained singing men and women for myself and the luxuries of the sons of men,
women of all sorts. So I became great 9

and increased more than all who were
before me in Jerusalem; yet my wisdom
10 stood by me. And nothing that my
eyes desired did I withhold from them.
I did not withhold my mind from any
mirth, but my mind found joy in all my
toil; for this was my portion from all
11 my toil. Then I reviewed all my works
which my hands had made and the toil
which I had expended in making them,
and lo, everything was vanity and
striving for the wind, and there was no
12 profit under the sun. So I turned again
to look upon wisdom, madness, and
folly; for what can the man do who
comes after the king? That which has
13 already been done! Then I saw that
wisdom is more profitable than folly,
even as light is preferable to darkness.
14 The wise man's eyes are in his head; but
the fool walks in darkness. But I realized that the same fate overtakes them
15 all. So I said to myself, 'As it befalls
the fool, so will it befall me; why, then,
should I be otherwise?' So I said to my-
16 self, 'This too is vanity!' For there is
no permanent record for either wise
man or fool, inasmuch as in the course
of the days to come everything is forgotten. How the wise and the fool alike
17 die! So I hated life; for everything that
is done under the sun seemed to me
wrong, for everything is vanity and
18 striving for the wind. I hated all my
toil at which I had toiled under the sun,
seeing that I must leave it to the man
19 who shall follow me. And who knows
whether he will be a wise man or a fool?
Yet he will have control of all the
product of my toil at which I have
toiled and of the wisdom which I have
won under the sun. This too is vanity.
20 So again I gave myself up to despair
concerning all the toil at which I had
21 toiled under the sun. For here is a man
whose toil has been done with wisdom,
knowledge, and success, but to a man
who has not toiled for it he gives it as
his portion. This too is vanity and a
22 great evil. For what does a man get for
all his toil and the striving of his mind
with which he has toiled under the sun?
23 For all his days are sorrowful and his
task is melancholy, and at night his
mind finds no rest. This too is vanity.
24 "There is nothing good for man but
that he eat and drink and find satisfaction in his work. This too have I seen,
25 that it is from the hand of God. For
who can eat and who can enjoy apart
from him? For to a man who is good 26
in his sight he gives wisdom, knowledge
and joy; but to the sinner he gives the
task of gathering and collecting that he
may give it to the one who is good in
God's sight. This too is vanity and
striving for the wind."

AN ORDERLY WORLD, 3:1–8

"For everything there is an appointed 3
time;
And there is a time for every purpose
under the heavens:
A time to be born, and a time to die; 2
A time for planting, and a time for up-
rooting;
A time to slay, and a time to heal; 3
A time to tear down, and a time to re-
build;
A time to weep, and a time to laugh; 4
A time to mourn, and a time to dance;
A time to scatter stones, and a time to 5
gather stones;
A time to embrace, and a time to re-
frain from embracing;
A time to seek, and a time to count as 6
lost;
A time to keep, and a time to throw
away;
A time to tear, and a time to sew; 7
A time to keep quiet, and a time to talk;
A time to love, and a time to hate; 8
A time for war, and a time for peace."

MAN'S LIMITATIONS, 3:9–15

"What does the maker gain from the 9
work which he has done? I see the task 10
which God has assigned to the sons of
men with which to occupy themselves.
He has made everything beautiful in 11
its season; but he has also implanted
ignorance in their mind, so that mankind cannot discover the work which
God has done from beginning to end. I 12
know that there is nothing good for
them but to be glad and to enjoy themselves while they live. Indeed, if any 13
man eats and drinks and enjoys himself
in all his work, it is a gift from God. I 14
know that whatsoever God does will be
forever; nothing may be added to it and
nothing may be withdrawn from it;
God has ordained it that they shall be
in awe before him. Whatever is has 15
been long ago and what is to be has
been long ago; and God seeks him who
has been persecuted."

MAN AND BEAST UPON THE SAME LEVEL, 3:16–22

16 "Furthermore, I saw under the sun
that wickedness took the place of
justice and wickedness took the place of
righteousness.
17 "I said to myself, 'God judges both
the righteous and the wicked, for he has
set a time for every purpose and for
18 every deed.' I said to myself regarding
the sons of men, 'It is that God may
test them and see that they are beasts.'
19 For there is one fate for both man and
beast—the same fate for them; as the
one dies, so dies the other; the same
breath is in all of them, and man has no
advantage over the beast; for every-
20 thing is vanity. All go to one place; all
are from the dust, and all return to the
21 dust. Who knows whether the spirit of
man goes upward and whether the
spirit of the beast goes downward to the
22 earth? So I saw that there is nothing
better than that man should rejoice in
his work, since that is his lot; for who
can bring him to see what shall be after
him?"

THIS TRANSITORY LIFE, 4:1–16

4 "So I considered once more all the
oppressions that are practiced under
the sun: for example, the tears of the
oppressed, with none to comfort them,
and the strength in the hands of their
oppressors, with none to comfort them.
2 So I congratulated the dead who were
already dead, rather than the living
3 who are still alive; and as happier than
both of them did I regard him who had
never been, who had not seen the
wicked work which is done under the
4 sun. Then I saw that all the labor and
all the hard work is due to men's
jealousy of one another. This too is
5 vanity and striving for the wind. The
fool folds his hands and devours his own
6 flesh. Better is one handful with quiet
than two handfuls with trouble and
7 striving after the wind. Then I saw
another case of vanity under the sun:
8 It is an individual without a companion; he has neither son, nor brother; and
yet there is no end to all his toil, nor is
his eye ever satisfied with riches. For
whom then should I toil and deny myself happiness? This too is vanity and
an evil task. Two are better than one, 9
for they get a good wage for their toil;
and if they fall, the one can lift up his 10
companion, but if a solitary person falls
there is no partner to lift him up. Like- 11
wise, if two sleep together, they keep
warm, but how can one alone keep
warm? And if somebody attacks one, 12
two can withstand him, and a threefold
cord is not quickly broken. Better is a 13
youth poor and wise than a king that
is old and foolish who no longer knows
how to take care of himself. For from a 14
household of rebels he came forth to be
king, even though in his own kingdom
he was born poor. I saw all the living 15
under the sun running with the youth
who was to stand in his place. There 16
was no end to all the people, to all at
whose head he was; yet those who come
later will not rejoice in him. For this
too is vanity and striving for the wind."

REGARDING VOWS, 5:1–9

"Guard your steps when you go to 5
the house of God; and to draw near to
obey is better than that fools should
offer sacrifice, for they know nothing
but to do wrong. Be not rash with your 2
mouth and let not your mind be in
haste to utter a word before God; for
God is in the heavens and you are on
the earth; so let your words be few. For 3
a dream comes through a mass of business, and the voice of a fool through a
mass of words. When you make a vow 4
to God do not delay in fulfilling it; for
he has no pleasure in fools! What you
vow, fulfil! It is better that you should 5
not vow than that you should vow and
not fulfil it. Let not your mouth bring 6
you into sin, and say not before the
messenger, 'It was a mistake.' Why
should God be angered at your voice
and destroy the work of your hands?
For through many empty dreams come 7
many vows. But do you fear God! If 8
you see the oppression of the poor, and
justice and right exploited in the province, be not amazed at the situation, for
one high official watches over another,
and there are those higher than both.
The ruthless has an advantage in every- 9
thing; he is king over the cultivated
land."

ABIDING SATISFACTION, 5:10–20

10 "He who loves money will not be satisfied with money;
Nor he who loves riches with gain.
This too is vanity.
11 When goods increase those who eat of them increase;
And what profit has their owner, but in looking at them?
12 Sweet is the sleep of the laborer, whether he eat little or much;
But the surfeit of the rich allows him no sleep.
13 There is a sore evil that I have seen under the sun—
Wealth kept by its owner to his own hurt.
14 And that wealth was lost in an unfortunate enterprise;
And he became the father of a son, without a thing in his hand.
15 Just as he emerged from his mother's womb,
Naked does he return, going even as he came;
And he carries away nothing of his toil which he can carry in his hand.
16 This, indeed, is a sore evil: just as he came, so will he go;
And what profit has he in that he toiled for the wind,
17 And spent all his days in darkness and mourning,
And in much trouble, sickness, and anger?

18 "So, the good which I see to be worth
while is that one should eat and drink
and get enjoyment out of all his toil at
which he toils under the sun during the
course of his life which God grants him;
19 for that is his lot. Every man to whom
God gives riches and wealth, and has
enabled him to eat of it and to bear his
lot and to rejoice in his toil—this is the
20 gift of God; for he will not recall much
the days of his life, because God responds to the joy of his heart."

FRUSTRATED DESIRE, 6:1–8

6 "There is an evil which I have seen
under the sun, and it is heavy upon
2 mankind: a man to whom God gives
riches, wealth, and honor, so that he lacks nothing of all which he desires, yet God does not permit him to partake of it; but a stranger partakes of it. This is vanity and an evil affliction. If a man becomes father of a hundred children and lives many years and many are the days of his years, but he is not satisfied with good, nor does he obtain burial, I say that a premature birth is better than he. Even though it comes in vain and goes out in darkness and its name is covered with darkness, and it does not see the sun or know it, this finds rest rather than the other. Even though he lives a thousand years twice over and gets no enjoyment—do not all go to one place?

"All a man's toil is for his mouth,
And yet his appetite is not satisfied.
For what advantage has the wise man over the fool,
And what has the poor man who knows how to walk before the living?
Better is the sight of the eyes than the wandering of desire;
This too is vanity and striving for the wind."

MAN HELPLESS BEFORE FATE, 6:10–12

"Whatever is, its name was called long ago, and what man is has been known; and he is unable to contend with him that is stronger than he. For the more words the greater is the vanity. What advantage has man? For who knows what is good for man in life, during the course of his empty life, since he spends them like a shadow? Who can tell a man what will be after him under the sun?"

A MEDLEY OF PROVERBS, 7:1–14

"A good name is better than good ointment,
And the day of death better than the day of one's birth.
It is better to go to the house of mourning than to go to the banquet-hall,
Inasmuch as that is every man's end, and the living will lay it to heart.
Better is sorrow than laughter,
For through a sad face the mind is improved.
The mind of the wise is in the house of mourning,

But the mind of fools is in the house of mirth.
5 It is better that a man should hear the rebuke of the wise,
Than that he should hear the song of fools.
6 For like the sound of thorns under the pot,
So is the laughter of the fool. This too is vanity.
7 For oppression makes the wise man mad,
And a gift destroys the mind.
8 Better is the end of a thing than its beginning;
Better is a patient spirit than a proud spirit.
9 Do not make haste in your spirit to be angry,
For anger rests in the bosom of fools.
10 Do not say, 'Why were the former days better than these?'
For it was not out of wisdom that you have asked about this.
11 Wisdom with an inheritance is good,
And an advantage to those who see the sun;
12 For in the protection of wisdom is the protection of money;
And the advantage of knowledge is that wisdom preserves the life of its owner.
13 Behold the work of God;
For who can straighten out what he has made crooked?
14 In the day of prosperity, be joyful,
And on the day of adversity, consider:
God has made one thing to balance another,
That man may not find out anything that is to be after him."

WORLDLY WISDOM, 7:15–29

15 "I have seen all sorts of things in my empty life:
For example, the righteous man perishing in his righteousness,
And the wicked prolonging his life in his wickedness.
16 Do not be over-righteous,
And be not excessively wise;
Why should you ruin yourself?
17 Be not over-wicked,
Nor play the fool;
Why should you die before your time?
18 It is well that you lay hold of one thing,
And also that your hand let not go of another;
For he who fears God will come forth with both.
Wisdom makes a wise man stronger 19
Than the ten rulers who are in the city.
For there is no man on earth so righteous 20
That he does good and never fails.
Do not give heed to all things that 21 men say,
Lest you hear your servant cursing you.
For you know that many times 22
You yourself have cursed others.

"All this I have tested by wisdom; I 23
said, 'I will be wise,' but it was far
from me. Whatever is is far off and 24
very deep; who can find it?

"I turned my mind to knowledge 25
and to searching and seeking wisdom
and substance, and to the knowledge
that wickedness is folly and foolishness
is madness. And one thing I find more 26
bitter than death: the woman whose
mind is snares and nets and her hands
fetters. He who is good in God's sight
will escape from her; but he who sins
will be caught by her.

"See, this is what I have found," says 27
Koheleth, "adding one to one to find
the total, which I have sought repeat- 28
edly, but not found; one man out of a
thousand have I found, but not a woman have I found among all these. Only 29
see this which I have found, that God
made mankind upright, but they have
sought out many contrivances."

THE CAPRICE OF RULERS, 8:1–9

"Who is like the wise man? 8
And who knows the explanation of a thing?
A man's wisdom illumines his face,
And his hard face is changed.
I obey the order of a king, because of 2 the divine oath.
Do not be in a hurry to leave his presence; 3
Do not stand firm in a bad cause,
For he does whatsoever he will;
Inasmuch as the word of a king is final; 4
And who can say to him, 'What are you doing?'

"He who keeps the command knows 5
nothing bad; and a wise mind knows

6 the time and judgment. For there is a
time and judgment for every matter;
for man's wickedness is heavy upon
7 him. For there is nobody who knows
what is to be, for who can tell him how
8 it shall be? There is nobody in authority over the wind to restrain the wind. Nor is there anybody in control of the day of death, nor is there release in war, nor can wickedness deliver its possessors. All this have I seen, having devoted my mind to all the work which is done under the sun, at a time when one man has power over another to injure
9 him.

THE LACK OF MORAL DISCRIMINATION IN HUMAN AFFAIRS, 8:10—9:6

10 "And so I have seen wicked men
carried to the tomb and praised from
the holy place and lauded in the city
where they had acted thus. This too is
11 vanity. Because the sentence upon an
evil deed is not quickly executed, therefore the minds of the sons of men are
12 fully determined to do evil. Even
though a sinner does wrong a hundred times and still continues living, yet I know that it shall be well with those who fear God, who are in awe before
13 him; but it shall not be well with the
wicked, nor shall he prolong his life like a shadow, since he is not awed in the presence of God.
14 "There is a vanity which is wrought
upon the earth, namely, that there are righteous men to whom it happens in accordance with what should be done to the wicked, and there are wicked men to whom it happens in accordance with what should be done to the righteous. I say that this too is vanity.
15 "So I commend mirth; for there is
nothing good for man under the sun except to eat, drink, and be merry; for this will stay by him in his toil during the course of his life which God gives
16 him under the sun. When I devoted my
mind to the knowledge of wisdom and to consideration of the work which is done upon the earth—for both day and
17 night his eyes see no sleep—then I saw
all God's work, that man is unable to discover the work which is done under the sun, inasmuch as man may labor in its search, but he will not find it; and even if the wise man thinks that he is on the point of knowing it, he will be unable to find it. For all this I laid upon 9
my mind and my mind considered all this, namely, that the righteous and the wise and their works are in the hand of God; no man knows whether it will be love or hatred. Everything in the past is vanity, inasmuch as there is one fate for all, for the righteous, for the wicked, and for the good; for the clean and the unclean, for him who offers sacrifice and for him who does not; as is the good, so is the sinner; he who takes an oath is as he who fears an oath. This is evil in all that is done under the sun, that there is one fate for all; and also that the mind of men is full of wickedness, and madness is in their minds while they are alive, and after that—to the dead! For whosoever is joined to all the living has hope; for as a living dog he is better than a dead lion. For the living know that they will die; but the dead know nothing at all, nor have they any longer any remembrance; for the memory of them is forgotten. Not only the love of them, but the hatred of them, and the envy of them have already perished, and they no longer have any share in anything that is done under the sun."

THE WRITER'S VIEW OF LIFE, 9:7—10:3

"Go, eat your food with gladness,
And drink your wine with a happy mind,
For God has already accepted your deeds.
At all times let your garments be white,
And let not oil be lacking upon your head.
Enjoy life with the wife whom you love
All the days of your empty life,
Which he has given you under the sun;
All your empty life.

"For that is your lot in life and in
your toil at which you toil under the
sun. Whatsoever your hand finds to do, 1
do it with your might; for there is no work or substance or knowledge or wisdom in Sheol whither you are going.
Once more I observed under the sun 1
that the race is not to the swift, nor the

battle to the strong; nor is there bread
for the wise, nor riches for the intelligent, nor favor for scholars; but time
2 and chance happen to all of them. For
man does not know his time; like fish
that are caught in an evil net, or like
birds caught in a snare, so are the sons
of men snared in an evil time as it falls
3 upon them suddenly. Also this have I
seen as an example of wisdom under the
4 sun and it greatly impressed me. There
was a small city, with few men in it, and
there came against it a great king and
surrounded it and built great siege-
5 works against it. But there was found
therein a poor, wise man, and he rescued the city by his wisdom; yet nobody remembered that poor, wise man.
5 But I say that wisdom is better than
strength, though the wisdom of the
poor man was despised and his words
7 were not heeded. The words of the wise
spoken quietly are heeded more than
8 the cry of a prince among fools. Wisdom is better than weapons of war, but
one sinner destroys much good. Dead
flies make the perfumer's precious ointment stink; so a little folly annuls great
2 wisdom. The wise man's mind makes
for his success; the fool's mind makes
3 for his failure. Also when a fool goes on
his way, his mind is lacking, and he
shows everybody that he is a fool."

MISCELLANEOUS MAXIMS, 10:4–20

"If the anger of the ruler rises against you, do not forget your place; for composure can pacify great offenses. There is an evil which I have seen under the sun, like an accidental error which comes forth from before a ruler.

"The fool is often set in high positions;
While the nobles dwell in low estate.
I have seen slaves upon horses,
While princes walked on the ground like slaves.
He who digs a pit may fall therein,
While him who breaks through a wall a serpent may bite.
He who quarries stones may be hurt by them,
While he who splits logs is endangered by them.
If the ax be dull,
And he do not sharpen its edge,
Then he must exert greater strength;
But wisdom is advantageous for winning success.
If the serpent bite before being charmed, 11
Then there is no profit to the charmer.
The words of a wise man's mouth are gracious, 12
But the lips of the fool destroy him.
The beginning of the words of his mouth is folly, 13
And the end of his utterance is wicked madness.
The fool multiplies words— 14
But man knows not what will be,
And who can tell him what will be after him?
When will the toil of the fool weary him 15
Who does not know enough to go to an interpreter?
Woe to you, O land, when your king is a boy, 16
And your princes feast in the morning!
Happy are you, O land, when your king is a noble, 17
And your princes feast at the proper time,
As men and not as sots!
Because of sloth the woodwork sinks, 18
And because of laziness the house leaks.
With mirth they make bread, 19
And wine gladdens life,
And money answers for everything.
Even on your couch do not defame a king, 20
Nor in your bed-chamber defame a rich man;
For a bird of the air may carry the sound,
And some winged creature may tell the thing."

THE UNCERTAINTY OF LIFE, 11:1–8

"Cast your bread upon the surface of the water, 11
For after many days you will find it.
Give one portion to seven or even to eight, 2
For you know not what evil shall happen on the earth.
If the clouds be filled with rain, 3
They will pour it out upon the earth;
And if a tree fall to the south or to the north,

In whatsoever place the tree falls,
there shall it be.
4 He who watches the wind will not
sow,
And he who observes the clouds will
not reap.
5 Even as you know not what the way
of the spirit is
Into the bones in the pregnant womb,
So you know not the work of God,
Who makes everything.
6 In the morning sow your seed,
And till the evening give your hand no
rest;
For you know not which shall prosper,
this or that,
Or whether both alike shall be good.
7 "Light is sweet, and it is good for the
8 eyes to see the sun. For if a man live
many years, and rejoice in them all,
let him remember that the days of
darkness will be many. Whatsoever
may come is vanity."

ADVICE TO THE YOUNG, 11:9—12:8

9 "Rejoice, O young man, in your youth,
And let your mind be glad in the days
of your vigor,
And walk in the ways of your mind
and in the sight of your eyes;
But know that for all these things
God will bring you into judgment.
10 And put away worry from your mind,
And remove evil from your flesh;
For youth and the prime of life are
vanity.
12 Remember your Creator in the days
of your vigor,
Before the evil days come,
And the years approach of which you
will say,
'I have no pleasure in them';
2 Before the sun becomes dark,
And the light, and the moon, and the
stars;
And the clouds return after the rain;
3 On the day when the guardians of the
house tremble,
And the strong men are bent,
And the grinding-maids cease because
they are few,
And the ladies peering through the
windows are darkened,
And the doors into the street are
closed;
When the sound of the mill is low,
And the sound of the bird is faint,
And all the notes of song sink low;
Also, he is afraid of a height,
And terrors are on the road;
And he rejects the almond,
And the locust is burdensome,
And the caper-berry is ineffectual;
Because man is going to his eternal
home,
And the mourners go about in the
street;
Before the silver cord is severed,
And the golden bowl broken,
And the jar shattered at the spring,
And the wheel broken at the cistern;
And the dust returns to the earth as
it was,
And the spirit returns to God who
gave it.
Vanity of vanities," says Koheleth,
"all is vanity."

CONCLUDING COMMENTS 12:9–13

In addition to the fact that Koheleth
was wise, he still taught the people
knowledge, and he composed, and
sought out, and arranged many proverbs. Koheleth sought to find pleasing
words, and what is written correctly,
namely, true things. The words of the
wise are like goads; and collections
which are given by one teacher are like
nails driven with a sledge. Furthermore, my son, take warning; of the
making of many books there is no end,
and much study is weariness of the flesh.
The conclusion of the matter, all
having been heard: Fear God and keep
his commands; for this concerns all
mankind, that God brings every work
into judgment with regard to everything concealed, whether it be good or
evil.

THE SONG OF SONGS

The Song of Songs, which is Solomon's.

THE MAIDEN TO THE YOUTH, 1:2–4

"Kiss me with kisses from your mouth,
For your love is better than wine;
The fragrance of your ointments is sweet;
Your very self is a precious ointment;
Therefore do the maidens love you.
Take me along with you, let us hasten;
Bring me, O king, into your chamber,
That we may exult and rejoice in you,
That we may praise your love more than wine;
Rightly are you loved."

THE MAIDEN TO THE DAUGHTERS OF JERUSALEM, 1:5, 6

"Blackened am I, but comely,
O daughters of Jerusalem,
Like the tents of Kedar,
like the hangings of Solomon.
Do not notice that I am blackened,
that the sun has scorched me,
my mother's son has burned me.
I was made keeper of the vineyards,
but my own vineyard I have not kept."

THE MAIDEN TO THE YOUTH, 1:7

"Tell me, you whom I love,
where you are pasturing your flock,
where you are making your fold at noon;
For why should I be like one veiled,
beside the flocks of your companions?"

TO THE MAIDEN, 1:8

"If you do not know,
O most beautiful of women,
Follow in the tracks of the flock,
And pasture your kids,
beside the tents of the shepherds."

THE YOUTH TO THE MAIDEN, 1:9–11

"To a steed in Pharaoh's chariot, 9
I compare you, my love.
Your cheeks are comely with bangles, 10
your neck with beads.
Bangles of gold we will make for you, 11
with studs of silver."

THE MAIDEN, 1:12–14

"While the king was on his couch, 12
his nard gave forth its fragrance.
A bunch of myrrh is my beloved to me, 13
as he lies at night between my breasts;
A cluster of henna is my beloved to me, 14
from the gardens of Engedi."

THE YOUTH TO THE MAIDEN, 1:15

"Ah, you are beautiful, my love· 15
ah, you are beautiful;
Your eyes are doves."

THE MAIDEN TO THE YOUTH, 1:16, 17

"Ah, you are beautiful, my beloved, 16
yea, lovely.
Yea, our couch is leafy,
The beams of our house are cedars, 17
our rafters cypresses."

THE MAIDEN, 2:1

"I am a saffron of the plain, 2
a hyacinth of the valleys."

THE YOUTH, 2:2

"Like a hyacinth among thistles, 2
so is my loved one among the maidens."

THE MAIDEN TO THE DAUGHTERS OF JERUSALEM, 2:3—3:5

3 "Like an apple tree among the trees of the forest,
so is my beloved among the youths.
In his shadow I long to sit,
and his fruit is sweet to my taste.
4 Bring me to the house of wine,
and look upon me with love.
5 Stay me with raisin-cakes,
refresh me with apples;
for I am sick with love.
6 Let his left hand be under my head,
and his right hand embrace me.

7 "I adjure you, O daughters of Jerusalem,
by the gazelles or by the hinds of the field,
That you rouse not, nor awaken love,
until it please.

8 "Hark! my beloved!
ah, here he comes,
Leaping over the mountains,
skipping over the hills.
9 My beloved is like a gazelle,
or a young stag.
Ah, here he stands,
behind our wall,
Looking through the windows,
peering through the lattices!
10 My beloved spoke up, and said to me,
'Rise, my love,
my beautiful one, come away;
11 For, see, the winter is past,
the rain is over and gone;
12 The flowers have appeared on the earth,
the time of song has come;
And the call of the turtle dove
is heard in our land;
13 The fig tree is putting forth its figs,
and the blossoming grapevines give forth fragrance.
Rise, my love,
my beautiful one, come away.
14 O my dove in the clefts of the rocks,
in the recesses of the cliffs,
Let me see your form,
let me hear your voice;
For your voice is sweet,
and your form is comely.'

15 "Catch for us the foxes,
the little foxes,
That are despoiling the vineyards,
since our vineyards are in bloom.

"My beloved belongs to me, and I to him,
who is pasturing his flock among the hyacinths.
Until the day blows,
and the shadows flee,
Gambol, my beloved,
like a gazelle or a young stag
upon the craggy mountains.

"Upon my bed at night,
I sought him whom I love;
I sought him, but could not find him;
I called him, but he did not answer me.
I will rise then, and go about the city,
in the streets and in the squares,
To seek him whom I love;
I sought him, but could not find him.
The watchmen who go about the city found me:
'Have you seen him whom I love?'
Scarcely did I get by them,
when I found him whom I love.
I held him and would not let him go,
until I brought him to my mother's house,
to the chamber of her who bore me.

"I adjure you, O daughters of Jerusalem,
by the gazelles or by the hinds of the field,
That you rouse not, nor awaken love,
until it please."

THE PROCESSION, 3:6–11

"What is this coming up from the wilderness,
like columns of smoke,
Perfumed with myrrh and frankincense,
made from all kinds of merchants' spices?
Ah, it is the litter of Solomon.
Sixty warriors are around it,
of the warriors of Israel,
All of them armed with swords,
trained in war

Each with his sword upon his hip,
against danger at night.
9 King Solomon made himself a palanquin,
from the woods of Lebanon.
10 He made its columns of silver,
its seat of gold,
Its body of purple,
its interior inlaid with ebony.
11 O daughters of Jerusalem, go forth,
and gaze upon King Solomon,
On the crown with which his mother crowned him
on the day of his nuptials,
on the day of his gladness of heart."

THE YOUTH TO THE MAIDEN, 4:1–15

4 "Ah, you are beautiful, my love;
ah, you are beautiful!
Your eyes are doves,
behind your veil.
Your hair is like a flock of goats,
streaming down from Mount Gilead.
2 Your teeth are like a flock of ewes ready for shearing,
that have come up from the washing,
All of which bear twins,
and none of which loses its young.
3 Your lips are like a thread of scarlet,
and your mouth is comely.
Your temple is like a slice of pomegranate,
behind your veil.
4 Your neck is like the tower of David,
built as an armory,
With a thousand bucklers hung upon it,
all kinds of warriors' shields.
5 Your two breasts are like two fawns,
twins of a gazelle,
that pasture among the hyacinths.
6 Until the day blows,
and the shadows flee,
I will betake myself to the mountain of myrrh,
and to the hill of frankincense.
7 You are altogether beautiful, my love,
and there is no blemish in you.
8 "Come from Lebanon, my bride;
come from Lebanon, come!
Descend from the top of Amana,
from the top of Senir (that is, Hermon),
From the dens of lions,
from the mountains of leopards.
You have heartened me, my sister, my bride, 9
you have heartened me,
With one glance of your eyes,
with one turn of your neck.
How beautiful is your love, 10
my sister, my bride!
How much better is your love than wine,
and the fragrance of your ointments than all kinds of perfume!
As for your lips, my bride, 11
they distil sweetness;
Honey and milk are under your tongue,
and the fragrance of your garments is like the fragrance of Lebanon.
A garden inclosed is my sister, my bride, 12
a garden inclosed, a fountain sealed,
A garden fountain, a well of fresh water, 15
and flowing streams from Lebanon.
Your products are a park of pomegranates, 13
together with choice fruits,
henna with nard,
Nard and saffron, calamus and cinnamon, 14
together with all kinds of frankincense woods,
Myrrh and aloes,
together with all the finest perfumes."

THE MAIDEN, 4:16

"Awake, northwind, 16
and come, southwind!
Blow upon my garden,
that its perfumes may distil,
That my beloved may come to his garden,
and eat its choice fruits."

THE YOUTH TO THE MAIDEN, 5:1a

"I have come to my garden, my sister, 5
my bride,

To gather my myrrh with my spice,
To eat my honeycomb with my honey,
To drink my wine with my milk."

TO THE LOVERS, 5:1*b*

"Eat, friends, drink,
and be drunk with love."

THE MAIDEN, 5:2–8

2 "I was asleep, but my fancy was alert;
hark! my beloved is knocking:
'Open to me, my sister, my love,
my dove, my perfect one;
For my head is filled with dew,
my locks with the mist of the night.'
3 'I have taken off my garments;
why should I put them on again?
I have washed my feet;
why should I soil them?'
4 My beloved put his hand through the hole,
and my heart yearned for him.
5 I rose to open to my beloved,
and my hands dripped myrrh,
And my fingers flowing myrrh,
upon the handles of the bar.
6 I opened to my beloved,
but my beloved had turned away, had passed by.
My heart sank when he turned his back;
I sought him, but could not find him;
I called him, but he did not answer me;
7 The watchmen who go about the city found me;
they smote me, they wounded me;
They stripped me of my mantle,
the guardians of the walls.

8 "I adjure you, O daughters of Jerusalem,
if you find my beloved,
That you tell him,
that I am sick with love."

TO THE MAIDEN, 5:9

9 "What is your lover but a lover,
O most beautiful of women?
What is your lover but a lover,
that you do so adjure us?"

THE MAIDEN, 5:10–16

"My beloved is fair and ruddy,
distinguished among myriads.
His head is fine gold,
his locks palm branches,
as black as a raven.
His eyes are like doves,
by streams of water,
Bathing in milk,
sitting by a pool.
His cheeks are like beds of spices,
exhaling perfumes.
His lips are hyacinths,
dropping flowing myrrh.
His hands are rods of gold,
studded with Tarshish-stones.
His body is a column of ivory,
adorned with sapphires.
His legs are pillars of marble,
set on bases of gold.
His form is like Lebanon,
as choice as cedars.
His mouth is sweet,
and he is altogether lovely.
Such is my beloved, and such my friend,
O daughters of Jerusalem."

TO THE MAIDEN, 6:1

"Whither has your beloved gone,
O most beautiful of women?
Whither has your beloved turned,
that we may seek him with you?"

THE MAIDEN, 6:2, 3

"My beloved has gone down to his garden,
to the beds of spices,
To pasture his flock in the gardens,
and gather hyacinths.
I belong to my beloved, and my beloved to me,
who pastures his flock among the hyacinths."

THE YOUTH TO THE MAIDEN, 6:4–10

"You are as beautiful as Tirzah, my love,
as comely as Jerusalem,
as august as the most renowned.

5 Turn your eyes away from me,
for they dazzle me.
Your hair is like a flock of goats,
streaming down from Gilead.
6 Your teeth are a flock of ewes,
that have come up from the washing,
All of which bear twins,
and none of which loses its young.
7 Your temple is like a slice of pomegranate,
behind your veil.
8 Sixty are the queens, and eighty the concubines,
and the maidens are numberless.
9 The only one is she,
my dove, my perfect one;
She is the only one of her mother;
she is the darling of her who bore her.
The maidens look upon her and bless her,
the queens and concubines praise her:
10 'Who is she that breaks forth like the dawn,
as beautiful as the moon,
As bright as the sun,
as august as the most distinguished?' "

THE MAIDEN, 6:11, 12

"I went down to the nut garden,
to look at the verdure of the valley,
To see whether the grapevine had budded,
whether the pomegranates had bloomed.
Before I knew it, my fancy set me
in the chariot of my ardent lover."

TO THE MAIDEN, 6:13—7:6

"Turn, turn, O Shulammite;
turn, turn, that we may gaze on you.
Ah, gaze on the Shulammite,
in the Mahanaim dance.
How beautiful are your steps in sandals,
O rapturous maiden!
The curves of your hips are like necklaces,
the handicraft of an artist

Your navel is a round bowl, 2
in which liquor is never lacking.
Your belly is a heap of wheat,
fenced in with hyacinths.
Your two breasts are like two fawns, 3
twins of a gazelle.
Your neck is like a tower of ivory, 4
your head upon it is like Carmel.
Your eyes are pools in Heshbon,
at the gate of Bath-rabbim.
Your nose is like a peak of Lebanon,
overlooking Damascus.
And the hair of your head is like purple, 5
in whose tresses a king is caught.
How beautiful, yea, how lovely you are, 6
beloved one, joyous maiden!"

THE YOUTH TO THE MAIDEN, 7:7–9

"Your very stature is like a palm tree, 7
and your breasts like clusters.
I said, 'Let me climb the palm tree, 8
let me take hold of its clusters,
And let your breasts be like clusters of the vine,
and the breath of your nose like apples,
And your palate like finest wine, 9
flowing pleasantly into my mouth,
stirring my lips and teeth.' "

THE MAIDEN, 7:10—8:4

"I belong to my beloved, 10
and his longing is for me.
Come, my beloved, let us go into the field, 11
let us rest among the henna flowers;
Let us go early to the vineyards, 12
to see whether the grapevine has budded,
Whether the vine blossoms have opened,
the pomegranates bloomed.
There I will give
my love to you.
The mandrakes give forth fragrance, 13
and at our doors are all kinds of choice fruits,
Both new and old,
which I have treasured for you,
my beloved.

8 "O that you were really my brother,
who had sucked the breasts of my mother,
That I might find you in the street, kiss you,
and no one then despise me;
2 That I might lead you, bring you to the house of my mother,
to the chamber of her who bore me;
That I might give you some spiced wine to drink,
some pomegranate juice;
3 That your left hand might be under my head,
and your right hand embrace me.

4 "I adjure you, O daughters of Jerusalem,
That you rouse not, nor awaken love,
until it please."

TO THE MAIDEN, 8:5a

5 "Who is this coming up from the wilderness,
leaning upon her beloved?"

THE MAIDEN TO THE YOUTH, 8:5b–7

"Under the apple tree I awakened you,
where your mother was in travail with you,
where she that bore you was in travail.
6 Place me like a seal upon your heart,
like a seal upon your arm;
For love is as mighty as death,
as strong as Sheol;
As for passion, its bolts are bolts of fire,
furious flames;
Many waters cannot quench love,
nor rivers overcome it.
If one were to offer all the substance of his house for love,
it would be utterly contemned."

TO THE MAIDEN, 8:8, 9

"Our sister is young,
and has no breasts.
What shall we do for our sister,
against the day when she will be spoken for?
If she is a wall,
we shall build a silver turret on her;
But if she is a door,
we shall secure her with cedar boards."

THE MAIDEN, 8:10–14

"If I were a wall,
and my breasts like towers,
Then would I be in his eyes,
like one who finds favor.

"Solomon had a vineyard at Baal-hamon;
He let the vineyard to caretakers.
Each was to bring a thousand shekels of silver for its fruit,
While my vineyard is my own.
The thousand shekels are yours, O Solomon,
While two hundred belong to the caretakers of the fruit.

"O you who sit in the gardens,
with companions listening,
let me hear your voice!
Hasten, my beloved,
be like a gazelle,
Or a young stag,
upon the mountains of spices!"

PART IV

THE BOOKS OF THE PROPHETS

THE MAJOR PROPHETS; Translated by Alex. R. Gordon

LAMENTATIONS; Translated by Theophile J. Meek

THE MINOR PROPHETS; Translated by J. M. Powis Smith

THE BOOK OF ISAIAH

SUPERSCRIPTION, 1:1

1 THE vision of Isaiah, the son of Amoz, which he saw concerning Judah and Jerusalem, in the days of Uzziah, Jotham, Ahaz, and Hezekiah, kings of Judah.

FAITHLESS CHILDREN, 1:2–3

2 Hear, O heavens, and give ear, O earth,
For the LORD has spoken:
"Sons have I reared and brought up,
But they have rebelled against me!
3 The ox knows its owner,
And the ass its master's crib;
But Israel does not know,
My people shows no understanding."

THE DESOLATION OF JUDAH, 1:4–9

4 Ah! sinful nation, guilt-laden people;
Brood of evildoers, children who deal corruptly;
Who have forsaken the LORD, and spurned the Holy One of Israel,
And gone back in estrangement from him!
5 Where will you still be smitten, that you continue in your defection?
The whole head is ailing, and the whole heart sick;
6 From the sole of the foot to the head there is no health in it—
Nought but blows and bruises and bleeding wounds,
That have not been pressed nor bound up nor softened with oil.
7 Your land is a desolation, your cities are burned;
Your soil—in your very presence aliens devour it;
It is a desolation like the overthrow of Sodom.
8 And the daughter of Zion is left like a booth in a vineyard,
Like a hut in a cucumber-field, like a watchman's tower.
Unless the LORD of hosts had left us a handful of survivors, 9
We should have become like Sodom, we should have resembled Gomorrah.

TRUE AND FALSE WORSHIP, 1:10–17

Hear the word of the LORD, 10
you rulers of Sodom;
Give ear to the instruction of our God,
you people of Gomorrah!
"Of what use is the multitude of your sacrifices to me," 11
says the LORD;
"I am sated with burnt-offerings of rams
and the fat of fed beasts;
In the blood of bullocks and lambs and he-goats
I take no delight.
When you come to visit me, 12
Who demands this of you—
the trampling of my courts?
Bring no more worthless offering! 13
the odor of sacrifice is an abomination to me.
New moon and sabbath,
the holding of assemblies—
Fasting and festival
I cannot endure.
Your new moons and your appointed seasons, 14
my whole being hates;
They are a burden upon me;
I am weary of bearing them.
So, when you spread out your hands, 15
I will hide my eyes from you;
Even though you make many a prayer,
I will not listen.
Your hands are full of bloodshed—
wash yourselves clean; 16
Put away the evil of your doings
from before my eyes;
Cease to do evil, 17
learn to do good;
Seek justice,
restrain the oppressor;
Uphold the rights of the orphan,
defend the cause of the widow!"

THE WAGES OF SIN, 1:18–20

18 "Come now, and let us reason together,"
says the LORD:
"If your sins be like scarlet,
can they become white as snow?
If they be red like crimson,
can they become as wool?
19 If you prove willing and obedient,
you shall eat the good of the land;
20 But if you refuse and rebel,
you shall taste the sword";
For the mouth of the LORD has spoken.

THE PURIFYING OF ZION, 1:21–31

21 How she has become a harlot,
the once faithful city;
She that was full of justice, in whom righteousness lodged,
but now murderers!
22 Your silver has become dross,
your wine is diluted with water:
23 Your rulers are unruly,
and associates of thieves;
Every one of them loves a bribe,
and runs after gifts;
They uphold not the rights of the orphan,
and the cause of the widow comes not to them.

24 Therefore this is the oracle of the Lord, the LORD of hosts,
the Mighty One of Israel:
"Ah! I will get satisfaction for myself on my enemies,
and avenge myself on my foes.
25 I will turn my hand against you;
And will smelt out your dross in the furnace,
and remove all your alloy.
26 Then will I restore your rulers as at first,
and your counselors as in the beginning;
And afterwards you shall be called,
'The stronghold of justice,
the faithful city.'"

27 Zion shall be redeemed by justice,
And her converts by righteousness;
28 But doom shall fall on rebels and sinners alike;
Those who forsake the LORD shall perish.
For you shall be put to shame through the terebinths in which you took pleasure, 29
And you shall be abashed through the gardens of which you made choice.
For you shall become like a terebinth whose leaves are withering, 30
Like a garden that has no water;
The strong one shall become tow, 31
And his work a spark;
And both of them shall burn together,
With none to quench.

THE MOUNTAIN OF THE LORD'S HOUSE, 2:1–4

The word that Isaiah, the son of 2
Amoz, received concerning Judah and
Jerusalem.
It shall come to pass in days to come, 2
That the mountain of the LORD'S house wil be
Established as the highest mountain,
And elevated above the hills.
All the nations will stream to it,
And many peoples will come and say: 3
"Come, let us go up to the mount of the LORD,
To the house of the God of Jacob;
That he may instruct us in his ways,
And that we may walk in his paths;
For from Zion goes forth instruction,
And the word of the LORD from Jerusalem."
Then shall he judge between the nations, 4
And arbitrate for many peoples;
And they shall beat their swords into plowshares,
And their spears into pruning-hooks.
Nation shall not lift up sword against nation,
Nor shall they learn war any more.

THE DAY OF THE LORD, 2:5–22

O house of Jacob, come and let us walk 5
In the light of the LORD!
For he has forsaken his people, 6
The house of Jacob;
Because they are full of diviners from the east,

And they practice soothsaying like the
Philistines,
And clasp hands with aliens.
7 Their land is filled with silver and gold,
And there is no end to their treasures;
Their land is filled with horses,
And there is no end to their chariots;
8 Their land is filled with idols;
They worship the work of their hands,
That which their fingers have made.
9 So mankind is humbled, and man is
brought low—
Forgive them not!

10 Go into the rock, and hide in the dust,
From before the dread presence of the
LORD,
And from his glorious majesty!
11 The haughty looks of man will be
brought low,
And the pride of man will be humbled,
And the LORD alone will be exalted on
that day.
12 For the LORD of hosts has a day
Against all that is proud and high,
And against all that is lofty and tall;
13 Against all the cedars of Lebanon, high
and lofty,
And against all the oaks of Bashan;
14 Against all the high mountains,
And against all the lofty hills;
15 Against every high tower,
And against every fortified wall;
16 Against all the ships of Tarshish,
And against all the gallant barks.
17 Then the haughtiness of man will be
humbled,
And the pride of man will be brought
low;
And the LORD alone will be exalted on
that day.

18 The idols will one and all vanish;
19 And men will go into the caves of the
rock,
And into the holes of the dust,
From before the dread presence of the
LORD,
And from his glorious majesty,
When he rises to strike terror on the
earth.
20 On that day will a man cast away,
To the moles and to the bats,
His idols of silver and his idols of gold,
Which he made for himself to worship—
21 To go into the rifts of the rocks,
And into the clefts of the crags,
From before the dread presence of the
LORD,
And from his glorious majesty,
When he rises to strike terror on the
earth.

Cease trusting man, in whose nostrils is 22
breath;
For of what account is he?

THE REIGN OF ANARCHY, 3:1–12

For see! the Lord, the LORD of hosts, 3
Is removing from Jerusalem and from
Judah both stay and staff—
All stay of bread and all stay of
water—
Soldier and warrior, judge and proph- 2
et, diviner and elder,
Captain of fifty, and man of rank, 3
Counselor, skilful magician, and ex-
pert enchanter.
And boys will I give them for princes, 4
And children shall rule over them;
And the people shall play the tyrant 5
over each other,
Everyone over his neighbor;
And rudely shall they behave, the
youth toward the old man,
And the base man toward the honor-
able.
When a man lays hold of his fellow in 6
his father's house:
"You have a mantle—you shall be our
leader,
And this heap of ruins shall be under
your hand";
On that day will he protest, saying, 7
"I will not be a healer;
For in my house there is neither bread
nor mantle;
You shall not make me leader of this
people!"
For Jerusalem has stumbled, 8
And Judah has fallen;
Because their words and their deeds 9
are against the LORD,
Provoking his glorious eyes.

Their partiality in judgment bears
witness against them,
And like Sodom they publish their sin
without concealment.
Woe to them! for ill have they done
to themselves.
Happy the righteous! for well shall 10
they fare;
For the fruit of their deeds they shall
eat.

11 Woe to the wicked! ill shall they fare;
For the work of their hands shall be paid back to them.
12 My people! babes are their masters,
And women rule them.
My people! your leaders mislead you,
And confuse the paths you should follow.

A JUDGMENT SCENE, 3:13–15

13 The LORD comes forward to plead,
He stands up to arraign his people;
14 The LORD will bring an indictment
Against the elders and princes of his people.
"It is you that have ravaged the vineyard;
The plunder of the poor is in your houses.
15 What mean you by crushing my people,
And grinding the face of the poor?"
Is the oracle of the Lord, the GOD of hosts.

THE DOOM OF THE DAUGHTERS OF ZION, 3:16—4:1

16 The LORD says:
"Because they have grown haughty, the daughters of Zion,
And walk with outstretched necks, and with ogling eyes,
Mincing along as they walk, and jingling with their feet—
The Lord shall smite with a scab
17 the scalps of the daughters of Zion,
and the LORD shall lay bare their brow.
18 [On that day will the Lord remove
the finery of the anklets and fillets and
19 crescents, the eardrops and bracelets
20 and veils, the headbands and armlets
and sashes, the perfume boxes and
21 amulets, the signet rings and nose
22 rings, the festival robes, the mantles
23 and shawls and satchels, the lace gowns
and linen vests, the turbans and capes.]
24 Instead of perfume there shall be rottenness,
And instead of a girdle, a rope;
Instead of curls, baldness,
And instead of a stately robe, a wrapping of sackcloth—
Branding instead of beauty.
Your men shall fall by the sword, 25
And your warriors in battle;
And the gates of Zion shall sorrow and sigh, 26
As she sits despoiled on the earth.
On that day shall seven women lay hold 4
On a single man,
Saying, 'We will provide our own food,
And will buy our own clothes;
Only let us be called by your name—
Take away our disgrace!'"

THE COMING GLORY OF ZION, 4:2–6

On that day will the vegetation of the 2
LORD be fair and glorious; and the fruit
of the land will be a pride and adornment to the survivors of Israel. And 3
those who remain in Zion and are left
in Jerusalem will be called holy—even
everyone who is enrolled among those
destined for life in Jerusalem—when 4
the Lord has washed away the filth of
the daughters of Zion, and has wiped
out the bloodstains of Jerusalem from
the midst of it, by the spirit of judgment and the spirit of destruction.
Then will the LORD create over the 5
whole site of Mount Zion, and over her
assemblies, a cloud of smoke by day
and the glow of a flaming fire by night;
for the glory of the LORD will be a canopy and a bower over all, serving as a 6
shade from the heat by day, and as a
refuge and shelter from storm and from
rain.

THE SONG OF THE VINEYARD, 5:1–7

Let me sing for my Loved One 5
My love song of his vineyard.

My Loved One had a vineyard
On a fertile hill;
He dug it, and cleared it of stones, 2
And planted it with choice vines;
He built a watchtower in the midst of it,
And hewed out a winevat;
And he expected it to yield grapes,
But it yielded wild grapes.

Now, O inhabitants of Jerusalem, and men of Judah, 3

Judge, I pray, between me and my
vineyard!
4 What more could have been done for
my vineyard
Than that which I have done for it?
Why, then, when I expected it to yield
grapes,
Did it yield wild grapes?

5 So now, I pray, let me tell you
What I will do to my vineyard:
I will remove its hedge, so that it shall
be ravaged;
I will break down its wall, so that it
shall be trampled down;
6 I will make it a waste, unpruned and
unhoed,
That shall spring up with briers and
thorns;
And the clouds will I command
That they rain no rain upon it.

7 For the vineyard of the LORD of hosts
is the house of Israel,
And the men of Judah are his cherished plantation;
He looked for justice, but lo! bloodshed,
For righteousness, but lo! a cry.

THE SIXFOLD WOE,
5:8–24

8 Woe to you who join house to house,
And add field to field,
Till there is no more room,
And you are left to dwell alone
In the midst of the land!
9 Therefore the LORD of hosts has
sworn in my hearing:
"Of a truth shall many houses become
a desolation,
Houses great and goodly, without an
inhabitant;
10 For ten acres of vineyard shall yield
but a bath,
And a homer of seed shall yield but an
ephah."

11 Woe to those who rise up early in the
morning,
To run after strong drink;
Who sit late into the twilight,
Till wine inflames them;
12 Whose feasts are lyre and harp,
Timbrel and flute and wine;
But the doing of the LORD they heed
not,
And the work of his hands they see not!
Therefore my people are gone into 13
exile,
For want of knowledge;
Their nobility is famished with
hunger,
And their rabble is parched with
thirst.

Therefore Sheol has enlarged her 14
appetite,
And opens her mouth without limit;
And down go the rank and the rabble
of Zion,
The noisy ones and the exultant in her.
[Mankind is humbled, and man is 15
brought low,
The eyes of the exalted are brought
low;
But the LORD of hosts is exalted 16
through justice,
The Holy God shows himself holy
through righteousness.]
Then lambs will graze as on their 17
pasture,
And fat kids will feed among the
ruins.

Woe to those who draw guilt on them- 18
selves with cords of ungodliness,
And the penalty of their sin as with
cart-ropes;
Who say, "Let his work speed on, 19
make haste,
That we may see it;
Let the purpose of the Holy One of
Israel draw near and come,
That we may know it!"

Woe to those who call evil good, 20
And good evil;
Who count darkness as light,
And light as darkness;
Who count bitter as sweet,
And sweet as bitter!

Woe to those who are wise in their own 21
eyes,
And in their own light intelligent!

Ah! the heroes at drinking wine, 22
And the warriors at blending liquor;
Who acquit the guilty for a bribe, 23
And wrest the rights of the innocent
from him!
Therefore, as a tongue of fire licks up 24
stubble,
And hay sinks down in the flame,
Their root will become like rottenness,

And their blossom will go up like dust;
Because they have scorned the instruction of the LORD of hosts,
And have spurned the word of the Holy One of Israel."[1]

THE VISION OF THE LORD, 6:1–13

6 In the year that King Uzziah died, I
saw the Lord sitting upon a throne,
high and uplifted, with the skirts of his
2 robe filling the temple. Over him stood
seraphim, each having six wings, with
two of which he covered his face, with
two he covered his loins, and with two
3 he hovered in flight. And they kept
calling to one another, and saying,
"Holy, holy, holy, is the LORD of hosts;
The whole earth is full of his glory."
4 And the foundations of the thresholds
shook at the sound of those who called,
and the house filled with smoke.
5 Then said I,
"Woe to me! for I am lost;
For I am a man of unclean lips,
And I dwell among a people of unclean lips;
For my eyes have seen the King,
The LORD of hosts."
6 Then flew one of the seraphim to me,
with a red-hot stone in his hand, which
he had taken with tongs from the altar;
7 and he touched my mouth with it, and
said,
"See! this has touched your lips;
So your guilt is removed, and your sin forgiven."
8 Then I heard the voice of the Lord,
saying,
"Whom shall I send,
And who will go for us?"
Whereupon I said,
"Here am I! send me."
9 So he said,
"Go and say to this people:
'Keep on hearing, but understand not;
And keep on seeing, but know not!'
10 Make the mind of this people gross,
Dull their ears, and besmear their eyes;
Lest they see with their eyes, and hear with their ears,
And have a mind to understand, and turn, and be healed."
11 Then I said,
"How long, O Lord?"
And he said,
"Till cities lie waste, without inhabitant,
And houses without man;
And the soil be left a desolation,
And the LORD have removed man far 12
away,
And many be the forsaken places in the midst of the land.
Even if a tenth remain in it, 13
This must pass through the fire again,
Like a terebinth, or an oak,
Whose stump remains when it is felled."
[A holy race is the stump of it.]

THE CHALLENGE OF FAITH, 7:1–9

Now in the days of Ahaz, the son of 7
Jotham, the son of Uzziah, king of
Judah, Rezin, the king of Syria, and
Pekah, the son of Remaliah, king of
Israel, went up to Jerusalem to war
against it, but they were not able to
come to blows with it. And when the 2
House of David was told, "The Syrians
lie encamped on Ephraimite territory,"
his heart and the heart of his people
shook as the trees of the forest shake
before the wind.
Then said the LORD to Isaiah, 3
"Go out now to meet Ahaz, you and
your son 'A remnant will return,' at
the end of the aqueduct from the upper
pool, on the highway to the laundrymen's field; and say to him, 'Take care, 4
and keep calm! Do not be afraid or
down-hearted because of these two
stumps of smoking firebrands, the fierce
anger of Rezin (with Syria) and the
son of Remaliah. Because Syria has 5
plotted mischief against you, with Ephraim and the son of Remaliah, saying, 6
"Let us go up against Judah, and throw
it into a panic, and make a schism in
it to our interest, and set up the son of
Tabeel as king in the midst of it," thus 7
says the Lord GOD:
"It shall not stand, and it shall not be!
For the head of Syria is Damascus, 8
And the head of Damascus is Rezin;
[And within sixty-five years Ephraim shall be broken in pieces, so as to be no longer a people.]
And the head of Ephraim is Samaria, 9
And the head of Samaria is the son of Remaliah.
If you do not hold fast,
Surely you shall not stand fast." ' "

[1] Vss. 25—30 will be found following 10:4 on p. 635.

THE SIGN OF "GOD IS WITH US," 7:10–25

10 Once more the LORD spoke to Ahaz, saying,
11 "Ask a sign of the LORD your God; make it deep as Sheol, or high as the heavens!"
12 But Ahaz said,
"I will not put the LORD to the test by asking such a thing."
13 So he said,
"Hear now, O House of David! Is it
too slight a thing for you to weary men,
that you must weary my God also?
14 Therefore the Lord himself will give
you a sign: Behold, a young woman is
with child, and is about to bear a son;
and she will call him Emmanuel [God is
15 with us]. Curds and honey will be his
food when he knows enough to refuse
16 the bad and choose the good. For before the child knows enough to refuse
the bad and choose the good, the land
before whose two kings you stand in
17 dread will be forsaken. The LORD will
bring upon you, and upon your people,
and upon your father's house, such
days as have not come since the day
that Ephraim parted from Judah, even
the king of Assyria."

18 It shall come to pass on that day,
That the LORD will whistle for the fly,
That is at the sources of the streams of Egypt,
And for the bee that is in the land of Assyria;
19 And they will come and settle, all of them,
In the precipitous ravines, and in the clefts of the crags,
And on all the thorn bushes, and on all the pasture grounds.

20 On that day will the Lord shave off,
With a razor hired from beyond the River, even the king of Assyria,
The hair of the head and the body;
The beard also will he sweep away.

21 And it shall come to pass on that day,
That one will rear a young cow and a couple of sheep;
22 And because of the abundant supply of milk
He will have curds for his food;
For curds and honey will be the food of everyone,
Who is left in the midst of the land.

And it shall come to pass on that day, 23
That every place where there used to be a thousand vines,
Worth a thousand silver shekels,
Will run to briers and thorns;
With arrows and bow will men come there, 24
For all the land will be briers and thorns.

And as for all the hills that used to be hoed with the hoe, 25
You will not be able to go there for fear of briers and thorns;
But they will become a place where oxen may be sent,
And where sheep may trample.

THE SIGN OF "SPEEDING TO THE SPOIL, HASTENING TO THE PREY," 8:1–10

Then said the LORD to me, 8
"Take a great tablet, and write upon
it in the ordinary script, 'Speeding is
the spoil, Hastening is the prey.' And 2
get for me reliable witnesses to attest
the writing, Uriah the priest, and
Zechariah, the son of Jeberechiah."
Then I went in to the prophetess, 3
and she conceived, and bore a son. So
the LORD said to me,
"Call him 'Speeding is the spoil,
Hastening is the prey'; for before the 4
child knows how to cry, 'My father!'
and 'My mother!' the wealth of Damascus and the spoil of Samaria shall be
carried away before the king of Assyria."

Once more the LORD spoke to me, 5
saying,
"Because this people have spurned 6
The waters of Shiloah, that flow gently,
And melt in fear before Rezin and the son of Remaliah,
Behold, the Lord is bringing up against them 7
The waters of the River, mighty and many,
Even the king of Assyria and all his glory;
And it shall rise over all its channels,
And shall pass over all its banks,
And shall sweep on through Judah, in an overwhelming flood, 8
And shall reach as high as the neck."
Yet his outspread wings shall fill the
breadth of your land, O Emmanuel!

9 Take knowledge, you peoples afar;
Give ear, all you distant parts of the earth!
Gird yourselves, and be dumbfounded;
Gird yourselves, and be dumbfounded!
10 Plan a plan—it shall come to nought;
Speak a word—it shall not stand!
For God is with us.

THE TEACHING AND THE TESTIMONY, 8:11–22

11 Thus spoke the LORD to me, while
he grasped me by the hand, and warned
me not to walk in the way of this
people:
12 "Nought that this people call holy
Shall you call holy;
And what they fear you shall not fear,
Nor shall you dread!
13 But the LORD of hosts—him shall you call holy;
He shall be your fear, and he your dread!
14 For to both the houses of Israel shall he prove a holy place,
A stone to strike against, and a rock to stumble upon,
A trap and a snare to the inhabitants of Jerusalem;
15 And many shall stumble thereon, and shall fall,
Shall be broken, and snared, and taken."

16 I will bind up my testimony, and seal
my teaching in the heart of my dis-
17 ciples. Then I will wait for the LORD,
who is hiding his face from the house of
18 Israel; I will set my hope on him, while
I and the children whom the LORD has
given me remain as signs and symbols
in Israel from the LORD of hosts, who
dwells on Mount Zion.

19 And when men say to you, "Consult
the ghosts and spirits that chirp and
gibber! Should not a people consult its
gods? On behalf of the living should
they not consult the dead for instruc-
20 tion and direction?"—of a truth, they
shall keep making a statement like this,
21 in which there is no light. And they
shall pass through the land, hard
pressed and hungry, and in their hunger they shall become mad with rage,
and shall curse their king and their
God, and shall look up to the heavens
22 and down again to the earth, but lo!
nought but distress and darkness, the
gloom of anguish, and impenetrable
murk.

THE PRINCE OF PEACE, 9:1–7

But there will be no more gloom to 9
her that was in anguish. As in days
gone by he brought contempt upon the
land of Zebulun and the land of Naphtali, so in the time to come will he bring
glory upon the land along the Sea Road,
beyond Jordan—the Circle of the Nations.

The people that walked in darkness 2
Have seen a great light;
Those who dwelt in a land of deep darkness—
On them has light shone.
Thou hast multiplied the nation, thou hast increased its joy; 3
They rejoice before thee as with the joy at harvest,
As men exult when they divide the spoil.
For the yoke that was their burden, 4
And the bars upon their shoulder,
The rod of their master,
Thou hast broken in pieces as on the day of Midian.
For every boot worn by booted warrior in the fray, 5
And war cloak stained with blood,
Will be for burning—food for the fire.
For a child is born to us, a son is given to us; 6
And the government will be upon his shoulder;
And his name will be called
"Wonderful counselor is God almighty,
Father forever, Prince of peace."
Of the increase of his government, and of peace, 7
There will be no end,
Upon the throne of David, and over his kingdom,
To establish it, and to uphold it,
In justice and in righteousness,
From henceforth, even forever.
The zeal of the LORD of hosts will do this.

THE LORD'S OUTSTRETCHED HAND, 9:8—10:4; 5:25–30

A word has the Lord sent into Jacob, 8
And it will light upon Israel;
And all the people will know it, 9

Ephraim and the inhabitants of Samaria,
Who have spoken in pride and boldness of heart, saying,
10 "Bricks have fallen, but with hewn stone will we rebuild;
Sycamores have been cut down, but with cedars will we replace them."
11 Therefore the LORD raised up their adversaries against them,
And spurred on their enemies,
12 The Syrians on the east, and the Philistines on the west,
Who devoured Israel with open mouth.
For all this his anger has not turned back,
But his hand is stretched out still.

13 The people turned not to him who smote them,
Nor sought the LORD of hosts;
14 Therefore the LORD cut off from Israel head and tail,
Palm-branch and reed in a single day—
15 The elder and the man of rank is the head,
And the prophet who teaches lies is the tail—
16 The leaders of this people were misleaders,
And those who were led by them were swallowed up;
17 Therefore the LORD will spare not their young men,
Nor will he have pity upon their orphans and widows;
Inasmuch as every one of them is godless and an evildoer,
And every mouth speaks impiety.
For all this his anger has not turned back,
But his hand is stretched out still.

18 Because wickedness burns like a fire,
Which devours briers and thorns,
Then kindles the thickets of the forest,
And they roll up in columns of smoke—
19 Through the wrath of the LORD of hosts the land was burned black,
And the people were as food for the fire.
No man spared his brother;
20 They carved on the right hand, but were hungry still,
They devoured on the left hand, but were not satisfied;
Each one devoured his neighbor's flesh,
Manasseh Ephraim, and Ephraim Manasseh, 21
While together they fell upon Judah.
For all this his anger has not turned back,
But his hand is stretched out still.

Woe to those who decree unrighteous decrees, 10
And the recorders who make mischievous records,
To thrust aside the needy from their rights, 2
And to rob my poor ones of justice,
That widows may become their spoil,
And that on orphans they may prey.
What will you do on the day of judgment, 3
In face of the storm which will come from afar?
To whom will you flee for help,
And where will you leave your wealth?
They can but crouch beneath the prisoners, 4
And fall beneath the slain!
For all this his anger has not turned back,
But his hand is stretched out still.

Therefore the anger of the LORD blazed against his people, 5 25
And he stretched out his hand against them, and smote them,
So that the mountains quaked;
And their dead bodies were like offal in the midst of the streets.
For all this his anger has not turned back,
But his hand is stretched out still.

So he will raise a signal to a nation afar, 26
He will whistle for him at the end of the earth;
And lo! speedily, swiftly will he come,
None weary, none stumbling in his ranks; 27
He will neither slumber nor sleep.
No loin-girdle of his is loosed,
No sandal-thong is snapped;
His arrows are sharpened, 28
His bows are all bent;
His horses' hoofs are counted like flint,
His wheels like the whirlwind.
His roar is like that of a lioness, 29
Like young lions will he roar and growl;
He will seize the prey, and will carry it off,
With none to deliver.

30 He will growl over them on that day
like the growling of the sea;
And if one look to the earth, lo! darkness full of distress,
The light is darkened in storm-clouds.

THE DOWNFALL OF ASSYRIA, 10:5–34

5 O Assyria, rod of my anger,
And staff of my fury!
6 Against a godless nation I send him,
And against the people of my wrath I charge him,
To despoil them, and to prey on them,
And to trample them down like mire of the streets.
7 But not so does he think,
And not so does he plan;
For destruction is in his mind,
And to cut off nations not a few.
8 For he says,
"Are not my captains all of them kings?
9 Is not Calno like Carchemish?
Is not Hamath like Arpad?
Is not Samaria like Damascus?
10 Inasmuch as my hand has reached to the kingdoms of the idols,
Whose carved images were more than those of Jerusalem and Samaria,
11 Shall I not do to Jerusalem and its images,
As I have done to Samaria and its idols?"

12 But when the Lord has finished all
his work on Mount Zion and Jerusalem,
he will punish the arrogant boasting of
the king of Assyria, and his vainglorious
13 pride. For he says,
"By the strength of my hand have I done it,
And by my wisdom, for I have understanding;
I have removed the boundaries of peoples,
And I have plundered their treasures;
I have brought down the inhabitants to the dust.
14 My hand has seized like a nest
The wealth of the peoples;
And as one gathers eggs that are left,
All the earth have I gathered;
And there was none that moved a wing,
Or opened the mouth, or chirped."
15 Shall an ax boast over the man that hews with it,
Or a saw lord itself over the man that plies it?
As though a rod were to sway the man that wields it,
Or a staff were to wield what is not wood!

Therefore the Lord, the LORD of hosts, 16
Will send wasting sickness into his fat,
And under his glory there will be kindled a kindling
Like the kindling of fire—
The Light of Israel will become a fire, 17
The Holy One of Israel a flame—
And the glory of his forest and garden land 18
It will consume, both body and soul,
As when a sick man wastes away;
And the remnant of his forest trees will be few, 19
So that a child may write them down.

On that day the remnant of Israel, 20
and the survivors of the house of Jacob,
will no more lean for support on the
enemy that smote them, but will lean in
loyal trust on the LORD, the Holy One
of Israel. A remnant will return—the 21
remnant of Jacob—to the Mighty God.
For though your people, O Israel, be 22
like the sand of the sea, only a remnant
of them will return. Destruction is decided upon, overwhelming in the force
of righteousness. For an act of destruc- 23
tion, complete and decisive, is the Lord,
the GOD of hosts, about to execute in
the midst of all the earth.

Therefore thus says the Lord, the 24
GOD of hosts:
"O people of mine who dwell in Zion,
be not afraid of Assyria, when he smites
you with the rod, and lifts up his staff
against you, as did the Egyptians! For 25
in a very little while my fury shall
cease, and my anger shall come to an
end. Then shall the LORD of hosts 26
brandish over him a scourge like that
with which he smote Midian at the
Rock of Oreb; and his staff that was
over the Sea shall he lift up against
him, as he did against the Egyptians.
And on that day shall his burden pass 27
from your shoulder, and his yoke be
removed from your neck."

He has gone up from Pene Rimmon,
He has come to Aiath; 28
He has passed through Migron,

At Michmash he stores his baggage;
29 He has crossed the Pass,
Geba is his bivouac;
Panic-stricken is Ramah,
Gibeah of Saul has fled.
30 Shriek aloud, O daughter of Gallim!
Hearken, O Laishah! Answer her, O Anathoth!
31 Madmenah has taken to flight,
The inhabitants of Gebim seek refuge.
32 This very day will he halt at Nob,
He will shake his fist at the mount of the daughter of Zion,
The hill of Jerusalem.

33 But see! the Lord, the LORD of hosts,
Is lopping his boughs with a terrible crash;
And the lofty of stature will be hewn down,
And the tall ones will tumble.
34 He will strike down the thickets of the forest with an iron ax,
And Lebanon will fall beneath the blows of a Mighty One.

THE AGE OF GOLD, 11:1–9

11 A shoot will spring from the stem of Jesse,
And a sprout from his roots will bear fruit.
2 And the spirit of the LORD will rest upon him,
The spirit of wisdom and understanding,
The spirit of counsel and might,
The spirit of knowledge and the fear of the LORD—
3 And his delight will be in the fear of the LORD.
He will not judge by that which his eyes see,
Nor decide by that which his ears hear;
4 But with justice will he judge the needy,
And with fairness decide for the poor of the land;
He will smite the ruthless with the rod of his mouth,
And with the breath of his lips will he slay the wicked.
5 Righteousness will be the girdle round his loins,
And faithfulness the girdle round his waist.
6 Then the wolf will lodge with the lamb,
And the leopard will lie down with the kid;
The calf and the young lion will graze together,
And a little child will lead them.
The cow and the bear will be friends, 7
Their young ones will lie down together;
And the lion will eat straw like the ox.
The suckling child will play on the hole of the asp, 8
And the weaned child will put his hand on the viper's den.
They will do no harm or destruction 9
On all my holy mountain;
For the land will have become full of the knowledge of the LORD,
As the waters cover the sea.

THE TRIUMPHANT RETURN OF THE EXILES, 11:10–16

It shall come to pass on that day that the root of Jesse, 10
Who will be standing as a signal to the peoples—
To him will the nations resort,
And his resting-place will be glorious.

On that day will the LORD once more 11
raise his hand to recover the remnant
that remains of his people, from Assyria
and from Egypt, from Pathros and
from Ethiopia, from Elam and from
Shinar, from Hamath and from the
coast-lands of the sea.

He will raise a signal to the nations, 12
And will gather the outcasts of Israel;
And the scattered daughters of Judah will he assemble
From the four corners of the earth.
Then all jealousy against Ephraim will cease, 13
And those who are hostile to Judah will be cut off;
Ephraim will not be jealous of Judah,
And Judah will not be hostile to Ephraim.
But they will swoop down on the shoulder of the Philistines on the west, 14
Together they will plunder the Kedemites;
Edom and Moab will be brought under their power,
And the sons of Ammon will become subject to them.

15 Then the LORD will dry up the tongue
of the Sea of Egypt,
With the glowing heat of his breath;
And he will shake his hand over the
River,
And will smite it into seven brooks,
And will enable men to cross it with
sandals.
16 So there will be a highway from Assyria
For the remnant that remains of his
people,
As there was for Israel
On the day that it went up from the
land of Egypt.

SONGS OF THANKSGIVING, 12:1–6

12 You shall say on that day:
"I will give thanks to thee, O LORD,
For thou wast angry with me,
But thine anger has turned back,
And thou hast comforted me.
2 See! God is my salvation—
I will trust, and will not be afraid;
For Yah the LORD is my strength and
my song,
And he has become my salvation."

3 Then you shall draw water with joy
4 from the wells of salvation, and shall
say on that day:
"Give thanks to the LORD, acclaim his
name!
Make known his doings among the
peoples,
Bear record that his name is exalted!
5 Sing praises to the LORD, for proudly
has he wrought;
Let this be known through all the
earth!
6 Cry aloud, and sing for joy, O inhabitants of Zion!
For great in your midst is the Holy
One of Israel."

13 AN ORACLE ON BABYLON, WHICH ISAIAH THE SON OF AMOZ RECEIVED, 13:1–22

2 On a bare hill raise a signal,
call aloud to them;
Wave the hand for them to enter
the gates of the nobles!
3 For I have commanded my consecrated ones,
I have summoned my warriors, my
proudly exulting ones,
to execute my anger.

Hark! a tumult on the mountains, 4
like that of a multitude of
people;
Hark! the uproar of kingdoms,
of nations assembled!
The LORD of hosts is mustering
a battle host.

They come from a distant land, 5
from the end of the heavens—
The LORD and his weapons of wrath,
to destroy the whole earth.

Wail! for the day of the LORD is at 6
hand;
as destruction from the Almighty will it come.
Therefore all hands will fall helpless, 7
And every man's heart will melt,
and they will be confounded; 8
Pangs and throes will seize them,
they will writhe like a woman
in travail;
They will look aghast at each other,
with their faces aflame.

See! the day of the LORD comes, 9
Pitiless, with wrath and fierce anger,
To make the earth a desolation,
And to destroy its sinners from off it.
For the stars of the heavens will veil 10
themselves,
And their constellations will not flash
out their light;
The sun will be dark when he rises,
And the moon will not shed her light.
I shall punish the world for the evil 11
thereon,
And the wicked for their guilt;
I shall still the pride of the arrogant,
And shall bring low the haughtiness of
tyrants;
I shall make man rarer than fine gold, 12
Mankind more rare than gold of Ophir.

Therefore the heavens will tremble, 13
And the earth will quake out of its
place,
Through the wrath of the LORD of
hosts,
On the day of his fierce anger.
And then, like a hunted gazelle, 14
Or a flock with none to gather it,
They will turn everyone to his people,
And will flee everyone to his land.
All who are found will be thrust 15
through,

And all who are caught will fall by the
sword;
16 Their babes will be dashed in pieces
before their eyes,
Their houses will be despoiled, and
their wives will be ravished.

17 See! I am stirring up the Medes
against them,
Who pay no regard to silver,
And take no pleasure in gold.
18 Their bows will dash the young men in
pieces,
And on the fruit of the womb will they
have no mercy,
Nor on children will their eye look
with pity.
19 And Babylon, the beauty of kingdoms,
The proud glory of the Chaldeans,
Will be as when God overthrew
Sodom and Gomorrah.

20 She will never more be inhabited,
Nor dwelt in throughout the ages;
No Arab will pitch his tent there,
No shepherds will fold their flocks
there;
21 But there desert demons will make
their lair,
And the houses will be full of jackals;
There ostriches will dwell,
And satyrs will dance there;
22 Goblins will howl in her palaces,
And jackals in her pleasant mansions.
Her time is nearly come,
And her days will not be prolonged.

THE RESTORATION OF ISRAEL, 14:1–2

14 For the LORD will have pity upon
Jacob, and will once more choose Israel,
and will settle them upon their own
soil; and aliens will join them, and will
become members of the house of Jacob.
2 For they will take them along with
them, and will bring them to their
place; and the house of Israel will give
them a foothold upon the LORD'S soil
as male and female slaves, thus making
captives of those who took them captive, and ruling over those who were
their masters.

SATIRE AGAINST THE KING OF BABYLON, 14:3–23

3 On the day that the LORD gives you
rest from your trouble and turmoil, and
from the hard service at which you
were made to serve, you will take up 4
this taunt-song against the king of
Babylon:
"How still has the tyrant become,
how still the terror!
The LORD has broken the staff of the 5
wicked,
the scepter of rulers,
Who smote the peoples in wrath 6
with smiting incessant,
And trampled the nations in anger
with trampling unchecked.
All the earth is at rest, is quiet, 7
they break into singing;
Even the cypresses rejoice at your 8
fate,
the cedars of Lebanon:
'Since you were laid low, there comes
up
no woodman against us.'

"Sheol beneath is thrilled 9
to greet your coming;
She stirs up for you the Shades,
all the rams of the earth;
She lifts from their thrones
all the kings of the nations.
All of them will answer, 10
and will say to you,
'So you too have become weak as we
are,
have been made like us!'
Brought down to Sheol is your pomp, 11
the noise of your harps;
Beneath you maggots are spread,
worms are your covering.

"How are you fallen from heaven, 12
O Lucifer, son of the dawn!
How are you hewn to the earth,
who laid waste all the nations!
You said to yourself,
'The heavens will I scale; 13
Above the stars of God
will I set up my throne;
I will sit on the Mount of Assembly,
in the recesses of the north;
I will scale the heights of the clouds, 14
I will match the Most High.'
But down to Sheol are you brought, 15
to the recesses of the Pit.

"Those who see you will gaze at you, 16
they will scan you closely:
'Is this the man who caused the earth
to quiver,
caused kingdoms to quake;

17 Who made the world like a desert,
and tore down its cities;
Who set not his prisoners free,
to return to their homes?'
18 All the kings of the nations,
They have all lain down in glory,
each in his house;
19 But you are cast forth, tombless,
like a hateful abortion,
Clothed with slain men gashed by the sword,
Who go down to the stones of the Pit,
like a trampled corpse.

20 "With them will you not be united in burial;
Because you have ruined your land,
you have slain your people.
And never more will be named
the race of evildoers;
21 So prepare for his sons a shambles
because of their fathers' guilt,
Lest they rise and take possession of the earth,
and fill the face of the world with cities!"

22 "I will rise up against them," is the
oracle of the LORD of hosts, "and will
cut off from Babylon race and remnant,
offspring and offshoot," is the oracle of
23 the LORD. "And I will make it the possession of the hedgehog—marshes of
water. And I will sweep it with the
broom of destruction," is the oracle of
the LORD of hosts.

THE PLAN OF THE LORD AGAINST ASSYRIA, 14:24–27

24 The LORD of hosts has sworn saying,
"Surely as I have planned, so shall it be;
And as I have purposed, so shall it stand—
25 That I will break Assyria in my land,
And will tread him down on my mountains;
Then his yoke shall move from off them,
And his burden shall move from off their shoulder.
26 This is the purpose that is formed
against all the earth;
And this is the hand that is stretched out
against all the nations.
27 For the LORD of hosts has formed a purpose;
then who can annul it?
And his hand is that which is stretched out;
then who can turn it back?"

THE FATE OF PHILISTIA, 14:28–32

In the year that king Ahaz died, 28
came this oracle:
"Rejoice not, O Philistia, all of you, 29
Because the rod that smote you is broken!
For out of the root of the snake shall come forth a viper,
And its fruit shall be a flying serpent.
The poor shall feed unmolested, 30
And the needy shall lie down in safety;
But your race will I kill by famine,
And your remnant will I slay.

"Wail, O gates; cry, O cities; 31
Melt with fear, O Philistia, all of you!
For out of the north comes the smoke of a war host,
With no straggler in its ranks.
What answer, then, shall one give 32
To the messengers of the nation?
'That the LORD has founded Zion,
And in her shall his afflicted people find refuge.' "

AN ORACLE ON MOAB, 15:1—16:14 15

Because in a night Ar-Moab
has been despoiled, has been ruined;
Because in a night Kir-Moab
has been despoiled, has been ruined—
The daughter of Dibon has scaled 2
the heights to weep;
On Nebo, and on Medeba,
Moab wails.
On every head is baldness,
every beard is shaved;
In their streets have they girded on sackcloth, 3
on their roofs is lamentation;
And in their squares does every one wail,
with tears running down.

Heshbon and Elealeh cry out, 4
As far as Jahaz their voice is heard;
Therefore the loins of Moab quiver,
The heart of him quivers.
My heart cries out for Moab, 5

As his fugitives press to Zoar, to the
third Eglath;
For up the ascent of Luhith weeping
they go,
And along the way to Horonaim the
cry of ruin they raise;
6 For the waters of Nimrim are a desolation,
The grass has withered, the herbage
has failed,
There is no green thing.

7 Therefore the gain that they acquired,
and that which they stored,
Over the Brook of the Willows they
carry away;
8 For the cry of distress has gone round
the border of Moab;
The wail of it reaches Eglaim, the wail
of it reaches Beer-elim;
9 For the waters of Dimon are full of
blood,
And I shall bring still more upon Dimon—
A lion for the survivors of Moab,
For the remnant of the land.

16 Then will the rulers of the land send
tribute of lambs,
From Selah, by way of the wilderness,
to the mount of the daughter of
Zion;
2 And like fluttering birds, like scattered
nestlings,
The daughters of Moab will gather at
the fords of the Arnon:
3 "Bring counsel, give decision;
Make your shade deep as night in the
height of noon!
Shelter the outcasts, betray not the
fugitives;
4 Let the outcasts of Moab sojourn
among you;
Be a shelter to them from the face of
the despoiler!"

When the oppressor has come to an
end, the despoiler has ceased,
The trampler-down has vanished out
of the land,
5 A throne will be established by kind-
ness,
And on it will sit in faithfulness,
In the tent of David,
A judge who seeks what is right,
And is swift to do justice.

6 We have heard of the pride of Moab,
how very proud he is—
Of his haughtiness and pride and insolence,
how baseless are his boastings!
Therefore Moab wails to Moab, 7
he wails altogether;
For the raisin-cakes of Kir-heres they
moan,
utterly stricken;
For the vineyards of Heshbon lan- 8
guish,
and the vine of Sibmah,
The red clusters of which laid prostrate
the lords of nations.
As far as Jazer they reached,
they strayed to the desert;
Her tendrils spread forth,
they passed over the sea.

Therefore I weep with Jazer 9
for the vine of Sibmah;
With my tears I drench you,
O Heshbon and Elealeh!
For the battle shout has fallen
on your fruits and on your harvest;
And joy and gladness vanish 10
out of the garden land;
No singing is heard in the vineyards,
no shout of joy is raised;
No grape-treader treads wine into the
vats,
the vintage-shout is stilled.
Therefore my bowels for Moab 11
moan like a harp,
And my heart for Kir-heres
wails like a flute.
And even though Moab appear and 12
weary himself with devotions on the
high place, or enter into his sanctuary
to pray, he will avail nothing.
This is the word that the LORD 13
spoke concerning Moab in days gone
by. But now the LORD has spoken, 14
saying,
"In three years, counting by the
years of a hireling, the glory of Moab
will be brought into contempt, in spite
of all its teeming multitude; and the
remnant will be very few and feeble."

AN ORACLE ON DAMASCUS, 17:1–11 17

"Lo! Damascus is removed from her
place among cities,
And will become a heap of ruins, deserted forever.
Her daughter-cities will be given over 2
to flocks,

Which will lie down in them, with none to make them afraid.
3 So the bulwark will be stripped from Ephraim,
And the sovereign power from Damascus;
And the remnant of Syria will perish—
They will be like the glory of the sons of Israel,"
Is the oracle of the LORD of hosts.

4 "It shall come to pass on that day,
That the glory of Jacob will wane,
And the fat of his flesh will grow lean;
5 It will be as when a reaper gathers the standing grain,
And his arm reaps the ears,
As when one gathers ears in the valley of Rephaim;
6 Or as when an olive tree is beaten, and gleanings are left on it,
Two or three berries on the uppermost branch,
Four or five on the boughs,"
Is the oracle of the LORD, the God of Israel.

7 On that day will a man look to his Maker,
And his eyes will turn to the Holy One of Israel;
8 He will look no more to the altars,
The work of his hands,
Nor turn to the sacred poles and incense altars,
Which his fingers have made.
9 On that day will your cities be deserted,
Like the deserted cities of the Amorites and Horites,
Which they deserted before the children of Israel,
And they will become a desolation.

10 Because you have forgotten the God of your salvation,
And have not been mindful of the Rock of your refuge,
Though you plant your gardens of Adonis,
And stock them with vine-slips of an alien god;
11 Though you make them grow on the day that you planted them,
And next morning bring your seedlings to blossom,
Yet the harvest will vanish on a day of sickness,
And incurable pain.

THE ROARING OF THE PEOPLES, 17:12–14

Ah! the roaring of many peoples, 12
That roar like the roaring of seas;
And the surging of nations, that surge
Like the surging of mighty waters!
The nations may surge like the surging of many waters, 13
But he will rebuke them, and they will flee far away,
And will be chased like chaff of the mountains before the wind,
Or like whirling dust before the hurricane.
At eventide, lo! terror; 14
Before morning, it is gone.
Such is the lot of those who despoil us,
And the fate of those who prey on us.

A MESSAGE TO ETHIOPIA, 18:1–7

Ah! land of the buzzing wings, 18
Which lies beyond the rivers of Ethiopia,
That sends ambassadors by sea, 2
In papyrus vessels on the face of the waters!
Go, you swift messengers,
To a nation tall and sleek,
To a people dreaded near and far,
A nation strong and triumphant,
Whose land the rivers divide!
All you inhabitants of the world, and you dwellers on earth, 3
When a signal is raised on the mountains, look!
When a trumpet is blown, hark!
For thus says the LORD to me: 4
"I will look on quietly in my dwelling-place,
Like shimmering heat in sunshine,
Like a cirrus cloud in the heat of harvest.
For before the harvest, when the blossom is over, 5
And the bud becomes a ripening grape,
The branches shall be lopped off with pruning-hooks,
And the tendrils shall be cut away;
They shall be left altogether to the mountain birds of prey, 6
And to the wild beasts of the land;
And the birds of prey shall summer upon them,
And all the wild beasts of the land shall winter upon them."

7 At that time shall a gift of homage be
brought to the LORD of hosts from a
people tall and sleek—from a people
dreaded near and far, a nation strong
and triumphant, whose land the rivers
divide—to Mount Zion, the place
where is the name of the LORD of hosts.

19 AN ORACLE ON EGYPT,
19:1–25

See! the LORD is riding on a swift
cloud,
And will come to Egypt;
And the idols of Egypt will quake before him,
And the heart of Egypt will melt within her.
2 "I will spur on Egypt against Egypt,
And they shall fight, brother against brother, and neighbor against neighbor,
City against city, and kingdom against kingdom.
3 And the spirit of Egypt shall be emptied out of her,
And her counsel will I confuse;
And they shall resort to idols and to mediums,
To ghosts and to spirits;
4 And I will hand over Egypt
To the power of a stern master;
And a ruthless king shall rule them,"
Is the oracle of the Lord, the LORD of hosts.

5 Then the waters will be drained from the sea,
And the river will be parched and dried up;
6 Its channels will become foul,
The Nile-arms of Egypt will dwindle and dry up;
Reed and rush will wither,
7 All the sedge-grass on the brink of the Nile will shrivel;
And all that is sown by the Nile
Will be dried up and driven into nothingness.
8 The fishermen also will mourn and lament,
Even all who cast hook in the Nile,
While those who spread nets on the water will languish.
9 The workers in flax will be put to shame—
The women who card and the men who weave cotton—
10 Her weavers will be crushed with grief,
All her workers for hire will be heartbroken.

11 Sheer fools are the princes of Zoan,
The wisest of Pharaoh's counselors are a senseless council;
How can you say to Pharaoh,
"A son of wise men am I, a son of ancient kings"?
12 Where, now, are your wise men,
That they may tell you,
And show what the LORD of hosts
Has planned against Egypt?
13 Befooled are the princes of Zoan,
Deluded are the princes of Memphis;
The cornerstones of her tribes have made Egypt reel.
14 The LORD has mingled within them a spirit of dizziness;
And they have made Egypt reel in all her work,
As a drunkard reels in his vomit;
15 And Egypt will have no work
Which head or tail can accomplish,
Palm-branch or reed.

On that day will Egypt be weak as a 16
woman, and she will tremble with dread
before the hand of the LORD of hosts,
which he will swing over her. And the 17
land of Judah will become a terror to
Egypt: whenever one mentions to her
the name of Judah, she will be filled
with dread because of the plan which
the LORD of hosts has formed against
her.
On that day there will be five cities 18
in the land of Egypt speaking the language of Canaan, and swearing allegiance to the LORD of hosts—the
name of one of them being "The city of
the sun."
On that day there will be an altar to 19
the LORD in the midst of the land of
Egypt, and a sacred pillar to the LORD
near its border. They will be a sign and 20
witness to the LORD of hosts in the
land of Egypt, so that when men cry to
the LORD because of oppressors, and
beseech him to send them a deliverer,
he will intervene and save them. And 21
the LORD will reveal himself to the
Egyptians, and the Egyptians will acknowledge the LORD on that day, and
will worship him with sacrifice and offering; they will also make vows to the
LORD, and will perform them. And 22

though the LORD may smite the Egyptians, he will smite only to heal; when they turn to the LORD, he will listen to their entreaties, and will heal them.
23 On that day there will be a highway from Egypt to Assyria; and the Assyrians will pass along it to Egypt, and the Egyptians to Assyria; and the Egyptians will worship the LORD along with the Assyrians.
24 On that day Israel will be a third
with Egypt and Assyria as a blessing in
25 the midst of the earth, which the LORD of hosts has blessed in these terms, "Blessed be Egypt my people, and Assyria the work of my hands, and Israel my heritage!"

THE SIGN OF THE CAPTIVITY OF EGYPT AND ETHIOPIA, 20:1–6

20 In the year that the commander-in-chief came to Ashdod, when he was sent by Sargon, king of Assyria, and fought against Ashdod, and took it
2 (now at that time the LORD had commanded Isaiah, the son of Amoz, saying, "Go and untie the sackcloth from your loins, and put off your sandals from your feet," and he had done so,
3 going naked and barefoot), the LORD said, "As my servant Isaiah has gone for three years naked and barefoot, as a sign and symbol against Egypt and
4 Ethiopia, so will the king of Assyria lead off the captives of Egypt and the exiles of Ethiopia, young and old, naked and barefoot, with buttocks uncovered,
5 to the shame of Egypt. Then men will be dismayed and put to shame because of Ethiopia their hope and Egypt their
6 pride. And the inhabitants of this coast-land will say on that day, 'See! this is the fate of those on whom we set our hope, and to whom we fled for help to save us from the king of Assyria; how then can we escape?' "

21 AN ORACLE ON THE DESERT OF THE SEA, 21:1–10

Like whirlwinds as they sweep through the Negeb,
It comes from the desert, from a terrible land.
2 A stern vision has been shown to me:
The robber robs, and the plunderer plunders.
"Go up, O Elam; lay siege, O Media!
All her groaning I bring to an end."
Therefore my loins are filled with anguish; 3
Pangs have seized me like those of a woman in travail.

I am tortured so that I cannot hear,
I am terror-stricken so that I cannot see.
My mind reels, shuddering assails me; 4
The twilight I delight in has been turned for me into trembling.
They lay out the tables, they spread the mats; 5
They eat, they drink.

"Arise, O princes, anoint the shields!"
For thus has the LORD spoken to me: 6
"Go, station the watchman,
Let him tell what he sees!
If he sees a troop, horsemen in pairs, 7
A troop of asses, a troop of camels,
Let him pay close heed, very close heed!"

Then he cried, 8
"Alas! on my watch-tower, O Lord,
I stand continually by day;
And at my guard-post I am stationed
Night after night."
When lo! there came a troop of men, 9
Horsemen in pairs.
Then he resumed and said,
"Fallen, fallen is Babylon;
And all the images of her gods are shattered to the earth."

O my threshed one, my child of the threshing-floor! 10
What I have heard from the LORD of hosts,
The God of Israel, I have made known to you.

AN ORACLE ON DUMAH, 21:11–12 11

Someone is calling to me from Seir:
"Watchman, what hour of the night is it?
Watchman, what hour of the night is it?"
The watchman says: 12
"Morning comes, but also night;
If you wish to know more, come again."

13 AN ORACLE, "IN THE ARABIAN DESERT," 21:13–17

Among the thickets in the Arabian
desert must you lodge,
O caravans of Dedanites!
14 Bring water to meet the thirsty,
Welcome the fugitives with bread,
O inhabitants of the land of Tema!
15 For before the sword they have fled,
Before the drawn sword;
And before the bent bow,
Before the stern press of battle.

16 For the LORD has said to me:
"In one more year, counting by the
years of a hireling, all the glory of
17 Kedar will come to an end; and the
number that is left of the warlike
archers of the sons of Kedar will be
few." For the LORD, the God of Israel,
has spoken.

22 AN ORACLE ON THE VALLEY OF VISION, 22:1–14

What is the matter with you, now,
that you have gone up,
all of you to the housetops,
2 You who are full of shoutings, a city
tumultuous,
a frenzied town?
Your slain are not slain by the sword,
nor dead in battle.
3 All your leaders fled together,
but were caught by the bowmen;
All your strong men were caught together,
though they fled afar.
4 Therefore I say, "Look away from me,
bitter tears let me shed;
Strive not to comfort me
for the ruin of the daughter of
my people!"
5 For a day of tumult and trampling and
confusion
has the Lord, the GOD of hosts,
In the Valley of Vision—a crashing of
walls,
and a cry to the mountains.

6 Elam took up the quiver,
Aram came riding on horses,
And Kir uncovered the shield.
7 Your choicest valleys were filled with
chariots,
And horsemen set themselves in array
against the gates,
And the defenses of Judah were laid 8
bare.
On that day you looked to the
weapons of war in the House of the
Forest, and paid attention to the many 9
breaches in the City of David; and you
collected the waters of the lower pool.
You also counted the houses of Jeru- 10
salem, and broke down a number of
them to fortify the walls; and you made 11
a reservoir between the two walls for
the waters of the old pool. But you
looked not to him who brought it about,
nor paid attention to him who planned
it long ago.

The Lord, the LORD of hosts, called 12
on that day
For weeping and wailing, for baldness
and girding with sackcloth;
But lo! joy and gladness, 13
Slaying cattle and killing sheep,
Eating flesh and drinking wine—
Eating and drinking, "for tomorrow
we may die."
But the LORD of hosts has revealed 14
himself in my hearing:
"Surely this guilt shall not be expiated
by you until you die!"
Says the Lord, the GOD of hosts.

SHEBNA AND ELIAKIM, 22:15–25

Thus says the Lord, the GOD of hosts: 15
"Come! go and say to this steward,
To Shebna, who is over the palace,
'What have you here, and whom have 16
you here,
That you have hewn a tomb for your-
self here,
Hewing your tomb on the height,
And carving for yourself a home on
the rock?
See! the LORD will toss you away, O 17
mighty man—
Gripping you fast,
And spinning you round and round— 18
Like a ball into a spacious land.
There shall you die,
And there shall your splendid chariots
go,
You disgrace of your master's house!'

"I will thrust you from your post, 19
And will pull you down from your
station.
And on that day will I call for my 20
servant,

Eliakim, the son of Hilkiah;
21 And I will invest him with your robe,
And will gird him with your sash;
And I will hand over your authority
to him,
And he shall become a father to the
inhabitants of Jerusalem
And to the house of Judah;
22 And I will place the key of the House
of David upon his shoulder,
And he shall open and no man shut,
And shall shut and no man open;
23 And I will fasten him like a peg in a
firm place,
And he shall become a throne of honor
to his father's house;
24 And they shall hang upon him the
whole weight of his father's house,
The offshoots and the offscourings,
even the meanest vessels,
Both bowls and pitchers of every
kind."
25 "On that day," is the oracle of the
LORD of hosts, "the peg that was fastened in a firm place shall give way and
be hewn down and fall, and the weight
that was upon it shall be cut off." For
the LORD has spoken.

23 AN ORACLE ON TYRE, 23:1-18

Wail, O ships of Tarshish!
for your stronghold has been
despoiled—
On their way from the land of Cyprus
the news was told to them—
2 Perished are the inhabitants of the
coast-land,
the merchants of Sidon,
Who traversed the sea, whose business
lay
3 on many waters,
Whose harvest was grain from the
Nile,
whose revenue was trade with
the nations.
4 Lament in shame, O Sidon, mother of
cities,
stronghold of the sea, saying,
"I am as one who has not travailed nor
given birth to children,
I am as one who has reared no young
men
nor brought up maidens."
5 [When the news reaches Egypt, the
news of Tyre,
they will writhe in pain.]

Pass over to Tarshish, wail, 6
you inhabitants of the coast-
land!
Is this your exultant city, 7
whose origin is of old,
Whose feet used to carry her
to settle afar?
Who has planned such a thing 8
against Tyre the crown-giver,
Whose merchants were princes,
whose traders were the honored
of the earth?
The LORD of hosts has planned it, 9
to desecrate all the pride,
To dishonor all the glory
of the honored of the earth.

Overflow your land like the Nile, O 10
daughter of Tarshish!
there is no more a barrier.
His hand has he stretched out over the 11
sea,
he has shaken the kingdoms;
The LORD has given a command
touching Canaan,
to destroy her strongholds.
He has said, "You shall no more exult, 12
O ravished one, virgin daugh-
ter of Sidon!
Arise, pass over to Cyprus;
even there shall you find no rest."
[It was, however, the Chaldeans, 13
and not the Assyrians, who gave her
over to the desert demons. They set up
their siegeworks, they razed her palaces, they made her a ruin.]
Wail, O ships of Tarshish! 14
for your stronghold has been
despoiled.
On that day will Tyre pass into ob- 15
livion for seventy years, like the days of
a certain king; but at the end of seventy
years will Tyre fare like the harlot in
the song:
"Take a harp, go round the city, 16
O harlot forgotten!
Play well, sing many a song,
that you may be remembered!"
For at the end of seventy years will 17
the LORD visit Tyre, and she will return to her hire, and will play the harlot
with all the kingdoms of the world on
the face of the earth. But her gain from 18
her hire will then be dedicated to the
LORD; it will not be stored up or
hoarded, but will be given over to those
who dwell in the presence of the LORD,
to supply them with abundant food and
stately clothing.

A VISION OF JUDGMENT, 24:1—27:13

24 See! the LORD is about to strip the earth, and lay it waste,
Its surface he will distort, and its inhabitants he will disperse;
2 Priest will share the fate of people, master of servant,
Mistress of maid, seller of buyer,
Borrower of lender, creditor of debtor.
3 The earth will be stripped bare,
The world will be plundered bare,
For the LORD has spoken this word.
4 The earth mourns, fades,
The world languishes, fades;
The high heavens languish with the earth.
5 The earth is polluted through the touch of its inhabitants,
Because they have transgressed laws, violated statutes,
Broken the everlasting covenant.
6 Therefore a curse has devoured the earth,
And its inhabitants have paid the penalty;
Therefore the inhabitants of the earth waste away,
And few are the mortals that are left.

7 The wine mourns, the vine languishes;
All the merry-hearted sigh.
8 The mirth of the timbrels is still,
The noise of the joyful has ceased,
The mirth of the harp is still.
9 With song will they no more drink wine;
Strong drink will be bitter to those who drink it.
10 Broken down is the city of chaos;
Every house is shut up, so that no one can enter;
11 In the streets there is outcry for wine.
All joy has reached its eventide,
The mirth of the world has gone;
12 Desolation is left in the city,
And its gates are battered to ruins.
13 For so will it be in the midst of the earth,
Among the peoples,
As when an olive tree is beaten, or at the gleaning of grapes,
When the vintage is over.
14 Yonder, men lift up their voice, they sing for joy,
At the majesty of the LORD they shout more loudly than the sea:

"Therefore glorify the LORD throughout the east, 15
On the coast-lands of the sea praise the name of the LORD,
The God of Israel!"
From the end of the earth have we heard songs of praise: 16
"Glory for the righteous!"
But I said, "I pine away;
I pine away. Woe is me!
The robbers rob,
The robbers run riot in robbery."

Terror and pit and snare 17
Are upon you, O inhabitants of the earth!
And he who flees from the noise of the terror 18
Will fall into the pit;
And he who escapes from the midst of the pit
Will be caught in the snare;
For windows on high are opened,
And the foundations of the earth tremble.
The earth breaks asunder, 19
The earth cracks asunder,
The earth shakes asunder;
The earth reels like a drunkard, 20
And sways like a hammock;
Its rebellion lies heavily upon it,
And it will fall, to rise no more.

It shall come to pass on that day, 21
That the LORD will punish
The host of the heights on high,
And the kings of the earth on the earth;
They will be gathered together like prisoners in a dungeon, 22
And will be imprisoned in a prison,
Until after many days they are punished.
Then will the moon turn pale with confusion, 23
And the sun will hide in shame;
For the LORD of hosts will be king on Mount Zion,
And will reveal his glory before his elders in Jeursalem.

O LORD, thou art my God, 25
I will exalt thee, I will give thanks to thy name;
For thou hast accomplished wonders—
Plans formed long ago, fulfilled in per fect faithfulness.
For thou has made of a city a heap, 2

Of a fortified town a ruin;
The stronghold of the proud is a city no more,
It will never more be rebuilt.
3 Therefore will barbarous peoples honor thee,
The cities of ruthless nations will reverence thee;
4 For thou hast been a stronghold to the weak,
A stronghold to the needy in his distress,
A refuge from the storm, a shade from the heat,
When the breath of the ruthless is like a storm in winter,
5 Like heat in a dry place, heat in the shade of a cloud.
The noise of the proud thou quellest,
The song of the ruthless thou stillest.

6 Then the LORD of hosts will prepare,
On this mountain for all the peoples,
A feast of fat things, a feast of wine on the lees,
Of fat things full of marrow, of wine on the lees well refined.
7 And he will destroy on this mountain
The veil that veils all the peoples,
And the web that is woven over all the nations;
8 He will destroy death forever.
So the Lord GOD will wipe away tears
From every face,
And will remove from all the earth
The reproach that lies on his people;
For the LORD has spoken.

9 And it will be said on that day,
"Lo! this is our God,
For whom we waited that he might save us;
This is the LORD for whom we waited;
Let us rejoice and be glad in his salvation!"
10 For the hand of the LORD will rest on this mountain,
But Moab will be trampled down where he stands,
As straw is trampled down in the water of a dung-pit;
11 And though he spread out his hands in the midst of it,
As a swimmer spreads out his hands to swim,
His pride will be laid low despite all the tricks of his hands.
12 The high fortress of his walls will be brought down,
Laid low, leveled to the earth, even to the dust.

On that day will this song be sung in the land of Judah: 26
"A strong city is ours; for safety he sets up
Walls and bulwarks.
Open the gates, that the righteous nation may enter— 2
Those who keep faith.
The steadfast mind thou keepest in perfect peace, 3
For it trusts in thee.
Trust in the LORD forever! for Yah the LORD 4
Is a rock everlasting.
For he has brought down the dwellers on high, 5
The lofty city.
He lays it low, lays it low to the earth,
He levels it to the dust.
The foot will trample it, the feet of the poor, 6
The steps of the needy."
The path of the upright is even, 7
The track of the righteous thou levelest;
In the path of thy judgments, O LORD, we have waited for thee; 8
Our heart's desire is for thy name and thy memorial.
I have yearned for thee in the night, 9
With all my heart I seek thee;
For when thy judgments come down to the earth,
The inhabitants of the world learn righteousness.
Though favor be shown to the wicked, 10
Yet will he not learn righteousness;
Even in the land of uprightness will he deal wrongfully,
And will not see the majesty of the LORD.

O LORD, thy hand is uplifted, but they see it not; 11
Now let them see to their shame thy zeal for thy people—
Let fire consume thine enemies!
O LORD, establish peace for us; 12
Since all our works thou hast wrought for us.
O LORD our God, other lords than thou have been our lords; 13
But thy name alone will we celebrate.
Dead men do not live, the Shades do not rise— 14

So hast thou visited them with destruction,
And wiped out all remembrance of them—
15 But the nation hast thou increased, O LORD,
The nation hast thou increased, and hast shown forth thy glory;
Thou hast enlarged all the bounds of the land.

16 In distress, O LORD, we sought thee;
We cried out because of oppression, when thy chastening was on us.
17 Like a woman with child, as she draws near to give birth,
As she writhes and cries out in her pangs,
So were we in thy presence, O LORD;
18 We were with child, we writhed in pain,
But we gave birth only to wind;
No deliverance did we achieve for the land,
No inhabitants of the world came to birth through us.
19 But thy dead will live, their bodies will rise,
Those who dwell in the dust will awake, and will sing for joy;
For thy dew is a dew of light,
And the earth will bring the Shades to birth.

20 Go, my people, enter your chambers,
And shut your doors behind you;
Hide yourselves for a little while,
Till the time of wrath go by.
21 For see! the LORD is coming out of his place,
To punish the inhabitants of the world for their guilt;
And the earth will uncover her blood,
And will no more conceal her slain.
27 On that day will the LORD punish,
With his sword which is hard and great and strong,
Leviathan the fleeing serpent, Leviathan the coiled serpent;
And he will slay the dragon that is in the sea.

2 On that day will it be said:
"A vineyard of delight—sing you of it!
3 I the LORD am its keeper,
Every moment I water it;
Lest anyone harm it,
I guard it night and day.
Wrath have I none; 4
But should I find briers and thorns,
In war would I march against them,
I would burn them altogether;
Or else let them cast themselves on my protection, 5
And make peace with me, make peace with me!"

On that day will Jacob take root, 6
Israel will blossom and bud;
And they will fill the face of the earth with fruit.

Has he smitten them as he smote those who smote them; 7
Or have they been slain like those who slew them?
By expulsion and exile did he proceed against them; 8
By his rough blast he swept them away on the day of the east wind.
Therefore on this condition may the guilt of Jacob be expiated— 9
This is all the return he expects for taking away their sin—
That they make all their altar stones like pounded chalkstones,
That their sacred poles and incense altars raise their heads no more.
For the fortified city is desolate,
A homestead forlorn and forsaken like the steppe; 10
There browses the calf,
There he lies down, and crops its branches;
And when its boughs are withered, they are broken off, 11
And women come, and make a fire of them.
For this is a people without understanding;
Therefore their Maker will show them no pity,
Their Creator will show them no favor.

On that day will the LORD thresh out the ears of grain, 12
From the River Euphrates to the River of Egypt;
And you will be picked up one by one,
O children of Israel!

On that day will a blast be blown on a great trumpet; 13
And those who were lost in the land of Assyria,

And those who were outcasts in the land of Egypt,
Will come and worship the LORD
On the holy mountain in Jerusalem.

THE FATE OF SAMARIA, 28:1–6

28 Woe to the proud crown of the drunkards of Ephraim,
And the fading flower of his glorious beauty,
That rests on the heads of those overcome with wine!
2 See! the LORD has one who is mighty and strong,
One like a storm of hail, or a destroying tempest,
Like a storm of mighty, overwhelming waters,
That beats down to the earth with violence.
3 And the proud crown of the drunkards of Ephraim
Will be trampled under foot;
4 And the fading flower of his glorious beauty,
That rests on the head of a fertile valley,
Will be like the early fig before summer,
Which, as soon as a man sees it,
While it is still in his hand, he swallows.

5 On that day will the LORD of hosts be a beautiful crown
And a glorious diadem to the remnant of his people—
6 A spirit of justice to those who preside over justice,
And of might to those who turn back the tide of battle to the gate.

A WARNING TO JUDAH, 28:7–22

7 But these also reel with wine,
And stagger with strong drink;
Priests and prophets reel with strong drink,
They are dazed with wine;
They stagger with strong drink, they reel amid their visions,
They stumble while giving judgment;
8 For all tables are full of filthy vomit,
No place is clean.

9 "To whom would he impart knowledge,
To whom explain the message?
Babes just weaned from the milk,
Just drawn from the breasts?
10 For it is rule by rule, rule by rule,
Line by line, line by line,
A little here, a little there!"

11 Yea, through barbaric lips,
And an alien tongue,
Will he speak to this people,
12 Who said to them,
"This is the rest you shall give to the weary,
And this the repose";
But they would not listen.
13 So the word of the LORD will be to them
Rule by rule, rule by rule,
Line by line, line by line,
A little here, a little there—
That when they go on their way, they may stumble backward,
And be broken, and snared, and taken.

14 Therefore hear the word of the LORD,
You scoffing men,
You satirists among this people
Who are in Jerusalem!
15 Because you say,
"We have struck a covenant with Death,
And have formed a compact with Sheol;
So, when the overwhelming scourge passes,
It will not reach us;
For lies have we made our refuge,
And under falsehood have we hidden"—
16 Therefore thus says the Lord GOD,
"Behold, I lay in Zion a stone,
A well-tested stone,
A precious stone, as the cornerstone of a sure foundation—
He who believes shall not be worried.
17 And I will make justice the measuring-line,
And righteousness the plummet."

Then hail will sweep away the refuge of lies,
And water will overwhelm the hiding-place;
18 Your covenant with Death will be annulled,
And your compact with Sheol will not stand.
When the overwhelming scourge passes,
You will be battered down by it;
19 As often as it passes, it will bear you away;

For morning by morning will it pass,
Both day and night;
And sheer terror will it be
To understand the message.
20 For the bed is too short to stretch one's self in,
And the covering is too narrow to wrap one's self in.
21 For the LORD will rise up as on Mount Perazim,
He will blaze out in wrath as in the valley of Gibeon,
To do his deed—strange is his deed!—
And to work his work—alien is his work!
22 Now, therefore, scoff no more,
Lest your bands be made firm;
For a sentence of doom, complete and decisive,
Have I heard from the Lord, the LORD of hosts,
Against all the land.

PLOWING AND THRESHING, 28:23–29

23 Give ear, and hear my voice;
Attend, and hear my speech!
24 Does the plowman keep plowing all the time,
Is he forever opening and harrowing his ground?
25 Does he not, after leveling its surface,
Scatter dill, and sow cummin,
And put in wheat and barley,
With spelt as their border?
26 For his God instructs and teaches him aright.
27 Dill is not threshed with a threshing-sledge,
Nor is the wagon-wheel turned on cummin;
But dill is beaten with a staff,
And cummin with a flail.
28 Is wheat crushed?
No! one does not thresh it forever,
But when he has rolled his wagon-wheel over it,
He spreads it out, and does not crush it.
29 This also comes from the LORD of hosts,
Whose counsel is wonderful, whose wisdom is great.

THE FATE OF ARIEL, 29:1–8

29 Woe to you, Ariel, Ariel,
The city against which David encamped!
Add year to year,
Let the cycle of festivals go round!
Then will I bring distress upon Ariel 2
[Altar-hearth],
And there shall be moaning and bemoaning,
And she shall be to me like an altar-hearth.
I will encamp against you round about, 3
And will hem you in with siegeworks,
And will set up forts against you.
Then low from the earth shall you 4
speak,
Deep from the dust shall your words come;
Like the voice of a ghost from the earth shall be your voice,
From the dust shall your words rise twittering.

But the horde of your enemies shall be- 5
come like fine dust,
The horde of the ruthless like passing chaff.
In an instant, suddenly,
From the LORD of hosts shall you be 6
visited
With thunder and earthquake and mighty noise,
With whirlwind and tempest and flame of devouring fire.
And all the horde of nations that war 7
against Ariel,
With all their siegeworks and forts and storming parties,
Shall be like a dream, a vision of the night.
As when a hungry man dreams that he 8
is eating,
And awakes with his craving unsatisfied;
Or when a thirsty man dreams that he is drinking,
And awakes faint, with his craving unquenched;
So shall it be with all the horde of nations,
That war against Mount Zion.

SPIRITUAL BLINDNESS AND PERVERSITY, 29:9–16

Daze yourselves, and be dazed, 9
Blind yourselves, and be blind,
You who are drunk, though not with wine,
You who reel, though not with strong drink!

10 For the LORD has poured upon you a
spirit of deep slumber,
He has tightly closed your eyes, and
has muffled your heads;
11 so that the revelation of all these things
has become to you like the words of a
scroll that is sealed, which if one hand
to a scholar with the request, "Pray
read this," he will say, "I cannot, for it
12 is sealed"; or if the scroll be handed to
one who is not a scholar, with the request, "Pray read this," he will say,
"I am not a scholar."

13 The LORD says:
"Because this people draw near me
with their mouth,
And honor me with their lips,
While their thoughts are far from me,
And their reverence for me is an injunction of men,
That is learned by rote,
14 Therefore, behold, I will once more
deal with this people
In a wonderful way,
In a wonderful and wondrous way,
And the wisdom of their wise men
shall perish,
And the intelligence of their intelligent men shall vanish."

15 Woe to them who make their plans
deep,
to hide them from the LORD,
Whose works are done in the dark,
and who say,
"Who sees us? Who knows us?"
16 O the perversity of you!
Is the potter of no more account than
the clay?
Shall the thing that is made say of its
maker,
"He made me not";
Or the thing that is molded say of its
molder,
"He has no intelligence?"

THE REDEMPTION OF ISRAEL, 29:17-24

17 Is there not still but a little while
Before Lebanon shall be turned into
garden land,
And the garden land be counted a
forest?
18 And on that day shall the deaf hear
the words of a book,
And out of gloom and darkness shall
the eyes of the blind see;
And the humble shall find new joy in 19
the LORD,
And the poorest shall exult in the
Holy One of Israel.
For the tyrant shall have vanished, 20
and the scoffer shall have ceased,
And all who are on the outlook for
evil shall have been cut off—
Those who bring condemnation upon 21
a man by a word,
Those who lay traps for the upholder
of justice at the gate,
And those who thrust aside the innocent on an empty plea.

Therefore thus says the LORD, 22
The God of the house of Jacob,
Who redeemed Abraham:
"Jacob shall never more be put to
shame,
And never more shall his face grow
pale;
For when his children see what my 23
hands have done in their midst,
They shall reverence my name;
They shall reverence the Holy One of
Jacob,
And shall stand in awe of the God of
Israel;
Those who have erred in judgment 24
shall arrive at understanding,
And those who murmured shall learn
instruction."

DENUNCIATION OF THE EGYPTIAN ALLIANCE, 30:1-5

"Woe to you rebellious children," is the 30
oracle of the LORD,
"Who carry out a purpose that comes
not from me,
And who form an alliance that is not
according to my mind—
Adding sin to sin—
Who set out on the way to Egypt, 2
Without asking my advice,
To take refuge in the protection of
Pharaoh,
And to take shelter in the shadow of
Egypt!
Therefore the protection you seek in 3
Pharaoh shall turn to your shame,
And the shelter you seek in the shadow of Egypt to your confusion.
For though his princes be at Zoan, 4

And his messengers arrive at Hanes,
5 All shall come to shame through a people that cannot benefit them,
That bring no help or benefit,
But only shame and disgrace."

6 AN ORACLE ON THE BEASTS OF THE NEGEB, 30:6–7

Through a land of trouble and anguish,
Of lioness and roaring lion,
Of viper and flying serpent,
They carry their wealth on the shoulders of young asses,
Their treasures on the humps of camels,
To a people that cannot benefit—
7 To Egypt, whose help is empty and vain,
Wherefore I have called her "Rahab Sit-still."

REBELLION AND RUIN, 30:8–17

8 Go now, write it on a tablet before them,
Inscribe it on a scroll,
That it may serve in days to come
As a witness forever;
9 For this is a rebellious people,
Faithless children,
Children who will not hear
The instruction of the LORD—
10 Who say to the seers, "You shall not see!"
And to the prophets, "You shall not prophesy to us right things!
Speak to us smooth things; prophesy delusions!
11 Get you out of the way; turn aside from the path!
Trouble us no more with the Holy One of Israel!"

12 Therefore thus says the Holy One of Israel:
"Because you have spurned this word,
And have trusted in cunning and crookedness,
And rely on them;
13 Therefore this guilt shall be to you like a descending rift,
Bulging out in a lofty wall,
Whose crash comes suddenly, in a moment,
14 Whose crash is like that of a potter's vessel,
Shattered beyond repair,
So that there cannot be found among the fragments a sherd,
To bring fire from the hearth,
Or to draw water from the cistern."

For thus said the Lord GOD, 15
The Holy One of Israel:
"By returning and resting shall you be saved,
In quietness and confidence shall be your strength."
But you refused to listen, and said, 16
"No! upon horses will we flee,"
Therefore you shall flee!
"And upon swift steeds will we ride,"
Therefore swift shall be your pursuers!
At the challenge of one a thousand shall flee, 17
At the challenge of five you shall flee,
Till you are left like a flagstaff on the top of a mountain,
Like a beacon on a hill.

FORGIVENESS AND PROSPERITY, 30:18–26

Therefore the LORD waits to be gracious to you, 18
And therefore he will arise to have pity upon you;
For the LORD is a God of justice—
Happy are all those who wait for him!
O people in Zion, who dwell at Jerusalem, 19
No more will you weep;
He will be gracious to you at the sound of your crying;
As soon as he hears, he will answer you.
Even though the LORD may have given you 20
Bread in short measure and water in scanty allowance,
Your Teacher will no more hide himself,
But your eyes will behold your Teacher.
And when you turn to right or to left, 21
Your ears will hear a voice behind you, saying,
"This is the way; walk in it!"
And you will defile your carved images overlaid with silver, 22
And your molten images plated with gold;
You will scatter them to the winds like an unclean thing,

You will say to them, "Begone!"
23 Then will he give you rain for your seed,
With which you sow the soil,
And wheat as the produce of the soil,
Which will be rich and nourishing.
On that day will your cattle graze in broad pastures,
24 And the oxen and young asses that till the soil
Will feed on salted fodder,
Which has been winnowed with shovel and fork.
25 And on every lofty mountain and on every high hill
There will be streams brimming with water,
On the day of the great slaughter,
When the towers fall.
26 And the light of the moon will be as the light of the sun,
And the light of the sun will be sevenfold,
As the light of seven days,
On the day when the LORD binds up the bruises of his people,
And heals the wounds with which they were smitten.

THE GLORIOUS TRIUMPH OF THE LORD, 30:27–33

27 See! the LORD comes from afar,
In blazing anger, and amid heavily rising banks of cloud,
His lips filled with fury,
And his tongue like devouring fire,
28 His breath like a sweeping torrent,
That reaches to the neck—
To sift the nations with the sieve of destruction,
And to place in the jaws of the peoples
A bridle that leads them to ruin.
29 But for you will there be a song,
As in the night when a sacred festival is held,
And gladness of heart, as when one sets out with a flute,
To go to the mount of the LORD, to the Rock of Israel.
30 For the LORD will cause his glorious voice to be heard,
And the descent of his arm to be seen,
In furious anger, and flame of devouring fire,
Amid cloud-burst, and rain-storm, and hail.
31 Assyria will be stricken with terror at the voice of the LORD,
When he smites with the rod;
And every stroke of the rod of chastisement, 32
Which the LORD lays upon them,
Will be accompanied by the strains of timbrel and harp,
As he assails them with brandished arm.
For a pyre is already laid out, 33
For the king it is prepared;
It is made both deep and wide;
It is piled up with fire and logs in abundance;
And the breath of the LORD, like a torrent of brimstone,
Is setting it on fire.

THE FOLLY OF RELIANCE ON EGYPT, 31:1–3

Woe to those who go down to Egypt for help, 31
And rely on horses;
Those who trust in chariots, because they are many,
And in horsemen, because they are very numerous;
But look not to the Holy One of Israel,
Nor consult the LORD!
Yet he is the wise one, and brings calamity, 2
And does not recall his words.
He will rise against the house of those who do evil,
And against the helpers of those who work mischief.
Now the Egyptians are men, and not God; 3
And their horses are flesh, and not spirit.
So, when the LORD stretches out his hand,
The helper will stumble, and the helped one will fall;
They will all of them perish together.

THE SALVATION OF JERUSALEM, 31:4–5

Thus says the LORD to me: 4
"As a lion or a young lion growls over his prey—
And, though a full band of shepherds be called out against him,
Is not dismayed at their shouting, nor pays any heed to their noise—
So will the LORD of hosts come down
To fight against Mount Zion, and against its hill.

5 Like hovering birds . . . .
[So will the LORD of hosts protect Jerusalem,
Protecting and delivering, sparing and saving]."

THE DOWNFALL OF ASSYRIA, 31:6–9

6 Return, O children of Israel,
To him against whom you have plunged deep in revolt!
7 For on that day each of you will cast away in contempt
The idols of silver and the idols of gold,
Which your hands made for yourselves as a sin.
8 Then Assyria will fall by the sword, not of man;
A sword, not of men, will devour him.
He will flee before the sword,
And his young men will be put to hard labor;
9 The rock of his strength will slip away through terror,
And his officers will desert the standard in panic.
This is the oracle of the LORD, whose fire is in Zion,
And whose furnace is in Jerusalem.

THE KINGDOM OF RIGHTEOUSNESS, 32:1–8

32 Behold! a king will reign in righteousness,
And princes will rule with justice;
2 And each of them will be like a hiding-place from the wind,
And a shelter from the storm,
Like streams of water in a dry place,
Like the shade of a great rock in a wearisome land.
3 Then the eyes of those who see will not be closed,
And the ears of those who hear will be attentive;
4 The mind of the hasty will have knowledge to apprehend,
And the tongue of the stammering will be quick to speak plainly.

5 No more will the fool be called noble,
Nor the knave be counted princely.
6 For the fool will speak folly,
And his mind will plot mischief,
So as to practice ungodliness,
And to utter falsehood regarding the LORD,
To leave the hungry unsatisfied,
And to hold back drink from the thirsty.
The arts also of the knave are evil; 7
He hatches plans
To ruin the needy with lying words,
Even when the poor man's plea is right.
But the noble man plans noble things, 8
And on noble things he takes his stand.

THE THOUGHTLESS WOMEN OF JERUSALEM, 32:9–14

You thoughtless women, rise up, hear my voice; 9
You complacent daughters, give ear to my words!
In little more than a year you will tremble, you complacent ones; 10
For the vintage will fail, the ingathering will not come.
Quake with fear, you thoughtless ones; 11
tremble, you complacent ones;
Strip, and make yourselves bare; gird sackcloth upon your loins!
Beat upon your breasts for the pleasant fields, 12
For the fruitful vines;
For the soil of my people, that will spring up with thorns and briers, 13
And for all the houses of mirth in the joyous city!
For the palace will be forsaken, the bustling city deserted; 14
Rampart and watchtower will become dens forever,
A joy of wild asses, a pasture of flocks.

RIGHTEOUSNESS AND PEACE, 32:15–20

Until the spirit be poured upon us from on high; 15
Then will the steppe become garden land,
And the garden land be counted an orchard.
And justice will dwell in the steppe, 16
And righteousness abide in the garden land;
And the effect of righteousness will be peace, 17
And the product of justice quietness and confidence forever.
My people will dwell in peaceful homes, 18
In secure abodes, and in quiet resting-places,

19 Even when the forest comes down with a crash,
And the city is laid in ruins.
20 Happy are you who sow beside all waters,
And let out freely the ox and the ass!

DISTRESS AND DELIVERANCE, 33:1–24

33 Woe to you despoiler, though you have not been despoiled;
And robber, though none has robbed you!
When you have made an end of despoiling, you will be despoiled;
And when you are weary of robbing, you will be robbed.

2 O LORD, be gracious to us!
We have waited for thee.
Be our arm of strength every morning,
Our salvation in time of distress!

3 At the sound of tumult the peoples flee,
When thou liftest thyself up the nations are scattered;
4 And thy people will gather the spoil as the locust gathers,
They will swarm upon it as grasshoppers swarm.

5 The LORD is exalted, for he dwells on high;
Zion he has filled with justice and righteousness—
6 Her fortune therefore will be secure—
With wealth of salvation, wisdom and knowledge,
With reverence for the LORD, which is her treasure.

7 Lo! the heroes of Ariel cry without,
The ambassadors of peace weep bitterly;
8 The highways lie waste, the travelers have ceased,
For the covenant has been broken, its witnesses have been mocked at;
No regard has been paid to man.
9 The earth languishes in mourning,
Lebanon withers in shame;
Sharon has become like the wilderness,
Bashan and Carmel are leafless.

10 "Now will I arise," says the LORD;
"Now will I mount on high, now will I lift myself up!
You are pregnant with chaff, you shall bring forth stubble; 11
Your breath is a fire that shall devour you.
And the peoples shall be like brands that are burned to a cinder, 12
Like thorns cut down, that are kindled with fire."

Hear what I have done, you who are afar; 13
And acknowledge my might, you who are near at hand!
The sinners in Zion are filled with dread; 14
Trembling has seized the godless:
"Who among us shall dwell with devouring fire,
Who among us shall dwell with eternal flames?"
He who walks uprightly, and speaks sincerely, 15
Who scorns the gain that is won by oppression,
Who keeps his hand free from the touch of a bribe,
Who stops his ears against hearing of bloodshed,
And closes his eyes against looking on evil—
He will dwell on the heights, 16
His stronghold will be rocky fastnesses;
His bread will be given to him, his water will be sure.

Your eyes will behold the King in his beauty, 17
They will see a land that stretches afar.
You will muse on the terror that is past: 18
"Where is he who counted, where is he who weighed,
Where is he who marked down the towers?"
You will see no more the savage people, 19
The people of obscure speech, which you cannot grasp,
Of barbaric tongue, which you cannot understand.
You will behold Zion, the city of our festal assemblies; 20
Your eyes will see Jerusalem,
A quiet home, an immovable tent,
Whose pegs will never be plucked up,
And none of whose cords will be snapped.

21 For there, in place of broad rivers and streams,
We shall have the River of the LORD,
On which no ship with oars will go,
No stately bark will pass.
22 For the LORD is our judge, the LORD our commander;
The LORD is our king, he will save us.
23 [Your tacklings hang loose: they
cannot hold the mast in its socket, nor
keep the sail spread out.]
Then will the blind share spoil in abundance,
And the lame will seize rich prey;
24 None who dwells there will say, "I am sick,"
For all her citizens will have had their sins forgiven.

THE DAY OF VENGEANCE, 34:1–17

34 You nations, draw near to listen;
You peoples, attend!
Let the earth hear, and that which fills it;
The world, and all that springs from it!
2 For the LORD is in anger against all the nations,
And in fury against all their host;
He has doomed them, he has given them up to the slaughter,
3 And their slain will be cast out;
The stench of their corpses will rise up,
The mountains will run with their blood,
4 And all the hills will flow with it.
The heavens will roll up like a scroll,
And all their host will fade,
As the foliage fades from the vine,
The falling leaf from the fig tree.

5 For in the heavens my sword has drunk its fill;
And see! it descends upon Edom,
For judgment upon the people whom I have doomed.
6 The sword of the LORD is glutted with blood,
It is gorged with fat,
With the blood of lambs and he-goats,
With the fat of the kidneys of rams.
For the LORD has a sacrifice in Bozrah,
A great slaughter in the land of Edom;
7 And wild oxen will fall down with fatlings,
And bullocks with steers;
And their land will be glutted with blood,
And their dust will be gorged with fat.

For the LORD has a day of vengeance, 8
A year of requital for the feud against Zion;
And the rivers of Edom will be turned into pitch, 9
And her dust into brimstone;
Her land will become burning pitch,
That will not be quenched night or day, 10
But whose smoke will rise forever;
It will lie waste from age to age,
None will pass through it forever and ever.
But the jackdaw and the hedgehog will take possession of it, 11
The owl and the raven will make their home in it;
And the LORD will stretch over it
The measuring-line of chaos and the plummet of desolation;
And satyrs will dwell there, 12
While her nobles will be no more.
Her name will be called "No kingdom there,"
And all her princes will become nothing.

Thorns will spring up in her palaces, 13
Nettles and thistles in her fortresses;
She will become a haunt of jackals,
An inclosure for ostriches;
Desert demons will join goblins, 14
And satyrs will meet one another;
There will the night hag repose,
And find herself a place of rest.
There will the screech owl nestle and lay, 15
Brood and hatch her eggs;
There will the vultures gather,
None without her mate.
Search and read it out of the book of the LORD— 16
None of these will be missing;
For the mouth of the LORD has given command,
And his spirit has gathered them.
He has cast the lot for them, 17
His hand has portioned it out to them with the line;
That they may possess it forever,
And dwell in it throughout the ages.

THE JOY OF THE REDEEMED, 35:1–10

The wilderness and the parched land shall be glad, 35
And the desert shall rejoice and blossom;
Like the crocus shall it blossom abundantly; 2
It shall rejoice with joy and singing.

The glory of Lebanon shall be given to it,
The splendor of Carmel and Sharon;
They shall see the glory of the LORD,
The splendor of our God.

3 Strengthen the feeble hands,
And the tottering knees make firm;
4 Say to those whose hearts beat wildly,
"Courage, fear not!
See! your God—with vengeance will he come,
With the recompense of God will he come to save you."

5 Then shall the eyes of the blind be opened,
And the ears of the deaf shall be unstopped;
6 Then shall the lame man leap like a hart,
And the tongue of the dumb shall sing.
For waters shall break out in the wilderness,
And streams in the desert;
7 The glowing sand shall become a pool,
And the thirsty ground springs of water;
In the haunt of jackals your flocks shall lie down,
And the inclosure of ostriches shall be filled with reeds and rushes.

8 And a highway shall be there and a road,
Which shall be called the Holy Way;
No unclean one shall pass over it—
But it shall be for his people as they go along the way—
And no fools shall wander there.
9 No lion shall be there,
No ravenous beast shall go up it;
They shall not be found there.
But the redeemed shall walk in it,
10 The ransomed of the LORD shall return by it;
They shall come to Zion with singing,
And with everlasting joy upon their heads;
They shall attain to joy and gladness,
And sorrow and sighing shall flee away.

THE INVASION OF SENNACHERIB, 36:1—37:38

36 Now in the fourteenth year of King
Hezekiah, Sennacherib, king of Assyria, came up against all the fortified
cities of Judah, and captured them.
Then the king of Assyria sent the field 2
marshal from Lachish to Jerusalem,
against King Hezekiah, with a large
army. And he took up his position by
the conduit of the upper pool, on the
highway to the laundrymen's field.
Then Eliakim, the son of Hilkiah, who 3
was steward of the palace, and Shebna,
the scribe, and Joah, the son of Asaph,
the recorder, went out to him. Then
the field marshal said to them, 4

"Say now to Hezekiah, 'Thus says
the great king, the king of Assyria:
"What confidence is this in which you
trust? Do you think that a mere word 5
of the lips is counsel and strength for
war? Now in whom do you trust that
you have rebelled against me? You 6
trust, evidently, in the staff of this
broken reed, Egypt, on which if a man
lean, it will run into his hand and
pierce it. So is Pharaoh, king of
Egypt, to all who trust in him! But if 7
you say to me, 'We trust in the LORD
our God,' is not he the one whose high
places and altars Hezekiah has taken
away, saying to Judah and Jerusalem,
'Before this altar shall you worship'?
And now, pray make a wager with my 8
master, the king of Assyria: I will give
you two thousand horses, if you are
able on your part to set riders upon
them! How then can you repulse the 9
attack of one of the least of my master's servants? Yet you trust in Egypt
for chariots and horsemen! Now have 10
I come up against this land to destroy
it without the LORD'S approval? The
LORD himself said to me, 'Go up
against this land and destroy it!'"'"

Then Eliakim, Shebna, and Joah 11
said to the field marshal,

"Speak now to your servants in
Aramaic, for we understand it; but do
not speak to us in Judean in the hearing
of the people who are on the wall."

But the field marshal said, 12

"Was it to your master and you that
my master sent me to speak these
words? Was it not rather to the men
who are sitting on the wall, doomed
with you to eat their own excrement
and to drink their own urine?"

Then the field marshal stood up and 13
cried with a loud voice in Judean, saying,

"Hear the words of the great king,
the king of Assyria! Thus says the 14
king: 'Do not let Hezekiah deceive

you; for he will not be able to deliver
15 you. Neither let Hezekiah cause you to
trust in the LORD by saying, "The
LORD will surely deliver us; this city
shall not be given into the hand of the
16 king of Assyria!" Do not listen to Hezekiah; for thus says the king of Assyria:
"Make peace with me and surrender to
me; and eat each of you from his own
vine and fig tree, and drink the water
17 of his own cistern, until I come and take
you away to a land like your own, a
land of grain and wine, a land of bread
18 and vineyards. Beware lest Hezekiah
lure you on by saying, 'The LORD will
deliver us!' Has any of the gods of the
nations delivered his land from the
19 hand of the king of Assyria? Where are
the gods of Hamath and Arpad? Where
are the gods of Sepharvaim? Where
are the gods of the land of Samaria?
Did they deliver Samaria from my
20 hand? Who were there among all the
gods of these lands that delivered their
land from my hand, that the LORD
should deliver Jerusalem from my
hand?' " ' "
21 Then they were silent and answered
him not a word; for the king's command was, "Do not answer him!"
22 Then Eliakim, the son of Hilkiah,
who was steward of the palace, and
Shebna, the scribe, and Joah, the son of
Asaph, the recorder, came to Hezekiah
with their garments torn, and told him
the words of the field marshal.
37 As soon as King Hezekiah heard it,
he tore his clothes, covered himself
with sackcloth, and went into the house
2 of the LORD. He also sent Eliakim,
who was steward of the palace, and
Shebna, the scribe, and the oldest of
the priests, covered with sackcloth, to
the prophet Isaiah, the son of Amoz.
3 They said to him,
"Thus says Hezekiah: 'This is a day
of distress, rebuke, and disgrace; for
children have come to the birth, and
4 there is no strength to bear them. It
may be that the LORD your God will
hear the words of the field marshal,
whom his master, the king of Assyria,
has sent to insult the living God, and
will rebuke the words which the LORD
your God has heard. Therefore lift up
a prayer for the remnant that is left!' "
5 But when the servants of King Heze-
6 kiah came to Isaiah, Isaiah said to
them,

"Thus shall you say to your master,
'Thus says the LORD: "Do not be
afraid of the words that you have
heard, with which the menials of the
king of Assyria have blasphemed me.
Behold, I will put a spirit in him, so 7
that when he hears a certain rumor he
shall return to his own land; and I will
cause him to fall by the sword in his
own land." ' "
Then the field marshal returned, and 8
found the king of Assyria warring
against Libnah; for he had heard that
he had left Lachish. But he heard con- 9
cerning Tirhakah, king of Ethiopia,
"He has come out to fight with you."
When he heard it, he sent messengers
to Hezekiah, saying,
"Thus shall you say to Hezekiah, 10
king of Judah: 'Do not let your God in
whom you trust deceive you, saying,
"Jerusalem shall not be given into the
hand of the king of Assyria!" You have 11
surely heard what the kings of Assyria
have done to all the lands in completely
destroying them, and will you be delivered? Did the gods of the nations 12
which my fathers destroyed deliver
them—Gozan, Haran, Rezeph, and the
Edenites who were in Telassar? Where 13
is the king of Hamath, the king of Arpad, and the king of the city of Sepharvaim, of Hena, and of Ivvah?' "
So Hezekiah received the letter from 14
the hand of the messengers and read it.
Then Hezekiah went up to the house of
the LORD and spread it out before the
LORD; and Hezekiah prayed to the 15
LORD, and said,
"O LORD of hosts, the God of Israel, 16
who art seated upon the cherubim,
thou art God, even thou alone, over all
the kingdoms of the earth; thou hast
made the heavens and the earth. In- 17
cline thine ear, O LORD, and hear;
open thine eyes, O LORD, and see, and
hear all the words of Sennacherib,
which he has sent to insult the living
God. Of a truth, O LORD, the kings of 18
Assyria have laid waste all the nations
and their lands, and have cast their 19
gods into the fire, for they were no gods,
but the work of men's hands, wood and
stone; and so they have destroyed
them. But now, O LORD our God, de- 20
liver us from his hand, that all the kingdoms of the earth may know that thou,
O LORD, art God alone."

21 Then Isaiah, the son of Amoz, sent to
Hezekiah, saying,
"Thus says the LORD, the God of
Israel: 'Because you have prayed to
me concerning Sennacherib, king of As-
22 syria, this is the word which the LORD
has spoken against him:
"She despises you, laughs at you—
the virgin daughter of Zion!
Behind you she wags the head—
the daughter of Jerusalem!
23 Whom have you insulted and blasphemed?
Against whom have you raised your
voice,
And lifted up your eyes on high?
against the Holy One of Israel!
24 By the hand of your servants
you have insulted the Lord,
and have said,
'With the multitude of my chariots
I ascended the mountain
heights,
the recesses of Lebanon;
And I felled its tallest cedars,
its choicest cypresses;
And I entered its remotest retreat,
its densest thicket.
25 I dug down,
and drank foreign waters;
With the soles of my feet I dried up
all the streams of Egypt.'
26 Have you not heard
how I prepared it long ago,
How I planned it in days of old,
and now have brought it to
pass—
That you should turn fortified cities
into ruin heaps,
27 While their inhabitants, shorn of their
strength,
are dismayed and confounded,
Are become like grass of the field,
like tender green grass,
Like grass on the housetops,
blasted before it is grown up.
28 I know your rising and sitting,
your going and coming,
and your raging against me.
29 Because you have raged against me
and your arrogance has come up
to my ears,
Therefore I will put my hook in your
nose,
and my bridle in your lips,
And I will cause you to return by the
way
by which you came."

" 'And this is the sign for you: This 3
year you shall eat what grows of itself,
and next year what springs from the
same; but in the third year sow and
reap, plant vineyards and eat their
fruit. The remnant that survives of the 3
house of Judah shall again strike root
downward and bear fruit upward; for a 3
remnant shall go forth from Jerusalem,
and a band of survivors from Mount
Zion. The zeal of the LORD of hosts
shall accomplish this.'
"Therefore thus says the LORD con- 3
cerning the king of Assyria: 'He shall
not enter this city, or shoot an arrow
there; neither shall he come before it
with shield, nor cast up a mound against
it. By the way that he came, by the 3
same he shall return; but he shall not
enter this city,' is the oracle of the
LORD. 'For I will defend and save this 3
city for my own sake, and for my servant
David's sake.' "
Then the angel of the LORD went 3
forth, and slew in the camp of the Assyrians one hundred and eighty-five
thousand; and when men rose early
next morning, they were all dead
bodies.
So Sennacherib, king of Assyria, set 3
out and went and returned home and
dwelt at Nineveh. But as he was wor- 3
shiping in the temple of Nisroch his
god, Adrammelech and Sarezer, his
sons, slew him with the sword, and they
escaped to the land of Ararat; and
Esarhaddon, his son, became king in
his stead.

HEZEKIAH'S SICKNESS AND RECOVERY, 38:1–9

In those days Hezekiah became dan- 3
gerously ill; and the prophet Isaiah, the
son of Amoz, came to him and said,
"Thus says the LORD: 'Set your affairs in order; for you shall die, and not
live.' "
Then Hezekiah turned his face to the
wall, and prayed to the LORD, saying,
"Remember now, O LORD, I pray
thee, how I have walked before thee in
truth and sincerity of heart, and have
done that which was good in thy sight."
And Hezekiah wept profusely.
Then the word of the LORD came to
Isaiah, saying,
"Go and say to Hezekiah, 'Thus says
the LORD, the God of David your

father: "I have heard your prayer, I
have seen your tears; behold, I will add
6 fifteen more years to your life, and I
will deliver you and this city from the
hand of the king of Assyria, and will
throw my shield over this city." ' "
21 Isaiah also said,
"Let them take a cake of figs, and
rub it upon the boil, so that he may
recover."
22 Then Hezekiah said,
"What will be the sign that I shall go
up to the house of the LORD?"
7 And he said,
"This will be the sign to you from the
LORD, that the LORD will do this thing
8 that he has promised: Behold, I will
turn back the shadow on the sundial of
Ahaz the ten steps which it has gone
down."
So the shadow of the sun turned back
the ten steps which it had gone down.

9 A PSALM OF HEZEKIAH KING OF JUDAH, 38:9–20

(Composed after he had been ill, and
had recovered from his illness.)

10 I said, "I must go hence
in the noontide of my days,
And be consigned to the gates of Sheol
for the rest of my years."
11 I said, "I shall no more see the LORD
in the land of the living;
I shall no more look upon man
among the inhabitants of the
world."
12 My dwelling is plucked up and stripped
from me
like a shepherd's tent;
Like a weaver has he rolled up my life,
he cuts me from the loom.
Day and night am I given over to suffering,
13 till morning I cry out in pain—
Like a lion he breaks all my bones—
Day and night am I given over to suffering,
14 Like a swift or a crane I twitter,
like a dove I moan.
My eyes look languishing upward:
O LORD, pay heed to me, become surety for me!
15 But what can I speak or say to him,
since he has done it?
I must go softly all my years
because of my bitterness of
heart.
O Lord, by these things men live, 16
And through all of them is the life of
my spirit sustained;
Therefore do thou restore me, and
bring me to life again!
Lo! it was for my welfare that I had 17
great bitterness;
And thou hast held me back from the
pit of destruction,
For thou hast cast all my sins behind
thy back.
Sheol cannot thank thee, death cannot 18
praise thee;
Those who go down to the Pit cannot
hope for thy love.
The living, the living man thanks thee, 19
as I do this day;
The father to the children makes
known thy faithfulness.
Be pleased, O LORD, to save me! 20
And we will play on stringed instruments all the days of our life,
Before the house of the LORD.[1]

ON THE EMBASSY FROM MERODACH-BALADAN, 39:1–8

At that time Merodach-baladan, the 39
son of Baladan, king of Babylon, sent
ambassadors with a present to Hezekiah; for he had heard that he had been
sick and had recovered. Hezekiah was 2
pleased with them, and showed them
his treasure-house, the silver, the gold,
the spices, the fine oil, and all his armory—all that was found among his
treasures: there was nothing in his
house or in all his kingdom that Hezekiah did not show them.
Then Isaiah the prophet came to 3
King Hezekiah, and said to him,
"What did these men say, and from
where have they come to you?"
Hezekiah said, 4
"They have come to me from a distant land, from Babylon."
"What did they see in your house?"
he said.
"They have seen all that is in my
house," said Hezekiah; "there was
nothing among my treasures that I did
not show them."
Then Isaiah said to Hezekiah, 5
"Hear the word of the LORD of
hosts: 'Behold, days are coming when 6
all that is in your house and that which

[1] Vss. 21 f. will be found following vs. 6 on this page.

your fathers have stored up to this day shall be carried away to Babylon; nothing shall be left,' says the LORD.
7 'Also some of your sons who shall be your issue, whom you shall beget, they shall take, and they shall become eunuchs in the palace of the king of Babylon.'"
8 Then Hezekiah said to Isaiah,
"Good is the word of the LORD, which you have spoken."
For he thought,
"At least there will be peace and security in my time."

VOICES FROM THE HEAVENS, 40:1–11

40 "Comfort, O comfort my people,"
says your God;
2 "Speak to the heart of Jerusalem,
and call to her,
That her time of service is ended,
that her guilt is paid in full,
That she has received of the LORD'S hand
double for all her sins."

3 Hark! one calls:
"In the wilderness clear the way of the LORD,
Make straight in the desert a highway for our God.
4 Let every valley be raised up,
And every mountain and hill brought low;
Let the uneven ground become a plain,
And the rugged heights a valley.
5 Then shall the glory of the LORD be revealed,
And all flesh shall see it together;
For the mouth of the LORD has spoken."

6 Hark! one says, "Call!"
And I said, "What shall I call?"
"All flesh is grass,
And all its beauty is like the flower of the field.
7 The grass withers, the flower fades,
When the breath of the LORD blows upon it—
Truly the people is grass—
8 The grass withers, the flower fades,
But the word of our God shall stand forever."

9 On a high mountain get you up,
O Zion, herald of good news!
Lift up your voice with strength,
O Jerusalem, herald of good news!
Lift it up, fear not;
Say to the cities of Judah,
"Behold your God!"
See! the Lord GOD is coming with might, 10
his own arm having won him the kingdom;
See! his reward is with him,
and his recompense before him.
Like a shepherd he tends his flock, 11
with his arm he gathers them;
The lambs he carries in his bosom,
and gently leads those who give suck.

THE GREATNESS AND GOODNESS OF THE LORD, 40:12–31

Who has measured the waters in the hollow of his hand, 12
And ruled off the heavens with a span,
And inclosed in a measure the dust of the earth,
And weighed the mountains with a balance,
And the hills in scales?
Who has directed the mind of the LORD, 13
And instructed him as his counselor?
With whom took he counsel for his enlightenment, 14
And who taught him the right path?
Who taught him knowledge,
And showed him the way of intelligence?
Lo! the nations are like a drop from a bucket, 15
Like fine dust in the scales are they counted.
Lo! the coast-lands weigh no more than a grain;
And Lebanon itself is not sufficient for fuel, 16
Nor are its beasts enough for burnt-offering.
All the nations are as nothing before him, 17
Blank ciphers he counts them.

To whom, then, would you liken God, 18
Or what likeness would you place over against him?
An idol! the smelter casts it, 19
And the goldsmith overlays it with gold,
And fastens it with silver links.

41 6 Each one helps his fellow,
And says to his comrade, "Have courage!"
7 The smelter cheers on the goldsmith,
He that smooths with the hammer him that strikes with the mallet,
Saying of the riveting, "It is good!"
As he fastens it with nails so that it cannot move.
40 20 He who would provide himself with an image of wood
Chooses a tree that will not rot;
Then seeks out a skilful workman
To set up an image that cannot move.

21 Do you not know? Do you not hear?
Has it not been told you from the beginning?
Have you not understood since the foundation of the earth?
22 It is he who sits enthroned above the circle of the earth,
So high that its inhabitants are like grasshoppers;
Who stretches out the heavens like a curtain,
And spreads them like a tent to dwell in;
23 Who brings princes to nothing,
And makes the rulers of the earth like a cipher—
24 Hardly have they been planted, hardly have they been sown,
Hardly has their stock taken root in the earth,
When he blows upon them, and they wither,
And the whirlwind carries them away like stubble.
25 "To whom, then, would you liken me,
That I should be equal," says the Holy One.
26 Lift up your eyes on high,
And see! who created these?
He who brought forth their host by number,
And called them all by name;
Through the greatness of his might,
And the strength of his power,
Not one is missing.

27 Why should you say, O Jacob,
And speak, O Israel:
"My way is hidden from the LORD,
And my rights are passed over by my God?"
28 Have you not known? Have you not heard?
The LORD is a God everlasting,
The Creator of the ends of the earth.
He does not faint, nor grow weary;
His insight is unfathomable.
He gives power to the fainting, 29
And to him that has no might he increases strength.
Though the youths faint and grow weary, 30
Though the young men fall prostrate,
They that wait on the LORD shall renew their strength, 31
They shall mount on wings like eagles,
They shall run and not be weary,
They shall walk and not faint.

AN APPEAL TO THE NATIONS, 41:1–4

Listen to me in silence, you coast-lands, 41
And let the nations await my argument;
Then let them approach, then let them speak,
And together let us draw near for judgment!
Who has roused one from the east, 2
Calling him in righteousness to his service,
Giving up nations before him,
And bringing down kings;
With his sword making them like dust,
Like driven stubble with his bow;
Pursuing them, and passing on safely, 3
By paths his feet have not trodden?
Who has wrought and done this, 4
Proclaiming at the beginning the generations to come?
I, the LORD, who am the first,
And am also with the last.

THE APPEAL TO ISRAEL, 41:5, 8–20

The coast-lands saw it, and were afraid; 5
The ends of the earth trembled,
They drew near, and came.[1]
But you, Israel my servant, 8
Jacob, whom I have chosen,
The descendants of Abraham my friend,
Whom I fetched from the ends of the earth, 9
And called from its corners,
To whom I said, "You are my servant;
I have chosen you, and have not spurned you";
Fear not, for I am with you; 10
Be not dismayed, for I am your God!

[1] Vss. 6–7 will be found after 40:19 on this page.

I will strengthen you, I will help you,
I will uphold you with my true right hand.
11 Behold, they shall all be ashamed and confounded
who are inflamed against you;
They shall perish like a thing of nought
who strive against you;
12 You shall seek but shall not find those
who contend against you;
They shall become like an empty cipher,
who war against you.
13 For I, the LORD your God,
have hold of your right hand,
I who say to you, "Fear not!
I am your helper."

14 "Fear not, O worm Jacob,
O insect Israel!
I am your helper," is the oracle of the LORD,
"And your redeemer is the Holy One of Israel.
15 Behold, I make of you a threshing-sledge,
A new one, armed with teeth;
You shall thresh the mountains, and crush them to dust,
And the hills you shall make like chaff;
16 You shall winnow them, and the wind shall carry them away,
The whirlwind shall scatter them;
But you shall exult in the LORD,
You shall glory in the Holy One of Israel.

17 "When the poor and the needy seek water in vain,
And their tongue is parched with thirst,
I the LORD will answer them,
I the God of Israel will not forsake them.
18 I will open rivers on the bare heights,
And wells in the midst of the valleys;
I will make the wilderness a pool,
And the parched land fountains of water.
19 I will plant in the wilderness the cedar,
The acacia, the myrtle, and the olive;
I will set in the desert the cypress,
The plane and the larch as well,
20 That men may see and know,
May consider and also understand,
That the hand of the LORD has done this,
That the Holy One of Israel has created it."

THE CHALLENGE TO THE GODS OF THE NATIONS, 41:21–29

"Present your case," 21
says the LORD;
"Bring forward your champions,"
says the King of Jacob.
"Let them approach and tell us 22
what is to happen:
Tell us what the former things were,
that we may lay them to heart;
Or the things that are coming announce to us,
that we may know their issue.
Tell us the things that are coming hereafter, 23
that we may know that you are gods;
That you can do good and do evil,
that we may be dismayed and frightened too.
But lo! you are nought, 24
And your work is a blank;
an abomination is he who chooses you."

I have roused one from the north, and he comes— 25
From the east he calls on my name;
He shall tread down rulers like mortar,
As the potter tramples clay.
Who foretold it from the first, that we might know, 26
And beforehand, that we might say, "Right"?
There was none that foretold, none that announced,
None that heard words from you.
I first told it to Zion, 27
And sent heralds of good news to Jerusalem;
But of these there was no one, of these no counselor, 28
That, when I asked them, could answer a word.
Lo! they are all of them nought, their deeds a blank, 29
Their molten images wind and waste.

THE MISSION OF THE SERVANT OF THE LORD, 42:1–4

See! my servant, whom I uphold; 42
My chosen one, in whom I delight.
I have put my spirit upon him,
He shall bring forth justice to the nations.
He shall not cry, nor shout, 2

Nor make his voice heard in the streets;
3 A bent reed shall he not break,
And a flickering wick shall he not quench.
Faithfully shall he bring forth justice;
4 He shall not flicker or bend,
Till he establish justice in the earth,
And the coast-lands wait for his teaching.

THE LIGHT OF THE NATIONS, 42:5–9

5 Thus says the LORD, the God,
Who created the heavens, and stretched them out,
Who made the earth and its products,
Who gives breath to the people upon it,
And spirit to those who walk in it:
6 "I the LORD have called you in righteousness,
And have grasped you by the hand;
I have kept you, and have made you a pledge to the people,
A light to the nations;
7 In opening blind eyes,
In bringing prisoners out of the dungeon,
Those who sit in darkness out of the prison.
8 I am the LORD, that is my name;
And my glory will I not give to another,
Nor my praise to carved images.
9 The former things, lo! they have come to pass,
And new things I foretell;
Before they spring into being,
I announce them to you."

A NEW SONG, 42:10–13

10 Sing to the LORD a new song,
His praise from the end of the earth;
Let the sea roar, and that which fills it,
The coast-lands, and those who dwell in them!
11 Let the desert rejoice, and her cities,
The villages that Kedar inhabits;
Let the crag-dwellers sing for joy,
Let them shout from the top of the mountains:
12 Let them give glory to the LORD,
And tell forth his praise through the coast-lands!

For the LORD will go forth like a warrior, 13
He will stir up his rage like a soldier;
He will shout, he will send forth the battle cry,
He will show himself a hero against his enemies.

THE INTERVENTION OF THE LORD, 42:14–17

I have long been silent, 14
I have kept still, and have restrained myself;
Now will I cry like a woman in travail,
I will gasp and pant together.
I will lay waste mountains and hills, 15
And will dry up all their herbage;
I will turn the rivers into deserts,
And will dry up the pools.
And I will lead the blind by a way that they know not, 16
By paths that they know not will I guide them;
I will make the darkness light before them,
And the rugged places a plain.
These are the things I will do,
And will not leave undone;
But they shall be turned backward, in utter shame, 17
Who trust in idols,
Who say to molten images,
"You are our gods."

THE BLINDNESS OF THE SERVANT, 42:18–25

Hear, you deaf ones, 18
And look, you blind ones, that you may see!
Who is blind but my servant, 19
And deaf like my messenger whom I send?
Who is as blind as my devoted one,
And as deaf as the servant of the LORD?
Many things have you seen, but you observe not; 20
With ears open, you hear not.
The LORD was pleased, for his righteousness' sake, 21
To make his instruction great and glorious;
But this is a people preyed upon and despoiled, 22
All of them snared in holes,

And hidden away in prisons;
They have become a prey, with none to deliver,
A spoil, with none to say, "Restore!"
23 And who among you pays heed to this,
Attends and hears for the time to come?
24 Who gave up Jacob to despoilers,
Israel to plunderers?
Was it not the LORD, against whom they sinned,
And in whose ways they would not walk,
And to whose instruction they did not listen?
25 So he poured upon them the heat of his anger,
And the fierceness of war,
Which wrapped them round in flames, although they understood it not,
And burned them, although they laid it not to heart.

REDEMPTION AND RESTORATION, 43:1-21

43 But now thus says the LORD,
Who created you, O Jacob, and formed you, O Israel:
"Fear not, for I have redeemed you,
I have called you by your name—you are mine!
2 When you pass through the waters, I will be with you,
And through the rivers, they shall not overwhelm you;
When you walk through the fire, you shall not be scorched,
Or through the flame, it will not burn you;
3 For I the LORD am your God,
I the Holy One of Israel am your savior.
Egypt I give as your ransom,
Ethiopia and Seba in exchange for you;
4 Because you are precious in my sight,
Honored and loved by me,
Lands I give in exchange for you,
And peoples instead of you.
5 Fear not, for I am with you;
From the east will I bring your descendants,
And from the west will I gather you;
6 I will say to the north, 'Give up!'
And to the south, 'Hold not back!
Bring my sons from afar,
And my daughters from the end of the earth;
Every one who is called by my name, 7
Whom I have created and formed,
And made for my glory.'"
Bring forth the people that are blind, 8
yet have eyes,
And are deaf, yet have ears!
All the nations are gathered together, 9
And the peoples are assembled;
Yet who among them could foretell this,
Could announce it to us beforehand?
Let them bring their witnesses to prove them in the right,
To hear their plea, and say, "It is true."
"You are my witnesses," is the oracle 10
of the LORD,
"My servants, whom I have chosen,
That they may know and believe me,
And understand that I am he.
Before me was no God formed,
And after me there shall be none:
I, I, am the LORD, 11
And apart from me there is no savior.
I foretold, and I saved, 12
I announced—I, and no alien god among you;
And you are my witnesses," is the oracle of the LORD.
"I am God from of old,
And from now onward the same. 13
There is none that can deliver out of my hand;
When I work, who can reverse it?"
Thus says the LORD, 14
Your Redeemer, the Holy One of Israel:
"For your sake will I send to Babylon,
And bring them all down as fugitives,
Namely, the Chaldeans, in their pleasure ships.
For I the LORD am your Holy One, 15
I the Creator of Israel am your King."
Thus says the LORD, 16
Who made a way through the sea,
A path through mighty waters;
Who led forth chariot and horse, 17
Army and warrior together—
And they lay down, and could not rise up,
They were extinguished and quenched like a wick:
"Remember not former things, 18
Nor pay heed to things long past.
Behold, I am doing a new thing, 19
Even now it is springing to light—

Do you not perceive it?
A way will I make in the wilderness,
And rivers in the desert;
20 The beasts of the field shall honor me,
The jackals and the ostriches,
Because I provide waters in the wilderness,
And rivers in the desert,
To give drink to my chosen people,
21 The people whom I formed for myself,
That they might recount my praise."

GRACE AND GLORY, 43:22—44:8

22 You have not called upon me, O Jacob,
Nor have you wearied yourself with me, O Israel.
23 Have you not brought me sheep for your burnt-offerings,
And honored me with your sacrifices?
Though I burdened you not with offerings,
Nor wearied you with frankincense,
24 Have you not bought me sweet cane with your money,
And sated me with the fat of your sacrifices,
While you have burdened me with your sins,
Wearied me with your iniquities?
25 I, I, am he who for my own sake blots out your transgressions,
And will remember your sins no more.
26 Recall the matter to me, and let us argue it out together;
Recount it, that you may be proved in the right!
27 Your first father sinned,
And your prophets rebelled against me;
28 Your princes also profaned my sanctuary;
Therefore I gave up Jacob to utter destruction,
And Israel to revilings.

44 Yet now hear, O Jacob my servant,
Israel, whom I have chosen!
2 Thus says the LORD, your Maker,
Who formed you from the womb, and will help you:
"Fear not, O Jacob my servant,
Jeshurun, whom I have chosen!
3 For I will pour water on the thirsty land,
And streams on the dry ground;
I will pour my spirit upon your children,
And my blessing upon your descendants;
4 And they shall grow up like grass in a swamp,
Like willows by running streams.
5 One shall say, 'I am the LORD'S,'
And another shall call himself by the name of Jacob;
Another shall inscribe on his hand, 'The LORD'S,'
And shall surname himself by the name of Israel."
6 Thus says the LORD, the King of Israel,
His Redeemer, the LORD of hosts:
"I am the first, and I the last;
Apart from me there is no God.
7 Who is like me? Let him proclaim it,
Let him declare it, and lay it out before me!
Who has announced from of old the things to come?
Let them tell the things that are to be!
8 Fear not, nor be disquieted!
Did I not of old announce and declare it to you,
With you as my witnesses?
Is there a God beside me,
Or a Rock of whom I know not?

THE FOLLY OF IDOLATRY, 44:9–20

9 The makers of idols are all of them
inane, their precious products are good
for nothing, and their devotees are
without sight or sense—that they may
10 be put to shame! Whoever, then,
fashions a god or casts an image that is
11 good for nothing, all who hold to it will
be put to shame, since the workmen are
but human beings. Let all of them assemble
and take their stand; they will
be put to terror and shame together.

12 The workman in iron works it over
the coals, and shapes it with hammers,
working it with his strong arm. Then
he becomes hungry, and loses his
strength; unless he drinks water, he
grows faint.

13 The workman in wood draws a
measuring-line over it, shapes it with a
pencil, works it with planes, shapes it
with compasses, and makes it into the
likeness of a man, with a beauty like

that of the human form—to sit in a
house!
14 A man cuts down a cedar, or takes a
plane or an oak, or lays hold of some
other tree of the forest, which the
LORD planted and the rain has
15 nourished for man to use as fuel. He
takes part of it and warms himself, he
kindles a fire and bakes bread; then he
makes a god and worships it, he molds
an image and prostrates himself before
16 it. Half of it he burns in the fire, and on
its embers he roasts flesh; he eats the
roast and is satisfied; he also warms
himself, and says, "Ha! ha! I am warm,
17 I feel the glow." And the rest of it he
makes into a god—his idol!—prostrates
himself before it, worships it, and prays
to it, saying, "Save me, for thou art my
god!"
18 They have no knowledge and no intelligence; for their eyes are besmeared
so that they cannot see, and their minds
are dulled so that they cannot under-
19 stand. No one has sense or knowledge
or intelligence to say, "Half of it have I
burned in the fire, and on its embers
have I baked bread, and I am roasting
flesh and eating it; and the rest of it
shall I make into an abomination, and
prostrate myself before a block of
wood?"
20 Feeder on ashes! A deluded mind has
led him astray, so that he cannot save
himself, or confess, "Am not I holding
to a delusion?"

JOY OVER ISRAEL'S REDEMPTION, 44:21–23

21 Remember these things, O Jacob,
Israel, for you are my servant!
I formed you, my servant you are,
O Israel, who will not be forgotten by
me.
22 I have blotted out your transgressions
like a mist,
Your sins like a cloud;
Return to me, for I have redeemed
you.
23 Sing, O heavens, for the LORD has
done it,
Shout, O depths of the earth;
Break into singing, O mountains,
O forest, and every tree in it!
For the LORD has redeemed Jacob,
And is revealing his glory in Israel.

THE CALL OF CYRUS, 44:24—45:13

Thus says the LORD, your Redeemer, 24
Who formed you from the womb:
"I, the LORD, the maker of all,
Who stretched out the heavens alone,
Who laid out the earth—who was with
me?
Who frustrates the omens of sooth- 25
sayers,
And makes diviners like madmen;
Who turns wise men backward,
And makes their knowledge folly;
But confirms the word of his servants, 26
And fulfils the predictions of his mes-
sengers—
I am he who says of Jerusalem, 'She
shall be inhabited,'
And of the cities of Judah, 'They shall
be built,
And their ruins will I raise up';
Who says to the deep, 'Be dry! 27
And all your streams will I drain';
Who says of Cyrus, 'My shepherd, 28
Who shall fulfil all my pleasure';
Who says of Jerusalem, 'She shall be
built,'
And of the temple, 'Your foundations
shall be laid.' "

Thus says the LORD to his anointed, 45
To Cyrus, whose right hand I have
grasped,
To bring down nations before him,
And to ungird the loins of kings,
To open doors before him,
And that gates may not be closed:
"I will go before you,
And will level the rugged heights;
The doors of bronze will I break in
pieces,
And the bars of iron will I cut asunder;
I will give you the treasures of dark- 3
ness,
The hoards of secret places;
That you may know that I am the
LORD,
That I who have called you by name
am the God of Israel.
For the sake of Jacob my servant,
And Israel my chosen one,
I have called you by name,
I have surnamed you, though you
knew me not.
I am the LORD, and there is no other; 5
Beside me there is no God.
I will gird you, though you knew me
not,

6 That men may know, from the east
And from the west, that beside me
there is none.
I am the LORD, and there is no other—
7 Who forms light, and creates darkness,
Who makes weal, and creates woe—
I the LORD am he who does all these
things.

8 "Pour down, O heavens, from above,
And let the clouds rain righteousness;
Let the earth open her womb,
And bring forth salvation;
Let her cause righteousness also to
spring up,
Since I the LORD have created it.

9 "Woe to him who strives with his
Maker—
A pot with the Potter!
Does the clay ask its potter, 'What are
you making?'
Or a man's work say to him, 'You have
no hands!'?
10 Woe to him who asks a father, 'What
are you begetting?'
Or a woman, 'With what are you in
labor?' "

11 Thus says the LORD,
The Holy One of Israel, who formed
it:
"Will you question me concerning my
children,
Or give me orders regarding the work
of my hands?
12 I made the earth,
And created man upon it;
My hands stretched out the heavens,
And all their host I marshaled;
13 I have roused one in righteousness,
And all his ways will I level;
He shall build my city,
And shall set my exiles free,
Not for price or reward,"
Says the LORD of hosts.

THE SALVATION OF THE WORLD, 45:14–25

14 Thus says the LORD:
"The laborers of Egypt, and the
merchants of Ethiopia,
and the stalwart men of Seba,
Shall pass over to your service,
and shall walk behind you in
fetters;
They shall pass over, and shall bow
down to you,
and shall pray to you,
'With you alone is God, and there is
no other,
no God besides;
15 Truly with you God hides himself,
the God of Israel is a savior.'
16 Ashamed and confounded are they all
together,
the makers of idols are driven
to confusion;
17 But Israel is saved by the LORD
with an everlasting salvation;
You shall not be put to shame or confounded
forever and ever."

18 For thus says the LORD who created
the heavens—
he is the God—
Who formed the earth and made it—
he established it—
He did not create it a chaos,
he formed it for a dwelling-
place:
"I am the LORD,
and there is no other.
19 I spoke not in secret,
in a land of darkness;
I said not to Jacob's descendants,
'Seek me in chaos!'
I the LORD speak what is right,
tell what is true.
20 Assemble and come, draw near together,
you survivors of the nations!
No knowledge have those who carry
about
their carved images of wood,
And offer their prayers to a god
that cannot save.
21 Let them take counsel together, then
let them show us,
and bring forward proof of it!
Who announced this of old,
foretold it long ago?
Was it not I the LORD—
no other God than I—
A righteous and a saving God—
none apart from me?
22 Turn to me, and be saved,
all ends of the earth!
For I am God, and there is no other—
23 by myself have I sworn—
Truth has gone out of my mouth,
a word that shall not return,
That to me every knee shall bow,
every tongue shall swear,
24 Saying, 'Only in the LORD
are righteousness and strength.'

To him shall come in confusion
all who were inflamed against him;
25 But in the LORD shall all the descendants of Israel
triumph and glory."

THE DOWNFALL OF THE GODS OF BABYLON, 46:1–13

46 Bel crouches, Nebo cowers;
Their idols are consigned to beasts,
They were laid as a load upon weary cattle.
2 They cower, they crouch together;
They cannot rescue the load,
But themselves go into captivity.

3 Listen to me, O house of Jacob,
All the remnant of the house of Israel,
Whom I have carried as a load from birth,
Whom I have borne as a burden from the womb—
4 And to old age I am still the same,
Till you are gray-headed will I carry you;
I have borne, and I will bear,
I will carry, and I will save:
5 "To whom will you liken me, to whom make me equal,
With whom will you compare me, that we should be like one another?
6 Those who pour gold from a bag,
And weigh out silver in a balance—
They hire a goldsmith to make a god of it,
Prostrate themselves before it, and worship it;
7 They bear it upon their shoulder,
Carry it, and set it down upon its feet,
Where it stands without moving from its place—
Though one cry to it, it will not answer,
Nor save him from his distress.
8 Think of this, and ponder over it,
Lay it to heart, you rebels!
9 Remember the former things of old,
For it is I who am God, and there is no other—
The God, and there is none like me;
10 Who tells the end from the beginning,
And from days of old that which is still undone;
Who says, 'My purpose shall stand,
And all my pleasure will I do';
11 Who calls from the east an agent of mine,
From a distant land the man of my purpose.
I have spoken, and I will bring it about;
I have purposed, and I will do it."

Listen to me, you stubborn of heart, 12
Who count yourselves far from righteousness:
"My triumph have I brought near, it is not far off, 13
And my salvation shall not lag;
I will put salvation in Zion,
Give to Israel my glory."

THE DOWNFALL OF BABYLON, 47:1–15

"Come down, and sit in the dust, 47
O virgin daughter of Babylon;
Sit throneless on the earth,
O daughter of the Chaldeans!
For no more shall you be called
tender and delicate.
Take millstones, and grind meal; 2
remove your veil,
Strip off the skirt, lay bare the leg,
pass through the rivers;
Let your nakedness be laid bare, 3
your shame be seen!
For vengeance inexorable will I take,"
says our Redeemer,
Whose name is the LORD of hosts,
the Holy One of Israel.
"Get into darkness, and sit silent, 5
O daughter of the Chaldeans!
For no more shall you be called
the mistress of kingdoms.
I was angry with my people, 6
I profaned my heritage;
I gave them into your hand,
you showed them no pity;
On the aged you made your yoke
to press very heavily.
And you said, 'I shall remain forever, 7
mistress for all time';
But you laid not these things to heart,
nor thought what their end would be.

"Now hear this, O voluptuous one, 8
you who sit complacently,
And say to yourself,
'I am, and there is none but me;
I shall not sit as a widow,
nor know loss of children!'
These two things shall come to you in 9
an instant,
in a single day;

Loss of children and widowhood, in
their full measure,
shall come upon you—
In spite of your many spells,
and your numerous enchantments—
10 Though you have trusted in your skill,
and have said, 'None sees me.'

"Your wisdom and your skill
have led you astray,
So that you said to yourself,
'I am, and there is none but me.'
11 Therefore disaster shall come upon
you,
which you shall not know how
to charm away;
And destruction shall fall upon you,
which you shall not be able to
appease;
And ruin shall swoop upon you,
which you shall not know how
to avert.
12 Stand, then, by your enchantments,
and your many spells,
with which you have wearied
yourself from your youth;
Perhaps you may yet succeed,
perhaps you may strike terror!

13 "You have wearied yourself with your
many counselors,
now let them stand up and save
you—
Those who map out the heavens,
and gaze at the stars,
And tell you month by month
what fortune will come to you.
14 Lo! they have become like stubble,
the fire burns them;
They cannot save themselves
from the power of the flame;
For it is no glowing coal to warm one's
self at,
no fire to sit before.
15 Such is the fate of those with whom
you have wearied yourself,
with whom you have trafficked
from your youth—
They stagger each his own way,
with none to save them."

PROPHECIES OLD AND NEW, 48:1–16

48 Hear this, O house of Jacob,
Who are called by the name of Israel,
And are sprung from the loins of Judah;
Who swear by the name of the LORD,
And invoke the God of Israel,
But not in good faith or sincerity;
Though they call themselves after the 2
holy city,
And lean on the God of Israel,
Whose name is the LORD of hosts:
"The former things I foretold of old, 3
They issued from my mouth, and I
announced them,
Then suddenly I did them, and they
came to pass;
Because I knew that you were obstinate, 4
That your neck was an iron band,
And your forehead bronze,
I foretold them to you of old, 5
I announced them to you before they
came,
Lest you should say, 'My idol did
them,
My carved image and my molten
image commanded them';
You heard this, and now that it is all 6
fulfilled,
Will you not bear witness to it?
From this time forth I announce to
you new things,
Hidden things, which you have not
known;
Only now have they been created, and 7
not of old,
Before this day you have not heard of
them,
Lest you should say, 'Lo! I knew
them';
You have neither heard nor known of 8
them,
Nor till now has your ear been opened
to them;
For I knew how treacherous you were,
How you had been known as a rebel
from your birth.
For my name's sake have I been 9
patient with you,
For my honor's sake have I bridled my
anger against you,
So as not to cut you off;
Lo! I refined you, but not like silver, 10
I tested you in the furnace of suffering.
For my own sake, my own sake, I do 11
this—
For how should my name be profaned!—
And my glory I yield to no other.
Listen to me, O Jacob, 12
Israel whom I called!
I, I, am the first,
I also am the last.

13 My hand laid the foundations of the earth,
My right hand spread out the heavens;
When I call to them, they stand up together.
14 Assemble, all of you, and listen!
Who among you foretold these things?
Since the LORD loves him, he will perform his pleasure on Babylon,
And his might on the Chaldeans.
15 I myself spoke, and called him;
I brought him, and made his way prosperous.
16 Draw near to me, listen to this!
From the first I spoke not in secret,
From the time that it happened I was there;
And now I the Lord GOD have sent him,
Endowed with my spirit."

THE FRUITS OF OBEDIENCE, 48:17–19

17 Thus says the LORD, your Redeemer,
The Holy One of Israel:
"I the LORD am your God,
Who teaches you for your profit,
And who leads you in the way by which you should go.
18 If only you had hearkened to my commands,
Then would your welfare have been like a river,
And your righteousness like the waves of the sea;
19 Your descendants would have been like the sand,
Your offspring like the dust of the earth;
And your name would not be cut off,
Nor destroyed from before me."

THE SUMMONS TO DEPART FROM BABYLON, 48:20–22

20 Go forth from Babylon, flee from Chaldea!
With a shout of joy tell, announce this,
Send it forth to the end of the earth!
Say, "The LORD has redeemed his servant Jacob."
21 They thirsted not when he led them through deserts;
Water from the rock he caused to flow for them;
He cleft the rock, and water gushed out.
"There is no peace," says the LORD, 22
"for the wicked."

THE DESTINY OF THE SERVANT, 49:1–6

Listen, you coast-lands, to me; 49
Hearken, you peoples afar!
The LORD called me from birth,
From my mother's womb he gave me my name.
He made my mouth like a sharp sword, 2
In the shadow of his hand he hid me;
He made me a polished arrow,
In his quiver he concealed me.
He said to me, "You are my servant, 3
Israel, through whom I will show forth my glory."
But I said, "In vain have I labored, 4
Idly and for nought have I spent my strength;
Nevertheless, my right is with the LORD,
And my reward with my God."
And now the LORD, 5
Who formed me from the womb to be his servant,
Says that he will bring back Jacob to himself,
And that Israel shall be gathered to him—
For I am honored in the eyes of the LORD,
And my God has become my strength—
He says, "It is too slight a thing for your being my servant 6
That I should but raise up the tribes of Jacob,
And restore the survivors of Israel;
So I will make you a light of the nations,
That my salvation may reach to the end of the earth."

THE RESTORATION OF ISRAEL, 49:7–13

Thus says the LORD, 7
The Redeemer and the Holy One of Israel,
To him who is despised by men, abhorred by people,
The slave of rulers:
"Kings shall see, and rise up,
Princes, and they shall bow down,

Because of the LORD, who is faithful,
The Holy One of Israel, who has chosen you."

8 Thus says the LORD:
"In a time of favor have I answered you,
On a day of salvation have I helped you;
I have kept you, and have made you a pledge to the people,
To restore the land,
To allot the desolate heritages,
9 Saying to the prisoners, 'Go forth!'
And to those in darkness, 'Show yourselves!'
On all roads shall they feed,
And on all bare heights shall be their pasture;
10 They shall not hunger or thirst,
And no hot wind or sun shall smite them;
For their merciful Friend shall lead them,
And shall guide them by fountains of water.
11 I will make all mountains a road,
And highways shall be raised for them.
12 Behold, these shall come from afar,
And these from the north and the west,
And these from the land of Syene."

13 Sing, O heavens, and exult, O earth;
Break into singing, O mountains!
For the LORD has comforted his people,
And has had pity upon his afflicted ones.

THE CONSOLATION OF ZION, 49:14—50:3

14 But Zion says, "The LORD has forsaken me,
The Lord has forgotten me!"
15 "Can a woman forget her sucking child,
So as not to have pity upon the son of her womb?
Even should these forget,
Yet I will not forget you.
16 See! I have carved you upon the palms of my hands;
Your walls are continually before me.
17 Already your builders make haste,
While those who destroyed you and laid you waste go forth from you.
18 Lift up your eyes round about, and see!
All of them gather, they come to you.
As I live," is the oracle of the LORD,
"All of them shall you put on as an ornament,
And shall gird about you like a bride.
For your waste and desolate places shall be restored, 19
And your land that was ravaged shall be filled with inhabitants.
For now shall you become too narrow for your inhabitants,
Since those who swallowed you up are far away.
The children that were born to you in your time of bereavement 20
Shall yet say in your ears,
'The place is too narrow for us;
Make room for us to dwell in!'
And you shall say to yourself, 21
'Who can have borne me these?
I was bereaved and barren, exiled and banished,
But these—who can have reared them?
Lo! I was left alone;
Whence can these have come?' "

Thus says the Lord GOD: 22
"Behold, I will lift up my hand to the nations,
And to the peoples will I raise my signal;
And they shall bring your sons in their bosom,
And your daughters shall be carried on their shoulders.
And kings shall be your foster fathers, 23
And their queens your nursing-mothers;
With their faces to the earth shall they bow down to you,
And shall lick the dust of your feet;
And you shall know that I am the LORD,
In whom none that trust shall be put to shame."

Can prey be taken from a warrior, 24
Or a tyrant's captives be rescued?
But thus says the LORD: 25
"Even should a warrior's captives be taken,
And a tyrant's prey be rescued,
Your opponents will I oppose,
And your children will I save.
I will cause your oppressors to eat their own flesh, 26
And they shall be drunk with their own blood as with new wine;

Then all flesh shall know that I the
LORD am your savior,
And that I the Mighty One of Jacob
am your redeemer."

50 Thus says the LORD:
"Where is your mother's writ of divorce,
With which I put her away?
Or who is the creditor of mine,
To whom I sold you?
Lo! it was for your sins that you were
sold,
And for her transgressions that your
mother was put away.
2 Why, then, was there no man, when I
came, to greet me,
None, when I called, to answer?
Is my hand too short to redeem,
Or have I no strength to save?
Lo! by my rebuke I dry up the sea,
I turn rivers into a desert;
Their fish are in distress for want of
water,
And die of thirst.
3 I clothe the heavens in mourning,
And sackcloth I make their covering."

THE DISCIPLINE OF THE SERVANT, 50:4–9

4 The Lord GOD has given me
a tongue for teaching
That I may know how to succor
the weary with a word.
Each morning he wakens, he wakens
my ear
to hear as disciples do;
5 The Lord GOD has opened my ear,
and I have not been rebellious,
I have not turned backward.
6 I gave my back to the smiters,
and my cheeks to the pluckers
of hair;
My face I hid not
from shame and spitting.
7 But the Lord GOD helps me,
therefore I have not been confounded;
I have set my face like a flint,
and I know that I shall not be
ashamed.
8 Near is my Vindicator; who will take
issue with me?
Let us stand up together!
Who will challenge my rights?
Let him draw near to me!
9 Behold, the Lord GOD helps me;
who will put me in the wrong?
Behold, they will all wear out like a
garment,
the moth will devour them.

THE FAITHFUL AND THE TREACHEROUS, 50:10–11

"Whoever among you fears the LORD, 10
and listens to the voice of his
servant—
Though he walk in darkness,
without a gleam of light,
Let him trust in the name of the
LORD,
and rely on his God!
But all you who kindle a fire, 11
and set brands aflame,
Begone to the flame of your fire,
and the brands you have kindled!
This is your fate at my hand:
to lie down in the place of torment."

THE NEARNESS OF DELIVERANCE, 51:1—52:12

"Listen to me, you who press after de- 51
liverance,
You who seek the LORD!
Look to the rock from which you were
hewn,
And the quarry from which you were
dug;
Look to Abraham your father,
And to Sarah who bore you!
For him alone did I call,
I blessed him, and multiplied him.
Even so shall the LORD comfort Zion,
He shall comfort all her ruins;
He shall make her wilderness like
Eden,
Her desert like the garden of the
LORD;
Joy and gladness shall be found in her,
Thanksgiving and the voice of singing.

"Hearken to me, O peoples;
O nations, give ear to me!
For instruction shall go forth from me,
And my truth as a light to the peoples.
My deliverance shall draw near in a
moment,
My salvation is on its way;
My arms shall rule the peoples,
The coast-lands shall wait for me,
And on my arm shall they put their
trust.

6 "Lift up your eyes to the heavens,
And look on the earth beneath!
For the heavens shall vanish like smoke,
And the earth shall wear out like a garment,
While its inhabitants shall likewise die;
But my salvation shall be forever,
And my triumph shall be unbroken.

7 "Listen to me, you who know what is right,
You people in whose hearts is my teaching!
Fear not the reproaches of mortal men,
Nor be dismayed at their revilings;
8 For the moth shall devour them like a garment,
And the worm shall devour them like wool;
But my triumph shall be forever,
And my salvation to all generations.

9 "Awake, awake, put on strength,
O arm of the LORD!
Awake, as in days of old,
as in generations long gone!
Was it not thou that didst hew Rahab in pieces,
that didst pierce the dragon?
10 Was it not thou that didst dry up the sea,
the waters of the mighty deep;
That didst make the depths of the sea a way
for the redeemed to pass over?
11 So the ransomed of the LORD will return by it,
And will come to Zion with singing,
And with everlasting joy upon their heads;
They will attain to joy and gladness,
And sorrow and sighing will flee away.

12 "I, I, am your comforter;
Why should you be afraid
Of man that dies, of mortal man,
That becomes like grass?
13 Why should you forget the LORD your Maker,
Who stretched out the heavens, and laid the foundations of the earth,
So that you live in continual dread
Of the fury of the oppressor, when he aims to destroy?
Where is the fury of the oppressor?
14 Soon shall the crouching captive be set at liberty;
He shall not sink down dead to the Pit,
Nor shall his bread fail.
For I the LORD am your God, 15
Who stirs up the sea, so that its billows roar—
The LORD of hosts is his name—
And I put my words in your mouth, 16
And hid you in the shadow of my hand,
When I stretched out the heavens, and laid the foundations of the earth,
And said to Zion, 'You are my people.' "

Rouse you, rouse you, 17
rise up, O Jerusalem,
Who have drunk at the hand of the LORD
the cup of his fury,
And have drained to the dregs
the bowl of intoxication!
There is none to guide her 18
of all the sons she has borne,
And there is none to take her by the hand
of all the sons she has reared.
These two things have befallen you— 19
who shall condole with you?—
Wreck and ruin, famine and sword—
who shall comfort you?—
Your sons lie swooning at all the street corners, 20
like an antelope in a net,
Filled with the fury of the LORD,
with the rebuke of your God.
Hear this, then, you afflicted one, 21
who are drunk, though not with wine!
Thus says your Lord, the LORD, 22
your God, who defends the cause of his people:
"See! I have taken from your hand
the cup of intoxication,
And you shall drink no more
of the bowl of my fury;
I will put it into the hand of your tormentors, 23
Those who said to you,
'Bow down, that we may pass over!'
And you made your back like the earth,
like a street for men to pass over."

Awake, awake, put on 52
your strength, O Zion;

Put on your beautiful garments,
O Jerusalem, the holy city!
For no more shall there come to you
an uncircumcised or unclean one.
2 Shake yourself from the dust, arise,
O captive Jerusalem;
Free yourself from the bonds on your neck,
O captive daughter of Zion!
3 For thus says the LORD:
"For nought were you sold,
and without money shall you be redeemed."
4 For thus says the Lord GOD:
"To Egypt went down my people at the first to sojourn there,
And the Assyrians oppressed them without cause;
5 But now what find I here?" is the oracle of the LORD.
"That my people have been taken captive for nought,
That their rulers howl over them," is the oracle of the LORD,
"And that all day long my name is despised!
6 Therefore my people shall know my name,
They shall know on that day that it is I who have spoken—
See! here I am."
7 How beautiful upon the mountains
are the feet of the heralds,
Who bring good news of peace,
news of salvation,
Who say to Zion,
"Your God has become king."
8 Hark! your watchmen lift up the voice,
together they sing;
For eye to eye they shall see,
when the LORD restores Zion.
9 Break into singing together,
you waste places of Jerusalem!
For the LORD has comforted his people,
he has redeemed Jerusalem.
10 The LORD has made bare his holy arm
in the eyes of all the nations;
And all the ends of the earth shall see
the salvation of our God.
11 Away! away! go out thence;
touch nothing unclean!
Go out of the midst of her; keep yourselves pure,
you who bear the vessels of the LORD!
For you shall not go out in haste,
nor depart in flight;
For the LORD shall go before you,
and the God of Israel shall be your rearguard.

THE SUFFERINGS AND THE TRIUMPH OF THE SERVANT, 52:13—53:12

Lo! my servant shall prosper,
He shall be exalted, and lifted up, and shall be very high.
As many were amazed at him—
So marred was his appearance beyond that of a man,
And his form beyond that of the sons of men—
So shall he startle many nations,
On account of him kings shall shut their mouths;
For what has not been told them shall they see,
And what they have not heard shall they contemplate.

"Who could have believed what we heard?
And the might of the LORD—to whom has it been revealed?
For he grew up like a sapling before us,
Like a root out of dry ground;
He had no form or charm, that we should look upon him,
No beauty, that we should admire him.
He was despised, and avoided by men,
A man of sorrows, and acquainted with pain;
And like one from whom men hide their faces,
He was despised, and we esteemed him not.

"Yet it was our pains that he bore,
Our sorrows that he carried;
While we accounted him stricken,
Smitten by God, and afflicted.
He was wounded for our transgressions,
He was crushed for our iniquities;
The chastisement of our welfare was upon him,
And through his stripes we were healed.
All we like sheep had gone astray,
We had turned everyone to his own way;

And the LORD made to light upon him
The guilt of us all.

7 "When he was oppressed, he humbled himself,
And opened not his mouth;
Like a sheep that is led to the slaughter,
Or like a ewe that is dumb before her shearers,
He opened not his mouth.
8 Through violence in judgment was he taken away,
And who gave thought to his fate—
How he was cut off from the land of the living,
For our transgressions was stricken to death?
9 They made his grave with the wicked,
His tomb with evildoers;
Although he had done no violence,
Nor was any deceit in his mouth."

10 Yet the LORD saw fit to crush him with pain,
So that, although he makes himself a guilt-offering,
He shall see posterity, shall prolong his life,
And the pleasure of the LORD shall prosper in his hand.
11 The fruit of his suffering shall he see,
In knowing himself righteous he shall be satisfied;
My servant shall bring righteousness to many,
And he shall himself bear their guilt.
12 Therefore will I divide him a portion with the great,
And with the strong shall he share the spoil;
Because he poured out his lifeblood to the utmost,
And was numbered with the transgressors,
And himself bore the sin of many,
And made intercession for the transgressors.

THE FUTURE GLORY OF JERUSALEM, 54:1–18

"Sing, O barren one, you who have borne no children;
Break into singing, and cry aloud, you who have not travailed!
For more are the children of her that is desolate
Than the children of her that is married," says the LORD.
"Enlarge the site of your tent, 2
And stretch without limit the curtains of your home;
Lengthen your cords, and make fast your pegs!
For to right and to left shall you spread abroad, 3
And your descendants shall take over the heritage of the nations,
And shall people the desolate cities.

"Fear not! for you shall not be put to shame; 4
And be not confounded! for you shall not be put to shame.
The shame of your youth shall you forget,
And the reproach of your widowhood shall you remember no more;
For your husband is your Maker, 5
Whose name is the LORD of hosts;
And your redeemer is the Holy One of Israel,
Who is called the God of all the earth;
For like a wife forsaken, and embittered in spirit, 6
The LORD has regarded you,
Like a wife of one's youth, when she is cast off,"
Says your God.

"For a little moment did I forsake you, 7
But with great pity will I bring you back to me;
In an outburst of wrath I hid my face 8
For a moment from you,
But with everlasting kindness will I have pity upon you,"
Says the LORD, your Redeemer.
"For like the days of Noah is this to me: 9
As I swore that the waters of Noah
Should no more pass over the earth,
So have I sworn no more to be angry with you,
Nor to rebuke you.
Though the mountains should be removed, 10
And the hills should waver,
My kindness shall not depart from you,
And my covenant of peace shall not waver,"
Says the LORD, who has pity upon you.

11 "O you afflicted one, storm-tossed, uncomforted,
Behold, I am setting your stones in emeralds,
And will lay your foundations in sapphires;
12 I will make your pinnacles of rubies,
Your gates of carbuncle stones,
And all your encircling wall of jewels.
13 All your sons shall be taught by the LORD,
And great shall be the prosperity of your children;
14 By righteousness shall you be established.
You shall be far from oppression, for you shall have nothing to fear,
And far from destruction, for it shall not come near you.
15 "If anyone stir up strife, it comes not from me;
He who stirs up strife with you shall fall to ruin upon you.
16 Behold, I have created the smith,
Who blows a fire of coals,
And brings forth a tool that is suited to its work;
I have created also the destroyer to make havoc,
17 And no weapon that is forged against you shall succeed,
And every tongue that is raised against you shall you confute.
This is the lot of the servants of the LORD,
And this their vindication at my hand," is the oracle of the LORD.

A CALL TO THE NEEDY, 55:1–13

55 "Ho! everyone that is thirsty, come to the waters,
And he that has no money, come, buy, and eat!
Come, buy grain without money,
And wine and milk without price!
2 Why should you spend money for what is not bread,
And your earnings for what does not satisfy?
If you but listen to me, you shall eat what is good,
And shall delight yourselves with rich nourishment.

3 "Incline your ear, and come to me;
Listen, that you may live!
For an everlasting covenant will I make with you,
The favor assured to David.
As once I made him a witness to peoples,
A leader and commander of peoples,
So you shall call nations you know not,
And nations that know you not shall run to you,
For the sake of the LORD your God,
The Holy One of Israel, because he has shed glory on you.

"Seek the LORD while he may be found,
Call upon him while he is near!
Let the wicked forsake his way,
And the unrighteous man his thoughts;
And let him return to the LORD, that he may have pity upon him,
And to our God, for he shall abundantly pardon.
For my thoughts are not your thoughts,
Nor are your ways my ways," is the oracle of the LORD;
"But as the heavens are higher than the earth,
So are my ways higher than your ways,
And my thoughts than your thoughts.

"For, as the rain comes down,
And the snow from heaven,
And returns not thither,
Without having watered the earth,
And made it bring forth and sprout,
Giving seed to the sower,
And bread to the eater,
So shall my word be that goes out of my mouth—
It shall not return to me fruitless,
Without having done the thing that I pleased,
And accomplishing the purpose for which I sent it.

"For with joy shall you go out,
And in peace shall you be led;
The mountains and the hills shall break into singing before you,
And all the trees of the field shall clap their hands.
Instead of the thorn shall come up the cypress,
And instead of the brier shall come up the myrtle;
And they shall be to the LORD a memorial,
An everlasting sign that shall not be cut off."

A WELCOME TO ALIENS AND EUNUCHS, 56:1–8

Thus says the LORD:
"Keep the law, and do what is right;
For my salvation is near at hand,
And my triumph is ready to be revealed.
Happy the man who does this,
The son of man who holds fast by it,
Who keeps the sabbath by not profaning it,
And keeps his hand from doing any evil!"

Let not the alien who has attached himself to the LORD say,
"The LORD will surely separate me from his people."
And let not the eunuch say,
"Lo! I am a dry tree."
For thus says the LORD:
"The eunuchs who keep my sabbaths,
And choose the things that I delight in,
And hold fast by my covenant—
To them will I give in my house and within my walls
A monument and a name better than sons and daughters;
I will give them an everlasting name,
One that shall not be cut off.
And the aliens who attach themselves to the LORD, to minister to him,
To love the name of the LORD, and to be his servants,
Even everyone who keeps the sabbath by not profaning it,
And holds fast by my covenant—
I will bring them to my holy mountain,
And will make them joyful in my house of prayer;
Their burnt-offerings and their sacrifices shall be welcome upon my altar,
For my house shall be called a house of prayer for all the peoples."

This is the oracle of the Lord GOD,
Who gathers the outcasts of Israel:
"I will yet gather to them
Those who were gathered against them."

THE FAITHLESS RULERS OF ISRAEL, 56:9–12

All you beasts of the field,
come to devour—
all you beasts in the forest!
My watchmen are all of them blind, 10
without any sense;
They are all of them dumb dogs,
that cannot bark,
But lie down dreaming,
loving to slumber.
And the dogs are greedy, 11
they cannot be satisfied—
Such are shepherds who have no intelligence—
They have turned all of them to their own way,
each without exception to his own gain:
"Come, let me fetch wine, 12
and let us fill ourselves with strong drink!
And tomorrow shall be as today,
a right royal day!"

THE UNTIMELY FATE OF THE RIGHTEOUS, 57:1–2

The righteous man perishes, 57
and none lays it to heart;
And godly men are swept away,
with none to give it a thought.
For in face of the evil the righteous man is swept away,
he enters into peace; 2
While they rest upon their beds,
he goes his righteous and upright way.

A WARNING TO THE IDOLATROUS, 57:3–13

But you—come hither, 3
you sons of a sorceress,
Offspring of an adulterer and a harlot!
against whom are you making merry? 4
Against whom are you opening the mouth wide,
and putting out the tongue?
Are you not apostate children,
a faithless brood—
You who inflame yourselves with lust among the terebinths, 5
under every spreading tree,
Who slaughter children in the valley,
among the clefts of the crags?
With the smooth stones of the valley your lot is cast; 6
they, they are your portion;
To them have you poured libations,
and offered cereal-offerings;

And for these things can I be appeased?
7 On a high and lofty mountain
you have set up your bed;
And thither have you climbed
to offer sacrifice.
8 Behind the door and the side posts
you have set up your phallic symbol;
And apart from me have you stripped and gone up,
you have distended your parts;
You have bargained for those
whose embraces you love;
And with them have you multiplied your harlotries,
while gazing on the phallus.
9 You have journeyed to Molech with oil,
and have offered many perfumes;
And you have sent your envoys afar,
even to the depths of Sheol.
10 You have wearied yourself with your many wanderings,
yet have not said, "It is hopeless!"
You found your strength renewed,
therefore you did not give up.
11 And of whom were you in such fear and dread
that you played the traitor,
And gave no thought to me,
nor paid any heed?
Was it not because I held my peace and closed my eyes
that you ceased to reverence me?
12 But I will expose this righteousness of yours,
these doings of yours;
13 And your loathsome idols shall not avail you when you cry,
nor save you in your time of distress:
The wind shall lift them all up,
a breath shall bear them away;
But he who takes refuge in me shall inherit the land,
and possess my holy mountain.

HEALING FOR THE WOUNDED SPIRIT, 57:14–21

14 One says:
"Grade up, grade up, clear the way;
Remove every obstacle from the way of my people!"
15 For thus says the high and exalted One,
Who dwells enthroned for ever, and whose name is Holy:
"I dwell enthroned on high, as the Holy One,
But with him also that is contrite and humble in spirit,
To revive the spirit of the humble,
And to revive the heart of the contrite.
16 For I will not contend for ever,
Nor be angry for all time;
For from me proceeds the spirit,
And the living being that I have made.
17 Because of their sin I was angry for a moment,
And I smote them, while I hid my face in wrath;
They went on rebelliously in the way of their own desires,
18 And I saw their doings," says the LORD.
"But now will I heal them, and guide them,
And will give full consolation to them and their mourners,
19 Producing as the utterance of the lips,
'Peace, peace to the far and the near.'
20 But the wicked are like the uptossed sea,
For it cannot rest,
But its waters toss up mire and filth.
21 There is no peace," says my God, "for the wicked."

TRUE AND FALSE FASTING, 58:1–12

58 "Call aloud, hold not back,
Lift up your voice like a trumpet;
Show my people their transgression,
The house of Jacob their sins!
2 Daily, indeed, they consult me,
And delight to know my ways,
Like a nation that does what is right,
And forsakes not the law of its God.
They ask me for righteous ordinances,
They delight to draw near to God:
3 'Why have we fasted, and thou seest not;
Why have we humbled ourselves, and thou heedest not?'

"If on your fast day you pursue your own business,
And press on with all your labors;
4 If you fast for the sake of strife and contention,
And to smite with godless fist;

You fast not on such a day
As to make your voice heard on high.
Can such be the fast I choose—
A day for a man to humble himself,
To bow down his head like a bulrush,
To grovel in sackcloth and ashes?
Will you call this a fast,
A day of pleasure to the LORD?

"Is not this the fast I choose—
To loose the bonds of wickedness,
To undo the knots of the yoke,
To let the oppressed go free,
And every yoke to snap?
Is it not to share your bread with the hungry,
And the homeless poor to bring home;
When you see the naked, to cover him,
And to hide not yourself from your own flesh?

"Then shall your light break out as the dawn,
And your healing shall spring forth speedily;
Your vindication shall go before you,
And the glory of the LORD shall be your rearguard.
You shall call, and the LORD will answer;
You shall cry, and he will say, 'Here I am!'

"If you remove from your midst the yoke,
The finger of scorn, and mischievous speech,
And share your bread with the hungry,
And satisfy the craving of the afflicted,
Then shall your light shine out in darkness,
And your gloom shall be as noonday;
And the LORD shall guide you continually,
And shall satisfy you with rich nourishment;
And your strength shall he renew,
And you shall be like a well-watered garden,
Or like a spring of water,
Whose waters fail not;
And your people shall rebuild the ancient ruins,
You shall raise up the foundations of many generations;
And you shall be called, 'The rebuilder of broken walls,
The restorer of streets to dwell in.'"

THE KEEPING OF THE SABBATH, 58:13–14

"If you turn back your foot from the sabbath, 13
Not doing your own business on my holy day;
If you call the sabbath a delight,
And the holy day of the LORD honorable;
If you honor it by not following your accustomed ways,
Nor doing your own business, nor indulging in idle talk—
Then shall you find your delight in the LORD, 14
And I will make you ride in triumph over the heights of the earth,
And will give you the heritage of Jacob your father to enjoy";
For the mouth of the LORD has spoken.

SIN, SORROW, CONFESSION, AND REDEMPTION, 59:1–21

See! the LORD's hand is not too short to save, **59**
Nor his ear too dull to hear;
But your iniquities have been a barrier 2
Between you and your God,
And your sins have hidden his face,
So that he could not hear you.
For your hands are stained with blood, 3
And your fingers with iniquity;
Your lips have spoken lies,
And your tongue utters untruth.
There is none who sues honestly, 4
None who pleads his case truthfully;
But each one trusts in vanity, and speaks lies,
Conceives wrong, and brings forth mischief.

Vipers' eggs they hatch, 5
And spiders' webs they weave;
He who eats of their eggs will die,
And the egg that is left uneaten will hatch out into an adder.
Their webs are useless for clothing, 6
With their products no man can cover himself;
Their works are works of mischief,
And deeds of violence are in their hands.

7 Their feet run to evil,
They make haste to shed innocent blood;
Their thoughts are thoughts of mischief,
Wreck and ruin are in their paths.
8 The way of peace they know not,
And no justice is in their tracks;
Their paths have they made crooked,
He who walks in them knows nothing of peace.

9 Therefore is justice far from us,
And righteousness does not reach us;
We look for light, but lo! darkness,
For the rays of dawn, but we walk in gloom.
10 We grope like blind men along a wall,
Like men without eyes we grope;
We stumble at noonday as in the twilight,
In the strength of manhood we are like the dead.
11 All of us growl like bears,
And sadly moan like doves;
We look for redress, but it comes not,
For salvation, but it remains far from us.
12 For many are our transgressions before thee,
And our sins bear witness against us;
Our transgressions are ever with us,
And our iniquities we know—
13 Rebellion, and unfaithfulness to the LORD,
Turning our backs on our God,
Speaking cruel and defiant words,
Conceiving and uttering lies from the heart.
14 Justice has been driven back,
And righteousness stands afar;
Truth stumbles in the public place,
And honesty can find no entrance;
15 Truth is not to be found,
And he who shuns evil makes himself an easy mark.

"The LORD saw with displeasure
That there was no justice;
16 And when he saw that there was no man—
When he saw with amazement that there was none to interpose—
His own arm helped him,
His righteous might upheld him.
17 He put on righteousness as a coat of mail,
With the helmet of salvation on his head;
He put on garments of vengeance for clothing,
And wrapped himself in fury as a cloak.
According to men's deserts shall he make recompense to them—
Wrath to his enemies, shame to his foes—
That men may revere the name of the LORD from the west,
And his glory from the rising of the sun;
For he shall come like a pent-up stream,
Which the breath of the LORD drives on;
But to Zion shall he come as redeemer,
And shall remove transgression from Jacob,"
Is the oracle of the LORD.

"As for me, this is my covenant with you," says the LORD: "My spirit which is upon you, and my words which I have put in your mouth, shall not depart from your mouth, nor from the mouth of your offspring, nor from the mouth of your offspring's offspring," says the LORD, "from henceforth, even forever."

THE GLORY OF THE NEW JERUSALEM, 60:1–22

Arise, shine! for your light has come,
And the glory of the LORD has risen upon you.
For lo! darkness shall cover the earth,
And thick darkness the peoples;
But upon you the LORD shall rise,
And upon you his glory shall appear;
And nations shall walk by your light,
And kings by the brightness of your rising.

Lift up your eyes round about, and see!
All of them gather, they come to you—
Your sons shall come from afar,
And your daughters shall be borne on the hip.
When you see it, you shall be radiant,
And your heart shall throb and swell;
For the riches of the sea shall be turned to you,
The wealth of the nations shall come to you.

A flood of camels shall cover you,
The young camels of Midian and Ephah;
All those of Sheba shall come;
Gold and frankincense shall they bring,
And shall herald the praises of the LORD.
All the flocks of Kedar shall gather to you,
The rams of Nebaioth shall minister to you;
They shall mount my altar as a well-pleasing sacrifice,
And my glorious house will I glorify.

Who are these that fly like a cloud,
Or like doves to their windows?
It is the ships which are gathering for me,
With the vessels of Tarshish in the van,
To bring your sons from afar,
Their silver and their gold with them,
In honor of the LORD your God,
The Holy One of Israel, because he has glorified you.

And aliens shall build your walls,
And their kings shall minister to you;
For though in my wrath I smote you,
In my favor will I have pity upon you.
And your gates shall be open continually,
Day and night shall they not be closed,
That men may bring to you the wealth of the nations,
With their kings conducted in state.
For the nation and the kingdom that will not serve you shall perish—
Utterly waste shall those nations be laid.

The glory of Lebanon shall come to you,
The cypress, the pine, and the larch together,
To glorify the place of my sanctuary,
And that I may do honor to my footstool.
Then the sons of those who oppressed you shall come bending to you,
And all those who scorned you shall bow down at the soles of your feet;
And they shall call you, "The city of the LORD,
The Zion of the Holy One of Israel."

Instead of your being forsaken and hated,
With none passing through you,
I will make you a pride forever,
A joy for all generations.
You shall suck the milk of the nations, 16
The breast of kings shall you suck;
And you shall know that I the LORD am your savior,
That your redeemer is the Mighty One of Jacob.

Instead of bronze will I bring gold, 17
And instead of iron will I bring silver;
And instead of wood, bronze,
And instead of stones, iron;
And Peace will I make your government,
And Righteousness your ruler.
No more shall news of violence be heard in your land, 18
Nor of wreck and ruin within your borders,
But you shall call your walls Salvation,
And your gates Praise.

No more shall the sun be your light by day, 19
Nor the moon by night shine upon you;
But the LORD shall be your unfailing light,
And your God your glory.
No more shall your sun set, 20
Nor shall your moon wane;
For the LORD shall be your unfailing light,
And your days of mourning shall be ended.

Your people shall be all of them righteous, 21
And shall possess the land forever,
As the shoot of my planting, the work of my hands,
With which I may glorify myself.
The least one shall become a tribe, 22
The smallest a mighty nation—
I the LORD will hasten it in its proper time.

THE YEAR OF THE LORD'S FAVOR, 61:1—62:12

The spirit of the Lord GOD is upon me, 61
For the LORD has anointed me;
He has sent me to bring good news to the lowly,
To bind up the broken-hearted,
To proclaim liberty to the captives,
And release to the prisoners;
To proclaim the year of the LORD'S favor, 2

And the day of our God's vengeance;
To comfort all mourners,
3 To provide for the mourners of Zion,
To give them a crown instead of ashes,
Oil of joy instead of a garment of mourning,
A song of praise instead of a drooping spirit,
That they may be called oak trees of righteousness,
The planting of the LORD, with which he may glorify himself.

4 Then shall they rebuild the ancient ruins,
They shall raise up the desolations of old;
They shall renew the wasted cities,
The desolations of age after age.
5 And strangers shall stand and feed your flocks,
Aliens shall be your plowmen and your vinedressers;
6 But you shall be called the priests of the LORD,
The ministers of our God shall you be named.
You shall enjoy the wealth of the nations,
And in their glory shall you revel.

7 Because their shame was in double measure,
And contempt was the lot they inherited,
Therefore in their land shall they inherit a double measure,
Everlasting joy shall be theirs.
8 For I the LORD love justice,
I hate robbery and crime;
So I will faithfully give them their recompense,
And an everlasting covenant will I make with them.
9 Their sons shall be known among the nations,
Their descendants in the midst of the peoples;
All who see them shall acknowledge them
As a race that the LORD has blessed.

10 I will greatly rejoice in the LORD,
I will exult in my God;
For he has clothed me in garments of salvation,
He has arrayed me in the robe of righteousness,
As a bridegroom puts on his crown,
And as a bride adorns herself with her jewels.
For as the earth puts forth her shoots,
And as a garden makes the seed that is sown in it to spring up,
So the Lord GOD shall make righteousness and praise
To spring up before all the nations.

For Zion's sake will I not keep silent,
And for Jerusalem's sake will I not rest,
Until her vindication come forth clear as light,
And her salvation as a burning torch.
Then the nations shall see your vindication,
And all kings your glory;
You shall be called by a new name,
Which the mouth of the LORD shall determine;
And you shall be a glorious crown in the hand of the LORD,
A royal diadem in the hand of your God.

No more shall you be named "Forsaken,"
nor your land be named "Desolate";
But you shall be called "My delight is in her,"
and your land "Married";
For the LORD delights in you,
and your land shall be married.
As a young man marries a maiden,
so shall your Builder marry you;
And as a bridegroom rejoices over his bride,
so shall your God rejoice over you.

Over your walls, O Jerusalem,
I have appointed watchmen,
Who never keep silent
by day or by night.
You who are the LORD'S remembrancers,
take no rest for yourselves,
And give him no rest,
until he establish
And make Jerusalem
a praise in the earth!
The LORD has sworn by his right hand,
and by his strong arm:
"No more will I give your grain
to be food for your enemies,

Nor shall aliens drink your vintage,
for which you have labored;
9 But those who have garnered the grain shall eat it,
and praise the LORD,
And those who have gathered the vintage shall drink it
in my holy courts."

0 Pass through, pass through the gates,
prepare the way of the people;
Grade up, grade up the highway,
clear it of stones;
raise a signal over the peoples.
1 See! the LORD has made proclamation
to the end of the earth:
"Say to the daughter of Zion,
'See! your salvation has come;
See! his reward is with him,
and his recompense before him.'
2 They shall be called, 'The holy people,
the redeemed of the LORD';
And you shall be called, 'Sought out,
the city unforsaken.'"

THE DAY OF THE LORD'S VENGEANCE, 63:1–6

3 "Who is this that comes from Edom,
In crimson garments from Bozrah,
This one in glorious apparel,
As he strides along in his strength?"

"It is I, who have promised vindication,
And am mighty to save."

2 "Why is thy clothing red,
Thy garments like his who treads in the wine press?"

3 "The wine trough I trod alone,
Of the peoples no one was with me.
I trod them in my anger,
And trampled them in my fury;
Their lifeblood besprinkled my garments,
And all my clothing I stained.
4 For a day of vengeance was in my heart,
And my year of redemption had come.
5 I looked, but there was none to help,
I looked in amazement, but there was none to uphold;
So my own arm helped me,
And my fury upheld me.

I trod down the peoples in my anger, 6
And shattered them in my fury;
And I brought down their glory to the earth."

PRAISE AND PRAYER, 63:7—64:11

The LORD'S gracious deeds will I recount 7
the praises of the LORD,
As befits all that the LORD has done for us,
even his great kindness to the house of Israel,
Which he showed them according to his pity,
according to the fulness of his love.
He said, "Surely they are my people, 8
sons who will not play me false";
So he became their savior
in all their distress. 9
It was no messenger or angel,
but his own presence that saved them;
In his love and in his pity
he redeemed them;
He took them up and carried them
all the days of old.
But they rebelled, 10
and grieved his holy spirit;
So he turned to be their enemy,
he fought against them.

Then one recalled the days of old, 11
of Moses and his people.
Where is he who brought up from the sea
the shepherd of his flock?
Where is he who put within him
his holy spirit;
He who caused his glorious arm to go 12
at Moses' right hand;
He who cleft the waters before them,
to make himself an everlasting name;
He who led them through the depths, 13
without their stumbling,
Like a horse through the steppe,
like cattle going down to the valley? 14
So did the spirit of the LORD guide them,
So didst thou lead thy people,
to make thyself a glorious name.

Look down from the heavens, and see, 15
From thy holy and glorious abode!

Where are thy zeal and thy might,
Thy yearning pity and mercy?
Restrain thyself not!
16 For thou art our Father.
Though Abraham know us not,
And Israel acknowledge us not,
Thou, O LORD, art our Father,
Our Redeemer from of old is thy name.
17 Why, O LORD, dost thou leave us to wander from thy ways;
Why dost thou harden our heart against reverence for thee?
Return, for the sake of thy servants,
The tribes of thy heritage!
18 Why have wicked men trampled upon thy holy hill;
Why have our enemies trodden down thy sanctuary?
19 We have become like those over whom thou hast not ruled from of old,
Like those who have not been called by thy name.

64 O that thou wouldst rend the heavens and come down,
That the mountains might quake at thy presence—
2 As when fire kindles brushwood,
And fire makes water to boil—
To make known thy name to thine enemies,
That the nations might tremble at thy presence,
3 While thou doest terrible things which we looked not for,
4 And which men have not heard from of old!
No ear has heard, no eye has seen
A god apart from thee, who works for those who wait for him.

5 But thou hast thwarted those who do right,
Who remember thy ways;
Thou wast angry, and we sinned,
Through our doings we fell into guilt.
6 We have all become like an unclean man,
And all our righteous deeds like a garment defiled;
We all fade like a leaf,
And our guilt bears us away like the wind.
7 There is none who calls on thy name,
Nor rouses himself to lay hold on thee;
For thou hast hidden thy face from us,
And hast delivered us into the power of our sins.

8 Yet now, O LORD, thou art our Father;
We are the clay, and thou art our potter;
We are all of us the work of thy hand.
Be not angry, O LORD, beyond measure,
Nor remember our guilt forever.
Look! we beseech thee—for we are all thy people—
Thy holy cities have become a wilderness, 1
Zion has become a wilderness,
Jerusalem a desolation;
Our holy and beautiful house, 1
Where our fathers praised thee,
Has been burned with fire,
And all that we cherished has been laid waste.
For these things, O LORD, wilt thou restrain thyself; 1
Wilt thou keep silent, and afflict us beyond measure?

JUDGMENT AND SALVATION, 65:1–25

I was ready to be consulted by those who asked me not, 6
I was ready to be found by those who sought me not;
I said, "Here am I! Here am I!"
To a nation that called not upon my name.
I spread out my hands all day long 2
To a rebellious people,
Who walk in a way that is not good,
After their own devices—
A people who provoke me 3
To my face continually,
Offering sacrifices in gardens,
And burning incense on tiles;
Who sit in graves, 4
And pass the night in caves,
Who eat the flesh of swine,
And in whose vessels is broth of unclean meats;
Who say, "Stand off; 5
Come not near me, lest I make you taboo!"
These men are a smoke in my nostrils,
A fire that burns continually.
See! it stands written before me: 6
"I will not keep silent, until I have requited—
Until I have requited on their bosom
Their own sins and the sins of their fathers as well," says the LORD,
"Who have offered sacrifices upon the mountains, 7
And have dishonored me upon the hills;
Therefore I will measure out their recompense on their bosom."

8 Thus says the LORD:
"As when vintage is found in the cluster,
And one says, 'Destroy it not,
For a blessing is in it,'
So will I do for my servants' sake,
That I may not destroy the whole.
9 I will bring out of Jacob a scion,
Out of Judah an heir to my mountains;
And my chosen ones shall inherit the land,
My servants shall dwell in it.
10 And Sharon shall become a fold for flocks,
And the valley of Achor a pasture for herds,
To my people who have sought me.
11 But as for you who forsake the LORD,
And forget my holy mountain,
Who spread a table for Fortune,
And fill cups of mixed wine for Destiny,
12 I will destine you for the sword,
And you shall all bow down to the slaughter;
Because, when I called, you did not answer,
When I spoke, you did not listen;
But you did what was evil in my eyes,
And chose what displeased me."

13 Therefore thus says the Lord GOD:
"Behold, my servants shall eat,
But you shall be hungry;
Behold, my servants shall drink,
But you shall be thirsty;
Behold, my servants shall rejoice,
But you shall be put to shame;
14 Behold, my servants shall sing for gladness of heart;
But you shall cry for sorrow of heart,
And shall wail for breaking of spirit;
15 And you shall leave your name as a curse for my chosen ones:
'So may the Lord GOD slay you!'
But my servants shall be called by another name.
16 Then he who prays for a blessing in the land shall pray
by the God of truth,
And he who swears an oath in the land shall swear
by the God of truth;
Because the former troubles shall have been forgotten,
and hidden from my eyes.
17 For behold, I am creating new heavens,
and a new earth;
And the former things shall not be remembered,
nor brought to mind;
But men shall rejoice and exult forever 18
in what I create;
For behold, I am creating Jerusalem
an exultation,
and my people a joy;
And I will exult over Jerusalem, 19
and rejoice in her people.
There shall no more be heard in her
the sound of weeping,
nor the sound of crying.
And there shall no more pass from her 20
young or old,
Without completing his full length of life;
But the youngest shall die a hundred years old,
While he who falls short of a hundred
shall be counted accursed.
And they shall build houses, and inhabit them; 21
And they shall plant vineyards, and
eat the fruit of them—
They shall not build, and another inhabit; 22
Nor shall they plant, and another eat—
For as the days of a tree shall be the
days of my people,
And the work of their hands shall my
chosen ones enjoy to the end.
They shall not labor in vain, 23
Nor bring forth children for destruction;
For they are a race of the LORD'S
blessed ones,
And their offspring shall remain with them.
Then, before they call, I will answer; 24
While they are still speaking, I will hear.
The wolf and the lamb shall feed together, 25
And the lion shall eat straw like the ox;
But the serpent—its food shall be dust!
They shall do no harm or destruction
On all my holy mountain," says the LORD.

THE NEW HEAVENS AND THE NEW EARTH, 66:1–24

Thus says the LORD: 66
"The heavens are my throne,
And the earth is my footstool;

What manner of house, then, would
you build for me,
What manner of place as my residence?
2 My hand made all these things,
And all these things are mine," is the
oracle of the LORD;
"Yet to this man will I have regard—
The one who is humble and contrite in
spirit,
And who trembles at my word.
3 But he who slaughters an ox, as well as
he who slays a man,
He who sacrifices a sheep, as well as he
who strangles a dog,
He who brings an oblation, as well as
he who sheds the blood of swine,
He who makes a memorial offering of
frankincense, as well as he who
blesses an idol—
These choose their own ways,
And delight in their abominations;
4 So will I also choose their torment,
And will bring upon them their terrors;
Because, when I called, no one answered,
When I spoke, they did not listen;
But they did what was evil in my eyes,
And chose what displeased me."

5 Hear the word of the LORD,
You who tremble at his word:
"Your brothers who hate you
And cast you from their midst,
For my name's sake have said,
'Let the LORD show forth his glory,
That we may look on your joy!';
But they shall be put to shame.

6 Hark! an uproar from the city,
a cry from the temple;
Hark! it is the LORD who is dealing out
recompense to his enemies.
7 But before she travailed,
she gave birth;
Before her pains came on her,
she was delivered of a son.
8 Who has heard the like of this,
who has seen the like?
Can a land pass through travail
in a single day?
Can a nation be brought to the birth
all at once?
But as soon as Zion travailed,
she gave birth to her children.
9 Shall I bring to the birth and not give
delivery?"
says the LORD.
"Or shall I who give delivery shut up
the womb?"
says your God.
"Rejoice with Jerusalem, and exult on 10
her account,
all you who love her;
Be very joyful with her,
all you who mourn for her;
That you may suck to your fill 11
from her soothing breast,
And nurse to your heart's delight
from her bountiful bosom!"
For thus says the LORD: 12
"Behold, I am extending to her prosperity like a river,
And the wealth of the nations like a
sweeping torrent;
And her sucklings shall be carried on
the hip,
And dandled on the knees.
Like one whom his mother comforts, 13
So will I comfort you—
Through Jerusalem shall you be comforted.
And when you see it, your heart shall 14
rejoice,
And your limbs shall flourish like
young grass.
So shall the power of the LORD be revealed toward his servants,
And his indignation toward his enemies.
For behold, the LORD shall come like 15
fire,
His chariots like a whirlwind,
To bring home his anger with fury,
His rebuke with flames of fire;
For the LORD shall hold judgment 16
upon all flesh
By fire and by his sword,
And the LORD'S slain shall be many.
Those who consecrate and purify 17
themselves for worship in the
gardens,
Following someone in the midst,
Who eat the flesh of swine,
Of vermin and of mice,
Shall come to an end together,"
Is the oracle of the LORD.
"For I know their works and their 18
thoughts,
And I am coming to gather all nations
and tongues;
They shall come, and see my glory,
And through them will I set up a sign. 19
Such of them as escape will I send to
the nations,

To Tarshish, Put, and Lydia, to
Meshech and Rosh,
To Tuval and Javan, the distant
coast-lands,
Which have not heard my fame, nor
seen my glory.
They shall proclaim my glory among
the nations,
20 And men shall bring all your brothers
from all the nations,
On horseback, in chariots and covered
wagons,
On mules and dromedaries,
For an offering to the LORD on my
holy mountain Jerusalem,"
Says the LORD,
"As the children of Israel bring an
offering
In a clean vessel to the house of the
LORD.
And some of these also will I take for 21
priests, for Levites,"
Says the LORD.
"For as the new heavens and the new 22
earth
Which I am making shall continue be-
fore me,"
Is the oracle of the LORD,
"So shall your race and your name con-
tinue.
And from new moon to new moon, and 23
from sabbath to sabbath,
All flesh shall come to worship before me,"
Says the LORD.
"And they shall go out and gaze on the 24
dead bodies of the men
Who have rebelled against me;
For their worm shall not die, nor shall
their fire be quenched,
But they shall be an abhorrence to all
flesh."

THE BOOK OF JEREMIAH

INTRODUCTION, 1:1–3

1 THE words of Jeremiah, the
son of Hilkiah, one of the priests
that were at Anathoth in the
2 land of Benjamin, to whom the
word of the LORD came in the days of
Josiah, the son of Amon, king of Judah,
3 in the thirteenth year of his reign, and
continued to come in the days of Jehoiakim, the son of Josiah, king of Judah, till the end of the eleventh year of
Zedekiah, the son of Josiah, king of Judah, when Jerusalem was carried into
exile in the fifth month.

THE CALL OF THE PROPHET, 1:4–19

4 The word of the LORD came to me,
saying,
5 "Before I formed you in the womb I knew you,
And before you were born I set you apart,
I appointed you a prophet to the nations."
6 Then said I,
"Ah, Lord GOD! I cannot speak;
For I am only a youth."
7 But the LORD said to me,
"Do not say, 'I am only a youth';
For to all to whom I send you shall you go,
And all that I command you shall you speak.
8 Do not be afraid of them;
For I am with you to deliver you,"
Is the oracle of the LORD.
9 Then the LORD stretched forth his
hand, and touched my mouth. And
the LORD said to me,
"See! I put my words in your mouth;
10 This day I give you authority over the nations and kingdoms,
To root up and to pull down, to wreck and to ruin,
To build and to plant."

11 The word of the LORD came to me,
saying,
"What do you see, Jeremiah?"
I said,
"I see a twig of an almond tree."
Then the LORD said to me, 12
"You have seen aright; for I am
watching over my word to put it into
effect."
A second time the word of the LORD 13
came to me, saying,
"What do you see?"
I said,
"I see a pot blown upon, and its
blower is in the north."
Then the LORD said to me, 14
"Out of the north shall trouble be
blown upon all the inhabitants of the
land. For behold, I am summoning all 15
the kingdoms of the north," is the oracle of the LORD; "and they shall come
and set up each his throne at the entrances of the gates of Jerusalem, and
against all her walls round about, and
against all the cities of Judah. And I 16
will pronounce my judgments against
them for all the wickedness they have
done in forsaking me, and offering sacrifices to other gods, and worshiping
the works of their own hands. You, 17
then, gird up your loins, and arise, and
speak to them all that I command you.
Do not be dismayed before them, lest I
dismay you before them. For behold, 18
I make you this day a fortified city, an
iron pillar, and a bronze wall, against
the whole land—the kings of Judah, its
princes and priests, and its common
people. They shall fight against you, 19
but they shall not overcome you; for I
am with you to deliver you," is the oracle of the LORD.

ISRAEL'S APOSTASY, 2:1—4:4

The word of the LORD came to me, 2
saying,
"Go and proclaim in the hearing of Jerusalem, 'Thus says the LORD: 2
"I recall your youthful devotion,
your bridal love,
How you followed me through the desert,
through a land unsown.

3 Israel was sacred to the LORD,
his firstfruits of harvest;
All who ate of it were held guilty—
trouble overtook them,"
is the oracle of the LORD.' "
4 Hear the word of the LORD, O house
of Jacob, even all the families of the
5 house of Israel. Thus says the LORD:
"What offense did your fathers find in
me,
That they went far from me,
And followed a thing of nought,
And themselves became nought?
6 They asked not, 'Where is the LORD
that brought us up
From the land of Egypt,
That led us through the desert,
Through a land of steppes and pits,
Through a land of drought and deep
darkness,
Through a land that no man traversed,
Where no man dwelt?'
7 I brought you to a garden land,
To eat its fruits and its good things;
But you came and defiled my land,
And made my heritage an abomination.
8 The priests asked not, 'Where is the
LORD?'
Those who handled the law cared
nothing about me;
The rulers rebelled against me,
And the prophets prophesied by the
Baal,
And followed things that were useless.
9 Yet against you too must I bring an
indictment,"
Is the oracle of the LORD,
"And against your children's children.
10 For pass over to the coast-lands of
Cyprus, and see,
Or send to Kedar, scan closely, and
see,
If ever there has been such a thing as
this!
11 Has a nation changed its gods,
Which are no gods?
Yet my people have changed their
Glory
For that which is useless.
12 Be aghast, O heavens, at this;
Be shocked, O earth, beyond words,"
Is the oracle of the LORD.
13 "For my people have committed two
crimes:
They have forsaken me, the fountain
of living water,
To hew for themselves cisterns, broken cisterns,
That can hold no water.

"Is Israel a slave; or a home-born serf? 14
Why, then, has he fallen a prey?
Against him the young lions have 15
roared,
They have lifted up their voice;
His land have they made a desolation,
His cities are destroyed and left without inhabitant.
The sons also of Memphis and Daphne 16
break the crown of your head;
But have you not brought this upon 17
yourself through your neglect of
the LORD your God,
At the time when he led you on the
way?
Now what business have you on the 18
road to Egypt,
To drink the water of the Nile?
Or what business have you on the road
to Assyria,
To drink the water of the River?
Your own wickedness will teach you, 19
And your own apostasy will convict
you;
You will know and see how bad and
bitter a thing it is
To forsake the LORD your God, and
to cherish no reverence for me,"
Is the oracle of the Lord, the GOD of
hosts.

"For long ago you broke your yoke, 20
you burst your bonds, and said
'I will not serve';
And on every high hill, and under
every spreading tree,
you reclined and played the
harlot.
Yet I planted you a choice vine, 21
all true seed;
How, then, are you changed to a rank
vine,
a wild plant?
Though you wash yourself with lye, 22
and use much soap,
Your guilt stands ingrained in my
sight,"
is the oracle of the Lord GOD.
"How can you say, 'I am not defiled, 23
nor have I run after the Baals'?
Look at your course in the Valley,
see what you have done!
You are a restive young camel, doubling on her tracks,
a wild ass used to the desert, 24

Sniffing the wind in her heat—
who can restrain her lust?
None that seek her need weary themselves;
in her month will they find her.
25 Keep your feet from running bare,
your throat from going dry;
But you say, 'It is hopeless! for I love alien gods,
and after them will I run.'

26 "As a thief is abashed when he is discovered,
so shall the house of Israel be abashed—
They, their kings, and their princes,
their priests, and their prophets,
27 Who say to a block of wood, 'You are my father,'
and to a stone, 'You have borne me'—
For they have turned to me their back,
and not their face;
Yet in their time of trouble they say,
'Arise, and save us!'
28 But where are your gods
whom you made for yourself?
Let them arise, and save you—if they can!—
in your time of trouble;
For as many in number as your cities
are your gods, O Judah!

29 "Why should you find fault with me,
since all of you have rebelled against me?"
is the oracle of the LORD.
30 "In vain did I smite your children,
you took no warning;
The sword devoured your prophets
like a ravening lion;
31 But you neither reverenced nor listened to
the word of the LORD.
Have I been a desert to Israel,
or a land of thick darkness?
Why, then, do my people say,
'We are our own masters,
we will come no more to thee'?
32 Can a girl forget her ornaments,
a bride her attire?
Yet my people have forgotten me
days without number.

33 "How finely you trim your way
to seek after love,
Teaching even the vilest women
the secret of your ways!
On your hands is found the blood 34
of the innocent poor—
Not breaking into houses did you find them,
but opposed to all such things.
Yet you say, 'I am innocent, 35
surely his anger has turned back from me.'
Behold, I condemn you for saying,
'I have not sinned.'

Why do you change your course 36
with so light a heart?
You shall be put to shame through Egypt also,
as you were through Assyria.
Thence also shall you go forth, 37
with your hands upon your head;
For the LORD has rejected those in whom you trust,
and you shall have no success with them.

"If a man divorce his wife, 3
and she leave him,
And become the wife of another man,
can she return to him again?
Is not that woman
wholly polluted?
But you have played the harlot with many lovers,
and would fain return to me!"
is the oracle of the LORD.

"Lift up your eyes to the bare heights, 2
and see—
where have you not been lain with?
By the waysides have you sat waiting for your lovers,
like an Arab in the desert;
And you have polluted the land with your harlotries
and with your vices;
So that the showers have been withheld, 3
and the spring rain has not come.
You have a harlot's brow,
and will not blush for shame.
Have you not now been calling to me, 4
'My father! the comrade of my youth!
Will he keep up his anger for ever, 5
will he retain it to the end?'
Thus have you spoken, but have done
all the evil that you could."

The LORD said to me in the days of 6
Josiah the king:

"Have you seen what apostate Israel
did, how she went up every high mountain and under every spreading tree, and
7 played the harlot there? I thought, 'After she has done all these things, she will
return to me'; but she did not return.
And though her faithless sister Judah
8 saw that, for all the adulteries that apostate Israel had committed, I put her
away, and gave her a writ of divorce,
yet her faithless sister Judah was not
afraid, but likewise went and played the
9 harlot, polluting the land with her wanton harlotry, and committing adultery
10 with stones and blocks of wood. In spite
of all that happened, her faithless sister
Judah did not return to me in sincerity,
but in sheer hypocrisy," is the oracle of
11 the LORD. So the LORD said to me,
"Apostate Israel has proved herself
more in the right than faithless Judah.
12 Go, then, and proclaim these words
toward the north:

'Return, apostate Israel,' is the oracle
of the LORD;
'I will frown no more upon you.
For I am full of kindness,' is the oracle
of the LORD;
'I will not keep up anger forever.
13 Only acknowledge your guilt,
How you have rebelled against the
LORD your God,
And have lavished your love upon
alien gods under every spreading
tree,
And have not listened to my voice,' is
the oracle of the LORD.

14 "Return, apostate children," is the
oracle of the LORD, "for I am your
Lord; and I will take you one from a
city, and two from a family, and will
15 bring you to Zion, and will give you
shepherds after my own mind, who
shall shepherd you with wisdom and
16 skill. And in those days, when you have
multiplied and increased in the land,"
is the oracle of the LORD, "men shall
no more speak of 'The ark of the covenant of the LORD'—it shall be neither
invoked, nor mentioned, nor resorted
17 to, nor made any more—but at that
time they shall call Jerusalem 'The
throne of the LORD,' and all the nations
shall gather there, to celebrate the
name of the LORD in Jerusalem, and
they shall no more follow the stubborn
18 promptings of their evil minds. In
those days the house of Judah shall join
the house of Israel, and they shall come
together from the land of the north to
the land that I gave your fathers for a
heritage.

"I thought, 'How I would rank you 19
among the sons,
And give you a pleasant land,
The goodliest heritage of all the na-
tions!'
And I thought, 'Surely you will call
me "Father,"
And will not turn back from me.'
But as a woman is faithless to her lover, 20
So were you faithless to me, O house
of Israel,"
Is the oracle of the LORD.

"Hark! on the bare heights is heard 21
the suppliant weeping of the
children of Israel;
For they have perverted their ways,
they have forgotten the LORD
their God.
Return, apostate children! 22
I will heal your apostasy."

"See! we come to thee;
for thou art the LORD our God.
Truly in vain is the clamor from the 23
hills,
the tumult on the mountains;
Truly on the LORD our God
rests the safety of Israel.
From our youth has the shameful 24
thing devoured
the fruits of our fathers' toil,
Their flocks and their herds,
their sons and their daughters;
So let us lie down in our shame, 25
and let our dishonor enfold us,
For against the LORD our God have
we sinned,
both we and our fathers,
from our youth even till now,
And we have not listened to the voice
of the LORD our God."

"If you return, O Israel," is the oracle 4
of the LORD,
"return to me;
If you put your detestable things out
of my sight,
and waver not;
If you swear, 'As the LORD lives,' in 2
truth,
in honesty, and in uprightness;
Then shall the nations invoke blessings on one another through him,
and in him shall they glory."

3 Thus says the LORD to the men of
Judah and to the inhabitants of Jerusalem:
"Break up your fallow ground,
And sow not among thorns;
4 Circumcise yourselves to the LORD,
And remove the foreskin of your heart,
You men of Judah and inhabitants of
Jerusalem;
Lest my fury break out like fire,
And burn with none to quench it,
Because of your evil deeds."

THE FOE FROM THE NORTH, 4:5—6:26

5 Declare in Judah, and make procla-
mation in Jerusalem, saying,
"Blow the trumpet through the land,
Proclaim aloud, saying,
'Gather and let us go
To the fortified cities!'
6 Raise a signal toward Zion,
Seek refuge, stay not;
For trouble I bring from the north,
Even dire destruction.
7 A lion has gone up from his thicket,
A destroyer of nations;
He has broken loose from his place,
To make your land a desolation,
That your cities may be ravaged,
And left without inhabitant.
8 Gird on sackcloth for this,
Lament, and wail;
For the fierce anger of the LORD
Has not turned back from us."

9 "On that day," is the oracle of the
LORD, "the courage of the king and the
princes shall fail, the priests shall stand
aghast, and the prophets shall be dazed
10 with horror. They shall say, 'Ah Lord
GOD! thou hast certainly deceived this
people and Jerusalem, saying, "All
shall be well with you," when the sword
was reaching the life.'
11 "At that time shall it be said of this
people, and of Jerusalem, 'A scorching
wind from the desert heights—no wind
12 to fan or cleanse, but one too strong for
this—comes at my command against
the daughter of my people; for now
I too pronounce judgment against
them.' "

13 See! he comes up like a cloud,
his chariots like a whirlwind;
His horses are swifter than eagles—
woe to us! for we are ruined.

O Jerusalem! wash your heart of wick- 14
edness,
that you may be saved!
How long shall your evil thoughts
find lodgment within you?
For hark! a messenger from Dan, 15
A bearer of bad news from Mount
Ephraim!
Make it known to the nations, 16
Announce it to Jerusalem:
"Leopards are coming from a distant
land,
They lift up their voice against the
cities of Judah;
Like keepers of a field, they ring her 17
about,
For she has rebelled against me," is
the oracle of the LORD.
"Your ways and your doings have 18
brought this upon you,
This is the fruit of your wickedness;
It is bitter, it reaches the heart."

O my soul, my soul! I writhe in an- 19
guish!
O the agony of my heart!
My heart beats wildly within me,
I cannot keep silent!
For I hear the sound of the trumpet,
the alarm of war.
Crash follows crash, 20
for the whole land is ruined;
In a moment my tents are ruined,
in an instant my curtains.
How long must I see the signal, 21
hear the sound of the trumpet?

"It is because my people are stupid, 22
and know me not;
They are sottish children,
and have no understanding;
They have skill to do evil,
but know not how to do good."

I looked at the earth, and lo! it was 23
chaos;
At the heavens, and their light was
gone.
I looked at the mountains, and lo! 24
they were quaking;
And all the hills swayed to and fro.
I looked, and lo! there was no man, 25
And all the birds of the air had flown.
I looked, and lo! the garden land was 26
desert,
And all its cities were ravaged before
the LORD,
Before his fierce anger.

27 For thus says the LORD:
"The whole land shall be a desolation,
Though I make not a full end.
28 For this shall the earth mourn,
And the heavens above put on black;
Because I have spoken, and will not retract,
I have purposed, and will not turn back."

29 At the rumor of horsemen and archers
The whole land is in flight;
They crawl into caves, they huddle in thickets,
They scale the crags;
Every city is forsaken,
And no man dwells in them.
30 And you, O ruined one, what mean you by dressing in scarlet,
And decking yourself with ornaments of gold,
And enlarging your eyes with paint?
In vain do you beautify yourself!
Your lovers scorn you—
They seek your life.
31 Hark! I hear a cry as of a woman in travail,
a cry of distress as of one who brings forth her first-born child.
It is the cry of the daughter of Zion,
as she gasps for breath,
and spreads out her hands,
Saying, "O woe to me! for I faint away
before the slaughterers."

5 Range through the streets of Jerusalem,
look and see!
Search her squares,
if you can find a man,
One who does justice, and aims at honesty,
that I may pardon her!
2 Even though they say, "As the LORD lives,"
yet they swear falsely.
3 O LORD, are not thine eyes set upon the truth?
Thou didst smite them,
but they smarted not;
Thou didst consume them,
but they would not take warning;
They made their faces harder than rock,
they would not return.

I said, "These are only the poor folk, 4
who are without sense;
For they know not the way of the LORD,
the rights of their God.
I will go to the great ones, 5
and will speak with them;
For they know the way of the LORD,
the rights of their God."
But they too had broken the yoke,
had burst the bonds.
Therefore a lion from the forest will 6
slay them,
A wolf from the desert will make havoc of them;
A leopard will prowl round their cities,
So that all who go out of them will be torn in pieces;
Because their transgressions are many,
Their apostasies are innumerable.

"How can I pardon you?" is the oracle 7
of the LORD;
"For your children have forsaken me,
And have sworn by them that are no gods.
When I fed them to the full, they committed adultery,
And trooped to the houses of harlots.
They are pampered horses, lusty stal- 8
lions,
Neighing each for his neighbor's wife.
For these things shall I not punish 9
them?" is the oracle of the LORD;
"And on a nation such as this shall I
not take vengeance?"

"Go up through her vine-rows, and 10
ravage,
And make a full end;
Lop off her tendrils,
For they are not the LORD'S.
For the house of Israel and the house 11
of Judah have played the traitor to me,"
Is the oracle of the LORD.
"They have belied the LORD, 12
Saying, 'Not he!
No harm shall befall us,
No sword or famine shall we see;
The prophets are mere wind, 13
And the word is not in them;
As they have spoken to us,
So let it be done to them!' "

Therefore thus says the LORD, the 14
God of hosts:
"Because you have spoken this word,
Behold, I am making my words in your mouth a fire,

And I am making this people wood,
and the fire shall devour them.
15 Behold, I am bringing upon you a nation from afar,
O house of Israel," is the oracle of the LORD—
"An ancient nation,
A very ancient nation,
A nation whose language you know not,
Whose speech you understand not.
16 Their quiver is like an open grave,
They are all men of war;
17 They shall eat up your harvest and your food,
They shall eat up your sons and your daughters;
They shall eat up your flocks and your herds,
They shall eat up your vines and your fig trees;
They shall batter down with the sword
Your fortified cities in which you trust."

18 "But even in those days," is the
oracle of the LORD, "I will not make a
19 full end of you. And when men ask,
'Why is it that the LORD our God has
done all these things to us?' you shall
say to them, 'Thus says the LORD: As
you have forsaken me, and served alien
gods in your land, so shall you serve
aliens in a land that is not yours.' "

20 Proclaim this in the house of Jacob,
And publish it in Judah:
21 "Hear this, O foolish and senseless people,
Who have eyes, but see not,
Ears, but hear not!
22 Do you not revere me?" is the oracle of the LORD,
"Do you not tremble before me?
I set the sand as a bound for the sea,
As an everlasting barrier, which it may not pass over—
Its waves may toss, but they cannot prevail,
Its billows may roar, but they cannot pass over—
23 Yet this people has a restive and rebellious mind,
They have swerved and gone off.
24 Nor do they say to themselves,
'Let us reverence the LORD our God,
Who gives us both winter and spring rain in its season,
And keeps for us the weeks appointed for harvest!'
25 Your crimes have upset this order,
And your sins have withheld the blessing from you.
26 For knaves are found among my people,
Who lie in wait as fowlers do,
And set a trap to catch men.
27 As a cage is full of birds,
Their houses are full of fraud;
So they become great and rich,
28 They grow fat and sleek.
They pass all bounds in wickedness,
They uphold not the cause of the orphan, to carry it to success,
And the rights of the needy they do not defend.
29 For these things shall I not punish them?" is the oracle of the LORD;
"And on a nation such as this shall I not take vengeance?"

30 An awful and appalling thing has happened in the land:
31 The prophets prophesy by false gods,
And the priests make profit through them;
My people love to have it so,
But what will you do when the end comes?

6 Flee for safety, O sons of Benjamin,
From the midst of Jerusalem!
In Tekoa blow the trumpet,
And on Beth-haccherem raise a signal!
For trouble is looming from the north,
Even dire destruction.
2 O the fair and luxuriant height
Of the daughter of Zion!
3 Against her shepherds will come,
They and their flocks;
They will pitch their tents around her,
And pasture each his plot.
4 "Prepare you war against her;
Up! let us storm her at noon!"
"Woe to us! the day declines,
The shadows of evening lengthen."
5 "Up! let us storm her by night,
And destroy her palaces!"

6 For thus says the LORD of hosts:
"Hew down trees,
And cast up a siege-mound against Jerusalem!
For she is a city of falsehood,
In whose midst there is nought but oppression.
7 As a fountain wells up its water,
So she wells up her wickedness.

Sounds of violence and robbery are
heard in her,
Sickness and wounds are ever before
me.
8 Take warning, O Jerusalem,
Lest I be alienated from you,
And make you a desolation,
An uninhabited land."

9 Thus says the LORD of hosts:
"Glean out as a vine
the remnant of Israel;
Pass your hand, like a grape-gatherer,
over its tendrils!"
10 But to whom shall I speak and give
warning,
that they may hear?
See! their ears are sealed,
and they cannot give heed;
See! the word of the LORD has become
to them scorn,
they find no pleasure in it.
11 Therefore I am full of the fury of the
LORD,
I am weary of holding it in.
"Pour it out on the children in the
street,
and on the gatherings of young
men also;
Both husband and wife shall be taken,
the old and the full-aged.
12 Their homes shall be turned over to
others,
their fields and their vineyards
also;
For I will stretch out my hand against
the inhabitants of the land,"
is the oracle of the LORD;
13 "Because from the least to the greatest
of them
each one traffics in ill-gotten
gain;
And from prophet to priest
each one deals in falsehood.
14 The wound of the daughter of my
people
they lightly heal,
Saying, 'All is well, all is well,'
when nought is well.
15 Were they ashamed when they did
their vile deeds?
they were not at all ashamed,
they knew not how to blush.
Therefore they shall fall among those
who fall,
they shall stumble in the hour
when I punish them,"
says the LORD.

Thus says the LORD: 16
"Stand by the ways, and look,
And ask for the ancient paths,
Where the good way is, and walk in it;
And find rest for yourselves.
But they said, 'We will not walk in it!'
So I set watchmen over them, saying, 17
'Give heed to the sound of the trum-
pet!'
But they said, 'We will not give heed!'
Therefore hear, O heavens, and learn 18
well
What shall befall them!
Hear, O earth; for behold, I am bring- 19
ing trouble upon this people,
The fruit of their own devices,
Because they have not given heed to
my words,
And have spurned my instruction.
What care I for the frankincense that 20
comes from Sheba,
Or the sweet cane from a distant land?
Your burnt-offerings are not accept-
able to me,
And your sacrifices bring me no pleas-
ure.
Therefore thus says the LORD: 21
'Behold, I am laying stumblingblocks
before this people,
And they shall stumble against them,
fathers and sons together,
And shall perish, both neighbor and
friend.' "

Thus says the LORD: 22
"Behold, a people is coming from the
north land,
A mighty nation is stirring from the
ends of the earth;
They lay hold on bow and javelin, 23
They are cruel and pitiless;
The sound of them is like that of the
sea when it roars,
And they ride upon horses—
Arrayed as a man for the battle
Against you, O daughter of Zion!"

We have heard the report of them, 24
and our hands fall helpless;
Anguish lays hold on us,
pain like that of a woman in
travail.
Go not out to the fields, 25
nor walk on the way!
For there is the sword of the enemy,
terror all around.
O daughter of my people, gird on sack- 26
cloth,
and wallow in ashes;

Take up mourning, as for an only son,
wailing most bitter!
For suddenly will come
the despoiler upon us.

THE PROPHET AS ASSAYER, 6:27–30

27 "I have made you an assayer and tester
among my people,
That you may prove and assay their
ways.
28 For they are all of them hardened
rebels,
Dealers in slander;
29 They are all of them bronze and iron,
Wholly corrupt.
29 The bellows are scorched with the fire,
The lead is consumed;
But in vain does the smelter keep on
smelting,
The dross is not drawn out.
30 'Refuse silver,' are they called,
For the LORD has refused them."

INSTRUCTIONS REGARDING THE TEMPLE ADDRESS, 7:1—8:13

7 The word that came to Jeremiah
from the LORD:
2 "Stand in the court of the house of
the LORD, and there proclaim this message: 'Hear the word of the LORD, all
you men of Judah, who enter by these
3 gates to worship the LORD! Thus says
the LORD of hosts, the God of Israel:
"Amend your ways and your doings,
that I may establish your home in this
4 place. Trust not in deceptive words,
such as 'The temple of the LORD, the
temple of the LORD, the temple of the
5 LORD is this!' For if you but amend
your ways and your doings—if you
practice strict justice toward one
6 another, if you do not oppress the resident alien, the orphan, and the widow,
nor shed innocent blood in this place,
nor run after other gods to your own
7 hurt—I will establish your home in this
place, in the land which I gave to your
8 fathers for all time. But, as it is, you
trust in deceitful words, that are of no
9 avail. What? Steal, murder, and commit adultery, swear falsely, offer sacrifices to the Baal, and run after other
10 gods, whom you do not know, and then
come and stand before me in this house
which bears my name, and say, 'We are
safe'—only to practice all these abominations! Has this house which bears 11
my name become a robbers' cave in
your eyes? Lo! I see through it," is the
oracle of the LORD. "For go, now, to 12
my sanctuary that was at Shiloh, where
I formerly established my name, and
see what I did to it because of the wickedness of my people Israel! So now, be- 13
cause you have done all these deeds,"
is the oracle of the LORD, "and I spoke
to you early and late, but you would
not listen, and I called you, but you
would not answer, I will do to this 14
house which bears my name, in which
you trust, and to the place which I gave
to you and your fathers, as I did to
Shiloh; and I will cast you out of my 15
sight, as I cast out all your kinsmen,
even the whole race of Ephraim." ' "

"As for you, intercede not for this 16
people, nor lift up cry or prayer on their
behalf, nor plead with me, for I will not
listen to you. Do you not see what they 17
are doing in the cities of Judah and in
the streets of Jerusalem? The children 18
are gathering wood, and the fathers are
kindling fires, and the women are
kneading dough, to make cakes for the
queen of the heavens; and they are
pouring libations to other gods, in order
to vex me. But is it me they are vex- 19
ing?" is the oracle of the LORD. "Is it
not their own selves, to the confusion
of their own faces?" Therefore thus 20
says the Lord GOD: "My anger and
my fury shall be poured out upon this
place—upon man and beast, upon the
trees of the field, and upon the fruits of
the ground—and it shall burn without
being quenched."

Thus says the LORD of hosts, the 21
God of Israel:

"Add your burnt-offerings to your
sacrifices, and eat the flesh of them!
For on the day that I brought your 22
fathers out of the land of Egypt, I did
not speak to them, nor give them
command regarding burnt-offering or
sacrifice; but this command I gave 23
them, 'Listen to my voice, and I will be
your God, and you shall be my people;
and walk in all the way that I command
you, that you may prosper!' Yet they 24
neither listened nor inclined their ears
to me, but followed the stubborn
promptings of their own evil minds, and
went backward instead of forward. And 25

though I sent all my servants the prophets, early and late, from the day that
your fathers came out of the land of
26 Egypt even to this day, they neither
listened nor inclined their ears to me,
but stiffened their necks, and behaved
27 worse than their fathers. Even though
you speak all these words to them, they
will not listen to you; though you call to
28 them, they will not answer you. Therefore you shall say to them:

'This is the nation that would not listen
To the voice of the LORD its God,
The nation that took no warning,
And from whose mouth honesty has completely gone.
29 Shear off your locks, and cast them away,
Raise a dirge on the bare heights;
For the LORD has spurned and cast off
The race that has roused him to wrath.'

30 "For the children of Judah have done
what is evil in my sight," is the oracle
of the LORD; "they have set up their
detestable things in the house which
31 bears my name, to defile it, and have
built the high place of Topheth, in the
valley of Ben-Hinnom, to burn their
sons and their daughters in the fire—a
thing which I never commanded, and
32 which never entered my mind. Therefore behold, days are coming," is the
oracle of the LORD, "when Topheth
shall no longer be called 'The valley of
Ben-Hinnom,' but 'The valley of
Slaughter,' for they shall bury in
33 Topheth till there is no more room; and
the dead bodies of this people shall be
food for the birds of the air and the
beasts of the field, with none to scare
34 them away; and I will banish from the
cities of Judah and from the streets of
Jerusalem the sound of mirth and the
sound of gladness, the voice of the
bridegroom and the voice of the bride,
for the land shall become a desolation.
8 At that time," is the oracle of the
LORD, "the bones of the kings of Judah, and the bones of its princes, the
bones of the priests, the bones of the
prophets, and the bones of the inhabitants of Jerusalem, shall be taken out of
2 their graves and spread before the sun,
the moon, and all the host of the
heavens, which they loved and served,
ran after, consulted, and worshiped;
they shall not be gathered up nor buried,
but shall be left as dung upon the face
of the ground. And death shall be pref- 3
erable to life for all the remnant that is
left of this evil race, in all the places to
which I have driven them," is the oracle of the LORD of hosts.

"You shall also say to them, 'Thus 4
says the LORD:

"If a man fall, does he not rise?
If he turn, does he not return?
Why, then, has this people of mine fallen into a perpetual apostasy? 5
They cling to deceit, they will not return!
I have given heed and listened, but none speaks the truth, 6
None repents of his wickedness, saying, 'What have I done?'
Each runs his own wayward course,
Like a horse plunging headlong in battle.
Even the stork in the heavens knows her seasons, 7
The turtle-dove, swift, and swallow keep the time of their coming;
But my people know not the ordinance of the LORD.
How can you say, 'We are wise, 8
And the law of the LORD is with us'?
When lo, the lying pen of the scribes
Has turned it into a lie!
So the wise shall be abashed, 9
They shall be dumbfounded and taken;
For lo, they have spurned the word of the LORD,
And what wisdom, then, have they?
Therefore I will give their wives to others, 10
Their fields to the conquerors;
Because from the least to the greatest of them
Each one traffics in ill-gotten gain;
From prophet to priest
Each one deals in falsehood.
The wound of the daughter of my people 11
They lightly heal,
Saying, 'All is well, all is well,'
When nought is well.
Were they ashamed when they did their vile deeds? 12
They were not at all ashamed, they knew not how to blush.
Therefore they shall fall among those who fall,
They shall stumble in the hour when I punish them," '
Says the LORD.
"If I seek to gather a harvest of them," 13

Is the oracle of the LORD,
"There is not a grape on the vine,
Nor a fig on the fig tree;
Even the leaves are withered,
All that I gave them is gone from them."

THE PEOPLE'S DESPAIR, 8:14–17

14 Why are we sitting still?
Gather and let us go to the fortified cities,
And there let us meet our doom!
For the LORD our God has doomed us to death,
And has given us poisoned water to drink;
Because we have sinned against the LORD.
15 We looked for prosperity, but no good has come,
For a time of healing, but lo! disaster.

16 "From Dan is heard the snorting of their horses,
At the neighing of their stallions the whole land quakes.
They come and devour the land and its produce,
The city and its inhabitants.
17 For behold, I am sending among you serpents,
Adders which cannot be charmed,
And they shall bite you,"
Is the oracle of the LORD.

THE PROPHET'S INCONSOLABLE GRIEF, 8:18—9:16

18 My pain is incurable,
My heart is sick within me.
19 Hark! the cry of the daughter of my people
Far and wide through the land:
"Is not the LORD in Zion?
Is not her King in her?"
"Yes! but why have they vexed me with their images,
With their foreign vanities?"
20 "The harvest is past, the summer is over,
And we are not saved."

21 For the wound of the daughter of my people I am wounded with grief,
I walk in mourning, horror has seized me.

Is there no balm in Gilead? 22
Is there no physician there?
Why, then, is there no recovery
for the health of the daughter of my people?
O that my head were waters, **9**
and my eyes a fountain of tears,
That I might weep day and night
for the slain of the daughter of my people!

O that I had in the desert 2
a traveler's inn,
That I might leave my people,
and be quit of them!
For they are all adulterers,
a company of traitors.
They stretch their tongue 3
like a treacherous bow;
And not in the interests of truth
have they grown strong in the land;
For they go on from crime to crime,
"And me they know not,"
is the oracle of the LORD.

Be on guard each one against his neighbor, 4
And let no one trust his brother!
For each brother is a sheer supplanter,
And each neighbor is a slanderer.
They cheat each one his neighbor, 5
And no one speaks the truth.
They have trained their tongue to speak lies,
They do wrong till they are weary.
They heap violence on violence, fraud on fraud, 6
"And me they refuse to know," is the oracle of the LORD.

Therefore thus says the LORD of hosts: 7
"Behold, I will smelt them, and test them,
For what else can I do,
In face of the wickedness of the daughter of my people?
Their tongue is a deadly arrow, 8
It speaks deceit;
With his mouth one speaks fair to his neighbor,
But in his mind he lays a trap for him.
For these things shall I not punish them?" is the oracle of the LORD; 9
"On a nation such as this shall I not take vengeance?

"Over the mountains raise weeping and wailing, 10

Over the pastures of the steppe a dirge!
Because they are laid waste, so that none passes through,
And none hears the lowing of cattle.
Both birds of the air and beasts have fled and gone.
11 I will make Jerusalem a heap of ruins, a lair of jackals;
And the cities of Judah will I make a desolation, without an inhabitant.
12 Who is the wise man, that he may understand this?
And who is he to whom the mouth of the LORD has spoken, that he may tell it?
Why is the land ruined and laid waste like a desert, so that none passes through?"

13 The LORD says:
"It is because they have forsaken my law, which I set before them,
And have not listened to my voice, nor walked by it;
14 But have followed the promptings of their own stubborn minds,
And have run after the Baals, which their fathers taught them to worship."
15 Therefore thus says the LORD of hosts, the God of Israel:
"Behold, I will feed them with wormwood,
And will give them poisoned water to drink;
16 And I will scatter them among the nations,
Whom neither they nor their fathers have known;
And after them will I send the sword,
Until I have consumed them."

THE DIRGE OF DEATH, 9:17–26

17 Thus says the LORD of hosts:
"Consider and call for the mourning women, that they may come,
And send for the skilful women, that they may make haste,
18 And raise a lament over us,
Till our eyes run down with tears,
And our eyelids gush with water!
19 For hark! a wail is heard from Zion:
'How we are ruined!
We are bitterly ashamed, because we have had to leave our land,
Because we have had to give up our dwellings.'

20 "Hear, you women, the word of the LORD,
Let your ears receive the word of his mouth;
And teach your daughters a lamentation,
Each one her neighbor a dirge:
21 'Death has climbed through our windows, has entered our halls,
Cutting off the children from the streets, the young men from the squares;
22 And the dead bodies of men shall fall like dung on the open field,
Like sheaves behind the reaper, with none to gather them.' "

23 Thus says the LORD:
"Let not the wise man boast of his wisdom,
Nor the strong man boast of his strength,
Nor the rich man boast of his riches!
24 But if one must boast, let him boast of this,
That he understands and knows me—
How I, the LORD, am he who practices kindness,
Justice, and righteousness on the earth;
For in these things I delight," is the oracle of the LORD.

25 "Behold, days are coming," is the
oracle of the LORD, "when I will
punish all who, though circumcised, are
26 really uncircumcised, Egypt and Edom,
Ammon and Moab, together with all
those who live in the desert who have
the corners of their hair clipped; for all
these nations are uncircumcised, and
all the house of Israel is uncircumcised
in heart."

THE FOLLY OF IDOLATRY, 10:1–16

10 Hear the word which the LORD has
spoken against you, O house of Israel!
2 Thus says the LORD:
"Follow not the way of the nations,
Nor be dismayed at the signs of the heavens,
When the nations are dismayed at them!

3 For the cults of the peoples are vanity—
They are but a timber which one cuts from the forest,
Which the carpenter's hands have wrought with the ax.
4 Men deck it with silver and gold,
Fasten it with hammer and nails,
And set it up, so that it cannot move.
5 They stand like scarecrows in a garden of cucumbers, and cannot speak;
They have to be carried, for they cannot walk.
Be not afraid of them! for they cannot do harm,
And also to do good is not in their power."

6 There is none like thee, O LORD!
Thou art great, and thy name is great in might.
7 Who would not reverence thee, O King of the nations?
For this is thy due, and there is none like thee
Among all the wise ones of the nations, and among all their royalties.
8 They are altogether stupid and senseless,
The core of their idols is but timber,
9 Overlaid with beaten silver brought from Tarshish
And with gold from Ophir,
The work of the carpenter and the goldsmith;
While their clothing is violet and purple,
All of it the work of skilled men.
11 [Thus shall you say of them: "The
gods that did not make the heavens and
the earth shall vanish from the earth
and from under the heavens!"]
10 But the Lord GOD is the true God,
He is the living God, the everlasting King;
At his wrath the earth quakes,
And his fury no nation can bear.
12 It is he who made the earth by his power,
Who established the world by his wisdom,
And stretched out the heavens by his skill.
13 When he thunders, there is a storm of waters in the heavens,
And he causes vapors to rise from the ends of the earth;
He makes lightnings for the rain,
And brings out the wind from his storehouses.

Every man is stupid and senseless, 14
Every goldsmith is put to shame through his images;
For his idols are frauds, which have no breath in them,
They are an empty mockery, 15
Which will break down in their time of trial.
Not such is the Portion of Jacob, 16
But he is the framer of all things,
And Israel is the tribe of his inheritance—
The LORD of hosts is his name.

THE APPROACHING DOOM, 10:17–25

Pick up your baggage from the land, 17
you who sit under siege!
For thus says the LORD: 18
"Behold, I am slinging out the inhabitants of the land
at a single shot;
And I will put them to sore distress,
so that they may pay for their guilt."

Woe is me! how hurt I am! 19
how grievous is my wound!
While I thought, "This is only a sickness,
which I can bear."
My tent is despoiled, 20
and all my cords are snapped;
My children have gone from me,
and are no more;
There is none to spread my tent again,
to set up my curtains.
For the shepherds are stupid, 21
and consult not the LORD;
Therefore they have had no success,
and their flock is all scattered.

Hark! a rumor! See! it comes! 22
A great commotion out of the north land!
To make the cities of Judah a desolation,
A lair of jackals.

I know, O LORD, that man's way is 23
not his own,
That it is not in man's power as he walks to control his steps.
Correct me, O LORD, but in just 24
measure,
Not in thy wrath, lest thou bring me to nothing.

25 Pour out thy wrath on the nations
that know thee not,
On the families that invoke not thy
name;
For they have devoured Jacob, and
have consumed him,
And they have laid waste his homestead.

THE PREACHING OF THE COVENANT, 11:1–17

11 The word that came to Jeremiah from
the LORD:
2 "Hear the words of this covenant,
and declare them to the men of Judah
3 and the inhabitants of Jerusalem, saying to them, 'Thus says the LORD, the
God of Israel: Cursed be the man who
heeds not the words of this covenant,
4 which I enjoined upon your fathers on
the day that I brought them out of that
iron furnace, the land of Egypt, saying,
"Listen to my voice, and do just as I
command you! So shall you be my
5 people, and I will be your God," in con-
firmation of the oath which I swore to
your fathers, when I promised to give
them a land flowing with milk and
honey, as it is this day.' "
I answered, saying,
"Yes, indeed, O LORD!"
6 Then the LORD said to me,
"Proclaim all these words in the cities
of Judah and in the streets of Jerusalem,
saying, 'Hear the words of this cove-
7 nant, and obey them! For I earnestly
appealed to your fathers on the day
that I brought them out of the land of
Egypt, and have appealed to them
early and late, even to this day, saying,
8 "Listen to my voice!" Yet they neither
listened nor inclined their ears, but
followed each the stubborn promptings of his own evil mind; so I brought
upon them all the threats of this covenant which I commanded them to observe, but which they did not observe.' "
9 The LORD further said to me,
"There is open treason among the
men of Judah and the inhabitants of
10 Jerusalem. They have returned to the
sins of their forefathers, who refused to
hear my words; and they have run after
other gods, to serve them. Both the
house of Israel and the house of Judah
have broken the covenant which I made
11 with their fathers. Therefore thus says
the LORD: 'Behold, I am bringing upon
them a disaster which they shall not be
able to escape. They may cry to me,
but I will not listen to them; the towns- 12
men of Judah and the inhabitants of
Jerusalem may likewise go and cry to
the gods to whom they offer sacrifices,
but they shall be utterly powerless to
help them in their time of trouble. For 13
as many in number as your cities are
your gods, O Judah; and as many in
number as the streets of Jerusalem are
the altars which you have set up to the
shameful thing—altars to offer sacrifices to the Baal.' And as for you, inter- 14
cede not for this people, nor lift up cry
or prayer on their behalf; for I will not
listen when they call to me in their time
of trouble."

"What right has my loved one in my 15
house,
when she has done such vile
deeds?
Can vows and holy flesh avert your
doom from you,
or through these things can you
escape?
The LORD called you a green olive 16
tree,
fair in appearance;
But to the roar of a mighty hurricane
he has set fire to it,
and its branches are burned."

"For the LORD of hosts, who planted 17
you, has pronounced evil against you,
because of the evil by which the house
of Israel and the house of Judah have
vexed me, by offering sacrifices to the
Baal!"

A PLOT AGAINST JEREMIAH, 11:18–23

The LORD informed me, and I knew; 18
I saw what they were doing.
But I was like an innocent lamb, 19
That is led to the slaughter;
I knew not that they had plotted
against me, saying,
"Let us destroy the tree with its sap,
Let us cut him off from the land of the
living,
That his name may be remembered no
more!"
O LORD of hosts, thou who judgest 20
righteously,
Who testest the heart and the con-
science,

Let me see thy vengeance upon them,
For to thee have I confided my cause!

21 Therefore thus says the LORD regarding the men of Anathoth who seek your life, saying, "You shall not prophesy in the name of the LORD, lest you die by our hands!"—thus says the LORD of hosts:

22 "Behold, I will punish them;
Their young men shall die by the sword,
And their sons and their daughters shall die by famine.
23 No remnant shall be left to them,
For I will bring trouble upon the men of Anathoth,
Even their year of reckoning."

THE PROPHET'S EXPOSTULATION, AND THE LORD'S REPLY, 12:1–6

12 Thou must be in the right, O LORD,
If I take issue with thee;
Yet would I lay my case before thee:
Why does the way of the wicked prosper?
Why do all the faithless live in comfort?
2 Thou plantest them, and they take root;
They grow, and they bring forth fruit;
Near art thou in their mouths,
But far from their thoughts.
3 Yet thou, O LORD, knowest me,
Thou seest me, and testest my mind toward thee.
Pull them out like sheep for the shambles,
And devote them to the day of slaughter!
4 How long must the land mourn,
And the grass of all the field wither?
Through the wickedness of those who dwell in it
Beast and bird are swept away;
For they say, "God is blind to our ways."

5 "If you have raced with men on foot,
and they have beaten you,
How will you compete with horses?
And if you take to flight in a safe land,
How will you do in the jungle of Jordan?
6 For even your brothers, those of your father's household—
Even they have played you false,
Even they are in full cry after you;
Trust them not, though they speak fair words to you!"

THE DESOLATION OF JUDAH, 12:7–13

"I have forsaken my house, 7
have abandoned my heritage;
I have given over my loved one
to the hand of her enemies.
My heritage has become to me 8
like a lion in the forest;
She has lifted up her voice against me;
therefore I hate her.
My heritage has become to me like a 9
speckled vulture,
with vultures circling against her;
Go, gather all beasts of the field,
bring them to devour!
Many shepherds have destroyed my 10
vineyard,
have trampled down my portion;
They have made my pleasant lot
a desolate waste.
They have made it a desolation, 11
in its desolation it mourns to me;
The whole land is made desolate,
yet no man lays it to heart.
Over all the bare heights in the desert 12
despoilers have come;
For the sword of the LORD has devoured
From end to end of the land,
So that no flesh is safe.
They have sown wheat, and have 13
reaped thorns;
They have worn themselves out, but gained no profit;
They are disappointed in their harvests
Because of the fierce anger of the LORD."

WARNING AND HOPE FOR THE NEIGHBORS OF JUDAH, 12:14–17

Thus says the LORD concerning all 14
my evil neighbors, who encroach upon
the heritage which I gave to my people
Israel:
"Behold, I am plucking them up from
their land, and I will pluck up from
their midst the house of Judah. But 15

after I have plucked them up, I will
once more have pity upon them, and
will restore them each to his own herit-
16 age, and each to his own land. And if
they learn the ways of my people—to
swear by my name, 'As the LORD
lives!'—even as they once taught my
people to swear by the Baal, they shall
be built up in the midst of my people.
17 But if any nation will not listen, I will
pluck it up completely and destroy it,"
is the oracle of the LORD.

PARABLE OF THE WAISTCLOTH, 13:1–11

13 The LORD spoke to me as follows:
"Go and buy a linen waistcloth, and
put it on your loins, without passing it
through water."
2 So I bought the waistcloth, in accordance with the word of the LORD, and
put it on my loins.
3 Then the word of the LORD came to
me a second time, saying,
4 "Take the waistcloth which you
bought, which is on your loins, and
arise, go to the Euphrates, and hide it
there in a crevice of the rock."
5 So I went and hid it by the Euphrates, as the LORD had bidden me.
6 After a number of days the LORD
said to me,
"Arise! Go to the Euphrates, and
bring thence the waistcloth which I
bade you hide there."
7 So I went to the Euphrates, and dug,
and got the waistcloth from the place
where I had hidden it. And lo! the
waistcloth was ruined, and good for
nothing.
8 Then the word of the LORD came to
me, saying,
9 "Thus says the LORD: So will I ruin
the pride of Judah and the great pride
10 of Jerusalem. This evil people, who will
not hear my words, but follow the stubborn promptings of their own minds,
and run after other gods, to serve and
worship them, shall be like this waist-
11 cloth, which is good for nothing. For,
as a waistcloth clings to the loins of a
man, so did I make the whole house of
Israel and the whole house of Judah
cling to me," is the oracle of the LORD,
"that they might become for me a
people of honor and praise and glory;
but they did not listen."

PARABLE OF THE JARS, 13:12–14

"Speak this word to them: 12
"Thus says the LORD, the God of
Israel, 'Every jar should be filled with
wine.' And if they say to you, 'Do we
not know quite well that every jar
should be filled with wine?' you shall 13
say to them, 'Thus says the LORD: Behold, I am filling with drunkenness all
the inhabitants of this land—the kings
who sit on David's throne, the priests,
the prophets, and all the inhabitants of
Jerusalem—and I will dash them against 14
one another, fathers and sons together,'
is the oracle of the LORD. 'No pity, or
mercy, or compassion, shall prevent
me from destroying them.'"

A SOLEMN WARNING, 13:15–17

Hear, and give ear! be not haughty; 15
for the LORD has spoken.
Give glory to the LORD your God, 16
before it grows dark,
Before your feet stumble
on the twilight mountains,
And while you look for light, he turn
it to gloom,
he make it thick darkness.
But if you will not listen, 17
I must weep in secret because
of your pride;
My eyes must weep much, they must
run down with tears,
because the flock of the LORD
has been taken captive.

LAMENT FOR THE KING AND THE QUEEN-MOTHER, 13:18–19

Say to the king and the queen-mother: 18
"Sit in the depths!
For down from your head has come
your beautiful crown."
The cities of the south are closed up, 19
with none to open them;
All Judah is swept into exile,
swept wholly into exile.

LAMENT FOR JERUSALEM, 13:20–27

"Lift up your eyes, and see, 20
how they come from the north.
Where is the flock that was given you,
your beautiful flock?

21 What will you say when they set
as heads over you
Those whom you yourself have trained
to be friends to you?
Will not pangs lay hold on you,
like those of a woman in travail?
22 And if you say to yourself,
'Why have these things befallen
me?'
It is for your many sins that your
skirts are stripped off,
that your person is outraged.
23 Can the Ethiopian change his skin,
or the leopard his spots?
Then may you also do good,
who are trained to do evil.
24 I will scatter you like drifting stubble
before the wind of the desert.
25 This is your lot, your portion assigned
by me,"
is the oracle of the LORD;
"Because you have forgotten me,
and have trusted in lies.
26 I will draw your skirts over your face,
and your shame shall be seen;
27 For I have seen your adulteries,
and your lustful neighings,
Your lewd intrigues, and your infamous deeds,
on the hills in the open field.
Woe to you, O Jerusalem! how long
will it be
till you are made clean?"

PROPHECIES ON THE DROUGHT, 14:1—15:9

14 The word of the LORD that came to
Jeremiah in regard to the drought:
2 "Judah mourns, and her gates languish;
Men cower in black to the ground, and
the cry of Jerusalem goes up.
3 Her nobles send their menials for
water;
They come to the cisterns, they find
no water;
They return with their pitchers empty;
Abashed and dejected, they cover their
heads.
4 The tillers of the soil are dismayed,
Because there is no rain in the land;
The plowmen are abashed, they cover
their heads.
5 Even the hind in the field calves and
abandons her young,
Because there is no grass;
6 And the wild asses stand on the bare
heights,
They gasp for air like crocodiles, their
eyes lose their luster,
Because there is no green thing.

"Though our sins bear witness against 7
us,
Act, O LORD, for thy name's sake!
For many are our backslidings,
Against thee have we sinned.
O thou who art the hope of Israel, 8
Its savior in time of trouble,
Why shouldst thou be like a stranger
in the land,
Like a traveler who turns aside to
lodge for a night?
Why shouldst thou be like a man overcome by sleep, 9
Like a warrior who is powerless to
help?
Yet thou, O LORD, art in the midst of
us,
And thy name we bear—abandon us
not!"

Thus says the LORD of this people: 10
"So do they love to wander,
Their feet they restrain not;
And the LORD cannot accept them;
Now will he remember their guilt,
And punish their sins."

The LORD said to me, 11
"Intercede not for the good of this
people! Though they fast, I will not 12
listen to their cry; and though they offer up burnt-offering and cereal-offering, I will not accept them; but I will
consume them by the sword, by famine,
and by pestilence."
Then said I, 13
"Ah, Lord GOD! the prophets keep
saying to them, 'You shall not see the
sword, nor shall famine visit you; but
assured peace will I give to you in this
place.' "
Then the LORD said to me, 14
"It is lies which the prophets prophesy
in my name. I neither sent them, nor
commissioned them, nor spoke to them.
What they prophesy to you is a lying
dream, an empty superstition, a deceptive invention of their own minds."
Therefore thus says the LORD: 15
"As regards the prophets who prophesy in my name—though I did not
send them—saying, 'Sword and famine
shall not visit this land,' by sword and
famine shall those prophets be consumed, while the people to whom they 16

prophesy shall be cast out in the streets
of Jerusalem, victims of famine and
sword, with none to bury them—themselves, their wives, their sons, and their
daughters—for I will pour out upon
them the trouble which they deserve.
17 And you shall speak this word to them:
'Let my eyes run down with tears,
And let them not cease by day or by night!
For the virgin daughter of my people is smitten with a sore wound,
With a very severe blow.
18 If I go out to the field, lo! those slain by the sword;
And if I enter the city, lo! the horrors of famine.
Both prophet and priest go begging through the land—
They know not where.' "

19 Hast thou utterly rejected Judah?
Hast thou a loathing for Zion?
Why, then, hast thou smitten us,
With no healing for us?
We looked for prosperity, but no good has come,
For a time of healing, but lo! disaster.
20 We acknowledge, O LORD, our wickedness, and the guilt of our fathers—
How we have sinned against thee.
21 Yet spurn us not, for thy name's sake,
Debase not thy glorious throne;
Remember, and break not thy covenant with us!
22 Are there any among the vanities of the nations that can bring rain?
Or can the heavens of themselves give showers?
Is it not thou, O LORD our God, on whom we set our hope?
For thou doest all these things.

15 Then the LORD said to me,
"Though Moses and Samuel stood
before me, I would show no favor toward
this people. Send them out of my sight,
2 and let them go! And if they ask you,
'Where shall we go?' you shall say to
them, 'Thus says the LORD:
"Those who are destined for death, to death;
And those who are destined for the sword, to the sword;
And those who are destined for famine, to famine;
And those who are destined for exile, to exile." ' "
3 "I will set over them four kinds of
fate," is the oracle of the LORD: "the
sword to slay, and the dogs to tear, the
birds of the air to devour, and the beasts
of the earth to destroy. And I will make 4
them a horror to all the kingdoms of the
earth, because of what Manasseh, the
son of Hezekiah, king of Judah, did in
Jerusalem."

"Who, then, will pity you, O Jerusalem? 5
Who will bemoan you?
Who will go out of his way to give you greeting?
You have cast me off," is the oracle of 6
the LORD,
"you have gone ever backward;
So I stretch out my hand to destroy you,
for I am weary of relenting.
I will winnow you with a winnowing-fork 7
in the gates of the land;
I will make my people childless, I will destroy them,
because of their perverse ways.
I will make their widows more numerous 8
than the sand of the sea;
I will bring on their mothers of young men
the despoiler at noonday;
I will cause to fall on them suddenly
terror and anguish.
The mother of seven shall languish 9
and swoon away;
Her sun shall set while it is still day,
ashamed and abashed shall she be.
And the rest of them will I give to the sword
before their enemies,"
is the oracle of the LORD.

THE PROPHET'S LONELINESS AND DESPONDENCY, 15:10—16:18, 21

Woe is me, my mother! that you bore me 10
As a man of strife and a man of contention to all the earth!
I have neither lent nor borrowed,
Yet all of them curse me.
So be it, O LORD, if I have failed to 11
entreat thee,
Or to plead with thee for the good of my enemies,
In their time of trouble and trial!

12 Have I an arm of iron,
Or a brow of bronze?
13 [Your riches and all your treasures will
I give for a spoil,
as the price of your sin, through
all your borders;
14 And I will make you serve your enemies
in a land which you know not;
For a fire is kindled in my wrath,
which shall burn against you
forever.][1]
15 Thou knowest, O LORD!
Think of me, and visit me;
Avenge me on my persecutors,
Through thy forbearance put me not off.
Know that for thy sake I have borne
reproach
16 From those who despise thy words.
As for me, thy word is my joy and delight;
For I bear thy name, O LORD, God of
hosts!
17 I sat not in the company of the sportive,
Nor made merry with them;
Under thy mighty power I sat alone,
For thou didst fill me with indignation.
18 Why is my pain unceasing, my wound
incurable,
Refusing to be healed?
Wilt thou really be to me like a treacherous brook,
Like waters that are not sure?

19 Therefore thus says the LORD:
"If you turn, I will restore you,
And you shall stand in my presence;
And if you bring forth what is precious, without anything base,
You shall be my mouthpiece.
They may turn to you,
But you shall not turn to them.
20 And I will make you toward this people
A fortified wall of bronze;
They may fight against you,
But they shall not overcome you;
For I am with you to help you,
And to deliver you," is the oracle of
the LORD.
21 "I will deliver you from the hand of the
wicked,
And will redeem you from the clutch
of the cruel."

[1] Vss. 13–14 are repeated, more fully, in their true context in 17:3–4.

The word of the LORD came to me, 16
saying,
"You shall not take a wife, nor have 2
sons and daughters in this place! For 3
thus says the LORD regarding the sons
and daughters that are born in this
place, and regarding the mothers that
bore them and the fathers that begot
them in this land:
'Of grievous deaths shall they die, 4
And shall be neither lamented nor
buried,
But they shall lie like dung on the
face of the ground.
They shall perish by sword and famine,
And their dead bodies shall be food
For the birds of the air and the beasts
of the earth.'"

Thus says the LORD: 5
"Do not enter the house of mourning,
nor go to lament,
nor bemoan them;
For I have withdrawn from this people
my good will,
my kindness and pity,"
is the oracle of the LORD.
"Both high and low shall die in this 6
place,
and shall not be buried;
None shall lament for them, nor gash
himself,
nor make himself bald for them;
None shall break bread for the 7
mourner,
to comfort him for the dead;
And none shall give him the cup of
consolation to drink,
for his father or mother.
Nor shall you enter the house of feast- 8
ing, to sit down with them,
to eat and to drink";
For thus says the LORD of hosts, 9
the God of Israel:
"Behold, I am banishing from this
place,
before your eyes, and in your
days,
The sound of mirth
and the sound of gladness,
The voice of the bridegroom
and the voice of the bride.

"And when you tell this people all 10
these things, and they ask you, 'Why
has the LORD pronounced all this great
evil upon us? And what offense or sin
have we committed against the LORD

11 our God?' you shall say to them, 'Because your fathers forsook me,' is the
oracle of the LORD, 'and ran after other
gods, and served and worshiped them,
while they forsook me, and did not obey
12 my law; and because you have behaved
worse than your fathers, following each
the stubborn promptings of his own
evil mind, without listening to me,
13 therefore I will hurl you out of this
land into a land which neither you nor
your fathers have known, and there
day and night shall you serve other
gods, who will show you no favor.' "
14 ["Therefore behold, days are coming," is the oracle of the LORD, "when
it shall no longer be said, 'As the LORD
lives, who brought up the children of
15 Israel from the land of Egypt,' but 'As
the LORD lives, who brought up the
children of Israel from the north land
and from all the other lands to which I
had driven them, and settled them on
their own land, which I had given to
their fathers.' "][1]

16 "Behold, I am sending for many fishers," is the oracle of the LORD,
"And they shall fish for them;
And afterward I will send for many hunters,
And they shall hunt them,
Out of every mountain and every hill,
Even from the crevices of the rocks.
17 For my eyes are upon all their ways,
They are not concealed from me,
Nor is their guilt wrapped up from my sight.
18 And I will doubly repay their guilt and their sin,
For with the lifeless bodies of their detestable things have they profaned my land,
And with their abominations have they filled my heritage.
21 Therefore behold, I will show them,
Once for all will I show them,
My power and my might,
And they shall know that the LORD is my name."

CONVERSION OF THE NATIONS, 16:19–20

19 "O LORD, my strength and my stronghold,
My refuge in time of trouble,
To thee shall the nations come
From the ends of the earth, saying,
'Our fathers inherited nought but lies,
Vain superstitions, which are good for nothing;
Can a man make gods for himself? 20
But such are no gods!' "

SIN AND DOOM, 17:1–4

"The sin of Judah is written 17
with an iron pen;
It is engraved with the point of a diamond
on the tablet of their heart;
It appears on the horns of their altars,
on their sacred pillars and sacred poles, 2
Under every spreading tree, and on every high hill,
on the mountains in the open field. 3
So your riches and all your treasures
will I give for a spoil,
as the price of your sin, through all your borders;
I will make you loosen your grip of the heritage 4
which I have given you,
And will make you serve your enemies
in a land which you know not;
For you have kindled my wrath to a fire,
which shall burn forever."

TRUST IN MAN AND TRUST IN GOD, 17:5–8

Thus says the LORD: 5
"Cursed is the man who trusts in man,
And makes flesh his arm of strength,
His mind being turned from the LORD!
He shall be like a scrub in the desert, 6
Unable to see the coming of good;
He shall dwell in the scorched lands of the wilderness,
In an uninhabited salt land.

"Blessed is the man who trusts in the LORD, 7
To whom the LORD is his confidence!
He shall be like a tree planted by waters, 8
That sends out its roots to the stream;
And is not afraid when heat comes,
For its leaves remain green;
Nor is anxious in a year of drought,
For it ceases not to bear fruit."

[1] Vss. 14–15 are repeated, with slight changes, in 23:7–8.

WORDS OF WISDOM, 17:9–18

9 The heart is treacherous above all
things, and desperately sick—
Who can understand it?
10 "I the LORD am a searcher of the
heart,
A tester of the conscience;
That I may give to every man according
to his ways,
According to the fruit of his doings."

11 Like a partridge hatching eggs which
she has not laid,
Is the man who amasses wealth which
he has not justly earned;
In the midst of his days he must leave
it,
And at the end he will prove himself a
fool.

12 A glorious throne, set on high from of
old,
Is the site of our sanctuary.
13 O LORD, thou hope of Israel,
All who forsake thee shall be put to
shame,
Those who prove faithless to thee in
the land shall be brought to confusion,
Because they have forsaken the
LORD,
The fountain of living water.

14 Heal me, O LORD, that I may be
healed;
Save me, that I may be saved;
For thou art my praise.
15 Lo! they keep saying to me,
'Where is the word of the LORD?
Pray, let it come!'
16 Yet I never urged thee to bring trouble
upon them,
Nor longed for the fatal day—
Thou knowest!
That which came out of my lips was
open before thee.
17 Be not a terror to me,
Thou who art my refuge on the day of
trouble!
18 Let them be put to shame that persecute
me,
But let me not be put to shame;
Let them be confounded,
But let me not be confounded;
Bring upon them the day of trouble,
With double destruction destroy
them!"

THE SANCTITY OF THE SABBATH, 17:19–27

Thus said the LORD to me: 19
"Go and stand at the Benjamin
Gate, by which the kings of Judah
pass in and out, and at all the other
gates of Jerusalem, by which the children of your people pass in and out, and 20
say to them: 'Hear the word of the
LORD, you kings of Judah, and all you
people of Judah and inhabitants of Jerusalem, who enter by these gates!
Thus says the LORD: As you value 21
your lives, be careful to carry no load
on the sabbath day. You shall bring no
load through the gates of Jerusalem,
nor carry one out of your houses, on the
sabbath day. And you shall do no work 22
at all on it, but shall keep the sabbath
day holy, as I commanded your fathers,
though they neither listened nor in- 23
clined their ears, but stiffened their
necks, refusing to listen or to take
warning. If you listen attentively to 24
me,' is the oracle of the LORD, 'and refrain from bringing any load through
the gates of this city on the sabbath
day, and if you keep the sabbath day
holy, and refrain from doing any work
on it, then shall there enter by the gates 25
of this city kings sitting on the throne
of David, riding in chariots and on
horses, they and their princes, together
with the people of Judah and the inhabitants of Jerusalem; and this city
shall be inhabited for ever. And people 26
shall come from the cities of Judah, and
from the districts around Jerusalem,
from the land of Benjamin, and from
the Shephelah, from the hill country,
and from the Negeb, bringing burnt-
offerings and sacrifices, cereal-offerings,
frankincense, and thank-offerings to
the house of the LORD. But if you do 27
not listen to me, in regard to keeping
the sabbath day holy by not carrying a
load or bringing it through the gates of
Jerusalem on the sabbath day, then
will I kindle in its gates a fire, which
shall devour the palaces of Jerusalem,
and shall not be quenched.' "

PARABLE OF THE POTTER, 18:1–17

The word that came to Jeremiah 18
from the LORD:
"Arise, and go down to the potter's 2

house; and there will I give you my
message."
3 So I went down to the potter's house
and found him engaged in work on the
4 wheels. And whenever the vessel at
which he was working became spoiled,
as clay is apt to do in the potter's hand,
he would turn it into another vessel,
such as seemed suitable in the potter's
own eyes.
5 Then the word of the LORD came to
me, saying,
6 "Cannot I deal with you like this
potter, O house of Israel?" is the oracle
of the LORD. "As the clay in the potter's hand, so are you in my hand, O
7 house of Israel! If at one moment I issue an order concerning a nation or
kingdom to pluck up, to tear down, and
8 to destroy, and if that nation against
which I issued the order turn from its
evil conduct, I will repent of the evil
9 which I planned to inflict upon it. And
if at another moment I issue an order
concerning a nation or kingdom to
10 build and to plant, and if it do what is
evil in my sight, by not listening to my
voice, I will repent of the good which I
11 intended to do to it. So now, speak to
the men of Judah and the inhabitants of
Jerusalem, saying, 'Thus says the
LORD: Behold, I am framing evil
against you, and am planning a scheme
against you. Turn, therefore, every
man from his evil course, and amend
12 your ways and your doings!' But they
will say, 'It is hopeless! for we will follow our own plans and will act each according to the stubborn promptings of
13 his own evil mind.' Therefore thus says
the LORD:

"Inquire among the nations!
who has heard the like of this?
The virgin Israel has done
a very dreadful thing.
14 Does the white snow vanish
from the crest of Sirion?
Does the cold flowing water
of the mountains run dry?
15 Yet my people have forgotten me,
and offer sacrifices to idols;
They stumble off their ways,
off the ancient tracks,
To walk in bypaths,
that have not been graded up,
16 Making their land a horror,
a perpetual scorn;
Everyone who passes by it is horrified,
and shakes his head.

Like the east wind will I scatter them 17
before the enemy;
I will show them my back, and not my
face,
on the day of their doom."

A FURTHER PLOT AGAINST JEREMIAH, 18:18–23

Then said they, 18
"Come and let us hatch a plot against
Jeremiah,
For instruction shall not pass from the
priest,
Nor counsel from the wise, nor the
word from the prophet;
Come and let us smite him for his
speech,
And let us pay no more heed to any of
his words!"

Pay thou heed to me, O LORD; 19
And listen to my plea!
Shall evil be repaid for good, 20
That they have dug a pit for my life?
Remember how I stood before thee
To intercede in their favor,
To avert thy wrath from them!
Therefore give up their children to 21
famine,
And hand them over to the sword;
Let their wives become childless wid-
ows,
And their men be slain by pestilence,
And their young men smitten by the
sword in battle!
Let a cry be heard from their houses, 22
When of a sudden thou bringest a
troop of raiders against them;
For they have dug a pit to catch me,
And have hidden snares for my feet.
But thou, O LORD, knowest 23
All their deadly scheme against me;
Therefore pardon not their guilt,
Nor blot out their sin from thy sight;
Let them be laid prostrate before thee,
Deal with them in thy time of anger!

PARABLE OF THE BROKEN FLASK, 19:1–13

Thus said the LORD: 19
"Go and get a potter's earthenware
flask, and take with you certain of the
elders and priests, and go out to the 2
valley of Ben-Hinnom, which is at the
entrance to the Potsherd Gate, and

there proclaim the message that I will
3 give you. Say, 'Hear the word of the
LORD, you men of Judah and inhabitants of Jerusalem! Thus says the
LORD of hosts, the God of Israel: Behold, I am bringing disaster upon this
place—such that the ears of everyone
who hears of it shall tingle—because
4 they have forsaken me, and have desecrated this place by offering sacrifices
to other gods whom neither they nor
their fathers have known, and because
the kings of Judah have filled this place
5 with the blood of innocent persons, and
have built high places to the Baal, in
order to burn their sons in the fire as
burnt-offerings to the Baal—a thing
which I never commanded, nor spoke
6 of, nor did it enter my mind. Therefore
behold, days are coming,' is the oracle
of the LORD, 'when this place shall no
longer be called "Topheth," nor "The
valley of Ben-Hinnom," but "The val-
7 ley of Slaughter," and I will break up
the plans of the men of Judah and Jerusalem in this place, and cause them to
fall by the sword before their enemies—
by the hand of those who seek their lives
—and give their dead bodies as food for
the birds of the air and the beasts of the
8 earth, and make this city a horror and a
scorn, so that everyone who passes by
it shall be horrified and shall hiss in
scorn because of all the blows that have
9 fallen upon it; and I will make them eat
the flesh of their sons and daughters,
and they shall eat each other's flesh,
through the stress of the siege which
their enemies—even those who seek
their lives—shall press upon them.'
10 Then break the flask before the eyes of
11 the men who accompany you, and say
to them, 'Thus says the LORD of hosts:
As the potter's vessel is broken and cannot be mended again, so will I break
this people and this city; and they shall
be buried in Topheth till there is no
12 more room to bury. For I will so act
toward this place and its inhabitants,'
is the oracle of the LORD, 'as to turn
13 this city into a Topheth; and the houses
of Jerusalem, including the houses of
the kings of Judah—even all the houses
on whose roofs they have offered sacrifices to all the host of the heavens, and
have poured libations to other gods—
shall be defiled like the site of Topheth.' "

JEREMIAH IN THE STOCKS, 19:14—20:6

Then Jeremiah returned from To- 14
pheth, where the LORD had sent him
to prophesy, and stood in the court of
the house of the LORD, and said to all
the people,
"Thus says the LORD of hosts, the 15
God of Israel: 'Behold, I am bringing
upon this city and upon all its towns the
full disaster that I pronounced against
it, because its people have stiffened
their necks so as not to listen to my
words.' "
Now when Pashhur, the son of Im- 20
mer the priest, who was chief overseer
in the house of the LORD, heard Jeremiah prophesying these things, Pash- 2
hur beat Jeremiah the prophet, and put
him in the stocks at the upper Benjamin Gate of the house of the LORD.
The next morning Pashhur released 3
Jeremiah from the stocks. Thereupon
Jeremiah said to him,
"The LORD calls you not Pashhur,
but 'Terror all around.' For thus says 4
the LORD: 'Behold, I am making you
a center of terror, to yourself and to all
your friends. You shall see them fall
by the sword of their enemies; and I
will give all Judah into the hand of the
king of Babylon, who shall carry them
captive to Babylon and shall slay them
by the sword. And I will give all the 5
wealth, all the gains, and all the goods
of this city, with all the treasures of the
kings of Judah, into the hand of their
enemies, who shall despoil them, and
take them, and carry them to Babylon.
And you, Pashhur, and all who live in 6
your house, shall go into exile. To
Babylon, shall you go, and there shall
you die, and there shall you be buried,
yourself and all your friends, to whom
you have prophesied falsely.' "

THE PROPHETIC IMPULSE, 20:7–13

Thou hast duped me, O LORD, and I 7
let myself be duped;
Thou hast been too strong for me, and
hast prevailed.
I have become a laughing-stock all
day long,
Everyone mocks me.
As often as I speak, I must cry out, 8
I must call, "Violence and spoil!"

For the word of the LORD has become
to me
A reproach and derision all day long.
9 If I say, "I will not think of it,
Nor speak any more in his name,"
It is in my heart like a burning fire,
Shut up in my bones;
I am worn out with holding it in—
I cannot endure it.
10 For I hear the whispering of many,
Terror all around.
"Denounce him! let us denounce him!"
Say all my intimate friends, who
watch for my tripping;
"Perhaps he will be duped, and we
shall prevail over him,
And shall take our revenge on him."
11 But the LORD is with me as a dreaded
warrior,
Therefore my persecutors shall stumble,
and shall not prevail,
They shall be put to bitter shame, because
they have not succeeded,
To everlasting confusion, which shall
not be forgotten.
12 O LORD of hosts, thou who testest the
right,
Who searchest the heart and the conscience,
Let me see thy vengeance on them,
For to thee have I confided my cause.
13 Sing to the LORD, praise the LORD;
For he has saved the life of the needy
From the hand of the wicked.

JEREMIAH CURSES HIS DAY, 20:14–18

14 Cursed be the day on which I was
born,
The day on which my mother bore
me—
Let it not be blessed!
15 Cursed be the man who brought the
good news to my father,
"A son is born to you"—
Wishing him much joy!
16 Let that man be like the cities
Which the LORD overthrew without
mercy;
Let him hear a cry in the morning,
And an alarm at noon;
17 Because he did not let me die in the
womb,
That my mother might have been my
grave,
And her womb have remained pregnant
forever!
Why came I out of the womb, 18
To see trouble and sorrow,
That my days might be spent in
shame?

THE WARNING TO KING ZEDEKIAH, 21:1–12

The word that came to Jeremiah 21
from the LORD, when King Zedekiah
sent to him Pashhur, the son of Malchiah,
and Zephaniah, the son of
Maaseiah the priest, saying, "Pray, in- 2
quire of the LORD on our behalf; for
Nebuchadrezzar, king of Babylon, has
opened hostilities against us. Perhaps
the LORD will deal with us in accordance
with all his wonderful works, and
will compel him to withdraw from us."
Then Jeremiah said to them, 3
"Thus shall you say to Zedekiah, 4
'Thus says the LORD, the God of Israel:
"Behold, I will turn the edge of
the weapons of war which are in your
hands, with which you fight against the
king of Babylon and the Chaldeans
who are besieging you outside the wall;
and I will bring them into the midst of
this city. And I myself will fight 5
against you with an outstretched hand
and with a strong arm, in anger, in
fury, and in great wrath. And I will 6
smite the inhabitants of this city, both
man and beast, with a great pestilence,
of which they shall die. And after- 7
wards," is the oracle of the LORD, "I
will give Zedekiah, king of Judah, his
servants, and the people that are left in
this city from pestilence, sword, and
famine, into the hand of Nebuchadrezzar,
king of Babylon, and into the
hand of their enemies—into the hand
of those who seek their lives—and they
shall put them to the sword, and shall
have neither mercy nor pity nor compassion
upon them." '
"And to this people say, 'Thus says 8
the LORD: "Behold, I set before you
the way of life and the way of death.
He who stays in this city shall die by 9
sword, famine, and pestilence; but he
who goes out and surrenders to the
Chaldeans who are besieging you shall
escape, and shall have his life as a prize
of war. For I have set my face against 10
this city for evil and not for good," is
the oracle of the LORD; "it shall be
given into the hand of the king of Babylon,
who shall burn it." '

11 "And to the household of the king
of Judah say, 'Hear the word of the
12 LORD, O House of David! Thus says
the LORD:
"Morning by morning give righteous
judgment,
And deliver the despoiled from the
hand of the oppressor;
Lest my fury go forth like fire,
And burn with none to quench it,
Because of your evil doings." ' "

THE PENALTY OF FALSE PRIDE, 21:13–14

13 "Behold, I am against you, O dweller
in the valley,
On the rock of the plain," is the oracle
of the LORD;
"You who say, 'Who shall come down
against us?
Who shall enter our haunts?'
14 I will punish you according to the
fruit of your doings,"
Is the oracle of the LORD;
"I will kindle a fire in her forest,
Which shall devour all that is round
about her."

PROPHECIES AGAINST THE KINGS OF JUDAH, 22:1–30

22 Thus says the LORD:
"Go down to the house of the king of
Judah, and there speak this word!
Say, 'Hear the word of the LORD, O
king of Judah, who sit on the throne of
David—you, your servants, and your
3 people, who enter by these gates! Thus
says the LORD: "Do justice and righteousness; deliver the despoiled from the
hand of the oppressor; commit no
wrong or violence against the resident
alien, the orphan, and the widow; and
do not shed innocent blood in this
4 place. For if you but do these things,
then shall there enter by the gates of
this house kings sitting on the throne
of David, riding in chariots and on
horses—they, their servants, and their
5 people. But if you do not listen to
these words, I swear by myself," is the
oracle of the LORD, "that this house
6 shall become a desolation." For thus
says the LORD concerning the house of
the king of Judah:
"Though you are as Gilead to me,
as the crest of Lebanon,
Yet will I make you a desert,
an uninhabited city.
I will bring destroyers against you,
each with his weapons;
They shall cut down your choicest
cedars,
and shall cast them into the
fire.
"And when people from many nations pass by this city, and ask one another, 'Why has the LORD done such a
thing to this great city?' they shall receive this answer, 'Because they forsook the covenant of the LORD their
God, and worshiped other gods, and
served them.' "

"Weep not for him that is dead, 10
Nor bemoan him;
But weep bitterly for him that goes
away,
For he shall return no more,
Nor see his native land!"
For thus says the LORD concerning 11
Shallum, the son of Josiah, king of Ju-
dah, who reigned instead of Josiah his
father, and went away from this place:
"He shall return no more to it, but 12
shall die in the place to which they car-
ried him captive, and he shall see this
land no more!"

"Woe to him that builds his house by 13
unrighteousness,
His upper chambers by injustice;
That makes his neighbor serve him
without pay,
And gives him not his wages;
That says, 'I will build myself a 14
roomy house,
With spacious chambers,'
And cuts out windows for it,
Panels it with cedar, and paints it
with vermilion!
Would you play the king by vying 15
with others in cedar?
Did not your father, as he ate and
drank,
Do justice and righteousness?
Then all went well with him.
He defended the cause of the poor and 16
needy;
Then all went well.
Is not that how to know me?"
Is the oracle of the LORD.
"But your eyes and your thoughts 17
Are set on nought but your ill-gotten
gain,
On the shedding of innocent blood,

And the practice of outrage and violence."

18 Therefore thus says the LORD concerning Jehoiakim, the son of Josiah, king of Judah:

"None shall lament for him,
'Ah my brother!' or 'Ah his brotherliness!'
None shall lament for him,
'Ah lord!' or 'Ah his highness!'
19 With the burial of an ass shall he be buried,
Dragged and flung out beyond the gates of Jerusalem."

20 "Go up Lebanon and cry,
In Bashan lift up your voice;
Cry from Abarim
That all your friends are exiled.
21 I spoke to you in your time of prosperity,
But you said, 'I will not listen!'
Such has been your way from your youth,
That you listened not to my voice.
22 All your neighbors shall be driven like sheep before the wind,
And your friends shall go into exile;
Then shall you be ashamed and confounded
Because of all your wickedness.
23 You who dwell in Lebanon, nestled among the cedars,
How you shall groan when pangs come upon you,
Pain as of a woman in travail!"

24 "As I live," is the oracle of the
LORD, "though Coniah, the son of
Jehoiakim, king of Judah, be the signet
ring on my right hand, I will pluck you
25 off, and give you into the hand of those
who seek your life—those of whom you
stand in dread—into the hand of
Nebuchadrezzar, king of Babylon, and
26 the hand of the Chaldeans. And I will
hurl you, together with the mother
who bore you, into another land, where
you were not born; and there shall you
27 die. And to the land to which you long
to return, you shall not return."

28 Is this man Coniah a contemptible, common utensil?
Is he an article that no one cares for?
Why, then, have he and his race been hurled and cast off
To a land that they know not?
29 O land, land, land,
Hear the word of the LORD!
Thus says the LORD: 30
"Write this man down as childless,
As a man who has no success with his sons;
For none of his race shall succeed
In sitting on the throne of David,
And ruling any more in Judah."

THE COMING OF THE TRUE KING, 23:1-8

"Woe to the shepherds who ruin and scatter 23
The sheep of my pasture!" is the oracle of the LORD.

Therefore thus says the LORD, the 2
God of Israel, concerning the shepherds
that tend my people:
"You have scattered my flock, you
have driven them away, and have not
taken care of them. Behold, I am taking care of you, to punish you for the
evil you have done," is the oracle of the
LORD. "Then will I gather the rem- 3
nant of my flock from all the lands to
which I have driven them, and I will
bring them back to their fold, where
they shall be fruitful and multiply.
And I will raise up shepherds over 4
them, who shall tend them; and they
shall no more be afraid, nor dismayed,
nor troubled," is the oracle of the
LORD.

"Behold, days are coming," is the oracle of the LORD, 5
"When I will raise up for David a righteous shoot;
And he shall reign as king with success,
Doing justice and righteousness in the land.
In his days shall Judah be saved, 6
And Israel shall live in security;
And this is the name they shall give him:
'The LORD is our vindicator.'

"Therefore behold, days are com- 7
ing," is the oracle of the LORD, "when
men shall no longer say, 'As the LORD
lives, who brought up the children of
Israel from the land of Egypt,' but 'As 8
the LORD lives, who brought up and
led the descendants of the house of Israel from the north land and from all
the other lands to which he had driven
them, and settled them on their own
land.' "

JUDGMENT ON THE PROPHETS OF JUDAH, 23:9–40

9 Concerning the prophets:
"My heart is broken within me,
All my bones are unstrung;
I am like a drunken man,
Like a man overcome by wine;
In the presence of the LORD,
And before his glorious majesty.
10 For the land is full of adulterers,
Because of whom the land mourns,
And the pastures of the steppe are parched;
Their course is evil,
And their might is not right.
11 Both prophet and priest are ungodly;
Even in my house have I met with their villainy,"
Is the oracle of the LORD.
12 "Therefore their way shall be to them
Like slippery ground in the dark,
Along which they shall be thrust till they fall.
For I will bring trouble upon them,
Their year of reckoning," is the oracle of the LORD.
13 "In the prophets of Samaria I saw an offensive thing:
They prophesied by the Baal, and misled my people Israel.
14 But in the prophets of Jerusalem have I seen a horrible thing:
They commit adultery, and walk in lies;
They strengthen the hands of evildoers,
So that no one turns from his evil ways;
To me they have all become like Sodom,
The citizens of Jerusalem like Gomorrah."
15 Therefore thus says the LORD of hosts concerning the prophets:
"Behold, I will feed them with wormwood,
And will give them poisoned water to drink;
For from the prophets of Jerusalem
Has ungodliness spread through all the land."

16 Thus says the LORD of hosts:
"Listen not to the words of the prophets
Who prophesy to you!
They fill you with vain hopes;
They speak a vision from their own minds,
Not from the mouth of the LORD,
Saying continually to those who despise the word of the LORD, 17
'All shall be well with you,'
While to everyone who follows the stubborn promptings of his own mind they say,
'No harm shall come upon you.'
For which of them has stood in the council of the LORD, 18
To see and hear his word?
Which of them has heeded and heard his word?
[See! the storm of the LORD has gone out in fury, 19
A sweeping storm, that will whirl on the head of the wicked.
The anger of the LORD will not turn back, 20
Until he has fully accomplished the designs of his mind;
In the end of the days you will understand it perfectly.][1]
I sent not the prophets, yet they ran; 21
I spoke not to them, yet they prophesied.
But if only they had stood in my council, 22
And had listened to my words,
They would have turned my people from their evil course,
And from their evil doings.

"Am I a God near at hand," is the oracle of the LORD, 23
"And not a God far off?
Can any man hide in secret places, 24
So that I cannot see him?" is the oracle of the LORD.
"Do not I fill the heavens and the earth?"
Is the oracle of the LORD.
"I have heard what the prophets say, 25
Who prophesy lies in my name, saying,
'I have dreamed, I have dreamed, I have dreamed!'
Will the mind of the prophets ever turn, 26
Who prophesy lies, who prophesy the delusion of their own minds,
Thinking to make my people forget my name— 27
Through their dreams which they tell one another—
As their fathers forgot my name for the Baal?

[1] Vss. 19–20 are repeated, with slight changes, in 30:23–24.

28 The prophet who has a dream,
Let him tell his dream!
And he who has my word,
Let him speak my word in sincerity!
What has the straw to do with the
wheat?"
Is the oracle of the LORD.
29 "Is not my word like fire,"
Is the oracle of the LORD;
"Or like a hammer that breaks the rock
in pieces?

30 "Therefore behold, I am against the
prophets," is the oracle of the LORD,
"who steal my words from one another.
31 Behold, I am against the prophets," is
the oracle of the LORD, "who use their
32 own tongues, and utter an oracle. Behold, I am against the prophets who
deal in lying dreams," is the oracle of
the LORD, "and tell them, and mislead
my people by their lies and their bom-
bast—when I neither sent them nor
commissioned them—and are of no use
at all to this people," is the oracle of the
LORD.
33 "And if anyone of this people, layman, or prophet, or priest, ask you,
'What is the burden of the LORD?' you
shall say to them, 'You are the burden,
and I will cast you off, is the oracle of
34 the LORD.' And if anyone, prophet, or
priest, or layman mention 'The burden
of the LORD,' I will punish that man
35 and his household. Thus shall you ask,
each of his neighbor, and each of his
brother, 'What has the LORD answered?' or 'What has the LORD spo-
36 ken?' But 'The burden of the LORD'
you shall mention no more; for every
man takes his own word as the burden,
and thus you distort the words of the
living God, the LORD of hosts, our
37 God! So you shall ask the prophet,
'What has the LORD answered?' or
38 'What has the LORD spoken?' But if
you mention 'The burden of the LORD,'
thus says the LORD, 'Because you have
used this phrase, "The burden of the
LORD," when I sent to you, saying,
"You shall not mention the burden of
39 the LORD," therefore behold, I will lift
you up, and will hurl you out of my
presence—you and the city that I gave
40 to you and your fathers—and I will lay
upon you everlasting reproach and
everlasting disgrace, that shall not be
forgotten.'"

PARABLE OF THE FIGS, 24:1–10

After Nebuchadrezzar, king of Baby- 24
lon, had carried Jeconiah, the son of
Jehoiakim, king of Judah, together
with the princes of Judah, the artisans,
and the smiths, into exile from Jerusalem, and brought them to Babylon, the
LORD showed me two baskets of figs
placed in front of the temple of the
LORD. One basket had very good figs, 2
like first-ripe ones, while the other
basket had very bad figs, so bad that
they could not be eaten. Then the 3
LORD said to me,
"What do you see, Jeremiah?"
And I said,
"Figs—the good figs very good, and
the bad ones very bad, so bad that they
cannot be eaten."
Then the word of the LORD came to 4
me, saying,
"Thus says the LORD, the God of 5
Israel: Like these good figs, so will I
regard with favor the exiles of Judah,
whom I sent from this place to the land
of the Chaldeans. I will look with 6
friendly eyes upon them, and will restore them to this land; I will build
them, and not tear them down; I will
plant them, and not pluck them up.
And I will give them a heart to know 7
me as the LORD; and they shall be my
people, and I will be their God; for they
shall turn to me with all their heart.
But like the bad figs, which are so bad 8
that they cannot be eaten," thus says
the LORD, "will I treat Zedekiah, king
of Judah, his princes, and the remnant
of Jerusalem which remains in this
land, together with those who live in
the land of Egypt. I will make them a 9
horror and offense to all the kingdoms
of the earth, a reproach and a byword,
a taunt and a curse, in all the places to
which I have driven them. And I will 10
send among them sword, famine, and
pestilence, till they are wiped off the
land which I gave to them and their
fathers."

WARNING TO JUDAH, 25:1–14

The word which came to Jeremiah 25
concerning all the people of Judah in
the fourth year of Jehoiakim, the son of

Josiah, king of Judah—that was the
first year of the reign of Nebuchadrez-
2 zar, king of Babylon—which Jeremiah
the prophet delivered to all the people
of Judah and all the inhabitants of Jerusalem:
3 "For these twenty-three years, from
the thirteenth year of Josiah, the son of
Amon, king of Judah, even to this day,
the word of the LORD has come to me,
and I have delivered it to you early and
4 late, but you did not listen—as in days
gone by the LORD sent all his servants
the prophets to you early and late, but
you neither listened nor inclined your
5 ears to listen—saying, 'Turn, I pray
you, each from his evil way and from
his evil doings, that you may live in the
land which the LORD gave to you and
6 your fathers forever and ever. And do
not run after other gods, to serve them
and worship them, nor vex me with the
work of your hands, that I may do you
7 no harm.' But you did not listen to
me," is the oracle of the LORD, "but
deliberately vexed me with the work of
8 your hands, to your own harm. Therefore thus says the LORD of hosts: 'Because you have not listened to my
9 words, behold, I am sending for a family from the north, and will bring them
against this land and its inhabitants,
and against all these nations round
about; and I will utterly destroy them,
and will make them a horror, a scorn,
10 and an everlasting reproach; and I will
banish from them the sound of mirth
and the sound of gladness, the voice of
the bridegroom and the voice of the
bride, the sound of the millstones and
11 the light of the lamp. And all this land
12 shall be a waste and a horror; and these
nations shall serve the king of Babylon
for seventy years. But when seventy
years are completed, I will punish the
king of Babylon and that nation for
their guilt,' " is the oracle of the LORD,
" 'and also the land of the Chaldeans,
and I will make it an everlasting deso-
13 lation. And I will bring upon that land
all my words which I have pronounced
against it—all that is written in this
book which Jeremiah prophesied against
14 all the nations. For they also shall serve
mighty nations and great kings, and I
will repay them according to their
deeds and according to the work of
their hands.' "

THE CUP OF WRATH, 25:15–38

Thus said the LORD, the God of Is- 15
rael, to me:
"Take from my hand this wine cup
of wrath, and make all the nations to
whom I am sending you drink it. And 16
when they drink it, let them reel, and
behave like madmen, because of the
sword which I am sending among
them."
So I took the cup from the LORD'S 17
hand, and made all the nations to
whom the LORD had sent me drink it—
Jerusalem and all the cities of Judah, 18
its kings and its princes, making them
a desolation, a horror, a hissing, and a
curse, as it is this day; Pharaoh, king of 19
Egypt, his servants, his princes, and all
his people, together with all the foreign 20
population; all the kings of the land of
Uz, and all the kings of the land of the
Philistines, of Askelon, Gaza, Ekron,
and the remnant of Ashdod; Edom, 21
Moab, and the Ammonites; all the 22
kings of Tyre and all the kings of Sidon,
and the kings of the coast-land which is
beyond the sea; Dedan, Tema, Buz, 23
and all those who have the corners of
their hair clipped; all the kings of Ara- 24
bia, and all the kings of the foreign
population that live in the desert; all 25
the kings of Zimri, all the kings of
Elam, and all the kings of the Medes;
all the kings of the north, far and near, 26
one with another; and all the kingdoms that are on the face of the earth.
Then the LORD said to me:
"The king of Sheshach shall drink
after them. And you shall say to them, 27
'Thus says the LORD of hosts, the God
of Israel: Drink yourselves drunk, till
you vomit, and fall to rise no more, because of the sword which I am sending
among you.' And if they refuse to take 28
the cup from your hand to drink, you
shall say to them, 'Thus says the
LORD of hosts: Drink you shall! For 29
if I begin my work of destruction with
the city which bears my name, how can
you go unpunished? You shall not go
unpunished; for I am summoning a
sword upon all the inhabitants of the
earth,' is the oracle of the LORD of
hosts.
"As for you, prophesy all these words 30
to them, and say to them:
'The LORD shall roar from on high,

From his holy abode shall he lift up
his voice;
With a mighty voice shall he roar
against his fold,
He shall raise a huzzah, like those who
tread the grapes,
Against all the inhabitants of the
earth.
31 The noise shall reach to the ends of
the earth,
For the LORD has a case against the
nations,
He has brought an indictment against
all flesh;
And the wicked shall be put to the
sword,'
Is the oracle of the LORD."
32 Thus says the LORD of hosts:
"Behold, trouble is spreading
from nation to nation,
A mighty tempest is stirring
from the ends of the earth.
33 "And those who are slain by the
LORD on that day shall extend from
one end of the earth to the other; they
shall not be mourned, nor gathered up,
nor buried, but shall lie like dung upon
the face of the ground.
34 "Wail, you shepherds, and cry,
Wallow in ashes, you lords of the
flock!
For your time for slaughter is ripe,
And you shall fall down slain like
choice lambs.
35 There shall be no means of flight for
the shepherds,
No escape for the lords of the flock.
36 Hark! the cry of the shepherds,
The wail of the lords of the flock!
For the LORD is despoiling their pasture,
37 And the peaceful folds are destroyed,
Because of the fierce anger of the
LORD.
38 The lions have left their covert,
For their land has become a waste,
Because of the sword of the LORD,
And because of his fierce anger."

THE TEMPLE ADDRESS, AND ITS CONSEQUENCES, 26:1–24

26 In the beginning of the reign of Jehoiakim, the son of Josiah, king of Judah, came this word from the LORD:
2 "Thus says the LORD: Stand in the
court of the house of the LORD, and
speak to all the people of Judah who
come to worship in the house of the
LORD all the words that I command
you to speak to them; keep not back
one word! Perhaps they may listen, 3
and turn each from his evil way, so that
I may repent of the evil which I am
planning to bring upon them because of
their evil doings. Say to them, 'Thus 4
says the LORD: If you do not listen to
me, by following my law which I have
set before you, and listening to the 5
words of my servants the prophets
whom I have been sending to you early
and late, but to whom you have not
listened, I will make this house like 6
Shiloh, and will make this city a curse
to all the nations of the earth.'"

Now the priests and the prophets, to- 7
gether with all the people, heard Jeremiah speaking these words in the house
of the LORD. So when Jeremiah had 8
finished speaking all that the LORD
had commanded him to speak to all the
people, the priests and the prophets
laid hold of him, saying,
"You shall die! How dare you 9
prophesy in the name of the LORD,
saying, 'This house shall become like
Shiloh, and this city shall become an
uninhabited waste'?"
Thereupon all the people crowded
round Jeremiah in the house of the
LORD.

When the princes of Judah heard the 10
news, they came up from the palace to
the house of the LORD, and took their
seats at the entrance to the new gate of
the house of the LORD. Then the 11
priests and the prophets addressed the
princes and all the people, saying,
"This man deserves to die; for he has
prophesied against this city in the
terms which you have heard."
Then Jeremiah addressed the princes 12
and all the people, saying,
"The LORD sent me to prophesy
against this house and this city all the
words which you have heard. But now, 13
if you amend your ways and your doings, and listen to the voice of the
LORD your God, the LORD will repent
of the evil which he has pronounced
against you. As for myself, see! I am 14
in your hands. Do to me as you think
right and proper. Only be well assured 15
of this, that, if you put me to death,
you will be bringing innocent blood
upon yourselves, upon this city, and

upon its people; for the LORD has
truly sent me to you, to speak all these
words in your hearing."
16 Then the princes and all the people
said to the priests and the prophets,
"This man does not deserve to die;
for he has spoken to us in the name of
the LORD our God."
17 Then certain of the elders of the land
rose and addressed the whole assembly
of the people, saying,
18 "Micah of Moresheth prophesied in
the days of Hezekiah, king of Judah;
and he said to all the people of Judah,
'Thus says the LORD of hosts:
"Zion shall be plowed like a field,
And Jerusalem shall become a ruin,
And the temple hill a high place in a
forest." '
19 "Did Hezekiah king of Judah and all
the people of Judah go the length of
putting him to death? Did they not
rather reverence the LORD, and entreat the favor of the LORD, so that the
LORD repented of the evil which he had
pronounced against them? We, on the
contrary, are in the act of bringing
great evil upon ourselves."
20 Now there was another man prophesying in the name of the LORD, Uriah,
the son of Shemaiah, from Kirjath-
jearim, who prophesied against this
city and this land just as Jeremiah had
21 done. And when King Jehoiakim, with
all his guardsmen and princes, heard
what he had said, the king sought to
put him to death. When Uriah heard
of it, he took fright, and fled to Egypt.
22 But King Jehoiakim dispatched men to
Egypt, Elnathan, the son of Achbor,
23 and some other men with him, who
brought Uriah from Egypt, and led
him to King Jehoiakim, who slew him
with the sword, and cast his dead body
24 into the public burying-ground. But
Jeremiah had the support of Ahikam,
the son of Shaphan, who saved him
from being handed over to the people
for execution.

THE YOKE OF THE KING OF BABYLON, 27:1–22

27 In the beginning of the reign of Zedekiah, the son of Josiah, king of Judah,
came this word to Jeremiah from the
LORD.
2 Thus said the LORD to me:
"Make yourself a yoke of thongs and
bars, and put it on your neck. Then 3
send to the king of Edom, the king of
Moab, the king of the Ammonites, the
king of Tyre, and the king of Sidon,
through their ambassadors who have
come to Jerusalem on a mission to Zedekiah, king of Judah, charging them 4
with this message to their masters,
'Thus says the LORD of hosts, the God
of Israel: Say to your masters, "I made 5
the earth, with the men and beasts that
are upon the face of the earth, by my
great power and by my outstretched
arm; and I give it to whom I please.
Now I have given all these lands into 6
the hand of Nebuchadnezzar, king of
Babylon, my servant, and I have likewise given him the beasts of the field to
serve him. And all the nations shall 7
serve him, his son, and his grandson,
until the time of his own land shall
come, when he shall serve mighty nations and great kings. And if any na- 8
tion or kingdom will not serve Nebuchadnezzar, king of Babylon, and will
not put its neck under the yoke of the
king of Babylon, I will punish that nation by sword, famine, and pestilence,"
is the oracle of the LORD, "until I have
given it into his hand. Do not listen, 9
then, to your prophets and diviners,
your dreamers, soothsayers, and sorcerers, who keep on saying to you,
'You shall not serve the king of Babylon!' For it is a lie which they are 10
prophesying to you, with the result
that you shall be removed far from
your land, and I shall have to drive you
away to perish. But if any nation will 11
bring its neck under the yoke of the
king of Babylon, and will serve him, I
will leave it on its own land," is the oracle of the LORD; "and it shall till the
land, and live in it." ' "
To Zedekiah, king of Judah, I also 12
spoke in the very same terms, saying,
"Bring your neck under the yoke of
the king of Babylon, and serve him and
his people that you may live! Why 13
should you and your people die by
sword, famine, and pestilence, as the
LORD has warned the nation that will
not serve the king of Babylon? Do not 14
listen to the words of the prophets who
say to you, 'You shall not serve the
king of Babylon!' For it is a lie which
they are prophesying to you. I did not 15
send them," is the oracle of the LORD,
"but they prophesy falsely in my name,

so that I shall have to drive you away
to perish, you and the prophets who are
prophesying to you."
16 And to the priests and to all this people I spoke, saying,
"Thus says the LORD: Do not listen
to the words of your prophets who
prophesy to you, saying, 'Lo! the vessels of the LORD'S house are very soon
to be brought back from Babylon'; for
it is a lie which they are prophesying to
17 you. Do not listen to them, but serve
the king of Babylon, that you may live.
Why should this city become a desola-
18 tion? If they be prophets, and if the
word of the LORD be with them, let
them entreat the LORD of hosts to prevent the vessels that are left in the
house of the LORD, and in the house of
the king of Judah, and in Jerusalem,
19 from going to Babylon. For thus says
the LORD of hosts concerning the pillars, the sea, the stands, and the rest of
the vessels that are left in this city—
20 those which Nebuchadnezzar, king of
Babylon, did not take away when he
carried Jeconiah, the son of Jehoiakim,
king of Judah, with all the nobles of
Judah and Jerusalem, into exile from
21 Jerusalem to Babylon—thus says the
LORD of hosts, the God of Israel, concerning the vessels that are left in the
house of the LORD, and in the house of
the king of Judah, and in Jerusalem:
22 'To Babylon shall they be brought, and
there shall they remain, until the day
that I take cognizance of them,' is the
oracle of the LORD, 'when I will bring
them up and restore them to this
place.'"

JEREMIAH AND HANANIAH, 28:1–17

28 Now that same year, in the beginning
of the reign of Zedekiah, king of Judah
—in the fourth year, the fifth month—
Hananiah, the son of Azzur, the prophet, who belonged to Gibeon, spoke to
me in the house of the LORD, in the
presence of the priests and all the people, saying,
2 "Thus says the LORD of hosts, the
God of Israel: 'I have broken the yoke
3 of the king of Babylon. Within two
years will I bring back to this place all
the vessels of the house of the LORD
which Nebuchadnezzar, king of Babylon, took away from this place and carried to Babylon. I will also bring back 4
to this place Jeconiah, the son of Jehoiakim, king of Judah, with all the exiles
of Judah who went to Babylon,' is the
oracle of the LORD; 'for I will break the
yoke of the king of Babylon."
Then Jeremiah the prophet an- 5
swered Hananiah the prophet, in the
presence of the priests and all the people who stood in the house of the LORD,
saying, 6
"Amen! The LORD do so! The
LORD fulfil the words which you have
prophesied, by bringing back the vessels of the LORD'S house, together with
all the exiles, from Babylon to this
place! Listen, however, to this word 7
which I speak in your hearing, and in
the hearing of all the people! The 8
prophets who preceded you and me,
from the very earliest times, when they
prophesied against mighty lands and
great kingdoms, prophesied of war,
famine, and pestilence. So when a 9
prophet prophesies of peace, that
prophet can be proved to be one whom
the LORD has truly sent only when the
word of the prophet is fulfilled."
Then Hananiah the prophet took the 10
yoke from the neck of Jeremiah the
prophet, and broke it. And Hananiah 11
said in the presence of all the people,
"Thus says the LORD: 'So will I
break the yoke of Nebuchadnezzar,
king of Babylon, from the neck of all
the nations within two years.'"
Then Jeremiah the prophet went on
his way.
But after Hananiah the prophet had 12
broken the yoke from the neck of Jeremiah the prophet, the word of the
LORD came to Jeremiah, saying,
"Go and say to Hananiah, "Thus 13
says the LORD: You have broken the
bars of wood, but I will replace them by
bars of iron. For thus says the LORD 14
of hosts, the God of Israel: I will put a
yoke of iron upon the neck of all these
nations, that they may serve Nebuchadnezzar, king of Babylon—and
serve him they shall—and I will give
him also the beasts of the field.'"
Then Jeremiah the prophet said to 15
Hananiah the prophet,
"Hear now, Hananiah! The LORD
has not sent you, but you are making
this people put their trust in a lie.
Therefore thus says the LORD; 'Be- 16
hold, I am sending you off the face of

the ground. This very year shall you
die; for you have spoken disloyalty
against the LORD.' "
17 So Hananiah the prophet died that
very year, in the seventh month.

THE LETTER TO THE EXILES, 29:1–23

29 These are the words of the letter
which Jeremiah the prophet sent from
Jerusalem to the elders among the exiles, and to the priests, the prophets,
and all the people whom Nebuchadnezzar had carried into exile from Jerusa-
2 lem to Babylon—after King Jeconiah,
with the queen-mother, the eunuchs,
the princes of Judah and Jerusalem, the
artisans, and the smiths, had left Jeru-
3 salem—by the hand of Elasah, the son
of Shaphan, and Gemariah, the son of
Hilkiah, whom Zedekiah, king of Judah, sent to Babylon on a mission to
Nebuchadnezzar, king of Babylon:
4 "Thus says the LORD of hosts, the
God of Israel, to all the exiles whom I
carried into exile from Jerusalem to
5 Babylon: 'Build houses, and live in
them; plant vineyards, and eat the
6 fruit of them; take wives, and beget
sons and daughters; take wives also for
your sons, and give your daughters to
husbands, that they may bear sons and
daughters; so let your numbers in-
7 crease, and not diminish. And seek the
welfare of the land to which I have carried you into exile, and pray to the
LORD on its behalf; for in its welfare
8 shall you find your welfare.' For thus
says the LORD of hosts, the God of Israel: 'Do not be deluded by the prophets and diviners who are in the midst of
you, nor listen to the dreams which
9 they dream; for they are prophesying
falsely to you in my name—I did not
send them,' is the oracle of the LORD.
10 For thus says the LORD: 'As soon as
Babylon has finished seventy years, I
will take cognizance of you, and will
fulfil my gracious promise to you, by
11 restoring you to this place. For I know
the thoughts that I cherish toward
you,' is the oracle of the LORD,
'thoughts of good and not of evil, to
12 give you a future and a hope. Then
you shall call me, and I will answer you;
you shall pray to me, and I will listen to
13 you; you shall seek me, and you shall
find me; for when you seek me with all
your heart, I will let myself be found by 14
you,' is the oracle of the LORD, 'and I
will restore your fortune, and will
gather you from all the nations and
places to which I have driven you
away,' is the oracle of the LORD, 'and I
will bring you back to the place from
which I carried you into exile.'
["For thus says the LORD concerning 16
the king who sits on the throne of David, and concerning all the people who
live in this city—your brothers who
have not gone out with you to exile—
thus says the LORD of hosts: 'Behold, I 17
am sending among them sword, famine,
and pestilence, and I will make them
like the bad figs which were so bad that
they could not be eaten; I will pursue 18
them with sword, famine, and pestilence, and I will make them a horror to
all the kingdoms of the earth—a curse
and a consternation, a scorn and a derision, among all the nations to which I
have driven them—because they did 19
not listen to my words,' is the oracle of
the LORD, 'with which I sent my servants the prophets early and late to
them, but they did not listen,' is the
oracle of the LORD. 'Therefore hear the 20
word of the LORD, all you exiles whom
I sent from Jerusalem to Babylon:]
"Because you say, 'The LORD has 15
raised us up prophets in Babylon,' thus 21
says the LORD of hosts, the God of Israel, concerning Ahab, the son of
Kolaiah, and Zedekiah, the son of
Maaseiah, who prophesy falsely to you
in my name: 'Behold, I am handing
them over to Nebuchadrezzar, king of
Babylon, who shall slay them before
your eyes; and from their fate shall all 22
the exiles of Judah in Babylon take a
curse—"May the LORD make you like
Zedekiah and Ahab, whom the king of
Babylon roasted in the fire!"—because 23
they have done godless deeds in Israel,
have committed adultery with their
neighbors' wives, and have spoken in
my name lying words which I did not
command them—I know it, and I bear
witness to it,' is the oracle of the
LORD."

THE MESSAGE TO SHEMAIAH, 29:24–32

To Shemaiah of Nehelam you shall 24
speak, saying,
"Thus says the LORD of hosts, the 25

God of Israel: 'Because you have sent
a letter in your own name to Zephaniah, the son of Maaseiah, the priest,
26 saying, "The LORD has made you
priest instead of Jehoiada the priest, to
exercise oversight in the house of the
LORD over every madman who plays
the prophet, and to put such a person
27 into the stocks and the collar. Now,
then, why have you not put a check on
Jeremiah of Anathoth, who has been
28 playing the prophet among you? For
he has actually sent a message to us in
Babylon, saying, 'Your exile shall be
prolonged; therefore build houses, and
live in them; plant vineyards, and eat
the fruit of them.' " ' "
29 When Zephaniah the priest had read
this letter in the hearing of Jeremiah
30 the prophet, the word of the LORD
31 came to Jeremiah, saying, "Send a
message to all the exiles, saying, 'Thus
says the LORD concerning Shemaiah
of Nehelam: Because Shemaiah has
prophesied to you, when I did not send
him, and has made you put your trust
32 in a lie, therefore thus says the LORD:
Behold, I will punish Shemaiah of
Nehelam and his family; not one man
shall he have living in the midst of this
people to see the good fortune which I
am bringing to my people,' is the oracle
of the LORD, 'for he has spoken disloyalty against the LORD.' "

THE HEALING OF THE WOUND, 30:1–22

The word that came to Jeremiah
from the LORD, as follows:
2 "Thus says the LORD, the God of
Israel: 'Write in a book all the words
that I have spoken to you. For behold,
days are coming,' is the oracle of the
LORD, 'when I will restore the fortune
of my people Israel and Judah,' says
the LORD, 'and will bring them back to
possess the land which I gave to their
fathers.' "
Now these are the words that the
LORD spoke concerning Israel and Judah.
"Thus says the LORD:
'I hear a sound of terror,
of dread and disaster.
Ask, now, and see
if a male may bear a child!
Why, then, do I see every man with
his hand on his loins,
like a woman in travail,
and every face turned to a
pallor?
Alas! for that day is great, 7
none is like it;
It is a time of distress for Jacob,
yet out of it shall he be saved.
On that day,' is the oracle of the 8
LORD of hosts,
'I will break the yoke from their neck,
and will burst their bonds;
And they shall serve aliens no more,
but shall serve the LORD their 9
God,
And David their king,
whom I will raise up for them.
So fear not, O Jacob my servant,' 10
is the oracle of the LORD,
'nor be dismayed, O Israel!
For behold, I will save you from afar,
and your race from the land of
their exile.
Then shall Jacob have once more
quiet and ease,
with none to make him afraid.
For I am with you to save you,' 11
is the oracle of the LORD;
'And I will make a full end of all the nations
among whom I scattered you;
But of you will I not make a full end; I
will correct you in just measure,
without leaving you wholly unpunished.'

"For thus says the LORD: 12
'Your wound is incurable,
your affliction sore;
There is no medicine for your wound, 13
no healing plaster.
All your friends have forgotten you, 14
they care no more for you;
For I have dealt you the blow of an
enemy,
the chastisement of a ruthless
foe;
Because your guilt is great,
your sins are flagrant.
Why do you cry out over your wound, 15
that your hurt is incurable?
It is because your guilt is great, your
sins are flagrant,
that I have done these things
to you.
Therefore all who devour you shall be 16
devoured,
And all your enemies shall go into exile;
Those who despoil you shall become a
spoil,

And all who prey on you will I give as
a prey.
17 For I will bring recovery to you,
And will heal you of your wounds,' is
the oracle of the LORD;
'Because they have called you "Outcasts,"
O Zion, for whom none cares.'"

18 "Thus says the LORD:
'Behold, I am restoring the tents of
Jacob,
And I will have pity upon his homes;
The city shall be built over its own
mound,
And the palace shall stand upon its
rightful site.
19 Out of them shall go songs of thanksgiving,
And the voices of those who make
merry.
I will multiply them, and they shall
not diminish;
I will increase them, and they shall not
dwindle away.
20 Their children shall be as in days of old,
And their congregation shall be established before me,
While I will punish all those who oppress them.
21 Their prince shall be one of themselves,
Their ruler shall come from the midst
of them;
And I will allow him to draw near and
approach me,
For who else would dare to approach
me?'
Is the oracle of the LORD.
22 'And you shall be my people,
And I will be your God.'"

THE STORM OF VENGEANCE, 30:23–24

23 See! the storm of the LORD has gone
out in fury,
A sweeping storm, that will whirl on
the head of the wicked.
24 The fierce anger of the LORD will not
turn back,
Until he has fully accomplished the designs of his mind;
In the end of the days you will understand it.

THE RESTORATION OF ISRAEL AND JUDAH, 31:1–26

31 "At that time," is the oracle of the
LORD, "I will be the God of all the
families of Israel, and they shall be my
people."

Thus says the LORD:
"The people that escapes from the
sword
Shall find grace in the wilderness;
When Israel goes to seek rest,
The LORD from afar shall appear to
him.
With an everlasting love have I loved
you,
Therefore with kindness will I draw
you to to me.
Once more will I build you, and you
shall be built,
O virgin of Israel!
Once more shall you take your
timbrels,
And go out in the dances of those who
make merry.
Once more shall you plant your vineyards
On the hills of Samaria;
The planters shall plant, and shall
raise their praises;
For a day shall come when the vintagers shall call
On the hills of Ephraim:
'Arise, and let us go up to Zion,
To the LORD our God!'"

For thus says the LORD:
"Raise a peal of gladness for Jacob,
And shout on the top of the mountains;
Publish, praise, and say,
'The LORD has saved his people,
The remnant of Israel.'
Behold, I am bringing them out of the
north land,
And will gather them from the uttermost parts of the earth,
Among them the blind and the lame,
The woman with child, and her that is
about to give birth—
A great company shall they return
hither.
With weeping they went away, but
with consolation will I bring them
back;
I will lead them to streams of water,
By a level way on which they shall not
stumble;
For I have become a father to Israel,
And Ephraim is my first-born.

"Hear the word of the LORD, O you
nations,

And announce it in distant coast-
lands;
Say, 'He who scattered Israel shall
gather him,
And shall keep him as a shepherd
keeps his flock.'
1 For the LORD has ransomed Jacob,
He has redeemed him from the hand
of those that were stronger than
he.
2 They shall come and be jubilant on
the height of Zion,
They shall be radiant at the goodness
of the LORD—
At the grain, the wine, and the oil,
At the young of the flock and the herd.
They shall be like a well-watered garden,
And they shall languish no more.
3 Then shall the maiden rejoice in the
dance,
And the young men and the old shall
make merry;
For I will turn their mourning to joy,
I will comfort them, and will give them
gladness instead of grief.
4 I will satisfy the priests with fat things,
And my people shall have their fill of
my goodness,"
Is the oracle of the LORD.

5 Thus says the LORD:
"Hark! in Ramah is heard lamentation,
bitter weeping!
It is Rachel weeping for her children,
Refusing to be comforted for her children,
because they are not."

6 Thus says the LORD:
"Restrain your voice from weeping,
And your eyes from tears!
For your labor shall have its reward,"
Is the oracle of the LORD;
"And they shall return from the land of
the enemy.
7 There is hope for your future,"
Is the oracle of the LORD;
"And your children shall return to their
own domain.

8 "Truly have I heard Ephraim bemoan-
ing:
'Thou hast chastened me, and I let
myself be chastened,
Like an untrained calf;
O restore me, that I may be restored!
For thou art the LORD my God.
9 Since I was exiled, I have repented,
And since I was disciplined, I have
smitten upon my thigh;
I am ashamed and confounded,
For I bear the disgrace of my youth.'

'Is Ephraim my precious son? 20
Is he my darling child?
For as often as I speak of him,
I cherish his memory still.
Therefore my heart yearns for him,
I must have pity upon him,"
Is the oracle of the LORD.

"Set up waymarks for yourself, 21
Make yourself guideposts;
Pay heed to the highway,
The way by which you went.
Return, O virgin of Israel,
Return to these your cities!
How long will you hesitate, 22
O backturning daughter?
For the LORD has created a new thing
on the earth—
The woman woos the man!"

Thus says the LORD of hosts, the 23
God of Israel:
"Once more shall they use this speech,
In the land and the cities of Judah,
When I have restored their fortune:
'The LORD bless you, O home of
righteousness,
O holy mountain!'
Yea, the people of Judah shall dwell 24
there,
And all her cities as well—
The plowmen, and those who wander
with flocks.
For I shall have satisfied the weary 25
spirit,
And every drooping spirit I shall have
filled."

Thereupon I awoke, and looked up; 26
and my dream was pleasant to me.

THE NEW COVENANT, 31:27–34

"Behold, days are coming," is the 27
oracle of the LORD, "when I will sow
the house of Israel and the house of
Judah with the seed of men and with
the seed of cattle; and as once I watched 28
over them to root up and to pull down,
to wreck, to ruin, and to harm, so will
I watch over them to build and to
plant," is the oracle of the LORD. "In 29
those days shall they say no more,
'The fathers have eaten sour grapes,
And the children's teeth are set on edge';

30 but everyone shall die for his own
guilt—everyone who eats the sour
grapes shall have his own teeth set on
edge.
31 "Behold, days are coming," is the
oracle of the LORD, "when I will make
a new covenant with the house of Israel
32 and with the house of Judah, not like
the covenant which I made with their
fathers on the day that I took them by
the hand to lead them out of the land of
Egypt—that covenant of mine which
they broke, so that I had to reject
33 them—but this is the covenant which I
will make with the house of Israel after
those days," is the oracle of the LORD:
"I will put my law within them, and
will write it on their hearts; and I will
be their God, and they shall be my
34 people. And they shall teach no more
every one his neighbor, and every one
his brother, saying, 'Know the LORD';
for all of them shall know me, from the
least of them to the greatest of them,"
is the oracle of the LORD; "for I will
pardon their guilt, and their sin will I
remember no more."

THE CERTAINTY OF ISRAEL'S REDEMPTION, 31:35–37

35 Thus says the LORD,
Who gives the sun for a light by day,
And the fixed orbs of moon and stars
for a light by night,
Who stirs up the sea till its waters
roar—
The LORD of hosts is his name:
36 "If these fixed orbs depart from my
sight,"
Is the oracle of the LORD,
"Then shall the race of Israel cease from
being a nation
Before me forever."

37 Thus says the LORD:
"If the heavens above can be measured,
Or the foundations of the earth below
can be fathomed,
Then will I too cast off all the race of
Israel
For all that they have done," is the
oracle of the LORD.

THE REBUILDING OF JERUSALEM, 31:38–40

38 "Behold, days are coming," is the
oracle of the LORD, "when the city
shall be rebuilt for the LORD from the
tower of Hananel to the corner-gate.
And the line shall go straight on from 39
there to the hill Gareb, and shall then
turn round to Goah. And all the valley 40
of Hinnom, with its dead bodies and
ashes, and all the fields extending to the
valley of Kidron, as far as the corner of
the horse-gate on the east, shall be
sacred to the LORD; it shall not be
pulled up nor torn down any more forever."

JEREMIAH'S PURCHASE OF THE FAMILY INHERITANCE, 32:1–44

The word that came to Jeremiah from 32
the LORD in the tenth year of Zedekiah, king of Judah—which was the
eighteenth year of Nebuchadrezzar—
at the time when the king of Babylon's 2
army was besieging Jerusalem, and
Jeremiah the prophet was shut up in
the guard-court of the palace of the
king of Judah, because Zedekiah, king
of Judah, had shut him up, saying,
"Why have you prophesied, saying,
'Thus says the LORD: Behold, I am
giving this city into the hand of the
king of Babylon, and he shall take it;
and Zedekiah, king of Judah, shall not 4
escape from the hand of the Chaldeans,
but shall most certainly be given into
the hand of the king of Babylon, and
shall speak with him face to face, and
shall see him eye to eye; and to Babylon 5
shall Zedekiah be led, and there shall he
remain until I visit him,' is the oracle of
the LORD; 'though you fight against
the Chaldeans, you shall have no success.' "
Jeremiah said, 6
"The word of the LORD came to me,
saying, 'Behold, Hanamel, the son of 7
your uncle Shallum, is coming to you,
to say, "Buy my field which is at Anathoth; for on you devolves the right of
redemption through purchase." ' According to the word of the LORD, then, 8
Hanamel, my uncle's son, came to me
in the guard-court, and said to me,
'Pray, buy my field which is at Anathoth, in the land of Benjamin; for yours
is the right of possession, since on you
devolves the right of redemption; buy
it for yourself.' So I recognized that
this was the word of the LORD, and I 9
bought the field which was at Anathoth

from Hanamel, my uncle's son, and weighed him out the money—seventeen shekels of silver. I signed the deed, and sealed it, got witnesses, and weighed the money with the scales. Then I took the sealed deed of purchase, containing the terms and conditions, together with an open copy of it, and handed them over to Baruch, the son of Neriah, the son of Mahseiah, in the presence of Hanamel, my uncle's son, and of the witnesses who had signed the deed of purchase, and of all the Jews who were seated in the guard-court. Then I charged Baruch in their presence, saying, 'Thus says the LORD of hosts, the God of Israel: "Take these deeds—this deed of purchase which is sealed, and this copy of it which is open—and place them in an earthenware jar, so that they may last for a long time to come." For thus says the LORD of hosts, the God of Israel: "Houses and fields and vineyards shall once more be bought in this land." ' "

Now after I had handed over the deed of purchase to Baruch, the son of Neriah, I prayed to the LORD, saying,

"Ah Lord GOD! Thou hast made the heavens and the earth by thy great power and by thine outstretched arm; nothing is too hard for thee. Thou showest kindness to thousands, and repayest the guilt of fathers upon the bosom of their children after them. Thou art the great and mighty God, whose name is the LORD of hosts—great in counsel and mighty in deed, whose eyes are open to all the ways of the children of men, rewarding each according to his ways and according to the fruit of his doings. Thou didst perform signs and wonders in the land of Egypt both toward Israel and toward other men, which are remembered to this day, and so thou didst win for thyself the renown which thou hast this day. Thou didst bring thy people Israel out of the land of Egypt with signs and wonders, with a strong hand and an outstretched arm, and with great terror; and thou gavest them this land which thou didst swear to their fathers to give them—a land flowing with milk and honey. But when they had entered into possession of it, they neither listened to thy voice, nor followed thine instruction; they did nothing that thou didst command them to do, and so thou
hast brought all this trouble upon them.
Lo! the siege-mounds for storming the 24
city have reached it; and through stress
of sword, famine, and pestilence the
city is as good as given into the hand of
the Chaldeans who are fighting against
it. What thou didst threaten has come,
as thou seest. Yet thou, O Lord GOD, 25
hast said to me: 'Buy the field for
money, and get witnesses,' when the
city is as good as given into the hand of
the Chaldeans!"

Then the word of the LORD came to 26
Jeremiah, saying,

"Since I am the LORD, the God of all 27
flesh, is anything too hard for me?
Therefore thus says the LORD: 'Be- 28
hold, I am giving this city into the hand
of the Chaldeans, and into the hand of
Nebuchadrezzar, king of Babylon; and
he shall take it. And the Chaldeans who 29
are fighting against this city shall come
and set this city on fire, and they shall
burn it, with the houses on whose roofs
men have offered sacrifices to the Baal
and poured libations to other gods, so
as to vex me. For the children of Israel 30
and the children of Judah, from their
youth up, have been doing nothing but
what was evil in my sight—they have
been doing nothing but vexing me with
the work of their hands,' is the oracle of
the LORD. 'For this city, from the day 31
that they built it, even to this day, has
roused my anger and my fury to the
point of removing it from my presence,
because of all the evil which the children 32
of Israel and the children of Judah have
done to vex me—they, their kings and
their princes, their priests and their
prophets, the men of Judah and the
inhabitants of Jerusalem. They have 33
turned to me their back, and not their
face; and though I taught them early
and late, they would not listen and take
warning, but have set up their detest- 34
able things in the house which bears my
name, to defile it, and have built the 35
high places of the Baal which are in the
valley of Ben-Hinnom, to offer up their
sons and their daughters as burnt-
offerings to Molech, which I did not
command them, nor did it enter my
mind that they would commit this
abomination, thus causing Judah to sin.
Now, therefore, thus says the LORD, 36
the God of Israel, concerning this city
of which you say, "Through stress of
sword, famine, and pestilence it is as

good as given into the hand of the king
37 of Babylon": Behold, I will gather
them from all the lands to which I have
driven them in my anger, my fury, and
my great wrath, and will bring them
back to this place, and will settle them
38 in security; and they shall be my people,
39 and I will be their God; and I will give
them a new heart and a new way, so
that they may revere me always, for
their own good, and for the good of their
40 children after them; and I will make an
everlasting covenant with them, never
to swerve from doing them good; and I
will put awe of me in their hearts, so
that they may not turn aside from me;
41 I will take delight in doing them good,
and will plant them on this land with
all the loyalty of my mind and heart.'
42 For thus says the LORD: 'As I have
brought upon this people all this great
trouble, so will I bring upon them all
43 the good that I promise them. And
fields shall be bought in this land of
which you say, "It is a desolation,
abandoned by man and beast, given
44 into the hand of the Chaldeans." Yes,
men shall buy fields for money, and
shall sign the deeds, seal them, and get
witnesses, in the land of Benjamin, in
the neighborhood of Jerusalem, and in
the cities of Judah—in the cities of the
hill country, the cities of the Shephelah,
and the cities of the Negeb—for I will
restore their fortune,' is the oracle of
the LORD."

FURTHER PROMISES OF RESTORATION, 33:1–26

33 A second time the word of the LORD
came to Jeremiah, while he was still
shut up in the guard-court, saying,
2 "Thus says the LORD, who made the
earth and formed it to stand fast—the
3 LORD is his name: 'Call to me, and I
will answer you, and will tell you great
and secret things, which you know not.'
4 For thus says the LORD, the God of
Israel, concerning the houses of this
city and the houses of the kings of
Judah, which have been broken down
5 for bulwarks and ramparts against the
Chaldeans who are coming to fight
against them, and to fill them with the
dead bodies of the men whom I will
slay in my anger and my fury, and for
whose manifold wickedness I will hide
6 my face from this city: 'Behold, I will

bring them complete recovery and healing, and will reveal to them abundance of peace and security. And I will restore the fortune of Judah and the fortune of Israel, and will build them up as at first; and I will cleanse them from all the guilt of their sin against me, and will pardon all the guilt of their sin and rebellion against me. Then this city shall be to me a joy and praise and glory among all the nations of the earth who shall hear of all the good that I will bring to her; and they shall fear and tremble because of all the good and all the prosperity that I will bring to her.'

"Thus says the LORD: 'In this place of which you say, "It is a ruin, abandoned by man and beast"—even in the cities of Judah and in the streets of Jerusalem, which are made a desolation, abandoned by man and beast—there shall once more be heard the sound of mirth and the sound of gladness, the voice of the bridegroom and the voice of the bride, the voice of those who say, as they bring thank-offerings to the house of the LORD,

"Give thanks to the LORD of hosts,
For the LORD is good,
For his kindness is everlasting."

For I will restore the fortune of the land to its former state,' says the LORD.

"Thus says the LORD of hosts: 'In this place which is a ruin, abandoned by man and beast, and in all its cities, there shall once more be homesteads of shepherds, resting their flocks. In the cities of the hill country, the cities of the Shephelah, and the cities of the Negeb, in the land of Benjamin, in the neighborhood of Jerusalem, and in the cities of Judah, flocks shall once more pass under the hands of those who count them,' says the LORD.

"Behold, days are coming," is the oracle of the LORD, "when I will fulfil the gracious promise which I made concerning the house of Israel and the house of Judah.

"In those days, and at that time,
I will raise up for David a righteous shoot,
Who shall do justice and righteousness in the land.
In those days shall Judah be saved,
And Jerusalem shall live in security;
And this is the name that they shall give him:
'The LORD is our Vindicator.'

17 "For thus says the LORD: 'David
shall never want a man to sit on the
18 throne of the house of Israel; nor shall
the Levitical priests want a man to
offer up burnt-offerings, to burn cereal-
offerings, or to make sacrifices in my
presence for all time to come.' "
19 The word of the LORD came to Jeremiah, saying,
20 "Thus says the LORD: 'If you can
break my covenant with the day and
my covenant with the night, so that
day and night shall no longer come at
21 their appointed time; then also shall my
covenant be broken with David my
servant—so that a son of his shall no
longer reign upon his throne—and with
22 the Levitical priests my ministers. Like
the host of the heavens which cannot be
numbered, and the sand of the sea
which cannot be measured, so will I
multiply the descendants of David my
servant and the Levites who minister
to me.' "
23 The word of the LORD came to Jeremiah, saying,
24 "Have you not observed what this
people have said, that 'the LORD has
cast off the two families whom he chose,
and has spurned his people so as to be
25 no longer a nation before him'? Therefore thus says the LORD: 'If my covenant be not maintained with the day and
the night, or if I do not uphold the fixed
ordinances of the heavens and the
26 earth, then also will I cast off the descendants of Jacob and of David my
servant, so as to take none of his descendants to be rulers over the descendants of Abraham, Isaac, and Jacob; but
I will restore their fortune, and will
have pity upon them.' "

JEREMIAH WARNS ZEDEKIAH OF HIS FATE, 34:1–7

1 The word that came to Jeremiah
from the LORD, when Nebuchadnezzar,
king of Babylon, and all his army, with
all the kingdoms and nations of the
earth that were under his sway, were
fighting against Jerusalem and all its
cities:
2 "Thus says the LORD, the God of
Israel: Go to Zedekiah, king of Judah,
and say to him, 'Thus says the LORD:
Behold, I am giving this city into the
hand of the king of Babylon, and he
shall burn it; and you yourself shall not 3
escape from his hand, but shall most
certainly be seized and given into his
hand, and shall see the king of Babylon
eye to eye, and shall speak with him
face to face; and to Babylon shall you
go. Yet hear the word of the LORD, O 4
Zedekiah, king of Judah! Thus says the
LORD concerning you: You shall not
die by the sword, but shall die in peace; 5
and they shall burn sweet spices for
you, as they burned them for your
fathers, the former kings that were before you; and they shall lament for you
with "Ah lord!" for I have spoken the
word,' is the oracle of the LORD."
So Jeremiah the prophet spoke all 6
these words to Zedekiah, king of Judah,
in Jerusalem, when the king of Baby- 7
lon's army was fighting against Jerusalem and all the cities of Judah that were
left, namely, Lachish and Azekah, for
these were the only cities of Judah that
remained as fortified cities.

ON THE BROKEN PLEDGE TO THE SLAVES, 34:8–22

The word that came to Jeremiah 8
from the LORD, after King Zedekiah
had made a covenant with all the
people that were in Jerusalem to make
them a proclamation of liberty that 9
each of them should liberate his Hebrew
slaves, both male and female, so that
none should hold his fellow-Jew in
slavery—and after all the princes and 10
people who had entered into the covenant to liberate their slaves, both male
and female, so that none should hold
them any longer in slavery, had obeyed
the covenant and liberated them, but 11
afterward turned round and brought
back the slaves that they had liberated,
both male and female, and reduced
them once more to slavery; then the 12
word of the LORD came to Jeremiah,
saying,
"Thus says the LORD, the God of 13
Israel: 'On the day that I brought your
fathers out of the land of Egypt, out of
a state of slavery, I made a covenant
with them, saying, "At the end of six 14
years you shall liberate each one his
fellow-Hebrew who has sold himself to
you, and has served you for six years—
you shall liberate him from your
service." But your fathers neither lis-

tened nor inclined their ears to me.
15 Just now you turned round, and did
what was right in my sight, by making
a proclamation of liberty to one another,
and entering into a covenant to this
effect before me in the house which
16 bears my name. But you have again
turned round and dishonored my name
by bringing back the slaves you had
liberated, both male and female, and
reducing them once more to slavery.'
17 Therefore thus says the LORD: 'Since
you have not listened to me in regard to
the proclamation of liberty to one
another, behold, I am making for you,'
is the oracle of the LORD, 'a proclamation of liberty to sword, pestilence, and
famine; and I will make you a horror to
18 all the kingdoms of the earth. And as
for the men who have broken my covenant—the men who have not carried
out the terms of the covenant which
they made in my presence, when they
cut the calf in two and passed between
19 the parts of it—even the princes of
Judah and Jerusalem, the eunuchs, the
priests, and all the people of the land,
who passed between the parts of the
20 calf—I will give them into the hand of
their enemies, into the hand of those
who seek their lives, and their dead
bodies shall be food for the birds of the
21 air and the beasts of the earth. And
Zedekiah, king of Judah, and his princes
will I give into the hand of their
enemies, into the hand of those who
seek their lives—into the hand of the
king of Babylon's army, which has
22 meanwhile gone away from you. Behold, I am issuing orders,' is the oracle
of the LORD, 'and will bring them back
to this city; and they shall fight against
it, and shall take it, and shall burn it;
and the cities of Judah will I make a
desolation, without an inhabitant.' "

THE FIDELITY OF THE RECHABITES, 35:1–19

35 The word that came to Jeremiah
from the LORD in the days of Jehoiakim, the son of Josiah, king of Judah,
as follows:
2 "Go to the household of the Rechabites, and talk with them, and bring
them to one of the chambers in the
house of the LORD, and offer them wine
to drink."

So I took Jaazaniah, the son of Jere-
miah, the son of Habazziniah, with his
brothers and all his sons, even the whole
household of the Rechabites, and
brought them to the house of the
LORD, to the chamber of the sons of
Hanan, the son of Igdaliah, the man of
God, which adjoined the chamber of
the princes, above the chamber of
Maaseiah, the son of Shallum, the keeper of the threshold; and I set before the
Rechabites a bowl full of wine, with
drinking cups, and said to them,
"Drink wine!"
But they said,
"We will drink no wine; for Jonadab,
the son of Rechab, our ancestor, laid a
charge upon us, saying, 'You shall drink
no wine, neither you nor your sons forever; and you shall build no house, nor
sow seed, nor plant or own a vineyard,
but shall live in tents all your days, so
that you may live long in the land
where you pass your days.' And we
have obeyed in every respect the charge
which Jonadab, the son of Rechab, our
ancestor, laid upon us, drinking no wine
all our lives—neither we, nor our wives,
nor our sons, nor our daughters—building no houses to live in, nor owning
vineyard, field, or seed, but living in 1
tents, acting in obedience to all the
charge which Jonadab our ancestor laid
upon us. It was only when Nebucha- 1
drezzar, king of Babylon, invaded the
land that we said, 'Come and let us go
up to Jerusalem before the advance of
the Chaldean and Syrian armies'; and
so we are living in Jerusalem."
Then the word of the LORD came to 1
Jeremiah, saying,
"Thus says the LORD of hosts, the 1
God of Israel: 'Go and say to the men
of Judah and the inhabitants of Jerusalem, Will you not learn the lesson of
obedience to my words?' is the oracle of
the LORD. 'The charge which Jonadab, 1
the son of Rechab, laid upon his sons,
to drink no wine, has been observed;
and in obedience to their ancestor's
charge they have drunk no wine to this
day. But though I spoke to you early
and late, you have not listened to me;
and though I sent all my servants the 15
prophets to you early and late, saying,
"Turn, I pray you, each from his evil
way, and amend your doings, and do
not run after other gods, to serve them,
that you may live in the land which I

gave to you and your fathers," you
have neither listened nor inclined your
5 ears to me. Therefore, because the sons
of Jonadab, the son of Rechab, have observed the charge which their father
laid upon them, while this people has
7 not listened to me, thus says the LORD,
the God of hosts, the God of Israel:
Behold, I am bringing upon Judah and
upon all the inhabitants of Jerusalem
all the evil which I pronounced against
them, because I spoke to them, but
they did not listen, and I called to them,
but they did not answer.' "
8 But to the household of the Rechabites, Jeremiah said,
"Thus says the LORD of hosts, the
God of Israel: 'Because you have been
obedient to the charge of Jonadab your
ancestor, and have kept all his instructions, and have done just as he charged
9 you, thus says the LORD of hosts, the
God of Israel: Jonadab, the son of
Rechab, shall not want a man to stand
in my presence forever.' "

THE BURNING OF THE SCROLL, 36:1–32

6 In the fourth year of Jehoiakim, the
son of Josiah, king of Judah, came this
word to Jeremiah from the LORD:
2 "Take a scroll, and write on it all the
words that I have spoken to you against
Israel, and Judah, and all the other
nations, from the day that I first spoke
to you in the days of Josiah even to this
3 day. Perhaps when the house of Israel
hears of all the evil that I am planning
to bring upon them, they will turn each
from his evil way, and will receive my
pardon for their guilt and their sin."
4 So Jeremiah called Baruch, the son
of Neriah; and at Jeremiah's dictation
Baruch wrote on a scroll all the words
that the LORD had spoken to him.
5 Then Jeremiah instructed Baruch, saying,
6 "I am debarred from going to the
house of the LORD. Go you, then, and
from the scroll which you have written
at my dictation read the words of the
LORD in the hearing of the people
gathered in the house of the LORD on
a fast day, as well as in the hearing of
all Judah who come from their cities.
7 Perhaps, as they present their supplication before the LORD, they will turn
each from his evil way, when they realize how great is the anger and fury
which the LORD has expressed against
this people."
So Baruch, the son of Neriah, did 8
just as Jeremiah the prophet instructed
him, reading from the book the words
of the LORD in the house of the LORD.
It was in the fifth year of Jehoiakim, 9
the son of Josiah, king of Judah, the
ninth month, the first day of the month,
when all the people in Jerusalem and all
those who came to Jerusalem from the
cities of Judah had proclaimed a fast
before the LORD, that Baruch in the 10
hearing of all the people read from the
book the words of Jeremiah in the house
of the LORD, from the chamber of
Gemariah, the son of Shaphan, the secretary, which was in the upper court,
at the entrance to the new gate of the
house of the LORD.
Now when Micaiah, the son of Gem- 11
ariah, the son of Shaphan, had heard
all the words of the LORD read from
the book, he went down to the palace, 12
to the secretary's chamber, where he
found all the princes seated—Elishama
the secretary, Delaiah, the son of Shemaiah, Elnathan, the son of Achbor,
Gemariah, the son of Shaphan, Zedekiah, the son of Hananiah, and all the
other princes. And Micaiah reported 13
to them all the words that he had heard
Baruch read from the book in the hearing of the people. Then all the princes 14
sent Jehudi, the son of Nethaniah, the
son of Shelemiah, the son of Cushi, to
Baruch with this message,
"Take with you the scroll from which
you have read in the hearing of the
people, and come to us."
So Baruch, the son of Neriah, took
the scroll with him, and went to them.
And they said to him, 15
"Read it once more in our hearing."
So Baruch read it in their hearing.
And when they had heard all the words, 16
they turned in alarm to one another,
and said to Baruch,
"We must certainly report all this to
the king."
Then they asked Baruch, 17
"Pray, tell us! How did you write all
these words? Was it at his dictation?"
And Baruch answered them, 18
"Yes! He dictated all these words to
me, and I wrote them with ink on the
scroll."
Then the princes said to Baruch, 19

"Go into hiding, you and Jeremiah,
and let no one know where you are."
20 When they had deposited the scroll
in the chamber of Elishama the secretary, they went to the king in his court,
and reported the whole matter in his
21 hearing. The king then sent Jehudi to
bring the scroll; and when he had
brought it from the chamber of Elishama the secretary, Jehudi read it in the
hearing of the king and of all the princes
who stood in attendance upon the king.
22 Since it was the ninth month, the king
was seated in the winter house, with a
23 fire burning in a brazier before him. As
Jehudi read three or four columns, the
king would cut it up with his penknife
and fling it into the fire that was in
the brazier, until the whole scroll was
consumed in the fire that was in the
24 brazier. Yet neither the king nor any
of his servants showed any alarm, nor
did they tear their clothes, as they heard
25 all these words. Even though Elnathan,
Delaiah, and Gemariah entreated the
king not to burn the scroll, he did not
26 listen to them. The king then ordered
Jerahmeel the royal prince, Seraiah, the
son of Azriel, and Shelemiah, the son of
Abdeel, to arrest Baruch the secretary
and Jeremiah the prophet. But the
LORD kept them concealed.
27 Now after the king had burned the
scroll containing the words that Baruch
had written at Jeremiah's dictation, the
word of the LORD came to Jeremiah,
saying,
28 "Take another scroll, and write on it
all the words that were on the first
scroll, which Jehoiakim, the king of
29 Judah, burned. And concerning Jehoiakim, king of Judah, you shall say, 'Thus
says the LORD: You have burned this
scroll, saying, "Why have you written
on it these words, 'The king of Babylon
will certainly come and destroy this
land, and will annihilate from it man
30 and beast'?" Therefore thus says the
LORD concerning Jehoiakim, king of
Judah: "No descendant of his shall sit
on the throne of David; and his dead
body shall be flung out to the heat by
31 day and to the cold by night. And I will
punish him, his family, and his servants,
for their guilt; and I will bring upon
them, and upon the inhabitants of Jerusalem, and upon the men of Judah,
all the evil that I pronounced against
them, though they did not listen."' "

So Jeremiah took another scroll, and 3
gave it to Baruch, the son of Neriah,
the secretary, who wrote on it at Jeremiah's dictation all the words of the
book which Jehoiakim, king of Judah,
had burned in the fire; and many words
of like nature were added to them.

A FURTHER WARNING TO ZEDEKIAH, 37:1–10

Zedekiah, the son of Josiah, whom
Nebuchadrezzar, king of Babylon had
made king in the land of Judah, reigned
as king in the place of Coniah, the
son of Jehoiakim. But neither he, nor
his servants, nor the people of the land,
listened to the words of the LORD
which he spoke through Jeremiah the
prophet. King Zedekiah, however, sent
Jehucal, the son of Shelemiah, and
Zephaniah, the son of Maaseiah the
priest, to Jeremiah the prophet, saying,
"Pray, intercede on our behalf with the
LORD our God." (For Jeremiah had
not yet been put in prison, but was still
coming and going freely among the
people; and when Pharaoh's army advanced out of Egypt, the Chaldeans
who were besieging Jerusalem, on hearing the news, raised the siege of Jerusalem.) Then the word of the LORD
came to Jeremiah the prophet, saying,
"Thus says the LORD, the God of Israel: 'Thus shall you say to the king of
Judah, who has sent you to consult me:
Behold, Pharaoh's army, which is advancing to your aid, shall return to the
land of Egypt; and the Chaldeans shall
come back to fight against this city, and
take it, and burn it.' Thus says the
LORD: 'Do not delude yourselves by
saying, "The Chaldeans are leaving us
for good"; for they shall not leave you.
Even if you defeated the whole Chal- 1
dean army that is fighting against you,
leaving but a few wounded men of them
in their several tents, they would rise
up and burn this city.' "

JEREMIAH ARRESTED AND IMPRISONED, 37:11–21

Now when the Chaldean army had 11
raised the siege of Jerusalem, because
of the advance of Pharaoh's army,
Jeremiah set out from Jerusalem on a 12

journey to the land of Benjamin, to
take possession of the property that belonged to him among the people there.
13 But just as he reached the Benjamin
Gate, a sentry who was posted there,
named Irijah, the son of Shemeliah, the
son of Hananiah, arrested Jeremiah the
prophet, saying,

"You are deserting to the Chaldeans."

14 Jeremiah replied,

"It is false; I am not deserting to the
Chaldeans."

But he would not listen to him. So
Irijah arrested Jeremiah, and brought
15 him to the princes. And the princes
were so angry with Jeremiah that they
beat him and put him in prison in the
house of Jonathan the secretary, which
16 had been turned into a prison. Having
thus come to the dungeon-cells, Jeremiah remained there for a number of
days.

17 Then King Zedekiah sent for him,
and received him; and the king asked
him secretly in his palace, "Is there any
word from the LORD?"

And Jeremiah said,

"There is. You shall be given into
the hand of the king of Babylon."

18 Then Jeremiah said to King Zedekiah,

"What wrong have I done to you, or
to your servants, or to this people, that
19 you have put me in prison? Where are
your prophets who prophesied to you,
saying, 'The king of Babylon shall not
come against you, nor against this
20 land?' So now, pray, listen to me, O my
lord the king; and give a favorable
hearing to my supplication, that I may
not be sent back to the house of Jonathan the secretary, and left to die
there!"

21 King Zedekiah then gave orders, and
Jeremiah was committed to the guard-
court, and given a loaf of bread daily
from the bakers' street, until all the
bread in the city was consumed. So
Jeremiah remained in the guard-court.

JEREMIAH RESCUED BY EBED-MELECH, 38:1–13

1 Now Shephatiah, the son of Mattan,
and Gedaliah, the son of Pashhur, and
Jucal, the son of Shelemiah, and Pashhur, the son of Malchiah, heard Jeremiah addressing all the people in these
terms,

"Thus says the LORD: 'He who re- 2
mains in this city shall die by sword,
famine, and pestilence; but he who surrenders to the Chaldeans shall have his
life given to him as a prize of war.' For 3
thus says the LORD: 'This city shall
certainly be given into the hand of the
king of Babylon's army, and they shall
take it.'"

So they said to the king, 4

"Pray, have this man put to death;
for he is disheartening the soldiers that
are left in this city, and all the people
as well, by addressing such words to
them; for this man is seeking not the
welfare of this people, but their ruin."

Whereupon King Zedekiah said, 5

"See! he is in your hand; for the king
can do nothing against you."

So they took Jeremiah, and cast him 6
into the cistern of Malchiah, the royal
prince, which was in the guard-court,
letting Jeremiah down with ropes. And
as there was no water in the cistern, but
only mud, Jeremiah sank in the mud.

But Ebedmelech the Ethiopian, a 7
eunuch in the service of the palace,
heard that they had put Jeremiah in
the cistern. The king being seated at
the Benjamin Gate, Ebedmelech set 8
out from the palace, and addressed the
king, saying,

"My lord the king, these men have 9
done wrong in treating Jeremiah as
they have done, casting him into the
cistern, to die where he is of famine, because there is no more bread in the
city."

The king then gave orders to Ebed- 10
melech the Ethiopian, saying,

"Take with you three men from here,
and draw Jeremiah the prophet out of
the cistern, before he die."

So Ebedmelech took the men with 11
him, and went to the wardrobe of the
palace, and took from there some torn
and tattered rags, and let them down
by ropes to Jeremiah in the cistern.
Then Ebedmelech the Ethiopian said 12
to Jeremiah,

"Pray, put these torn and tattered
rags below your armpits under the
ropes."

Jeremiah did so, and then they drew 13
Jeremiah up with the ropes, and
brought him up from the cistern. And
Jeremiah remained in the guard-court.

THE SECRET MEETING WITH ZEDEKIAH, 38:14–28*a*

14 Then King Zedekiah sent for Jeremiah the prophet, and received him at the third entrance to the house of the LORD; and the king said to Jeremiah, "I am going to ask you a question, and you must conceal nothing from me."

15 Jeremiah said to Zedekiah,
"If I tell you the truth, are you not sure to put me to death? And if I give you advice, you will not listen to me."

16 So King Zedekiah swore an oath in secret to Jeremiah, saying,
"As the LORD lives, who made this life of ours, I will neither put you to death, nor hand you over to these men who are seeking your life."

17 Then Jeremiah said to Zedekiah,
"Thus says the LORD, the God of hosts, the God of Israel: 'If you but surrender to the officers of the king of Babylon, your life shall be spared, and this city shall not be burned; both yourself and your household shall be spared.
18 But if you do not surrender to the officers of the king of Babylon, this city shall be handed over to the Chaldeans, who shall burn it; and you yourself shall not escape from their hand.'"

19 Then King Zedekiah said to Jeremiah,
"I am afraid of the Jews who have gone over to the Chaldeans, lest I be handed over to them, and they subject me to indignity."

20 But Jeremiah said,
"You shall not be handed over. Pray, then, listen to the voice of the LORD, as I declare it to you, that your life may be spared, and all may be well with you.
21 But if you refuse to surrender, this is
the word that the LORD has revealed
22 to me: all the women who are left in
the palace of the king of Judah shall be led out to the officers of the king of Babylon, saying,

'Your bosom friends have deceived you,
and have overreached you;
They have sunk your feet in the mire,
and have turned away from you.'

23 All your wives and children shall be led out to the Chaldeans, while you yourself shall not escape from their hand, but shall be captured by the king of Babylon; and this city shall be burned."

24 Then Zedekiah said to Jeremiah,
"Let no one know of this conversation, on pain of death. And if the princes hear that I have been talking with you, and come and say to you, 'Pray, tell us what you said to the king, and what the king said to you; conceal nothing from us, on pain of death,' you shall say to them, 'I was presenting my petition to the king, that he would not send me back to Jonathan's house, to die there.'"

So when all the princes came to Jeremiah, and questioned him, he answered them in accordance with all these instructions that the king had given; and they pressed him no further, for the conversation had not been overheard. Jeremiah then remained in the guard-court till the day that Jerusalem was taken.

THE CAPTURE OF JERUSALEM, 39:1–2, 4–10[1]

In the ninth year of Zedekiah, king of Judah, in the tenth month, Nebuchadrezzar, king of Babylon, and all his army advanced against Jerusalem and besieged it; and in the eleventh year of Zedekiah, in the fourth month, on the ninth day of the month, the city was breached. When Zedekiah, king of Judah and all the soldiers saw what had happened, they left the city by night, and fled by way of the king's garden, through the gate between the two walls, and made for the Jordan valley. But the Chaldean army pursued them, and overtook Zedekiah in the steppes of Jericho; and they arrested him, and brought him up to Nebuchadnezzar, king of Babylon, at Riblah in the land of Hamath, where he pronounced judgment against him. And the king of Babylon slew the sons of Zedekiah at Riblah before his eyes. The king of Babylon likewise slew all the nobles of Judah. Then he put out the eyes of Zedekiah, and bound him with chains, to carry him to Babylon. The Chaldeans also burned the house of the king and the houses of the people, and demolished the walls of Jerusalem. Then Nebuzaradan, the commander of the guard, carried captive to Babylon the rest of the people that were left in the city, and the deserters who had surrendered to him, together with the artisans that were left. But Nebuzara-

[1] **38:28*b* and 39:3 will be found in the next section.**

dan, the commander of the guard, left in
the land of Judah a number of the poor
people, who had nothing, and at the
same time gave them vineyards and
fields.

THE RELEASE OF JEREMIAH, 38:28*b*, 39:3, 11–14

28*b* When Jerusalem had been taken, all
the officials of the king of Babylon—
3 Nergal-sharezer, the chief councilor,
Nebushazban, the chief eunuch, and all
the rest of the officials of the king of
Babylon—came and took their seats at
1 the middle gate. Now Nebuchadrezzar,
king of Babylon, had given orders regarding Jeremiah to Nebuzaradan, the
2 commander of the guard, saying, "Take
him, and look well after him; do him no
harm, but treat him as he tells you."
3 So Nebuzaradan, the commander of the
guard, issued orders, and Nebushazban,
the chief eunuch, Nergal-sharezer, the
chief councilor, and all the chief officials
4 of the king of Babylon sent and took
Jeremiah out of the guard-court, and
handed him over to Gedaliah, the son of
Ahikam, the son of Shaphan, to have
him conveyed to his home. So he
stayed among the people.

THE PROMISE TO EBEDMELECH, 39:15–18

5 While Jeremiah was still shut up in
the guard-court, the word of the LORD
came to him saying,
6 "Go and say to Ebedmelech the
Ethiopian, 'Thus says the LORD of
hosts, the God of Israel: Behold, I am
about to fulfil the words that I have
spoken concerning this city—for evil
and not for good—and you shall see
7 them fulfilled on that day. But I will
deliver you on that day,' is the oracle
of the LORD, 'and you shall not be
handed over to the men of whom you
8 stand in dread. For I will most certainly save you from falling by the sword,
and your life shall be given to you as a
prize of war, because you have put your
trust in me,' is the oracle of the LORD."

JEREMIAH WITH GEDALIAH, 40:1–12

0 The word that came to Jeremiah from
the LORD, after his release from Ramah
by Nebuzaradan, the commander of
the guard, who had found him bound
with chains among all the exiles of Jerusalem and Judah who were being carried captive to Babylon.
Now the commander of the guard 2
had taken Jeremiah and said to him,
"The LORD your God pronounced 3
this doom upon this place, and the
LORD has fulfilled his word, and has
done as he said, because you sinned
against the LORD, and did not listen to
his voice—therefore this thing has come
upon you. But now, see! I release you 4
this day from the chains that are upon
your hands. If you are disposed to
come with me to Babylon, come, and I
will look well after you; but if you are
not disposed to come with me to Babylon, think no more of it. See! the whole
land is before you. Go wherever you
think right and proper. Go back, if you 5
wish, to Gedaliah, the son of Ahikam,
the son of Shaphan, whom the king of
Babylon has appointed governor over
the cities of Judah, and stay with him
among the people; or go wherever else
you please."
The commander of the guard then
gave him an allowance of victuals and
released him. So Jeremiah came to Ged- 6
aliah, the son of Ahikam, at Mizpeh,
and stayed with him among the people
that were left in the land.
Now when all the commanders of the 7
forces that were in the field, together
with their men, heard that the king of
Babylon had appointed Gedaliah, the
son of Ahikam, governor of the land,
and that he had intrusted to his charge
the men, women, and children, of the
poorest classes of the land, who had not
been carried captive to Babylon, they 8
came to Gedaliah at Mizpeh—Ishmael,
the son of Nethaniah, Johanan, the son
of Kareah, Seraiah, the son of Tanhumeth, the sons of Ephai of Netophah,
and Jezaniah, the son of the Maacathite—together with their men. Then 9
Gedaliah, the son of Ahikam, the son
of Shaphan, swore an oath to them and
their men, saying,
"Do not be afraid of the Chaldean
officials. If you stay in the land, and
serve the king of Babylon, all shall be
well with you. As for myself, I intend 10
to stay at Mizpeh, to represent your interests before the Chaldeans who may
visit us; but you may gather wine, fruit,

and oil, store them in your vessels, and
stay in the cities which you choose to
occupy."
11 Likewise, all the Jews who were in
Moab, Ammon, Edom, and all the other
countries, when they heard that the
king of Babylon had left a remnant in
Judah, and that he had appointed Gedaliah, the son of Ahikam, the son of
12 Shaphan, governor over them, returned
from all the places to which they had
been driven, and came to the land of
Judah—to Gedaliah at Mizpeh—and
gathered wine and fruit in great abundance.

MURDER OF GEDALIAH, 40:13—41:18

13 Now Johanan, the son of Kareah,
and all the commanders of the forces
that were in the field, came to Gedaliah
14 at Mizpeh, and said to him,
"Are you at all aware that Ballis,
king of the Ammonites, has sent Ishmael, the son of Nethaniah, to take
your life?"
But Gedaliah, the son of Ahikam, did
not believe them.
15 Then Johanan, the son of Kareah,
spoke secretly to Gedaliah at Mizpeh,
saying,
"Pray, let me go and slay Ishmael,
the son of Nethaniah, without anyone
knowing it. Why should he take your
life, and cause all the Jews who are
gathered round you to be scattered, and
the remnant of Judah to perish?"
16 But Gedaliah, the son of Ahikam,
said to Johanan, the son of Kareah,
"You shall do no such thing. For you
are speaking falsely of Ishmael."
41 In the seventh month, however, Ishmael, the son of Nethaniah, the son of
Elishama, a member of the royal family,
accompanied by ten men, came to Gedaliah, the son of Ahikam, at Mizpeh.
2 As they dined together at Mizpeh, Ishmael, the son of Nethaniah, and the ten
men who were with him arose, and
smote with the sword, and slew Gedaliah, the son of Ahikam, whom the
king of Babylon had appointed govern-
3 or over the land. Ishmael also smote all
the Jews who were with him at Mizpeh,
as well as the Chaldean soldiers who
happened to be there.
4 The day after the murder of Gedaliah,
5 before anyone was aware of it, certain
men from Shechem, Shiloh, and Samaria—eighty in all—with their beards
shaved, their clothes rent, and their
bodies gashed, came bearing cereal-
offerings and frankincense, to present
them in the house of the LORD. Ishmael, the son of Nethaniah, went out
from Mizpeh to meet them, as they
came along weeping; and when he met
them, he said to them,
"Come to Gedaliah, the son of Ahikam."
When they reached the middle of the
city, Ishmael, the son of Nethaniah,
and the the men who were with him
slew them, and cast them into a cistern.
There were ten of their number, however, who said to Ishmael,
"Do not put us to death; for we have
stores of wheat, barley, oil, and honey,
buried in the fields."
So he let them alone, and did not put
them to death with their fellows.
Now the cistern into which Ishmael
cast all the dead bodies of the men
whom he had slain was a great cistern
which King Asa had made as a means
of defense against Baasha, king of Israel; this cistern Ishmael, the son of
Nethaniah, filled with the slain.
Ishmael then carried away captive 1
all the rest of the people that were at
Mizpeh—the king's daughters, and all
the people that remained at Mizpeh,
whom Nebuzaradan, the commander
of the guard, had committed to the
charge of Gedaliah, the son of Ahikam—
all these Ishmael, the son of Nethaniah,
carried away captive, and started to
cross over to the Ammonites. But when 1
Johanan, the son of Kareah, and all the
commanders of the forces that were
with him, heard of all the crimes that
Ishmael, the son of Nethaniah, had
committed, they took all their men, 1
and set out to fight with Ishmael, the
son of Nethaniah, overtaking him by
the great waters that are at Gibeon.
And when all the people that were with 1
Ishmael saw Johanan, the son of Kareah, and all the commanders of the
forces that were with him, they were
filled with joy; and all the people whom 1
Ishmael had carried captive from Mizpeh turned round and went back to
Johanan, the son of Kareah. But Ish- 1
mael, the son of Nethaniah, with eight
men, escaped from Johanan, and made
his way to the Ammonites.

16 Then Johanan, the son of Kareah,
and all the commanders of the forces
that were with him, took all the remnant of the people whom Ishmael, the
son of Nethaniah, had carried captive
from Mizpeh, after he had slain Gedaliah, the son of Ahikam—men, women,
children, and eunuchs, whom he had
17 brought back from Gibeon—and they
went and stayed at Chimham's Inn, in
the neighborhood of Bethlehem, intend-
18 ing to go on to Egypt, through fear of
the Chaldeans; for they were afraid of
them, because Ishmael, the son of
Nethaniah, had slain Gedaliah, the son
of Ahikam, whom the king of Babylon
had appointed governor over the land.

THE MIGRATION TO EGYPT, 42:1—43:13

Then all the commanders of the
forces, including Johanan, the son of
Kareah, and Azariah, the son of Hoshaiah, with all the people from the
least to the greatest, approached Jere-
2 miah the prophet, and said to him,
"Give a favorable hearing to our supplication, and pray to the LORD your
God for us, even for all this remnant—
for we are left but a few out of many, as
3 you can see with your own eyes—that
the LORD your God may show us the
way we should go and the thing we
should do."
4 Then Jeremiah the prophet said to
them,
"I have heard your petition. I will
pray to the LORD your God, as you
request; and whatever answer the
LORD may give you, I will tell you—
I will hold nothing back from you."
5 They said to Jeremiah,
"The LORD be a true and faithful
witness against us, if we do not act in
accordance with all the word which the
6 the LORD your God may send to us!
Whether it be pleasant or unpleasant,
we will obey the voice of the LORD our
God, to whom we are sending you, that
we may prosper through obeying the
voice of the LORD our God."
7 At the end of ten days the word of
8 the LORD came to Jeremiah. So he
summoned Johanan, the son of Kareah,
and all the commanders of the forces
that were with him, and all the people
9 from the least to the greatest; and he
said to them,

"Thus says the LORD, the God of
Israel, to whom you sent me to present
your supplication before him: 'If you 10
stay on in this land, I will build you up
and not tear you down, and I will plant
you and not uproot you; for I regret the
harm that I have done to you. Do not 11
be afraid of the king of Babylon, of
whom you are afraid; do not be afraid
of him,' is the oracle of the LORD; 'for
I am with you to save you, and to deliver you out of his hand. I will have 12
pity upon you, and will inspire him
with pity for you, so that he may allow
you to stay in your own land. But if 13
you say, "We will not stay in this
land," refusing to obey the voice of the
LORD your God, and saying, "No, we 14
will go to the land of Egypt, where we
shall see no war, and shall hear no
sound of trumpet, and shall have no
hunger for bread; and there will we
stay," then hear the word of the LORD, 15
O remnant of Judah!' Thus says the
LORD of hosts, the God of Israel: 'If
you are determined to go to Egypt, and
if you go to settle there, the sword 16
which you fear shall overtake you there
in the land of Egypt, and the famine
which you dread shall cling to your
heels there in Egypt; and there shall
you die. All the men who are deter- 17
mined to go to Egypt, to settle there,
shall die by sword, famine, and pestilence, not one of them surviving or escaping from the doom that I am bringing upon them.' For thus says the 18
LORD of hosts, the God of Israel: 'As
my anger and my fury have been
poured out upon the inhabitants of Jerusalem, so shall my fury be poured out
upon you when you enter Egypt; and
you shall be an execration and a horror,
a curse and a scorn; and you shall see
this place no more.' So this is the word 19
that the LORD has spoken to you, O
remnant of Judah: 'Do not go to
Egypt!' And be certain of this—for I 20
warn you this day that you will wrong
your own selves if, after sending me to
the LORD your God, saying, 'Pray to
the LORD our God for us; and whatever
the LORD our God may say, tell us, and
we will do it,' and if, after I have told it 21
to you this day, you do not listen to the
voice of the LORD your God in regard
to anything that he has sent me to tell
you—now be certain of this, that you 22
shall die by sword, famine, and pesti-

lence, in the place where you desire to
go to settle there."
43 When Jeremiah had finished speaking to all the people all the words of the
LORD their God, even all these words
which the LORD their God had sent
2 him to speak to them, Azariah, the
son of Hoshaiah, Johanan, the son of
Kareah, and all the proud and defiant
men said to Jeremiah,
"You are telling a lie. The LORD our
God did not send you to say, 'You
shall not go to Egypt to settle there';
3 but Baruch, the son of Neriah, has been
egging you on against us, to deliver us
into the hand of the Chaldeans, that
they may put us to death, or carry us
captive to Babylon."
4 So Johanan, the son of Kareah, and
all the commanders of the forces, and
all the people, did not listen to the
voice of the LORD by staying in the
5 land of Judah; but Johanan, the son of
Kareah, and all the commanders of the
forces, took all the remnant of Judah
that had returned from all the nations
to which they had been driven, to settle
6 in the land of Judah—the men, women,
and children, the king's daughters,
every person whom Nebuzaradan, the
commander of the guard, had left with
Gedaliah, the son of Ahikam, the son of
Shaphan, including Jeremiah the proph-
7 et and Baruch, the son of Neriah—and,
not listening to the voice of the LORD,
they came to the land of Egypt, and
arrived at Daphne.
8 Then the word of the LORD came to
Jeremiah at Daphne, saying,
9 "Take some large stones, and bury
them among the mortar under the
pavement in the gateway of Pharaoh's
palace at Daphne, in the sight of
10 certain Jews. Then say to them,
'Thus says the LORD of hosts, the God
of Israel: Behold, I am sending for
Nebuchadrezzar, king of Babylon, my
servant, who shall set his throne above
these stones which you have buried,
and shall spread his royal pavilion over
11 them. And he shall come and smite the
land of Egypt, devoting to death those
who are doomed to death, to exile those
who are doomed to exile, and to the
sword those who are doomed to the
12 sword. And he shall kindle a fire in the
houses of the gods of Egypt, and shall
burn them and carry them away captive; and he shall purge the land of
Egypt as a shepherd purges his mantle
of vermin, and shall go from it unmolested. Also he shall break in pieces the
obelisks at Heliopolis, in the land of
Egypt, and shall burn the houses of the
gods of Egypt.'"

JEREMIAH'S LAST APPEAL TO HIS PEOPLE,
44:1–30

The word that came to Jeremiah concerning all the Jews living in the land of Egypt—at Migdol, Daphne, Memphis, and in the land of Pathros—as follows:
"Thus says the LORD of hosts, the God of Israel: 'You have seen all the trouble that I have brought upon Jerusalem and all the other cities of Judah, so that they are now an uninhabited waste, because of the wickedness by which they vexed me, by going off to sacrifice and render worship to other gods, whom neither they nor you nor your fathers knew. Though I sent all my servants the prophets to you early and late, saying, "Pray, do not do this abominable thing which I hate," they neither listened nor inclined their ears, to turn from their wickedness by not offering sacrifices to other gods, so that my fury and my anger were poured out and blazed in the cities of Judah and the streets of Jerusalem, and they became a waste and a desolation, as they are this day.' And now thus says the LORD, the God of hosts, the God of Israel: 'Why are you doing yourselves a great wrong, cutting off man and woman, child and suckling, from the midst of Judah, without leaving a remnant behind you, by vexing me with the work of your hands, in offering sacrifices to other gods in the land of Egypt, where you have gone to settle, and so making yourselves a curse and a scorn among all the nations of the earth? Have you forgotten the crimes of your fathers, the crimes of the kings of Judah, the crimes of your princes, the crimes of yourselves, and the crimes of your wives, which they committed in the land of Judah and in the streets of Jerusalem? To this day they have neither humbled themselves, nor been afraid, nor followed my law and my

statutes which I set before you and
1 your fathers.' Therefore thus says the
LORD of hosts, the God of Israel: 'I am
determined to bring ruin upon you, and
2 to cut off the whole of Judah. So I will
take the remnant of Judah that were
determined to go to the land of Egypt
to settle there, and they shall all be
consumed in the land of Egypt; they
shall fall by the sword and be consumed by famine; from the least to the
greatest shall they die by sword and
famine, and they shall be an execration
3 and a horror, a curse and a scorn. I will
punish those who live in the land of
Egypt, as I punished Jerusalem, by
4 sword, famine, and pestilence, so that
none of the remnant of Judah that have
gone to the land of Egypt to settle there
shall escape or survive to return to the
land of Judah where they long to return
to live there; for none shall return but a
handful of fugitives.' "
5 Then all the men who knew that
their wives were offering sacrifices to
other gods, and all the women who
stood by—even all the people who
lived in the land of Egypt and in Pathros, a great multitude—answered Jeremiah, saying,
6 "As regards the word that you have
spoken to us in the name of the LORD,
7 we will not listen to you, but will assuredly carry out every word that has
gone from our own mouths, by offering
sacrifices to the queen of the heavens,
and by pouring libations to her, as we
did, both we and our fathers, our kings
and our princes, in the cities of Judah
and in the streets of Jerusalem. For
then we had plenty to eat, and were
8 well, and met with no trouble; but
since we gave up offering sacrifices to
the queen of the heavens, and pouring
libations to her, we have been destitute
of all things, and have been consumed
by sword and famine."
9 The women also said,
"And when we were offering sacrifices to the queen of the heavens, and
pouring libations to her, was it without
the approval of our husbands that we
made for her cakes stamped with her
image, and poured libations to her?"
0 Then Jeremiah spoke to all the people, both men and women—all the people that had given him this answer—
saying,

"As regards the sacrifices that you 21
offered in the cities of Judah and in the
streets of Jerusalem, you and your
fathers, your kings and your princes, as
well as your common people, did they
not rankle in the mind and thought of
the LORD, so that the LORD could no 22
longer bear your wicked and abominable deeds, and so your land became an
uninhabited waste, horror, and curse, as
it is this day? It is just because you 23
offered these sacrifices, and sinned
against the LORD, by not listening to
the voice of the LORD, nor following his
law, his statutes, and his decrees, that
this present trouble has befallen you."
Jeremiah further said to all the peo- 24
ple, and to all the women,
"Hear the word of the LORD, all you
people of Judah who are in the land of
Egypt! Thus says the LORD of hosts, 25
the God of Israel: 'You and your wives
have pledged your word, and have fulfilled it in actual deed, saying, "We will
assuredly carry out the vows we have
taken, to offer sacrifices to the queen of
the heavens, and to pour libations to
her." By all means keep your word,
and carry out your vows! Hear, how- 26
ever, the word of the LORD, all you
people of Judah who live in the land of
Egypt! I have sworn by my great
name,' says the LORD, 'that never
more shall my name be invoked by any
man of Judah in all the land of Egypt,
saying, "As the Lord GOD lives!" Be- 27
hold, I am watching over them for evil
and not for good; and all the men of
Judah who are in the land of Egypt
shall be consumed by sword and famine, until an end is made of them. And 28
those who escape from the sword—few
in number—shall return from the land
of Egypt to the land of Judah. Then all
the remnant of Judah, who came to the
land of Egypt to settle there, shall
know whose word shall stand—mine, or
theirs! And this is the sign for you,' is 29
the oracle of the LORD, 'that I will punish you in this place, so that you may
know that my words shall stand against
you for evil. Thus says the LORD: Be- 30
hold, I am giving Pharaoh Hophra,
king of Egypt, into the hand of his enemies, into the hand of those who seek
his life, as I gave Zedekiah, king of Judah, into the hand of Nebuchadrezzar,
king of Babylon, his enemy, who sought
his life.' "

THE ORACLE TO BARUCH, 45:1–5

45 The word that Jeremiah the prophet
spoke to Baruch, the son of Neriah,
when he had written these words on a
scroll at the dictation of Jeremiah, in
the fourth year of Jehoiakim, the son of
Josiah, king of Judah.
2 Thus says the LORD, the God of Israel, concerning you, O Baruch:
3 "You have said, 'Woe to me!
For the LORD has added sorrow to my
pain;
I am weary with my groaning,
I can find no rest.'
4 Say to him, 'Thus says the LORD:
Behold, I am tearing down what I
have built,
And I am rooting up what I have
planted.
[That is the whole earth.]
5 Do you seek great things for yourself?
Seek them not; for behold, I am bring-
ing trouble
Upon all flesh,' is the oracle of the
LORD.
'But your life will I give to you as a
prize of war
In every place where you go.' "

ORACLES ON EGYPT, 46:1–28

46 The word of the LORD that came to
Jeremiah the prophet concerning the
nations.
2 On Egypt: concerning the army of
Pharaoh Necho, king of Egypt, en-
camped at Carchemish by the River
Euphrates, which was defeated by
Nebuchadrezzar, king of Babylon, in
the fourth year of Jehoiakim, the son of
Josiah, king of Judah.
3 "Set buckler and shield in array,
And advance to battle;
4 Harness the steeds, and mount, you
horsemen,
Stand forth with your helmets;
Unsheathe the spears, don the breast-
plates!
5 Why do I see them dismayed, turned
back,
And their warriors beaten?
Why have they fled apace, without
looking back,
With terror on every side?"
Is the oracle of the LORD.
6 "The swift cannot flee,
Nor the strong man escape;
To the north, by the River Euphrates,
They stumble and fall.
"Who is this rising up like the Nile,
Like rivers whose waters toss?
Egypt rises up like the Nile,
Like rivers whose waters toss.
He says, 'I will rise up, I will cover the
earth,
I will destroy its inhabitants.'
Up, you steeds; rage, you chariots;
March forth, you warriors—
Cush and Put, that handle the shield,
And the Lydians, that bend the bow.
"But that day shall be for the Lord, the 1
GOD of hosts,
A day of vengeance, to avenge himself
on his enemies;
And the sword shall devour till it is
sated,
And shall drink its fill of their blood.
For the Lord, the GOD of hosts, shall
hold a sacrifice
In the north land, by the River Eu-
phrates.
Go up to Gilead, and take balm, 1
O virgin daughter of Egypt!
In vain do you multiply medicines;
For you there is no healing.
The nations have heard your cry, 1
The earth is full of your wailing;
For warrior stumbles on warrior,
Both of them fall together."

The word that the LORD spoke to 1
Jeremiah the prophet, in regard to the
coming of Nebuchadrezzar, king of
Babylon, to smite the land of Egypt:
"Tell it in Migdol, 1
And publish it in Memphis;
Say, 'Stand to arms, and make ready,
For the sword devours round about
you.'
Why has Apis fled, and your bull god 1
not held his ground?
Because the LORD has thrust him
down.
The foreigners among you stumble 1
and fall,
They say to one another,
'Up, and let us return to our people,
To the land of our birth, before the
deadly sword.'
"Call Pharaoh, king of Egypt, 'Bluster- 1
er,
Who has let the hour go by!'

18 As I live," is the oracle of the King,
Whose name is the LORD of hosts,
"One shall come like Tabor among the mountains,
Or like Carmel by the sea.
19 Get ready your baggage for exile,
O daughter that dwells in Egypt!
For Memphis shall become a desolation,
A waste without an inhabitant.

20 "A graceful heifer is Egypt;
But a wasp from the north has attacked her.
21 Even the hired soldiers within her are like calves of the stall—
Even they have turned and fled together,
Without making a stand;
For their day of doom has come upon them,
Their time of reckoning.
22 She hisses like a serpent,
As her enemies advance in force;
With axes they come against her,
Like fellers of trees.
23 They shall cut down her forest," is the oracle of the LORD,
"Although it is impenetrable;
For they are more in number than locusts,
They cannot be counted.

24 "Put to shame is the daughter of Egypt,
Handed over to the people of the north.
25 Says the LORD of hosts, the God of Israel:
'Behold, Amon of Thebes will I punish,
And Pharaoh, and those who trust in him.
26 I will hand them over to those who seek their lives,
To Nebuchadrezzar, king of Babylon, and his servants;
Though afterward she shall be inhabited,
As in the days of old,'" is the oracle of the LORD.

27 "So fear not, O Jacob my servant,
Nor be dismayed, O Israel!
For behold, I will save you from afar,
And your race from the land of their exile.
Then shall Jacob have once more quiet and ease,
With none to make him afraid.

Fear not, O Jacob my servant," is the oracle of the LORD, 28
"For I am with you;
And I will make a full end of all the nations
Among whom I drove you away,
But of you will I not make a full end;
But I will correct you in just measure,
Not leaving you wholly unpunished."

ON THE PHILISTINES, 47:1–7

The word of the LORD that came to 47
Jeremiah the prophet concerning the
Philistines, before Pharaoh smote Gaza.
Thus says the LORD: 2
"Behold, waters are rising from the north,
And shall become a raging torrent;
They shall overflow the land and all that fills it,
The cities and those who dwell in them.
Men shall cry out,
All the inhabitants of the land shall wail.
At the noise of the gallop of the hoofs of his steeds, 3
At the rush of his chariots, the rumble of his wheels,
The fathers look not back to their children,
So slack are their hands;
Because of the day that is coming 4
To despoil all the Philistines,
To cut off from Tyre and Sidon
Every helper that remains;
For the LORD is about to despoil the Philistines,
The remnant of the coast-land of Caphtor.
Baldness has come upon Gaza, 5
Ruined is Askelon;
How long must you gash yourselves,
O remnant of the Anakim?
Ah, sword of the LORD! when will you be at peace? 6
Get back to your scabbard; rest and be still!
But how can it be at peace, 7
Since the LORD has given it a charge,
Has made it an appointment
Against Askelon and the seashore?"

ON MOAB, 48:1–46 48

Thus says the LORD of hosts, the
God of Israel:

"Woe to Nebo! because it is despoiled;
Kirjathaim is shamed, is taken;
The bulwark is shamed, is discomfited.
2 No more is the fame of Moab,
In Heshbon they plotted her ruin:
'Come, let us cut her off from her place
among nations!'
You also, O Madmen, shall be silenced;
The sword shall pursue you.

3 "Hark! a cry from Horonaim,
'Havoc and dire destruction!'
4 Moab is ruined;
As far as Zoar they send out the cry.
5 For up the ascent of Luhith weeping
they go;
And down the pass to Horonaim the
cry of ruin they raise:
6 'Flee, save yourselves,
Though you be like a scrub in the
desert!'

7 "Because you trusted in your works
and in your treasures,
You also shall be taken;
And Chemosh shall go into exile,
Along with his priests and his princes.
8 The despoiler shall come upon every
city,
And no city shall escape;
The valley shall perish, and the plateau shall be destroyed,
As the LORD has said.

9 "Give wings to Moab,
For fain would she fly away,
While her cities become a desolation,
With none to dwell in them.
10 Cursed be he who does the work of the
LORD with slackness,
And cursed be he who holds back his
sword from bloodshed!

11 "Moab has been at ease from his
youth,
He has settled on his lees;
He has not been emptied from vessel
to vessel,
Nor has he gone into exile;
So his taste remains in him,
And his scent is unchanged.
12 Therefore behold, days are coming,"
is the oracle of the LORD,
"When I will send tilters to him, who
shall tilt him,
And empty his vessels, and dash his
jars in pieces.

Then shall Moab be put to shame 13
through Chemosh,
As the house of Israel was put to shame
Through Bethel, in whom they trusted.

"How can you say, 'We are heroes, 14
And mighty men of war,'
When the despoiler of Moab has come 15
up against him,
And the flower of his youth has gone
down to the slaughter?"
Is the oracle of the King, whose name
is the LORD of hosts.
"Near at hand is the doom of Moab, 16
And his fate speeds on apace.
Bemoan him, all you who are round 17
about him,
All you who know his name;
Say, 'How is the strong staff broken,
The beautiful rod!'

"Come down from your throne of 18
glory, and sit in the mire,
O daughter that dwells in Dibon;
For the despoiler of Moab has come
up against you,
has destroyed your fortresses.
Stand by the wayside, and watch, 19
you who dwell in Aroer;
Ask him that flees, and her that escapes,
'What has happened?'
Moab is shamed, is discomfited; 20
wail and cry!
Tell the news in Arnon,
that Moab is despoiled.

So judgment has come on the table- 2
land: on Holon, Jahzah, and Me-
phaath; on Dibon, Nebo, and Beth- 2
diblathaim; on Kirjathaim, Beth- 2
gamul, and Beth-meon; on Kerioth and 2
Bozrah, and on all the cities of the land
of Moab, far and near.
"Hewn off is the horn of Moab, 2
And broken is his arm," is the oracle
of the LORD.
"Make him drunk, for against the 2
LORD has he magnified himself;
Moab has clapped his hands,
So he too shall be held in derision.
Was not Israel a derision to you? 2
Was he found in the company of
thieves,
That as often as you speak of him,
you shake your head?
Leave the cities, and occupy the 2
crags,
You who dwell in Moab;

Be like the doves that nest
In the sides of the cavern's mouth!

29 "We have heard of the pride of Moab—
How very proud he is—
Of his haughtiness and pride and arrogance—
The lordliness of his mind.
30 I know his insolence," is the oracle of the LORD,
"How baseless are his boastings, accomplishing nothing.
31 Therefore I wail for Moab,
I cry for all Moab,
I moan for the men of Kir-heres.

32 "With Jazer I weep for you,
O vine of Sibmah!
Your branches passed over the sea,
reached as far as Jazer;
Now on your fruits and your vintage
the despoiler has fallen,
33 And joy and gladness vanish
from the garden land of Moab,
The wine have I stopped from the winepresses,
no grape-treader treads them,
The shout is the shout of battle,
not the shout of joy.

34 "Heshbon and Elealeh cry out,
As far as Jahaz they send forth their voice,
From Zoar to Horonaim and the third Eglath;
For even the waters of Nimrim are a desolation.
35 And I will bring to an end in Moab,"
is the oracle of the LORD,
"Him that goes up to the high place,
and offers sacrifices to his god.
36 Therefore my heart for Moab moans like a flute,
My heart for the men of Kir-heres moans like a flute,
Because the gain that they acquired has perished.

37 "Every head is bald, and every beard is clipped;
On every hand are gashes, and on every loin is sackcloth.
38 On all the housetops of Moab, and on all its squares,
There is universal mourning;
For I have broken Moab like a worthless vessel,"
Is the oracle of the LORD.

"How is Moab discomfited! how he wails! 39
How he turns his back in shame!
So shall Moab become a derision and a horror
To all who are round about him."

For thus says the LORD: 40
"One like a vulture shall swoop down,
And spread his wings against Moab.
The cities shall be taken, and the strongholds be seized; 41
And the heart of the warriors of Moab on that day
Shall be like the heart of a woman in travail.
And Moab shall be destroyed from being a people, 42
Because he has magnified himself against the LORD.
Terror, and pit, and snare 43
Are upon you, O inhabitants of Moab."
Is the oracle of the LORD.
"And he who flees from the terror shall fall into the pit, 44
And he who escapes from the pit shall be caught in the snare;
For these things will I bring upon Moab
In their year of reckoning," is the oracle of the LORD.

"In the shadow of Heshbon there stand 45
Fugitives without strength;
For a fire has gone out of Heshbon,
A flame from the city of Sihon;
It devours the brow of Moab,
The crown of the sons of tumult.
Woe to you, O Moab! 46
The people of Chemosh is perished.
Your sons have been taken captive,
And your daughters have been led into exile;
Though I will restore the fortune of Moab 47
In the end of the days," is the oracle of the LORD.

Thus far is the judgment on Moab.

ON THE AMMONITES, 49:1–6 49

Thus says the LORD:
"Has Israel no sons?
Has he no heir?
Why, then, has Milcom taken over the inheritance of Gad?

And why do his people dwell in its
cities?
2 Therefore behold, days are coming,"
is the oracle of the LORD,
"When I will cause the shout of battle
to be heard
Against Rabbah of the children of
Ammon;
And she shall become a desolate
mound,
And her daughter cities shall be
burned;
Then shall Israel take over the inheritance
of those who took over
his inheritance,"
Says the LORD.

3 "Wail, O Heshbon!
for the city has been despoiled.
Cry, O daughters of Rabbah!
gird on sackcloth, lament,
and lacerate yourselves with
gashes;
For Milcom shall go into exile,
along with his priests and
princes.

4 "Why do you boast of your valleys,
O daughter that lives at ease,
Trusting in your treasures, and saying,
'Who shall come against me?'
5 Behold, I am bringing terror upon
you,"
is the oracle of the Lord, the
GOD of hosts,
"from all who are round about
you;
And you shall be driven each one in
headlong flight,
with none to rally the fugitives;
6 Though afterward I will restore
the fortune of the children of
Ammon,"
is the oracle of the LORD.

7 ON EDOM, 49:7–22

Thus says the LORD of hosts:
"Is wisdom no more in Teman?
Is the counsel of the sages gone?
Is their wisdom scattered to the
winds?
8 Flee, hide yourselves in inaccessible
haunts,
You who live in Dedan!
For the doom of Esau am I bringing
upon him,
His time of reckoning.

If grape-gatherers came to you, 9
They would leave no gleanings behind;
If robbers came by night,
They would destroy to their heart's
content.
So I strip Esau bare, 10
His retreats I uncover,
So that he cannot conceal himself.
He is despoiled by the arm of his brothers
and neighbors,
With none to help him.
Leave your orphans, I will keep them 11
alive;
And your widows—let them put their
trust in me!"

For thus says the LORD: 12
"If those who did not deserve to
drink the cup must yet drink it, shall
you go unpunished? You shall not go
unpunished, but drink you shall. For 13
by myself have I sworn," is the oracle
of the LORD, "that Bozrah shall become
a horror and a scorn, a waste and
a curse, and all her daughter cities shall
become perpetual wastes."

A message have I heard from the 14
LORD,
And an envoy is sent through the nations:
"Gather, and go against her,
And advance to the battle!
For behold, I make you small among 15
the nations,
And despised among men.
The terror you inspired has deceived 16
you,
Your pride of heart—
You who dwell in the clefts of the
crags,
Who hold the heights of the hills!
Though you build your nest as high as
the eagle,
Even thence will I bring you down,"
is the oracle of the LORD.
"Then shall Edom become a horror; 17
Everyone who passes by her shall hiss
with horror
At all her wounds.
As when Sodom and Gomorrah were 18
overthrown,
Along with their neighbors," says the
LORD,
"No man shall dwell there,
No mortal man shall stay in her.
Like a lion coming up from the jungle 19
of Jordan

Against the peaceful sheepfold,
So will I chase them in a moment from their place,
And whom I choose I will set upon it.
For who is like me? and who will challenge me?
What shepherd is there who will face me?
0 Therefore hear the purpose that the LORD has formed against Edom,
And the plans that he has laid against the inhabitants of Teman!
Even the youngest of the flock shall be dragged away,
And their fold shall be shocked at their fate.
1 At the sound of their fall the earth shall quake,
And the noise of their crying shall be heard as far as the Red Sea.
2 Behold, one like a vulture shall mount up and swoop down,
And spread his wings against Bozrah;
And the heart of the warriors of Edom on that day
Shall be like the heart of a woman in travail."

ON DAMASCUS, 49:23–27

3 Hamath and Arpad are put to shame,
For bad news have they heard;
They melt in fear, they are in turmoil like the sea,
Which cannot rest.
4 Damascus is unstrung, she turns to flee,
Trembling seizes her;
Anguish and pangs lay hold on her,
Like a woman in travail.
5 How forlorn is the famous city,
The joyous town!
So her young men shall fall in her squares,
And all her warriors shall be silenced on that day,"
Is the oracle of the LORD of hosts.
"And I will kindle a fire in the wall of Damascus,
Which shall devour the palaces of Benhadad."

ON KEDAR AND THE KINGDOM OF HAZOR, WHICH NEBUCHADREZZAR KING OF BABYLON SMOTE, 49:28–33

Thus says the LORD:
"Arise, go up against Kedar,
And despoil the Kedemites.
29 Their tents and their flocks shall be taken,
Their curtains and all their goods;
Their camels also shall be borne away,
While men shout at them, 'Terror all around!'
30 Scatter in flight to inaccessible haunts,
You inhabitants of Hazor," is the oracle of the LORD;
"For Nebuchadrezzar, king of Babylon, has formed a purpose against you,
And has laid a plan against you.

31 "Arise, go up against a nation at ease,
That dwells in security," is the oracle of the LORD,
"A nation that has neither gates nor bars,
That lives alone.
32 Their camels shall fall a prey,
And their throngs of cattle shall become a spoil;
I will scatter to all the winds those who have the corners of their hair clipped,
And from every side of them will I bring doom upon them,"
Is the oracle of the LORD.
33 "And Hazor shall become a haunt of jackals,
A desolation forever;
No man shall dwell there,
No mortal man shall stay in her."

ON ELAM, 49:34–39

34 The word of the LORD that came to Jeremiah the prophet concerning Elam, in the beginning of the reign of Zedekiah, king of Judah.
35 Thus says the LORD of hosts:
"Behold, I am breaking the bow of Elam,
The mainstay of their might;
36 And I will bring upon Elam four winds
From the four quarters of the heavens,
And will scatter them to all these winds,
So that there shall be no nation
To which the outcasts of Elam shall not come.
37 And I will discomfit Elam before their enemies,
Before those who seek their lives;
And I will bring trouble upon them,
Even my fierce anger," is the oracle of the LORD.

38 "And I will send the sword after them,
Until I have consumed them;
And I will set my throne in Elam,
And thence will I destroy both king
and princes,"
Is the oracle of the LORD;
39 "Though in the end of the days I will
restore the fortune of Elam,"
Is the oracle of the LORD.

ON BABYLON, 50:1—51:58

50 The word that the LORD spoke concerning Babylon and the land of the
Chaldeans by Jeremiah the prophet:
2 "Tell among the nations, publish the
news,
Raise a signal, publish without concealment;
Say, 'Babylon is taken,
Bel is put to shame, Merodach is discomfited,
Her images are put to shame, her idols
are discomfited.'
3 For against her has come up a people
from the north,
That shall make her land a desolation,
So that none shall dwell in it—
Both man and beast shall have fled
and gone.

4 "In those days, and at that time,"
Is the oracle of the LORD,
"The children of Israel shall come,
Along with the children of Judah,
Weeping as they go,
To seek the LORD their God.
5 They shall ask the way to Zion,
With their faces turned to it,
And they shall come and join them-
selves to the LORD
In an everlasting covenant that shall
not be forgotten.

6 "Lost sheep have my people been,
Their shepherds have misled them,
They have turned them astray on the
mountains;
From mountain to hill have they gone,
Forgetting their fold.
7 All who found them devoured them—
While their enemies said, 'We are
guiltless'—
Because they sinned against the
LORD, the fold of righteousness,
Against the LORD, the hope of their
fathers.

8 "Flee from the midst of Babylon,
Go out of the land of the Chaldeans,
Like he-goats before the flock.
For behold, I am rousing and raising 9
against Babylon
A muster of mighty nations from the
north land,
Who shall set themselves in array
against her,
Till she is taken from her place.
Their arrows shall be like those of a
skilful warrior,
Who returns not with empty hands;
And Chaldea shall be a spoil— 10
All who despoil her shall have their
fill,"
Is the oracle of the LORD.

"Though you rejoice and exult, 11
you who plunder my heritage,
Though you gambol like calves at grass,
and neigh like stallions,
Your mother shall be bitterly 12
ashamed,
she who bore you shall be
abashed;
Behold, the last of the nations shall
become a wilderness,
a dry land, and a desert;
Through the wrath of the LORD she 1
shall not be inhabited,
but shall become an utter desolation;
Everyone who passes by Babylon shall
hiss in horror
at all her wounds.

"Set yourselves in array against Babylon round about,
all you who bend the bow;
Shoot at her, spare not your arrows,
for she has sinned against the
LORD.
Shout against her round about,
'She gives way,
Her buttresses have fallen,
her walls are torn down!'
Because it is the vengeance of the
LORD,
therefore take vengeance upon
her,
do to her as she has done.
Cut off from Babylon both him that 1
sows
and him that wields the sickle
in time of harvest;
While from the presence of the deadly
sword
they turn everyone to his people,
and flee everyone to his land.

7 "A scattered flock is Israel,
Chased away by lions.
First the king of Assyria devoured him,
And now at the last Nebuchadrezzar, king of Babylon, has gnawed his bones."
8 Therefore thus says the LORD of hosts, the God of Israel:
"Behold, I am punishing the king of Babylon and his land,
As I punished the king of Assyria;
9 And I will bring back Israel to his fold,
And he shall pasture on Carmel and Bashan,
And shall browse to his heart's content on Mount Ephraim and Gilead.
In those days, and at that time,"
Is the oracle of the LORD,
"Men shall search for the guilt of Israel, but shall find none,
And for the sins of Judah, but shall discover none;
For I will pardon those whom I leave as a remnant.

"Go up against the land of Merathaim,
And against the inhabitants of Pekod;
Slay and destroy them utterly,"
Is the oracle of the LORD;
"Do just as I have commanded you.
Hark! the sound of battle in the land,
The sound of dire destruction!
How the hammer of all the earth
Is hewn and broken in pieces!
How Babylon is become
A horror among the nations!
I set a snare for you, O Babylon,
And you have been taken unawares;
You have been found, you have been caught,
Because you have challenged the LORD.
The LORD has opened his armory,
And has brought forth his weapons of wrath;
For the Lord, the GOD of hosts,
Has a work to do in the land of the Chaldeans.

"Come upon her from every quarter, throw open her granaries,
Pile her up like heaps of grain, destroy her utterly,
Let nothing of her be left!
Slay all her bullocks, let them go down to the slaughter;
Woe to them! for their day has come,
Their time of reckoning.
Hark! they flee, they escape from the land of Babylon, 28
To tell in Zion of the vengeance which the LORD our God has taken,
The vengeance he has taken for his temple.

"Summon against Babylon archers, 29
All who bend the bow;
Encamp against her round about,
Let none of her escape!
Repay her for her deeds,
Do to her just as she has done;
For she has been insolent to the LORD,
The Holy One of Israel.
Therefore her young men shall fall in the squares, 30
And all her warriors shall be silenced on that day,"
Is the oracle of the LORD.

"Lo! I am against you, O Insolence!" 31
Is the oracle of the Lord, the GOD of hosts;
"For your day has come, your time of reckoning.
Insolence shall stumble and fall, 32
With none to lift him up;
And I will kindle a fire in his cities,
Which shall devour all who are round about him."

Thus says the LORD of hosts: 33
"The children of Israel are crushed,
Along with the children of Judah;
And all who took them captive hold them fast,
They refuse to let them go.
But their vindicator is strong, 34
He whose name is the LORD of hosts;
He will surely defend their cause,
That he may bring rest to the earth,
But unrest to the inhabitants of Babylon.

"A sword upon the Chaldeans," is the oracle of the LORD, 35
"Upon the inhabitants of Babylon, upon her princes and her sages;
A sword upon her soothsayers, that they may become fools, 36
A sword upon her soldiers, that they may be discomfited:
A sword upon her horses, and upon her chariots, 37

And upon all the foreign people in the midst of her, that they may be turned into women;
A sword upon her treasures, that they may be plundered,
38 A sword upon her waters, that they may be dried up;
For she is a land of images,
And with idols they make themselves mad.

39 "Therefore desert demons and goblins shall dwell there,
And ostriches shall inhabit her;
She shall be peopled no more forever,
Nor occupied throughout the ages.
40 As when God overthrew Sodom and Gomorrah,
Along with their neighbors," is the oracle of the LORD,
"No man shall dwell there,
No mortal man shall stay in her.

41 "Behold, a people is coming from the north,
A great nation and mighty kings are stirring from the ends of earth;
42 They lay hold on bow and javelin,
They are cruel and pitiless;
The sound of them is like that of the sea when it roars,
And they ride upon horses—
Arrayed as a man for the battle
Against you, O daughter of Zion!
43 The king of Babylon has heard the report of them,
And his hands fall helpless;
Anguish lays hold on him,
Pain like that of a woman in travail.

44 "Behold, like a lion coming up from the jungles of Jordan,
Against the peaceful sheepfold,
So will I chase them in a moment from their place,
And whom I choose I will set over it.
For who is like me? and who will challenge me?
What shepherd is there who will face me?
45 Therefore hear the purpose that the LORD has formed against Babylon,
And the plans that he has laid against the land of the Chaldeans!
Even the youngest of the flock shall be dragged away,
And their fold shall be shocked at their fate.

At the sound of the capture of Baby- 4
lon the earth shall quake,
And her cry shall be heard through the nations."

Thus says the LORD: 5
"Behold, I am rousing against Babylon,
And against the people of Leb-kamai,
the spirit of a destroyer;
And I will send to Babylon winnowers who shall winnow her,
and shall clean her land bare;
Then woe betide her on every side
on her day of trouble!
Let the archer bend his bow,
and stand up in his coat of mail;
Spare not her young men,
but utterly destroy all her host;
Let them lie down slain in the land of the Chaldeans,
thrust through in her streets!
For their land is full of guilt
against the Holy One of Israel;
But Israel and Judah have not been left widows
by their God, the LORD of hosts.

"Flee from the midst of Babylon,
save everyone his life;
Perish not through her guilt,
for this is the LORD'S time of vengeance—
due recompense is he repaying to her.
Babylon was a cup of gold in the hand of the LORD,
that made all the earth drunk;
Of her wine the nations drank,
so that the nations went mad.
Suddenly Babylon falls and is broken;
wail over her!
Take balm for her wound;
perhaps she may be healed!
We would fain have healed Babylon,
but she is not healed.
Leave her, and let us go
each to his land;
For her judgment touches the heavens,
and reaches the skies.
The LORD has vindicated our rights;
Come, and let us recount in Zion
What the LORD our God has done.

"Polish the arrows, prepare the shields;
For the LORD has roused the spirit of the king of the Medes,

He has formed a design against Babylon, to destroy it;
For such is the vengeance the LORD will take,
The vengeance he will take for his temple.
Against the walls of Babylon raise a signal,
Strengthen the blockades, set blockaders,
Prepare the ambushes;
For the LORD has both designed and done
What he spoke concerning the inhabitants of Babylon.
O you who dwell by many waters,
And are rich in treasures,
Your end has come, your ill-gotten gains are gone;
For the LORD of hosts has sworn by himself:
'I will fill you with men, swarming like locusts,
Who shall raise against you the shout of victory.'

"It is he who made the earth by his power,
Who established the world by his wisdom,
And stretched out the heavens by his skill.
When he thunders, there is a storm of waters in the heavens,
And he causes vapors to rise from the ends of the earth;
He makes lightnings for the rain,
And brings out the wind from his storehouses.
Every man is stupid and senseless,
Every goldsmith is put to shame through his images;
For his idols are frauds, which have no breath in them,
They are a mockery, a delusion,
Which will break down in their time of trial.
Not such is the Portion of Jacob,
But he is the framer of all things,
And Israel is the tribe of his inheritance—
The LORD of hosts is his name.

'You are my maul, my weapon of war,
With you I shatter nations,
With you I destroy kingdoms;
With you I shatter horse and rider,
With you I shatter chariot and driver;
With you I shatter man and woman,
With you I shatter old man and boy,
With you I shatter young man and maiden;
With you I shatter shepherd and flock, 23
With you I shatter plowman and team,
With you I shatter governor and deputy.
And I will requite Babylon and all the 24
inhabitants of Chaldea, before your
eyes, for all the wrong that they have
done in Zion," is the oracle of the
LORD.

"Behold, I am against you, O destroying mountain, 25
That destroyed all the earth," is the oracle of the LORD;
"I will stretch out my hand against you,
And will roll you down from the crags,
And will make you a burning mountain.
No cornerstone shall be taken from you, 26
No foundation stone;
But you shall be a perpetual desolation,"
Is the oracle of the LORD.
"Raise a signal on the earth, 27
Blow a trumpet among the nations;
Prepare the nations for war against her,
Summon against her the kingdoms of Ararat,
Minni and Ashkenaz;
Appoint a field marshal against her,
Bring up horses like bristling locusts.
Prepare the nations for war against her, 28
The king of the Medes, his governors, and all his deputies,
With all the land which he rules.
The earth quakes and writhes in pain, 29
For the purposes of the LORD against Babylon stand,
To make the land of Babylon a desolation,
Without an inhabitant.

"The warriors of Babylon have ceased to fight, 30
They stay in their strongholds;
Their strength is exhausted, they are turned into women;
Her dwellings are ablaze, her bars are broken.
Runners run to meet runner, 31

Messenger to meet messenger,
To tell the king of Babylon
That his city is taken from end to end,
32 That the fords have been seized,
That the outworks are burned,
And that the men of war are discomfited.
33 For thus says the LORD of hosts, the God of Israel:
'The daughter of Babylon is like a threshing-floor
after it has been trodden,
And in a little while the time of harvest
shall come for her.'

34 "Nebuchadrezzar, king of Babylon, has devoured me,
he has consumed me;
He has set me down as an empty vessel,
he has swallowed me like a monster;
He has filled his maw with my dainties,
he has rinsed me out.
35 'The violence done to my flesh be upon Babylon!'
let the inhabitants of Zion say;
'My blood be upon the inhabitants of Chaldea!'
let Jerusalem say.
36 Therefore thus says the LORD:
'Behold, I am defending your cause,
and will take vengeance for you;
I will dry up her sea,
and will drain her fountain.
37 And Babylon shall become a heap of ruins,
a haunt of jackals,
A horror and a hissing,
without an inhabitant.'

38 "Though they roar together like young lions,
And growl like lions' whelps,
39 With poison will I prepare them a feast,
And I will make them drunk till they swoon away,
And sleep a perpetual sleep,
And never awake," is the oracle of the LORD.
40 "I will bring them down to the slaughter like lambs,
Like rams and he-goats.

41 "How is Sheshach taken,
The praise of the whole earth seized!
How has Babylon become
A horror among the nations!
42 The sea has come up on Babylon,
With the surge of its waves is she covered;
43 Her cities have become a waste,
A dry land, and a desert,
A land where no man dwells,
Through which no mortal passes.
44 Bel also will I punish in Babylon,
And out of his mouth will I bring forth
what he has swallowed;
Then no more shall the nations stream to him,
For the wall of Babylon is fallen.

45 "Go out of the midst of her, O my people!
Save everyone his life
From the fierce anger of the LORD.
46 Be not downhearted or fearful
At the rumors heard in the land;
When one rumor comes in one year,
And another in the next;
When violence reigns in the land,
And ruler stands against ruler.
47 Therefore behold, days are coming,
When I will punish the images of Babylon,
And all her land shall be put to shame,
And all her slain shall lie in the midst of her.
48 Then the heavens and the earth, and all that is in them,
Shall ring out their joy over Babylon;
For out of the north shall the despoilers come to her,"
Is the oracle of the LORD;
49 "And Babylon also must fall for the slain of Israel,
As for Babylon have fallen the slain of all the earth.

50 "You that escape from the sword,
Go, stand not still;
Remember the LORD from afar,
And think of Jerusalem:
51 'We are put to shame, for reproach have we heard;
Confusion has covered our faces,
For strangers have entered the sanctuary
Of the house of the LORD.'
52 Therefore behold, days are coming,"
Is the oracle of the LORD,
"When I will punish her images,
And all through her land the slain shall lie.
53 Though Babylon scale the heavens,

And fortify her stronghold on high,
Yet from me shall despoilers come to
her,"
Is the oracle of the LORD.

"Hark! a cry from Babylon,
The sound of dire destruction from
the land of the Chaldeans!
For the LORD is despoiling Babylon,
And stills her mighty voice.
They roar like many waters,
The din of their voice is raised;
For the despoiler has come upon Baby-
lon,
And her warriors are taken, their
bows are broken in pieces;
For the LORD is a God of recom-
pense,
He will surely requite.
Her princes and her sages will I make
drunk,
Her governors, her deputies, and her
soldiers;
And they shall sleep a perpetual sleep,
And shall never awake," is the oracle
of the King,
Whose name is the LORD of hosts.

Thus says the LORD of hosts:
'The broad wall of Babylon shall be
razed to the ground,
And her lofty gates shall be burned;
So the peoples shall toil for nought,
And the nations shall weary them-
selves for the fire."

THE MESSAGE TO SERAIAH, 51:59–64

The word with which Jeremiah the
rophet charged Seraiah, the son of
Neriah, the son of Mahseiah, when he
vent with Zedekiah, king of Judah, to
Babylon in the fourth year of his reign,
Seraiah being quarter-master.
When Jeremiah had written on a spe-
ial scroll a record of all the trouble
hat was to come upon Babylon—even
ll these words that he had written con-
erning Babylon—Jeremiah said to
Seraiah,
"When you reach Babylon, see that
ou read all these words, and say,
Thou, O LORD, hast declared concern-
ng this place, that thou wilt cut it off,
o that neither man nor beast may
well in it, but that it will be a perpetu-
l desolation.' And when you have fin-
hed reading this scroll, tie a stone to
it, and throw it into the middle of the
Euphrates, and say, 'Thus shall Baby- 64
lon sink, to rise no more, because of the
trouble that I am bringing upon her.'"
Thus far are the words of Jeremiah.

THE FALL OF JERUSALEM, 52:1–30

Zedekiah was twenty-one years old 52
when he became king, and he reigned
in Jerusalem for eleven years. His
mother's name was Hamutal, the
daughter of Jeremiah of Libnah. He 2
did what was evil in the sight of the
LORD, just as Jehoiakim had done; and 3
the anger of the LORD blazed against
Jerusalem and Judah until he had cast
them out of his presence.
Then Zedekiah rebelled against the
king of Babylon. Accordingly, in the 4
ninth year of his reign, in the tenth
month, on the tenth day of the month,
Nebuchadrezzar, king of Babylon, with
all his army came against Jerusalem,
encamped against it, and built a siege-
wall against it round about; and the 5
city remained under siege till the
eleventh year of King Zedekiah. In the 6
fourth month, on the ninth day of the
month, when the famine in the city was
so severe that there was no food for the
common people, the city was breached, 7
and the king and all the soldiers fled
and left the city by night by way of the
gate between the two walls, which was
by the king's garden, while the Chaldeans were beleaguering the city, and
went in the direction of the Arabah.
But the Chaldean army pursued the 8
king, and overtook Zedekiah in the
steppes of Jericho, his whole army having scattered from him. Then they 9
took the king and brought him up to
the king of Babylon at Riblah in the
land of Hamath, and he pronounced
judgment against him. Also the king of 10
Babylon slew the sons of Zedekiah before his eyes. He likewise slew all the
princes of Judah at Riblah. Then the 11
king of Babylon put out the eyes of
Zedekiah, bound him in fetters, carried
him to Babylon, and put him in prison,
where he remained till the day of his
death.
In the fifth month, on the tenth day 12
of the month—this was the nineteenth
year of King Nebuchadrezzar, king
of Babylon—Nebuzaradan, the com-

mander of the guard, a minister in attendance on the king of Babylon, came
13 to Jerusalem, and burned the house of
the LORD and the king's house; and
all the houses of Jerusalem, even every
14 great house, he burned. The whole
Chaldean army that was with the commander of the guard broke down all the
the walls of Jerusalem round about.
15 Then Nebuzaradan, the commander of
the guard, carried captive the rest of
the people that were left in the city, and
the deserters who had deserted to the
king of Babylon, together with the arti-
16 sans that were left. But some of the
poorest of the land Nebuzaradan, the
commander of the guard, left as vine-
17 dressers and plowmen. Moreover, the
bronze pillars, the stands, and the
bronze sea that were in the house of the
LORD, the Chaldeans broke up and
carried all the bronze from them to
18 Babylon. Also the pots, the shovels,
the snuffers, the basins, the pans, and
all the vessels of bronze with which the
service was conducted, they took away.
19 Likewise the cups, the firepans, the basins, the pots, the lampstands, the pans,
and the bowls, what was of gold, the
commander of the guard took away as
gold, and what was of silver, as silver—
20 besides the two columns, the sea, the
twelve bronze bulls that were under the
sea, and the stands, which King Solomon
had made for the house of the LORD,
the bronze of all these vessels being be-
21 yond weight. The columns were each
eighteen cubits in height, twelve cubits
in circumference, and four fingers in di-
22 ameter, the center being hollow. A
bronze capital surmounted each, and
the height of each capital was five cubits, with network and pomegranates
round about the capital, all of bronze;
and the second column had the same
23 network and pomegranates. On the
network round about there were
ninety-six pomegranates on the outside, one hundred in all.
24 Then the commander of the guard
took Seraiah, the chief priest, and
Zephaniah, the second priest, with the three keepers of the threshold; he took also from the city a eunuch who had charge of the soldiers, and seven of the personal companions of the king who were found in the city, the scribe of the commander of the army who mustered the people of the land, and sixty of the people of the land who were found in the city. Having taken them, Nebuzaradan, the commander of the guard, brought them to the king of Babylon at Riblah. Then the king of Babylon struck them down and put them to death at Riblah in the land of Hamath. Thus was Judah carried captive from its land.

This is the sum-total of the people whom Nebuchadrezzar carried captive: in the seventh year, three thousand and twenty-three Jews; in the eighteenth year of Nebuchadrezzar, eight hundred and thirty-two persons from Jerusalem; in the twenty-third year of Nebuchadrezzar, seven hundred and forty-five Jews, carried captive by Nebuzaradan, the commander of the guard; in all, four thousand six hundred persons.

THE DELIVERANCE OF JEHOIACHIN,
52:31–34

In the thirty-seventh year of the exile of Jehoiachin, king of Judah, in the twelfth month, on the twenty-fifth day of the month, Evil-Merodach, king of Babylon, in the first year of his reign, summoned Jehoiachin and brought him from prison. He spoke kindly to him, and set his throne above that of the other kings who were with him in Babylon. So he changed his prison dress, and dined in his presence regularly all the days of his life; and for his provision, a regular allowance was given him from the king of Babylon, a portion for each day, all the days of his life, till the day of his death.

THE BOOK OF LAMENTATIONS

THE DESOLATION AND MISERY OF CONQUERED JERUSALEM, 1:1–22

א

How lonely the city sits,
once so crowded with people!
She has become like a widow,
once so great among the nations;
She that was a princess among the cities
has become a vassal.

ב

2 She weeps bitterly by night,
with her tears upon her cheeks;
She has no comforter
out of all her lovers;
All her friends have betrayed her;
they have become her enemies.

ג

3 Judah has been carried into exile,
to suffer tribulation and hard servitude;
She has to live among the nations,
she can find no home;
Her pursuers have all overtaken her
in the midst of her troubles.

ד

4 The roads to Zion mourn,
without pilgrims to the feasts;
All her gates are desolate;
her priests moan;
Her maidens have been dragged off,
while she is left disconsolate.

ה

5 Her oppressors have become supreme;
her enemies have triumphed;
For the LORD has afflicted her
for the multitude of her sins;
Her children have gone forth,
as captives before the oppressor.

ו

6 Gone too from the daughter of Zion
is all her splendor;
Her princes have become like stags,
that can find no pasture,
But flee exhausted
before the hunter.

ז

Jerusalem recalls, 7
in the time of her affliction and misery,
All her glory,
which she had in days of old,
Now that her people have fallen at the hands of the oppressor,
with none to help her;
The oppressors gaze at her,
they laugh at her downfall.

ח

Jerusalem sinned greatly, 8
and so has become filthy;
All her late admirers despise her,
because they see her condition;
Whereas she herself moans,
and turns away.

ט

Her uncleanness clung to her skirts; 9
she took no thought of her future;
So she has fallen most horribly,
with none to comfort her.
"See, O LORD, my affliction,
how the enemy triumphs."

י

The oppressor has laid his hand 10
upon all her treasures;
For she has seen the nations
enter her sanctuary,
Those whom thou didst command
not to enter thine assembly place.

כ

Her people are all moaning, 11
in their search for bread;
They give of their treasures for food,
to keep themselves alive.
"See, O LORD, and behold,
how abased I am."

ל

12 "Ho, all you who pass along the road,
look and see,
If there is any pain like my pain,
which has been dealt to me,
With which the LORD has afflicted me
in the day of his fierce anger.

מ

13 "From above he has hurled fire;
into my bones he has made it descend;
He has spread a net for my feet;
he has tripped me up;
He has made me desolate,
miserable all the time.

נ

14 "Watch has been kept over my transgressions;
by his hand they are bound together;
They have come upon my neck;
he has shattered my strength;
The Lord has delivered me
into the power of those that I cannot withstand.

ס

15 "The Lord in my midst
has set at nought all my warriors;
He has called an assembly against me,
to crush my young men;
The Lord has trodden as in a winepress
the virgin daughter of Judah.

ע

16 "For all these things I weep;
my eyes shed tears;
For a comforter is far from me,
someone to console me;
My children are distraught,
for the enemy has prevailed."

פ

17 Zion spreads out her hands,
with none to comfort her;
The LORD has given command regarding Jacob,
that his neighbors are to be his oppressors;
Jerusalem has become
abhorrent to them.

צ

18 "The LORD is right,
for I have rebelled against his word;
Yet hear, all you peoples,
and look at my pain:
How my youths and maidens
have gone into captivity.

ק

"I called on my lovers,
but they repudiated me;
My priests and elders
perished in the city,
When they sought food
to keep themselves alive.

ר

"See, O LORD, how I am in distress,
how my spirits are troubled;
How my heart is upset within me,
because I have been so rebellious.
On the street the sword has caused bereavement,
even as death in the house.

ש

"They hear how I moan,
with none to comfort me;
All my enemies have heard of my plight;
they rejoice that thou hast done it;
That thou hast brought the day which thou didst announce;
but they are like me.

ת

"Let all their wickedness come before thee,
and do unto them,
As thou hast done unto me
for all my transgressions;
For my sorrow is great,
and my heart is miserable."

GOD'S JUDGMENT ON JERUSALEM, 2:1–22

א

How the Lord in his anger has brought disgrace
upon the daughter of Zion!
He has cast down from heaven to earth
the glory of Israel;
And has given no heed to his footstool
in the day of his anger.

ב

The Lord has consumed without mercy
all the habitations of Jacob;

He has thrown down in his wrath
the strongholds of the daughter of Judah;
He has struck to the ground,
he has degraded her king and her princes.

ג

He has cut off in fierce anger
all of Israel's strength;
He has drawn back their right hand
from the enemy;
And has burned throughout Jacob,
like a flaming fire which consumes the neighborhood.

ד

He has bent his bow like an enemy,
with his right hand set like an adversary;
And he has slain all the notables
in the tents of the daughter of Zion;
He has vented his fury like fire.

ה

The Lord has become like an enemy;
he has consumed Israel;
He has consumed all his palaces;
he has demolished his fortresses;
And he has heaped on the daughter of Judah
mourning and moaning.

ו

He has torn down his pavilion like that of a garden;
he has demolished his meeting place;
The LORD has abolished in Zion
festival and sabbath;
And he has repudiated in the heat of his anger
king and priest.

ז

The Lord has spurned his altar;
he has rejected his sanctuary;
He has surrendered into the power of the enemy
the walls of her palaces;
There was shouting in the temple of the LORD,
as on a day of festival.

ח

8 The LORD had determined
to destroy the wall of the daughter of Zion;
He stretched out a line;
he did not restrain his hand from consuming;
So rampart and wall mourn;
they lament together.

ט

Her gates are sunk to the ground; 9
he has destroyed and broken her bars;
Her king and princes are among the nations;
government has ceased;
Neither do her prophets receive
any visions from the LORD.

י

Silent on the ground sit 10
the elders of the daughter of Zion;
They have thrown dust on their heads;
they have put on sackcloth;
The maidens of Jerusalem
hang their heads to the ground.

כ

My eyes are spent with tears; 11
my spirits are troubled.
My grief is poured out on the ground,
over the downfall of the daughter of my people;
Because of the swooning of babes and sucklings
in the city squares.

ל

To their mothers they keep saying, 12
"Where is there grain and wine?"
While they swoon like one wounded
in the city squares;
While their lives ebb away
on their mother's bosoms.

מ

To what can I liken you; 13
what can I compare with you,
O daughter of Jerusalem?
What can I liken to you,
that I may comfort you, O virgin daughter of Zion?
For your ruin is as vast as the sea;
who can heal you?

נ

Your prophets have divined for you 14
stuff and nonsense;

And instead of denouncing your iniquity,
to restore your fortune,
They have divined for you oracles,
vain and misleading.

ס

15 All who pass along the road
clap their hands at you;
They hiss and wag their heads
at the daughter of Jerusalem:
"Is this the city
that was called perfect in beauty,
the joy of all the earth?"

פ

16 All your enemies
revile you;
They hiss and gnash their teeth;
they say, "We have consumed her;
This is indeed the day that we looked for;
we have found it; we see it."

ע

17 The LORD has done what he planned;
he has carried out his word,
As he decreed long ago;
he has devastated without mercy,
And he has let the enemy rejoice over you;
he has exalted the strength of your oppressors.

צ

18 Cry unto the Lord;
wail, O daughter of Zion;
Weep tears like a torrent,
day and night;
Give yourself no respite;
let your tears cease not.

ק

19 Rise, cry out in the night,
at the beginning of the watches;
Pour out your heart like water
in the presence of the Lord;
Lift up your hands to him
for the life of your children,
Who faint for hunger
at the head of every street.

ר

20 See, O LORD, and behold;
to whom else hast thou done thus:
Whether it be women devouring their own offspring,
their petted children;
Or priest and prophet
slain in the sanctuary of the LORD?

ש

Prostrate on the ground in the streets lie
both the young and the old;
My youths and maidens
have fallen by the sword;
Thou hast slain them in the day of thine anger;
thou hast slaughtered them without mercy.

ת

Thou didst invite them as though it were a feast day,
to my guest chamber from the neighborhood;
But in the day of the LORD's anger
there was none
that escaped or survived;
Those whom I fondled and reared,
my enemy exterminated.

JERUSALEM'S LAMENT AND PRAYER, 3:1–66

א

"I am a person who has seen affliction
by the rod of his wrath;
He has led me and made me walk
in darkness and not light.
Against me alone he has repeatedly turned
his hand all the time.

ב

"He has wasted my flesh and my skin;
he has broken my bones.
He has fenced me in,
and encompassed me with bitterness and hardship.
He has made me live in the dark,
like those long dead.

ג

"He has walled me in so that I cannot get out;
he has loaded me with chains.
Also, whenever I have cried, and called for help,
he has ignored my prayer.

9 He has walled up my ways with hewn stones;
he has made my paths crooked.

ד

10 "He has been a lurking bear to me,
a lion in ambush.
11 He has waylaid me, and mangled me;
he has made me desolate.
12 He has bent his bow,
and set me up as a target for his arrows.

ה

13 "He has driven into my vitals
the shafts of his quiver;
14 I have become the butt of all peoples,
their taunt-song all the time.
15 He has filled me with bitterness;
he has sated me with anguish.

ו

16 "He has broken my teeth with gravel stones;
he has made me cower in ashes;
17 And he has robbed me of happiness;
I have forgotten what prosperity is;
18 So I said, 'Gone is my strength,
and my hope in the LORD.'

ז

19 "The thought of my affliction and bitterness
is anguish and misery.
20 I am indeed thinking of it,
and I am crushed in spirit.
21 But this I call to mind,
and so I have hope:

ח

22 "That the gracious deeds of the LORD never cease,
his compassion never fails;
23 They are fresh every morning;
great is his faithfulness.
24 'The LORD is my heritage,' I said;
'therefore will I hope in him.'

ט

25 "The LORD is good to him who craves him,
to the person who seeks him.
26 It is good that one should wait quietly
for help from the LORD;
27 It is good for a man,
that he should bear the yoke in his youth.

י

"Let him sit alone in silence, 28
since it has been laid upon him.
Let him lay his mouth in the dust; 29
perhaps there may be hope.
Let him offer his cheek to the smiter; 30
let him be sated with disgrace;

כ

"For the Lord forever 31
will not spurn him.
Though he cause grief, 32
he will have compassion in accordance with his abundant kindness;
For he does not willingly afflict, 33
nor grieve mankind.

ל

"To crush under foot 34
all prisoners of the earth,
To deprive a man of his rights, 35
in the face of the Almighty,
To subvert man in his cause, 36
the Lord does not countenance.

מ

"Who is there that can order anything into being, 37
when the Lord has not decreed it?
Is it not by decree of the Most High, 38
that good and evil come?
Of what can living man complain, 39
each one because of his sins?

נ

"Let us search, and examine our ways, 40
and return to the LORD;
Let us lift up our hearts with our hands 41
to God in the heavens:
'We have transgressed and rebelled; 42
but thou hast not pardoned.

ס

" 'Thou hast enveloped thyself in anger, and pursued us; 43
thou hast slain without mercy;
Thou hast enveloped thyself in a cloud, 44
so that no prayer can pass through;
Thou hast made us scum and refuse 45
among the peoples.

פ

46 " 'All our enemies
have reviled us;
47 Desolation and destruction
have become terror and calamity to us.'
48 My eyes shed torrents of water,
over the downfall of the daughter of my people.

ע

49 "My eyes will flow unceasingly,
without any respite,
50 Until the LORD from the heavens
looks down, and sees.
51 My eyes give me pain,
because of all the maidens of my city.

צ

52 "They who had no reason to be my enemies
hunted me like a bird;
53 They threw me into a pit to die,
and cast stones on me.
54 Water flowed over my head;
I said, 'I am lost.'

ק

55 "I called on thy name, O LORD,
out of the depths of the pit.
56 Thou didst hear my cry,
'Close not thine ear to my supplication, to my cry';
57 Thou didst draw near when I called on thee;
thou didst say, 'Fear not.'

ר

58 "O LORD, thou didst plead my cause,
thou didst redeem my life.
59 O LORD, thou hast seen the wrong done me;
give me justice.
60 Thou hast seen all their vengeance,
all their plots against me.

ש

61 "Thou hast heard their insults, O LORD,
all their plots against me,
62 The utterances of my assailants,
and their muttering against me all day long.
63 Whether they are idle or busy,
see how I am their taunt-song.

ת

64 "Repay them, O LORD,
as their deeds deserve;
Give them blindness of heart; 65
let thy curse be on them;
Pursue them in anger, 66
and destroy them from under thy heavens, O LORD!"

THE CONTRAST BETWEEN JERUSALEM'S PAST AND PRESENT, 4:1–22

א

How dim the gold has become, 4
how changed the finest gold!
The sacred stones are being thrown out
at the head of every street.

ב

The precious children of Zion, 2
comparable to fine gold,
Count, alas, as earthen pots,
the work of a potter's hands!

ג

Even the jackals present their breasts, 3
they suckle their young;
But the daughter of my people has become cruel,
like the ostriches of the desert.

ד

The tongue of the suckling child cleaves 4
to his palate for thirst;
The children are begging bread,
with none to offer it to them.

ה

They that did feast on dainties 5
are perishing in the streets;
They that were reared amid purple
have to take to dunghills.

ו

So the iniquity of the daughter of my people must be greater 6
than the sin of Sodom,
That was overthrown as in a moment,
without any hands being laid on her.

ז

Her princes were purer than snow; 7
they were whiter than milk;
They were ruddier in body than corals;
a sapphire was their form.

ח

8 But their appearance has become blacker than coal;
they are not recognized on the streets;
Their skin has shriveled on their bones;
it has become as dry as a stick.

ט

9 Better off are those stricken by the sword
than those stricken by hunger;
For they can eat, even though wounded,
of the fruits of the field.

י

10 Tender-hearted women with their own hands
have cooked their children;
They became their food,
at the downfall of the daughter of my people.

כ

11 The LORD has spent his fury;
he has vented his fierce anger;
And he has kindled a fire in Zion,
that has consumed her foundations.

ל

12 No kings of the earth believed,
nor any of the inhabitants of the world,
That the oppressor and enemy could enter
the gates of Jerusalem.

מ

13 It was for the sins of her prophets,
the iniquities of her priests,
Who shed in her midst
the blood of the righteous.

נ

14 They stagger blindly through the streets;
they are defiled with blood;
That which they should not,
they touch with their clothes.

ס

15 "Away! Unclean!" they cry of themselves;
"Away! Away! Touch not!"
For they are fugitives, wanderers among the nations;
they no longer have a home.

פ

Those whose heritage was the LORD, 16
he no longer notices;
He does not honor the priests;
he does not respect the prophets.

ע

Our eyes still strain 17
after help for us that is vain;
In our watching we have watched
for a nation that will not save.

צ

Men dog our footsteps, 18
so that we cannot walk in our public squares;
Our end is near; our days are finished;
for our end has come.

ק

Our pursuers were swifter 19
than the eagles of the heavens;
They chased us on the mountains;
they lay in wait for us in the wilderness.

ר

Our breath of life, the LORD'S anointed, 20
was captured in their pits,
Of whom we had said,
"Under his protection we shall live among the nations."

ש

Rejoice and be glad, O daughter of Edom, 21
living in the land of Uz!
To you also shall the cup pass;
you shall become drunk, and be stripped naked.

ת

Your iniquity is absolved, O daughter of Zion; 22
he will no longer keep you in captivity.
He will punish your iniquity, O daughter of Edom;
he will lay bare your sins.

THE NATION'S PRAYER FOR COMPASSION, 5:1–22

"Mark, O LORD, what has befallen us; 5
Look, and see our disgrace.
Our heritage has been turned over to aliens, 2

Our homes to foreigners.
3 We have become orphans, without a father;
Our mothers are like widows.
4 Our drinking-water we have to buy;
Our wood comes only by purchase.
5 With a yoke on our necks we are persecuted;
We toil without rest.
6 We have stretched out our hands to Egypt,
To Assyria in order to get food enough.
7 Our fathers sinned, and are no more;
While we have to bear their guilt.
8 Slaves rule over us,
With none to free us from their power;
9 At the peril of our lives we win our bread,
Because of the sword in the wilderness.
10 Our skin glows like a fire pot,
With the fever heat of famine.
11 Women are ravished in Zion,
Girls in the cities of Judah.
12 Princes are hanged by their hands;
Elders are not respected.
13 Young men have to carry the mill,
And youths stumble under loads of wood.
The elders have left the gate, 14
The young men their music.
Our joy of heart has vanished; 15
Our dance has been turned into mourning.
The crown has fallen from our head; 16
Woe to us! for we have sinned.
For this our heart has become faint; 17
For these things our eyes have grown dim;
Because of Mount Zion which lies desolate, 18
With jackals prowling upon it.
But thou, O LORD, art enthroned forever; 19
Thy throne endures throughout the ages.
Why wilt thou forget us forever, 20
Forsake us for life?
Restore us, O LORD, to thyself, so that we may return; 21
Renew our days as of old;
For if thou wert to reject us completely, 22
Thou wouldst be going too far in thine anger against us."

THE BOOK OF EZEKIEL

THE CALL OF THE PROPHET, 1:1—3:15

1 IN THE thirtieth year, in the fourth
month, on the fifth day of the
month, as I was among the exiles
by the river Chebar, the heavens
2 opened, and I saw visions of God. [It
was on the fifth day of the month, in the
fifth year of the exile of King Jehoia-
3 chin, that the word of the LORD came
to Ezekiel, the son of Buzi, the priest, in
the land of the Chaldeans, by the river
Chebar, and the hand of the LORD was
upon him there.]
4 I looked, and lo! there came from the
north a violent gale, accompanied by a
great cloud, with fire flashing through
it, and a radiance round about it, while
out of the midst of it gleamed something with a luster like that of shining
5 metal. Out of the midst of it emerged
the semblance of four living creatures,
and this was their appearance: their
6 form was like that of a man. Each,
however, had four faces and four wings.
7 Their legs, too, were straight, while the
soles of their feet resembled the sole of a
calf's foot; and they sparkled like bur-
8 nished bronze. Under their wings, on
their four sides, were the hands of a
9 man. The wings of the four of them
were linked one to another; and their
faces turned not as they went, but each
10 went straight forward. As for the appearance of their faces, the four of them
had the face of a man in front, the face
of a lion on the right, the face of an ox
on the left, and the face of an eagle be-
11 hind. The wings of the four of them
were outstretched, one pair being
linked to those of the next creature, and
12 the other pair covering the body. Each
went straight forward; wherever the
spirit wished to go, they went, not turn-
13 ing as they went. And in the midst of the
creatures was an appearance like burning coals of fire, resembling torches, moving to and fro among the creatures; and
14 the fire had a radiance, while out of the
fire went lightning, running to and fro.

As I looked at the creatures, lo! there 15
was a wheel on the ground beside each
of the four of them. The color of the 16
wheels was like topaz; and the four of
them had the same shape, their construction being as if one wheel were
within another. When they went, they 17
went on their four sides, not turning as
they went. The wheels had felloes; and 18
as I looked at them, lo! the felloes of
the four of them were full of eyes round
about. When the creatures went, the 19
wheels went beside them; and when the
creatures rose from the earth, the
wheels also rose. Wherever the spirit 20
wished to go, they went; for the spirit
of the creatures was in the wheels.
When these went, they went; and when 21
these stood still, they stood still; and
when these rose from the earth, the
wheels rose along with them; for the
spirit of the creatures was in the
wheels.

Over the heads of the creatures was 22
the semblance of a firmament, glittering
like transparent ice, stretched above
their heads. Under the firmament one 23
pair of their wings touched those of the
next creature, while the other pair covered the body. And when they went, 24
the sound of their wings sounded to me
like the sound of mighty waters, or like
the voice of the Almighty—it was a
sound of tumult like that of an armed
camp—and when they stood still, they 25
let down their wings. Above the firma- 26
ment that was over their heads was the
semblance of a throne, colored like sapphire; and upon the semblance of the
throne was a semblance like that of a
man sitting above it. From the appear- 27
ance of his loins upward I saw something with a luster like that of shining metal; and from the appearance of
his loins downward I saw something
resembling fire, with a radiance round
about it, resembling the bow that ap- 28
pears in the clouds on a rainy day.

Such was the semblance of the glory
of the LORD, as it appeared to me. And
when I saw it, I fell upon my face. Then

I heard the voice of someone speaking.
2 And he said to me,
"O mortal man, stand upon your
feet, that I may speak with you!"
2 As he spoke to me, a spirit entered
3 me, and set me upon my feet. And I
heard him that spoke to me saying,
"O mortal man, I am sending you to
the children of Israel, that nation of
rebels who have rebelled against me—
they and their fathers have sinned
4 against me to this very day, the children also are hard-faced and stubborn—
I am sending you to them, and you shall
say to them, 'Thus says the Lord GOD!'
5 And whether they listen or decline to
listen—for they are a rebellious house
—they shall know that there is a
6 prophet among them. And you, O
mortal man, fear them not, nor be dismayed at them; even when thistles and
thorns are round about you, and you
dwell among scorpions, fear not their
words, nor be dismayed at their looks—
7 for they are a rebellious house. You
shall speak what I say to them, whether
they listen or decline to listen—for they
8 are a rebellious house. And you, O
mortal man, hear what I say to you; be
not rebellious like that rebellious house.
Open your mouth, and eat what I give
you!"
9 Then I looked, and lo! there was a
hand stretched out to me; and lo! there
10 was in it a scroll. And he unrolled it before me; and it was covered with writing on both sides—words of lamentation, mourning, and woe were written
3 on it. Then he said to me,
"O mortal man, eat what you find
here; eat this scroll, then go and speak
to the house of Israel!"
2 So I opened my mouth, and he gave
3 me the scroll to eat, saying to me,
"O mortal man, eat and digest this
scroll which I am giving you!"
And when I ate the scroll, it was as
4 sweet as honey in my mouth. Then he
said to me,
"O mortal man, go to the house of Israel, and speak what I say to them.
5 For it is not to a people of unintelligible
speech or difficult language that you are
6 sent, but to the house of Israel—not to
many peoples of unintelligible speech or
difficult language, whose words you
cannot understand. If I sent you to
them, they would certainly listen to
7 you. But the house of Israel will not
listen to you; for they will not listen to
me; for the whole house of Israel is
hard-faced and stubborn. But I will 8
make you as hard-faced and stubborn
as they; I will make you like adamant, 9
harder than flint. Fear them not, nor
be dismayed before them—for they are
a rebellious house."
He said further to me, 10
"O mortal man, all the words that I
shall speak to you receive and attend
to. Then go to the exiles, your fellow- 11
countrymen, and speak to them, and
say, 'Thus says the Lord GOD!' whether they hear or decline to hear."
Then a spirit lifted me up (and as the 12
glory of the LORD rose from its place,
I heard behind me the sound of a great 13
rustling; it was the sound of the wings
of the creatures as they touched one another, and the sound of the wheels beside them, that caused the great rustling), a spirit lifted me up and carried 14
me away, and I went with my spirit
in a fierce glow—the hand of the LORD
pressing hard upon me—and came to 15
the exiles who lived at Tel-abib, by the
River Chebar, and stayed with them
there for seven days in a state of stupor.

THE PROPHET AS WATCHMAN, 3:16–21

At the end of seven days the word of 16
the LORD came to me, saying,
"O mortal man, I appoint you a 17
watchman to the house of Israel; and
whenever you hear a word from my
mouth, you shall warn them from me.
If I say to the wicked, 'You shall surely 18
die,' and you fail to warn him—if you
say nothing to warn the wicked man
from his wicked way, in order to save
his life—he being wicked shall die for
his iniquity, but his blood will I require
at your hand. If, however, you warn 19
the wicked man, and he turn not from
his wicked conduct and his wicked way,
he shall die for his iniquity, but you will
have saved yourself. Or if a righteous 20
man turn from his righteousness, and
do what is wrong, and I make that the
occasion for bringing about his downfall, he shall die; because you did not
warn him, he shall die for his sin, and
the righteous deeds which he has done
shall not be remembered, but his blood
will I require at your hand. If, how- 21

ever, you warn the righteous man not
to sin, and he do not sin, he shall live,
because he took warning; and you will
have saved yourself."

THE SEALING OF THE PROPHET'S LIPS, 3:22–27

22 Then the hand of the LORD came
there upon me, and he said to me,
"Arise, go out to the plain, and there
will I speak with you."
23 So I arose, and went out to the plain;
and lo! there stood the glory of the
LORD, like the glory which I had seen
by the River Chebar; and I fell upon
24 my face. But a spirit entered me, and
set me upon my feet; and he spoke with
me, and said to me,
"Go, shut yourself up in your house.
25 And see! O mortal man, I will place
cords upon you, and will bind you with
them, so that you cannot go out in pub-
26 lic. And I will make your tongue cleave
to your palate, so that you shall be
dumb, and unable to reprove them—for
27 they are a rebellious house. But when
I speak with you, I will open your
mouth, and you shall say to them,
'Thus says the Lord GOD!'—let him
hear who will, and let him decline to
hear who will—for they are a rebellious
house."

SYMBOLS OF THE SIEGE AND FALL OF JERUSALEM, 4:1—5:17

4 "And you, O mortal man, take a
brick, and place it before you, and trace
2 upon it a city—Jerusalem—and lay en-
trenchments against it, build a siege-
wall against it, throw up a mound
against it, pitch camps against it, and
set battering-rams against it round
3 about. Then take an iron griddle, and
place it as an iron wall between you and
the city; and set your face toward it,
bringing it under a state of siege, and
press on the siege against it. This is a
sign for the house of Israel.
4 "Then lie upon your left side, and
bear upon it the guilt of the house of
Israel—as many days as you lie upon it
5 you shall bear their guilt. For the years
of their punishment I assign you an
equal number of days—three hundred
and ninety days—during all of which
you shall bear the guilt of the house of
Israel. And when you have completed 6
these, you shall next lie upon your right
side, and shall bear the guilt of the
house of Judah—forty days I assign
you, each day representing a year. And 7
you shall set your face and your bared
arm toward the siege of Jerusalem, and
shall prophesy against it. And behold, 8
I will place cords upon you, and you
shall not turn from side to side until
you have completed the days of your
siege.
"Then take wheat, barley, beans, 9
lentils, millet, and spelt; put them into
a pot, and make them into bread; and
during all the days that you are lying
upon your side—three hundred and
ninety days—you shall eat it. And the 10
food that you eat shall be weighed out,
twenty shekels a day, to be eaten at a
fixed hour each day. Water also shall 11
you drink by measure, a sixth of a hin
a day, to be drunk at a fixed hour each
day. And your food shall be in the form 12
of barley-cakes, which you shall bake on
human excrement in the presence of the
people."
Then the LORD said, 13
"So shall the children of Israel eat
their bread unclean among the nations
to which I will drive them."
Whereupon I said, 14
"Ah Lord GOD! I have never yet
defiled myself with uncleanness; from
my boyhood up till now I have not eat-
en what died a natural death or was
torn by wild beasts, nor has unclean
flesh entered my mouth."
So he said to me, 15
"See! I allow you cow's dung instead
of human excrement, on which to prepare your food."
He said further to me, 16
"O mortal man, behold, I am breaking the staff of bread in Jerusalem; and
they shall eat bread by weight, in anxious fear, and shall drink water by
measure, in dire dismay, till from want 17
of bread and water they fall together
into a stupor, and pine away under
their punishment.
"And you, O mortal man, take a 5
sharp sword, and use it as a barber's
razor, passing it over your head and
beard; then take scales for weighing,
and divide the hair. One-third you shall 2
burn in the fire that will rage within the
city when the days of the siege are over;

one-third you shall smite with the
sword round about the city; and one-
3 third you shall scatter to the wind. But
take a few of these, and wrap them in
4 the skirts of your robe; and take some
of these again, and cast them into the
midst of the fire, and burn them in the
fire; and say to the whole house of
Israel,
5 "Thus says the LORD: 'This is a
symbol of the fate of Jerusalem. I set
her in the midst of the nations, with
6 lands round about her. Yet she has
wickedly rebelled against my ordinances and statutes more than the nations and lands that are round about
her; for her people have scorned my
ordinances and have not followed my
7 statutes.' Therefore thus says the Lord
GOD: 'Because you have been more rebellious than the nations that are round
about you, by not following my statutes, nor obeying my ordinances, nor
even conforming to the practices of the
nations that are round about you'—
8 therefore thus says the Lord GOD: 'Behold, I am against you—even I—and I
will execute judgments in the midst of
9 you in the sight of the nations. Because
of all your abominable deeds I will do
among you what I have never done before, and the like of which I will never
10 do again. On this account fathers shall
eat their sons and sons shall eat their
fathers in the midst of you; and I will
execute judgments among you, and will
scatter to all the winds all who remain
11 of you. As I live,' is the oracle of the
Lord GOD, 'because you have defiled
my sanctuary with all your detestable
and abominable deeds, I will cut you
12 down without mercy or pity. One-
third of you shall die of pestilence or
perish with famine in the midst of you;
one-third shall fall by the sword round
about you; and one-third will I scatter
to all the winds, and after them will I
13 draw the sword. So shall my anger
spend itself, and my fury will I satisfy
upon you, and be appeased; and you
shall know that I the LORD have spoken—through my zeal when I spend my
14 fury upon you. I will make you also a
waste among the nations that are round
about you, and a reproach in the sight
15 of every passer-by. You shall be a reproach and a contempt, a warning and
a horror, to the nations that are round
about you, when I execute judgments
among you with furious chastisements
—I the LORD have spoken. And I will 16
send my deadly arrows against you—
the arrows intended for destruction
which I will send to destroy you—and I
will bring repeated attacks of famine
upon you, and break your staff of
bread. I will send against you famine 17
and wild beasts to rob you of your children; and pestilence and bloodshed
shall pass through you; and I will bring
the sword upon you—I the LORD have
spoken.'"

A PROPHECY AGAINST THE MOUNTAINS OF ISRAEL, 6:1–14

The word of the LORD came to me, 6
saying,
"O mortal man, set your face toward 2
the mountains of Israel, and prophesy
against them, and say, 'O mountains of 3
Israel, hear the word of the Lord GOD!
Thus says the Lord GOD to the mountains and the hills, the ravines, and the
valleys: Behold, I am bringing a sword
upon you, and I will destroy your high
places; your altars shall be demolished, 4
and your incense altars broken; and I
will bring down your slain before your
idols; I will lay the dead bodies of the 5
children of Israel before their idols, and
I will scatter your bones round about
your altars. In all your settlements the 6
cities shall be laid waste and the high
places demolished, so that your altars
may be laid waste and made desolate,
your idols broken and annihilated, your
incense altars cut down, and your
works blotted out. Your slain also shall 7
fall in the midst of you; and you shall
know that I am the LORD, when I leave 8
but a few of you who escape from the
sword among the nations, scattered
through the lands. Then those of you 9
who escape shall remember me among
the nations to which they are carried
captive, when I have broken their heart
which has apostatized from me, and
blinded their eyes which have run wantonly after their idols; and they shall
loathe themselves for the evil deeds
they have done—even for all their
abominations—and they shall know 10
that it was not without purpose that I
the LORD threatened to do all this evil
to them.'"

Thus says the Lord GOD: "Clench your fists, stamp your feet, and say, 'Alas!' over all the vile abominations of the house of Israel, for which they shall fall by sword, famine, and pestilence. He who is far off shall die of pestilence; he who is near at hand shall fall by the sword; and he who remains under siege shall perish with famine—so will I spend my fury upon them. And they shall know that I am the LORD, when their slain lie among their idols round about their altars, on every high hill, and on every mountain top, under every spreading tree, and under every leafy terebinth—the sanctuaries where they offered soothing odors to all their idols. And I will stretch out my hand against them, and will make the land a desolation and a waste, through the whole extent of their settlements, from the desert to Riblah; so shall they know that I am the LORD."

THE DAY OF DOOM, 7:1–27

Again the word of the LORD came to me, saying,

"And you, O mortal man, say, 'Thus says the Lord GOD to the land of Israel: An end has come—the end has come—upon the four corners of the land. Now has the end come upon you; I will send my anger against you, and will judge you in accordance with your ways, and repay you for all your abominations. My eye shall not spare you, nor will I pity; but I will repay you for your ways, while your abominations are right in the midst of you; and you shall know that I the LORD am smiting.'

"Thus says the Lord GOD: 'Woe upon woe! See, it comes! An end has come—the end has come—it awakes against you. See, it comes! Doom comes upon you, O inhabitants of the land! The time has come, the day is near—it shall not tarry, nor delay. Soon will I pour out my fury upon you, and spend my wrath upon you; I will judge you in accordance with your ways, and repay you for all your abominations. My eye shall not spare you, nor will I pity; but I will repay you for your ways, while your abominations are right in the midst of you; and you shall know that I the LORD am smiting.'

"Behold, the day! See, it comes! 10
Doom advances. Pride has blossomed,
insolence has budded, violence has 11
grown into a shoot of wickedness; yet
nothing comes of them, their tumult, or
their turmoil—there is no commanding
power among them.

"The time has come, the day draws 12
near! Let not the buyer rejoice, nor the
seller lament; for wrath falls upon all
their teeming multitude. The seller 13
shall not recover what he has sold, nor
the buyer secure what he has bought.
They have sounded the trumpet, they 14
have made all ready; but none advances to the battle, for my wrath falls
upon all their teeming multitude.
Without is the sword, and within are 15
pestilence and famine; he who is in the
open field shall die by the sword, and he
who is in the city shall be devoured by
famine and pestilence; and if any sur- 16
vivors escape, they shall be like doves
of the valleys upon the mountains, all
of them moaning over their guilt. All 17
hands shall fall helpless, and all knees
shall run with water. They shall gird on 18
sackcloth, and be covered with dismay;
shame shall be on every face, and baldness on every head. Their silver shall 19
they fling into the streets, and their
gold shall become to them as an unclean thing; for their silver and their
gold shall not be able to save them on
the day of the LORD'S wrath; it shall
neither satisfy their craving, nor stay
their hunger, because it was the temptation that led them into sin. They 20
prided themselves on its beauty, and
made of it images of their abominable
and detestable things, on which account I will make it an unclean thing to
them. And I will hand it over to aliens 21
as a prey, to the most godless of the
earth as a spoil; and they shall make a
common chain of it. And I will turn my 22
face from them, and my treasured place
shall be profaned; robbers shall enter it,
and profane it. For the country is full 23
of bloody crimes, and the city is full of
violence. Therefore I will bring in the 24
worst of the nations, and they shall take
possession of their houses; I will also silence the stronghold on which they prided themselves, and their sanctuaries
shall be profaned. Panic shall come; and 25
they shall seek peace, but in vain. Woe 26
upon woe shall come, rumor upon rumor; and they shall seek a vision from

the prophet, but in vain. Instruction
also shall pass from the priest, and
27 counsel from the aged. The king shall
go into mourning, and the prince shall
clothe himself with garments of despair,
while the hands of the common people
shall be palsied with terror; for in accordance with their ways will I treat
them, and in accordance with their
practices will I judge them; so shall
they know that I am the LORD."

VISIONS OF IDOLATRY IN JERUSALEM, 8:1–18

8 In the sixth year, in the sixth month,
on the fifth day of the month, as I was
sitting in my house, with the elders of
Judah sitting before me, the hand of
2 the Lord GOD fell upon me there. I
looked, and lo! there was a form of the
appearance of a man, from his loins
downward of the appearance of fire,
and from his loins upward of the appearance of a luster like that of shining
3 metal. He reached out the form of a
hand, and caught me by a lock of my
hair; and a spirit lifted me up between
earth and heaven, and brought me in
visions of God to Jerusalem, to the door
of the north gate leading into the inner
court, where stood the image of resent-
4 ment, that arouses resentment. And
lo! there was the glory of the God of
Israel, in the same appearance as I had
5 seen it in the plain. And he said to me,
"O mortal man, raise your eyes to
the north."
So I raised my eyes to the north, and
lo! north of the altar-gate, at the entrance, stood this image of resentment.
6 Then he said to me,
"O mortal man, do you see what they
are doing? Do you see the great abominations which the house of Israel are
doing here, forcing me away from my
sanctuary? You shall see still greater
abominations than these."
7 So he brought me to the door of the
court. And I looked, and lo! there was
8 a hole in the wall. Then he said to me,
"O mortal man, dig through the
wall."
So I dug through the wall. And lo!
9 there was a door. Then he said to me,
"Go in, and see the vile abominations
which they are doing here."
10 So I went in, and looked, and lo!
there were all sorts of loathsome forms
of reptiles and beasts, together with all
the idols of the house of Israel, depicted
upon the wall all around. And there
were seventy of the elders of the house
of Israel, with Jaazaniah, the son of
Shaphan, in the midst of them, standing in front of the pictures, each with
his censer in his hand, from which rose
the odor of a cloud of incense. Then he
said to me,
"O mortal man, do you see what the
elders of the house of Israel are doing in
the dark, each in his picture-chamber,
thinking, 'The LORD cannot see us, for
the LORD has forsaken the land?'"
Then he said to me,
"You shall see still greater abominations which they are doing."
So he brought me to the door of the
northward gate of the house of the
LORD. And lo! there sat women weeping for Tammuz. Then he said to me,
"Do you see this, O mortal man?
You shall see still greater abominations
than these."
So he brought me to the inner court
of the house of the LORD. And lo! at
the door of the temple of the LORD, between the vestibule and the altar, there
were about twenty-five men, with their
backs to the temple of the LORD, and
their faces to the east, worshiping the
sun in the east. Then he said to me,
"Do you see this, O mortal man? Is
it too slight a thing for the house of Judah to do the abominations which they
are doing here, that they must needs
fill the land with lawlessness, and vex
me still more? See! they are thrusting
their obscenity against my very nostrils. Therefore will I on my part act in
fury. My eye shall not spare, nor will I
pity; even though they call aloud in my
hearing, I will not listen to them."

THE DESTRUCTION OF THE IDOLATERS, 9:1–11

Then he called aloud in my hearing,
and said,
"Come forward, you officers of the
city, armed each with his weapon of
destruction!"
And lo! there came from the direction
of the upper gate, facing the north, six
men armed each with his weapon for
slaughter, and in the midst of them another man clothed in linen, with a
writer's inkhorn at his side. And they

came and stood beside the bronze altar.
3 Now the glory of the God of Israel had
gone up from the cherubim on which it
rested to the threshold of the house.
Then he called to the man clothed in
linen, with the writer's inkhorn at his
4 side, and said to him,
"Pass through the city—through
Jerusalem—and set a mark upon the
foreheads of the men who sigh and cry
for all the abominations that are done
in the midst of it."
5 And to the others he said in my hearing,
"Pass through the city after him, and
6 slay without mercy or pity. Old men,
young men and maidens, little children
and women—strike them all dead! But
touch no one on whom is the mark.
And begin at my sanctuary!"
So they began with the elders in
7 front of the house. Then he said to
them,
"Defile the house, and fill the courts
with the slain. Then go out, and slay in
the city!"
8 As they went on slaying, and I was
left alone, I fell upon my face, and cried
out, saying,
"Ah Lord GOD! wilt thou destroy all
that remains of Israel, in this outpour-
ing of thy fury upon Jerusalem?"
9 So he said to me,
"The guilt of the house of Israel and
Judah is immeasurable. The land is full
of bloodshed, and the city is full of oppression; for they think, 'The LORD
has forsaken the land, and the LORD
10 does not see us.' Therefore I on my
part will show no mercy or pity; I will
requite their doings upon their heads."
11 And lo! the man clothed in linen,
with the inkhorn at his side, brought
back the report,
"I have done as thou didst command
me."

THE DEPARTURE OF THE GLORY OF THE LORD, 10:1–22

10 Then I looked, and lo! upon the
firmament that was over the head of
the cherubim there appeared the semblance of a throne, colored like sap-
2 phire. And he spoke to the man clothed
in linen, and said,
"Go in among the wheelwork under
the cherubim, and fill both your hands
with blazing coals from between the
cherubim, and scatter them over the
city."
So he went in before my eyes. Now, 3
as the man went in, the cherubim were
standing on the right side of the house,
and the cloud filled the inner court; for 4
when the glory of the LORD had gone
up from the cherubim to the threshold
of the house, the house was filled with
the cloud, while the court was filled
with the radiance of the glory of the
LORD. And the sound of the wings of 5
the cherubim was heard as far as the
outer court, as loud as the voice of God
Almighty when he speaks. So, when he 6
had commanded the man clothed in
linen, saying, "Take fire from among
the wheelwork, from between the cherubim," the man went and stood beside a
wheel. Then he reached out his hand to 7
the fire that was between the cherubim,
and took some of it, and went out.
(And there appeared among the cheru- 8
bim the form of a man's hand under
their wings.) Then I looked, and lo! 9
there were four wheels beside the cherubim—one wheel beside one cherub,
and another wheel beside another cherub—and the color of the wheels was like
topaz. The four of them were similar in 10
appearance, as if one wheel were within
another. When they went, they went 11
upon their four sides, not turning as
they went; for they followed the direction where their front faced, not turning as they went. And the whole bodies 12
of the four of them, their backs and
hands and wings, together with the
wheels, were full of eyes round about.
And their wheels were called wheel- 13
work in my hearing. And each of the 14
cherubim had four faces: the first face
that of an ox, the second that of a man,
the third that of a lion, and the fourth
that of an eagle. They were the same 15
creatures that I had seen by the River
Chebar. And when the cherubim went, 16
the wheels went beside them; and when
the cherubim lifted their wings to rise
from the earth, the wheels never left
their side; when these stood still, they 17
stood still; and when these rose, they
rose with them; for the spirit of the
creatures was in them.
Then the glory of the LORD left the 18
threshold of the house, and stood over
the cherubim. And the cherubim lifted 19
their wings, and rose from the earth be-

fore my eyes, the wheels remaining beside them as they went on their way.
And they stood at the door of the east
gate of the house of the LORD, the glory
of the God of Israel resting above them.
20 They were the same creatures that I
had seen underneath the God of Israel
by the River Chebar; and I recognized
21 them as cherubim. Each had four faces
and four wings; and underneath their
wings was the semblance of human
22 hands. As for the semblance of their
faces, they were the same faces that I
had seen by the River Chebar; and
each went straight forward.

DENUNCIATION OF THE FALSE COUNSELORS OF ISRAEL, 11:1–12

11 Then a spirit lifted me up, and
brought me to the east gate of the house
of the LORD, looking east; and lo! at
the door of the gate there were twenty-
five men, among whom I saw Jaazaniah, the son of Azzur, and Pelatiah, the
son of Benaiah, princes of the people.
2 Then the LORD said to me,
"O mortal man, these are the men
who are planning mischief and offering
3 evil counsel in this city, saying, 'Is it
not full time for us to build houses?
This city is the pot, and we are the
4 flesh.' Therefore prophesy against
them, prophesy, O mortal man!"
5 Then the spirit of the LORD fell upon
me, and he said to me,
"Say, Thus says the LORD: 'So you
think, O house of Israel, and I know
6 your thoughts. You have slain many a
man in this city, and have filled its
7 streets with the slain.' Therefore thus
says the Lord GOD: 'Your slain men
whom you have laid in the midst of it—
they are the flesh, and it is the pot; but
as for you, I will take you out of the
8 midst of it. You are afraid of the sword,
and the sword will I bring upon you,' is
9 the oracle of the Lord GOD. 'I will take
you out of the midst of it, and will hand
you over to strangers, and execute judg-
10 ments upon you. By the sword shall
you fall, and over all the borders of Israel will I execute judgments upon you;
so shall you know that I am the LORD.
11 This city shall be no pot for you, and
you shall be no flesh in the midst of it.
Over all the borders of Israel will I exe-
12 cute judgments upon you; and you
shall know that I am the LORD, whose
statutes you have not followed, and
whose ordinances you have not obeyed,
but have conformed to the practices of
the nations that are round about
you.'"

A PROMISE OF RESTORATION, 11:13–21

As I delivered this prophecy, Pela- 1
tiah, the son of Benaiah, died; whereupon I fell upon my face, and cried
aloud, saying,
"Ah Lord GOD, wilt thou make a
complete end of the remnant of Israel?"
Then the word of the LORD came to 1
me, saying,
"O mortal man, the inhabitants of 1
Jerusalem say of your kinsmen, your
fellow-exiles, even the whole house of
Israel, 'They are far from the LORD; to
us the land is given as a possession.'
Therefore say, 'Thus says the Lord 1
GOD: Though I have sent them afar
among the nations, and though I have
scattered them over the lands, and have
been but little of a sanctuary to them
among the lands where they have gone,
yet will I gather them from the peoples, 1
and assemble them from the lands
where they have been scattered; I will
give them the land of Israel, and they 1
shall return there, and shall remove
from it all its loathsome and abominable impurities; and I will give them a 1
new heart, and will put a new spirit
within them; I will remove the heart of
stone from their flesh, and will give
them a heart of flesh, so that they may 2
follow my statutes, and keep my ordinances, and obey them; then shall they
be my people, and I will be their God.
But as for those whose heart is set upon 2
their loathsome and abominable impurities, I will requite their doings upon
their heads,' is the oracle of the LORD."

THE GLORY OF THE LORD LEAVES THE CITY, 11:22–25

Then the cherubim lifted their wings 2
—the wheels remaining beside them,
and the glory of the LORD resting above 2
them—and the glory of the LORD rose
from the midst of the city, and stood
upon the mountain east of the city.

4 And the spirit lifted me up, and
brought me in visions of God back to
the exiles in Chaldea. So the vision
5 that I had seen passed from me. Then
I told the exiles all that the LORD had
shown me.

SYMBOLS OF EXILE, 12:1–20

1 The word of the LORD came to me,
saying,
2 "O mortal man, you are living in the
midst of the rebellious house, who have
eyes to see but see not, and have ears to
hear but hear not—for they are a rebel-
3 lious house. Therefore, O mortal man,
prepare yourself baggage for exile in
the daytime before their eyes; then go
like an exile from your own place to another before their eyes—perhaps they
will see that they are a rebellious house.
4 Carry out your baggage, as though it
were real baggage for exile, in the daytime before their eyes; then go out
yourself, as though you were really going into exile, in the evening before
5 their eyes. Dig a hole through the wall
6 before their eyes, and go out by it; carry your baggage upon your shoulders
before their eyes, and take it out in the
dark; cover your face, so that you may
not see the ground; for I am making
you an omen to the house of Israel."
7 So I did as I had been commanded. I
brought out my baggage, as though it
were real baggage for exile, in the daytime; then in the evening I dug a hole
through the wall with my hand, and
went out in the dark, carrying my baggage upon my shoulders before their
eyes.
8 Next morning the word of the LORD
came to me, saying,
9 "O mortal man, has not the house
of Israel—that rebellious house—been
asking you, 'What are you doing?'
10 Say to them, 'Thus says the Lord GOD:
This sign applies to Jerusalem and the
whole house of Israel who are in the
11 midst of it.' Say, 'I am an omen to
them. As I have done, so shall they
have to do; they shall go into exile—
12 into captivity. And the prince who is in
the midst of them shall carry his baggage upon his shoulders, and go out in
the dark; he shall dig a hole through the
wall, to go out by it; he shall cover his
face, so that he may not see the ground
13 with his eyes. And I will spread a net
for him, and he shall be caught in my
toils; and I will bring him to Babylon,
in the land of the Chaldeans—though
he shall not see it—and there shall he
die. And all his retinue, his supporters, 14
and all his troops, will I scatter to every
wind; and after them will I draw the
sword. And they shall know that I am 15
the LORD, when I have scattered them
among the nations, and dispersed them
over the lands. But a few of them will I 16
save from sword, famine, and pestilence, that they may recount all their
abominable deeds among the nations
where they go; so shall they know that
I am the LORD.' "
Again the word of the LORD came to 17
me, saying,
"O mortal man, eat your bread with 18
quaking, and drink your water with
trembling and anxiety; and say to the 19
people of the land, 'Thus says the Lord
GOD concerning the inhabitants of
Jerusalem, in the land of Israel: They
shall eat their bread with anxiety, and
shall drink their water with dismay; for
the land shall be stripped bare of all
that it contains, because of the lawlessness of all those who live in it, and the 20
inhabited cities shall be laid waste, and
the land shall become a desolation; so
shall you know that I am the LORD.' "

PROPHECY AND FULFILMENT, 12:21–28

The word of the LORD came to me, 21
saying,
"O mortal man, what is this proverb 22
which you have in the land of Israel,
'The days go on, and every vision
comes to nothing'? Therefore say to 23
them, 'Thus says the Lord GOD: I will
put an end to this proverb, and they
shall no longer repeat it in Israel.' Instead of it, say to them, 'The days are
at hand when every vision shall be fulfilled. No longer shall there be any 24
empty vision nor any flattering divination in the midst of the house of Israel.
For I the LORD will speak a word, and 25
it shall be fulfilled—it shall no longer be
delayed—for in your days, O rebellious
house, I will both speak a word and fulfil it,' is the oracle of the Lord GOD."
Again the word of the LORD came to 26
me, saying,
"O mortal man, the house of Israel 27
keep saying to themselves, 'The vision

which he sees is for many days hence;
he is prophesying of times far off.'
28 Therefore say to them, 'Thus says the
Lord GOD: None of my words shall
be any longer delayed; when I speak a
word, it shall be fulfilled,' is the oracle
of the Lord GOD."

PROPHECIES AGAINST THE PROPHETS OF ISRAEL, 13:1–23

13 The word of the LORD came to me,
saying,
2 "O mortal man, prophesy against the
prophets of Israel, prophesy and say to
them, 'Hear the word of the LORD!
3 Thus says the Lord GOD: Woe to the
fools of prophets who follow the
promptings of their own spirits, with-
4 out seeing a vision! O Israel, your
prophets are like jackals among ruins.
5 They have not mounted the breaches,
nor built a wall for the house of Israel,
that they may stand fast in battle on
6 the day of the LORD. They see empty
visions and lying divinations, who say,
"It is the oracle of the LORD," when
the LORD has not sent them. Yet they
7 expect the word to be fulfilled! Is it not
an empty vision which you see, and a
lying divination which you speak, when
you say, "It is the oracle of the LORD,"
8 and I have not spoken? Therefore thus
says the Lord GOD: Because you have
spoken empty words, and have seen lying visions, therefore behold, I am
against you,' is the oracle of the LORD,
9 'and my hand shall be against the
prophets who see empty visions and utter lying divinations; they shall have no
place in the council of my people, nor
be enrolled in the register of the house
of Israel, nor be allowed to enter the
land of Israel; so shall you know that I
10 am the Lord GOD. Because they mislead my people, saying, "All is well,"
when nought is well— and if anyone
build a flimsy wall, they daub it with
11 whitewash—therefore say to those who
daub the wall with whitewash, "A lashing rain shall come, and hailstones shall
fall, and a violent gale shall break out;
12 and lo! the wall shall fall, and then you
shall be asked, Where is the daubing
13 with which you daubed it?" Therefore
thus says the Lord GOD: I will let loose
a violent gale in my wrath, and there
shall come a lashing rain in my anger,
and hailstones shall fall in my fury; and 1
I will break down the wall which you
daubed with whitewash, and will bring
it to the ground, so that its foundations
may be laid bare; and when it falls, you
shall perish in the midst of it; so shall
you know that I am the LORD. Thus 1
will I spend my fury upon the wall, and
upon those who daubed it with whitewash; and you shall be asked, "Where
is the wall? And where are those who
daubed it, the prophets of Israel who 1
prophesied of Jerusalem, and who saw
for her visions of welfare when nought
was well?" is the oracle of the LORD.
"Also, O mortal man, set your face 1
against the daughters of your people,
who prophesy out of their own imagination, prophesy against them, and say, 1
'Thus says the Lord GOD: Woe to the
women who sew bands on everyone's
wrists, and make veils for the heads of
people of every stature—hunting for
lives! Would you hunt for the lives of
my people to make a living for yourselves, by profaning my name among 1
my people for handfuls of barley and
morsels of bread, by bringing death to
those who ought not to die, and life to
those who ought not to live, through
the lies which you tell to my people
who listen to your lies? Therefore thus 2
says the Lord GOD: Behold, I am
against your bands with which you
hunt for lives, and I will tear them from
their arms, and will set free the lives for
which you hunt; I will likewise tear off 2
your veils, and will rescue my people
from your hands, that they may no
longer remain in your hands to be hunted; so shall you know that I am the
LORD. Because with your lies you have 2
disheartened the righteous, when I did
not dishearten him, and have encouraged the wicked, that he might not turn
from his evil way and be saved alive,
therefore you shall no longer see empty 2
visions nor utter lying divinations; and
I will rescue my people from your
hands; so shall you know that I am the
LORD.' "

THE PUNISHMENT OF IDOLATERS, 14:1–11

Then certain of the elders of Israel
came to me, and sat down in front of

2 me. And the word of the LORD came
to me, saying,
3 "O mortal man, these men have set
up idols in their minds, and have placed
temptations to sin in front of them;
what right have they to consult me?
4 Therefore speak with them, and say to
them, 'Thus says the Lord GOD: If
anyone of the house of Israel who sets
up idols in his mind, and places temptations to sin in front of him, go to a
prophet, that he may consult me
through him, I the LORD will answer
him myself according to the number of
5 his idols, that I may catch the house of
Israel in their own devices, because
they have all become estranged from
6 me by their idols.' Therefore say to the
house of Israel, 'Thus says the Lord
GOD: Repent, and turn from your
idols, and from all your abominations!
7 For if anyone of the house of Israel, or
of the aliens residing in Israel, who sev-
ers himself from allegiance to me, and
sets up idols in his mind, and places
temptations to sin in front of him, go to
a prophet, that he may consult me
through him, I the LORD will answer
8 him myself; I will set my face against
that man, and make him a sign and a
byword, and cut him off from the midst
of my people; so shall you know that I
9 am the LORD. And if the prophet be
enticed into speaking a word, I the
LORD have enticed that prophet; and I
will stretch out my hand against him,
and destroy him from the midst of my
0 people Israel. They shall both suffer
for it—the punishment of the prophet
shall be like the punishment of the man
1 who consulted him—that the house of
Israel may no longer apostatize from
me, nor any longer defile themselves
with all their transgressions, but may
become my people, and I their God,' is
the oracle of the Lord GOD."

THE INEXORABLE DOOM OF JERUSALEM, 14:12–23

2 The word of the LORD came to me,
saying,
3 "O mortal man, if a land sin against
me by acting treacherously, and I
stretch out my hand against it, and
break its staff of bread, and send
famine upon it, and cut off from it man
4 and beast, even though these three
men were in the midst of it—Noah,
Daniel, and Job—they would by their
righteousness save but themselves," is
the oracle of the Lord GOD.
"Or if I send wild beasts over the 15
land, and they depopulate it, so that it
becomes a desolation, with none passing through it because of the wild beasts,
even though these three men were in 16
the midst of it, as I live," is the oracle
of the Lord GOD, "they would save
neither sons nor daughters—they would
save but themselves alone—and the
land would be left a desolation.
"Or if I bring a sword upon that land, 17
saying, 'Let the sword pass through the
land!' and cut off from it man and
beast, even though these three men 18
were in the midst of it, as I live," is the
oracle of the Lord GOD, "they would
save neither sons nor daughters—they
would save but themselves alone.
"Or if I send pestilence into that 19
land, and pour out my fury upon it in
bloodshed, cutting off from it man and
beast, even though Noah, Daniel, and 20
Job were in the midst of it, as I live," is
the oracle of the Lord GOD, "they
would save neither son nor daughter—
they would by their righteousness save
but themselves.
"Therefore thus says the Lord GOD: 21
How much more when I send against
Jerusalem my four deadly judgments—
sword, famine, wild beasts, and pestilence—to cut off from it man and beast!
Nevertheless, if there be any survivors 22
left in it, sons and daughters who shall
make good their escape to you, you
shall be consoled for the trouble that I
have brought upon Jerusalem—even
for all that I have brought upon it—
when you see their ways and their doings; they shall console you when you 23
see their ways and their doings, and
you shall know that it was not without
cause that I did all that I have done in
it," is the oracle of the Lord GOD.

THE ALLEGORY OF THE WORTHLESS VINE, 15:1–8

The word of the LORD came to me, **15**
saying,
"O mortal man, in what respect is 2
the wood of the vine better than the
rank growth from any other tree of the

3 forest? Is timber taken from it to make
anything? Is even a peg taken from it
4 to hang any kind of vessel on? No! It
is thrown into the fire as fuel; and when
its two ends are devoured by the fire,
and the middle of it is burned black, is
5 it good for anything? Even when it
was whole, it was good for nothing;
how much less when the fire has devoured it, and it is burned black!
6 Therefore thus says the Lord GOD: As
the wood of the vine is that of one of
the trees of the forest which I give up to
the fire as fuel, so do I give up the in-
7 habitants of Jerusalem. I will set my
face against them; and though they
have come out of the fire, the fire shall
consume them; and they shall know
that I am the LORD, when I set my face
8 against them. And I will make the land
a desolation, because they have acted
treacherously," is the oracle of the Lord
GOD.

THE ALLEGORY OF THE FAITHLESS WIFE, 16:1–63

16 The word of the LORD came to me,
saying,
2 "O mortal man, acquaint Jerusalem
3 with her abominable deeds, and say,
'Thus says the Lord GOD to Jerusalem:
By origin and birth you belong to the
land of the Canaanites. Your father
was an Amorite, and your mother a
4 Hittite. But as for your birth, on the
day you were born your navel-string
was not cut, nor were you washed with
water to cleanse you, nor were you
salted or wrapped in swaddling clothes
5 —no eye had pity enough upon you to
do any of these things out of compassion for you—but you were cast upon
the open field, with no regard for your
6 life, on the day you were born. Then I
passed by you, and saw you weltering
in your blood; and I said to you, as you
7 lay weltering in your blood, 'Live, and
grow like a plant of the field!' So you
grew big and strong, till you reached
the time of your maturity. Your
breasts were formed, and your hair appeared; yet you remained naked and
8 bare. Again I passed by you, and saw
that you had reached the age of love; so
I spread the skirts of my robe over you,
and covered your nakedness; and I
plighted my troth to you, and entered
into a covenant with you," is the oracle
of the Lord GOD. "So you became
mine. Then I bathed you with water,
and washed your blood from you; and I
anointed you with oil. I clothed you 10
with embroidered robes, shod you with
shoes of porpoise skin, wrapped you in
fine linen, and swathed you in silk. I 11
adorned you with ornaments, putting
bracelets upon your arms, and a chain
round your neck, a ring upon your nose, 12
pendants upon your ears, and a splendid crown upon your head. Thus were 13
you adorned with gold and silver, and
clothed with fine linen, silk, and embroidery; you lived on choice flour,
honey, and oil; you grew very, very
beautiful, and became fit for a throne;
and your reputation for beauty went 14
out through the nations, for your beauty was perfect because of the splendor
that I had bestowed upon you," is the
oracle of the Lord GOD.
"But you trusted in your beauty, and 15
played the harlot on your reputation;
you lavished your harlotries on everyone who passed by. You took off your 16
garments, and made yourself gaily
decked shrines, on which you played
the harlot. You took also your splendid 17
ornaments of gold and silver, which I
had given you, and made yourself
images of men, with which you played
the harlot. And you took your em- 18
broidered robes, and wrapped them in
these. My oil and my incense you set
before them; my bread which I had 19
given you—the choice flour, oil, and
honey with which I had fed you—you
set before them as a soothing odor," is
the oracle of the Lord GOD. "And you 20
took your sons and daughters, whom
you had borne to me, and offered them
as sacrifices to be devoured by them.
Was your harlotry so slight a thing
that you must also slaughter my chil- 21
dren, and offer them up as burnt-offerings to them? And with all your abom- 22
inable harlotries you did not remember
your youthful days, when you were
naked and bare, and lay weltering in
your blood.
"After all your wickedness—woe, 23
woe to you!" is the oracle of the Lord
GOD—"you built yourself a shrine, and 24
made yourself a public resort in every
street; you built your resorts at every 25
street corner, and there you prostituted
your beauty, offering yourself to every

passer-by, and multiplying your har-
26 lotries. You played the harlot with
your gross neighbors, the Egyptians,
multiplying your harlotries to vex me.
27 So I stretched out my hand against
you, reduced your allowance, and handed you over to the will of your enemies,
the daughters of the Philistines, who
were ashamed of your lewd conduct.
28 But you played the harlot with the
Assyrians, being still unsated; and
when you had played the harlot with
29 them, you were still unsated. So you
multiplied your harlotries with that
land of traders, Chaldea, and even then
30 you were unsated. What name can I
find to describe your conduct," is the
oracle of the Lord GOD, "in doing all
these things, acting like an abandoned
31 harlot, building your shrines at every
street corner, and making your resorts
in every open space, though you were
not like a harlot in collecting hire—
32 adulterous wife that you are, preferring
33 strangers to your husband! To every
harlot men give a gift; but you gave
your gifts to all your lovers, bribing
them to come from every quarter to in-
34 dulge in harlotry with you. In this respect, then, you were in contrast to
other women, that you solicited men to
harlotry, while you were not solicited,
and that you paid hire to them, while
no hire was paid to you—in this respect
you were a contrast.

35 "Therefore, O harlot, hear the word
36 of the LORD! Thus says the Lord GOD:
For the pouring out of your effrontery,
and for the exposing of your nakedness
in harlotry with your lovers, for the
worship of all your abominable idols,
and for the bloodshed of your children
37 whom you gave to them, behold, I am
assembling all your lovers, whose embraces you have enjoyed—all whom
you loved, as well as all for whom you
cared nothing—I will assemble them
against you from every quarter, and
will expose your nakedness for them to
38 gaze at. I will judge you, as women are
judged who break wedlock and shed
blood, and I will turn you over to my
39 bloody fury and indignation; I will
hand you over to your lovers, and they
shall tear down your shrines and demol-
ish your resorts; they shall strip you of
your clothing, and take away your
splendid ornaments, leaving you naked
40 and bare; they shall bring an assemblage of people against you, who shall
stone you and slash you with their
swords; and they shall burn your 41
houses, and execute judgments upon
you in the sight of many women; so will
I put a stop to your harlotry, and you
shall no longer pay hire to your lovers;
then I will stay my fury against you, 42
and my indignation shall pass from
you; I will be quiet, and no longer angry. Because you did not remember 43
your youthful days, but roused me to
wrath with all these things, I on my
part will requite your doings upon your
head," is the oracle of the Lord GOD,
"because you have added lewdness to
all your other abominations.

"Behold, everyone who quotes prov- 44
erbs shall quote this proverb against
you, 'As the mother, so her daughter!' 45
You are the daughter of a mother who
loathed her husband and her children;
and you are the sister of sisters who
loathed their husbands and their children. Your mother was a Hittite, and 46
your father an Amorite; your elder sister was Samaria, who lived with her
daughters to the north of you; and your
younger sister was Sodom, who lived
with her daughters to the south of you.
But you were not content to follow 47
their ways, nor to copy their abominations—that were too slight a thing for
you!—but you acted more corruptly in
all your ways than they. As I live," is 48
the oracle of the Lord GOD, "your sister Sodom and her daughters have not
done as you and your daughters have
done. Behold, this was the sin of your 49
sister Sodom: she and her daughters
lived in pride, plenty, and thoughtless
ease; they supported not the poor and
needy; they grew haughty, and com- 50
mitted abomination before me; so I
swept them away, as you have seen.
Nor was Samaria guilty of half your 51
sins. You have committed more abominations than they; and through all the
abominations which you have committed you have placed your sisters in the
right. In thus giving judgment in favor 52
of your sisters, you must bear the burden of your shame; through the more
abominable sins which you have committed, they are more in the right than
you; and because you have placed your
sisters in the right, you must bear the
burden of your ignominy and shame.

"But I will restore their fortune—the 53

fortune of Sodom and her daughters,
and the fortune of Samaria and her
daughters—and I will restore your for-
54 tune along with theirs, that you may
feel ashamed and abashed for all that
55 you did to rouse me to wrath. Then
your sisters, Sodom with her daughters,
and Samaria with her daughters, shall
return to their former state; and you
with your daughters shall return to
56 your former state. As the name of your
sister Sodom was never heard on your
57 lips in your heyday of pride—before
your nakedness was exposed—so have
you now become the reproach of the
daughters of Edom, and all who are
round about her, together with the
daughters of the Philistines, and all
those round about them who hold you
58 in contempt. You are bearing the consequences of your abominable lewdness," is the oracle of the LORD.
59 "But thus says the Lord GOD: Though
I must repay you for what you have
done, in scorning the oath and breaking
60 the covenant with me, yet will I remember the covenant which I made
with you in the days of your youth, and
I will establish an everlasting covenant
61 with you. Then shall you also remember your ways, and shall feel ashamed
when I take your sisters, the elder and
the younger, and give them to you as
daughters—but not because of your
62 covenant with me. And I will establish
my covenant with you; and you shall
63 know that I am the LORD, so that you
may remember, and feel ashamed, and
never again open your mouth for shame,
when I forgive you for all that you have
done," is the oracle of the Lord GOD.

THE ALLEGORY OF THE EAGLES AND THE VINE, 17:1-24

17 The word of the LORD came to me,
saying,
2 "O mortal man, put a riddle, and
propound an allegory, to the house of
3 Israel; and say, 'Thus says the LORD:
"A great eagle, with great wings,
And long pinions,
In full plumage, of diverse colors,
Came to Lebanon;
He took the tip of a cedar,
Plucked the topmost of its twigs,
4 And carried it to a land of traders,
Set it in a city of merchants;
He took also of the seed of the land, 5
And planted it in a fertile field;
He placed it beside many waters,
Set it as a slip,
That it might sprout, and become a spreading vine 6
Of lowly height,
Whose tendrils might turn toward him,
And its roots be under him.
So it became a vine, and put forth branches,
And sent out boughs.

"But there was another great eagle, with great wings, 7
And thick plumage;
And lo! this vine bent its roots
In his direction—
It sent out its tendrils for him to water,
From the bed in which it was planted;
Yet it was planted on good soil, 8
Beside many waters,
That it might put forth branches, and bear fruit,
And become a noble vine."
Say, then, 'Thus says the Lord GOD: 9
Can it prosper?
Shall he not pluck up its roots,
And strip off its fruit,
That all its sprouting leaves may wither?
Nor will it require much strength or many people
To heave it from its roots.
It is planted, indeed, but can it prosper? 10
As soon as the east wind strikes it, shall it not wither away—
Wither away on the bed in which it grows?' "

Then the word of the LORD came to 11
me, saying,
"Say to the rebellious house, 'Do you 12
not know what these things mean?'
Then say, 'Lo! the king of Babylon
came to Jerusalem, and took its king
and its princes, and carried them home
with him to Babylon. And he took one 13
of the royal family, and made a covenant with him, and put him under an
oath—while he carried away the leading men of the land—so that the king- 14
dom might be a lowly one, not daring to
lift up its head, but holding its ground
by keeping the covenant. But he re- 15
belled against him, and sent ambassadors to Egypt, asking for horses and a
strong army. Now can a man who does

these things prosper? Can he escape
his doom? Can he break a covenant,
16 and yet escape? As I live,' is the oracle
of the Lord GOD, 'in the land of the
king who made him king—of the king
whose oath he scorned and whose covenant he broke—at his home in Baby-
17 lon shall he die. And Pharaoh with his
great army and strong force shall do
nothing for him on the day of battle,
when mounds are thrown up and siege-
18 walls built to cut off many a life. He
scorned the oath, and broke the covenant; he pledged his word, and yet did
all these things. Therefore he cannot
19 escape.' Thus says the Lord GOD: 'As
I live, my oath which he scorned, and
my covenant which he broke—I will re-
20 quite upon his own head. I will spread
my net for him, and he shall be taken
in my toils; I will carry him to Babylon,
and there will I take proceedings
against him for the treason which he
21 has committed against me. And all the
flower of all his ranks shall fall by the
sword, and those who remain shall fly
to every wind; so shall you know that
I the LORD have spoken.

22 "Thus says the Lord GOD:
'I too will take from the tip of the
cedar,
From its topmost twigs will I pluck a
tender one,
And will plant it on a high and commanding mountain,
23 On the lofty mountain of Israel will I
plant it;
And it shall put forth branches ,and
bear fruit,
And shall become a noble cedar;
Under it shall nestle birds of every
feather,
In the shadow of its branches shall
they nestle.
24 And all the trees of the field shall know
that I the LORD
Bring down the tall tree, raise up the
low tree,
Dry up the green tree, bring blossom
to the dry tree—
I the LORD have spoken, and I will do
it.' "

THE PRINCIPLE OF PERSONAL RESPONSIBILITY, 18:1–32

18 The word of the LORD came to me,
saying,
"What mean you by quoting this 2
proverb in the land of Israel:
'The fathers eat sour grapes,
And the children's teeth are set on
edge'?
As I live," is the oracle of the Lord 3
GOD, "you shall have no more occasion
to quote this proverb in Israel. Be- 4
hold, all lives are mine—the life of the
son is mine equally with that of the father—the person who sins shall die.

"If a man be righteous, and do what 5
is lawful and right—if he eat no flesh 6
with the blood in it, nor lift up his eyes
to the idols of the house of Israel; if he
defile not his neighbor's wife, nor approach a woman in her time of uncleanness; if he oppress no one, but con- 7
scientiously restore the debtor's pledge;
if he commit no robbery, but share his
bread with the hungry, and cover the
naked with a garment; if he lend no
money at interest, nor take increase for 8
himself; if he withhold his hand from
crime, observe strict justice between
man and man, follow my statutes, and 9
be careful to observe my ordinances—
he is righteous, and shall surely live," is
the oracle of the Lord GOD.

"If he beget a son, a violent man, and 10
a shedder of blood, who does none of 11
these things, but eats flesh with the
blood in it, defiles his neighbor's wife,
oppresses the poor and needy, commits 12
robbery, does not restore the debtor's
pledge, lifts up his eyes to the idols,
commits abomination, lends on interest 13
and takes increase—that son shall by
no means live; because he commits all
these abominations, he shall surely die,
and his blood shall be upon his own
head.

"But if this man beget a son who sees 14
all the sins that his father has done, and
is afraid, and does not act likewise—
does not eat flesh with the blood in it, 15
nor lift up his eyes to the idols of the
house of Israel, does not defile his
neighbor's wife, oppresses no one, ex- 16
acts no pledge, commits no robbery,
shares his bread with the hungry, and
covers the naked with a garment, with- 17
holds his hand from crime, takes no
interest or increase, obeys my ordinances, and follows my statutes—that
son shall not die for the iniquity of his
father, but shall surely live. His father 18
died for his iniquity, because he practiced oppression, robbed his fellow-

man, and did what was evil among his
19 people; and you ask, 'Why should not
the son bear the consequences of his father's iniquity?' If the son do what
is lawful and right by being careful to
observe all my statutes, he shall surely
20 live. He who sins shall die; the son
shall not bear the consequences of the
father's iniquity, nor the father bear
the consequences of the son's iniquity;
the righteousness of the righteous shall
be put to his own account, and the
wickedness of the wicked shall be put
to his.
21 "Or if the wicked man turn from all
the sins which he has committed, and
keep all my statutes, and do what is
lawful and right, he shall surely live,
22 and not die. None of the transgressions
which he has committed shall be remembered against him; for the righteousness which he has done he shall
23 live. Have I any pleasure at all in the
death of the wicked?" is the oracle of
the Lord GOD; "and not rather in this,
that he turn from his way and live?
24 "But if the righteous man turn from
his righteousness, and commit iniquity,
acting in accordance with all the abominations which the wicked man practices, none of the righteous deeds which
he has done shall be remembered; for
the treason which he has committed,
and the sin which he has done, he shall
25 die. Yet you say, 'The way of the Lord
is not fair.' Hear, then, O house of Israel! Is my way not fair? Is it not your
26 ways that are not fair? If a righteous
man turn from his righteousness, and
commit iniquity, he shall die; for the
iniquity which he has committed he
27 shall die. But if a wicked man turn
from the wickedness which he has committed, and do what is lawful and
28 right, he shall save his life; because he
is afraid, and turns from all the transgressions which he has committed, he
29 shall surely live, and not die. Yet the
house of Israel says, 'The way of the
Lord is not fair.' Are my ways not fair,
O house of Israel? Is it not your ways
30 that are not fair? Therefore, O house
of Israel, I will judge you each in accordance with his ways," is the oracle
of the Lord GOD. "Repent, then, and
turn from all your transgressions, lest
31 your iniquity bring you to ruin. Cast
away from you all the transgressions
which you have committed against me;
and get yourselves a new heart and a
new spirit. Why should you die, O
house of Israel? For I have no pleasure 32
in the death of anyone who dies," is the
oracle of the Lord GOD. "Turn, then,
and live!"

LAMENT FOR THE ROYAL PRINCES, 19:1–9

And you, raise a dirge over the 19
princes of Israel, and say,
"Ah! your mother was a lioness 2
in the midst of lions;
She couched among young lions,
she reared her whelps.
She brought up one of her whelps, 3
a young lion he became;
He learned to catch the prey,
mankind he devoured.
The nations raised a clamor against 4
him,
in their pit was he taken;
They led him away with hooks
to the land of Egypt.

"When she saw that she was foiled, 5
that her hope was gone,
She took another of her whelps,
a young lion she made him.
He stalked among lions, 6
a young lion he became;
He learned to catch the prey,
mankind he devoured.
He ravaged their palaces, 7
and their cities he laid waste;
The land was awed and all who were in
it,
at the sound of his roaring.

"Against him the nations placed 8
their snares round about;
They spread their net for him,
in their pit was he taken.
They placed him in a cage, 9
they brought him under guard;
And they led him away with hooks
to the king of Babylon;
That his voice might be heard no
more
on the mountains of Israel."

LAMENT FOR THE MOTHER, 19:10–14

"Your mother was like a vine in a vine- 10
yard,
planted by waters;

She was fruitful, and full of branches,
because of waters many.
11 A strong branch she had
for a royal scepter;
It rose in its height
among the thick foliage,
And was seen in its stateliness
with a mass of tendrils.
12 But she was plucked up in fury,
she was cast to the ground;
The east wind parched her,
tore off her fruit;
And her strong branch withered away,
the fire devoured it.
13 Now she is planted in the desert,
in a dry and thirsty land;
14 And fire has gone out from her branch,
has devoured her boughs;
And she has no strong branch
as a royal scepter."

This is a dirge, and it became current as a dirge.

PUNISHMENT AND PARDON, 20:1–44

20 In the seventh year, in the fifth
month, on the tenth day of the month,
certain of the elders of Israel came to
consult the LORD, and sat down before
2 me. Then the word of the LORD came
to me, saying,
3 "O mortal man, speak to the elders
of Israel, and say to them, 'Thus says
the Lord GOD: Have you come to consult me? As I live, I will not be consulted by you,' is the oracle of the Lord
4 GOD. Would you pass judgment upon
them, O mortal man? Would you pass
judgment upon them? Then acquaint
them with the abominable deeds of
5 their fathers, and say to them, 'Thus
says the Lord GOD: On the day that I
chose Israel, and swore by uplifted
hand to the descendants of the house of
Jacob, revealing myself to them in the
land of Egypt, and swearing by uplifted
hand to them, saying, "I am the LORD
6 your God"—on that day I swore by uplifted hand to them, that I would bring
them out of the land of Egypt to a land
that I had given to them, a land flowing
with milk and honey, a land which is
7 the glory of all lands; and I said to
them, "Cast away each of you the detestable things which you love, and do
not defile yourselves with the idols of
Egypt, since I am the LORD your
God." But they rebelled against me, 8
and would not listen to me; they did
not cast away each one the detestable
things which they loved, nor did they
forsake the idols of Egypt. So I resolved to pour out my fury upon them,
to vent my anger against them in the
midst of the land of Egypt. But in deal- 9
ing with them I had regard for my hon-
or, that it might not be profaned in the
sight of the nations among whom they
lived, and in whose sight I had revealed
myself to them, promising to bring
them out of the land of Egypt. So I 10
brought them out of the land of Egypt,
and led them into the desert. I gave 11
them my statutes, and taught them my
ordinances, by observing which man
may enjoy life. I gave them also my 12
sabbaths, as a sign between me and
them, that they might know that it was
I the LORD that set them apart for myself. But the house of Israel rebelled 13
against me in the desert; they did not
follow my statutes, but scorned my ordinances, by observing which man may
enjoy life; my sabbaths also they grossly profaned. So I resolved to pour out
my fury upon them in the desert by
making a complete end of them. But 14
in dealing with them I had regard for
my honor, that it might not be profaned in the sight of the nations in
whose sight I had brought them out. I 15
did, however, swear by uplifted hand to
them in the desert, that I would not
bring them to the land that I had given
to them—a land flowing with milk and
honey, a land which is the glory of all
lands—because they had scorned my 16
ordinances, and did not follow my statutes, but profaned my sabbaths; for
their hearts were set upon their idols.
But I took pity upon them by refrain- 17
ing from destroying them, and I did not
make a complete end of them in the
desert. Then I said to their children in 18
the desert, "Do not follow the statutes
of your fathers, nor keep their ordinances, nor defile yourselves with their
idols! Since I am the LORD your God, 19
follow my statutes, and be careful to
observe my ordinances; keep my sab- 20
baths holy, and let them be a sign between me and you, that you may know
that I am the LORD your God." But 21
the children rebelled against me; they

did not follow my statutes, nor were
they careful to observe my ordinances,
by obeying which man may enjoy life;
they profaned my sabbaths. So I resolved to pour out my fury upon them,
to vent my anger against them in the
22 desert. But I withdrew my hand, and
in dealing with them I had regard for
my name, that it might not be profaned
in the sight of the nations in whose
23 sight I had brought them out. I did,
however, swear by uplifted hand to
them in the desert, that I would scatter
them among the nations, and disperse
24 them over the lands, because they had
not obeyed my ordinances, but had
scorned my statutes, and profaned my
sabbaths, and kept their eyes upon the
25 idols of their fathers. I gave them also
statutes that were not good, and ordinances by which they could not enjoy
26 life; and I made them defile themselves
by their very gifts—the sacrifice of their
first-born children as burnt-offerings—
that I might destroy them, and they
might know that I am the LORD.'

27 "Therefore, O mortal man, speak to
the house of Israel, and say to them,
'Thus says the Lord GOD: In still another way did your fathers blaspheme
me—by dealing treacherously with me.
28 When I brought them to the land that
I had sworn by uplifted hand to give
to them, as often as they saw any high
hill or any leafy tree, there they offered
their sacrifices, and there they presented their offensive gifts; there they set
forth their soothing odors, and there
29 they poured their libations. Then I said
to them, "What kind of high place is this
to which you go?" So it has been called
"high place" to this day.'

30 "Therefore say to the house of
Israel, 'Thus says the Lord GOD: When
you pollute yourselves after the manner
of your fathers by running wantonly
31 after their detestable things, and when,
in offering your gifts, in making your
sons pass through the fire, you continue
to pollute yourselves with all your idols
down to this very day—shall I be consulted by you, O house of Israel? As I
live' is the oracle of the Lord GOD, 'I
32 will not be consulted by you. And
when you say, "We will be like the nations, the races of the lands, in serving
wood and stone," what you have in
33 mind shall not be. As I live,' is the oracle of the Lord GOD, 'with a strong
hand, with an outstretched arm, and
with outpoured fury, will I be king over
you. And with a strong hand, with an 34
outstretched arm, and with outpoured
fury, will I bring you out of the peoples,
and gather you from the lands over
which you are scattered; and I will 35
bring you into the desert of the peoples, and there take proceedings against
you face to face. As I took proceedings 36
against your fathers in the desert of the
land of Egypt, so will I take proceedings against you,' is the oracle of the
LORD GOD. 'I will make you pass 37
under the rod, and bring you into the
purging-trough; and I will purge from 38
among you the rebels, and those who
transgress against me. I will bring them
out of the land where they sojourn, but
they shall not enter the land of Israel;
so shall you know that I am the LORD.
And as for you, O house of Israel, 39
thus says the Lord GOD: Go, destroy
each his idols; and afterwards you shall
surely listen to me, and no longer profane my holy name by your gifts and
your idols. But on my holy mountain, 40
on the mountain of the height of Israel,'
is the oracle of the Lord GOD, 'there
shall all the house of Israel worship me
in the land; there will I accept you, and
there will I ask for your contributions,
and for the choicest of your gifts, in all
your sacred things. As a soothing odor 41
will I accept you when I bring you out
from the peoples, and gather you from
the lands over which you are scattered;
and through you will I reveal my holiness in the sight of the nations. And 42
you shall know that I am the LORD,
when I bring you to the land of Israel,
to the land which I swore by uplifted
hand to give to your fathers. And there 43
shall you remember your ways, and all
those doings of yours by which you
have polluted yourselves; and you shall
loathe yourselves for all the evil things
that you have done. And you shall 44
know that I am the LORD, when I have
dealt with you for my name's sake, and
not in accordance with your evil ways
and your corrupt doings, O house of
Israel,' is the oracle of the Lord GOD."

FIRE AND SWORD, 20:45—21:32

The word of the LORD came to me, 45
saying,

46 "O mortal man, set your face toward
the south, and inveigh against the
47 south; prophesy against the forest land
of the south, and say to the forest of the
south, 'Hear the word of the LORD!
Thus says the Lord GOD: Behold, I am
kindling a fire in you, which shall devour every green tree and every dry tree
in you; the flaming flame shall not be
quenched, and every face from south
48 to north shall be scorched by it. And all
flesh shall see that I the LORD have
kindled it, so that it may not be
quenched.'"
49 Then said I,
"Ah Lord GOD! they say of me, 'Is
he not a maker of allegories?'"
21 Then the word of the LORD came to
me, saying,
2 "O mortal man, set your face toward
Jerusalem, and inveigh against her
sanctuaries; prophesy against the land
3 of Israel, and say to the land of Israel,
'Thus says the LORD: Behold, I am
against you, and I will draw my sword
from its sheath, and will cut off from
4 you righteous and wicked alike. And
because I cut off from you righteous
and wicked alike, my sword shall go out
from its sheath against all flesh from
5 south to north; and all flesh shall know
that I the LORD have drawn my sword
from its sheath, to return no more.'
6 Sigh, therefore, O mortal man; sigh
before them with heartbreaking, bitter
7 grief. And when they ask you, 'Why do
you sigh?' say, 'Because of news, at the
coming of which every heart shall melt,
every hand shall fall helpless, every
spirit shall be faint, and every knee
shall run with water; lo! it comes, and it
shall be,' is the oracle of the Lord GOD."
8 Again the word of the LORD came to
me, saying,
9 "O mortal man, prophesy, and say,
'Thus says the LORD:
"A sword, a sword,
Is whetted and polished;
10 It is whetted for slaughter,
It is polished to flash as lightning.
[Or shall we make mirth, O rod of my
son, despising every tree?]
11 It is given to the slayer,
To grasp with the hand;
The sword is whetted and polished,
To be put in the hand of the slayer."'
12 "Cry, and wail, O mortal man!
For it has fallen upon my people,
And upon all the princes of Israel;
Together with my people have they
been handed over to the sword.
Smite, therefore, upon your thigh,
For there is a trial in store; 13
And who can despise the rod of my
wrath?"
Is the oracle of the Lord GOD.

"Prophesy, therefore, O mortal man, 14
And clench your fists;
Let the sword come down a second
time, let it come down a third
time,
The sword of the slain, the great sword
of the slain!
Bring terror upon them, till their 15
hearts melt,
And many of them fall dead at all their
gates,
Given over to the point of the sword,
Which is made to flash as lightning,
and is whetted for slaughter!
Turn, O sword, to the rear, to the 16
right, to the front, to the left,
Wherever your face is set!
I also will clench my fists, 17
And I will sate my fury—
I the LORD have spoken."
Again the word of the LORD came to 18
me, saying,
"And you, O mortal man, set two 19
roads for the sword of the king of Babylon to take—both of them starting from
the same country—and make a sign- 20
post, to guide the sword on its way, at
the fork of the roads leading on the one
hand to Rabbah of the children of Ammon, and on the other to Jerusalem in
the heart of Judah. For the king of 21
Babylon stands at the parting of the
ways, at the fork of the two roads,
practicing divination; he shakes the arrows, he consults the teraphim, he inspects the liver. Into his right hand 22
falls the lot marked 'Jerusalem,' calling
for slaughter, for the shout of battle,
for the planting of battering-rams
against the gates, for the throwing up of
mounds, for the building of a siege-wall.
To them, indeed, it will seem a false 23
divination—for they count on weeks
upon weeks—but it keeps me in remembrance of their guilt, so that they may
be taken.
"Therefore thus says the Lord GOD: 24
'Because you keep me in remembrance of
your guilt, through your flagrant transgressions, and the sins that are mani-

fest in all your doings—because you are
kept in remembrance through them,
25 you shall be taken by force.' And as
for you, who are destined to be slain,
you wicked one, the prince of Israel,
whose hour has come, on the final day
26 of doom, thus says the Lord GOD:
'Away with the diadem; off with the
crown! Leave nothing alone; lift up
what is low, bring down what is high!
27 A ruin, a ruin, a ruin, will I make it;
and nothing shall be changed until he
comes to whom it rightfully belongs—
to him will I give it.'

28 "And you, O mortal man, prophesy,
and say, 'Thus says the Lord GOD concerning the Ammonites and their reviling:

"A sword, a sword,
Is unsheathed for slaughter,
Is polished to flash as lightning;
29 Because men showed you false visions,
gave you lying divinations,
Commanding you to wield it on the
necks of wicked men destined to
be slain,
Whose hour had come, on the final day
of doom.
30 Return it to its sheath!
For in the place of your birth,
In the land of your origin will I judge
you.
31 I will pour out my fury upon you,
With the fire of my wrath will I blow
upon you;
And I will hand you over to barbarous
men,
Who are forgers of destruction.
32 You shall be food for the fire,
And your blood shall fill the land;
You shall be remembered no more,
For I the LORD have spoken." ' "

THE CITY OF BLOOD, 22:1–31

22 The word of the LORD came to me,
saying,
2 "O mortal man, would you pass
judgment, would you pass judgment,
upon the city of blood? Then acquaint
3 her with all her abominable deeds,
and say, 'Thus says the Lord GOD:
O city, that sheds blood in the midst
of her, so that her time of doom
may come upon her, and that makes
idols for herself, so that she may
4 be defiled! You have become guilty
of the blood which you have shed,
and have become defiled through the
idols which you have made; you have
brought near your day of doom, and
have drawn forward your time of reckoning; therefore I make you a reproach to the nations, and a ridicule to
all the lands. Both those who are near 5
you and those who are far from you
shall ridicule you, O infamous one,
rank with disorder. Behold, the princes 6
of Israel within you give all their
strength to the shedding of blood; fa- 7
ther and mother within you men despise, the resident alien within you they
treat oppressively, the orphan and widow they wrong. My holy things you 8
despise, and my sabbaths you profane.
There are those within you who slander 9
in order to shed blood, those within you
who eat flesh with the blood in it, those
within you who commit lewdness; with- 10
in you men take their fathers' concubines, within you they lie with women
in their time of uncleanness; within you 11
they commit abomination each with his
neighbor's wife, within you they lewdly
defile each his daughter-in-law, and lie
each with his sister, his father's daughter; within you men take bribes in order 12
to shed blood; they take interest and
increase; they oppress their neighbors
by extortion. And me you forget!' " is
the oracle of the Lord GOD.

"Behold, I clench my fists in anger 13
at the extortion which you practice, and
at the bloodshed which is in the midst
of you. Will your heart remain firm, 14
and your hands keep strong, in the days
when I deal with you? I the LORD
have spoken the word, and I will do it.
I will scatter you among the nations, 15
and disperse you over the lands; I will
consume your uncleanness out of you,
and you shall be dishonored in the sight 16
of the nations; so shall you know that
I am the LORD."

Again the word of the LORD came to 17
me, saying,
"O mortal man, the house of Israel 18
has become dross to me; they are all of
them bronze, tin, iron, and lead, in the
midst of the furnace—dross of silver
they are. Therefore thus says the Lord 19
GOD: Because you have all become
dross, behold, I will gather you into the
midst of Jerusalem. As one gathers 20
silver, bronze, iron, lead, or tin into the
midst of the furnace, to blow fire upon

it, and melt it, so will I gather you in
my anger and fury, and I will cast you
21 in, and melt you; I will gather you together, and will blow upon you with
the fire of my wrath, and you shall be
22 melted in the midst of the city. As silver is melted in the midst of the furnace, so shall you be melted in the
midst of it; and you shall know that I
the LORD have poured out my fury
upon you."

23 Again the word of the LORD came to
me, saying,

24 "O mortal man, say to her: 'You are
a land on which no rain or shower shall
25 fall on the day of my indignation. For
the rulers in the midst of the land are
like a roaring lion that rends his prey;
they devour men's lives, they seize
treasure and wealth, they make many
26 widows in the midst of her. Her priests
also violate my law, and profane my
holy things; they make no difference
between sacred and secular, and teach
no difference between unclean and
clean; they shut their eyes to my sabbaths, so that I am profaned among
27 them. The princes in the midst of her
are like wolves that rend the prey, shedding blood, and destroying lives, to get
28 dishonest gain. Her prophets also daub
their walls with whitewash, showing
them empty visions, and giving them
lying divinations, saying, "Thus says
the Lord GOD," when the LORD has
29 not spoken. The common people practice oppression, and commit robbery;
they wrong the poor and needy, and
treat the resident alien with injustice.
30 When I sought among them for a man
who would build up the wall, and hold
the breach before me in defense of the
land, to prevent my destroying it, I
31 found no one. Therefore I pour out my
indignation upon them; with the fire of
my wrath I consume them; their ways
I requite upon their heads!'" is the
oracle of the Lord GOD.

THE ALLEGORY OF THE TWO SISTERS, 23:1–49

3 The word of the LORD came to me,
saying,

2 "O mortal man, there were two wom-
3 en, daughters of one mother. In their
girlhood they played the harlot, they
played the harlot in Egypt. There men
pressed their bosoms, there men bruised
their virgin breasts. Their names were 4
Oholah, the elder, and Oholibah, her
sister. They became my wives, and bore
sons and daughters. The name Oholah
signifies Samaria, and Oholibah Jerusalem.

"Although she was my wife, Oholah 5
played the harlot, and doted on her
lovers the Assyrians—lords clothed in 6
purple, governors and deputies, all of
them handsome young men, knights
riding on horseback—she bestowed her 7
favors on them, the flower of the Assyrians all of them, and defiled herself
with all the idols of all on whom she
doted, not giving up the harlotries she 8
committed in Egypt, since in her girlhood men lay with her, and bruised her
virgin breasts, and lavished their lust
upon her. So I handed her over to 9
her lovers the Assyrians, on whom
she doted. They uncovered her nak- 10
edness, they took away her sons and
daughters, her own self they slew with
the sword; and by reason of the judgments which they executed upon her,
she became a byword among women.

"But although her sister Oholibah 11
saw this, she carried on her doting and
her harlotries worse than her sister.
She doted on the Assyrians, governors 12
and deputies, lords clothed in purple,
knights riding on horseback, all of them
handsome young men. And although I 13
saw how she defiled herself—how both
of them took the same way—she went 14
still further in her harlotries. For she
saw portraits of men on the wall, figures of Chaldeans portrayed in vermilion, with girdles round their loins, and 15
flowing turbans upon their heads, all of
them looking like officers, portraits of
Babylonians, whose native land was
Chaldea; and when she saw them, she 16
doted on them, and sent messengers to
them in Chaldea. And the Babylonians 17
came to visit her on the bed of love, and
defiled her with their lust, till she was
sated, and became disgusted with them.
And because she flaunted her harlotries, 18
and exposed her nakedness, I became
disgusted with her, as I had become disgusted with her sister. Yet she went on 19
with her harlotries, remembering the
days of her girlhood, when she played
the harlot in the land of Egypt. She 20
doted on her paramours, whose lust was
as gross as that of asses or stallions, re- 21

peating the lewdness of her youth,
when the Egyptians bruised her
breasts, and pressed her girlish bosom.
22 "Therefore, O Oholibah, thus says
the Lord GOD: 'Behold, I am rousing
your lovers against you—the lovers
with whom you became disgusted—
and I will bring them against you from
23 every side: the Babylonians, and all the
Chaldeans, men of Pekod, Shoa, and
Koa, together with all the Assyrians,
handsome young men, all of them governors and deputies, officers and councilors, all of them riding on horseback.
24 And they shall come against you with
an army of chariots and wheels, and
with a host of men on foot; they shall
array themselves against you on every
side with buckler, shield, and helmet; I
will intrust to them the execution of
judgment, and they shall execute their
25 judgments upon you. I will stamp you
with the seal of my indignation, and
they shall deal with you in fury; they
shall cut off your nose and ears, and
what remains of you shall fall by the
sword; they shall take away your sons
and daughters, and what remains of
26 you shall be devoured by fire; they shall
strip you of your clothes, and shall take
27 away your splendid jewels. Thus will I
put a stop to your lewd harlotries, committed ever since you were in the land
of Egypt, so that you may no longer
set your eyes upon them, nor remember
Egypt any more.'
28 "For thus says the Lord GOD: 'Behold, I am handing you over to those
whom you hate—those with whom you
29 became disgusted—and they shall deal
with you in hatred, and shall take away
all the fruits of your labor, leaving you
naked and bare. So shall the shame of
your harlotry be exposed—your lewd
30 harlotry. It shall bring these things
upon you, because you have played the
harlot with the nations in defiling your-
31 self with their idols. You have gone the
same way as your sister; so I will hand
her cup over to you.'
32 "Thus says the Lord GOD:
'You shall drink your sister's cup,
Which is deep and large;
You shall become a scorn and derision,
For it is full to the brim.
33 You shall be filled with pain and sorrow,
For a cup of horror and awe
Is the cup of your sister Samaria.
You shall drink it, and drain it— 34
You shall drain it to the dregs;
And your breasts you shall tear,
For I have spoken,'
Is the oracle of the Lord GOD.
"Therefore thus says the Lord GOD: 35
'Because you have forgotten me, and
cast me behind your back, you must
bear the consequences of your lewd
harlotries.'"
The LORD further said to me, 36
"O mortal man, would you pass judgment upon Oholah and Oholibah? Then
acquaint them with their abominable
deeds! For they have committed 37
adultery, and there is bloodshed upon
their hands; with their idols have they
committed adultery, and to them have
they sacrificed as burnt-offerings the
sons whom they bore to me. This also 38
have they done to me: they have defiled my sanctuary, and have profaned
my sabbaths. For when they had sacri- 39
ficed their sons to their idols, they went
that same day to my sanctuary to profane it. This was what they did within
my house. Still worse, you sent for men 40
from a far country—you sent a messenger to them, and they came—and for
them you bathed yourself, painted
your eyes, adorned yourself with ornaments, and sat on a stately couch, with 41
a table spread in front of it, on which
you set my incense and my oil. Sounds 42
of revelry were heard there, the revelry
of thoughtless men, including drunkards from the desert, who had been
brought together in hosts, and who had
bracelets placed upon their arms, and
splendid crowns upon their heads. I 43
said, 'Now will they commit adultery
and play the harlot with them.' And 44
they went in to them, as one goes in to a
harlot; so they went in to those lewd
women, Oholah, and Oholibah. But 45
honest men shall condemn them to the
punishment due to adulterous women,
and such as shed blood; for they have
committed adultery, and there is bloodshed upon their hands.
"For thus says the Lord GOD: 46
'Bring up an assemblage against them,
and give them over to pillage and spoil.
Let the assemblage stone them, and cut 47
them off with the sword; let them slay
their sons and daughters, and burn
their houses. Thus will I put a stop to 48
lewdness in the land; and all women
shall take warning, and not follow your

49 lewd example. Your lewdness shall be
brought home to you, and you shall
bear the consequences of your sinful
idolatry; so shall you know that I am
the Lord GOD.' "

THE ALLEGORY OF THE RUSTY POT, 24:1–14

24 In the ninth year, in the tenth
month, on the tenth day of the month,
the word of the LORD came to me, saying,
2 "O mortal man, write down the name
of this day; for on this very day the
king of Babylon has invested Jerusa-
3 lem. And propound an allegory to the
rebellious house, and say to them,
'Thus says the Lord GOD:
"Set on the pot, set it on,
And pour water into it;
4 Put into it the pieces,
All the good pieces, the thigh and the
shoulder;
Fill it with the choicest bones,
5 Taken from the choicest of the flock;
Pile wood under it, let it boil well,
That the bones also may be seethed in
the midst of it." '
6 "Therefore thus says the Lord GOD:
'Woe to the bloody city, a pot full of
filth, whose filth never leaves her! On
each of her pieces she sets her stain,
7 without a lot falling upon them. For she
has blood in the midst of her; and on the
bare rock she places it, instead of pouring it upon the ground, so that it may
8 be covered with dust; to stir up fury,
to bring on vengeance, she has put
blood on the bare rock, so that it may
not be covered.'
9 "Therefore thus says the Lord GOD:
'Woe to the bloody city! I myself will
10 make the pile great; I will heap on the
wood, and kindle the fire; I will cook
the flesh, and brew the broth, till the
11 bones are burned. Then I will set it
empty upon the embers, so that it may
be heated, and its bottom may glow,
that its impurity may be melted in the
midst of it, and its filth may be con-
12 sumed. But however hotly it burns, its
13 thick filth will not leave it. Therefore,
O filthy one, defiled by impurity, because I sought to cleanse you, and you
would not be cleansed, you shall no
more be cleansed from your impurity
14 till I have spent my fury upon you. I
the LORD have spoken the word, and I
will do it. I will not hold back, nor pity,
nor relent; in accordance with your
ways and your doings will I punish you,'
is the oracle of the Lord GOD."

DEATH OF THE PROPHET'S WIFE, 24:15–27

The word of the LORD came to me, 15
saying,
"O mortal man, behold, I am taking 16
away from you the delight of your eyes
by a stroke; but you shall neither lament, nor weep, nor drop a tear. Sigh 17
in silence; make no mourning for the
dead; wind your turban round your
head, and put your sandals upon your
feet; cover not your beard, and eat no
mourning bread."
That evening my wife died; and in 18
the morning I did as I had been commanded. The same morning I spoke to
the people; and the people said to me, 19
"Will you not tell us what these
things mean? Is it for us that you are
acting so?"
Then I said to them, 20
"The word of the LORD came to me,
saying, 'Say to the house of Israel, Thus 21
says the Lord GOD: Behold, I am
about to profane my sanctuary, the
pride of your strength, the delight of
your eyes, and the pride of your heart;
and the sons and daughters whom you
leave behind you shall fall by the sword.
Then shall you do as I have done: you 22
shall not cover your beards, nor eat
mourning bread; your turbans shall re- 23
main upon your heads, and your sandals upon your feet; you shall not lament or weep, but shall pine away in
your sins, and shall moan to one
another. Ezekiel shall be a sign to you: 24
just as he has done shall you do when
the time comes; so shall you know that
I am the Lord GOD.
" 'And as for you, O mortal man, on 25
the day when I take from them their
stronghold, their proud joy, the delight
of their eyes, that upon which their
heart is set, together with their sons
and daughters, on that day shall a fugi- 26
tive come to you with news, and on the 27
same day that the fugitive comes your
mouth shall be opened, and you shall
speak, and shall no longer be dumb. So
shall you be a sign to them; and they
shall know that I am the LORD.' "

ORACLES AGAINST AMMON, MOAB, EDOM, AND THE PHILISTINES, 25:1–17

25 The word of the LORD came to me,
saying,
2 "O mortal man, set your face toward
the Ammonites, and prophesy against
3 them, and say to the Ammonites, 'Hear
the word of the Lord GOD!' Thus says
the Lord GOD: 'Because you cried
"Aha!" over my sanctuary when it was
profaned, and over the land of Israel
when it was made desolate, and over
the house of Judah when it went into
4 exile, behold, I am handing you over
as a possession to the Kedemites, and
they shall pitch their camps and make
their settlements in you, they shall eat
5 your fruit and drink your milk. And I
will make Rabbah a pasture for camels,
and the cities of Ammon a fold for
flocks; so shall you know that I am the
6 LORD.' For thus says the Lord GOD:
'Because you clenched your fists and
stamped your feet and rejoiced with all
the maliciousness of your heart over the
7 land of Israel, behold, I stretch my
hand over you, and will give you as a
spoil to the nations, I will cut you off
from the peoples, and will blot you out
from the lands—I will destroy you utterly; so shall you know that I am the
LORD.'
8 "Thus says the Lord GOD: 'Because
Moab said, "Behold, the house of Judah
9 has become like other nations," behold,
I am laying open the flank of Moab,
from the cities on its frontier to Beth-
10 jeshimoth, Baal-meon, and Kirjathaim,
the glory of the land, and I will give
Moab along with Ammon as a possession to the Kedemites, so that it
may no longer be remembered among
11 the nations. Thus will I execute judgments upon Moab; and they shall know
that I am the LORD.'
12 "Thus says the Lord GOD: 'Because
Edom acted revengefully against the
house of Judah, and incurred grievous
guilt by taking revenge upon them,
13 therefore thus says the Lord GOD: I
will stretch my hand over Edom, and
will cut off from it man and beast; I will
make it a waste from Teman, and to
14 Dedan shall they fall by the sword. I
will wreak my vengeance upon Edom
by the hand of my people Israel, and
they shall deal with Edom in accordance with my anger and fury; and they
shall know my vengeance," is the oracle
of the Lord GOD.
"Thus says the Lord GOD: 'Because 15
the Philistines acted revengefully
against the house of Judah, and took
malicious revenge upon them, seeking
to destroy them by a perpetual enmity,
therefore thus says the Lord GOD: Be- 16
hold, I am stretching my hand over the
Philistines, and I will cut off the Cherethites, and destroy the people of the
seacoast to the last remnant; I will 17
wreak upon them sore vengeance, by
acts of furious chastisement; and they
shall know that I am the LORD, when
I carry out my vengeance upon them.'"

ORACLE AGAINST TYRE, 26:1–21

In the eleventh year, in the eleventh 26
month, on the first day of the month,
the word of the LORD came to me, say-
ing,
"O mortal man, because Tyre has 2
said against Jerusalem,
'Aha! the gate of the peoples is broken,
She is thrown open to me;
I shall be filled, while she is laid waste,'
Therefore thus says the Lord GOD: 3
'Behold, I am against you, O Tyre,
And will bring up many nations
against you,
As the sea brings up its waves;
They shall destroy the walls of Tyre, 4
And shall tear down her towers.
I will scrape her very dust from her,
And will make her a bare rock;
She shall be a place for the spreading 5
of nets
In the heart of the sea;
For I have spoken it,' is the oracle of
the Lord GOD,
'And she shall become a spoil to the
nations.
Her daughters also on the mainland 6
shall be slain by the sword,
And they shall know that I am the
LORD.'

"For thus says the Lord GOD: 7
'Behold, I am bringing upon Tyre from
the north
Nebuchadrezzar, king of Babylon,
king of kings,
With horses and chariots, horsemen,
and a host of men on foot.

8 Your daughters on the mainland shall
he slay by the sword;
And a siege wall shall he place against
you,
And a mound shall he throw up against
you,
And a buckler shall he set up against
you;
9 His battering-rams shall he place
against your walls,
And with his axes shall he break down
your towers.
10 From the multitude of his horses the
dust shall cover you,
And with the noise of his horsemen,
his wheels, and his chariots,
Your walls shall shake when he enters
your gates,
As one enters a city that is breached.
11 With the hoofs of his horses shall he
trample all your streets,
Your people shall he slay by the sword,
And your strong pillars shall he bring
to the ground.
12 Your wealth shall be plundered, and
your merchandise made a prey;
Your walls shall be torn down, and
your happy homes destroyed;
Your stones and timber and dust shall
be sunk in the heart of the waters.
13 I will silence the noise of your songs,
And the sound of your harps shall be
heard no more.
14 I will make you a bare rock,
You shall be a place for the spreading
of nets,
You shall be built no more;
For I the LORD have spoken it,'
Is the oracle of the Lord GOD.
15 "Thus says the Lord GOD to Tyre:
'Shall not the coast-lands quake at the
sound of your downfall, when the
wounded groan, and slaughter is rife in
16 the midst of you? Then shall all the
princes of the sea come down from their
thrones, and lay aside their robes, and
strip off their embroidered garments;
they shall clothe themselves in mourning weeds; they shall sit upon the ground,
and tremble every moment, and shud-
17 der over you. And they shall raise a
dirge over you, and say to you:
"How you have perished, have vanished
from the sea,
O city renowned,
That was strong upon the sea,
herself and her people,
That struck the terror of her might
upon all who dwelt there!

Now the coast-lands quake 18
on the day of your downfall,
The coast-lands by the sea
are dismayed at your passing.'"
"For thus says the Lord GOD: 'When 19
I make you a desolate city, like the
cities that are uninhabited, when I
bring the deep over you, and the mighty
waters cover you, then will I thrust 20
you down, with those who go down to
the Pit, to the people of ancient times,
and will make you dwell in the underworld, in the primeval wastes, with
those who go down to the Pit, so that
you may remain uninhabited, and may
no more take your place in the land of
the living; I will bring you to an awful 21
end, and you shall be no more; though
you be sought for, you shall be found
no more,' is the oracle of the Lord GOD."

LAMENT OVER TYRE, 27:1–36

The word of the LORD came to me, 27
saying,
"And you, O mortal man, raise a 2
dirge against Tyre, and say to Tyre, 3
that sits at the gateway of the sea, the
merchant of the peoples along many a
coast-land, 'Thus says the Lord GOD:
"O Tyre, you have said,
'I am perfect in beauty';
Your domain was in the heart of the 4
seas,
your builders made you perfect
in beauty.
Of cypresses from Senir 5
they fashioned all your planks;
A cedar they took from Lebanon
to make you a mast.
Of oaks from Bashan 6
they made your oars;
Your deck they made of larch
from the coast-lands of Cyprus.
Of fine linen from Egypt, richly em- 7
broidered,
was your sail,
serving you as an ensign;
Your awning was of blue and purple
from the coast-lands of Elishah.
The inhabitants of Sidon and Arvad 8
were rowers for you;
Your skilled men, O Tyre, were in you,
serving as your steersmen.
The elders of Gebel and her skilled 9
men were in you,
repairing your leaks;

All the ships of the sea with their sailors were in you,
to handle your wares.
10 Men of Persia, Lud, and Put were in your army,
serving as your soldiers;
Shield and helmet they hung on you,
they displayed your glory.
11 The sons of Arvad and Helech manned your walls round about,
And the men of Gammad were in your towers;
They hung their shields upon your walls round about,
they made perfect your beauty.

12 "Tarshish traded with you because
of your abundant wealth of every kind;
she bartered with you silver, iron, tin,
13 and lead. Javan, Tubal, and Meshech
traded with you; they supplied you with
14 slaves and bronze utensils. Those of the
house of Togarmah bartered with
15 you horses, horsemen, and mules. The
men of Rhodes traded with you; the
people of many a coast-land were at
your service; ivory tusks and ebony
16 they brought you as tribute. Edom
traded with you because of your abundant resources; she bartered with you
garnets, purple dyes, embroidered work,
17 fine linen, coral, and rubies. Judah and
the land of Israel traded with you; they
supplied you with wheat from Minnith,
18 wax, honey, oil, and balsam. Damascus
traded with you because of your abundant resources, your abundant wealth
of every kind; she bartered with you
wine from Helbon and white wool.
19 The men of Uzal supplied you with
20 wrought iron, cassia, and calamus. Dedan sold you saddlecloths for riding.
21 Arabia and all the chiefs of Kedar were
at your service; they sold you lambs,
22 rams, and goats. The merchants of
Sheba and Raamah traded with you;
they bartered with you the finest of all
kinds of spices, and the finest of all
23 kinds of precious stones and gold. Haran, Canneh, and Eden, Assyria, and all
24 the Medes traded with you; they sold
you choice fabrics, richly embroidered
mantles of blue, stuffs of various colors,
25 and strongly twisted skeins. Ships of
Tarshish carried your merchandise.

"So you were filled, and became heavily laden,
in the heart of the seas.
Your rowers brought you
into deep waters; 26
The east wind wrecked you
in the heart of the seas.
Your wealth, your wares, and your merchandise, 27
your sailors and your steersmen,
Your caulkers, your traders, and all your soldiers aboard you—
even all the crowd within you—
Shall sink in the heart of the seas
on the day of your downfall.
At the sound of your steersmen's cry 28
the pasture-lands shall quake;
And all oarsmen and sailors, 29
all steersmen of the deep,
Shall come down from their ships,
and shall stand upon the shore;
They shall raise their voices over you, 30
and shall cry out bitterly;
They shall cast up dust on their heads,
they shall wallow in ashes;
They shall shave their heads for you, 31
and gird on sackcloth;
They shall weep for you in bitterness of heart,
with bitter lamentation;
Their daughters shall raise a dirge for you, 32
and lament over you:
'Who has been ruined like Tyre
in the heart of the sea?
When your merchandise came from the seas, 33
you supplied many peoples;
With the abundance of your wealth and your wares
you enriched the kings of the earth.
Now you are wrecked in the seas, 34
in the depths of the waters;
Your cargo and all your crew
are sunk in the heart of you.
All the inhabitants 35
are appalled at your fate;
Their kings are aghast with horror,
their faces are convulsed;
The merchants among the peoples hiss you to scorn, 36
for you have come to an awful end,
and shall be no more forever.' " ' "

ORACLE AGAINST THE KING OF TYRE, 28:1–10

The word of the LORD came to me, 28
saying,

2 "O mortal man, say to the prince of
Tyre, 'Thus says the Lord GOD:
"Because you are puffed up with pride,
And have said, 'I am a god,
I sit in the seat of the gods
In the heart of the seas,'
When you are but a man, and no god,
Though you count yourself wise as a
god—
3 You are wiser, forsooth, than Daniel,
No secret thing can they hide from
you!
4 By your shrewdness and your skill
you have won yourself wealth,
You have gathered gold and silver
into your treasuries;
5 By your great shrewdness in trade you
have increased your wealth,
And because of your wealth you are
puffed with pride"—
6 Therefore thus says the Lord GOD:
"Because you count yourself wise as a
god,
7 Behold, I am bringing aliens against
you,
The most ruthless of nations;
And they shall draw their swords
against your subtle beauty,
And shall stain your splendor.
8 They shall bring you down to the Pit,
And you shall die the death of the
slain
In the heart of the seas.
9 Will you then venture to say, 'I am
a god,'
In the presence of those who slay you,
When you are but a man, and no god,
In the hands of those who pierce you?
10 You shall die the death of the uncircumcised
By the hands of aliens;
For I have spoken it," ' is the oracle of
the Lord GOD."

DIRGE OVER THE KING OF TYRE, 28:11–19

11 Again the word of the LORD came to
me, saying,
12 "O mortal man, raise a dirge over the
king of Tyre, and say of him, 'Thus
says the Lord GOD: You were the seal
of perfection, full of wisdom, and com-
13 plete in beauty. You dwelt in Eden,
the garden of God. You had a shield of
every kind of precious stone, the ruby,
topaz, and emerald, the beryl, onyx,
and jasper, the sapphire, garnet, chrysolite, and gold; and on your clothing was
a wealth of fine gold. On the day when
you were created, I placed you with the 14
guardian cherubim on the holy hill of
God; and you walked amidst stones of
fire. You were perfect in your ways 15
from the day when you were created,
till guilt was discovered in you. Through 16
the greatness of your trade you filled
your mind with lawlessness, and you
fell into sin; therefore I cast you out as
a profane thing from the hill of God,
and the guardian cherubim drove you
from the midst of the stones of fire.
You were puffed up with pride through 17
your beauty, you ruined your wisdom
by reason of your splendor; therefore I
flung you to the ground, and exposed
you for kings to gaze at. Through the 18
greatness of your guilt, through the sins
of your trade, you profaned your sacredness; therefore I brought forth fire from
the midst of you, and I reduced you to
ashes upon the ground in the sight of all
who saw you. All who knew you among 19
the nations are appalled at your fate;
for you have come to an awful end, and
shall be no more forever.' "

ORACLE AGAINST SIDON, 28:20–26

The word of the LORD came to me, 20
saying,
"O mortal man, set your face toward 21
Sidon, and prophesy against her, and 22
say, 'Thus says the Lord GOD:
"Behold, I am against you, O Sidon,
And will reveal my glory in the midst
of you;
Then shall you know that I am the
LORD,
When I execute judgments in the
midst of you,
And reveal my holiness through you.
For I will send pestilence into you, 23
And bloodshed into your streets;
And the slain shall fall in the midst of
you,
By the sword that descends upon you
from every side;
And you shall know that I am the
LORD.

"Then the house of Israel shall no 24
more find a pricking brier or a piercing
thorn among all the malicious peoples
that surround them on every side; and
they shall know that I am the Lord
GOD."

25 'Thus says the Lord GOD: "When I
have gathered the house of Israel from
the peoples among whom they are scattered, and have revealed my holiness
through them in the sight of the nations, then shall they live in their own
land, which I gave to my servant Jacob;
26 they shall live securely in it, and shall
build houses and plant vineyards; they
shall live securely in it, when I have
executed judgments upon all the malicious peoples that surround them on
every side; and they shall know that I
am the LORD their God." ' "

ORACLE AGAINST PHARAOH, 29:1–16

29 In the tenth year, in the tenth month,
on the twelfth day of the month, the
word of the LORD came to me, saying,
2 "O mortal man, set your face against
Pharaoh, king of Egypt, and prophesy
against him, and against Egypt, the
3 whole of it; speak, and say, 'Thus says
the Lord GOD:

"Behold, I am against you, O Pharaoh,
King of Egypt,
The great crocodile that lies
In the midst of its streams,
That says, 'This stream of mine is my
own—
It was I that made it.'
4 I will put hooks in your jaws,
And will make the fish of your streams
cleave to your scales;
And I will draw you out of the midst
of your streams,
With all the fish of your streams that
cleave to your scales.
5 And I will cast you into the desert,
Yourself and all the fish of your
streams;
On the open field shall you lie,
Ungathered and unburied;
To the beasts of the earth and the
birds of the air
Will I leave you for food.
6 Then all the inhabitants of Egypt shall
know
That I am the LORD,
Because you have been a staff of reed
To the house of Israel—
7 When they grasped you by the hand,
you snapped,
And tore all their hand;
And when they leaned upon you, you
broke,
And made all their loins quake."

'Therefore thus says the Lord GOD: 8
"Behold, I am bringing a sword upon
you, and I will cut off from you man
and beast, and the land of Egypt shall 9
be a desolation and a waste; so shall
they know that I am the LORD. Because you have said, 'The stream is my
own; it was I that made it,' therefore 10
behold, I am against you, and against
your stream; and I will make the land
of Egypt a waste and a desolation, from
Migdol to Syene, even to the border of
Ethiopia. No foot of man shall cross it, 11
no foot of beast shall cross it; for forty
years shall it remain uninhabited. I will 12
make the land of Egypt a desolation in
the midst of lands that are made desolate, and for forty years shall her cities
remain a desolation in the midst of
cities that are laid waste; and I will
scatter the Egyptians among the nations, and disperse them over the lands."

'Thus says the Lord GOD: "At the 13
end of forty years I will gather the
Egyptians from the peoples among
whom they are scattered; and I will re- 14
store the fortune of Egypt, and will
bring them back to their native land of
Pathros, and there shall they form a
lowly kingdom. It shall be the lowliest 15
of all kingdoms, and shall no more raise
its head above the nations; for I will
keep them so small that they shall not
be able to rule over the nations. And 16
they shall no more be a ground of confidence to the house of Israel, recalling
sin to mind when they turn to them;
and they shall know that I am the Lord
GOD." ' "

EGYPT AS WAGES FOR NEBUCHADREZZAR, 29:17–21

In the twenty-seventh year, in the 17
first month, on the first day of the
month, the word of the LORD came to
me, saying,
"O mortal man, Nebuchadrezzar, 18
king of Babylon, engaged his army in a
great campaign against Tyre. Every
head was rubbed bald, and every shoulder was peeled bare; yet neither he nor
his army won any return from the campaign which he directed against Tyre.
Therefore thus says the Lord GOD: 19
'Behold, I am giving the land of Egypt
to Nebuchadrezzar, king of Babylon;
and he shall carry off her abundance,
and shall despoil her and prey upon her,

to pay his army. As a return for the campaign which he directed against Tyre, I am giving him the land of Egypt, because they rendered a service to me,' is the oracle of the Lord GOD.

"On that day will I cause a horn to sprout for the house of Israel; and I will enable you to speak freely in the midst of them; and they shall know that I am the LORD."

THE DESOLATION OF EGYPT, 30:1–26

The word of the LORD came to me, saying,

"O mortal man, prophesy, and say,
'Thus says the Lord GOD:
"Wail, 'Woe for the day!'
For the day is near,
The day of the LORD is near,
A day of clouds, the time of doom for the nations.
A sword shall descend upon Egypt,
And there shall be writhing in Ethiopia,
When the slain fall in Egypt,
And her abundance is carried off,
And her foundations are torn up.'

[Ethiopia, Put, and Lud, all the Arabians, the Lybians, and the Chereth-ites with them, shall fall by the sword.]

" 'Thus says the LORD:
"Those who uphold Egypt shall fall,
And her proud strength shall come down;
From Migdol to Syene shall they fall by the sword in her,"
Is the oracle of the Lord GOD.
"She shall be desolate in the midst of lands that are made desolate,
And her cities shall lie in the midst of cities that are laid waste.
And they shall know that I am the LORD,
When I have kindled a fire in Egypt,
And all her helpers are shattered.
On that day shall messengers go forth from my presence in ships,
To strike terror upon Ethiopia in its security;
And writhing shall seize them on the day of Egypt's doom;
For lo! it comes."
Thus says the Lord GOD:
"I will make an end of the abundance of Egypt
By the hand of Nebuchadrezzar, king of Babylon.
He and his people with him, the most ruthless of nations, 11
Shall be brought in to destroy the land;
They shall draw their swords against Egypt,
And shall fill the land with the slain.
I will make the streams a waste, 12
And I will sell the land to evil men;
I will make the land and all that is in it a desolation,
By the hand of aliens—
I the LORD have spoken it."
Thus says the Lord GOD: 13
"I will destroy the magnates of Memphis,
And no more shall there be a prince in the land of Egypt;
I will put fear on the land of Egypt,
And will make Pathros a desolation, 14
And will kindle a fire in Zoan,
And will execute judgments upon Thebes;
I will pour out my fury on Pelusium, 15
the stronghold of Egypt,
And I will cut off the teeming multitude of Thebes;
I will kindle a fire in Egypt, 16
And Pelusium shall writhe in anguish,
Thebes shall be split asunder, and Memphis reduced to gravel;
The young men of On and Bubastis 17
shall fall by the sword,
And their maidens shall go into exile;
At Daphne the day shall be dark, 18
When I break there the scepter of Egypt;
And her proud strength shall fail her,
A cloud shall cover her,
While her daughters go into exile.
Thus will I execute judgments upon 19
Egypt;
And they shall know that I am the LORD." ' "

THE BREAKING OF PHARAOH'S ARMS, 30:20–26

In the eleventh year, in the first 20
month, on the seventh day of the
month, the word of the LORD came to
me, saying,
"O mortal man, I have broken the 21
arm of Pharaoh, king of Egypt, and behold, it shall not be bound up, so that
healing applications may be used and
bandages put on, to make it strong
enough to grasp the sword.
"Therefore thus says the Lord GOD: 22

'Behold, I am against Pharaoh, king of
Egypt, and will break his arms, both
the strong one and the broken one, and
I will make the sword fall from his
23 hand. And I will scatter the Egyptians
among the nations, and disperse them
24 over the lands. And I will strengthen
the arms of the king of Babylon, and
will put my sword in his hand, while I
break the arms of Pharaoh, making him
groan before him like a man mortally
25 wounded. I will strengthen the arms of
the king of Babylon, while the arms of
Pharaoh fall; and they shall know that
I am the LORD, when I put my sword
into the hand of the king of Babylon,
and he stretches it over the land of
26 Egypt. So I will scatter the Egyptians
among the nations, and disperse them
over the lands; and they shall know
that I am the LORD.' "

THE CEDAR OF EGYPT, 31:1-18

31 In the eleventh year, in the third
month, on the first day of the month,
the word of the LORD came to me, saying,

2 "O mortal man, say to Pharaoh, king
of Egypt, and to his teeming multitude:
'Whom are you like in your greatness?
3 Like a stately cedar in Lebanon,
With graceful branches, and a thick shade of foliage,
Lofty in height, with its top among the clouds.
4 Waters nourished it, the deep made it grow,
Pouring her streams round its plantation,
And sending her channels to all the trees of the field.
5 So it towered aloft above all the trees of the field,
Its boughs increased in number, and its branches in length,
Through the wealth of water in its rills.
6 Among its boughs all the birds of the air made their nests,
And under its branches all the beasts of the field bore their young,
While within its shadow all mighty nations lived.
7 It was fair in its greatness, with the length of its branches;
For its root was by many waters.
8 The cedars in the garden of God could not eclipse it,
The cypresses could not match it in boughs,
Nor the plane-trees compare with it in branches;
There was no tree in the garden of God to match it in beauty.
9 By the wealth of its branches I made it fair,
So that all the trees of Eden, in the garden of God, envied it.'

10 "Therefore thus says the Lord GOD:
'Because it towered aloft, and raised its
top to the clouds, and prided itself on
11 its height, I am handing it over to the
mightiest of the nations, who shall surely deal with it in accordance with its
12 wickedness; and aliens, the most ruthless of the nations, shall cut it down,
and cast it upon the mountains; and its
branches shall fall into all the valleys,
and its boughs shall lie broken in all the
ravines of the land; and all the peoples
of the earth shall depart from its shadow in terror. Upon its fallen trunk shall
13 all the birds of the air nestle, and upon
its branches shall all the beasts of the
field be found, in order that no trees
14 nourished by water may tower aloft, or
raise their tops to the clouds—that no
trees feeding on water may rival them
in height—for all of them are doomed
to death, doomed to descend to the underworld, in the midst of the children
of men, with those who go down to the
Pit.'

15 "Thus says the Lord GOD: 'On the
day when it goes down to Sheol, I will
darken the deep, and check its streams
till the mighty waters are stayed; I will
clothe Lebanon in black for it, and all
the trees of the field shall droop in sorrow for it. I will make the nations
16 quake at the sound of its downfall,
when I bring it down to Sheol with
those who go down to the Pit. And all
the trees of Eden, the choicest and best
trees of Lebanon, all that feed on water,
shall be comforted in the underworld;
17 they also shall go down with it to Sheol,
to those who are slain by the sword,
while those who lived under its shadow
among the nations, shall likewise perish.

18 "Whomsoever, then, among the trees
of Eden you may resemble in glory and
greatness, you shall be brought down to
the underworld with the trees of Eden,
and shall lie in the midst of the uncircumcised with those who are slain by

the sword. Such shall be the fate of
Pharaoh and all his teeming multitude,'
is the oracle of the Lord GOD."

DIRGE OVER PHARAOH, 32:1–16

1 In the eleventh year, in the twelfth
month, on the first day of the month,
the word of the LORD came to me, saying,
2 "O mortal man, raise a dirge over
Pharaoh, king of Egypt, and say to him:
'To a young lion of the nations you
likened yourself,
When you are nought but a dragon in
the seas,
spouting water from your nostrils,
Troubling the waters with your feet,
and fouling their streams.'
3 "Thus says the Lord GOD:
'I will spread my net over you,
With a host of mighty peoples,
And I will draw you up in my seine,
4 And will cast you on the ground;
On the open field will I toss you.
I will cause all the birds of the air to
settle upon you,
And with you will I glut all the beasts
of the earth;
5 I will lay out your flesh on the mountains,
And with your bones will I fill the valleys;
6 I will drench the earth, to the mountain tops, with your flowing blood,
And the ravines shall be full of you.
7 And when I have done with you, I will
veil the heavens,
And will darken their stars;
I will veil the sun with a cloud,
And the moon shall not give her light;
8 All the shining lights of the heavens
will I darken over you,
And I will throw blackness upon your
land,'
Is the oracle of the Lord GOD.

9 "I will trouble the hearts of many
peoples when I announce your downfall
among the nations, to lands which you
10 never knew. I will make many peoples
appalled at your fate; and their kings
shall shudder with terror over you,
when I brandish my sword in their
sight. They shall tremble every moment, each for his own life, on the day
of your downfall.

"For thus says the Lord GOD: 11
'The sword of the king of Babylon shall
descend upon you,
And your teeming multitude will I 12
cause to fall by the swords of war-
riors,
All of them the most ruthless of nations.
They shall despoil the pride of Egypt,
And all her teeming multitude shall be
destroyed.
I will destroy likewise all her beasts 13
From beside many waters;
And no foot of man shall trouble them
any more,
Nor shall hoof of cattle trouble them.
Then will I cause their waters to settle, 14
And their rivers to flow with oil,'
Is the oracle of the Lord GOD.
'And when I have made the land of 15
Egypt a desolation,
When the land has been stripped of all
that fills it,
When I have smitten all who dwell in
it,
They shall know that I am the LORD.
This is the dirge which they shall chant, 16
Which the daughters of all the nations
shall chant,
Which they shall chant over Egypt
and all her teeming multitude,'
Is the oracle of the Lord GOD."

DIRGE OVER EGYPT, 32:17–32

In the twelfth year, in the first 17
month, on the fifteenth day of the
month, the word of the LORD came to
me, saying,
"O mortal man, wail over the teem- 18
ing multitude of Egypt, and with this
dirge send them down, you and the
daughters of mighty nations, to the underworld, with those who go down to
the Pit:
'Though you are incomparable in 19
beauty,
Go down, and be laid with the uncircumcised;
In the midst of those who are slain by 20
the sword
Lie down, you and all your teeming
multitude!'
Then out of the midst of Sheol shall the 21
mightiest of warriors speak of her and
her helpers:
'They have come down, and lie with
the uncircumcised
In the midst of those who are slain by
the sword.'

22 There is Assyria, with all her company
round about her grave, all of them slain,
23 fallen by the sword; her grave was made
in the recesses of the Pit, and her company
is round about her grave, all of
them slain, fallen by the sword, who
struck terror into the land of the living.
24 There is Elam, with all her teeming
multitude round about her grave, all of
them slain, fallen by the sword, gone
down uncircumcised to the underworld,
who struck terror into the land of the
living; and they bear the burden of
their shame with those who go down to
25 the Pit. In the midst of the slain a bed
was made for her and all her teeming
multitude round about her grave, all of
them uncircumcised, slain by the sword,
because they struck terror into the land
of the living; and they bear the burden
of their shame with those who go down
to the Pit; in the midst of the slain are
26 they placed. There are Meshech and
Tubal, with all their teeming multitude
round about their graves, all of them
uncircumcised, slain by the sword, because
they struck terror into the land of
27 the living. They lie not with the fallen
warriors of old, who went down to Sheol
with their weapons of war, whose
swords were laid under their heads, and
their shields upon their bodies, because
the terror of their might was on the land
28 of the living. So shall you also lie
among the uncircumcised, with those
29 who are slain by the sword. There is
Edom, her kings and all her princes,
who for all their might are laid with
those who are slain by the sword; they
lie with the uncircumcised, with those
30 who go down to the Pit. There are all
the princes of the north, and all the
Sidonians, who have gone down with
the slain, in shame, for all the terror of
their might, and lie uncircumcised with
those who are slain by the sword, and
bear the burden of their shame with
31 those who go down to the Pit. These
shall Pharaoh see, and be comforted for
all his teeming multitude who are slain
by the sword, even Pharaoh and all his
army," is the oracle of the Lord GOD.
32 "Because he struck terror into the land
of the living, he shall be laid in the
midst of the uncircumcised, with those
who are slain by the sword, even Pharaoh
and all his teeming multitude," is
the oracle of the Lord GOD.

THE PROPHET AS WATCHMAN, 33:1–20

The word of the LORD came to me, saying,
"O mortal man, speak to your fellow-countrymen, and say to them: 'If, when I bring the sword upon a land, the people of the land take one of their number, and appoint him their watchman; and if, when he sees the sword coming upon the land, he blow the trumpet, and warn the people; then whosoever hears the sound of the trumpet but does not take warning—when the sword does come and take him away, his blood shall be upon his own head. He heard the sound of the trumpet but did not take warning, therefore his blood shall be upon his own head; whereas, if he had taken warning, he would have saved himself. But if the watchman, when he sees the sword coming, blow not the trumpet, and the people be not warned—when the sword does come and take away one of their number, that man is taken away for his iniquity, but his blood will I require at the watchman's hand. So you, O mortal man, I appoint as a watchman to the house of Israel; and whenever you hear a word from my mouth, you shall warn them from me. If I say to the wicked, 'O wicked man, you shall surely die,' and you say nothing to warn the wicked man from his way, that wicked man shall die for his iniquity, but his blood will I require at your hand. If, however, you warn the wicked man to turn from his way, and he turn not from his way, he shall die for his iniquity, but you shall have saved yourself.'

"Therefore, O mortal man, say to the house of Israel: 'Because you say, "Our transgressions and our sins lie upon us, and under them we waste away; how then can we live?" as I live,' is the oracle of the Lord GOD, 'I have no pleasure in the death of the wicked, but rather in this, that the wicked man turn from his way and live. Turn, O turn, from your evil ways! Why should you die, O house of Israel?'

"And you, O mortal man, say to your fellow-countrymen: 'The righteousness of the righteous man shall not save him on the day of his transgression; and the wickedness of the wicked man shall not

bring about his downfall on the day
when he turns from his wickedness.
The righteous man shall not be able to
save himself by his righteousness on the
13 day when he falls into sin. If I say to
the righteous man, "You shall surely
live," and he trust in his righteousness,
and do wrong, none of his righteous
deeds shall be remembered, but for the
wrong which he has done he shall die.
14 And if I say to the wicked man, "You
shall surely die," and he turn from his
sin, and do what is lawful and right—
15 if the wicked man restore the pledge,
repay what he has taken by robbery,
follow the statutes that lead to life, and
do no wrong, he shall surely live, and
16 not die. None of the sins which he has
committed shall be remembered against
him; because he has done what is lawful
17 and right, he shall surely live. Yet your
fellow-countrymen say, "The way of
the Lord is not fair," when it is their
18 way which is not fair! If the righteous
man turn from his righteousness, and
19 do wrong, he shall die for it. And if the
wicked man turn from his wickedness,
and do what is lawful and right, he shall
20 live by it. Yet you say, "The way of
the Lord is not fair." O house of Israel,
I will judge you each according to his
ways.' "

NEWS OF THE CAPTURE OF JERUSALEM, 33:21–33

21 In the eleventh year of our exile, in
the tenth month, on the fifth day of the
month, a fugitive from Jerusalem came
to me, saying,
"The city is smitten."
22 Now the hand of the LORD had been
upon me the evening before the fugitive
came; but he opened my mouth at the
moment when he came to me in the
morning, and when my mouth was
23 opened I was no longer dumb. Then the
word of the LORD came to me, saying,
24 "O mortal man, those who inhabit
these ruins in the land of Israel keep on
saying, 'Abraham was but one man,
yet he received possession of the land;
now, we being many, the land will
surely be given to us as a possession.'
25 Therefore say to them, 'Thus says the
Lord GOD: You eat flesh with the
blood in it, you lift up your eyes to your
idols, you shed blood, and shall you
26 have possession of the land? You resort
to the sword, you commit abominations, you defile one another's wives, and
shall you have possession of the land?'
Say to them, 'Thus says the Lord GOD: 27
As I live, those in the ruins shall fall by
the sword, and those in the open field
will I give to the beasts as food, and
those in the fastnesses and caves shall
die of pestilence. And I will make the 28
land a desolation and a waste; its proud
strength shall fail, and the mountains
of Israel shall be desolate, with none to
cross them. And they shall know that 29
I am the LORD, when I make the land
a desolation and a waste, because of all
the abominations which they have
committed.'
"As for you, O mortal man, your fel- 30
low-countrymen who talk of you by the
walls and at the doors of the houses say
to one another, 'Come and hear what
the word is that comes from the LORD!'
They come to you, as my people used to 31
come; and they sit before you, as if they
were still my people: they listen to your
words, but they will not obey them; for
with their mouths they make a show of
love, but their minds are set upon their
own selfish gain. You are to them like 32
a singer of love songs, with a beautiful
voice, and able to play well on the instrument; they listen to your words,
but they will not obey them. Only when 33
the hour comes—and it is coming—
they shall know that a prophet has been
in the midst of them."

PROPHECY AGAINST THE SHEPHERDS OF ISRAEL, 34:1–31

The word of the LORD came to me, 34
saying,
"O mortal man, prophesy against the 2
shepherds of Israel; prophesy, and say
to them, 'Thus says the Lord GOD:
Woe to the shepherds of Israel, who
have attended to themselves! Should
not shepherds attend to the flock? But 3
you have fed on the milk, and have
clothed yourselves with the wool; you
have slaughtered the fatlings, and have
not tended the flock. You have neither 4
strengthened the weak, nor healed the
sick, nor bound up the wounded, nor
brought back the strayed, nor sought
out the lost; and with rigor have you
ruled the strong. So my flock was scat- 5
tered for want of a shepherd, and became food to all the beasts of the field;

6 my flock wandered over all the mountains, and over every high hill; my flock
was scattered over all the face of the
earth, with none to seek or search for
them.'
7 "Therefore, O shepherds, hear the
8 word of the LORD! 'As I live,' is the
oracle of the Lord GOD, 'since my flock
has become a prey, and my flock has
become food to all the beasts of the
field, for want of a shepherd—because
the shepherds did not care for my flock,
but attended to themselves, and did not
attend to my flock'—therefore, O shep-
9 herds, hear the word of the LORD!
10 'Thus says the Lord GOD: Behold, I
am against the shepherds, and will require my flock at their hand; I will stop
them from attending to my flock, so
that the shepherds may no longer attend to themselves; and I will save my
flock from their mouths, so that they
may not be food to them.'
11 "For thus says the Lord GOD: 'Behold, here am I, and I will seek and
12 search for my flock. As a shepherd
searches for his flock on a day of whirlwind, when his sheep are scattered, so
will I search for my flock, and rescue
them from all the places to which they
have been scattered on the day of clouds
13 and thick darkness. I will lead them
out of the nations, and gather them
from the lands; and I will bring them
to their own country, and tend them on
the mountains of Israel, in the valleys,
14 and in all the best places of the land. In
good pasture will I tend them, and on
the high mountains of Israel shall be
their fold; there shall they lie down in a
good fold, and on rich pasture shall they
15 graze on the mountains of Israel. I myself will tend my flock, and I myself
will lead them to their pasture,' is the
16 oracle of the Lord GOD. 'I will seek out
the lost, I will bring back the strayed,
I will bind up the wounded, I will
strengthen the sick; and I will watch
over the fat and strong ones, tending
17 them rightly.' And as for you, O my
flock, thus says the Lord GOD: 'Behold, I will judge between sheep and
18 sheep. But as for the rams and he-
goats, is it not enough for you to graze
on the good pasture, that you must
trample the rest of the pasture beneath
your feet; and to drink of the clear
water, that you must foul the rest with
your feet, compelling my flock to graze
on that which you have trampled beneath your feet, and to drink that
which you have fouled with your feet?'
"Therefore thus says the Lord GOD
to them: 'Behold, here am I, and I will
judge between the fat sheep and the
lean sheep. Because you push with side
and shoulder, and butt at all the weak
ones with your horns, till you have scattered them abroad, I will save my sheep,
so that they may no longer be a prey,
and I will judge between sheep and
sheep. And I will set up one shepherd
over them, to tend them, even my
servant David, who shall tend them,
and be a shepherd to them. I the LORD
will be their God, and my servant
David shall be prince among them—I
the LORD have spoken it. I will make
with them a covenant of peace, and I
will remove wild beasts out of the land,
so that they may live securely in the
steppes, and sleep in the woods. And I
will bless them round about my hill,
and will send down the showers in their
season—showers of blessing shall they
be. Then the trees of the field shall
yield their fruit, and the earth shall
yield her produce; they shall live securely on their land; and they shall
know that I am the LORD, when I
break the bars of their yoke, and rescue
them from the hands of those who enslaved them. And they shall no longer
be a prey to the nations, nor shall the
beasts of the earth devour them; but
they shall live securely, with none to
make them afraid. I will provide for
them a soil renowned for fruitfulness,
and they shall no longer be consumed
with hunger in the land, and no longer
bear the reproach of the nations. Thus
they shall know that I, the LORD, am
their God, and that they, the house of
Israel, are my people,' is the oracle of
the Lord GOD. 'And you my flock are
the flock of my pasture, and I the
LORD am your God,' is the oracle of
the Lord GOD."

PROPHECY AGAINST MOUNT SEIR, 35:1–15

The word of the LORD came to me,
saying,
"O mortal man, set your face against
Mount Seir, and prophesy against it,
and say to it, 'Thus says the Lord GOD:

Behold, I am against you, O Mount
Seir; and I will stretch out my hand
against you, and make you a desolation
4 and a waste; your cities will I lay waste,
and you shall be a desolation; so shall
5 you know that I am the LORD. Because you kept up a perpetual enmity
against the children of Israel, and
handed them over to the sword at the
time of their calamity—the time of
6 their final doom; therefore as I live,' is
the oracle of the Lord GOD, 'I will hold
you guilty of bloodshed, and blood shall
7 pursue you. I will make Mount Seir a
desolation and a waste; I will cut off from
it him that comes and him that goes,
8 and will fill its mountains with its slain;
over your hills and valleys, and over all
your ravines, shall men fall slain by the
9 sword. I will make you a perpetual desolation, and your cities shall remain
uninhabited; so shall you know that I
10 am the LORD. Because you said, "The
two nations and the two lands shall be
mine, and I will take possession of
11 them"—when the LORD was in them;
therefore as I live,' is the oracle of the
Lord GOD, 'I will treat you in accordance with the anger and indignation
with which you treated them in your
hatred against them, and I will reveal
my character among you when I punish
12 you. And you shall know that I the
LORD have heard all the insults which
you have uttered against the mountains
of Israel, saying, "They are our possession; they are given to us as food."
13 And because you spoke many boastful
words against me with your mouth—
14 and I heard them—therefore thus says
the Lord GOD: When the whole earth
rejoices, I will make you a desolation.
15 As you rejoiced over the heritage of the
house of Israel, because it was a desolation, so will I deal with you. A desolation shall you be, O Mount Seir, and
the whole of Edom a ruin; so shall they
know that I am the LORD.' "

THE RESTORATION OF THE LAND OF ISRAEL, 36:1–15

36 "And you, O mortal man, prophesy
to the mountains of Israel, and say, 'O
mountains of Israel, hear the word of
2 the LORD! Thus says the Lord GOD:
"Because the enemy jeered over you,
saying, 'Aha! the ancient heights have
become our possession,' " ' therefore 3
prophesy and say, 'Thus says the Lord
GOD: Because you have been snarled
and snapped at from every side, to become the possession of the rest of the
nations, and made the subject of talk
and gossip to the people, therefore, O 4
mountains of Israel, hear the word of
the Lord GOD! Thus says the Lord
GOD to the mountains and the hills, the
ravines and the valleys, the desolate
wastes and the deserted cities, which
have become a prey and derision to the
rest of the nations that are round about:
In the fire of my indignation I speak 5
against the rest of the nations, and
against Edom, the whole of it, who with
intense glee and maliciousness of heart
took over my land as a possession for
themselves, to hold it as a prey.' There- 6
fore prophesy over the land of Israel,
and say to the mountains and the hills,
the ravines and the valleys, 'Thus says
the Lord GOD: "Behold, I speak in my
indignation and fury, because you have
borne the reproach of the nations.
Therefore thus says the Lord GOD: I 7
swear by uplifted hand that the nations
which are round about you shall bear
their reproach. But you, O mountains 8
of Israel, shall put forth your branches
and bear your fruit for my people Israel,
because they shall shortly come. For 9
behold, I am for you, and will look to
you, and will see that you are tilled and
sown. And I will plant upon you a large 10
population, even the whole house of
Israel, so that the cities may be re-
peopled and the waste places rebuilt. I 11
will plant upon you a large population
of men and beasts, who shall increase
and be fruitful; and I will settle you as
in former days, and treat you better
than at first; so shall you know that I
am the LORD. And I will cause men to 12
be born upon you, my people Israel,
and they shall have possession of you,
and you shall be their heritage, and
shall no longer make them childless.
Thus says the Lord GOD: Because men 13
keep saying to you, 'You are a devourer
of men, you make your people childless,' therefore you shall no longer de- 14
vour men, and shall no longer make
your people childless," ' is the oracle of
the Lord GOD; 'and I will no longer 15
permit the taunts of the nations to be
heard against you, and no longer shall
you have to bear the reproach of the

peoples, for no longer shall you make
your people childless,' is the oracle of
the Lord GOD."

THE REGENERATION OF THE PEOPLE, 36:16–38

16 The word of the LORD came to me,
saying,
17 "O mortal man, when the house of
Israel lived in their own land, they defiled it by their ways and their doings;
like the foulness of a woman in her time
of uncleanness were their ways in my
18 sight. So I poured out my fury upon
them for the blood which they had shed
upon the land, and for the defilement
which they had brought upon it through
19 their idols. I scattered them among the
nations, and dispersed them over the
lands: in accordance with their ways
20 and their doings I punished them. But
when they arrived among the nations to
which they came, and caused my holy
name to be profaned, in that men said
of them, 'These are the people of the
LORD, and they have gone out of his
21 land,' I was grieved for my holy name
which the house of Israel had caused to
be profaned among the nations to which
22 they came. Therefore say to the house
of Israel, 'Thus says the Lord GOD: It
is not for your sake that I am about to
act, O house of Israel, but for my holy
name which you have caused to be profaned among the nations to which you
23 came. I will restore the holiness of my
great name which has been profaned
among the nations—the name which
you have caused to be profaned in the
midst of them—and when I restore my
holiness in their sight, through my dealings with you, the nations shall know
that I am the LORD,' is the oracle of
24 the Lord GOD. 'For I will take you out
of the nations, and gather you from all
the lands; and I will bring you to your
25 own land. I will sprinkle pure water
over you, and you shall be pure: from
all your impurities, and from all your
26 idolatries, will I purify you. I will give
you a new heart, and will put within
you a new spirit; I will remove the
heart of stone out of your flesh, and will
27 give you a heart of flesh; and I will put
my spirit within you, and make you
follow my statutes and be careful to
28 observe my ordinances. You shall live
in the land which I gave to your
fathers; and you shall be my people,
and I will be your God. I will save you
from all your impurities. And I will call
to the grain, and make it abundant,
allowing no famine to come upon you.
I will also make the fruit of the trees
and the produce of the fields abundant,
so that you may no longer bear among
the nations the reproach of famine.
Then shall you remember your evil 3
ways, and your doings that were not
good; and you shall loathe yourselves
for your sinful and abominable deeds.
But be it known to you, it is not for 3
your sake that I am doing this,' is the
oracle of the Lord GOD; 'therefore be
ashamed and abashed for your ways, O
house of Israel!'
"Thus says the Lord GOD: On the 3
day when I purify you from all your
iniquities, I will have the cities re-
peopled, and the waste places rebuilt.
And the land that was desolate shall be 3
tilled once more, instead of lying a
desolation under the eyes of every passer-by; and men shall say, 'Yonder land 3
that was desolate has become like the
garden of Eden; and the cities that were
waste, desolate, and ruined are now
fortified and inhabited.' Then the na- 3
tions that are left round about you shall
know that I the LORD have rebuilt the
ruined cities, and replanted the desolate
wastes. I the LORD have spoken it, and
I will do it.
"Thus says the Lord GOD: This also 3
will I let the house of Israel ask me to
do for them—to make their people as
numerous as a flock. Like the flock for 3
a sacrifice, like the flock at Jerusalem
during her festivals, so shall the cities
that were laid waste be filled with a
flock of men; and they shall know that
I am the LORD."

THE VISION OF THE VALLEY, 37:1–14

The hand of the LORD was upon me; 3
and the LORD carried me out by the
spirit, and set me down in the midst of
a valley which was full of bones. He led
me all round them, and lo! there were
very many of them on the surface of the
valley, and lo! they were very dry.
Then he said to me,
"O mortal man, can these bones
live?"
And I answered,

"O Lord GOD, thou knowest."
4 Then he said to me,
"Prophesy over these bones, and say
to them, 'O dry bones, hear the word of
5 the LORD! Thus says the Lord GOD to
these bones: Behold, I am causing
breath to enter you, and you shall live.
6 I will put sinews upon you, and will
clothe you with flesh, and cover you
with skin; then I will put breath into
you, and you shall live; and you shall
know that I am the LORD.' "
7 So I prophesied as I had been commanded; and as I prophesied, there was
a sound; and lo! there followed a rustling; and the bones came together, bone
8 to its bone. And as I looked, lo! there
were sinews upon them, and flesh came
up, and skin covered them over; but
9 there was no breath in them. Then he
said to me,
"Prophesy to the breath; prophesy,
O mortal man, and say to the breath,
'Thus says the Lord GOD: Come from
the four winds, O breath, and breathe
into these slain men, that they may
live!' "
10 So I prophesied as he had commanded me; and the breath came into them,
and they lived, and stood upon their
11 feet—an exceedingly great host. Then
he said to me,
"O mortal man, these bones are the
whole house of Israel. Behold, they
keep saying, 'Our bones are dried up,
and our hope is lost; we are completely
12 cut off.' Therefore prophesy, and say
to them, 'Thus says the Lord GOD:
Behold, I am opening your graves, and
will raise you out of your graves, O my
people, and will bring you into the land
13 of Israel. And when I open your graves,
and raise you out of your graves, O my
people, you shall know that I am the
14 LORD. Then I will put my spirit into
you, and you shall live; and I will settle
you on your own land; and you shall
know that I am the LORD. I have
spoken it, and I will do it,' is the oracle
of the LORD."

THE ALLEGORY OF THE TWO STICKS, 37:15–28

15 The word of the LORD came to me,
saying,
"O mortal man, take a stick, and 16
write on it, 'Of Judah and the children
of Israel associated with him'; then
take another stick, and write on it, 'Of
Joseph and all the house of Israel associated with him.' Join them together, so 17
as to form a single stick in your hand.
And when your fellow-countrymen ask 18
you, 'Will you not tell us what you mean
by these things?' say to them, 'Thus 19
says the Lord GOD: Behold, I am taking the stick of Joseph (which is in the
hand of Ephraim) and the tribes of Israel associated with him, and I will
unite it with the stick of Judah, making
them a single stick in my hand.' And, 20
keeping the sticks on which you have
written in your hand before their eyes,
say to them, 'Thus says the Lord GOD: 21
Behold, I am taking the children of Israel from the midst of the nations to
which they have gone, and I will gather
them from every side, and bring them
into their own land; and I will make 22
them a single nation in the land, upon
the mountains of Israel; and a single
king shall be king over them all—they
shall no longer be two nations, and shall
no longer be divided into two kingdoms. And they shall no longer defile 23
themselves with their idolatries, their
foul practices, and all their other transgressions; for I will save them from all
their sinful apostasies, and will keep
them pure; so shall they be my people,
and I will be their God. And my serv- 24
ant David shall be king over them—
there shall be a single shepherd for all of
them—and they shall follow my ordinances and be careful to observe my
statutes. And they shall live on the 25
land that I gave to Jacob my servant,
the land in which their fathers lived;
they and their children and their children's children shall live on it forever,
and David my servant shall be their
prince forever. I will make with them a 26
covenant of peace—an everlasting covenant shall it be with them—and I will
bless them and multiply them. I will
set my sanctuary in the midst of them
forever, and my dwelling-place shall be 27
with them; and I will be their God, and
they shall be my people. And when my 28
sanctuary is set in the midst of them
forever, the nations shall know that I
the LORD am setting Israel apart for
myself.' "

THE OVERTHROW OF GOG,
38:1—39:29

38 The word of the LORD came to me,
saying,
2 "O mortal man, set your face toward
Gog, of the land of Magog, the great
prince of Meshech and Tubal, and
3 prophesy against him, and say, 'Thus
says the Lord GOD: Behold, I am
against you, O Gog, the great prince of
4 Meshech and Tubal; I will turn you
round, and put hooks in your jaws; and
I will lead you out, with all your army,
horses, and horsemen, all of them in
full panoply, a mighty host, equipped
with buckler and shield, all of them
5 wielding the sword—Persia, Cush, and
Put, all of them equipped with shield
6 and helmet, together with Gomer and
all his hordes, the house of Togarmah
and all their hordes, from the farthest
7 north—many a people with you. Be
ready, and keep ready, you and all your
host mustered about you; keep yourself
8 in reserve for me. For after many days
you shall be called up for service, in the
end of the years you shall march
against a land restored from desolation,
and inhabited by a people gathered
from many a nation, against the mountains
of Israel that were once a perpetual
waste, but are now inhabited by a
people brought home from the nations,
9 all of them living in security—you shall
advance like a storm, you shall come
like a cloud covering the land, you and
all your hordes, and many a people
with you.
10 "Thus says the Lord GOD: On that
day shall thoughts come into your
mind, and you shall plan a mischievous
11 scheme, saying, 'I will march against
this land of open villages, I will fall
upon these quiet people who live in security,
all of them undefended by wall or
12 bar or gates,' to despoil them, and prey
upon them, to bring down your hand
against the re-inhabited wastes, and
against the people gathered from the
nations, who are peacefully acquiring
cattle and goods, as they live at the
13 center of the earth. Sheba and Dedan,
the merchants of Tarshish, and all her
magnates, shall say to you, 'Was it to
despoil them that you came? Was it to
prey upon them that you mustered
your host? Was it to carry off silver
and gold, to seize cattle and goods, to
take great spoil?' Therefore prophesy,
O mortal man, and say to Gog, 'Thus
says the Lord GOD: On that day when
my people Israel are living in security,
shall you not bestir yourself and come
from your place in the farthest north—
you and many a people with you, all of
them riding on horseback, a great host,
a mighty army—and fall upon my people
Israel like a cloud covering the land?
It shall come to pass in the end of the
days that I will bring you against my
land, so that the nations may know me,
when I reveal my holiness in their sight,
through my dealings with you, O Gog.'

"Thus says the Lord GOD: 'You are
the one whom in former days, through
my servants the prophets of Israel,
who prophesied in those days, I threatened
to bring against them. But on
that day when Gog shall invade the
land of Israel,' is the oracle of the Lord
GOD, 'my fury shall rise in my nostrils.
In my indignation and the fire of my
wrath, I swear: On that day there shall
be an earthquake in the land of Israel,
so great that the fish of the sea, the
birds of the air, the beasts of the field,
all the reptiles that creep upon the
ground, and every human being upon
the surface of the earth, shall tremble
at my presence, the mountains shall be
torn down, the cliffs shall tumble, and
every wall shall fall to the ground. I
will summon against him every kind of
terror,' is the oracle of the Lord GOD,
'and every man's sword shall be against
his brother; I will proceed against him
also with pestilence and bloodshed; and
I will rain upon him and his hordes, and
upon the many peoples that are with
him, a lashing rain, accompanied by
hailstones, fire, and brimstone. So will
I reveal my greatness and my holiness,
and will make myself known in the sight
of many nations; and they shall know
that I am the LORD.'

"And you, O mortal man, prophesy
against Gog, and say, 'Thus says the
Lord GOD: Behold, I am against you,
O Gog, the great prince of Meshech and
Tubal; I will turn you round, and drive
you on; I will bring you up from the
farthest north, and lead you against the
mountains of Israel; then I will strike
your bow from your left hand, and spill
your arrows from your right hand. You
shall fall upon the mountains of Israel,
you and all your hordes, and the peo-

ples that are with you; to ravenous
birds of every sort, and to the beasts of
5 the field, will I leave you as food. On
the open field shall you lie; for I have
spoken it,' is the oracle of the Lord
6 GOD. 'And I will send fire against Magog, and against those who live securely
in the coast-lands; so shall they know
7 that I am the LORD. I will reveal my
holy name in the midst of my people Israel, and no longer allow my holy name
to be profaned; so shall the nations
know that I am the LORD, the Holy
8 One of Israel. Lo! it comes, and it shall
be,' is the oracle of the Lord GOD:
9 'this is the day of which I spoke. Then
shall those who live in the cities of Israel go out and make firewood of the
weapons—the shields and bucklers, the
bows and arrows, the handpikes and
spears—for seven years shall they make
10 firewood of them, and shall not need to
take wood from the fields, nor to cut it
from the forests, because they shall
make firewood of the weapons; so shall
they despoil those who despoiled them,
and prey upon those who preyed upon
them,' is the oracle of the Lord GOD.
11 "And on that day will I give Gog a
burial place that shall bear his name in
Israel, even the valley of Abarim, east
of the Dead Sea: men shall stop up the
valley of Abarim, and there shall they
bury Gog and all his mob; and they
shall call it, 'The Valley of Gog's mob.'
12 For seven months shall the house of Israel be engaged in burying them, in
13 order to purify the land—all the people
of the land shall be engaged in burying
them—and it shall bring them fame on
the day when I reveal my glory," is the
14 oracle of the Lord GOD. "And they
shall set apart a standing commission of
men who shall pass through the land,
searching for those who remain unburied on the surface of the land, to
purify it. At the end of seven months
15 shall they begin the search. And when
they pass through the land, and one of
them sees a man's body, he shall set up
a mark beside it, till the burial parties
have buried it in the valley of Gog's
16 mob. There shall they bury the whole
mob, and thus purify the land.
17 "And as for you, O mortal man, thus
says the Lord GOD: Say to the birds of
every sort, and to all the beasts of the
field, 'Assemble and come, gather from
every quarter, to the sacrificial feast
which I am preparing for you upon the
mountains of Israel, a great sacrificial
feast, at which you shall eat flesh and
drink blood; you shall eat the flesh of 18
warriors, and drink the blood of princes
of the earth, all of them rams, lambs,
and he-goats, bullocks, and fatlings of
Bashan; you shall eat fat till you are 19
glutted, and drink blood till you are
drunk, at the sacrificial feast which I
prepare for you; at my table you shall 20
be glutted with horses and horsemen,
warriors and soldiers of every sort,' is
the oracle of the Lord GOD. Thus will 21
I manifest my glory among the nations;
and all the nations shall see the judgments that I execute, and the hand that
I lay upon them. And from that day 22
onward the house of Israel shall know
that I am the LORD their God. The na- 23
tions also shall know that the house of
Israel went into exile for their iniquity,
because they dealt treacherously with
me, for which reason I hid my face from
them, and handed them over to their
adversaries, and they fell all of them by
the sword; in accordance with their un- 24
cleanness and their transgressions I
dealt with them, and hid my face from
them. Therefore thus says the Lord 25
GOD: Now will I restore the fortune of
Jacob, and have pity upon the whole
house of Israel, and be zealous for my
holy name. They shall forget their 26
shame, and all the treason which they
committed against me, when they live
securely on their own land, with none to
make them afraid, when I have brought 27
them back from the peoples, and have
gathered them out of the lands of their
enemies, and have revealed my holiness
in the sight of many nations through
my dealings with them. And they shall 28
know that I am the LORD their God in
that I sent them into exile among the
nations, but now have gathered them
into their own land, and will no longer
leave any of them in exile, nor any long- 29
er hide my face from them; for I have
poured out my spirit upon the house of
Israel,' is the oracle of the Lord GOD."

THE NEW TEMPLE,
40:1—42:20

In the twenty-fifth year of our exile, 40
in the first month of the year, on the
tenth day of the month—this was the
fourteenth year after the city had been

smitten—on that very day the hand of
2 the LORD was upon me, and he brought
me in visions of God to the land of Israel, and set me on a very high mountain, on which was a building laid out
3 like a city over against me. He brought
me there, and lo! there was a man
whose appearance was like bronze,
with a line of flax and a measuring rod
4 in his hand, standing at the gate. And
the man said to me,

"O mortal man, look, listen, and attend to all that I show you—for you
were brought here in order that I might
show them to you—then tell the house
of Israel all that you see."

5 And lo! there was a wall running all
round the outside of the building. And
the man measured it with the measuring-rod in his hand, which was six cubits long, each cubit being equivalent
to a cubit and a handbreadth; and he
found it one rod in breadth and one rod
in height.

6 Then he brought me to the gate looking east; and when he had climbed the
steps of it, he measured the threshold of
the gate, which was one rod broad.
7 Each of the guard-rooms was one rod
long, and one rod broad; and between
the guard-rooms was a space of five
8 cubits. The threshold also of the gate
at the vestibule leading into the build-
9 ing was one rod. Then he measured the
vestibule, which was eight cubits broad,
with its jambs each two cubits broad.
10 The guard-rooms of the east gate were
three on each side, all of the same size;
while the jambs on each side were also
11 of the same size. Then he measured the
breadth of the gateway, ten cubits; and
the length of the gateway, thirteen cu-
12 bits. In front of each guard-room was a
platform, one cubit square, the guard-
rooms themselves being six cubits
13 square. Then he measured the gate
from the back of one guard-room to the
back of the other, a breadth of twenty-
14 five cubits, from door to door. Then he
measured the length of the vestibule,
twenty cubits, where the inner court
15 abutted on the vestibule. Thus from
the outside front of the gate to the inside front of the vestibule were fifty cu-
16 bits. And the guard-rooms had latticed
windows on the inside of the gateway
round about; the vestibule also had
windows on the inside round about;
while on each jamb were palm trees.

Then he brought me to the outer 17
court; and lo! there was a pavement
round about the court, with thirty
chambers fronting on it. The pavement 18
ran along the sides of the gates, and
was as broad as they were long—this
was the lower pavement. And he meas- 19
ured the breadth from the inside front
of the outer gate to the outside front of
the inner court, a hundred cubits.

Then he brought me to the north 20
gate of the outer court, and measured
its length and its breadth. This gate 21
had three guard-rooms on each side,
with jambs and vestibule, of the same
size as those of the first gate. It was
fifty cubits in length, and twenty-five
cubits in breadth. It had windows, ves- 22
tibule, and palm trees, of the same size
as those of the east gate. It was reached
by a stairway of seven steps; and its
vestibule was on the inside. And the 23
inner court had a gate opposite this
north gate, corresponding to the gate
on the east; and he measured from gate
to gate, a hundred cubits.

Then he led me southward; and lo! 24
there was a gate looking south. He
measured its jamb and vestibule, and
found them of the same size as the
others. The gate and its vestibule had 25
windows round about, of the same size
as the others. It was fifty cubits in
length, and twenty-five cubits in
breadth. It also had a stairway of sev- 26
en steps; and its vestibule was on the
inside. It had palm trees on its jambs,
one on each side. And the inner court 27
had a gate opposite this south gate; and
he measured from gate to gate, a hundred cubits.

Then he brought me to the inner 28
court by the south gate; and he measured the south gate, with its guard- 29
rooms, jambs, and vestibule, and found
them of the same size as the others.
The gate and its vestibule had windows
round about; and it was fifty cubits in
length, and twenty-five cubits in
breadth. Its vestibule was twenty cu- 30
bits long, and five cubits broad; and the 31
vestibule faced the inner court. Palm
trees were on its jambs; and its stairway had eight steps.

Then he brought me to the inner 32
court on the east side; and he measured
the gate, with its guard-rooms, jambs, 33
and vestibule, and found them of the
same size as the others. The gate and

its vestibule had windows round about;
and it was fifty cubits in length, and
34 twenty-five cubits in breadth. Its vestibule faced the outer court; and palm
trees were on its jambs, on each side;
and its stairway had eight steps.
35 Then he brought me to the north
gate, and measured it, with its guard-
36 rooms, jambs, and vestibule, and found
them of the same size as the others. It
also had windows round about. It was
fifty cubits in length, and twenty-five
37 cubits in breadth. Its vestibule faced
the outer court; and palm trees were on
its jambs, on either side; and its stairway had eight steps.
38 There was a chamber opening into
the vestibule of the gate, in which they
39 were to wash the burnt-offerings. And
in the vestibule of the gate there were
two tables on each side, for the purpose
of slaughtering the burnt-offerings, the
sin-offerings, and the guilt-offerings;
40 and outside the vestibule, as one approached the entrance of the north
gate, there were two tables on each side
41 —that is, four tables inside, and four
tables outside the gateway—eight tables in all, on which they were to
42 slaughter the sacrifices. In addition,
there were four tables of hewn stone,
each a cubit and a half long, a cubit and
a half broad, and a cubit high, on which
they were to lay the instruments for
slaughtering the burnt-offerings and
43 the sacrifices. And pegs, a handbreadth
long, were fastened on the walls round
about, on which to hang the flesh of the
sacrifices.
44 Then he brought me through the gate
to the inner court; and lo! there were
two chambers in the inner court, one by
the north gate, facing south, and the
other by the south gate, facing north.
45 And he said to me,
"This chamber, facing south, is for
the priests who have charge of the
46 house; and the other chamber, facing
north, is for the priests who have charge
of the altar, that is, for the sons of
Zadok, who alone among the sons of
Levi may approach the LORD, to minister to him."
47 Then he measured the court, and
found it a hundred cubits long, and a
hundred cubits broad—a square. And
the altar stood in front of the house.
48 Then he brought me to the vestibule
of the house, and measured the jambs
of the vestibule, which were five cubits
broad on each side. The gate was fourteen cubits broad, and the sides of the
gate were each three cubits broad. The 49
length of the vestibule was twenty cubits, and the breadth twelve cubits. It
was reached by a stairway of ten steps.
And pillars stood beside the jambs, one
on each side.
Then he brought me to the nave of 41
the house, and measured the jambs,
which were six cubits broad on each
side. The breadth of the door was ten 2
cubits, the leaves of the door being five
cubits each. Then he measured the
nave, which was forty cubits long and
twenty cubits broad.
Then he entered the inner room, and 3
measured the jambs of the door, which
were two cubits each; while the breadth
of the door was six cubits, the leaves of
the door being three cubits each. Then 4
he measured the room, which was twenty cubits long, and twenty cubits
broad, in front of the nave. And he said
to me,
"This is the most sacred place."
Then he measured the wall of the 5
house, which was six cubits broad, with
side chambers four cubits broad all
round the house. These side chambers 6
were in three stories, thirty in each
story; and there were rebatements in
the wall, all round the house, for the
chambers to rest on, so that they might
not rest on the flat wall of the house.
The side chambers increased in breadth 7
as they rose upward; for the rebatements round about the house increased
in depth as they rose upward, causing
the wall of the house to contract in
breadth as it rose upward. From the
lowest story one rose through the middle story to the upper. And round 8
about the house ran a raised platform,
a full rod of six cubits and six handbreadths high, which formed the foundation of the side chambers. The out- 9
side wall of the side chambers was five
cubits broad; and between the side 10
chambers of the house and the row of
chambers in the court lay a yard, twenty cubits broad, all round the house.
The doors of the side chambers opened 11
on a free space, one door to the north,
and another to the south; and the free
space was five cubits broad round
about. On the west side of the yard was 12
a building seventy cubits broad; and the

wall surrounding the building was five
cubits broad, and ninety cubits long.
13 Then he measured the house, a hundred cubits long; and the yard, with its
building and walls, a hundred cubits
14 long; while the east front of the house,
with the yard, was a hundred cubits
15 broad. Then he measured the building
on the west side of the yard, with its
walls on either side, a hundred cubits
long.
16 The nave, the inner room, and the
vestibule were roofed over; and all
three had latticed windows round
about. The inside walls of the house
were paneled with wood round about,
from the floor to the windows, and
17 from the windows to the roof, as well as
over the door leading to the inner
room, within and without. And on all
the walls round about, in the inner
18 room and in the nave, there were
carved cherubim and palm trees, palm
tree alternating with cherub, and each
19 cherub with two faces, a man's face
looking to the palm tree on one side,
and a lion's face to the palm tree on the
other side. These were carved all round
20 the house; from the floor to the roof
there were carved cherubim and palm
21 trees. The wall of the shrine was a
square; and in front of the shrine was
22 something resembling an altar of wood,
three cubits high, two cubits long, and
two cubits broad, its corners, base, and
sides being all of wood. And he said to
me,
"This is the table which stands before the LORD."
23 The nave and the shrine had each a
24 double door, each door having two
swinging leaves, one pair for each door.
25 Cherubim and palm trees were carved
on these, as they were carved on the
walls. There was also a canopy of wood
26 outside in front of the vestibule. And
there were cherubim and palm trees on
both side walls of the vestibule, and on
the canopy.
42 Then he led me to the inner court on
the north, and brought me to a row of
chambers facing the yard and its build-
2 ings on the north. Their length was a
hundred cubits, and their breadth fifty
3 cubits. On opposite sides of the row,
facing respectively the yard of twenty
cubits in the inner court, and the pavement in the outer court, galleries rose
4 in three stories. In front of the chambers was a passage, ten cubits broad,
and a hundred cubits long; and the
doors of the chambers opened on it to
the north. The chambers in the upper 5
story were narrower than the others;
for the galleries detracted their size
as compared with those in the lower
and middle stories of the building. For 6
they were built in three stories, and had
no pillars like those in the outer court;
hence more room was taken from the
chambers in the upper and middle
stories than from those on the ground
floor. The outer wall, bounding the 7
chambers along the side of the outer
court, was fifty cubits in length; for the 8
length of the row of chambers in the
outer court was fifty cubits, while in
front of the temple it was a hundred cubits. And below these chambers, as one 9
approached them from the outer court,
was the eastward entrance, at the head
of the outer wall.
On the south side, in front of the 10
yard and its buildings, was another
row of chambers, with a passage in 11
front of them, similar to the chambers
on the north, of the same length and
breadth, with the same exits and arrangements, and with doors corre- 12
sponding to theirs, only facing the
south. There was likewise a door at the
head of the passage, in front of the outer wall, as one approached it on the
east. And he said to me, 13
"The north and the south chambers
facing the yard are the sacred chambers where the priests who approach the
LORD shall eat the most sacred things,
and where they shall lay the most sacred things, the cereal-offerings, the
sin-offerings, and the guilt-offerings;
for the place is sacred. When the priests 14
enter the sacred place, they shall
not pass from it to the outer court
without laying there the robes in which
they have ministered (for they are sacred), and putting on other garments
in which they shall approach the part of
the building that is open to the people."
When he had finished measuring the 15
inner house, he brought me out by the
gate looking east, and measured the
whole building round about. First he 16
measured the east side, five hundred
cubits by the measuring-rod. Then he 17
turned to the north side, and measured
it, five hundred cubits by the measuring-rod. Then he turned to the south 18

side, and measured it, five hundred cu-
9 bits by the measuring-rod. Then he
turned to the west side, and measured
it, five hundred cubits by the measur-
0 ing-rod. On all four sides he measured
the building, which had a wall round
about it, five hundred cubits in length,
and five hundred cubits in breadth, to
separate the sacred from the secular.

THE RETURN OF THE GLORY OF THE LORD, 43:1–4

3 Then he brought me to the gate look-
2 ing east; and lo! the glory of the God of
Israel came from the direction of the
east. The sound of his coming was like
the sound of many waters; and the
3 earth shone with his glory. The appearance which I saw was like the appearance which I had seen when he came to
destroy the city, or like the appearance
which I had seen by the River Chebar;
4 and I fell upon my face. And the glory
of the LORD entered the house by the
gate looking east.

REGULATIONS FOR THE TEMPLE AND ITS WORSHIP, 43:5—46:24

5 Then a spirit raised me up, and
brought me into the inner court; and
lo! the glory of the LORD filled the
6 house. And while the man still stood
beside me, I heard one speaking to me
7 from the house, and saying to me,
"O mortal man, this is the place of
my throne, and this is the place for the
soles of my feet, where I will dwell in
the midst of the children of Israel forever. And the house of Israel shall no
longer defile my holy name, neither
they, nor their kings, by their idolatry,
and by the dead bodies of their kings,
8 by placing their threshold against my
threshold, and their doorpost beside
my doorpost, with only a wall between
me and them, and by defiling my holy
name by the abominations which they
have committed, and on account of
which I have devoured them in my an-
9 ger. Now let them put far from me
their idolatry, and the dead bodies of
their kings; and I will dwell in the
midst of them forever.
10 "And you, O mortal man, show the
house of Israel the house, its plan and
its pattern, that they may be ashamed
of all that they have done; acquaint 11
them with the form and structure of the
house, its exits and entrances, and all
its forms, regulations, and rules; and
write it all down in their sight, so that
they may observe all its forms and
regulations, and follow them.
"This is the rule for the house: The 12
whole territory round about the top of
the mountain shall be most sacred. Lo!
this is the rule for the house.
"And these are the dimensions of the 13
altar in cubits of a cubit and a handbreadth: Its pedestal shall be one cubit high, and one cubit broad, with a
rim round its edge one span broad—
this shall be the base of the altar. And 14
from the top of the pedestal to the lower ledge shall be two cubits, and the
breadth one cubit; and from the smaller
ledge to the greater ledge shall be four
cubits, and the breadth one cubit. And 15
the altar-hearth shall be four cubits
high; and above the altar-hearth shall
be four horns, each one cubit long.
The altar-hearth shall be square on all 16
four sides—twelve cubits long by
twelve cubits broad. The upper ledge 17
also shall be square on all four sides—
fourteen cubits long by fourteen cubits
broad—with a rim round it half a cubit
broad. And the pedestal shall be one
cubit square. And the steps of the altar
shall look east."
Then he said to me, 18
O mortal man, thus says the Lord
GOD: 'These are the regulations for the
altar: On the day when it is erected,
for the purpose of offering burnt-offerings and splashing blood upon it, you 19
shall give a young bullock as a sin-offering to the Levitical priests who belong
to the family of Zadok, and who alone
may approach my presence to minister
to me,' is the oracle of the Lord GOD.
'You shall take some of the blood, and 20
apply it to the four horns of the altar, to
the four corners of the ledge, and to the
rim round about it; thus you shall
cleanse and purify the altar. Then you 21
shall take the bullock for the sin-offering, and have it burned at the proper
place in the temple grounds, outside
the sanctuary. Then on the second day 22
you shall offer an unblemished he-goat
as a sin-offering, and thus the altar
shall be cleansed as it was cleansed by
the bullock. And when you have fin- 23

ished cleansing it, you shall offer an unblemished bullock and an unblemished
24 ram from the flock. When you offer
them before the LORD, the priests shall
sprinkle salt upon them, and offer
them up as a burnt-offering to the
25 LORD. For seven days shall you provide daily a he-goat as a sin-offering,
also an unblemished bullock and an un-
26 blemished ram from the flock. Thus
for seven days shall they continue purifying and cleansing the altar, conse-
27 crating it for worship. At the end of
these days, from the eighth day onward, the priests shall offer your burnt-
offerings and your thank-offerings upon
the altar; and I will accept you,' is the
oracle of the Lord GOD."

44 Then he brought me back to the outer gate of the sanctuary, looking east,
2 which was closed. And the LORD said
to me,

"This gate shall remain closed: it
shall not be opened, nor shall any man
enter by it; for the LORD, the God of
Israel, has entered by it; therefore it
3 shall remain closed. The prince alone
may sit in it, to eat bread before the
LORD; he shall enter by way of the
vestibule of the gate, and shall depart
the same way."

4 Then he brought me by way of the
north gate to the front of the house;
and I looked, and lo! the glory of the
LORD filled the house of the LORD;
5 and I fell upon my face. And the LORD
said to me,

"O mortal man, mark, see, and hear
all that I say to you regarding all the
rules and regulations of the house of the
LORD; mark also the entrances and ex-
6 its of the sanctuary. And say to these
rebels of the house of Israel, 'Thus
says the Lord GOD: Let us have no
more of the abominations which you
7 have committed, O house of Israel, by
introducing into my sanctuary aliens
uncircumcised in heart and flesh, to
profane my house, when you offered me
the fat and blood that are my food!
You have broken my covenant with all
8 your abominations, and have not kept
charge of my sacred things, but have
introduced these aliens to keep charge
9 in my sanctuary. Therefore thus says
the Lord GOD: No alien, uncircumcised
in heart and flesh, of all the aliens that
are in the midst of the children of Is-
10 rael, shall enter my sanctuary. And
the Levites, who went far from me
when Israel went astray—who went
astray from me after their idols—shall
bear the consequences of their guilt, by 11
being ministers in my sanctuary, having oversight at the gates of the house,
and ministering in the house, slaughtering the burnt-offerings and sacrifices for
the people, and standing before the people to minister to them. Because they 12
ministered to them before their idols,
and thus caused the house of Israel to
fall into sin, I have sworn by uplifted
hand concerning them,' is the oracle of
the Lord GOD, 'that they shall bear the
consequences of their guilt by no longer 13
approaching me, to act as priests to me,
or to touch any of my sacred things, my
most sacred things—so shall they bear
the burden of their shame for the
abominations which they have committed—but I will give them charge of 14
the house, to do all the service and all
the work that is to be done in it. But 15
the Levitical priests, the sons of Zadok,
who kept charge of my sanctuary when
the children of Israel went astray from
me, they shall approach me to minister
to me, and shall stand before me to
offer me the fat and the blood,' is the
oracle of the Lord GOD; 'they shall 16
enter my sanctuary, and shall approach
my table to minister to me, and shall
keep my charge. And when they enter 17
the gates of the inner court, they shall
wear linen garments; they shall have no
wool upon them while they are ministering within the gates of the inner
court, or anywhere in the sanctuary;
they shall have linen turbans upon 18
their heads, and linen breeches upon
their loins; they shall cover themselves
with nothing that causes sweat. And 19
when they go out to join the people in
the outer court, they shall put off the
garments in which they have been ministering, and lay them in the sacred
chambers; and they shall put on other
garments, lest they make the people taboo by their garments. And they shall 20
neither shave their heads, nor let their
hair grow long; they shall only clip
their hair. No priest shall drink wine 21
when he enters the inner court. And 22
none shall marry a layman's widow, or a
divorced woman, but only a virgin of
the stock of the house of Israel, or the
widow of a priest. They shall teach my 23
people the difference between the sa-

cred and the secular, and show them how to distinguish between the unclean and the clean. In a case at court they shall act as judges, and shall decide the case according to my laws; and they shall observe my rules and regulations at all my festivals, and shall maintain the sacredness of my sabbaths. No priest shall defile himself by approaching a dead person, except in the case of a father or mother, a son or daughter, a brother or unmarried sister; and if he should suffer defilement in this way, he shall let seven days elapse, after which he shall be clean; and when he enters the inner court, to minister in the sanctuary, he shall offer a sin-offering for himself,' is the oracle of the Lord GOD. 'And the priests shall have no heritage, since I am their heritage; and no property shall be given to them in Israel, since I am their property. The cereal-offerings, the sin-offerings, and the guilt-offerings shall be their food; and everything devoted to the LORD in Israel shall go to them. The best of all the firstfruits of everything, and all the contributions of everything which you offer, shall be for the priests; and your first batch of baking shall you give to the priest, so that a blessing may rest on your homes. But of nothing that dies a natural death, or has been torn to pieces, whether bird or beast, shall the priests eat.

" 'And when you allot the land for inheritance, you shall set apart as an allotment to the LORD a sacred portion of the land, twenty-five thousand cubits long, and twenty thousand cubits broad, which shall be sacred through its whole extent. And from this area you shall measure off a section, twenty-five thousand cubits long, and ten thousand cubits broad, as the most sacred portion of the land; it shall be for the priests who minister in the sanctuary, and approach the LORD to minister to him, providing room for their houses and grounds. Of this section there shall be reserved for the sanctuary a square block, five hundred cubits in length by five hundred cubits in breadth, with an open space of fifty cubits round about it. Another section, twenty-five thousand cubits long, and ten thousand cubits broad, shall be for the Levites who minister in the sanctuary; it shall be theirs for houses to live in. And alongside of the sacred allotment you shall
provide the city property, five thousand cubits broad and twenty-five
thousand cubits long, which shall belong to the whole house of Israel. And 7
the prince shall have the land on both
sides of the sacred allotment and the
city property, facing the sacred allotment and the city property west and
east, along a length equal to that of one
of the tribal lots, from the west to the
east border of the land; this shall be his 8
property in Israel. And my princes
shall no longer oppress my people, but
shall assign the land to the house of Israel according to their tribes.' "

Thus says the Lord GOD: 9
"Enough, O princes of Israel! Have
done with violence and spoil; practice
justice and right; cease evicting my
people from their homes," is the oracle
of the Lord GOD. "You shall have just 10
scales, a just ephah, and a just bath.
The ephah and the bath shall be of the 11
same measure—the bath containing
the tenth of a homer, and the ephah the
tenth of a homer, the homer being the
standard of measurement. And the 12
shekel shall be twenty gerahs (five
shekels shall be five shekels, and ten
shekels shall be ten shekels), and your
mana shall be twenty shekels.

"This is the contribution which you 13
shall offer: the sixth of an ephah out of
every homer of wheat, and the sixth of
an ephah out of every homer of barley; 14
a proportion of oil amounting to the
tenth of a bath out of every kor, ten
baths making a kor; and one sheep out 15
of every flock of two hundred—from all
the families of Israel—to provide for
the cereal-offering, the burnt-offering,
and the thank-offerings, that atonement may be made for them," is the
oracle of the Lord GOD. "All the peo- 16
ple of the land shall offer this contribution to the prince in Israel. And it 17
shall be the prince's duty to provide
the burnt-offering, the cereal offering,
and the libation, at the various festivals—the new moons, the sabbaths,
and all the other fixed festivals of the
house of Israel—at which he shall provide the sin-offering, the cereal-offering, the burnt-offering, and the thank-
offerings, to make atonement for the
house of Israel."

Thus says the Lord GOD: 18
"In the first month, on the first day

of the month, you shall take an un-
blemishd bullock, and purify the sanc-
19 tuary. And the priest shall take part
of the blood of the sin-offering, and
apply it to the doorposts of the house,
the four corners of the ledge of the altar, and the posts of the gate of the in-
20 ner court. In the seventh month, on
the first day of the month, you shall do
the same for anyone who has sinned
through error or ignorance, and purify
21 the house. And in the first month, on the
fifteenth day of the month, you shall
hold the festival of Passover; and for sev-
en days you shall eat unleavened bread.
22 On that day the prince shall provide for
himself and all the people of the land a
23 bullock as a sin-offering; and during the
seven days of the festival he shall provide seven unblemished bullocks and
seven unblemished rams daily as a
burnt-offering to the LORD, with a he-
24 goat daily as a sin-offering. And as a
cereal-offering he shall provide an
ephah for each bullock, and an ephah
for each ram, with a hin of oil for each
25 ephah. In the seventh month, on the
fifteenth day of the month, and during
the seven days of the festival, he shall
make the same provision, alike for the
sin-offering, the burnt-offering, the
cereal-offering, and the oil."

46 Thus says the Lord GOD:
"The gate of the inner court looking
east shall remain closed during the six
working days; but it shall be opened on
the sabbath day and the day of the new
2 moon. And the prince shall enter from
without by way of the vestibule of the
gate, and shall remain standing by the
post of the gate, while the priests offer
his burnt-offering and his thank-offerings; he shall worship at the threshold
of the gate, and then go out, though the
gate shall not be closed till evening.
3 The common people also shall worship
before the LORD at the door of the
same gate on the sabbaths and at the
4 new moons. The burnt-offering which
the prince shall offer to the LORD on
the sabbath day shall be six unblemished lambs and one unblemished ram,
5 the cereal-offering being an ephah for
the ram, and as much as he can afford
for the lambs, with a hin of oil for each
6 ephah. On the day of the new moon it
shall be an unblemished bullock, six unblemished lambs, and one unblemished
7 ram; and as a cereal-offering he shall
provide an ephah for the bullock, an
ephah for the ram, and as much as he
can afford for the lambs, with a hin of
oil for each ephah. When the prince
enters, he shall do so by way of the
vestibule of the gate; and he shall go
out the same way. But when the common people enter the presence of the
LORD, at the fixed festivals, he who
enters for worship by way of the north
gate shall go out by the south gate,
while he who enters by way of the
south gate shall go out by the north
gate; he shall not return by way of the
gate by which he entered, but shall go
straight ahead of him. When they enter, the prince shall enter in the midst
of them; and when they go out, he shall
go out with them. At the feasts and
fixed festivals the cereal-offering shall
be an ephah for the bullock, an ephah
for the ram, and as much as he can afford for the lambs, with a hin of oil for
each ephah. And when the prince offers
a voluntary offering (a burnt-offering
or thank-offerings as a voluntary offering to the LORD) the eastward gate
shall be opened for him, and he shall
offer his burnt-offering or his thank-
offerings as he does on the sabbath
day; then he shall go out, and the gate
shall be closed after him. And each
day he shall provide an unblemished
lamb, one year old, as a burnt-offering
to the LORD; morning by morning
shall he provide it. And as a cereal-
offering he shall provide with it morning by morning the sixth of an ephah of
fine flour, with the third of a hin of oil
to moisten it, as a cereal-offering to the
LORD. This shall be a standing order
for the regular burnt-offering; he shall
provide the lamb, the cereal-offering,
and the oil, morning by morning, for
the regular burnt-offering."
Thus says the Lord GOD:
"If the prince make a gift of part of
his inheritance to one of his sons, it
shall belong to that son; it is his property by right of inheritance. But if he
make a gift of part of his inheritance to
one of his servants, it shall remain in
his possession till the year of release,
when it shall return to the prince;
whereas the inheritance that goes to a
son shall belong to him. And the prince
shall not rob the people of their property, by taking any part of their inheritance; out of his own property shall he

endow his sons, so that none of my people may be driven out of his property."
Then he brought me, through the entrance beside the gate, to the north
row of the priests' sacred chambers;
and lo! there was a place at the extreme west of it. And he said to me,
"This is the place where the priests
shall boil the guilt-offering and the sin-
offering, and where they shall bake the
cereal-offering, to prevent their bringing them into the outer court, and thus
making the people taboo."
Then be brought me to the outer
court, and led me past the four corners
of the court; and lo! at each corner of
the court there was another court—at
the four corners of the court four small
courts, all four of the same size, each
forty cubits long, and thirty broad.
Round each of the four of them ran a
row of masonry, with boiling-ranges
built under each of the rows round
about. And he said to me,
"These are the boilers where the
ministers of the temple shall boil the
sacrifices for the people."

THE STREAM FROM THE TEMPLE, 47:1–12

Then he brought me back to the door
of the house; and lo! there was water
flowing from under the threshold of the
house eastward—for the front of the
house was eastward—and the water
came down on the south side of the
house, south of the altar. Then he
brought me out by way of the north
gate, and led me round the outside of
the building to the outer gate looking
east; and lo! the water was trickling
down on the south side. Passing eastward, with the measuring-line in his
hand, the man measured a thousand
cubits, and made me cross the water,
which came up to my ankles. Again he
measured a thousand, and made me
cross the water, which came up to my
knees. Again he measured a thousand,
and made me cross the water, which
came up to my loins. Again he measured a thousand and it was a stream
which I could not cross; for the water
had risen deep enough to swim in; it
was a stream which could not be
crossed. Then he said to me,
"Do you see this, O mortal man?"
Then he led me back along the bank
of the stream; and as I went back, lo! 7
on the bank of the stream, along both
sides of it, there were very many trees.
Then he said to me, 8
"These waters are going out to the
eastern region—and they shall descend
upon the Arabah; and when they enter
the Sea, with its brackish water, the
water shall become fresh. Wherever 9
the stream goes, all sorts of swarming
creatures shall live in it, and fish shall
be there in very great numbers; for this
stream goes there for the very purpose
that, wherever it goes, the water may
become fresh, and creatures may live in
it. And fishermen shall stand on its 10
shore, all the way from Engedi to En-
eglaim, and shall spread their nets on
it; and its fish of all sorts shall be very
plentiful, like those of the Great Sea.
Only its marshes and swamps shall not 11
become fresh; they shall be left for the
supply of salt. On the bank of the 12
stream, along both sides of it, there
shall grow all sorts of trees for food, the
leaves of which shall not wither, nor
their fruit fail, but they shall bear fresh
fruit every month, because the water
that feeds them flows from the sanctuary; and their fruit shall serve for food,
and their leaves for healing."

THE DIVISION OF THE LAND, 47:13—48:35

Thus says the Lord GOD: 13
"These are the frontiers by which
you shall divide the land for inheritance
among the twelve tribes of Israel. Except that a double portion shall go to
Joseph, you shall divide it equally. As 14
I swore by uplifted hand to give this
land to your fathers, it shall fall to you
as a heritage. These, then, are the 15
frontiers of the land:
"On the north: from the Great Sea,
by way of Hethlon, to the pass of
Hamath, as far as Zedad, thence to 16
Berothah, Sibraim, on the frontier between Damascus and Hamath, and
Hazer-enon, on the frontier of Hauran.
The frontier, then, shall run from the 17
sea to Hazer-enon, on the frontier of
Damascus, and to Ziphron on the north
and the frontier of Hamath. This is the
northern frontier.
"On the east: the Jordan, from the 18

frontier between Hauran and Damascus, and along between Gilead and Israel, that is, from the northern frontier
to the Eastern Sea, as far as Tamar.
This is the eastern frontier.
19 "On the south: from Tamar to the
waters of Meribath-kadesh, thence
along the Brook to the Great Sea. This
is the southern frontier.
20 "On the west: the Great Sea, from
the southern frontier to a point opposite the pass of Hamath. This is the
western frontier.
21 "So shall you divide this land among
you according to the tribes of Israel.
22 And you shall allot it as a heritage for
yourselves, and for the aliens who reside among you and have begotten children among you, since they are to be
treated by you like native-born children of Israel, and are to be allotted a
heritage along with you among the
23 tribes of Israel. In whatever tribe the
alien resides, there shall you assign him
his heritage," is the oracle of the Lord
GOD.

48 "These are the names of the tribes:
"At the northern end, from the Sea,
by way of Hethlon, to the pass of
Hamath, as far as Hazer-enon, bordering on the territory of Damascus, near
Hamath, on the north, running from
east to west, Dan—one portion.
2 "Bordering on Dan, from east to
west, Asher—one portion.
3 "Bordering on Asher, from east to
west, Naphtali—one portion.
4 "Bordering on Naphtali, from east
to west, Manasseh—one portion.
5 "Bordering on Manasseh, from east
to west, Ephraim—one portion.
6 "Bordering on Ephraim, from east
to west, Reuben—one portion.
7 "Bordering on Reuben, from east
to west, Judah—one portion.
8 "Bordering on Judah, from east to
west, shall be the allotment which you
shall set apart—twenty-five thousand
cubits broad, and in length equal to one
of the tribal portions, from east to
west—with the sanctuary in the midst
9 of it. The allotment which you shall
set apart for the LORD shall be twenty-
five thousand cubits in length, and
10 twenty thousand cubits in breadth. Of
this sacred allotment the priest shall
have a section, twenty-five thousand
cubits in length from east to west, and
ten thousand cubits in breadth from

north to south, with the sanctuary of the LORD in the midst of it; this section shall be for the holy priests, the sons of Zadok, who kept my charge, and did not go astray, as the Levites did, when the children of Israel went astray; it shall be a special allotment to them, out of the total allotment of the land, a most sacred place, adjoining the frontier of the Levites. And alongside the border of the priests, the Levites shall have a section, twenty-five thousand cubits in length, and ten thousand cubits in breadth. Thus the whole shall be twenty-five thousand cubits in length, and twenty thousand cubits in breadth. And none of this choice portion of the land shall be sold, or exchanged, or alienated; for it is sacred to the LORD. The five thousand cubits, which remain in breadth of the twenty-five thousand, shall be common land, for the city, for dwellings, and for pasture-lands, with the city lying in the midst of it. And these shall be the dimensions of the city: four thousand five hundred cubits on the north, four thousand five hundred on the south, four thousand five hundred on the east, and four thousand five hundred on the west. And the city shall have pasture-lands extending two hundred and fifty cubits to the north, two hundred and fifty to the south, two hundred and fifty to the east, and two hundred and fifty to the west. The remaining length of ten thousand cubits to the east, and ten thousand to the west, alongside the sacred allotment, shall belong to the city; its produce shall supply food for the workers in the city, and it shall be cultivated by the workers in the city from all the tribes of Israel. The whole allotment—that is, the sacred allotment, together with the city property—you shall make twenty-five thousand cubits square. What remains shall belong to the prince; that is, the land on either side of the sacred allotment and the city property, extending east of the allotment of twenty-five thousand cubits as far as the eastern border, and west of the allotment of twenty-five thousand cubits as far as the western border, parallel to the tribal portions, shall belong to the prince. Thus the sacred allotment—that is, the temple sanctuary and the Levites' property—together with the city property shall be in the midst of the prince's portion. And the prince's portion shall be between the frontiers of Judah and Benjamin.

"And the rest of the tribes:

"From east to west, Benjamin—one portion.

"Bordering on Benjamin, from east to west, Simeon—one portion.

"Bordering on Simeon, from east to west, Issachar—one portion.

"Bordering on Issachar, from east to west, Zebulun—one portion.

"Bordering on Zebulun, from east to west, Gad—one portion.

"And to the south of Gad the frontier shall run from Tamar to the waters of Meribath-kadesh, thence along the Brook to the Great Sea. This is the land which you shall allot as a heritage to the tribes of Israel; and these are their portions," is the oracle of the Lord GOD.

"And these shall be the gates of the 30
city, each gate being named after one
of the tribes of Israel:

"On the north side, four thousand 31
five hundred cubits by measure, three
gates—the gate of Reuben, the gate of
Judah, and the gate of Levi.

"On the east side, four thousand five 32
hundred cubits, three gates—the gate
of Joseph, the gate of Benjamin, and
the gate of Dan.

"On the south side, four thousand 33
five hundred cubits, three gates—the
gate of Simeon, the gate of Issachar,
and the gate of Zebulun.

"On the west side, four thousand five 34
hundred cubits, three gates—the gate
of Gad, the gate of Asher, and the gate
of Naphtali.

"The circumference shall be eighteen 35
thousand cubits. And the name of the
city from that day onward shall be
'The LORD is there.'"

THE BOOK OF DANIEL

THE FOUR JEWISH YOUTHS, 1:1–21

1 IN THE third year of the reign of
Jehoiakim, king of Judah, Nebuchadnezzar, king of Babylon, came
2 to Jerusalem, and besieged it. And
the Lord gave Jehoiakim, king of Judah, into his hand, with the choicest of
the vessels of the house of God; and he
brought them to the land of Shinar, to
the house of his god, and placed the
3 vessels in the treasury of his god. Then
the king instructed Ashpenaz, the chief
of his eunuchs, to bring certain of the
Israelites, who belonged to the royal
4 family and the nobility—youths who
had no defect in them, but were handsome in appearance, and skilled in all
branches of learning, equipped with
knowledge, and endowed with intelligence, such as were capable of standing
in the palace of the king—and to teach
them the literature and language of the
5 Chaldeans. And the king assigned
them a daily portion of the king's delicacies, and of the wine which he drank.
For three years they were to be trained,
and at the end of that time they were
to stand in the presence of the king.
6 Among them were certain Jews, Daniel, Hananiah, Mishael, and Azariah.
7 And the chief of the eunuchs gave
names to them, naming Daniel Belteshazzar, Hananiah Shadrach, Mishael Meshach, and Azariah Abednego.
8 Now Daniel determined that he
would not defile himself with the king's
delicacies, nor with the wine which he
drank; so he asked permission of the
chief of the eunuchs not to defile him-
9 self. But though God had given Daniel
favor and sympathy in the eyes of the
10 chief of the eunuchs, the chief of the
eunuchs said to Daniel,

"I am afraid of my lord, the king, who has assigned your food and your drink, lest he find you looking more haggard than the youths of your own age, in which case you would forfeit my head to the king."

Then Daniel said to the steward, whom the chief of the eunuchs had placed over Daniel, Hananiah, Mishael, and Azariah,

"Pray, try your servants for ten days, letting us have vegetables to eat, and water to drink; then compare our appearance with the appearance of the youths who eat of the king's delicacies, and deal with your servants in accordance with what you see."

So he listened to them in this regard, and tried them for ten days. And at the end of ten days they were better in appearance, and fatter in flesh, than all the youths who ate of the king's delicacies. So the steward removed their delicacies, and the wine that they were to drink; and he gave them vegetables.

As for these four youths, God gave them knowledge and skill in all branches of literature and learning, while Daniel was accomplished in all kinds of visions and dreams. Now at the end of the days which the king had appointed for bringing them in, the chief of the eunuchs brought them in to the presence of Nebuchadnezzar; and when the king conversed with them, he found none among them all like Daniel, Hananiah, Mishael, and Azariah. So they became attendants of the king. And in all matters of learning and knowledge, about which the king questioned them, he found them ten times better than all the magicians and enchanters that were in all his kingdom. And Daniel retained his position till the first year of King Cyrus.

NEBUCHADNEZZAR'S DREAM, 2:1–49

In the second year of the reign of Nebuchadnezzar, Nebuchadnezzar dreamed a dream; and his spirit was disturbed, and his sleep left him. Then the king gave orders to summon the magicians, the enchanters, the sorcerers, and the Chaldeans, that they might tell the king his dream. So they came and stood before the king, whereupon the king said to them,

"I have dreamed a dream; and my spirit is troubled in the effort to understand the dream."

Then the Chaldeans spoke to the king in Aramaic,

"O king, live forever! Tell your servants the dream, and we will give the interpretation."

The king answered the Chaldeans, saying,

"I am fully resolved that, if you do not make known to me the dream and its interpretation, you shall be hewn limb from limb, and your houses shall be made a dunghill. But if you tell me the dream and its interpretation, you shall receive from me gifts and rewards and great honor. So tell me the dream and its interpretation."

A second time they answered, saying,

"Let the king tell his servants the dream, and we will give the interpretation."

The king answered, saying,

"I know quite well that you are trying to gain time, because you see how fully resolved I am that, if you do not make known to me the dream, there is but one fate for you; and you have conspired together to speak false and deceitful words to me, hoping that a change may come. So tell me the dream, and I shall know that you can give me its interpretation."

The Chaldeans answered the king, saying,

"There is not a man on the earth who can tell the king what he asks; for no king, however great and mighty, has asked such a thing of any magician, enchanter, or Chaldean. The king is asking a hard thing, and none can tell the king what he asks, except the gods whose dwelling is not with mortal flesh."

At this answer the king became so angry and so very furious that he gave orders to destroy all the wise men of Babylon. So the decree went forth that the wise men were to be slain; and Daniel and his companions would have been slain.

Then Daniel made a wise and tactful answer to Arioch, the captain of the king's guard, who had gone to slay the wise men of Babylon; he answered Arioch, the king's captain, saying,

"Why is the king's decree so harsh?"
When Arioch had explained the mat- 16
ter to Daniel, Daniel went in, and asked
the king to grant him time, and he
would give the king the interpretation.
Then Daniel went home, and explained 17
the matter to his companions, Hananiah, Mishael, and Azariah, in order that 18
they might ask mercy of the God of the
heavens concerning this secret, and so
Daniel and his companions might not
perish with the rest of the wise men of
Babylon. Then the secret was revealed 19
to Daniel in a vision of the night. Then
Daniel blessed the God of the heavens;
Daniel spoke, saying, 20

"Blessed be the name of God from ever-
lasting to everlasting,
For wisdom and might are his!
He changes the seasons and times,
He removes kings, and he sets up 21
kings;
He gives wisdom to the wise,
And knowledge to those who are en-
dowed with understanding.
He reveals things deep and secret, 22
He knows what is in the darkness,
And with him dwells the light.
I thank thee, and praise thee, O God 23
of my fathers,
Who hast given me wisdom and might,
And hast now made known to me
what we asked of thee,
For thou hast made known to us the
concern of the king."

So Daniel went to Arioch, whom the 24
king had appointed to destroy the wise
men of Babylon; he went and spoke to
him as follows:

"Do not destroy the wise men of
Babylon; bring me before the king, that
I may give the king the interpretation."
Then Arioch brought Daniel before 25
the king in haste, and spoke to him as
follows:

"I have found a man, among the
exiles of Judah, who can make known
the interpretation to the king."
The king spoke to Daniel, whose 26
name was Belteshazzar, saying,

"Are you able to make known to me
the dream that I have seen, and its interpretation?"
Daniel answered the king, saying, 27

"No wise men, enchanters, magicians,
or astrologers are able to tell the king
the secret which the king has asked;
but there is a God in the heavens who 28
reveals secrets, and he makes known to

King Nebuchadnezzar what shall be in
the end of the days. Your dream, and
the visions of your head on your bed,
were as follows:
29 "You, O king, lay in bed, wondering
what should be in the future; and he
who reveals secrets makes known to
30 you what shall be. As for myself, this
secret has not been revealed to me by
virtue of any wisdom that I possess
more than any other living man, but in
order that the interpretation may be
made known to the king, and that you
may understand the thoughts of your
mind.
31 "You, O king, looked, and lo! there
was a great image. This image, which
was of vast size and surpassing brightness, stood before you; and its appear-
32 ance was terrible. As for that image, its
head was of fine gold, its breast and
arms were of silver, its belly and thighs
33 of bronze, its legs of iron, its feet partly
34 of iron, and partly of clay. You looked
till you saw a stone hewn from a mountain without hands, which smote the
image on its feet of iron and clay, break-
35 ing them in pieces. Then the iron, the
clay, the bronze, the silver, and the
gold were broken in pieces together,
and became like chaff from summer
threshing-floors, and were carried away
by the wind, so that no trace of them
could be found; while the stone that
smote the image became a great moun-
36 tain, filling all the earth. This was the
dream, and we will tell the king the interpretation of it.
37 "You, O king, the king of kings, to
whom the God of the heavens has given
the kingdom, the power, the strength,
38 and the glory, and into whose hand he
has put the children of men, the beasts
of the field, and the birds of the air,
wherever they dwell, making you rule
over them all—you are the head of
39 gold. After you shall arise another kingdom, inferior to you; then a third kingdom, of bronze, which shall rule over all
40 the earth. And the fourth kingdom
shall be as strong as iron; for as iron
breaks in pieces and beats down all
things, and as iron crushes all things, so
41 shall it break in pieces and crush. And
as you saw the feet and toes partly of
potter's clay, and partly of iron, it shall
be a divided kingdom; there shall be
something of the firmness of iron in it,
as you saw iron mixed with muddy
clay; but as the toes of the feet were
partly iron, and partly clay, the kingdom shall be partly strong, and partly
brittle. As you saw iron mixed with
muddy clay, they shall mix together
in marriage; but they shall not hold
together, as iron does not mix with clay.
In the days of those kings the God of
the heavens shall set up a kingdom
which shall never be destroyed, nor
shall the kingdom be left to another
people; it shall break in pieces and annihilate all these kingdoms, but it shall
stand forever, as you saw how a stone
was hewn from a mountain without
hands, which broke in pieces the iron,
the bronze, the clay, the silver, and the
gold. A great God makes known to the
king what shall be in the future; the
dream is certain, and its interpretation
sure."

Then King Nebuchadnezzar fell upon
his face, and prostrated himself before
Daniel, and commanded sacrifice and
soothing odors to be offered to him.
And the king spoke to Daniel, saying,

"Truly, your God is the God of gods,
and the Lord of kings; and he is a re-
vealer of secrets, inasmuch as you have
been able to reveal this secret."

Then the king promoted Daniel, and
gave him many great gifts; he made
him ruler over the whole province of
Babylon, and chief prefect over all the
wise men of Babylon. At Daniel's request, the king appointed Shadrach,
Meshach, and Abednego in charge of
the affairs of the province of Babylon;
but Daniel remained at the gate of the
king.

THE FURNACE OF FIRE, 3:1–30

King Nebuchadnezzar made an image of gold, sixty cubits in height, and six cubits in breadth, which he set up on the plain of Dura, in the province of Babylon. Then King Nebuchadnezzar sent to assemble the satraps, the prefects, the governors, the councilors, the treasurers, the judges, the justices, and all the officials of the provinces, to come to the dedication of the image which King Nebuchadnezzar had set up. And when the satraps, the prefects, the governors, the councilors, the treasurers, the judges, the justices, and all the officials of the provinces were assembled

for the dedication of the image which
4 King Nebuchadnezzar had set up, the
herald called aloud,
"To you is given a command, O
5 peoples, nations, and tongues, that as
soon as you hear the sound of the horn,
the pipe, the lyre, the trigon, the harp,
the bagpipe, and every other kind of
musical instrument, you shall fall down
and prostrate yourselves before the
image of gold which King Nebuchad-
6 nezzar has set up; and whoever does
not fall down and prostrate himself
shall forthwith be cast into the midst of
a furnace of flaming fire."
7 As soon, then, as all the peoples
heard the sound of the horn, the pipe,
the lyre, the trigon, the harp, and every
other kind of musical instrument, all
the peoples, nations, and tongues fell
down and prostrated themselves before
the image of gold which King Nebu-
8 chadnezzar had set up. Thereupon certain Chaldeans came forward, and laid
9 an accusation against the Jews, saying
to King Nebuchadnezzar,
10 "O king, live forever! You, O king,
have made a decree that every man
who hears the sound of the horn, the
pipe, the lyre, the trigon, the harp, the
bagpipe, and every other kind of musical instrument, shall fall down and
prostrate himself before the image of
11 gold; and whoever does not fall down
and prostrate himself shall be cast into
the midst of a furnace of flaming fire.
12 Now there are certain Jews whom you
have appointed in charge of the affairs
of the province of Babylon, Shadrach,
Meshach, and Abednego; these men, O
king, pay no regard to you; they do not
serve your gods, nor do they prostrate
themselves before the image of gold
which you have set up."
13 Then Nebuchadnezzar, in rage and
fury, ordered Shadrach, Meshach, and
Abednego to be brought; and when
these men were brought before the king,
14 Nebuchadnezzar addressed them, saying,
"Is it true, O Shadrach, Meshach,
and Abednego, that you do not serve
my gods, nor prostrate yourselves before the image of gold which I have set
15 up? Now if you are ready, as soon as
you hear the sound of the horn, the
pipe, the lyre, the trigon, the harp, the
bagpipe, and every other kind of musical instrument, to fall down and prostrate yourselves before the image which
I have made, well and good; but if you
will not prostrate yourselves, you shall
forthwith be cast into the midst of a
furnace of flaming fire; and what god
is there who shall deliver you out of my
hands?"
Shadrach, Meshach, and Abednego 16
answered the king, saying,
"O Nebuchadnezzar, we need not
waste words in discussing this matter
with you. If our God, whom we serve, 17
is able to deliver us, he will deliver us
out of the furnace of flaming fire, and
out of your hand, O king; but even if 18
not, be it known to you, O king, we will
not serve your gods, nor prostrate ourselves before the image of gold which
you have set up."
At these words Nebuchadnezzar was 19
filled with fury, and his face was distorted with rage against Shadrach, Meshach, and Abednego. He ordered the
furnace to be heated seven times more
than it was usual for it to be heated;
then he ordered certain of the strongest 20
men in his army to bind Shadrach, Meshach, and Abednego, and to cast them
into the furnace of flaming fire. There- 21
upon these men were bound in their
cloaks, their tunics, their hats, and their
other clothes, and were cast into the
midst of the furnace of flaming fire. So 22
sharp was the king's order, and so very
hot was the furnace, that the flame of
the fire slew the men who took up
Shadrach, Meshach, and Abednego.
But these three men, Shadrach, Me- 23
shach, and Abednego, fell down bound
into the midst of the furnace of flaming
fire.
Then King Nebuchadnezzar became 24
alarmed; and he rose up hastily, and
addressed his ministers, saying,
"Did we not cast three men bound
into the midst of the fire?"
They answered the king, saying,
"Certainly, O king."
He answered, saying, 25
"Well, I see four men loose, walking
in the midst of the fire, quite unscathed;
and the appearance of the fourth resembles one of the gods."
Then King Nebuchadnezzar ap- 26
proached the mouth of the furnace of
flaming fire, and spoke, saying,
"O Shadrach, Meshach, and Abednego, servants of the Most High God,
come out, and come here!"

Then Shadrach, Meshach, and Abednego came out of the midst of the fire;
27 and when the assembled satraps, prefects, governors, and king's ministers
saw that the fire had had no effect on
the persons of these men, that the hair
of their heads had not been singed, nor
their cloaks damaged, and that no smell
28 of burning had settled on them, Nebuchadnezzar spoke, saying,
"Blessed be the God of Shadrach,
Meshach, and Abednego, who has sent
his angel to deliver his servants who
trusted in him, and frustrated the
king's order, by surrendering their own
persons, rather than serve and worship
29 any god, except their own God! Therefore I make a decree that any people,
nation, or tongue, that speaks a word
against the God of Shadrach, Meshach,
and Abednego, shall be hewn limb from
limb, and their houses made a dunghill;
for there is no other god who is able to
deliver in this manner."
30 Then the king promoted Shadrach,
Meshach, and Abednego in the province
of Babylon.

NEBUCHADNEZZAR'S MADNESS, 4:1–37

4 King Nebuchadnezzar to all the
peoples, nations, and tongues, that live
in all the earth: Peace be multiplied to
2 you! It is my pleasure to tell of the
signs and wonders that the Most High
God has wrought toward me.
3 How great are his signs,
And how mighty his wonders!
His kingdom is an everlasting kingdom,
And his dominion endures throughout
the ages.
4 I, Nebuchadnezzar, was living at
ease in my house, enjoying prosperity
5 in my palace, when I saw a dream that
alarmed me, fancies upon my bed and
6 visions of my head that upset me. So I
made a decree that all the wise men of
Babylon should be brought before me,
to make known to me the interpreta-
7 tion of the dream. Then came in the
magicians, the enchanters, the Chaldeans, and the astrologers; but when I
told them the dream, they could not
make known to me the interpretation
8 of it. At last there came in before me
Daniel, whose name is Belteshazzar—
after the name of my god—a man in
whom is the spirit of the holy gods; and
I told him my dream, as follows:
"O Belteshazzar, chief of the magi- 9
cians, inasmuch as I know that the
spirit of the holy gods is in you, and
that no secret is a trouble to you, I will
tell you the visions that I have seen in
my dream, and you shall give me the
interpretation of them. As for the vis- 10
ions of my head that I saw in bed,
I looked, and lo! there was a tree in
the midst of the earth,
And its height was great;
The tree had grown great and strong, 11
So that its height reached to the
heavens,
And its bound of vision to the end of
the earth.
Its leaves were fair, and its fruit was 12
abundant,
Providing food for all;
The beasts of the field were sheltering
under its shadow,
And the birds of the air were nestling
among its branches,
And all flesh was fed from it.
"In the visions of my head on my bed 13
I looked, and lo! there was a guardian,
a holy one, who came down from the
heavens, and called aloud, saying, 14
'Hew down the tree, and lop off its
branches,
Shake off its leaves, and scatter its
fruit;
Drive away the beasts from under its
shadow,
And the birds from among its branches.
Yet leave the stump of its roots in the 15
earth,
Secured by a band of iron and bronze,
Among the tender grass of the field;
Let him be drenched by the dew of the
heavens,
And let him have his share with the
beasts of the field;
Let his mind be changed from a man's, 16
And the mind of a beast be given to
him,
And let seven years pass over him.
By the decision of the guardians is the 17
decree,
And through the instruction of the
holy ones is the sentence,
In order that all who live may know
That the Most High rules the kingdom
of men,
Giving it to whomsoever he will,
And setting up over it the lowliest of
men.'

18 "I, King Nebuchadnezzar, saw this
dream; and you, O Belteshazzar, tell
me the interpretation of it, inasmuch
as all the wise men of my kingdom are
unable to make known to me the interpretation of it, but you are able, because the spirit of the holy gods is in
you."

19 Then Daniel, whose name was Belteshazzar, was stunned for a moment, as
his thoughts upset him. But the king
addressed him, saying,

"O Belteshazzar, let not the dream
and its interpretation upset you!"

Belteshazzar answered, saying,

"My lord, may the dream be for
those who hate you, and its interpreta-
20 tion for your enemies! The tree which
you saw, which grew great and strong;
whose height reached to the heavens,
and its bound of vision to the very end
21 of the earth; whose leaves were fair,
and whose fruit was abundant, providing food for all; under whose shadow
the beasts of the field were sheltering,
and among whose branches the birds of
22 the air were nestling—it is yourself, O
king, who have grown so great and
strong, that your greatness reaches to
the heavens, and your dominion to the
23 very end of the earth. And as the king
saw a guardian, a holy one, coming
down from the heavens, and saying,
'Hew down the tree, and destroy it; yet
leave the stump of its roots in the earth,
secured by a band of iron and bronze,
among the tender grass of the field; and
let him be drenched by the dew of the
heavens, and let him share with the
beasts of the field, till seven years pass
24 over him'—this is the interpretation, O
king, that there is a decision of the
Most High, which has gone out against
25 my lord the king, that you shall be
driven from among men, and shall have
your dwelling with the beasts of the
field, and shall be forced to eat grass
like an ox, and shall be drenched by the
dew of the heavens, till seven years pass
over you, and you learn that the Most
High rules the kingdom of men, giving
26 it to whomsoever he will. And as instructions were given to leave the stump
of the roots of the tree, your kingdom
shall be assured to you from the moment you learn that it is the Heavens
27 who rule. Therefore, O king, be pleased
to accept my advice, and break off your
sins by practicing almsgiving, and your
guilt by showing mercy to the poor;
then perhaps your prosperity may be
prolonged."

Now all this befell King Nebuchad- 28
nezzar. At the end of twelve months, 29
as he was walking on the roof of the
royal palace of Babylon, the king said 30
to himself,

"Is not this great Babylon, which I
have built as a royal residence, by my
own mighty power, and for my own
glorious majesty?"

While the words were still in the 31
king's mouth, a voice fell from the
heavens:

"O King Nebuchadnezzar, sentence
is passed upon you; the kingdom is
gone from you! You shall be driven 32
from among men, and shall have your
dwelling with the beasts of the field;
you shall be forced to eat grass like an
ox, and seven years shall pass over you,
till you learn that the Most High rules
the kingdom of men, giving it to whomsoever he will."

Forthwith the sentence upon King 33
Nebuchadnezzar was executed. He was
driven from among men, and had to eat
grass like an ox; his person was
drenched by the dew of the heavens, till
his hair grew as long as the feathers of
an eagle, and his nails as the claws of a
bird.

At the end of the days I, Nebuchad- 34
nezzar, lifted my eyes to the heavens,
and my reason returned to me; then I
blessed the Most High, praising and
honoring him who lives forever:

"For his dominion is an everlasting dominion,
And his kingdom endures throughout
the ages;
All the inhabitants of the earth are 35
persons of no account to him;
He does what he will among the host
of the heavens,
And among the inhabitants of the
earth;
And there is none who can stay his
hand,
Or say to him, 'What doest thou?' "

At that very moment my reason re- 36
turned to me; and for the glory of my
kingdom, my majesty and my splendor
returned to me, my ministers and my
lords came to consult me, I was established in my kingdom, and surpassing greatness was added to me. Now I, 37
Nebuchadnezzar, praise and exalt and

honor the King of the heavens; for all his works are right, and his ways are just; and those who walk in pride he is able to abase.

BELSHAZZAR'S FEAST, 5:1–31

5 King Belshazzar made a great feast
for a thousand of his lords, and drank
2 wine before the thousand. Inflamed by
the taste of the wine, Belshazzar gave
orders to bring in the vessels of gold and
silver, which his father Nebuchadnezzar had taken away from the temple at
Jerusalem, that the king and his lords,
his consorts and his concubines, might
3 drink out of them. So they brought in
the vessels of gold and silver, which had
been taken away from the temple at
Jerusalem; and the king and his lords,
his consorts and his concubines, drank
4 out of them. As they drank the wine,
they praised the gods of gold and silver,
5 bronze, iron, wood, and stone. Forthwith there appeared the fingers of a
man's hand, which wrote on the plaster
of the wall of the king's palace, opposite
the lampstand; and the king saw the
6 palm of the hand as it wrote. Then the
king's face changed color, as his
thoughts upset him; the joints of his
loins relaxed, and his knees knocked
7 against each other. The king called
aloud for the enchanters, the Chaldeans, and the astrologers to be brought
in; and the king addressed the wise men
of Babylon, saying,
"Whosoever reads this writing, and
gives me the interpretation of it, shall
be clothed with purple, and shall have
a chain of gold round his neck, and shall
be third ruler in the kingdom."
8 But when all the king's wise men
came in, they could not read the writing, nor make known to the king the
9 interpretation of it. Then was King
Belshazzar greatly upset, and he
changed color; his lords also were
10 thrown into consternation. At the cries
of the king and his lords, the queen-
mother came into the banqueting-hall;
and the queen-mother addressed him,
saying,
"O king, live forever! Let not your
thoughts upset you, nor your face
11 change color. There is in your kingdom
a man in whom is the spirit of the holy
gods. In the days of your father there
was found in him light, and understanding, and wisdom, like the wisdom
of the gods, so that King Nebuchadnezzar, your father, made him chief of the
magicians, enchanters, Chaldeans, and
astrologers, because there was found in 12
this Daniel, whom the king named
Belteshazzar, surpassing ability, knowledge, understanding, and skill in in-
terpreting dreams, solving riddles, and
unraveling knots. Let Daniel be called
in, then, and he will give the interpretation."
So Daniel was brought in before the 13
king; and the king addressed Daniel,
saying,
"You are Daniel, of the exiles of Judah, whom my father the king brought
from Judah! I have heard of you, that 14
the spirit of the gods is in you, and that
light, and understanding, and surpassing wisdom are found in you. Now the 15
wise men, the enchanters, have been
brought in before me, that they might
read this writing, and make known to
me the interpretation of it; but they
could not give the interpretation of the
matter. I have heard of you, however, 16
that you can give interpretations, and
unravel knots. Now, if you can read
the writing, and make known to me the
interpretation of it, you shall be clothed
with purple, and shall have a chain of
gold round your neck, and shall be third
ruler in the kingdom."
Then Daniel answered the king, say- 17
ing,
"Keep your gifts for yourself, and give
your rewards to another; but I will read
the writing to the king, and make known
to him the interpretation of it. O king,
the Most High God gave Nebuchadnez- 18
zar your father the kingdom, with its
greatness, its glory, and its majesty; and
because of the greatness that he gave him,
all the peoples, nations, and tongues
trembled in fear before him; whom
he would he slew, and whom he would 19
he kept alive, whom he would he raised
up, and whom he would he put down.
But when his mind was lifted up, and his 20
spirit became obstinate, so that he bore
himself proudly, he was deposed from
his kingly throne, and deprived of his
glory, he was driven from among men, 21
and his mind was made like that of the
beasts, his dwelling was with the wild
asses, he was given grass to eat like an
ox, and his person was drenched by the

dew of the heavens, till he learned that
the Most High God rules the kingdom
of men, setting over it whom he will.
22 And you his son, O Belshazzar, have
not humbled yourself, though you knew
23 all this, but have lifted yourself up
against the Lord of the heavens, in that
you have had the vessels of his house
brought in before you, and have drunk
wine out of them—you and your lords,
your consorts and your concubines—
and have praised the gods of silver and
gold, bronze, iron, wood, and stone,
which can neither see nor hear nor understand, and have not glorified the
God in whose hand your breath is, and
24 to whom belong all your ways. From
him, then, has the palm of the hand
been sent, and this writing inscribed.
25 This is the writing that has been in-
26 scribed: *Mene, Tekel,* and *Peres.* And
this is the interpretation of the matter:
Mene—God has numbered your king-
27 dom, and brought it to an end; *Tekel*—
you have been weighed in the scales,
28 and found wanting; *Peres*—your kingdom is divided, and given to the Medes
and Persians."
29 Then Belshazzar gave orders, and
Daniel was clothed with purple, and
had a chain of gold put round his neck,
while a proclamation was made concerning him, that he should be third
ruler in the kingdom.
30 That night Belshazzar, the king of
31 Chaldea, was slain; and Darius, the
Mede, received the kingdom, being
then about sixty-two years of age.

THE DEN OF LIONS, 6:1–28

6 It pleased Darius to set over the
kingdom a hundred and twenty satraps,
2 to administer the whole kingdom, and
over them three presidents, of whom
Daniel was one, that the satraps might
be responsible to them, and the king
3 might suffer no loss. And Daniel distinguished himself above all the presidents and satraps, because surpassing
ability was in him; and the king was
disposed to set him over the whole
kingdom.
4 Then the presidents and satraps
sought to find some ground of complaint
against Daniel in connection with his
administration of the kingdom; but
they could find no ground of complaint
or fault, because he was faithful, and
no error or fault was to be found in him.
So these men said, 5
"We shall find no ground of complaint
against this Daniel, unless we find it in
connection with the law of his God."
Then these presidents and satraps 6
thronged to the king, and addressed
him as follows:
"O King Darius, live forever! All the 7
presidents of the kingdom, the prefects
and the satraps, the ministers and the
governors, have agreed in council that
the king should lay down a statute, and
pass a strict interdict, to the effect that
whosoever shall offer a petition to any
god or man for thirty days, except to
you, O king, shall be cast into the den
of lions. Now, O king, lay down the 8
interdict, and sign the document, so
that it may not be changed, in accordance with the law of the Medes and
Persians, which is unalterable."
Accordingly, King Darius signed the 9
document containing the interdict.
Now, when Daniel learned that the 10
document had been signed, he went to
his house, which had windows in its
upper chamber open toward Jerusalem,
and three times a day he continued
kneeling upon his knees, praying, and
giving thanks before his God, as formerly he used to do. Then these men 11
thronged in, and found Daniel offering
petitions and supplications before his
God. So they approached the king, and 12
questioned him concerning the king's
interdict,
"Did you not sign an interdict, to the
effect that whosoever should offer a
petition to any god or man for thirty
days, except to you, O king, should be
cast into the den of lions?"
The king answered, saying,
"The thing stands fast, in accordance
with the law of the Medes and Persians,
which is unalterable."
Then they answered the king, saying, 13
"This Daniel, of the exiles of Judah,
pays no regard to yourself, O king, nor
to the interdict which you have signed,
but three times a day he continues offering his own petitions."
When the king heard these words, he 14
was deeply grieved, and applied his
mind to saving Daniel; till sunset he
exerted himself to rescue him. Then 15
these men thronged to the king, and
said to the king,
"You are aware, O king, that it is a

law of the Medes and Persians that no
interdict or statute which the king lays
down can be changed."
16 So the king gave orders, and Daniel
was brought forward, and cast into the
den of lions. Then the king spoke to
Daniel, saying,
"May your God, whom you worship
so regularly, save you!"
17 Then a stone was brought forward,
and laid upon the mouth of the den;
and the king sealed it with his own
signet, as well as with the signet of his
lords, so that no change might be made
18 in respect to Daniel. Then the king
went to his palace, and spent the night
fasting; no diversions were brought to
19 him, and his sleep fled from him. Then
at dawn, as soon as it was light, the
king arose, and went in haste to the den
20 of lions. When he came near the den,
where Daniel was, the king cried out
with a sorrowful voice, and spoke to
Daniel, saying,
"O Daniel, servant of the living God,
has your God, whom you worship so
regularly, been able to save you from
the lions?"
21 Then Daniel answered the king, saying,
22 "O king, live forever! My God has
sent his angel, and has shut the mouths
of the lions, so that they have not injured me; because I was found innocent
before him, and before you also, O king,
have I done no injury."
23 At these words the king was exceedingly glad, and gave orders that Daniel
should be taken out of the den. And
when Daniel was taken out of the den,
no kind of injury was found on him,
because he had trusted in his God.
24 Then the king gave orders, and the men
who had accused Daniel were brought
forward—they, and their children, and
their wives—and cast into the den of
lions; and before they had reached the
bottom of the den, the lions fell upon
them, and crushed all their bones to
25 pieces. Then King Darius wrote as follows to all the peoples, nations, and
tongues, that live in all the earth:
26 "Peace be multiplied to you! I hereby make a decree that throughout all
the kingdom which I rule men shall
tremble in reverence before the God of
Daniel;
For he is the living God,
Immutable forever;
His kingdom is one that shall never be
overthrown,
And his dominion is one that shall endure to the end;
He saves, and he delivers, 27
He does signs and wonders
In the heavens and in the earth;
It is he who has saved Daniel
From the power of the lions."
So this Daniel prospered during the 28
reign of Darius, and during the reign of
Cyrus the Persian.

THE VISION OF THE FOUR BEASTS, 7:1–28

In the first year of Belshazzar, king 7
of Babylon, Daniel had a dream and
visions of his head on his bed; then he
wrote down the dream, and told the gist
of the matter, as follows:
"In my visions by night I saw the
four winds of the heavens stirring up
the great sea. Then out of the sea rose
four great beasts, different from one
another. The first was like a lion, with
the wings of an eagle; I watched till its
wings were plucked off, and it was
raised from the earth, and made to
stand on two feet like a man, while the
mind of a man was given to it. And lo!
there was a second beast, like a bear,
raised up on one side, with three ribs in
its mouth between its teeth; and this
order was given to it, 'Arise, devour
much flesh!' Then I looked, and lo!
there was another beast, like a leopard,
with four wings of a bird on its sides;
the beast had also four heads, and dominion was given to it. Then, in the
visions of the night, I looked, and lo!
there was a fourth beast, dreadful and
terrible, exceedingly strong, with great
iron teeth, which devoured and tore in
pieces, trampling what remained under
its feet. It was different from all the
beasts that were before it; and it had
ten horns. As I watched the horns, lo!
there came up among them another
horn, a little one, before which three of
the first horns were plucked up by the
roots; and lo! in this horn there were
eyes like the eyes of a man, and a mouth
speaking great things. I watched
Till thrones were placed,
And a Venerable One took his seat;
His clothing was white as snow,
And the hair of his head like pure wool;
His throne was a flame of fire,

Whose wheels were blazing fire;
10 A stream of fire went forth,
And flowed from before him;
A thousand thousands ministered to him,
And ten thousand times ten thousand stood before him;
The court took its seat,
And the books were opened.

11 "I watched till—on account of the
great words that the horn had spoken—
the beast was slain, and its body destroyed, and handed over to be burned
12 by fire. As for the rest of the beasts,
their dominion was taken away, but
their lives were spared for a season and
13 a time. Then in the visions of the night
I looked,
And lo! with the clouds of the heavens
There came one like a man,
Who advanced toward the Venerable One,
And was brought near his presence.
14 To him was given dominion, and glory, and kingly power,
That all peoples, and nations, and tongues should serve him;
His dominion was to be an everlasting dominion, that should not pass away,
And his kingdom one that should not be overthrown.

15 "As for me, Daniel, my spirit was distressed by these things; for the visions
16 of my head upset me. So I approached
one of those who stood by, and asked
him to tell me the truth regarding all
this. And he answered me, and made
known to me the interpretation of the
things, as follows:
17 'These great beasts, four in number, are four kings,
Who shall arise out of the earth;
18 But the saints of the Most High shall receive the kingdom,
And shall retain the kingdom forever, even forever and ever.'

19 "Then I desired to know the truth
regarding the fourth beast, which was
different from all the others, exceedingly dreadful, with iron teeth and bronze
claws, which devoured and tore in
pieces, trampling what remained under
20 its feet; as well as regarding the ten
horns which were on its head, and the
other horn which came up, and before
which three of them fell, the horn
which had eyes, and a mouth speaking
great things, which appeared greater
than its fellows, the horn which I saw 21
waging war with the saints, and pre-
vailing against them, till the Venerable 22
One came, and the court took its seat,
and dominion was given to the saints
of the Most High, and the time came
for the saints to have possession of the
kingdom. And he answered as follows: 23
'The fourth beast shall be a fourth kingdom on the earth,
Which shall be different from all the other kingdoms;
It shall devour the whole earth,
And shall trample it down, and tear it in pieces.
As for the ten horns, out of this king- 24
dom shall arise ten kings,
And after them shall arise another king,
Who shall be different from the former kings,
And shall put down three of them.
He shall speak words against the Most 25
High,
And shall wear out the saints of the Most High;
He shall plan to change the sacred seasons and the law,
And they shall be handed over to him for a year, two years, and half a year.
Then the court shall take its seat, and 26
his dominion shall be taken away,
To be consumed and destroyed for all time;
And the kingdom, the dominion, and 27
the greatness of the kingdoms under the whole heavens
Shall be given to the people of the saints of the Most High;
Their kingdom shall be an everlasting kingdom,
And all dominions shall serve and obey them.'

"This was the end of the matter. As 28
for me, Daniel, my thoughts greatly upset me, and my face changed color; but
I kept the matter in my mind."

THE VISION OF THE RAM AND THE HE-GOAT, 8:1–27

In the third year of the reign of King 8
Belshazzar a vision appeared to me,
Daniel, of the same nature as that
which had previously appeared to me.
In my vision I found myself at the 2
citadel of Susa, in the province of Elam,
beside the stream Ulai. I raised my 3

eyes, and looked, and lo! standing in
front of the stream there was a ram
with two horns, both of them high,
though one was higher than the other,
and the higher came up behind the
4 other. I saw the ram butting westward,
northward, and southward; none of the
beasts could stand before him, nor
could anyone rescue from his power; he
did as he pleased, and accomplished
great exploits.
5 As I was considering the matter, lo!
a he-goat from the west advanced over
the whole face of the earth, without
touching the earth; and the goat had a
conspicuous horn between his eyes.
6 When he came to the ram with the two
horns, which I had seen standing in
front of the stream, he ran at him in the
7 impetus of his might. As I saw him
come close to the ram, he was moved by
fierce rage against him, and he smote
the ram, and broke his two horns; and
as the ram had no power to stand before
him, he cast him down to the ground,
and trampled upon him, there being
none to rescue the ram from his power.
8 Then the he-goat accomplished very
great exploits; but when he had reached
the height of his power, the great horn
was broken, and in its place there came
up four other horns, facing the four
winds of the heavens.
9 Out of one of them there emerged
another horn, a little one, which grew
very great toward the south, the east,
10 and the glorious land. It became as
great as the host of the heavens; and
some of the starry host it cast down to
the ground, and trampled under foot.
11 It made itself even as great as the
Prince of the host, whose regular offering was taken away from him, and the
site of whose sanctuary was profaned.
12 Thus was the regular offering treated
with criminal violence, and the truth
cast down to the ground, while it worked
13 its will, and prospered. Then I heard a
holy one speak; and another holy one
asked this one who spoke,
"How long shall be the vision of the
regular offering taken away, the desolating crime put in its place, and the sanctuary and the host of the heavens
trampled under foot?"
14 And he answered him,
"For two thousand three hundred
evenings and mornings; then shall the
wrongs of the sanctuary be righted."

Now when I, Daniel, had seen the vi- 15
sion, and was seeking to understand it,
lo! there stood before me a human-like
form, while from between the banks of 16
the Ulai I heard a human voice, calling,
and saying,
"O Gabriel, make this man understand the vision."
So he came near where I stood; and 17
when he came, I was terrified, and fell
upon my face. But he said to me,
"Understand, O mortal man! for the
vision relates to the time of the end."
As he spoke with me, I remained in a 18
swoon with my face to the ground. But
he touched me, and set me upon my
feet. Then he said, 19
"Behold, I am making known to you
what shall be at the end of the time of
wrath; for the vision relates to the appointed end of all. The ram which you 20
saw, with the two horns, is the king of
Media and Persia. The he-goat is the 21
king of Greece; and the great horn between his eyes is the first king. As the 22
horn was broken, and four others arose
in its place, so four kingdoms shall arise
from his nation, though not with a
power like his. And at the close of these 23
kingdoms, when crimes have reached
their height, there shall arise a king of
fierce countenance, with an understanding of secret wiles. He shall at- 24
tain to great power, though not by his
own power; he shall cause fearful destruction, and shall prosper in what he
does, destroying powerful rivals. He 25
shall form designs against the saints,
and shall cause treachery to prosper
under his hand; he shall devise great
things in his own mind, and shall destroy many unawares; he shall even
rise up against the Prince of princes,
but shall be broken by no human hand.
The vision which has been told of the 26
mornings and evenings is true; but keep
the vision a secret, for it relates to the
distant future."
Thereupon I, Daniel, was faint and 27
sick for a number of days; then I rose
up, and carried on the king's business.
But I was disquieted by the vision, for
I did not understand it.

THE PROPHECY OF THE SEVENTY WEEKS, 9:1–27

In the first year of Darius, the son of
Xerxes, of the race of the Medes, who

had been made king over the realm of
2 the Chaldeans, in the first year of his
reign, I, Daniel, observed in the Scriptures the number of the years which the
word of the LORD had revealed to Jeremiah, the prophet, for the full accomplishment of the desolations of Jerusa-
3 lem, namely, seventy years. So I turned
my face toward the Lord GOD, applying myself to prayer and supplications,
4 with fasting, sackcloth, and ashes; and
I interceded with the LORD my God,
and made confession, saying,
"Ah now, O Lord, the great and revered God, who keeps loving faith with
those who love him and keep his com-
5 mands, we have sinned, we have acted
wrongfully and wickedly, we have rebelled and turned aside from thy com-
6 mands and ordinances, and we have not
listened to thy servants, the prophets,
who spoke in thy name to our kings and
princes, our leaders, and all the com-
7 mon people. To thee, O Lord, pertains
the right, but to us confusion of face, as
at this day—to the men of Judah and
the inhabitants of Jerusalem, as well as
to all Israel, near and far, in all the
lands to which thou hast driven them,
because of the treason which they com-
8 mitted against thee. To us, O Lord,
pertains confusion of face—to our
kings, our princes, and our leaders, be-
9 cause we have sinned against thee. But
to the Lord our God pertain compassion and forgiveness, because we have
10 rebelled against him, and have not
listened to the voice of the LORD our
God in following the laws which he set
before us by his servants the prophets.
11 All Israel, indeed, has broken thy law,
and turned aside from listening to thy
voice; therefore thou hast poured out
upon us the curse embodied in the oath
which is written in the law of Moses,
12 the servant of God. Because we have
sinned against him, he has fulfilled his
word, which he spoke against us, and
against our rulers who ruled us, by
bringing upon us a disaster so great
that under the whole heavens there has
not been done the like of what has been
13 done in Jerusalem. All this disaster has
come upon us, as it is written in the law
of Moses; yet we have not sought the
favor of the LORD our God by turning
from our offenses and gaining discern-
14 ment in thy truth. Therefore the LORD
has been vigilant in bringing this disaster upon us; for the LORD our God is
righteous in all the works that he has
done, while we have not listened to his
voice. And now, O Lord our God, who 15
didst bring thy people out of the land of
Egypt by a mighty hand, and didst
gain for thyself the renown which thou
hast this day, we have sinned, we have
done wickedly. O LORD, in accordance 16
with all thy righteous deeds, pray, let
thine anger and fury turn from Jeru
salem thy city, thy holy hill, because
for our sins, and for the offenses of our
fathers, Jerusalem and thy people have
become a reproach to all who are round
about us. And now, O our God, listen 17
to the prayer and supplications of thy
servant, and for thine own sake, O Lord,
make thy face shine upon thy sanctuary which is desolate. O my God! 18
Incline thine ear, and listen. Open thine
eyes, and see our desolations—the city
which bears thy name—for it is not on
account of our own righteousness that
we present our supplications before
thee, but on account of thy great compassion. O Lord, hear; O Lord, forgive; 19
O Lord, attend, and act—do not delay—for thine own sake, O my God,
because thy city and thy people bear
thy name."
While I was still speaking, and pray- 20
ing, confessing my sin and the sin of my
people Israel, and presenting my supplication before the LORD my God for
the holy hill of my God, while I was still 21
speaking in prayer, the man Gabriel,
whom I had seen in the previous vision,
being sped in swift flight, approached
me about the time of the evening sacrifice; and he came and spoke with me, 22
saying,
"O Daniel, I have come expressly to
enlighten you. While you were at the 23
beginning of your supplications, a word
went forth, and I have come to make it
known to you; for you are a man greatly beloved. Therefore pay heed to the
word, and give attention to the vision:
'Seventy weeks of years are destined 24
for your people and for your holy
city,
To finish the crime, to end the sin, to
expiate the guilt,
To bring in everlasting righteousness,
to confirm prophetic vision,
And to consecrate the most sacred
place.'
"Learn, therefore, and understand: 25

'From the going forth of the word to
restore and rebuild Jerusalem,
Till there comes a prince, an anointed
one, there shall be seven weeks;
Then for sixty-two weeks it shall stay
rebuilt, with its squares and
streets;
26 And at the end of the times, after the
sixty-two weeks,
The anointed one shall be cut off,
leaving none to succeed him;
The city and the sanctuary shall be
destroyed along with the prince,
And the end shall come in a flood, with
war raging to the end;
27 Then for one week the covenant shall
be abandoned by many,
And for half of the week sacrifice and
offering shall cease,
While in their place there shall be a
desolating abomination,
Till at the end the doom that is determined shall be poured out upon
the desolating thing.' "

THE CONFLICT OF KINGDOMS, 10:1—12:13

10 In the third year of Cyrus, king of
Persia, a word was revealed to Daniel
whose name was Belteshazzar—a true
word concerning a great warfare—and
he paid heed to the word, and gave attention to the vision.
2 In those days I, Daniel, continued in
3 mourning for three whole weeks; I ate
no appetizing food, no flesh or wine
entered my mouth, nor did I anoint
myself at all, till three whole weeks
were ended. Then, on the twenty-fourth
4 day of the first month, as I stood on the
5 bank of the great river, the Tigris, I
raised my eyes, and looked, and lo!
there was a man clothed in linen, his
6 loins girded with fine gold of Ophir, his
body flashing like a topaz, his face like
lightning, and his eyes like torches of
fire, his arms and legs gleaming like
burnished bronze, and the sound of his
7 words like the sound of a multitude. I,
Daniel, alone saw the vision; for the
men who were with me did not see the
vision, but a great trembling had fallen
upon them, so that they fled to hide
8 themselves. So I was left alone to see
this great vision, and no strength was
left in me; my vigor was turned into
weakness, and I retained no strength.
I heard the sound of his words; but as 9
I heard the sound of his words, I fell
in a swoon, with my face to the ground.
And lo! a hand touched me, and set me 10
tottering upon my knees and the palms
of my hands. Then he said to me, 11
"O Daniel, greatly beloved, stand
upright, and pay heed to the words that
I speak to you; for I have been sent expressly to you."
So when he had spoken this word to
me, I stood up trembling. Then he said 12
to me,
"Fear not, O Daniel! for ever since
you applied your mind to gain understanding, and to humble yourself before
your God, your prayers have been
heard, and I have come in answer to
your prayers. For twenty-one days, in- 13
deed, the guardian angel of the kingdom of Persia opposed me; but Michael,
one of the archangels, came to help me,
so I left him there with the angel of the
kingdom of Persia, and have come to
enlighten you as to what shall befall
your people in the end of the days; for
the vision relates to the still distant
future."
When he had spoken to me in these 15
terms, I bent my face to the earth, and
remained dumb. Then lo! one like a 16
man touched my lips; and I opened my
mouth, and spoke to him who stood
before me, saying,
"O my lord, by reason of the vision
my pangs have come writhing upon me,
and I retain no strength. So how can 17
such a servant of my lord as I talk with
such a one as my lord? As it is, no
strength remains in me, and no breath
is left in me."
Then the one like a man touched me 18
again, and put strength into me. And 19
he said,
"Fear not, O greatly beloved! Peace
be with you! Be strong, and be brave!"
When he had spoken to me, I felt
strengthened, and said,
"Let my lord speak; for you have
strengthened me."
Then he said, 20
"Do you know why I have come to
you? Presently I must return to fight
with the angel of Persia; and when I
have done with him, the angel of Greece
will come. There is none to support me 21
against these, except your angel Michael, who stands up to support and
defend me. However, I will tell you 1

what is inscribed in the book of truth—
2 here and now I will tell you the truth:
"There shall arise three more kings
in Persia, then a fourth, who shall be
far richer than all of them; and when he
has grown strong through his riches, he
shall set all his forces in motion against
3 the kingdom of Greece. Then a warlike
king shall arise, who shall rule with
great power, and shall do as he pleases.
4 But when he has grown strong, his kingdom shall be broken up, and divided
toward the four winds of the heavens;
it shall not pass to his posterity, nor
shall it retain the power with which he
ruled; but his kingdom shall be plucked
up, and given to others than these.
5 "Then the king of the south shall be
strong; but one of his captains shall be
stronger than he, and shall rule over a
6 kingdom greater than his. After a number of years they shall form an alliance;
and the daughter of the king of the
south shall come to the king of the
north, to seal the treaty of peace. But
her influence shall be of no avail, nor
shall her influence last; for she shall be
given up, together with her suite, her
son, and her husband.
7 "In those days there shall arise in his
place a scion from her roots, who shall
come with an army, and shall enter the
stronghold of the king of the north, and
shall throw him and his people into a
8 panic, and shall overcome them, and
shall carry captive to Egypt their gods,
their molten images, and their precious
vessels of silver and gold. For a number
of years he shall refrain from attacking
9 the king of the north. Then the latter
shall invade the kingdom of the king of
the south, though he shall return to his
10 own country. But his son shall bestir
himself, and shall muster an array of
great forces, and shall advance against
him, sweeping along like an overwhelming flood, and in his turn shall press
11 forward to his stronghold. Then the
king of the south, moved by fierce rage,
shall march out and fight with him,
that is, with the king of the north, who
shall raise a great army. But the army
shall be given into his hand, and shall
12 be carried away captive. Then his heart
shall be lifted up, and he shall put down
tens of thousands, though he shall not
13 make good his success. For the king of
the north shall raise another army,
greater than the former one, and after
a number of years he shall advance
against him in great force and with
abundant supplies. In those days many 14
shall rise up against the king of the
south, and violent men among your
own people shall lift themselves up, in
order to fulfil the vision; but they shall
fall to the ground. Then the king of the 15
north shall come, and throw up a
mound, and take a well-fortified city;
and the forces of the south shall make
no stand against him; even their picked
troops shall have no strength to stand.
The invader shall do as he pleases, with 16
none to stand against him; he shall
stand in the glorious land, holding it all
in his hand. Then he shall set his face 17
to advance against the king of the south
with the full strength of his kingdom,
but shall have to make terms with him;
and he shall give him his daughter in
marriage, so as to gain control of the
land; but this also shall not stand, nor
succeed with him. Then he shall turn 18
his face toward the coast-lands, and
shall take many of them; but a certain
commander shall put an end to his insolence, and shall repay his insolence
sevenfold. Then he shall turn his face 19
toward the strongholds of his own land;
but he shall stumble and fall, and shall
be found no more.
"In his place there shall arise one 20
who shall send an exactor of tribute
through the most glorious part of the
kingdom; but within a few days he shall
be crushed, though not by open violence, nor in battle.
"In his place there shall arise a con- 21
temptible person, on whom the royal
dignity has not been conferred, but who
shall come by stealth, and shall win the
kingdom by intrigues. Armed forces 22
shall be utterly overwhelmed before
him, and the prince of the covenant
shall also be crushed. And as soon as 23
one makes an alliance with him, he shall
practice treachery, and shall rise to
great power, though he has but a handful of people, by means of stealth. Then 24
he shall assail the richest men of the
provinces, and shall do what neither his
fathers nor his fathers' fathers have
done—he shall lavish among them
plunder and spoil and goods; and he
shall hatch his plots against fortresses,
though only for a time. By means of a 25
great army he shall raise his might and
courage against the king of the south;

and the king of the south shall bestir
himself to battle against him with a
very great and powerful army, but shall
not make a stand, for plots shall be
26 hatched against him; even those who
eat of his delicacies shall crush him, and
his army shall be swept away, and
27 many shall fall down dead. Each of the
kings shall have his mind bent on mischief, and shall speak lies at a common
table; but it shall not avail, for an end
awaits them at the time appointed.
28 Then he shall return to his own land
laden with goods; and his mind being
set against the holy covenant, he shall
work his will, and return to his own land.
29 "At the time appointed he shall again
invade the south; but this time it shall
30 not be as in former times; for Roman
ships shall come against him, and he
shall be cowed. Then he shall be inflamed once more with rage against the
holy covenant; and having come to an
understanding with those who have forsaken the holy covenant, he shall once
31 more work his will. Armed forces shall
be raised by him, and they shall desecrate the stronghold of the sanctuary,
and shall abolish the regular offering,
and shall put in its place the desolating
32 abomination. By his intrigues he shall
corrupt those who have violated the
covenant; but the people who know
their God shall be steadfast, and shall
33 accomplish exploits. Such as are wise
among the people shall bring understanding to the multitude, though for
many days they shall fall victims to
sword and flame, to captivity and plun-
34 der. While they fall, they shall receive
a little help; and many shall attach
35 themselves to them in hypocrisy. But
those of the wise who fall shall do so in
order to be refined, and purified, and
made white, with a view to the time of
the end; for the time appointed is still
36 to come. And the king shall do as he
pleases; he shall uplift and exalt himself
above every god, and shall speak monstrous things against the God of gods;
and he shall prosper till the time of
wrath is ended, for what is determined
37 shall be done. He shall have no regard
even for the gods of his fathers—no regard for the Delight of women, nor for
any other god; for he shall exalt himself
38 above all. Instead of them, he shall
honor the god of strongholds; a god
whom his fathers did not know he shall
honor with gold and silver, precious
stones and costly gifts. He shall man 39
his strongest fortresses with worshipers of an alien god; and on those who
acknowledge this god he shall bestow
great honor, making them rulers over
many, and allotting them land as a reward.
"At the time of the end the king of 40
the south shall thrust at him; but the
king of the north shall burst upon him
like a whirlwind, with chariots, and
horsemen, and many ships, and shall
sweep through many lands like an overwhelming flood. He shall invade the 41
glorious land, and myriads shall fall;
but these shall escape from his hand—
Edom, and Moab, and the remnant of
the Ammonites. As he stretches his 42
hand over the countries, the land of
Egypt shall not escape, but he shall lay 43
his hand upon the treasures of gold and
silver, and upon all the precious things
of Egypt, with the Lybians and Ethiopians in his train. Then news from the 44
east and the north shall upset him, and
he shall withdraw in great fury to destroy and annihilate many, and shall 45
pitch his royal pavilion between the sea
and the glorious holy mountain; and he
shall come to his end, with none to help
him.
"At that time shall Michael arise— 12
the archangel who stands on guard over
your fellow-countrymen—and there
shall be a time of trouble such as there
has never been since there was a nation;
but at that time your people shall be delivered, even everyone whose name is
found written in the book. And many of 2
those who sleep in the land of dust shall
awake, some to everlasting life, and
others to everlasting reproach and contempt. Then those who are wise shall 3
shine like the brightness of the firmament, those who have led the multitude
to righteousness like the stars forever
and ever. And now, O Daniel, bind up 4
the words, and seal the book, till the
time of the end; for many shall prove
disloyal, and troubles shall be many."
Then I, Daniel, looked, and lo! two 5
others were standing, one on this bank
of the river, and one on that bank of the
river. And I said to the man clothed in 6
linen, who appeared above the waters
of the river,
"How long shall it be till the end of
these wonders?"

7 Then I heard the man clothed in
linen, who appeared above the waters
of the river, as he raised his right hand
and his left hand toward the heavens,
swear by him who lives forever, that it
should be for a year, years, and half a
year, and that after the power of him
who shattered the holy people should
be ended, all these things should be
8 ended. I heard, but I did not understand. So I said,
"O my lord, what will the latter end
of these things be?"
9 But he said,
"Go your way, O Daniel! for the
words are bound up and sealed till the
time of the end. Many shall purify 10
themselves, and make themselves
white, and be refined; but the wicked
shall carry on their wickedness, and
none of the wicked shall understand;
only the wise shall understand. From 11
the time that the regular offering is
abolished, and the desolating abomination put in its place, there shall be a
thousand two hundred and ninety days.
Happy is he who waits till he reaches 12
the thousand three hundred and thirty-
five days! So go your way, and rest till 13
the end comes; then you shall rise to enjoy your portion at the end of the
days."

THE BOOK OF HOSEA

THE SUPERSCRIPTION, 1:1

1 THE word of the LORD that came to Hosea, the son of Beeri, in the days of Uzziah, Jotham, Ahaz, and Hezekiah, kings of Judah, and in the days of Jeroboam, the son of Joash, king of Israel.

THE MARRIAGE OF HOSEA, 1:2–9

2 In the beginning, when the LORD
spoke through Hosea, then the LORD
said to Hosea,

"Go, and take to yourself a harlotrous wife, and harlotrous children;
For the land has committed great harlotry, turning from following the LORD."

3 So he went and took Gomer, the
daughter of Diblaim, and she became
4 pregnant and bore him a son. Then the
LORD said to him,

"Call him Jezreel; for but a little while,
And I will demand the blood of Jezreel from the house of Jehu;
And I will bring to an end the dominion of the house of Israel.
5 And it shall come to pass on that day,
That I will break the bow of Israel, in the valley of Jezreel."

6 When she became pregnant again
and bore a daughter, he said to him,

"Call her 'She-who-is-unpitied'; for I will not again
Have pity upon the house of Israel, that I should ever forgive them.
7 But upon the house of Judah I will have pity;
And I will deliver them through the LORD, their God;
And I will not deliver them by bow,
Nor by sword, nor by war,
Nor by horses and horsemen."

8 Then she weaned "She-who-is-unpitied," and became pregnant, and bore
9 a son. And he said,

"Call him, 'Not-my-people';
For you are not my people,
And I am not your God."

GLIMPSES OF FUTURE GLORY, 1:10—2:1

"Then the number of the children of Israel shall be like the sands of the sea, 10
Which can be neither measured nor numbered;
And whereas it was said to them, 'You are not my people,'
It shall be said to them, 'Sons of the living God.'
Then the children of Judah and the children of Israel shall be gathered together, 11
And they shall appoint over themselves one head;
And they shall go up from the land, for great shall be the day of Jezreel.
Say to your brother, 'My-people,' 2
And to your sister, 'She-that-is-pitied.' "

DENUNCIATION OF ISRAEL AS A FAITHLESS WIFE, 2:2–13

"Reason with your mother, reason— 2
For she is not my wife,
And I am not her husband—
That she put away her harlotry from before her,
And her adultery from between her breasts;
Lest I strip her naked, 3
And place her as in the day she was born,
And make her like the desert,
And set her like a parched land,
And slay her with thirst.
And upon her children I will have no pity, 4
Because they are harlot's children.
For their mother played the harlot; 5
She who bore them acted shamelessly.
For she said, 'I will go after my lovers,
Who give me my bread and my water,
My wool and my flax, my oil and my drink.'
Therefore, lo, I am going to hedge up her way with thorns; 6

And I will erect a wall against her,
So that she cannot find her paths.
7 And she shall run after her lovers,
But not overtake them,
And seek them, but not find them.
And she shall say, 'I will go back to my first husband,
For it was better with me then than now.'
8 But she did not know
That it was I who gave her
The grain and the wine and the oil,
And the silver, which I multiplied for her,
And the gold, worked for the Baal.
9 Therefore I will hold back my grain in its time,
And my wine in its season;
And I will snatch away my wool and my flax,
So that she cannot cover her nakedness.
10 And now I will lay bare her shame to the eyes of her lovers,
And none shall rescue her from my hand.
11 And I will bring to an end all her mirth,
Her festival, her new moon, her sabbath, and all her fixed festivals.
12 And I will lay waste her vine and her fig tree of which she said,
'They are my hire,
Which my lovers have given me.'
And I will make them a wilderness,
And the beasts of the field shall devour them.
13 So I will punish her for the days of the Baals to whom she offered sacrifice,
And decked herself with nose-ring and necklace,
And went after her lovers,
But forgot me," is the oracle of the LORD.

PICTURES OF RESTORATION AND BLESSING, 2:14–23

14 "Therefore I am going to persuade her,
And lead her to the wilderness,
And speak to her heart.
15 Then I will give back her vineyards there,
And the valley of Achor as a door of hope.
And she shall respond there as in the days of her youth,
As in the day when she came up from the land of Egypt.
On that day it shall come to pass," is the oracle of the LORD, 16
"That you will call me, 'My husband,'
And you will no longer call me, 'My Baal.'
For I will put away the names of the Baals from her mouth, 17
And they shall no longer be invoked by their name.
On that day I will make a league for them 18
With the beasts of the field, the birds of the air, and the reptiles of the ground;
And the bow, the sword, and war I will break off from the land;
And I will make them lie down in security."

"And I will betroth you to myself forever; 19
I will betroth you to myself in righteousness and justice,
And in kindness and mercy.
And I will betroth you to myself in faithfulness; 20
And you shall know the LORD.
It shall come to pass on that day," is the oracle of the LORD, 21
"That I will answer the heavens,
And they shall answer the earth;
And the earth shall answer the grain, the wine, and the oil; 22
And they shall answer Jezreel;
And I will sow her for myself in the land, 23
And I will pity 'Her-who-is-unpitied';
And I will say to 'Not-my-people,'
'You are my people';
And he shall say, 'My God.'"

HOSEA'S OWN ACCOUNT OF HIS MARRIAGE AND ITS MEANING, 3:1–5

"The LORD said to me again, 3
'Go, love a woman that is beloved
of a paramour, and is an adulteress;
even as the LORD loves the Israelites,
though they turn to other gods and are
lovers of raisin-cakes.'
"So I bought her for myself for fifteen 2
shekels of silver and a homer and a half
of barley. Then I said to her, 3
'Many days you must dwell as mine;

You must not play the harlot, nor have
a husband; nor will I myself come
near you.'
4 "For the Israelites shall abide many
days with no king, no prince, no sacrifice, no sacred pillar, no ephod, and no
5 teraphim. Afterward, the Israelites
shall return and seek the LORD, their
God, and David their king; and they
shall hasten eagerly toward the LORD,
and his goodness in the days to come."

THE IDOLATROUS APOSTASY OF ISRAEL, 4:1–19

4 "Hear the word of the LORD, O Israelites!
For the LORD has a quarrel with the inhabitants of the land;
Because there is no fidelity, no kindness, and no knowledge of God in the land.
2 Cursing, lying, murder, theft, and adultery—
They break out, and one crime follows hard upon another.
3 Therefore the land mourns, and everything that dwells therein languishes,
Even to the beasts of the earth, and the birds of the air;
And the fish of the sea also are swept away.

4 "Yet, let no one make charges, and let no one accuse;
For with you is my quarrel, O priest;
5 And you shall stumble by day;
The prophet also shall stumble with you by night;
And I will destroy your people.
6 My people are destroyed for want of knowledge—
Because you have rejected knowledge,
I will reject you from being my priest.
Since you have forgotten the law of your God,
I likewise will forget your children.

7 "The more they increased, the more they sinned against me;
They have exchanged their glory for shame.
8 They feed on the sin of my people,
And for their guilt they whet their appetite.
9 So it has become 'like people, like priest';
And I will visit his ways upon him,
And requite his deeds to him.
10 And they shall eat, but not be satisfied;
They shall play the harlot, but not be fruitful;
Because they have forsaken the LORD, to practice harlotry.

11 "Wine and liquor take away the understanding.
12 My people inquire of their block of wood,
And their staff instructs them.
For a harlotrous spirit has led them astray,
And they have become apostates from their God.
13 Upon the tops of the mountains they sacrifice,
And upon the hills they make offerings,
Beneath oak, poplar, and terebinth,
Because their shade is good.

"Therefore your daughters play the harlot,
And your sons' wives commit adultery.
14 I will not punish your daughters when they play the harlot,
Nor your sons' wives when they commit adultery;
For they themselves go apart with harlots,
And sacrifice with temple-prostitutes,
And a people without insight must come to ruin.

15 "Though you play the harlot, O Israel,
Let not Judah incur guilt.
Do not come to Gilgal,
Nor go up to Bethaven,
Nor take oath at Beersheba, 'As the LORD lives.'
16 But like a wild heifer, Israel is wild;
Can the LORD feed them now like a lamb at large?"

17 "A maker of images is Ephraim;
He has set up for himself a fat bull!
18 They have grossly apostatized;
They love shame more than their glory.
19 A wind shall carry them away in its wings;
And they shall be ashamed of their altars."

THE GUILT OF ISRAEL AND JUDAH AND ITS PUNISHMENT, 5:1–14

5 "Hear this, O priests!
Give heed, O house of Israel!
Listen, O house of the king!
For the judgment pertains to you;
For you have been a snare at Mizpeh,
And a net spread out upon Tabor.
2 And they have dug deep the pit of Shittim;
But I am a restraint to them all.

3 "I know Ephraim,
And Israel is not hidden from me.
For you have played the harlot, O Ephraim;
Israel is defiled.
4 Their deeds will not permit them
To return to their God.
For an apostate spirit is within them,
And they do not know the LORD.

5 "The pride of Israel shall testify to his face;
And Israel and Ephraim shall stumble in their guilt;
Judah, also, shall stumble with them.
6 With their flocks and their herds, they shall go
To seek the LORD, but shall not find him—
He has departed from them.
7 They have been faithless to the LORD;
For they have borne illegitimate children.
Now he will devour them,
The plowmen and their fields.

8 "Blow the horn in Gibeah,
the trumpet in Ramah;
Sound the alarm at Bethaven;
startle Benjamin!
9 Ephraim shall become a ruin
on the day of punishment.
Among the tribes of Israel,
I announce what is sure.

10 "The princes of Judah have become
Like those who move a boundary line.
Upon them I will pour out
My wrath like water.
11 Ephraim is oppressed, crushed in judgment,
Because Israel went after idols.
12 But I am like a moth unto Ephraim,
And like rottenness unto the house of Judah.

"When Ephraim saw his sickness, 13
And Judah his wound,
Then Ephraim went to Assyria,
And sent to the great king.
But he is not able to heal you;
Nor can he relieve you of your wound.
For I will be like a lion unto Ephraim, 14
And like a young lion to the house of Judah.
I will rend and be gone;
I will carry off, with none to rescue."

ISRAEL'S DEEP DEPRAVITY BELIES HER FACILE REPENTANCE, 5:15—6:11*a*

"I will go back to my place, 15
Until they realize their guilt, and seek my face;
In their trouble they will seek me:
'Come, let us return unto the LORD; 6
For he has torn, but he will heal us;
He smote, but he will bind us up;
He will revive us in two or three days; 2
He will raise us up that we may live before him.
Let us know, let us press on to know 3
the LORD;
As soon as we seek him, we shall find him;
He will come to us like the winter rain,
Like the spring rain that waters the land.'

"What shall I do with you, O Ephraim? 4
What shall I do with you, O Judah?
For your piety is like a morning cloud,
Or like the dew that leaves early.
Therefore will I hew them by the prophets; 5
I will slay them by the words of my mouth,
And my judgment will go forth like the light.
For I delight in piety, not sacrifice; 6
And in the knowledge of God, rather than burnt-offerings.

"But they broke the agreement at Admah; 7
There they dealt faithlessly with me.
Gilead is a city of wrong-doers, 8
Tracked with bloody footprints.
Like troops of men lying in wait, 9
So the priests hid themselves;
On the way to Shechem they committed murder,

They practiced vice.
10 In Bethel, I saw a horrible thing;
There Ephraim played the harlot,
Israel was defiled.
11[a] For you too, O Judah, a harvest is appointed."

ISRAEL'S INTERNAL CORRUPTION, 6:11*b*—7:7

11[b] "When I would restore the fortune of my people,
7 When I would heal Israel,
The guilt of Ephraim is revealed,
And the sin of Samaria;
For they have wrought falsehood,
And the thief comes in;
Gangs prowl about.
2 But they never realize
That I shall remember all their wickedness,
That now their deeds encircle them,
That they are before my face.
3 Through their wickedness they rejoice the king,
And through their treachery princes.
4 They are all adulterers;
They are like a burning oven,
Whose baker ceases stirring,
From the time the dough is kneaded until it is leavened.
5 From the day he became king, the princes have made him sick with the heat of wine;
Worthless men have made him drunk.
6 For their heart glows like an oven, with their trickery;
All night through their anger sleeps;
In the morning it blazes like a flaming fire.
7 They are all hot like an oven,
And they devour their rulers.
All their kings have fallen;
There is no one among them who calls upon me."

ISRAEL'S DISLOYAL FOREIGN POLICY, 7:8–16

8 "Ephraim wastes away among the peoples;
Ephraim is a cake unturned.
9 Strangers devour his strength, without his knowledge;
Gray hairs are scattered upon him, without his knowledge.
10 And the pride of Israel witnesses against him;
But they do not return to the LORD, their God,
Nor seek him for all this.

"For Ephraim has become like a silly dove, without sense; 11
They call to Egypt, they go to Assyria.
As they go, I will spread my net over them; 12
Like birds of the air, I will bring them down;
I will bind them on account of their wickedness.
Woe to them that they have wandered away from me! 13
Ruin to them that they have rebelled against me!
Can I redeem them,
While they speak lies against me?

"They do not cry unto me from their hearts, 14
But wail upon their couches for grain and wine;
They cut themselves and rebel against me.
Yet it was I who trained and strengthened their arms, 15
While against me they plan wickedness.
They turn to the Baal; 16
They are like a treacherous bow.
Their princes shall fall by the sword,
Because of their stumbling speech in the land of Egypt."

IDOLATRY AND DISLOYALTY SPELL DESTRUCTION, 8:1–14

"Set the trumpet to your lips, 8
Like a watchman, against the house of the LORD!
Because they have broken my covenant,
And sinned against my law.
To me they shall cry, 'My God, we, Israel, know thee.' 2
Israel has abhorred the good; 3
An enemy shall pursue him.

"They made kings; but it was not of my doing; 4
They made princes; but without my knowledge.
Of their silver and their gold they made
Idols for themselves, that they might be cut off.

5 I loathe your bull, O Samaria;
My anger blazes against them;
How long will they be incapable of innocence?
6 For from Israel is it;
A mechanic made it;
And it is not God.
Indeed, Samaria's bull
Shall become splinters.

7 "For they sowed the wind;
And they shall reap the whirlwind.
The standing grain which has no sprout shall yield no meal;
If it should yield, foreigners would devour it.
8 Israel shall be devoured;
Soon shall they be among the nations
Like a worthless thing.
9 For they have gone up to Assyria,
Like a wild ass wandering by itself;
Ephraim gives love-gifts.
10 But though they hire among the nations,
I will soon gather them up;
And they shall cease a while from anointing a king and princes.

11 "Though Ephraim has multiplied altars,
They have become to him altars for sinning.
12 I will write him down as an opponent of my law;
He shall be considered as a foreigner.
13 They love sacrifice and they sacrifice
Flesh, and they eat it.
The LORD is not pleased with them;
Soon will he remember their guilt,
And punish their sin;
They shall return to Egypt.
14 For Israel forgot his maker and built palaces;
And Judah multiplied fortified cities;
But I will send a fire upon his cities,
And it shall devour his palaces."

ISRAEL MUST GO INTO EXILE, 9:1–9

9 "Do not rejoice, O Israel!
Do not exult, like the peoples!
For you have become apostates from your God;
You have loved a harlot's hire
Upon all threshing-floors for grain.

2 "But threshing-floor and wine-vat shall not know them,
And wine shall fail them.
They shall not remain in the land of the LORD, 3
But Ephraim shall return to Egypt,
And in Assyria they shall eat unclean food.

"They shall not pour libations of wine to the LORD; 4
Nor shall they prepare their sacrifices for him.
Their food shall be like mourners' food,
In that all who eat of it will defile themselves;
For their food is for themselves only;
It may not come into the house of the LORD.

"What will you do on the festival day, 5
And on the day of the feast of the LORD?
For lo, they shall go to Assyria; 6
Egypt shall gather them,
Memphis shall bury them.
Their desirable places nettles shall possess;
Thorns shall be in their tents.
The days of punishment will come; 7
The days of requital will come;
Israel shall know.

"The prophet is distracted,
The man of the spirit is crazed,
Because of your great guilt;
Great is the opposition to the watchman of Ephraim, the people of my God. 8
The prophet—the fowler's snare is upon all his ways;
Opposition is in the house of his God.
They have dug a deep pit for him, 9
As in the days of Gibeah.
He will remember their guilt,
He will punish their sins."

IRREPARABLE RUIN, 9:10–17

"Like grapes in the wilderness, 10
I found Israel.
Like the first ripe fig on the fig tree, in its first season,
I saw your fathers.
But they came to Baal-peor;
And dedicated themselves to the Baal,
And became an abhorrence like the thing which they loved.

11 "Ephraim's glory flies away like a bird,
So that there will be no births, no motherhood, no conception.
12 Even if they do rear their children,
I will bereave them to a man.
But woe, indeed, to them when I depart from them!
13 As I foresaw, Ephraim's sons must become a prey,
Ephraim must bring out his sons to the slaughter."
14 Give them—O LORD, what canst thou give?
Give them a miscarrying womb,
And dry breasts.

15 "All their wickedness is in Gilgal,
For there I conceived hatred for them.
Because of their wicked deeds,
I will drive them out of my house.
I will no longer love them,
Since all their princes are rebels.

16 "Ephraim is stricken;
Their root is dried up;
They shall bear no fruit.
Even if they do have children,
I will slay the darlings of their womb.
17 My God shall reject them,
Because they have not listened to him;
And they shall become wanderers among the nations."

IDOLATRY AND ITS PUNISHMENT, 10:1–8

10 "Israel is a spreading vine;
His fruit renders him confident;
The more his fruit increased,
The more altars he made;
The more prosperous his land became,
The finer did he make his sacred pillars.
2 Their heart is false; soon must they atone;
Their altars shall be desecrated,
And their sacred pillars destroyed.

3 "For they will soon be saying,
'We have no king;
For we do not revere the LORD;
And as for that, what could the king do for us?'
4 They speak mere words; they swear false oaths;
They make leagues; and judgment will blossom forth,
Like weeds in the furrows of the field.
For the calf of Bethaven, 5
The inhabitants of Samaria shall be anxious;
His people and his priestlings shall mourn for him;
They shall wail for his honor,
Because it has gone into exile from him.
He himself, too, shall be carried to Assyria, 6
As tribute to the great king.
Ephraim shall receive disgrace,
And Israel shall be ashamed of his idol.

"The king of Samaria shall be destroyed, 7
Like a chip upon the surface of the water.
And the high places of Aven shall be destroyed, 8
The sin of Israel;
Thorn and thistle shall spring up upon their altars;
And they shall say to the mountains, 'Cover us';
And to the hills, 'Fall upon us.'"

MORAL FAILURE IS POLITICAL RUIN, 10:9–15

"From the days of Gibeah, you have sinned, O Israel; 9
There they said that war would not overtake them in Gibeah.
I will come against the wicked people and punish them; 10
And peoples shall be gathered together against them,
When they are chastened for their two crimes.
Ephraim was a trained heifer that loved to thresh; 11
But I put a yoke upon her fair neck.
I harnessed Ephraim; Judah ploughed;
Jacob harrowed for himself.

"Sow for yourselves righteousness; 12
Reap the fruit of piety;
Break up your fallow ground;
For it is time to seek the LORD,
Till he come and rain righteousness upon you.
You have ploughed wickedness, you have harvested wrong; 13
You have eaten the fruit of lies,
In that you trusted in your chariots, and in your great might.

14 "But revolt shall arise among your peoples,
And all your fortresses shall be destroyed,
As Shalman destroyed Beth-arbel on the day of battle;
The mother was dashed in pieces with the children.
15 Thus will I do to you, O house of Israel, because of your wickedness!
In the storm, the king of Israel shall be utterly destroyed."

GOD'S LOVE FOR ISRAEL SPURNED BUT TRIUMPHANT, 11:1–11

11 "When Israel was a child, I came to love him,
And from Egypt I called him.
2 The more I called them,
The more they went away from me;
They sacrificed to the Baals,
And made offerings to idols.
3 "But it was I who taught Ephraim to walk;
I took them up in my arms;
But they did not know that I cared for them.
4 With human lines I led them,
With loving cords;
And I became for them like him who lifts the yoke from their jaws;
And I bent toward them and fed them.
5 "Ephraim shall return to Egypt,
And Assyria shall be his king,
Because they have refused to return to me.
6 The sword shall begin upon his cities,
And make an end of his fields,
And shall devour his fortresses.
7 For my people are dependent upon a change in me;
And if they call upon me because of the yoke,
Will I not, nevertheless, raise it up?
8 "How can I give you up, O Ephraim!
How surrender you, O Israel!
How can I treat you like Admah!
How make you like Zeboim!
My mind turns against me;
My sympathies also grow hot.
9 I will not carry out my fierce anger;
Nor will I again destroy Ephraim;
For I am God and not man,
The holy one in the midst of you;
And I will not destroy.
"They shall go after the LORD; 10
Like a lion he will roar;
Yea, he will roar;
And his sons shall come trembling from the west,
They shall come fluttering like a bird 11
from Egypt,
And like a dove from the land of Assyria;
And I will bring them back to their homes,"
Is the oracle of the LORD.

ISRAEL'S FAITHLESSNESS AND ITS PUNISHMENT, 11:12—12:14

"Ephraim surrounds me with lies, 12
And the house of Israel with deceit;
But Judah still seeks after God,
And is loyal to the holy one.
Ephraim feeds upon wind, 12
And pursues the east wind all the time;
They multiply lies and falsehood;
They make a treaty with Assyria,
And carry oil to Egypt.
"The LORD has a quarrel with Judah; 2
And he will punish Jacob according to his ways;
According to his deeds will he requite him.
In the womb he seized his brother's 3
heel,
And in his full vigor he strove with God.
Then he fought against an angel and 4
prevailed;
He wept and entreated him for mercy.
At Bethel he found him,
And there he talked with him.
Then Jacob fled to the field of Aram, 12
And Israel worked for a wife,
And for a wife he watched sheep.
"But the LORD, the God of hosts, 5
The LORD, is his name.
Therefore do you return to your God, 6
Practice kindness and justice,
And wait for your God continually.
"A Canaanite, in whose hands are false 7
balances,
He loves to oppress.
But Ephraim says, 'Indeed, I am rich; 8

I have found power for myself.'
All his gain will not suffice
For the guilt which he has incurred.
9 I am the LORD, your God,
From the land of Egypt;
I will again make you dwell in tents,
As in the days of old.

10 "I spoke to the prophets,
And I gave many visions,
And through the prophets I gave parables.
11 Gilead, indeed, is wickedness; yea, they are falsehood;
In Gilgal they sacrifice to demons;
Their altars, also, are like heaps,
Upon the furrows of the field.
13 By a prophet the LORD brought Israel up from Egypt,
And by a prophet he was kept.
14 Ephraim has provoked him bitterly;
So he will hurl his blood upon him;
And his disgrace his Lord will requite to him."

ISRAEL'S DESTRUCTION NOTWITHSTANDING IDOLS AND KINGS, 13:1–16

13 "Whenever Ephraim spoke there used to be awe;
He was a prince in Israel.
Then he transgressed through the Baal and died.
2 And now they sin more and more,
In that they make for themselves molten images,
And of their silver, through their skill, idols,
Wholly the product of mechanics.
'To such,' they say, 'sacrifice.'
Men kissing calves!
3 Therefore they shall be like a morning cloud,
Or like the dew which leaves early;
Like the chaff that whirls up from the threshing-floor,
Or like the smoke from the window.

4 "But I am the LORD, your God
From the land of Egypt;
And you know no God but me;
And there is no deliverer, except me.
5 I fed you in the wilderness,
In the land of drought;
6 But when they had fed themselves full,
Their heart became arrogant,
And so they forgot me.
7 So I will be unto them like a lion,
Or like a leopard by the road I will lurk.
8 I will rend them like a bear robbed of its cubs,
And I will tear off the covering of their chest,
And I will devour them there like a lion;
The beast of the field shall mangle them.

9 "I am your destruction, O Israel;
Who can help you?
10 Where now is your king, that he may deliver you?
And all your princes that they may rule you,
Of whom you said,
'Give me a king and princes'?
11 I gave you a king in my anger,
And I took him away in my wrath.
12 The guilt of Israel is bound up;
His sin is stored away.
13 The pangs of a woman in child-birth shall come upon him,
But he is a foolish son;
For it is no time to stand
In the mouth of the womb.

14 "Shall I rescue them from the power of Sheol?
Shall I redeem them from death?
Where are your plagues, O Death?
Where is your destruction, O Sheol?
Repentance is hid from my eyes.
15 It indeed shall separate brothers;
The east wind, a wind of the LORD, shall come from the wilderness;
It shall come up and his fountain shall dry up,
And his spring shall be parched.
He shall spoil the treasury
Of every desirable thing.
16 Samaria must bear her guilt;
For she has rebelled against her God;
They must fall by the sword,
Their children be dashed in pieces,
And their pregnant women be ripped open."

AN INVITATION AND A PROMISE, 14:1–9

1 Return, O Israel, to the LORD, your God;
For you have stumbled in your guilt.
2 Take with you words,

And return to the LORD.
Say to him, "Wholly forgive guilt;
And we will take what is good,
And requite thee with the fruits of our lips.
3 Assyria shall not deliver us;
Nor will we ride upon war-horses;
Nor will we say any longer, 'Our God,'
To the work of our own hands;
For in thee the orphan finds mercy.

4 "I will heal their backsliding;
I will love them voluntarily;
For my anger has turned away from them.
5 I will be like the dew to Israel,
So that he will blossom like the lily,
And his roots will spread like the poplar;
6 His tendrils will spread out;
And his beauty will be like the olive tree,
And his fragrance like that of Lebanon.
7 Those who shall again dwell beneath his shadow,
Shall raise grain,
And they shall blossom like a vine,
Whose fragrance shall be like the wine of Lebanon.

8 "What more has Ephraim any need of idols?
I am his Anath and his Asherah;
I am like a green fir-tree;
From me is his fruit found."

9 Whoever is wise, let him understand these things,
Whoever is discerning, let him know them;
That the ways of the LORD are right,
And the righteous walk in them,
While sinners stumble in them.

THE BOOK OF JOEL

THE LOCUST PLAGUE AND THE DROUGHT, 1:1–19

1 THE word of the LORD, which
came to Joel, the son of Pethuel:
2 Hear this, O elders;
And listen, all you dwellers in
the land!
Has such a thing ever been in your
days,
Or in the days of your fathers?
3 Tell of it to your sons,
And your sons to their sons in turn,
And their sons to the next generation.

4 What the shearer left, the locust ate,
And what the locust left, the hopper
ate,
And what the hopper left, the stripper
ate.
5 Rouse yourselves, you topers, and
weep;
And wail, all you drinkers of wine,
Because of the new wine; for it is cut
off from your mouth.

6 For a nation has come up against my
land,
Strong and innumerable;
His teeth are a lion's teeth,
And the fangs of a lioness are his.
7 He has made my vine a waste,
And blighted my fig tree;
He has stripped off its bark and
thrown it away;
Its branches are whitened.

8 Wail, like a virgin girded with sack-
cloth
For the bridegroom of her youth.
9 Cut off are the offering and the liba-
tion
From the house of the LORD.
The priests mourn,
The ministers of the LORD.

10 The field is devastated;
The ground mourns;
Because the grain is laid waste,
The wine is dried up,
The oil fails.
The farmers are disappointed, 11
The vine-dressers lament,
For the wheat and the barley;
Because the harvest of the field is lost.
The vine withers, 12
And the fig tree wilts.
The pomegranate, palm, and apple—
All the trees of the field dry up;
So that mirth has withered away
From the sons of men.

Gird yourselves with sackcloth and 13
mourn, O priests;
Wail, O ministers of the altar!
Come, spend the night in sackcloth,
O ministers of my God!
Because the sacrifice and libation are
withheld
From the house of your God.
Sanctify a fast; 14
Call a convocation!
Gather, O elders,
All the inhabitants of the land
Into the house of the LORD your God;
And cry unto the LORD.
Alas for the day! 15
For the day of the LORD is near,
And as destruction from the Almighty
it comes.
Has not food been cut off 16
From before our eyes?
From the house of our God,
Gladness and joy?

The mules stamp at their stalls; 17
The granaries are devastated;
The barns are ruined;
Because the grain has failed.
What can we put in them? 18
The herds of cattle wander about,
Because they have no pasture;
The flocks of sheep, also, are dis-
mayed.

Unto thee, O LORD, do I cry, 19
Because fire has consumed the pastures of the steppe,
And flame has scorched all the trees of
the field.

The beasts of the field, also, cry out
unto thee;
Because the streams of water are dry,
And fire has consumed the pastures of
the steppe.

THE LOCUSTS AND THE DAY OF THE LORD, 2:1–11

2 Blow the trumpet in Zion;
Raise the alarm on my holy mountain!
Let all the inhabitants of the land
tremble;
For the day of the LORD comes!
2 For near is the day of darkness and
gloom,
The day of clouds and deep darkness.

Like blackness spread over the moun-
tains,
Is the great and powerful people.
The like of them has not been from of
old;
Nor will there be any again after them,
Throughout the years of successive
generations.

3 Before them a fire devours,
And after them a flame scorches.
Like the garden of Eden was the land
before them,
And after them it is a desert waste;
And nothing escapes them.

4 They look like horses,
And they run like war-horses.
5 Like the rattle of chariots,
They leap on the tops of the moun-
tains;
Like the crackling of a flame of fire,
That devours the stubble;
Like a mighty people,
Arrayed for battle.
6 Before them peoples are in anguish,
All faces grow pale.
7 Like warriors they run;
Like men of war they climb the wall.
They go each his own way,
And do not entangle their paths.
8 They do not push one another;
Each goes his own road.
And though they fall into a stream,
They do not sink.
9 They rush upon the city;
They run upon the wall;
They go up into the houses;
Through the windows they enter like
a thief.

Before them the land trembles; 10
The heavens quake;
Sun and moon grow dark,
And the stars withhold their bright-
ness.
The LORD thunders at the head of his 11
army;
For very great is his host;
He that executes his command is pow-
erful.
For great is the day of the LORD,
And exceedingly terrible; and who can
withstand it?

A CALL TO PENITENCE, 2:12–17

"Yet even now," is the oracle of the 12
LORD,
"Return to me with your whole heart,
And with fasting, and weeping, and
mourning."
And rend your heart and not your gar- 13
ments,
And return to the LORD, your God;
For he is gracious and merciful,
Slow to anger and abounding in kind-
ness,
And relenting of evil.
Who knows but that he will again re- 14
lent,
And leave behind him a blessing,
An offering and a libation
To the LORD, your God?

Blow the trumpet in Zion; 15
Order a sacred fast; call a holy assem-
bly;
Assemble the people; order a holy con- 16
vocation;
Gather in the elders; collect the chil-
dren,
And the infants at the breast!
Let the bridegroom go forth from his
chamber,
And the bride from her pavilion!

Between the porch and the altar, 17
Let the priests, the ministers of the
LORD, weep;
And let them say, "Spare thy people,
O LORD,
And make not thy heritage a re-
proach,
That they should become a by-word
among the nations.
Why should they say among the peo-
ples,
'Where is their God?'"

FORGIVENESS AND PROMISE, 2:18–27

18 Then the LORD became solicitous for his land,
And had pity upon his people.
19 And the LORD answered and said to his people,
"Lo, I am going to send you
The grain, the wine, and the oil,
And you will be satisfied therewith;
And I will no more make you a reproach among the nations.
20 And I will remove the Northerner far from you;
And I will drive him out into a parched and waste land;
His van into the eastern sea,
And his rear into the western sea;
And the stench of him will arise and the foul smell of him will ascend;
Though he has done great things.

21 "Fear not, O land;
Exult and rejoice;
For the LORD has done great things!
22 Fear not, O beasts of the field;
For the pastures of the steppe are green,
The tree bears its fruit,
The fig-tree and the grape-vine yield their increase.

23 "And do you, O sons of Zion, exult,
And rejoice in the LORD, your God;
For he gave you a warning,
Teaching righteousness;
And he has sent down to you rain,
The winter and the spring rains as of old.

24 "And the threshing-floors shall be full of grain;
And the wine-vats shall overflow with wine and oil;
25 And I will repay you for the years
Which the locust devoured,
The hopper, the stripper, and the shearer,
My great army, which I sent upon you.

26 "And you shall eat to the full and be satisfied,
And you shall praise the name of the LORD, your God,
Who has done wonders for you;
And my people shall never again be put to shame,
And you shall know that I am in the midst of Israel. 27
I, the LORD, am your God, and there is none else;
So my people shall never again be put to shame."

THE DAY OF THE LORD AND ITS MANIFESTATIONS, 2:28–32

"It shall come to pass afterward, 28
That I will pour out my spirit upon all flesh;
Your sons and your daughters shall prophesy;
Your old men shall dream dreams,
And your young men shall see visions.
Furthermore, upon the male and female slaves, 29
In those days I will pour out my spirit.

"And I will set portents in the heavens and on the earth, 30
Blood, and fire, and columns of smoke.
The sun shall be changed to darkness and the moon to blood, 31
Before the coming of the day of the LORD, great and terrible.
But everyone that calls upon the name of the LORD shall be delivered; 32
For in Mount Zion and in Jerusalem there shall be those that escape";
As the LORD has said.
And the escaped will be those whom the LORD proclaims.

JUDGMENT UPON THE NATIONS, 3:1–8

"For behold, in those days and at 3
that time, when I restore the fortune of
Judah and Jerusalem, I will gather all
the nations, and bring them down to
the valley of Jehoshaphat; and I will
enter into judgment with them there,
on account of my people and my heritage, Israel, whom they have scattered among the nations. They have divided my land, and cast lots upon my people, and given a boy for a harlot, and sold a girl for wine, and drunk it.

"Moreover, what are you to me, O Tyre, and Sidon, and all the districts of Philistia? Are you paying me back for something I have done? Or are you doing something to me? Right speedily will I requite your deed upon your own head! For you have taken my silver and my gold; and my goodly treasures

you have brought into your palaces.
6 The people of Judah, and the people of
Jerusalem, you have sold to the Greeks,
so as to remove them far from their
7 own territory. Behold, I am going to
rouse them up from the place into which
you have sold them; and I will requite
8 your deed upon your own head. I will
sell your sons and your daughters into
the hand of the people of Judah, and
they will sell them to the Sabeans, to a
distant nation." For the LORD has
spoken.

THE WORLD-JUDGMENT, 3:9–13

9 Proclaim this among the nations:
Hallow war! Arouse the warriors!
Let the fighting men approach and
ascend!
10 Beat your plowshares into swords,
And your pruning hooks into lances!
Let the weakling say, "I am a warrior."
11 Haste and come, all you nations,
And gather yourselves there from
every side.
Bring down thy warriors, O LORD!
12 Let the nations rouse themselves and
come up
To the valley of Jehoshaphat;
For there I will sit to judge
All the nations from every side.
13 Put in the sickle,
For the harvest is ripe!
Go in, tread;
For the wine-press is full!
The vats overflow!
For their wickedness is great.

THE GOLDEN AGE, 3:14–21

14 Multitudes upon multitudes are in the
valley of decision,
For the day of the LORD is near in the
valley of decision.
The sun and the moon are darkened, 15
And the stars withhold their brightness.

For the LORD roars from Zion, 16
And from Jerusalem he utters his
voice;
And the heavens and the earth quake.
But the LORD is a refuge to his people,
And a stronghold to the children of
Israel.

"And you shall know that I, the LORD, 17
your God,
Am dwelling in Zion, my holy mountain.
And Jerusalem shall be holy,
And aliens shall not again pass
through her.

"And it shall come to pass on that day, 18
That the mountains shall drip sweet
wine,
And the hills shall flow with milk,
And all the river-beds of Judah shall
flow with water;
And a spring shall go forth from the
house of the LORD,
And water the valley of Shittim.

"Egypt shall become a waste, 19
And Edom shall be a barren steppe;
Because of the wrong done to the children of Judah,
In that they shed innocent blood in
their land.
But Judah shall abide forever, 20
And Jerusalem throughout the ages.
And I will avenge their blood; I will 21
not leave it unpunished."
For the LORD dwells in Zion.

THE BOOK OF AMOS

TITLE AND PURPOSE OF THE BOOK, 1:1–2

1 THE words of Amos, who was one of the shepherds of Tekoa, which he received regarding Israel, in the days of Uzziah, king of Judah, and in the days of Jeroboam, the son of Joash, king of Israel, two years before the earthquake; saying,

2 "The LORD roars from Zion,
And from Jerusalem he utters his voice;
So that the pastures of the shepherds mourn,
And the top of Carmel withers."

DOOM UPON THE SURROUNDING NATIONS, 1:3—2:5

3 Thus says the LORD:
"For the three transgressions of Damascus,
And for the four, I will not turn it back;
Because they have threshed Gilead
With threshing-tools of iron.
4 So I will send a fire upon the house of Hazael,
And it shall devour the palaces of Ben-hadad;
5 And I will break the bar of Damascus,
And cut off the inhabitants from the valley of Aven,
And the holder of the scepter from Beth-eden;
And the people of Syria shall go captive to Kir."
Says the LORD.

6 Thus says the LORD:
"For the three transgressions of Gaza,
And for the four, I will not turn it back;
Because they carried into exile a whole people,
To hand them over to Edom.
7 So I will send a fire upon the wall of Gaza,
And it shall devour her palaces;
And I will cut off the inhabitants from Ashdod, 8
And the holder of the scepter from Askelon,
And I will turn my hand against Ekron,
And the remnant of the Philistines shall perish."
Says the Lord GOD.

Thus says the LORD:
"For the three transgressions of Tyre,
And for the four, I will not turn it back;
Because they handed over a whole people as captives to Edom,
And did not remember the covenant of brotherhood.
So I will send a fire upon the wall of Tyre,
And it shall devour her palaces."

Thus says the LORD:
"For the three transgressions of Edom,
And for the four, I will not turn it back;
Because he pursued his brother with the sword,
And stifled his pity,
So that his anger raged perpetually,
And his wrath stormed continually.
So I will send a fire upon Teman,
And it shall devour the palaces of Bozrah."

Thus says the LORD:
"For the three transgressions of the Ammonites,
And for the four, I will not turn it back;
Because they ripped up the pregnant women of Gilead,
That they might enlarge their boundary.
So I will kindle a fire upon the wall of Rabbah,
And it shall devour her palaces;
With shouting on the day of battle,
With a storm on the day of tempest;
And their king shall live in exile,
He and his princes together."
Says the LORD.

2 Thus says the LORD:
"For the three transgressions of Moab,
And for the four, I will not turn it back;
Because he burned the bones
Of the king of Edom to lime.
2 So I will send a fire against Moab,
And it shall devour the palaces of Kerioth;
And Moab shall die with uproar,
With shouting and the sound of the trumpet;
3 And I will cut off the chieftain from the midst of her,
And slay all her princes with him."
Says the LORD.

4 Thus says the LORD:
"For the three transgressions of Judah,
And for the four, I will not turn it back;
Because they have rejected the instruction of the LORD,
And have not kept his statutes;
But their lies have led them astray,
After which their fathers walked.
5 So I will send a fire upon Judah,
And it shall devour the palaces of Jerusalem."

THE SIN AND DOOM OF ISRAEL, 2:6–16

6 Thus says the LORD:
"For the three transgressions of Israel,
And for the four, I will not turn it back;
Because they have sold the innocent for silver,
And the needy in exchange for a pair of sandals;
7 They who trample upon the heads of the poor,
And thrust aside the humble from the way.
A man and his father go in to the harlots,
Thereby profaning my holy name.
8 Garments taken in pledge they spread out
Beside every altar;
And the wine of those who have been fined they drink
In the houses of their gods.

9 "Yet it was I who destroyed the Amorite from before them,
Whose height was like that of the cedars,
And he was as strong as the oaks;
But I destroyed his fruit above,
And his roots below.
And it was I too who brought you up from the land of Egypt, 10
And led you through the wilderness for forty years,
That you might seize the land of the Amorites.
Also I raised up some of your sons as prophets, 11
And some of your young men as Nazirites.
Is this not indeed so, O Israelites?"
The oracle of the LORD.
"But you made the Nazirites drink wine; 12
And you laid command upon the prophets, saying, 'You shall not prophesy.'

"Behold, I am going to make a groaning under you, 13
As a wagon groans that is loaded with sheaves.
Flight shall perish from the swift, 14
And the strong shall not exert his strength,
And the warrior shall not save himself;
And he who handles the bow shall not stand firm, 15
Nor shall the swift of foot save himself,
Nor shall he who rides upon horseback save himself;
And the stoutest of heart among the warriors 15
Shall flee away naked on that day."
The oracle of the LORD.

THE CATEGORICAL IMPERATIVE, 3:1–8

Hear this word which the LORD speaks against you, O Israelites, against the whole family that I brought up from the land of Egypt, saying, 3
"You only have I known, 2
of all the families of the earth";
Therefore will I punish you
for all your wrongdoing.

Do two men walk together, 3
unless they have made an appointment?
Does a lion roar in the forest, 4
when he has no prey?
Does a young lion send forth his voice from his lair,
unless he has seized something?

5 Does a bird fall to the ground,
when there is no snare for it?
Does a trap spring from the ground,
when it has taken nothing at all?
6 If a trumpet be blown in a city,
do the people not tremble?
If there be disaster in a city,
has not the LORD caused it?
7 Surely, he will do nothing,
the Lord GOD,
Except he reveal his purpose
to his servants the prophets.
8 When the lion roars,
who does not fear?
When the Lord GOD speaks,
who will not prophesy?

THE DOOM OF SAMARIA, 3:9—4:3

9 Make proclamation over the palaces in Assyria,
And over the palaces in the land of Egypt,
And say, "Assemble yourselves upon the mountains of Samaria
And see the great confusion in the midst of her,
And the oppression within her."
10 "For they do not know how to do right," is the oracle of the LORD,
"Who treasure up violence and robbery in their palaces."

11 Therefore thus says the Lord GOD:
"The foe shall surround the land,
And strip you of your strength;
And your palaces shall be plundered."

12 Thus says the LORD:
"Just as a shepherd rescues from the
mouth of a lion two shank-bones or a
piece of an ear, so will the Israelites be
rescued, who dwell in Samaria, along
with the corner of a couch, and the leg
of a bed."

13 "Hear and testify against the house of Jacob,"
Is the oracle of the Lord GOD, the God of hosts,
14 "That on the day when I punish Israel for its offenses,
I will inflict punishment upon the altars of Bethel,
And the horns of the altar shall be cut off and fall to the ground.
And I will smite both winter house and summer house, 15
And the ivory houses shall be ruined;
And many houses shall come to an end."
The oracle of the LORD.

"Hear this word, you cows of Bashan, 4
You who are on the mount of Samaria,
Who oppress the weak, who crush the needy,
Who say to their lords, 'Bring that we may drink.'

"The Lord GOD has sworn by his holiness, 2
That there are days coming upon you,
When they will drag you away with hooks,
And what is left of you with fish-hooks;
And through the breaches you will go, each straight ahead, 3
And you will be cast upon the refuse heap."
The oracle of the LORD.

THE SACRILEGE OF SACRIFICE, 4:4, 5

"Come to Bethel, and—transgress! 4
To Gilgal, and multiply your transgressions!
Bring your sacrifices every morning,
And every three days, your tithes!
Burn a thank-offering of leavened bread, 5
And proclaim voluntary offerings; publish them!
For so you love to do, O Israelites."
The oracle of the Lord GOD.

REPEATED CHASTISEMENTS ARE FUTILE, 4:6–11

"And yet, it was I that gave you 6
Cleanness of teeth in all your cities,
And lack of bread in all your places.
But you did not return to me."
The oracle of the LORD.

"Still further, it was I that withheld from you the rain, 7
While there were yet three months till harvest;
And I sent rain upon one city,
But upon another I sent no rain;
One field was rained upon,

But the field upon which there was no rain dried up,
8 So that two or three towns went begging to one town,
That they might get water to drink, and were not satisfied.
But you did not return to me."
The oracle of the LORD.

9 "I smote you with blight and mildew;
I laid waste your gardens and your vineyards;
And your fig trees and olive trees the locust devoured.
But you did not return to me."
The oracle of the LORD.

10 "I sent a pestilence among you after the manner of Egypt;
I slew your young men with the sword,
Together with your captured horses;
And I brought up the stench of your camp into your nostrils.
But you did not return to me."
The oracle of the LORD.

11 "I overthrew some of you,
As when God overthrew Sodom and Gomorrah;
And you were like a brand snatched from the burning.
But you did not return to me."
The oracle of the LORD.

12 "Therefore, thus will I do to you, O Israel.
Because I will do this to you,
Prepare to meet your God, O Israel."

13 For behold, he who formed the mountains and created the wind;
He who tells man what his thought is,
He who makes dawn and darkness,
And treads upon the heights of the earth;
The LORD, the God of hosts, is his name.

ISRAEL'S DESTRUCTION AND ITS CAUSES, 5:1–17

5 "Hear this word that I am taking up
concerning you, a dirge, O house of
Israel:
"Fallen, never to rise again,
2 is the virgin Israel;
Prostrate on her own soil,
with none to raise her up."

For thus says the Lord GOD: "The 3
city that sent forth a thousand shall
have but a hundred left; and the one
that sent forth a hundred shall have but
ten left, for the house of Israel."

For thus says the LORD to the house 4
of Israel:
"Seek me, that you may live;
And seek not Bethel. 5
You shall not go to Gilgal,
Nor cross over to Beersheba.
For Gilgal shall go into galling captivity,
And Bethel shall become a delusion."

Seek the LORD, that you may live; 6
Lest he set the house of Joseph on fire,
And it devour, with no one to quench it for Bethel;
You who turn justice to gall, 7
And cast down righteousness to the earth.

He who made the Pleiades and Orion, 8
Who turns dense darkness to dawn,
And darkens day into night;
Who summons the waters of the sea,
And pours them out upon the face of the earth—
The LORD is his name—
He who causes ruin to burst forth upon the strong, 9
And brings destruction upon the fortress.

They hate him who reproves in the gate, 10
And loathe him who speaks the truth.
Therefore because you trample upon the weak, 11
And take from him exactions of grain,
Though you have built houses of hewn stone,
You shall not dwell in them;
Though you have planted pleasant vineyards,
You shall not drink their wine.

For I know that your transgressions are many, 12
And your sins countless,
You who oppress the innocent, take bribes,
And thrust aside the needy at the gate.
Therefore he who is prudent will be silent at such time; 13
For it will be an evil time.

14 Seek good and not evil that you may live and that it may be so, that the LORD, the God of hosts, is with you, as you have said.

15 Hate evil, and love good
And establish justice at the gate;
Perhaps, the LORD, the God of hosts,
Will be gracious to a remnant of Joseph.

16 Therefore thus says the LORD, the God of hosts, the Lord:
"In all squares shall be lamentation;
And in all the streets, they shall say, 'Woe! Woe!'
17 And they shall call the plowman to mourning,
And to lamentation, all who know how to wail.
And in all vineyards there shall be lamentation,
When I pass through the midst of you," says the LORD.

THE TERRORS OF THE DAY OF THE LORD, 5:18–27

18 "Woe to you who desire the day of the LORD!
What, then, does the day of the LORD mean to you?
It is darkness, and not light;
19 As though a man were fleeing from a lion,
And a bear should meet him!
Or as if he entered his house and rested his hand upon the wall,
And a serpent bit him!
20 Is not the day of the LORD darkness and not light,
And blackness, with no brightness in it?

21 "I hate, I spurn your feasts,
And I take no pleasure in your festal gatherings.
22 Even though you offer me burnt-offerings,
And your cereal-offerings, I will not accept them;
And the thank-offerings of your fatted beasts I will not look upon.
23 "Take away from me the noise of your songs,
And to the melody of your lyres I will not listen.
24 But let justice roll down like waters,
And righteousness like a perennial stream.
Was it sacrifices and offerings that you brought me 25
In the wilderness for forty years, O house of Israel?
But you have carried around Sakkuth, your king, 26
And Kaiwan, the star of your god,
Your images which you have made for yourselves.
So I will carry you into exile beyond Damascus," 27
Says the LORD, whose name is the God of hosts.

DESTRUCTION TO SAMARIA, 6:1–14

"Woe to them who are at ease in Zion, 6
And self-confident on the mount of Samaria;
Distinguished as the chief of the nations,
To whom the house of Israel resorts.
Pass over to Calneh and see; 2
And go thence to Hamath, the great;
And go down to Gath of the Philistines!
Are they any better than these kingdoms?
Or is their territory greater than yours,
O, you who put off the evil day, 3
And bring near the seat of violence?

"They who lie upon ivory couches, 4
And stretch themselves out upon divans;
And eat lambs from the flock,
And calves from the midst of the stall;
They who sing to the accompaniment of the lyre, 5
And compose songs for themselves like David;
They who drink chalices of wine, 6
And anoint themselves with the finest oils;
But they are not heart-sick over the ruin of Joseph.
Therefore they shall be the first of the exiles to go into exile, 7
And the shout of the revelers shall pass away,"
Is the oracle of the LORD, the God of hosts. 8

The Lord GOD has sworn by himself: 8

8c "I abhor the pride of Jacob,
And his palaces I hate;
So I will deliver up the city and everything in it."

9 And it shall be that if there be left
ten men in one house, and they die, one
10 being left over; then his uncle, who is to
burn a sacrifice for him, will take him
up, to bring forth the bones from the
house, and will say to whoever may be
in the rear of the house, "Is there still
anyone with you?" and he will say,
"No one"; and he will say, "Silence,"
for one must not invoke the name of the
LORD.

11 For behold, the LORD is about to command
That the great house be smitten into ruins,
And the small house into fragments.
12 Can horses run upon rocks?
Or can one plow the sea with oxen,
That you should turn justice into poison,
And the fruit of righteousness into wormwood?
13 You who delight in that which is not,
Who say, "Have we not, by our own strength,
Acquired power for ourselves?"
14 "For lo, I am raising up against you, O house of Israel,"
Is the oracle of the LORD, God of hosts, "a nation;
And they shall crush you from the entrance of Hamath
Unto the brook of the Arabah."

THREE VISIONS OF DESTRUCTION, 7:1–9

7 Thus the Lord GOD showed me; and
lo, he was forming locusts, at the beginning
of the coming up of the aftermath
(now it was the aftermath after the
2 king's mowings); and when they had
finished eating the grass of the earth, I
said,
"O Lord GOD, forgive, I pray;
How can Jacob stand?
For he is so small."
3 The LORD relented of this.
"It shall not be," said the LORD.

4 Thus the Lord GOD showed me; and
lo, the Lord GOD was summoning to a
trial by fire; and it had devoured the
great deep, and was about to devour
the plow-land.
Then I said, 5
"O Lord GOD, cease, I pray;
How can Jacob stand?
For he is so small."
The LORD relented of this. 6
"Neither shall it be," said the Lord GOD.

Thus he showed me; and lo, the Lord 7
was standing upon a wall, with a
plumb-line in his hand. Then the 8
LORD said to me,
"What do you see, Amos?"
And I said,
"A plumb-line."
Then the LORD said,
"Behold I am setting a plumb-line,
In the midst of my people Israel;
I will never again pass them by.
The high places of Isaac shall be laid waste; 9
And the sanctuaries of Israel shall be ruined;
And I will rise against the house of Jeroboam with the sword."

PRIEST AGAINST PROPHET, 7:10–17

Then Amaziah, the priest of Bethel, 10
sent to Jeroboam, king of Israel, saying,
"Amos has conspired against you in
the midst of the house of Israel. The
land is unable to endure all his words.
For thus says Amos: 11
'By the sword shall Jeroboam die,
And Israel shall surely be carried into exile away from its soil.' "
Then Amaziah said to Amos, 12
"O seer, go away, off with you to the land of Judah,
And there earn your living, by prophesying there;
But never again prophesy at Bethel, 13
For this is the king's sanctuary, and the royal palace."
Then Amos replied to Amaziah, say- 14
ing,
"I am no prophet, nor am I a member of a prophetic order;
But I am a shepherd and a dresser of sycamores.
And the LORD took me from behind the flock, 15

And the LORD said to me,
'Go, prophesy to my people Israel.'
16 And now hear the word of the LORD.
You are saying, 'You shall not prophesy against Israel,
Nor drop a word against the house of Isaac.'
17 Therefore thus says the LORD:
'Your wife shall practice harlotry in the city,
Your sons and your daughters shall fall by the sword,
Your land shall be parceled out by measure,
And you yourself shall die upon unclean soil,
And Israel shall surely be carried into exile away from its soil.'"

SOCIAL WRONGS SPELL NATIONAL RUIN, 8:1–14

8 Thus the Lord GOD showed me;
And lo, a basket of summer fruit!
2 And he said, "What do you see, Amos?"
And I said, "A basket of summer fruit."
Then the LORD said to me,
"The end has come to my people Israel;
I will never again pass them by.
3 The songs of the palace shall become dirges on that day,"
Is the oracle of the Lord GOD;
"Many shall be the carcasses; in every place they shall be cast out."
4 Hear this, you who trample upon the needy,
And would bring the poor of the land to an end,
5 Saying, "When will the new moon pass
That we may sell grain,
And the Sabbath that we may offer wheat for sale,"
Making the ephah small and the price great,
And falsifying the scales;
6 Buying the poor for silver,
And the needy in exchange for a pair of sandals,
And selling the refuse of the grain.
7 The LORD has sworn by the pride of Jacob,
"I will never forget all their deeds!"
8 Shall not the land tremble because of this,
And all who dwell therein mourn;
And all of it rise up like the Nile,
And be shaken and sink like the Nile of Egypt?

9 "And it shall come to pass on that day,"
Is the oracle of the Lord GOD,
"That I will cause the sun to set at noon,
And I will darken the earth in broad daylight;
10 And I will turn your festivals into mourning,
And all your songs into dirges;
And I will put sackcloth upon all loins,
And baldness on every head;
And I will make it like the mourning for an only son,
And the end of it like a bitter day."

11 "Behold days are coming,"
Is the oracle of the Lord GOD,
"When I will send famine upon the land;
Not a famine of bread,
Nor a thirst for water,
But for hearing the words of the LORD.
12 And they shall wander from sea to sea,
And run from north to east,
To seek the word of the LORD;
But shall not find it.

13 "On that day they shall faint,
The fair maidens and the young men, for thirst;
14 They who swear by Ashimah of Samaria,
And say, 'As your god lives, O Dan,'
And 'As your Dod lives, O Beersheba';
They shall fall, never to rise again."

A VISION OF TOTAL DESTRUCTION, 9:1–8

9 I saw the Lord, standing upon the altar,
And he said, "Smite the capitals, so that the thresholds may shake,
And smash them on the heads of them all;
And what may be left of them I will slay with the sword;

Not a single one of them shall get away,
Nor shall a single one escape.

2 "Though they dig into Sheol,
Thence shall my hand take them;
And though they mount up to the heavens,
Thence will I bring them down;
3 Though they hide themselves on the top of Carmel,
Thence will I search them out and take them;
Though they hide themselves from my eyes on the floor of the sea,
There will I command the serpent, that it bite them;
4 Though they go into captivity before their foes,
There will I command the sword, that it slay them;
And I will set my eye upon them
For evil, and not for good."

5 For the Lord GOD of hosts
Is he who touches the earth and it melts,
And all who live therein mourn;
And it rises like the Nile,
And sinks like the Nile of Egypt;
6 The one who builds his chambers in the heavens,
And founds his vault upon the earth,
Who summons the waters of the sea,
And pours them out upon the surface of the earth;
The LORD is his name.

7 "Are you not like the Ethiopians to me,
O Israelites?" is the oracle of the LORD.
"Did I not bring up Israel from the land of Egypt,
Also the Philistines from Caphtor, and the Syrians from Kir?
8 Behold, the eyes of the Lord GOD are upon the sinful kingdom;
And I will destroy it from off the face of the ground,
Except that I will not wholly destroy the house of Jacob."
The oracle of the LORD.

ULTIMATE RESTORATION, 9:9–15

"For, behold, I am about to give command, 9
And I will shake the house of Israel among all the nations,
Just as one shakes the sieve,
But not a kernel shall fall to the ground.
By the sword all the sinners of my people shall die, 10
Those who say, 'Disaster shall not reach or overtake us.'

"On that day I will raise up the fallen hut of David, 11
And I will wall up its ruins,
And raise up its breaches,
And rebuild it as in the days of old;
In order that they may possess the remnant of Edom and all the nations, 12
Over whom my name is called."
The oracle of the LORD, who does this.

"Behold the days are coming," is the oracle of the LORD, 13
"When the plowman shall overtake the reaper,
And the treader of grapes him who sows the seed;
And the mountains shall drip new wine,
And all the hills shall melt;
And I will restore the fortune of my people Israel, 14
So that they shall rebuild the ruined cities,
And dwell in them and plant vineyards,
And drink their wine,
And make gardens, and eat their fruit;
And I will plant them upon their own soil, 15
And they shall never again be rooted up,
From off their soil which I have given them."
Says the LORD, your God.

THE BOOK OF OBADIAH

DIRE VENGEANCE UPON EDOM

1 The Vision of Obadiah

THUS says the Lord GOD regarding Edom:
"We have heard a message from the LORD,
And a messenger has been sent forth among the nations:
'Arise! Let us rise up against her for battle.'
2 Behold, I have set you as the least among the nations,
Contemptible are you among men.
3 The pride of your heart has deceived you,
You who dwell in the clefts of the cliff,
And set your dwelling on high,
And say to yourself,
'Who can bring me down to the earth?'
4 Though you build your nest high like the eagle,
And set your nest even among the stars,
From there I will bring you down," is the oracle of the LORD.

5 "If robbers came to you,
Or burglars by night—how you are ruined!
Would they not steal only what they could handle?
If grape gatherers came to you,
Would they not leave some gleanings?
6 How Esau is ransacked,
And his treasures plundered!
7 They have driven you to the very border;
All those who were in league with you have betrayed you.
The men who were at peace with you have overpowered you;
Your associates have put a foreign people in your place."
[There is no meaning in it.]

8 "On that day," is the oracle of the LORD,
"I will surely destroy the wise men from Edom,
And intelligence from Mount Esau.
And your warriors shall be appalled, O Teman,
So that every fighting man shall be cut off from Mount Esau.
For the violence done to your brother Jacob, 10
Shame shall cover you and you shall be cut off forever.
On the day when you stood by, 11
While aliens carried off his goods,
And foreigners entered his gates,
And cast lots upon Jerusalem,
You, too, were as one of them."

"You should not have gloated over your brother, 12
on the day of his adversity.
You should not have rejoiced over the Judeans,
on the day of their ruin.
You should not have made a wide mouth,
on the day of trouble.
You should not have entered the gate of my people, 13
on the day of their calamity.
You should not have gloated over his misfortune,
on the day of his calamity.
You should not have put forth your hand upon his goods,
on the day of his calamity.
Nor should you have stood at the breach, 14
to cut off his fugitives,
Nor have delivered up his refugees,
on the day of his trouble.

"For the day of the LORD is near, 15
Upon all the nations.
As you have done, it shall be done to you;
Your deed shall return upon your own head.
For just as you have drunk upon my holy mountain, 16
So all the nations shall drink wine;
They shall drink and gulp down,
And become as though they had not existed.

17 "But in Mount Zion there shall be a
group of fugitives,
And it shall be holy;
And the house of Jacob shall possess
their own possessions.
18 And the house of Jacob shall be a fire,
And the house of Joseph a flame;
And the house of Esau shall be stubble,
And they shall lick them up and devour them;
And there shall be no survivor to the
house of Esau."
For the LORD has spoken.

They shall possess the Negeb (the 19
hills of Esau) and the Shephelah (the
Philistines); and they shall possess the
fields of Ephraim (the fields of Samaria
and Benjamin) and Gilead; and the ex- 20
iles from Halah and Habor shall possess
the land of the Canaanites as far as
Zarephath; and the exiles of Jerusalem, who are in Sepharad, shall possess the cities of the Negeb; and
conquerors shall go up into Mount
Zion to rule over the hill country of
Esau. For the LORD shall have dominion.

THE BOOK OF JONAH

THE GREAT REFUSAL, 1:1–16

1 THE word of the LORD came to
Jonah, the son of Amittai, as
follows:
2 "Arise, go to Nineveh, that
great city, and preach against it; for
their wickedness has come up before
me."
3 But Jonah arose to flee to Tarshish,
from the presence of the LORD. So he
went down to Joppa, where he found a
ship, bound for Tarshish. He paid his
fare, and went aboard, to go with them
to Tarshish, from the presence of the
LORD.
4 But the LORD hurled a great wind
upon the sea, so that there was a great
storm on the sea; and it was thought
5 that the ship would be broken up. Then
the sailors were frightened, and they
cried each to his god; and they threw
overboard the stuff that was in the ship,
in order to lighten it.
But Jonah had gone down into the
hold of the ship, and was lying fast
6 asleep. So the captain approached him,
and said to him,
"Why are you sleeping? Get up; call
upon your god. Perhaps that god will
bethink himself of us, that we perish
not."
7 Then they said, one to another,
"Come, let us cast lots, that we may
know upon whose account this disaster
has befallen us."
So they cast lots; and the lot fell upon
8 Jonah. Then they said to him,
"Tell us, now, for what reason this
disaster has befallen us. What is your
business? Whence do you come? What
is your country? And from what people are you?"
9 So he said to them,
"I am a Hebrew; and I stand in awe
of the LORD, the God of the heavens,
who made both the sea and the dry
land."
10 Then the men were exceedingly terrified, and said to him,
"What a wicked thing you have
done!"
For the men knew that he was fleeing
from the presence of the LORD, because he had told them. Whereupon 1
they said to him,
"What shall we do with you, that the
sea may become calm for us?"
For the sea was running higher and
higher. Then he said to them, 1
"Pick me up, and cast me into the
sea, so that the sea may be calm for
you; for I know that this great storm is
upon you because of me."
But the men rowed hard to bring the
ship back to the dry land, yet could not;
for the sea was running higher and
higher against them. So they cried unto
the LORD, saying,
"O LORD, we beseech thee, let us not
perish for this man's life; and lay not
up against us innocent blood; for thou,
O LORD, dost do as thou pleasest."
Then they picked up Jonah and
threw him overboard; and the sea
ceased from its raging.
Thereupon the men feared the LORD
profoundly; and they sacrificed to the
LORD and made vows.

JONAH'S REPENTANCE, 1:17—2:10

Now, the LORD had assigned a great
fish to swallow up Jonah; and Jonah
was in the belly of the fish three days
and three nights. Then Jonah prayed
to the LORD, his God, from the belly of
the fish, saying,
"Out of my trouble I called unto the
LORD, and he answered me;
From the heart of Sheol I called for
help; thou didst hear my voice.
For thou hadst cast me into the
depths, into the heart of the sea,
And a flood encompassed me.
All thy breakers and thy waves passed
over me.
Then I said, 'I am cast out of thy
sight;
How shall I ever again look upon thy
holy temple?'
The waters closed in over my life; the
deep surrounded me;

Sea-weed was wound around my head.
6 To the roots of the hills I went down;
The earth with its bars was against me
forever.
But thou didst bring up my life from
the Pit, O LORD, my God!
7 When I was losing consciousness, I remembered the LORD;
And my prayer unto thee entered thy
holy temple.
8 Those who heed false vanities forsake
their piety,
9 But I will sacrifice to thee with the
voice of thanksgiving;
What I have vowed, I will pay.
Deliverance belongs to the LORD."
10 Then the LORD commanded the fish,
and it vomited Jonah forth upon the
dry land.

JONAH'S MISSION AND ITS RESULT, 3:1–10

3 Then the word of the LORD came to
Jonah a second time, as follows:
2 "Arise, go to Nineveh, that great
city, and proclaim unto it the proclamation which I am about to tell you."
3 So Jonah arose, and went to Nineveh, as the LORD had said. Now Nineveh was an exceedingly great city, the
walk through it requiring three days.
4 Now Jonah had gone a day's journey
into the city, when he made proclamation, saying,
"Forty days more, and Nineveh shall
be overthrown."
5 Whereupon the men of Nineveh believed God, and proclaimed a fast, and
clothed themselves in sackcloth, from
the greatest unto the least of them.
6 When the news reached the king of
Nineveh, he rose from his throne, put
off his robe, put on sackcloth, and sat
7 upon the ash-heap. He also sent messengers through Nineveh, saying,
"By decree of the king and his nobles,
as follows: Let neither man nor beast,
cattle nor sheep, taste a thing; let them
not feed, and let them not drink water.
8 But let them put on sackcloth, both
man and beast, and let them call aloud
unto God; and let each one turn from
his wicked way, and from whatsoever
9 violence he has in hand. Who knows
but that God will turn and relent, turning from his fierce anger, so that we perish not."

Then God saw their actions, that 10
they had turned from their wicked way.
So God relented of the evil which he
had said he would do unto them, and
he did it not.

JONAH REBUKED, 4:1–11

But Jonah was greatly displeased 4
and very angry. So he prayed to the 2
LORD, saying,
"O LORD, is not this what I said
while I was still upon my own soil?
Therefore I hastened to flee to Tarshish. For I knew that thou wast a
gracious God, and merciful, slow to
anger, and abounding in kindness, and
relenting of evil. Now, therefore, O 3
LORD, take my life, I pray thee, from
me. For I am better off dead than
alive!"
Then the LORD said, 4
"Are you so very angry?"
Then Jonah went forth from the city, 5
and sat down to the east of the city;
and he made a booth for himself there,
and sat under it in the shade, until he
should see what would happen in the
city. So the LORD God gave orders to 6
a gourd, and it grew up above Jonah so
as to be a shade over his head, to save
him from his discomfort; and Jonah
was very glad because of the gourd.
Then God ordered a worm, when the 7
dawn came up on the morrow, to smite
the gourd, so that it wilted. And when 8
the sun arose, God ordered a burning
east wind; and the sun smote down
upon Jonah's head so that he fainted,
and asked that he might die, and said,
"I am better off dead than alive!"
Then God said to Jonah, 9
"Are you so very angry over the
gourd?"
And he replied,
"I am angry enough to die!"
Then the LORD said, 10
"You have had pity on the gourd,
for which you did not toil; nor did you
raise it; which grew in a night, and perished in a night! And should not I, 11
indeed, have pity on Nineveh, that
great city, in which are more than a
hundred and twenty thousand infants,
that cannot distinguish between their
right hand and their left, and many
cattle?"

THE BOOK OF MICAH

THE SUPERSCRIPTION, 1:1

1 THE word of the LORD which came to Micah, the Morashtite, in the days of Jotham, Ahaz, and Hezekiah, kings of Judah, which he received concerning Samaria and Jerusalem.

THE DOWNFALL OF ISRAEL, 1:2–9

2 Hear, O peoples, all of you!
Give heed, O earth, and everything in it!
And let the Lord GOD be a witness against you,
The Lord from his holy temple.

3 For, lo, the LORD is coming forth from his place,
And he will descend and tread upon the heights of the earth;
4 And the mountains shall melt under him,
And the valleys be split asunder,
Like wax before the fire,
Like waters poured down a precipice.

5 For the transgression of Jacob is all this,
And for the sin of the house of Judah.
What is Jacob's transgression?
Is it not Samaria?
And what is Judah's sin?
Is it not Jerusalem?

6 So I will turn Samaria into a ruin of the field,
Into a planted vineyard.
And I will pour down her stones into the valley,
And lay bare her foundations.

7 All her carved images shall be smashed to pieces,
And all her images shall be burned;
And all her idols I will lay waste.
For from the harlot's hire they were gathered,
And unto the harlot's hire they shall return.

For this let me lament and wail; 8
Let me go barefoot and stripped.
Let me make lamentation like the jackals,
And mourning like the ostriches.

For her stroke is incurable; 9
For it has come even to Judah;
It reaches the gate of my people,
Even to Jerusalem.

A DIRGE FOR ISRAEL, 1:10–16

Tell it not in Gath! 10
Weep bitterly in Bethel;
roll yourselves in dust.
They sound the trumpet abroad for you, 11
O inhabitant of Shaphir.
From her city she comes not forth,
the inhabitant of Zaanan.
Beth-ezel is taken from its foundations,
from the site where it stood.
How can she hope for good, 12
the inhabitant of Maroth?
For disaster will come down from the LORD,
to the gate of Jerusalem.
Harness the steed to the chariot, 13
O inhabitant of Lachish—
The beginning of sin was she
to the daughter of Zion—
For in you are found
the transgressions of Israel.
Therefore you shall give parting gifts 14
to Moresheth Gath.
Beth-achzib has become a snare
to the kings of Israel.
I will again bring the conqueror to you, 15
O inhabitant of Mareshah.
Unto Adullam shall come
the glory of Israel.
Make yourself bald, tear out your hair, 16
for the children you delight in;
Enlarge your baldness like the eagle's,
for they will go into exile from you.

RICH OPPRESSORS SHALL BE OPPRESSED, 2:1–11

2 Woe to them who devise wrong,
And work out wickedness upon their beds.
In the morning light they do it,
Because it is in their power.
2 They covet fields and seize them,
And houses, and carry them off.
So they crush a yeoman and his house,
A man and his possessions.

3 Therefore thus says the LORD:
"Behold, I am planning evil against this family,
Which you will be unable to remove from your necks,
Nor will you be able to walk erect;
For it will be an evil time."

4 On that day a taunt-song shall be sung over you,
And a lamentation shall be wailed, as follows:
"The possession of my people is parceled out,
with none to restore it;
To our captors our soil is allotted;
we are utterly ruined."
5 Therefore you shall have no one stretching the line,
Or casting the lot, in the assembly of the LORD.
6 "Do not keep on harping," they harp;
"One should not be harping upon such things;
Shame will not overtake us,"
7 Says the house of Jacob.
"Is the LORD'S spirit impatient,
Or are such things his deeds?
Do not his words mean good
To his people Israel?"

8 But you are my people's foe;
You rise against those who are at peace.
You strip off from those who pass through in confidence
Spoils of war.
9 The women of my people you expel
From their comfortable homes.
From their children you take away
My glory forever.

10 Arise, and go!
For this is not your resting place!
For the sake of a mere trifle,
You take a heavy mortgage.

If a man, walking in a false spirit, should lie, 11
"I will prophesy to you of wine and strong drink,"
He would be this people's prophet!

A WORD OF PROMISE, 2:12, 13

I will completely assemble Jacob, all of him; 12
I will fully gather the remnant of Israel.
Moreover, I will make them like a flock of Bozrah,
Like a herd in the midst of the pasture;
And they shall go forth from Edom.
The breaker shall go up before them; 13
They shall break through the gate and go forth thereby;
Their king shall pass on before them,
With the LORD at their head.

THE DOWNFALL OF PROPHETS, PRIESTS, AND PRINCES, 3:1–12

Then I said, 3
"Hear now, you heads of Jacob,
And rulers of the house of Israel,
Is it not your place to know justice,
You who hate the good, and love wickedness, 2
Snatching their skin from upon them,
And their flesh from upon their bones?"

They eat the flesh of my people, 3
And strip them of their flesh,
And lay bare their bones and break them,
Like meat in the pot and flesh within the cauldron.

Then shall they cry unto the LORD, 4
And he will not answer them,
But will hide his face from them, at that time,
Inasmuch as they have done wicked deeds.

Thus has the LORD said, 5
Regarding the prophets who lead my people astray,
Who preach prosperity when their mouth is filled;

But if one does not put something in their mouths,
They declare war against him!

6 "Therefore, it shall be night for you, without vision,
And darkness for you, without divination.
For the sun shall set upon the prophets,
And the day shall become dark over them.

7 "The seers shall be abashed,
And the diviners shall blush;
And they shall all cover the upper lip,
Because there is no answer from God."

8 But I am full of power,
The spirit of the LORD, justice, and strength,
To declare to Jacob his crimes,
And to Israel his sins.

9 Hear this, now, you heads of the house of Jacob,
And rulers of the house of Israel,
Who abhor justice,
And distort everything that is right;
10 Who build Zion with blood,
And Jerusalem with guilt.

11 Her chiefs pronounce judgment for a bribe,
And her priests declare oracles for hire,
And her prophets divine for cash.
Yet they lean upon the LORD, saying,
"Is not the LORD in the midst of us?
No misfortune can befall us."

12 Therefore, because of you,
Zion shall be plowed like a field,
And Jerusalem shall become a ruin,
And the temple hill a high place in a forest.

THE GOLDEN AGE, 4:1–5

4 It shall come to pass in days to come,
That the mountain of the LORD'S house will be
Established as the highest mountain,
And elevated above the hills.
Peoples will stream unto it,
2 And many nations will come, and say:
"Come, let us go up to the mount of the LORD,
To the house of the God of Jacob;
That he may instruct us in his ways,
And that we may walk in his paths;
For from Zion goes forth instruction,
And the word of the LORD from Jerusalem."

Then shall he judge between many peoples, 3
And arbitrate for great nations, at a distance;
And they shall beat their swords into plowshares,
And their spears into pruning-hooks.
Nation shall not lift up sword against nation,
Nor shall they learn war any more.

And they shall sit each under his vine, 4
And under his fig tree, with none to frighten them;
For the mouth of the LORD of hosts has spoken.
For all the peoples walk, 5
Each in the name of his god;
But we will walk in the name of the LORD,
Our God, forever and ever.

EXILE AND RESTORATION, 4:6–10

"On that day," is the oracle of the LORD, 6
"I will gather the lame,
And assemble the outcast,
And her whom I have afflicted.
And I will make the lame a remnant; 7
And the sick, a strong nation,
And the LORD shall rule over them in Mount Zion,
From now on and forever.
And you, O tower of the flock, 8
Height of the daughter of Zion,
To you shall come the former dominion,
The kingdom of the daughter of Jerusalem.

Why, now, do you cry so loud? 9
Is there no king among you?
Or has your counselor perished,
That agony has laid hold of you like a woman in travail?
Writhe and bring forth, 10
O daughter of Zion, like a woman in travail;
For soon you must go forth from the city,
And dwell in the field,
And go to Babylon.
There you shall be rescued;
There the LORD will ransom you,
From the power of your foes."

THE DOWNFALL OF THE NATIONS, 4:11—5:1

1 Soon there shall be gathered against
you
Many nations, saying, "Let her be desecrated,
And let our eyes fasten upon Zion."
2 But they know not the purposes of the
LORD,
Nor do they understand his plan,
That he has gathered them like grain
to the threshing-floor.

3 Arise and thresh, O daughter of Zion;
For I will make your horn iron,
And your hoofs will I make bronze.
You shall crush many peoples,
And devote their spoil to the LORD,
And their wealth to the Lord of all the
earth.

5 Now you will cut yourselves deeply;
They will lay siege against us;
With the rod they will strike upon the
cheek
The ruler of Israel.

THE MESSIANIC KING, 5:2–4

2 And you, O Bethlehem Ephrathah,
Too little to be among the clans of
Judah,
From you, one shall come forth for
me,
Who shall be ruler over Israel,
Whose origins are from of old,
From ancient days.
3 Therefore he will give them up
Until the time when she who is with
child shall have borne;
And the rest of his brothers shall return to the Israelites.
4 But he shall stand fast and feed his
flock in the strength of the LORD,
In the majesty of the name of the
LORD, his God.
And they shall endure;
For then shall he be great unto the
ends of the earth.

ISRAEL'S PROTECTORS AGAINST INVASION, 5:5–6

5 And this shall be our protection from
Assyria:
When he comes into our land,
And treads upon our soil,
Then we will raise up against him
seven shepherds
And eight princes of men;
And they shall shepherd the land of 6
Assyria with the sword,
And the land of Nimrod with the
drawn sword;
And they shall rescue us from Assyria,
When he comes into our land,
And treads upon our border.

THE DIVINE ORIGIN AND IRRESISTIBLE POWER OF THE REMNANT, 5:7–9

The remnant of Jacob shall be 7
In the midst of many peoples,
Like the dew from the LORD,
Like the showers upon the grass,
Which waits not for man,
Nor tarries for the sons of men.

And the remnant of Jacob shall be 8
among the nations,
In the midst of many peoples,
Like the lion among the beasts of the
forest,
Like the young lion among the flocks
of sheep,
Who, if he passes through,
Tramples and tears, with none to deliver.

Your hand shall be high above your 9
foes,
And all your enemies shall be cut off.

PUNITIVE PURIFICATION, 5:10–15

"It shall come to pass on that day," 10
Is the oracle of the LORD,
"That I will cut off your horses from
the midst of you,
And destroy your chariots.
And I will cut off the cities of your 11
land,
And lay waste all your fortresses.
I will cut off the sorceries from your 12
hand,
And you shall have no soothsayers.
And I will cut off your images 13
And your sacred pillars from the
midst of you;
And you shall bow down no more
To the work of your hands.
And I will uproot your sacred poles 14
from the midst of you,
And destroy your cities.

15 And I will wreak vengeance in anger and wrath,
Upon the nations that have not hearkened."

THE CASE OF THE LORD AGAINST ISRAEL, 6:1–5

6 Hear, now, what the LORD says,
"Arise, present your case before the mountains,
And let the hills hear your voice!
2 Hear, O mountains, the argument of the LORD,
And give ear, O foundations of the earth.
For the LORD has an argument with his people,
And a controversy with Israel.

3 "My people, what have I done to you?
And how have I wearied you? Answer me!
4 For I brought you up from the land of Egypt,
And delivered you from the prison house;
And I sent before you Moses,
Aaron, and Miriam.

5 "My people, remember, now, what Balak, king of Moab, planned;
And what Balaam, son of Beor, answered him,
From Shittim to Gilgal;
That you may understand the righteous deeds of the LORD."

TRUE RELIGION, 6:6–8

6 With what shall I come before the LORD,
And bow myself before God most high?
Shall I come before him with burnt-offerings,
With calves a year old?
7 Will the LORD be pleased with thousands of rams,
With myriads of streams of oil?
Shall I give my first-born for my transgression,
The fruit of my body for the sin of my soul?
8 You have been told, O man, what is good,
And what the LORD requires of you:
Only to do justice, and to love kindness,
And to walk humbly with your God?

THE CITY'S SIN AND ITS PUNISHMENT, 6:9–16

Hark! the LORD calls to the city— 9
And "success" is fearing thy name!—
"Hear, O tribe, and assembly of the city,
Whose rich men are full of violence; 12
Whose inhabitants speak falsehood,
And whose tongue is deceit in their mouths.

"Can I forget the wicked treasures in the house of the wicked, 10
And the short measure that is accursed?
Can I treat as pure him with the wicked scales, 11
And with the bag of false weights?

"So I will begin to smite you, 13
To lay you in ruins because of your sins.
You shall eat, but not be satisfied. 14
You shall conceive, but not bear;
And what you may bear, I will give to the sword.
You shall sow, but not reap; 15
You shall trample the olives, but not anoint yourselves with oil;
And tread out the grapes, but drink no wine.

"For you have kept the decrees of Omri, 16
And all the doings of the house of Ahab;
And you have walked by their counsels,
So that I may give you over to ruin,
And your inhabitants to scorn;
The mockery of the peoples you shall bear."

THE MORAL COLLAPSE OF ISRAEL, 7:1–6

Woe is me! For I am become 7
Like those that gather summer fruit,
In the gleanings of the vintage,
When there is not a cluster to eat,
Nor an early fig that my appetite craves.

The godly has perished from the land, 2
And there is none righteous among men.
They all lie in wait for blood;
Each hunts his brother with a net.

3 They solemnly swear that bad is good;
The prince and the judge demand a bribe;
And the great man expresses his desire;
And so they pervert justice.

4 The best of them are like a brier;
The most upright of them are like a hedge.
The day of their watchmen, their punishment, is come;
Soon shall be their havoc.

5 Put no confidence in a friend;
Trust not an intimate.
From her who lies in your bosom
Guard the doors of your mouth.

6 For the son insults his father;
The daughter rises up against her mother,
The daughter-in-law against her mother-in-law;
A man's foes are the members of his own household.

THE OVERTHROW OF ISRAEL'S ENEMIES, 7:7–10

7 But I shall wait confidently for the LORD;
I shall hope for the God of my deliverance;
My God will hear me.

8 Rejoice not, O my foe, over me!
Though I have fallen, I shall arise.
Though I sit in darkness,
The LORD will be my light.

9 The anger of the LORD I must bear—
For I have sinned against him—
Until he shall take up my case,
And do me justice.

He will bring me forth to the light;
I shall see his vindication.
10 My foe shall see,
And shame shall cover her.

She that said unto me,
"Where is the LORD, your God?"
My eyes will gaze upon her;
Soon shall she be trampled upon,
Like the mud of the streets.

JERUSALEM RESTORED, 7:11–13

There shall be a day for rebuilding your walls; 11
On that day the frontier shall be far distant.
A day there shall be when unto you they will come 12
From Assyria even unto Egypt,
From Egypt even to the River;
From sea to sea,
And from mountain to mountain.
But the earth shall become a waste, 13
Because of its inhabitants,
On account of the fruit of their deeds.

A PRAYER FOR THE HELP OF THE LORD, 7:14–20

Shepherd thy people with thy staff, 14
the flock of thine inheritance,
That dwells alone, a jungle
in the midst of a garden.
May they feed in Bashan and in Gilead,
as in the days of old.
As in the days when thou didst come forth from the land of Egypt, 15
show us wonderful things.
May the nations see, and be ashamed of all their power. 16
May they lay their hand upon their mouths,
and may their ears be deaf.
May they lick the dust like the serpent, 17
like crawling things of the earth.
May they come trembling from their dens unto the LORD, our God;
may they quake and fear because of thee.

Who is god like thee, 18
forgiving iniquity,
and passing over transgression?
Against the remnant of his heritage,
he will not hold his anger forever,
for he delights in kindness.
He will again show us mercy, 19
he will tread down our iniquities.
Thou wilt cast into the depths of the sea all their sins.
Thou wilt show faithfulness to Jacob, 20
kindness toward Abraham,
As thou hast sworn to our fathers,
from days of old.

THE BOOK OF NAHUM

THE SUPERSCRIPTION, 1:1

1 An oracle on Nineveh: the book of the vision of Nahum, the Elkoshite.

THE AVENGING WRATH OF THE LORD, 1:2–10

2 A jealous and avenging God is the LORD;
The LORD is avenging and full of wrath.
The LORD takes vengeance upon his enemies,
And lays up wrath for his foes.
3 The LORD is slow to anger and great in power,
But the LORD will by no means leave guilt unpunished.
In storm and tempest is his way,
And clouds are the dust of his feet.
4 He rebukes the sea, and dries it up,
And all the rivers he makes dry.
Bashan and Carmel wither,
And the bud of Lebanon languishes.
5 The mountains quake at him,
And the hills melt.
The earth is laid waste before him,
The world with all its inhabitants.
6 Who can stand before his wrath?
Who can endure his fierce anger?
His fury is poured out like fire,
And the rocks are burst open by him.
7 The LORD is good to those that wait for him,
A stronghold on the day of trouble;
He knows those that take refuge in him.
8 But with an overflowing flood
He will make an end of his adversaries;
And his foes he will pursue into the darkness.
9 What are you planning against the LORD?
He is about to execute complete destruction;
He will not take vengeance twice upon his enemies.
10 They are thorns cut down and dried out;
They will be consumed like dry stubble.

THREATS AND PROMISES, 1:11—2:2

Did not one go forth from you plotting evil against the LORD, 1
Counseling rascality?
Thus says the LORD: 1
"When many days are completed,
They shall be cut off and shall pass away.
I have afflicted you, but I will never again afflict you.
And now I will break his rod from upon you, 1
And burst asunder your bonds."
For the LORD has given command regarding you, 1
"There shall be sown of your name no longer.
From the house of your gods I will cut off the carved and the molten images.
I will make your grave a disgrace."

Behold, upon the mountains, the feet of a herald, 1
one proclaiming prosperity!
Celebrate your feasts, O Judah,
fulfil your vows.
For never again will ruin pass through you;
he will be wholly cut off.
For the LORD will restore the vine of Jacob, 2
likewise, the vine of Israel;
Though devastators have devastated them,
and laid waste their branches.

THE SACK OF NINEVEH, 2:1, 3–13

The shatterer has come up against you; 1
Keep the rampart;
Watch the road; brace your loins;
Strengthen your forces to the utmost.

The shield of his warriors is reddened;
The mighty men are clothed in scarlet,
Like the flame of torches.

They will make ready the chariot on
that day,
And the chargers will prance.
4 The chariots will rage in the streets,
Dashing to and fro in the open spaces.
Their appearance will be like that of
torches,
Darting about like lightning.
5 He summons his nobles; they stumble
as they go.
They hasten to the wall,
And the battering ram is set up.

6 The gates of the rivers are opened,
And the palace melts away.
7 Its mistress is brought forth; she goes
into captivity,
While her maidens mourn,
Moaning like the sound of doves,
Beating upon their breasts.
8 And Nineveh is like a pool of water,
Whose water escapes.
"Halt, halt!" they cry,
But no one turns back.
9 "Plunder silver, plunder gold;
For there is no end to the stores,
An abundance of all sorts of valuable
articles."

10 There is emptiness, desolation, and
waste,
And a melting heart and trembling
knees;
And anguish is in all loins,
And the faces of all of them become
livid.
11 Where is the den of the lions,
And the cave of the young lions,
Whither the lion went, bringing in
prey,
The lion's cub, with none to disturb?
12 Where the lion tore enough prey for
his cubs,
And rended for his lionesses,
Filling his den with prey,
And his lair with booty?

13 "Behold, I am against you,"
Is the oracle of the LORD of hosts;
"And I will burn up your chariots with
smoke,
And the sword shall devour your
young lions;
And I will cut off your prey from the
land,
And the voice of your messengers shall
be heard no more."

THE IMMINENT AND INEVITABLE END, 3:1–19

Woe to the city, bloody throughout, 3
Full of lies and booty!
Prey ceases not.
The crack of the whip, and the noise 2
of the rumbling wheel,
And the galloping horse, and the jolting chariot;
The charging horseman, and the 3
flashing sword,
And the glittering spear, and a multitude of slain,
And a mass of bodies, and no end to
the corpses!
They stumble over the corpses!
Because of the many harlotries of a 4
harlot
Of goodly favor and a mistress of
spells,
Who sells nations by her harlotries,
And clans by her spells.

"Behold, I am against you," 5
Is the oracle of the LORD of hosts,
"And I will strip off your skirts to your
face,
And I will show nations your nakedness,
And kingdoms your shame.
And I will throw vile things at you, 6
And treat you with contempt, and
make you a horror;
So that everyone that sees you will 7
flee from you,
Saying, 'Nineveh is destroyed;
Who will mourn for her?
Whence can I seek comforters for
her?'

"Are you any better than Thebes, 8
That sat by the great Nile,
With water all around her,
Whose rampart was the sea,
Whose wall was water?
Ethiopia was her strength, and Egypt, 9
And there was no end to it;
Put and the Libyans were her help;
Yet even she became an exile; 10
She went into captivity;
Even her children were dashed in
pieces
At the head of every street;
And upon her honored ones they cast
lots,
And all her great men were bound in
chains.

11 "You too shall reel and swoon;
You too shall seek refuge from the foe.
12 All your fortresses shall be fig trees with the first ripe figs;
If they be shaken they fall into the mouth of the eater.
13 Behold, your people shall be but women in the midst of you;
To your foes the gates of your land will be opened wide;
Fire will devour your barriers.

14 "Draw yourself water for the siege; strengthen your forts;
Plunge into the mud, and trample the clay;
Lay hold of the brick-mold!
15 There fire shall devour you,
The sword shall cut you off;
It shall devour you as the locust does.
Multiply yourselves like the locust;
Multiply yourselves like the locust-swarm.

16 "Increase your merchants more than the stars of the heavens!
Locusts spread the wing and fly away!
17 Your watchers are like locust-swarms;
Your scribes like clouds of locusts,
That settle in the hedges in the cool of the day.
When the sun arises, they flee,
And their location is unknown.

18 "Your shepherds slumber, O king of Assyria;
your nobles sleep!
Your people are scattered upon the hilltops,
with none to gather them.
19 There is no healing for your wound;
your hurt is incurable.
Everyone who shall hear the news about you,
will clap his hands over you.
For against whom has not your malice continually gone forth?"

THE BOOK OF HABAKKUK

THE SUPERSCRIPTION 1:1

1 The oracle which Habakkuk, the prophet, received.

THE PROPHET'S PROBLEM AND ITS ANSWER, 1:2—2:20

2 How long, O LORD, must I cry for help,
and thou not hear?
Call out to thee, "Violence,"
and thou not save?
3 Why dost thou show me wrongdoing,
and make me look upon trouble?
Destruction and violence are before me,
and there is strife,
and opposition arises.
4 Therefore the law is paralyzed,
And judgment never goes forth.
But the wicked circumvent the innocent;
Therefore judgment goes forth perverted.

5 "Look out upon the nations and see,
And be utterly amazed!
For a deed is being done in your days
That you would not believe, were it told you.
6 For behold, I am raising up the Chaldeans,
That savage and impetuous nation,
That marches through the breadth of the earth,
To seize habitations that are not his own.

7 "Terrible and dreadful is he;
Judgment and destruction go forth from him.
8 Swifter than leopards are his horses,
And keener than wolves of the desert.
His horses prance,
And his horsemen come from afar;
They swoop down like a vulture hastening to devour.
9 "Wholly for violence does he come;
Terror marches before him;
And he gathers up captives like sand.
He makes scorn of kings, 10
And rulers are a joke to him!
He laughs at all fortresses,
And heaps up dirt and captures them.
Then he changes like the wind and passes on, 11
And he makes strength his god."

Art not thou from of old, 12
O LORD, my holy God?
Thou diest not!
O LORD, thou hast made him for judgment!
And thou, O Rock, hast established him for chastisement!
Too pure of eyes art thou to look upon wickedness, 13
And thou canst not gaze upon wrongdoing.
Why then dost thou gaze upon faithless men,
And keep silent when the wicked swallows up
Him that is more righteous than himself?
For thou makest men like fish of the sea, 14
Like reptiles, with no ruler.

He brings them all up with the hook; 15
He drags them away with his net,
And he gathers them up in his seine.
So he rejoices and exults;
So he sacrifices to his net, 16
And makes offerings to his seine;
For through them his portion is fat,
And his food is abundant.
Shall he keep on emptying his net forever, 17
And never cease slaying the nations?

I will take my stand upon my watchtower, 2
And station myself upon the rampart;
And watch to see what he will say to me,
And what answer he will make to my complaint.
Then the LORD answered me, saying, 2
"Write the vision clearly upon the tablets,

That one may read it on the run.
3 For the vision is a witness for the appointed time,
And speaks of the end, and does not lie.
If it tarry, wait for it;
For it will surely come without delay.

4 "Verily, the wicked man—I take no pleasure in him;
But the righteous lives by reason of his faithfulness.
5 How much less shall the faithless man live,
And the arrogant man who is restless,
Who enlarges his appetite like Sheol,
And is as insatiable as death;
For he gathers to himself all nations,
And assembles to himself all peoples.

6 "Shall not all these take up a taunt-song against him,
And a sharp satire against him, saying,
'Woe to him who enriches himself with what is not his own—
How long?—and loads himself with debts!'
7 Will not your creditors rise up suddenly,
And those awake who will make you quake?
And you will become spoil for them.
8 Because you have despoiled many nations,
All the rest of the peoples shall despoil you;
Because of human bloodshed, and the violence done to the land,
The city and all that dwelt therein."

9 Woe to him who acquires unjust gain for his household,
Setting his nest on high, that he may be delivered from the power of disaster.
10 You have devised disgrace for your household,
By cutting off many peoples, thus forfeiting your life.
11 For the stone from the wall cries out,
And the beam from the woodwork answers it.

12 Woe to him who builds a city by bloodshed,
And establishes a town by wrong!
13 Are not these things from the LORD of hosts,
That peoples exhaust themselves for the fire,
And nations wear themselves out for nought?
But the earth shall be filled with the knowledge of the glory of the LORD, 14
As the waters cover the sea.

Woe to him who makes his friend drink 15
From the cup and the wineskin, till he makes him drunk,
So as to gaze upon his shame!
You shall be sated with shame rather than honor; 16
Drink yourself and be disgraced!
The cup of the right hand of the LORD shall come round to you,
And disgrace upon your glory.
For the violence done to Lebanon shall cover you, 17
And the destruction wrought upon Hamath shall terrify you;
Because of human bloodshed, and the violence done to the land,
The city and all that dwelt therein.

Of what use is an idol when its designer has designed it, 18
Or a molten image, and a teacher of lies?
For he who designed his own image trusts in it,
So that he makes dumb nonentities!

Woe to him who says to wood, "Wake up," 19
To a dumb stone, "Arise."
Can it give oracles?
Lo, it is encased with gold and silver;
And there is no breath within it!
But the LORD is in his holy temple; 20
Be silent before him, all the earth!

A PSALM, 3:1–19

[A prayer of Habakkuk, the prophet: upon *Shigyonoth*]

O LORD, I have heard the report of thee;
I have seen thy work, O LORD.
In the midst of the years, declare it!
In the midst of the years, make it known!
In wrath, remember to be merciful!

God went forth from Teman,
And the Holy One from Mount Paran. *Selah*

His glory covered the heavens,
And his praise filled the earth.
4 A brilliance like light was under him;
Rays of light were at his side;
And he made them the veil of his majesty.
5 Before him went the pestilence,
And the plague ran at his heels.
6 He stood firm, and shook the earth;
He looked, and made the nations quake.
And the everlasting mountains were shattered,
And the ancient hills bowed low.
Such were his ways of old.

7 The tent-hangings of Cushan were torn to shreds;
The hangings of the land of Midian fluttered wildly.
8 Did thine anger burn against the rivers, O LORD,
Or against the mountains,
Or thy rage against the sea,
When thou didst ride upon thy steeds,
Upon thy victorious chariots?

9 Thou didst wholly uncover thy bow;
Thou didst fill thy quiver full of arrows. *Selah*
Thou didst split the earth with rivers;
10 The mountains saw thee; they writhed with pain.
The clouds poured down water;
The abyss uttered its voice.
The sun forgot his appointments,
11 The moon stood still in its habitation,
At the light of thine arrows as they flew,
At the glittering flash of thy spear.

Thou didst bestride the earth in fury; 12
Thou didst trample the nations in anger.
Thou didst go forth to deliver thy people, 13
To deliver thine anointed.
Thou didst smite the head from the house of the wicked,
Laying bare the foundation even to the rock. *Selah*
Thou didst pierce his head with thine arrows; 14
His chargers were routed.
[The violent set nets so as to devour the lowly in secret.]
Thou didst tread the sea with thy horses, 15
The turmoil of great waters.

I have heard and my body trembles; 16
My lips quiver at the sound.
Decay enters my bones,
And my steps totter beneath me.
I will wait for the day of trouble
To come upon the people that oppresses us.

Though the fig tree do not flourish, 17
And there be no fruit on the vines;
Though the product of the olive fail,
And the fields yield no food;
Though the flock be cut off from the fold,
And there be no cattle in the stalls;
Yet will I exult in the LORD; 18
I will rejoice in my victorious God!
GOD, the Lord, is my strength; 19
And he makes my feet like the feet of hinds,
And makes me walk upon my heights.

[For the director. On my stringed instruments]

THE BOOK OF ZEPHANIAH

THE SUPERSCRIPTION, 1:1

1 THE word of the LORD which came to Zephaniah, the son of Cushi, the son of Gedaliah, the son of Amariah, the son of Hezekiah, in the days of Josiah, the son of Amon, king of Judah.

A DAY OF DOOM UPON THE WORLD, 1:2–6

2 "I will utterly sweep away everything
From upon the face of the ground," is the oracle of the LORD.
3 "I will sweep away man and beast;
I will sweep away the birds of the air, and the fish of the sea.
And I will cause the wicked to stumble,
And I will cut off mankind from off the face of the ground,"
Is the oracle of the LORD;
4 "And I will stretch out my hand against Judah,
And against all the inhabitants of Jerusalem.
And from this place I will cut off the Baal to the last remnant;
The name of the priestlings, along with the priests;
5 And those who prostrate themselves upon the roofs
To the host of the heavens;
And those who prostrate themselves before the LORD
And swear by Milcom;
6 And those who have withdrawn from following the LORD,
And those who have not sought the LORD,
Nor inquired after him."

THE TERRORS OF THE DAY OF THE LORD, 1:7–18

7 Silence before the Lord GOD,
For the day of the LORD is near at hand!
For the LORD has prepared a sacrifice;
He has sanctified his guests!
It shall come to pass on the day of the LORD'S sacrifice,
That I will punish the princes and the king's sons,
And everyone that clothes himself in foreign garments.
And I will punish everyone that leaps over the threshold on that day,
Those filling their master's house with violence and deceit.

"It shall come to pass on that day," is the oracle of the LORD, 10
"That there will be the sound of a cry from the Fish-Gate,
And a wail from the New Town;
And there will be a great crash from the hills.
Wail, O inhabitants of the Mortar! 11
For all the people of Canaan shall be ruined;
All who weigh out silver shall be cut off.

"At that time I will search Jerusalem with lamps, 12
And will punish those who are at ease,
Thickened upon their lees, who say to themselves,
'The LORD does neither good nor bad.'
And their property shall become a ruin, 13
And their houses a desolation.
And they shall build houses, but not inhabit them;
And plant vineyards, but not drink their wine."

Near at hand is the great day of the LORD; 14
Near and speeding fast!
Near at hand is the bitter day of the LORD,
On which the warrior will cry in terror!
A day of wrath is that day; 15
A day of trouble and distress,
A day of desolation and waste,
A day of darkness and gloom,
A day of cloud and thundercloud;
A day of the trumpet and battle-cry, 16

Against the fortified cities,
And against the lofty battlements.

7 "And I will bring trouble upon mankind so that they shall walk like blind men";
Because they have sinned against the LORD.
And their blood shall be poured out like dust,
And their flesh like dung.
8 Neither their silver nor their gold
Will be able to rescue them.
On the day of the wrath of the LORD, and in the fire of his zeal,
All the earth shall be consumed;
For a complete destruction, indeed a frightful one, will he make
Of all the inhabitants of the earth.

THE DAY OF DOOM UPON PHILISTIA, 2:1–7

1 Gather yourselves in crowds,
O nation without shame;
2 Before you move far off,
Like the chaff which passes away;
Before there come upon you
The fierce anger of the LORD;
Before there come upon you,
The day of the anger of the LORD!

3 Seek the LORD, all you meek of the earth,
Who do his will;
Seek righteousness, seek humility;
Perhaps you may be hidden on the day of the anger of the LORD.

4 For Gaza shall be deserted,
And Askelon a waste.
Ashdod—at noon they shall expel her,
And Ekron shall be uprooted.

5 Woe to those who dwell by the sea-coast,
The nation of the Cherethites!
The word of the LORD is against you,
O Canaan, land of the Philistines!
And I will destroy you so that there shall be no inhabitant.

6 And the sea-coast shall become pastures (with cisterns) for shepherds,
And folds for flocks;
7 And the sea-coast will belong to the remnant of the house of Judah.
By the sea shall they feed;
In the houses of Askelon at evening shall they lie down.
For the LORD, their God, shall visit them,
And restore their fortune.

VENGEANCE UPON MOAB AND AMMON, 2:8–11

"I have heard the taunts of Moab, 8
And the revilings of the Ammonites,
Wherewith they have taunted my people,
And vaunted themselves against their territory.
Therefore, as I live," is the oracle of 9
the LORD of hosts,
The God of Israel,
"Moab shall become like Sodom,
And the Ammonites like Gomorrah;
A land overrun by weeds and salt-pits,
And a desolation forever.
The remnant of my people shall prey upon them,
And the survivors of my nation shall possess them."

This shall be their lot in return for 10
their arrogance,
Because they taunted and vaunted themselves
Against the people of the LORD of hosts.
The LORD will be terrible against 11
them;
For he will famish all the gods of the earth,
So that there shall bow down to him, each from its place,
All the coast-lands of the nations.

DOOM UPON ETHIOPIA AND ASSYRIA, 2:12–15

You, too, O Ethiopians, 12
shall be slain by my sword!
And he will stretch out his hand 13
against the north,
and destroy Assyria.
And he will make Nineveh a desolation,
a drought like the desert;
And herds shall lie down in the midst 14
of her,
every beast of the field.
Both jackdaw and hedgehog
shall lodge in her capitals;

The owl shall hoot in the window,
the bustard on the threshold;
for I will destroy her city.
15 This is the exultant city,
that dwelt in security!
That said to itself,
"I am, and there is none else."
How she has become a ruin,
a lair for wild beasts!
Everyone that passes by her hisses,
and shakes his fist!

SIN AND JUDGMENT, 3:1–7

3 Woe to the defiant and defiled one, the oppressing city!
2 She has listened to no voice;
She has accepted no correction!
In the LORD she has not trusted;
To her God she has not drawn near!

3 Her princes within her are roaring lions;
Her judges are wolves of the night,
Who long not for the morning.
4 Her prophets are reckless, treacherous men;
Her priests profane holy things;
They do violence to the law.

5 The LORD is righteous within her;
He will do no wrong.
Every morning he brings his judgment to light;
He does not fail;
But the wicked knows no shame.

6 I have cut off nations; their battlements are destroyed.
I have made their streets desolate,
with none passing by.
Their cities have been laid waste,
without a man, without an inhabitant.
7 I said, "Surely she will fear me; she will accept correction;
And there shall not be cut off from her sight
Anything which I have laid upon her.
But they have zealously made
All their doings corrupt."

JERUSALEM DELIVERED, 3:8–13

8 "Therefore wait for me," is the oracle of the LORD,
"against the day when I arise as a witness.
For it is my decision to gather nations,
to assemble kingdoms,
That I may pour out my wrath upon them,
all the heat of my anger.
For in the fire of my zeal,
all the earth shall be consumed.
"For then I will turn the speech of the peoples
into a purified speech;
So that all of them may call upon the name of the LORD,
and serve him with one accord.
From beyond the rivers of Ethiopia,
to the farthest regions of the north,
they shall bring offerings to me.

"On that day you shall not be put to shame by any of your deeds,
wherein you have rebelled against me;
For then I will remove from the midst of you
your proudly exulting ones;
And you shall no more be haughty
in my holy mountain;
For I will leave in the midst of you
a people humble and poor.

"And in the name of the LORD shall they seek refuge—
the remnant of Israel.
They shall do no wrong,
nor shall they tell lies;
Nor shall there be found in their mouth
a deceitful tongue;
For they shall feed and lie down,
with none to disturb them."

ISRAEL'S WORLD-WIDE RENOWN, 3:14–20

Cry aloud, O daughter of Zion;
shout, O Israel!
Be glad and rejoice with your whole heart,
O daughter of Jerusalem!
The LORD has routed your opponents,
he has removed your foes.
The king of Israel, the LORD, is in the midst of you;
you shall see disaster no more.
On that day it shall be said to Jerusalem, "Fear not, O Zion;
let not your hands relax.

17 The LORD, your God, is in the midst of you,
a victorious warrior.
He will rejoice over you with gladness,
he will renew you in his love.
He will exult over you with a shout,
18 as in the days of a festival.

"I will gather up those that smite you,
and those bringing reproach upon you.
19 Lo, I will deal with all your oppressors
at that time.
And I will deliver the lame,
and gather the outcast.
And I will make them renowned and praised
in all the earth.

"At that time I will bring you, 20
And at that time I will gather you;
For I will make you renowned and praised
Among all the peoples of the earth;
When I restore your fortune before your very eyes,"
Says the LORD.

THE BOOK OF HAGGAI

BEGINNING THE REBUILDING OF THE TEMPLE,

1:1–15*a*

1 IN THE second year of Darius, the
king, in the sixth month, on the
first day of the month, the word of
the LORD came through Haggai,
the prophet, to Zerubbabel, the son of
Shealtiel, governor of Judah, and to
Joshua, the son of Jehozadak, the chief
priest, saying:
2 "Thus spoke the LORD of hosts,
saying, 'This people say, "The time
has not yet come to rebuild the house of
the LORD." ' "
3 The word of the LORD came through
Haggai, the prophet, saying,
4 "Is it a time for you yourselves to
live in your paneled houses, while this
house lies waste?"
5 "But now," thus says the LORD of
6 hosts, "give thought to your ways. You
have sown much, but reaped little; you
have eaten, but not to repletion; you
have drunk, but not your fill; you have
put on clothes, but there was no
warmth in them; and he who earned
wages put it into a bag with a hole in
it."
7 Thus says the LORD of hosts:
8 "Give thought to your ways. Go up
to the hills, and bring lumber, and rebuild the house, that I may be pleased
with it and be honored," says the
9 LORD. "You expected much, and it
was but little; and you brought it home,
and I blew it away! For what reason?"
is the oracle of the LORD of hosts. "Because of my house which lies waste,
while you yourselves run each to his
10 own house. Therefore the heavens
above you withhold their dew, and the
11 earth withholds its increase. For I
called for a drought upon the land, and
upon the hills, upon the grain and the
wine and the oil, and upon everything
that the ground yields; and upon man
and beast, and every product of labor."
12 So Zerubbabel, the son of Shealtiel,
and Joshua, the son of Jehozadak, the
chief priest, and all the remnant of the
people, listened to the voice of the
LORD, their God, and to the words of
the prophet Haggai, inasmuch as the
LORD, their God, had sent him; and
the people were afraid because of the
LORD. Whereupon Haggai, the messenger of the LORD, with the message
of the LORD to the people, spoke, saying,
" 'I am with you,' is the oracle of the
LORD."
So the LORD aroused the spirit of
Zerubbabel, the son of Shealtiel, governor of Judah, and the spirit of Joshua, the son of Jehozadak, the chief
priest, and the spirit of all the remnant
of the people, so that they came and
went to work upon the house of the
LORD of hosts, their God, on the twenty-fourth day of the sixth month.

WORDS OF ENCOURAGEMENT TO THE BUILDERS,

1:15*b*—2:9

In the second year of Darius, the
king, in the seventh month, on the
twenty-first day of the month, the word
of the LORD came through Haggai, the
prophet, saying,
"Say, now, to Zerubbabel, the son of
Shealtiel, the governor of Judah, and to
Joshua, the son of Jehozadak, the chief
priest, and to the remnant of this people, thus:
'Who is there left among you that
saw this house in its ancient splendor?
And how it looks to you now! Does it
not seem to you like nothing at all?
But now, be strong, O Zerubbabel,' is
the oracle of the LORD, 'and be strong,
O Joshua, the son of Jehozadak, the
chief priest, and be strong, all the people of the land,' is the oracle of the
LORD, 'and work; for I am with you,'
is the oracle of the LORD of hosts; 'it is
the promise that I made you when you
came forth from Egypt; and my spirit
is standing in the midst of you; fear
not.' "

6 For thus says the LORD of hosts:
"A little while longer, and I will shake
the heavens and the earth, the sea and
7 the dry land. And I will shake all the
nations, and the treasures of all the nations shall come in, and I will fill this
house with splendor," says the LORD of
8 hosts. "Mine is the silver and mine is
the gold," is the oracle of the LORD of
9 hosts. "The future splendor of this
house shall be greater than the past,"
says the LORD of hosts; "and upon this
place I will bestow prosperity," is the
oracle of the LORD of hosts.

PROMISES OF AN IMMEDIATE CHANGE FOR THE BETTER, 2:10–23

10 On the twenty-fourth day of the
ninth month, in the second year of
Darius, the word of the LORD came
through Haggai, the prophet, as follows:
11 "Thus says the LORD of hosts: 'Ask
the priests, now, for a decision, saying,
12 "If a man carrying holy flesh in the
skirt of his clothing touch with his
skirt bread, or pottage, or wine, or oil,
or any kind of food, will it become
holy?" ' "
And the priests answered, saying,
"No!"
13 Then said Haggai, the prophet,
"If one who is unclean through contact with a corpse touch any one of
these, will it become unclean?"
And the priests answered, saying,
"It will!"
14 Then Haggai responded, saying,
"So is this people, and so is this nation before me," is the oracle of the
LORD, "and so is all the work of their
hands; and what they offer there is
unclean.
"But, now, pray lay it to heart from 15
this day and henceforth. Since the time
when one stone was not yet laid upon
another in the temple of the LORD,
how have you fared? When one came 16
to a heap of twenty measures, there
were but ten; and when one came to the
wine-vat to draw off fifty measures
from the wine-press, there were only
twenty. I smote you with blight and 17
with mildew, and all the products of
your hands with hail. And yet you did
not return unto me," is the oracle of the
LORD.
"Pray, lay it to heart; from this day 18
forward, from the twenty-fourth day
of the ninth month, from the day when
the temple of the LORD was founded;
lay it to heart. Is the seed yet in the 19
barn? And do the vine, the fig trees,
the pomegranate, and the olive tree
still yield nothing? From this day on
I will bless you."
Then the word of the LORD came a 20
second time to Haggai, on the twenty-
fourth of the month, saying,
"Say unto Zerubbabel, governor of 21
Judah, as follows: 'I will shake the
heavens and the earth. And I will over- 22
turn the throne of the kingdoms, and I
will destroy the strength of the kingdoms of the nations; and I will overturn the chariot with its riders, so that
the horses and their riders shall go down
each by the sword of his fellow.' On 23
that day," is the oracle of the LORD of
hosts, "I will take you, O Zerubbabel,
son of Shealtiel, my servant," is the
oracle of the LORD, "and I will make
you like a seal ring; for I have chosen
you," is the oracle of the LORD of
hosts.

THE BOOK OF ZECHARIAH

A LESSON FROM THE PAST, 1:1–6

1 IN THE eighth month in the second
year of Darius, the word of the
LORD came to Zechariah, the son
of Berechiah, the son of Iddo, the
prophet, saying,
2 "The LORD was very angry at your
3 fathers. Say to them, 'Thus says the
LORD of hosts: "Return to me," is the
oracle of the LORD of hosts, "that I
may return to you," says the LORD of
4 hosts.' Be not like your fathers, to
whom the former prophets preached,
saying, 'Thus says the LORD of hosts:
"Turn now from your wicked ways and
from your wicked deeds." ' But they
did not hearken, nor did they give heed
to me," is the oracle of the LORD.
5 "Your fathers—where are they? And
the prophets—do they live forever?
6 Yet did not my words and my statutes
with which I charged my servants, the
prophets, overtake your fathers? So
they turned and said, 'Even as the
LORD of hosts had purposed to do to
us, in accordance with our ways and our
deeds, so has he treated us.' "

A VISION OF RESTORATION, 1:7–17

7 On the twenty-fourth day of the
eleventh month (namely, the month of
Shebat), in the second year of Darius,
the word of the LORD came to Zechariah,
the son of Berechiah, the son of
Iddo, the prophet, saying,
8 "I saw by night, and there was a man
riding upon a red horse, and he was
standing among the myrtle trees which
are in the hollow, and behind him were
9 red, sorrel, and white horses. Whereupon
I said, 'What are these, sir?' Then
the angel that was talking with me said
to me, 'I will show you what these are.'
10 And the man who was standing among
the myrtles answered, saying, 'These
are those whom the LORD sent forth to
11 patrol the earth.' Then they answered
the angel of the LORD, who was standing
among the myrtle trees, saying, 'We
have patrolled the earth; and lo, the
whole earth is resting peacefully.' Then 12
the angel of the LORD spoke, saying, 'O
LORD of hosts, for how long wilt thou
have no mercy upon Jerusalem and the
cities of Judah, with which thou hast
been angry now for seventy years?'
Then the LORD answered the angel 13
who was talking with me, with gracious
words, comforting words. So the angel 14
who was talking with me said to me,
'Proclaim as follows: "Thus says the
LORD of hosts: 'I am very greatly concerned
about Jerusalem and Mount
Zion, and I am exceedingly angry at the 15
easy-going nations; for while I was
angry but a little, they furthered the
disaster.'
Therefore thus says the LORD: 16
"I will return to Jerusalem in mercy;
My house shall be rebuilt therein,"
Is the oracle of the LORD of hosts;
"And a line shall be stretched over Jerusalem."
"Again proclaim, saying, 17
'Thus says the LORD of hosts:
"My cities shall again overflow with prosperity,
And the LORD shall again have pity upon Zion
And again choose Jerusalem."' "

A VISION OF FOUR HORNS AND THEIR DESTROYERS, 1:18–21

I raised my eyes and looked; and lo, 18
there were four horns! Then I said to 19
the angel who was talking with me,
"What are these?"
And he said to me,
"These are the horns which dispersed
Judah, Israel, and Jerusalem."
Then the LORD showed me four 20
blacksmiths. Whereupon I said,
"What are these coming to do?" 21
And he spoke, saying,
"These are the horns which dispersed
Judah, so that not a man raised his
head; and these have come to terrify

them, to cast down the horns of the nations, who lifted up the horn against the land of Judah in order to scatter it."

A VISION OF A MAN WITH A MEASURING-LINE, 2:1–5

2 I raised my eyes and looked, and lo,
there was a man with a measuring-line
2 in his hand! Then I said,
"Where are you going?"
He said to me,
"To measure Jerusalem, to see how broad and how long it should be."
3 And lo, as the angel who talked with
me was going away, another angel came
4 forth to meet him. And he said to him,
"Run, speak to that young man yonder, saying, 'Jerusalem shall be inhabited like unwalled villages, because of the mass of men and beasts within
5 her.' And I will be unto her," is the
oracle of the LORD, "a wall of fire round about her, and I will be the splendor within her."

A SUMMONS TO THE EXILES, 2:6–13

6 "Ho, ho! flee from the land of the north,"
Is the oracle of the LORD;
"For like the four winds of the heavens,
I will make you fly,"
Is the oracle of the LORD.
7 "Ho! O Zion! Escape, O inhabitants of Babylon."
8 For thus says the LORD of hosts
(hereafter he will send me forth with honor) regarding the nations that have plundered you (he who touches you touches the apple of his eye!):
9 "Verily I will wave my hand over
them, and they shall become plunder for their slaves."
Thus you shall know that the LORD of hosts has sent me.

10 "Shout with joy, and rejoice, O daughter of Zion!
For lo, I am coming to dwell in the midst of you,"
Is the oracle of the LORD.
11 Many nations will attach themselves to the LORD on that day;
And they will become his people,
And he will dwell in the midst of you;
And you will know that the LORD of hosts has sent me unto you.
And the LORD will take possession of Judah, 12
His portion upon the holy land;
And he will again choose Jerusalem.
Silence, all flesh, in the presence of the LORD! 13
For he rouses himself from his holy dwelling.

JOSHUA ACCUSED BY SATAN AND VINDICATED BY THE LORD, 3:1–10

Then he showed me Joshua, the chief 3
priest, standing before the angel of the LORD; and the Satan was standing at his right hand in order to oppose him.
So the angel of the LORD said to the 2
Satan,
"The LORD rebuke you, O Satan! May the LORD who has chosen Jerusalem rebuke you! Is not this a brand snatched from the fire?"
Now Joshua was dressed in dirty 3
clothes, as he stood before the angel.
So he spoke, and told those standing 4
before him, as follows:
"Take away the dirty clothes from upon him."
Then he said to him,
"See! I have removed your guilt from upon you; and have clothed you with festal garments."
Then he said, 5
"Let them put a clean turban upon his head."
So they clothed him with clean garments while the angel of the LORD
stood by. Then the angel of the LORD 6
warned Joshua, saying,
"Thus says the LORD of hosts: 'If 7
you walk in my ways, and if you keep my charge, then you shall rule my house and have charge of my courts; and I will give you free access among those who stand here.'
"Hear now, O Joshua, the chief 8
priest, you, and all your friends who sit in your presence, are men of good omen; for lo, I will bring in my servant,
the Branch. For behold the stone which 9
I have set before Joshua; upon a single stone with seven facets I will engrave its inscription," is the oracle of the LORD of hosts. "And I will remove the guilt of that land on one day."

10 "On that day," is the oracle of the
LORD of hosts, "everyone of you will
invite his friend under the vine and
under the fig tree."

THE VISION OF THE LAMP AND THE OLIVE TREES, 4:1–14

4 Then the angel who was talking with
me roused me again like a man who is
2 aroused from his sleep. Then he said to
me,

"What do you see?"

And I said,

"I see, and lo, a lampstand that is all
gold; and a bowl upon the top of it; and
seven lights upon it, and seven pipes to
3 the lights which are upon its top. And
there are two olive trees upon it, one on
the right of the bowl, and one on its
left."

4 Then I spoke again to the angel who
was talking with me, saying,

"What are these, sir?"

5 So the angel who was talking with me
answered me, saying,

"You do not know what these are?"

And I said,

"No, sir."

6a Then he answered, saying to me,

10b "These seven are the eyes of the
LORD which range over the whole
earth."

11 Then I replied, saying to him,

"What are these two olive trees, upon
the right of the lampstand, and upon its
left?"

12 And I spoke a second time, and said
to him,

"What are the two olive branches
which are held by the two golden pipes
which empty into the golden bowl?"

13 Then he answered me, saying,

"Do you not know what these are?"

And I said,

"No, sir."

14 So he said,

"These are the two anointed ones
who stand by the Lord of all the
earth."

SPIRITUAL DELIVERANCE, 4:6b–10

6b This is the word of the LORD to Zerubbabel, saying,

"Not by arms, nor by force, but by
my spirit," says the LORD of hosts.

"What are you, O great mountain? 7
Before Zerubbabel, become a plain!
And he shall bring forth the top-stone
With shouts of 'Grace, grace, to it.' "

The word of the LORD came to me, 8
saying,

"The hands of Zerubbabel founded 9
this house, and his hands shall complete
it."

So you shall know that the LORD of
hosts has sent me unto you. For who 10a
has despised a day of small things?
They shall rejoice when they see the
plummet in the hand of Zerubbabel.

VISIONS OF THE FLYING ROLL AND THE WOMAN IN THE MEASURE, 5:1–11

I raised my eyes again and looked; 5
and lo, there was a flying roll!

He said to me, 2

"What do you see?"

I answered,

"I see a flying roll, the length of
which is twenty cubits and its width ten
cubits."

Then he said to me, 3

"This is the curse that is going forth
over the surface of the whole land. For
how long now have all thieves remained
unpunished? And how long now have
those forsworn remained unpunished?
I will send it forth," is the oracle of the 4
LORD of hosts, "and it shall enter the
house of the thief and the house of him
who swears falsely by my name, and it
shall settle in the midst of his house and
consume it with its woodwork and its
stonework."

Then the angel that was talking with 5
me went forth, and he said to me,

"Raise your eyes now and see what
this is that goes forth."

And I said,

"What is it?" 6

Then he said,

"This is the ephah-measure that is
going forth."

He also said,

"This is their guilt throughout all the
earth."

Then a leaden lid was raised, and 7
there sat a woman within the measure!

Then he said, 8

"This is Wickedness!"

And he pushed her down into the
middle of the measure, and cast the
9 leaden weight upon its opening. Then I
raised my eyes and looked, and there
were two women coming out, with the
wind in their wings, having wings like
those of a stork. And they lifted the
measure up between the earth and the
10 sky. Then I said to the angel that was
talking with me,
"Where are they taking the measure?"
11 And he answered me,
"To build a house for it in the land of
Shinar. And when it is erected, they
will set it down there upon its base."

THE VISION OF THE FOUR CHARIOTS, 6:1–8

6 I raised my eyes again, and looked;
and there were four chariots coming out
from between the two mountains; and
the mountains were mountains of cop-
2 per. In the first chariot, there were bay
3 horses; in the second, black horses; in
the third, white horses; and in the
4 fourth, dappled horses. So I said again
to the angel that was talking with me,
"What are these, sir?"
5 The angel answered me, saying,
"These are for the four winds of the
heavens that are going out after standing before the LORD of all the earth.
6 That wherein are the black horses will
go to the north land; the white will go
to the west; the dappled will go to the
7 south land; and the bays will go to the
land of the east."
They were straining to go forth to
patrol the earth. So he said,
"Go, patrol the earth."
8 So they patrolled the earth. Then he
called me, and spoke to me saying,
"Look at those going forth to the
north land; they will give rest to the
spirit of the LORD in the north land."

THE CORONATION OF ZERUB-BABEL, 6:9–15

9 The word of the LORD came to me,
saying,
10 "Take the offering from the exiles,
from Heldai, Tobiah, and Jedaiah, who
have come from Babylon; and do you
go in on that day, and enter the house
of Josiah, the son of Zephaniah; and 11
take silver and gold and make a crown
and place it upon the head of Zerubbabel, the son of Shealtiel, the governor.
Then speak to them, saying, 'Thus spoke 12
the LORD of hosts, saying, "Behold a
man whose name is Branch; and he
shall branch forth from his place and
shall rebuild the temple of the LORD.
He shall rebuild the temple of the 13
LORD; and he shall bear the honor, and
shall sit and reign upon his throne. And
Joshua, the priest, shall be on his right
hand; and there shall be peaceful counsel between them both." '
"The crown shall be for Heldai and 14
for Tobiah and for Jedaiah and for Josiah, the son of Zephaniah, as a memorial in the temple of the LORD. Also 15
those from afar shall come and rebuild
the temple of the LORD, that you may
know that the LORD of hosts has sent
me unto you. And it shall come to pass
if you hearken closely to the voice of
the LORD your God. . . ."

A LESSON FROM THE PAST, 7:1–14

In the fourth year of Darius, the king, 7
on the fourth day of the ninth month,
in Chislev, the word of the LORD came
to Zechariah. Now Bethel-sar-ezer had 2
sent Regem-melek and his men to propitiate the LORD; saying to the priests 3
that belonged to the house of the LORD
of hosts, and to the prophets thus:
"Shall I weep in the fifth month and
fast, as I have done now for many
years?"
The words of the LORD of hosts came 4
to me, saying,
"Speak to all the people of the land 5
and to the priests, saying, 'When you
fasted and mourned in the fifth and in
the seventh months the past seventy
years, was it for me that you fasted so
strictly? And when you eat, and when 6
you drink, do you not yourselves eat
and yourselves drink? Are not these 7
the words which the LORD proclaimed
through the former prophets, when Jerusalem was inhabited and prosperous,
with her towns round about her, and
the Negeb and the Shephelah were inhabited?' "
Then the word of the LORD came to 8
Zechariah, saying, "Thus spoke the 9

LORD of hosts, saying, 'Render true
judgments, and practice kindness and
10 mercy each toward his brother. Do not
oppress the widow and the orphan, the
resident alien, and the poor; and let
none of you devise in your heart wick-
11 edness against your brother.' But they
refused to give heed, and turned a stubborn shoulder, and made their ears dull
12 so that they could not hear; and they
made their minds insensate so that they
could not hear the teaching and the
words which the LORD of hosts sent by
his spirit, through the former prophets.
So there was great wrath on the part of
13 the LORD of hosts. As he called and
they did not listen, so 'they shall call
and I will not listen,' said the LORD of
14 hosts. So he scattered them among all
the nations that they had not known;
and the land was desolate after them,
so that none passed by and none returned; and they made the lovely land
a ruin."

WORDS OF PROMISE, 8:1–17

8 The word of the LORD of hosts came,
2 saying, "Thus says the LORD of hosts:
'I have been very indignant over Zion;
I have been aroused to great wrath
over her.' "
3 Thus says the LORD:
"I will return to Zion,
And I will dwell in the midst of Jerusalem;
And Jerusalem shall be called, 'The
faithful city,'
And the mountain of the LORD of
hosts, 'The holy mountain.' "
4 Thus says the LORD of hosts:
"Aged men and women shall again dwell
in the streets of Jerusalem,
Each with his staff in his hand by reason of his great age;
5 And the streets of the city shall be
filled
With boys and girls, playing in its
streets."
6 Thus says the LORD of hosts:
"If it seem incredible in the sight of the
remnant of this people in those
days,
In my sight also will it seem incredible?"
Is the oracle of the LORD of hosts.
7 Thus says the LORD of hosts:
"Behold, I am about to deliver my
people
From the land of the rising, and the
land of the setting sun;
And I will bring them in, and they
shall dwell in the midst of Jerusalem.
And they shall be my people, and I
will be their God,
In faithfulness and righteousness."
Thus says the LORD of hosts:
"Let your hands be strong, you who
are listening in these days to these
words from the mouth of the prophets
that were on the day when the foundation of the house of the LORD of hosts,
the temple, was laid that it might be
built. For before those days there was 1
no wages for man or beast; nor was
there safety from the foe either for him
who went out or for him who came in;
for I had sent forth every man, each
against his fellow. But now, I am not 1
as in the former days toward the remnant of this people," is the oracle of the
LORD of hosts. "For I will sow pros- 1
perity; the vine shall yield its fruit, and
the land shall yield its increase, and the
heavens shall yield their dew; and I will
make the remnant of this people possess
all these things. And it shall come to 1
pass that even as you have been a curse
among the nations, O house of Judah
and house of Israel, just so will I deliver
you, and you shall become a blessing.
Fear not; let your hands be strong!"
For thus says the LORD of hosts: 1
"Even as I purposed to do harm to
you, when your fathers angered me, and
I did not relent; so likewise will I pur- 1
pose again in these days to do good to
Jerusalem and to the house of Judah;
fear not!
"These are the things that you must
do. Speak truth one with another. Give
true and just decisions in your courts.
Let none of you devise evil in your 1
thoughts against your friend, and do
not love perjury. For all these things I
loathe," is the oracle of the LORD.

THE WORLD-WIDE RENOWN OF THE JEWS, 8:18–23

The word of the LORD of hosts came 1
to me, saying, "Thus says the LORD of 1
hosts: 'The fast of the fourth month,
and the fast of the fifth, and the fast of
the seventh, and the fast of the tenth,
shall become for the house of Judah occasions of joy and gladness, and goodly

festivals. So, love faithfulness and
20 peace.' Thus says the LORD of hosts:
'Peoples shall yet come, even the citi-
21 zens of many cities. And the citizens of
one city shall go to another, saying,
"Let us go at once to propitiate the
LORD and to seek the LORD of hosts!"
22 "I certainly will go." Thus many
peoples and strong nations shall come
to seek the LORD of hosts in Jerusalem,
23 and to propitiate the LORD.' Thus says
the LORD of hosts: 'In those days, ten
men, from nations of every language,
shall lay hold of him who is a Jew, saying, "Let us go with you; for we have
heard that God is with you!"' "

THE COMING DESTRUCTION OF JUDAH'S NEIGHBORS, 9:1–8

9 An Oracle.
The word of the LORD is against the
land of Hadrach,
And Damascus will be its resting-place.
For the cities of Syria belong to the
LORD,
As well as all the tribes of Israel;
2 And Hamath, too, which borders there-
on;
Tyre and Sidon, though they be very
clever.
3 But Tyre built herself a stronghold,
And heaped up silver like dust,
And gold like the mud of the streets.
4 The LORD, however, will dispossess her,
And smite her wealth into the sea,
And she shall be consumed by fire.

5 Askelon shall see and be afraid;
Gaza too, and shall be in great anguish;
Ekron also, because her hope has been
put to shame;
And the king shall perish from Gaza.
Askelon shall be uninhabited;
6 And mongrels shall dwell in Ashdod;
And I will cut down the pride of the
Philistines.
7 And I will take away its blood from its
mouth,
And its hateful things from between its
teeth;
It, too, shall remain for our God,
And shall be like a family in Judah,
And Ekron shall be like the Jebusites.

8 Then I will encamp by my house as a
guard, that none pass to and fro;
So that an oppressor shall not pass over
them again;
For now have I seen with my own eyes.

THE MESSIAH AND HIS DOMINION, 9:9–17

Exult greatly, O daughter of Zion; 9
Shout with joy, O daughter of Jerusalem.
Lo, your king comes to you;
Vindicated and victorious is he;
Humble, and riding upon an ass,
Even upon a colt, the foal of an ass.
He shall cut off the chariot from 10
Ephraim,
And the horse from Jerusalem;
And the bow of war shall be cut off,
And he shall command peace upon the
nations.
His dominion shall be from sea to sea,
And from the river to the ends of the
earth.

You, also—because of the blood of your 11
covenant,
I will send forth your captives from the
waterless pit.
Return to the stronghold, you prisoners 12
of hope;
This very day do I announce that I will
restore double to you.
For I will bend Judah as my bow; 13
I will fill it with Ephraim.
And I will stir up your sons, O Zion,
against your sons, O Greece;
And I will make you like a warrior's
sword.
And the LORD shall be manifested over 14
you,
And his arrow shall go forth like light-
ning.
For the Lord GOD will blow the trum-
pet,
And will march forth amid the storms
of the south.

The LORD of hosts will protect them, 15
And they shall devour and trample
down the stone-slingers;
And they shall drink their blood like
wine,
And they shall be filled, like the sacrifi-
cial basin, like the corners of the
altar.
For the LORD their God shall deliver 16
them on that day;
Like a flock shall he shepherd them
upon his own land;
For they shall be conspicuous like the
stones of a diadem;
For how good and how fair it shall be! 17
Grain shall make the young men flourish,
And wine the maidens.

THE TRIUMPHANT RESTORATION OF ISRAEL AND JUDAH, 10:1—11:3

10 "Ask rain from the LORD, in the season of the spring rain,
From the LORD who makes the lightning,
And gives them showers of rain,
To everyone grass in the field.
2 For the teraphim speak nonsense;
The soothsayers divine lies;
And the dreamers speak falsehoods,
And give empty consolation.
Therefore they move on like sheep;
They roam about because there is no shepherd.
3 "My wrath shall blaze forth against the shepherds,
And I will punish the leaders.
For the LORD of hosts will visit his flock, the house of Judah,
And will make them like his splendid steed in battle.
4 From them shall come the cornerstone, from them the tent-pin,
From them the bow for war, and from them all the officers.
5 And they shall be like warriors trampling in the mire of the streets in battle;
And they shall fight because the LORD is with them,
And shall put to shame those riding upon horses.
6 "I will strengthen the house of Judah,
And deliver the house of Joseph.
I will bring them back because I have pity on them,
And they shall be as though I had not spurned them;
For I am the LORD, their God, and I will answer them.
7 And Ephraim shall be like a warrior;
And their hearts shall exult as with wine.
Their children shall see and rejoice,
And their hearts shall exult in the LORD.
8 "I will whistle for them and gather them in;
For I will rescue them, and they shall be as numerous as ever.
9 Though I sowed them among the peoples,
Yet in far-away places they shall remember me,
And shall rear their children and return.
10 For I will bring them back from the land of Egypt,
And from Assyria I will gather them;
And to the land of Gilead and Lebanon I will bring them in,
Till there be no more room for them.

11 "And they shall pass over the sea of Egypt,
And he will smite the waves in the sea.
And all the depths of the Nile shall be dried up,
And the pride of Assyria shall be brought low,
And the scepter shall depart from Egypt.
12 I will strengthen them in the LORD,
And they shall praise his name,"
Is the oracle of the LORD.

11 Open your doors, O Lebanon,
That the fire may devour your cedars!
2 Wail, O cypress, for the cedar has fallen;
For the glorious ones are laid low!
Wail, O oaks of Bashan,
For the impenetrable forest has fallen!
3 Hark! the cry of the shepherds,
Because their glory is ruined!
Hark! the roar of the young lions,
Because the pride of the Jordan is ruined!

THE FOOLISH SHEPHERDS, 11:4–17 and 13:7–9

4 Thus said the LORD, my God:
"Become a shepherd of the flock to
5 be slaughtered. For those who buy
them slay them, and are not condemned; and those who sell them say,
'Blessed be the LORD, for I have become rich!' And their own shepherds
6 have no mercy on them. For I will have
no mercy any more upon the inhabitants of the land," is the oracle of the
LORD; "for lo, I will cause men to come
each into the power of his shepherd,
and each into the power of his king;
and they shall subdue the land, and I
will not deliver it from their power."
7 So I became a shepherd of the flock
to be slaughtered for the merchants of
the flock; and took for myself two rods.
The one I called Delight; and the other
I called Union. So I became a shepherd
8 of the flock. (I destroyed the three

shepherds in one month.) Then my
wrath burned against them; and they
9 loathed me. So I said,
"I will not be your shepherd. What
is to die, may die; what is to be lost,
may be lost; and those that are left
shall devour each the flesh of her neighbor."
10 So I took my rod, Delight, and I cut
it in two, thus breaking the contract I
11 had made with all the peoples. So it
was broken on that day. Then the merchants of the flock who were watching
me knew that it was the word of the
12 LORD. Then I said to them,
"If it seem good to you, pay me my
wages, but if not, let it go!"
So they weighed out my wages, thirty
13 shekels of silver. But the LORD said to
me,
"Cast it into the treasury, that fine
price at which you have been valued by
them."
So I took the thirty shekels of silver,
and cast it into the treasury in the
14 house of the LORD. Then I broke my
second rod, Union, to signify the breaking of the brotherhood between Judah
15 and Israel. Then the LORD said to me,
"Take to yourself again the gear of a
16 foolish shepherd. For lo, I am about to
raise up in the land a shepherd; for that
which is lost he will not search; that
which is scattered, he will not seek;
that which is wounded, he will not heal;
and that which is vigorous, he will not
nourish. But the flesh of the fatling he
will devour, and their hoofs he will
break off.

17 "Woe unto my foolish shepherd,
who forsakes the flock!
A sword upon his arm,
and his right eye!
May his arm utterly wither,
and his right eye become wholly blind!

13 7 "Up, sword, against my shepherd,
And against the man, my associate!"
Is the oracle of the LORD of hosts.
"I will smite the shepherd, so that the
sheep be scattered;
And I will turn my hand against the
little ones.
8 And it shall come to pass in all the land,"
Is the oracle of the LORD,
"That two-thirds shall be cut off there-
in, and die,
And one-third shall survive therein.
And I will bring that third through fire, 9
And I will refine them as silver is refined,
And test them as gold is tested.
They will call upon my name,
And I will answer them.
I will say, 'They are my people';
And they will say, 'The LORD is my
God.' "

ASPECTS OF JUDAH'S FUTURE, 12:1–14 and 13:1–6

The oracle of the word of the LORD 12
against Israel.
The oracle of the LORD who spread
out the heavens and laid the foundations of the earth and formed the spirit
of mankind within them:
"Lo, I am about to make Jerusalem 2
an intoxicating bowl unto all the peoples
around. Moreover, the cities of Judah
will be under siege along with Jerusalem.
And it shall come to pass on that day, 3
that I will make Jerusalem a heavy
stone for all the peoples. All who try
to lift it will hurt themselves seriously;
and all the nations of the earth will be
gathered against it. On that day," is 4
the oracle of the LORD, "I will smite
every horse with the staggers, and its
rider with madness. But I will open the
eyes of the house of Judah, while I
smite all the horses of the peoples with
blindness.
"Then the families of Judah shall say 5
to themselves, 'There is strength for the
inhabitants of Jerusalem in the LORD
of hosts, their God.' On that day I will 6
make the families of Judah like a pot of
fire in the woods, and like a lighted
torch among sheaves; and they shall
devour upon the right hand and upon
the left all the peoples around; while
Jerusalem shall again be inhabited on
its own site, namely, in Jerusalem. And 7
the LORD will deliver the households of
Judah first, in order that the glory of
the house of David and the glory of the
inhabitants of Jerusalem over Judah be
not too great.
"On that day the LORD will protect 8
the inhabitants of Jerusalem; and he
who stumbles among them shall be, on
that day, like David; and the house of
David shall be like God, like the angel
of the LORD before them.
"It shall come to pass on that day, 9
that I will seek to destroy all the nations that come against Jerusalem. And 10

I will pour out upon the house of David
and upon the inhabitants of Jerusalem
a spirit of favor and of prayer; and they
shall look at him whom they have
stabbed to death; and they shall mourn
for him like the mourning for an only
child, and they shall weep bitterly for
him, like the bitter weeping over the
first-born.
11 "On that day there shall be a great
mourning in Jerusalem, like the mourning for Hadadrimmon in the plain of
12 Megiddo. The clans shall mourn, each
clan apart; the clan of the house of
David apart, and their wives apart; the
clan of the house of Nathan apart, and
13 their wives apart; the clan of the house
of Levi apart, and their wives apart;
the clan of Shimei apart, and their
14 wives apart; all the clans that are left,
each one apart, and their wives apart.
13 "On that day a fountain shall be
opened for the house of David and for
the inhabitants of Jerusalem for the
2 cleansing of sin and uncleanness. And
it shall come to pass on that day," is the
oracle of the LORD of hosts, "that I will
cut off the names of the idols from the
land, so that they will no longer be
named. I will drive away the prophets
and the spirit of uncleanness from the
3 land. So it shall come to pass that if
anybody still prophesies, his father and
his mother who bore him will say to
him, 'You shall not remain alive, for
you have spoken lies in the name of the
LORD.' So his father and his mother
who bore him will stab him to death as
he prophesies.
4 "It shall come to pass on that day,
that the prophets will each be ashamed
of his vision when he prophesies; nor
will he clothe himself with a hairy
5 mantle in order to deceive people. And
he will say, 'No prophet am I! I am a
tiller of the soil. The land has been my
6 occupation from my youth.' And when
someone says to him, 'What mean these
scars on your back?' He will say, 'I
was wounded in the house of my
lovers.' "[1]

JERUSALEM AND THE NATIONS, 14:1–21

14 Lo, a day is coming for the LORD,
when your spoil will be divided in the
2 midst of you. For I will gather all the
nations against Jerusalem to battle,
and the city shall be taken, and the
houses plundered, and the women violated; and one-half of the city shall go
into exile; but the rest of the people
shall not be cut off from the city. Then 3
the LORD shall go forth and fight
against those nations, as on the day
when he fought on the day of battle.
His feet shall stand, on that day, upon
the mount of Olives (which is in front
of Jerusalem on the east); and the
mount of Olives shall be split in two
from east to west by a very wide valley;
and half of the mountain shall move
northward, and the other half southward. And the valley of Hinnom shall 5
be blocked, for the valley of Hinnom
shall touch its side. And you shall flee,
just as you fled from before the earthquake in the days of Uzziah, king of
Judah. Then the LORD, your God, shall
come, and all the holy ones with him.
It shall come to pass on that day, 6
that there shall be neither heat, nor
cold, nor frost. And there shall be con- 7
tinuous day (it is understood of the
LORD!), not day and night; but there
shall be light at night-time.
It shall come to pass on that day, 8
that living waters shall go forth from
Jerusalem, half of them toward the
Eastern Sea, and half toward the Western Sea, continuing in summer and in
winter. Then the LORD shall become 9
king over all the earth. On that day the
LORD shall be one; and his name, one.
All the land shall be turned into a 10
region like the Arabah, from Geba to
Rimmon, south of Jerusalem. It, however, shall be high and be inhabited
upon its site, from the gate of Benjamin unto the place of the former gate,
unto the corner gate, and from the
tower of Hananel as far as the royal
wine-press. And the people shall live 11
there; and there shall be no more curse;
but Jerusalem shall be inhabited in
security.
This shall be the kind of plague with 12
which the LORD will plague all the
peoples who made war upon Jerusalem:
their flesh he will cause to rot, as they
stand upon their feet; their eyes shall
rot in their sockets; and their tongues
shall rot in their mouths.
So also, like this plague shall be the 15
plague upon the horse, the mule, the

[1] For 13:7–9 see p. 877.

camel, and the ass, and whatsoever
beasts may be in those camps.
3 It shall come to pass on that day,
that there will be a great terror from
the LORD among them; and they will
lay hold each of the hand of his fellow;
and the hand of one will be lifted
4 against the hand of another. (Even Judah will fight against Jerusalem.) And
the wealth of all the nations around
shall be gathered together, gold, silver,
and clothing in great abundance.
6 And it shall come to pass that any
that are left of all the nations that went
up against Jerusalem, shall go up from
year to year to worship the king, the
LORD of hosts, and to celebrate the
7 feast of booths. And it shall come to
pass that if anyone of the clans of the
earth does not go up to Jerusalem to
worship the king, the LORD of hosts,
there shall be no rain upon them. Also 18
if the clan of Egypt does not go up or
enter, then upon them there shall fall
the plague with which the LORD will
plague the nations who do not go up to
celebrate the feast of booths. This shall 19
be the punishment of Egypt and the
punishment of all the nations that go
not up to celebrate the feast of booths.

On that day there shall be upon the 20
bells of the horses, "Holy to the LORD."
And the pots in the house of the LORD
shall be like the sacrificial bowls before
the altar, since every pot in Jerusalem 21
and in Judah shall be holy to the LORD
of hosts; and all who sacrifice shall
come and take of them to boil the flesh
in them. And there shall no longer be a
trader in the house of the LORD of
hosts on that day.

THE BOOK OF MALACHI

THE SUPERSCRIPTION, 1:1

1 The oracle of the word of the LORD to Israel through Malachi.

A PROOF OF GOD'S LOVE FOR ISRAEL, 1:2–5

2 "I have loved you," says the LORD.
But you say, "How hast thou loved us?"
"Was not Esau the brother of Jacob?"
is the oracle of the LORD.
3 "Yet I loved Jacob, but Esau I hated;
And I have made his mountains a waste,
And his heritage one for jackals of the steppe.
4 If Edom says, 'We are laid prostrate,
But we will rebuild the ruins,' "
Thus says the LORD of hosts:
"They may build, but I will tear down;
And they shall be called 'The wicked region,'
And 'The people with whom the LORD is angry perpetually.'
5 And your eyes shall see and you yourselves shall say,
'The LORD is great beyond the region of Israel.' "

THE LORD HONORS THOSE WHO HONOR HIM, 1:6—2:9

6 "A son honors his father, and a servant his master.
But if I be a father, where is my honor?
And if I be a master, where is my reverence?"
Says the LORD of hosts to you,
O priests, who despise my name.

7 "But you say, 'How have we despised thy name?'
You bring upon my altar polluted food.
Then you say, 'How have we polluted it?'
In that you say, 'The table of the LORD is contemptible.'
"And when you bring the blind for sacrifice, is there no harm?
And when you bring the lame and the sick, is there no harm?
Bring it, now, to your governor; will he accept you,
Or receive you graciously?" says the LORD of hosts.
"But seek now the favor of God that he may be gracious to us—
From your hand has this come to be—
Will he be gracious toward you?"
Says the LORD of hosts.

"O that there were one among you that would close the doors,
That you might not kindle fire on my altar in vain.
I have no pleasure in you,"
Says the LORD of hosts;
"And I will accept no offering from your hand.

"For from the rising of the sun, even to its setting, 11
My name is great among the nations;
And in every place an offering is made, is presented to my name,
And a pure offering.
For my name is great among the nations,"
Says the LORD of hosts;
"But you are defiling it, 12
In that you say, 'The table of the LORD is defiled,
And his food, its product, is despicable.'
"And you say, 'What a weariness it is!' 13
And you sniff at it," says the LORD of hosts;
"And you bring the mangled, the lame and the sick;
You bring it as an offering!
Can I accept it from your hand?"
Says the LORD.

"Cursed be the cheat, in whose flock there is a male, 14
And he vows it, but sacrifices a blemished victim to the LORD.

For a great king am I," says the LORD of hosts;
"And my name is feared among the nations.

2 "Now this command is for you, O priests.
2 If you do not hearken, nor lay it to heart,
To give honor to my name,"
Says the LORD of hosts;
"Then I will send the curse upon you,
And I will turn your blessing into a curse;
I will indeed make it a curse, because you pay no heed.

3 "Lo, I will rebuke posterity for you,
And I will strew dung upon your faces, the dung of your feasts;
And I will carry you away from beside me,
4 That you may know that I sent this charge to you;
Seeing that my covenant was with Levi,"
Says the LORD of hosts.
5 "My covenant was with him;
Life and prosperity—I gave them to him,
Fear, and he feared me,
And stood in awe of my name.
6 True instruction was in his mouth,
And no wrong was upon his lips.
In peace and uprightness he walked with me,
And many did he turn from guilt.

7 "For the lips of a priest should preserve knowledge;
And instruction should they seek at his mouth;
For he is the messenger of the LORD of hosts.
8 But you have turned aside from the way;
You have made many stumble through the instruction;
You have violated the covenant of Levi,"
Says the LORD of hosts.
9 "So I too will make you
Despised and abased before all the people;
Inasmuch as you are not keeping my ways,
But are showing partiality through the oracle."

A PROTEST AGAINST DIVORCE, 2:10–16

Have we not all one father? 10
Did not one God create us?
Why then do we play one another false,
By violating the covenant of our fathers?
Judah has played false, and an abominable thing 11
Has been done in Israel and in Jerusalem.
For Judah has profaned the sanctuary of the LORD which he loved,
And has married the daughter of an alien god.
May the LORD cut off for the man 12 who does this,
Awaker and answerer from the tents of Jacob,
And him who brings an offering to the LORD of hosts.
And this again you do: 13
You cover the altar of the LORD with tears, with weeping and groaning,
Because there is no longer any looking toward the offering,
Or any receiving of favor at your hand.

And you say, "For what reason?" 14
Because the LORD is a witness between you
And the wife of your youth,
Whom you have played false,
Though she is your comrade and the wife of your youth.

But not one has done this 15
Who had a remnant of spirituality.
And what was that one seeking?
Godly offspring?
So take heed to your spiritual life,
And let none be faithless to the wife of his youth.

"For one who hates and divorces," 16
Says the LORD God of Israel,
"Covers his clothing with violence,"
Says the LORD of hosts.
"So take heed of your spiritual life, and do not be faithless."

THE NEAR APPROACH OF THE DAY OF JUDGMENT, 2:17—3:5

You have wearied the LORD with 17 your statements.

Yet you say, "How have we wearied him?"
In that you say, "Everyone who does evil
Is good in the eyes of the LORD,
And he takes pleasure in them";
Or "Where is the God of justice?"

3 "Behold, I will send forth my messenger,
And he shall prepare the way before me!
And suddenly to his temple shall come
The Lord whom you are seeking!
And the messenger of the covenant in whom you delight—
Behold, he comes," says the LORD of hosts.

2 "Who can endure the day of his coming?
And who can stand when he appears?
For he shall be like a refiner's fire,
And like fullers' soap.
3 And he shall sit down as a refiner and cleanser of silver,
And shall cleanse the sons of Levi.

"He shall purify them like gold and silver,
So that they shall become for the LORD men who bring him offerings in righteousness.
4 Then the offering of Judah and Jerusalem shall be pleasing to the LORD,
As in days of old and as in former years.

5 "Then I will draw near to you for judgment,
And I will be a swift witness
Against the sorcerers and adulterers,
And against those who swear to falsehood;
And against those who oppress the hireling in his wages,
The widow and the orphan;
And those who defraud the resident alien,
And do not fear me," says the LORD of hosts.

THE PAYMENT OF TITHES WINS THE FAVOR OF GOD, 3:6–12

6 "Though I, the LORD, change not,
You, O sons of Jacob, are not destroyed.
7 From the days of your fathers you have revolted
From my statutes, and have not kept them.
Return unto me, that I may return to you,"
Says the LORD of hosts.

"But you say, 'How shall we return?'
8 Should man rob God?
Yet you are robbing me!
But you say, 'How have we robbed thee?'
In the tithe and the contribution!
9 With a curse are you accursed;
For you are robbing me; this whole nation!

10 Bring the whole tithe into the storehouse,
That there may be food in my house,
And test me now in this way," says the LORD of hosts,
"And see if I will not open for you the windows of the heavens,
And pour out for you a blessing until there is no more need.

11 "Then I will rebuke the devourer for you,
So that he shall not destroy for you the products of the soil.
Nor shall the vine in the field cast its grapes for you,"
Says the LORD of hosts.
12 "And all the nations shall call you blessed,
For you shall be a land of delight,"
Says the LORD of hosts.

THE FINAL TRIUMPH OF THE RIGHTEOUS, 3:13—4:6

13 "Your words have been stout against me," says the LORD.
"But you say, 'How have we spoken against thee?'
14 You say, 'It is useless to serve God;
And what profit is it that we have kept his charge,
And have walked in mourning before the LORD of hosts?
15 So now we are deeming the arrogant fortunate;
The doers of wickedness, indeed, are built up;
In fact, they test God, and escape!'"

16 Thus did those who reverence the LORD talk

To one another,
So that the LORD gave heed and listened,
And a book of remembrance was written before him,
Concerning those who revere the LORD and think upon his name.
17 "So they shall be mine," says the LORD of hosts,
"On the day that I am about to make—my very own;
And I will spare them even as a man spares his son who serves him.
18 Then shall you again distinguish between the righteous and the wicked,
Between him who serves God, and him who serves him not.

4 "For behold, the day shall come burning like an oven,
And all the arrogant and every doer of wickedness shall be stubble,
And the day that comes shall burn them up," says the LORD of hosts,
"So that it will leave them neither root nor branch.
But for you who revere my name, there will arise 2
The sun of righteousness, with healing in its wings.
And you shall go forth skipping like calves from the stall,
And you shall trample upon the wicked; 3
For they shall be dust under the soles of your feet,
On the day that I am about to make," says the LORD of hosts.

"Remember the law of Moses, my servant, 4
Which I commanded him in Horeb for all Israel—
Statutes and ordinances.
Behold, I will send you Elijah the prophet, 5
Before the coming of the great and terrible day of the LORD;
And he shall turn the hearts of fathers toward their sons, 6
And the hearts of sons toward their fathers,
Lest I come and smite the land with a curse."

THE APOCRYPHA

AN AMERICAN TRANSLATION

by

EDGAR J. GOODSPEED

PREFACE

THE Apocrypha formed an integral part of the King James Version of 1611, as they had of all the preceding English versions from their beginning in 1382. But they are seldom printed as part of it any longer, still more seldom as part of the English Revised Version, and were not included in the American Revision. This is partly because the Puritans disapproved of them; they had already begun to rop them from printings of their Geneva Bible by 1600, and began to demand copies f the King James Version omitting them, as early as 1629. And it is partly because we ıoderns discredit them because they did not form part of the Hebrew Bible and most of hem have never been found in any Hebrew forms at all.

But they were part of the Bible of the early church, for it used the Greek version of he Jewish Bible, which we call the Septuagint, and these books were all in that version. 'hey passed from it into Latin and the great Latin Bible edited by St. Jerome about .D. 400, the Vulgate, which became the Authorized Bible of western Europe and Engınd and remained so for a thousand years. But Jerome found that they were not in he Hebrew Bible, and so he called them the Apocrypha, the hidden or secret books.

It must not be supposed, however, that Jerome gathered them into a group and put hem at the end of his Old Testament version. On the contrary, they are scattered here nd there through the Vulgate, much as they are through the Greek Bible. They are also cattered through the versions made from the Vulgate—the Wyclif-Purvey English ranslations and the old German Bible, both products of the fourteenth century. It reıained for Luther to take the hint Jerome had dropped eleven hundred years before, nd to separate them in his German Bible of 1534 from the rest of the Old Testament, nd put them after it. This course was followed the next year by Coverdale, in the first rinted English Bible, of 1535; and the English Authorized Bibles, the Great Bible, the ishops' and the King James, all followed the same course. The Catholic English Old 'estament of 1610, however, followed the Vulgate arrangement and left them scattered mong the books which we include in our Old Testament. It still contains them, but on he Protestant side both British and American Bible societies more than a hundred years go (1827) took a definite stand against their publication, and they have since almost isappeared.

Great values reside in the Apocrypha: the Prayer of Manasseh is a notable piece of turgy; I Maccabees is of great historical value for its story of Judaism in the second entury before Christ, the heroic days of Judas Maccabeus and his brothers, when harisaism had its rise. The additions to Esther impart a religious color to that roıantic story; Judith, Susanna, and Tobit, while fascinating pieces of fiction, were meant y their writers to teach important lessons to their contemporaries. Wisdom and Ec'esiasticus are among the masterpieces of the Jewish sages.

But to us this appendix of the Old Testament is important as forming a very necesıry link between the Old Testament and the New; and if we had no Old Testament at ll, the Apocrypha would still be indispensable to the student of the New Testament, of 'hich it forms the prelude and background. This is why I have prepared an American ranslation of the Apocrypha, to complete our American translation of the Bible, and

to make its various books more intelligibly accessible to college and university student
and to the general reader. The strong contrast they present in sheer moral values to th
New Testament is most instructive. And they form an indispensable part of the histori
Christian Bible, as it was known in the ancient Greek and Latin churches, in the Ref
ormation and the Renaissance, and in all Authorized English Bibles, Catholic an
Protestant.

The excellent critical Greek text of the Septuagint recently published at Stuttgart b
Alfred Rahlfs has in general been followed in this translation, supplemented, of course
by other studies on the Apocrypha, especially the volumes edited by R. H. Charles a
Oxford in 1913. For II Esdras, for which only a Latin text buttressed by oriental version
survives, I have made use of the critical labors of Bensly, James, Box, and Violet. Th
Revised Version and the translations of individual books by some of the contributors t
Charles's volumes (*Apocrypha and Pseudepigrapha*) and others have greatly helpe
the translator. In the vexed matter of the numbering of the verses the King James Bibl
of 1611 has been followed. The bracketed verse-numbers in II Esdras 7:[36–105] mar
the missing portion discovered by Bensly at Amiens and published in 1875. My brothe
Charles T. B. Goodspeed, has very kindly read the translation through in proof.

On the whole, the translation of the Apocrypha has been surprisingly neglected. Th
translators of the Septuagint, Thomson in 1808 and Brenton in 1844, studiously omitte
the apocryphal books they encountered in it, and not all of Charles's associates in hi
impressive volumes made new translations. Single books have here and there been trans
lated from the Greek by individual scholars, but, while Bissell ably revised the Kin
James Apocrypha in 1880, I cannot find that the Apocrypha as a whole have been trans
lated into English since Coverdale in 1535 and Gregory Martin in 1582 translated the
from the Latin Vulgate (Martin's version remained unpublished until 1610); or tha
the Greek Apocrypha as a whole, that is, all the books except II Esdras, have ever befor
been directly translated from Greek into English.

Coverdale's translation of the Apocrypha in his Bible of 1535 was made from th
Latin Vulgate, with the aid of Pagninus' Latin and of recent German translations, es
pecially Luther's. Coverdale's Bible became the basis of successive revisions—Matthew
the Great Bible, the Bishops', and the King James. The Geneva revisers of 1560, how
ever, knew Greek, and contributed retranslations from the Greek of two of the book
along with revisions of the others. Revision of the translation in the light of the Gree
continued to some degree in the Bishops' and the King James Bibles; in the Englis
Revised Version of 1895 six more books appear virtually retranslated from the Greek
and the rest revised. But even in it, five books remain revisions, however faithful, c
Coverdale's translation of the Vulgate, so that our standard versions of the Apocryph
(and aside from Bissell's revision there are no others), though three or four times revised
still to a substantial degree rest ultimately upon the Latin Vulgate.

In contrast with them, the translation here presented is, except for the Latin II Esdras
based directly upon the Greek text.

EDGAR J. GOODSPEED

THE FIRST BOOK OF ESDRAS

1 WHEN Josiah celebrated the
Passover festival in Jerusalem to his Lord, he sacrificed the Passover on the
2 fourteenth day of the first month, placing the priests in their divisions, clad in
their vestments, in the temple of the
3 Lord. And he ordered the Levites, the
temple slaves of Israel, to consecrate
themselves to the Lord, when they put
the holy chest of the Lord in the house
of the Lord, which Solomon the king,
4 the son of David, had built; and he said,
"You will not have to carry it on
your shoulders any more; so now worship the Lord your God, and serve his
people, Israel, and prepare yourselves
5 by your families and kindreds, as
David, king of Israel, wrote, and with
all the magnificence of Solomon his
son; and take your places in the temple,
according to your ancestral groups as
Levites before your brothers, the Isra-
6 elites, in proper order, and sacrifice the
Passover, and get the sacrifices ready
for your brothers, and observe the
Passover, in accordance with the Lord's
command which was given to Moses."
7 And Josiah gave the people that
were present thirty thousand lambs and
kids, and three thousand calves; these
were given out of the king's revenues,
as he promised, to the people and the
8 priests and Levites. And Hilkiah and
Zechariah and Jehiel, the rulers of the
temple, gave the priests for the Passover two thousand, six hundred sheep
9 and three hundred calves. And Jeconiah and Shemaiah and Nathanael,
his brother, and Asabiah and Ochiel
and Joram, colonels of regiments, gave
the Levites for the Passover five thousand sheep and seven hundred calves.
10 And it was done; the priests and
Levites, with the unleavened bread,
11 stood in proper order, according to their
kindreds and their family divisions,
before the people, to make the offering
to the Lord, as it is prescribed in the
book of Moses; this they did in the
12 morning. They roasted the Passover
with fire in the proper way, and boiled
the sacrifices in caldrons and basins,
with savory odors, and set them before 13
all the people. Afterward they prepared some for themselves and their
brothers the priests, the sons of Aaron;
for the priests were offering the fat until 14
late, so the Levites prepared meat for
themselves and for their brothers the
priests, the sons of Aaron. The sacred 15
musicians, too, the sons of Asaph,
were in their places, according to the
regulations of David, with Asaph and
Zechariah and Eddinus, who were of
the king's circle, and the doorkeepers 16
stood at each door. No one needed to
interrupt his duties for the day, for
their brothers, the Levites, prepared
meat for them. So the things that had 17
to do with the Lord's sacrifices were
carried out that day, in celebrating the
Passover and offering the sacrifices on 18
the altar of the Lord, as King Josiah
commanded. So the Israelites who were 19
present at that time observed the Passover and the festival of Unleavened
Bread for seven days. No such Pass- 20
over had been celebrated in Israel since
the times of the prophet Samuel, and
none of the kings of Israel had cele- 21
brated such a Passover as Josiah and
the priests and the Levites and the
Jews celebrated with all the Israelites
that were present in their dwellings in
Jerusalem. It was in the eighteenth 22
year of the reign of Josiah that this
Passover was observed. And the do- 23
ings of Josiah were upright in the
Lord's sight, for his heart was full of
piety. And the events of his times have 24
been recorded in the past about those
who sinned and acted wickedly toward
the Lord, beyond any other nation or
kingdom, and how they grieved him
keenly, so that the words of the Lord
rose up to condemn Israel.
After all these doings of Josiah, it hap- 25
pened that Pharaoh, king of Egypt,
came to make war at Carchemish on
the Euphrates, and Josiah went out to
encounter him. And the king of Egypt 26
sent word to him, saying,
"What do you want of me, King of 27

Judah? I was not sent against you by
the Lord God, for my war is on the Euphrates. And now the Lord is with me!
The Lord is with me, urging me on; depart and do not oppose the Lord."
28 But Josiah would not turn back to
his chariot, but tried to fight with him,
disregarding the words of Jeremiah the
prophet, spoken by the mouth of the
29 Lord, and joined battle with him in the
plain of Megiddo, and the leaders
30 fought against King Josiah. And the
king said to his servants,
"Take me away from the battle, for
I am very sick."
And his servants immediately took
31 him out of the fray. And he got into
his second chariot, and was taken back
to Jerusalem, and departed this life,
and was buried in the tomb of his fore-
32 fathers. And they grieved for Josiah
all over Judah, and Jeremiah the
prophet lamented for Josiah, and the
principal men, with the women, have
mourned him to this day; and it was ordained that this should always be done,
throughout all the nation of Israel.
33 This is recorded in the scroll of the histories of the kings of Judah; and every
one of the deeds of Josiah, and his
splendor, and his understanding of the
Law of the Lord, and what he had done
before, and these present deeds, are
told in the scroll of the kings of Israel
and Judah.
34 And the men of the nation took
Jeconiah, the son of Josiah, and made
him king, to succeed Josiah his father,
when he was twenty-three years old.
35 And he reigned three months in Judah
and Jerusalem. Then the king of Egypt
deposed him from reigning in Jerusa-
36 lem, and he assessed the nation a
hundred talents of silver and one talent
37 of gold. And the king of Egypt appointed Jehoiakim, his brother, king of
38 Judah and Jerusalem. And Jehoiakim
put the nobles in prison and seized his
brother Zarius and brought him back
from Egypt.
39 Jehoiakim was twenty-five years old
when he became king of Judah and
Jerusalem, and he did what was wrong
40 in the sight of the Lord. And Nebuchadnezzar, the king of Babylon, came
against him, and put him in chains of
41 brass and took him to Babylon. (And
Nebuchadnezzar took some of the
sacred dishes of the Lord and carried
them off and set them up in his temple
in Babylon. But the stories about him 42
and his uncleanness and his impious
behavior are written in the chronicles of
the kings.)
And Jehoiachin, his son, became king 43
in his stead; for when he was made
king, he was eighteen years old, and he 44
reigned three months and ten days in
Jerusalem, and did what was wrong in
the sight of the Lord. And a year later, 45
Nebuchadnezzar sent and removed him
to Babylon, with the sacred dishes of
the Lord, and appointed Zedekiah king 46
of Judah and Jerusalem, when Zedekiah was twenty-one years old. And he
reigned eleven years. And he did what 47
was wrong in the sight of the Lord, and
disregarded the words that were spoken
by Jeremiah the prophet, from the
mouth of the Lord. And although King 48
Nebuchadnezzar had made him swear
by the name of the lord, he broke his
oath and rebelled, and he hardened his
neck and his heart and transgressed
the laws of the Lord, the God of Israel.
And the leaders of the people and of the 49
priests did many impious acts and surpassed in lawlessness all the unclean
acts of all the heathen, and polluted
the temple of the Lord that had been
consecrated in Jerusalem. And the God 50
of their forefathers sent by his messenger to call them back, for he would
have spared them and his dwelling;
but they mocked his messengers, and 51
whenever the Lord spoke to them, they
made sport of his prophets, until he 52
grew angry with his people because of
their ungodliness and ordered the kings
of the Chaldeans to be brought against
them. These killed their young men 53
with the sword around their holy
temple, and did not spare youth or
maiden, old man or child, for he delivered them all into their hands. And 54
all the sacred dishes of the Lord, great
and small, and the chests of the Lord,
and the royal treasures they took, and
carried them off to Babylon. And they 55
burned the house of the Lord, and tore
down the walls of Jerusalem, and
burned down their towers, and com- 56
pletely ruined all her glories. And those
who survived the sword he removed to
Babylon. And they were his servants 57
and those of his children, until the
Persians began to reign; to fulfil what
the Lord said by the mouth of Jeremiah,

58 "Until the land enjoys its sabbaths,
all the time of her desolation she shall
keep the sabbath, until the lapse of
seventy years."
2 In the first year that Cyrus reigned
over Persia, to fulfil what the Lord said
2 by the mouth of Jeremiah, the Lord
stirred the heart of Cyrus, king of
Persia, and he made a proclamation
throughout all his kingdom, and put it
3 in writing, saying,
"Thus speaks Cyrus, king of Persia:
The Lord of Israel, the Lord Most
High, has made me king of the world,
4 and directed me to build him a house
5 in Jerusalem, in Judah. So if any one of
you is of his people, his Lord be with
him, and let him go up to Jerusalem, in
Judah, and build the house of the Lord
of Israel; he is the Lord who lives in
6 Jerusalem. So let a man's neighbors,
who live in each place, help him with
7 gold and silver, with presents, with
horses and cattle, beside the other
things added as vows for the temple of
the Lord in Jerusalem."
8 Then the heads of families of the
tribe of Judah and the tribe of Benjamin arose, and the priests and the
Levites, and all whose hearts the Lord
had stirred to go up to build the house
9 in Jerusalem for the Lord. And their
neighbors helped them with everything,
with silver and gold, with horses and
cattle, and a great many vows from
many whose hearts were stirred.
10 And King Cyrus brought out the
sacred dishes of the Lord, which Nebuchadnezzar had carried off from Jerusalem, and deposited in the temple of
11 his idols; but Cyrus, king of Persia,
brought them out, and delivered them
12 to his treasurer Mithridates, and they
were turned over by him to Shesh-
13 bazzar, the governor of Judah. And
this was the number of them: a thousand gold cups, a thousand silver cups,
twenty-nine silver censers, thirty gold
bowls, two thousand, four hundred
and ten silver bowls, and a thousand
14 other dishes. So all the dishes, gold and
silver, five thousand, four hundred and
15 sixty-nine, were taken and carried back
by Sheshbazzar, along with those who
had been in captivity, from Babylon to
Jerusalem.
16 But in the times of Artaxerxes, king
of Persia, Bishlam, Mithridates, Tabeel, Rehum, the recorder, and Shimshai, the scribe, and the others associated with them, living in Samaria
and other places, wrote him the following letter, against those who lived in
Judah and Jerusalem:
"To King Artaxerxes our Lord, your 17
servants Rehum, the recorder, and
Shimshai, the scribe, and the other
judges of their court in Coelesyria and
Phoenicia; now be it known to our lord 18
the king, that the Jews who have come
up to us from you have reached Jerusalem and are rebuilding that rebellious
and wicked city and repairing its
bazaars and walls and laying the
foundations of a temple. Now if this 19
city is rebuilt and its walls completed,
they will not submit to paying tribute,
but will even resist the kings. And 20
since the matter of the temple is now
under way, we think it right not to
neglect such a matter, but to address 21
our lord the king, so that, if you approve, a search may be made in the
records of your forefathers; for you will 22
find in their chronicles what is written
about them, and you will learn that
this city was rebellious, troublesome to
kings and towns, and that the Jews 23
were rebels and organizers of warfare
in it from ancient times; that was why
the city was laid waste. We now there- 24
fore inform you, lord king, that if this
city is rebuilt, and its walls restored,
you will no longer have a way of access
to Coelesyria and Phoenicia."
Then the king wrote in reply to 25
Rehum, the recorder, and Shimshai, the
scribe, and their associates, who lived
in Samaria, Syria, and Phoenicia, as
follows:
"I have read the letter which you 26
sent me. I accordingly ordered search
to be made, and it was found that this
city from ancient times used to rebel
against the kings, and the people cre- 27
ated revolts and wars in it, and that
stern and powerful kings ruled in
Jerusalem, and took tribute from
Coelesyria and Phoenicia. Therefore I 28
have now given orders to prevent these
men from rebuilding the city, and to
take measures that nothing further be
done and that these wicked undertak- 29
ings go no farther, to the annoyance of
the kings."
When the message of King Arta- 30
xerxes was read, Rehum and Shimshai, the scribe, and their associates

proceeded in haste to Jerusalem, with
horsemen and a crowd of troops and
began to hinder the builders. So the
rebuilding of the temple in Jerusalem
was suspended until the second year of
the reign of Darius, king of Persia.
3 Now King Darius made a great
banquet for all his subjects, and all his
domestics, and all the nobles of Media
2 and Persia, and all the viceroys and
provincial and district governors under
his sway, in the hundred and twenty-
seven provinces from India to Ethiopia.
3 And they ate and drank, and when they
were satisfied, they went home, but
Darius the king went to his bedroom,
4 and fell asleep, and then awoke. Then
the three young men of his bodyguard,
who kept guard over the person of the
king, said to one another,
5 "Let us each say what one thing is
strongest, and Darius the king will give
rich presents and great honors to the
6 one whose words seem the wisest, and
have him dressed in purple, and drink
from gold plate, and sleep on a gold
bed, and give him a chariot with gold
bridles, and a linen headdress, and a
7 necklace around his neck, and because
of his wisdom he shall sit next to
Darius, and be called Darius' kinsman."
8 Then they each wrote his own answer and put his seal on it, and put
them under the pillow of King Darius,
9 and said,
"When the king wakes up, they will
give him the writing, and the one whose
choice the king and the three princes
of Persia judge the wisest, shall be considered the victor in what he has written."
10 The first wrote,
"Wine is strongest."
11 The second wrote,
"The king is strongest."
12 The third wrote,
"Women are strongest, but truth
prevails over everything."
13 So when the king awoke, they took
the writing and gave it to him and he
14 read it. Then he sent and summoned
all the nobles of Persia and Media, and
the governors and officers and magis-
15 trates and officials, and he took his
seat in the council chamber, and what
was written was read before them.
16 And he said,
"Summon the young men, and let
them show their reasons."
And they were summoned, and came 17
in. And they said to them,
"Explain to us about what you have
written."
So the first one, who had told of the 18
strength of wine, began and said,
"Gentlemen, how supremely strong
wine is! It leads the minds of all who
drink it astray. It makes the mind of 19
the king and the mind of the fatherless
child alike; the mind of the menial and
the freeman, of the poor and the rich.
It turns every thought to mirth and 20
merrymaking, and forgets all grief and
debt. It makes all hearts rich, and for- 21
gets kings and governors, and makes
everybody talk in thousands. And 22
when they drink, they forget to be
friendly to friends and brothers, and
very soon they draw their swords. And 23
when they recover from their wine,
they cannot remember what they have
done. Gentlemen, is not wine supreme- 24
ly strong, since it forces them to act
so?"
When he had said this, he stopped.
Then the second, who had told of the 4
king's might, began to speak:
"Gentlemen, are not men strongest, 2
because they control land and sea, and
all that is in them? But the king is su- 3
premely strong, and is lord and master
of them, and every command he gives
them they obey. If he orders them to 4
make war on one another, they do so;
and if he sends them out against the
enemy, they go, and surmount mountains, walls, and towers. They kill and 5
are killed, but they do not disobey the
king's command. And if they are victorious, they bring everything to the
king, the spoils they take and all the
rest. And those who do not go to war or 6
fight, but till the soil, again, when they
sow and reap, bring it to the king, and
they compel one another to pay taxes
to the king. He is only one man; but 7
if he orders them to kill, they kill; if he
orders them to release, they release;
if he orders them to strike down, they 8
strike; if he orders them to lay waste,
they lay waste; if he orders them to
build, they build; if he orders them to 9
cut down, they cut down; if he orders
them to plant, they plant. So all his 10
people and his troops obey him. Besides, he reclines at table, he eats and

11 drinks and sleeps, and they keep watch
about him, and they cannot any of
them go away and look after his own
12 affairs, or disobey him at all. Gentlemen, how can the king not be strongest,
when he is so obeyed?"

And he stopped.

13 Then the third, who had spoken of
women and of truth—his name was
Zerubbabel—began to speak:

14 "Gentlemen, is not the king great,
and are not men many, and is not wine
strong? Who is it then that rules over
them and masters them? Is it not
15 women? Women have borne the king
and all the people, who are lords of
16 sea and land; from them they are
sprung, and they brought them up, to
plant the vineyards, from which the
17 wine comes. They make men's clothes,
they make men's splendor, and men
18 cannot exist without women. Why, if
men amass gold and silver, and everything of beauty, and then see one
woman remarkable for looks and
19 beauty, they let all these things go,
and gape at her, and stare at her with
open mouths, and would all rather have
her than gold or silver or any thing of
20 beauty. A man will leave his own
father, who brought him up, and his
own country, and be united to his wife.
21 With his wife he ends his days, and
remembers neither his father nor his
22 mother nor his country. Hence you
must recognize that women rule over
men. Do you not toil and labor, and
bring it all and give it to your wives?
23 A man takes his sword and goes out on
expeditions to rob and steal, and to sail
24 the sea and the rivers; he faces the lion
and walks in the darkness, and when he
steals and robs and plunders, he brings
25 it back to the woman he loves. So a man
loves his wife better than his father or
26 mother. Many have lost their heads
completely for the sake of women, and
27 become slaves for their sakes. Many
have perished, or failed, or sinned for
28 the sake of women. Now do you not
believe me? Is not the king great in
his power? Do not all lands fear even
29 to touch him? Yet I have seen him
with Apame, the king's concubine, the
daughter of the noble Bartacus, sitting
30 at the king's right hand, and taking the
crown from the king's head, and putting
it on her own, and she slapped the king
31 with her left hand. At this the king
stared at her open-mouthed. If she
smiled at him, he laughed; if she grew
angry at him, he flattered her, so that
she might be reconciled to him again.
Gentlemen, how can women not be 32
mighty, when they act like that?"

Then the king and the nobles looked 33
at one another; and he began to speak
about truth:

"Gentlemen, are not women mighty? 34
The earth is vast, and heaven is high,
and the sun is swift in his course, for he
circles about the heavens and hastens
back to his own starting-point in a
single day. Is he not great who does 35
these things? So truth is great, and
mightier than all other things. The 36
whole earth calls upon truth, and
heaven blesses her; all his works quake
and tremble, there is no wrongdoing
with him. Wine is not upright, the king 37
is not upright, women are not upright,
all the sons of men are not upright,
and all their doings, all such things, are
not upright; there is no truth in them,
and through their unrighteousness they
will perish. But truth endures and is 38
strong forever, and lives and reigns forever and ever. There is no partiality or 39
preference with her, but she does what
is right, rather than all that is wrong
and wicked. All men approve her doings, and there is no injustice in her 40
judgment. To her belongs power and
the royal dignity and authority and
majesty in all the ages; blessed be the
God of truth!"

When he stopped speaking, all the 41
people shouted and said,

"Truth is great and supremely
strong."

Then the king said to him, 42

"Ask whatever you please, beyond
what is written here, and we will give it
to you, since you have been found the
wisest. You shall sit next to me, and
be called my kinsman."

Then he said to the king, 43

"Remember the vow that you made,
the day you succeeded to your throne,
to rebuild Jerusalem and send back all 44
the dishes taken from Jerusalem, which
Cyrus set aside, when he vowed to
destroy Babylon, and to send them
back there. And you vowed to rebuild 45
the house, which the Edomites burned,
when Jerusalem had been laid waste by
the Chaldeans. So now, my lord the 46
king, that is what I ask and request of

you, and this is the princely liberality
to come from you: I beg you to carry
out the vow that you vowed with your
own lips to the King of Heaven that
you would carry out."
47 Then Darius, the king, got up and
kissed him, and he wrote letters for
him to all his managers and magistrates and officers and governors, to
escort him in safety with all who were
going up with him to rebuild Jerusalem.
48 And he wrote letters to all the magistrates in Coelesyria and Phoenicia and
to those in the Lebanon, to bring
cedar timbers from the Lebanon to
Jerusalem and that they should help
49 him to rebuild the city. And he wrote
in the interest of all the Jews who were
going up from his kingdom to Judah,
to secure their freedom, that no noble
or governor or magistrate or manager
50 should forcibly enter their doors, and
that all the country which they were to
occupy they should possess free from
tribute; and that the Edomites should
give up the Jewish villages which they
51 controlled, and that twenty talents a
year should be given for the rebuilding
of the temple, until it was completed,
52 and ten talents a year besides, to provide burnt offerings to be offered daily
upon the altar, in accordance with the
command they had to offer seventeen,
53 and that all who came up from Babylonia to rebuild the city should have
their freedom, they and their children
54 and all the priests who came up. He
wrote providing their expenses also,
and the priestly vestments in which
55 they officiate. And he wrote that the
Levites' expenses should be provided
until the day when the house should be
56 finished and Jerusalem rebuilt. And
he wrote that lots of land and wages
should be given to all who guarded the
57 city. And he sent back all the dishes
from Babylon, which Cyrus had set
aside; and all that Cyrus had ordered
done he commanded them to do and to
send back to Jerusalem.
58 When the young man went out, he
lifted his face to heaven toward Jerusalem, and praised the King of Heaven,
59 saying,
"From you comes victory, from you
comes wisdom; to you belongs glory,
60 and I am your servant. Blessed are
you, who have given me wisdom; I
praise you, Lord of my forefathers."

And he took the letters and went to 6
Babylon, and reported it to all his
brothers. And they blessed the God of 6
their forefathers, because he had given
them relief and liberty to go up and re- 6
build Jerusalem and the temple which
was called by his name; and they
banqueted with music and gladness for
seven days.
After this the heads of families were 5
chosen to go up, according to their
clans, with their wives and sons and
daughters, and their male and female
slaves, and their cattle. And Darius
sent with them a thousand horsemen,
to escort them back to Jerusalem in
peace, with music of drums and flutes
(for all their brothers made merry);
he made them go up with them.
These are the names of the men who
went up, by their families within their
tribes, for their priestly office: of the
priests, the sons of Phineas, the son of
Aaron; Jeshua, the son of Jozadak, the
son of Seraiah, and Joakim, the son of
Zerubbabel, the son of Salathiel, of the
house of David, of the line of Phares,
of the tribe of Judah, who uttered wise
sayings before Darius, the king of
Persia, in the second year of his reign,
in the month of Nisan, the first month.
These are those from Judah who
went up after their sojourn in captivity,
whom Nebuchadnezzar, king of Babylon, had removed to Babylon, and who
returned to Jerusalem and the rest of
Judah, each one to his own town, going
with Zerubbabel and Jeshua, Nehemiah, Seraiah, Resaiah, Bigvai, Mordecai, Bilshan, Mispar, Reeliah, Rehum,
and Baanah, their leaders; the numbers
of those of the nation, and their leaders: the descendants of Parosh, two
thousand, one hundred and seventy-
two; of the descendants of Shephatiah,
four hundred and seventy-two; the 1
descendants of Arah, seven hundred
and fifty-six; the descendants of 1
Pahath-moab, of the descendants of
Jeshua and Joab, two thousand, eight
hundred and twelve; the descendants of 1
Elam, one thousand, two hundred and
fifty-four; the descendants of Zattu,
nine hundred and forty-five; the descendants of Chorbe, seven hundred and
five; the descendants of Binnui, six
hundred and forty-eight; the descend- 1
ants of Bebai, six hundred and twenty-
three; the descendants of Azgad, one

thousand, three hundred and twenty-
14 two; the descendants of Adonikam, six
hundred and sixty-seven; the descendants of Bigvai, two thousand and sixty-
six; the descendants of Adin, four
15 hundred and fifty-four; the descendants of Ater, the son of Hezekiah,
ninety-two; the descendants of Kilan
and Azetas, sixty-seven; the descendants of Azuru, four hundred and
16 thirty-two; the descendants of Annias,
one hundred and one; the descendants
of Arom: the descendants of Bezai,
three hundred and twenty-three; the
descendants of Jorah, one hundred and
17 twelve; the descendants of Baiterus,
three thousand and five; the descendants of Bethlehem, one hundred and
18 twenty-three; the men of Netophah,
fifty-five; the men of Anathoth, one
hundred and fifty-eight; the men of
19 Bethasmoth, forty-two; the men of
Kirjath-jearim, twenty-five; the men of
Chephirah and Beeroth, seven hundred
20 and forty-three; the Chadiasans and
Ammidians, four hundred and twenty-
two; the men of Ramah and Geba,
21 six hundred and twenty-one; the men
of Michmash, one hundred and twenty-
two; the men of Bethel-Ai, fifty-two;
the descendants of Magbish, one hun-
22 dred and fifty-six; the descendants of
the other Elam and Ono, seven hundred and twenty-five; the descendants
of Jericho, three hundred and forty-
23 five; the descendants of Senaah, three
thousand, three hundred and thirty.
24 Of the priests: the descendants of
Jedaiah, of the house of Jeshua, among
the descendants of Anasib, nine hundred and seventy-two; the descendants of Immer, one thousand and fifty-
25 two; the descendants of Pashhur, one
thousand, two hundred and forty-
seven; the descendants of Harim, one
thousand and seventeen.
26 Of the Levites: the descendants of
Jeshua and Kadmiel and Bannas and
27 Sudias, seventy-four; of the sacred
singers: the descendants of Asaph, one
hundred and twenty-eight; of the door-
28 keepers: the descendants of Shallum,
the descendants of Ater, the descendants of Tolman, the descendants of
Akkub, the descendants of Hatita, the
descendants of Shobai—in all, one hundred and thirty-nine.
29 Of the temple slaves: the descendants of Ziha, the descendants of Hasupha, the descendants of Tabbaoth, the
descendants of Keros, the descendants
of Siaha, the descendants of Padon, the
descendants of Lebanah, the descendants of Hagabah, the descendants of 30
Akkub, the descendants of Uthai, the
descendants of Ketab, the descendants
of Hagab, the descendants of Shamlai,
the descendants of Hanan, the descendants of Cathua, the descendants of
Gahar, the descendants of Reaiah, the
descendants of Rezin, the descendants 31
of Nekoda, the descendants of Chezib,
the descendants of Gazzan, the descendants of Uzza, the descendants of
Paseah, the descendants of Hasrah,
the descendants of Besai, the descendants of Asnah, the descendants of the
Meunites, the descendants of Nephisim, the descendants of Bakbuk, the
descendants of Hakupha, the descendants of Asur, the descendants of
Pharakim, the descendants of Bazluth,
the descendants of Mehida, the de- 32
scendants of Cutha, the descendants
of Charea, the descendants of Barkos,
the descendants of Sisera, the descendants of Temah, the descendants of
Neziah, the descendants of Hatipha.
Of the descendants of Solomon's 33
servants: the descendants of Hassophereth, the descendants of Peruda,
the descendants of Jaalah, the descendants of Lozon, the descendants of
Giddel, the descendants of Shephatiah,
the descendants of Hattil, the descend- 34
ants of Pochereth-hazzabaim, the descendants of Sarothie, the descendants
of Masiah, the descendants of Gas, the
descendants of Addus, the descendants
of Subas, the descendants of Apherra,
the descendants of Barodis, the descendants of Shaphat, the descendants
of Ami. In all, the temple slaves and 35
the descendants of the servants of
Solomon were three hundred and
seventy-two.
These are those who went up from 36
Telmelah and Telharsha, under the
leadership of Cherub, Adan, and Immer, but were not able to show by their 37
families or lineage that they belonged
to Israel: the descendants of Delaiah
the descendant of Tobiah, the descendants of Nekoda, six hundred and
fifty-two. And of those of the priests 38
who had assumed the priesthood but
were not found registered: the descendants of Habaiah, the descendants

of Hakkoz, the descendants of Jaddus
who married Agia, one of the daughters
of Barzillai, and was called by his name.
39 And when the ancestry of these men
was looked for in the register, and could
not be found, they were excluded from
40 officiating as priests. And Nehemiah
and the governor told them not to
share in the consecrated things until a
high priest should appear clothed in
the Manifestation and the Truth.
41 In ail, there were: of Israel, over
twelve years of age, besides male and female slaves, forty-two thousand, three
42 hundred and sixty; of their male and female slaves, seven thousand, three hundred and thirty-seven; of musicians and
singers, two hundred and forty-five.
43 There were four hundred and thirty-
five camels, and seven thousand and
thirty-six horses, two hundred and
forty-five mules, and five thousand, five
hundred and twenty-five asses.
44 And some of the principal heads of
families, when they reached the temple
of God in Jerusalem, vowed that they
would erect the house in its old place,
45 to the best of their ability, and that
they would give to the sacred building
fund a thousand minas in gold and five
thousand minas in silver, and a hundred
priest's garments.
46 So the priests and the Levites and
some of the people settled in Jerusalem
and the country, and the sacred singers
and the doorkeepers and all Israel
settled in their villages.
47 When the seventh month came, and
the Israelites were all at home, they
gathered as one man in the square in
front of the first gate toward the east.
48 And Jeshua, the son of Jozadak, and
his brothers the priests, and Zerubbabel, the son of Salathiel, and his
brothers took their places and prepared the altar of the God of Israel,
49 in order to offer on it burnt offerings, as
is directed in the book of Moses, the
50 man of God. And they were joined by
some of the other peoples of the land,
and they erected the altar in its place;
for though they had been hostile to
them, all the people in the land supported them, and brought sacrifices at
the proper times, and the morning and
evening burnt offerings for the Lord,
51 and they kept the Camping Out festival, as it is prescribed in the Law, and
they brought sacrifices every day,
when it was proper, and besides these 52
the regular offerings and sacrifices on
sabbaths and new moons and all the
sacred festival days. And all who had 53
made voluntary gifts to God began to
offer sacrifices to God, beginning with
the new moon of the seventh month,
though the temple of God was not yet
rebuilt. And they paid money to the 54
masons and carpenters, and gave food 55
and drink and carts to the Sidonians
and Tyrians, to bring cedar timbers
from the Lebanon and convey them in
rafts to the harbor of Joppa, as Cyrus,
the king of Persia, had commanded
them in writing.
In the second year Zerubbabel, the 56
son of Salathiel, came to the temple of
God in Jerusalem, and in the second
month he began with Jeshua, the son of
Jozadak, and their brothers, and the
Levitical priests and all who had come
back from the exile to Jerusalem, and 57
they laid the foundation of the temple
of God on the new moon of the second
month, in the second year, after they
came to Judah and Jerusalem. And 58
they appointed the Levites who were
over twenty years old to have charge of
the work of the Lord. And Jeshua rose up
and his sons and his brothers and Kadmiel his brother and the sons of Jeshua
Emadabun and the sons of Joda, the
son of Iliadun, with their sons and
brothers, all the Levites, as one man
pressing forward the work on the house
of God.
And the builders built the sanctuary 59
of the Lord, and the priests stood in
their robes, with musical instruments
and trumpets, and the Levites, the sons
of Asaph, with their cymbals, praising 60
the Lord and blessing him, according to
the directions of David, king of Israel,
and they sang loudly, giving thanks 61
to the Lord with hymns, because all
Israel enjoys his goodness and his
glory forever. And all the people 62
sounded trumpets and gave a great
shout, praising the Lord for the erection of the house of the Lord. And some 63
of the Levitical priests and the older
men among the heads of their families,
who had seen the house that preceded
this one, came to the building of this
house with outcries and loud lamentation, while many came with trumpets 64
and a great shout of joy, so that the 65
people could not hear the trumpets on

account of the lamentation, for the
multitude sounded the trumpets loudly, so that it was heard a long way off.
66 And when the enemies of the tribe of
Judah and Benjamin heard it, they
came to find out what the sound of the
67 trumpets meant. And they learned
that those who had returned from
captivity were building the sanctuary
68 for the Lord, the God of Israel, and
they went to Zerubbabel and Jeshua
and the heads of families, and said to
them,
69 "We will help you build, for we, like
you, obey your Lord, and have sacrificed to him from the days of Esarhaddon, king of Assyria, who brought us
here."
70 Then Zerubbabel and Jeshua and the
heads of families of Israel said to them,
"It is not for you and us to build the
71 house for the Lord our God, for we will
build it by ourselves for the Lord of
Israel, as Cyrus, the king of Persia, has
commanded us."
72 But the heathen of the land pressed
upon those who were in Judea, and,
blockading them, hindered them from
73 building, and by making plots and
stirring up the people and uprisings
they prevented the completion of the
building all the lifetime of King Cyrus.
So they were kept from building for two
years, until the reign of Darius.
6 But in the second year of the reign
of Darius, the prophets Haggai and
Zechariah, the son of Iddo, prophesied
to the Jews who were in Judea and
Jerusalem, prophesying to them in the
name of the Lord, the God of Israel.
2 Then Zerubbabel, the son of Salathiel,
and Jeshua, the son of Jozadak, got up
and began to build the house of the
Lord that was in Jerusalem, while the
prophets of the Lord joined them and
helped them.
3 At that very time there came to
them Sisinnes, the governor of Syria
and Phoenicia, and Sathrabuzanes and
their companions, and said to them,
4 "By whose orders are you building
this house, and completing this roof
and all these other things? And who
are the builders who are carrying this
out?"
5 Still the elders of the Jews were
shown favor, for the Lord had regard
6 for the captives, and they were not
prevented from building until Darius
was informed about them and orders
were issued.
This is the copy of a letter which 7
Sisinnes, the governor of Syria and
Phoenicia, and Sathrabuzanes and
their companions wrote and sent to
Darius:
"Greetings to King Darius. Let it all 8
be known to our lord the king that
when we went to the country of Judea
and entered the city of Jerusalem, we
found the elders of the Jews, who had
been in captivity, building in the city of 9
Jerusalem a great, new house for the
Lord, of costly hewn stone, with timbers set in the walls, and we found this 10
work proceeding with haste, and the
undertaking prospering in their hands,
and being completed with all glory and
diligence. Then we inquired of these 11
elders and said,
" 'At whose command are you building this house, and laying the foundations of these works?'
"Then in order to inform you and 12
write to you, we inquired of them what
men were the leaders, and asked them
for a list of the names of those who
were taking the lead. And they an- 13
swered and said,
" 'We are servants of the Lord who
created the heaven and the earth. And 14
the house was built many years ago by
a king of Israel who was great and
strong, and was finished. And when 15
our forefathers sinned against the
heavenly Lord of Israel and provoked
him, he delivered them into the hands
of Nebuchadnezzar, the king of Babylon, the king of the Chaldeans; and 16
they tore the house down and burned
it, and carried the people away as
captives to Babylon. But in the first 17
year of the reign of Cyrus over Babylonia, Cyrus the king wrote an order
that this house be rebuilt. And the 18
sacred dishes of gold and silver that
Nebuchadnezzar had carried away from
the house at Jerusalem, and set up in
his own sanctuary, Cyrus the king
brought forth again from the sanctuary
in Babylon, and they were given to
Zerubbabel and Sheshbazzar, the governor, and he was instructed to carry 19
all these dishes back and put them back
in the sanctuary in Jerusalem, and that
this sanctuary of the Lord should be
rebuilt on the same spot. Then this 20
Sheshbazzar, after coming here, laid

the foundations of the house of the
Lord that is in Jerusalem, and although
it has been under construction from
then until now it has not reached com-
21 pletion.' Now therefore, if it meets
your approval, O king, let search be
made in the royal archives of our lord
22 the king in Babylon, and if it is found
that the building of the house of the
Lord in Jerusalem was done with the
consent of Cyrus the king, and it meets
the approval of our lord the king, let
him give us orders about this."
23 Then King Darius ordered a search
to be made in the royal archives that
were deposited in Babylon. And in the
castle of Ecbatana, in the land of
Media, was found a roll in which this
was recorded:
24 "In the first year of the reign of
Cyrus, King Cyrus ordered the rebuilding of the house of the Lord in Jerusalem, where they sacrifice with per-
25 petual fire; the height of it to be ninety
feet, the width ninety feet, with three
courses of hewn stone and a course of
new native timber, and the cost to be
provided from the house of Cyrus the
26 king; and that the sacred dishes of the
house of the Lord, of gold and silver,
which Nebuchadnezzar carried away
from the house in Jerusalem and removed to Babylon, be restored to the
house in Jerusalem to be placed where
27 they were." And he further ordered
that Sisinnes, the governor of Syria
and Phoenicia, and Sathrabuzanes and
their companions and the local governors appointed in Syria and Phoenicia
should take care to let the place alone,
and to permit Zerubbabel, the servant
of the Lord and governor of Judea,
and the elders of the Jews, to build the
house of the Lord in its old place.
28 "And I command that it be completely
built and that they seek earnestly to
help the returned captives of Judea,
until the house of the Lord is finished;
29 and that a grant from the tribute of
Coelesyria and Phoenicia be particularly given these men for sacrifices to
the Lord, that is, to Zerubbabel, the
governor, for bulls and rams and lambs,
30 and likewise wheat and salt and wine
and oil, regularly every year, without
objection, as the priests in Jerusalem
31 indicate they are daily used, so that
libations may be offered to the Most
High God for the King and his children,
and that they may pray for their lives."
And he commanded further that, if 32
any transgressed or disregarded any of
the things said above or added below, a
beam should be taken from his house
and he should be hung on it, and his
property be taken for the king. "There- 33
fore may the Lord, whose name is called
upon there, destroy any king and nation that shall stretch out their hands
to hinder or damage that house of the
Lord in Jerusalem. I, King Darius, 34
have decreed that it be done in exactly
this way."
Then Sisinnes, the governor of 7
Coelesyria and Phoenicia, and Sathrabuzanes and their companions obeying
the orders of Darius the king, looked 2
after the holy work very attentively,
assisting the elders of the Jews and
the governors of the temple. And the 3
holy work progressed, while the prophets Haggai and Zechariah prophesied;
and they completed it at the command
of the Lord, the God of Israel; and with
the consent of Cyrus and Darius and
Artaxerxes, the kings of Persia, the holy 5
house was finished by the twenty-third
day of the month of Adar, in the sixth
year of King Darius. And the Israelites 6
and the priests and the rest of the returned exiles who had joined them did
according to what was in the book of
Moses. And they offered at the dedica- 7
tion of the temple of the Lord a
hundred bulls, two hundred rams, four
hundred lambs, and twelve he-goats 8
for the sin of all Israel, to correspond
to the number of the twelve princes
of the tribes of Israel; and the priests 9
and the Levites stood robed, by tribes,
in charge of the service of the Lord God
of Israel in accordance with the book
of Moses, and the doorkeepers stood at
each gate.
And the Israelites who had returned 10
from exile held the Passover on the
fourteenth day of the first month, for
the priests and the Levites had been
purified together, but all the returned 11
exiles had not been purified, for the
Levites had all been purified together,
so they sacrificed the Passover for all 12
the returned exiles and their brothers
the priests and themselves. And the 13
Israelites who had returned from exile,
and who had separated themselves from
the accursed doings of the heathen of

the land and sought the Lord, ate it.
14 And they observed the festival of Unleavened Bread for seven days, rejoic-
15 ing before the Lord, because he had
changed the attitude of the king of
Assyria toward them, so as to strength-
en their hands for the service of the
Lord, the God of Israel.
8 Afterward, in the reign of Artaxerxes,
the king of Persia, there came Ezra,
the son of Seraiah, the son of Azariah,
the son of Hilkiah, the son of Shallum,
2 the son of Zadok, the son of Ahitub,
the son of Amariah, the son of
Uzzi, the son of Bukki, the son of
Abishua, the son of Phineas, the son
of Eleazar, the son of Aaron, the chief
3 priest. This Ezra came up from Babylon as a scribe, skilled in the law of
Moses, which was given by the God of
4 Israel, and the king showed him honor,
for he found favor before him in all
5 that he asked. And there came with
him to Jerusalem some of the Israelites
and the priests and Levites and holy
singers and doorkeepers and temple
6 slaves, in the seventh year of the reign
of Artaxerxes, in the fifth month (that
was the king's seventh year); for they
left Babylon on the new moon of the
first month, and they reached Jerusalem on the new moon of the fifth month,
so prosperous a journey had the Lord
7 given them for his sake. For Ezra possessed great knowledge, so that he neglected nothing that was in the Law of
the Lord or the commandments, but
taught all Israel all the statutes and
ordinances.

8 Now the written commission came
from Artaxerxes, the king, to Ezra,
the priest and reader of the Law of the
Lord, and the following is a copy of it:
9 "King Artaxerxes sends greeting to
Ezra, the priest and reader of the Law
10 of the Lord. As I have taken a friendly
attitude, I have given orders that those
of the Jewish nation who wish to do so,
and of the priests and Levites and of the
others in our realm shall, if they choose
11 to, go to Jerusalem with you. So let all
who think of doing so, set out with you,
as I and the seven friends and counci-
12 lors have decided, to look into matters
in Judea and Jerusalem, in accordance
with what is in the Law of the Lord,
13 and to carry to the Lord of Israel in
Jerusalem the gifts that I and the
friends have promised; and that all the
gold and silver that can be found in the
country of Babylonia for the Lord in
Jerusalem, with what has been given 14
by the nation for the temple of their
Lord at Jerusalem be collected, both
gold and silver for bulls and rams and
lambs and the things incident to them,
so as to offer offerings upon the altar 15
of their Lord that is in Jerusalem. And 16
all that you with your brothers wish
to do with gold and silver carry out,
according to the will of your God, and 17
deliver the sacred dishes of the Lord
that have been given you for the use of
the temple of your God that is in
Jerusalem. And anything else that oc- 18
curs to you as necessary for the temple
of your God, you are to give from the
royal treasury; and I, Artaxerxes the 19
king, have commanded the treasurers
of Syria and Phoenicia that whatever
Ezra, the priest and reader of the Law
of the Most High God, sends for, they
shall take care to give him, up to a 20
hundred talents of silver, and likewise
up to a hundred measures (fifteen hundred bushels) of wheat and a hundred
measures (a thousand gallons) of wine
and salt in abundance; and let every- 21
thing prescribed in the Law of God be
scrupulously performed to the Most
High God, so that wrath may not come
upon the realm of the king and his sons.
You are also instructed to lay no tribute 22
or any other tax upon any priests or
Levites or sacred singers or porters or
temple slaves or persons employed in
this temple, and that no one has authority to lay any such tax upon them.
And you, Ezra, must appoint justices 23
and judges to judge all through Syria
and Phoenicia all who know the Law of
your God; and those who do not know
it you must teach. And all who trans- 24
gress the Law of your God and of the
king will be suitably punished, either
with death, or by some other punishment, a fine or imprisonment."

Blessed be the only Lord, who put 25
this into the king's heart, to glorify
his house in Jerusalem, and gave me 26
honor in the sight of the king and his
councilors and all his friends and
grandees. So I was encouraged by the 27
help of the Lord, my God, and I
gathered men from Israel to go up with
me.

These are the principal men, by their 28
families and their groups, who came up

with me from Babylon, in the reign of
29 Artaxerxes the king: of the descend-
30 ants of Phineas, Gershom; of the descendants of Ithamar, Gamael; of the
descendants of David, Hattush, the
31 son of Shecaniah; of the descendants of
Parosh, Zechariah, and with him a
32 hundred and fifty men enrolled; of the
descendants of Pahath-moab, Eliohenai, the son of Zerahiah, and with
him two hundred men; of the descendants of Zattu, Shecaniah, the son of
Jahaziel, and with him three hundred
men; of the descendants of Adin, Obed,
the son of Jonathan, and with him
33 two hundred and fifty men; of the
descendants of Elam, Jeshaiah, the
son of Gotholiah, and with him seventy
34 men; of the descendants of Shephatiah,
Zeraiah, the son of Michael, and with
35 him seventy men; of the descendants of
Joab, Obadiah, the son of Jehiel, and
with him two hundred and twelve
36 men; of the descendants of Bani, Shelomith, the son of Josiphiah, and with
37 him a hundred and sixty men; of the
descendants of Bebai, Zechariah, the
son of Bebai, and with him twenty-
38 eight men; of the descendants of Azgad,
Johanan, the son of Hakkatan, and
with him a hundred and ten men;
39 of the descendants of Adonikam, those
who came last, and these were their
names: Eliphelet, Jeuel, and Shemaiah,
40 and with them seventy men; and of the
descendants of Bigvai, Uthai, the son
of Istalcurus, and with him seventy
men.

41 So I assembled them at the river
called Theras, and we camped there
for three days, and I observed them.
42 And when I found none of the descendants of the priests or of the
43 Levites there, I sent to Eleazar and
44 Iduel and Maasmas and Elnathan and
Shemaiah and Jarib, Nathan, Elnathan, Zechariah, and Meshullam, who
45 were leaders and intelligent men, and
I told them to go to Iddo, who was in
command at the place of the treasury,
46 and ordered them to tell Iddo and his
kinsmen and the treasurers at that
place to send us men to serve as priests
47 in the house of our Lord. And by the
mighty hand of our Lord they brought
us competent men of the descendants
of Mahli, the son of Levi, the son of
Israel, Sherebiah and his sons and his
48 kinsmen, eighteen in all; and Hashabiah and with him Jeshaiah, his
brother, of the descendants of Hananiah, and his sons, making twenty
men; and of the temple slaves, whom 49
David and the princes had given to
work for the Levites, two hundred and
twenty temple slaves; their names were
all listed.

Then I proclaimed a fast there for 50
the young men before our Lord, to seek
from him a safe journey for us and our
children and our cattle that were with
us. For I was ashamed to ask the king 51
for foot soldiers and cavalry and an
escort to make us safe from those who
opposed us; for we had told the king, 52
"The power of our Lord will be with
those who seek him, and will give them
every support."

And we prayed to our Lord again 53
about these things, and we found him
merciful. Then I set apart twelve men 54
of the chiefs of the priests, Sherebiah
and Hashabiah, and ten of their kinsmen with them, and I weighed out to 55
them the silver and the gold and the
sacred dishes, of the house of our Lord,
which the king himself and his councilors and the grandees of all Israel had
given. And I weighed and turned over 56
to them six hundred and fifty talents
of silver, and silver dishes to the value
of a hundred talents, and a hundred
talents of gold, and twenty gold bowls, 57
and twelve bronze dishes of fine bronze
that glittered like gold. And I said to 58
them,

"You are holy to the Lord and the
dishes are holy, and the silver and gold
are a gift to the Lord, the Lord of our
forefathers. Be watchful and guard 59
them until you deliver them to the
chiefs of the priests and the Levites
and to the heads of the families of
Israel in Jerusalem, in the chambers of
the house of our Lord."

And the priests and the Levites took 60
the silver and the gold and the dishes
which had been in Jerusalem, and carried them into the temple of the Lord.

And we set out from the river Theras 61
on the twelfth day of the first month,
and entered Jerusalem, because the
mighty hand of our Lord was upon us,
and he saved us from every enemy on
the way, and we reached Jerusalem.
And when our third day there came, 62
the silver and gold were weighed and
turned over in the house of our Lord to

63 Meremoth, the son of Uriah, the priest,
who had with him Eleazar, the son of
Phineas, and they had with them Jozabad, the son of Jeshua, and Moeth, the
64 son of Binnui, the Levites; it was all
counted and weighed, and the total
weight of it was immediately recorded.
65 And those who had come back from
captivity offered as sacrifices to the
Lord, the God of Israel, twelve bulls for
66 all Israel, ninety-six rams, seventy-two
lambs, twelve he-goats for a thank-
offering—all as a sacrifice to the Lord.
67 And they delivered the king's orders
to the royal treasurers and to the
governors of Coelesyria and Phoenicia,
and they showed honor to the people
and the temple of the Lord.

68 When this was accomplished, the
principal men came to me and said,
69 "The people of Israel and the leaders
and the priests and the Levites have not
separated from the alien heathen of the
land and the impurities of them, the
Canaanites and Hittites and Perizzites
and Jebusites and Moabites and
70 Egyptians and Idumaeans, for they
and their sons have married their
daughters, and the holy race has been
mixed with the alien heathen of the
land, and from the beginning of this
matter, the princes and nobles have
shared in this iniquity."

71 As soon as I heard this, I tore open
my clothes and my sacred mantle, and
pulled out some of my hair and beard,
and sat down gloomy and grieved.
72 And all who were moved at the word
of the Lord of Israel gathered about
me, as I grieved over this iniquity, and
I sat grief-stricken until the evening
73 sacrifice. Then I got up from my fast
with my clothes and my sacred mantle
torn, and I knelt down and stretched
74 out my hands to the Lord, and said,

"Lord, I am ashamed, I am abashed
75 before you. For from the times of our
forefathers, our sins have risen higher
than our heads, and our mistakes have
76 mounted up to heaven, and we have
been involved in grievous sin, even to
77 this day. And because of our sins and
those of our forefathers, we have been
delivered with our brothers and our
kings and our priests to the kings of the
earth, to be slain and taken captive and
78 plundered, in shame, unto this day. And
yet how great has been your mercy to
us, Lord, that a root and a name should
be left to us in the place of your sanctuary, and that a light has been disclosed 79
to us in the house of our Lord, and that
food is given us in the time of our
bondage. Even in our bondage we have 80
not been forsaken by our Lord, but he
has brought us into favor with the kings
of Persia, so that they have given us
food and glorified the temple of our 81
Lord, and raised Zion up from its desolation, to give us a stronghold in Judea
and Jerusalem. And now, Lord, what 82
can we say, when we have these things?
For we have disobeyed your commands,
which you gave through your servants
the prophets, when you said, 'The land 83
which you enter to possess is a land that
has been polluted with the pollution of
the aliens of the land, and they have
filled it with their impurity. So now 84
you must not marry your daughters to
their sons, and you must not take their
daughters for your sons; and you must 85
not seek ever to have peace with them,
so that you may grow strong and eat
the good things of the land, and bequeath it to your descendants forever.'
And all that has happened to us has 86
happened because of our wicked deeds
and our great sins. For you, Lord, have
lightened our sins, and have given us 87
such a root as this, but we have turned
back again, to transgress your law, to
mingle with the impurity of the heathen
of the land. Are you not angry enough 88
with us to destroy us, until there is left
no root or stock or name of ours? Lord 89
of Israel, you are true; for we are left,
a root, today. Now here we are before 90
you, in all our iniquity, for in view of it
we cannot any longer stand before
you."

Now while Ezra was praying and 91
making his confession, lying on the
ground before the temple weeping,
there gathered about him an immense
throng from Jerusalem, men, women,
and children, for there was great
lamentation among the multitude. And 92
Shecaniah, the son of Jehiel, one of the
Israelites, called out and said to Ezra,

"We have sinned against the Lord,
and have married foreign women from
the heathen of the land, yet there is still
hope for Israel. Let us make oath to 93
the Lord about this, that we will expel
all our wives who are of foreign origin,
with their children, as you and all who 94
obey the Law of the Lord decide. Get 95

up and take action, for it is your business, and we will support you in taking
vigorous action."
96 Then Ezra got up, and made the
chiefs of the priests and Levites of all
Israel swear to do this, and they swore
9 to it. Then Ezra got up from the court
of the temple, and went to the priestly
2 chamber of Jehohanan, the son of
Eliashib, and spent the night, and he
would not eat bread or drink water, but
mourned over the great iniquity of the
3 multitude. And a proclamation was
made all over Judea and Jerusalem to
all who had returned from the captivity
that they should gather in Jerusalem;
4 and if anyone failed to meet there within two or three days in accordance with
the decision of the ruling elders, his
cattle should be confiscated, and he
should be excluded from the multitude
of those who had returned from exile.
5 And the men of the tribe of Judah
and Benjamin gathered in three days
at Jerusalem (it was the ninth month,
on the twentieth day of the month),
6 and all the multitude sat in the square
before the temple, trembling because
7 of the winter weather. And Ezra got
up and said to them,
"You have broken the Law, and
have married foreign women, to in-
8 crease Israel's sins. Now make your
confession and give glory to the Lord
9 God of our forefathers, and do his will,
and separate from the heathen of the
land and from the foreign women."
10 Then all the multitude shouted and
said in a loud voice,
11 "We will do as you say. But the
crowd is great and it is wintertime, and
we are not able to stand out-of-doors,
and cannot do so, and this is not a thing
we can do in a day or two, for we have
12 sinned too much in this matter. So let
the princes of the people remain, and
let all those in our settlements that
have foreign wives come at the times
13 appointed, with the elders and judges
of each place, until we free ourselves
from the Lord's wrath over this
matter."
14 Jonathan, the son of Asahel, and
Jahzeiah, the son of Tikvah, undertook
the matter on these terms, and Meshullam and Levi and Shabbethai sat with
15 them as judges. And the returned exiles
acted in accordance with all this.
16 And Ezra the priest picked out for
himself the leading men of their families, all of them by name, and on the
new moon of the tenth month they
held a sitting to inquire into the matter.
And the case of the men who had 17
foreign wives was brought to an end by
the new moon of the first month.
And among the priests the ones who 18
presented themselves who were found
to have foreign wives were: of the de- 19
scendants of Jeshua, the son of Jozadak, and his brothers: Maaseiah and
Eleazar and Jarib and Jodan; they 20
pledged themselves to cast off their
wives, and gave rams in atonement for
their mistake. And of the descendants 21
of Immer: Hanani and Zebadiah and
Maaseiah and Shemaiah and Jehiel and
Azariah. And of the descendants of 22
Pashur: Elioenai, Maaseiah, Ishmael,
and Nathanael, Gedaliah, and Elasah.
And of the Levites: Jozabad and 23
Shimei and Kelaiah, who was Kelita,
and Pethahiah and Judah and Jonah.
And of the sacred singers: Eliashib 24
and Zaccur. Of the porters: Shallum 25
and Telem.
Of Israel: of the descendants of 26
Parosh, Ramiah, Izziah, Malchijah,
Mijamin, and Eleazar, and Asibias,
and Benaiah; of the descendants of 27
Elam, Mattaniah and Zechariah, Jehiel
and Abdi, and Jeremoth and Elijah.
And of the descendants of Zattu, Elio- 28
enai, Eliashib, Othoniah, Jeremoth,
and Zabad and Zerdaiah. And of the 29
descendants of Bebai, Jehohanan and
Hananiah and Zabbai and Emathis;
and of the descendants of Bani: 30
Meshullam, Malluch, Adaiah, Jashub,
and Sheal and Jeremoth. And of the 31
descendants of Addi: Naathus and
Moossias, Laccunus and Naidus, and
Bescaspasmys and Sesthel, and Bal-
nuus and Manasseas. And of the de- 32
scendants of Annan: Elionas and
Asaias and Melchias and Sabbaias and
Simon Chosamaeus. And of the de- 33
scendants of Hashum: Mattenai and
Mattattah and Zabad and Eliphelet
and Manasseh and Shimei. And of the 34
descendants of Bani: Jeremai, Maadai,
Amram, Joel, Mamdai and Bedeiah
and Vaniah, Carabasion and Eliashib
and Machnadebai, Eliasis, Binnui,
Elialis, Shimei, Shelemiah, Nethaniah.
And of the descendants of Ezora:
Shashai, Azarel, Azael, Shemaiah,
Amariah, Joseph. And of the descend- 35

ants of Nebo: Mattithiah, Zabad, Iddo,
36 Joel, Benaiah. These had all married
foreign women, and they cast them off
with their children.
37 So the priests and the Levites and the
men of Israel settled in Jerusalem and
in the country. On the new moon of the
seventh month, when the Israelites
38 were in their communities, the whole
multitude gathered under a common
impulse in the square before the east
39 gate of the temple and told Ezra, the
high priest and reader, to bring the
Law of Moses, which had been given
him by the Lord, the God of Israel.
40 And Ezra, the high priest, brought the
Law for all the multitude, men and
women, and all the priests to hear, on
the new moon of the seventh month.
41 And he read aloud in the square before
the gate of the temple from morning
till noon, in the presence of both men
and women, and the whole multitude
42 gave attention to the Law. And Ezra,
the priest and reader of the Law, stood
in the wooden pulpit which had been
43 prepared, and beside him stood Mattithiah, Shema, Anaiah, Azariah, Uriah,
Hezekiah, and Baalsamus, at his right,
44 and at his left, Pedaiah, Mishael,
Malchijah, Lothasubus, Nabariah, and
45 Zechariah. Then Ezra took up the book
of the Law before the multitude, for
he was seated in a conspicuous place
before them all, and when he opened 46
the Law, they all stood up. And Ezra
blessed the Lord, the Most High God,
the God of Hosts, the Almighty, and 47
all the multitude shouted "Amen."
And they lifted up their hands and fell
on the ground, and worshipped the
Lord. Jeshua and Anniuth and Shere- 48
biah, Jamin, Akkub, Shabbethai, Hodiah, Masseiah and Kelita, Azariah and
Jozabad, Hanan, Pelaiah, the Levites,
taught the Law of the Lord, and read
the Law of the Lord to the multitude,
putting life into the reading.
Then the governor said to Ezra, the 49
high priest and reader, and to the
Levites who were teaching the multitude, to all,
"This day is sacred to the Lord" (and 50
they were all weeping as they heard the
Law) "so go and eat the fat and drink 51
the sweet, and send portions to those
who have none, for the day is sacred
to the Lord. Do not mourn, for the 52
Lord will honor you."
And the Levites commanded all the 53
people, saying,
"This day is sacred; do not mourn."
And they all went off to eat and 54
drink and enjoy themselves, and to
give portions to those who had none,
and to hold a great celebration, for they 55
had been inspired by the words which
they had been taught, and for which
they had come together.

THE SECOND BOOK OF ESDRAS

1 THE Second Book of Ezra the
Prophet, the son of Seraiah,
the son of Azariah, the son of
Hilkiah, the son of Shallum,
the son of Zadok, the son of Ahitub,
2 the son of Achiah, the son of Phineas,
the son of Heli, the son of Amariah, the son of Azariah, the son of
Meraioth, the son of Arna, the son
of Uzzi, the son of Borith, the son of
Abishua, the son of Phineas, the son
3 of Eleazar, the son of Aaron, of the
tribe of Levi, who was a captive in
the country of the Medes in the reign
of Artaxerxes, king of Persia.
4 And the word of the Lord came to
me, saying,
5 "Go and declare to my people their
crimes and to their sons their iniquities which they have committed
against me, so that they may tell
them to their children's children.
6 For the sins of their parents have increased in them, for they have forgotten me and have offered sacrifice
7 to strange gods. Was it not I who
brought them out of the land of
Egypt, out of the house of bondage?
But they have angered me, and
8 scorned my counsels. Shake out the
hair of your head and hurl all evils
upon them, because they have not
obeyed my law, but they are a
9 rebellious people. How long shall I
bear with them, when I have con-
10 ferred such benefits upon them? I
have overthrown many kings for
them; I struck down Pharaoh with
11 his servants, and all his army. I destroyed all nations before them, and
I scattered the people of two provinces in the east, Tyre and Sidon, and
12 I slew all their enemies. But you
must speak to them and say,
13 " 'Thus says the Lord: Surely it
was I who brought you across the
sea and produced broad highways for
you where there was no road; I gave
you Moses for a leader and Aaron for
14 a priest; I gave you light from a pillar
of fire, and did great wonders among
you; but you forgot me, says the
Lord.
" 'Thus says the Lord Almighty: 15
The quail were a sign to you; I gave
you camps to protect you, yet you
grumbled in them; and you have not 16
triumphed for my sake over the destruction of your enemies, but even
now you still grumble. Where are the 17
kindnesses I have shown you? When
you were hungry and thirsty in the
desert did you not cry out to me,
saying, "Why have you brought us 18
into this wilderness to kill us? It
would have been better for us to serve
the Egyptians than to die in this
desert." I pitied your groaning and 19
gave you manna for food; you ate
the bread of angels. When you were 20
thirsty, did I not split open the rock,
and waters flowed out in abundance?
On account of the heat I covered you
with the leaves of trees. I divided 21
fertile lands among you; the Canaanites, the Perizzites, and the
Philistines I drove out before you.
What more can I do for you? says
the Lord. Thus says the Lord Al- 22
mighty: When you were in the desert,
at the bitter river, thirsty and blaspheming my name, I did not give you 23
fire for your blasphemy, but I put
wood into the water and made the
river sweet.
" 'What shall I do to you, Jacob? 24
You would not obey me, Judah. I
will turn to other nations, and give
them my name, so that they may
observe my precepts. Since you have 25
forsaken me, I will forsake you.
When you seek mercy from me, I will
not have pity on you. When you call 26
upon me, I will not hear you; for you
have stained your hands with blood,
and your feet are quick to commit
murder. It is not as though you had 27
forsaken me, but yourselves, says the
Lord. Thus says the Lord Almighty: 28
Have I not begged you as a father
begs his sons, or a mother her daughters, or a nurse her little ones, to be 29

my people, and that I should be your
God, and you should be my sons and
30 I should be your father? I gathered
you as a hen gathers her brood under
her wings. But now what shall I do
to you? I will cast you out from be-
31 fore my face. When you make offerings to me, I will turn my face away
from you, for I have repudiated your
feast days, and new moons, and cir-
32 cumcisions of the flesh. I sent my
servants the prophets to you, and
you took them and killed them, and
tore their bodies in pieces; and their
blood I will require of you, says the
Lord.
33 " 'Thus says the Lord Almighty:
Your house is desolate; I will drive
you forth as the wind drives stubble;
34 and your children shall have no children, because they with you have
neglected my command, and have
35 done what is evil in my sight. I will
give your houses to a people that is to
come, who without having heard me
believe. Those to whom I have
showed no signs will do what I have
36 commanded. They have not seen the
prophets, yet they will call to mind
37 their uprightness. I call to witness the
gratitude of the people that is to
come, whose little ones rejoice with
gladness, though they do not see me
with physical eyes, but in spirit they
will believe the things I have said.' "
38 And now, Father, look upon me
with glory, and see the people coming
39 from the east, to whom I will give to
lead them Abraham and Isaac and
Jacob, and Hosea and Amos and
Micah, and Joel, and Obadiah and
40 Jonah, and Nahum and Habakkuk,
Zephaniah, Haggai, Zechariah, and
Malachi, who is also called the Messenger of the Lord.

2 " 'Thus says the Lord: I brought
that people out of bondage, and gave
them commandments through my
servants the prophets; but they would
not listen to them, but made my
2 counsels void. The mother that bore
them said to them, "Go, my children,
for I am a widow and deserted;
3 I brought you up in gladness, but in
grief and sorrow I have lost you, for
you have sinned before the Lord God
and done what is evil in my sight.
4 But now what can I do for you? For
I am a widow and deserted. Go, my
children, and ask for mercy from the
Lord." I call you, father, as a witness, 5
in addition to the mother of the children, because they would not keep my
agreement, to bring confusion upon 6
them, and to give their mother up to
pillage, so that they may have no
descendants. Let them be scattered 7
among the heathen, let their names
be blotted out from the earth, because they have scorned my agreement.

" 'Alas for you, Assyria, who con- 8
ceal the unrighteous with you. O
wicked nation, remember what I did
to Sodom and Gomorrah, whose land 9
lies in lumps of pitch and heaps of
ashes. So I will make those who
would not listen to me, says the Lord
Almighty.'

"Thus speaks the Lord to Ezra: 10
Tell my people that I will give them
the kingdom of Jerusalem, which I
was going to give to Israel. And I 11
will take back to myself their glory,
and I will give to these the everlasting dwellings which I had prepared
for those others. The tree of life will 12
give them fragrant perfume, and they
will not toil or be weary. Ask, and 13
you will receive; pray for few days
for yourselves, that they may be
shortened; the kingdom is already
prepared for you; be on the watch.
Call heaven and earth to witness; call 14
them to witness, for I have left out
evil and created good, because I live,
says the Lord.

"Mother, embrace your sons, bring 15
them up in gladness like a dove,
strengthen their feet, for I have
chosen you, says the Lord. And I will 16
raise up the dead from their places,
and bring them out of their tombs,
because I recognize my name in
them. Do not fear, mother of sons, 17
for I have chosen you, says the Lord.
I will send to help you my serv- 18
ants Isaiah and Jeremiah, for whose
counsel I have consecrated and prepared for you twelve trees loaded with
different fruits, and an equal number 19
of springs flowing with milk and
honey, and seven huge mountains on
which roses and lilies grow, with
which I will fill your sons with joy.
Do justice to the widow, judge the 20
fatherless, give to the needy, protect
the orphan, clothe the naked, cure the 21

injured and the weak, do not laugh
at a lame man, defend the maimed,
and let the blind man behold my
22 glory. Preserve the old man and the
23 youth within your walls. When you
find any who are dead, give them
burial and mark the place, and I will
give you the first place in my resur-
24 rection. Pause and be quiet, my peo-
25 ple, for your rest will come. Good
nurse, nourish your sons, for you
26 must strengthen their feet. As for
the slaves whom I have given you,
not one of them shall perish, for I will
require them from your number.
27 Do not worry, for when the day of
affliction and anguish comes, others
will lament and be sad, but you will
28 be joyful and rich. The heathen will
be jealous, but they will be not able
to do anything against you, says the
29 Lord. My hands will cover you, so
that your sons will not see the Pit.
30 Be joyful, mother, with your sons, for
I will rescue you, says the Lord.
31 Remember your sons who are asleep,
for I will bring them forth from the
hiding-places of the earth and show
mercy to them, for I am merciful,
32 says the Lord Almighty. Embrace
your children until I come, and proclaim mercy to them, for my springs
run over, and my favor will not fail."
33 I, Ezra, received a command from
the Lord on Mount Horeb, to go to
Israel; but when I went to them, they
refused me and rejected the Lord's
34 command. Therefore I say to you,
heathen, who hear and understand,
expect your shepherd; he will give
you everlasting rest, for he is close at
hand, who will come at the end of the
35 world. Be ready for the rewards of
the kingdom, for everlasting light will
36 shine upon you forever. Flee from
the shadow of this world, receive the
enjoyment of your glory. I call my
37 Savior to witness publicly. Receive
the approval of the Lord, and rejoice,
with thanksgiving to him who has
38 called you to heavenly realms. Get
up and stand and see the number of
those who are marked with his seal
39 at the feast of the Lord. Those who
have removed from the shadow of the
world have received splendid gar-
40 ments from the Lord. Receive your
number, Zion, and close the list of
your people who are clothed in white,

who have fulfilled the Law of the
Lord. The number of your sons whom 41
you desired is full; intreat the Lord's
power that your people which was
called from the beginning may be
made holy.
I, Ezra, saw on Mount Zion a great 42
throng which I could not count, and
they all praised the Lord with songs.
And in the midst of them was a 43
youth of lofty stature, taller than all
the rest, and he put crowns upon the
heads of each of them, and he was
still more exalted. But I was possessed with wonder. Then I asked 44
the angel, and said,
"Who are these, sir?"
And he answered and said to me, 45
"These are those who have laid
aside their mortal clothing, and have
put on immortal, and have confessed
the name of God; now they are
crowned and receive palms."
And I said to the angel, 46
"Who is that young man, who puts
the crowns on them and the palms
in their hands?"
He answered and said to me, 47
"He is the Son of God, whom they
confessed in the world."
Then I began to glorify those who
had stood firmly for the name of the
Lord. Then the angel said to me, 48
"Go, tell my people what kind of
wonders of the Lord you have seen,
and how great they are."
In the thirtieth year after the de- **3**
struction of the city, I, Salathiel, who
am Ezra, was in Babylon, and I was
troubled as I lay on my bed, and my
thoughts filled my mind, because I 2
saw the desolation of Zion, and the
wealth of those who lived in Babylon.
And my spirit was agitated, and I be- 3
gan to utter devout words to the
Most High, and I said,
"O Sovereign Lord, was it not you 4
who in the beginning when you
formed the earth, and all alone too,
spoke and commanded the dust, and
it gave you Adam, a dead body? But 5
he was both himself a formation of
your hands, and you breathed into
him the breath of life, and he was
made alive before you. And you led 6
him into Paradise which your right
hand planted before the earth appeared; and you enjoined upon him 7
your one concern, and he transgressed

it, and you immediately ordained
death for him and his peoples; and
there sprang from him nations and
tribes, peoples and clans without
8 number. And every nation followed
its own will and behaved wickedly
in your sight, and you did not hinder
9 them. But again, in time, you
brought the flood upon the inhabitants of the world, and destroyed
10 them. And the same fate befell them;
as Adam experienced death, they ex-
11 perienced the flood. But you left one
of them, Noah, with his household,
all the upright people that were
descended from him.
12 "And it came to pass that when
the inhabitants of the earth began
to multiply, and sons and peoples
and nations grew very numerous,
that they began again to be more un-
13 godly than their predecessors. And it
came to pass that when they did what
was wrong in your sight, you chose for
yourself one of them, whose name was
14 Abraham, and you loved him, and to
him alone you revealed the end of the
15 times, secretly at night. And you
made an everlasting agreement with
him, and told him that you would
16 never forsake his descendants; and
you gave him Isaac, and to Isaac you
gave Jacob and Esau. And you set
Jacob apart for yourself, but you cut
off Esau, and Jacob became a great
17 multitude. And it came to pass, when
you led his descendants out to Egypt,
that you brought them to Mount Sinai.
18 And you bent the heavens, and shook
the earth, and moved the universe,
and made the deeps tremble, and dis-
19 turbed the world. And your glory
passed through the four gates of fire
and earthquake and wind and cold,
so that you might give the Law to
Jacob's descendants, and your command to the posterity of Israel.
20 "Yet you did not take from them
their wicked heart, so that your Law
21 might bear fruit among them. For
the first Adam, burdened with a
wicked heart, transgressed and was
overcome, as were also all who were
22 descended from him. So weakness became permanent, and the Law was in
the heart of the people with the evil
root; and what was good departed,
23 and what was evil remained. So the
times passed and the years came to
an end, and you raised up for yourself
a slave named David. And you told 24
him to build a city to bear your name,
and to offer to you offerings of your
own in it. This was done for many 25
years; then those who lived in the city
sinned, acting in all respects just as 26
Adam and his posterity had done, for
they too had the wicked heart. And 27
you delivered your city into the hands
of your enemies. Then I said to my- 28
self, 'Do those who live in Babylon
do any better? and is it on this account that she has conquered Zion?'
"For it came to pass, when I had 29
come here, that I saw acts of ungodliness without number, and in this
thirtieth year my soul saw many
sinning, and my heart sank, for I have 30
seen how you bear with them when
they sin, and have spared those who
act wickedly, and have destroyed
your people, and preserved your
enemies, and you have not shown 31
anyone at all how this way should be
given up. Does Babylon do better
deeds than Zion? Or has any other 32
nation known you except Israel? Or
what tribes have believed your agreements like that of Jacob? Yet their 33
reward has not appeared, and their
labor has not borne fruit. For I have
gone all about the nations, and I have
seen them abounding in wealth, yet
unmindful of your commandments.
Now therefore weigh our iniquities 34
and those of the inhabitants of the
world on the scales; and which way
the movement of the pointer turns
will be found out. Or when did the 35
inhabitants of the earth not sin in
your sight? Or what nation has kept
your commandments so well? You 36
will find names of men who have
kept your commandments, but you
will not find nations."
And the angel who had been sent 4
to me, whose name was Uriel, an- 2
swered and said to me,
"Your mind has utterly failed in
this world and do you expect to
understand the way of the Most
High?"
And I said, 3
"Yes, my lord."
And he answered me and said,
"I was sent to show you three ways,
and to set three figures before you.
If you can solve one of these for me, 4

I will show you the way you want to
see and teach you why the heart is
wicked."
5 And I said,
"Go on, my lord."
And he said to me,
"Come, weigh me the weight of fire,
or measure me a measure of wind,
or call back for me the day that is
past."
6 And I answered and said,
"Who that is born can do that,
that you should ask such things of
me?"
7 And he said to me,
"If I had asked you, 'How many
dwellings are there in the heart of
the sea, or how many streams at the
source of the deep, or how many
ways above the firmament, or what
are the ways of leaving Paradise?'
8 perhaps you would have said to me,
'I have never gone down into the
deep, nor into Hades, nor have I ever
9 climbed up into the heavens.' But
now I have only asked you about fire
and wind and the day, through all of
which you have passed, and without
which you cannot live, and you have
given me no answer about them!"
10 And he said to me, "Your own things
that grow up with you, you cannot
11 understand; and how can your frame
grasp the way of the Most High, or
one already worn out by the corrupt
world understand incorruption?"
12 And when I heard this, I fell on my
face and said to him,
"It would have been better that we
should not be here than to come here
and live in ungodliness, and suffer,
without understanding why."
13 And he answered me and said,
"I went to a forest of trees of the
14 field, and they took counsel and said,
'Come, let us go and make war on the
sea, so that it may retire before us,
and we may make more forests for
15 us.' In like manner the waves of the
sea themselves also took counsel and
said, 'Come, let us go up and conquer
the forest of the field, so that there
also we may win ourselves more
16 territory.' And the thought of the
forest was in vain, for the fire came
17 and consumed it; so was the thought
of the sea waves, for the sand stood
18 firm and stopped them. Now if you
were their judge, which of them would
you have undertaken to justify, and
which to condemn?"
And I answered and said, 19
"It was a foolish plan that both
formed, for the land is given to the
forest, and the place of the sea is given
it to bear its waves."
And he answered me and said, 20
"You have judged rightly; and
why have you not judged so in your
own case? For just as the land is 21
given to the forest, and the sea to its
waves, so those who live on the earth
can understand only the things that
are on the earth, and those who are
above the heavens, the things that
are above the height of the heavens."
Then I answered and said, 22
"I beseech you, sir, to what end has
the capacity for understanding been
given me? For I did not mean to ask 23
about ways above, but about those
things which pass by us every day:
why Israel is given up to the heathen
in disgrace; the people whom you
loved are given up to godless tribes;
and the law of our forefathers is made
of no effect, and the written agreements are no more. And we pass from 24
the world like locusts, and do not deserve to obtain mercy. But what will 25
he do for his name, by which we are
called? It is about these things that I
have asked."
And he answered me and said, 26
"If you live, you will see, and if you
survive, you will often marvel; for
the age is hurrying fast to its end;
for it will not be able to bear the 27
things that are promised to the upright in the appointed times; for this
age is full of sorrow and weakness.
For the evil about which you ask me 28
is sown, but the harvest of it has not
yet come. So unless what has been 29
sown is reaped, and unless the place
where the evil was sown passes away,
the field where the good is sown cannot come. For a grain of evil seed 30
was sown from the beginning in the
heart of Adam, and how much ungodliness it has produced up to this
time and will produce before the judgment comes. Estimate for yourself 31
how great a crop of ungodliness a
grain of evil seed has produced. And 32
when ears without number are sown,
how great a threshing-floor they will
inevitably fill!"

33 And I answered and said,
"How long and when shall this
be? Why are our years few and evil?"
34 And he answered me and said,
"You cannot hurry faster than the
Most High, for you hurry for your
own self, but he who is above hurries
35 for many. Did not the souls of the upright ask about these things in their
rooms, saying, 'How long must I
hope thus? And when will the har-
36 vest of our reward come?' And Jere-
miel, the archangel, answered them
and said, 'When the number of those
who are like you is complete, for he
has weighed the world in the balance,
37 and has measured the times with a
measure, and carefully counted the
hours, and he will not move or disturb them, until the prescribed measure is reached.' "
38 And I answered and said,
"O Sovereign Lord, but all even of
39 us are full of ungodliness. And let
not the harvest of the upright be
perchance kept back, on account of
the sins of those who live on the
earth."
40 And he answered me and said,
"Go and ask a woman who is with
child if when she has completed her
nine months her womb can keep the
child within her any longer."
41 And I said,
"No, sir, it cannot."
And he said to me,
42 "In Hades the storehouses of
souls are like the womb; for just as a
woman who is bearing a child makes
haste to escape the inevitable birth,
so these places also make haste to
give up those things that were in-
43 trusted to them from the beginning.
Then those things which you desire to
see will be disclosed to you."
44 And I answered and said,
"If I have found favor in your sight,
and if it is possible, and if I am fit
45 for it, show me this also, whether
there is more to come than is past,
or the greater part has gone by us.
46 For what is past I know, but I do not
know what is to come."
47 And he said to me,
"Stand at my right and I will show
you the meaning of a figure."
48 And I stood there and looked, and
behold, a burning furnace passed before me, and it came to pass, when
the flame had gone by, that I looked
and, behold, the smoke remained.
After that, a cloud full of water 49
passed before me, and stormily sent
down a heavy rain, and when the
rainstorm had passed, the drops remained in it. And he said to me, 50
"Consider for yourself; for as the
rain is more than the drops, and the
fire is more than the smoke, so the
quantity that has past has far ex-
ceeded, but the drops and the smoke
remained."
Then I prayed and said, 51
"Do you think I shall live until
that time?"
He answered me and said, 52
"About the signs of which you
ask me, I can tell you of them in
part, but as to your life I was not
sent to tell you, but I do not know.
"But about the signs: Behold, the 5
days will come, when those who
live on the earth will be seized with
great dismay, and the way of truth
will be hidden, and the land will be
barren of faith. And iniquity will be 2
increased beyond what you yourself
see, and beyond what you ever heard
of. And the country which you now 3
see ruling will be waste and untrod-
den, and men shall see it deserted.
But if the Most High grants you life, 4
you will see it after the third day
thrown into confusion, and the sun
will shine suddenly in the night and
the moon in the daytime. Blood shall 5
trickle out of wood, and a stone will
utter its voice, and peoples will be
troubled, and the courses will be
changed. And one will reign for whom 6
those who live on the earth do not
hope, and the birds will fly away together, and the Sea of Sodom will cast 7
forth fish, and one whom the many
do not know will utter his voice in
the night, but all will hear his voice.
And there will be darkness in many 8
places, and fire will often break out,
and wild animals will go outside their
haunts, and women in their uncleanness will bear monsters. And salt 9
waters will be found in sweet, and all
friends will conquer one another, and
intelligence will hide itself, and understanding retire to its room; and it will 10
be sought by many and will not be
found, and unrighteousness and lack
of self-control will increase on the

11 earth. And one country will ask its
neighbor, and say, 'Has uprightness,
or a man who does right, passed
through you?' and it will answer,
12 'No.' At that time, it will happen
that men will hope and not obtain;
they will work, but their ways will
not prosper. These signs I am per-
13 mitted to tell you, but if you pray
again and weep as you do now, and
fast seven days, you will again hear
greater things than these."

14 Then I awoke, and my body
shuddered violently, and my soul was
15 troubled, so that it fainted. But the
angel who came and talked with me
held me fast, and strengthened me
16 and set me on my feet. And on the
second night it came to pass that
Phaltiel, the captain of the people,
came to me and said to me.

17 "Where have you been and why is
your face so sad? Or do you not
know that Israel has been intrusted
to you in the land of their exile?
18 Get up therefore and eat some bread,
so that you may not forsake us, as a
shepherd leaves his flock in the power
of wicked wolves."

19 Then I said to him,

"Go away from me, and do not
come near me for seven days, and
then you can come to me."

And he listened to what I said, and
went away from me.

20 So I fasted for seven days, wailing
and lamenting, just as the angel Uriel
21 commanded me. And it came to pass
after seven days that the thoughts of
my mind were very painful to me
again. And my soul received the
22 spirit of understanding again, and I
began again to utter words before the
23 Most High, and said,

"Sovereign Lord, from all the
24 forests on the earth and from all its
trees you chose one vine, and from
all the lands in the world you chose
for yourself one garden, and from all
the flowers in the world you chose for
25 yourself one lily, and from all the
depths of the sea you filled yourself
one river, and of all the cities that
have been built you consecrated Zion
26 to yourself, and of all the birds that
have been created you named for
yourself one dove, and of all the cattle
that have been formed you provided
27 for yourself one sheep, and of all the
peoples that have multiplied you got
yourself one people, and you gave to
this people that you desired a law
that was approved by all. And now, 28
Lord, why have you given this one
up to the many, and after preparing
one root above the others have you
scattered your only one among the
many? And those who opposed 29
your promises have trampled on those
who believed your agreements. For 30
if you really hate your people it
ought to be punished with your own
hands."

And it came to pass when I had 31
uttered these words that the angel
who had come to me on a previous night was sent to me. And he 32
said to me,

"Listen to me, and I will instruct
you; attend to me, and I will tell you
more."

And I said,

"Speak, my lord." 33

And he said to me,

"Are you so very much distracted
over Israel, or do you love him more
than his Maker does?"

And I said, 34

"No, sir, but I spoke from grief,
for my heart pains me every hour,
while I strive to understand the way
of the Most High, and to inquire into
what his decree apportions."

And he said to me, 35

"You cannot."

And I said,

"Why, sir, then why was I born?
And why did not my mother's womb
become my grave, so that I might not
see the trouble of Jacob, and the
exhaustion of the posterity of Israel?"

And he said to me, 36

"Count up for me those that have
not yet come, and gather the scattered raindrops for me, and make the
withered flowers green again for me,
and open the closed chambers for 37
me, and bring out for me the winds
shut up in them, or show me the picture of a voice, and then I will show
you the mark you ask to see."

And I said, 38

"Sovereign Lord, who is there who
can know these things except he
whose dwelling is not with men?
But I am foolish, and how can I speak 39
of these things about which you have
asked me?"

40 And he said to me,
"Just as you cannot do one of these
things that were mentioned, so you
cannot find out my judgment, or the
end of the love that I have promised
my people."
41 And I said,
"But behold, sir, you protect those
who are alive at the end, but what
will those who were before us do, or
we, or those who come after us?"
42 And he said to me,
"I will compare my judgment to a
crown; just as there is no slowness on
the part of those who are last, there
is no swiftness on the part of those
who are first."
43 And I answered and said,
"Could you not have created at
one time those who have been created, and those who are now, and
those who are to be, so that you
might show your judgment sooner?"
44 And he answered me and said,
"The creation cannot make more
haste than the Creator, and the world
cannot at one time hold all who have
been created in it."
45 Then I said,
"How could you say to your slave
that you would surely make the
creation created by you alive all together? If therefore they are all to
live at once, it can support them all
at once now."
46 And he said to me,
"Ask a woman's womb and say to
it, 'If you bring forth ten children,
why do so at intervals?' Ask it therefore to produce ten at once."
47 And I said,
"Of course it cannot, but can do it
only in time."
48 And he said to me,
"And I have made the earth the
womb for those who are at intervals
49 engendered in it. For just as an infant cannot bear, or as one who is old
cannot do it any more, so I have
organized the world that I created."
50 And I asked him and said,
"Since you have now shown me
the way, I will speak before you. For
is our mother, of whom you have
told me, still young, or is she now approaching old age?"
51 And he answered me and said,
"Ask a woman who bears children,
and she will tell you. For if you say
to her, 'Why are those whom you 52
have borne lately not like those whom
you bore before but smaller in
stature?' she herself will tell you, 53
'Those who were born in the vigor
of youth are of one kind, and those
who were born in old age, when the
womb was failing, are of another.'
So you too must consider that you 54
are smaller in stature than those who
were before you, and those who come 55
after you will be smaller than you,
for the creation is already growing
old, as it were, and past the strength
of youth."
And I said, 56
"I beseech you, sir, if I have found
favor in your sight, show your slave
by whom you will visit your creation."
And he said to me, 6
"As for the beginning of the world
of the earth, before the outlets of the
world were fixed, and before the assembled winds blew, and before the 2
voices of the thunders sounded, and
before the lightning flashes shone,
and before the foundations of Paradise were laid, and before the beauti- 3
ful flowers were seen, and before the
moving forces were established, and
before the innumerable companies
of angels were gathered, and before 4
the heights of the air were raised aloft,
and before the dimensions of the
firmaments were named, and before
Zion was appointed his footstool,
and before the years of the present 5
were discovered, and before the wiles
of present-day sinners were cut off,
and those who had treasured the
faith were sealed; even then I con- 6
sidered it, and these things were made
through me, and through no other,
just as their end also shall come
through me, and through no other."
And I answered and said, 7
"What will mark the parting of the
times? Or when will the end of the
first or the beginning of the second
be?"
And he said to me, 8
"From Abraham to Abraham, for
from him sprang Jacob and Esau, but
Jacob's hand held Esau's heel from
the beginning. For Esau is the end 9
of this age, and Jacob is the beginning
of the one that follows. For the be- 10
ginning of a man is his hand, and the

end of a man in his heel. Between the
heel and the hand look for nothing
else, Ezra!"
11 Then I answered and said,
"O Sovereign Lord, if I have
12 found favor in your sight, show your
slave the end of your signs, some part
of which you showed me the other
night."
13 And he answered and said to me,
"Rise to your feet, and you will
14 hear a very loud voice. And if the
place where you stand is violently
15 shaken, you must not be terrified
when it speaks, for what it says is
about the end, and the foundations of
the earth will understand that the
16 speech concerns them; they will
tremble and quake, for they know
that at the end they must be
changed."
17 And it came to pass that, when I
heard, I rose to my feet and listened,
and, behold, a voice was speaking,
and the sound of it was like the noise
18 of many waters. And it said,
"Behold, the days are coming, and
it shall be, when I begin to draw near
to visit those who live on the earth,
19 and when I begin to require their
wrongdoing from those who have
done it, and when the humiliation
20 shall be complete, and when the age
which is beginning to pass away shall
be sealed, I will perform these signs:
the books will be opened before the
face of the firmament, and they shall
21 all see it together; and infants a year
old shall talk, and women with child
will bring forth untimely infants at
22 three or four months, and they will
live and dance, and sown ground will
suddenly appear unsown, and full
storehouses will suddenly be found
empty, and the trumpet will sound,
23 and when all men hear it, they will
24 suddenly be terrified. And it will
come to pass at that time that friends
will make war on their friends like
enemies, and the earth and those who
live on it will be greatly terrified, and
the sources of the springs will stop,
so that for three hours they will not
25 run. And it shall be that whoever
shall have survived all these things
that I have foretold to you shall himself be saved and shall see my salva-
26 tion and the end of my world. And
they will see the men who were taken
up, who from their birth have not
tasted death, and the heart of the
earth's inhabitants will be changed
and converted to a different spirit.
For evil will be destroyed and deceit 27
will be abolished, but faith will
flourish, and corruption be conquered,
and truth, which has been without 28
fruit so long, will be disclosed."
And it came to pass, while he 29
talked with me, that behold, little
by little the place where I stood was
moved upon itself. And he said to me, 30
"I have come to show you these
things and things to come, this night.
If therefore you will pray again and 31
fast again for seven days, I will again
declare to you even greater things
than these by day. For your voice has 32
surely been heard before the Most
High, for the Mighty One has seen
your uprightness, and has remarked
your purity, which you have maintained from your youth. And be- 33
cause of this he sent me to show you
all these things and to say to you,
'Believe and do not fear; and do not 34
be in haste to engage in idle speculations over the former times, so that
you may not have to hasten in the
last times.' "
And it came to pass after this that 35
again I wept and fasted seven days
as before, to complete the three
weeks, as I had been told. And it 36
came to pass on the eighth night that
my heart was again troubled within
me, and I began to speak before the
Most High. For my spirit was greatly 37
excited and my soul was distressed.
And I said, 38
"O Lord, at the beginning of the
creation you surely spoke, and said
on the first day, 'Let heaven and
earth be made,' and your word performed the work. Then the spirit 39
was hovering, and darkness and
silence were all around; the sound of
man's voice you had not yet heard.
Then you ordered a ray of light to be 40
brought out of your storehouses, so
that your works might then appear.
Again, on the second day, you cre- 41
ated the spirit of the firmament, and
commanded it to divide and make a
division between the waters, so that
one part might go up and one part
remain below. On the third day you 42
commanded the waters to be gathered

together in the seventh part of the
earth, but six parts you dried up and
kept them so that some of them
might be planted and cultivated and
43 serve before you. For your word went
forth, and the work was immediately
44 done. For suddenly there came forth
fruit in immeasurable abundance,
and of manifold appeal to the taste,
and flowers of inimitable hues, and
odors of unfathomable fragrance.
These were made on the third day.
45 But on the fourth day you commanded the brightness of the sun to
come into being, the light of the
moon, and the order of the stars,
46 and you commanded them to serve
47 man who was still to be formed. But
on the fifth day you ordered the
seventh part, where the water was
gathered, to bring forth living things,
48 birds and fish, and it was done, the
mute, lifeless water producing living
creatures, as it was commanded, so
that nations might tell of your
49 wondrous works because of it. Then
you preserved two living creatures;
one you named Behemoth, and the
50 other you named Leviathan, and you
separated them from each other, for
the seventh part, where the water
was gathered together, could not hold
51 them both. And you gave Behemoth
one part, which had dried up on the
third day, to live in, in which there
52 are a thousand mountains; but to
Leviathan you gave a seventh part
that is moist; and you preserved
them to be devoured by whomsoever
you please, and when you please.
53 But on the sixth day, you commanded
the earth to create before you cattle
54 and wild animals and reptiles, and
over them Adam, whom you appointed leader over all the works that
you had made, and from him we are
all descended whom you have chosen
55 to be your people. I have said all this
before you, Lord, because you have
said that it was for our sakes that
56 you made this first-born world. But
as for the rest of the nations which
are sprung from Adam, you have said
that they are nothing and are like
spittle, and you have compared their
abundance to a drop in a bucket.
57 And now, Lord, behold, these nations
that are counted as nothing rule over
58 us and devour us. But we, your people, whom you called your first-born,
only-begotten, chosen and beloved,
are delivered into their hands. If it 59
was for our sakes that the world was
created, why do we not possess the
world as our inheritance? How long
shall this be?"

And it came to pass, when I had 7
finished saying these words, that the
angel was sent to me who had been
sent to me on the former nights, and 2
he said to me,

"Get up, Ezra, and hear the words
which I have come to say to you."

And I said, 3

"Speak, my lord."

And he said to me,

"Suppose a sea lies in a broad expanse, so that it is wide and vast,
but the entrance to it is located in a 4
narrow space, so that it is like a
river; if anyone is determined to reach 5
the sea, to see it or master it, how can
he reach the broad water unless he
passes through the narrows? Another 6
illustration: Suppose a city is built
and located on level ground, and is
full of all good things, but the approach to it is narrow and precipi- 7
tous so that there is fire on the right
hand and deep water on the left, and 8
there is only one path lying between
them, that is, between the fire and the
water, so that the path can support
the steps of only one man. Now if 9
that city is given to a man as an inheritance, if the heir does not pass
through the danger that lies before it,
how can he receive his inheritance?"

And I said, 10

"True, sir."

And he said to me,

"Israel's destiny is like that. For I 11
made the world for their sakes, and
when Adam transgressed my statutes,
what has now happened was decreed;
and the ways of entering this world 12
were made narrow, grievous, and
toilsome, and few and evil, full of
dangers and burdened with great
hardships. But the approaches to the 13
greater world are broad and safe and
produce the fruit of immortality. Un- 14
less therefore the living have really
entered these narrow and fruitless
experiences, they cannot obtain the
things that are destined for them.
But now why are you disturbed, 15
though you are to perish? And why

are you so moved, though you are
16 mortal? And why do you not take
into consideration what is future, but
only what is present?"
17 And I answered and said,
"Sovereign Lord, you have ordained in your law that the upright
shall possess these things, but the un-
18 godly shall perish. So the upright can
endure straitened circumstances in
the hope of ample ones, but those
who have done wickedly endure the
straitened circumstances and will not
see the ample ones."
19 And he said to me,
"You are not a better judge than
God, or more intelligent than the
20 Most High! For let the many that
exist perish, rather than that the
Law of God which has been set before
21 them be disregarded. For God strictly commanded those who came, at
their coming, as to what they should
do to live, and what they should observe to escape being punished. But
22 they disobeyed and opposed him, and
they devised foolish thoughts and
23 conceived wicked wiles, and went so
far as to say that the Most High did
24 not exist, and they ignored his ways,
and scorned his law, and denied his
agreements, and had no faith in his
statutes, and did not complete his
25 work. Therefore, Ezra, the empty
have emptiness, and the full, fulness.
26 For behold the time will come, and it
will be that when the signs come
which I have foretold to you, the city
that appears as a bride will appear,
and the land which is now hidden will
27 be seen. And whoever is delivered from
the evils I have predicted will see my
28 wonders. For my son the Christ will
be revealed with those who are with
him, and he will make glad those who
29 are left, in four hundred years. And
it will be after those years that my
son Christ will die, and all who draw
30 human breath. And the world will be
turned into its ancient silence for
seven days, as it was in the first beginning, so that no one will be left.
31 And it will be after seven days that
the world which is not yet awake will
be wakened, and what is corruptible
32 will perish. And the earth will give
up those who are asleep in it, and the
dust those who are silent in it, and
the chambers will give up the souls
that have been committed to them.
And the Most High will be revealed 33
on his judgment seat, and pity will
pass away, and long-suffering be
withdrawn, and judgment alone will 34
remain, and truth will stand, and
faithfulness be strong, and work will 35
be rewarded, and its wages appear,
and uprightness will awake and
iniquity will not sleep. And the lake [36]
of torment will appear, and over
against it will be a place of rest; the
furnace of the Pit will appear, and
over against it the paradise of joy.
Then the Most High will say to the [37]
heathen that have been raised up,
'See and understand whom you have
denied, or whom you have refused
to serve, or whose commands you
have scorned. Look at this side and [38]
at that; on this side, joy and rest, and
on that, fire and torment.' So he
will speak to them on the Day of
Judgment; a day that has no sun [39]
or moon or stars, or cloud, or thunder, [40]
or lightning, or wind or water or air, [41]
or darkness or evening or morning, or
summer or heat or winter or frost
or cold, or hail or rain or dew, or noon [42]
or night, or dawn or sunshine or
brightness or light, only the splendor
of the glory of the Most High, by
which all will begin to see what is
destined for them. For it will last as [43]
though for a week of years. This is [44]
my judgment and its arrangement;
and to you alone have I shown this."
And I answered, [45]
"I said then, Lord, and I say now,
blessed are those who live and keep
your commandments! But about [46]
those for whom I prayed, who is there
of those who live who has not sinned,
or who is there that is born who
has not transgressed your agreement?
And now I see that the world to come [47]
will bring joy to few but torment to
many. For an evil heart has grown up [48]
in us, which has alienated us from
these commands, and has led us off to
corruption and the ways of death,
and shown us the paths of perdition,
and removed us far from life, and
that, not just a few, but almost all
who have been created!"
And he answered me and said, [49]
"Listen to me, and I will instruct
you, and I will admonish you a
second time. It was on this account [50]

that the Most High made not one
[51] world but two. For because you have
said that the upright are not many
but few, and the ungodly abound,
[52] hear the answer to this. If you have a
very few precious stones, will you
increase their number with lead and
clay?"
[53] And I said,
"Lord, how can that be?"
[54] And he said to me,
"Not only that, but ask the earth
and she will tell you; intreat her, and
[55] she will inform you. For you must
say to her, 'You produce gold and
silver and copper and also iron and
[56] lead and clay. But silver is more
abundant than gold, and copper than
silver, and iron than copper, lead than
[57] iron, and clay than lead. So consider
which things are precious and to be
desired, what is abundant, or what is
rare?'"
[58] And I said,
"Sovereign Lord, what is plentiful
is cheaper, for what is more rare is
more precious."
[59] And he answered me and said,
"Consider with yourself what you
have thought, for he who has what
is hard to get rejoices more than he
[60] who has what is plentiful. It is so
with the judgment that I have
promised; for I will rejoice over the
few who will be saved, because it is
they who have made my glory to prevail more now, and through whom my
[61] name has now been honored. And I
will not grieve over the great number
of those who perish, for they are the
ones who are now like vapor, and
counted as flame and smoke; they
have burned and glowed and gone
out."
[62] And I answered and said,
"O earth, why have you brought
forth, if the understanding is made
out of dust like other creatures!
[63] For it would have been better if the
dust itself had not been born, so
that the intelligence might not have
[64] sprung from it. But now the intelligence grows with us, and it is on this
account that we are tormented, because we must perish, and we know
[65] it! Let the human race lament, and
the wild beasts rejoice; let all who
are born lament, but the four-footed
[66] creatures and the cattle be glad. For
they are much better off than we, for
they do not look for a judgment, and
they do not know of any torment
or salvation promised to them after
death. But what benefit is it to us [67]
that we are preserved alive but
cruelly tormented? For all who are [68]
born are involved in iniquities and
full of sins and weighed down with
offenses. And if we were not to come [69]
to judgment after death, perhaps it
would have been better for us."
And he answered me and said, [70]
"When the Most High made the
world, and Adam and all who came
from him, he first prepared the judgment and the things that belong to
the judgment. And now understand [71]
from your own words, for you said
that the intelligence grows with us.
So those who live on the earth will be [72]
tortured on this account because,
though they had intelligence, they
did iniquity, and though they received commandments, they did not
keep them, and though they had obtained the Law, they broke it. What [73]
will they have to say then at the
judgment, or how will they answer in
the last times? For how long the [74]
Most High has shown long-suffering
to those who inhabit the world, and
not for their sakes, but for the sake
of the times that he has fixed!"
Then I answered and said, [75]
"If I have found favor in your
sight, Sovereign, show this also to
your slave; whether after death as
soon as each one of us gives up his
soul, we shall be faithfully kept at rest
until those times come when you begin to renew the creation, or shall be
tortured at once."
And he answered me and said, [76]
"I will show you that also; but you
must not associate with those who
have shown scorn, or count yourself
among those who are tortured. For [77]
you have a treasure of works laid up
with the Most High, but it will not
be shown to you until the last times.
For about death, the teaching is:
When the final sentence goes forth [78]
from the Most High that a man is to
die, when the soul departs from the
body to return again to him who
gave it, first of all it prays to the glory
of the Most High; if it was one of [79]
those who scorned and did not ob-

serve the way of the Most High, and
of those who have despised his law,
and of those who hate those who fear
[80] God, such spirits shall not enter
dwellings but wander about thenceforth in torment, always grieving and
[81] sad, in seven ways: The first way is
that they have scorned the Law of the
[82] Most High. The second way is that
they can no longer make a good re-
[83] pentance, so that they may live. The
third way is that they will see the
reward destined for those who have
believed the agreements of the Most
[84] High. The fourth way is that they
will consider the torment destined for
[85] them in the last days. The fifth way
is that they will see that the dwelling-
places of the others are guarded by
[86] angels in profound silence. The sixth
way is that they will see that some
of them will pass over to be tormented
[87] henceforth. The seventh way, which
is worse than all the ways that have
been mentioned, is that they will
waste away in shame and be consumed in disgrace, and wither with
fear, at seeing the glory of the Most
High before whom they sinned while
they lived, and before whom they
are destined to be judged in the last
times.

[88] "But of those who have observed
the ways of the Most High, this is the
order, when they shall be separated
[89] from this fragile jar. In the time when
they lived in it, they carefully served
the Most High, though they were
in danger every hour, so as to keep
the Law of the Lawgiver perfectly.
[90] Therefore this is the teaching about
[91] them: First of all, they see with
great rapture the glory of him who
takes them up, for they will rest in
[92] seven orders. The first order is that
they have striven with much toil to
conquer the wicked thought that was
formed with them, so that it should
not lead them away from life to
[93] death. The second order is that they
see the labyrinth in which the souls of
the ungodly wander, and the punish-
[94] ment that awaits them. The third
order is that they see the testimony
that he who formed them has borne
to them, because when they were
alive they faithfully observed the Law
[95] which was given them. The fourth
order is that they understand the rest
which they now enjoy, gathered in
their chambers, in great quietness,
watched over by angels, and the
glory that awaits them in the last
days. The fifth order is that they [96]
exult that they have now escaped
what is corruptible and will possess
the future as their inheritance, and
besides perceive the narrowness and
toilsomeness from which they have
been freed and the spaciousness they
are destined to receive and enjoy in
immortality. The sixth order is that [97]
it is shown to them how their face is
destined to shine like the sun, and
how they are to be made like the
light of the stars, and be incorruptible thenceforth. The seventh order, [98]
which is greater than all those that
have been mentioned, is that they
will exult boldly, and that they will
trust confidently, and rejoice fearlessly, for they hasten to see the face
of him whom they served in life, and
from whom they are to receive their
reward when they are glorified. These [99]
are the orders of the souls of the upright, as henceforth proclaimed, and
the above ways of torture are those
which those who would not give heed
will henceforth suffer."

And I answered and said, [100]
"Then will time be given the souls
after they are separated from the
bodies, to see what you have told me
of?"

And he said to me, [101]
"They have freedom for seven
days, to see on the seven days the
things you have been told, and afterward they will be gathered in their
dwellings."

And I answered and said, [102]
"If I have found favor in your
sight, show me, your slave, further,
whether on the Day of Judgment the
upright will be able to intercede for
the ungodly, or to beseech the Most
High on their behalf, fathers for sons,
or sons for parents, brothers for [103]
brothers, relatives for their kinsmen,
and friends for those who are most
dear to them."

And he answered me and said, [104]
"Since you have found favor in my
sight, I will show you this also. The
Day of Judgment is final and shows
to all the stamp of truth. Just as now
a father cannot send his son or a son

his father or a master his slave or a
friend his dearest friend to be sick for
[105]him, or sleep or eat or be cured, so no
one can pray for another then, or lay
a burden on another, for they must
all bear everyone his own iniquity or
uprightness then."
36 And I answered and said,
"How then do we now find that
first Abraham prayed for the men of
Sodom, and Moses for our forefathers
37 who sinned in the desert, and Joshua after him for Israel in the days
38 of Achan, and Samuel in the days of
Saul, and David for the plague, and
Solomon for those in the sanctuary,
39 and Elijah for those who received the
rain, and for one who was dead, that
40 he might live, and Hezekiah for the
people in the days of Sennacherib, and
41 many others for many? So if now,
when corruption has increased and
wrong has multiplied, the upright
have prayed for the ungodly, why
will it not be so then also?"
42 And he answered me and said,
"The present world is not the end,
and its glory is not lasting; therefore
those who were strong prayed for the
43 weak. But the Day of Judgment will
be the end of this world, and the beginning of the immortal world to
come, in which corruption has passed
44 away, immorality is ended, unbelief
is abolished, uprightness has increased, and truth has appeared.
45 So no one will then be able to pity one
who is condemned in the judgment, or
harm one who is victorious."
46 And I answered and said,
"This is my first and last word: for
it would have been better for the
earth not to have produced Adam,
or when it had produced him com-
47 pelled him not to sin. For what good
is it to all men to live in sorrow and
48 expect punishment after death? O
Adam, what have you done? For although it was you who sinned, the
fall was not yours alone, but also ours,
49 for we are descended from you. For
what good does it do us if the eternal
world is promised to us, but we have
50 done deeds that bring death? And
that an imperishable hope is proclaimed to us, but we have miserably
51 failed? And that safe and healthy
habitations are reserved for us, but
52 we have lived wickedly? And that
the glory of the Most High is going
to protect those who have lived purely, but we have walked in the most
wicked ways? And that a Paradise 53
will be revealed the fruit of which endures uncorrupted, which contains
plenty and healing, but we cannot
enter it, for we have lived in unseem- 54
ly ways? And that the faces of those 55
who have practiced abstinence will
shine brighter than the stars, but our
faces will be blacker than darkness?
For when we were alive and committed 56
iniquity, we did not consider what
we were to suffer after death."
And he answered and said, 57
"This is the meaning of the battle
that every man born on earth must
fight, that, if he is beaten, he will 58
suffer what you have said, but if he is
victorious, he will receive what I
say. For this is the way of which 59
Moses spoke, when he was alive, saying to the people, 'Choose life for
yourself, so that you may live!' But 60
they would not believe him or the
prophets after him, or yet me who
have spoken to them, so there will be 61
not so much grief at their destruction
as joy over those who have been persuaded of salvation."
And I answered and said, 62
"I know, sir, that the Most High
is now called merciful, because he has
mercy on those who have not yet
come into the world, and gracious, be- 63
cause he is gracious to those who turn
to his Law, and long-suffering, because 64
he is long-suffering to those who
have sinned as his creatures, and 65
bountiful, because he had rather give
than exact, and of great mercy, be- 66
cause he multiplies mercies more and
more to those who are alive and those
who have passed away and those who
are to be, for if he did not multiply 67
them, the world with those who live
in it would not be made alive, and a 68
giver, for if he did not give in his
goodness, so that those who have
committed iniquities might be relieved of them, not one ten-thou-
sandth of mankind could have life;
and a judge, for if he did not pardon 69
those who were created by his word,
and erase a multitude of offenses,
there would probably be left only very 70
few of the innumerable multitude."
And he answered me and said, 8

"The Most High made this world
for the sake of many, but the world to
2 come, for the sake of few. But I will
tell you a parable, Ezra. Just as, if
you ask the earth, it will tell you that
it produces much more soil from
which earthenware is made, but little
dust from which gold comes, that is
3 the way with the present world; many
have been created, but few will be
saved."
4 And I answered and said,
"Then drink down understanding,
my soul, and devour wisdom, my
5 heart! For not of your own will you
came, and against your will you go,
for you have been given only a short
6 time to live. O Lord above us, if you
will only allow your slave to pray before you, and would give us seed for
the heart and cultivation of the understanding so that fruit may be produced, by which a corruptible being,
who bears the image of man, may
7 live! For you stand alone, and we are
one creation of your hands, as you
8 have said. And when you bring to
life a body formed in the womb, and
provide its members, what you have
created is preserved in fire and water,
and for nine months what you have
formed endures your creation which
9 has been created in it. But that
which preserves and that which is
preserved are both preserved by your
preserving. And when the womb
gives up what has been created in it,
10 you have commanded that from the
members themselves, that is from
the breasts, milk, the fruit of the
11 breasts, be given, so that what has
been formed may be nourished for a
time. And afterward you develop it
12 in your mercy. You nourish it in your
uprightness, and instruct it through
your Law, and bring it up in your wis-
13 dom. You put it to death as your
creation, and make it live as your
14 work. If then you lightly destroy
him who was formed with such pains,
at your command, why was he made at
15 all? And now I will speak out: About
all mankind you know best; but it is
about your people that I am grieved,
16 and it is for your inheritance that I
mourn, and about Israel that I am
sad, and about the posterity of Jacob
17 that I am disturbed. Therefore I will
begin to pray before you for myself
and for them, for I see the failings of
us who live in the land and I have 18
heard of the strictness of the judgment that is to come. Therefore hear 19
my voice, and consider my words,
and I will speak before you."

The beginning of the words of the
prayer of Ezra, before he was taken
up. And he said,

"Lord, who inhabit eternity, whose 20
are the highest heavens, and whose
upper chambers are in the air, whose 21
throne is immeasurable, and whose
glory is beyond comprehension, before whom the hosts of angels stand
trembling, and at your command are 22
changed to wind and fire, whose word
is sure and whose utterances are
certain, whose command is mighty
and whose orders are terrible, whose 23
look dries up the depths, and whose
indignation melts the mountains, and
whose truth endures forever, hear, 24
Lord, the prayer of your slave, and
listen to the petition of your creature,
and heed my words; for as long as I 25
live I must speak, and as long as I
have my reason I must answer. Do 26
not look at the sins of your people,
but at those who have served you in
truth! And do not notice the pursuits 27
of the ungodly, but those who have
observed your agreements under torture. And do not think of those who 28
have behaved wickedly in your sight,
but remember those who have willingly acknowledged your fear. And do 29
not will the destruction of those who
have the ways of cattle, but have regard for those who have so finely
taught your Law. And do not be in- 30
dignant at those who are deemed
worse than beasts, but love those
who have always trusted in your
glory. For we and our forefathers 31
have followed ways that bring death,
but it is because of us sinners that you
are called merciful. For if you desire 32
to have pity on us, you will be called
merciful, for we have no deeds of uprightness to show. For the upright, 33
who have many good deeds laid up
with you, will receive their reward
in consequence of their own deeds.
For what is man, that you are in- 34
dignant at him, or what is a corruptible race, that you are so bitter
toward it? For in truth there is no 35
one among those who were ever born

who has not acted wickedly, or among
those who have grown up who has not
36 sinned. For in this, Lord, your uprightness and goodness will be declared, if you have mercy on those
who have no stock of good deeds."
37 And he answered me and said,
"Some things you have said well,
and it will come to pass in accordance
38 with your words. For indeed I will
not think about the forming of those
who have sinned, or their death or
39 judgment or destruction, but I will
rejoice over the fashioning of the upright, over their pilgrimage also, and
their salvation and the reward they
40 will receive. So it is as I have said.
41 For just as the farmer sows many
seeds upon the ground, and plants a
multitude of plants, and yet not all
that was sown will be saved in due
time, and not all that were planted
will take root, so those who are sown
in the world will not all be saved."
42 And I answered and said,
"If I have found favor before you,
43 I will speak. For if the farmer's seed
does not come up, because it has not
received your rain in season, or if it
has been spoiled by an excess of rain,
44 it perishes; but man, who was formed
by your hands and is called your
image, because he is made like you—
for whose sake you formed everything—do you compare him to the
45 farmer's seed? No, Lord above us,
but spare your people and have pity
on your inheritance, for you pity your
own creation."
46 And he answered me and said,
"The present for those who are
now, and the future for those who
47 shall be. For you are far from able to
love what I have created more than I.
But you have often counted yourself
48 among the ungodly. Never! But for
this you will be commended before
49 the Most High, because you humbled
yourself, as was fitting, and did not
count yourself among the upright,
so as to glorify yourself too much.
50 For those who inhabit the world in
the last times will be afflicted with
many great miseries, because they
51 have walked in great pride. But you
must think of yourself and ask about
the glory of those who are like your-
52 self. For it is for you that Paradise is
opened, the tree of life is planted, the
age to come is prepared, plenty is
provided, a city is built, a rest is
ordained, good deeds completed, wisdom perfected beforehand. The root 53
of evil is sealed up from you, for you
sickness is extinct, and death has departed; Hades has fled, and corruption has gone into oblivion; sorrows 54
have passed away, and the treasure
of immortality is finally displayed.
So do not ask any more questions 55
about the great number of those who
perish. For though they had re- 56
ceived liberty, they scorned the Most
High and despised his Law, and forsook his ways. Moreover they tram- 57
pled upon his saints and said in their 58
hearts that there was no God, though
they knew well that they must die.
For just as the things I have spoken 59
of await you, so the thirst and torment which are prepared await them.
For the Most High did not wish man
to perish, but those who were cre- 60
ated have themselves defiled the
name of him who made them, and
proved ungrateful to him who prepared life for them. Therefore my 61
judgment is now drawing near, but I 62
have not revealed it to all men, but
only to you and a few like you."
And I answered and said,
"Behold, Lord, you have revealed 63
to me the great number of signs
which you are going to perform in the
last days, but you have not revealed
to me at what time you will do this."
And he answered me and said, 9
"Measure it carefully within yourself, and it will be that when you see
that a certain part of the signs which
have been foretold have passed, then 2
you will understand that it is the very
time when the Most High is to visit
the world that was made by him.
So when there shall appear in the 3
world earthquakes, the tumult of
peoples, plots of the heathen, wavering of leaders, and confusion of
princes, then you will understand that 4
it was of these things that the Most
High spoke from the days that were
of old, from the beginning. For just 5
as with everything that has happened in the world, the beginning is
plain and the end manifest, so also 6
are the times of the Most High; the
beginnings are signalized by wonders
and mighty works, and the end by

7 acts and signs. And it will be that
everyone who will be saved, and who
is able to escape by reason of his
deeds or his faith, by which he be-
8 lieved, will survive the dangers I
have foretold, and will see my salvation in my land, and within my
borders which I have consecrated to
9 myself from eternity. Then those
who have now neglected my ways
will be amazed, and those who have
rejected them with contempt will
10 abide in torment. For as many as
failed to acknowledge me in their
lifetime, though they received my
11 benefits, and as many as disdained
my Law, while they still had freedom,
and while an opportunity to repent
was still open to them, did not under-
12 stand but scorned it, these must
recognize it after death, through tor-
13 ment. So you must no longer be
curious as to how the ungodly will be
punished, but ask how the righteous
will be saved, to whom that age belongs and for the sake of whom it was
made."
14 I answered and said,
15 "I said before, and say now, and
will say again, there are more that
16 perish than that will be saved, as a
wave is greater than a drop of water."
17 And he answered me and said,
"As is the field, so is the seed,
and as are the flowers, so are the
colors, and as is the work, so is it
judged, and as is the farmer, so is the
threshing-floor. For there was a time
18 in the ages of eternity, when I was
preparing for those who now are, before the world was made for them to
19 live in, and no one opposed me then,
for there was no one else; but now
those who have been created in this
world which is provided with an unfailing table and an inexhaustible
pasture, have become corrupt in their
20 characters. So I considered my world,
and, behold, it was lost; and my universe, and, behold, it was in danger,
because of the devices of those who
21 had come into it. And I saw, and
spared them, not very greatly, and
saved myself one grape out of a
cluster, and one plant out of a forest.
22 So let the multitude perish, that were
born in vain, but let my grape be
saved, and my plant, because with
much labor I have perfected them.
But if you will let seven days more 23
pass but not fast in them, but go to a 24
flowery field, where no house is built,
and eat only of the flowers of the
field, and taste no meat and drink no
wine, but only flowers, and will pray 25
to the Most High continually, I will
come and talk with you."
So I went as he told me, to the field 26
called Ardat, and I sat there among
the flowers, and ate the wild plants,
and the food they afforded satisfied
me. And it came to pass after seven 27
days that as I lay on the grass my
heart was troubled as it had been before. Then my mouth was opened, 28
and I began to speak before the
Most High, and said,
"O Lord, you surely showed your- 29
self to our forefathers in the desert
when they came out of Egypt and
went into the desert, which was un-
trodden and unproductive, and you 30
surely said, 'Israel, hear me, and
mark my words, posterity of Jacob.
For behold, I sow my Law in you, and 31
it will bring forth fruit in you, and
you will be glorified through it forever.' But our forefathers who re- 32
ceived the Law did not keep it, and
did not observe the statutes, yet the
fruit of the Law did not perish, for it
could not, because it was yours;
but those who had received it per- 33
ished, because they had not kept
what had been sown in them. And, 34
behold, it is the rule that when the
earth has received seed, or the sea a
ship, or any dish food or drink, and
when it comes about that what was
sown or what was launched or what
was put in is destroyed, they are de- 35
stroyed, but the things which contained them remain. But with us it
has not been so; we who received the 36
Law will perish because we sinned,
along with our heart which received
it; but the Law does not perish, but 37
abides in its glory."
When I said this to myself, I lifted 38
up my eyes and saw a woman at my
right, and behold, she was weeping
and wailing aloud, and was deeply
grieved at heart, and her clothes were
torn, and she had ashes on her head.
And I dismissed the thoughts I had 39
been thinking, and turned to her
and said to her, 40

"Why do you weep, and why are
you grieved at heart?"
41 And she said to me,
"Let me weep over myself, my
lord, and continue to mourn, for I am
greatly embittered in spirit and deeply afflicted."
42 And I said to her,
"What has happened to you? Tell
me."
43 And she said to me,
"Your servant was barren and had
no child, though I had a husband for
44 thirty years. And every day and
hour, those thirty years, I prayed to
45 the Most High, night and day. Then
after thirty years it came about that
God heard your servant, and looked
on my affliction and gave heed to my
distress and gave me a son. And I rejoiced greatly over him, I and my husband and all my neighbors, and we
paid great honor to the Mighty One.
46 And I brought him up with great
47 care. And it came about, when he
was grown up, that I proceeded to
take a wife for him, and made a marriage feast.
10 "And it came about that when my
son entered his wedding chamber, he
2 fell down and died. And we all overturned the lights, and all my neighbors rose up to comfort me, and I was
quiet until evening the second day.
3 And it came about, when they had all
stopped comforting me, to quiet me,
that I got up in the night, and fled,
and came to this field, as you see.
4 And now I plan not to return to the
city, but to stay here, and I will not
eat or drink, but mourn and fast
continually until I die."
5 Then I broke off the reflections
with which I was still occupied, and
answered her in anger and said,
6 "You most foolish of all women,
can you not see our sorrow, and what
7 has happened to us? For Zion, the
mother of us all, is afflicted with grief
8 and in deep humiliation. Now lament
bitterly, for we are all lamenting, and
be sad, for we are all sad, but you
9 sorrow for just one son. For ask the
earth, and she will tell you that it is
she who ought to mourn over so many
who have come into being upon her.
10 And from the beginning all have been
born of her and others will come, and,
behold, almost all of them go to perdition, and the most of them are
destined to destruction. Who there- 11
fore ought to mourn more, if not she,
who has lost such a multitude, rather
than you, who sorrow for only one?
But if you say to me, 'My lamenta- 12
tion is not like the earth's, for I have
lost the fruit of my womb, which I
bore with pain and brought forth
with sorrow; but it is with the earth 13
after the manner of the earth; the
multitude that is now in it goes as it
came'; then I say to you, 'As you 14
brought forth with pain, so the earth
also has from the beginning given her
fruit, man, to him who made her.'
So keep your sorrow to yourself, and 15
bear bravely the misfortunes that
have overtaken you. For if you ac- 16
cept the judgment of God, you will
receive your son back in due time,
and be praised among women. So go 17
into the city to your husband."
And she said to me, 18
"I will not do it, or enter the city,
but I will die here."
Then I proceeded to speak to her 19
further, and said,
"Do not do that, but let yourself be 20
persuaded because of the misfortunes
of Zion, and be comforted because of
the sorrow of Jerusalem. For you see 21
that our sanctuary has been laid
waste, and our altar torn down, and
our temple destroyed, and our harp 22
is brought low, and our song is silenced, and our rejoicing has ceased,
and the light of our lamp is put out,
and the chest of our agreement is
plundered, and our sacred things are
polluted, and the name by which we
have been called is profaned, our children are abused, and our priests are
burned, and our Levites have gone
into captivity, and our girls are defiled, and our wives are ravished, and
our upright men are carried off, and
our little ones are exposed, and our
young men are enslaved, and our
strong men are made weak. And 23
worst of all is the seal of Zion, for she
is now sealed up from her glory, and
delivered into the hands of those who
hate us. So shake off your great sad- 24
ness and lay aside your many sorrows,
so that the Mighty One may become
gracious to you, and the Most High
may give you rest, and relief from
your troubles."

25 And it came to pass, as I spoke to
her, that her face suddenly shone exceedingly
and the look of her countenance
flashed like lightning, so that
I was too greatly frightened to go
near her, and wondered what it could
26 mean. And behold, she suddenly
gave a loud and fearful cry, so that
27 the earth shook at the sound. And I
looked, and behold the woman no
longer appeared to me, but a city was
being built and a place of huge
foundations showed itself; and I was
afraid, and cried aloud and said,
28 "Where is the angel Uriel, who
came to me at first? For it was he
who brought me into this great bewilderment;
my end has become corruption,
and my prayer a reproach!"
29 And as I said this, behold, the
angel who had come to me at first,
30 came to me, and saw me; and, behold,
I lay there like a corpse, and I had
lost my reason, and he took my right
hand, and steadied me, and helped
me to my feet, and said to me,
31 "What is the matter with you, and
why are you troubled, and why are
your understanding and the thinking
of your mind confused?"
32 And I said,
"Because you utterly abandoned
me. I did as you told me, and went
out to the field, and behold, I looked,
and I saw what I cannot describe."
33 And he said to me,
"Stand up like a man, and I will instruct you."
34 And I said,
"Speak, my lord, only do not
abandon me, so that I may not die in
35 vain. For I have seen what I did not
know, and I heard what I do not
36 understand. Is my mind deceived, or
37 my soul dreaming? Now therefore I
beseech you to explain to your slave
about this confusion."
38 And he answered me and said,
"Listen to me, and I will teach you,
and tell you about the things of which
you are afraid, for the Most High has
39 revealed many secrets to you. For he
has seen your rectitude, and that you
have sorrowed continually for your
people and lamented bitterly over
40 Zion. This then is the meaning of the
41 vision: The woman who appeared to
you a little while ago, whom you saw
42 mourning and began to comfort, but
whom you then saw not in the form of
a woman, but she appeared to you as
a city that was being built, and as to 43
what she told you about the misfortune
of her son, this is the explanation:
The woman that you saw, 44
whom you now see as a city that is
built, is Zion! And as for her telling 45
you that she was barren for thirty
years, that was because there were
three thousand years when no offering
was yet offered in her; and it came 46
to pass that after three thousand
years Solomon built the city and
offered sacrifices; it was then that the
barren woman bore a son. And as for 47
her telling you that she brought him
up with care, that was the period of
residence in Jerusalem. And as for 48
her saying to you, 'As my son was
going into the marriage chamber, he
died,' and that misfortune had overtaken
her, that was the fall of Jerusalem
that has taken place. And, be- 49
hold, you saw her face and how she
mourned for her son, and you began
to comfort her for what had happened.
And now the Most High see- 50
ing that you are deeply grieved, and
are whole-heartedly distressed for her,
has shown you the splendor of her
glory and the charm of her beauty.
It was on this account that I told you 51
to stay in the field where no house
was built, for I knew that the Most 52
High was going to reveal these things
to you. That was why I told you to 53
go into the field, where there was no
foundation of a building, for no work 54
built by man could stand in the place
where the city of the Most High was
to be revealed. So do not be afraid, 55
or terrified at heart, but go in, and
see the splendor and greatness of the
building, as far as the sight of your
eyes can see. And afterward you will 56
hear as much as the hearing of your
ears can hear. For you are more 57
blessed than many, and you have
been called by the Most High as few
have been. But tomorrow night you 58
must stay here, and the Most High 59
will show you in dreams those visions
of what the Most High is going to do
in the last days to those who live on
the earth."

So I slept that night and the following
one, as he had commanded me.
And it came to pass on the second **11**

night that I had a dream, and behold,
there came up out of the sea an eagle,
with twelve feather-covered wings
2 and three heads. And I looked, and
behold he spread his wings over the
whole earth, and all the winds of
heaven blew upon him, and the clouds
3 gathered about him. And I looked,
and out of his wings grew additional
wings, and they became small, dwarf-
4 ish wings. But his heads were resting;
the middle head was greater than the
other heads, but it was resting like
5 them. And I looked, and behold, the
eagle flew with his wings, to reign over
the earth, and over those who live
6 on it. And I saw that everything
under heaven was subject to him,
and no one opposed him, nor any
creature that was on the earth.
7 And I looked and, behold, the eagle
rose upon his talons, and uttered his
voice to his wings, saying,
8 "Do not all watch at once, sleep
each in his own place, and watch by
9 turns; but let the heads be reserved
for the last."
10 And I looked, and behold, the
voice did not come from his heads but
11 from the midst of his body. And I
counted his additional wings, and be-
12 hold, there were eight of them. And
I looked, and behold, on the right
side, one wing arose and it reigned
13 over the whole earth. And it came to
pass, after it had reigned, that it
came to an end, and disappeared,
so that even the place where it had
been could not be seen. Then the
second arose and reigned, and it ruled
14 a long time. And it came to pass,
after it had reigned, that it also came
to an end, so that it disappeared like
15 the first. And behold a voice was
heard, saying to it,
16 "Listen, you who have ruled the
earth so long, I make this proclamation to you before you begin to disap-
17 pear: No one after you will rule as
long as you have ruled, or even half
as long!"
18 Then the third wing raised itself
up, and ruled like the former ones,
19 and it also disappeared. And so it fell
to all the wings, one by one to be
emperor, and then to disappear again.
20 And I looked, and behold, in due
time, the additional wings on the
right side raised themselves up, in
order to be emperor, and there were
some of them who succeeded but immediately disappeared, and some of 21
them raised themselves up, but did
not remain emperor. And afterward 22
I looked, and behold, the twelve
wings and two little wings disappeared, and nothing was left on the 23
eagle's body except the three heads
that were resting and six little wings.
And I looked, and behold, from the 24
six little wings two separated, and
stayed under the head that was on the
right side; but four stayed in their
places. And I looked, and behold, 25
these four additional wings planned
to raise themselves up and be emper-
ors. And I looked, and behold, one 26
raised itself up, and immediately disappeared; and a second, and it dis- 27
appeared more quickly than the first.
And I looked, and behold, the two 28
that were left also planned to reign;
but while they were planning it, be- 29
hold, the one of the resting heads
that was in the middle awoke, for it
was greater than the other two
heads; and I saw how the two heads 30
were united with it; and behold, the 31
head turned with the ones that were
with it, and it ate up the additional
wings which planned to reign. More- 32
over, this head made itself master of
the whole earth, and ruled very oppressively over its inhabitants, and it
had more power over the world than
all the wings that had gone before.
And afterward I looked, and behold, 33
the middle head suddenly disappeared, just as the wings had done.
But the two heads remained, and 34
they also reigned over the earth and
over its inhabitants. And I looked, 35
and behold, the head on the right
side ate up the one on the left.
Then I heard a voice saying to me, 36
"Look before you, and think about
what you see."
And I looked, and behold, what 37
seemed to be a lion rose out of the
forest roaring, and I heard how he
uttered a man's voice to the eagle,
and spoke saying,
"Listen, and I will speak to you. 38
The Most High says to you, 'Are you 39
not all that is left of the four animals
that I made to reign in my world, so
that through them the end of my
times might come? And you are the 40

fourth to come, and you have conquered all the animals that are past,
and you have held the world in subjection in great terror, and the whole
earth with harsh oppression, and you
have lived so long in the world with
41 deceit; and you have not judged the
42 earth with truth. You have persecuted the meek and hurt the peaceable, you have hated those who tell
the truth, and loved liars, and you
have destroyed the dwellings of the
fruitful, and torn down the walls of
43 those who did you no harm. And
your insolence has reached the Most
High and your pride the Mighty One.
44 And the Most High has looked at his
times, and behold, they are ended,
45 and his ages are completed! Therefore you will surely disappear, you
eagle, and your dreadful wings, and
your wicked additional wings, and
your malignant heads, and your cruel
talons, and your whole worthless
46 body, so that the whole earth may be
freed from your violence, and be refreshed and relieved, and hope for
the justice and mercy of him who
made her."

12 And it came to pass, while the lion
was saying these words to the eagle
2 that I looked, and behold, the head
that had been left disappeared, and
the two wings which had gone over
to it lifted themselves up to reign,
and their reign was short and full
3 of uproar. And I looked, and behold,
they also disappeared, and the whole
body of the eagle was burned, and
the earth was panic-stricken.

Then, because of great disturbance
of mind and great fear, I awoke, and
I said to my spirit,

4 "Behold, you have brought this
upon me, because you try to search
out the ways of the Most High!
5 Behold, I am still weary in mind and
very weak in my spirit, and there is
not the least strength left in me, because of the great fear which I felt
6 this night. So now I will intreat the
Most High to strengthen me to the
end."

7 And I said,

"Sovereign Lord, if I have found
favor in your sight, and if I am
counted upright by you beyond
many, and if my prayer has indeed
8 come up before your face, strengthen
me, and show your slave the meaning and explanation of this dreadful
vision, so as to comfort my soul fully.
For you have thought me worthy to 9
be shown the end of the times and the
last of them."

And he said to me, 10

"This is the meaning of this vision
that you have seen: As for the eagle 11
that you saw rising from the sea, it is
the fourth kingdom that appeared in
a vision to your brother Daniel. But 12
it was not explained to him as I now
explain it to you or have explained
it. Behold, the days are coming when 13
a kingdom will rise on the earth, and
it will be more terrible than all the
kingdoms that were before it. More- 14
over, twelve kings will reign over it,
one after another. But the second 15
who is to reign will rule longer than
the twelve. This is the meaning of the 16
twelve wings that you saw. And as 17
for your hearing a voice that spoke,
that came not from his heads but
from the middle of his body, this is
the meaning: In the midst of the 18
time of the kingdom no small strug-
gles will arise, and it will be in danger
of falling, but it will not fall then,
but will regain its former power.
And as for your seeing eight addition- 19
al wings springing from his wings,
this is the meaning. For eight kings 20
will rise in it, whose times will be
short and whose years will be fleeting,
and two of them will fall when the 21
middle of its time draws near; but
four will be preserved for the time
when the time of its end begins to
approach; but two will be kept until
the end. And as for your seeing the 22
three heads resting, this is the meaning: In its last days the Most High 23
will raise up three kings, and they
will renew many things in it, and will
distress the earth and those who live 24
in it, with greater oppression than all
who were before them. That is why
they are called the eagle's heads. For 25
it is they that will bring his wickedness to a head and will bring him to
his end. And as for your seeing the 26
greater head disappear—one of them
will die in his bed, but in torment.
But as for the two who were left, the 27
sword will devour them. For the 28
sword of one of them will devour the
one who was with him, but he too will

29 fall by the sword in the last days. And
as for your seeing two additional
wings crossing over to the head on
30 the right side, this is the meaning: It
is these that the Most High has kept
for the eagle's end, for their reign was
short and full of disturbance, as you
31 saw. And as for the lion that you saw
roused roaring out of the forest, and
speaking to the eagle, and rebuking
him for his wickedness and all his
32 words that you have heard, he is the
Anointed One, whom the Most High
has kept until the end of the days,
who will spring from the posterity of
David and come and talk with them.
He will charge them with their ungodliness and rebuke them for their
wickedness, and reproach them to
their faces with their transgressions.
33 For first he will set them alive before
his judgment seat, and when he has
rebuked them, he will destroy them.
34 But my people who remain he will
mercifully set free, who remain in my
borders, and he will make them glad
until the end comes, the Day of Judgment, of which I told you at the be-
35 ginning. This is the dream that you
36 had, and this is its meaning. But you
alone were worthy to know the secret
37 of the Most High. So write all that
you have seen in a book, and put it in
38 a secret place, and teach them to the
wise among your people, whose hearts
you know can receive and keep these
39 secrets. But you must stay here sev-
en days more, so that you may be
shown whatever it pleases the Most
High to show you."
40 Then he departed from me. And it
came about that when all the people
had heard that the seven days had
passed and I had not returned to the
city, they all gathered together, from
the least to the greatest, and came to
me and spoke to me saying,
41 "How have we sinned against you,
and what harm have we done you,
that you have entirely abandoned us,
42 and stay in this place? For of all the
prophets, you alone are left to us,
like a grape cluster out of the vintage,
and like a lamp in a dark place, and
like a safe harbor for a ship in a
43 storm. Are not the evils that have
44 befallen us enough? So if you abandon us, how much better it would have
been for us if we too had been burned
in the burning of Zion! For we are no 45
better than those who died there."
And they wept aloud.
And I answered them and said,
"Have courage, Israel, and do not 46
be sorrowful, you house of Jacob.
For you are remembered before the 47
Most High, and the Mighty One will
never forget you. For I have not 48
abandoned you or withdrawn from
you, but I came to this place to pray
over the desolation of Zion, and to
ask for mercy in view of the degrada-
tion of our sanctuary. And now go 49
home, every one of you, and when
these days are over, I will come to
you."
And the people went back to the 50
city, as I told them to do. But I 51
stayed in the field for seven days, as
he had commanded me, and I ate
only of the flowers of the field: my
food was vegetables in those days.
And it came about after seven days 13
that in the night I dreamed a dream,
and behold a wind arose from the 2
sea, so that it stirred up all its waves.
And I looked, and behold, the wind 3
brought out of the heart of the sea
something like the figure of a man,
and this man flew with the clouds of
heaven, and wherever he turned his
face to look, everything that was
seen by him trembled, and wherever 4
the voice went from his mouth, all
who heard his voice melted as wax
melts when it feels the fire. And after 5
that I looked, and behold, an innumerable multitude of men was gathered together from the four winds of
heaven, to make war upon the man
who had come up out of the sea. And 6
I looked, and behold, he carved himself out a great mountain, and flew
up upon it. But I sought to see the 7
region or place from which the mountain had been carved, and I could
not. And after that I looked, and be- 8
hold, all who had gathered together
against him, to fight with him, were
much afraid, but dared to fight.
And behold, when he saw the onset of 9
the multitude that approached, he
did not raise his hand, or hold a
sword, or any weapon of war, but I 10
saw only how he sent out of his
mouth what looked like a flood of
fire, and out of his lips a flaming
breath, and from his tongue he sent

11 forth a storm of sparks. These were
all mixed together, the flood of fire,
and the flaming breath, and the
mighty storm, and it fell upon the
onset of the multitude which was
ready to fight, and burned them all
up, so that suddenly there was nothing to be seen of the countless multitude but the dust of their ashes and
the smell of smoke. When I saw it, I
12 was amazed. Afterward I saw this
man come down from the mountain,
and call to him another multitude
13 that was peaceable. Then many people came to him, some joyful, some
sorrowful, some in fetters, some bringing offerings.

Then in an excess of fear I awoke,
and besought the Most High, and
said,

14 "You have shown your slave these
wonders from the beginning, and
have thought me worthy to have my
15 prayer heard by you. Now show me
further the meaning of this dream!
16 For as I think of it in my mind, alas
for those who will be left in those
days, and alas much more for those
17 who are not left! For those who are
18 not left will be sad, since they know
what is reserved for the last days,
but cannot attain them. But alas
19 for those who are left, too, for this
reason, for they must experience
great dangers and much distress, as
20 these dreams show. Yet it is better,
for all the danger, to attain these
things, than to pass from the world
like a cloud, and not to see what will
happen at the end."

And he answered me and said,

21 "I will tell you the meaning of the
vision, and I will reveal to you the
22 things of which you speak. As for
what you say about those who are
23 left, this is the meaning: He who occasions the danger at that time will
guard those who are exposed to danger, who have works, and faith in the
24 Almighty. So you must understand
that those who are left are more
blessed than those who have died.
25 This is the meaning of the vision: As
for your seeing a man come up from
26 the heart of the sea, he is the one
whom the Most High has kept a long
time, through whom he will redeem
his creation; and he will organize
27 those who are left. And as for your
seeing wind and fire and storm issue
from his mouth, and as for his not 28
holding a sword or a weapon of war,
but destroying the onset of the multitude that came to subdue him, this is
the meaning: Behold, the days are 29
coming when the Most High is going
to deliver those who are on the earth,
and amazement will come upon those 30
who live on the earth, and they will 31
plan to make war one upon another,
city upon city and place upon place,
people upon people, and kingdom
upon kingdom. And it will come 32
about, when this happens, that the
signs will occur which I showed you
before, and my Son will be revealed,
whom you saw as a man coming up.
And it will come about, when all the 33
nations hear his voice, that every man
will leave his country and the wars
that they have with one another, and 34
a countless multitude such as you
saw will be gathered together, wishing to come and subdue him. But he 35
will stand on the top of Mount Zion.
And Zion will come and be revealed 36
to all men, made ready and built, like
the mountain that you saw carved
out without hands. And my Son will 37
charge the heathen who have come
with their ungodliness (this was symbolized by the storm), and will up- 38
braid them to their face with their
evil thoughts and the tortures with
which they are to be tortured (which
were symbolized by the flame), and
he will destroy them without effort
by the Law (which is symbolized by
the fire). And as for your seeing him 39
gather about himself another multitude that was peaceable, these are the 40
ten tribes that in the days of King
Hoshea were carried away from their
own land into captivity, whom Shalmaneser, king of Assyria, made captives, and carried beyond the river;
they were carried off to another country. But they formed this plan among 41
themselves, to leave the heathen population, and go to a more distant region, where the human race had never
lived, so that there perhaps they 42
might keep their statutes, which they
had not kept in their own country.
And they went in by the narrow pas- 43
sages of the Euphrates River. For the 44
Most High then did wonders for
them, for he held back the sources of

the river until they had passed over.
45 But it was a long journey of a year
and a half to that country, and that
46 country is called Arzareth. There
they have lived until the last time,
and now, when they are about to
47 come again, the Most High will hold
back the sources of the river again,
so that they can cross over. It is on
that account that you saw the multitude gathered together in peace.
48 But those also who are left of your
people, who are found within my
49 holy borders, will live. Therefore it
will be that when he destroys the
multitude of the nations that are
gathered together, he will protect the
50 people that remain, and then he will
show them many, many wonders."

51 And I said,

"Sovereign Lord, show me this—
why I saw a man come up from the
heart of the sea."

52 And he said to me,

"Just as no one can seek out or
know what is in the depth of the sea,
so no one on earth can see my Son, or
those who are with him, except at the
53 time of his Day. This is the meaning
of the dream that you had. And you
alone have been enlightened about
54 these things, because you have forsaken your own affairs and devoted
yourself to mine, and have sought
55 after my Law, for you have devoted
your life to wisdom and called under-
56 standing your mother. That is why
I have shown you this, for there is reward with the Most High! For it
will be that after three more days I
will say other things to you, and declare weighty and wonderful matters
to you."

57 Then I went away and walked in
the field, greatly glorifying and praising the Most High for the wonders
58 that he does from time to time, and
because he directs the times and the
things that take place in the times.
And I stayed there three days.

14 And it came to pass on the third
day, as I sat under an cak, behold, a
voice came from a bush in front of
me, and said,

"Ezra, Ezra!"

2 And I said,

"Here I am, sir!"

3 And I rose to my feet, and he said
to me,

"I revealed myself visibly in the
bush, and talked with Moses, when
my people was in slavery in Egypt,
and I sent him, and led my people 4
out of Egypt, and brought them to
Mount Sinai, and kept him with me
many days, and told him many won- 5
derful things, and showed him the
secrets of the times, and the end of
the times, and commanded him, saying,

" 'These words you must publish 6
openly, and those you must keep secret.' And now I tell you, the signs 7, 8
that I have shown you, and the
dreams that you have had, and the
meaning of them that you have
heard, lay up in your heart! For you 9
will be taken up from among men,
and henceforth you will live with my
Son and those who are like you, until
the times are ended. For the world 10
has lost its youth, and the times are
beginning to grow old. For the life 11
of the world is divided into twelve
parts, and nine parts and half of the
tenth part are already past, and there 12
are left two parts and half of the
tenth part. Now therefore put your 13
house in order, and warn your people,
comfort the humble among them,
and teach those who are wise, and
now renounce the life that perishes,
and dismiss from your mind mortal 14
considerations, and throw off the
burdens of human existence, and lay
aside your weak nature, and put 15
away your perplexities, and hasten
to escape from these times. For worse 16
evils are still to come than those you
have seen happen. For the more the 17
world grows weak with age, the more
evils will increase upon those who live
in it. Truth will more and more re- 18
tire, and falsehood draw near. For
the eagle that you saw in your vision
is already hastening to come."

And I answered and said, 19

"Let me speak before you, sir! For 20
behold, I will go away, as you have
commanded me, and I will warn the
people who are now living; but who
will warn those who are still to be
born? For the world lies in darkness,
and those who live in it have no light;
for your Law is burnt, and so no one 21
knows what has been done by you or
what is going to be done. But if I 22
have found favor before you, impart

to me the holy Spirit, and I will write
all that has happened in the world
since the beginning, which were written in your Law, so that men can
find the path, and those who wish to
live in the last times may live."
23 And he answered me and said,
"Go, gather the people together,
and tell them not to look for you for
24 forty days. But you must prepare for
yourself many writing tablets, and
take with you Seraiah, Dabria,
Shelemiah, Elkanah, and Asiel, who
25 are able to write swiftly. And you
are to come here, and I will light the
lamp of understanding in your heart,
and it will not be put out until the
things you are to write are finished.
26 And when you have finished, some
things you shall publish and some you
shall hand down secretly to the wise.
At this hour tomorrow you shall begin to write."
27 And I went as he commanded me,
and gathered all the people together,
and said,
28,29 "Israel, hear these words. Our forefathers lived in Egypt as strangers at
first, and they were delivered from
30 there, and received the Law of life,
which they did not observe, which
you also transgressed after them.
31 Then land was given you to possess
in the country of Zion, but you and
your forefathers acted unrighteously
and did not observe the ways which
the Most High commanded you to
32 keep; and, as he is an upright judge,
he took from you what he had given
33 you in his own time. And now you
are here, and your brothers are in the
34 interior. If therefore you will rule
your mind and instruct your heart,
you will be preserved while you live,
35 and obtain mercy after death. For
after death will come the judgment,
when we will live again, and then the
names of the upright will appear and
the deeds of the ungodly will be dis-
36 closed. But let no one come near me
now, or look for me for forty days."
37 Then I took the five men, as he
commanded me, and we went to the
38 field, and stayed there. And it came
to pass the next day that a voice
called me, and said,
"Ezra, open your mouth, and
drink what I give you to drink."
39 And I opened my mouth, and, behold, a full cup was offered me. It
was full of what looked like water,
but the color of it was like fire. And 40
I took it, and drank, and when I
had drunk it, my heart gushed forth
understanding, and wisdom grew in
my breast, for my spirit retained its
memory, and my mouth opened and 41
was no longer closed. Moreover, the 42
Most High gave understanding to the
five men, and they wrote what was
said, one after another, in letters that
they did not know. And they stayed
forty days; they wrote in the daytime, and ate their bread at night; but 43
I spoke by day and was not silent
at night. In forty days ninety-four 44
books were written. And it came to 45
pass, when the forty days were over,
that the Most High spoke to me and
said,
"Publish the twenty-four books
that you wrote first, for the worthy
and the unworthy to read, but keep 46
the seventy books that were written
last, to hand down to the wise men
among your people, for in them is the 47
source of understanding, and the
spring of wisdom, and the stream of
knowledge." And I did so, [in the 48
seventh year, in the sixth week, after
five thousand years of the creation,
and three months and twelve days.

Then Ezra was caught up, and
taken to the land of those who were
like him, after he had written all this.
And he was called the scribe of the
knowledge of the Most High forever
and ever.]

(*The oriental versions end with this bracketed conclusion, which is absent from the Latin.*)

"Behold, speak in the hearing of my 15
people the words of prophecy which
I will put in your mouth," says the
Lord, "and have them written on 2
paper, for they are trustworthy and
true. Do not fear what they imagine 3
against you, or let the unbelief of
those who oppose you trouble you.
For all unbelievers will die in their un- 4
belief.
"Behold," says the Lord, "I will 5
bring evils upon the whole world, the
sword and famine and death and destruction. For wickedness has spread 6
over the whole earth, and their harmful doings are complete. Therefore," 7
says the Lord, "I will not be silent 8

any longer about their ungodly acts
which they impiously commit, or endure them in their wicked practices.
Behold, innocent and upright blood
cries to me, and the souls of the up-
9 right cry out continually. I will certainly avenge them," says the Lord,
"and all innocent blood I will require
10 of them for myself. Behold, my people is led to slaughter like a flock; I
will not suffer them to live in the
11 land of Egypt any longer, but I will
bring them out with a strong hand
and an outstretched arm, and I will
strike Egypt with plague as I did be-
12 fore, and destroy all its land. Let
Egypt lament, and its foundations,
for the plague of punishment and correction that the Lord will bring upon
13 it. Let the farmers who cultivate the
soil lament, for their grain will fail,
and their trees will be destroyed by
14 blight and hail and a fearful star. Alas
for the world and those who live in
15 it! For the sword and their destruction have drawn near, and nation will
rise against nation to fight, with
16 swords in their hands. For there will
be inconstancy among men; they
will grow strong, one party against
another, and have no regard for their
king or the chief of their princes, in
17 their strength. For a man will want
to enter a city, and will not be able.
18 For because of their pride, the cities
will be in confusion, the houses will
be wiped out, men will be afraid.
19 A man will not have pity on his neighbor, when it comes to making an attack on their houses with the sword,
and plundering their property, because of hunger for bread, and because of great distress.

20 "Behold, I will call together," says
God, "all the kings of the earth, to
fear me, from the sunrise and from
the south, from the east and from
Lebanon, to turn and give back what
21 they have given them. For as they
have done unto this day to my chosen,
I will do, and will pay it back into
their laps." This is what the Lord
22 God says: "My right hand will not
spare the sinners, and my sword will
not cease from those who shed inno-
23 cent blood on the earth." And a fire
went forth from his wrath, and consumed the foundations of the earth
and the sinners like burnt straw.
"Alas for those who sin, and do not 24
keep my commandments," says the
Lord; "I will not spare them. Begone, 25
you rebellious sons, do not pollute
my sanctuary." For the Lord knows 26
all who offend against him, therefore
he has given them up to die and to be
killed. For now disasters have come 27
upon the whole world, and you will
stay among them, for God will not deliver you, because you have sinned
against him.

Behold, a dreadful vision, appear- 28
ing from the east! And the nations of 29
Arabian serpents will come out with
many chariots, and from the day they
set out, their hissing will be carried
over the earth, so that all who hear
them will fear and tremble. The Car- 30
monians will come out frantic with
anger, like wild boars from the forest,
and they will come in great strength,
and engage them in battle, and will
lay waste a part of the land of Assyria
with their teeth. And afterward the 31
serpents, mindful of their origin, will
prevail, and if they conspire in great
strength and turn to pursue them,
they also will be thrown into confu- 32
sion and be silenced by their strength,
and turn and flee. And from the land 33
of Assyria a waylayer will beset them
and destroy one of them, and fear
and trembling will come upon their
army, and indecision upon their
kings.

Behold, clouds from the east, and 34
from the north to the south, and
their appearance is very dreadful, full
of wrath and storm; and they will 35
strike against one another, and will
shed an abundance of stars upon the
earth, and their own star, and there
will be blood from the sword up to a
horse's belly and a man's thigh and a 36
camel's hock, and there will be great 37
fear and trembling on the earth, and
those who witness that wrath will
shudder, and trembling will seize
them. And, after that, heavy rain- 38
storms will come from the south and
the north, and another part from the
west. And winds from the east will 39
grow strong, and will reveal it, and
the cloud that he raised in his wrath,
and the star will be driven violently
from the east to the south and west
to produce destruction. And great 40
clouds will rise, huge and angry, with

the star, to destroy all the earth and
its inhabitants, and they will pour
over every deep and height a dread-
41 ful star, fire and hail and flying
swords and floods of water, so that
all the fields and streams will be
filled with the abundance of those
42 waters. And they will break down
cities and walls and mountains and
hills and forest trees and grass in the
43 meadows and their grain. And they
will cross over steadily to Babylon
44 and destroy her. They will come to
her and surround her and pour out
the star and all its wrath upon her,
and the dust and smoke will go up to
heaven, and they will all lament her,
45 round about her. And those who survive will serve those who have destroyed her.
46 And you, Asia, partner of the
beauty of Babylon, and the glory of
47 her person, alas for you, poor wretch,
because you have become like her;
you have ornamented your daughters
in immorality to please and glory in
your lovers, who have always desired
48 you! You have imitated that hateful
adulteress in all her deeds and devices. Therefore, God says,
49 "I will send misfortunes upon you,
widowhood, poverty, famine, the
sword, pestilence, to lay waste your
houses and bring them to destruction
50 and death. And the glory of your
strength will dry up like a flower,
when the heat that is directed upon
51 you rises. And you will grow weak
like a poor creature beaten with
stripes and wounds, so that you cannot receive your heroes and lovers.
52 Would I act against you with such
53 zeal," says the Lord, "if you had not
always killed my chosen, exulting and
clapping your hands, and speaking
over their dead bodies, drunk as you
54 were? So adorn the beauty of your
55 face! A prostitute's wages will be in
your lap, so you will receive your rec-
56 ompense. As you shall do to my
chosen," says the Lord, "so God will
do to you, and he will deliver you to
57 misfortunes. And your children will
die of hunger, and you will fall by the
sword, and your cities will be destroyed and all your people in the
58 country will fall by the sword, and
those who are in the mountains will
perish with hunger, and will eat their
own flesh and drink their own blood
in their hunger for bread and thirst
for water. Unhappy beyond others, 59
you will come and endure fresh afflictions. And as they pass by they will 60
crush the unprofitable city, and destroy a part of your land, and do
away with a portion of your glory, as
they return from the destruction of
Babylon. And you will be demol- 61
ished by them like stubble, and they
will be like fire to you. And they will 62
devour you and your cities, your land
and your mountains, all your forests
and fruit trees they will burn with
fire. They will carry your sons away 63
as captives, and take your wealth as
plunder, and spoil the beauty of your
face."
Alas for you, Babylon and Asia! 16
Alas for you, Egypt and Syria! Put 2
on sackcloth and haircloth, and bewail your sons and lament them, for
your destruction is at hand. The 3
sword has been sent upon you, and
who is there to turn it aside? A fire 4
has been sent upon you, and who is
there to put it out? Misfortunes have 5
been sent upon you, and who is there
to drive them away? Can one drive 6
off a hungry lion in a forest, or put
out a fire in the stubble, when it has
once begun to burn? Can one turn 7
back an arrow shot by a strong
archer? If the Lord God sends mis- 8
fortunes, who can turn them back?
When fire goes out from his wrath, 9
who is there to put it out? When he 10
lightens, who will not fear? When he
thunders, who will not shudder?
When the Lord threatens, who will 11
not be utterly destroyed at his presence? The earth trembles to its foun- 12
dations, the sea is stirred to its depths,
and its waves are thrown into confusion, and its fish also, at the presence
of the Lord, and the glory of his
might. For his right arm that bends 13
the bow is strong, his arrows that he
shoots are sharp; they will not miss
when they begin to be shot to the
ends of the earth. Behold, disasters 14
are shot forth, and they will not return until they come upon the earth.
A fire is lighted, and will not be put 15
out, until it consumes the foundations of the earth. Just as an arrow 16
shot by a strong archer does not come
back, so the disasters which shall be

shot at the earth will not turn back.
17 Alas for me! Who will deliver me in
those days?
18 It is the beginning of sorrows,
when there will be great mourning;
the beginning of famine, when many
will perish; the beginning of wars,
when powers will fear; the beginning
of disasters, when all will tremble.
What will they do in these circum-
19 stances, when disasters come? Behold, famine and pestilence and distress and anguish are sent as scourges
20 to correct men. But in spite of all
these things they will not turn from
their wickedness, or ever remember
21 the scourges. Behold, grain will be so
cheap on the earth that they will
think they are sure of peace, and
then disasters will spring up on the
earth—the sword, famine, and great
22 disorder. For many who live on the
earth will die of hunger, and the rest
who survive the famine the sword will
23 destroy. And the dead will be thrown
out like dung, and there will be no one
to comfort them; for the earth will be
left desolate, and its cities will be
24 torn down. There will be nobody left
to cultivate the ground and sow it.
25 The trees will bear fruit, but who will
26 gather it? The grapes will ripen, but
who will tread them? For there will
be a great deserting of the land here
27 and there. For one man will long to
see another, or to hear his voice.
28 For ten will be left, out of a city, and
two, out of a field, who have hidden
in the thick woods and the clefts of
29 the rocks. Just as in an olive orchard,
three or four olives may be left on
30 each tree, or when the grapes are
gathered in a vineyard, some clusters
are left by those who search the vine-
31 yard carefully, so in those days three
or four will be left by those who
search their houses with the sword.
32 And the earth will be left desolate,
and its fields will be given up to
briars, and all its roads and paths will
grow thorns, because no sheep will go
33 along them. Girls will grieve, because
they have no bridegrooms, women
will grieve because they have no husbands, their daughters will grieve be-
34 cause they have no help. Their
bridegrooms will be destroyed in war,
and their husbands will die of hunger.
35 But listen to these things, and understand them, you slaves of the
Lord! Behold, it is the word of the 36
Lord; receive it, do not disbelieve the
things of which the Lord says, "Be- 37
hold, disasters are approaching and
they are not delayed." Just as a 38
woman with child, in the ninth month,
when the hour of her delivery draws
near, two or three hours before it, is
seized with agonizing pains about her
womb, and when the child comes
forth from the womb it will not delay
for a moment, so these disasters will 39
not delay in coming upon the earth,
and the world will groan and pains
will envelop it.
"Hear my word, my people, pre- 40
pare for battle, and in the midst of
these disasters be like strangers in the
earth; let him who sells do it as 41
though he would have to flee; and let
him who buys do it as though he
would lose it; let him who trades do it 42
as though he would get no profit; and
let him who builds build as though he
were not going to live in what he
builds; let him who sows do it as 43
though he were not to reap, and let
him who prunes do it as though he
were not to gather the grapes; let 44
those who marry do it as though they
were not to have sons, and those who
do not marry as though they were
widowed. Because those who toil, 45
toil in vain, for strangers will gather 46
their fruits, and plunder their property, and overthrow their houses and
take their sons captive, for they produce their children for captivity and
famine. And those who do business 47
do it to be plundered; the more they
adorn their cities and their houses
and their possessions and their persons, the angrier I will be with them 48
for their sins," says the Lord. Just 49
as a respectable and virtuous woman
abhors a prostitute, so uprightness 50
will abhor wickedness, when she
adorns herself, and will accuse her to
her face, when he comes who is to defend him who seeks out every sin on
the earth.
Therefore do not be like her or her 51
works. For behold, in a little while, 52
wickedness will be removed from the
earth, and uprightness will reign over
us. Let no sinner say he has not 53
sinned, for he will burn fiery coals
upon the head of him who says, "I

have not sinned before God and his
54 glory." Behold, the Lord knows all
the doings of men, and their devices,
and their thoughts and their hearts.
55 When he said, "Let the earth be
made," it was made, and "Let the
56 heaven be made," it was made. At
his command the stars were established, and he knows the number of
57 the stars. He searches the deep and
its treasuries; he has measured the sea
58 and what it holds. He has shut up
the sea in the midst of the waters,
and by his command he has hung
59 the earth upon the water. He has
stretched the heaven like an arch
60 and based it upon the waters. He has
put springs of water in the desert, and
lakes upon the tops of the mountains,
so as to send rivers from the heights
61 so that the earth may drink. He
formed man, and put a heart in the
midst of his body, and imparted to
him breath and life and understanding, and the spirit of Almighty God,
62 who created all things and searches
out things hidden in secret places.
63 He certainly knows your devices, and
what you think in your hearts. Alas
for sinners and those who want to
64 hide their sins! Because the Lord
will closely examine all their doings,
65 and prove you all guilty. And you
will be put to shame when your sins
are brought out into the sight of men,
and your iniquities rise up to accuse
you on that day. What will you do?
66 Or how will you hide your sins in the
presence of God and his angels? Be- 67
hold, God is the judge; fear him.
Give up your sins, and forget your
iniquities, and never practice them
again; then God will lead you forth
and deliver you from all distress.
For behold, the hot anger of the 68
great multitude is kindled over you,
and some of you they will carry off
and make you eat what is sacrificed to
idols. And those who give them their 69
consent they will hold in derision and
contempt and trample on them. For 70
there will be disturbances here and
there, and in near-by cities a great
uprising against those who fear the
Lord. They will be like madmen, 71
sparing no one, in plundering and
pillaging those who still fear the
Lord. For they will pillage and plun- 72
der their property, and drive them
out of their houses. Then will appear 73
the testing of my chosen, like gold
which is tested by fire.
"Listen, my chosen," says the
Lord. "Behold, the days of persecu- 74
tion are here, and I will deliver you
from them. Do not fear or doubt, for 75
God is your guide. And you who keep 76
my commandments and precepts,"
says the Lord God, "let not your sins
drag you down, or your wickedness
prevail over you. Alas for those who 77
are bound by their sins and covered
with their wickedness, as a field is
overgrown with woods, and its grain
so covered with thorns that no one
can get through. It is shut out, and 78
left to be consumed by fire."

THE BOOK OF TOBIT

1 THE story of Tobit, the son of
Tobiel, the son of Hananiel, the
son of Aduel, the son of Gabael,
of the stock of Asael, of the tribe
2 of Naphtali, who in the days of Shalmaneser, king of Assyria, was carried into
captivity from Thisbe, which is to the
south of Kedesh Naphtali in Galilee
above Asher.
3 I, Tobit, walked all the days of my
life in ways of truth and uprightness. I
did many acts of charity for my
brothers and my nation who were taken
to the land of the Assyrians, to Nine-
4 veh, with me. And when I was in my
own country, in the land of Israel, when
I was young, the whole tribe of my
forefather Naphtali revolted from the
house in Jerusalem, which had been
chosen from all the tribes of Israel for
all the tribes to offer sacrifice in, and in
which the temple of the dwelling of the
Most High had been dedicated and
built for all ages.
5 So all the tribes which had revolted
with it would offer sacrifice to the
6 heifer Baal. But I alone went many a
time to Jerusalem for the festivals, as
the Scripture commands all Israel in
an everlasting decree, taking with me
the first fruits and the tenth parts of my
crops and my first shearings, and I
would give them to the priests, the sons
7 of Aaron, at the altar. A tenth part of
all my produce I would give to the sons
of Levi, who officiated at Jerusalem,
and another tenth I would sell, and go
and spend the proceeds in Jerusalem
8 each year, and a third tenth I would
give to those to whom it was fitting to
give it, as Deborah my grandmother
had instructed me—for I was left an
orphan by my father.
9 When I became a man, I married
Hannah, who was of the stock of our
10 family, and by her I had a son, Tobias.
And when I was carried into captivity
to Nineveh, all my brothers and rela-
11 tives ate the food of the heathen, but I
12 kept myself from eating it, because I
remembered God with all my heart.

And the Most High gave me favor and 13
standing with Shalmaneser, and I became his buyer. I made a journey to 14
Media, and deposited ten talents of
silver with Gabael, the brother of
Gabrias, in Ragae, in Media. But when 15
Shalmaneser died, his son Sennacherib
became king in his place, and the highways were unsafe, so that I could no
longer travel to Media.
In the times of Shalmaneser I used to 16
do many acts of charity for my brothers.
I would give my bread to the hungry
and my clothes to the naked, and if I 17
saw one of my people dead and thrown
outside the wall of Nineveh, I would
bury him. And if Sennacherib the king 18
killed anyone who had come as a fugitive from Judea, I buried them secretly,
for he killed many in his anger, and
their bodies were looked for by the king
and could not be found. But one of the 19
Ninevites went and informed the king
about me, that I was burying them, and
I hid, and when I learned that I was
being sought for, to be put to death, I
was frightened and escaped. Then all 20
my property was seized, and nothing
was left me but my wife Hannah and
my son Tobias.
Before fifty days had passed, his two 21
sons killed him, and fled into the mountains of Ararat, and Esarhaddon his son
became king in his place. He appointed
Ahikar, my brother Hanael's son, to
have charge of all the accounting of
his kingdom and all its administration.
And Ahikar asked for me, and I went 22
to Nineveh. Ahikar was cupbearer and
keeper of the signet and had charge of
administration and of the accounts;
Esarhaddon appointed him second to
himself, and he was my nephew.
When I reached my home and my 2
wife Hannah was restored to me, and
Tobias my son, at the Harvest Festival,
which is the feast of the Seven Weeks,
a good dinner was prepared for me, and
I sat down to eat. And I saw the 2
abundance of food, and I said to my
son,

"Go and bring any poor man of our
brothers whom you can find, who remembers the Lord, and I will wait for
you."
3 And he came back and said,
"Father, one of our race has been
strangled and thrown out in the bazaar!"
4 Then before I tasted anything I
rushed out and brought him into a room
5 until the sun set. Then I returned and
washed myself and ate my food in sad-
6 ness; and I remembered the prophecy
of Amos, as he said,

"Your feasts will be turned into sorrow,
And all your good cheer into lamentation."

7 And I wept aloud.
And when the sun was set, I went
and dug a grave and buried him.
8 And my neighbors laughed at me and
said, "He is not yet afraid of being put
to death for doing this. He ran away,
and here he is burying the dead again."
9 That same night, after I had buried
him, I returned, and as I was ceremonially defiled, I lay down to sleep by
the wall of the courtyard, with my face
10 uncovered. And I did not know that
there were sparrows in the wall above
me, and, as my eyes were open, the
sparrows' droppings fell into my eyes
and produced white films on them; and
I went to the physicians, and they could
not help me. But Ahikar supported me
for two years, until he went to Elymais.
11 Then my wife Hannah found em-
12 ployment at women's work, and sent
the work back to its owners, and they
paid her wages, and gave her a kid be-
13 sides. But when she came home to me,
the kid began to bleat. And I said to
her,
"Where did this kid come from? Is
it stolen? Give it back to its owners,
for we have no right to eat anything
that is stolen."
14 But she said to me,
"It was given me as a gift, in addition
to my wages."
But I would not believe her, and told
her to give it back to its owners, and I
blushed for her. Then she answered
and said to me,
"And where are your charities?
Where is your uprightness? Of course
you know everything!"
3 Then I was grieved, and wept, and I
prayed sorrowfully, and said,

"Lord, you are upright, and all your
doings and all your ways are mercy and
truth, and you always judge truly and
justly. Remember me and look upon
me; do not take vengeance on me for
my sins and my ignorant acts, and for
those of my forefathers, which they
committed in your sight, for they disobeyed your commands. You have giv-
en us up to pillage and captivity and
death, and made us a proverb and a
reproach among all the nations among
whom we have been scattered. And
now your judgments which are many
are right, in exacting from me for my
sins and those of my forefathers, because we did not keep your commandments, for we have not walked uprightly before you. So now deal with me according to your pleasure; command my
spirit to be taken from me, so that I
may be released and return to dust, for
I had rather die than live, because I
have had to listen to false reproaches,
and have felt great sorrow. Command
me to be released from this distress and
taken to my everlasting place of abode;
do not turn your face away from me."
On that very day, it happened to
Sarah, the daughter of Raguel, in
Ecbatana in Media, that she too was
reproached by her father's maids, because she had been married to seven
husbands, and the wicked demon As-
modeus had killed them before they had
been with her as is customary with
wives. They said to her,
"Do you not know that you strangle
your husbands? You have already had
seven, and you have not borne the
name of one of them. Why do you tor- 9
ment us? If they are dead, go after
them! May we never see son or
daughter of yours!"
When she heard these things, she was 10
deeply hurt, and wished to hang herself,
but she said,
"I am my father's only child; if I do
this, it will disgrace him, and I will
bring his old age down to the grave in
sorrow."
And she prayed by her window, and 11
said,
"Blessed are you, O Lord, my God,
and blessed be your holy and honored
name forever; may all your works bless
you forever. And now, Lord, I turn my 12
face and my eyes to you; command 13
me to be released from the earth and

4 to hear reproach no more. You know,
Lord, that I am innocent of any sin
5 with man; I have never defiled my
name, or the name of my father, in
the land of my captivity. I am my
father's only child; he has no other
child to be his heir. He has no brother
near him or nephew whom I should
keep myself to marry. I have already
lost seven husbands; why must I live
any longer? And if it is not your
pleasure to kill me, command that some
regard be had for me, and some pity be
shown me, and that I no more may
have to listen to reproach."
6 And the prayer of both of them was
heard in the presence of the glory of the
7 great Raphael, and he was sent to cure
them both; for Tobit, to remove the
white films, and to give Sarah, the
daughter of Raguel, to Tobit's son
Tobias, as his wife, and to bind As-
modeus, the wicked demon, because
Tobias was entitled to possess her. So
at the same time, Tobit went into his
house, and Sarah, the daughter of
Raguel, came down from her upstairs
room.
4 On that day Tobit remembered the
money that he had deposited with
2 Gabael in Ragae in Media. And he said
to himself,
"I have asked for death; why should
I not call my son Tobias, to explain to
him before I die?"
3 So he called him, and said,
"My boy, when I die, bury me, and
do not neglect your mother; provide for
her as long as you live; do what is
pleasing to her, and do not grieve her
4 in anything. Remember, my boy, that
she faced many dangers for you before
your birth, and when she dies, bury her
5 beside me in one grave. All your life,
my boy, remember the Lord, our God;
do not consent to sin and transgress
his commands. Act uprightly all your
life, and do not walk in the ways of
wrongdoing.
6 "For if you do right, prosperity will
attend your undertakings. To all who
act uprightly, give charity from your
property, and do not let your eye begrudge what you give to charity. Do
not turn your face away from any poor
man, and God's face will not be turned
7 away from you. Give to charity in pro-
8 portion to what you have; if you have
little, do not be afraid to give sparingly

to charity, for then you will lay up a 9
good treasure for yourself against a day
of adversity; for charity will save you 10
from death, and keep you from going
down into darkness. Charity is a good 11
offering in the sight of the Most High
for all who give it.
"My boy, beware of any immoral- 12
ity. First, take a wife who is of the
stock of your forefathers; do not marry
an alien, who does not belong to your
father's tribe, for we are the sons of
the prophets. Remember, my boy, that
Noah, Abraham, Isaac, and Jacob, our
forefathers of old, all married wives
from among their kindred, and were
blessed in their children, and their
posterity will possess the land. Now, 13
my boy, love your kindred, and do not
disdain your brothers and the sons and
daughters of your people and refuse to
marry one of them. For such disdain
leads to ruin and great distress, and
worthlessness brings loss and great
want, for worthlessness is the mother of
famine. The wages of any man who 14
works for you, you must not retain
overnight, but you must pay him immediately. If you serve God, you will
be rewarded. Take care, my boy, in all
that you do, and be well disciplined in
all your conduct. Do not do to anyone 15
else what you hate. Do not drink wine
to the point of intoxication; drunkenness must not go with you on your
way. Give some of your bread to the 16
hungry and of your clothes to the
naked. Give all your surplus to charity, and do not let your eye begrudge
what you give to charity. Scatter your 17
bread on the graves of the upright, but
do not give to sinners.
"Ask advice of every wise man, and 18
do not think lightly of any useful advice. Always bless the Lord God, and 19
ask him to make your ways straight
and your paths and plans prosper. For
no heathen nation possesses understanding, but the Lord gives all good
things, and he humbles whoever he
pleases, as he chooses.
"Now, my boy, remember my commands; do not let them be blotted from
your mind. And now I must inform 20
you of the ten talents of silver that I
deposited with Gabael, son of Gabrias,
in Ragae in Media. Do not be afraid, 21
my boy, because we have become poor.
You are well off, if you fear God and

refrain from any sin, and do what is
pleasing in his sight."

5 Then Tobias answered and said to
him,
2 "Father, I will do all that you have
commanded me. But how can I get the
money, when I do not know him?"
3 So he gave him the receipt, and said
to him,
"Seek out a man to go with you, and
I will pay him wages, as long as I live;
so go and get the money."
4 And he went to look for a man, and
found Raphael, who was an angel,
5 though Tobias did not know it. And he
said to him,
"Can I go with you to Ragae in
Media, and do you know that region?"
6 And the angel said to him,
"I will go with you, for I know the
way, and I have stayed with our
brother Gabael."
7 And Tobias said to him,
"Wait for me, and I will tell my
father."
8 And he said to him,
"Go, and do not delay."
And he went in and said to his father,
"Here I have found a man who will
go with me."
And he said,
"Call him to me, so that I may find out
what tribe he belongs to and whether
he is a reliable man to go with you."
9 So he called him, and he came in,
10 and they greeted each other. And Tobit
said to him,
"Brother, to what tribe and to what
family do you belong? Inform me."
11 And he said to him,
"Are you in search of a tribe and
family, or a hired man to go with your
son?"
And Tobit said to him,
"I only want to learn your connec-
tions and your name, brother."
12 And he said,
"I am Azariah, the son of Hananiah
the older, one of your kinsmen."
13 And he said to him,
"Welcome, brother! Do not be angry with me for trying to learn your
tribe and your family; you are a kinsman of mine, and come of a fine, good
lineage. For I came to know Hananiah
and Jathan, the sons of Shemaiah the
older, when we used to travel to Jerusalem together to worship and offer our
first-born cattle and the tenths of our
produce, for they did not go astray when our brothers did; you come of a fine stock, brother. But tell me what wages I am to give you; a drachma a day and your expenses and my son's? And I will add to your wages besides, if you come back safe and sound."

So they agreed on these terms. And he said to Tobias,

"Get ready for the journey, and farewell."

So his son made his preparations for the journey, and his father said to him,

"Go with this man, and God who lives in heaven will prosper your journey, and let his angel go with you."

And they both went out to start, and the boy's dog followed them.

And his mother Hannah wept, and she said to Tobit,

"Why have you sent our child away? Is he not our walking-stick when he goes in and out before us? Do not let money be added to money, but let it be as dirt in comparison with our child. For while the Lord lets us live, that is enough for us."

And Tobit said to her,

"Do not be troubled, my sister. He will come back safe and sound, and your eyes will see him. For a good angel will go with him, and he will have a prosperous journey, and will come back safe and sound."

So she stopped crying.

And they went on their way and came toward evening to the river Tigris and there they spent the night. And the boy went to wash himself, and a fish jumped out of the river and would have swallowed the boy. But the angel said to him,

"Take hold of the fish!"

And the boy seized the fish and threw it up on the land. And the angel said to him,

"Cut the fish up, and take its heart and liver and gall and keep them safe."

And the boy did as the angel told him, and they cooked the fish and ate it. And they both traveled on until they drew near Ecbatana. And the boy said to the angel,

"Brother Azariah, what are the liver and heart and gall of the fish good for?"

And he said to him,

"As for the heart and the liver, if anyone is troubled with a demon or an evil spirit, you must make a smoke of

them before the man or the woman,
and they will be troubled no more.
8 And as for the gall, if you rub it on a
man who has white films over his eyes,
he will be cured."
9 When they approached Ragae, the
10 angel said to the boy,
"Brother, we will stop today with
Raguel, for he is your relative. He has
an only daughter, named Sarah. I am
going to tell him to give her to you in
11 marriage, for you have a right to have
12 her, for you are her only relative, and
she is beautiful and sensible. So now
if you will listen to me, I will speak to
her father, and when we come back
from Ragae, we will perform the marriage.
For I know that by the law of
Moses Raguel cannot marry her to anyone
else under pain of death, for it is
your right and no one else's to possess
her."
13 Then the boy said to the angel,
"Brother Azariah, I have heard that
this girl has been given in marriage to
seven husbands and they all perished
14 in the bridal chamber. Now I am my
father's only child, and I am afraid that
if I go in, I will die like the others, for
a demon is in love with her, and he
harms only those who approach her.
So I am afraid that I would die and
bring my father's and my mother's life
to the grave in sorrow over me; and
they have no other son to bury them."
15 And the angel said to him,
"Don't you remember the commands
your father gave you, about your taking
a wife from your own relatives?
Now you must listen to me, brother,
for she must be your wife, and don't be
concerned about the demon, for she
will be given to you tonight to be your
16 wife. And when you go into the bridal
chamber, you must take some of the
ashes of the incense, and put on them
some of the heart and the liver of the
17 fish, and make a smoke, and the demon
will smell it and will flee and never
come back. And when you go up to her,
you must both rise up and cry out to
the merciful God, and he will save you
and have mercy on you. Have no fear,
for she was destined for you from the
beginning, and you will save her, and
she will go home with you, and I suppose
you will have children by her."
When Tobias heard this, he loved
her, and he became deeply attached to
her.

When they arrived at Ecbatana, 7
they went to the house of Raguel, and
Sarah met them and welcomed them,
and they greeted her, and she took
them into the house. And Raguel said 2
to Edna his wife,
"How much this young man resembles
my cousin Tobit!"
And Raguel asked them, 3
"Where are you from, brothers?"
And they said to him,
"We belong to the sons of Naphtali
who are in captivity in Nineveh."
And he said to them, 4
"Do you know our kinsman Tobit?"
And they said,
"We do."
And he said to them,
"Is he well?"
And they said, 5
"He is alive and well."
And Tobias said,
"He is my father!"
Then Raguel sprang up and kissed 6
him, and he wept, and blessed him, and 7
said to him,
"You are the son of that fine, good
man!"
And when he heard that Tobit had
lost his eyesight, he was grieved, and
wept, and his wife Edna and his 8
daughter Sarah wept too. And they
welcomed them warmly, and they
slaughtered a ram from the flock, and
set food before them in abundance.
Then Tobias said to Raphael,
"Brother Azariah, speak about the
things you talked of on our journey,
and let that matter be settled."
So he communicated the matter to 9
Raguel, and Raguel said to Tobias,
"Eat, drink and be merry, for you 10
have the right to take my child. But I
must reveal the truth to you. I have 11
given my child to seven husbands, and
whenever they approached her, they
died the same night. Still, for the
present be merry."
And Tobias said,
"I will eat nothing here until you
make a binding agreement with me to
do this."
Then Raguel said, 12
"Take her at once according to the
ordinance; you are her relative, and she
belongs to you; and the merciful God
will give you the greatest prosperity."

13 And he called in his daughter Sarah,
and he took her by the hand and gave
her to Tobias to be his wife, and said,
"Here, take her according to the law
of Moses, and take her back to your
father."
14 And he gave them his blessing. And
he called in Edna his wife, and he took
a scroll and wrote an agreement, and
15 they put their seals to it. Then they
began to eat.
16 Then Raguel called Edna his wife
aside and said to her,
"My sister, get the other bed
chamber ready, and take her into it."
17 And she did as he told her, and took
her into it, and she wept. And she let
her daughter weep on her shoulder, and
she said to her,
18 "Courage, my child! The Lord of
heaven and earth show you favor instead of this grief of yours! Courage,
my daughter!"
8 When they had finished supper, they
2 took Tobias in to her. And as he went,
he remembered what Raphael had said,
and took the ashes of the incense and
put the heart and the liver of the fish
3 on them and made a smoke. And when
the demon smelled the smoke, he fled
to the farthest parts of Upper Egypt,
4 and the angel bound him there. When
they were both shut in together,
Tobias got up from the bed and said,
"Get up, my sister, and let us pray
that the Lord will have mercy upon us."
5 And he began to say,
"Blessed are you, God of our forefathers, and blessed be your holy and
glorious name forever. Let the heavens
6 and all your creation bless you. You
made Adam and gave him his wife Eve
as a helper and support, and from them
came the human race. You said, 'It is
not good that the man should be alone;
let us make him a helper like himself.'
7 Now, Lord, it is not because of lust
that I take my sister here, but in truth.
Have mercy on me, and let me grow old
with her."
8 And she said "Amen" with him;
9 and they both slept all night.
And Raguel got up and went and
dug a grave, for he said,
10 "Perhaps he will die too."
11 Then Raguel went into his house
12 and said to his wife Edna,
"Send one of the maids and let them
see whether he is alive, and if he is not,
let us bury him without letting anyone
know."
And the maid opened the door and 1
went in, and found them both asleep.
And she came out and told them that he 1
was alive. Then Raguel blessed God, 1
and said,
"Blessed are you, O God, with every 1
pure and holy blessing! Let your saints
and all your creation bless you, and let
all your angels and your chosen people
bless you forever. You are blessed be- 1
cause you have had mercy on two only
children; Lord, show them mercy; grant
that they may live to the end in health,
with gladness and mercy."
Then he ordered his servants to fill up 1
the grave. And he made them a mar- 1
riage feast that lasted fourteen days.
And Raguel swore to him before the 2
days of the marriage feast were over
that he must not leave until the fourteen days of the marriage feast were
past, and then he should take half of 2
Raguel's property and return in safety
to his father. "The rest," he said, "will
be yours when I and my wife die."
And Tobias called Raphael and said 9
to him,
"Brother Azariah, take with you a
servant and two camels, and go to
Gabael, in Ragae in Media, and get me
the money and bring him to the marriage feast. For Raguel has sworn that
I must not leave, and my father is
counting the days, and if I delay long,
he will be greatly grieved."
So Raphael went and spent the
night with Gabael, and gave him the
receipt, and he brought out the bags
with their seals unbroken, and gave
them to him. And they got up early in
the morning together, and came to the
marriage feast; and Tobias blessed his
wife.
Now his father Tobit was counting 1
each day. And when the days required
for the journey were past and they did
not come back, he said,
"Is it possible that they have been
disappointed? Or is Gabael perhaps
dead, and there is no one to give him
the money?"
And he was greatly distressed. And
his wife said to him,
"The child has perished; that is why
he has taken so long."
And she began to bewail him, and
said,

5 "Do I not care, my child, because I
let you go, you light of my eyes?"
6 And Tobit said to her,
"Be quiet, have no concern; he is all
right."
7 And she said to him,
"Be quiet, do not deceive me; my
child has perished."
And every day she would go down
the road by which he had left, and in
the daytime she refused to eat, and
through the night she never ceased to
bewail her son Tobias until the fourteen days of the marriage feast, which
Raguel had sworn he must spend there,
were over.
Then Tobias said to Raguel,
"Let me go, for my father and my
mother are giving up all hope of ever
seeing me again."
8 But his father-in-law said to him,
"Stay with me, and I will send to
your father, and they will explain to
him about you."
9 And Tobias said,
"No, send me to my father."
10 Then Raguel got up and gave him
his wife Sarah and half of his property,
11 slaves and cattle and money. And he
blessed them as he let them go, and
said,
"The God of heaven will give you
prosperity, my children, before I die."
12 And he said to his daughter,
"Respect your father-in-law and
your mother-in-law, they are now your
parents. Let me hear a good report of
you."
And he kissed her. And Edna said to
Tobias,
"May the Lord of heaven bring you
back safely, dear brother, and grant
that I may see your children by my
daughter Sarah, so that I may be glad
before the Lord. Here I solemnly intrust my daughter to you; do not hurt
her feelings."
11 After that, Tobias set off, praising
God, because he had prospered him on
his journey, and he blessed Raguel and
his wife Edna.
2 He went on until they approached
Nineveh. And Raphael said to Tobias,
"Do you not know, brother, how
3 you left your father? Let us run ahead,
before your wife, and get the house
4 ready. But take the gall of the fish in
your hand."
So they went, and the dog went along
after them.
And Hannah sat looking down the 5
road for her boy. And she saw him 6
coming, and she said to his father,
"Here comes your son, and the man
who went with him!"
And Raphael said, 7
"I know that your father will open
his eyes; so you rub the gall on his eyes, 8
and he will feel the sting and will rub
them, and remove the white films, and
he will see you."
And Hannah ran to meet them and 9
fell on her son's neck and said to him,
"Now that I have seen you, my child,
I am ready to die."
And they both wept. And Tobit 10
came out to the door, and he stumbled,
and his son ran up to him and he took 11
hold of his father and sprinkled the gall
on his father's eyes, saying,
"Courage, father!"
And when his eyes began to smart, he 12
rubbed them, and the white films 13
scaled off from the corners of his eyes.
And when he saw his son, he fell on his
neck and wept, and said, 14
"Blessed are you, O God, and
blessed is your name forever, and
blessed are all your holy angels. For 15
though you have flogged me, you have
had mercy on me; here I can see
Tobias, my son."
And his son went in rejoicing, and
told his father the wonderful things
that had happened to him in Media.
So Tobit went out rejoicing to meet 16
his daughter-in-law, at the gate of
Nineveh. And those who saw him go
were amazed, because he had received
his sight. And Tobit gave thanks be- 17
fore them, because God had had mercy
on him. And when Tobit came up to
Sarah his daughter-in-law, he blessed
her, saying,
"Welcome, daughter! Blessed is God,
who has brought you to us, and blessed
are your father and your mother."
And there was rejoicing among all his
brothers in Nineveh. And Ahikar and 18
Nasbas his nephew came, and Tobias' 19
marriage feast was held for seven days,
with great gladness.
Then Tobit called his son Tobias and 12
said to him,
"My child, see to the wages of the
man who went with you, for we must
give him more."

2 And he said to him,
"Father, I can afford to give him half
3 of what I brought back, for he has
brought me back to you safe and
sound, and he cured my wife and he
brought me the money, and besides
he has cured you."
4 And the old man said,
"It is due him."
5 And he called the angel and said to
him,
"Accept half of all that you brought
back."
6 Then he called them both and said
to them in private,
"Bless God and give thanks to him.
Ascribe majesty to him, and before all
the living acknowledge how he has dealt
with you. It is a good thing to bless
God and exalt his name, declaring
God's works and doing them honor, so
do not be slow to give him thanks.
7 It is wise to keep a king's secret, but
the works of God should be gloriously
revealed. Do good, and evil will not
8 overtake you. Prayer is good if accompanied with fasting, charity, and uprightness. A little with uprightness is
better than much with wickedness. It is
better to give to charity than to lay up
9 gold. For charity will save a man from
death; it will expiate any sin. Those
who give to charity and act uprightly
10 will have their fill of life; but those who
commit sin are the enemies of their own
11 lives. I will not conceal anything from
you; as I said, it is wise to keep a king's
secret, but the works of God should be
12 gloriously revealed. So now, when you
and your daughter-in-law Sarah prayed,
I brought the remembrance of your
prayer before the Holy One. And when
you buried the dead, I was still with
13 you. And when you did not shrink
from getting up and leaving your dinner
to go and lay out the dead, your good
deed did not escape me, but I was with
14 you. So God sent me to cure you and
15 your daughter-in-law Sarah. For I am
Raphael, one of the seven holy angels,
who offer up the prayers of God's
people and go into the presence of the
glory of the Holy One!"
16 And they were both confounded, and
fell on their faces, for they were terri-
17 fied. And he said to them,
"Do not be afraid; peace be with
18 you. Bless God forever. For not
through any favor on my part but by
the will of God I came to you. Therefore bless him forever. All these days 1
that I appeared to you, I did not eat or
drink, but you beheld a vision. Now 2
give thanks to God, for I must go up
to him who sent me, and you must
write all that has happened on a
scroll."
And when they got up, they no 2
longer saw him. And they acknowl- 2
edged the great, wonderful doings of
God, and how the angel of the Lord had
appeared to them.
Then Tobit wrote a prayer of rejoic- 1
ing, and said,

"Blessed be God who lives forever,
and blessed be his kingdom,
For he flogs, and he has mercy,
He takes men down to Hades, and he
brings them up,
And there is no one who can escape
his hand.
Give thanks to him, Israelites, before
the heathen,
For he has scattered you among
them.
Show his majesty there;
Exalt him in the presence of every
living being,
For he is our Lord and God,
He is our father forever.
He will flog us for our wrongdoing,
And he will show mercy again and
gather us from all the heathen
Wherever you are scattered.
If you turn to him with all your
heart,
And with all your soul, to act truly
in his sight,
Then he will turn to you,
And he will not hide his face from
you.
See how he will deal with you,
And give him thanks with your full
voice.
Bless the Lord of Righteousness
And exalt the King of the Ages.
In the land of my captivity I give
him thanks,
And I show his might and his
majesty to a nation of sinners:
'Turn to him, you sinners, and do
what is right in his sight;
Who knows but he will be pleased
with you, and show you mercy?'
I exalt my God,
My soul exalts the king of heaven,
And exults in his majesty.

8 Let all men speak and give him
thanks in Jerusalem.
9 O Jerusalem, the holy city,
He will flog you for the doings of
your sons,
And again he will have mercy on the
sons of the upright.
10 Give thanks to the Lord in goodness,
And bless the King of the Ages,
That his tent may be rebuilt in you
with joy.
May he make glad in you those who
are captives,
And the miserable may he love in
you,
To all generations, forever.
11 Many nations will come from afar to
the name of the Lord God,
Bearing gifts in their hands, gifts for
the king of heaven.
Generations of generations will bring
you exultation.
12 Cursed be all who hate you!
Blessed forever shall be all who love
you.
13 Rejoice and exult in the sons of the
upright,
For they will be gathered together,
and they will bless the Lord of
the upright.
14 Blessed are those who love you!
They will rejoice in your peace.
Blessed are those who grieved over
all your stripes,
For they will be glad about you,
when they see all your glory,
And they will rejoice forever.
15 Let my soul bless God, the great
King,
16 For Jerusalem will be built of sapphire and emerald,
And her walls of precious stones,
And her towers and battlements of
pure gold;
17 And the streets of Jerusalem will be
paved with beryl and ruby and
stones of Ophir,
18 And all her lanes shall say 'Hallelujah,' and shall utter praise,
saying, 'Blessed be God, who has
raised you up forever.' "

14 And Tobit ended his thanksgiving.
2 He was fifty-eight years old when he
lost his sight, and eight years later he
recovered it; and he gave to charity and
continued to fear the Lord his God and
3 to give thanks to him. And when he
had grown very old, he called his son
and his son's sons to him and said to
him,
"My child, take your sons; here I
have grown old and will soon depart this
life. Go to Media, my child, for I firmly 4
believe what Jonah the prophet said
about Nineveh, that it will be destroyed, but in Media there will be
peace, rather than here, for a while, and
that our brothers will be scattered from
the good land over the earth, and Jerusalem will be desolate, and the house of
God in it will be burned down, and will
be desolate for a time; and then God 5
will have mercy on them again, and
bring them back to their land; and they
will build the house, though not as it
was before, until the times of that age
are passed. And afterward they will
return from the places of their captivity
and rebuild Jerusalem in splendor, and
the house of God will be rebuilt in it
gloriously, for all generations forever,
as the prophets said of it. And all the 6
heathen will turn to fear the Lord God
in truth, and they will bury their idols,
and all the heathen will bless the Lord. 7
And his people will thank God, and the
Lord will uplift his people, and all who
love the Lord God in truth and uprightness will rejoice and show mercy
to our brothers. And now, my child, 8
leave Nineveh, for what the prophet
Jonah said will surely happen. But 9
keep the law and the ordinances, and
be merciful and upright, so that you
may prosper. Bury me properly and 10
my wife beside me. And do not live
any longer in Nineveh. My child, see
what Haman did to Ahikar, who had
brought him up—how he plunged him
from light into darkness and how he requited him! Yet Ahikar was saved and
the other was recompensed and disappeared in darkness himself. Manasseh
gave to charity, and escaped the fatal
snare which Haman set for him, but
Haman fell into the trap and perished.
See, my children, what charity can do, 11
and how uprightness can save!"

As he said this, he breathed his last
there in his bed. He was a hundred and
fifty-eight years old; and they gave him
a splendid funeral.

When Hannah died, he buried her 12
beside his father. Then Tobias went
back with his wife and his sons to

Ecbatana, to Raguel his father-in-law.
13 And he reached an honored old age,
and he gave his father-in-law and his
mother-in-law splendid funerals, and he
inherited their property and his father
14 Tobit's. And he died in Ecbatana in
Media, at the age of a hundred and
twenty-seven. But before he died he 15
heard of the destruction of Nineveh,
which Nebuchadnezzar and Ahasuerus
had captured. So before he died he rejoiced over Nineveh.

THE BOOK OF JUDITH

1 IN THE twelfth year of the reign of
Nebuchadnezzar, who ruled over
the Assyrians in the great city of
Nineveh, in the days when Arphaxad ruled over the Medes in Ecba-
2 tana, Arphaxad built around Ecbatana
walls of hewn stones four and a half
feet wide and nine feet long. He built
the walls a hundred and five feet high
3 and seventy-five feet wide, and at the
gates he built towers a hundred and
fifty feet high, with foundations ninety
4 feet wide; and he made its gates, gates
that rose to a height of a hundred and
five feet, and were sixty feet wide, so
that his host of warriors could march
5 out and his infantry could form. So in
those days King Nebuchadnezzar made
war on King Arphaxad in the Great
Plain; this plain is on the borders of
6 Ragae. He was joined by all the inhabitants of the hill country and all
who lived along the Euphrates and
Tigris and Hydaspes, and on the plains
of Arioch, king of Elymais, and many
nations joined the army of the Chaldeans.

7 Then Nebuchadnezzar, king of Assyria, sent to all the inhabitants of
Persia and to all who lived toward the
west, who were settled in Cilicia and
Damascus and the Lebanon and the
8 Antilebanon, and to all who lived along
the seacoast, and to the inhabitants of
Carmel and Gilead that were heathen,
and to Upper Galilee and the great
9 plain of Esdraelon, and to all that were
in Samaria and its towns, and beyond
Jordan as far as Jerusalem and Betane
and Chelous and Kadesh, and the river
of Egypt, Tahpanhes and Raamses and
10 all the land of Goshen, until you pass
Tanis and Memphis, and to all who
lived in Egypt, until you reach the
11 borders of Ethiopia. But all the inhabitants of the land paid no attention
to the command of Nebuchadnezzar,
king of Assyria, and would not go with
him to the war, for they were not afraid
of him, but regarded him as just a single man, and they sent his messengers
back disappointed and in disgrace.

Then Nebuchadnezzar was very an- 12
gry with that whole country, and he
swore by his throne and his kingdom
that he would certainly take vengeance
upon all the regions of Cilicia, Damascus, and Syria, and kill with the sword
all the inhabitants of the land of Moab
and the Ammonites and all Judea and
everybody in Egypt, until you come to
the coasts of the two seas. So in the 13
seventeenth year he made war on King
Arphaxad, and he overcame him and
put Arphaxad's whole army and all his
cavalry and all his chariots to flight,
and he took possession of his cities and 14
reached Ecbatana and took its towers
and plundered its bazaars and turned
its glory into shame. Then he took 15
Arphaxad captive among the mountains of Ragae, and struck him down
with his spears and utterly destroyed
him, unto this day. Then he returned 16
with the spoils and all his motley
army, a very great body of soldiers,
and there he and his army took their
ease and feasted for a hundred and
twenty days.

In the eighteenth year of his reign, 2
on the twenty second day of the first
month, it was proposed in the palace of
Nebuchadnezzar, king of Assyria, to
take vengeance on all the land, just as
he had said. He called together all his 2
ministers and all his nobles and set
before them his secret purpose and
fully related all the wickedness of the
land with his own lips, and they de- 3
creed that all who had not obeyed the
command the king had uttered should
be destroyed. When he had complet- 4
ed his plan, Nebuchadnezzar, king of
Assyria, summoned Holofernes, the
general of his army, who was second
to himself, and said to him,

"Thus says the Great King, the Lord 5
of all the earth: When you go from
my presence, you must take with you
men confident in their strength to the
number of a hundred and twenty
thousand infantry and twelve thousand mounted men, and you must go 6
out to attack all the western country,

because they have disobeyed the com-
7 mand that I uttered. You must call
upon them to prepare earth and water,
in token of submission, for I will go
against them in my anger and I will
cover the whole face of the earth with
the feet of my army and I will give
8 them up to them to plunder, and their
ravines will be filled with their wounded, and every brook and dashing river
9 will be filled with their dead, and I will
send them as captives to the ends of
10 all the earth. But you must go and
take all their frontiers for me in advance, and they must give themselves
up to you, and you must hold them for
me till the day of their punishment.
11 But as for those who disobey, your eye
must not spare them, but you must
give them up to be slain and plundered
12 in all your land. For as surely as I am
alive, by the power of my kingdom, I
have spoken and I will do this with
13 my hand. You must not transgress any
of your lord's commands, but you must
carry them out in full, as I have ordered you to do; you must not put off
doing them."

14 So Holofernes left his master's presence and called in all the marshals and
generals and officers of the Assyrian
15 army, and he mustered picked soldiers,
as his master had ordered him to do,
to the number of a hundred and twenty
thousand and twelve thousand mount-
16 ed archers, and he marshaled them as a
17 great army is marshaled. He took camels and asses and mules, an immense
number, for their transport, and sheep
and cattle and goats without number
18 to provision them, and food in abundance for every man, beside a great
deal of gold and silver from the king's
19 palace. And he set off with his entire
army to go ahead of King Nebuchadnezzar and to cover the whole face of the
land toward the west with their chariots
and horsemen and picked foot soldiers,
20 and there went out with them a motley
host like locusts, like the dust of the
earth; they could not be counted, they
were so many.

21 They marched three days' journey
from Nineveh, to the edge of the plain
of Bectileth and they encamped opposite Bectileth, near the mountain that
22 is to the north of Upper Cilicia. And
he took his whole army, his infantry
and cavalry and chariots, and moved
into the mountainous country and rav- 2
aged Put and Lud and plundered all
the sons of Rassis and the sons of
Ishmael who lived along the desert, to
the south of the country of Cheleon.
Then he crossed the Euphrates and 2
passed through Mesopotamia and tore
down all the high-walled towns on the
river Abron, until you come to the sea.
He took possession of the frontiers of 2
Cilicia, and cut down all who resisted
him, and went as far as the southern
frontiers of Japheth, facing Arabia.
He encircled all the sons of Midian, 2
burning their tents and plundering their
flocks. He went down into the plain of 2
Damascus during the wheat harvest
and set all their fields on fire and destroyed their flocks and herds and
plundered their cities and devastated
their lands and smote all their young
men with the edge of the sword.

So fear and horror of him fell on all 2
the inhabitants of the seacoast who
were in Sidon and Tyre and those who
lived in Sur and Ocine and all who lived
in Jamnia, and the inhabitants of Ashdod and Askelon were exceedingly
afraid of him. So they sent messengers 3
and said in peaceful terms,

"Here we servants of Nebuchadnezzar the Great King lie before you; use
us as you please. Our dwellings and all
our land and every wheatfield, our
flocks and herds and all our tent-folds
lie before you; use them as you please.
Our cities and their inhabitants are
your slaves; come and treat them as you
see fit."

So the men went to Holofernes and
told him all these things. And he
went down to the seacoast with his
army and put garrisons in the high-
walled towns and took picked men from
them for allies, and the people and all
the country round welcomed him with
garlands and dances and music. And
he broke down all their frontier land-
marks and cut down their groves, and
he succeeded in destroying all the gods
of the country, in order that all the nations should worship Nebuchadnezzar
alone, and that all their tongues and
tribes should call upon him as god.

Then he came toward Esdraelon,
near Dothan, which is opposite the
main ridge of Judea, and they pitched 10
their camp between Geba and Scythopolis, and he remained there a whole

month, in order to gather together all
the transport of his army.
4 Then the Israelites who lived in
Judea heard all that Holofernes, the
commander-in-chief of Nebuchadnezzar, king of Assyria, had done to the
heathen, and how he had plundered all
2 their temples and destroyed them, and
they were dreadfully afraid of him and
disturbed about Jerusalem and the
3 temple of the Lord their God. For
they had recently come back from their
captivity, and all the people of Judea
had gathered together not long before,
and the sacred dishes and the altar and
the temple had been consecrated after
4 their profanation. So they sent into
all the borders of Samaria and to
Cona and Bethhoron and Belmain and
Jericho and to Choba and Aesora and
5 the valley of Salem and occupied in advance all the summits of the high
mountains and fortified the villages
that were on them and stored up food
in preparation for war, for their fields
6 had lately been reaped. And Joakim
the high priest, who was in Jerusalem
at that time, wrote to the inhabitants
of Bethulia and Betomesthaim which is
opposite Esdraelon facing the plain
7 near Dothan, telling them to seize
the passes of the mountains, because
through them Judea could be entered,
and it was easy to prevent any from
approaching, as the way was narrow,
with room for two men at most.
8 So the Israelites did as they were
ordered by Joakim the high priest and
the council of all the people of Israel
9 who live in Jerusalem. And every man
of Israel cried to God with great earnestness, and they humbled themselves
10 with great sincerity. They and their
wives and their children and their cattle and every visitor and hired man and
11 slave put sackcloth on their loins. And
every man and woman of Israel who
lived in Jerusalem, with their children,
fell down before the temple and threw
ashes on their heads and spread out
their sackcloth before the Lord. And
they covered the altar with sackcloth
12 and cried earnestly in concert to the
God of Israel praying that he would
not permit their children to be plundered and their wives to be pillaged
and the cities they had inherited to be
destroyed, and the sanctuary to be profaned and reviled, to the delight of the
heathen. Then the Lord heard their 13
voice and regarded their affliction. The
people continued to fast for several
days all over Judea and Jerusalem before the sanctuary of the Lord Almighty. And Joakim the high priest 14
and all the priests who officiated before the Lord and ministered to the
Lord offered the continual burnt offering and the vows and the freewill offerings of the people with sackcloth upon
their loins and ashes upon their miters, 15
and they cried to the Lord with all
their might to look with favor upon all
the house of Israel.
Then Holofernes, the commander-in- 5
chief of the Assyrian army, was told
that the Israelites had prepared for war,
and had closed the passes of the mountains and fortified every mountain top
and put barricades in the level country, and he was exceedingly angry, and 2
he summoned all the princes of Moab
and the generals of Ammon and all the
governors of the seacoast, and said to 3
them,
"Tell me, you Canaanites, what is
this people that occupies the mountain
country, and what cities do they inhabit? How large is their army, and
in what does their power or strength
lie? What king has risen over them as
leader of their army, and why have 4
they alone of all the inhabitants of the
west refused to come and meet me?"
Then Achior, the commander of all 5
the Ammonites, said to him,
"Now let my lord hear what is said
by the mouth of your servant, and I
will tell you the truth about this nation which inhabits this mountain region near you; nothing false shall proceed from your servant's mouth. This 6
nation is descended from the Chaldeans. In former times they lived for 7
a while in Mesopotamia, because they
would not follow the gods of their forefathers who were in the country of the
Chaldeans. But they left the ways of 8
their ancestors and worshipped the
God of heaven, a god whom they had
come to know, and their parents drove
them out from the presence of their
gods, and they fled to Mesopotamia
and lived there a long time. Then their 9
God told them to leave the place where
they were living and go to the land of
Canaan. So they settled there and
grew rich in gold and silver and very

10 many cattle. Then they went down
into Egypt, for a famine spread over
the face of the land of Canaan, and
they stayed there until they were
grown up. There they became a great
multitude; their nation could not be
11 counted. The king of Egypt took
measures against them and took advantage of them, making them work at
making bricks; they degraded them and
12 made them slaves. Then they cried to
their God, and he afflicted all the land
of Egypt with incurable plagues; and
the Egyptians drove them out from
13 among them. God made the Red Sea
14 dry up before them, and he set them on
the road to Sinai and Kadesh Barnea,
and they drove out all the inhabitants
15 of the desert and lived in the country of
the Amorites, and they were so strong
that they destroyed all the people of
Heshbon, and they crossed the Jordan
and took possession of all the mountain
16 region. They drove out before them
Canaanite and Perizzite and Jebusite,
and Shechem and all the Gergesites,
and they settled there for a long time.
17 As long as they did not sin against
their God, they prospered, for God who
18 hates wrongdoing was with them. But
when they abandoned the way he had
determined for them, they were utterly
destroyed through many wars and carried off as captives to a country that
was not their own, and the Temple of
their God was leveled to the ground,
and their cities were taken by their
19 enemies. Now they have turned to
their God and have come back from
their dispersion that they suffered and
they have taken possession of Jerusalem where their sanctuary is, and
they have settled in the mountain re-
20 gion, for it was unoccupied. Now, your
Majesty, if there is any fault of ignorance in this nation, and they are sinning
against their God, and we perceive that
they are guilty of this offense, then we
21 can go up and defeat them. But if
there is no disobedience to law in their
nation, then my lord must pass by
them, or their Lord will protect them
and their God defend them, and we
shall be disgraced in the eyes of the
whole earth."
22 When Achior finished saying these
things, all the people who stood around
about the tent objected, and the officers
of Holofernes and all the inhabitants of
the seacoast and of Moab advised putting him to death, "For," they said, 2
"we must not be afraid of the Israelites,
for behold they are a people with no
strength or might in real warfare. So 2
now we must advance and they will be
devoured by all your army, Lord Holofernes."

When the disturbance made by the
men around the council had ceased,
Holofernes, the commander-in-chief of
the Assyrian army, said to Achior and
all the Moabites before all the body of
heathen,

"And who are you, Achior, and you
mercenaries of Ephraim, that you
should act the prophet among us as you
have done today, and tell us not to
make war upon the people of Israel, because their God will protect them?
What god is there except Nebuchadnezzar? He will put forth his strength
and destroy them off the face of the
earth, and their God will not save them,
but we who are his slaves will strike
them down as one man, and they will
not withstand the might of our horses.
For with them we will consume them,
and their mountains will be drunk with
their blood and their plains will be
filled with their dead bodies. The track
of their feet will not stand before us
but they will utterly perish, says King
Nebuchadnezzar, the Lord of the whole
earth, for he said the words he had
spoken would not be in vain.

"But you, Achior, you hireling of
Ammon, who have said these things in
the time of your inquity, you shall not
see my face again from this day until
I take vengeance on the nation of those
that came out of Egypt. Then the
sword of my army and my host of
servants will pierce your sides and you
will fall among their wounded when I
return. Now my slaves will take you
into the mountains and put you in one
of the hill cities, and you will not perish
until you are destroyed with them.
If you hope in your heart that they will
not be taken, your face must not be
downcast; I have spoken and none of
the things that I have said will fail to
be fulfilled."

Then Holofernes ordered his slaves
who were standing by in his tent to
seize Achior and take him away to
Bethulia and turn him over to the
Israelites. And his slaves seized him

and took him out of the camp into the
plain and brought him out of the midst
of the plain into the hilly country and
reached the springs which were below
2 Bethulia. When the men of the town
saw them, they caught up their weapons and came out of the town to the
crest of the hill and all the slingers prevented them from coming up, hurling
3 stones upon them. So they slipped under the hill and bound Achior and left
him lying at the foot of the hill, and
went off to their master.
4 Then the Israelites went down from
their town and came upon him. And
they unbound him and took him
back to Bethulia and brought him before the magistrates of their town,
5 who in those days were Uzziah, the son
of Micah, of the tribe of Symeon, and
Chabris, the son of Gothoniel, and
6 Charmis, the son of Melchiel. They
assembled all the elders of the city, and
all their young men and their women
hurried together to the meeting, and
they put Achior in the midst of all their
people, and Uzziah asked him what
7 had happened. And he answered and
told them what had happened in the
council of Holofernes, and all that he
had said in the presence of the leaders
of the Assyrians, and how Holofernes
had boasted against the house of Israel.
8 Then the people fell down and worshiped God, and cried out,
9 "Lord God of Heaven, look down on
their arrogance and take pity on the
humiliation of our nation, and look this
day upon the face of those who are consecrated to you."
20 Then they consoled Achior and
21 praised him highly, and Uzziah took
him from the meeting to his house and
gave a banquet for the elders, and they
called upon the God of Israel for help
all that night.

7 The next day Holofernes ordered all
his army and all his people who had
come to his support to move against
Bethulia and to seize the mountain
passes and to make war on the Israel-
2 ites. And every able-bodied man of
them moved that day; their strength
was a hundred and seventy thousand
infantry and twelve thousand cavalry,
besides the baggage and the footmen
among them, a very great multitude.
3 They encamped in the valley near
Bethulia, by the spring, and they
spread in breadth over Dothaim as far
as Belbaim and in length from Bethulia
to Cyamon which faces Esdraelon.
But the Israelites, when they saw 4
their great numbers, were greatly troubled and said to one another,
"These people will lick up the face of
the whole country, and neither the
high mountains nor the valleys nor the
hills will bear their weight."
And each one took up his weapons 5
and they kindled fires on their towers
and stayed on guard all that night.
On the second day Holofernes led out 6
all his cavalry before the Israelites who
were in Bethulia, and he reconnoitered 7
the approaches to their city and located
the springs of water and seized them
and set guards of soldiers over them,
and returned to his army.
Then all the rulers of the sons of 8
Esau and all the leaders of the people
of Moab and the commanders of the
seacoast came to him and said,
"Let our master listen to what we 9
have to say, in order that there may
not be any disaster to your army. For 10
these people of the Israelites do not rely
on their spears, but on the mountain
heights in which they live, for it is not
easy to reach the tops of their mountains. So now, master, do not fight 11
against them in battle array, and not a
man of your army will fall. Remain 12
in your camp, and keep every man of
your force safe, and let your servants
take possession of the spring of water
that flows from the foot of the mountain, for from it all the inhabitants of 13
Bethulia get their water. Then thirst
will destroy them, and they will surrender their town. We and our people
will go up to the neighboring mountain
summits to prevent anyone from getting out of the town. And they and 14
their wives and their children will be
consumed with hunger, and before the
sword is drawn against them they will
be laid low in the streets where they
live. So you will repay them with evil 15
because they rebelled and did not receive you peaceably."
Their words pleased Holofernes and 16
all his attendants, and he gave orders to
do as they said. And the camp of the 17
sons of Ammon moved along with five
thousand of the Assyrians, and they
encamped in the valley and seized the
water supply and the springs of the

18 Israelites. And the sons of Esau and
the sons of Ammon went up and encamped in the mountainous country
opposite Dothaim, and they sent some
of them southward and eastward toward Akraba, near Chus, on the Brook
Mochmur. The rest of the army of the
Assyrians encamped in the plain, and
they covered the whole face of the country, and their tents and their baggage
train encamped in a great multitude,
and they made a very great host.
19 Then the Israelites cried out to the
Lord their God, for their courage failed,
because all their enemies had surrounded them and there was no way to es-
20 cape from the midst of them. The
whole army of Assyria, their infantry,
and chariots and cavalry, remained in a
circle around them for thirty-four days,
and all the buckets of water of all the
21 inhabitants of Bethulia failed, and their
cisterns were empty, and they had not
a full supply of water to drink for one
day, for they measured it out to them
22 to drink. Their little children were disheartened, and the women and the
young men fainted with thirst and fell
down in the streets of the town and in
the roadways through the gates, and
there was no strength left in them any
longer.
23 Then all the people, the young men,
the women, and the children, gathered
together against Uzziah and the rulers
of the town, and they cried aloud and
said before all the elders,
24 "May God be judge between you and
us, for you have done us a great wrong
in not making peace with the As-
25 syrians. Now we have no one to help
us, but God has sold us into their
hands, to be laid low before them with
26 thirst and utter destruction. Now call
them in and surrender the whole town
to the people of Holofernes and to all
27 his army to be plundered. It is better
for us to be plundered by them, for we
shall become slaves and our lives will
be preserved and we shall not see our
babies die before our eyes, and our
28 wives and children expire. We call to
witness against you heaven and earth,
and our God, the Lord of our forefathers; let him not do what we have
said today."
29 Great lamentation arose from all of
them alike in the midst of the meeting,
and they cried aloud to the Lord God.
Then Uzziah said to them, 3
"Courage, brothers! Let us hold out
five days longer; by that time the Lord
our God will show us his mercy, for he
will not utterly forsake us. But if these 3
pass and no help comes to us, I will do
as you say." So he dismissed the people 3
to their respective stations, and they
went away to the walls and towers of
their town, and sent their wives and
children home, and there was great de-
pression in the town.
In those days news of it came to
Judith the daughter of Merari, the son
of Ox, the son of Joseph, the son of
Oziel, the son of Elkiah, the son of
Ananias, the son of Gideon, the son of
Raphaim, the son of Ahitub, the son
of Elijah, the son of Hilkiah, the son of
Eliab, the son of Nathanael, the son of
Salamiel, the son of Sarasadai, the son
of Israel. Her husband Manasseh belonged to her tribe and family, and he
had died in the days of the barley harvest. For as he was overseeing the men
who were binding sheaves on the plain,
the heat affected his head, and he threw
himself upon his bed and died in his
town Bethulia, and they buried him
with his forefathers in the field that is
between Dothaim and Balamon. Judith had been a widow and remained in
her house for three years and four
months. She built herself a tent on the
top of her house, and she wore sackcloth next to her skin and her widow's
mourning. She fasted all the days of
her widowhood except the day before
the sabbath and the sabbath and the
day before the new moon and the new
moon, and the feasts and the joyful cele-
brations of the house of Israel. She
was very beautiful and fair to see, and
her husband Manasseh had left her
gold and silver, and male and female
slaves, and cattle and lands, and she
lived on them. There was nobody who
spoke ill of her, for she feared God with
all her heart.
She heard the wicked words the people had spoken against the governor because they fainted for lack of water,
and Judith heard all the things that
Uzziah said to them, how he swore to
them that he would surrender the town
to the Assyrian at the end of five days,
and she sent her maid who was in 1
charge of all that she had and sum-

moned Chabris and Charmis, the elders
11 of her town. They came to her, and she
said to them,
"Listen to me, rulers of the inhabitants of Bethulia, for the thing is not
right that you have said before the
people today, and have confirmed with
this oath that you have sworn between
God and you, saying that you will surrender the town to our enemies, unless
the Lord turns and helps us within that
12 time. Now who are you, who have tried
God today, and who set yourselves up
in place of God among the sons of men?
13 You investigate the Lord Almighty, and
14 will never learn anything. You cannot
sound the depth of a man's mind, and
you cannot grasp the thoughts of his
understanding. How can you examine
God, who made all these things, and
understand his mind and perceive his
thought? No, no, do not provoke the
15 Lord our God. For if he does not wish
to help us within these five days, he
has power to protect us within whatever time he pleases, or to destroy us
16 before our enemies. But you must not
treat the counsels of the Lord our God
as pledged, for God is not like a man, to
be threatened, or like a son of man, to
17 be cajoled. Therefore let us wait for the
deliverance that comes from him, and
call upon him to help us, and he will
18 hear our cry, if it pleases him. For
there has not arisen in our age nor is
there today a tribe or family or people
or town of our stock that worships gods
made with hands, as they did in former
19 times, because of which our forefathers
were given up to the sword and to be
despoiled and fell in a great disaster be-
20 fore our enemies. We have known no
other god than him, and so we hope
that he will not neglect us, nor any of
21 our nation. For if we are taken, all
Judea will be taken, and our sanctuary
will be plundered, and he will hold our
blood responsible for the profanation of
22 it, and the slaughter of our brothers
and the capture of the land and the
desolation of our inheritance he will
bring back upon our heads among the
heathen wherever we are in slavery,
and we will become an offense and a
reproach in the sight of our masters.
23 For our slavery will not develop into
favor, but the Lord our God will turn
it into disgrace. Now, brothers, let us
24 set an example to our brothers, for their
lives depend on us, and the sanctuary
and the temple and the altar rest upon
us. Notwithstanding all this, let us 25
give thanks to the Lord our God, who
is making trial of us as he did of our
forefathers also. Remember how he 26
dealt with Abraham, and how he dealt
with Isaac, and what happened to
Jacob in Syrian Mesopotamia, when he
was keeping the sheep of his uncle Laban. For he has not tried us with fire, 27
as he did them, to search their hearts,
and he has not taken vengeance upon
us, but the Lord scourges those who
come near him, to instruct them."
Then Uzziah said to her, 28
"All that you have said, you have
spoken with a pure heart, and there is
no one who can oppose your words.
For today is not the first time that your 29
wisdom has been displayed, but from
the beginning of your life all the people
have known your good sense, for what
your mind designs is good. But the 30
people were exceedingly thirsty and
they compelled us to do as we told them
we would, and to put ourselves under
an oath, which we cannot break. Now 31
pray for us, for you are a devout woman, and the Lord will send rain to fill
our cisterns, and we will not faint any
more."
Then Judith said to them, 32
"Listen to me, and I will do something that will go down to the sons of
our nation for endless generations. You 33
must stand at the gate tonight, and I
will go out with my maid, and before
the days are over after which you said
you would surrender the town to our
enemies, the Lord will deliver Israel by
my hand. But you must not inquire 34
about my act, for I will not tell you
what I am going to do until it is done."
Then Uzziah and the rulers said to 35
her,
"Farewell, and the Lord God go before you, to take vengeance upon our
enemies." And they returned from the 36
tent and went to their posts.

But Judith fell upon her face and put **9**
ashes on her head, and she stripped off
the sackcloth that she had put on, and
just as the incense offering of that evening was being offered in Jerusalem in
the house of God, Judith cried aloud
and said,
"Lord God of my father Symeon, in 2
whose hand you put a sword to take

vengeance on the aliens who had loosened a maiden's headdress to defile her
and stripped her thigh to shame her,
and profaned her womb to disgrace
3 her; for you said, 'It must not be done,'
yet they did it. So you gave up their
rulers to be killed, and their bed, which
was ashamed of the deceit they had
practiced, to be stained with blood, and
you struck down slaves upon princes
4 and princes upon their thrones, and
you gave up their wives to plunder and
their daughters to captivity and all
their spoils to be divided among your
beloved sons, who were very zealous
for you and abhorred the pollution of
their blood and called on you for help.
5 O God, my God, listen to a widow like
me. For you made what preceded those
things, and those things, and what followed them, and you design the present
and the future, and what you meditate
6 comes to pass. The things you plan
present themselves and say, 'Here we
are.' For all your ways stand ready,
and you judge with foreknowledge.
7 For here the Assyrians are multiplied
in their might, they are exalted over
horse and rider, they glory in the arm of
the foot soldiers, they place their hope
in shield and spear and bow and sling,
and do not know that you are a lord
8 that crushes wars. The Lord is your
name; break their strength with your
might, and shatter their force in your
anger, for they plan to profane your
sanctuary, to pollute the tent where
your glorious name rests, to strike down
the horn of your altar with the sword.
9 Look at their arrogance, direct your
anger upon their heads, put in the
hand of a widow like me the strength
10 to do what I have planned. With my
deceitful lips strike down the slave with
the ruler and the ruler with his servant,
break down their state with a woman's
11 hand. For your strength is not in numbers nor your might in the strong, but
you are the God of the lowly, the helper
of the inferior, the champion of the
weak, the protector of the neglected,
12 the savior of the despairing. Yes, God
of my father, and God of the inheritance of Israel, Lord of the heavens and
the earth, creator of the waters, king of
13 all your creation, hear my prayer and
make my deceitful words the wound
and stripe of those who have planned
such cruelty against your agreement
and your consecrated house, and Mount
Zion and the house your sons possess.
Make your whole nation and every
tribe to know and understand that you
are God, the God of all power and
might, and that the nation of Israel has
no protector but you."

It came to pass, when she had ceased calling on the God of Israel and had finished saying all these things, that she rose from her prostrate position and called her maid, and went down into the house, where she lived on the sabbaths and on her feast days, and she took off the sackcloth which she had put on and she took off her widow's mourning and washed herself with water and anointed herself with rich ointment, and braided her hair and put on a headdress and she dressed herself in festal attire which she used to wear when her husband Manasseh was alive. She took sandals for her feet, and put on her anklets and bracelets and rings and earrings and all her ornaments and made herself very beautiful to attract the eyes of any men who might see her. Then she gave her maid a leather bottle of wine and a jar of oil, and she filled a bag with parched grain and figs and pure bread, and she packed all her dishes and had her carry them.

Then they went out to the gate of the town of Bethulia and they found Uzziah standing at the gate with Chabris and Charmis, the elders of the town. When they saw her, and that her face was altered and her dress changed, they admired her beauty very greatly, and they said to her,

"May the God of our forefathers win you favor and fulfil your designs, to the gratification of the sons of Israel and the exaltation of Jerusalem."

And she worshiped God, and said to them,

"Order them to open the gate of the town for me, and I will go out to carry out the things of which you talked with me."

Then they ordered the young men to open the gate for her as she had said, and they did so. And Judith went out, she and her maid with her; and the men of the town watched her until she had gone down the mountain and had gone through the valley and they could see her no more.

They went straight on through the

valley, and an outpost of the Assyrians
12 met her; and they took her into custody
and asked her,
"To what people do you belong and
where do you come from, and where are
you going?"
And she said,
"I am a daughter of the Hebrews, and
I am escaping from their presence because they are going to be given to you
13 to devour. I am going to the presence of
Holofernes, the commander-in-chief of
your army, to give him a true report,
and I will show him a way by which he
can go and become master of all the
hilly country without losing from his
men one living body or spirit."
14 When the men heard her words and
observed her face, they regarded it as
wonderfully beautiful, and they said to
her,
15 "You have saved your life by hurrying to come down to the presence of our
lord. So now go to his tent, and some of
us will escort you until they deliver you
16 into his charge. But if you stand before
him, have no fear in your heart but report to him what you have said, and he
will treat you well."
17 Then they chose a hundred men of
their number and had them escort her
and her maid, and they conducted
them to the tent of Holofernes.
18 And they ran together from the
whole camp, for the news of her coming
had spread among the tents, and they
came and gathered about her as she
stood outside the tent of Holofernes,
waiting until they told him about her.
19 And they wondered at her beauty, and
admired the Israelites, judging by her,
and they said to one another,
"Who can despise these people, when
they have such women among them?
For it is not right to leave one man of
them alive, for if we let them go they
will be able to beguile the whole earth."
20 Then those who reclined with Holofernes and all his attendants came out
21 and took her into the tent. Now Holofernes was resting on his bed, under the
canopy, which was woven of purple and
gold and emeralds and precious stones.
22 And they told him about her, and he
came forward into the space before the
tent, with silver lamps preceding him.
23 But when Judith came before him and
his attendants, they all wondered at
the beauty of her face, and she fell on
her face and made obeisance to him,
and his slaves raised her up.
Then Holofernes said to her, 11
"Take courage, lady, do not be afraid
in your heart, for I never hurt anyone
who has chosen to serve Nebuchadnezzar, the king of the whole earth. And 2
now, if your people that inhabit the
hilly country had not slighted me, I
would not have raised my spear against
them. But they have brought this upon
themselves. Now tell me why you have 3
escaped from them and come to us, for
you have come to save yourself. Take
courage, for you shall live tonight and
henceforth. No one will hurt you but 4
everybody will treat you well, as they
treat the slaves of my lord, King Nebuchadnezzar."
And Judith said to him, 5
"Accept the words of your slave, and
let your maidservant speak before you,
and I will declare nothing false to my
lord tonight. If you follow out the 6
words of your maidservant, God will
fully carry out the matter with you, and
my lord will not fall short of his designs. For by the life of Nebuchad- 7
nezzar, king of the whole earth, and by
the might of him who has sent you to
correct every soul, not only do men
serve him because of you, but also the
wild animals and cattle and wild birds,
through your might, shall live under
the sway of Nebuchadnezzar and all his
house. For we have heard of your wis- 8
dom and the cleverness of your mind,
and the whole earth has been told that
you are the only man in the whole kingdom who is competent, and able in
knowledge and wonderful in the arts of
war. Now as to what Achior said in 9
your council, we have heard his words,
for the men of Bethulia saved him, and
he told them all that he had said before
you. Therefore, my lord and master, 10
do not disregard what he said, but
treasure it in your heart, for it is true;
for our nation cannot be punished, the
sword cannot prevail against them, unless they sin against their God. And 11
now, that my lord may not be defeated
and disappointed, death is about to
fall upon them, for a sin has overtaken
them by which they will anger their
God, when they shall do what they
should not. When food failed them, 12
and all their water grew scanty, they
planned to resort to their cattle and re-

solved to consume all that God by his
13 laws had forbidden them to eat. The
first fruits of the wheat, and the tenths
of the wine and the oil which they
had consecrated and reserved for the
priests who stand before the face of our
God in Jerusalem, which none of the
people is permitted even to touch with
their hands, they decided to consume.
14 They have sent men to Jerusalem, because those who live there have also
done this, to bring them permission
15 from the senate. The result will be that
when the answer reaches them and they
do this, on that day they will be de-
16 livered up to you to be destroyed. So
when I, your slave, learned all this, I
made my escape from their presence,
and God sent me to perform things
with you at which the whole earth, as
many as shall hear of them, shall be as-
17 tonished. For your slave is devout and
serves the God of heaven night and
day. Now I will stay with you, my
lord, and every night your slave will go
out into the valley and I will pray to
God and he will tell me when they have
18 committed their sins. And I will come
and report it to you also and you shall
go out with your whole army, and not
19 one of them will oppose you. I will lead
you through the heart of Judea until
you face Jerusalem, and I will set your
throne in the midst of her, and you
shall drive them like sheep that have no
shepherd, and no dog shall so much as
growl at you; for this was told me to
give me foreknowledge; it was declared
to me, and I was sent to tell you."

20 Her words pleased Holofernes and all
his attendants, and they wondered at
her wisdom and said,

21 "There is not such a woman from one
end of the earth to the other, for beauty
and intelligence."

22 And Holofernes said to her,
"God did well to send you before the
people, to put strength in our hands,
and bring destruction upon those who
23 have slighted my lord. You are beautiful, and you speak well, for if you do as
you have said, your God shall be my
God, and you shall live in the house
of King Nebuchadnezzar and be renowned over the whole earth."

12 Then he commanded them to bring
her in where his silver dishes were,
and gave orders that they should set
some of his own food before her, and
that she should drink his wine. But 2
Judith said,
"I cannot eat them, for it might give
offense, but I will be supplied with the
things I have brought with me."
Holofernes said to her, 3
"If what you have with you gives
out, where can we get more like it to
give you?"
And Judith said to him, 4
"As surely as you are alive, my lord,
your slave will not use up the things I
have with me before the Lord carries
out by my hand the things he has resolved upon."
So Holofernes' attendants brought 5
her into the tent, and she slept until
midnight. And toward the morning
watch she got up, and sent to Holo- 6
fernes, saying,
"Now let my lord give orders that
your slave be permitted to go out to
pray."
And Holofernes ordered his body- 7
guards not to hinder her. And she remained in the camp three days, and at
night she went out into the valley of
Bethulia and washed herself at the
spring in the camp. And when she came 8
up from the water, she prayed the Lord
God of Israel to make her way straight
so that she might raise up the sons of
his people. Then she went in clean and 9
stayed in the tent until she had her
food toward evening.
It happened that on the fourth day 10
Holofernes gave a banquet for his
slaves only, and invited none of those
on duty. And he said to Bagoas, the 11
eunuch who had charge of all he had,
"Go now, and persuade this Hebrew
woman who is in your charge, to come
to us and eat and drink with us. For it 12
is a disgrace to our dignity if we let such
a woman go without having her company, for if we do not draw her to us
she will laugh at us."
So Bagoas went out from the pres- 13
ence of Holofernes and went in to her
and said,
"This beautiful maidservant must
not hesitate to come to my lord and to
be honored in his presence and to drink
wine and be merry with us, and to become today like a daughter of the Assyrians who wait in the house of Nebuchadnezzar."
Then Judith said to him,
"And who am I, to refuse my lord?

For I will make haste to do everything
that is pleasing in his sight, and this
will be my boast to the day of my
death."
15 And she got up and dressed herself
beautifully with all her feminine finery,
and her slave went and spread fleeces
on the ground for her before Holofernes, which she had received from
Bagoas for her daily use, so that she
might recline on them and eat.
16 So Judith went in and lay down, and
Holofernes' mind was amazed at her
and his heart was stirred, and he was
exceedingly desirous of intimacy with
her, for he had been watching for an
opportunity to deceive her ever since
he had seen her.
17 And Holofernes said to her,
"Drink now, and be merry with us."
18 And Judith said,
"Certainly I will drink, my lord, for
my life means more to me today than in
all the days since I was born."
19 Then she took what her slave had
prepared, and ate and drank before
20 him. And Holofernes was delighted
with her, and he drank a very great
deal of wine, more than he had ever
drunk on one day since he was born.
13 But when evening came on, his
slaves hastened to withdraw. And
Bagoas went out to the tent and closed
it, and dismissed the attendants from
his master's presence, and they went
off to their beds, for they were all tired,
because the banquet had been so long.
2 But Judith was left alone in the tent,
with Holofernes prostrate upon his bed,
3 for he was drenched with wine. Judith
had told her slave to stand outside her
bed chamber and wait for her to come
out, as usual; for she had said that she
would go out to offer her prayer; and
she had told Bagoas the same thing.
4 So they all went out from his presence, and there was no one, small or
great, left in the bed chamber. And
Judith stood beside his bed and said in
her heart,
"Lord, God of all power, look favorably at this hour upon the works of
my hands for the exaltation of Jeru-
5 salem. For now is the time to help
your inheritance and to carry out my
undertaking for the destruction of the
enemies who have risen up against us."
6 And she went up to the rail of the
bed, which was at Holofernes' head,
and took down from it his scimitar,
and she went close to the bed and 7
grasped the hair of his head, and said
"Give me strength, Lord, God of
Israel, today!"
And she struck him on the neck 8
twice, with all her might, and severed
his head from his body. Then she 9
rolled his body off the bed, and pulled
the canopy down from the pillars, and
after a little while she went out and
gave Holofernes' head to her maid,
and she put it in her bag of food, and 10
they both went out together as they
were accustomed to do, to offer their
prayer. They passed through the camp
and skirted that valley, and went up
the mountain to Bethulia and came to
its gates.
And Judith called from a long way 11
off to the watchmen at the gates,
"Open, open the gate! God, our God
is with us, to show his strength in
Israel, and his might against our enemies, as he has done today."
And it happened that when her 12
townmen heard her voice, they hastened down to the gate of their town,
and called the elders of the town together. And they all ran together, 13
small and great, for it seemed strange
to them that she should come, and they
opened the gate and welcomed them,
and they kindled a fire for light, and
gathered about them. And she said to 14
them in a loud voice,
"Praise God, praise him! Praise God
who has not withdrawn his mercy from
the house of Israel, but has shattered
our enemies by my hand this very
night!"
Then she took the head out of the 15
bag and showed it, and she said to
them,
"Here is the head of Holofernes, the
commander of the army of Assyria, and
here is the canopy under which he lay
in his drunkenness. For the Lord has
struck him down by a woman's hand.
And as surely as the Lord lives, who 16
protected me on the way I went, my
face deceived him to his destruction,
and he committed no sin with me, to
pollute and disgrace me."
All the people were greatly aston- 17
ished, and they bowed down and worshiped God, and said under a common
impulse,
"Blessed are you, our God, who have

brought to nought the enemies of your
people today."
18 And Uzziah said to her,
"Blessed are you, my daughter, beyond all the women on earth in the
sight of the Most High God, and blessed
is the Lord God, who created the heavens and the earth, who guided you to
strike the leader of our enemies on the
19 head. Your hope shall never disappear
from the minds of men when they re-
20 member the strength of God. May
God make this an eternal glory to you
and reward you with blessings, because
on account of the affliction of our nation you did not spare your own life,
but you anticipated our calamity, going
straight on before our God."
And all the people said,
"Be it so! Be it so!"
14 Then Judith said to them,
"Listen to me, brothers. Take this
head and hang it on the battlement of
2 your wall. And when the day breaks,
and the sun rises on the earth, you must
take up your weapons, each of you, and
every valiant man go out of the town,
and you must put a captain over them
as though you were going down on the
plain against the outpost of the Assyrians, but you must not go down.
3 Then they will take up their arms and
go into their camp and awaken the
officers of the Assyrian army; and they
will hurry to the tent of Holofernes, and
they will not find him. Then fear will
fall upon them and they will flee before
4 you. And you and all who inhabit all
the borders of Israel must follow them
5 up and destroy them as they go. But
before you do this, bring Achior the
Ammonite to me, so that he may see
and recognize the man who despised
the house of Israel and who sent him
to us as though to his death."
6 Then they summoned Achior from
the house of Uzziah. And when he
came and saw the head of Holofernes
in the hand of a man in the gathering
of people, he fell on his face and his
7 spirit failed. And when they raised him
up, he fell at Judith's feet, and made
obeisance to her, and said,
"Blessed are you in every tent of
Judah, and in every nation those who
8 hear your name will be alarmed. Now
tell me all that you have done in these
days."
So Judith related to him in the presence of the people all that she had done
from the day that she went out of the
town until the time she was speaking
to them. And when she stopped speak- 9
ing, the people uttered a great shout
and gave a joyful cry in their town.
And when Achior saw all that the God 10
of Israel had done, he believed in God
with all his heart, and accepted circumcision and was adopted into the
household of Israel, and remained so
unto this day.
When the dawn came, they hung 11
Holofernes' head from the wall, and
every man took up his weapons and
they went out in companies toward
the approaches to the mountain. But 12
when the Assyrians saw them, they
sent word to their officers, and they
went to the generals and colonels and
all their officers. And they came to the 13
tent of Holofernes and said to him who
had charge of all that he had,
"Wake our lord up, for these slaves
have dared to come down against us to
battle, so that they may be utterly
destroyed."
Then Bagoas went and knocked at 14
the curtain of the tent, for he supposed
that he was sleeping with Judith. When 15
no one answered, he drew the curtain
aside and went into the bed chamber,
and found him thrown down dead
upon the step, and his head had been
cut off and was gone. And he cried out 16
aloud, with lamentation and groaning
and a great shout, and tore open his
clothing. And he went into the tent 17
where Judith stayed, and could not
find her, and he rushed out to the people
and shouted,
"The slaves have deceived us; one 18
Hebrew woman has brought disgrace
upon the house of Nebuchadnezzar, for
here is Holofernes lying on the ground,
and his head is not on his shoulders."
But when the leaders of the Assyrian 19
army heard these words, they tore open
their shirts and their souls were dreadfully dismayed, and they raised an exceedingly loud crying and shouting in
the midst of the camp. And when the 1
men in the tents heard it, they were
amazed at what had happened, and
fear and trembling came upon them,
and not a man waited to face his comrade, but streaming out under a common impulse they fled by every way of
the plain and of the hilly country.

3 Those who had encamped in the hilly
country around Bethulia also turned
and fled. Then the Israelites, every
soldier among them, streamed after
4 them. And Uzziah sent men to Beto-
masthaim and Bebai and Chobai and
Kola and all the borders of Israel, to
tell of what had been accomplished,
and to order them all to stream out
after their enemies to destroy them.
5 And when the Israelites heard, under a
common impulse they all fell upon
them, and cut them in pieces as far as
Chobai. Those of Jerusalem and of all
the hilly country also came, for they
had been told what had happened to
the camp of their enemies, and those in
Gilead and in Galilee fell upon their
flank with great slaughter until they
6 passed Damascus and its borders. The
remaining inhabitants of Bethulia fell
upon the Assyrian camp and pillaged it,
7 and were made very rich. And the
Israelites when they returned from the
slaughter took possession of what remained, and the villages and hamlets
in the hilly country and in the plain got
a great quantity of spoil, for there was
a very great amount of it.
8 Then Joakim, the high priest, and
the senate of the Israelites who lived in
Jerusalem came to witness the blessings
which the Lord had conferred upon
Israel and to see Judith and greet her.
9 And when they went to see her, they
all blessed her with one accord, and
said to her,
"You are the exaltation of Jerusalem,
you are the great glory of Israel, you
10 are the great boast of our nation. You
have done all this with your hand; you
have done Israel good, and God is well
pleased with it. The Omnipotent Lord
bless you forever."
And all the people said,
"Be it so!"
11 And all the people plundered the
camp for thirty days; and they gave
Judith the tent of Holofernes and all
his silver dishes and his beds and his
bowls and all his furniture, and she
took them and put them on her mule,
and she harnessed her wagons and piled
them on them.
12 And all the women of Israel came to
see her, and they blessed her and made
a dance in her honor, and she took
branches in her hands and gave them
13 to the women that were with her, and
they crowned themselves with olive,
she and the women with her, and she
went before all the people in the dance,
leading all the women, and all the men
of Israel in their armor, with garlands
and with songs on their lips. And Ju- 16
dith began this thanksgiving before all
Israel, and all the people loudly sang
this song of praise. And Judith said, 2

"Begin to play unto my God with tambourines,
Sing unto my Lord to the sound of cymbals,
Raise hymn and praise for him,
Exalt his name, and call upon it,
For the Lord is a God that shatters wars, 3
For he brought me into his camp, in the midst of the people,
Rescuing me from the hands of my pursuers.
Assyria came from the north out of the mountains, 4
He came with the myriads of his host,
Their multitude blocked up the torrents,
And their cavalry covered the hills.
He said he was going to burn up my borders, 5
And kill my young men with the sword,
And throw my babies upon the ground,
And take my children as spoils,
And my girls as plunder.
The Lord Almighty brought them to nought 6
By the hand of a woman.
For their champion did not fall at the hands of young men, 7
The sons of the Titans did not strike him down,
Nor the tall giants set upon him,
But Judith, the daughter of Merari,
Made him faint with the beauty of her face.
For she took off her widow's mourning, 8
To lift up those who were in distress in Israel.
She anointed her face with ointment,
And arranged her hair in a headdress,
And put on a linen dress to deceive him.
Her sandal ravished his eye, 9
And her beauty captivated his soul.
The scimitar passed through his neck.
Persians shuddered at her daring, 10
And Medes were daunted at her boldness.

11 Then my oppressed people cried out,
My weak people were terrified and cowered down,
They lifted up their voices and turned to flee.
12 The sons of their maidservants stabbed them,
And wounded them like runaways' children;
They perished before the army of my Lord.
13 I will sing to my God a new song;
Lord, you are great and glorious,
Wonderfully strong, unconquerable.
14 Let all your creation serve you,
For you but spoke, and they were created,
You sent forth your Spirit, and it formed them,
And there is no one that can resist your voice.
15 For mountains will be moved from their foundations like waters,
And rocks will melt like wax before you,
But to those who fear you
You will continue to show mercy.
16 For any sacrifice for a fragrant odor is a small thing,
And any fat for a whole burnt offering is insignificant in your sight,
But he that fears the Lord is great forever.
17 Alas for the heathen that rise up against my nation.
The Lord Almighty will take vengeance on them in the day of judgment,
To apply fire and worms to their bodies,
And they will feel them and wail forever."

When they reached Jerusalem, they 18
worshiped God, and when the people
were purified, they offered their whole
burnt offerings and their freewill offerings and their gifts. And Judith dedi- 19
cated to God all the dishes of Holofernes, which the people had given her,
and the canopy which she had taken
for herself from his bed chamber she
gave as a gift to God; and the people 20
continued to celebrate in Jerusalem before the sanctuary for three months,
and Judith stayed with them.

After those days everyone traveled 21
back to his own inheritance, and Judith
returned to Bethulia and remained on
her estate, and she was famous all over
the land in her time. Many men de- 22
sired to marry her, but no man had relations with her, all her life long, from
the day Manasseh her husband died
and was gathered to his people. She 23
became greater and greater and she
grew old in her husband's house until
she was a hundred and five. She set her
maid free, and died in Bethulia, and
they buried her in the cave of her
husband Manasseh. And the house of 24
Israel mourned for her for seven days.
Before she died she divided her property among all the nearest relations of
her husband Manasseh and her own
nearest relatives. No one could terrify 25
the Israelites in Judith's days, nor for
a long time after she died.

THE ADDITIONS TO THE BOOK OF ESTHER

12 IN THE second year of the reign of
Artaxerxes the Great, on the first
day of Nisan, Mordecai the son of
Jair, the son of Shimei, the son of
Kish, of the tribe of Benjamin, had a
3 dream. He was a Jew, and lived in the
city of Susa, an important man, in at-
4 tendance at the royal court; he was one
of the captives that Nebuchadnezzar,
king of Babylon, had brought from
Jerusalem, with Jeconiah, king of
5 Judah. And this was his dream: behold, noise and tumult, thunders and
6 earthquake, uproar on the earth. And
here came two great dragons, both
ready to wrestle, and they uttered a
7 great roar. And at their roar every nation made ready for war, to fight
against the nation of the upright.
8 And behold, a day of darkness and
gloom, affliction and anguish, distress
9 and great tumult upon the earth. And
the whole upright nation was troubled,
10 fearing their own hurt, and they prepared to perish; and they cried out to
God. And at their cry there arose as
though from a tiny spring, a great river,
11 with abundant water; light came, and
the sun rose, and the humble were exalted and consumed the glorious.

12 When Mordecai, who had had this
dream, and had seen what God had
resolved to do, awoke, he kept it in his
mind, and all day sought by all means
to understand it.

2 Now Mordecai took his rest in the
court with Gabatha and Tharra, the two
royal eunuchs who kept watch in the
2 court. He overheard their reflections,
and inquired into their designs, and
found out that they were preparing to
lay hands on King Artaxerxes, and he
3 informed the king about them. And
the king examined the two eunuchs,
and when they confessed, they were led
4 off to execution. And the king wrote a
memorandum about this matter, and
5 Mordecai also wrote about it. And the
king ordered Mordecai to be in attendance at the court, and he made him
6 presents because of it. But Haman,
the son of Ammedatha, a Bougaean,
was in high honor with the king, and he
set out to injure Mordecai and his
people, because of the two royal
eunuchs.

(*Esther 1:1—3:13 follows here in the Greek.*)

And this is the copy of the letter: 13
"The Great King, Artaxerxes, to the
rulers of a hundred and twenty-seven
provinces, from India to Ethiopia, and
to the subordinate governors, writes
thus: Having become ruler of many 2
nations, and come to have dominion
over the whole world, I desire, not because I am elated by the presumption
of power, but behaving always with
mildness and moderation, to insure that
my subjects shall live in unbroken tranquillity, and in order to make my kingdom peaceable and open for travel in
all its extent, to re-establish the peace
which all men desire. When I asked my 3
counselors how this end might be accomplished, Haman, who excels among
us in soundness of judgment, and is distinguished for his unfailing loyalty and
steadfast fidelity, and has attained the
second rank in the kingdom, pointed 4
out to us, that among all the nations
of the world there is scattered an ill-
disposed people, with laws contrary to
those of every nation, which continually disregards the royal ordinances, so
that the unifying of our realm, directed
by us with the best intentions, cannot
be effected. Understanding therefore 5
that this nation, and it alone, stands
in constant opposition to all men, perversely following a strange manner of
life and laws, and ill-disposed to our
administration, doing all the harm it
can, so that our rule may not be made
secure, we have decreed that the per- 6
sons designated in the letters sent to
you by Haman, who is in charge of our
administration, and is a second father
to us, shall all, with their wives and
children, be destroyed, root and branch,
by the sword of their enemies, without
pity or mercy, on the fourteenth day of

the twelfth month, Adar, of this pres-
7 ent year; so that they who all along
have been disaffected, may in a single day go down through violence to
Hades, and leave our government secure and undisturbed for the future."
(*Esther 3:14—4:17 follows here
in the Greek.*)
8 And he besought the Lord, calling
to mind all the doings of the Lord, and
said,
9 "Lord, you King, who rule over all,
for all is in your power, and there is no
one who can oppose you when you
10 choose to save Israel, for you made
heaven and earth, and every wonderful
11 thing under heaven, and you are Lord
of all, and there is no one who can resist
12 you, who are the Lord; you know all
things; you know, Lord, that it was not
in insolence or arrogance or vainglory
that I did this, and refused to bow
13 down to this proud Haman, for I would
have been willing to kiss the soles of his
14 feet, to save Israel. But I did it so as
not to set the glory of man above the
glory of God, and I will bow down to no
one but you, my Lord, and I will not
15 do it in pride. Now, Lord God and
King, God of Abraham, spare your
people, for they are looking at us to consume us, and they desire to destroy the
inheritance that has been yours from
16 the beginning. Do not be indifferent to
your portion, which you ransomed for
17 yourself from the land of Egypt. Hear
my prayer, and have mercy on your
heritage; turn our mourning into feasting, so that we may live, and sing
praise to your name, Lord; do not destroy the mouth of those who praise
you."
18 And all Israel cried out with all their
might, for death was before their eyes.
14 Then Esther, the queen, overwhelmed with deadly anxiety, fled to
2 the Lord; she took off her splendid
clothing and put on garments of distress and mourning, and instead of the
rarest perfumes, she covered her head
with ashes and dung, and she abased
her body utterly, and every part that
she delighted to adorn she covered with
3 her tangled hair. And she prayed to
the Lord and said,
"My Lord, our King, you stand
alone; help me who am alone, and have
4 no helper but you; for my danger is in
5 my hand. Ever since I was born, I have
heard in the tribe of my family that
you, Lord, took Israel from among all
the nations, and our forefathers from
among all their ancestors for an everlasting possession, and that you did for
them all that you promised. But now
we have sinned before you, and you
have handed us over to our enemies,
because we glorified their gods; you are
upright, Lord. And now they are not
satisfied that we are in bitter captivity
but they have made an agreement with
their idols to abolish what your mouth
has ordained, and destroy your possession, and stop the mouths of those
who praise you and quench the glory
of your house, and your altar, and open 10
the mouths of the heathen to praise unreal gods, so that a mortal king may be
magnified forever. Lord, do not give up 11
your scepter to those who have no
being, and do not let them mock at our
fall, but turn their plan against themselves, and make an example of the
man who has begun this against us. Re- 12
member, Lord; make yourself known
in this time of our affliction and give
me courage, king of the gods and
holder of all dominion. Put eloquent 13
speech in my mouth, before this lion,
and change his heart to hate the man
who is fighting against us, so that there
may be an end of him, and of those
who support him. But save us by your 14
hand, and help me, who stand alone,
and have no one but you, Lord. You 15
know everything, and you know that I
hate the splendor of the wicked, and
abhor the bed of the uncircumcised and
of any alien. You know what I am 16
forced to do—that I abhor the symbol
of my proud position, which is placed
upon my head on the days when I appear in public; I abhor it like a filthy
rag, and never wear it in private. Your 17
slave has not eaten at Haman's table,
and I have not honored the king's feast,
or drunk the wine of the libations.
Your slave has had no joy from the day 18
I was brought here until now, except in
you, Lord God of Abraham. O God, 19
whose might is over all, hear the voice
of the despairing, and save us from the
hands of evil-doers, and save me from
what I fear."
And it came to pass on the third day, **1**
when she had ceased to pray, that she
took off the clothes in which she had
worshiped, and dressed herself in splen- 2

dor. When she was magnificently clad,
she invoked the aid of the all-seeing
God and Savior, and took with her her
3 two maids; on one she leaned languish-
4 ingly, while the other followed her,
5 carrying her train. She was radiant
with her perfect beauty, and her face
was happy as it was lovely, but her
6 heart was in an agony of fear. When
she had gone through all the doors, she
stood before the king. He was seated
on his royal throne, clad in all his
magnificence, and covered with gold
and precious stones; he was an awe-
7 inspiring sight. And he raised his face,
burning with splendor, and looked at
her with the fiercest anger; and the
queen fell down and turned pale and
fainted, and she collapsed upon the
head of the maid who went before her.
8 Then God changed the king's spirit
to mildness, and in great anxiety he
sprang from his throne and caught her
in his arms, until she came to herself,
and he reassured her with soothing
words, and said to her,
9 "What is it, Esther? I am your
10 brother. Courage, you shall not die, for
our command is only for the people;
come near."
11 Then he lifted the gold scepter and
12 laid it upon her neck, and he embraced
her and said,
"Tell me!"
13 And she said to him,
"I saw you, my lord, like an angel of
God, and my mind was dismayed with
14 awe at your splendor; you are wonderful, my lord, and your face is full of
graciousness."
15 But as she spoke, she fell fainting;
16 and the king was troubled, and all his
train tried to reassure her.

(*Esther 5:3—8:12 follows here in the Greek.*)

16 Of this letter the following is a copy:
"The Great King, Artaxerxes, sends
greeting to the rulers of countries in a
hundred and twenty-seven provinces,
from India to Ethiopia, and to those
2 who are loyal to our rule. The more
frequently they are honored by the
excessive favor of their benefactors, the
3 prouder many men become, and not
only seek to injure our subjects, but, in
their inability to bear prosperity, they
undertake designs against their own
4 benefactors, and not only uproot gratitude from among men, but intoxicated
by the boasts of foolish men they suppose they will escape the evil-hating
justice of the ever all-seeing God. And 5
often many of those who occupy places
of authority have by the persuasiveness
of the friends who have been intrusted
with the conduct of affairs, been made
accomplices in the shedding of innocent
blood, and been involved in irremedi-
able disasters, when such men by the 6
specious fallacies of their vicious natures beguile the sincere good will of
their sovereigns. And what has been 7
impiously accomplished by the baneful
conduct of those who exercise authority unworthily, you can see not so much
from the venerable histories which have
come down to us, as from the scrutiny
of matters close at hand. And in order 8
to make our kingdom in the future tranquil and peaceful for all men, we will 9
change our attitude, and always decide
the matters that fall under our notice
with more considerate attention. For 10
Haman, the son of Hammedathi, a
Macedonian, an alien indeed from the
Persian blood, and widely removed
from our kindliness, being entertained
as a guest by us, enjoyed the humanity 11
that we extend to every nation to such
a degree that he was called our father,
and was continually bowed down to by
all, as a person second only to the royal
throne. But he in his unbearable arro- 12
gance designed to deprive us of our
kingdom, and to compass the death of 13
our preserver and perpetual benefactor
Mordecai, and of Esther, our blameless
partner in the kingdom, together with
their whole nation, demanding with
intricate deceptions and intrigues that
they be destroyed. For he thought by 14
these means that he would find us
deserted and would transfer the domi-
nation of the Persians to the Macedonians. But we find that the Jews, 15
who were consigned to annihilation by
this thrice sinful man, are no evil-doers
but are governed by most just laws,
and are sons of the Most High, Most 16
Mighty Living God, who has directed
the kingdom for us and for our forefathers with most excellent guidance.
Therefore please pay no further atten- 17
tion to the letters sent you by Haman,
the son of Hammedathi, because the 18
very man who was active in this has
been hung with all his house at the
gates of Susa, for God, who governs all

things, has speedily inflicted on him the
19 punishment he deserved. Therefore put
up the copy of this letter publicly
everywhere, and let the Jews live under
20 their own laws, and reinforce them, so
that on the thirteenth day of the
twelfth month, Adar, on that very day
they may defend themselves against
those who assail them at the time of
21 their affliction. For God, who governs
all things, has made this day a joy to
them instead of proving the destruction
22 of the chosen race. So you must observe
it as a notable day among your
commemorative festivals, and all good
23 cheer, so that both now and hereafter
it may mean preservation to us and to
the loyal Persians, but to those who
plot against us it may serve as a re-
24 minder of destruction. But any city or
country without exception, which shall
fail to act in accordance with this, shall
be utterly destroyed in wrath with
fire and sword; it will be made not only
impassable for men, but also hateful to
wild animals and birds for all time.

(*This is followed in the Greek by 8:13—10:3, where the Hebrew Esther ends. The Greek version adds the following:*)

10 4 And Mordecai said,
5 "This came from God. For I remember the dream that I had about these
things; for none of them has failed to
6 be fulfilled. As for the tiny spring that
became a river, when light came, and
the sun shone and there was an abundance
of water, the river is Esther, whom
the king married and made queen.
And I and Haman are the two dragons.
And those who gathered to destroy the
name of the Jews are the heathen.
And my nation, which cried out to
God and was saved, is Israel; for the
Lord has saved his people, the Lord has
delivered us from all these evils, and
God has wrought great signs and wonders, such as never happened among the
heathen. That is why he made two lots,
one for the people of God and one for
all the heathen, and these two lots
came to the hour and time and day
when God should judge among all the
nations. And God remembered his people, and he acquitted his inheritance. So
these days in the month of Adar, on
the fourteenth and fifteenth of that
month, will be observed by them with
assembling together and joy and gladness before God from generation to generation, forever, among his people
Israel."

In the fourth year of the reign of Ptolemy and Cleopatra, Dositheus, who said he was a priest and Levite, and Ptolemy his son, brought in (to Egypt) this preceding letter of Purim, which they said was true, and had been translated by Lysimachus the son of Ptolemy, one of the residents of Jerusalem.

THE WISDOM OF SOLOMON

1 LOVE uprightness, you who judge the land,
Think of the Lord with goodness,
And seek him with sincerity of heart.
2 For he is found by those who do not try him,
And is manifested to those who do not disbelieve him.
3 For crooked reasonings separate from God,
And when his power is tested, it exposes fools.
4 For wisdom cannot enter a deceitful soul,
Or live in a body in debt to sin.
5 For the holy spirit of instruction will flee from deceit,
And will rise and leave at unwise reasoning,
And be put to confusion at the approach of wrong.
6 For wisdom is a kindly spirit,
And will not acquit a blasphemer of what he says,
For God is a witness of his heart,
And a truthful observer of his mind,
And a hearer of his tongue.
7 For the spirit of the Lord fills the world,
And that which embraces all things knows all that is said.
8 Therefore no one who utters what is wrong will go unobserved,
Nor will justice, in its investigation, pass him by.
9 For there will be an inquiry into the designs of the ungodly,
And the sound of his words will reach the Lord,
To convict him of his transgressions.
10 For a jealous ear hears everything,
And the sound of grumbling is not hidden.
11 So beware of useless grumbling,
And spare your tongue from slander;
For no secret word goes for naught,
And a lying mouth destroys the soul.
12 Do not invite death by the error of your life,
Or incur destruction by the work of your hands;
For God did not make death, 13
And he does not enjoy the destruction of the living.
For he created everything to exist, 14
And the generative forces of the world are wholesome,
And there is no poisonous drug in them,
And the kingdom of Hades is not on earth.
For uprightness is immortal. 15
But ungodly men by their acts and words have summoned him, 16
They thought him their friend, and softened,
And made an agreement with him,
For they are fit to belong to his party.
For they did not reason soundly, but said to themselves, 2
"Our life is short and miserable,
And there is no cure when man comes to his end,
And no one has been known to return from Hades.
For we were born at a venture, 2
And hereafter we shall be as though we had never existed,
Because the breath in our nostrils is smoke,
And reason is a spark in the beating of our hearts;
When it is quenched, the body will turn to ashes, 3
And the spirit will dissolve like empty air.
And in time our name will be forgotten, 4
And no one will remember what we have done,
And our life will pass away like the traces of a cloud,
And be scattered like mist
Pursued by the sun's rays
And overcome by its heat.
For our life is a fleeting shadow, 5
And there is no way to recall our end,
For it is sealed up and no one can bring it back.

6 So come, let us enjoy the good things that exist,
And eagerly make use of the creation as we did in our youth.
7 Let us have our fill of costly wine and perfumes,
And let us not miss the spring flowers.
8 Let us crown ourselves with rosebuds before they wither;
9 Let none of us miss his share in our revelry;
Everywhere let us leave the signs of our gladness;
For this is our portion and this our lot.
10 Let us oppress the upright poor;
Let us not spare the widow,
Or respect the venerable gray head of the aged.
11 But let our strength be our law of uprightness,
For weakness is proved useless.
12 Let us lie in wait for the upright, for he inconveniences us
And opposes our doings,
And reproaches us with our transgressions of the Law,
And charges us with sins against what we have been taught;
13 He professes to possess knowledge of God,
And calls himself a child of the Lord;
14 We have found him a reproof of our thoughts,
He is wearisome to us even to see,
15 For his life is not like others,
And his ways are strange.
16 He considers us counterfeit,
And avoids our ways as unclean.
He calls the end of the upright happy,
And boasts that God is his father.
17 Let us see whether what he says is true,
And let us test what will happen at his departure.
18 For if the upright man is a son of God, he will help him,
And save him from the hands of his adversaries.
19 Let us test him with insults and torture,
So that we may learn his patience,
And prove his forbearance.
20 Let us condemn him to a shameful death,
For he will be watched over, from what he says!"
21 So they reasoned, but they went astray,
For their wickedness blinded them,
And they did not know God's secrets, 2
Or hope for the reward of holiness,
Or recognize the prize of blameless souls.
For God created man for immortality, 2
And made him the image of his own eternity,
But through the devil's envy death 2
came into the world,
And those who belong to his party experience it.

But the souls of the upright are in the hand of God,
And no torment can reach them.
In the eyes of foolish people they seemed to die,
And their decease was thought an affliction,
And their departure from us their ruin,
But they are at peace.
For though in the sight of men they are punished,
Their hope is full of immortality,
And after being disciplined a little, they will be shown great kindness.
For God has tried them,
And found them worthy of himself.
He has tested them like gold in a furnace,
And accepted them like the sacrifice of a whole burnt offering.
They will shine out, when he visits them,
And spread like sparks among the stubble.
They will judge nations and rule peoples,
And the Lord will reign over them forever.
Those who trust in him will understand the truth,
And those who are faithful will cling to him in love,
For his chosen will find favor and mercy.
But the ungodly will be punished according to their reasonings,
For they disregarded what was right and turned away from the Lord,
For the man who makes light of wisdom and instruction is wretched,
And there is nothing in their hope, and their labors are unprofitable,
And what they do is useless.
Their wives are silly,

And their children bad;
There is a curse on their birth.
13 For happy is the barren woman who is undefiled,
Who has not experienced a sinful union;
She will have fruit when God examines men's souls.
14 And happy is the eunuch who has not transgressed the Law with his hand,
Nor imagined wicked things against the Lord,
For special favor shall be shown him for his faith,
And a more delightful share in the Lord's sanctuary.
15 For good work brings renown,
And the root of understanding is unerring.
16 But the children of adulterers will not grow up,
And the offspring of an illicit union will disappear.
17 For if they are long-lived, they will be thought of no account,
And, at the last, their old age will be unhonored.
18 If they die early, they will have no hope
Or comfort on the day of decision.
19 For the fate of an unrighteous generation is hard.

4 It is better to be childless but virtuous,
For in the memory of virtue there is immortality,
For it is recognized by both God and men;
2 When it is present, men imitate it,
And they long for it when it is gone.
And it marches in triumph, wearing a wreath forever,
Victorious in the contest for prizes that are undefiled.
3 But the numerous brood of the ungodly will be unprofitable,
And with its base-born slips will not strike its roots deep,
Or establish a secure foundation.
4 For though it flourishes with branches for a while,
It stands insecurely and will be shaken by the wind,
And uprooted by the force of the winds.
5 The twigs will be broken off before they are grown,
And their fruit will be useless, not ripe enough to eat,
And good for nothing.
For children born of unlawful slumbers 6
Will be witnesses to their parents' guilt when they are examined.
But an upright man, if he dies before his time, will be at rest, 7
For an honored old age does not depend on length of time, 8
And is not measured by the number of one's years,
But understanding is gray hair for men, 9
And a blameless life is old age.
Because he pleased God well, he was loved by him, 10
And while living among sinners he was taken up.
He was caught up, so that wickedness might not alter his understanding, 11
Or guile deceive his soul.
For the spell of wickedness obscures what is good, 12
And the instability of desire perverts the innocent mind.
Being perfected in a little while he has fulfilled long years, 13
For his soul pleased the Lord; 14
Therefore he hurried from the midst of wickedness.
The peoples saw yet did not perceive
Or take such a thing to heart,
For favor and mercy are with his chosen, 15
And he watches over his saints.
But an upright man who has fallen asleep will condemn the ungodly who are still alive, 16
And youth that is soon perfected, the great age of the unrighteous.
For they see the wise man's end, 17
And do not perceive what the Lord's purpose about him was,
And for what he kept him safe;
They see, and make light of him; 18
But the Lord will laugh them to scorn.
And afterward they will become a dishonored corpse, 19
And be insulted among the dead forever;
He will burst them open, dumb and swollen,
And will shake them from their foundations,
And they will be utterly dried up,
And they will suffer anguish,
And the memory of them will perish.

20 They will come like cowards at the reckoning-up of their sins,
And their transgressions will convict them to their face.
5 Then the upright man will stand with great boldness
Face to face with his oppressors
And with those who set his labors at nought.
2 They will be dreadfully dismayed at the sight,
And amazed at the unexpectedness of his deliverance.
3 They will talk to themselves in repentance,
And in their distress of mind they will groan and say,
4 "This is the man we fools once laughed at,
And made a byword of reproach.
We thought his life was madness,
And his end dishonored.
5 How did he come to be reckoned among the sons of God,
And why is his lot among the saints?
6 Then we must have wandered from the true way,
And the light of uprightness did not light us,
And the sun did not rise upon us.
7 We were full of paths of lawlessness and destruction,
And traveled through trackless deserts,
But we did not recognize the Lord's road.
8 What good did our arrogance do us?
And what have wealth and ostentation done for us?
9 They have all passed away like a shadow,
And like a messenger running by;
10 Like a ship crossing the billowing water,
And when it is gone there is no track to be found
Or path of its keel in the waves;
11 Or as when a bird flies through the air,
It leaves no sign of its passage;
The light air, whipped by the beat of its wings,
And torn apart by the force of its speed,
Is traversed as its wings move,
And afterward no sign of its passage is found there.
12 Or as when an arrow is shot at a mark,
The air is pierced and immediately returns to itself,
So that its course is unknown;
So we also, as soon as we were born, 13
ceased to be,
And had no sign of virtue to show,
But were consumed in our wickedness.
For the ungodly man's hope is like 14
chaff carried by the wind,
And like hoarfrost driven away by a storm,
It is dissipated like smoke before the wind,
And passes by like the memory of a stranger who stays but a night.
But the upright live forever, 15
And their reward is with the Lord,
And the Most High takes care of them.
Therefore they will receive the glo- 16
rious kingdom,
And the beautiful diadem from the Lord's hand,
For he will cover them with his right hand,
And shield them with his arm.
He will take his jealousy for his 17
armor,
And will make creation his weapons to repulse his foes.
He will put on uprightness for a 18
corselet,
And wear unfeigned justice for a helmet.
He will take holiness for an invincible 19
shield,
And sharpen his stern anger for a 20
sword;
And with him the world will go to war against the madmen.
Well-aimed flashes of lightning will 21
fly,
And will leap to the mark from the clouds, as from a well-bent bow,
And from a catapult hailstones full of 22
wrath will be hurled.
The water of the sea will be angry with them,
And the rivers will roll relentlessly over them.
A mighty wind will oppose them, 23
And winnow them like a tempest.
And lawlessness will lay waste the whole earth,
And wrongdoing overturn the thrones of princes.
Listen therefore, kings, and under- 6
stand:
Learn this, judges of the ends of the earth;
Pay attention, rulers of the people, 2

Who boast of multitudes of nations;
3 For your dominion was given you from the Lord,
And your sovereignty from the Most High.
He will examine your works and inquire into your plans;
4 For though you are servants of his kingdom, you have not judged rightly,
Or kept the Law,
Or followed the will of God.
5 He will come upon you terribly and swiftly,
For a stern judgment overtakes those in high places.
6 For the humblest man may be forgiven through mercy,
But the mighty will be mightily tested,
7 For the Lord of all will show no partiality,
And will not respect greatness,
For it was he who made small and great,
And he takes thought for all alike,
8 But a rigorous inquiry is in store for the powerful.
9 My words are addressed to you, therefore, you monarchs,
So that you may learn wisdom and not go astray;
10 For those who observe holy things in holiness will be made holy,
And those who are taught them will have a defense to offer;
11 So desire my words,
Long for them, and you will be instructed.
12 Wisdom is bright and unfading,
And she is easily seen by those who love her,
And found by those who search for her.
13 She forestalls those who desire her, by making herself known first.
14 The man who rises early to seek her will not have to toil,
For he will find her sitting at his gates.
15 For to think of her is the highest understanding,
And the man who is vigilant for her sake will soon be free from care.
16 For she goes about in search of those who are worthy of her,
And she graciously appears to them in their paths,
And meets them in every thought.

For the truest beginning of her is the desire for instruction, 17
And concern for instruction is love of her,
And love for her is the observance of her laws, 18
And adherence to her laws is assurance of immortality,
And immortality brings men near to God; 19
So the desire for wisdom leads to a kingdom. 20
If therefore you take pleasure in thrones and scepters, monarchs of the people, 21
Honor wisdom, so that you may reign forever.
But what wisdom is and how she came to be, I will declare, 22
And I will not hide these secrets from you,
But I will trace her out from the beginning of creation,
And make the knowledge of her clear,
And I will not pass by the truth;
I will not travel with futile envy, 23
For it cannot associate with wisdom.
The multitude of the wise is the salvation of the world, 24
And a prudent king is the stability of his people.
So be instructed by my words and you will be benefited. 25
I too am a mortal man, like all men, 7
And a descendant of that first-formed man, who sprang from the earth,
And I was shaped into flesh in my mother's womb, 2
Solidified in blood in ten months
From man's seed and the pleasure of marriage.
And when I was born I breathed in the common air, 3
And fell on the kindred earth,
Giving the same first cry as all the rest.
I was carefully wrapped up and nursed, 4
For no king has any other beginning of existence; 5
But all men have one entrance upon life, and the same way of leaving it. 6
Therefore I prayed, and understanding was given me; 7
I called, and the spirit of wisdom came to me.
I preferred her to scepters and thrones, 8

And I thought wealth of no account
compared with her.
9 I did not think a priceless stone her
equal,
For all the gold, in her presence, is
just a little sand,
And silver is no better than mud,
before her.
10 I loved her more than health and
good looks,
And I preferred her even to light,
And her radiance is unceasing.
11 But all blessings came to me along
with her,
And uncounted wealth is in her hands.
12 And I rejoiced over them all, because
wisdom ruled them,
For I did not know that she was their
mother.
13 I learned honestly, and I share ungrudgingly,
I will not hide her wealth away,
14 For it is an unfailing treasure for men,
And those who get it make friends
with God,
Being commended to him by the
gifts that come from her discipline.
15 May God grant to me to speak
properly,
And to have thoughts worthy of what
he has given;
For it is he that guides wisdom
And directs the wise.
16 For in his hand are we and our words,
All understanding and knowledge of
trades.
17 For it is he that has given me unerring knowledge of what is,
To know the constitution of the world
and the working of the elements;
18 The beginning and end and middle of
periods of time,
The alternations of the solstices and
the changes of the seasons,
19 The cycles of the years and the positions of the stars,
20 The natures of animals, and the dis-
positions of wild beasts,
The powers of spirits and the designs
of men,
The varieties of plants and the virtues
of roots;
21 All that was secret or manifest I
learned,
22 For wisdom, the fashioner of all
things, taught me.
For there is in her a spirit that is
intelligent, holy,

Unique, manifold, subtle,
Mobile, clear, undefiled,
Distinct, beyond harm, loving the
good, keen,
Unhindered, beneficent, philanthropic, 23
Firm, sure, free from care,
All-powerful, all-seeing,
And interpenetrating all spirits
That are intelligent, pure, and most
subtle.
For wisdom is more mobile than any 24
motion,
And she penetrates and permeates
everything, because she is so
pure;
For she is the breath of the power of 25
God,
And a pure emanation of his al-
mighty glory;
Therefore nothing defiled can enter
into her.
For she is a reflection of the everlast- 26
ing light,
And a spotless mirror of the activity
of God,
And a likeness of his goodness.
Though she is one, she can do all 27
things,
And while remaining in herself, she
makes everything new.
And passing into holy souls, genera-
tion after generation,
She makes them friends of God, and
prophets.
For God loves nothing but the man 28
who lives with wisdom.
For she is fairer than the sun, 29
Or any group of stars;
Compared with light, she is found
superior;
For night succeeds to it, 30
But evil cannot overpower wisdom.
For she reaches in strength from one 8
end of the earth to the other,
And conducts everything well.
I loved her and sought after her 2
from my youth up,
And I undertook to make her my
bride,
And I fell in love with her beauty.
She glorifies her high birth in living 3
with God,
For the Lord of all loves her.
For she is initiated into the knowledge 4
of God,
And is a searcher of his works.
But if the possession of wealth is to be 5
desired in life,

What is richer than wisdom, which operates everything?
6 And if understanding works,
Who in all the world is a greater craftsman than she?
7 And if a man loves uprightness,
Her labors are virtues;
For she teaches self-control and understanding,
Uprightness and courage;
Nothing in life is more useful to men than these.
8 But if a man longs for much experience,
She knows antiquity and can forecast the future,
She understands the tricks of language and the solving of riddles;
She knows the meaning of signs and portents,
And the outcomes of seasons and periods.
9 So I decided to bring her to live with me,
Knowing that she would give me good counsel,
And encouragement in cares and grief.
10 Because of her I will have glory among the multitude,
And honor with the elders, though I am young,
11 I will be found keen in judgment,
And I will be admired in the presence of monarchs.
12 When I am silent, they will wait for me to speak,
And when I speak, they will pay attention,
And if I talk at some length,
They will put their hands over their mouths.
13 Because of her, I will have immortality,
And leave an everlasting memory to those who come after me.
14 I will govern peoples, and nations will be subject to me.
15 Dread sovereigns will be frightened when they hear of me;
Among the people I will appear good and in war brave.
16 When I enter my house, I will find rest with her,
For intercourse with her has no bitterness,
And living with her no grief,
But gladness and joy.
17 When I considered these things with myself,
And reflected in my mind
That in kinship with wisdom there is immortality,
18 And in her friendship there is pure delight,
And unfailing wealth in the labors of her hands,
And understanding in the experience of her company,
And glory in sharing in her words,
I went about seeking how to win her for myself.
19 I was a well-formed child,
And a good soul fell to me,
20 Or rather, I was good and entered an undefiled body.
21 But I perceived that I could not win her unless God gave her to me
(And this too came of understanding, to know from whom the favor came).
I appealed to the Lord and besought him,
And said with all my heart:
9 "God of my forefathers and merciful Lord,
Who created all things by your word,
2 And by your wisdom formed man
To rule over the creatures you had made,
3 And manage the world in holiness and uprightness,
And pass judgment in rectitude of soul,
4 Give me the wisdom that sits by your throne,
And do not reject me as unfit to be one of your servants.
5 For I am your slave and the son of your maidservant,
A man weak and short-lived,
And inferior in my understanding of judgment;
6 For even if one among the sons of men is perfect,
If the wisdom that comes from you is lacking, he will count for nothing.
7 You have chosen me out to be king of your people,
And to be judge of your sons and daughters;
8 You told me to build a sanctuary on your holy mountain,
And an altar in the city where you dwell,
A copy of the holy tent which you prepared in the beginning;
9 And with you is wisdom, which knows your works,

And was present when you made the
world,
And understands what is pleasing in
your sight,
And what is in accord with your commands.
10 Send her forth from the holy heavens
And dispatch her from your glorious
throne,
To be with me and toil,
And so that I may know what is
pleasing to you.
11 For she knows and understands all
things,
And she will guide me with good sense
in my actions,
And will guard me with her splendor.
12 Then my doings will be acceptable,
And I will judge your people uprightly,
And be worthy of the throne of my
father.
13 For what man can know the counsel of
God,
Or who can decide what the Lord
wills?
14 For the calculations of mortals are
timid,
And our designs are likely to fail,
15 For a perishable body weighs down
the soul,
And its earthy tent burdens the
thoughtful mind.
16 We can hardly guess at things upon
the earth,
And we have hard work finding the
things that are just at hand,
But who has tracked out the things in
heaven?
17 And who has learned your counsel
unless you gave him wisdom,
And sent your holy spirit from on
high?
18 So the paths of those who were on the
earth were straightened,
And men were taught the things that
please you,
And were saved by wisdom."

10 It was she that protected the first-
formed father of the world,
In his loneliness, after his creation,
And rescued him from his transgression,
2 And gave him strength to master all
things.
3 And when an unrighteous man abandoned her in his anger,
He perished in his fratricidal rage.
4 When the earth was deluged because
of him, wisdom again saved
The upright man, steering him with a
cheap piece of wood.
It was she that when the nations were 5
confused, in their wicked conspiracy,
Recognized the upright man, and preserved him blameless before God,
And kept him steadfast against having pity on his child.
When the ungodly were perishing, she 6
saved an upright man,
Who fled from the fire that descended
on the Five Towns;
To their wickedness a smoking waste
Still bears lasting witness, 7
As do trees that bear fruit that never
ripens,
And a pillar of salt that stands as a
memorial of an unbelieving soul.
For because they passed wisdom by, 8
They were not only made incapable
of recognizing what was good,
But also left behind them to life a
memorial of their folly,
So that their faults could not pass un-
noticed.
But wisdom delivered those who 9
served her from their troubles.
An upright man, who was a fugitive 10
from a brother's wrath,
She guided in straight paths;
She showed him God's kingdom,
And gave him knowledge of holy
things;
She made him prosper in his toils
And increased the fruit of his labors;
When those who oppressed him were 11
covetous, she stood by him,
And made him rich.
She protected him from his enemies, 12
And kept him safe from those who lay
in wait for him,
And decided his hard contest in his
favor,
So that he should know that godliness
is stronger than anything.
When an upright man was sold, she 13
did not abandon him,
But delivered him from sin;
She went down into the pit with him,
And she did not leave him in prison, 14
Until she brought him the scepter of a
kingdom,
And power over those who lorded it
over him;
She showed that they were false who
had blamed him,
And she gave him everlasting honor.

15 She delivered from a nation of oppressors
A holy people and a blameless race;
16 She entered the soul of a servant of the Lord,
And withstood awe-inspiring kings with portents and signs;
17 She paid to holy men a reward for their toils,
She guided them along a wonderful way,
And became a shelter for them in the daytime,
And a flame of stars at night.
18 She brought them over the Red Sea,
And led them through deep waters.
19 But their enemies she overwhelmed,
And cast them up from the bottom of the deep.
20 Therefore the upright despoiled the ungodly,
And they sang, Lord, of your holy name,
And praised with one accord your defending hand.
21 For wisdom opens the mouth of the dumb,
And makes the tongues of babes speak plainly.

11 She made their doings prosper by means of a holy prophet.
2 They traveled through an uninhabited desert,
And pitched their tents in trackless places.
3 They withstood their enemies and repulsed their foes.
4 They grew thirsty and called upon you,
And water was given them out of a rocky cliff,
And a cure for their thirst out of the hard stone.
5 For the means by which their enemies were punished
Benefited them in their time of need.
6 Instead of the fountain of an ever flowing river,
Stirred up with filthy blood,
7 As a rebuke for the decree to kill the babes,
You gave them plenty of water, in a way unlooked for,
8 Showing through their thirst at that time
How you punished their adversaries.
9 For when they were tried, although they were only disciplined in mercy,
They learned how the ungodly were tormented, when they were judged in wrath.
For these you tested like a father, 10
warning them,
But those you examined like a stern king, condemning them.
Whether absent or present, they were 11
harassed alike;
For a double grief seized them, 12
And groaning over the memory of the past.
For when they heard that through 13
their punishments
The others were benefited, they felt it was the Lord.
For the man who had long before 14
been cast forth and exposed, and whom they had rejected with scorn,
As events resulted, they admired,
When they felt thirst in a different way from the upright.
But for the foolish fancies of their un- 15
righteousness,
Misled by which they worshiped unreasoning reptiles and worthless vermin,
You sent a multitude of unreasoning creatures upon them to punish them,
So that they should know that a man 16
is punished by the things through which he sins.
For your all-powerful hand, which 17
created the world out of formless matter,
Did not lack means to send upon them a multitude of bears, or bold lions,
Or newly created wild animals, un- 18
known before, and full of rage,
Either puffing out a fiery breath,
Or scattering a roar of smoke,
Or flashing dreadful sparks from their eyes,
Which could not only have destroyed 19
them utterly by the harm they did,
But have made them die of fright at the very sight of them.
Why, without these, they might have 20
been felled by a single breath,
Being pursued by justice,
And scattered by the breath of your power.
But you ordered everything by measure and number and weight.
For it is always yours to have great 21
strength,

And who can withstand the might of your arm?
22 For in your sight the whole world is like what turns the scale in a balance,
And like a drop of dew that comes down on the earth in the morning.
23 But you have mercy on all men, because you can do all things,
And you overlook men's sins to lead them to repent,
24 For you love all things that exist,
And abhor none of the things that you have made;
For you would never have formed anything if you hated it.
25 And how could anything have endured, if you had not willed it,
Or what had not been called forth by you have been preserved?
26 But you spare all, because they are yours, Lord, lover of life,
12 For your imperishable spirit is in all things.
2 Therefore you correct little by little those who go astray,
And you admonish them by reminding them of the things through which they sin;
So that they may escape from their wickedness and believe in you, Lord.
3 For those who long ago inhabited your holy land
4 You hated for acting most hatefully,
Practicing enchantments and unholy rites,
5 Merciless killing of children,
And cannibal feasting on human flesh and blood.
6 Initiates from the midst of a pagan brotherhood,
And parents who were murderers of helpless lives,
You determined to destroy by the hands of our forefathers,
7 So that the land which you prized above all others
Might receive a worthy colony of God's children.
8 But even these, as being men, you spared,
And you sent wasps as forerunners of your host,
To destroy them little by little.
9 Not that you were unable to make the upright defeat the ungodly in battle,
Or to destroy them at one blow with terrible wild animals or a stern command,
But in judging them little by little you gave them opportunity to repent, 10
For you were not ignorant that their origin was evil,
And their wickedness inborn,
And that their manner of thought would never change.
For they were a race accursed from the beginning, 11
And it was not through fear of any man that you left them unpunished for their sins.
For who can say, "What have you done?" 12
Or who can oppose your judgment?
And who can accuse you of the destruction of the nations which you made?
Or who will come to stand before you as the avenger of unrighteous men?
For neither is there any god but you, who care for all men, 13
To show that you do not judge unrighteously,
Nor will any king or monarch be able to face you about those whom you have punished. 14
But since you are upright, you conduct all things uprightly, 15
Considering it inconsistent with your power
To condemn the man who does not deserve to be punished.
For your strength is the beginning of uprightness 16
And the fact that you are Lord of all makes you spare all.
For when men disbelieve in the perfection of your power, you display your strength, 17
And in the case of those that know, you rebuke their rashness.
But you, being master of your strength, judge us with fairness 18
And govern us with great forbearance.
For the power is at your command, whenever you wish it.
By such deeds you taught your people 19
That the upright man must be humane,
And you made your sons be of good hope,
Because you give repentance for sins,

20 For if you punished with such care
and indulgence
Those who were the enemies of your
servants, and deserved death,
Giving them time and opportunity to
escape from their wickedness,
21 With what exactness you have judged
your sons,
To whose forefathers you gave oaths
and agreements promising them
good!
22 So when you discipline us, you flog
our enemies ten thousand fold,
So that when we judge we may reflect
on your goodness,
And when we are judged we may look
for mercy.
23 Therefore you tormented through
their own abominable practices
Those who lived wickedly, in a life of
folly,
24 For they went astray far beyond the
ways of error,
Accepting as gods the lowest and
basest of animals,
Being deceived like foolish babies.
25 Therefore you sent your judgment in
mockery of them,
As though to unreasoning children.
26 But those who cannot be admonished
by mockeries of correction,
Will experience a judgment worthy of
God.
27 For because through what they suffered they became indignant
At those whom they considered
gods, being punished by means
of them,
They saw and recognized as the true
God him whom they had before
refused to know.
Therefore the very height of condemnation overtook them.

13 For all men are foolish by nature,
and had no perception of God,
And from the good things that were
visible they had not the power
to know him who is,
Nor through paying attention to his
works did they recognize the
workman,
2 But either fire, or wind, or swift air,
Or the circle of the stars, or rushing
water,
Or the heavenly luminaries, the rulers
of the world, they considered
gods.
And if through delight in their beauty
they supposed that these were 3
gods,
Let them know how far superior is
the Lord of these,
For the originator of beauty created
them;
But if it was through awe at their 4
power and operation,
Let them conclude from them how
much mightier he who formed
them is.
For from the greatness and beauty 5
of what is created,
The originator of them is correspond-
ingly perceived.
But yet little blame attaches to these 6
men,
For perhaps they just go astray
In their search for God and their de-
sire to find him;
For living among his works they 7
search
And believe the testimony of their
sight, that what they see is
beautiful.
But again, even they are not to be 8
excused;
For if they had power to know so 9
much
That they could try to make out the
world,
Why did they not sooner find the
Lord of all this?
For they are miserable, and their 10
hopes are set on the dead,
Who have called the works of men's
hands gods,
Gold and silver, the subject of art,
And likenesses of animals,
Or useless stone, worked by some
ancient hand.
But if some carpenter saws down a 11
tree he can handle,
And skilfully strips off all its bark,
And shaping it nicely
Makes a dish suited to the uses of life,
And burns the chips of his work 12
To prepare his food, and eats his fill;
But the worst of them, which is good 13
for nothing,
A crooked piece, full of knots,
He takes and carves to occupy his
spare time,
And shapes it with understanding
skill;
He makes it a copy of a human form,
Or makes it like some common ani- 14
mal,

Smearing it with vermilion, and painting its surface red,
And coating every blemish in it;
15 And making an abode for it worthy of it,
He fixes it on the wall, and fastens it with iron.
16 So he plans for it, so that it will not fall down,
For he knows that it cannot help itself;
For it is only an image and needs help.
17 But he prays to it about his property and his marriage and his children,
And is not ashamed to speak to a lifeless thing,
18 And appeals to something that is weak, for health,
And asks something that is dead, for life,
And supplicates what is itself utterly inexperienced, for aid,
And something that cannot even take a step, about a journey,
19 And he asks strength for gain and business and success in what he undertakes
From something whose hands are most feeble.

14 Again, a man setting out on a voyage, and about to travel over wild waves,
Calls upon a piece of wood more unsound than the ship that carries him.
2 For it was designed through the desire for gain,
And wisdom was the craftsman that built it.
3 And your providence, Father, pilots it,
For you give a way even in the sea,
And a safe path through the waves,
4 Showing that you can save from anything,
So that even without skill a man may go to sea.
5 But it is your will that the works of your wisdom should not be idle;
Therefore men trust their lives to even the smallest plank,
And cross the flood on a raft and get safely over.
6 For in the beginning, when the haughty giants perished,
The hope of the world took refuge on a raft,
And steered by your hand left to the world a generating germ.

For blessed is wood through which uprightness comes, 7
But what is made with hands is accursed, along with the man who made it, 8
Because he shaped it, and what was perishable was called a god.
For the ungodly man and his ungodliness are equally hateful to God. 9
For what is done must be punished with the man who did it. 10
Therefore there will be an examination of the idols of the heathen, 11
For, although part of God's creation, they became an abomination,
And snares to the souls of men,
And a trap for the feet of the foolish.
For the devising of idols is the beginning of fornication, 12
And the invention of them is the corruption of life.
For they did not exist from the beginning, and they will not last forever; 13
For through the vanity of men they came into the world, 14
And therefore a speedy end for them was designed.
For a father afflicted with untimely grief 15
Made a likeness of his child, that had been quickly taken from him,
And presently honored as a god him who was once a dead man,
And handed down to his subjects mysteries and rites.
Then the ungodly practice, strengthened by time, came to be observed as law, 16
And by the orders of monarchs carved images were worshiped.
And when men could not honor them in their presence, because they lived far away, 17
They imagined how they looked, far away,
And made a visible image of the king they honored,
So as by their zeal to flatter the absent one as though he were present.
But the ambition of the artist stimulated 18
Even those who did not know the subject to intensified worship;
For he, perhaps wishing to gratify someone in authority, 19
Elaborated the likeness by his art into greater beauty;

20 And the multitude, attracted by the charm of his workmanship,
Now regarded as an object of worship the one whom they had recently honored as a man.
21 And this proved an ambush for man's life,
Because men in bondage to misfortune or royal authority
Clothed stick and stones with the Name that cannot be shared with others.
22 And then it was not enough for them to go astray about the knowledge of God,
But though living in a great war of ignorance,
They call such evils peace.
23 For neither while they murder children in their rites nor celebrate secret mysteries,
Nor hold frenzied revels with alien laws
24 Do they keep their lives or marriages pure,
But one man waylays another and kills him, or grieves him by adultery.
25 And it is all a confusion of blood and murder, theft and fraud,
Depravity, faithlessness, discord, perjury,
26 Clamor at the good, forgetfulness of favors,
Defilement of souls, confusion of sex,
Irregularity in marriage, adultery, and indecency.
27 For the worship of the unspeakable idols
Is the beginning and cause and end of every evil.
28 For they either rejoice in madness, or prophesy falsely,
Or live unrighteously, or readily forswear themselves.
29 For since they believe in lifeless idols,
They do not expect to be harmed for swearing wickedly.
30 But justice will overtake them for both matters,
Because they thought wickedly of God and gave heed to idols,
And because they swore unrighteously to deceive, in disregard of holiness.
31 For it is not the power of the gods men swear by,
But the penalty of those who sin
That always pursues the transgression of the unrighteous.

But you, our God, are kind and true, 15
You are long-suffering, and govern everything in mercy.
For even if we sin, we are yours, and know your might; 2
But we will not sin, for we know that we are accounted yours.
For to know you is perfect uprightness, 3
And to recognize your might is the root of immortality.
For no artful device of men has led us astray, 4
Nor the fruitless labor of scene-painters,
A figure smeared with varied colors,
The appearance of which leads to desire in fools, 5
And they long for the lifeless form of a dead image.
Lovers of evil and deserving of such hopes 6
Are those who make them and those who feel desire for them and those who worship them.
For a potter, molding the soft earth, 7
Laboriously shapes each object for our use;
Why, from the same clay he forms
Dishes to serve clean purposes,
And those of the opposite kind, all alike;
But of what use shall be made of either,
The potter is the judge.
And with misdirected toil he shapes a futile god out of the same clay, 8
And having shortly before sprung from the earth,
After a little goes to that from which he was taken,
When he is called upon to return the soul that was lent him.
But he is concerned, not because he will grow tired, 9
Nor because his life is short,
But he competes with gold- and silversmiths,
And copies those who mold brass,
And thinks it a glory that he can form counterfeits.
His heart is ashes, and his hope cheaper than dirt, 10
And his life more worthless than clay,
For he has not recognized the one who formed him, 11
And inspired him with an active soul,
And breathed into him the breath of life.

12 But they consider our existence play,
And life a lucrative fair,
For, they say, one must make money any way one can, even by evil.
13 For this man knows better than all others that he sins,
Producing from earthy material fragile dishes and carved images.
14 But most foolish, and more wretched than a baby's soul,
Are all those enemies of your people, who oppress them,
15 For they consider all the idols of the heathen gods,
Which can neither use eyes to see with,
Nor noses to inhale the air,
Nor ears to hear with,
Nor fingers on their hands to feel with,
And their feet are of no use to walk on.
16 For a man made them,
And one whose own spirit is borrowed formed them;
For no man can form a god like him;
17 For mortal as he is, what he makes with his lawless hands is dead;
For he is better than the things he worships,
For of the two, he has life, but they never had it.
18 Why, they worship even the most hateful animals;
For by comparison, they are worse than the other animals in their lack of intelligence;
19 Nor are they in their appearance as animals so beautiful as to be desired,
But they have escaped both the praise of God and his blessing.

16 Therefore they were punished as they deserved, by similar animals,
And tormented with a multitude of vermin.
2 And instead of this punishment, you benefited your people,
And to satisfy the desire of their appetite, you prepared something with a strange taste—
Quails for food,
3 So that those others, when they desired food,
Because of the hideousness of the things sent among them,
Should lose even the smallest appetite,
While they, after being in want for a little while,
Should partake of something with a strange taste.
4 For it was necessary that an unescapable want should come upon those others for their tyrannical behavior,
But these should only be shown how their enemies were tormented.
5 For when the terrible fury of wild animals came upon them,
And they were perishing by the bites of wriggling snakes,
Your wrath did not continue to the uttermost,
6 But they were harassed for a little while to admonish them,
For they had a token of preservation to remind them of the commandment of your law;
7 For the one who turned toward it was saved not because of what he saw,
But because of you, who are the preserver of all.
8 And by this you persuaded our enemies
That you are the one who saves from every evil.
9 For they were killed by the bites of locusts and flies,
And no cure was found for their life,
For they deserved to be punished by such means.
10 But not even the teeth of venomous serpents could overcome your sons,
For your mercy came to help them and healed them.
11 For it was to remind them of your oracles that they were stung,
And they were quickly delivered,
To keep them from falling into deep forgetfulness
And becoming sundered from your kindness.
12 For it was no plant or plaster that cured them,
But your word, Lord, that heals all men.
13 For you have power over life and death,
And you take men down to the gates of Hades and bring them up again.
14 A man may kill in his wickedness,
But the spirit once it is gone out he cannot bring back,
Nor can he release the imprisoned soul.
15 But it is impossible to escape your hand,
16 For ungodly men, refusing to know you,

Were flogged with the strength of your
arm,
Pursued by unusual rains and hail-
storms and relentless showers,
And utterly consumed by fire.
17 For, strangest of all, on the water,
which quenches everything,
The fire had the greater effect,
For the universe is the champion of
the upright;
18 For now the flame was quieted,
So that it should not burn up the
animals sent against the ungodly,
But that they, when they saw it,
might recognize that they were
pursued by the judgment of God;
19 And again it blazed up in the midst of
the water, with more than fiery
power,
To destroy the products of an unrighteous land.
20 Instead of these you gave your people
angels' food,
And untiringly supplied them with
bread from heaven, ready to eat,
Strong in all enjoyment and suited
to every taste;
21 For your support manifested your
sweetness toward your children,
And the bread, responding to the
desire of the man that took it,
Was changed to what each one desired.
22 But snow and ice endured fire without
melting,
So that they should know that fire
was destroying the crops of their
enemies,
Blazing in the hail,
And flashing in the rain;
23 And that this again, in order that upright men might be fed,
Had forgotten its power.
For creation, serving you who made
24 it,
Strains against the unrighteous, to
punish them,
But relaxes on behalf of those who
trust in you, to benefit them.
25 Therefore even then, assuming all
forms,
It served your all-sustaining bounty,
In response to the desire of those who
were in need,
26 So that your sons, whom you have
loved, Lord, might learn
That it is not the production of the
crops that supports man,
But that it is your word that preserves
those who believe in you.
For what the fire could not destroy 27
Melted away when it was simply
warmed by a fleeting sunbeam,
So that it might be known that we 28
must rise before the sun to give
you thanks,
And appeal to you at the rising of the
light.
For the unthankful man's hope will 29
melt like the wintry hoarfrost,
And run off like useless water.
For your judgments are great and **17**
hard to set forth;
Therefore uninstructed souls went
astray.
For when lawless men thought they 2
were oppressing a holy nation
They lay shut up under their roofs,
exiled from the eternal providence,
Prisoners of darkness and captives of
the long night.
For when they thought they were 3
hidden in their secret sins
By a dark veil of forgetfulness,
They were scattered, terribly fright-
ened,
And appalled by specters.
For even the inner chamber that held 4
them did not protect them from
fear,
But appalling sounds rang around
them,
And somber ghosts appeared, with
gloomy faces.
And no fire was strong enough to suc- 5
ceed in giving them light,
Nor could the bright flames of the
stars
Undertake to illumine that hateful
night.
Only there shone on them 6
A fearful flame, of itself,
And though dreadfully frightened at
that sight when it could not be
seen,
They thought the things they beheld
still worse.
And the delusions of magic art were 7
prostrate,
And their boasted wisdom suffered a
contemptuous rebuke,
For those who claimed to drive away 8
fears and troubles from sick souls
Were sick themselves with ridiculous
fear.

9 For if nothing alarming frightened them,
Yet scared by the creeping of vermin and the hissing of reptiles
10 They died of fright,
Refusing even to look upon the air, which could not be escaped on any side.
11 For wickedness is a cowardly thing, condemned by a witness of its own,
And being distressed by conscience, has always exaggerated hardships;
12 For fear is nothing but the giving up of the reinforcements that come from reason,
13 And as the expectation of them from within is deficient,
It reckons its ignorance worse than the cause of the torment.
14 But they, all through the night, which was really powerless,
And came upon them from the recesses of a powerless Hades,
Sleeping the same sleep,
15 Were now driven by monstrous phantoms,
And now paralyzed by their soul's surrender;
For they were drenched in sudden, unlooked-for fear.
16 Then whoever was there fell down
And so was shut up and guarded in a prison not made of iron;
17 For whether a man was a farmer or a shepherd,
Or a laborer whose work was in a wilderness,
He was overtaken and suffered the unavoidable fate,
For they were all bound with one chain of darkness.
18 Whether there was a whistling wind,
Or a melodious sound of birds in spreading branches,
Or the regular noise of rushing water,
19 Or a harsh crashing of rocks thrown down,
Or the unseen running of bounding animals,
Or the sound of the most savage wild beasts roaring,
Or an echo thrown back from a hollow in the mountains,
It paralyzed them with terror.
20 For the whole world was bathed in bright light,
And occupied in unhindered work;
Only over them was spread a heavy night,
A picture of the darkness that was to receive them.
But heavier than the darkness were they to themselves.
18 But your holy ones enjoyed a very great light;
And the others, hearing their voices but not seeing their forms,
Thought them happy, because they had not suffered,
2 But they were thankful because the others, though they had before been wronged, did not hurt them.
And prayed to be separated from them.
3 Therefore you provided a blazing pillar
As guide on their unknown journey,
And an unharmful sun for their honorable exile.
4 For they deserved to be deprived of light and imprisoned in darkness
Who had kept your sons shut up,
Through whom the imperishable light of the Law was to be given to the world.
5 When they plotted to kill the babies of the holy ones,
Though one child had been exposed and saved,
To rebuke them you took from them a multitude of their children,
And destroyed them all together in a mighty flood.
6 That night was made known to our forefathers beforehand,
So that they should know certainly what oaths they had believed, and rejoice.
7 The preservation of the upright and the destruction of their enemies
Were expected by your people;
8 For in punishing their adversaries,
You called us to you and glorified us.
9 For in secret the holy children of good men offered the sacrifice,
And with one accord agreed to the divine law,
That they should share alike
The same blessings and dangers,
And were already beginning to sing the praises of their forefathers,
10 When there echoed back the discordant shout of their enemies,
And the piteous sound of lamentation for children spread abroad;
11 But slave was punished with master, with the same penalty,

And the commoner suffered the same
as the king,
12 And all of them together under one
form of death
Had countless corpses.
For those who were alive were not
even enough to bury them,
For in one instant their most valued
children were destroyed.
13 For though they disbelieved everything because of their enchantments,
When the first-born were destroyed,
they acknowledged that the people was God's son.
14 For when gentle silence enveloped
everything,
And night was midway of her swift
course,
15 Your all-powerful word leaped from
heaven, from the royal throne,
A stern warrior, into the midst of the
doomed land,
16 Carrying for a sharp sword your un-
disguised command,
And stood still, and filled all things
with death,
And touched heaven but walked upon
the earth.
17 Then suddenly apparitions in dreadful
dreams startled them,
And unlooked-for fears assailed them,
18 And one thrown here half-dead, another there,
Showed why they were dying,
19 For the dreams that had alarmed
them warned them of it,
So that they should not perish without knowing why they suffered.
20 But the experience of death affected the upright also,
And a multitude were destroyed in the
desert.
But the wrath did not continue long.
21 For a blameless man hurried to fight in
their defense,
Bringing the great shield of his ministering,
Prayer and the propitiation of incense;
He withstood that wrath and put an
end to the disaster,
Showing that he was a servant of
yours;
22 But he overcame that anger not by
bodily strength,
Nor by force of arms,
But by his word he subdued the
chastiser,
When he appealed to the oaths and
agreements given to the forefathers.
For when the dead had already fallen 23
on one another in heaps,
He stood between and cut the wrath
short
And cut off its way to the living.
For on his long robe was the whole 24
world,
And the glories of the forefathers were
in the carving of the four rows of
stones,
And your majesty was on the diadem
upon his head.
Before these the destroyer gave way, 25
and these he feared,
For that experience of wrath was
enough by itself.
But, on the ungodly, pitiless anger 19
came to the uttermost,
For he knew their future also beforehand,
That after permitting them to go 2
away,
And sending them off in haste,
They would change their minds and
pursue them.
For while they were still busy with 3
their mourning,
And were lamenting beside the graves
of the dead,
They involved themselves in another
foolish design,
And pursued as runaways those whom
they had driven out with en-
treaties.
For the fate they deserved dragged 4
them on to this end,
And made them forget what had
happened,
So that they should make up the
punishment that their torments
lacked,
And your people should experience an 5
incredible journey,
While they themselves should find a
strange death.
For the whole creation in its own kind 6
was reshaped anew,
In obedience to your commands,
So that your servants might be protected unharmed.
The cloud was seen that over- 7
shadowed the camp,
And the emergence of dry land where
water had stood before,
An unobstructed road out of the Red
Sea,

And a grassy plain out of the raging billow;
8 Through which those who were protected by your hand passed over as a nation,
Witnessing marvelous portents.
9 For they ranged like horses
And skipped like lambs,
Praising you, Lord, who had delivered them.
10 For they still remembered the things in their sojourning,
How instead of the birth of animals the earth brought forth gnats,
And instead of aquatic creatures the river vomited up a host of frogs.
11 But later they saw a new production of birds also,
When moved by appetite they asked for delicacies;
12 For quails came up from the sea to their relief.
13 And those punishments came upon the sinners
Not without premonitory signs, in the violence of the thunders;
For they suffered justly through their own wickedness,
For they exhibited a more bitter hatred of strangers.
14 For some would not receive men who did not know them, when they came to them,
But these men made slaves of strangers who showed them kindness.
15 And not only so, but those others shall have some consideration,
For the men they received with such hostility were aliens;

But these men, though they had welcomed them with feasting, 16
Afflicted those who had already shared the same rights with them, with dreadful labors.
And they were stricken with loss of sight too, 17
Like those others, at the upright man's door,
When, surrounded with yawning darkness,
Each one sought the way through his own doors.
For the elements changed in order with one another, 18
Just as on a harp the notes vary the character of the time,
Yet keep the pitch,
As one may accurately infer from the observation of what happened;
For land animals were turned into water creatures, 19
And swimming things changed to the land;
Fire retained its power in water, 20
And water forgot its quenching property.
Contrariwise, flames did not wither the flesh 21
Of perishable animals that walked about among them,
Nor was the easily melting ice-like kind of immortal food melted.
For in everything, you, Lord, magnified and glorified your people, 22
And you did not neglect them, but stood by them at every time and place.

THE WISDOM OF SIRACH

1 ALL wisdom comes from the Lord,
And remains with him forever.
2 The sand of the seas, and the drops of rain,
And the days of eternity—who can count them?
3 The height of the heavens, and the breadth of the earth,
And the deep, and wisdom—who can track them out?
4 Wisdom was created before them all,
And sound intelligence from eternity.
6 To whom has the source of wisdom been revealed?
And who knows her devices?
8 There is but one who is wise, a very terrible one,
Seated upon his throne;
9 The Lord himself created her;
He saw her and counted her,
And poured her out upon all he made;
10 Upon all mankind, as he chose to bestow her;
But he supplied her liberally to those who loved him.
11 To fear the Lord is a glory and a ground of exultation;
A joy, and a crown of ecstasy.
12 To fear the Lord delights the heart,
And brings gladness and joy and long life.
13 The man who fears the Lord will have a happy end,
And be blessed in the day of his death.
14 To fear the Lord is the source of wisdom,
And she was created with the faithful in the womb.
15 She has built her nest among men as a foundation from eternity,
And among their posterity she will be held in trust.
16 To fear the Lord is to be satisfied with wisdom,
For she intoxicates them with her fruits.
17 She will fill all their houses with desirable things,
And their storehouses with her produce;
18 To fear the Lord is a crown of wisdom,
Making peace and healing health flourish.
He beheld her and counted her;
He rained down understanding and sound knowledge, 19
And increased the glory of those who possessed her.
To fear the Lord is the root of wisdom, 20
And her branches are long life.
Unrighteous anger can never be excused, 22
For the weight of a man's anger drags him down.
A patient man will control himself for a while, 23
And afterward joy will break out.
He will repress his words for a time, 24
And the lips of many will tell of his understanding.
In the storehouses of wisdom there are wise proverbs, 25
But godliness is a detestation to the irreligious.
If you desire wisdom, keep the commandments, 26
And the Lord will supply you with her liberally.
For to fear the Lord is wisdom and education, 27
And faith and meekness win his approval.
Do not disobey the fear of the Lord, 28
And do not approach it with a divided heart.
Do not be a hypocrite in the mouths of men, 29
And take heed to your own lips.
Do not exalt yourself, or you may fall, 30
And bring disgrace upon yourself;
And the Lord will reveal your secrets
And prostrate you before all the congregation,
Because you did not come to the fear of the Lord,
But your heart was full of deceit.
My child, if you come to serve the Lord, 2
Prepare yourself to be tried.
Set your heart right and be firm, 2
And do not be hasty when things go against you;

3 Hold fast to him, and do not forsake him,
So that you may be honored when your life ends.
4 Accept whatever happens to you,
And be patient in humiliating vicissitudes.
5 For gold is tested with fire,
And men who are approved must be tested in the furnace of humiliation.
6 Have faith in him, and he will help you;
Make your ways straight, and put your hope in him.
7 You who fear the Lord, wait for his mercy,
And do not turn aside, or you will fall.
8 You who fear the Lord, have faith in him,
And you will not lose your reward.
9 You who fear the Lord, hope for his blessings,
And for everlasting joy and mercy.
10 Look at the generations of antiquity and see,
Who that put his trust in the Lord was ever put to shame?
Or who that continued to fear him was ever forsaken?
Or who that called upon him was overlooked by him?
11 For the Lord is merciful and has pity,
And forgives sins and delivers in times of affliction.
12 Alas for cowardly hearts and palsied hands!
And for a sinner who follows two paths!
13 Alas for a faint heart, for it does not believe;
Therefore it will not be protected.
14 Alas for you, who have lost your steadfastness!
What will you do when the Lord visits you?
15 Those who fear the Lord will not disobey his words,
And those who love him will keep his ways.
16 Those who fear the Lord will seek his favor,
And those who love him will be filled with the Law.
17 Those who fear the Lord will prepare their hearts,
And will humble their souls before him.
18 "Let us fall into the Lord's hands,
And not into the hands of men."
For as his majesty is,
So is his mercy also.

Listen to me, your father, children,
And act in such a way that you may be preserved.
For the Lord has glorified the father above his children,
And he has established the rights of the mother over her sons.
He who provides for his father atones for his sins,
And he who shows his mother honor is like a man who lays up treasure.
He who provides for his father will be gladdened by his children,
And will be heard on the day that he prays.
He who shows his father honor will have a long life,
And he who listens to the Lord will refresh his mother,
And will serve his parents as his masters.
Honor your father in word and deed,
So that his blessing may attend you.
For a father's blessing establishes the houses of his children,
But a mother's curse uproots their foundations.
Do not glorify yourself by dishonoring your father,
For your father's disgrace is no glory to you.
For a man's glory arises from honoring his father,
And a neglected mother is a reproach to her children.
My child, help your father in his old age,
And do not grieve him, as long as he lives.
If his understanding fails, be considerate,
And do not humiliate him, when you are in all your strength.
Charity given to a father will not be forgotten,
And will build you up a further atonement for your sins.
When you are in trouble, you will be remembered;
Like frost in sunshine your sins will melt away.
He who deserts his father is like a blasphemer,
And he who angers his mother is cursed by the Lord.

17 My child, carry on your business in humility,
And you will be loved by men whom God accepts.
18 The greater you are, the more you must practice humility,
And you will find favor with the Lord.
20 For the Lord's power is great,
And he is glorified by the humble-minded.
21 Do not seek for what is too hard for you,
And do not investigate what is beyond your strength;
22 Think of the commands that have been given you,
For you have no need of the things that are hidden.
23 Do not waste your labor on what is superfluous to your work,
For things beyond man's understanding have been shown you.
24 For many have been led astray by their imagination,
And a wicked fancy has made their minds slip.
26 It will go hard with an obstinate heart at the end,
And the man who loves danger will perish through it.
27 An obstinate heart will be loaded with troubles,
And the irreligious man will add one sin to another.
28 There is no cure for the misfortune of the proud,
For a wicked plant has taken root in him.
29 An intelligent man's mind can understand a proverb;
And a wise man desires a listening ear.
30 As water will quench a blazing fire,
So charity will atone for sin.
31 He who returns favors is remembered afterward,
And when he totters, he will find a support.

4 My child, do not defraud the poor man of his living,
And do not make the eyes of the needy wait.
Do not pain a hungry heart,
2 And do not anger a man who is in want.
3 Do not increase the troubles of a mind that is incensed,
And do not put off giving to a man who is in need.
Do not refuse a suppliant in his trouble, 4
And do not avert your face from the poor.
Do not turn your eyes away from a beggar, 5
And do not give anyone cause to curse you,
For if he curses you in the bitterness of his spirit, 6
His creator will hear his prayer.
Make yourself beloved in the congregation, 7
And bow your head to a great personage;
Listen to what a poor man has to say, 8
And give him a peaceful and gentle answer.
Rescue a man who is being wronged from the hand of the wrongdoer, 9
And do not be faint-hearted about giving your judgment.
Be like a father to the fatherless, 10
And take the place of a husband to their mother.
Then you will be like a son of the Most High,
And he will show you more than a mother's love.
Wisdom makes her sons exalted, 11
And lays hold of those who seek her.
Whoever loves her loves life, 12
And those who seek her early will be filled with joy.
Whoever holds her fast will win glory; 13
The Lord will bless every house he enters.
Those who serve her serve the Holy One, 14
And the Lord loves those who love her.
Whoever obeys her will judge the heathen, 15
And whoever attends to her will dwell in security.
If he trusts in her, he will possess her, 16
And his descendants will retain possession of her.
For at first she will go with him in devious ways, 17
She will bring fear and cowardice upon him,
And torment him with her discipline,
Until she can trust in his soul,
And test him with her judgments.
Then she will come straight back to him again, and make him glad, 18
And reveal her secrets to him.
If he wanders off, she will forsake him, 19

And hand him over to his downfall.
20 Watch your opportunity and guard against evil,
And do not have to feel shame for your soul.
21 For there is a shame that brings sin,
And there is a shame that is glory and favor.
22 Show regard for no one at the expense of your soul,
And respect no one, to your own downfall.
23 Do not refrain from speaking when it is needed;
For wisdom is known through speech,
24 And instruction through the spoken word.
25 Do not contradict the truth,
But feel shame for your want of education.
26 Do not be ashamed to confess your sins,
And do not try to force back the current of a river.
27 Do not make yourself a bed for a fool,
And do not show partiality for a ruler;
28 Contend for the truth to the death,
And the Lord will fight for you.
29 Do not be rash in speech,
But slothful and slack in action.
30 Do not be like a lion at home,
And unreasonable with your servants.
31 Do not stretch your hand out to receive,
But close it when you should repay.
5 Do not set your heart on your money,
And do not say, "It is enough for me."
2 Do not follow your soul and your strength
And pursue the desires of your heart.
3 Do not say, "Who can have power over me?"
For the Lord will certainly take vengeance.
4 Do not say, "I sinned, and what happened to me?"
For the Lord is long-suffering.
5 As for atonement, do not be unafraid
To add one sin to another,
6 And do not say, "His mercy is great,
He will make atonement for the multitude of my sins."
For mercy and wrath are both with him,
And his anger will rest upon sinners,
7 Do not put off turning to the Lord,
And do not postpone it from day to day;
For the Lord's wrath will suddenly come forth,
And in the time of vengeance you will perish.
Do not set your heart on unrighteous gain, 8
For it will be of no benefit to you in the time of misfortune.
Do not winnow in every wind, 9
And do not follow every path;
That is what the deceitful sinner does.
Be steadfast in your understanding, 10
And let what you say be one.
Be quick to hear, 11
And make your reply with patience.
If you possess understanding, answer your neighbor, 12
But if you do not have it, keep your hand over your mouth!
Both glory and disgrace come from speaking, 13
And a man's tongue is his downfall.
Do not be known as a whisperer, 14
And do not set an ambush with your tongue,
For shame rests upon the thief,
And evil condemnation on the double-tongued.
Do not be ignorant in great matters or in small, 15
And do not prove an enemy instead of a friend; **6**
For an evil name incurs disgrace and reproach;
So does a sinner who is double-tongued.
Do not exalt yourself in your soul's designs, 2
So that your soul may not be torn in pieces like a bull;
If you eat up your leaves, you will destroy your fruit, 3
And leave yourself like a dried-up tree.
A wicked heart will destroy its possessor, 4
And fill his enemies with malignant joy.
Sweet speech makes many friends, 5
And a polite tongue multiplies courtesy.
Let those who are at peace with you be many, 6
But let your advisers be one in a thousand.
If you make a friend, make one only after testing him, 7
And do not be in a hurry to confide in him.
There are friends who are so when it suits their convenience, 8

Who will not stand by you when you
are in trouble.
9 And there are friends who turn into
enemies,
And reveal quarrels to your discredit.
10 And there are friends who will sit at
your table,
But will not stand by you when you
are in trouble.
11 They will make themselves at home,
as long as you are prosperous,
And will give orders to your servants;
12 If you come down in the world, they
will take sides against you,
And hide themselves from your presence.
13 Separate yourself from your enemies,
And beware of your friends.
14 A faithful friend is a strong protection;
A man who has found one has found
a treasure.
15 A faithful friend is beyond price,
And his value cannot be weighed.
16 A faithful friend is a life-giving medicine,
And those who fear the Lord will find
it.
17 The man who fears the Lord will make
genuine friendships,
For to him his neighbor is like himself.
18 My child, from your youth up cultivate education,
And you will keep on finding wisdom
until you are gray.
19 Approach her like a man who plows
and sows,
And wait for her abundant crops.
For in cultivating her, you will toil but
little,
And soon you will eat her produce.
20 She seems very harsh, to the undisciplined,
And a thoughtless man cannot abide
her.
21 She will rest on him like a great stone
to test him,
And he will not delay to throw her off.
22 For wisdom is what her name implies,
And to most men she is invisible.
23 Listen, my child, and accept my
opinion,
And do not refuse my advice.
24 Put your feet into her fetters,
And your neck into her collar.
25 Put your shoulder under her and
carry her,
And do not weary of her chains;
26 Come to her with all your heart,
And follow her ways with all your
might.
Inquire and search, and she will be 27
made known to you,
And when you have grasped her, do
not let her go.
For at last you will find the rest she 28
gives,
And you will find her turning into
gladness.
Her fetters will become your strong 29
defense,
And her collars a splendid robe.
She wears gold ornaments, 30
And her chains are purple thread;
You will put her on like a splendid robe, 31
And put her on your head like a
victor's wreath.
My child, if you wish, you can be 32
educated,
And if you devote yourself to it, you
can become shrewd.
If you love to hear, you will receive, 33
And if you listen, you will be wise.
Take your stand in the throng of 34
elders;
Which of them is wise? Attach yourself to him.
Be willing to listen to every godly discourse, 35
And do not let any wise proverbs
escape you.
If you see a man of understanding, go 36
to him early,
And let your feet wear out his doorstep.
Think about the statutes of the Lord, 37
And constantly meditate on his commandments.
He will strengthen your mind,
And the wisdom you desire will be
given you.
Do no evil, and evil will not overtake you. 7
Avoid what is wrong, and it will turn
away from you.
My son, do not sow among the furrows of iniquity, 2
And you will not reap them sevenfold. 3
Do not ask the Lord for pre-eminence, 4
Or the king for a seat of honor.
Do not justify yourself in the sight of 5
the Lord,
Or show off your wisdom before the
king;
Do not seek to be made a judge, 6
Or you may not be able to put down
wrongdoing;

Or you may show partiality to a man
of influence,
And put a stumbling block in the way
of your own uprightness.
7 Do not sin against the multitude of
the city,
And do not throw yourself down in the
throng.
8 Do not repeat a sin,
For with even one offense you are not
innocent.
9 Do not say, "He will consider the
number of my offerings,
And when I sacrifice to the Most
High God, he will accept it."
10 Do not be discouraged about your
prayers,
And do not fail to give to charity.
11 Do not laugh at a man when he is in
bitterness of spirit;
For there is one who can humble and
can exalt!
12 Do not sow a lie against your brother,
Or do such a thing to your friend.
13 Do not consent to utter any lie,
For the practice of it is not beneficial.
14 Do not indulge in idle talk in the
throng of elders,
And do not repeat yourself when you
pray.
15 Do not hate hard work,
Or farming, which was created by the
Most High.
16 Do not be counted in the crowd of
sinners;
Remember that wrath will not delay.
17 Humble your heart exceedingly,
For fire and worms are the punishment of the ungodly.
18 Do not exchange a friend for an
advantage,
Or a real brother for the gold of Ophir.
19 Do not fail a wise, good wife,
For her favor is worth more than gold.
20 Do not ill-treat a servant who does his
work faithfully,
Or a hired man who is devoting his life
to you.
21 Let your soul love an intelligent
servant;
Do not defraud him of his freedom.
22 If you have cattle, look after them,
And if they are profitable to you, keep
them.
23 If you have children, discipline them,
And from their youth up bend their
necks.
24 If you have daughters, look after their
persons,
And do not look too favorably upon
them.
If you give your daughter in marriage, 25
you will have done a great thing,
But bestow her on a man of understanding.
If you have a wife after your own 26
heart, do not cast her out,
But do not trust yourself to one whom
you hate.
Honor your father with your whole 27
heart,
And do not forget the pangs of your
mother.
Remember that it was of them you 28
were born,
And how can you requite them for
what they have done for you?
Honor the Lord with all your soul, 29
And revere his priests.
Love him who made you with all your 30
strength,
And do not forsake his ministers.
Fear the Lord and honor the priest, 31
And give him his portion, as you were
commanded,
The first fruits, and the sin offering,
and the gift of the shoulders,
And the sacrifice of consecration, and
the first fruits of holy things.
Stretch out your hand to the poor 32
also,
That your blessing may be accom-
plished.
A present pleases every man alive, 33
And in the case of the dead, do not
withhold your kindness.
Do not be wanting to those who weep, 34
But mourn with those who mourn.
Do not hesitate to visit a man who is 35
sick,
For you will be loved for such acts.
In all that you say remember your 36
end,
And you will never commit a sin.
Do not quarrel with a powerful 8
man,
Or you may fall into his hands.
Do not contend with a rich man, 2
Or he may outweigh you.
Gold has been the destruction of
many,
And perverted the minds of kings.
Do not quarrel with a garrulous man, 3
And do not add fuel to the fire.
Do not make sport of an uneducated 4
man,
Or you may dishonor your own fore-
fathers.

5 Do not reproach a man when he turns from his sin;
Remember that we are all liable to punishment.
6 Do not treat a man with disrespect when he is old,
For some of us are growing old.
7 Do not exult over a man who is dead;
Remember that we are all going to die.
8 Do not neglect the discourse of wise men,
But busy yourself with their proverbs;
For from them you will gain instruction,
And learn to serve great men.
9 Do not miss the discourse of old men,
For they learned it from their fathers.
For from them you will gain understanding,
And learn to return an answer in your time of need.
10 Do not kindle the coals of a sinner,
Or you may be burned with the flame of his fire.
11 Do not start up before an insolent man,
So that he may not lie in ambush for what you say.
12 Do not lend to a man who is stronger than you,
Or if you do, act as though you had lost it.
13 Do not give surety beyond your means,
And if you give surety, regard it as something you will have to pay.
14 Do not go to law with a judge;
For in view of his dignity they will decide for him.
15 Do not travel with a reckless man,
So that he may not overburden you.
For he will do just as he pleases,
And you will perish through his folly.
16 Do not have a fight with a hot-tempered man,
And do not travel across the desert with him,
For bloodshed is as nothing in his eyes,
And where there is no help, he will strike you down.
17 Do not take counsel with a fool,
For he will not be able to keep the matter secret.
18 Do not do a secret thing before a stranger,
For you do not know what he will bring forth.

Do not open your heart to every man, 19
And do not accept a favor from him.

Do not be jealous about the wife of 9
your bosom,
And do not teach her an evil lesson, to your own hurt.
Do not give your soul to a woman, 2
So that she will trample on your strength.
Do not meet a prostitute, 3
Or you may fall into her snares.
Do not associate with a woman singer, 4
Or you may be caught by her wiles.
Do not look closely at a girl, 5
Or you may be entrapped in penalties on her account.
Do not give yourself to prostitutes, 6
So that you may not lose your inheritance.
Do not look around in the streets of 7
the city,
And do not wander about the unfrequented parts of it.
Avert your eyes from a beautiful 8
woman,
And do not look closely at beauty that belongs to someone else.
Many have been led astray by a woman's beauty,
And love is kindled by it like a fire.
Do not ever sit at table with a married 9
woman,
And do not feast and drink with her,
Or your heart may turn away to her,
And you may slip into spiritual ruin.
Do not forsake an old friend, 10
For a new one is not equal to him.
A new friend is new wine;
When it grows old, you will enjoy drinking it.
Do not envy the glory of a sinner; 11
For you do not know what disaster awaits him.
Do not share in the satisfaction of un- 12
godly men,
Remember that until death they will not be found upright.
Keep far from a man who has the 13
power of life and death,
And you will have no suspicion of the fear of death.
If you do approach him, do not offend him,
So that he may not take away your life.
Understand that you are striding along among traps,
And walking on the city battlements.

14 As far as you can, guess at your
neighbors,
And take counsel with those who are
wise.
15 Let your discussion be with men of
understanding,
And all your discourse about the Law
of the Most High.
16 Make upright men your companions
at table,
And your exultation be over the fear
of the Lord.
17 It is for the skill of the craftsmen that
a piece of work is commended,
And a ruler of the people must be wise
in what he says.
18 A talkative man is dreaded in his city,
And a man who is rash in speech is
hated.

10 A wise judge will instruct his people,
And the rule of a man of understanding is well ordered.
2 Like the judge of a people are his
officers,
And like the governor of a city are all
who live in it.
3 An uneducated king ruins his people,
But a city becomes populous through
the understanding of its rulers.
Authority over the earth is in the
hands of the Lord,
4 And in due time he will set over it one
who will serve his purpose.
5 A man's prosperity is in the hands of
the Lord,
And he makes his glory rest on the
person of the scribe.
6 Do not get angry with your neighbor
for any misdeed,
And do not gain your end by acts of
violence.
7 Pride is detested in the sight of the
Lord and of men,
And injustice is wrong in the sight of
both.
8 Sovereignty passes from one nation
to another
Because of injustice and violence and
greed for money.
Why are dust and ashes proud?
9 For while a man is still alive, his
bowels decay;
10 There is a long illness—the doctor
makes light of it;
A man is a king today, and dead tomorrow.
11 For when a man dies,
Reptiles, animals, and worms become
his portion.

A man begins to be proud when he 12
departs from the Lord,
And his heart forsakes his Creator.
For pride begins with sin, 13
And the man who clings to it will rain
down abominations.
For this reason, the Lord brings un-
heard-of calamities upon them,
And overturns them utterly.
The Lord tears down the thrones of 14
rulers,
And seats the humble-minded in their
places.
The Lord plucks up nations by the 15
roots,
And plants the lowly in their places.
The Lord overturns heathen countries, 16
And destroys them down to the foun-
dations of the earth.
He takes some of them away, and 17
destroys them,
And makes the memory of them cease
from the earth.
Pride was not created for men, 18
Nor fierce anger for those who are
born of women.
What is an honorable posterity? A
human posterity!
What is an honorable posterity? Men 19
who fear the Lord.
What is a base posterity? A human
posterity!
What is a base posterity? Men who
break the commandments.
Among his brothers, their leader is 20
honored,
And those who fear the Lord are
honored in his eyes.
Rich, and distinguished, and poor 21
alike—
Their glory is the fear of the Lord. 22
It is not right to slight a poor man 23
who has understanding,
And it is not proper to honor a sinful
man.
Prince, judge, and ruler are honored, 24
But none of them is greater than the
man who fears the Lord.
Free men will wait on a wise servant, 25
And the intelligent man will not ob-
ject.
Do not parade your wisdom when 26
you are at work,
And do not commend yourself when
you are in need;
It is better to work and have plenty of 27
everything,
Than to go about commending your-
self but in want of bread.

28 My child, glorify your soul with meekness,
And show it such honor as it deserves.
29 Who can justify a man who sins against his own soul?
And who can honor a man who disgraces his own life?
30 A poor man is honored for his knowledge,
And a rich man is honored for his wealth.
31 If a man is honored in poverty, how much more will he be in wealth?
And if a man is dishonored when he is rich, how much more will he be when he is poor?
1 The wisdom of a humble person will lift up his head,
And make him sit among the great.
2 Do not praise a man for his good looks,
And do not detest a man for his appearance.
3 The bee is one of the smallest of winged creatures,
But what she produces is the greatest of sweets.
4 Do not boast of the clothes you wear,
And do not be uplifted when you are honored,
For the works of the Lord are marvelous,
And his doings are hidden from men.
5 Many sovereigns have had to sit on the ground,
While a man who was never thought of has assumed the diadem.
6 Many rulers have been utterly disgraced,
And men of renown have been delivered into the hands of others,
7 Do not find fault before you investigate;
First understand, and then rebuke.
8 Do not answer before you hear,
And do not interrupt in the middle of what is being said.
9 Do not quarrel about a matter that does not concern you,
And when sinners judge, do not sit in council with them.
10 My child, do not busy yourself about many things.
If you multiply your activities, you will not be held guiltless,
And if you pursue, you will not overtake,
And you will not escape by running away.
One man toils and labors and hurries, 11
And is all the worse off.
Another is slow, and needs help; 12
Lacks strength and has plenty of poverty,
Yet the eyes of the Lord look favorably on him,
And he lifts him up out of his low position 13
And lifts up his head,
And many wonder at him.
Good and evil, life and death, 14
Poverty and wealth, are from the Lord,
What the Lord gives stays by the godly, 17
And what he approves will always prosper.
One man grows rich by carefulness and greed, 18
And this will be his reward:
When he says, "Now I can rest, 19
And enjoy my goods,"
He does not know when the time will come
When he will die and leave them to others.
Stand by your agreement, and attend to it, 20
And grow old in your work.
Do not wonder at the doings of the sinner, 21
But trust in the Lord and stick to your work.
For it is easy in the Lord's eyes
Swiftly and suddenly to make a poor man rich.
The blessing of the Lord rests on the wages of the godly; 22
And he quickly makes his blessing flourish.
Do not say, "What do I need, 23
And from this time on what can benefit me?"
Do not say, "I have enough, 24
And from this time on how can I be injured?"
In prosperity one forgets misfortune, 25
For it is easy in the Lord's sight when a man dies 26
To repay him according to his ways.
An hour of hardship makes one forget enjoyment, 27
And when a man dies, what he has done is disclosed.
Count no one happy before his death, 28
And a man will be known by his children.

29 Do not bring any and every man to your home,
For a treacherous man has many wiles.
30 A proud man's heart is like a decoy partridge in a cage,
And like a spy he looks for your downfall;
31 For he tries to entrap you, turning good into evil,
And he finds fault with your favorite things.
32 A spark of fire kindles a whole heap of coals,
And a sinful man lies in wait for blood.
33 Beware of an evil-doer, for he contrives wickedness,
Or he will bring blame on you forever.
34 If you entertain a stranger, he will disturb and torment you,
And he will estrange you from your home.

12 If you do a kindness, know to whom you are doing it,
And you will be thanked for your good deeds.
2 If you do a kindness to a godly man, you will be repaid,
If not by him, yet by the Most High.
3 The man who persists in evil will not prosper,
Nor the man who will not give to charity.
4 Give to the godly man, and do not help the sinner;
5 Do kindnesses to the humble-minded, and do not give to the ungodly;
Hold back his bread, and do not give it to him,
So that he may not come to control you with it;
For you will experience twice as much evil
For all the good you do him.
6 For the Most High hates sinners,
And will take vengeance on the ungodly.
7 Give to the good man, and do not help the sinner.
8 A friend cannot be proved in prosperity,
Nor an enemy concealed in adversity.
9 When a man prospers, his enemies are grieved,
And when he is unfortunate, even his friend separates from him.
10 Never trust your enemy,
For his wickedness is like bronze that rusts;
Even if he acts humbly, and goes about bent over, 11
Look out for yourself, and be on your guard against him.
You must be to him like a man who wipes a mirror clean,
And you must make sure that it is not all covered with rust.
Do not place him at your side, 12
Or he may overthrow you and take your place.
Do not seat him at your right hand,
Or he may try to get your seat,
And you may at last learn the truth of what I say,
And be stung by my words.
Who pities a snake-charmer when he is bitten, 13
Or all those who have to do with wild animals?
In the same way you will pity a man who approaches a sinner, 14
And mingles with his sins?
He will stay with you for a while, 15
But if you fall, he will not hold out.
An enemy will speak sweetly with his lips, 16
But in his heart he will plan to throw you into a pit.
An enemy will shed tears with his eyes,
But if he gets a chance, he cannot get blood enough.
If misfortune overtakes you, you will find him there before you, 17
And while he is pretending to help you, he will trip you up.
He will shake his head, and clap his hands, 18
And whisper a great deal, and change his expression toward you.
The man who touches pitch will get his hands dirty, 13
And the man who associates with a proud person will become like him.
Do not lift a load that is too heavy for you, 2
And do not associate with a man stronger or richer than you are.
What relation can an earthen pot have with a kettle?
The kettle knocks against it, and it is broken in pieces.
When a rich man does a wrong, he adds a threat; 3

When a poor man suffers a wrong, he
must beg pardon.
4 If you can be useful, he makes you
work for him,
And if you are in want, he abandons
you.
5 As long as you have anything, he will
live with you,
And will strip you bare, but he will
feel no distress.
6 If he needs you, he will deceive you,
And smile upon you, and raise your
hopes.
He will speak you fair and say, "Is
there anything you need?"
7 He will shame you with his food,
Until he has impoverished you again
and again,
And finally he will mock you.
Afterward when he sees you he will
pass you by,
And shake his head at you.
8 Take care not to be misled,
And humbled through your own folly.
9 When a leading man invites you,
be retiring,
And he will invite you all the more.
10 Do not press upon him, or you may be
pushed away;
But do not stand too far off, or you
may be forgotten.
11 Do not aim to speak to him as an
equal,
But do not believe all he says;
For he will test you with much conversation,
And will examine you with a smile.
12 He who does not keep to himself what
is said to him is unmerciful,
And will not hesitate to hurt and to
bind.
13 Keep them to yourself, and take great
care,
For you are walking with your own
downfall.
15 Every creature loves its like,
And every man loves his neighbor.
16 All living beings gather with their own
kind,
And a man associates with another
like himself.
17 What companionship can a wolf have
with a lamb?
Just as much as a sinner with a godly
man.
18 What peace can there be between a
hyena and a dog?
And what peace between a rich man
and a poor one?

Wild asses are the prey of lions in the 19
wilderness,
Just as the poor are pasture for the
rich.
Humility is detestable to the proud, 20
Just as a poor man is detestable to a
rich one.
When a rich man is shaken, he is 21
steadied by his friends,
But when a poor man falls down, his
friends push him away.
When a rich man falls, there are many 22
to help him;
He tells secrets, and they justify him.
When a humble man falls, they add
reproaches.
He speaks with understanding, but
no place is made for him.
When a rich man speaks, everyone 23
keeps silent,
And they extol what he says to the
clouds.
When a poor man speaks, they say,
"Who is that?"
And if he stumbles, they will help to
throw him down.
Wealth is good if it carries with it no 24
sin,
And poverty is called evil by the un-
godly.
A man's disposition affects his ap- 25
pearance,
Both for good and for evil.
A cheerful face is a sign of a happy 26
heart,
But it takes painstaking thought to
compose proverbs!
How happy is the man who makes no **14**
slip with his mouth,
And is not stabbed with sorrow for his
sins!
Happy is the man whose heart does 2
not condemn him,
And who has not given up hope.
Wealth does not become a niggard- 3
ly man,
And what use is money to an envious
man?
The man who withholds from himself 4
amasses for others,
And others will enjoy his goods.
If a man is evil to himself, to whom 5
will he be good?
For he will not take any pleasure in his
own money.
There is nobody worse than the man 6
who is grudging to himself,
And that is the penalty of his wicked-
ness.

7 If he does any good, he does it
through forgetfulness,
And shows his wickedness in the end.
8 He is a wicked man who has an envious eye,
Turning away his face, and pretending not to see human souls.
9 A covetous man's eye is never satisfied with what he gets,
And wicked injustice dries up the heart.
10 An evil eye begrudges bread,
And is in want of it at his own table.
11 My child, if you have any means, provide well for yourself,
And make suitable offerings to the Lord.
12 Remember that death will not delay,
And the agreement of Hades has not been shown to you.
13 Treat your friend well before you die,
And reach out and give to him as much as your strength permits.
14 Do not miss your time of prosperity,
And do not let the good fortune that you desire escape you.
15 Will you not leave the fruit of your labors to someone else,
And the result of your toil to be cast lots for?
16 Give and take, and deceive your soul,
For there is no looking for luxury in Hades.
17 Human life grows old like a cloak,
For from the beginning the decree has read, "You will surely die."
18 Like the thick leaves on a flourishing tree,
Which drops some and puts forth others,
Are the generations of flesh and blood;
One dies, and another is born;
19 Everything made will decay and disappear,
And the man who has made it will depart with it.
20 Happy is the man who meditates on wisdom,
Who reasons with his understanding;
21 Who considers her ways in his mind,
And reflects on her secrets;
(Go after her like a hunter
22 And lie in wait by her ways!)
23 Who peers in at her windows,
And listens at her doorways;
24 Who lodges close to her house,
And fastens his pegs in her walls;
25 Who pitches his tent close beside her,
And finds comfortable lodgings;
Who puts his children under her shelter, 2
And spends the night under her branches;
He will be sheltered by her from the heat, 2
And will lodge in her splendors.
The man who fears the Lord will do this, 1
And he who masters the Law will win her.
She will meet him like a mother,
And receive him like a bride.
She will feed him with the bread of understanding,
And give him the water of wisdom to drink;
He will lean on her, and not fall,
And will rely on her, and not be disappointed.
She will exalt him above his neighbors,
And open his mouth in the midst of the assembly;
He will find joy and a crown of gladness,
And possess eternal renown.
Men with no understanding will not win her,
And sinners will not see her.
She is far from pride,
And liars give no heed to her.
Praise is not becoming on the lips of a sinner,
For it was not sent him from the Lord.
For praise must be uttered in wisdom, 1
And the Lord will make it prosper.
Do not say, "It was because of the Lord that I fell away," 1
For he will not do things that he hates.
Do not say, "It was he that led me astray," 1
For he has no need of a sinner.
The Lord hates anything abominable; 1
And it is not loved by those who fear him.
It was he who made man in the beginning, 1
And left him in the hands of his own decision;
If you will, you can keep the commandments, 1
And acting faithfully rests on your own good pleasure.
He has set fire and water before you; 1
Stretch out your hand for whichever you wish.
Life and death are before a man, 1
And whichever he chooses will be given him.

18 For the wisdom of the Lord is great;
He is mighty in strength, and beholds all things.
19 His eyes rest on those who fear him,
And he knows everything man does.
20 He has not commanded anyone to be ungodly,
And he has given no one permission to sin.

16 Do not desire a multitude of unprofitable children,
Nor delight in ungodly sons.
2 If they multiply, do not rejoice in them,
Unless the fear of the Lord is with them.
3 Do not put your trust in their lives,
And do not rely on their number;
For one is better than a thousand,
And to die childless than to have children that are ungodly.
4 For from one man of understanding, a city will be peopled,
But a tribe of lawless men will be destroyed.
5 Many such things my eyes have seen,
And mightier things than these my ears have heard.
6 In a gathering of sinners a fire is kindled,
And in a disobedient nation wrath burns.
7 He did not forgive the giants of old,
Who rebelled in their strength;
8 He did not spare the people among whom Lot was living,
Whom he detested for their pride.
9 He did not have mercy on the doomed nation,
Who were dispossessed for their sins;
10 Or on the six hundred thousand men on foot,
Who gathered against him in their obstinacy.
11 Why, if there is one stiff-necked man,
It is a wonder if he goes unpunished;
For both mercy and wrath are with him,
12 He is mighty in forgiveness, and yet pours out his wrath;
Great as is his mercy, so great is his correction also;
He will judge a man by his doings.
13 A sinner will not escape with his booty,
And the steadfastness of the godly man will not be disappointed.
He will make room for all mercy, 14
Yet what every man receives will be governed by what he has done,
Do not say, "I will be hidden from 17
the Lord,
And on high who will remember me?
Among so many people I will not be noticed,
And what is my soul in a boundless creation?
Behold the heaven and the heaven of 18
heavens,
The abyss and the earth shake when he inspects them;
Yes, the mountains and the founda- 19
tions of the earth
Shake and tremble when he looks at them.
No mind can think about them, 20
And who can grasp his ways?
There are hurricanes which no man 21
sees,
And the most of his doings are done in secret.
Who can declare his upright deeds, 22
Or who can endure them? For his agreement is far from me."
A man who is wanting in understand- 23
ing thinks in this way,
And a senseless, misguided man has these foolish thoughts.
Listen to me, my child, and receive 24
instruction,
And apply your mind to what I say;
I will disclose instruction by weight, 25
And declare knowledge with exactness.
When the Lord created his works in 26
the beginning,
After he made them, he fixed their several divisions.
He organized his works in a system 27
forever,
And their divisions for all their generations.
They do not grow hungry or tired,
And they do not stop working.
None of them crowds his neighbor 28
aside,
And they never disobey his command.
After that, the Lord looked at the 29
earth,
And filled it with his blessings.
He covered the face of it with every 30
living creature,
And to it they return.
The Lord created man out of the 17
ground,
And made him return to it again.

2 He set a limit to the number of their
days,
And gave them dominion over what
was on the earth.
3 He clothed them with strength like
his own,
And made them in his own image.
4 He put fear of them in every living
creature,
And made them masters of the wild
animals and birds.
6 He gave them reason and speech and
sight,
Hearing, and a mind for thought.
7 He filled them with the knowledge of
understanding,
And showed them good and evil.
8 He put his eyesight in their minds
To show them the majesty of his
works,
9 So that they would praise his holy
name
And declare the majesty of his works.
11 He gave them knowledge also,
And gave them a law of life as an inheritance.
12 He made an everlasting agreement
with them,
And showed them his decrees.
13 Their eyes saw his glorious majesty,
And their ears heard the glory of his
voice.
14 He said to them, "Beware of anything
that is wrong,"
And he gave everyone of them commands about his neighbor.
15 Their ways are always before him;
They cannot be hidden from his eyes.
17 For every nation he appointed a ruler,
But Israel is the Lord's own portion.
19 All their doings are as clear as the
sun before him,
And his eyes rest continually upon
their ways.
20 Their iniquities are not hidden from
him,
And all their sins are before the Lord.
22 A man's charity is like a signet with
him,
And a man's liberality he will preserve
like the apple of his eye.
23 Afterward he will rise up and requite
them,
And pay back their recompense upon
their heads.
24 But to those who repent he has given
a way to return,
And he encourages those whose endurance fails

Turn to the Lord, and forsake your 2
sins;
Offer a prayer before him, and lessen
your offense.
Draw near to the Most High, and 2
turn away from iniquity,
And hate bitterly what he abhors.
Who will praise the Most High in 2
Hades,
Compared with those who give him
thanks while they still live?
Thanksgiving from the dead perishes 2
as though he were not;
It is the man who is alive and well
that should praise the Lord.
How great is the mercy of the Lord, 2
And his forgiveness for those who turn
to him!
For everything cannot exist in men, 3
For man is not immortal.
What is brighter than the sun? Yet 3
it is eclipsed;
So flesh and blood devise evil.
He looks after the power of the very 3
height of heaven,
But all men are only dust and ashes.
He who lives forever has created all 1
things alike;
The Lord alone can be thought up-
right.
He has permitted no one to declare
his works,
And who can track out his mighty
deeds?
Who can compute the power of his
majesty?
And who can in addition detail his
mercies?
It is not possible to take from them or
to add to them,
Or to track out the wonders of the
Lord.
Where man ends, he begins,
And when man stops, will he be per-
plexed?
What is man, and of what use is he?
What is the good of him, and what is
the evil?
The length of a man's days
Is great at a hundred years,
Like a drop of water from the sea, or 1
a grain of sand,
Are a few years in the day of eternity.
Therefore the Lord has been patient 1
with them,
And he has poured out his mercy upon
them.
He sees and recognizes that their end 1
is evil,

So he increases his forgiveness.
A man has mercy on his neighbor,
But the mercy of the Lord is for all
mankind,
Reproving and training and teaching
them,
And bringing them back as a shep-
herd does his flock.
On those who accept his training he
has mercy,
And on those who eagerly seek his
decrees.
My child, do not spoil your good
deeds,
Or when you make any gift cause
pain by what you say.
Does not the dew assuage the scorch-
ing heat?
So a word is more potent than a gift.
Why, is not a word better than a gift?
Both mark the charitable man;
A fool ungraciously abuses people,
And a present from a grudging man
makes one cry his eyes out.
Learn before you speak,
And take care of yourself before you
get sick;
Examine yourself before you are
judged,
And at the time of visitation you will
find forgiveness.
Humble yourself before you fall sick,
And when you would sin, show re-
pentance instead.
Let nothing prevent you from paying
your vows in time,
And do not wait till you die to be
justified.
Prepare yourself before you make a
vow,
And do not be like a man who tests
the Lord.
Think of his wrath in later days,
And the time of vengeance, when he
turns away his face.
Remember the time of famine in the
time of plenty,
Poverty and want in the days of
wealth.
Between morning and evening the
situation changes,
And it all passes swiftly in the sight
of the Lord.
A wise man is always reverent,
And in days of sin he is careful not to
offend;
Every man of understanding recog-
nizes wisdom,
And will thank the man who finds her.

Men skilled in the use of words com- 29
pose cleverly themselves,
And pour forth apt proverbs.
Do not follow your impulses, 30
But restrain your longings.
If you give assent to the impulse of 31
your heart,
It will make you a laughingstock to
your enemies.
Do not indulge in too much luxury, 32
Do not be tied to its expense.
Do not be impoverished from feasting 33
on borrowed money
When you have nothing in your purse.
A workman who is a drunkard will 19
never get rich;
The man who despises little things will
gradually fail;
Wine and women make men of under- 2
standing stand aloof;
And the man who is devoted to
prostitutes is reckless.
Worms and decay will eventually pos- 3
sess him,
And the rash soul will be destroyed.
The man who trusts people quickly 4
is light-minded;
And he who sins offends against his
own soul.
The man who is merry of heart will 5
be condemned,
And he who hates loquacity has the 6
less malice.
If you never repeat what you are told, 7
You will fare none the worse.
Before friend or foe do not recount it, 8
And unless it would be sinful of you,
do not reveal it.
For someone has heard you and 9
watched you,
And when the time comes he will hate
you.
If you hear something said, let it die 10
with you,
Have courage, it will not make you
burst!
A fool to express a thought suffers 11
such pangs
As a woman in childbirth suffers to
bear a child.
Like an arrow sticking in the flesh of 12
the thigh
Is a word in the heart of a fool.
Question a friend; perhaps he did 13
not do it;
Or if he did, so that he will not do it
again.
Question your neighbor; perhaps he 14
did not say it;

Or if he did, so that he may not repeat it.
15 Question a friend, for often there is slander,
And you must not believe everything that is said.
16 A man may make a slip without intending to—
Who has not sinned with his tongue?
17 Question your neighbor before you threaten him,
And leave room for the Law of the Most High.
20 The fear of the Lord is the sum of wisdom,
And in all wisdom the Law is fulfilled.
22 The knowledge of wickedness is not wisdom,
And where the counsel of sinners is, there is no understanding.
23 There is a cunning that is detestable,
And there is a foolish man who is only deficient in wisdom.
24 A man who is inferior in understanding but fears God is better
Than one who abounds in prudence but transgresses the Law.
25 There is an exact kind of shrewdness that is wrong,
And there is a man who acts crookedly to gain a judgment.
26 There is a kind of villain that bends mournfully,
But inwardly is full of deceit.
27 He covers his face, and pretends to be deaf,
But when no one is looking, he will take advantage of you.
28 And though for lack of strength he may be prevented from sinning,
If he finds an opportunity, he will do you harm.
29 A man is known by his appearance,
And an intelligent man can be told by the expression of his face.
30 A man's clothes and a broad smile,
And the way he walks tell what he is.

20 There is a rebuke that is uncalled for,
And a time when the man who keeps silent is wise.
2 How much better it is to rebuke someone than to get angry,
For the man who makes full confession will be kept from failure.
4 Like a eunuch's craving to ravish a girl
Is the man who would do right by violence.

One man keeps silence and is considered wise; 5
While another is hated for his loquacity.
One man keeps silence because he has nothing to say; 6
And another keeps silence because he knows it is the time for it.
A wise man will keep silence till his time comes, 7
But a boaster and a fool miss the fitting time.
The man who talks excessively is detested, 8
And he who takes it on himself to speak is hated.
There are advantages that come to a man in adversity, 9
And there are gains that result in loss.
There are gifts that will do you no good, 10
And there are gifts that are returned double.
There are humiliations for the sake of gaining glory, 11
And there are men who rise from low conditions.
One man buys much for little, 12
And yet pays for it seven times over.
A man who speaks wisely makes himself beloved; 13
But the pleasant speeches of fools are thrown away.
A present from a fool will do you no good, 14
For his eyes are not one but many.
He gives little but finds a great deal of fault, 15
And opens his mouth like a town-crier.
He will lend today and ask it back tomorrow;
Such a man is hateful.
The fool says, "I have not got a friend; 16
And I get no thanks for my good deeds."
Those who eat his bread are evil-tongued;
How many will laugh at him, and how often! 17
A slip on the ground is better than a slip of the tongue; 18
So the fall of the wicked will come quickly.
A disagreeable man and an unseasonable story— 19
They will both be constantly on the lips of the uneducated.

20 A proverb on the lips of a fool will be refused,
For he will not utter it at the proper time.
21 One man is kept from sinning through poverty,
So his conscience does not prick him when he goes to rest.
22 Another loses his own life from sheer embarrassment,
And destroys it by his senseless expression.
23 Another out of embarrassment makes promises to his friend,
And so makes him his enemy for nothing.
24 A lie is a bad blot in a man;
It is continually found on the lips of the ignorant.
25 A thief is better than a habitual liar,
But they are both doomed to destruction.
26 Dishonor is habitual with a liar,
And his shame attends him continually.
27 A man who speaks wisely makes his way in the world,
And a man of good sense pleases the great.
28 The man who cultivates the soil makes his heap high,
And the man who pleases the great atones for wrongdoing.
29 Gifts and presents can blind the eyes of wise men,
And avert reproofs like a muzzle on the mouth.
30 Hidden wisdom and concealed treasure—
What is the use of either of them?
31 A man who conceals his folly is better
Than a man who conceals his wisdom.
21 My child, if you have sinned, do not do it again,
And pray over your former sins.
2 Flee from sin as from the face of a snake;
For if you approach it, it will bite you.
Its teeth are lion's teeth,
And destroy the souls of men.
3 All iniquity is like a two-edged sword;
A blow from it cannot be healed.
4 Terror and violence lay waste riches;
So the house of a proud man will be laid waste.
5 The prayer from a poor man's mouth reaches his ears,
And his judgment comes speedily.
6 A man who hates reproof is walking in the sinner's steps,
But he who fears the Lord will turn to him in his heart.
A man who is mighty in tongue is known afar off, 7
But a thoughtful man knows when he slips.
The man who builds his house with other men's money 8
Is like one who gathers stones for winter.
An assembly of wicked men is like tow wrapped together; 9
For their end is a blazing fire.
The way of sinners is made smooth with stones, 10
But at the end of it is the pit of Hades.
The man who keeps the Law controls his thoughts, 11
And wisdom is the consummation of the fear of the Lord.
The man who is not shrewd will not be instructed, 12
But there is a shrewdness that spreads bitterness.
A wise man's knowledge abounds like a flood, 13
And his counsel is like a living spring.
The heart of a fool is like a broken dish;
It will hold no knowledge. 14
If a man of understanding hears a wise saying, 15
He commends it, and adds to it;
A self-indulgent man hears it, and it displeases him,
And he throws it behind his back.
The discourse of a fool is like a burden on a journey; 16
But enjoyment is found on the lips of a man of understanding.
The utterance of a sensible man will be asked for in an assembly, 17
And what he says they will think over in their minds.
To a fool wisdom is like a ruined house, 18
And the knowledge of a man without understanding is words that will not bear investigation.
To the foolish man, instruction is fetters on his feet, 19
And handcuffs on his right hand.
A fool raises his voice when he laughs, 20
But a shrewd man will hardly even smile quietly.
To a sensible man instruction is like a gold ornament, 21
And like a bracelet on his right arm.

22 The foot of a fool is quick to enter a house,
But an experienced man waits respectfully before it.
23 A senseless person peeps into a house through the door,
But a cultivated man stands outside.
24 It is stupidity in a man to listen at a door;
But a man of sensibility it would overwhelm with disgrace.
25 The lips of strangers will talk of these things,
But the words of sensible men are weighed on the scales.
26 The minds of fools are in their mouths,
But the mouth of wise men is their mind.
27 When an ungodly man curses his adversary,
He curses his own soul.
28 A whisperer pollutes his own soul,
And will be hated in the neighborhood.

22 A slothful man is like a filthy stone,
And everybody hisses at his disgrace.
2 A slothful man is like the filth of a dunghill;
Anyone who picks it up shakes out his hand.
3 It is a disgrace to be the father of an ignorant son,
And to have a daughter is a disadvantage.
4 A sensible daughter will get a husband of her own,
But one who brings disgrace is a grief to her father.
5 She who is bold disgraces her father and her husband,
And will be despised by both.
6 Unseasonable talk is music in a time of mourning;
But blows and discipline in wisdom are always in order.
7 The man who teaches a fool is gluing a potsherd together,
Or rousing a sleeper out of a deep sleep.
8 The man who lectures to a fool lectures to one who is dozing,
And at the conclusion he will say, "What was it?"
11 Weep for one who is dead, for light has failed him;
And weep over a fool, for understanding has failed him.
Weep less bitterly over the dead, for he has gone to rest;
But the fool's life is worse than death.
The mourning for the dead lasts seven days, 12
But that for a fool or an ungodly man lasts all the days of his life.
Do not talk much with a senseless man, 13
Or go to see a man of no understanding;
Beware of him, or you may have trouble,
And do not be dirtied when he shakes himself.
Avoid him, and you will find rest,
And you will not be wearied by his senselessness.
What is heavier than lead? 14
What can you call it but Fool?
Sand and salt and a lump of iron 15
Are easier to bear than a man without understanding.
A wooden girder fastened in a building 16
Is not loosened by an earthquake;
So a mind established on well-considered thought
Will not be afraid in an emergency.
A mind fixed on understanding thought 17
Is like a plaster ornament on a smooth wall.
Fences set up in the air 18
Will not stand against the wind;
So a cowardly heart with foolish thoughts
Will not stand against any fear.
The man who pricks the eye makes tears fall, 19
And the man who pricks the heart makes it show feeling.
The man who throws a stone at the birds scares them away, 20
And the man who abuses a friend destroys a friendship.
Even if you draw the sword against your friend, 21
Do not despair, for there is a way to repent;
If you open your mouth against your friend, 22
Do not be afraid, for there is such a thing as reconciliation;
But when it comes to abuse and arrogance and telling a secret and a treacherous blow—
At such treatment any friend will take to flight.
Win your neighbor's confidence when he is poor, 23

So that when he prospers you may
be filled likewise.
Stand by him in time of trouble,
So that you may share his inheritance
with him.
24 The vapor and smoke from the furnace
precede the fire;
So abuse precedes bloodshed.
25 I will not shrink from giving shelter
to a friend,
And I will not hide myself from him,
26 And if misfortune overtakes me on his
account
Everyone who hears of it will beware
of him.
27 Who will set a guard over my
mouth,
And put a skilful seal upon my lips,
So that I may not fall because of them,
And my tongue may not destroy me?
23 O Lord, Father and Master of my life,
Do not abandon me to their designs;
Do not let me fall because of them.
2 Who will set scourges over my mind,
And the discipline of wisdom over my
heart,
So that they may not spare me for my
errors of ignorance,
And it may not pass over my sins,
3 So that my acts of ignorance may
not become numerous,
And my sins multiply,
And I fall before my adversaries,
And my enemy rejoice over me?
4 O Lord, Father and God of my life,
Do not give me roving eyes,
And avert evil desire from me;
6 Let not sensual appetite and intercourse master me,
And do not give me up to a shameless
mind.
7 Listen, my children, to the discipline of the mouth,
For he who observes it will not be
taken captive.
8 It is through his lips that the sinner
is caught,
And the abusive and the proud are
tripped up by them.
9 Do not accustom your mouth to an
oath,
And do not form the habit of uttering
the name of the Holy One;
10 For just as a servant who is constantly being questioned
Does not lack the marks of a blow,
11 So the man who constantly swears and
utters the Name
Cannot be absolved from sin.
A man who swears a great deal will be
filled with iniquity,
And the scourge will never leave his
house.
If he offends, his sin rests upon him,
And if he disregards it, he sins doubly;
And if he has sworn needlessly, he is
not justified,
For his house will be filled with
misery.
There is a way of speaking that may 12
be compared with death;
It must not be found in the inher-
itance of Jacob.
For all this will be far from the godly,
And they will not wallow in sin.
Do not accustom your mouth to foul 13
rudeness,
For that is sinful speech.
Remember your father and mother, 14
When you sit in council with the great,
Or you may forget yourself in their
presence,
And seem like a fool through the
habit you have formed,
So that you will wish you had never
been born,
And curse the day of your birth.
A man who forms the habit of abusive 15
speech
Will never be educated as long as he
lives.
There are two kinds of men that 16
multiply sins,
And a third that incurs wrath:
A spirit hot as a burning fire;
It cannot be quenched until it is con-
sumed;
One who is a fornicator in his physical
body;
He will not stop until the fire burns
him up;
To the fornicator all bread is sweet; 17
He will not tire until he dies;
A man who goes astray from his own 18
bed,
And says to himself, "Who can see
me?
Darkness is around me, and the walls
hide me;
So no one can see me; what risk do
I run?
The Most High will not remember my
sins."
The eyes of men are his only fear, 19
And he does not know that the eyes
of the Lord
Survey all the ways of men,
And observe the secret places.

20 All things were known to him before
they were created,
So was it also after they were completed.
21 Such a man will be punished in the
streets of the city,
And caught where he least suspects it.
22 It is so also with a wife who leaves
her husband,
And provides an heir by a stranger.
23 For, first, she disobeys the law of the
Most High,
And, second, she wrongs her husband,
And, third, she commits adultery
through her fornication,
And provides children by a stranger.
24 She will be brought before the assembly,
And her sin will be visited upon her
children.
25 Her children will not take root,
And her branches will not bear fruit.
26 She will leave her memory for a curse,
And her reproach will not be blotted
out,
27 And those who are left behind will
know
That there is nothing better than the
fear of the Lord,
And nothing more pleasant than observing the Lord's commandments.

24 Wisdom is her own recommendation,
And exults in the midst of her people.
2 She opens her mouth in the assembly
of the Most High,
And in the presence of his might she
utters her boast:
3 "I issued from the mouth of the Most
High,
And covered the earth like a mist.
4 I lived on the heights,
And my throne was on the pillar of
cloud.
5 I alone compassed the circuit of
heaven,
And I walked in the depth of the
abyss.
6 I owned the waves of the sea and the
whole earth
And every people and nation.
7 Among all these I sought a resting-place;
In whose possession should I lodge?
8 Then the Creator of all gave me his
command;
And he who created me made my tent
rest,
And said, 'Pitch your tent in Jacob,
And find your inheritance in Israel.'
He created me from the beginning, 9
before the world,
And I shall never cease.
I ministered before him in the holy 10
tent,
And so I was established in Zion.
He made me rest likewise in the be- 11
loved city,
And I had authority over Jerusalem.
I took root in the glorified people, 12
In the portion of the Lord, and of his
inheritance.
I was exalted like a cedar in the 13
Lebanon,
Or a cypress in the mountains of
Hermon;
I was exalted like a palm tree in 14
Engadi,
Or like the rose bushes in Jericho;
Like a fine olive tree in the field;
I was exalted like a plane tree.
I gave forth a perfume like cinnamon 15
and camel's thorn,
And I spread fragrance like choice
myrrh;
Like galbanum, onycha, and stacte,
And like the smoke of frankincense in
the tent.
I stretched out my branches like a 16
terebinth,
My branches were glorious, graceful
branches.
I made grace grow like a vine, 17
And my blossoms produced fame and
wealth.
Come to me, you who desire me, 19
And fill yourselves with my produce.
For the memory of me is sweeter than 20
honey,
And the possession of me, than the
honeycomb.
Those who eat me will still be hungry, 21
And those who drink me will still be
thirsty.
He who obeys me will not be put to 22
shame,
And those who work with me will
commit no sin."
All this is the book of the agreement 23
of the Most High God,
The Law which Moses ordained for us
As an inheritance for the congregations of Jacob;
Which fills men with wisdom like the 25
Pishon,
And like the Tigris in the days of the
new wheat;

5 Which overflows with understanding like the Euphrates,
And like the Jordan in harvest time;
7 Which makes instruction shine forth like light,
Like the Gihon in the days of the vintage.
8 Just as the first man did not know her perfectly,
The last one will not track her out.
9 For her thinking is fuller than the sea,
And her counsel than the great deep.
0 I came out like a canal from the river,
And like a watercourse in a garden.
1 I said, "I will water my garden,
And drench my flower bed."
And behold, my canal became a river,
And my river became a sea.
2 I will again make instruction dawn like the daybreak,
And make it shine forth afar.
3 I will pour out teaching again like prophecy,
And leave it behind for endless generations.
4 Observe that I have not labored for myself only,
But for all who seek her out.
1 In three things I show my beauty and stand up in beauty
Before the Lord and men;
Harmony among brothers, and friendship among neighbors,
And wife and husband suited to each other.
2 But three kinds of men my soul hates,
And I am greatly angered at their existence:
A poor man who is proud, and a rich man who lies,
And an old man who is an adulterer and lacks understanding.
3 If you have not gathered in your youth,
How can you find anything in your old age?
4 How beautiful judgment is for hoary hair,
And the knowledge of what to advise for the elderly!
5 How beautiful is the wisdom of old men,
And consideration and counsel in men of distinction!
6 Rich experience is the crown of old men,
And their boast is the fear of the Lord.

Nine things I have thought of and considered happy: 7
And I can mention a tenth with my tongue:
A man who is happy in his children;
One who lives to see his enemies fall;
Blessed is the man who lives with a wife of understanding; 8
And the one who does not slip with his tongue;
And the one who is not a slave to his inferior;
Blessed is the man who finds good sense; 9
And the one who discourses to the ears of men who listen;
How great the man is who finds wisdom; 10
But there is no one greater than the man who fears the Lord.
The fear of the Lord surpasses everything; 11
To what can the man who possesses it be compared?
Any wound but a wounded heart! 13
And any wickedness but the wickedness of a woman!
Any calamity but a calamity brought about by those who hate you; 14
And any vengeance but the vengeance of your enemies!
There is no head higher than a snake's head, 15
And no anger greater than an enemy's.
I had rather keep house with a lion and a serpent 16
Than keep house with a wicked woman.
A woman's wickedness changes her looks, 17
And darkens her face like a bear;
Her husband sits at table among his neighbors, 18
And involuntarily groans bitterly.
Any malice is small to a woman's malice; 19
May the lot of the sinner befall her!
Like a sandy climb to an old man's feet 20
Is a talkative wife to a quiet man.
Do not fall down before a woman's beauty, 21
And do not greatly desire her for a wife.
It means anger and impudence and great disgrace. 22
If a woman supports her husband.
A humbled mind and a downcast face, 23

And a wounded heart mean a wicked wife.
A woman who does not make her husband happy
Means palsied hands and paralyzed knees.
24 Sin began with a woman,
And because of her we all die.
25 Do not give water an outlet
Nor a wicked woman freedom to speak.
26 If she does not act as you would have her,
Cut her off from your person.

26 Happy is the man who has a good wife!
The number of his days is doubled.
2 A noble wife gladdens her husband,
And he lives out his years in peace.
3 A good wife is good fortune;
She falls to the lot of those who fear the Lord.
4 Whether rich or poor, he has a stout heart;
And always has a cheerful face.
5 There are three things my heart is afraid of,
And a fourth person that I fear:
Town gossip, and the gathering of a mob,
And a false accusation—these are all worse than death.
6 It is heartache and sorrow when one wife is the rival of another,
And a tongue-lashing that exposes things to everybody.
7 A wicked woman is a chafing ox-yoke;
Taking hold of her is like grasping a scorpion.
8 A drunken woman gets very angry,
And does not even cover up her own shame.
9 A woman's immorality is revealed by her roving looks,
And by her eyelids.
10 Keep a close watch over a headstrong daughter,
For if she is allowed her liberty, she may take advantage of it.
11 Keep watch over a roving eye,
And do not be surprised if it offends against you.
12 Like a thirsty traveler who opens his mouth
And drinks of any water that is near,
She will sit down before every tent peg,
And open her quiver to the arrow.
13 The grace of a wife delights her husband,
And her knowledge fattens his bones.
A silent wife is a gift from the Lord, 1
And a well-trained spirit is beyond estimation.
A modest wife is blessing after blessing, 1
And a self-controlled spirit no scales can weigh.
Like the sun rising on the Lord's loftiest heights, 1
Is the beauty of a good woman as she keeps her house in order.
Like a lamp shining on the holy lampstand, 1
Is a beautiful face on a good figure.
Like gold pillars on silver bases
Are beautiful feet with shapely heels.
Over two things my heart is grieved, 2
And over a third anger overcomes me:
A soldier in poverty and want,
And men of understanding who are treated like dirt,
And the man who turns back from uprightness to sin—
The Lord will prepare a sword for him!
A merchant can hardly keep himself from doing wrong, 2
And a storekeeper cannot be acquitted of sin.
Many sin for the sake of gain, 2
And the man who is intent on increasing what he has, has to shut his eyes.
A peg will stick between the joints of stones,
And between buying and selling, sin is ground out.
Unless a man earnestly holds on to the fear of the Lord,
His house will soon be overturned.
When a sieve is shaken, the refuse remains in it;
So, when a man reasons, his filth remains.
The furnace tests the potter's dishes,
And the test of a man is in his reasoning.
Its fruit shows how a tree has been cultivated;
So does the expression of the thought of a man's mind.
Do not praise a man before you hear him reason,
For that is the way men are tested.
If you pursue what is right, you will overtake it,
And put it on like a splendid robe.
Birds roost with their own kind,

And truth comes back to those who practice it.
10 The lion lies in wait for his prey,
And so does sin for those who do wrong.
11 The discourse of a godly man is always wise,
But the foolish man changes like the moon.
12 Among unintelligent people watch your opportunity to leave,
But among thoughtful people stay on.
13 The discourse of fools is offensive,
And their laughter is wanton sinfulness.
14 A profane man's talk makes your hair stand on end,
And their quarreling makes you stop your ears.
15 When arrogant men quarrel, there is bloodshed,
And their abuse of one another is dreadful to hear.
16 The man who tells secrets destroys confidence,
And will not find a friend to his mind.
17 If you love your friend, keep faith with him,
But if you tell his secrets, do not pursue him.
18 For sure as a man loses his dead,
You have lost your neighbor's friendship,
19 And as you let a bird out of your hand,
You have let your neighbor out, and you will never catch him.
Do not go after him, for he is far away,
20 And has made his escape like a gazelle from a trap.
21 For you can bind up a wound,
And be reconciled after abuse,
But for the man who tells secrets there is no hope.
22 A man who winks his eye plots mischief,
And no one can keep it from him.
23 Face to face with you he speaks sweetly,
And will show respect for what you say;
But afterward he will twist his lips,
And make a stumbling block of your words.
24 I have hated many things, but found nothing like him,
And the Lord hates him too.
25 The man who throws a stone into the air is throwing it on his own head,
And a treacherous blow wounds both.

The man who digs a hole will fall into it, 26
And the man who sets a trap will be caught in it.
If a man does wicked things, they will roll on him, 27
And he will not know where they come from.
Mockery and abuse overtake arrogant men, 28
And vengeance lies in wait for them like a lion.
Those who enjoy the downfall of the godly will be caught in a trap, 29
And pain will consume them before they die.
Wrath and anger are also detestable, 30
And the sinful man clings to them.
The man who takes vengeance will have vengeance taken on him by the Lord, 28
And he will keep close watch of his sins.
Forgive your neighbor his wrongdoing; 2
Then your sins will be forgiven when you pray.
Shall one man cherish anger against another, 3
And yet ask healing from the Lord?
Does he have no mercy on a man like himself, 4
And yet pray for his own sins?
If he, though he is flesh and blood, cherishes anger, 5
Who will atone for his sins?
Remember your end and give up your enmity; 6
Think of death and destruction, and stand by the commandments.
Remember the commandments, and do not be angry with your neighbor; 7
Think of the agreement of the Most High, and overlook men's ignorance.
Keep from quarreling, and you will reduce your sins, 8
For a passionate man kindles quarrels.
A sinful man creates dissension among friends, 9
And arouses enmity among those who are at peace.
The more fuel, the more the fire will burn, 10
And the more obstinate the quarrel, the more it will burn.
The stronger a man is, the greater is his anger,

And the richer he is, the haughtier
will his wrath be.
11 A hurried dispute kindles a fire,
And a hasty quarrel means bloodshed.
12 If you blow on a spark, it will blaze,
And if you spit on it, it will be put out;
Yet both come out of your mouth.
13 Curse the whisperer and the deceitful man;
For he has destroyed many who were
at peace.
14 A third person's tongue has stirred
many up,
And removed them from one nation
to another;
It has torn down strongly fortified
cities,
And overthrown the houses of the
great.
15 A third person's tongue has driven
out noble women,
And robbed them of the fruit of their
labors.
16 The man who listens to it will find no
rest,
And will not live in peace.
17 The blow of a whip leaves a bruise,
But the blow of a tongue breaks the
bones.
18 Many have fallen by the edge of the
sword,
But not so many as have fallen by the
tongue.
19 Happy is the man who is protected
from it,
Who does not feel its anger,
Who does not bear its yoke,
And is not bound with its chains.
20 For its yoke is an iron yoke,
And its chains are brazen chains;
21 Its death is a cruel death,
And Hades is better than it.
22 It will not control godly men,
And they will not be burned in its fire.
23 Those who forsake the Lord will fall
into it,
And it will burn at them and not be
put out;
It will be sent upon them like a lion,
And ravage them like a leopard.
24 If you see to hedging your property in
with thorns,
And shut up your silver and gold,
25 Make balances and scales to weigh
your words,
And make a barred door for your
mouth.
26 Take heed not to make a slip with it,
Or you will fall before someone lying
in wait for you.
The man who shows mercy will lend 29
to his neighbor,
And the man who takes him by the
hand keeps the commandments.
Lend to your neighbor when he is in 2
need,
And pay your neighbor back again
when it is time.
Keep your word and keep faith with 3
him,
And in every emergency you will find
what you need.
Many consider a loan as a windfall, 4
And bring trouble on those who help
them.
A man will kiss another man's hands 5
until he gets it;
And speak humbly about his neighbor's money;
But when payment is due, he extends
the time,
And answers indifferently,
And finds fault about the time of payment.
If a man succeeds, he will hardly get 6
half of it,
And he will consider that a windfall.
If he does not, the other has defrauded him of his money,
And needlessly made him his enemy;
He will pay him with curses and abuse,
And repay him with insults instead of
honor.
Many refuse to lend, not from their 7
wickedness,
But they are afraid of being needlessly
defrauded.
But be patient with a poor man, 8
And do not make him wait for charity.
For the commandment's sake help the 9
needy man,
And, in view of his need, do not send
him away unsatisfied.
Lose your money for the sake of a 10
brother or a friend,
And do not let it rust to ruin under a
stone.
Lay up your treasure according to 11
the commandments of the Most
High,
And it will be more profitable to you
than gold.
Store up gifts to charity in your store- 12
rooms,
And it will deliver you from all harm.
Better than a mighty shield and a 13
ponderous spear,

It will fight for you against your
enemy.
14 A good man will go surety for his
neighbor,
But the man who has lost his sense
of shame will abandon him.
15 Do not forget the favor your surety
has done you,
For he has put himself in your place.
16 A sinner will disregard the service
done him by his surety,
17 And an ungrateful man will forsake
the man who saved him.
18 Going surety has ruined many prosperous men,
And shaken them like an ocean wave.
It has driven influential men out of
their houses,
And made them wander among foreign
nations.
19 A sinner fails in acting as security,
And the man who pursues profits falls
into lawsuits.
20 Help your neighbor to the best of
your ability,
But take heed that you do not fall.
21 The basis of life is water and bread
and clothing,
And a house to cover one's nakedness.
22 The life of a poor man under a shelter
of logs is better
Than splendid fare in someone else's
house.
23 Be contented with much or little,
And you will not hear the reproach of
being a stranger.
24 It is a miserable life to go from house
to house;
And where you are a stranger, you
cannot open your mouth.
25 If you entertain others and give them
drink, you will have no thanks,
And besides that you will have bitter
things to hear:
26 "Come in, stranger, set the table,
And if you have anything with you,
let me have it to eat."
27 "Get out, stranger, here is somebody
more important;
My brother has come to be my guest;
I need my house."
28 These things are trying to a man of
sensibility:
The reproach of a household and the
abuse of a creditor.
30 The man who loves his son will continually beat him,
So that he may be glad at the end.
The man who disciplines his son will 2
profit by him,
And boast of him among his acquaintances;
The man who teaches his son will 3
make his enemy jealous,
And exult over him before his friends.
When his father dies, it is as though 4
he were not dead,
For he leaves behind him one like
himself.
In his lifetime he sees him and re- 5
joices,
And in death he does not grieve.
He has left one to avenge him upon 6
his enemies,
And to repay the kindness of his
friends.
The man who spoils his son will have 7
to bind up his wounds,
And his heart will tremble at every
cry.
An unbroken horse turns out stub- 8
born,
And a son left to himself grows up
headstrong.
If you pamper your child, he will 9
astonish you.
Play with him, and he will grieve you;
Do not laugh with him, so that you 10
may not have to mourn with
him
And gnash your teeth over him at
last.
Do not allow him liberty in his youth; 11
Bruise his sides while he is a child, 12
So that he will not become stubborn
and disobey you.
Discipline your son and take pains 13
with him,
So that he will not distress you with
his bad behavior.
A poor man who is well and has a 14
strong constitution is better off
Than a rich man who is afflicted in
body.
Health and a good constitution are 15
better than any amount of gold,
And a strong body than untold riches.
There is no greater wealth than health 16
of body,
And there is no greater happiness than
gladness of heart.
Death is better than a wretched life, 17
And eternal rest than continual sickness.
Good things spread out before a 18
mouth that is closed
Are like piles of food laid on a grave.

19 What good is an offering of fruit to an
idol?
It can neither eat nor smell.
That is the way with a man who is
afflicted by the Lord:
20 He sees things with his eyes and
groans
Like a eunuch embracing a girl!
21 Do not give yourself up to sorrow,
And do not distress yourself of your
own accord.
22 Gladness of heart is a man's life.
And exultant joy prolongs his days.
23 Be kind to yourself and comfort your
heart,
And put sorrow far from you;
For sorrow has destroyed many,
And there is no profit in it.
24 Envy and anger shorten a man's days,
And worry brings on old age before its
time.
25 A heart that is cheerful and good
Will pay attention to the food he eats.
31 Anxiety about wealth makes a man
waste away,
And his worry about it drives away
his sleep.
2 Wakefulness and worry banish drowsiness
As a serious illness dispels sleep.
3 A rich man toils to amass money,
And when he stops to rest, he enjoys
luxury;
4 A poor man toils for the want of a
livelihood,
And if he stops to rest, he finds himself in want.
5 The man who loves gold cannot be
called upright,
And the man who pursues profits will
be led astray by them,
6 Many have been brought to their
downfall because of gold
And have been brought face to face
with ruin.
7 It is a stumbling block to those who
are possessed by it,
And every foolish man is taken captive by it.
8 Happy is the rich man who is found
blameless,
And does not go after gold;
9 Who is he?—that we may congratulate him,
For he has worked wonders among his
people.
10 Who has been tested by it and found
perfect?
He has a right to boast.
Who has been able to transgress and
has not transgressed,
And to do wrong and has not done it?
His prosperity will be lasting,
And the congregation will talk of his
charities.
Do you sit at a great table?
Do not gulp at it,
And do not say, "How much there is
on it!"
Remember that an envious eye is
wrong.
What has been created that is worse
than the eye?
That is why it sheds tears on every
face.
Do not reach out your hand wherever
it looks,
And do not crowd your neighbor in
the dish;
Be considerate of him of your own accord,
And be thoughtful in everything.
Eat like a human being what is served
to you,
Do not champ your food, or you will
be detested.
Be the first to leave off for good manners' sake,
And do not be greedy, or you will give
offense.
Even though you are seated in a large
company,
Do not be the first to help yourself.
How adequate a little is for a well-bred man!
He does not have to gasp upon his
bed!
Healthy sleep results from moderation
in eating;
One gets up in the morning, in good
spirits.
The distress of sleeplessness and indigestion
And colic attend the greedy man.
If you are compelled to eat,
Get up in the middle of the meal and
stop eating.
Listen to me, my child, and do not disregard me.
And in the end you will find my words
true:
Be industrious in all your work,
And no disease will overtake you.
The man who is generous with his
bread men's lips will bless,
And their testimony to his goodness
can be relied on.

24 The town will grumble at the man
who is grudging with his bread,
And their testimony to his niggardliness is correct.
25 Do not play the man about wine,
For wine has been the ruin of many.
26 The furnace proves the steel's temper
by dipping it;
So wine tests hearts when proud men
quarrel.
27 Wine is like life to men
If you drink it in moderation;
What life has a man who is without
wine?
For it was created to give gladness to
men.
28 An exhilaration to the heart and gladness to the soul
Is wine, drunk at the proper time and
in sufficient quantity;
29 Bitterness to the soul is much drinking of wine
Amidst irritation and conflict.
30 Drunkenness increases the anger of a
foolish man to his injury,
Reducing his strength and causing
wounds.
31 Do not rebuke your neighbor at a
banquet,
And do not despise him in his mirth.
Do not say a reproachful word to him,
And do not press him to repay you.
32 If they make you master of the
feast, do not be uplifted;
Behave like one of them among them.
Look after them, and then take your
seat;
2 When you have performed your duties, take your place,
So that you may rejoice on their account,
And be crowned with a wreath for
your efficiency.
3 Speak, elder, for that is your part,
With sound understanding, and do not
interfere with the music.
4 When there is to be entertainment, do
not talk volubly,
And do not philosophize when it is inopportune.
5 A carbuncle signet in a gold setting
Is a musical concert at a banquet.
6 An emerald signet richly set in gold
Is the melody of music with the taste
of wine.
7 Speak, young man, if you are
obliged to,
And only if you are asked repeatedly.

Speak concisely; say much in few 8
words;
Act like a man who knows more than
he says.
When among great men do not act like 9
an equal;
And when another man is speaking,
do not talk much.
The lightning hastens before the 10
thunder,
And approval opens the way for a
modest man.
Leave in good season and do not bring 11
up the rear;
Hurry home and do not linger.
Amuse yourself there, and do what 12
you please,
But do not sin through proud speech.
For all these things bless your Maker, 13
Who makes you drink his blessings
till you are satisfied.
The man who fears the Lord will 14
accept his discipline,
And those who rise early to seek him
will gain his approval.
The man who pursues the Law will get 15
his fill of it,
But the hypocrite will be tripped up
by it.
Those who fear the Lord will discern 16
his judgment,
And will kindle upright acts like the
light.
A sinful man will shun reproof, 17
And will find a legal decision to his
liking.
A man of discretion will not neglect 18
thought;
An alien or a proud man will not
cower from fear;
Do nothing without consideration; 19
And when you do a thing, do not
change your mind.
Do not walk in a path full of obstacles, 20
And do not stumble over stony
ground.
Do not trust an untried way, 21
And guard against your children. 22
In every act have faith in yourself, 23
For that is the keeping of the commandments.
The man who has faith in the Law 24
heeds the commandments,
And the man who trusts in the Lord
will not fail.
No evil will befall the man who 33
fears the Lord
But in trial he will deliver him again
and again.

2 A wise man will not hate the Law,
But the man who is hypocritical about
it is like a ship in a storm.
3 A man of understanding will trust in
the Law,
And he trusts the Law as he would a
decision by the sacred lot.
4 Prepare what you have to say, and
then you will be listened to;
Knit your instruction together and
give your answer.
5 The heart of a fool is a wagon wheel;
And his thought is like a turning axle.
6 A stallion is like a mocking friend;
He neighs under everyone who mounts
him.
7 Why is one day better than another,
When the light of every day in the
year is from the sun?
8 By the Lord's knowledge they have
been separated,
And he has made the various seasons
and festivals.
9 Some of them he has exalted and
made sacred,
And some he has made ordinary days.
10 All men are from the ground,
And Adam was created out of earth.
11 In the wealth of his knowledge the
Lord has distinguished them,
And made their ways different.
12 Some of them he has blessed and
exalted,
And some he has made holy and
brought near himself.
Some of them he has cursed and
humbled,
And thrown down from their position.
13 Like clay in the hand of the potter—
For all his ways are guided by his
good pleasure—
So men are in the hands of their
Creator,
To be repaid as he decides.
14 As good is the opposite of evil,
And life the opposite of death,
So the sinner is the opposite of the
godly man.
15 So look upon all the works of the
Most High,
In pairs, one the opposite of the other.
16 I was the last to wake up,
Like one who gleans after the grape-gatherers;
By the blessing of the Lord I got
ahead,
And like a grape-gatherer I filled my
winepress.

Observe that I have not labored for 17
myself only,
But for all who seek instruction.
Hear me, you leaders of the people, 18
And you rulers of the assembly, listen
to me.
To a son or a wife, to a brother or a 19
friend,
Do not give power over yourself as
long as you live,
And do not give your money to someone else,
So that you may not change your
mind and have to ask for it.
As long as you live and have breath 20
in your body,
Do not sell yourself to anybody.
For it is better that your children 21
should ask from you,
Than that you should look to the
clean hands of your sons.
In all that you do retain control, 22
So that you will not put any stain
upon your reputation.
When the days of your life reach their 23
end,
At the time of your death distribute
your property.
Fodder and a stick and loads for an 24
ass,
Bread and discipline and work for a
servant.
Put your slave to work, and you will 25
have rest;
Leave his hands idle, and he will seek
his liberty.
The yoke and the strap will bend his 26
neck,
And racks and tortures are for a servant who is a wrongdoer.
Put him to work, so that he will not 27
be idle,
For idleness teaches much evil.
Set him such work as is suited to him, 28
And if he does not obey, load him with
fetters.
But do not be overbearing to anybody, 29
And do not do anything without consideration.
If you have a servant, regard him as 30
yourself,
Because you have bought him with
blood.
If you have a servant, treat him like 31
a brother,
For you need him as you do your own
life.

If you ill-treat him, and he leaves
and runs away,
Where will you look for him?
34 Vain and delusive are the hopes of
a man of no understanding,
And dreams give wings to fools!
2 Like a man who catches at a shadow,
and chases the wind,
Is the man who is absorbed in dreams.
3 A vision of dreams is this against that,
The likeness of one face before another.
4 From an unclean thing what can be
clean?
And from something false what can
be true?
5 Divinations and omens and dreams
are folly,
And fancies of the mind like those
of a woman in travail.
6 Unless they are sent from the Most
High as a warning,
Do not pay any attention to them,
7 For dreams have deceived many,
And setting their hopes on them has
led to their downfall.
8 The Law must be observed without
any such falsehoods,
And wisdom finds perfection in truthful lips.
9 A well-taught man knows a great
deal,
And a man of experience will discourse
with understanding.
10 The man who has not been tested
knows little,
But the man who has wandered far
gains great ingenuity.
11 I have seen much in my travels,
And I understand more than I can
describe;
12 I have often been in danger of death,
But I have been saved by these qualities.
13 The spirit of those who fear the Lord
will live,
For their hope is in him who can save
them.
14 The man who fears the Lord will have
no dread,
And will not be afraid, for he is his
hope.
15 Happy is the soul of the man who
fears the Lord!
Whom does he regard? And who is
his support?
16 The eyes of the Lord rest on those
who love him,
A mighty shield, a strong support,

A shelter from the hot wind and the
noonday heat,
A guard against stumbling and a
defense against falling.
He lifts up the soul and gives light 17
to the eyes,
And bestows healing, life, and blessing.
If a man offers a sacrifice that was 18
wrongfully obtained, it is blemished,
And the gifts of sinful men are not
acceptable.
The Most High is not pleased with 19
the offerings of ungodly men,
And a man cannot atone for his sins
with a great number of sacrifices.
The man who offers a sacrifice from 20
the property of the poor
Sacrifices a son before his father's eyes.
Scanty fare is the living of the poor; 21
The man who deprives them of it is a
murderous man.
The man who takes away his neigh- 22
bor's living murders him,
And the man who deprives a hired
man of his wages is guilty of
bloodshed.
One man builds and another tears 23
down;
What do they gain but toil?
One man prays and another curses; 24
Which one's voice will the Lord listen
to?
If a man washes himself after touch- 25
ing a corpse and then touches it
again,
What good has his bath done him?
That is the way with a man who fasts 26
for his sins,
And goes and does the same things
over.
Who will listen to his prayer?
And what has he gained by humiliating himself?
The man who keeps the Law will 35
make many offerings;
He who gives heed to the commandments will offer a thanksgiving
sacrifice,
The man who returns a kindness will 2
offer a meal offering,
And the man who gives to charity will
offer the sacrifice of praise.
Avoiding wickedness wins the Lord's 3
approval,
And avoiding wrongdoing is atonement.
Do not appear before the Lord 4
empty-handed,

5 For all these things must be done because they are commanded.
6 The offering of an upright man enriches the altar,
And its fragrance reaches the Most High.
7 The sacrifice of an upright man is acceptable,
And the memory of it will not be forgotten.
8 Glorify the Lord with a generous eye,
And do not stint the first fruits of your hands.
9 In all your giving show a joyful face,
And dedicate your tithes with gladness.
10 Give to the Most High as he has given to you,
With a generous eye, and as your hand has found.
11 For the Lord is one who repays,
And he will repay you seven times over.
12 Do not try to bribe him, for he will not accept it,
And do not rely on an ill-gotten sacrifice;
For the Lord is a judge,
And there is no partiality with him.
13 He will show no partiality against the poor,
But he will listen to the prayer of the man who is wronged.
14 He will not disregard the supplication of the orphan,
Or the widow, if she pours out her story.
15 Do not the widow's tears run down her cheeks,
While she utters her complaint against the man who has caused them to fall?
16 The man who serves God with good will is welcomed,
And his prayer reaches to the clouds.
17 The prayer of the humble pierces the clouds,
And until it reaches God, he will not be consoled.
He will not leave off until the Most High considers him,
And does justice to the upright, and passes judgment.
18 And the Lord will not delay,
Or be slow about them,
Until he crushes the loins of the unmerciful,
And takes vengeance on the heathen;
Until he destroys the multitude of the insolent,
And breaks the scepters of the unrighteous;
Until he repays a man for his doings, 1
And repays men's deeds according to their thoughts;
Until he judges the case of his people,
And makes them glad with his mercy.
Mercy is as beautiful in a time of 2
trouble
As rain clouds in a time of drought.

Have mercy upon us, Lord God of 3
all, and look upon us,
And cast fear of you upon all the heathen.
Raise your hand against alien peoples,
And let them see your might.
As you have been sanctified before them, in us,
May you be magnified before us, in them;
And let them know, as we have known,
That there is no god, Lord, but you.
Show signs again, and show other wonders,
Make your hand and your right arm glorious.
Arouse your anger and pour out your wrath,
Destroy the adversary and wipe out the enemy.
Hasten the time and remember your oath;
And let them relate your mighty acts.
Let him that would save himself be consumed in furious fire,
And let those who harm your people meet destruction.
Crush the heads of the enemy's rulers, 1
Who say, "There is no one but ourselves!"
Gather all the tribes of Jacob, 1
And give them their inheritance, as it was of old.
Have mercy, Lord, on the people that 1.
has borne your name,
And on Israel, whom you compared to your first-born.
Have pity on the city of your sanctu- 1
ary,
Jerusalem, the place where you rest.
Fill Zion with the celebration of your 1
goodness,
And your people with your glory.
Bear witness to those whom you cre- 1.
ated in the beginning,
And fulfil the prophecies made in your name.
Give those who wait for you their 1
reward,

And let men trust in your prophets.
17 Hear, Lord, the prayer of your suppliants,
With Aaron's blessing on your people,
And all the people on the earth will know
That you are the Lord, the eternal God.
18 The stomach will eat any food,
Yet one food is better than another.
19 As the mouth tastes the meat of game,
An intelligent mind detects false words.
20 A perverse mind causes pain,
But an experienced man will pay him back.
21 A woman can receive any man,
Yet one girl surpasses another.
22 A woman's beauty gladdens one's countenance,
And exceeds every desire man has.
23 If mercy and meekness are on her lips,
Her husband is not like the sons of men.
24 The man who gets a wife enters upon a possession,
A helper like himself, and a pillar of support.
25 Where there is no hedge, a piece of property will be plundered,
And where there is no wife, a man will wander about and groan.
26 For who will trust an active robber
Who bounds from one city to another?
So who will trust a man who has no nest,
And spends the night wherever evening overtakes him?
1 Every friend will say, "I am your friend";
But sometimes a friend is a friend only in name.
2 Is it not a sorrow like that for death itself
When a companion and friend turns into an enemy?
3 O wicked thought! Why were you shaped
To cover the earth with deceit?
4 There are companions who rejoice in their friends' happiness,
But, when trouble comes, are against them.
5 There are companions who labor with a friend for their stomach's sake,
Who will take up the shield in the face of war.

Do not forget your friend in your heart, 6
And do not be unmindful of him in your wealth.
Every adviser praises good counsel, 7
But some give advice in their own interests.
Be on your guard against advisers 8
And first find out what is for their advantage—
For they will take thought for themselves—
Or they will cast the lot against you,
And say to you, "Your way is good," 9
And will stand over against you to see what will happen to you.
Do not consult with the man who looks suspiciously at you, 10
And conceal your purpose from those who are jealous of you;
With a woman about her rival, 11
Or with a coward about a war;
With a merchant about business,
Or with a buyer about selling;
With an envious man about gratitude,
Or with a merciless man about kindliness;
With an idler about any piece of work.
Or with a man hired by the year about finishing his work;
With a lazy servant about a large undertaking;
Do not look to these for any advice,
But stay all the time with a godly man, 12
Who you know keeps the commandments;
Whose heart is at one with your heart,
And who will sorrow with you if you fail.
And hold fast the counsel of your own mind, 13
For you have nothing more to be depended on than it.
For a man's soul is sometimes wont to bring him news 14
Better than seven watchmen sitting high on a watchtower.
And, above all this, intreat the Most High 15
To direct your way in truth.
Every undertaking begins with reason, 16
And consideration precedes every work.
If we trace the changes of the mind, 17
Four parts appear, 18
Good and evil, life and death.

But it is the tongue that continually
rules them.
19 A man may be shrewd and the instructor of many,
And yet be unprofitable to himself
20 A man skilful in his use of words may
be hated;
He will fail to get any food.
21 For agreeableness has not been given
him by the Lord,
Because he has been deprived of all
wisdom.
A man may be wise for himself,
22 And the products of his understanding may be trustworthy on his
lips;
23 A wise man will instruct his own people,
And the products of his understanding will be trustworthy;
24 A wise man will be satisfied with
blessing,
And all who see him will call him
happy.
25 A man's life is numbered by days,
But the days of Israel are unnumbered.
26 The wise man will obtain the trust of
his people,
And his name will live forever.
27 My child, test your soul while you
live,
And see what hurts it, and do not give
it that.
28 For not everything is good for everyone,
And not everybody enjoys everything.
29 Do not be insatiable about any luxury,
And do not be carried away with food,
30 For sickness comes with excessive eating,
And greediness leads to severe illness.
31 Many have died of greediness,
But the man who guards against it
prolongs his life.

38 Show the physician due honor in
view of your need of him,
For the Lord has created him;
2 Healing comes from the Most High,
And he will receive presents from the
king.
3 The skill of the physician exalts him,
And he is admired among the great.
4 The Lord has created medicines out
of the earth,
And a sensible man will not refuse
them.
5 Was not water made sweet by wood,
So that its strength might be shown?
And he has given men knowledge
So that he might be glorified for his
wonderful works.
With them he cures and takes away
pain.
The druggist makes a mixture of them.
His works will never end,
And from him peace spreads over the
face of the earth.
My child, do not be negligent when
you are sick,
But pray to the Lord, and he will cure
you.
Renounce wrongdoing and make your
hands do right,
And cleanse your heart from every sin.
Offer a fragrant offering and a memorial sacrifice of fine flour,
And make your offering rich, as
though you were no longer to
live,
And leave room for the physician, for
the Lord has created him,
And he must not desert you, for you
need him.
There is a time when your welfare depends upon them,
For they too will pray the Lord
To guide them to bringing relief
And effecting a cure and restoration
to health.
As for the man who sins in the sight of
his Maker,
May he fall into the hands of the
physician!
My child, for the dead let your tears
fall,
And like one who is suffering terribly
begin your lament.
Wrap his body up fittingly,
And do not neglect his burial.
Weep bitterly and wail passionately
And show your grief as he may deserve,
For one day or perhaps two, to avert
criticism;
Then be comforted for your sorrow.
For death comes of sorrow,
And sorrow of heart prostrates one's
strength.
In misfortune grief will continue,
And the life of the poor saddens the
heart.
But do not resign your heart to grief;
Dismiss it, but remember your end.
Do not forget it, for he will not come
back;
You cannot help him, and you will
harm yourself;

"Remember my judgment, for yours will be like it;
Mine today, and yours tomorrow!"
When the dead is at rest, let his memory rest,
And be comforted for him when his spirit departs.
A scribe attains wisdom through the opportunities of leisure,
And the man who has little business to do can become wise.
How can the man who holds the plow become wise,
Who glories in handling the ox-goad,
Who drives oxen, and guides them at their work,
And whose discourse is with the sons of bulls?
He sets his mind on turning his furrows,
And his anxiety is about fodder for heifers.
It is so with every craftsman and builder,
Who keeps at work at night as well as by day.
Some cut carved seals,
And elaborate variety of design;
Another puts his mind on painting a likeness,
And is anxious to complete his work.
It is so with the smith sitting by his anvil,
And expert in working in iron;
The smoke of the fire reduces his flesh,
And he exerts himself in the heat of the furnace.
He bends his ear to the sound of the hammer,
And his eyes are on the pattern of the implement.
He puts his mind on completing his work,
And he is anxious to finish preparing it.
It is so with the potter, as he sits at his work,
And turns the wheel with his foot;
He is constantly careful about his work,
And all his manufacture is by measure;
He will shape the clay with his arm,
And bend its strength with his feet;
He puts his mind on finishing the glazing,
And he is anxious to make his furnace clean.

All these rely on their hands; 31
And each one is skilful in his own work;
Without them, no city can be inhabited, 32
And men will not live in one or go about in it.
But they are not sought for to advise the people, 33
And in the public assembly they do not excel.
They do not sit on the judge's seat,
And they do not think about the decision of lawsuits;
They do not utter instruction or judgment,
And they are not found using proverbs.
Yet they support the fabric of the world, 34
And their prayer is in the practice of their trade.
It is not so with the man who applies himself, 39
And studies the Law of the Most High.
He searches out the wisdom of all the ancients,
And busies himself with prophecies;
He observes the discourse of famous men, 2
And penetrates the intricacies of figures.
He searches out the hidden meaning of proverbs, 3
And acquaints himself with the obscurities of figures.
He will serve among great men, 4
And appear before rulers.
He will travel through the lands of strange peoples,
And test what is good and what is evil among men.
He will devote himself to going early 5
To the Lord his Maker,
And will make his entreaty before the Most High.
He will open his mouth in prayer,
And make entreaty for his sins.
If the great Lord pleases, 6
He will be filled with the spirit of understanding,
He will pour out his wise sayings,
And give thanks to the Lord in prayer;
He will direct his counsel and knowledge, 7
And study his secrets.

8 He will reveal instruction in his teaching,
And will glory in the Law of the Lord's agreement.
9 Many will praise his understanding,
And it will never be blotted out.
His memory will not disappear,
And his name will live for endless generations.
10 Nations will repeat his wisdom,
And the congregation will utter his praise.
11 If he lives long, he will leave a greater name than a thousand,
And if he goes to rest, his fame is enough for him.
12 I have reflected further, and I will utter it,
And I am full as the full moon.
13 Listen to me, you holy sons, and bud
Like a rose that grows by a water-course;
14 Exhale fragrance like a frankincense tree,
And blossom like a lily.
Give forth an odor and sing a song,
Bless the Lord for all his works.
15 Magnify his name,
And confess him with praise,
With songs on your lips and with lyres,
And this is what you are to say in your thanksgiving:
16 "The works of the Lord are all extremely good,
And every command of his will be obeyed in its proper season."
17 No one can say "What does this mean? Why is that?"
For in his good time they will all be searched out,
At his command the waters stood in a heap,
And the reservoirs of water at the word he uttered.
18 At his order all that he pleases is done,
And there is no one who can interfere with his saving power.
19 The doings of all mankind are before him,
And it is not possible to be hidden from his eyes.
20 From everlasting to everlasting he beholds them,
And nothing is marvelous to him.
21 No one can say, "What does this mean? Why is that?"
For everything has been created for its use.
His blessing covers the land like a river,
And saturates the dry land like a flood.
As he turns fresh water into salt water,
So the heathen will experience his wrath.
To his people his ways are straight,
Just as they are stumbling blocks to the disobedient.
From the beginning good things have been created for the good,
Just as evils have been created for sinners.
The elements necessary for man's life
Are water and fire and iron and salt,
And wheat flour and milk and honey,
The blood of the grape, and olive oil and clothing.
All these things prove good to the godly,
Just as they turn into evils for the sinful.
There are winds which have been created for vengeance,
And, when he is angry, they make their scourges strong;
When the consummation comes, they will pour out their strength,
And calm the anger of their Creator.
Fire and hail and famine and death—
These have all been created for vengeance.
The teeth of wild animals, and scorpions and vipers,
And the sword that drives the ungodly to destruction—
They will rejoice when he commands,
And be made ready on the earth for their functions.
And they will not disobey his word, at their proper times.
Therefore from the beginning I have become assured,
And have reached this conclusion and left it in writing:
The works of the Lord are all good,
And will supply every need when it arises,
And no one can say, "This is worse than that,"
For they will all prove good in their season.
So now sing praise with all your heart and voice,
And bless the name of the Lord.
Much occupation is appointed for every man,

And a heavy yoke rests on the sons of
Adam
From the day they come out of their
mother's womb
Until the day when they return to the
mother of us all,
Their perplexities and anxiety of
mind,
Their apprehension, and the day of
their end!
From the man who sits on his splendid throne
To the one who is abased in dust and
ashes,
From the man who wears purple and
a crown
To the one who is clad in coarse linen,
There is wrath and envy and trouble
and perplexity
And fear of death and anger and strife,
And when a man rests upon his bed,
His sleep at night confuses his knowledge.
He gets little or no rest,
And afterward in his sleep, he is like a
watchman on duty,
Bewildered by the vision of his mind
Like a man who has escaped from
the front of battle.
In the moment of his extremity he
wakes up,
And wonders that his fear came to
nothing.
It is so with all flesh, man and beast;
And with sinners seven times more;
Death and blood and strife and sword,
Misfortunes, famine and affliction and
plague—
All these were created for the wicked,
And because of them the flood came.
All that comes from the earth returns
to the earth,
And what comes from the waters turns
back to the sea.
All bribery and injustice will be
blotted out,
But good faith will stand forever.
The property of unrighteous men will
dry up like a river,
And explode like a clap of thunder in a
rain.
As surely as an open-handed man is
glad,
Transgressors will utterly fail.
The children of the ungodly will not
put forth many branches;
They are unclean roots on a precipitous rock.
Sedge by any water or riverbank
Will be plucked up before any grass.
Kindness is like a garden of blessing, 17
And charity endures forever.
The life of a self-supporting man or 18
of a workman is made sweet,
But a man who finds a treasure is
better off than both of them.
Children or the building of a city 19
perpetuate a man's name,
But an irreproachable wife is counted
better than both of them.
Wine and music delight the heart, 20
But the love of wisdom is better than
both of them.
The flute and the lute make sweet 21
melody,
But a pleasant tongue is better than
both of them.
The eye desires grace and beauty, 22
But more than both of them the
springing grain.
A friend and a comrade meet opportunely, 23
But a wife with her husband is better
than both of them.
Brothers and help are for a time of 24
trouble,
But charity is a better deliverer than
both of them.
Gold and silver make a man stand 25
firm,
But good counsel is more approved
than both of them.
Money and vigor elate the mind, 26
But the fear of the Lord is better than
both of them.
There is no flaw in the fear of the
Lord,
And with it there is no need to seek
for help.
The fear of the Lord is like a garden 27
of blessing,
And covers a man better than any
glory.
My child, do not lead a beggar's 28
life;
It is better to die than to beg.
When a man looks to another man's 29
table,
His existence cannot be considered life.
He pollutes his soul with another
man's food,
But a man who is intelligent and well-instructed will beware of it.
In a shameless man's mouth begging 30
is sweet,
But it kindles a fire in his heart.
O death, how bitter is the remembrance of you 41

To a man at peace among his possessions,
To a man who is free from distractions
and prosperous in everything,
And is still vigorous enough to enjoy
his food!
2 O death, your sentence is good
For a needy man of failing strength,
In extreme old age, and distracted
about everything;
Who is contrary, and has lost his
patience.
3 Do not fear the sentence of death;
Remember those who went before you
and those who come after.
This is the sentence of the Lord upon
all flesh and blood,
4 And how can you refuse what is the
will of the Most High?
Whether it was ten or a hundred or a
thousand years,
There is no reproach about life in
Hades.
5 The children of sinners are detestable children,
And live in the circles of the ungodly.
6 The possessions of the children of sinners will be lost,
And perpetual reproach will follow
their posterity.
7 His children will blame an ungodly
father
Because they are reproached on his
account.
8 Alas for you, ungodly men,
Who have forsaken the law of the
Most High God!
9 When you are born, you are born to a
curse,
And when you die, a curse will be
your lot.
10 Everything that springs from the
earth will go back to the earth;
Just as surely the ungodly go from a
curse to destruction.
11 Men grieve about their bodies,
But the name of sinners is not good
and will be blotted out.
12 Take heed about your name, for you
retain it longer
Than a thousand great stores of gold.
13 The days of a good life are numbered,
But a good name lasts forever.
14 Children, maintain instruction and be
at peace;
Concealed wisdom and invisible treasure—
What is the use of either?
15 A man who hides his folly is better
Than a man who hides his wisdom.
Therefore regard what I say;
For not every kind of shame is it well
to maintain,
And not everything is approved in
good faith by all.
Be ashamed of a father and mother,
for immorality,
And of a prince and a ruler, for a lie;
Of a judge and a magistrate, for an
offense,
And of an assembly and the people,
for disregard for the Law;
Of a partner and a friend, for unjust
dealing,
And of the place where you are living,
for theft;
Respect the truth of God and his
agreement,
Be ashamed to lean on your elbow at
table;
To be contemptuous about giving
back what you have received;
And to keep silent before those who
greet you;
To look at a woman who is a courtesan,
And to turn your face away from a
relative;
To take someone's portion or present,
And to stare at a married woman;
To meddle with another man's maid
(And do not stand over her bed);
To utter words of abuse before friends
(And after you make a gift do not
add abuse);
To repeat what you have heard,
And to tell things that are secret.
Then you will be really modest,
And win the approval of everyone.
Do not be ashamed of these things,
And do not show partiality, so as to
sin:
Of the Law of the Most High and his
agreement,
And of judgment, to punish the ungodly;
Of having a reckoning with a partner
and fellow-travelers,
And of a present from what is inherited by your companions;
Of the accuracy of scales and weights,
And of the acquisition of much or
little;
Of profit from dealing with merchants,
And of the careful training of children;
And of staining the side of a bad
servant with blood.
It is well to put a seal on a wicked
wife,

And where there are many hands,
lock things up.
Whatever you hand over, let it be by
number and weight;
And in giving and receiving, let everything be in writing.
Do not be ashamed to instruct the
senseless and foolish,
Or an aged man who is charged with
immorality.
Then you will be really instructed,
And approved in the eyes of every
man alive.
A daughter is a secret cause of
sleeplessness to her father,
And his concern for her robs him of his
rest;
In her youth, for fear she will pass her
prime,
And when she is married, for fear
she will be hated;
When she is a girl, for fear she will be
profaned,
And be with child in her father's
house;
When she has a husband, for fear she
will transgress;
And when she is married, for fear she
will be childless.
Keep a close watch over a headstrong
daughter,
For fear she will fill your enemies with
malignant joy,
And make you the talk of the town
and notorious among the people,
And disgrace you before the multitude.
2 Do not look at anybody for her
beauty,
And do not sit among women,
3 For as a moth comes out of clothing,
A woman's wickedness comes from a
woman.
4 A man's wickedness is better than a
beneficent woman,
Or a woman that disgraces you
shamefully.
5 I will call to mind the doings of the
Lord,
And recount the things that I have
seen.
By the commands of the Lord his
works are done;
6 The light-giving sun looks down on
everything,
And his work is full of the glory of the
Lord.
7 He has not permitted the saints of the
Lord

To recount all his wonders,
Which the Lord, the Almighty, has
firmly established,
So that the universe might stand fast
through his glory.
He searches out the great deep and 18
the human mind,
And he understands their designs;
For the Most High possesses all knowl-
edge,
And looks upon the portent of eter-
nity,
And declares the things that are past 19
and the things that are to come,
And uncovers the tracks of hidden
things.
No thought escapes him, 20
Not one word is hidden from him,
He has ordained the majesty of his 21
wisdom,
For he is from everlasting to ever-
lasting.
It cannot be increased or diminished,
And he has no need of any counselor.
How much to be desired are all his 22
works,
And how sparkling they are to see.
All these things live and last forever, 23
With all their functions, and they are
all obedient.
They are all in pairs, one facing an- 24
other,
Not one of them is missing.
One confirms the good of the other, 25
And who can have too much of be-
holding his glory?
The glory of the height is the firma- 43
ment in its purity,
The sight of the heavens with the
spectacle of their splendor.
The sun, when he appears, making 2
proclamation as he goes forth,
Is a wonderful instrument, the work
of the Most High;
At noonday he dries up the country, 3
And who can withstand his burning
heat?
A man who blows a furnace works in 4
the midst of heat,
But the sun three times as much,
burning up the mountains.
He breathes out fiery vapors,
And shoots forth his beams, blinding
men's eyes.
Great is the Lord who made him, 5
At whose command he hurries on his
course.
The moon, too, he places in its 6
position at its season,

To mark times and be an everlasting sign;
7 The moon gives the sign for the festival,
A light that wanes after reaching the full.
8 The month is named after her;
She increases marvelously as she changes,
An instrument of the hosts on high,
Shining in the firmament of the heavens.
9 The beauty of heaven is the glory of the stars,
A system giving light in the highest places of the Lord.
10 At the command of the Holy One they take their places as he decrees,
And they will not fail in their watches.
11 See the rainbow, and bless him who made it
Surpassingly beautiful in its brightness.
12 It curves over the heaven in a glorious circle,
The hands of the Most High have stretched it out.
13 By his command he brings the hurrying snow,
And makes swift the lightnings of his judgment;
14 Because of it, the storehouses are opened,
And the clouds fly out like birds.
15 In his majesty he makes the clouds thick,
And the hailstones are broken in pieces.
16 When he appears, the mountains shake,
At his wish the south wind blows.
17 His voice in the thunder rebukes the earth;
So do the hurricane from the north and the whirlwind.
He sprinkles the snow like birds fluttering down,
It comes down like locusts settling;
18 The eye is amazed at the beauty of its whiteness,
And the mind is astonishing at its raining.
19 He pours hoarfrost over the earth like salt,
And, when it freezes, it becomes points of thorns.
20 The cold north wind blows,
And the ice freezes on the water;
It lodges on every pool of water,
And the water puts it on like a breastplate.
It consumes the mountains and burns up the wilderness,
And shrivels the green herbage like fire.
A mist coming quickly heals everything;
The dew falling refreshes things after the heat.
By his counsel he has stilled the deep,
And planted islands in it.
Those who sail the sea tell of its danger,
And we wonder at what we hear with our ears.
There are strange and wonderful works in it,
All kinds of living things, the whale creation.
Because of him his messenger prospers on his way,
And through his command all things consist.
We may say more, but we will not reach the end,
And the conclusion of what we have to say is: He is the whole.
Where can we find strength to glorify him?
For he is greater than all his works.
The Lord is terrible and exceedingly great,
And his power is wonderful.
Glorify the Lord and exalt him
As much as you can, for even then he will surpass it.
When you exalt him put forth all your strength;
Do not grow weary, for you will not reach the end.
Who has ever seen him, so that he can describe him?
And who can tell his greatness as it really is?
Many things greater than these still remain hidden,
For we have seen but few of his works.
For the Lord has made all things,
And he has given wisdom to the godly.
Let us now praise distinguished men,
Our forefathers before us.
They are a great glory to the Lord who created them;
They have shown his majesty from of old.

3 Men who exercised authority in their
reigns,
And were renowned for their might!
They gave their counsel with understanding,
And brought men tidings through
their prophecy—
4 Leaders of the people in deliberation
and understanding,
Men of learning for the people,
Wise in their words of instruction;
5 Composers of musical airs,
Authors of poems in writing;
6 Rich men, endowed with strength,
Who lived in peace upon their lands—
7 All these were honored in their generation,
And were a glory in their day.
8 There are some of them who have
left a name,
So that men declare their praise;
9 And there are some who have no
memorial,
And have perished as though they
had not lived,
And have become as though they had
not been,
With their children after them.
10 Yet these were merciful men,
And their uprightness has not been
forgotten.
11 With their descendants it will remain,
A good inheritance for their posterity.
12 Their descendants stand by the agreements,
And their children also for their sakes;
13 Their posterity will endure forever,
And their glory will not be blotted out.
14 Their bodies are buried in peace,
But their name lives to all generations.
15 Peoples will recite their wisdom,
And the congregation declare their
praise!
16 Enoch pleased the Lord and was
taken up from the earth,
A pattern of repentance for all generations.
17 Noah was found perfect and upright;
In the time of God's anger he was
taken in exchange.
On his account a remnant was left to
the earth
When the flood occurred.
18 Everlasting agreements were made
with him,
That all life should never be blotted
out by a flood.
19 Abraham was the great father of a
multitude of nations,
And no one has been found equal to
him in glory.
He observed the Law of the Most 20
High,
And entered into an agreement with
him.
He certified the agreement in his flesh,
And, when he was tested, he proved
faithful.
For that reason he assured him with 21
an oath
That nations would be blessed through
his posterity,
And that he would make him as nu-
merous as the dust of the earth,
And would raise his posterity as high
as the stars,
And that they should possess
From sea to sea,
And from the river to the end of the
earth.
He guaranteed it to Isaac also in like 22
manner,
Because of his father Abraham.
The blessing of all mankind and the
agreement
He made to rest upon the head of 23
Jacob.
He acknowledged him with his bless-
ings,
And gave them to him as his in-
heritance.
And he divided his portions,
And distributed them among twelve
tribes.
From his posterity he brought a 45
man of mercy,
Who found favor in the sight of all
mankind,
And was beloved by God and man—
Moses, whose memory is blessed.
He made him equal to his holy ones in 2
glory,
And made him great in the fears of his
enemies.
By his words he brought wonders to 3
pass;
He made him glorious in the sight of
kings.
He gave him commands for his people,
And showed him some of his glory.
Through faithfulness and meekness he 4
sanctified him,
He chose him out of all mankind.
He made him hear his voice; 5
He brought him into the thick dark-
ness,
And gave him his commandments face
to face,

The law of life and knowledge,
To teach Jacob his agreement,
And Israel his decrees.
6 He exalted Aaron, a holy man like him,
Who was his brother, from the tribe of Levi.
7 He made him an everlasting ordinance,
And gave him the priesthood of the people.
He blessed him with stateliness,
And put on him a splendid robe;
8 He clothed him with glorious perfection,
And strengthened him with garments of authority,
The drawers, the robe, and the apron,
9 And he surrounded him with pomegranates,
With very many gold bells all around
To ring out as he walked,
To make their sound heard in the temple,
To remind the sons of his people;
10 With a holy garment, with gold and violet
And purple, a work of embroidery;
With the oracle of judgment, the decider of truth.
11 With twisted scarlet, the work of an artist;
With precious stones, engraved like signets,
In a setting of gold, the work of an engraver,
For a reminder, in carved letters,
Giving the number of the tribes of Israel;
12 With a gold crown upon his turban,
Engraved like a signet with "Sacredness":
A glorious distinction, a work of might,
The desire of the eyes, richly adorned.
13 Before him, there never were such beautiful things,
No alien will ever put them on,
But his sons alone
And their posterity forever.
14 His sacrifices will be wholly consumed
Twice every day perpetually.
15 Moses filled his hands,
And anointed him with sacred oil;
It became an everlasting agreement with him
And his posterity all the days of heaven,
To minister to him and act as priest
And bless the people in his name.
He chose him out of all the living
To offer sacrifice to the Lord,
Incense and fragrance for a memorial sacrifice,
To make atonement for your people.
In his commandments he gave him
Authority over the agreements about judgments,
To teach Jacob the decrees
And to enlighten Israel with his law.
Strangers conspired against him,
And envied him in the desert;
The men with Dathan and Abiram,
And the company of Korah, in their wrath and anger.
The Lord saw it and was not pleased,
And they were destroyed by his fierce anger;
He executed signs upon them,
To devour them with his blazing fire.
And he increased Aaron's glory,
And gave him his inheritance;
He apportioned to him the very first of the first fruits;
He prepared the Presentation Bread in abundance,
For they are to eat the sacrifices of the Lord,
Which he gave to him and his posterity.
But he has no share in the land of the people,
And he has no portion among the people,
For he himself is your portion and your inheritance.
Phineas, the son of Eleazar, is the third in glory,
For he was zealous for the fear of the Lord,
And stood fast, when the people turned away,
In the goodness and eagerness of his soul,
And made atonement for Israel.
Therefore an agreement of peace was established with him,
That he should be the leader of the saints and of his people,
That he and his posterity should possess
The dignity of the priesthood forever.
And an agreement was made with David,
The son of Jesse, of the tribe of Judah;
As the king's inheritance passes only from son to son,
The inheritance of Aaron is for his posterity.

26 May he give you wisdom of mind
To judge his people with uprightness
So that their prosperity may not come
to an end,
But their glory may last through all
their generations.
46 Joshua, the son of Nun, was mighty
in war,
And the successor of Moses in prophesying.
He became, as his name describes him,
Great to save his chosen,
To take vengeance on the enemies
that rose up against them,
So that he might give Israel their
possessions.
2 How glorious he was when he lifted
up his hands,
And pointed his sword at the towns!
3 Before him who ever stood so fast?
For he carried on the wars of the Lord.
4 Was not the sun stayed by his hand,
And one day increased to two?
5 He called on the Most High Ruler,
When his enemies pressed upon him
on all sides,
And the great Lord answered him
6 With hailstones of mighty power.
He made war burst upon that nation,
And at the descent he destroyed his
opponents,
So that the heathen might recognize
his armor,
And know that he fought in the sight
of the Lord.
This champion was followed by one
7 Who in the days of Moses did an act
of piety,
No other than Caleb, the son of
Jephunneh,
Who stood opposed to the community,
And restrained the people from sin,
And quieted their wicked grumbling.
These two alone were preserved
8 Out of six hundred thousand people
on foot,
To bring them into their possessions,
To a land running with milk and honey.
9 And the Lord gave Caleb strength,
And it remained with him until he
was old,
So that he climbed the heights of the
land,
And his posterity obtained a heritage,
10 So that all the sons of Israel might see
That it is good to follow after the
Lord.
11 The judges too, with their various
names,

All whose hearts did not fall into
idolatry,
And who did not turn away from the
Lord—
May their memory be blessed!
May their bones revive where they 12
lie,
And their names be transmitted
To the descendants of their renown.
There was Samuel, beloved by his 13
Lord;
A prophet of the Lord, he established
the kingdom,
And anointed princes over his people.
By the Law of the Lord he judged the 14
community,
And the Lord showed regard for
Jacob.
By his faithfulness he was proved a 15
prophet,
And he was known to be trustworthy
through the words of his vision,
And he called upon the Lord, his 16
Master,
When his enemies pressed him on
every side,
And he offered him a suckling lamb;
Then the Lord thundered from 17
heaven,
And made his voice heard with a loud
noise,
And he wiped out the rulers of the 18
Tyrians
And all the princes of the Philistines.
And before he fell asleep forever, 19
He called them to witness, before the
Lord and his anointed,
"From no human being have I taken
his property,
Even as much as a pair of shoes,"
And no one accused him.
Even after he fell asleep he prophe- 20
sied,
And showed the king his end,
And lifted his voice out of the earth
In prophecy, to blot out the wicked-
ness of the people.
After him Nathan arose, 47
To prophesy in the days of David.
Just as the fat is separated from the 2
offering,
David was separated from the Israel-
ites.
He played with lions as though they 3
were kids,
And with bears as though they were
lambs of the flock.
In his youth did he not kill a giant, 4
And relieve the people of reproach,

When he lifted his hand with a stone
in the sling,
And brought down the boasting of
Goliath?
5 For he called on the Lord, the Most
High,
And he gave strength to his right hand
To slay a mighty warrior,
And to exalt the strength of his
people.
6 So they lauded him for his ten thousands,
And praised him for the blessings of
the Lord,
When the glorious diadem was
brought to him.
7 For he wiped out his enemies on every
side,
And annihilated his adversaries the
Philistines,
He crushed their strength, unto this
day.
Over all that he did he gave thanks
8 To the Holy One, the Most High,
with words of praise.
He sang praise with his whole heart,
And he loved his Maker.
9 He placed singers before the altar,
To make sweet melody with their
voices.
10 He gave dignity to the festivals,
And set the seasons in order throughout the year,
While they praised God's holy name,
And the sanctuary rang with it from
early morning.
11 The Lord took away his sins,
And exalted his strength forever,
And gave him the agreement about
the kings,
And a glorious throne in Israel.
12 After him arose his wise son,
Who lived in wide borders because of
him;
13 Solomon reigned in days of peace,
And God gave him rest on every side,
So that he might erect a house in his
name,
And provide a sanctuary forever.
14 How wise you became in your youth,
And how full of understanding, like a
river!
15 Your soul covered the earth,
And you filled it with puzzling proverbs.
16 Your name reached distant islands,
And you were loved for your peaceful
sway.

For your songs and proverbs and fig- 1
ures,
And your expositions, the countries
wondered at you.
Through the name of the Lord God, 1
Who is called the God of Israel,
You gathered gold like tin,
And accumulated silver like lead.
You laid your flanks beside women, 1
And were brought into subjection by
your body.
You brought a stain upon your fame, 2
And polluted your posterity,
So that you brought wrath upon your
children,
And they were grieved at your folly,
So that the sovereignty was divided, 2
And a disobedient kingdom arose out
of Ephraim.
But the Lord will not forsake his 2
mercy,
And he will not prove false to any of
his words,
Nor will he blot out the descendants
of his chosen,
Nor destroy the posterity of him who
loved him.
For he gave Jacob a remnant,
And David a root sprung from him.
So Solomon rested with his fore- 2
fathers,
And left behind him one of his own
children,
"The people's folly," a man wanting in
understanding,
Rehoboam, who by his counsel made
the people revolt.
And there was Jeroboam, the son of
Nebat, who made Israel sin,
And showed Ephraim a sinful way.
Their sins became so exceedingly 24
many
That they dislodged them from their
land.
For they sought out every kind of 2
wickedness,
Until vengeance should come upon
them.
Then the prophet Elijah arose like 4
fire,
And his word burned like a torch;
He brought a famine upon them, 2
And made them few by his zeal,
By the word of the Lord he shut up 3
heaven;
In the same way, he brought down
fire three times.
How glorified you were, Elijah, in 4
your wonderful acts,

And who can glory like you?
5 You who raised one who was dead, from death,
And from Hades, by the word of the Most High;
6 Who brought kings down to destruction,
And distinguished men from their beds.
7 Who heard rebukes at Sinai,
And judgments of vengeance at Horeb;
8 Who anointed kings to exact retribution,
And prophets to succeed him;
9 Who were taken up in a whirlwind of fire,
In a chariot with fiery horses;
10 Who, it is written, is to come in rebuke at the appointed time,
To quiet anger before it becomes wrath,
To turn the heart of the father to his son,
And to reform the tribes of Jacob.
11 Happy are those who saw you,
And those who fell asleep in love;
For we will surely live.
12 When Elijah was sheltered by the whirlwind,
Elisha was filled with his spirit.
In all his days he was not shaken by any ruler
And no one overmastered him.
13 Nothing was too wonderful for him,
And when he had fallen asleep, his body prophesied.
14 In his life he did signs,
And after his death he worked wonders.
15 For all this the people did not repent,
And did not forsake their sins,
Until they were carried away captive from their land,
And scattered over all the earth.
And the people were left very few in number,
But a prince remained in the house of David.
16 Some of them did what was right,
And some of them sinned more and more.
17 Hezekiah fortified his city,
And brought water into the midst of it;
He dug the sheer rock with iron,
And built wells for water.
18 In his days Sennacherib came up,
And sent the commander, and departed.
And he raised his hand against Zion,
And uttered great boasts in his arrogance;
19 Then their hearts and hands were shaken,
And they suffered like women in travail
20 Then they called upon the Lord, who is merciful,
Spreading out their hands to him,
And the Holy One heard them speedily from heaven,
And delivered them by the hand of Isaiah.
21 He struck the camp of the Assyrians,
And his angel wiped them out.
22 For Hezekiah did what pleased the Lord,
And was strong in the ways of his forefather David,
Which the prophet Isaiah commanded,
Who was great and faithful in his prophetic vision.
23 In his days the sun went back,
And prolonged the life of the king.
24 Through the spirit of might he foresaw the future,
And comforted those who mourned in Zion.
25 He revealed the things that were to be, forever,
And the hidden things, before they came to pass.

49 The memory of Josiah is like a blending of incense
Carefully prepared by the perfumer;
Everyone finds it sweet as honey to the taste,
And like music at a banquet.
2 He succeeded in converting the people,
And abolished the wicked abominations.
3 He made his heart right with the Lord,
In the days of wicked men he encouraged godliness.
4 Except David and Hezekiah and Josiah,
They all sinned greatly,
For they forsook the Law of the Most High.
The kings of Judah failed utterly,
5 For they gave their strength to others,
And their glory to a foreign nation.
6 They set fire to the city chosen for the sanctuary,
And made her streets desolate,

7 For the sake of Jeremiah; for they
had misused him;
Though he was consecrated before
his birth to be a prophet,
To root up and injure and ruin,
Likewise to build and to plant.
8 It was Ezekiel who saw the glorious
vision,
Which he showed him upon the
chariot borne by the winged
creatures.
9 For he remembers his enemies with
rain,
And to do good to those who make
their paths straight.
10 And may the bones of the Twelve
Prophets revive out of their place,
For they comforted Jacob,
And delivered them with their confident hope.
11 How shall we magnify Zerubbabel?
For he was like a signet on the right
hand;
So was Jeshua, the son of Jozadak,
12 For they in their days rebuilt the
house,
And raised a temple holy to the Lord,
Prepared for everlasting glory.
13 The memory of Nehemiah also is lasting,
For he raised up for us the walls which
had fallen,
And set up barred gates,
And rebuilt our houses.
14 No one was ever created on earth
like Enoch
For he was taken up from the earth;
15 Nor was a man ever born like Joseph,
The leader of his brothers, the support of the people;
And his bones were cared for.
16 Shem and Seth were greatly honored
above other men,
But above every living thing was
Adam in his creation.

50 It was Simon, the son of Onias, the
great priest,
Who in his lifetime repaired the house,
And in his days strengthened the
sanctuary.
2 He laid the foundation for the height
of the double wall,
The lofty substructure for the temple
inclosure.
3 In his days a water cistern was hewed
out,
A reservoir in circumference like the
sea.

He took thought for his people to keep 4
them from calamity,
And fortified the city against siege.
How glorious he was, surrounded by 5
the people,
As he came out of the sanctuary!
Like the morning star among the 6
clouds,
Like the moon when it is full;
Like the sun shining forth upon the 7
sanctuary of the Most High;
Like the rainbow, showing itself
among glorious clouds,
Like roses in the days of first fruits, 8
Like lilies by a spring of water,
Like a sprig of frankincense, on summer days,
Like fire and incense in the censer, 9
Like a dish of beaten gold,
Adorned with all kinds of precious
stones;
Like an olive putting forth its fruit, 10
And like a cypress towering among
the clouds.
When he assumed his glorious robe, 11
And put on glorious perfection,
And when he went up to the holy
altar,
He made the court of the sanctuary
glorious.
And when he received the portions 12
from the hands of the priests,
As he stood by the hearth of the altar,
With his brothers like a wreath about
him,
He was like a young cedar on Lebanon,
And they surrounded him like the
trunks of palm trees,
All the descendants of Aaron in their 13
splendor,
With the Lord's offering in their
hands,
Before the whole assembly of Israel;
And when he finished the service at 14
the altars,
To adorn the offering of the Most
High, the Almighty,
He stretched out his hand to the cup, 15
And poured out some of the blood of
the grape;
He poured it out at the foot of the
altar,
A fragrant odor unto the Most High,
the King of All.
Then the descendants of Aaron 16
shouted;
They sounded the trumpets of beaten
work;

They made a great sound heard,
For a reminder, before the Most High.
17 Then all the people made haste together,
And fell upon their faces on the ground,
To worship their Lord,
The Almighty, the Most High.
18 The singers too praised him with their voices;
They made sweet music in the fullest volume.
19 And the people intreated the Lord Most High,
With prayer before him who is merciful,
Until the worship of the Lord should be finished,
And they completed his service.
20 Then he came down and lifted his hands
Over the whole assembly of the descendants of Israel,
To pronounce the blessing of the Lord with his lips,
And to exult in his name.
21 And they prostrated themselves a second time,
To receive the blessing from the Most High.
22 Now bless the God of all,
Who in every way does great things;
Who exalts our days from our birth,
And deals with us according to his mercy.
23 May he give us gladness of heart,
And may there be peace in our days
In Israel, and through the days of eternity.
24 May he intrust his mercy to us,
And let him deliver us in our days.
25 With two nations my soul is vexed,
And the third is no nation;
26 They who live on the mountain of Samaria, and the Philistines,
And the foolish people that live in Shechem.
Instruction in understanding and knowledge
27 Has Jeshua, son of Sirach, son of Eleazar, of Jerusalem,
Written in this book,
Who poured forth wisdom from his mind.
28 Happy is he who concerns himself with these things,
And he that lays them up in his mind will become wise.

For if he does them, he will be strong 29
for all things,
For the light of the Lord is his path.
I will give thanks to you, Lord and 51
King,
And praise you as God my Savior.
I give thanks to your name,
For you have been my protector and 2
helper,
And have delivered my body from destruction,
And from the snare of a slanderous tongue.
From lips that utter lies,
And before those who stood by,
You were my helper and delivered me, 3
In the greatness of your mercy and of your name,
From the gnashing of teeth when I was about to be devoured,
From the hand of those who sought my life,
From the numerous troubles that I had,
From choking fire all around me, 4
And from the midst of a flame which I had not kindled,
From the depth of the heart of Hades, 5
And from the unclean tongue and the lying speech.
An unrighteous tongue uttered slander 6
to the king;
My soul drew nigh to death,
And my life was near to Hades beneath;
They surrounded me on every side, 7
and there was no one to help me;
I looked for the help of men, and there was none.
Then I remembered your mercy, Lord, 8
And your work which has been from of old,
For you deliver those who wait for you,
And save them from the hand of their enemies.
And I sent up my supplication from 9
the earth,
And prayed for deliverance from death.
I besought the Lord, the father of my 10
lord,
Not to forsake me in my days of trouble,
At the time when there is no help against the proud.
I said, "I will praise your name con- 11
tinually,
And praise you with thanksgiving."
And my prayer was heard,

12 For you saved me from destruction,
And delivered me from my emergency.
Therefore I will give thanks to you and praise you,
And bless the name of the Lord.
13 When I was very young, before I went on my wanderings,
I sought wisdom expressly in my prayer;
14 In front of the temple I asked for her,
And I will search for her unto the end.
15 From her flower as from her ripening grape,
My heart delighted in her.
My foot trod in uprightness;
From my youth I followed her steps.
16 I bowed my ear a little and received her,
And found much instruction for myself.
17 I made progress in her;
And to him who gave me wisdom I will give glory.
18 For I resolved to practice her,
And I was zealous for the good, and I shall not be disappointed.
19 My soul grappled with her,
And in the fulfilment of the Law I was very strict.
I spread out my hands to heaven above,
And lamented my ignorance of her.
20 I directed my soul to her,
And through purification I found her.
I gained my purpose with her from the beginning;
Therefore I will not be forsaken.
My heart was stirred to seek her; 2
Therefore I obtained a good possession.
The Lord gave me the power to speak as my reward, 2
And I will praise him with it.
Come to me, you who are untaught, 2
And pass the night in the house of instruction.
Why do you say you are wanting in these things, 2
And that your souls are very thirsty?
I opened my mouth and said, 2
Get her for yourselves without money,
Put your neck under her yoke, 2
And let your soul receive instruction.
She is to be found close by.
See with your own eyes that I have worked but little, 2
And yet found myself much repose.
Get some instruction with a great sum in silver, 2
And you will gain much gold with it.
Let your soul delight in his mercy, 2
And may you not be disappointed for praising him.
Finish your work in time, 3
And in his own time he will give you your reward.

THE BOOK OF BARUCH

THESE are the words of the book
that Baruch the son of Neriah,
the son of Mahseiah, the son of
Zedekiah, the son of Hasadiah,
2 the son of Hilkiah, wrote in Babylon, in
the fifth year, on the seventh day of the
month, at the time when the Chaldeans
took Jerusalem and burned it with fire.
3 And Baruch read the words of this
book in the hearing of Jeconiah, the
son of Jehoiakim, king of Judah, in the
hearing of all the people who came to
4 hear the book read, and in the hearing
of the nobles and the princes, and in
the hearing of the elders, and in the
hearing of all the people, small and
great—in fact, of all who lived in Baby-
5 lon, by the River Sud. Then they wept,
and fasted, and prayed before the Lord;
6 and they raised money, each one giving
7 what he could, and they sent it to
Jerusalem, to Jehoiakim the high priest,
the son of Hilkiah, the son of Shallum,
and to the priests, and to all the people
that were found with him in Jerusalem,
8 when he took the plate of the house of
the Lord that had been carried away
from the temple, to return it to the
land of Judah—the silver dishes which
Zedekiah the son of Josiah, king of
9 Judah, had made, after Nebuchadnezzar, king of Babylon, had carried off
Jeconiah and the officers and captives
and nobles and the common people
from Jerusalem, and taken him to
10 Babylon. And they said,
"Here we send you money, so buy
with the money burnt offerings and sin
offerings and incense and prepare a grain
offering, and offer them upon the altar
11 of the Lord our God, and pray for the
life of Nebuchadnezzar, king of Babylon, and for the life of Belshazzar his
son, that their days may be like the
12 days of heaven, upon the earth. And
the Lord will give us strength, and he
will give sight to our eyes, and we will
live under the shadow of Nebuchadnezzar, king of Babylon, and under the
shadow of Belshazzar his son, and we
will serve them for a long time and find
favor in their sight. Pray for us to the 13
Lord our God, for we have sinned
against the Lord our God, and to this
day the anger of the Lord and his
wrath have not turned away from us.
So read this scroll, which we send to 14
you, to make your confession in the
house of the Lord, on festival days and
on days of assembly. And you shall say, 15
"'Uprightness belongs to the Lord
our God, but confusion of face, as on
this day, befits us, the men of Judah,
and the residents of Jerusalem, and our 16
kings and our officials, and our priests
and our prophets, and our forefathers;
for we have sinned before the Lord, 17
and disobeyed him, and we have not 18
obeyed the voice of the Lord our God,
so as to follow the commands of the
Lord which he set before us. From 19
the day when the Lord brought our
fathers out of the land of Egypt, until
today, we have been disobedient to the
Lord our God, and we have been neg-
lectful, in not obeying his voice. And 20
misfortunes have attended us, and the
curse has come upon us which the Lord
agreed upon with Moses his servant, on
the day when he brought our forefathers out of the land of Egypt, to
give us a land that ran with milk and
honey, as they have this day. And we 21
did not obey the voice of the Lord our
God, expressed in all the words of the
prophets whom he sent to us, but we 22
followed each one the design of his own
wicked heart so as to serve other gods,
and do what was evil in the eyes of the
Lord our God. So the Lord made good **2**
his word which he uttered against us,
and against our judges who judged
Israel, and against our kings and
against our officials and against the
men of Israel and Judah. Nowhere 2
under heaven have such calamities occurred as he has brought upon Jerusalem, as it was written in the Law of
Moses, so that one of us ate the flesh 3
of his son, and another of us ate the
flesh of his daughter. He has made us 4
subject to all the kingdoms around us,

to be a reproach and a desolation
among all the peoples about us, where
5 the Lord has scattered them. They
were brought low and not raised up,
because we had sinned against the Lord
our God, in not obeying his voice.
6 " 'Uprightness belongs to the Lord
our God, but confusion of face befits us
and our forefathers, as it does this day.
7 All the calamities with which the Lord
8 threatened us have overtaken us. Yet
we have not besought the Lord by turning away, each of us, from the designs
9 of his wicked heart. And the Lord has
watched for these calamities and has
brought them upon us, for the Lord is
upright in all his doings which he has
10 commanded us to imitate. Yet we have
not obeyed his voice and followed the
Lord's commands, which he has set
before us.
11 " 'And now, Lord God of Israel, who
brought your people out of Egypt with
a strong hand and with portents and
wonders, and with great power and an
uplifted arm, and made yourself such
12 a name as yours is today, we have
sinned, we have been ungodly, we have
done wrong, Lord our God, in the face
13 of all your ordinances. Let your anger
be turned away from us, for few of us
are left, among the heathen, where you
14 have scattered us. Listen, Lord, to our
prayer and our petition, and for your
sake deliver us, and grant us favor in
the eyes of those who have led us into
15 captivity, so that the whole earth may
know that you are the Lord our God,
for Israel and his descendants are
16 called by your name. Lord, look down
from your holy dwelling, and think
about us. Turn your ear to us, Lord,
17 and hear us; open your eyes and see;
for the dead, who are in Hades, whose
breath has been taken from their
bodies, cannot ascribe glory and up-
18 rightness to the Lord, but the soul that
grieves greatly, that goes about bent
over and sick, with failing sight—the
soul that hungers will ascribe glory and
19 uprightness to you, Lord. For it is not
for the upright acts of our forefathers
and of our kings that we present our
prayer for pity before you, O Lord our
20 God. For you have inflicted your
anger and your wrath upon us, just as
you promised through your servants
the prophets to do, when you said,
21 "Thus says the Lord: Bow your
shoulders and work for the king of
Babylon, and stay in the land which I
gave to your forefathers. But if you 2
will not obey the voice of the Lord, and
serve the king of Babylon, I will put 2
an end to the sound of joy and the
sound of gladness, the voice of bridegroom and the voice of bride, in the
towns of Judah and in Jerusalem, and
the whole country will become un-
trodden and uninhabited."
" 'But we did not obey your voice 2
and serve the king of Babylon, and you
made good your words that you had
spoken through your servants the
prophets, that the bones of our kings
and the bones of our forefathers should
be taken out of their places, and behold 2
they are thrown out to the heat by day
and to the frost by night; and they
perished in great misery, by famine
and the sword and expulsion. And the 2
house that was called by your name
you have made as it is today, because
of the wickedness of the house of
Israel and of the house of Judah. Yet 2
you have dealt with us, O Lord our
God, with all your forbearance and all
your great compassion, as you promised 2
through your servant Moses to do,
when you commanded him to write the
Law before the sons of Israel, and said,
" ' "Unless you obey my voice, this 2
great buzzing multitude will surely
turn into a small number among the
heathen where I will scatter them.
For I know that they will not listen to 3
me, for they are a stiff-necked people.
But in the land to which they are
carried away they will come to themselves, and they will know that I am 3
the Lord their God. I will give them
minds and ears to listen, and they will 3
praise me in the land to which they are
carried away, and they will remember
my name, and they will turn from their 3
obstinacy and their wicked doings, for
they will remember what befell their
forefathers who sinned in the sight of
the Lord. Then I will restore them to 3
the land that I swore to give to their
forefathers, Abraham and Isaac and
Jacob, and they will possess it; and I
will multiply them, and they will not
be despised. And I will make an everlasting agreement with them that I
shall be their God and they shall be
my people. And I will never again re-

move my people Israel from the land
which I have given them."
3 "'O Lord Almighty, God of Israel,
the soul in anguish and the wearied
2 spirit cry out to you. Listen, Lord, and
have mercy, for we have sinned in your
3 sight. For you abide forever, and we
4 perish forever. O Lord Almighty, God
of Israel, hear the prayer of the dead in
Israel, and of the sons of those who
sinned in your sight, who did not obey
the voice of the Lord their God, so
5 that calamities have pursued us. Do
not remember the iniquities of our
forefathers, but remember your power
6 and your name at this time, for you are
the Lord our God, and we will praise
7 you, O Lord. For you have put your
fear into our hearts for this reason,
that we should call upon your name,
and we will praise you in our exile, for
we have put out of our hearts all the
iniquity of our forefathers, who sinned
8 in your sight. Here we are today in
exile, where you have scattered us, to
be reproached and cursed and condemned for all the iniquities of our
forefathers who rebelled against the
Lord our God.'"

9 Hear the commandments of life, O Israel;
Listen, and learn wisdom.
10 Why is it, Israel, that you are in the land of your enemies,
That you have grown old in a strange land,
That you have been polluted with the dead,
11 That you are counted among those in Hades?
12 You have forsaken the spring of wisdom.
13 If you had walked in the way of God,
You would have lived in peace forever.
14 Learn where wisdom is, where strength is,
Where understanding is, so that you may at the same time learn
Where length of days and life are,
Where there is light for the eyes, and peace.
15 Who can find her location,
And who can get into her storehouses?
16 Where are the rulers of the heathen,
And those who master the animals of the earth,
17 Who have their sport with the wild birds,
And lay up silver and gold,
In which men trust,
And have property without end;
Who work in silver and anxious care, 18
And whose works defy investigation?
They have vanished and gone to Hades, 19
And others have taken their places.
A younger generation has seen the light 20
And settled on the earth,
But they have not learned the way to knowledge,
Nor understood its paths, 21
Nor laid hold of it.
Their sons have strayed far out of their way;
It was never heard of in Canaan, 22
Or seen in Teman;
The sons of Hagar, who seek for understanding on the earth, 23
The merchants of Merran and Teman,
The story-tellers and the searchers for understanding
Have not found the way to wisdom,
Or remembered its paths.
O Israel, how great is the house of God, 24
And how vast the region that he possesses!
It is great, it has no end; 25
It is immeasurably high.
There were born the giants, famous of old, 26
Tall in stature, expert in war.
God did not choose them 27
Or give them the way of knowledge.
So they perished, because they had no understanding; 28
They perished through their own folly.
Who ever went up to heaven and got her, 29
And brought her down from the clouds?
Who ever crossed the sea and found her, 30
And will buy her with fine gold?
No one knows the way to her, 31
Or concerns himself with the path to her.
But he who knows all things knows her, 32
He has discovered her through his understanding.
He who created the earth forever,
Filled it with four-footed creatures;
He who sends forth the light, and it goes; 33
He called it, and it obeyed him in fear;

34 The stars shone in their watches, and were glad;
He called them, and they said, "Here we are!"
They shone with gladness for him who made them.
35 He is our God;
No other can be compared with him!
36 He found out the whole way to knowledge,
And has given it to Jacob his servant
And to Israel, whom he loved.
37 After that, she appeared on the earth
And mingled with men.
4 This is the book of the commandments of God,
And the Law, that will endure forever.
All those who hold fast to it will live,
But those who forsake it will die.
2 Come back, Jacob, and take hold of it;
Approach the radiance from her light.
3 Do not give your glory to another,
And your benefits to an alien people.
4 Blessed are we, Israel,
Because we know the things that please God.
5 Have no fear, my people,
For the memorial of Israel;
6 You have been sold to the heathen,
Not to be destroyed,
But because you had angered God
You were handed over to your adversaries.
7 For you provoked him who made you
By sacrificing to demons, and not to God.
8 You forgot the everlasting God, who had brought you up,
And you grieved Jerusalem, that had reared you,
9 For she saw the anger that has come upon you from God, and said,
"Listen, you women who live in Zion.
God has brought great sorrow upon me.
10 For I have witnessed the capture of my sons and daughters,
Which the Everlasting has brought upon them.
11 For I nursed them in gladness,
But I have sent them away with weeping and sorrow.
12 Let no one exult over a widow like me,
Forsaken by so many;
I have been left desolate because of the sins of my children,
Because they turned away from the Law of God.
13 But they would not learn his ordinances,
Or walk in the ways of God's commands,
Or follow the paths of correction in his uprightness.
Let the women who live in Zion come, 14
And remember the taking captive of my sons and daughters,
Which the Everlasting has brought upon them.
For he brought a nation from far away 15 against them,
A ruthless nation, of strange speech,
Who had no respect for an old man
And no pity for a child,
And they led the widow's beloved sons 16 away,
And left the lonely woman bereft of her daughters.
"But how can I help you? 17
For he who has brought these calami- 18 ties upon you
Will deliver you from the hands of your enemies.
Go, my children, go, 19
For I am left desolate.
I have taken off the clothing of peace, 20
And put on the sackcloth of my supplication;
I will cry out to the Everlasting all my days.
Have courage, my children, cry out to 21 God,
And he will save you from subjection, from the hands of your enemies;
For I have set on the Everlasting my 22 hope that he will save you.
And joy has come to me from the Holy One for the mercy
Which will soon come to you, from your everlasting Savior.
For I sent you out with sorrow and 23 weeping,
But God will give you back to me with joy and gladness forever.
For just as the women who live in 24 Zion have just now seen your deportation,
So they will soon see your deliverance come from your God,
Which will come upon you with the great glory and splendor of the Everlasting.
My children, endure patiently the 25 anger that has come upon you from God,
For your enemy has overtaken you;
But you will soon witness his destruction,
And put your feet upon their necks.

26 My luxurious ones have traveled rough roads,
They have been taken away like a flock carried off by enemies.
27 Have courage, my children, and cry out to God,
For you will be remembered by him who brought this upon you.
28 For as the thought once came to you to go astray from God,
You must return and seek him with tenfold fervor.
29 For he who has brought these calamities upon you
Will bring you everlasting joy with your deliverance."
30 Take courage, Jerusalem,
For he who named you will comfort you.
31 Those who did you harm and rejoiced at your fall will be miserable;
32 The towns which enslaved your children will be miserable;
She who received your sons will be miserable.
33 For as she rejoiced at your fall,
And was glad of your ruin,
So she shall be grieved at her own desolation.
34 And I will take away her exultation in her great population,
And her boasting will be turned to sorrow.
35 For from the Everlasting fire will descend upon her for many days,
And she will be a habitation of demons for a long time.
36 Look away eastward, Jerusalem,
And see the gladness that is coming to you from God.
37 See, your sons are coming, whom you sent away,
They are coming, gathered from east to west, at the command of the Holy One,
Rejoicing in the glory of God.
5 Take off the clothes of your sorrow and your harsh treatment, Jerusalem,
And put on forever the beauty of the glory that is from God.
2 Put on the cloak of the uprightness that is from God,
Put on your head the headdress of the glory of the Everlasting.
3 For God will show your splendor to all that is under heaven.
4 For your name will forever be called by God
The Peace of Uprightness and the Glory of Godliness.
Arise, Jerusalem, and stand upon the height, 5
And look away to the east,
And see your children gathered from the setting of the sun to its rising, at the command of the Holy One,
Rejoicing that God has remembered them.
For they went forth from you being led away on foot by their enemies, 6
But God will bring them in to you
Carried aloft in glory, like a royal throne.
For God has ordained that every high mountain and the everlasting hills shall be made low, 7
And the valleys filled up to make level ground,
So that Israel may go safely, to the glory of God.
And the woods and every fragrant tree have shaded Israel, at God's command, 8
For God will lead Israel with joy, by the light of his glory, 9
With the mercy and uprightness that come from him.

THE LETTER OF JEREMIAH

A copy of a letter which Jeremiah 6
sent to the captives who were to be
taken to Babylon by the king of Babylon, to report to them as he had been
commanded by God.
Because of the sins which you have 2
committed in the sight of God, you will
be taken to Babylon as captives by
Nebuchadnezzar, king of Babylon. So 3
when you reach Babylon, you will stay
there for many years, and for a long
time, seven generations; but afterward
I will bring you away from there in
peace. Now in Babylon you will see 4
gods made of silver and gold and wood,
carried on men's shoulders, inspiring
fear in the heathen. So beware of be- 5
coming just like the foreigners, and
being filled with awe at them, when
you see the throng before and behind
them worshiping them, but say in your 6
heart, "Lord, we must worship you."
For an angel is with you, and he cares 7
for your lives.
For their tongues are polished by a 8
carpenter, and they are gilded and

silvered, but they are deceptions and
9 cannot speak. And as though for a girl
fond of ornament, they take gold and
make crowns for the heads of their
10 gods, and sometimes the priests secretly withdraw gold and silver from
their gods and lavish it upon them-
11 selves, and give some of it even to the
prostitutes upon the housetop. And
they adorn them with clothes, like
men, these gods of silver, gold, and
12 wood, though they cannot save themselves from being corroded with rust.
When they have dressed them in purple
13 clothing, they wipe their faces because
of the dust from the house which lies
14 thick upon them. He carries a scepter
like a local human judge, though he
cannot destroy anyone who sins against
15 him. He holds a dagger in his right
hand and an ax, but he cannot save
16 himself from war and robbers. Therefore it is manifest that they are not
gods, so you must not stand in awe of
them.

17 For just as a man's dish is useless
when it is broken, so are their gods,
when they have been set down in their
houses. Their eyes are full of dust
raised by the feet of those who come in.
18 And just as the courtyard doors are
shut upon a man who has offended
against a king, as though sentenced to
death, the priests close their houses
securely with doors and locks and bars,
so that they will not be plundered by
19 robbers. They burn lamps, and more
than they themselves need, though
20 their gods can see none of them. They
are just like one of the beams of the
house, but men say their hearts are
eaten out, and when vermin from the
ground devour them and their cloth-
21 ing, they do not perceive it; their faces
are blackened by the smoke from the
22 temple. Bats, swallows, and birds light
on their bodies and on their heads; so
23 do cats also. Therefore you may be
sure they are not gods, so you must
not stand in awe of them.

24 As for the gold which they wear for
ornament, they will not shine unless
someone wipes off the rust; for even
when they were being cast, they did
25 not feel it. They are bought at great
cost, but there is no breath in them.
26 As they have no feet, they are carried
on men's shoulders, thus exposing their
27 own disgrace to men. Even those who
attend them are ashamed, because if
one of them falls on the ground, it cannot get up by itself. And if someone
sets it up, it cannot move of itself, and
if it is tipped, it cannot straighten itself
up; but gifts are offered to them as if
they were dead. What is sacrificed to 28
them their priests sell and use the proceeds of; and in like manner their
wives preserve some of them, but give
none of them to the poor or the helpless. A woman in her sickness or in 29
childbed can touch their sacrifices.
Therefore, being assured from these
facts that they are not gods, you must
not stand in awe of them.

For how can they be called gods? 30
For women set the tables for gods of
silver, gold, and wood; and in their 31
temples the priests sit apart with their
clothes torn open, and their heads and
beards shaved and their heads uncovered, and they howl and shout be- 32
fore their gods as some do at a wake
over a dead man. The priests take some 33
of their clothes from them and put
them on their wives and children. And 34
if they experience any injury or any
benefit from anyone, they cannot repay it; they cannot set up a king, or put
one down. In like manner, they cannot 35
bestow wealth or money; if someone
makes a vow to them and does not fulfil it, they will not exact it. They can- 36
not save a man from death, nor rescue
the weak from the strong. They can- 37
not restore a blind man's sight, they
cannot deliver a man who is in distress.
They cannot take pity on a widow, or 38
do good to an orphan. These things 39
made of wood and plated with gold or
silver are like stones from the mountain, and those who attend them will be
put to shame. Why then should anyone 40
think them gods, or call them so?

Besides, even the Chaldeans themselves dishonor them, for when they 41
see a dumb man, who cannot speak,
they bring him to Bel and pray that
he may speak—as though Bel were
able to understand. Yet they cannot 42
perceive this and abandon them, for
they have no understanding themselves. And the women with ropes on 43
sit by the wayside, burning chaff for
incense, and when one of them is
dragged off by one of the passers-by and
lain with, she derides her companion,
because she has not been as much de-

sired as herself, and has not had her
44 rope broken. Everything that is done
to them is a deception. So why should
anyone think them gods, or call them
so?
45 They are made by carpenters and
goldsmiths; they can be nothing but
what the craftsmen wish them to be.
46 The very men who make them cannot
last long; then how can the things that
47 are made by them be gods? For they
have only deceptions and reproach for
48 those who come after. For when war or
calamity overtakes them, the priests
consult together as to where they can
49 hide themselves and their gods. How
therefore can one fail to see that they
are not gods, since they cannot save
50 themselves from war or disaster? For
since they are made of wood and
covered with gold or silver, it will
eventually be found out that they are a
51 deception. It will be evident to all the
heathen and their kings that they are
not gods at all but the work of men's
hands, and that there is no work of God
52 in them. Who then can be ignorant
that they are not gods?
53 For they cannot set up a king over a
54 country, or give men rain; they cannot
decide a case, or give relief to a man
who is wronged; for they have no
power; for like crows they are between
55 heaven and earth. For when a temple
of wooden gods, or gilded or silvered
ones, catches fire, their priests flee and
save themselves, but they themselves
56 are burnt in two like beams. They can
offer no resistance to a king or any
enemies. Why then should anyone believe or suppose that they are gods?
57 Gods made of wood, silvered or
gilded, cannot save themselves from
58 thieves or robbers, and the gold and
silver on them, and the clothes they
have on, those who are strong enough
will strip from them and carry off, and
they will not be able to help themselves.
So it is better to be a king who can 59
show his courage, or a household dish,
that serves its owner's purpose, than
such false gods; or even a house door
that keeps what is in the house safe,
than such false gods; or a wooden pillar in a palace, than such false gods.
For sun, moon, and stars shine, and 60
when they are sent to perform a service,
they obey; in like manner lightning, 61
when it flashes, is widely visible, and
in the same way the wind blows in
every land; and when God commands 62
the clouds to spread over the whole
world, they carry out his order. And 63
the fire sent from above to consume
mountains and forests does as it is
ordered. But these cannot be compared with them in their manifesta-
tions or their powers. Therefore you 64
must not think that they are gods, or
call them so, since they are unable to
decide cases or to benefit men. So as 65
you know that they are not gods, you
must not stand in awe of them.
For they can neither curse kings nor 66
bless them; they cannot show portents 67
in the heavens before the nations, or
shine like the sun, or give light like the
moon. The wild animals are better 68
than they are, for they can flee to
cover and help themselves. So in no 69
way is it evident to us that they are
gods; therefore you must not stand in
awe of them.
For just as a scarecrow in a cucumber 70
bed gives no protection, their wooden,
gilded, and silvered gods give none.
In like manner, their wooden, gilded, 71
and silvered gods are like a white thorn
in a garden, on which every bird
settles; and like a corpse, thrown out
into the darkness. From the purple and 72
fine linen that rot upon them, you can
tell that they are not gods; and they
will finally be consumed themselves,
and be despised in the land. An upright 73
man who has no idols is far better, for
he will be far above reproach.

THE STORY OF SUSANNA

1 THERE once lived in Babylon
2 a man named Joakim. He married a wife named Susanna, the
daughter of Hilkiah, a very
3 beautiful and pious woman. Her parents also were upright people and instructed their daughter in the Law of
4 Moses. Joakim was very rich, and he
had a fine garden adjoining his house;
and the Jews used to come to visit him
because he was the most distinguished
of them all.
5 That year two of the elders of the
people were appointed judges—men of
the kind of whom the Lord said,
"Lawlessness came forth from Babylon, from elders who were judges, who
were supposed to guide the people."
6 These men came constantly to
Joakim's house, and all who had cases
7 to be decided came to them there. And
it happened that when the people left
at midday, Susanna would go into her
8 husband's garden and walk about. So
the two elders saw her every day, as she
went in and walked about, and they
9 conceived a passion for her. So their
thoughts were perverted and they
turned away their eyes, so as not to
look up to heaven or consider justice in
10 giving judgment. They were both smitten with her, but they could not disclose
11 their pain to each other, for they were
ashamed to reveal their passion, for
they desired to have relations with her,
12 and they watched jealously every day
13 for a sight of her. And they said to one
another,
"Let us go home, for it is dinner-time."
14 So they went out of the garden and
parted from one another; then they
turned back and encountered one another. And when they cross-questioned
one another as to the explanation, they
admitted their passion. Then they
agreed together upon a time when they
would be able to find her alone.
15 Now it happened, as they were
watching for an opportunity, that she
went in one day as usual with no one
but her two maids, and wished to bathe
in the garden, as it was very hot.
And there was no one there except the 16
two elders who had hidden themselves
and were watching her. And she said to 17
her maids,
"Bring me olive oil and soap, and
close the doors of the garden, so that I
can bathe."
And they did as she told them, and 18
shut the doors of the garden, and went
out at the side doors to bring what
they had been ordered to bring, and
they did not see the elders, for they
were hidden. And when the maids went 19
out, the two elders got up and ran to her
and said,
"Here the doors of the garden are 20
shut and no one can see us, and we are
in love with you, so give your consent
and lie with us. If you do not, we will 21
testify against you that there was a
young man with you, and that was why
you dismissed your maids."
And Susanna groaned and said, 22
"I am in a tight place. For if I do
this, it means my death; but if I refuse,
I cannot escape your hands. I had 23
rather not do it and fall into your hands
than commit sin in the Lord's sight!"
Then Susanna gave a loud scream, 24
and the two elders shouted against her.
And one of them ran and opened the 25
garden doors. And when the people in 26
the house heard the shouting in the
garden, they rushed through the side
doors to see what had happened to her.
And when the elders told their story, 27
her slaves were deeply humiliated, for
such a thing had never been said about
Susanna.

The next day, when the people came 28
together to her husband, Joakim, the
two elders came, full of their wicked
design to put Susanna to death. And 29
they said before the people,

"Send for Susanna, the daughter of
Hilkiah, Joakim's wife."
30 And they did so. And she came, with
her parents and her children, and all her
31 relatives. Now Susanna was accustomed to luxury and was very beauti-
32 ful. And the lawbreakers ordered her
to be unveiled, for she was wearing a
veil, so that they might have their fill
33 of her beauty. And the people with her
34 and all who saw her wept. And the two
elders stood up in the midst of the
people and laid their hands on her head,
35 and she wept and looked up to heaven,
36 for her heart trusted in the Lord. And
the elders said,
"As we were walking by ourselves in
the garden, this woman came in with
two maids, and shut the doors of the
37 garden and dismissed her maids, and
a young man, who had been hidden,
came to her, and lay down with her.
38 And we were in the corner of the
garden, and when we saw this wicked
39 action, we ran up to them, and though
we saw them together, we could not
hold him, because he was stronger than
we, and opened the doors and rushed
40 out. But we laid hold of this woman
and asked her who the young man was;
and she would not tell us. This is our
testimony."
41 Then the assembly believed them,
as they were elders of the people and
judges, and they condemned her to
42 death. But Susanna uttered a loud cry,
and said,
"Eternal God, you who know what
is hidden, who know all things before
43 they happen, you know that what they
have testified to against me is false,
and here I am to die when I have done
none of the things they have so wickedly charged me with."
44 And the Lord heard her cry,
45 and as she was being led away to be
put to death, God stirred up the holy
spirit of a young man named Daniel,
46 and he loudly shouted,
"I am clear of the blood of this
woman."
47 And all the people turned to him and
said,
"What does this mean, that you have
said?"
And he took his stand in the midst of 48
them and said,
"Are you such fools, you Israelites,
that you have condemned a daughter
of Israel without any examination or
ascertaining of the truth? Go back to 49
the place of trial. For these men have
borne false witness against her."
So all the people hurried back. And 50
the elders said to him,
"Come, sit among us and inform us,
for God has given you the right to do
so."
And Daniel said to them, 51
"Separate them widely from one another, and I will examine them."
And when they were separated from 52
each other, he called one of them to
him, and said to him,
"You ancient of wicked days, how
your sins have overtaken you, that you
committed before, making unjust de- 53
cisions, condemning the innocent and
acquitting the guilty, although the
Lord said, 'You shall not put an innocent and upright man to death.' So 54
now, if you saw this woman, tell us,
under which tree did you see them
meet?"
He answered,
"Under a mastic tree."
And Daniel said, 55
"You have told a fine lie against your
own life, for already the angel of God
has received the sentence from God,
and he will cut you in two."
And he had him removed and ordered 56
them to bring in the other. And he said
to him,
"You descendant of Canaan and not
of Judah, beauty has beguiled you, and
desire has corrupted your heart! This 57
is how you have been treating the
daughters of Israel, and they yielded
to you through fear, but a daughter of
Judah would not endure your wickedness. So now tell me, Under which tree 58
did you catch them embracing each
other?"
And he said,
"Under a liveoak tree."
And Daniel said to him, 59
"You have also told a fine lie against
your own life! For the angel of God is
waiting with his sword to saw you in
two, to destroy you both."

60 And the whole company uttered a
great shout and blessed God who saves
61 those who hope in him. And they threw
themselves upon the two elders, for
Daniel had convicted them out of their
own mouths of having borne false wit-
62 ness, and treated them as they had
wickedly planned to treat their neighbor; they obeyed the Law of Moses and
killed them. And innocent blood was
saved that day.

And Hilkiah and his wife praised 63
God for their daughter Susanna and so
did Joakim her husband and all her
relatives, because she had done nothing
immodest. And from that day onward, 64
Daniel had a great reputation in the
eyes of the people.

THE SONG OF THE THREE CHILDREN

AND they walked about in the
midst of the fire, singing
hymns to God and blessing
1 the Lord. And Azariah stood
still and uttered this prayer; in the
midst of the fire he opened his mouth
and said,
2 "Blessed are you, Lord God of our
forefathers, and worthy of praise!
Your name is glorified forever!
3 For you are upright in all that you
have done;
All your works are true, and your
ways straight,
And all your judgments are true.
The sentences that you passed were
just
4 In all that you have brought upon us,
And upon Jerusalem, the Holy City
of our forefathers.
For in truth and justice you have
brought all these things upon us
because of our sins.
5 For we have sinned and done wrong
in forsaking you,
6 We have sinned grievously in everything, and have disobeyed your
commands;
We have not observed them or done
As you commanded us to do, for our
own good.
7 All that you have brought upon us,
and all that you have done to us,
You have done in justice.
8 You have handed us over to enemies
without law, to hateful rebels,
And to a ruthless king, the most wicked
ruler in all the world,
9 Yet we cannot open our mouths.
Shame and disgrace have overtaken
your slaves and your worshipers.
10 For the sake of your name, do not
surrender us utterly;
Do not cancel your agreement,
11 And do not withdraw your mercy
from us,
For the sake of Abraham whom you
loved,
And for the sake of Isaac, your slave,
And for the sake of Israel, your holy
one,
12 To whom you spoke, and promised
That you would make their descendants as many as the stars of
heaven,
Or the sand that is on the seashore.
For, Master, we have become fewer 13
than all the heathen,
And we are humiliated everywhere,
because of our sins.
And now there is no prince, or 14
prophet, or leader,
No burnt offering, or sacrifice, or
offering, or incense;
No place to make an offering before
you, or to find mercy.
But may we be accepted through a 15
contrite heart and a humble
spirit,
As though it were through whole 16
burnt offerings of rams and bulls,
And through tens of thousands of fat
lambs.
So let our sacrifice rise before you
today,
And fully follow after you,
For those who trust in you will not be
disappointed.
So now we follow you with all our 17
hearts; we revere you
And seek your face. Do not disap- 18
point us,
But deal with us in your forbearance
And your abundant mercy.
Deliver us in your wonderful way, 19
And glorify your name, Lord;
May all who do your slaves harm be
disgraced;
May they be put to shame and lose all 20
their power and might,
And may their strength be broken.
Let them know that you are the Lord 21
God alone,
Glorious over the whole world."
Now the king's servants who threw 22
them in never ceased feeding the
furnace fires with naphtha, pitch, tow,
and faggots, and the flame streamed 23
out above the furnace for forty-nine
cubits (seventy-three feet). It even 24
spread, and burned up those Chaldeans
whom it found about the furnace. But 25
the angel of the Lord came down to
join Azariah and his companions in the
furnace, and drove the fiery blaze out of
the furnace, and made the middle of 26

the furnace as though a moist wind was
whistling through it, and the fire did
not touch them at all, or harm or
trouble them.
27 Then all three, as with one mouth,
praised, glorified, and blessed God in
the furnace, and said,
28 "Blessed are you, Lord God of our
forefathers,
And to be praised and greatly exalted forever.
29 And blessed is your glorious, holy
name,
And to be highly praised and greatly exalted forever.
30 Blessed are you in the temple of your
holy glory,
And to be highly praised and greatly
glorified forever.
31 Blessed are you who sit upon winged
creatures, and look into the
depths,
And to be praised and greatly
exalted forever.
32 Blessed are you on your kingly
throne,
And to be highly praised and greatly exalted forever.
33 Blessed are you in the firmament of
heaven,
And to be praised and glorified forever.
34 Bless the Lord, all you works of the
Lord,
Sing praise to him and greatly exalt
him forever.
35 Bless the Lord, you heavens,
Sing praise to him and greatly exalt
him forever.
36 Bless the Lord, you angels of the Lord,
Sing praise to him and greatly exalt
him forever.
37 Bless the Lord, all you waters above
the heaven,
Sing praise to him and greatly
exalt him forever.
38 Bless the Lord, all you powers,
Sing praise to him and greatly exalt
him forever.
39 Bless the Lord, sun and moon;
Sing praise to him and greatly exalt
him forever.
40 Bless the Lord, you stars of heaven,
Sing praise to him and greatly exalt
him forever.
41 Bless the Lord, all rain and dew,
Sing praise to him and greatly exalt
him forever.

Bless the Lord, all you winds, 42
Sing praise to him and greatly exalt
him forever.
Bless the Lord, fire and heat, 43
Sing praise to him and greatly exalt
him forever.
Bless the Lord, cold and warmth, 44
Sing praise to him and greatly exalt
him forever.
Bless the Lord, dews and snows, 45
Sing praise to him and greatly exalt
him forever.
Bless the Lord, nights and days, 46
Sing praise to him, and greatly exalt
him forever.
Bless the Lord, light and darkness, 47
Sing praise to him and greatly exalt
him forever.
Bless the Lord, ice and cold, 48
Sing praise to him and greatly exalt
him forever.
Bless the Lord, frosts and snows, 49
Sing praise to him and greatly exalt
him forever.
Bless the Lord, lightnings and clouds, 50
Sing praise to him and greatly exalt
him forever.
Let the earth bless the Lord, 51
Let it sing praise to him and greatly
exalt him forever.
Bless the Lord, you mountains and 52
hills,
Sing praise to him and greatly exalt
him forever.
Bless the Lord, all things that grow 53
on the earth,
Sing praise to him and greatly exalt
him forever.
Bless the Lord, seas and rivers, 55
Sing praise to him and greatly exalt
him forever.
Bless the Lord, you springs, 54
Sing praise to him and greatly exalt
him forever.
Bless the Lord, you whales and all the 56
things that move in the waters,
Sing praise to him and greatly exalt
him forever.
Bless the Lord, all you wild birds, 57
Sing praise to him and greatly exalt
him forever.
Bless the Lord, all you animals and 58
cattle,
Sing praise to him and greatly exalt
him forever.
Bless the Lord, you sons of men, 59
Sing praise to him and greatly exalt
him forever.

60 Bless the Lord, O Israel,
Sing praise to him and greatly exalt him forever.
61 Bless the Lord, you priests of the Lord,
Sing praise to him and greatly exalt him forever.
62 Bless the Lord, you slaves of the Lord,
Sing praise to him and greatly exalt him forever.
63 Bless the Lord, spirits and souls of the upright,
Sing praise to him and greatly exalt him forever.
64 Bless the Lord, you who are holy and humble in heart,
Sing praise to him and greatly exalt him forever.
Bless the Lord, Hananiah, Azariah, and Mishael, 65
Sing praise to him and greatly exalt him forever.
For he has rescued us from Hades and saved us from the hand of death,
And delivered us from the burning fiery furnace;
From the midst of the fire he has delivered us.
Give thanks to the Lord, for he is kind, 66
For his mercy endures forever.
Bless him, all you who worship the Lord, the God of gods, 67
Sing praise to him and give thanks to him,
For his mercy endures forever."

THE STORY OF BEL AND THE DRAGON

1 WHEN King Astyages was
gathered to his fathers,
Cyrus the Persian suc-
2 ceeded to his kingdom. And
Daniel was a companion of the king,
and was distinguished above all his
3 other friends. Now the Babylonians
had an idol called Bel, and every day
they bestowed on it twelve bushels of
fine flour and forty sheep and fifty
4 gallons of wine. And the king revered
it and went every day to worship it,
but Daniel worshiped his own God.
And the king said to him,
"Why do you not worship Bel?"
5 And he said,
"Because I do not revere artificial
idols, but the living God, who created
heaven and earth and is sovereign over
all mankind."
6 And the king said to him,
"Do you not think that Bel is a living God? Do you not see how much he
eats and drinks every day?"
7 And Daniel laughed and said,
"Do not be deceived, O king, for it
is only clay inside and bronze outside,
and never ate or drank anything."
8 Then the king was angry and called
Bel's priests, and said to them,
"If you cannot tell me who it is that
eats up these provisions, you shall die,
9 but if you can show me that Bel eats
them, Daniel shall die, because he has
uttered blasphemy against Bel."
And Daniel said to the king,
"It shall be as you say."
10 Now the priests of Bel were seventy
in number, beside their wives and
children. So the king went with Daniel
11 to the temple of Bel. And the priests
of Bel said,
"See, we will go outside, and you, O
king, must put the food on the table,
and mix the wine and put it on, and
shut the door and seal it with your
12 signet. And when you come back in
the morning, if you do not find that it
is all eaten up by Bel, we will die; or
Daniel will, who is making these false
13 charges against us." For they scorned
him, because they had made a secret
entrance under the table, and through
it they used to go in regularly and devour the offerings.
So it happened that when they had 14
gone, the king put the food for Bel on
the table. Then Daniel ordered his
servants to bring ashes, and they
scattered them over the whole temple,
in the presence of the king alone. Then
they went out, and shut the door, and
sealed it with the king's signet, and
went away. And the priests came in 15
the night as usual, with their wives and
children, and ate and drank it all up.
And the king rose early the next 16
morning, and Daniel came with him.
And the king said, 17
"Are the seals unbroken, Daniel?"
And he said,
"They are unbroken, O king."
And as soon as he opened the doors, 18
the king looked at the table, and
shouted loudly,
"You are great, O Bel, and there is
no deception at all about you."
But Daniel laughed and held the 19
king back from going in, and said to
him,
"Look at the floor and observe
whose footprints these are."
And the king said, 20
"I see the footprints of men, women,
and children!"
Then the king was enraged, and he 21
seized the priests and their wives and
children, and they showed him the
secret doors by which they got in and
devoured what was on the table. So 22
the king killed them, and he turned Bel
over to Daniel, and he destroyed it and
its temple.
Now there was a great serpent in that 23
place, and the Babylonians worshiped
it. And the king said to Daniel, 24
"You cannot deny that it is a living
god, so worship it."
And Daniel said, 25
"I will worship the Lord my God,
for he is a living God. But with your 26
permission, O king, I will kill this
serpent without sword or stick."
And the king said,

"You have my permission."
7 And Daniel took pitch, fat, and hair
and boiled them together, and made
lumps of them, and he put them into
the serpent's mouth, and it ate them
and burst open. And he said,
"See the objects of your worship!"
8 When the Babylonians heard it, they
were very indignant and made a conspiracy against the king, saying,
"The king has become a Jew! He has
overturned Bel, and killed the serpent,
and slaughtered the priests."
9 So they went to the king and said,
"Give Daniel up to us, or else we will
kill you and your household."
0 And the king saw that they were
pressing him hard, and he was forced
1 to give Daniel up to them. And they
threw him into the lions' den and he re-
2 mained there six days. There were
seven lions in the den; and they had
been given two human bodies and two
sheep every day; but now these were
not given them, so that they might devour Daniel.
3 Now the prophet Habakkuk was in
Judea, and he had cooked a stew and
crumbled bread into a bowl, and was
going into the field to carry it to the
4 reapers, when the angel of the Lord said
to Habakkuk,
"Carry the dinner that you have to
Babylon, to Daniel, in the lions' den."
And Habakkuk said, 35
"Sir, I have never seen Babylon, and
I do not know the den."
Then the angel of the Lord took hold 36
of the crown of his head, and lifted him
up by his hair and with the speed of
the wind set him down in Babylon,
right over the den. And Habakkuk 37
shouted,
"Daniel! Daniel! Take the dinner
which God has sent you."
And Daniel said, 38
"You have remembered me, O God,
and have not forsaken those who love
you."
Then Daniel arose and ate. And the 39
angel of God immediately put Habakkuk back in his own place again.
On the seventh day, the king came to 40
mourn for Daniel; and he came to the
den and looked in, and there sat Daniel.
Then the king shouted loudly, 41
"You are great, Lord God of Daniel,
and there is no other beside you!"
And he lifted him out, and the men 42
who had tried to bring about his destruction he threw into the den; and
they were instantly devoured before
his eyes.

THE PRAYER OF MANASSEH

ALMIGHTY LORD,
God of our forefathers,
Abraham, Isaac, and Jacob,
And of their upright descendants;
You who have made the heaven and the
earth with all their system;
Who have fettered the sea with your word
of command;
Who have shut up the great deep, and
sealed it with your terrible, glorious
name;
Before whom all things shudder, and
tremble before your power,
For the majesty of your glory is unbear-
able,
And the anger of your threatening against
sinners is unendurable,
Immeasurable and unsearchable is the
mercy you promise,
For you are the Lord Most High,
Tender-hearted, long-suffering, and most
merciful,
And regretful of the wickedness of men.
You therefore, Lord God of the upright,
Have not ordained repentance for the
upright,
For Abraham, Isaac, and Jacob, who did
not sin against you;
You have ordained repentance for a sinner
like me,
For my sins are more numerous than the
sands of the sea,
My transgressions are multiplied, Lord,
they are multiplied!
I am unworthy to look up and see th
height of heaven,
For the multitude of my iniquities.
I am weighed down with many an iro
fetter,
So that I bend beneath my sins,
And I have no relief,
Because I have provoked your anger,
And done what is wrong in your sight,
Setting up abominations and multiplyin
offenses.
Now therefore I bend the knee of m
heart, begging you for kindness.
I have sinned, Lord, I have sinned,
And I know my transgressions.
I earnestly beseech you,
Forgive me, Lord, forgive me!
Do not destroy me in the midst of m
transgressions!
Do not be angry with me forever and la
up evil for me,
Or condemn me to the lowest parts of th
earth.
For you, Lord, are the God of those wh
repent,
And you will manifest your goodnes
toward me,
For unworthy as I am, you will save m
in the abundance of your mercy,
And I will praise you continually as lon
as I live,
For all the host of heaven sings your praise
And yours is the glory forever. Amen.

THE FIRST BOOK OF MACCABEES

1 IT CAME to pass after Alexander
of Macedon, the son of Philip, who
came from the land of Chittim,
had utterly defeated Darius, the
king of the Medes and Persians, that he
reigned in his stead, as he had before
2 reigned over Greece. And he waged
many wars and captured fortresses and
3 slaughtered the kings of the earth; and
he made his way to the ends of the
earth and despoiled a multitude of nations. The whole earth was silent before
him, and he became exalted, and his
4 heart was uplifted. He mustered a very
mighty army and ruled over the lands
and rulers of the heathen, and they
5 paid him tribute. Afterward he fell
sick, and knew that he was going to die.
6 So he called in his distinguished servants who had been brought up with
him, and divided his kingdom among
7 them while he was still alive. Alexander
had reigned twelve years when he died.
8 His servants succeeded him, each in
9 his own domain. After his death they
all put on crowns, as did their sons after
them, for many years, and they did
much evil on the earth.
10 There sprang from them a sinful
shoot named Antiochus Epiphanes, the
son of King Antiochus; he had been a
hostage in Rome and he became king in
the one hundred and thirty-seventh
year of the Greek kingdom.
11 In those days there arose out of
Israel lawless men who persuaded
many, saying,
"Let us go and make a treaty with
the heathen around us, for ever since
the time we became separated from
them, many misfortunes have overtaken us."
12 The plan seemed good in their eyes,
13 and some of the people went eagerly to
the king, and he authorized them to
introduce the practices of the heathen.
14 And they built a gymnasium in Jerusa-
15 lem, in the heathen fashion, and submitted to uncircumcision, and disowned
the holy agreement; they allied themselves with the heathen and became
the slaves of wrongdoing.
When his rule appeared to Antiochus 16
to be established, he conceived the
idea of becoming king of the land of
Egypt, so that he might reign over the
two kingdoms. So he entered Egypt 17
with a strong force, with chariots and
elephants and cavalry and a great fleet.
And he made war on Ptolemy, king of 18
Egypt, and Ptolemy turned and fled
before him, and many fell wounded.
And they captured the walled cities in 19
the land of Egypt, and he plundered
the land of Egypt.
After subduing Egypt, in the one 20
hundred and forty-third year, Antiochus turned back and came up against
Israel and entered Jerusalem with a
strong force. And in his arrogance he 21
went into the sanctuary and took the
gold altar and the lampstand for the
light, and all its furniture and the table 22
for the Presentation Bread and the
cups and the bowls and the gold censers
and the curtain and the crowns and the
gold ornamentation on the front of the
temple, for he stripped it all off. And 23
he took the silver and the gold, and the
choice dishes, and he took the secret
treasures, which he found; he took them 24
all and went back to his own country.
He massacred people and spoke with
great arrogance.
And there was great mourning 25
everywhere throughout Israel. Rulers 26
and elders groaned, girls and young
men fainted away, and the beauty of
the women was altered. Every bride- 27
groom began to lament, and she that
sat in the bridal chamber grieved.
The very earth was shaken over its 28
inhabitants, and the whole household
of Jacob was covered with shame.
After two years the king sent an 29
officer to collect tribute, to the towns
of Judah, and he entered Jerusalem
with a strong force. And he spoke to 30
them craftily in peaceful terms, and
they trusted him. Then he suddenly
fell upon the city and struck it a great

blow and destroyed many of the people
31 in Israel. He plundered the city, and
burned it down, and tore down the
houses in it and the walls around it.
32 And they took the women and children
captive and possessed themselves of the
33 cattle. Then they fortified the City of
David with a great, strong wall, with
strong towers, and it became their cita-
34 del. And they put sinful heathen there,
who did not obey the law, and they
35 entrenched themselves there. And they
stored up weapons and provisions, and
they collected the spoils of Jerusalem
and laid them up there, and they be-
36 came a great threat, and it proved a
place of ambush against the sanctuary
and a wicked adversary to Israel constantly.

37 And they shed innocent blood all
around the sanctuary,
And polluted the sanctuary itself.
38 The inhabitants of Jerusalem fled away
because of them,
And she became a place where
strangers lived,
And she became strange to her own
offspring,
And her children forsook her.

39 Her sanctuary became desolate like a
wilderness,
Her feasts were turned into grief,
Her sabbaths became a reproach,
And her honor became contempt.
40 Her dishonor was as great as her glory
had been,
And her exaltation was turned into
grief.

41 Then the king wrote to his whole
kingdom that they should all become
42 one people, and everyone should give
up his particular practices. And all the
heathen assented to the command of
43 the king. And many from Israel
agreed to his kind of worship and
offered sacrifice to idols and broke the
44 sabbath. And the king sent word by
messengers to Jerusalem and the towns
of Judah to follow practices foreign to
45 the country and put a stop to whole
burnt offerings and sacrifices and drink
offerings at the sanctuary, and to break
the sabbaths and profane the feasts
46 and pollute sanctuary and sanctified; to
47 build altars and sacred precincts and idol
temples and sacrifice hogs and unclean
48 cattle; and to leave their sons uncircumcised and defile themselves with

every unclean and profane practice, so that they might forget the Law and change all their religious ordinances; and anyone who did not obey the command of the king should die. He wrote to his whole kingdom, to this effect, and he appointed inspectors over all the people, and he ordered the towns of Judah every one of them to offer sacrifice. And many of the people and everyone who was ready to forsake the Law joined with them and they did wrong in the land, and forced Israel to hide in every hiding-place they had.

On the fifteenth day of Chislev, in the one hundred and forty-fifth year, he erected a dreadful desecration upon the altar, and in the towns of Judah round about they built altars, and at the doors of their houses and in the squares they burned incense, and wherever they found the book of the Law, they tore them up and burned them, and if anyone was found to possess a book of the agreement or respected the Law, the king's decree condemned him to death. The Israelites who appeared from month to month in the towns they treated with force. On the twenty-fifth of the month they offered sacrifice upon the altar which was set up on the altar of burnt offering. The women who had circumcised their children they put to death under the decree, hanging the babies around their necks, and destroying their families and the men who had circumcised them. Yet many in Israel stood firm and resolved in their hearts not to eat what was unclean; they preferred death to being polluted with food or profaning the sacred agreement, and so they died. And Israel suffered intensely.

In those days Mattathias, the son of John, the son of Simeon, a priest of the descendants of Joarib, removed from Jerusalem, and settled in Modin. He had five sons, John, surnamed Gaddi, Simon, called Thassi, Judas, called Maccabeus, Eleazar, called Avaran, and Jonathan, called Apphus. He saw the impious things that were going on in Judah and Jerusalem, and he said,

"Alas! Why was I born to witness the ruin of my people and the ruin of the holy city, and to sit by while it is being given up to its enemies, and the sanctuary to aliens?

8 "Her temple has come to be like a man
disgraced,
9 Her glorious furniture has been
captured and carried off,
Her infant children have been killed
in her streets,
Her young men with the enemy's
sword.
10 What nation has not appropriated,
What kingdom has not seized, her
spoils?
11 Her adornment has all been taken
away.
Instead of a free woman, she has
become a slave.
12 Behold, our sanctuary and our beauty
And our glory have been laid waste,
And the heathen have profaned them!
13 Why should we live any longer?"
14 And Mattathias and his sons tore
open their clothes and put on sackcloth
and grieved bitterly.
15 Then the king's officers who were
forcing the people to give up their religion, came to the town of Modin, to
16 make them offer sacrifice. And many
Israelites went to them, and Mattathias
17 and his sons gathered together. Then
the king's messengers answered and
said to Mattathias,
"You are a leading man, great and
distinguished in this town, surrounded
18 with sons and brothers; now be the first
to come forward and carry out the
king's command as all the heathen and
the men of Judah and those who are
left in Jerusalem have done, and you
and your sons will be counted among
the Friends of the king, and you and
your sons will be distinguished with
presents of silver and gold and many
royal commissions."
19 Then Mattathias answered and said
in a loud voice,
"If all the heathen in the king's
dominions listen to him and forsake
each of them the religion of his forefathers, and choose to follow his com-
20 mands instead, yet I and my sons and
my brothers will live in accordance
with the agreement of our forefathers.
21 God forbid that we should abandon the
22 Law and the ordinances. We will not
listen to the message of the king, or depart from our religion to the right hand
or to the left."
23 As he ceased to utter these words, a
Jew went up before the eyes of all of
them to offer sacrifice as the king commanded, on the altar in Modin. And 24
Mattathias saw him and was filled with
zeal, and his heart was stirred, and he
was very properly roused to anger, and
ran up and slaughtered him upon the
altar. At the same time he killed the 25
king's officer who was trying to compel
them to sacrifice, and he tore down the
altar. Thus he showed his zeal for the 26
Law, just as Phineas did to Zimri, the
son of Salom. Then Mattathias cried 27
out in a loud voice in the town and
said,
"Let everybody who is zealous for
the Law and stands by the agreement
come out after me."
And he and his sons fled to the 28
mountains and left all they possessed
in the town.
Then many seekers for uprightness 29
and justice went down into the wilderness to settle, with their sons and their 30
wives and their cattle, because their
hardships had become so severe. And 31
news reached the king's agents and the
forces that were in Jerusalem, in the
City of David, that men who had disregarded the king's order had gone
down to the hiding-places in the wilderness. And they pursued them in force 32
and overtook them, and pitched their
camp against them and prepared to
attack them on the sabbath day. And 33
they said to them,
"Enough! Come out and do as the
king commands, and you will live."
And they said, 34
"We will not come out nor do as the
king commands, and break the sabbath."
Then they hastened to attack them. 35
And they made no response to them; 36
they did not throw a stone at them nor
block up their hiding-places, for they 37
said,
"Let us all die guiltless. We call
heaven and earth to witness that you
destroy us unlawfully."
So they attacked them on the sab- 38
bath, and they died, with their wives
and their children and their cattle, to
the number of a thousand people.
And Mattathias and his friends 39
learned of it, and they grieved bitterly
over them. And one said to another, 40
"If we all do as our brothers have
done, and refuse to fight against the
heathen for our lives and what we be-

lieve is right, they will very soon destroy us from the face of the earth."
41 On that day they reached this decision:
"If anyone attacks us on the sabbath day, let us fight against him and
not all die, as our brothers died in the
hiding-places."
42 Then they were joined by a company
of Hasideans, war-like Israelites, every
43 one a volunteer for the Law. And all
who had fled to escape harsh treatment
44 joined them and reinforced them. And
they mustered a force and struck down
sinners in their anger, and in their
wrath those who disobeyed the Law,
and the rest fled to the heathen to save
45 themselves. And Mattathias and his
friends went about and tore down the
46 altars, and forcibly circumcised all the
uncircumcised children that they found
47 within the limits of Israel. And they
drove the arrogant before them, and
the work prospered in their hands.
48 So they rescued the Law from the
hands of the heathen and their kings,
and would not let the sinner triumph.
49 When the time drew near for Mattathias to die, he said to his sons,
"Arrogance and reproach have now
grown strong; it is a time of disaster
50 and hot anger. Now, my children, you
must be zealous for the Law, and give
your lives for the agreement of our fore-
51 fathers. Remember the deeds of our
forefathers which they did in their generations, and you will win great glory
52 and everlasting renown. Was not Abraham found faithful when he was tried,
and it was credited to him as upright-
53 ness? Joseph in his time of distress
observed the commandment and be-
54 came master of Egypt. Phineas our
forefather for his intense zeal obtained
the promise of an everlasting priest-
55 hood. Joshua for carrying out his
56 orders became a judge in Israel. Caleb
for bearing witness before the congregation obtained an inheritance in the
57 land. David for being merciful in-
58 herited a royal throne forever. Elijah
for his intense zeal for the Law was
59 caught up into heaven. Hananiah,
Azariah, and Mishael had faith in God
60 and were saved from the fire. Daniel
for his innocence was delivered from
61 the mouths of the lions. Observe this
from generation to generation, that
none who hope in him will fail in

strength. Do not be afraid of the words 62
of a sinful man, for his glory will turn
to dung and worms. Today he will be 63
exalted, and tomorrow he will be
nowhere to be found, for he has returned to dust, and what he plotted
will perish. My children, be manful and 64
strong for the Law, for by it you will
obtain glory. Now here is Simon your 65
brother; I know that he is a man of
discretion. You must always listen to
him; he will be a father to you. And 66
Judas Maccabeus has been warlike
from his youth; he will be your captain
and conduct the people's warfare. And 67
you must gather about you all who observe the Law, and avenge the wrongs
of your people. Pay back the heathen 68
for what they have done, and give heed
to what the Law commands."
Then he blessed them and was gath- 69
ered to his forefathers. He died in the 70
one hundred and forty-sixth year and
was buried in the tombs of his forefathers in Modin, and all Israel made
loud lamentation for him.
Then his son Judas, who was called 3
Maccabeus, arose in his stead, and all 2
his brothers and all who had stood by
his father helped him, and with gladness carried on Israel's war. And he in- 3
creased the glory of his people, and put
on a breastplate like a giant, and he
belted on his weapons and organized
campaigns, protecting his camp with
the sword. He was like a lion in his ac- 4
tions, and like a cub roaring for its
prey. He pursued and hunted out those 5
who disobeyed the Law, and those
who harassed his people he consumed.
Those who disobeyed the Law were 6
convulsed with fear of him and all who
broke the Law were dismayed and deliverance was accomplished by his
hand. He angered many kings and 7
gladdened Jacob by his deeds, and his
memory will be blessed forever. He 8
went among the towns of Judah and
destroyed the ungodly and cast them
out of her, and averted wrath from
Israel. He was renowned to the ends 9
of the earth, and rallied those who were
perishing.
Then Apollonius gathered the hea- 10
then together, with a large force from
Samaria, to make war on Israel. And 11
Judas learned of it and went out to
meet him and he struck him down and
killed him. And many fell wounded,

12 and the rest made their escape. And
they took their spoils, and Judas took
the sword of Apollonius and fought
with it all his life.
13 Then Seron, the commander of the
Syrian army, heard that Judas had
gathered a following and a company of
the faithful about him, and of men used
14 to going out to war. And he said,
"I will make myself a reputation and
gain distinction in the kingdom, and I
will make war on Judas and those who
are with him, who set the king's command at naught."
15 And with him there went up again
a strong body of ungodly men, to help
him to take vengeance on the Israelites.
16 And he approached the pass of Beth-
horon. And Judas went out with very
17 few men to meet him. But when they
saw the army coming to meet them,
they said to Judas,
"How can we, few as we are, fight
with such a strong host? Besides we
are faint, for we have had nothing to
eat today."
18 And Judas said,
"It is easy for many to be inclosed
in the hands of a few, and there is no
difference in the sight of heaven between saving through many or through
19 few, for victory in war does not depend
upon the size of the force, but strength
20 comes from heaven. They come against
us full of violence and lawlessness, to
destroy us and our wives and our chil-
21 dren, and to plunder us, but we are
fighting for our lives and our laws.
22 He himself will crush them before us,
and you must not be afraid of them."
23 When he ceased to speak, he fell
suddenly upon them, and Seron and
24 his army were crushed before him, and
they pursued him from the pass of
Bethhoron to the plain, and eight
hundred of them fell, and the rest
made their escape into the country of
25 the Philistines. So the fear of Judas and
his brothers and the dread of them began to fall upon the heathen around
26 them, and his fame reached even the
king, and the heathen talked of the
tactics of Judas.
27 When King Antiochus heard these
reports, he was very angry, and he sent
and gathered all the forces of his king-
28 dom, a very strong army. And he
opened his treasury and gave his
forces a year's pay, and ordered them
to be in readiness for any need that
might arise. And he saw that the 29
money in his treasuries was exhausted,
and the tribute of the country was small
because of the division and distress that
he had brought upon the land in doing
away with the laws which had been in
effect from the earliest times, and he 30
feared that he would not have enough,
as he formerly had, for his expenses
and for the presents which he had been
used to give before with a lavish hand,
beyond the kings that went before him.
So he was very much perplexed and 31
resolved to go to Persia and get the
tribute of those countries and raise a
large sum of money. And he left 32
Lysias, a man of distinction, of the
royal blood, to have charge of the king's
affairs from the river Euphrates to the
borders of Egypt, and to take care of 33
Antiochus his son until his return.
He turned over to him half his forces 34
and his elephants and gave him orders
about everything he wanted done, and
about the inhabitants of Judea and Jerusalem, against whom he was to send a 35
force to crush out and destroy the
strength of Israel and what was left of
Jerusalem, and to efface their memory
from the place, and settle aliens in all 36
their borders, and distribute their land
among them.
Then the king took the remaining 37
half of his forces and set off from
Antioch, his royal city, in the one
hundred and forty-seventh year and
crossed the Euphrates River and went
through the interior.
Then Lysias chose Ptolemy, son of 38
Dorymenes, and Nicanor and Gorgias,
warlike men among the Friends of the
king, and he sent with them forty thou- 39
sand men and seven thousand horse to
go to the land of Judah and destroy it,
as the king had commanded. And he 40
set off with all his force, and they came
and encamped near Emmaus in the
level country. And the merchants of 41
the country heard about them and
they took a great quantity of silver and
gold, and fetters, and came to the camp
to get the Israelites for slaves. And
they were joined by forces from Syria
and the land of the Philistines.
And Judas and his brothers saw that 42
the situation was very grave and that
the forces were encamped within their
borders, and they knew what the king

had said, when he ordered them to
inflict utter destruction on the people,
43 and they said to one another,
"Let us repair the destruction of our
people, and let us fight for our people
and for the sanctuary."
44 And the congregation gathered together to make ready for war and to
pray and ask for mercy and compassion.
45 Jerusalem was uninhabited like a
wilderness,
There was not one of her children
who came in or went out,
The sanctuary was trodden down,
The sons of aliens were in the citadel,
it was a stopping-place for heathen.
Joy vanished from Jacob,
And the flute and harp ceased to
play.
46 Then they gathered together and
went to Mizpeh, opposite Jerusalem,
for Israel formerly had a praying-place
47 in Mizpeh. And they fasted that day
and put on sackcloth, and sprinkled
ashes upon their heads, and tore open
48 their clothes. And they unrolled the
roll of the Law, such as the heathen
used to hunt out and look through for
49 pictures of their idols. And they
brought out the priestly garments and
the first fruits and the tithes and they
gathered the Nazirites who had ful-
50 filled their vows, and they called aloud
to heaven,
"What are we to do to these men,
51 and where can we take them, when
your sanctuary is trodden down and
profaned, and your priests are grieved
52 and humiliated? Here the heathen are
gathered together against us to destroy
us; you know their designs against us.
53 How can we make a stand before them
unless you help us?"
54 And they sounded the trumpets and
55 gave a great shout. Then Judas appointed officers over the people, colonels and captains and lieutenants
56 and sergeants. And he ordered those
who were building houses or planting
vineyards or betrothed to women or
were afraid, every one of them to
return home, as the Law provided. And
57 the army moved and encamped to the
58 south of Emmaus. And Judas said,
"Prepare yourselves and be brave
men and be ready in the morning to
fight these heathen who are gathered
together against us, to destroy us and
our sanctuary, for it is better for us to 59
die in battle than to witness the ruin of
our nation and our sanctuary. But he 60
will do just as shall be the will of
heaven."
Then Gorgias took five thousand 4
men and a thousand picked horse, and
his army moved under cover of night
so as to fall upon the camp of the Jews 2
and attack them suddenly; and the
men of the citadel were his guides. And 3
Judas heard of it and he and his gallant
men moved to attack the king's force in
Emmaus, while the forces were still 4
scattered from the camp. And Gorgias 5
came into the camp of Judas in the
night, and found no one there, and he
hunted for them in the mountains, for
he said,
"They are fleeing from us!"
And at daybreak Judas appeared in 6
the plain with three thousand men,
though they did not have such armor
and swords as they wished. And they 7
saw the camp of the heathen strongly
fortified, with horsemen patrolling it,
and these, expert in war. And Judas 8
said to the men who were with him,
"Do not be afraid of their numbers,
and do not fear their charge. Remem- 9
ber how our forefathers were saved at
the Red Sea, when Pharaoh pursued
them with an armed force. So now let 10
us cry to heaven, if perhaps he will
accept us and remember his agreement
with our forefathers, and crush this
camp before us today. Then all the 11
heathen will know that there is one who
ransoms and preserves Israel."
Then the aliens lifted up their eyes 12
and saw them coming against them,
and they came out of the camp to 13
battle. And Judas' men sounded the
trumpets and attacked, and the hea- 14
then broke and fled to the plain, and all 15
the hindmost fell by the sword. And
they pursued them as far as Gazara
and the plains of Idumea and Ashdod
and Jamnia, and there fell of them fully
three thousand men.
And Judas and his force returned 16
from the pursuit of them, and he said 17
to the people,
"Do not set your hearts on plunder,
for there is a battle before us, for 18
Gorgias and his army are near us, in the
mountain. Now stand your ground
against our enemies, and fight them,

and afterward you can take their spoils
boldly."
19 Before Judas had finished saying this,
a detachment of them appeared recon-
20 noitering from the mountain, and they
saw that they had been routed and that
they were burning the camp, for the
sight of the smoke showed them what
21 had happened. And when they perceived this, they were very much
alarmed, and seeing Judas' army in the
22 plain ready to attack, they all fled to
23 the land of the Philistines. And Judas
turned back to plunder the camp, and
they took a great deal of gold and
silver, and sapphire and sea-purple
24 stuffs, and great wealth. And they returned singing and blessing heaven, for
he is good, for his mercy endures for-
25 ever. So Israel had a great deliverance
that day.
26 Those of the aliens who escaped went
and reported to Lysias all that had
27 happened. And when he heard it, he
was dismayed and discouraged, because it was not at all what he wished
that had happened to Israel, and it had
not turned out as the king had ordered.
28 So in the following year he gathered together sixty thousand picked men, to
29 conquer them. And they came into
Idumea and encamped at Bethsura,
and Judas met them with ten thousand
30 men. And he saw that their camp was
strong, and he prayed and said,

"Blessed are you, Savior of Israel,
who stopped the rush of the champion
by the hand of your slave David, and
delivered the camp of the Philistines
into the hands of Jonathan, the son of
31 Saul, and of his armor-bearer. In like
manner shut up this camp in the hand
of your people Israel, and let them be
ashamed of their army and their horse-
32 men. Make them cowardly and melt
the boldness of their strength, and let
them tremble at their destruction.
33 Strike them down with the sword of
those that love you, and let all who
know your name praise you with
hymns."
34 Then they joined battle, and there
fell of the army of Lysias fully five
thousand men; they fell right before
35 them. But when Lysias saw that his
army had been routed, and that Judas
had grown bold, and that they were
ready either to live or to die nobly, he
withdrew to Antioch and hired soldiers
in the greatest numbers, to come again
to Judea.
And Judas and his brothers said, 36
"Now that our enemies are crushed,
let us go up to purify the sanctuary
and rededicate it."
And the whole army gathered to- 37
gether, and they went up to Mount
Zion. And they found the sanctuary 38
desolated and the altar polluted and
the doors burned up, and weeds growing in the courts as they do in a wood
or on some mountain, and the priests'
quarters torn down. And they tore 39
open their clothes and uttered great
lamentation and covered themselves
with ashes, and fell on their faces on 40
the ground, and sounded the ceremonial
trumpets, and cried out to heaven.
Then Judas appointed men to fight 41
the garrison in the citadel, until he
should purify the sanctuary. And he 42
appointed priests that were without
blemish and adherents of the Law,
and they purified the sanctuary and 43
carried out the stones that had defiled
it to an unclean place. And they de- 44
liberated as to what they should do
about the altar of burnt offering, which
had been polluted. And a good idea 45
occurred to them—to take it down, so
that it might never be thrown up to
them that the heathen had polluted it;
so they took down the altar, and de- 46
posited the stones in the temple mountain, in a suitable place, until a prophet
should come and declare what should
be done with them. And they took 47
whole stones, as the Law required, and
built a new altar like the former one.
And they built the sanctuary and the 48
interior of the temple and consecrated
the courts. And they made new holy 49
dishes and they brought the lampstand
and the altar of incense and the table
into the temple. And they burned in- 50
cense on the altar, and lighted the
lamps on the lampstand, and they
lighted the temple. And they put the 51
loaves of bread on the table and hung
up the curtains, and completed all the
work they had undertaken.

And they arose early on the twenty- 52
fifth day of the ninth month, that is,
the month of Chislev, in the one
hundred and forty-eighth year, and 53
offered sacrifice according to the Law
upon the new altar of burnt offering
which they had made. At the time and 54

on the day the heathen had polluted it,
it was rededicated with songs and harps
55 and lutes and cymbals. And all the
people fell on their faces and blessed
heaven which had prospered them.
56 And they celebrated the rededication
of the altar for eight days and offered
burnt offerings with joy, and offered a
57 sacrifice of deliverance and praise. And
they decorated the front of the temple
with gold crowns and small shields and
rededicated the gates and the priests'
quarters, and fitted them with doors.
58 And there was very great joy among
the people, and the reproach the heathen had cast upon them was wiped
59 out. And Judas and his brothers and
all the congregation of Israel decreed
that the days of the rededication of the
altar should be observed at their season,
every year, for eight days, beginning
with the twenty-fifth of the month of
60 Chislev, with gladness and joy. At
that time they built high walls and
strong towers around Mount Zion, so
that the heathen might not come and
tread them down as they had done be-
61 fore. And he established a force there
to hold it, and he fortified Bethsura to
hold it, so that the people might have
a stronghold facing Idumea.

5 It happened when the heathen round
about heard that the altar had been
rebuilt and the sanctuary rededicated
as before, that it made them very
2 angry, and they resolved to destroy the
descendants of Jacob that were among
them, and they began to kill and ravage
3 among the people. And Judas fought
against the sons of Esau in Idumea, and
against Akrabattene, because they beset Israel, and he dealt them a severe
blow and crushed them, and plundered
4 them. And he remembered the wickedness of the sons of Baean, who became
a snare and stumbling block to the people, lying in wait for them upon the
5 roads. And he shut them up in their
towers, and he encamped against them
and utterly destroyed them, and
burned her towers with fire, and all
6 who were in them. He passed on to
the Ammonites, and there he found a
strong arm, and a large body of people,
with Timotheus in command of them.
7 And he fought many battles with them,
and they were crushed before him, and
8 he struck them down. And he occupied
Jazer and its villages, and returned to
Judea.

Then the heathen in Gilead gathered 9
together against Israel, to destroy those
who were in their borders, and they
fled to the stronghold of Dathema, and 10
sent a letter to Judas and his brothers,
saying,

"The heathen around us have gathered together against us to destroy us,
and they are preparing to come and 11
seize this stronghold in which we have
taken refuge, and Timotheus is the
leader of their force. So come and 12
rescue us from his hand, for a great
many of us have fallen, and all our 13
brothers who were in the district of
Tob have been put to death, and they
have carried off their wives and children as captives, with their property,
and they have destroyed a regiment of
men there."

They were still reading the letter 14
when other messengers arrived from
Galilee, with their clothes torn open,
with a report to the same effect, saying 15
that people from Ptolemais and Tyre
and Sidon, and all Galilee of the aliens
had gathered against them, they said,
"to destroy us." When Judas and the 16
people heard this message, a great
meeting was held to decide what they
should do for their brothers who were
in such distress and were being attacked by them. And Judas said to his 17
brother Simon,

"Choose men for yourself and go and
save our brothers who are in Galilee,
and I and my brother Jonathan will go
into Gilead."

And he left Joseph, the son of Zecha- 18
riah, and Azariah, a leader of the people, with the remainder of the force, in
Judea, to guard it. And he gave them 19
their orders, saying,

"Take command of these people, and
do not join battle with the heathen until we return."

Simon was allotted three thousand 20
men, to go into Galilee, and Judas eight
thousand men, to go into Gilead. And 21
Simon went into Galilee, and engaged
in many battles with the heathen, and
the heathen were beaten before him,
and he pursued them to the very gate
of Ptolemais. There fell of the heathen 22
fully three thousand men, and he
plundered them. And he took with him 23
those who were in Galilee and in Ar-

batta with their wives and children and
all that they had, and brought them
back to Judea with great rejoicing.
24 And Judas Maccabeus and his brother Jonathan crossed the Jordan, and
marched three days' journey into the
25 wilderness. And they encountered the
Nabateans and met them peaceably,
and told them all that had happened
26 to their brothers in Gilead, and that
many of them were shut up in Bosorra
and Bosor, in Alema, Chaspho, Maked,
and Karnaim—all large, fortified towns
27 —and that they were shut up in the
other towns of Gilead, and that they
planned on the next day to attack the
strongholds and take them, and destroy
28 all these men in one day. And Judas
and his army turned suddenly by the
wilderness road to Bosorra, and he took
the town and killed every male in it
with the sword, and he took all their
29 spoils, and burned it with fire. And he
left there by night, and they arrived
30 at the stronghold. And at daybreak
they looked up, and there was a crowd
of people without number, bringing
ladders and engines to take the stronghold, and they were attacking them.
31 And Judas saw that the battle had begun, and the cry from the city went up
to heaven, with trumpets and loud
32 shouting, and he said to the men of his
force,

"Fight for our brothers today!"

33 And he went out after them in three
companies, and they sounded the
trumpets and cried aloud in prayer.
34 And the army of Timotheus saw that
it was Maccabeus, and they fled before
him, and he struck them a severe blow,
and there fell of them that day fully
35 eight thousand men. Then he turned
aside to Alema and fought against it
and took it, and he killed every male
in it, and plundered it and burned it
36 with fire. Then he moved on and seized
Chaspho, Maked, and Bosor and the
other towns of Gilead.

37 After that, Timotheus gathered another army, and he pitched his camp
opposite Raphon, on the other side of
38 the torrent. And Judas sent men to
reconnoiter the camp, and they reported to him,

"All the heathen around us have
gathered and joined him, an im-
39 mensely great force, and they have
hired Arabs to help them, and they are
encamped across the torrent, in readiness to attack you."

And Judas went to meet them. Then 40
Timotheus said to the officers of his
army, when Judas and his army approached the stream,

"If he crosses over to us first, we will
not be able to stand against him, for he
will easily defeat us. But if he is afraid 41
and pitches his camp on the other side
of the river, we will cross over to him
and defeat him."

When Judas came near the stream, 42
he stationed the officers of the people
by the stream, and gave them their
orders, saying,

"Do not permit anyone to encamp,
but let them all advance to battle."

And he crossed over against them 43
first, with all the people after him, and
all the heathen were beaten before
them, and they threw away their arms
and fled to the temple inclosure of
Karnaim. Then they took the town, 44
and burned the temple inclosure with
all who were in it. So Karnaim was conquered, and they could not make a
stand before Judas any longer.

And Judas gathered all the Israelites 45
that were in Gilead, from the least to
the greatest, with their wives and children and their belongings, a very great
body of people, to go to the land of
Judah. And they reached Ephron; it 46
was a large town, strongly fortified, on
their way; they could not turn aside
from it to the right or left, but had to
go through the center of it. And the 47
people of the town shut them out and
blocked up the gates with stones. And 48
Judas sent them a peaceful message,
saying,

"We are going through your country
to reach our country, and no one will do
you any harm, we will simply pass by
on foot."

But they would not open to him.
Then Judas ordered proclamation to be 49
made throughout the body that everyone should encamp where he was. So 50
the men of the army encamped, and he
fought against the city all that day and
all that night, and the town was delivered into his hands. And he de- 51
stroyed every male with the sword, and
he destroyed it and plundered it, and
he passed through the city over the
slain. And they crossed the Jordan to 52
the great plain opposite Bethshean.

53 And Judas kept gathering up those
who fell behind and encouraging the
people, all the way until he reached the
54 land of Judah. And they went up to
Mount Zion with gladness and joy, and
offered whole burnt offerings because
not one of them had fallen before they
returned in peace.
55 In the days when Judas and Jonathan were in the land of Gilead and
Simon his brother was in Galilee, oppo-
56 site Ptolemais, Joseph, the son of Zechariah, and Azariah, the leaders of the
forces, heard of the warlike exploits
57 they had performed, and they said,
"Let us also make a name for ourselves, and let us go and fight the
heathen around us."
58 And he gave orders to the part of the
army that was with them, and they
59 marched to Jamnia. And Gorgias came
out of the town with his men to meet
60 them in battle. And Joseph and Azariah were routed, and they were pursued to the borders of Judea. And there
fell that day of the people of Israel fully
61 two thousand men. And there was a
great rout among the people, because
they had not listened to Judas and his
brothers, but thought they would per-
62 form some exploit. They did not belong to the family of those who were
permitted to save Israel with their
hands.
63 This man Judas and his brothers
were greatly renowned in all Israel
and among all the heathen, wherever
64 their name was heard of; and men
gathered about them commending
them.
65 And Judas and his brothers went
forth and made war on the sons of Esau
in the country to the south, and he
struck down Hebron and its villages,
and he tore down its fortifications and
66 burned its towers around it. And he set
off to go to the land of the Philistines,
67 and reached Mareshah. Some priests
fell in battle that day, when they went
out to war without due consideration,
because they wished to distinguish
68 themselves. And Judas turned aside to
Ashdod, to the land of the Philistines,
and he tore down their altars and
burned up the carved images of their
gods and plundered the towns, and
returned to the land of Judah.
6 As King Antiochus was making his
way through the interior, he heard that
there was in Persia a town called
Elymais, renowned for its wealth, its
silver and gold. The temple in it was 2
very rich, and there were there gold
shields and breastplates and arms left
there by Alexander, the son of Philip,
king of Macedon, who was the first to
reign over the Greeks. And he went 3
and tried to take the town, and plunder
it, but he could not do it, because his
design became known to the men of the
town, and they opposed him in battle, 4
and he fled and set out from there in
great distress to return to Babylon.
And someone came to him in Persia to 5
bring him word that the forces that
had marched into the land of Judah had
been routed, and that Lysias had gone 6
at first with a strong force, and had
been put to flight before them, and
that they had grown strong by reason
of the quantity of arms and spoils they
had taken from the armies they had
destroyed, and that they had taken 7
down the horror which he had built on
the altar in Jerusalem, and had surrounded the sanctuary with high walls,
as it had been before, and also his town
of Bethsura. And it happened when the 8
king heard these accounts, that he was
astounded and dreadfully shaken, and
he took to his bed, and fell sick with
grief, for matters had not gone as he
intended. He was sick for a long time, 9
for his grief was intensified, and he con-
cluded that he was going to die. So he 10
called in all his Friends and said to
them,
"Sleep departs from my eyes, and my 11
heart fails with anxiety. I have said to
myself, 'What distress I have reached,
and what a great flood I am now in.'
For I was gracious and beloved in my
exercise of power. But now I remem- 12
ber the wrongs which I did in Jerusalem, when I took away all the gold and
silver dishes that were in it, and sent
to destroy the inhabitants of Judah
without any cause. I know that it is be- 13
cause of this that these misfortunes
have overtaken me. Here I am dying
of grief in a strange land."
And he summoned Philip, one of his 14
Friends, and put him in charge of his
whole kingdom. He gave him his dia- 15
dem and his robe and his signet ring, so
that he might educate his son Antiochus
and bring him up to be king. And King 16
Antiochus died there in the one hun-

17 dred and forty-ninth year. And when
Lysias learned that the king was dead,
he set up Antiochus his son to reign,
whom he had taken care of as a boy,
and he named him Eupator.
18 The men in the citadel kept hemming
Israel in about the sanctuary, harassing
them continually and giving support
19 to the heathen. So Judas planned to
destroy them, and he called all the
people together to lay siege to them.
20 And they assembled and laid siege to
it in the one hundred and fiftieth year,
and he built siege towers and engines.
21 And some of them escaped from the
blockade, and some ungodly Israelites
22 joined them, and they made their way
to the king and said,
"How long will you delay doing jus-
23 tice and avenging our brothers? We
agreed to serve your father and to conduct ourselves in accordance with his
24 orders and to follow his commands. On
account of this the sons of our people
have besieged it and become hostile to
us. Such of us as they found, they put
to death, and they have plundered our
25 property. They have stretched out
their hands not only against us but
against all the lands on their borders.
26 Here today they have encamped
against the citadel in Jerusalem to capture it, and they have fortified the
27 sanctuary and Bethsura. And unless
you act against them quickly, they will
do greater things than these, and you
will not be able to check them."
28 When the king heard this, he was
angry, and he gathered all his Friends,
the officers of his army, and those in
29 charge of the cavalry. And mercenary
forces came to him from other kingdoms and from the islands in the sea.
30 And his forces numbered a hundred
thousand infantry and twenty thousand cavalry, and thirty-two elephants
31 trained for war. And they passed
through Idumea and pitched their camp
against Bethsura and fought against it
for a long time, and built engines of
war. And they sallied out and burned
them down, and fought bravely.
32 Then Judas left the citadel and
pitched his camp at Beth-zechariah,
33 opposite the king's camp. And the
king got up early in the morning and
moved his army precipitately along the
road to Beth-zechariah, and his forces
armed themselves for battle, and
sounded the trumpets. And they showed 34
the elephants the juice of grapes and
mulberries to incite them to battle.
They distributed the animals among 35
the phalanxes and stationed with each
elephant a thousand men in chain
armor with brass helmets on their
heads, and five hundred picked horsemen were assigned to each animal.
These were posted in advance wherever 36
the animal was to be, and wherever it
went they accompanied it; they did
not leave it. There were wooden towers 37
upon them, strong and covered over,
on each animal, ingeniously fastened
on, and on each one were four powerful
men who fought on them, beside the
Indian driver. The rest of the cavalry 38
he stationed on this side and on that,
on the two wings of the army, threatening the enemy and again finding shelter
among the phalanxes. And when the 39
sun fell on the gold and brass shields,
the mountains flashed back and shone
like blazing torches. One wing of the 40
king's army spread over the high mountains, while some were on low ground,
but they advanced steadily, in good
order. And all who heard the noise of 41
their multitude and of the marching of
the multitude and the rattle of their
arms trembled, for the army was very
great and strong.
Then Judas and his army advanced 42
to battle, and six hundred men from
the king's army fell. And Eleazar Ava- 43
ran saw that one of the animals was
armed with royal armor, and stood
higher than all the other animals, and
he thought that the king was on it;
and he gave his life to save his people 44
and win everlasting renown for himself.
For he ran boldly up to it in the midst 45
of the phalanx slaying to right and left,
and they opened before him on this
side and on that, and he slipped under 46
the elephant and stabbed it underneath
and killed it, and it fell to the earth
upon him, and he died there. And when 47
they saw the strength of the kingdom
and the impetuosity of its forces, they
gave way before them.
But the men of the king's army went 48
up to Jerusalem to meet them, and the
king pitched his camp in Judea, and
opposite Mount Zion. And he made 49
peace with the men of Bethsura, and
they evacuated the town, because they
had no food there to support a siege,

50 for it was a sabbatical year. So the king
occupied Bethsura and stationed a gar-
51 rison there to hold it. And he encamped
against the sanctuary for a long time,
and set up siege towers there and war
engines and machines to throw fire and
stones, and ballistas to shoot arrows,
52 and slings. And they also built war
engines against their war engines and
53 fought for a long time. But there were
no provisions in the storerooms, because it was a sabbatical year, and
those who had taken refuge in Judea
from the heathen had consumed what
54 was left of the stores. And there were
few men left in the sanctuary, for the
famine had been too much for them,
and they had scattered, each man to his
home.

55 Then Lysias heard that Philip, whom
King Antiochus before his death had
appointed to bring up his son to be
56 king, had returned from Persia and
Media, with the forces that had gone
with the king, and that he was seeking
57 to get control of the government. So he
hastily agreed to withdraw, and he said
to the king and the officers of the army
and the men,

"We are growing weaker every day,
and our provisions are getting short and
the place we are besieging is strong,
and the affairs of the kingdom depend
58 upon us, so let us now come to terms
with these men, and make peace with
59 them and with all their nation, and
make an agreement with them that
they shall follow their own laws, as they
used to do, for it was on account of their
laws which we abolished that they became angry and did all this."

60 And the proposal pleased the king
and his officers, and he sent to them, to
61 make peace, and they agreed. And the
king and the officers made oath to
them; then they evacuated the strong-
62 hold. But when the king went into
Mount Zion and saw the strength of the
place, he broke the oath that he had
sworn, and gave orders to tear down the
63 wall that encircled it. Then he departed in haste and returned to Antioch
and found Philip in possession of the
city, and he fought against him and
took the city by force.

7 In the one hundred and fifty-first
year Demetrius, the son of Seleucus,
came out from Rome and went with a
few men to a seaside town and became
king there. And it happened when he
sought to enter the royal city of his
forefathers, that the troops seized
Antiochus and Lysias, to bring them
before him. When the matter was made
known to him, he said,

"Do not let me see their faces."

So the soldiers killed them, and 4
Demetrius took his seat upon his royal
throne. And all the lawless and un- 5
godly men of Israel came to him, and
Alcimus who wished to be high priest
was their leader. And they accused the 6
people to the king, and said,

"Judas and his brothers have destroyed all your Friends, and have
scattered us out of our land. So now 7
send a man in whom you have confidence, and let him go and see all the
damage he has done to us and to the
king's country and let him punish
them and all their helpers."

And the king chose Bacchides, one 8
of the king's Friends, who was governor
of the country beyond the river, and
was a great man in the kingdom, and
faithful to the king. And he sent him 9
and the ungodly Alcimus, and assured
him of the high priesthood, and ordered
him to take vengeance on the Israelites.
And they set forth and came with a 10
strong force to the land of Judah, and
he sent messengers to Judas and his
brothers, with a peaceful message, but
in guile. But they paid no attention to 11
their message, for they saw that they
had come with a strong force. And a 12
body of scribes gathered before Alcimus
and Bacchides, to ask for justice. The 13
foremost among the Israelites that
asked for peace from them were the
Hasideans, for they said, 14

"A priest of the blood of Aaron has
come with the forces, and he will not do
us any wrong."

And he talked peaceably with them, 15
and made oath to them, saying,

"We will not attempt to injure you
or your friends."

And they trusted him. And he ar- 16
rested sixty of them and killed them in
a single day, just as he said who wrote,

"The flesh and blood of your saints 17
they scattered
Around Jerusalem, and they had no
one to bury them."

Then the fear and dread of them fell 18
upon all the people, for they said,

"There is no truth or justice in them,

for they broke the agreement and the
oath that they swore."
19 And Bacchides left Jerusalem and
pitched his camp in Bethzaith and he
set and seized many of the deserters
that had been with him, and some of
the people, and he slaughtered them
20 and threw them into the great pit. And
he established Alcimus over the country, and left a force with him to help
him. Then Bacchides went back to the
king.
21 Alcimus strove to maintain his high
22 priesthood. And all those who harassed
their people gathered about him, and
they took possession of the land of
Judah and did great harm in Israel.
23 And Judas saw all the damage that
Alcimus and his men had done to the
Israelites, more even than the heathen
24 had, and he went out into all the outer
borders of Judea and took vengeance
on the men who had deserted him, and
kept them from going out into the coun-
25 try. But when Alcimus saw that Judas
and his men were growing strong, and
realized that he could not withstand
them, he returned to the king and made
wicked charges against them.
26 Then the king sent Nicanor, one of
his distinguished officers, who hated
Israel bitterly, and ordered him to de-
27 stroy the people. And Nicanor went to
Jerusalem with a strong force, and he
deceitfully sent a peaceful message to
Judas and his brothers, saying,
28 "Let us have no battle between me
and you. I will come with a few men
to have a peaceable personal meeting."
29 So he came to Judas, and they
greeted one another peaceably. But
the enemy were ready to kidnap Judas.
30 And the fact that he had come to him
in deceit became known to Judas, and
he was very much afraid of him and
31 would not meet him again. And Nicanor knew that his plan had been discovered, and he went out to meet
32 Judas in battle at Caphar-salama, and
about five hundred of Nicanor's men
fell, and they fled to the City of David.
33 After this, Nicanor went up to Mount
Zion, and some of the priests came out
of the sanctuary with some of the
elders of the people to greet him peaceably, and show him the whole burnt
offering that was being offered for the
34 king. And he jeered at them and
laughed at them and polluted them,
and spoke arrogantly and swore angrily, 35
"If Judas and his army are not immediately delivered into my hands, it
will happen that if I return safely, I
will burn this house up!"
And he went away in great anger.
And the priests went in and stood be- 36
fore the altar and the sanctuary and
they wailed and said,
"You chose this house to bear your 37
name, to be a house for prayer and
petition for your people. Take venge- 38
ance on this man and on his army, and
let them fall by the sword. Remember
their sacrilegious words and let them
not continue."
And Nicanor set out from Jerusalem 39
and pitched his camp in Bethhoron, and
the Syrian army met him there. And
Judas encamped in Adasa with three 40
thousand men, and Judas prayed and
said,
"When the king's men uttered 41
blasphemy, your angel went forth and
struck down a hundred and eighty-five
thousand of them. Crush this army be- 42
fore us today, in the same way, and let
the rest know that he spoke wickedly
against your sanctuary, and judge him
as his wickedness deserves."
And the armies met in battle on the 43
thirteenth of the month of Adar, and
Nicanor's army was beaten, and he
himself was the first to fall in the battle.
But when his army saw that Nicanor 44
had fallen, they threw down their arms
and fled. And they pursued them a 45
day's journey, from Adasa until you
come to Gazara, and they sounded
the ceremonial trumpets behind them.
And people came forth out of all the 46
villages of Judea around, and hemmed
them in, and turned them back toward
the pursuers, and they all fell by the
sword; not one of them was left. And 47
they took the spoils and the plunder,
and they cut off Nicanor's head and his
right hand, which he had stretched out
so arrogantly, and brought them and
displayed them at Jerusalem. And the 48
people rejoiced greatly, and they observed that day as a day of great gladness. And they decreed that that day 49
should be annually observed, on the
thirteenth of Adar. Then the land of 50
Judah was quiet for a short time.
And Judas heard of the reputation of 8
the Romans, that they were powerful,
and favored all who joined them, and

established friendly relations with those
who approached them, and were power-
2 ful. And they told him about their wars
and the exploits they had performed
among the Gauls, and how they had
subdued them and made them pay
3 tribute, and what they had done in the
land of Spain, in getting possession of
4 the silver and gold mines there, and
how by their planning and patience
they had become masters of that whole
region, though it was very far away
from them, and about the kings who
had come against them from the ends
of the earth, until they had crushed
them and inflicted great losses upon
them, and how the rest paid them
5 tribute every year; and how they had
crushed Philip and Perseus, the king of
Chittim, and those who had opposed
them they had beaten in battle and
6 subdued; and how Antiochus, the great
king of Asia, had marched against them
with a hundred and twenty elephants
and horses and chariots and a very
great force, and had been beaten by
7 them, and they had captured him alive
and had required him and those who
succeeded him to pay a great tribute
8 and give hostages, and a section of
country, in India, Media, and Lydia,
of the best lands, and they had taken
them from him and given them to King
9 Eumenes; and how the men of Greece
had planned to come and destroy them,
10 and they had learned of the matter, and
they sent one general against them, and
they fought with them and many of
them fell wounded, and they took their
wives and children captive and they
plundered them and conquered the
land and tore down their strongholds
11 and enslaved them unto this day; and
how they had destroyed and enslaved
all the other kingdoms and islands that
12 had ever opposed them, but had maintained friendly relations with their
friends and those who relied upon them;
and how they had conquered kings far
and near, and all who heard their name
13 were afraid of them. Those whom they
wished to help and make kings, became
kings, and those whom they wished,
they deposed; and they were greatly
14 exalted. Yet with all this they never
any of them put on a diadem, or wore
purple, as a mark of magnificence.
15 And they had built themselves a senate
house, and every day three hundred
and twenty men deliberated, constantly
planning for the people, that they might
conduct themselves properly, and they 16
intrusted the government to one man
every year, and the authority over all
their country, and they all obeyed that
one man, and there was no envy or
jealousy among them.

And Judas chose Eupolemus, the 17
son of John, the son of Hakkoz, and
Jason, the son of Eleazar, and sent
them to Rome, to establish friendly
relations and an alliance with them,
so that they might relieve them of their 18
yoke, for they saw that the rule of the
Greeks was reducing Israel to slavery.
And they went to Rome, though the 19
journey was very long, and they went
into the senate house and answered and
said,

"Judas, who is called Maccabeus, 20
and his brothers and the Jewish people
have sent us to you, to make an alliance
and firm peace with you, and that we
may be enrolled as allies and friends of
yours."

They were pleased with the proposal, 21
and this is a copy of the letter which 22
they wrote in answer, on brass tablets,
and sent to Jerusalem, to remain there
among them, as a memorial of peace
and alliance.

"Good fortune to the Romans and 23
to the Jewish nation by sea and land,
forever! May sword and foe be far
from them! But if war is made on 24
Rome first, or on any of their allies,
in all her dominion, the Jewish nation 25
will act as their allies, as the occasion
shall demand of them, with all their
hearts. And to those who make the 26
war they shall not give or supply wheat,
arms, money, or ships, as Rome decides,
and they shall observe their obligations,
accepting nothing from the other side.
In like manner, if war is made on the 27
Jewish nation first, the Romans will
heartily act as their allies as occasion
demands, and no wheat, arms, money, 28
or ships will be supplied to the allies,
as Rome decides, and they shall observe
these obligations in good faith. On 29
these terms the Romans have made a
treaty with the Jewish people. But if 30
hereafter one party or the other decides
to add or subtract anything, they shall
do as they choose, and whatever they
add or subtract shall be valid. And 31
about the wrongs that King Demetrius

is doing you, we have written to him,
saying, 'Why have you made your yoke
heavy upon our friends and allies the
32 Jews? So if they appeal to us against
you again, we will do them justice and
make war upon you by land and sea.' "
9 When Demetrius heard that Nicanor
and his troops had fallen in battle, he
sent Bacchides and Alcimus into the
land of Judah again a second time,
2 with the right wing of his army. And
they marched by the Gilgal road, and
pitched their camp against Mesaloth, in
Arbela, and took it, and destroyed
3 many people. And in the first month of
the one hundred and fifty-second year
they encamped against Jerusalem.
4 Then they set out and marched to
Berea with twenty thousand men and
5 two thousand horse. And Judas was
encamped at Elasa, and had three
6 thousand picked men with him. And
they saw that the number of the troops
was great and they were greatly terrified, and many slipped out of the camp;
not more than eight hundred men were
7 left. And Judas saw that his army had
slipped away, and that the battle
was imminent, and he was troubled in
mind, for he had no time to rally them.
8 And in desperation he said to those who
were left,
"Let us get up and go against our
opponents; perhaps we can fight against
them."
9 And they tried to dissuade him, saying,
"We certainly cannot; but let us
save our lives now, and come back with
our brothers and fight against them;
we are so few."
10 And Judas said,
"I will never do this thing, and flee
from them; and if our time has come,
let us die bravely for our brothers, and
not leave a stain upon our honor."
11 So the army set out from the camp
and formed its lines to join battle, and
the cavalry was divided into two parts,
and the slingers and archers marched
before the army, and all the powerful
12 men who formed the front line. But
Bacchides was on the right wing. And
the phalanx advanced on the two sides,
13 and they sounded their trumpets, and
Judas' men also sounded their trumpets, and the earth shook with the
shout of the armies, and the battle
14 raged from morning till evening. And
when Judas saw that Bacchides and the
strength of his army were on the right
wing, all the stout-hearted went with
him, and the right wing was beaten 15
back by them, and he pursued them as
far as Mount Azotus. And the men on 16
the left wing saw that the right wing was
beaten back, and they turned and followed the track of Judas and his men
from behind. And the fight became 17
desperate, and many on both sides fell
wounded. And Judas fell and the rest 18
fled. And Jonathan and Simon took 19
their brother Judas and buried him in
the tombs of his forefathers in Modin.
And they wept over him, and all Israel 20
lamented him greatly and mourned for
a long time, saying,
"What a hero is fallen, the Savior of 21
Israel!"
The rest of the deeds of Judas, and 22
his wars, and the exploits that he performed, and his greatness are un-
recorded, for they were very many.
It happened after the death of Judas 23
that those who had no regard for the
Law raised their heads all over Israel,
and all the wrongdoers reappeared. In 24
those days there was a very great
famine, and the country went over to
their side. And Bacchides chose the un- 25
godly men and appointed them masters
of the country. And they searched and 26
sought out the friends of Judas and
brought them to Bacchides, and he
punished them and mocked them. And 27
there was great distress in Israel, such
as there had not been since the time
when the prophets ceased to appear to
them. And all the friends of Judas 28
gathered together and said to Jonathan,
"Since the death of your brother 29
Judas, there has been no one like him
to go in and out against our enemies and
Bacchides and among those of our nation who are hostile. So now we have 30
chosen you today to be our ruler and
leader in his place, to carry on our war."
And Jonathan accepted the com- 31
mand at that time, and took the place
of his brother Judas.
And Bacchides learned of this, and 32
tried to kill him. And Jonathan and his 33
brother Simon and all his men learned
of it, and they fled into the wild country
about Tekoa, and they pitched their
camp by the waters of the pool of
Asphar. And Bacchides learned of it on 34

the sabbath, and he and all his army
came across the Jordan.
35 Now Jonathan had sent his brother,
a leader of the multitude, and entreated
the Nabateans, as his friends,
to let them leave with them their baggage,
of which there was a great deal.
36 But the sons of Jambri, from Medaba,
came out and seized John and all that
37 he had, and went off with it. Afterward,
news came to Jonathan and his
brother Simon that the sons of Jambri
were making a great wedding, and were
conducting the bride, the daughter of
one of the great nobles of Canaan, with
38 a great retinue, from Nadabath. And
they remembered the blood of their
brother John, and they went up and
hid under the shelter of the mountain.
39 And they looked up and saw, and there
was confusion, and a great deal of baggage,
for the bridegroom had come out
with his friends and his kinsmen to
meet them, with drums and musicians
40 and many weapons. Then they fell
upon them from their ambush and
killed them, and many fell wounded,
and the survivors fled into the moun-
41 tain, and they took all their spoils. So
the wedding was turned into grief and
the voice of their musicians into lamen-
42 tation. And when they had fully
avenged their brother's blood, they
turned back to the marshes of the
Jordan.
43 And Bacchides heard of it, and he
came on the sabbath to the banks of the
44 Jordan, with a strong force. And Jonathan
said to his men,
"Let us get up now and fight for our
lives, for today is not like yesterday or
45 the day before, for here is the battle in
front of us and behind us, and on one
side the water of the Jordan, and on the
other marsh and thicket, and there is
46 no room to retreat. So now, cry out to
heaven that you may be delivered from
the hands of our enemies."
47 And the battle was joined, and
Jonathan stretched out his hand to
strike Bacchides down, and he gave
48 ground before him. Then Jonathan and
his men jumped into the Jordan and
swam over to the other side; and they
did not cross the Jordan in pursuit of
49 them. And fully a thousand of Bacchides'
men fell that day.
50 And he returned to Jerusalem, and
they built fortified towns in Judea; the
stronghold in Jericho, and Emmaus,
and Bethhoron, and Bethel, and Timnath
Pharathon, and Tephon, with
high walls and barred gates; and he put 51
garrisons in them to harass Israel. And 52
he fortified the town of Bethsura, and
Gazara, and the citadel, and he put
troops in them, and stores of provisions.
And he took the sons of the 53
principal men of the country as hostages,
and put them in custody in the
citadel at Jerusalem.
In the one hundred and fifty-third 54
year, in the second month, Alcimus
gave orders to tear down the wall of the
inner court of the sanctuary; he thus
destroyed the work of the prophets,
but he began to tear it down. At that 55
very time, Alcimus was stricken, and
his work hindered and his mouth
stopped, and he was paralyzed and
could no longer utter a word, or give
orders about his household. So Alcimus 56
died at that time, in great agony. And 57
when Bacchides saw that Alcimus was
dead, he went back to the king, and the
land of Judah was quiet for two years.
Then all those who disregarded the 58
Law plotted, saying,
"Here Jonathan and his men are living
undisturbed and secure, so now we
will bring Bacchides back, and he will
arrest them all in a single night."
And they went and consulted him. 59
And he set out and came with a strong 60
force and he sent letters secretly to all
his allies in Judea to arrest Jonathan
and his men, but they could not because
their plan became known to
them. And they seized fully fifty of the 61
men of the country who were ringleaders
in this wickedness, and killed
them. And Jonathan and Simon and 62
their men withdrew to Bethbasi, in the
wild country, and he rebuilt the parts
that had been torn down, and they
strengthened it. And Bacchides learned 63
of it, and he gathered all his host and
sent word to the men of Judea, and he 64
came and pitched his camp against
Bethbasi, and fought against it for a
long time and set up siege engines.
Then Jonathan left his brother 65
Simon in the town and went out into
the country, and he went with a small
force. And he struck down Odomera 66
and his brothers, and the sons of
Phasiron in their tent, and they began 67
to strike and attacked with their forces.

And Simon and his men went out of the
town and set fire to the siege engines,
68 and they fought with Bacchides, and he
was beaten by them, and they pressed
him very hard, for his plan and his
69 attack were in vain. And he was very
angry with the men who disregarded
the Law who had advised him to come
into the country, and he killed many of
them, and resolved to go back to his
70 country. And Jonathan learned of it,
and he sent envoys to him to make
peace with him, and obtain the release
71 of his prisoners. And he agreed and
did as he promised and made oath to
him that he would not seek to injure
72 him so long as he lived. And he released to him the prisoners that he had
taken before from the land of Judea, and
he went away and returned to his own
country, and did not come into their
73 borders again. So the sword ceased in
Israel. And Jonathan lived in Michmash. And Jonathan began to judge
the people, and he destroyed the ungodly out of Israel.

0 In the one hundred and sixtieth year,
Alexander Epiphanes, the son of Antiochus, went up and took possession of
Ptolemais, and they welcomed him, and
2 he became king there. When King Demetrius heard of it, he mustered very
strong forces and went out to meet him
in battle.

3 And Demetrius sent letters to Jonathan in peaceful terms to flatter him,
4 for he said to himself,

"Let us be the first to make peace
with them, before he makes peace with
5 Alexander against us, for he will remember all the wrongs we have done
him and his brothers and his nation."

6 And he gave him authority to
muster troops, and to procure arms
and to be his ally, and he gave orders
that they should turn over to him the
7 hostages that were in the citadel. So
Jonathan went up to Jerusalem, and
read the letters in the hearing of all
the people, and of the men who were in
8 possession of the citadel; and they were
dreadfully frightened when they heard
that the king had given him author-
9 ity to muster troops. And the men in
the citadel turned over the hostages to
Jonathan, and he gave them back to
10 their parents. And Jonathan lived in
Jerusalem, and he began to build and
11 renovate the city. And he ordered those
who did the work to build the walls and
encircle Mount Zion with four-foot
stones for its fortification, and they did
so. And the foreigners who were in the 12
strongholds that Bacchides had built
fled; each one left his post and went 13
back to his own country, except that in 14
Bethsura there were left some of those
who had forsaken the Law and the
commandments, for it served as a
refuge for them.

And King Alexander heard of all the 15
promises that Demetrius had sent to
Jonathan, and they related to him the
battles and exploits that he and his
brothers had performed, and the troubles they had endured, and he said to 16
himself,

"Can we find another man like him?
Now we must make him our friend and
ally."

So he wrote letters and sent them to 17
him, in the following terms:

"King Alexander sends greetings to 18
his brother Jonathan. We have heard 19
that you are a valiant warrior, and fit
to be our friend. Now we have today 20
appointed you to be high priest of your
nation and to be called a Friend of the
king" (and he sent him a purple robe
and a gold crown) "and to side with us
and maintain friendly relations with
us."

So Jonathan put on the holy vest- 21
ments in the seventh month of the one
hundred and sixtieth year, at the
Camping Out festival, and he mustered troops and provided arms in
abundance.

And Demetrius heard of these things, 22
and he was annoyed, and said,

"Why have we brought it about that 23
Alexander has gotten ahead of us in
establishing friendly relations with the
Jews, to strengthen his position? I too 24
will write them a message of encouragement and distinction, with promises of
gifts, so that they may become a support for me."

So he sent one to them in these 25
terms:

"King Demetrius sends greetings to
the Jewish nation. Since you have kept 26
your agreement with us, and remained
true to our friendship, and have not
gone over to our enemies, we have rejoiced to hear of it. So now continue to 27
keep faith with us, and we will deal
favorably with you in return for your

28 dealings with us, and we will grant you
many exemptions and make you pres-
29 ents. So I do now free you and I release
all the Jews from paying tribute and
from the salt tax and the crown tax.
30 And instead of one-third of the grain and
instead of half of the fruit of the trees,
which it falls to me to receive, I surrender from this day forward the right
to take them from the land of Judea
and from the three districts which are
attached to it from Samaria and
Galilee, from this day forth and for all
31 time. Let Jerusalem and her territory,
her tithes and her taxes, be holy and
32 free. I relinquish also my authority
over the citadel in Jerusalem, and I give
it to the high priest, in order that he
may put men whom he shall choose in
33 possession of it, to garrison it. And
every Jewish person who has been
carried into captivity from the land of
Judea into any part of my kingdom, I
set at liberty without payment, and let
all officials cancel the taxes upon their
34 cattle also. And let all the festivals and
sabbaths and new moons and appointed
days, and three days before each festival, and three days after each festival,
be days of exemption and immunity for
35 all the Jews in my kingdom, and no one
shall have authority to exact anything
from any of them or to trouble any of
36 them about any matter. And among
the king's forces at least thirty thousand Jews shall be enrolled, and they
shall receive pay, as all the king's forces
37 have a right to do. And some of them
shall be stationed in the king's great
strongholds, and some shall be put in
positions of trust in the kingdom. And
those who are set over them and those
who govern them shall be of their own
number, and they shall follow their
own laws, as the king has commanded
38 in the land of Judea. And the three districts that have been added to Judea
from the country of Samaria shall be
added to Judea so that they may be
considered as under one man, and not
obey any other authority than the
39 high priest. Ptolemais and the land pertaining to it I have presented to the
sanctuary in Jerusalem, for the ex-
40 penses incident to the sanctuary. And
I will give fifteen thousand silver
shekels every year, from the king's
revenues, from such places as are con-
41 venient. And the additional grant,
which the administration has not paid
over as it formerly did, they shall henceforth pay in full toward the service of
the temple. In addition, the five thou- 42
sand silver shekels which they used to
take out of the dues of the temple, from
the revenue every year, is also canceled,
for it rightfully belongs to the priests
who conduct the worship. And who- 43
ever takes refuge in the temple at Jerusalem, and in any of its precincts, who
owes money to the king or any other
obligation shall be released from it, with
all his property in my realm. The cost 44
of rebuilding and renovating the fabric
of the sanctuary shall be provided out
of the king's revenue. The cost of re- 45
building the walls of Jerusalem and of
fortifying it all around, and of building
the walls in Judea, shall also be provided out of the king's revenue."

But when Jonathan and the people 46
heard these terms, they did not believe
them or accept them, for they remembered the great injury he had done
to Israel, and that he had distressed
them intensely. And they took Alex- 47
ander's side, for he had been first in
addressing them in peaceful terms, and
they always remained his allies.

Then King Alexander gathered large 48
forces and pitched his camp against
Demetrius. And the two kings joined 49
battle, and the army of Demetrius fled,
and Alexander pursued him and defeated them, and he pressed the fighting 50
hard, until sunset, and Demetrius fell
that day.

Then Alexander sent envoys to 51
Ptolemy, king of Egypt, with this
message:

"Since I have returned to my king- 52
dom, and have taken my seat on the
throne of my forefathers, and have
taken over the government, and have
defeated Demetrius and taken possession of our country—for I have met 53
him in battle, and he and his army were
defeated by us, and we have taken our
seat on the throne of his kingdom—
let us now establish friendly relations 54
with one another, so give me your
daughter to be my wife, and I will be
your son-in-law, and give you and her
gifts worthy of you."

And King Ptolemy answered, 55
"It was a happy day when you returned to the country of your forefathers and took your seat on the

5 throne of their kingdom. I will now do
for you what you wrote, but meet me
in Ptolemais, so that we may see each
other, and I will be your father-in-law,
as you have said."
7 So Ptolemy came up from Egypt,
with his daughter Cleopatra, and
reached Ptolemais in the one hundred
8 and sixty-second year. And King Alexander met him, and he gave him his
daughter Cleopatra in marriage, and he
celebrated her wedding at Ptolemais
with great pomp, as kings do.
9 Then King Alexander wrote to
0 Jonathan to come to meet him. And he
went in splendor to Ptolemais and met
the two kings, and gave them and their
Friends silver and gold and many gifts,
1 and was well received by them. Some
malcontents from Israel, who disregarded the Law, gathered against him,
to lay charges against him, but the king
2 paid no attention to them. And the
king gave orders, and they took Jonathan's clothes off and clothed him in
3 purple; they did as he ordered. And the
king made him sit beside him, and said
to his officers,
"Go out with him into the middle of
the city, and make a proclamation that
no one is to appeal against him on any
ground, and no one must interfere with
him on any account."
4 So it happened that when those who
were complaining of him saw the distinction with which he was treated, as
the herald proclaimed, and saw him
5 clothed in purple, they all fled. And the
king treated him with distinction, and
enrolled him among his Best Friends,
and made him general and governor.
6 So Jonathan returned to Jerusalem in
peace and gladness.
7 In the one hundred and sixty-fifth
year, Demetrius' son Demetrius came
from Crete to the country of his fore-
8 fathers. When King Alexander heard
of it, he was greatly disturbed and re-
9 turned to Antioch. And Demetrius appointed Apollonius who was in command of Coelesyria, and he gathered a
strong force and pitched his camp at
Jamnia, and sent to Jonathan the high
priest saying,
0 "You are all alone in resisting us, but
I am laughed at and reproached because of you. Why do you claim your
authority against us up in the moun-
1 tains? If you really trust in your
troops, come down into the plain to us
and let us measure our strength together there, for I have control of the
towns. So inquire and find out who I 72
am, and who the others are who help
us, and they will tell you that you will
have no foothold before us, for your
forefathers have been routed twice in
their land. So now you will not be able 73
to stand against the cavalry and such
a force as this on the plain, where there
is no stone or pebble, or place to escape
to."
When Jonathan heard the message of 74
Apollonius, his heart was stirred, and he
chose ten thousand men, and set out
from Jerusalem, and his brother Simon
joined him to help him. And he pitched 75
his camp against Joppa, and the men
of the town shut him out, for Apollonius had a garrison in Joppa; and they 76
fought against it. Then the men of the
town were frightened and they opened
the gates, and Jonathan took possession
of Joppa. And Apollonius heard of it, 77
and he mustered three thousand horsemen and a strong force and he marched
to Ashdod as though he meant to travel
on, but at the same time he advanced
into the plain, because he had a large
force of cavalry and relied upon it. And 78
he pursued him to Ashdod, and the
armies joined battle. And Apollonius 79
had left a thousand horse in hiding in
their rear, and Jonathan learned that 80
there was an ambuscade in his rear.
And they surrounded his army and
showered their arrows upon the people
from morning till evening, but the 81
people stood fast, as Jonathan had
ordered, while the enemy's horses were
tired out. Then Simon advanced his 82
force and joined battle with the phalanx, for the cavalry were exhausted,
and they were defeated by him, and
fled, and the cavalry were scattered 83
over the plain. And they fled to Ashdod and took refuge in Beth-dagon, their
idol's temple. And Jonathan burned 84
Ashdod and the towns around it, and
plundered them, and he burned up the
temple of Dagon and those who had
taken refuge in it. And those who had 85
fallen by the sword, together with those
who were burned up came to fully eight
thousand men. And Jonathan set forth 86
and pitched his camp against Askelon
and the men of the town came out
to meet him with great pomp. Then 87

Jonathan returned to Jerusalem with
his men, with a great quantity of
88 plunder. And it happened that, when
King Alexander heard of these things,
he treated Jonathan with still more dis-
89 tinction, and he sent him a gold buckle,
such as are usually given to the members of the royal family; and he gave
him Ekron and all that district for
settlement.

11 And the king of Egypt gathered
strong forces, like the sand on the seashore, and many ships, and undertook
to possess himself of Alexander's kingdom by deceit, and to add it to his own
2 kingdom. And he set out for Syria with
peaceful professions, and the people of
the towns opened their gates to him,
and met him, for King Alexander had
ordered them to meet him, as he was
3 his father-in-law. But when Ptolemy
entered the towns, he placed a garrison
4 of his troops in each town. And when
they reached Ashdod, they showed him
the temple of Dagon burned, and Ashdod and its suburbs torn down and
corpses lying about, and those who had
been burned, whom he had burned in
the war, for they had piled them in heaps
5 in his way. And they told the king
what Jonathan had done, in order to
throw blame on him, and the king was
6 silent. And Jonathan met the king with
pomp at Joppa, and they greeted one
another and spent the night there.
7 And Jonathan traveled with the king
as far as the river called the Eleutherus,
8 and then returned to Jerusalem. But
Ptolemy made himself master of the
coast towns all the way to Seleucia
which is by the sea, and formed wicked
9 designs about Alexander. And he sent
envoys to King Demetrius, saying,
"Come, let us make an agreement
with each other, and I will give you my
daughter, whom Alexander had, and
you shall reign over your father's king-
10 dom. For I regret having given him
my daughter, for he has undertaken to
kill me."
11 But he threw blame on him because
12 he coveted his kingdom. So he took his
daughter away from him, and gave her
to Demetrius, and was estranged from
Alexander, and their enmity became
13 manifest. And Ptolemy entered Antioch, and assumed the diadem of Asia,
so he put two diadems upon his head,
that of Egypt and that of Asia.

But King Alexander was in Cilicia, 1
at that time, for the people of those
regions were in revolt. When Alexander 1
heard of it, he marched against him.
And Ptolemy led out his army and met
him with a strong force, and routed
him. And Alexander fled to Arabia to 1
find shelter, but King Ptolemy was
triumphant. And Zabdiel the Arab cut 1
off Alexander's head and sent it to
Ptolemy. Three days later King Ptol- 1
emy died, and his men in the strongholds were destroyed by the men of the
strongholds. And in the one hundred 1
and sixty-seventh year, Demetrius became king.
In those days Jonathan mustered the 2
men of Judea to attack the citadel, and
he set up many siege engines against it.
And some breakers of the Law, who 2
hated their own nation, went to the
king and reported to him that Jonathan
was besieging the citadel. When he 2
heard of it, he was angry, but upon
hearing it he immediately set out and
came to Ptolemais, and wrote Jonathan
not to continue the siege but to meet
him as soon as possible at Ptolemais,
for a conference. When Jonathan heard 2
this, he gave orders to continue the
siege, and he selected some of the
elders of Israel and of the priests and
put himself in danger, for he took silver 2
and gold and clothing and a great many
other presents, and went to the king,
at Ptolemais, and he pleased the king.
And when some of the men of his nation 2
who disregarded the Law complained
of him, the king treated him just as his 2
predecessors had done, and showed him
great honor in the presence of all his
Friends. He confirmed him in the high 2
priesthood, and all the other honors he
had received before, and made him
chief of his Best Friends. Jonathan 2
asked the king to free Judea and the
three provinces and Samaria from
tribute, and promised him three hundred talents. The king agreed, and 2
wrote a letter to Jonathan on all these
matters as follows:
"King Demetrius sends greetings to 3
his brother Jonathan and to the Jewish
nation. This copy of the letter which 3
we have written to Lasthenes our kinsman, we have written to you also, so
that you may be acquainted with it.
'King Demetrius sends greeting to his 3
father Lasthenes. We have determined 3

to favor the Jewish nation, who are
friends of ours, and observe their obligations to us, because of the good will
34 they have shown us. So we have recognized as theirs the territory of Judea
and the three districts of Aphaerema,
Lydda, and Ramathaim (they were
transferred from Samaria to Judea) and
everything pertaining to them, for all
those who offer sacrifice in Jerusalem,
instead of the royal dues which the
king formerly took from them annually
from the produce of the land and the
35 fruit of the trees. And the other things
that fall to us, of the tithes and dues
that fall to us, and the salt pits and the
crown tax that fall to us, all these we
will from henceforth make over to them.
36 And not one of these things shall be
annulled from this time forth forever.
37 So now take care to make a copy of
this, and have it given to Jonathan
and set up in a prominent place on
the holy mount.' "
38 And King Demetrius saw that the
country was quiet before him, and that
there was no opposition to him, and he
dismissed all his troops, every man to
his home, except the foreign forces that
he had hired from the islands of the
heathen, so the old soldiers of his
39 fathers had a grudge against him. Now
Trypho was one of Alexander's old
party, and when he saw that all the
troops were grumbling at Demetrius,
he went to Imalkue the Arab who was
bringing up Antiochus, the little son
40 of Alexander, and he insisted that he
should turn him over to him, to become
king in his father's place. And he reported to him all that Demetrius had
done, and told him of the animosity his
troops felt for him; and he stayed
with him a long time.
41 Then Jonathan sent to King Demetrius asking him to expel the garrison of the citadel from Jerusalem, and
the garrisons from the strongholds, for
42 they kept fighting against Israel. And
Demetrius sent to Jonathan and said,
"I will not only do this for you and
your nation, but I will greatly honor
you and your nation if I find an op-
43 portunity. So now please send me men
who will fight for me, for all my troops
are in revolt."
44 So Jonathan sent three thousand
able-bodied men to Antioch, and they
came to the king, and he was glad they
had come. And the people of the city, 45
fully a hundred and twenty thousand
of them, gathered in the midst of the
city, and wanted to kill the king. And 46
the king fled to the palace, and the
people of the city seized the thoroughfares of the city, and began to fight.
Then the king summoned the Jews to 47
his aid, and they all together rallied
about him, and scattered over the city
and killed that day fully a hundred
thousand people. And they set the city 48
on fire, and took a great quantity of
spoil that day, and saved the king.
When the people of the city saw that 49
the Jews controlled the city as they
pleased, their hearts failed them, and
they cried out to the king in entreaty,
saying,
"Give us your pledge and make the 50
Jews stop fighting against us and the
city."
And they threw down their arms and 51
made peace. And the Jews were in high
honor with the king, and with all his
subjects, and they returned to Jerusalem with a great quantity of spoil. And 52
King Demetrius sat on his royal throne,
and the land was quiet before him. But 53
he lied in all that he had said, and became estranged from Jonathan and did
not return the favors he had done him,
but treated him very harshly.
Now after this Trypho returned, 54
bringing with him the little child
Antiochus. And he became king and
assumed the diadem. And all the troops 55
that Demetrius had cast off rallied
about him, and they fought against
Demetrius and he was routed, and fled.
And Trypho took the animals and took 56
possession of Antioch. And the youth- 57
ful Antiochus wrote to Jonathan, saying,
"I confirm you in the high priesthood
and appoint you over the four districts,
and to be one of the king's Friends."
And he sent him gold plate and 58
table service, and gave him the right
to drink from gold goblets, and dress in
purple and wear a gold buckle. And he 59
made his brother Simon governor from
the Ladder of Tyre to the frontier of
Egypt. And Jonathan set out and 60
traveled across the river and among the
towns, and the whole army of Syria
rallied about him, to ally themselves with
him. And he went to Askelon, and the 61
people of the town received him with

honor. And he went from there to
Gaza, but the people of Gaza shut their
gates against him, so he laid siege to it,
and fired its suburbs and plundered
62 them. Then the people of Gaza asked
for terms, and he gave them his pledge
and took the sons of their leaders as
hostages, and sent them to Jerusalem;
and he went through the country as far
as Damascus.
63 And Jonathan heard that the officers
of Demetrius were at Kadesh in Galilee,
with a strong force, wishing to remove
64 him from his office, so he went to meet
them, but he left his brother Simon in
65 the country. And Simon pitched his
camp against Bethsura, and fought
against it a long time, and shut it in.
66 And they asked him to give them
pledges and he did so; and he put them
out of it and took possession of the
town and put a garrison in it.
67 And Jonathan and his army pitched
their camp by the water of Gennesaret,
and early in the morning they went to
the Plain of Hazor. And, behold, the
army of the foreigners met him in the
68 plain; they had set an ambush for him
in the mountains, but they themselves
69 met him face to face. But the ambush
rose out of their places and joined battle, and all who were on Jonathan's side
70 fled; not one was left of them except
Mattathias, the son of Absalom, and
Judas, the son of Chalphi, who were
71 captains of the forces. And Jonathan
tore open his clothes and threw dust on
72 his head and prayed. And he turned
against them again in battle and routed
73 them, and they fled. Those who were
fleeing on his side saw it and returned
to him and pursued them with him as
far as Kadesh all the way to their
camp, and they pitched their camp
74 there. And there fell of the foreigners
that day fully three thousand men.
And Jonathan returned to Jerusalem.

12 And Jonathan saw that the time was
favorable, and he selected men and sent
them to Rome to confirm and renew
2 friendly relations with them. And he
sent letters to the Spartans and to other
3 places to the same effect. And they
went to Rome and went into the senate
house and said,
"Jonathan the high priest and the
Jewish people have sent us to renew
friendly relations and alliance on their
behalf, as they have been heretofore."

And they delivered to them in each
place letters addressed to them, asking
them to see them off for the land of
Judah in peace.
This is the copy of the letter that
Jonathan wrote to the Spartans:
"Jonathan, the high priest, and the
council of the nation and the priests
and the rest of the Jewish people send
greeting to their brothers the Spartans.
In former times a letter was sent to the
high priest Onias from Arius who was
then king among you, to say that you
are our kinsmen, as the copy of it that
is appended to this shows. And Onias
showed honor to the man who was sent
to him, and accepted the letter, which
contained a declaration of alliance and
friendliness. So, though we are in no
need of these, since we find our encouragement in the sacred books that
are in our keeping, we have undertaken
to send to renew relations of brotherhood and friendliness with you, so that
we may not become entirely estranged
from you, for it is a long time since you
sent to us. So we on every occasion un-
remittingly at our festivals and on other
appropriate days remember you at the
sacrifices that we offer and in our
prayers, as it is right and proper to
remember kinsmen. We rejoice in your
renown. But many hardships and wars 1
have beset us, and the kings around us
have made war on us. We have not
wished to trouble you or our other allies
and friends about these wars, for we
have the help that comes from heaven
to aid us, and we have been saved from
our enemies, and our enemies have been
humbled. So we have chosen Numenius, the son of Antiochus, and Antipater, the son of Jason, and have sent
them to the Romans to renew our
former relations of friendliness and alliance with them. So we have instructed them to go to you also and
greet you, and to deliver to you our
letter about the renewal of our fraternal
relations. Now please reply to us about 1
this."
And this is the copy of the letter 1
which they had sent to Onias:
"Arius, king of the Spartans, sends 2
greetings to Onias, the chief priest. It 2
has been found in a writing concerning
the Spartans and Jews, that they are
kinsmen, and that they are descended
from Abraham. Now since we have 2

learned this, please write us about your
3 welfare. We for our part write you that
your cattle and property are ours and
ours are yours. So we command them
to report to you to this effect."
4 And Jonathan heard that Demetrius'
officers had returned with a stronger
force than before to make war on him.
5 And he set out from Jerusalem and met
them in the country of Hamath, for he
did not give them time to make their
6 way into his own country. And he sent
spies into their camp and they came
back and reported to him that they
were forming in a certain way so as to
7 fall upon him that night. But when the
sun set, Jonathan ordered his men to
be on the watch and to remain under
arms so as to be ready for battle all
night long, and he stationed outposts
8 around the camp. And his adversaries
heard that Jonathan and his men were
ready for battle, and they were frightened and were terrified at heart, and
9 they lighted fires in their camp. But
Jonathan and his men did not know of
it until morning, for they saw the fires
0 burning. Then Jonathan pursued them,
but he could not overtake them, for
they had crossed the river Eleutherus.
1 So Jonathan turned aside against the
Arabs who are called Zabadeans, and
he defeated them and plundered them.
2 And he set forth and went to Damascus,
and traveled all through the country.
3 And Simon set out and made his way
to Askelon, and the strongholds near
it, and he turned aside to Joppa and
4 took it by surprise, for he had heard
that they wanted to turn over the
stronghold to Demetrius' men, and he
stationed a garrison there to hold it.
5 When Jonathan returned, he called
together the elders of the people, and
planned with them to build strong-
6 holds in Judea, and to increase the
height of the walls of Jerusalem, and to
build a great mound between the citadel
and the city, to separate it from the
city, so that it might be by itself, so
that they could not buy or sell in it.
7 So they gathered together to build up
the city, and part of the east wall by
the ravine collapsed, and he replaced it
8 with the so-called Chaphenatha. And
Simon built Adida in the lowlands and
he fortified it and fitted it with barred
gates.
9 And Trypho undertook to become
king of Asia and assume the diadem,
and to raise his hand against King
Antiochus. But he was afraid that 40
Jonathan would not permit him to, but
would fight against him, so he undertook to seize him, in order to destroy
him. And he set out and came to
Bethshean. And Jonathan went out to 41
meet him with forty thousand picked
fighting men, and came to Bethshean.
And Trypho saw that he had come with 42
a strong force, and he was afraid to
raise his hand against him, so he re- 43
ceived him with honor, and he introduced him to all his Friends, and gave
him presents, and instructed his Friends
and his forces to obey him as they
would himself. And he said to Jona- 44
than,
"Why have you burdened all these
people, when there is no war between
us? Come, send them home, and choose 45
yourself a few men to remain with you,
and come with me to Ptolemais and I
will turn it over to you, together with
the rest of the strongholds and the rest
of the forces and all the officials, and I
will go back again, for it was for this
that I came."
And he trusted him and did as he 46
said and dismissed his forces, and they
returned to the land of Judah. He left 47
himself three thousand men, two thousand of whom he left in Galilee, and one
thousand went with him. But when 48
Jonathan entered Ptolemais, the people
of Ptolemais closed the gates and seized
him, and all who had come in with
him they put to the sword. And Try- 49
pho sent forces and cavalry to Galilee
and the great plain to destroy all
Jonathan's men. And they found out 50
that he had been taken and had
perished with his men, but they encouraged one another and marched
away in close order, ready to fight. And 51
when their pursuers saw that they
were ready to fight for their lives, they
turned back. And they all reached the 52
land of Judah unmolested, but they
mourned over Jonathan and his men,
and they were greatly frightened; and
all Israel mourned for him bitterly.
And all the heathen around them tried 53
to destroy them utterly, for they said,
"They have no leader or helper, so
now let us make war on them and
destroy their memory from among
men."

13 And Simon heard that Trypho had
gathered a strong force to invade the
land of Judah and destroy it utterly.
2 And he saw that the people were
trembling and alarmed, and he went up
to Jerusalem and gathered the people
3 together and encouraged them and said
to them,
"You know yourselves all that I and
my brothers and my father's house
have done for the laws and the sanctuary, and the wars and hardships we
4 have been through. As a result, my
brothers have all perished for Israel's
5 sake, and I alone am left. Now I never
want to spare my own life in any
emergency, for I am no better than my
6 brothers. But I will avenge my nation
and the sanctuary and your wives and
children, because all the heathen have
gathered out of hatred, to destroy us
utterly."
7 And when they heard these words,
8 the spirit of the people revived, and
they answered with a great shout,
"You are our leader, in the place of
Judas and Jonathan your brothers.
9 Carry on our war, and we will do all
that you tell us."
10 So he called together all the fighting
men, and made haste to finish the walls
of Jerusalem and put fortifications
11 around it. And he sent Jonathan, the
son of Absalom, with a considerable
force to Joppa, and he drove out the
men who were in it and remained there
in possession.
12 Then Trypho set out from Ptolemais
with a strong force to invade Judah,
taking Jonathan with him in custody.
13 But Simon pitched his camp in Adida
14 facing the plain. And Trypho learned
that Simon had risen to take the place
of his brother Jonathan and that he
was going to make war on him, and he
sent envoys to him, saying,
15 "It is for money that your brother
Jonathan owed the royal treasury in
connection with the offices that he held,
16 that we are holding him. So now send a
hundred talents of silver and two of his
sons as hostages, so that when he is released he will not revolt against us, and
we will let him go."
17 And Simon knew that they were
speaking to him treacherously, but he
sent to get the money and the children,
so that he should not incur deep ani-
18 mosity on the part of the people, and
they should say, "Because I did not
send him the money and the children,
he perished." So he sent the children 19
and the hundred talents. But Trypho
played him false and would not let
Jonathan go. After this he came to
invade the country, and destroy it, and
they went around by the road to Adora,
and Simon and his army kept abreast
of him everywhere he went. And the 21
men in the citadel sent envoys to
Trypho urging him to come to them by
way of the wild country and send them
provisions. And Trypho got all his 22
cavalry ready to go, but that night
there was a very heavy snow, and he
could not go because of the snow, so he
set forth and went into Gilead. And 23
when he approached Bascama, he
killed Jonathan, and he was buried
there. And Trypho went back to his 24
own country again.
And Simon sent and got the bones 25
of his brother Jonathan, and buried
him in Modin, the town of his forefathers. And all Israel lamented him 26
greatly and mourned over him for a
long time. And Simon built a monu- 27
ment over the grave of his father and
his brothers, and made it high so that
it could be seen, with polished stone
on back and front. And he erected 28
seven pyramids in a row, for his father
and his mother and his four brothers.
And he made devices for these, setting 29
up great columns and putting on the
columns trophies of armor for an everlasting memorial, and beside the armor
carved prows of ships, so that they
could be seen by all who sailed the sea.
Such was the monument that he built 30
at Modin, and that still stands today.
Now Trypho dealt treacherously 31
with King Antiochus the younger and
killed him and became king in his 32
place and assumed the diadem of Asia,
and brought great calamity upon the
country. But Simon built the strong- 33
holds of Judea and surrounded them
with high towers and thick walls and
barred gates, and he stored up provisions in the strongholds. And Simon 34
chose men and sent them to King
Demetrius so that he should give the
country relief, because all that Trypho
did was to plunder. And King Deme- 35
trius sent him a message in these terms,
and answered him and wrote a letter,
as follows:

"King Demetrius sends greeting to
Simon, the high priest and the Friend
of kings, and to the Jewish elders and
nation. The gold crown and the palm
branch which you sent we have received, and we are ready to make a
lasting peace with you, and to write
to our officials to grant you the im-
38 munities you ask. The things we have
guaranteed to you stand assured, and
the strongholds which you have built
39 shall be yours. Any oversights and de-
ficiencies up to this time we forgive, as
well as the crown tax that you owe, and
if any other tax was collected in Jerusalem, it shall no longer be collected.
40 And if any of you are suitable persons
to be enrolled at our court, they shall
be so enrolled, and there shall be peace
between us."
41 It was in the one hundred and
seventieth year that the yoke of the
42 heathen was lifted from Israel. And the
people began to write in their contracts
and agreements, "In the first year of
Simon, the great high priest and governor and commander of the Jews."
43 In those days he pitched his camp
against Gazara, and surrounded it with
troops; and he built a siege engine and
brought it up to the town and attacked
44 a tower and took it. And the men who
were on the engine sprang out into the
45 town. And there was a great stir in
the town, and the people of the town
with their wives and children went up
on the wall with their clothes torn open
and cried with a great shout asking
46 Simon to treat with them, and they
said,
"Do not treat us as our wickedness
deserves, but have mercy on us."
47 So Simon came to terms with them
and did not fight them, but he put them
out of the city and purified the houses
in which the idols were, and then he
48 entered it with songs and praise. And
he expelled all impurity from it, and
settled men in it who observed the
Law, and he fortified it more strongly
and built himself a dwelling there.
49 But the men in the citadel in Jerusalem were being kept from going in and
out of the country to buy and sell, and
they were famished and a good many
50 of them died of starvation. And they
cried out to Simon to make terms with
them, and he did so. And he expelled
them from it and purified the citadel
from its defilements. And they took 51
possession of it on the twenty-third day
of the second month in the one hundred
and seventy-first year, with praise
and palm branches and with lyres and
cymbals and harps, and with hymns
and songs, because a great enemy had
been destroyed out of Israel. And he 52
decreed that they should observe that
day with gladness every year. And the
temple mount facing the citadel he
fortified more strongly, and he and
his men lived there. And Simon saw 53
that his son John was now a man and
he made him commander of all his
forces; and he lived in Gazara.
In the one hundred and seventy- **14**
second year King Demetrius gathered
his forces and marched into Media to
obtain help so that he could fight
against Trypho. And Arsaces, king of 2
Persia and Media, heard that Demetrius had entered his territory and
he sent one of his officers to take him
alive. And he went and defeated De- 3
metrius' army and captured him and
brought him to Arsaces, and he put
him under guard.
And the land of Judah was at peace 4
as long as Simon lived; he sought the
good of his nation; his rule and his renown pleased them all his life. With 5
all his other glories, he took Joppa for a
port and made it a way of access to the
islands of the sea. He enlarged the 6
territory of his nation, and became
master of the land. He gathered many 7
captives and made himself master of
Gazara and Bethsura and the citadel,
and he removed from it what defiled it,
and there was no one who could resist
him. And they cultivated their land in 8
peace, and the land yielded its produce,
and the trees in the plains bore their
fruit. The old men sat in the streets; 9
they all talked together of their well-
being; and the young men put on
splendid warlike attire. He supplied the 10
towns with provisions, and he furnished
them with fortifications, until his renown was spoken of to the ends of the
earth. He made peace in the land, and 11
Israel rejoiced with great joy. Each 12
man sat under his vine and his fig tree,
and there was no one that could make
them afraid. There was no one left in 13
the land to fight them, and the kings
were destroyed in those days. He re- 14
established all those of his people who

had been humbled; he sought out the
Law, and removed everyone who was
15 lawless and wicked. He made the
sanctuary glorious and increased the
equipment of the sanctuary.
16 It was reported in Rome and as far
as Sparta that Jonathan was dead, and
17 they grieved bitterly. But when they
heard that his brother Simon had been
made high priest in his place, and that
he was in control of the country and
18 the towns in it, they wrote to him on
brass tablets to renew with him the
friendly relations and alliance they had
established with his brothers Judas and
19 Jonathan; and they were read before
20 the assembly in Jerusalem. And this is
the copy of the letter which the Spartans sent:

"The chief magistrates and the city
of the Spartans send greeting to Simon,
the chief priest, and to the elders and
the priests and the rest of the Jewish
21 people, our kinsmen. The envoys that
were sent to our people told us of your
spendor and wealth, and we were glad
22 of their coming. We have recorded
what they said in the decrees of the
people, as follows:

" 'Numenius, the son of Antiochus,
and Antipater, the son of Jason, envoys of the Jews, came to us to renew
23 their friendly relations with us. And
the people were pleased to receive the
men with honor and to deposit the copy
of what they said among the public
records, so that the Spartan people may
have a record of it. And they sent a
copy of this to Simon the high priest.' "
24 After this Simon sent Numenius to
Rome with a great gold shield weighing
a thousand pounds, to confirm their
alliance with them.
25 But when the people heard these
things, they said,

"How shall we thank Simon and his
26 sons? For he and his brothers and his
father's house have stood fast, and
have fought and driven from them the
enemies of Israel, and secured his
freedom."
27 So they engraved it on brass tablets
and set it on pillars on Mount Zion.
And this is the copy of what they wrote:

"On the eighteenth day of Elul, in
the one hundred and seventy-second
year—that is, the third year of the
28 high priesthood of Simon, the prince
of God's people—in a great congregation of priests and people and leaders
of the nation and elders of the country,
this has been reported to us: On the 29
frequent occasions when wars have
arisen in the country, Simon, the son
of Mattathias the priest, of the descendants of Joarib, and his brothers
have exposed themselves to danger and
resisted the adversaries of their nation
so that their sanctuary and their law
might be upheld, and they have reflected great glory upon their nation.
Jonathan rallied their nation and be- 30
came their high priest, and was gathered to his people. And when their 31
enemies resolved to invade their country, and attack their sanctuary, Simon 32
resisted them, and fought for his nation, and spent a great deal of money
of his own, and armed the warlike men
of his nation, and gave them wages.
And he fortified the towns of Judea 33
and Bethsura on the borders of Judea,
where their enemies formerly kept their
arms, and he stationed a garrison of
Jews there. And he fortified Joppa, on 34
the seacoast, and Gazara, on the borders of Ashdod, where their enemies
formerly lived, and he settled Jews
there, and all that was necessary for
the restoration of them he put in them.
And when the people saw Simon's 35
faithfulness and the glory that he designed to bring to his nation, they made
him their leader and high priest, because he had done all these things and
because of the uprightness and fidelity
he had shown to his nation, and because he had sought in every way to
exalt his people. In his days matters 36
prospered in his hands so that the
heathen were driven out of their country, as well as those in the City of
David, in Jerusalem, who had built
themselves a citadel, from which they
would go out and pollute the surroundings of the sanctuary, and did great
damage to its purity. He settled Jews 37
in it and fortified it to make the land
and the city safe, and he made the walls
of Jerusalem high. In view of these 38
things, King Demetrius confirmed him
in the high priesthood, and made him 39
one of his Friends, and treated him
with great honor. For he had heard 40
that the Jews had been addressed by
the Romans as friends and allies and
kinsmen, and that they had received
Simon's envoys with great honor. And 41

the Jews and their priests resolved that
Simon should be their leader and high
priest forever until a true prophet
42 should appear, and that he should be
their general, to appoint them to their
duties, and to set them over the country and over the arms and over the
fortifications; and that he should take
care of the sanctuary, and that all
43 should obey him, and that all contracts
in the country should be dated in his
reign and that he should be clothed in
44 purple and wear gold. And no one of
the people or of the priests shall be allowed to set aside any of these things,
or to contradict what he shall say or
to gather an assembly in the country
without him, or to be clothed in purple
45 or pin on a gold buckle. Whoever disobeys these actions or disregards any
of them shall be liable to punishment."
46 And all the people agreed to decree
that they should do these things to
47 Simon, and Simon accepted them and
agreed to be high priest and general and
governor of the Jews and the priests, and
48 to preside over them all. And they ordered that this decree should be inscribed on brass tablets and that they
should be set up in a conspicuous place in
the sanctuary enclosure, and that copies
49 of it be deposited in the treasury, so that
Simon and his sons might have it.

15 And Antiochus, the son of King Demetrius, sent a letter from the islands
of the sea to Simon, the priest and
governor of the Jews, and to the whole
2 nation, and it ran as follows:
"King Antiochus sends greeting to
Simon, the chief priest and governor,
3 and to the Jewish nation. As some
ruffians have made themselves masters
of the kingdom of our forefathers, and
I wish to claim the kingdom, so that I
may restore it to its former state, and
have raised a large force of mercenaries
4 and prepared ships of war, and propose
to land in the country to go in search
of the men who have ruined our country and have laid waste many towns
5 in my kingdom, I now guarantee to
you all the immunities which the kings
before me have granted you, and whatever other gifts they have released you
6 from. And I give you authority to coin
money for your country with your own
7 stamp, and Jerusalem and the sanctuary shall be free, and all the arms you
have prepared and the strongholds you
have built and now hold, shall remain
yours. And any royal obligation and all 8
future royal obligations shall be re-
mitted for you from this time forth
forever. And when we get possession of 9
our kingdom, we will greatly glorify
you and your nation and the temple so
that your glory will be visible to the
whole earth."
In the one hundred and seventy- 10
fourth year Antiochus went forth into
the country of his forefathers, and all
the troops joined him, so there were
very few left with Trypho. And Antio- 11
chus pursued him, and he came in his
flight to Dor by the sea, for he knew 12
that misfortune had overtaken him
and his troops had deserted him. And 13
Antiochus pitched his camp against
Dor with a hundred and twenty thousand soldiers and eight thousand horse.
And he surrounded the town, and ships 14
joined in the attack from the sea, and
he pressed the town hard by land and
sea, and did not allow anyone to go out
or in.
And Numenius and his companions 15
came back from Rome with letters to
the kings and the countries, in which
this was written:
"Lucius, consul of the Romans, sends 16
greeting to King Ptolemy. The envoys 17
of the Jews have come to us as our
friends and allies, to renew the old friendly relations and alliance, having been
sent by Simon, the high priest, and the
Jewish people, and they have brought 18
a gold shield weighing a thousand
pounds. It is our pleasure therefore to 19
write to the kings and the countries not
to injure them or fight them or their
towns or their country, and not to ally
themselves with those who fight against
them. And we have determined to ac- 20
cept the shield from them. So if any 21
miscreants flee from their country to
you, hand them over to Simon, the
high priest, so that he may punish them
in accordance with their law."
He wrote the same message to King 22
Demetrius and to Attalus, and to
Ariarathes, and to Arsaces, and to all 23
the countries, and to Sampsames and
the Spartans, and to Delos, and to
Myndos, and to Sicyon, and to Caria,
and to Samos, and to Pamphylia, and
to Lycia, and to Halicarnassus, and to
Rhodes, and to Phaselis, and to Cos,
and to Side, and to Aradus and Gortyna

and Cnidus and Cyprus and Cyrene.
24 And they wrote a copy for Simon, the
high priest.
25 And King Antiochus attacked Dor
on the second day, continually throwing his forces against it, and erecting
war engines, and he prevented Trypho
26 from going in or out. And Simon sent
him two thousand picked men to fight
for him, and silver and gold and a
27 quantity of war material. But he would
not accept them but disregarded all the
agreements he had made with him before, and he was estranged from him.
28 And he sent one of his Friends named
Athenobius to him, to confer with him,
saying,
"You are holding Joppa and Gazara,
and the citadel in Jerusalem, cities of my
29 kingdom. You have laid waste their
territories and done great injury to the
country, and you have taken possession
30 of many places in my kingdom. So now
give up the towns that you have seized,
and the tribute of the places you have
taken possession of outside the borders
31 of Judea, or else give me five hundred
talents of silver for them, and five
hundred talents of silver more, for the
damage you have done and for the
tribute of the towns; or else we will
come and make war on you."
32 So Athenobius the king's Friend
came to Jerusalem, and saw Simon's
splendor, and the sideboard with gold
and silver plate and his great pomp, and
he was amazed; and he gave him the
33 king's message. And Simon said to him
in reply,
"We have neither taken other men's
land, nor are we in possession of other
34 men's property, but of the inheritance of
our forefathers; it was wrongfully held
by our enemies at one time, but we,
grasping our opportunity, hold firmly
35 the inheritance of our forefathers. But
as for Joppa and Gazara, which you
demand, while they have done great
damage to our people and in our country, we will give a hundred talents for
them."
36 He made him no answer, but went
back to the king in anger, and reported
these words to him, and Simon's
splendor and all that he had seen, and
the king was extremely angry.
37 But Trypho embarked on a ship
38 and fled to Orthosia. And the king
appointed Cendebaeus commander-in-
chief of the seacoast, and gave him
infantry and cavalry, and ordered him 39
to pitch his camp before Judea, and he
ordered him to wall Kedron and fortify
its gates and fight against the people,
but the king pursued Trypho. And 40
Cendebaeus arrived at Jamnia, and
began to provoke the people and to invade Judea, and to take the people captive and to kill them. And he built the 41
walls of Kedron, and he stationed
cavalry and other forces there, so that
they might go out and make raids on
the highways of Judea, as the king
had ordered him to do.

And John went up from Gazara and 1
told his father Simon what Cendebaeus
had done. And Simon called in his two 2
eldest sons, Judas and John, and said
to them,
"I and my brothers and my father's
house have fought the battles of Israel
from our youth until today, and we
have succeeded in delivering Israel
many times. But now I am old, and 3
you by his mercy are old enough; you
must take my place and my brother's,
and go out and fight for our nation,
and the help that comes from heaven
be with you!"
And he chose twenty thousand 4
soldiers and cavalry from the country,
and they marched against Cendebaeus
and spent the night at Modin. And 5
they got up in the morning and
marched into the plain, and here a
great force came to meet them, horse
and foot, and there was a stream between them. And he encamped oppo- 6
site them, with his people. And he saw
that his people were afraid to cross the
stream, so he crossed first; and his men
saw him and they crossed after him.
And he divided the people, putting the 7
cavalry in the midst of the infantry, for
the enemy's cavalry were very numerous. And they sounded the trumpets, 8
and Cendebaeus and his army were
routed, and many of them fell wounded,
and those who were left fled to the
stronghold. At that time Judas, John's 9
brother, was wounded, but John pursued them until he came to Kedron,
which had been walled. And they fled 10
to the towers in the fields of Ashdod,
and he burned it up, and fully two thousand of them fell. And he returned to
Judea in peace.
Now Ptolemy, the son of Abubus, 11

had been appointed governor over the
plain of Jericho, and he had a great deal
12 of silver and gold, for he was the son-
13 in-law of the high priest. And his heart
was elated and he plotted deceitfully
against Simon and his sons, to remove
14 them. Simon was making visits to the
towns in the country, and providing for
their care. And he went down to
Jericho with his sons Mattathias and
Judas, in the one hundred and seventy-
seventh year, in the eleventh month,
15 the month of Shebat. And Abubus' son
deceitfully entertained them in the
fortress called Dok, which he had built,
and he had a great banquet for them,
16 and he had men hidden there. And
when Simon and his sons were drunk,
Ptolemy and his men got up and got
their weapons and went to the banquet
hall to attack Simon and killed him and
his two sons and some of his servants.
17 So he committed an act of great
treachery and returned evil for good.
18 And Ptolemy wrote of this and sent it
to the king, so that he might send
troops to his aid, and that he might
turn over to him their country and
towns. And he sent others to Gazara to 19
make away with John, and he sent
letters to the colonels, telling them to
come to him, so that he might give
them silver and gold and presents; and 20
he sent others to take possession of
Jerusalem, and the temple mount. And 21
a man ran ahead to Gazara and informed John that his father and his
brothers had perished, and said,

"He has sent to kill you also!"

He was greatly amazed when he 22
heard it, and he seized the men who
came to destroy him and killed them,
for he knew that they meant to destroy
him.

The rest of the acts of John, and his 23
wars and the exploits that he performed, and the building of the walls
that he effected, and his deeds—be- 24
hold, they are written in the chronicles
of his high priesthood, from the time
that he became high priest after his
father.

THE SECOND BOOK OF MACCABEES

1 TO THE Jewish brothers in
Egypt, the Jewish brothers in
Jerusalem and the land of Judea
send greetings and wish you per-
2 fect peace. May God bless you, and remember his agreement with Abraham,
3 Isaac, and Jacob, his faithful slaves, and
give you all a mind to worship him and
do his will with a stout heart and a will-
4 ing spirit. May he open your mind with
his Law and his statutes, and make
5 peace and listen to your prayers and
be reconciled to you, and not forsake
6 you in adversity. This is our prayer for
7 you here. In the reign of Demetrius, in
the one hundred and sixty-ninth year,
we Jews wrote you in the extreme distress that overtook us in those years,
from the time that Jason and his men
revolted from the holy land and the
8 kingdom, and set fire to the gateway
and shed innocent blood. And we besought the Lord, and were heard, and
we offered sacrifice and the meal offering, and we lighted the lamps, and set
9 out the Presentation Loaves. And you
must keep the Camping Out festival in
10 the month of Chislev. The one hundred
and eighty-eighth year.

Those who are in Jerusalem and
those in Judea and the senate and
Judas send greetings and good wishes to
Aristobulus, the teacher of King Ptolemy, who is of the stock of the anointed
11 priests, and to the Jews in Egypt. As
we have been saved by God from great
dangers, we offer devout thanks to him
as men who array themselves against
12 a king; for he drove out those who arrayed themselves against him in the
13 holy city. For when their leader reached
Persia, with an army about him that
seemed irresistible, they were cut down
in the temple of Nanaea, through
treachery on the part of the priests
14 of Nanaea. For Antiochus with his
Friends came to the place on the pretext of marrying her, in order to get a
large sum of money by way of dowry.
15 And when the priests of the temple of
Nanaea had brought out the money,
and he had come with a few followers
inside the wall of the temple inclosure,
they shut the temple when Antiochus
had gone in, and opened the secret door 16
in the ceiling, and threw stones and
struck down the leader, and dismem-
bered him and threw their heads to the
people who were outside. (Blessed in 17
every way be our God who brought the
impious to justice!)

As we are about to celebrate the 18
purification of the temple, on the
twenty-fifth day of the month of Chislev, we think it necessary to inform
you, so that you too may observe the
Camping Out festival and the kindling
of the fire, when Nehemiah, who built
the temple and the altar, offered sacrifices. For when our forefathers were 19
being taken to Persia, the pious priests
of that day took some of the fire on the
altar and hid it secretly in the hollow
of an empty cistern, where they made
it secure, so that the place was unknown to anyone. Many years after, 20
when it pleased God, Nehemiah was
commissioned by the king of Persia,
and sent the descendants of the priests
who had hidden the fire to get it. But
when they reported to us that they
could not find any fire but only muddy
water, he ordered them to dip some out 21
and bring it to him. And when the
things to be sacrificed had been put in
place, Nehemiah ordered the priests to
sprinkle the water on the wood and
the things that were laid on it. And 22
when this was done and some time had
passed, and the sun, which had been
clouded over, shone out, a great blaze
was kindled, so that they all wondered.
And the priests uttered a prayer while 23
the sacrifice was being consumed—the
priests and all present, Jonathan leading and the rest responding, as Nehemiah did. And this was the prayer: 24

"O Lord, Lord God, creator of all
things, who are terrible and strong and
upright and merciful, who alone are
king and good, the only patron, who 25
alone are upright and almighty and
eternal, who save Israel from every evil,
who chose our forefathers and sancti-

26 fied them, accept this sacrifice on behalf of all your people Israel, and
watch over your allotment, and make
27 it holy. Gather together our scattered
people, set at liberty those who are in
slavery among the heathen, look upon
those who are despised and abhorred,
and let the heathen know that you are
28 our God. Afflict our oppressors and
those who are violent in their arro-
29 gance. Plant your people in your holy
place, as Moses said."
30 Then the priests struck up the
31 hymns. And when the things that were
sacrificed were consumed, Nehemiah
ordered them to pour the water that
32 was left on large stones. And when this
was done, a flame was kindled, but
when the light shone back from the
33 altar, it went out. And when the thing
became known, and the king of Persia
was told that in the place where the
priests that were deported had hidden
the fire, water had appeared, and with
it Nehemiah's people had burned up
34 the things they sacrificed, the king,
after investigating the matter, made
35 the place a sacred inclosure, and the
king exchanged many different gifts
36 with his favorites. Nehemiah's people
called this Nephthar, which is translated "Purification," but most people
call it Nephthai.

2 It is also found in the records that
the prophet Jeremiah ordered those
who were carried away to take some of
2 the fire, as has been described, and that
after giving them the Law, the prophet
charged those who were carried away
not to forget the Lord's commands, and
not to be led astray in their minds
when they saw gold and silver idols and
3 their ornamentation. And with other
similar exhortations he told them that
the Law should not pass from their
4 hearts. It was also in the writing that
the prophet, in obedience to a revelation, gave orders that the tent and the
ark should accompany him, and that he
went away to the mountain where
Moses went up and beheld God's in-
5 heritance. And Jeremiah came and
found a cave-dwelling, and he took the
tent and the ark and the incense altar
into it, and he blocked up the door.
6 And some of those who followed him
came up to mark the road, and they
7 could not find it. But when Jeremiah
found it out, he blamed them and said,

"The place shall be unknown until
God gathers the congregation of his
people together and shows his mercy.
Then the Lord will show where they 8
are, and the glory of the Lord will appear, as they were shown in the days of
Moses, and when Solomon asked that
the place might be made very sacred."
It was also stated that he, in his wis- 9
dom, offered a dedicatory sacrifice at
the completion of the temple, and just 10
as Moses prayed to the Lord, and fire
came down from heaven and consumed
the offerings, so Solomon also prayed,
and the fire came down and burned up
the whole burnt offerings. And Moses 11
said,
"Because the sin offering had not
been eaten, it was consumed."
In like manner Solomon also kept the 12
eight days.
The same thing was related also in 13
the records and memoirs about Nehemiah, and that he founded a library and
collected the books about the kings
and the prophets, and the works of
David, and royal letters about sacred
gifts. In like manner Judas also collect- 14
ed for us all the books that had been
scattered because of the outbreak of
war, and they are in our hands. So, if 15
you want them, send men to get them
for you.
So as we are about to celebrate the 16
Purification, we write to you. Please
observe these days. It is God that has 17
saved all his people and given them
back their heritage and kingdom and
priesthood and consecration, as he 18
promised through the Law; for in God
we have hope that he will speedily have
mercy on us, and gather us together
from under heaven to the holy place,
for he has delivered us from great misfortunes and has purified the place.
Now the story of Judas Maccabeus 19
and his brothers, and the purification
of the great temple, and the rededication of the altar, and also of the wars 20
with Antiochus Epiphanes and his son
Eupator, and the heavenly manifesta- 21
tions shown to those who zealously
championed the Jewish religion, so
that few as they were, they plundered
the whole country and drove out the
barbarian hordes and recovered the 22
world-renowned temple, and freed the
city, and restored the laws which were
on the point of being destroyed, since

the Lord, with great forbearance had
23 shown mercy to them—all this, as related by Jason of Cyrene in five books,
we will try to condense into one vol-
24 ume. For in view of the flood of sta-
tistics and the difficulty created by the
abundance of the material, for those
who wish to plunge into the historical
25 narratives, we have aimed at attracting
those who like to read, and at making
it easy for those who are disposed to
memorize, and at being of use to all
26 our readers. For us, who have taken
upon ourselves the painful task of
abridgment, the thing is not easy, and
27 takes sweat and midnight oil, just as it
is no easy matter for a man who prepares a banquet and strives to benefit
others. Still, to win the gratitude of so
many, we will gladly endure the painful
28 task, leaving to the historian the investigation of details, but taking pains
29 to follow the lines of an epitome. For
as the builder of a new house must have
the whole structure in mind, while the
man who undertakes to decorate and
paint it has only to seek out what is
suitable for its adornment, so I think
30 it is with us. To enter upon the subject
and discuss matters fully and elaborate
the details is the task of the original
31 historian, but one who re-writes it must
be permitted to seek brevity of expression, and to forego the labored
32 treatment of the matter. Here then let
us begin the story, without adding
more to what has already been said; for
it is foolish to write a long preface to
the history and then abbreviate the
history itself.

3 When the holy city was inhabited
in perfect peace, and the laws were
strictly observed, because of the piety
of Onias, the high priest, and his hatred
2 of wickedness, it came to pass that even
the kings themselves did honor to the
place, and glorified the temple with
3 most noble gifts, so that even Seleucus,
king of Asia, from his own revenues
provided all the expense of the sacri-
4 ficial service. But a man named Simon,
of the tribe of Benjamin, who had been
appointed governor of the temple, had
a difference with the high priest about
5 the conduct of the city market. When
he failed to carry his point against
Onias, he went to Apollonius of Tarsus,
who was at that time governor of
6 Coelesyria and Phoenicia, and reported
to him that the treasury in Jerusalem
was full of such untold quantities of
money that the amount of the funds
was beyond computation; and that
they did not belong to the account of the
sacrifices and they might fall under the
control of the king. When Apollonius 7
met the king, he informed him of the
money that had been pointed out to
him. And he appointed Heliodorus,
who was his chancellor, and sent him
with instructions to effect the removal
of this money. Heliodorus immediate- 8
ly set out on his journey, under the
guise of visiting the towns of Coelesyria and Phoenicia, but in reality to
carry out the king's design.

When he reached Jerusalem, and had 9
been cordially welcomed by the high
priest and the city, he laid before them
the disclosure that had been made to
him, and explained why he had come,
and inquired whether this was really
true. The high priest pointed out that 10
some deposits belonged to widows and
orphans, and one belonged to Hyrca- 11
nus, son of Tobias, a man of very high
position—so falsely had the impious
Simon spoken; that it all amounted to
four hundred talents of silver and two
hundred of gold, and that it was abso- 12
lutely impossible that those who were
relying on the sacredness of the place
and on the sanctity and inviolability
of the temple, which was respected all
over the world, should be wronged.

But Heliodorus, because of the royal 13
orders he had received, said that anyway this must be confiscated for the
royal treasury. So he set a day, and 14
went in to conduct an inspection of
these funds; and there was no little
distress all over the city. The priests 15
in their priestly robes threw themselves down before the altar, and called
to heaven on him who had given the
law about deposits to keep these safe
for those who had deposited them. One 16
could not observe the appearance of the
high priest without being pierced to
the heart, for his expression and his
change of color revealed the anguish
of his soul. For terror and bodily 17
shuddering had come over the man,
which plainly showed to those who
looked at him the pain that was in his
heart. Moreover the people in the 18
houses came flocking out to make a
general supplication because the place

was on the point of being treated with
19 contempt. The women, with sackcloth
girt under their breasts, thronged the
streets, while maidens who were kept
indoors ran together, some to the gate-
ways, some to the walls, and some
20 looked out from the windows; and all
raised their hands to heaven and
21 uttered their supplication. One could
not help pitying the multitude, all
prostrating themselves in a body, and
the anxiety of the high priest in his
great anguish.
22 While they therefore called upon the
Almighty Lord to keep the things that
had been intrusted to him in perfect
security for those who had intrusted
23 them to him, Heliodorus was carrying
24 out what had been decided upon. But
no sooner had he and his guards arrived before the treasury than the
Sovereign of spirits and of all authority
caused a great manifestation so that
all who had been daring enough to come
with him were appalled at the power of
25 God and fainted with terror. For there
appeared to them a horse with a dreadful rider, adorned with magnificent trappings, and rushing swiftly at Heliodorus
26 it struck at him with its forefeet. His
rider seemed clad in golden armor. Two
young men also appeared to him, re-
markably strong and gloriously beautiful and splendidly dressed, who stood
on each side of him and flogged him
continually, inflicting many stripes on
27 him. He fell suddenly to the ground
and was enveloped in deep darkness,
and men picked him up and put him
on a stretcher and carried him off—
28 the man that had just entered that
treasury with a great retinue and his
whole guard but was now rendered
helpless—and they clearly recognized
29 the sovereign power of God. So through
the divine intervention he lay prostrate,
30 bereft of all hope of deliverance, while
they blessed the Lord who had marvel-
lously honored his own place; and the
temple, which a little while before had
been full of fear and commotion, now
that the Almighty Lord had manifested himself was filled with joy and
gladness.
31 Some of the intimate friends of Heliodorus soon asked Onias to call upon
the Most High and grant him his life, as
32 he lay at his very last gasp. The high
priest suspected that the king might
form the opinion that some villainy had
been practiced upon Heliodorus by the
Jews, and offered a sacrifice for the
man's recovery. But as the high priest 33
was offering the sacrifice of propitiation, the same young men again appeared to Heliodorus, clad in the same
clothes, and they stood beside him and
said,
"Be very grateful to Onias the high
priest, for the Lord has spared your
life for his sake; and since you have 34
been flogged from heaven, proclaim
to all men the sovereign power of God."
When they had said this, they van- 35
ished. So Heliodorus offered a sacrifice to the Lord and made very great
vows to him who had saved his life, and
after a friendly meeting with Onias
marched back to the king. And he bore 36
witness before all men to the deeds of
the supreme God which he had seen.
When the king asked Heliodorus 37
what kind of man was suitable to be
sent once more to Jerusalem, he said,
"If you have an enemy or a con- 38
spirator against the government, send
him there, and you will get him back
soundly flogged, if he escapes with his
life, for there is certainly some divine
power about the place. For he whose 39
dwelling is in heaven watches over that
place and helps it, and strikes down
and destroys those who come to injure
it."
This was the way the matter of 40
Heliodorus and the protection of the
treasury turned out.
But this Simon who had informed 4
about the money and against his country, made accusations against Onias,
saying that he had incited Heliodorus
and had been the actual author of these
troubles. He dared to charge with con- 2
spiracy against the government the
benefactor of the city, the protector of
his countrymen, and the champion of
the laws! But when his enmity reached 3
such a point that murders were committed by one of Simon's trusted men,
Onias, becoming aware of the danger 4
of their contention, and that Apollonius, the son of Menestheus, the governor of Coelesyria and Phoenicia, was
increasing Simon's malice, resorted to 5
the king, not to be an accuser of his
fellow-citizens, but as looking after the
welfare, public and private, of all the
people; for he saw that without the 6

king's interest it was impossible for the
government to secure peace again, and
that Simon would not abandon his
folly.
7 But when Seleucus departed this
life and Antiochus, who was called
Epiphanes, succeeded to the kingdom,
Onias' brother Jason obtained the high
8 priesthood by corruption, promising the
king in his petition three hundred and
sixty talents of silver, and eighty tal-
9 ents from other revenues. Besides this
he promised to pay a hundred and fifty
more, if he was given authority to set
up a gymnasium and a training place
for youth there and to enrol the people
of Jerusalem as citizens of Antioch.
10 When the king had consented, and
he had taken office, he immediately
brought his countrymen over to the
11 Greek way of living. He set aside the
royal ordinances especially favoring
the Jews, secured through John, the
father of Eupolemus, who went on the
mission to the Romans to establish
friendly relations and an alliance with
them, and abrogating the lawful ways
of living he introduced new customs
12 contrary to the Law. For he willingly
established a gymnasium right under
the citadel, and he made the finest of
the young men wear the Greek hat.
13 And to such a pitch did the cultivation
of Greek fashions and the coming-in
of foreign customs rise, because of the
excessive wickedness of this godless
Jason, who was no high priest at all,
14 that the priests were no longer earnest
about the services of the altar, but dis-
daining the sanctuary and neglecting
the sacrifices, they hurried to take part
in the unlawful exercises in the wres-
tling school, after the summons to the
15 discus-throwing, regarding as worthless the things their forefathers valued, and thinking Greek standards the
16 finest. As a result, they found themselves in a trying situation, for those
whose mode of life they cultivated, and
whom they wished to imitate exactly,
became their enemies and punished
17 them. For it is no small matter to sin
against the laws of God, as the period
that followed will show.
18 Now when the quinquennial games
were being held at Tyre, and the king
19 was present, the vile Jason sent envoys
who were citizens of Antioch to represent
Jerusalem, to carry three hundred silver
drachmas for the sacrifice to Hercules.
But even those who carried it thought
it should not be used for a sacrifice,
as that was not fitting, but should be
spent in some other way. So this money 20
intended by its sender for the sacrifice
to Hercules, was applied because of
those who carried it to the fitting out of
triremes.
When Apollonius, the son of Menes- 21
theus, was sent into Egypt to attend
the coronation of King Philometor,
Antiochus, learning that the latter was
disaffected toward his government,
took measures for his own security, so
he came to Joppa and visited Jerusalem. He was magnificently welcomed 22
by Jason and received with torches
and acclamations. Then he marched
into Phoenicia.
After the lapse of three years, Jason 23
sent Menelaus, the brother of this
Simon, to take the money to the king
and to present papers relating to necessary business. But he, on being pre- 24
sented to the king, extolled him with
such apparent authority that he obtained the high priesthood for himself,
outbidding Jason by three hundred
talents of silver. Upon receiving the 25
royal commission, he came back, possessing nothing that qualified him for
the high priesthood, but with the passions of a savage tyrant and the rage of
a wild beast. So Jason, who had sup- 26
planted his own brother, was sup-
planted by another, and driven as a
fugitive into the country of the Ammonites. So Menelaus held the office, but 27
he did not pay any of the money he
had promised to the king, and when
Sostratus, the governor of the citadel,
demanded it, for it was his duty to col- 28
lect the revenues, the two men were
summoned by the king to appear before
him on account of it. Menelaus left his 29
brother Lysimachus to act in his place
in the high priesthood, and Sostratus
left Crates, the viceroy of Cyprus, to
act in his.
In this state of things, the people of 30
Tarsus and Mallus made an insurrec-
tion because they had been given as a
present to Antiochis, the king's mistress. So the king went in haste to 31
Cilicia to adjust matters there, leaving
a man of high rank named Andronicus
to act in his place. Then Menelaus, 32
thinking he had found a favorable open-

ing, presented Andronicus with some
gold dishes from the temple, which he
had appropriated; he had already sold
others at Tyre and the neighboring
33 towns. When Onias was certain of this,
he sternly rebuked him, after retiring to
a place of sanctuary at Daphne, near
34 Antioch. So Menelaus took Andronicus aside and urged him to arrest
Onias. And he went to Onias, and
having been persuaded to use treachery, offered him sworn pledges and
gave him his right hand, and persuaded
him, notwithstanding his suspicions,
to leave his sanctuary, and immediately without regard to justice put him in
35 prison. This made not only Jews but
many people of other nationalities indignant and angry over the wicked
36 murder of the man. And when the
king came back from Cilicia, the Jews
in the city, with the support of the
Greeks who abhorred the crime, appealed to him about the unjustifiable
37 killing of Onias. So Antiochus, as he
was sincerely sorry, and moved to pity,
and shed tears over the sober and well-
38 ordered life of the departed, in a fiery
passion stripped the purple robe from
Andronicus and tore off his under-
clothes and led him about through the
whole city to the very place where he
had sinned against Onias, and there he
dispatched the murderer, and the Lord
rendered him the punishment he deserved.
39 When many thefts from the temple
had been committed in the city by
Lysimachus with the connivance of
Menelaus, and the report of them
spread abroad, the people gathered
against Lysimachus, as a great deal of
gold plate had already been scattered.
40 But when the people made an uprising
and were inflamed with anger, Lysimachus armed about three thousand
men, and commenced hostilities with a
man named Avaranus, who was as
foolish as he was aged, in command.
41 And when they were aware of Lysimachus' attack, some picked up stones
and others sticks of wood and others
caught up handfuls of the ashes that
were lying about, and flung them pell-
42 mell at Lysimachus and his men. As a
result, they wounded many of them,
and felled many, and put them all to
flight, and the temple-robber himself
they killed beside the treasury.

Charges were made against Menelaus 43
about this affair, and when the king 44
visited Tyre, the three men sent by the
senate presented the case before him.
Menelaus was now facing defeat, but 45
he promised a large sum of money to
Ptolemy, son of Dorymenes, to prevail
upon the king. So Ptolemy took the 46
king aside into a colonnade, as if to
take the air, and persuaded him to
change his mind, and he acquitted 47
Menelaus, who was to blame for all the
trouble, of the charges against him, and
condemned to death the wretched men
who would have been dismissed as innocent if they had pleaded even before
Scythians. So the advocates of the 48
city and the people and the sacred plate
promptly suffered this unjust punishment. This caused some Tyrians, in 49
their detestation of the crime, to provide magnificently for their burial. But 50
Menelaus, because of the covetousness
of the authorities, remained in power,
increasing in wickedness and persistently plotting against his fellow-citizens.
About that time Antiochus made his **5**
second attack upon Egypt. And it hap- 2
pened that all over the city for about
forty days, there appeared horsemen
charging in mid-air, in robes inwrought
with gold, fully armed, in companies,
with spears and drawn swords; squad- 3
rons of cavalry drawn up, charges and
countercharges taking place on this
side and on that, with brandishing of
shields, forests of spears, showers of
missiles, the flash of gold trappings, and
armor of every kind. Therefore all men 4
prayed that the manifestation beto-
kened good.
There arose a false rumor that Antio- 5
chus had departed this life, and Jason
took fully a thousand men and made a
sudden attack upon the city. As the
troops upon the walls gave way, and
the city was already virtually captured,
Menelaus took refuge in the citadel.
Then Jason unsparingly slaughtered 6
his fellow-citizens, regardless of the
fact that success gained over one's
kindred is the greatest failure, and
fancying that he was winning trophies
from his enemies, not from his countrymen. He did not get control of the 7
government, however, and in the end
got only shame from his conspiracy,
and had to take refuge again as a fugitive in the country of the Ammonites.

8 So finally he met a miserable end; accused before Aretas, the sovereign of
the Arabians, fleeing from city to city,
pursued by all men, hated as an apostate from the laws, and abhorred as the
butcher of his country and his fellow-
9 citizens, he was driven into Egypt, and
he who had sent many from their own
country into exile died in a strange
land, crossing the sea to the Lacedae-
monians hoping to find protection
there because of his relationship to
10 them. So he who had thrown many out
to lie unburied had none to mourn for
him, and had no funeral at all and no
place in the tomb of his forefathers.
11 When news of what had happened
reached the king, he thought that
Judea was in revolt; so he set out from
Egypt like a wild beast and took the
12 city by storm. And he ordered his
soldiers to cut down without distinction
anyone they met and to slay those who
13 took refuge in their houses. Then there
was a massacre of young and old, an
annihilation of boys, women and children, a slaughter of girls and babies.
14 In no more than three days eighty
thousand people were destroyed, forty
thousand of them in hand-to-hand encounter, and as many were sold into
15 slavery as were slain. Not content with
this, he dared to go into the most holy
temple in all the world, guided by
Menelaus who had betrayed both the
16 laws and his country; and took the
sacred plate in his polluted hands, and
with his profane hands he swept away
what had been dedicated by other kings
to enhance the glory and honor of the
17 place. In the elation of his spirit,
Antiochus did not realize that it was
because of the sins of the inhabitants
of the city that the Lord was angered
for a little, so that he had not had re-
18 gard for the place. But if they had not
happened to be entangled in so many
sins this man, like Heliodorus, who was
sent by King Seleucus to inspect the
treasury, would have been flogged and
turned back from his presumptuous
19 purpose as soon as he approached. But
the Lord did not select the nation for
the sake of the place, but the place for
20 the sake of the nation. Therefore the
place itself, after sharing in the misfortunes that overtook the nation, par-
ticipated afterward in its benefits; and
what was forsaken by the Almighty
in his wrath was restored in all its
glory when its great Master became
reconciled to it.

So Antiochus carried away eighteen
hundred talents from the temple, and
hurried off to Antioch, thinking in his
arrogance that he would make the land
navigable and the sea traversable on
foot, he was so intoxicated in mind.
And to harass the people he left governors—in Jerusalem, Philip, a Phrygian
by nationality, but in character more
barbarous than the man who appointed
him; in Gerizim, Andronicus, and besides these, Menelaus, who was worse
than the others in his overbearing
treatment of his townsmen. In his hostile attitude to the Jewish citizens, he
sent Apollonius, the Mysian captain,
with a force of twenty-two thousand,
with orders to slay all the grown men,
and to sell the women and younger men
as slaves. When this man arrived at
Jerusalem, he pretended to be peacefully disposed, and waited till the holy
sabbath day; then finding the Jews
refraining from work, he ordered his
men to parade under arms and put to
the sword all those who came out to
see them, and rushing into the city with
his armed men he destroyed them in
great multitudes. But Judas Maccabeus with some nine others got away
to the wild country and kept himself
alive with his comrades in the mountains as wild animals do, and they lived
on what grew wild rather than suffer
pollution with the rest.

Not long after, the king sent an old
Athenian to force the Jews to forsake
the laws of their forefathers and cease
to live according to the laws of God,
but to pollute the temple in Jerusalem
and to call it that of the Olympian
Zeus, and to call the one in Gerizim
that of Zeus the Hospitable, in keeping
with the character of those who lived
there. This harshly and most grievously intensified the evil. For the heathen
filled the temple with profligacy and
revelry, amusing themselves with prostitutes and lying with women within
the sacred precincts, and bringing into
it things that were forbidden. The altar
was covered with abominable offerings,
which the laws forbade. A man could
not keep the sabbath or celebrate the
festivals of his forefathers, or admit he
was a Jew at all. On the monthly cele-

bration of the king's birthday, they
were taken by bitter necessity to taste
the sacrifices, and when the festival of
Dionysus was celebrated, they were
compelled to wear wreaths of ivy and
8 march in procession in his honor. At
Ptolemy's suggestion a decree was issued to the neighboring Greek towns,
that they should adopt the same policy
toward the Jews and make them taste
9 the sacrifices, and that they should slay
any who would not agree to adopt
Greek customs. So anyone could see
10 how their misery was intensified. For
two women were brought in for circum-
cising their children, and they led them
publicly about the city with their
babies hanging at their breasts, and
then threw them down from the top of
11 the wall. Others who had gathered in
caves near by, to keep the seventh day
in secret, were betrayed to Philip and
all burned together, because they had
scruples about defending themselves,
in their respect for the dignity of that
most holy day.

12 So I beseech those who read this book
not to be cast down by such misfortunes but to consider that these
punishments were meant not for the
destruction of our people but for their
13 correction. For it is a mark of great
benevolence not to let the impious alone
for a long time but to punish them
14 promptly. For in the case of other nations, the Master is long-suffering and
waits before he punishes them until
they have reached the full measure of
15 their sins; but in our case he has decided differently, so that he may not
take vengeance on us afterward when
our sins have reached their height.
16 So he never withdraws his mercy from
us, and although he disciplines us with
misfortune, he does not abandon his
17 own people. This much let us say by
way of reminder; after these few words
we must resume our story.

18 Eleazar, one of the leading scribes,
a man of advanced age and fine appearance, was being forced to open his
19 mouth and eat pork. But he, welcoming a glorious death in preference to a
life of pollution went up of his own
20 accord to the torture wheel, setting an
example of how those should come forward who are steadfast enough to refuse food which it is wrong to taste even
21 for the natural love of life. Those who
were in charge of that unlawful sacrificial meal, because of their long-stand-
ing acquaintance with the man, took
him aside, and privately urged him to
bring meat provided by himself, which
he could properly make use of, and pretend that he was eating the meat of the
sacrifice, as the king had ordered, so 22
that by doing this he might escape the
death penalty, and on account of his
lifelong friendship with them be kindly
treated. But he, making a high resolve, 23
worthy of his years and the dignity of
his age and the hoary hair which he had
reached with such distinction, and his
admirable life even from his childhood,
and still more of the holy and divine
legislation, declared himself in accord
with these, telling them to send him
down to Hades at once.

"For," said he, "it does not become 24
our time of life to pretend, and so lead
many young people to suppose that
Eleazar when ninety years old has
gone over to heathenism, and to be led 25
astray through me, because of my
pretense for the sake of this short and
insignificant life, while I defile and disgrace my old age. For even if for the 26
present I escape the punishment of
men, yet whether I live or die I shall
not escape the hands of the Almighty.
Therefore by manfully giving up my 27
life now, I will prove myself worthy of
my great age, and leave to the young a 28
noble example of how to die willingly
and nobly for the sacred and holy
laws."

With these words he went straight 29
to the torture wheel, while those who so
shortly before had felt kindly toward
him became hostile to him, because the
words he had uttered were in their
opinion mere madness. As he was about 30
to die under the strokes, he said with a
groan,

"The Lord, in his holy knowledge,
knows that, though I might have
escaped death, I endure dreadful pains
in my body from being flogged; but in
my heart I am glad to suffer this, because I fear him."

And so he died, leaving in his death 31
a pattern of nobility and a memorial of
virtue not only to the young but to the
mass of his nation.

It happened that seven brothers were 7
also arrested with their mother, and
were tortured with whips and thongs by

the king, to force them to taste of the
2 unlawful swine's meat. One of them
made himself their advocate and said,
"What do you expect to ask and
learn from us? For we are ready to die,
rather than transgress the laws of our
forefathers."
3 The king was infuriated and gave
orders that pans and caldrons should be
4 heated. And when they were immediately heated, he commanded that the
tongue of the one who had been their
advocate should be cut out, and that
they should scalp him and cut off his
extremities, while his brothers and his
5 mother looked on. And when he was
utterly crippled, he ordered them to
bring him to the fire and fry him. And
as the vapor from the pan spread
thickly, they with their mother encouraged one another to die nobly,
saying,
6 "The Lord God is looking on, and
he truly relents toward us, as Moses
declared in his Song, which bore witness against them face to face, when
he said,
'And he will relent toward his
slaves.' "
7 When the first one had departed in
this manner, they brought the second
one to be mocked, and they tore off the
skin of his head with the hair, and
asked him,
"Will you eat, or have your body
punished limb by limb?"
8 But he replied in the language of his
forefathers and answered,
"No."
So he also underwent the same series
9 of tortures as the first suffered. But
when he was at his last gasp, he said,
"You wretch, you release us from this
present life, but the king of the world
will raise us up, because we have died
for his laws, to an everlasting renewal
of life."
10 After him, the third was mocked,
and when he was told to put out his
tongue, he did so quickly, and coura-
11 geously stretched out his hands, and
said nobly,
"I got these from heaven, and for the
sake of its laws I disregard them, and
from it I hope to receive them back
12 again," so that the king himself and
those who were with him were amazed
at the young man's spirit, because he
made light of his sufferings.

And when he had departed, they
tortured and maltreated the fourth in
the same way. And when he was near
his end, he spoke thus:
"It is better to die by men's hands
and look for the hopes God gives of
being raised again by him; for you will
have no resurrection to life."
Next they brought up the fifth and
maltreated him. But he looked at him
and said,
"Since you have authority among
men, though you are mortal, you do
what you please; but do not suppose
that our race has been abandoned by
God. But follow your course and see
how his mighty power will torment you
and your posterity."
After him they brought the sixth.
And when he was at the point of death,
he said,
"Do not be falsely deceived; for we
suffer these things because of ourselves,
for we sin against our own God, so these
amazing things have happened. But
you must not suppose that you will go
unpunished for having attempted to
fight against God."
But their mother was surpassingly
wonderful, and deserves a blessed
memory, for though she saw her seven
sons perish within a single day, she
bore it with good courage, because of
her hope in the Lord. And she encouraged each of them in the language
of their forefathers, for she was filled
with a noble spirit and stirred her
woman's heart with manly courage, and
said to them,
"I do not know how you appeared
in my womb, for it was not I that gave
you life and breath, and it was not I
that brought into harmony the elements of each. Therefore the creator
of the world, who formed the human
race and arranged the generation of all
things, will give you back again life and
breath in his mercy, as you now are
regardless of yourselves for the sake of
his laws."
Now Antiochus, thinking that he was
being treated with contempt, and suspecting her reproachful cry, as the
youngest still survived, not only appealed to him in words but also promised him with oaths that he would make
him rich and envied, if he would give
up the ways of his forefathers, and
would make him his Friend and intrust

25 him with office. But when the young
man paid no attention to him, the king
called the mother to him and urged her
to advise the boy to save himself.
26 After he had labored with her a long
time, she undertook to persuade her
27 son. She bent over him, and mocking
the cruel tyrant, she spoke thus, in the
language of her forefathers:
"My son, have pity on me, who carried you nine months in the womb, and
nursed you for three years, and brought
you up and brought you to your present
28 age, and supported you. I beseech you,
my child, to look up at the heaven and
the earth, and see all that is in them,
and perceive that God did not make
them out of the things that existed,
and in that way the human race came
29 into existence. Do not be afraid of this
butcher, but show yourself worthy of
your brothers, and accept death, so
that by God's mercy I may get you
back again with your brothers."
30 Before she could finish, the young
man said,
"What are you waiting for? I will
not obey the command of the king,
but I obey the command of the Law
that was given to our forefathers
31 through Moses. But you, who have
designed every kind of evil against the
Hebrews, will not escape the hands of
32 God. For we are suffering because of
33 our own sins. And though our living
Lord is angry for a little while, to rebuke and discipline us, he will be recon-
34 ciled with his own slaves again. But
you, impious man, the vilest of all men,
do not foolishly buoy yourself up in
your insolence with uncertain hopes,
when you raise your hand against the
35 children of heaven; for you have not yet
escaped the judgment of the Almighty
36 all-seeing God. For our brothers after
enduring a brief suffering have drunk
everlasting life, under the agreement of
God. But you, by the judgment of God,
will receive the rightful penalty of your
37 arrogance. I, like my brothers, give up
body and soul for the laws of my forefathers, calling upon God speedily to
show mercy to our nation, and to lead
you to confess, in trials and plagues,
38 that he alone is God; and to stay
through me and my brothers the wrath
of the Almighty, which has justly fallen
on our whole nation."
39 But the king was infuriated and
treated him worse than the others, being embittered at his mockery. So he 40
passed away unpolluted, trusting firmly in the Lord. Last of all, the mother 41
met her end, after her sons.
So much then for the eating of sacri- 42
fices and excessive barbarities.
But Judas, who was called Macca- 8
beus, and his followers secretly entered
the villages and called on their kinsmen
to join them, and by enlisting those
who had clung to the Jewish religion,
they mustered as many as six thousand. And they called upon the Lord to 2
look upon the people who were oppressed by all men and to have pity on
the sanctuary which had been profaned
by the godless, and to have mercy on 3
the city which was being ruined and
would soon be leveled with the ground,
and to hearken to the blood that cried
to them, and to remember the lawless 4
destruction of the innocent babies and
the blasphemies uttered against his
name, and to hate their wickedness.
And as soon as Maccabeus got them 5
organized, the heathen found him irresistible, for the wrath of the Lord
now turned to mercy. He would go un- 6
expectedly to towns and villages and
set fire to them, and in recovering advantageous positions and putting to
flight not a few of the enemy, he found 7
the nights especially favorable for such
attacks. And the country rang with
talk of his valor.
When Philip saw that the man was 8
gaining ground little by little, and that
his successful advances were becoming
more frequent, he wrote to Ptolemy,
the governor of Coelesyria and Phoenicia, to support the king's side. And 9
he promptly selected Nicanor, the son
of Patroclus, one of the king's chief
Friends and sent him, putting him in
command of not less than twenty thousand heathen of various nationalities,
to wipe out the whole race of Judea.
And he associated with him Gorgias, a
general and a man of experience in
military service. But Nicanor resolved 10
by taking the Jews captive to make up
for the king the tribute which he owed
to the Romans, which amounted to two
thousand talents. And he immediately 11
sent to the coast towns, inviting them
to buy Jewish slaves, and promising to
deliver them at ninety for a talent,

little expecting the judgment from the
Almighty that was to overtake him.
12 When news of Nicanor's advance
reached Judas, and when he informed
his followers of the arrival of the army,
13 those who were cowardly and doubtful
about the judgment of God ran away
14 and took themselves off. And others
sold everything they had left and besought the Lord together to deliver
those who had been sold in advance by
15 the impious Nicanor; if not for their
own sakes, for the sake of the agreements made with their forefathers, and
because they had been called by his
16 revered and glorious name. And Maccabeus gathered his men together, to the
number of six thousand, and exhorted
them not to be panic-stricken at the
enemy, or to fear the vast multitude
of the heathen who were coming against
them wrongfully, but to fight nobly,
17 keeping before their eyes the lawless
outrage they had committed against
the holy place, and the tormenting of
the derided city, and besides, the destruction of their ancestral mode of
18 life. "For they," he said, "trust in
arms and daring, but we trust in the
Almighty God, for he is able with a
mere nod to strike down not only our
enemies but the whole world."
19 And he told them besides of the times
when help had been given them in the
days of their forefathers, and how in the
time of Sennacherib a hundred and
20 eighty-five thousand had perished, and
the help that came in Babylonia, in
the battle with the Galatians, when
they went into the affair eight thousand
in all, with four thousand Macedonians, and when the Macedonians were
hard pressed, the eight thousand destroyed the hundred and twenty thousand, because of the help that came
to them from heaven, and took a great
21 quantity of booty. When he had revived their courage with these words,
and made them ready to die for their
laws and their country, he divided his
22 army into four parts. He put his
brothers Simon and Joseph and Jonathan each in command of a division,
putting fifteen hundred men under
23 each, besides Eleazar also, and he read
aloud from the holy book, and gave
"the Help of God" as the watchword,
and taking command of the first division himself, he joined battle with
Nicanor.

And the Almighty was their ally,
and they slaughtered more than nine
thousand of the enemy, and wounded
and disabled most of Nicanor's army,
and forced them all to flee. And they captured the money of those who had come
to buy them. And after pursuing them
for a considerable distance, they were
obliged to turn back because of the
time of day; for it was the day before
the sabbath, and for that reason they
could not prolong their pursuit of them.
But after collecting the enemy's arms
and stripping them of their spoils, they
busied themselves about the sabbath,
fervently blessing and thanking the
Lord who had preserved them to see
that day, because he had begun to show
them mercy. After the sabbath, they
gave some of the spoils to the wounded
and to the widows and orphans and
divided the rest with their children.
When they had accomplished this, they
made a common supplication, and besought the merciful Lord to be wholly
reconciled to his slaves.

When they encountered the forces of
Timotheus and Bacchides, they killed
more than twenty thousand of them,
and obtained possession of some exceedingly high strongholds, and they divided a great amount of plunder, giving shares equal to their own to the
wounded and orphans and widows,
and also to the older people as well.
And they carefully collected all their
own arms and deposited them in the
advantageous places, and the rest of
the spoils they carried to Jerusalem.
And they killed the cavalry commander
of Timotheus' forces, a most impious
man, who had greatly injured the Jews.
And in celebrating their victory in the
city of their forefathers, they burned
those who had set fire to the sacred
gates, and Callisthenes, who had taken
refuge in a cottage; so he received the
proper reward for his impious conduct.
But the thrice-accursed Nicanor, who
had brought the thousand slave-dealers
to buy the Jews, after being humbled
through the Lord's help by those whom
he had thought of no account, took off
his fine clothes and going alone like a run-
away across country reached Antioch,
having been supremely successful—in
destroying his army! So the man who

had undertaken to secure tribute for
the Romans by the capture of the
people of Jerusalem proclaimed that
the Jews had a champion, and that the
Jews were invulnerable because of their
way of life, because they followed the
laws laid down by him.
Now about that time it happened
that Antiochus returned in disorder
2 from the region of Persia. For he had
entered the city called Persepolis, and
tried to rob the temples and get control
of the city. At this the people naturally had swift recourse to arms, and they
were routed, and the result was that
Antiochus was put to flight by the
people of the country, and left in dis-
3 grace. And while he was at Ecbatana,
news came to him of what had happened to Nicanor and the forces of
4 Timotheus. And excited by anger, he
thought he would fasten upon the Jews
the injury done him by those who had
put him to flight, so he ordered his
charioteer to drive without stopping
until he finished the journey, although
the judgment of heaven accompanied
him. For in his arrogance he said,
"I will make Jerusalem the common
graveyard of the Jews, when I get
there."
5 But the All-seeing Lord, the God of
Israel, struck him down with an incurable but unseen blow, for he had hardly
uttered the words when he was seized
with an incurable pain in his bowels
6 and sharp internal pains—very justly,
for he had tormented the bowels of
7 others with many unusual miseries. He
did not desist at all from his insolence,
but was more and more filled with arrogance, breathing fire in his fury against
the Jews, and giving orders to hasten
the journey. But it happened that he
fell out of his chariot as it was rushing
along, and was racked in every part of
8 his body from the fall. And the man
who just now presumed to command
the waves of the sea, in his superhuman
boastfulness, and thought he could
weigh the mountain heights in his
scales, was flat on the ground and had
to be carried in a litter—making the
9 power of God manifest to all men; so
that worms swarmed from the impious
creature's body, and while he was still
alive in anguish and pain, his flesh fell
off, and because of the stench the whole
army turned from his corruption in dis-
gust. The man who shortly before 10
thought he could touch the stars of
heaven, no one could now bear to
carry, because of his intolerable stench.
So it was then that, broken in spirit, he 11
began for the most part to give up his
arrogance, and under the scourge of
God to attain some knowledge, for he
was tortured with pain every instant.
And when he could not even endure his 12
own stench, he said this:
"It is right to submit to God and,
since man is mortal, not to think he is
God's equal."
And the vile fellow made a vow to 13
the Lord who would no longer have
mercy on him, stating that he declared 14
the holy city, which he was hastening
to level with the ground and to make a
common graveyard, free; and as for the 15
Jews, who he had decided were unworthy of burial, but should be thrown
out with their children to the wild animals, for the birds to pick, that he
would make them all equal to citizens
of Athens; and the holy sanctuary, 16
which before he had plundered, he
would adorn with the finest offerings,
and he would give back all the sacred
dishes many times over, and the expenses incident to the sacrifices he
would supply from his own revenues;
and in addition to this, he would be- 17
come a Jew and visit every inhabited
place to proclaim the power of God.
But when his suffering by no means 18
ceased, for God's judgment had come
justly upon him, in despair about himself he wrote the Jews the following
letter, assuming the attitude of a suppliant. It ran thus:
"To the esteemed Jewish citizens, 19
Antiochus, the king and general, sends
hearty greetings and wishes for their
health and prosperity. If you and your 20
children are well and your affairs are
going as you wish, I am glad. As my 21
hope is in heaven, I remember with
affection your esteem and good will.
On my way back from the regions of
Persia, I have been taken seriously ill,
so I have thought it necessary to plan
for the general welfare of all. Not that 22
I despair of myself, for I have strong
hopes of recovering from my sickness.
But observing that my father, on the 23
occasions when he campaigned in the
upper country, appointed his successor,
so that, if anything unexpected hap- 24

pened, or any disturbing news came,
the people at home, knowing to whom
the government was left, should not be
25 disturbed; and in addition to this, perceiving that the adjacent princes, who
are neighbors to the kingdom, watch
for opportunities and are expectant of
what may turn up, I have appointed
my son Antiochus king, whom I have
often committed and commended to
most of you, when I hurried off to the
upper provinces; and I have written
26 him what is written below. So I beg
and beseech you to remember the public and private services rendered you
and to continue your good will to me
27 and my son. For I am convinced that
he will follow my policy with mildness
and kindness, in his relations with
you."
28 So the murderer and blasphemer,
after the most intense sufferings, such
as he had inflicted on other people,
ended his life most pitiably, among the
29 mountains, in a foreign land. And his
foster-brother Philip took his body
home, and then, as he feared the son of
Antiochus, he went over to Ptolemy
Philometor in Egypt.
10 Now Maccabeus and his followers
under the Lord's leadership regained
2 the temple and the city, and tore down
the altars that had been built by the
aliens in the public square, and also
3 the sacred inclosures. And when they
had purified the sanctuary, they built
another altar of sacrifice, and striking
flints and getting fire from them, they
offered sacrifices, after an interval of
two years, and they burned incense and
lighted lamps and set out the Presenta-
4 tion Loaves. And when they had done
this, they fell on their faces and besought the Lord that they might never
again encounter such misfortune, but
that, if they should ever sin, he would
discipline them with forbearance, and
not hand them over to blasphemous and
5 barbarous heathen. And it came about
that on the very same day on which the
sanctuary had been profaned by aliens,
the purification of the sanctuary took
place, that is, on the twenty-fifth day
of the same month, which was Chislev.
6 And they celebrated it for eight days
with gladness, like the Camping Out
festival, and recalled how, a little while
before, during the Camping Out festival
they had been wandering in the mountains and caverns like wild animals.
So carrying wands wreathed with leaves
and beautiful branches and palm leaves
too they offered hymns of praise to him
who had brought to pass the purifying
of his own place. And they passed a
public ordinance and decree that the
whole Jewish nation should observe
these days every year. Such was the
end of Antiochus, who was called
Epiphanes.
We will now set forth what took
place under Antiochus Eupator, who
was the son of that godless man, sum-
marizing the principal disasters of the
wars. For this man, upon succeeding
to the kingdom, appointed one Lysias to
have charge of the government, and to
be governor-in-chief of Coelesyria and
Phoenicia. For Ptolemy who was called
Macron instituted the practice of showing justice to the Jews because of the
wrong that had been done them, and
attempted to carry on his dealings with
them amicably. As a result, he was accused before Eupator by the king's
Friends, and on all sides heard himself
called a traitor, because he had abandoned Cyprus which Philometor had
intrusted to him, and gone over to
Antiochus Epiphanes, and, as he could
not maintain the dignity of his office,
he took poison and ended his life.
But Gorgias, when he became governor of the region, maintained mercenaries and kept on warring against the
Jews at every turn. In addition to that,
the Idumeans, who held important
forts, were harassing the Jews, and
enlisting those from Jerusalem who
took refuge there, they sought to continue the war. But Maccabeus and
his men made a supplication and besought God to be their ally, and then
threw themselves upon the forts of the
Idumeans, and attacking them vigorously they made themselves masters of
the positions, and fought off those who
manned the wall, and slaughtered those
whom they encountered, killing not less
than twenty thousand. As fully nine
thousand had taken refuge in two very
strong towers well supplied for a siege,
Maccabeus left Simon and Joseph and
in addition Zaccheus and his men, making a force strong enough to besiege
them, and set off for places that were
more urgent. But the men with Simon
were covetous and were bribed by some

of the men in the towers, and on receiving seventy thousand drachmas let
21 some of them escape. But when news
of what had happened reached Maccabeus, he gathered the leaders of the
people together, and charged them with
having sold their brothers for money,
by freeing their enemies to fight them.
22 So he killed those men for having
proved traitors, and immediately cap-
23 tured the towers. And as he was successful in arms in everything he undertook, he destroyed more than twenty
thousand men in the two forts.
24 But Timotheus, who had been defeated by the Jews before, gathered
enormous mercenary forces, and mustering no small number of Asiatic
cavalry, came as though he would take
25 Judea by storm. But when he approached, Maccabeus and his men
sprinkled earth on their heads and put
26 sackcloth on their loins, and falling
down upon the step before the altar
begged him to favor them and be the
enemy of their enemies, and oppose
their adversaries, as the Law declares.
27 And when they had ended their prayer,
they took their arms, and advanced a
considerable distance from the city, and
when they got near the enemy, they
28 halted. And just as the dawn was
breaking, the two armies joined battle,
those on one side having besides their
valor their assurance of success and
victory in having taken refuge with the
Lord, while those on the other followed
their passions as leader in the contest.
29 And when the fighting had become
fierce, there appeared to the enemy
from heaven five splendid figures on
horses with gold bridles, leading the
30 Jews, and they surrounded Maccabeus,
and protected him with their armor
and kept him unhurt, while they shot
arrows and hurled thunderbolts at the
enemy, so that, confused and blinded,
they were thrown into disorder and
31 cut to pieces. Twenty thousand five
hundred were slaughtered, and six
32 hundred horsemen. Timotheus himself took refuge in a stronghold called
Gazara, which was strongly garrisoned
and under the command of Chaereas.
33 Then Maccabeus and his men were
glad, and they besieged the fort for four
34 days. And those who were inside, relying on the strength of the place,
blasphemed dreadfully and uttered
impious speeches. But at dawn the 35
fifth day, twenty young men in the
army of Maccabeus, fired with anger
by these blasphemies, manfully as-
saulted the wall and in savage fury cut
down everyone they met. Others who 36
had climbed up in the same way, in the
confusion over those who had gotten
in, set the towers on fire and starting
fires burned the blasphemers alive. Still
others broke open the gates, and let in
the rest of the force, capturing the city.
They killed Timotheus, who was hidden 37
in a cistern, and his brother Chaereas
and Apollophanes. When they had ac- 38
complished this, with hymns and
thanksgivings they blessed the Lord
who does great services to Israel, and
gives them victory.

A very short time after, Lysias, the 11
guardian and relative of the king, who
was in charge of the government, being
greatly annoyed at what had happened,
mustered about eighty thousand men 2
and all his cavalry, and came against
the Jews, with the intention of making
the city a place for Greeks to live in,
and of imposing tribute on the temple, 3
as they did on the other sacred places
of the heathen, and of offering the high
priesthood for sale every year, taking 4
no account at all of the power of God,
but uplifted by his tens of thousands
of infantry, and his thousands of cavalry, and his eighty elephants. And he 5
entered Judea, and approached Bethsura, a fortified place about five-eighths
of a mile from Jerusalem, and pressed
it hard.

But when Maccabeus and his men 6
got news that he was besieging the
strongholds, with lamentations and
tears they and the people besought the
Lord to send some valiant angel to save
Israel. Maccabeus himself was the first 7
to take up arms and called on the
others to risk their lives with him and
go to the aid of their brothers. So they
hurried off eagerly together. But there, 8
while they were still near Jerusalem, a
rider, clothed in white, appeared at
their head, brandishing gold weapons.
And they all blessed the merciful God 9
together, and their hearts were strengthened, and they felt equal to overcoming
not only men but the fiercest animals
and iron walls. So they advanced in 10
good order with their heavenly ally,
for the Lord had had mercy on them.

11 And flying at the enemy like lions, they
killed eleven thousand of them and
sixteen hundred horsemen, and forced
12 all the rest to flee. The most of them
got away stripped and wounded, and
Lysias himself escaped only by a dis-
13 graceful flight. But as he was not without understanding, he thought over the
defeat he had met with, and perceived
that the Hebrews were invincible, because the mighty God was their ally, so
14 he sent to them and persuaded them
to come to a general settlement on just
terms, because he would persuade the
king and prevail upon him to become
15 their friend. And Maccabeus agreed to
all that Lysias proposed, thus looking
out for the common good, for the king
granted all the demands that Maccabeus made in writing to Lysias for the
Jews.
16 For the letter written to the Jews by
Lysias was as follows:
"Lysias sends greeting to the Jewish
17 people. Your emissaries John and Absalom have presented the accompanying petition and asked about the mat-
18 ters set forth in it. So I informed the
king of the matters that needed to be
laid before him, and he has agreed to
19 all that was possible. If then you will
continue your loyalty to the government, I will endeavor to further your
20 interests in the future. But about the
details of these matters, I have ordered
these men and my representatives to
21 confer with you. Goodbye. The hundred and forty-eighth year, Dioscorin-
thius twenty-fourth."
22 The king's letter ran thus:
"King Antiochus sends greeting to
23 his brother Lysias. Now that our father
has departed to the gods, we desire the
subjects of the kingdom to be unmolested and to busy themselves with the
24 care of their own affairs, and as we have
heard that the Jews will not agree to
our father's policy of making them
adopt Greek practices, but prefer their
own way of living, and ask to be allowed to follow their own customs, we
wish this nation also to be undisturbed,
25 and our decision is that their temple be
returned to them, and that they follow
26 their ancestral customs. Please send
messengers to them therefore, and give
them assurances, so that they may
know our purpose and be of good cheer,
and contentedly go about the conduct
of their affairs."
The king's letter to the nation ran 27
as follows:
"King Antiochus sends greeting to
the Jewish senate and to the rest of the
Jews. If you are well, it is what we de- 28
sire; we too are well. Menelaus has in- 29
formed us that you want to go home
and look after your own affairs. There- 30
fore those who go home by the thirtieth
of Xanthicus will have our assurance
that the Jews can fearlessly enjoy their 31
own food and laws, as before; and none
of them shall be molested in any way
for what he may have ignorantly done.
I have sent Menelaus also to cheer you. 32
Goodbye. The hundred and forty- 33
eighth year, Xanthicus fifteenth."
The Romans also sent them a letter 34
to this effect:
"Quintus Memmius and Titus Ma-
nius, envoys of the Romans, send greeting to the Jewish people. With regard 35
to what Lysias, the king's relative, has
granted you, we also give our approval.
But as to the matters which he decided 36
should be referred to the king, as soon
as you have considered the matter, send
us word, so that we may take proper
action. For we are going to Antioch; so 37
make haste and send men to us, so that
we also may know what your intentions are. Goodbye. The hundred and 38
forty-eighth year, Xanthicus fifteenth."
After this agreement was reached, 12
Lysias went back to the king, and the
Jews went about their farming. But 2
some of the local governors, Timotheus and Apollonius, the son of Gen-
naeus, besides Hieronymus and Demo-
phon, as well as Nicanor, the governor
of Cyprus, would not leave them alone
and let them live in peace. Some peo- 3
ple of Joppa also perpetrated the following outrage. They invited the Jews
who lived among them to embark with
their wives and children on boats they
had provided, with no hint of any ill
will toward them, but in accordance 4
with the public regulations of the town.
And when they accepted, as they
wished to live peaceably and had no
suspicion, they took them out to sea
and drowned fully two hundred of
them.
When Judas got news of the cruelty 5
that had been practiced on his countrymen, he called his men together, and 6

calling on God, the righteous judge, he
attacked the murderers of his brothers,
and one night set the harbor on fire and
burned the boats, and put those who
had taken refuge there to the sword.
7 But as the town shut its gates against
him, he retired, meaning to come back
and exterminate the whole community
8 of Joppa. But learning that the people
of Jamnia meant to treat the Jews there
9 in the same way, he attacked the people
of Jamnia in the night, and set fire to
the harbor as well as the fleet, so that
the glow of the fire was visible in Jerusalem, thirty miles away.
10 When they had gone more than a
mile from there, on their march against
Timotheus, fully five thousand Arabs
with five hundred horsemen attacked
11 them. After a hard fight, by the help
of God Judas and his men were victorious, and the nomads, being worsted,
besought Judas to make friends with
them, promising to give him cattle and
12 to help them in other ways. Judas
thought they would really be useful in
many ways, and agreed to make peace
with them, so after receiving his assurances, they left for their camp.
13 He also attacked a town strengthened with earthworks and encircled
with walls, inhabited by heathen of all
14 sorts, and named Caspin. Its occu-
pants, relying on the strength of their
walls and their stores of provisions,
scoffed madly at Judas and his men,
and went so far as to blaspheme and
15 make impious speeches. But Judas and
his men called upon the great Sovereign
of the world, who without rams or war
engines threw down the walls of Jericho in the days of Joshua, and rushed
16 furiously upon the walls. And by the
will of God they took the city, and
slaughtered untold numbers, so that
the neighboring lake, a quarter of a mile
wide, seemed to be filled with running
blood.
17 When they had gone ninety-five
miles from there, they reached Charax,
and the Jews who are called Tybiani.
18 They could not find Timotheus in those
regions, for he had gone away unsuc-
cessful, but leaving behind him in one
19 place a very strong garrison. But Dositheus and Sosipater, who were captains
under Maccabeus, marched out and destroyed the force Timotheus had left in
the stronghold, more than ten thousand
men. Maccabeus however arranged his 20
army in divisions and put them in command of the divisions and hurried after
Timotheus, who had with him a hundred and twenty thousand infantry and
two thousand, five hundred cavalry.
But when Timotheus learned of the 21
advance of Judas, he sent the women
and children and the rest of the baggage
train ahead to a place called Carnaim,
for that stronghold was hard to besiege
or to reach, because of the difficulty of
all that region. But when Judas' first 22
division appeared and terror came over
the enemy and fear came upon them
at the manifestation of him who beholds all things, they hastily fled in all
directions, so that in many cases they
were hurt by their own men and
wounded by the points of their swords.
But Judas pressed the pursuit increas- 23
ingly, putting the wretches to the
sword, and destroyed fully thirty thousand men.
But Timotheus himself, falling into 24
the hands of Dositheus and Sosipater
and their men, besought them with
much guile to spare his life and let him
go, because he had the parents of many
of them and the brothers of some in his
power, and it would go hard with these.
So when he had most fully guaranteed 25
to restore them unharmed, to save
their brothers they let him go.
Then Judas marched against Car- 26
naim and the temple of Atargatis, and
slaughtered twenty-five thousand people. After the rout and destruction of 27
these, he marched against Ephron, a
fortified town, where Lysias lived and
multitudes of all nationalities. Hardy
young men posted before the walls
vigorously defended it, and large quantities of war engines and missiles were
kept there. But they called upon the 28
Sovereign who forcibly shatters the
might of his enemies, and took the
town, and slew fully twenty-five thousand of those who were in it.
Then they set out from there and 29
marched rapidly to Scythopolis, which
is seventy-five miles from Jerusalem.
But when the Jews there bore witness 30
to the good will shown them by the
people of Scythopolis, and their kind
treatment of them in times of misfortune, they thanked them and ex- 31
horted them to be well disposed to
their race in the future also. Then, as

the festival of Weeks was close at hand,
they went up to Jerusalem.
32 After the festival called Pentecost
they marched hurriedly against Gorgias,
33 the governor of Idumea. And he came
out with three thousand infantry and
34 four hundred cavalry. And when they
joined battle, it happened that a few
35 of the Jews fell. But a man named
Dositheus, one of Bacenor's men, a
mounted man of great strength, caught
hold of Gorgias and grasping his cloak
was dragging him off by main strength,
meaning to take the accursed rascal
alive, when one of the Thracian horsemen bore down upon him and disabled
his shoulder, so that Gorgias escaped
and reached Mareshah.
36 But as Esdris and his men had been
fighting a long time and were tired out,
Judas called upon the Lord to show
himself their ally and leader in the
37 fight; then raising the war cry and war
songs in their ancestral language, he
charged Gorgias' men unexpectedly and
put them to flight.
38 Then Judas assembled his army and
went to the town of Adullam. And as
the next day was the seventh day, they
purified themselves as they were accustomed to do, and kept the sabbath.
39 On the following day, as by that time it
had become necessary, Judas' men went
to gather up the bodies of the fallen,
and bring them back to lie with their
relatives in the graves of their fore-
40 fathers. But on every one of the dead,
under the shirt, they found amulets of
the idols of Jamnia, which the Law for-
bids the Jews to war; and it became
clear to all that this was why they had
41 fallen. So they all blessed the ways of
the Lord, the righteous Judge, who
reveals the things that are hidden, and
42 fell to supplication, begging that the
sin that had been committed should be
wholly blotted out. And the noble
Judas exhorted the people to keep
themselves free from sin, after having
seen with their own eyes what had happened because of the sin of those who
43 had fallen. He also took a collection,
amounting to two thousand silver
drachmas, each man contributing, and
sent it to Jerusalem, to provide a sin
offering, acting very finely and properly in taking account of the resurrec-
44 tion. For if he had not expected that
those who had fallen would rise again,
it would have been superfluous and
foolish to pray for the dead; or if it was 4
through regard for the splendid reward
destined for those who fall asleep in
godliness, it was a holy and pious
thought. Therefore he made atonement for the dead, so that they might be
set free from their sin.
In the hundred and forty-ninth year, 1
news reached Judas and his men that
Antiochus Eupator had come with great
hosts against Judea, bringing with him
Lysias, his guardian, who had charge
of the government, each with a Greek
force of a hundred and ten thousand
infantry, and five thousand three hundred cavalry, and twenty-two elephants
and three hundred chariots armed with
scythes. Menelaus also joined them,
and with loud pretenses encouraged
Antiochus, not to save his country, but
because he thought he would be put in
charge of the government. But the
King of kings aroused the anger of
Antiochus against the rascal, and when
Lysias informed him that this man was
to blame for all the trouble, he ordered
them to take him to Berea and to put
him to death in the way that is customary there. For there is a tower there
seventy-five feet high, filled with ashes,
and it had an arrangement running all
around it dropping straight into the
ashes. There they all push a man guilty
of sacrilege or notorious for other
crimes to destruction. By such a fate
it came to pass that Menelaus the
transgressor died, not even getting
burial in the ground. And very justly,
for as he had committed many sins
against the altar, the fire and ashes of
which were holy, through ashes he came
by his death.
But the king, enraged in mind, was
coming to inflict on the Jews the worst
of the things they had suffered in his
father's time. And when Judas got
news of it, he ordered the people to call
on the Lord all day and all night now if
ever to help those who were on the
point of losing their Law and their
country and the holy temple, and not to
let the people who had just begun to
revive fall into the hands of profane
heathen. And when they had all done
this together and besought the merciful
Lord for three days without ceasing,
with weeping and fasting and prostra-
tions, Judas encouraged them and

13 ordered them to rally to him. After a
private meeting with the elders, he decided that they should march out and
decide the matter by the help of God
before the king could get his army into
Judea and get possession of the city.
14 So committing the decision to the creator of the world and encouraging his
men to fight nobly to the death for laws,
temple, city, country, and government,
15 he pitched his camp at Modin. And
giving his men "God's Victory," for the
watchword, he threw himself upon the
camp in the night and reached the
royal tent, and killed fully two thousand men, and stabbed the leading
16 elephant and his driver, and finally
filled the camp with terror and con-
17 fusion, and got away successfully. This
happened by the Lord's help and protection, just as day was dawning.
18 After this taste of the Jews' hardihood, the king resorted to stratagem
19 in attempting their positions. He advanced against Bethsura, a strong Jewish fort; he was turned back, stumbled,
20 failed. Judas sent what was necessary
21 in to the garrison. But Rhodocus, a
man of the Jewish force, gave secret
information to the enemy; he was found
22 out, arrested, and put in prison. The
king again approached the people in
Bethsura, gave assurances, received
them, withdrew, attacked Judas and
23 his men, was worsted, got news that
Philip, who had been left in charge of
the government at Antioch, had gotten
desperate, was dismayed, conciliated
the Jews, yielded, and swore to do all
that was just, settled with them and
offered sacrifice, honored the sanctu-
24 ary and respected the holy place, received Maccabeus, left Hegemonides as
governor in control from Ptolemais to
25 Gerar. He went to Ptolemais; the people of Ptolemais were angry about the
treaty, for they were so indignant that
they wanted to annul the agreements.
26 Lysias appeared to speak publicly,
made as good a defense as was possible,
convinced them, appeased them, won
them over, and set out for Antioch.
This was the course of the king's attack
and withdrawal.

14 Three years later, news reached
Judas and his men that Demetrius, the
son of Seleucus, had sailed into the harbor of Tripolis with a strong force and a
fleet, and had made away with Antiochus and his guardian Lysias and taken 2
possession of the country. But Alci- 3
mus, who had formerly been high priest,
but had polluted himself of his own accord in the days when there was no
communication with the heathen, considering that there was no way for him
to save himself or to obtain access to
the holy altar, went to King Demetrius 4
in the hundred and fifty-first year, and
presented him with a gold crown and
palm, and in addition to them some of
the customary olive branches from the
temple; and he kept silence that day.
But when he found an opportunity 5
favorable to his mad purpose, being invited by Demetrius to a council, and
asked about the temper and intentions
of the Jews, he answered,
"It is the Jews who are called Hasi- 6
daeans, under the leadership of Judas
Maccabeus, that keep the war alive,
and stir up sedition, and will not let the
kingdom enjoy tranquillity. That is 7
why, renouncing my ancestral glory
(I mean the high priesthood), I have
now come here, first, because I am 8
genuinely concerned for the king's
interests, and secondly out of regard for
my fellow-citizens; for through the inconsiderate behavior of those whom I
have mentioned, our whole nation is in
no small misfortune. Inform yourself, 9
O king, about these things in detail, and
act in the interests of our country and
our hard-pressed nation, with the
courteous consideration that you show
to all. For as long as Judas lives, it is 10
impossible for the government to find
peace."
When he said this, the rest of the 11
Friends, who were hostile to Judas, immediately inflamed Demetrius further
against him. He immediately chose 12
Nicanor, who had been master of the
elephants, and appointed him governor
of Judea, and sent him out with orders 13
to make away with Judas himself, and
scatter his men, and instal Alcimus as
high priest of the sublime temple. And 14
all the heathen in Judea who had driven
Judas into exile flocked to join Nicanor, thinking that the reverses and
disasters of the Jews would be to their
advantage.
But when they heard of Nicanor's 15
expedition and the attack of the heathen, they sprinkled themselves with
earth and intreated him who had estab-

lished his own people forever, and always upholds his own portion by mani-
16 festing himself. Then, when the leader
gave the order, he set forth at once
from there and joined battle with them
17 at the village of Adasa. Simon, Judas'
brother, had encountered Nicanor, and
had recently been checked because of
the consternation his antagonists in-
18 spired. Still Nicanor, hearing of the
valor of Judas and his men, and their
courage in their battles for their country, hesitated to decide the matter by
19 the sword. So he sent Posidonius and
Theodotus and Mattathias to propose
20 terms. After full consideration of these,
when each leader had communicated
them to his people, and their judgment
proved favorable, they agreed to the
21 treaty. So they fixed a day on which to
meet by themselves, a chariot advanced
from each side, couches were placed in
22 position; Judas posted armed men in
readiness at suitable points, through
fear that some treachery might suddenly develop on the part of the enemy;
they held the appropriate conference.
23 Nicanor stayed in Jerusalem, and did
nothing improper, but sent home the
thronging crowds that had gathered.
24 He kept Judas constantly in his company; he had become warmly attached
25 to the man; he urged him to marry and
have children. He did marry, settled
down, took his part in life.
26 But when Alcimus realized their
good understanding with each other,
and got hold of the treaty they had
made, he went to Demetrius and told
him that Nicanor was disloyal to the
government, for he had appointed
Judas, the conspirator against the king-
27 dom, as his successor. The king was
excited and incensed by the rascal's accusations, and wrote to Nicanor stating
that he was dissatisfied with the treaty,
and ordering him to send Maccabeus
as a prisoner to Antioch without delay.
28 When Nicanor received the message,
he was troubled and annoyed at having
to cancel the agreement when the man
29 had done no wrong. But as it was not
possible to oppose the king, he watched
for an opportunity to accomplish this
30 by strategy. But Maccabeus observed
that Nicanor began to treat him more
stiffly and was acting more rudely than
usual, and concluding that this stiffness
was not a very good sign, he mustered
no small number of his men and went
into hiding from Nicanor.
When the latter realized that he had 31
been splendidly outmaneuvered by the
man, he went to the great and holy
temple as the priests were offering the
customary sacrifices, and ordered them
to deliver the man up. And when they 32
protested with oaths that they did
not know where the man he sought
was, he stretched out his right hand 33
toward the sanctuary and uttered this
oath:
"If you do not hand Judas over to me
as a prisoner, I will level this sacred
precinct of God with the ground and
tear down the altar, and build here a
splendid temple to Dionysus."
With these words he left. But the 34
priests stretched out their hands to
heaven and called upon him who always fights for our nation, and said,
"Lord of all, who are self-sufficient, 35
you consented to have a temple for your
habitation among us; now therefore, 36
holy Lord of all consecration, keep undefiled forever this house that has been
so lately purified."
Now one of the elders of Jerusalem 37
named Razis was reported to Nicanor
as a man who loved his countrymen and
was very well thought of, and was
called father of the Jews for his benevolence. For in former times, when there 38
was no communication with the Gen-
tiles, he had been accused of Judaism,
and had most zealously risked soul and
body for it. And Nicanor, wishing to 39
manifest the enmity he felt for the
Jews, sent more than five hundred
soldiers to arrest him; for he thought 40
that in arresting him he would be doing
them an injury. But when this force 41
was on the point of capturing the tower
and was forcing the courtyard door and
demanding that fire be brought and
the doors set on fire, as he was surrounded he fell upon his sword, pre- 42
ferring to die nobly rather than to fall
into the wretches' hands and suffer outrages unworthy of his rank. But he 43
missed his stroke in the haste of the
struggle, and with the crowd streaming
in through the doors, he ran gallantly
up on the wall and bravely threw himself down into the crowd. But as they 44
quickly drew back, and a space opened,
he fell in the middle of the open space.
But being still alive and fired with 45

anger he got up and with his blood
gushing out, though severely wounded,
he ran through the crowd and standing
46 on a steep rock, as he was losing the last
of his blood, he pulled out his bowels
with both hands and hurled them at the
crowd, and so expired, calling upon him
who is lord of life and spirit, to give
these back to him again.

15 But Nicanor, getting word that Judas and his men were in the region of
Samaria, resolved to attack them in
2 perfect safety, on the day of rest. And
when the Jews who were forced to follow him said,

"Do not destroy them savagely and
barbarously like this, but show respect
for the day which has been pre-emi-
nently honored with holiness by him
3 who beholds all things," the thrice-
accursed wretch asked if there was a
sovereign in heaven who had commanded them to keep the sabbath day;
4 and when they declared,

"It is the living Lord himself, the
Sovereign in heaven, who bade us ob-
5 serve the seventh day," he said,

"I am a sovereign too, on earth, and
I command you to take up arms and
finish the king's business."

Nevertheless, he did not succeed in
carrying out his cruel purpose.

6 And Nicanor in his utter haughtiness and pretense had determined to
erect a public monument of victory
7 over Judas and his men. But Maccabeus did not cease to trust with perfect
confidence that he would get help from
8 the Lord, and he exhorted his men not
to fear the attack of the heathen but to
keep in mind all the help that had come
to them before from heaven, and to
look now for the victory which would
9 come to them from the Almighty. And
encouraging them from the Law and
the prophets and reminding them of
the battles they had fought, he made
10 them more eager. And when he had
aroused their courage, he gave his
orders, and at the same time pointed
out the perfidy of the heathen and their
11 breaking of their oaths. Then he armed
each one, not so much with the security
of shields and spears as with the encouragement of brave words, and
cheered them all by telling a dream that
was worthy of belief, a kind of vision.

12 The sight he saw was this: Onias, the
former high priest, a fine, good man, of
dignified appearance, but mild in manner and one who spoke fittingly, and
trained from childhood in all that belongs to character, with outstretched
hands praying for the whole Jewish
community; then in the same fashion 13
another man appeared, distinguished
by his gray hair and dignity, and
wrapped in marvelous, most majestic
sublimity; and Onias answered and 14
said,

"This is Jeremiah, the prophet of
God, who loves the brothers, and prays
fervently for the people and the holy
city."

And Jeremiah stretched out his right 15
hand and delivered to Judas a gold
sword, and as he gave it to him, he addressed him thus:

"Take this holy sword as a gift from 16
God, with which you will strike down
your adversaries."

Encouraged by Judas' words, which 17
were so fine, and so fitted to rouse men
to valor and to stir the souls of the
young to manliness, they determined
not to carry on a campaign but to
charge gallantly and engaging them
hand to hand with the utmost manful-
ness to decide the matter, because the
city and the sanctuary and the temple
were in peril. For they were not so 18
much alarmed about wives and children, or about brothers and relatives,
but first and foremost about the consecrated sanctuary. And those who 19
were left in the city felt no slight distress, for they were anxious about the
encounter in the open.

When they were all now awaiting the 20
decisive moment, and the enemy had
already joined battle, and the army was
drawn up and the animals had been
posted in a convenient position, and
the cavalry stationed on the wings,
Maccabeus, realizing the hosts before 21
him, and the elaborate supply of arms,
and the fierceness of the animals,
stretched out his hands to heaven and
called upon the Lord who works wonders, for he knew that it is not won by
arms but that as he decides he gains the
victory for those who deserve it. And 22
he called upon him in these words:

"It was you, Lord, who sent your
angel in the time of Hezekiah, king of
Judah, and he destroyed fully a hundred and eighty-five thousand in the
camp of Sennacherib. So now also, 23

Sovereign of the heavens, send forth a
brave angel to carry fear and terror
24 before us. By the might of your arm
may those who blasphemously come
against your holy people be struck
down."
25 With these words he ended. But
Nicanor and his men advanced with
26 trumpets and battle songs. And Judas
and his men met the enemy with en-
27 treaties and prayers. So fighting with
their hands and praying to God with
their hearts, they laid low no less than
thirty-five thousand, being greatly
cheered by God's manifest aid.
28 When the business was over, and
they were joyfully returning, they recognized Nicanor, lying dead, in his
29 armor. And there was shouting and
tumult, and they blessed the Sovereign
in the language of their forefathers.
30 Then the man who was in body and
soul the perfect champion of his fellow-
citizens, who maintained the good will
of his youth toward his fellow-citizens,
ordered them to cut off Nicanor's head
and arm and carry them to Jerusalem.
31 And when he arrived there, and had
called his countrymen together, and
stationed the priests before the altar,
he sent for those who were in the cita-
32 del. And he showed them the vile
Nicanor's head and the wretch's hand,
which he had boastfully stretched forth
against the holy house of the Almighty,
and he cut out the impious Nicanor's 33
tongue, and said he would give it piece-
meal to the birds, and hang up the reward of his folly in front of the sanctuary. And they all looked up to heaven 34
and blessed the Lord who had so manifested himself, and said,
"Blessed be he who has kept his own
place from being defiled."
And he hung Nicanor's head from 35
the citadel, a clear and conspicuous
proof to all of the Lord's help. And 36
they all decreed by popular vote of the
people never to let this day go by without observing it, but to celebrate the
thirteenth day of the twelfth month—
which is called Adar in Aramaic—the
day before Mordecai's day.
So this was the way Nicanor's efforts 37
turned out; and as the city was held by
the Hebrews from that time, I too will
here conclude my account. If it has 38
been well and pointedly written, that
is what I wanted; but if it is poor,
mediocre work, that was all I could do.
For just as it is harmful to drink wine 39
by itself, or again to drink water by itself, while wine mixed with water is
delicious and enhances one's enjoyment, so the style in which an account
is composed delights the ears of those
who read the work.
So this will be the end.

THE NEW TESTAMENT

AN AMERICAN TRANSLATION

By

EDGAR J. GOODSPEED

PREFACE

THE New Testament was written not in classical Greek, nor in the "biblical" Greek of the Greek version of the Old Testament, nor even in the literary Greek of its own day, but in the common language of everyday life. This fact has been fully established by the Greek papyrus discoveries and the grammatical researches of the last twenty-five years. It follows that the most appropriate English form for the New Testament is the simple, straightforward English of everyday expression.

The invitation of the University Press to provide such a translation was accepted by the present translator in the hope that it might result in a version with something of the ease, boldness, and unpretending vigor which mark the original Greek. The writers of the New Testament had for the most part little use for literary art. The principal figure among them, the apostle Paul, said this in so many words. They put their message in the simplest and most direct terms they could command, so that it spoke directly to the common life of their day. The great passages in the New Testament owe their greatness more to the trenchant vigor of their thought, or the moral sublimity of their ideas, than to the graces of rhetoric.

The translation of such a book demands, first, the understanding of what the several writers meant to say, and second, the casting of their thought in the simplest and clearest of present-day English. It is the meaning, not the dress, of the New Testament that is of principal importance. For many of us the familiar expressions of the Authorized Version are richly freighted with memories and associations. But few indeed sit down and read the New Testament in that version continuously and understandingly, a book at a time, as it was written to be read. The antique diction, the mechanical method of translation, and the disturbing verse division retard and discourage the reader. The aim of the present translation has been to present the meaning of the different books as faithfully as possible, without bias or prejudice, in English of the same kind as the Greek of the original, so that they may be continuously and understandingly read. There is no book in the New Testament that cannot easily be read at a sitting. For American readers, especially, who have had to depend so long upon versions made in Great Britain, there is room for a New Testament free from expressions which, however familiar in England or Scotland, are strange to American ears.

The progress of recent years in the study of the text, grammar, lexicography, and interpretation of the New Testament, together with the discoveries of Greek papyri made chiefly since 1897, offers a wealth of material to the translator. The grammatical works of Blass, Burton, Moulton, and Robertson, and the new lexicons of Preuschen (1910), Zorell (1911), Ebeling (1913), Souter (1916), and Abbott-Smith (1922), with the lexical studies of Moulton and Milligan (1914—) greatly facilitate the work of the interpreter.

I have closely followed the Greek text of Westcott and Hort, now generally accepted. Every scholar knows its great superiority to the late and faulty Greek texts from which the early English translations from Tyndale to the Authorized Version were made. In a few instances, I have accepted the emendations suggested by Dr. Hort himself in his *Notes on Select Readings*. Under the influence of more recent investigations, I have departed from Westcott and Hort in John 19:29; Acts 6:9; 19:28, 34; James 1:17; and Revelation 13:1; and I have adopted the striking suggestion of Rendel Harris, that by an error of the eye the name of Enoch has dropped out of the text in I Peter 3:19. The passages marked by Westcott and Hort as interpolations have been omitted from this translation, as being no part of the original text.

The generous co-operation of the University Press has made it possible to print the translation as one would a modern book, with all those aids of quotation marks and paragraphing which make an open and inviting page, and so facilitate reading, reference, and understanding. The translator has not interspersed the text with footnotes or captions of his own devising, preferring to leave it to make its own impression upon the reader. Nor has he prefaced the several books with historical introductions, which might aid in their understanding. For such aids, he would refer to his *Story of the New Testament,* which the studious reader may find a helpful companion to the present translation.

It has been truly said that any translation of a masterpiece must be a failure, but if this translation can in any measure bring home the great, living messages of the New Testament a little more widely and forcibly to the life of our time, the translator will be well content.

EDGAR J. GOODSPEED

The University of Chicago
August 31, 1923

PREFACE

TO

THE 1948 EDITION

THE twenty-five years that have passed since *An American Translation* wa first printed, in 1923, have been full of significance for the history of the English New Testament. The flood of criticism it called forth offered an opportunity for presenting the literary and linguistic arguments for modern-speech versions and these have more and more won the day. Modern-speech translations have multiplied and the New Testament in modern speech has found general acceptance with lovers of the Bible. Even the Catholic revised New Testament of 1941 has relinquished the antique forms of the third person singular—goeth, bloweth, and the like—and the *Revised Standard Version* of 1946 has accepted the modern forms of the second person singular which were as a matter of fact in general use even when the King James Version wa published in 1611, as Shakespeare shows. The Bishop of London in an effort to promote the reading and understanding of the New Testament epistles has translated them into the most fearless and vigorous modern spoken English. The general translation picture has in fact altered importantly since 1923. While much had been done before that date in Britain and America in this direction, the American Translation was at first treated a a voice crying in the wilderness, but better knowledge of the situation and more respec for it now prevail.

While the general cast of the translation remains unchanged, further research and reflection, coupled with a wealth of friendly suggestions, have made some improvement in it possible. Substantial lexical and grammatical progress has marked these years. Th great Liddell-Scott-Jones Greek lexicon, which began to appear at Oxford in 1925, has reached completion (1940). Preisigke's dictionary of the Greek papyri has come out in three volumes, 1925–31. Walter Bauer's great New Testament lexicon has appeared and reached a third edition (1936). The Moulton and Howard New Testament gramma was finished in 1929, and Moulton and Milligan's *Vocabulary of the Greek Testament* reached completion in 1930. The Chester Beatty and Michigan papyri, which began to come to light in 1930, have been published (1933–37). The mysterious word "racha" ha been found in a significant connection in a Greek papyrus letter of 257 B.C. We may hope the quarter-century that lies before us will be no less rich in research and discovery. A new generation of New Testament scholars has arisen to explore it, and we older worker wish them every satisfaction and all success.

The response to this translation has from the first been far greater than the transla tor ever anticipated. To the host of readers who have so generously welcomed it, he offer his sincerest thanks.

EDGAR J. GOODSPEED

Bel-Air, Los Angeles

THE GOSPEL ACCORDING TO MATTHEW

1 THE ancestry of Jesus Christ,
who was descended from David,
who was descended from
Abraham.
2 Abraham was the father of Isaac,
and Isaac of Jacob, and Jacob of Judah
3 and his brothers, and Judah of Perez
and Zerah, whose mother was Tamar.
And Perez was the father of Hezron,
4 and Hezron of Aram, and Aram of
Aminadab, and Aminadab of Nahshon,
5 and Nahshon of Salmon, and Salmon of
Boaz, whose mother was Rahab. And
Boaz was the father of Obed, whose
mother was Ruth. And Obed was the
6 father of Jesse, and Jesse of King
David.
David was the father of Solomon,
7 whose mother was Uriah's wife. And
Solomon was the father of Rehoboam,
and Rehoboam of Abijah, and Abijah
8 of Asa, and Asa of Jehoshaphat, and
Jehoshaphat of Joram, and Joram of
9 Uzziah, and Uzziah of Jotham, and
Jotham of Ahaz, and Ahaz of Hezekiah,
10 and Hezekiah of Manasseh, and Manasseh
of Amon, and Amon of Josiah,
11 and Josiah of Jeconiah and his brothers,
at the period of the Babylonian
Exile.
12 After the Babylonian Exile, Jeconiah
had a son named Shealtiel, and Sheal-
13 tiel was the father of Zerubbabel, and
Zerubbabel of Abiud, and Abiud of Eli-
14 akim, and Eliakim of Azor, and Azor
of Zadok, and Zadok of Achim, and
15 Achim of Eliud, and Eliud of Eleazar,
and Eleazar of Matthan, and Matthan
16 of Jacob, and Jacob of Joseph, the husband
of Mary, who was the mother of
Jesus called Christ.
17 So the whole number of generations
from Abraham to David is fourteen,
and from David to the Babylonian Exile,
fourteen, and from the Babylonian
Exile to the Christ, fourteen.

18 Now the birth of Jesus Christ came
about this way. Mary, his mother, was
engaged to Joseph, but before they
were married it was found that she
was about to become a mother through
the influence of the holy Spirit. But 19
her husband, Joseph, was an upright
man and did not wish to disgrace her,
and he decided to break off the engagement
privately. But while he was think- 20
ing of doing this, an angel of the Lord
appeared to him in a dream, and
said,
"Joseph, descendant of David, do
not fear to take Mary, your wife, to
your home, for it is through the influence
of the holy Spirit that she is to become
a mother. She will have a son, 21
and you are to name him Jesus, for it is
he who is to save his people from their
sins."
All this happened in fulfilment of 22
what the Lord said through the prophet,

"The maiden will be pregnant and 23
will have a son,
And they will name him Immanuel"
—a word which means "God with us."
So when Joseph awoke from his sleep, 24
he did as the angel of the Lord had directed
him, and took his wife to his
home. But he did not live with her as 25
a husband until she had had a son, and
he named the child Jesus.
Now after the birth of Jesus at Beth- 2
lehem in Judea, in the days of King
Herod, astrologers from the east arrived
at Jerusalem, and asked, 2
"Where is the newly born king of the
Jews? For we have seen his star rise
and we have come to do homage to
him."
When King Herod heard of this, he 3
was troubled, and all Jerusalem with
him. So he called together all the high 4
priests and scribes of the people and
asked them where the Christ was to be
born. They said,
"At Bethlehem in Judea, for this is 5
what the prophet wrote:
" 'And you, Bethlehem in Judah's 6
land,
You are by no means least important
among the leaders of
Judah,
For from you will come a leader

Who will be the shepherd of my
people Israel.' "
7 Then Herod secretly sent for the astrologers, and found out from them the
exact time when the star appeared.
8 And he sent them to Bethlehem, and
said to them,
"Go and inquire particularly about
the child, and when you have found
him, bring me word, so that I may go
and do homage to him too."
9 So they obeyed the king and went,
and the star which they had seen rise
led them on until it reached the place
where the child was, and stopped above
10 it. When they saw the star, they were
11 very glad, and they went into the house
and saw him with his mother, Mary,
and they threw themselves down and
did homage to him. They opened their
treasure boxes and presented the child
with gifts of gold, frankincense, and
12 myrrh. Then, as they had been divinely
warned in a dream not to go back to
Herod, they returned to their own country by another way.
13 When they were gone, an angel of
the Lord appeared to Joseph in a
dream, and said,
"Wake up! Take the child and his
mother and make your escape to
Egypt, and stay there until I tell you
to leave. For Herod is going to look for
the child in order to make away with
him."
14 Then he awoke and took the child
and his mother by night and took ref-
15 uge in Egypt, to fulfil what the Lord
said by the prophet, "I called my son
from Egypt."
16 Then Herod saw that he had been
tricked by the astrologers, and he was
very angry, and he sent and made away
with all the boys in Bethlehem and in
all that neighborhood who were two
years old or under, for that was the
time he had learned from the astrologers
17 by his inquiries. Then the saying was
fulfilled which was uttered by the
prophet Jeremiah,
18 "A cry was heard in Ramah!
Weeping and great lamenting!
Rachel weeping for her children,
And inconsolable because they were
gone."
19 But when Herod died, an angel of the
Lord appeared in a dream to Joseph in
20 Egypt and said,
"Wake up! Take the child and his
mother and go to the land of Israel, for
those who sought the child's life are
dead."
Then he awoke, and took the child 21
and his mother and went to the land of
Israel. But hearing that Archelaus was 22
reigning over Judea in the place of his
father Herod, he was afraid to return
there; and being warned in a dream, he
took refuge in the region of Galilee, and 23
he went and settled in a town called
Nazareth, in fulfilment of the saying of
the prophets,
"He shall be called a Nazarene."

In those days John the Baptist ap- 3
peared, and preached in the desert of
Judea.
"Repent!" he said, "for the King- 2
dom of Heaven is coming!"
It was he who was spoken of by the 3
prophet Isaiah, when he said,
"Hark! Someone is shouting in the
desert,
'Get the Lord's way ready!
Make his paths straight!' "
John wore clothing made of hair cloth, 4
and he had a leather belt around his
waist, and he lived on dried locusts and
wild honey. Then Jerusalem and all 5
Judea and the whole Jordan valley
went out to him, and they were bap- 6
tized by him in the Jordan River, in
acknowledgment of their sins. But 7
when he saw many of the Pharisees and
Sadducees coming for baptism, he said
to them,
"You brood of snakes! Who warned
you to escape from the wrath that is
coming? Then produce fruit that will 8
be consistent with your professed repentance! Do not suppose that you can 9
say to yourselves, 'We have Abraham
for our forefather,' for I tell you God
can produce descendants for Abraham
right out of these stones! But the axe 10
is already lying at the roots of the trees.
Any tree that fails to produce good
fruit is going to be cut down and
thrown into the fire. I am baptizing 11
you in water in token of your repentance, but he who is coming after me is
stronger than I am, and I am not fit to
carry his shoes. He will baptize you in
the holy Spirit and in fire. His winnow- 12
ing fork is in his hand, and he will clean
up his threshing-floor, and store his
wheat in his barn, but he will burn up
the chaff with inextinguishable fire."

13 Then Jesus came from Galilee to the
Jordan, to John, to be baptized by him.
14 But John dissuaded him, and said,
"I need to be baptized by you, and
do you come to me?"
15 But Jesus answered,
"Let it be so this time, for it is right
for us to do everything that God requires."
16 Then John consented. And when Jesus was baptized, he went right up out
of the water, and the heavens opened,
and he saw the Spirit of God come down
17 like a dove and light upon him, and a
voice from heaven said,
"This is my Son, my Beloved! This
is my Chosen."
4 Then Jesus was guided by the Spirit
into the desert, to be tempted by the
2 devil. And he fasted forty days and
nights, and afterwards he was fam-
3 ished. And the tempter came up and
said to him,
4 "If you are God's son, tell these
stones to turn into bread!"
But he answered,
"The Scripture says, 'Not on bread
alone is man to live, but on every word
that comes from the mouth of God!'"
5 Then the devil took him to the holy
city, and made him stand on the sum-
6 mit of the Temple, and said to him,
"If you are God's son, throw yourself down, for the Scripture says,
"'He will give his angels orders
about you,
And they will lift you up with
their hands
So that you may never strike
your foot against a stone!'"
7 Jesus said to him,
"The Scripture also says, 'You shall
not try the Lord your God.'"
8 Again the devil took him to a very
high mountain, and he showed him all
the kingdoms of the world and their
9 splendor, and said to him,
"I will give all this to you, if you will
fall on your knees and do homage to
me."
10 Then Jesus said to him,
"Begone, Satan! For the Scripture
says, 'You must do homage to the Lord
your God, and worship him alone!'"
11 Then the devil left him, and angels
came and waited on him.
12 But when Jesus heard that John had
been arrested, he retreated to Galilee.
13 And he left Nazareth and went and settled in Capernaum, by the sea, in the
district of Zebulon and Naphtali, in ful- 14
filment of what was said by the prophet Isaiah,
"Zebulon's land, and Naphtali's 15
land,
Along the road to the sea, across the
Jordan,
Galilee of the heathen!
The people that were living in dark- 16
ness
Have seen a great light,
And on those who were living in the
land of the shadow of death
A light has dawned!"
From that time Jesus began to preach 17
and say,
"Repent! for the Kingdom of Heav-
en is coming!"
As he was walking by the Sea of Gali- 18
lee, he saw two brothers, Simon, who
was afterward called Peter, and his
brother, Andrew, casting a net into the
sea, for they were fishermen. He said to 19
them,
"Come and follow me, and I will
make you fish for men!"
They immediately dropped their 20
nets and went with him. And he went 21
on a little further and saw two other
men who were brothers, James, the son
of Zebedee, and his brother, John, in
the boat with Zebedee, their father,
putting their nets in order, and he
called them. And they immediately 22
left the boat and their father, and went
with him.
Then he went all over Galilee, teach- 23
ing in their synagogues and proclaiming the good news of the kingdom, and
curing any disease or sickness among
the people. Word went all through 24
Syria about him, and people brought to
him all who were suffering with any
kind of disease, or who were in great
pain—demoniacs, epileptics, and paralytics—and he cured them. Great 25
crowds followed him about, from Galilee and the Ten Towns and Jerusalem
and Judea and from the other side of
the Jordan.
When he saw the crowds of people he **5**
went up on the mountain. There he
seated himself, and when his disciples
had come up to him, he opened his lips 2
to teach them. And he said,
"Blessed are those who feel their 3
spiritual need, for the Kingdom of
Heaven belongs to them!

4 “Blessed are the mourners, for they
will be consoled!
5 “Blessed are the humble-minded, for
they will possess the land!
6 “Blessed are those who are hungry
and thirsty for uprightness, for they
will be satisfied!
7 “Blessed are the merciful, for they
will be shown mercy!
8 “Blessed are the pure in heart, for
they will see God!
9 “Blessed are the peacemakers, for
they will be called God’s sons!
10 “Blessed are those who have endured
persecution for their uprightness, for
the Kingdom of Heaven belongs to
them!
11 “Blessed are you when people abuse
you, and persecute you, and falsely say
everything bad of you, on my account.
12 Be glad and exult over it, for you will
be richly rewarded in heaven, for that
is the way they persecuted the prophets who went before you!
13 “You are the salt of the earth! But
if salt loses its strength, how can it be
made salt again? It is good for nothing
but to be thrown away and trodden
14 underfoot. You are the light of the
world! A city that is built upon a hill
15 cannot be hidden. People do not light
a lamp and put it under a peck-measure; they put it on its stand and it gives
16 light to everyone in the house. Your
light must burn in that way among
men so that they will see the good you
do, and praise your Father in heaven.
17 “Do not suppose that I have come to
do away with the Law or the Prophets.
I have not come to do away with them
18 but to complete them. For I tell you, as
long as heaven and earth endure, not
one dotting of an *i* or crossing of a *t* will
be dropped from the Law until it is
19 all observed. Anyone, therefore, who
weakens one of the slightest of these
commands, and teaches others to do so,
will be ranked lowest in the Kingdom
of Heaven; but anyone who observes
them and teaches others to do so will
be ranked high in the Kingdom of
20 Heaven. For I tell you that unless your
uprightness is far superior to that of the
scribes and Pharisees, you will never
even enter the Kingdom of Heaven!
21 “You have heard that the men of old
were told ‘You shall not murder,’ and
‘Whoever murders will have to answer
22 to the court.’ But I tell you that anyone who gets angry with his brother will
have to answer to the court, and anyone who speaks abusively to his
brother will have to answer to the great
council, and anyone who says to his
brother ‘You cursed fool!’ will have to
answer for it in the fiery pit! So when 23
you are presenting your gift at the altar, if you remember that your brother
has any grievance against you, leave 24
your gift right there before the altar
and go and make up with your brother;
then come back and present your gift.
Be quick and come to terms with your 25
opponent while you are on the way to
court with him, or he may hand you
over to the judge, and the judge may
hand you over to the officer, and you
will be thrown into prison. I tell you, 26
you will never get out again until you
have paid the last penny!
“You have heard that men were told 27
‘You shall not commit adultery.’ But I 28
tell you that anyone who looks at a
woman with desire has already committed adultery with her in his heart.
But if your right eye makes you fall, 29
tear it out and throw it away, for you
might better lose one part of your body
than have it all thrown into the pit! If 30
your right hand makes you fall, cut it
off and throw it away, for you might
better lose one part of your body than
have it all go down to the pit!
“They were told, ‘Anyone who di- 31
vorces his wife must give her a certificate of divorce.’ But I tell you that 32
anyone who divorces his wife on any
ground, except unfaithfulness, makes
her commit adultery, and anyone who
marries her after she is divorced commits adultery.
“Again, you have heard that the 33
men of old were told, ‘You shall not
swear falsely, but you must fulfil your
oaths to the Lord.’ But I tell you not 34
to swear at all, either by heaven, for it is
God’s throne, or by the earth, for it is 35
his footstool, or by Jerusalem, for it is
the city of the great king. You must 36
not swear by your own head, for you
cannot make one single hair white or
black. But your way of speaking must 37
be ‘Yes’ or ‘No.’ Anything that goes
beyond that comes from the evil one.
“You have heard that they were told, 38
‘An eye for an eye and a tooth for a
tooth.’ But I tell you not to resist in- 39
jury, but if anyone strikes you on your

right cheek, turn the other to him too;
40 and if anyone wants to sue you for your
41 shirt, let him have your coat too. And
if anyone forces you to go one mile, go
42 two miles with him. If anyone begs
from you, give to him, and when anyone wants to borrow from you, do not
turn away.
43 "You have heard that they were
told, 'You must love your neighbor
44 and hate your enemy.' But I tell you,
love your enemies and pray for your
45 persecutors, so that you may show
yourselves true sons of your Father in
heaven, for he makes his sun rise on
bad and good alike, and makes the rain
fall on the upright and the wrongdoers.
46 For if you love only those who love
you, what reward can you expect? Do
not the very tax-collectors do that?
47 And if you are polite to your brothers
and no one else, what is there remarkable in that? Do not the very heathen
48 do that? So you are to be perfect, as
your heavenly Father is.
6 "But take care not to do your good
deeds in public for people to see, for, if
you do, you will get no reward from
2 your Father in heaven. So when you
are going to give to charity, do not
blow a trumpet before yourself, as the
hypocrites do, in the synagogues and
the streets, to make people praise them.
I tell you, that is all the reward they
3 will get! But when you give to charity,
your own left hand must not know
4 what your right hand is doing, so that
your charity may be secret, and your
Father who sees what is secret will reward you.
5 "When you pray, you must not be
like the hypocrites, for they like to
pray standing in the synagogues and in
the corners of the squares, to let people
see them. I tell you, that is all the re-
6 ward they will get! But when you pray,
go into your own room, and shut the
door, and pray to your Father who is
unseen, and your Father who sees what
7 is secret will reward you. And when you
pray, do not repeat empty phrases as
the heathen do, for they imagine that
their prayers will be heard if they use
8 words enough. You must not be like
them. For God, who is your Father,
knows what you need before you ask
9 him. This, therefore, is the way you
are to pray:
'Our Father in heaven,
Your name be revered!
Your kingdom come! 10
Your will be done
On earth as well as in heaven!
Give us today bread for the day, 11
And forgive us our debts, as we 12
have forgiven our debtors.
And do not subject us to tempta- 13
tion,
But save us from the evil one.'
For if you forgive others when they of- 14
fend you, your heavenly Father will
forgive you too. But if you do not for- 15
give others when they offend you, your
heavenly Father will not forgive you
for your offenses.
"When you fast, do not put on a 16
gloomy look, like the hypocrites, for
they neglect their personal appearance
to let people see that they are fasting.
I tell you, that is all the reward they
will get. But when you fast, perfume 17
your hair and wash your face, so 18
that no one may see that you are fasting, except your Father who is unseen,
and your Father who sees what is secret, will reward you.
"Do not store up your riches on 19
earth, where moths and rust destroy
them, and where thieves break in and 20
steal them, but store up your riches in
heaven, where moths and rust cannot
destroy them, and where thieves cannot
break in and steal them. For wherever 21
your treasure is, your heart will be also.
The eye is the lamp of the body. So 22
if your eye is sound, your whole
body will be light, but if your eye is unsound, your whole body will be dark. 23
If, therefore, your very light is darkness, how deep the darkness will be!
No slave can belong to two masters, for 24
he will either hate one and love the
other, or stand by one and make light
of the other. You cannot serve God
and money. Therefore, I tell you, do not 25
worry about your life, wondering what
you will have to eat or drink, or about
your body, wondering what you will
have to wear. Is not life more important than food, and the body than
clothes? Look at the wild birds. They 26
do not sow or reap, or store their food
in barns, and yet your heavenly Father
feeds them. Are you not of more account than they? But which of you 27
with all his worry can add a single hour
to his life? Why should you worry 28
about clothing? See how the wild flow-

ers grow. They do not toil or spin, and
29 yet I tell you, even Solomon in all his
splendor was never dressed like one of
30 them. But if God so beautifully dresses
the wild grass, which is alive today and
is thrown into the furnace tomorrow,
will he not much more surely clothe
31 you, you who have so little faith? So
do not worry and say, 'What shall we
have to eat?' or 'What shall we have to
drink?' or 'What shall we have to
32 wear?' For these are all things the
heathen are in pursuit of, and your
heavenly Father knows well that you
33 need all this. But you must make his
kingdom, and uprightness before him,
your greatest care, and you will have all
34 these other things besides. So do not
worry about tomorrow, for tomorrow
will have worries of his own. Let each
day be content with its own ills.
7 "Pass no more judgments upon other
people, so that you may not have judg-
2 ment passed upon you. For you will be
judged by the standard you judge by,
and men will pay you back with the
same measure you have used with
3 them. Why do you keep looking at the
speck in your brother's eye, and pay no
attention to the beam that is in your
4 own? How can you say to your brother, 'Just let me get that speck out of
your eye,' when all the time there is a
5 beam in your own? You hypocrite!
First get the beam out of your own eye,
and then you can see to get the speck
out of your brother's eye.
6 "Do not give what is sacred to dogs,
and do not throw your pearls before pigs, or they will trample them under their feet and turn and tear you in
7 pieces. Ask, and what you ask will be
given you. Search, and you will find
what you search for. Knock, and the
8 door will open to you. For it is always
the one who asks who receives, and the
one who searches who finds, and the
one who knocks to whom the door
9 opens. Which of you men when his son
asks him for some bread will give him a
10 stone? Or if he asks for a fish, will he
11 give him a snake? So if you, bad as you
are, know enough to give your children
what is good, how much more surely
will your Father in heaven give what is
good to those who ask him for it!
12 Therefore, you must always treat other
people as you would like to have them
treat you, for this sums up the Law and
the Prophets.
"Go in at the narrow gate. For the 13
road that leads to destruction is broad
and spacious, and there are many who
go in by it. But the gate is narrow and 14
the road is hard that leads to life, and
there are few that find it.
"Beware of the false prophets, who 15
come to you disguised as sheep but are
ravenous wolves underneath. You can 16
tell them by their fruit. Do people pick
grapes off thorns, or figs off thistles?
Just so any sound tree bears good fruit, 17
but a poor tree bears bad fruit. No 18
sound tree can bear bad fruit, and no
poor tree can bear good fruit. Any tree 19
that does not bear good fruit is cut
down and burned. So you can tell them 20
by their fruit. It is not everyone who 21
says to me 'Lord! Lord!' who will get
into the Kingdom of Heaven, but only
those who do the will of my Father in
heaven. Many will say to me on that 22
Day, 'Lord! Lord! Was it not in your
name that we prophesied, and by your
name that we drove out demons, and
by your name that we did many mighty
acts?' Then I will say to them plainly, 23
'I never knew you! Go away from me,
you who do wrong!'
"Everyone, therefore, who listens to 24
this teaching of mine and acts upon it,
will be like a sensible man who built his
house on rock. And the rain fell, and 25
the rivers rose, and the winds blew, and
beat about that house, and it did not go
down, for its foundations were on rock.
And anyone who listens to this teach- 26
ing of mine and does not act upon it,
will be like a foolish man who built his
house on sand. And the rain fell, and 27
and the rivers rose, and the winds blew
and beat about that house, and it went
down, and its downfall was complete."
When Jesus had finished this dis- 28
course, the crowds were astounded at his
teaching, for he taught them like one 29
who had authority and not like their
scribes.
When Jesus came down from the 8
mountain, great crowds of people followed him. And a leper came up to 2
him and fell on his knees before him,
saying,
"If you only choose, sir, you can cure
me!"
So he stretched out his hand and 3
touched him, saying,

"I do choose! Be cured!"
And his leprosy was immediately
4 cured. Then Jesus said to him,
"See that you tell nobody, but go! Show yourself to the priest, and in proof of your cure, offer the gift that Moses prescribed."
5 When he got back to Capernaum, a
Roman captain came up and appealed
6 to him, saying,
"My servant, sir, is lying sick with paralysis at my house, in great distress."
7 He said to him,
"I will come and cure him."
8 But the captain answered,
"I am not a suitable person, sir, to
have you come under my roof, but simply say the word, and my servant will
9 be cured. For I am myself under the
orders of others and I have soldiers under me, and I tell one to go, and he goes, and another to come, and he comes, and my slave to do something, and he does it."
10 When Jesus heard this he was astonished, and said to his followers,
"I tell you, I have not found anyone
11 in Israel with such faith as this. And I
tell you, many will come from the east and from the west and take their places at the feast with Abraham, Isaac, and Jacob, in the Kingdom of Heaven,
12 while the heirs to the kingdom will be
driven into the darkness outside, there to weep and grind their teeth!"
13 Then Jesus said to the captain,
"Go! You shall find it just as you believe!"
And the servant was immediately cured.
14 Jesus went into Peter's house, and
there he found Peter's mother-in-law
15 sick in bed with fever. And he touched
her hand and the fever left her, and she got up and waited on him.
16 In the evening they brought to him
many who were possessed by demons, and he drove the spirits out with a
17 word, and cured all who were sick, in
fulfilment of the words of the prophet Isaiah, "He took our sickness and carried away our diseases."
18 Then Jesus, seeing a crowd about
him, gave orders to cross to the other
19 side. And a scribe came up and said to
him,
"Master, I will follow you wherever you are going!"

And Jesus said to him, 20
"Foxes have holes and wild birds have nests, but the Son of Man has nowhere to lay his head!"
And another of his disciples said to 21
him,
"Let me first go, sir, and bury my father."
But Jesus said to him, 22
"Follow me, and leave the dead to bury their own dead!"
And he got into the boat, and his dis- 23
ciples went with him. And suddenly a 24
terrific storm came up on the sea, so that the waves broke over the boat, but
he remained asleep. And they came 25
and woke him up, saying,
"Save us, sir! We are lost!"
And he said to them, 26
"Why are you afraid? You have so little faith!"
Then he got up and reproved the wind and the sea, and there was a great
calm. And the men were amazed and 27
said,
"What kind of man is this? For the very winds and sea obey him!"
When he reached the other side, in 28
the region of Gadara, two men possessed by demons came out of the tombs and confronted him; they were so extremely violent that nobody could
go along that road. And they suddenly 29
screamed out,
"What do you want of us, you Son of God? Have you come here before the appointed time to torture us?"
Now at some distance from them 30
there was a great drove of pigs feeding.
And the demons entreated him, saying, 31
"If you are going to drive us out, send us into the drove of pigs."
And he said to them, 32
"Begone!"
And they came out and went into the pigs. And suddenly the whole drove rushed over the steep bank into the sea,
and perished in the water. And the 33
men who tended them ran away and went off to the town and told it all, and the news about the men possessed by
demons. And the whole town came 34
out to meet Jesus, and when they saw him they begged him to go away from their district.
So he got into the boat and crossed 9
the sea, and returned to his own city.
Some people came bringing to him 2
on a bed a man who was paralyzed.

Seeing their faith, Jesus said to the
paralytic,
"Courage, my son! Your sins are forgiven."
3 Some of the scribes said to themselves,
"This man is talking blasphemy!"
4 Jesus knew what they were thinking,
and he said,
"Why do you have such wicked
5 thoughts in your hearts? For which is
easier, to say, 'Your sins are forgiven,'
6 or to say, 'Get up and walk'? But I
would have you know that the Son of
Man has authority to forgive sins on
earth." Then he said to the paralytic,
"Get up, pick up your bed and go
home!"
7 And he got up and went home. And
8 when the crowd saw it, they were filled
with awe, and praised God for giving
such power to men.
9 Afterward, as Jesus was passing
along from there, he saw a man called
Matthew sitting at the tollhouse, and
he said to him,
"Follow me!"
And he got up and followed him.
10 While Jesus was at home at table, a
number of tax-collectors and irreligious
people came in and joined Jesus and his
11 disciples at table. And the Pharisees
observed it, and they said to his disciples,
"Why does your master eat with tax-collectors and irreligious people?"
12 But he heard it, and said,
"It is not the well but the sick who
13 have to have the doctor! Go and
learn what the saying means, 'It is
mercy, not sacrifice, that I care for.'
I did not come to invite the pious but
the irreligious."
14 Then the disciples of John came up
to him and said,
"Why is it that we and the Pharisees
are keeping the fast, while your disciples are not keeping it?"
15 Jesus said to them,
"Can wedding guests mourn as long
as the bridegroom is with them? But a
time will come when the bridegroom
will be taken from them, and they will
16 fast then. But no one sews a patch of
unshrunken cloth on an old coat, for the
patch will tear away from the coat, and
17 make the hole worse than ever. And
people do not put new wine into old
wine-skins, or if they do, the skins
burst, and the wine runs out and the
skins are spoiled. But people put new
wine into fresh wine skins, and so both
are saved."
Just as he said this to them, an offi- 18
cial came up and bowing low before him
said to him,
"My daughter has just died. But
come! Lay your hand on her and she
will come to life!"
And Jesus got up and followed him, 19
with his disciples. And a woman who 20
had had a hemorrhage for twelve years
came up behind him and touched the
tassel of his cloak. For she said to her- 21
self, "If I can just touch his cloak, I will
get well." And Jesus turned and saw 22
her, and he said,
"Courage, my daughter! Your faith
has cured you!" And from that time the
woman was well.
When Jesus reached the official's 23
house, and saw the flute-players and
the disturbance the crowd was making,
he said, 24
"Go away, for the girl is not dead;
she is asleep." And they laughed at
him. But when he had driven the people 25
out, he went in and grasped her hand,
and the girl got up. And the news of 26
this spread all over that part of the
country.
As Jesus was passing along from 27
there, two blind men followed him,
calling out,
"Take pity on us, you Son of David!"
When he had gone indoors, the blind 28
men came up to him, and Jesus said to
them,
"Do you believe that I can do this?"
They said to him.
"Yes, sir."
Then he touched their eyes and said, 29
"Have what your faith expects!"
And their sight was restored. Jesus 30
sternly warned them, "Do not let anyone know." But they went off and 31
spread the news about him all over that
part of the country.
But just as they were going out, 32
some people brought to him a dumb
man who was possessed by a demon,
and as soon as the demon was driven 33
out, the dumb man was able to speak.
And the crowds were amazed, and
said,
"Nothing like this was ever seen in
Israel!"
But the Pharisees said, 34

"It is by the aid of the prince of the
demons that he drives them out."
35 Jesus went round among all the
towns and villages, teaching in their
synagogues, and proclaiming the good
news of the kingdom, and curing every
disease and illness.
36 But the sight of the crowds of people
filled him with pity for them, because
they were bewildered and dejected, like
37 sheep that have no shepherd. Then he
said to his disciples,
"The harvest is abundant enough,
38 but the reapers are few. So pray to the
owner of the harvest to send reapers to
gather it."
10 Then he called his twelve disciples to
him, and gave them power over the
foul spirits so that they could drive
them out, and so that they could heal
any disease or illness.
2 These are the names of the twelve
apostles: first, Simon, who was called
Peter, and his brother Andrew, and
James the son of Zebedee and his broth-
3 er John, Philip and Bartholomew,
Thomas and Matthew the tax-collector, James the son of Alpheus and
4 Thaddeus, Simon the Zealot and Judas
Iscariot who afterward betrayed him.
5 Jesus sent these twelve out, after
giving them these directions:
"Do not go among the heathen, or to
6 any Samaritan town, but proceed instead to the lost sheep of Israel's house.
7 And as you go about, preach and say,
'The Kingdom of Heaven is at hand!'
8 Cure the sick, raise the dead, heal lepers, drive out demons. Give without
payment, just as you received without
9 payment. Do not take gold or silver
or copper money in your purses, and
10 do not take a bag for your journey,
nor two shirts, nor shoes, nor a staff, for
11 the workman deserves his food! Whatever town or village you come to, inquire for some suitable person, and stay
with him till you leave the place.
12 And as you go into his house, wish it
13 well. If the house deserves it, the peace
you wish it will come over it, but if it
does not deserve it, let your blessing
14 come back upon yourselves. And where
no one will welcome you, or listen to
you, leave that house or town and
15 shake off its very dust from your feet. I
tell you, the land of Sodom and Gomorrah will fare better on the Day of Judgment than that town.

"Here I am sending you out like 16
sheep among wolves. So you must be
wise like serpents, and guileless like
doves. But be on your guard against 17
men, for they will give you up to their
courts, and have you flogged in their
synagogues, and you will be brought 18
before governors and kings on my
account, to bear your testimony before
them and the heathen. But when they 19
give you up, you must have no anxiety
about how to speak or what to say, for
you will be told at the very moment
what you ought to say, for it is not you 20
who will speak, it is the Spirit of your
Father that will speak through you.
One brother will give up another to 21
death, and a father his child, and children will turn against their parents,
and have them put to death. You will 22
be hated by everybody on my account,
but the man who holds out to the very
end will be saved. But when they per- 23
secute you in one town, make your escape to another, for I tell you, you will
not have gone through all the towns of
Israel before the Son of Man arrives. A 24
pupil is not better than his teacher, nor
a slave better than his master. A pupil 25
should be satisfied to come to be like his
teacher, or a slave, to come to be like
his master. If men have called the
head of the house Beelzebub, how much
worse names will they give to the members of his household! So do not be 26
afraid of them. For there is nothing
covered up that is not going to be uncovered, nor secret that is not going to
be known. What I tell you in the dark 27
you must say in the light, and what you
hear whispered in your ear, you must
proclaim from the housetops. Have no 28
fear of those who kill the body, but cannot kill the soul. You had better be
afraid of one who can destroy both soul
and body in the pit. Do not sparrows 29
sell two for a cent? And yet not one of
them can fall to the ground against
your Father's will! But the very hairs 30
on your heads are all counted. You 31
must not be afraid; you are worth more
than a great many sparrows! There- 32
fore everyone who will acknowledge me
before men I will acknowledge before
my Father in heaven, but anyone who 33
disowns me before men, I will disown
before my Father in heaven.
"Do not think that I have come to 34
bring peace to the earth. I have not

come to bring peace but a sword.
35 For I have come to turn a man against
his father and a daughter against her
mother and a daughter-in-law against
36 her mother-in-law, and a man's ene-
37 mies will be in his own household. No
one who loves father or mother more
than he loves me is worthy of me, and
no one who loves son or daughter more
38 than he loves me is worthy of me, and
no one who will not take up his cross
39 and follow me is worthy of me. Whoever gains his life will lose it, and whoever loses his life for my sake will gain
it.
40 "Whoever welcomes you welcomes
me, and whoever welcomes me wel-
41 comes him who has sent me. Whoever
welcomes a prophet because he is a
prophet will have the same reward as a
prophet, and whoever welcomes an upright man because he is upright will
have the same reward as an upright
42 man. And no one who will give the
humblest of my disciples even a cup of
cold water because he is my disciple, I
tell you, can ever fail of his reward."

11 When Jesus had finished giving his
twelve disciples these instructions, he
went on from there to teach and preach
in their towns.
2 Now when John heard in prison of
what the Christ was doing, he sent by
3 his disciples and said to him,
"Are you the one who was to come,
or should we look for someone else?"
4 Jesus answered them,
"Go and report to John what you
5 hear and see. The blind are regaining
their sight and the lame can walk, the
lepers are being cured and the deaf can
hear, the dead are being raised and
good news is being preached to the
6 poor. And blessed is the man who finds
nothing that repels him in me."
7 But as they were going away, Jesus
began to speak to the crowds about
John.
"What was it that you went out into
the desert to look at? A reed swaying
8 in the wind? Then what did you go out
there to see? A man luxuriously
dressed? Men who dress in that way
9 you find in the palaces of kings. Then
why did you go out there? Was it to
see a prophet? Yes, I tell you, and far
10 more than a prophet! This is the man
of whom the Scripture says,

" 'Here I send my messenger on before you;
He will prepare the road ahead of
you.'
"I tell you, among men born of wom- 11
en no one greater than John the Baptist has ever appeared. And yet those
who are of little importance in the
Kingdom of Heaven are greater than
he. But from the time of John the Bap- 12
tist until now men have been taking the
Kingdom of Heaven by storm and im-
petuously crowding into it. For up to 13
the time of John all the Prophets and
the Law itself prophesied about it, and, 14
if you are ready to accept the idea, he is
himself Elijah who was to come. Let 15
him who has ears listen! But to what 16
can I compare this present age? It is
like children sitting about in the bazaars and calling out to their play-
mates,
" 'We have played the flute for you, 17
and you would not dance!
We have wailed and you would
not beat your breasts!'
For when John came, he neither ate nor 18
drank, and people said, 'He has a demon!' Now that the Son of Man has 19
come, he does eat and drink, and people
say, 'Look at him! A glutton and a
drinker, the companion of tax-collectors and irreligious people!' And yet
Wisdom is vindicated by her actions!"
Then he began to reproach the towns 20
in which most of his wonders had been
done, because they did not repent.
"Alas for you, Chorazin! Alas for 21
you, Bethsaida! For if the wonders that
have been done in you had been done
in Tyre and Sidon, they would have repented in sackcloth and ashes long ago!
But I tell you, Tyre and Sidon will fare 22
better on the Day of Judgment than
you will! And you, Capernaum! Are 23
you to be exalted to the skies? You will
go down among the dead! For if the
wonders that have been done in you
had been done in Sodom, it would have
stood until today. But I tell you that 24
the land of Sodom will fare better on
the Day of Judgment than you will!"
At that same time Jesus said, 25
"I thank you, Father, Lord of heaven
and earth, for hiding all this from the
learned and intelligent and revealing it
to children. Yes, I thank you, Father, 26
for choosing to have it so. Everything 27
has been handed over to me by my Fa-

ther, and no one understands the Son
but the Father, nor does anyone understand the Father but the Son and anyone to whom the Son chooses to reveal
28 him. Come to me, all of you who toil
and are burdened, and I will let you
29 rest. Let my yoke be put upon you, and
learn from me, for I am gentle and
humble-minded, and your hearts will
30 find rest, for the yoke I offer you is a
kindly one, and the load I ask you to
bear is light."

12 At that same time Jesus walked one
Sabbath through the wheat fields, and
his disciples became hungry and began
to pick the heads of wheat and eat
2 them. But the Pharisees saw it and
said to him,

"Look! Your disciples are doing
something which it is against the Law
to do on the Sabbath!"

3 But he said to them,

"Did you never read what David
did, when he and his companions were
4 hungry? How is it that he went into
the House of God and that they ate
the Presentation Loaves which it was
against the Law for him and his companions to eat, or for anyone except the
5 priests? Or did you never read in the
Law how the priests in the Temple are
not guilty when they break the Sab-
6 bath? But I tell you, there is something greater than the Temple here!
7 But if you knew what the saying
means, 'It is mercy, not sacrifice, that I
care for,' you would not have con-
8 demned men who are not guilty. For
the Son of Man is master of the Sabbath."

9 And he left the place and went into
10 their synagogue. There was a man
there with one hand withered. And in
order to get a charge to bring against
him, they asked him,

"Is it right to cure people on the
Sabbath?"

11 But he said to them,

"Who among you if he has one
sheep and it falls into a hole on the
Sabbath, will not take hold of it and
12 lift it out? And how much more a man
is worth than a sheep! Therefore, it is
right to do people good on the Sabbath."

13 Then he said to the man,

"Hold out your hand!"

And he held it out, and it was restored and became as well as the other.
But the Pharisees left the synagogue 14
and consulted about him, with a view
to putting him to death.

But Jesus knew of this, and he left 15
that place. And numbers of people followed him about, and he cured them
all, and warned them not to say any- 16
thing about him—in fulfilment of what 17
was said by the prophet Isaiah,

"Here is my servant whom I have 18
selected,
My beloved, who delights my
heart!
I will endow him with my Spirit,
And he will announce a judgment
to the heathen.
He will not wrangle or make an 19
outcry,
And no one will hear his voice in
the streets;
He will not break off a bent reed, 20
And he will not put out a smolder-
ing wick,
Until he carries his judgment to
success.
The heathen will rest their hopes 21
on his name!"

At that time some people brought to 22
him a man blind and dumb, who was
possessed by a demon, and he cured
him, so that the dumb man could speak
and see. And all the crowds of people 23
were astounded, and said,

"Can this be the Son of David?"

But when the Pharisees heard of it 24
they said,

"This man cannot drive out demons
except by the aid of Beelzebub, the
prince of the demons."

But he knew what they were think- 25
ing, and he said to them,

"Any kingdom that is disunited is on
the way to destruction, and any city or
household that is disunited cannot last.
If Satan is driving Satan out, he is dis- 26
united, and so how can his kingdom
last? And if I am driving the demons 27
out by Beelzebub's aid, by whose aid
do your sons drive them out? Therefore let them be your judges. But if I 28
am driving the demons out by the aid
of God's Spirit, then the Kingdom of
God has overtaken you. How can any- 29
one get into a strong man's house and
carry off his property unless he first
binds the strong man? After that he
can plunder his house. Anyone who is 30
not with me is against me, and anyone
who does not join me in gathering,

31 scatters. Therefore, I tell you, men
will be forgiven for any sin or abusive
speech, but abusive speech about the
32 Spirit cannot be forgiven. And whoever speaks against the Son of Man will
be forgiven for it, but whoever speaks
against the holy Spirit cannot be forgiven for it, either in this world or in
the world to come.

33 "Either make the tree sound and
its fruit sound, or make the tree bad
and its fruit bad; a tree is known by
34 its fruit. You brood of snakes! how
can you, bad as you are, utter anything good? For the mouth says only
35 what the heart is full of. A good man,
out of the good he has accumulated,
brings out things that are good, and
a bad man, out of what he has accumulated that is bad, brings out things
36 that are bad. But I tell you, for every
careless word that men utter they will
have to answer on the Day of Judg-
37 ment. For it is by your words that you
will be acquitted, or by your words that
you will be condemned."

38 Then some of the scribes and Pharisees addressed him, saying,

"Master, we would like to have you
show us some sign."

39 But he answered,

"Only a wicked and faithless age insists upon a sign, and no sign will be
given it but the sign of the prophet Jo-
40 nah. For just as Jonah was in the stomach of the whale for three days and
nights, the Son of Man will be three
days and nights in the heart of the
41 earth. Men of Nineveh will rise with
this generation at the judgment and
condemn it, for when Jonah preached
they repented, and there is more than
42 Jonah here! The queen of the south will
rise with this generation at the judgment and condemn it, for she came
from the very ends of the earth to listen
to Solomon's wisdom, and there is more
than Solomon here!

43 "When a foul spirit goes out of a
man, it roams through deserts in search
44 of rest and can find none. Then it says,
'I will go back to my house that I left,'
and it goes and finds it unoccupied,
45 cleaned, and all in order. Then it goes
and gets seven other spirits more wicked than itself, and they go in and live
there, and in the end the man is worse
off than he was before. That is the way
it will be with this present wicked generation."

While he was still speaking, his 46
mother and his brothers came up and
stood outside the crowd, wanting to
speak to him. But he said to the man 48
who told him,

"Who is my mother, and who are my
brothers?"

And he pointed to his disciples and 49
said,

"Here are my mother and my brothers! For whoever does the will of my 50
Father in heaven is my brother and sister and mother!"

That same day Jesus went out of his **13**
house and was sitting on the seashore.
And such great crowds gathered about 2
him that he got into a boat and sat
down in it, while all the people stood on
the shore. And he told them many 3
things in figures, and said to them,

"A sower went out to sow, and as he 4
was sowing, some of the seed fell by the
path and the birds came and ate it up,
and some fell on rocky ground where 5
there was not much soil and it sprang
up at once, because the soil was not
deep, but when the sun came up it was 6
scorched and withered up, because it
had no root. And some of it fell among 7
the thorns, and the thorns grew up and
choked it out. And some fell on good 8
soil, and yielded some a hundred, some
sixty, and some thirty-fold. Let him 9
who has ears listen!"

His disciples came up and said to 10
him,

"Why do you speak to them in figures?"

He answered, 11

"You are permitted to know the secrets of the Kingdom of Heaven, but
they are not. For people who have will 12
have more given them, and will be
plentifully supplied, and from people
who have nothing even what they have
will be taken away. This is why I speak 13
to them in figures, because though they
look they do not see, and though they
listen they do not hear or understand.
They are a fulfilment of Isaiah's 14
prophecy,

" 'You will listen and listen, and never understand,
And you will look and look, and
never see!
For this nation's mind has grown 15
dull,

And they hear faintly with their
ears,
And they have shut their eyes,
So as never to see with their eyes,
And hear with their ears,
And understand with their minds,
and turn back,
And let me cure them!'
16 But blessed are your eyes, for they do
see, and your ears, for they do hear.
17 For I tell you, many prophets and upright men have longed to see what you
see, and could not see it, and to hear
what you hear, and could not hear it.
18 "You must listen closely then to
19 the figure of the sower. When anyone
hears the teaching of the kingdom and
does not understand it, the evil one
comes and robs him of the seed that has
been sown in his mind. That is what
20 was sown along the path. And what
was sown upon the rocky soil means the
man who hears the message and at once
21 accepts it joyfully, but it takes no real
root in him, and lasts only a little while,
and when trouble or persecution comes
because of the message, he gives it up
22 at once. And what was sown among the
thorns means the man who listens to
the message, and then the worries of
the time and the pleasure of being rich
choke out the message, and it yields
23 nothing. And what was sown in good
ground means the man who listens to
the message and understands it, and
yields one a hundred, and another sixty, and another thirty-fold."
24 Another figure which he used in
speaking to them was this:
"The Kingdom of Heaven is like a
man who sowed good seed in his field,
25 but while men slept his enemy came
and sowed weeds among the wheat,
26 and went away. And when the wheat
came up and ripened, the weeds ap-
27 peared too. And the owner's slaves
came to him and said, 'Was not the
seed good that you sowed in your field,
sir? So where did these weeds come
28 from?' He said to them, 'This is some
enemy's doing.' And they said to him,
'Do you want us to go and gather them
29 up?' But he said, 'No, for in gathering
up the weeds you may uproot the
30 wheat. Let them both grow together
until harvest time, and when we harvest I will direct the reapers to gather
up the weeds first and tie them up in
bundles to burn, but get the wheat into my barn.'"
Another figure which he used in 31
speaking to them was this:
"The Kingdom of Heaven is like a
mustard seed which a man took and
sowed in his field. It is the smallest of 32
all seeds, but when it is grown it is the
largest of plants and grows into a tree,
so that the wild birds come and roost
in its branches."
Another figure which he used with 33
them was this:
"The Kingdom of Heaven is like
yeast, which a woman took and buried
in a bushel of flour until it had all
risen."
Jesus said all this to the crowds in 34
figures, and told them nothing except
in figures, to fulfil what was said by 35
the prophet,
"I will open my mouth in figures,
I will utter things that have been
hidden since the creation."
Then he left the crowds and went 36
into his house. And his disciples came
up to him and said,
"Explain to us the figure of the
weeds in the field."
He answered, 37
"The sower who sows the good seed
is the Son of Man. The field is the 38
world. The good seed is the sons of the
kingdom. The weeds are the sons of the
evil one. The enemy who sowed them is 39
the devil. The harvest is the close of
the age, and the reapers are angels. So 40
just as the weeds are gathered up and
burned, this is what will happen at the
close of the age; the Son of Man will 41
send out his angels, and they will gather up out of his kingdom all the causes
of sin and the wrongdoers and throw 42
them into the blazing furnace; there
they will wail and grind their teeth.
Then the upright will shine out like the 43
sun, in their Father's kingdom. Let him
who has ears listen!
"The Kingdom of Heaven is like a 44
hoard of money, buried in a field,
which a man found, and buried again.
And he was overjoyed, and went and
sold everything he had and bought the
field.
"Again, the Kingdom of Heaven is 45
like a dealer in search of fine pearls.
He found one costly pearl, and went 46
and sold everything he had, and bought
it.

47 "Again, the Kingdom of Heaven is
like a net that was let down into the
48 sea, and inclosed fish of all kinds. When
it was full, they dragged it up on the
beach, and sat down and sorted the
good fish into baskets and threw the
49 bad away. That is what will happen at
the close of the age. The angels will go
out and remove the wicked from among
50 the upright, and throw them into the
blazing furnace. There they will wail
and grind their teeth.

51 "Do you understand all this?"
They said to him,
"Yes."
52 He said to them,
"That is why every scribe who has
become a disciple of the Kingdom of
Heaven is like a householder who can
supply from his storeroom new things
as well as old."

53 When Jesus had finished these fig-
54 ures, he left that place, and went to his
own part of the country. And he taught
the people in their synagogue in such a
way that they were astonished, and
said,
"Where did he get this wisdom, and
55 the power to do these wonders? Is he
not the carpenter's son? Is not his
mother named Mary, and are not his
brothers named James, Joseph, Simon,
56 and Judas? And do not all his sisters
live here among us? Then where did he
get all this?"
57 And they took offense at him. But
Jesus said to them,
"A prophet is not refused honor anywhere except in his native place and at
his home."
58 And he did not do many wonders
there, because of their want of faith.

14 At that time, Herod the governor
2 heard the reports about Jesus, and he
said to his attendants,
"This man must be John the Baptist. He has risen from the dead, and
that is why wonderful powers are working through him."
3 For Herod had seized John and
bound him and put him in prison, on
account of Herodias, his brother Phil-
4 ip's wife, for John said to him,
"It is not right for you to be living
with her."
5 And while he wanted him killed, he
was afraid of the people; for they con-
6 sidered him a prophet. But when Herod's birthday came, Herodias' daughter
danced before the company. And Herod was delighted with her, and swore that he would give her anything she asked for. But she, at her mother's instigation, said,

"Give me John the Baptist's head here on a platter!"

And the king was sorry, but because he had sworn to do it, and because of the guests who were present, he ordered it to be given to her. And he sent and had John beheaded in the prison. And his head was brought back on a platter and given to the girl, and she took it to her mother. John's disciples came and took his body away, and buried him, and then they went and reported it to Jesus.

When Jesus heard it, he quietly retired by boat to a secluded place. And the crowds heard of it and followed him on foot from the towns. So when he got out of the boat he found a great crowd gathered, and his heart was touched at the sight of them, and he cured those of them that were sick. And when it was evening, the disciples came up to him and said,

"This is a lonely place and the day is over. Send the crowds off to the villages to buy themselves food."

But Jesus said to them,

"They do not need to go away. Give them food yourselves."

They said to him,

"We have nothing here but five loaves and two fish."

He said,

"Bring them here to me."

Then he ordered the crowds to sit down on the grass, and he took the five loaves and the two fish and looked up to heaven and blessed them, and he broke the loaves in pieces and gave them to the disciples and they gave them to the people. And they all ate and had enough. And the pieces left over that they gathered up filled twelve baskets. There were about five thousand men who were fed, besides women and children.

And he immediately made his disciples get into the boat and cross before him to the other side while he dismissed the crowds. After he had dismissed them he went up the hill by himself to pray. And when evening came on he was there alone, but the boat was by

this time a long way from shore, strug-
gling with the waves, for the wind was
25 against them. Toward morning he
went out to them, walking on the sea.
26 And the disciples saw him walking on
the sea, and they were terrified and said,
"It is a ghost!"
27 And they screamed with fear. But
Jesus immediately spoke to them and
said,
"Take courage! It is I. Do not be
afraid."
28 Peter answered,
"If it is you, Master, order me to
come to you on the water."
29 And he said,
"Come!"
And Peter got out of the boat and
walked on the water and went to Jesus.
30 But when he felt the wind he was
frightened, and beginning to sink, he
cried out,
"Master, save me!"
31 Jesus immediately stretched out his
hand and caught hold of him, and said
to him,
"Why did you waver? You have so
little faith!"
32 When they got into the boat, the
33 wind went down. And the men in the
boat fell down before him and said,
"You are certainly God's Son!"
34 And they crossed over to the other
35 side and came to Gennesaret. And the
men of the place recognized him, and
sent all over that district and brought
36 to him all who were sick, and they
begged him to let them touch just the
tassel of his cloak, and all who touched
it were cured.

15 Then some Pharisees and scribes
came to Jesus from Jerusalem, and said
to him,
2 "Why do your disciples break the
rules handed down by our ancestors?
For they eat their bread without first
washing their hands."
3 But he answered,
"Why do you too break God's command for the sake of what has been
4 handed down to you? For God said,
'Honor your father and mother,' and
'He who abuses his father or mother
5 must be put to death.' But you say,
'Whoever tells his father or mother,
"Anything of mine that might have
been of use to you is given to God,"
6 does not have to provide for his father.'
So you have nullified what God has
said, for the sake of what has been
handed down to you. You hypocrites! 7
Isaiah prophesied finely about you
when he said,
" 'This people honor me with their 8
lips,
Yet their hearts are far away from
me.
But their worship of me is all in 9
vain,
For the lessons they teach are but
human precepts.' "
And he called the people to him and 10
said to them,
"Listen to this, and grasp it! It is not 11
what goes into a man's mouth that pollutes him; it is what comes out of his
mouth that pollutes a man."
Then his disciples came up to him 12
and said to him,
"Do you know that the Pharisees
were shocked to hear you say that?"
But he answered, 13
"Any plant that my heavenly Father
did not plant must be uprooted! Leave 14
them alone. They are blind guides!
But if one blind man leads another,
they will both fall into the ditch!"
Peter said to him, 15
"Explain the figure for us."
He said, 16
"Have even you no understanding
yet? Can you not see that whatever 17
goes into the mouth passes into the
stomach and then is disposed of? But 18
the things that come out of the mouth
come from the heart, and they pollute
a man. For out of the heart come wick- 19
ed designs, murder, adultery, immorality, stealing, false witness, impious
speech. It is these things that pollute a 20
man, but not eating with unwashed
hands!"
And Jesus left that place and retired 21
to the neighborhood of Tyre and Sidon.
And a Canaanite woman of that dis- 22
trict came out and screamed,
"Son of David, take pity on me, sir!
My daughter is dreadfully possessed by
a demon!"
But he would not answer her a word. 23
And his disciples came up and urged
him, saying,
"Send her away, for she keeps
screaming after us."
But he answered, 24
"I am sent only to the lost sheep of
Israel's house."

25 And she came and fell down before
him, and said,
"Help me, sir!"
26 He answered,
"It is not right to take the children's
bread and throw it to the dogs!"
27 But she said,
"O yes, sir! For even dogs eat the
scraps that fall from their masters'
table!"
28 Then Jesus answered,
"You have great faith! You shall
have what you want."
And her daughter was cured from
that time.
29 Jesus left that place and went along
the shore of the Sea of Galilee, and went
up on the hillside, and sat down there.
30 Then great crowds came to him bringing with them those who were lame,
crippled, blind, or dumb, and many
others. And they laid them down at his
31 feet, and he cured them, so that the
people were astonished to see the dumb
speak, the lame walk, and the blind see.
And they praised the God of Israel.
32 Then Jesus called his disciples to him
and said,
"I pity these people for they have
been staying with me three days now
and they have nothing left to eat, and
I do not mean to send them away hungry, for they may give out on the way."
33 The disciples said to him,
"Where can we get bread enough in
this solitude to feed such a crowd?"
34 Jesus said to them,
"How many loaves have you?"
They said,
"Seven, and a few small fish."
35 Then he ordered the people to take
36 their places on the ground, and he took
the seven loaves and the fish and gave
thanks and he broke them in pieces and
gave them to his disciples, and the dis-
37 ciples gave them to the people. And
they all ate and satisfied their hunger.
And the pieces that they left that were
38 picked up filled seven baskets. There
were four thousand men who were fed,
39 besides women and children. And he
dismissed the people and got into the
boat and went to the district of Maga-
dan.
16 The Pharisees and Sadducees came
up and to test him asked him to show
2 them a sign from heaven. He answered,
4 "It is a wicked and faithless age that
insists on a sign, and no sign will be
given it but the sign of Jonah."
And he left them and went away.
When the disciples went across the 5
lake, they forgot to take any bread.
And Jesus said to them, 6
"Look out, and be on your guard
against the yeast of the Pharisees and
Sadducees!"
But they were debating with one 7
another, and saying,
"We have not brought any bread!"
Jesus noticed it and said, 8
"Why are you discussing with one
another your being without bread?
You have so little faith! Do you not 9
understand yet? Do you not remember
the five loaves for the five thousand,
and how many baskets full you gathered up? Nor the seven loaves for the 10
four thousand, and how many baskets
full you gathered up? Why do you not 11
see that I was not talking to you about
bread? But be on your guard against
the yeast of the Pharisees and Sadducees!"
Then they understood that he was 12
warning them not against yeast but
against the teaching of the Pharisees
and Sadducees.
When Jesus reached the district of 13
Caesarea Philippi, he asked his disciples,
"Who do people say that the Son of
Man is?"
They said, 14
"Some say John the Baptist, others
Elijah, and still others Jeremiah or one
of the prophets."
He said to them, 15
"But who do you say that I am?"
Simon Peter answered, 16
"You are the Christ, the Son of the
living God!"
Jesus answered, 17
"Blessed are you, Simon, son of
Jonah, for human nature has not dis-
closed this to you, but my Father in
heaven! But I tell you, your name is 18
Peter, a rock, and on this rock I will
build my church, and the powers of
death shall not subdue it. I will give 19
you the keys of the Kingdom of Heav-
en, and whatever you forbid on earth
will be held in heaven to be forbidden,
and whatever you permit on earth will
be held in heaven to be permitted."
Then he warned the disciples not to 20
tell anyone that he was the Christ.

21 It was then that Jesus Christ for the
first time explained to his disciples that
he had to go to Jerusalem and endure
great suffering there at the hands of the
elders, high priests, and scribes, and be
killed, and be raised to life on the third
22 day. And Peter took him aside and began to reprove him for it, saying,
"God bless you, Master! that can
never happen to you!"
23 But he turned and said to Peter,
"Get out of my sight, you Satan! You
hinder me, for you do not side with
God, but with men!"
24 Then Jesus said to his disciples,
"If anyone wants to go with me, he
must disregard himself and take his
25 cross and follow me. For whoever
wants to preserve his own life will lose
it, and whoever loses his life for me will
26 find it. For what good will it do a man
if he gains the whole world at the cost
of his life? What can a man give to
27 buy back his life? For the Son of Man
is going to come with his angels in his
Father's glory, and then he will repay
28 everyone for what he has done. I tell
you, some of you who stand here will
not taste death before they see the Son
of Man come to reign!"

17 Six days after this, Jesus took Peter
and James and his brother John, and
led them up on a high mountain, by
2 themselves. And his appearance underwent a change in their presence and
his face shone like the sun, and his
3 clothes became as white as light. And
Moses and Elijah appeared to them,
4 talking with him. And Peter spoke,
and said to Jesus,
"Master, how good it is that we are
here! If you wish, I will make three
huts here, one for you, and one for
Moses, and one for Elijah."
5 As he spoke a bright cloud overshadowed them and a voice from the cloud
said,
"This is my Son, my Beloved. He is
my Chosen. Listen to him!"
6 When the disciples heard it, they
were dreadfully frightened and fell
7 upon their faces. And Jesus came and
touched them, and said,
"Get up and do not be afraid."
8 When they looked up, they saw no
9 one but Jesus himself. And as they
were going down the mountain, Jesus
cautioned them, saying,
"Do not tell anyone of the vision you
have seen until the Son of Man is raised
from the dead."
The disciples asked him, 10
"Then why do the scribes say that
Elijah has to come first?"
He answered, 11
"Elijah does come and is to reform
everything, but I tell you, Elijah has 12
come already, and they would not recognize him, but treated him just as they
pleased. It is in just that way that the
Son of Man is going to be treated by
them!"
Then the disciples understood that 13
he was speaking to them of John the
Baptist.
When they came to the people again, 14
a man came up to him and fell on his
knees, saying,
"Master, take pity on my son, for he 15
has epilepsy, and is very wretched; he
often falls into the fire or into the water.
And I brought him to your disciples and 16
they have not been able to cure him."
Jesus answered, 17
"O you unbelieving, obstinate people! How long must I be with you?
How long must I put up with you?
Bring him here to me!"
And Jesus reproved the demon and it 18
came out of him, and from that moment
the boy was cured. Afterward, when he 19
was alone, the disciples went to Jesus
and said to him,
"Why could we not drive it out?"
He said to them, 20
"Because you have so little faith. For
I tell you, if you have faith the size of
a grain of mustard, you can say to this
mountain, 'Move from here over to
there!' and it will move, and nothing
will be impossible for you."
As they were going about in Galilee, 22
Jesus said to them,
"The Son of Man is going to be handed over to men, and they will kill him, 23
but on the third day he will be raised
to life again." And they were greatly
distressed.
When they reached Capernaum, the 24
collectors of the temple-tax came and
said to Peter,
"Does not your Master pay the temple-tax?"
He said, 25
"Yes."
But when he went home, Jesus spoke
of it first and said,
"What do you think, Simon? From

whom do earthly kings collect duties
and taxes? From their own people, or
from aliens?"
26 He said,
"From aliens."
Jesus said to him,
"Then their own people are exempt.
27 But rather than give offense to them,
go down to the sea and throw in a hook.
Take the first fish that comes up, open
its mouth and you will find in it a dollar. Take that and pay the tax for us
both."
18 Just at that time the disciples came
up and asked Jesus,
"Who is really greatest in the Kingdom of Heaven?"
2 He called a child to him and had him
3 stand among them, and he said,
"I tell you, unless you change and
become like children, you will never get
into the Kingdom of Heaven at all.
4 Anyone, therefore, who is as unassum-
ing as this child is the greatest in the
5 Kingdom of Heaven, and anyone who
welcomes one child like this on my ac-
6 count welcomes me. But whoever hin-
ders one of these little ones who believe
in me might better have a great millstone hung around his neck and be
7 sunk in the open sea. Alas for the world
for such hindrances! They have to
come, but alas for the man who causes
them!
8 "But if your own hand or your own
foot makes you fall, cut it off and throw
it away. You might better enter upon
life maimed or crippled than keep both
hands and feet but be thrown into the
9 everlasting fire. And if your own eye
makes you fall, dig it out and throw it
away. You might better enter upon life
with only one eye than be thrown with
both eyes into the fiery pit.
10 "Beware of feeling scornful of one
single little child, for I tell you that in
heaven their angels have continual ac-
12 cess to my Father in heaven. What do
you think? If a man has a hundred
sheep and one of them strays away,
will he not leave the ninety-nine on the
hills, and go in search of the one that is
13 astray? And if he happens to find it,
I tell you he rejoices more over it than
he does over the ninety-nine that did
14 not stray. In just that way, it is not
the will of my Father in heaven that a
single one of these little ones be lost.
15 "But if your brother wrongs you, go
to him and show him his fault while you
are alone with him. If he listens to you,
you have won back your brother. But 16
if he will not listen, take one or two others with you, so that everything may be
supported by the testimony of two or
three witnesses. If he refuses to listen 17
to them, tell the congregation. And if
he refuses to listen to it, treat him as a
heathen or a tax-collector.
"I tell you, whatever you forbid on 18
earth will be held in heaven to be forbidden, and whatever you permit on
earth will be held in heaven to be permitted. Again, I tell you, if even two 19
of you here on earth agree about what
they shall pray for, it will be given them
by my Father in heaven. For wherever 20
two or three are gathered as my followers, I am there among them."
Then Peter came to him and said, 21
"Master, how many times am I to
forgive my brother when he wrongs me?
Seven times over?"
Jesus said to him, 22
"Not seven times over, I tell you, but
seventy-seven times over! For this rea- 23
son the Kingdom of Heaven may be
compared to a king, who resolved to
settle accounts with his slaves. And 24
when he set about doing so, a man was
brought in who owed him ten million
dollars. And as he could not pay, his 25
master ordered him to be sold, with his
wife and children and all he had, in payment of the debt. So the slave threw 26
himself down before him and implored
him, 'Give me time, and I will pay you
all of it.' And his master's heart was 27
touched, and he let the slave go and
canceled the debt. But when the slave 28
went out he met a fellow-slave of his
who owed him a hundred dollars, and
he caught him by the throat, saying,
'Pay me what you owe!' So his fellow-
slave threw himself down before him, 29
and begged him, 'Give me time, and
I will pay you.' But he refused and
went and had him put in prison until 30
he should pay the debt. When his
fellow-slaves saw what had happened, 31
they were greatly distressed, and they
went to their master and reported the
whole matter to him. Then his master
called him in and said to him, 'You 32
wicked slave! I canceled all that debt
of yours when you entreated me.
Ought you not to have taken pity on 33
your fellow-slave, as I did on you?' So 34

his master in his anger handed him over
to the jailers, until he should pay all he
5 owed him. That is what my heavenly
Father will do to you, if you do not
each forgive your brothers from your
hearts!"

9 When Jesus had finished this discourse, he left Galilee and went to the
part of Judea that is on the other side of
2 the Jordan. Great crowds followed him
about and he cured them there.
3 And some Pharisees came up to him
to test him, and they said,
"Is it right for a man to divorce his
wife for any cause?"
4 But he answered,
"Did you never read that the Creator
at the beginning made them male and
5 female, and said, 'For this reason a
man shall leave his father and mother
and be united to his wife, and the two
of them shall become one'? So they are
6 no longer two but one. Therefore, what
God has joined together, man must not
try to separate."
7 They said to him,
"Then why did Moses command us
to draw up a written divorce-notice and
give it to her?"
8 He said to them,
"It was on account of your perversity
that Moses permitted you to divorce
your wives, but it was not so at the be-
9 ginning. I tell you that whoever divorces his wife on any ground but her
unfaithfulness, and marries another
woman, commits adultery."
10 The disciples said to him,
"If that is a man's relation to his
wife, it is better not to marry!"
11 He said to them,
"It is not everyone who can accept
that, but only those who have a special
12 gift. For some are incapable of marriage from their birth, and some have
been made so by men, and some have
made themselves so for the sake of the
Kingdom of Heaven. Let him accept
it who can."
13 Then some children were brought up
to him so that he might lay his hands on
them and pray, but his disciples re-
14 proved the people for it. But Jesus said,
"Let the children alone, and do not
try to keep them from coming to me,
for the Kingdom of Heaven belongs to
such as they."
15 And he laid his hands on them and
went on.

A man came up to him and said, 16
"Master, what good deed must I do
to obtain eternal life?"
But he said to him, 17
"Why do you ask me about what is
good? There is only one who is good.
But if you want to enter that life, keep
the commandments."
He said to him, 18
"Which ones?"
Jesus said,
"These 'You shall not murder, You
shall not commit adultery, You shall
not steal, You shall not bear false witness, Honor your father and mother,' 19
and 'You shall love your neighbor as
you do yourself.'"
The young man said to him, 20
"I have obeyed all these commandments. What do I still lack?"
Jesus said to him, 21
"If you want to be perfect, go! Sell
your property and give the money to
the poor, and you will have riches in
heaven. Then come back and be a follower of mine."
But when the young man heard that, 22
he went away much cast down, for he
had a great deal of property.
Jesus said to his disciples, 23
"I tell you, it will be hard for a rich
man to get into the Kingdom of Heav-
en! And again I tell you, it is easier for 24
a camel to get through a needle's eye
than for a rich man to get into the
Kingdom of God!"
But when the disciples heard this, 25
they were completely astounded and
said,
"Then who can be saved?"
But Jesus looked at them and said, 26
"For men it is impossible, but anything is possible for God!"
Then Peter spoke and said to him, 27
"Here we have left all we had and followed you. What are we to have?"
Jesus said to them, 28
"In the new world, I tell you, when
the Son of Man takes his seat on his
glorious throne, you who have followed
me will also sit upon twelve thrones,
and judge the twelve tribes of Israel!
And anyone who has given up houses or 29
brothers or sisters or father or mother
or children or land for my sake will receive many times as much, and make
sure of eternal life. But many who are 30
first now will be last then, and many
who are now last will be first. For the 20

Kingdom of Heaven is like an employer
who went out early in the morning to
2 hire laborers for his vineyard. He
agreed with the laborers to pay them a
dollar a day, and sent them to his vine-
3 yard. He went out about nine o'clock
and saw others standing in the bazaar
4 with nothing to do. And he said to
them, 'You go to my vineyard, too, and I
will pay you whatever is right.' So they
5 went. He went out again about twelve
and about three, and did the same.
6 About five he went out and found
others standing about and he said to
them, 'Why are you standing about
7 here all day doing nothing?' They
said to him, 'Because nobody has
hired us.' He said to them, 'You go to
8 my vineyard, too.' When evening came,
the owner of the vineyard said to his
foreman, 'Call the laborers and pay
them their wages, beginning with the
9 last and ending with the first.' When
those who were hired about five o'clock
10 came they received a dollar apiece. And
when those who were hired first came
they expected to get more, but they too
11 got a dollar apiece. And when they got
it they grumbled at their employer,
12 and said, 'These men who were hired
last worked only one hour, and you
have put them on the same footing
with us who have done the heavy work
of the day and have stood the midday
13 heat.' But he answered one of them,
'My friend, I am doing you no injustice. Did you not agree with me on a
14 dollar? Take what belongs to you and
go. I wish to give the last man hired as
15 much as I give you. Have I no right to
do what I please with what is mine?
Or do you begrudge my generosity?'
16 So those who are last now will be first
then, and those who are first will be
last."

17 When Jesus was about to go up to
Jerusalem, he took the Twelve off by
themselves, and as they were on the
way, he said to them,

18 "We are going up to Jerusalem, and
the Son of Man will be handed over to
the high priests and scribes, and they
19 will condemn him to death, and hand
him over to the heathen to be mocked
and flogged and crucified, and on the
third day he will be raised to life."

20 Then the mother of Zebedee's sons
came up to him with her sons, bowing
21 low, to ask a favor of him. He said to her,

"What do you want?"

She said to him,

"Give orders that these two sons of
mine sit one at your right and one at
your left, when you are king!"

But Jesus answered, 2

"You do not know what you are asking for! Can you drink what I am going
to drink?"

They answered,

"Yes, we can."

He said to them, 2

"Then what I drink you shall drink,
but as for sitting at my right and my
left, that is not mine to give, but belongs to those for whom it is destined
by my Father."

When the other ten heard of this, 2
they were very indignant at the two
brothers. But Jesus called them to 2
him and said,

"You know that the rulers of the
heathen lord it over them, and their
great men tyrannize over them. It is 2
not to be so among you, but whoever
wants to be great among you must be
your servant, and whoever wants to 27
hold the first place among you must be
your slave, just as the Son of Man has 28
come not to be waited on, but to wait
on other people, and to give his life to
ransom many others."

As they were going out of Jericho, a 29
great crowd followed him. And two 30
blind men sitting by the roadside, hearing that it was Jesus who was passing,
called out,

"You Son of David! Take pity on us,
sir!"

The crowd told them to be still, but 31
they called all the louder,

"You Son of David! Take pity on us,
sir!"

And Jesus stopped and called them, 32
and said,

"What do you want me to do for
you?"

They said to him, 33

"Sir, have our eyes opened!"

And Jesus took pity on them and 34
touched their eyes, and they immediately regained their sight, and followed
him.

When they were near Jerusalem and 21
had come to Bethphage and the Mount
of Olives, Jesus sent two disciples on
ahead, saying to them, 2

"Go to the village that lies in front of
you, and you will at once find an ass

tied there, and a colt with her. Untie
3 her and bring them to me. If anyone
says anything to you, you are to say
'The Master needs them'; then he will
send them at once."
4 Now this happened in fulfilment of
what was said by the prophet,
5 "Tell the daughter of Zion,
'Here is your king coming to you,
Gentle, and riding on an ass,
And on the foal of a beast of burden.'"
6 So the disciples went and did as Jesus
7 had directed them; they brought the
ass and the colt, and laid their coats
upon them, and Jesus seated himself
8 upon them. And most of the crowd
spread their coats in his way, and others
cut branches from the trees and scat-
6 tered them before him. And the crowds
that went in front of him and that followed him shouted,
"God bless the Son of David!
Blessed be he who comes in the
Lord's name.
God bless him from on high!"
10 When he came into Jerusalem, the
whole city was stirred, and everyone
asked,
"Who is he?"
11 The crowd answered,
"It is Jesus, the prophet of Nazareth
in Galilee!"
12 And Jesus went into the Temple and
drove out all who were buying or selling things in it, and he upset the money-changers' tables and the pigeon-
13 dealers' seats, and he said to them,
"The Scripture says, 'My house shall
be called a house of prayer,' but you
make it a robbers' den."
14 And blind and lame people came up
to him in the Temple, and he cured
15 them. But when the high priests and
the scribes saw the wonders that he did
and saw the boys shouting in the Temple, "God bless the Son of David!" they
16 were indignant, and said to him,
"Do you hear what they are saying?"
Jesus said to them,
"Yes. Did you never read, 'You have
drawn praise from the mouths of children and infants'?"
17 And he left them, and went out of the
city to Bethany, and spent the night
there.
18 In the morning as he went back to
19 the city, he grew hungry, and seeing a
fig tree by the roadside, he went up to
it, but found nothing on it but leaves.

And he said to it,
"No more fruit shall ever grow on
you!"
And the fig tree withered up at once. 20
When the disciples saw it, they were
amazed and said,
"How did the fig tree come to wither
up immediately?"
Jesus answered, 21
"I tell you, if you have faith and have
no doubt, you will not only do what I
have done to the fig tree, but even if
you say to this mountain, 'Get up and
throw yourself into the sea,' it will be
done. And everything that you pray 22
for with faith, you will obtain."
When he had entered the Temple, 23
and was teaching, the high priests and
the elders of the people came up to him,
and said,
"What authority have you for doing
as you do, and who gave you this authority?"
Jesus answered, 24
"Let me ask you one question, and if
you answer it, I will tell you what authority I have for doing as I do. Where 25
did John's baptism come from? Was it
from heaven, or from men?"
And they argued with one another,
"If we say, 'It was from heaven,' he
will say to us, 'Then why did you not
believe him?' But if we say, 'From 26
men,' we have the people to fear, for
they all consider John a prophet."
And they answered Jesus, 27
"We do not know."
He said to them,
"Nor will I tell you what authority I
have for doing as I do. But what do you 28
think? There was a man who had two
sons. He went to the first and said,
'My son, go and work in the vineyard
today.' And he answered, 'I will, sir.' 29
but he did not go. Then the man went 30
to the second son, and told him the
same thing. And he answered, 'I will
not!' But afterward he changed his
mind and went. Which of the two did 31
what his father wanted?"
They said,
"The second one."
Jesus said to them,
"I tell you, the tax-collectors and
prostitutes are going into the Kingdom
of God ahead of you. For John came to 32
you with a way of uprightness, and you
would not believe him. The tax-collectors and prostitutes believed him,

but even after seeing that, you would
not change your minds and believe him!
33 "Listen to another figure. There was
a land owner who planted a vineyard
and fenced it in, and hewed out a wine-
vat in it, and built a watch-tower, and
leased it to tenants, and left the neigh-
34 borhood. When the time for the vintage
approached he sent his slaves to the
35 tenants to receive his share. But the
tenants took his slaves and beat one
and killed another and stoned a third.
36 Again he sent other slaves and more of
them than he had sent at first, and they
36 treated them in the same way. Finally
he sent his son to them, thinking, 'They
38 will respect my son.' But when the
tenants saw his son, they said to one
another, 'This is his heir! Come on, let
39 us kill him, and get his inheritance!' So
they took him and drove him out of the
40 vineyard and killed him. When the
owner of the vineyard comes back,
therefore, what will he do to these tenants?"
41 They said to him,
"He will put the wretches to a miserable death, and let the vineyard to other tenants who will give him his share of
the vintage when it is due."
42 Jesus said to them,
"Did you never read in the Scriptures,
" 'That stone which the builders rejected
Has become the cornerstone;
This came from the Lord,
And seems marvelous to us'?
43 "That, I tell you, is why the Kingdom of God will be taken away from
you, and given to a people that will pro-
44 duce its proper fruit. Whoever falls on
that stone will be shattered, but whoever it falls upon will be scattered like
chaff."
45 When the high priests and the Pharisees heard his figures, they knew that
46 he was speaking about them, and they
wanted to have him arrested, but they
were afraid of the people, for the people considered him a prophet.
22 And Jesus spoke to them again in
figures, and said,
2 "The Kingdom of Heaven is like a
king, who gave a wedding banquet for
3 his son. And he sent his slaves to summon those who had been invited to the
4 banquet, and they would not come. He
sent other slaves a second time, and
said to them, 'Tell those who have been
asked, "Here I have my banquet all
ready, my bullocks and fat cattle are
killed, and everything is ready. Come
to the banquet!" ' But they took no 5
notice of it, and went off, one to his
estate, and another to his business, and 6
the rest seized his slaves, and ill treated
them and killed them. This made the 7
king angry, and he sent his troops and
put those murderers to death and
burned their city. Then he said to his 8
slaves, 'The banquet is ready, but those
who were invited have proved unworthy of it. So go out where the roads 9
leave the city and invite everyone you
find to the banquet.' So his slaves went 10
out on the roads, and got together all
the people they could find, good or bad,
and the hall was filled with guests. But 11
when the king came in to view the
guests, he saw among them a man who
did not have on wedding clothes. And 12
he said to him, 'My friend, how did you
happen to come here without wedding
clothes?' But he had nothing to say.
Then the king said to his attendants, 13
'Bind him hand and foot and throw
him out into the darkness, there to
weep and grind his teeth.' For many 14
are invited but few chosen."
Then the Pharisees went and made a 15
plot to entrap him in argument. So 16
they sent their disciples to him with the
Herodians, to say to him,
"Master, we know that you tell the
truth, and teach the way of God with
sincerity, regardless of the consequences, for you are impartial. So give 17
us your opinion: Is it right to pay the
poll-tax to the emperor, or not?"
But he saw their malice, and said, 18
"Why do you put me to such a test, 19
you hypocrites? Show me the poll-tax
coin!"
And they brought him a denarius.
And he said to them, 20
"Whose head and title is this?"
They answered, 21
"The emperor's."
Then he said to them,
"Then pay the emperor what belongs
to the emperor, and pay God what belongs to God!"
And when they heard it they were 22
amazed, and they went away and left
him.
On the same day some Sadducees 23
came up to him, claiming that there is

no resurrection, and they asked him
this question:
24 "Master, Moses said, 'If a man dies
without children his brother shall marry his widow, and raise up a family for
25 him.' Now there were seven brothers
among us. The first of them married
and died, and as he had no children, he
26 left his wife to his brother; so did the
second, and the third, and the rest of
27 the seven. After them all the woman
28 died. At the resurrection which one's
wife will she be? For they all married
her."
29 Jesus answered them,
"You are wrong, because you do not
understand the Scriptures nor the pow-
30 er of God. For after the resurrection
there is no marrying or being married,
but they live as angels do in heaven.
31 But as to the resurrection of the dead,
did you never read what was said to
32 you by God, 'I am the God of Abraham, the God of Isaac, and the God of
Jacob'? He is not the God of dead men
but of living!"
33 When the crowd heard this, they
were astounded at his teaching.
34 And when the Pharisees heard that
he had silenced the Sadducees, they
35 gathered together, and one of them, an
expert in the Law, to test him, asked,
36 "Master, what command is greatest
in the Law?"
37 And he said to him,
" 'You must love the Lord your God
with your whole heart, your whole soul,
38 and your whole mind.' That is the
39 great, first command. There is a second like it: 'You must love your neigh-
40 bor as you do yourself.' These two commands sum up the whole of the Law
and the Prophets."
41 While the Pharisees were still gathered there, Jesus asked them,
42 "What do you think about the
Christ? Whose son is he?"
They said to him,
"David's."
43 He said to them,
"How is it then that David under
the Spirit's influence calls him lord,
and says,
44 " 'The Lord has said to my lord, "Sit
at my right hand,
Until I put your enemies under
your feet" '?
45 So if David calls him lord, how can
he be his son?"
And no one could make him any an- 46
swer, and from that day no one ventured to ask him any more questions.
Then Jesus said to the crowds and to 23
his disciples,
"The scribes and Pharisees have tak- 2
en Moses' seat. So do everything they 3
tell you, and observe it all, but do not
do as they do, for they talk but do not
act. They tie up heavy loads and have 4
them put on men's shoulders, but they
will not lift a finger to move them. They 5
do everything they do to have men see
it. They wear wide Scripture texts as
charms, and they wear large tassels,
and they like the best places at dinners 6
and the front seats in the synagogues,
and to be saluted with respect in pub- 7
lic places, and to have men call them
'Rabbi.' But you must not let people 8
call you 'Rabbi,' for you have only one
teacher, and you are all brothers. And 9
you must not call anyone on earth your
father, for you have only one father,
your heavenly Father. And you must 10
not let men call you master, for you
have only one master, the Christ. But 11
he who is greatest among you must be
your servant. Whoever exalts himself 12
will be humbled and whoever humbles
himself will be exalted.
"But alas for you, you hypocritical 14
scribes and Pharisees, for you lock the
doors of the Kingdom of Heaven in
men's faces, for you will neither go in
yourselves nor let those enter who are
trying to do so. Alas for you, you hypo- 15
critical scribes and Pharisees, for you
scour land and sea to make one convert,
and when he is converted you make
him twice as fit for the pit as you are.
Alas for you, you blind guides, who say, 16
'If anyone swears by the sanctuary,
that is nothing, but if anyone swears
by the gold of the sanctuary, it is binding.' Blind fools! which is greater, the 17
gold, or the sanctuary that makes the
gold sacred? You say, 'If anyone 18
swears by the altar, that is nothing,
but if anyone swears by the offering
that is on it, it is binding.' You blind 19
men! Which is greater, the offering, or
the altar that makes the offering sacred? Anyone who swears by the altar 20
is swearing by it and by everything
that is on it, and anyone who swears 21
by the sanctuary is swearing by it and
by him who dwells in it; and anyone 22
who swears by heaven is swearing by

the throne of God and by him who sits
upon it.
23 "Alas for you, you hypocritical
scribes and Pharisees, for you pay tithes
on mint, dill, and cummin, and you
have let the weightier matters of the
Law go—justice, mercy, and integrity.
But you should have observed these,
24 without overlooking the others. You
blind guides! straining out the gnat,
25 and yet swallowing the camel! Alas for
you, you hypocritical scribes and Pharisees, for you clean the outside of the
cup and the dish, but inside they are
26 full of greed and self-indulgence. You
blind Pharisee! You must first clean
the inside of the cup and the dish, so
27 that the outside may be clean too. Alas
for you, you hypocritical scribes and
Pharisees, for you are like white-washed
tombs! They look well on the outside,
but inside they are full of the bones of
28 the dead, and all that is unclean. So
you outwardly appear to men to be upright, but within you are full of hypocrisy and wickedness.
29 "Alas for you, you hypocritical
scribes and Pharisees, for you build
tombs for the prophets, and decorate
30 the monuments of the upright, and say,
'If we had been living in the times of
our fathers, we would not have joined
them in the murder of the prophets.'
31 So you bear witness against yourselves
that you are descended from the mur-
32 derers of the prophets. Go on and fill
up the measure of your forefathers'
33 guilt. You serpents! You brood of
snakes! How can you escape being sen-
34 tenced to the pit? This is why I am going to send you prophets, wise men and
scribes, some of whom you will kill and
crucify, and some you will flog in your
synagogues and hunt from one town to
35 another; it is that on your heads may
come all the innocent blood shed on the
earth from the blood of Abel the upright to the blood of Zechariah, Barach-
iah's son, whom you murdered between
36 the sanctuary and the altar! I tell you,
all this will come upon this age!
37 "O Jerusalem, Jerusalem! murdering
the prophets, and stoning those who are
sent to her, how often I have longed to
gather your children around me, as a
hen gathers her brood under her wings,
38 but you refused! Now I leave you to
39 yourselves. For I tell you, you will never see me again until you say, 'Blessed
be he who comes in the Lord's name!'"
And Jesus left the Temple and was 24
going away, when his disciples came up
to him to call his attention to the Temple buildings. But he answered, 2
"Do you see all this? I tell you, not
one stone will be left here upon another
but shall be torn down."
As he was sitting on the Mount of 3
Olives, the disciples came up to him by
themselves, and said to him,
"Tell us when this is to happen, and
what will be the sign of your coming,
and of the close of the age."
Jesus answered, 4
"Take care that no one misleads you
about this. For many will come under 5
my name, and say, 'I am the Christ,'
and many will be misled by them. You 6
will hear of wars and rumors of war; do
not let yourselves be alarmed. They
have to come, but that is not the end.
For nation will rise in arms against 7
nation, and kingdom against kingdom,
and there will be famines and earthquakes here and there. All this is only 8
the beginning of the sufferings. Then 9
they will hand you over to persecution
and they will put you to death, and you
will be hated by all the heathen because
you bear my name. Then many will 10
fall away and betray one another and
hate one another. Many false prophets 11
will appear, and many will be misled by
them, and because of the increase of 12
wickedness, most men's love will grow
cold. But he who holds out to the end 13
will be saved. And this good news of 14
the kingdom will be preached all over
the world, to testify to all the heathen,
and then the end will come.
"So when you see the dreadful dese- 15
cration, of which the prophet Daniel
spoke, set up in the Holy Place"—the
reader must take note of this—"then 16
those who are in Judea must fly to the
hills; a man on the housetop must not 17
go down to get things out of the house,
and a man in the field must not turn 18
back to get his coat. But alas for wom- 19
en who are with child at that time or
who have babies! And pray that you 20
may not have to fly in winter or on the
Sabbath, for there will be greater mis- 21
ery then than there has ever been from
the beginning of the world until now, or
ever will be again. If those days had 22
not been cut short, nobody would have

escaped, but for the sake of God's people those days will be cut short.
23 "If anyone says to you at that time,
'Look! here is the Christ!' or 'There he
24 is!' do not believe it, for false Christs
and false prophets will appear, and
they will show great signs and wonders
to mislead God's chosen people if they
25 can. Here I have told you beforehand.
26 So if they say to you, 'There he is, in
the desert!' do not go out there; 'Here
he is, in a room in here!' do not believe
27 it. For just as the lightning starts in
the east and flashes to the west, so the
coming of the Son of Man will be.
28 Wherever there is a dead body, the vultures will flock.
29 "But immediately after the misery of
those days, the sun will be darkened,
and the moon will not shed its light,
and the stars will fall from the sky, and
30 the forces of the sky will shake. Then
the sign of the Son of Man will appear
in the sky, and all the nations of the
earth will lament when they see the
Son of Man coming on the clouds of the
31 sky, in all his power and splendor. And
he will send out his angels with a loud
trumpet-call, and they will gather his
chosen people from the four winds,
from one end of the sky to the other.
32 "Let the fig tree teach you the lesson.
As soon as its branches grow soft and
put forth leaves, you know that sum-
33 mer is coming. So when you see all
these things, you must know that he is
34 just at the door. I tell you, before the
present generation passes away, these
35 things will all happen. Earth and sky
will pass away but my words will never
36 pass away. But about that day or hour
no one knows, not even the angels in
heaven nor the Son, but only the
37 Father. For just as it was in the time of
Noah, it will be at the coming of the
38 Son of Man. For just as in those days
before the flood people were eating and
drinking, marrying and being married,
until the very day Noah entered the
39 ark, and knew nothing about it until the
flood came and destroyed them all, so it
will be at the coming of the Son of Man.
40 Two men will be in the field; one will be
41 taken and one left. Two women will be
grinding with the handmill; one will be
42 taken and one left. So you must be on
the watch, for you do not know on what
43 day your Master is coming. But you
may be sure of this, that if the master
of the house had known in what part of
the night the thief was coming, he
would have been on the watch, and
would not have let his house be broken
into. Therefore you must be ready too, 44
for the Son of Man is coming at a time
when you do not expect him.
"Who then will be the faithful, 45
thoughtful slave whom his master put
in charge of his household, to give the
members of it their supplies at the
proper time? Blessed is that slave if his 46
master when he returns finds him doing
it. I tell you, he will put him in charge 47
of all his property. But if he is a bad 48
slave and says to himself, 'My master
is going to stay a long time,' and begins 49
to beat the other slaves, and eats and
drinks with drunkards, that slave's 50
master will come back some day when
he does not expect him, and at some
time of which he does not know and 51
will cut him in two, and put him with
the hypocrites, to weep and grind his
teeth.
"Then the Kingdom of Heaven will 25
be like ten bridesmaids who took their
lamps and went out to meet the bridegroom. Now five of them were foolish 2
and five were sensible. For the foolish 3
ones brought their lamps but brought
no oil with them, but the sensible ones 4
with their lamps brought oil in their
flasks. As the bridegroom was slow in 5
coming, they all grew drowsy and fell
asleep. But in the middle of the night 6
there was a shout 'Here is the bridegroom! Come out and meet him!' Then 7
all the bridesmaids awoke, and trimmed
their lamps. And the foolish ones said 8
to the sensible ones, 'Give us some of
your oil, for our lamps are going out.'
But the sensible ones answered, 'There 9
may not be enough for us and you.
You had better go to the dealers and
buy yourselves some.' But while they 10
were gone to buy it, the bridegroom arrived, and the ones that were ready
went in with him to the wedding banquet, and the door was closed. After- 11
ward the other bridesmaids came and 12
said, 'Sir! Sir! Open the door for us!'
But he answered, 'I tell you, I do not
know you!' So you must be on the 13
watch, for you do not know either the
day or the hour.
"For it is just like a man who was go- 14
ing on a journey, and called in his
slaves, and put his property in their

15 hands. He gave one five thousand dollars, and another two thousand, and another one thousand; to each according
16 to his ability. Then he went away. The
man who had received the five thousand dollars immediately went into
business with the money, and made five
17 thousand more. In the same way the
man who had received the two thou-
18 sand made two thousand more. But
the man who had received the one thousand went away and dug a hole in the
ground and hid his master's money.
19 Long afterward, their master came
back and settled accounts with them.
20 And the man who had received the five
thousand dollars came up bringing him
five thousand more, and said, 'Sir, you
put five thousand dollars in my hands;
here I have made five thousand more.'
21 His master said to him, 'Well done, my
excellent, faithful slave! you have been
faithful about a small amount; I will
put a large one into your hands. Come,
22 share your master's enjoyment!' And
the man who had received the two
thousand came up and said, 'Sir, you
put two thousand dollars into my
hands; here I have made two thousand
23 more.' His master said to him, 'Well
done, my excellent, faithful slave! you
have been faithful about a small
amount; I will put a large one into your
hands. Come! share your master's en-
24 joyment.' And the man who had received the one thousand came up and
said, 'Sir, I knew you were a hard man,
who reaped where you had not sown,
and gathered where you had not
25 threshed, and I was frightened, and I
went and hid your thousand dollars in
26 the ground. Here is your money!' His
master answered, 'You wicked, lazy
slave! You knew that I reaped where I
had not sown and gathered where I had
27 not threshed? Then you ought to have
put my money in the bank, and then
when I came back I would have gotten
28 my property with interest. So take the
thousand dollars away from him, and
give it to the man who has the ten
29 thousand, for the man who has will
have more given him, and will be plentifully supplied, and from the man who
has nothing even what he has will be
30 taken away. And put the good-for-
nothing slave out into the darkness
outside, to weep and grind his teeth
there.'

"When the Son of Man comes in his 31
splendor, with all his angels with him,
he will take his seat on his glorious
throne, and all the nations will be gath- 32
ered before him, and he will separate
them from one another, just as a shepherd separates his sheep from his goats,
and he will put the sheep at his right 33
hand and the goats at his left. Then 34
the king will say to those at his right,
'Come, you whom my Father has
blessed, take possession of the kingdom
which has been destined for you from
the creation of the world. For when I 35
was hungry, you gave me food, when I
was thirsty you gave me something to
drink, when I was a stranger, you invited me to your homes, when I had no 36
clothes, you gave me clothes, when I
was sick, you looked after me, when I
was in prison, you came to see me.'
Then the upright will answer, 'Lord, 37
when did we see you hungry and give
you food, or thirsty, and give you something to drink? When did we see you a 38
stranger, and invite you home, or without clothing, and supply you with it?
When did we see you sick or in prison, 39
and go to see you?' The king will an- 40
swer, 'I tell you, in so far as you did it
to one of the humblest of these brothers
of mine, you did it to me.' Then he will 41
say to those at his left, 'Begone, you accursed people, to the everlasting fire
destined for the devil and his angels!
For when I was hungry, you gave me 42
nothing to eat, and when I was thirsty
you gave me nothing to drink, when I 43
was a stranger, you did not invite me
home, when I had no clothes, you did
not supply me, when I was sick and in
prison, you did not look after me.'
Then they in their turn will answer, 44
'Lord, when did we see you hungry, or
thirsty, or a stranger, or in need of
clothes, or sick, or in prison, and did not
wait upon you?' Then he will answer, 45
'I tell you, in so far as you failed to do it
for one of these people who are humblest, you failed to do it for me.' Then 46
they will go away to everlasting punishment, and the upright to everlasting
life."

When Jesus had finished this dis- 26
course he said to his disciples,

"You know that in two days the 2
Passover Festival will come, and the
Son of Man will be handed over to be
crucified."

3 Then the high priests and the elders
of the people gathered in the house of
the high priest, whose name was Caia-
4 phas, and plotted to arrest Jesus by
5 stealth and put him to death. But they
said,

"It must not be during the festival,
or there may be a riot."

6 When Jesus got back to Bethany, to
7 the house of Simon the leper, a woman
came up to him with an alabaster flask
of very expensive perfume and poured
it upon his head, while he was at table.
8 When his disciples saw it, they said indignantly,

"What was the use of wasting it like
9 that? It might have been sold for a
large sum, and the money given to the
poor."

0 But Jesus observed this and said to
them,

"Why do you bother the woman? It
is a fine thing that she has done to me.
1 For you always have the poor among
you, but you will not always have me.
2 In pouring this perfume on me she has
done something to prepare me for buri-
3 al. I tell you, wherever this good news
is preached all over the world, what she
has done will also be told, in memory of
her."

4 Then one of the Twelve, named Judas Iscariot, went to the high priests,
5 and said,

"What will you give me if I hand
him over to you?"

And they counted him out thirty sil-
6 ver pieces. And from that time he
watched for a good opportunity to hand
him over to them.

7 On the first day of the festival of Unleavened Bread, the disciples came to
Jesus and said,

"Where do you wish us to make the
preparations for you to eat the Passover supper?"

8 And he said,

"Go into the city, to a certain man,
and say to him, 'The Master says, "My
time is near. I am going to keep the
Passover at your house with my disciples." ' "

9 So the disciples did as Jesus directed
them, and prepared the Passover
supper.

0 When evening came, he took his
place at table with the twelve disciples.
1 And as they were eating, he said,

"I tell you, one of you will betray
me!"

They were deeply hurt and began to 22
say to him one after another,

"Can it be I, Master?"

He answered, 23

"The man who just dipped his hand
in the same dish with me is going to betray me. The Son of Man is to go away 24
as the Scriptures say of him, but alas
for the man by whom the Son of Man is
betrayed! It would have been better
for that man if he had never been
born!"

Judas, who betrayed him, said, 25

"Can it be I, Master?"

He said to him,

"You are right!"

As they were eating Jesus took a loaf 26
and blessed it, and he broke it in pieces
and gave it to his disciples, saying,

"Take this and eat it. It is my
body!"

And he took the wine-cup and gave 27
thanks and gave it to them, saying,

"You must all drink from it, for this 28
is my blood which ratifies the agreement, and is to be poured out for many
people, for the forgiveness of their sins.
And I tell you I will never drink this 29
product of the vine again till the day
when I shall drink the new wine with
you in my Father's kingdom!"

After singing the hymn, they went 30
out of the city and up the Mount of
Olives.

Then Jesus said to them, 31

"You will all desert me tonight, for
the Scriptures say, 'I will strike the
shepherd, and the sheep of the flock
will be scattered.' But after I am raised 32
to life again, I will go back to Galilee
before you."

Peter answered, 33

"If they all desert you, I will never
do it!"

Jesus said to him, 34

"I tell you, tonight, before a cock
crows, you will disown me three times!"

Peter said to him, 35

"Even if I have to die with you, I
will never disown you!" All the disciples said so too.

Then Jesus came with them to a 36
place called Gethsemane, and he said to
the disciples,

"Sit down here while I go over yonder and pray."

And he took Peter and Zebedee's two 37

sons with him, and he began to show
38 grief and distress of mind. Then he said
to them,
"My heart is almost breaking. You
must stay here and keep watch with
me."
39 And he went on a little way, and
threw himself on his face, and prayed,
saying,
"My Father, if it is possible, let this
cup pass by me. Yet not as I please but
as you do!"
40 When he went back to the disciples
he found them asleep. And he said to
Peter,
"Then were you not able to watch
41 with me for one hour? You must all
watch, and pray that you may not be
exposed to trial! One's spirit is eager,
but flesh and blood are weak!"
42 He went away again a second time
and prayed, saying,
"My Father, if it cannot pass by me
without my drinking it, your will be
done!"
43 When he came back he found them
asleep again, for they could hardly keep
44 their eyes open. And he left them and
went away again and prayed a third
45 time, in the same words as before. Then
he came back to the disciples and said
to them,
"Are you still sleeping and taking
your rest? See, the time has come for
the Son of Man to be handed over to
46 wicked men! Get up! Let us be going!
Look! Here comes my betrayer!"
47 Just as he was speaking, Judas, one
of the Twelve, came up, and with him a
great crowd with swords and clubs,
from the high priests and the elders of
48 the people. Now the man who betrayed
him gave them a signal, saying
"The one I kiss is the man. Seize
him!"
49 And he went straight up to Jesus and
said,
"Good evening, Master!" and kissed
him affectionately.
50 Jesus said to him,
"My friend, what are you here for?"
Then they came up and laid hands on
51 Jesus and secured him. One of the men
with Jesus put out his hand and drew
his sword, and striking at the high
52 priest's slave, cut his ear off. Then
Jesus said to him,
"Put your sword back where it belongs! For all who draw the sword will
die by the sword. Do you suppose I 53
cannot appeal to my Father, and he
would at once furnish me more than
twelve legions of angels? But then how 54
are the Scriptures to be fulfilled, which
say that this must happen?"
At that same time Jesus said to the 55
crowd,
"Have you come out to arrest me
with swords and clubs, as though I were
a robber? Day after day I have sat in
the Temple preaching, and you never
seized me. But this has all taken place 56
in fulfilment of the writings of the
prophets."
Then all the disciples left him and
made their escape.
The men who had seized Jesus took 57
him away to Caiaphas, the high priest,
at whose house the scribes and elders
had gathered. And Peter followed 58
him at a distance as far as the courtyard of the high priest's house, and he
went inside and sat down among the attendants to see how it came out. Now 59
the high priests and the whole council
were trying to get false testimony
against Jesus, so that they might put
him to death. And they could not, al- 60
though many false witnesses presented
themselves. But finally two came forward and said, 61
"This man said, 'I can tear down the
sanctuary of God, and build it up in
three days.'"
And the high priest got up and said 62
to him,
"Have you no answer to make?
What about their evidence against
you?"
But Jesus was silent. And the high 63
priest said to him,
"I charge you, on your oath, by the
living God, tell us whether you are the
Christ, the son of God."
Jesus said to him, 64
"It is true. Why, I tell you you will
soon see the Son of Man seated at the
right hand of the Almighty and coming
upon the clouds of the sky!"
Then the high priest tore his clothing 65
and said,
"He has uttered blasphemy! What
do we want of witnesses now? Here
you have heard his blasphemy! What 66
is your decision?"
They answered,
"He deserves death."

67 Then they spat in his face and struck
68 him, and others slapped him, saying,
"Show us you are a prophet, you
Christ! Who was it that struck you?"
69 Now Peter was sitting outside in the
courtyard, and a maid came up to him,
and said,
"You were with Jesus the Galilean,
too!"
70 But he denied it before them all, and
said,
"I do not know what you mean."
71 And he went out into the gateway,
and another maid saw him, and said to
the men there,
"This fellow was with Jesus the Nazarene!"
72 He denied it again, with an oath, and
said,
"I do not know the man!"
73 A little while after the bystanders
came up to Peter and said,
"You are certainly one of them too,
for your accent shows it!"
74 Then he started to swear with the
strongest oaths,
"I do not know the man!"
And at that moment a cock crowed.
75 And Peter remembered Jesus' words
when he had said,
"Before a cock crows, you will disown me three times!" And he went outside and wept bitterly.

27 When it was morning, all the high
priests and elders of the people held a
consultation about Jesus, with a view
2 to putting him to death. And they
bound him and led him away and handed him over to Pilate the governor.
3 Then Judas who had betrayed him,
when he saw that he had been condemned, in his remorse brought back
the thirty silver pieces to the high
4 priests and elders, and said,
"I did wrong when I handed an innocent man over to death!"
They said,
"What is that to us? See to it
yourself."
5 And he threw down the silver and
left the Temple and went off and hung
6 himself. The high priests gathered up
the money, and they said,
"It is not legal to put this into the
Temple treasury, for it is blood
money."
7 So after consultation they bought
with it the Potter's Field as a burial
8 ground for strangers. That is why that
piece of ground has ever since been
called the Field of Blood. So the words 9
spoken by the prophet Jeremiah were
fulfilled: "They took the thirty silver
pieces, the price of the one whose price
had been fixed, on whom some of the
Israelites has set a price, and gave them 10
for the Potter's Field as the Lord directed me."
Now Jesus stood before the governor, 11
and the governor asked him,
"Are you the king of the Jews?"
Jesus said,
"Yes."
And while the high priests and elders 12
were making their charges against him,
he made no answer. Then Pilate said 13
to him,
"Do you not hear what evidence
they are bringing against you?"
And he made him no reply to even a 14
single accusation, so that the governor
was greatly surprised. Now at festival 15
time the governor was accustomed to
release for the people any prisoner
whom they chose, and at this time 16
there was a notorious prisoner named
Barabbas. So when they gathered to 17
ask this, Pilate said to them,
"Which one do you want me to release for you, Barabbas, or Jesus, the
so-called Christ?"
For he knew that they had handed 18
him over to him out of envy. Now 19
while he was on the bench his wife sent
to him to say,
"Do not have anything to do with
that innocent man, for I have just had a
painful experience in a dream about
him."
But the high priests and the elders 20
prevailed on the crowd to ask for Barabbas, and to have Jesus put to death.
And the governor answered, 21
"Which of the two do you want me
to release for you?"
They said,
"Barabbas."
Pilate said to them, 22
"Then what am I to do with Jesus,
the so-called Christ?"
They all said,
"Have him crucified!"
He said, 23
"Why, what has he done that is
wrong?"
But they shouted all the louder,
"Have him crucified!"
When Pilate saw that he was accom- 24

plishing nothing but that a riot was
beginning instead, he took some water
and washed his hands in the presence
of the crowd, saying,
"I am not responsible for this man's
death; you must see to it yourselves."
25 And all the people answered,
"His blood be on us and on our children!"
26 Then he released Barabbas for them,
and he had Jesus flogged and handed
him over to be crucified.
27 Then the governor's soldiers took Jesus into the governor's house, and got
the whole battalion together about him.
28 And they stripped him and put a red
29 cloak on him, and made a wreath of
thorns and put it on his head, and they
put a stick in his hand, and knelt down
before him in mockery, saying,
"Long live the king of the Jews!"
30 And they spat at him, and took the
31 stick and struck him on the head. And
when they had finished making sport of
him, they took off the cloak, and put
his own clothes on him, and led him
away to be crucified.
32 As they went out of the city they
came upon a Cyrenian named Simon,
and they forced him to carry Jesus'
33 cross. When they came to a place called
Golgotha, which means the Place of the
34 Skull, they offered him a drink of wine
mixed with gall, and when he tasted it
35 he would not drink it. And they crucified him and divided his clothes among
36 them by drawing lots, and sat down
37 there to keep watch of him. They put
above his head the charge against him,
which read,
"This is Jesus, the king of the Jews."
38 There were two robbers crucified
with him at the time, one at his right
39 and one at his left. And the passers-by
40 jeered at him, shaking their heads and
saying,
"You who would tear down the
temple, and build one in three days,
save yourself! If you are the Son of
God, come down from the cross!"
41 The high priests, too, made sport of
him with the scribes and elders, and
said,
42 "He saved others, but he cannot
save himself! He is King of Israel; let
him come down from the cross now, and
43 we will believe in him. He trusts in
God; let God deliver him if he cares for
him, for he said he was God's son."

Even the robbers who were crucified 44
with him abused him in the same way.
Now from noon there was darkness 45
over the whole country until three
o'clock. And about three, Jesus called 46
out loudly,
"Eloi, Eloi, lema sabachthani?" that
is, "My God! My God! Why have you
forsaken me?"
Some of the bystanders when they 47
heard it said,
"The man is calling for Elijah!"
And one of them ran off at once and 48
got a sponge and soaked it in sour wine
and put it on the end of a stick and held
it up to him to drink. But the others 49
said,
"Let us see whether Elijah will come
to save him."
But Jesus cried out again loudly, and 50
gave up his spirit. And at once the cur- 51
tain of the sanctuary was torn in two
from top to bottom. The earth shook,
the rocks split, the tombs opened, and 52
many of the saints who had fallen
asleep rose and left their tombs and 53
after his resurrection went into the holy
city and showed themselves to many
people. And the captain and the men 54
with him who were watching Jesus,
when they saw the earthquake and all
that was happening, were dreadfully
frightened and said,
"He surely must have been a son of
God!"
There were several women there 55
watching from a distance who had followed Jesus from Galilee to wait upon
him, among them Mary of Magdala, 56
Mary the mother of James and Joseph,
and the mother of Zebedee's sons.
In the evening a rich man named Jo- 57
seph, from Arimathea, who had himself been a disciple of Jesus, came. He 58
went to Pilate and asked him for Jesus'
body. Then Pilate ordered it to be giv-
en to him. And Joseph took the body 59
and wrapped it in a piece of clean linen,
and laid it in a new tomb that belonged 60
to him, that he had cut in the rock, and
he rolled a great stone over the doorway of the tomb, and went away. And 61
Mary of Magdala and the other Mary
remained there, sitting before the tomb.
On the next day, that is, the day af- 62
ter the Preparation Day, the high
priests and Pharisees went in a body to
Pilate and said, 63
"Sir, we remember that when this

impostor was alive he said, 'After three
64 days I will rise again!' Give orders,
therefore, to have the tomb closely
guarded till the third day, so that his
disciples cannot come and steal him,
and then tell the people that he is risen
from the dead, and that delusion be
worse than the other was."
65 Pilate said to them,
"Take a guard of soldiers, and go and
make it as secure as you can."
66 And they went and set the guard and
put a seal on the stone.
28 After the Sabbath, as the first day of
of the week was dawning, Mary of
Magdala and the other Mary went to
2 look at the tomb. And there was a
great earthquake. For an angel of the
Lord came down from heaven and went
and rolled the stone back and sat upon
3 it. His appearance was like lightning
and his clothing was as white as snow.
4 The men on guard trembled with fear of
5 him, and became like dead men. And
the angel said to the women,
"You need not be afraid. I know that
you are looking for Jesus who was cru-
6 cified. He is not here, he has risen, as he
said he would do. Come and see the
7 place where he was lying. Now go
quickly and tell his disciples, 'He has
risen from the dead, and is going back
to Galilee before you. You will see him
there.' Now I have given you my message."
8 And they hurried away from the
tomb frightened and yet overjoyed, and
9 ran to tell the news to his disciples. And
Jesus himself met them, and said,
"Good morning!"
And they went up to him and clasped
his feet, and bowed to the ground before him. Jesus said to them, 10
"You need not be afraid. Go and tell
my brothers to go to Galilee and they
will see me there."
While they were on their way, some 11
of the guard went into the city and reported to the high priests all that had
happened. And they got together and 12
consulted with the elders, and gave the
soldiers a large sum of money, and said 13
to them,
"Tell people that his disciples came
in the night and stole him away while
you were asleep. And if news of it 14
reaches the governor, we will satisfy
him, and see that you do not get into
trouble."
So they took the money and did as 15
they were told. And this story has been
current among the Jews ever since.
And the eleven disciples went to Gal- 16
ilee to the mountain to which Jesus had
directed them. There they saw him and 17
bowed down before him, though some
were in doubt about it.
And Jesus came up to them and 18
said,
"Full authority in heaven and on the
earth has been given to me. Therefore 19
go and make disciples of all the heath-
en, baptize them in the name of the
Father, the Son, and the holy Spirit,
and teach them to observe all the com- 20
mands that I have given you. I will always be with you, to the very close of
the age."

THE GOSPEL ACCORDING TO MARK

1 THE beginning of the good news
of Jesus Christ.
2 As it is written in the prophet
Isaiah,
"Here I send my messenger on before you;
He will prepare your way;
3 Hark! Someone is shouting in the
desert,
'Get the Lord's way ready,
Make his paths straight,'"
4 John the baptizer appeared in the desert, and preached repentance and baptism in order to obtain the forgiveness
5 of sins. And all Judea and everybody
in Jerusalem went out to him there,
and accepted baptism from him in the
Jordan River, acknowledging their sins.
6 John's clothing was made of hair cloth,
and the belt around his waist was leather, and he lived on dried locusts and
7 wild honey. And this was his message:
"After me there is coming one stronger than I am, one whose shoes I am not
8 fit to stoop down and untie. I have baptized you in water, but he will baptize
you in the holy Spirit."

9 It was in those days that Jesus came
from Nazareth in Galilee, and was bap-
10 tized by John in the Jordan. And just
as he was coming up out of the water he
saw the heavens torn open and the
Spirit coming down like a dove to enter
11 into him, and out of the heavens came
a voice:
"You are my Son, my Beloved! You
are my Chosen!"
12 The spirit immediately drove him
13 out into the desert. And he remained
in the desert for forty days, and Satan
tried to tempt him there; and he was
among the wild animals; and the angels
waited on him.
14 After John was arrested, Jesus went
into Galilee proclaiming the good news
15 from God, saying,
"The time has come and the reign of
God is near; repent, and believe this
good news."
16 As he was passing along the shore of
the Sea of Galilee, he saw Simon and his
brother Andrew casting their nets in
the sea, for they were fishermen. Jesus 17
said to them,
"Come, follow me, and I will make
you fish for men."
They immediately abandoned their 18
nets and followed him. He went on a 19
little further and saw James, the son of
Zebedee, and his brother John; they
too were in their boat putting their nets
in order. He immediately called them. 20
And they left their father Zebedee in
the boat with the hired men and went
off after him.
They proceeded to Capernaum, and 21
on the very first Sabbath he went to the
synagogue and taught. And they were 22
amazed at his teaching, for he taught
them like one who had authority, and
not like the scribes. Just then there 23
was in their synagogue a man under the
control of a foul spirit, and he cried out,
"What do you want of us, Jesus, you 24
Nazarene? Have you come to destroy
us? I know who you are, you are God's
holy One!"
Jesus reproved him, and said, 25
"Silence! Get out of him!"
The foul spirit convulsed the man 26
and gave a loud cry and went out of
him. And they were all so amazed that 27
they discussed it with one another, and
said,
"What does this mean? It is a new
teaching! He gives orders with authority even to the foul spirits, and they
obey him!"
And his fame immediately spread in 28
all directions through the whole neighborhood of Galilee.
As soon as they left the synagogue, 29
they went with James and John to the
house of Simon and Andrew. Simon's 30
mother-in-law was in bed, sick with a
fever, and they immediately told him
about her. And he went up to her, and 31
grasping her hand, he made her rise.
And the fever left her, and she waited
on them.
In the evening, after sunset, they 32
brought to him all who were sick or
possessed by demons, and the whole 33

34 town was gathered at the door. And he
cured many who were sick with various
diseases, and drove out many demons,
and he would not let the demons speak,
because they knew that he was Christ.
35 Early in the morning, long before
daylight, he got up and left the house
and went off to a lonely spot, and
36 prayed there. And Simon and his companions sought him out and found him,
37 and said to him,

"They are all looking for you!"

38 He said to them,

"Let us go somewhere else, to the neighboring country towns, so that I may preach in them, too, for that is why I came out here."

39 So he went all through Galilee, preaching in their synagogues and driving out the demons.

40 There came to him a leper appealing to him on his knees, saying to him,

"If you only choose, you can cure me."

41 And he pitied him and stretched out his hand and touched him, and said to him,

"I do choose! Be cured!"

42 And the leprosy immediately left
43 him, and he was cured. And Jesus immediately drove him away with a
44 stern warning, saying to him,

"See that you say nothing about this to anybody, but begone! show yourself to the priest, and in proof of your cure make the offerings for your purification which Moses prescribed."

45 But he went off and began to talk so much about it, and to spread the story so widely, that Jesus could no longer go into a town openly, but stayed out in unfrequented places, and people came to him from every direction.

2 Some days later he came back to Capernaum, and people heard that he was
2 at home, and such a crowd gathered
that after a while there was no room
even around the door, and he was tell-
3 ing them his message. And some people came bringing to him a man who
was paralyzed, four of them carrying
4 him. As they could not get him near
Jesus on account of the crowd, they
broke open the roof just over his head,
and through the opening they lowered
the mat with the paralytic lying on it.
5 When Jesus saw their faith, he said to
the paralytic,

"My son, your sins are forgiven."

There were some scribes sitting there 6
pondering and saying to themselves,

"Why does this man talk so? This is 7
blasphemy. Who can forgive sins but
God alone?"

Jesus, at once perceiving by his spirit 8
that they were pondering over this,
said to them,

"Why do you ponder over this in
your minds? Which is easier, to say to 9
this paralytic, 'Your sins are forgiven,'
or to say to him, 'Get up and pick up
your mat and walk'? But to let you 10
know that the Son of Man has authority to forgive sins on earth," turning to
the paralytic he said, "I tell you, get 11
up, pick up your mat, and go home!"

And he got up, and immediately 12
picked up his mat and went out before
them all, so that they were all astonished and acknowledged the power of
God, saying,

"We never saw anything like this before."

He went out of the town again and 13
along the shore, and all the people
came to him and he taught them. And 14
as he was passing along he saw Levi,
the son of Alpheus, sitting at the tollhouse, and he said to him,

"Follow me."

And he got up and followed him.

He was at table in his house, and 15
many tax-collectors and irreligious people were there at table with him and his
disciples, for there were many of them
among his followers. And when the 16
scribes who were of the Pharisees' party
saw that he was eating with irreligious
people and tax-collectors, they said to
his disciples,

"Why does he eat with tax-collectors and irreligious people?"

Jesus heard it, and said to them, 17

"It is not well people but the sick who have to have the doctor. I did not come to invite the pious but the irreligious."

Now John's disciples and the Phari- 18
sees were keeping a fast. And people
came and asked him,

"Why is it that when John's disciples and the disciples of the Pharisees are keeping the fast, yours are not keeping it?"

Jesus said to them, 19

"Can wedding guests fast while the bridegroom is with them? As long as they have the bridegroom with them

20 they cannot fast. But a time will come
when the bridegroom will be taken
from them, and when that day comes,
21 they will fast. No one sews a patch of
unshrunken cloth on an old coat; or if
he does, the patch tears away, the new
from the old, and makes the hole worse
22 than ever. And no one pours new wine
into old wine-skins; or if he does, the
wine bursts the skins, and the wine is
lost, and the skins too. New wine has
to be put into fresh skins."

23 He happened to be passing through
the wheat fields on the Sabbath, and his
disciples began to pick the heads of
wheat as they made their way through.
24 And the Pharisees said to him,

"Look! Why are they doing what it
is against the law to do on the Sabbath?"

25 He said to them,

"Did you never read what David did,
when he was in need and hungry, he
26 and his men? How is it that he went
into the house of God when Abiathar
was high priest, and ate the Presentation Loaves, which it is against the law
for anyone but the priests to eat, and
gave some to his companions too?"

27 And he said to them,

"The Sabbath was made for man,
28 not man for the Sabbath, and so the
Son of Man is master even of the Sabbath."

3 He went again to a synagogue, and
there was a man there with one hand
2 withered. And they were watching him
closely, to see whether he would cure
him on the Sabbath, in order to get a
3 charge to bring against him. He said to
the man with the withered hand,

"Get up and come forward."

4 And he said to them,

"Is it allowable to do people good on
the Sabbath, or to do them harm? To
save life or kill?" But they made no
5 answer. And he looked around at them
with anger, hurt by their obstinacy,
and he said to the man,

"Hold out your hand!"

And he held it out, and his hand was
6 cured. Then the Pharisees left the synagogue and immediately consulted
with the Herodians about Jesus, with a
view to putting him to death.

7 So Jesus retired with his disciples to
the seashore, and a great many people
from Galilee followed him, and from
8 Judea and Jerusalem and Idumea and
from the other side of the Jordan and
from the neighborhood of Tyre and
Sidon a great many who had heard of
the things he was doing came to him.
He told his disciples to have a boat always ready for his use, to prevent his
being crushed by the crowd. For he 10
cured so many people that all who had
any ailments pressed up to him to
touch him. And whenever the foul spir- 11
its saw him, they fell down before him
and screamed out,

"You are the Son of God!" And he 12
warned them repeatedly not to tell who
he was.

And he went up the mountain and 13
summoned those whom he wanted,
and they went to him. He appointed 14
twelve of them, whom he called apostles, to be with him and to be sent out
to preach, with power to drive out the 15
demons. These were the twelve he appointed: Peter, which was the name he 16
gave to Simon, James the son of Zebe- 17
dee, and John, James's brother (he
named them Boanerges, that is, Sons of
Thunder), Andrew, Philip, Bartholo- 18
mew, Matthew, Thomas, James the 19
son of Alpheus, Thaddeus, Simon the
Zealot, and Judas Iscariot, who betrayed him.

Then he went home. And again the 20
crowd gathered in such numbers that
there was no chance for them even to
have their meals. His relatives heard of 21
it and came over to stop him, for they
said that he was out of his mind. And 22
the scribes who had come down from
Jerusalem said that he was possessed
by Beelzebub and drove out demons by
the help of the prince of demons. So he 23
called them to him and spoke to them
in figures, saying,

"How can Satan drive Satan out? If 24
a kingdom is disunited, that kingdom
cannot last. And if a household is dis- 25
united, that household cannot last.
And if Satan has rebelled against him- 26
self and become disunited, he cannot
last but is coming to his end. But no 27
one can go into a strong man's house
and carry off his property unless he
first binds the strong man; after that he
can plunder his house. I tell you, men 28
will be forgiven for everything, for all
their sins and all the abusive things
they say. But whoever reviles the holy 29
Spirit can never be forgiven, but is
guilty of an unending sin."

30 This was because they said, "He is
possessed by a foul spirit."
31 And his mother and his brothers
came. And they stood outside the
house and sent word in to him to come
32 outside to them. There was a crowd
sitting around him when they told him,
"Your mother and your brothers are
outside asking for you."
33 He answered,
"Who are my mother and my
brothers?"
34 And looking around at the people
sitting about him, he said,
"Here are my mother and my broth-
35 ers! Whoever does the will of God is
my brother and sister and mother."
4 Then he began again to teach by the
seashore. And a crowd gathered around
him so great that he got into a boat and
sat in it, a little way from the shore,
while all the people were on the land
2 close to the water. He taught them
many lessons in figures, and said to
them in the course of his teaching,
3 "Listen: A sower went out to sow,
4 and as he was sowing, some of the seed
chanced to fall by the path, and the
5 birds came and ate it up. Some of it fell
on rocky ground, and where there was
not much soil, and it sprang up at once
6 because the soil was not deep, but when
the sun came up, it was scorched, and
withered up, because it had no root.
7 Some of the seed fell among the thorns,
and the thorns grew up and choked it
8 out, and it yielded no grain. And some
fell on good soil, and came up and grew
and yielded thirty, sixty, even a hundredfold."
9 And he said,
"Let him who has ears be sure to
listen!"
10 When he was by himself, those who
stayed about him with the Twelve
asked him about the figures he had
11 used. And he said to them,
"To you has been intrusted the secret of the reign of God, but to those
outsiders, everything is offered in fig-
12 ures, so that
" 'They may look and look and yet
not see,
And listen and listen and yet not
understand,
Lest possibly they should turn and
be forgiven.' "
13 And he said to them,
"If you do not understand this figure,
then how will you understand my other
figures? What the sower sows is the 14
message. The ones by the path are 15
those into whose hearts the message
falls, and as soon as they hear it Satan
comes and carries off the message that
has been sown in their hearts. It is so 16
too with the ones sown on the rocky
ground; they gladly accept the message
as soon as they hear it, but it takes no 17
real root in them and they last only a
little while; then when trouble or persecution comes because of the message
they give it up at once. It is different 18
with those sown among the thorns.
They are people who listen to the message, but the worries of the time and 19
the pleasure of being rich and passions
for other things creep in and choke the
message out and it yields nothing. And 20
the ones sown in good ground are the
people who listen to the message and
welcome it and yield thirty, sixty, even
a hundredfold.
"Do people get out the lamp," he 21
said to them, "and then put it under
the peck-measure, or under the bed, instead of putting it up on the lampstand?
For no one hides anything except for the 22
purpose of sometimes bringing it to
light again, and people keep things
secret only to reveal them some day. If 23
anyone has ears let him be sure to listen.
"Take care what you hear," he said 24
to them. "The measure you give will
be given to you, and even more besides.
For a man who has will have more 25
given him, and from a man who has
nothing, even what he has will be
taken away.
"The reign of God," he said, "is like 26
a man scattering seed on the ground,
and then sleeping at night and getting 27
up by day, while the seed sprouts and
comes up, without his knowing it. The 28
ground of itself is productive, putting
forth first a blade, then a head, then
fully developed wheat in the head. But 29
as soon as the crop will let him, the man
goes in with his sickle, for the harvest
time has come.
"How can we find any comparison," 30
he said, "for the reign of God, or what
figure can we use to describe it? It is 31
like a mustard seed, which, when sown
in the ground, though it is the smallest
of all the seeds in the world, yet once 32
sown, comes up and grows to be the
largest of all the plants, and produces

branches so large that the wild birds
can roost under the shelter of it."
33 With many such figures he told them
the message, as far as they were able to
34 receive it. He said nothing to them except in figures, but in private he explained everything to his own disciples.
35 That same day when it was evening
he said to them,
"Let us cross to the other side."
36 So they left the crowd and took him
away in the boat in which he was sitting. There were other boats with him.
37 And a heavy squall of wind came on
and the waves dashed into the boat, so
38 that it was beginning to fill. He was in
the stern, asleep on the cushion. And
they woke him up and said to him,
"Master, does it make no difference
to you that we are sinking?"
39 Then he awoke and reproved the
wind, and said to the sea,
"Hush! Silence!"
And the wind went down and there
40 was a great calm. And he said to them,
"Why are you afraid? Have you still
no faith?"
41 And they were very much frightened,
and said to one another,
"Who can he be? For even the wind
and the sea obey him."
5 So they reached the other side of the
sea, and landed in the region of Gerasa.
2 As soon as he got out of the boat, a man
possessed by a foul spirit came out of
the burial places near by to meet him.
3 This man lived among the tombs, and
no one could any longer secure him
4 even with a chain, for he had often been
fastened with fetters and chains and
had snapped the chains and broken the
fetters; and there was no one strong
5 enough to master him, and night and
day he was always shrieking among the
tombs and on the hills and cutting him-
6 self with stones. And catching sight of
Jesus in the distance he ran up and
7 made obeisance to him and screamed out,
"What do you want of me, Jesus, son
of the Most High God? In God's name,
8 I implore you, do not torture me." For
he was saying to him,
"You foul spirit, come out of this
man."
9 He asked him,
"What is your name?"
He said,
"My name is Legion, for there are
many of us."

And they begged him earnestly not 10
to send them out of that country.
Now there was a great drove of pigs 11
feeding there on the hillside. And they 12
implored him,
"Send us among the pigs, let us go
into them."
So he gave them permission. And the 13
foul spirits came out and went into the
pigs, and the drove of about two thousand rushed over the steep bank into
the sea, and were drowned in the sea.
And the men who tended them ran 14
away and spread the news in the town
and in the country around, and the people came to see what had happened.
When they came to Jesus and found the 15
demoniac sitting there with his clothes
on and in his right mind—the same man
who had been possessed by Legion—
they were frightened. And those who 16
had seen it told them what had happened to the demoniac, and all about
the pigs. And they began to beg him to 17
leave their district. As he was getting 18
into the boat, the man who had been
possessed begged to be allowed to go
with him. And he would not permit it, 19
but said to him,
"Go home to your own people, and
tell them all the Lord has done for you
and how he took pity on you." And he 20
went off and began to tell everybody in
the Ten Towns all Jesus had done for
him; and they were all astonished.
When Jesus had crossed again in 21
the boat to the other side, a great
crowd gathered about him as he stood
on the shore. And a man named Jairus, 22
the leader of a synagogue, came up and
seeing him threw himself at his feet,
and appealed to him, saying, 23
"My little daughter is at the point of
death. Come, lay your hands on her, so
that she may get well and live!"
So he went with him. And a great 24
crowd followed him and pressed around
him. And a woman who had had a 25
hemorrhage for twelve years, and had 26
had a great deal of treatment from various doctors and had spent all that she
had and had not been benefited at all
but had actually grown worse, had 27
heard about Jesus. And she came up in
the crowd behind him and touched his
coat, for she said, 28
"If I can only touch his clothes, I
shall get well."
The hemorrhage stopped at once, 29

and she felt in her body that she was
0 cured. Jesus instantly perceived that
healing power had passed from him,
and he turned around in the crowd and
said,
"Who touched my clothes?"
1 His disciples said to him,
"You see the crowd pressing around
you, and yet you ask, 'Who touched
me?'"
2 But he still looked around to see the
3 person who had done it. The woman,
knowing what had happened to her,
came forward frightened and trembling,
and threw herself down at his feet
4 and told him the whole truth. And he
said to her,
"My daughter, it is your faith that
has cured you. Go in peace and be free
from your disease."
5 Even as he spoke people came from
the house of the leader of the synagogue
and said,
"Your daughter is dead. Why should
you trouble the Master any further?"
6 But Jesus paid no attention to what
they said, but said to the leader of the
synagogue,
"Do not be afraid, just have faith."
7 He let no one go with him but Peter,
8 James, and James's brother John. They
came to the house of the leader of the
synagogue, and there he found everything
in confusion, and people weeping
9 and wailing loudly. And he went into
the house and said to them,
"What is the meaning of all this confusion
and crying? The child is not
0 dead, she is asleep." And they laughed
at him. But he drove them all out, and
took the child's father and mother and
the men who were with him and went
into the room where the child was lying.
1 And he grasped her hand and said
to her,
"Taleitha, koum!"—that is to say,
"Little girl, I tell you, get up!"
2 And the little girl immediately got up
and walked about, for she was twelve
years old. The moment they saw it
3 they were utterly amazed. And he
strictly forbade them to let anyone
know of it, and told them to give her
something to eat.

6 Leaving there he went, followed by
his disciples, to his own part of the
2 country. When the Sabbath came he
began to teach in the synagogue. And
the people were astonished when they
heard him, and said,
"Where did he get all this? How does
he come to have such wisdom? How
are such marvelous things done through
him? Is he not the carpenter, Mary's 3
son, and the brother of James, Joses,
Judas, and Simon? And do not his sisters
live here among us?"
And they took offense at him. Jesus 4
said to them,
"A prophet is treated with honor
everywhere except in his native place
and among his relatives and at his
home."
He could not do any wonder there, 5
except that he put his hands on a few
sick people and cured them. And he 6
wondered at their want of faith.
Then he went around among the villages
teaching. And he called the 7
Twelve to him and sent them off two
by two, giving them power over the
foul spirits. He forbade them to take 8
anything for the journey except a staff
—no bread, no bag, no small change
even in their girdles; they were to go in 9
sandals, and not to wear two shirts.
And he said to them, 10
"Whenever you go to stay at a house
remain in it till you leave that place.
If any place refuses to receive you or to 11
listen to you, when you leave it shake
off the very dust from the soles of your
feet as a warning to them."
So they went out and preached that 12
men should repent, and drove out 13
many demons, and anointed many sick
people with oil and cured them.
King Herod heard of him, for his 14
name was now well known, and people
were saying that John the baptizer had
risen from the dead, and that that was
why he was endowed with these extraordinary
powers. But others said he 15
was Elijah, and still others that he was
a prophet of the old prophetic kind.
But when Herod heard of him he said, 16
"John, whom I beheaded, has risen
from the dead."
For it was Herod who had sent and 17
seized John and bound him and put
him in prison, on account of Herodias,
his brother Philip's wife, because Herod
had married her. For John said to Herod, 18
"It is not right for you to be living
with your brother's wife."
Herodias felt bitterly toward him 19
and wanted to kill him. But she could

20 not do it, for Herod stood in awe of
John, knowing that he was an upright
and holy man, and he protected him.
And when he heard him talk he was
very much disturbed, and yet he liked
21 to hear him. When a holiday came and
Herod on his birthday gave a banquet
to his courtiers and officers and to the
22 leading men of Galilee, Herodias' own
daughter came in and danced for them.
And Herod and his guests were delighted, and the king said to the girl,
23 "Ask me for anything you like and I
will give it to you." And he made oath
to her,

"I will give you whatever you ask
me for, up to half my kingdom."
24 When she had left the room she said
to her mother,

"What shall I ask him for?"

But she said,

"The head of John the baptizer."
25 And she hurried back at once to the
king and asked him for it, saying,

"I want you right away to give me
John the Baptist's head on a platter."
26 The king was exceedingly sorry, but
on account of his oath and his guests he
did not like to break his word to her,
27 and he immediately sent one of his
guard with orders to get John's head.
28 And he went off and beheaded him in
the prison and brought back his head on
a platter and gave it to the girl, and the
29 girl gave it to her mother. When his
disciples heard of it they came and took
his body away and put it in a tomb.
30 The apostles rejoined Jesus and reported to him all they had done and
31 taught. And he said to them,

"Come away by yourselves to some
quiet place, and rest a little while."

For people were coming and going in
large numbers, and they had no time
32 even for meals. So they set off by themselves in their boat for a secluded place.
33 And many people saw them start and
knew of it, and hurried around by land
from all the neighboring towns, and got
34 ahead of them. So when he got out of
the boat, he found a great crowd gathered, and his heart was touched at the
sight of them, because they were like
sheep that have no shepherd; and he
proceeded to teach them a great deal.
35 When it grew late his disciples came up
to him and said,

"This is a lonely place and it is get-
36 ting late. Send the people off to the
farms and villages around to buy themselves something to eat."

But he answered, 37

"Give them food yourselves."

They said to him,

"Can we go and buy forty dollars'
worth of bread and give it to them to
eat?"

But he said to them, 38

"How many loaves have you? Go
and see."

They looked, and told him.

"Five, and two fish."

And he directed them all to sit down 39
in parties on the fresh grass. And they 40
threw themselves down in groups, in
hundreds and in fifties. Then he took 41
the five loaves and the two fish and
looked up to heaven and blessed the
loaves and broke them in pieces and
gave them to the disciples to pass to the
people; and he divided the two fish
among them all. And they all ate and 42
had enough. And the pieces they gath- 43
ered up filled twelve baskets, besides
the pieces of the fish. There were five 44
thousand men who ate the loaves.

He immediately had his disciples get 45
into the boat and cross before him to
the other side toward Bethsaida, while
he was dismissing the crowd. When he 46
had taken leave of the people he went
up on the mountain to pray. When 47
evening came on, the boat was in the
middle of the sea, and he was alone on
shore. And he saw that they were strain- 48
ing at the oars, for the wind was against
them, and toward morning he went out
to them, walking on the sea, and was
going to pass them. When they saw him 49
walking on the sea, they thought it was
a ghost and screamed aloud, for they all 50
saw him and were terrified. But he
immediately spoke to them and said,

"Take courage, it is I. Do not be
afraid."

Then he went up to them and got in- 51
to the boat. And the wind fell. And
they were perfectly beside themselves,
for they had not understood about the 52
loaves, but their minds were blinded.

They crossed over to the other side 53
and came to Gennesaret and moored
the boat. As soon as they came ashore, 54
the people recognized Jesus, and they 55
hurried all over the countryside and began to bring the sick to him on their
mats, wherever they heard he was. And 56
whatever village or town or farm he

went to, they would lay their sick in the
streets and beg him to let them
touch just the tassel of his cloak, and
all who touched it were cured.

7 The Pharisees gathered about him
with some scribes who had come from
2 Jerusalem. They had noticed that some
of his disciples ate their food without
first giving their hands a ceremonial
3 washing to purify them. For the Pharisees and all the Jews observe the rules
handed down from their ancestors, and
will not eat until they have washed
4 their hands in a particular way, and
they will not eat anything from the
market without first purifying it by
sprinkling it, and they have a number
of other observances which have come
down to them, in the way of washing
5 cups, pitchers, and basins. And the
Pharisees and the scribes asked him,

"Why do your disciples not observe
the rules handed down by our ancestors, but eat food without purifying
their hands?"

6 But he said to them,

"It was about you hypocrites that
Isaiah prophesied so finely, in the
words,

" 'This people honor me with their
lips,
Yet their hearts are far away from
me.
7 But their worship of me is all in
vain,
For the lessons they teach are but
human precepts.'

8 "You give up what God has commanded and hold fast to what men have
handed down."

9 "How skilful you are," he said to
them, "in nullifying what God has commanded in order to observe what has
10 been handed down to you. For Moses
said, 'Honor your father and your
mother,' and again, 'Whoever abuses
his father or mother must be put to
11 death.' But you say, 'If a man says to
his father or mother, "Anything of mine
that might have been of use to you is
Korban," ' that is, consecrated to God,
12 you let him off from doing anything
13 more for his father or mother, and so
you nullify what God has said by what
you have handed down. You have
many such practices."

14 He called the people to him again
and said to them,

"Listen to me, all of you, and understand this. Nothing that goes into a 15
man from outside can pollute him. It
is what comes out of a man that pollutes him."

When he had left the crowd and gone 17
home, his disciples asked him what he
meant by this figure. And he said to 18
them,

"Have not even you any understanding then? Do you not see that nothing
that goes into a man from outside can
pollute him, since it does not go into his 19
heart but into his stomach and then is
disposed of?" So he declared all food
clean. He went on to say, 20

"It is what comes out of a man that
pollutes him. For it is from inside, from 21
men's hearts, that designs of evil come;
immorality, stealing, murder, adultery,
greed, malice, deceit, indecency, envy, 22
abusiveness, arrogance, folly—all these 23
evils come from inside, and they pollute a man."

He left that place and went to the 24
neighborhood of Tyre and Sidon. And
he went into a certain house, and wanted no one to know of it. And he could
not keep it secret, but a woman whose 25
little daughter was possessed by a foul
spirit immediately heard about him and
came and threw herself at his feet. Now 26
the woman was a Greek, of Syrophoenician birth. And she begged him to drive
the demon out of her daughter. He said 27
to her,

"Let the children first eat all they
want, for it is not right to take the children's bread and throw it to the dogs."

But she answered, 28

"True, sir! and still the dogs under
the table eat what the children leave!"

He said to her, 29

"If you can say that, go home; the
demon has left your daughter."

And she went home and found the 30
child lying on the bed, and the demon
gone.

He left the neighborhood of Tyre 31
again and went by way of Sidon to the
Sea of Galilee, crossing the district of
the Ten Towns. And they brought to 32
him a man who was deaf and hardly
able to speak, and they begged him to
lay his hand on him. He took him off 33
by himself away from the crowd, and
put his fingers in the man's ears, and
touched his tongue with saliva. And he 34
looked up to heaven and sighed, and
said to him,

"Ephphatha!"—which means
"Open."
35 And his ears were opened and his
tongue was released and he talked
36 plainly. And Jesus forbade them to
tell anyone about it, but the more he
forbade them the more they spread the
37 news far and wide. And people were
utterly amazed, and said,

"How well he has done everything! He even makes the deaf hear and the dumb speak!"

8 In those days when a great crowd had gathered again and they had nothing to eat, he called his disciples to him and said to them,

2 "I pity these people, for they have
been staying with me three days now,
3 and they have nothing left to eat. And
if I send them home hungry they will
give out on the way, for some of them
come from a distance."

4 His disciples replied,

"Where can anyone get bread enough, here in this solitude, to satisfy these people's hunger?"

5 "How many loaves have you?" he
asked.

"Seven," they said.

6 Then he ordered the people to take
their places on the ground. And he took
the seven loaves and gave thanks and
broke them in pieces and gave them
to his disciples to pass, and they passed
7 them to the people. They had a few
small fish, and he blessed them and told
the disciples to pass them also to the
8 people. And they ate and satisfied
their hunger. And the pieces that they
left, that were picked up, filled seven
9 baskets. There were about four thousand of the people. And he dismissed
10 them. Then he immediately got into
the boat with his disciples and went to
the district of Dalmanutha.

11 The Pharisees came out and began a
discussion with him, testing him by
asking him to show them a sign
12 from heaven. And he sighed deeply
and said,

"Why do the men of this day ask for a sign? I tell you, no sign will be given them."

13 And he left them and got into the
boat again and crossed to the other side.
14 Now they had forgotten to bring any
bread, and they had only one loaf with
15 them in the boat. And he warned them,
saying,

"Look out! Be on your guard against the yeast of the Pharisees and the yeast of Herod!"

They were discussing with one an- 16
other their being without bread. And 17
he noticed it and said to them,

"Why do you discuss your being
without bread? Do you not yet see nor
understand? Are your minds so dull?
When you have eyes can you not see, 18
and when you have ears can you not
hear? Do you not remember how many 19
baskets of pieces you picked up when
I broke the five loaves in pieces for
those five thousand men?"

They said to him,

"Twelve."

"When I broke the seven loaves in 20
pieces for the four thousand, how many
baskets of pieces did you pick up?"

They said to him,

"Seven."

He said to them, 21

"Do you not understand yet?"

And they came to Bethsaida. And 22
people brought a blind man to him and
begged him to touch him. He took the 23
blind man by the hand and led him outside of the village, and spitting in his eyes
he laid his hands on him and asked him,

"Do you see anything?"

He looked up and said, 24

"I can see people, for they look to me like trees, only they are moving about."

Then he laid his hands on his eyes 25
again, and he looked steadily and was
cured, and saw everything plainly. And 26
he sent him home and said to him,

"Do not even go into the village."

Then Jesus and his disciples went 27
away to the villages around Caesarea
Philippi. On the way he questioned his
disciples and said to them,

"Who do people say that I am?"

They said to him, 28

"John the Baptist; others say Elijah, and others that you are one of the prophets."

And he asked them, 29

"But who do you say that I am?"

Peter answered and said to him,

"You are the Christ."

And he warned them not to say this 30
about him to anyone.

Then he explained to them for the 31
first time that the Son of Man must go
through much suffering, and be refused
by the elders and the high priests and
the scribes, and be killed, and rise again

2 three days after. He told them this
plainly. And Peter took him aside, and
3 began to reprove him for it. But turning and seeing his disciples he reproved
Peter, and said,
"Get out of my sight, you Satan! for
you do not side with God, but with
men."
4 And he called the people and his disciples to him and said to them,
"If anyone wants to go with me, he
must disregard himself, and take his
5 cross and follow me. For whoever
wants to preserve his own life will lose
it, and whoever loses his life for me and
6 for the good news will preserve it. For
what good does it do a man to gain the
whole world and yet part with his life?
7 For what can a man give to buy back
8 his life? For if anyone is ashamed of
me and my teachings in this unfaithful
and sinful age, then the Son of Man
will be ashamed of him, when he comes
back in his Father's glory, with the holy
9 angels." And he said to them, "I tell
you, some of you who stand here will
certainly live to see the reign of God
come in its might."
2 Six days after this Jesus took Peter,
James, and John with him, and led
them up on a high mountain, off by
themselves. And his appearance under-
3 went a change in their presence, and his
clothes shone whiter than any earthly
4 bleaching could make them. And Elijah appeared to them, accompanied by
Moses, and they talked with Jesus.
5 Then Peter spoke, and said to Jesus,
"Master, how good it is that we are
here! Let us put up three huts, one for
you and one for Moses and one for Eli-
6 jah." For he did not know what to say,
7 they were so frightened. And a cloud
came and overshadowed them, and
from the cloud came a voice,
"This is my Son, my Beloved. Listen
to him."
8 And suddenly, on looking around,
they saw that there was now no one
9 with them but Jesus alone. As they
were going down the mountain, he cautioned them to let no one know what
they had seen, until the Son of Man
10 should rise from the dead. And they
did not forget what he said, but discussed with one another what he meant
11 by the rising from the dead. And they
asked him,

"Why do the scribes say that Elijah
has to come first?"
He said to them, 12
"Elijah does come first, and reforms
everything, and does not the Scripture
say of the Son of Man that he will suffer much and be refused? Why, I tell 13
you, not only has Elijah come, but people have treated him just as they
pleased, as the Scripture says about
him."
When they came to the disciples, 14
they saw a great crowd around them,
and some scribes arguing with them.
And all the people were amazed when 15
they saw him, and they ran up to him
and greeted him. And he asked them, 16
"What are you discussing with
them?"
One of the crowd answered, 17
"Master, I brought my son to you,
for he is possessed by a dumb spirit,
and wherever it seizes him it throws him 18
on the ground, and he foams at the
mouth and grinds his teeth; and he is
wasting away. I told your disciples
to drive it out, and they could not do it."
He answered them and said, 19
"O you unbelieving people, how long
must I be with you? How long must I
put up with you? Bring him here to me!"
And they brought the boy to him. 20
As soon as the spirit saw him, it convulsed the boy, and he fell down on the
ground and rolled about, foaming at the
mouth. Jesus asked the boy's father, 21
"How long has he been like this?"
And he said,
"From his childhood, and many a 22
time it has thrown him into the fire or
into the water, to put an end to him.
But if there is anything you can do,
take pity on us and help us!"
Jesus said to him, 23
"'If there is anything I can do!'
Everything is possible for one who has
faith!"
The boy's father immediately cried 24
out,
"I have faith! Help my want of
faith!"
Then Jesus, seeing that a crowd was 25
rapidly gathering, reproved the foul
spirit and said to it,
"You deaf and dumb spirit, get out
of him, I charge you, and never enter
him again!"
And it gave a cry and convulsed him 26
terribly, and went out of him.

And the boy was like a corpse, so that
most of them said that he was dead.
27 But Jesus grasped his hand and made
28 him rise, and he stood up. When he
had gone home, and his disciples were
alone with him, they asked him,
"Why could not we drive it out?"
29 He said to them,
"This kind of thing can be driven out
only by prayer."
30 And they left that place and made
their way through Galilee, and he did
31 not wish anyone to know it; for he was
teaching his disciples, saying to them,
"The Son of Man is to be handed
over to men, and they will kill him, and
three days after he is killed he will rise
again."
32 But they did not understand what he
meant, and they were afraid to ask him
about it.
33 And they reached Capernaum. When
he got home, he asked them,
"What was it that you were discussing on the way?"
34 But they made no answer, for on the
way they had been discussing with one
another which of them was the great-
35 est. And he sat down and called the
Twelve in, and said to them,
"If anyone wishes to be first, he must
be the last of all and the servant of all."
36 And he took a child and made him
stand among them, and he put his arms
around him, and said to them,
37 "Whoever welcomes one child like
this on my account is welcoming me,
and whoever welcomes me, welcomes
not me but him who has sent me."
38 John said to him,
"Master, we saw a man driving out
demons with your name, and we told
him not to do so, for he was not one of
our followers."
39 But Jesus said,
"Do not tell him not to do so, for
there is no one who will use my name to
do a mighty act, and be able soon after
40 to abuse me. For the man who is not
41 against us is for us. For whoever gives
you a cup of water to drink, on the
ground that you belong to Christ, I tell
you, will certainly not fail to be repaid.
42 And whoever causes one of these humble believers to fall might better have a
great millstone hung around his neck
43 and be thrown into the sea. If your
hand makes you fall, cut it off. You
might better enter upon life maimed,
than go with both your hands to the pit,
into the fire that cannot be put out.
And if your foot makes you fall, cut it 45
off. You might better enter upon life
crippled, than be thrown with both
your feet into the pit. And if your eye 47
makes you fall, tear it out. You might
better get into the Kingdom of God
with only one eye than be thrown with
both your eyes into the pit, where the 48
worm that feeds upon them never dies
and the fire is never put out. Every- 49
one must be seasoned with fire. Salt is 50
a good thing, but if salt loses its
strength, what will you use to season
it? You must have salt within you, and
live in peace with one another."
And he left that place and went into 10
the district of Judea and crossed the
Jordan, and crowds of people again
gathered about him, and again he
taught them as he was accustomed to
do. Some Pharisees came up, and in 2
order to test him asked him whether a
man should be allowed to divorce his
wife. But he answered, 3
"What has Moses commanded you
to do?"
They said, 4
"Moses permits a man to divorce his
wife by drawing up a written divorce-
notice."
But Jesus said to them, 5
"It was on account of your perversity that he laid down that law for you.
But from the beginning of the creation, 6
'God made them male and female.
Therefore a man must leave his father 7
and mother, and he and his wife must
become one,' and so they are no longer 8
two but one. Therefore what God has 9
joined together man must not try to
separate."
When they reached the house the 10
disciples asked him about this again.
And he said to them, 11
"Anyone who divorces his wife and
marries another woman commits adultery against his former wife, and if a 12
woman divorces her husband and marries another man, she is an adulteress."
And people brought children to him 13
to have him touch them, but the disciples reproved them for it. When Jesus 14
saw it, he was indignant, and said to
them,
"Let the children come to me; do not
try to stop them, for the Kingdom of
God belongs to such as they. I tell you, 15

whoever does not accept the Kingdom
of God like a child shall not enter it at
all."
6 And he took the children in his arms
and laid his hands on them and blessed
them.
7 As he was starting again on his journey, a man came running up to him,
and knelt at his feet and asked him,
"Good master, what must I do to
make sure of eternal life?"
8 But Jesus said to him,
"Why do you call me good? No one
9 is good but God himself. You know the
commandments—'Do not murder, Do
not commit adultery, Do not steal, Do
not bear false witness, Do not defraud,
Honor your father and mother.' "
0 But he said to him,
"Master, I have obeyed all these
commandments ever since I was a
child."
1 And Jesus looked at him and loved
him, and he said to him,
"There is one thing that you lack.
Go, sell all you have, and give the
money to the poor, and then you will
have riches in heaven; and come back
and be a follower of mine."
2 But his face fell at Jesus' words, and
he went away much cast down, for he
had a great deal of property.
3 And Jesus looked around and said to
his disciples,
"How hard it will be for those who
have money to enter the Kingdom of
God!"
4 But the disciples were amazed at
what he said. And Jesus said to them
again,
"My children, how hard it is to enter
25 the Kingdom of God! It is easier for a
camel to get through the eye of a needle
than for a rich man to get into the
Kingdom of God!"
26 They were perfectly astounded and
said to him,
"Then who can be saved?"
27 Jesus looked at them and said,
"For men it is impossible, but not for
God, for anything is possible for God."
28 Peter started to say to him,
"Well, we have left all we had, and
have followed you."
29 Jesus said,
"I tell you, there is no one who has
given up home or brothers or sisters or
mother or father or children or land for
30 me and for the good news, but will receive now in this life a hundred times
as much in homes, brothers, sisters,
mothers, children, and lands, though
not without persecution—and in the
coming age eternal life. But many who 31
are first now will be last then, and the
last will be first."
As they went on their way up to Jeru- 32
salem, Jesus walked ahead of them, and
they were in dismay, and those who still
followed were afraid. And he took the
Twelve aside again and began to tell
them what was going to happen to him.
"See!" he said, "we are going up to 33
Jerusalem, and the Son of Man will be
handed over to the high priests and
scribes, and they will condemn him to
death and hand him over to the heathen and they will ridicule him and spit 34
on him and flog him and kill him; and
three days after he will rise again."
And Zebedee's two sons, James and 35
John, came up to him and said,
"Master, we want you to do for us
whatever we ask."
He said to them, 36
"What do you want me to do for
you?"
They said to him, 37
"Let us sit one at your right hand
and one at your left, in your triumph."
Jesus said to them, 38
"You do not know what you are asking for. Can you drink the cup that I
am drinking, or undergo the baptism
that I am undergoing?"
They said to him, 39
"Yes, we can."
Jesus said to them,
"Then you shall drink the cup that I
am drinking, and you shall undergo the
baptism that I am undergoing; but as 40
for sitting at my right or at my left,
that is not mine to give, but belongs to
those for whom it is destined."
When the other ten heard of this they 41
were at first very indignant at James
and John. And Jesus called them to 42
him, and said to them,
"You know that those who are supposed to rule the heathen lord it over
them, and their great men tyrannize
over them; but it is not to be so among 43
you. Whoever wants to be great among
you must be your servant, and whoever 44
wants to hold the first place among you
must be everybody's slave. For the 45
Son of Man himself has not come to be

waited on, but to wait on other people,
and to give his life to free many others."
46 And they came to Jericho. As he was
leaving the town with his disciples and
a great crowd, Timaeus' son Barti-
maeus, a blind beggar, was sitting at
47 the roadside. When he heard that it
was Jesus of Nazareth he began to cry
out,
"Jesus, you son of David, take pity
on me!"
48 Many of the people rebuked him and
told him to be still. But he cried out
all the louder,
"You son of David, take pity on
me!"
49 Jesus stopped and said,
"Call him here."
And they called the blind man and
said to him,
"Courage now! Get up, he is calling
you!"
50 And he threw off his coat and sprang
51 to his feet and went up to Jesus. Jesus
spoke to him and said,
"What do you want me to do for
you?"
The blind man said to him,
"Master, let me regain my sight!"
52 Jesus said to him,
"Go your way. Your faith has cured
you."
And he immediately regained his
sight and followed Jesus along the road.
11 When they were getting near Jerusalem, and had come to Bethphage and
Bethany near the Mount of Olives,
Jesus sent two of his disciples on ahead,
2 and said to them,
"Go to the village that lies in front of
you, and as soon as you enter it you
will find tied there a colt that has never
been ridden. Untie it and bring it here.
3 And if anybody says to you, 'Why are you
doing that?' say 'The Master needs it,
and will send it back here directly.'"
4 And they set off and found a colt tied
in the street at the door of a house, and
5 they untied it. Some of the bystanders
said to them,
"What are you doing, untying the
colt?"
6 But they answered them as Jesus
had told them to do, and the men let
7 them take it. So they brought the colt
to Jesus, and they threw their coats
8 over it and Jesus mounted it. And
many of the people spread their coats
in the road, and others cut straw from
the fields and scattered it in his path.
And those in front and those behind
shouted,
"God bless him!
Blessed be he who comes in the
Lord's name!
Blessed be the reign of our father 10
David which is coming!
God bless him from on high!"
And he came into Jerusalem and into 11
the Temple, and looked it all over;
then, as it was already late, he went out
with the Twelve to Bethany.
On the next day, after they had left 12
Bethany, he felt hungry. And he saw 13
in the distance a fig tree covered with
leaves, and he went up to it to see if he
could find any figs on it. When he
reached it he found nothing but leaves,
for it was not the time for figs. And he 14
spoke to the tree and said to it,
"May no one ever eat fruit from you
any more!"
And his disciples heard it.
When they reached Jerusalem, he 15
went into the Temple, and began to
drive out of it those who were buying or
selling things in it, and he upset the
money-changers' tables and the pigeon-
dealers' seats, and he would not allow 16
anyone to carry anything through the
Temple. And he taught them, and said, 17
"Does not the Scripture say, 'My
house shall be called a house of prayer
for all the nations'? But you have made
it a robbers' den."
The high priests and the scribes 18
heard of this, and they cast about for a
way of destroying him, for they were
afraid of him, for all the people were
amazed at what he taught. So when 19
evening came, he and his disciples used
to go out of the city.
In the morning as they were passing 20
along, they saw that the fig tree was
withered, to its very roots. And Peter 21
remembered about it and said to him,
"Look, Master! The fig tree that you
cursed is withered up!"
Jesus answered and said to them, 22
"Have faith in God! I tell you, who- 23
ever says to this mountain, 'Get up and
throw yourself into the sea!' and has no
doubt in his mind, but has faith that
what he says will happen, shall have it.
Therefore I tell you, whenever you pray 24
or ask for anything, have faith that it
has been granted you, and you shall
have it. And whenever you stand up to 25

pray, if you have a grievance against
anyone, forgive him, so that your Father in heaven too may forgive you your
offenses."
27 Then they went into Jerusalem
again. And as Jesus was walking about
in the Temple, the high priests, scribes,
28 and elders came up and said to him,
"What authority have you for doing
as you do? And who gave you a right
to do as you are doing?"
29 Jesus said to them,
"Let me ask you one question, and if
you answer me, I will tell you what au-
30 thority I have for doing as I do. Was
John's baptism from heaven or from
men? Answer me."
31 And they argued with one another,
"If we say, 'It was from heaven,' he
will say, 'Then why did you not believe
32 him?' Yet can we say, 'It was from
men'?" For they were afraid of the
people, because all the people thought
33 John was really a prophet. So they answered Jesus,
"We do not know."
Jesus said to them,
"Nor will I tell you what authority I
have for doing as I do."

12 Then he began to speak to them in
figures.
"A man once planted a vineyard and
fenced it in and hewed out a wine-vat
and built a watch tower, and he leased
it to tenants and left the neighborhood.
2 At the proper time he sent a slave to
the tenants to get from them a share of
3 the vintage. And they took him and
beat him and sent him back empty-
4 handed. And again he sent another
slave to them. And they beat him over
the head and treated him shamefully.
5 And he sent another; and him they
killed; and so with many others, some
6 they beat and some they killed. He still
had one left to send, a dearly loved son.
He sent him to them last of all, think-
7 ing, 'They will respect my son.' But
the tenants said to one another, 'This
is his heir! Come on, let us kill him, and
8 the property will belong to us!' So they
took him and killed him, and threw his
9 body outside of the vineyard. What
will the owner of the vineyard do? He
will come back and put the tenants to
death and give the vineyard to others.
10 Did you never read this passage of
Scripture:

"'That stone which the builders rejected
Has become the cornerstone;
This came from the Lord 11
And seems marvelous to us'?"
And they tried to have him arrested, 12
but they were afraid of the people, for
they knew that the illustration was
aimed at them. And they left him and
went away.
They sent some Pharisees and Herod- 13
ians to him to entrap him in argument.
And they came up and said to him, 14
"Master, we know that you tell the
truth regardless of the consequences,
for you are not guided by personal con-
siderations, but teach the way of God
with sincerity. Is it right to pay the
poll tax to the emperor or not? Should 15
we pay it, or refuse to pay it?"
But he saw through their pretense,
and said to them,
"Why do you put me to such a test?
Bring me a denarius to look at."
And they brought him one. He said 16
to them,
"Whose head and title is this?"
And they told him,
"The emperor's."
And Jesus said, 17
"Pay the emperor what belongs to
the emperor, and pay God what belongs
to God!"
And they were astonished at him.
Some of the Sadducees, who say there 18
is no resurrection, came to him and
asked him a question.
"Master," they said, "Moses made 19
us a law that if a man's brother died,
leaving a wife but no child, the man
should marry the widow and raise up a
family for his brother. There were once 20
seven brothers. And the eldest married
a wife and died, leaving no child. And 21
the second married her, and died without leaving any child, and so did the
third. And none of the seven left any 22
child. Finally, the woman died too. At 23
the resurrection, which one's wife will
she be? For all seven of them married
her."
Jesus said to them, 24
"Does not this show that you are
wrong, and do not understand either
the Scriptures or the power of God?
For when people rise from the dead, 25
there is no marrying or being married,
but they live as angels do in heaven.
But as to the dead being raised, have 26

you never read in the Book of Moses, in
the passage about the bush, how God
said to him, 'I am the God of Abraham,
the God of Isaac, and the God of Ja-
27 cob'? He is not God of dead men but
of living! You are entirely wrong."
28 One of the scribes came up and heard
them arguing. He saw that Jesus had
answered them well, and he asked him,
"Which is the first of all the commands?"
29 Jesus answered,
"The first one is, 'Hear, Israel! The
30 Lord our God is one lord, and you must
love the Lord your God with your
whole heart, your whole soul, your
whole mind, and your whole strength.'
31 And this is the second: 'You must love
your neighbor as you do yourself.' No
other command is greater than these."
32 The scribe said to him,
"Really, Master, you have finely
said that he stands alone, and there is
33 none but he, and to love him with one's
whole heart, one's whole understanding, and one's whole strength, and to
love one's neighbor as one's self is far
more than all these burnt-offerings and
sacrifices."
34 And Jesus saw that he answered
thoughtfully, and he said to him,
"You are not far from the Kingdom
of God!"
And no one ventured to ask him any
more questions.
35 As Jesus was teaching in the Temple,
he answered them and said,
"How can the scribes say that the
36 Christ is a son of David? David himself, under the influence of the holy
Spirit, said,
" 'The Lord has said to my lord, "Sit
at my right hand
Until I put your enemies under
your feet." '
37 David himself calls him lord, and how
can he be his son?"
The mass of the people liked to hear
38 him. And in the course of his teaching
he said to them,
"Beware of the scribes who like to go
about in long robes and to be saluted
39 with respect in public places, and to
have the front seats in the synagogues
40 and the best places at dinners—men
that eat up widows' houses and to cover
it up make long prayers! They will get
a far heavier sentence!"
41 And he sat down facing the treasury
and watched the people dropping money into it; and many rich people were
putting in large sums. A poor widow 42
came up and dropped in two little copper coins which make a cent. And he 43
called his disciples to him and said,
"I tell you that this poor widow has
put in more than all these others who
have been putting money into the treasury. For they all gave of what they had 44
to spare, but she in her want has put in
everything she possessed—all she had
to live on."
As he was leaving the Temple, one of 13
his disciples said to him,
"Look, Master! What wonderful
stones and buildings!"
Jesus said to him, 2
"Do you see these great buildings?
Not one stone shall be left here upon
another that shall not be torn down."
As he was sitting on the Mount of 3
Olives opposite the Temple, Peter,
James, John, and Andrew asked him,
apart from the others,
"Tell us when this is to happen, and 4
what the sign will be when it is all just
going to be carried out."
And Jesus said to them, 5
"Take care that no one misleads you
about this. Many will come under my 6
name and say 'I am he,' and many will
be misled by them. But when you hear 7
of wars and rumors of war, you must
not be alarmed. They have to come,
but it is not yet the end. For nation 8
will rise in arms against nation and
kingdom against kingdom; there will
be earthquakes here and there, there
will be famines. This is only the beginning of the sufferings. But you must be 9
on your guard; they will hand you over
to courts and you will be taken into
synagogues and beaten, and you will
be brought before governors and kings
on my account, to testify to them. For 10
before the end the good news must be
preached to all the heathen. When they 11
are taking you off to trial do not worry
beforehand about what you ought to
say, but say whatever is given you when
the time comes, for it is not you that
will speak, but the holy Spirit. Brother 12
will give up brother to be put to death,
and the father his child, and children
will turn against their parents and have
them put to death. You will be hated 13
by everyone, because you bear my
name. But he who holds out to the end

14 will be saved. But as soon as you see
the dreadful desecration standing where
he has no right to stand" (the reader
must take note of this), "then those
15 who are in Judea must fly to the hills; a
man on the housetop must not go
down or go into his house to get any-
16 thing out of it, and a man in the field
17 must not turn back to get his coat. Alas
for women who are with child at that
18 time, or who have babies! Pray that it
19 may not be winter when it comes, for
there will be such misery in those days
as there has never been since the beginning of God's creation until now,
20 and never will be again. If the Lord
had not cut those days short, nobody
would have escaped, but for the sake
of his own chosen people he has cut the
21 days short. If anyone says to you at
that time, 'Look! Here is the Christ!'
or 'Look! There he is!' do not believe
22 it. For false Christs and false prophets
will appear, and they will show signs
and wonders to mislead God's chosen
23 people if they can. But you must be
on your guard; I have told you all
24 about it beforehand. But in those days,
when that misery is over, the sun will
be darkened and the moon will not shed
25 its light and the stars will fall from the
sky and the forces in the sky will shake.
26 Then they will see the Son of Man coming on the clouds with great power and
27 glory, and then he will send out the angels and gather his chosen people from
the four winds, from one end of the
world to the other.
28 "Let the fig tree teach you the lesson.
As soon as its branches grow soft and
put forth leaves you know that summer
29 is coming. So when you see these things
happening, you must know that he is
30 just at the door. I tell you, these things
will all happen before the present age
31 passes away. Earth and sky will pass
32 away, but my words will not. But
about that day or hour no one knows,
not even the angels in heaven, nor the
33 Son; only the Father. You must look
out and be on the alert, for you do not
34 know when it will be time; just as a
man when he leaves home to go on a
journey, and puts his slaves in charge,
each with his duties, gives orders to the
35 watchman to keep watch. So you must
be on the watch, for you do not know
when the master of the house is coming
—in the evening or at midnight or toward daybreak or early in the morning
—for fear he should come unexpectedly 36
and find you asleep. And what I am 37
telling you I mean for all—Be on the
watch!"

It was now two days before the festi- 14
val of the Passover and of Unleavened
Bread. And the high priests and scribes
were casting about for a way to arrest
him by stealth and put him to death,
for they said, 2
"It must not be during the festival,
or there may be a riot."

Jesus was in Bethany, at the house of 3
Simon the leper, and as he was at table,
a woman came in, with an alabaster
flask of liquid spikenard perfume, very
expensive; she broke the flask and
poured the perfume on his head. But 4
there were some who said indignantly
to themselves,
"What was the use of wasting the
perfume like that? It might have been 5
sold for more than sixty dollars, and the
money have been given to the poor."
And they grumbled at her. But Jesus 6
said,
"Leave her alone. Why do you bother her? It is a fine thing that she has
done to me. For you always have the 7
poor among you, and whenever you
please you can do for them, but you will
not always have me. She has done all 8
she could; she has perfumed my body in
preparation for my burial. I tell you, 9
wherever the good news is preached all
over the world, what she has done will
also be told in memory of her."

Then Judas Iscariot, one of the 10
Twelve, went to the high priests to betray Jesus to them. They were delight- 11
ed to hear it and promised to pay him
for it. So he was watching for an opportunity to betray him to them.

On the first day of the festival of Un- 12
leavened Bread, on which it was customary to kill the Passover lamb, Jesus'
disciples said to him,
"Where do you wish us to go and
make the preparations for you to eat
the Passover supper?"
So he sent away two of his disciples, 13
saying to them,
"Go into the city, and you will meet
a man carrying a pitcher of water. Fol- 14
low him, and whatever house he goes
into, say to the man of the house, 'The
Master says, "Where is my room where
I can eat the Passover supper with my

15 disciples?"' And he will show you a
large room upstairs, furnished and
ready. Make your preparations for us
there."
16 So the disciples started and went into
the city, and found everything just as
he had told them; and they prepared
the Passover supper.
17 When it was evening he came with
18 the Twelve. And when they were at
the table eating, Jesus said,

"I tell you, one of you is going to betray me—one who is eating with me."

19 And they were hurt, and said to him
one after another,

"Can it be I?"

20 He said to them,
"It is one of the Twelve, who is dipping his bread in the same dish with
21 me. For the Son of Man is indeed to
go away as the Scriptures say of him,
but alas for the man by whom the Son
of Man is betrayed! It would have been
better for that man if he had never been
born."
22 As they were eating, he took a loaf
and blessed it, and he broke it in pieces
and gave it to them saying,

"Take this. It is my body."

23 And he took the wine cup and gave
thanks and gave it to them and they all
24 drank from it. And he said to them,
"This is my blood which ratifies the
agreement, and is to be poured out for
25 many people. I tell you, I will never
drink the product of the vine again till
the day when I shall drink the new
wine in the Kingdom of God."
26 After singing the hymn they went out
of the city and up the Mount of Olives.
27 And Jesus said to them,
"You will all desert me, for the Scriptures say, 'I will strike the shepherd,
28 and the sheep will be scattered.' But
after I am raised to life again I will go
back to Galilee before you."
29 But Peter said to him,

"Even if they all desert you, I will not!"

30 Jesus said to him,

"I tell you, this very night before the cock crows twice you yourself will disown me three times!"

31 But he persisted vehemently,

"If I have to die with you, I will never disown you."

And they all said the same thing.

32 They came to a place called Gethsemane, and he said to his disciples,

"Sit down here while I pray."

And he took Peter, James, and John 33
along with him, and he began to feel
distress and dread, and he said to them, 34
"My heart is almost breaking. You
must stay here and keep watch." And 35
he went on a little way and threw himself on the ground and prayed that if it
were possible he might be spared the
hour of trial, and he said, 36
"Abba!" that is, Father, "anything
is possible for you! Take this cup away
from me! Yet not what I please but
what you do!"
When he went back he found them 37
asleep and he said to Peter,
"Simon, are you asleep? Were you
not able to watch for one hour? Keep 38
awake, and pray that you may not be
subjected to trial. One's spirit is eager,
but human nature is weak."
He went away again and prayed in 39
the same words as before. When he 40
came back he found them asleep again,
for they could hardly keep their eyes
open; and they did not know what answer to make to him. When he came 41
back for the third time, he said to them,
"Are you still sleeping and taking
your rest? Enough of this! The time
has come. See! the Son of Man is betrayed into the hands of wicked men.
Get up, let us be going. Look, here 42
comes my betrayer!"
Just at that moment, while he was 43
still speaking, Judas, who was one of
the Twelve, came up, and with him a
crowd of men with swords and clubs,
from the high priests, scribes, and
elders. Now the man who betrayed 44
him had given them a signal, saying,

"The one I kiss is the man. Seize him and take him safely away."

So when he came he went straight up 45
to Jesus and said, "Master!" and kissed
him affectionately.
And they laid hands on him and 46
seized him. But one of the bystanders 47
drew his sword and struck at the high
priest's slave and cut his ear off. And 48
Jesus spoke and said to them,
"Have you come out to arrest me
with swords and clubs, as though I were
a robber? I have been among you day 49
after day in the Temple teaching, and
you never seized me. But let the
Scriptures be fulfilled!"
Then all the disciples left him and 50
made their escape.

51 And a young man followed him with
nothing but a linen cloth about his
52 body; and they seized him, but he left
the cloth behind and ran away naked.
53 They took Jesus away to the high
priest, and all the high priests, elders,
54 and scribes came together. And Peter
followed him at a distance, right into
the courtyard of the high priest and sat
down with the attendants and warmed
55 himself at the fire. The high priests
and the whole council tried to get evidence against Jesus in order to put him
56 to death, and they could find none, for
while many gave false testimony
against him their evidence did not
57 agree. Then some got up and gave false
testimony against him to this effect:
58 "We ourselves have heard him say, 'I
will tear down this sanctuary built by
men's hands, and in three days I will
build another, made without hands.'"
59 And even then their evidence did not
60 agree. Then the high priest got up and
came forward into the center and asked
Jesus,
"Have you no answer to make?
What about their evidence against
you?"
61 But Jesus was silent and made no
answer. The high priest again questioned him and said to him,
"Are you the Christ, the son of the
Blessed One?"
62 But Jesus said,
"I am! and you will see the Son of
Man seated at the right hand of the Almighty and coming in the clouds of the
sky!"
63 Then the high priest tore his clothing,
and said,
"What do we want of witnesses now?
64 Did you hear his blasphemy? What is
your decision?"
And they all condemned him as de-
65 serving to be put to death. And some
started to spit at him and to blindfold
him and strike him, and say to him,
"Now show that you are a prophet!"
And the attendants slapped him as
they took charge of him.
66 While Peter was down in the courtyard, one of the high priest's maids
67 came up, and seeing Peter warming
himself, she looked at him and said,
"You were with this Jesus of Nazareth too!"
68 But he denied it, saying,
"I do not know or understand what
you mean."
He went out into the gateway. And 69
the maid saw him there and began
again to tell the bystanders,
"This fellow is one of them!"
But he denied it again. And again a 70
little while after, the bystanders said to
Peter,
"You certainly are one of them, for
you are a Galilean!"
But he began to swear with the 71
strongest oaths,
"I do not know this man that you are
talking about!"
At that moment for the second time 72
a cock crowed. And Peter remembered
how Jesus had said to him, "Before the
cock crows twice, you will disown me
three times!" And at that, he wept
aloud.
As soon as it was daylight, the high **15**
priests held a consultation with the
elders and scribes, and they and the
whole council bound Jesus and took
him away and handed him over to Pilate. Pilate asked him, 2
"Are you the king of the Jews?"
He answered,
"Yes."
And the high priests kept heaping 3
accusations upon him. But Pilate 4
again asked him,
"Have you no answer to make? See
what charges they are making against
you."
But Jesus made no further answer 5
at all, so that Pilate wondered. Now at 6
festival time he used to set free for them
one prisoner, whom they petitioned for.
There was in prison a man called Ba- 7
rabbas, among some revolutionaries who
in their outbreak had committed murder. And a crowd of people came up 8
and started to ask him for the usual
favor. Pilate asked them, 9
"Do you want me to set the king of
the Jews free for you?"
For he knew that the high priests had 10
handed him over to him out of envy.
But the high priests stirred up the 11
crowd to get him to set Barabbas free
for them instead. And Pilate again said 12
to them,
"Then what shall I do with the man
you call the king of the Jews?"
They shouted back, 13
"Crucify him!"
And Pilate said to them, 14

"Why, what has he done that is
wrong?"
But they shouted all the louder,
"Crucify him!"
15 And as Pilate wanted to satisfy the
crowd, he set Barabbas free for them,
and after having Jesus flogged handed
him over to be crucified.
16 Then the soldiers took him inside the
courtyard, that is, of the governor's
residence, and they called the whole
17 battalion together. And they dressed
him up in a purple cloak, and made a
wreath of thorns and crowned him with
18 it, and they began to acclaim him,
"Long live the king of the Jews!"
19 And they struck him on the head
with a stick and spat at him, and they
knelt down and did homage to him.
20 When they had finished making sport
of him, they took off the purple cloak
and put his own clothes on him.
21 Then they took him out of the city to
crucify him. And they forced a passer-
by, who was coming in from the country, to carry his cross—one Simon, a
Cyrenian, the father of Alexander and
22 Rufus. And they took him to the place
called Golgotha, which means the
23 Place of the Skull. They offered him
drugged wine, but he would not take
24 it. Then they crucified him, and divided
up his clothes, drawing lots for them to
25 see what each of them should have. It
was nine in the morning when they
26 crucified him. And the notice of the
charge against him read, "The king of
27 the Jews." They crucified two robbers
along with him, one at his right and one
29 at his left. And the passers-by jeered
at him, shaking their heads and saying,
"Aha! you who would tear down the
sanctuary and build one in three days!
30 Come down from the cross and save
yourself!"
31 The high priests too made sport of
him to one another with the scribes and
said,
"He saved others, but he cannot save
32 himself! Let this Christ, the king of
Israel, come down from the cross now,
so that we may see it and believe!" And
the men who were crucified with him
abused him.
33 At noon darkness spread over the
whole country, and lasted until three
34 in the afternoon. And at three o'clock
Jesus called out loudly,
"Eloi, Eloi, lama sabachthani?"
which means, "My God, my God, why
have you forsaken me?"
Some of the bystanders, when they 35
heard it, said,
"See! He is calling for Elijah!"
One man ran off and soaked a sponge 36
in common wine, and put it on the end
of a stick and held it up to him to drink,
saying,
"Let us see whether Elijah does come
to take him down!"
But Jesus gave a loud cry, and ex- 37
pired. And the curtain of the sanctuary 38
was torn in two, from top to bottom.
And when the captain who stood facing 39
him saw how he expired he said,
"This man surely must have been a
son of God!"
There were some women also watch- 40
ing from a distance, among them Mary
of Magdala, Mary the mother of the
younger James and of Joseph, and Salome, who used to accompany him and 41
wait on him when he was in Galilee—
besides many other women who had
come up to Jerusalem with him.
Although it was now evening, yet 42
since it was the Preparation Day, that
is, the day before the Sabbath, Joseph 43
of Arimathea, a highly respected member of the council, who was himself living in expectation of the reign of God,
made bold to go to Pilate and ask for
Jesus' body. Pilate wondered whether 44
he was dead already, and he sent for
the captain and asked whether he was
dead yet, and when he learned from the 45
captain that he was, he gave Joseph
permission to take the body. And he 46
bought a linen sheet and took him down
from the cross and wrapped him in the
sheet, and laid him in a tomb that had
been hewn out of the rock, and rolled a
stone against the doorway of the tomb.
And Mary of Magdala and Mary, 47
Joses' mother, were looking on and saw
where he was put.
When the Sabbath was over, Mary 16
of Magdala, Mary, James's mother, and
Salome bought spices, in order to go
and anoint him. Then very early on the 2
first day of the week they went to the
tomb, when the sun had just risen. And 3
they said to one another,
"Who will roll the stone back from
the doorway of the tomb for us?"
And they looked up and saw that the 4
stone had been rolled back, for it was
very large. And when they went into 5

the tomb they saw a young man in a
white robe sitting at the right, and they
6 were utterly amazed. But he said to
them,
"You must not be amazed. You are
looking for Jesus of Nazareth who was
crucified. He has risen, he is not here.
7 See! This is where they laid him. But
go and say to his disciples and to Peter,
'He is going before you to Galilee; you
will see him there, just as he told you.' "
8 And they fled out of the tomb, for
they were all trembling and bewildered,
and they said nothing about it to anyone, for they were afraid to do so.

AN ANCIENT APPENDIX

But they reported briefly to Peter and his companions all they had been told. And afterward Jesus himself sent out by them from the east to the west the sacred and incorruptible message of eternal salvation.

ANOTHER ANCIENT APPENDIX

9 Now after he had risen, early on the
first day of the week, he appeared first
to Mary of Magdala, from whom he
10 had driven out seven evil spirits. She
went and told his old companions, while
they were mourning and weeping.
11 When they heard that he was alive and
that she had seen him, they would not
believe it. Afterward he showed him- 12
self in a different form to two of them
as they were walking along, on their
way into the country. They went back 13
and told the rest, but they would not
believe them. Still later he appeared to 14
the Eleven themselves when they were
at table, and reproached them for their
obstinacy and want of faith, because
they had not believed those who had
seen him after he had been raised from
the dead. And he said to them, 15
"Go to the whole world and proclaim
the good news to all the creation. He 16
who believes it and is baptized will be
saved, but he who does not believe it
will be condemned. And signs like these 17
will attend those who believe: with my
name they will drive out demons; they
will speak in foreign tongues; they will 18
take snakes in their hands, and if they
drink poison it will not hurt them; they
will lay their hands on the sick, and
they will get well."
So the Lord Jesus, after he had spok- 19
en to them, was caught up into heaven
and took his seat at God's right hand.
And they went out and preached every- 20
where, while the Lord worked with
them and confirmed their message by
the signs that attended it.

THE GOSPEL ACCORDING TO LUKE

1 MANY writers have undertak-
en to compose accounts of
the movement which has
2 developed among us, just as
the original eye-witnesses who became
teachers of the message have handed it
3 down to us. For that reason, Theophilus, and because I have investigated it
all carefully from the beginning, I have
determined to write a connected ac-
4 count of it for Your Excellency, so that
you may be reliably informed about the
things you have been taught.

5 In the days when Herod was king of
Judea, there was a priest named Zechariah who belonged to the division of
Abijah. His wife was also a descendant
of Aaron, and her name was Elizabeth.
6 They were both upright in the sight of
God, blamelessly observing all the
Lord's commands and requirements.
7 They had no children, for Elizabeth
was barren; and they were both advanced in life.
8 Once when he was acting as priest
before God, when his division was on
9 duty, it fell to his lot, according to the
priests' practice, to go into the sanctuary of the Lord and burn the incense,
10 while all the throng of people was outside, praying at the hour of the incense
11 offering. And an angel of the Lord appeared to him, standing at the right of
12 the altar of incense. When Zechariah
saw him he was startled and overcome
13 with fear. And the angel said to him,
"Do not be afraid, Zechariah, for
your prayer has been heard. Your wife
Elizabeth will bear you a son, and you
14 are to name him John. This will bring
gladness and delight to you, and many
15 will rejoice over his birth. For he will
be great in the sight of the Lord. He
will drink no wine or strong drink, but
he will be filled with the holy Spirit
16 from his very birth, and he will turn
many of Israel's descendants to the
17 Lord their God. He will go before him
with the spirit and the power of Elijah,
to reconcile fathers to their children,
and to bring the disobedient back to the
wisdom of upright men, to make a people perfectly ready for the Lord."
Zechariah said to the angel, 18
"How am I to know that this is so?
For I am an old man, and my wife is
advanced in life."
The angel answered, 19
"I am Gabriel. I stand in the very
presence of God. I have been sent to
speak to you and to tell you this good
news. Now you will keep silent and be 20
unable to speak until the day when this
happens, because you have not believed
what I have said, for it will all be fulfilled in due time."
The people were waiting for Zecha- 21
riah, and wondering that he stayed so
long in the sanctuary. But when he 22
came out he could not speak to them,
and they knew that he had seen a vision
in the sanctuary. For his part, he kept
making signs to them, and remained
dumb. And when his period of service 23
was over, he went back to his home.
Soon afterward his wife Elizabeth 24
began to expect a child, and she kept
herself in seclusion for five months.
"This is what the Lord has done for 25
me," she said, "now that he has deigned
to remove the disgrace I have endured."
In the sixth month the angel Gabriel 26
was sent by God to a town in Galilee
called Nazareth, to a maiden there who 27
was engaged to be married to a man
named Joseph, a descendant of David.
The maiden's name was Mary. And the 28
angel went into the town and said to
her,
"Good morning, favored woman!
The Lord be with you!"
But she was startled at what he said, 29
and wondered what this greeting
meant. And the angel said to her, 30
"Do not be afraid, Mary, for you
have gained God's approval. You are 31
to become a mother and you will give
birth to a son, and you are to name him
Jesus. He will be great and will be 32
called the Son of the Most High. The
Lord God will give him the throne of
his forefather David, and he will reign 33

over Jacob's house forever; his reign
will have no end."
Mary said to the angel,
"How can this be, when I have no
husband?"
The angel answered,
"The holy Spirit will come over you,
and the power of the Most High will
overshadow you. For that reason your
child will be called holy, and the Son of
God. And your relative, Elizabeth, although she is old, is going to give birth
to a son, and this is the sixth month
with her who was said to be barren.
For nothing is ever impossible for
God."
And Mary said,
"I am the Lord's slave. Let it be as
you say."
Then the angel left her.
In those days Mary set out and hurried to the hill-country, to a town in
Judah, and she went to Zechariah's
house and greeted Elizabeth. When
Elizabeth heard Mary's greeting, the
babe stirred within her. And Elizabeth
was filled with the holy Spirit and she
gave a great cry, and said,

"You are the most favored of women,
And blessed is your child!
Who am I,
To have the mother of my Lord come to me?

"For the moment your greeting reached my ears,
The child stirred with joy within me!
Blessed is she who has believed,
For what the Lord has promised her will be fulfilled!"

And Mary said,

"My heart extols the Lord,
My spirit exults in God my Savior.
For he has noticed his slave in her humble station,
For from this time all the ages will think me favored!

"For the Almighty has done wonders for me,
How holy his name is!
He shows his mercy age after age
To those who fear him.

"He has done mighty deeds with his arm, 51
He has routed the proud-minded,
He has dethroned monarchs and exalted the poor, 52
He has satisfied the hungry with good things, and sent the rich away empty-handed. 53

"He has helped his servant Israel, 54
Remembering his mercy,
As he promised our forefathers 55
To have mercy on Abraham and his descendants forever!"

So Mary stayed with her about three 56
months, and then returned home.
Now the time came for Elizabeth's 57
child to be born, and she gave birth to
a son. Her neighbors and relatives 58
heard of the great mercy the Lord had
shown her, and they came and congratulated her. On the eighth day they 59
came to circumcise the child, and they
were going to name him Zechariah,
after his father. But his mother said, 60
"No! He is to be named John."
They said to her, 61
"There is no one among your relatives who bears that name."
But they made signs to the child's 62
father and asked him what he wished to
have the child named. He asked for a 63
writing tablet, and wrote,
"His name is John."
And they were all amazed. Then his 64
voice and the use of his tongue were
immediately restored, and he blessed
God aloud. And all their neighbors 65
were overcome with fear, and all over
the hill-country of Judea all these stories were told, and everyone who heard 66
them kept them in mind, and said,
"What is this child going to be?"
For the Lord's hand was with him.
And his father Zechariah was filled 67
with the holy Spirit and he uttered a
divine message, saying,

"Blessings on the Lord, the God of Israel, 68
Because he has turned his attention to his people, and brought about their deliverance,
And he has produced a mighty Savior for us 69
In the house of his servant David.
"By the lips of his holy prophets he promised of old to do this— 70

71 To save us from our enemies and
from the hands of all who hate
us,
72 Thus showing mercy to our forefathers,
And keeping his sacred agreement,
73 "And the oath that he swore to our
forefather Abraham,
74 That we should be delivered from
the hands of our enemies,
75 And should serve him in holiness
and uprightness, unafraid,
In his own presence all our lives.

76 "And you, my child, will be called
a prophet of the Most High,
For you will go before the Lord to
make his way ready,
77 Bringing his people the knowledge
of salvation
Through the forgiveness of their
sins.
78 "Because the heart of our God is
merciful,
And so the day will dawn upon us
from on high,
79 To shine on men who sit in darkness and the shadow of death,
And guide our feet into the way to
peace."

80 And the child grew up and became
strong in the Spirit, and he lived in the
desert until the day when he proclaimed
himself to Israel.

2 In those days an edict was issued by
the Emperor Augustus that a census of
2 the whole world should be taken. It
was the first census, taken when Quir-
3 inius was governor of Syria. So everyone went to his own town to register.
4 And Joseph went up from Galilee from
the town of Nazareth to Judea to the
city of David called Bethlehem, because he belonged to the house and fam-
5 ily of David, to register with Mary,
who was engaged to him and who was
6 soon to become a mother. While they
were there, the time came for her child
7 to be born, and she gave birth to her
first-born son; and she wrapped him up,
and laid him in a manger, for there was
no room for them at the inn.
8 There were some shepherds in that
neighborhood keeping watch through
the night over their flock in the open
fields. And an angel of the Lord stood by them, and the glory of the Lord shone around them, and they were terribly frightened. The angel said to them,

"Do not be frightened, for I bring you good news of a great joy that is to be felt by all the people, for today, in the town of David, a Savior for you has been born who is your Messiah and Lord. And this will prove it to you: You will find a baby wrapped up and lying in a manger."

Suddenly there appeared with the angel a throng of the heavenly army, praising God, saying,

"Glory to God in heaven and on
earth!
Peace to the men he favors!"

When the angels left them and returned to heaven, the shepherds said to one another,

"Come! Let us go over to Bethlehem, and see this thing that has happened, that the Lord has told us of!"

And they hurried there, and found Mary and Joseph, with the baby lying in the manger. When they saw this, they told what had been said to them about this child. And all who heard it were amazed at what the shepherds told them, but Mary treasured up all they had said, and pondered over it. And the shepherds went back glorifying God and praising him for all that they had heard and seen in fulfilment of what they had been told.

When he was eight days old and it was time to circumcise him, he was named Jesus, as the angel had named him, before his birth was first expected.

When their purification period under the Law of Moses was over, they took him up to Jerusalem to present him to the Lord, in fulfilment of the requirement of the Law of the Lord, "Every first-born male shall be considered consecrated to the Lord," and to offer the sacrifice prescribed in the Law of the Lord, "A pair of turtle-doves or two young pigeons."

Now there was a man in Jerusalem named Symeon, an upright, devout man, who was living in expectation of the comforting of Israel, and under the influence of the holy Spirit. It had been revealed to him by the holy Spirit that he should not die without seeing the Lord's Messiah. And under the Spirit's

influence he went into the Temple, and
when Jesus' parents brought the child
there to do for him what the Law re-
8 quired, Symeon also took him in his
arms and blessed God, and said,
9 "Now, Master, you will let your
slave go free
In peace, as you promised,
0 For my eyes have seen your salvation
1 Which you have set before all the
nations,
2 A light of revelation for the heathen,
And a glory to your people Israel!"
3 The child's father and mother were
4 astonished at what Symeon said about
him. And he gave them his blessing, and
said to Mary, the child's mother,
"This child is destined to cause the
fall and rise of many in Israel, and to be
a portent that will be much debated—
5 you yourself will be pierced to the heart
—and so the thoughts of many minds
will be revealed."
5 There was also a prophetess there
named Hannah, the daughter of Phan-
uel, who belonged to the tribe of Asher.
She was very old, for after her girlhood
she had been married for seven years,
and she had been a widow until she was
now eighty-four. She never left the
Temple, but worshipped night and day
with fasting and prayer. She came up
just at that time and gave thanks to
God and spoke about the child to all
who were living in expectation of the
liberation of Jerusalem.
When they had done everything that
the Law of the Lord required, they returned to Galilee, to their own town of
Nazareth.
And the child grew up and became
strong and filled with wisdom, with
God's blessing resting on him.
His parents used to go to Jerusalem
every year at the Passover Festival.
And when he was twelve years old, they
went up as usual to the festival and
made their customary stay. When they
started back the boy Jesus stayed behind in Jerusalem without his parents'
knowledge. They supposed that he was
somewhere in the party, and traveled
until the end of the first day's journey,
and then they looked everywhere for
him among their relatives and acquaintances. As they could not find him, they
went back to Jerusalem in search of
him. And on the third day they found 46
him in the Temple, sitting among the
teachers, listening to them and asking
them questions, and everyone who 47
heard him was astonished at his intelligence and at the answers he made.
When his parents saw him they were 48
amazed, and his mother said to him.
"My child, why did you treat us like
this? Here your father and I have been
looking for you, and have been very
anxious."
He said to them, 49
"How did you come to look for me?
Did you not know that I must be at my
Father's house?"
But they did not understand what he 50
told them. And he went back with 51
them to Nazareth and obeyed them.
And his mother treasured all these
things up in her mind.
As Jesus grew older he gained in wis- 52
dom and won the approval of God and
men.

In the fifteenth year of the reign of **3**
the Emperor Tiberius, when Pontius
Pilate was governor of Judea, and Herod governor of Galilee, while his brother Philip was governor of the territory
of Iturea and Trachonitis, and Lysanias
was the governor of Abilene, in the high 2
priesthood of Annas and Caiaphas, a
message from God came to Zechariah's
son John in the desert. And he went all 3
through the Jordan Valley preaching
repentance and baptism in order to obtain the forgiveness of sins, as the book 4
of the sermons of the prophet Isaiah
says,
"Hark! Someone is shouting in the
desert,
Get the Lord's way ready!
Make his paths straight.
Every hollow must be filled up, 5
And every mountain and hill leveled.
What is crooked is to be made
straight,
And the rough roads are to be
made smooth,
And all mankind is to see how God 6
can save!"
So he would say to the crowds that 7
came out there to be baptized by him,
"You brood of snakes! Who warned
you to fly from the wrath that is coming? Then produce fruit that will be 8
consistent with your professed repent-

ance! And do not begin to say to yourselves, 'We have Abraham for our forefather,' for I tell you, God can produce
descendants for Abraham right out of
9 these stones! But the axe is already lying at the roots of the trees. Any tree
that fails to produce good fruit is going
to be cut down and thrown into the
fire."
10 The crowds would ask him,
"Then what ought we to do?"
11 And he answered,
"The man who has two shirts must
share with the man who has none, and
the man who has food must do the
same."
12 Even tax-collectors came to be baptized, and they said to him,
"Master, what ought we to do?"
13 He said to them,
"Do not collect any more than you
are authorized to."
14 And soldiers would ask him,
"And what ought we to do?"
He said to them,
"Do not extort money or make false
charges against people, but be satisfied
with your pay."
15 As all this aroused people's expecta-
tions, and they were all wondering in
their hearts whether John was the
16 Christ, John said to them all,
"I am only baptizing you in water,
but someone is coming who is stronger
than I am, whose shoes I am not fit to
untie. He will baptize you in the holy
17 Spirit and in fire. He has his winnowing
fork in his hand, to clean up his threshing-floor, and store his wheat in his
barn, but he will burn up the chaff with
inextinguishable fire."
18 So with many varied exhortations he
would preach the good news to the peo-
19 ple, but Herod the governor, whom he
condemned because of Herodias, his
brother's wife, and all the wicked things
20 Herod had done, crowned them all by
putting John in prison.
21 Now when all the people were baptized and when Jesus also after his bap-
22 tism was praying, heaven opened and
the holy Spirit came down upon him in
the material shape of a dove, and there
came a voice from heaven,
"You are my Son, my Beloved! You
are my Chosen!"
23 Jesus himself was about thirty years
old when he began his work. He was
the son, it was supposed, of Joseph, the

son of Eli, the son of Matthat, the son
of Levi, the son of Melchi, the son of
Jannai, the son of Joseph, the son of
Mattathias, the son of Amos, the son of
Nahum, the son of Esli, the son of Nag-
gai, the son of Maath, the son of Mattathias, the son of Semein, the son of
Josech, the son of Joda, the son of Jo-
hanan, the son of Resa, the son of Ze-
rubbabel, the son of Salathiel, the son of
Neri, the son of Melchi, the son of Addi,
the son of Cosam, the son of Elmadam,
the son of Er, the son of Jesus, the son
of Eliezer, the son of Jorim, the son of
Matthat, the son of Levi, the son of Symeon, the son of Judah, the son of
Joseph, the son of Jonam, the son of
Eliakim, the son of Melea, the son of
Menna, the son of Mattatha, the son of
Nathan, the son of David, the son of
Jesse, the son of Obed, the son of Boaz,
the son of Salmon, the son of Nahshon,
the son of Amminadab, the son of Ram,
the son of Hezron, the son of Perez, the
son of Judah, the son of Jacob, the son
of Isaac, the son of Abraham, the son of
Terah, the son of Nahor, the son of
Serug, the son of Reu, the son of Peleg,
the son of Heber, the son of Shelah,
the son of Kenan, the son of Arphaxad,
the son of Shem, the son of Noah, the
son of Lamech, the son of Methuselah,
the son of Enoch, the son of Jared, the
son of Mahalalel, the son of Kenan, the
son of Enosh, the son of Seth, the son
of Adam, the son of God.

Jesus returned from the Jordan full
of the holy Spirit, and he was led about
in the desert for forty days by the Spirit, and was tempted by the devil. In all
those days he ate nothing, and when
they were over he was famished. And
the devil said to him,
"If you are God's son, tell this stone
to turn into bread!"
Jesus answered,
"The Scripture says, 'Not on bread
alone is man to live!'"
And he took him up and showed him
in an instant all the kingdoms of the
world. And the devil said to him,
"I will give you all this power and
their splendor, for it has been turned
over to me, and I can give it to anyone
I please. If you will do homage before
me, it shall all be yours."
Jesus answered,
"The Scripture says, 'You must do

homage before the Lord your God, and
worship him alone.' "
9 And he took him to Jerusalem, and
made him stand on the summit of the
Temple, and said to him,
"If you are God's son, throw your-
10 self down from here, for the Scripture
says, 'He will give his angels orders
11 about you, to protect you,' and, 'They
will lift you up with their hands, so
that you may never strike your foot
against a stone.' "
12 Jesus answered,
"We have been told, 'You shall not
try the Lord your God.' "
13 When the devil had tried every kind
of temptation he left him till another
time.
14 Under the power of the Spirit Jesus
returned to Galilee, and news of him
15 went all over that region. And he
taught in their synagogues, and was
honored by them all.
16 And he came to Nazareth, where he
had been brought up, and on the Sabbath he went to the synagogue, as he
was accustomed to do, and stood up to
17 read the Scriptures. And the roll of the
prophet Isaiah was handed to him, and
he unrolled it and found the place
where it says,
18 "The spirit of the Lord is upon me,
For he has consecrated me to
preach the good news to the
poor,
He has sent me to announce to the
prisoners their release and to the
blind the recovery of their sight,
To set the down-trodden at liberty,
19 To proclaim the year of the Lord's
favor!"
20 And he rolled up the roll and gave it
back to the attendant and sat down.
The eyes of everyone in the synagogue
21 were fixed upon him. And he began by
saying to them,
"This passage of Scripture has been
fulfilled here in your hearing today!"
22 And they all spoke well of him and
were astonished at the winning words
that fell from his lips, and they said,
"Is he not Joseph's son?"
23 He said to them,
"No doubt you will quote this proverb to me: 'Doctor, cure yourself! Do
the things here in your own country
24 that we hear you did at Capernaum.' I
tell you," said he, "no prophet is welcome in his own country. But I tell 25
you, there were plenty of widows in Israel in Elijah's time, when the sky was
closed for three years and a half, and
there was a great famine all over the
land, and Elijah was not sent to one of 26
them, but to a widow at Zarephath in
Sidon. And there were plenty of lepers 27
in Israel in the time of the prophet Elisha, and none of them was cured, but
Naaman the Syrian."
And when the people in the syna- 28
gogue heard this, they were all very
angry, and they got up and drove him 29
out of the town and took him to the
brow of the hill on which their town
was built, intending to throw him down
from it. But he made his way through 30
the midst of them and went on.
And he came down to Capernaum, a 31
town in Galilee. And he taught them
on the Sabbath, and they were amazed 32
at his teaching, for he spoke with authority. There was a man in the syna- 33
gogue who was possessed by the spirit
of a foul demon and he cried out loudly,
"Ha! What do you want of us, Jesus, 34
you Nazarene? Have you come to destroy us? I know who you are! You
are God's Holy One!"
Jesus reproved him and said, 35
"Silence! Get out of him!"
And the demon threw the man down
in the midst of them, and came out of
him, without doing him any harm. And 36
they were all amazed and said to one
another,
"What is the meaning of this teaching? For he gives orders authoritative-
ly and effectually to the foul spirits, and
they come out." And news of him 37
spread to every place in that region.
When he got up and left the syna- 38
gogue, he went to Simon's house. And
Simon's mother-in-law was suffering
with a severe attack of fever, and they
asked him about her. And he stood 39
over her and reproved the fever and it
left her, and she immediately got up
and waited on them.
As the sun went down all who had 40
friends sick with various diseases
brought them to him, and he laid his
hands on every one of them and cured
them. And demons came out of many 41
people, crying out,
"You are the Son of God!"
But he reproved them and forbade

them to speak, because they knew he
was the Christ.
42 When it was day, he left the house
and made his way to a lonely spot, and
crowds of people went in search of him,
and overtook him and tried to keep him
43 from leaving them. But he said to
them,
"I must preach the good news of the
Kingdom of God to the other towns
also, for that is what I was sent to do."
44 So he went about Judea, preaching in
the synagogues.
5 Once as the crowd was pressing about
him to hear God's message, he happened to be standing by the Lake of
2 Gennesaret, and he saw two boats on
the shore of the lake, for the fishermen
had gotten out of them and were wash-
3 ing their nets. And he got into one of
the boats, which belonged to Simon,
and asked him to push out a little from
the shore. Then he sat down and
taught the crowds of people from the
4 boat. When he stopped speaking, he
said to Simon,
"Push out into deep water, and then
put down your nets for a haul."
5 Simon answered,
"Master, we worked all night and
caught nothing, but as you tell me to do
it, I will put down the nets."
6 So they did so, and inclosed such a
shoal of fish that their nets began to
7 break. And they signaled to their comrades in the other boat to come and
help them. And they came, and they
filled both boats so full that they began
8 to sink. When Simon Peter saw it, he
fell down at Jesus' feet and said,
"Leave me, Lord, for I am a sinful
man."
9 For he and all the men with him were
perfectly amazed at the haul of fish
10 they had made, and so were Zebedee's
sons, James and John, who were Simon's partners. Jesus said to Simon,
"Do not be afraid. From now on you
are to catch men!"
11 And they brought the boats to land
and left everything and followed him.
12 When he was in one of the towns, he
came upon a man covered with leprosy.
And when he saw Jesus he fell down on
his face, and begged him, saying,
"If you only choose, sir, you can cure
me!"
13 And he stretched out his hand and
touched him, saying,

"I do choose! Be cured!"
And the leprosy immediately left
him. Then he warned him to tell no- 14
body,
"But go," he said, "show yourself to
the priest, and in proof of your cure
make the offerings for your purification, just as Moses prescribed."
Yet the news about him spread more 15
and more, and great crowds gathered
to hear him and to be cured of their
diseases. But Jesus himself would re- 16
tire into the desert and pray.
One day as he was teaching, there 17
were some Pharisees and experts in the
Law sitting near by, who had come
from every village in Galilee and Judea
and from Jerusalem. The power of the
Lord was there, so that he might cure
people. Some men came up carrying on 18
a bed a man who was paralyzed, and
they tried to get him in and lay him before Jesus. And as they could find no 19
way to get him in, on account of the
crowd, they went up on the roof and
let him down with his mat through the
tiles, among the people in front of Jesus. When he saw their faith, he said, 20
"Friend, your sins are forgiven!"
And the scribes and the Pharisees be- 21
gan to debate and say,
"Who is this man who talks blasphemy? Who can forgive sins but God
alone?"
But Jesus saw what they were dis- 22
cussing, and said to them,
"What are you pondering over in
your minds? Which is easier, to say, 23
'Your sins are forgiven,' or to say, 'Get
up and walk'? But to let you know 24
that the Son of Man has authority to
forgive sins on earth"—turning to the
man who was paralyzed he said to him
—"I tell you, get up, pick up your mat,
and go home!"
And he got up at once before them 25
all, and picked up what he had been lying on, and went home, praising God.
They were all seized with astonishment, 26
and praised God, and filled with awe
they said,
"We have seen something wonderful
today!"
After this he went out, and he saw a 27
tax-collector named Levi sitting at the
tollhouse, and he said to him,
"Follow me!"
And he left everything and got up 28
and followed him. Then Levi gave a 29

great entertainment for him in his
house, and there was a great throng of
tax-collectors and others who were at
30 table with them. And the Pharisees
and their scribes grumbled about it to
his disciples, and said,
"Why do you eat and drink with tax-collectors and irreligious people?"
31 Jesus answered them,
"It is not well people but the sick
32 who have to have the doctor. I have
not come to invite the pious but the irreligious to repentance!"
33 They said to him,
"John's disciples observe frequent
fasts and offer prayers, and so do the
disciples of the Pharisees, but your disciples eat and drink."
34 Jesus said to them,
"Can you make wedding guests fast
while the bridegroom is with them?
35 But other days will come, and when the
bridegroom is taken away from them,
in those days they will fast."
36 He used this figure also in speaking
to them:
"No one tears a piece from a new
coat and sews it on an old one, or if he
does, he will both tear the new one and
the piece from the new one will not
37 match the old one. And nobody puts
new wine into old wine-skins, or if he
does, the new wine will burst the skins
and run out, and the skins will be
38 spoiled. New wine has to be put into
39 fresh skins. No one after drinking old
wine wants new, for he says, 'The old is
better!'"
6 One Sabbath he happened to be passing through the wheat fields, and his
disciples were picking the heads of
wheat, and eating them, rubbing them
2 in their hands. And some of the Pharisees said,
"Why do you do what it is against
the Law to do on the Sabbath?"
3 Jesus answered,
"Have you not read even what David did, when he and his companions
4 were hungry? How he went into the
house of God and took the Presentation
Loaves, which it was against the Law
for anyone but the priests to eat, and
5 ate them with his companions?" And
he said to them, "The Son of Man is
master of the Sabbath."
6 On another Sabbath he happened to
go to the synagogue and teach. There
was a man there whose right hand was
withered. And the scribes and the 7
Pharisees were on the watch to see
whether he would cure people on the
Sabbath, in order to find a charge to
bring against him. But he knew what 8
they were thinking, and he said to the
man with the withered hand,
"Get up and stand in front."
And he got up and stood there. Jesus 9
said to them,
"I want to ask you, Is it allowable on
the Sabbath to do people good or to do
them harm? to save life or to destroy
it?"
And he looked around at them all 10
and said to the man,
"Hold out your hand!"
And he did so, and his hand was restored.
But they were perfectly furious, and 11
discussed with one another what they
could do to Jesus.
It was in those days that he went up 12
on the mountain to pray, and passed
the whole night in prayer to God.
When day came, he called his disciples 13
to him, and chose twelve of them whom
he named apostles: Simon, whom he 14
named Peter, his brother Andrew,
James, John, Philip, Bartholomew,
Matthew, Thomas, James, the son of 15
Alphaeus, Simon, who was called the
Zealot, Judas, the son of James, and 16
Judas Iscariot, who turned out a traitor. And he came down with them and 17
took his stand on a level place with a
great throng of his disciples, and a great
crowd of people from all over Judea
and from Jerusalem and the seacoast
district of Tyre and Sidon, who had
come to hear him and to be cured of
their diseases. And those who were 18
troubled with foul spirits were cured.
And all the people tried to touch him, 19
because power went forth from him and
cured them all. Then he fixed his eyes 20
on his disciples, and said,
"Blessed are you who are poor, for
the Kingdom of God is yours!
"Blessed are you who are hungry 21
now, for you will be satisfied!
"Blessed are you who weep now, for
you will laugh!
"Blessed are you when people hate 22
you and exclude you and denounce you
and spurn the name you bear as evil, on
account of the Son of Man. Be glad 23
when that happens, and leap for joy,
for you will be richly rewarded in heav-

en, for that is the way their forefathers
treated the prophets.
24 "But alas for you who are rich, for
you have had your comfort!
25 "Alas for you who have plenty to eat
now, for you will go hungry!
"Alas for you who laugh now, for you
will mourn and weep!
26 "Alas for you when everyone speaks
well of you, for that is the way their
forefathers treated the false prophets!
27 "But I tell you who hear me, love
your enemies, treat those who hate you
28 well, bless those who curse you, pray
29 for those who abuse you. To the man
that strikes you on the cheek, turn the
other also, and from the man who takes
away your coat, do not keep back your
30 shirt either. Give to everyone that
asks of you, and if anyone takes away
what is yours, do not demand it back.
31 And treat men just as you wish them to
32 treat you. If you love only those who
love you, what merit is there in that?
For even godless people love those who
33 love them. And if you help only those
who help you, what merit is there in
that? Even godless people act in that
34 way. And if you lend only to people
from whom you expect to get something, what merit is there in that?
Even godless people lend to godless
people, meaning to get it back again in
35 full. But love your enemies, and help
them and lend to them, never despairing, and you will be richly rewarded,
and you will be sons of the Most High,
for he is kind even to the ungrateful and
36 the wicked. You must be merciful, just
37 as your Father is. Do not judge others,
and they will not judge you. Do not
condemn them, and they will not condemn you. Excuse others and they will
38 excuse you. Give, and they will give to
you; good measure, pressed down, shaken together, and running over, they
will pour into your lap. For the measure you use with others they in turn will
use with you."
39 And he used a figure saying,
"Can one blind man lead another?
40 Will they not both fall into a hole? A
pupil is not better than his teacher, but
every pupil when he is fully trained will
41 be like his teacher. Why do you keep
looking at the speck in your brother's
eye, and pay no attention to the beam
42 that is in your own? How can you say
to your brother, 'Brother, just let me
get that speck out of your eye,' when
you cannot see the beam in your own
eye? You hypocrite! First get the
beam out of your own eye, and then
you can see to get out the speck in your
brother's eye. For sound trees do not 43
bear bad fruit, nor bad trees sound
fruit. Every tree is known by its fruit. 44
They do not pick figs off thorns, or
gather grapes from brambles. A good 45
man, out of the good he has accumulated in his heart, produces good, and a
bad man, out of what he has accumulated that is bad, produces what is bad.
For his mouth says only what his heart
is full of. Why do you call me: 'Lord! 46
Lord!' and not do what I tell you? If 47
anyone comes to me and listens to this
teaching of mine and acts upon it, I will
show you whom he is like. He is like a 48
man who was building a house, who dug
deep and laid his foundation upon the
rock, and when there was a flood the
torrent burst upon that house and
could not shake it, because it was well
built. But the man who listens to it, 49
and does not act upon it, is like a man
who built a house on the ground without any foundation. The torrent burst
upon it, and it collapsed at once, and
the wreck of that house was complete."
When he had finished saying all this 7
in the hearing of the people, he went to
Capernaum.
A Roman captain had a slave whom 2
he thought a great deal of, and the slave
was sick and at the point of death.
When the captain heard about Jesus, he 3
sent some Jewish elders to him, to ask
him to come and save his slave's life.
And they went to Jesus and urged him 4
strongly to do it, and said,
"He deserves to have you do this for
him, for he loves our nation, and it was 5
he who built us our synagogue."
So Jesus went with them. But when 6
he was not far from the house, the captain sent some friends to him, to say to
him,
"Master, do not take any more trouble, for I am not a suitable person to
have you under my roof. That is why I 7
did not think I was fit to come to you.
But simply say the word, and have my
servant cured. For I am myself under 8
the orders of others, and I have soldiers
under me, and I tell one to go, and he
goes, and another to come, and he

comes, and my slave to do something,
and he does it."
9 When Jesus heard this, he was astonished at him, and turning to the crowd
that was following him, he said,
"I tell you, I have not found such
faith as this even in Israel!"
10 And when the messengers went back
to the house, they found the slave well.
11 Soon afterward he happened to go to
a town called Nain, and his disciples
and a great throng of people went with
12 him. As he came up to the gate of the
town, a dead man was being carried
out; he was his mother's only son, and
she was a widow. A crowd of the towns-
13 people was with her. And when the
Lord saw her, he pitied her, and said
to her,
"Do not weep."
14 And he went up and touched the bier,
and the bearers stopped. And he said,
"Young man, I tell you, wake up!"
15 And the dead man sat up and began
to speak, and he gave him back to his
16 mother. And they were all overcome
with awe, and they praised God, and
said,
"A great prophet has appeared
among us!" and "God has not forgotten
his people!"
17 This story about him spread all over
Judea and all the country around.
18 John's disciples told him of all this,
19 and he called two of them to him, and
sent them to the Lord to ask him,
"Are you the one who was to come,
or should we look for someone else?"
20 And the men went to him and said,
"John the Baptist sent us to you to
ask, 'Are you the one who was to come,
or should we look for someone else?' "
21 Just then he cured many of diseases
and ailments and evil spirits, and he
gave sight to many who were blind.
22 And he answered them,
"Go and report to John what you
have seen and heard. The blind are regaining their sight, the lame can walk,
the lepers are being cured and the deaf
can hear, the dead are being raised and
good news is being preached to the
23 poor. And blessed is the man who finds
nothing that repels him in me."
24 When John's messengers were gone,
he began to speak to the crowds about
John,
"What was it that you went out into
the desert to look at? A reed swaying
in the wind? Then what did you go out 25
there to see? A man luxuriously
dressed? Men who wear fine clothes
and live in luxury you find in palaces.
Then what did you go out there to see? 26
A prophet? Yes, I tell you, and far
more than a prophet! This is the man 27
of whom the Scripture says,
" 'Here I send my messenger on before you,
He will prepare the road ahead of
you!'
"I tell you, among men born of wom- 28
en there is none greater than John; and
yet one who is of little importance
in the Kingdom of God is greater than
he. And all the people, even the tax- 29
collectors, when they heard him, acknowledged the justice of God's demands, by accepting baptism from
John, but the Pharisees and experts in 30
the Law thwarted God's purpose for
themselves, by refusing to be baptized
by him. So what is there to which I can 31
compare the men of this age? What are
they like? They are like children sit- 32
ting about in the bazaar and calling out
to one another,
" 'We have played the flute for you,
and you would not dance!
We have wailed and you would
not weep!'
"For when John the Baptist came, he 33
did not eat any bread or drink any
wine, and you said, 'He has a demon!'
Now that the Son of Man has come, he 34
does eat and drink, and you say, 'Look
at him! A glutton and a drinker, the
companion of tax-collectors and irreligious people!' So wisdom is vindicated 35
by all who are really wise."
One of the Pharisees asked him to 36
have dinner with him, and he went to
the Pharisee's house and took his place
at the table. Now there was a woman 37
in the town who was leading a sinful
life, and when she learned that he was
having dinner at the Pharisee's house,
she got an alabaster flask of perfume,
and came and stood behind him at his 38
feet, weeping, and began to wet his feet
with her tears, and she wiped them with
her hair, and kissed them, and put the
perfume on them. When the Pharisee 39
who had invited him saw this, he said
to himself,
"If this man were really a prophet, he
would know who and what the woman

is who is touching him, for she leads a
wicked life."
40 Jesus answered him, and said to him,
"Simon, there is something I want to
say to you."
He said,
"Proceed, Master."
41 "Two men were in debt to a money-
lender. One owed him a hundred dol-
42 lars and the other ten. As they could
not pay him, he canceled what they
owed him. Now which of them will be
more attached to him?"
43 Simon answered,
"The one, I suppose, for whom he
canceled most."
44 "You are right," he said. And turning to the woman, he said to Simon,
"Do you see this woman? I came to
your house; you did not give me any
water for my feet, but she has wet my
feet with tears and wiped them with her
45 hair. You did not give me a kiss, but
from the moment I came in she has not
46 stopped kissing my feet. You did not
put any oil upon my head, but she has
47 put perfume upon my feet. Therefore,
I tell you, her sins, many as they are,
are forgiven, for she has loved me so
much. But the man with little to be
forgiven loves me but little."
48 And he said to her,
"Your sins are forgiven!"
49 The men at table with him began to
say to themselves,
"Who is this man, who even forgives
sins?"
50 But he said to the woman,
"It is your faith that has saved you.
Go in peace."
8 Soon afterward he went about
among the towns and villages preaching
and telling the good news of the Kingdom of God. The Twelve went with
2 him, and some women who had been
cured of evil spirits and sickness—
Mary, who was called Mary of Magdala, out of whom seven demons had
3 been driven, and Joanna, the wife of
Chuza, Herod's manager, and Susanna,
and many others, who provided for
them with their means.
4 When a great throng was gathering
and people were coming to him from
one town after another, he said in his
figurative way,
5 "A sower went out to sow his seed.
As he was sowing, some of the seed fell
by the path and was trodden on, and
the wild birds ate it up. And some of it 6
fell upon the rock, and when it sprang
up it withered, because it had no moisture. And some fell among the thorns, 7
and the thorns grew up with it and
choked it out. And some fell on good 8
soil, and grew up and yielded a hundred fold!"
As he said this he called out,
"Let him who has ears to hear with,
listen!"
His disciples asked him what this 9
figure meant. And he said, 10
"You are permitted to know the secrets of the Kingdom of God, but they
are given to others in the form of figures, so that they may look and yet not
see, and hear and yet not understand.
This is what the figure means. The 11
seed is God's message. The ones by the 12
path are those who hear, and then the
devil comes and carries off the message
from their hearts, so that they may not
believe it and be saved. The ones on 13
the rock are those who receive the message joyfully when they first hear it,
but it takes no real root. They believe
for a little while, and then in the time
of trial they draw back. And what falls 14
among the thorns means those who listen and pass on, and the worries and
wealth and pleasures of life stifle them
and they yield nothing. But the seed 15
in the good soil means those who listen
to the message and keep it in good,
true hearts, and yield unfailingly.
"Nobody lights a lamp and then 16
covers it with a dish or puts it under
a bed, but he puts it on its stand, so
that those who come in may see the
light. For there is nothing hidden that 17
shall not be disclosed, nor kept secret
that shall not be known and come to
light. So take care how you listen. For 18
people who have will have more given
to them, and from people who have
nothing, even what they think they
have will be taken away."
His mother and his brothers came to 19
him, but they could not get near him,
on account of the crowd. And the 20
word came to him,
"Your mother and your brothers are
standing outside; they want to see
you."
He answered, 21
"My mother and my brothers are
those who listen to God's message and
obey it!"

22 It happened one day that he got into
a boat with his disciples, and said to
them,
"Let us cross to the other side of the
lake."
23 So they set sail. As they sailed along,
he fell asleep. And a squall of wind
came down upon the lake, and they
were being swamped and were in peril.
24 And they went to him and woke him
up, and said to him,
"Master! Master! We are lost!"
Then he awoke and reproved the
wind and the rough water, and they
25 ceased, and there was a calm. And he
said to them,
"Where is your faith?"
But they were frightened and
amazed, and said to one another,
"Who can he be? For he gives orders
even to the winds and the water, and
they obey him!"
26 They made a landing in the neighborhood of Gerasa, which is just across the
27 lake from Galilee. And when he landed,
he met a man possessed by demons,
who was coming out of the town. He
had worn no clothing for a long time,
and did not live in a house but in the
28 tombs. When he saw Jesus he cried out
and threw himself down before him,
and said in a loud voice,
"What do you want of me, Jesus,
Son of the Most High God? I beg you
not to torture me!"
29 For he was commanding the foul spirit to get out of the man. For it had often seized him, and though he had been
fastened with chains and fetters, and
was closely watched, he would snap his
bonds and the demon would drive him
30 away to the desert. And Jesus asked
him,
"What is your name?"
He said,
"Legion!" For many demons had
31 gone into him. And they begged him
not to order them off to the bottomless
32 pit. Now there was a large drove of
pigs feeding there on the hillside, and
they begged him to give them leave to
33 go into them. And he did so. Then the
demons came out of the man and went
into the pigs, and the drove rushed over
the steep bank into the lake, and were
34 drowned. When the men who tended
them saw what had happened, they ran
away and spread the news in the town
35 and in the country around. And the
people came out to see what had happened, and they came to Jesus and
found the man out of whom the demons
had gone sitting there, at Jesus' feet,
with his clothes on and in his right
mind, and they were frightened. And 36
those who had seen it told them how the
man who had been possessed was cured.
Then all the people of the neighborhood 37
of Gerasa asked him to go away from
them, for they were terribly frightened.
And he got into a boat and went back.
The man out of whom the demons had 38
gone begged to go with him, but Jesus
sent him away, and said,
"Go back to your home, and tell all 39
that God has done for you."
And he went and told all over the
town what Jesus had done for him.
When Jesus returned, the people 40
welcomed him, for they were all watching for him. And a man named Jairus 41
came up—he was leader of the synagogue—and he fell down at Jesus' feet
and begged him to come to his house,
because he had an only daughter, about 42
twelve years old, and she was dying.
As he was going, the crowds of people
almost crushed him. And a woman who 43
had had a hemorrhage for twelve years,
and whom nobody had been able to
cure, came up behind him and touched 44
the tassel of his cloak, and the hemorrhage stopped at once. Jesus said, 45
"Who was it who touched me?"
And as everyone denied having done
so, Peter said,
"Master, the people are all around
you and they are crowding you."
But Jesus said, 46
"Somebody touched me, for I know
that power passed from me."
When the woman saw that she had 47
not escaped his notice, she came forward trembling, and fell down before
him, and before all the people told why
she had touched him, and how she had
been cured at once. And he said to 48
her,
"My daughter, it is your faith that
has cured you. Go in peace."
Even as he spoke someone came from 49
the house of the leader of the synagogue
and said,
"Your daughter is dead. Do not
trouble the Master any more."
But Jesus heard it and said to him, 50
"Do not be afraid; just have faith,
and she will get well."

51 When he reached the house, he let no
one go in with him but Peter, John, and
James, and the child's father and moth-
52 er. And they were all wailing and beating their breasts for her. But he said,
"Stop wailing! For she is not dead,
she is asleep."
53 And they laughed at him, for they
54 knew that she was dead. But he
grasped her hand and called out,
"Get up, my child!"
55 And her spirit returned and she stood
up immediately, and he directed them
56 to give her something to eat. And her
parents were amazed, but he ordered
them not to tell anyone what had happened.

9 Then he called the Twelve together,
and gave them power and authority
over all the demons, and to cure dis-
2 eases, and he sent them out to proclaim
the Kingdom of God and to cure the
3 sick. He said to them,
"Do not take anything for your journey, no staff nor bag nor bread nor
4 money, nor an extra shirt. Whatever
house you go to stay in, remain there,
5 and start on again from it. And where
they will not welcome you, leave that
town and shake off the very dust from
your feet as a protest against them."
6 And they set forth and went from
village to village, telling the good news
and curing people everywhere.
7 Herod the governor heard of all that
was happening, and he was perplexed
because some people said that John had
8 risen from the dead, and some that Elijah had appeared, and others that one
of the ancient prophets had come back
to life. But Herod said,
"John I have beheaded, but who can
this be about whom I hear such reports?"
And he endeavored to see him.
10 Then the apostles came back and told
Jesus what they had done. And he took
them and quietly retired to a town
11 called Bethsaida. But the crowds
learned of it and followed him, and he
welcomed them and spoke to them
about the Kingdom of God, and he
cured those who needed to be cured.
12 When the day began to decline, the
Twelve came up and said to him,
"Send the crowd away to the villages
and farms around to find food and shelter, for we are in a lonely place here."
13 But he said to them,

"Give them food yourselves!"
And they said,
"We have only five loaves and two
fish, unless we go ourselves and buy
food for all these people." For there 14
were about five thousand men.
But he said to his disciples,
"Have them sit down in groups of
about fifty each."
And they did so, and made them all 15
sit down. Then he took the five loaves 16
and the two fish and looked up to heav-
en and blessed them, and he broke
them in pieces and gave them to the disciples to pass to the people. And they 17
all ate and had enough, and the pieces
left over that were gathered up filled
twelve baskets.
Once when he was praying by him- 18
self, with only the disciples near him,
he asked them,
"Who do the people say that I am?"
They answered, 19
"John the Baptist, though others say
Elijah, and others that one of the old
prophets has come back to life."
And he said to them, 20
"But who do you say that I am?"
Peter answered,
"The Christ of God!"
But he warned them particularly not 21
to tell this to anyone, and said, 22
"The Son of Man must endure great
suffering and be refused by the elders,
the high priests, and the scribes, and be
killed, and be raised to life on the third
day."
And he said to everyone, 23
"If anyone wants to go with me, he
must disregard himself, and take his
cross day after day and follow me. For 24
whoever wants to preserve his life will
lose it, and whoever loses his life for me
will preserve it. What good does it do 25
a man to gain the whole world and lose
or forfeit himself? For if anyone is 26
ashamed of me and my teaching the
Son of Man will be ashamed of him,
when he comes in his glory and the
glory of his Father and of the holy angels. I tell you, some of you who stand 27
here will certainly not taste death until
they see the Kingdom of God!"
It was about eight days after Jesus 28
said this that he took Peter, John, and
James, and went up on the mountain
to pray. And as he was praying, the 29
look of his face changed and his clothes
turned dazzling white. And two men 30

were talking with him. They were
31 Moses and Elijah, and they appeared
in glory and spoke of his departure
which he was to go through with at
32 Jerusalem. Peter and his companions
had been overcome by sleep, but wak-
ing up they saw his glorious appearance
33 and the two men standing by him. Just
as they were parting from him, Peter
said to Jesus,
"Master, how good it is that we are
here! Let us put up three huts, one for
you and one for Moses and one for
Elijah!" For he did not know what
he was saying.
34 But as he said it, a cloud came and
overshadowed them, and they were
frightened as they passed under the
35 cloud. And from the cloud came a
voice that said,
"This is my Son, my Chosen! Listen
to him!"
36 At the sound of the voice, they saw
that Jesus was alone. And they kept
silence, and said nothing about what
they had seen to anyone at that time.
37 The next day, when they had come
down from the mountain, a great crowd
38 met him. And a man in the crowd
shouted,
"Master, I beg you to look at my son,
for he is my only child, and all at once
39 a spirit seizes him, and he suddenly
cries out, and it convulses him until he
foams at the mouth, and it leaves him,
40 after a struggle, badly bruised. And I
begged your disciples to drive it out,
and they could not."
41 Jesus answered,
"O you unbelieving, obstinate people! How long must I be with you and
put up with you? Bring your son here!"
42 Even while the boy was coming, the
demon threw him down and convulsed
him, but Jesus reproved the foul spirit
and cured the boy and gave him back
43 to his father. And they were all amazed
at the power of God.
While everybody was full of wonder
at all that he was doing, he said to his
disciples,
44 "You must store up these teachings
in your minds, for the Son of Man is going to be handed over to men."
45 But they did not understand what he
meant, indeed it was concealed from
them, in order that they might not comprehend it, and they were afraid to ask
him what he meant.

A discussion arose among them as to 46
which of them would be the greatest.
But Jesus knew the question that was 47
in their minds and he took a child and
made him stand by his side, and said 48
to them,
"Whoever welcomes this child on my
account is welcoming me, and whoever
welcomes me, welcomes him who has
sent me. For it is the lowliest among
you all who is really great."
John answered, 49
"Master, we saw a man driving out
demons with your name, and we told
him not to do so, for he does not go
with us."
Jesus said to him, 50
"Do not try to stop him, for the man
who is not against you is for you."
As the time approached when he was 51
to be taken up to heaven, he set his face
toward Jerusalem, and sent messengers 52
before him. They started out and went
into a Samaritan village, to make preparations for him. And the people there 53
would not receive him, because he was
going to Jerusalem. When the disciples, 54
James and John, saw this, they said,
"Master, will you have us order fire
to come down from heaven and consume them?"
But he turned and reproved them. 55
And they went on to another village. 56
As they were going along the road, a 57
man said to him,
"I will follow you wherever you go."
Jesus said to him, 58
"Foxes have holes, and wild birds
have nests, but the Son of Man has no-
where to lay his head!"
He said to another, 59
"Follow me."
But he said,
"Let me first go and bury my fath-
er."
Jesus said to him, 60
"Leave the dead to bury their own
dead; you must go and spread the news
of the Kingdom of God!"
Yet another man said to him, 61
"Lord, I am going to follow you, but
let me first say goodbye to my people
at home."
Jesus said to him, 62
"No one who puts his hand to the
plough, and then looks back, is fitted
for the Kingdom of God."
After this the Lord appointed sev- 10
enty-two others, and sent them on be-

fore him, two by two, to every town or
place to which he intended to come.
2 And he said to them,
"The harvest is abundant enough,
but the reapers are few. So pray to the
owner of the harvest to send reapers to
3 gather it. Now go. Here I send you out
4 like lambs among wolves. Carry no
purse nor wallet nor shoes, and do not
stop to exchange civilities with anyone
5 on the way. Whenever you go to stay
at a house, first say, 'Peace to this
6 household!' If there is anyone there
who loves peace, your blessing will rest
upon him, but if there is not, it will
7 come back to you. Stay at the same
house, eating and drinking what they
offer you, for the workman deserves
his pay. Do not change from one house
8 to another. Whenever you come to a
town and they welcome you, eat what
9 is offered you, and cure the sick there,
and say to them, 'The Kingdom of God
10 is close upon you!' But whenever you
come to a town and they do not welcome
you, go out into the open streets
11 and say, 'The very dust of your town
that sticks to our feet we wipe off in
protest. But understand this: the
12 Kingdom of God is at hand!' I tell you,
on that Day Sodom will fare better
13 than that town! Alas for you, Chorazin!
Alas for you, Bethsaida! For if
the wonders that have been done in you
had been done in Tyre and Sidon, they
would have repented long ago, sitting
14 in sackcloth and ashes! But Tyre and
Sidon will fare better than you at the
15 Judgment! And you, Capernaum! Are
you to be exalted to the skies? You will
16 go down among the dead! Whoever listens
to you listens to me, and whoever
disregards you disregards me, and whoever
disregards me disregards him who
sent me."
17 The seventy-two came back delighted,
and said,
"Lord, when we use your name the
very demons submit to us!"
18 He said to them,
"I saw Satan fall from heaven like a
19 flash of lightning! Here I have given
you the power to tread on snakes and
scorpions, and to trample on all the
power of the enemy. Nothing will hurt
20 you at all. But do not be glad that the
spirits submit to you, but be glad that
your names are enrolled in heaven."

At that moment he was inspired with 21
joy, and said,
"I thank you, Father, Lord of heaven
and earth, for hiding all this from the
learned and intelligent, and revealing
it to children! Yes, I thank you, Father,
for choosing to have it so! Every- 22
thing has been handed over to me by
my Father, and no one knows who the
Son is but the Father, nor who the
Father is but the Son, and anyone to
whom the Son chooses to reveal him."
And he turned to his disciples when 23
they were alone, and said,
"Blessed are the eyes that see what
you see! For I tell you, many prophets 24
and kings have wished to see what you
see, and could not see it, and to hear
what you hear, and could not hear it!"
Then an expert in the Law got up to 25
test him and said,
"Master, what must I do to make
sure of eternal life?"
Jesus said to him, 26
"What does the Law say? How does
it read?"
He answered, 27
"'You must love the Lord your God
with your whole heart, your whole soul,
your whole strength, and your whole
mind,' and 'your neighbor as you do
yourself.'"
Jesus said to him, 28
"You are right. Do that, and you
will live."
But he, wishing to justify his ques- 29
tion, said,
"And who is my neighbor?"
Jesus replied, 30
"A man was on his way down from
Jerusalem to Jericho, when he fell into
the hands of robbers, and they stripped
him and beat him and went off leaving
him half dead. Now a priest happened 31
to be going that way, and when he saw
him, he went by on the other side of the
road. And a Levite also came to the 32
place, and when he saw him, he went
by on the other side. But a Samaritan 33
who was traveling that way came upon
him, and when he saw him he pitied
him, and he went up to him and dressed 34
his wounds with oil and wine and bound
them up. And he put him on his own
mule and brought him to an inn and
took care of him. The next day he took 35
out two dollars and gave it to the innkeeper
and said, 'Take care of him, and
whatever more you spend I will pay

36 you for on my way back.' Which of
these three do you think proved himself a neighbor to the man who fell into
the robbers' hands?"
37 He said,
"The man who took pity on him."
Jesus said to him,
"Go and do so yourself!"
38 As they continued their journey, he
came to a certain village, and a woman
named Martha welcomed him to her
39 house. She had a sister named Mary,
who seated herself at the Master's feet,
and listened to what he was saying.
40 But Martha was worried with all she
had to do for them, and she came up
and said,
"Master, does it make no difference
to you that my sister has left me to do
all the work alone? Tell her to help
me."
41 The Master answered,
"Martha, Martha, you are worried
and anxious about many things, but
42 our wants are few, indeed there is only
one thing we need. For Mary has chos-
en the right thing, and it must not be
taken away from her."
11 Once as he was praying in a certain
place, when he stopped, one of his disciples said to him,
"Lord, teach us to pray, as John
taught his disciples."
2 He said to them,
"When you pray, say, 'Father, your
name be revered! Your kingdom come!
3 Give us each day our bread for the day,
4 and forgive us our sins, for we ourselves
forgive anyone who is our debtor; and
do not subject us to temptation.'"
5 And he said to them,
"Suppose one of you has a friend, and
goes to him in the middle of the night,
and says to him, 'Friend, lend me three
6 loaves, for a friend of mine has just
come to my house after a journey, and
7 I have nothing for him to eat,' and he
answers from inside, 'Do not bother
me; the door is now fastened, and my
children and I have gone to bed; I can-
8 not get up and give you any.' I tell you,
even if he will not get up and give him
some because he is his friend, yet because of his persistence he will rouse
9 himself and give him all he needs. So I
tell you, ask, and what you ask will be
given you. Search, and you will find
what you search for. Knock, and the
10 door will open to you. For it is always
the one who asks who receives, and the
one who searches who finds, and the
one who knocks to whom the door
opens. Which of you fathers, if his son 11
asks him for a fish will give him a snake
instead? Or if he asks for an egg, will 12
give him a scorpion? So if you, bad as 13
you are, know enough to give your children what is good, how much more surely will your Father in heaven give the
holy Spirit to those who ask him for
it!"
Once he was driving out a dumb 14
demon, and when the demon was gone
the dumb man spoke. And the people
were amazed. But some of them said, 15
"It is with the aid of Beelzebub, the
prince of the demons, that he drives the
demons out."
Others to test him asked him for a 16
sign from heaven. But he knew what 17
they were thinking, and he said to
them,
"Any kingdom that is disunited is on
the way to destruction, and one house
falls after another. And if Satan is dis- 18
united, how can his kingdom last? Because you say that I drive out demons
with Beelzebub's aid. But if it is with 19
his aid that I drive out demons, by
whose do your sons drive them out?
Therefore, they shall be your judges.
But if it is with the finger of God that 20
I am driving the demons out, then the
Kingdom of God has overtaken you.
When a strong man fully armed guards 21
his own dwelling, his property is undisturbed. But when somebody stronger 22
than he attacks him and overcomes
him, he strips him of the arms that he
relied on, and divides up the spoils.
Anyone who is not with me is against 23
me, and anyone who does not join me
in gathering, scatters. When a foul 24
spirit goes out of a man, it roams
through deserts in search of rest, and
when it finds none, it says, 'I will go
back to my house that I left.' And it 25
goes and finds it unoccupied, cleaned,
and all in order. Then it goes and gets 26
seven other spirits more wicked than itself, and they go in and live there, and
in the end the man is worse off than he
was before."
As he said this, a woman in the crowd 27
raised her voice and said to him,
"Blessed is the mother who bore you
and nursed you!"
But he said, 28

"You might better say, 'Blessed are
those who hear God's message and observe it!'"
29 As the crowds pressed around him,
he went on to say,
"This is a wicked age! It demands a
sign, and no sign will be given it but
30 the sign of Jonah. For just as Jonah
became a sign to the people of Nineveh,
so the Son of Man will be a sign to this
31 age. The queen of the south will rise
with the men of this generation at the
Judgment and will condemn them, for
she came from the very ends of the
earth to listen to Solomon's wisdom,
and there is more than Solomon here!
32 Men of Nineveh will rise with this generation at the Judgment and will condemn it, for they repented at Jonah's
preaching, and there is more than Jo-
33 nah here! No one lights a lamp and
puts it in the cellar or under a peck
measure; he puts it on its stand, so that
people who come in can see the light.
34 Your eye is the lamp of your body.
When your eye is sound, your whole
body is light, but when it is unsound,
35 your body is dark. So take care! Your
36 very light may be darkness! If, therefore, your whole body is light with no
darkness in it at all, it will all be as light
as a lamp makes things for you by its
light."
37 When he said this, a Pharisee asked
him to lunch with him, and he went to
his house and took his place at table.
38 The Pharisee noticed that he did not
wash before luncheon, and he was sur-
39 prised. But the Lord said to him,
"You Pharisees clean the outside of
cups and dishes, but inside you are full
40 of greed and wickedness. You fools!
Did not the Creator of the outside make
41 the inside too? But give your inmost
life as charity, and you will immediate-
42 ly find everything clean. But alas for
you Pharisees! For you pay tithes on
mint, rue, and every tiny herb, and disregard justice and the love of God. But
you should have observed these, with-
43 out neglecting the others. Alas for you
Pharisees! For you love to have the
front seat in the synagogues and to be
saluted with respect in public places.
44 Alas for you! For you are like un-
marked graves which men tread upon
without knowing it."
45 At this, one of the experts in the Law
said to him,

"Master, when you say that, you affront us too."
But he said, 46
"Yes, alas for you experts in the Law
too! For you load men with burdens
they can hardly carry, and you will not
touch them yourselves with a single
finger. Alas for you! For you build 47
monuments for the prophets, whom
your forefathers killed. So you testify 48
to what your fathers did and approve
it, for they killed them and you build
their monuments. This is why the Wis- 49
dom of God said, 'I will send prophets
and apostles to them, and some of them
they will kill and some they will persecute'—so that this age may be charged 50
with the blood of all the prophets that
has been shed since the creation of the
world, from the blood of Abel to the 51
blood of Zechariah, who perished between the altar and the sanctuary. Yes,
I tell you! This age will be charged
with it all! Alas for you experts in the 52
Law! For you have taken the key to
the door of knowledge, but you have
not entered it yourselves, and you have
kept out those who tried to enter."
After he left the house, the scribes 53
and the Pharisees began to watch him
closely and to try to draw him out on
many subjects, plotting to entrap him 54
in something he might say.
Meanwhile as the people gathered in **12**
thousands, until they actually trod on
one another, he proceeded to say to his
disciples first of all,
"Beware of the yeast of the Pharisees, that is, hypocrisy. There is noth- 2
ing covered up that is not going to be
uncovered, nor secret that is not going
to be known. For what you say in the 3
darkness will be heard in the light, and
what you whisper in someone's ear, behind closed doors, will be proclaimed
from the housetops. I tell you, who are 4
my friends, have no fear of those who
kill the body, and after that can do no
more. I will show you whom to fear: 5
fear him who, after killing you, has
power to hurl you into the pit. Yes,
fear him, I tell you. Do not sparrows 6
sell five for two cents? And yet not one
of them is forgotten in God's sight. But 7
the very hairs on your heads are all
counted! You must not be afraid, you
are worth more than a great many sparrows! I tell you, everyone who will ac- 8
knowledge me before men, the Son of

Man will acknowledge before the an-
9 gels of God, but anyone who disowns
me before men will be disowned before
10 the angels of God. And anyone who
speaks against the Son of Man will be
forgiven for it, but no one who reviles
11 the holy Spirit will be forgiven. When
they bring you before the synagogues
or the magistrates or the authorities,
you must have no anxiety about how to
12 defend yourselves or what to say, for
at the very moment the holy Spirit will
teach you what you ought to say."
13 Someone in the crowd said to him,
"Master, tell my brother to give me
my share of our inheritance."
14 But he said to him,
"Who made me a judge or arbitrator
of your affairs?"
15 And he said to them,
"Take care! You must be on your
guard against every form of greed, for
a man's life does not belong to him, no
matter how rich he is."
16 And he told them this story:
"A certain rich man's lands yielded
17 heavily. And he said to himself, 'What
am I going to do, for I have nowhere to
18 store my crops?' Then he said, 'This is
what I will do; I will tear down my
barns and build larger ones, and in
them I will store all my grain and my
19 goods. And I will say to my soul, "Soul,
you have great wealth stored up for
years to come. Now take your ease;
20 eat, drink, and enjoy yourself." ' But
God said to him, 'You fool! This very
night your soul will be demanded of
you. Then who will have all you have
21 prepared?' That is the way with the
man who lays up money for himself,
and is not rich with God."
22 And he said to his disciples,
"Therefore, I tell you, do not worry
about life, wondering what you will
have to eat, or about your body, won-
23 dering what you will have to wear. Life
is more important than food, and the
24 body than clothes. Think of the crows!
They do not sow or reap, and they have
no storehouses or barns, and God feeds
them. How much more you are worth
25 than the birds! Which of you with all
his worry can add a single hour to his
26 life? So if you cannot do the least good,
why should you worry about the rest?
27 See how the lilies grow. They do not
toil or spin, but, I tell you, even Solomon in all his splendor was never
dressed like one of them. But if God so 28
dresses the wild grass, which is alive today, and is thrown into the furnace tomorrow, how much more surely will he
clothe you, who have so little faith? So 29
you must not ask what you are to have
to eat or drink, and you must not be
anxious about it. For these are all 30
things the nations of the world are in
pursuit of, and your Father knows well
that you need them. But you must 31
strive to find his kingdom, and you will
have these other things besides. Do not 32
be afraid, little flock, for your Father
has chosen to give you the kingdom.
Sell what belongs to you, and give away 33
the money! Get yourselves purses that
will never wear out, inexhaustible riches
in heaven, where thieves cannot get
near nor moths destroy. For wherever 34
your treasure is, your heart will be too.
You must be ready with your lamps 35
burning, like men waiting for their mas- 36
ter to come home from a wedding, so
that when he comes and knocks, they
can open the door for him at once.
Blessed are the slaves whom their mas- 37
ter will find on the watch when he
comes. I tell you, he will gird up his
robe and make them take their places
at table, and go around and wait on
them. Whether he comes late at night 38
or early in the morning and finds them
on the watch, they are blessed. But you 39
may be sure of this, that if the master
of the house had known what time the
thief was coming, he would have been
on the watch, and would not have let
his house be broken into. You must be 40
ready too, for the Son of Man is coming
at a time when you do not expect him."
Peter said to him, 41
"Lord, do you mean this figure for
us, or is it for everybody?"
And the Lord said, 42
"Who then will be the faithful,
thoughtful manager, whom his master
will put in charge of his household, to
give the members of it their supplies at
the proper time? Blessed is that slave 43
if his master when he returns finds him
doing it. I tell you, he will put him in 44
charge of all his property. But if the 45
slave says to himself, 'My master is not
coming back for a long time,' and begins to beat the men and women slaves
and to eat and drink and get drunk,
that slave's master will come back 46
some day when he does not expect him,

and at some time of which he does not
know, and will cut him in two, and put
47 him with the unbelievers. The slave
who knows his master's wishes, but
does not get ready or act upon them,
48 will be severely punished. But one who
does wrong without knowing them will
be lightly punished. From anyone who
has been given much, much will be required, and of the man to whom people
have intrusted much, they will demand
49 even more. I have come to bring fire
down to the earth, and how I wish it
50 were kindled already! I have a baptism to undergo, and how distressed I
51 am till it is over! Do you think I have
come to bring peace to the earth? Not
52 peace, I tell you, but discord! For from
now on if there are five people in a
house they will be divided three against
53 two and two against three. Father will
be against son, and son against father,
mother against daughter and daughter
against mother, mother-in-law against
her daughter-in-law and daughter-in-
law against her mother-in-law."

54 And he said to the crowds,

"When you see a cloud rise in the
west, you say at once, 'It is going to
55 rain,' and it does. And when you see
the south wind blowing, you say, 'It is
56 going to be very hot,' and it is so. You
hypocrites! You know how to interpret
the look of the earth and sky; and why
can you not interpret this present
57 time? Why do you not decide what is
58 right yourselves? For when you are
going before the magistrate with your
opponent, do your best on the way to
get rid of him, or he may hurry you off
to the judge and the judge hand you
over to the constable and the constable
59 throw you into prison. I tell you, you
will never get out again until you have
paid the last cent!"

13 Just then some people came up to
bring him word of the Galileans whose
blood Pilate had mingled with that of
2 their sacrifices. And he answered,

"Do you think, because this happened to them, that these Galileans
were worse sinners than any other Gali-
3 leans? No, I tell you; unless you re-
4 pent, you will all perish as they did! Or
those eighteen people at Siloam who
were killed when the tower fell upon
them—do you think they were worse
offenders than all the other people who
5 live in Jerusalem? No, I tell you; unless you repent, you will all perish as
they did!"

He used this figure: 6

"A man had a fig tree growing in his
garden, and he went to look for fruit
on it, and could not find any. And he 7
said to the gardener, 'Here I have come
three years to look for fruit on this fig
tree, without finding any. Cut it down.
Why should it waste the ground?' He 8
answered, 'Let it stand this one year
more, sir, till I dig around it and manure it; perhaps it will bear fruit next 9
year. But if it does not, you can have
it cut down.'"

One Sabbath he was teaching in one 10
of the synagogues, and there was a 11
woman there who for eighteen years
had had a sickness caused by a spirit.
She was bent double and could not
straighten herself up at all. When Jesus 12
saw her he called to her,

"You are freed from your sickness!"

And he laid his hands on her, and she 13
instantly became erect, and praised
God. But the leader of the synagogue, 14
in his vexation because Jesus had cured
her on the Sabbath, spoke out and said
to the crowd,

"There are six days on which it is
right to work. Come on them and be
cured, but not on the Sabbath day."

But the Lord answered, 15

"You hypocrites! Does not every
one of you untie his ox or his donkey
from the stall on the Sabbath and lead
him away to water? And ought not 16
this woman, who is a descendant of
Abraham, whom Satan has kept bound
for eighteen years, to be released from
those bonds on the Sabbath day?"

When he said this, all his opponents 17
were humiliated, and all the people
were delighted at all the splendid things
that he did.

He said, therefore, 18

"What is the Kingdom of God like,
and to what can I compare it? It is like 19
a mustard seed that a man took and
dropped in his garden, and it grew and
became a tree, and the wild birds roost-
ed on its branches."

And he went on, 20

"To what can I compare the Kingdom of God? It is like yeast that a 21
woman took and hid in a bushel of
flour, till it all rose."

So he went about among the towns 22
and villages, teaching and making his

23 way toward Jerusalem. And someone
said to him,
"Are only a few to be saved, Master?"
He said to them,
24 "You must strain every nerve to get
in through the narrow door, for I tell
you many will try to get in, and will not
25 succeed, when the master of the house
gets up and shuts the door, and you begin to stand outside and to knock on
the door, and say, 'Open it for us, sir!'
Then he will answer you and say, 'I do
26 not know where you come from.' Then
you will go on to say, 'We have been
entertained with you, and you have
27 taught in our streets!' And he will say
to you, 'I do not know where you come
from. Get away from me, all you
28 wrongdoers!' There you will weep and
grind your teeth when you see Abraham and Isaac and Jacob and all the
prophets in the Kingdom of God, while
29 you are put outside. People will come
from the east and west and the north
and south, and take their places in the
30 Kingdom of God. There are those now
last who will then be first, and there are
those now first who will be last."
31 Just then some Pharisees came up
and said to him,
"Go! Get away from here, for Herod
wants to kill you!"
32 He said to them,
"Go and say to that fox, 'Here I am,
driving out demons and performing
cures, today and tomorrow, and on the
33 third day I will be through. But I must
go on today and tomorrow and the next
day, for it is not right for a prophet to
34 die outside Jerusalem.' O Jerusalem!
Jerusalem! murdering the prophets,
and stoning those who are sent to her,
how often I have longed to gather your
children around me, as a hen gathers
her brood under her wings, but you re-
35 fused! Now I leave you to yourselves.
And I tell you, you will never see me
again until you say, 'Blessed be he who
comes in the Lord's name!'"

14 One Sabbath, when he went to take
a meal at the house of a member of the
council who was a Pharisee, they were
2 watching him. There was a man be-
3 fore him who had dropsy. And Jesus
said to the Pharisees and the experts
in the Law,
"Is it right to cure people on the Sabbath or not?"

But they made no answer. And he 4
took hold of the man and cured him and
sent him away. Then he said to them, 5
"Who among you, if his child or his
ox falls into a well, will not pull him out
at once on the Sabbath?" And they 6
could make no reply to this.
He noticed that the guests picked out 7
the best places, and he gave them this
illustration:
"When someone invites you to a 8
wedding supper, do not take the best
place, for someone more distinguished
than you may have been invited, and
his host and yours will come and say to
you 'Make room for this man,' and then 9
you will proceed in confusion to take
the poorest place. But when you are in- 10
vited anywhere, go and take the poorest place, so that when your host comes
in, he will say to you, 'My friend, come
to a better place.' So you will be shown
consideration before all the other
guests. For everyone who exalts him- 11
self will be humbled, but the man who
humbles himself will be exalted."
And he said to the man who had in- 12
vited him,
"When you give a luncheon or a dinner, do not invite your friends or your
brothers or your relatives or your rich
neighbors, for then they will invite you
in return and you will be repaid. But 13
when you give an entertainment, invite
people who are poor, maimed, lame, or
blind. Then you will be blessed, be- 14
cause they cannot repay you; for you
will be repaid at the resurrection of the
upright."
One of the other guests heard this, 15
and said to him,
"Blessed is the man who shall be at
the banquet in the Kingdom of God!"
He said to him, 16
"A man once gave a great dinner, and
invited a large number to it, and when
the dinner hour came, he sent around 17
his slave, to say to those who were invited, 'Come! for it is now ready!' And 18
they all immediately began to excuse
themselves. The first one said to him,
'I have bought a piece of land, and I
must go and look at it. Please have me
excused.' Another said, 'I have bought 19
five yoke of oxen, and I am going to examine them. Please have me excused.'
Another said, 'I have married, and so I 20
cannot come.' So the slave went back, 21
and reported this to his master. Then

the master of the house was angry and
said to his slave, 'Hurry out into the
streets and squares of the city, and
bring the poor, the maimed, the blind,
22 and the lame in here!' And the slave
said, 'What you ordered, sir, has been
23 done, and there is still room.' And the
master said to the slave, 'Go out on the
roads, and among the hedges, and make
them come in, so that my house may be
24 full. For I tell you that none of those
men who were invited shall taste of
my dinner!' "

25 There were great crowds accompanying him, and once he turned and said
to them,
26 "If anyone comes to me without hating his own father and mother and wife
and children and brothers and sisters,
and his very life too, he cannot be a dis-
27 ciple of mine. For no one who does not
take up his own cross and come after
28 me can be a disciple of mine. What man
among you if he wishes to build a tower
does not first sit down and estimate the
cost of it, to see whether he has enough
29 to complete it? Or else when he has laid
his foundation and cannot finish the
building, everyone who sees it will be-
30 gin to ridicule him, and say, 'This man
started to erect a building, and could
31 not finish it!' Or what king, if he is going to meet another king in battle, does
not sit down first and consider whether
he is able with ten thousand men to
meet the other who is coming against
32 him with twenty thousand? And if he
cannot, while the other is still far away,
he sends envoys to him and asks on
33 what terms he will make peace. In just
that way, no one of you who does not
say goodbye to all he has can be a dis-
34 ciple of mine. Salt is good; but if salt
loses its strength, what can it be sea-
35 soned with? It is fit neither for the
ground nor the manure heap; people
throw it away. Let him who has ears
to hear with, listen!"

15 All the tax-collectors and irreligious
people were crowding up to hear him.
2 And the Pharisees and scribes grumbled, and said,
"This man welcomes irreligious people, and even eats with them!"
3 So in speaking to them he used this
figure:
4 "What man among you, if he has a
hundred sheep, and loses one of them,
does not leave the ninety-nine in the
wilderness, and go in search of the one
that is lost, until he finds it? And when 5
he finds it, he puts it on his shoulders
with joy, and when he reaches home, he 6
calls in his friends and neighbors, and
says to them, 'Congratulate me, for I
have found my lost sheep!' I tell you, 7
in just that way there will be more joy
in heaven over one sinful person who repents, than over ninety-nine upright
people who do not need any repentance. Or what woman who has ten sil- 8
ver coins and loses one, does not light
the lamp and sweep the house and look
carefully until she finds it? And when 9
she finds it, she calls in her friends and
neighbors, and says to them, 'Congratulate me, for I have found the coin
that I lost!' In just that way, I tell 10
you, there is joy among the angels of
God over one sinful person who repents!"

And he said, 11
"A man had two sons. The younger 12
of them said to his father, 'Father, give
me my share of the property.' So he
divided his property between them.
Not many days later, the younger son 13
gathered up all he had, and went away
to a distant country, and there he
squandered his property by fast living.
After he had spent it all, a severe fam- 14
ine arose in that country, and he began
to be in want. And he went and hired 15
himself out to a resident of the country,
and he sent him into his fields to tend
pigs. And he was ready to fill himself 16
with the pods the pigs were eating, and
no one would give him anything. When 17
he came to himself he said, 'How many
hired men my father has, who have
more than enough to eat, and here I
am, dying of hunger! I will get up, and 18
go to my father, and say to him, "Father, I have sinned against heaven and in
your eyes; I no longer deserve to be 19
called your son; treat me like one of
your hired men!" ' And he got up and 20
went to his father. But while he was
still a long way off, his father saw him,
and pitied him, and ran and fell on his
neck, and kissed him. His son said to 21
him, 'Father, I have sinned against
heaven, and in your eyes; I no longer
deserve to be called your son; treat me
like one of your hired men!' But his 22
father said to his slaves, 'Make haste
and get out the best robe, and put it on
him, and put a ring on his hand, and

23 shoes on his feet; and get the calf we are
fattening, and kill it, and let us feast
24 and celebrate, for my son here was
dead, and he has come to life; he was
lost, and he is found!' So they began to
25 celebrate. But his elder son was in the
field. When he came in and approached
the house, he heard music and dancing,
26 and he called one of the servants to him
27 and asked him what it meant. He said
to him, 'Your brother has come, and
your father has killed the calf he has
been fattening, because he has gotten
28 him back alive and well.' But he was
angry and would not go into the house.
And his father came out and urged him.
29 And he said to his father, 'Here I have
served you all these years, and have
never disobeyed an order of yours, and
you have never given me a kid, so that
30 I could entertain my friends. But when
your son here came, who has eaten up
your property with women of the
street, for him you killed the calf you
31 have been fattening!' But he said to
him, 'My child, you have been with me
all the time, and everything I have is
32 yours. But we had to celebrate and be
glad, because your brother was dead,
and has come to life, and was lost and
is found!' "

16 And he said to his disciples,
"There was a rich man who had a
manager, and it was reported to him
that this man was squandering his
2 property. So he called him in and said
to him, 'What is this that I hear about
you? Make an accounting for your conduct of my affairs, for you cannot be
3 manager any longer!' Then the manager said to himself, 'What am I going
to do, because my master is going to
take my position away from me? I can-
4 not dig; I am ashamed to beg. I know
what I will do, so that when I am removed from my position people will
5 take me into their homes.' Then he
called in each of his master's debtors,
and he said to the first one, 'How much
6 do you owe my master?' He said,
'Eight hundred gallons of oil.' And he
said to him, 'Here is your agreement;
sit right down and write four hundred!'
7 Then he said to another, 'And how
much do you owe?' He answered, 'Fifteen hundred bushels of wheat.' He
said to him, 'Here is your agreement;
8 write twelve hundred.' And his master
praised the dishonest manager, because
he had acted shrewdly. For the sons of
this age are shrewder in their relation
to their own age than the sons of the
light. So I tell you, make friends for 9
yourselves with your ill-gotten wealth,
so that when it fails, they may take you
into the eternal dwellings. The man 10
who can be trusted in a very small matter can be trusted in a large one, and
the man who cannot be trusted in a
very small matter cannot be trusted in
a large one. So if you have proved un- 11
trustworthy in using your ill-gotten
wealth, who will trust you with true
riches? And if you have been untrust- 12
worthy about what belonged to someone else, who will give you what belongs
to you? No servant can belong to two 13
masters, for he will either hate one and
love the other, or he will stand by one
and make light of the other. You cannot serve God and money!"

The Pharisees, who were avaricious, 14
heard all this, and they ridiculed him.
And he said to them, 15
"You are the men who parade your
uprightness before people, but God
knows your hearts. For what men consider great is detestable in the sight of
God. Until John came, it was the Law 16
and the Prophets. From that time the
Kingdom of God has been proclaimed,
and everyone has been crowding into
it. But it is easier for heaven and earth 17
to pass away than for one dotting of an
i in the Law to go unfulfilled. Anyone 18
who divorces his wife and marries another woman commits adultery, and
whoever marries a woman who has been
divorced from her husband commits
adultery.

"There was once a rich man, who 19
used to dress in purple and fine linen,
and to live in luxury every day. And a 20
beggar named Lazarus was put down at
his gate covered with sores and eager to 21
satisfy his hunger with what was
thrown away from the rich man's table.
Why, the very dogs came and licked his
sores. And it came about that the beg- 22
gar died and was carried away by the
angels to the companionship of Abraham, and the rich man too died and was
buried. And in Hades he looked up, 23
tormented as he was, and saw Abraham
far away, with Lazarus beside him.
And he called to him and said, 'Father 24
Abraham! take pity on me, and send
Lazarus to dip the tip of his finger in

water and cool my tongue, for I am in
25 torment, here in the flames!' And Abraham said, 'My child, remember that
you received your blessings in your lifetime, and Lazarus had his misfortunes
in his; and now he is being comforted
26 here, while you are in anguish. Besides
there is a great chasm set between you
and us, so that those who want to go
over from this side to you cannot, and
they cannot cross from your side to
27 us.' And he said, 'Then I beg you, father, to send him to my father's house,
28 for I have five brothers; let him warn
them so that they will not also come to
29 this place of torture.' Abraham answered, 'They have Moses and the
30 prophets; let them listen to them.' But
he said, 'No! Father Abraham, but if
someone will go to them from the dead,
31 they will repent!' He answered, 'If they
will not listen to Moses and the prophets, they will not be convinced even if
someone rises from the dead!'"

17 And he said to his disciples,
"It is inevitable that hindrances
should arise, but alas for the man who
2 causes them! he might better have a
millstone hung around his neck, and be
thrown into the sea, than be a hindrance to one of these humble people.
3 Be on your guard! If your brother
wrongs you, remonstrate with him, and
4 if he repents, forgive him. And if he
wrongs you seven times a day, and seven times turns to you and says, 'I am
sorry,' you must forgive him."

5 The apostles said to the Lord,
"Give us more faith."

6 And the Lord said,
"If your faith is as big as a mustard
seed, you could have said to this mulberry tree, 'Be pulled up by the roots
and planted in the sea,' and it would
have obeyed you!

7 "What man among you, if he has a
servant ploughing or keeping sheep,
will say to him when he comes in from
the field, 'Come at once and sit down at
8 the table,' instead of saying to him,
'Get my supper ready, and dress yourself, and wait on me while I eat and
drink, and you can eat and drink after-
9 ward'? Is he grateful to the slave for
doing what he has been ordered to do?
10 So you also, when you do all you have
been ordered to do, must say, 'We are
good-for-nothing slaves! We have done
only what we ought to have done!'"

On his way to Jerusalem, he passed 11
through Samaria and Galilee. And as
he was going into one village he met ten 12
lepers, and they stood at a distance,
and raising their voices, said, 13
"Jesus, Master, take pity on us!"

And when he saw them, he said to 14
them,
"Go and show yourselves to the
priests."

And as they went they were cured.
But one of them, when he saw that he 15
was cured, came back, loudly praising
God, and fell on his face at Jesus' feet, 16
and thanked him. He was a Samaritan.
And Jesus said, 17
"Were not all ten cured? Where are
the other nine? Was no one found to 18
return and give thanks to God except
this foreigner?"

And he said to him, 19
"Stand up and go! Your faith has
cured you."

He was once asked by the Pharisees 20
when the Kingdom of God would come,
and he answered,
"The Kingdom of God is not coming
visibly, and people will not say, 'Look! 21
here it is!' or 'There it is!' for the Kingdom of God is within you."

And he said to his disciples, 22
"The time will come when you will
long to see one of the days of the Son
of Man, and you will not be able to do
so. Men will say to you, 'Look! There 23
he is!' or, 'Look! Here he is!' Do not
go off in pursuit of him, for just as when 24
the lightning flashes, it shines from one
end of the sky to the other, that will be
the way with the Son of Man. But first 25
he must go through much suffering,
and be refused by this age. In the time 26
of the Son of Man it will be just as
it was in the time of Noah. People 27
went on eating, drinking, marrying,
and being married up to the very day
that Noah got into the ark and the
flood came and destroyed them all. Or 28
as it was in Lot's time; they went on
eating, drinking, buying, selling, planting, and building, but the day Lot left 29
Sodom, it rained fire and brimstone
from heaven and destroyed them all.
It will be like that on the day when the 30
Son of Man appears. A man who is on 31
the housetop that day, with his goods
in the house, must not go down to get
them, and a man in the field, too,

32 must not turn back. Remember Lot's
33 wife! Whoever tries to preserve his life
will lose it, and whoever loses his life
34 will preserve it. I tell you, there will be
two men in the same bed that night;
one will be taken and the other left.
35 There will be two women grinding together; one will be taken and the other
left!"
37 They said to him,
"Where will this be, Master?"
And he said to them,
"Wherever there is a dead body the
vultures will flock!"
18 He gave them an illustration to show
that they must always pray and not
2 give up, and he said,
"There was once in a city a judge
who had no fear of God and no respect
3 for men. There was a widow in the city
and she came to him and said, 'Protect
4 me from my opponent.' And he would
not for a time, but afterward he said to
himself, 'Though I have no fear of God
5 nor respect for men, yet because this
widow bothers me, I will protect her, or
she will finally wear me out with her
coming.'"
6 And the Master said,
"Listen to what this dishonest judge
7 said! Then will not God provide protection for his chosen people, who cry out to
8 him day and night? Is he slow to help
them? I tell you, he will make haste to
provide it! But when the Son of Man
comes, will he find faith on earth?"
9 To some who were confident of their
own uprightness, and thought nothing
of others, he used this illustration:
10 "Two men went up to the Temple to
pray; one was a Pharisee and the other
11 a tax-collector. The Pharisee stood up
and uttered this prayer to himself:
'O God, I thank you that I am not like
other men, greedy, dishonest, or adul-
12 terous, or like that tax-collector. I fast
two days in the week; I pay tithes on
13 everything I get.' But the tax-collector
stood at a distance and would not even
raise his eyes to heaven, but struck his
breast, and said, 'O God, have mercy
14 on a sinner like me!' I tell you, it was
he who went back to his house with
God's approval, and not the other. For
everyone who exalts himself will be
humbled, but the man who humbles
himself will be exalted."
15 People brought babies to him for
him to touch, but the disciples, when
they saw it, reproved them for it. But 16
Jesus called them up to him and said,
"Let the children come to me and do
not try to stop them, for the Kingdom
of God belongs to such as they. I tell 17
you whoever does not accept the Kingdom of God like a child will not enter it
at all."
A member of the council asked him, 18
"Good master, what must I do to
make sure of eternal life?"
Jesus said to him, 19
"Why do you call me good? No one
is good but God himself. You know the 20
commandments, 'Do not commit adultery, Do not kill, Do not steal, Do not
bear false witness, Honor your father
and mother.'"
And he said, 21
"I have obeyed all these commandments ever since I was a child."
When Jesus heard this, he said to 22
him,
"There is one thing that you still
lack. Sell all that you have, and divide
the money among the poor, and then
you will have riches in heaven; and
come back and be a follower of mine."
But when he heard that, he was 23
much cast down, for he was very rich.
And when Jesus saw it, he said, 24
"How hard it will be for those who
have money to get into the Kingdom of
God! It is easier for a camel to get 25
through the eye of a needle than for a
rich man to get into the Kingdom of
God!"
And those who heard it said, 26
"Then who can be saved?"
And he said, 27
"The things that are impossible for
men are possible for God!"
Peter said, 28
"Here we have left home and fol-
lowed you."
And he said to them, 29
"I tell you, there is no one who has
given up home or wife or brothers or
parents or children for the Kingdom of
God who will not receive many times 30
more in this time, and in the coming age
eternal life."
And he took the Twelve aside and 31
said to them,
"See! we are going up to Jerusalem,
and everything written in the prophets
about the Son of Man will be fulfilled.
For he will be handed over to the hea- 32
then, and ridiculed and insulted and

33 spat upon, and they will flog him and
kill him, and on the third day he will
rise again."
34 And they did not understand any of
this; the words were obscure to them,
and they did not know what he meant.
35 As he approached Jericho, a blind
man happened to be sitting by the
36 roadside begging. And hearing a crowd
37 going by he asked what it meant. They
told him that Jesus of Nazareth was
38 coming by. And he shouted,
"Jesus, you Son of David, take pity
on me!"
39 And those who were in front reproved him and told him to be quiet,
but he cried out all the louder,
"You Son of David, take pity on
me!"
40 And Jesus stopped and ordered the
man to be brought to him. When he
came up, Jesus asked him,
41 "What do you want me to do for
you?"
He answered,
"Master, let me regain my sight!"
42 And Jesus said to him,
"Regain your sight! Your faith has
cured you!"
43 And he regained his sight immediately, and followed Jesus, giving thanks
to God. And all the people saw it and
praised God.

19 And he went into Jericho and was
2 passing through it. Now there was a
man named Zaccheus, the principal
3 tax-collector, a rich man, who wanted
to see who Jesus was, and he could not
because of the crowd, for he was a small
4 man. So he ran on ahead and climbed
up into a sycamore tree, to see him, for
5 Jesus was coming that way. When Jesus reached the place, he looked up and
said to him,
"Zaccheus, come down quickly! for I
must stay at your house today."
6 And he came down quickly and wel-
7 comed him gladly. And when they saw
this, everyone complained, and said,
"He has gone to stay with an irreligious man!"
8 But Zaccheus stopped and said to the
Lord,
"See, Lord! I will give half my
property to the poor, and if I have defrauded anyone of anything, I will pay
him four times as much."
9 Jesus said to him,
"Salvation has come to this house
today, for he too is a descendant of
Abraham. For the Son of Man has 10
come to search for what was lost and to
save it."
As they were listening to this, Jesus 11
went on to give them an illustration,
because he was near Jerusalem and
they supposed that the Kingdom of
God was immediately going to appear.
So he said, 12
"A nobleman once went to a distant
country to secure his appointment to a
kingdom and then return. And he 13
called in ten of his slaves and gave
them each twenty dollars and told them
to trade with it while he was gone. But 14
his countrymen hated him, and they
sent a delegation after him to say, 'We
do not want this man made king over
us.' And when he had secured the ap- 15
pointment and returned, he ordered the
slaves to whom he had given the money
to be called in, so that he could find
out how much they had made. The 16
first one came in and said, 'Your twenty dollars has made two hundred, sir!'
And he said to him, 'Well done, my ex- 17
cellent slave! You have proved trustworthy about a very small amount, you
shall be governor of ten towns.' The 18
second came in and said, 'Your twenty
dollars has made a hundred, sir!' And 19
he said to him, 'And you shall be governor of five towns!' And the other one 20
came in and said, 'Here is your twenty
dollars, sir. I have kept it put away in
a handkerchief, for I was afraid of you, 21
for you are a stern man. You pick up
what you did not lay down, and reap
what you did not sow.' He said to him, 22
'Out of your own mouth I will convict
you, you wretched slave! You knew,
did you, that I was a stern man, and
that I pick up what I did not lay down,
and harvest what I did not sow? Then 23
why did you not put my money in the
bank, so that when I came back I could
have gotten it with interest?' And he 24
said to the bystanders, 'Take the twenty dollars away from him, and give it to
the man who has the two hundred!'
They said to him, 'He has two hundred, 25
sir!'—'I tell you, the man who has will 26
have more given him, and from the man
who has nothing, even what he has will
be taken away! But bring those ene- 27
mies of mine here who did not want me
made king over them, and slaughter
them in my presence!' "

28 With these words he went on ahead
of them, on his way to Jerusalem.
29 When he was near Bethphage and
Bethany by the hill called the Mount
of Olives, he sent two of his disciples
30 and said to them,
"Go to the village that lies in front of
you, and as you enter it you will find
tied there a colt that has never been
31 ridden. Untie it and bring it here. And
if anyone asks you why you are untying
it, you are to say, 'The Master needs
it.'"
32 And the messengers went and found
33 it just as he had told them. And as they
were untying the colt, its owners said to
them,
"Why are you untying the colt?"
34 And they said,
"The Master needs it!"
35 And they brought it to Jesus. And
they threw their coats on the colt and
36 mounted Jesus on it. And as he went
on, people spread their coats in the
37 road. Just as he was coming down the
Mount of Olives and approaching the
city, the whole throng of his disciples
began to praise God loudly and joyfully, for all the wonders they had seen,
38 and to say,
"Blessed is the king who comes in
the Lord's name,
Peace be in heaven and glory on
high!"
39 Some Pharisees in the crowd said to
him,
"Master, reprove your disciples!"
40 And he answered,
"I tell you, if they keep silence, the
stones will cry out!"
41 As he approached the city and saw it,
42 he wept over it, and said,
"If you yourself only knew today the
conditions of peace! But as it is, they
43 are hidden from you. For a time is coming upon you when your enemies will
throw up earthworks about you and
surround you and shut you in on all
44 sides, and they will throw you and your
children within you to the ground, and
they will not leave one stone upon another within you because you did not
know when God visited you!"
45 Then he went into the Temple and
proceeded to drive out those who were
46 selling things there, and he said to
them,
"The Scripture says, 'And my house
shall be a house of prayer,' but you
have made it a robbers' den!"
Every day he taught in the Temple, 47
and the high priests and scribes and the
leading men of the people were trying
to destroy him, but they could not find 48
any way to do it, for all the people hung
upon his words.

One day as he was teaching the peo- 20
ple in the Temple, and preaching the
good news, the high priests and scribes
came up with the elders and said to 2
him,
"Tell us what authority you have for
doing as you do, or who gave you any
such authority?"
He said to them, 3
"I will ask you a question too. Tell 4
me, did John's baptism come from
heaven or from men?"
And they argued with one another, 5
and said,
"If we say 'From heaven,' he will
say, 'Why did you not believe him?'
But if we say, 'From men,' all the peo- 6
ple will stone us to death, for they are
convinced that John was a prophet."
So they answered that they did not 7
know where it came from. And Jesus 8
said to them,
"Nor will I tell you what authority I
have for doing as I do."
Then he went on to give the people 9
this illustration:
"A man once planted a vineyard, and
leased it to tenants, and went away for
a long absence. At the proper time 10
he sent a slave to the tenants to have
them give him a share of the vintage,
but the tenants beat him, and sent him
back empty-handed. And again he sent 11
another slave, and they beat him also
and mistreated him and sent him back
empty-handed. And again he sent a 12
third, but they wounded him too, and
threw him outside. Then the owner of 13
the vineyard said, 'What can I do? I
will send them my dear son; perhaps
they will respect him.' But when the 14
tenants saw him, they argued with one
another, 'This is his heir! Let us kill
him, so that the property will belong to
us!' So they drove him out of the vine- 15
yard and killed him. Now what will the
owner of the vineyard do to them? He 16
will come and put those tenants to
death, and give the vineyard to
others."
When they heard this they said,

"Heaven forbid!"
17 He looked at them and said,
"Then what does this saying of Scripture mean,
" 'That stone which the builders rejected
Has become the cornerstone'?
18 Whoever falls on that stone will be
shattered, but whoever it falls upon
will be scattered like chaff."
19 And the scribes and high priests
wanted to arrest him then and there,
but they were afraid of the people, for
they knew that he had aimed this illus-
20 tration at them. So they kept watch of
him and set some spies who pretended
to be honest men to fasten on something that he said, so that they might
hand him over to the control and au-
21 thority of the governor. And they
asked him,
"Master, we know that you are right
in what you say and teach, and that
you show no favor, but teach the way
22 of God in sincerity. Is it right for us to
pay taxes to the emperor, or not?"
23 But he detected their trickery, and
said to them,
24 "Show me a denarius. Whose head
and title does it bear?"
They said,
"The emperor's."
25 He said to them,
"Then pay the emperor what belongs to the emperor, and pay God
what belongs to God!"
26 So they could not fasten on what he
said before the people, and they were
amazed at his answer, and said nothing
more.
27 Then some of the Sadducees, who say
that there is no resurrection, came up
and asked him,
28 "Master, Moses made us a law that
if a man's brother die leaving a wife but
no children, the man should marry the
widow and raise up a family for his
29 brother. Now there were seven broth-
30 ers. And the eldest married a wife and
31 died childless. And the second married
her, and the third, and all the seven
married her and died without leaving
32 any child. Afterward the woman died
33 too. Now at the resurrection, which
one's wife will the woman be? For all
seven of them married her."
34 Jesus said to them,
"The people of this world marry and
35 are married, but those who are thought
worthy to attain that other world and
the resurrection from the dead, neither
marry nor are married. For they can- 36
not die again; they are like the angels,
and through sharing in the resurrection, they are sons of God. But that the 37
dead are raised to life, even Moses indicated in the passage about the bush,
when he calls the Lord 'the God of
Abraham, the God of Isaac, and the
God of Jacob.' He is not the God of 38
dead men but of living, for all men are
alive to him."
Some of the scribes replied, 39
"Master, that was a fine answer!"
For they did not dare to ask him any 40
more questions.
But he said to them, 41
"How can they say that the Christ
is a son of David? For David himself 42
says in the Book of Psalms,
" 'The Lord has said to my lord,
"Sit at my right hand,
Until I make your enemies a foot- 43
stool for your feet!" '
David then calls him lord. So how can 44
he be his son?"
While all the people were listening, 45
he said to his disciples,
"Beware of the scribes who like to go 46
about in long robes, and love to be saluted with respect in public places, and
to have the front seats in the synagogues and the best places at banquets
—men who eat up widows' houses and 47
to cover it up make long prayers! They
will get all the heavier sentence!"
And looking up, he saw the rich peo- **21**
ple dropping their gifts into the treasury. And he saw a poor widow drop in 2
two coppers. And he said, 3
"I tell you, this poor widow has put
in more than all the rest. For they all 4
gave from what they had to spare, but
she in her want has put in all she had to
live on."
When some spoke about the Temple 5
and its decoration with costly stone and
votive offerings, he said,
"As for all this that you are looking 6
at, the time is coming when not one
stone will be left here upon another
that will not be torn down!"
Then they asked him, 7
"Master, when will this happen, and
what will be the sign that it is going to
take place?"
And he said, 8
"Take care not to be misled. For

many will come under my name, and
say, 'I am he,' and 'The time is at
9 hand.' Do not follow them. But when
you hear of wars and outbreaks, do not
be alarmed. These have to come first,
but the end does not follow immediately."
10 Then he said to them,
"Nation will rise in arms against nation, and kingdom against kingdom.
11 There will be great earthquakes, and
pestilence and famine here and there.
There will be horrors and great signs in
12 the sky. But before all this, men will
arrest you and persecute you, and hand
you over to synagogues and prisons and
have you brought before kings and
13 governors on my account. It will all
14 lead to your testifying. So make up
your minds not to prepare your de-
15 fense, for I will give you such wisdom
of utterance as none of your opponents
16 will be able to resist or dispute. You
will be betrayed even by your parents
and brothers and kinsmen and friends
and they will put some of you to death,
17 and you will be hated by everyone be-
18 cause you bear my name. Yet not a
19 hair of your head will perish! It is by
your endurance that you will win your
20 souls. But when you see Jerusalem being surrounded by armies, then you
must understand that her devastation
21 is at hand. Then those who are in Judea must fly to the hills, those who are
in the city must get out of it, and those
who are in the country must not go into
22 it, for those are the days of vengeance,
when all that is written in the Scrip-
23 tures will be fulfilled. But alas for wom-
en who are with child at that time, or
who have babies, for there will be great
misery in the land and anger at this
24 people. They will fall by the edge of
the sword, and be carried off as prisoners among all nations, and Jerusalem
will be trampled under foot by the
heathen, until the time of the heathen
25 comes. There will be signs too in sun,
moon, and stars, and on earth dismay
among the heathen, bewildered at the
26 roar of the sea and the waves. Men
will swoon with fear and foreboding of
what is to happen to the world, for the
27 forces in the sky will shake. Then they
will see the Son of Man coming in a
28 cloud with great power and glory. But
when this begins to happen, look up
and raise your heads, for your deliverance will be at hand."
And he gave them an illustration: 29
"See the fig tree and all the trees. As 30
soon as they put out their leaves, you
see them and you know without being
told that summer is coming. So when 31
you see these things happen, you must
know that the Kingdom of God is at
hand. I tell you, it will all happen be- 32
fore the present generation passes
away. Earth and sky will pass away, 33
but my words will not. But take care 34
that your hearts are not loaded down
with self-indulgence and drunkenness
and worldly cares, and that day takes
you by surprise, like a trap. For it will 35
come on all who are living anywhere on
the face of the earth. But you must be 36
vigilant and always pray that you may
succeed in escaping all this that is going
to happen, and in standing in the presence of the Son of Man."
He would spend the days teaching in 37
the Temple, but at night he would go
out of the city and stay on the hill
called the Mount of Olives. And in the 38
morning all the people would come to
him in the Temple to listen to him.
Now the festival of Unleavened 22
Bread, which is called the Passover, was
approaching. And the high priests and 2
the scribes were casting about for a
way to put him to death, for they were
afraid of the people.
But Satan entered into Judas, who 3
was called Iscariot, a member of the
Twelve. And he went off and discussed 4
with the high priests and captains of
the Temple how he could betray him to
them. And they were delighted and 5
agreed to pay him for it. And he ac- 6
cepted their offer, and watched for an
opportunity to betray him to them
without a disturbance.
When the day of Unleavened Bread 7
came, on which the Passover lamb had
to be sacrificed, Jesus sent Peter and 8
John, saying to them,
"Go and make preparations for us to
eat the Passover."
They said to him, 9
"Where do you want us to prepare
it?"
He said to them, 10
"Just after you enter the city, you
will meet a man carrying a pitcher of
water. Follow him to the house to
which he goes, and say to the man of 11

the house, 'Our Master says to you,
"Where is the room where I can eat the
Passover supper with my disciples?"'
12 And he will show you a large room upstairs with the necessary furniture.
Make your preparations there."
13 So they went and found everything
just as he had told them, and they prepared the Passover supper.
14 When the time came, he took his
place at the table, with the apostles
15 about him. And he said to them,
"I have greatly desired to eat this
Passover supper with you before I suf-
16 fer. For I tell you, I will never eat one
again until it reaches its fulfilment in
the Kingdom of God."
17 And when he was handed a cup, he
thanked God, and then said,
"Take this and share it among you,
18 for I tell you, I will not drink the product of the vine again until the Kingdom
of God comes."
19 And he took a loaf of bread and
thanked God, and broke it in pieces,
and gave it to them, saying,
21 "This is my body. Yet look! The
hand of the man who is betraying me is
22 beside me on the table! For the Son of
Man is going his way, as it has been decreed, but alas for the man by whom
he is betrayed!"
23 And they began to discuss with one
another which of them it was who was
24 going to do this. A dispute also arose
among them, as to which one of them
ought to be considered the greatest.
25 But he said to them,
"The kings of the heathen lord it
over them, and their authorities are
26 given the title of Benefactor. But you
are not to do so, but whoever is greatest among you must be like the young-
27 est, and the leader like a servant. For
which is greater, the man at the table,
or the servant who waits on him? Is
not the man at the table? Yet I am like
28 a servant among you. But it is you
29 who have stood by me in my trials. So
just as my Father has conferred a king-
30 dom on me I confer on you the right to
eat and drink at my table in my kingdom, and to sit on thrones and judge
31 the twelve tribes of Israel! O Simon,
Simon! Satan has obtained permission
32 to sift all of you like wheat, but I have
prayed that your own faith may not
fail. And afterward you yourself must
turn and strengthen your brothers."

Peter said to him, 33
"Master, I am ready to go to prison
and to death with you!"
But he said, 34
"I tell you, Peter, the cock will not
crow today before you deny three times
that you know me!"
And he said to them, 35
"When I sent you out without any
purse or bag or shoes, was there any-
thing you needed?"
They said,
"No, nothing."
He said to them, 36
"But now, if a man has a purse let
him take it, and a bag too. And a man
who has no sword must sell his coat
and buy one. For I tell you that this 37
saying of Scripture must find its fulfilment in me: 'He was rated an outlaw.'
Yes, that saying about me is to be fulfilled!"
But they said, 38
"See, Master, here are two swords!"
And he said to them,
"Enough of this!"
And he went out of the city and up 39
on the Mount of Olives as he was accustomed to do, with his disciples following him. And when he reached the 40
spot, he said to them,
"Pray that you may not be subjected
to trial."
And he withdrew about a stone's 41
throw from them, and kneeling down he
prayed and said, 42
"Father, if you are willing, take this
cup away from me. But not my will
but yours be done!"
When he got up from his prayer, he 45
went to the disciples and found them
asleep from sorrow. And he said to 46
them,
"Why are you asleep? Get up, and
pray that you may not be subjected to
trial!"
While he was still speaking, a crowd 47
of people came up, with the man called
Judas, one of the Twelve, at their head,
and he stepped up to Jesus to kiss him.
Jesus said to him, 48
"Would you betray the Son of Man
with a kiss?"
Those who were about him saw what 49
was coming and said,
"Master, shall we use our swords?"
And one of them did strike at the 50
high priest's slave and cut his right ear
off. But Jesus answered, 51

"Let me do this much!"
And he touched his ear and healed
52 him. And Jesus said to the high priests,
captains of the Temple, and elders who
had come to take him,
"Have you come out with swords and
53 clubs as though I were a robber? When
I was among you day after day in the
Temple you never laid a hand on me!
But you choose this hour, and the cover
of darkness!"
54 Then they arrested him and led him
away and took him to the house of the
high priest. And Peter followed at a
55 distance. And they kindled a fire in the
middle of the courtyard and sat about
56 it, and Peter sat down among them. A
maid saw him sitting by the fire and
looked at him and said,
"This man was with him too."
57 But he denied it, and said,
"I do not know him."
58 Shortly after, a man saw him and
said,
"You are one of them too!"
But Peter said,
"I am not!"
59 About an hour later, another man insisted,
"This man was certainly with him
too, for he is a Galilean!"
60 But Peter said,
"I do not know what you mean."
And immediately, just as he spoke,
61 a cock crowed. And the Lord turned
and looked at Peter, and Peter remembered the words the Lord had said to
him—"Before the cock crows today,
62 you will disown me three times." And
he went outside and wept bitterly.
63 The men who had Jesus in custody
64 flogged him and made sport of him, and
they blindfolded him, and asked him,
"Show that you are a prophet! Who
65 was it that struck you?" And they said
many other abusive things to him.
66 As soon as it was day, the elders of
the people, the high priests and scribes,
assembled, and brought him before
their council, and said to him,
67 "If you are the Christ, tell us so."
But he said to them,
"If I tell you, you will not believe me,
68 and if I ask you a question, you will not
69 answer me. But from this time on, the
Son of Man will be seated at the right
hand of God Almighty!"
70 And they all said,
"Are you the Son of God then?"

And he said to them,
"I am, as you say!"
Then they said, 71
"What do we want of testimony
now? We have heard it ourselves from
his own mouth!"
Then they arose in a body and took 23
him to Pilate, and they made this 2
charge against him:
"Here is a man whom we have found
misleading our nation, and forbidding
the payment of taxes to the emperor,
and claiming to be an anointed king
himself."
And Pilate asked him, 3
"Are you the king of the Jews?"
He answered,
"Yes."
And Pilate said to the high priests 4
and the crowd,
"I cannot find anything criminal
about this man."
But they persisted and said, 5
"He is stirring up the people all over
Judea by his teaching. He began in
Galilee and he has come here."
When Pilate heard this, he asked if 6
the man were a Galilean and learning 7
that he belonged to Herod's jurisdiction
he turned him over to Herod, for Herod
was in Jerusalem at that time. When 8
Herod saw Jesus he was delighted, for
he had wanted for a long time to see
him, because he had heard about him
and he hoped to see some wonder done
by him. And he questioned him at some 9
length, but he made him no answer.
Meanwhile the high priests and the 10
scribes stood by and vehemently accused him. And Herod and his guards 11
made light of him and ridiculed him,
and they put a gorgeous robe on him
and sent him back to Pilate. And Her- 12
od and Pilate became friends that day,
for they had been at enmity before.
Pilate summoned the high priests 13
and the members of the council and the
people, and said to them, 14
"You brought this man before me
charged with misleading the people,
and here I have examined him before
you and not found him guilty of any of
the things that you accuse him of. Nei- 15
ther has Herod, for he has sent him
back to us. You see he has done nothing to call for his death. So I will teach 16
him a lesson and let him go."
But they all shouted out, 18

"Kill him, and release Barabbas for
us!"
19 (He was a man who had been put in
prison for a riot that had taken place in
20 the city and for murder.) But Pilate
wanted to let Jesus go, and he called
21 out to them again. But they kept on
shouting,
"Crucify him! Crucify him!"
22 And he said to them a third time,
"Why, what has he done that is
wrong? I have found nothing about
him to call for his death. So I will teach
him a lesson and let him go."
23 But they persisted with loud outcries
in demanding that he be crucified, and
24 their shouting won. And Pilate pronounced sentence that what they asked
25 for should be done. He released the
man they asked for, who had been put
in prison for riot and murder, and handed Jesus over to their will.
26 As they led him away, they seized a
man named Simon, from Cyrene, who
was coming in from the country, and
put the cross on his back, for him to
27 carry behind Jesus. He was followed by
a great crowd of people and of women
who were beating their breasts and la-
28 menting him. But Jesus turned to them
and said,
"Women of Jerusalem, do not weep
for me but weep for yourselves and for
29 your children, for a time is coming
when they will say, 'Happy are the
childless women, and those who have
30 never borne or nursed children!' Then
people will begin to say to the mountains, 'Fall on us!' and to the hills,
31 'Cover us up!' For if this is what they
do when the wood is green, what will
happen when it is dry?"
32 Two criminals were also led out to
execution with him.
33 When they reached the place called
the Skull, they crucified him there, with
the criminals one at his right and one at
34 his left. But Jesus said,
"Father, forgive them, for they do
not know what they are doing!"
And they divided up his clothes
among them by drawing lots for them,
35 while the people stood looking on. Even
the councilors jeered at him, and said,
"He has saved others, let him save
himself, if he is really God's Christ, his
Chosen One!"
36 The soldiers also made sport of him,
coming up and offering him sour wine,
saying, 37
"If you are the king of the Jews, save
yourself!" For there was a notice above 38
his head, "This is the king of the Jews!"
One of the criminals who were hang- 39
ing there, abused him, saying,
"Are you not the Christ? Save yourself and us too!"
But the other reproved him and said, 40
"Have you no fear even of God when
you are suffering the same penalty?
And we are suffering it justly, for we 41
are only getting our deserts, but this
man has done nothing wrong."
And he said, 42
"Jesus, remember me when you come
into your kingdom!"
And he said to him, 43
"I tell you, you will be in Paradise
with me today!"
It was now about noon, and darkness 44
came over the whole country, and lasted until three in the afternoon, as the 45
sun was in eclipse. And the curtain before the sanctuary was torn in two.
Then Jesus gave a loud cry, and said, 46
"Father, I intrust my spirit to your
hands!"
With these words he expired.
When the captain saw what had hap- 47
pened he praised God, and said,
"This man must really have been
innocent!"
And all the crowds that had collected 48
for the sight, when they saw what happened, returned to the city beating
their breasts. And all his acquaintances 49
and the women who had come with
him from Galilee, stood at a distance
looking on.
Now there was a man named Joseph, 50
a member of the council, a good and upright man, who had not voted for the 51
plan or action of the council. He came
from the Jewish town of Arimathea and
lived in expectation of the Kingdom of
God. He went to Pilate and asked for 52
Jesus' body. Then he took it down 53
from the cross and wrapped it in linen
and laid it in a tomb hewn in the rock,
where no one had yet been laid. It was 54
the Preparation Day, and the Sabbath
was just beginning. The women who 55
had come with Jesus from Galilee followed and saw the tomb and how his
body was put there. Then they went 56
home, and prepared spices and perfumes.

24 On the Sabbath they rested in obedience to the commandment, but on the
first day of the week, at early dawn,
they went to the tomb, taking spices
2 they had prepared. But they found the
3 stone rolled back from the tomb, and
when they went inside they could not
4 find the body. They were in great perplexity over this, when suddenly two
men in dazzling clothing stood bes de
5 them. The women were frightened and
bowed their faces to the ground, but the
men said to them,
"Why do you look among the dead
6 for him who is alive? Remember what
he told you while he was still in Galilee,
7 when he said that the Son of Man must
be handed over to wicked men and be
crucified and rise again on the third
day."
8 Then they remembered his words,
9 and they went back from the tomb and
told all this to the eleven and all the
10 rest. They were Mary of Magdala and
Joanna and Mary, the mother of James;
the other women with them also told
11 this to the apostles. But the story
seemed to them to be idle talk and they
would not believe them.
13 That same day two of them were going to a village called Emmaus, about
14 seven miles from Jerusalem, and they
were talking together about all these
15 things that had happened. And as they
were talking and discussing them, Jesus
himself came up and went with them,
16 but they were prevented from recogniz-
17 ing him. And he said to them,
"What is all this that you are discussing with each other on your way?"
18 They stopped sadly, and one of them
named Cleopas said to him,
"Are you the only visitor to Jerusalem who does not know what has happened there lately?"
19 And he said,
"What is it?"
They said to him,
"About Jesus of Nazareth, who in
the eyes of God and of all the people
was a prophet mighty in deed and
20 word, and how the high priests and the
members of our council gave him up to
be sentenced to death, and had him
21 crucified. But we were hoping that he
was to be the deliverer of Israel. Why,
besides all this, it is three days since it
22 happened. But some women of our
number have astounded us. They went
to the tomb early this morning and 23
could not find his body, but came back
and said that they had actually seen a
vision of angels who said that he was
alive. Then some of our party went to 24
the tomb and found things just as the
women had said, but they did not see
him."
Then he said to them, 25
"How foolish you are and how slow
to believe, after all that the prophets
have said! Did not the Christ have to 26
suffer thus before entering upon his
glory?"
And he began with Moses and all the 27
prophets and explained to them the
passages all through the Scriptures that
referred to himself. When they reached 28
the village to which they were going, he
acted as though he were going on, but 29
they urged him not to, and said,
"Stay with us, for it is getting toward
evening, and the day is nearly over."
So he went in to stay with them. And 30
when he took his place with them at table, he took the bread and blessed it
and broke it in pieces and handed it to
them. Then their eyes were opened and 31
they knew him, and he vanished from
them. And they said to each other, 32
"Did not our hearts glow when he
was talking to us on the road, and was
explaining the Scriptures to us?"
And they got up immediately and 33
went back to Jerusalem, and found the
eleven and their party all together, say- 34
ing that the Master had really risen and
had been seen by Simon. And they told 35
what had happened on the road, and
how they had known him when he
broke the bread in pieces.
While they were still talking of these 36
things, he himself stood among them.
They were startled and panic-stricken, 37
and thought they saw a ghost. But he 38
said to them,
"Why are you so disturbed, and why
do doubts arise in your minds? Look at 39
my hands and feet, for it is I myself!
Feel of me and see, for a ghost has not
flesh and bones, as you see I have."
But they could not yet believe it for 41
sheer joy and they were amazed. And
he said to them,
"Have you anything here to eat?"
And they gave him a piece of broiled 42
fish, and he took it and ate it before 43
their eyes.
Then he said to them, 44

"This is what I told you when I was
still with you—that everything that is
written about me in the Law of Moses
and the Prophets and the Psalms must
come true."
45 Then he opened their minds to the
46 understanding of the Scriptures, and
said to them,

"The Scriptures said that Christ
should suffer as he has done, and rise
47 from the dead on the third day, and
that repentance leading to the forgiveness
of sins should be preached to all
the heathen in his name. You are to be 48
witnesses to all this, beginning at Jerusalem.
And I will send down upon you 49
what my Father has promised. Wait
here in the city until you are clothed
with power from on high."

And he led them out as far as Beth- 50
any. Then he lifted up his hands and
blessed them. And as he was blessing 51
them, he parted from them. And they 52
went back with great joy to Jerusalem,
and were constantly in the Temple, 53
blessing God.

THE GOSPEL ACCORDING TO JOHN

1 IN THE beginning the Word existed. The Word was with God, and
the Word was divine.
2 It was he that was with God in
3 the beginning. Everything came into existence through him, and apart from him
4 nothing came to be. It was by him that
life came into existence, and that life
5 was the light of mankind. The light is
still shining in the darkness, for the
darkness has never put it out.
6 There appeared a man by the name
7 of John, with a message from God. He
came to give testimony, to testify to the
light, so that everyone might come to
8 believe in it through him. He was not
the light; he came to testify to the light.
9 The real light, which sheds light upon
everyone, was just coming into the
10 world. He came into the world, and
though the world came into existence
through him, the world did not recog-
11 nize him. He came to his home, and his
12 own family did not welcome him. But
to all who did receive him and believe
in him he gave the right to become chil-
13 dren of God, owing their birth not to
nature nor to any human or physical
impulse, but to God.
14 So the Word became flesh and blood
and lived for a while among us, abounding in blessing and truth, and we saw
the honor God had given him, such
honor as an only son receives from his
15 father. (John testified to him and cried
out—for it was he who said it—"He
who was to come after me is now ahead
of me, for he existed before me!")
16 For from his abundance we have all
had a share, and received blessing after
17 blessing. For while the Law was given
through Moses, blessing and truth
18 came to us through Jesus Christ. No
one has ever seen God; it is the divine
Only Son, who leans upon his Father's
breast, that has made him known.
19 Now this is the testimony that John
gave when the Jews sent priests and
Levites to him from Jerusalem to ask
20 him who he was. He admitted—he
made no attempt to deny it—he ad-
mitted that he was not the Christ.
Then they asked him, 21
"What are you then? Are you Eli-
jah?"
He said,
"No, I am not."
"Are you the Prophet?"
He answered,
"No."
Then they said to him, 22
"Who are you? We must have some
answer to give those who sent us here.
What have you to say for yourself?"
He said, 23
"I am a voice of one shouting in the
desert, 'Straighten the Lord's way!' as
the prophet Isaiah said."
Now the messengers were Pharisees. 24
And they asked him, 25
"Then why are you baptizing people,
if you are not the Christ, nor Elijah,
nor the Prophet?"
"I am only baptizing in water," John 26
answered, "but someone is standing
among you of whom you do not know.
He is to come after me, and I am not 27
worthy to undo his shoe!"
This took place at Bethany, on the 28
farther side of the Jordan, where John
was baptizing.
The next day he saw Jesus coming 29
toward him, and he said,
"There is God's lamb, who is to remove the world's sin! This is the man 30
of whom I spoke when I said, 'After me
there is coming a man who is even now
ahead of me, for he existed before me.'
I did not know him, but it is in order 31
that he may be made known to Israel
that I have come and baptized people
in water."
And John gave this testimony: 32
"I saw the Spirit come down from
heaven like a dove, and it remained
upon him. I did not know him, but he 33
who sent me to baptize in water said to
me, 'The one on whom you see the Spirit come down and remain, is the one
who is to baptize in the holy Spirit.'
And I did see it, and I testify that he is 34
the Son of God."
Again the next day John was stand- 35

36 ing with two of his disciples, and looking at Jesus as he passed, he said,
"There is God's lamb!"
37 The two disciples heard him say this,
38 and they followed Jesus. But Jesus turned, and seeing them following him he said,
"What do you want?"
They said to him,
"Rabbi"—that is to say, Master—"Where are you staying?"
39 He said to them,
"Come and you will see."
So they went and saw where he was staying, and they spent the rest of the day with him. It was about four in the afternoon.
40 Andrew, Simon Peter's brother, was one of the two who heard what John
41 said and followed Jesus. Andrew immediately sought out his own brother Simon and said to him,
"We have found the Messiah!"—that is to say, the Christ.
42 He took him to Jesus. Jesus looked at him and said,
"You are Simon, son of John. You shall be called Cephas"—that is, Peter, which means rock.
43 The next day Jesus decided to leave for Galilee. And he sought out Philip and said to him,
"Come with me."
44 Now Philip came from Bethsaida,
45 the town of Andrew and Peter. Philip sought out Nathanael, and said to him,
"We have found the one about whom Moses wrote in the Law and about whom the prophets wrote; it is Jesus, the son of Joseph, who comes from Nazareth!"
46 Nathanael said to him,
"Can anything good come from Nazareth?"
Philip said to him,
"Come and see!"
47 Jesus saw Nathanael coming toward him, and he said of him,
"Here is really an Israelite without any deceit in him!"
48 Nathanael said to him,
"How do you know me?"
Jesus answered,
"Before Philip called you, while you were still under that fig tree, I saw you."
49 Nathanael answered,
"Master, you are the Son of God! You are king of Israel!"
Jesus answered, 50
"Do you believe in me because I told you that I had seen you under that fig tree? You will see greater things than
that!" And he said to him, "I tell you 51
all, you will see heaven opened and God's angels going up and coming down upon the Son of Man!"
Two days later there was a wedding 2
at Cana in Galilee, and Jesus' mother
was present. Jesus and his disciples 2
were also invited to the wedding. The 3
wine gave out, and Jesus' mother said to him,
"They have no more wine!"
Jesus said to her, 4
"Do not try to direct me. It is not yet time for me to act."
His mother said to the servants, 5
"Do whatever he tells you."
Now there were six stone water jars 6
there, for the ceremonial purification practiced by the Jews, each large enough to hold twenty or thirty gal-
lons. Jesus said to them, 7
"Fill these jars with water."
So they filled them full. And he said 8
to them,
"Now draw some out and take it to the master of the feast."
And they did so. When the master of 9
the feast tasted the water which had now turned into wine, without knowing where it had come from—though the servants who had drawn the water
knew—he called the bridegroom and 10
said to him,
"Everyone else serves his good wine first, and his poorer wine after people have drunk deeply, but you have kept back your good wine till now!"
This, the first of the signs of his mis- 11
sion, Jesus showed at Cana in Galilee. By it he showed his greatness, and his disciples believed in him.
After this Jesus went down to Caper- 12
naum with his mother, his brothers, and his disciples, and they stayed there for a few days.
Now the Jewish Passover was ap- 13
proaching, and Jesus went up to Jerusalem. In the Temple he found the 14
dealers in cattle, sheep, and pigeons, and the money-changers sitting at their tables. And he made a lash out of rope, 15
and drove them all, sheep and cattle, out of the Temple, and scattered the money-changers' coins on the ground,

16 and overturned their tables. And he
said to the pigeon-dealers,
"Take these things away! Do not
turn my Father's house into a market!"
17 His disciples remembered that the
Scriptures said, "My zeal for your
house will consume me!"
18 Then the Jews addressed him and said,
"What sign have you to show us, for
acting in this way?"
19 Jesus answered,
"Destroy this sanctuary, and I will
raise it in three days!"
20 The Jews said,
"It has taken forty-six years to build
this sanctuary, and are you going to
raise it in three days?"
21 But he was speaking of his body as
22 the sanctuary. So afterward when he
had risen from the dead, his disciples
remembered that he had said this, and
they believed the passage of Scripture
and what Jesus had said.
23 Now while he was in Jerusalem, at
the Passover Festival, many, when
they saw the signs that he showed,
24 came to believe in him. But Jesus on
his part would not trust himself to
25 them, for he knew them all, and had no
need of anybody's evidence about men,
for he knew well what was in their
hearts.

3 Among the Pharisees there was a
man named Nicodemus, a member of
2 the Jewish Council. This man went to
Jesus one night, and said to him,
"Master, we know that you are a
teacher who has come from God, for no
one can show the signs that you do, unless God is with him."
3 Jesus answered him,
"I tell you, unless a man is born
over again from above, he can never
see the Kingdom of God!"
4 Nicodemus said to him,
"How can a man be born when he is
old? Can he enter his mother's womb
over again and be born?"
5 Jesus answered,
"I tell you, if a man does not owe his
birth to water and spirit, he cannot get
6 into the Kingdom of God. Whatever
owes its birth to the physical is physical, and whatever owes its birth to the
7 Spirit is spiritual. Do not wonder at my
telling you that you must be born over
8 again from above. The wind blows
wherever it pleases, and you hear the
sound of it, but you do not know where
it comes from or where it goes. That is
the way with everyone who owes his
birth to the Spirit."
Nicodemus said to him, 9
"How can that be?"
Jesus answered, 10
"Are you the teacher of Israel and
yet ignorant of this? I tell you, we 11
know what we are talking about and
we have seen the things we testify to,
yet you all reject our testimony. If you 12
will not believe the earthly things that
I have told you, how can you believe
the heavenly things I have to tell? Yet 13
no one has gone up into heaven except
the Son of Man who came down from
heaven. And just as Moses in the des- 14
ert lifted the serpent up in the air, the
Son of Man must be lifted up, so that 15
everyone who believes in him may have
eternal life."

For God loved the world so much 16
that he gave his only Son, so that no
one who believes in him should be lost,
but that they should all have eternal
life. For God did not send his Son into 17
the world to pass judgment upon the
world, but that through him the world
might be saved. No one who believes in 18
him has to come up for judgment. Anyone who does not believe stands condemned already, for not believing in
God's only Son. And the basis of the 19
judgment is this, that the light has
come into the world, and yet, because
their actions were wicked, men have
loved the darkness more than the light.
For everyone who does wrong hates 20
the light and will not come to it, for fear
his actions will be exposed. But every- 21
one who is living the truth will come to
the light, to show that his actions have
been performed in dependence upon
God.

After this Jesus went into the coun- 22
try of Judea with his disciples, and
stayed there with them and baptized.
John too was baptizing at Aenon, near 23
Salim, for there was plenty of water
there, and people came there and were
baptized. For John had not yet been 24
put in prison. So a discussion arose be- 25
tween John's disciples and a Jew, about
purification. And they went to John 26
and said to him,
"Master, the man who was with you
across the Jordan, and to whom you
yourself gave testimony, is baptizing,
and everybody is going to him."

27 John answered,
"A man cannot get anything unless
28 it is given to him from heaven. You
will bear me witness that I said, 'I am
not the Christ; I have been sent in ad-
29 vance of him.' It is the bridegroom
who has the bride; but the bridegroom's
friend who stands outside and listens
for his voice is very glad when he hears
the bridegroom speak. So this happi-
30 ness of mine is now complete. He must
grow greater and greater, but I less and
less."
31 He who comes from above is above
all others. A son of earth belongs to
earth and speaks of earth. He who
comes from heaven is above all others.
32 It is to what he has seen and heard that
he gives testimony, and yet no one ac-
33 cepts his testimony. Whoever does accept it has thereby acknowledged that
34 God is true. For he whom God has sent
speaks God's words, for God gives him
35 his Spirit without measure. The Father loves his Son, and has put every-
36 thing in his hands. Whoever believes
in the Son possesses eternal life, but
whoever disobeys the Son will not experience life, but will remain under the
anger of God.
4 So when the Lord learned that the
Pharisees had been told that he was
gaining and baptizing more disciples
2 than John—though it was not Jesus
himself who baptized them, but his dis-
3 ciples—he left Judea and went back
4 again to Galilee. Now he had to pass
5 through Samaria. So he came to a town
in Samaria called Sychar, near the field
6 that Jacob gave to his son Joseph, and
Jacob's spring was there. So Jesus,
tired with his journey, sat down just as
he was by the spring. It was about
7 noon. A Samaritan woman came to
draw water. Jesus said to her,
"Give me a drink."
8 For his disciples had gone into the
9 town to buy some food. So the Samaritan woman said to him,
"How is it that a Jew like you asks a
Samaritan woman like me for a drink?"
For Jews have nothing to do with Sam-
10 aritans. Jesus answered,
"If you knew what God has to give,
and who it is that said to you, 'Give me
a drink,' you would have asked him,
and he would have given you living
water."
11 She said to him,

"You have nothing to draw water
with, sir, and the well is deep. Where
can you get your living water? Are you 12
a greater man than our forefather Jacob, who gave us this well, and drank
from it himself, with his sons and his
flocks?"
Jesus answered, 13
"Anyone who drinks this water will 14
be thirsty again, but anyone who drinks
the water that I will give him will never
be thirsty, but the water that I will give
him will become a spring of water within him, bubbling up for eternal life."
The woman said to him, 15
"Give me this water, sir, so that I
may never be thirsty, nor have to come
all this way to draw water."
He said to her, 16
"Go and call your husband and come
back here."
The woman answered, 17
"I have no husband."
Jesus said to her,
"You are right when you say you 18
have no husband, for you have had five
husbands and the man you are now living with is not your husband. What
you say is true."
The woman said to him, 19
"I see that you are a prophet, sir.
Our forefathers worshiped God on this 20
mountain, and yet you Jews say that
the place where people must worship
God is in Jerusalem."
Jesus said to her, 21
"Believe me, the time is coming when
you will worship the Father neither on
this mountain nor at Jerusalem. You 22
worship something you know nothing
about; we know what we worship, for
salvation comes from the Jews. But a 23
time is coming—it is already here!—
when the true worshipers will worship
the Father in spirit and sincerity, for
the Father wants such worshipers. God 24
is spirit, and his worshipers must worship him in spirit and in sincerity."
The woman said to him, 25
"I know that the Messiah is coming
—he who is called the Christ. When he
comes, he will tell us everything!"
Jesus said to her, 26
"I who am talking to you am he!"
Just then his disciples came back, 27
and they were surprised to find him
talking with a woman, yet no one of
them asked him what he wanted or
why he was talking with her. So the 28

woman left her pitcher and went back
to the town, and said to the people,
29 "Come, here is a man who has told
me everything I ever did! Do you suppose he is the Christ?"
30 The people left the town and went to
him.
31 Meanwhile the disciples urged him,
saying,
"Master, eat something."
32 But he said to them,
"I have food to eat of which you do
not know."
33 So the disciples said to one another,
"Do you suppose that someone has
brought him something to eat?"
34 Jesus said to them,
"My food is doing the will of him
who has sent me, and finishing his work.
35 Are you not saying, 'Four months more
and the harvest will come'? Look, I
tell you! Raise your eyes and see the
fields, for they are white for harvest-
36 ing. The reaper is already being paid
and gathering the harvest for eternal
life, so that the sower may be glad with
37 the reaper. For here the saying holds
38 good, 'One sows, another reaps.' I have
sent you to reap a harvest on which you
have not worked. Other men have
worked and you have profited by their
work."
39 Many of the Samaritans in that town
came to believe in him because of the
testimony the woman gave when she
said, "He has told me everything I ever
40 did!" So when the Samaritans came to
Jesus, they asked him to stay with
them, and he did stay there two days.
41 And a great many more believed be-
42 cause of what he said, and they said to
the woman,
"It is no longer because of your statement that we believe, for we have heard
him ourselves, and we know that he is
really the Savior of the world."
43 When the two days were over, Jesus
44 went on to Galilee, for he himself declared that a prophet is not honored in
45 his own country. So when he reached
Galilee, the Galileans welcomed him,
for they had seen everything he had
done in Jerusalem, at the festival, for
they too had gone to the festival.
46 So he came again to Cana in Galilee,
where he had made the water into
wine. There was at Capernaum one of
the king's officials whose son was sick.
47 When he heard that Jesus had come
back from Judea to Galilee, he went to
him and begged him to come down and
cure his son, for he was at the point of
death. Jesus said to him, 48
"Unless you see signs and marvels
you will never believe!"
The official said to him, 49
"Come down, sir, before my child is
dead!"
Jesus said to him, 50
"You can go home. Your son is going
to live."
The man believed what Jesus said to
him and went home. While he was on 51
the way, his slaves met him and told
him that his boy was going to live. So 52
he asked them at what time he had begun to get better, and they said to him,
"Yesterday at one o'clock the fever
left him."
So the father knew that it was the 53
very time when Jesus had said to him
"Your son is going to live." And he
and his whole household believed in
Jesus. This second sign Jesus showed 54
after coming back from Judea to Galilee.

After this there was a Jewish festival 5
and Jesus went up to Jerusalem. Now 2
there is in Jerusalem near the Sheep-
gate a pool called in Hebrew Bethzatha,
which has five colonnades. In these 3
there used to lie a great number of people who were sick, blind, lame, or paralyzed. There was one man there who 5
had been sick for thirty-eight years.
Jesus saw him lying there, and finding 6
that he had been in this condition for a
long time, he said to him,
"Do you want to get well?"
The sick man answered, 7
"I have nobody, sir, to put me into
the pool when the water stirs, but while
I am getting down someone else steps in
ahead of me."
Jesus said to him, 8
"Get up, pick up your mat, and
walk!"
And the man was immediately cured, 9
and he picked up his mat and walked.
Now it was the Sabbath. So the Jews 10
said to the man who had been cured,
"It is the Sabbath, and it is against
the Law for you to carry your mat."
But he answered, 11
"The man who cured me said to me,
'Pick up your mat and walk.'"
They asked him, 12

"Who was it that said to you, 'Pick
it up and walk'?"
13 But the man who had been cured did
not know who it was, for as there was a
crowd there, Jesus had left the place.
14 Afterward Jesus found him in the Temple, and said to him,
"See! You are well again. Give up
sin, or something worse may happen to
you."
15 The man went and told the Jews that
16 it was Jesus who had cured him. This
was why the Jews used to persecute
Jesus, because he did things like this
17 on the Sabbath. But he answered
them,
"My Father is still at work, and I
work too."
18 On account of this the Jews were all
the more eager to kill him, because he
not only broke the Sabbath but actually called God his Father, thus putting himself on an equality with God.
19 So Jesus answered them,
"I tell you, the Son cannot do anything of his own accord, but only what
he sees the Father doing. For whatever
20 the Father does, the Son also does. For
the Father loves the Son and lets him
see everything that he himself is doing,
and he will let him see greater deeds
21 than these, to make you wonder. For
just as the Father awakens the dead
and brings them to life, the Son brings
22 anyone he chooses to life. For the
Father passes judgment on no one, but
he has committed the judgment entire-
23 ly to the Son, so that all men may
honor the Son just as they honor the
Father. Whoever refuses to honor the
Son refuses to honor the Father who
24 sent him. I tell you, whoever listens
to my message and believes him who
has sent me, possesses eternal life, and
will not come to judgment, but has al-
25 ready passed out of death into life. I
tell you, the time is coming—it is
here already!—when those who are
dead will listen to the voice of the Son
of God, and those who listen to it will
26 live. For just as the Father is self-
existent, he has given self-existence to
27 the Son, and he has given him the authority to act as judge, because he is a
28 son of man. Do not be surprised at
this, for the time is coming when all
who are in their graves will listen to his
29 voice, and those who have done right
will come out to resurrection and life,
and those who have done wrong, to
resurrection and judgment. I cannot do 30
anything of my own accord. I pass judgment just as I am told to do, and my
judgment is just, for I am not seeking
to do what I please, but what pleases
him who has sent me.
"If I testify to myself, my testimony 31
is not true. It is someone else who testi- 32
fies to me, and I know that the testimony that he gives about me is true.
You yourselves sent to John, and he 33
testified to the truth. But the testi- 34
mony that I accept is not from any
man; I only speak of this that you
may be saved. He was the lamp that 35
burned and shone, and you were ready
to be gladdened for a while by his light.
But I have higher testimony than 36
John's, for the things that my Father
has intrusted to me to accomplish, the
very things that I am doing, are proof
that my Father has sent me, and my 37
Father who has sent me has thus borne
witness to me. You have never heard
his voice or seen his form, and you do 38
not keep his message in your hearts, for
you do not believe the messenger whom
he has sent. You pore over the Scrip- 39
tures, for you think that you will find
eternal life in them, and these very
Scriptures testify to me, yet you refuse 40
to come to me for life. I do not accept 41
any honor from men, but I know well 42
that you have not the love of God in
your hearts. I have come in my Fa- 43
ther's name, and you refuse to accept
me. If someone else comes in his own
name you will accept him. Yet how can 44
you believe in me, when you accept
honor from one another, instead of seeking the honor that comes from the one
God? Do not suppose that I will accuse 45
you to the Father. It is Moses that
accuses you—Moses, on whom you
have fixed your hopes! For if you really 46
believed Moses, you would believe me,
for it was about me that he wrote. But
if you refuse to believe what he wrote, 47
how are you ever to believe what I say?"
After this Jesus went to the other side 6
of the Sea of Galilee, or Tiberias, and
a great crowd followed him, because 2
they could see the signs he showed
in what he did for the sick. But Jesus 3
went up on the hill, and sat down there
with his disciples. Now the Jewish 4
festival of the Passover was at hand. So 5
Jesus, raising his eyes and seeing that

a great crowd was coming up to him,
said to Philip,
"Where can we buy food for these
people to eat?"
6 Now he said this to test him, for he
7 knew what he meant to do. Philip answered,
"Two hundred dollars' worth of
bread would not be enough for each of
them to have even a little."
8 Andrew, Simon Peter's brother, another of his disciples, said to him,
9 "There is a boy here who has five
barley loaves and a couple of fish, but
what is that among so many people?"
10 Jesus said,
"Make the people sit down."
There was plenty of grass there, so
the men threw themselves down, about
11 five thousand of them. Then Jesus took
the loaves, and gave thanks, and distributed them among the people who
were resting on the ground, and in the
same way as much of the fish as they
12 wanted. When they were satisfied, he
said to his disciples,
"Pick up the pieces that are left, so
that nothing may be wasted."
13 So they picked them up, and they
filled twelve baskets with pieces of the
five barley loaves that were left after
the people had eaten.
14 When the people saw the signs that
he showed, they said,
"This is really the Prophet who was
to come into the world!"
15 So Jesus, seeing that they meant to
come and carry him off to make him
king, retired again to the hill by himself.
16 But in the evening his disciples went
17 down to the sea and got into a boat and
started across the sea for Capernaum.
By this time it was dark, and Jesus had
18 not yet joined them; a strong wind was
blowing and the sea was growing rough.
19 When they had rowed three or four
miles, they saw Jesus walking on the
sea and approaching the boat, and they
20 were terrified. But he said to them,
"It is I; do not be afraid!"
21 Then as soon as they consented to
take him into the boat, the boat was at
the shore they had been trying to
reach.
22 Next day the people who had stayed
on the other side of the sea saw that
there had been only one boat there, and
that Jesus had not embarked in it with
his disciples, but that the disciples had
gone away by themselves. But some 23
boats from Tiberias landed near the
place where they had eaten the bread
after the Lord had given thanks for it.
So when the people saw that neither 24
Jesus nor his disciples were any longer
there, they got into the boats and went
to Capernaum in search of him. And 25
when they had crossed the sea and
found him, they said to him,
"When did you get here, Master?"
Jesus answered, 26
"I tell you, it is not because of the
signs you have seen that you have come
in search of me, but because you ate
that bread and had all you wanted of it.
You must not work for the food that 27
perishes, but for that which lasts for
eternal life, which the Son of Man will
give you, for God the Father has authorized him to do so."
Then they said to him, 28
"What must we do to carry out God's
work?"
Jesus answered them, 29
"The work God has for you is to believe in the messenger that he has sent
to you."
Then they said to him, 30
"Then what sign do you show for us
to see and so come to believe you?
What work are you doing? Our fore- 31
fathers in the desert had manna to eat;
as the Scripture says, 'He gave them
bread out of heaven to eat!' "
Jesus said to them, 32
"I tell you, Moses did not give you
the bread out of heaven, but my Father
gives you the true bread out of heaven, 33
for it is God's bread that comes down
out of heaven and gives life to the
world."
Then they said to him, 34
"Give us that bread always, sir!"
Jesus said to them, 35
"I am the bread that gives life. No
one who comes to me will ever be hungry, and no one who believes in me will
ever be thirsty. But as I have told you, 36
although you have seen me, you will
not believe. All that my Father gives 37
to me will come to me, and I will never
refuse anyone who comes to me, for I 38
have come down from heaven not to do
what I please but what pleases him who
has sent me. And the purpose of him 39
who has sent me is this, that I should
lose nothing of all that he has given

me, but should raise them to life on the
40 Last Day. For it is the purpose of my
Father that everyone who sees the Son
and believes in him shall have eternal
life, and that I shall raise him to life on
the Last Day."
41 The Jews complained of him for saying, "I am the bread that has come out
42 of heaven," and they said,
"Is he not Joseph's son, Jesus, whose
father and mother we know? How can
he now say, 'I have come down out of
heaven'?"
43 Jesus answered,
"Do not complain to one another.
44 No one can come to me unless the Father who sent me draws him to me; then
I myself will raise him to life on the
45 Last Day. In the prophets it is written,
'And all men will be taught by God!'
Everyone who listens to the Father and
46 learns from him will come to me. Not
that anyone has ever seen the Father,
except him who is from God; he has
47 seen the Father. I tell you, whoever
believes already possesses eternal life.
48 I am the bread that gives life. Your
49 forefathers in the desert ate the manna
50 and yet they died. But this bread that
comes down out of heaven is such that
51 no one who eats it will ever die. I am
this living bread that has come down
out of heaven. Whoever eats this bread
will live forever, and the bread that I will
give for the world's life is my own flesh!"
52 This led the Jews to dispute with one
another. They said,
"How can he give us his flesh to eat?"
53 Then Jesus said to them,
"I tell you, unless you eat the flesh
of the Son of Man and drink his blood,
54 you have no self-existent life. Whoever
lives on my flesh and drinks my blood
possesses eternal life, and I will raise
55 him to life on the Last Day. For my
flesh is real food and my blood is real
56 drink. Whoever lives on my flesh and
drinks my blood remains united to me
57 and I remain united to him. Just as the
living Father has sent me, and I live
because of the Father, so he who lives
58 on me will live because of me. This is
the bread that has come down out of
heaven—not like that which your forefathers ate and yet died. Whoever lives
on this bread will live forever."
59 Jesus said all this while he was teaching in the synagogue at Capernaum.

Many of his disciples on hearing it said, "This is a harsh teaching! Who can listen to it?"

But Jesus, knowing that his disciples were complaining about this, said to them,

"Does this stagger you? Then what if you see the Son of Man go up where he was before? The Spirit is what gives life; flesh is of no use at all. The things that I have said to you are spirit and they are life. Yet there are some of you who will not believe." For Jesus knew from the first who would not believe, and who was going to betray him. And he added,

"This is why I said to you, 'No one can come to me unless he is enabled to do so by the Father.'"

In consequence of this many of his disciples drew back and would not go about with him any longer. So Jesus said to the Twelve,

"Do you mean to go away too?"

Simon Peter answered,

"To whom can we go, Lord? You have a message of eternal life, and we believe and are satisfied that you are the Holy One of God."

Jesus answered them,

"Did I not myself select all twelve of you? And even of you, one is an informer." He meant Judas the son of Simon Iscariot, for he, though he was one of the Twelve, was going to betray him.

After this Jesus went from place to place in Galilee, for he would not do so in Judea, because the Jews were making efforts to kill him. But the Jewish camping festival was coming. So his brothers said to him,

"You ought to leave here and go to Judea, to let your disciples also see the things you are doing. For no one acts in secret when he desires to be publicly known. If you are going to do these things, let the world see you." For even his brothers did not believe in him. Then Jesus said to them,

"It is not yet time for me to act, but any time is suitable for you. It is impossible for the world to hate you, but it does hate me for testifying that its ways are wrong. As for you, go up to the festival; I am not going up to this festival as yet, for it is not quite time for me to go."

9 That was what he told them, and he
stayed on in Galilee.
10 But after his brothers had gone up
to the festival, then Jesus went up also,
not publicly, but as though he did not
11 wish to be observed. Now the Jews
were looking for him at the festival and
12 asking where he was, and there was a
great deal of muttering about him
among the crowds, some saying that he
was a good man, and others that he was
not, but was imposing on the people.
13 But no one spoke of him in public, for
fear of the Jews.
14 But when the festival was half over,
Jesus went up to the Temple and be-
15 gan to teach. This astonished the
Jews.
"How is it that this man knows his
letters?" they said, "when he has never
gone to school?"
16 So Jesus answered,
"My teaching is not my own; it
comes from him who has sent me. Any-
17 one who resolves to do his will will
know whether my teaching comes from
18 God, or originates with me. Whoever
speaks simply for himself is looking for
honor for himself, but whoever looks
for honor for the person who has sent
him shows his sincerity; there is no dis-
19 honesty about him. Was it not Moses
who gave you the Law? Yet not one of
you obeys the Law. Why are you trying to kill me?"
20 The crowd answered,
"You must be possessed! Who is
trying to kill you?"
21 Jesus answered,
"I have done just one deed, and you
22 are all astonished at it. Yet Moses gave
you the rite of circumcision—not that
it began with Moses but with your forefathers—and you practice it even on the
23 Sabbath. But if a person undergoes
circumcision on a Sabbath, to avoid
breaking the Law of Moses, are you
angry at me for making a man perfectly
24 well on a Sabbath? You must not judge
so externally; you must judge justly!"
25 Some of the people of Jerusalem said,
"Is not this the man they want to
26 kill? And here he is speaking publicly,
and they say nothing to him! Can the
authorities really have found that he
27 is the Christ? But then, we know where
this man comes from, but when the
Christ comes, no one will know where
he is from."

So Jesus, as he was teaching in the 28
Temple, cried out,
"You do know me and you do know
where I come from, and I have not
come of my own accord but someone
who is very real, whom you do not
know, has sent me. I do know him, be- 29
cause I come from him, and he has sent
me here."
Then they tried to arrest him, and 30
yet no one laid hands on him, because
he was not yet ready. But many of the 31
people believed in him, and said,
"Will the Christ show more signs
when he comes than this man has
shown?"
The Pharisees heard the people say- 32
ing these things about him in whispers,
and the high priests and the Pharisees
sent attendants to arrest him. Jesus 33
said,
"I am to be with you a little while
longer, and then I am going to him who
has sent me. You will look for me and 34
you will not find me, and you will not
be able to go where I shall be."
Then the Jews said to one another, 35
"Where is he going, that we shall not
find him? Is he going to our people
scattered among the Greeks, and will he
teach the Greeks? What does he mean 36
by saying 'You will look for me and you
will not find me, and you will not be
able to go where I shall be'?"
Now on the last day, the great day of 37
the festival, Jesus stood up and cried
out,
"If anyone is thirsty, let him come to
me and drink. If anyone believes in 38
me, streams of living water, as the
Scripture says, shall flow forth from his
heart."
He meant by this the Spirit which 39
those who believed in him were to receive—for the Spirit had not yet come,
because Jesus had not yet been glorified. So some of the people, when they 40
heard these words, said,
"This is certainly the Prophet!"
Others said, 41
"This is the Christ!"
But they rejoined,
"What! Is the Christ to come from
Galilee? Do not the Scriptures say 42
that the Christ is to spring from the
descendants of David and to come from
the village of Bethlehem where David
lived?"
So the people were divided about 43

44 him, and some of them wanted to arrest him, yet no one laid hands on him.
45 The attendants went back to the high priests and Pharisees, and they said to the attendants,
"Why have you not brought him?"
46 The attendants answered,
"No man ever talked as he does!"
47 The Pharisees answered,
"Have you been imposed upon too?
48 Have any of the councilors or of the
49 Pharisees believed in him? But these common people who do not know the Law are doomed!"
50 One of them, Nicodemus, who had previously gone to Jesus, said to them,
51 "Does our Law condemn the accused without first hearing what he has to say, and finding out what he has done?"
52 They answered,
"Are you from Galilee too? Study and you will find that no prophet is to appear from Galilee."
8 12 Then Jesus spoke to them again and said,
"I am the light of the world. Whoever follows me will not have to walk in darkness but will have the light of life."
13 The Pharisees said to him,
"You are testifying to yourself. Your testimony is not true."
14 Jesus answered,
"Even if I am testifying to myself, my testimony is true, for I know where I have come from and where I am going; but you do not know where I come from
15 or where I am going. You judge by material standards, but I am judging no-
16 body. But even if I do judge, my decision is just, because I am not by myself, but the Father who sent me is with me.
17 Why, in your own Law it is stated that the testimony of two persons is valid.
18 Here I am testifying to myself, and the Father who has sent me testifies to me."
19 Then they said to him,
"Where is your Father?"
Jesus answered,
"You do not know either me or my Father. If you knew me, you would know my Father too."
20 He said these things in the treasury, as he was teaching in the Temple, and no one arrested him, because he was not yet ready.
21 Then he said to them again,
"I am going away, and you will look for me, but you will die in the midst of your sin. You cannot come where I am going."
So the Jews said, 22
"Is he going to kill himself, and is that why he says, 'You cannot come where I am going'?"
He said to them, 23
"You are from below; I am from above. You belong to this world; I do
not belong to this world. That is why 24
I said to you that you would die in the midst of your sins, for unless you believe that I am what I say, you will die in the midst of your sins."
They said to him, 25
"Who are you?"
Jesus said to them,
"Why do I even talk to you at all? I 26
have a great deal to say about you and to condemn in you, yet he who sent me is truthful, and the things that I say to the world are things that I have learned from him."
They did not understand that he was 27
speaking to them of the Father. So 28
Jesus said,
"When you lift the Son of Man up in the air, then you will know that I am what I say, and that I do nothing of my own accord, but speak as the Father
has instructed me. And he who has sent 29
me is with me; he has not left me alone, for I always do what pleases him."
As he said this, many believed in him. 30
So Jesus said to the Jews who had 31
believed in him,
"If you abide by what I teach, you
are really disciples of mine, and you 32
will know the truth and the truth will set you free."
They answered, 33
"We are descended from Abraham, and have never been anyone's slaves. How can you say to us, 'You will be set free'?"
Jesus answered, 34
"I tell you, everyone who commits
sin is a slave to sin. Now a slave does 35
not belong to a household permanently; but a son does. So if the Son sets 36
you free you will be really free. I know 37
that you are descended from Abraham, yet you want to kill me, because there is no room in your hearts for my teaching. It is what I have seen in the pres- 38
ence of my Father that I tell, and it is what you have heard from your father that you do."

39 They answered,
"Our father is Abraham."
Jesus said to them,
"If you are Abraham's children, then
40 do what Abraham did. But instead you
are trying to kill me, a man who has
told you the truth he has heard from
God. Abraham would not have done
41 that. You are doing as your father
does."
They said to him,
"We are not illegitimate children.
We have one father, God himself."
42 Jesus said to them,
"If God were your father, you would
love me, for I have come from God. I
have not come of my own accord, but
43 he has sent me. Why is it that you do
not understand what I say? It is because you cannot bear to listen to my
44 message. The devil is the father you
are sprung from, and you want to carry
out your father's wishes. He was a
murderer from the first, and he has
nothing to do with the truth, for there
is no truth in him. When he tells a lie,
he speaks in his true character, for he is
45 a liar and the father of them. But because I tell the truth you will not be-
46 lieve me. Who among you can prove
me guilty of sin? But if I tell you the
truth, why do you refuse to believe me?
47 Whoever is sprung from God listens to
God's words. The reason you refuse to
listen is that you are not sprung from
God."
48 The Jews answered,
"Are we not right in saying that you
are a Samaritan and are possessed?"
49 Jesus answered,
"I am not possessed, but I have respect for my Father, and you have no
50 respect for me. But I do not seek hon-
or for myself; there is someone who
seeks it for me, and is the judge of it.
51 I tell you, if anyone observes my
teaching, he will never experience
death."
52 The Jews said to him,
"Now we are sure that you are possessed! Abraham is dead and so are
the prophets, and yet you say, 'If anyone observes my teaching, he will never
53 know what death is!' Are you a greater
man than our forefather Abraham?
Yet he is dead and the prophets are
dead. What do you claim to be?"
54 Jesus answered,
"If I show special honor to myself,
such honor counts for nothing. It is
my Father who shows me honor. You
say he is your God, yet you have never 55
come to know him. But I know him. If
I say I do not know him, I will be a liar
like yourselves. No! I do know him,
and I am faithful to his message. Your 56
forefather Abraham exulted at the
thought of seeing my coming. He has
seen it, and it has made him glad."
The Jews said to him, 57
"You are not fifty years old, and
have you seen Abraham?"
Jesus said to them, 58
"I tell you, I existed before Abraham
was born!"
At that, they picked up stones to 59
throw at him, but Jesus disappeared
and made his way out of the Temple.
As he passed along, he saw a man 9
who had been blind from his birth. His 2
disciples asked him,
"Master, for whose sin was this man
born blind? For his own, or for that of
his parents?"
Jesus answered, 3
"It was neither for his own sin nor
for that of his parents, but to let what
God can do be illustrated in his case.
We must carry on the work of him who 4
has sent me while the daylight lasts.
Night is coming, when no one can do
any work. As long as I am in the world, 5
I am a light for the world."
As he said this he spat on the ground 6
and made clay with the saliva, and he
put the clay on the man's eyes, and 7
said to him,
"Go and wash them in the Pool of
Siloam"—a name which means One
who has been sent. So he went and
washed them, and went home able to
see.
Then his neighbors and people who 8
had formerly seen him begging, said,
"Is not this the man who used to sit
and beg?"
Some said, 9
"Yes! It is he!"
Others said,
"No! but he looks like him."
He himself said,
"I am the man."
So they said to him, 10
"Then how does it happen that you
can see?"
He answered, 11
"The man they call Jesus made some
clay and smeared it on my eyes, and said

to me, 'Go to Siloam and wash them.'
So I went and when I had washed them
I could see."
12 They said to him,
"Where is he?"
He answered,
"I do not know."
13 They took the man who had been
14 blind to the Pharisees. Now it was on
the Sabbath that Jesus had made the
15 clay and made him able to see. So once
more the Pharisees asked him how he
had become able to see, and he said to
them,
"He put some clay on my eyes, and I
washed them, and I can see."
16 Then some of the Pharisees said,
"This man does not come from God,
for he does not keep the Sabbath."
But others said,
"How can a sinful man show such
signs as this?"
And there was a division of opinion
17 among them. So they asked the blind
man again,
"What have you to say about him,
because he has made you able to see?"
He said,
"He is a prophet!"
18 But the Jews would not believe that
he had been blind and had become able
to see until they summoned the parents
of the man who had been given his
19 sight, and asked them,
"Is this your son, who you say was
born blind? How is it that he can see
now?"
20 His parents answered,
"We know that this is our son, and
21 that he was born blind. But we do not
know how it is that he can see now, or
who has made him able to see. You
must ask him. He is grown up. Let him
tell you about himself."
22 His parents said this because they
were afraid of the Jews, for the Jews
had already made an agreement that if
anyone acknowledged Jesus as the
Christ, he should be excluded from the
23 synagogues. That was why his parents
said, "He is grown up; you must ask
24 him." So they again summoned the
man who had been blind, and they said
to him,
"Give God the praise. This man we
know is a sinful man."
25 He answered,
"I do not know about his being a sinful man. All I know is that I was blind
before and now I can see."
They said to him, 26
"What did he do to you? How did
he make you able to see?"
He answered, 27
"I have already told you and you
would not listen. Why do you want to
hear it again? Do you want to become
disciples of his too?"
Then they sneered at him, and said, 28
"You are a disciple of his yourself,
but we are disciples of Moses. We know 29
that God spoke to Moses, but we do
not know where this man came from."
The man answered, 30
"There is something very strange
about this! You do not know where he
came from, and yet he has made me
able to see! We know that God does 31
not listen to sinful people, but if a man
is devout and obeys God, God will listen to him. It was never heard of in 32
this world that anyone made a man
born blind able to see. If this man were 33
not from God, he could not do anything."
They answered, 34
"You were born in utter sin, and are
you trying to teach us?"
So they excluded him from the synagogue.
Jesus learned that they had excluded 35
him, and he found the man and said to
him,
"Do you believe in the Son of Man?"
The man answered, 36
"Who is he, sir? Tell me, so that I
may believe in him."
Jesus said to him, 37
"You have seen him already, and it
is he who is now talking to you."
He said, 38
"I believe, sir!" and he fell on his
knees before him.
And Jesus said, 39
"I have come into this world to judge
men, that those who cannot see may
see, and that those who can see may become blind."
Some Pharisees who were present 40
heard this, and they said to him,
"Then are we blind too?"
Jesus said to them, 41
"If you were blind, you would be
guilty of no sin, but as it is, you say
'We can see'; so your sin continues.
"I tell you, any man who does not 10
enter the sheepfold by the door, but

climbs over at some other place, is a
2 thief and robber. But the man who
enters by the door is the shepherd of
3 the flock. The watchman opens the
door to him, and the sheep obey his
voice, and he calls to his own sheep and
4 leads them out. When he gets his own
flock all out, he goes in front of them,
and the sheep follow him, because they
5 know his voice. But they will never
follow a stranger but will run away
from him, because they do not know the
voices of strangers."
6 This was the figure Jesus used in
speaking to them, but they did not understand what he meant by it.
7 So Jesus said again,
8 "I tell you, I am the door of the
sheep. All who have come before me
are thieves and robbers, but the sheep
9 would not obey them. I am the door.
Whoever enters through me will be
saved, and will pass in and out and
10 find pasture. A thief comes only to,
steal and kill and destroy; I have come
to let them have life, and to let them
11 have it in abundance. I am the good
shepherd. A good shepherd will give his
12 life for his sheep. A hired man who is
not a shepherd and does not own the
sheep, when he sees a wolf coming, will
leave the sheep and run away, and the
wolf will carry them off and scatter the
13 flock. For he is only a hired man, and
14 does not care about the sheep. I am the
good shepherd. I know my sheep and
15 my sheep know me, just as the Father
knows me and I know the Father, and
16 I am giving my life for my sheep. I
have other sheep too that do not belong
to this fold. I must lead them too, and
they will obey my voice, and they will
all become one flock, with one shep-
17 herd. This is why the Father loves me,
because I am giving my life, but giving
18 it to take it back again. No one has
taken it from me, but I am giving it of
my own accord. I have power to give
it, and I have power to take it back
again. These are the orders I have received from my Father."
19 These words caused a fresh division
20 of opinion among the Jews. Many of
them said,
"He is possessed and mad! Why do
you listen to him?"
21 Others said,
"These are not the words of a man
who is possessed. Can a madman make
blind men see?"
That was the time of the Rededica- 22
tion Festival at Jerusalem. It was winter time and Jesus was walking up and 23
down inside the Temple, in Solomon's
Colonnade. So the Jews gathered 24
around him and said to him,
"How much longer are you going to
keep us in suspense? If you are really
the Christ, tell us so frankly!"
Jesus answered, 25
"I have told you so, and you will not
believe it. The things I have been doing by my Father's authority are my
credentials, but you do not believe it 26
because you do not belong to my sheep.
My sheep listen to my voice, and I 27
know them and they follow me, and I 28
give them eternal life, and they shall
never be lost, and no one shall tear
them out of my hands. What my Fa- 29
ther has intrusted to me is of more importance than everything else, and no
one can tear anything out of the Father's hands. The Father and I are 30
one."
The Jews again picked up stones to 31
stone him with. Jesus answered, 32
"I have let you see many good things
from the Father; which of them do you
mean to stone me for?"
The Jews answered, 33
"We are not stoning you for doing
anything good, but for your impious
talk, and because you, a mere man,
make yourself out to be God."
Jesus answered, 34
"Is it not declared in your Law, 'I
said, "You are gods" '? If those to 35
whom God's message was addressed
were called gods—and the Scripture
cannot be set aside—do you mean to 36
say to me whom the Father has consecrated and made his messenger to the
world, 'You are blasphemous,' because
I said, 'I am God's Son'? If I am not 37
doing the things my Father does, do not
believe me. But if I am doing them, 38
then even if you will not believe me, believe the things I do, in order that you
may realize and learn that the Father is
in union with me, and I am in union
with the Father."
In consequence of this they again 39
tried to arrest him, and he withdrew
out of their reach.
He went across the Jordan again to 40
the place where John used to baptize at

41 first, and there he stayed. And people
came to him in great numbers, and they
said of him,
"John did not show any sign in proof
of his mission, but all that he said about
this man was true."
42 And many became believers in him
in that place.
11 Now a man named Lazarus was sick;
he lived in Bethany, the village of Mary
2 and her sister Martha. It was the Mary
who poured perfume upon the Lord
and wiped his feet with her hair, whose
3 brother Lazarus was sick. So the sisters
sent word to Jesus: "Master, he whom
4 you love is sick." When Jesus received
it he said,
"This sickness is not to end in death,
but is for the honor of God, that
through it the Son of God may be honored."
5 Jesus loved Martha and her sister
6 and Lazarus. So when he heard that
Lazarus was sick, he stayed on for two
7 days in the place where he was, and
then afterward said to his disciples,
"Let us go back to Judea."
8 The disciples said to him,
"Master, the Jews have just been trying to stone you, and are you going back
there again?"
9 Jesus answered,
"Is not the day twelve hours long?
If a man travels by day he will not
stumble, for he can see the light of this
10 world; but if he travels at night he will
stumble because he has no light."
11 He told them this, and then he added,
"Our friend Lazarus has fallen asleep,
but I am going there to wake him."
12 The disciples said to him,
"Master, if he has fallen asleep he
will recover."
13 Now Jesus had referred to his death.
But they supposed that he meant a
14 natural falling asleep. So Jesus then
told them plainly,
15 "Lazarus is dead, and for your sake
I am glad that I was not there, so that
you may learn to believe in me. But let
us go to him."
16 So Thomas the Twin said to his fel-
low-disciples,
"Let us go also, and die with him."
17 When Jesus arrived he found that
Lazarus had been buried for four days.
18 Now Bethany is only about two miles
19 from Jerusalem, and a number of Jews

had come out to see Mary and Martha,
to condole with them about their brother. When Martha heard that Jesus was 2
coming she went out to meet him, but
Mary remained at home. Martha said 2
to Jesus,
"Master, if you had been here, my
brother would not have died! Even 2
now I know that anything you ask God
for, he will give you." 2
Jesus said to her,
"Your brother will rise."
Martha said to him, 2
"I know that he will rise at the resurrection, on the Last Day."
Jesus said to her, 2
"I myself am Resurrection and Life.
He who believes in me will live on, even
if he dies, and no one who is alive and 2
believes in me will ever die. Do you believe that?"
She said to him, 2
"Yes, Master, I do indeed believe
that you are the Christ, the Son of God,
who was to come into the world."
With these words she went and called 2
her sister Mary, whispering to her,
"Here is the Master, asking for
you."
When she heard it she sprang up and 2
went to him, for Jesus had not yet come 3
into the village, but was still at the
place where Martha had met him. The 3
Jews who were sitting with her in the
house, condoling with her, when they
saw Mary spring up and go out, supposed that she was going to weep at the
tomb, and followed her. When Mary 3
came where Jesus was and saw him, she
fell at his feet, and said,
"Master, if you had been here, my
brother would not have died!"
When Jesus saw her weep and the 3
Jews who had come with her weeping
too, repressing a groan, and yet showing
great agitation, he said, 3
"Where have you laid him?"
They answered,
"Come and see, Master."
Jesus shed tears. So the Jews said, 3
"See how much he loved him!" 3
But some of them said, 37
"Could not this man, who opened the
eyes of that blind man, have kept Laz-
arus from dying?"
Again repressing a groan, Jesus went 3
to the tomb. It was a cave with a stone
laid against the mouth of it. Jesus 39
said,

"Move the stone away."
The dead man's sister, Martha, said
to him,
"Master, by this time he is decaying,
for he has been dead four days."
40 Jesus said to her,
"Have I not promised you that if
you will believe in me you will see the
glory of God?"
41 So they moved the stone away. And
Jesus looked upward and said,
"Father, I thank you for listening to
42 me, though I knew that you always listen to me. But I have said this for the
sake of the people that are standing
around me that they may believe that
you have made me your messenger."
43 After saying this he called out in a
loud voice,
"Lazarus, come out!"
44 The dead man came out, bound hand
and foot with wrappings, and with his
face muffled with a handkerchief. Jesus
said to them,
"Unbind him and let him go."
45 So it came about that many of the
Jews who had come to visit Mary and
saw what Jesus did, came to believe in
46 him, but some of them went back to
the Pharisees and told them what he
had done.
47 Then the high priests and the Pharisees called a meeting of the council, and
they said,
"What are we to do about the fact
that this man is showing so many
48 signs? If we let him go on, everybody
will believe in him, and then the Romans will come and put an end to our
holy place and our people."
49 But one of them, Caiaphas, who was
high priest that year, said to them,
50 "You know nothing about it. You do
not realize that it is to your interest
that one man should die for the people,
instead of the whole nation being destroyed."
51 Now he was not self-moved in saying
this, but as high priest for that year he
was inspired to say that Jesus was to
52 die for the nation—and not only for the
nation but also for the purpose of unit-
53 ing the scattered children of God. So
from that day they planned to kill Jesus.
54 In consequence of this, Jesus did not
appear in public among the Jews any
longer, but he left that neighborhood
and went to the district near the desert,
to a town called Ephraim, and stayed
there with his disciples. Now the Jew- 55
ish Passover Festival was approaching
and many people went up from the
country to Jerusalem before the Passover, to purify themselves. So they were 56
looking for Jesus there, and saying to one
another as they stood about the Temple,
"What do you think? Do you think
he will not come to the festival at all?"
For the high priests and the Phari- 57
sees had given orders that anyone who
found out where he was should let them
know, so that they might arrest him.
Six days before the Passover Jesus 12
came to Bethany, where Lazarus,
whom he had raised from the dead, was
living. They gave a dinner for him 2
there, and Martha waited on them,
while Lazarus was one of those at the
table with him. And Mary took a pound 3
of liquid spikenard perfume, very costly, and poured it on Jesus' feet, and
then wiped his feet with her hair, and
the whole house was filled with the
fragrance of the perfume. But Judas 4
Iscariot, one of his disciples, who was
going to betray him, said,
"Why was this perfume not sold for 5
sixty dollars, and the money given to
the poor?"
But he did not say this because he 6
cared about the poor, but because he
was a thief and when he had charge of
the purse he used to take what was put
in it. Jesus said, 7
"Let her alone; let her keep it for the
day of my funeral, for you always have 8
the poor among you, but you will not
always have me."
A great crowd of the Jews found out 9
that he was there, and they came not
only to see Jesus but also to see Lazarus, whom he had raised from the dead.
But the high priests planned to kill 10
Lazarus also, for because of him many 11
of the Jews were leaving them and becoming believers in Jesus.
On the following day the great throng 12
that had come up to the festival, hearing that Jesus was coming to Jerusalem,
got palm branches and went out to 13
meet him, shouting,
"Bless him!
Bless him who comes in the Lord's
name!
Bless the king of Israel!"
And Jesus found a young ass and 14
mounted it, in accordance with the
Scripture,

15 "Do not be afraid, Daughter of Zion!
See, your king is coming
Mounted on an ass's colt!"
16 His disciples did not understand this
at the time but after Jesus was glorified
they remembered that this was said of
him in Scripture and that they had
17 done this to him. The crowd that had
been with him when he called Lazarus
out of the tomb and raised him from
18 the dead bore witness to it. That was
why the crowd went out to meet him,
because they heard that he had showed
19 that sign. So the Pharisees said to one
another,
"You see, you cannot do anything!
The whole world has run after him!"
20 There were some Greeks among those
who had come up to worship at the
21 festival, and they went to Philip, who
was from Bethsaida in Galilee, and
made this request to him:
"Sir, we want to see Jesus."
22 Philip went and told Andrew, and
Andrew and Philip went to Jesus and
23 told him. Jesus answered,
"The time has come for the Son of
24 Man to be glorified. I tell you, unless a
grain of wheat falls on the ground and
dies, it remains just one grain. But if
25 it dies, it yields a great harvest. Whoever loves his life loses it, and whoever
hates his life in this world will preserve
26 it for eternal life. If anyone serves me,
he must follow me, and wherever I am,
my servant must be also. If anyone
serves me, my Father will show him
27 honor. Now my heart is troubled; what
can I say? Father, save me from this
trial! And yet it was for this very pur-
28 pose that I have come to this trial.
Father, honor your own name!"
Then there came a voice from
heaven,
"I have honored it, and I will honor
it again!"
29 The crowd of bystanders heard it and
said it was thunder. Others said,
"An angel spoke to him!"
30 Jesus answered,
"It was not for my sake that the
31 voice came, but for yours. The judgment of this world is now in progress.
Its evil genius is now to be expelled,
32 and if I am lifted up from the ground,
I will draw all men to myself."
33 He said this to show the kind of death
34 he was going to die. The crowd answered,

"We have heard from the Law that
the Christ is to remain here forever.
So how can you say that the Son of
Man must be lifted up? Who is this
Son of Man?"
Jesus said to them, 35
"You will have the light only a little
while longer. Go on while you still have
the light, so that darkness may not
overtake you, for those who go about
in the dark do not know where they are
going. While you have the light believe 36
in the light, that you may become sons
of light."
With these words Jesus went away,
and disappeared from them. But for 37
all the signs he had shown among them,
they would not believe in him, in fulfil- 38
ment of the saying of the prophet
Isaiah,
"Lord, who has believed our account?
And to whom has the Lord's
arm been unveiled?"
So they could not believe; for Isaiah 39
says again,
"He has made their eyes blind and 40
their minds dull,
To keep them from seeing with
their eyes, and understanding
with their minds,
And turning to me to be cured."
Isaiah said this because he saw his 41
glory; it was of him that he spoke. Yet 42
for all that, even among the members of
the Council, many came to believe in
him, but on account of the Pharisees
they would not acknowledge it, for fear
of being expelled from the synagogues,
for they cared more for the approval of 43
men than for the approval of God.
But Jesus cried loudly, 44
"Whoever believes in me, believes
not in me but in him who has sent me;
and whoever sees me, sees him who has 45
sent me. I have come into the world as 46
a light, so that no one who believes in
me may have to remain in darkness.
If anyone hears my words and disre- 47
gards them, it is not I that judge him,
for I have not come to judge the world
but to save the world. Whoever rejects 48
me and refuses to accept my teachings
is not without his judge; the very message I have given will be his judge on
the Last Day, for I have not spoken on 49
my account, but the Father who has
sent me has himself given me orders
what to tell and what to say. And I 50

know his orders mean eternal life. So
whatever I say, I say only as the
Father has told me."
13 Before the Passover Festival began,
Jesus knew that the time had come for
him to leave this world and go to the
Father, but he had loved those who
were his own in the world, and he loved
2 them to the last. So at supper—the
devil having by this time put the
thought of betraying Jesus into the
mind of Judas Iscariot, Simon's son—
3 Jesus, fully aware that the Father had
put everything into his hands, and that
he had come from God and was going
4 back to God, rose from the table, took
off his outer clothing, and fastened a
5 towel about his waist. Then he poured
water into the basin and began to wash
the disciples' feet, wiping them with the
6 towel that was about his waist. So he
came to Simon Peter. He said to him,
"Master, are you going to wash my
feet?"
7 Jesus answered,
"You cannot understand now what
I am doing, but you will learn by and
by."
8 Peter said to him,
"You shall never wash my feet!"
Jesus answered,
"You will have no share with me unless I wash you."
9 Simon Peter said to him,
"Master, wash not only my feet but
my hands and my face too!"
10 Jesus said to him,
"Anyone who has bathed only needs
to have his feet washed to be altogether
clean. And you are already clean—
11 though not all of you." For he knew
who was going to betray him; that was
why he said, "You are not all of you
clean."
12 When he had washed their feet and
put on his clothes and taken his place,
he said to them again,
"Do you understand what I have
13 been doing to you? You call me Teacher and Master, and you are right, for
14 that is what I am. If I then, your Master and Teacher, have washed your feet,
you ought to wash one another's feet
15 too. For I have set you an example, in
order that you may do what I have
16 done to you. I tell you, no slave is superior to his master, and no messenger
is greater than the man who sends him.
17 Now that you have this knowledge, you
will be blessed if you act upon it. I do 18
not mean all of you; I know whom I
have chosen; but let the Scripture be
fulfilled:
" 'He who is eating my bread
Has raised his heel against me.'
From now on I will tell you things be- 19
fore they happen, so that when they do
happen you may believe that I am what
I say. I assure you, whoever welcomes 20
any messenger of mine welcomes me
and whoever welcomes me welcomes
him who has sent me."
After Jesus had said this he was 21
greatly moved and said solemnly,
"I tell you, it is one of you that will
betray me!"
The disciples looked at one another 22
in doubt as to which of them he meant.
Next to Jesus, at his right at the table, 23
was one of his disciples whom Jesus especially loved. So Simon Peter nodded 24
to him and said to him,
"Tell us whom he means."
He leaned back from where he lay, on 25
Jesus' breast, and said to him,
"Master, who is it?"
Jesus answered, 26
"It is the one to whom I am going to
give this piece of bread when I have
dipped it in the dish." So he dipped the
piece of bread and took it and gave it to
Judas, Simon Iscariot's son. After he 27
took the bread, Satan took possession
of him. Then Jesus said to him,
"Be quick about your business."
But no one else at the table knew 28
what he meant by telling him this, for 29
some of them thought that as Judas
had the purse Jesus meant to say to
him, "Buy what we need for the festival," or to have him give something to
the poor. So immediately after taking 30
the piece of bread he went out. It was
then night.
When he was gone, Jesus said, 31
"Now the Son of Man has been honored, and God has been honored, through
him, and God will through himself honor 32
him; he will honor him immediately. My 33
children, I am to be with you only a little
longer. You will look for me, but, as I
said to the Jews, 'Where I am going you
cannot follow,' I now say to you. I give 34
you a new command: Love one another.
Just as I have loved you, you must love
one another. By this they will all know 35
that you are my disciples—by your love
for one another."

36 Simon Peter said to him,
"Master, where are you going?"
Jesus answered,
"I am going where you cannot follow me now, but you will follow me later."
37 Peter said to him,
"Master, why cannot I follow you now? I will lay down my life for you."
38 Jesus answered,
"You will lay down your life for me? I tell you, before a cock crows, you will disown me thrice over!

14 "Your minds must not be troubled; you must believe in God, and believe in
2 me. There are many rooms in my Father's house; if there were not, I would have told you, for I am going away to
3 make ready a place for you. And if I go and make it ready, I will come back and take you with me, so that you may be
4 where I am. You know the way to the place where I am going."
5 Thomas said to him,
"Master, we do not know where you are going; how can we know the way?"
6 Jesus said to him,
"I am Way and Truth and Life. No one can come to the Father except
7 through me. If you knew me, you would know my Father also. From now on you do know him and you have seen him."
8 Philip said to him,
"Master, let us see the Father, and it will satisfy us."
9 Jesus said to him,
"Have I been with you so long, and yet you, Philip, have not recognized me? Whoever has seen me has seen the Father. How can you say, 'Let us see
10 the Father'? Do you not believe that I am in union with the Father and the Father is in union with me? I am not the source of the words that I say to you, but the Father who is united with
11 me is doing these things himself. You must believe that I am in union with the Father and that the Father is in union with me, or else you must believe
12 because of the things themselves. I tell you, whoever believes in me will do such things as I do, and things greater yet, because I am going to the Father.
13 Anything you ask for as followers of mine I will grant, so that the Father
14 may be honored through the Son. I will grant anything you ask me for as my followers.

"If you really love me, you will ob- 15
serve my commands. And I will ask the 16
Father and he will give you another
Helper to be with you always. It is the 17
Spirit of Truth. The world cannot obtain it, because it does not see it or recognize it; you recognize it because it
stays with you and is within you. I am 18
not going to leave you friendless. I am 19
coming back to you. In a little while the world will not see me any more, but you will still see me, because I shall live
on, and you will live on too. When that 20
day comes you will know that I am in union with my Father and you are with
me and I am with you. It is he who 21
has my commands and observes them that really loves me, and whoever loves me will be loved by my Father, and I will love him, and show myself to him."
Judas (not Judas Iscariot) said to 22
him,
"Master, how does it happen that you are going to show yourself to us and not to the world?"
Jesus answered, 23
"Anyone who loves me will observe my teaching, and my Father will love him and we will come to him and live
with him. No one who does not love 24
me will observe my teaching, and yet the teaching you are listening to is not mine but is that of him who has sent me.
"I have told you this while I am still 25
staying with you, but the Helper, the 26
holy Spirit which the Father will send in my place, will teach you everything and remind you of everything that I
have told you. I leave you peace; 27
I give you my own peace. I do not give it to you as the world gives. Your minds must not be troubled or afraid.
You have heard me say that I am going 28
away and am coming back to you; if you loved me you would be glad that I am going to the Father, for the Father
is greater than I. And I have told you 29
of it now before it happens, in order that when it happens you may believe
in me. I shall not talk much more with 30
you, for the evil genius of the world is
coming. He has no power over me, but 31
he is coming that the world may know that I love the Father and am doing what he has commanded me to do. Come, let us go away.

"I am the true vine, and my Father **15**

2 is the cultivator. Any branch of mine
that does not bear fruit he trims away,
and he prunes every branch that bears
3 fruit, to make it bear more. You are
pruned already because of the teaching
4 that I have given you. You must remain united to me and I will remain
united to you. Just as no branch can
bear fruit by itself unless it remains
united to the vine, you cannot unless
5 you remain united to me. I am the
vine, you are the branches. Anyone
who remains united to me, with me
united to him, will be very fruitful, for
you cannot do anything apart from me.
6 Anyone who does not remain united to
me is thrown away like a branch and
withers up, and they gather them and
throw them into the fire and burn
7 them. If you remain united to me and
my words remain in your hearts, ask
for whatever you please and you shall
8 have it. When you are very fruitful and
show yourselves to be disciples of mine,
9 my Father is honored. I have loved
you just as the Father has loved me.
10 You must retain my love. If you keep
my commands you will retain my love,
just as I have observed the Father's
11 commands and retain his love. I have
told you all this so that you may have
the happiness that I have had, and your
12 happiness may be complete. The command that I give you is to love one an-
13 other just as I have loved you. No one
can show greater love than by giving up
14 his life for his friends. You are my
friends if you do what I command you
15 to do. I do not call you slaves any longer, for a slave does not know what his
master is doing, but now I call you
friends, for I have made known to you
everything that I have learned from
16 my Father. It was not you who chose
me, it is I who have chosen you, and
appointed you to go and bear fruit—
fruit that shall be lasting, so that the
Father may grant you whatever you
ask him for as my followers.

17 "What I command you to do is to
18 love one another. If the world hates
you, remember that it hated me first.
19 If you belonged to the world, the world
would love what was its own. But it is
because you do not belong to the world,
but I have selected you from the world,
20 that the world hates you. Remember
what I said to you: No slave is greater
than his master. If they have persecuted me they will persecute you too. If
they have observed my teaching, they
will observe yours too. But they will do 21
all this to you on my account, because
they do not understand who has sent
me. If I had not come and spoken to 22
them, they would not have been guilty
of sin, but as it is, they have no excuse
for their sin. Whoever hates me hates 23
my Father also. If I had not done 24
things before them that no one else
ever did they would not be guilty of sin.
But as it is, they have both seen and
hated both me and my Father. But the 25
saying of their Law, 'They hated me
without cause,' must be fulfilled. When 26
the Helper comes whom I will send to
you from the Father—that Spirit of
Truth that comes from the Father—he
will bear testimony to me, and you must
bear testimony too, because you have 27
been with me from the first.

"I have told you this to keep you 16
from faltering. They will exclude you 2
from their synagogues; why, the time is
coming when anyone who kills you will
think he is doing religious service to
God. They will do this because they 3
do not know the Father or me. But I 4
have told you about these things in order that when the time comes for them
to happen, you may remember that I
told you of them. I did not tell you this
at first because I was still staying with
you. But now I am going away to him 5
who sent me, and not one of you asks
me where I am going, but your minds 6
are full of sorrow because I have told
you this. Yet it is only the truth when 7
I tell you that it is better for you that I
should go away. For if I do not go, the
Helper will not come to you, but if I go
I will send him to you. When he comes, 8
he will bring conviction to the world
about sin and uprightness and judgment; about sin, as shown in their not 9
believing in me; about uprightness, 10
as shown by my going away to the Father, where you can no longer see me;
and about judgment, as shown by the 11
condemnation of the evil genius of this
world. I have much more to tell you, 12
but you cannot take it in now, but 13
when the Spirit of Truth comes, he will
guide you into the full truth, for he will
not speak for himself but will tell what
he hears, and will announce to you the
things that are to come. He will do hon- 14

or to me, for he will take what is mine
15 and communicate it to you. All that
the Father has belongs to me. That is
why I said that he will take what is
mine and communicate it to you.
16 "In a little while you will not see me
any longer, and a little while after, you
will see me again."
17 Then some of his disciples said to one
another,
"What does he mean when he tells
us, 'In a little while you will not see me
any longer, and a little while after, you
will see me again,' and 'Because I am
18 going away to the Father'?" So they
kept saying "What does he mean by 'In
a little while'? We do not know what he
is talking about."
19 Jesus saw that they wanted to ask
him a question, and he said to them,
"Are you asking one another about
my saying 'In a little while you will not
see me any longer, and a little while af-
20 ter, you will see me again'? I tell you,
you will weep and wail while the world
will be happy; you will grieve, but your
21 grief will change to happiness. When a
woman is in labor she is sorrowful, for
her time has come; but when the child
is born, she forgets her pain in her joy
that a human being has been brought
22 into the world. So you, too, are sorrowful now; but I will see you again, and
your hearts will be happy, and no one
23 can rob you of your happiness. When
that time comes, you will not ask me
any question; I tell you, whatever you
ask the Father for, he will give you as
24 my followers. Hitherto you have not
asked for anything as my followers, but
now ask, and you will receive, so that
your happiness may be complete.
25 "I have said all this to you in figures,
but a time is coming when I shall not
do so any longer, but will tell you
26 plainly about the Father. When that
time comes you will ask as my followers,
and I do not promise to intercede with
27 the Father for you, for the Father loves
you himself because you love me and
believe that I have come from the
28 Father. I did come from the Father
and enter the world. Now I am leaving
the world again and going back to the
Father."
29 His disciples said,
"Why, now you are talking plainly
and not speaking figuratively at all.
30 Now we know that you know everything and do not need to have anyone
ask you questions. This makes us believe that you have really come from
God."
Jesus answered, 31
"Now do you believe that? Why, a 32
time is coming—it is already come!—
when you will all be scattered to your
homes and will leave me alone. And
yet I am not alone, for the Father is
with me. I have told you all this, so 33
that through me you may find peace.
In the world you have trouble; but take
courage! I have conquered the world."
When Jesus had said all this he raised 1
his eyes to heaven and said,
"Father, the time has come. Do hon-
or to your son, that your son may do
honor to you, just as you have done in 2
giving him power over all mankind, so
that he may give eternal life to all
whom you have given him. And eter- 3
nal life means knowing you as the only
true God, and knowing Jesus your messenger as Christ. I have done honor to 4
you here on earth, by completing the
work which you gave me to do. Now, 5
Father, do such honor to me in your
presence as I had done me there before
the world existed.
"I have revealed your real self to the 6
men you gave me from the world. They
were yours and you gave them to me,
and they have obeyed your message.
Now at last they know that all that you 7
have given me comes from you, for I 8
have given them the truths that you
gave me, and they have accepted them
and been convinced that I came from
you, and they believe that you sent me.
I have a request to make for them. I 9
make no request for the world, but only
for those whom you have given me, for
they are yours—all that is mine is yours 10
and what is yours is mine—and they
have done me honor. Now I am to be 11
no longer in this world, but they are to
remain in the world, while I return to
you. Holy Father, keep them by your
power which you gave me, so that they
may be one just as we are. As long as I 12
was with them I kept them by your
power which you gave me, and I protected them, and not one of them was
lost (except the one who was destined
to be lost), so that what the Scripture
says might come true. But now I am 13
coming to you, and I say this here in
this world in order that they may have

the happiness that I feel fully realized
14 in their own hearts. I have given them
your message, and the world has come
to hate them, for they do not belong to
the world any more than I belong to the
15 world. I do not ask you to take them
away from the world, but to keep them
16 from the evil one. They do not belong to
the world any more than I belong to
17 the world. Consecrate them by truth.
18 Your message is truth. Just as you sent
me to the world, I have sent them to
19 the world. And it is for their sake that
I consecrate myself, that they also may
be consecrated by the truth.

20 "It is not for them only that I make
this request. It is also for those who
through their message come to believe
21 in me. Let them all be one. Just as
you, Father, are in union with me and
I am with you, let them be in union
with us, so that the world may believe
22 that you sent me. I have given them
the glory that you gave me, so that
23 they may be one just as we are, I in
union with them and you with me, so
that they may be perfectly unified, and
the world may recognize that you sent
me and that you love them just as you
24 loved me. Father, I wish to have those
whom you have given me with me
where I am, to see my glory that you
have given me, for you loved me before
25 the creation of the world. Righteous
Father, though the world did not know
you, I knew you, and these men knew
26 that you had sent me. I have made
your self known to them and I will do
so still, so that the love which you have
had for me may be in their hearts, and
I may be there also."

18 When Jesus had said this, he went
out with his disciples to the other side
of the Ravine of the Cedars where there
was a garden, and he went into it with
2 his disciples. Judas who betrayed him
also knew the place, for Jesus often met
3 his disciples there. So Judas got out the
garrison and some attendants from the
high priests and Pharisees, and came
there with lanterns, torches, and weap-
4 ons. Then Jesus, as he knew everything
that was going to happen to him, came
forward and said to them,

"Whom are you looking for?"
5 They answered,
"Jesus of Nazareth."
He said to them,
"I am he."
Judas who betrayed him was standing among them. When Jesus said to 6
them, "I am he," they drew back and
fell to the ground. Then he asked them 7
again,

"Whom are you looking for?"
They said,
"Jesus of Nazareth."
Jesus answered, 8
"I have told you that I am he, so if
you are looking for me, let these men
go." This was to fulfil the saying he 9
had uttered, "I have not lost one of
those whom you have given me."

Then Simon Peter, who had a sword 10
with him, drew it and struck at the
high priest's slave and cut off his right
ear. The slave's name was Malchus.
Then Jesus said to Peter, 11

"Put your sword back into the
sheath. Shall I not drink the cup which
the Father has offered me?"

So the garrison and the colonel and 12
the attendants of the Jews seized Jesus
and bound him, and they took him first 13
to Annas. For he was the father in-law
of Caiaphas, who was high priest that
year. Now it was Caiaphas who had 14
advised the Jews that it was to their
interest that one man should die for the
people.

But Simon Peter and another disciple 15
followed Jesus. This other disciple was
an acquaintance of the high priest, and
he went on with Jesus into the high
priest's courtyard, while Peter stood 16
outside at the door. So this other disciple, the acquantance of the high priest,
went out and spoke to the woman at
the door and brought Peter in. The 17
maid at the door said to Peter,

"Are you also one of this man's disciples?"
He said,
"No, I am not."
As it was cold the slaves and attend- 18
ants had made a charcoal fire, and stood
about it warming themselves. And Peter also was among them, standing and
warming himself.

Then the high priest questioned Je- 19
sus about his disciples and his teaching.
Jesus answered, 20
"I have spoken openly to the world.
I have always taught in synagogues or
in the Temple where all the Jews meet
together, and I have said nothing in secret. Why do you question me? Ask 21
those who have heard me what it was

that I said to them. They will know
what I have said."
22 When he said this, one of the attendants who stood near struck him and said,

"Is that the way you answer the high priest?"

23 Jesus replied,

"If I have said anything wrong, testify to it; but if what I have said is true, why do you strike me?"

24 So Annas sent him over still bound to Caiaphas the high priest.

25 But Simon Peter still stood warming himself. So they said to him,

"Are you also one of his disciples?"

He denied it and said,

"No, I am not."

26 One of the high priest's slaves, a relative of the man whose ear Peter had cut off, said,

"Did I not see you with him in the garden?"

27 Peter again denied it, and at that moment a cock crowed.

28 Then they took Jesus from Caiaphas to the governor's house. It was early in the morning, and they would not go into the governor's house themselves, to avoid being ceremonially defiled and to be able to eat the Passover supper.

29 So Pilate came out to them, and said,

"What charge do you make against this man?"

30 They answered,

"If he were not a criminal, we would not have turned him over to you."

31 Pilate said to them,

"Take him yourselves, and try him by your law."

The Jews said to him,

"We have no authority to put anyone to death."

32 This was to fulfil what Jesus said when he declared how he was to die.

33 So Pilate went back into the governor's house and called Jesus and said to him,

"Are you the king of the Jews?"

34 Jesus answered,

"Did you think of that yourself, or have other people said it to you about me?"

35 Pilate answered,

"Do you take me for a Jew? Your own people and the high priests handed you over to me. What offense have you committed?"

Jesus answered, 36

"My kingdom is not a kingdom of this world. If my kingdom were a kingdom of this world, my men would have fought to keep me from being handed over to the Jews. But as it is, my kingdom has no such origin."

Pilate said to him, 37

"Then you are a king?"

Jesus answered,

"Yes, I am a king. It was for this that I was born and for this that I came to the world, to give testimony for truth. Everyone who is on the side of truth listens to my voice."

Pilate said to him, 38

"What is truth!"

With these words he went out again to the Jews, and said to them,

"I can find nothing to charge him
with. But it is your custom to have me 39
release one man for you at Passover time. Do you want me therefore to release the king of the Jews for you?"

Then they shouted back, 40

"No! Not him, but Barabbas!"

Now Barabbas was a robber.

Then Pilate took Jesus and had him 19
flogged. And the soldiers made a 2
wreath out of thorns and put it on his head, and put a purple coat on him, and
they marched up to him, saying, 3

"Long live the king of the Jews!"
each one giving him a blow. And Pilate 4
went out again and said to the Jews,

"See! I will bring him out to you, to show you that I can find nothing to charge him with."

So Jesus came out, still wearing the 5
wreath of thorns and the purple coat. And Pilate said to them,

"Here is the man!"

When the high priests and their at- 6
tendants saw him, they shouted,

"Crucify him! Crucify him!"

Pilate said to them,

"Take him yourselves and crucify him, for I can find nothing to charge him with."

The Jews answered, 7

"We have a law, and by our law he deserves death, for declaring himself to be a son of God."

When Pilate heard that, he was more 8
frightened than before and he went 9
back into the governor's house and said to Jesus,

"Where do you come from?"
10 But Jesus made him no answer. Then
Pilate said to him,
"Do you refuse to speak to me? Do
you not know that it is in my power to
release you or to crucify you?"
11 Jesus answered him,
"You would have no power at all
over me, if it were not given to you
from above. So you are less guilty than
the man who betrayed me to you."
12 This made Pilate try to find a way to
let him go, but the Jews shouted,
"If you let him go, you are no friend
of the emperor's! Anyone who calls
himself a king utters treason against
the emperor!"
13 When Pilate heard that, he brought
Jesus out and had him sit in the
judge's seat in the place they call the
Stone Platform, or in Hebrew, Gabba-
14 tha. It was the day of Preparation for
the Passover, and it was about noon.
And Pilate said to the Jews,
"There is your king!"
15 At that they shouted,
"Kill him! Kill him! Crucify him!"
Pilate said to them,
"Am I to crucify your king?"
The high priests answered,
"We have no king but the emperor!"
16 Then Pilate handed him over to
them to be crucified.
17 So they took Jesus, and he went out
carrying the cross by himself to a place
called the Place of the Skull, or in He-
18 brew, Golgotha. There they crucified
him, with two others, one on each side
19 and Jesus in the middle. Pilate wrote
a placard and put it on the cross; it
read "Jesus the Nazarene, the king of
20 the Jews." Many of the Jews read this
placard, for the place where Jesus was
crucified was near the city, and it was
written in Hebrew, Latin, and Greek.
21 So the Jewish high priests said to Pilate,
"Do not write 'The king of the
Jews,' but write 'He said, I am king of
the Jews.' "
22 Pilate answered,
"What I have written, I have written!"
23 When the soldiers had crucified Jesus, they took his clothes and divided
them into four parts, one for each soldier, besides his shirt. Now his shirt had
no seam; it was woven in one piece from
24 top to bottom. So they said to one another,

"Let us not tear it, but let us draw
for it, to see who gets it." This was to
fulfil what the Scripture says:
"They divided my garments among
them,
And for my clothing they cast
lots."
This was what the soldiers did. Near 25
Jesus' cross stood his mother and her
sister, Mary, the daughter of Clopas,
and Mary of Magdala. So Jesus, seeing 26
his mother and the disciple whom he
loved standing near, said to his mother,
"There is your son!"
Then he said to his disciple, 27
"There is your mother!"
And from that time his disciple took
her into his home.
After that, Jesus, knowing that 28
everything was now finished, to fulfil
the saying of Scripture, said,
"I am thirsty."
A bowl of sour wine was standing 29
there. So they put a sponge soaked in
the wine on a pike and held it to his lips.
When Jesus had taken the wine, he 30
said,
"It is finished!"
Then bowing his head he gave up his
spirit.
As it was the day of Preparation for 31
the Passover, in order that the bodies
might not be left on the crosses over the
Sabbath, for that Sabbath was an especially important one, the Jews asked
Pilate to have the men's legs broken
and the bodies removed. So the soldiers 32
went and broke the legs of the first man
and then of the other who had been
crucified with him. But when they 33
came to Jesus they saw that he was
dead already, and they did not break
his legs, but one of the soldiers thrust a 34
lance into his side, and blood and water
immediately flowed out. The man who 35
saw it testifies to it—his testimony is
true; he knows that he is telling the
truth—to lead you also to believe. For 36
this happened to fulfil what the Scripture says:
"Not one of its bones shall be broken." Moreover, it says in another 37
place,
"They will look at the man whom
they pierced."
After this, Joseph, of Arimathea, 38
who was a disciple of Jesus, but a secret one, because of his fear of the Jews,

asked Pilate to let him remove Jesus'
body, and Pilate gave him permission.
So Joseph went and took the body
39 down. And Nicodemus also, who had
first come to Jesus at night, went, taking a roll of myrrh and aloes weighing
40 about a hundred pounds. So they took
Jesus' body, and wrapped it with the
spices in bandages, in the Jewish way
41 of preparing bodies for burial. There
was a garden at the place where Jesus
had been crucified, and in the garden
was a new tomb in which no one had
42 yet been laid. So because it was the
Jewish Preparation day, and the tomb
was close by, they put Jesus there.

20 On the day after the Sabbath, very
early in the morning while it was still
dark, Mary of Magdala went to the
tomb, and she saw that the stone had
2 been removed from it. So she ran away
and went to Simon Peter and the other
disciple who was dear to Jesus, and said
to them,

"They have taken the Master out of
the tomb, and we do not know where
they have put him."

3 So Peter and the other disciple went
out of the city and started for the
4 tomb. And they both ran, and the
other disciple ran faster than Peter and
5 got to the tomb first. And he stooped
down and saw the bandages lying on
6 the ground, but he did not go in. Then
Simon Peter came up behind him, and
he went inside the tomb, and saw the
7 bandages lying on the ground, and the
handkerchief that had been over Jesus'
face not on the ground with the band-
8 ages, but folded up by itself. Then the
other disciple who had reached the
tomb first went inside too, and saw and
9 was convinced. For they did not yet
understand the statement of Scripture
10 that he must rise from the dead. So
the disciples went back to their homes.
11 But Mary stood just outside the
tomb, weeping. And as she wept she
12 looked down into the tomb, and saw
two angels in white sitting where Jesus'
body had been, one at his head and one
13 at his feet. And they said to her,

"Why are you weeping?"

She said to them,

"They have taken my Master away,
and I do not know where they have put
him."

14 As she said this she turned around
and saw Jesus standing there, but she
did not know that it was he. Jesus said 15
to her,

"Why are you weeping? Who are
you looking for?"

She, supposing that he was the gardener, said to him,

"If it was you, sir, that carried him
away, tell me where you have put him,
and I will take him away."

Jesus said to her, 16

"Mary!"

She turned and said to him in Hebrew,

"Rabbouni!" which means Master.

Jesus said to her, 17

"You must not cling to me, for I have
not yet gone up to my Father, but go to
my brothers and say to them, 'I am
going up to my Father and your Father,
to my God and your God.'"

Mary of Magdala went and declared 18
to the disciples,

"I have seen the Master!"

and she told them that he had said this
to her.

When it was evening on the first day 19
after the Sabbath, and the doors of the
house where the disciples met were
locked for fear of the Jews, Jesus came
in and stood among them and said to
them,

"Peace be with you!"

Then he showed them his hands and his 20
side, and the disciples were full of joy at
seeing the Master. Jesus said to them 21
again,

"Peace be with you! Just as my Father sent me forth so I now send you."

As he said this he breathed upon 22
them, and said,

"Receive the holy Spirit! If you for- 23
give any men's sins, they are forgiven
them, and if you fix any men's sins
upon them, they will remain fixed."

But Thomas, one of the Twelve, who 24
was called the Twin, was not with them
when Jesus came in. So the rest of the 25
disciples said to him,

"We have seen the Master!"

But he said to them,

"Unless I see the marks of the nails
in his hands, and put my finger into
the marks of the nails, and put my hand
into his side, I will never believe it!"

A week later, his disciples were again 26
in the house, and Thomas was with
them. Although the doors were locked,
Jesus came in and stood among them,
and said,

"Peace be with you!"

Then he said to Thomas,

"Put your finger here and look at my hands, and take your hand and put it in my side, and be no longer unbelieving, but believe!"

Thomas answered him,

"My Master and my God!"

Jesus said to him,

"Is it because you have seen me that you believe? Blessed be those who have not seen me and yet believe!"

There were many other signs that Jesus showed before his disciples which are not recorded in this book. But these have been recorded so that you may believe that Jesus is the Christ, the Son of God, and through believing you may have life as his followers.

After this Jesus again showed himself to the disciples at the Sea of Tiberias, and he did so in this way. Simon Peter, Thomas called the Twin, Nathanael, of Cana in Galilee, the sons of Zebedee, and two other disciples of Jesus were all together. Simon Peter said to them,

"I am going fishing."

They said to him,

"We will go with you."

They went out and got into the boat, and that night they caught nothing. But just as day was breaking, Jesus stood on the beach, though the disciples did not know that it was he. So Jesus said to them,

"Children, have you any fish?"

They answered,

"No."

"Throw your net in on the right of the boat," he said to them, "and you will find them."

They did so, and they could not haul it in for the quantity of fish in it. Then the disciple who was dear to Jesus said to Peter,

"It is the Master!"

When Simon Peter heard that it was the Master, he put on his clothes, for he had taken them off, and sprang into the sea. The rest of the disciples followed in the boat, for they were not far from land, only about a hundred yards, dragging in the net full of fish. When they landed they saw a charcoal fire burning, with a fish on it, and some bread. Jesus said to them,

"Bring some of the fish you have just caught."

So Simon Peter got into the boat, and 11
hauled the net ashore, full of large fish,
a hundred and fifty-three of them, and
though there were so many, the net was
not torn. Jesus said to them, 12

"Come and have breakfast."

None of the disciples dared to ask him
who he was, for they knew it was the
Master. Jesus went and got the bread 13
and gave it to them, and the fish also.
This was the third time that Jesus 14
showed himself to his disciples, after he
had risen from the dead.

When they had finished breakfast, 15
Jesus said to Simon Peter,

"Simon, son of John, are you more devoted to me than these others?"

Peter said to him,

"Yes, Master, you know that I love you."

He said to him,

"Then feed my lambs!"

Again he said to him a second time, 16

"Simon, son of John, are you devoted to me?"

He said to him,

"Yes, Master, you know that I love you."

He said to him,

"Then tend my sheep!"

He said to him the third time, 17

"Simon, son of John, do you love me?"

Peter was hurt because the third time Jesus asked him if he loved him, and he answered,

"Master, you know everything, you can see that I love you."

Jesus said to him,

"Then feed my sheep! I tell you, 18
when you were young, you used to gird
yourself and go where you pleased,
but when you grow old, you will stretch
out your hands and someone else will
gird you and take you where you do
not wish to go."

He said this to show the kind of 19
death by which Peter was to honor
God; and after he had said it he said to
Peter,

"Follow me!"

Peter turned and saw following them 20
the disciple who was dear to Jesus, who
at the supper leaned back on Jesus'
breast and said, "Master, who is it that

21 is going to betray you?" When Peter
saw him, he said to Jesus,
"But, Master, what about him?"
22 Jesus said to him,
"If I wish him to wait till I come,
what does it matter to you? You must
follow me."
23 So the story spread among the brothers that this disciple was not going to
die. But Jesus did not tell him that he
was not going to die; he said, "If I wish
him to wait till I come, what does it
matter to you?"

It is this disciple who testifies to these things and who wrote them down, and we know that his testimony is true.

There are many other things that Jesus did, so many in fact that if they were all written out, I do not suppose that the world itself would hold the books that would be written.

THE ACTS OF THE APOSTLES

1 IN MY first volume, Theophilus, I
dealt with all that Jesus did and
2 taught from the beginning until
the day when through the holy
Spirit he gave the apostles he had chos-
en their instructions, and was taken up
3 to heaven. He had shown himself alive
to them after he had suffered, in many
convincing ways, appearing to them
through forty days, and telling them
4 about the Kingdom of God. And once
when he ate with them, he instructed
them not to leave Jerusalem, but to
wait for what the Father had promised.
"You have heard me speak of it," he
5 said, "for John baptized people in water, but in a few days you will be baptized in the holy Spirit."
6 So those who were present asked him,
"Master, is this the time when you
are going to re-establish the kingdom for
Israel?"
7 He said to them,
"It is not for you to know times and
dates which the Father has fixed by his
8 own authority, but you will be given
power when the holy Spirit comes upon
you, and you will be witnesses for me in
Jerusalem and all over Judea and
Samaria and to the very ends of the
earth."
9 As he said this, he was caught up before their eyes and a cloud took him up
10 from their sight. And while they were
gazing after him into the sky, two men
dressed in white suddenly stood beside
11 them, and said to them,
"Men of Galilee, why do you stand
looking up into the sky? This very Jesus who has been caught up from you
into heaven will come in just the way
that you have seen him go up to heav-
en."
12 Then they went back to Jerusalem
from the hill called the Olive-orchard,
which is near Jerusalem, half a mile
away.
13 When they entered the city they
went to the upstairs room where they
were staying. There were Peter, John,
James and Andrew, Philip and Thomas, Bartholomew and Matthew, James,
the son of Alpheus, Simon the Zealot,
and Judas, the son of James. They were 14
all devoting themselves with one mind
to prayer, with the women and Mary,
Jesus' mother, and his brothers.
It was at that time that Peter got up 15
among the brothers—there were about
a hundred and twenty persons present
—and said,
"Brothers, the prediction of the 16
Scriptures had to come true that the
holy Spirit uttered by the lips of David,
about Judas, who acted as guide for the
men that arrested Jesus—for he was 17
one of our number and a share in this
ministry of ours fell to his lot." (This 18
man bought a piece of land with the
money paid him for his treachery, and
his body swelled up and burst open in
the middle and all his vitals poured out.
This fact was well known to all the resi- 19
dents of Jerusalem, so that the piece of
land came to be called in their language
Akeldamach, the bloody field.) "For in 20
the Book of Psalms it is written,

" 'Let his estate be desolate, with no
one to live on it,'

and

" 'Let someone else take his position.'

"So one of the men who has been as- 21
sociated with us all the time that the
Lord Jesus moved about among us,
from his baptism by John to the time 22
when he was caught up from us, must
join us as a witness to his resurrection."
Then they proposed two men, Joseph 23
called Barsabbas, who was known as
Justus, and Matthias. And they 24
prayed, saying,
"Lord, you who know all hearts,
show us which one of these two you
have chosen to take this place of serv- 25
ice as an apostle which Judas left to go
where he belonged."
Then they drew lots between them, 26
and the lot fell on Matthias, and he was
added to the eleven apostles.

On the day of the Harvest Festival, **2**
they were all meeting together, when 2

suddenly there came from the sky a
sound like a violent blast of wind, and
it filled the whole house where they
3 were sitting. And they saw tongues like
flames separating and settling one on
4 each of them, and they were all filled
with the holy Spirit and began to say
in foreign languages whatever the
Spirit prompted them to utter.

5 Now there were devout Jews from
every nation under heaven living in
6 Jerusalem. And when this sound was
heard, the crowd gathered in great
excitement, because each one heard
them speaking in his own language.
7 They were amazed and said in their
astonishment,

"Are not all these men who are
8 speaking Galileans? Then how is it
that each of us hears his own native
9 tongue? Parthians, Medes, Elamites,
residents of Mesopotamia, and Judea
10 and Cappadocia, of Pontus, and Asia,
of Phrygia, and Pamphylia, of Egypt
and the district of Africa about Cyrene,
visitors from Rome, Jews and pro-
11 selytes, Cretans and Arabs—we all hear
them tell in our native tongues the
mighty deeds of God."

12 And they were all amazed and bewildered and said to one another,

"What can this mean?"

13 But others said derisively,

"They have had too much new wine!"

14 Then Peter stood up with the eleven
around him, and raising his voice addressed them.

"Men of Judea," he said, "and all
you residents of Jerusalem, let me explain this to you, and pay attention to
15 what I say. These men are not drunk
as you suppose, for it is only nine in the
16 morning. But this is what was predicted by the prophet Joel,

17 " 'It will come about in the last days, God says,
That I will pour out my Spirit upon all mankind;
Your sons and daughters will become prophets,
Your young men will have visions,
And your old men will have dreams.
18 Even on my slaves, both men and women,
I will pour out my Spirit in those days,
And they will become prophets.
I will show wonders in the sky above,
And signs on the earth below,
Blood and fire and thick smoke.
The sun will turn to darkness,
And the moon to blood,
Before the coming of the great, splendid Day of the Lord.
Then everyone who calls on the name of the Lord will be saved.'

"Men of Israel, listen to what I say.
Jesus of Nazareth, as you know, was a
man whom God commended to you by
the wonders, portents, and signs that
God did right among you through him.
But you, by the fixed purpose and intention of God, handed him over to
wicked men, and crucified and killed
him. But God set aside the pain of death
and raised him up, for death could not
control him. For David says of him,

" 'I constantly regarded the Lord before me,
For he is at my right hand, so that I may not be displaced.
Therefore my heart is glad, and my tongue rejoices,
And my body will still live in hope.
For you will not desert my soul in death,
You will not let your Holy One see destruction.
You have made the ways of life known to me,
And you will fill me with joy in your presence.'

"Brothers, one may say to you confidently of the patriarch David that he
died and was buried, and his grave is
here among us to this very day. But as
he was a prophet, and knew that God
had promised him with an oath that he
would put one of his descendants upon
his throne, he foresaw the resurrection
of the Christ and told of it, for he was
not deserted in death and his body did
not see destruction. This Jesus, God
raised from the dead, and to his resurrection we are all witnesses. So he has
been exalted to God's right hand, and
has received from his Father the promise of the holy Spirit and has poured out
what you see and hear.

"For David did not go up to heaven,
but he said,

" 'The Lord said to my lord, Sit at my right hand,
Until I make your enemies your footstool.'

6 "Therefore the whole nation of Israel must know beyond doubt that
God has declared this Jesus whom you
crucified both Lord and Christ."
7 When they heard this, they were
stung to the heart, and they said to
Peter and the rest of the apostles,
"Brothers, what shall we do?"
8 Peter said to them,
"Repent, and be baptized every one
of you in the name of Jesus Christ, in
order to have your sins forgiven; then
you will receive the gift of the holy
9 Spirit. For the promise of it belongs
to you and your children, as well as to
all those far away whom the Lord our
God calls to him."
0 He said much more besides in giving
his testimony, and exhorted them,
saying,
"Save yourselves from this crooked
generation."
1 So they welcomed his message and
were baptized, and about three thou-
2 sand people joined them that day. And
they devoted themselves to the teaching and the society of the apostles, the
breaking of bread, and the prayers.
3 Everyone felt a sense of awe, and
many wonders and signs were done by
4 the apostles. The believers all shared
everything they had with one another,
5 and sold their property and belongings,
and divided the money with all the
rest, according to their special needs.
6 Day after day they all went regularly
to the Temple, they broke their bread
together in their homes, and they ate
their food with glad and simple hearts,
7 praising God and respected by all the
people. And every day the Lord added
people who were saved to their number.
3 Peter and John were on their way
up to the Temple for the three o'clock
2 hour of prayer, when a man who had
been lame from his birth was carried
by. He used to be placed every day at
what was known as the Beautiful Gate
of the Temple, to beg from the people
3 on their way into the Temple, and
when he saw Peter and John on the
point of going into the Temple he asked
4 them to give him something. Peter
fixed his eyes on him, as John did also,
and said to him,
"Look at us!"
5 He looked at them, supposing that
they were going to give him something.
6 But Peter said,
"I have no silver or gold, but I will
give you what I have. In the name of
Jesus Christ of Nazareth, walk!"
And he took him by the right hand 7
and raised him up, and his feet and
ankles immediately became strong, and 8
he sprang to his feet and began to walk,
and he went into the Temple with
them, walking, leaping, and praising
God. When all the people saw him 9
walking about, praising God, and rec- 10
ognized him as the man who used to sit
and beg at the Beautiful Gate of the
Temple, they were filled with wonder
and astonishment at what had happened to him.
And as he still clung to Peter and 11
John, all the people crowded about
them in the utmost astonishment in
what was known as Solomon's Colonnade. When Peter saw this, he said to 12
the people,
"Men of Israel, why are you so surprised at this? Why do you stare so at
us, as though it were by some power or
some piety of ours that we had made
him able to walk? The God of Abra- 13
ham, Isaac, and Jacob, the God of our
forefathers, has done this honor to his
servant Jesus, whom you betrayed and
disowned before Pilate, when he had
decided to let him go. But you dis- 14
owned the Holy, Righteous One. You
asked to have a murderer released for
you, and killed the very source of life. 15
But God raised him from the dead, as
we can testify. It is his power that 16
through faith has made this man whom
you see and recognize strong again,
and it is faith inspired by him that has
given him the perfect health you all see.
Yet I know, brothers, that you did 17
not know what you were doing, any
more than the members of your council
did; but it was in this way that God 18
fulfilled what he by all the prophets
foretold that his Christ must suffer. So 19
repent and turn to God, to have your
sins wiped out, that happier times may
come from the presence of the Lord,
and that he may send Jesus, your des- 20
tined Christ. Yet he must remain in 21
heaven till the time for the universal ref-
ormation of which God told in ancient
times by the lips of his holy prophets.
Moses said, 'The Lord God will raise up 22
a prophet for you from among your
brothers, as he raised me up. You must
listen to everything that he tells you.

23 Anyone that will not listen to that
prophet will be annihilated from
24 among the people.' Why, all the prophets from Samuel down, who have spo-
25 ken, have also foretold these days. You
are the descendants of the prophets and
the heirs of the agreement that God
made with your forefathers when he
said to Abraham, 'Through your posterity all the families of the earth will
26 be blessed.' It was to you that God
first sent his servant after he had raised
him from the dead, to bless you by
making every one of you turn from his
wickedness."

4 As they were talking to the people,
the high priests, the commander of the
Temple, and the Sadducees came up
2 to them, greatly disturbed because they
were teaching the people and declaring
that in the case of Jesus there had been
3 a resurrection from the dead. They arrested them, and as it was already
evening, they shut them up until next
4 morning. But many of those who had
heard what they said believed it, and
the number of men grew to be about
five thousand.

5 On the next day the leading members
of the council, the elders, and the
6 scribes met in Jerusalem, with Annas
the high priest, Caiaphas, John, Alexander, and all who belonged to the high
7 priest's family. They had the apostles
brought before them and demanded of
them,

"By what power or authority have
men like you done this?"

8 Then Peter, filled with the holy Spirit, said to them,

"Members of the council and elders
9 of the people, if it is for benefiting a
helpless man, and as to how he was
cured, that we are called to account
10 here today, you and the people of Israel
must all know that it is through the
power of Jesus Christ of Nazareth
whom you crucified but whom God
raised from the dead, that he stands
11 here before you well. He is the stone
that you builders rejected, which has
12 become the cornerstone. There is no
salvation through anyone else, for
there is no one else in the world who has
been named to men as our only means
of being saved."

13 They were amazed to see how out-
spoken Peter and John were, and to
find that they were uneducated, ordinary men. They recognized them as
companions of Jesus, and seeing the 14
man who had been cured standing beside them, they had nothing to say.
But they ordered them out of the pres- 15
ence of the council and conferred together. They said, 16

"What can we do with these men?
For it is plain to everyone in Jerusalem
that an extraordinary wonder has been
done by them. We cannot deny that.
But to keep it from spreading farther 17
among the people, let us warn them to
say nothing to anyone else at all about
this person."

So they called them in and ordered 18
them not to speak or teach at all about
the name of Jesus. But Peter and John 19
answered them,

"You must decide whether it is right
in the sight of God to obey you instead
of him, for we cannot help telling of 20
what we have seen and heard."

But after further threats they let 21
them go, as they could find no way to
punish them, on account of the people,
for they were all giving honor to God
for what had happened, for the man on 22
whom this wonder of healing had been
done was more than forty years old.

After being released, they went 23
back to their friends, and told them
what the high priests and elders had
said to them. When they heard it, with 24
one impulse they all raised their voices
to God and said,

"Master, it was you who made heav-
en, earth, and sea, and everything that
is in them, and who said through the 25
holy Spirit by the lips of our forefather
David, your servant,

" 'Why did the heathen rage,
And the peoples form vain de-
signs?
The kings of the earth stood by, 26
And the rulers assembled
Against the Lord and against his
Christ.'

For indeed they have assembled here in 27
this city against your holy servant
Jesus, whom you had consecrated—
Herod and Pontius Pilate, with the
heathen and the peoples of Israel, to 28
carry out what your hand and will had
destined should happen. And now, Lord, 29
take note of their threats, and give your
slaves the power to utter your message
fearlessly, when you stretch out your 30
hand to heal, and signs and wonders are

done by the power of your holy servant
Jesus."
1 When they had prayed, the place
where they were gathered shook, and
they were all filled with the holy Spirit,
and fearlessly uttered God's message.
2 There was but one heart and soul in
the multitude who had become believers, and not one of them claimed anything that belonged to him as his own,
but they shared everything they had
3 with one another. The apostles gave
their testimony to the resurrection of
the Lord Jesus with great power, and
God's favor rested richly upon them.
4 No one among them was in any want,
for any who owned lands or houses
would sell them and bring the proceeds
of the sale and put them at the disposal
5 of the apostles; then they were shared
with everyone in proportion to his need.
6 Joseph, a Levite, and a native of Cyprus, whom the apostles had named
Barnabas, which means Son of Encour-
7 agement, sold a piece of land that belonged to him, and brought the money
and put it at the disposal of the
apostles.
5 But a man named Ananias, who,
with his wife Sapphira, had sold a piece
2 of property, with his wife's connivance
appropriated some of the price received,
and brought only a part of it and put it
3 at the disposal of the apostles. And
Peter said,
"Ananias, why has Satan taken such
possession of your heart that you
should lie to the holy Spirit, by appro-
priating part of the price of your land?
4 As long as it was unsold was it not
yours, and after it was sold was not the
money under your control? How could
you think of doing such a thing? You
did not lie to men but to God!"
5 When Ananias heard these words he
fell down and expired, and everyone
who heard them spoken was appalled.
6 The younger men got up and wrapping
him up carried him out and buried him.
7 About three hours later, his wife came
in, without having learned what had
8 happened. Peter said to her,
"Tell me, did you sell the land for
such and such a sum?"
"Yes," she said, "that was it."
9 Peter said to her,
"How could you two agree to test the
Spirit of the Lord? There at the door
are the footsteps of the men who have
buried your husband, and they will
carry you out."
She instantly fell down at his feet 10
and expired. When the young men
came in they found her dead, and they
carried her out and buried her beside
her husband. And the whole church 11
and all who heard this were appalled.
They would all meet together in Solo- 12
mon's Colonnade. None of the others 13
dared to associate with them, but the
people made much of them, and men 14
and women in increasing numbers believed in the Lord and came over to
their side.
Signs and wonders in great numbers
continued to be done among the people
by their hands, so that people would 15
carry their sick right out into the
streets, and lay them down on beds and
mats, to have at least Peter's shadow
fall on some of them as he went by.
Even from the towns around Jerusalem 16
crowds would come in bringing sick people and those who were troubled with
foul spirits, and they were all cured.
This aroused the high priest and all 17
his supporters, the party of the Sadducees, and filled them with jealousy,
and they arrested the apostles and put 18
them in the common jail. But an angel 19
of the Lord opened the jail doors in the
night and let them out, and said to
them,
"Go, take your stand in the Temple, 20
and tell the people all about this new
life."
And they obeyed, and about day- 21
break went into the Temple and began
to teach. The high priest and his party
came over and called together the council and indeed the whole senate of the
Israelites, and sent to the prison to
have the apostles brought in. But the 22
attendants who went for them could
not find them in the jail, and they came
back and reported, 23
"We found the prison securely locked
up, with the sentries on duty at the
doors, but on opening the doors we
found no one inside."
When the commander of the Temple 24
and the high priests heard this report,
they were very much at a loss as to
what would come of it. Someone came 25
over and reported to them,
"The men that you put in jail are
standing right here in the Temple,
teaching the people!"

26 Then the commander and his men
went and brought them back, but without using violence, for they were afraid
27 of being stoned by the people. So they
brought them before the council and
the high priest questioned them.
28 "We strictly forbade you," he said,
"to teach on this authority, and here
you have filled Jerusalem with your
teaching, and propose to hold us responsible for this man's death!"
29 Peter and the apostles answered,
"We must obey God rather than
30 men. The God of our forefathers raised
Jesus to life when you had hung him
31 on a tree and killed him. God took
him up to his right hand as leader and
savior, in order to give repentance
32 and forgiveness of sins to Israel. We
and the holy Spirit which God has giv-
en to those who obey him are witnesses
to these things."
33 When they heard this, they were furi-
34 ous, and wanted to kill them. But a
Pharisee named Gamaliel, a teacher of
the Law highly regarded by all the people, got up in the council and ordered
35 the men to be removed for a while, and
then said,
"Men of Israel, take care what you
36 propose to do with these men. For
some time ago Theudas appeared,
claiming to be a person of importance,
and a group of men numbering some
four hundred joined him. But he was
killed and all his followers were dis-
37 persed and disappeared. After him, at
the time of the census, Judas of Galilee
appeared, and raised a following, but
he too perished, and all his followers
38 were scattered. So in the present case,
I tell you, keep away from these men
and let them alone, for if this idea or
movement is of human origin, it will
39 come to naught, but if it is from God,
you will not be able to stop it. You may
actually find yourselves fighting God!"
40 They were convinced by him, and
they called the apostles in and had
them flogged, and warned them not to
speak about the name of Jesus, and
41 then let them go. So they went out
from before the council, glad that they
had been thought worthy to bear dis-
42 grace for the sake of Jesus, and they
did not for a single day stop teaching
and preaching in the Temple and in
private houses the good news of Jesus,
the Christ.

In those days, as the number of the
disciples was increasing, complaints
were made by the Greek-speaking Jews
against the native Jews that their widows were being neglected in the daily
distribution of food. So the Twelve
called in the whole body of disciples
and said to them,
"It is not desirable that we should
give up preaching the word of God to
keep accounts. You, brothers, must
pick out from your number seven men
of good standing, who are wise and full
of the Spirit, and we will put them in
charge of this matter, while we devote
ourselves to prayer and to delivering
the message."
This plan met the approval of the
whole body, and they selected Stephen,
a man full of faith and of the holy
Spirit, with Philip, Prochorus, Nicanor,
Timon, Parmenas, and Nicholas of
Antioch, who had been a convert to
Judaism. They brought these men before the apostles, and they prayed and
laid their hands upon them.
So God's message continued to
spread; the number of the disciples in
Jerusalem increased rapidly, and a
great many priests accepted the faith.
Stephen, greatly strengthened by
God's favor, did remarkable signs and
wonders among the people. But members of the synagogue known as that of
the Libyans, Cyreneans, and Alexan-
drians, and men from Cilicia and Asia
undertook to debate with Stephen, but 10
they could not meet his wisdom and the
inspiration with which he spoke. So 11
they instigated people to say,
"We have heard him use abusive
language about Moses and about God."
They aroused the people, the elders, 12
and the scribes, and they set upon him
and seized him, and brought him before
the council. Then they brought forward 13
false witnesses, who said,
"This man is constantly saying
things against this holy place and
against the Law, for we have heard him 14
say that Jesus of Nazareth will tear
this place down and change the customs that have been handed down to us
by Moses."
Everyone who sat in the council fixed 15
his eyes on him, and they saw that his
face was like that of an angel. The high 7
priest said,
"Is this so?"

2 He answered,
"Brothers and fathers, listen. The
glorious God appeared to our forefather
Abraham when he was in Mesopotamia,
3 before he settled in Haran, and he said
to him, 'Leave your country and your
relatives and come to the country that
4 I will show you.' So he left the country
of the Chaldeans and went to live in
Haran, and from there after the death
of his father, God caused him to move
into this country where you now live.
5 He gave him no property in it, not a
single foot, but he promised to give it
to him and his posterity after him permanently, though he had no children at
6 that time. This was what God said:
'His descendants will be strangers, living in a foreign land, and they will be
enslaved and misused for four hundred
7 years, and I will sentence the nation
that has enslaved them,' God said, 'and
afterward they will leave that country
8 and worship me on this spot.' And he
made the agreement of circumcision
with him, and so Abraham became the
father of Isaac and circumcised him on
the eighth day, and Isaac became the
father of Jacob, and Jacob of the twelve
9 patriarchs. The patriarchs became jealous of Joseph and sold him into slavery
10 in Egypt. But God was with him, and
rescued him from all his troubles, and
enabled him to win favor and to show
wisdom when he stood before Pharaoh,
king of Egypt, and he appointed him
governor of Egypt and of his whole
11 household. Then a famine spread all
over Egypt and Canaan, and there was
great suffering, and our forefathers
12 could not find any food. But Jacob
heard that there was food in Egypt,
and he sent our forefathers on their
13 first visit there. On their second visit,
Joseph made himself known to his
brothers, and Pharaoh learned of Jo-
14 seph's parentage. Then Joseph sent and
15 invited his father Jacob and all his relatives, seventy-five in all, and Jacob
came down to Egypt. There he and our
16 forefathers died, and they were carried
back to Shechem, and laid in the tomb
that Abraham had bought for a sum of
money from the sons of Hamor in She-
17 chem. As the time drew near for the
fulfilment of the promise God had made
to Abraham, the people became more
18 and more numerous in Egypt, until another king, who knew nothing about
Joseph, became ruler of Egypt. He took 19
advantage of our people and oppressed
our forefathers, making them abandon
their infant children, so that they
should not live. It was at this time that 20
Moses was born. He was a wonderfully
beautiful child, and for three months he
was taken care of in his father's house.
When he was abandoned, the daughter 21
of Pharaoh adopted him and brought
him up as her own son. So Moses was 22
educated in all the Egyptian culture;
he was strong in speech and action.
When he was forty years old, it oc- 23
curred to him to visit his brothers, the
descendants of Israel. Seeing one of 24
them being imposed upon, he interfered
and defended the man who was being
ill treated, striking down the Egyptian.
He supposed that his brothers would 25
understand that God was using him as
the means of delivering them, but they
did not. The next day, he came across 26
two of them fighting and tried to pacify
them. He said to them, 'You are brothers. Why should you injure each other?'
But the aggressor thrust him off, say- 27
ing, 'Who made you our ruler and
judge? Do you mean to kill me as you 28
did that Egyptian yesterday?' At those 29
words Moses fled, and went and lived
for a time in Midian, and two sons were
born to him there. When forty years 30
had passed, an angel appeared to him in
the desert of Mount Sinai, in the flame
of a burning bush. When Moses saw it 31
he wondered at the sight, and when he
went up to see what it was, the voice of
the Lord said, 'I am the God of your 32
forefathers, the God of Abraham, Isaac,
and Jacob.' Moses was terrified and
did not dare to look at it. Then the 33
Lord said to him, 'Take off your shoes,
for the place where you are standing is
holy ground. I have certainly seen the 34
oppression of my people in Egypt, and
I have heard their groans, and I have
come down to save them. So come! I
will make you my messenger to Egypt!'
The Moses whom they had refused, 35
saying to him, 'Who made you our ruler
and judge?' God sent both to rule and
to deliver them, with the help of the
angel who had appeared to him in the
bush. It was he who brought them out 36
of Egypt, and did wonders and signs
there, and at the Red Sea, and for forty
years in the desert. This was the Moses 37
who said to the descendants of Israel,

'God will raise up a prophet for you
from among your brothers, just as he
38 raised me up.' It was he who with
the congregation in the desert went
between the angel who spoke to him
on Mount Sinai and our forefathers,
and received and communicated to
39 you utterances that still live. Yet
our forefathers would not listen to him,
but thrust him off, and their hearts
40 turned back to Egypt, for they said to
Aaron, 'Make us gods to march in front
of us, for as for this Moses, who brought
us out of Egypt, we do not know what
41 has become of him!' They even made a
calf in those days, and offered sacrifice
to their idol, and held a celebration over
42 what their own hands had made. So
God turned his back on them and left
them to worship the starry host, just as
the Book of the Prophets says,

"'Was it to me that you offered victims and sacrifices, O house of Israel,
Those forty years in the desert?
43 You took up the tent of Moloch and the star of your god Rompha,
The images you had made to worship!
So I will deport you beyond Babylon.'

44 In the desert our forefathers had the
Tent of the Testimony built like the
model Moses had seen, just as he who
45 spoke to him told him to make it. This
tent was handed down to our forefathers and they brought it here with
them when under Joshua they dispossessed the nations that God drove out
before them, and it existed until the
46 time of David. He won the approval of
God and begged to be allowed to provide a dwelling for the God of Jacob,
47 and Solomon actually built a house for
48 him. But the Most High does not live in
buildings made by human hands. As the
prophet says,

49 "'The sky is my throne,
And the earth a footstool for my feet.
What house can you build for me? says the Lord,
Or what place is there where I can rest?
50 Was it not my hand that made it all?

51 You stubborn people, with heathen
hearts and ears, you are always opposing the holy Spirit, just as your forefathers did! Which of the prophets did 52
your forefathers not persecute? They
killed the men who foretold the coming
of the Righteous One, whom you have
now betrayed and killed—you who had 53
the Law given to you by angels, and did
not obey it!"

When they heard that, they were en- 54
raged and ground their teeth at him.
But he, full of the holy Spirit, looked up 55
to heaven and saw God's glory and
Jesus standing at God's right hand.
And he said, 56

"Look! I can see heaven open, and
the Son of Man standing at God's right
hand!"

But they uttered a great shout and 57
stopped their ears, and they rushed
upon him all together, and dragged 58
him out of the city and stoned him, the
witnesses throwing down their clothes
at the feet of a young man named Saul.
As they stoned Stephen, he prayed, 59

"Lord Jesus, receive my spirit!"

Then falling on his knees, he cried 60
out,

"Lord, do not lay this sin up against
them!"

With these words he fell asleep. And 8
Saul entirely approved of his being put
to death.

A great persecution of the church in
Jerusalem broke out that day, and they
were all scattered over Judea and
Samaria except the apostles. Some pi- 2
ous men buried Stephen and loudly lamented him. But Saul harassed the 3
church. He went into one house after
another, and dragging out men and
women, put them in prison.

Those who were scattered went from 4
place to place preaching the good news
of the message. Philip reached the city 5
of Samaria, and proclaimed the Christ
to them. When the people heard Philip 6
and saw the signs that he showed they
were all interested in what he had to
say, for with loud cries foul spirits came 7
out of many who had been possessed
by them, and many paralytics and
lame people were cured. So there was 8
great rejoicing in that city.

There was a man named Simon in the 9
town, who had been amazing the Samaritan people by practicing magic
there, and making great pretensions.
Everyone there, high and low, made 10
much of him, and said,

"He must be what is known as the
Great Power of God!"
11 They made much of him because for
a long time he had amazed them with
12 his magic. But when they believed
Philip's preaching of the good news of
the Kingdom of God and the name of
Jesus Christ, men and women alike ac-
13 cepted baptism. Even Simon himself
believed and after his baptism attached
himself to Philip, and he was amazed at
seeing such signs and great wonders
taking place.
14 When the apostles at Jerusalem
heard that Samaria had accepted God's
message, they sent Peter and John
15 there. When they came, they prayed
that the Samaritans might receive the
16 holy Spirit, for it had not yet come
upon any of them; they had simply
been baptized in the name of the Lord
17 Jesus. Then they laid their hands on
them, and they received the holy Spirit.
18 But when Simon saw that the holy
Spirit was imparted through the laying
on of the apostles' hands, he offered
19 them money, saying,
"Give me also this power to communicate the holy Spirit to anyone I lay
my hands upon."
20 But Peter said to him,
"Go to destruction with your money,
for thinking you could buy God's gift
21 with it! You have no share or part in
this movement, for your heart is not
22 honest in the sight of God. So repent
of this wickedness of yours, and pray to
the Lord, to see if you may not be for-
23 given for thinking of such a thing. For
I see that you are a bitter poison and a
bundle of iniquity!"
24 Simon answered,
"You must pray to the Lord for me,
that none of the things you have said
may happen to me!"
25 After they had given their testimony
and delivered the Lord's message, they
went back to Jerusalem, telling the
good news in many Samaritan villages
on the way.
26 But an angel of the Lord said to
Philip,
"Get up and go south, by the road
that runs from Jerusalem to Gaza."
(The town is now deserted.)
27 So he got up and went. Now there
was an Ethiopian eunuch, a member of
the court of Candace, queen of Ethiopia, her chief treasurer, who had come
up to Jerusalem to worship, and was on 28
his way home. He was sitting in his car,
reading the prophet Isaiah. Then the 29
Spirit said to Philip,
"Go up and stay by that car."
Philip ran up and heard him reading 30
the prophet Isaiah, and he said to him,
"Do you understand what you are
reading?"
"Why, how can I," he answered, 31
"unless someone explains it to me?"
And he invited Philip to get in and sit
beside him. This was the passage of 32
Scripture that he was reading:
"Like a sheep he was led away to be
slaughtered,
And just as a lamb is dumb before
its shearer,
He does not open his mouth.
His sentence ended in his humilia- 33
tion.
Who will tell the story of his posterity?
For his life is perished from the
earth."
"Tell me, of whom is the prophet 34
speaking?" said the eunuch to Philip,
"Of himself, or of someone else?"
Then Philip began, and starting from 35
this passage, he told him the good news
about Jesus. As they went on along 36
the road, they came to some water, and
the eunuch said,
"Here is some water! What is there
to prevent my being baptized?"
So he ordered the car to stop, and 38
Philip and the eunuch both went down
into the water, and Philip baptized
him. When they came up out of the 39
water, the Spirit of the Lord hurried
Philip away, and the eunuch saw nothing more of him. Full of joy, he went on 40
with his journey, while Philip found
himself at Ashdod and went on telling
the good news in all the towns all the
way to Caesarea.
Now Saul, still breathing murderous 9
threats against the Lord's disciples,
went to the high priest, and asked him 2
for letters to the synagogues in Damascus, so that if he found any men or
women there who belonged to the Way,
he might bring them in chains to Jerusalem. But on his journey, as he was 3
approaching Damascus, a sudden light
flashed around him from heaven, and 4
he fell to the ground. Then he heard a
voice saying to him,

"Saul! Saul! Why do you persecute
me?"
5 "Who are you, sir?" he asked.
"I am Jesus, whom you are persecut-
6 ing," said the voice. "But get up and
go into the city, and there you will be
told what you ought to do."
7 Saul's fellow-travelers stood speech-
less, for they heard the voice but could
8 not see anyone. When Saul got up from
the ground and opened his eyes he could
see nothing. They had to take him by
the hand and lead him into Damascus,
9 and for three days he could not see, and
neither ate nor drank.
10 There was at Damascus a disciple
named Ananias, and the Lord said to
him in a vision,
"Ananias!"
And he answered,
"Yes, Lord!"
11 The Lord said to him,
"Get up and go to the street called
the Straight Street, and ask at the
house of Judas for a man named Saul,
from Tarsus, for he is there praying.
12 He has had a vision and seen a man
named Ananias come in and lay his
hands on him, to restore his sight."
13 But Ananias answered,
"Lord, I have heard many people tell
of this man, and the harm he has done
14 to your people in Jerusalem. He is here
with authority from the high priests to
arrest everyone who calls upon your
name."
15 The Lord said to him,
"Go! This man is the means I have
chosen for carrying my name among the
heathen and their kings, and among the
16 descendants of Israel. For I am going
to show him all he will have to endure for my sake."
17 Ananias set out and went to the
house, and there he laid his hands upon
Saul, and said to him,
"Saul, my brother, I have been sent
by the Lord Jesus, who appeared to
you on the road by which you came,
so that you may regain your sight and
be filled with the holy Spirit."
18 Something like scales immediately
dropped from his eyes, and his sight
was restored, and he got up and was
19 baptized, and, after taking some food,
regained his strength.
Saul stayed for some time with the
20 disciples at Damascus, and began at
once to declare in the synagogues that
Jesus was the Son of God. Everyone 21
who heard him was astonished, and said,
"Is not he the man who made such
havoc of the people in Jerusalem who
call upon that name, and who came
here especially for the purpose of arresting such persons and taking them before the high priests?"
But Saul grew more and more power- 22
ful, and bewildered the Jews who lived
in Damascus by his proofs that Jesus
was the Christ.
After some time had passed, the Jews 23
made a plot to kill him, but Saul found
out about the plot. They watched the 24
city gates day and night, in order to
kill him, but his disciples took him one 25
night and let him down over the wall,
lowering him in a basket.
When he reached Jerusalem he tried 26
to join the disciples, and they were all
afraid of him, for they could not believe
that he really was a disciple. But Bar- 27
nabas got hold of him and introduced
him to the apostles, and he told them
how on his journey he had seen the
Lord, and that he had spoken to him,
and how boldly he had spoken for the
cause of Jesus at Damascus. After that, 28
he associated with them freely in Jerusalem, and spoke boldly for the Lord's 29
cause, talking and debating with the
Greek-speaking Jews. But they tried
to kill him. When the brothers found 30
this out, they took him down to Caesarea, and sent him away to Tarsus.
So the church all over Judea, Galilee, 31
and Samaria was at peace and became
established. It lived in reverence for
the Lord and, stimulated by the holy
Spirit, it grew steadily in numbers.
As Peter was traveling about among 32
them all, he happened to visit God's
people at Lydda. There he found a man 33
named Aeneas, a paralytic who had
been bedridden for eight years. Peter 34
said to him,
"Aeneas, Jesus Christ cures you! Get
up, and make your bed!"
And he got up immediately. And 35
everybody who lived in Lydda and in
Sharon saw him, and they turned to the
Lord.
Among the disciples at Joppa there 36
was a woman named Tabitha, which is
in Greek Dorcas, that is, gazelle. She
had devoted herself to doing good and
to acts of charity. Just at that time it 37
happened that she had been taken ill

and had died, and they had washed her
body and laid her out in a room up-
38 stairs. As Joppa was near Lydda, the
disciples heard that Peter was there,
and they sent two men to him, urging
39 him to come over to them without delay. Peter went with them at once.
When he arrived, they took him up to
the room and all the widows stood
around him crying and showing him the
shirts and coats that Dorcas had made
40 when she was still with them. But
Peter put them all out of the room.
Then he knelt down and prayed, and
then turning to the body he said,
"Tabitha, stand up!"
She opened her eyes, and seeing
41 Peter, she sat up. He gave her his hand
and raised her to her feet, and calling
in the believers and the widows, he gave
42 her back to them alive. This became
known all over Joppa, and many came
43 to believe in the Lord. So it came about
that Peter stayed for some time in
Joppa, at the house of a tanner named
Simon.

10 There was at Caesarea a man named
Cornelius, a captain in what was known
2 as the Italian regiment. He was a devout man, who feared God, as did all
the members of his household. He was
liberal in charities to the people, and
3 always prayed to God. One afternoon,
about three o'clock, he had a vision,
and distinctly saw an angel of God
come into his room and say to him,
"Cornelius!"
4 He stared at him in terror, and said,
"What is it, sir?"
"Your prayers and charities," the angel answered, "have gone up and been
5 remembered before God. Now send
men to Joppa, for a man named Simon,
6 who is also called Peter. He is being
entertained at the house of a tanner
named Simon, which is close to the
sea."
7 When the angel who had spoken to
him was gone, Cornelius called two
of his servants, and a devout soldier
who was one of his personal attendants,
8 and after telling them the whole story,
sent them to Joppa.
9 The next day, while they were still
on their way, and were just getting
near the town, Peter went up on the
10 housetop about noon to pray. He got
very hungry, and wanted something to
eat. While they were getting it ready,
he fell into a trance, and saw the sky 11
opened and a thing like a great sheet
coming down, lowered to the ground by
the four corners, with all kinds of quad- 12
rupeds, reptiles, and wild birds in it.
And a voice came to him, 13
"Get up, Peter! Kill something and
eat it!"
But Peter said,
"Never, sir! For I have never eaten 14
anything that was common and unclean."
The voice came to him again a sec- 15
ond time,
"Do not call what God has cleansed
unclean."
This happened three times; then the 16
thing was taken right up into the sky.
While Peter was still wondering what 17
the vision he had had could mean, the
men whom Cornelius had sent had
asked the way to Simon's house and
reached the door, and they called out 18
to ask if Simon who was called Peter
was staying there. As Peter was pon- 19
dering over his vision, the Spirit said
to him,
"There are two men looking for you.
Get up and go down, and go with them 20
without any hesitation, for I have sent
them."
Then Peter went down to see the 21
men, and said to them,
"I am the man you are asking for.
What is the reason for your coming?"
They answered, 22
"Cornelius, who is a captain, and an
upright and God-fearing man, and who
has a good reputation with the whole
Jewish nation, was directed by a holy
angel to send for you to come to his
house, and to listen to what you have
to say."
So Peter invited them in and enter- 23
tained them. The next day he started
off with them, accompanied by some of
the brothers from Joppa, and the day 24
after, he reached Caesarea. Cornelius
had invited in his relatives and his intimate friends and was waiting for
them. When Peter actually arrived, 25
Cornelius met him and fell at his feet
and made obeisance to him. But Peter 26
raised him to his feet, and said,
"Get up! I am only human myself."
So he went in talking with him, 27
and he found that many people had
gathered, and he said to them, 28
"You know that it is against the Law

for a Jew to associate with a foreigner
or to visit one; but God has taught me
not to call anyone common or unclean.
29 That was why, when I was sent for, I
came without any hesitation. And now
I want to ask why you sent for me."
30 Cornelius answered,
"Three days ago, just at this time of
day, I was praying in my house about
three o'clock, when a man in dazzling
31 clothing stood before me, and said,
'Cornelius, your prayer has been heard,
and your charities have been recalled
32 to mind by God. So send to Joppa and
invite Simon who is called Peter to
come here. He is staying at the house
of a tanner named Simon, close to the
33 sea.' So I sent for you immediately,
and you have very kindly come. Now
we are all here in God's presence, to
hear everything that the Lord has instructed you to say."
34 Then Peter began and said,
"Now I really understand that God
35 shows no partiality, but welcomes the
man of any nation who reveres him and
does what is right. He has sent his mes-
36 sage to Israel's descendants, and made
the good news of peace known to them
through Jesus Christ. He is Lord of us
37 all. You know the story that has gone
all over Judea, starting from Galilee
after the baptism that John proclaimed,
38 about Jesus of Nazareth, and how God
endowed him with the power of the
holy Spirit, and he went about doing
good and curing all who were in the
power of the devil, because God was
39 with him. We are witnesses of everything that he did in the country of the
Jews and in Jerusalem. Yet they hung
40 him on a tree and killed him. But
God raised him to life on the third day
41 and caused him to be plainly seen, not
by all the people, but by witnesses
whom God had designated beforehand,
that is, by us, who ate and drank with
him after he had risen from the dead.
42 He also directed us to announce to the
people and bear solemn testimony that
he is the one whom God has appointed
to be the judge of the living and the
43 dead. It is of him that all the prophets
bear witness that everyone that believes in him will have his sins forgiven
through his name."
44 Before Peter had finished saying
these words, the holy Spirit fell on all
45 who were listening to his message. The
Jewish believers who had come with
Peter were amazed because the gift of
the holy Spirit had been showered upon
the heathen too, for they heard them 46
speaking in foreign languages and declaring the greatness of God. Then
Peter said,
"Can anyone refuse the use of water 47
to baptize these people when they have
received the holy Spirit just as we did?"
And he directed that they should be 48
baptized in the name of Jesus Christ.
Then they asked him to stay on there a
few days.
The apostles and brothers all over 11
Judea heard that the heathen had also
accepted God's message, and when 2
Peter returned to Jerusalem, the advocates of circumcision took him to task,
charging him with having visited and 3
eaten with men who were uncircumcised. Then Peter explained the matter 4
to them from beginning to end. He said,
"I was praying in the town of Joppa, 5
and while in a trance I had a vision.
Something like a great sheet came down
out of the sky, lowered by its four corners. It came right down to me, and 6
when I looked at it, I saw in it quadrupeds, wild animals, reptiles, and wild
birds. And I heard a voice say to me, 7
'Get up, Peter! Kill something and
eat it!' But I said, 'Never, sir! For 8
nothing that was common or unclean
has ever passed my lips.' Then the voice 9
from heaven answered again, 'Do not
call what God has cleansed unclean!'
This happened three times; then it was 10
all drawn back again into the sky. Just 11
at that moment three men, who had
been sent to me from Caesarea, reached
the house where we were staying, and 12
the Spirit told me not to hesitate to
go with them. These six brothers here
also went with me, and we went to
the man's house. Then he told us how 13
he had seen the angel stand in his house
and say, 'Send to Joppa for a man
named Simon who is also called Peter,
and he will tell you things that will 14
save you and your whole household.'
When I began to speak to them, the 15
holy Spirit fell upon them just as it did
upon us at the beginning, and I remem- 16
bered the saying of the Lord, 'John
baptized in water, but you will be
baptized in the holy Spirit.' So if God 17
had given them the same gift that we
received when we believed in the Lord

Jesus Christ, who was I, to be able to
interfere with God?"
18 When they heard this, they made no
further objection, but they gave honor
to God, and said,

"Then God has given even the heathen repentance and the hope of life!"

19 The fugitives from the persecution
that had broken out over Stephen went
all the way to Phoenicia, Cyprus, and
Antioch, but they told the message to
20 none but Jews. There were some men
from Cyprus and Cyrene among them,
however, who when they reached
Antioch spoke to the Greeks also, and
told them the good news about the Lord
21 Jesus. The Lord's hand was with them,
and there were a great many who be-
22 lieved and turned to the Lord. The
news about them came to the ears of
the church in Jerusalem, and they sent
23 Barnabas all the way to Antioch. When
he reached there and saw the favor God
had shown them, he was delighted, and
encouraged them all to be resolute and
steadfast in their devotion to the Lord,
24 for he was an excellent man, full of the
holy Spirit and faith. So a considerable
number of people came over to the
25 Lord. Then Barnabas went over to
26 Tarsus to look for Saul, and when he
found him he brought him to Antioch.
The result was that for a whole year
they met with the church, and taught
large numbers of people, and it was at
Antioch that the disciples first came to
be known as Christians.

27 About that time some prophets from
28 Jerusalem came down to Antioch, and
one of them named Agabus got up and
under the influence of the Spirit revealed the fact that there was going to
be a great famine all over the world.
This was the famine that occurred in
29 the reign of Claudius. The disciples
determined to make up a contribution,
each according to his ability, and send
it to the brothers who lived in Judea,
30 and this they did, sending it to the
elders by Barnabas and Saul.

12 About that time King Herod laid violent hands upon some who belonged to
2 the church. He had John's brother,
3 James, beheaded, and when he saw that
this gratified the Jews, he proceeded to
arrest Peter too, at the time of the fes-
4 tival of Unleavened Bread. He had
him seized and put in jail, with four
squads of soldiers to guard him, meaning after the Passover to bring him out
before the people. So Peter was kept in 5
the jail, but the church was praying
earnestly to God for him. The night 6
before Herod was going to bring him
out, Peter was asleep between two
soldiers, and fastened with two chains,
and watchmen were at the door, guard-
ing the jail, when an angel of the Lord 7
stood at his side, and a light shone in
the room, and striking Peter on the
side, he woke him, and said to him,

"Get up quickly!"

The chains dropped from his hands,
and the angel said to him, 8

"Put on your belt and your sandals!"

And he did so. Then he said to him,

"Put on your coat and follow me!"

So he followed him out without 9
knowing that what the angel was doing
was real, for he thought he was having
a vision. They passed the first guard 10
and then the second, and came to the
iron gate that led into the city. It
opened to them of itself, and they
passed out and went along one street,
when suddenly the angel left him. Then 11
Peter came to himself, and he said,

"Now I am certain that the Lord sent his angel and rescued me from the power of Herod and all that the Jewish people were expecting."

When he realized his situation, he 12
went to the house of Mary, the mother
of John who was also called Mark,
where a number of people were gathered, praying. When he knocked at the 13
outer door, a maid named Rhoda came
to answer it, and when she recognized 14
Peter's voice, in her joy she did not stop
to open the door, but ran in and told
them that Peter was standing outside.
But they said to her, 15

"You are mad!"

But she insisted that it was so. Then they said,

"Then it is his guardian angel!"

But Peter kept on knocking. And 16
when they opened the door and saw
him they were amazed. He motioned 17
to them to be quiet, and then related to
them how the Lord had brought him
out of the prison.

"Tell all this to James and the brothers," he said.

Then he left them and went somewhere else. But when morning came, 18
there was no little commotion among

the soldiers as to what could have be-
19 come of Peter. Herod had inquiries
made for him, and when he could not
find him, he examined the guards and
ordered them to be put to death. Then
he left Judea for Caesarea, and stayed
there.
20 Herod was very angry with the people of Tyre and Sidon. So they came
before him in a body, and after winning
over Blastus, the king's chamberlain,
they asked for a reconciliation, because
their country depended upon the king's
21 dominions for its food supply. So a day
was fixed and on it Herod, dressed in
his robes of state, took his seat on the
throne, and made them an address,
22 and the people shouted in applause,
"It is a god's voice, not a man's!"
23 But the angel of the Lord struck him
down immediately, because he did not
give the honor to God; and he was eaten
24 by worms and died. But the Lord's
message continued to grow and spread.
25 When Barnabas and Saul had performed their mission to Jerusalem, they
went back, taking John who was called
Mark with them.

13 There were at Antioch in the church
there a number of prophets and teachers—Barnabas, Symeon who was called
Niger, Lucius the Cyrenian, Manaen,
who had been brought up with Herod
2 the governor, and Saul. As they were
engaged in worshiping the Lord and in
fasting, the holy Spirit said,
"Set Barnabas and Saul apart for
me, for the work to which I have called
them."
3 So after fasting and prayer, they laid
their hands upon them and let them go.
4 Being sent out in this way by the
holy Spirit, they went down to Seleucia
5 and sailed from there to Cyprus. When
they reached Salamis, they proclaimed
God's message in the Jewish synagogues. They had John with them as
their assistant.
6 They went through the whole island
as far as Paphos, and there they came
across a Jewish magician and false
7 prophet named Barjesus. He was attached to the governor, Sergius Paulus,
who was an intelligent man. He sent
for Barnabas and Saul and asked them
8 to let him hear God's message. But
Elymas the magician—for that is the
meaning of his name—opposed them,
and tried to keep the governor from accepting the faith. But Saul, who was 9
also called Paul, was filled with the holy
Spirit, and looked at him and said, 10
"You monster of underhandedness
and cunning! You son of the devil!
You enemy of all that is right! Will
you never stop trying to make the
Lord's straight paths crooked? The 11
Lord's hand is right upon you, and you
will be blind and unable even to see the
sun for a time."
Instantly a mist of darkness fell upon
him, and he groped about for someone
to lead him by the hand. Then the 12
governor, seeing what had happened,
believed, and was thunderstruck at the
Lord's teaching.
Paul and his companions sailed from 13
Paphos and went to Perga in Pamphylia. There John left them and returned to Jerusalem, but they went on 14
from Perga and reached Antioch near
Pisidia. On the Sabbath they went to
the synagogue there and took seats.
After the reading of the Law and the 15
Prophets, the leaders of the synagogue
sent to them, saying,
"Brothers, if you have any appeal
to make to the people, proceed."
Then Paul got up, and motioning 16
with his hand, said,
"Men of Israel, and you who reverence God, listen! The God of this peo- 17
ple of Israel chose our forefathers, and
made the people great during their stay
in Egypt, and then with uplifted hand
led them out of Egypt. Then after he 18
had taken care of them for forty years
in the desert, he destroyed seven na- 19
tions in Canaan, and settled them upon
their land for about four hundred and
fifty years. After that he gave them 20
judges, down to the time of the prophet
Samuel. Then they demanded a king 21
and for forty years God gave them
Saul, the son of Kish, a man of the tribe
of Benjamin. Then he removed him and 22
raised David up to be their king, bearing this testimony to him: 'I have
found in David the son of Jesse a man
after my own heart, who will do all that
I desire.' It is from his descendants 23
that God has brought to Israel as he
promised to do, a savior in Jesus, in 24
preparation for whose coming John
had preached to all the people of Israel
baptism in token of repentance. To- 25
ward the end of his career, John said,

'What do you suppose that I am? I am
not he! No! Someone is coming after
me, the shoes on whose feet I am not
26 fit to untie!' Brothers! Descendants
of the house of Abraham, and those
others among you who reverence God!
It is to us that this message of salva-
27 tion has been sent. For the people of
Jerusalem and their leaders refused to
recognize him, and condemned him,
thus fulfilling the very utterances of the
prophets which are read every Sab-
28 bath, and though they could find no
ground for putting him to death, they
demanded of Pilate that he be executed.
29 When they had carried out everything
that had been said about him in the
Scriptures, they took him down from
30 the cross and laid him in a tomb. But
31 God raised him from the dead, and for
many days he appeared to those who
had come up to Jerusalem with him
from Galilee, and they are now wit-
32 nesses for him to the people. So we now
33 bring you the good news that God has
fulfilled to us, their children, the promise that he made to our forefathers, by
raising Jesus to life, just as the Scripture says in the second psalm, 'You are
my Son! Today I have become your
34 Father!' Now as evidence that he has
raised him from the dead, never again
to return to decay, he said this: 'I will
fulfil to you my sacred promises to Da-
35 vid.' For in another psalm he says,
'You will not let your Holy One under-
36 go decay.' Now David, after serving
God's purposes in his own generation,
fell asleep and was laid among his fore-
37 fathers and did undergo decay, but he
whom God raised to life did not under-
38 go it. You must understand therefore,
my brothers, that through him the forgiveness of your sins is announced to
39 you, and that through union with him
everyone who believes is cleared of
every charge of which the Law of Moses
40 could not clear you. Take care, therefore, that what is said in the prophets
does not prove true of you:

41 " 'Look, you scoffers! Then wonder and begone!
For I am doing something in your times
Which you will never believe even when it is related to you!' "

42 As they were going out, the people
begged to have all this said to them
again on the following Sabbath, and 43
after the congregation had broken up,
many of the Jews and the devout converts to Judaism went away with Paul
and Barnabas, and they talked with
them, and urged them to rely on the
favor of God.

The next Sabbath almost all the town 44
gathered to hear God's message. But 45
when the Jews saw the crowds, they
were very jealous, and they contradict-
ed what Paul said and abused him.
Then Paul and Barnabas spoke out 46
plainly, and said,

"God's message had to be told to
you first, but since you thrust it off and
judge yourselves unworthy of eternal
life, we now turn to the heathen. For 47
these are the orders the Lord has given
us:

" 'I have made you a light for the heathen,
To be the means of salvation to the very ends of the earth!' "

When the heathen heard this they 48
were delighted, and praised God's message, and all who were destined for
eternal life believed, and the Lord's 49
message spread all over the country.
But the Jews stirred up the well-to-do 50
religious women and the leading men of
the town, and they started a persecution against Paul and Barnabas, and
drove them out of their district. They 51
shook off the dust from their feet in
protest, and went to Iconium. But the 52
disciples continued to be full of joy and
of the holy Spirit.

At Iconium in the same way, they 14
went to the Jewish synagogue and
spoke with such power that a great
number of both Jews and Greeks believed. But the Jews who refused their 2
message stirred up the heathen and
poisoned their minds against the brothers. They spent some time there, 3
speaking fearlessly and relying upon
the Lord, who bore witness to his gracious message by letting signs and wonders be done by them. But the people 4
of the town were divided, some siding
with the Jews and some with the apostles. And when there was a movement 5
on the part of both the heathen and the
Jews with the authorities to insult and
stone them, and they became aware 6
of it, they made their escape to the
Lycaonian towns of Lystra and Derbe

7 and the country around, and there they
went on preaching the good news.
8 In the streets of Lystra a man used to
sit who had not the use of his feet. He
had been lame from his birth, and had
9 never been able to walk. He was listening to Paul as he talked, when Paul
looked at him and, seeing that he had
10 faith that he would be cured, said to
him loudly,
"Stand on your feet!"
And he sprang up and began to walk.
11 The crowds, seeing what Paul had done,
shouted in the Lycaonian language,
"The gods have come down to us in
human form!"
12 They called Barnabas Zeus, and
Paul, because he was the principal
13 speaker, Hermes. The priest of the
temple of Zeus that stood at the entrance to the town came with crowds of
people to the gates, bringing bulls and
garlands, meaning to offer sacrifice to
14 them. But when the apostles, Barnabas
and Paul, heard of it, they rushed into
15 the crowd, tearing their clothes and
shouting,
"Friends, why are you doing this?
We are only human beings like you,
and we bring you the good news that
you should turn from these follies to a
living God, who made heaven and
earth and sea and all that they con-
16 tain. In ages past he let all the heathen
17 follow their own ways; though he did
not fail to give some evidence about
himself, through his kindnesses to you,
in sending you rain from heaven and
fruitful seasons, giving you food and
happiness to your heart's content."
18 Even with these words they could
hardly restrain the people from offering
sacrifice to them.
19 But some Jews came from Antioch
and Iconium, and won the people over,
and they stoned Paul and dragged him
out of the town, thinking that he was
20 dead. But the brothers gathered about
him, and he got up and re-entered the
town. The next day he went on with
21 Barnabas to Derbe. They proclaimed
the good news in that town and made
a number of disciples. Then they returned to Lystra, Iconium, and Anti-
22 och, reassuring the disciples and encouraging them to stand by the faith
and reminding them that we have to
undergo many hardships to get into the
23 Kingdom of God. They appointed elders for them in each church, and with
prayer and fasting they committed
them to the Lord in whom they had believed. Then they crossed Pisidia and 24
entered Pamphylia. They told their 25
message in Perga, then went on to At-
talia, and from there they sailed back to 26
Antioch, where they had first been commended to God's favor for the work
which they had now finished. When 27
they arrived there, they called the
church together, and reported how God
had worked with them, and how he had
opened the way to faith for the hea- 28
then. There they stayed for a long time
with the disciples.

Some people came down from Judea **15**
and began to teach the brothers that
unless they were circumcised as Moses
prescribed, they could not be saved.
This created a disturbance and a seri- 2
ous discussion between Paul and Barnabas and them, and it was agreed that
Paul and Barnabas and some others of
their number should go up to Jerusalem
to confer with the apostles and elders
about this question.
The church saw them off upon their 3
journey, and as they traveled through
Phoenicia and Samaria they told of the
conversion of the heathen, and caused
great rejoicing among all the brothers.
When they reached Jerusalem, they 4
were welcomed by the church, the apostles, and the elders, and they reported
how God had worked with them. But 5
some members of the Pharisees' party
who had become believers got up and
said that such converts ought to be circumcised and told to obey the Law of
Moses.
The apostles and elders had a meet- 6
ing to look into this matter. After a 7
long discussion, Peter got up and said to
them,
"Brothers, you know that in the early
days God chose that of you all I should
be the one from whose lips the heathen
should hear the message of the good
news and believe it. And God who 8
knows men's hearts testified for them
by giving them the holy Spirit just as
he had done to us, making no difference 9
between us and them, but cleansing
their hearts by faith. Then why do you 10
now try to test God, by putting on the
necks of these disciples a yoke that
neither our forefathers nor we have
been able to bear? Why, we believe 11

that it is by the mercy of the Lord Jesus
that we are saved just as they are."
12 This quieted the whole meeting, and
they listened while Barnabas and Paul
told of the signs and wonders which
God had done among the heathen
13 through them. When they finished
James made this response:
14 "Brothers, listen to me. Symeon has
told how God first showed an interest
in taking from among the heathen a
15 people to bear his name. And this
agrees with the predictions of the
prophets which say,
16 " 'Afterward I will return, and rebuild David's fallen dwelling.
I will rebuild its very ruins, and set it up again,
17 So that the rest of mankind may seek the Lord,
And all the heathen who are called by my name,
18 Says the Lord, who has been making this known from of old.'
19 In my opinion, therefore, we ought not
to put obstacles in the way of those of
the heathen who are turning to God,
20 but we should write to them to avoid
anything that has been contaminated
by idols, immorality, the meat of strangled animals, and the tasting of blood.
21 For Moses for generations past has had
his preachers in every town, and has
been read aloud in the synagogues
every Sabbath."
22 Then the apostles and elders with the
whole church resolved to select representatives and send them with Paul and
Barnabas to Antioch. They were Judas
who was called Barsabbas, and Silas,
both leading men among the brothers.
23 They were the bearers of this letter:
"The apostles and the brothers who are
elders send greeting to the brothers of
heathen birth in Antioch, Syria, and
24 Cilicia. As we have heard that some of
our number, without any instructions
from us, have disturbed you by their
25 teaching and unsettled your minds, we
have unanimously resolved to select
representatives and send them to you
with our dear brothers Barnabas and
26 Paul, who have risked their lives for the
27 sake of our Lord Jesus Christ. So we
send Judas and Silas to you, to give
you this same message by word of
28 mouth. For the holy Spirit and we have
decided not to lay upon you any burden
29 but this indispensable one, that you
avoid whatever has been sacrificed to
idols, the tasting of blood and of the
meat of animals that have been strangled, and immorality. You will do well
to keep yourselves free from these
things. Goodbye."
So the delegates went down to Anti- 30
och and gathered the congregation together and delivered the letter; and 31
when they read it they were delighted
with the encouragement it gave them.
Judas and Silas were themselves proph- 32
ets, and gave the brothers much encouragement and strength by their
words. After they had stayed some 33
time, the brothers let them go, with a
greeting to those who had sent them.
But Paul and Barnabas stayed on in 35
Antioch and taught, and with many
others preached the good news of the
Lord's message.
Some time after, Paul said to Bar- 36
nabas,
"Come, let us go back and revisit the
brothers in each of the towns where we
made the Lord's message known, to see
how they are getting on."
Now Barnabas wanted to take John 37
who was called Mark with them. But 38
Paul did not approve of taking with
them a man who had deserted them in
Pamphylia instead of going on with
them to their work. They differed so 39
sharply about it that they separated,
and Barnabas took Mark and sailed for
Cyprus. But Paul selected Silas and set 40
out, the brothers commending him to 41
the Lord's favor. He traveled through
Syria and Cilicia and strengthened the
churches.
He went to Derbe and Lystra also. **16**
At Lystra there was a disciple named
Timothy whose mother was a Jewish
Christian while his father was a Greek,
and who was highly thought of by the 2
brothers in Lystra and Iconium. Paul 3
wished to take this man on with him,
and so on account of the Jews in that
district he had him circumcised, for
they all knew that his father was a
Greek. As they traveled on from one 4
town to another, they passed on to the
brothers for their observance the decisions that had been reached by the
apostles and elders at Jerusalem. So 5
the churches became stronger and
stronger in the faith, and their numbers
increased from day to day.
Thus they crossed Phrygia and Gala- 6

tia. The holy Spirit prevented them
from delivering the message in Asia,
7 and when they reached Mysia they
tried to get into Bithynia, but the Spir-
8 it of Jesus would not permit it, and
they passed Mysia and came down to
9 Troas. There Paul had a vision one
night; a Macedonian was standing appealing to him and saying,

"Come over to Macedonia and help
us."

10 As soon as he had this vision, we
made efforts to get on to Macedonia,
concluding that God had called us to
tell them the good news.

11 So we sailed from Troas, and ran a
straight course to Samothrace, and next
12 day to Neapolis. From there we went
to Philippi, a Roman garrison town,
and the principal place in that part of
Macedonia.

In this town we stayed for some days.
13 On the Sabbath we went outside the
gates, to the bank of the river where
we supposed there was a praying place,
and we sat down and talked with the
14 women who gathered there. One of our
hearers was a woman named Lydia, a
dealer in purple goods, from the town of
Thyatira. She was a believer in God,
and the Lord touched her heart, and led
15 her to accept Paul's teaching. When
she and her household were baptized,
she appealed to us, and said,

"If you are really convinced that I
am a believer in the Lord, come and
stay at my house." And she insisted
upon our coming.

16 Once as we were on our way to the
praying place a slave-girl met us who
had the gift of ventriloquism, and made
her masters a great deal of money by
her fortune-telling. This girl would follow Paul and the rest of us, crying out,

"These man are slaves of the Most
High God, and they are making known
to you a way of salvation."

18 She did this for a number of days,
until Paul, very much annoyed, turned
and said to the spirit in her,

"In the name of Jesus Christ I order
you to come out of her!" And it came
out instantly.

19 But when her masters saw that their
hopes of profits were gone, they seized
Paul and Silas, dragged them to the
20 public square, to the authorities, and
brought them before the chief magistrates.

"These men," they said, "are Jews,
and they are making a great disturbance in our town. They are advocating 21
practices which it is against the law for
us as Romans to adopt or observe."

The crowd also joined in the attack 22
on them, and the magistrates had them
stripped and beaten. After beating 23
them severely, they put them in jail,
and gave the jailer orders to keep close
watch of them. He, having had such 24
strict orders, put them into the inner
cell, and fastened their feet in the
stocks. But about midnight, as Paul 25
and Silas were praying and singing
hymns of praise to God, and the prisoners were listening to them, suddenly 26
there was such an earthquake that the
jail shook to its foundations; all the
doors flew open, and everybody's
chains were unfastened. It woke up the 27
jailer, and when he saw that the doors
of the jail were open, he drew his sword
and was just going to kill himself, supposing that the prisoners had escaped.
But Paul shouted out, 28

"Do not do yourself any harm! We
are all here!"

Then he called for lights and rushed 29
in, and fell trembling at the feet of Paul
and Silas. He led them out of the jail 30
and said to them,

"Gentlemen, what must I do to be
saved?"

"Believe in the Lord Jesus," they 31
said, "and you and your household will
be saved!"

Then they told God's message to him 32
and to all the members of his household. And right then in the night, he 33
took them and washed their wounds,
and he and all his household were baptized immediately. Then he took them 34
up to his house and offered them food,
and he and all his household were very
happy over their new faith in God. In 35
the morning the magistrates sent policemen with instructions to let the men
go. The jailer reported this message to 36
Paul, saying,

"The magistrates have sent orders
that you are to be released. So you can
take your leave and go unmolested."

But Paul said to them, 37

"They had us beaten in public without giving us a trial, and put us in jail,
although we are Roman citizens! And
now are they going to dismiss us secret-

ly? By no means! Have them come
here themselves and take us out!"
38 The policemen delivered this message to the magistrates, and they were
alarmed when they heard that they
39 were Roman citizens, and came and
conciliated them, and took them out of
the jail, and begged them to leave the
40 town. After leaving the jail they went
to Lydia's house, and saw the brothers
and encouraged them. Then they left
the town.

17 After passing through Amphipolis
and Apollonia, they reached Thessalonica, where the Jews had a synagogue.
2 Paul went to it as he was accustomed to
do, and for three Sabbaths he discussed
3 the Scriptures with them, explaining
them and showing that the Christ had
to suffer and rise from the dead.

"Jesus," he said, "of whom I am telling you, is the Christ!"

4 He convinced some of them, and
they joined Paul and Silas, along with a
great many devout Greeks and a num-
5 ber of the principal women. This offended the Jews and they gathered
some unprincipled loafers, formed a
mob and started a riot in the town.
They attacked Jason's house, to find
them and bring them out among the
6 people. As they could not find them,
they dragged Jason and some of the
brothers before the town magistrates,
shouting,

"The men who have made trouble all
7 over the world have come here too, and
Jason has taken them in. They all disobey the emperor's decrees, and claim
that someone else called Jesus is king."

8 The crowd and the magistrates were
9 very much excited at hearing this, and
they put Jason and the others under
bonds before they let them go.

10 The brothers sent Paul and Silas
away immediately, in the course of the
following night, to Berea. On arriving
there they went to the Jewish syna-
11 gogue. The Jews there were more highminded than those at Thessalonica, and
received the message with great eagerness and studied the Scriptures every
day, to find out whether it was true.
12 Many of them became believers and so
did no small number of Greek women
13 of position, and men too. But when the
Jews at Thessalonica found out that
God's message had been delivered at
Berea by Paul, they came there too, to
excite and stir up the populace. Then 14
the brothers immediately sent Paul off
to the coast, while Silas and Timothy
stayed behind. The men who went with 15
Paul took him all the way to Athens,
and came back with instructions for
Silas and Timothy to rejoin him as
soon as possible.

While Paul waited for them at 16
Athens, he was exasperated to see how
idolatrous the city was. He had discus- 17
sions at the synagogue with the Jews
and those who worshiped with them,
and every day in the public square
with any whom he happened to find.
Some of the Epicurean and Stoic philos- 18
ophers debated with him. Some of
them said,

"What is this rag-picker trying to
make out?"

Others said,

"He seems to be preaching some foreign deities."

This was because he was telling the
good news of Jesus and the resurrection. So they took him and brought 19
him to the council of the Areopagus and
said,

"May we know just what this new
teaching of yours is? Some of the 20
things you tell us sound strange to us,
and we want to know just what they
mean."

For all Athenians and all visitors 21
there from abroad used to spend all
their time telling or listening to something new.

Then Paul stood up in the middle of 22
the council and said,

"Men of Athens, from every point of
view I see that you are extremely religious. For as I was going about and 23
looking at the things you worship, I
even found an altar with this inscription: 'To an Unknown God.' So it is
what you already worship in ignorance
that I am now telling you of. God who 24
created the world and all that is in it,
since he is Lord of heaven and earth,
does not live in temples built by human
hands, nor is he waited on by human 25
hands as though he were in need of
anything, for he himself gives all men
life and breath and everything. From
one forefather he has created every na- 26
tion of mankind, and made them live
all over the face of the earth, fixing their
appointed times and the limits of their
lands, so that they might search for 27

God, and perhaps grope for him and
find him, though he is never far from
28 any of us. For it is through union with
him that we live and move and exist, as
some of your poets have said,
" 'For we are also his offspring.'
29 So if we are God's children we ought not
to imagine that the divine nature is like
gold or silver or stone, wrought by hu-
30 man art and thought. While God overlooked those times of ignorance, he now
calls upon all men everywhere to re-
31 pent, since he has fixed a day on which
he will justly judge the world through a
man whom he has appointed, and
whom he has guaranteed to all men by
raising him from the dead."
32 When they heard of the resurrection
of the dead, some of them sneered, but
others said,
"We should like to hear you again on
this subject."
33 So Paul left the council. Some per-
34 sons joined him, however, and became
believers, among them Dionysius, a
member of the council, and a woman
named Damaris, and some others.
18 After this he left Athens and went to
2 Corinth. There he found a Jew named
Aquila, a native of Pontus, who had recently come from Italy with his wife
Priscilla, because Claudius had ordered
all Jews to leave Rome. Paul went to
3 see them, and as they practiced the
same trade, he stayed with them, and
they worked together, for they were
4 tent-makers. Every Sabbath he would
preach in the synagogue, and try to
convince both Jews and Greeks.
5 By the time Silas and Timothy arrived from Macedonia, Paul was absorbed in preaching the message, emphatically assuring the Jews that Jesus
6 was the Christ. But as they contradict-
ed and abused him, he shook his clothes
in protest, and said to them,
"Your blood be on your own heads!
I am not to blame for it! After this I
will go to the heathen."
7 So he moved to the house of a worshiper of God named Titus Justus,
which was next door to the synagogue.
8 But Crispus, the leader of the synagogue, believed in the Lord, and so did
all his household, and many of the
people of Corinth heard Paul and be-
9 lieved and were baptized. One night the
Lord said to Paul in a vision,
"Do not be afraid! Go on speaking
and do not give up, for I am with you, 10
and no one shall attack you or injure
you, for I have many people in this
city."
So he settled there for a year and a 11
half, and taught them God's message.
When Gallio was governor of Greece 12
the Jews made a concerted attack upon
Paul, and brought him before the governor.
"This fellow," they said, "is trying 13
to induce people to worship God in
ways that are against the law."
Before Paul could open his lips, Gal- 14
lio said to the Jews,
"If some misdemeanor or rascality
were involved, Jews, you might reasonably expect me to listen to you. But as 15
it is only a question of words and titles
and your own law, you must look after
it yourselves. I refuse to decide such
matters."
And he drove them away from the 16
court. Then they all seized Sosthenes, 17
the leader of the synagogue, and beat
him in front of the court. But Gallio
paid no attention to it.
Paul stayed some time longer, and 18
then bade the brothers goodbye and
sailed for Syria, with Priscilla and
Aquila, after having his hair cut at
Cenchreae, because of a vow he had
been under. When they reached Ephe- 19
sus he left them there while he went to
the synagogue and had a discussion
with the Jews. They asked him to stay 20
longer, but he would not consent. He 21
bade them goodbye, saying,
"I will come back to you again if it is
God's will."
Then he sailed from Ephesus. When 22
he reached Caesarea, he went up to
Jerusalem and paid his respects to the
church, and then went on to Antioch.
After spending some time there, he 23
started out again, and traveled sys-
tematically through Galatia and Phrygia, reassuring all the disciples.
A Jew named Apollos, a native of 24
Alexandria, came to Ephesus. He was
an eloquent man, skilful in the use of
the Scriptures. He had had some in- 25
struction about the Way of the Lord,
and glowing with the Spirit he talked
and taught painstakingly about Jesus,
though he knew of no baptism but
John's. He spoke very confidently in 26
the synagogue at first, but when Priscilla and Aquila heard him, they took

him home and explained the Way of
27 God to him more correctly. As he
wanted to cross to Greece, the brothers
wrote to the disciples there, urging them
to welcome him. On his arrival there he
was of great service to those who
through God's favor had become be-
28 lievers, for he vigorously refuted the
Jews in public, and showed from the
scriptures that Jesus was the Christ.
19 It was while Apollos was in Corinth
that Paul, after passing through the interior, reached Ephesus. Finding some
2 disciples there, he said to them,
"Did you receive the holy Spirit
when you became believers?"
"No," they said to him, "we never
even heard that there was a holy Spirit."
3 "How then were you baptized?" he
asked.
"With John's baptism," they answered.
4 "John's baptism was a baptism in
token of repentance," said Paul, "and
he told the people to believe in him who
was to follow him, that is, in Jesus."
5 When they heard this, they were
baptized in the name of the Lord Jesus,
6 and when Paul laid his hands on them,
the holy Spirit came on them, and they
spoke in foreign tongues and with
7 prophetic inspiration. There were
about twelve of them in all.
8 He went to the synagogue there, and
for three months spoke confidently,
holding discussions and trying to persuade them about the Kingdom of God.
9 But as some of them were obstinate and
refused to believe, finding fault with the
Way before the people, he left them,
and withdrew the disciples, and held
daily discussions in the lecture-hall of
10 Tyrannus. This went on for two years,
so that everyone who lived in Asia,
Greeks as well as Jews, heard the Lord's
message.
11 God did such extraordinary wonders
12 by means of Paul, that people took to
the sick handkerchiefs or aprons he had
used, and they were cured of their diseases, and the evil spirits went out of
13 them. Some Jews who went from place
to place casting out demons tried to use
the name of the Lord Jesus in the cases
of people who had evil spirits in them,
saying,
"I command you in the name of Jesus whom Paul preaches!"

A Jewish high priest named Sceva 14
had seven sons who were doing this.
But the evil spirit answered, 15
"I know Jesus, and I know of Paul,
but who are you?"
And the man in whom the evil spirit 16
was sprang at them, and overpowered
them all, with such violence that they
ran out of the house tattered and
bruised. This came to be known to 17
everyone who lived in Ephesus, Greeks
as well as Jews, and great awe came
over them all, and the name of the Lord
Jesus came to be held in high honor.
Many who became believers would 18
come and confess and reveal their
former practices. A number of people 19
who had practiced magic brought out
their books and burned them publicly.
The value of these was estimated and
found to be ten thousand dollars. So 20
the Lord's message went on growing
wonderfully in influence and power.
After these events, Paul, under the 21
Spirit's guidance, resolved to go to Jerusalem, and to revisit Macedonia and
Greece on the way.
"After I have gone there," he said,
"I must see Rome also."
He sent two of his assistants, Timo- 22
thy and Erastus, to Macedonia, while
he stayed on for a while in Asia.
Just at that time a great commotion 23
arose about the Way. A silversmith 24
named Demetrius was making large
profits for his workmen by the manufacture of silver shrines of Artemis. He 25
got the workmen in that and similar
trades together, and said to them,
"Men, you know that this business is
the source of our prosperity, and you 26
see and hear that not only in Ephesus
but almost all over Asia, this man Paul
has persuaded and drawn away numbers of people, telling them that gods
made by human hands are not gods at
all. There is danger, therefore, not only 27
that this business of ours will be dis-
credited, but also that the temple of the
great goddess Artemis will be neglected
and the magnificence of her whom all
Asia and the world worship will be a
thing of the past!"
When they heard this, they became 28
very angry, and cried,
"Great is Artemis of Ephesus!"
So the commotion spread all over 29
the city, and by a common impulse the
people rushed to the theater, dragging

with them two Macedonians, Gaius and
Aristarchus, Paul's traveling compan-
30 ions. Paul wanted to go before the people himself, but the disciples would not
31 let him. Some of the religious authorities of Asia also, who were friends of his,
sent to him and begged him not to ven-
32 ture into the theater. Meanwhile the
people were shouting, some one thing
and some another, for the meeting was
in confusion, and most of them had no
33 idea why they had come together. Some
of the crowd called upon Alexander, as
the Jews had pushed him to the front,
and he made a gesture with his hand and
was going to speak to the people in their
34 defense. But when they saw that he was
a Jew, a great shout went up from them
all, and they cried for two hours,
"Great is Artemis of Ephesus!"
35 At last the recorder quieted the mob
and said,
"Men of Ephesus, who in the world
does not know that the city of Ephesus
is the guardian of the temple of the
great Artemis, and of the stone that
36 fell down from the sky? So as these
facts are undeniable, you must be calm,
37 and not do anything reckless. For you
have brought these men here, though
they have not been guilty of disloyalty
nor uttered any blasphemy against our
38 goddess. If Demetrius and his fellow-
craftsmen have a charge to bring
against anyone, there are the courts
and the governors; let them take legal
39 action. But if you require anything beyond that, it must be settled before the
40 regular assembly. For we are in danger
of being charged with rioting in connection with today's events, though
there is really nothing about this commotion that we will not be able to explain."
41 With these words he dismissed the
assembly.
20 When the confusion was over, Paul
sent for the disciples and encouraged
them. Then he bade them goodbye and
2 started for Macedonia. After traveling
through those districts and giving the
people a great deal of encouragement,
3 he went on to Greece where he stayed
for three months. Just as he was going
to sail for Syria, the Jews made a plot
against him, and he made up his mind
4 to return by way of Macedonia. He
was accompanied by Sopater of Berea,
the son of Pyrrhus, Aristarchus and Se-
cundus, from Thessalonica, Gaius of
Derbe and Timothy, and Tychicus and
Trophimus, from Asia. They went on 5
to Troas and waited for us there, while 6
we sailed from Philippi after the festival of Unleavened Bread, and joined
them at Troas five days later. There
we stayed a week.
On the first day of the week, when 7
we had met for the breaking of bread,
Paul addressed them, as he was going
away the next morning, and he prolonged his address until midnight.
There were a great many lamps in the 8
upstairs room where we met and a 9
young man named Eutychus, who was
sitting at the window, became very
drowsy as Paul went on talking, and
finally went fast asleep and fell from
the third story to the ground, and was
picked up for dead. But Paul went 10
downstairs, and threw himself upon
him, and put his arms around him.
"Do not be alarmed," he said, "he is
still alive."
Then he went upstairs again, and 11
broke the bread, and ate, and after a
long talk with them that lasted until
daylight, he went away. They took the 12
boy home alive, and were greatly comforted.
We had already gone on board the 13
ship and sailed for Assos, intending to
take Paul on board there, for that was
the arrangement he had made, as he intended to travel there by land. So 14
when he met us at Assos, we took him
on board and went on to Mitylene. Sail- 15
ing from there, we arrived off Chios on
the following day. On the next we
crossed to Samos, and on the next we
reached Miletus. For Paul had decided 16
to sail past Ephesus, so that he would
not have to lose any time in Asia, for he
was hurrying to reach Jerusalem, if possible, by the day of the Harvest Festival.
From Miletus he sent to Ephesus for 17
the elders of the church. When they 18
came, he said to them,
"You know well enough how I lived
among you all the time from the first
day I set foot in Asia, and how I served 19
the Lord most humbly and with tears,
through all the trials that I encountered because of the plots of the Jews.
I never shrank from telling you any- 20
thing that was for your good, nor from

teaching you in public or at your
21 houses, but earnestly urged Greeks as
well as Jews to turn to God in repentance
and to believe in our Lord Jesus.
22 I am here now on my way to Jerusalem,
for the Spirit compels me to go there,
though I do not know what will happen
23 to me there, except that in every town
I visit, the holy Spirit warns me that
imprisonment and persecution are
24 awaiting me. But my life does not matter,
if I can only finish my race and do
the service intrusted to me by the Lord
Jesus, of declaring the good news of
25 God's favor. Now I know perfectly
well that none of you among whom I
went about preaching the Kingdom of
26 God will ever see my face again. Therefore
I declare to you today that I am
not responsible for the blood of any of
27 you, for I have not shrunk from letting
you know God's purpose without re-
28 serve. Take care of yourselves and of
the whole flock, of which the holy Spirit
has made you guardians, and be shepherds
of the church of God, which he
29 got at the cost of his own life. I know
that after I am gone savage wolves will
get in among you and will not spare the
30 flock, and from your own number men
will appear and teach perversions of the
truth in order to draw the disciples
31 away after them. So you must be on
your guard and remember that for
three years, night and day, I never
stopped warning each one of you, even
32 with tears. Now I commit you to the
Lord, and to the message of his favor,
which will build you up and give you a
place among those whom God has con-
33 secrated. I have never coveted anyone's
34 gold or silver or clothes. You know well
enough that these hands of mine provided
for my needs and my compan-
35 ions. I showed you in every way that
by hard work like that we must help
those who are weak and remember the
words of the Lord Jesus, for he said, 'It
makes one happier to give than to be
given to.' "

36 With these words, he knelt down
37 with them all and prayed. They all
wept aloud, and throwing their arms
about Paul's neck they kissed him af-
38 fectionately, for they were especially
saddened at his saying that they would
never see his face again. Then they accompanied
him to the ship.

21 When the parting was over and we
had sailed, we made a straight run to
Cos and the next day to Rhodes and
from there to Patara. There we found 2
a ship bound for Phoenicia, and we
went on board and sailed on it. After 3
sighting Cyprus and leaving it on our
left, we sailed for Syria, and put in at
Tyre, for the ship was to unload her
cargo there. So we looked up the disci- 4
ples there and stayed a week with
them. Instructed by the Spirit, they
warned Paul not to set foot in Jerusalem. But when our time was up, we left 5
there and went on, and all of them with
their wives and children escorted us out
of the town. There we knelt down on
the beach and prayed; then we bade 6
one another goodbye, and we went on
board the ship, and they went home.

After making the run from Tyre, we 7
landed at Ptolemais, where we greeted
the brothers and spent a day with
them. The next day we left there and 8
went on to Caesarea, where we went
to the house of Philip the missionary,
who was one of the Seven, and stayed
with him. He had four unmarried 9
daughters who had the gift of prophecy.
We spent a number of days there, and 10
in the course of them a prophet named
Agabus came down from Judea. He 11
came to see us and took Paul's belt and
bound his own feet and hands with it,
and said,

"This is what the holy Spirit says:
'The Jews at Jerusalem will bind the
man who owns this belt like this, and
will hand him over to the heathen!' "

When we heard this, we and the peo- 12
ple there begged him not to go up to
Jerusalem. Then Paul answered, 13

"What do you mean by crying and
breaking my heart? I am ready not
only to be bound at Jerusalem but to
die there for the sake of the Lord Jesus."

So as he would not yield, we gave up 14
urging him, and said,

"The Lord's will be done!"

After those days we made our prepa- 15
rations and started for Jerusalem. Some 16
of the disciples from Caesarea went
with us and took us to the house of
Mnason, a man from Cyprus, one of
the early disciples, to spend the night.
When we reached Jerusalem, the bro- 17
thers there gave us a hearty welcome.
On the next day we went with Paul to 18
see James, and all the elders came in.

19 Paul greeted them warmly and gave a
detailed account of what God had done
among the heathen through his efforts.
20 They praised God when they heard it,
and they said to him,
"You see, brother, how many thousand believers there are among the
Jews, all of them zealous upholders of
21 the Law. They have been told that you
teach all Jews who live among the
heathen to turn away from Moses, and
that you tell them not to circumcise
their children nor to observe the old
22 customs. What then? They will be
23 sure to hear that you have come. So do
what we tell you. We have four men
24 here who are under a vow. Join them,
undergo the rites of purification with
them, and pay their expenses so that
they can have their heads shaved.
Then everybody will understand that
there is no truth in the stories about
you, but that you yourself observe the
25 Law. As for the heathen who have become believers, we have written them
our decision that they must avoid anything that has been contaminated by
idols, the tasting of blood, the meat of
strangled animals, and immorality."
26 Then Paul joined the men and went
through the rites of purification with
them and the next day went to the
Temple to give notice of the time when,
upon the offering of the sacrifice for
each one of them, their days of purification would be over.
27 The seven days were almost over
when the Jews from Asia caught sight
of him in the Temple, and stirred up all
28 the crowd and seized him, shouting,
"Men of Israel, help! This is the man
who teaches everybody everywhere
against our people and the Law and
this place, and besides he has actually
brought Greeks into the Temple and
desecrated this sacred place."
29 For they had previously seen Trophimus of Ephesus with him in the city,
and they supposed that Paul had
30 brought him into the Temple. The
whole city was thrown into confusion,
and the people hurried together, and
seized Paul and dragged him outside of
the Temple, the gates of which were im-
31 mediately shut. They were trying to
kill him when the news reached the colonel of the regiment that all Jerusalem
32 was in a tumult. He immediately got
some officers and men and hurried down
among them, and when they saw the
colonel and the soldiers they stopped
beating Paul. Then the colonel came 33
up and arrested him, and ordered him
to be bound with two chains, and then
inquired who he was and what he had
been doing. Some of the crowd shouted
one thing and some another, and as he
could not find out the facts on account
of the confusion, he ordered him to be
taken into the barracks. When Paul 35
got to the steps, he was actually carried
by the soldiers, on account of the vio- 36
lence of the mob, for the mass of people
followed them shouting,
"Kill him!"
Just as they were going to take him 37
into the barracks, Paul said to the
colonel,
"May I say something to you?"
"Do you know Greek?" the colonel
asked. "Are you not the Egyptian who 38
some time ago raised the four thousand
cut-throats and led them out into the
desert?"
"I am a Jew," Paul answered, "from 39
Tarsus, in Cilicia, a citizen of no insignificant city. I beg you to let me speak
to the people."
He gave him permission, and Paul 40
standing on the steps made a gesture to
the people, and when they had become
quiet he spoke to them in Hebrew.
"Brothers and fathers," he said, "lis- 22
ten to what I have to say in my defense."
When they heard him speak to them 2
in Hebrew, they became even more
quiet, and he said,
"I am a Jew, and I was born in Tar- 3
sus in Cilicia, but was brought up here
in this city, and thoroughly educated
under the teaching of Gamaliel in the
Law of our forefathers. I was zealous
for God, just as all of you are today. I 4
persecuted this Way even to the death,
and bound both men and women and
put them in prison, as the high priest 5
and the whole council will bear me witness. In fact, they gave me letters to
the brothers in Damascus and I went
there to bind those who were there and
bring them back to Jerusalem to be
punished. But on my way, as I was ap- 6
proaching Damascus, suddenly about
noon, a blaze of light flashed around
me from heaven, and I fell upon the 7
ground and heard a voice say to me,
'Saul! Saul! Why do you persecute

8 me?' I answered, 'Who are you, sir?'
'I am Jesus of Nazareth,' he said,
9 'whom you are persecuting.' The men
who were with me saw the light, but
they did not hear the voice of the one
10 who was speaking to me. Then I said,
'What am I to do, sir?' The Lord said
to me, 'Get up and go into Damascus.
There you will be told of all you are des-
11 tined to do.' As I could not see, because of the dazzling light, my companions had to lead me by the hand,
12 and so I reached Damascus. There a
man named Ananias, a devout observer
of the Law, highly respected by all the
13 Jews who lived there, came to see me,
and standing by my side, said to me,
'Saul, my brother, regain your sight!'
Then instantly I regained my sight and
14 looked at him, and he said, 'The God of
our forefathers has appointed you to
learn his will and to see his Righteous
15 One and hear him speak, for you shall
be his witness before all men of what
16 you have seen and heard. And now,
why do you delay? Get up and be baptized, and wash away your sins, calling
17 on his name.' After I had returned to
Jerusalem, one day when I was praying
18 in the Temple, I fell into a trance, and
saw him saying to me, 'Make haste and
leave Jerusalem at once, for they will
not accept your evidence about me.'
19 And I said, 'Lord, they know that I
used to go through one synagogue after
another, and to imprison and flog those
20 who believed in you, and when the
blood of your witness Stephen was being shed, I stood by and approved it,
and took charge of the clothes of the
21 men who killed him.' But he said to
me, 'Go! I will send you far away to
the heathen.' "

22 They had listened to him until he
said that, but then they shouted,

"Kill him and get him out of the
world! A creature like that ought not
to be allowed to live!"

23 As they were shouting and throwing
their clothes about and flinging dust in-
24 to the air, the colonel ordered Paul
brought into the barracks, and gave directions that he should be examined
under the lash, so that he might find
out why they made such an outcry
25 against him. But when they had
strapped him up, Paul said to the officer who was standing near,

"Is it legal for you to flog a Roman
citizen, and without giving him a
trial?"

Upon hearing this, the officer went to 26
the colonel and reported it.

"What do your propose to do?" he
said. "This man is a Roman citizen."

Then the colonel came to Paul and 27
said,

"Tell me, are you a Roman citizen?"

"Yes," he said.

"I had to pay a large sum for my 28
citizenship," said the colonel.

"But I am a citizen by birth," said
Paul.

Then the men who had been going to 29
examine him immediately left him, and
the colonel himself was alarmed to find
that Paul was a Roman citizen and
that he had had him bound.

The next day, as he wished to find 30
out the real reason why the Jews denounced him, he had him unbound and
ordered the high priests and the whole
council to assemble, and took Paul
down and brought him before them.
Paul looked steadily at the council and **23**
said,

"Brothers, I have done my duty to
God with a perfectly clear conscience
up to this very day."

At this the high priest Ananias or- 2
dered the people who were standing
nearest to him to strike him on the
mouth. Then Paul said to him, 3

"God will strike you, you white-
washed wall! Do you sit there to try
me by the Law, and order them to
strike me in violation of the Law?"

But the people who stood near him 4
said,

"Do you mean to insult God's high
priest?"

"I did not know, brothers," said 5
Paul, "that he was high priest, for the
Scripture says, 'You shall not say anything against any ruler of your people.' "

Knowing that part of them were Sad- 6
duces and part of them Pharisees, Paul
called out in the council,

"Brothers, I am a Pharisee, and the
son of Pharisees! It is for my hope for
the resurrection of the dead that I am
on trial!"

When he said that, a dispute arose 7
between the Pharisees and the Sadducees, and the meeting was divided. For 8
the Sadducees hold that there is no
resurrection and that there are no an-

gels or spirits, while the Pharisees be-
9 lieve in all three. So there was a great
uproar, and some scribes of the Pharisees' party got up and insisted,
"We find nothing wrong with this
man. Suppose some spirit or angel really spoke to him!"
10 As the dispute was becoming violent,
the colonel began to be afraid that they
would tear Paul in pieces, and ordered
the soldiers to go down and get him
away from them and bring him into the
barracks.
11 On the following night the Lord
stood beside him and said,
"Courage! For just as you have testified for me in Jerusalem, you must
testify in Rome also."
12 In the morning, the Jews made a
conspiracy and took an oath not to eat
13 or drink till they had killed Paul. There
were more than forty of them involved
14 in this plot, and they went to the high
priests and elders and said to them,
"We have taken a solemn oath not to
touch anything to eat till we have killed
15 Paul. Now you and the council must
suggest to the colonel that he should
have Paul brought down to you, as
though you meant to look into his case
more carefully, and we will be ready to
kill him before he gets down."
16 But Paul's nephew heard of the plot,
and he came and got into the barracks,
17 and told Paul. Paul called one of the
officers and said to him,
"Take this young man to the colonel,
for he has something to tell him."
18 So he took him to the colonel, and
said,
"The prisoner Paul called me to him
and asked me to bring this young man
to you, as he has something to say to
you."
19 So the colonel took him by the arm
and stepping aside where they could be
alone, asked,
"What is it that you have to tell
me?"
20 "The Jews," he answered, "have
agreed to ask you to bring Paul down
to the council tomorrow, with the intention of having a fuller inquiry
21 made into his case. But do not let
them persuade you, for more than forty
of them are lying in wait for him, and
they have taken an oath not to eat or
drink till they have killed him. They

are all ready now, and are only waiting
to get your promise."
So the colonel sent the youth away, 22
directing him not to tell anyone that he
had given him this information. Then 23
he called in two of his officers and said
to them,
"Get two hundred men ready to
march to Caesarea, with seventy
mounted men and two hundred spear-
men, by nine o'clock tonight." They 24
were also to provide horses for Paul to
ride, so that they might take him in
safety to Felix, the governor, to whom 25
he wrote a letter to this effect:
"Claudius Lysias sends greetings to 26
his Excellency Felix, the governor.
This man had been seized by the Jews 27
and they were just going to kill him
when I came upon them with my men
and rescued him, as I had learned that
he was a Roman citizen. As I wanted 28
to learn what charge they made against
him, I had him brought before their
council, and found that their accusa- 29
tions had to do with questions about
their Law, but that he was not charged
with anything that would call for his
death or imprisonment. As I have been 30
informed that a plot against him is
brewing, I am sending him on to you at
once, and directing his accusers to present their charges against him before
you."
Then the soldiers took Paul, as they 31
had been ordered to do, and escorted
him as far as Antipatris that night. The 32
next day, they returned to the barracks, leaving the mounted men to go
on with him, and they on reaching Caes- 33
area delivered the letter to the governor and handed Paul over to him.
After reading the letter, he asked Paul 34
what province he belonged to, and
when he learned that he was from Cilicia, he said, 35
"I will hear your case as soon as your
accusers arrive."
And he gave orders that he should be
kept in Herod's palace.
Five days later, the high priest Ana- 24
nias came down with some of the elders
and an attorney named Tertullus, and
they presented their case against Paul
before the governor. When Paul had 2
been summoned, Tertullus began the
prosecution.
"Your Excellency Felix," he said,
"since through your efforts we enjoy

perfect peace, and through your fore-
sight this nation is securing needed re-
3 forms, we always and everywhere acknowledge this with profound grati-
4 tude. But—not to detain you too long
—I beg you to be kind enough to give
5 us a brief hearing. For we have found
this man a pest and a disturber of the
peace among Jews all over the world.
He is a ringleader of the Nazarene sect,
6 and actually tried to desecrate the
8 Temple, but we caught him. If you will
examine him yourself you will be able
to find out from him all about the
things we charge him with."
9 The Jews also joined in these charges,
and said that the statement was true.
10 The governor made a sign to Paul to
speak, and he answered,
"As I know that for many years you
have acted as judge for this nation, I
11 cheerfully undertake my defense, for it
is not more than twelve days ago, as
you can easily satisfy yourself, that I
12 went up to worship at Jerusalem, and
they have never found me debating
with anyone in the Temple, or creating
a disturbance among the people in the
13 synagogues or about the city, and they
cannot sustain the charges they have
14 just made against me. I admit that in
worshiping the God of my forefathers I
follow the way of life that they call a
sect, but I believe everything that is
taught in the Law or written in the
15 prophets, and I have the same hope in
God that they themselves hold, that
there is to be a resurrection of the up-
16 right and the wicked. Therefore I strive
always to have a clear conscience be-
17 fore God and men. After an absence of
several years, I had come to bring charitable donations for my nation, and to
offer sacrifice. I had undergone the rites
of purification and was occupied with
these matters when they found me in
the Temple, with no crowd or disturb-
18 ance at all. But there were some Jews
19 from Asia who ought to be here before
you and to present their charges if they
20 have any to make against me. Or let
these men themselves tell what they
found wrong in me when I appeared be-
21 fore the council—unless it was the one
thing I shouted out as I stood among
them—'It is on the question of the resurrection of the dead that I am here on
trial before you today!'"
22 Then Felix, who was somewhat well
informed about the Way, adjourned the
trial, telling them,
"When Lysias, the colonel, comes
down here, I will decide your case."
He ordered the officer to keep Paul 23
in custody, but to allow him some
liberty, and not to prevent his friends
from looking after him.
Some days later Felix came with his 24
wife Drusilla, who was a Jewess, and
sent for Paul and heard what he had to
say about faith in Christ Jesus. But as 25
he talked of uprightness, self-control,
and the coming judgment, Felix became
alarmed, and said,
"You may go for the present. I will
find time later to send for you."
At the same time he hoped to get 26
money from Paul, and for that reason
he used to send for him very often and
talk with him.
But when two whole years had 27
passed, Felix was succeeded by Porcius
Festus, and as he wanted to gratify the
Jews, Felix left Paul in prison.
Three days after his arrival in the **25**
province, Festus went up from Caesarea to Jerusalem, and the high priests 2
and Jewish leaders presented their
charges against Paul, and begged him 3
as a favor to order Paul to come to Jerusalem, plotting to kill him on the
way. Festus answered that Paul was 4
being kept in custody at Caesarea, and
that he himself was going there soon.
"So have your principal men go down 5
with me," he said, "and present charges
against the man, if there is anything
wrong with him."
After staying only eight or ten days 6
there, he went down to Caesarea, and
the next day took his seat on the bench,
and ordered Paul brought in. When he 7
came, the Jews who had come down
from Jerusalem surrounded him, and
made a number of serious charges
against him, which they could not
substantiate. Paul said in his own de- 8
fense,
"I have committed no offense against
the Jewish Law or the Temple or the
emperor."
Then Festus, wishing to gratify the 9
the Jews, said to Paul,
"Will you go up to Jerusalem and be
tried there before me on these
charges?"
But Paul said, 10
"I am standing before the emperor's

court, where I ought to be tried. I have
done the Jews no wrong, as you can eas-
11 ily see. If I am guilty and have done
anything that deserves death, I do not
refuse to die; but if there is no truth in
the charges that these men make
against me, no one can give me up to
them; I appeal to the emperor."
12 Then Festus after conferring with
the council answered,
"You have appealed to the emperor,
and to the emperor you shall go!"
13 Some time after, King Agrippa and
Bernice came to Caesarea on a state
14 visit to Festus, and as they stayed
there several days, Festus laid Paul's
case before the king.
"There is a man here," he said, "who
15 was left in prison by Felix, and when I
was at Jerusalem the Jewish high
priests and elders presented their case
against him, and asked for his convic-
16 tion. I told them that it was not the
Roman custom to give anybody up until the accused met his accusers face to
face and had a chance to defend himself
17 against their accusations. So they came
back here with me and the next day
without losing any time I took my
seat on the bench and ordered the
18 man brought in. But when his accusers got up, they did not charge him
with any such crimes as I had expected.
19 Their differences with him were about
their own religion and about a certain
Jesus who had died but who Paul said
20 was alive. I was at a loss as to how to
investigate such matters, and I asked
him if he would like to go to Jerusalem
and be tried on these charges there.
21 But Paul appealed to have his case reserved for his Majesty's decision, and I
have ordered him kept in custody until
I can send him to the emperor."
22 "I should like to hear the man myself," Agrippa said to Festus.
"You shall hear him tomorrow," Festus answered.
23 So the next day, Agrippa and Bernice came with great pomp and went
into the audience-room attended by
officers and the leading citizens of the
town, and at the command of Festus
24 Paul was brought in. Then Festus said,
"King Agrippa and all who are present, you see here the man about whom
the whole Jewish people have applied
to me both at Jerusalem and here,
clamoring that he ought not to live any
longer. I could not find that he had 25
done anything for which he deserved
death, but as he appealed to his Majesty I decided to send him to him. Yet I 26
have nothing definite to write to our
sovereign about him. So I have brought
him before you all, and especially before you, King Agrippa, in order to get
from your examination of him something to put in writing. For it seems to 27
me absurd to send a prisoner on, without stating the charges against him."
Then Agrippa said to Paul, 26
"You are at liberty to speak in your
own defense."
So Paul stretched out his hand and
began his defense.
"I think myself fortunate, King 2
Agrippa," said he, "that it is before you
that I am to defend myself today
against all the things the Jews charge
me with, especially because you are so 3
familiar with all the Jewish customs
and questions. I beg you, therefore, to
listen to me with patience. The way I 4
lived from my youth up, spending my
early life among my own nation and at
Jerusalem, is well known to all Jews, for 5
they have known from the first, if they
are willing to give evidence, that I was
a Pharisee and my life was that of the
strictest sect of our religion. Even now 6
it is for my hope in the promise that
God made to our forefathers that I
stand here on trial, the promise in the 7
hope of seeing which fulfilled our twelve
tribes serve God zealously night and
day. It is about this hope, your Majesty, that I am accused by some Jews.
Why do you think it incredible that 8
God should raise the dead? I once 9
thought it my duty vigorously to oppose the cause of Jesus of Nazareth.
That was what I did at Jerusalem when 10
on the authority of the high priests I
put many of God's people in prison.
When they were put to death, I cast my 11
vote against them, and many a time in
all the synagogues I had them punished, and tried to force them to say
impious things. In my mad rage
against them I even pursued them to
distant towns. I was once going to 12
Damascus on this business, authorized
and commissioned by the high priests,
when on the road at noon, your Majes- 13
ty, I saw a light from heaven brighter
than the sun flash around me and my
fellow-travelers. We all fell to the 14

ground, and I heard a voice say to me
in Hebrew, 'Saul! Saul! Why do you
persecute me? You cannot kick against
15 the goad!' 'Who are you, sir?' said I.
The Lord said, 'I am Jesus, whom you
16 are persecuting. But get up and stand
on your feet, for I have appeared to you
for the express purpose of appointing
you to serve me and to testify to what
you have seen and to the visions you
17 will have of me. I will save you from
your people and from the heathen, to
18 whom I will send you to open their
eyes and turn them from darkness to
light and from Satan's control to God,
so that they may have their sins forgiven and have a place among those
who are consecrated through faith in
19 me.' Therefore, King Agrippa, I did
20 not disobey that heavenly vision, but
first to the people of Damascus and Jerusalem and then all over Judea, and
even to the heathen I preached that
they must repent and turn to God
and live as men who have repented
21 should. That is why the Jews seized
me in the Temple and tried to kill me.
22 To this day I have had God's help and
I stand here to testify to high and low
alike, without adding a thing to what
Moses and the prophets declared would
23 happen, if the Christ was to suffer and
by being the first to rise from the dead
was to proclaim the light to our people
and to the heathen."

24 As he said this in his defense, Festus
called out,

"You are raving, Paul! Your great
learning is driving you mad!"

25 "I am not raving, your Excellency
Festus," said Paul, "I am telling the
26 sober truth. The king knows about
this, and I can speak to him with freedom. I do not believe that he missed
any of this, for it did not happen in a
27 corner! King Agrippa, do you believe
the prophets? I know that you do!"

28 "You are in a hurry to persuade me
and make a Christian of me!" Agrippa
said to Paul.

29 "In a hurry or not," said Paul, "I
would to God that not only you, but all
who hear me today, might be what I
am—except for these chains!"

30 Then the king rose, with the governor and Bernice and those who had sat
31 with them, and after leaving the room,
in talking the matter over together, they
said,

"This man has not done anything to
deserve death or imprisonment."

"He might have been set at liberty," 32
said Agrippa to Festus, "if he had not
appealed to the emperor."

When it was decided that we were to 27
sail for Italy, Paul and some other prisoners were turned over to an officer of
the Imperial regiment, named Julius.
We went on board an Adramyttian ship 2
bound for the ports of Asia, and put to
sea. We had a Macedonian from Thessalonica, named Aristarchus, with us.
The next day we put in at Sidon, and 3
Julius kindly allowed Paul to go and see
his friends and be taken care of. Put- 4
ting to sea from there, we sailed under
the lee of Cyprus, as the wind was
against us, and after traversing the Ci- 5
lician and Pamphylian waters, we
reached Myra in Lycia. There the offi- 6
cer found an Alexandrian ship bound
for Italy, and put us on board. For a 7
number of days we made slow progress
and had some difficulty in arriving off
Cnidus. Then as the wind kept us from
going on, we sailed under the lee of
Crete, off Cape Salmone, and with 8
difficulty coasted along it and reached
a place called Fair Havens, near the
town of Lasea.

As a great deal of time had now 9
passed, and navigation had become
dangerous, for the autumn fast was already over, Paul began to warn them.

"Gentlemen," he said, "I see that 10
this voyage is likely to end in disaster
and heavy loss, not only to ship and
cargo but to our own lives also."

But the officer was more influenced 11
by the pilot and the captain than by
what Paul had to say, and as the harbor 12
was not fit to winter in, the majority
favored putting to sea again, in the
hope of being able to reach and winter
in Phoenix, a harbor in Crete facing
west-south-west and west-north-west.
When a moderate south wind sprang 13
up, thinking their object was within
reach, they weighed anchor, and ran
close along the coast of Crete. But very 14
soon a violent wind which they call a
Northeaster rushed down from it. The 15
ship was caught by it and could not
face the wind, so we gave way and let
her run before it. As we passed under 16
the lee of a small island called Cauda,
we managed with great difficulty to secure the ship's boat. After hoisting it 17

on board, they used ropes to brace the
ship, and as they were afraid of being
cast on the Syrtis banks, they lowered
18 the sail, and let the ship drift. The
next day, as the storm continued to be
violent, they began to throw the cargo
19 overboard, and on the next, they threw
the ship's tackle overboard with their
20 own hands. For a number of days neither the sun nor the stars were visible,
and the storm continued to rage, until
at last we gave up all hope of being
21 saved. Then, when they had gone a
long time without food, Paul got up
among them, and said,

"Gentlemen, you ought to have listened to me and not to have sailed from
Crete and incurred this disaster and loss.
22 Even now, I beg you to keep up your
courage, for there will be no loss of life
23 among you, but only of the ship. For
last night an angel of the God I belong
24 to and serve stood before me, and said,
'Do not be afraid, Paul! You must
stand before the emperor, and see! God
has given you the lives of all the people
25 who are on the ship with you.' So keep
up your courage, gentlemen! For I
have faith in God that it will be just as
26 I was told. But we are to be stranded
on some island."

27 It was the fourteenth night of the
storm, and we were drifting through
the Adriatic when about midnight the
sailors began to suspect that there was
28 land ahead. On taking soundings, they
found a depth of twenty fathoms, and
a little later, taking soundings again,
29 they found a depth of fifteen. Then as
they were afraid we might go on the
rocks, they dropped four anchors from
the stern and waited anxiously for day-
30 light. The sailors wanted to escape from
the ship, and actually lowered the boat
into the sea, pretending that they were
31 going to run out anchors from the bow,
but Paul said to the officers and the
soldiers,

"Unless these men stay on board,
you cannot be saved."

32 Then the soldiers cut the ropes that
33 held the boat and let it drift away. Until daybreak Paul kept urging them all
to take something to eat.

"For fourteen days," he said, "you
have been constantly on the watch,
34 without taking anything to eat. I beg
you to eat something; it is necessary for
your safety. For not one of you will
lose even a hair of his head."

With these words he took some 35
bread and after thanking God for it before them all, he broke it in pieces and
began to eat it. This raised the spirits 36
of all of them, and they took something
to eat. There were about seventy-six 37
of us on board. When they had had 38
enough to eat, they threw the wheat
into the sea, in order to lighten the ship.
When daylight came they could not 39
recognize the coast, but they saw a bay
with a beach and determined to run the
ship ashore there if possible. So they 40
cast off the anchors and left them in the
sea, at the same time they undid the
lashings of the steering oars, and hoisting the foresail to the wind, they made
for the beach. But they struck a shoal 41
and ran the ship aground. The bow
struck and could not be moved, while
the stern began to break up under the
strain. The soldiers proposed to kill the 42
prisoners, for fear some of them might
swim ashore and escape, but the officer 43
wanted to save Paul, and so he prevented them from doing this, and ordered all who could swim to jump overboard first and get to land, and the rest 44
to follow on planks or other pieces of
wreckage. So they all got safely to
land.

After our escape we learned that the **28**
island was called Malta. The natives 2
showed us remarkable kindness, for
they made a fire and welcomed us all, because of the rain that had come on and
the cold. Paul gathered a bundle of 3
sticks and put them on the fire, when a
viper crawled out of them because of
the heat and fastened on his hand.
When the natives saw the creature 4
hanging from his hand, they said to one
another,

"This man is undoubtedly a murderer, for though he has been saved from
the sea, justice will not let him live."

But he only shook the creature off in- 5
to the fire and was unharmed. They ex- 6
pected to see him swell up or suddenly
fall dead, but after waiting a long time
and seeing nothing unusual happen to
him, they changed their minds and said
that he was a god.

The governor of the island, whose 7
name was Publius, had estates in that
part of the island, and he welcomed us
and entertained us hospitably for three

8 days. Publius' father happened to be
sick in bed with fever and dysentery,
and Paul went to see him and after
praying laid his hands on him and
9 cured him. After that, the other sick
people on the island came and were
10 cured. They made us many presents,
and when we sailed, they provided us
with everything that we needed.
11 Three months later, we sailed on an
Alexandrian ship named the Dioscuri,
12 which had wintered at the island. We
put in at Syracuse and stayed there
13 three days, then we weighed anchor and
reached Rhegium. A day later, a south
wind sprang up and the following day
14 we arrived at Puteoli. There we found
some of the brothers, and they urged
us to spend a week with them. Then
15 we went on to Rome. The brothers
there had had news of our coming, and
came as far as Appius' Forum and
Three Taverns to meet us, and when
Paul saw them he thanked God and
was greatly encouraged.
16 When we reached Rome, Paul was
given permission to live by himself,
with a soldier to guard him.
17 Three days later, he invited the leading Jews to come to see him, and when
they came he said to them,

"Brothers, I have done nothing
against our people, or the customs of
our forefathers, yet I was turned over to
the Romans as a prisoner at Jerusalem.
18 They examined me and were ready to
let me go, as I was innocent of any
19 crime that deserved death. But the
Jews objected, and I was obliged to appeal to the emperor—not that I had
any charge to make against my own
20 nation. That is why I asked to see you
and speak with you, for it is on account
of Israel's hope that I have to wear this
chain."
21 "We have had no letters about you
from Judea," they answered, "and none
of the brothers who have come here has
reported or said anything against you.
But we want to hear you state your 22
views, for as far as this sect is concerned, we understand that everywhere
it is denounced."

So they fixed a day, and came in even 23
larger numbers to the place where he
was staying, and from morning till
night he explained to them the Kingdom of God and gave his testimony,
trying to convince them about Jesus
from the Law of Moses and the Prophets. Some of them were convinced by 24
what he said, but others would not believe. As they could not agree among 25
themselves, they started to leave, when
Paul added one last word.

"The holy Spirit put it finely," he
said, "when it said to your forefathers
through the prophet Isaiah,

" 'Go to this Nation and say to them, 26
"You will listen, and listen, and never understand,
And you will look, and look, and never see!
For this nation's mind has grown dull, 27
And they hear faintly with their ears,
And they have shut their eyes,
So as never to see with their eyes,
And hear with their ears,
And understand with their minds, and turn back,
And let me cure them!" '

"Understand then that this message 28
of God's salvation has been sent to the
heathen. They will listen to it!"

So he stayed for two full years in 30
rented lodgings of his own, and welcomed everybody who came to see him,
preaching the Kingdom of God to them 31
and teaching about the Lord Jesus
Christ openly and unhindered.

THE LETTER TO THE ROMANS

1 PAUL, a slave of Jesus Christ,
called as an apostle, set apart to
2 declare God's good news, which
he promised long ago through his
3 prophets in the holy Scriptures, about
his Son, who was physically descended
4 from David, and decisively declared
Son of God in his holiness of spirit, by
being raised from the dead—Jesus
5 Christ our Lord, through whom we
have received God's favor and been
commissioned in his name to urge obedience and faith upon all the heathen,
6 including you who have been called to
7 belong to Jesus Christ—to all those in
Rome whom God loves, who are called
to be his people; God our Father and
the Lord Jesus Christ bless you and
give you peace.
8 First I thank my God through Jesus
Christ about you all, because the news
of your faith is spreading all over the
9 world. As God is my witness, whom I
serve in my spirit in spreading the good
news of his Son, I never fail to men-
10 tion you when I pray, and to ask that
somehow by God's will I may some day
11 at last succeed in reaching you. For I
long to see you, to convey to you some
spiritual gift that will strengthen you;
12 in other words, that you and I may be
mutually encouraged by one another's
13 faith. I want you to understand, brothers, that I have often intended to come
to see you (though thus far I have been
prevented) in order to produce some results among you, as well as among the
14 rest of the heathen. I owe a debt both
to Greeks and to foreigners, to the cul-
15 tivated and the uncultivated. So, for
my part, I am eager to preach the good
16 news to you at Rome also. For I am
not ashamed of the good news, for it is
God's power for the salvation of everyone who has faith, of the Jew first and
17 then of the Greek. In it God's way of
uprightness is disclosed through faith
and for faith, just as the Scripture says,
"The upright will have life because of
his faith."

For God's anger is breaking forth 18
from heaven against all the impiety and
wickedness of the men who in their
wickedness are suppressing the truth.
For all that can be known of God is 19
clearly before them; God has shown it
to them. Ever since the creation of the
world, his invisible nature—his eternal 20
power and divine character—have been
clearly perceptible through what he has
made. So they have no excuse, for, 21
though they knew God, they have not
honored him as God or given thanks to
him, but they have indulged in futile
speculations, until their stupid minds
have become dark. They called them- 22
selves wise, but they have turned into
fools, and for the splendor of the im- 23
mortal God they have substituted images in the form of mortal man, birds,
animals, and reptiles.
So God abandoned them, with their 24
heart's cravings, to impurity, and let
them degrade their own bodies. For 25
they had exchanged the truth of God
for what was false, and worshiped and
served what he had created, instead of
the Creator, who is blessed forever!
Amen! That is why God has abandoned 26
them to degrading passions. Their
women have exchanged their natural
function for one that is unnatural, and 27
men too in the same way have disregarded the natural function of women
and been consumed with passion for one
another, men with men, acting in-
decently, and experiencing in their
own persons the inevitable penalty of
their mistake. And just as they refused 28
to recognize God any longer, God has
abandoned them to unworthy impulses
and indecent conduct. They revel in 29
every kind of wrong-doing, wickedness,
greed, and depravity. They are full of
envy, murder, quarreling, deceit, and
ill-nature. They are gossips, slanderers, 30
abhorrent to God, insolent, overbearing, boastful, ingenious in evil, undutiful, conscienceless, treacherous, unlov- 31
ing, and unpitying. They know God's 32
decree that those who act in this way

deserve to die, yet they not only do it,
but applaud any who do.
2 Therefore you have no excuse, my
friend, whoever you are, if you pose as a
judge, for when you pass judgment on
someone else, you are condemning yourself, for you, who sit in judgment, do
2 the very same things yourself. We know
that God's judgment rightfully falls
upon those who do such things as these.
3 And do you suppose, my friend, who
sit in judgment upon those who do such
things and yet do them yourself, that
you will escape the judgment of God?
4 Do you think so lightly of his wealth of
kindness, forbearance, and patience,
and fail to see that God's kindness
5 ought to induce you to repent? But in
your obstinacy and impenitence you are
storing up wrath for yourself on the
Day of Wrath, when the justice of God
6 will burst forth. For he will pay every
7 man for what he has done. Those who
by persistently doing right strive for
glory, honor, and immortality will
8 have eternal life, but self-seeking people
who are disloyal to the truth and responsive only to what is wrong will ex-
9 perience anger and fury, crushing distress and anguish, every human soul of
them that actually does what is wrong
10 —the Jew first, and the Greek also; but
there will be glory, honor, and peace for
everyone who does right, the Jew first,
11 and the Greek also, for God shows no
partiality.
12 All who sin without having the Law
will perish without regard to the Law,
and all who sin under the Law will be
13 judged by the Law. For merely hearing
the Law read does not make a man upright in the sight of God; men must
obey the Law to be made upright.
14 When heathen who have no Law in-
stinctively obey what the Law demands, even though they have no law
15 they are a law to themselves, for they
show that what the Law demands is
written on their hearts, and their consciences will testify for them, and with
their thoughts they will either accuse or
16 perhaps defend themselves, on that
Day when, as the good news I preach
teaches, God through Christ Jesus
judges what men have kept secret.
17 Suppose you call yourself a Jew, and
18 rely on law, and boast about God, and
can understand his will, and from hearing the Law read can tell what is right,
and you are sure that you can guide the 19
blind, enlighten people who are in the
dark, train the foolish, teach the young, 20
since you have knowledge and truth
formulated in the Law—why, then, 21
will you teach others and refuse to
teach yourself? Will you preach
against stealing, and yet steal yourself?
Will you warn men against adultery, 22
and yet practice it yourself? Will you
pretend to detest idols, and yet rob
their temples? Will you boast of the 23
Law and yet dishonor God by breaking
it? For, as the Scripture says, the very 24
name of God is abused among the heathen, because of you! Circumcision 25
will help you only if you observe the
Law; but if you are a lawbreaker, you
might as well be uncircumcised. So if 26
people who are uncircumcised observe
the requirements of the Law, will they
not be treated as though they were circumcised? And if, although they are 27
physically uncircumcised, they obey
the Law, they will condemn you, who
break the Law, although you have it in
writing, and are circumcised. For the 28
real Jew is not the man who is one outwardly, and the real circumcision is not
something physical and external. The 29
real Jew is the man who is one inwardly, and real circumcision is a matter of
the heart, a spiritual, not a literal,
thing. Such a man receives his praise
not from men, but from God.
What advantage is there then in be- 3
ing a Jew, and what is the use of circumcision? A great deal, from every 2
point of view. In the first place, the
Jews were intrusted with the utterances of God. What if some of them 3
have shown a lack of faith? Can their
lack of it nullify the faithfulness of
God? By no means! God must prove 4
true, though every man be false; as the
Scripture says,

"That you may be shown to be right
in what you say,
And win your case when you go into
court."

But if our wrongdoing brings out the 5
uprightness of God, what are we to say?
Is it wrong in God (I am putting it in
ordinary human terms) to inflict punishment? By no means, for then how 6
could he judge the world? But, you 7
say, if a falsehood of mine has brought
great honor to God by bringing out his
truthfulness, why am I tried for being

8 a sinner? And why not say, as people
abuse us for saying and charge us with
saying, "Let us do evil that good may
come out of it"? Such people will be
condemned as they deserve!

9 What does this mean? Are we Jews
at a disadvantage? Not at all. We have
already charged Jews and Greeks all
alike with being under the control of
10 sin. As the Scripture says,

"There is not a single man who is
upright,
11 No one understands, no one
searches for God.
12 All have turned away, they are one
and all worthless,
No one does right, not a single one!
13 Their throats are like open graves,
They use their tongues to deceive;
The venom of asps is behind their
lips,
14 And their mouths are full of bitter
curses.
15 Their feet are swift when it comes
to shedding blood,
16 Ruin and wretchedness mark their
paths,
17 They do not know the way of
peace.
18 There is no reverence for God before
their eyes!"

19 Now we know that everything the
Law says is addressed to those under
its authority, so that every mouth may
be shut, and the whole world be made
20 accountable to God. For no human being
can be made upright in the sight of
God by observing the Law. All that the
Law can do is to make man conscious of
21 sin. But now God's way of uprightness
has been disclosed without any reference
to law, though the Law and the
22 Prophets bear witness to it. It is God's
way of uprightness and comes through
having faith in Jesus Christ, and it is
for all who have faith, without distinc-
23 tion. For all men sin and come short
24 of the glory of God, but by his mercy
they are made upright for nothing, by
the deliverance secured through Christ
25 Jesus. For God showed him publicly
dying as a sacrifice of reconciliation to
be taken advantage of through faith.
This was to vindicate his own justice
(for in his forbearance, God passed over
26 men's former sins)—to vindicate his
justice at the present time, and show
that he is upright himself, and that he
makes those who have faith in Jesus
upright also.

Then what becomes of our boasting? 27
It is shut out. On what principle?
What a man does? No, but whether a
man has faith. For we hold that a man 28
is made upright by faith; the observance
of the Law has nothing to do
with it. Does God belong to the Jews 29
alone? Does he not belong to the heathen
too? Of course he belongs to the
heathen too; there is but one God, and 30
he will make the circumcised upright
on the ground of their faith and the
uncircumcised upright because of theirs. 31
Is this using faith to overthrow law?
Far from it. This confirms the Law.

Then what are we to say about our 4
ancestor Abraham? For if he was made 2
upright by what he did, it is something
to be proud of. But not to be proud of
before God, for what does the Scrip- 3
ture say? "Abraham had faith in God,
and it was credited to him as uprightness." Now paying a workman is not 4
considered a favor, but an obligation,
but a man who has no work to offer, but 5
has faith in him who can make the ungodly upright, has his faith credited to
him as uprightness. So David himself 6
says of the happiness of those to whom
God credits uprightness without any
reference to their actions,

"Happy are they whose violations 7
of the Law have been forgiven,
whose sins are covered up!
Happy is the man whose sin the 8
Lord will take no account of!"

Does this happiness apply to those who 9
are circumcised, or to those who are
uncircumcised as well? What we say
is, Abraham's faith was credited to him
as uprightness. In what circumstances? 10
Was it after he was circumcised or before? Not after he was circumcised, but
before; and he was afterward given the 11
mark of circumcision as the stamp of
God's acknowledgment of the uprightness based on faith that was his before
he was circumcised, so that he should
be the forefather of all who, without
being circumcised, have faith and so
are credited with uprightness, and the 12
forefather of those circumcised persons
who not only share his circumcision but
follow our forefather Abraham's example in the faith he had before he was circumcised.

For the promise made to Abraham 13

and his descendants that the world
should belong to him did not come to
him or his descendants through the
Law, but through the uprightness that
14 resulted from his faith. For if it is the
adherents of the Law who are to possess
it, faith is nullified and the promise
15 amounts to nothing! For the Law only
brings down God's wrath; where there
is no law, there is no violation of it.
16 That is why it all turns upon faith; it
is to make it a matter of God's favor, so
that the promise may hold good for all
Abraham's descendants, not only those
who are adherents of the Law, but also
those who share the faith of Abraham.
17 For he is the father of all of us; as the
Scripture says, "I have made you the
father of many nations." The promise
is guaranteed in the very sight of God
in whom he had faith, who can bring
the dead to life and call into being what
18 does not exist. Abraham, hoping
against hope, had faith, and so became
the father of many nations, in fulfilment of the Scripture, "So countless
19 shall your descendants be." His faith
did not weaken, although he realized
that his own body was worn out, for he
was about a hundred years old, and
that Sarah was past bearing children.
20 He did not incredulously question
God's promise, but his faith gave him
21 power and he praised God in the full
assurance that God was able to do what
22 he had promised. That was why it
was credited to him as uprightness.
23 It was not on his account alone that
these words, "it was credited to him,"
24 were written, but also on ours, for it is
to be credited also to us who have faith
in him who raised from the dead our
25 Lord Jesus, who was given up to death
to make up for our offenses, and raised
to life to make us upright.

5 So as we have been made upright by
faith, let us live in peace with God
2 through our Lord Jesus Christ, by
whom we have been introduced through
faith to the favor of God that we now
enjoy, and let us glory in our hope of
3 sharing the glory of God. More than
that, we ought to glory in our troubles,
for we know that trouble produces en-
4 durance, and endurance, character, and
5 character, hope, and hope will not disap-
point us. For, through the holy Spirit
that has been given us, God's love has
6 flooded our hearts. For when we were
still helpless, at the decisive moment
Christ died for us godless men. Why, a 7
man will hardly give his life for an upright person, though perhaps for a
really good man some may be brave
enough to die. But God proves his love 8
for us by the fact that Christ died for
us when we were still sinners. So if we 9
have already been made upright by the
shedding of his blood, it is far more certain that through him we shall be saved
from God's anger! If, when we were 10
God's enemies, we were reconciled to
him through the death of his Son, it is
far more certain that now that we are
reconciled we shall be saved through
sharing in his life! More than that, we 11
actually glory in God through our Lord
Jesus Christ, to whom we owe our reconciliation.

It is just like the way in which 12
through one man sin came into the
world, and death followed sin, and so
death spread to all men, because all
men sinned. It is true sin was in the 13
world before the Law was given, and
men are not charged with sin where
there is no law. Still death reigned from 14
Adam to Moses, even over those who
had not sinned as Adam had, in the face
of an express command. So Adam
foreshadowed the one who was to come.
But there is no comparison between 15
God's gift and that offense. For if one
man's offense made the mass of mankind die, God's mercy and his gift giv-
en through the favor of the one man
Jesus Christ have far more powerfully
affected mankind. Nor is there any 16
comparison between the gift and the
effects of that one man's sin. That sentence arose from the act of one man,
and was for condemnation; but God's
gift arose out of many offenses and results in acquittal. For if that one man's 17
offense made death reign through that
one man, all the more will those who
receive God's overflowing mercy and
gift of uprightness live and reign
through the one individual Jesus
Christ.

So as one offense meant condemna- 18
tion for all men, just so one righteous
act means acquittal and life for all men.
For just as that one man's disobedience 19
made the mass of mankind sinners, so
this one's obedience will make the mass
of them upright. Then law slipped in, 20
and multiplied the offense. But greatly

as sin multiplied, God's mercy has far
21 surpassed it, so that just as sin had
reigned through death, mercy might
reign through uprightness and bring
eternal life through Jesus Christ our
Lord.
6 Then what shall we conclude? Are
we to continue to sin to increase the
2 spread of mercy? Certainly not! When
we have died to sin, how can we live in
3 it any longer? Do you not know that
all of us who have been baptized into
union with Christ Jesus have been bap-
4 tized into his death? Through baptism
we have been buried with him in death,
so that just as he was raised from the
dead through the Father's glory, we too
5 may live a new life. For if we have
grown into union with him by undergoing a death like his, of course we shall
do so by being raised to life like him,
6 for we know that our old self was crucified with him, to do away with our sinful body, so that we might not be en-
7 slaved to sin any longer, for when a man
is dead he is free from the claims of sin.
8 If we have died with Christ, we believe
9 that we shall also live with him, for we
know that Christ, once raised from the
dead, will never die again; death has
10 no more hold on him. For when he died,
he became once for all dead to sin; the
life he now lives is a life in relation to
11 God. So you also must think of yourselves as dead to sin but alive to God,
through union with Christ Jesus.
12 So sin must not reign over your mortal bodies, and make you obey their
13 cravings, and you must not offer the
parts of your bodies to sin as the instruments of wrong, but offer yourselves to
God as men brought back from death
to life, and offer the parts of your bodies
to him as instruments of uprightness.
14 For sin must no longer control you, for
you live not under law but under mercy.
15 What follows, then? Are we to sin,
because we live not under law but under
16 mercy? Certainly not! Do you not
know that when you submit to being
someone's slaves, and obeying him, you
are the slaves of the one whom you
obey, whether your slavery is to sin,
and leads to death, or is to obedience,
17 and leads to uprightness? But, thank
God! though you were once slaves of
sin, you have become obedient from
your hearts to the standard of teaching
18 that you received, and so you have been
freed from sin, and made slaves of uprightness. I use these familiar human 19
terms because of the limitations of your
nature. For just as you before gave up
the parts of your bodies in slavery to
vice and greater and greater license,
you must now give them up in slavery
to uprightness, which leads to consecration. For when you were slaves of sin, 20
you were free as far as uprightness was
concerned. What good did you get from 21
doing the things you are now ashamed
of? Why, they result in death! But 22
now that you have been freed from sin
and have become slaves of God, the
benefit you get is consecration, and the
final result is eternal life. For the wages 23
sin pays is death, but the gift God gives
is eternal life through union with Christ
Jesus our Lord.
Do you not know, brothers—for I 7
am speaking to men who know what
law is—that law governs a man only as
long as he lives? For a married woman 2
is bound by law to her husband while he
lives, but if he dies, the marriage law
no longer applies to her. So if she mar- 3
ries another man while her husband is
alive, she is called an adulteress, but if
her husband dies, she is free from that
law, and can marry someone else without being an adultress. So you, in turn, 4
my brothers, in the body of Christ have
become dead as far as the Law is concerned, so that you may belong to another husband, who was raised from the
dead in order that we might bear fruit
for God. For when we were living mere 5
physical lives the sinful passions, awakened by the Law, operated through the
organs of our bodies to make us bear
fruit for death. But now the Law no 6
longer applies to us; we have died to
what once controlled us, so that we can
now serve in the new Spirit, not under
the old letter.
Then what shall we conclude? That 7
the Law is sin? Certainly not! Yet, if
it had not been for the Law, I should
never have learned what sin was; I
should not have known what it was to
covet if the Law had not said, "You
must not covet." That command gave 8
sin an opening, and it led me to all sorts
of covetous ways, for sin is lifeless without law. I was once alive and without 9
law, but when the command came, sin
awoke and then I died; and the com- 10
mand that should have meant life in my

11 case proved to mean death. The command gave sin an opening and sin de-
12 ceived me and killed me with it. So the
Law itself is holy, and each command
is holy, just, and good.
13 Did what was good, then, prove the
death of me? Certainly not! It was sin
that did so, so that it might be recognized as sin, because even through
something that was good it effected my
death, so that through the command it
might appear how immeasurably sinful
14 sin was. We know that the Law is
spiritual, but I am physical, sold into
15 slavery to sin. I do not understand
what I am doing, for I do not do what
I want to do; I do things that I hate.
16 But if I do what I do not want to do, I
17 acknowledge that the Law is right. In
reality, it is not I that do these things;
it is sin, which has possession of me.
18 For I know that nothing good resides in
me, that is, in my physical self; I can
19 will, but I cannot do what is right. I do
not do the good things that I want to
do; I do the wrong things that I do not
20 want to do. But if I do the things
that I do not want to do, it is not I that
am acting, it is sin, which has possession
21 of me. I find the law to be that I who
want to do right am dogged by what is
22 wrong. My inner nature agrees with
23 the divine law, but all through my body
I see another principle in conflict with
the law of my reason, which makes me
a prisoner to that law of sin that runs
24 through my body. What a wretched
man I am! Who can save me from this
25 doomed body? Thank God! it is done
through Jesus Christ our Lord! So
mentally I am a slave to God's law, but
physically to the law of sin.
8 So there is no condemnation any more
for those who are in union with Christ
2 Jesus. For the life-giving law of the
Spirit through Christ Jesus has freed
you from the Law of sin and death.
3 For though it was impossible for the
Law to do it, hampered as it was by our
physical limitations, God, by sending
his own Son in our sinful physical form,
as a sin-offering put his condemnation
upon sin through his physical nature,
4 so that the requirement of the Law
might be fully met in our case, since we
live not on the physical but on the
5 spiritual plane. People who are controlled by the physical think of what is
physical, and people who are controlled by the spiritual think of what is
spiritual. For to be physically minded 6
means death, but to be spiritually
minded means life and peace. For to be 7
physically minded means hostility to
God, for it refuses to obey God's law, indeed it cannot obey it. Those who are 8
physical cannot please God. But you 9
are not physical but spiritual, if God's
Spirit has really taken possession of
you; for unless a man has Christ's spirit, he does not belong to Christ. But if 10
Christ is in your hearts, though your
bodies are dead in consequence of sin,
your spirits have life in consequence of
uprightness. If the Spirit of him who 11
raised Jesus from the dead has taken
possession of you, he who raised Christ
Jesus from the dead will also give your
mortal bodies life through his Spirit
that has taken possession of you.
So, brothers, we are under obliga- 12
tions, but not to the physical nature, to
live under its control, for if you live 13
under the control of the physical you
will die, but if, by means of the Spirit,
you put the body's doings to death,
you will live. For all who are guided 14
by God's Spirit are God's sons. It is not 15
a consciousness of servitude that has
been imparted to you, to fill you with
fear again, but the consciousness of
adoption as sons, which makes us cry,
"Abba!" that is, Father. The Spirit it- 16
self testifies with our spirits that we are
God's children, and if children, heirs 17
also; heirs of God, and fellow-heirs with
Christ, if we really share his sufferings
in order to share his glory too.
For I consider what we suffer now not 18
to be compared with the glory that is
to burst upon us. For creation is wait- 19
ing with eager longing for the sons of
God to be disclosed. For it was not the 20
fault of creation that it was frustrated;
it was by the will of him who condemned it to that, and in the hope that 21
creation itself would be set free from its
bondage to decay, and have the glorious
freedom of the children of God. We 22
know that all creation has been groaning in agony together until now. More 23
than that, we ourselves, though we
have in the Spirit a foretaste of the future, groan to ourselves as we wait to
be declared God's sons, through the redemption of our bodies. It was in this 24
hope that we were saved. But a hope
that can be seen is not a hope, for who

25 hopes for what he sees? But when we
hope for something that we do not see,
we wait persistently for it.
26 In the same way the Spirit helps us
in our weakness, for we do not know
how to pray as we should, but the Spirit itself pleads for us with inexpressible
27 yearnings, and he who searches our
hearts knows what the Spirit means, for
it pleads for God's people in accord-
28 ance with his will. We know that in
everything God works with those who
love him, whom he has called in accordance with his purpose, to bring
29 about what is good. For those whom
he had marked out from the first he
predestined to be made like his Son, so
that he should be the eldest of many
30 brothers; and those whom he has predestined he calls, and those whom he
calls he makes upright, and those
whom he makes upright he glorifies.
31 Then what shall we conclude from
this? If God is for us, who can be
32 against us? Will not he who did not
spare his own Son, but gave him up for
us all, with that gift give us every-
33 thing? Who can bring any accusation
against those whom God has chosen?
34 God pronounces them upright; who
can condemn them? Christ Jesus who
died, or rather who was raised from the
dead, is at God's right hand, and actu-
35 ally pleads for us. Who can separate us
from Christ's love? Can trouble or misfortune or persecution or hunger or
36 destitution or danger or the sword? As
the Scripture says,

"For your sake we are being put to
death all day long,
We are treated like sheep to be
slaughtered."

37 But in all these things we are more than
victorious through him who loved us.
38 For I am convinced that neither death
nor life nor angels nor their hierarchies
39 nor the present nor the future nor any
supernatural forces either of height or
depth nor anything else in creation will
be able to separate us from the love God
has shown in Christ Jesus our Lord!

9 I am telling the truth as a Christian,
it is no falsehood, for my conscience
under the holy Spirit's influence bears
2 me witness in it, when I say that I am
greatly pained and my heart is con-
3 stantly distressed, for I could wish myself accursed and cut off from Christ
for the sake of my brothers, my natural
kindred. For they are Israelites, and to 4
them belong the rights of sonship,
God's glorious presence, the divine
agreements and legislation, the Temple
service, the promises, and the patri- 5
archs, and from them physically Christ
came—God who is over all be blessed
forever! Amen. Not that God's mes- 6
sage has failed. For not everybody
who is descended from Israel really belongs to Israel, nor are they all children 7
of Abraham because they are descended
from him, but he was told, "The line of
Isaac will be called your descendants."
That is to say, it is not his physical 8
descendants who are children of God,
but his descendants born in fulfilment
of the promise who are considered his
true posterity. For this is what the 9
promise said: "When I come back at
this time next year, Sarah will have a
son." And that is not all, for there was 10
Rebecca too, when she was about to
bear children to our forefather Isaac.
For before the children were born or 11
had done anything either good or bad,
in order to carry out God's purpose of
selection, which depends not on what
men do but on his calling them, she was 12
told, "The elder will be the younger's
slave." As the Scripture says, "I loved 13
Jacob, but I hated Esau."
What do we conclude? That God is 14
guilty of injustice? By no means. He 15
said to Moses, "I will have mercy on
the man on whom I choose to have
mercy, and take pity on the man on
whom I choose to take pity." So it de- 16
pends not on human will or exertion,
but on the mercy of God. The Scrip- 17
ture says to Pharaoh, "I have raised
you to your position for the very purpose of displaying my power in dealing
with you, and making my name known
all over the world." So he has mercy 18
on anyone he pleases, and hardens the
heart of anyone he pleases.
"Why, then," you will ask, "does he 19
still find fault? For who can resist his
will?" On the contrary, who are you, 20
my friend, to answer back to God? Can
a thing that is molded say to its
maker, "Why did you make me like
this?" Has not the potter with his 21
clay the right to make from the same
lump one thing for exalted uses and another for menial ones? Then what if 22
God, though he wanted to display his
anger and show his power, has shown

great patience toward the objects of
his anger, already ripe for destruction,
23 so as to show all the wealth of his glory
in dealing with the objects of his mercy,
whom he has prepared from the begin-
24 ning to share his glory, including us
whom he has called not only from
among the Jews but from among the
25 heathen? Just as he says in Hosea,

"I will call a people that was not
mine, my people,
And her who was not beloved, my
beloved,
26 And in the very place where they
were told, 'You are no people of
mine,'
They shall be called sons of the living God."

27 And Isaiah cries out about Israel,
"Although the sons of Israel are as numerous as the sand of the sea, only a
28 remnant of them will be saved, for the
Lord will execute his sentence rigorous-
29 ly and swiftly on the earth." As Isaiah
foretold,

"If the Lord of Hosts had not left
us children,
We would have been like Sodom,
and have resembled Gomorrah!"

30 Then what do we conclude? That
heathen who were not striving for uprightness attained it, that is, an uprightness which was produced by faith;
31 while Israel, straining after a law that
should bring uprightness, did not come
32 up to it. And why? Because they did
not seek it through faith, but through
doing certain things. They stumbled
over that stone that makes people
33 stumble, as the Scripture says,

"See, I will put a stone on Zion to
make people stumble, and a rock
to trip over,
But no one who has faith in it will
be disappointed."

10 Brothers, my heart is full of good
will toward them; my prayer to God is
2 that they may be saved. I can testify
to their sincere devotion to God, but
3 it is not an intelligent devotion. For in
their ignorance of God's way of uprightness and in the attempt to set up
one of their own, they refused to con-
4 form to God's way of uprightness. For
Christ marks the termination of law, so
that now anyone who has faith may at-
5 tain uprightness. Moses wrote that anyone who carried out the uprightness the
Law prescribed would find life through
it. But this is what the uprightness 6
that springs from faith says: "Do not
say to yourself, 'Who will go up to 7
heaven?'" that is, to bring Christ
down; or "'Who will go down into the
depths?'" that is, to bring Christ up
from the dead. No! This is what it 8
says: "God's message is close to you,
on your lips and in your mind"—that
is, the message about faith that we
preach. For if with your lips you ac- 9
knowledge the message that Jesus is
Lord, and with your mind you believe
that God raised him from the dead, you
will be saved. For with their minds men 10
believe and are made upright, and with
their lips they make the acknowledgment and are saved. For the Scripture 11
says, "No one who has faith in him will
be disappointed." There is no distinc- 12
tion between Jew and Greek for they
all have the same Lord, and he is generous to all who call upon him. For every- 13
one who calls upon the name of the
Lord will be saved. But how are they 14
to call upon him if they have not believed in him? And how are they to
believe him if they have never heard
him? And how are they to hear unless
someone preaches to them? And how 15
are men to preach unless they are sent
to do it? As the Scripture says, "How
welcome is the coming of those who
bring good news!"

It is true, they have not all accepted 16
the good news, for Isaiah says, "Lord,
who has believed what we have told?"
So faith comes from hearing what is 17
told, and that hearing comes through
the message about Christ. But I ask, 18
had they no opportunity to hear it? On
the contrary,

"Their voices have gone all over the
earth,
And their words to the ends of the
world."

But I ask again, did Israel fail to un- 19
derstand? Why, to begin with, Moses
said,

"I will make you jealous of what is
no nation at all,
I will exasperate you at a senseless
nation."

Then Isaiah broke out boldly and said, 20

"I have been found by men who
were not looking for me,
I have shown myself to men who
were not questioning me."

But of Israel he said, 21

"All day long I have held out my
hands to a disobedient and obstinate people."
11 I ask then, has God repudiated his
people? By no means. Why, I am an
Israelite myself, I am descended from
Abraham, and I belong to the tribe of
2 Benjamin. God has not repudiated his
people, which he had marked out from
the first. Do you not know what the
Scripture says in speaking of Elijah,
how he appealed to God against Israel?
3 "Lord, they have killed your prophets,
they have demolished your altars, I am
the only one left and they are trying to
4 take my life." But what is God's reply? "I have left myself seven thousand men who have never knelt to
5 Baal!" So too at the present time there
is a remnant selected by God's mercy.
6 But if it is by his mercy, it is not for
anything they have done. Otherwise,
his mercy would not be mercy at all.
7 What follows? Israel failed to get what
it sought, but those whom God selected
8 got it. The rest became callous; as the
Scripture says, "God has thrown them
into a state of spiritual insensibility,
with eyes that cannot see and ears that
cannot hear, that has lasted down to
9 this day." And David said,
"Let their feasting prove a snare and
a trap to them,
Their ruin and their retribution.
10 Let their eyes be darkened, so that
they cannot see;
Make their backs bend forever under their burden!"
11 I ask then, has their stumbling led to
their absolute ruin? By no means.
Through their false step salvation has
gone to the heathen, so as to make the
12 Israelites jealous. But if their false step
has so enriched the world, and their defeat has so enriched the heathen, how
much more good the addition of their
full number will do!
13 But it is to you who are of the heathen that I am speaking. So far then as
I am an apostle to the heathen, I make
14 the most of my ministry, in the hope of
making my countrymen jealous, and
15 thus saving some of them. For if their
rejection has meant the reconciling of
the world, what can the acceptance of
16 them mean but life from the dead? If
the first handful of dough is consecrated, the whole mass is, and if the root of
a tree is consecrated, so are its branches.

If some of the branches have been 17
broken off, and you who were only a
wild olive shoot have been grafted in,
in place of them, and made to share the
richness of the olive's root, you must 18
not look down upon the branches. If
you do, remember that you do not support the root; the root supports you.
"But," you will say, "branches were 19
broken off so that I could be grafted in!"
That is true; but it was for their want 20
of faith that they were broken off, and
it is through your faith that you stand
where you do. You ought not to feel
proud; you ought to be afraid, for if 21
God did not spare the natural branches,
he will not spare you. Observe then the 22
goodness and the severity of God—
severity to those who have fallen, but
goodness to you, provided you abide by
his goodness, for otherwise, you in your
turn will be pruned away. Those others 23
too, if they do not cling to their unbelief, will be grafted in, for God has the
power to graft them in again. For if 24
you were cut from a wild olive and un-
naturally grafted upon a cultivated
one, how much easier it will be to graft
them upon the olive to which they
properly belong!
For to keep you from thinking too 25
well of yourselves, brothers, I do not
want you to miss this secret, that only
partial insensibility has come upon
Israel, to last until all the heathen have
come in, and then all Israel will be 26
saved, just as the Scripture says,
"The deliverer will come from Zion,
He will drive all ungodliness away
from Jacob,
And this will be my agreement 27
with them,
When I take away their sins."
From the point of view of the good 28
news they are treated as enemies of
God on your account; but from the
point of view of God's choice, they are
dear to him because of their forefathers,
for God does not change his mind about 29
those to whom he gives his blessings or
sends his call. For just as you once dis- 30
obeyed God, but now have had mercy
shown you because they disobeyed, so 31
they are now disobedient in order that
they in turn may experience the same
mercy as you. For God has made all 32
men prisoners of disobedience so as to
have mercy upon them all. How inex- 33
haustible God's resources, wisdom, and

knowledge are! How unfathomable his
decisions are, and how untraceable his
ways!
34 "Who has ever known the Lord's
thoughts, or advised him?
35 "Or who has advanced anything to
him, for which he will have to be repaid?"
36 For from him everything comes;
through him everything exists; and in
him everything ends! Glory to him forever! Amen.
12 I appeal to you, therefore, brothers,
by this mercy of God, to offer your
bodies in a living sacrifice that will be
holy and acceptable to God; that is your
2 rational worship. You must not adopt
the customs of this world but by your
new attitude of mind be transformed
so that you can find out what God's will
is—what is good, pleasing, and perfect.
3 By the favor that God has shown me,
I would tell every one of you not to
think too highly of himself, but to
think reasonably, judging himself by
the degree of faith God has allowed
4 him. For just as there are many parts
united in our human bodies, and the
parts do not all have the same function,
5 so, many as we are, we form one body
through union with Christ, and we are
6 individually parts of one another. We
have gifts that differ with the favor that
God has shown us, whether it is that
of preaching, differing with the meas-
7 ure of our faith, or of practical service,
differing in the field of service, or the
teacher who exercises his gift in teach-
8 ing, the speaker, in his exhortation, the
giver of charity, with generosity, the
office-holder, with devotion, the one
who does acts of mercy, with cheerful-
9 ness. Your love must be genuine. Hate
what is wrong, and hold to what is right.
10 Be affectionate in your love for the
brotherhood, eager to show one another
11 honor, not wanting in devotion, but on
12 fire with the Spirit. Serve the Lord. Be
happy in your hope, steadfast in time of
13 trouble, persistent in prayer. Supply
the needs of God's people, be unfailing
14 in hospitality. Bless your persecutors;
15 bless them; do not curse them. Rejoice
with those who rejoice, weep with those
16 who weep. Live in harmony with one
another. Do not be too ambitious, but
accept humble tasks. Do not be con-
17 ceited. Do not pay anyone back with
evil for evil. See that you are above
reproach in the eyes of everyone. If 18
possible, for your part, live peaceably
with everybody. Do not take your 19
revenge, dear friends, but leave room
for God's anger, for the Scripture says,
"Vengeance belongs to me; I will pay
them back, says the Lord." No! If 20
your enemy is hungry, feed him! If he
is thirsty, give him something to drink!
For if you do, you will heap burning
coals upon his head! Do not be con- 21
quered by evil, but conquer evil with
good.
Everyone must obey the authorities 13
that are over him, for no authority can
exist without the permission of God;
the existing authorities have been established by him, so that anyone who 2
resists the authorities sets himself in
opposition to what God has ordained,
and those who oppose him will bring
down judgment upon themselves. The 3
man who does right has nothing to fear
from the magistrates, as the wrongdoer
has. If you want to have no fear of the
authorities, do right, and they will commend you for it, for they are God's 4
agents to do you good. But if you
do wrong you may well be afraid, for
they do not carry swords for nothing.
They are God's servants, to execute his
wrath upon wrongdoers. You must 5
obey them, therefore, not only to escape God's wrath, but as a matter of
principle, just as you pay your taxes; 6
they are God's ministers, devoting
themselves to this service. Pay them 7
all what is due them—tribute to the
man entitled to receive it, taxes to the
man entitled to receive them, respect to
the man entitled to it, and honor to the
man entitled to it. Owe nobody any- 8
thing—except the duty of mutual love,
for whoever loves his fellow-men has
fully satisfied the Law. For the com- 9
mandments, "You must not commit
adultery, You must not murder, You
must not steal, You must not covet,"
and any other commandments there
are, are all summed up in one saying,
"You must love your neighbor as you
do yourself." Love never wrongs a 10
neighbor, and so love fully satisfies the
Law.
All this especially, because you know 11
this critical time and that it is time for
you to wake from your sleep, for our
salvation is nearer to us now than when
we first believed. The night is nearly 12

over; the day is at hand. So let us throw
aside the deeds of darkness, and put on
13 the armor of light. Let us live honorably, as in the light of day, not in carousing and drunkenness, or in immorality and indecency, or in quarreling
14 and jealousy. But clothe yourselves
with the Lord Jesus Christ, and do not
think about gratifying your physical
cravings.

14 Treat people who are overscrupulous
in their faith like brothers; do not criti-
2 cize their views. One man's faith allows him to eat anything, while the
overscrupulous man eats nothing but
3 vegetables. The man who will eat anything must not look down on the man
who abstains from some things, and the
man who abstains from them must not
criticize the one who does not, for God
4 has accepted him. Who are you to
criticize someone else's servant? It is
for his own master to say whether he
succeeds or fails; and he will succeed,
for the Master can make him do so.
5 One man thinks one day better than
another, while another thinks them all
alike. Everybody must be fully con-
6 vinced in his own mind. The man who
observes the day does it in the Lord's
honor. The man who eats does it in the
Lord's honor, for he gives God thanks,
and the man who abstains does it in the
Lord's honor, and gives him thanks.
7 None of us lives only to himself, and
8 none of us dies only to himself; if we
live, we are responsible to the Lord,
and if we die, we are responsible to him;
so whether we live or die, we belong to
9 the Lord. For Christ died and returned
to life for the very purpose of being
Lord of both the dead and the living.
10 What business have you to criticize
your brother? What business have you
to look down upon your brother? We
shall all have to stand before God for
11 judgment. For the Scripture says,

"As surely as I live, says the Lord,
every knee will bend before me,
And every tongue will make its
confession to God."

12 So each one of us must give an account
of himself to God.

13 Therefore let us not criticize one another any more. You must resolve instead never to put any hindrance or ob-
14 stacle in your brother's way. I know
and as a follower of the Lord Jesus I am
convinced that nothing is unclean in itself; a thing is unclean only to the man
who regards it as unclean. For if your 15
brother's feelings are hurt by what you
eat, your life is not governed by love.
You must not, by what you eat, ruin a
man for whom Christ died. The thing 16
you have a right to do must not become
a cause of reproach. The Kingdom of 17
God is not a matter of what we eat or
drink, but of uprightness, peace, and
happiness through the possession of the
holy Spirit. Whoever serves Christ in 18
that way pleases God and gains the approval of men. Let us, therefore, keep 19
before us whatever will contribute to
peace and the development of one another. You must not, just for the sake 20
of food, undo the work of God. It is
true, everything is clean, but it is wrong
for a man to hurt the consciences of
others by what he eats. The right 21
thing to do is to eat no meat at all and
to drink no wine or do anything else if
it hurts your brother's conscience. For 22
your part, you must keep the faith you
have to yourself, as between God and
you. He is a happy man who has no
fault to find with himself in following
the course that he approves, but the 23
man who has misgivings about eating,
and then eats, is thereby condemned,
for he is not following his convictions,
and anything that does not rest on conviction is wrong.

It is the duty of us who are strong to **15**
put up with the weaknesses of those
who are immature, and not just suit
ourselves. Everyone of us must try to 2
please his neighbor, to do him good, and
help in his development. Christ did not 3
please himself, but as the Scripture
says, "The reproaches of those who reproach you have fallen on me." For 4
everything that was written in earlier
times was written for our instruction,
so that by being steadfast and through
the encouragement the Scriptures give,
we might hold our hope fast. May God, 5
from whom steadfastness and encouragement come, give you such harmony
with one another, in following the example of Christ Jesus, that you may 6
praise the God and Father of our Lord
Jesus Christ with one accord and one
voice.

Therefore, treat one another like 7
brothers, in God's honor, just as Christ
has treated you. I hold that Christ has 8
become an agent of circumcision to

show God's truthfulness in carrying out
the promises made to our forefathers,
9 and causing the heathen to praise God
for his mercy; as the Scripture says,

"I will give thanks to you for this
among the heathen,
And sing in honor of your name."

10 And again,

"Rejoice, you heathen, with his people!"

11 And again,

"Praise the Lord, all you heathen,
And let all nations sing his
praises."

12 Again Isaiah says,

"The descendant of Jesse will
come,
The one who is to rise to rule the
heathen;
The heathen will set their hopes on
him."

13 May God, the source of hope, fill you
with perfect happiness and peace in
your faith, so that you may have overflowing
hope through the power of the
holy Spirit.

14 For my part, as far as you are concerned,
my brothers, I am convinced
that you are already full of goodness of
heart, endowed with perfect knowledge,
and well qualified to instruct one
15 another. But, just to refresh your
memories, I have written you pretty
16 boldly on some points, because of the
favor God has shown men in making
me a minister of Christ Jesus among
the heathen, to act as a priest of God's
good news, to see that the heathen are
an acceptable sacrifice, consecrated by
17 the holy Spirit. So as a follower of
Christ Jesus I have reason to be proud
18 of my work for God. For I will venture
to speak only of what Christ has accomplished
through me in winning the
heathen to obedience, by word and ac-
19 tion, by the force of signs and marvels,
and by the power of the holy Spirit,
with the result that I have completed
the preaching of the good news of
Christ all the way from Jerusalem
20 around to Illyricum. In all this it has
been my ambition to preach the good
news only where Christ's name was unknown,
so as not to build on founda-
21 tions other men had laid. As the Scripture
says,

"They who have never been told of
him will see,
And they who have never heard
will understand!"

This is why I have so often been pre- 22
vented from coming to see you. But 23
now there is no more work for me in this
part of the world, and as I have had a
great desire for many years to come to
see you, when I go to Spain I hope to 24
see you on my way there, and to have
you see me off on my journey, after I
have enjoyed being with you for a
while. Just now I am starting for Jeru- 25
salem, to take help to God's people.
For Macedonia and Greece have deter- 26
mined to make a contribution for the
poor among God's people in Jerusalem.
They determined to do it, and they 27
really are indebted to them, for if the
heathen have shared their spiritual
blessings, they ought to do them a service
in material ways. So when I have 28
finished this matter, and seen this contribution
safely into their possession, I
will start for Spain, and come to you on
the way, and I know that when I do 29
come to see you, I will come with
Christ's fullest blessing.

I beg you, brothers, for the sake of 30
our Lord Jesus Christ, and of the love
that the Spirit inspires, join me in most
earnest prayer to God for me. Pray 31
that I may escape from those in Judea
who are disobedient, and that the help
I am taking to Jerusalem may be well
received by God's people, so that, if it is 32
God's will, I may come with a glad
heart to see you and enjoy a visit with
you. God who gives peace be with you 33
all! Amen.

I want to introduce to you our sister 16
Phoebe, who is a helper in the church
at Cenchreae. Welcome her as a Chris- 2
tian, as God's people should welcome
one another, and give her whatever help
she may need from you. For she has
herself been a protector of many, including
myself.

Remember me to Prisca and Aquila, 3
my fellow-workers in the cause of
Christ Jesus, who risked their necks to 4
save my life. Not only I but also all the
churches among the heathen thank
them. Remember me also to the church 5
that meets at their house. Remember
me to my dear Epaenetus, who was the
first man in Asia to turn to Christ. Re- 6
member me to Mary, who has worked

7 so hard for you. Remember me to Andronicus and Junias, my fellow-countrymen, who went to prison with me.
They are noted men among the missionaries, and they became Christians
8 before I did. Remember me to Amplia-
9 tus, my dear Christian friend. Remember me to Urbanus, our fellow-worker
in Christ's cause, and to my dear
10 Stachys. Remember me to that veter-
an Christian, Apelles. Remember me
to those who belong to the household of
11 Aristobulus. Remember me to my fellow-countryman, Herodion. Remember
me to the Christians in the household of
12 Narcissus. Remember me to Tryph-
aena and Tryphosa, those hard workers
in the Lord's cause. Remember me to
my dear Persis, who has worked so hard
13 for the Lord. Remember me to Rufus,
that eminent Christian, and to his
mother, who has been a mother to me.
14 Remember me to Asyncritus, Phlegon,
Hermes, Patrobas, Hermas, and the
15 brothers who meet with them. Remember me to Philologus and Julia, to Ne-
reus and his sister, and to Olympas, and
all God's people who meet with them.
16 Greet one another with a sacred kiss.
All the churches of Christ wish to be remembered to you.

17 I beg you, brothers, to be on the
watch for those who introduce divisions
and difficulties, in opposition to the instruction that you were given, and to
avoid them. Such men are not serving 18
our Lord Christ, but their own base
passions, and with their plausible and
flattering talk they deceive simple-
minded people. Everyone has heard of 19
your obedience, and I am very happy
about you, but I want you to be wise
about what is good and guileless about
what is bad. And God, who is the 20
source of peace, will soon crush Satan
under your feet.

The blessing of our Lord Jesus be
with you.

My fellow-worker, Timothy, wishes 21
to be remembered to you, and so do Lucius, Jason, and Sosipater, my fellow-
countrymen. I, Tertius, who write this 22
letter, wish to be remembered to you as
a fellow-Christian. My host, Gaius, the 23
host of the whole church, wishes to be
remembered to you. Erastus, the city-
treasurer, and our brother Quartus wish
to be remembered to you.

To him who can make you strong by 25
the good news I bring and the preaching about Jesus Christ, through the disclosure of the secret kept back for long
ages but now revealed, and at the com- 26
mand of the eternal God made known
through the writings of the prophets to
all the heathen, to lead them to obedience and faith—to the one wise God 27
be glory forever through Jesus Christ.
Amen.

THE FIRST LETTER TO THE CORINTHIANS

1 PAUL, by the will of God called as
an apostle of Jesus Christ, and
2 our brother Sosthenes, to the
church of God at Corinth, to
those who are consecrated by union
with Christ Jesus, and called as God's
people, like all those anywhere who call
on the name of Jesus Christ, their Lord
3 as well as ours; God our Father and the
Lord Jesus Christ bless you and give
you peace.
4 I am always thanking God about
you, for the blessing God has given you
5 through Christ Jesus. For you have
grown rich in everything through union
with him—in power of expression and
6 in capacity for knowledge. So your experience has confirmed the testimony
7 that I bore to Christ, and there is no
gift that you lack even while you are
waiting for our Lord Jesus Christ to re-
8 appear, and at the Day of our Lord Jesus Christ he will insure your complete
9 vindication. God can be depended on,
and it was he who called you to this fellowship with his Son, Jesus Christ our
Lord.
10 But I urge you all, brothers, for the
sake of our Lord Jesus Christ, to agree
in what you say, and not to allow fac-
tions among you, but to be perfectly
11 united in mind and judgment. For I
have been informed, my brothers, by
Chloe's people, that quarrels are going
12 on among you. What I mean is this,
that one of you says, "I am a follower
of Paul," another, "And I, of Apollos,"
another, "And I, of Cephas," and an-
13 other, "And I, of Christ!" Christ has
been divided up! But was it Paul who
was crucified for you? Or were you
14 baptized in the name of Paul? I
am thankful that I never baptized any
15 of you except Crispus and Gaius,
so that no one could say that you
16 were baptized in my name. And I
did baptize the members of the household of Stephanas too; I do not know
whether I baptized anyone else besides.
For Christ did not send me to baptize, 17
but to preach the good news—but not
with fine language, or the cross of
Christ might seem an empty thing.
For to those who are on the way to 18
destruction, the story of the cross is
nonsense, but to us who are to be saved,
it means all the power of God. For the 19
Scripture says,

"I will destroy the wisdom of the
wise,
And I will thwart the shrewdness
of the shrewd!"

Where now is your philosopher? 20
Your scribe? Your reasoner of today?
Has not God made a fool of the world's
wisdom?
For since in God's providence the 21
world with all its wisdom did not come
to know God, God chose, through the
folly of the gospel message, to save
those who had faith in him. For Jews 22
insist upon miracles, and Greeks demand philosophy, but we proclaim a 23
Christ who was crucified—an idea that
is revolting to Jews and absurd to the
heathen, but to those whom God has 24
called, whether they are Jews or
Greeks, a Christ who is God's power
and God's wisdom. For God's folly is 25
beyond the wisdom of men, and God's
weakness is beyond their strength.
For consider, brothers, what hap- 26
pened when God called you. Not many
of you were what men call wise, not
many of you were influential, not many
were of high birth. But it was what the 27
world calls foolish that God chose to
put the wise to shame with, and it was
what the world calls weak that God
chose to shame its strength with, and it 28
was what the world calls low and insignificant and unreal that God chose to
nullify its realities, so that in his pres- 29
ence no human being might have anything to boast of. But you are his chil- 30
dren, through your union with Christ
Jesus, whom God has made our wisdom
—our uprightness and consecration and

31 redemption, so that, as the Scripture
says, "Let him who would boast, boast
of the Lord!"

2 So when I came to you, brothers, I
did not come and tell you the secret
purpose of God in superior, philosophi-
2 cal language, for I resolved, while I was
with you, to forget everything but Je-
3 sus Christ and his crucifixion. For my
part, I came among you in weakness and
with a great deal of fear and trembling,
4 and my teaching and message were not
put in plausible, philosophical language, but they were attended with
5 convincing spiritual power, so that your
faith might rest, not on human philosophy, but on the power of God.

6 Yet there is a wisdom that we impart
when we are with people who have a
mature faith, but it is not what this
world calls wisdom, nor what the authorities of this world, doomed as they
7 are to pass away, would call so. But it
is a mysterious divine wisdom that we
impart, hitherto kept secret, and destined by God before the world began
8 for our glory. It is a wisdom unknown
to any of the authorities of this world,
for otherwise they would never have
9 crucified our glorious Lord. But, as the
Scripture says, there are things

"Which no eye ever saw and no ear
ever heard,
And never occurred to the human
mind,
Which God has provided for those
who love him."

10 For God revealed them to us through
his Spirit, for the Spirit fathoms everything, even the depths of God himself.
11 For what human being can understand
a man's thoughts except the man's own
spirit within him? Just so no one understands the thoughts of God but the
12 spirit of God. But the Spirit we have
received is not that of the world, but
the Spirit that comes from God, which
we have to make us realize the blessings
13 God has given us. These disclosures we
impart, not in the set phrases of human
philosophy, but in words the Spirit
teaches, giving spiritual truth a spiritu-
14 al form. A material man will not accept
what the Spirit of God offers. It seems
mere folly to him, and he cannot understand it, because it takes spiritual in-
15 sight to see its true value. But the spiritual man is alive to all true values, but
his own true value no unspiritual man
can see. For who has ever known the 16
Lord's thoughts, so that he can instruct
him? But we share the thoughts of
Christ.

So, for my part, brothers, I could not 3
treat you as spiritual persons; I had to
treat you just as creatures of flesh and
blood, as babies in Christian living. I 2
fed you with milk, not solid food, for
you were not ready for it.

Why, you are not ready for it now,
for you are still worldly. For when 3
there are still jealousy and quarrels
among you, are you not worldly and
living on a merely human level? For 4
when one man says, "I am a follower of
Paul," and another, "I am a follower of
Apollos," are you not simply human?
What is Apollos? Or what is Paul? 5
Just servants through whom you came
to have faith, as the Lord gave each of
us opportunity. I did the planting, 6
Apollos the watering, but it was God
who made the plants grow. So neither 7
the planter nor the waterer counts for
anything, but only God who makes the
plants grow. The planter and the wa- 8
terer are all one, though each of us will
be paid for his own work. For we are 9
fellow-laborers for God, and you are
God's farm, God's building.

Like an expert builder, I laid a foun- 10
dation, as God commissioned me to do,
and now someone else is building upon
it. But let everyone be careful how he
does so. For no one can lay any other 11
foundation than the one that is laid,
that is, Jesus Christ himself. And 12
whether one uses gold or silver or costly
stone in building on the foundation, or
wood or hay or straw, the quality of 13
everyone's work will appear, for the
Day will show it. For the Day will
break in fire, and the fire will test the
quality of everyone's work. If what 14
a man has built on the foundation
stands the test, he will have his pay. If 15
a man's work is burned up, he must
stand the loss, though he himself will be
saved, but as one who has passed
through the fire.

Do you not know that you are God's 16
temple and that God's Spirit makes its
home in you? If anyone destroys the 17
temple of God, God will destroy him.
For the temple of God is sacred, and
that is what you are.

Let no one of you deceive himself. If 18
any one of you imagines that he is wiser

than the rest of you, in what this world
calls wisdom, he had better become a
19 fool, so as to become really wise. For
this world's wisdom is foolishness to
God. For the Scripture says, "He who
catches the wise with their own cun-
20 ning," and "The Lord knows that the
deliberations of the wise are fruitless."
21 So no one should boast about men. For
22 it all belongs to you—Paul, Apollos,
Cephas, the world, life, death, the present, the future—all of it belongs to you.
23 But you belong to Christ, and Christ
belongs to God.

4 The right way for a man to think of
us is as Christ's servants, and managers
authorized to distribute the secret
2 truths of God. Now further, what is always demanded of managers is that
3 they can be depended on. I for my part
care very little about being examined
by you or by any human court. I do
not even offer myself for investigation.
4 For while my conscience does not trouble me at all, that does not prove that I
am innocent. It is the Lord who must
5 examine me. Do not form any premature judgments, therefore, but wait until the Lord comes back. For he will
light up the darkness that now hides
things and show what the motives in
people's minds are, and then everyone
will get from God the praise he deserves.

6 Now, brothers, for your benefit I
have applied all this only to Apollos
and myself, by using us as illustrations
to teach you the old lesson, "Never go
beyond the letter," and to keep any of
you from boasting of one teacher at the
7 expense of another. For who sees anything special in you? And what have
you got that you have not been given?
But if it has been given you, why do
you boast as though it had not been?
8 Are you satisfied already? Have you
become rich already? Have you entered your kingdom without waiting for
us? I wish you had entered it, so that
9 we might share it with you! For it
seems to me, God has exhibited us apostles at the very end of the procession,
like the men condemned to die in the
arena. For we have become a spectacle
to the whole universe, angels as well as
10 men. We are made fools of, for the sake
of Christ, while you are men of sense,
through being united with him. We are
weak, you are strong. You are distinguished, we are despised. To this day 11
we have gone hungry, thirsty, and
shabby; we have had rough usage, we
have had no home, we have worked 12
with our hands for a living. When people abuse us, we bless them, when they
persecute us, we put up with it, when 13
they slander us, we try to conciliate
them. We have come to be like the
scum of the earth, the dregs of the
world, and we are so now.

I do not write this to you to make 14
you ashamed, but to instruct you as
my dear children. For no matter how 15
many guides you may have in the
Christian life, you will not have many
fathers; for in this matter of union with
Christ, I became your father, through
preaching the good news to you. So I 16
urge you, follow my example. This is 17
why I have sent Timothy to you. He is
a dear child of mine, in the service of
the Lord, and one on whom you can depend, and he will help you to keep in
mind my methods in the service of
Christ Jesus, which I follow everywhere in every church.

Some of you seem to think that I am 18
not coming to visit you, and are putting
on airs about it. But I am coming very 19
soon to see you, if the Lord is willing,
and then I will find out, not what these
conceited people have to say, but what
they can actually do. For the kingdom 20
of God is not a matter of words but of
power. Which will you have? Shall I 21
come to you with a stick, or in a loving
and gentle spirit?

Immorality is actually notorious **5**
among you, and immorality of a kind
unknown even among the heathen—that
a man has taken his father's wife. And 2
can you put on airs, instead of being
overwhelmed with grief at having to
expel from your number the man who
has done this? For my part, though I 3
have been absent from you in person, I
have been present with you in spirit,
and as thus present I have already
passed judgment upon the man who has
done this, and meeting with you, in 4
spirit, with the power of our Lord Jesus, by the authority of our Lord Jesus 5
I have handed the man over to Satan,
for his physical destruction, in order
that his spirit may be saved on the Day
of the Lord. Certainly this is nothing 6
for you to boast of. Do you not know
that a little yeast will affect all the

7 dough? You must clean out the old
yeast and become fresh dough, free
from the old as you really are. For our
Passover lamb is already sacrificed; it
8 is Christ himself. So let us keep the festival, not with old yeast nor with the
yeast of vice and wickedness, but with
the unleavened bread of purity and
truth.

9 I wrote you in my letter not to asso-
10 ciate with immoral people—not that
you are to have nothing whatever to do
with the immoral people of the world,
any more than with its greedy and
grasping people or idolaters, for then
you would have to leave the world alto-
11 gether. What I meant was that you
are not to associate with anyone who is
supposed to be a Christian brother, and
yet is immoral or greedy or idolatrous
or abusive or drunken or grasping—
with such a person you must not even
12 eat. For what have I to do with judging outsiders? Is it not your part to
judge those who are inside the church,
and God's, to judge those who are out-
13 side? Drive the wrongdoer out from
among you.

6 When one of you has a disagreement
with his neighbor, does he dare to bring
the matter before a heathen court, instead of laying it before God's people?
2 Do you not know that God's people are
to be the judges of the world? And
if the world is to come before you for
judgment, are you unfit to decide the
3 most trivial cases? Do you not know
that we are to be the judges of angels,
to say nothing of ordinary matters?
4 If then you have ordinary matters to
be settled, will you submit them for
judgment to men who are nothing in
5 the church? I ask it to shame you.
Has it come to this, that there is not
a single wise man among you who could
settle a disagreement between one
6 brother and another, but one brother
has to go to law with another, and be-
7 fore unbelievers too? Having lawsuits
with one another at all means your
utter failure, to begin with. Why not
rather be wronged? Why not rather be
8 robbed? But it is you who wrong and
rob others, and your own brothers at
9 that! Do you not know that wrongdoers will not have any share in God's
kingdom? Do not let anyone mislead
you. People who are immoral or idolaters or adulterers or sensual or given
to unnatural vice or thieves or greedy— 10
drunkards, abusive people, robbers—
will not have any share in God's kingdom. Some of you used to be like that; 11
but you have washed it all away, you
have been consecrated, you have
become upright, by the power of our
Lord Jesus Christ and through the
Spirit of our God.

I may do anything I please, but not 12
everything I may do is good for me. I
may do anything I please; but I am not
going to let anything master me. It is 13
true, food is meant for the stomach,
and the stomach for the food, but God
will put an end to both of them. But
the body is not meant for immorality,
but for the service of the Lord, and the
Lord is for the body to serve. And as 14
God raised the Lord to life, he will raise
us also by his power. Do you not know 15
that your bodies are parts of Christ's
body? Am I then to take away from
Christ parts of his body, and make
them parts of a prostitute's? Never!
Or do you not know that a man who 16
has to do with a prostitute makes one
body with her? For "The two," says
the Scripture, "shall become physically
one." But whoever is united with the 17
Lord is one with him in spirit. Fly 18
from immorality! Any other sin a man
commits is something outside his body,
but the immoral man sins against his
own body. Or do you not know that 19
your body is a temple of the holy Spirit
that is within you, which you have received from God? Besides, you are not
your own; you have been bought and 20
paid for. Therefore, honor God with
your bodies.

As to the matters of which you wrote 7
me, it is an excellent thing for a man to
remain unmarried. But there is so 2
much immorality that every man had
better have a wife of his own, and every
woman a husband of her own. The hus- 3
band must give his wife what is due her,
and the wife must do the same by her
husband. A wife cannot do as she likes 4
with her own person; it is her husband's; and in the same way a husband
cannot do as he likes with his own person; it is his wife's. You must not re- 5
fuse each other what is due, unless you
agree to do so for a while, to devote
yourselves to prayer, and then to come
together again, so that Satan may not
tempt you through your lack of self-

6 control. But I mean this as a conces-
7 sion, not a command. I should like to
have everyone be just as I am myself;
but each one has his own special gift
from God, one of one kind, and one of
another.
8 To all who are unmarried and to widows, I would say this: It is an excellent thing if they can remain single as I
9 am. But if they cannot control themselves, let them marry. For it is better
to marry than to be on fire with pas-
10 sion. To those already married my instructions are—and they are not mine,
but the Lord's—that a wife is not to
11 separate from her husband. If she does
separate, she must remain single or else
become reconciled to him. And a hus-
12 band must not divorce his wife. To
other people I would say, though not as
Christ's command, if a Christian has a
wife who is not a believer, and she is
willing to live with him, he must not
13 divorce her, and a woman who has a
husband who is not a believer, but is
willing to live with her, must not di-
14 vorce her husband. For the husband
who is not a believer is consecrated
through union with his wife, and the
woman who is not a believer is consecrated through union with her Christian husband, for otherwise your children would be unblest, but, as it is,
15 they are consecrated. But if the one
who is not a believer wishes to separate,
let the separation take place. In such
cases the brother or sister is not a slave;
16 God has called you to live in peace. For
how do you wives know whether you
will save your husbands? Or how do
you husbands know whether you will
save your wives?
17 Only, everyone must continue in the
station which the Lord has appointed
for him, and in which he was when
God's call came to him. This is the rule
18 I make in all the churches. If a man
was circumcised when he was called, he
must not try to alter it. If a man was uncircumcised when he was called, he must
19 not have himself circumcised. Being
circumcised or being uncircumcised
does not make any difference; all that
matters is keeping God's commands.
20 Everyone ought to remain in the sta-
21 tion in which he was called. If you were
a slave when you were called, never
mind. Even if you can gain your freedom, make the most of your present
condition instead. For a slave who has 22
been called to union with the Lord is a
freedman of the Lord, just as a free man
who has been called is a slave of Christ.
You have been bought and paid for; 23
you must not let yourselves become
slaves to men. Brothers, everyone 24
must remain in fellowship with God in
the station in which he was called.
About unmarried women I have no 25
command of the Lord to give you, but I
will give you my opinion as that of one
on whom through the Lord's mercy you
can depend.
This, then, is my opinion in view of 26
the present distress—that it is a good
thing for a man to remain just as he is.
If you are united to a wife, do not seek 27
to be released. If you are not, do not
seek a wife. But if you do marry, there 28
is no sin in that. And if a girl marries,
it is no sin. But those who marry will
have worldly trouble, which I would
like to spare you. But this I do say, 29
brothers. The appointed time has
grown very short. From this time on
those who have wives should live as
though they had none, and those who 30
mourn as though they did not mourn,
and those who are glad as though they
were not glad, and those who buy anything as though they did not own it,
and those who mix in the world, as 31
though they were not absorbed in it.
For the present shape of the world is
passing away. I want you to be free 32
from all anxiety. An unmarried man is
concerned about the Lord's work, and
how he can please the Lord. A married 33
man is concerned about worldly affairs,
and how he can please his wife, and so
his interests are divided. An unmar- 34
ried woman or a girl is concerned about
the Lord's work, so as to be consecrated
in body and spirit, but the woman who
marries is concerned with wordly affairs, and how she can please her husband. It is for your benefit that I say 35
this, not to put a halter on you, but to
promote good order, and to secure your
undivided devotion to the Lord.
But if a man thinks he is not acting 36
properly toward the girl to whom he is
engaged, if his passions are too strong,
and that is what ought to be done, let
him do as he pleases; it is no sin; let
them be married. But a man who has 37
definitely made up his mind, under no
constraint of passion but with full self-

control, and who has decided in his own
mind to keep her as she is, will be doing
38 what is right. So the man who marries
her does what is right, and the man
who refrains from doing so does even
better.
39 A wife is bound to her husband as
long as he lives. If her husband dies,
she is free to marry anyone she pleases
40 so long as he is a Christian. But she will
be happier, in my judgment, if she remains as she is, and I think I have
God's spirit as well as other people.
8 About food that has been offered to
idols, it is true, as you say, that we all
have some knowledge on that matter.
Knowledge gives people airs; love is
2 what builds up character. If a man
thinks he has acquired some knowledge,
he does not yet know it as well as he
3 ought to know it. But if one loves
4 God, one is known by him. As to eating things, then, that have been offered
to idols, we all know that no idol has
any real existence, and that there is no
5 God but one. For supposing there are
so-called gods in heaven or on earth—
and indeed there are plenty of such gods
6 and lords—yet for us there is just one
God, the Father, who is the source of
all things, and for whom we live, and
just one Lord, Jesus Christ, through
whom everything was made and
7 through whom we live. But it is not
everyone that has this knowledge; for
some, through being long accustomed
to idols, still eat meat that has been
sacrificed to them as really offered to an
idol, and their consciences, being over-
8 sensitive, are troubled. But food is not
going to affect our standing with God.
We are none the worse if we do not eat
9 it, and none the better if we do. But
you must take care that this right of
yours does not prove a hindrance to the
10 overscrupulous. For if somebody sees
you, who have this knowledge, attending a dinner in an idol's temple,
will not he, with his sensitive conscience, be led to eat meat that is of-
11 fered to idols? For this overscrupulous
brother, for whom Christ died, is ruined
12 by what you call your knowledge. But
in sinning against your brothers in this
way and wounding their too scrupulous
consciences, you are really sinning
13 against Christ. Therefore, if what I eat
makes my brother fall, I will never eat
meat again, rather than make my
brother fall.
Am I not free? Am I not an apostle? 9
Have I not seen Jesus our Lord? Are
you not the product of my work in the
Lord's service? If I am not an apostle 2
to other people, I certainly am one to
you, for you yourselves, in your relation to the Lord, are the certificate of
my apostleship.
My answer to those who want to in- 3
vestigate me is this: Have we not a 4
right to our food and drink? Have we 5
not a right to take a Christian wife
about with us, like the rest of the apostles and the Lord's brothers and Cephas? Or is it only Barnabas and I 6
that have no right to give up working
for a living? What soldier ever pays his 7
expenses out of his own pay? Who
plants a vineyard and does not eat any
of the grapes? Who tends a flock and
does not get any of the milk? Am I 8
saying only what men say? Does not
the Law say so too? For in the Law of 9
Moses it reads, "You shall not muzzle
an ox that is treading out the grain."
Is it about the oxen that God is concerned? Is he not clearly speaking in 10
our interests? Of course this law was
written in our interests, because the
plowman ought to plow, and the
thresher to thresh, in the expectation
of sharing in the crop. If it was we who 11
sowed the spiritual seed among you, is
it too much if we reap material benefits
from you? If others enjoy such rights 12
over you, have we not a still better
claim? But, you say, we have never
availed ourselves of this right. No, we
will stand anything rather than put
any hindrance in the way of the good
news of the Christ. Do you not know 13
that those who do the work about the
Temple get their living from the Temple, and those who attend to the altar
divide the sacrifices with the altar? In 14
just that way the Lord directed that
those who preach the good news should
get their living from it. But I have not 15
availed myself of any of these rights.
And I am not writing this now so that I
may become an illustration of this; I
had rather die than do that. No one
shall deprive me of this boast of mine.
As far as preaching the good news is 16
concerned, that is nothing for me to
boast of, for I cannot help doing it. For
I am ruined if I do not preach. For if I 17

do it of my own accord, I have my pay,
but if I do it because I must, it is still a
responsibility that I am charged with.
18 What pay then do I get? Why, that in
my preaching I can offer the good news
without cost, and so not take full advantage of my rights as a preacher.
19 Though I am free from anyone's control, I have made myself everyone's
20 slave, so as to win over all the more. To
the Jews I have become like a Jew, to
win Jews over; to men under the Law I
have become like a man under the Law,
though I am not myself under the Law,
so as to win over those who are under
21 the Law. To those who have no law I
have become like a man without any
law—though I am not without the law
of God, but under the law of Christ—
so as to win over those who are without
22 any law. To the overscrupulous I have
become overscrupulous, so as to win the
overscrupulous; I have become everything to everybody, so as by all means
23 to save some of them. And I do it all
for the sake of the good news, so that I
may share in its blessings along with
the rest.
24 Do you not know that in a race the
runners all compete, but only one wins
the prize? That is the way you must
25 run, so as to win. Any man who enters
an athletic contest goes into strict
training, to win a wreath that will soon
wither, but the one we compete for will
26 never wither. So that is the way I run,
unswervingly. That is the way I fight,
27 not punching the air. But I beat and
bruise my body and make it my slave,
so that after I have called others to the
contest I may not be disqualified myself.

10 For I would not have you forget,
brothers, that though our forefathers
were all protected by the cloud, and all
2 passed safely through the sea, and in
the cloud and the sea all, as it were, accepted baptism as followers of Moses,
3 and all ate the same supernatural food
4 and drank the same supernatural drink
—for they used to drink from a supernatural rock which attended them, and
5 the rock was really Christ—still most of
them disappointed God, for they were
struck down in the desert.
6 Now these things happened to warn
us, so that we should not long for what
7 is evil as they did. You must not become idolaters, like some of them, for
the Scripture says, "The people sat
down to eat and drink and got up to
dance." Let us not practice immoral- 8
ity, like some of them, twenty-three
thousand of whom fell dead in one day.
Let us not try the Lord's patience too 9
far, as some of them did, for they were
killed for it by the snakes. You must 10
not grumble, as some of them did, for
they were destroyed for it by the destroying angel. These things happened 11
to them as a warning to others, but
they were written down to instruct us,
in whose days the ages have reached
their climax.
So the man who thinks he can stand 12
must be on his guard against a fall. It 13
is no superhuman temptation that you
have had. And God can be depended
on not to let you be tried beyond your
strength, but when temptation comes,
to give you a way out of it, so that you
can withstand it.
Therefore, my dear brothers, have 14
nothing to do with the worship of idols.
I appeal to your good sense. Make up 15
your minds about what I say. Does 16
not the consecrated cup which we bless
mean that in drinking it we share in the
blood of Christ? Does not the bread
that we break mean that in eating it we
share in the body of Christ? Because 17
there is one loaf, we, many as we are,
are one body, for we all share the one
loaf. Think of the Israelites' practices. 18
Do not those who eat what is sacrificed
have fellowship at the sacrificial altar?
What am I saying then? That there 19
is any such thing as being offered to
an idol, or any such thing as an idol?
No, but that what the heathen sacri- 20
fice they offer to demons and not to
God, and I do not want you to have
fellowship with demons. You cannot 21
drink the cup of the Lord and the cup
of demons. You cannot eat at the table
of the Lord and at the table of demons.
Or are we trying to arouse the Lord to 22
jealousy? Are we stronger than he is?
We are free to do anything, but not 23
everything is good for us. We are free
to do anything, but not everything
builds up character. No one should 24
look after his own advantage but after
that of his neighbor.
Eat anything for sale in the meat 25
market without raising any question,
as far as conscience is concerned, for the 26
earth and everything in it belongs to

27 the Lord. If one of the unbelievers invites you to dinner, and you wish to go,
eat whatever is served, without raising
any question, as far as conscience is
28 concerned. But if someone says to you,
"This meat has been offered in sacrifice," let it alone, on account of the man
who told you and his conscientious
29 scruples; his scruples, I say, not yours.
For why should my liberty of action be
30 limited by another's scruples? If I give
thanks for what I eat, why should
I be denounced for eating what I give
thanks over?
31 So whether you are eating or drinking or doing anything else, do it all to
32 the honor of God. You must not be
hindrances to Jews or Greeks or to the
33 church of God either, just as I for my
part try to please everyone in all I do,
not aiming at my own advantage, but
11 at that of people generally, in order
that they may be saved. Follow my
example in this, as I am following
Christ's.
2 I appreciate your always remembering me, and your standing by the things
I passed on to you, just as you received
3 them. But I want you to understand
that Christ is the head of every man,
while a woman's head is her husband,
4 and Christ's head is God. Any man
who offers prayer or explains the will of
God with anything on his head dis-
5 graces his head, and any woman who
offers prayer or explains the will of God
bareheaded disgraces her head, for it is
just as though she had her head shaved.
6 For if a woman will not wear a veil, let
her cut off her hair too. But if it is a
disgrace for a woman to have her hair
cut off or her head shaved, let her wear
7 a veil. For a man ought not to wear
anything on his head, for he is the image of God and reflects his glory; while
woman is the reflection of man's glory.
8 For man was not made from woman,
9 but woman from man, and man was
not created for woman, but woman was
10 for man. That is why she ought to
wear upon her head something to symbolize her subjection, on account of the
11 angels, if nobody else. But in union
with the Lord, woman is not inde-
pendent of man nor man of woman.
12 For just as woman was made from man,
man is born of woman, and it all real-
13 ly comes from God. Judge for yourselves. Is it proper for a woman to
offer prayer to God with nothing on
her head? Does not nature itself teach 14
you that for a man to wear his hair long
is degrading, but a woman's long hair is 15
her pride? For her hair is given her as
a covering. But if anyone is disposed 16
to be contentious about it, I for my
part recognize no other practice in worship than this, and neither do the
churches of God.
But while I am on this subject, I can- 17
not approve of your meetings, because
they are doing you more harm than
good. For, in the first place, when you 18
meet as a congregation, I hear that you
divide into sets, and in a measure I believe it. Doubtless there must be par- 19
ties among you, if those who are right
are to be recognized among you. So 20
when you hold your meetings, it is not
the Lord's Supper that you eat, for each 21
of you hurries to get his own supper and
eat it, and one goes hungry while another gets drunk. Have you no houses 22
to eat and drink in? Or do you mean to
show your contempt for the church of
God, and to humiliate those who have
nothing? What can I say to you? Can I
approve of you? Not in this matter
certainly. For I myself received from 23
the Lord the account that I passed on
to you, that the Lord Jesus the night he
was betrayed took some bread and gave 24
thanks for it and then broke it in pieces,
saying, "This is my body which takes
your place. Do this in memory of me."
He took the cup, too, after supper, in 25
the same way, saying, "This cup is the
new agreement ratified by my blood.
Whenever you drink it, do so in memory of me." For until the Lord comes 26
back, every time you eat this bread and 27
drink from the cup, you proclaim his
death. Hence anyone who eats the
bread or drinks from the Lord's cup in
a way that is unworthy of it will be
guilty of profaning the body and the
blood of the Lord. A man should exam- 28
ine himself, and only when he has done
so should he eat the bread or drink
from the cup. For anyone who eats 29
and drinks, eats and drinks a judgment upon himself if he does not recognize the body. This is why many of you 30
are sick and ill and a number have fall-
en asleep. But if we recognized our 31
own condition, we would not incur this
judgment. But since we do incur it, we 32
are disciplined by the Lord, so that we

may not be condemned along with the
33 world. So, my brothers, when you come
together to eat, wait for one another.
34 If anyone is hungry, let him eat at
home, so that your meetings may not
bring down a judgment upon you. The
details I will settle when I come.
12 About spiritual gifts, brothers, I do
2 not want you to be misinformed. You
know that when you were heathen you
would stray off, as impulse directed, to
3 idols that could not speak. Therefore,
I must tell you that no one who is
speaking under the influence of the
Spirit of God ever says, "Curse Jesus!"
and no one can say, "Jesus is Lord!"
without being under the influence of
the holy Spirit.
4 Endowments vary, but the Spirit is
5 the same, and forms of service vary, but
6 it is the same Lord who is served, and
activities vary, but God who produces
7 them all in us all is the same. Each one
is given his spiritual illumination for
8 the common good. One man receives
through the Spirit the power to speak
wisely, another, by the same Spirit, receives the power to express knowledge,
9 another, from his union with the same
Spirit receives faith, another, by one
and the same Spirit, the ability to cure
10 the sick, another, the working of wonders, another, inspiration in preaching,
another, the power of distinguishing
the true Spirit from false ones, another,
various ecstatic utterances, and another, the ability to explain them.
11 These are all produced by one and the
same Spirit, and apportioned to each of
us just as the Spirit chooses.
12 For just as the body is one and yet
has many parts, and all the parts of the
body, many as they are, form one body,
13 so it is with Christ. For we have all—
Jews or Greeks, slaves or free men—
been baptized in one spirit to form one
body, and we have all been saturated
14 with one Spirit. For the body does not
15 consist of one part but of many. If the
foot says, "As I am not a hand, I am
not a part of the body," that does not
make it any less a part of the body.
16 And if the ear says, "As I am not an
eye, I am not a part of the body," that
does not make it any less a part of the
17 body. If all the body were eye, how
would we hear? If it were all ear, how
18 could we have a sense of smell? As it is,
God has arranged the parts, every one
of them in the body as he wished them
to be. If they were all one part, where 19
would the body be? As it is, there are 20
many parts, but one body. The eye 21
cannot say to the hand, "I do not need
you," or the head to the feet, "I do not
need you." On the contrary, the parts 22
of the body that are considered most
delicate are indispensable, and the 23
parts of it that we think common, we
dress with especial care, and our unpresentable parts receive especial attention which our presentable parts do not 24
need. God has so adjusted the body
and given such especial distinction to
its inferior parts that there is no clash 25
in the body, but its parts all alike care
for one another. If one part suffers, all 26
the parts share its sufferings. If a part
has honor done it, all the parts enjoy it
too. Now you are Christ's body, and 27
individually parts of it. And God has 28
placed people in the church, first as
apostles, second as inspired preachers,
third as teachers, then wonder-workers;
then come ability to cure the sick, helpfulness, administration, ecstatic speaking. Is everyone an apostle? Is every- 29
one an inspired preacher? Is everyone
a teacher? Is everyone a wonder-worker? Is everyone able to cure the sick? 30
Can everyone speak ecstatically? Can
everyone explain what it means? But 31
you must cultivate the higher endowments.
I will show you a far better way. If I 13
can speak the languages of men and
even of angels, but have no love, I am
only a noisy gong or a clashing cymbal.
If I am inspired to preach and know all 2
the secret truths and possess all knowledge, and if I have such perfect faith
that I can move mountains, but have
no love, I am nothing. Even if I give 3
away everything I own, and give myself up, but do it in pride, not love, it
does me no good. Love is patient and 4
kind. Love is not envious or boastful.
It does not put on airs. It is not rude. 5
It does not insist on its rights. It does
not become angry. It is not resentful.
It is not happy over injustice, it is only 6
happy with truth. It will bear any- 7
thing, believe anything, hope for anything, endure anything. Love will nev- 8
er die out. If there is inspired preaching, it will pass away. If there is ecstatic speaking, it will cease. If there is
knowledge, it will pass away. For our 9

knowledge is imperfect and our preach-
10 ing is imperfect. But when perfection
comes, what is imperfect will pass
11 away. When I was a child, I talked like
a child, I thought like a child, I reasoned like a child. When I became a
12 man, I put aside my childish ways. For
now we are looking at a dim reflection
in a mirror, but then we shall see face to
face. Now my knowledge is imperfect,
but then I shall know as fully as God
13 knows me. So faith, hope, and love endure. These are the great three, and
the greatest of them is love.

14 You must pursue love, while you are
cultivating the spiritual endowments,
2 and especially inspired preaching. For
anyone who speaks ecstatically is
speaking not to men but to God, for no
one can understand him, though by the
Spirit he is uttering secret truths. But
3 the inspired preacher does his fellow-
men good and encourages and comforts
4 them. Anyone who speaks ecstatically
does himself good, but the inspired
5 preacher does a congregation good. I
want you all to speak ecstatically, but I
especially want you to be inspired to
preach. The man who is inspired to
preach is more useful than the one who
speaks ecstatically—unless he can explain what he says so that it may do the
church some good.

6 But as it is, brothers, if I come back
to you and speak ecstatically, what
good will I do you, unless I have some
revelation or special knowledge or mes-
7 sage or teaching to give you? Even in-
animate things, like the flute or the
harp, may produce sound, but if there
is no difference in the notes, how can
8 you tell what is being played? If the
bugle does not sound a clear call, who
9 will prepare for battle? So if you in
your ecstatic speaking utter words no
one can understand, how will people
know what you are saying? You will be
10 talking to the empty air! There are
probably ever so many different languages in the world, each with its own
11 meaning. So if I do not know the meaning of the language, I shall seem to the
man who is speaking to be a foreigner,
and he will seem to me to be one too.
12 So since you are ambitious for spiritual
endowments, you must try to excel in
them in ways that will do good to the
13 church. Therefore, the man who can
speak ecstatically should pray for the
power to explain what he says. For if I 14
pray ecstatically, it is my spirit that
prays, but my mind is helping nobody.
Then what am I to do? I will sing ec- 15
statically, but I will sing intelligently
too. For if you utter blessings in ecstat- 16
ic speech, how is an ordinary man to
say Amen to your thanksgiving? For
he does not know what you are saying.
You are giving thanks well enough, but 17
it is doing him no good. Thank God, I 18
speak in ecstasy more than any of you.
But in public worship I would rather 19
say five words with my understanding
so as to instruct others also than ten
thousand words in an ecstasy.

Brothers, you must not be children 20
mentally. In evil be babies, but mentally be mature. In the Law it says, 21
"By men of strange languages and by
the lips of foreigners I will speak to this
nation, and not even then will they listen to me, says the Lord." So this ec- 22
static speaking is meant as a sign not to
those who believe but to unbelievers,
but inspired preaching is a sign not to
unbelievers but to those who believe.
Hence, if the whole church assembles 23
and they all speak ecstatically, and ordinary people or unbelievers come in,
will they not say that you are mad?
But if they are all inspired to preach 24
and some unbeliever or outsider comes
in, he is convinced of his sin by them
all, he is called to account by them all,
the secrets of his heart are exposed, and 25
he will fall down on his face and worship God, and declare that God is really
among you.

Then what is the right course, broth- 26
ers? When you meet together, suppose every one of you has a song, a
teaching, a revelation, an ecstatic utterance, or an explanation of one; it
must all be for the good of all. If there 27
is any ecstatic speaking, let it be limited to two or three people at the most,
and have one speak at a time and someone explain what he says. But if there 28
is no one to explain it, have him keep
quiet in church, and talk to himself and
to God. And let two or three who are 29
inspired to preach speak, while the rest
weigh what is said; and if anything is 30
revealed to another who is seated, the
one who is speaking must stop. For in 31
this way you can all preach one after
another, as you are inspired to, so that
everyone may be instructed and stimu-

32 lated, for the spirits of prophets will
33 give way to prophets, for God is not a
God of disorder but of peace.
34 As in all the churches of God's people, women are to keep quiet in church,
for they are not allowed to speak.
They must take a subordinate place, just
35 as the Law says. If they want to find
out about anything, they should ask
their husbands at home, for it is disgraceful for a woman to speak in
36 church. Did God's message start from
you Corinthians? Or are you the only
people it has reached?
37 If anyone claims to be inspired to
preach, or to have any other spiritual
endowment, let him understand that
what I am now writing you is a com-
38 mand from the Lord. If anyone pays
no attention to it, pay no attention to
39 him. So, my brothers, set your hearts
on being inspired to preach, and yet do
not hinder people from speaking ecstat-
40 ically. But let everything be done in a
proper and orderly way.
15 Now I want to remind you, brothers,
of the form in which I presented to you
the good news I brought, which you ac-
2 cepted and have stood by, and through
which you are to be saved, if you hold
on, unless your faith has been all for
3 nothing. For I passed on to you, as of
first importance, the account I had received, that Christ died for our sins, as
4 the Scriptures foretold, that he was
buried, that on the third day he was
raised from the dead, as the Scriptures
5 foretold, and that he was seen by Ce-
6 phas, and then by the Twelve. After
that he was seen by more than five hundred brothers at one time, most of
whom are still alive, although some of
7 them have fallen asleep. Then he was
seen by James, then by all the apostles,
8 and finally he was seen by me also, as
though I were born at the wrong time.
9 For I am the least important of the
apostles, and am not fit to be called an
apostle, because I once persecuted
10 God's church. But by God's favor I
have become what I am, and the favor
he showed me has not gone for nothing,
but I have worked harder than any of
them, although it was not really I but
11 the favor God showed me. But whether
it was I or they, this is what we preach,
and this is what you believed.
12 Now if what we preach about Christ
is that he was raised from the dead,
how can some of you say that there is
no such thing as a resurrection of the
dead? If there is no resurrection of the 13
dead, then Christ was not raised, and if 14
Christ was not raised, there is nothing
in our message; there is nothing in our
faith either, and we are found guilty of 15
misrepresenting God, for we have testified that he raised Christ, when he did
not do it, if it is true that the dead are
never raised. For if the dead are never 16
raised, Christ was not raised; and if 17
Christ was not raised, your faith is a delusion; you are still under the control of
your sins. Yes, and those who have fall- 18
en asleep in trust in Christ have perished. If we have centered our hopes 19
on Christ in this life, and that is all, we
are the most pitiable people in the
world.
But the truth is, Christ was raised 20
from the dead, the first to be raised of
those who have fallen asleep. For since 21
it was through a man that we have
death, it is through a man also that we
have the raising of the dead. For just 22
as because of their relation to Adam all
men die, so because of their relation to
Christ they will all be brought to life
again. But each in his own turn; Christ 23
first, and then at Christ's coming those
who belong to him. After that will 24
come the end, when he will turn over
the kingdom to God his Father, bringing to an end all other government,
authority, and power, for he must re- 25
tain the kingdom until he puts all his
enemies under his feet. The last enemy 26
to be overthrown will be death, for 27
everything is to be reduced to subjection and put under Christ's feet. But
when it says that everything is subject
to him, he is evidently excepted who
reduced it all to subjection to him. And 28
when everything is reduced to subjection to him, then the Son himself will
also become subject to him who has reduced everything to subjection to him,
so that God may be everything to
everyone.
Otherwise, what do people mean by 29
having themselves baptized on behalf
of their dead? If the dead do not rise at
all, why do they have themselves baptized on their behalf? Why do we our- 30
selves run such risks every hour? By 31
the very pride I take in you, brothers,
through our union with Christ Jesus
our Lord, I face death every day. From 32

the human point of view, what good is
it to me that I have fought wild animals
here in Ephesus? If the dead do not
rise at all, "Let us eat and drink, for we
33 will be dead tomorrow!" Do not be
misled. Bad company ruins character.
34 Return to your sober sense as you
ought, and stop sinning, for some of
you are utterly ignorant about God.
To your shame I say so.
35 But someone will say, "How can the
dead rise? What kind of a body will
36 they have when they come back?" You
foolish man, the very seed you sow nev-
37 er comes to life without dying first; and
when you sow it, it has not the form it
is going to have, but is a naked kernel,
perhaps of wheat or something else;
38 and God gives it just such a form as he
pleases, so that each kind of seed has a
39 form of its own. Flesh is not all alike;
men have one kind, animals another,
40 birds another, and fish another. There
are heavenly bodies, and there are
earthly bodies, but the beauty of the
heavenly bodies is of one kind, and the
beauty of the earthly bodies is of an-
41 other. The sun has one kind of beauty,
and the moon another, and the stars
another; why, one star differs from an-
42 other in beauty. It is so with the resur-
43 rection of the dead. The body is sown
in decay, it is raised free from decay. It
is sown in humiliation, it is raised in
splendor. It is sown in weakness, it is
44 raised in strength. It is a physical body
that is sown, it is a spiritual body that
is raised. If there is a physical body,
45 there is a spiritual body also. This is
45 also what the Scripture says: "The
first man Adam became a living creature." The last Adam has become a
46 life-giving Spirit. It is not the spiritual
that comes first, but the physical, and
47 then the spiritual. The first man is of
the dust of the earth; the second man is
48 from heaven. Those who are of the
earth are like him who was of the earth,
and those who are of heaven are like
49 him who is from heaven, and as we have
been like the man of the earth, let us
also be like the man from heaven.
50 But I can tell you this, brothers: flesh
and blood cannot share in the Kingdom
of God, and decay will not share in
51 what is imperishable. I will tell you a
secret. We shall not all fall asleep, but
52 we shall all be changed, in a moment,
in the twinkling of an eye, at the sound

of the last trumpet. For the trumpet
will sound, and the dead will be raised
free from decay, and we shall be
changed. For this perishable nature 53
must put on the imperishable, and this
mortal nature must put on immortality. And when this mortal nature puts 54
on immortality, then what the Scripture says will come true—"Death has
been triumphantly destroyed. Where, 55
Death, is your victory? Where, Death,
is your sting?" Sin is the sting of 56
death, and it is the Law that gives
sin its power. But thank God! He gives 57
us victory through our Lord Jesus
Christ. So my dear brothers, be firm 58
and unmoved, and always devote yourselves to the Lord's work, for you know
that through the Lord your labor is not
thrown away.

About the collection for God's peo- **16**
ple, I want you to do as I told the
churches of Galatia to do. On the first 2
of every week each of you is to put aside
and store up whatever he gains, so that
money will not have to be collected
after I come. When I come I will send 3
whatever persons you authorize with
credentials, to carry your gift to Jerusalem. And if it seems worth while for 4
me to go myself, they can go with me.
I will come to you after passing 5
through Macedonia, for I am going
through Macedonia, and I will proba- 6
bly stay some time with you, or even
pass the winter, so that you may start
me off for wherever I may be going.
For I do not want to see you now just 7
in passing, for I hope to spend some
time with you if the Lord permits it.
But I shall stay in Ephesus until the 8
Harvest Festival, for I have a great and 9
promising opportunity here, as well as
many opponents.

If Timothy reaches you, put him at 10
his ease among you, for he is devoted to
the Lord's work, just as I am. So no one 11
is to slight him. But see him off cordially when he comes back to me, for
I am expecting him with the other
brothers.

As for our brother Apollos, I have 12
often urged him to visit you with the
other brothers, and he is quite unwilling to come now, but he will come when
he has a good opportunity.

Be on the watch. Stand firm in your 13
faith. Act like men. Show yourselves
strong. Do everything with love. 14

15 Now I urge you, brothers—you know
that the family of Stephanas was the
first to be converted in Greece, and
that they have devoted themselves to
16 the service of God's people—I want you
to enlist under such leaders, and under
anyone who joins with you and works
17 hard. And I am glad that Stephanas,
Fortunatus, and Achaicus have come
here, for they have made up for your
18 absence. They have cheered my heart,
and yours too. You should appreciate
such men.

The churches of Asia wish to be re- 19
membered to you. Aquila and Prisca,
with the congregation that meets at
their house, send you their special
Christian greetings. All the brothers 20
wish to be remembered to you. Greet
one another with a sacred kiss.

This farewell I, Paul, add in my own 21
hand. A curse upon anyone who has no 22
love for the Lord. Lord, come quickly!
The blessing of the Lord Jesus be with 23
you! My love be with you all through 24
Christ Jesus.

THE SECOND LETTER TO THE CORINTHIANS

1 PAUL, by God's will an apostle of
Christ Jesus, and Timothy our
brother, to the church of God
that is at Corinth, and all God's
2 people all over Greece; God our Father
and the Lord Jesus Christ bless you and
give you peace.
3 Blessed be the God and Father of our
Lord Jesus Christ, the merciful Father,
and the God always ready to comfort!
4 He comforts me in all my trouble, so
that I can comfort people who are in
any trouble with the comfort with
which I myself am comforted by God.
5 For if I have a liberal share of Christ's
sufferings, through Christ I have a lib-
6 eral share of comfort too. If I am in
trouble, it is to bring you comfort and
salvation, and if I am comforted, it is
for the sake of the comfort which you
experience when you steadfastly endure
such sufferings as I also have to bear.
7 My hopes for you are unshaken. For I
know that just as surely as you share
my sufferings, just so surely you will
8 share my comfort. For I do not want
you, brothers, to misunderstand the
distress that I experienced in Asia, for
I was so utterly and unendurably
crushed, that I actually despaired of
9 life itself. Why, I felt in my heart that
the end must be death. That was to
keep me from relying on myself instead
of on God, who can even raise the dead.
10 So deadly was the peril from which he
saved me, as he will save me again! It
is on him that I have set my hope that
11 he will save me again. You must help
me by your prayers, so that many will
give thanks to God on my behalf for the
blessing granted me in answer to many
prayers.
12 For my boast is what my conscience
tells me, that my relations to the world
and still more to you have been marked
by pure motives and godly sincerity,
not by worldly shrewdness but by the
13 favor of God. For what I am writing
to you is only what you can read and
understand, and I hope that you will
understand it fully, as some of you have 14
come to understand me, and that you
will understand that you have a right to
be proud of me, as I have of you, on the
Day of our Lord Jesus.
It was because I was sure of this that 15
I wanted to come to see you before going anywhere else, to give you a double
pleasure; I was going to visit you on my 16
way to Macedonia, and then to come
back to you from Macedonia and have
you see me off for Judea. Was it vacil- 17
lating of me to want to do that? Do I
make my plans like a worldly man,
ready to say "Yes" and "No" in the
same breath? As surely as God can be 18
relied on, there has been no equivoca-
tion about our message to you. The 19
Son of God, Christ Jesus, whom we proclaimed among you, Silvanus, Timothy,
and I, you have not found wavering
between "Yes" and "No." With him it
has always been "Yes," for to all the 20
promises of God he supplies the "Yes"
that confirms them. That is why we
utter the "Amen" through him, when
we give glory to God. But it is God 21
who guarantees us and you to Christ;
he has anointed us and put his seal upon 22
us and given us his Spirit in our hearts,
as his guarantee.
But upon my soul I call God to wit- 23
ness that it is simply to spare you that
I have stayed away from Corinth. Not 24
that we are the masters of you and your
faith; we are working with you to make
you happy, for in your faith you stand
firm enough.
For I made up my mind not to make 2
you another painful visit. For if I hurt 2
your feelings, who is there to cheer me
up but the man whose feelings I hurt?
This is what I said in my letter, so that 3
I might avoid coming and having my
feelings hurt by the very people who
might have been expected to make me
happy, for I felt sure about you all, that
what made me happy would make you

4 all happy. For I was in great trouble
and distress of mind when I wrote you,
and I shed many tears as I did it, yet
it was not to hurt your feelings, but to
make you realize the extraordinary affection I have for you.
5 But if anyone has hurt anybody's
feelings, it is not so much mine, as
yours, or at least those of some of you,
6 not to be too hard upon all of you. For
that individual, this censure by the
majority of you is punishment enough,
7 and so you must now turn around and
forgive and comfort him, or he may be
8 overwhelmed by his remorse. So I beg
you to restore him to his place in your
9 affections. For that is why I wrote you
—to find out how you would stand the
test, and see if you would obey me ab-
10 solutely. When you forgive a man, I
forgive him too. For anything I had to
forgive has been forgiven on your account, and as in the very presence of
11 Christ, to keep Satan from getting the
better of us. For we know what he is
after.
12 When I went to Troas to preach the
good news of the Christ there, I found a
13 good opening for the Lord's work, but
my mind could not rest because I did
not find my brother Titus there. So I
said goodbye to them and went on to
14 Macedonia. But thank God! he always leads me in his triumphal train,
through Christ, and spreads the perfume of knowledge of him everywhere
15 through me as his censer-bearer. Yes,
I am the fragrance of Christ to God,
diffused among those who are being
saved and those who are perishing
16 alike; to the one, a deathly, deadly
odor, to the other a vital, life-giving
17 one. Who is qualified for this task? I
am! For I am no peddler of God's message, like most men, but like a man of
sincerity, commissioned by God and in
his presence, in union with Christ I utter his message.

3 Am I falling into self-recommenda-
tion again? Do I, like some people,
need letters of recommendation to you
2 or from you? You are my recommen-
dations, written on my heart, for every-
3 body to read and understand. You
show that you are a letter from Christ
delivered by me, written not in ink, but
in the Spirit of the living God, and not
on tablets of stone, but on the human
heart.

Such is the confidence that I have 4
through Christ in my relations to God.
Not that I am of myself qualified to 5
claim anything as originating with me.
My qualification is from God, and he 6
has qualified me to serve him in the interests of a new agreement, not in writing but of spirit. For what is written
kills, but the Spirit gives life.
But if the religion of death, carved in 7
letters of stone, was ushered in with
such splendor, so that the Israelites
could not look at Moses' face on account of the brightness that was fading from it, why should not the religion 8
of the Spirit be attended with much
greater splendor? If there was splendor 9
in the religion of condemnation, the religion of uprightness must far surpass
it in splendor. For in comparison with 10
its surpassing splendor, what was splendid has come to have no splendor at all.
For if what faded away came with 11
splendor, how much more splendid
what is permanent must be!
So since I have such a hope, I speak 12
with great frankness, not like Moses, 13
who used to wear a veil over his face,
to keep the Israelites from gazing at the
fading of the splendor from it. Their 14
minds were dulled. For to this day,
that same veil remains unlifted, when
they read the old agreement, for only
through union with Christ is it removed. Why, to this day, whenever 15
Moses is read, a veil hangs over their
minds, but "whenever a man turns to 16
the Lord, the veil is removed." Now the 17
Lord here means the Spirit, and wherever the Spirit of the Lord is, there is
freedom. And all of us, reflecting the 18
splendor of the Lord in our unveiled
faces, are being changed into likeness
to him, from one degree of splendor to
another, for this comes from the Lord
who is the Spirit.

So since by the mercy of God I am 4
engaged in this service, I never lose
heart. I disown disgraceful, under- 2
handed ways. I refuse to practice cunning or to tamper with God's message.
It is by the open statement of the truth
that I would commend myself to every
human conscience in the sight of God.
If the meaning of my preaching of the 3
good news is veiled at all, it is so only
in the case of those who are on the way
to destruction. In their case, the god of 4
this world has blinded the minds of the

unbelievers, to keep the light of the
good news of the glorious Christ, the
likeness of God, from dawning upon
5 them. For it is not myself but Christ
Jesus that I am proclaiming as Lord;
I am only a slave of yours for Jesus'
6 sake. For God who said, "Let light
shine out of darkness," has shone in
my heart, to give me the light of the
knowledge of God's glory, that is on
the face of Christ.
7 But I have this treasure in a mere
earthen jar, to show that its amazing
power belongs to God and not to me.
8 I am hard pressed on every side, but
never cut off: perplexed, but not driv-
9 en to despair; routed, but not abandoned; struck down, but not destroyed;
10 never free from the danger of being put
to death like Jesus, so that in my body
11 the life of Jesus also may be seen. For
every day I live I am being given up to
death for Jesus' sake, so that the life
of Jesus may be visible in my mortal
12 nature. So it is death that operates in
my case, but life that operates in
13 yours. In the same spirit of faith as his
who said, "I believed, and so I spoke,"
14 I too believe, and so I speak, sure that
he who raised the Lord Jesus from the
dead will raise me also like Jesus, and
bring me side by side with you into his
15 presence. For it is all for your benefit,
in order that as God's favor reaches
greater and greater numbers, it may result in more and more thanksgiving in
praise of God.
16 So I never lose heart. Though my
outer nature is wasting away, my inner
17 is being renewed every day. For this
slight, momentary trouble is piling up
for me an eternal blessedness beyond
18 all comparison, because I keep my eyes
not on what is seen but what is unseen.
5 For what is seen is transitory, but what
is unseen is eternal. For I know that if
this earthly tent that I live in is taken
down, God will provide me a building in
heaven to live in, not built by human
2 hands but eternal. This makes me sigh
with longing to put on my heavenly
3 dwelling, for if I do, I shall never find
4 myself disembodied. For I who am still
in my tent sigh with anxiety, because I
do not want to be stripped of it, but to
put on the other over it, so that what is
only mortal may be absorbed in life.
5 It is God himself who has prepared me
for this change, and he has given me the
Spirit as his guarantee.
So I am confident. I know well that 6
as long as I am at home in the body I
am away from the Lord (for I have to 7
guide my steps by faith, not by what is
seen)—yet I am confident, and I pre- 8
fer to leave my home in the body and
make my home with the Lord. So 9
whether I am at home or away from it,
it is my ambition to please him. For we 10
must all appear in our true characters
before the tribunal of the Christ, each
to be repaid with good or evil for the
life he has lived in the body.
It is with this knowledge of what the 11
fear of the Lord means that I appeal to
men. My true character is perfectly
plain to God, and I hope to your consciences too. I am not trying to recom- 12
mend myself to you again. I am giving
you cause to be proud of me, to use in
answering men who pride themselves
on external advantages and not on sincerity of heart. For if I was out of my 13
senses, as they say, it was between God
and me; and if I am in my right mind,
it is for your good. It is Christ's love 14
that controls me, for I have become
convinced that as one has died for all,
all have died, and he died for all that 15
those who live might no longer live for
themselves, but for him who died for
them and rose again.
So from that time on, I have esti- 16
mated nobody at what he seemed to be
outwardly; even though I once estimated Christ in that way, I no longer
do so. So if anyone is in union with 17
Christ, he is a new being; the old state
of things has passed away; there is a
new state of things. All this comes from 18
God, who through Christ has reconciled me to himself, and has commissioned me to proclaim this reconciliation—how God through Christ recon- 19
ciled the world to himself, refusing to
count men's offenses against them, and
intrusted me with the message of reconciliation.
It is for Christ, therefore, that I am 20
an envoy, seeing that God makes his
appeal through me. On Christ's behalf
I beg you to be reconciled to God. He 21
made him who knew nothing of sin to
be sin, for our sake, so that through
union with him we might become God's
uprightness.

6 As God's fellow-worker, I appeal to
you, too, not to accept the favor of
2 God and then waste it. For he says,
"I have listened to you at a welcome
time,
And helped you on a day of deliverance!"
Now the welcome time has come!
3 This is the day of deliverance! I put no
obstacles in anyone's path, so that no
4 fault may be found with my work. On
the contrary, as a servant of God I try
in every way to commend myself to
them, through my great endurance in
5 troubles, difficulties, hardships, beatings, imprisonments, riots, labors,
6 sleepless nights, and hunger, through
my purity of life, my knowledge, my
patience, my kindness, my holiness of
7 spirit, my genuine love, the truth of my
teaching, and the power of God; with
the weapons of uprightness for the
8 right hand and the left, in honor or dis-
9 honor, in praise or blame; considered
an impostor, when I am true, obscure,
when I am well known, at the point of
death, yet here I am alive, punished,
10 but not dead yet, pained, when I am always glad, poor, when I make many
others rich, penniless, when really I
own everything.
11 I have kept nothing back from you,
men of Corinth; I have opened my
12 heart to you. It is not that I am cramp-
13 ing you, it is your own affections. To
pay me back, I tell you, my children,
you must open your hearts too.
14 Do not get into close and incongruous
relations with unbelievers. What partnership can uprightness have with iniquity, or what can light have to do
15 with darkness? How can Christ agree
with Belial? Or what has a believer in
16 common with an unbeliever? What
bargain can a temple of God make with
idols? For we are a temple of the living
God, just as God said,
"I will live in them and move among
them,
And I will be their God and they
will be my people."
17 Therefore,
"Come out from them,
And separate from them, says the
Lord,
And touch nothing that is unclean.
Then I will welcome you,
18 I will become a father to you,
And you shall become my sons and
daughters,
Says the Lord Almighty."
So since we have promises like these, 7
dear friends, let us cleanse ourselves of
everything that can defile body or spirit, and by reverence for God make our
consecration complete.
Make room for me in your hearts. I 2
have not wronged or harmed or got the
better of anybody. I do not mean this 3
as a reflection upon you, for as I said
before, you will always have a place in
my heart whether I live or die. I have 4
the greatest confidence in you. I take
the greatest pride in you. I am fully
comforted. After all my trouble, I am
overjoyed.
For even when I reached Macedonia, 5
my poor human nature could get no relief—there was trouble at every turn;
fighting without, and fear within. But 6
God, who comforts the downcast, comforted me by the coming of Titus, and 7
not only by his coming, but by the comfort you had given him, for he told me
how you longed to see me, how sorry
you were, and how you took my part,
which made me happier still. For even 8
if I did hurt your feelings with that letter, I cannot regret it; even if I did regret it, when I saw that the letter had
hurt your feelings perhaps for a while, I 9
am glad of it now; not because you had
your feelings hurt, but because having
them hurt led you to repent, for you
took it as God meant you to do, so that
you should not lose anything at all
through me. For the pain that God ap- 10
proves results in a repentance that leads
to salvation and leaves no regrets; but
the world's pain results in death. See 11
how earnest this God-given pain has
made you! how eager to clear yourselves, how indignant, how alarmed,
how eager to see me, how zealous, how
avenging! At every point you have
proved that you are clear of this matter. So although I did write to you, it 12
was not on account of the offender, nor
of the injured man, but in the sight of
God to reveal to you your devotion to
me. That is why I am so comforted. 13
With all my own comfort, I was still
more overjoyed at the gladness of Titus, for his mind has been set at rest by
you all. If I did express some pride in 14
you to him, I have had no reason to be
ashamed of it, but just as all I said to

you was true, my boasting before Titus
15 has also proved true. His heart goes out
all the more to you, as he recalls how
you all obeyed him, and with what reverence and trembling you received him.
16 I am glad that I can feel perfect confidence in you.

8 I must tell you, brothers, how the
favor of God has been shown in the
2 churches of Macedonia, for in spite of a
severe ordeal of trouble, their extraordinary gladness, combined with their extreme poverty, has overflowed in a
3 wealth of generosity. For they have
given to the utmost of their ability, as I
can bear them witness, and beyond
4 it, and begged me most earnestly, of
their own accord, to let them share in
5 the support of God's people. They
did far more than I hoped, for first
in obedience to God's will, they gave
themselves to the Lord, and to me.
6 This has led me to urge Titus to complete the arrangements he had formerly begun among you for this gra-
7 cious undertaking. Just as you excel in
everything else — faith, expression,
knowledge, perfect devotion, and the
love we have awakened in you—you
must excel in this generous undertaking
too.

8 I do not mean this as a command. I
only want to test the genuineness of
your love by the devotion of others.
9 You know how gracious the Lord Jesus
Christ was. Though he was rich, he became poor for your sake, in order that
by his poverty you might become rich.
10 But I will tell you what I think about
it. For this is the best way to deal with
you, for you were the first not only to
do anything about this, but to want to
do anything, and that was last year.
11 Now finish doing it, so that your readiness to undertake it may be equaled by
the way you finish it up, as well as your
12 means permit. If a man is willing to
give, the value of his gift is in its proportion to what he has, not to what he
13 has not. I do not mean to be easy upon
14 others and hard upon you, but to equal-
ize the burden, and in the present situation to have your plenty make up for
what they need, so that some day their
plenty may make up for what you need,
15 and so things may be made equal—as
the Scripture says, "The man who got
much did not have too much, and the
man who got little did not have too
little."

Thank God, he puts the same devo- 16
tion to you that I feel into Titus' heart,
for he has responded to my appeal, but 17
he goes to you really of his own accord,
he is so devoted to you. I am sending 18
with him his brother, who is famous in
all the churches for his work in spreading the good news. What is more, he 19
has been appointed by the churches to
travel with me in the interests of this
generous undertaking, which I am
superintending to honor the Lord and
to show our readiness to help. I mean 20
to have no one able to find any fault
with the way I handle this munificence.
I intend to do what is right not only in 21
the Lord's sight but in the eyes of men.
I send with them another brother of 22
ours whose devotion we have often tested in many ways, which is now greater
than ever, because of his perfect confidence in you. So as far as Titus is con- 23
cerned, he is my partner and comrade
in my work for you, while these brothers of ours represent the churches, and
are a credit to Christ. So you must give 24
proof to them before all the churches of
your love, and justify my pride in you.

It is really unnecessary for me to 9
write to you about this fund for your
fellow-Christians, for I know how will- 2
ing you are to help in it; I boast of you
for it to the people in Macedonia, telling them that Greece has been ready
since last year, and your enthusiasm
has been a stimulus to most of them.
But I send the brothers so that our 3
pride in you may not have a fall in this
matter, but you may be all ready as I
have told them you will; for if some 4
people from Macedonia come with me,
and find that you are not ready, it will
humiliate me—to say nothing of you—
for having expressed such confidence.
So I have thought it necessary to ask 5
these brothers to go on to you ahead of
me, to arrange in advance for this gift
you have promised, so as to have it
ready, like an expression of your good-
will, not of your avarice.

Remember this: The man who sows 6
sparingly will reap sparingly, and the
man who sows generously will reap generously. Everyone must give what he 7
has made up his mind to give, not re-
luctantly or under compulsion; God
loves a man who is glad to give. God is 8

able to provide you with every blessing
in abundance so that you will always
have enough for every situation, and
ample means for every good enterprise:
9 as the Scripture says,
"He scatters his gifts to the poor;
His uprightness will never be forgotten."
10 He who supplies the sower with seed
and so with bread to eat will supply you
with seed, and multiply it and enlarge
11 the harvest of your uprightness. You
will grow rich in every way, so that
through me you can show perfect liberality
that will make men thank God for
12 it. For the rendering of this service
does more than supply the wants of
God's people; it results in a wealth of
13 thanksgiving to God. The way you
stand the test of this service must do
honor to God, through your fidelity to
what you profess as to the good news
of Christ, and through the liberality of
your contributions for them and for all
14 others; then they will long for you and
pray for you, because of the extraordi-
15 nary favor God has shown you. Thank
God for his indescribable gift!

10 I appeal to you personally, by the
gentleness and forbearance of Christ—
the Paul who is so humble when face to
face with you, but so bold in dealing
2 with you when he is far away! I beg
you not to make me take as bold an attitude
when I come, as I count on taking
toward some people who suspect me
3 of acting from worldly motives. For
though I do live an earthly life, I am
4 not carrying on an earthly war, for the
weapons I use are not earthly ones, but
divinely strong for destroying for-
5 tresses. I destroy arguments and every
obstacle that is raised against the
knowledge of God, and I take captive
every thought and make it obey Christ,
6 and am prepared to punish any trace of
disobedience when you have made your
7 obedience perfectly clear. You look at
things externally. If anyone is sure he
belongs to Christ, let him think again
and understand that I belong to Christ
8 just as much as he. For suppose I do
boast a little too much of my authority
—which the Lord gave me to build you
up, not to pull you down—I will not
9 have to blush for it. I do not want to
10 seem to scare you with my letters. For
they say, "His letters are impressive
and telling, but his personal appearance
is insignificant and as a speaker he
amounts to nothing." Such people had 11
better understand that when I arrive
and take action I will do just as I say
I will in my letters when I am far away.
I do not indeed venture to class or com- 12
pare myself with certain individuals
who approve of themselves. But when
they measure themselves by one another
and compare themselves with one
another, they do not show good sense.
But my boasting will not be extrava- 13
gant, nor exceed the limits God has allowed
me, which reach all the way to
you. It is no strain for me to do this, as 14
it might be for people who had never
got so far, for I was the first to come all
the way to you with the good news of
the Christ. I do not indulge in extrava- 15
gant boasts over work done by others,
but I do hope that as your faith increases,
my influence may be immensely
enlarged through you, and I may 16
preach the gospel in the lands beyond
you without having to boast over work
already done in another's field. But 17
let the man who boasts, boast about the
Lord. For it is not the man who ap- 18
proves of himself who is really approved;
it is the man of whom the Lord
approves.

I wish you would put up with a little 11
folly from me. Do put up with it! I 2
feel a divine jealousy about you, for I
betrothed you to Christ, to present you
as a pure bride to her one husband. But 3
I am afraid that just as the serpent
by his cunning deceived Eve, your
thoughts will be led astray from their
single-hearted fidelity to Christ. For 4
when somebody comes along and
preaches another Jesus than the one I
preached, or you receive a different
spirit from the one you received or a
different gospel from the one you accepted,
you put up with it well enough!
For I think that I am not in the least 5
inferior to these superfine apostles of
yours. Even if I have no particular 6
gifts in speaking, I am not wanting in
knowledge. Why, I have always made
that perfectly clear in my dealings with
you.

Do you think that I did wrong in de- 7
grading myself to uplift you, because I
preached God's good news to you without
any compensation? I robbed other 8
churches, letting them pay me so that I
could work for you! And when I was 9

with you and wanted money, I did not
burden any of you, for when the brothers came from Macedonia they supplied what I needed. So I kept myself,
as I shall always do, from being a bur-
10 den to you in any way. By the truth of
Christ that is in me, this boast of mine
shall not be silenced anywhere in
11 Greece. And why? Because I do not
love you? God knows I do.
12 And I shall go on doing as I do, so as
to cut the ground from under those who
want to make out that in their boasted
apostleship they work on the same
13 terms that I do. Such men are sham
apostles, dishonest workmen, masquer-
14 ading as apostles of Christ. And no
wonder, for even Satan himself mas-
15 querades as a shining angel. So it is
nothing strange if his servants also mas-
querade as servants of uprightness. But
their doom will fit their actions.
16 I repeat, no one should think me a
fool, but if you do, show me at least the
patience you would show a fool, and let
me have my little boast like the others.
17 When I boast in this reckless way, I do
not say what I am saying for the Lord,
18 but as a fool would talk. Since many
are so human as to boast, I will do it
19 also. For you like to put up with fools,
20 you are so wise yourselves! For you
put up with it if a man makes you his
slaves, or lives on you, or takes you in,
or puts on airs, or gives you a slap in
21 the face. To my shame I must admit
that I was too weak for that sort of
thing. But whatever anyone else dares
to boast of—I am playing the part of
22 a fool—I will dare to boast of too. If
they are Hebrews, so am I! If they are
Israelites, so am I! If they are de-
23 scended from Abraham, so am I! If
they are Christian workers—I am talking like a madman!—I am a better one!
with far greater labors, far more imprisonments, vastly worse beatings, and
24 in frequent danger of death. Five times
I have been given one less than forty
25 lashes, by the Jews. I have been beaten
three times by the Romans, I have been
stoned once, I have been shipwrecked
three times, a night and a day I have
26 been adrift at sea; with my frequent
journeys, in danger from rivers, danger
from robbers, danger from my own people, danger from the heathen, danger
in the city, danger in the desert, danger
at sea, danger from false brothers,
through toil and hardship, through 27
many a sleepless night, through hunger
and thirst, often without food, and exposed to cold. And besides everything 28
else, the thing that burdens me every
day is my anxiety about all the
churches. Who is weak without my be- 29
ing weak? Whose conscience is hurt
without my being fired with indignation? If there must be boasting, I will 30
boast of the things that show my weakness! The God and Father of the Lord 31
Jesus, he who is forever blessed, knows
that I am telling the truth. When I was 32
at Damascus, the governor under King
Aretas had the gates of Damascus
watched in order to catch me, but I was 33
lowered in a basket from a window in
the wall, and got out of his clutches.
I have to boast. There is nothing to 12
be gained by it, but I will go on to visions and revelations given me by the
Lord. I know of a man fourteen years 2
ago—whether in the body or out of it,
I do not know, God knows—being actually caught up to the third heaven. And 3
I know that this man—I do not know
whether it was in the body or out of it,
God knows—was caught up into Para- 4
dise, and heard things that must not be
told, which no human being can repeat.
On this man's account I am ready to 5
boast, but about myself I will boast
only of my weaknesses. Though if I 6
do choose to boast, I will not be such a
fool, for I will only be telling the truth.
But I will refrain from it, for I do not
want anyone to be influenced by the
wonderful character of these revelations
to think more of me than is justified by
my words or conduct. So to keep me 7
from being too much elated a bitter
physical affliction was sent to me, a
very messenger of Satan, to harass me,
to keep me from being too much elated.
Three times I have prayed to the Lord 8
about this, begging that it might leave
me, and he said to me, "My favor is 9
enough for you, for only where there is
weakness is perfect strength developed."
So I am perfectly willing to boast of
all my weakness, so that the strength
of Christ may shelter me. That is why 10
I am pleased with weaknesses, insults,
hardships, persecutions, and difficulties, when they are endured for Christ's
sake, for it is when I am weak that I am
strong.

11 I have been making a fool of myself,
but you forced me to do it, when you
ought to have been expressing your approval of me. For I am not a bit inferior to your superfine apostles, even
12 if I am nobody! The signs that mark a
true apostle were most patiently shown
when I was among you, in signs, won-
13 ders, and marvels. For what is there in
which the other churches had the better
of you, except in the fact that I would
not permit myself to be a burden to
you? You must forgive me that wrong!
14 Here it is the third time that I have
been ready to come to see you, and I
do not intend to be a burden to you
now; for it is not your money but yourselves that I want; for children are not
expected to lay up money for their parents, but parents for their children.
15 And I will be glad to spend all I have
and all I am for your sake. Are you
going to love me the less for loving you
16 so intensely? But granting that I did
not burden you myself, I was clever
about it, you say, and took you in by a
17 trick. Yet did I make anything out of
18 you by anybody that I sent to you? I
asked Titus to go and I sent his brother
with him. Did Titus make anything
out of you? Did not he and I act in the
same spirit, and take the very same
steps?
19 Have you been supposing all along
that it is before you I have been defending myself? It is in the sight of God and
as a follower of Christ that I have been
speaking. But it is all to do you good,
20 dear friends, for I am afraid that perhaps when I come I may find you not as
I want to find you, and that you may
find me not as you want to find me. I
am afraid that perhaps there may be
quarreling, jealousy, bad feeling, rivalry, slander, gossip, conceit, and disor-
21 der, and that when I come back my
God may humiliate me before you, and
I may have to mourn over many who
have kept on in their old sins and have
never repented of the impurity, immorality, and sensuality in which they have
indulged.

This will be my third visit to you. 13
Any charge must be sustained by the
evidence of two or three witnesses.
Those who have kept on in their old 2
sins and all the rest I have warned, and
I warn them now while I am still away,
as I did on my second visit, that if I
come back I will spare nobody—since 3
you demand proof that Christ really
speaks through me. He is not weak in
dealing with you. On the contrary,
right among you he exhibits his power.
Even if he was crucified through weak- 4
ness, by the power of God he is alive.
For we are weak as he was, but you will
find that by the power of God we will
be alive as he is. It is yourselves you 5
must test, to see whether you are holding to the faith. It is yourselves you
must examine. Do you not know that
Jesus Christ is within you? Unless you
fail to stand the test! I hope you will 6
see that I do not fail to stand it. But I 7
pray to God that you may not do wrong
—not to prove me equal to the test, but
that you should do right even if I fail to
stand it. For I cannot do anything 8
against the truth, but only for it. I am 9
glad to be weak, if you are strong! That
is what I pray for—the perfecting of
your characters. That is why I write 10
this while I am away from you, so that
when I come, I may not have to be
harsh in my use of the authority the
Lord has given me, for it was to build
you up, not to pull you down.

Now brothers, goodbye! Be what you 11
ought to be, listen to my appeal, agree
with one another, live in peace, and
God the source of love and peace will
be with you. Greet one another with a 12
sacred kiss. All God's people wish to 13
be remembered to you.

The blessing of the Lord Jesus Christ, 14
the love of God and the participation
in the holy Spirit be with you all.

THE LETTER TO THE GALATIANS

1 PAUL, an apostle not from men
nor sent by any man, but by
Jesus Christ and God the Father
who raised him from the dead—
2 and all the brothers who are here with
3 me, to the churches of Galatia; blessing
and peace to you from God our Father
4 and the Lord Jesus Christ, who to save
us from the present wicked world gave
himself for our sins at the will of our
5 God and Father. To him be glory forever and ever! Amen.
6 I am amazed that you are so quickly
turning away from him who called you
by the mercy of Christ, to some differ-
7 ent good news—not that there is any
other, only that there are some people
who are trying to unsettle you and want
to turn the good news of the Christ
8 around. But even if we or an angel from
heaven preach to you good news that
contradicts the good news we have
9 preached to you, a curse upon him! We
have said it before, and I repeat it now
—if anyone is preaching to you good
news that contradicts the good news
you have already received, a curse upon
him!
10 Is that appealing to men's weaknesses, or to God? Is that trying to suit
men? If I were still doing that, I would
11 be no slave of Christ. For I tell you
plainly, brothers, that the good news
that I preached is not a human affair.
12 I did not receive it from any man, and I
was not taught it, but it came to me
through a revelation of Jesus Christ.
13 You have heard of my former conduct when I was attached to the Jewish
religion—how furiously I used to persecute the church of God and ravage it,
14 and how I surpassed many of my own
age among my people in my devotion
to Judaism, I was so fanatically devoted to what my forefathers had handed
15 down. And when God, who had set me
apart from my birth and had called me
16 in his mercy, saw fit to reveal his Son to
me, so that I might preach the good
news about him to the heathen, immediately, instead of consulting with
any human being, or going up to Jeru- 17
salem to see those who had been apostles before me, I went off to Arabia, and
on my return came back to Damascus.
Then three years later I went up to 18
Jerusalem, to become acquainted with
Cephas, and I spent two weeks with
him; but I did not see any other apostle, 19
except James, the Lord's brother. (In 20
writing you this, I call God to witness
that I am telling the truth!) After that, 21
I went to the districts of Syria and
Cilicia. I was still personally unknown 22
to the Christian churches of Judea;
they only heard people say, "The man 23
who once persecuted us is now preaching the good news of the faith he tried
to destroy," and they praised God for 24
me. Then, fourteen years later, I went 2
up to Jerusalem again, with Barnabas,
and took Titus also with me. It was in 2
obedience to a revelation that I went.
I laid before them the good news that I
preach to the heathen, presenting it
privately to the leaders, for fear my efforts might be or might have been futile. But they did not insist that even 3
my companion Titus, although he was
a Greek, should be circumcised, to grat- 4
ify the false brothers who had been
smuggled in, who sneaked in to spy
upon the freedom we enjoy in Christ
Jesus, so as to reduce us to slavery
again. But we did not submit to them 5
for a moment, in order that the truth
of the good news might remain yours.
Those who were regarded as the leaders 6
—what they once were makes no difference to me; God shows no partiality—
the leaders contributed nothing new
to me. On the contrary, when they 7
saw that I had been intrusted with
the good news for the heathen, just
as Peter had been intrusted with it
for the Jews—for he who actuated 8
Peter to be an apostle to the Jews also
actuated me to be one to the heathen—
and when they recognized the favor 9
God had shown me, James, Cephas,
and John, who were regarded as
pillars of the church, pledged Barna-

bas and me their co-operation, with the
understanding that we should work
among the heathen and they among
10 the Jews. Only, we were to remember
the poor, and that I have taken pains to
11 do. But when Cephas came to Antioch, I opposed him to his face, for his
12 own conduct condemned him. For until some people came from James, he
used to eat with the heathen, but after
they came, he began to draw back and
hold aloof, for fear of the party of cir-
13 cumcision. The other Jewish Christians
followed his example in concealing their
real views, so that even Barnabas was
14 carried away by their pose. But when
I saw that they were not straightforward about the truth of the good news,
I said to Cephas, right before them all,
"If you live like a heathen and not like
a Jew, though you are a Jew yourself,
why should you try to make the heathen live like Jews?"
15 We who are Jews by birth, and not
16 sinful heathen, but who know that a
man is not made upright by doing what
the Law commands, but by faith in
Christ Jesus—even we believed in
Christ Jesus, so as to be made upright
by faith in Christ and not by doing
what the Law commands—for by doing
what the Law commands no one can be
17 made upright. If through our efforts to
be made upright through Christ, we
have ourselves been proved as much
"sinners" as the heathen, does that
make Christ encourage sin? By no
18 means. I really convict myself of
wrongdoing when I start to rebuild
19 what I tore down. For it is through the
Law that I have become dead to the
20 Law, so that I may live for God. I have
been crucified with Christ, and it is no
longer I that live, but Christ that lives
in me. The life I am now living in the
body I am living by faith in the Son of
God who loved me and gave himself for
21 me. I refuse to nullify the mercy of
God. For if uprightness could be secured through law, then Christ died for
nothing!

3 You senseless Galatians! Who has
bewitched you, when you had Jesus
Christ shown crucified right before
2 your eyes? This is all I want to ask
you: Did you receive the Spirit
through doing what the Law commands, or through believing the mes-
3 sage you heard? Are you so senseless?
Did you begin with the Spirit only to
end now with the flesh? Have you gone 4
through so much, all for nothing?—if
it really is for nothing! When he sup- 5
plies you with the Spirit and works
wonders among you, is it because you
do what the Law commands, or because
you believe the message you heard?
Just as Abraham had faith in God and 6
it was credited to him as uprightness.

So you see, the real descendants of 7
Abraham are the men of faith. The 8
Scripture foresaw that God would accept the heathen as upright in consequence of their faith, and preached the
good news in advance to Abraham in
the words, "All the heathen will be
blessed through you." So the men of 9
faith share the blessing of Abraham and
his faith.

For there is a curse upon all who rely 10
on obedience to the Law, for the Scripture says, "Cursed be anyone who does
not stand by everything that is written
in the Book of the Law and obey it."
That no one is accepted as upright by 11
God for obeying the Law is evident because "the upright will have life because
of his faith," and the Law has nothing 12
to do with faith; it teaches that it is the
man who does these things that will find
life by doing them. Christ ransomed us 13
from the Law's curse by taking our
curse upon himself (for the Scripture
says, "Cursed be anyone who is hung
on a tree") in order that the blessing 14
given to Abraham might through Jesus
Christ reach the heathen, so that
through faith we might receive the
promised Spirit.

To take an illustration, brothers, 15
from daily life: even a human agreement, once ratified, no one annuls or alters. Now the promises were made to 16
Abraham and his line. It does not say,
"and to your lines," in the plural, but in
the singular, "and to your line," that
is, Christ. My point is this: An agree- 17
ment already ratified by God cannot be
annulled and its promise canceled by
the Law, which arose four hundred and
thirty years later. If our inheritance 18
rests on the Law, it has nothing to do
with the promise. Yet it was as a promise that God bestowed it upon Abraham.

Then what about the Law? It was a 19
later addition, designed to produce
transgressions, until the descendant to

which the promise was made should
come, and it was enacted by means of
20 angels, through an intermediary; though
an intermediary implies more than one
21 party, while God is but one. Is the Law
then contrary to God's promises? By
no means. For if a law had been given
that could have brought life, uprightness would really have come through
22 law. But the Scripture describes all
mankind as the prisoners of sin, so
that the promised blessing might on
the ground of faith in Jesus Christ be
given to those who have faith.
23 But before this faith came, we were
kept shut up under the Law, in order to
obtain the faith that was to be revealed.
24 So the Law has been our attendant on
our way to Christ, so that we might be
25 made upright through faith. But now
that faith has come, we are no longer in
the charge of the attendant.
26 For in Christ Jesus you are all sons of
27 God through your faith. For all of you
who have been baptized into union with
Christ have clothed yourselves with
28 Christ. There is no room for "Jew" and
"Greek"; there is no room for "slave"
and "freeman"; there is no room for
"male" and "female"; for in union with
29 Christ Jesus you are all one. And if you
belong to Christ, then you are true descendants of Abraham and his heirs
under the promise.

4 I mean this: As long as the heir is a
minor, he is no better than a slave, although he is the owner of all the prop-
2 erty, but he is under guardians and
trustees until the time fixed by his fa-
3 ther. So when we were minors, we were
slaves to material ways of looking at
4 things, but when the proper time came,
God sent his Son, born of a woman, and
5 made subject to law, to ransom those
who were subject to law, so that we
might receive adoption.
6 And because you are sons, God has
sent into our hearts the spirit of his
Son, with the cry, "Abba!" that is,
7 Father. So you are no longer a slave,
but a son; and if a son, then an heir,
made so by God.
8 But formerly, in your ignorance of
God, you were slaves to gods that really
9 did not exist, but now that you know
God, or rather have come to be known
by him, how can you turn back to the
old, crude notions, so poor and weak,
and wish to become slaves to them
again? You are observing days, 10
months, seasons, and years! I begin to 11
be afraid that perhaps the labor I spent
on you was wasted.
Take my position, I beg you, broth- 12
ers, just as I once took yours! You took
no advantage of me then; though you 13
know that it was because of an illness
that I preached the good news to you
that first time; and yet what must have 14
tried you in my physical condition, you
did not scorn and despise, but you welcomed me like an angel of God, like
Christ Jesus himself. What has become 15
of that satisfaction of yours? For I can
bear witness that you would have torn
out your very eyes, if you could, and
given them to me! Have I turned into 16
an enemy to you, by telling you the
truth? These men are making much of 17
you, but not with honorable intentions.
They want to shut you out, so that you
will have to make much of them. But 18
it is a finer thing to be made much of
honestly and constantly—not just
when I can be with you, my children— 19
you for whom I am enduring a mother's
pains again, until Christ is formed in
you. I wish I could be with you now, 20
and use a different tone with you, for I
do not know which way to turn about
you.
Tell me this, you who want to be sub- 21
ject to law: Will you not listen to the
Law? For the Scripture says that Abra- 22
ham had two sons, one by the slave-
girl, and one by the free woman. But 23
the child of the slave-girl was born in
the ordinary course of nature, while the
child of the free woman was born in fulfilment of the promise. This is an alle- 24
gorical utterance. For the women are
two agreements, one coming from
Mount Sinai, bearing children that are
to be slaves; that is, Hagar (and Hagar 25
means Mount Sinai, in Arabia), and
corresponds to the present Jerusalem,
for Jerusalem is in slavery with her children. But the Jerusalem above is free, 26
and she is our mother. For the Scrip- 27
ture says,

"Rejoice, childless woman, who bear
no children,
Break into shouting, you who have
no birthpains!
For the desolate woman has more
children than the married one!"

Now we, brothers, are like Isaac, 28
children born in fulfilment of the prom-

29 ise. But just as then the child born in
the ordinary course of nature persecuted the one born through the influ-
30 ence of the Spirit, so it is today. Yet
what does the Scripture say? "Drive
the slave-girl and her son away, for the
slave-girl's son shall not share the inheritance with the son of the free wom-
31 an." So, brothers, we are children not
of a slave but of one who is free.

5 This is the freedom with which Christ
has freed us. So stand firm in it, and do
not get under a yoke of slavery again.
2 Why, I, Paul, tell you that if you let
yourselves be circumcised, Christ can
3 do nothing for you. I insist again to any
man who lets himself be circumcised,
that he is under obligation to obey the
4 whole Law. You people who propose
to be made upright by law have finished
with Christ; you have lost your hold
5 upon God's favor. But we, by the Spirit, through faith wait for the upright-
6 ness we hope for. For in union with
Christ Jesus, neither circumcision nor
the want of it counts for anything, but
only faith acting through love.

7 You were making such progress!
Who has stopped your obeying the
8 truth? That kind of persuasion never
9 came from him who called you! A little
10 yeast will make all the dough rise. I
am confident in the Lord that you will
not take a different view. The man
who is unsettling you will have to pay
the penalty for it, no matter who he
11 is. And I, brothers, if I am still preaching circumcision, why am I still being
persecuted? If that is the case, the
cross has ceased to be an obstacle, I
12 suppose! I wish the people who are up-
setting you would go on, and mutilate
themselves!

13 For you, brothers, have been called
to freedom; only do not make your
freedom an excuse for the physical, but
14 in love be slaves to one another. For
the whole Law is summed up in one saying: "You must love your neighbor as
15 you do yourself." But if you bite one
another and eat one another, take care,
or you will be destroyed by one another.

16 I mean this: Live by the Spirit, and
then you will not indulge your physical
17 cravings. For the physical cravings are
against the Spirit, and the cravings of
the Spirit are against the physical; the
two are in opposition, so that you cannot do anything you please. But if you 18
are guided by the Spirit, you are not
subject to law. The things our physical 19
nature does are clear enough—immorality, impurity, licentiousness, idolatry, 20
sorcery, enmity, quarreling, jealousy,
anger, selfishness, dissension, party-
spirit, envy, drunkenness, carousing, 21
and the like. I warn you as I did before
that people who do such things will
have no share in the Kingdom of God.
But what the Spirit produces is love, 22
joy, peace, patience, kindness, goodness, faithfulness, gentleness, self-con- 23
trol. There is no law against such
things! Those who belong to Jesus the 24
Christ have crucified the physical nature with its propensities and cravings.

If we live by the Spirit, let us be guid- 25
ed by the Spirit. Let us not in our van- 26
ity challenge one another or envy one
another. But if a man is caught doing 6
something wrong, brothers, you are
spiritual, and you must set him right,
in a spirit of gentleness. Think of yourself, for you may be tempted too. Bear 2
one another's burdens, and in that way
carry out the law of the Christ. For if 3
anyone thinks he is somebody when he
is really nobody, he is deceiving himself. Every man ought to test his own 4
work, and then whatever satisfaction he
has will be with reference to himself,
and not in comparison with someone
else. For everyone will have to carry 5
his own load.

Those who are taught the message 6
must share all their goods with their
teacher. Do not be deceived. God is 7
not to be sneered at. A man will reap
just what he sows. The man who sows 8
to gratify his physical cravings will
reap destruction from them, and the
man who sows to benefit the spirit will
reap eternal life from the Spirit. Let 9
us not get tired of doing right, for at the
proper time we shall reap, if we do not
give out. So then whenever we have an 10
opportunity, let us do good to all men,
especially to those who belong to the
family of the faith.

See what large letters I make, when 11
I write to you with my own hand!
These men who are trying to force you 12
to let yourselves be circumcised want to
present a good appearance externally,
to save themselves from having to
stand persecution for the cross of Jesus

13 the Christ. Why, even those who let
themselves be circumcised do not observe the Law themselves! But they
want you to let yourselves be circumcised so that they can boast of that
14 physical fact about you! But I never
want to boast of anything but the cross
of our Lord Jesus Christ, on which the
world has been crucified to me and I
15 have been to the world. For neither
circumcision nor the want of it is of any
importance, but only a new creation.
Peace and mercy be on all who will fol- 16
low this rule, and on the true Israel of
God.

Let nobody interfere with me after 17
this, for I bear on my body the scars
that mark me as a slave of Jesus.

The blessing of our Lord Jesus Christ 18
be with your spirit, brothers. Amen.

THE LETTER TO THE EPHESIANS

1 PAUL, by God's will an apostle of
Christ Jesus, to God's people
who are steadfast in Christ
2 Jesus; God our Father and the
Lord Jesus Christ bless you and give
you peace.
3 Blessed be the God and Father of our
Lord Jesus Christ, who through Christ
has blessed us with every spiritual
4 blessing in the heavenly realm. Through
him he chose us out before the creation
of the world, to be consecrated and
5 above reproach in his sight in love. He
foreordained us to become his sons
through Jesus Christ, in fulfilment of
6 his generous purpose, so that we might
praise the splendid blessing which he
has given us through his beloved Son.
7 It is through union with him and
through his blood that we have been
8 delivered and our offenses forgiven, in
the abundance of his mercy which he
9 has lavished upon us. He has given us
perfect insight into his secret purpose
and understanding of it, in following
out the design he planned to carry out
10 in Christ, and in arranging, when the
time should have fully come, that everything in heaven and on earth should be
11 unified in Christ—the Christ through
whom it is our lot to have been predestined by the design of him who in
everything carries out the purpose of
12 his will, to win praise for his glory, by
having been the first to believe in
13 Christ. You also have heard the message of the truth, the good news of your
salvation, and believed in him, and
through union with him you have been
marked with the seal of the holy Spirit
14 that was promised, which is the guarantee of our inheritance, so that we
may get full possession of it, and praise
his glory for it.
15 This is why I, for my part, since I
have heard of the faith in the Lord
Jesus that prevails among you and
16 among all God's people, never cease to
thank God for you when I mention you
17 in my prayers that the God of our
Lord Jesus Christ, the glorious Father,
may grant you the Spirit of wisdom and
revelation through the knowledge of
himself, enlightening the eyes of your 18
mind so that you may know what the
hope is to which he calls you, and how
gloriously rich his inheritance is among
God's people, and how surpassingly 19
great his power is for us who believe;
like the mighty strength he exerted in 20
raising Christ from the dead, and seat-
ing him at his right hand in heaven,
far above all hierarchies, authorities, 21
powers, and dominions, and all titles
that can be bestowed not only in this
world but in the world to come. He has 22
put everything under his feet and made
him the indisputable head of the
church, which is his body, filled by him 23
who fills everything everywhere. You 2
also were dead because of the offenses 2
and sins in the midst of which you once
lived under the control of the present
age of the world, and the master-spirit
of the air, who is still at work among the
disobedient. We all lived among them 3
once, indulging our physical cravings
and obeying the impulses of our lower
nature and its thoughts, and by nature
we were doomed to God's wrath like
other men. But God is so rich in mercy 4
that because of the great love he had for
us, he made us, dead as we were through 5
our offenses, live again with the Christ.
It is by his mercy that you have been
saved. And he raised us with Christ, 6
and through our union with Christ
Jesus made us sit down with him in
heaven, to show the incomparable 7
wealth of his mercy throughout the
ages to come by his goodness to us
through Christ Jesus. For it is by his 8
mercy that you have been saved
through faith. It is not by your own
action, it is the gift of God. It has not 9
been earned, so that no one can boast
of it. For he has made us, creating us 10
through our union with Christ Jesus for
the life of goodness which God had
predestined us to live.
So remember that you were once 11
physically heathen, and called uncir-

cumcised by those who called themselves circumcised, though only physi-
12 cally, by human hands. At that time
you had no connection with Christ, you
were aliens to the commonwealth of Israel, and strangers to the agreements
about God's promise; with no hope and
13 no God in all the world. But now through
your union with Christ Jesus you who
were once far away have through the
14 blood of Christ been brought near. For
he is himself our peace. He has united
the two divisions, and broken down the
15 barrier that kept us apart, and through
his human nature put an end to the
feud between us, and abolished the Law
with its rules and regulations, in order
to make peace and create out of the two
parties one new man by uniting them
16 with himself, and to kill the feud between them and his cross and in one
body reconcile them both to God with
17 it. He came with the good news of
peace for you who were far away and
18 for those who were near; for it is through
him that we both with one Spirit are
19 now able to approach the Father. So
you are no longer foreigners or strangers,
but you are fellow-citizens of God's
20 people and members of his family. You
are built upon the apostles and prophets
as your foundation, and Christ Jesus
21 himself is the cornerstone. Through him
every part of the building is closely
united and grows into a temple sacred
22 through its relation to the Lord, and
you are yourselves built up into a
dwelling for God through the Spirit.

3 This is why I, Paul, whom Jesus the
Christ has made a prisoner for the sake
2 of you heathen—if at least you have
heard how I dealt with the mercy of
3 God that was given me for you, and
how the secret was made known to me
by revelation, as I have briefly writ-
4 ten. As you read that, you will be
able to understand the insight I have
5 into the secret of the Christ (which in
past ages was not disclosed to mankind
as fully as it has now been revealed
through the Spirit to his holy apostles
6 and prophets) that through union with
Christ Jesus the heathen are fellow-
heirs with the Jews, belong to the same
body and share the promise with them,
7 through the good news for which I became a worker by virtue of the gift of
God's mercy which by the exercise of
8 his power he has given me. To me, the
very least of all his people, his favor
has been given, of preaching to the
heathen the inexhaustible wealth of
the Christ, and making clear how the 9
secret purpose is to be worked out
which has been hidden away for ages in
God the creator of all things, so that the 10
many-sided wisdom of God may now
through the church be made known to
the rulers and authorities in heaven,
fulfilling the eternal purpose which God 11
carried out in Christ Jesus our Lord.
Through union with him and through 12
faith in him, we have courage to approach God with confidence. So I ask 13
that what I am having to suffer for
your sake may not make me lose heart,
for it does you honor.

For this reason I kneel before the 14
Father from whom every family in 15
heaven or on earth takes its name, and 16
beg him out of his wealth of glory to
strengthen you mightily through his
Spirit in your inner nature and through 17
your faith to let Christ in his love make
his home in your hearts. Your roots
must be deep and your foundations
strong, so that you and all God's people 18
may be strong enough to grasp what
breadth, length, height, and depth
mean, and to understand Christ's love, 19
so far beyond our understanding, so
that you may be filled with the very
fulness of God. To him who by the ex- 20
ertion of his power within us can do un-
utterably more than all we ask or
imagine, be glory through the church 21
and through Christ Jesus through all
generations forever and ever. Amen.

So I, the prisoner for the Lord's sake, **4**
appeal to you to live lives worthy of the
summons you have received; with per- 2
fect humility and gentleness, with patience, bearing with one another lovingly. Make every effort to maintain the 3
unity of the Spirit through the tie of
peace. There is but one body and one 4
Spirit, just as there is but one hope that
belongs to the call you received. There 5
is but one Lord, one faith, one baptism,
one God and Father of all, who is 6
above us all, pervades us all, and is
within us all. But each one of us has 7
been given mercy in Christ's generous
measure. So it says, 8

"When he went up on high, he led a
host of captives,
And gave gifts to mankind."

What does "he went up" mean, except 9

that he had first gone down to the under
10 parts of the earth? It is he who went
down who has also gone up above all
11 the heavens, to fill the universe. And he
has given us some men as apostles, some
as prophets, some as missionaries, some
12 as pastors and teachers, in order to fit
his people for the work of service, for
13 building the body of Christ, until we all
attain unity in faith, and in the knowledge of the Son of God, and reach mature manhood, and that full measure of
14 development found in Christ. We must
not be babies any longer, blown about
and swung around by every wind of
doctrine through the trickery of men
with their ingenuity in inventing error.
15 We must lovingly hold to the truth and
grow up into perfect union with him
16 who is the head—Christ himself. For it
is under his control that the whole system, adjusted and united by each liga-
ment of its equipment, develops in proportion to the functioning of each particular part, and so builds itself up
through love.

17 So what I mean and insist upon in
the Lord's name is this: You must no
longer live like the heathen, with their
frivolity of mind and darkened under-
18 standing. They are estranged from the
life of God because of the ignorance
that exists among them and their ob-
19 stinacy of heart, for they have become
callous, and abandoned themselves to
sensuality, greedily practicing every
20 kind of vice. That is not the way you
have been taught what Christ means,
21 at least if you have really become acquainted with him and been instructed
in him, and in union with him have been
taught the truth as it is found in Jesus.
22 You must lay aside with your former
habits your old self which is going to
ruin through its deceptive passions.
23 You must adopt a new attitude of
24 mind, and put on the new self which
has been created in likeness to God,
with the uprightness and holiness that
belong to the truth.

25 So you must lay aside falsehood and
each tell his neighbor the truth, for we
26 are parts of one another. Be angry, but
do not sin. The sun must not go down
27 upon your anger; you must not give the
28 devil a chance. The man who stole
must not steal any more; he must work
with his hands at honest toil instead, so
as to have something to share with
those who are in need. No bad word 29
must ever pass your lips, but only
words that are good and suited to im-
prove the occasion, so that they will be
a blessing to those who hear them. You 30
must not offend God's holy Spirit, with
which you have been marked for the
Day of Redemption. You must give up 31
all bitterness, rage, anger, and loud,
abusive talk, and all spite. You must be 32
kind to one another, you must be tender-hearted, and forgive one another
just as God through Christ has forgiven
you. So follow God's example, like his 5
dear children, and lead loving lives, 2
just as Christ loved you and gave himself for you, as a fragrant offering and
sacrifice to God.

But immorality or any form of vice 3
or greed must not be so much as mentioned among you; that would not be
becoming in God's people. There must 4
be no indecency or foolish or scurrilous
talk—all that is unbecoming. There
should be thanksgiving instead. For 5
you may be sure that no one who is immoral, or impure, or greedy for gain
(for that is idolatry) can have any
share in the Kingdom of Christ and God.

Whatever anyone may say in the way 6
of worthless arguments to deceive you,
these are the things that are bringing
God's anger down upon the disobedient. Therefore have nothing to do 7
with them. For once you were sheer 8
darkness, but now, as Christians, you
are light itself. You must live like children of light, for light leads to perfect 9
goodness, uprightness, and truth; you 10
must make sure what pleases the Lord.
Have nothing to do with the profitless 11
doings of the darkness; expose them
instead. For while it is degrading even 12
to mention their secret practices, yet 13
when anything is exposed by the light,
it is made visible, and anything that is
made visible is light. So it says, 14

"Wake up, sleeper!
Rise from the dead,
And Christ will dawn upon you!"

Be very careful, then, about the way 15
you live. Do not act thoughtlessly, but
like sensible men, and make the most of 16
your opportunity, for these are evil
times. So do not be foolish, but under- 17
stand what the Lord's will is. Do not 18
get drunk on wine, for that is profligacy, but be filled with the Spirit, and 19
speak to one another in psalms, hymns,

and sacred songs. Sing praise to the
20 Lord with all your hearts; always give
thanks for everything to God our
Father, as followers of our Lord Jesus
21 Christ, and subordinate yourselves to
one another out of reverence to Christ.
22 You married women must subordinate yourselves to your husbands, as
23 you do to the Lord, for a husband is the
head of his wife, just as Christ is the
head of the church, which is his body,
24 and is saved by him. Just as the church
is in subjection to Christ, so married
women must be, in everything, to their
25 husbands. You who are husbands must
love your wives, just as Christ loved the
26 church and gave himself for her, to consecrate her, after cleansing her with the
bath in water through her confession of
27 him, in order to bring the church to
himself in all her beauty, without a flaw
or a wrinkle or anything of the kind,
but to be consecrated and faultless.
28 That is the way husbands ought to love
their wives—as if they were their own
bodies; a man who loves his wife is
29 really loving himself, for no one ever
hates his own person, but he feeds it
and takes care of it, just as Christ does
30 with the church, for we are parts of his
31 body. Therefore a man must leave his
father and mother and attach himself
to his wife, and they must become one.
32 This is a great secret, but I understand
33 it of Christ and the church. But each
one of you must love his wife just as he
loves himself, and the wife, too, must
respect her husband.

6 Children, as Christians obey your
2 parents, for that is right. "You must
honor your father and mother"—that
is the first commandment accompanied
3 with a promise—"so that you may pros-
4 per and have a long life on earth." You
fathers, too, must not irritate your children, but you must bring them up with
Christian training and instruction.

5 You who are slaves, obey your earthly masters, in reverence and awe, with
sincerity of heart, as you would the
6 Christ, not with mere external service,
as though you had only men to please,
but like slaves of Christ, carrying out
7 the will of God. Do your duties heartily and willingly, as though it were for
the Lord, not for men, for you know 8
that everyone, slave or free, will be rewarded by the Lord for his good conduct. You who are masters, too, must 9
treat your slaves in the same way, and
cease to threaten them, for you know
that their Master and yours is in heav-
en, and that he will show no partiality.

Henceforth you must grow strong 10
through union with the Lord and
through his mighty strength. You must 11
put on God's armor. so as to be able to
stand up against the devil's stratagems.
For we have to struggle, not with 12
enemies of flesh and blood, but with the
hierarchies, the authorities, the master-
spirits of this dark world, the spirit-
forces of evil on high. So you must take 13
God's armor, so that when the evil day
comes you will be able to make a stand,
and when it is all over to hold your
ground. Stand your ground, then, with 14
the belt of truth around your waist, and
put on uprightness as your coat of mail,
and on your feet put the readiness the 15
good news of peace brings. Besides all 16
these, take faith for your shield, for
with it you will be able to put out all
the flaming missiles of the evil one, and 17
take salvation for your helmet, and for
your sword the Spirit, which is the voice
of God. Use every kind of prayer and 18
entreaty, and at every opportunity
pray in the Spirit. Be on the alert
about it; devote yourselves constantly
to prayer for all God's people and for 19
me, that when I open my lips I may be
given a message, so that I may boldly
make known the secret of the good
news, for the sake of which I am an 20
envoy, and in prison. Pray that, when
I tell it, I may have the courage to
speak as I ought.

In order that you also may know how 21
I am, our dear brother Tychicus, a
faithful helper in the Lord's service,
will tell you all about it. That is the 22
very reason I am sending him, to let
you know how I am, and to cheer your
hearts.

God our Father and the Lord Jesus 23
Christ give the brothers peace and love,
with faith. God's blessing be with all 24
who have an unfailing love for our Lord
Jesus Christ.

THE LETTER TO THE PHILIPPIANS

1 PAUL and Timothy, slaves of
Christ Jesus, to all God's people in union with Christ Jesus
who are in Philippi, with the
2 superintendents and assistants; God
our Father and the Lord Jesus Christ
bless you and give you peace.
3 I never think of you without thank-
4 ing my God, and always whenever I
5 pray for you all I do it with joy over
your co-operation in the good news
from the day you first received it until
6 now. For I am certain that he who has
begun the good work in you will finish
7 it for the Day of Jesus Christ. And I
have a right to feel in this way about
you all, because both when I am in
prison and when I am defending and
vindicating our right to preach the
good news, I have you in my heart as
8 all sharing that privilege with me. For
God is my witness how I yearn for you
all with the affection of Christ Jesus
9 himself. And it is my prayer that your
love may grow richer and richer in
10 knowledge and perfect insight, so that
you may have a sense of what is vital,
and may be men of transparent character and blameless life, in preparation
11 for the Day of Christ, with your lives
filled with the fruits which uprightness
produces through Jesus Christ, to the
honor and praise of God.
12 Now I want to assure you, brothers,
that what has happened to me has
actually resulted in furthering the
13 preaching of the good news. Thus it is
generally known throughout the Imperial Guard and elsewhere that it is
for the sake of Christ that I am in pris-
14 on, and so most of the Christian brothers have been exceedingly encouraged
by my imprisonment to declare God's
message without any fear of the consequences.
15 Some of them, it is true, are actually
preaching the Christ from jealousy and
partisanship, but there are others who
16 are doing it out of good-will. These latter do it from love for me, for they know
that God has put me where I am to defend our right to preach the good news.
But the others are preaching the Christ 17
not sincerely but for their own ends,
imagining that they are making my imprisonment harder to bear.
But what difference does it make? 18
All that matters is that, in one way or
another, from false motives or honest
ones, Christ is being made known; I am
glad of that. Yes, and I expect to be
glad, for I know that through your 19
prayers and the help of the Spirit of
Jesus Christ, all this will turn out for
my highest welfare, for I eagerly and 20
confidently hope that I shall never disgrace myself but that this time as always hitherto, living or dying, I shall
do Christ credit by my unfailing courage.
For, as I see it, living means Christ 21
and dying something even better. But 22
if living on here means having my labor
bear fruit, I cannot tell which to choose.
I am undecided between the two, for I 23
long to depart and be with Christ, for
that is far, far better, and yet your 24
needs make it very necessary for me to
stay on here. I am convinced of this, 25
and so I know that I shall stay on and
serve you all, to help you to develop
and to be glad in your faith. So you will 26
find in me fresh cause for Christian exultation, through having me with you
again.
Whatever happens, show yourselves 27
citizens worthy of the good news of the
Christ, so that whether I come and see
you or am kept away and only hear
news of you, I may know that you are
standing firm with one spirit, one purpose, fighting side by side for faith in
the good news. Never for a moment 28
falter before your opponents, for your
fearlessness will be a sure sign for them
of their coming destruction, but to you
it will be an omen, from God himself, of
your deliverance. For you have been 29
granted the privilege not only of trusting in Christ but of suffering for him.
Take your part in the same struggle 30
that you have seen me engage in and
that you hear I am still keeping up.
So by whatever appeal there is in our 2

relation to Christ, by whatever incen-
tive there is in love, by whatever participation there is in the Spirit, what-
2 ever affection and sympathy, make me
perfectly happy by living in harmony,
with the same attitude of love, with the
3 same feeling and purpose. Do not act
for selfish ends or from vanity, but
modestly treat one another as your su-
4 periors. Do not take account of your
own interests, but of the interests of
5 others as well. Have the same attitude
6 that Christ Jesus had. Though he possessed the nature of God, he did not
7 grasp at equality with God, but laid it
aside to take on the nature of a slave
8 and become like other men. When he
had assumed human form, he still further humbled himself and carried his
obedience so far as to die, and to die
9 upon the cross. That is why God has
so greatly exalted him, and given him
10 the name above all others, so that in the
name of Jesus everyone should kneel, in
heaven and on earth and in the under-
11 world, and everyone should acknowledge Jesus Christ as Lord, and thus
glorify God the Father.

12 So, my dear friends, as you have always been obedient, with reverence and
awe make every effort to insure your
salvation, not simply as though I were
with you, but all the more because I am
13 away. For it is God who in his good-
will is at work in your hearts, inspiring
14 your will and your action. Do everything without any grumbling or disput-
15 ing, so that you will be blameless and
honest, faultless children of God in the
midst of a crooked and perverted age,
in which you appear like stars in a dark
16 world, offering men the message of life.
Then I will have reason to boast of you
on the Day of Christ, because my exertion and labor have not been wasted.
17 Even if my life is to be poured out as a
libation as you offer your faith in a service of sacrifice to God, I am glad to
have it so, and I congratulate you upon
18 it, just as you must be glad and congratulate me.

19 I hope, with the help of the Lord
Jesus, to send Timothy to you soon, so
that I, too, may be cheered by having
20 news about you. For I have no one like
him who would take such a real interest
21 in you. For they are all looking out for
their own interests, not for those of
22 Jesus Christ. But you know his character, and how like a son helping his
father he has worked like a slave with
me in preaching the good news. So I 23
hope to send him to you just as soon as
I can see how my case is going to turn
out. I trust the Lord to enable me to 24
come to you myself before long. But I 25
feel that I must send back to you Epaphroditus, my brother, fellow-laborer,
and fellow-soldier, whom you sent to
look after my needs. For he has been 26
longing to see you all, and has been
greatly distressed because you heard
that he was sick. For he was sick, and 27
nearly died, but God took pity on him,
and not only on him, but on me, to save
me from having one sorrow after
another. So I am all the more eager to 28
send him, so that you may have the
pleasure of seeing him again, and I may
feel more relieved. So give him a hearty 29
Christian welcome, and value men like
him very highly, for he came near dying
for the Lord's work, and risked his life 30
to make up for what was lacking in the
service you have done me.

Now, my brothers, goodbye, and the **3**
Lord be with you. I do not mind writing the same thing over and over to
you; it is necessary for your safety.

Look out for those dogs, those mis- 2
chief-makers, with their amputation!
We are the true circumcision, who wor- 3
ship God by his Spirit, priding ourselves only on Christ Jesus, and not
relying on physical advantages, though 4
I at least am entitled to rely on them.

If anyone thinks he can rely on his
physical advantages, still more can I!
I was circumcised when I was eight 5
days old. I am a descendant of Israel.
I belong to the tribe of Benjamin. I
am a Hebrew, and the son of Hebrews.
As to the Law, I was a Pharisee; as to 6
my zeal, I was a persecutor of the
church; and by the Law's standard of
uprightness, no fault could be found
with me. But for the sake of Christ I 7
have come to count my former gains as
loss. Why, I count everything as loss 8
compared with the supreme advantage
of knowing Christ Jesus my Lord. For
his sake I have lost everything, and
think it rubbish, in order to gain Christ
and be known to be united to him, with 9
any uprightness I may have not based
on law but coming through faith in
Christ—the uprightness that comes
from God through faith. I want to 10

know him in the power of resurrection,
and to share his sufferings and even his
11 death, in the hope of attaining resur-
12 rection from the dead. Not that I have
secured it yet, or already reached perfection, but I am pressing on to see if I
can capture it, because I have been cap-
13 tured by Jesus Christ. Brothers, I do
not consider that I have captured it
yet, only, forgetting what is behind me,
and straining toward what lies ahead,
14 I am pressing toward the goal, for the
prize to which God through Christ Je-
15 sus calls us upward. Let as many of us
therefore as are mature have this attitude. If you have any different attitude, God will make this clear to you.
16 Only we must live up to what we have
already attained.
17 Follow my example, brothers, all of
you, and notice those who follow the
18 pattern we have set you. For there are
many who live, as I have often told
you, and tell you now with tears, like
19 enemies of the cross of Christ. They
are doomed to destruction: their appe-
tites are their god; they glory in their
shame; they are absorbed in earthly
20 matters. But the commonwealth to
which we belong is in heaven, and
from it we are eagerly awaiting the
coming of a savior, the Lord Jesus
21 Christ. He will make our poor bodies
over to resemble his glorious body, by
exerting the power he has to subject
everything to himself.

4 So, my dear brothers whom I so long
to see, my joy and pride, stand firm in
the Lord, dear friends.
2 I appeal to Euodia and I appeal to
Syntyche to agree together, as Chris-
3 tians. And I beg you, my true comrade,
help them, for they toiled at my side in
spreading the good news, with Clement
and the rest of my fellow-workers,
whose names are in the book of life.
4 Goodbye, and the Lord be with you
5 always. Again I say, goodbye. Let all
men see your forbearing spirit. The
6 Lord is coming soon. Have no anxiety
about anything, but make all your
wants known to God in prayer and en-
7 treaty, and with thanksgiving. Then,
through your union with Christ Jesus,
the peace of God, so far above any human thought, will guard your minds
and thoughts.
Now, brothers, let your minds dwell 8
on what is true, what is worthy, what
is right, what is pure, what is amiable,
what is kindly—on everything that is
excellent or praiseworthy. Do the 9
things that you learned, received, and
heard from me, and that you saw me
do. Then God who gives peace will be
with you.
I was very glad, as a Christian, to 10
have your interest in me revive again
after so long; for you have always been
interested, but you have had no opportunity to show it. Not that I have any- 11
thing to complain of, for I have learned
how to be contented with the condition
I am in. I know how to live humbly 12
and I know how to enjoy plenty. I
have learned the secret, in any and all
conditions, of being well-fed and of going hungry, of having plenty and of going without. I can do anything through 13
him who gives me strength. But it was 14
very kind of you to share my difficulties. And you at Philippi know as well 15
as I do, that in the early days of the
good news, after I left Macedonia, no
church but yours went into partnership
and opened an account with me. Even 16
when I was at Thessalonica you sent
money more than once for my needs.
Not that I want your gifts, but I want 17
you to have the profits that will accu-
mulate to your credit. You have paid 18
me in full, and more too. I am fully
supplied with what I have received
from you through Epaphroditus. It is
like fragrant incense, just such a sacrifice as God welcomes and approves.
My God will gloriously supply all your 19
needs with his wealth, through your
union with Christ Jesus. Glory to our 20
God and Father forever and ever.
Amen.
Remember me to all my fellow- 21
Christians. The brothers who are with
me wish to be remembered to you. All 22
God's people wish to be remembered to
you, especially those who belong to the
emperor's household.
The blessing of our Lord Jesus Christ 23
be with your spirits.

THE LETTER TO THE COLOSSIANS

1 PAUL, by God's will an apostle of
Christ Jesus, and our brother
2 Timothy, to the devoted and
steadfast Christian brothers in
Colossae; God our Father bless you and
give you peace.
3 We never pray for you without
thanking God, the Father of our Lord
4 Jesus Christ, for what we have heard of
your faith in Christ Jesus, and of the
5 love you have for all God's people, and
for the hope of what is stored up for you
in heaven. You first heard of it long
6 ago when the true message of the gospel
came among you, to thrive and bear its
fruit among you, as it does all over the
world, from the time when you first
heard about the mercy of God, and
7 really came to know it, in the form in
which Epaphras, my dear fellow-slave,
taught it to you. He is my faithful rep-
8 resentative as a servant of Christ, and
it is he who has told me of the love the
9 Spirit has awakened in you. That is
why, from the day I first heard of it, I
have never given up praying for you
and asking God to fill you, through
full spiritual wisdom and insight, with
10 a clear knowledge of what his will is, so
that the lives you live may be worthy
of your Master and wholly pleasing to
him, and you may be fruitful in all
kinds of good deeds, and may grow
11 into fuller knowledge of God. Then, so
mighty is his majesty, he will nerve you
perfectly with strength for the cheerful
exercise of endurance and forbearance
12 in every situation, and you will thank
the Father who has entitled you to
share the lot of God's people in the
13 realm of light. He has rescued us from
the dominion of darkness, and has
transferred us into the realm of his
14 dear Son, by whom we have been ransomed from captivity through having
15 our sins forgiven. He is a likeness of the
unseen God, born before any creature,
16 for it was through him that everything
was created in heaven and on earth, the
seen and the unseen, angelic thrones,
dominions, principalities, authorities—
all things were created through him and
for him. He existed before all things 17
and he sustains and embraces them all.
He is the head of the church, it is his 18
body; for he is the beginning, the first-
born from among the dead—that he
might come to stand first in everything.
For all the divine fulness chose to dwell 19
in him, and through him to reconcile to 20
God all things on earth or in heaven, making this peace through his blood shed on
the cross. And it has brought you, who 21
were once estranged from him, hostile
in attitude and engaged in doing wrong
(though now he has reconciled you
through dying in his human body) in 22
holiness, and free from reproach or
blame, into God's presence—if at least 23
you continue firm and steadfast in the
exercise of faith, and never shift from
the hope held out in the good news to
which you listened, which has been
preached all over the world, and for
which I, Paul, became a worker.
At present I am glad to be suffering 24
in your interest, and I am making up
in my own person what is lacking in
Christ's sufferings for the church, which
is his body. In it, by divine appoint- 25
ment, I became a worker, that I might
preach among you the message of God
in its fulness—that secret, hidden from 26
the ages and generations, but now disclosed to those who are consecrated to
him, to whom God has chosen to make 27
known among the heathen how glorious
this mystery of Christ in you, the promise of glorification, really is. And in 28
spreading the news of him, we warn
everyone and teach everyone all our
wisdom, in order to bring everyone to
Christian perfection. That is what I 29
am working for, fighting with all the
energy with which he so mightily en-
dows me.
For I want you to know what a fight 2
I am putting up for you and for our
brothers in Laodicea, and for all who do
not know me personally, that your 2
hearts may be cheered. I want you to
be united by love, and to have all the

benefit of assured knowledge in coming
3 to know Christ—that divine mystery
in which all treasures of wisdom and
4 knowledge are to be found. What I
mean is, let nobody mislead you by
5 specious arguments. For though I am
absent from you in person I am with
you in spirit, and I am glad to observe
your harmony and the solidity of your
faith in Christ.

6 So just as you once accepted the
Christ, Jesus, as your Lord, you must
7 live in vital union with him. You must
be rooted and built up in him and made
strong in faith, just as you were taught
to be, overflowing with it in your gratitude.

8 Take care that nobody exploits you
through the pretensions of philosophy,
guided by human tradition, following
material ways of looking at things, in-
9 stead of following Christ. For it is in
him that all the fulness of God's nature
10 lives embodied, and in union with him
you too are filled with it. He is the head
of all your principalities and dominions.
11 Through your relation to him you have
received not a physical circumcision,
but a circumcision effected by Christ,
in stripping you of your material na-
12 ture, when in your baptism you were
buried with him, and raised to life with
him through your faith in the power of
God who raised him from the dead.
13 Yes, you who were dead through your
misdeeds and physically uncircumcised, God raised to life with Christ.
14 He forgave us all our misdeeds, canceled the bond which stood against us,
with its requirements, and put it out of
our way when he nailed it to the cross.
15 He disarmed the principalities and dominions and displayed them openly,
triumphing over them through him.

16 So no one can call you to account for
what you eat or drink, or do about annual or monthly feasts or Sabbaths.
17 That was all only the shadow of something that was to follow; the reality is
18 found in Christ. No one can put you in
the wrong by persisting in studied humility and the worship of angels, being
absorbed in the visions he has seen, and
groundlessly conceited over his mere
19 human mind. Such people lose their
connection with the head, from which
the whole body through its ligaments
and sinews must be governed and
united if it is to grow in the divine way.

If you have died with Christ to ma- 20
terial ways of looking at things, why do
you act as though you still belonged to
the world, and submit to rules like
"You must not handle," "You must 21
not taste," "You must not touch"—
referring to things that are all meant to 22
be used up and destroyed? This is to
follow mere human rules and regulations. Such practices pass for wisdom, 23
with their self-imposed devotions, their
self-humiliation, and their ascetic discipline, but they carry with them no
real distinction, they are really only a
catering to the flesh.

If, then, you have been raised to life 3
with Christ, set your hearts on the
things that are where Christ is, above,
seated at God's right hand. Fix your 2
thoughts on the things that are above,
not on those that are on earth. For 3
you have died, and your life now lies
hidden with Christ in God. When 4
Christ, who is our true life, shall make
his appearance, then you also will appear glorified with him.

So treat as dead your physical na- 5
ture, as far as immorality, impurity,
passion, evil desire, and greed are concerned; for it is really idolatry. It is on 6
account of these things that God's
anger is coming. And you once prac- 7
ticed them as others do, when you lived
that old earthly life. But now you too 8
must put them all aside—anger, rage,
spite, rough, abusive talk—these must
be banished from your lips. You must 9
not lie to one another. For you have
stripped off your old self with its ways
and have put on that new self newly 10
made in the likeness of its Creator, to
know him fully. Here, what matters 11
is not "Greek" and "Jew," the circumcised and the uncircumcised, barbarian,
Scythian, slave, freeborn, but Christ is
everything and in us all.

As persons chosen by God, then, con- 12
secrated and dearly loved, you must
clothe yourselves with tenderness of
heart, kindness, humility, gentleness,
forbearance. You must bear with one 13
another and forgive one another, if anyone has reason to be offended with anyone else. Just as the Lord has forgiven 14
you, so you must forgive. And over all
these put on love, which completes
them and fastens them all together.
Let the ruling principle in your hearts 15
be Christ's peace, for in becoming

members of one body you have been
called under its sway. And you must be
16 thankful. Let the message of Christ
live in your hearts in all its wealth of
wisdom. Teach it to one another and
train one another in it with thankful-
ness, with psalms, hymns, and sacred
songs, and sing to God with all your
17 hearts. And whatever you have to say
or do, do it all as followers of the Lord
Jesus, and offer your thanksgiving to
God the Father through him.
18 You married women must subordinate yourselves to your husbands, for
19 that is your duty as Christians. You
who are husbands must love your wives
and not be harsh to them.
20 Children, always obey your parents,
for that is commendable in Christians.
21 Fathers, do not irritate your children,
or they may lose heart.
22 You who are slaves must always
obey your earthly masters, not with
mere external service, as though you
had only men to please, but with sincerity of heart, because you fear the
23 Lord. Work at everything you do with
all your hearts, as work done not for
24 men only but for the Lord, for you
know that it is from him that you are to
receive that inheritance which is to be
your reward. Think of Christ as the
25 master you are working for. For the
man who wrongs anyone will be paid
back for the wrong he has done; there
4 will be no exceptions. You who are
masters must treat your slaves justly
and fairly, and remember that you
have a Master too, in heaven.
2 Be persistent in prayer and wide
awake about it when you give thanks.
3 Pray for me too, that God may give me
an opening for the message, and let me
tell the secret of Christ on account of
4 which I am kept in prison until I can
make clear to the authorities why I
5 cannot help telling it. Use wisdom in
dealing with outsiders, making the
most of your opportunities. Always 6
put your message attractively, and yet
pointedly, and be prepared to give
every inquirer a fitting answer.
Our dear brother Tychicus, my faith- 7
ful helper and fellow-servant in the
Lord's work, will tell you all about me.
I am sending him to you for the express 8
purpose of letting you know my circumstances, and of cheering your
hearts. And with him I send my dear, 9
faithful brother Onesimus, who is one
of your own number. They will tell you
all about matters here.
Aristarchus, my fellow-prisoner, 10
wishes to be remembered to you, and so
does Barnabas' cousin Mark. (About
him you have had instructions; if he
comes to see you, make him welcome.)
So also does Jesus who is called Justus. 11
They are the only ones among the converts from Judaism who have worked
with me for the reign of God who have
proved a comfort to me. Epaphras, one 12
of your own number, a slave of Christ
Jesus, wishes to be remembered to you.
He is always standing up for you in his
prayers that you may stand fast, like
men of mature convictions, whatever
God's will for you may be. I can testify 13
how anxious he is about you and the
brothers in Laodicea and Hierapolis.
Our dear Luke, the doctor, and Demas 14
wish to be remembered to you. Re- 15
member me to the brothers in Laodicea
and to Nympha and the church that
meets at her house. When this letter 16
has been read to you, have it read to
the church at Laodicea also, and see
that you read the letter that is coming
from there. And tell Archippus, "See 17
that you perform the Christian service
you have been assigned."
This farewell is in my own hand, 18
from Paul. Remember that I am in prison. God bless you.

THE FIRST LETTER TO THE THESSALONIANS

1 PAUL, Silvanus, and Timothy to
the Thessalonian church in union
with God the Father and the
Lord Jesus Christ; God bless you
and give you peace.
2 We always thank God for you all when
3 we mention you in our prayers, for we can
never forget before our God and Father
your energetic faith, your loving service, and your unwavering expectation
4 of our Lord Jesus Christ. For we know,
brothers whom God so loves, that he
5 has chosen you, for our preaching of the
good news did not come to you as mere
words but with power and the holy
Spirit and full conviction—you know
the kind of life we lived among you for
6 your good. And you followed the example set by us and by the Lord, for
though our message brought you great
trouble, you welcomed it with joy in-
7 spired by the holy Spirit, so that you
set an example to all the believers in
8 Macedonia and Greece. For the Lord's
message has rung out from you not only
over Macedonia and Greece, but the
story of your belief in God has gone
everywhere, so that we never need to
9 mention it. For when people speak of
us, they tell what a welcome you gave
us, and how you turned from idols to
God, to serve a true and living God,
10 and to wait for the coming from heaven
of his Son, whom he raised from the
dead—Jesus, our deliverer from God's
coming wrath.

2 You know yourselves, brothers, that
our visit to you was far from ineffectu-
2 al. We had just been through ill-treatment and insults at Philippi, as you remember, but, in the face of great opposition, we took courage by the help of
our God, and told you God's good
3 news. For our appeal does not rest on
a delusion, nor spring from any impure
4 motive; there is no fraud about it. God
has thought us fit to be intrusted with
the good news, and so we tell it, making
no effort to please men, but to please
5 God, who tests our hearts. We never
used flattery, as you know, or found
pretexts for making money, as God is
our witness. We never sought praise 6
from men, either from you or anyone
else, though as Christ's apostles we
might have stood on our dignity. We 7
were children when we were with you;
we were like a mother nursing her children. That was the kind of affection 8
we had for you, which made us ready
to share with you not only God's good
news but our own lives too, because
you were so dear to us. You remember, 9
brothers, how we toiled and labored.
We worked night and day, when we
preached the good news to you, in order
not to be a burden to any of you. You 10
will testify, and God will, how pure and
upright and irreproachable our relations were with you who believed.
You know how, like a father with his 11
children, we used to urge, encourage,
and implore you to make your lives 12
worthy of God who invites you into his
kingdom and his glory.

We for our part constantly thank 13
God for another reason too—because
when you received God's message from
our lips, you welcomed it not as the
message of men but as the message of
God, as it really is, which does its work
in the hearts of you believers. For you, 14
brothers, followed the example of God's
churches in Judea that are in union
with Christ Jesus, for you in your turn
had to bear the same ill-treatment
from your neighbors as they did from
the Jews, who killed the Lord Jesus and 15
persecuted the prophets and us; who
displease God, and in their hostility to
all mankind try to keep us from speak- 16
ing to the heathen so that they may be
saved, so as always to fill up the measure of their sins. But God's wrath has
overtaken them at last!

For our part, brothers, when we were 17
separated from you for a little while—
in person, though not in spirit—we
were extremely eager and longed intensely to see you. For we resolved to 18
come to see you—I, Paul, did so again
and again—but Satan held us back.

19 For what hope or happiness shall we
have or what prize to be proud of in the
presence of our Lord Jesus when he
20 comes, except you? You are our pride
and our joy.

3 So when I could not bear it any longer, I made up my mind to stay behind
2 alone at Athens, and I sent my brother
Timothy, a servant of God in preaching the good news of the Christ, to
3 strengthen you in your faith and encourage you not to be led astray, any
of you, in all these troubles. You know
yourselves that this is what we must
4 expect, for when we were with you, we
told you beforehand that we were going
to have trouble, and it came true, as
5 you know. That was why, when I could
not bear it any longer, I sent to find out
about your faith, for I was afraid that
the tempter might have tempted you
6 and all our labor might be lost. But
now that Timothy has just come back
to me from you, and brought me good
news of your faith and love, and told
me how kindly you think of me and
that you long to see me just as much as
7 I long to see you, I feel encouraged,
brothers, about you, in spite of all my
8 distress and trouble, at your faith, for
now I can really live, since you are
9 standing firm in the Lord. For how can
I thank God enough for you, for all the
happiness you make me feel in the
10 presence of our God, as I pray night
and day with intense earnestness that
I may see your faces and supply what
is lacking in your faith?

11 May our God and Father himself and
our Lord Jesus open my way to you!
12 May the Lord make your love for one
another and for all men wide and full
13 like my love for you, so that your hearts
may be strong and faultlessly pure in
the sight of our God and Father, when
our Lord Jesus appears with all his
saints!

4 Now, brothers, we ask and entreat
you, in the name of the Lord Jesus, to
live as you learned from us that you
must live, to please God—as indeed you
are doing, only do it more and more.
2 For you remember what instructions
we gave you on the authority of the
Lord Jesus.
3 It is God's will that you should be
consecrated, that you abstain from im-
4 morality, that each of you learn to take
a wife for himself from pure and honorable motives, not to gratify his passion, 5
like the heathen who know nothing of
God. No one is to wrong or defraud his 6
brother in this matter, for the Lord
avenges all such things, as we told you
before, in the most solemn terms. God 7
has not called us to an unclean life, but
to a pure one. So whoever disregards 8
this is not disregarding man, but God,
who gives you his holy Spirit.

You do not need to have anyone 9
write to you about brotherly love, for
you have yourselves been taught by
God to love one another, and you are 10
doing it to all the brothers all over
Macedonia.

But we do entreat you, brothers, to 11
surpass yourselves in striving to live
quietly and mind your own affairs, and
work with your hands, as we directed
you, so that you may have the respect 12
of the outsiders, and not be dependent
upon anybody.

We do not want you to be under any 13
misapprehension, brothers, about those
who are falling asleep. You must not
grieve for them, as others do who have
no hope. For if we believe that Jesus 14
died and rose again, then by means of
Jesus God will bring back with him
those who have fallen asleep. For we 15
can assure you, on the Lord's own authority, that those of us who will still
be living when the Lord comes will
have no advantage over those who have
fallen asleep. For the Lord himself, at 16
the summons, when the archangel calls
and God's trumpet sounds, will come
down from heaven, and first those who
died in union with Christ will rise; then 17
those of us who are still living will be
caught up with them on clouds into the
air to meet the Lord, and so we shall be
with the Lord forever. Therefore, en- 18
courage one another with this truth.

But as to times and dates, brothers, 5
you do not need to have anyone write
to you, for you yourselves know per- 2
fectly well that the Day of the Lord is
to come like a thief in the night. When 3
people say, "What peace and security!" then suddenly destruction will be
upon them, like birth-pains upon a
woman about to give birth to a child,
and there will be no escape. But you 4
are not in darkness, brothers, so that
that Day should surprise you like
thieves. You all belong to the light and 5
the day. We have nothing to do with

6 night or with darkness. So we must not
sleep like other men, but we must be
7 vigilant and composed. For those who
sleep sleep at night and those who get
8 drunk do so at night, but we who belong to the day must be composed,
wearing faith and love for a coat of
mail, and helmeted with the hope of
9 salvation. For God has not destined us
for his wrath, but to gain salvation
10 through our Lord Jesus Christ, who
died for us so that whether we are still
alive or fall asleep we may live with
11 him. Therefore encourage one another
and strengthen one another, just as you
are doing.

12 We beg you, brothers, to respect
those who work with you and who lead
you in the service of the Lord, and
13 teach you. Hold them in the highest
esteem and affection for what they do.
14 Live at peace with one another. We
beg you, brothers, warn the idlers,
cheer up the despondent, keep hold of
the weak, be patient with everybody.
Take care that none of you ever pays 15
back evil for evil, but always try to 16
treat one another and everybody with
kindness. Always be joyful. Never 17
give up praying. Thank God whatever 18
happens. For this is what God through
Christ Jesus wants you to do. Do not 19
stifle the Spirit. Do not disregard the 20
utterances it inspires, but test them all, 21
retaining what is good and avoiding 22
every kind of evil.

May God himself, the giver of peace, 23
consecrate you through and through.
Spirit, soul, and body, may you be kept
sound, and be found irreproachable
when our Lord Jesus Christ comes. He 24
who calls you can be relied on, and he
will do this.

Brothers, pray for us. 25

Greet all the brothers with a sacred 26
kiss. I charge you in the Lord's name to 27
have this letter read to all the brothers.

The blessing of our Lord Jesus Christ 28
be with you.

THE SECOND LETTER TO THE THESSALONIANS

1 PAUL, Silvanus, and Timothy to
the Thessalonian church in union
with God our Father and the
2 Lord Jesus Christ; God the Father and the Lord Jesus Christ bless
you and give you peace.
3 We always have to thank God for
you, brothers, as it is right that we
should, because your faith is growing
so wonderfully and the love of every
one of you for one another is increasing.
4 As a result, we ourselves speak of you
with pride in the churches of God for
your steadfastness and faith in the face
of all the persecutions and troubles you
5 are having to endure. This is a proof of
God's justice in judging, and it is to
prove you worthy of the Kingdom of
God, for the sake of which you are suf-
6 fering, since God considers it only just
to repay with suffering those who are
7 making you suffer and to give rest to
you who are suffering and to us, when
our Lord Jesus appears from heaven,
8 with his mighty angels in a blaze of fire,
and takes vengeance on the godless who
will not listen to the good news of our
9 Lord Jesus. They will be punished with
eternal ruin and exclusion from the
presence of the Lord and his glorious
10 might, when on that Day he comes to
be honored in his people, and wondered
at in all who believe in him—because
our testimony has been confirmed in
you.
11 To this end we always pray for you
too, asking our God to find you worthy
of the call he has given you, and by his
power to fulfil every desire you may
have for goodness, and every effort of
12 your faith, so that the name of our
Lord Jesus may be glorified in you and
you in him, by the blessing of our God
and the Lord Jesus Christ.
2 As to the coming of our Lord Jesus
Christ, brothers, and our assembling to
2 meet him, we beg you not to let your
minds be too easily unsettled or
wrought up, by any message of the
Spirit or any utterance or letter pur-
porting to be from me, to the effect that
the Day of the Lord has already come.
You must not let anyone deceive you at 3
all. For that is not until the rebellion
takes place and the embodiment of disobedience makes his appearance—he
who is doomed to destruction, the ad- 4
versary of every being that is called a
god or an object of worship, and so
overbearing toward them as to enter
God's sanctuary and take his seat
there, proclaiming himself to be God—
do you not remember that when I was 5
with you, I used to tell you this? So 6
now you know what it is that is holding
him back from making his appearance
before the appointed time arrives. For 7
disobedience is already secretly at
work, but only until he who is now
holding it in check is gotten out of the
way. Then the embodiment of disobe- 8
dience will make his appearance, and
the Lord Jesus will destroy him with
the breath of his mouth and annihilate
him by his appearance and arrival.
The other's appearance, by the contriv- 9
ance of Satan, will be full of power and
pretended signs and wonders, and full 10
of wicked deception for men who are
going to destruction, because they refused to love the truth and be saved.
This is why God sends upon them a 11
misleading influence, to make them believe what is false, so that all who have 12
refused to believe the truth but have
preferred disobedience may be condemned.

We always have to thank God for 13
you, brothers whom the Lord so loves,
because God chose you from the beginning to be saved through consecration
by the Spirit and through faith in the
truth, and called you to it through our 14
preaching of the good news, so that you
may share in the glory of our Lord Jesus Christ. So stand firm, brothers, and 15
hold fast to the instructions you have
received from us, whether by letter or

16 by word of mouth. May our Lord Jesus
Christ himself and God our Father,
who has loved us and kindly given us
unfailing encouragement and a well-
17 founded hope, encourage you and
strengthen you to do and say everything that is right.

3 Now, brothers, pray for us, that the
Lord's message may spread rapidly and
2 gloriously as it did among you, and
that we may be saved from unjust and
wicked men; for not everybody has
faith.
3 But the Lord is to be relied on, and
he will give you strength and protect
4 you from the evil one. We have faith
in you through the Lord that you are
doing and will keep doing what we di-
5 rect you to do. May the Lord guide
your hearts into a sense of God's love
and into a steadfastness like Christ's.
6 We charge you, brothers, in the
name of the Lord Jesus Christ, to keep
away from any brother who lives in
idleness, instead of following the teach-
7 ing you received from us. For you
know yourselves what you must do to
follow my example, for I was not idle
8 when I was with you; I did not eat
anybody's bread without paying for it,
but with toil and labor I worked night
and day, in order not to be a burden to
any of you. Not that I had not a right 9
to my support, but to give you in my
own conduct an example to imitate.
When I was with you, I gave you this 10
rule: "If anyone refuses to work,
give him nothing to eat!" For we hear 11
that some of you are living in idleness,
mere busybodies, not doing any work.
Now with the authority of the Lord 12
Jesus Christ we charge and exhort such
people to keep quiet and do their work
and earn their own living. But you, 13
brothers, must not get tired of doing
right. If anyone refuses to obey what 14
we have said in this letter, mark the
man and do not have anything to do
with him, to make him feel ashamed.
Do not look upon him as an enemy but 15
warn him as a brother. And may the 16
Lord of peace himself always give you
peace in every way. The Lord be with
you all.
This greeting is in my own hand, 17
Paul's; it is the mark in every letter of
mine. This is the way I write. The 18
blessing of our Lord Jesus Christ be
with you all.

THE FIRST LETTER TO TIMOTHY

1 PAUL, an apostle of Christ Jesus
by order of God our Savior and
2 of Jesus Christ our hope, to Timothy, my true child in faith; God
the Father and Christ Jesus our Lord
bless you and be merciful to you, and
give you peace.
3 As I asked you to do when I was on
my way to Macedonia, stay on in
Ephesus in order to warn certain people
4 there not to teach strange views nor to
devote themselves to fictions and inter-
minable pedigrees; such things lead to
controversy instead of the divine sys-
5 tem which operates through faith. The
aim of your instruction must be love
that springs from a pure heart and from
a good conscience and from a sincere
6 faith. Some people have failed in these
things and been diverted into fruitless
7 talk. They would like to be teachers of
law although they do not understand
the words they use or the matters they
insist upon.
8 I agree that the Law is excellent—
9 provided it is legitimately used, with
the understanding that law is not intended for upright men but for the lawless and disorderly, the godless and irreligious, the irreverent and profane,
men who kill their fathers or mothers,
10 murderers, immoral people, men sexu-
ally perverted, kidnappers, liars, per-
jurers, or whatever else is contrary to
11 sound teaching, as set forth in the glorious good news of the blessed God with
which I have been intrusted.
12 I thank Christ Jesus our Lord who
has given me the strength for it, for
thinking me trustworthy and putting
13 me into his service, though I once used
to abuse, persecute, and insult him.
But he had mercy on me, because I had
14 acted in ignorance and unbelief, and
the blessing of our Lord has been given
me in the greatest abundance, together
with faith and love that union with
15 Christ Jesus brings. It is a trustworthy
saying, entitled to the fullest acceptance, that Christ Jesus came into the
world to save sinners. And I am the
16 foremost of them, but God had mercy
on me in order that in my case as the
foremost, Christ Jesus might display
his perfect patience, as an example to
those who would later believe in him
and find eternal life. To the eternal 17
King, immortal and invisible, the one
God, be honor and glory forever and
ever! Amen.
These are the instructions that I in- 18
trust to you, my son Timothy, and they
are in accordance with the predictions
made long ago about you. Fight the
good fight with their aid, keeping hold 19
of faith and a good conscience. For
some people have let that go and have
had their faith ruined, like Hymenaeus 20
and Alexander, whom I turned over to
Satan, to be taught not to blaspheme.
First of all, then, I urge that en- 2
treaties, prayers, petitions, and thanksgivings be offered for all men, for emper- 2
ors and all who are in authority, so that
we may live tranquil, quiet lives, with
perfect piety and probity. It is right to 3
do this, and it pleases God our Savior,
who wants all men to be saved and to 4
come to know the truth.
For there is but one God, and one 5
intermediary between God and men—
the man Christ Jesus, who gave himself 6
as a ransom for all men. This is what
was testified to at the proper times, and 7
I was appointed a herald and apostle of
it—I am telling the truth, I am not lying—to teach the heathen faith and
truth.
I want the men everywhere to offer 8
prayer, lifting to heaven hands that are
holy, without any angry disputes.
Women for their part are to dress mod- 9
estly and sensibly in proper clothes, not
adorning themselves by braiding their
hair or with gold or pearls or expensive
clothing, but, as is appropriate for 10
women who profess to be religious,
with good actions.
Women must listen quietly in church 11
and be perfectly submissive. I do not 12
allow women to teach or to domineer
over men; they must keep quiet. For 13
Adam was formed first, and then Eve;
and it was not Adam who was deceived, 14

it was the woman who was deluded and
15 fell into sin. But they will be saved
through motherhood, if they continue
to have faith and to be loving and holy,
3 and sensible as well. This is a trustworthy saying.
Whoever aspires to the office of superintendent sets his heart on a fine
2 work. A superintendent must be a man
above reproach, only once married,
temperate, sensible, a man of good be-
3 havior, hospitable, able to teach; not
addicted to drink or pugnacious, but a
man of moderation and peace, not
4 avaricious, managing his own house
well, and keeping his children under
5 control and perfectly respectful—for if
a man does not know how to conduct
his own household, how can he look
6 after a church of God? He must not be
a new convert, or he may grow conceited and incur criticism from slander-
7 ous people. He must also be a man of
good standing with outsiders, or he
may get into disgrace and be entrapped
8 by the slanderers. Assistants, in turn,
must be serious, straightforward men,
not addicted to wine or dishonest gain,
9 but holding the divine truth of the
10 faith with a clear conscience. They
should first be tested, and afterward, if
there is no fault to be found with them,
11 they can serve as assistants. Their
wives too must be serious, not gossips;
they must be temperate, and perfectly
12 trustworthy. The assistants must be
only once married, and manage their
children and their households well.
13 For those who do good service as assistants gain a good standing for themselves and great confidence in their
faith in Christ Jesus.
14 I hope to come to you soon, but I am
15 writing you all this so that if I am delayed, you may know how we are to
conduct ourselves in the household of
God, for it is the church of the living
God, the pillar and foundation of the
16 truth. No one can deny the profundity
of the divine truth of our religion!
"He was revealed in flesh,
He was vindicated by the Spirit,
He was seen by the angels,
He was proclaimed among the
heathen,
He was believed in throughout the
world,
He was taken up into glory."
4 The Spirit distinctly says that in
later times some will turn away from
the faith, and devote their attention to
deceitful spirits and the things that demons teach through the pretensions of 2
liars—men with seared consciences who 3
forbid people to marry and insist on abstinence from certain kinds of food
that God created for men who believe
and understand the truth to enjoy and
give thanks for. For everything God 4
has created is good, and nothing need
be refused, provided it is accepted with
thanksgiving, for then it is consecrated 5
by prayer and the Scripture used in it.
If you point this out to the brothers, 6
you will be a good servant of Christ
Jesus, living on the principles of the
faith and the excellent teaching you
have had. But let worldly fictions and 7
old wives' tales alone. Train yourself
for the religious life. Physical training 8
is of some service, but religion is of
service in every way, for it carries with
it the promise of life here and hereafter.
This is a trustworthy saying, entitled 9
to the fullest acceptance. It is for this 10
that we toil and struggle, for we have
fixed our hopes on the living God, the
Savior of all men, especially those who
believe.
This is what you must urge and 11
teach. Let no one look down on you 12
because you are young, but set those
who believe an example in speech, conduct, love, faith, and purity. Until I 13
come, devote yourself to the public
reading of Scripture, preaching, and
teaching. Do not neglect the gift you 14
have, that was given you with predictions of your work, when the elders laid
their hands upon you. Cultivate these 15
things, devote yourself to them, so that
everyone will see your progress. Look 16
out for yourself and for your teaching.
Persevere in your work, for if you do
you will save both yourself and those
who listen to you.
Never reprove an older man, but ap- 5
peal to him as to a father. Treat
younger men like brothers, older wom- 2
en like mothers, younger ones like sisters, with absolute purity. Look after 3
widows who are really dependent. If a 4
widow has children or grandchildren,
let them learn first to show piety in the
treatment of their own families, and to
return the care of those who brought
them up, for that is what God approves. But a woman who is really a 5

widow, and has no children, has fixed
her hope on God, and devotes herself to
prayers and entreaties night and day.
6 A widow who gives herself up to pleas-
7 ure is dead while she is still alive. Insist
upon these points, so that people may
8 be irreproachable. Whoever fails to
provide for his own relatives, and particularly for members of his own family,
has disowned the faith and is worse
9 than an unbeliever. No one under sixty
years of age should be put on the list of
widows. A widow must have been mar-
10 ried but once, and have a good reputation for Christian service, such as bringing up children, being hospitable to
strangers, washing the feet of God's
people, helping people in distress, or
devoting herself to any form of doing
11 good. Do not put young women on the
list of widows, for when their youthful
vigor comes between them and Christ,
12 they want to marry, and become guilty
13 of breaking their previous pledge. Besides, as they go about from house to
house they learn to be idle, and not
only idle but gossips and busybodies,
and talk of things they ought not to
14 mention. So I would have young wom-
en marry and have children and keep
house and avoid giving our opponents
15 any excuse for abusing us. For some
widows have already turned aside to
16 follow Satan. Any Christian woman
who has widowed relatives should look
after them, and relieve the church, so
that it can look after widows who are
really dependent.

17 Elders who do their duties well
should be considered as deserving twice
as much as they get, particularly those
who work at preaching and teaching.
18 For the Scripture says, "You must not
muzzle an ox when it is treading out the
grain," and the workman deserves his
19 wages. Do not listen to an accusation
made against an elder, unless it is supported by two or three witnesses.
20 Those who are found guilty you must
reprove publicly, as a warning to
21 others. I charge you before God and
Christ Jesus and the chosen angels to
observe these rules without any dis-
crimination, and to be perfectly impar-
22 tial. Never ordain anyone hastily; do
not make yourself responsible for the
23 sins of others; keep your life pure. Stop
drinking nothing but water; take a little wine for the good of your digestion
and for your frequent attacks of illness.
Some men's sins are perfectly evident, 24
and lead them right on to judgment,
but there are others whose sins only
dog their steps. Good deeds too are 25
evident enough, or when they are not,
they cannot be wholly concealed.

All who are under the yoke of slavery 6
must treat their masters with the
greatest respect, so that the name of
God and our teaching may not be
abused. Those who have Christian 2
masters must not think lightly of them
because they are brothers; they must
serve them all the more faithfully, because those who benefit by it are believers and hence dear to them.

These are the things you must teach
and preach. Anyone who teaches differ- 3
ent views and does not agree with the
wholesome instruction which comes from
our Lord Jesus Christ, and with reli- 4
gious teaching is a conceited, ignorant
person, with a morbid craving for speculations and arguments which result
only in envy, quarreling, abuse, base
suspicions, and mutual irritation be- 5
tween people of depraved minds, who
are lost to the truth and think of religion only as a means of gain. And reli- 6
gion with contentment is a great means
of gain. For we bring nothing into 7
the world, and we can take nothing out
of it. If we have food and clothing we 8
will be satisfied. But men who want to 9
get rich fall into temptations and snares
and many foolish, harmful cravings,
that plunge people into destruction and
ruin. For love of money is the root of 10
all the evils, and in their eagerness to
get rich, some men wander away from
the faith and pierce themselves to the
heart with many a pang.

But you, man of God, must fly from 11
these things. Strive for uprightness,
godliness, faith, love, steadfastness,
gentleness. Take part in the great con- 12
test of faith! Take hold of eternal life, to
which God called you, when before
many witnesses you made the great
profession of faith. Before God who 13
maintains all life, and before Christ
Jesus who in testifying before Pontius
Pilate made his great profession, I
charge you to keep his command stain- 14
less and irreproachable until the appearance of our Lord Jesus Christ,
which will be brought about in his own 15

time by the blessed, only Sovereign,
the King of kings and Lord of lords,
16 who alone possesses immortality and
dwells in unapproachable light, whom
no man has ever seen or can see. To
him be honor and eternal dominion.
Amen.

17 Charge the rich of this world not to
be arrogant, nor to set their hopes on
such an uncertain thing as riches, but
on God who richly provides us with
18 everything for our enjoyment. Charge
them to do good, to be rich in good
deeds, open-handed and generous,
storing up a valuable treasure for 19
themselves for the future, so as to grasp
the life that is life indeed.

Timothy, guard what has been in- 20
trusted to you. Keep away from the
worldly, empty phrases and contradic-
tions of what they falsely call knowledge, through professing which some 21
people have made a failure of the faith.
God bless you all.

THE SECOND LETTER TO TIMOTHY

1 PAUL, by God's will an apostle of
Christ Jesus in fulfilment of the
promise of that life which is
found in union with Christ Jesus,
2 to my dear child Timothy; God the
Father and Christ Jesus our Lord bless
you and be merciful to you and give
you peace.

3 I thank God, whom I, like my forefathers, worship with a clear conscience, when I remember you, as I
4 constantly do, in my prayers. When I
remember the tears you shed I long
night and day to see you again, and
5 have the perfect happiness of being re-
minded of your genuine faith, a faith
that was seen first in your grandmother
Lois and in your mother Eunice; I am
6 sure it is in you also. For this reason I
would remind you to rekindle the divine gift that you received when I laid
7 my hands upon you. For the Spirit
God has given us is a spirit not of timid-
ity but of power, love, and self-disci-
8 pline. So you must not be ashamed
to testify to our Lord, nor be ashamed
of me who am in prison for his sake, but
join with me in suffering for the good
9 news, through the power of God. He
saved us and called us to a consecrated
life, not for anything we had done, but
of his own accord and out of the mercy
which he bestowed upon us ages ago
10 through Christ Jesus, which has now
been revealed through the appearance
of our Savior Christ Jesus. He has tak-
en away the power of death and
brought life and immortality to light
11 through the good news, of which I have
been appointed a herald, apostle and
12 teacher. This is why I am suffering as
I am, but I am not ashamed of it, for I
know whom I have trusted and I am sure
that he is able to guard what I have in-
13 trusted to him for that Day. As your
example in wholesome instruction, keep
before you what you learned from me,
in the faith and love that come through
14 union with Christ Jesus. Guard that
splendid trust through the holy Spirit
that lives in our hearts.

You know that everyone in the 15
province of Asia has deserted me, including Phygelus and Hermogenes.
May the Lord show mercy to the house- 16
hold of Onesiphorus, for he often
cheered me and was not ashamed of my
being in prison. Why, when he arrived 17
in Rome, he took pains to inquire for
me and found me. The Lord grant that 18
he may be shown mercy by the Lord on
that Day! And you know well enough
how he helped me at Ephesus.

So you, my son, must find strength 2
in the blessing that comes through
Christ Jesus. The things you learned 2
from me before many witnesses you
must commit to trustworthy men who
will be capable of teaching others.
Share my hardships like a good soldier 3
of Christ Jesus. Anyone who is in the 4
army keeps from being involved in
business affairs, so as to please the officer who enlisted him. No one who com- 5
petes in the games is awarded a crown
unless he obeys the rules. The farmer 6
who does the work ought to be the first
to have some of the produce. Think 7
over what I say. For the Lord will help
you to understand it perfectly. Re- 8
member Jesus Christ as risen from the
dead, and descended from David, as I
preach the good news, for the sake of 9
which I even suffer imprisonment as a
criminal. But God's message is not imprisoned! For that reason I am ready 10
to submit to anything for the sake of
those whom God has chosen, so that
they too may gain the salvation that
comes through Christ Jesus and brings
eternal glory. How true those words 11
are! "If we have died with him, we
will live with him! If we endure, we 12
will reign with him! If we disown him,
he will also disown us! If we are un- 13
faithful, he will remain faithful, for he
cannot be false to himself!"

Remind men of these things. Charge 14
them before God to avoid idle arguments which do no one any good and
only bring destruction on those who
listen to them. Do your best to win 15

God's approval as a workman who has
nothing to be ashamed of, but rightly
16 shapes the message of truth. Leave
worldly, empty phrases alone, for they
lead people deeper and deeper into god-
17 lessness, and their teaching spreads like
a cancer; men like Hymenaeus and
18 Philetus, who have missed the truth
and say that the resurrection has taken
place already, thus undermining peo-
19 ple's faith. Yet God's solid foundation
stands unshaken, bearing this inscription, "The Lord knows those who belong to him," and "Everyone who uses
the name of the Lord must give up
20 evil." In any large house there are not
only gold and silver dishes but also
wooden and earthen ones, some for
great occasions and some for ordinary
21 use. So if a man will cleanse himself
from these things, he will be put to
great uses, consecrated and used by the
master of the house himself, and ready
22 for any good use. Fly from the cravings
of youth, and go in pursuit of uprightness, faith, love, and peace, in company
with those who call upon the Lord with
23 pure hearts. Avoid foolish, crude speculations; you know they only lead to
24 quarrels, and a slave of the Lord must
not quarrel, but treat everyone kindly;
he must be persuasive and unresentful,
25 correcting his opponents with gentleness; for God may possibly let them re-
26 pent and acknowledge the truth, and
they may yet return to their senses and
escape from the toils of the devil, who
has caught them to make them do his
will.

3 Understand this, that in the last days
2 there are going to be hard times. People will be selfish, avaricious, boastful,
arrogant, abusive, undutiful, ungrate-
3 ful, irreverent, unfeeling, irreconcilable, slanderous, with no self-control,
brutal, with no love for what is good,
4 treacherous, reckless, conceited, caring
5 more for pleasure than for God, keeping up the forms of religion, but resisting its influence. Avoid such people.
6 They are the kind of men who make
their way into people's houses and
make captives of poor, weak women,
loaded down with their sins and under
7 the control of all sorts of impulses, always ready to learn but never able to
8 comprehend the truth. Just as Jannes
and Jambres opposed Moses, these people in turn oppose the truth; they are
men of depraved minds and counterfeit faith. But they will not make much 9
progress, for everyone will perceive
their folly, just as they did that of those
others. But you have closely followed 10
my teaching, my conduct, my aim, my
faith, my patience, my love, my steadfastness, my persecutions, my sufferings
—the things that happened to me at 11
Antioch, Iconium, and Lystra, the persecutions I endured; yet the Lord
brought me safely out of them all. But 12
everyone who wants to live a godly life
as a follower of Christ Jesus will be persecuted, and bad men and impostors 13
will go on from bad to worse, deceiving
others and deceived themselves. But you 14
must stand by what you have learned
and been convinced of, and remember
from whom you learned it, and how 15
from childhood you have known the
Scriptures which can give you the wisdom that through faith in Christ Jesus
leads to salvation. All Scripture is di- 16
vinely inspired, and useful in teaching,
in reproof, in correcting faults, and in
training in uprightness, so that the man 17
of God will be adequate, and equipped
for any good work.

I charge you in the sight of God and **4**
Christ Jesus who is to judge the living
and the dead, and by his appearing and
his kingdom, preach the message; be at 2
it in season and out of season; convince,
reprove, exhort people, with perfect
patience and willingness to teach. For 3
a time will come when they will not listen to wholesome instruction, but will
overwhelm themselves with teachers to
suit their whims and tickle their fancies, and they will turn from listening 4
to the truth and wander off after fictions. But you must always be com- 5
posed; do not shrink from hardship; do
your work as a missionary, and your
whole duty as a minister.

My life is already being poured out, 6
and the time has come for my departure. I have had a part in the great 7
contest, I have run my race, I have preserved my faith. Now the crown of up- 8
rightness awaits me, which the Lord,
the upright judge, will award me on
that Day, and not only me but also all
who have loved and hoped for his appearing.

Do your best to come to me soon, for 9
Demas has deserted me for love of the 10

present world, and has gone to Thessalonica. Crescens has gone to Galatia,
11 and Titus to Dalmatia. No one but
Luke is with me. Get Mark and bring
him with you, for he is of great assist-
12 ance to me, and I have sent Tychicus
13 to Ephesus. When you come, bring the
cloak that I left with Carpus at Troas,
and the books, especially the parch-
14 ments. Alexander, the metal-worker,
did me a great deal of harm. The Lord
15 will repay him for what he did. You too
must be on your guard against him, for
he vehemently opposed my teaching.
16 At my first appearance in court no one
came to help me; everybody deserted
me. May it not be laid up against
17 them! But the Lord stood by me, and
gave me strength, so that I might make
a full presentation of the message and
let all the heathen hear it. So I was
saved from the jaws of the lion. The 18
Lord will rescue me from any harm and
bring me safely to his heavenly kingdom. To him be glory forever and ever.
Amen.

Remember me to Prisca and Aquila, 19
and to the members of the household of
Onesiphorus. Erastus stayed in Cor- 20
inth. I left Trophimus sick at Miletus
Do your best to come before winter. 21

Eubulus wishes to be remembered to
you, and so do Pudens, Linus, Claudia,
and all the brothers.

The Lord be with your spirit. God 22
bless you all.

THE LETTER TO TITUS

1 PAUL, a slave of God, and an
apostle of Jesus Christ, to arouse
faith in those whom God has
chosen, and the comprehension
2 of religious truth, in the hope of eternal
life, which God who never lies promised
3 ages ago, and revealed at the proper
time in his message, through the
preaching with which I have been intrusted at the command of God our
4 Savior, to Titus, my true child in our
common faith; God our Father and
Christ Jesus our Savior bless you and
give you peace.
5 I left you behind in Crete expressly
to correct what defects there were, and
to appoint elders in each town, as I
6 directed you—men of irreproachable
character, who have been married only
once, whose children are Christians,
free from any suspicion of profligacy or
7 disobedience. For as God's overseer a
superintendent must be irreproachable,
not arrogant or quick-tempered or giv-
en to drink or pugnacious or addicted
8 to dishonest gain, but hospitable, a
lover of goodness, sensible, upright, of
9 holy life, self-controlled, standing by
the message that can be relied on, just
as he was taught it, so that he may be
qualified both to encourage others with
wholesome teaching and to show the
error of those who oppose him.
10 For there are many undisciplined
people, who deceive themselves with
their empty talk, especially those of the
11 party of circumcision. They must be
silenced, for such men upset whole
households by teaching things they
ought not to teach, for the sake of dis-
12 honest gain. It was a Cretan, a prophet of their own, who said,

"Cretans are always liars, savage
brutes, lazy gluttons,"

13 and that statement is true. Therefore
correct them rigorously, to make them
14 have a healthy faith, and not study
Jewish fictions or commands given by
15 men who reject the truth. To the pure
everything is pure, but to the evil-
minded and unbelieving nothing is
pure, but their very minds and consciences are unclean. They profess to 16
know God, but they disown him by
what they do; they are detestable, disobedient men, worthless for any good
purpose.

But you must teach people the things **2**
that properly belong to wholesome
teaching. Teach the older men to be 2
temperate, serious, and sensible—men
of vigorous faith, love, and steadfastness. Teach the older women, too, to 3
be reverent in their behavior, and not
to gossip or be slaves of drink, but to 4
be teachers of what is right, so as to
train the younger women to be loving
wives and mothers, and to be sensible, 5
pure-minded, domestic, kind, and submissive to their husbands, so as not to
bring reproach on God's message. Urge 6
the younger men, too, to be sensible. In 7
every way set them an example of good
conduct yourself. Teach with sincerity
and seriousness, and present a whole- 8
some, unobjectionable message, so that
your opponent may be put to shame at
finding nothing bad to say about us.
Tell slaves always to obey their masters 9
and try to please them, not to oppose 10
them or steal from them, but to show
such perfect good faith as to do credit
to the teaching about God our Savior,
by everything they do.
For God's mercy has appeared with 11
salvation for all men, training us to 12
renounce godless ways and worldly
passions, and live serious, upright,
and godly lives in this world, while we 13
wait for the fulfilment of our blessed
hope in the glorious appearing of our
great God and Savior Christ Jesus. He 14
gave himself for us, to free us from all
wickedness and purify for himself a
people of his own, eager to do right.
This is what you must teach and urge 15
and insist upon with full authority. No **3**
one is to look down on you. Remind
men to accept and obey the constituted
authorities, to be ready for any useful
service, to abuse nobody, to be peace- 2
able and reasonable, showing perfect

3 gentleness to everyone. For we ourselves were once without understanding,
disobedient, deluded, enslaved to all
kinds of passions and pleasures. Our
minds were full of malice and envy.
Men hated us and we hated one another.
4 But when the goodness and kindness of
God our Savior were revealed, he saved
5 us, not for any upright actions we had
performed, but from his own mercy,
through the bath of regeneration and
6 renewal by the holy Spirit, which he
has poured out upon us abundantly
7 through Jesus Christ our Savior, so that
we might be made upright through his
mercy and become possessors of eternal
8 life in fulfilment of our hope. This is a
trustworthy teaching, and I want you
to insist on these things, so that those
who believe in God may make it their
business to do good. All this is right
9 and beneficial to mankind. But have
nothing to do with foolish controver-
sies, pedigrees, strife, and wrangles
about the Law, for they are profitless
and futile. If a man is inclined to a sect, 10
after warning him once or twice, have
nothing more to do with him. You may 11
be sure that a man of that kind is corrupt and sinful, for his own actions condemn him.

When I send Artemas or Tychicus to 12
you, do your best to come to me at
Nicopolis, for I have decided to settle
there for the winter. Do all you can to 13
help Zenas the expert in the Law and
Apollos on with their journey, and see
that they have everything they need.
Have our people learn to make it their 14
business to do good, so as to meet these
pressing demands and not live unfruitful lives.

All who are with me wish to be re- 15
membered to you. Remember me to all
believers who love me. God bless you
all.

THE LETTER TO PHILEMON

1 PAUL, a prisoner for Jesus Christ,
and brother Timothy, to our
dear fellow-worker Philemon,
2 and our sister Apphia, and our
fellow-soldier Archippus, and the church
3 that meets in your house; God our
Father and the Lord Jesus Christ bless
you and give you peace.
4 I never mention you in my prayers
5 without thanking my God for what I
hear of the love and faith you have in
6 the Lord Jesus and all his people, and I
pray that through coming to know
every good thing about us as Christians
they may effectually share your faith.
7 I have been greatly pleased and encouraged over your love, for the hearts
of God's people have been cheered, my
brother, by you.
8 So although as a Christian I feel
quite free to order you to do what ought
9 to be done, I prefer to appeal to you in
the name of love, simply as what I
am—Paul, no less an envoy of Christ
Jesus, though now a prisoner for him.
10 I appeal to you for my child Onesimus,
whose father I have become here in
11 prison. Once you found him useless,
but now he has become useful to you
12 and to me, and now that I send him
back to you, it is like sending my very
13 heart. I would have liked to keep him
with me, to wait on me in your place
while I am in prison for the good news,
but I do not wish to do anything with- 14
out your consent, so that your kindness
might be voluntary, and not have the
appearance of compulsion. For perhaps 15
this is why you and he were parted for a
while, that you might have him back
forever, not as a slave any longer but 16
more than a slave, a dear brother—dear
especially to me, but how much dearer
to you, both as a man and as a Christian! So if you regard me as a comrade, 17
welcome him as you would me. And if 18
he has caused you any loss or owes you
anything, charge it to my account. I, 19
Paul, write this with my own hand: I
will repay it—not to mention the fact
that you owe me your very self besides.
Come, brother, let me make something 20
out of you, in a Christian sense! Cheer
my heart as a Christian.
I write you in full reliance upon your 21
obedience; I know that you will do even
more than I ask. And get ready to en- 22
tertain me too, for I hope that I shall
be restored to you, in answer to your
prayers.
Epaphras, my fellow-prisoner for 23
Christ Jesus, wishes to be remembered
to you, and so do my fellow-workers,
Mark, Aristarchus, Demas, and Luke. 24
The blessing of the Lord Jesus Christ 25
be with your spirits.

THE LETTER TO THE HEBREWS

1 IT WAS little by little and in different ways that God spoke in old
times to our forefathers through
2 the prophets, but in these latter
days he has spoken to us in a Son,
whom he had destined to possess everything, and through whom he had made
3 the world. He is the reflection of God's
glory, and the representation of his being, and bears up the universe by his
mighty word. He has effected man's
purification from sin, and has taken his
seat on high at the right hand of God's
4 Majesty, showing himself to be as much
greater than the angels as his title is
5 superior to theirs. For to what angel
did God ever say,
"You are my Son! I have today become your Father"?
Or again,
6 "I will become his Father, and he
shall become my Son"? But of the time
when he is to bring his firstborn Son
back to the world he says,
"And let all God's angels bow before
him."
7 In speaking of the angels he says,
"He who changes his angels into
winds,
And his attendants into blazing
fire!"
8 But of the Son he says,
"God is your throne forever and
ever!
And a righteous scepter is the scepter of his kingdom!
9 You have loved right and hated
wrong!
That is why God, your God, has
anointed you with exhilarating
oil beyond all your comrades."
10 And
"You, Lord, in the beginning founded the earth,
And the sky is the work of your
hands!
11 They will perish, but you continue!
And they will all wear out like a
coat,
12 And you will fold them up like a
mantle,
And change them as one changes
his coat.
But you are always the same, and
your years will have no end!"
But to what angel did he ever say, 13
"Sit at my right hand,
Until I make your enemies a footstool for you"?
Are not the angels all spirits in serv- 14
ice, whom he sends on his errands for
the good of those who are destined to
possess salvation?
This is why we must give the very 2
closest attention to the message we
have heard, to keep from ever losing
our hold upon it. For if the message 2
delivered by angels proved to be au-
thentic, and every violation or neglect
of it led to a corresponding penalty,
how can we escape if we pay no atten- 3
tion to such a salvation as this? It was
first proclaimed by the Lord himself,
and it was guaranteed to us by those
who heard him, while God himself cor- 4
roborated their testimony with signs,
portents, and various wonders, and by
impartations of the holy Spirit when he
saw fit.
For it was not for angels that he des- 5
tined the control of that world to be,
that we are speaking of. For someone 6
has somewhere solemnly declared,
"What is man? for you think of
him;
Or any man? for you care for him.
You made him for a little while in- 7
ferior to angels;
Yet you have crowned him with
glory and honor,
And you have put him in charge of
the works of your hands!
You have put everything under his 8
feet!"
In thus making everything subject to
man, God left nothing that was not subjected to him. But we do not as yet see
everything made subject to him, but we 9
do see Jesus, who was "made for a little
while inferior to angels, crowned with
glory and honor" because he suffered
death, so that by the favor of God he
might taste the bitterness of death on

10 behalf of every human being. For it was
appropriate that he who is the great
First Cause of the universe should, in
guiding his many children to his glorious salvation, make their leader in it
fully qualified through what he suf-
11 fered. For both he who purifies them
and they who are purified spring from
one source. That is why he is not
ashamed to call them brothers, and
say,
"I will tell your name to my brothers,
In the midst of the congregation I
will sing your praise";
13 and again
"I will put my trust in God";
and again,
"Here I am with the children that
God has given me."
14 Therefore since these children referred to have the same mortal nature,
Jesus also shared it, like them, in order
that by his death he might dethrone the
15 lord of death, the devil, and free from
their slavery men who had always
16 lived in fear of death. For of course it
was not angels but the descendants of
17 Abraham that he came to help. And so
he had to be made like his brothers in
every respect, so that he might prove a
compassionate high priest as well as
one faithful in his service to God, in
18 order to forgive the people's sins. For
because he has himself been tempted
in what he has suffered he is able to
help others who are in trial.
3 Therefore, my fellow-Christians, who
have likewise heard the heavenly invitation, observe how faithful Jesus, the
commissioner and high priest of our re-
2 ligion, has been to the God who appointed him, just as Moses was, in all
3 the house of God. For Jesus is entitled
to as much more honor than Moses as
the builder of a house is than the house
4 he builds. For every house has a builder, and the builder of the universe is
5 God. Now the faithfulness of Moses in
all the house of God was that of a servant, in faithfully repeating what he was
6 told to say; but Christ's faithfulness
was that of a son set over the house of
God. And we are that house, if we keep
up our courage and our triumphant
hope to the very end.
7 Therefore, as the holy Spirit says,
"If you hear his voice today,
8 Do not harden your hearts as your
forefathers provoked me by doing,
As in that time of trial in the desert,
Where your forefathers put my do- 9
ings to the proof for forty years,
Though they saw them all the
time.
That was why I was angry with 10
that generation,
And I said, 'Their minds are always wandering,
And they have never found my
paths.'
But as I made oath in my anger, 11
They shall never be admitted to
my Rest!"
See to it, my brothers, that no one of 12
you has a wicked, unbelieving heart,
that turns away from the ever-living
God, but encourage one another every 13
day, as long as we can still speak of Today, so that no one of you may have his
heart hardened by the pleasantness of
sin. For we are true partners with 14
Christ if we really keep the conviction
that we had at first unshaken to the
very end. So while we can still speak of 15
Today, if you hear him speak, do not
harden your hearts, as they provoked
him by doing. For who was it that 16
heard him speak and yet provoked him?
Was it not all those who had escaped
from Egypt under Moses' leadership?
And who was it with whom God was 17
angry forty whole years? Was it not
with those who had sinned, who
dropped dead in the desert? And who 18
was it to whom God made oath that
they should not be admitted to his
Rest, if it was not to those who had disobeyed him? So we see that it was 19
their unbelief that kept them from be- 4
ing admitted to it. We ought therefore
to fear that when the promise of admis-
sion to his Rest is still open, some one
of you may be found to have failed to
reach it. For we have had good news 2
preached to us, just as they did, but the
message they heard did them no good
because they did not agree through
faith with what they heard. For we 3
who have believed are admitted to that
Rest, of which he said,
"As I made oath in my anger,
They shall never be admitted to
my Rest!"
And yet God's work was finished at the

4 creation of the world, for he says somewhere of the seventh day,
"On the seventh day God rested after all his work,"
5 while here he says again,
"They shall never be admitted to my Rest!"
6 Since then it is still true that somebody
will be admitted to it, and those who
had a gospel preached to them before
were not admitted because of their dis-
7 obedience, he again fixes a new Today,
saying long afterward through David,
as already quoted,
"If you hear his voice today,
Do not harden your hearts!"
8 For if Joshua had really brought them
rest God would not afterward have
9 spoken of another day. So there must
still be a promised Sabbath of Rest for
10 God's people. For all who are admitted
to God's Rest rest after their work, just
11 as God did after his. Let us, therefore,
make every effort to be admitted to
that Rest, so that none of us may fail
through such disobedience as theirs.
12 For the message of God is a living and
active force, sharper than any double-edged sword, piercing through soul and
spirit, and joints and marrow, and keen
in judging the thoughts and purposes
13 of the mind. No being created can escape God's sight, but everything is bare
and helpless before the eyes of him with
whom we have to reckon.

14 Since then we have in Jesus, the Son
of God, a great high priest who has
gone up into heaven, let us keep firm
15 hold of our religion. For our high priest
is not one who is incapable of sympathy
with our weaknesses, but he has been
tempted in every way just as we have,
16 without committing any sin. So let us
come with courage to God's throne of
grace to receive his forgiveness and find
him responsive when we need his help.

5 For every high priest who is chosen
from among men is appointed to represent his fellow-men in their relations
with God, and to offer gifts and sin-
2 offerings. He can sympathize with the
ignorant and misguided because he is
3 himself subject to weakness, and on
this account he is obliged to offer sacrifices for sin, not only for the people but
4 for himself as well. And no one takes
the office upon himself, but men assume
it only when called to it by God, as
5 Aaron was. So even Christ did not
claim for himself the dignity of the high
priesthood, but he was appointed to it
by him who said to him,
"You are my Son! I have today become your Father!"
For he says in another passage, 6
"You are a priest forever of the priesthood of Melchizedek."
For Jesus in his life on earth offered 7
prayers and entreaties, crying aloud
with tears, to him who was able to save
him from death, and because of his
piety his prayer was heard. And al- 8
though he was a son, he learned to obey,
through what he suffered, and when he 9
was fully qualified, he became a source
of unending salvation for all who obey
him, since God pronounced him a high 10
priest of the priesthood of Melchizedek.

I have much to say to you about this, 11
but it is difficult to make it clear to you,
because you have become so slow of apprehension. For although from the 12
length of your Christian experience you
ought to be teaching others, you actually need someone to teach you over
again the very elements of Christian
truth, and you have come to need milk
instead of solid food. For anyone who 13
is limited to milk is unacquainted with
Christian teaching, for he is only an infant. But full-grown men have a right 14
to solid food, for their faculties are
trained by practice to distinguish right 6
and wrong. Let us therefore leave elementary Christian teaching alone and
advance toward maturity. We must not
be always relaying foundations, of repentance for wrong-doing, and of faith
in God, with the teaching of baptism 2
and the laying on of hands, the resurrection of the dead and final judgment.
And we will advance if God permits it. 3
For it is impossible to arouse people to 4
a fresh repentance when they have once
for all come into the light and had a
taste of the gift from heaven, and
shared in the holy Spirit and felt the 5
goodness of the word of God and the
strong influences of the coming age,
and yet have fallen back, for they cruci- 6
fy the Son of God on their own account,
and hold him up to contempt. Ground 7
that drinks in frequent showers and
produces vegetation that is of use to
those for whom it is cultivated receives
God's blessing. But if it yields thorns 8
and thistles, it is thought worthless and

almost cursed, and it will finally be
burned.
9 But about you, dear friends, even
though we say this, we are sure of bet-
10 ter things that promise salvation. For
God is not so unjust as to forget the
work you have done and the love you
have showed for his cause, in giving
help to your fellow-Christians as you
11 still do. But we want each of you to
exhibit this same earnestness to the
very end with regard to your confidence
12 in your hope, so that you may never
grow careless, but may learn to follow
the example of those who through their
faith and endurance are the possessors
of God's promises.
13 For when God made his promise to
Abraham, since there was no one greater for him to make oath by, he did so by
14 himself, and said,

"I will certainly bless you richly, and
15 greatly increase your numbers." And
so after waiting patiently, he received
16 what God had promised him. For men
make oath by something greater than
themselves, and they accept an oath as
settling finally any disagreement they
17 may have. Therefore, God in his desire
to make it perfectly clear to those to
whom he made his promise, that his
purpose was unalterable, bound him-
18 self with an oath, so that by these two
unalterable things, which make it impossible for God to break his promise,
we who have taken refuge with him
may be greatly encouraged to seize
19 upon the hope that is offered to us. This
hope is like an anchor for our souls. It
reaches up secure and strong into the
sanctuary behind the heavenly curtain,
20 where Jesus has gone ahead of us, and
become forever a high priest of the
priesthood of Melchizedek.

7 For this man Melchizedek, king of
Salem and priest of the Most High God,
who met Abraham as he was on his way
back from defeating the kings, and gave
2 him his blessing, to whom Abraham apportioned one tenth of all the spoil, who
is first, as his name shows, king of righteousness and then king of Salem, which
3 means king of peace—with no father or
mother or ancestry, and with no beginning to his days nor end to his life, but
like no one but the Son of God, continues as priest forever.
4 Now see how great this man must
have been to have the patriarch Abraham give him a tenth of the spoil.
Those of the descendants of Levi who 5
are appointed to the priesthood are directed by the Law to collect tithes from
the people, that is, from their own
brothers, although they are descended
from Abraham like themselves. But 6
this man, whose ancestry is not connected with theirs, collected tithes from
Abraham himself, and gave his blessing
to the man who had received the promises from God. But, beyond any doubt, 7
it is the inferior that is blessed by the
superior. In the one case, mortal men 8
collect tithes; but in the other, one who,
it is intimated, lives on. In one way of 9
putting it, Levi himself, the collector of
the tithes, through Abraham paid him
tithes, for none of Abraham's posterity 10
was yet begotten at the time of his
meeting with Melchizedek.

Now if anything final had been really 11
accomplished through the Levitical
priesthood, for even the giving of the
Law was based upon it, what further
need would there have been of appointing a different priest of the priesthood
of Melchizedek, instead of choosing
one of the priesthood of Aaron? For 12
when there is a change in the priesthood, a change necessarily takes place
in the Law as well. For he of whom all 13
this was said was related to a tribe no
member of which ever officiated at the
altar. For it is perfectly clear that our 14
Lord sprang from the tribe of Judah,
with reference to which Moses said
nothing at all about priests. The point 15
is still more clear in view of the fact that
the appointment of the new priest resembles that of Melchizedek, for he is 16
appointed not for possessing any legal
physical qualifications, but by virtue
of a life that cannot end. For the 17
psalm bears witness,

"You are a priest forever, of the
priesthood of Melchizedek!"

So an earlier regulation is abrogated be- 18
cause it was poor and ineffective (for 19
there was nothing final about the Law),
and a better hope begins to dawn,
through which we may approach God.
And in proportion as Jesus was not ap- 20
pointed priest without God's making
oath to it, the agreement which he 22
guarantees is better than the old one,
for God took no oath in appointing the
old priests, but he made oath to his 21
appointment, when he said to him,

"The Lord has sworn it and he will
not change:
You are a priest forever!'"
23 The old priests too had to be numerous,
because death prevented their continu-
24 ing in office. But he continues forever,
and so his priesthood is untransferable.
25 Therefore, he is forever able to save all
who come to God through him, because
he always lives and intercedes for them.
26 Such a high priest we needed—godly,
blameless, unstained, removed from sinful men and raised above the very heav-
27 ens; who does not need, as the old high
priests did, to offer sacrifices every day,
first for his own sins and then for those
of the people—for this last he has done
28 once for all, in offering up himself. For
the Law appoints to the high priesthood
men full of imperfection; but this utterance about the making of the oath,
which came long after the Law, appoints a son, fully qualified to be high
priest forever.
8 Now the main point in what I am
saying is this: We have such a high
priest as this, and he has taken his seat
in heaven at the right hand of God's
2 Majesty, to officiate as priest in the
sanctuary and in that true tent of worship which not man but the Lord him-
3 self set up. But every high priest is appointed to offer gifts and sacrifices, and
so this high priest also must have some
4 sacrifice to offer. Further, if he were
still on earth, he would not be a priest
at all, for there are priests enough provided to offer the gifts the Law pre-
5 scribes—though the service they engage in is only a shadow and imitation
of that in heaven. For when Moses was
going to make the tent of worship he
was warned, "Be sure to make it all
just like the pattern you were shown on
6 the mountain." But, as it is, the priestly service to which Christ has been appointed is as much better than the old
as the agreement established by him
and the promises on which it is based
7 are superior to the former ones. For if
that first agreement had been perfect,
there would have been no occasion for a
8 second one. But in his dissatisfaction
with them he says,
" 'See! the time is coming,' says the
Lord,
'When I will conclude a new agreement with the house of Israel
and with the house of Judah,
Not like the one that I made with 9
their forefathers,
On the day when I took them by
the hand to lead them out from
the land of Egypt,
For they would not abide by their
agreement with me,
So I paid no attention to them,'
says the Lord.
'For this is the agreement that I 10
will make with the house of
Israel,
In those later days,' says the Lord;
'I will put my laws into their minds,
And write them on their hearts,
And they will have me for their
God,
And I will have them for my peo-
ple.
And they will not have to teach 11
their townsmen and their brothers to know the Lord,
For they will all know me,
From the lowest to the highest.
For I will be merciful to their misdeeds, 12
And I will no longer remember
their sins.' "
Now when he speaks of a new agree- 13
ment, he is treating the first one as obsolete; but whatever is obsolete and
antiquated is almost ready to disappear.
Even the first agreement provided 9
regulations for worship, and a sanctuary that was fully equipped. For a tent 2
was erected, with the lamp and the table and the presentation bread in the
outer part, which was called the sanctuary. And beyond the second curtain, 3
in the part called the inner sanctuary,
stood the gold incense-altar and the 4
chest that contained the agreement,
entirely covered with gold, with the
gold jar in it that held the manna, and
Aaron's staff that budded, and the
tablets containing the agreement; and 5
above the chest were the winged creatures of the Divine Presence overshadowing the lid on which the blood was
sprinkled—of which I cannot now
speak in detail. With these arrange- 6
ments for worship, the priests used constantly to go into the outer part of the
tent, in the performance of their rites,
but only the high priest could enter the 7
inner part, and he but once a year, and
never without taking some victim's
blood, to offer on his own behalf and for
the sins committed through ignorance

8 by the people. In all this the holy
Spirit was seeking to show that there
was no free access to the sanctuary
while the outer tent was still standing.
9 And all this looked toward the present
time and was symbolic of the fact that
the mere offering of material gifts and
sacrifices cannot inwardly qualify the
10 worshiper to approach God, since they
have to do only with food and drink
and various washings—material regulations in force only until the time for
the new order.

11 But when Christ came, as the high
priest of the better system under which
we live, he went once for all, through
that greater, more perfect tent of worship not made by human hands nor a
part of our material creation, into the
12 sanctuary, taking with him no blood of
goats and calves, but his own, and se-
13 cured our permanent deliverance. For
if sprinkling ceremonially defiled persons with the blood of bulls and goats
and with the ashes of a heifer purifies
14 them physically, how much more surely will the blood of the Christ, who with
the eternal Spirit made himself an unblemished offering to God, purify our
consciences from the old wrongdoing
for the worship of the ever-living God?

15 And this is why he is the negotiator of
a new agreement, in order that as someone has died to deliver them from the
offenses committed under the old agreement, those who have been offered it
may receive the unending inheritance
16 they have been promised. For where a
will is involved, the death of the one
17 who made it must be established, for a
will is valid only in the case of a person
who is dead; it has no force as long as
18 the testator is alive. So even the old
agreement could not be ratified without
19 the use of blood. For when Moses had
told all the regulations of the Law to all
the people, he took calves' and goats'
blood, along with water, crimson wool,
and a bunch of hyssop, and sprinkled
the roll of the Law and all the people,
20 saying, "This blood ratifies the agreement which God has commanded me to
21 make with you." The tent too and all
the appliances used in the priestly service he sprinkled with blood in the same
22 way. In fact, under the Law, almost
everything is purified with blood, and
unless blood is poured out nothing is
forgiven.

By such means, therefore, these 23
things that were only copied from the
originals in heaven had to be purified,
but the heavenly originals themselves
required far better sacrifices than these.
For it was not a sanctuary made by hu- 24
man hands and only copied after the
true one that Christ entered, but he
went into heaven itself, in order to appear now on our behalf in the very presence of God. Nor does he go in to offer 25
himself over and over again, like the
high priest who enters the sanctuary
year after year, taking with him blood
that is not his own, for then he would 26
have had to suffer death over and over,
ever since the creation of the world.
But, as it is, once for all at the close of
the age he has appeared, to put an end
to sin by his sacrifice. And just as men 27
are destined to die once and after that
to be judged, so the Christ too, after 28
being offered in sacrifice once for all to
carry away the sins of many, will appear again but without any burden of
sin, to those who are eagerly waiting for
him to come and save them.

For while the Law foreshadowed the **10**
blessings that were to come, it did not
fully express them, and so the priests
by offering the same sacrifices endlessly
year after year cannot wholly free those
who come to worship from their sins.
Otherwise, would they not have ceased 2
to offer these sacrifices, because those
who offered them, having once been
purified, would have had no further
consciousness of sin? They really only 3
serve to remind the people annually of
the sins they have committed, for bulls' 4
and goats' blood is powerless to remove
sin. That is why the Christ, when he 5
was coming into the world, said,

"You have not wished sacrifice or
offering, but you have provided
a body for me.
You never cared for burnt-offer- 6
ings and sacrifices for sin!
So I said, 'See, I have come! as the 7
Book of the Law says of me,
O God, to do your will!' "

At first he says, "You never wished or 8
cared for sacrifices or offerings, or
burnt-offerings or sacrifices for sin"—
all of which the Law prescribes—and 9
then he adds, "See, I have come to do
your will!" He is taking away the old
to put the new in its place. And it is 10
through his doing of God's will that we

have been once for all purified from sin
through the offering of the body of
11 Jesus Christ in sacrifice. Every other
priest stands officiating day after day,
offering over and over again the same
sacrifices, though they were powerless
12 ever to remove people's sins. But
Christ has offered for all time one sacrifice for sin, and has taken his seat at
13 God's right hand, from that time waiting for his enemies to be made his foot-
14 stool. For by that one sacrifice he has
forever qualified those who are purified
15 from sin to approach God. And we
have the testimony of the holy Spirit to
this, for after saying,
16 " 'This is the agreement that I will
make with them
In those later days,' says the Lord,
'I will put my laws into their minds,
And write them upon their
hearts,' "
he goes on,
17 " 'And their sins and their misdeeds
I will no longer remember.' "
18 But when these are forgiven, there is no
more need of offerings for sin.
19 Since then, brothers, we have free
access to the sanctuary through the
20 blood of Jesus, by the new, living way
which he has opened for us, through the
curtain, that is, his physical nature,
21 and since in him we have a great priest
22 set over the house of God, let us draw
near to God in sincerity of heart and
with perfect faith, with our hearts
cleansed from the sense of sin, and our
23 bodies washed with clean water. Let us
hold unwaveringly to the hope that we
profess, for he who has given us his
24 promise may be trusted. By observing
one another, let us arouse ourselves to
rival one another's love and good deeds.
25 Let us not neglect meeting together as
some do, but let us encourage one another, all the more as you can see that
the great Day is coming nearer.
26 For if we choose to go on sinning after
we have so fully learned the truth, there
is no sacrifice left to be offered for our
27 sins, but only the dreadful prospect of
judgment and that blazing indignation
28 which is to devour God's enemies. Anyone who breaks the Law of Moses is
put to death without any show of pity,
on the evidence of only two or three
29 witnesses. How much worse a punishment do you think will anyone deserve
who tramples the Son of God underfoot.
and treats as worthless the blood of the
agreement by which he has been purified, and outrages God's spirit of
mercy? For we know who it is that has 30
said,
"Vengeance belongs to me! I will
pay back!"
and in another place,
"The Lord will be the judge of his
people!"
It is a fearful thing to fall into the hands 31
of the living God!
But you must remember those early 32
days when after you had received the
light you had to go through a great
struggle with persecution, sometimes 33
being actually exposed as a public spectacle to insults and violence, and sometimes showing yourselves ready to share
the lot of those in that condition. For 34
you showed sympathy with those who
were in prison, and you put up with it
cheerfully when your property was
taken from you, for you knew that you
had in yourselves a greater possession
that was lasting. You must not lose 35
your courage, for it will be richly rewarded, but you will need endurance if 36
you are to carry out God's will and
receive the blessing he has promised.
For 37
"In a very little while
He who is to come will come and
not delay,
And he whom I accept as righteous 38
will find life through his faith.
But if a man draws back, my heart
can take no pleasure in him."
But we will not draw back and perish, 39
but we will have faith and save our
souls.
Faith means the assurance of what **11**
we hope for; it is our conviction about
things that we cannot see. For it was 2
by it that the men of old gained God's
approval.
It is faith that enables us to see that 3
the universe was created at the command of God, so that the world we see
did not simply arise out of matter.
Faith made Abel's sacrifice greater in 4
the sight of God than Cain's; through
faith he gained God's approval as an
upright man, for God himself approved
his offering, and through faith even
when he was dead he still spoke. Faith 5
caused Enoch to be taken up from the
earth without experiencing death; he
could not be found, because God had

taken him up. For before he was taken
up there is evidence that he pleased
6 God, but without faith it is impossible
to please him; for whoever would approach God must have faith in his existence and in his willingness to reward
7 those who try to find him. Faith led
Noah, when he was warned by God of
things no one then saw, in obedience to
the warning to build an ark in which to
save his family, and by such faith he
condemned the world, and came to possess that uprightness which faith pro-
8 duces. Faith enabled Abraham to
obey when God summoned him to leave
his home for a region which he was to
have for his own, and to leave home
without knowing where he was going.
9 Faith led him to make a temporary
home as a stranger in the land he had
been promised, and to live there in his
tents, with Isaac and Jacob, who shared
10 the promise with him. For he was looking forward to that city with the sure
foundations, designed and built by
11 God. Faith made even Sarah herself
able to have a child, although she was
past the time of life for it, because she
thought that he who had made the
12 promise would keep it. And so from one
man, for any prospect of descendants
as good as dead, there sprang a people
in number like the stars in the heavens
or the countless sands on the seashore.
13 All these people lived all their lives
in faith, and died without receiving
what had been promised; they only saw
it far ahead and welcomed the sight of
it, recognizing that they themselves
were only foreigners and strangers here
14 on earth. For men who recognize that
show that they are in search of a coun-
15 try of their own. And if it had been the
country from which they had come to
which their thoughts turned back, they
would have found an opportunity to
16 return to it. But, as it is, their aspira-
tions are for a better, a heavenly country! That is why God is not ashamed
to be called their God, for he has prepared a city to receive them.
17 Faith enabled Abraham, when he was
put to the test, to offer Isaac as a sacrifice. He who had accepted God's promises was ready to sacrifice his only son,
18 of whom he had been told, "Your pos-
19 terity is to arise through Isaac!" For
he believed that God was able to raise
men even from the dead, and from the
dead he did indeed, to speak figuratively, receive him back. Faith enabled 20
Isaac to bequeath to Jacob and Esau
blessings that were still to be. Faith 21
made Jacob when he was dying give a
blessing to each of Joseph's sons, and
bow in worship even while leaning on
his staff. Faith inspired Joseph when he 22
was dying to tell of the future migration
of the Israelites, and to give instructions about his own body. Faith led 23
Moses' parents to hide him for three
months after his birth, because they
saw that he was a beautiful child and
they would not respect the edict of the
king. Faith made Moses, when he was 24
grown up, refuse to be known as a son of
Pharaoh's daughter, for he preferred 25
sharing the hardships of God's people
to a short-lived enjoyment of sin, and 26
thought such contempt as the Christ
endured was truer wealth than the
treasures of Egypt, for he was looking
forward to the coming reward. Faith 27
made him leave Egypt, unafraid of the
king's anger, for he persevered as
though he saw him who is unseen.
Faith made him institute the Passover 28
and splash the blood upon the door-
posts, to keep the angel that destroyed
the firstborn from touching them.
Faith enabled them to cross the Red 29
Sea as though it were dry land, although the Egyptians when they tried
to follow them across it were drowned.
Faith made the walls of Jericho fall, 30
after they had marched around them
each day for seven days. Faith saved 31
Rahab the prostitute from being destroyed with those who disobeyed God,
because she had given a friendly welcome to the scouts.
And why should I go on? For my 32
time would fail me if I told of Gideon,
Barak, Samson, Jephthah, David,
Samuel, and the prophets, who by 33
their faith conquered kingdoms, attained uprightness, received new promises, shut the mouths of lions, put out 34
furious fires, escaped death by the
sword, found strength in their time of
weakness, proved mighty in war, put
foreign armies to flight. Women had 35
their dead restored to them by resurrection. Others endured torture, and
refused to accept release, that they
might rise again to the better life. Still 36
others had to endure taunts and blows,
and even fetters and prison. They were 37

stoned to death, they were tortured to
death, they were sawed in two, they
were killed with the sword. Clothed in
the skins of sheep or goats, they were
driven from place to place, destitute,
38 persecuted, misused—men of whom the
world was not worthy wandering in
deserts, mountains, caves, and holes in
the ground.
39 Yet though they all gained God's approval by their faith, they none of them
40 received what he had promised, for
God had resolved upon something still
better for us, that they might not reach
the fulfilment of their hopes except with
us.
12 Therefore, let us too, with such a
crowd of witnesses about us, throw off
every impediment and the entangle-
ment of sin, and run with determination
2 the race for which we are entered, fixing
our eyes upon Jesus, our leader and example in faith, who in place of the happiness that belonged to him, submitted
to a cross, caring nothing for its shame,
and has taken his seat at the right hand
3 of the throne of God. Think of the opposition that he encountered from those
sinners against themselves, if you would
4 not grow weary and faint-hearted. You
have not yet resisted unto death in your
5 struggle with sin, and you have forgotten the challenge addressed to you as
God's sons,

"My son, do not think lightly of the
Lord's discipline,
Or give up when he corrects you.
6 For it is those whom the Lord loves
that he disciplines,
And he chastises every son that he
acknowledges."

7 You must submit to it as discipline.
God is dealing with you as his sons. For
where is there a son whom his father
8 does not discipline? But if you have
none of that discipline which all sons
undergo, you are illegitimate children,
9 and not true sons. When our earthly
fathers disciplined us we treated them
with respect; should we not far more
submit to the Father of our spirits, and
10 so have life? For they disciplined us
for a short time and as they thought
proper, but he does it for our good, to
11 make us share his holiness. Discipline
is never pleasant at the time; it is painful; but to those who are trained by it,
it afterward yields the peace of char-
12 acter. So tighten your loosening hold!
Stiffen your wavering stand! And keep 13
your feet in straight paths, so that
limbs that are lame may not be dislocated but instead be cured.
Try to be at peace with everyone, 14
and strive for that consecration without
which no one can see the Lord. Be 15
careful that no one fails to gain God's
favor, or some poisonous root may come
up to trouble and contaminate you all
—some immoral or godless person like 16
Esau, who sold his very birthright for
one single meal. For you know how, 17
when he afterward wished to claim the
blessing, he was refused it, although he
begged for it with tears, for he had no
opportunity to repent of what he had
done.
For it is no tangible blazing fire that 18
you have come up to, no blackness and
darkness and storm, no trumpet blast 19
and voice whose words made those who
heard them beg to be told no more, for 20
they could not bear the order, "Even a
wild animal, if it touches the mountain,
must be stoned to death," and so awful 21
was the sight that Moses said, "I am
aghast and appalled!" But you have 22
come up to Mount Zion, to the city of
the living God, the heavenly Jerusalem,
to countless angels, to the solemn gath- 23
ering of all God's elder sons, enrolled as
citizens in heaven, to a judge who is the
God of all, to the spirits of upright men
now at last enjoying the fulfilment of
their hopes, to Jesus the negotiator of a 24
new agreement, and to sprinkled blood
that speaks more powerfully than even
Abel's. Take care not to refuse to listen 25
to him who is speaking. For if they
could not escape because they would
not listen to him who warned them
here on earth, how much less can we,
who reject him who is from heaven!
Then his voice shook the earth, but now 26
his promise is, "But once more I will
make not only the earth but the very
heaven to tremble!" Now the words 27
"But once more" indicate the final removal of all that is shaken, as only created, leaving only what is unshaken to
be permanent. Let us, therefore, be 28
thankful that the kingdom given to us
cannot be shaken, and so please God
by worshiping him with reverence and
awe; for our God is a consuming fire. 29
Your love for the brotherhood must 13
continue. Do not forget to be hospita- 2
ble to strangers, for by being so some,

without knowing it, have had angels as
3 their guests. Remember those who are
in prison as though you were in prison
with them, and those who are ill-treated as being yourselves liable to the same
4 trials. Marriage should be respected by
everyone, and the marriage relation
kept sacred, for vicious and immoral
5 people God will punish. You must not
be avaricious; you must be content
with what you have, for God himself
has said, "I will never let go of you or
6 desert you!" So that we can confidently say,

"The Lord is my helper; I will not
be afraid.
What can men do to me?"

7 Do not forget your former leaders,
the men who brought you God's message. Remember how they ended their
lives and imitate their faith.
8 Jesus Christ is the same today that
he was yesterday, and he will be so for-
9 ever. You must not be carried away
with strange varieties of teaching. The
true way to steadfastness of heart is
through God's mercy, not through
scruples about food, which have never
10 done their adherents any good. Our altar is one at which those who serve the
tent of worship have no right to eat.
11 For the bodies of the animals whose
blood is taken into the sanctuary by the
high priest are burned outside the
12 camp. And so Jesus too, in order to
purify the people by his blood, suffered
13 death outside the city gate. Let us,
therefore, go out to him, outside the
camp, sharing the contempt that he
14 endured, for we have no permanent
city here on earth, but we are in search
of the city that is to come. In his name 15
let us continually offer praise as our
sacrifice to God—the utterance of lips
that glorify God's name. But do not 16
forget to be helpful and generous, for
that is the kind of sacrifice that pleases
God.

Obey your leaders and give way to 17
them, for they are keeping watch in
defense of your souls, as men accountable for the trust. Make their work a
joy and not a grief, for that would be
the worse for you.

Pray for me, for I am sure I have a 18
clear conscience, and I mean in every
way to live an upright life. I ask this of 19
you more especially that I may be
brought back to you the sooner.

May God, the giver of peace, who 20
brought back from the dead our Lord
Jesus who through the blood by which
he ratified the everlasting agreement
has become the great shepherd of the
sheep, fit you by every blessing to do his 21
will, and through Jesus Christ carry
out in us what will please him. To him
be glory forever and ever. Amen.

I beg you brothers, to listen patient- 22
ly to this appeal, for I have written you
but briefly.

You must know that our brother 23
Timothy has been released from prison.
If he comes here soon, we will see you
together.

Remember us to all your leaders and 24
to all your fellow-Christians. The
brothers from Italy wish to be remembered to you.

God bless you all! 25

THE LETTER OF JAMES

1 JAMES, a slave of God and of the
Lord Jesus Christ, sends greeting
to the twelve tribes that are scattered over the world.
2 You must find the greatest joy,
my brothers, in being involved in
3 various trials, for you know that the
4 testing of your faith leads to steadfastness, and steadfastness must have full
play, so that you may be fully and perfectly developed without any defect.
5 If any one of you is deficient in wisdom, let him ask God who gives generously to everyone, and does not reproach one with it afterward, and he
6 will give it to him. But he must ask
with faith, and without any doubt, for
the man who doubts is like the billowing sea, driven and blown about by the
7 wind. Such a man must not expect to
8 get anything from the Lord—an irreso-
lute person like him, who is uncertain
9 about everything he does. A brother of
low position ought to be proud of his
10 eminence, but one who is rich ought to
rejoice at being reduced in circumstances, for the rich will disappear like
11 a wild flower. For the sun comes up
with its scorching heat and dries up the
grass, and the flower withers, and all
its beauty is gone. That is the way a
rich man will fade and die in the midst
of his pursuits.
12 Blessed is the man who endures trial,
for when he stands the test, he will be
given the crown of life, which God has
13 promised to those who love him. No
one should think when he is tempted
that his temptation comes from God,
for God is incapable of being tempted
by what is evil, and he does not tempt
14 anyone. When anyone is tempted, it is
by his own desire that he is enticed and
15 allured. Then desire conceives and gives
birth to sin, and when sin is mature, it
16 brings forth death. Do not be misled,
17 my dear brothers. Every good gift and
every perfect present is from heaven,
and comes down from the Father of the
heavenly lights, about whom there is no
18 variation of changing shadow. Of his
own accord he brought us into being
through the message of truth, so that
we might be a kind of first-fruits among
his creatures.
You must understand this, my dear 19
brothers. Everyone must be quick to
hear, slow to speak, slow to be angry,
for men's anger does not produce the 20
uprightness God wishes. So strip your- 21
selves of everything that soils you, and
of every evil growth, and in a humble
spirit let the message that has the power
to save your souls be planted in your
hearts. Obey the message; do not mere- 22
ly listen to it, and deceive yourselves.
For anyone who merely listens to the 23
message without obeying it is like a
man who looks in a mirror at the face
that nature gave him; he looks at him- 24
self and then goes off and immediately
forgets what he looked like. But 25
whoever looks at the faultless law that
makes men free and keeps looking, so
that he does not just listen and forget,
but obeys and acts upon it, will be
blessed in what he does. If anyone 26
thinks he is religious, and does not
bridle his tongue, but deceives himself,
his religious observances are of no account. A religious observance that is 27
pure and stainless in the sight of God
the Father is this: to look after orphans
and widows in their trouble, and keep
one's self unstained by the world.
My brothers, do you try to combine 2
faith in our glorious Lord Jesus Christ
with acts of partiality? For if a finely 2
dressed man with a gold ring comes into
your meeting, and a poor man in shabby
clothes comes in also, and you pay at- 3
tention to the man in the fine clothes
and say to him, "Sit here; this is a good
place!" and say to the poor man,
'Stand up, or sit on the floor at my
feet," have you not wavered and shown 4
that your judgments are guided by base
motives? Listen, my dear brothers. 5
Has not God chosen the world's poor to
be rich in faith, and to possess the kingdom that he promised to those who love
him? But you humiliate the poor. Are 6
not the rich your oppressors? Is it not

7 they who drag you into court? Is it not
they who slander the noble name you
8 bear? If you really obey the supreme
law where the Scripture says, "You
must love your neighbor as you do
9 yourself," you are doing right, but if
you show partiality, you are committing a sin, and stand convicted before
10 the Law as law breakers. For anyone
who obeys the whole of the Law but
makes one single slip is guilty of break-
11 ing it all. For he who said, "You must
not commit adultery," said also, "You
must not commit murder." Now if you
abstain from adultery, but commit murder, you are still a violator of the Law.
12 You must talk and act like men who
expect to be judged by the law that
13 treats men as free. For the merciless
will be mercilessly judged; but mercy
will triumph over judgment.
14 My brothers, what is the good of a
man's saying he has faith, if he has no
good deeds to show? Can faith save
15 him? If some brother or sister has no
clothes and has not food enough for a
16 day, and one of you says to them,
"Goodbye, keep warm and have plenty
to eat," without giving them the neces-
17 saries of life, what good does it do? So
faith by itself, if it has no good deeds to
18 show, is dead. But someone may say,
"You have faith, and I good deeds."
Show me your faith without any good
deeds, and I will show you my faith by
19 my good deeds. Do you believe in one
God? Very well! So do the demons,
20 and they shudder. But do you want
proof, my senseless friend, that faith
without good deeds amounts to nothing?
21 Was not our forefather Abraham made
upright for his good deeds, for offering
22 his son Isaac on the altar? You see that
in his case faith and good deeds worked
together; faith found its highest ex-
23 pression in good deeds, and so the
Scripture came true that says, "Abraham had faith in God, and it was credited to him as uprightness, and he was
24 called God's friend." You see a man is
made upright by his good deeds and not
25 simply by having faith. Was not even
Rahab the prostitute made upright for
her good deeds, in entertaining the
scouts and sending them off by a dif-
26 ferent road? Just as the body without
the spirit is dead, faith is dead without
good deeds.

3 Not many of you should become
teachers, my brothers, for you know
that we who teach will be judged with
greater strictness. For we all make 2
many mistakes. Anyone who never
makes a mistake in what he says has a
character that is fully developed and is
able to control his whole body as well.
If we put bits into horses' mouths to 3
make them obey us, we can guide their
whole bodies. Even ships, great as they 4
are, and driven by strong winds, are
steered with a very small rudder wherever the pilot pleases. So the tongue is 5
a little organ and yet very boastful.
What a great forest a spark will set on
fire! And the tongue is a fire, a world 6
of wrong the tongue proves in our
bodies, soiling the whole body and setting fire to the whole round of nature,
and set on fire itself by hell. For every 7
kind of animal and bird, reptile and sea
creature, can be tamed and has been
tamed by man, but no human being can 8
tame the tongue. It is an irreconcilable
evil, full of deadly poison. With it we 9
bless the Lord our Father, and with it
we curse men made in God's likeness.
Blessing and cursing issue from the 10
same mouth! This is not right, my
brothers. Does a spring pour forth fresh 11
and brackish water from the same
crevice? Can a fig tree produce olives, 12
my brothers, or a grape vine figs? A
salt spring cannot give fresh water.
What wise, intelligent man is there 13
among you? Let him show by his good
life that what he does is done in the humility of wisdom. But if you cherish 14
bitter feelings of jealousy and rivalry in
your hearts, do not pride yourselves on
it and thus belie the truth. Such wis- 15
dom does not come from above. It is
earthly, animal, demon-like. For wher- 16
ever jealousy and rivalry exist, there
will be confusion and every low action.
The wisdom that is from above is first 17
of all pure, then peaceable, considerate,
willing to yield, full of compassion and
good deeds, whole-hearted, straightforward. The harvest uprightness yields 18
must be sown in peace, by peacemakers.

What causes wars and fights among 4
you? Is it not your cravings, which are
at war within your bodies? You crave 2
things, and cannot have them, and so
you commit murder. You covet things,
and cannot get them, and so you quarrel and fight. You do not have things
because you do not ask for them. You 3

ask and fail to get them because you
ask with wrong motives, to spend them
4 on your pleasures. You renegades! Do
you not know that the friendship of the
world means enmity with God? So
whoever wishes to be the world's friend
5 declares himself God's enemy. Do you
suppose the Scripture means nothing
when it says, "He yearns jealously over
the Spirit he has put in our hearts?"
6 But he gives all the greater blessing. As
the Scripture says, "God opposes
haughty persons, but he blesses humble-
7 minded ones." Therefore, submit to
God. Resist the devil and he will fly
8 from you. Approach God, and he will
approach you. Wash your hands, you
sinners! Make your hearts pure, you
9 doubters! Be miserable, grieve, and
weep aloud! Turn your laughter into
grief and your happiness into gloom.
10 Humble yourselves before the Lord,
and he will raise you up.

11 Do not talk against one another,
brothers. Whoever talks against a
brother or condemns his brother talks
against the Law, and condemns the
Law. But if you condemn the Law you
are not an observer of the Law but its
12 judge. There is only one lawgiver and
judge—he who has the power to save
and to destroy; who are you, to judge
your neighbor?

13 Come now, you who say, "Today or
tomorrow we are going to such and such
a town, to stay a year and go into busi-
14 ness and make money," when you do
not know what your life will be like tomorrow! You are just a mist, which appears for a little while and then disap-
15 pears. This, instead of saying, "If it is
the Lord's will, we shall live to do this
16 or that." But, as it is, you pride yourselves on your pretensions. All such
17 pride is wrong. So when a man knows
what is right and fails to do it, he is
guilty of sin.

5 Come now, you rich people! weep
aloud and howl over the miseries that
2 are going to overtake you! Your wealth
has rotted, your clothes are moth-eaten,
3 your gold and silver are rusted, and
their rust will testify against you and
eat into your very flesh, for you have
4 stored up fire for the last days. Why, the
wages you have withheld from the laborers who have reaped your harvests
cry aloud, and the cries of the harvesters have reached the ears of the Lord of
Hosts. You have lived luxuriously and 5
voluptuously here on earth; you have
fattened your hearts for the day of
slaughter. You have condemned and 6
murdered the upright. Will he make no
resistance?

So be patient, brothers, until the 7
coming of the Lord. The farmer has to
wait for the precious crop from the
ground, and be patient with it, until it
gets the early and the late rains. You 8
must have patience too; you must keep
up your courage, for the coming of the
Lord is close at hand. Do not complain 9
of one another, brothers, or you will be
judged. The judge is standing right at
the door! As an example, brothers, of 10
ill-treatment patiently endured, take
the prophets, who have spoken in the
name of the Lord. Why, we call those 11
who showed such endurance happy!
You have heard of the steadfastness of
Job, and you have seen what the Lord
brought out of it, for the Lord is very
kind and merciful.

Above all, my brothers, do not swear 12
an oath, either by heaven or by the
earth, or by anything else; let your
"Yes" be a plain Yes, and your "No" a
plain No, or you will fall under condemnation.

If any one of you is in trouble, he 13
should pray. If any one is in good
spirits, he should sing a hymn. If any 14
one is sick, he should call in the elders
of the church and have them pray over
him, and pour oil on him in the name of
the Lord, and the prayer offered in faith 15
will save the sick man; the Lord will restore him to health, and if he has committed sins, he will be forgiven. So con- 16
fess your sins to one another and pray
for one another, so that you may be
cured. An upright man can do a great
deal by prayer when he tries. Elijah 17
was a man like us, and he prayed earnestly that it might not rain, and for
three years and six months there was no
rain in the land. Then he prayed again, 18
and the heavens yielded rain and the
earth produced crops. My brothers, if 19
any one of you is led astray from the
truth, and someone brings him back,
you may be sure that whoever brings a 20
sinner back from his misguided way will
save the man's soul from death, and
cover up a host of sins.

THE FIRST LETTER OF PETER

1 PETER, an apostle of Jesus Christ
to those who are scattered as
foreigners over Pontus, Galatia,
Cappadocia, Asia, and Bithynia,
2 whom God the Father has chosen and
predestined by the consecration of the
Spirit to be obedient to Jesus Christ,
and to be sprinkled with his blood; God
bless you and give you perfect peace.
3 Blessed be the God and Father of our
Lord Jesus Christ! In his great mercy
he has caused us to be born anew to a
life of hope through the resurrection of
4 Jesus Christ from the dead, and to an
imperishable, unsullied, and unfading
inheritance, which is kept safe for you in
5 heaven, and you by God's power are
being protected through faith to receive
a salvation that is now ready to be dis-
6 closed at the last time. Rejoice over
this, although just now perhaps distressed for a little while by various
7 trials; they are to show that your faith
when tested is found to be more precious than gold, which though it is
perishable is tested with fire, and they
will bring you praise, glory, and honor
8 when Jesus Christ is revealed. Love him,
though you have not seen him, but since
you believe in him though you do not
now see him, rejoice with triumphant,
9 unutterable joy to attain the goal of
faith, the salvation of your souls.
10 About this salvation the prophets
who prophesied of the blessing that was
destined for you made the most careful
11 investigation, trying to learn for what
possible time the spirit of Christ within
them in predicting the sufferings destined for Christ intended them and the
12 glories that were to follow them. It was
disclosed to them that they were serving not themselves but you in dealing
with these things, which have now been
told you by those who through the holy
Spirit sent from heaven brought you
the good news; things into which
angels long to look!
13 Therefore, prepare your minds for
action, and with perfect calmness fix
your hopes on the mercy that you are to
experience when Jesus Christ is revealed. Like obedient children, do not 14
adapt yourselves to the cravings you
used to follow when you were ignorant,
but like the holy Being who has called 15
you, you must also be holy in all
your conduct, for the Scripture says, 16
"You must be holy,
Because I am holy."
And if you address him as Father who 17
judges everyone impartially by what
he does, you must live reverently all the
time you stay here, for you know that 18
you have not been ransomed with anything perishable like silver or gold, from
the futile way of living in which you
were brought up, but with precious 19
blood, like that of an unblemished,
spotless lamb, the blood of Christ, who 20
was predestined for this before the
foundation of the world, but was revealed only at the end of the ages, for 21
the sake of you who through him trust
in God, who raised him from the dead
and showed him honor; and so your
faith and hope rest on God.
Now that by obeying the truth you 22
have purified your souls for sincere love
of the brotherhood, you must love one
another intensely and heartily, for you 23
have been born anew from a germ not
perishable, but imperishable, through
the message of the living, everlasting
God. For 24
"All flesh is like grass,
And all its glory like the flowers of
the grass.
The grass withers,
And the flower fades,
But the word of the Lord will last 25
forever."
That word is the good news that has
been brought to you.

Free yourselves, therefore, from all 2
malice, deceit, hypocrisy, envy, and
slander of any kind, and like newborn 2
babes crave the pure spiritual milk that
will make you grow up to salvation,
since you have tasted the Lord's kind- 3
ness. Come to him, as to a living stone 4
rejected by men, but chosen and prized

5 in the sight of God, and build yourselves up as living stones into a spiritual
house for a consecrated priesthood, so
as to offer spiritual sacrifices that
through Jesus Christ will be acceptable
6 to God. For it says in Scripture,

"Here I lay a choice stone in Zion, a
costly cornerstone;
No one who believes in it will ever
be disappointed!"

7 It is you, therefore, who believe who see
its value, but for men who do not
believe,

"The stone which the builders refused has been made a cornerstone,"

8 and

"A stone to stumble over, and a rock
to trip them up."

They stumble over the message because
they will not obey it; that is their des-
9 tiny. But you are the chosen race, the
royal priesthood, the consecrated nation, his own people, so that you may
declare the virtues of him who has
called you out of darkness into his won-
10 derful light; you who were once "no
people" but are now "God's people";
once "unpitied" but now "pitied indeed."

11 Dear friends, I beg you, as aliens
and exiles here, not to indulge the
physical cravings that are at war with
12 the soul. Live upright lives among the
heathen, so that even if they charge you
with being evildoers, they may from
observing the uprightness of your conduct come to praise God on the Day of
Judgment.

13 Submit to all human authority, for
the Master's sake; to the emperor, as
14 supreme, and to governors, as sent by
him to punish evil-doers, and to en-
15 courage those who do right. For it is
the will of God that by doing right you
should silence the ignorant charges of
16 foolish people. Live like free men, only
do not make your freedom an excuse for
doing wrong, but be slaves of God.
17 Treat everyone with respect. Love the
brotherhood, be reverent to God, respect the emperor.

18 You servants must be submissive to
your masters and perfectly respectful
to them; not only to those who are kind
and considerate, but also to those who
19 are unreasonable. For God approves a
man if from a sense of duty he endures
20 suffering unjustly inflicted—for what
credit is there in your enduring being
beaten for doing wrong? But if you endure suffering for doing what is right,
you have God's approval. That is the 21
life to which you have been called, for
Christ himself suffered for you, leaving
you an example so that you might follow his footsteps. He committed no sin, 22
and deceit was never on his lips. He 23
was abused but he did not retort. He
suffered but he did not threaten, but
committed his case to him who judges
justly. He carried the burden of our 24
sins in his own body on the tree, in
order that we might die to sin and live
for uprightness. By his wounds you
have been healed. For you were astray 25
like sheep, but now you have returned
to the shepherd and guardian of your
souls.

You married women, in the same **3**
way, must be submissive to your husbands, so that any who refuse to believe
the message may be won over without
argument through the behavior of their
wives when they see how chaste and 2
submissive you are. You must not 3
adopt the external attractions of arranging the hair and wearing jewelry
and dress; yours must be the inner 4
beauty of character, the imperishable
attraction of a quiet and gentle spirit,
which has great value in the sight of
God. It was in that way in ancient 5
times that those pious women who set
their hopes on God made themselves
attractive. They were submissive to
their husbands, like Sarah, who obeyed 6
Abraham, and called him Master. You
are true daughters of hers, if you do
right and are unafraid.

You married men also must be con- 7
siderate in living with your wives. You
must show deference to women as the
weaker sex, sharing the gift of life with
you, so that there may be nothing to
interfere with your prayers.

Finally, you must all be harmonious, 8
sympathizing, loving, tender-hearted,
modest, not returning evil for evil, or 9
abuse for abuse. You must bless them
instead. It is for this that you were
called—to obtain blessing. For

"Let him who would enjoy life 10
And see happy days,
Keep his tongue from evil,
And his lips from uttering deceit.
Let him turn away from evil and 11
do right,

Let him seek peace and go after it.
12 For the eyes of the Lord are upon
upright men,
And his ears are open to their
entreaty,
But the Lord's face is set against
men that do wrong."
13 And who is there that can hurt you if
14 you are eager to do what is right? Even
if you should suffer for uprightness, you
are blessed. But do not be afraid of
15 them, nor be troubled, but reverence
Christ in your hearts as Lord, and always be ready to make your defense to
anyone who calls you to account for
the hope that you have. But do so
16 gently and respectfully, and keep your
conscience clear, so that those who
abuse your upright Christian conduct
may be made ashamed of their slanders.
17 For it is better to suffer for doing right,
if that should be God's will, than for
18 doing wrong. For Christ himself died
once for all, for sin, an upright man for
unrighteous men, to bring you to God,
and was physically put to death, but he
19 was made alive in the Spirit. In it
Enoch went and preached even to those
20 spirits that were in prison, who had
once been disobedient, when in Noah's
time God in his patience waited for the
ark to be made ready, in which a few
people, eight in all, were brought safely
21 through the water. Baptism, which corresponds to it, now saves you also (not
as the mere removing of physical stain,
but as the craving for a conscience right
with God)—through the resurrection of
22 Jesus Christ, who has gone to heaven
and is at God's right hand, with angels,
hierarchies, and powers made subject
to him.

4 Since Christ therefore has suffered in
our physical nature, you must also arm
yourselves with the same resolve. For
he who suffers in his physical nature has
2 done with sin, and no longer lives by
what men desire, but for the rest of his
3 earthly life by what God wills. You
have spent time enough in the past in
doing as the heathen like to do, indulging in sensuality, passion, drunkenness,
carousing, dissipation, and detestable
4 idolatry. They are amazed that you no
longer join them in plunging into the
same flood of dissipation, and they
5 abuse you for it; but they will have to
answer for it to him who is ready to
6 judge living and dead. This is why the
good news was preached to the dead
also, that though they are judged in
their physical nature as men are, they
may yet live, like God, in the Spirit.
But the end of all things is near. Be 7
serious and collected, therefore, and
pray. Above all keep your love for one 8
another strong, because love covers up
a host of sins. Be ungrudgingly hos- 9
pitable to one another. Whatever the 10
endowment God has given you, use it in
service to one another, like good dis-
pensers of God's varied mercy. If one 11
preaches, let him do it like one who utters the words of God; if one does some
service, let him do it as with strength
which God supplies, so that in everything God may be glorified through
Jesus Christ. To him belong glory and
dominion forever and ever. Amen.

Dear friends, do not be surprised that 12
a test of fire is being applied to you, as
though a strange thing were happening
to you, but be glad that you are in a 13
measure sharing the sufferings of the
Christ, so that when his glory is revealed you may be triumphantly happy. If you are being abused for the sake 14
of Christ, you are blessed, because the
glorious Spirit of God is resting upon
you. For no one of you must suffer as a 15
murderer or thief or criminal or revolu-
tionist, but if a man suffers for being a 16
Christian, he must not be ashamed of it,
but must do honor to God through that
name. For the time has come for the 17
judgment to begin with the household
of God, and if it begins with us, what
will be the end of those who refuse
God's good news? If it is hard for the 18
upright man to be saved, what will become of the godless and sinful? There- 19
fore, those who suffer by the will of God
must intrust their souls to a Creator
who is faithful, and continue to do what
is right.

I appeal therefore to those who are 5
elders among you; I am their brother-
elder and a witness to what the Christ
suffered, and I am to share in the glory
that is to be revealed—be shepherds of 2
the flock of God that is among you, not
as though it were forced upon you but
of your own free will, and not from base
love of gain but freely, and not as tyr- 3
annizing over those in your charge but
proving models for the flock; and when 4
the chief shepherd appears, you will receive the glorious wreath that will never

5 fade. You younger men must show
deference to the elders. And you must
all clothe yourselves in humility toward
one another, for God opposes the proud,
6 but shows mercy to the humble. Submit humbly, therefore, to God's mighty
hand, so that he may in due time raise
7 you up. Throw all your anxiety upon
8 him, for he cares for you. Be calm and
watchful. Your opponent the devil is
prowling about like a roaring lion, want-
9 ing to devour you. Resist him and be
strong in the faith, for you know that
your brotherhood all over the world is
having the same experience of suffering.
10 And God, the giver of all mercy, who
through your union with Christ has
called you to his eternal glory, after you
have suffered a little while will himself
make you perfect, steadfast, and strong.
His be the dominion forever. Amen. 11
By Silvanus, our faithful brother, as 12
I think him, I have written you this
short letter to encourage you and bear
my testimony that this is what the true
mercy of God means. Stand fast in it.
Your sister-church in Babylon, chosen 13
like you, and Mark my son wish to be
remembered to you. Greet one another 14
with a kiss of love.

Peace to all of you that are in union
with Christ.

THE SECOND LETTER OF PETER

1 SIMON PETER, a slave and apostle of Jesus Christ, to those who
through the uprightness of our
God and Savior Jesus Christ
have been given a faith as privileged
2 as ours; God bless you and give you
perfect peace through the knowledge
3 of God and of Jesus our Lord. For
his divine power has given us every
requisite for life and piety, through
our coming to know him who through
his glory and excellence called us to
4 him. Thus he has given us his precious and splendid promises so that
through them you may escape the cor-
rupting influences that exist in the
world through passion, and come to
5 share in the divine nature. For this
very reason make every effort to sup-
plement your faith with goodness, good-
6 ness with knowledge, knowledge with
self-control, self-control with steadfast-
7 ness, steadfastness with piety, piety
with a spirit of brotherhood, and the
8 spirit of brotherhood with love. For if
you have these qualities in their fulness,
they will make you neither idle nor unproductive when it comes to the under-
9 standing of our Lord Jesus Christ. For
whoever lacks these qualities is blind or
near-sighted, and has forgotten that he
has been cleansed from his former sins.
10 Therefore, brothers, make all the greater efforts to make God's call and choice
of you certain. For if you have these
11 qualities, you will never stumble, for
then you will be triumphantly admitted
to the eternal kingdom of our Lord and
Savior Jesus Christ.
12 Therefore I will always remind you
of this, although you know it and are
firmly grounded in the truth that you
13 have. Yet I think it right, as long as I
live in my present tent, to arouse you
14 by a reminder, for I know that I must
soon put it away, as our Lord Jesus
15 Christ has shown me. I will also take
care that after I am gone you will be
able at any time to call these things to
16 mind. For they were no fictitious
stories that we followed when we informed you of the power of our Lord
Jesus Christ and of his coming, but we
had been eye-witnesses of his majesty.
For when he was so honored and glori- 17
fied by God the Father and from the
supreme glory there were borne to him
such words as these: "This is my Son,
my Beloved! He is my Chosen!"—we 18
heard these words borne from heaven
when we were with him on that sacred
mountain. So we have the message of 19
the prophets more fully guaranteed.
Please pay attention to that message as
to a lamp shining in a dark place, until
the day dawns and the morning star
rises in your hearts. You must under- 20
stand this in the first place, that no
prophecy in Scripture can be understood through one's own powers, for no 21
prophecy ever originated in the human
will, but under the influence of the holy
Spirit men spoke for God.
There were false prophets too among 2
the people, just as there will be false
teachers among you, who will introduce
destructive sects and deny the Master
who has bought them, thus bringing on
themselves swift destruction. Many 2
people will follow their immoral ways,
and they will cause the true way to be
maligned. In their greed they will ex- 3
ploit you with pretended arguments.
From of old their condemnation has not
been idle, and their destruction has not
slumbered. For if God did not spare 4
angels when they sinned, but plunged
them into Tartarus, and committed
them to dark dungeons to await their
doom, and if he did not spare the 5
ancient world, but preserved Noah, a
preacher of righteousness, and seven
others, when he brought the flood upon
the godless world; and if he condemned 6
the cities of Sodom and Gomorrah, and
overwhelmed them with ashes, as a
warning to ungodly men of what was to
come, and saved the upright Lot who 7
was so distressed by the immoral conduct of unprincipled men—for as long 8
as that upright man lived among them,
day after day his upright soul was tor-

mented by what he saw and heard of
9 their lawless actions—then the Lord
knows how to rescue God-fearing people from trial and to punish wrongdoers
while they are being kept for the Day
10 of Judgment, especially those who yield
to their physical nature and indulge in
passions that defile them, and despise
authority. Rash, headstrong men!
11 They stand in no awe of majesty, but
deride beings against whom even angels
far superior to these beings in strength
and power bring no abusive charge be-
12 fore the Lord. These men, like unreasoning animals, mere creatures of
instinct created to be caught and killed,
abuse what they do not understand and
will be destroyed like animals, suffering
wrong as the reward for their wrong-
13 doing. They find pleasure in the indulgence of the moment; they are a stain
and a disgrace, and they revel in their
deceit while they join in your meals.
14 They have eyes for nobody but adulterous women—eyes insatiable in sin.
They lure unsteadfast souls. Their
hearts are trained in greed. They are
15 accursed! They have left the straight
path and gone astray. They have followed the path of Balaam, the son of
Beor, who set his heart on dishonest
16 gain, but he was rebuked for his offense; a dumb animal spoke with a human voice and checked the prophet's
17 madness. Such men are dried-up
springs, clouds driven before the storm,
and they are doomed to utter darkness.
18 They utter arrogant nonsense and use
physical cravings to lure into immorality men who are just escaping from
19 among those who live in error; promising them freedom when they are themselves slaves of destruction; for a man
is the slave of whatever overcomes him.
20 For if after men have escaped the cor-
rupting influences of the world through
the knowledge of the Lord and Savior
Jesus Christ, they again become entangled in them and are overcome by
them, their final condition is worse than
21 their former one. For it would have
been better for them never to have
known the way of uprightness than after knowing it to have turned their
backs upon the sacred command with
22 which they had been intrusted. What
has happened to them shows the truth
of the proverb, "A dog returns to what
he has vomited up, and a sow that has
washed goes back to wallow in the
mire."

This is the second letter, dear friends, 3
that I have now written to you, in the
effort to arouse your unsullied minds to 2
remember the things foretold by the
holy prophets, and the command of the
Lord and Savior through your apostles.
First of all, you must understand this, 3
that in the last days mockers will come
with their mockeries, going where their
passions lead and saying, "Where is his 4
promised coming? For ever since our
forefathers fell asleep everything has remained as it was from the beginning of
creation!" For they wilfully ignore the 5
fact that long ago there existed heavens
and an earth which had been formed at
God's command out of water and by
water, by which also that world was de- 6
stroyed, through being flooded with
water. But by the same command the 7
present heavens and earth are stored up
for fire, and are kept for the day when
godless men are to be judged and destroyed.

But do not overlook this one fact, 8
dear friends, that with the Lord one
day is like a thousand years and a
thousand years are like one day. The 9
Lord is not slow about his promise, in
the sense that some men think; he is
really showing his patience with you,
because he does not want any to perish,
but wishes all men to be brought to repentance. The Day of the Lord will 10
come like a thief; on it the heavens will
pass away with a roar, the heavenly
bodies will burn up and be destroyed,
and the earth and all its works will melt
away. If all these things are to be dis- 11
solved in this way, what holy and pious
lives you ought to lead, while you await 12
and hasten the coming of the Day of
God, which will cause the heavens to
burn up and dissolve and the heavenly
bodies to blaze and melt. In fulfilment 13
of his promise we expect new heavens
and a new earth, where uprightness will
prevail.

Therefore, dear friends, while waiting 14
for this, make every effort to be found
by him unstained, irreproachable, and
at peace. Look upon our Lord's pa- 15
tience as salvation, just as our dear
brother Paul, with the wisdom that
God gave him, wrote you to do, speak- 16
ing of it as he does in all his letters.

There are some things in them hard to
understand, which ignorant, unsteadfast people twist to their own ruin, just
17 as they do the rest of the Scriptures. So
you, dear friends, now that you are
forewarned, must be on your guard
against being led away by the errors of
unprincipled men and losing your present firmness. You must grow in the 18
blessing and knowledge of our Lord and
Savior Jesus Christ. Glory to him now
and forever.

THE FIRST LETTER OF JOHN

1 IT IS what existed from the beginning, that we announce; what we
have heard, what we have seen
with our own eyes, what we have
beheld, and touched with our hands; it
2 is the very message of life—for life has
been revealed, and we have seen it and
testify to it and announce to you that
eternal life that was with the Father
3 and has been revealed to us—it is what
we have seen and heard that we announce to you also, so that you may
share our fellowship, for our fellowship
is with the Father and with his Son
4 Jesus Christ, and we write this to you to
make your happiness complete.
5 This is the message that we heard
from him and announce to you: God is
light; there is no darkness at all in
him.
6 If we say, "We have fellowship with
him," and yet live in darkness, we are
7 lying and not living the truth. But if
we live in the light, just as he is in the
light, we have fellowship with one another, and the blood of Jesus his Son
8 cleanses us from every sin. If we say,
"We are without any sin," we are deceiving ourselves, and there is no
9 truth in our hearts. If we acknowledge
our sins, he is upright and can be depended on to forgive us our sins and
10 cleanse us from everything wrong. If
we say, "We have not sinned," we are
making him a liar, and his message is
not in our hearts.
2 My dear children, I am writing you
this so that you may not sin; yet if anyone does sin, we have in Jesus Christ
one who is upright and will intercede for
2 us with the Father. He is himself an
atoning sacrifice for our sins, and not
only for ours but also for the whole
3 world. This is how we can be sure that
we know him—by obeying his com-
4 mands. Whoever says, "I know him,"
but does not obey his commands, is a
liar, and there is no truth in his heart;
5 but whoever obeys his message really
has the love of God in perfection in his
heart. This is the way we can be sure
that we are in union with him; whoever 6
says, "I am always in union with him"
must live just as he lived.
Dear friends, it is no new command 7
that I am writing you, but an old one
that you have had from the beginning.
That old command is the message you
have heard. Yet it is a new command 8
that I am writing you; it is newly realized in him and in yourselves, for the
darkness is passing and the true light is
already shining.
Whoever says, "I am in the light," 9
and yet hates his brother, is still in
darkness. Whoever loves his brother is 10
always in the light and puts no hindrance in anyone's way. But whoever 11
hates his brother is in darkness, and is
living in darkness, and he does not
know where he is going, for the darkness has blinded his eyes.
I am writing to you, dear children, 12
because your sins have been forgiven
for his sake. I am writing to you, fa- 13
thers, because you know him who has
existed from the beginning. I am writing to you, young men, because you
have been victorious over the evil one.
I write to you, children, because you
know the Father. I write to you, fa- 14
thers, because you know him who has
existed from the beginning. I write to
you, young men, because you are
strong, and God's message is always in
your hearts, and you have been victorious over the evil one. Do not love the 15
world or what is in the world. If anyone loves the world, there is no love for
the Father in his heart, for all that there 16
is in the world, the things that our
physical nature and our eyes crave, and
the proud display of life—these do not
come from the Father, but from the
world; and the world with its cravings 17
is passing away, but whoever does
God's will will endure forever.
Children, it is the last hour. You 18
have heard that Antichrist is coming,
and many Antichrists have indeed appeared. So we may be sure that it is the
last hour. They have gone out from our 19

number, but they did not really belong
to us. For if they had belonged to us,
they would have stayed with us. It was
to make it clear that none of them
really belonged to us that they with-
20 drew. But you have been anointed by
the Holy One. You all know the truth;
21 I do not write to you because you do
not know it, but because you do know
it, and because no lie can come from the
truth.

22 Who is such a liar as the man who
denies that Jesus is the Christ? He is
the real Antichrist—the man who dis-
23 owns the Father and the Son. No one
who disowns the Son can have the
Father. Whoever acknowledges the Son
24 has the Father too. Keep what you
have heard from the beginning in your
hearts. If you keep what you have
heard from the beginning in your
hearts, you will always be in union with
25 the Son and the Father. And what he
himself has promised us is eternal life.
26 I write you this with reference to
those who are trying to mislead you.
27 You still retain in your hearts the
anointing with the Spirit that you received from him, and you do not need
to have anyone teach you. But just as
that anointing of his teaches you about
everything, and as it is true and no
falsehood, keep in union with him just
28 as it has taught you to do. Now, dear
children, keep in union with him, so
that if he appears, we may have confidence and not shrink from him in
29 shame when he comes. If you know
that he is upright, you may be sure
that everyone who acts uprightly is his
child.

3 Think what love the Father has had
for us, in letting us be called God's
children, for that is what we are. This
is why the world does not know what
we are—because it has never come to
2 know him. Dear friends, we are God's
children now; it has not yet been disclosed what we are to be. We know that
if he appears, we shall be like him, for
3 we shall see him as he is. And everyone
who possesses this hope in him tries to
make himself as pure as he is.

4 Whoever commits sin disobeys law;
5 sin is disobedience to law. You know
that he appeared to take our sins away,
6 and that there is no sin in him. No one
who keeps in union with him sins. Anyone who sins has never seen him or
come to know him. Dear children, let 7
no one mislead you; whoever acts uprightly is upright, just as he is upright.
Whoever commits sin is a child of the 8
devil, for the devil has sinned from the
beginning. This is why the Son of God
appeared—to undo the devil's work.

No one who is a child of God com- 9
mits sin, for God's nature remains in his
heart, and he cannot sin, because he is
a child of God. This is how the chil- 10
dren of God and those of the devil can
be distinguished: No one who does not
act uprightly or who does not love his
brother is a child of God. For the mes- 11
sage you have heard from the beginning is this: We must love one another.
We must not be like Cain who was a 12
child of the evil one, and butchered his
brother. And why did he butcher him?
Because his own actions were wicked
and his brother's upright.

You must not be surprised, brothers, 13
if the world hates you! We know that 14
we have passed out of death into life,
because we love our brothers. Anyone 15
who does not love is still in death.
Whoever hates his brother is a murderer, and you know that no murderer
can have eternal life remain in his heart.
We know what love means from the 16
fact that he laid down his life for us; so
we also ought to lay down our lives for
our brothers. But if someone who is 17
rich sees his brother in need and closes
his heart against him, how can he have
any love for God in his heart? Dear 18
children, let us love not with words or
lips only but in deed and truth.

From that we can be sure that we 19
are on the side of the truth, and satisfy
our consciences in God's sight, if they 20
condemn us for anything, for God is
greater than our consciences, and he
knows all. Dear friends, if our con- 21
sciences do not condemn us, we approach God with confidence, and we ob- 22
tain from him whatever we ask for, because we are obeying his commands
and doing the things that please him.
His command is this—that we are to 23
believe in his Son Jesus Christ, and
love one another, as he has commanded us to do. All who obey his com- 24
mands keep in union with him, and he
does with them; and this is how we
know that he keeps in union with us—
by the Spirit which he has given us.

4 Dear friends, do not believe every
inspired utterance, but test the utterances to see whether they come from
God, for many false prophets have
2 come out into the world. You can tell
the Spirit of God in this way: every inspired utterance that acknowledges
that Jesus Christ has come in human
3 form comes from God, and any inspired
utterance that does not acknowledge
Jesus does not come from God; it is the
inspiration of the Antichrist. You have
heard that it was coming, and here it is
already in the world.
4 You are children of God, dear children, and you have been victorious over
these men, for he who is in our hearts is
greater than he who is in the world.
5 They are children of the world; that is
why they speak as the world directs,
6 and the world listens to them. We are
God's children. Whoever knows God
listens to us; whoever is not a child of
God will not listen to us. In this way
we can tell what is inspired by truth
from what is inspired by error.
7 Dear friends, let us love one another, for love comes from God, and
everyone who loves is a child of God
8 and knows God. Whoever does not
love does not know God, for God is
9 love. God's love for us has been revealed in this way—that God has sent
his only Son into the world, to let us
10 have life through him. The love con-
sists not in our having loved God, but
in his loving us and sending his Son as
an atoning sacrifice for our sins.
11 Dear friends, if God has loved us so,
12 we ought to love one another. No one
has ever seen God; yet if we love one
another, God keeps in union with us
and love for him attains perfection in
13 our hearts. This is the way we know
that we keep in union with him and he
does with us—because he has given us
14 some of his Spirit. We have seen and
can testify that the Father has sent the
15 Son to be Savior of the world. If anyone acknowledges that Jesus Christ is
the Son of God, God keeps in union
16 with him and he with God. So we
know and believe in the love God has
for us.
God is love, and whoever continues
to love keeps in union with God, and
17 God with him. Love attains perfection
in us, when we have perfect confidence
about the Day of Judgment, because
here in this world we are living as he
lives. There is no fear in love, but per- 18
fect love drives out fear. For fear sug-
gests punishment and no one who feels
fear has attained perfect love. We love 19
because he loved us first. If anyone 20
says, "I love God," and yet hates his
brother, he is a liar; for whoever does
not love his brother whom he has seen
cannot love God whom he has not seen.
This is the command that we get from 21
him, that whoever loves God must love
his brother also.
Everyone who believes that Jesus is 5
the Christ is a child of God, and everyone who loves the Father loves his
child. This is how we can be sure that 2
we love the children of God: it is by loving God and obeying his commands.
For loving God means obeying his 3
commands, and his commands are not
burdensome, for every child of God is 4
victorious over the world. The victory
that has triumphed over the world is
our faith. For who is there that is 5
victorious over the world except the
man who believes that Jesus is the Son
of God? It was he, Jesus Christ him- 6
self, who came in water and in blood;
not in water only, but in water and in
blood. The Spirit also testifies to this,
for the Spirit is truth. For there are 8
three that testify to it, the Spirit, the
water, and the blood, and the three are
at one. If we accept the testimony of 9
men, the testimony of God is stronger
still; for the value of God's testimony
lies in this, that he has testified to his
Son. Whoever believes in the Son of 10
God possesses that testimony in his
heart. Anyone who will not believe
God has made him a liar, for he has refused to believe the testimony that
God has borne to his Son. And that tes- 11
timony is that God has given us eternal
life, and that this life is found in his
Son. Whoever has the Son has life; 12
whoever has not the Son has not life.
I write this to you so that you who 13
believe in the Son of God may know
that you have eternal life. And we have 14
confidence in him, that if we ask him for
anything that is in accordance with his
will, he will listen to us. And if we know 15
that he listens to whatever we ask him
for, we know that the requests we have

16 made of him are granted. If anyone
sees his brother committing any sin except a deadly one, he will ask and obtain life for him—provided the sin is
not a deadly one. There is such a thing
as deadly sin; I do not say that a man
17 should pray about that. Any wrongdoing is sin, but there are sins that are
not deadly.
18 We know that no child of God commits sin, but that he who was born of
God protects him, and the evil one
cannot touch him. We know that we 19
are children of God, while the whole
world is in the power of the evil one.
And we know that the Son of God has 20
come, and has given us power to recognize him who is true; and we are in
union with him who is true, through his
Son, Jesus Christ. He is the true God
and eternal life. Dear children, keep 21
away from idols.

THE SECOND LETTER OF JOHN

1 THE Elder to the chosen lady and
her children, whom I truly love
—and not only I but all who
2 know the truth—because of the
truth that stays in our hearts and will
3 be with us forever; blessing, mercy, and
peace be with us from God the Father
and Jesus Christ, the Father's Son, in
truth and love.
4 It makes me exceedingly happy to
find that some of your children are
guided by truth, just as we have been
5 commanded to be by the Father. And
now I beg you, my lady—not as though
I were writing you any new command,
but one which we have had from the
beginning—let us love one another.
6 Love means this, that we be guided by
his commands. The command, as you
have heard from the beginning, is to be
7 guided by love. For many impostors
have gone out into the world—men who
do not acknowledge the coming of Jesus
Christ in human form. That is the
mark of the impostor and the Antichrist. Look out for yourselves, take 8
care not to lose what we have worked
for, but that you are paid for it in full.
Anyone who goes too far and does not 9
keep to the teaching of Christ has not
God. It is the man who holds to the
teaching who has both the Father and
the Son. If anyone comes to you with- 10
out bringing this teaching, do not let
him come into the house or bid him
good morning. For anyone who bids 11
him good morning shares in his wicked
work.
Though I have a great deal to write 12
to you, I would rather not write it with
paper and ink, but I hope to come to
see you, and talk with you face to face,
so that your happiness may be complete. The children of your chosen sis- 13
ter wish to be remembered to you.

THE THIRD LETTER OF JOHN

1 THE Elder to my dear friend
Gaius, whom I truly love.
2 Dear friend, it is my prayer
that everything is going well
with you and that you are well; I know
3 it is well with your soul. For it makes
me exceedingly happy when some
brothers come and testify to the truth
of your life, for you are guided by truth.
4 I know of no greater blessing than hearing that my children are being guided
by the truth.
5 Dear friend, it is loyal of you to do
anything you can for the brothers, es-
6 pecially as they are strangers; they
have testified before the church to your
love. Please see them off on their journey in a way appropriate to God's
7 service. For they have started out for
the sake of the cause, and they are ac-
8 cepting nothing from the heathen. So
we ought to support such men, so
that we may co-operate with the truth.

I have written to the church, but 9
Diotrephes who likes to be their leader
will not accept what I say. So if I come, 10
I will bring up the things that he is
doing, and how he is maliciously accus-
ing me. Not content with that, he refuses to welcome the brothers himself,
and he is interfering with those who
want to do so, and has them put out of
the church.
Dear friend, do not initiate evil, but 11
good. The man who does right is a
child of God; the man who does wrong
has never seen God. Everybody testi- 12
fies to Demetrius; the truth itself does;
I testify to him too, and you know
that my testimony to him is true.
I have a great deal to write to you, 13
but I do not want to write it with pen
and ink; I hope to see you very soon 14
and we will talk face to face. Goodbye. Our friends wish to be remembered to you. Remember me to our
friends, every one.

THE LETTER OF JUDE

1 JUDE, a slave of Jesus Christ, and
the brother of James, to those who
have been called, who are dear to
God the Father and have been
kept through union with Jesus
2 Christ; may mercy, peace, and
love be granted you in abundance.
3 Dear friends, I was just on the point
of writing to you about our common
salvation, when it became necessary for
me to write and appeal to you to come
to the defense of the faith that has once
for all been intrusted to God's people.
4 For some people have sneaked in
among us—their doom was foretold
long ago—godless persons, who turn
the mercy of our God into an excuse for
immorality, and disown our only
Master and Lord, Jesus Christ.
5 Now I want to remind you, though
you know it all already, that he who
brought the people safely out of the
land of Egypt afterward destroyed the
6 ones who did not believe, and the angels who neglected their responsibilities
and abandoned their homes he has put
in everlasting chains to be kept in darkness for the judgment of the great Day,
7 just as Sodom and Gomorrah and the
neighboring towns which like them indulged in immorality and unnatural
vice stand as a warning, in undergoing
the punishment of eternal fire.
8 In that same way these dreamers defile the body, make light of authority,
9 and deride majesty. The archangel
Michael himself, when he had the dispute with the devil about Moses' body,
did not venture to condemn him for
blasphemy; he only said, "May the
10 Lord rebuke you!" But these people
deride anything they do not understand, and the things they know by instinct, like unreasoning animals, they
11 use for their own destruction. Alas for
them, for they follow Cain's path, they
plunge into Balaam's error for gain,
and they perish in rebelliousness like
12 Korah's. They are stains on your religious meals, where they carouse together, boldly attending to no one but
themselves; rainless clouds driven before the wind; leafless trees without
fruit, doubly dead, and uprooted; wild 13
sea waves foaming up their own shame;
wandering stars doomed forever to utter darkness.

Of them also Enoch, in the seventh 14
generation from Adam, prophesied,
when he said, "See! The Lord comes
with his holy myriads to execute judg- 15
ment upon all, and to convict all the
godless of all the godless deeds they
have done, and of all the harsh things
that godless sinners have said against
him."

These men are grumblers, dissatis- 16
fied with life. They go where their passions lead, their talk is arrogant and
they cultivate people in the hope of
gain.

But you, dear friends, must remem- 17
ber what was foretold by the apostles
of our Lord Jesus Christ, for they said 18
to you, "In the last times there will be
mockers who will go where their own
godless passions lead." These are the 19
men who create division; they are animal and devoid of the Spirit. But you, 20
dear friends, must build yourselves up
on your most holy faith and pray
in the holy Spirit, keep in the love of 21
God, and wait for the mercy of our
Lord Jesus Christ, to bring you to
eternal life. Those whom you pity in 22
their uncertainty, save, snatching them 23
out of the fire, and look on others with
pity mixed with fear, loathing even the
clothes their animal nature has stained.

Now to him who is able to keep you 24
from stumbling and to make you stand
in his presence irreproachable and triumphant—to the one God our Savior 25
be glory, majesty, power, and authority through Jesus Christ our Lord before
time began and now and forever and
ever. Amen.

THE REVELATION OF JOHN

1 A REVELATION made by Jesus
Christ which God gave him
to disclose to his slaves of
what must very soon happen.
He sent and communicated it by his
2 angel to his slave John, who testifies to
what he saw—to the message of God
and the testimony of Jesus Christ.
3 Blessed be the man who reads this
prophecy and those who hear it read
and heed what is written in it, for the
time is near.

4 John to the seven churches in Asia,
blessing and peace to you from him
who is and was and is coming, and
from the seven spirits before his throne,
5 and from Jesus Christ the trustworthy
witness, the firstborn of the dead, and
the sovereign of the kings of the earth.
To him who loves us and has released
6 us from our sins by his blood—he has
made us a kingdom of priests for his
God and Father—to him be glory and
7 power forever. Amen. See! He is coming on the clouds, and every eye will see
him, even the men who pierced him,
and all the tribes of the earth will lament over him. So it is to be. Amen.
8 "I am the Alpha and the Omega,"
says the Lord God, who is and was and
is coming, the Almighty.
9 I, John, your brother and companion
in the distress, the kingdom, and the
endurance that Jesus brings, found
myself on the island called Patmos, for
uttering God's message and testifying
10 to Jesus. On the Lord's day I fell into
a trance, and I heard a loud voice like
11 a trumpet behind me say,
"Write what you see in a roll and
send it to the seven churches—to Ephesus, Smyrna, Pergamum, Thyatira,
Sardis, Philadelphia, and Laodicea."
12 I turned to see whose voice it was
that was speaking to me, and when I
turned I saw seven gold lampstands,
13 and among the lampstands a being like
a man, wearing a long robe, with a gold
14 belt around his breast. His head and
hair were as white as white wool, as
white as snow; his eyes blazed like fire;
his feet were like bronze, refined in a 15
furnace, and his voice was like the
noise of mighty waters. In his right 16
hand he held seven stars; from his
mouth came a sharp double-edged
sword, and his face shone like the sun
at noonday. When I saw him, I fell at 17
his feet like a dead man. But he laid
his right hand upon me, and said,
"Do not be afraid. I am the first and
the last, the living one. I was dead, yet 18
here I am alive forever and ever. I
hold the keys of death and the underworld. So write what you have seen, 19
what is now and what is to happen
hereafter. The secret meaning of the 20
seven stars that you saw in my right
hand, and of the seven gold lampstands
is this: The seven stars are the guardian angels of the seven churches and the
seven lampstands are the seven
churches.
"To the angel of the church in 2
Ephesus write:
" 'He who holds the seven stars in his
right hand and goes about among the
seven gold lampstands speaks thus: I 2
know what you have done; your hard
work and your endurance. I know that
you cannot tolerate wicked men, and
that you have tested those who claimed
to be apostles when they were not, and
have found them to be impostors. You 3
show endurance; you have undergone
much for my sake, and you have not
grown weary. But I hold it against you 4
that you do not love as you did at first.
So remember how far you have fallen, 5
and repent and do as you did at first,
or else I will come to you and take your
lampstand from its place, if you do not
repent. But it is in your favor that you 6
hate the practices of the Nicolaitans, as
I do. Let everyone who can hear listen 7
to what the Spirit says to the churches.
I will permit him who is victorious to
eat the fruit of the tree of life that
stands in the Paradise of God.'
"To the angel of the church in 8
Smyrna write:
" 'The first and the last, who died
and came to life again, speaks thus:

9 I know of your distress and poverty—
though you are rich!—I know how you
are slandered by those who claim to be
Jews when they are not, but only a
10 synagogue of Satan! Do not be afraid
of what you are going to suffer. See!
The devil is going to put some of you
into prison to be tested there, and for
ten days to endure persecution. Prove
faithful even unto death and I will give
11 you the crown of life. Let everyone
who can hear listen to what the Spirit
says to the churches. He who is victorious will not be hurt by the second
death.'

12 "To the angel of the church in Pergamum write:

" 'He who wields the sharp, double-
13 edged sword speaks thus: I know
where you live; where Satan has his
throne! Yet you cling to my name and
did not renounce your faith in me even
in the days when my faithful Antipas,
my witness, was put to death among
14 you—where Satan lives. Yet I hold it
somewhat against you that you have
among you some adherents of the
teaching of Balaam, who taught Balak
to entrap the children of Israel into
eating meat that had been sacrificed
to idols, and into immoral practices.
15 So you also have among you some
who hold the teaching of the Nico-
16 laitans. So repent, or else I will come
to you quickly and make war upon
them with the sword that is in my
17 mouth. Let everyone who can hear listen to what the Spirit says to the
churches. I will give him who is victorious some of the hidden manna, and
I will give him a white pebble with a
new name written on it which no one
knows except the man who receives it.'

18 "To the angel of the church in Thyatira write:

" 'The Son of God, whose eyes blaze
like fire, and whose feet are like gilded
19 bronze, speaks thus: I know the things
you do, your love and faithfulness and
helpfulness and endurance, and I know
that you are now doing more than you
20 did at first. But I hold it against you
that you tolerate that Jezebel of a
woman who claims to be inspired and
who is misleading my slaves and teaching them to practice immorality and
to eat meat that has been sacrificed to
21 idols. I have given her time to repent,
but she refuses to repent of her immorality. See! I am going to lay her on a 22
sick bed, and to bring great distress
upon those who share her immorality,
unless they repent of her practices, and 23
I will strike her children dead. Then all
the churches will know that I am he
who searches men's hearts and minds,
and I will repay each of you for what
you have done. But to the rest of you 24
at Thyatira, who do not hold this teaching and have not learned the "deep
things" of Satan, as they call them—
to you I say, I have no fresh burden to
lay on you, but keep hold of what you 25
have, until I come. To him who is vic- 26
torious and continues to the end to do
the things that please me, I will give authority over the heathen—just such 27
authority as I received from my Father; he will shepherd them with an
iron staff, and shatter them like earthen
jars!—and I will give him the morning 28
star. Let everyone who can hear listen 29
to what the Spirit says to the churches.'

"To the angel of the church in Sardis 3
write:

" 'He who holds the seven spirits of
God and the seven stars speaks thus:
I know what you are doing; you are
supposed to be alive, but you are dead.
Wake up, and strengthen what is left, 2
although it is already on the point of
death, for I have found nothing you
have done complete in the sight of my
God. So remember what you received 3
and heard, and obey it, and repent. If
you do not wake up, I will come like a
thief, and you will not know at what
hour I am coming upon you. Yet you 4
have a few at Sardis who have not soiled
their clothes. They will walk with me
clad in white, for they deserve to. He 5
who is victorious will be clothed thus, in
white clothing, and I will not erase his
name from the book of life, but I will acknowledge him as mine in the presence
of my Father and his angels. Let every- 6
one who can hear listen to what the
Spirit says to the churches.'

"To the angel of the church in Phila- 7
delphia write:

" 'He who is holy and true, who carries the key of David, who opens and
no one shall shut, and shuts and no one
shall open, speaks thus: I know what 8
you are doing. See! I have put before
you an open door that no one can close.
I know that you have little strength,
but you have obeyed my message and

9 you have not disowned my name. I
will make some who belong to that
synagogue of Satan and claim to be
Jews when they are not so, but are lying—I will make them come and bow
down at your feet, and learn that I
10 loved you. Because you have kept in
mind the message of what I endured, I
also will keep you safe in the time of
testing that is going to come upon the
whole world, to test the inhabitants of
11 the earth. I am coming soon. Keep
hold of what you have, so that no one
12 may deprive you of your crown. I will
make him who is victorious a pillar in
the temple of my God; he shall never go
out of it again. I will write on him the
name of my God and the name of the
city of my God—the new Jerusalem,
which is to come down out of heaven
13 from my God—and my new name. Let
everyone who can hear listen to what
the Spirit says to the churches.'

14 "To the angel of the church in Laodicea write:

" 'The Amen, the true and faithful
witness, the origin of God's creation,
15 speaks thus: I know what you are doing, and that you are neither hot nor
cold. I wish you were either hot or
16 cold! As it is, since you are tepid and
neither hot nor cold, I am going to spit
17 you out of my mouth! Because you
say, "I am rich, I have become wealthy,
I need nothing," and you do not know
that it is you that are wretched, piti-
18 able, poor, blind, and naked, I advise
you to buy of me gold that has been
tested with fire, so that you may be
rich, and white clothes to put on, to
keep your shameful nakedness from
being seen, and salve to put on your
19 eyes, to make you see. I reprove and
20 discipline all whom I love. So be earnest
and repent. Here I stand knocking at
the door. If anyone listens to my voice
and opens the door, I will be his guest
21 and dine with him, and he with me. I
will permit him who is victorious to
take his seat beside me on my throne,
just as I have been victorious and
taken my seat beside my Father on his
22 throne. Let everyone who can hear
listen to what the Spirit says to the
churches.' "

4 Afterward I had another vision:
There was a door standing open in the
heavens and the first voice like a trumpet that I had heard speak to me, said,
"Come up here, and I will show you
what must take place."

Immediately after this I found my- 2
self in a trance, and there stood a
throne in heaven with a being seated
on it. The one who was seated on it 3
looked like jasper and sardius, and
around the throne was a halo of the
color of an emerald. Around the throne 4
were twenty-four thrones, with twenty-
four elders seated on them, clothed in
white and with gold crowns on their
heads. Out from the throne came flash- 5
es of lightning, rumblings, and peals of
thunder. In front of the throne seven
blazing lamps were burning: they are
the seven spirits of God. In front of the 6
throne was what looked like a sea of
glass, like crystal. Around the throne,
in the middle of each side, were four
animals covered with eyes in front and
behind. The first animal was like a 7
lion, the second was like an ox, the
third had a face like a man's, and the
fourth was like an eagle flying. The 8
four animals have each of them six
wings, and they are covered with eyes
all over and underneath their wings.
And day and night they never cease to
say,

"Holy, holy, holy is the Lord God,
the Almighty, who was and is and is
coming."

And whenever the animals offer 6
glory, honor, and thanksgiving to him
who is seated on the throne, who lives
forever and ever, the twenty-four eld- 10
ers fall down before him who is seated
on the throne, and worship him who
lives forever and ever, and they throw
down their crowns before the throne,
and say,

"You are worthy, our Lord and God, 11
to receive glory, honor, and power, for
you created all things; by your will
they existed and were created."

Then I saw lying in the right hand of 5
him who was seated on the throne a
roll with writing on both sides, sealed
with seven seals. And I saw a mighty 2
angel announcing in a loud voice,

"Who is fit to open the roll and
break its seals?"

But no one in heaven or on earth or 3
underneath the earth could open the
roll or look into it. Then I cried bitter- 4
ly because no one could be found fit to
open the roll or look into it. But one of 5
the elders said to me,

"Do not cry! See! The lion who is of
the tribe of Judah, of the line of David,
has been victorious so that he can open
the roll and break its seals."
6 Then I saw standing in the center of
the throne and of the four animals and
of the elders a Lamb which seemed to
have been slaughtered. He had seven
horns and seven eyes; these are the
seven spirits of God, which are sent on
7 errands to all parts of the earth. He
came and took the roll from the right
hand of him who was seated on the
8 throne. When he took the roll, the four
animals and the twenty-four elders fell
down before the Lamb, each with a
harp and gold bowls full of incense,
that is, of the prayers of God's people.
9 Then they sang a new song:
"You deserve to take the roll and
open its seals, for you have been
slaughtered, and with your blood have
bought for God men from every tribe,
10 tongue, people, and nation, and have
made them a kingdom of priests for our
God, and they are to reign over the
earth."
11 Then in my vision I heard the voices
of many angels surrounding the throne,
the animals, and the elders, numbering
myriads of myriads and thousands of
12 thousands, saying in a loud voice,
"The Lamb that was slaughtered deserves to receive power, wealth, wisdom, might, honor, glory, and blessing."
13 Then I heard every creature in heaven, on earth, underneath the earth, and on the sea, and all that they contain, say,
"Blessing, honor, glory, and power to him who is seated on the throne and to the Lamb forever and ever!"
14 The four animals said,
"Amen!"
And the elders fell down and worshiped.
6 In my vision, when the Lamb broke the first of the seven seals, I heard the first of the four animals say with a voice like thunder,
"Come!"
2 Then I saw a white horse, and its
rider carried a bow. He was given a
crown, and he rode forth as a victor to
3 conquer. When he broke the second
seal, I heard the second animal say,
"Come!"
4 And another horse came forth,
bright red, and its rider was given power to take peace away from the earth, and make men slaughter one another; he was given a great sword.
When he broke the third seal, I heard 5
the third animal say,
"Come!"
And there I saw a black horse, and
its rider had a pair of scales in his hand,
and I heard a voice which seemed to 6
come from the midst of the four animals say,
"Wheat at a dollar a quart, and barley three quarts for a dollar, but you must not injure the oil and wine!"
When he broke the fourth seal, I 7
heard the voice of the fourth animal
say,
"Come!"
And there I saw a livid horse, and 8
its rider's name was Death, and
Hades followed him. They were given power over one quarter of the earth, to kill the people with sword, famine, death, and the wild animals of the earth.
When he broke the fifth seal, I saw 9
underneath the altar the souls of those
who have been slaughtered on account
of God's message and for adhering to
the testimony. They cried out in a 10
loud voice,
"Holy and true Master, how long is it to be before you judge the inhabitants of the earth and avenge our blood?"
Then each of them was given a white 11
robe and they were told to be quiet a
little while longer, until the number of
their fellow-slaves and their brothers,
who were to be killed as they had been,
should be complete.
When he broke the sixth seal I saw 12
that there was a great earthquake.
The sun turned black as sackcloth; the
full moon became like blood; the stars 13
of the sky fell upon the earth just as a
fig tree drops its unripe figs when it is
shaken by a strong wind; the sky was 14
torn apart and rolled up like a roll; and
every mountain and island was dislodged from its place. The kings of the 15
earth, the nobles, the officers, the rich,
the strong—everybody, slave and free
—hid themselves in the caves and
among the rocks of the mountains.
And they said to the mountains and the 16
rocks,
"Fall on us, and conceal us from the

sight of him who is seated on the
throne, and from the anger of the
17 Lamb, for the great day of their anger
has come, and who can escape?"
7 After that I saw four angels standing
at the four corners of the earth holding
back the four winds of the earth, so
that no wind should blow on the earth
2 or on the sea or on any tree. Then I
saw another angel ascend from the east
with the seal of the living God, and he
cried out in a loud voice to the four angels who had it in their power to harm
the earth and the sea,
3 "Do not harm the earth or the sea or
the trees until we mark the slaves of our
God on their foreheads."
4 I heard that the number of those
that were marked with the seal was
144,000. They were from every tribe of
5 the children of Israel: 12,000 from the
tribe of Judah that were marked;
12,000 from the tribe of Reuben;
6 12,000 from the tribe of Gad; 12,000
from the tribe of Asher; 12,000 from the
tribe of Naphtali; 12,000 from the tribe
7 of Manasseh; 12,000 from the tribe of
Symeon; 12,000 from the tribe of Levi;
12,000 from the tribe of Issachar;
8 12,000 from the tribe of Zebulon;
12,000 from the tribe of Joseph; 12,000
from the tribe of Benjamin.
9 After that I saw a great crowd which
no one could count from every nation,
tribe, people, and language, standing
before the throne and before the Lamb,
wearing white robes, with palm branch-
10 es in their hands, and they cried in a
loud voice,
"Our deliverance is the work of our
God who is seated on the throne, and of
the Lamb!"
11 Then all the angels stood around the
throne and the elders and the four animals, and fell on their faces before the
12 throne and worshiped God, saying,
"Amen! Blessing, glory, wisdom,
thanksgiving, honor, power, and
strength be to our God forever and
ever. Amen!"
13 Then one of the elders addressed me
and said,
"Who are these people dressed in
white robes, and where do they come
from?"
14 I said to him,
"You know, my lord."
He said to me,
"They are the people who come
through the great persecution, who
have washed their robes white in the
blood of the Lamb. That is why they 15
are before the throne of God, and serve
him day and night in his temple, and
he who is seated on the throne will
shelter them. They will never be hun- 16
gry or thirsty again, and never again
will the sun or any burning heat distress them, for the Lamb who is in the 17
center of the throne will be their shepherd, and will guide them to springs of
living water, and God will wipe every
tear from their eyes."
When he broke the seventh seal, 8
there was silence in heaven for about
half an hour. Then I saw the seven an- 2
gels who stand before God, and seven
trumpets were given to them.
Then another angel with a gold cen- 3
ser came and stood at the altar, and he
was given a great quantity of incense so
that he might mingle it with the prayers of all the saints on the altar of gold
that stood before the throne. So the 4
smoke of the incense went up before
God from the angel's hand for the
prayers of his people. Then the angel 5
took the censer and filled it with fire
from the altar, and emptied it upon the
earth, and there followed peals of
thunder, rumblings, flashes of lightning, and an earthquake.
Then the seven angels with the seven 6
trumpets prepared to blow them.
The first blew his trumpet, and there 7
was a storm of hail and fire mixed with
blood, and it fell upon the earth, and
one third of the earth was burned up,
and one third of the trees were burned
up, and all the green grass was burned
up.
Then the second angel blew his 8
trumpet, and what looked like a great
mountain ablaze with fire was thrown
into the sea, and one third of the sea
turned into blood, and one third of all 9
the live creatures in the sea perished,
and one third of the ships were destroyed.
Then the third angel blew his trum- 10
pet, and there fell from the sky a great
star blazing like a torch, and it fell upon
one third of the streams and the springs
of water. The star is called Apsinthus, 11
that is, Wormwood. Then one third of
the waters turned to wormwood, and
numbers of people died of the waters,
for they had turned bitter.

12 Then the fourth angel blew his
trumpet, and one third of the sun was
blasted, and one third of the moon and
one third of the stars, so that one third
of them were darkened, and there was
no light for one third of the day and of
the night.
13 Then in my vision I heard an eagle
flying in midair say in a loud voice,
"Alas! Alas! Alas for the inhabitants
of the earth, because of the other
blasts of the three angels who are going
to blow their trumpets!"
9 Then the fifth angel blew his trumpet, and I saw a star that had fallen on
the earth from the sky. He was given
2 the key to the pit of the abyss, and he
opened the pit of the abyss, and smoke
like the smoke of a great furnace poured
up out of the pit, and the sun and the
air were darkened by the smoke from
3 the pit. Out of the smoke locusts descended upon the earth, but with powers like those of earthly scorpions.
4 They were told not to harm the grass
of the earth or any plant or tree, but
only the men who did not have the
mark of God's seal upon their fore-
5 heads. They were not allowed to kill
anyone, but only to torture them for
five months, and the torture they inflicted was like that caused by a scor-
6 pion when it stings a man. In those
days men will seek death and never
find it. They will want to die, but
7 death will fly from them. In appearance the locusts were like war-horses
armed for battle; on their heads were
what appeared to be crowns like gold;
8 their faces were like human faces; they
had hair like a woman's; their teeth
9 were like those of lions; their breasts
were like iron breast-plates, and the
noise of their wings was like the noise
of a great number of chariots and
10 horses rushing into battle. They had
tails and stings like scorpions; it was in
their tails that their power lay to harm
11 men for five months. They had over
them as king the angel of the abyss,
whose name in Hebrew is Abaddon,
but in Greek he is called Apollyon.
12 The first woe is past. See! Two woes
are yet to come.
13 Then the sixth angel blew his trumpet, and I heard a voice from the corners of the altar of gold that was before
14 God say to the sixth angel who had the
trumpet,

"Release the four angels that are
bound at the great river Euphrates."
Then the four angels who were held 15
in readiness for that hour and day and
month and year were let loose to kill
one third of mankind. The number of 16
the hosts of horsemen was twice 10,000
times 10,000; I heard their number.
And this was how the horses and their 17
riders looked in my vision: Their
breast-plates were fire red, dark blue,
and yellow. The horses' heads were
like lions' heads, and fire, smoke, and
sulphur poured from their mouths. One 18
third of mankind were killed by these
three plagues—the fire, smoke, and
sulphur that poured from their mouths.
For the power of the horses lay in their 19
mouths and their tails; their tails were
like snakes, and they had heads with
which they hurt people. Yet what was 20
left of mankind, those who escaped being killed by these plagues, did not repent of the works of their hands and
give up worshiping demons and gold,
silver, bronze, stone, and wooden idols,
which cannot either see or hear or
move, and they did not repent of their 21
murders, or their magic arts, or their
immorality, or their thefts.
Then I saw another mighty angel de- 10
scend from heaven. He was clothed in
a cloud, and there was a rainbow above
his head. His face was like the sun, his
legs were like pillars of fire, and he had 2
a little scroll open in his hand. He set
his right foot on the sea and his left
foot on the land, and he uttered a great
shout like the roar of a lion; and when 3
he shouted, the seven thunders raised
their voices. When the seven thunders 4
had spoken I was going to write it
down, but I heard a voice from heaven
say,
"Seal up what the seven thunders
have said! Do not write it down!"
Then the angel, whom I had seen 5
standing on the sea and on the land,
raised his right hand to heaven, and 6
swore by him who lives forever and
ever, who created the heavens and all
that is in them, the earth and all that
is in it, and the sea and all that is in it,
that there should be no more delay, but 7
at the time when the seventh angel
spoke, when he should blow his trumpet, then God's mysterious purpose,
the good news of which he gave to his
slaves the prophets, would be accom-

8 plished. Then the voice that I had
heard from heaven spoke to me again,
and said,
"Go and take the scroll that lies
open in the hand of the angel who is
standing on the sea and on the land."
9 So I went up to the angel and told
him to give me the little scroll. And he
said to me,
"Take it and eat it; it will be bitter
in your stomach, but in your mouth it
will taste as sweet as honey."
10 So I took the little scroll from the
angel's hand and ate it, and it did taste
as sweet as honey, but when I had eaten
11 it, it made my stomach bitter. Then
they said to me,
"You must prophesy again about
many peoples, nations, languages, and
kings!"

11 Then I was given a measuring rod
like a staff, and I was told,
"Rise and measure the temple of
God and the altar, and count those
2 who worship there, but leave out the
court outside the temple; do not measure that, for it has been given up to the
heathen, and for forty-two months they
3 will trample upon the holy city. And I
will permit my two witnesses, clothed
in sackcloth, to prophesy for 1,260
days."
4 They are the two olive trees and the
two lampstands that stand before the
5 Lord of the earth. If anyone tries to
hurt them fire comes out of their
mouths and consumes their enemies; if
anyone tries to hurt them, he will cer-
6 tainly be killed in that way. They have
the power to shut up the sky, so that no
rain will fall during the days when they
are prophesying, and they have power
to turn the waters into blood and to
smite the earth with any plague when-
7 ever they please. When they finish
their testimony, the animal that comes
up out of the abyss will make war on
them and conquer them and kill them,
8 and their bodies will lie in the street of
the great city that is figuratively called
Sodom and Egypt—where their Lord
9 also was crucified. For three days and
a half, men of all peoples, tribes, languages, and nations will look at their
bodies, and will not let them be buried.
10 The inhabitants of the earth will gloat
over them and celebrate by sending
presents to one another, for these two
prophets were a torment to the inhabitants of the earth. After three days 11
and a half, the breath of life from God
entered them, and they stood on their
feet, and terror seized those who saw
them. And they heard a loud voice 12
from heaven say to them,
"Come up here."
And they went up to heaven in a
cloud, before the eyes of their enemies.
At that moment there was a great 13
earthquake, and one tenth of the city
was destroyed. Seven thousand people
were killed in the earthquake, and the
rest were filled with awe, and acknowledged the glory of the God of heaven.
The second woe is past. See! The 14
third woe is soon to come.
Then the seventh angel blew his 15
trumpet, and loud voices were heard in
heaven, saying,
"The sovereignty of the world has
passed into the possession of our Lord
and his Christ, and he will reign forever and ever."
Then the twenty-four elders who 16
were seated on their thrones before
God fell on their faces and worshiped
God, saying, 17
"We give you thanks, Lord God Almighty, who are and were, because you
have assumed your great power and begun to reign. The heathen were en- 18
raged, but now your anger has come,
and the time for the dead to be judged,
and for rewarding your slaves the
prophets and your people high and low
who revere your name, and for destroying the destroyers of the earth!"
Then the temple of God in heaven 19
was thrown open, and the chest containing his agreement was seen inside
his temple, and there were flashes of
lightning, rumblings, peals of thunder,
an earthquake, and a great storm of
hail.

Then a great portent appeared in the 12
sky—a woman clothed in the sun, with
the moon under her feet, and on her
head a crown of twelve stars. She was 2
soon to have a child, and she cried out
with pain and agony in giving birth to
it. Another portent appeared in the sky 3
—there was a great red dragon with
seven heads and ten horns, with seven
diadems on his heads. His tail swept 4
away one third of the stars of heaven
and flung them down upon the earth.
The dragon stood in front of the woman

who was about to give birth to a child in
order to devour her child as soon as it
5 was born. She gave birth to a son, a
male child, who is to shepherd all the
heathen with a staff of iron; and her
child was caught up to God, to his
6 throne. Then the woman fled into the
desert, where there was a place prepared by God for her, where she was to
be taken care of for 1,260 days.
7 Then war broke out in heaven, Michael and his angels fighting with the
dragon. The dragon and his angels
8 fought but they were defeated, and
there was no place for them any longer
9 in heaven. So the great dragon, the ancient serpent who is called the devil and
Satan, who deceives the whole world,
was hurled down to the earth, and his
angels were hurled down with him.
10 Then I heard a loud voice in heaven
say,

"The deliverance and power and
reign of our God, and the authority of
his Christ have now come, for the accuser of our brothers, who kept bringing charges against them day and night
before our God, has been hurled down.
11 They have conquered him because of
the Lamb's blood, and the message to
which they bore testimony, for they did
not cling to life even in the face of
12 death. Therefore, rejoice, you heavens
and you who live in them! But alas for
the earth and the sea, for the devil has
descended upon you in a great rage, for
he knows that his time is short."

13 When the dragon saw that he had
been hurled down to the earth, he went
in pursuit of the woman who had given
14 birth to the male child. But the woman was given the two wings of a great
eagle, so that she might fly from the
serpent to her place in the desert, where
she is to be taken care of for a time,
15 times, and a half-time. Then the serpent poured water from his mouth after
the woman like a river, to sweep her
16 away. But the earth helped the woman,
for the earth opened its mouth and
swallowed the river which the dragon
17 had poured out of his mouth. So the
dragon was enraged at the woman, and
he went off to make war on the rest of
her children—those who obey God's
commands and adhere to the testimony
of Jesus.

13 Then I stood on the sand of the seashore, and I saw an animal come up out
of the sea with ten horns and seven
heads, and with ten diadems on its
horns, and blasphemous titles on its
heads. The animal I saw was like a 2
leopard, its feet were like a bear's and
its mouth was like a lion's mouth. The
dragon gave it his own power and his
throne and great authority. One of its 3
heads seemed to have received a mortal
wound, but its mortal wound had been
healed. And the whole earth followed
the animal in wonder, and worshiped 4
the dragon for having given the animal
his authority, and they worshiped the
animal, and said,

"Who is there like the animal? Who
can fight with it?"

It was allowed to utter great boasts 5
and blasphemies, and to exert authority for forty-two months. It opened its 6
mouth in blasphemies against God,
blaspheming his name and his dwelling-
place, that is, those who live in heaven.
It was allowed to make war on God's 7
people and to conquer them, and it was
given authority over every tribe, people, language, and nation. All the in- 8
habitants of the earth whose names
have not from the foundation of the
world been written in the slain Lamb's
book of life, will worship it. Let every- 9
one who can hear listen. Whoever is 10
destined for captivity will go into captivity; whoever kills with the sword
must be killed with the sword. On this
fact rests the endurance and fidelity of
God's people.

Then I saw another animal come up 11
out of the land. It had two horns like a
lamb, but it spoke like a dragon. It ex- 12
ercises the full authority of the first animal on its behalf. It makes the earth
and its inhabitants worship the first
animal, whose mortal wound had been
healed. It performs great wonders, 13
even making fire come down from
heaven to earth before men's eyes. It 14
leads the inhabitants of the earth
astray by the wonders it is allowed to
do on behalf of the animal, telling the
inhabitants of the earth to erect a statue to the animal that bears the mark
of the sword-thrust and yet lives. It is 15
also allowed to impart life to the animal's statue so that the animal's statue
can speak, and to have all who do not
worship the animal's statue killed.
And it makes everyone, high and low, 16
rich and poor, freemen and slaves, have

a mark stamped on their right hands or
17 on their foreheads, and permits no one
to buy or sell anything unless he bears
the mark, that is, the animal's name or
the number corresponding to its name.
18 There is wisdom hidden here! Let
everyone of intelligence calculate the
animal's number, for it indicates a certain man; its number is 666.

14 Then in my vision I saw the Lamb
standing on Mount Zion, and with him
144,000 people who had his name and his
Father's name written on their fore-
2 heads. And I heard a sound from heav-
en, like the sound of many waters, and
like the sound of mighty thunders. The
sound I heard was like that of harpists
3 playing on their harps. They were singing a new song before the throne and
the four animals and the elders, and no
one could learn the song except the
144,000 who had been ransomed from
4 the earth. They are the men who have
not been defiled by relations with
women; they are celibates. It is they
who follow the Lamb wherever he goes.
They have been ransomed from among
men as the first-fruits for God and the
5 Lamb, and they have never been known
to utter a lie; they are irreproachable.
6 Then I saw another angel flying in
midair, with eternal good news to announce to the inhabitants of the earth,
to every nation, tribe, language, and
7 people. He cried in a loud voice,
"Fear God and give him glory, for
the hour for his judgment has come.
Worship him who made heaven and
earth and sea and the springs of
water."
8 A second angel followed, saying,
"She is fallen! Mighty Babylon is
fallen, who made all the heathen drink
the wine of the passion of her immorality!"
9 A third angel followed them, saying
in a loud voice,
"Whoever worships the animal and
its statue and lets its mark be put on
10 his forehead or on his hand shall drink
the wine of God's wrath, poured un-
mixed into the cup of his anger, and be
tortured with fire and brimstone before
the eyes of the holy angels and the
11 Lamb. The smoke of their torture will
go up forever and ever, and they will
have no rest night or day—these worshipers of the animal and its statue,
and any who bear the mark of its
name." On this fact rests the endur- 12
ance of God's people, who obey God's
commands and cling to their faith in
Jesus.
Then I heard a voice from heaven 13
say,
"Write: Blessed are the dead who
from this time forth die as Christians!"
"Yes!" answers the Spirit, "Let them
rest from their toil, for what they have
done will go with them!"
Then I saw a white cloud, and seated 14
on it a being like a man, with a gold
crown on his head and a sharp sickle in
his hand.
And another angel came out of the 15
temple and cried in a loud voice to him
who was seated on the cloud,
"Use your sickle and reap. The time
has come to reap, for the earth's harvest is ripe."
So he who was seated on the cloud 16
swung his sickle over the earth, and the
earth was reaped.
Another angel came out of the tem- 17
ple in heaven, and he too had a sharp
sickle. And another angel came forth 18
from the altar, who presided over the
fire, and he called in a loud voice to the
one who had the sharp sickle,
"Use your sharp sickle and gather
the bunches of grapes from the earth's
vine, for the grapes on it are ripe."
So the angel swung his sickle on the 19
earth and gathered the fruit of the
earth's vine, and flung it into the
great winepress of God's wrath. The 20
grapes were trodden in the winepress
outside the city, and blood poured out
of the winepress in a stream so deep
that for 200 miles it came up to the
horses' bridles.

Then I saw another great, marvelous 15
portent in heaven. There were seven
angels with seven plagues which are to
be the last, for with them the expression
of God's wrath is ended.
And I saw what looked like a sea of 2
glass mixed with fire, and standing
upon the sea of glass those who had
come off victorious from the animal and
its statue and the number corresponding to its name. They had harps that
God had given them, and they were 3
singing the song of Moses, the slave of
God, and the song of the Lamb:
"Great and marvelous are your doings, Lord God Almighty! Upright and
true are your ways, King of the Ages!

4 Who will not fear and give glory to
your name, Lord? For you alone are
holy. All the heathen will come and
worship before you, for the justice of
your sentences has now been shown."
5 Afterward I saw the temple, that is,
the tent of the testimony, thrown open
6 in heaven, and the seven angels with
the seven plagues came out of the temple.
They were clothed in clean, glistening
linen and had gold belts around
7 their breasts. Then one of the four animals
gave the seven angels seven gold
bowls full of the wrath of God who
8 lives forever and ever, and the temple
was filled with smoke from the glory
and power of God, and no one could go
into the temple until the seven plagues
16 of the seven angels were over. Then I
heard a loud voice from the temple say
to the seven angels,

"Go and empty the seven bowls of
God's wrath upon the earth!"

2 So the first angel went and emptied
his bowl upon the earth, and loathsome,
painful sores attacked the men
who bore the mark of the animal and
worshiped its statue.

3 The second emptied his bowl upon
the sea, and it turned into blood like a
dead man's, and every live thing in the
sea died.

4 The third emptied his bowl upon the
rivers and the springs of water, and
5 they turned into blood. Then I heard
the angel of the waters say,

"You are just in pronouncing this
sentence, you who are and were, the
6 Holy One; for they shed the blood of
your people and prophets, and you
have given them blood to drink, as they
deserve."

7 And I heard the altar answer,

"Yes, Lord God Almighty! Your
sentences are true and just."

8 The fourth emptied his bowl upon
the sun, and it was allowed to scorch
9 mankind with its heat, and they were
dreadfully scorched, but they reviled
the name of God who had control of
these plagues, and would not repent
and give him glory.

10 The fifth emptied his bowl upon the
animal's throne, and its kingdom was
plunged in darkness, and men gnawed
11 their tongues in anguish and reviled the
God of heaven for their sufferings and
sores, but they would not repent of
what they had done.

The sixth emptied his bowl upon the 12
great river Euphrates, and its waters
dried up to make the way ready for the
kings from the east. Then I saw three 13
foul spirits like frogs emerge from the
mouth of the dragon and from the
mouth of the animal and from the
mouth of the false prophet. They are 14
demon spirits that perform wonders,
and they go out to the kings all over the
world to muster them for the battle on
the great Day of God the Almighty.
(See, I am coming like a thief! Blessed 15
is he who keeps awake, and keeps hold
of his clothes, so that he will not have to
go naked and be put to shame!) So 16
they mustered the kings at the place
called in Hebrew Armageddon.

The seventh emptied his bowl upon 17
the air, and a loud voice came out of the
temple from the throne, saying,

"It is all over!"

Then there were flashes of lightning, 18
rumblings and peals of thunder, and
there was a great earthquake; there has
never been such an earthquake since
man first existed upon the earth, it was
so great. The great city broke into 19
three pieces, the cities of the heathen
fell, and God remembered to give
mighty Babylon the cup of the wine of
his fierce anger. Every island vanished, 20
the mountains disappeared, huge hail- 21
stones of a hundred pounds weight fell
on mankind from heaven, and men reviled
God because of the plague of hail,
the plague of it was so terrible.

Then one of the seven angels with 17
the seven bowls came and spoke to me.

"Come," he said, "I will show you
the doom of the great idolatress who is
seated on many waters, in whose idol- 2
atry the kings of the earth have joined,
and with the wine of whose idolatry the
inhabitants of the earth have been intoxicated."

So he carried me away in a trance to 3
a desert, and I saw a woman seated on
a scarlet animal all covered with blasphemous
titles; it had seven heads and
ten horns. The woman was dressed in 4
purple and scarlet, and glittered with
gold, precious stones, and pearls. She
had in her hand a gold cup full of accursed
things, and the impurities of her
immorality. On her forehead there was 5
written a name that was symbolic:
"Mighty Babylon, mother of idolatresses
and of earth's abominations."

6 I saw that the woman was drunk with
the blood of God's people, and the
blood of the witnesses of Jesus. When
7 I saw her I was utterly amazed, but the
angel said to me,
"Why are you amazed? I will explain to you what the woman and the
animal with seven heads and ten horns
8 that carries her symbolize. The animal
that you saw was, and is no more; it is
going to come up out of the abyss, but
it is to go to destruction. The inhabitants of the earth, whose names from
the foundation of the world have not
been written in the book of life, will be
amazed when they see that the animal
was, and is no more, and yet is to come.
9 Here is a problem for a profound mind!
The seven heads are seven hills, on
10 which the woman is seated. They are
also seven kings; five have fallen, one is
reigning, the other has not yet come,
and when he does his stay must be
11 brief. The animal that was, and is no
more, is also an eighth king, although it
is one of the seven, and it is to go to
12 destruction. The ten horns that you
saw are also ten kings, who have not yet
begun to reign, but for a single hour
they receive authority as kings along
13 with the animal. They have one purpose, they give their power and author-
14 ity to the animal. They will make war
upon the Lamb, and the Lamb with
his elect, chosen, and faithful followers
with him will conquer them, for he is
Lord of lords and King of kings.
15 "The waters that you saw," he said
to me, "on which the idolatrous woman
was seated, are peoples, multitudes,
16 nations, and languages. The ten horns
that you saw and the animal will hate
the idolatrous woman and make her
desolate and naked, and eat her flesh
17 and burn her up with fire. For God has
put it into their hearts to carry out his
purpose by having a common purpose
and giving up their authority to the
animal until God's decrees are carried
18 out. And the woman that you saw is
the great city that has dominion over
the kings of the earth."

18 Afterward I saw another angel come
down from heaven. He possessed great
authority and his splendor lighted up
2 the earth. He cried out with a mighty
voice.
"She is fallen! Mighty Babylon is
fallen! She has become the haunt of demons, and a dungeon for every foul
spirit and every unclean and loathsome
bird, for after drinking the wine of 3
the passion of her immorality all the
heathen have fallen; the kings of the
earth have joined in her idolatry, and
the traders of the earth have grown
rich from her excessive luxury!"
Then I heard another voice from 4
heaven say,
"Come out of her, my people, so that
you may not share in her sins, and suffer from her plagues. For her sins are 5
piled up to the sky, and God has remembered her crimes. Pay her back in 6
her own coin, and give her double for
what she has done. In the cup she
mixed for others, mix her a double
draught. The more she has given her- 7
self to pride and luxury the more you
must give her torture and grief. Because she says to herself, 'I sit on a
throne; I am not a widow, I shall never
have any sorrow,' her plagues will over- 8
take her in one day, death, grief, and
famine, and she will be burned up with
fire; for the Lord God who has judged
her is mighty. The kings of the earth 9
who have joined in her idolatry and
luxury will weep and lament over her
when they see the smoke from her
burning. They will stand a long way off 10
for fear of her torture and say, 'Alas!
Alas for the great city, for Babylon the
mighty city, for in a single hour your
judgment has overtaken you!' The 11
merchants of the earth will weep and
mourn over her, for no one will buy
their cargoes any more—cargoes of 12
gold, silver, precious stones, pearls,
fine linen, purple, silk, and scarlet, all
kinds of citron wood, all kinds of objects of ivory and costly wood, bronze,
iron, and marble, and cinnamon, spices, 13
incense, perfume, frankincense, wine,
olive oil, flour, wheat, cattle, sheep,
horses, carriages, slaves—and human
lives! The fruit of your soul's desire is 14
gone, your luxury and splendor have
perished, and people will never find
them again. The dealers in these 15
things, who had grown rich from their
trade with her, for fear of her torture will stand a long way off, weeping
and mourning, and say, 'Alas! Alas for 16
the great city that was dressed in fine
linen, purple, and scarlet, and glittered
with gold, precious stones, and pearls,

17 for in a single hour this vast wealth has
been laid waste!' All navigators and all
who travel by sea, sailors and sea-
18 faring men, stood a long way off and
cried out when they saw the smoke
from her burning, 'What city was like
19 the great city?' They threw dust on
their heads and wept and mourned, crying out, 'Alas! Alas for the great city,
where all who had ships on the sea grew
rich through her extravagance! For in
a single hour she has been laid waste!'
20 Gloat over her, heaven! and all you
people of God, apostles, and prophets,
for God has avenged you upon her!"
21 Then a mighty angel caught up a
stone like a great millstone and threw it
into the sea, saying,
"With such violence will Babylon the
great city be hurled to destruction and
22 never be seen again! The sound of
harpists and musicians, flute-players
and trumpets will never be heard in you
again. No craftsman of any kind will
ever be found in you again, no sound
of the millstone will ever be heard in
23 you again; no light of any lamp will
ever shine in you again; no voice of
bride or bridegroom will ever be heard
in you again. For your merchants were
the great men of the earth; by your
magic all the heathen have been led
24 astray, and in you was found the blood
of prophets, God's people, and all who
have been slaughtered on the earth."

19 After that I heard what sounded like
the loud shout of a great multitude in
heaven saying,
"Praise the Lord! Salvation, glory,
2 and power belong to our God, for his
judgments are sound and upright. For
he has passed judgment upon the great
idolatress who corrupted the earth with
her idolatry, and he has avenged the
blood of his slaves upon her!"
3 Then they said again,
"Praise the Lord! For smoke will go
up from her forever and ever!"
4 Then the twenty-four elders and the
four animals fell down and worshiped
God who was seated upon the throne.
"Amen!" they said, "Praise the
Lord!"
5 And there came a voice from the
throne, saying,
"Praise our God, all you slaves of his,
high and low, who fear him!"
6 Then I heard what sounded like the
shout of a great multitude and the noise
of many waters and the sound of
mighty thunders, saying,
"Praise the Lord; for the Lord our
God, the Almighty now reigns! Let us 7
be glad and triumphant and give him
glory, for the marriage of the Lamb has
come, and his bride has made herself
ready. She has been permitted to wear 8
clean, glistening linen, for linen represents the upright deeds of God's people."
Then he said to me, 9
"Write: 'Blessed are they who are
invited to the marriage supper of the
Lamb.' These," he said to me, "are the
true words of God."
I fell at his feet to worship him, but 10
he said to me,
"You must not do that. I am only a
fellow-slave of yours and of your
brothers who have accepted the testimony of Jesus. Worship God! For the
testimony of Jesus is what inspires
prophecy."
Then I saw heaven thrown open and 11
there appeared a white horse. His rider
was called Faithful and True, and he
judges and wages war in uprightness.
His eyes blazed like fire. There were 12
many diadems on his head, and there
was a name written on him which no
one knew but himself. The garment he 13
wore was spattered with blood, and his
name was the Word of God. The ar- 14
mies of heaven followed him mounted
on white horses and clothed in pure
white linen. From his mouth came a 15
sharp sword with which he is to strike
down the heathen. He will shepherd
them with a staff of iron, and will
tread the winepress of the fierce anger
of God the Almighty. On his clothing 16
and his thigh he has this title written:
King of kings and Lord of lords.
Then I saw an angel standing on the 17
sun, and shouting in a loud voice to all
the birds that fly in midair,
"Come! Gather for God's great banquet, and eat the bodies of kings, com- 18
manders, and mighty men, of horses
and their riders—the bodies of all men,
slaves and freemen, high and low."
Then I saw the animal and the kings 19
of the earth and their armies gather to
make war on him who was mounted
upon the horse and on his army.
And the animal was captured and 20
with it the false prophet who performed
wonders on its behalf by means of

which he led astray those who had let
the animal's mark be put on them and
who worshiped its statue. Both of
them were flung alive into the fiery lake
21 of burning brimstone. The rest were
killed with the sword that came out of
the mouth of him who sat on the horse,
and all the birds gorged themselves
upon their bodies.
20 Then I saw an angel come down
from heaven with the key of the abyss
2 and a great chain in his hand. He
seized the dragon, the ancient serpent,
who is the devil and Satan, and bound
3 him for a thousand years, and hurled
him into the abyss and he closed it and
sealed it over him, to keep him from
leading the heathen astray any longer,
until the thousand years are over; after
that he must be released for a little
while.
4 Then I saw thrones with beings seated on them, who were empowered to
act as judges. And I saw the souls of
those who had been beheaded on account of the testimony of Jesus and the
message of God, who refused to worship the animal and its statue, and
would not have its mark put on their
foreheads or on their hands. They were
restored to life and reigned with the
5 Christ a thousand years. The rest of
the dead were not restored to life until
the thousand years were over. This is
6 the first resurrection. Blessed and holy
is the man who experiences the first
resurrection! The second death has no
power over them; they will be priests of
God and the Christ, and reign with him
for the thousand years.
7 When the thousand years are over,
Satan will be released from his prison,
8 and will go out to lead astray the
heathen in the four corners of the earth,
Gog and Magog, and to muster them
for battle, in numbers like the sand of
9 the sea. They came up on the broad
plain of the earth and surrounded the
encampment of God's people, and the
beloved city. Then fire came down from
10 heaven and consumed them, and the
devil who led them astray was flung
into the fiery, sulphurous lake, where
the animal and the false prophet were,
there to be tortured day and night
forever and ever.
11 Then I saw a great white throne with
a being seated on it from whose presence earth and sky fled so far that they
could not be found. I saw the dead, 12
high and low, standing before the
throne, and books were opened. Then
another book was opened; it was the
book of life. And the dead were judged
by what was written in the books about
what they had done. The sea gave up 13
the dead that were in it, and death and
the underworld gave up the dead that
were in them, and they were all judged
by what they had done. Then death 14
and Hades were flung into the fiery
lake. This is the second death—the
fiery lake. Anyone whose name was 15
not found written in the book of life
was flung into the fiery lake.
Then I saw a new heaven and a new 21
earth, for the first heaven and the first
earth had passed away, and there was
no longer any sea. And I saw the holy 2
city, a new Jerusalem, come down out
of heaven from God, like a bride
dressed and ready to meet her husband. I heard a loud voice from the 3
throne say,
"See! God's dwelling is with men,
and he will live with them. They will
be his people and God himself will be
with them, and he will wipe every tear 4
from their eyes. There will be no death
any longer, nor any grief or crying or
pain. The old order has passed away."
Then he who sat upon the throne 5
said,
"See! I am making everything new!
Write this," he said, "for these words
are trustworthy and true. It is all 6
over!" he told me, "I am the Alpha
and the Omega, the beginning and the
end. I will give anyone who is thirsty
water without cost from the spring of
the water of life. He who is victorious 7
will possess all this, and I will be his
God and he will be my son. But the 8
cowardly, unfaithful, and polluted—
murderers, immoral people, those who
practice magic or idolatry, and all liars
will find themselves in the burning lake
of fire and brimstone. This is the
second death."
Then one of the seven angels who had 9
the seven bowls full of the seven last
plagues came and spoke to me.
"Come," he said, "I will show you
the bride, the wife of the Lamb."
He carried me away in a trance to a 10
great, high mountain, and showed me
Jerusalem, the holy city, coming down
out of heaven from God, in all the glory 11

of God. It shone with a radiance like
that of some very precious stone, like
12 jasper, clear as crystal. It had a great,
high wall with twelve gates, and twelve
angels at the gates, which had carved
upon them the names of the twelve
13 tribes of the sons of Israel. There were
three gates on the east, three gates on
the north, three gates on the south, and
14 three gates on the west. The wall of
the city had twelve foundation stones,
and on them were the twelve names of
15 the twelve apostles of the Lamb. He
who talked with me had a gold measuring rod, with which to measure the city
16 and its gates and wall. The city was a
square, its length the same as its
breadth. He measured the city with his
rod, and it was 12,000 furlongs. Its
length, breadth, and height were the
17 same. He measured the wall and it was
about 144 cubits (216 feet), as men
measure, for that was the way the angel
18 measured. The material of the wall was
jasper, but the city was pure gold, as
19 transparent as glass. The foundation
stones of the wall of the city were ornamented with all kinds of precious
stones. The first foundation stone was
jasper, the second sapphire, the third
20 chalcedony, the fourth emerald, the
fifth sardonyx, the sixth sardius, the
seventh chrysolite, the eighth beryl, the
ninth topaz, the tenth chrysoprase, the
eleventh jacinth, the twelfth amethyst.
21 The twelve gates were twelve pearls;
each gate made of a single pearl. The
principal street of the city was pure
22 gold, as transparent as glass. I saw no
temple in it, for the Lord God the Almighty and the Lamb are its temple.
23 The city does not need the sun nor the
moon to shine in it, for the glory of God
lighted it, and the Lamb is its lamp.
24 The heathen will walk by its light. The
kings of the earth will bring their splen-
25 dor to it. Its gates will never be shut by
day—for there will be no night there
26 and they will bring the splendor and the
27 wealth of the heathen into it. Nothing
unclean will ever enter it, nor anyone
who indulges in abominable practices
and falsehoods, but only those who are
22 written in the Lamb's book of life. Then
he showed me a river of living water,
clear as crystal, which issued from the
2 throne of God and of the Lamb, and ran
through the middle of the principal
street of the city. On both sides of the
river grew the tree of life. It bore
twelve kinds of fruit, yielding a different kind each month, and the leaves of
the tree were a cure for the heathen.
There will no longer be anything that is 3
accursed. The throne of God and of the
Lamb will be in the city, and his slaves
will worship him; they will see his face, 4
and his name will be on their foreheads.
There will no longer be any night and 5
they will have no need of lamplight or
sunlight, for the Lord God will shine on
them, and they will reign forever and
ever.

"These words are trustworthy and 6
true," he said to me; "for the Lord, the
God of the spirits of the prophets, sent
his angel to show his slaves what must
happen very soon. See! I am coming 7
very soon! Blessed is he who heeds the
words of prophecy that are in this
book."

It was I, John, who heard and saw 8
these things. When I heard and saw
them, I fell at the feet of the angel who
showed them to me, to worship him.
But he said to me,

"You must not do that. I am only a 9
fellow-slave of yours and of your
brothers the prophets and the men who
heed the words of this book. Worship
God!

"Do not seal up the words of prophe- 10
cy that are in this book," he said to me,
"for the time of their fulfilment is very
near. Let the evil-doer still do evil, let 11
the base man still be base, let the upright man still be upright, and the man
who is holy still be holy."

"See! I am coming very soon, bring- 12
ing with me my rewards, to repay
everyone for what he has done. I am 13
the Alpha and the Omega, the first and
the last, the beginning and the end.
Blessed are those who wash their robes, 14
so as to have the right to approach the
tree of life and to enter the gates of the
city. The dogs, those who practice 15
magic or immorality, murderers, idolaters, and anyone who loves falsehood
or tells lies will be shut out of it.

"I, Jesus, sent my angel to give you 16
this testimony for the churches. I am of
the line and family of David, I am the
bright morning star."

"Come," say the Spirit and the bride. 17
Let everyone who hears this say,

"Come!"

Let everyone who is thirsty come.
Let anyone who wants it come and take
without cost living water.
18 I warn everyone who hears the message of prophecy in this book read, that
if anyone adds anything to it, God will
inflict upon him the plagues that are
19 described in this book; and if anyone
removes from this book any of the prophetic messages it contains, God will
remove from him his share in the tree of
life and the holy city which are described in this book.
He who testifies to all this says, 20
"It is true! I am coming very soon!"
Amen! Come, Lord Jesus!
The blessing of the Lord Jesus Christ 21
be with his people.

PRINTED IN U·S·A·